NCAA FOOTBALL

THE OFFICIAL 1994 COLLEGE FOOTBALL RECORDS BOOK

NATIONAL COLLEGIATE ATHLETIC ASSOCIATION

THE NATIONAL COLLEGIATE ATHLETIC ASSOCIATION
6201 College Boulevard, Overland Park, Kansas 66211-2422
913/339-1906

July 1994

Compiled By:
Richard M. Campbell, *Assistant Statistics Coordinator.*
John D. Painter, *Assistant Statistics Coordinator.*
Sean W. Straziscar, *Assistant Statistics Coordinator.*

Edited By:
J. Gregory Summers, *Assistant Director of Publishing.*

Typesetting/Production By:
Pamela G. Carr, *Typesetter.*

Cover Design By:
Wayne O. Davis, *Assistant Publishing Production Coordinator.*

Cover Photograph By:
Doug Adams/Allsport.

Contents

Division I-A Records

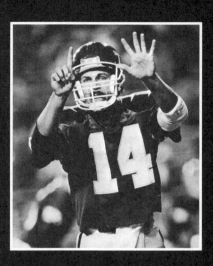

Individual Records

Under a three-division reorganization plan adopted by the special NCAA Convention of August 1973, teams classified major-college in football on August 1, 1973, were placed in Division I. College-division teams were divided into Division II and Division III. At the NCAA Convention of January 1978, Division I was divided into Division I-A and Division I-AA for football only.

From 1937, when official national statistics rankings began, through 1969, individual rankings were by totals. Beginning in 1970, most season individual rankings were by per-game averages. In total offense, rushing and scoring, it is yards or points per game; in receiving, catches per game and yards per game; in interceptions, catches per game; and in punt and kickoff returns, yards per return. Punting always has been by average, and all team rankings have been per game. Beginning in 1979, passers were rated in all divisions on "efficiency rating points," which are derived from a formula that compares passers to the national averages for 14 seasons of two-platoon Division I football starting with the 1965 season. One hundred points equals the 14-year averages for all players in Division I. Those averages break down to 6.29 yards per attempt, 47.14 percent completions, 3.97 percent touchdown passes and 6.54 percent interceptions. The formula assumes that touchdowns are as good as interceptions are bad; therefore, these two figures offset each other for the average player. To determine efficiency rating points, multiply a passer's yards per attempt by 8.4, add his completion percentage, add his touchdown percentage times 3.3, then subtract his interception percentage times two.

Passers must have a minimum of 15 attempts per game to determine rating points because fewer attempts could allow a player to win the championship with fewer than 100 attempts in a season. A passer must play in at least 75 percent of his team's games to qualify for the rankings (e.g., a player on a team with a nine-game season could qualify by playing in seven games); thus, a passer with 105 attempts could qualify for the national rankings.

All individual and team records and rankings include regular-season games only. Career records of other players who played in both Division I and Division II or III—such as Grambling's Doug Williams—will be found where they played the majority of their career. Williams played three of his four seasons in Division II; thus, his career records are in the Division II section.

Statistics in some team categories were not tabulated until the advent of the computerized statistics program in 1966. The records listed in those categories begin with the 1966 season and are so indicated.

In 1954, the regular-season schedule was limited to a maximum of 10 games, and in 1970, to a limit of 11 games, excluding postseason competition.

A player whose career includes statistics for parts of five seasons (or an active player who will have five seasons) because he was granted an additional season of competition for reasons of hardship (Bylaw 14.2.5) or a freshman red-shirt (Bylaw 14.2.1) are denoted by "$".

COLLEGIATE RECORDS

Individual collegiate records are determined by comparing the best records in all four divisions (I-A, I-AA, II and III) in comparable categories. Included are career records of players who played half of their careers in two divisions (such as Dennis Shaw of San Diego State, Howard Stevens of Randolph-Macon and Louisville, and Tom Ehrhardt of LIU-C. W. Post and Rhode Island). For individual collegiate career leaders, see page 173.

Total Offense

(Rushing Plus Passing)
MOST PLAYS
Quarter
35—Mike Romo, Southern Methodist vs. Rice, Nov. 10, 1990 (4th; 31 passes, 4 rushes); Chris Rowland, Washington vs. California, Oct. 6, 1973 (4th; 31 passes, 4 rushes)

Half
53—Matt Vogler, Texas Christian vs. Houston, Nov. 3, 1990 (2nd; 47 passes, 6 rushes)

Game
94—Matt Vogler, Texas Christian vs. Houston, Nov. 3, 1990 (696 yards)

Season
704—David Klingler, Houston, 1990 (5,221 yards)

2 Yrs
1,294—David Klingler, Houston, 1990-91 (8,447 yards)

3 Yrs
1,548—Ty Detmer, Brigham Young, 1988-91 (13,456 yards)

Career
(4 yrs.) 1,795—Ty Detmer, Brigham Young, 1988-91 (14,665 yards)

MOST PLAYS PER GAME
Season
64.0—David Klingler, Houston, 1990 (704 in 11)

2 Yrs
61.6—David Klingler, Houston, 1990-91 (1,294 in 21)

Career
48.5—Doug Gaynor, Long Beach St., 1984-85 (1,067 in 22)

MOST PLAYS BY A FRESHMAN
Game
76—Sandy Schwab, Northwestern vs. Michigan, Oct. 23, 1982 (431 yards)

Season
504—Sandy Schwab, Northwestern, 1982 (2,555 yards)
Also holds per-game record at 45.8 (504 in 11)

MOST YARDS GAINED
Quarter
340—Andre Ware, Houston vs. Southern Methodist, Oct. 21, 1989 (2nd)

Half
510—Andre Ware, Houston vs. Southern Methodist, Oct. 21, 1989 (1st)

Game
732—David Klingler, Houston vs. Arizona St., Dec. 2, 1990 (716 passing, 16 rushing)

Season
5,221—David Klingler, Houston, 1990 (81 rushing, 5,140 passing)

2 Yrs
9,455—Ty Detmer, Brigham Young, 1989-90 (-293 rushing, 9,748 passing)

3 Yrs
10,664—Ty Detmer, Brigham Young, 1988-90 (-336 rushing, 11,000 passing)

Career
(4 yrs.) 14,665—Ty Detmer, Brigham Young, 1988-91 (-366 rushing, 15,031 passing)

MOST YARDS GAINED PER GAME
Season
474.6—David Klingler, Houston, 1990 (5,221 in 11)

2 Yrs
402.2—David Klingler, Houston, 1990-91 (8,447 in 21)

Career
320.9—Chris Vargas, Nevada, 1992-93 (6,417 in 20)

MOST YARDS GAINED, FIRST TWO SEASONS
6,710—Doug Gaynor, Long Beach St., 1984-85
Also holds per-game record at 305.0

MOST SEASONS GAINING 4,000 YARDS OR MORE
3—Ty Detmer, Brigham Young, 1989-91

MOST SEASONS GAINING 3,000 YARDS OR MORE
3—Ty Detmer, Brigham Young, 1989-91

MOST SEASONS GAINING 2,500 YARDS OR MORE
3—Shane Matthews, Florida, 1990-92; Ty Detmer, Brigham Young, 1989-91; Shawn Moore, Virginia, 1988-90; Erik Wilhelm, Oregon St., 1986-88; Brian McClure, Bowling Green, 1983-85; Randall Cunningham, Nevada-Las Vegas, 1982-84; Doug Flutie, Boston College, 1982-84; John Elway, Stanford, 1980-82

MOST YARDS GAINED BY A FRESHMAN
Game
458—Bob Hoernschemeyer, Indiana vs. Nebraska, Oct. 9, 1943 (37 plays)

Season
2,975—Todd Ellis, South Caro., 1986 (436 plays)
Also holds per-game record at 270.5

MOST YARDS GAINED BY A SOPHOMORE
Game
625—Scott Mitchell, Utah vs. Air Force, Oct. 15, 1988 (631 passing, -6 rushing)

Season
4,433—Ty Detmer, Brigham Young, 1989 (12 games, 497 plays)
Per-game record—390.8, Scott Mitchell, Utah, 1988

MOST YARDS GAINED IN FIRST GAME OF CAREER
483—Billy Stevens, UTEP vs. North Texas, Sept. 18, 1965

MOST YARDS GAINED IN TWO, THREE AND FOUR CONSECUTIVE GAMES
2 Games
1,310—David Klingler, Houston, 1990 (578 vs. Eastern Wash., Nov. 17; 732 vs. Arizona St., Dec. 2)

3 Games
1,651—David Klingler, Houston, 1990 (341 vs. Texas, Nov. 10; 578 vs. Eastern Wash., Nov. 17; 732 vs. Arizona St., Dec. 2)

4 Games
2,276—David Klingler, Houston, 1990 (625 vs. Texas Christian, Nov. 3; 341 vs. Texas, Nov. 10; 578 vs. Eastern Wash., Nov. 17; 732 vs. Arizona St., Dec. 2)

MOST GAMES GAINING 300 YARDS OR MORE
Season
12—Ty Detmer, Brigham Young, 1990

Career
33—Ty Detmer, Brigham Young, 1988-91

MOST CONSECUTIVE GAMES GAINING 300 YARDS OR MORE
Season
12—Ty Detmer, Brigham Young, 1990

Career
19—Ty Detmer, Brigham Young, 1989-90

MOST GAMES GAINING 400 YARDS OR MORE
Season
9—David Klingler, Houston, 1990
Career
13—Ty Detmer, Brigham Young, 1988-91

MOST CONSECUTIVE GAMES GAINING 400 YARDS OR MORE
Season
5—Ty Detmer, Brigham Young, 1990
Also holds career record at 5

MOST YARDS GAINED AGAINST ONE OPPONENT
Career
1,483—Ty Detmer, Brigham Young vs. San Diego St., 1988-91

MOST YARDS GAINED PER GAME AGAINST ONE OPPONENT
Career
(Min. 3 games) 383.7—Gary Schofield, Wake Forest vs. Maryland, 1981-83 (1,151 yards)
(Min. 4 games) 370.8—Ty Detmer, Brigham Young vs. San Diego St., 1988-91 (1,483 yards)

MOST YARDS GAINED BY TWO OPPOSING PLAYERS
Game
1,321—Matt Vogler, Texas Christian (696) & David Klingler, Houston (625), Nov. 3, 1990

GAINING 1,000 YARDS RUSHING AND 1,000 YARDS PASSING
Season
Michael Carter (QB), Hawaii, 1991 (1,092 rushing, 1,172 passing); Brian Mitchell (QB), Southwestern La., 1989 (1,311 rushing, 1,966 passing); Dee Dowis (QB), Air Force, 1989 (1,286 rushing, 1,285 passing); Darian Hagan (QB), Colorado, 1989 (1,004 rushing, 1,002 passing); Bart Weiss (QB), Air Force, 1985 (1,032 rushing, 1,449 passing); Reggie Collier (QB), Southern Miss., 1981 (1,005 rushing, 1,004 passing); Johnny Bright (HB), Drake, 1950 (1,232 rushing, 1,168 passing)

A QUARTERBACK GAINING 2,000 YARDS RUSHING AND 4,000 YARDS PASSING
Career
Major Harris, West Va., 1987-89 (2,030 rushing, 4,834 passing); Brian Mitchell, Southwestern La., 1986-89 (3,335 rushing, 5,447 passing); Rickey Foggie, Minnesota, 1984-87 (2,038 rushing, 4,903 passing); John Bond, Mississippi St., 1980-83 (2,280 rushing, 4,621 passing); Prince McJunkins, Wichita St., 1979-82 (2,047 rushing, 4,544 passing)

A QUARTERBACK GAINING 300 YARDS PASSING AND 100 YARDS RUSHING
Game
Donald Douglas, Houston vs. Southern Methodist, Oct. 19, 1991 (319 passing, 103 rushing); Randy Welniak, Wyoming vs. Air Force, Sept. 24, 1988 (359 passing, 108 rushing); Ned James, New Mexico vs. Wyoming, Nov. 1, 1986 (406 passing, 118 rushing)

A QUARTERBACK GAINING 200 YARDS RUSHING AND 200 YARDS PASSING
Game
Brian Mitchell, Southwestern La. vs. Colorado St., Nov. 21, 1987 (271 rushing, 205 passing); Steve Gage, Tulsa vs. New Mexico, Nov. 8, 1986 (212 rushing, 209 passing); Reds Bagnell, Pennsylvania vs. Dartmouth, Oct. 14, 1950 (214 rushing, 276 passing)

TEAMS HAVING A 3,000-YARD PASSER, 1,000-YARD RUSHER AND 1,000-YARD RECEIVER IN THE SAME YEAR
6 teams. Most recent: Wyoming, 1993 (Joe Hughes [3,135 passer], Ryan Yarborough [1,512 receiver] and Ryan Christopherson [1,014 rusher]); San Diego St., 1993 (Tim Gutierrez [3,033 passer], Marshall Faulk [1,530 rusher] and Darnay Scott [1,262 receiver])

HIGHEST AVERAGE GAIN PER PLAY
Game
(Min. 37-62 plays) 12.8—Chris Vargas, Nevada vs. Nevada-Las Vegas, Oct. 2, 1993 (42 for 537)
(Min. 63 plays) 9.9—David Klingler, Houston vs. Texas Christian, Nov. 3, 1990 (63 for 625)
Season
(Min. 3,000 yards) 8.9—Ty Detmer, Brigham Young, 1989 (497 for 4,433)
Career
(Min. 7,500 yards) 8.2—Ty Detmer, Brigham Young, 1988-91 (1,795 for 14,665)

MOST TOUCHDOWNS RESPONSIBLE FOR
(TDs Scored and Passed For)
Game
11—David Klingler, Houston vs. Eastern Wash., Nov. 17, 1990 (passed for 11)
Season
55—David Klingler, Houston, 1990 (scored 1, passed for 54)
2 Yrs
85—David Klingler, Houston, 1990-91 (scored 2, passed for 83)
3 Yrs
122—Ty Detmer, Brigham Young, 1989-91 (scored 14, passed for 108)
Career
135—Ty Detmer, Brigham Young, 1988-91 (scored 14, passed for 121)

MOST TOUCHDOWNS RESPONSIBLE FOR PER GAME
Season
5.0—David Klingler, Houston, 1990 (55 in 11)
2 Yrs
4.0—David Klingler, Houston, 1990-91 (85 in 21)
3 Yrs
3.4—Ty Detmer, Brigham Young, 1989-91 (122 in 36)
Career
2.9—Ty Detmer, Brigham Young, 1988-91 (135 in 46)
Collegiate record—3.6, Dennis Shaw, San Diego St., 1968-69 (72 in 20)

MOST POINTS RESPONSIBLE FOR
(Points Scored and Passed For)
Game
66—David Klingler, Houston vs. Eastern Wash., Nov. 17, 1990 (passed for 11 TDs)
Season
334—David Klingler, Houston, 1990 (scored 1 TD, passed for 54 TDs, accounted for 2 two-point conversions)
2 Yrs
514—David Klingler, Houston, 1990-91 (scored 2 TDs, passed for 83 TDs, accounted for 2 two-point conversions)
3 Yrs
582—Ty Detmer, Brigham Young, 1988-90 (scored 10 TDs, passed for 86 TDs, accounted for 3 two-point conversions)
Career
820—Ty Detmer, Brigham Young, 1988-91 (scored 14 TDs, passed for 121 TDs, accounted for 5 two-point conversions)

MOST POINTS RESPONSIBLE FOR PER GAME
Season
30.4—David Klingler, Houston, 1990 (334 in 11)
2 Yrs
22.8—Jim McMahon, Brigham Young, 1980-81 (502 in 22)
3 Yrs
17.1—Ty Detmer, Brigham Young, 1988-90 (582 in 34)
Career
17.8—Ty Detmer, Brigham Young, 1988-91 (820 in 46)
Collegiate record—21.6, Dennis Shaw, San Diego St., 1968-69 (432 in 20)

SCORING 200 POINTS AND PASSING FOR 200 POINTS
Career
Rick Leach, Michigan, 1975-78 (scored 204, passed for 270)

MOST RUSHES
Quarter
20—Kent Kitzmann, Minnesota vs. Illinois, Nov. 12, 1977 (3rd); Steve Owens, Oklahoma vs. Oklahoma St., Nov. 29, 1969 (3rd); O. J. Simpson, Southern Cal vs. Oregon St., Nov. 16, 1968 (4th)
Half
34—Tony Sands, Kansas vs. Missouri, Nov. 23, 1991 (2nd, 240 yards)
Game
58—Tony Sands, Kansas vs. Missouri, Nov. 23, 1991 (396 yards)
Season
403—Marcus Allen, Southern Cal, 1981 (2,342 yards)
2 Yrs
757—Marcus Allen, Southern Cal, 1980-81 (3,905 yards)
Career
(3 yrs.) 994—Herschel Walker, Georgia, 1980-82 (5,259 yards)
(4 yrs.) 1,215—Steve Bartalo, Colorado St., 1983-86 (4,813 yards)

MOST RUSHES PER GAME
Season
39.6—Ed Marinaro, Cornell, 1971 (356 in 9)
2 Yrs
36.0—Marcus Allen, Southern Cal, 1980-81 (757 in 21)
Career
34.0—Ed Marinaro, Cornell, 1969-71 (918 in 27)

MOST RUSHES BY A FRESHMAN
Game
45—James McDougal, Wake Forest vs. Clemson, Oct. 9, 1976 (249 yards)
Season
292—Steve Bartalo, Colorado St., 1983 (1,113 yards)

MOST RUSHES PER GAME BY A FRESHMAN
Season
29.2—Steve Bartalo, Colorado St., 1983 (292 in 10)

MOST CONSECUTIVE RUSHES BY SAME PLAYER
Game
16—William Howard, Tennessee vs. Mississippi, Nov. 15, 1986 (during two possessions)

MOST RUSHES IN TWO CONSECUTIVE GAMES
Season
102—Lorenzo White, Michigan St., 1985 (53 vs. Purdue, Oct. 26; 49 vs. Minnesota, Nov. 2)

MOST YARDS GAINED
Quarter
214—Andre Herrera, Southern Ill. vs. Northern Ill., Oct. 23, 1976 (1st, 17 rushes)
Half
287—Stacey Robinson, Northern Ill. vs. Fresno St., Oct. 6, 1990 (1st; 114 in first quarter, 173 in second quarter; 20 rushes)
Game
396—Tony Sands, Kansas vs. Missouri, Nov. 23, 1991 (58 rushes) (240 yards on 34 carries, second half)
Season
2,628—Barry Sanders, Oklahoma St., 1988 (344 rushes, 11 games)
2 Yrs
3,905—Marcus Allen, Southern Cal, 1980-81 (757 rushes)
Career
(3 yrs.) 5,259—Herschel Walker, Georgia, 1980-82 (994 rushes)
(4 yrs.) 6,082—Tony Dorsett, Pittsburgh, 1973-76 (1,074 rushes)

MOST YARDS GAINED PER GAME
Season
238.9—Barry Sanders, Oklahoma St., 1988 (2,628 in 11)
2 Yrs
186.0—Marcus Allen, Southern Cal, 1980-81 (3,905 in 21)

Career

174.6—Ed Marinaro, Cornell, 1969-71 (4,715 in 27)

MOST YARDS GAINED BY A FRESHMAN
Game

386—Marshall Faulk, San Diego St. vs. Pacific (Cal.), Sept. 14, 1991 (37 rushes)

Season

1,616—Herschel Walker, Georgia, 1980 (274 rushes)

Per-game record—158.8, Marshall Faulk, San Diego St., 1991 (1,429 in 9)

MOST YARDS GAINED BY A SOPHOMORE
Game

342—Charlie Davis, Colorado vs. Oklahoma St., Nov. 13, 1971 (34 rushes)

Season

1,908—Lorenzo White, Michigan St., 1985 (386 rushes)

Also holds per-game record at 173.5 (1,908 in 11)

FRESHMEN GAINING 1,000 YARDS OR MORE
Season

By 35 players (see chart after Annual Rushing Champions. Most recent: Terrell Willis, Rutgers, 1993 (1,261); Charles Henley, Kansas, 1993 (1,127); Marquis Williams, Arkansas St., 1993 (1,060); Leon Johnson, North Caro., 1993 (1,012); Winslow Oliver, New Mexico, 1992 (1,063); Deland McCullough, Miami (Ohio), 1992 (1,026)

TWO FRESHMEN, SAME TEAM, GAINING 1,000 YARDS OR MORE
Season

Mike Smith (1,062) & Gwain Durden (1,049), Tenn.-Chatt., 1977

EARLIEST GAME A FRESHMAN REACHED 1,000 YARDS
Season

7—Marshall Faulk, San Diego St., 1991 (1,157 vs. Colorado St., Nov. 9); Emmitt Smith, Florida, 1987 (1,011 vs. Temple, Oct. 17)

FIRST PLAYER TO GAIN 1,000 YARDS OR MORE
Season

Byron "Whizzer" White, Colorado, 1937 (1,121)

EARLIEST GAME GAINING 1,000 YARDS OR MORE
Season

5—Marcus Allen, Southern Cal, 1981 (1,136); Ernest Anderson, Oklahoma St., 1982 (1,042); Ed Marinaro, Cornell, 1971 (1,026); Ricky Bell, Southern Cal, 1976 (1,008); Barry Sanders, Oklahoma St., 1988 (1,002)

MOST YARDS GAINED BY A QUARTERBACK
Game

308—Stacey Robinson, Northern Ill. vs. Fresno St., Oct. 6, 1990 (22 rushes)

Season

1,443—Stacey Robinson, Northern Ill., 1989 (223 rushes)

Also holds per-game record at 131.2 (1,443 in 11)

Career

3,612—Dee Dowis, Air Force, 1986-89 (543 rushes)

Per-game record—109.1, Stacey Robinson, Northern Ill., 1988-90 (2,727 in 25)

LONGEST GAIN BY A QUARTERBACK
Game

98—Mark Malone, Arizona St. vs. Utah St., Oct. 27, 1979 (TD)

MOST GAMES GAINING 100 YARDS OR MORE
Season

11—By 9 players. Most recent: Barry Sanders, Oklahoma St., 1988

Career

33—Tony Dorsett, Pittsburgh, 1973-76 (43 games); Archie Griffin, Ohio St., 1972-75 (42 games)

MOST GAMES GAINING 100 YARDS OR MORE BY A FRESHMAN
Season

9—Tony Dorsett, Pittsburgh, 1973; Ron "Po" James, New Mexico St., 1968

Consecutive record 8 by James

MOST CONSECUTIVE GAMES GAINING 100 YARDS OR MORE
Career

31—Archie Griffin, Ohio St. Began Sept. 15, 1973 (vs. Minnesota), ended Nov. 22, 1975 (vs. Michigan)

MOST GAMES GAINING 200 YARDS OR MORE
Season

8—Marcus Allen, Southern Cal, 1981

Career

11—Marcus Allen, Southern Cal, 1978-81 (in 21 games during 1980-81)

MOST GAMES GAINING 200 YARDS OR MORE BY A FRESHMAN
Season

4—Herschel Walker, Georgia, 1980

MOST CONSECUTIVE GAMES GAINING 200 YARDS OR MORE
Season

5—Barry Sanders, Oklahoma St., 1988 (320 vs. Kansas St., Oct. 29; 215 vs. Oklahoma, Nov. 5; 312 vs. Kansas, Nov. 12; 293 vs. Iowa St., Nov. 19; 332 vs. Texas Tech, Dec. 3); Marcus Allen, Southern Cal, 1981 (210 vs. Tennessee, Sept. 12; 274 vs. Indiana, Sept. 19; 208 vs. Oklahoma, Sept. 26; 233 vs. Oregon St., Oct. 3; 211 vs. Arizona, Oct. 10)

MOST GAMES GAINING 300 YARDS OR MORE
Season

4—Barry Sanders, Oklahoma St., 1988

Career

4—Barry Sanders, Oklahoma St., 1986-88

MOST YARDS GAINED IN TWO, THREE, FOUR AND FIVE CONSECUTIVE GAMES
2 Games

626—Mike Pringle, Cal St. Fullerton, 1989 (357 vs. New Mexico St., Nov. 4; 269 vs. Long Beach St., Nov. 11)

3 Games

937—Barry Sanders, Oklahoma St., 1988 (312 vs. Kansas, Nov. 12; 293 vs. Iowa St., Nov. 19; 332 vs. Texas Tech, Dec. 3)

4 Games

1,152—Barry Sanders, Oklahoma St., 1988 (215 vs. Oklahoma, Nov. 5; 312 vs. Kansas, Nov. 12; 293 vs. Iowa St., Nov. 19; 332 vs. Texas Tech, Dec. 3)

5 Games

1,472—Barry Sanders, Oklahoma St., 1988 (320 vs. Kansas St., Oct. 29; 215 vs. Oklahoma, Nov. 5; 312 vs. Kansas, Nov. 12; 293 vs. Iowa St., Nov. 19; 332 vs. Texas Tech, Dec. 3)

MOST SEASONS GAINING 1,500 YARDS OR MORE
Career

3—Herschel Walker, Georgia, 1980-82; Tony Dorsett, Pittsburgh, 1973, 1975-76

MOST SEASONS GAINING 1,000 YARDS OR MORE
Career

4—Amos Lawrence, North Caro., 1977-80; Tony Dorsett, Pittsburgh, 1973-76

Collegiate record tied by Howard Stevens, Randolph-Macon, 1968-69, Louisville, 1971-72

TWO PLAYERS, SAME TEAM, EACH GAINING 1,000 YARDS OR MORE
Season

22 times. Most recent: North Caro., 1993—Curtis Johnson (1,034) & Leon Johnson (1,012)

TWO PLAYERS, SAME TEAM, EACH GAINING 200 YARDS OR MORE
Game

Gordon Brown, 214 (23 rushes) & Steve Gage (QB), 206 (26 rushes), Tulsa vs. Wichita St., Nov. 2, 1985

TWO OPPOSING I-A PLAYERS EACH GAINING 200 YARDS OR MORE
Game

Barry Sanders, Oklahoma St. (215) & Mike Gaddis, Oklahoma (213), Nov. 5, 1988; George Swarn, Miami (Ohio) (239) & Otis Cheathem, Western Mich. (219), Sept. 8, 1984

MOST YARDS GAINED BY TWO OPPOSING PLAYERS
Game

553—Marshall Faulk, San Diego St. (386) & Ryan Benjamin, Pacific (Cal.) (167), Sept. 14, 1991

MOST YARDS GAINED BY TWO PLAYERS, SAME TEAM
Game

476—Tony Sands (396) & Chip Hilleary (80), Kansas vs. Missouri, Nov. 23, 1991

Season

2,997—Barry Sanders (2,628) & Gerald Hudson (Sanders' backup, 369), Oklahoma St., 1988

Also hold per-game record at 272.5

Career

8,193—Eric Dickerson (4,450) & Craig James (3,743), Southern Methodist, 1979-82 (alternated at the same position during the last 36 games)

MOST YARDS GAINED IN FIRST GAME OF CAREER

220—Alan Thompson, Wisconsin vs. Oklahoma, Sept. 20, 1969

MOST YARDS GAINED BY A FRESHMAN IN FIRST GAME OF CAREER

212—Greg Hill, Texas A&M vs. Louisiana St., Sept. 14, 1991 (30 carries)

LONGEST RUSH BY A FRESHMAN IN FIRST GAME OF CAREER

98—Jerald Sowell, Tulane vs. Alabama, Sept. 4, 1993

MOST YARDS GAINED IN OPENING GAME OF SEASON

343—Tony Jeffery, Texas Christian vs. Tulane, Sept. 13, 1986 (16 rushes)

MOST YARDS GAINED AGAINST ONE OPPONENT
Career

(4 yrs.) 754—Tony Dorsett, Pittsburgh vs. Notre Dame, 1973-76 (96 rushes)

(3 yrs.) 690—Mike Gaddis, Oklahoma vs. Oklahoma St., 1988-89, 1991 (82 rushes)

MOST YARDS GAINED PER GAME AGAINST ONE OPPONENT
Career

(Min. 2 games) 256.0—Marshall Faulk, San Diego St. vs. Hawaii, 1991, 1992 (512 yards, 65 rushes)

(Min. 3 games) 230.0—Mike Gaddis, Oklahoma vs. Oklahoma St., 1988-89, 1991 (690 yards, 82 rushes)

HIGHEST AVERAGE GAIN PER RUSH
Game

(Min. 8-14 rushes) 30.2—Kevin Lowe, Wyoming vs. South Dak. St., Nov. 10, 1984 (10 for 302)

(Min. 15-25 rushes) 21.4—Tony Jeffery, Texas Christian vs. Tulane, Sept. 13, 1986 (16 for 343)

(Min. 26 rushes) 13.7—Eddie Lee Ivery, Georgia Tech vs. Air Force, Nov. 11, 1978 (26 for 356)

Season

(Min. 101-213 rushes) 9.6—Chuck Weatherspoon, Houston, 1989 (119 for 1,146)

(Min. 214-281 rushes) 7.8—Mike Rozier, Nebraska, 1983 (275 for 2,148)

(Min. 282 rushes) 7.6—Barry Sanders, Oklahoma St., 1988 (344 for 2,628)

Glenn Davis, Army, 1945, holds the record for a minimum of 75 rushes—11.5 (82 for 944)

Career

(Min. 300-413 rushes) 8.3—Glenn Davis, Army, 1943-46 (358 for 2,957)

(Min. 414-780 rushes) 7.2—Mike Rozier, Nebraska, 1981-83 (668 for 4,780)

(Min. 781 rushes) 6.1—Archie Griffin, Ohio St., 1972-75 (845 for 5,177)

MOST TOUCHDOWNS SCORED BY RUSHING
Game

8—Howard Griffith, Illinois vs. Southern Ill., Sept. 22, 1990 (5, 51, 7, 41, 5, 18, 5, 3 yards; Griffith scored three touchdowns [51, 7, 41] on consecutive carries and scored four touchdowns in the third quarter)

Season

37—Barry Sanders, Oklahoma St., 1988 (11 games)

Also holds per-game record at 3.36 (37 in 11)

Career
64—Anthony Thompson, Indiana, 1986-89

MOST GAMES SCORING TWO OR MORE TOUCHDOWNS BY RUSHING
Season
11—Barry Sanders, Oklahoma St., 1988

MOST CONSECUTIVE GAMES SCORING TWO OR MORE TOUCHDOWNS BY RUSHING
Career
12—Barry Sanders, Oklahoma St. (last game of 1987, all 11 in 1988)

MOST TOUCHDOWNS SCORED BY RUSHING BY A FRESHMAN
Game
7—Marshall Faulk, San Diego St. vs. Pacific (Cal.), Sept. 14, 1991
Season
21—Marshall Faulk, San Diego St., 1991
Also holds per-game record at 2.3 (21 in 9)

MOST RUSHING TOUCHDOWNS SCORED BY A QUARTERBACK
Game
6—Dee Dowis, Air Force vs. San Diego St., Sept. 1, 1989 (55, 28, 12, 16, 60, 17 yards; 249 yards rushing on 13 carries)
Season
19—Stacey Robinson, Northern Ill., 1990, 1989; Brian Mitchell, Southwestern La., 1989; Fred Solomon, Tampa, 1974
Career
47—Brian Mitchell, Southwestern La., 1986-89 (in 43 games)

MOST TOUCHDOWNS SCORED IN ONE QUARTER
4—Howard Griffith, Illinois vs. Southern Ill., Sept. 22, 1990 (all rushing, 3rd quarter); Dick Felt, Brigham Young vs. San Jose St., Nov. 8, 1952 (all rushing, 4th quarter)

MOST QB TOUCHDOWNS OVER TWO CONSECUTIVE SEASONS
38—Stacey Robinson, Northern Ill., 1989-90 (19 and 19)

MOST YARDS GAINED BY TWO BROTHERS
Season
3,690—Barry Sanders, Oklahoma St. (2,628) & Byron Sanders, Northwestern (1,062), 1988

Passing

HIGHEST PASSING EFFICIENCY RATING POINTS
Game
(Min. 12-24 atts.) 403.4—Tim Clifford, Indiana vs. Colorado, Sept. 26, 1980 (14 attempts, 11 completions, 0 interceptions, 345 yards, 5 TD passes)
(Min. 25-49 atts.) 273.8—Tom Tunnicliffe, Arizona vs. Pacific (Cal.), Oct. 23, 1982 (28 attempts, 21 completions, 0 interceptions, 427 yards, 6 TD passes)
(Min. 50 atts.) 197.8—David Klingler, Houston vs. Eastern Wash., Nov. 17, 1990 (58 attempts, 41 completions, 2 interceptions, 572 yards, 11 TD passes)
Season
(Min. 15 atts. per game) 176.9—Jim McMahon, Brigham Young, 1980 (445 attempts, 284 completions, 18 interceptions, 4,571 yards, 47 TD passes)
Career
(Min. 200 comps.) 162.73—Ty Detmer, Brigham Young, 1988-91 (1,530 attempts, 958 completions, 65 interceptions, 15,031 yards, 121 TD passes)

HIGHEST PASSING EFFICIENCY RATING POINTS BY A FRESHMAN
Season
(Min. 15 atts. per game) 148.0—Kerwin Bell, Florida, 1984 (184 attempts, 98 completions, 7 interceptions, 1,614 yards, 16 TD passes)

MOST PASSES ATTEMPTED
Quarter
32—Jack Trudeau, Illinois vs. Purdue, Oct. 12, 1985 (4th, completed 14)

Half
48—David Klingler, Houston vs. Southern Methodist, Oct. 20, 1990 (1st, completed 32)
Game
79—Matt Vogler, Texas Christian vs. Houston, Nov. 3, 1990 (completed 44)
Season
643—David Klingler, Houston, 1990 (11 games, completed 374)
2 Yrs
1,140—David Klingler, Houston, 1990-91 (completed 652)
3 Yrs
1,377—Ty Detmer, Brigham Young, 1989-91 (completed 875)
Career
(4 yrs.) 1,530—Ty Detmer, Brigham Young, 1988-91 (completed 958)

MOST PASSES ATTEMPTED PER GAME
Season
58.5—David Klingler, Houston, 1990 (643 in 11)
Career
39.6—Mike Perez, San Jose St., 1986-87 (792 in 20)

MOST PASSES ATTEMPTED BY A FRESHMAN
Game
71—Sandy Schwab, Northwestern vs. Michigan, Oct. 23, 1982 (completed 45)
Season
503—Mike Romo, Southern Methodist, 1989 (completed 282)

MOST PASSES COMPLETED
Quarter
21—Mike Romo, Southern Methodist vs. Rice, Nov. 10, 1990 (4th, attempted 31)
Half
32—David Klingler, Houston vs. Southern Methodist, Oct. 20, 1990 (1st, attempted 48)
Game
48—David Klingler, Houston vs. Southern Methodist, Oct. 20, 1990 (attempted 76)
Season
374—David Klingler, Houston, 1990 (11 games, attempted 643)
2 Yrs
652—David Klingler, Houston, 1990-91 (attempted 1,140)
Also holds per-game record at 31.0 (652 in 21)
3 Yrs
875—Ty Detmer, Brigham Young, 1989-91 (attempted 1,377)
Per-game record—24.8, David Klingler, Houston, 1989-91 (720 in 29)
Career
(4 yrs.) 958—Ty Detmer, Brigham Young, 1988-91 (attempted 1,530)

MOST PASSES COMPLETED PER GAME
Season
34.0—David Klingler, Houston, 1990 (374 in 11)
Career
25.9—Doug Gaynor, Long Beach St., 1984-85 (569 in 22)

MOST PASSES COMPLETED BY A FRESHMAN
Game
45—Sandy Schwab, Northwestern vs. Michigan, Oct. 23, 1982 (attempted 71)
Season
282—Mike Romo, Southern Methodist, 1989 (attempted 503)
Also holds per-game record at 25.6 (282 in 11)

MOST CONSECUTIVE PASSES COMPLETED
Game
22—Chuck Long, Iowa vs. Indiana, Oct. 27, 1984
Season
22—Chuck Long, Iowa vs. Indiana, Oct. 27, 1984; Steve Young, Brigham Young, 1982 (completed last 8 attempts vs. Utah St., Oct. 30, and first 14 vs. Wyoming, Nov. 6)

MOST PASSES COMPLETED IN TWO, THREE AND FOUR CONSECUTIVE GAMES
2 Games
82—David Klingler, Houston, 1990 (48 vs. Southern Methodist, Oct. 20; 34 vs. Arkansas, Oct. 27) and

1990 (41 vs. Eastern Wash., Nov. 17; 41 vs. Arizona St., Dec. 2)
3 Games
118—David Klingler, Houston, 1990-91 (41 vs. Eastern Wash., Nov. 17, 1990; 41 vs. Arizona St., Dec. 2, 1990; 36 vs. Louisiana Tech, Aug. 31, 1991) and 1990 (48 vs. Southern Methodist, Oct. 20; 34 vs. Arkansas, Oct. 27; 36 vs. Texas Christian, Nov. 3)
4 Games
144—Andre Ware, Houston, 1989 (42 vs. Texas Christian, Nov. 4; 29 vs. Texas, Nov. 11; 37 vs. Texas Tech, Nov. 25; 36 vs. Rice, Dec. 2)

HIGHEST PERCENTAGE OF PASSES COMPLETED
Game
(Min. 20-29 comps.) 92.6%—Rick Neuheisel, UCLA vs. Washington, Oct. 29, 1983 (25 of 27)
(Min. 30-39 comps.) 83.3%—Todd Santos, San Diego St. vs. Utah, Sept. 12, 1987 (35 of 42)
(Min. 40 comps.) 81.1%—Rich Campbell, California vs. Florida, Sept. 13, 1980 (43 of 53)
Season
(Min. 150 atts.) 71.3%—Steve Young, Brigham Young, 1983 (306 of 429)
Career
(Min. 875-999 atts.) 65.2%—Steve Young, Brigham Young, 1981-83 (592 of 908)
(Min. 1,000-1,099 atts.) 64.6%—$Chuck Long, Iowa, 1981-85 (692 of 1,072)
(Min. 1,100 atts.) 63.9%—Jack Trudeau, Illinois, 1981, 1983-85 (736 of 1,151)

$ See page 6 for explanation.

HIGHEST PERCENTAGE OF PASSES COMPLETED BY A FRESHMAN
Season
(Min. 200 atts.) 66.2%—Grady Benton, Arizona St., 1992 (149 of 225)

MOST PASSES HAD INTERCEPTED
Game
9—John Reaves, Florida vs. Auburn, Nov. 1, 1969 (attempted 66)
Season
34—John Eckman, Wichita St., 1966 (attempted 458)
Also holds per-game record at 3.4 (34 in 10)
Career
(3 yrs.) 68—Zeke Bratkowski, Georgia, 1951-53 (attempted 734)
(4 yrs.) 73—Mark Herrmann, Purdue, 1977-80 (attempted 1,218)
Per-game record—2.3, Steve Ramsey, North Texas, 1967-69 (67 in 29)

LOWEST PERCENTAGE OF PASSES HAD INTERCEPTED
Season
(Min. 150-349 atts.) 0.0%—Matt Blundin, Virginia, 1991 (0 of 224)
(Min. 350 atts.) 1.1%—Charlie Ward, Florida St., 1993 (4 of 380)
Career
(Min. 600-799 atts.) 1.7%—Damon Allen, Cal St. Fullerton, 1981-84 (11 of 629)
(Min. 800-1,049 atts.) 2.3%—Anthony Calvillo, Utah St., 1992-93 (19 of 829)
(Min. 1,050 atts.) 2.9%—Brett Favre, Southern Miss., 1987-90 (34 of 1,169)

MOST PASSES ATTEMPTED WITHOUT AN INTERCEPTION
Game
68—David Klingler, Houston vs. Baylor, Oct. 6, 1990 (completed 35)
Entire Season
224—Matt Blundin, Virginia, 1991 (completed 135)

MOST CONSECUTIVE PASSES ATTEMPTED WITHOUT AN INTERCEPTION
Season
271—Trent Dilfer, Fresno St., 1993
Career
271—Trent Dilfer, Fresno St., 1993

MOST CONSECUTIVE PASSES ATTEMPTED WITH JUST ONE INTERCEPTION
Career
329—Damon Allen, Cal St. Fullerton, 1983-84 (during

16 games; began Oct. 8, 1983, vs. Nevada, ended Nov. 3, 1984, vs. Fresno St. Interception occurred vs. Idaho, Sept. 15, 1984)

MOST CONSECUTIVE PASSES ATTEMPTED WITHOUT AN INTERCEPTION AT THE START OF CAREER
138—Mike Gundy, Oklahoma St., 1986 (during 8 games)

MOST YARDS GAINED
Quarter
340—Andre Ware, Houston vs. Southern Methodist, Oct. 21, 1989 (2nd)
Half
517—Andre Ware, Houston vs. Southern Methodist, Oct. 21, 1989 (1st, completed 25 of 41)
Game
716—David Klingler, Houston vs. Arizona St., Dec. 2, 1990 (41 of 70)
Season
(12 games) 5,188—Ty Detmer, Brigham Young, 1990 (completed 361 of 562)
(11 games) 5,140—David Klingler, Houston, 1990 (completed 374 of 643)
2 Yrs
9,748—Ty Detmer, Brigham Young, 1989-90 (completed 626 of 974)
3 Yrs
13,779—Ty Detmer, Brigham Young, 1989-91 (completed 875 of 1,377)
Career
(4 yrs.) 15,031—Ty Detmer, Brigham Young, 1988-91 (completed 958 of 1,530)

MOST YARDS GAINED PER GAME
Season
467.3—David Klingler, Houston, 1990 (5,140 in 11)
2 Yrs
406.2—Ty Detmer, Brigham Young, 1989-90 (9,748 in 24)
3 Yrs
382.8—Ty Detmer, Brigham Young, 1989-91 (13,779 in 36)
Career
326.8—Ty Detmer, Brigham Young, 1988-91 (15,031 in 46)

MOST YARDS GAINED BY A FRESHMAN
Game
469—Ben Bennett, Duke vs. Wake Forest, Nov. 8, 1980
Season
3,020—Todd Ellis, South Caro., 1986
Also holds per-game record at 274.5 (3,020 in 11)

MOST YARDS GAINED BY A SOPHOMORE
Game
631—Scott Mitchell, Utah vs. Air Force, Oct. 15, 1988
Season
4,560—Ty Detmer, Brigham Young, 1989
Per-game record—392.9, Scott Mitchell, Utah, 1988 (4,322 in 11)

MOST SEASONS GAINING 2,000 YARDS OR MORE
Career
4—Glenn Foley, Boston College, 1990-93 (2,189—2,225—2,231—3,397); Alex Van Pelt, Pittsburgh, 1989-92 (2,527—2,427—2,796—3,163); T. J. Rubley, Tulsa, 1987-89, 1991 (2,058—2,497—2,292—2,054); Tom Hodson, Louisiana St., 1986-89 (2,261—2,125—2,074—2,655); Todd Santos, San Diego St., 1984-87 (2,063—2,877—2,553—3,932); Kevin Sweeney, Fresno St., 1983-86 (2,359—3,259—2,604—2,363)

MOST YARDS GAINED IN TWO, THREE AND FOUR CONSECUTIVE GAMES
2 Games
1,288—David Klingler, Houston, 1990 (572 vs. Eastern Wash., Nov. 17; 716 vs. Arizona St., Dec. 2)
3 Games
1,798—David Klingler, Houston, 1990-91 (572 vs. Eastern Wash., Nov. 17, 1990; 716 vs. Arizona St., Dec. 2, 1990; 510 vs. Louisiana Tech, Aug. 31, 1991)
4 Games
2,150—David Klingler, Houston, 1990 (563 vs. Texas Christian, Nov. 3; 299 vs. Texas, Nov. 10; 572 vs. Eastern Wash., Nov. 17; 716 vs. Arizona St., Dec. 2)

MOST GAMES GAINING 200 YARDS OR MORE
Season
12—Ty Detmer, Brigham Young, 1990, 1989; Robbie Bosco, Brigham Young, 1985, 1984
Career
38—Ty Detmer, Brigham Young, 1988-91

MOST CONSECUTIVE GAMES GAINING 200 YARDS OR MORE
Season
12—Ty Detmer, Brigham Young, 1990, 1989; Robbie Bosco, Brigham Young, 1984
Career
27—Ty Detmer, Brigham Young (from Sept. 2, 1989, to Sept. 21, 1991)

MOST GAMES GAINING 300 YARDS OR MORE
Season
12—Ty Detmer, Brigham Young, 1990, 1989
Career
33—Ty Detmer, Brigham Young, 1988-91

MOST CONSECUTIVE GAMES GAINING 300 YARDS OR MORE
Season
12—Ty Detmer, Brigham Young, 1990, 1989
Career
24—Ty Detmer, Brigham Young (from Sept. 2, 1989, to Dec. 1, 1990)

MOST GAMES GAINING 400 YARDS OR MORE
Season
9—David Klingler, Houston, 1990
Career
12—Ty Detmer, Brigham Young, 1988-90

MOST YARDS GAINED BY TWO OPPOSING PLAYERS
Game
1,253—Matt Vogler, Texas Christian (690) & David Klingler, Houston (563), Nov. 3, 1990

TWO PLAYERS, SAME TEAM, EACH PASSING FOR 250 YARDS OR MORE
Game
Andre Ware (517) & David Klingler (254), Houston vs. Southern Methodist, Oct. 21, 1989; Steve Cottrell (311) & John Elway (270), Stanford vs. Arizona St., Oct. 24, 1981

MOST YARDS GAINED IN OPENING GAME OF SEASON
511—Scott Mitchell, Utah vs. Idaho St., Sept. 10, 1988

MOST YARDS GAINED AGAINST ONE OPPONENT
Career
1,495—Ty Detmer, Brigham Young vs. New Mexico, 1988-91

MOST YARDS GAINED PER GAME AGAINST ONE OPPONENT
Career
(Min. 3 games) 410.7—Gary Schofield, Wake Forest vs. Maryland, 1981-83 (1,232 yards)
Career
(Min. 4 games) 373.8—Ty Detmer, Brigham Young vs. New Mexico, 1988-91 (1,495 yards)

MOST YARDS GAINED PER ATTEMPT
Game
(Min. 25-39 atts.) 15.4—Glenn Foley, Boston College vs. Virginia Tech, Nov. 6, 1993 (29 for 448)
(Min. 40-59 atts.) 14.1—John Walsh, Brigham Young vs. Utah St., Oct. 30, 1993 (44 for 619)
(Min. 60 atts.) 10.5—Scott Mitchell, Utah vs. Air Force, Oct. 15, 1988 (60 for 631)
Season
(Min. 412 atts.) 11.1—Ty Detmer, Brigham Young, 1989 (412 for 4,560)
Career
(Min. 1,000 atts.) 9.8—Ty Detmer, Brigham Young, 1988-91 (1,530 for 15,031)

MOST YARDS GAINED PER COMPLETION
Game
(Min. 22-41 comps.) 22.9—John Walsh, Brigham Young vs. Utah St., Oct. 30, 1993 (27 for 619)
(Min. 42 comps.) 15.7—Matt Vogler, Texas Christian vs. Houston, Nov. 3, 1990 (44 for 690)
Season
(Min. 109-204 comps.) 18.2—Doug Williams, Grambling, 1977 (181 for 3,286)
(Min. 205 comps.) 17.2—Ty Detmer, Brigham Young, 1989 (265 for 4,560)
Career
(Min. 275-399 comps.) 17.3—J. J. Joe, Baylor, 1990-93 (347 for 5,995)
(Min. 400 comps.) 15.7—Shawn Moore, Virginia, 1987-90 (421 for 6,629)

MOST TOUCHDOWN PASSES
Quarter
6—David Klingler, Houston vs. Louisiana Tech, Aug. 31, 1991 (2nd)
Half
7—Dennis Shaw, San Diego St. vs. New Mexico St., Nov. 15, 1969 (1st)
Game
11—David Klingler, Houston vs. Eastern Wash., Nov. 17, 1990
Season
54—David Klingler, Houston, 1990 (11 games)
2 Yrs
83—David Klingler, Houston, 1990-91
Also holds per-game record at 4.0 (83 in 21)
3 Yrs
108—Ty Detmer, Brigham Young, 1989-91
Career
121—Ty Detmer, Brigham Young, 1988-91

MOST TOUCHDOWN PASSES PER GAME
Season
4.9—David Klingler, Houston, 1990 (54 in 11)
Career
2.8—David Klingler, Houston, 1988-91 (91 in 32)
Collegiate record—2.9, Dennis Shaw, San Diego St., 1968-69 (58 in 20)

HIGHEST PERCENTAGE OF PASSES FOR TOUCHDOWNS
Season
(Min. 175-374 atts.) 11.6%—Dennis Shaw, San Diego St., 1969 (39 of 335)
(Min. 375 atts.) 10.6%—Jim McMahon, Brigham Young, 1980 (47 of 445)
Career
(Min. 400-499 atts.) 9.7%—Rick Leach, Michigan, 1975-78 (45 of 462)
(Min. 500 atts.) 9.1%—Danny White, Arizona St., 1971-73 (59 of 649)

MOST CONSECUTIVE GAMES THROWING A TOUCHDOWN PASS
Career
35—Ty Detmer, Brigham Young (from Sept. 7, 1989, to Nov. 23, 1991)

MOST CONSECUTIVE PASSES COMPLETED FOR TOUCHDOWNS
Game
6—Brooks Dawson, UTEP vs. New Mexico, Oct. 28, 1967 (first six completions of the game)

MOST TOUCHDOWN PASSES IN FIRST GAME OF CAREER
5—John Reaves, Florida vs. Houston, Sept. 20, 1969

MOST TOUCHDOWN PASSES BY A FRESHMAN
Game
6—Bob Hoernschemeyer, Indiana vs. Nebraska, Oct. 9, 1943
Season
22—Danny Wuerffel, Florida, 1993

MOST TOUCHDOWN PASSES IN FRESHMAN AND SOPHOMORE SEASONS
45—Ty Detmer, Brigham Young, 1988 (13) & 1989 (32)

MOST TOUCHDOWN PASSES BY A SOPHOMORE
32—Jimmy Klingler, Houston, 1992; Ty Detmer, Brigham Young, 1989

MOST TOUCHDOWN PASSES AT CONCLUSION OF JUNIOR YEAR
86—Ty Detmer, Brigham Young, 1988 (13), 1989

(32) & 1990 (41)

MOST TOUCHDOWN PASSES, SAME PASSER AND RECEIVER
Season
19—Elvis Grbac to Desmond Howard, Michigan, 1991; Andre Ware to Manny Hazard, Houston, 1989
Career
33—Troy Kopp to Aaron Turner, Pacific (Cal.), 1989-92

MOST PASSES ATTEMPTED WITHOUT A TOUCHDOWN PASS
Season
266—Stu Rayburn, Kent, 1984 (completed 125)

FEWEST TIMES SACKED ATTEMPTING TO PASS
Season
(Min. 300 atts.) 4—Steve Walsh, Miami (Fla.), 1988, in 390 attempts. Last 4 games of the season: Tulsa, 1 for -8 yards; Louisiana St., 1 for -2; Arkansas, 1 for -12; Brigham Young, 1 for -9.

Receiving

MOST PASSES CAUGHT
Game
22—Jay Miller, Brigham Young vs. New Mexico, Nov. 3, 1973 (263 yards)
Season
142—Manny Hazard, Houston, 1989 (1,689 yards)
Career
(2 yrs.) 220—Manny Hazard, Houston, 1989-90 (2,635 yards)
(3 yrs.) 261—Howard Twilley, Tulsa, 1963-65 (3,343 yards)
(4 yrs.) 266—Aaron Turner, Pacific (Cal.), 1989-92 (4,345 yards)

MOST PASSES CAUGHT PER GAME
Season
13.4—Howard Twilley, Tulsa, 1965 (134 in 10)
Career
10.5—Manny Hazard, Houston, 1989-90 (220 in 21)

MOST PASSES CAUGHT BY TWO PLAYERS, SAME TEAM
Season
212—Howard Twilley (134) & Neal Sweeney (78), Tulsa, 1965 (2,662 yards, 24 TDs)
Career
453—Mark Templeton (262) & Charles Lockett (191), Long Beach St., 1983-86 (4,871 yards, 30 TDs)

MOST PASSES CAUGHT IN CONSECUTIVE GAMES
38—Manny Hazard, Houston, 1989 (19 vs. Texas Christian, Nov. 4; 19 vs. Texas, Nov. 11)

MOST CONSECUTIVE GAMES CATCHING A PASS
Career
46—Carl Winston, New Mexico, 1990-93 (every game)

MOST PASSES CAUGHT BY A TIGHT END
Game
17—Jon Harvey, Northwestern vs. Michigan, Oct. 23, 1982 (208 yards); Emilio Vallez, New Mexico vs. UTEP, Oct. 27, 1967 (257 yards)
Season
73—Dennis Smith, Utah, 1989 (1,089 yards)
Career
181—Kelly Blackwell, Texas Christian, 1988-91 (2,155 yards)

MOST PASSES CAUGHT PER GAME BY A TIGHT END
Season
6.4—Mark Dowdell, Bowling Green, 1983 (70 in 11); Chuck Scott, Vanderbilt, 1983 (70 in 11)
Career
5.4—Gordon Hudson, Brigham Young, 1980-83 (178 in 33)

MOST PASSES CAUGHT BY A RUNNING BACK
Game
18—Mark Templeton, Long Beach St. vs. Utah St., Nov. 1, 1986 (173 yards)

Season
99—Mark Templeton, Long Beach St., 1986 (688 yards)
Career
262—Mark Templeton, Long Beach St., 1983-86 (1,969 yards)

MOST PASSES CAUGHT BY A FRESHMAN
Game
18—Richard Woodley (WR), Texas Christian vs. Texas Tech, Nov. 10, 1990 (180 yards)
Season
61—Jason Wolf, Southern Methodist, 1989 (676 yards)
Also holds per-game record at 5.5

CATCHING AT LEAST 50 PASSES AND GAINING AT LEAST 1,000 YARDS RUSHING
Season
By 10 players. Most recent: Ryan Benjamin, Pacific (Cal.), 1991 (51 catches and 1,581 yards rushing) Darrin Nelson, Stanford, holds record for most seasons at 3 (1977-78, 1981)

CATCHING AT LEAST 60 PASSES AND GAINING AT LEAST 1,000 YARDS RUSHING
Johnny Johnson, San Jose St., 1988 (61 catches and 1,219 yards rushing); Brad Muster, Stanford, 1986 (61 catches and 1,053 yards rushing); Darrin Nelson, Stanford, 1981 (67 catches and 1,014 yards rushing)

MOST YARDS GAINED
Game
349—Chuck Hughes, UTEP vs. North Texas, Sept. 18, 1965 (caught 10)
Season
1,779—Howard Twilley, Tulsa, 1965 (caught 134)
Career
4,357—Ryan Yarborough, Wyoming, 1990-93 (caught 229)

MOST YARDS GAINED PER GAME
Season
177.9—Howard Twilley, Tulsa, 1965 (1,779 in 10)
Career
128.6—Howard Twilley, Tulsa, 1963-65 (3,343 in 26)

MOST YARDS GAINED BY A TIGHT END
Game
259—Gordon Hudson, Brigham Young vs. Utah, Nov. 21, 1981 (caught 13)
Season
1,156—Chris Smith, Brigham Young, 1990 (caught 68)
Career
2,484—Gordon Hudson, Brigham Young, 1980-83 (caught 178)

MOST YARDS GAINED PER GAME BY A TIGHT END
Season
102.0—Mike Moore, Grambling, 1977 (1,122 in 11)
Career
75.3—Gordon Hudson, Brigham Young, 1980-83 (2,484 in 33)

MOST YARDS GAINED BY A FRESHMAN
Game
243—Darnay Scott, San Diego St. vs. Brigham Young, Nov. 16, 1991 (caught 8)
Season
870—Cormac Carney, Air Force, 1978 (caught 57)
Also holds per-game record at 79.1

MOST GAMES GAINING 100 YARDS OR MORE
Season
11—Aaron Turner, Pacific (Cal.), 1991
Also holds consecutive record at 11
Career
23—Aaron Turner, Pacific (Cal.), 1989-92 (in 44 games played)

MOST GAMES GAINING 200 YARDS OR MORE
Season
5—Howard Twilley, Tulsa, 1965
Also holds consecutive record at 3

MOST YARDS GAINED BY TWO PLAYERS, SAME TEAM
Game
640—Rick Eber (322) & Harry Wood (318), Tulsa vs. Idaho St., Oct. 7, 1967 (caught 33, 6 TDs)
Season
2,662—Howard Twilley (1,779) & Neal Sweeney (883), Tulsa, 1965

TWO PLAYERS, SAME TEAM, EACH GAINING 1,000 YARDS
Bryan Reeves (1,362; 91 catches) & Michael Stephens, (1,062; 80 catches), Nevada, 1993; Charles Johnson (1,149; 57 catches) & Michael Westbrook (1,060; 76 catches), Colorado, 1992; Andy Boyce (1,241; 79 catches) & Chris Smith (1,156; 68 catches), Brigham Young, 1990; Patrick Rowe (1,392; 71 catches) & Dennis Arey (1,118; 68 catches), San Diego St., 1990; Jason Phillips (1,443; 108 catches) & James Dixon (1,103; 102 catches), Houston, 1988

TWO PLAYERS, SAME TEAM, RANKED NO. 1 & NO. 2 IN FINAL RECEIVING RANKINGS
Season
Jason Phillips (No. 1, 9.8 catches per game) & James Dixon (No. 2, 9.3 catches per game), Houston, 1988

THREE PLAYERS, SAME TEAM, EACH CATCHING 60 PASSES OR MORE
Patrick Rowe (71), Dennis Arey (68) & Jimmy Raye (62), San Diego St., 1990

MOST 1,000-YARD RECEIVING SEASONS
3—Ryan Yarborough, Wyoming, 1991-93 (1,081 in 1991; 1,351 in 1992; 1,512 in 1993); Aaron Turner, Pacific (Cal.), 1990-92 (1,264 in 1990; 1,604 in 1991; 1,171 in 1992); Clarkston Hines, Duke, 1987-89 (1,084 in 1987; 1,067 in 1988; 1,149 in 1989); Marc Zeno, Tulane, 1985-87 (1,137 in 1985; 1,033 in 1986; 1,206 in 1987)

HIGHEST AVERAGE GAIN PER RECEPTION
Game
(Min. 3-4 receps.) 72.7—Terry Gallaher, East Caro. vs. Appalachian St., Sept. 13, 1975 (3 for 218; 82, 77, 59 yards)
(Min. 5-9 receps.) 52.6—Alexander Wright, Auburn vs. Pacific (Cal.), Sept. 9, 1989 (5 for 263; 78, 60, 41, 73, 11 yards)
(Min. 10 receps.) 34.9—Chuck Hughes, UTEP vs. North Texas, Sept. 18, 1965 (10 for 349)
Season
(Min. 30-49 receps.) 27.9—Elmo Wright, Houston, 1968 (43 for 1,198)
(Min. 50 receps.) 24.4—Henry Ellard, Fresno St., 1982 (62 for 1,510)
Career
(Min. 75-104 receps.) 25.7—Wesley Walker, California, 1973-76 (86 for 2,206)
(Min. 105 receps.) 22.0—Herman Moore, Virginia, 1988-90 (114 for 2,504)

HIGHEST AVERAGE GAIN PER RECEPTION BY A TIGHT END
Season
(Min. 30 receps.) 22.6—Jay Novacek, Wyoming, 1984 (33 for 745)
Career
(Min. 75 receps.) 19.2—Clay Brown, Brigham Young, 1978-80 (88 for 1,691)

MOST TOUCHDOWN PASSES CAUGHT
Game
6—Tim Delaney, San Diego St. vs. New Mexico St., Nov. 15, 1969 (16 receptions)
Season
22—Manny Hazard, Houston, 1989 (142 receptions)
Per-game record—2.3, Tom Reynolds, San Diego St. 1969 (18 in 8)
Career
43—Aaron Turner, Pacific (Cal.), 1989-92 (266 receptions)

MOST GAMES CATCHING A TOUCHDOWN PASS
Season
10—Ryan Yarborough, Wyoming, 1993; Desmond Howard, Michigan, 1991; Aaron Turner, Pacific

(Cal.), 1991; Herman Moore, Virginia, 1990; Manny Hazard, Houston, 1989
Career
27—Ryan Yarborough, Wyoming, 1990-93 (caught a total of 42 in 46 games)

MOST CONSECUTIVE GAMES CATCHING A TOUCHDOWN PASS
Season
10—Desmond Howard, Michigan, 1991
Career
12—Desmond Howard, Michigan (last two games of 1990 and first 10 games of 1991); Aaron Turner, Pacific (Cal.) (last three games of 1990 and first nine games of 1991)

MOST TOUCHDOWN PASSES CAUGHT BY A TIGHT END
Season
18—Dennis Smith, Utah, 1989 (73 receptions)
Career
24—Dennis Smith, Utah, 1987-89 (156 receptions); Dave Young, Purdue, 1977-80 (172 receptions)

HIGHEST PERCENTAGE OF PASSES CAUGHT FOR TOUCHDOWNS
Season
(Min. 10 TDs) 58.8%—Kevin Williams, Southern Cal, 1978 (10 of 17)
Career
(Min. 20 TDs) 35.3%—Kevin Williams, Southern Cal, 1977-80 (24 of 68)
Also holds record for touchdown frequency: 1 TD every 2.8 catches

HIGHEST AVERAGE YARDS PER TOUCHDOWN PASS
Season
(Min. 10) 56.1—Elmo Wright, Houston, 1968 (11 for 617 yards; 87, 50, 75, 2, 80, 79, 13, 67, 61, 43, 60 yards)
Career
(Min. 15) 46.5—Charles Johnson, Colorado, 1990-93 (15 for 697 yards)

MOST TOUCHDOWN PASSES CAUGHT, 50 YARDS OR MORE
Season
8—Henry Ellard, Fresno St., 1982 (68, 51, 80, 61, 67, 72, 80, 72 yards); Elmo Wright, Houston, 1968 (87, 50, 75, 80, 79, 67, 61, 60 yards)

MOST CONSECUTIVE PASSES CAUGHT FOR TOUCHDOWNS
6—Gerald Armstrong, Nebraska, 1992 (1 vs. Utah, Sept. 5; 1 vs. Arizona St., Sept. 26; 1 vs. Oklahoma St., Oct. 10; 1 vs. Colorado, Oct. 31; 2 vs. Kansas, Nov. 7); Carlos Carson, Louisiana St., 1977 (5 vs. Rice, Sept. 24; 1 vs. Florida, Oct. 1; first receptions of his career)

MOST TOUCHDOWN PASSES CAUGHT BY A FRESHMAN
Season
10—Dwight Collins, Pittsburgh, 1980

Punting

MOST PUNTS
Game
36—Charlie Calhoun, Texas Tech vs. Centenary (La.), Nov. 11, 1939 (1,318 yards; 20 were returned, 8 went out of bounds, 6 were downed, 1 was blocked [blocked kicks counted against the punter until 1955] and 1 went into the end zone for a touchback. Thirty-three of the punts occurred on first down during a heavy downpour in the game played at Shreveport, Louisiana)
Season
101—Jim Bailey, Va. Military, 1969 (3,507 yards)
Career
(3 yrs.) 276—Jim Bailey, Va. Military, 1969-71 (10,127 yards)
(4 yrs.) 320—Cameron Young, Texas Christian, 1976-79 (12,947 yards)

HIGHEST AVERAGE PER PUNT
Game
(Min. 5-9 punts) 60.4—Lee Johnson, Brigham Young vs. Wyoming, Oct. 8, 1983 (5 for 302; 53, 44, 63, 62, 80 yards)
(Min. 10 punts) 53.6—Jim Benien, Oklahoma St. vs. Colorado, Nov. 13, 1971 (10 for 536)
Season
(Min. 40-49 punts) 49.8—Reggie Roby, Iowa, 1981 (44 for 2,193)
(Min. 50-74 punts) 48.2—Ricky Anderson, Vanderbilt, 1984 (58 for 2,793)
(Min. 75 punts) 45.8—Bucky Scribner, Kansas, 1982 (76 for 3,478)
Career
(Min. 150-199 punts) 45.6—Reggie Roby, Iowa, 1979-82 (172 for 7,849)
(Min. 200-249 punts) 44.7—Ray Guy, Southern Miss., 1970-72 (200 for 8,934)
(Min. 250 punts) 44.3—Bill Smith, Mississippi, 1983-86 (254 for 11,260)

HIGHEST AVERAGE PER PUNT BY A FRESHMAN
Season
(Min. 40 punts) 47.0—Tom Tupa, Ohio St., 1984 (41 for 1,927)

MOST YARDS ON PUNTS
Game
1,318—Charlie Calhoun, Texas Tech vs. Centenary (La.), Nov. 11, 1939 (36 punts)
Season
4,138—Johnny Pingel, Michigan St., 1938 (99 punts)
Career
12,947—Cameron Young, Texas Christian, 1976-79 (320 punts)

MOST GAMES WITH A 40-YARD AVERAGE OR MORE
Career
(Min. 4 punts) 36—Bill Smith, Mississippi, 1983-86 (punted in 44 games)

MOST PUNTS, 50 YARDS OR MORE
Season
31—Chuck Ramsey, Wake Forest, 1973 (87 punts); Marv Bateman, Utah, 1971 (68 punts)
Career
(2 yrs.) 51—Marv Bateman, Utah, 1970-71 (133 punts)
(3 yrs.) 61—Russ Henderson, Virginia, 1976-78 (226 punts)
(4 yrs.) 88—Bill Smith, Mississippi, 1983-86 (254 punts)

MOST CONSECUTIVE GAMES WITH AT LEAST ONE PUNT OF 50 YARDS OR MORE
Career
32—Bill Smith, Mississippi, 1983-86

MOST PUNTS IN A CAREER WITHOUT HAVING ONE BLOCKED
300—Tony DeLeone, Kent, 1981-84
Also holds consecutive record at 300

LONGEST PUNT
99—Pat Brady, Nevada vs. Loyola Marymount, Oct. 28, 1950

RANKING IN TOP 12 IN BOTH PUNTING AND FIELD GOALS
Daron Alcorn, Akron, 1992 (No. 11 in punting, 43.6-yard average and tied for No. 9 in field goals, 1.64 per game); Dan Eichloff, Kansas, 1991 (No. 12 in punting, 42.3-yard average and No. 3 in field goals, 1.64 per game); Chris Gardocki, Clemson, 1990 (No. 4 in punting, 44.3-yard average and No. 4 in field goals, 1.73 per game), 1989 (No. 10 in punting, 42.7-yard average and No. 6 in field goals, 1.82 per game); Rob Keen, California, 1988 (No. 11 in punting, 42.6-yard average and No. 3 in field goals, 1.91 per game); Steve Little, Arkansas, 1977 (No. 4 in punting, 44.3-yard average and No. 2 in field goals, 1.73 per game)

Interceptions

MOST PASSES INTERCEPTED
Game
5—Dan Rebsch, Miami (Ohio) vs. Western Mich., Nov. 4, 1972 (88 yards); Byron Beaver, Houston vs. Baylor, Sept. 22, 1962 (18 yards); Walt Pastuszak, Brown vs. Rhode Island, Oct. 8, 1949 (47 yards); Lee Cook, Oklahoma St. vs. Detroit Mercy, Nov. 28, 1942 (15 yards)
Season
14—Al Worley, Washington, 1968 (130 yards)
Career
29—Al Brosky, Illinois, 1950-52 (356 yards)

MOST PASSES INTERCEPTED PER GAME
Season
1.4—Al Worley, Washington, 1968 (14 in 10)
Career
1.1—Al Brosky, Illinois, 1950-52 (29 in 27)

MOST PASSES INTERCEPTED BY A LINEBACKER
Season
9—Bill Sibley, Texas A&M, 1941 (57 yards)

MOST PASSES INTERCEPTED BY A FRESHMAN
Game
3—Torey Hunter, Washington St. vs. Arizona St., Oct. 19, 1991 (22 yards); Shawn Simms, Bowling Green vs. Toledo, Oct. 24, 1981 (46 yards)
Season
13—George Shaw, Oregon, 1951 (136 yards)
Also holds per-game record at 1.3 (13 in 10)

MOST YARDS ON INTERCEPTION RETURNS
Game
182—Ashley Lee, Virginia Tech vs. Vanderbilt, Nov. 12, 1983 (2 interceptions)
Season
302—Charles Phillips, Southern Cal, 1974 (7 interceptions)
Career
501—Terrell Buckley, Florida St., 1989-91 (21 interceptions)

MOST TOUCHDOWNS SCORED ON INTERCEPTION RETURNS
Game
3—Johnny Jackson, Houston vs. Texas, Nov. 7, 1987 (31, 53, 97 yards)
Season
3—By many players. Most recent: Johnny Jackson, Houston, 1987 (8 interceptions); Erik McMillan, Missouri, 1987 (5 interceptions)
Career
5—Ken Thomas, San Jose St., 1979-82 (14 interceptions); Jackie Walker, Tennessee, 1969-71 (11 interceptions)

HIGHEST AVERAGE GAIN PER INTERCEPTION
Game
(Min. 2 ints.) 91.0—Ashley Lee, Virginia Tech vs. Vanderbilt, Nov. 12, 1983 (2 for 182)
Season
(Min. 5 ints.) 50.6—Norm Thompson, Utah, 1969 (5 for 253)
Career
(Min. 15 ints.) 26.5—Tom Pridemore, West Va., 1975-77 (15 for 398)

MOST CONSECUTIVE GAMES INTERCEPTING A PASS
15—Al Brosky, Illinois, began Nov. 11, 1950 (vs. Iowa), ended Oct. 18, 1952 (vs. Minnesota)

Punt Returns

MOST PUNT RETURNS
Game
20—Milton Hill, Texas Tech vs. Centenary (La.), Nov. 11, 1939 (110 yards)
Season
55—Dick Adams, Miami (Ohio), 1970 (578 yards)
Also holds per-game record at 5.50
Career
153—Vai Sikahema, Brigham Young, 1980-81, 1984-85 (1,312 yards)

MOST YARDS ON PUNT RETURNS
Game
219—Golden Richards, Brigham Young vs. North Texas, Sept. 10, 1971 (5 returns)
Season
791—Lee Nalley, Vanderbilt, 1948 (43 returns)
Also holds per-game record at 79.1

Career

1,695—Lee Nalley, Vanderbilt, 1947-49 (109 returns)

HIGHEST AVERAGE GAIN PER RETURN

Game

(Min. 3-4 rets.) 59.7—Chip Hough, Air Force vs. Southern Methodist, Oct. 9, 1971 (3 for 179)

(Min. 5 rets.) 43.8—Golden Richards, Brigham Young vs. North Texas, Sept. 10, 1971 (5 for 219)

Season

(Min. 1.2 rets. per game) 25.9—Bill Blackstock, Tennessee, 1951 (12 for 311)

(Min. 1.5 rets. per game) 25.0—George Sims, Baylor, 1948 (15 for 375)

Career

(Min. 1.2 rets. per game) 23.6—Jack Mitchell, Oklahoma, 1946-48 (39 for 922)

(Min. 1.5 rets. per game) 20.5—Gene Gibson, Cincinnati, 1949-50 (37 for 760)

MOST TOUCHDOWNS SCORED ON PUNT RETURNS

Game

2—By many players. Most recent: Andre Parvis, North Caro. vs. Tulane, Nov. 13, 1993 (fell on two blocked punts in end zone); Jeff Sweitzer, Akron vs. Northern Ariz., Nov. 4, 1989 (53 and 70 yards in first and second quarters)

Season

4—James Henry, Southern Miss., 1987; Golden Richards, Brigham Young, 1971; Cliff Branch, Colorado, 1971

Career

7—Johnny Rodgers, Nebraska, 1970-72 (2 in 1970, 3 in 1971, 2 in 1972); Jack Mitchell, Oklahoma, 1946-48 (3 in 1946, 1 in 1947, 3 in 1948)

Kickoff Returns

MOST KICKOFF RETURNS

Game

11—Trevor Cobb, Rice vs. Houston, Dec. 2, 1989 (166 yards)

Season

44—Frank Collins, Utah, 1974 (907 yards)

Career

114—Joe Redding, Southwestern La., 1985-88 (2,642 yards)

MOST RETURNS PER GAME

Season

4.6—Dwayne Owens, Oregon St., 1990 (41 in 9)

Career

3.0—Steve Odom, Utah, 1971-73 (99 in 33)

MOST YARDS ON KICKOFF RETURNS

Game

241—Jerry Blitz, Harvard vs. Princeton, Nov. 8, 1952 (7 returns)

Season

1,014—Dwayne Owens, Oregon St., 1990 (41 returns)

Career

2,642—Joe Redding, Southwestern La., 1985-88 (114 returns)

MOST YARDS RETURNED PER GAME

Season

112.7—Dwayne Owens, Oregon St., 1990 (1,014 in 9)

Career

78.2—Steve Odom, Utah, 1971-73 (2,582 in 33)

HIGHEST AVERAGE GAIN PER RETURN

Game

(Min. 3 rets.) 72.7—Anthony Davis, Southern Cal vs. Notre Dame, Dec. 2, 1972 (3 for 218)

Season

(Min. 1.2 rets. per game) 40.1—Paul Allen, Brigham Young, 1961 (12 for 481)

(Min. 1.5 rets. per game) 38.2—Forrest Hall, San Francisco, 1946 (15 for 573)

Career

(Min. 1.2 rets. per game) 36.2—Forrest Hall, San Francisco, 1946-47 (22 for 796)

(Min. 1.5 rets. per game) 31.0—Overton Curtis, Utah St., 1957-58 (32 for 991)

MOST TOUCHDOWNS SCORED ON KICKOFF RETURNS

Game

2—Leeland McElroy, Texas A&M vs. Rice, Oct. 23, 1993 (93 & 88 yards); Stacey Corley, Brigham Young vs. Air Force, Nov. 11, 1989 (99 & 85 yards); *Raghib Ismail, Notre Dame vs. Michigan, Sept. 16, 1989 (88 & 92 yards); Raghib Ismail, Notre Dame vs. Rice, Nov. 5, 1988 (87 & 83 yards); Anthony Davis, Southern Cal vs. Notre Dame, Dec. 2, 1972 (97 & 96 yards); Ollie Matson, San Francisco vs. Fordham, Oct. 20, 1951 (94 & 90 yards); Ron Horwath, Detroit Mercy vs. Hillsdale, Sept. 22, 1950 (96 & 96 yards); Paul Copoulos, Marquette vs. Iowa Pre-Flight, Nov. 6, 1943 (85 & 82 yards)

Season

3—Leeland McElroy, Texas A&M, 1993; Terance Mathis, New Mexico, 1989; Willie Gault, Tennessee, 1980; Anthony Davis, Southern Cal, 1974; Stan Brown, Purdue, 1970; Forrest Hall, San Francisco, 1946

Career

6—Anthony Davis, Southern Cal, 1972-74

*Ismail is the only player in history to score twice in two games.

SCORING A TOUCHDOWN ON TEAM'S OPENING KICKOFF OF TWO SEASONS

Season

Barry Sanders, Oklahoma St., 1988 (100 yards vs. Miami, Ohio, Sept. 10) & 1987 (100 yards vs. Tulsa, Sept. 5)

Total Kick Returns

(Combined Punt and Kickoff Returns)

MOST KICK RETURNS

Game

20—Milton Hill, Texas Tech vs. Centenary, Nov. 11, 1939 (20 punts, 110 yards)

Season

70—Keith Stephens, Louisville, 1986 (28 punts, 42 kickoffs, 1,162 yards); Dick Adams, Miami (Ohio), 1970 (55 punts, 15 kickoffs, 944 yards)

Career

199—Tony James, Mississippi St., 1989-92 (121 punts, 78 kickoffs, 3,194 yards)

MOST YARDS ON KICK RETURNS

Game

247—Tyrone Hughes, Nebraska vs. Kansas St., Oct. 6, 1991 (8 returns); Golden Richards, Brigham Young vs. North Texas, Sept. 10, 1971 (7 returns)

Season

1,228—Steve Odom, Utah, 1972

Per-game record—116.2, Dion Johnson, East Caro., 1990 (1,046 yards, with 167 on punt returns and 879 on kickoff returns in 9 games)

Career

3,194—Tony James, Mississippi St., 1989-92 (1,332 on punts, 1,862 on kickoffs)

GAINING 1,000 YARDS ON PUNT RETURNS AND 1,000 YARDS ON KICKOFF RETURNS

Career

Tony James, Mississippi St., 1989-92 (1,332 & 1,862); Willie Drewrey, West Va., 1981-84 (1,072 & 1,302); Anthony Carter, Michigan, 1979-82 (1,095 & 1,504); Devon Ford, Appalachian St., 1973-76 (1,197 & 1,761); Troy Slade, Duke, 1973-75 (1,021 & 1,757)

HIGHEST AVERAGE PER KICK RETURN

(Min. 1.2 Punt Returns and 1.2 Kickoff Returns Per Game)

Season

27.2—Erroll Tucker, Utah, 1985 (40 for 1,087; 16 for 389 on punt returns, 24 for 698 on kickoff returns)

HIGHEST AVERAGE PER KICK RETURN

(Min. 1.3 Punt Returns and 1.3 Kickoff Returns Per Game)

Career

22.0—Erroll Tucker, Utah, 1984-85 (79 for 1,741; 38 for 650 on punt returns, 41 for 1,091 on kickoff returns)

AVERAGING 20 YARDS EACH ON PUNT RETURNS AND KICKOFF RETURNS

(Min. 1.2 Returns Per Game Each)

Season

By 7 players. Most recent: Lee Gissendaner, Northwestern, 1992 (21.8 on punt returns, 15 for 327; 22.4 on kickoff returns, 17 for 381)

MOST TOUCHDOWNS SCORED ON KICK RETURNS

(Must Have at Least One Punt Return and One Kickoff Return)

Game

2—By 5 players. Most recent: Eric Blount, North Caro. vs. William & Mary, Oct. 5, 1991 (1 punt, 1 kickoff)

Season

5—Robert Woods, Grambling, 1977 (3 punts, 2 kickoffs); Pinky Rohm, Louisiana St., 1937 (3 punts, 2 kickoffs)

Career

8—Johnny Rodgers, Nebraska, 1970-72 (7 punts, 1 kickoff); Cliff Branch, Colorado, 1970-71 (6 punts, 2 kickoffs)

WINNING BOTH PUNT RETURN AND KICKOFF RETURN CHAMPIONSHIPS

Season

Erroll Tucker, Utah, 1985

Career

Erroll Tucker, Utah, 1985; Ira Matthews, Wisconsin, kickoff returns (1976) and punt returns (1978)

All Runbacks

(Combined Interceptions, Punt Returns and Kickoff Returns)

SCORING MORE THAN ONE TOUCHDOWN IN EACH CATEGORY

Season

Erroll Tucker, Utah, 1985 (3 interceptions, 2 punt returns, 2 kickoff returns)

SCORING ONE TOUCHDOWN IN EACH CATEGORY

Season

Scott Thomas, Air Force, 1985; Mark Haynes, Arizona St., 1974; Dick Harris, South Caro., 1970

HIGHEST AVERAGE PER RUNBACK

Season

(Min. 40 rets.) 28.3—Erroll Tucker, Utah, 1985 (6 for 216 on interceptions, 16 for 389 on punt returns, 24 for 698 on kickoff returns; total 46 for 1,303)

HIGHEST AVERAGE PER RUNBACK

(At Least 7 Interceptions and Min. 1.3 Punt Returns and 1.3 Kickoff Returns Per Game)

Career

22.6—Erroll Tucker, Utah, 1984-85 (8 for 224 on interceptions, 38 for 650 on punt returns, 41 for 1,091 on kickoff returns; total 87 for 1,965)

MOST TOUCHDOWNS ON INTERCEPTIONS, PUNT RETURNS AND KICKOFF RETURNS

(Must Have at Least One Touchdown in Each Category)

Season

7—Erroll Tucker, Utah, 1985 (3 interceptions, 2 punt returns, 2 kickoff returns)

Career

8—Erroll Tucker, Utah, 1984-85 (3 interceptions, 3 punt returns, 2 kickoff returns)

Opponent's Kicks Blocked

MOST OPPONENT'S PUNTS BLOCKED BY

Game

4—Ken Irvin, Memphis vs. Arkansas, Sept. 26, 1992 (4 punts)

Season

8—James Francis (LB), Baylor, 1989 (11 games); Jimmy Lisko, Arkansas St., 1975 (11 games)

MOST OPPONENT'S PAT KICKS BLOCKED BY

Season

5—Ray Farmer, Duke, 1993

MOST OPPONENT'S TOTAL KICKS BLOCKED BY
(Includes Punts, PAT Attempts, FG Attempts)
Game
4—Ken Irvin, Memphis vs. Arkansas, Sept. 26, 1992 (4 punts)
Career
19—James Ferebee, New Mexico St., 1978-81 (8 FG attempts, 6 PAT attempts, 5 punts)

MOST TOUCHDOWNS SCORED ON BLOCKED PUNTS
Season
3—Joe Wessel, Florida St., 1984

All-Purpose Yards
(Yardage Gained From Rushing, Receiving and All Runbacks)
MOST PLAYS
Game
58—Tony Sands, Kansas vs. Missouri, Nov. 23, 1991 (58 rushes)
Season
432—Marcus Allen, Southern Cal, 1981 (403 rushes, 29 receptions)
Career
(3 yrs.) 1,034—Herschel Walker, Georgia, 1980-82 (994 rushes, 26 receptions, 14 kickoff returns)
(4 yrs.) 1,347—Steve Bartalo, Colorado St., 1983-86 (1,215 rushes, 132 receptions)

MOST YARDS GAINED
Game
422—Marshall Faulk, San Diego St. vs. Pacific (Cal.), Sept. 14, 1991 (386 rushing, 11 receiving, 25 kick-off returns)
Season
3,250—Barry Sanders, Oklahoma St., 1988 (2,628 rushing, 106 receiving, 95 punt returns, 421 kickoff returns; 11 games)
Career
(3 yrs.) 5,749—Herschel Walker, Georgia, 1980-82 (5,259 rushing, 243 receiving, 247 kickoff returns; 1,034 plays)
(4 yrs.) 7,172—$Napoleon McCallum, Navy, 1981-85 (4,179 rushing, 796 receiving, 858 punt returns, 1,339 kickoff returns; 1,138 plays)
Collegiate record—7,564, Howard Stevens, Randolph-Macon, 1968-69, and Louisville, 1971-72 (5,297 rushing, 738 receiving, 781 punt returns, 748 kick-off returns)

$ See page 6 for explanation.

MOST YARDS GAINED PER GAME
Season
295.5—Barry Sanders, Oklahoma St., 1988 (3,250 in 11 games)
Career
237.8—Ryan Benjamin, Pacific (Cal.), 1990-92 (5,706 in 24 games; 3,119 rushing, 1,063 receiving, 100 punt returns, 1,424 kickoff returns)

MOST YARDS GAINED BY A FRESHMAN
Game
422—Marshall Faulk, San Diego St. vs. Pacific (Cal.), Sept. 14, 1991 (386 rushing, 11 receiving, 25 kick-off returns)
Season
2,026—Terrell Willis, Rutgers, 1993 (1,261 rushing, 61 receiving, 704 kickoff returns; 234 plays)
Per-game record—184.8, Marshall Faulk, San Diego St., 1991 (1,663 in 9)

MOST SEASONS WITH 2,000 OR MORE YARDS
2—Ryan Benjamin, Pacific (Cal.), 1991 (2,995) & 1992 (2,597); Glyn Milburn, Stanford, 1990 (2,222) & 1992 (2,121); Sheldon Canley, San Jose St., 1989 (2,513) & 1990 (2,213); Chuck Weatherspoon, Houston, 1989 (2,391) & 1990 (2,038); Napoleon McCallum, Navy, 1983 (2,385) & 1985 (2,330); Howard Stevens, Randolph-Macon, 1968 (2,115) & Louisville, 1972 (2,132)

HIGHEST AVERAGE GAIN PER PLAY
Season
(Min. 1,500 yards, 100-124 plays) 18.5—Henry Bailey, Nevada-Las Vegas, 1992 (1,883 on 102)

(Min. 1,500 yards, 125 plays) 15.7—Terance Mathis, New Mexico, 1989 (2,138 on 136)
Career
(Min. 5,000 yards, 275-374 plays) 17.4—Anthony Carter, Michigan, 1979-82 (5,197 on 298)
(Min. 5,000 yards, 375 plays) 14.6—Terance Mathis, New Mexico, 1985-87, 1989 (6,691 on 457)

MOST YARDS GAINED BY TWO PLAYERS, SAME TEAM
Career
10,253—Marshall Faulk (5,595) & Darnay Scott (4,658), San Diego St., 1991-93

Scoring
MOST POINTS SCORED
(By Non-Kickers)
Game
48—Howard Griffith, Illinois vs. Southern Ill., Sept. 22, 1990 (8 TDs on runs of 5, 51, 7, 41, 5, 18, 5, 3 yards)
Game vs. Major-College Opponent
44—Marshall Faulk, San Diego St. vs. Pacific (Cal.), Sept. 14, 1991 (7 TDs, 1 two-point conversion)
Season
234—Barry Sanders, Oklahoma St., 1988 (39 TDs in 11 games)
2 Yrs
312—Barry Sanders, Oklahoma St., 1987-88 (52 TDs in 22 games)
Career
(3 yrs.) 376—Marshall Faulk, San Diego St., 1991-93 (62 TDs, 2 two-point conversions)
(4 yrs.) 394—Anthony Thompson, Indiana, 1986-89 (65 TDs, 4 PATs)

MOST POINTS SCORED PER GAME
Season
21.3—Barry Sanders, Oklahoma St., 1988 (234 in 11)
2 Yrs
14.2—Barry Sanders, Oklahoma St., 1987-88 (312 in 22)
Career
12.1—Marshall Faulk, San Diego St., 1991-93 (376 in 31)

MOST POINTS SCORED BY A FRESHMAN
Game
44—Marshall Faulk, San Diego St. vs. Pacific (Cal.), Sept. 14, 1991 (7 TDs, 1 two-point conversion)
Season
140—Marshall Faulk, San Diego St., 1991 (23 TDs, 1 two-point conversion)
Also holds per-game record at 15.6 (140 in 9)

MOST TOUCHDOWNS SCORED
Game
8—Howard Griffith, Illinois vs. Southern Ill., Sept. 22, 1990 (all 8 by rushing on runs of 5, 51, 7, 41, 5, 18, 5, 3 yards)
Game vs. Major-College Opponent
7—Marshall Faulk, San Diego St. vs. Pacific (Cal.), Sept. 14, 1991; Arnold "Showboat" Boykin, Mississippi vs. Mississippi St., Dec. 1, 1951
Season
39—Barry Sanders, Oklahoma St., 1988 (11 games)
Also holds per-game record at 3.5 (39 in 11)
2 Yrs
52—Barry Sanders, Oklahoma St., 1987-88 (22 games)
Also holds per-game record at 2.4 (52 in 22)
Career
(3 yrs.) 62—Marshall Faulk, San Diego St., 1991-93 (57 rushing, 5 pass receptions)
Also holds per-game record at 2.0 (62 in 31)
(4 yrs.) 65—Anthony Thompson, Indiana, 1986-89 (64 rushing, 1 pass reception)

MOST TOUCHDOWNS SCORED IN TWO AND THREE CONSECUTIVE GAMES
2 Games
11—Kelvin Bryant, North Caro., 1981 (6 vs. East Caro., Sept. 12; 5 vs. Miami, Ohio, Sept. 19)
3 Games
15—Kelvin Bryant, North Caro., 1981 (6 vs. East

Caro., Sept. 12; 5 vs. Miami, Ohio, Sept. 19; 4 vs. Boston College, Sept. 26)

MOST TOUCHDOWNS SCORED BY A FRESHMAN
Game
7—Marshall Faulk, San Diego St. vs. Pacific (Cal.), Sept. 14, 1991 (all by rushing)
Season
23—Marshall Faulk, San Diego St., 1991 (21 rushing, 2 pass receptions)
Also holds per-game record at 2.6 (23 in 9)

MOST CONSECUTIVE GAMES SCORING A TOUCHDOWN
Career
23—Bill Burnett, Arkansas (from Oct. 5, 1968, through Oct. 31, 1970; 47 touchdowns)

MOST GAMES SCORING A TOUCHDOWN
Season
11—By many players. Most recent: Barry Sanders, Oklahoma St., 1988
Career
31—Ted Brown, North Caro. St., 1975-78; Tony Dorsett, Pittsburgh, 1973-76; Glenn Davis, Army, 1943-46

MOST GAMES SCORING TWO OR MORE TOUCHDOWNS
Season
11—Barry Sanders, Oklahoma St., 1988
Career
17—Tony Dorsett, Pittsburgh, 1973-76; Steve Owens, Oklahoma, 1967-69; Glenn Davis, Army, 1943-46

MOST CONSECUTIVE GAMES SCORING TWO OR MORE TOUCHDOWNS
Season
11—Barry Sanders, Oklahoma St., 1988
Career
13—Barry Sanders, Oklahoma St. (from Nov. 14, 1987, through 1988)

MOST GAMES SCORING THREE OR MORE TOUCHDOWNS
Season
9—Barry Sanders, Oklahoma St., 1988

MOST CONSECUTIVE GAMES SCORING THREE OR MORE TOUCHDOWNS
Season
5—Barry Sanders, Oklahoma St., 1988 (from Sept. 10 through Oct. 15); Paul Hewitt, San Diego St., 1987 (from Oct. 10 through Nov. 7)

MOST TOUCHDOWNS AND POINTS SCORED BY TWO PLAYERS, SAME TEAM
Season
54 and 324—Barry Sanders (39-234) & Hart Lee Dykes (15-90), Oklahoma St., 1988
Career
97 and 585—Glenn Davis (59-354) & Doc Blanchard (38-231), Army, 1943-46

PASSING FOR A TOUCHDOWN AND SCORING TOUCHDOWNS BY RUSHING AND RECEIVING
Game
By many players. Most recent: Keith Byars, Ohio St. vs. Iowa, Sept. 22, 1984

PASSING FOR A TOUCHDOWN AND SCORING ON A PASS RECEPTION AND PUNT RETURN
Game
By many players. Most recent: Scott Schwedes, Syracuse vs. Temple, Oct. 26, 1985

MOST EXTRA POINTS ATTEMPTED BY KICKING
Game
14—Terry Leiweke, Houston vs. Tulsa, Nov. 23, 1968 (13 made)
Season
71—Kurt Gunther, Brigham Young, 1980 (64 made)
Career
222—Derek Mahoney, Fresno St., 1990-93 (216 made)

MOST EXTRA POINTS MADE BY KICKING
Game
13—Derek Mahoney, Fresno St. vs. New Mexico, Oct. 5, 1991 (13 attempts); Terry Leiweke, Houston vs. Tulsa, Nov. 23, 1968 (14 attempts)
Season
67—Cary Blanchard, Oklahoma St., 1988 (67 attempts)
Also holds per-game record at 6.1 (67 in 11)
Career
216—Derek Mahoney, Fresno St., 1990-93 (222 attempts)
Per-game record—5.2, Al Limahelu, San Diego St., 1969-70 (103 in 20)

BEST PERFECT RECORD OF EXTRA POINTS MADE
Season
67 of 67—Cary Blanchard, Oklahoma St., 1988

HIGHEST PERCENTAGE OF EXTRA POINTS MADE
Career
(Min. 100 atts.) 100%—David Browndyke, Louisiana St., 1986-89 (109 of 109); Pete Stoyanovich, Indiana, 1985-88 (101 of 101); Van Tiffin, Alabama, 1983-86 (135 of 135)

MOST CONSECUTIVE EXTRA POINTS MADE
Game
13—Derek Mahoney, Fresno St. vs. New Mexico, Oct. 5, 1991 (13 attempts)
Season
67—Cary Blanchard, Oklahoma St., 1988 (67 attempts)
Career
157—Carlos Huerta, Miami (Fla.), 1988-91

MOST POINTS SCORED BY KICKING
Game
24—Mike Prindle, Western Mich. vs. Marshall, Sept. 29, 1984 (7 FGs, 3 PATs)
Season
131—Roman Anderson, Houston, 1989 (22 FGs, 65 PATs)
Also holds per-game record at 11.9 (131 in 11)
Career
423—Roman Anderson, Houston, 1988-91 (70 FGs, 213 PATs)
Also holds per-game record at 9.6 (423 in 44)

HIGHEST PERCENTAGE OF EXTRA POINTS AND FIELD GOALS MADE
Season
(Min. 30 PATs and 15 FGs made) 98.3%—Chuck Nelson, Washington, 1982 (34 of 34 PATs, 25 of 26 FGs)
(Min. 40 PATs and 20 FGs made) 97.3%—Chris Jacke, UTEP, 1988 (48 of 48 PATs, 25 of 27 FGs)
Career
(Min. 100 PATs and 50 FGs made) 93.3%—John Lee, UCLA, 1982-85 (116 of 117 PATs, 79 of 92 FGs)

Washington's Jeff Jaeger holds the Division I-A record for career field goals with 80.

MOST TWO-POINT ATTEMPTS MADE
Game
6—Jim Pilot, New Mexico St. vs. Hardin-Simmons, Nov. 25, 1961 (all by running, attempted 7)
Season
6—Howard Twilley, Tulsa, 1964 (all on pass receptions); Jim Pilot, New Mexico St., 1961 (all by running); Pat McCarthy, Holy Cross, 1960 (all by running)
Career
13—Pat McCarthy, Holy Cross, 1960-62 (all by running)

MOST SUCCESSFUL TWO-POINT PASSES
Season
12—John Hangartner, Arizona St., 1958 (attempted 21)
Career
19—Pat McCarthy, Holy Cross, 1960-62 (attempted 33)

Defensive Extra Points

MOST DEFENSIVE EXTRA POINTS SCORED
Game
1—By 23 players. Most recent: Lee Rubin, Penn St. vs. Pittsburgh, Nov. 21, 1992 (kick return)
Season
1—By 23 players. Most recent: Lee Rubin, Penn St. vs. Pittsburgh, Nov. 21, 1992 (kick return)

LONGEST RETURN OF A DEFENSIVE EXTRA-POINT ATTEMPT
Game
100—William Price (CB), Kansas St. vs. Indiana St., Sept. 7, 1991 (intercepted pass three yards deep in Indiana St. end zone); Curt Newton (LB), Washington St. vs. Oregon St., Oct. 20, 1990 (returned conversion pass attempt from Washington St. goal line); Quintin Parker (DB), Illinois vs. Wisconsin, Oct. 28, 1989 (returned kick from Illinois goal line); Lee Ozmint (SS), Alabama vs. Louisiana St., Nov. 11, 1989 (intercepted pass at Alabama goal line)

FIRST DEFENSIVE EXTRA-POINT ATTEMPT
Season
Thomas King (S), Southwestern La. vs. Cal St. Fullerton, Sept. 3, 1988 (returned blocked kick 6 yards)

MOST DEFENSIVE EXTRA-POINT KICKS BLOCKED
Game
2—Nigel Codrington (DB), Rice vs. Notre Dame, Nov. 5, 1988 (1 resulted in a score)
Also holds season record at 2

Fumble Returns

(Since 1992)

MOST FUMBLE RETURNS
Game
1—By many players

Field Goals

MOST FIELD GOALS ATTEMPTED
Game
9—Mike Prindle, Western Mich. vs. Marshall, Sept. 29, 1984 (7 made)
Season
38—Jerry DePoyster, Wyoming, 1966 (13 made)
Also holds per-game record at 3.8
Career
(3 yrs.) 93—Jerry DePoyster, Wyoming, 1965-67 (36 made)
Also holds per-game record at 3.1
(4 yrs.) 105—Philip Doyle, Alabama, 1987-90 (78 made); Luis Zendejas, Arizona St., 1981-84 (78 made)
Doyle holds per-game record at 2.4 (105 in 43)

MOST FIELD GOALS MADE
Quarter
4—By 4 players. Most recent: David Hardy, Texas A&M vs. Texas-Arlington, Sept. 18, 1982 (2nd)
Half
5—Dat Ly, New Mexico St. vs. Kansas, Oct. 1, 1988 (1st); Dale Klein, Nebraska vs. Missouri, Oct. 19, 1985 (1st)
Game
7—Dale Klein, Nebraska vs. Missouri, Oct. 19, 1985 (32, 22, 43, 44, 29, 43, 43 yards), 7 attempts; Mike Prindle, Western Mich. vs. Marshall, Sept. 29, 1984 (32, 44, 42, 23, 48, 41, 27 yards), 9 attempts
Season
29—John Lee, UCLA, 1984 (33 attempts)
2 Yrs
50—John Lee, UCLA, 1984-85 (57 attempts)
Career
80—Jeff Jaeger, Washington, 1983-86 (99 attempts)

MOST FIELD GOALS MADE PER GAME
Season
2.6—John Lee, UCLA, 1984 (29 in 11)
Career
1.8—John Lee, UCLA, 1982-85 (79 in 43)

BEST PERFECT RECORD OF FIELD GOALS MADE
Game
7 of 7—Dale Klein, Nebraska vs. Missouri, Oct. 19, 1985

MOST FIELD GOALS MADE BY A FRESHMAN
Game
6—*Mickey Thomas, Virginia Tech vs. Vanderbilt, Nov. 4, 1989 (6 attempts)
Season
23—Collin Mackie, South Caro., 1987 (30 attempts)

Conventional-style kicker.

HIGHEST PERCENTAGE OF FIELD GOALS MADE
Season
(Min. 15 atts.) 96.2%—Chuck Nelson, Washington, 1982 (25 of 26)
Career
(Min. 45-54 atts.) 87.8%—Bobby Raymond, Florida, 1983-84 (43 of 49)
(Min. 55 atts.) 85.9%—John Lee, UCLA, 1982-85 (79 of 92)

MOST CONSECUTIVE FIELD GOALS MADE
Season
25—Chuck Nelson, Washington, 1982 (first 25, missed last attempt of season vs. Washington St., Nov. 20)
Career
30—Chuck Nelson, Washington, 1981-82 (last 5 in 1981, from Southern Cal, Nov. 14, and first 25 in 1982, ending with last attempt vs. Washington St., Nov. 20)

MOST GAMES KICKING A FIELD GOAL
Career
40—Gary Gussman, Miami (Ohio), 1984-87 (in 44 games played)

MOST CONSECUTIVE GAMES KICKING A FIELD GOAL
19—Gary Gussman, Miami (Ohio), 1986-87; Larry Roach, Oklahoma St., 1983-84

MOST FIELD GOALS MADE, 60 YARDS OR MORE
Game
2—Tony Franklin, Texas A&M vs. Baylor, Oct. 16, 1976 (65 & 64 yards)
Season
3—Russell Erxleben, Texas, 1977 (67 vs. Rice, Oct. 1; 64 vs. Baylor, Oct. 16; 60 vs. Texas Tech, Oct. 29) (4 attempts)
Career
3—Russell Erxleben, Texas, 1975-78 (see Season Record above)

MOST FIELD GOALS ATTEMPTED, 60 YARDS OR MORE
Season
5—Tony Franklin, Texas A&M, 1976 (2 made)
Career
11—Tony Franklin, Texas A&M, 1975-78 (2 made)

MOST FIELD GOALS MADE, 50 YARDS OR MORE
Game
3—Sergio Lopez-Chavero, Wichita St. vs. Drake, Oct. 27, 1984 (54, 54, 51 yards); Jerry DePoyster, Wyoming vs. Utah, Oct. 8, 1966 (54, 54, 52 yards)
Season
8—Fuad Reveiz, Tennessee, 1982 (10 attempts)
Career
20—Jason Hanson, Washington St., 1988-91 (35 attempts)

MOST FIELD GOALS ATTEMPTED, 50 YARDS OR MORE
Season
17—Jerry DePoyster, Wyoming, 1966 (5 made)
Career
38—Tony Franklin, Texas A&M, 1975-78 (16 made)

HIGHEST PERCENTAGE OF FIELD GOALS MADE, 50 YARDS OR MORE
Season
(Min. 10 atts.) 80.0%—Fuad Reveiz, Tennessee, 1982 (8 of 10)
Career
(Min. 15 atts.) 60.9%—Max Zendejas, Arizona, 1982-85 (14 of 23)

MOST FIELD GOALS MADE, 40 YARDS OR MORE
Game
5—Alan Smith, Texas A&M vs. Arkansas St., Sept. 17, 1983 (44, 45, 42, 59, 57 yards)
Season
14—Chris Jacke, UTEP, 1988 (16 attempts)
Career
39—Jason Hanson, Washington St., 1988-91 (66 attempts) (19 of 31, 40-49 yards; 20 of 35, 50 or more yards)

MOST FIELD GOALS ATTEMPTED, 40 YARDS OR MORE
Season
25—Jerry DePoyster, Wyoming, 1966 (6 made)
Career
66—Jason Hanson, Washington St., 1988-91 (39 made)

HIGHEST PERCENTAGE OF FIELD GOALS MADE, 40 YARDS OR MORE
Season
(Min. 10 made) 90.9%—John Carney, Notre Dame, 1984 (10 of 11)
Career
(Min. 20 made) 69.4%—John Lee, UCLA, 1982-85 (25 of 36)

HIGHEST PERCENTAGE OF FIELD GOALS MADE, 40-49 YARDS
Season
(Min. 10 made) 100%—John Carney, Notre Dame, 1984 (10 of 10)
Career
(Min. 15 made) 82.6%—Jeff Jaeger, Washington, 1983-86 (19 of 23)

MOST CONSECUTIVE FIELD GOALS MADE, 40-49 YARDS
Career
12—John Carney, Notre Dame, 1984-85

HIGHEST PERCENTAGE OF FIELD GOALS MADE, UNDER 40 YARDS
Season
(Min. 16 made) 100%—Philip Doyle, Alabama, 1989 (19 of 19); Scott Slater, Texas A&M, 1986 (16 of 16); Bobby Raymond, Florida, 1984 (18 of 18); John Lee, UCLA, 1984 (16 of 16); Randy Pratt, California, 1983 (16 of 16); Paul Woodside, West Va., 1982 (23 of 23)
Career
(Min. 30-39 made) 97.0%—Bobby Raymond, Florida, 1983-84 (32 of 33)
(Min. 40 made) 96.4%—John Lee, UCLA, 1982-85 (54 of 56)

LONGEST AVERAGE DISTANCE FIELD GOALS MADE
Game
(Min. 4 made) 49.5—Jeff Heath, East Caro. vs. Texas-Arlington, Nov. 6, 1982 (58, 53, 42, 45 yards)
Season
(Min. 10 made) 50.9—Jason Hanson, Washington St., 1991 (10 made)
Career
(Min. 25 made) 42.4—Russell Erxleben, Texas, 1975-78 (49 made)

LONGEST AVERAGE DISTANCE FIELD GOALS ATTEMPTED
Season
(Min. 20 atts.) 51.2—Jason Hanson, Washington St., 1991 (22 attempts)
Career
(Min. 40 atts.) 44.7—Russell Erxleben, Texas, 1975-78 (78 attempts)

MOST TIMES KICKING TWO OR MORE FIELD GOALS IN A GAME
Season
10—Paul Woodside, West Va., 1982
Career
27—Kevin Butler, Georgia, 1981-84

MOST TIMES KICKING THREE OR MORE FIELD GOALS IN A GAME
Season
6—Joe Allison, Memphis St., 1992; Luis Zendejas, Arizona St., 1983
Career
13—Luis Zendejas, Arizona St., 1981-84

MOST TIMES KICKING FOUR OR MORE FIELD GOALS IN A GAME
Season
4—Matt Bahr, Penn St., 1978
Career
6—John Lee, UCLA, 1982-85
Also holds career record for most times kicking four or more field goals in a game at 8

LONGEST FIELD GOAL MADE
67—Joe Williams, Wichita St. vs. Southern Ill., Oct. 21, 1978; Steve Little, Arkansas vs. Texas, Oct. 15, 1977; Russell Erxleben, Texas vs. Rice, Oct. 1, 1977

LONGEST INDOOR FIELD GOAL MADE
57—Juan Carrillo, Cal St. Fullerton vs. Northern Ariz., Oct. 15, 1977 (in Northern Arizona's Walkup Skydome)

LONGEST FIELD GOAL MADE WITHOUT USE OF A KICKING TEE
62—Jason Hanson, Washington St. vs. Nevada-Las Vegas, Sept. 28, 1991

LONGEST FIELD GOAL MADE BY A FRESHMAN
59—Barry Childers, Marshall vs. Western Caro., Oct. 25, 1980; Tony Franklin, Texas A&M vs. Rice, Nov. 15, 1975

LONGEST FIELD GOAL MADE ON FIRST ATTEMPT OF CAREER
61—Ralf Mojsiejenko, Michigan St. vs. Illinois, Sept. 11, 1982

MOST FIELD GOALS MADE IN FIRST GAME OF CAREER
5—Jose Oceguera, Long Beach St. vs. Kansas St., Sept. 3, 1983 (5 attempts); Nathan Ritter, North Caro. St. vs. East Caro., Sept. 9, 1978 (6 attempts); Joe Liljenquist, Brigham Young vs. Colorado St., Sept. 20, 1969 (6 attempts)

MOST GAMES IN WHICH FIELD GOAL(S) PROVIDED THE WINNING MARGIN
Season
6—Henrik Mike-Mayer, Drake, 1981
Career
10—Jeff Ward, Texas, 1983-86; John Lee, UCLA, 1982-85; Dan Miller, Miami (Fla.), 1978-81

Team Records

SINGLE GAME—Offense

Total Offense

MOST PLAYS
112—Montana vs. Montana St., Nov. 1, 1952 (475 yards)

MOST PLAYS, BOTH TEAMS
196—San Diego St. (99) & North Texas (97), Dec. 4, 1971 (851 yards)

FEWEST PLAYS
12—Texas Tech vs. Centenary (La.), Nov. 11, 1939 (10 rushes, 2 passes, -1 yard)

FEWEST PLAYS, BOTH TEAMS
33—Texas Tech (12) & Centenary (La.) (21), Nov. 11, 1939 (28 rushes, 5 passes, 30 yards)

MOST YARDS GAINED
1,021—Houston vs. Southern Methodist, Oct. 21, 1989 (250 rushing, 771 passing, 86 plays)

MOST YARDS GAINED, BOTH TEAMS
1,563—Houston (827) & Texas Christian (736), Nov. 3, 1990 (187 plays)

FEWEST YARDS GAINED
Minus 47—Syracuse vs. Penn St., Oct. 18, 1947 (-107 rushing, gained 60 passing, 49 plays)

FEWEST YARDS GAINED, BOTH TEAMS
30—Texas Tech (-1) & Centenary (La.) (31), Nov. 11, 1939 (33 plays)

MOST YARDS GAINED BY A LOSING TEAM
736—Texas Christian vs. Houston, Nov. 3, 1990 (lost 35-56)

BOTH TEAMS GAINING 600 YARDS OR MORE
In 12 games. Most recent: Houston (684) & Texas Tech (636), Nov. 30, 1991 (182 plays); Brigham Young (767) & San Diego St. (695), Nov. 16, 1991 (168 plays); San Jose St. (616) & Pacific (Cal.) (603), Oct. 19, 1991 (157 plays)

FEWEST YARDS GAINED BY A WINNING TEAM
22—Citadel vs. Davidson, Nov. 23, 1946 (won 21-13)

HIGHEST AVERAGE GAIN PER PLAY (Min. 75 Plays)
11.9—Houston vs. Southern Methodist, Oct. 21, 1989 (86 for 1,021)

MOST TOUCHDOWNS SCORED BY RUSHING AND PASSING
15—Wyoming vs. Northern Colo., Nov. 5, 1949 (9 rushing, 6 passing)

Rushing

MOST RUSHES
99—Missouri vs. Colorado, Oct. 12, 1968 (421 yards)

MOST RUSHES, BOTH TEAMS
141—Colgate (82) & Bucknell (59), Nov. 6, 1971 (440 yards)

FEWEST RUSHES
5—Houston vs. Texas Tech, Nov. 25, 1989 (36 yards)

FEWEST RUSHES, BOTH TEAMS
28—Texas Tech (10) & Centenary (La.) (18), Nov. 11, 1939 (23 yards)

MOST YARDS GAINED
768—Oklahoma vs. Kansas St., Oct. 15, 1988 (72 rushes)

MOST YARDS GAINED, BOTH TEAMS
1,039—Lenoir-Rhyne (837) & Davidson (202), Oct. 11, 1975 (111 plays)

FEWEST YARDS GAINED, BOTH TEAMS
Minus 24—San Jose St. (-102) & UTEP (78), Oct. 22, 1966 (75 rushes)

MOST YARDS GAINED, BOTH TEAMS, MAJOR-COLLEGE OPPONENTS
956—Oklahoma (711) & Kansas St. (245), Oct. 23, 1971 (111 rushes)

MOST YARDS GAINED WITHOUT LOSS
677—Nebraska vs. New Mexico St., Sept. 18, 1982 (78 rushes)

MOST YARDS GAINED BY A LOSING TEAM
525—Air Force vs. New Mexico, Nov. 2, 1991 (70 rushes, lost 32-34)

HIGHEST AVERAGE GAIN PER RUSH
(Min. 50 Rushes)
11.9—Alabama vs. Virginia Tech, Oct. 27, 1973 (63 for 748)

MOST PLAYERS ON ONE TEAM EACH GAINING 100 YARDS OR MORE
4—Army vs. Montana, Nov. 17, 1984 (Doug Black 183, Nate Sassaman 155, Clarence Jones 130, Jarvis Hollingsworth 124); Alabama vs. Virginia Tech, Oct. 27, 1973 (Jimmy Taylor 142, Wilbur Jackson 138, Calvin Culliver 127, Richard Todd 102); Texas vs. Southern Methodist, Nov. 1, 1969 (Jim Bertelsen 137, Steve Worster 137, James Street 121, Ted Koy 111); Arizona St. vs. Arizona, Nov. 10, 1951 (Bob Tarwater 140, Harley Cooper 123, Duane Morrison 118, Buzz Walker 113)

MOST TOUCHDOWNS SCORED BY RUSHING
12—UTEP vs. New Mexico St., Nov. 25, 1948

Passing

MOST PASSES ATTEMPTED
81—Houston vs. Southern Methodist, Oct. 20, 1990 (completed 53)

MOST PASSES ATTEMPTED, BOTH TEAMS
135—Texas Christian (79) & Houston (56), Nov. 3, 1990 (completed 81)

FEWEST PASSES ATTEMPTED
0—By many teams. Most recent: Baylor vs. Southern Methodist, Oct. 9, 1993 (91 rushes)

FEWEST PASSES ATTEMPTED, BOTH TEAMS
1—Michigan St. (0) & Maryland (1), Oct. 20, 1944 (not completed)

MOST PASSES ATTEMPTED WITHOUT COMPLETION
18—West Va. vs. Temple, Oct. 18, 1946

MOST PASSES ATTEMPTED WITHOUT INTERCEPTION
72—Houston vs. Texas Christian, Nov. 4, 1989 (completed 47)

MOST PASSES ATTEMPTED WITHOUT INTERCEPTION, BOTH TEAMS
114—Illinois (67) & Purdue (47), Oct. 12, 1985 (completed 67)

MOST CONSECUTIVE PASSES ATTEMPTED WITHOUT A RUSHING PLAY
32—North Caro. St. vs. Duke, Nov. 11, 1989 (3rd & 4th quarters, completed 16)

MOST PASSES COMPLETED
53—Houston vs. Southern Methodist, Oct. 20, 1990 (attempted 81)

MOST PASSES COMPLETED, BOTH TEAMS
81—Texas Christian (44) & Houston (37), Nov. 3, 1990 (attempted 135)

BEST PERFECT GAME (1.000 Pct.)
11 of 11—North Caro. vs. William & Mary, Oct. 5, 1991; Air Force vs. Northwestern, Sept. 17, 1988; Oregon St. vs. UCLA, Oct. 2, 1971; Southern Cal vs. Washington, Oct. 9, 1965

HIGHEST PERCENTAGE OF PASSES COMPLETED
(Min. 15-24 comps.) 95.0%—Mississippi vs. Tulane, Nov. 6, 1982 (19 of 20)
(Min. 25-34 comps.) 92.6%—UCLA vs. Washington, Oct. 29, 1983 (25 of 27)
(Min. 35 comps.) 81.1%—California vs. Florida, Sept. 13, 1980 (43 of 53)

HIGHEST PERCENTAGE OF PASSES COMPLETED, BOTH TEAMS
(Min. 40 Completions)
84.6%—UCLA & Washington, Oct. 29, 1983 (44 of 52)

MOST PASSES HAD INTERCEPTED
10—California vs. UCLA, Oct. 21, 1978 (52 attempts); Detroit Mercy vs. Oklahoma St., Nov. 28, 1942

MOST YARDS GAINED
771—Houston vs. Southern Methodist, Oct. 21, 1989 (completed 40 of 61)

MOST YARDS GAINED, BOTH TEAMS
1,253—Texas Christian (690) & Houston (563), Nov. 3, 1990 (135 attempts)

FEWEST YARDS GAINED, BOTH TEAMS
Minus 13—North Caro. (-7 on 1 of 3 attempts) & Pennsylvania (-6 on 2 of 12 attempts), Nov. 13, 1943

MOST YARDS GAINED PER ATTEMPT
(Min. 30-39 atts.) 14.6—Arizona St. vs. Stanford, Oct. 24, 1981 (35 for 511)
(Min. 40 atts.) 15.9—UTEP vs. North Texas, Sept. 18, 1965 (40 for 634)

MOST YARDS GAINED PER COMPLETION
(Min. 15-24 comps.) 31.9—UTEP vs. New Mexico, Oct. 28, 1967 (16 for 510)
(Min. 25 comps.) 25.4—UTEP vs. North Texas, Sept. 18, 1965 (25 for 634)

MOST TOUCHDOWN PASSES
11—Houston vs. Eastern Wash., Nov. 17, 1990

MOST TOUCHDOWN PASSES, MAJOR-COLLEGE OPPONENTS
10—Houston vs. Southern Methodist, Oct. 21, 1989; San Diego St. vs. New Mexico St., Nov. 15, 1969

MOST TOUCHDOWN PASSES, BOTH TEAMS
14—Houston (11) & Eastern Wash. (3), Nov. 17, 1990

MOST TOUCHDOWN PASSES, BOTH TEAMS, MAJOR-COLLEGE OPPONENTS
13—San Diego St. (10) & New Mexico St. (3), Nov. 15, 1969

Punting

MOST PUNTS
39—Texas Tech vs. Centenary (La.), Nov. 11, 1939 (1,377 yards)
38—Centenary (La.) vs. Texas Tech, Nov. 11, 1939 (1,248 yards)

MOST PUNTS, BOTH TEAMS
77—Texas Tech (39) & Centenary (La.) (38), Nov. 11, 1939 (2,625 yards) (The game was played in a heavy downpour in Shreveport, Louisiana. Forty-two punts were returned, 19 went out of bounds, 10 were downed, 1 went into the end zone for a touchback, 4 were blocked and 1 was fair caught. Sixty-seven punts [34 by Texas Tech and 33 by Centenary] occurred on first-down plays, including 22 consecutively in the third and fourth quarters. The game was a scoreless tie.)

FEWEST PUNTS
0—By many teams. Most recent: Wisconsin vs. Michigan St., Dec. 5, 1993 (won 41-20); North Caro. vs. Duke, Nov. 26, 1993 (won 38-24)

FEWEST PUNTS BY A LOSING TEAM
0—By many teams. Most recent: New Mexico St. vs. UTEP, Sept. 14, 1991 (lost 21-22)

HIGHEST AVERAGE PER PUNT
(Min. 5-9 punts) 60.4—Brigham Young vs. Wyoming, Oct. 8, 1983 (5 for 302)
(Min. 10 punts) 53.6—Oklahoma St. vs. Colorado, Nov. 13, 1971 (10 for 536)

HIGHEST AVERAGE PER PUNT, BOTH TEAMS
(Min. 10 Punts)
55.3—Brigham Young & Wyoming, Oct. 8, 1983 (11 for 608)

Punt Returns

MOST PUNT RETURNS
22—Texas Tech vs. Centenary (La.), Nov. 11, 1939 (112 yards)

MOST PUNT RETURNS, BOTH TEAMS
42—Texas Tech (22) & Centenary (La.) (20), Nov. 11, 1939 (233 yards)

MOST YARDS ON PUNT RETURNS
319—Texas A&M vs. North Texas, Sept. 21, 1946 (10 returns)

HIGHEST AVERAGE GAIN PER RETURN
(Min. 5 Returns)
44.2—Denver vs. Colorado Col., Sept. 17, 1954 (6 for 265)

MOST TOUCHDOWNS SCORED ON PUNT RETURNS
3—Holy Cross vs. Brown, Sept. 21, 1974; Louisiana St. vs. Mississippi, Dec. 5, 1970; Wichita St. vs. Northern St., Oct. 22, 1949; Wisconsin vs. Iowa, Nov. 8, 1947

Kickoff Returns

MOST KICKOFF RETURNS
14—Arizona St. vs. Nevada, Oct. 12, 1946 (290 yards)

MOST YARDS ON KICKOFF RETURNS
295—Cincinnati vs. Memphis, Oct. 30, 1971 (8 returns)

HIGHEST AVERAGE GAIN PER RETURN
(Min. 6 Returns)
46.2—Southern Cal vs. Washington St., Nov. 7, 1970 (6 for 277)

MOST TOUCHDOWNS SCORED ON KICKOFF RETURNS
2—By many teams. Most recent: Brigham Young vs. Air Force, Nov. 11, 1989; Notre Dame vs. Michigan, Sept. 16, 1989; New Mexico St. vs. Drake, Oct. 15, 1983 (consecutive returns)

TOUCHDOWNS SCORED ON BACK-TO-BACK KICKOFF RETURNS, BOTH TEAMS
2—By many teams. Most recent: Wisconsin & Northern Ill., Sept. 14, 1985

Total Kick Returns

(Combined Punt and Kickoff Returns)

MOST YARDS ON KICK RETURNS
376—Florida St. vs. Virginia Tech, Nov. 16, 1974 (9 returns)

HIGHEST AVERAGE GAIN PER RETURN
(Min. 7 Returns)
41.8—Florida St. vs. Virginia Tech, Nov. 16, 1974 (9 for 376)

Scoring

MOST POINTS SCORED
103—Wyoming vs. Northern Colo. (0), Nov. 5, 1949 (15 TDs, 13 PATs)

MOST POINTS SCORED AGAINST A MAJOR-COLLEGE OPPONENT
100—Houston vs. Tulsa (6), Nov. 23, 1968 (14 TDs, 13 PATs, 1 FG)

MOST POINTS SCORED, BOTH TEAMS
124—Oklahoma (82) & Colorado (42), Oct. 4, 1980

MOST POINTS SCORED BY A LOSING TEAM
56—Purdue vs. Minnesota (59), Oct. 9, 1993

MOST POINTS, BOTH TEAMS IN A TIE GAME
104—Brigham Young (52) & San Diego St. (52), Nov. 16, 1991

MOST POINTS SCORED IN ONE QUARTER
49—Fresno St. vs. New Mexico, Oct. 5, 1991 (2nd quarter); Davidson vs. Furman, Sept. 27, 1969 (2nd quarter); Houston vs. Tulsa, Nov. 23, 1968 (4th quarter)

MOST POINTS SCORED IN ONE HALF
76—Houston vs. Tulsa, Nov. 23, 1968 (2nd half)

MOST TOUCHDOWNS SCORED
15—Wyoming vs. Northern Colo., Nov. 5, 1949 (9 rushing, 6 passing)

MOST TOUCHDOWNS SCORED, BOTH TEAMS
18—Oklahoma (12) & Colorado (6), Oct. 4, 1980

MOST EXTRA POINTS MADE BY KICKING
13—Fresno St. vs. New Mexico, Oct. 5, 1991 (attempted 13); Houston vs. Tulsa, Nov. 23, 1968 (attempted 14); Wyoming vs. Northern Colo., Nov. 5, 1949 (attempted 15)

MOST TWO-POINT ATTEMPTS SCORED
7—Pacific (Cal.) vs. San Diego St., Nov. 22, 1958 (attempted 9)

MOST DEFENSIVE EXTRA-POINT ATTEMPTS
2—Northern Ill. vs. Akron, Nov. 3, 1990 (2 interception returns); Rice vs. Notre Dame, Nov. 5, 1988 (2 kick returns; 1 scored)

MOST DEFENSIVE EXTRA-POINT ATTEMPTS SCORED
1—By many teams

MOST FIELD GOALS MADE
7—Nebraska vs. Missouri, Oct. 19, 1985 (attempted 7); Western Mich. vs. Marshall, Sept. 29, 1984 (attempted 9)

MOST FIELD GOALS MADE, BOTH TEAMS
9—Southwestern La. (5) & Central Mich. (4), Sept. 9, 1989 (attempted 11)

MOST FIELD GOALS ATTEMPTED
9—Western Mich. vs. Marshall, Sept. 29, 1984 (made 7)

MOST FIELD GOALS ATTEMPTED, BOTH TEAMS
12—Clemson (6) & Georgia (6), Sept. 17, 1983 (made 6)

MOST FIELD GOALS MISSED
7—Louisiana St. vs. Florida, Nov. 25, 1972 (attempted 8)

First Downs

MOST FIRST DOWNS
44—Nebraska vs. Utah St., Sept. 7, 1991 (33 rush, 10 pass, 1 penalty)

MOST FIRST DOWNS, BOTH TEAMS
72—New Mexico (37) & San Diego St. (35), Sept. 27, 1986

FEWEST FIRST DOWNS BY A WINNING TEAM
0—Michigan vs. Ohio St., Nov. 25, 1950 (won 9-3); North Caro. St. vs. Virginia, Sept. 30, 1944 (won 13-0)

MOST FIRST DOWNS BY RUSHING
36—Nebraska vs. New Mexico St., Sept. 18, 1982

MOST FIRST DOWNS BY PASSING
30—Brigham Young vs. Colorado St., Nov. 7, 1981; Tulsa vs. Idaho St., Oct. 7, 1967

Fumbles

MOST FUMBLES
17—Wichita St. vs. Florida St., Sept. 20, 1969 (lost 10)

MOST FUMBLES, BOTH TEAMS
27—Wichita St. (17) & Florida St. (10), Sept. 20, 1969 (lost 17)

MOST FUMBLES LOST
10—Wichita St. vs. Florida St., Sept. 20, 1969 (17 fumbles)

MOST FUMBLES LOST, BOTH TEAMS
17—Wichita St. (10) & Florida St. (7), Sept. 20, 1969 (27 fumbles)

MOST FUMBLES LOST IN A QUARTER
5—San Diego St. vs. California, Sept. 18, 1982 (1st quarter); East Caro. vs. Southwestern La., Sept. 13, 1980 (3rd quarter on 5 consecutive possessions)

Penalties

MOST PENALTIES AGAINST
24—San Jose St. vs. Fresno St., Oct. 4, 1986 (199 yards)

MOST PENALTIES, BOTH TEAMS
36—San Jose St. (24) & Fresno St. (12), Oct. 4, 1986 (317 yards)

FEWEST PENALTIES, BOTH TEAMS
0—By many teams. Most recent: Army & Navy, Dec. 6, 1986

MOST YARDS PENALIZED
238—Arizona St. vs. UTEP, Nov. 11, 1961 (13 penalties)

MOST YARDS PENALIZED, BOTH TEAMS
421—Grambling (16 for 216 yards) & Texas Southern (17 for 205 yards), Oct. 29, 1977

Turnovers

(Number of Times Losing the Ball on Interceptions and Fumbles)

MOST TURNOVERS LOST
13—Georgia vs. Georgia Tech, Dec. 1, 1951 (8 interceptions, 5 fumbles)

MOST TURNOVERS, BOTH TEAMS
20—Wichita St. (12) & Florida St. (8), Sept. 20, 1969 (17 fumbles, 3 interceptions)

MOST TOTAL PLAYS WITHOUT A TURNOVER (Rushes, Passes, All Runbacks)
110—Baylor vs. Rice, Nov. 13, 1976; California vs. San Jose St., Oct. 5, 1968 (also did not fumble)

MOST TOTAL PLAYS WITHOUT A TURNOVER, BOTH TEAMS
184—Arkansas (93) & Texas A&M (91), Nov. 2, 1968

MOST TOTAL PLAYS WITHOUT A TURNOVER OR A FUMBLE, BOTH TEAMS
158—Stanford (88) & Oregon (70), Nov. 2, 1957

MOST TURNOVERS BY A WINNING TEAM
11—Purdue vs. Illinois, Oct. 2, 1943 (9 fumbles, 2 interceptions; won 40-21)

MOST PASSES HAD INTERCEPTED BY A WINNING TEAM
7—Pittsburgh vs. Army, Nov. 15, 1980 (54 attempts; won 45-7)

MOST FUMBLES LOST BY A WINNING TEAM
9—Arizona St. vs. Utah, Oct. 14, 1972 (10 fumbles; won 59-48); Purdue vs. Illinois, Oct. 2, 1943 (10 fumbles; won 40-21)

SINGLE GAME—Defense

Total Defense

FEWEST PLAYS ALLOWED
12—Centenary (La.) vs. Texas Tech, Nov. 11, 1939 (10 rushes, 2 passes; -1 yard)

FEWEST YARDS ALLOWED
Minus 47—Penn St. vs. Syracuse, Oct. 18, 1947 (-107 rushing, 60 passing; 49 plays)

MOST YARDS ALLOWED
1,021—Southern Methodist vs. Houston, Oct. 21, 1989 (250 rushing, 771 passing)

Rushing Defense

FEWEST RUSHES ALLOWED
5—Texas Tech vs. Houston, Nov. 25, 1989 (36 yards)

FEWEST RUSHING YARDS ALLOWED
Minus 109—Toledo vs. Northern Ill., Nov. 11, 1967 (33 rushes)

Pass Defense

FEWEST ATTEMPTS ALLOWED
0—By many teams. Most recent: Colorado vs. Oklahoma, Nov. 15, 1986

FEWEST COMPLETIONS ALLOWED
0—By many teams. Most recent: Southern Cal vs. Oregon St., Oct. 16, 1993 (5 attempts)

LOWEST COMPLETION PERCENTAGE ALLOWED (Min. 10 Attempts)
.000—San Jose St. vs. Cal St. Fullerton, Oct. 10, 1992 (0 of 11 attempts); Temple vs. West Va., Oct. 18, 1946 (0 of 18 attempts)

FEWEST YARDS ALLOWED
Minus 16—Va. Military vs. Richmond, Oct. 5, 1957 (2 completions)

MOST PASSES INTERCEPTED BY
11—Brown vs. Rhode Island, Oct. 8, 1949 (136 yards)

MOST PASSES INTERCEPTED BY AGAINST A MAJOR-COLLEGE OPPONENT
10—UCLA vs. California, Oct. 21, 1978; Oklahoma St. vs. Detroit Mercy, Nov. 28, 1942

MOST PASSES INTERCEPTED BY A LOSING TEAM
7—Kentucky vs. Florida, Sept. 11, 1993 (52 attempts)

MOST YARDS ON INTERCEPTION RETURNS
240—Kentucky vs. Mississippi, Oct. 1, 1949 (6 returns)

MOST TOUCHDOWNS ON INTERCEPTION RETURNS
4—Houston vs. Texas, Nov. 7, 1987 (198 yards; 3 TDs in the fourth quarter)

First Downs

FEWEST FIRST DOWNS ALLOWED
0—By many teams. Most recent: North Caro. St. vs. Western Caro., Sept. 1, 1990

Opponent's Kicks Blocked

MOST OPPONENT'S PUNTS BLOCKED
4—Memphis vs. Arkansas, Sept. 26, 1992 (10 attempts); Michigan vs. Ohio St., Nov. 25, 1950; Southern Methodist vs. Texas-Arlington, Sept. 30, 1944

MOST OPPONENT'S PUNTS BLOCKED, ONE QUARTER
3—Purdue vs. Northwestern, Nov. 11, 1989 (4 attempts)

Turnovers Gained

(Number of Times Gaining the Ball on Interceptions and Fumbles)

MOST TURNOVERS GAINED
13—Georgia Tech vs. Georgia, Dec. 1, 1951 (8 interceptions, 5 fumbles)

MOST CONSECUTIVE OPPONENT'S SERIES RESULTING IN TURNOVERS
7—Florida vs. Florida St., Oct. 7, 1972 (3 interceptions, 4 fumbles lost; first seven series of the game)

Fumble Returns

(Since 1992)

MOST TOUCHDOWNS ON FUMBLE RETURNS
2—Arizona vs. Illinois, Sept. 18, 1993; Toledo vs. Arkansas St., Sept. 5, 1992

LONGEST RETURN OF A FUMBLE
97 yards—East Caro. vs. West Va., Nov. 7, 1992

Defensive Extra Points

MOST DEFENSIVE EXTRA POINTS SCORED AGAINST
1—By many teams. Most recent: Pittsburgh vs. Penn St., Nov. 21, 1992 (kick return)

MOST DEFENSIVE EXTRA-POINT ATTEMPTS AGAINST
2—Akron vs. Northern Ill., Nov. 3, 1990 (2 interception returns); Notre Dame vs. Rice, Nov. 5, 1988 (2 blocked kick returns, 1 scored)

SEASON—Offense

Total Offense

MOST YARDS GAINED PER GAME
624.9—Houston, 1989 (6,874 in 11)

MOST YARDS GAINED
6,874—Houston, 1989 (11 games)

HIGHEST AVERAGE GAIN PER PLAY
7.9—Army, 1945 (526 for 4,164)

GAINING 300 YARDS OR MORE PER GAME RUSHING AND 200 YARDS OR MORE PER GAME PASSING
Arizona St., 1973 (310.2 rushing, 255.3 passing); Houston, 1968 (361.7 rushing, 200.3 passing)

MOST PLAYS PER GAME
92.4—Notre Dame, 1970 (924 in 10)

MOST TOUCHDOWNS RUSHING AND PASSING
84—Nebraska, 1983
Also holds per-game record at 7.0

Rushing

MOST YARDS GAINED PER GAME
472.4—Oklahoma, 1971 (5,196 in 11)

HIGHEST AVERAGE GAIN PER RUSH
7.6—Army, 1945 (424 for 3,238)

HIGHEST AVERAGE GAIN PER RUSH (Min. 500 Rushes)
6.8—Oklahoma, 1971 (761 for 5,196)

MOST RUSHES PER GAME
73.9—Oklahoma, 1974 (813 in 11)

MOST TOUCHDOWNS RUSHING PER GAME
5.1—Texas, 1970, 1969; Oklahoma, 1956 (each 51 in 10)

Passing

MOST YARDS GAINED PER GAME
511.3—Houston, 1989 (5,624 in 11)

MOST YARDS GAINED
5,624—Houston, 1989 (11 games)

HIGHEST AVERAGE GAIN PER ATTEMPT (Min. 350 Attempts)
10.9—Brigham Young, 1989 (433 for 4,732)

HIGHEST AVERAGE GAIN PER COMPLETION
(Min. 100-174 comps.) 19.1—Houston, 1968 (105 for 2,003)
(Min. 175-224 comps.) 18.0—Grambling, 1977 (187 for 3,360)
(Min. 225 comps.) 17.0—Brigham Young, 1989 (279 for 4,732)

MOST PASSES ATTEMPTED PER GAME
63.1—Houston, 1989 (694 in 11)

MOST PASSES COMPLETED PER GAME
39.4—Houston, 1989 (434 in 11)

HIGHEST PERCENTAGE COMPLETED (Min. 150 Attempts)
70.8%—Long Beach St., 1985 (323 of 456)

LOWEST PERCENTAGE HAD INTERCEPTED
(Min. 300-399 atts.) 1.1%—Georgia, 1991 (4 of 355)
(Min. 400 atts.) 1.2%—Southern Cal, 1993 (5 of 432)

MOST TOUCHDOWN PASSES PER GAME
5.0—Houston, 1989 (55 in 11)

MOST TOUCHDOWN PASSES
55—Houston, 1989 (11 games)

FEWEST TOUCHDOWN PASSES
0—By 6 teams since 1975. Most recent: Vanderbilt, 1993 (11 games, 157 attempts)

HIGHEST PASSING EFFICIENCY RATING POINTS (Min. 150 Attempts)
174.45—Brigham Young, 1989 (433 attempts, 279 completions, 15 interceptions, 4,732 yards, 33 TD passes)

A TEAM WITH A 3,000-YARD PASSER, 1,000-YARD RECEIVER AND 1,000-YARD RUSHER
San Diego St., 1993 (Tim Gutierrez 3,033 passing, Darnay Scott 1,262 receiving, Marshall Faulk 1,530 rushing); Wyoming, 1993 (Joe Hughes 3,135 passing, Ryan Yarborough 1,512 receiving, Ryan Christopherson 1,014 rushing); Houston, 1989 (Andre Ware 4,699 passing, Manny Hazard 1,689 receiving, Chuck Weatherspoon 1,146 rushing); Colorado St., 1983 (Terry Nugent 3,319 passing, Jeff Champine 1,002 receiving, Steve Bartalo 1,113 rushing); Southern Methodist, 1968 (Chuck Hixson 3,103 passing, Jerry LeVias 1,131 receiving, Mike Richardson 1,034 rushing)

A TEAM WITH TWO 1,000-YARD RECEIVERS
Nevada, 1993 (Bryan Reeves, 1,362 & Michael Stephens, 1,062); Colorado, 1992 (Charles Johnson, 1,149 & Michael Westbrook, 1,060); San Diego St., 1990 (Patrick Rowe, 1,392 & Dennis Arey, 1,118); Brigham Young, 1990 (Andy Boyce, 1,241 & Chris Smith, 1,156); Houston, 1988 (Jason Phillips, 1,444 & James Dixon, 1,103)

A TEAM WITH THE NO. 1 & NO. 2 RECEIVERS
Houston, 1988 (Jason Phillips, No. 1, 9.82 catches per game & James Dixon, No. 2, 9.27 catches per game)

MOST 100-YARD RECEIVING GAMES IN A SEASON, ONE TEAM
19—San Diego St., 1990 (Patrick Rowe 9, Dennis Arey 8 & Jimmy Raye 2)

Punting

MOST PUNTS PER GAME
13.9—Tennessee, 1937 (139 in 10)

FEWEST PUNTS PER GAME
2.0—Nevada, 1948 (18 in 9)

HIGHEST PUNTING AVERAGE
50.6—Brigham Young, 1983 (24 for 1,215 yards)

HIGHEST PUNTING AVERAGE (Min. 40 Punts)
47.6—Vanderbilt, 1984 (59 for 2,810)

HIGHEST NET PUNTING AVERAGE
45.0—Brigham Young, 1983 (24 for 1,215 yards, 134 yards in punts returned)

HIGHEST NET PUNTING AVERAGE (Min. 40 Punts)
44.4—Colorado St., 1976 (72 for 3,323, 123 yards in punts returned)

Punt Returns

MOST PUNT RETURNS PER GAME
6.9—Texas A&M, 1943 (69 in 10)

FEWEST PUNT RETURNS PER GAME
0.5—Iowa, 1971 (6 in 11)

MOST PUNT-RETURN YARDS PER GAME
114.5—Colgate, 1941 (916 in 8)

HIGHEST AVERAGE GAIN PER RETURN
(Min. 15-29 rets.) 25.2—Arizona St., 1952 (18 for 454 yards)
(Min. 30 rets.) 22.4—Oklahoma, 1948 (43 for 963)

MOST TOUCHDOWNS SCORED ON PUNT RETURNS (From 1966)
7—Southern Miss., 1987 (on 46 returns)

Kickoff Returns

MOST KICKOFF RETURNS PER GAME
7.3—Cal St. Fullerton, 1990 (80 in 11)

FEWEST KICKOFF RETURNS PER GAME
0.7—Boston College, 1939 (7 in 10)

MOST KICKOFF-RETURN YARDS PER GAME
134.7—Virginia Tech, 1973 (1,482 in 11)

HIGHEST AVERAGE GAIN PER RETURN
(Min. 25-34 rets.) 30.3—Florida St., 1992 (27 for 819)
(Min. 35 rets.) 27.5—Rice, 1973 (39 for 1,074)

MOST TOUCHDOWNS SCORED ON KICKOFF RETURNS (From 1966)
4—Dayton, 1974 (on 44 returns)

Scoring

MOST POINTS PER GAME
56.0—Army, 1944 (504 in 9)

MOST POINTS SCORED
624—Nebraska, 1983 (12 games)

HIGHEST SCORING MARGIN
52.1—Army, 1944 (scored 504 points for 56.0 average and allowed 35 points for 3.9 average in 9 games)

MOST POINTS SCORED, TWO CONSECUTIVE GAMES
177—Houston, 1968 (77-3 vs. Idaho, Nov. 16, and 100-6 vs. Tulsa, Nov. 23)

MOST TOUCHDOWNS PER GAME
8.2—Army, 1944 (74 in 9)

MOST TOUCHDOWNS
89—Nebraska, 1983 (12 games)

MOST EXTRA POINTS MADE BY KICKING
77—Nebraska, 1983 (77 in 12, attempted 85)
Also holds per-game record at 6.4

MOST CONSECUTIVE EXTRA POINTS MADE BY KICKING
67—Oklahoma St., 1988 (attempted 67)

MOST TWO-POINT ATTEMPTS MADE PER GAME
2.2—Rutgers, 1958 (20 in 9, attempted 31)

MOST DEFENSIVE EXTRA-POINT ATTEMPTS
3—Rice, 1988 (1 vs. Southwestern La., Sept. 24, blocked kick return; 2 vs. Notre Dame, Nov. 5, 2 blocked kick returns, 1 scored)

MOST DEFENSIVE EXTRA-POINT ATTEMPTS SCORED
1—By 23 teams. Most recent: Penn St., 1992 (kick return vs. Pittsburgh, Nov. 21)

MOST FIELD GOALS PER GAME
2.6—UCLA, 1984 (29 in 11)

First Downs

MOST FIRST DOWNS PER GAME
30.9—Brigham Young, 1983 (340 in 11)

MOST RUSHING FIRST DOWNS PER GAME
21.4—Oklahoma, 1974 (235 in 11)

MOST PASSING FIRST DOWNS PER GAME
19.8—Brigham Young, 1990 (237 in 12)

Fumbles

MOST FUMBLES
73—Cal St. Fullerton, 1992 (lost 41)

MOST FUMBLES LOST
41—Cal St. Fullerton, 1992 (fumbled 73 times)

FEWEST OWN FUMBLES LOST
2—Bowling Green, 1993; Dayton, 1968; UCLA, 1952; Tulsa, 1942; Washington, 1941

MOST CONSECUTIVE FUMBLES LOST
14—Oklahoma, 1983 (during 5 games, Oct. 8-Nov. 5)

Penalties

MOST PENALTIES PER GAME
12.9—Grambling, 1977 (142 in 11, 1,476 yards)

MOST YARDS PENALIZED PER GAME
134.2—Grambling, 1977 (1,476 in 11, 142 penalties)

Turnovers (Giveaways)

(Passes Had Intercepted and Fumbles Lost)

FEWEST TURNOVERS
8—Miami (Ohio), 1966 (4 interceptions, 4 fumbles lost)

FEWEST TURNOVERS PER GAME
0.8—Miami (Ohio), 1966 (8 in 10 games)

MOST TURNOVERS
61—Tulsa, 1976 (24 interceptions, 37 fumbles lost); North Texas, 1971 (33 interceptions, 28 fumbles lost)

MOST TURNOVERS PER GAME
6.1—Mississippi St., 1949 (55 in 9 games; 25 interceptions, 30 fumbles lost)

SEASON—Defense

Total Defense

FEWEST YARDS ALLOWED PER GAME
69.9—Santa Clara, 1937 (559 in 8)

FEWEST RUSHING AND PASSING TOUCHDOWNS ALLOWED PER GAME
0.0—Tennessee, 1939; Duke, 1938

LOWEST AVERAGE YARDS ALLOWED PER PLAY
1.7—Texas A&M, 1939 (447 for 763)

LOWEST AVERAGE YARDS ALLOWED PER PLAY
(Min. 600-699 plays) 2.5—Nebraska, 1967 (627 for 1,576)
(Min. 700 plays) 2.7—Toledo, 1971 (734 for 1,795)

MOST YARDS ALLOWED PER GAME
553.0—Maryland, 1993 (6,083 in 11)

Rushing Defense

FEWEST YARDS ALLOWED PER GAME
17.0—Penn St., 1947 (153 in 9)

MOST YARDS LOST BY OPPONENTS PER GAME
70.1—Wyoming, 1968 (701 in 10, 458 rushes)

LOWEST AVERAGE YARDS ALLOWED PER RUSH
(Min. 240-399 rushes) 0.6—Penn St., 1947 (240 for 153)
(Min. 400-499 rushes) 1.3—North Texas, 1966 (408 for 513)
(Min. 500 rushes) 2.1—Nebraska, 1971 (500 for 1,031)

Pass Defense

FEWEST YARDS ALLOWED PER GAME
13.1—Penn St., 1938 (105 in 8)

FEWEST YARDS ALLOWED PER ATTEMPT
(Min. 200-299 atts.) 3.4—Toledo, 1970 (251 for 856)
(Min. 300 atts.) 3.8—Notre Dame, 1967 (306 for 1,158)

FEWEST YARDS ALLOWED PER COMPLETION
(Min. 100-149 comps.) 9.4—Oklahoma, 1986 (128 for 1,198)
(Min. 150 comps.) 9.5—Notre Dame, 1993 (263 for 2,502)

LOWEST COMPLETION PERCENTAGE ALLOWED
(Min. 150-199 atts.) 31.1%—Virginia, 1952 (50 of 161)
(Min. 200 atts.) 33.3%—Notre Dame, 1967 (102 of 306)

FEWEST TOUCHDOWNS ALLOWED BY PASSING
0—By many teams. Most recent: Louisiana St., 1959; North Texas, 1959

LOWEST PASS EFFICIENCY DEFENSIVE RATING (From 1990)
74.99—Texas A&M, 1993 (292 attempts, 116 completions, 13 interceptions, 1,339 yards, 5 TDs)

MOST PASSES INTERCEPTED BY PER GAME
4.1—Pennsylvania, 1940 (33 in 8)

HIGHEST PERCENTAGE INTERCEPTED BY (Min. 200 Attempts)
17.9%—Army, 1944 (36 of 201)

MOST YARDS GAINED ON INTERCEPTION RETURNS
782—Tennessee, 1971 (25 interceptions)

MOST INTERCEPTION YARDS PER GAME
72.5—Texas, 1943 (580 in 8)

HIGHEST AVERAGE PER INTERCEPTION RETURN
(Min. 10-14 ints.) 36.3—Oregon St., 1959 (12 for 436)
(Min. 15 ints.) 31.3—Tennessee, 1971 (25 for 782)

MOST TOUCHDOWNS ON INTERCEPTION RETURNS
7—Tennessee, 1971 (25 interceptions; 287 pass attempts against)

Punting

MOST OPPONENT'S PUNTS BLOCKED BY
11—Arkansas St., 1975 (11 games, 95 punts against)

Punt Returns

FEWEST RETURNS ALLOWED
5—Notre Dame, 1968 (52 yards)

FEWEST YARDS ALLOWED
2—Miami (Fla.), 1989 (12 returns)

LOWEST AVERAGE YARDS ALLOWED PER PUNT RETURN
0.2—Miami (Fla.), 1989 (12 for 2 yards)

Kickoff Returns

LOWEST AVERAGE YARDS ALLOWED PER KICKOFF RETURN
8.3—Richmond, 1951 (23 for 192 yards)

Opponent's Kicks Blocked

MOST PAT KICKS BLOCKED
Season
6—Duke, 1993

Scoring

FEWEST POINTS ALLOWED PER GAME
0.0—Tennessee, 1939 (10 games); Duke, 1938 (9 games)

MOST POINTS ALLOWED AND POINTS ALLOWED PER GAME
544 and 49.5—UTEP, 1973 (11 games)

Fumbles

MOST OPPONENT'S FUMBLES RECOVERED
36—Brigham Young, 1977; North Texas, 1972

MOST TOUCHDOWNS SCORED ON FUMBLE RETURNS
3—Tulane, 1993

Turnovers (Takeaways)

(Opponent's Passes Intercepted and Fumbles Recovered)

MOST OPPONENT'S TURNOVERS
57—Tennessee, 1970 (36 interceptions, 21 fumbles lost)

MOST OPPONENT'S TURNOVERS PER GAME
5.4—UCLA, 1954 (49 in 9); UCLA, 1952 (49 in 9); Pennsylvania, 1950 (49 in 9); Wyoming, 1950 (49 in 9)

HIGHEST MARGIN OF TURNOVERS PER GAME OVER OPPONENTS
4.0—UCLA, 1952 (36 in 9; 13 giveaways vs. 49 takeaways)
Also holds total-margin record at 36

HIGHEST MARGIN OF TURNOVERS PER GAME BY OPPONENTS
3.1—Southern Miss., 1969 (31 in 10; 45 giveaways vs. 14 takeaways)

Defensive Extra Points

MOST DEFENSIVE EXTRA-POINT ATTEMPTS AGAINST
2—Notre Dame, 1988 (2 kick returns, 1 scored); Southwestern La., 1988 (2 kick returns, none scored)

MOST DEFENSIVE EXTRA POINTS SCORED AGAINST
2—Oklahoma, 1992 (vs. Texas Tech, Sept. 3, and vs. Oklahoma St., Nov. 14)

Consecutive Records

MOST CONSECUTIVE VICTORIES
47—Oklahoma, 1953-57

MOST CONSECUTIVE GAMES WITHOUT DEFEAT
48—Oklahoma, 1953-57 (1 tie)

MOST CONSECUTIVE LOSSES
34—Northwestern, from Sept. 22, 1979, vs. Syracuse through Sept. 18, 1982, vs. Miami (Ohio)
Ended with 31-6 victory over Northern Ill., Sept. 25, 1982

MOST CONSECUTIVE GAMES WITHOUT A VICTORY ON THE ROAD
46—Northwestern (including one tie), from Nov. 23, 1974, through Oct. 30, 1982

MOST CONSECUTIVE GAMES WITHOUT A TIE
(Includes Bowl Games)
311—Miami (Fla.) (current), from Nov. 11, 1968

MOST CONSECUTIVE GAMES WITHOUT BEING SHUT OUT
246—UCLA, from Oct. 2, 1971, to Oct. 24, 1992 (ended by Arizona St. with 20-0 victory)

MOST CONSECUTIVE SHUTOUTS
(Regular Season)
17—Tennessee, from Nov. 5, 1938, through Oct. 12, 1940

MOST CONSECUTIVE QUARTERS OPPONENTS HELD SCORELESS
(Regular Season)
71—Tennessee, from 2nd quarter vs. Louisiana St., Oct. 29, 1938, to 2nd quarter vs. Alabama, Oct. 19, 1940

MOST CONSECUTIVE VICTORIES AT HOME
57—Miami (Fla.) (Orange Bowl), from Oct. 12, 1985 (current); Alabama (at Tuscaloosa), from Oct. 26, 1963, through Oct. 23, 1982

MOST CONSECUTIVE WINNING SEASONS
32—Nebraska (current), from 1962

MOST CONSECUTIVE NON-LOSING SEASONS
49—Penn St., 1939-1987

MOST CONSECUTIVE NON-WINNING SEASONS
28—Rice, 1964-91

MOST CONSECUTIVE SEASONS WINNING NINE OR MORE GAMES
25—Nebraska (current), from 1969

MOST CONSECUTIVE SEASONS PLAYING IN A BOWL GAME
25—Nebraska (current), from 1969; Alabama, from 1959 through 1983

MOST CONSECUTIVE GAMES SCORING ON A PASS
37—Brigham Young, from Nov. 31, 1981, through Sept. 7, 1985

MOST CONSECUTIVE GAMES PASSING FOR 200 YARDS OR MORE
64—Brigham Young, from Sept. 13, 1980, through Oct. 19, 1985

MOST CONSECUTIVE GAMES WITHOUT A SHUTOUT
216—Tulane, from Dec. 29, 1973, to Sept. 11, 1993 (34-0 shutout by Rice)

MOST CONSECUTIVE EXTRA POINTS MADE
262—Syracuse, from Nov. 18, 1978, to Sept. 9, 1989. (By the following kickers: Dave Jacobs, last PAT of 1978; Gary Anderson, 72 from 1979 through 1981; Russ Carpentieri, 17 in 1982; Don McAulay, 62 from 1983 through 1985; Tim Vesling, 71 in 1986 and 1987; Kevin Greene, 37 in 1988; John Biskup, 2 in 1989.)

MOST CONSECUTIVE STADIUM SELLOUTS
195—Nebraska (current), from 1962

Additional Records

HIGHEST-SCORING TIE GAME
52-52—Brigham Young & San Diego St., Nov. 16, 1991

MOST TIE GAMES IN A SEASON
4—Central Mich., 1991 (11 games); UCLA, 1939 (10 games); Temple, 1937 (9 games)

MOST SCORELESS TIE GAMES IN A SEASON
4—Temple, 1937 (9 games)

MOST CONSECUTIVE SCORELESS TIE GAMES
2—Alabama, 1954 vs. Georgia, Oct. 30 & vs. Tulane, Nov. 6; Georgia Tech, 1938 vs. Florida, Nov. 19 & vs. Georgia, Nov. 26

LAST SCORELESS TIE GAME
Nov. 19, 1983—Oregon & Oregon St.

MOST POINTS OVERCOME TO WIN A GAME
(Between Division I-A Teams)
31—Ohio St. (41), Minnesota (37), Oct. 28, 1989 (trailed 0-31 with 4:29 remaining in 2nd quarter); Maryland (42), Miami (Fla.) (40), Nov. 10, 1984 (trailed 0-31 with 12:35 remaining in 3rd quarter)
30—California (42), Oregon (41), Oct. 2, 1993 (trailed 0-30 in 2nd quarter)

MOST POINTS SCORED IN FOURTH QUARTER TO WIN A GAME
28—Washington St. (49) vs. Stanford (42), Oct. 20, 1984 (trailed 14-42 with 5:38 remaining in third quarter and scored 35 consecutive points)

MOST POINTS SCORED IN A BRIEF PERIOD OF TIME
41 in 2:55 of possession time during six drives—Nebraska vs. Colorado, Oct. 15, 1983 (6 TDs, 5 PATs in 3rd quarter. Drives occurred during 9:10 of total playing time in the period)
21 in 1:24 of total playing time—San Jose St. (42) vs. Fresno St. (7), Nov. 17, 1990 (3 TDs, 3 PATs in second quarter; 1:17 of possession time on two drives and one intercepted pass returned for a TD)

MOST IMPROVED WON-LOST RECORD
8 games—Purdue, 1943 (9-0) from 1942 (1-8); Stanford, 1940 (10-0, including a bowl win) from 1939 (1-7-1)

MOST IMPROVED WON-LOST RECORD AFTER WINLESS SEASON
7 games—Florida, 1980 (8-4-0, including a bowl win) from 1979 (0-10-1)

Annual Champions, All-Time Leaders

Total Offense

CAREER YARDS PER GAME
(Minimum 5,500 yards)

Player, Team	Years	G	Plays	Yards	TDR‡	Yd. PG
Chris Vargas, Nevada	§1992-93	20	872	6,417	48	*320.9
Ty Detmer, Brigham Young	1988-91	46	*1,795	*14,665	*135	318.8
Mike Perez, San Jose St.	1986-87	20	875	6,182	37	309.1
Doug Gaynor, Long Beach St.	1984-85	22	1,067	6,710	45	305.0
Tony Eason, Illinois	1981-82	22	1,016	6,589	43	299.5
David Klingler, Houston	1988-91	32	1,431	9,327	93	291.5
Steve Young, Brigham Young	1981-83	31	1,177	8,817	74	284.4
Doug Flutie, Boston College	1981-84	42	1,558	11,317	74	269.5
Brent Snyder, Utah St.	1987-88	22	1,040	5,916	43	268.9
Anthony Calvillo, Utah St.	1992-93	22	983	5,838	43	265.4
Shane Matthews, Florida	1989-92	35	1,397	9,241	82	264.0
Joe Hughes, Wyoming	1992-93	23	911	6,007	49	261.2
Larry Egger, Utah	1985-86	22	903	5,651	42	256.9
Jim Plunkett, Stanford	1968-70	31	1,174	7,887	62	254.4
Troy Kopp, Pacific (Cal.)	1989-92	40	1,595	10,037	90	250.9
Randall Cunningham, Nevada-Las Vegas	1982-84	33	1,330	8,224	67	249.2
Erik Wilhelm, Oregon St.	1985-88	37	1,689	9,062	55	244.9
Todd Dillon, Long Beach St.	1982-83	23	1,031	5,588	38	243.0
Bernie Kosar, Miami (Fla.)	1983-84	23	847	5,585	48	242.8
Alex Van Pelt, Pittsburgh	1989-92	45	1,570	10,814	58	240.3
Jack Trudeau, Illinois	1981, 83-85	34	1,318	8,096	56	238.1
Chuck Hixson, Southern Methodist	1968-70	29	1,358	6,884	50	237.4
Robbie Bosco, Brigham Young	1983-85	35	1,159	8,299	72	237.1
Dan McGwire, Iowa/San Diego St.	1986-87, 89-90	32	1,067	7,557	50	236.2
Johnny Bright, Drake	1949-51	25	825	5,903	64	236.1

Stanford quarterback Jim Plunkett finished his collegiate career in 1970 as the all-time major-college leader in total offensive yards per game. His mark of 254.4 still ranks 14th.

Boston College quarterback Doug Flutie's 11,317 yards of total offense ranks second on the Division I-A career list.

Player, Team	Years	G	Plays	Yards	TDR‡	Yd. PG
Jeff Garcia, San Jose St.	1991-93	31	1,146	7,274	63	234.6
Brian McClure, Bowling Green	1982-85	42	1,630	9,774	67	232.7
Marc Wilson, Brigham Young	1977-79	33	1,183	7,602	68	230.4
Todd Santos, San Diego St.	1984-87	46	1,722	10,513	71	228.5
Pat Sullivan, Auburn	1969-71	30	970	6,844	71	228.1
John Reaves, Florida	1969-71	32	1,258	7,283	58	227.6

Record. ‡Touchdowns-responsible-for are player's TDs scored and passed for. §Competed two years in Division I-A and two years in Division I-AA. Four-year totals: 8,184 yards and 233.8 average.

SEASON YARDS PER GAME

Player, Team	Year	G	Plays	Yards	TDR‡	Yd. PG
David Klingler, Houston	†1990	11	*704	*5,221	*55	*474.6
Andre Ware, Houston	†1989	11	628	4,661	49	423.7
Ty Detmer, Brigham Young	1990	12	635	5,022	45	418.5
Steve Young, Brigham Young	†1983	11	531	4,346	41	395.1
Chris Vargas, Nevada	†1993	11	535	4,332	35	393.8
Scott Mitchell, Utah	†1988	11	589	4,299	29	390.8
Jim McMahon, Brigham Young	†1980	12	540	4,627	53	385.6
Ty Detmer, Brigham Young	1989	12	497	4,433	38	369.4
Troy Kopp, Pacific (Cal.)	1990	9	485	3,276	32	364.0
Jim McMahon, Brigham Young	†1981	10	487	3,458	30	345.8
Jimmy Klingler, Houston	†1992	11	544	3,768	34	342.5
Anthony Dilweg, Duke	1988	11	539	3,713	26	337.6
Bill Anderson, Tulsa	†1965	10	580	3,343	35	334.3
Ty Detmer, Brigham Young	†1991	12	478	4,001	39	333.4
Dan McGwire, San Diego St.	1990	11	484	3,664	28	333.1
Mike McCoy, Utah	1993	12	529	3,969	21	330.8
Mike Perez, San Jose St.	†1986	9	425	2,969	14	329.9
Robbie Bosco, Brigham Young	†1984	12	543	3,932	35	327.7
Doug Flutie, Boston College	1984	11	448	3,603	30	327.5
Jim Everett, Purdue	†1985	11	518	3,589	24	326.3
Todd Dillon, Long Beach St.	†1982	11	585	3,587	23	326.1
Marc Wilson, Brigham Young	†1979	11	488	3,580	32	325.5

Record. †National champion. ‡Touchdowns-responsible-for are player's TDs scored and passed for.

CAREER YARDS

Player, Team	Years	Plays	Yards Rush	Yards Pass	Total	Avg.
Ty Detmer, Brigham Young	1988-91	*1,795	-366	*15,031	*14,665	#8.17
Doug Flutie, Boston College	1981-84	1,558	738	10,579	11,317	7.26
Alex Van Pelt, Pittsburgh	1989-92	1,570	-99	10,913	10,814	6.89
Todd Santos, San Diego St.	1984-87	1,722	-912	11,425	10,513	6.11
Kevin Sweeney, Fresno St.	$1982-86	1,700	-371	10,623	10,252	6.03
Troy Kopp, Pacific (Cal.)	1989-92	1,595	-221	10,258	10,037	6.29
Brian McClure, Bowling Green	1982-85	1,630	-506	10,280	9,774	6.00
Jim McMahon, Brigham Young	1977-78, 80-81	1,325	187	9,536	9,723	7.34
Glenn Foley, Boston College	1990-93	1,440	-340	10,042	9,702	6.74
Terrence Jones, Tulane	1985-88	1,620	1,761	7,684	9,445	5.83
David Klingler, Houston	1988-91	1,431	-103	9,430	9,327	6.52
Shawn Jones, Georgia Tech	1989-92	1,609	855	8,441	9,296	5.78
Shane Matthews, Florida	1989-92	1,397	-46	9,287	9,241	6.61
T. J. Rubley, Tulsa	1987-89, 91	1,541	-244	9,324	9,080	5.89
Brad Tayles, Western Mich.	1989-92	1,675	354	8,717	9,071	5.42
John Elway, Stanford	1979-82	1,505	-279	9,349	9,070	6.03
Erik Wilhelm, Oregon St.	1985-88	1,689	-331	9,393	9,062	5.37
Ben Bennett, Duke	1980-83	1,582	-553	9,614	9,061	5.73
Chuck Long, Iowa	$1981-85	1,410	-176	9,210	9,034	6.41
Todd Ellis, South Caro.	1986-89	1,517	-497	9,519	9,022	5.95
Tom Hodson, Louisiana St.	1986-89	1,307	-177	9,115	8,938	6.84
Scott Mitchell, Utah	1987-89	1,306	-145	8,981	8,836	6.77
Steve Young, Brigham Young	1981-83	1,177	1,084	7,733	8,817	7.49
Brian Mitchell, Southwestern La.	1986-89	1,521	3,335	5,447	8,782	5.77
Marvin Graves, Syracuse	1990-93	1,373	286	8,466	8,752	6.37
Jeremy Leach, New Mexico	1988-91	1,695	-762	9,382	8,620	5.09
Robert Hall, Texas Tech	1990-93	1,341	581	7,908	8,489	6.33
Mark Herrmann, Purdue	1977-80	1,354	-744	9,188	8,444	6.24
Robbie Bosco, Brigham Young	1983-85	1,158	-101	8,400	8,299	7.17
Troy Taylor, California	1986-89	1,490	110	8,126	8,236	5.53
Randall Cunningham, Nevada-Las Vegas	1982-84	1,330	204	8,020	8,224	6.18
Steve Slayden, Duke	1984-87	1,546	125	8,004	8,129	5.26
Jack Trudeau, Illinois	1981, 83-85	1,318	-50	8,146	8,096	6.14
Mark Barsotti, Fresno St.	1988-91	1,192	768	7,321	8,089	6.79
Gene Swick, Toledo	1972-75	1,579	807	7,267	8,074	5.11
Andre Ware, Houston	1987-89	1,194	-144	8,202	8,058	6.75
Len Williams, Northwestern	1990-93	1,614	542	7,486	8,028	4.97
Joe Adams, Tennessee St.	1977-80	1,256	-677	8,649	7,972	6.35
Rodney Peete, Southern Cal	1985-88	1,226	309	7,640	7,949	6.48
Stan White, Auburn	1990-93	1,481	-96	8,016	7,920	5.35
Shawn Moore, Virginia	1987-90	1,177	1,268	6,629	7,897	6.71
Jim Plunkett, Stanford	1968-70	1,174	343	7,544	7,887	6.72
Art Schlichter, Ohio St.	1978-81	1,316	1,285	6,584	7,869	5.98
Mike Gundy, Oklahoma St.	1986-89	1,275	-248	8,072	7,824	6.14
John Holman, Northeast La.	1979-82	1,376	-25	7,827	7,802	5.67

Player, Team	Years	Plays	Yards Rush	Pass	Total	Avg.
Gino Torretta, Miami (Fla.)	1989-92	1,101	32	7,690	7,722	7.01
Jack Thompson, Washington St.	1975-78	1,345	-120	7,818	7,698	5.72
Dan Marino, Pittsburgh	1979-82	1,185	-270	7,905	7,635	6.44
Brett Favre, Southern Miss.	1987-90	1,362	-89	7,695	7,606	5.58
Marc Wilson, Brigham Young	1977-79	1,183	-35	7,637	7,602	6.43

*Record. $See page 6 for explanation. #Record for minimum of 6,500 yards. (Note: Chris Vargas of Nevada competed two years in Division I-A and two years in Division I-AA. Four-year total: 8,184 yards.)

CAREER YARDS RECORD PROGRESSION

(Record Yards—Player, Team, Seasons Played)

3,481—Davey O'Brien, Texas Christian, 1936-38; **3,882**—Paul Christman, Missouri, 1938-40; **4,602**—Frank Sinkwich, Georgia, 1940-42; **4,627**—Bob Fenimore, Oklahoma St., 1943-46; **4,871**—Charlie Justice, North Caro., 1946-49; **5,903**—Johnny Bright, Drake, 1949-51; **6,354**—Virgil Carter, Brigham Young, 1964-66; **6,568**—Steve Ramsey, North Texas, 1967-69; **7,887**—Jim Plunkett, Stanford, 1968-70; **8,074**—Gene Swick, Toledo, 1972-75; **8,444**—Mark Herrmann, Purdue, 1977-80; **9,723**—Jim McMahon, Brigham Young, 1977-78, 1980-81; **11,317**—Doug Flutie, Boston College, 1981-84; **14,665**—Ty Detmer, Brigham Young, 1988-91.

SEASON YARDS

Player, Team	Year	G	Plays	Yards Rush	Pass	Total	Avg.
David Klingler, Houston	†1990	11	*704	81	5,140	*5,221	7.42
Ty Detmer, Brigham Young	1990	12	635	-106	*5,188	5,022	7.91
Andre Ware, Houston	†1989	11	628	-38	4,699	4,661	7.42
Jim McMahon, Brigham Young	†1980	12	540	56	4,571	4,627	8.57
Ty Detmer, Brigham Young	1989	12	497	-127	4,560	4,433	@8.92
Steve Young, Brigham Young	†1983	11	531	444	3,902	4,346	8.18
Chris Vargas, Nevada	†1993	11	535	67	4,265	4,332	8.10
Scott Mitchell, Utah	†1988	11	589	-23	4,322	4,299	7.30
Robbie Bosco, Brigham Young	1985	13	578	-132	4,273	4,141	7.16
Ty Detmer, Brigham Young	†1991	12	478	-30	4,031	4,001	8.37
Mike McCoy, Utah	1993	12	529	109	3,860	3,969	7.50
Robbie Bosco, Brigham Young	†1984	12	543	57	3,875	3,932	7.24
Jimmy Klingler, Houston	†1992	11	544	-50	3,818	3,768	6.93
Anthony Dilweg, Duke	1988	11	539	-111	3,824	3,713	6.89
Todd Santos, San Diego St.	†1987	12	562	-244	3,932	3,688	6.56
Troy Kopp, Pacific (Cal.)	1991	12	496	-81	3,767	3,686	7.43
Dan McGwire, San Diego St.	1990	11	484	-169	3,833	3,664	7.57
Doug Flutie, Boston College	1984	11	448	149	3,454	3,603	8.04
Jim Everett, Purdue	†1985	11	518	-62	3,651	3,589	6.93
Todd Dillon, Long Beach St.	†1982	11	585	70	3,517	3,587	6.13
Marc Wilson, Brigham Young	†1979	11	488	-140	3,720	3,580	7.34
Sam King, Nevada-Las Vegas	1981	12	507	-216	3,778	3,562	7.03
Matt Kofler, San Diego St.	1981	11	594	191	3,337	3,528	5.94
Steve Young, Brigham Young	1982	11	481	407	3,100	3,507	7.29
Eric Zeier, Georgia	1993	11	484	-43	3,525	3,482	7.19
John Kaleo, Maryland	1992	11	588	80	3,392	3,472	5.90
Doug Gaynor, Long Beach St.	1985	12	589	-96	3,563	3,467	5.89
Jim McMahon, Brigham Young	1981	10	487	-97	3,555	3,458	7.10

*Record. †National champion. @ Record for minimum of 3,000 yards.

SINGLE-GAME YARDS

Yds.	Rush	Pass	Player, Team (Opponent)	Date
732	16	716	David Klingler, Houston (Arizona St.)	Dec. 2, 1990
696	6	690	Matt Vogler, Texas Christian (Houston)	Nov. 3, 1990
625	62	563	David Klingler, Houston (Texas Christian)	Nov. 3, 1990
625	-6	631	Scott Mitchell, Utah (Air Force)	Oct. 15, 1988
612	-1	613	Jimmy Klingler, Houston (Rice)	Nov. 28, 1992
603	4	599	Ty Detmer, Brigham Young (San Diego St.)	Nov. 16, 1991
601	37	564	Troy Kopp, Pacific, Cal. (New Mexico St.)	Oct. 20, 1990
599	86	513	Virgil Carter, Brigham Young (UTEP)	Nov. 5, 1966
597	-22	619	John Walsh, Brigham Young (Utah St.)	Oct. 30, 1993
594	-28	622	Jeremy Leach, New Mexico (Utah)	Nov. 11, 1989
585	-36	621	Dave Wilson, Illinois (Ohio St.)	Nov. 8, 1980
582	11	571	Marc Wilson, Brigham Young (Utah)	Nov. 5, 1977
578	6	572	David Klingler, Houston (Eastern Wash.)	Nov. 17, 1990
562	25	537	Ty Detmer, Brigham Young (Washington St.)	Sept. 7, 1989
552	-13	565	Jim McMahon, Brigham Young (Utah)	Nov. 21, 1981
548	12	536	Dave Telford, Fresno St. (Pacific, Cal.)	Oct. 24, 1987
540	-45	585	Robbie Bosco, Brigham Young (New Mexico)	Oct. 19, 1985
540	104	436	Archie Manning, Mississippi (Alabama)	Oct. 4, 1969
539	1	538	Jim McMahon, Brigham Young (Colorado St.)	Nov. 7, 1981
537	65	472	Anthony Calvillo, Utah St. (Brigham Young)	Oct. 30, 1993
537	-1	538	Chris Vargas, Nevada (Nevada-Las Vegas)	Oct. 2, 1993
537	2	535	Shane Montgomery, North Caro. St. (Duke)	Nov. 11, 1989
537	-24	561	Tony Adams, Utah St. (Utah)	Nov. 11, 1972
536	58	478	Tim Schade, Minnesota (Penn St.)	Sept. 4, 1993
536	28	508	Mike Perez, San Jose St. (Pacific, Cal.)	Oct. 25, 1986
532	0	532	Jeff Van Raaphorst, Arizona St. (Florida St.)	Nov. 3, 1984
531	13	518	Jeff Graham, Long Beach St. (Hawaii)	Oct. 29, 1988
528	-40	568	David Lowery, San Diego St. (Brigham Young)	Nov. 16, 1991
528	-2	530	Dan McGwire, San Diego St. (New Mexico)	Nov. 17, 1990
527	-17	544	Eric Zeier, Georgia (Southern Miss.)	Oct. 9, 1993

When Purdue quarterback Mark Herrmann finished his collegiate career in 1980, his 8,444 yards of total offense was the major-college record.

Utah quarterback Scott Mitchell was the 1988 Division I-A leader in total offense with 390.8 yards per game.

Yds.	Rush	Pass	Player, Team (Opponent)	Date
527	17	510	David Klingler, Houston (Louisiana Tech)	Aug. 31, 1991
525	-29	554	Greg Cook, Cincinnati (Ohio)	Nov. 16, 1968
524	118	406	Ned James, New Mexico (Wyoming)	Nov. 1, 1986
521	-39	560	Ty Detmer, Brigham Young (Utah St.)	Nov. 24, 1990
521	57	464	Whit Taylor, Vanderbilt (Tennessee)	Nov. 28, 1981
519	-14	533	David Klingler, Houston (Texas Tech)	Nov. 30, 1991
517	45	472	Doug Flutie, Boston College (Miami, Fla.)	Nov. 23, 1984
517	73	444	Matt Kofler, San Diego St. (Iowa St.)	Oct. 10, 1981

ANNUAL CHAMPIONS

					Yards		
Year	Player, Team		Class	Plays	Rush	Pass	Total
1937	Byron "Whizzer" White, Colorado		Sr.	224	1,121	475	1,596
1938	Davey O'Brien, Texas Christian		Sr.	291	390	1,457	1,847
1939	Kenny Washington, UCLA		Sr.	259	811	559	1,370
1940	Johnny Knolla, Creighton		Sr.	298	813	607	1,420
1941	Bud Schwenk, Washington (Mo.)		Sr.	354	471	1,457	1,928
1942	Frank Sinkwich, Georgia		Sr.	341	795	1,392	2,187
1943	Bob Hoernschemeyer, Indiana		Fr.	355	515	1,133	1,648
1944	Bob Fenimore, Oklahoma St.		So.	241	897	861	1,758
1945	Bob Fenimore, Oklahoma St.		Jr.	203	1,048	593	1,641
1946	Travis Tidwell, Auburn		Fr.	339	772	943	1,715
1947	Fred Enke, Arizona		So.	329	535	1,406	1,941
1948	Stan Heath, Nevada		Sr.	233	-13	2,005	1,992
1949	Johnny Bright, Drake		So.	275	975	975	1,950
1950	Johnny Bright, Drake		Jr.	320	1,232	1,168	2,400
1951	Dick Kazmaier, Princeton		Sr.	272	861	966	1,827
1952	Ted Marchibroda, Detroit Mercy		Sr.	305	176	1,637	1,813
1953	Paul Larson, California		Jr.	262	141	1,431	1,572
1954	George Shaw, Oregon		Sr.	276	178	1,358	1,536
1955	George Welsh, Navy		Sr.	203	29	1,319	1,348
1956	John Brodie, Stanford		Sr.	295	9	1,633	1,642
1957	Bob Newman, Washington St.		Jr.	263	53	1,391	1,444
1958	Dick Bass, Pacific (Cal.)		Jr.	218	1,361	79	1,440
1959	Dick Norman, Stanford		Jr.	319	55	1,963	2,018
1960	Bill Kilmer, UCLA		Sr.	292	803	1,086	1,889
1961	Dave Hoppmann, Iowa St.		Jr.	320	920	718	1,638
1962	Terry Baker, Oregon St.		Sr.	318	538	1,738	2,276
1963	George Mira, Miami (Fla.)		Sr.	394	163	2,155	2,318
1964	Jerry Rhome, Tulsa		Sr.	470	258	2,870	3,128
1965	Bill Anderson, Tulsa		Sr.	580	-121	3,464	3,343
1966	Virgil Carter, Brigham Young		Sr.	388	363	2,182	2,545
1967	Sal Olivas, New Mexico St.		Sr.	368	-41	2,225	2,184
1968	Greg Cook, Cincinnati		Sr.	507	-62	3,272	3,210
1969	Dennis Shaw, San Diego St.		Sr.	388	12	3,185	3,197

Beginning in 1970, ranked on per-game (instead of total) yards

						Yards			
Year	Player, Team		Class	G	Plays	Rush	Pass	Total	Avg.
1970	Pat Sullivan, Auburn		Jr.	10	333	270	2,586	2,856	285.6
1971	Gary Huff, Florida St.		Jr.	11	386	-83	2,736	2,653	241.2
1972	Don Strock, Virginia Tech		Sr.	11	480	-73	3,243	3,170	288.2
1973	Jesse Freitas, San Diego St.		Sr.	11	410	-92	2,993	2,901	263.7
1974	Steve Joachim, Temple		Sr.	10	331	277	1,950	2,227	222.7
1975	Gene Swick, Toledo		Sr.	11	490	219	2,487	2,706	246.0
1976	Tommy Kramer, Rice		Sr.	11	562	-45	3,317	3,272	297.5
1977	Doug Williams, Grambling		Sr.	11	377	-57	3,286	3,229	293.5
1978	Mike Ford, Southern Methodist		So.	11	459	-50	3,007	2,957	268.8
1979	Marc Wilson, Brigham Young		Sr.	11	488	-140	3,720	3,580	325.5
1980	Jim McMahon, Brigham Young		Jr.	12	540	56	4,571	4,627	385.6
1981	Jim McMahon, Brigham Young		Sr.	10	487	-97	3,555	3,458	345.8
1982	Todd Dillon, Long Beach St.		Jr.	11	585	70	3,517	3,587	326.1
1983	Steve Young, Brigham Young		Sr.	11	531	444	3,902	4,346	395.1
1984	Robbie Bosco, Brigham Young		Jr.	12	543	57	3,875	3,932	327.7
1985	Jim Everett, Purdue		Sr.	11	518	-62	3,651	3,589	326.3
1986	Mike Perez, San Jose St.		Jr.	9	425	35	2,934	2,969	329.9
1987	Todd Santos, San Diego St.		Sr.	12	562	-244	3,932	3,688	307.3
1988	Scott Mitchell, Utah		So.	11	589	-23	4,322	4,299	390.8
1989	Andre Ware, Houston		Jr.	11	628	-38	4,699	4,661	423.7
1990	David Klingler, Houston		Jr.	11	*704	81	5,140	*5,221	*474.6
1991	Ty Detmer, Brigham Young		Sr.	12	478	-30	4,031	4,001	333.4
1992	Jimmy Klingler, Houston		So.	11	544	-50	3,818	3,768	342.5
1993	Chris Vargas, Nevada		Sr.	11	535	67	4,265	4,332	393.8

*Record.

Rushing

CAREER YARDS PER GAME

(Minimum 2,500 yards)

Player, Team	Years	G	Plays	Yards	TD	Yd. PG
Ed Marinaro, Cornell	1969-71	27	918	4,715	50	*174.6
O. J. Simpson, Southern Cal	1967-68	19	621	3,124	33	164.4
Herschel Walker, Georgia	1980-82	33	994	5,259	49	159.4
LeShon Johnson, Northern Ill.	1992-93	22	592	3,314	18	150.6
Marshall Faulk, San Diego St.	1991-93	31	766	4,589	57	148.0
Tony Dorsett, Pittsburgh	1973-76	43	1,074	*6,082	55	141.4
Mike Rozier, Nebraska	1981-83	35	668	4,780	49	136.6
Howard Stevens, Louisville	§1971-72	20	509	2,723	25	136.2
Jerome Persell, Western Mich.	1976-78	31	842	4,190	39	135.2
Rudy Mobley, Hardin-Simmons	1942,46	19	414	2,543	32	133.8
Vaughn Dunbar, Indiana	1990-91	22	565	2,842	24	129.2
Steve Owens, Oklahoma	1967-69	30	905	3,867	56	128.9
Charles White, Southern Cal	1976-79	44	1,023	5,598	46	127.2
Johnny Bright, Drake	1949-51	25	513	3,134	39	125.4
Woody Green, Arizona St.	1971-73	30	601	3,754	33	125.1
Archie Griffin, Ohio St.	1972-75	42	845	5,177	25	123.3
Anthony Thompson, Indiana	1986-89	41	1,089	4,965	*64	121.1
Mark Kellar, Northern Ill.	1971-73	31	743	3,745	32	120.8
Paul Gipson, Houston	1966-68	23	447	2,769	25	120.4
John Cappelletti, Penn St.	‡1972-73	22	519	2,639	29	120.0
Steve Bartalo, Colorado St.	1983-86	41	*1,215	4,813	46	117.4
Louie Giammona, Utah St.	1973-75	30	756	3,499	21	116.6
Paul Palmer, Temple	1983-86	42	948	4,895	39	116.5
Bill Marek, Wisconsin	1972-75	32	719	3,709	44	115.9
Darren Lewis, Texas A&M	1987-90	44	909	5,012	44	113.9
Dick Jauron, Yale	1970-72	26	515	2,947	27	113.3
Bo Jackson, Auburn	1982-85	38	650	4,303	43	113.2
Joe Morris, Syracuse	1978-81	38	813	4,299	25	113.1
Eugene "Mercury" Morris, West Tex. A&M	1966-68	30	541	3,388	34	112.9

**Record. §Competed two years in Division I-A and two years in Division II (Randolph-Macon, 1968-69). Four-year totals: 5,297 yards, 139.4 average. ‡Defensive back in 1971.*

SEASON YARDS PER GAME

Player, Team	Year	G	Plays	Yards	TD	Yd. PG
Barry Sanders, Oklahoma St.	†1988	11	344	*2,628	*37	*238.9
Marcus Allen, Southern Cal	†1981	11	*403	2,342	22	212.9
Ed Marinaro, Cornell	†1971	9	356	1,881	24	209.0
Charles White, Southern Cal	†1979	10	293	1,803	18	180.3
LeShon Johnson, Northern Ill.	†1993	11	327	1,976	12	179.6
Mike Rozier, Nebraska	†1983	12	275	2,148	29	179.0
Tony Dorsett, Pittsburgh	†1976	11	338	1,948	21	177.1
Ollie Matson, San Francisco	†1951	9	245	1,566	20	174.0
Lorenzo White, Michigan St.	†1985	11	386	1,908	17	173.5
Herschel Walker, Georgia	1981	11	385	1,891	18	171.9
O. J. Simpson, Southern Cal	†1968	10	355	1,709	22	170.9
Ernest Anderson, Oklahoma St.	†1982	11	353	1,877	8	170.6
Ricky Bell, Southern Cal	†1975	11	357	1,875	13	170.5

**Record. †National champion.*

CAREER YARDS

Player, Team	Years	Plays	Yards	Avg.	Long
Tony Dorsett, Pittsburgh	1973-76	1,074	*6,082	5.66	73
Charles White, Southern Cal	1976-79	1,023	5,598	5.47	79
Herschel Walker, Georgia	1980-82	994	5,259	5.29	76
Archie Griffin, Ohio St.	1972-75	845	5,177	††6.13	75
Darren Lewis, Texas A&M	1987-90	909	5,012	5.51	84
Anthony Thompson, Indiana	1986-89	1,089	4,965	4.56	52
George Rogers, South Caro.	1977-80	902	4,958	5.50	80
Trevor Cobb, Rice	1989-92	1,091	4,948	4.54	79
Paul Palmer, Temple	1983-86	948	4,895	5.16	78
Steve Bartalo, Colorado St.	1983-86	*1,215	4,813	3.96	39
Mike Rozier, Nebraska	1981-83	668	4,780	#7.16	93
Ed Marinaro, Cornell	1969-71	918	4,715	5.14	79
Marcus Allen, Southern Cal	1978-81	893	4,682	5.24	45
Ted Brown, North Caro. St.	1975-78	860	4,602	5.35	95
Thurman Thomas, Oklahoma St.	1984-87	898	4,595	5.12	66
Marshall Faulk, San Diego St.	1991-93	766	4,589	5.99	71
Terry Miller, Oklahoma St.	1974-77	847	4,582	5.41	81
Darrell Thompson, Minnesota	1986-89	911	4,518	4.96	98
Lorenzo White, Michigan St.	1984-87	991	4,513	4.55	73
Eric Dickerson, Southern Methodist	1979-82	790	4,450	5.63	80
Earl Campbell, Texas	1974-77	765	4,443	5.81	‡‡83
Amos Lawrence, North Caro.	1977-80	881	4,391	4.98	62
Bo Jackson, Auburn	1982-85	650	4,303	6.62	80
Joe Morris, Syracuse	1978-81	813	4,299	5.29	75
Reggie Taylor, Cincinnati	1983-86	876	4,242	4.48	‡‡68
Mike Mayweather, Army	1987-90	832	4,212	5.06	52
Jerome Persell, Western Mich.	1976-78	842	4,190	4.98	86
Napoleon McCallum, Navy	$1981-85	908	4,179	4.60	60
Tico Duckett, Michigan St.	1989-92	824	4,176	5.07	88
George Swarn, Miami (Ohio)	1983-86	881	4,172	4.74	98
Errict Rhett, Florida	$1989-93	873	4,163	4.77	49
Curtis Adams, Central Mich.	1981-84	761	4,162	5.47	87
Allen Pinkett, Notre Dame	1982-85	889	4,131	4.65	76
James Gray, Texas Tech	1986-89	742	4,066	5.48	72
Robert Lavette, Georgia Tech	1981-84	914	4,066	4.45	83
Stump Mitchell, Citadel	1977-80	756	4,062	5.37	77
Dalton Hilliard, Louisiana St.	1982-85	882	4,050	4.59	66
Charles Alexander, Louisiana St.	1975-78	855	4,035	4.72	64
Darrin Nelson, Stanford	1977-78, 80-81	703	4,033	5.74	80
Joe Washington, Oklahoma	1972-75	656	3,995	6.09	71
Mike Voight, North Caro.	1973-76	826	3,971	4.81	84
Jamie Morris, Michigan	1984-87	742	3,944	5.32	74
Eric Bieniemy, Colorado	1987-90	699	3,940	5.64	69
Emmitt Smith, Florida	1987-89	700	3,928	5.61	96
Ron "Po" James, New Mexico St.	1968-71	818	3,884	4.75	69
Steve Owens, Oklahoma	1967-69	905	3,867	4.27	‡‡49
Mike Williams, New Mexico	1975-78	857	3,862	4.51	36
Sonny Collins, Kentucky	1972-75	777	3,835	4.94	66
Eric Wilkerson, Kent	1985-88	735	3,830	5.21	74
Billy Sims, Oklahoma	$1975-79	538	3,813	7.09	‡‡71
James McDougald, Wake Forest	1976-79	880	3,811	4.33	62
Tony Sands, Kansas	1988-91	778	3,788	4.87	66

**Record. $See page 6 for explanation. ‡‡Did not score. ††Record for minimum of 781 carries. #Record for minimum of 414 carries.*

CAREER YARDS RECORD PROGRESSION

(Record Yards—Player, Team, Seasons Played)

1,961—Marshall Goldberg, Pittsburgh, 1936-38; **2,105**—Tom Harmon, Michigan, 1938-40; **2,271**—Frank Sinkwich, Georgia, 1940-42; **2,301**—Bill Daley, Minnesota, 1940-42, Michigan, 1943; **2,957**—Glenn Davis, Army, 1943-46; **3,095**—Eddie Price, Tulane, 1946-49; **3,238**—John Papit, Virginia, 1947-50; **3,381**—Art Luppino, Arizona, 1953-56; **3,388**—Eugene "Mercury" Morris, West Tex. A&M, 1966-68; **3,867**—Steve Owens, Oklahoma, 1967-69; **4,715**—Ed Marinaro, Cornell, 1969-71; **5,177**—Archie Griffin, Ohio St., 1972-75; **6,082**—Tony Dorsett, Pittsburgh, 1973-76.

SEASON YARDS

Player, Team	Year	G	Plays	Yards	Avg.
Barry Sanders, Oklahoma St.	†1988	11	344	*2,628	‡7.64
Marcus Allen, Southern Cal	†1981	11	*403	2,342	5.81
Mike Rozier, Nebraska	†1983	12	275	2,148	#7.81
LeShon Johnson, Northern Ill.	†1993	11	327	1,976	6.04
Tony Dorsett, Pittsburgh	†1976	11	338	1,948	5.76
Lorenzo White, Michigan St.	†1985	11	386	1,908	4.94
Herschel Walker, Georgia	1981	11	385	1,891	4.91
Ed Marinaro, Cornell	†1971	9	356	1,881	5.28
Ernest Anderson, Oklahoma St.	†1982	11	353	1,877	5.32
Ricky Bell, Southern Cal	†1975	11	357	1,875	5.25
Paul Palmer, Temple	†1986	11	346	1,866	5.39
Charles White, Southern Cal	†1979	10	293	1,803	6.15
Anthony Thompson, Indiana	†1989	11	358	1,793	5.01
Obie Graves, Cal St. Fullerton	1978	12	275	1,789	6.51
Bo Jackson, Auburn	1985	11	278	1,786	6.42
George Rogers, South Caro.	†1980	11	297	1,781	6.00
Billy Sims, Oklahoma	†1978	11	231	1,762	7.63
Charles White, Southern Cal	1978	12	342	1,760	5.15
Robert Newhouse, Houston	1971	11	277	1,757	6.34
Byron Morris, Texas Tech	1993	11	298	1,752	5.88
Herschel Walker, Georgia	1982	11	335	1,752	5.23
Earl Campbell, Texas	†1977	11	267	1,744	6.53
Mike Pringle, Cal St. Fullerton	1989	11	296	1,727	5.83
Don McCauley, North Caro.	1970	11	324	1,720	5.31

**Record. †National champion. ‡Record for minimum of 282 carries. #Record for minimum of 214 carries.*

SINGLE-GAME YARDS

Yds.	Player, Team (Opponent)	Date
396	Tony Sands, Kansas (Missouri)	Nov. 23, 1991
386	Marshall Faulk, San Diego St. (Pacific, Cal.)	Sept. 14, 1991
377	Anthony Thompson, Indiana (Wisconsin)	Nov. 11, 1989
357	Mike Pringle, Cal St. Fullerton (New Mexico St.)	Nov. 4, 1989
357	Rueben Mayes, Washington St. (Oregon)	Oct. 27, 1984
356	Eddie Lee Ivery, Georgia Tech (Air Force)	Nov. 11, 1978
350	Eric Allen, Michigan St. (Purdue)	Oct. 30, 1971
349	Paul Palmer, Temple (East Caro.)	Oct. 11, 1986
347	Ricky Bell, Southern Cal (Washington St.)	Oct. 9, 1976
347	Ron Johnson, Michigan (Wisconsin)	Nov. 16, 1968
343	Tony Jeffery, Texas Christian (Tulane)	Sept. 13, 1986
342	Roosevelt Leaks, Texas (Southern Methodist)	Nov. 3, 1973
342	Charlie Davis, Colorado (Oklahoma St.)	Nov. 13, 1971
340	Eugene "Mercury" Morris, West Tex. A&M (Montana St.)	Oct. 5, 1968
332	Barry Sanders, Oklahoma St. (Texas Tech)	Dec. 3, 1988
329	John Leach, Wake Forest (Maryland)	Nov. 20, 1993
328	Derrick Fenner, North Caro. (Virginia)	Nov. 15, 1986
326	George Swarn, Miami, Ohio (Eastern Mich.)	Nov. 16, 1985
326	Fred Wendt, UTEP (New Mexico St.)	Nov. 25, 1948
322	LeShon Johnson, Northern Ill. (Southern Ill.)	Oct. 2, 1993
322	Greg Allen, Florida St. (Western Caro.)	Oct. 31, 1981
321	Frank Mordica, Vanderbilt (Air Force)	Nov. 18, 1978
320	Barry Sanders, Oklahoma St. (Kansas St.)	Oct. 29, 1988
319	Andre Herrera, Southern Ill. (Northern Ill.)	Oct. 23, 1976
319	Jim Pilot, New Mexico St. (Hardin-Simmons)	Nov. 25, 1961
316	Emmitt Smith, Florida (New Mexico)	Oct. 21, 1989
316	Mike Adamle, Northwestern (Wisconsin)	Oct. 18, 1969
312	Mark Brus, Tulsa (New Mexico St.)	Oct. 27, 1990
312	Barry Sanders, Oklahoma St. (Kansas)	Nov. 12, 1988
310	Tony Alford, Colorado St. (Utah)	Oct. 28, 1989
310	Mitchell True, Pacific, Cal. (UC Davis)	Nov. 18, 1972
308	Stacey Robinson (QB), Northern Ill. (Fresno St.)	Oct. 6, 1990
307	Curtis Kuykendall, Auburn (Miami, Fla.)	Nov. 24, 1944
306	LeShon Johnson, Northern Ill. (Iowa)	Nov. 6, 1993
304	Barry Sanders, Oklahoma St. (Tulsa)	Oct. 1, 1988
304	Sam Dejarnette, Southern Miss. (Florida St.)	Sept. 25, 1982
304	Bill Marek, Wisconsin (Minnesota)	Nov. 23, 1974
303	Tony Dorsett, Pittsburgh (Notre Dame)	Nov. 15, 1975
302	Jason Davis, Louisiana Tech (Southwestern La.)	Sept. 29, 1990
302	Kevin Lowe, Wyoming (South Dak. St.)	Nov. 10, 1984
300	Marshall Faulk, San Diego St. (Hawaii)	Nov. 14, 1992

ANNUAL CHAMPIONS

Year	Player, Team	Class	Plays	Yards
1937	Byron "Whizzer" White, Colorado	Sr.	181	1,121
1938	Len Eshmont, Fordham	So.	132	831
1939	John Polanski, Wake Forest	So.	137	882
1940	Al Ghesquiere, Detroit Mercy	Sr.	146	957
1941	Frank Sinkwich, Georgia	Jr.	209	1,103
1942	Rudy Mobley, Hardin-Simmons	So.	187	1,281
1943	Creighton Miller, Notre Dame	Sr.	151	911
1944	Wayne "Red" Williams, Minnesota	Jr.	136	911
1945	Bob Fenimore, Oklahoma St.	Jr.	142	1,048
1946	Rudy Mobley, Hardin-Simmons	Sr.	227	1,262
1947	Wilton Davis, Hardin-Simmons	So.	193	1,173
1948	Fred Wendt, UTEP	Sr.	184	1,570
1949	John Dottley, Mississippi	Jr.	208	1,312
1950	Wilford White, Arizona St.	Sr.	199	1,502
1951	Ollie Matson, San Francisco	Sr.	245	1,566
1952	Howie Waugh, Tulsa	Sr.	164	1,372
1953	J. C. Caroline, Illinois	So.	194	1,256
1954	Art Luppino, Arizona	So.	179	1,359
1955	Art Luppino, Arizona	Jr.	209	1,313
1956	Jim Crawford, Wyoming	Sr.	200	1,104
1957	Leon Burton, Arizona St.	Sr.	117	1,126
1958	Dick Bass, Pacific (Cal.)	Jr.	205	1,361
1959	Pervis Atkins, New Mexico St.	Jr.	130	971
1960	Bob Gaiters, New Mexico St.	Sr.	197	1,338
1961	Jim Pilot, New Mexico St.	So.	191	1,278
1962	Jim Pilot, New Mexico St.	Jr.	208	1,247
1963	Dave Casinelli, Memphis	Sr.	219	1,016
1964	Brian Piccolo, Wake Forest	Sr.	252	1,044
1965	Mike Garrett, Southern Cal	Sr.	267	1,440
1966	Ray McDonald, Idaho	Sr.	259	1,329
1967	O. J. Simpson, Southern Cal	Jr.	266	1,415
1968	O. J. Simpson, Southern Cal	Sr.	355	1,709
1969	Steve Owens, Oklahoma	Sr.	358	1,523

Beginning in 1970, ranked on per-game (instead of total) yards

Year	Player, Team	Class	G	Plays	Yards	Avg.
1970	Ed Marinaro, Cornell	Jr.	9	285	1,425	158.3
1971	Ed Marinaro, Cornell	Sr.	9	356	1,881	209.0
1972	Pete VanValkenburg, Brigham Young	Sr.	10	232	1,386	138.6
1973	Mark Kellar, Northern Ill.	Sr.	11	291	1,719	156.3
1974	Louie Giammona, Utah St.	Jr.	10	329	1,534	153.4
1975	Ricky Bell, Southern Cal	Jr.	11	357	1,875	170.5
1976	Tony Dorsett, Pittsburgh	Sr.	11	338	1,948	177.1
1977	Earl Campbell, Texas	Sr.	11	267	1,744	158.5
1978	Billy Sims, Oklahoma	Jr.	11	231	1,762	160.2
1979	Charles White, Southern Cal	Sr.	10	293	1,803	180.3
1980	George Rogers, South Caro.	Sr.	11	297	1,781	161.9
1981	Marcus Allen, Southern Cal	Sr.	11	*403	2,342	212.9
1982	Ernest Anderson, Oklahoma St.	Jr.	11	353	1,877	170.6
1983	Mike Rozier, Nebraska	Sr.	12	275	2,148	179.0
1984	Keith Byars, Ohio St.	Jr.	11	313	1,655	150.5
1985	Lorenzo White, Michigan St.	So.	11	386	1,908	173.5
1986	Paul Palmer, Temple	Sr.	11	346	1,866	169.6
1987	Elbert "Ickey" Woods, Nevada-Las Vegas	Sr.	11	259	1,658	150.7
1988	Barry Sanders, Oklahoma St.	Jr.	11	344	*2,628	*238.9
1989	Anthony Thompson, Indiana	Sr.	11	358	1,793	163.0
1990	Gerald Hudson, Oklahoma St.	Sr.	11	279	1,642	149.3
1991	Marshall Faulk, San Diego St.	Fr.	9	201	1,429	158.8
1992	Marshall Faulk, San Diego St.	So.	10	265	1,630	163.0
1993	LeShon Johnson, Northern Ill.	Sr.	11	327	1,976	179.6

*Record.

FRESHMAN 1,000-YARD RUSHERS

Player, Team	Year	Yards
Ron "Po" James, New Mexico St.	1968	1,291
Tony Dorsett, Pittsburgh	1973	1,586
James McDougald, Wake Forest	1976	1,018
Mike Harkrader, Indiana	1976	1,003
Amos Lawrence, North Caro.	1977	1,211
Darrin Nelson, Stanford	1977	1,069
Mike Smith, Tenn.-Chatt.	1977	1,062
Gwain Durden, Tenn.-Chatt.	1977	1,049
Allen Ross, Northern Ill.	1977	1,036
Allen Harvin, Cincinnati	1978	1,238
Joe Morris, Syracuse	1978	1,001
Ron Lear, Marshall	1979	1,162
Herschel Walker, Georgia	1980	*1,616
Kerwin Bell, Kansas	1980	1,114
Joe McIntosh, North Caro. St.	1981	1,190
Steve Bartalo, Colorado St.	1983	1,113
Spencer Tillman, Oklahoma	1983	1,047
D. J. Dozier, Penn St.	1983	1,002
Eddie Johnson, Utah	1984	1,021
Darrell Thompson, Minnesota	1986	1,240
Emmitt Smith, Florida	1987	1,341
Reggie Cobb, Tennessee	1987	1,197
Bernie Parmalee, Ball St.	1987	1,064
Curvin Richards, Pittsburgh	1988	1,228
Chuck Webb, Tennessee	1989	1,236
Robert Smith, Ohio St.	1990	1,064
Marshall Faulk, San Diego St.	1991	1,429
Greg Hill, Texas A&M	1991	1,216
David Small, Cincinnati	1991	1,004
Winslow Oliver, New Mexico	1992	1,063
Deland McCullough, Miami (Ohio)	1992	1,026
Terrell Willis, Rutgers	1993	1,261
Charles Henley, Kansas	1993	1,127
Marquis Williams, Arkansas St.	1993	1,060
Leon Johnson, North Caro.	1993	1,012

*Record for freshman.

Quarterback Rushing

SEASON YARDS

Player, Team	Year	G	Plays	Yards	TD	Avg.
Stacey Robinson, Northern Ill.	1989	11	223	*1,443	*19	6.47
Dee Dowis, Air Force	1987	12	194	1,315	10	6.78
Brian Mitchell, Southwestern La.	1989	11	237	1,311	*19	5.53
Fred Solomon, Tampa	1974	11	193	1,300	*19	6.74
Dee Dowis, Air Force	1989	12	172	1,286	18	*7.48
Stacey Robinson, Northern Ill.	1990	11	193	1,238	*19	6.41
Rob Perez, Air Force	1991	12	233	1,157	10	4.97
Jack Mildren, Oklahoma	1971	11	193	1,140	17	5.91
Nolan Cromwell, Kansas	1975	11	218	1,124	9	5.16
Michael Carter, Hawaii	1991	12	221	1,092	16	4.94
Tory Crawford, Army	1986	11	*244	1,075	15	4.41
Bart Weiss, Air Force	1985	12	180	1,032	12	5.73
Jimmy Sidle, Auburn	1963	10	185	1,006	10	5.44
Reggie Collier, Southern Miss.	1981	11	153	1,005	12	6.57
Darian Hagan, Colorado	1989	11	186	1,004	17	5.40

*Record.

CAREER YARDS

Player, Team	Years	G	Plays	Yards	TD	Avg.
Dee Dowis, Air Force	1986-89	47	543	*3,612	41	76.9
Brian Mitchell, Southwestern La.	1986-89	43	678	3,335	*47	77.6
Fred Solomon, Tampa	1971-74	43	557	3,299	39	76.7
Stacey Robinson, Northern Ill.	1988-90	25	429	2,727	38	*109.1
Jamelle Holieway, Oklahoma	1985-88	38	505	2,699	30	71.0
Bill Hurley, Syracuse	1975-79	46	*685	2,551	19	55.5
Michael Carter, Hawaii	1990-93	46	574	2,534	39	55.1
Bill Deery, William & Mary	1972-74	33	443	2,401	19	72.8
Reggie Collier, Southern Miss.	1979-82	39	446	2,304	26	59.1
John Bond, Mississippi St.	1980-83	44	572	2,280	24	51.8
Tory Crawford, Army	1984-87	31	495	2,255	34	72.7
Tom Parr, Colgate	1971-73	30	435	2,221	31	74.0
Alton Grizzard, Navy	1987-90	38	599	2,174	15	57.2
Gary Wood, Cornell	1961-63	27	433	2,156	19	79.9
Roy DeWalt, Texas-Arlington	1975, 77-79	38	468	2,136	27	56.2
Bucky Richardson, Texas A&M	1987-88, 90-91	41	370	2,095	30	51.1
Rocky Long, New Mexico	1969-71	31	469	2,071	21	66.8
Steve Davis, Oklahoma	1973-75	33	515	2,069	33	62.7
Steve Taylor, Nebraska	1985-88	37	429	2,065	30	55.8
Rick Leach, Michigan	1975-78	43	440	2,053	34	47.7
Prince McJunkins, Wichita St.	1979-82	44	613	2,047	27	46.5
Rickey Foggie, Minnesota	1984-87	41	510	2,038	24	49.7
Major Harris, West Va.	1987-89	33	386	2,030	18	51.5
Steve Gage, Tulsa	1983-84, 86	33	522	2,029	30	61.5
Harry Gilmer, Alabama	1944-47	40	390	2,025	19	50.6
Darian Hagan, Colorado	1988-91	41	489	2,007	27	49.0

*Record.

Passing

SAMPLE COMPILATION OF NCAA PASSING EFFICIENCY RATING

Player		G	Att.	Cmp.	Yds.	TD	Int.
Ty Detmer, Brigham Young		46	1,530	958	15,031	121	65

Completion Percentage:	62.61	
Yards Per Attempted Pass:	9.82	
Percent of Passes for TDs:	7.91	
Percent of Passes Intercepted:	4.25	

ADD the first three factors:

		Rating Points
Completion Percentage:	62.61	62.61
Yards Per Attempted Pass:	9.82 times 8.4	82.49
Percent of Passes for TDs:	7.91 times 3.3	26.10
		171.20

SUBTRACT the last factor:

Percent of Passes Intercepted:	4.25 times 2	-8.50
	Round off to:	**162.7**

Syracuse's Marvin Graves finished his collegiate career last season with a passing efficiency rating of 142.4, the seventh-best career mark in Division I-A history.

CAREER PASSING EFFICIENCY
(Minimum 500 Completions)

Player, Team	Years	Att.	Cmp.	Int.	Pct.	Yds.	TD	Pts.
Ty Detmer, Brigham Young	1988-91	*1,530	*958	65	.626	*15,031	*121	*162.7
Jim McMahon, Brigham Young	1977-78, 80-81	1,060	653	34	.616	9,536	84	156.9
Steve Young, Brigham Young	1981-83	908	592	33	**.652	7,733	56	149.8
Robbie Bosco, Brigham Young	1983-85	997	638	36	.640	8,400	66	149.4
Chuck Long, Iowa	$1981-85	1,072	692	46	‡.646	9,210	64	147.8
Andre Ware, Houston	1987-89	1,074	660	28	.615	8,202	75	143.3
Marvin Graves, Syracuse	1990-93	943	563	45	.597	8,466	48	142.4
Doug Gaynor, Long Beach St.	1984-85	837	569	35	.680	6,793	35	141.6
Steve Stenstrom, Stanford	1991-93	987	616	30	.624	7,709	56	140.7
Dan McGwire, Iowa/San Diego St.	1986-87, 89-90	973	575	30	.591	8,164	49	140.0
Chris Vargas, Nevada	§1992-93	806	502	34	.623	6,359	47	139.4
John Elway, Stanford	1979-82	1,246	774	39	.621	9,349	77	139.3
David Klingler, Houston	1988-91	1,261	726	38	.576	9,430	91	138.2
Scott Mitchell, Utah	1987-89	1,165	669	38	.574	8,981	68	137.7
Shane Matthews, Florida	1989-92	1,202	722	46	.601	9,287	74	137.6
Marc Wilson, Brigham Young	1977-79	937	535	46	.571	7,637	61	137.2
Randall Cunningham, Nevada-Las Vegas	1982-84	1,029	597	29	.580	8,020	59	136.8
Kerwin Bell, Florida	1984-87	953	549	35	.576	7,585	56	136.5
Tom Hodson, Louisiana St.	1986-89	1,163	674	41	.580	9,115	69	136.3
Rodney Peete, Southern Cal	1985-88	972	571	32	.587	7,640	52	135.8

Nebraska quarterback Jerry Tagge's career passing efficiency rating of 140.1 ranks fourth among Division I-A quarterbacks with 325 to 399 completions.

Player, Team	Years	Att.	Cmp.	Int.	Pct.	Yds.	TD	Pts.
Troy Kopp, Pacific (Cal.)	1989-92	1,374	798	47	.581	10,258	87	134.9
Joe Adams, Tennessee St.	1977-80	1,100	604	60	.549	8,649	81	134.4
Mike Gundy, Oklahoma	1986-89	1,037	606	37	.584	8,072	54	133.9
Todd Santos, San Diego St.	1984-87	1,484	910	57	.613	11,425	70	133.9
Tony Eason, Illinois	1981-82	856	526	29	.615	6,608	37	133.8
Danny McCoin, Cincinnati	1984-87	899	544	26	.605	6,801	39	132.6
Rich Campbell, California	1977-80	891	574	42	.644	6,933	33	132.6
Jim Everett, Purdue	$1981-85	923	550	30	.596	7,158	40	132.5
Matt Rodgers, Iowa	1988-91	844	516	30	.611	6,308	40	132.5
Doug Flutie, Boston College	1981-84	1,270	677	54	.533	10,579	67	132.2
Gino Torretta, Miami (Fla.)	1989-92	991	555	24	.560	7,690	47	132.0
Robert Hall, Texas Tech	1990-93	997	548	28	.550	7,908	48	131.9
Jack Trudeau, Illinois	1981, 83-85	1,151	736	38	†.639	8,146	51	131.4
Kevin Sweeney, Fresno St.	$1982-86	1,336	731	48	.547	10,623	66	130.6
Bill Musgrave, Oregon	1987-90	1,018	582	38	.572	7,631	55	130.6
Glenn Foley, Boston College	1990-93	1,275	703	60	.551	10,042	72	130.5
Gene Swick, Toledo	1972-75	938	556	45	.593	7,267	44	130.3
Jason Verduzco, Illinois	1989-92	986	622	29	.631	6,974	40	130.0
Brian McClure, Bowling Green	1982-85	1,427	900	58	.631	10,280	63	130.0

(400-499 Completions)

Player, Team	Years	Att.	Cmp.	Int.	Pct.	Yds.	TD	Pts.
Vinny Testaverde, Miami (Fla.)	1982, 84-86	674	413	25	.613	6,058	48	152.9
Trent Dilfer, Fresno St.	1991-93	774	461	21	.596	6,944	51	151.2
Troy Aikman, Oklahoma/UCLA	1984-85, 87-88	637	401	18	.630	5,436	40	149.7
Chuck Hartlieb, Iowa	1985-88	716	461	17	.643	6,269	34	148.9
Elvis Grbac, Michigan	1989-92	754	477	29	.633	5,859	64	148.9
Gifford Nielsen, Brigham Young	1975-77	708	415	29	.586	5,833	55	145.3
Tom Ramsey, UCLA	1979-82	691	411	33	.595	5,844	48	143.9
Shawn Moore, Virginia	1987-90	762	421	32	.552	6,629	55	143.8
Jerry Rhome, Southern Methodist/Tulsa	1961, 63-64	713	448	23	.628	5,472	47	142.6
Charlie Ward, Florida St.	1989, 91-93	759	474	21	.625	5,747	49	141.8
Bernie Kosar, Miami (Fla.)	1983-84	743	463	29	.623	5,971	40	139.8
Craig Erickson, Miami (Fla.)	1987-90	752	420	22	.559	6,056	44	137.8
Dave Yarema, Michigan St.	$1982-86	727	447	29	.615	5,569	41	136.5
Gary Huff, Florida St.	1970-72	796	436	42	.548	6,378	52	133.1
Joe Hughes, Wyoming	1992-93	744	424	25	.570	5,841	38	133.1
Jeff Francis, Tennessee	1985-88	768	476	26	.620	5,867	31	132.7
Mike Perez, San Jose St.	1986-87	792	471	30	.595	6,194	36	132.6
Cale Gundy, Oklahoma	1990-93	751	420	31	.559	6,142	36	132.2

(325-399 Completions)

Player, Team	Years	Att.	Cmp.	Int.	Pct.	Yds.	TD	Pts.
Jim Harbaugh, Michigan	1983-86	582	368	19	.632	5,215	31	149.6
Danny White, Arizona St.	1971-73	649	345	36	.532	5,932	59	148.9
Jim Karsatos, Ohio St.	1983-86	573	330	19	.576	4,698	36	140.6
Jerry Tagge, Nebraska	1969-71	581	348	19	.599	4,704	33	140.1
Garrett Gabriel, Hawaii	1987-90	661	356	31	.539	5,631	47	139.5
Rick Mirer, Notre Dame	1989-92	698	377	23	.540	5,996	41	139.0
Gary Sheide, Brigham Young	1973-74	594	358	31	.603	4,524	45	138.8
Dan Speltz, Cal St. Fullerton	1988-89	583	350	19	.600	4,595	33	138.4
Don McPherson, Syracuse	$1983-87	687	367	25	.534	5,812	46	138.1
Joe Youngblood, Central Mich.	1990-93	572	331	28	.579	4,718	35	137.6
Sam King, Nevada-Las Vegas	1979-81	625	360	29	.576	5,393	30	136.6
J. J. Joe, Baylor	1990-93	665	347	28	.522	5,995	31	134.9
Jesse Freitas, Stanford/San Diego St.	1970, 72-73	547	338	33	.618	4,408	28	134.3
Jeff Blake, East Caro.	1988-91	667	360	20	.540	5,133	43	133.9

*Record. **Record for minimum of 875 attempts. ‡Record for minimum of 1,000 attempts. †Record for minimum of 1,100 attempts. $See page 6 for explanation. §Vargas played two years in Division I-A and two years in Division I-AA.

SEASON PASSING EFFICIENCY
(Minimum 15 Attempts Per Game)

Player, Team	Year	G	Att.	Cmp.	Int.	Pct.	Yds.	TD	Pts.
Jim McMahon, Brigham Young	#†1980	12	445	284	18	.638	4,571	47	*176.9
Ty Detmer, Brigham Young	†1989	12	412	265	15	.643	4,560	32	175.6
Trent Dilfer, Fresno St.	†1993	11	333	217	4	.652	3,276	28	173.1
Jerry Rhome, Tulsa	#†1964	10	326	224	4	.687	2,870	32	172.6
Elvis Grbac, Michigan	†1991	11	228	152	5	.667	1,955	24	169.0
Ty Detmer, Brigham Young	#1991	12	403	249	12	.618	4,031	35	168.5
Steve Young, Brigham Young	#†1983	11	429	306	10	*.713	3,902	33	168.5
Vinny Testaverde, Miami (Fla.)	†1986	10	276	175	9	.634	2,557	26	165.8
Brian Dowling, Yale	1968	9	160	92	10	.575	1,554	19	165.8
Dave Barr, California	1993	11	275	187	12	.680	2,619	21	164.5
Don McPherson, Syracuse	†1987	11	229	129	11	.563	2,341	22	164.3
Dave Wilson, Ball St.	1977	11	177	115	7	.650	1,589	17	164.2
Bob Berry, Oregon	1963	10	171	101	7	.591	1,675	16	164.0
Jim Harbaugh, Michigan	†1985	11	212	139	6	.656	1,913	18	163.7
Troy Aikman, UCLA	1987	11	243	159	6	.654	2,354	16	163.6
Turk Schonert, Stanford	†1979	11	221	148	6	.670	1,922	19	163.0
Brian Broomell, Temple	1979	11	214	120	11	.561	2,103	22	162.3
Dennis Shaw, San Diego St.	†1969	10	335	199	26	.594	3,185	39	162.2
Timm Rosenbach, Washington St.	†1988	11	302	199	10	.659	2,791	23	162.0
Davey O'Brien, Texas Christian	¢#†1938	10	167	93	4	.557	1,457	19	161.7

Player, Team	Year	G	Att.	Cmp.	Int.	Pct.	Yds.	TD	Pts.
Chuck Hartlieb, Iowa	1987	12	299	196	8	.656	2,855	19	161.4
Darrell Bevell, Wisconsin	1993	11	256	177	10	.691	2,294	19	161.1
David Brown, Duke	1989	9	163	104	6	.638	1,479	14	161.0
Shawn Moore, Virginia	†1990	10	241	144	8	.598	2,262	21	160.7
Chuck Long, Iowa	1983	10	236	144	8	.610	2,434	14	160.4
Jeff Garcia, San Jose St.	1991	9	160	99	5	.619	1,519	12	160.1
Matt Blundin, Virginia	1991	9	224	135	0	.603	1,902	19	159.6
Kerwin Bell, Florida	1985	11	288	180	8	.625	2,687	21	159.4
Mike Gundy, Oklahoma St.	1988	11	236	153	12	.648	2,163	19	158.2
Charlie Ward, Florida St.	1993	11	380	264	4	.695	3,032	27	157.8
Maurice DeShazo, Virginia Tech	1993	11	230	129	7	.561	2,080	22	157.5
Danny White, Arizona St.	1973	11	265	146	12	.551	2,609	23	157.4
Heath Shuler, Tennessee	1993	11	285	184	8	.646	2,354	25	157.3
Stan Heath, Nevada	#†1948	9	222	126	9	.568	2,005	22	157.2
Glenn Foley, Boston College	1993	11	363	222	10	.612	3,397	25	157.0
Jim Harbaugh, Michigan	1986	11	254	167	8	.658	2,557	10	157.0
Chris Vargas, Nevada	#1993	11	490	331	18	.676	4,265	34	156.2
Shawn Moore, Virginia	1989	11	221	125	7	.566	2,078	18	156.1
Dan Speltz, Cal St. Fullerton	1989	11	309	214	11	.693	2,671	20	156.1
John Walsh, Brigham Young	1993	11	397	244	15	.615	3,727	28	156.0
Ty Detmer, Brigham Young	1990	12	562	361	28	.642	*5,188	41	155.9
Rob Johnson, Southern Cal	1993	12	405	278	5	.686	3,285	26	155.5
Doug Williams, Grambling	#1977	11	352	181	18	.514	3,286	38	155.2
John Huarte, Notre Dame	1964	10	205	114	11	.556	2,062	16	155.1
Jim McMahon, Brigham Young	#†1981	10	423	272	7	.643	3,555	30	155.0
Elvis Grbac, Michigan	†1992	9	169	112	12	.663	1,465	15	154.2
Steve Sloan, Alabama	1965	10	160	97	3	.606	1,453	10	153.8
Tom Ramsey, UCLA	†1982	11	311	191	10	.614	2,824	21	153.5
Martin Vaughn, Pennsylvania	1973	9	206	114	8	.553	1,926	17	153.3
Dick Doheny, Fordham	1949	8	140	87	5	.621	1,127	13	153.3

Terry Baker of Oregon State was the 1962 passing efficiency leader (minimum 15 attempts per game) with a rating of 146.5. He also won the Heisman Trophy that season.

*Record. †National pass-efficiency champion. #National total-offense champion. ¢Available records before 1946 do not include TD passes except for O'Brien and relatively few other passers; thus, passing efficiency points cannot be compiled for those players without TD passes.

ANNUAL PASSING EFFICIENCY LEADERS

(% Minimum 11 Attempts Per Game)

1946—Bill Mackrides, Nevada, 176.9; **1947**—Bobby Layne, Texas, 138.9; **1948**—Stan Heath, Nevada, 157.2 (#); **1949**—Bob Williams, Notre Dame, 159.1; **1950**—Claude Arnold, Oklahoma, 157.3; **1951**—Dick Kazmaier, Princeton, 155.3 (#); **1952**—Ron Morris, Tulsa, 177.4; **1953**—Bob Garrett, Stanford, 142.2; **1954**—Pete Vann, Army, 166.5; **1955**—George Welsh, Navy, 146.1 (#); **1956**—Tom Flores, Pacific (Cal.), 147.5; **1957**—Lee Grosscup, Utah, 175.5; **1958**—John Hangartner, Arizona St., 150.1; **1959**—Charley Johnson, New Mexico St., 135.7; **1960**—Eddie Wilson, Arizona, 140.8; **1961**—Ron DiGravio, Purdue, 140.1; **1962**—John Jacobs, Arizona St., 153.9; **1963**—Bob Berry, Oregon, 164.0; **1964**—Jerry Rhome, Tulsa, 172.6 (#).

(Minimum 15 Attempts Per Game)

1946—Ben Raimondi, Indiana, 117.0; **1947**—Charley Conerly, Mississippi, 125.8; **1948**—Stan Heath, Nevada, 157.2 (#); **1949**—Dick Doheny, Fordham, 153.3; **1950**—Dick Doheny, Fordham, 149.5; **1951**—Babe Parilli, Kentucky, 130.8; **1952**—Gene Rossi, Cincinnati, 149.7; **1953**—Bob Garrett, Stanford, 142.2; **1954**—Len Dawson, Purdue, 145.8; **1955**—George Welsh, Navy, 146.1 (#); **1956**—Bob Reinhart, San Jose St., 121.3; **1957**—Bob Newman, Washington St., 126.5 (#); **1958**—Randy Duncan, Iowa, 135.1; **1959**—Charley Johnson, New Mexico St., 135.7; **1960**—Charley Johnson, New Mexico St., 134.1; **1961**—Eddie Wilson, Arizona, 134.2; **1962**—Terry Baker, Oregon St., 146.5 (#); **1963**—Bob Berry, Oregon, 164.0; **1964**—Jerry Rhome, Tulsa, 172.6 (#).

(Minimum 15 Attempts Per Game)

Year	Player, Team	G	Att.	Cmp.	Int.	Pct.	Yds.	TD	Pts.
1965	Steve Sloan, Alabama	10	160	97	3	.606	1,453	10	153.8
1966	Dewey Warren, Tennessee	10	229	136	7	.594	1,716	18	142.2
1967	Bill Andrejko, Villanova	10	187	114	6	.610	1,405	13	140.6
1968	Brian Dowling, Yale	9	160	92	10	.575	1,554	19	165.8
1969	#Dennis Shaw, San Diego St.	10	335	199	26	.594	3,185	39	162.2
1970	Jerry Tagge, Nebraska	11	165	104	7	.630	1,383	12	149.0
1971	Jerry Tagge, Nebraska	12	239	143	4	.598	2,019	17	150.9
1972	John Hufnagel, Penn St.	11	216	115	8	.532	2,039	15	148.0
1973	Danny White, Arizona St.	11	265	146	12	.551	2,609	23	157.4
1974	#Steve Joachim, Temple	10	221	128	13	.579	1,950	20	150.1
1975	James Kubacki, Harvard	8	137	77	9	.562	1,273	11	147.6
1976	Steve Haynes, Louisiana Tech	10	216	120	11	.556	1,981	16	146.9
1977	Dave Wilson, Ball St.	11	177	115	7	.650	1,589	17	164.2
1978	Paul McDonald, Southern Cal	11	194	111	7	.572	1,667	18	152.8

(See page 34 for annual leaders beginning in 1979)
#National total-offense champion. %In many seasons during 1946-64, only a few passers threw as many as 15 passes per game; thus, a lower minimum was used.

Bernie Kosar made the most of his two seasons at Miami (Florida), averaging 259.6 passing yards per game to rank 10th on the Division I-A career list.

CAREER YARDS

Player, Team	Years	Att.	Cmp.	Int.	Pct.	Yds.	TD	Long
Ty Detmer, Brigham Young	1988-91	*1,530	*958	65	.626	*15,031	*121	76
Todd Santos, San Diego St.	1984-87	1,484	910	57	.613	11,425	70	84
Alex Van Pelt, Pittsburgh	1989-92	1,463	845	59	.578	10,913	64	91
Kevin Sweeney, Fresno St.	$1982-86	1,336	731	48	.547	10,623	66	95
Doug Flutie, Boston College	1981-84	1,270	677	54	.533	10,579	67	80
Brian McClure, Bowling Green	1982-85	1,427	900	58	.631	10,280	63	90
Troy Kopp, Pacific (Cal.)	1989-92	1,374	798	47	.581	10,258	87	80
Glenn Foley, Boston College	1990-93	1,275	703	60	.551	10,042	72	78
Ben Bennett, Duke	1980-83	1,375	820	57	.596	9,614	55	88
Jim McMahon, Brigham Young	1977-78, 80-81	1,060	653	34	.616	9,536	84	80
Todd Ellis, South Caro.	1986-89	1,266	704	66	.556	9,519	49	97
David Klingler, Houston	1988-91	1,261	726	38	.576	9,430	91	95
Erik Wilhelm, Oregon St.	1985-88	1,480	870	61	.588	9,393	52	‡74
Jeremy Leach, New Mexico	1988-91	1,432	735	62	.513	9,382	50	82
John Elway, Stanford	1979-82	1,246	774	39	.621	9,349	77	70
T. J. Rubley, Tulsa	1987-89, 91	1,336	682	54	.510	9,324	73	75
Shane Matthews, Florida	1989-92	1,202	722	46	.601	9,287	74	70
Chuck Long, Iowa	$1981-85	1,072	692	46	‡‡.646	9,210	64	89
Mark Herrmann, Purdue	1977-80	1,218	717	*73	.589	9,188	62	75
Tom Hodson, Louisiana St.	1986-89	1,163	674	41	.580	9,115	69	80
Scott Mitchell, Utah	1987-89	1,165	669	38	.574	8,981	68	72
Brad Tayles, Western Mich.	1989-92	1,370	663	67	.484	8,717	49	84
Joe Adams, Tennessee St.	1977-80	1,100	604	60	.549	8,649	81	71
Marvin Graves, Syracuse	1990-93	943	563	45	.597	8,466	48	84
Shawn Jones, Georgia Tech	1989-92	1,217	652	50	.536	8,441	51	82
Robbie Bosco, Brigham Young	1983-85	997	638	36	.640	8,400	66	‡89
Andre Ware, Houston	1987-89	1,074	660	28	.615	8,202	75	87
Dan McGwire, Iowa/San Diego St.	1986-87, 89-90	973	575	30	.591	8,164	49	71
Jack Trudeau, Illinois	1981, 83-85	1,151	736	38	†.639	8,146	51	83
Troy Taylor, California	1986-89	1,162	683	46	.588	8,126	51	79
Mike Gundy, Oklahoma St.	1986-89	1,037	606	37	.584	8,072	54	‡84
Jeff Graham, Long Beach St.	1985-88	1,175	664	42	.565	8,063	42	85
Randall Cunningham, Nevada-Las Vegas	1982-84	1,029	597	29	.580	8,020	59	69
Stan White, Auburn	1990-93	1,231	659	52	.535	8,016	40	78
Steve Slayden, Duke	1984-87	1,204	699	53	.581	8,004	48	73
Robert Hall, Texas Tech	1990-93	997	548	28	.550	7,908	48	95
Dan Marino, Pittsburgh	1979-82	1,084	626	64	.577	7,905	74	65
John Holman, Northeast La.	1979-82	1,201	593	54	.494	7,827	51	85
Jack Thompson, Washington St.	1975-78	1,086	601	49	.553	7,818	53	80
Bobby Fuller, Appalachian St./South Caro.	1987-88, 90-91	1,061	596	32	.562	7,746	52	79
Steve Young, Brigham Young	1981-83	908	592	33	**.652	7,733	56	63
Steve Stenstrom, Stanford	1991-93	987	616	30	.624	7,709	56	92
Brett Favre, Southern Miss.	1987-90	1,169	613	34	.524	7,695	52	80
Gino Torretta, Miami (Fla.)	1989-92	991	555	24	.560	7,690	47	99
Terrence Jones, Tulane	1985-88	1,042	570	41	.547	7,684	46	76
John Paye, Stanford	1983-86	1,198	715	44	.597	7,669	38	80
Rodney Peete, Southern Cal	1985-88	972	571	32	.587	7,640	52	‡68

*Record. $See page 6 for explanation. ‡Did not score. †Record for minimum of 1,100 attempts. ‡‡Record for minimum of 1,000 attempts. **Record for minimum of 875 attempts.

CAREER YARDS RECORD PROGRESSION
(Record Yards—Player, Team, Seasons Played)

3,075—Billy Patterson, Baylor, 1936-38; **3,777**—Bud Schwenk, Washington (Mo.), 1939-41; **4,004**—Johnny Rauch, Georgia, 1945-48; **4,736**—John Ford, Hardin-Simmons, 1947-50; **4,863**—Zeke Bratkowski, Georgia, 1951-53; **5,472**—Jerry Rhome, Southern Methodist, 1961, Tulsa, 1963-64; **6,495**—Billy Stevens, UTEP, 1965-67; **7,076**—Steve Ramsey, North Texas, 1967-69; **7,544**—Jim Plunkett, Stanford, 1968-70; **7,549**—John Reaves, Florida, 1969-71; **7,818**—Jack Thompson, Washington St., 1975-78; **9,188**—Mark Herrmann, Purdue, 1977-80; **9,536**—Jim McMahon, BrighamYoung, 1977-78, 80-81; **9,614**—Ben Bennett, Duke, 1980-83; **10,579**—Doug Flutie, Boston College, 1981-84; **10,623**—Kevin Sweeney, Fresno St., $1982-86; **11,425**—Todd Santos, San Diego St., 1984-87; **15,031**—Ty Detmer, Brigham Young, 1988-91.

$See page 6 for explanation.

CAREER YARDS PER GAME
(Minimum 5,000 yards)

Player, Team	Years	G	Att.	Cmp.	Int.	Pct.	Yds.	TD	Yd.PG
Ty Detmer, Brigham Young	1988-91	46	*1,530	*958	65	.626	*15,031	*121	*326.8
Chris Vargas, Nevada	§1992-93	20	806	502	34	.623	6,359	47	318.0
Mike Perez, San Jose St.	1986-87	20	792	471	30	.595	6,194	36	309.7
Doug Gaynor, Long Beach St.	1984-85	22	837	569	35	.680	6,793	35	308.8
Tony Eason, Illinois	1981-82	22	856	526	29	.614	6,608	37	300.4
David Klingler, Houston	1988-91	32	1,261	726	38	.576	9,430	91	294.7
Brent Snyder, Utah St.	1987-88	22	875	472	36	.539	6,105	39	277.5
Shane Matthews, Florida	1989-92	35	1,202	722	46	.601	9,287	74	265.3
Larry Egger, Utah	1985-86	22	799	470	31	.588	5,749	39	261.3
Bernie Kosar, Miami (Fla.)	1983-84	23	743	463	29	.623	5,971	40	259.6

*Record. §Vargas played two years in Division I-A and two years in Division I-AA.

CAREER TOUCHDOWN PASSES

Player, Team	Years	G	TD Passes
Ty Detmer, Brigham Young	1988-91	46	*121
David Klingler, Houston	1988-91	32	91
Troy Kopp, Pacific (Cal.)	1989-92	40	87
Jim McMahon, Brigham Young	1977-78, 80-81	44	84
Joe Adams, Tennessee St.	1977-80	41	81
John Elway, Stanford	1979-82	43	77
Andre Ware, Houston	1987-89	29	75
Shane Matthews, Florida	1989-92	35	74
Dan Marino, Pittsburgh	1979-82	40	74
T. J. Rubley, Tulsa	1987-89, 91	47	73
Glenn Foley, Boston College	1990-93	44	72
Todd Santos, San Diego St.	1984-87	46	70
Tom Hodson, Louisiana St.	1986-89	44	69
Steve Ramsey, North Texas	1967-69	29	69
Scott Mitchell, Utah	1987-89	33	68
Doug Flutie, Boston College	1981-84	42	67
Kevin Sweeney, Fresno St.	1983-86	47	66
Robbie Bosco, Brigham Young	1983-85	35	66
Elvis Grbac, Michigan	1989-92	41	64
Alex Van Pelt, Pittsburgh	1989-92	45	64
Chuck Long, Iowa	$1981-85	45	64

*Record. $See page 6 for explanation.

SEASON YARDS

Player, Team	Year	G	Att.	Cmp.	Int.	Pct.	Yards	TD	Long
Ty Detmer, Brigham Young	1990	12	562	361	28	.642	*5,188	41	69
David Klingler, Houston	1990	11	*643	*374	20	.582	5,140	*54	95
Andre Ware, Houston	1989	11	578	365	15	.631	4,699	46	87
Jim McMahon, Brigham Young	†1980	12	445	284	18	.638	4,571	47	80
Ty Detmer, Brigham Young	†1989	12	412	265	15	.643	4,560	32	67
Scott Mitchell, Utah	1988	11	533	323	15	.606	4,322	29	72
Robbie Bosco, Brigham Young	1985	13	511	338	24	.661	4,273	30	‡89
Chris Vargas, Nevada	1993	11	490	331	18	.676	4,265	34	78
Ty Detmer, Brigham Young	1991	12	403	249	12	.618	4,031	35	97
Todd Santos, San Diego St.	1987	12	492	306	15	.622	3,932	26	74
Steve Young, Brigham Young	†1983	11	429	306	10	*.713	3,902	33	63
Robbie Bosco, Brigham Young	1984	12	458	283	11	.618	3,875	33	54
Mike McCoy, Utah	1993	12	430	276	10	.642	3,860	21	87
Dan McGwire, San Diego St.	1990	11	449	270	7	.601	3,833	27	71
Anthony Dilweg, Duke	1988	11	484	287	18	.593	3,824	24	65
Jimmy Klingler, Houston	1992	11	504	303	18	.601	3,818	32	82
Sam King, Nevada-Las Vegas	1981	12	433	255	19	.589	3,778	18	71
Troy Kopp, Pacific (Cal.)	1991	12	449	275	16	.612	3,767	37	68
John Walsh, Brigham Young	1993	11	397	244	15	.615	3,727	28	69
Marc Wilson, Brigham Young	1979	12	427	250	15	.585	3,720	29	‡76
Dan McGwire, San Diego St.	1989	12	440	258	19	.586	3,651	16	57
Jim Everett, Purdue	1985	11	450	285	11	.633	3,651	23	70
Bernie Kosar, Miami (Fla.)	1984	12	416	262	16	.630	3,642	25	85
Steve Stenstrom, Stanford	1993	11	455	300	14	.659	3,627	27	91
Jeremy Leach, New Mexico	1989	12	511	282	20	.552	3,573	22	82
Doug Gaynor, Long Beach St.	1985	12	452	321	18	.710	3,563	19	57
Jim McMahon, Brigham Young	†1981	10	423	272	7	.643	3,555	30	‡67
Eric Zeier, Georgia	1993	11	425	269	7	.633	3,525	24	80
Todd Dillon, Long Beach St.	1982	11	504	289	21	.573	3,517	19	‡73

*Record. †National pass-efficiency champion. ‡Did not score.

SEASON YARDS PER GAME

Player, Team	Year	G	Att.	Cmp.	Int.	Pct.	Yards	TD	Yd.PG
David Klingler, Houston	1990	11	*643	*374	20	.582	5,140	*54	*467.3
Ty Detmer, Brigham Young	1990	12	562	361	28	.642	*5,188	41	432.3
Andre Ware, Houston	1989	11	578	365	15	.631	4,699	46	427.2
Scott Mitchell, Utah	1988	11	533	323	15	.606	4,322	29	392.9
Chris Vargas, Nevada	1993	11	490	331	18	.676	4,265	34	387.7
Jim McMahon, Brigham Young	†1980	12	445	284	18	.638	4,571	47	380.9
Ty Detmer, Brigham Young	†1989	12	412	265	15	.643	4,560	32	380.0
Troy Kopp, Pacific (Cal.)	1990	9	428	243	14	.568	3,311	31	367.9
Jim McMahon, Brigham Young	†1981	10	423	272	7	.643	3,555	30	355.5
Steve Young, Brigham Young	†1983	11	429	306	10	*.713	3,902	33	354.7
Dan McGwire, San Diego St.	1990	11	449	270	7	.601	3,833	27	348.5
Anthony Dilweg, Duke	1988	11	484	287	18	.593	3,824	24	347.6
Jimmy Klingler, Houston	1992	11	504	303	18	.601	3,818	32	347.1
Bill Anderson, Tulsa	†1965	10	509	296	14	.582	3,464	30	346.4
David Klingler, Houston	1991	10	497	278	17	.559	3,388	29	338.8
Marc Wilson, Brigham Young	1979	12	427	250	15	.585	3,720	29	338.2

*Record. †National pass-efficiency champion.

Troy Kopp of Pacific (California) threw 87 touchdown passes in his four-year career, a total that ranks third in Division I-A history.

Texas Christian's Matt Vogler passed for 690 yards, the second-best single-game total in Division I-A history, in a game against Houston November 3, 1990.

SEASON TOUCHDOWN PASSES

Player, Team	Year	G	TD Passes
David Klingler, Houston	1990	11	*54
Jim McMahon, Brigham Young	1980	12	47
Andre Ware, Houston	1989	11	46
Ty Detmer, Brigham Young	1990	12	41
Dennis Shaw, San Diego St.	1969	10	39
Doug Williams, Grambling	1977	11	38
Troy Kopp, Pacific (Cal.)	1991	12	37
Ty Detmer, Brigham Young	1991	12	35
Chris Vargas, Nevada	1993	11	34
Dan Marino, Pittsburgh	1981	11	34
Robbie Bosco, Brigham Young	1984	12	33
Steve Young, Brigham Young	1983	11	33
Jimmy Klingler, Houston	1992	11	32
Ty Detmer, Brigham Young	1989	12	32
Jerry Rhome, Tulsa	1964	10	32
Troy Kopp, Pacific (Cal.)	1990	9	31

*Record.

SINGLE-GAME YARDS

Yds.	Player, Team (Opponent)	Date
716	David Klingler, Houston (Arizona St.)	Dec. 2, 1990
690	Matt Vogler, Texas Christian (Houston)	Nov. 3, 1990
631	Scott Mitchell, Utah (Air Force)	Oct. 15, 1988
622	Jeremy Leach, New Mexico (Utah)	Nov. 11, 1989
621	Dave Wilson, Illinois (Ohio St.)	Nov. 8, 1980
619	John Walsh, Brigham Young (Utah St.)	Oct. 30, 1993
613	Jimmy Klingler, Houston (Rice)	Nov. 28, 1992
599	Ty Detmer, Brigham Young (San Diego St.)	Nov. 16, 1991
585	Robbie Bosco, Brigham Young (New Mexico)	Oct. 19, 1985
572	David Klingler, Houston (Eastern Wash.)	Nov. 17, 1990
571	Marc Wilson, Brigham Young (Utah)	Nov. 5, 1977
568	David Lowery, San Diego St. (Brigham Young)	Nov. 16, 1991
565	Jim McMahon, Brigham Young (Utah)	Nov. 21, 1981
564	Troy Kopp, Pacific, Cal. (New Mexico St.)	Oct. 20, 1990
563	David Klingler, Houston (Texas Christian)	Nov. 3, 1990
561	Tony Adams, Utah St. (Utah)	Nov. 11, 1972
560	Ty Detmer, Brigham Young (Utah St.)	Nov. 24, 1990
558	Chuck Hartlieb, Iowa (Indiana)	Oct. 29, 1988
554	Greg Cook, Cincinnati (Ohio)	Nov. 16, 1968
544	Eric Zeier, Georgia (Southern Miss.)	Oct. 9, 1993
538	Chris Vargas, Nevada (Nevada-Las Vegas)	Oct. 2, 1993
538	Jim McMahon, Brigham Young (Colorado St.)	Nov. 7, 1981
537	Ty Detmer, Brigham Young (Washington St.)	Sept. 7, 1989
536	Dave Telford, Fresno St. (Pacific, Cal.)	Oct. 24, 1987
536	Todd Santos, San Diego St. (Stanford)	Oct. 17, 1987
536	David Spriggs, New Mexico St. (Southern Ill.)	Sept. 30, 1978
535	Shane Montgomery, North Caro. St. (Duke)	Nov. 11, 1989
534	Paul Justin, Arizona St. (Washington St.)	Oct. 28, 1989
533	David Klingler, Houston (Texas Tech)	Nov. 30, 1991
532	Jeff Van Raaphorst, Arizona St. (Florida St.)	Nov. 3, 1984

CAREER YARDS PER ATTEMPT
(Minimum 900 Attempts)

Player, Team	Years	Att.	Cmp.	Pct.	Yards	Yards Per Cmp.	Yards Per Att.
Ty Detmer, Brigham Young	1988-91	*1,530	*958	.626	*15,031	*15.69	*9.82
Jim McMahon, Brigham Young	1977-78, 80-81	1,060	653	.616	9,536	14.60	9.00
Marvin Graves, Syracuse	1990-93	943	563	.597	8,466	15.04	8.98
Chuck Long, Iowa	$1981-85	1,072	692	#.646	9,210	13.31	8.59
Steve Young, Brigham Young	1981-83	908	592	††.652	7,733	13.06	8.52
Robbie Bosco, Brigham Young	1983-85	997	638	.640	8,400	13.17	8.43
Dan McGwire, Iowa/San Diego St.	1986-87, 89-90	973	575	.591	8,164	14.20	8.39
Doug Flutie, Boston College	1981-84	1,270	677	.533	10,579	15.63	8.33
Marc Wilson, Brigham Young	1977-79	937	535	.571	7,637	14.27	8.15
Kerwin Bell, Florida	1984-87	953	549	.576	7,585	13.82	7.96
Kevin Sweeney, Fresno St.	$1982-86	1,336	731	.547	10,623	14.53	7.95
Robert Hall, Texas Tech	1990-93	997	548	.550	7,908	14.43	7.93
Glenn Foley, Boston College	1990-93	1,275	703	.551	10,042	14.28	7.88
Joe Adams, Tennessee St.	1977-80	1,100	604	.549	8,649	14.32	7.86
Rodney Peete, Southern Cal	1985-88	972	571	.587	7,640	13.38	7.86
Tom Hodson, Louisiana St.	1986-89	1,163	674	.580	9,115	13.52	7.84
Jim Plunkett, Stanford	1968-70	962	530	.551	7,544	14.23	7.84
Steve Stenstrom, Stanford	1991-93	987	616	.624	7,709	12.51	7.81

*Record. $See page 6 for explanation. #Record for minimum of 1,000 attempts. ††Record for minimum of 875 attempts.

SINGLE-GAME ATTEMPTS

No.	Player, Team (Opponent)	Date
79	Matt Vogler, Texas Christian (Houston)	Nov. 3, 1990
76	David Klingler, Houston (Southern Methodist)	Oct. 20, 1990
75	Chris Vargas, Nevada (McNeese St.)	Sept. 19, 1992
73	Jeff Handy, Missouri (Oklahoma St.)	Oct. 17, 1992
73	Troy Kopp, Pacific, Cal. (Hawaii)	Oct. 27, 1990
73	Shane Montgomery, North Caro. St. (Duke)	Nov. 11, 1989
72	Matt Vogler, Texas Christian (Texas Tech)	Nov. 10, 1990
71	Jimmy Klingler, Houston (Rice)	Nov. 28, 1992
71	Sandy Schwab, Northwestern (Michigan)	Oct. 23, 1982
70	David Klingler, Houston (Texas Tech)	Nov. 30, 1991
70	David Klingler, Houston (Arizona St.)	Dec. 2, 1990
70	Dave Telford, Fresno St. (Utah St.)	Nov. 14, 1987
69	Dave Wilson, Illinois (Ohio St.)	Nov. 8, 1980
69	Chuck Hixson, Southern Methodist (Ohio St.)	Sept. 28, 1968
68	David Klingler, Houston (Baylor)	Oct. 6, 1990
68	Jeremy Leach, New Mexico (Utah)	Nov. 11, 1989
68	Steve Smith, Stanford (Notre Dame)	Oct. 7, 1989
68	Andre Ware, Houston (Arizona St.)	Sept. 23, 1989
67	Mike Hohensee, Minnesota (Ohio St.)	Nov. 7, 1981
66	Chuck Clements, Houston (Cincinnati)	Nov. 13, 1993
66	Tim Schade, Minnesota (Penn St.)	Sept. 4, 1993
66	Drew Bledsoe, Washington St. (Montana)	Sept. 5, 1992
66	Jack Trudeau, Illinois (Purdue)	Oct. 12, 1985
66	John Reaves, Florida (Auburn)	Nov. 1, 1969
65	Eric Zeier, Georgia (Florida)	Oct. 30, 1993
65	Jimmy Klingler, Houston (Texas Christian)	Oct. 31, 1992
65	Scott Mitchell, Utah (UTEP)	Oct. 1, 1988
65	Mike Bates, Miami, Ohio (Toledo)	Oct. 24, 1987
65	Craig Burnett, Wyoming (San Diego St.)	Nov. 15, 1986
65	Gary Schofield, Wake Forest (Maryland)	Oct. 16, 1982
65	Jim McMahon, Brigham Young (Colorado St.)	Nov. 7, 1981
65	Brooks Dawson, UTEP (UC Santa Barb.)	Sept. 14, 1968
65	Bill Anderson, Tulsa (Southern Ill.)	Oct. 30, 1965
65	Bill Anderson, Tulsa (Memphis)	Oct. 9, 1965

SINGLE-GAME COMPLETIONS

No.	Player, Team (Opponent)	Date
48	David Klingler, Houston (Southern Methodist)	Oct. 20, 1990
46	Jimmy Klingler, Houston (Rice)	Nov. 28, 1992
45	Sandy Schwab, Northwestern (Michigan)	Oct. 23, 1982
44	Matt Vogler, Texas Christian (Houston)	Nov. 3, 1990
44	Chuck Hartlieb, Iowa (Indiana)	Oct. 29, 1988
44	Jim McMahon, Brigham Young (Colorado St.)	Nov. 7, 1981
43	Jeff Handy, Missouri (Oklahoma St.)	Oct. 17, 1992
43	Chris Vargas, Nevada (McNeese St.)	Sept. 19, 1992
43	Gary Schofield, Wake Forest (Maryland)	Oct. 17, 1981
43	Dave Wilson, Illinois (Ohio St.)	Nov. 8, 1980
43	Rich Campbell, California (Florida)	Sept. 13, 1980
42	Jimmy Klingler, Houston (Texas Christian)	Oct. 31, 1992
42	Troy Kopp, Pacific, Cal. (Hawaii)	Oct. 27, 1990
42	Andre Ware, Houston (Texas Christian)	Nov. 4, 1989
42	Dan Speltz, Cal St. Fullerton (Utah St.)	Oct. 7, 1989
42	Robbie Bosco, Brigham Young (New Mexico)	Oct. 19, 1985
42	Bill Anderson, Tulsa (Southern Ill.)	Oct. 30, 1965
41	David Klingler, Houston (Texas Tech)	Nov. 30, 1991
41	David Klingler, Houston (Arizona St.)	Dec. 2, 1990
41	David Klingler, Houston (Eastern Wash.)	Nov. 17, 1990
41	Jeremy Leach, New Mexico (Utah)	Nov. 11, 1989
41	Scott Mitchell, Utah (UTEP)	Oct. 1, 1988
41	Doug Gaynor, Long Beach St. (Utah St.)	Sept. 7, 1985
40	Mike Romo, Southern Methodist (Rice)	Nov. 10, 1990
40	Andre Ware, Houston (Arizona St.)	Sept. 23, 1989
40	Dave Telford, Fresno St. (Utah St.)	Nov. 14, 1987
40	Todd Santos, San Diego St. (Stanford)	Oct. 17, 1987
40	Larry Egger, Utah (UTEP)	Nov. 29, 1986
40	John Paye, Stanford (San Diego St.)	Oct. 5, 1985
40	Gary Schofield, Wake Forest (Maryland)	Oct. 16, 1982
40	Jim McMahon, Brigham Young (North Texas)	Nov. 8, 1980

Missouri's Jeff Handy attempted 73 passes, the fourth-highest total in Division I-A history, in an October 17, 1992, game against Oklahoma State. His 43 completions ranks seventh on the all-time list.

Rice's Tommy Kramer was the major-college passing champion in 1976 with 24.5 completions per game.

ANNUAL CHAMPIONS

Year	Player, Team	Class	Att.	Cmp.	Int.	Pct.	Yds.	TD
1937	Davey O'Brien, Texas Christian	Jr.	234	94	18	.402	969	—
1938	Davey O'Brien, Texas Christian	Sr.	167	93	4	.557	1,457	—
1939	Kay Eakin, Arkansas	Sr.	193	78	18	.404	962	—
1940	Billy Sewell, Washington St.	Sr.	174	86	17	.494	1,023	—
1941	Bud Schwenk, Washington (Mo.)	Sr.	234	114	19	.487	1,457	—
1942	Ray Evans, Kansas	Jr.	200	101	9	.505	1,117	—
1943	Johnny Cook, Georgia	Fr.	157	73	20	.465	1,007	—
1944	Paul Rickards, Pittsburgh	So.	178	84	20	.472	997	—
1945	Al Dekdebrun, Cornell	Sr.	194	90	15	.464	1,227	—
1946	Travis Tidwell, Auburn	Fr.	158	79	10	.500	943	5
1947	Charlie Conerly, Mississippi	Sr.	233	133	7	.571	1,367	18
1948	Stan Heath, Nevada	Sr.	222	126	9	.568	2,005	22
1949	Adrian Burk, Baylor	Sr.	191	110	6	.576	1,428	14
1950	Don Heinrich, Washington	Jr.	221	134	9	.606	1,846	14
1951	Don Klosterman, Loyola Marymount	Sr.	315	159	21	.505	1,843	9
1952	Don Heinrich, Washington	Sr.	270	137	17	.507	1,647	13
1953	Bob Garrett, Stanford	Sr.	205	118	10	.576	1,637	17
1954	Paul Larson, California	Sr.	195	125	8	.641	1,537	10
1955	George Welsh, Navy	Sr.	150	94	6	.627	1,319	8
1956	John Brodie, Stanford	Sr.	240	139	14	.579	1,633	12
1957	Ken Ford, Hardin-Simmons	Sr.	205	115	11	.561	1,254	14
1958	Buddy Humphrey, Baylor	Sr.	195	112	8	.574	1,316	7
1959	Dick Norman, Stanford	Jr.	263	152	12	.578	1,963	11
1960	Harold Stephens, Hardin-Simmons	Sr.	256	145	14	.566	1,254	3
1961	Chon Gallegos, San Jose St.	Sr.	197	117	13	.594	1,480	14
1962	Don Trull, Baylor	Jr.	229	125	12	.546	1,627	11
1963	Don Trull, Baylor	Sr.	308	174	12	.565	2,157	12
1964	Jerry Rhome, Tulsa	Sr.	326	224	4	.687	2,870	32
1965	Bill Anderson, Tulsa	Sr.	509	296	14	.582	3,464	30
1966	John Eckman, Wichita St.	Jr.	458	195	*34	.426	2,339	7
1967	Terry Stone, New Mexico	Jr.	336	160	19	.476	1,946	9
1968	Chuck Hixson, Southern Methodist	So.	468	265	23	.566	3,103	21
1969	John Reaves, Florida	So.	396	222	19	.561	2,896	24

Beginning in 1970, ranked on per-game (instead of total) completions

Year	Player, Team	Class	G	Att.	Cmp.	Avg.	Int.	Pct.	Yds.	TD
1970	Sonny Sixkiller, Washington	So.	10	362	186	18.6	22	.514	2,303	15
1971	Brian Sipe, San Diego St.	Sr.	11	369	196	17.8	21	.531	2,532	17
1972	Don Strock, Virginia Tech	Sr.	11	427	228	20.7	27	.534	3,243	16
1973	Jesse Freitas, San Diego St.	Sr.	11	347	227	20.6	17	.654	2,993	21
1974	Steve Bartkowski, California	Sr.	11	325	182	16.5	7	.560	2,580	12
1975	Craig Penrose, San Diego St.	Sr.	11	349	198	18.0	24	.567	2,660	15
1976	Tommy Kramer, Rice	Sr.	11	501	269	24.5	19	.537	3,317	21
1977	Guy Benjamin, Stanford	Sr.	10	330	208	20.8	15	.630	2,521	19
1978	Steve Dils, Stanford	Sr.	11	391	247	22.5	15	.632	2,943	22

Beginning in 1979, ranked on passing efficiency rating points (instead of per-game completions)

Year	Player, Team	Class	G	Att.	Cmp.	Int.	Pct.	Yds.	TD	Pts.
1979	Turk Schonert, Stanford	Sr.	11	221	148	6	.670	1,922	19	163.0
1980	Jim McMahon, Brigham Young	Jr.	12	445	284	18	.638	4,571	47	*176.9
1981	Jim McMahon, Brigham Young	Sr.	10	423	272	7	.643	3,555	30	155.0
1982	Tom Ramsey, UCLA	Sr.	11	311	191	10	.614	2,824	21	153.5
1983	Steve Young, Brigham Young	Sr.	11	429	306	10	*.713	3,902	33	168.5
1984	Doug Flutie, Boston College	Sr.	11	386	233	11	.604	3,454	27	152.9
1985	Jim Harbaugh, Michigan	Jr.	11	212	139	6	.656	1,913	18	163.7
1986	Vinny Testaverde, Miami (Fla.)	Sr.	10	276	175	9	.634	2,557	26	165.8
1987	Don McPherson, Syracuse	Sr.	11	229	129	11	.563	2,341	22	164.3
1988	Timm Rosenbach, Washington St.	Jr.	11	302	199	10	.659	2,791	23	162.0
1989	Ty Detmer, Brigham Young	So.	12	412	265	15	.643	4,560	32	175.6
1990	Shawn Moore, Virginia	Sr.	10	241	144	8	.598	2,262	21	160.7
1991	Elvis Grbac, Michigan	Jr.	11	228	152	5	.667	1,955	24	169.0
1992	Elvis Grbac, Michigan	Sr.	9	169	112	12	.663	1,465	15	154.2
1993	Trent Dilfer, Fresno St.	Jr.	11	333	217	4	.652	3,276	28	173.1

*Record.

Receiving

CAREER CATCHES PER GAME
(Minimum 20 Games)

Player, Team	Years	G	Rec.	Yards	TD	Rec.PG
Manny Hazard, Houston	1989-90	21	220	2,635	31	*10.5
Howard Twilley, Tulsa	1963-65	26	261	3,343	32	10.0
Jason Phillips, Houston	1987-88	22	207	2,319	18	9.4
Bryan Reeves, Nevada	§1991-93	31	234	3,407	32	7.6
David Williams, Illinois	1983-85	33	245	3,195	22	7.4
James Dixon, Houston	1987-88	22	161	1,762	14	7.3
John Love, North Texas	1965-66	20	144	2,124	17	7.2
Fred Gilbert, UCLA/Houston	1989, 91-92	22	158	1,672	14	7.2
Ron Sellers, Florida St.	1966-68	30	212	3,598	23	7.1
Barry Moore, North Texas	1968-69	20	140	2,183	12	7.0
Mike Kelly, Davidson	1967-69	23	156	2,114	17	6.8
Guy Liggins, San Jose St.	1986-87	22	149	2,191	16	6.8
Dave Petzke, Northern Ill.	1977-78	22	148	1,960	16	6.7
Loren Richey, Utah	1985-86	21	140	1,746	13	6.7
Chris Penn, Tulsa	1991, 93	22	142	2,370	17	6.5
Tim Delaney, San Diego St.	1968-70	29	180	2,535	22	6.2
Larry Willis, Fresno St.	1983-84	23	142	2,260	14	6.2
Phil Odle, Brigham Young	1965-67	30	183	2,548	25	6.1
Aaron Turner, Pacific (Cal.)	1989-92	44	*266	*4,345	*43	6.0
Mike Mikolayunas, Davidson	1968-70	29	175	1,768	14	6.0
Terance Mathis, New Mexico	1985-87, 89	44	263	4,254	36	6.0
Michael Stephens, Nevada	1992-93	21	125	1,712	15	6.0
Rick Eber, Tulsa	1966-67	20	119	1,902	15	6.0
Hugh Campbell, Washington St.	1960-62	30	176	2,453	22	5.9
Vern Burke, Oregon St.	1962-63	20	117	1,801	19	5.9

*Record. §Played 1991 season in Division I-AA.

SEASON CATCHES PER GAME

Player, Team	Year	G	Rec.	Yards	TD	Rec.PG
Howard Twilley, Tulsa	†1965	10	134	*1,779	16	*13.4
Manny Hazard, Houston	†1989	11	*142	1,689	*22	12.9
Jason Phillips, Houston	†1988	11	108	1,444	15	9.8
Fred Gilbert, Houston	†1991	11	106	957	7	9.6
Chris Penn, Tulsa	†1993	11	105	1,578	12	9.5
Jerry Hendren, Idaho	†1969	10	95	1,452	12	9.5
Howard Twilley, Tulsa	†1964	10	95	1,178	13	9.5
Sherman Smith, Houston	†1992	11	103	923	6	9.4
James Dixon, Houston	1988	11	102	1,103	11	9.3
David Williams, Illinois	†1984	11	101	1,278	8	9.2
Bryan Reeves, Nevada	1993	10	91	1,362	17	9.1
Glenn Meltzer, Wichita St.	†1966	10	91	1,115	4	9.1
Jay Miller, Brigham Young	†1973	11	100	1,181	8	9.1

*Record. †National champion.

CAREER CATCHES

Player, Team	Years	Rec.	Yards	Avg.	TD
Aaron Turner, Pacific (Cal.)	1989-92	*266	4,345	16.3	*43
Terance Mathis, New Mexico	1985-87, 89	263	4,254	16.2	36
Mark Templeton, Long Beach St. (RB)	1983-86	262	1,969	7.5	11
Howard Twilley, Tulsa	1963-65	261	3,343	12.8	32
David Williams, Illinois	1983-85	245	3,195	13.0	22
Marc Zeno, Tulane	1984-87	236	3,725	15.8	25
Jason Wolf, Southern Methodist	1989-92	235	2,232	9.5	17
Bryan Reeves, Nevada	§1991-93	234	3,407	14.6	32
Ryan Yarborough, Wyoming	1990-93	229	*4,357	‡19.0	42
Manny Hazard, Houston	1989-90	220	2,635	12.0	31
Darrin Nelson, Stanford (RB)	1977-78, 80-81	214	2,368	11.1	16
Ron Sellers, Florida St.	1966-68	212	3,598	17.0	23
Jason Phillips, Houston	1987-88	207	2,319	11.2	18
Hart Lee Dykes, Oklahoma St.	1985-88	203	3,171	15.6	29
Carl Winston, New Mexico	1990-93	202	2,972	14.7	14
Keith Edwards, Vanderbilt	1980, 82-84	200	1,757	8.8	3
Bobby Slaughter, Louisiana Tech	1987-90	198	2,544	12.9	14
Richard Buchanan, Northwestern	1987-90	197	2,474	12.6	22
Gerald Harp, Western Caro.	1977-80	197	3,305	16.8	26
Matt Bellini, Brigham Young (RB)	1987-90	196	2,544	13.0	13
Brad Muster, Stanford (FB)	1984-87	196	1,669	8.5	6
Greg Primus, Colorado St.	1989-92	192	3,200	16.7	16
Charles Lockett, Long Beach St.	1983-86	191	2,902	15.1	19
Lloyd Hill, Texas Tech	1990-93	189	3,059	16.2	20
Clarkston Hines, Duke	1986-89	189	3,318	17.6	38
Wil Ursin, Tulane	1990-93	188	2,466	13.1	17
Ricky Proehl, Wake Forest	1986-89	188	2,949	15.6	25
Boo Mitchell, Vanderbilt	1985-88	188	2,964	15.8	9
Monty Gilbreath, San Diego St.	1986-89	187	2,241	12.0	8
Eric Henley, Rice	1988-91	186	2,200	11.8	16

Player, Team	Years	Rec.	Yards	Avg.	TD
Johnnie Morton, Southern Cal	1990-93	185	2,957	16.0	21
Jeff Champine, Colorado St.	1980-83	184	2,811	15.3	21
Wendell Davis, Louisiana St.	1984-85	183	2,708	14.8	19
Phil Odle, Brigham Young	1965-67	183	2,548	13.9	25
Mark Szlachcic, Bowling Green	1989-92	182	2,507	13.8	18
Kelly Blackwell, Texas Christian (TE)	1988-91	181	2,155	11.9	13
Tim Delaney, San Diego St.	1968-70	180	2,535	14.1	22
Michael Smith, Kansas St.	1988-91	179	2,457	13.7	11
Darnay Scott, San Diego St.	1991-93	178	3,139	17.6	25
Walter Murray, Hawaii	1982-85	178	2,865	16.1	20
Gordon Hudson, Brigham Young (TE)	1980-83	178	2,484	14.0	22
Rick Beasley, Appalachian St.	1978-80	178	3,124	17.6	23
Bryan Rowley, Utah	$1989-93	177	3,143	17.8	25

*Record. $See page 6 for explanation. ‡Record for minimum of 200 catches. §Played 1991 season in Division I-AA.

SEASON CATCHES

Player, Team	Year	G	Rec.	Yards	TD
Manny Hazard, Houston	†1989	11	*142	1,689	*22
Howard Twilley, Tulsa	†1965	10	134	*1,779	16
Jason Phillips, Houston	†1988	11	108	1,444	15
Fred Gilbert, Houston	†1991	11	106	957	7
Chris Penn, Tulsa	†1993	11	105	1,578	12
Sherman Smith, Houston	†1992	11	103	923	6
James Dixon, Houston	1988	11	102	1,103	11
David Williams, Illinois	†1984	11	101	1,278	8
Jay Miller, Brigham Young	†1973	11	100	1,181	8
Jason Phillips, Houston	†1987	11	99	875	3
Mark Templeton, Long Beach St. (RB)	†1986	11	99	688	2
Rodney Carter, Purdue	†1985	11	98	1,099	4
Keith Edwards, Vanderbilt	†1983	11	97	909	0
Jerry Hendren, Idaho	†1969	10	95	1,452	12
Howard Twilley, Tulsa	†1964	10	95	1,178	13
Richard Buchanan, Northwestern	1989	11	94	1,115	9
Aaron Turner, Pacific (Cal.)	1991	11	92	1,604	18
Bryan Reeves, Nevada	1993	10	91	1,362	17
Dave Petzke, Northern Ill.	†1978	11	91	1,217	11
Glenn Meltzer, Wichita St.	†1966	10	91	1,115	4

*Record. †National champion.

SEASON TOUCHDOWN RECEPTIONS

Player, Team	Year	G	TD
Manny Hazard, Houston	1989	11	*22
Desmond Howard, Michigan	1991	11	19
Aaron Turner, Pacific (Cal.)	1991	11	18
Dennis Smith, Utah	1989	12	18
Tom Reynolds, San Diego St.	1971	10	18
Bryan Reeves, Nevada	1993	10	17
J. J. Stokes, UCLA	1993	11	17
Mario Bailey, Washington	1991	11	17
Clarkston Hines, Duke	1989	11	17
Ryan Yarborough, Wyoming	1993	11	16
Dan Bitson, Tulsa	1989	11	16
Howard Twilley, Tulsa	1965	10	16
Jason Phillips, Houston	1988	11	15
Henry Ellard, Fresno St.	1982	11	15

*Record.

SINGLE-GAME CATCHES

No.	Player, Team (Opponent)	Date
22	Jay Miller, Brigham Young (New Mexico)	Nov. 3, 1973
20	Rick Eber, Tulsa (Idaho St.)	Oct. 7, 1967
19	Manny Hazard, Houston (Texas)	Nov. 11, 1989
19	Manny Hazard, Houston (Texas Christian)	Nov. 4, 1989
19	Ron Fair, Arizona St. (Washington St.)	Oct. 28, 1989
19	Howard Twilley, Tulsa (Colorado St.)	Nov. 27, 1965
18	Richard Woodley, Texas Christian (Texas Tech)	Nov. 10, 1990
18	Mark Templeton, Long Beach St. (RB) (Utah St.)	Nov. 1, 1986
18	Howard Twilley, Tulsa (Southern Ill.)	Oct. 30, 1965
17	Loren Richey, Utah (UTEP)	Nov. 29, 1986
17	Keith Edwards, Vanderbilt (Georgia)	Oct. 15, 1983
17	Jon Harvey, Northwestern (Michigan)	Oct. 23, 1982
17	Don Roberts, San Diego St. (California)	Sept. 18, 1982
17	Tom Reynolds, San Diego St. (Utah St.)	Oct. 22, 1971
17	Mike Mikolayunas, Davidson (Richmond)	Oct. 11, 1969
17	Jerry Hendren, Idaho (Southern Miss.)	Oct. 4, 1969
17	Emilio Vallez, New Mexico (New Mexico St.)	Oct. 27, 1967
17	Chuck Hughes, UTEP (Arizona St.)	Oct. 30, 1965

CAREER YARDS

Player, Team	Years	Rec.	Yards	Avg.	TD
Ryan Yarborough, Wyoming	1990-93	229	*4,357	#19.0	42
Aaron Turner, Pacific (Cal.)	1989-92	*266	4,345	16.3	*43
Terance Mathis, New Mexico	1985-87, 89	263	4,254	16.2	36
Marc Zeno, Tulane	1984-87	236	3,725	15.8	25
Ron Sellers, Florida St.	1966-68	212	3,598	17.0	23
Bryan Reeves, Nevada	§1991-93	234	3,407	14.6	32
Elmo Wright, Houston	1968-70	153	3,347	‡21.9	34
Howard Twilley, Tulsa	1963-65	261	3,343	12.8	32
Clarkston Hines, Duke	1986-89	189	3,318	17.6	38
Gerald Harp, Western Caro.	1977-80	197	3,305	16.8	26
Dan Bitson, Tulsa	1987-89, 91	163	3,300	20.2	29
Greg Primus, Colorado St.	1989-92	192	3,200	16.7	16
David Williams, Illinois	1983-85	245	3,195	13.0	22
Hart Lee Dykes, Oklahoma St.	1985-88	203	3,171	15.6	29
Bryan Rowley, Utah	$1989-93	177	3,143	17.8	25
Darnay Scott, San Diego St.	1991-93	178	3,139	17.6	25
Rick Beasley, Appalachian St.	1978-80	178	3,124	17.6	23
Eric Drage, Brigham Young	1990-93	162	3,065	18.9	29
Lloyd Hill, Texas Tech	1990-93	189	3,059	16.2	20
Carl Winston, New Mexico	1990-93	202	2,972	14.7	14
Johnnie Morton, Southern Cal	1990-93	185	2,957	16.0	21
Ricky Proehl, Wake Forest	1986-89	188	2,949	15.7	25
Henry Ellard, Fresno St.	1979-82	138	2,947	21.4	25
Kendal Smith, Utah St.	1985-88	169	2,943	17.4	25
Charles Lockett, Long Beach St.	1983-86	191	2,902	15.1	19
Chuck Hughes, UTEP	1964-66	162	2,882	17.8	19
Walter Murray, Hawaii	1982-85	178	2,865	16.1	20

*Record. $See page 6 for explanation. ‡Record for minimum of 105 catches. #Record for minimum of 200 catches. §Played 1991 season in Division I-AA.

CAREER YARDS PER GAME
(Minimum 20 Games)

Player, Team	Years	G	Yards	Yd.PG
Manny Hazard, Houston	1989-90	21	2,635	*125.5
Ron Sellers, Florida St.	1966-68	30	3,598	119.9
Elmo Wright, Houston	1968-70	30	3,347	111.6
Howard Twilley, Tulsa	1963-65	30	3,343	111.4
Bryan Reeves, Nevada	‡1991-93	31	3,407	109.9
Chris Penn, Tulsa	1991, 93	22	2,370	107.7
Jason Phillips, Houston	1987-88	22	2,319	105.4
Aaron Turner, Pacific (Cal.)	1989-92	44	4,345	98.8
Rick Beasley, Appalachian St.	†1977-80	32	3,124	97.6
David Williams, Illinois	1982-85	33	3,195	96.8
Terance Mathis, New Mexico	1985-87, 89	44	4,254	96.7
Ryan Yarborough, Wyoming	1990-93	46	*4,357	94.7
Darnay Scott, San Diego St.	1991-93	34	3,139	92.3
Lloyd Hill, Texas Tech	1990-93	34	3,059	90.0
Marc Zeno, Tulane	1984-87	44	3,725	84.7
Tim Delaney, San Diego St.	1968-70	30	2,535	84.5

‡Played 1991 season in Division I-AA. †Played defensive back in 1977.

CAREER TOUCHDOWN RECEPTIONS

Player, Team	Years	G	TD
Aaron Turner, Pacific (Cal.)	1989-92	44	*43
Ryan Yarborough, Wyoming	1990-93	46	42
Clarkston Hines, Duke	1986-89	44	38
Terance Mathis, New Mexico	1985-87, 89	44	36
Elmo Wright, Houston	1968-70	30	34
Bryan Reeves, Nevada	§1991-93	31	32
Steve Largent, Tulsa	1973-75	30	32
Howard Twilley, Tulsa	1963-65	30	32
Manny Hazard, Houston	1989-90	21	31
Sean Dawkins, California	1990-92	33	30
Desmond Howard, Michigan	1989-91	33	30
Jade Butcher, Indiana	1967-69	30	30
Eric Drage, Brigham Young	1990-93	46	29
Dan Bitson, Tulsa	1987-89, 91	44	29
Hart Lee Dykes, Oklahoma St.	1985-88	41	29

*Record. §Played 1991 season in Division I-AA.

SEASON YARDS

Player, Team	Year	Rec.	Yards	Avg.	TD
Howard Twilley, Tulsa	†1965	134	*1,779	13.3	16
Manny Hazard, Houston	†1989	*142	1,689	11.9	*22
Aaron Turner, Pacific (Cal.)	†1991	92	1,604	17.4	18
Chris Penn, Tulsa	†1993	105	1,578	15.0	12
Chuck Hughes, UTEP	1965	80	1,519	19.0	12
Ryan Yarborough, Wyoming	1993	67	1,512	22.6	16
Henry Ellard, Fresno St.	1982	62	1,510	††24.4	15
Ron Sellers, Florida St.	†1968	86	1,496	17.4	12
Jerry Hendren, Idaho	†1969	95	1,452	15.3	12
Jason Phillips, Houston	†1988	108	1,444	13.4	15

*Record. †National champion. ††Record for minimum of 50 catches.

SINGLE-GAME YARDS

Yds.	Player, Team (Opponent)	Date
349	Chuck Hughes, UTEP (North Texas)	Sept. 18, 1965
322	Rick Eber, Tulsa (Idaho St.)	Oct. 7, 1967
318	Harry Wood, Tulsa (Idaho St.)	Oct. 7, 1967
316	Jeff Evans, New Mexico St. (Southern Ill.)	Sept. 30, 1978
297	Brian Oliver, Ball St. (Toledo)	Oct. 9, 1993
290	Tom Reynolds, San Diego St. (Utah St.)	Oct. 22, 1971
289	Wesley Walker, California (San Jose St.)	Oct. 2, 1976
288	Mike Siani, Villanova (Xavier, Ohio)	Oct. 30, 1971
285	Thomas Lewis, Indiana (Penn St.)	Nov. 6, 1993
284	Don Clune, Pennsylvania (Harvard)	Oct. 30, 1971
283	Chris Castor, Duke (Wake Forest)	Nov. 6, 1982
282	Larry Willis, Fresno St. (Montana St.)	Nov. 17, 1984
278	Derek Graham, Princeton (Yale)	Nov. 14, 1981

ANNUAL CHAMPIONS

Year	Player, Team	Class	Rec.	Yards	TD
1937	Jim Benton, Arkansas	Sr.	47	754	—
1938	Sam Boyd, Baylor	Sr.	32	537	—
1939	Ken Kavanaugh, Louisiana St.	Sr.	30	467	—
1940	Eddie Bryant, Virginia	So.	30	222	2
1941	Hank Stanton, Arizona	Sr.	50	820	—
1942	Bill Rogers, Texas A&M	Sr.	39	432	—
1943	Neil Armstrong, Oklahoma St.	Fr.	39	317	—
1944	Reid Moseley, Georgia	So.	32	506	—
1945	Reid Moseley, Georgia	Jr.	31	662	—
1946	Neil Armstrong, Oklahoma St.	Sr.	32	479	1
1947	Barney Poole, Mississippi	Jr.	52	513	8
1948	Johnny "Red" O'Quinn, Wake Forest	Jr.	39	605	7
1949	Art Weiner, North Caro.	Sr.	52	762	7
1950	Gordon Cooper, Denver	Jr.	46	569	8
1951	Dewey McConnell, Wyoming	Sr.	47	725	9
1952	Ed Brown, Fordham	Sr.	57	774	6
1953	John Carson, Georgia	Sr.	45	663	4
1954	Jim Hanifan, California	Sr.	44	569	7
1955	Hank Burnine, Missouri	Sr.	44	594	2
1956	Art Powell, San Jose St.	So.	40	583	5
1957	Stuart Vaughan, Utah	Sr.	53	756	5
1958	Dave Hibbert, Arizona	Jr.	61	606	4
1959	Chris Burford, Stanford	Sr.	61	756	6
1960	Hugh Campbell, Washington St.	So.	66	881	10
1961	Hugh Campbell, Washington St.	Jr.	53	723	5
1962	Vern Burke, Oregon St.	Jr.	69	1,007	10
1963	Lawrence Elkins, Baylor	Jr.	70	873	8
1964	Howard Twilley, Tulsa	Jr.	95	1,178	13
1965	Howard Twilley, Tulsa	Sr.	134	*1,779	16
1966	Glenn Meltzer, Wichita St.	So.	91	1,115	4
1967	Bob Goodridge, Vanderbilt	Sr.	79	1,114	6
1968	Ron Sellers, Florida St.	Sr.	86	1,496	12
1969	Jerry Hendren, Idaho	Sr.	95	1,452	12

Beginning in 1970, ranked on per-game (instead of total) catches

Year	Player, Team	Class	G	Rec.	Avg.	Yards	TD
1970	Mike Mikolayunas, Davidson	Sr.	10	87	8.7	1,128	8
1971	Tom Reynolds, San Diego St.	Sr.	10	67	6.7	1,070	7
1972	Tom Forzani, Utah St.	Sr.	11	85	7.7	1,169	8
1973	Jay Miller, Brigham Young	So.	11	100	9.1	1,181	8
1974	Dwight McDonald, San Diego St.	Sr.	11	86	7.8	1,157	7
1975	Bob Farnham, Brown	Jr.	9	56	6.2	701	2
1976	Billy Ryckman, Louisiana Tech	Sr.	11	77	7.0	1,382	10
1977	Wayne Tolleson, Western Caro.	Sr.	11	73	6.6	1,101	7
1978	Dave Petzke, Northern Ill.	Sr.	11	91	8.3	1,217	11
1979	Rick Beasley, Appalachian St.	Jr.	11	74	6.7	1,205	12
1980	Dave Young, Purdue	Sr.	11	67	6.1	917	8
1981	Pete Harvey, North Texas	Sr.	9	57	6.3	743	3
1982	Vincent White, Stanford	Sr.	10	68	6.8	677	8
1983	Keith Edwards, Vanderbilt	Jr.	11	97	8.8	909	8
1984	David Williams, Illinois	Jr.	11	101	9.2	1,278	8

Year	Player, Team	Class	G	Rec.	Avg.	Yards	TD
1985	Rodney Carter, Purdue	Sr.	11	98	8.9	1,099	4
1986	Mark Templeton, Long Beach St. (RB)	Sr.	11	99	9.0	688	2
1987	Jason Phillips, Houston	Jr.	11	99	9.0	875	3
1988	Jason Phillips, Houston	Sr.	11	108	9.8	1,444	15
1989	Manny Hazard, Houston	Jr.	11	*142	12.9	1,689	*22

Beginning in 1990, ranked on both per-game catches and yards per game

PER-GAME CATCHES

Year	Player, Team	Class	G	Rec.	Avg.	Yards	TD
1990	Manny Hazard, Houston	Sr.	10	78	7.8	946	9
1991	Fred Gilbert, Houston	Jr.	11	106	9.6	957	7
1992	Sherman Smith, Houston	Jr.	11	103	9.4	923	6
1993	Chris Penn, Tulsa	Sr.	11	105	9.6	1,578	12

YARDS PER GAME

Year	Player, Team	Class	G	Rec.	Yards	Avg.	TD
1990	Patrick Rowe, San Diego St.	Jr.	11	71	1,392	126.6	8
1991	Aaron Turner, Pacific (Cal.)	Jr.	11	92	1,604	145.8	18
1992	Lloyd Hill, Texas Tech	Jr.	11	76	1,261	114.6	12
1993	Chris Penn, Tulsa	Sr.	11	105	1,578	143.5	12

*Record.

Scoring

CAREER POINTS PER GAME

(Minimum 19 Games)

Player, Team	Years	G	TD	XPt.	FG	Pts.	Pt.PG
Marshall Faulk, San Diego St.	1991-93	31	‡62	4	0	‡376	*12.1
Ed Marinaro, Cornell	1969-71	27	52	6	0	318	11.8
Bill Burnett, Arkansas	1968-70	26	49	0	0	294	11.3
Steve Owens, Oklahoma	1967-69	30	56	0	0	336	11.2
Eddie Talboom, Wyoming	1948-50	28	34	99	0	303	10.8
O. J. Simpson, Southern Cal	1967-68	19	33	0	0	198	10.4
Rudy Mobley, Hardin-Simmons	1942, 46	19	32	0	0	192	10.1
Howard Twilley, Tulsa	1963-65	26	32	67	0	259	10.0
Blaise Bryant, Iowa St.	1989-90	20	32	6	0	198	9.9
Tom Harmon, Michigan	1938-40	24	33	33	2	237	9.9
Jackie Parker, Mississippi St.	1952-53	19	24	41	0	185	9.7
Roman Anderson, Houston	1988-91	44	0	*213	70	*423	9.6
Anthony Thompson, Indiana	1986-89	41	*65	4	0	394	9.6
Johnny Bright, Drake	1949-51	25	40	0	0	240	9.6
Glenn Davis, Army	1943-46	37	59	0	0	354	9.6
Mack Herron, Kansas St.	1968-69	20	31	2	0	188	9.4
Stacey Robinson, Northern Ill. (QB)	1988-90	25	38	6	0	234	9.4
Pervis Atkins, New Mexico St.	1959-60	20	29	13	0	187	9.4
Bernard White, Bowling Green	1984-85	22	34	0	0	204	9.3
Floyd Little, Syracuse	1964-66	30	46	2	0	278	9.3
Felix "Doc" Blanchard, Army	1944-46	25	38	3	0	231	9.2
Bobby Reynolds, Nebraska	1950-52	23	28	40	1	211	9.2
Anthony Davis, Southern Cal	1972-74	33	50	2	0	302	9.2

*Record. ‡Three-year totals record.

SEASON POINTS PER GAME

Player, Team	Year	G	TD	XPt.	FG	Pts.	Pt.PG
Barry Sanders, Oklahoma St.	†1988	11	*39	0	0	*234	*21.3
Bobby Reynolds, Nebraska	†1950	9	22	25	0	157	17.4
Art Luppino, Arizona	†1954	10	24	22	0	166	16.6
Ed Marinaro, Cornell	†1971	9	24	4	0	148	16.4
Lydell Mitchell, Penn St.	1971	11	29	0	0	174	15.8
Marshall Faulk, San Diego St.	†1991	9	23	2	0	140	15.6
Byron "Whizzer" White, Colorado	†1937	8	16	23	1	122	15.3

*Record. †National champion.

CAREER POINTS

(Non-Kickers)

Player, Team	Years	TD	XPt.	FG	Pts.
Anthony Thompson, Indiana	1986-89	*65	4	0	*394
Marshall Faulk, San Diego St.	1991-93	‡62	4	0	‡376
Tony Dorsett, Pittsburgh	1973-76	59	2	0	356
Glenn Davis, Army	1943-46	59	0	0	354
Art Luppino, Arizona	1953-56	48	49	0	337
Steve Owens, Oklahoma	1967-69	56	0	0	336
Wilford White, Arizona St.	1947-50	48	27	4	327
Barry Sanders, Oklahoma St.	1986-88	54	0	0	324
Allen Pinkett, Notre Dame	1982-85	53	2	0	320
Pete Johnson, Ohio St.	1973-76	53	0	0	318
Ed Marinaro, Cornell	1969-71	52	6	0	318
Herschel Walker, Georgia	1980-82	52	2	0	314
James Gray, Texas Tech	1986-89	52	0	0	312
Mike Rozier, Nebraska	1981-83	52	0	0	312
Ted Brown, North Caro. St.	1975-78	51	6	0	312

Player, Team	Years	TD	XPt.	FG	Pts.
John Harvey, UTEP	1985-88	51	0	0	306
Eddie Talboom, Wyoming	1948-50	34	99	0	303
Anthony Davis, Southern Cal	1972-74	50	2	0	302
Dalton Hilliard, Louisiana St.	1982-85	50	0	0	300
Billy Sims, Oklahoma	$1975-79	50	0	0	300
Charles White, Southern Cal	1976-79	49	2	0	296
Nolan Jones, Arizona St.	1958-61	30	77	13	296
Steve Bartalo, Colorado St.	1983-86	49	0	0	294
Bill Burnett, Arkansas	1968-70	49	0	0	294
Brian Mitchell, Southwestern La.	1986-89	47	4	0	286
Rick Badanjek, Maryland	1982-85	46	10	0	286
Keith Byars, Ohio St.	1982-85	48	0	0	286

*Record. $See page 6 for explanation. ‡Three-year totals record.

CAREER POINTS

(Kickers)

Player, Team	Years	PAT	PAT Att.	FG	FG Att.	Pts.
Roman Anderson, Houston	1988-91	213	217	70	101	*423
Carlos Huerta, Miami (Fla.)	1988-91	178	181	73	91	397
Jason Elam, Hawaii	$1988-92	158	161	79	100	395
Derek Schmidt, Florida St.	1984-87	174	178	73	102	393
Luis Zendejas, Arizona St.	1981-84	134	135	78	*105	368
Jeff Jaeger, Washington	1983-86	118	123	*80	99	358
John Lee, UCLA	1982-85	116	117	79	92	353
Max Zendejas, Arizona	1982-85	122	124	77	104	353
Kevin Butler, Georgia	1981-84	122	125	77	98	353
Derek Mahoney, Fresno St.	1990-93	*216	*222	45	63	351
Philip Doyle, Alabama	1987-90	105	108	78	*105	%345
Andy Trakas, San Diego St.	1989-92	170	178	56	82	338
Barry Belli, Fresno St.	1984-87	116	123	70	99	326
Jason Hanson, Washington St.	1988-91	136	141	62	95	322
R. D. Lashar, Oklahoma	1987-90	194	200	42	60	320
Collin Mackie, South Caro.	1987-90	112	113	69	95	319
Cary Blanchard, Oklahoma St.	1987-90	150	151	54	73	#314
Fuad Reveiz, Tennessee	1981-84	101	103	71	95	314
Sean Fleming, Wyoming	1988-91	150	155	54	92	312
Van Tiffin, Alabama	1983-86	135	135	59	87	312
Jess Atkinson, Maryland	1981-84	128	131	60	82	308
Gary Gussman, Miami (Ohio)	1984-87	102	104	68	94	306
Greg Cox, Miami (Fla.)	1984-87	162	169	47	64	303
Dan Eichloff, Kansas	1990-93	116	119	62	87	302
Scott Sisson, Georgia Tech	1989-92	119	121	60	88	299
Rusty Hanna, Toledo	1989-92	94	99	68	99	298
Tim Lashar, Oklahoma	1983-86	168	170	43	65	297
John Biskup, Syracuse	1989-92	125	132	57	78	296
Quin Rodriguez, Southern Cal	1987-90	139	146	52	68	295

*Record. $See page 6 for explanation. %Includes one TD reception. #Includes one two-point conversion.

SEASON POINTS

Player, Team	Year	TD	XPt.	FG	Pts.
Barry Sanders, Oklahoma St.	†1988	*39	0	0	*234
Mike Rozier, Nebraska	†1983	29	0	0	174
Lydell Mitchell, Penn St.	1971	29	0	0	174
Art Luppino, Arizona	†1954	24	22	0	166
Bobby Reynolds, Nebraska	†1950	22	25	0	157
Anthony Thompson, Indiana	†1989	25	4	0	154
Fred Wendt, UTEP	†1948	20	32	0	152
Pete Johnson, Ohio St.	†1975	25	0	0	150

*Record. †National champion.

SINGLE-GAME POINTS

No.	Player, Team (Opponent)	Date
48	Howard Griffith, Illinois (Southern Ill.)	Sept. 22, 1990
44	Marshall Faulk, San Diego St. (Pacific, Cal.)	Sept. 14, 1991
43	Jim Brown, Syracuse (Colgate)	Nov. 17, 1956
42	Arnold "Showboat" Boykin, Mississippi (Mississippi St.)	Dec. 1, 1951
42	Fred Wendt, UTEP (New Mexico St.)	Nov. 25, 1948
38	Dick Bass, Pacific (Cal. (San Diego St.)	Nov. 22, 1958
37	Jimmy Nutter, Wichita St. (Northern St.)	Oct. 22, 1949
36	Calvin Jones, Nebraska (Kansas)	Nov. 9, 1991
36	Blake Ezor, Michigan St. (Northwestern)	Nov. 18, 1989
36	Dee Dowis, Air Force (San Diego St.)	Sept. 2, 1989
36	Kelvin Bryant, North Caro. (East Caro.)	Sept. 12, 1981
36	Andre Herrera, Southern Ill. (Northern Ill.)	Oct. 23, 1976
36	Anthony Davis, Southern Cal (Notre Dame)	Dec. 2, 1972
36	Tim Delaney, San Diego St. (New Mexico St.)	Nov. 15, 1969
36	Tom Francisco, Virginia Tech (Va. Military)	Nov. 24, 1966
36	Howard Twilley, Tulsa (Louisville)	Nov. 6, 1965
36	Pete Pedro, West Tex. A&M (UTEP)	Sept. 30, 1961
36	Tom Powers, Duke (Richmond)	Oct. 21, 1950

ANNUAL CHAMPIONS

Year	Player, Team	Class	TD	XPt.	FG	Pts.
1937	Byron "Whizzer" White, Colorado	Sr.	16	23	1	122
1938	Parker Hall, Mississippi	Sr.	11	7	0	73
1939	Tom Harmon, Michigan	Jr.	14	15	1	102
1940	Tom Harmon, Michigan	Sr.	16	18	1	117
1941	Bill Dudley, Virginia	Sr.	18	23	1	134
1942	Bob Steuber, Missouri	Sr.	18	13	0	121
1943	Steve Van Buren, Louisiana St.	Sr.	14	14	0	98
1944	Glenn Davis, Army	So.	20	0	0	120
1945	Felix "Doc" Blanchard, Army	Jr.	19	1	0	115
1946	Gene Roberts, Tenn.-Chatt.	Sr.	18	9	0	117
1947	Lou Gambino, Maryland	Jr.	16	0	0	96
1948	Fred Wendt, UTEP	Sr.	20	32	0	152
1949	George Thomas, Oklahoma	Sr.	19	3	0	117
1950	Bobby Reynolds, Nebraska	So.	22	25	0	157
1951	Ollie Matson, San Francisco	Sr.	21	0	0	126
1952	Jackie Parker, Mississippi St.	Jr.	16	24	0	120
1953	Earl Lindley, Utah St.	Jr.	13	3	0	81
1954	Art Luppino, Arizona	So.	24	22	0	166
1955	Jim Swink, Texas Christian	Jr.	20	5	0	125
1956	Clendon Thomas, Oklahoma	Jr.	18	0	0	108
1957	Leon Burton, Arizona St.	Jr.	16	0	0	96
1958	Dick Bass, Pacific (Cal.)	Jr.	18	8	0	116
1959	Pervis Atkins, New Mexico St.	Jr.	17	5	0	107
1960	Bob Gaiters, New Mexico St.	Sr.	23	7	0	145
1961	Jim Pilot, New Mexico St.	So.	21	12	0	138
1962	Jerry Logan, West Tex. A&M	Sr.	13	32	0	110
1963	Cosmo Iacavazzi, Princeton	Jr.	14	0	0	84
	Dave Casinelli, Memphis	Sr.	14	0	0	84
1964	Brian Piccolo, Wake Forest	Sr.	17	9	0	111
1965	Howard Twilley, Tulsa	Sr.	16	31	0	127
1966	Ken Hebert, Houston	Jr.	11	41	2	113
1967	Leroy Keyes, Purdue	Jr.	19	0	0	114
1968	Jim O'Brien, Cincinnati	Jr.	12	31	13	142
1969	Steve Owens, Oklahoma	Sr.	23	0	0	138

Beginning in 1970, ranked on per-game (instead of total) points

Year	Player, Team	Class	G	TD	XPt.	FG	Pts.	Avg.
1970	Brian Bream, Air Force	Jr.	10	20	0	0	120	12.0
	Gary Kosins, Dayton	Jr.	9	18	0	0	108	12.0
1971	Ed Marinaro, Cornell	Sr.	9	24	4	0	148	16.4
1972	Harold Henson, Ohio St.	So.	10	20	0	0	120	12.0
1973	Jim Jennings, Rutgers	Sr.	11	21	2	0	128	11.6
1974	Bill Marek, Wisconsin	Jr.	9	19	0	0	114	12.7
1975	Pete Johnson, Ohio St.	Jr.	11	25	0	0	150	13.6
1976	Tony Dorsett, Pittsburgh	Sr.	11	22	2	0	134	12.2
1977	Earl Campbell, Texas	Sr.	11	19	0	0	114	10.4
1978	Billy Sims, Oklahoma	Jr.	11	20	0	0	120	10.9
1979	Billy Sims, Oklahoma	Sr.	11	22	0	0	132	12.0
1980	Sammy Winder, Southern Miss.	Jr.	11	20	0	0	120	10.9
1981	Marcus Allen, Southern Cal	Sr.	11	23	0	0	138	12.5
1982	Greg Allen, Florida St.	So.	11	21	0	0	126	11.5
1983	Mike Rozier, Nebraska	Sr.	12	29	0	0	174	14.5
1984	Keith Byars, Ohio St.	Jr.	11	24	0	0	144	13.1
1985	Bernard White, Bowling Green	Jr.	11	19	0	0	114	10.4
1986	Steve Bartalo, Colorado St.	Sr.	11	19	0	0	114	10.4
1987	Paul Hewitt, San Diego St.	Jr.	12	24	0	0	144	12.0
1988	Barry Sanders, Oklahoma St.	Jr.	11	*39	0	0	*234	*21.3
1989	Anthony Thompson, Indiana	Sr.	11	25	4	0	154	14.0
1990	Stacey Robinson, Northern Ill. (QB)	Sr.	11	19	6	0	120	10.9
1991	Marshall Faulk, San Diego St.	Fr.	9	23	2	0	140	15.6
1992	Garrison Hearst, Georgia	Jr.	11	21	0	0	126	11.5
1993	Byron Morris, Texas Tech	Jr.	11	22	2	0	134	12.2

*Record.

Interceptions

CAREER INTERCEPTIONS

Player, Team	Years	No.	Yards	Avg.
Al Brosky, Illinois	1950-52	*29	356	12.3
Martin Bayless, Bowling Green	1980-83	27	266	9.9
John Provost, Holy Cross	1972-74	27	470	17.4
Tracy Saul, Texas Tech	1989-92	25	425	17.0
Tony Thurman, Boston College	1981-84	25	221	8.8
Tom Curtis, Michigan	1967-69	25	440	17.6
Jeff Nixon, Richmond	1975-78	23	377	16.4
Bennie Blades, Miami (Fla.)	1984-87	22	355	16.1
Jim Bolding, East Caro.	1973-76	22	143	6.5
Terrell Buckley, Florida St.	1989-91	21	*501	23.9

Player, Team	Years	No.	Yards	Avg.
Chuck Cecil, Arizona	1984-87	21	241	11.5
Barry Hill, Iowa St.	1972-74	21	202	9.6
Mike Sensibaugh, Ohio St.	1968-70	21	226	10.8
Kevin Smith, Texas A&M	1988-91	20	289	14.5
Mark Collins, Cal St. Fullerton	1982-85	20	193	9.7
Anthony Young, Temple	1981-84	20	230	11.5
Chris Williams, Louisiana St.	1977-80	20	91	4.6
Charles Jefferson, McNeese St.	1975-78	20	95	4.8
Artimus Parker, Southern Cal	1971-73	20	268	13.4
Dave Atkinson, Brigham Young	1971-73	20	222	11.1
Jackie Wallace, Arizona	1970-72	20	250	12.5
Tom Wilson, Colgate	1964-66	20	215	10.8
Lynn Chandnois, Michigan St.	1946-49	20	410	20.5
Bobby Wilson, Mississippi	1946-49	20	369	18.5

*Record.

SEASON INTERCEPTIONS

Player, Team	Year	No.	Yards
Al Worley, Washington	†1968	*14	130
George Shaw, Oregon	†1951	13	136
Terrell Buckley, Florida St.	†1991	12	238
Cornelius Price, Houston	†1989	12	187
Bob Navarro, Eastern Mich.	†1989	12	73
Tony Thurman, Boston College	†1984	12	99
Terry Hoage, Georgia	†1982	12	51
Frank Polito, Villanova	†1971	12	261
Bill Albrecht, Washington	1951	12	140
Hank Rich, Arizona St.	†1950	12	135

*Record. †National champion.

ANNUAL CHAMPIONS

Year	Player, Team	Class	No.	Yards
1938	Elmer Tarbox, Texas Tech	Sr.	11	89
1939	Harold Van Every, Minnesota	Sr.	8	59
1940	Dick Morgan, Tulsa	Jr.	7	210
1941	Bobby Robertson, Southern Cal	Sr.	9	126
1942	Ray Evans, Kansas	Jr.	10	76
1943	Jay Stoves, Washington	Sr.	7	139
1944	Joe Stuart, California	Jr.	7	76
1945	Jake Leicht, Oregon	So.	9	195
1946	Larry Hatch, Washington	So.	8	114
1947	John Bruce, William & Mary	Jr.	9	78
1948	Jay Van Noy, Utah St.	Jr.	8	228
1949	Bobby Wilson, Mississippi	Sr.	10	70
1950	Hank Rich, Arizona St.	Sr.	12	135
1951	George Shaw, Oregon	Fr.	13	136
1952	Cecil Ingram, Alabama	Jr.	10	163
1953	Bob Garrett, Stanford	Sr.	9	80
1954	Gary Glick, Colorado St.	Jr.	8	168
1955	Sam Wesley, Oregon St.	Jr.	7	61
1956	Jack Hill, Utah St.	Sr.	7	132
1957	Ray Toole, North Texas	Sr.	7	133
1958	Jim Norton, Idaho	Jr.	9	222
1959	Bud Whitehead, Florida St.	Jr.	6	111
1960	Bob O'Billovich, Montana	Jr.	7	71
1961	Joe Zuger, Arizona St.	Sr.	10	121
1962	Byron Beaver, Arizona St.	Sr.	10	56
1963	Dick Kern, William & Mary	Sr.	8	116
1964	Tony Carey, Notre Dame	Jr.	8	121
1965	Bob Sullivan, Maryland	Sr.	10	61
1966	Henry King, Utah St.	Sr.	11	180
1967	Steve Haterius, West Tex. A&M	Sr.	11	90
1968	Al Worley, Washington	Sr.	*14	130
1969	Seth Miller, Arizona St.	Sr.	11	63

Beginning in 1970, ranked on per-game (instead of total) number

Year	Player, Team	Class	G	No.	Avg.	Yards
1970	Mike Sensibaugh, Ohio St.	Sr.	8	8	1.00	40
1971	Frank Polito, Villanova	So.	10	12	1.20	261
1972	Mike Townsend, Notre Dame	Jr.	10	10	1.00	39
1973	Mike Gow, Illinois	Jr.	11	10	0.91	142
1974	Mike Haynes, Arizona St.	Jr.	11	10	0.91	115
1975	Jim Bolding, East Caro.	Jr.	10	10	1.00	51
1976	Anthony Francis, Houston	Jr.	11	10	0.91	118
1977	Paul Lawler, Colgate	Sr.	9	7	0.78	53
1978	Pete Harris, Penn St.	Jr.	11	10	0.91	155
1979	Joe Callan, Ohio	Sr.	9	9	1.00	110

Year	Player, Team	Class	G	No.	Avg.	Yards
1980	Ronnie Lott, Southern Cal	Sr.	11	8	0.73	166
	Steve McNamee, William & Mary	Sr.	11	8	0.73	125
	Greg Benton, Drake	Sr.	11	8	0.73	119
	Jeff Hipp, Georgia	Sr.	11	8	0.73	104
	Mike Richardson, Arizona St.	So.	11	8	0.73	89
	Vann McElroy, Baylor	Jr.	11	8	0.73	73
1981	Sam Shaffer, Temple	Sr.	10	9	0.90	76
1982	Terry Hoage, Georgia	Jr.	10	12	1.20	51
1983	Martin Bayless, Bowling Green	Sr.	11	10	0.91	64
1984	Tony Thurman, Boston College	Sr.	11	12	1.09	99
1985	Chris White, Tennessee	Sr.	11	9	0.82	168
	Kevin Walker, East Caro.	Sr.	11	9	0.82	155
1986	Bennie Blades, Miami (Fla.)	Jr.	11	10	0.91	128
1987	Keith McMeans, Virginia	Fr.	10	9	0.90	35
1988	Kurt Larson, Michigan St. (LB)	Sr.	11	8	0.73	78
	Andy Logan, Kent	Sr.	11	8	0.73	54
1989	Cornelius Price, Houston	Jr.	11	12	1.09	187
	Bob Navarro, Eastern Mich.	Jr.	11	12	1.09	73
1990	Jerry Parks, Houston	Jr.	11	8	0.73	124
1991	Terrell Buckley, Florida St.	Jr.	12	12	1.00	238
1992	Carlton McDonald, Air Force	Sr.	11	8	0.73	109
1993	Orlanda Thomas, Southwestern La.	Jr.	11	9	0.82	84

*Record.

Punting

CAREER AVERAGE
(Minimum 150 Punts)

Player, Team	Years	No.	Yards	Avg.	Long
Reggie Roby, Iowa	1979-82	172	7,849	*45.6	69
Greg Montgomery, Michigan St.	1985-87	170	7,721	45.4	86
Tom Tupa, Ohio St.	1984-87	196	8,854	45.2	75
Barry Helton, Colorado	1984-87	153	6,873	44.9	68
Ray Guy, Southern Miss.	1970-72	200	8,934	44.7	93
Bucky Scribner, Kansas	1980-82	217	9,670	44.6	70
Greg Horne, Arkansas	1983-86	180	8,002	44.5	72
Ray Criswell, Florida	1982-85	161	7,153	44.4	73
Russell Erxleben, Texas	1975-78	214	9,467	44.2	80
Mark Simon, Air Force	1984-86	156	6,898	44.2	64
Johnny Evans, North Caro. St.	1974-77	185	8,143	44.0	81
Chuck Ramsey, Wake Forest	1971-73	205	9,010	44.0	70
Jimmy Colquitt, Tennessee	1981-84	201	8,816	43.9	70
John Teltschik, Texas	1982-85	217	9,496	43.8	81

(Minimum 250 Punts)

Player, Team	Years	No.	Yards	Avg.	Long
Bill Smith, Mississippi	1983-86	254	11,260	*44.3	92
Jim Arnold, Vanderbilt	1979-82	277	12,171	43.9	79
Ralf Mojsiejenko, Michigan St.	1981-84	275	11,997	43.6	72
Jim Miller, Mississippi	1976-79	266	11,549	43.4	82
Russ Henderson, Virginia	1975-78	276	11,957	43.3	74
Maury Buford, Texas Tech	1978-81	293	12,670	43.2	75
Chris Becker, Texas Christian	1985-88	265	11,407	43.0	77
Mark Bounds, West Tex. A&M/Texas Tech.	√1988-91	252	10,842	43.0	89
Ron Keller, New Mexico	1983-86	252	10,737	42.6	77
James Gargus, Texas Christian	1981-84	255	10,862	42.6	74

*Record. √Transferred to Texas Tech after West Tex. A&M dropped football program in 1990.

SEASON AVERAGE
(Qualifiers for Championship)

Player, Team	Year	No.	Yards	Avg.
Reggie Roby, Iowa	†1981	44	2,193	*49.8
Kirk Wilson, UCLA	†1956	30	1,479	49.3
Zack Jordan, Colorado	†1950	38	1,830	48.2
Ricky Anderson, Vanderbilt	†1984	58	2,793	‡48.2
Reggie Roby, Iowa	†1982	52	2,501	48.1
Marv Bateman, Utah	†1971	68	3,269	48.1
Owen Price, UTEP	†1940	30	1,440	48.0
Jack Jacobs, Oklahoma	1940	31	1,483	47.8
Bill Smith, Mississippi	1984	44	2,099	47.7
Ed Bunn, UTEP	†1992	41	1,955	47.7

*Record. †National champion. ‡Record for minimum of 50 punts.

ANNUAL CHAMPIONS

Year	Player, Team	Class	No.	Yards	Avg.
1937	Johnny Pingel, Michigan St.	Jr.	49	2,101	42.9
1938	Jerry Dowd, St. Mary's (Cal.)	Sr.	62	2,711	43.7
1939	Harry Dunkle, North Caro.	So.	37	1,725	46.6
1940	Owen Price, UTEP	Jr.	30	1,440	48.0
1941	Owen Price, UTEP	Sr.	40	1,813	45.3
1942	Bobby Cifers, Tennessee	Jr.	37	1,586	42.9
1943	Harold Cox, Arkansas	Fr.	37	1,518	41.0
1944	Bob Waterfield, UCLA	Sr.	60	2,575	42.9
1945	Howard Maley, Southern Methodist	Sr.	59	2,458	41.7
1946	Johnny Galvin, Purdue	Sr.	30	1,286	42.9
1947	Leslie Palmer, North Caro. St.	Sr.	65	2,816	43.3
1948	Charlie Justice, North Caro.	Jr.	62	2,728	44.0
1949	Paul Stombaugh, Furman	Sr.	57	2,550	44.7
1950	Zack Jordan, Colorado	So.	38	1,830	48.2
1951	Chuck Spaulding, Wyoming	Jr.	37	1,610	43.5
1952	Des Koch, Southern Cal	Jr.	47	2,043	43.5
1953	Zeke Bratkowski, Georgia (QB)	Sr.	50	2,132	42.6
1954	A. L. Terpening, New Mexico	Sr.	41	1,869	45.6
1955	Don Chandler, Florida	Sr.	22	975	44.3
1956	Kirk Wilson, UCLA	So.	30	1,479	49.3
1957	Dave Sherer, Southern Methodist	Jr.	36	1,620	45.0
1958	Bobby Walden, Georgia	So.	44	1,991	45.3
1959	John Hadl, Kansas	So.	43	1,960	45.6
1960	Dick Fitzsimmons, Denver	So.	25	1,106	44.2
1961	Joe Zuger, Arizona St.	Sr.	31	1,305	42.1
1962	Joe Don Looney, Oklahoma	Jr.	34	1,474	43.4
1963	Danny Thomas, Southern Methodist	Jr.	48	2,110	44.0
1964	Frank Lambert, Mississippi	Sr.	50	2,205	44.1
1965	Dave Lewis, Stanford	Jr.	29	1,302	44.9
1966	Ron Widby, Tennessee	Sr.	48	2,104	43.8
1967	Zenon Andrusyshyn, UCLA	So.	34	1,502	44.2
1968	Dany Pitcock, Wichita St.	Sr.	71	3,068	43.2
1969	Ed Marsh, Baylor	Jr.	68	2,965	43.6
1970	Marv Bateman, Utah	Jr.	65	2,968	45.7
1971	Marv Bateman, Utah	Sr.	68	3,269	48.1
1972	Ray Guy, Southern Miss.	Sr.	58	2,680	46.2
1973	Chuck Ramsey, Wake Forest	Sr.	87	3,896	44.8
1974	Joe Parker, Appalachian St.	So.	63	2,788	44.3
1975	Tom Skladany, Ohio St.	Jr.	36	1,682	46.7
1976	Russell Erxleben, Texas	So.	61	2,842	46.6
1977	Jim Miller, Mississippi	So.	66	3,029	45.9
1978	Maury Buford, Texas Tech	Fr.	71	3,131	44.1
1979	Clay Brown, Brigham Young	Jr.	43	1,950	45.3

Beginning in 1980, ranked on minimum 3.6 punts per game

Year	Player, Team	Class	No.	Yards	Long	Avg.
1980	Steve Cox, Arkansas	Sr.	47	2,186	86	46.5
1981	Reggie Roby, Iowa	Jr.	44	2,193	68	*49.8
1982	Reggie Roby, Iowa	Sr.	52	2,501	66	48.1
1983	Jack Weil, Wyoming	Sr.	52	2,369	86	45.6
1984	Ricky Anderson, Vanderbilt	Sr.	58	2,793	82	@48.2
1985	Mark Simon, Air Force	Jr.	53	2,506	71	47.3
1986	Greg Horne, Arkansas	Sr.	49	2,313	65	47.2
1987	Tom Tupa, Ohio St. (QB)	Sr.	63	2,963	72	47.0
1988	Keith English, Colorado	Sr.	51	2,297	77	45.0
1989	Tom Rouen, Colorado	So.	36	1,651	63	45.8
1990	Cris Shale, Bowling Green	Sr.	66	3,087	81	46.8
1991	Mark Bounds, Texas Tech	Sr.	53	2,481	78	46.8
1992	Ed Bunn, UTEP	Sr.	41	1,955	73	47.7
1993	Chris MacInnis, Air Force	Sr.	49	2,303	74	47.0

*Record. @ Record for minimum of 50 punts.

Punt Returns

CAREER AVERAGE
(Minimum 1.2 Returns Per Game)

Player, Team	Years	No.	Yards	TD	Long	Avg.
Jack Mitchell, Oklahoma	1946-48	39	922	**7	70	*23.6
Gene Gibson, Cincinnati	1949-50	37	760	4	75	20.5
Eddie Macon, Pacific (Cal.)	1949-51	48	907	4	**100	18.9
Jackie Robinson, UCLA	1939-40	37	694	2	89	18.8
Mike Fuller, Auburn	1972-74	50	883	3	63	17.7
Bobby Dillon, Texas	1949-51	47	830	1	84	17.7
Erroll Tucker, Utah	1984-85	38	650	3	89	17.1
George Hoey, Michigan	1966-68	31	529	1	60	17.1
Jack Christiansen, Colorado St.	1948-50	37	626	2	89	16.9
Henry Pryor, Rutgers	1948-49	37	625	1	85	16.9
Adolph Bellizeare, Pennsylvania	1972-74	33	557	3	73	16.9
Ken Hatfield, Arkansas	1962-64	70	1,135	5	95	16.2
Gene Rossides, Columbia	1945-48	53	851	3	70	16.1
Bill Hillenbrand, Indiana	1941-42	65	1,042	2	88	16.0

*Record. **Record tied.

SEASON AVERAGE
(Minimum 1.2 Returns Per Game)

Player, Team	Year	No.	Yards	Avg.
Bill Blackstock, Tennessee	1951	12	311	*25.9
George Sims, Baylor	1948	15	375	25.0
Gene Derricotte, Michigan	1947	14	347	24.8
Erroll Tucker, Utah	†1985	16	389	24.3
George Hoey, Michigan	1967	12	291	24.3
Floyd Little, Syracuse	1965	18	423	23.5

*Record. †National champion.

ANNUAL CHAMPIONS
(Ranked on Total Yards Until 1970)

Year	Player, Team	Class	No.	Yards	Avg.
1939	Bosh Pritchard, Va. Military	So.	42	583	13.9
1940	Junie Hovious, Mississippi	Sr.	33	498	15.1
1941	Bill Geyer, Colgate	Sr.	33	616	18.7
1942	Bill Hillenbrand, Indiana	Jr.	23	481	20.9
1943	Marion Flanagan, Texas A&M	Jr.	49	475	9.7
1944	Joe Stuart, California	Jr.	39	372	9.5
1945	Jake Leicht, Oregon	So.	28	395	14.1
1946	Harry Gilmer, Alabama	Jr.	37	436	11.8
1947	Lindy Berry, Texas Christian	So.	42	493	11.7
1948	Lee Nalley, Vanderbilt	Jr.	43	*791	18.4
1949	Lee Nalley, Vanderbilt	Sr.	35	498	14.2
1950	Dave Waters, Wash. & Lee	Jr.	30	445	14.8
1951	Tom Murphy, Holy Cross	So.	25	533	21.3
1952	Horton Nesrsta, Rice	Jr.	44	536	12.2
1953	Paul Giel, Minnesota	Sr.	17	288	16.9
1954	Dicky Maegle, Rice	Sr.	15	293	19.5
1955	Mike Sommer, Geo. Washington	So.	24	330	13.8
1956	Bill Stacy, Mississippi St.	Jr.	24	290	12.1
1957	Bobby Mulgado, Arizona St.	Sr.	14	267	19.1
1958	Howard Cook, Colorado	Sr.	24	242	10.1
1959	Pervis Atkins, New Mexico St.	Jr.	16	241	15.1
1960	Lance Alworth, Arkansas	Jr.	18	307	17.1
1961	Lance Alworth, Arkansas	Sr.	28	336	12.0
1962	Darrell Roberts, Utah St.	Sr.	16	333	20.8
1963	Ken Hatfield, Arkansas	Jr.	21	350	16.7
1964	Ken Hatfield, Arkansas	Sr.	31	518	16.7
1965	Nick Rassas, Notre Dame	Sr.	24	459	19.1
1966	Vic Washington, Wyoming	Jr.	34	443	13.0
1967	Mike Battle, Southern Cal	Jr.	47	570	12.1
1968	Roger Wehrli, Missouri	Sr.	41	478	11.7
1969	Chris Farasopoulous, Brigham Young	Jr.	35	527	15.1

Beginning in 1970, ranked on average per return (instead of total yards)‡

Year	Player, Team	Class	No.	Yards	TD	Long	Avg.
1970	Steve Holden, Arizona St.	So.	17	327	2	94	19.2
1971	Golden Richards, Brigham Young	Jr.	33	624	**4	87	18.9
1972	Randy Rhino, Georgia Tech	So.	25	441	1	96	17.6
1973	Gary Hayman, Penn St.	Sr.	23	442	1	83	19.2
1974	John Provost, Holy Cross	Sr.	13	238	2	85	18.3
1975	Donnie Ross, New Mexico St.	Sr.	21	338	1	#81	16.1
1976	Henry Jenkins, Rutgers	Sr.	30	449	0	#40	15.0
1977	Robert Woods, Grambling	Sr.	††11	279	3	72	25.4
1978	Ira Matthews, Wisconsin	Sr.	16	270	3	78	16.9
1979	Jeffrey Shockley, Tennessee St.	Sr.	27	456	1	79	16.9
1980	Scott Woerner, Georgia	Sr.	31	488	1	67	15.7
1981	Glen Young, Mississippi St.	Jr.	19	307	2	87	16.2
1982	Lionel James, Auburn	Jr.	25	394	0	#63	15.8
1983	Jim Sandusky, San Diego St.	Sr.	20	381	1	90	19.0
1984	Ricky Nattiel, Florida	So.	22	346	1	67	15.7
1985	Erroll Tucker, Utah	Sr.	16	389	2	89	24.3
1986	Rod Smith, Nebraska	Jr.	‡‡12	227	1	63	18.9
1987	Alan Grant, Stanford	Jr.	27	446	2	77	16.5
1988	Deion Sanders, Florida St.	Sr.	33	503	1	76	15.2
1989	Larry Hargrove, Ohio	Sr.	17	309	1	83	18.2
1990	Dave McCloughan, Colorado	Sr.	32	524	2	90	16.4
1991	Bo Campbell, Virginia Tech	Jr.	15	273	0	45	18.2
1992	Lee Gissendaner, Northwestern	Jr.	15	327	1	72	21.8
1993	Aaron Glenn, Texas A&M	Sr.	17	339	2	76	19.9

*Record. **Record tied. #Did not score. ††Declared champion; with three more returns (making 1.3 per game) for zero yards still would have highest average. ‡Ranked on minimum 1.5 returns per game, 1970-73; 1.2 from 1974. ‡‡Declared champion; with two more returns (making 1.2 per game) for zero yards still would have highest average.

ANNUAL PUNT RETURN LEADERS (1939-69)
BASED ON AVERAGE PER RETURN
(Minimum 1.2 Returns Per Game)

1939—Jackie Robinson, UCLA, 20.0; **1940**—Jackie Robinson, UCLA, 21.0; **1941**—Walt Slater, Tennessee, 20.4; **1942**—Billy Hillenbrand, Indiana, 20.9; **1943**—Otto Graham, Northwestern, 19.7; **1944**—Glenn Davis, Army, 18.4; **1945**—Jake Leicht, Oregon, 14.8; **1946**—Harold Griffin, Florida, 20.1; **1947**—Gene Derricotte, Michigan, 24.8; **1948**—George Sims, Baylor, 25.0; **1949**—Gene Evans, Wisconsin, 21.8; **1950**—Lindy Hanson, Boston U., 22.5; **1951**—Bill Blackstock, Tennessee, 25.9; **1952**—Gil Reich, Kansas, 17.2; **1953**—Bobby Lee, New Mexico, 19.4; **1954**—Dicky Maegle, Rice, 19.5; **1955**—Ron Lind, Drake, 21.1; **1956**—Ron Lind, Drake, 19.1; **1957**—Bobby Mulgado, Arizona St., 19.1; **1958**—Herb Hallas, Yale, 23.4; **1959**—Jacque MacKinnon, Colgate, 17.5; **1960**—Pat Fischer, Nebraska, 21.2; **1961**—Tom Larscheid, Utah St., 23.4; **1962**—Darrell Roberts, Utah St., 20.8; **1963**—Rickie Harris, Arizona, 17.4; **1964**—Ken Hatfield, Arkansas, 16.7; **1965**—Floyd Little, Syracuse, 23.5; **1966**—Don Bean, Houston, 20.2; **1967**—George Hoey, Michigan, 24.3; **1968**—Rob Bordley, Princeton, 20.5; **1969**—George Hannen, Davidson, 22.4.

Kickoff Returns

CAREER AVERAGE
(Minimum 1.2 Returns Per Game)

Player, Team	Years	No.	Yards	Avg.
Forrest Hall, San Francisco	1946-47	22	796	*36.2
Anthony Davis, Southern Cal	1972-74	37	1,299	35.1
Overton Curtis, Utah St.	1957-58	32	991	31.0
Fred Montgomery, New Mexico St.	1991-92	39	1,191	30.5
Altie Taylor, Utah St.	1966-68	40	1,170	29.3
Stan Brown, Purdue	1968-70	49	1,412	28.8
Henry White, Colgate	1974-77	41	1,180	28.8
Donald Dennis, West Tex. A&M	1964-65	27	777	28.8
Bobby Ward, Memphis	1973-74	27	770	28.5
Paul Loughran, Temple	1970-72	40	1,123	28.1
Jim Krieg, Washington	1970-71	31	860	27.7

*Record.

SEASON AVERAGE
(Minimum 1.2 Returns Per Game)

Player, Team	Year	No.	Yards	Avg.
Paul Allen, Brigham Young	1961	12	481	*40.1
Leeland McElroy, Texas A&M	†1993	15	590	39.3
Forrest Hall, San Francisco	†1946	15	573	**38.2
Tony Ball, Tenn.-Chatt.	†1977	13	473	36.4
George Marinkov, North Caro. St.	1954	13	465	35.8
Bob Baker, Cornell	1964	11	386	35.1

*Record. †National champion. **Record for minimum of 1.5 returns per game.

ANNUAL CHAMPIONS
(Ranked on Total Yards Until 1970)

Year	Player, Team	Class	No.	Yards	Avg.
1939	Nile Kinnick, Iowa	Sr.	15	377	25.1
1940	Jack Emigh, Montana	Sr.	18	395	21.9
1941	Earl Ray, Wyoming	So.	23	496	21.6
1942	Frank Porto, California	Sr.	17	483	28.4
1943	Paul Copoulos, Marquette	So.	11	384	34.9
1944	Paul Copoulos, Marquette	Jr.	14	337	24.1
1945	Al Dekdebrun, Cornell	Sr.	14	321	22.9
1946	Forrest Hall, San Francisco	Jr.	15	573	*38.2
1947	Doak Walker, Southern Methodist	So.	10	387	38.7
1948	Bill Gregus, Wake Forest	Jr.	19	503	26.5
1949	Johnny Subda, Nevada	Sr.	18	444	24.7
1950	Chuck Hill, New Mexico	Jr.	27	729	27.0
1951	Chuck Hill, New Mexico	Sr.	17	504	29.6
1952	Curly Powell, Va. Military	Sr.	27	517	19.1
1953	Max McGee, Tulane	Sr.	17	371	21.8
1954	Art Luppino, Arizona	So.	20	632	31.6
1955	Sam Woolwine, Va. Military	Jr.	22	471	21.4
1956	Sam Woolwine, Va. Military	Sr.	18	503	27.9
1957	Overton Curtis, Utah St.	Jr.	23	695	30.2
1958	Sonny Randle, Virginia	Sr.	21	506	24.1
1959	Don Perkins, New Mexico	Sr.	15	520	34.7
1960	Bruce Samples, Brigham Young	Sr.	23	577	25.1
1961	Dick Mooney, Idaho	Sr.	23	494	21.5
1962	Donnie Frederick, Wake Forest	Sr.	29	660	22.8
1963	Gary Wood, Cornell	Sr.	19	618	32.5
1964	Dan Bland, Mississippi St.	Jr.	20	558	27.9
1965	Eric Crabtree, Pittsburgh	Sr.	25	636	25.4
1966	Marcus Rhoden, Mississippi St.	Sr.	26	572	22.0
1967	Joe Casas, New Mexico	Sr.	23	602	26.2
1968	Mike Adamle, Northwestern	So.	34	732	21.5
1969	Stan Brown, Purdue	Jr.	26	698	26.8

Beginning in 1970, ranked on average per return (instead of total yards)‡

Year	Player, Team	Class	No.	Yards	Avg.
1970	Stan Brown, Purdue	Sr.	19	638	33.6
1971	Paul Loughran, Temple	Jr.	15	502	33.5
1972	Larry Williams, Texas Tech	So.	16	493	30.8
1973	Steve Odom, Utah	Sr.	21	618	29.4
1974	Anthony Davis, Southern Cal	Sr.††11		467	42.5
1975	John Schultz, Maryland	Sr.	13	403	31.0
1976	Ira Matthews, Wisconsin	So.	14	415	29.6
1977	Tony Ball, Tenn.-Chatt.	Fr.	13	473	36.4
1978	Drew Hill, Georgia Tech	Sr.	19	570	30.0
1979	Stevie Nelson, Ball St.	Fr.	18	565	31.4
1980	Mike Fox, San Diego St.	So.	†11	361	32.8
1981	Frank Minnifield, Louisville	Jr.	11	334	30.4
1982	Carl Monroe, Utah	Sr.	14	421	30.1
1983	Henry Williams, East Caro.	Jr.	19	591	31.1
1984	Keith Henderson, Texas Tech	Fr.	13	376	28.9
1985	Erroll Tucker, Utah	Sr.	24	698	29.1
1986	Terrance Roulhac, Clemson	Sr.	17	561	33.0
1987	Barry Sanders, Oklahoma St.	So.	14	442	31.6
1988	Raghib Ismail, Notre Dame	Fr.	#12	433	36.1
1989	Tony Smith, Southern Miss.	So.	14	455	32.5
1990	Dale Carter, Tennessee	Jr.	17	507	29.8
1991	Fred Montgomery, New Mexico St.	Jr.	25	734	29.4
1992	Fred Montgomery, New Mexico St.	Sr.	14	457	32.6
1993	Leeland McElroy, Texas A&M	Fr.	15	590	39.3

*Record. #Declared champion; with two more returns (making 1.3 per game) for zero yards still would have highest average. †Declared champion; with one more return (making 1.2 per game) for zero yards still would have highest average. ††Declared champion; with three more returns (making 1.3 per game) for zero yards still would have highest average. ‡Ranked on minimum 1.5 returns per game, 1970-73; 1.2 from 1974.

ANNUAL KICKOFF RETURN LEADERS (1939-69) BASED ON AVERAGE PER RETURN
(Minimum 1.2 Returns Per Game)

1939—Nile Kinnick, Iowa, 25.1; **1940**—Bill Geyer, Colgate, 27.0; **1941**—Vern Lockard, Colorado, 24.4; **1942-45**—Not compiled; **1946**—Forrest Hall, San Francisco, 38.2; **1947**—Skippy Minisi, Pennsylvania, 28.8; **1948**—Jerry Williams, Washington St., 29.9; **1949**—Billy Conn, Georgetown, 31.1; **1950**—Johnny Turco, Holy Cross, 27.4; **1951**—Bob Mischak, Army, 31.3; **1952**—Carroll Hardy, Colorado, 32.2; **1953**—Carl Bolt, Wash. & Lee, 27.1; **1954**—George Marinkov, North Caro. St., 35.8; **1955**—Jim Brown, Syracuse, 32.0; **1956**—Paul Hornung, Notre Dame, 31.0; **1957**—Overton Curtis, Utah St., 30.2; **1958**—Marshall Starks, Illinois, 26.3; **1959**—Don Perkins, New Mexico, 34.7; **1960**—Tom Hennessey, Holy Cross, 33.4; **1961**—Paul Allen, Brigham Young, 40.1; **1962**—Larry Coyer, Marshall, 30.2; **1963**—Gary Wood, Cornell, 32.5; **1964**—Bob Baker, Cornell, 35.1; **1965**—Tom Barrington, Ohio St., 34.3; **1966**—Frank Moore, Louisville, 27.9; **1967**—Altie Taylor, Utah St., 31.9; **1968**—Kerry Reardon, Iowa, 32.1; **1969**—Chris Farasopoulous, Brigham Young, 32.2.

All-Purpose Yards

CAREER YARDS PER GAME
(Minimum 3,500 yards)

Player, Team	Years	Rush	Rcv.	Int.	PR	KOR	Yds.	Yd.PG
Ryan Benjamin, Pacific (Cal.)	1990-92	3,119	1,063	0	100	1,424	5,706	*237.8
Sheldon Canley, San Jose St.	1988-90	2,513	828	0	5	1,800	5,146	205.8
Howard Stevens, Louisville	§1971-72	2,723	389	0	401	360	3,873	193.7
O. J. Simpson, Southern Cal	1967-68	3,124	235	0	0	307	3,666	192.9
Ed Marinaro, Cornell	1969-71	4,715	225	0	0	0	4,940	183.0
Marshall Faulk, San Diego St.	1991-93	4,589	973	0	0	33	5,595	180.5
Herschel Walker, Georgia	1980-82	5,259	243	0	0	247	5,749	174.2
Louie Giammona, Utah St.	1973-75	3,499	171	0	188	1,345	5,203	173.4

*Record. §Competed two years in Division I-A and two years in Division II (Randolph-Macon, 1968-69). Four-year average: 199.1.

SEASON YARDS PER GAME

Player, Team	Year	Rush	Rcv.	Int.	PR	KOR	Yds.	Yd.PG
Barry Sanders, Oklahoma St.	†1988	*2,628	106	0	95	421	*3,250	*295.5
Ryan Benjamin, Pacific (Cal.)	†1991	1,581	612	0	4	798	2,995	249.6
Byron "Whizzer" White, Colorado	†1937	1,121	0	103	587	159	1,970	246.3
Mike Pringle, Cal St. Fullerton	†1989	1,727	249	0	0	714	2,690	244.6
Paul Palmer, Temple	†1986	1,866	110	0	0	657	2,633	239.4
Ryan Benjamin, Pacific (Cal.)	†1992	1,441	434	0	96	626	2,597	236.1
Marcus Allen, Southern Cal	†1981	2,342	217	0	0	0	2,559	232.6
Sheldon Canley, San Jose St.	1989	1,201	353	0	0	959	2,513	228.5
Ollie Matson, San Francisco	†1951	1,566	58	18	115	280	2,037	226.3
Art Luppino, Arizona	†1954	1,359	50	84	68	632	2,193	219.3
Chuck Weatherspoon, Houston	1989	1,146	735	0	715	95	2,391	217.4
Anthony Thompson, Indiana	1989	1,793	201	0	0	394	2,388	217.1
Napoleon McCallum, Navy	†1983	1,587	166	0	272	360	2,385	216.8
Ed Marinaro, Cornell	†1971	1,881	51	0	0	0	1,932	214.7
Howard Stevens, Louisville	†1972	1,294	221	0	337	240	2,132	213.2
Napoleon McCallum, Navy	†1985	1,327	358	0	157	488	2,330	211.8
Keith Byars, Ohio St.	†1984	1,655	453	0	0	176	2,284	207.6
Mike Rozier, Nebraska	1983	2,148	106	0	0	232	2,486	207.2

*Record. †National champion.

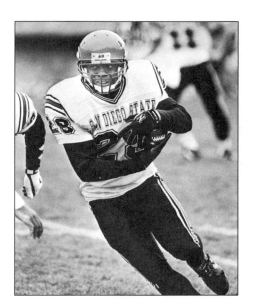

San Diego State running back Marshall Faulk averaged 180.5 all-purpose yards per game during his three seasons with the Aztecs.

Oklahoma State running back Barry Sanders set Division I-A single-season marks for rushing yardage (2,628) and all-purpose yards (3,250) in 1988.

CAREER YARDS

Player, Team	Years	Rush	Rcv.	Int.	PR	KOR	Yds.	Yd.PP
Napoleon McCallum, Navy	$1981-85	4,179	796	0	858	1,339	*7,172	6.3
Darrin Nelson, Stanford	1977-78, 80-81	4,033	2,368	0	471	13	6,885	7.1
Terance Mathis, New Mexico	1985-87, 89	329	*4,254	0	115	1,993	6,691	14.6
Tony Dorsett, Pittsburgh	1973-76	*6,082	406	0	0	127	6,615	5.9
Paul Palmer, Temple	1983-86	4,895	705	0	12	997	6,609	6.1
Charles White, Southern Cal	1976-79	5,598	507	0	0	440	6,545	6.0
Trevor Cobb, Rice	1989-92	4,948	892	0	21	651	6,512	5.3
Glyn Milburn, Oklahoma/Stanford	1988, 90-92	2,302	1,495	0	1,145	1,246	6,188	8.1
Anthony Thompson, Indiana	1986-89	4,965	713	0	0	412	6,090	5.1
Archie Griffin, Ohio St.	1972-75	5,177	286	0	0	540	6,003	6.7
Ron "Po" James, New Mexico St.	1968-71	3,884	217	0	8	1,870	5,979	6.5
Eric Wilkerson, Kent	1985-88	3,830	506	0	0	1,638	5,974	7.0
Steve Bartalo, Colorado St.	1983-86	4,813	1,079	0	0	0	5,892	4.4
Wilford White, Arizona St.	1947-50	3,173	892	212	798	791	5,866	9.2
Joe Washington, Oklahoma	1972-75	3,995	253	0	807	726	5,781	7.3
Herschel Walker, Georgia	1980-82	5,259	243	0	0	247	‡5,749	5.6
George Swarn, Miami (Ohio)	1983-86	4,172	1,057	0	0	498	5,727	5.6
Chuck Weatherspoon, Houston	1987-90	3,247	1,375	0	611	482	5,715	9.7
Ryan Benjamin, Pacific (Cal.)	1990-92	3,119	1,063	0	100	1,424	‡5,706	8.8
Eric Metcalf, Texas	1985-88	2,661	1,394	0	1,076	574	5,705	6.7
George Rogers, South Caro.	1977-80	4,958	371	0	0	339	5,668	5.9
Jamie Morris, Michigan	1984-87	3,944	703	0	0	984	5,631	6.4
Joe Morris, Syracuse	1978-81	4,299	278	0	0	1,023	5,600	6.3
James Brooks, Auburn	1977-80	3,523	219	0	128	1,726	5,596	7.6
Marshall Faulk, San Diego St.	1991-93	4,589	973	0	0	33	‡5,595	6.6
Johnny Rodgers, Nebraska	1970-72	745	2,479	0	1,515	847	‡5,586	13.8
Thurman Thomas, Oklahoma St.	1984-87	4,595	551	0	143	237	5,526	5.5
Mike Rozier, Nebraska	1981-83	4,780	216	0	0	449	‡5,445	7.7

*Record. $See page 6 for explanation. ‡Three-year totals.

SEASON YARDS

Player, Team	Year	Rush	Rcv.	Int.	PR	KOR	Yds.	Yd.PP
Barry Sanders, Oklahoma St.	†1988	*2,628	106	0	95	421	*3,250	8.3
Ryan Benjamin, Pacific (Cal.)	†1991	1,581	612	0	4	798	2,995	9.6
Mike Pringle, Cal St. Fullerton	†1989	1,727	249	0	0	714	2,690	7.6
Paul Palmer, Temple	†1986	1,866	110	0	0	657	2,633	6.8
Ryan Benjamin, Pacific (Cal.)	†1992	1,441	434	0	96	626	2,597	8.1
Marcus Allen, Southern Cal	†1981	2,342	217	0	0	0	2,559	5.9
Sheldon Canley, San Jose St.	1989	1,201	353	0	0	959	2,513	7.4
Mike Rozier, Nebraska	1983	2,148	106	0	0	232	2,486	8.4
Chuck Weatherspoon, Houston	1989	1,146	735	0	415	95	2,391	10.7
Anthony Thompson, Indiana	1989	1,793	201	0	0	394	2,388	5.8
Napoleon McCallum, Navy	†1983	1,587	166	0	272	360	2,385	6.1
Napoleon McCallum, Navy	†1985	1,327	358	0	157	488	2,330	6.3
Keith Byars, Ohio St.	†1984	1,655	453	0	0	176	2,284	6.4
Glyn Milburn, Stanford	†1990	729	632	0	267	594	2,222	8.4
Vaughn Dunbar, Indiana	1991	1,699	252	0	0	262	2,213	5.9
Sheldon Canley, San Jose St.	1990	1,248	386	0	5	574	2,213	6.3
Johnny Johnson, San Jose St.	1988	1,219	668	0	0	315	2,202	7.1
Art Luppino, Arizona	†1954	1,359	50	84	68	632	2,193	10.4
Rick Calhoun, Cal St. Fullerton	1986	1,398	125	0	138	522	2,183	7.0
Marshall Faulk, San Diego St.	1993	1,530	644	0	0	0	2,174	6.3
Terance Mathis, New Mexico	1989	38	1,315	0	0	785	2,138	15.7
Howard Stevens, Louisville	†1972	1,294	221	0	377	240	2,132	6.4

*Record. †National champion.

ALL-PURPOSE SINGLE-GAME HIGHS

Yds.	Player, Team (Opponent)	Date
422	Marshall Faulk, San Diego St. (Pacific, Cal.)	Sept. 14, 1991
417	Paul Palmer, Temple (East Caro.)	Nov. 10, 1986
417	Greg Allen, Florida St. (Western Caro.)	Oct. 31, 1981
416	Anthony Thompson, Indiana (Wisconsin)	Nov. 11, 1989
411	John Leach, Wake Forest (Maryland)	Nov. 20, 1993
402	Ryan Benjamin, Pacific, Cal. (Utah St.)	Nov. 21, 1992
401	Chuck Hughes, UTEP (North Texas) (349 on receptions)	Sept. 18, 1965
397	Eric Allen, Michigan St. (Purdue)	Oct. 30, 1971
388	Ryan Benjamin, Pacific, Cal. (Cal St. Fullerton)	Oct. 5, 1991
387	Kendal Smith, Utah St. (San Jose St.)	Oct. 22, 1988
387	Ron Johnson, Michigan (Wisconsin)	Nov. 16, 1968
386	Barry Sanders, Oklahoma St. (Kansas)	Nov. 12, 1988
379	Glyn Milburn, Stanford (California)	Nov. 17, 1990
375	Rueben Mayes, Washington St. (Oregon St.)	Nov. 3, 1984
374	Tony Dorsett, Pittsburgh (Penn St.)	Nov. 22, 1975
373	Barry Sanders, Oklahoma St. (Oklahoma)	Nov. 5, 1988
372	Chuck Weatherspoon, Houston (Eastern Wash.)	Nov. 17, 1990

ANNUAL CHAMPIONS

Year	Player, Team	Class	Rush	Rcv.	Int.	PR	KOR	Yds.	Yd.PG
1937	Byron "Whizzer" White, Colorado	Sr.	1,121	0	103	587	159	1,970	246.3
1938	Parker Hall, Mississippi	Sr.	698	0	128	0	594	1,420	129.1
1939	Tom Harmon, Michigan	Jr.	868	110	98	0	132	1,208	151.0
1940	Tom Harmon, Michigan	Sr.	844	0	20	244	204	1,312	164.0
1941	Bill Dudley, Virginia	Sr.	968	60	76	481	89	1,674	186.0
1942	records not available	—	—	—	—	—	—	—	—
1943	Stan Koslowski, Holy Cross	Fr.	784	63	50	438	76	1,411	176.4
1944	Red Williams, Minnesota	Jr.	911	0	0	242	314	1,467	163.0
1945	Bob Fenimore, Oklahoma St.	Jr.	1,048	12	129	157	231	1,577	197.1
1946	Rudy Mobley, Hardin-Simmons	Sr.	1,262	13	79	273	138	1,765	176.5
1947	Wilton Davis, Hardin-Simmons	So.	1,173	79	0	295	251	1,798	179.8
1948	Lou Kusserow, Columbia	Sr.	766	463	19	130	359	1,737	193.0
1949	Johnny Papit, Virginia	Jr.	1,214	0	0	0	397	1,611	179.0
1950	Wilford White, Arizona St.	Sr.	1,502	225	0	64	274	2,065	206.5
1951	Ollie Matson, San Francisco	Sr.	1,566	58	18	115	280	2,037	226.3
1952	Billy Vessels, Oklahoma	Sr.	1,072	165	10	120	145	1,512	151.2
1953	J. C. Caroline, Illinois	So.	1,256	52	0	129	33	1,470	163.3
1954	Art Luppino, Arizona	So.	1,359	50	84	68	632	2,193	219.3
1955	Jim Swink, Texas Christian	Jr.	1,283	111	46	64	198	1,702	170.2
	Art Luppino, Arizona	Jr.	1,313	74	0	62	253	1,702	170.2
1956	Jack Hill, Utah St.	Sr.	920	215	132	21	403	1,691	169.1
1957	Overton Curtis, Utah St.	Jr.	616	193	60	44	695	1,608	160.8
1958	Dick Bass, Pacific (Cal.)	Jr.	1,361	121	5	164	227	1,878	187.8
1959	Pervis Atkins, New Mexico St.	Jr.	971	301	23	241	264	1,800	180.0
1960	Pervis Atkins, New Mexico St.	Sr.	611	468	23	218	293	1,613	161.3
1961	Jim Pilot, New Mexico St.	So.	1,278	20	0	161	147	1,606	160.6
1962	Gary Wood, Cornell	Jr.	889	7	0	69	430	1,395	155.0
1963	Gary Wood, Cornell	Sr.	818	15	0	57	618	1,508	167.6
1964	Donny Anderson, Texas Tech	Jr.	966	396	0	28	320	1,710	171.0
1965	Floyd Little, Syracuse	Jr.	1,065	248	0	423	254	1,990	199.0
1966	Frank Quayle, Virginia	So.	727	420	0	30	439	1,616	161.6
1967	O. J. Simpson, Southern Cal	Jr.	1,415	109	0	0	176	1,700	188.9
1968	O. J. Simpson, Southern Cal	Sr.	1,709	126	0	0	131	1,966	196.6
1969	Lynn Moore, Army	Sr.	983	44	0	223	545	1,795	179.5
1970	Don McCauley, North Caro.	Sr.	1,720	235	0	0	66	2,021	183.7
1971	Ed Marinaro, Cornell	Sr.	1,881	51	0	0	0	1,932	214.7
1972	Howard Stevens, Louisville	Sr.	1,294	221	0	377	240	2,132	213.2
1973	Willard Harrell, Pacific (Cal.)	Jr.	1,319	18	0	88	352	1,777	177.7
1974	Louie Giammona, Utah St.	Jr.	1,534	79	0	16	355	1,984	198.4
1975	Louie Giammona, Utah St.	Sr.	1,454	33	0	124	434	2,045	185.9
1976	Tony Dorsett, Pittsburgh	Sr.	1,948	73	0	0	0	2,021	183.7
1977	Earl Campbell, Texas	Sr.	1,744	111	0	0	0	1,855	168.6
1978	Charles White, Southern Cal	Jr.	1,760	191	0	0	145	2,096	174.7
1979	Charles White, Southern Cal	Sr.	1,803	138	0	0	0	1,941	194.1
1980	Marcus Allen, Southern Cal	Jr.	1,563	231	0	0	0	1,794	179.4
1981	Marcus Allen, Southern Cal	Sr.	2,342	217	0	0	0	2,559	232.6
1982	Carl Monroe, Utah	Sr.	1,507	108	0	0	421	2,036	185.1
1983	Napoleon McCallum, Navy	Jr.	1,587	166	0	272	360	2,385	216.8
1984	Keith Byars, Ohio St.	Jr.	1,655	453	0	0	176	2,284	207.6
1985	Napoleon McCallum, Navy	Sr.	1,327	358	0	157	488	2,330	211.8
1986	Paul Palmer, Temple	Sr.	1,866	110	0	0	657	2,633	239.4
1987	Eric Wilkerson, Kent	Jr.	1,221	269	0	0	584	2,074	188.6
1988	Barry Sanders, Oklahoma St.	Jr.	*2,628	106	0	95	421	*3,250	*295.5
1989	Mike Pringle, Cal St. Fullerton	Sr.	1,727	249	0	0	714	2,690	244.6
1990	Glyn Milburn, Stanford	So.	729	632	0	267	594	2,222	202.0
1991	Ryan Benjamin, Pacific (Cal.)	Jr.	1,581	612	0	4	798	2,995	249.6
1992	Ryan Benjamin, Pacific (Cal.)	Sr.	1,441	434	0	96	626	2,597	236.1
1993	LeShon Johnson, Northern Ill.	Sr.	1,976	106	0	0	0	2,082	189.3

*Record.

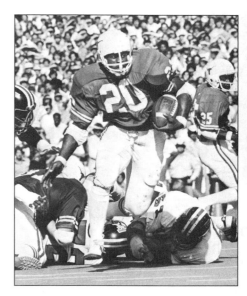

Texas running back Earl Campbell totaled 1,855 all-purpose yards in 1977 and led Division I-A with a per-game average of 168.6.

Field Goals

CAREER FIELD GOALS

(One-inch tees were permitted in 1949, two-inch tees were permitted in 1965, and use of tees was eliminated in 1989. The goal posts were widened from 18 feet, 6 inches to 23 feet, 4 inches in 1959 and were narrowed back to 18 feet, 6 inches in 1991. In 1993, the hash marks were moved 6 feet, 8 inches closer to the center of the field, to 60 feet from each sideline.)

Player, Team	Years	Total	Pct.	Under 40 Yds.	40 Plus	Long	‡Won
Jeff Jaeger, Washington (S)	1983-86	*80-99	.808	59-68	21-31	52	5
John Lee, UCLA (S)	1982-85	79-92	*.859	54-56	25-36	52	**10
Jason Elam, Hawaii (S)	$1988-92	79-100	.790	50-55	29-45	56	3
Philip Doyle, Alabama (S)	1987-90	78-*105	.743	57-61	21-44	53	6
Luis Zendejas, Arizona St. (S)	1981-84	78-*105	.743	53-59	25-46	55	1
Kevin Butler, Georgia (S)	1981-84	77-98	.786	50-56	27-42	60	7
Max Zendejas, Arizona (S)	1982-85	77-104	.740	47-53	30-51	57	7
Carlos Huerta, Miami (Fla.) (S)	1988-91	73-91	.802	56-60	17-31	52	3
Derek Schmidt, Florida St. (S)	1984-87	73-104	.702	44-55	29-49	54	1
Fuad Reveiz, Tennessee (S)	1981-84	71-95	.747	45-53	26-42	60	7

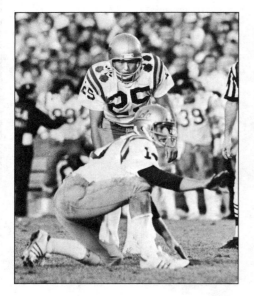

UCLA's John Lee kicked 29 field goals in 1984 to set a Division I-A single-season record.

Player, Team	Years	Total	Pct.	Under 40 Yds.	40 Plus	Long	‡Won
Roman Anderson, Houston (S)	1988-91	70-101	.802	*61-*72	9-29	53	3
Barry Belli, Fresno St. (S)	1984-87	70-99	.707	47-53	23-46	55	5
Collin Mackie, South Caro. (S)	1987-90	69-95	.726	48-57	21-38	52	5
Gary Gusman, Miami (Ohio) (S)	1984-87	68-94	.723	50-57	18-37	53	2
Rusty Hanna, Toledo (S)	1989-92	68-99	.687	51-58	17-41	51	3
Larry Roach, Oklahoma St. (S)	1981-84	68-101	.673	46-54	22-47	56	5
Paul Woodside, West Va. (S)	1981-84	65-81	.802	45-49	20-32	55	5
John Diettrich, Ball St. (S)	1983-86	63-90	.700	42-50	21-40	62	5
Jason Hanson, Washington St. (S)	1988-91	63-96	.656	24-30	*39-*66	62	4
Dan Eichloff, Kansas (S)	1990-93	62-87	.713	40-50	22-37	61	5
Kenny Stucker, Ball St. (S)	1988-91	62-87	.713	45-51	17-36	52	4
David Browndyke, Louisiana St. (S)	1986-89	61-75	.813	49-53	12-22	52	3
Todd Gregoire, Wisconsin (S)	1984-87	61-81	.753	48-56	13-25	54	6
Todd Wright, Arkansas (S)	1989-92	60-79	.759	41-47	19-32	50	2
Jess Atkinson, Maryland (S)	1981-84	60-82	.732	40-48	20-34	50	5
Scott Sisson, Georgia Tech (S)	1989-92	60-88	.682	45-53	15-35	51	6
Obed Ariri, Clemson (S)	1977-80	60-92	.652	47-55	13-37	57	5
Chuck Nelson, Washington (S)	1980-82	59-72	.819	47-53	12-19	51	5
Van Tiffin, Alabama (S)	1983-86	59-87	.678	32-38	27-49	57	4
John Hopkins, Stanford (S)	1987-90	59-88	.670	43-50	16-38	54	4
Jeff Ward, Texas (S)	1983-86	58-78	.744	36-41	22-37	57	**10
Jeff Shudak, Iowa St. (S)	1987-90	58-79	.734	38-45	20-34	55	5

*Record. **Record tied. $See page 6 for explanation. ‡Number of games in which his field goal(s) provided the winning margin. (S) Soccer-style kicker.

SEASON FIELD GOALS

Player, Team	Year	Total	Pct.	Under 40 Yds.	40 Plus	Long	‡Won
John Lee, UCLA (S)	†1984	*29-33	.879	16-16	13-17	51	5
Paul Woodside, West Va. (S)	†1982	28-31	.903	23-23	5-8	45	2
Luis Zendejas, Arizona St. (S)	†1983	28-37	.757	19-22	9-15	52	1
Fuad Reveiz, Tennessee (S)	1982	27-31	.871	14-14	13-17	60	2
Chuck Nelson, Washington (S)	1982	25-26	*.962	22-23	3-3	49	1
Chris Jacke, UTEP (S)	1988	25-27	.926	11-11	*14-16	52	2
John Diettrich, Ball St. (S)	†1985	25-29	.862	16-17	9-12	54	2
Kendall Trainor, Arkansas (S)	†1988	24-27	.889	14-15	10-12	58	4
Carlos Reveiz, Tennessee (S)	1985	24-28	.857	12-14	12-14	52	2
Chris White, Illinois (S)	1984	24-28	.857	16-17	8-11	52	1
Philip Doyle, Alabama (S)	†1990	24-29	.828	16-17	8-12	47	2
Bruce Kallmeyer, Kansas (S)	1983	24-29	.828	13-14	11-15	57	1
Mike Prindle, Western Mich. (S)	1984	24-30	.800	17-20	7-10	56	1
Joe Allison, Memphis (S)	†1992	23-25	.920	13-14	10-11	51	1
Bobby Raymond, Florida (S)	1984	23-26	.885	18-18	5-8	51	1
Mike Bass, Illinois (S)	1982	23-26	.885	12-13	11-13	53	1
Kevin Butler, Georgia (S)	1984	23-28	.821	12-14	11-14	60	2
Collin Mackie, South Caro. (S)	†1987	23-30	.767	17-21	6-9	49	0
Obed Ariri, Clemson (S)	†1980	23-30	.767	18-19	5-11	52	3
Derek Schmidt, Florida St. (S)	†1987	23-31	.742	16-21	7-10	53	0

*Record. †National champion. ‡Number of games in which his field goal(s) provided the winning margin. (S) Soccer-style kicker.

SINGLE-GAME FIELD GOALS

No.	Player, Team (Opponent)	Date
7	Dale Klein, Nebraska (Missouri)	Oct. 19, 1985
7	Mike Prindle, Western Mich. (Marshall)	Sept. 29, 1984
6	Rusty Hanna, Toledo (Northern Ill.)	Nov. 21, 1992
6	Philip Doyle, Alabama (Southwestern La.)	Oct. 6, 1990
6	Sean Fleming, Wyoming (Arkansas St.)	Sept. 15, 1990
6	Bobby Raymond, Florida (Kentucky)	Nov. 17, 1984
6	John Lee, UCLA (San Diego St.)	Sept. 8, 1984
6	Bobby Raymond, Florida (Florida St.)	Dec. 3, 1983
6	Alan Smith, Texas A&M (Arkansas St.)	Sept. 17, 1983
6	Al Del Greco, Auburn (Kentucky)	Oct. 9, 1982
6	Vince Fusco, Duke (Clemson)	Oct. 16, 1976
6	Frank Nester, West Va. (Villanova)	Sept. 9, 1972
6	Charley Gogolak, Princeton (Rutgers)	Sept. 25, 1965

ANNUAL CHAMPIONS

(From 1959-90, goal posts were 23 feet, 4 inches; and from 1991, narrowed to 18 feet, 6 inches.)

Year	Player, Team	Total	PG	Pct.	Under 40 Yds.	40 Plus	Long	‡Won
1959	Karl Holzwarth, Wisconsin (C)	7-8	0.8	.875	7-8	0-0	29	4
1960	Ed Dyas, Auburn (C)	13-18	1.3	.722	13-17	0-1	37	2
1961	Greg Mather, Navy (C)	11-15	1.1	.733	9-12	2-3	45	1
1962	Bob Jencks, Miami (Ohio) (C)	8-11	0.8	.727	7-9	1-2	52	3
	Al Woodall, Auburn (C)	8-20	0.8	.400	8-13	0-7	35	0
1963	Billy Lothridge, Georgia Tech (C)	12-16	1.2	.750	10-14	2-2	41	3
1964	Doug Moreau, Louisiana St. (C)	13-20	1.3	.650	13-20	0-0	36	0
1965	Charley Gogolak, Princeton (S)	16-23	1.8	.696	7-10	9-13	54	0
1966	Jerry DePoyster, Wyoming (C)	13-*38	1.3	.342	7-13	6-*25	54	1
1967	Gerald Warren, North Caro. St. (C)	17-22	1.7	.773	13-14	4-8	47	1
1968	Bob Jacobs, Wyoming (C)	14-29	1.4	.483	10-15	4-14	51	2
1969	Bob Jacobs, Wyoming (C)	18-27	1.8	.667	13-16	5-11	43	2

Beginning in 1970, ranked on per-game (instead of total) made

Year	Player, Team	Total	PG	Pct.	Under 40 Yds.	40 Plus	Long	‡Won
1970	Kim Braswell, Georgia (C)	13-17	1.3	.765	11-14	2-3	43	0
1971	Nick Mike-Mayer, Temple (S)	12-17	1.3	.706	8-10	4-7	48	1
1972	Nick Mike-Mayer, Temple (S)	13-20	1.4	.650	10-11	3-9	44	3
1973	Rod Garcia, Stanford (S)	18-29	1.6	.621	10-14	8-15	59	2
1974	Dave Lawson, Air Force (C)	19-31	1.7	.613	13-14	6-17	60	1
1975	Don Bitterlich, Temple (S)	21-31	1.9	.677	13-14	8-17	56	0
1976	Tony Franklin, Texas A&M (S)	17-26	1.6	.654	9-12	8-14	65	0
1977	Paul Marchese, Kent (S)	18-27	1.8	.667	13-15	5-12	51	2
1978	Matt Bahr, Penn St. (S)	22-27	2.0	.815	19-20	3-7	50	3
1979	Ish Ordonez, Arkansas (S)	18-22	1.6	.818	12-14	6-8	50	2
1980	Obed Ariri, Clemson (S)	23-30	2.1	.767	18-19	5-11	52	3
1981	Bruce Lahay, Arkansas (S)	19-24	1.7	.792	12-15	7-9	49	4
	Kevin Butler, Georgia (S)	19-26	1.7	.731	11-14	8-12	52	0
	Larry Roach, Oklahoma St. (S)	19-28	1.7	.679	12-14	7-14	56	3
1982	Paul Woodside, West Va. (S)	28-31	2.6	.903	23-23	5-8	45	2
1983	Luis Zendejas, Arizona St. (S)	28-37	2.6	.757	19-22	9-15	52	1
1984	John Lee, UCLA (S)	*29-33	*2.6	.879	16-16	13-17	51	5
1985	John Diettrich, Ball St. (S)	25-29	2.3	.862	16-17	9-12	54	2
1986	Chris Kinzer, Virginia Tech (C)	22-27	2.0	.815	14-17	8-10	50	5
1987	Collin Mackie, South Caro. (S)	23-30	2.1	.767	17-21	6-9	49	0
	Derek Schmidt, Florida St. (S)	23-31	2.1	.742	16-21	7-10	53	0
1988	Kendall Trainor, Arkansas (S)	24-27	2.2	.889	14-15	10-12	58	4
1989	Philip Doyle, Alabama (S)	22-25	2.0	.880	19-19	3-6	44	2
	Gregg McCallum, Oregon (S)	22-29	2.0	.759	15-15	7-14	47	2
	Roman Anderson, Houston (S)	22-34	2.0	.647	17-20	5-14	51	0
1990	Philip Doyle, Alabama (S)	24-29	2.2	.828	16-17	8-12	47	2
1991	Doug Brien, California (S)	19-28	1.7	.679	15-20	4-8	50	2
1992	Joe Allison, Memphis (S)	23-25	2.1	.920	13-14	10-11	51	1
1993	Michael Proctor, Alabama (S)	22-29	1.8	.759	15-20	7-9	53	0

*Record. ‡Number of games in which his field goal(s) provided the winning margin. (C) Conventional kicker. (S) Soccer-style kicker.

Last season, Ohio State defensive back Marlon Kerner became one of 61 major-college players since 1941 to race from goal line to goal line with an interception.

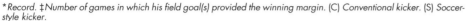

All-Time Longest Plays

Since 1941, official maximum length of all plays fixed at 100 yards.

RUSHING

Yds.	Player, Team (Opponent)	Year
99	Jerald Sowell, Tulane (Alabama)	1993
99	Kelsey Finch, Tennessee (Florida)	1977
99	Ralph Thompson, West Tex. A&M (Wichita St.)	1970
99	Max Anderson, Arizona St. (Wyoming)	1967
99	Gale Sayers, Kansas (Nebraska)	1963
98	Darrell Thompson, Minnesota (Michigan)	1987
98	George Swarn, Miami, Ohio (Western Mich.)	1984
98	Mark Malone, Arizona St. (Utah St.)	1979
98	Stanley Howell, Mississippi St. (Southern Miss.)	1979
98	Steve Atkins, Maryland (Clemson)	1978
98	Granville Amos, Va. Military (William & Mary)	1964
98	Jim Thacker, Davidson (Geo. Washington)	1952
98	Bill Powell, California (Oregon St.)	1951
98	Al Yannelli, Bucknell (Delaware)	1946
98	Meredith Warner, Iowa St. (Iowa Pre-Flight)	1943

PASSING

Yds.	Passer-Receiver, Team (Opponent)	Year
99	John Paci-Thomas Lewis, Indiana (Penn St.)	1993
99	Gino Torretta-Horace Copeland, Miami, Fla. (Arkansas)	1991
99	Scott Ankrom-James Maness, Texas Christian (Rice)	1984
99	Cris Collinsworth-Derrick Gaffney, Florida (Rice)	1977
99	Terry Peel-Robert Ford, Houston (San Diego St.)	1972
99	Terry Peel-Robert Ford, Houston (Syracuse)	1970
99	Colin Clapton-Eddie Jenkins, Holy Cross (Boston U.)	1970
99	Bo Burris-Warren McVea, Houston (Washington St.)	1966
99	Fred Owens-Jack Ford, Portland (St. Mary's, Cal.)	1947
98	Tom Dubs-Richard Hill, Ohio (Kent)	1991
98	Paul Oates-Sean Foster, Long Beach St. (San Diego St.)	1989
98	Barry Garrison-Al Owens, New Mexico (Brigham Young)	1987
98	Kelly Donohoe-Willie Vaughn, Kansas (Colorado)	1987
98	Jeff Martin-Mark Flaker, Drake (New Mexico St.)	1976
98	Pete Woods-Joe Stewart, Missouri (Nebraska)	1976
98	Dan Hagemann-Jack Steptoe, Utah (New Mexico)	1976
98	Bruce Shaw-Pat Kenney, North Caro. St. (Penn St.)	1972
98	Jerry Rhome-Jeff Jordan, Tulsa (Wichita St.)	1963
98	Bob Dean-Norman Dawson, Cornell (Navy)	1947

INTERCEPTION RETURNS

Since 1941, 61 players have returned interceptions 100 yards. The most recent:

Yds.	Player, Team (Opponent)	Year
100	Marlon Kerner, Ohio St. (Purdue)	1993
100	Ray Jackson, Colorado St. (UTEP)	1993
100	John Hardy, California (Wisconsin)	1990
100	Ed Givens, Army (Lafayette)	1990

PUNT RETURNS

Yds.	Player, Team (Opponent)	Year
100‡	Richie Luzzi, Clemson (Georgia)	1968
100‡	Don Guest, California (Washington St.)	1966
100	Jimmy Campagna, Georgia (Vanderbilt)	1952
100	Hugh McElhenny, Washington (Southern Cal)	1951
100	Frank Brady, Navy (Maryland)	1951
100	Bert Rechichar, Tennessee (Wash. & Lee)	1950
100	Eddie Macon, Pacific, Cal. (Boston U.)	1950

‡Return of field-goal attempt.

KICKOFF RETURNS

Since 1941, 170 players have returned kickoffs 100 yards. The most recent:

Yds.	Player, Team (Opponent)	Year
100	Leroy Gallman, Duke (Tennessee)	1993
100	Jack Jackson, Florida (Mississippi St.)	1993
100	Charles Henley, Kansas (Colorado)	1993
100	Leeland McElroy, Texas A&M (Texas)	1993
100	Fred Montgomery, New Mexico St. (Long Beach St.)	1991
100	Anthony Prior, Washington St. (Southern Cal)	1991
100	Ricky Turner, Pittsburgh (West Va.)	1990

PUNTS

Yds.	Player, Team (Opponent)	Year
99	Pat Brady, Nevada (Loyola Marymount)	1950
96	George O'Brien, Wisconsin (Iowa)	1952
94	John Hadl, Kansas (Oklahoma)	1959
94	Carl Knox, Texas Christian (Oklahoma St.)	1947
94	Preston Johnson, Southern Methodist (Pittsburgh)	1940

FUMBLE RETURNS
(Since 1992)

Yds.	Player, Team (Opponent)	Year
97	Mike Collins, West Va. (Missouri)	1993
97	Ernie Lewis, East Caro. (West Va.)	1992
96	Jeff Arneson, Illinois (Ohio St.)	1992
93	Parrish Foster, New Mexico St. (Nevada)	1993
92	David Thomas, Miami (Ohio) (Akron)	1993
91	Michael Barber, Clemson (Tenn.-Chatt.)	1992
91	Cassius Ware, Mississippi (Auburn)	1992

FIELD GOALS

Yds.	Player, Team (Opponent)	Year
67	Joe Williams, Wichita St. (Southern Ill.)	1978
67	Steve Little, Arkansas (Texas)	1977
67	Russell Erxleben, Texas (Rice)	1977
65	Tony Franklin, Texas A&M (Baylor)	1976
64	Russell Erxleben, Texas (Oklahoma)	1977
64	Tony Franklin, Texas A&M (Baylor)	1976
63	Morten Andersen, Michigan St. (Ohio St.)	1981
63	Clark Kemble, Colorado St. (Arizona)	1975
62†	Jason Hanson, Washington St. (Nevada-Las Vegas)	1991
62	John Diettrich, Ball St. (Ohio)	1986

Yds.	Player, Team (Opponent)	Year
62	Chip Lohmiller, Minnesota (Iowa)	1986
62	Tom Whelihan, Missouri (Colorado)	1986
62	Dan Christopulos, Wyoming (Colorado St.)	1977
62	Iseed Khoury, North Texas (Richmond)	1977
62	Dave Lawson, Air Force (Iowa St.)	1975
61	Dan Eichloff, Kansas (Ball St.)	1992
61	Mark Porter, Kansas St. (Nebraska)	1988
61	Ralf Mojsiejenko, Michigan St. (Illinois)	1982
61	Steve Little, Arkansas (Tulsa)	1976
61	Wayne Latimer, Virginia Tech (Florida St.)	1975
61	Ray Guy, Southern Miss. (Utah St.)	1972
60	Joe Nedney, San Jose St. (Wyoming)	1992
60	Don Shafer, Southern Cal (Notre Dame)	1986
60	Steve DeLine, Colorado St. (Air Force)	1985
60	Kevin Butler, Georgia (Clemson)	1984
60	Chris Perkins, Florida (Tulane)	1984
60	Fuad Reveiz, Tennessee (Georgia Tech)	1982
60	Russell Erxleben, Texas (Texas Tech)	1977
60	Bubba Hicks, Baylor (Rice)	1975
60	Dave Lawson, Air Force (Colorado)	1974
60	Tony Di Rienzo, Oklahoma (Kansas)	1973
60	Bill McClard, Arkansas (Southern Methodist)	1970

†Longest collegiate field goal without use of a kicking tee. Also longest field goal with narrower (18'6") goal posts.

Team Champions

Annual Offense Champions

TOTAL OFFENSE

Year	Team	Avg.
1937	Colorado	375.4
1938	Fordham	341.6
1939	Ohio St.	309.3
1940	Lafayette	368.2
1941	Duke	372.2
1942	Georgia	429.5
1943	Notre Dame	418.0
1944	Tulsa	434.7
1945	Army	462.7
1946	Notre Dame	441.3
1947	Michigan	412.7
1948	Nevada	487.0
1949	Notre Dame	434.8
1950	Arizona St.	470.4
1951	Tulsa	480.1
1952	Tulsa	466.6
1953	Cincinnati	409.5
1954	Army	448.7
1955	Oklahoma	410.7
1956	Oklahoma	481.7
1957	Arizona St.	444.9
1958	Iowa	405.9
1959	Syracuse	451.5
1960	New Mexico St.	419.6
1961	Mississippi	418.7
1962	Arizona St.	384.4
1963	Utah St.	395.3
1964	Tulsa	461.8
1965	Tulsa	427.8
1966	Houston	437.2
1967	Houston	427.9
1968	Houston	562.0
1969	San Diego St.	532.2
1970	Arizona St.	514.5
1971	Oklahoma	566.5
1972	Arizona St.	516.5
1973	Arizona St.	565.5
1974	Oklahoma	507.7
1975	California	458.5
1976	Michigan	448.1
1977	Colgate	486.1
1978	Nebraska	501.4
1979	Brigham Young	521.4
1980	Brigham Young	535.0
1981	Arizona St.	498.7

Year	Team	Avg.
1982	Nebraska	518.6
1983	Brigham Young	584.2
1984	Brigham Young	486.5
1985	Brigham Young	500.2
1986	San Jose St.	481.4
1987	Oklahoma	499.7
1988	Utah	526.8
1989	Houston	*624.9
1990	Houston	586.8
1991	Fresno St.	541.9
1992	Houston	519.5
1993	Nevada	569.1

*Record.

RUSHING OFFENSE

Year	Team	Avg.
1937	Colorado	310.0
1938	Fordham	297.1
1939	Wake Forest	290.3
1940	Lafayette	306.4
1941	Missouri	307.7
1942	Hardin-Simmons	307.4
1943	Notre Dame	313.7
1944	Army	298.6
1945	Army	359.8
1946	Notre Dame	340.1
1947	Detroit Mercy	319.7
1948	UTEP	378.3
1949	UTEP	333.2
1950	Arizona St.	347.0
1951	Arizona St.	334.8
1952	Tulsa	321.5
1953	Oklahoma	306.9
1954	Army	322.0
1955	Oklahoma	328.9
1956	Oklahoma	391.0
1957	Colorado	322.4
1958	Pacific (Cal.)	259.6
1959	Syracuse	313.6
1960	Utah St.	312.0
1961	New Mexico St.	299.1
1962	Ohio St.	278.9
1963	Nebraska	262.6
1964	Syracuse	251.0
1965	Nebraska	290.0
1966	Harvard	269.0
1967	Houston	270.9
1968	Houston	361.7
1969	Texas	363.0
1970	Texas	374.5
1971	Oklahoma	*472.4
1972	Oklahoma	368.8
1973	UCLA	400.3

Year	Team	Avg.
1974	Oklahoma	438.8
1975	Arkansas St.	340.5
1976	Michigan	362.6
1977	Oklahoma	328.9
1978	Oklahoma	427.5
1979	East Caro.	368.5
1980	Nebraska	378.3
1981	Oklahoma	334.3
1982	Nebraska	394.3
1983	Nebraska	401.7
1984	Army	345.3
1985	Nebraska	374.3
1986	Oklahoma	404.7
1987	Oklahoma	428.8
1988	Nebraska	382.3
1989	Nebraska	375.3
1990	Northern Ill.	344.6
1991	Nebraska	353.2
1992	Nebraska	328.2
1993	Army	298.5

*Record.

PASSING OFFENSE

Year	Team	Avg.
1937	Arkansas	185.0
1938	Texas Christian	164.1
1939	Texas Christian	148.5
1940	Cornell	186.3
1941	Arizona	177.7
1942	Tulsa	233.9
1943	Brown	133.1
1944	Tulsa	206.3
1945	St. Mary's (Cal.)	161.3
1946	Nevada	198.1
1947	Michigan	173.9
1948	Nevada	255.0
1949	Fordham	183.4
1950	Southern Methodist	214.6
1951	Loyola Marymount	210.6
1952	Fordham	225.8
1953	Stanford	179.5
1954	Purdue	177.3
1955	Navy	185.1
1956	Washington St.	206.8
1957	Utah	195.2
1958	Army	172.2
1959	Stanford	227.8
1960	Washington St.	185.5
1961	Wisconsin	188.4
1962	Tulsa	199.3
1963	Tulsa	244.8
1964	Tulsa	317.9
1965	Tulsa	346.4

DIVISION I-A

Year	Team	Avg.
1966	Tulsa	272.0
1967	UTEP	301.1
1968	Cincinnati	335.8
1969	San Diego St.	374.2
1970	Auburn	288.5
1971	San Diego St.	251.4
1972	Virginia Tech	304.4
1973	San Diego St.	305.0
1974	Colorado St.	261.8
1975	San Diego St.	291.3
1976	Brigham Young	307.8
1977	Brigham Young	341.6
1978	Southern Methodist	276.2
1979	Brigham Young	368.3
1980	Brigham Young	409.8
1981	Brigham Young	356.9
1982	Long Beach St.	326.8
1983	Brigham Young	381.2
1984	Brigham Young	346.2
1985	Brigham Young	354.5
1986	San Jose St.	312.5
1987	San Jose St.	338.1
1988	Utah	395.9
1989	Houston	*511.3
1990	Houston	473.9
1991	Houston	372.8
1992	Houston	407.1
1993	Nevada	397.5

*Record.

SCORING OFFENSE

Year	Team	Avg.
1937	Colorado	31.0
1938	Dartmouth	28.2
1939	Utah	28.4
1940	Boston College	32.0
1941	Texas	33.8
1942	Tulsa	42.7
1943	Duke	37.2
1944	Army	*56.0
1945	Army	45.8
1946	Georgia	37.2
1947	Michigan	38.3
1948	Nevada	44.4
1949	Army	39.3
1950	Princeton	38.8
1951	Maryland	39.2
1952	Oklahoma	40.7
1953	Texas Tech	38.9
1954	UCLA	40.8
1955	Oklahoma	36.5
1956	Oklahoma	46.6
1957	Arizona St.	39.7
1958	Rutgers	33.4
1959	Syracuse	39.0
1960	New Mexico St.	37.4
1961	Utah St.	38.7
1962	Wisconsin	31.7
1963	Utah St.	31.7
1964	Tulsa	38.4
1965	Arkansas	32.4
1966	Notre Dame	36.2
1967	UTEP	35.9
1968	Houston	42.5
1969	San Diego St.	46.4
1970	Texas	41.2
1971	Oklahoma	44.9
1972	Arizona St.	46.6
1973	Arizona St.	44.6
1974	Oklahoma	43.0
1975	Ohio St.	34.0
1976	Michigan	38.7
1977	Grambling	42.0
1978	Oklahoma	40.0
1979	Brigham Young	40.6
1980	Brigham Young	46.7
1981	Brigham Young	38.7
1982	Nebraska	41.1
1983	Nebraska	52.0
1984	Boston College	36.7
1985	Fresno St.	39.1
1986	Oklahoma	42.4
1987	Oklahoma	43.5
1988	Oklahoma St.	47.5
1989	Houston	53.5
1990	Houston	46.5
1991	Fresno St.	44.2
1992	Fresno St.	40.5
1993	Florida St.	43.2

*Record.

Annual Defense Champions

TOTAL DEFENSE

Year	Team	Avg.
1937	Santa Clara	*69.9
1938	Alabama	77.9
1939	Texas A&M	76.3
1940	Navy	96.0
1941	Duquesne	110.6
1942	Texas	117.3
1943	Duke	121.7
1944	Virginia	96.8
1945	Alabama	109.9
1946	Notre Dame	141.7
1947	Penn St.	76.8
1948	Georgia Tech	151.3
1949	Kentucky	153.8
1950	Wake Forest	163.2
1951	Wisconsin	154.8
1952	Tennessee	166.7
1953	Cincinnati	184.3
1954	Mississippi	172.3
1955	Army	160.7
1956	Miami (Fla.)	189.4
1957	Auburn	133.0
1958	Auburn	157.5
1959	Syracuse	96.2
1960	Wyoming	149.6
1961	Alabama	132.6
1962	Mississippi	142.2
1963	Southern Miss.	131.2
1964	Auburn	164.7
1965	Southern Miss.	161.1
1966	Southern Miss.	163.7
1967	Nebraska	157.6
1968	Wyoming	206.8
1969	Toledo	209.1
1970	Toledo	185.8
1971	Toledo	179.5
1972	Louisville	202.5
1973	Miami (Ohio)	177.4
1974	Notre Dame	195.2
1975	Texas A&M	183.8
1976	Rutgers	179.2
1977	Jackson St.	207.0
1978	Penn St.	203.9
1979	Yale	175.4
1980	Pittsburgh	205.5
1981	Pittsburgh	224.8
1982	Arizona St.	228.9
1983	Texas	212.0
1984	Nebraska	203.3
1985	Oklahoma	193.5
1986	Oklahoma	169.6
1987	Oklahoma	208.1
1988	Auburn	218.1
1989	Miami (Fla.)	216.5
1990	Clemson	216.9
1991	Texas A&M	222.4
1992	Alabama	194.2
1993	Mississippi	234.5

*Record.

RUSHING DEFENSE

Year	Team	Avg.
1937	Santa Clara	25.3
1938	Oklahoma	43.3
1939	Texas A&M	41.5
1940	Texas A&M	44.3
1941	Duquesne	56.0
1942	Boston College	48.9
1943	Duke	39.4
1944	Navy	53.8
1945	Alabama	33.9
1946	Oklahoma	58.0
1947	Penn St.	*17.0
1948	Georgia Tech	74.9
1949	Oklahoma	55.6
1950	Ohio St.	64.0
1951	San Francisco	51.6
1952	Michigan St.	83.9
1953	Maryland	83.9
1954	UCLA	73.2
1955	Maryland	75.9
1956	Miami (Fla.)	106.9
1957	Auburn	67.4
1958	Auburn	79.6
1959	Syracuse	19.3
1960	Wyoming	82.4
1961	Utah St.	50.8
1962	Minnesota	52.2
1963	Mississippi	77.3
1964	Washington	61.3
1965	Michigan St.	45.6
1966	Wyoming	38.5
1967	Wyoming	42.3
1968	Arizona St.	57.0
1969	Louisiana St.	38.9
1970	Louisiana St.	52.2
1971	Michigan	63.3
1972	Louisville	82.1
1973	Miami (Ohio)	77.0
1974	Notre Dame	102.8
1975	Texas A&M	80.3
1976	Rutgers	83.9
1977	Jackson St.	67.8
1978	Penn St.	54.5
1979	Yale	75.0
1980	Pittsburgh	65.3
1981	Pittsburgh	62.4
1982	Virginia Tech	49.5
1983	Virginia Tech	69.4
1984	Oklahoma	68.8
1985	UCLA	70.3
1986	Oklahoma	60.7
1987	Michigan St.	61.5
1988	Auburn	63.2
1989	Southern Cal	61.5
1990	Washington	66.8
1991	Clemson	53.4
1992	Alabama	55.0
1993	Arizona	30.1

*Record.

PASSING DEFENSE

Year	Team	Avg.$
1937	Harvard	31.0
1938	Penn St.	*13.1
1939	Kansas	34.1
1940	Harvard	33.3
1941	Purdue	27.1
1942	Harvard	45.4
1943	North Caro.	36.5
1944	Michigan St.	26.7
1945	Holy Cross	37.7
1946	Holy Cross	53.7
1947	North Caro. St.	39.3
1948	Northwestern	54.1
1949	Miami (Fla.)	54.7
1950	Tennessee	67.5
1951	Wash. & Lee	67.9
1952	Virginia	50.3
1953	Richmond	40.3
1954	Alabama	45.8
1955	Florida	42.0
1956	Villanova	43.8
1957	Georgia Tech	33.4
1958	Iowa St.	39.0
1959	Alabama	45.7
1960	Iowa St.	30.2
1961	Pennsylvania	56.9
1962	New Mexico	56.8
1963	UTEP	43.8
1964	Kent	53.6
1965	Toledo	69.8
1966	Toledo	70.4

Year	Team	Avg.$
1967	Nebraska	90.1
1968	Kent	107.6
1969	Dayton	90.0
1970	Toledo	77.8
1971	Texas Tech	60.1
1972	Vanderbilt	80.3
1973	Nebraska	39.9
1974	Iowa	65.7
1975	Va. Military	51.1
1976	Western Mich.	78.5
1977	Tennessee St.	67.9
1978	Boston College	65.1
1979	Western Caro.	77.5
1980	Kansas St.	91.4
1981	Nebraska	100.1
1982	Missouri	123.5
1983	Ohio	115.3
1984	Texas Tech	114.8
1985	Oklahoma	103.6
1986	Oklahoma	108.9
1987	Oklahoma	102.4
1988	Baylor	117.8
1989	Kansas St.	129.3
1990	Alabama	82.47
1991	Texas	77.37
1992	Western Mich.	83.16
1993	Texas A&M	74.99

*Record. $Beginning in 1990, ranked on passing-efficiency defense rating points instead of per-game yardage allowed.

SCORING DEFENSE

Year	Team	Avg.
1937	Santa Clara	1.1
1938	Duke	**0.0
1939	Tennessee	**0.0
1940	Tennessee	2.6
1941	Duquesne	2.9
1942	Tulsa	3.2
1943	Duke	3.8
1944	Army	3.9
1945	St. Mary's (Cal.)	4.0
1946	Notre Dame	2.7
1947	Penn St.	3.0
1948	Michigan	4.9
1949	Kentucky	4.8
1950	Army	4.4
1951	Wisconsin	5.9
1952	Southern Cal	4.7
1953	Maryland	3.1
1954	UCLA	4.4
1955	Georgia Tech	4.6
1956	Georgia Tech	3.3
1957	Auburn	2.8
1958	Oklahoma	4.9
1959	Mississippi	2.1
1960	Louisiana St.	5.0
1961	Alabama	2.2
1962	Louisiana St.	3.4
1963	Mississippi	3.7
1964	Arkansas	5.7
1965	Michigan St.	6.2
1966	Alabama	3.7
1967	Oklahoma	6.8
1968	Georgia	9.8
1969	Arkansas	7.6
1970	Dartmouth	4.7
1971	Michigan	6.4
1972	Michigan	5.2
1973	Ohio St.	4.3
1974	Michigan	6.8
1975	Alabama	6.0
1976	Michigan	7.4
	Rutgers	7.4
1977	North Caro.	7.4
1978	Ball St.	7.5
1979	Alabama	5.3
1980	Florida St.	7.7
1981	Southern Miss.	8.1
1982	Arkansas	10.5
1983	Virginia Tech	8.3
1984	Nebraska	9.5
1985	Michigan	6.8
1986	Oklahoma	6.6

Year	Team	Avg.
1987	Oklahoma	7.5
1988	Auburn	7.2
1989	Miami (Fla.)	9.3
1990	Central Mich.	8.9
1991	Miami (Fla.)	9.1
1992	Arizona	8.9
1993	Florida St.	9.4

**Record tied.

Other Annual Team Champions

PUNTING

Year	Team	#Avg.
1937	Iowa	43.0
1938	Arkansas	41.6
1939	Auburn	43.3
1940	Auburn	42.3
1941	Clemson	42.3
1942	Tulsa	41.3
1943	Michigan	39.2
1944	UCLA	43.0
1945	Miami (Fla.)	39.9
1946	UTEP	41.2
1947	Duke	41.9
1948	North Caro.	44.0
1949	Furman	44.7
1950	Colorado	45.1
1951	Alabama	41.8
1952	Colorado	44.3
1953	Georgia	41.2
1954	New Mexico	42.6
1955	Michigan St.	41.2
1956	Colorado St.	42.2
1957	Utah St.	40.1
1958	Georgia	41.9
1959	Brigham Young	43.2
1960	Georgia	43.7
1961	Arizona St.	42.1
1962	Wyoming	42.6
1963	Southern Methodist	41.4
1964	Mississippi	44.1
1965	Arizona St.	44.0
1966	Tennessee	43.4
1967	Houston	44.4
1968	Wichita St.	43.2
1969	Georgia	43.5
1970	Utah	45.0
1971	Utah	46.7
1972	Southern Miss.	45.1
1973	Wake Forest	44.1
1974	Ohio St.	44.9
1975	Ohio St.	44.1
1976	Colorado St.	**44.4
1977	Mississippi	43.4
1978	Texas	41.7
1979	Mississippi	42.4
1980	Florida St.	42.6
1981	Michigan	43.1
1982	Vanderbilt	42.1
1983	Brigham Young	*45.0
1984	Ohio St.	44.0
1985	Colorado	43.6
1986	Michigan	43.1
1987	Ohio St.	40.7
1988	Brigham Young	42.9
1989	Colorado	43.8
1990	Pittsburgh	41.2
1991	Texas Tech	40.6
1992	Nebraska	41.7
1993	New Mexico	41.8

#Beginning in 1975, ranked on net punting average. *Record for net punting average. **Record for net punting average, minimum of 40 punts.

PUNT RETURNS

Year	Team	Avg.
1937	—	—
1938	—	—
1939	UCLA	16.3
1940	UCLA	16.2
1941	Colgate	18.7

Year	Team	Avg.
1942	—	—
1943	Columbia	20.9
1944	New York U.	22.0
1945	—	—
1946	Columbia	16.8
1947	Florida	19.7
1948	Oklahoma	†22.4
1949	Wichita St.	18.3
1950	Texas A&M	17.6
1951	Holy Cross	18.1
1952	Arizona St.	‡25.2
1953	Kansas St.	23.8
1954	Miami (Fla.)	19.7
1955	North Caro.	22.5
1956	Cincinnati	17.7
1957	North Texas	17.5
1958	Notre Dame	17.6
1959	Wyoming	16.6
1960	Arizona	17.7
1961	Memphis	17.4
1962	West Tex. A&M	18.4
1963	Army	18.1
1964	UTEP	16.9
1965	Georgia Tech	23.0
1966	Brown	21.0
1967	Memphis	16.3
1968	Army	17.4
1969	Davidson	21.3
1970	Wichita St.	28.5
1971	Mississippi St.	20.8
1972	Georgia Tech	17.3
1973	Utah	23.4
1974	Auburn	16.6
1975	New Mexico St.	15.3
1976	Wichita St.	15.0
1977	Grambling	16.9
1978	McNeese St.	15.7
1979	Tennessee St.	16.9
1980	Georgia	16.5
1981	North Caro. St.	13.4
1982	Auburn	15.8
1983	San Diego St.	17.0
1984	Florida	13.8
1985	Utah	20.7
1986	Arizona St.	17.9
1987	Stanford	15.4
1988	Florida St.	15.5
1989	Ohio	18.2
1990	Michigan	15.6
1991	Alabama	16.9
1992	Northwestern	21.8
1993	Texas A&M	17.9

†Record for minimum of 30 punt returns. ‡Record for minimum of 15 punt returns.

KICKOFF RETURNS

Year	Team	Avg.
1937	—	—
1938	—	—
1939	Wake Forest	32.9
1940	Minnesota	36.4
1941	Tulane	32.1
1942	—	—
1943	Navy	28.8
1944	—	—
1945	—	—
1946	William & Mary	31.7
1947	Southern Methodist	31.4
1948	Wyoming	27.4
1949	Army	34.1
1950	Wyoming	29.3
1951	Marquette	25.0
1952	Wake Forest	25.1
1953	Texas Tech	23.8
1954	Arizona	26.1
1955	Southern Cal	25.8
1956	Georgia Tech	24.6
1957	Notre Dame	27.6
1958	Tulsa	25.8
1959	Auburn	25.8
1960	Yale	26.7
1961	Harvard	25.9
1962	Alabama	28.9
1963	Memphis	27.7

Year	Team	Avg.
1964	Cornell	27.1
1965	Dartmouth	28.7
1966	Notre Dame	29.6
1967	Air Force	25.3
1968	Louisville	25.7
1969	Brigham Young	28.7
1970	South Caro.	26.5
1971	Miami (Fla.)	24.1
1972	Michigan	26.9
1973	Rice	†27.5
1974	Southern Cal	25.7
1975	Maryland	$29.5
1976	South Caro.	27.0
1977	Miami (Ohio)	24.6
1978	Utah St.	26.7
1979	Brigham Young	26.3
1980	Oklahoma	33.2
1981	Iowa	29.1
1982	Utah	25.5
1983	Tennessee	28.8
1984	Texas Tech	25.2
1985	Air Force	27.0
1986	Clemson	26.1
1987	Oklahoma St.	23.7
1988	Notre Dame	24.2
1989	Colorado	26.1
1990	Nebraska	27.8
1991	New Mexico St.	25.2
1992	Florida St.	30.3
1993	Texas A&M	31.2

†Record for minimum of 35 kickoff returns. $Record for minimum of 25 kickoff returns.

Toughest-Schedule Annual Leaders

The NCAA's toughest-schedule program (which began in 1977) is based on what all Division I-A opponents did against other Division I-A teams when not playing the team in question. Games against non-I-A teams are deleted, and nine intradivision games are required to qualify. (Bowl games are not included.) The leaders:

Year	Team (†Record)	W	L	T	¢Opponents' Record Pct.
1977	Miami (Fla.) (3-8-0)	66	42	2	.609
	Penn St. (10-1-0)	61	39	2	.608
1978	Notre Dame (8-3-0)	77	31	2	.709
	Southern Cal (11-1-0)	79	40	1	.663
1979	UCLA (5-6-0)	71	37	2	.655
	South Caro. (8-3-0)	69	38	2	.642
1980	Florida St. (10-1-0)	70	34	0	.673
	Miami (Fla.) (8-3-0)	64	33	1	.658
1981	Penn St. (9-2-0)	71	33	2	.679
	Temple (5-5-0)	71	33	2	.669
1982	Penn St. (10-1-0)	63	34	2	.646
	Kentucky (0-10-1)	63	34	5	.642
1983	Auburn (10-1-0)	70	31	3	.688
	UCLA (6-4-1)	68	37	5	.641
1984	Penn St. (6-5-0)	58	36	3	.613
	Georgia (7-4-0)	60	39	4	.602
1985	Notre Dame (5-6-0)	72	29	3	.707
	Alabama (8-2-1)	65	32	5	.662
1986	Florida (6-5-0)	64	29	3	.682
	Louisiana St. (9-2-0)	67	36	2	.648
1987	Notre Dame (8-3-0)	71	34	2	.673
	Florida St. (10-1-0)	60	29	4	.667
1988	Virginia Tech (3-8-0)	74	36	0	.673
	Arizona (7-4-0)	70	37	3	.650

†Not including bowl games. ¢When not playing the team listed.

Top 10 Toughest-Schedule Leaders for 1989-93

1989

Team	¢Opp. Record	Pct.
1. Notre Dame	74-38-4	.655
2. Louisiana St.	67-41-1	.619
3. Colorado St.	67-42-3	.612
4. Florida St.	65-41-2	.611
	Texas	65-41-2	.611
6. South Caro.	57-36-2	.611
7. Auburn	64-42-1	.603
8. Oregon St.	64-42-3	.601
9. Maryland	62-41-2	.600
	Tennessee	62-41-2	.600

1990

Team	¢Opp. Record	Pct.
1. Colorado	72-42-3	.628
2. Stanford	67-39-4	.627
3. Purdue	60-36-3	.621
4. Notre Dame	63-38-5	.618
5. Texas	65-40-3	.616
6. Miami (Fla.)	65-41-5	.608
7. Virginia Tech	59-38-3	.605
8. Georgia	62-41-2	.600
9. Maryland	60-40-2	.598
10. Penn St.	63-43-4	.591

1991

Team	¢Opp. Record	Pct.
1. South Caro.	57-31-2	.644
2. Florida	66-37-1	.639
3. Louisiana St.	60-38-0	.612
4. Florida St.	64-40-3	.612
5. Maryland	62-39-3	.611
6. Southern Cal	67-43-0	.609
7. Oklahoma St.	62-40-3	.605
8. Northern Ill.	44-30-4	.590
9. Tennessee	63-44-0	.589
10. Houston	61-43-2	.585

1992

Team	¢Opp. Record	Pct.
1. Southern Cal	68-38-4	.636
2. Stanford	73-43-4	.625
3. Florida	72-46-1	.609
4. Northwestern	64-41-7	.603
5. Arizona	64-43-1	.597
6. Missouri	55-37-5	.593
7. Arkansas	58-40-0	.592
8. Oregon St.	65-46-0	.586
	Louisiana St.	64-45-2	.586
10. Iowa	65-46-7	.581

1993

Team	¢Opp. Record	Pct.
1. Louisiana St.	67-38-5	.632
2. Purdue	66-38-3	.631
3. Miami (Fla.)	62-36-2	.630
4. Maryland	68-40-0	.630
5. Florida	72-42-5	.626
6. Pittsburgh	65-39-3	.621
7. Southern Cal	73-46-1	.613
8. Northwestern	65-41-2	.611
9. UCLA	67-43-0	.609
10. Florida St.	71-46-0	.607

†Not including bowl games. ¢When not playing the team listed.

Annual Most-Improved Teams

Year	Team	$Games Improved	From		To		Coach
1937	California	4½	1936	6-5-0	1937	*10-0-1	Stub Allison
	Syracuse	4½	1936	1-7-0	1937	5-2-1	#Ossie Solem
1938	Texas Christian	5½	1937	4-4-2	1938	*11-0-0	Dutch Meyer
1939	Texas A&M	5½	1938	4-4-1	1939	*11-0-0	Homer Norton
1940	Stanford	8	1939	1-7-1	1940	*10-0-0	#Clark Shaughnessy
1941	Vanderbilt	4½	1940	3-6-1	1941	8-2-0	Red Sanders
1942	Utah St.	5½	1941	0-8-0	1942	6-3-1	Dick Romney
1943	Purdue	8	1942	1-8-0	1943	9-0-0	Elmer Burnham
1944	Ohio St.	6	1943	3-6-0	1944	9-0-0	#Carroll Widdoes
1945	Miami (Fla.)	7	1944	1-7-1	1945	*9-1-1	Jack Harding
1946	Illinois	5	1945	2-6-1	1946	*8-2-0	Ray Eliot
	Kentucky	5	1945	2-8-0	1946	7-3-0	#Paul "Bear" Bryant
1947	California	6½	1946	2-7-0	1947	9-1-0	#Lynn "Pappy" Waldorf
1948	Clemson	6	1947	4-5-0	1948	*11-0-0	Frank Howard
1949	Tulsa	5	1948	0-9-1	1949	5-4-1	J. O. Brothers
1950	Brigham Young	5	1949	0-11-0	1950	4-5-1	Chick Atkinson
	Texas A&M	5	1949	1-8-1	1950	*7-4-0	Harry Stiteler
1951	Georgia Tech	6	1950	5-6-0	1951	*11-0-1	Bobby Dodd
1952	Alabama	4½	1951	5-6-0	1952	*10-2-0	Harold "Red" Drew
1953	Texas Tech	7	1952	3-7-1	1953	*11-1-0	DeWitt Weaver
1954	Denver	5	1953	3-5-2	1954	9-1-0	Bob Blackman
1955	Texas A&M	6½	1954	1-9-0	1955	7-2-1	Paul "Bear" Bryant
1956	Iowa	5	1955	3-5-1	1956	*9-1-0	Forest Evashevski

The legend of Paul "Bear" Bryant includes coaching the nation's most-improved major-college team in two different seasons—1946 (Kentucky) and 1955 (Texas A&M).

Led by freshman sensation Tony Dorsett, Pittsburgh posted a 6-5-1 record in 1973 after finishing 1-10-0 the year before. Three seasons later, the Panthers captured the mythical national championship.

Year	Team	$Games Improved	From		To		Coach
1957	Notre Dame	5	1956	2-8-0	1957	7-3-0	Terry Brennan
	Texas	5	1956	1-9-0	1957	†6-4-1	#Darrell Royal
1958	Air Force	6	1957	3-6-1	1958	‡9-0-1	#Ben Martin
1959	Washington	6½	1958	3-7-0	1959	*10-1-0	Jim Owens
1960	Minnesota	5½	1959	2-7-0	1960	†8-2-0	Murray Warmath
	North Caro. St.	5½	1959	1-9-0	1960	6-3-1	Earle Edwards
1961	Villanova	6	1960	2-8-0	1961	*8-2-0	Alex Bell
1962	Southern Cal	6	1961	4-5-1	1962	*11-0-0	John McKay
1963	Illinois	6	1962	2-7-0	1963	*8-1-1	Pete Elliott
1964	Notre Dame	6½	1963	2-7-0	1964	9-1-0	#Ara Parseghian
1965	UTEP	6½	1964	0-8-2	1965	*8-3-0	#Bobby Dobbs
1966	Dayton	6½	1965	1-8-1	1966	8-2-0	John McVay
1967	Indiana	7	1966	1-8-1	1967	†9-2-0	John Pont
1968	Arkansas	5	1967	4-5-1	1968	*10-1-0	Frank Broyles
1969	UCLA	5½	1968	3-7-0	1969	8-1-1	Tommy Prothro
1970	Tulsa	5	1969	1-9-0	1970	6-4-0	#Claude Gibson
1971	Army	5	1970	1-9-1	1971	6-4-0	Tom Cahill
	Georgia	5	1970	5-5-0	1971	*11-1-0	Vince Dooley
1972	Pacific (Cal.)	5	1971	3-8-0	1972	8-3-0	Chester Caddas
	Southern Cal	5	1971	6-4-1	1972	*12-0-0	John McKay
	UCLA	5	1971	2-7-1	1972	8-3-0	Pepper Rodgers
1973	Pittsburgh	5	1972	1-10-0	1973	†6-5-1	#Johnny Majors
1974	Baylor	5½	1973	2-9-0	1974	†8-4-0	Grant Teaff
1975	Arizona St.	5	1974	7-5-0	1975	*12-0-0	Frank Kush
1976	Houston	7	1975	2-8-0	1976	*10-2-0	Bill Yeoman
1977	Miami (Ohio)	7	1976	3-8-0	1977	10-1-0	Dick Crum
1978	Tulsa	6	1977	3-8-0	1978	9-2-0	John Cooper
1979	Wake Forest	6½	1978	1-10-0	1979	†8-4-0	John Mackovic
1980	Florida	7	1979	0-10-1	1980	*8-4-0	Charley Pell
1981	Clemson	5½	1980	6-5-0	1981	*12-0-0	Danny Ford
1982	New Mexico	6	1981	4-7-1	1982	10-1-0	Joe Morrison
	Southwestern La.	6	1981	1-9-1	1982	7-3-1	Sam Robertson
1983	Kentucky	5½	1982	0-10-1	1983	†6-5-1	Jerry Claiborne
	Memphis	5½	1982	1-10-0	1983	6-4-1	Rex Dockery
1984	Army	6	1983	2-9-0	1984	*8-3-1	Jim Young
1985	Colorado	5½	1984	1-10-0	1985	†7-5-0	Bill McCartney
	Fresno St.	5½	1984	6-6-0	1985	*11-0-1	Jim Sweeney
1986	San Jose St.	7	1985	2-8-1	1986	*10-2-0	Claude Gilbert
1987	Syracuse	6	1986	5-6-0	1987	‡11-0-1	Dick MacPherson
1988	West Va.	5	1987	6-6-0	1988	†11-1-0	Don Nehlen
	Washington St.	5	1987	3-7-1	1988	*9-3-0	Dennis Erickson
1989	Tennessee	5½	1988	5-6-0	1989	*11-1-0	Johnny Majors
1990	Temple	6	1989	1-10-0	1990	7-4-0	Jerry Berndt
1991	Tulsa	6½	1990	3-8-0	1991	*10-2-0	Dave Rader
1992	Hawaii	6	1991	4-7-1	1992	*11-2-0	Bob Wagner
1993	Southwestern La.	6	1992	2-9-0	1993	8-3-0	Nelson Stokley
	Virginia Tech	6	1992	2-8-1	1993	*9-3-0	Frank Beamer

$To determine games improved, add the difference in victories between the two seasons to the difference in losses, then divide by two; ties not counted. Bowl victory (*), loss (†), tie (‡) included in record. #First year as head coach at that college.

All-Time Most-Improved Teams

Games	Team (Year)	Games	Team (Year)
8	Purdue (1943)	6½	Tulsa (1991)
8	Stanford (1940)	6½	Wake Forest (1979)
7	San Jose St. (1986)	6½	Toledo (1967)
7	Florida (1980)	6½	Dayton (1966)
7	Miami (Ohio) (1977)	6½	UTEP (1965)
7	Houston (1976)	6½	Notre Dame (1964)
7	Indiana (1967)	6½	Washington (1959)
7	Texas Tech (1953)	6½	Texas A&M (1955)
7	Miami (Fla.) (1945)	6½	California (1947)

1993 Most-Improved Teams

College (Coach)	1992	1993	$Games Improved
Southwestern La. (Nelson Stokley)	2-9-0	8-3-0	6
Virginia Tech (Frank Beamer)	2-8-1	9-3-0	6
Auburn (Terry Bowden)	5-5-1	11-0-0	5½
Cincinnati (Tim Murphy)	3-8-0	8-3-0	5
Wisconsin (Barry Alvarez)	5-6-0	10-1-1	5
West Va. (Don Nehlen)	5-4-2	11-1-0	4½
California (Keith Gilbertson)	4-7-0	9-4-0	4
Kansas St. (Bill Snyder)	5-6-0	9-2-1	4
Arizona (Dick Tomey)	6-5-1	10-2-0	3½
Clemson (Ken Hatfield)	5-6-0	9-3-0	3½
Louisville (Howard Schnellenberger)	5-6-0	9-3-0	3½
Ball St. (Paul Schudel)	5-6-0	8-3-1	3
Eastern Mich. (Ron Cooper)	1-10-0	4-7-0	3
Louisiana St. (Curley Hallman)	2-9-0	5-6-0	3
Navy (George Chaump)	1-10-0	4-7-0	3
New Mexico (Dennis Franchione)	3-8-0	6-5-0	3
Ohio (Tom Lichtenberg)	1-10-0	4-7-0	3
Penn St. (Joe Paterno)	7-5-0	10-2-0	3
Wyoming (Joe Tiller)	5-7-0	8-4-0	3

$To determine games improved, add the difference in victories between the two seasons to the difference in losses; ties not counted.

All-Time Team Won-Lost Records

Classified as Division I-A for the last 10 years. Won-lost-tied record includes bowl games.

PERCENTAGE (TOP 26)

Team	Yrs.	Won	Lost	Tied	Pct.†	*Bowls W-L-T	Total Games
Notre Dame#	105	723	211	41	.762	13-6-0	975
Michigan	114	739	242	36	.749	12-13-0	1,017
Alabama	99	691	237	44	.734	26-17-3	972
Oklahoma	99	659	240	52	.720	20-10-1	951
Texas	101	687	273	32	.709	16-16-2	992
Ohio St.	104	659	265	53	.702	13-13-0	977
Southern Cal	101	630	254	52	.701	23-13-0	936
Nebraska$	104	673	290	40	.691	14-18-0	1,003
Penn St.	107	674	291	41	.690	18-10-2	1,006
Tennessee	97	636	276	53	.687	18-16-0	965
Central Mich.	93	480	255	36	.646	3-1-0	771
Florida St.√	47	316	176	16	.638	14-7-2	508
Washington√	104	562	310	49	.637	12-8-1	921
Army	104	588	327	50	.635	2-1-0	965
Miami (Ohio)	105	546	308	42	.633	5-2-0	896
Louisiana St.√	100	573	325	46	.631	11-16-1	944
Georgia	100	589	333	53	.631	15-13-3	975
Arizona St.	81	444	255	24	.631	9-5-1	723
Auburn√	101	558	335	46	.619	12-9-2	939
Colorado	104	557	348	36	.611	6-12-0	941
Miami (Fla.)	67	411	260	19	.609	10-10-0	690
Michigan St.	97	521	328	43	.608	5-6-0	892
Bowling Green	75	389	242	52	.608	2-3-0	683
UCLA	75	437	280	37	.604	10-8-1	754
Minnesota	110	555	359	43	.602	2-3-0	957
Fresno St.	72	431	280	28	.602	7-2-0	739

ALPHABETICAL LISTING

Team	Yrs.	Won	Lost	Tied	Pct.†	*Bowls W-L-T	Total Games
Air Force	38	210	197	13	.515	6-5-1	420
Alabama	99	691	237	44	.734	26-17-3	972
Arizona	89	459	313	33	.591	3-6-1	805
Arizona St.	81	444	255	24	.631	9-5-1	723
Arkansas	100	550	361	40	.599	9-15-3	951
Army	104	588	327	50	.635	2-1-0	965
Auburn√	101	558	335	46	.619	12-9-2	939
Ball St.	69	324	258	31	.554	0-3-1	613
Baylor	91	468	402	43	.536	8-7-0	913
Boston College	95	497	351	35	.583	4-5-0	883
Bowling Green	75	389	242	52	.608	2-3-0	683
Brigham Young	69	370	308	26	.544	5-12-1	704
California	98	530	379	51	.579	5-6-1	960
Central Mich.	93	480	255	36	.646	3-1-0	771
Cincinnati	106	445	456	51	.494	1-1-0	952
Clemson	98	526	356	45	.592	12-7-0	927
Colorado	104	557	348	36	.611	6-12-0	941
Colorado St.	95	357	434	33	.453	1-1-0	824
Duke	81	414	321	31	.561	3-4-0	766
East Caro.	58	282	269	12	.512	2-0-0	563
Eastern Mich.	101	368	379	46	.493	1-0-0	793
Florida	87	491	332	39	.592	10-11-0	862
Florida St.√	47	316	176	16	.638	14-7-2	508
Fresno St.	72	431	280	28	.602	7-2-0	739
Georgia	100	589	333	53	.631	15-13-3	975
Georgia Tech	101	555	369	43	.596	17-8-0	967
Hawaii	78	414	287	25	.587	1-1-0	726
Houston	48	282	218	15	.562	7-5-1	515
Illinois	104	496	407	49	.547	4-6-0	952
Indiana	106	382	488	44	.442	3-5-0	914
Iowa	105	465	432	38	.518	6-6-1	935
Iowa St.	102	421	460	45	.479	0-4-0	926
Kansas	104	477	453	58	.512	2-5-0	988
Kansas St.√	98	326	537	42	.383	1-1-0	905
Kent	71	257	359	27	.421	0-1-0	643
Kentucky√	103	490	447	44	.522	5-3-0	981
Louisiana St.√	100	573	325	46	.631	11-16-1	944
Louisville√	75	325	349	17	.483	3-1-0	691
Maryland	101	505	438	42	.534	6-9-2	985
Memphis√	78	355	347	32	.505	1-0-0	734

Team	Yrs.	Won	Lost	Tied	Pct.†	*Bowls W-L-T	Total Games
Miami (Fla.)	67	411	260	19	.609	10-10-0	690
Miami (Ohio)	105	546	308	42	.633	5-2-0	896
Michigan	114	739	242	36	.749	12-13-0	1,017
Michigan St.	97	521	328	43	.608	5-6-0	892
Minnesota	110	555	359	43	.602	2-3-0	957
Mississippi√	99	513	380	35	.572	14-11-0	928
Mississippi St.√	94	406	429	39	.487	4-4-0	874
Missouri	103	507	425	51	.542	8-11-0	983
Navy	113	546	425	57	.559	3-4-1	1,028
Nebraska$	104	673	290	40	.691	14-18-0	1,003
Nevada-Las Vegas	26	162	122	4	.569	1-0-0	288
New Mexico	95	361	419	31	.464	2-2-1	811
New Mexico St.	98	363	428	32	.461	2-0-1	823
North Caro.	103	548	395	54	.577	7-11-0	997
North Caro. St.	102	434	433	55	.501	7-8-1	922
Northern Ill.	92	418	353	11	.540	1-0-0	822
Northwestern	106	371	523	42	.419	1-0-0	936
Notre Dame#	105	723	211	41	.762	13-6-0	975
Ohio	98	421	407	47	.508	0-2-0	875
Ohio St.	104	659	265	53	.702	13-13-0	977
Oklahoma	99	659	240	52	.720	20-10-1	951
Oklahoma St.	92	410	427	47	.490	9-3-0	884
Oregon	98	433	405	46	.516	3-6-0	884
Oregon St.	97	392	441	50	.472	2-2-0	883
Pacific (Cal.)	75	337	384	23	.468	3-1-1	744
Penn St.	107	674	291	41	.690	18-10-2	1,006
Pittsburgh	104	567	384	42	.592	8-10-0	993
Purdue	106	471	407	45	.535	4-1-0	923
Rice√	82	351	442	31	.445	4-3-0	824
Rutgers	124	530	482	41	.523	0-1-0	1,053
San Diego St.	71	400	273	32	.590	2-3-0	705
San Jose St.	75	379	315	38	.544	4-3-0	732
South Caro.	100	444	436	43	.504	0-8-0	923
Southern Cal	101	630	254	52	.701	23-13-0	936
Southern Methodist@	77	391	354	53	.523	4-6-1	798
Southern Miss.√	77	416	288	26	.588	2-6-0	730
Southwestern La.	86	406	386	32	.512	0-1-0	824
Stanford	87	480	329	47	.581	8-7-1	856
Syracuse	104	583	381	49	.599	8-6-1	1,015
Temple	95	367	391	52	.485	1-1-0	810
Tennessee	97	636	276	53	.687	18-16-0	965
Texas	101	687	273	32	.709	16-16-2	992
Texas A&M	99	549	361	47	.598	10-10-0	957
Texas Christian	97	440	446	56	.497	4-9-1	942
Texas Tech	69	385	321	32	.543	4-14-1	738
Toledo	73	345	322	22	.517	4-1-0	689
Tulane√	100	418	458	38	.478	2-6-0	914
Tulsa	89	474	319	27	.595	4-7-0	820
UCLA	75	437	280	37	.604	10-8-1	754
Utah	100	473	364	31	.563	2-1-0	868
Utah St.	96	417	365	31	.532	1-4-0	813
UTEP	76	291	399	29	.425	5-3-0	719
Vanderbilt	104	502	428	50	.522	1-1-1	980
Virginia	104	501	459	48	.521	2-4-0	1,008
Virginia Tech	100	513	380	46	.571	2-5-0	939
Wake Forest	92	326	488	33	.404	2-2-0	847
Washington√	104	562	310	49	.637	12-8-1	921
Washington St.	97	401	398	45	.502	3-2-0	844
West Va.	101	557	399	45	.591	8-8-0	981
Western Mich.	88	413	309	24	.570	0-1-0	746
Wisconsin	104	478	401	50	.541	2-5-0	929
Wyoming	96	390	404	28	.491	4-5-0	822

The following are not listed above because of reclassification to Division I-A (year joined I-A):

Team	Yrs.	Won	Lost	Tied	Pct.†	*Bowls W-L-T	Total Games
Akron (1987)	93	414	360	36	.533	0-0-0	810
Arkansas St. (1992)	79	347	323	37	.517	0-0-0	707
Louisiana Tech (1989)	90	453	315	37	.586	0-0-1	805
Nevada (1992)	83	388	333	32	.537	0-1-0	753
Northeast La. (1994)	43	205	233	8	.469	5-3-0	446

VICTORIES

Team	Wins	Team	Wins
Michigan	739	Arizona St.	444
Notre Dame	723	South Caro.	444
Alabama	691	Texas Christian	440
Texas	687	UCLA	437
Penn St.	674	North Caro. St.	434
Nebraska$	673	Oregon	433
Ohio St.	659	Fresno St.	431
Oklahoma	659	Iowa St.	421
Tennessee	636	Ohio	421
Southern Cal	630	Northern Ill.	418
Georgia	589	Tulane√	418
Army	588	Utah St.	417
Syracuse	583	Southern Miss.√	416
Louisiana St.√	573	Duke	414
Pittsburgh	567	Hawaii	414
Washington√	562	Western Mich.	413
Auburn√	558	Miami (Fla.)	411
Colorado	557	Oklahoma St.	410
West Va.	557	Mississippi St.√	406
Georgia Tech	555	Southwestern La.	406
Minnesota	555	Washington St.	401
Arkansas	550	San Diego St.	400
Texas A&M	549	Oregon St.	392
North Caro.	548	Southern Methodist@	391
Miami (Ohio)	546	Wyoming	390
Navy	546	Bowling Green	389
California	530	Texas Tech	385
Rutgers	530	Indiana	382
Clemson	526	San Jose St.	379
Michigan St.	521	Northwestern	371
Mississippi√	513	Brigham Young	370
Virginia Tech	513	Eastern Mich.	368
Missouri	507	Temple	367
Maryland	505	New Mexico St.	363
Vanderbilt	502	New Mexico	361
Virginia	501	Colorado St.	357
Boston College	497	Memphis√	355
Illinois	496	Rice√	351
Florida	491	Toledo	345
Kentucky√	490	Pacific (Cal.)	337
Central Mich.	480	Kansas St.√	326
Stanford	480	Wake Forest	326
Wisconsin	478	Louisville√	325
Kansas	477	Ball St.	324
Tulsa	474	Florida St.√	316
Utah	473	UTEP	291
Purdue	471	East Caro.	282
Baylor	468	Houston	282
Iowa	465	Kent	257
Arizona	459	Air Force	210
Cincinnati	445	Nevada-Las Vegas	162

The following are not listed above because of reclassification to Division I-A:

Louisiana Tech	453
Akron	414
Nevada	388
Arkansas St.	347
Northeast La.	205

†Ties computed as half won and half lost. *Record in a major bowl game only (i.e., a team's opponent was classified as a major-college team that season or it was classified as a major-college team at the time.) #Leader since 1948. Notre Dame displaced all-time leader Yale .8082 to .8081 after the 1947 season. $Record adjusted in 1989 (8 less victories, 1 less defeat). @ Football program suspended 1987-88. √Includes games forfeited or changed by action of the NCAA Council.

Records in the 1990s

(1990-91-92-93, Including Bowls and Playoffs)

PERCENTAGE

Team	W-L-T	Pct.†	Team	W-L-T	Pct.†
Florida St.	44-6-0	.880	Arizona St.	22-22-0	.500
Miami (Fla.)	42-6-0	.875	Mississippi St.	22-22-2	.500
Texas A&M	41-8-1	.830	Utah	24-24-0	.500
Notre Dame	40-8-1	.827	Utah St.	22-22-1	.500
Alabama	40-9-1	.810	Virginia Tech	22-22-1	.500
Washington	38-9-0	.809	Kansas	22-23-1	.489
Nebraska	38-9-1	.802	Michigan St.	22-23-1	.489
Florida	39-10-0	.796	Memphis	21-22-1	.489
Michigan	36-9-3	.781	Oregon	22-24-0	.478
Colorado	36-9-4	.776	Southern Miss.	21-23-1	.478
Tennessee	36-10-3	.765	Tulsa	21-23-1	.478
Nevada*	39-12-0	.765	Wisconsin	21-23-1	.478
Penn St.	37-12-0	.755	Akron	20-22-2	.477
Fresno St.	35-12-1	.740	Army	21-23-0	.477
Ohio St.	33-12-3	.719	Rice	21-23-0	.477
Syracuse	33-12-3	.719	Colorado St.	22-25-0	.468
Clemson	33-13-1	.713	Texas Tech	21-24-0	.467
Bowling Green	30-11-4	.711	Washington St.	21-24-0	.467
Northeast La.**	33-14-1	.698	Rutgers	20-24-0	.455
Oklahoma	31-13-2	.696	Houston	19-24-1	.443
North Caro.	32-14-0	.691	South Caro.	18-24-2	.432
Auburn	29-14-2	.667	Texas Christian	18-25-1	.420
North Caro. St.	32-16-1	.663	Arkansas	17-26-2	.400
Virginia	30-16-1	.649	Southwestern La.	17-26-1	.398
Brigham Young	32-17-2	.647	Louisiana St.	17-27-0	.386
Western Mich.	27-15-2	.636	Nevada-Las Vegas	17-27-0	.386
California	30-17-1	.635	Northern Ill.	17-27-0	.386
Georgia Tech	29-17-0	.628	Kentucky	17-28-0	.378
Iowa	29-18-1	.615	Cincinnati	16-28-0	.364
Georgia	28-18-0	.609	Wake Forest	16-29-0	.356
Mississippi	28-18-0	.609	Pittsburgh	15-29-1	.344
UCLA	28-18-0	.609	Iowa St.	14-28-2	.341
Toledo	26-17-1	.602	Pacific (Cal.)	15-30-0	.333
West Va.	26-17-2	.600	Minnesota	14-30-0	.318
Ball St.	26-18-1	.589	Missouri	13-29-2	.318
Texas	26-18-1	.589	New Mexico St.	14-30-0	.318
Central Mich.	24-16-5	.589	Vanderbilt	14-30-0	.318
Kansas St.	26-18-1	.589	Duke	13-30-1	.307
Arizona	27-19-1	.585	New Mexico	14-32-0	.304
Hawaii	28-20-1	.582	Maryland	13-31-1	.300
Baylor	26-19-1	.576	Oklahoma St.	11-31-2	.273
Louisville	26-19-1	.576	Navy	11-33-0	.250
Indiana	26-19-2	.574	Purdue	11-33-0	.250
Stanford	27-20-0	.574	Temple	11-33-0	.250
Air Force	28-21-0	.571	Eastern Mich.	10-33-1	.239
San Jose St.	24-19-2	.556	Northwestern	10-34-0	.227
Boston College	25-20-1	.554	Southern Methodist	9-33-2	.227
San Diego St.	25-20-2	.553	Tulane	10-35-0	.222
Wyoming	26-21-1	.552	UTEP	9-36-1	.207
Louisiana Tech	23-19-3	.544	Ohio	8-34-2	.205
Illinois	25-21-1	.543	Arkansas St.*	7-34-2	.186
Southern Cal	25-22-2	.531	Oregon St.	7-36-1	.170
East Caro.	23-22-0	.511	Kent	5-39-0	.114
Miami (Ohio)	21-20-3	.511			

VICTORIES

(Minimum 30 Victories)

Team	Wins	Team	Wins
Florida St.	44	Fresno St.	35
Miami (Fla.)	42	Clemson	33
Texas A&M	41	Northeast La.**	33
Alabama	40	Ohio St.	33
Notre Dame	40	Syracuse	33
Florida	39	Brigham Young	32
Nevada*	39	North Caro.	32
Nebraska	38	North Caro. St.	32
Washington	38	Oklahoma	31
Penn St.	37	Bowling Green	30
Colorado	36	California	30
Michigan	36	Virginia	30
Tennessee	36		

†Ties counted as half won and half lost. *Joined I-A in 1992. **Joined I-A in 1994.

Winningest Teams by Decade

(By Percentage; Bowls and Playoffs Included)

1980-89

Rank	Team	W-L-T	Pct.†	Rank	Team	W-L-T	Pct.†
1.	Nebraska	93-17-0	.846	11.	Florida St.	77-26-3	.741
2.	Miami (Fla.)	87-19-0	.821	12.	Auburn	76-29-1	.722
3.	Brigham Young	92-23-0	.800	13.	Washington	75-29-1	.717
4.	Oklahoma	84-21-2	.794	14.	Alabama	75-30-2	.710
5.	Georgia	82-21-4	.785		Arkansas	75-30-2	.710
6.	Penn St.	81-24-1	.769	16.	Ohio St.	74-31-2	.701
7.	UCLA	78-23-5	.759	17.	Florida	69-32-3	.678
8.	Southern Meth.	61-19-1	.759	18.	Fresno St.	69-33-1	.675
9.	Clemson	76-23-4	.757	19.	Southern Cal	69-33-2	.673
10.	Michigan	79-27-2	.741	20.	Arizona St.	67-32-3	.672

1970-79

Rank	Team	W-L-T	Pct.†	Rank	Team	W-L-T	Pct.†
1.	Oklahoma	102-13-3	.877	11.	Arizona St.	90-28-0	.763
2.	Alabama	103-16-1	.863	12.	Yale@	67-21-2	.756
3.	Michigan	96-16-3	.848	13.	San Diego St.	82-26-2	.755
4.	Tennessee St.*	85-17-2	.827	14.	Miami (Ohio)	80-26-2	.750
5.	Nebraska	98-20-4	.820	15.	Central Mich.#	80-27-3	.741
6.	Penn St.	96-22-0	.814	16.	Arkansas	79-31-5	.709
7.	Ohio St.	91-20-3	.811	17.	Houston	80-33-2	.704
8.	Notre Dame	91-22-0	.805	18.	Louisiana Tech#	77-34-2	.690
9.	Southern Cal	93-21-5	.803	19.	McNeese St.#	75-33-4	.688
10.	Texas	88-26-1	.770	20.	Dartmouth@	60-27-3	.683

1960-69

Rank	Team	W-L-T	Pct.†	Rank	Team	W-L-T	Pct.†
1.	Alabama	85-12-3	.865	11.	Memphis	70-25-1	.734
2.	Texas	80-18-2	.810	12.	Arizona St.	72-26-1	.732
3.	Arkansas	80-19-1	.805	13.	Louisiana St.	70-25-5	.725
4.	Mississippi	72-20-6	.765		Nebraska	72-27-1	.725
5.	Bowling Green	71-22-2	.758	15.	Wyoming	69-26-4	.717
6.	Dartmouth@	68-22-0	.756	16.	Princeton@	64-26-0	.711
	Ohio St.	67-21-2	.756	17.	Utah St.	68-29-3	.695
8.	Missouri	72-22-6	.750	18.	Purdue	64-28-3	.689
	Southern Cal	73-23-4	.750	19.	Syracuse	68-31-0	.687
10.	Penn St.	73-26-0	.737	20.	Florida	66-30-4	.680
					Miami (Ohio)	66-30-4	.680
					Tennessee	65-29-6	.680

†Ties computed as half won and half lost. *In I-A less than 8 years, now a member of I-AA. @Now a member of I-AA. #A member of I-A less than 8 years.

National Poll Rankings

National Champion Major Selectors (1869 to Present)

Selector	Selection Format	Active Seasons First	Active Seasons Last	Active Seasons Total	Predated Seasons	Total Rankings
Frank Dickinson	Math	1926	1940	15	1924-25	17
Deke Houlgate	Math	1927	1958	32	1885-1926	72
Dick Dunkel	Math	1929	1993	65		65
William Boand	Math	1930	1960	31	1919-29	42
Paul Williamson	Math	1932	1963	32		32
Parke Davis	Research	1933	1933	1	1869-1932	65
Edward Litkenhous	Math	1934	1984	51		51
Richard Poling	Math	1935	1984	50	1924-34	61
Associated Press	Poll	1936	1993	58		58
Helms Athletic Foundation	Poll	1941	1982	42	1883-1940	100
Harry Devold	Math	1945	1993	49	1939-44	55
United Press International	Poll	1950	1990	41		41
Football Writers Association	Poll	1954	1993	40		40
Football News	Poll	1958	1993	36		36
National Football Foundation	Poll	1959	1990	32		32
Herman Mathews	Math	1966	1993	27		27
Sporting News	Poll	1975	1993	19		19
New York Times	Math	1979	1993	15		15
National Championship Foundation	Poll	1980	1993	14	1869-1979	124
Sports Illustrated	Poll	1981	1993	13		13
College Football Researchers Association	Poll	1982	1992	11	1919-81	74
USA Today/CNN	Poll	1982	1993	12		12
UPI/National Football Foundation	Poll	1991	1992	2		2
USA Today/National Football Foundation	Poll	1993	1993	1		1

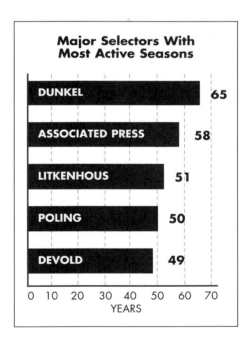

Major Selectors With Most Active Seasons

- DUNKEL — 65
- ASSOCIATED PRESS — 58
- LITKENHOUS — 51
- POLING — 50
- DEVOLD — 49

(x-axis: 0 10 20 30 40 50 60 70 — YEARS)

POLL SYSTEMS HISTORY

Associated Press (1936-present), the first major nationwide poll for ranking college football teams was voted on by sportswriters and broadcasters. It continues to this day and is probably the most well-known and widely circulated among all of history's polls.

Boand System (1930-60), known as the Azzi Ratem System developed by William Boand of Tucson, Arizona. He moved to Chicago in 1932. Appeared in many newspapers as well as Illustrated Football Annual (1932-42) and weekly in Football News (1942-44, 1951-60). Predated national champions from 1919-29.

College Football Researchers Association (1982-92), founded by Anthony Cusher of Reeder, North Dakota, and Robert Kirlin of Spokane, Washington. Announced its champion in its monthly bulletin and No. 1 team determined by top-10 vote of membership on a point system. Predated national champions from 1919-81.

Devold System (1945-present), a mathematical rating system developed by Harry Devold from Minneapolis, Minnesota, a former football player at Cornell. He eventually settled in the Detroit, Michigan, area and worked in the real estate business. The ratings have appeared in The Football News since 1962. Predated national champions from 1939-44.

Behind Heisman Trophy-winning quarterback Charlie Ward, Florida State was chosen national champion by all major selectors in 1993.

Dickinson System (1926-40), a mathematical point system devised by Frank Dickinson, a professor of economics at Illinois. The annual Dickinson ratings were emblematic of the national championship and the basis for awarding the Rissman National Trophy and the Knute K. Rockne Intercollegiate Memorial Trophy. Notre Dame gained permanent possession of the Rissman Trophy (named for Jack F. Rissman, a Chicago clothing manufacturer) after its third victory in 1930. Minnesota retired the Rockne Trophy (named in honor of the famous Notre Dame coach) after winning it for a third time in 1940. Subsequently, The Associated Press annual national champions were awarded the Williams Trophy and the Reverend J. Hugh O'Donnell Trophy. In 1947, Notre Dame retired the Williams Trophy (named after Henry L. Williams, Minnesota coach, and sponsored by the M Club of Minnesota). In 1956, Oklahoma retired the O'Donnell Trophy (named for Notre Dame's president and sponsored by Notre Dame alumni). Beginning with the 1957 season, the award was known as the AP Trophy, and since 1983 the award has been known as the Paul "Bear" Bryant Trophy.

Dunkel System (1929-present), a power index system devised by Dick Dunkel Sr. (1929-71); from 1972 by Dick Dunkel Jr.

Football News (1958-present), weekly poll of its staff writers has named a national champion since 1958.

Football Writers Association of America (1954-present), the No. 1 team of the year is determined by a five-person panel representing the nation's football writers. The national championship team named receives the Grantland Rice Award.

Helms Athletic Foundation (1941-82), originally known by this name from 1936-69 and established by the founding sponsor, Paul H. Helms, Los Angeles sportsman and philanthropist. After Helms' death in 1957, United Savings & Loan Association became its benefactor during 1970-72. A merger of United Savings and Citizen Savings was completed in 1973, and the Athletic Foundation became known as Citizens Savings Athletic Foundation. In 1982, First Interstate Bank assumed sponsorship for its final rankings. In 1941, Bill Schroeder, managing director of the Helms Athletic Foundation, retroactively selected the national football champions for the period beginning in 1883 (the first year of a scoring system) through 1941. Thereafter, Schroeder, who died in 1988, then chose, with the assistance of a Hall Board, the annual national champion after the bowl games.

Houlgate System (1927-58), a mathematical rating system developed by Deke Houlgate of Los Angeles, California. His ratings were syndicated in newspapers and published in Illustrated Football and the Football Thesaurus (1946-58).

Litkenhous (1934-84), a difference-by-score formula developed by Edward E. Litkenhous, a professor of chemical engineering at Vanderbilt, and his brother, Frank.

Mathews Grid Ratings (1966-present), a mathematical rating system developed by college mathematics professor Herman Mathews of Middlesboro, Kentucky. Has appeared in newspapers and The Football News.

National Championship Foundation (1980-present), established by Mike Riter of Germantown, New York. Issues annual report. Predated national champions from 1869-1979.

National Football Foundation (1959-90), the National Football Foundation and Hall of Fame named its first national champion in 1959. Headquartered in Larchmont, New York, the present National Football Foundation was established in 1954 to promote amateur athletics in America. The national champion was awarded the MacArthur Bowl from 1959-90. In 1991 and 1992, the NFF/HOF joined with UPI to award the MacArthur Bowl, and in 1993 the NFF/HOF joined with USA Today to present the Sears MacArthur Bowl.

New York Times (1979-present), a mathematical rating system introduced by this major newspaper.

Parke Davis (1933), a noted college football historian, Parke H. Davis, went back and named the championship teams from 1869 through the 1932 season. He also named a national champion at the conclusion of the 1933 season. Interestingly, the years 1869-75 were identified by Davis as the Pioneer Period; the years 1876-93 were called the Period of the American Intercollegiate Football Association, and the years 1894-1933 were referred to as the Period of Rules Committees and Conferences.

Poling System (1935-84), a mathematical rating system for college football teams developed by Richard Poling from Mansfield, Ohio, a former football player at Ohio Wesleyan. Poling's football ratings were published annually in the Football Review Supplement and in various newspapers. Predated national champions from 1924-34.

Sporting News (1975-present), voted on annually by the staff of this St. Louis-based nationally circulated sports publication.

Sports Illustrated (1981-present), voted on annually by a committee of writers representing various regions of the country for this nationally circulated sports magazine.

United Press International (1950-90), in 1950, the United Press news service began its poll of football coaches (replaced as coaches' poll after 1990 season). When the United Press merged with the International News Service in 1958, it became known as United Press International. The weekly UPI rankings were featured in newspapers and on radio and television nationwide. UPI and the National Football Foundation formed a coalition for 1991 and 1992 to name the MacArthur Bowl national champion.

USA Today/Cable News Network (1982-present), introduced a weekly poll of sportswriters in 1982 and ranked the top 25 teams in the nation with a point system. The poll results are featured in USA Today, a national newspaper, and on the Cable News Network, a national cable television network. Took over as the coaches' poll in 1991. USA Today also formed a coalition with the National Football Foundation in 1993 to name the MacArthur Bowl national champion.

Williamson System (1932-63), a power rating system chosen by Paul Williamson of New Orleans, Louisiana, a geologist and member of the Sugar Bowl committee.

Thanks from the NCAA Statistics Service to Robert A. Rosiek of Dearborn Heights, Michigan, who researched much of the former polls' history.

National Poll Champions, 1869-1899

Year	Parke Davis	Helms	Houlgate	National Championship Foundation
1869	Princeton/Rutgers			Princeton
1870	Princeton			Princeton
1871	*			*
1872	Princeton/Yale			Princeton
1873	Princeton			Princeton
1874	Yale/Harvard/Princeton			Yale
1875	Harvard/Colgate/Princeton			Harvard
1876	Yale			Yale
1877	Yale/Princeton			Yale
1878	Princeton			Princeton
1879	Princeton/Yale			Princeton
1880	Princeton/Yale			Princeton
1881	Yale/Princeton			Yale
1882	Yale			Yale
1883	Yale	Yale		Yale
1884	Yale/Princeton	Yale		Yale
1885	Princeton	Princeton	Princeton	Princeton
1886	Yale/Princeton	Yale	*	Yale
1887	Yale	Yale	Yale	Yale
1888	Yale	Yale	Yale	Yale
1889	Princeton	Princeton	Princeton	Princeton
1890	Harvard	Harvard	Harvard	Harvard
1891	Yale	Yale	Yale	Yale
1892	Yale	Yale	Yale	Yale
1893	Yale	Princeton	Princeton	Princeton
1894	Yale/Pennsylvania	Yale	Princeton	Yale
1895	Pennsylvania/Yale	Pennsylvania	Pennsylvania	Pennsylvania
1896	Princeton/Lafayette	Princeton	Princeton	Lafayette
1897	Pennsylvania/Yale	Pennsylvania	Pennsylvania	Pennsylvania
1898	Princeton	Harvard	Harvard	Harvard
1899	Princeton	Harvard	Harvard	Harvard

*No national champion selected.

Most National Championships Won or Shared, 1869-1899

PRINCETON – 20

YALE – 19

HARVARD – 5

PENNSYLVANIA – 3

National Poll Champions, 1900-1929

Year	Board	Football Research	Parke Davis	Helms	Houlgate	National Championship Foundation	Dickinson	Dunkel	Poling
1900			Yale	Yale	Yale	Yale			
1901			Yale	Michigan	Michigan	Michigan			
1902			Michigan/Yale	Michigan	Michigan	Michigan			
1903			Princeton	Princeton	Princeton	Princeton			
1904			Pennsylvania	Pennsylvania	Pennsylvania	Michigan			
1905			Yale	Chicago	Chicago	Chicago			
1906			Yale	Princeton	*	Princeton			
1907			Yale	Yale	Yale	Yale			
1908			Pennsylvania	Pennsylvania	Pennsylvania	Louisiana St.			
1909			Yale	Yale	Yale	Yale			
1910				Harvard	Harvard	Pittsburgh			
1911			Princeton	Princeton	Princeton	Penn St.			
1912			Harvard	Harvard	Harvard	Penn St.			
1913			Harvard/Chicago	Harvard	Harvard	Harvard			
1914			Army/Illinois	Army	Army	Army			
1915			Cornell/Pittsburgh	Cornell	Cornell	Cornell			
1916			Pittsburgh/Army	Pittsburgh	Pittsburgh	Pittsburgh			
1917				Georgia Tech	Georgia Tech	Georgia Tech			
1918				Pittsburgh	Pittsburgh	Michigan			
1919	Illinois	Harvard/Illinois	Harvard/Illinois/Notre Dame	Harvard	Harvard	Notre Dame			
1920	Princeton/Harvard	California	Princeton/Notre Dame	California	California	California			
1921	California/Lafayette/Wash. & Jeff.	California	Cornell/Lafayette/Iowa	Cornell	Cornell	Cornell			
1922	Princeton	Princeton	Princeton/Cornell	Cornell	California	California			
1923	Illinois	Illinois	Illinois	Illinois	California	Michigan			
1924	Notre Dame	Notre Dame	Pennsylvania	Notre Dame	Notre Dame	Notre Dame	Notre Dame		Notre Dame
1925	Alabama	Alabama	Dartmouth	Alabama	Alabama	Alabama	Dartmouth		Alabama
1926	Navy	Alabama	Lafayette	Alabama/Stanford	Navy	Alabama	Stanford		Alabama
1927	Georgia	Yale	Illinois	Illinois	Notre Dame	Illinois	Illinois		Georgia
1928	Georgia Tech	Georgia Tech	Georgia Tech/Detroit Mercy	Georgia Tech	Georgia Tech	Georgia Tech	Southern Cal		Georgia Tech
1929	Notre Dame	Notre Dame	Pittsburgh	Notre Dame	Southern Cal	Notre Dame	Notre Dame	Notre Dame	Notre Dame

National Poll Champions, 1930-1949

Year	AP	UPI	FW	NFF	Dickinson	Dunkel	Helms	Litkenhous	Williamson
1930					Notre Dame	Notre Dame	Notre Dame		
1931					Southern Cal	Southern Cal	Southern Cal		Southern Cal
1932					Michigan	Southern Cal	Southern Cal		Southern Cal
1933					Michigan	Ohio St.	Michigan		Southern Cal
1934					Minnesota	Alabama	Minnesota	Minnesota	Alabama
1935					Southern Methodist	Princeton	Minnesota	Minnesota	Louisiana St.
1936	Minnesota				Minnesota	Minnesota	Minnesota	Minnesota	Louisiana St.
1937	Pittsburgh				Pittsburgh	California	California	Pittsburgh	Pittsburgh
1938	Texas Christian				Notre Dame	Tennessee	Texas Christian	Tennessee	Texas Christian
1939	Texas A&M				Southern Cal	Texas A&M	Texas A&M	Cornell	Texas A&M
1940	Minnesota				Minnesota	Tennessee	Stanford	Minnesota	Tennessee
1941	Minnesota					Minnesota	Minnesota	Minnesota	Texas
1942	Ohio St.					Ohio St.	Wisconsin	Georgia	Georgia
1943	Notre Dame					Notre Dame	Notre Dame	Notre Dame	Notre Dame
1944	Army					Army	Army	Army	Army
1945	Army					Army	Army	Army	Army
1946	Notre Dame					Notre Dame	Army/Notre Dame	Notre Dame	Georgia
1947	Notre Dame					Michigan	Michigan/Notre Dame	Michigan	Notre Dame
1948	Michigan					Michigan	Michigan	Michigan	Michigan
1949	Notre Dame					Notre Dame	Notre Dame	Notre Dame	Notre Dame

OTHER POLLS

Year	Board	Football Research	Parke Davis	Devold	Houlgate	National Championship Foundation	Poling
1930	Notre Dame	Alabama	Notre Dame/Alabama		Notre Dame	Notre Dame	Notre Dame
1931	Southern Cal	Southern Cal	Pittsburgh/Purdue		Southern Cal	Southern Cal	Southern Cal
1932	Southern Cal	Southern Cal	Southern Cal/Michigan/Colgate		Southern Cal	Southern Cal	Southern Cal
1933	Michigan	Michigan	Michigan/Princeton		Michigan	Michigan	Michigan
1934	Minnesota	Minnesota			Alabama	Minnesota	Alabama
1935	Minnesota	Minnesota			Southern Methodist	Minnesota	Minnesota
1936	Pittsburgh	Pittsburgh			Pittsburgh	Minnesota	Minnesota
1937	Pittsburgh	Pittsburgh			Pittsburgh	Pittsburgh	Pittsburgh
1938	Tennessee	Tennessee			Tennessee	Texas Christian	Tennessee
1939	Texas A&M	Texas A&M		Texas A&M	Texas A&M	Texas A&M	Texas A&M
1940	Minnesota	Minnesota		Minnesota	Minnesota	Minnesota	Stanford
1941	Minnesota	Minnesota		Minnesota	Alabama	Minnesota	Minnesota
1942	Ohio St.	Ohio St.		Georgia	Georgia	Ohio St.	Georgia
1943	Notre Dame	Notre Dame		Notre Dame	Notre Dame	Notre Dame	Notre Dame
1944	Army	Army		Army	Army	Army	Army
1945	Army	Army		Army	Army	Army	Army
1946	Notre Dame/Army	Army		Notre Dame	Army	Notre Dame	Notre Dame/Army
1947	Michigan	Michigan		Michigan	Michigan	Michigan	Michigan
1948	Michigan	Michigan		Michigan	Michigan	Michigan	Michigan
1949	Notre Dame	Oklahoma		Notre Dame	Notre Dame	Notre Dame	Notre Dame

National Poll Champions, Since 1950

The national champion was selected before bowl games as follows: AP (1936-64 and 1966-67); UP-UPI (1950-73); FWAA (1954); NFF-HF (1959-70). In all other latter-day polls, champions were selected after bowl games.

Year	AP	UPI	FW	NFF	USA/CNN	UPI/NFF	USA/NFF
1950	Oklahoma	Oklahoma					
1951	Tennessee	Tennessee					
1952	Michigan St.	Michigan St.					
1953	Maryland	Maryland					
1954	Ohio St.	UCLA	UCLA				
1955	Oklahoma	Oklahoma	Oklahoma				
1956	Oklahoma	Oklahoma	Oklahoma				
1957	Auburn	Ohio St.	Ohio St.				
1958	Louisiana St.	Louisiana St.	Iowa				
1959	Syracuse	Syracuse	Syracuse	Syracuse			
1960	Minnesota	Minnesota	Mississippi	Minnesota			
1961	Alabama	Alabama	Ohio St.	Alabama			
1962	Southern Cal	Southern Cal	Southern Cal	Southern Cal			
1963	Texas	Texas	Texas	Texas			
1964	Alabama	Alabama	Arkansas	Notre Dame			
1965	Alabama	Michigan St.	Michigan St./Alabama	Michigan St.			
1966	Notre Dame	Notre Dame	Notre Dame	Notre Dame/Michigan St.			
1967	Southern Cal	Southern Cal	Southern Cal	Southern Cal			
1968	Ohio St.	Ohio St.	Ohio St.	Ohio St.			
1969	Texas	Texas	Texas	Texas			
1970	Nebraska	Texas	Nebraska	Texas/Ohio St.			
1971	Nebraska	Nebraska	Nebraska	Nebraska			
1972	Southern Cal	Southern Cal	Southern Cal	Southern Cal			
1973	Notre Dame	Alabama	Notre Dame	Notre Dame			
1974	Oklahoma	Southern Cal	Southern Cal	Southern Cal			

DIVISION I-A

Year	AP	UPI	FW	NFF	USA/CNN	UPI/NFF	USA/NFF
1975	Oklahoma	Oklahoma	Oklahoma	Oklahoma			
1976	Pittsburgh	Pittsburgh	Pittsburgh	Pittsburgh			
1977	Notre Dame	Notre Dame	Notre Dame	Notre Dame			
1978	Alabama	Southern Cal	Alabama	Alabama			
1979	Alabama	Alabama	Alabama	Alabama			
1980	Georgia	Georgia	Georgia	Georgia			
1981	Clemson	Clemson	Clemson	Clemson			
1982	Penn St.	Penn St.	Penn St.	Penn St.	Penn St.		
1983	Miami (Fla.)	Miami (Fla.)	Miami (Fla.)	Miami (Fla.)	Miami (Fla.)		
1984	Brigham Young	Brigham Young	Brigham Young	Brigham Young	Brigham Young		
1985	Oklahoma	Oklahoma	Oklahoma	Oklahoma	Oklahoma		
1986	Penn St.	Penn St.	Penn St.	Penn St.	Penn St.		
1987	Miami (Fla.)	Miami (Fla.)	Miami (Fla.)	Miami (Fla.)	Miami (Fla.)		
1988	Notre Dame	Notre Dame	Notre Dame	Notre Dame	Notre Dame		
1989	Miami (Fla.)	Miami (Fla.)	Miami (Fla.)	Miami (Fla.)	Miami (Fla.)		
1990	Colorado	Georgia Tech	Colorado	Colorado	Colorado		
1991	Miami (Fla.)		Washington		Washington	Washington	
1992	Alabama		Alabama		Alabama	Alabama	
1993	Florida St.		Florida St.		Florida St.		Florida St.

(Legend of Present Major Selectors: Associated Press (AP) from 1950-present; United Press International (UPI) from 1950-90, United Press, 1950-57, UPI from 1958 after merger with International News Service; Football Writers Association of America (FW) from 1954-present; National Football Foundation and Hall of Fame (NFF) from 1959-90; USA Today/Cable News Network (USA/CNN) from 1982-present; United Press International/National Football Foundation and Hall of Fame (UPI/NFF) from 1991-92; USA Today/National Football Foundation and Hall of Fame (USA/NFF) from 1993. The Associated Press has been the designated media poll since 1936. United Press International served as the coaches' poll from 1950 to 1991 when it was taken over by USA Today/Cable News Network. In 1991-92, the No. 1 team in the final UPI/NFF ratings received the MacArthur Bowl as the national champion by the NFF. Beginning in 1993, the No. 1 team in the USA Today/NFF final poll received the Sears MacArthur Bowl.)

OTHER POLLS

Year	Dunkel	Helms	Litkenhous	Williamson	Board	Football Research	Devold	FB News
1950	Tennessee	Oklahoma	Oklahoma	Oklahoma	Princeton	Tennessee	Tennessee	
1951	Maryland	Michigan St.	Tennessee	Tennessee	Georgia Tech/Illinois	Maryland	Maryland	
1952	Michigan St.	Michigan St.	Michigan St.	Michigan St.	Michigan St.	Michigan St.	Michigan St.	
1953	Notre Dame	Notre Dame	Notre Dame	Notre Dame	Notre Dame	Oklahoma	Notre Dame	
1954	UCLA	UCLA/Ohio St.	UCLA	Ohio St.	Ohio St.	Ohio St./UCLA	Ohio St.	
1955	Oklahoma	Oklahoma	Oklahoma	Oklahoma	Michigan St.	Oklahoma	Oklahoma	
1956	Oklahoma	Oklahoma	Oklahoma	Oklahoma	Oklahoma	Iowa	Oklahoma	
1957	Michigan St.	Auburn	Ohio St.	Auburn	Ohio St.	Auburn	Ohio St.	
1958	Louisiana St.	Louisiana St.	Louisiana St.	Louisiana St.	Louisiana St.	Louisiana St.	Louisiana St.	Louisiana St.
1959	Mississippi	Syracuse	Syracuse	Syracuse	Syracuse	Syracuse	Syracuse	Syracuse
1960	Mississippi	Washington	Iowa	Mississippi	Iowa	Mississippi	Mississippi	Minnesota
1961	Alabama	Alabama	Alabama	Alabama		Alabama	Alabama	Alabama
1962	Southern Cal	Southern Cal	Texas	Southern Cal		Southern Cal	Southern Cal	Southern Cal
1963	Texas	Texas	Texas	Texas		Texas	Texas	Texas
1964	Michigan	Arkansas	Alabama			Arkansas	Notre Dame	Notre Dame
1965	Michigan St.	Michigan St.	Michigan St.			Alabama	Michigan St.	Michigan St.
1966	Notre Dame	Notre Dame/Michigan St.	Notre Dame			Michigan St.	Notre Dame	Notre Dame
1967	Notre Dame	Southern Cal	Tennessee			Southern Cal	Southern Cal	Southern Cal
1968	Ohio St.	Ohio St.	Georgia			Ohio St.	Texas	Ohio St.
1969	Texas	Texas	Texas			Texas	Texas	Texas
1970	Nebraska	Nebraska	Texas			Nebraska	Nebraska	Nebraska
1971	Nebraska	Nebraska	Nebraska			Nebraska	Nebraska	Nebraska
1972	Southern Cal	Southern Cal	Southern Cal			Southern Cal	Southern Cal	Southern Cal
1973	Oklahoma	Notre Dame				Oklahoma	Oklahoma	Notre Dame
1974	Oklahoma	Oklahoma/Southern Cal	Oklahoma			Oklahoma	Oklahoma	Oklahoma
1975	Oklahoma	Ohio St./Oklahoma				Oklahoma	Oklahoma	Oklahoma
1976	Southern Cal	Pittsburgh				Southern Cal	Southern Cal	Pittsburgh
1977	Notre Dame	Notre Dame				Notre Dame/Alabama	Notre Dame	Notre Dame
1978	Oklahoma	Alabama/Oklahoma/Southern Cal	Oklahoma			Alabama	Oklahoma	Southern Cal
1979	Alabama	Alabama				Southern Cal	Alabama	Alabama
1980	Oklahoma	Georgia				Pittsburgh	Pittsburgh	Georgia
1981	Penn St.	Clemson	Clemson			Clemson	Clemson	Clemson
1982	Penn St.	Penn St./Southern Methodist	Penn St.			Penn St.	Penn St.	Penn St.
1983	Miami (Fla.)		Nebraska			Auburn	Nebraska	Miami (Fla.)
1984	Florida		Nebraska			Brigham Young	Florida	Washington
1985	Oklahoma					Oklahoma	Oklahoma	Oklahoma
1986	Oklahoma					Oklahoma	Oklahoma	Penn St.
1987	Miami (Fla.)					Miami (Fla.)	Miami (Fla.)	Miami (Fla.)
1988	Notre Dame					Notre Dame	Notre Dame	Notre Dame
1989	Miami (Fla.)					Miami (Fla.)	Miami (Fla.)	Miami (Fla.)
1990	Georgia Tech					Colorado	Colorado	Colorado
1991	Washington					Miami (Fla.)	Miami (Fla.)	Washington
1992	Alabama					Alabama	Alabama	Alabama
1993	Florida St.					Florida St.	Florida St.	Florida St.

OTHER POLLS (BEGAN IN 1966)

Year	Mathews	NY Times	Sports Ill.	Sporting News
1966	Notre Dame			
1967	Southern Cal			
1968	Texas			
1969	Ohio St.			
1970	Notre Dame			

Year	Mathews	NY Times	Sports Ill.	Sporting News
1971	Nebraska			
1972	Southern Cal			
1973				
1974	Ohio St.			
1975	Alabama/ Ohio St.			Arizona St.
1976	Southern Cal			Pittsburgh
1977	Notre Dame			Notre Dame
1978	Oklahoma			Southern Cal
1979	Alabama	Alabama		Alabama
1980	Oklahoma	Pittsburgh		Georgia
1981	Clemson	Clemson	Clemson	Clemson
1982	Penn St.	Penn St.	Penn St.	Penn St.
1983	Nebraska	Auburn	Miami (Fla.)	Miami (Fla.)
1984	Florida	Florida	Brigham Young	Florida
1985	Michigan	Oklahoma	Oklahoma	Oklahoma
1986	Penn St.	Oklahoma	Penn St.	Penn St.
1987	Miami (Fla.)	Miami (Fla.)	Miami (Fla.)	Miami (Fla.)
1988	Notre Dame	Notre Dame	Notre Dame	Notre Dame
1989	Miami (Fla.)	Miami (Fla.)	Miami (Fla.)	Miami (Fla.)
1990	Colorado	Miami (Fla.)	Colorado	Colorado
1991	Washington	Miami (Fla.)	Washington	Miami (Fla.)
1992	Alabama	Alabama	Alabama	Alabama
1993	Florida St.	Florida St.	Florida St.	Florida St.

Bowls Hosting Most National Champions, Since 1900

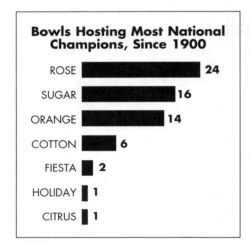

ROSE	24
SUGAR	16
ORANGE	14
COTTON	6
FIESTA	2
HOLIDAY	1
CITRUS	1

National Champions in Bowl Games

Year	Team	Coach (Years†)	Record	Bowl (Result)
1900	Yale	Malcolm McBride	12-0-0	None
1901	Michigan	Fielding Yost	11-0-0	Rose (beat Stanford, 49-0)
1902	Michigan	Fielding Yost	11-0-0	None
1903	Princeton	Art Hillebrand	11-0-0	None
1904	Pennsylvania	Carl Williams	12-0-0	None
1905	Chicago	Amos Alonzo Stagg	11-0-0	None
1906	Princeton	Bill Roper	9-0-1	None
1907	Yale	William Knox	9-0-1	None
1908	Pennsylvania	Sol Metzer	11-0-1	None
1909	Yale	Howard Jones	10-0-0	None
1910	Harvard	Percy Haughton	8-0-1	None
1911	Princeton	Bill Roper	8-0-2	None
1912	Harvard	Percy Haughton	9-0-0	None
1913	Harvard	Percy Haughton	9-0-0	None
1914	Army	Charley Daly	9-0-0	None
1915	Cornell	Al Sharpe	9-0-0	None
1916	Pittsburgh	Glenn "Pop" Warner	8-0-0	None
1917	Georgia Tech	John Heisman	9-0-0	None
1918	Pittsburgh	Glenn "Pop" Warner	4-1-0	None
1919	Harvard	Robert Fisher	9-0-1	Rose (beat Oregon, 7-6)
1920	California	Andy Smith	9-0-0	Rose (beat Ohio St., 28-0)
1921	Cornell	Gil Dobie	8-0-0	None
1922	Cornell	Gil Dobie	8-0-0	None
1923	Illinois	Robert Zuppke	8-0-0	None
1924	Notre Dame	Knute Rockne	10-0-0	Rose (beat Stanford, 27-10)
1925	Alabama	Wallace Wade	10-0-0	Rose (beat Washington, 20-19)
	Dartmouth	Jesse Hawley	8-0-0	None
1926	Alabama	Wallace Wade	9-0-1	Rose (tied Stanford, 7-7)
	Stanford	Glenn "Pop" Warner	10-0-1	Rose (tied Alabama, 7-7)
1927	Illinois	Robert Zuppke	7-0-1	None
1928	Georgia Tech	Bill Alexander	10-0-0	Rose (beat California, 8-7)
	Southern Cal	Howard Jones	9-0-1	None
1929	Notre Dame	Knute Rockne	9-0-0	None
1930	Notre Dame	Knute Rockne	10-0-0	None
1931	Southern Cal	Howard Jones	10-1-0	Rose (beat Tulane, 21-12)
1932	Michigan	Harry Kipke	8-0-0	None
	Southern Cal	Howard Jones	10-0-0	Rose (beat Pittsburgh, 35-0)
1933	Michigan	Harry Kipke	7-0-1	None
1934	Minnesota	Bernie Bierman	8-0-0	None
1935	Minnesota	Bernie Bierman	8-0-0	None
	Southern Methodist	Matty Bell	12-1-0	Rose (lost to Stanford, 0-7)
1936	Minnesota	Bernie Bierman (5-15)	7-1-0	None
1937	Pittsburgh	Jock Sutherland (13-18)	9-0-1	None
1938	Texas Christian	Dutch Meyer (5-5)	11-0-0	Sugar (beat Carnegie Mellon, 15-7)
1939	Texas A&M	Homer Norton (6-16)	11-0-0	Sugar (beat Tulane, 14-13)
1940	Minnesota	Bernie Bierman (9-19)	8-0-0	None
1941	Minnesota	Bernie Bierman (10-20)	8-0-0	None
1942	Ohio St.	Paul Brown (2-2)	9-1-0	None
1943	Notre Dame	Frank Leahy (3-5)	9-1-0	None
1944	Army	Earl "Red" Blaik (4-11)	9-0-0	None

Year	Team	Coach (Years†)	Record	Bowl (Result)
1945	Army	Earl "Red" Blaik (5-12)	9-0-0	None
1946	Notre Dame	Frank Leahy (4-6)	8-0-1	None
1947	Notre Dame	Frank Leahy (5-7)	9-0-0	None
1948	Michigan	Bennie Oosterbaan (1-1)	9-0-0	None
1949	Notre Dame	Frank Leahy (7-9)	10-0-0	None
1950	Oklahoma	Bud Wilkinson (4-4)	10-1-0	Sugar (lost to Kentucky, 7-13)
1951	Tennessee	Robert Neyland (20-20)	10-0-0	Sugar (lost to Maryland, 13-28)
1952	Michigan St.	Clarence "Biggie" Munn (6-9)	9-0-0	None
1953	Maryland	Jim Tatum (7-9)	10-1-0	Orange (lost to Oklahoma, 0-7)
1954	Ohio St.	Woody Hayes (4-9)	10-0-0	Rose (beat Southern Cal, 20-7)
	UCLA	Red Sanders (6-12)	9-0-0	None
1955	Oklahoma	Bud Wilkinson (9-9)	11-0-0	Orange (beat Maryland, 20-6)
1956	Oklahoma	Bud Wilkinson (10-10)	10-0-0	None
1957	Auburn	Ralph "Shug" Jordan (7-7)	10-0-0	None
	Ohio St.	Woody Hayes (7-12)	9-1-0	Rose (beat Oregon, 10-7)
1958	Louisiana St.	Paul Dietzel (4-4)	11-0-0	Sugar (beat Clemson, 7-0)
	Iowa	Forest Evashevski (5-8)	8-1-1	Rose (beat California, 38-12)
1959	Syracuse	Ben Schwartzwalder (11-14)	11-0-0	Cotton (beat Texas, 23-14)
1960	Minnesota	Murray Warmath (7-9)	8-2-0	Rose (lost to Washington, 7-17)
	Mississippi	Johnny Vaught (14-14)	10-0-1	Sugar (beat Rice, 14-6)
1961	Alabama	Paul "Bear" Bryant (4-17)	11-0-0	Sugar (beat Arkansas, 10-3)
	Ohio St.	Woody Hayes (11-16)	8-0-1	None
1962	Southern Cal	John McKay (3-3)	11-0-0	Rose (beat Wisconsin, 42-37)
1963	Texas	Darrell Royal (7-10)	11-0-0	Cotton (beat Navy, 28-6)
1964	Alabama	Paul "Bear" Bryant (7-20)	10-1-0	Orange (lost to Texas, 17-21)
	Arkansas	Frank Broyles (3-4)	11-0-0	Cotton (beat Nebraska, 10-7)
	Notre Dame	Ara Parseghian (1-14)	9-1-0	None
1965	Alabama	Paul "Bear" Bryant (8-21)	9-1-1	Orange (beat Nebraska, 39-28)
	Michigan St.	Duffy Daugherty (12-12)	10-1-0	Rose (lost to UCLA, 12-14)
1966	Michigan St.	Duffy Daugherty (13-13)	9-0-1	None
	Notre Dame	Ara Parseghian (3-17)	9-0-1	None
1967	Southern Cal	John McKay (8-8)	10-1-0	Rose (beat Indiana, 14-3)
1968	Ohio St.	Woody Hayes (18-23)	10-0-0	Rose (beat Southern Cal, 27-16)
1969	Texas	Darrell Royal (13-16)	11-0-0	Cotton (beat Notre Dame, 21-17)
1970	Nebraska	Bob Devaney (9-14)	11-0-1	Orange (beat Louisiana St., 17-12)
	Ohio St.	Woody Hayes (20-25)	9-1-0	Rose (lost to Stanford, 17-27)
	Texas	Darrell Royal (14-17)	10-1-0	Cotton (lost to Notre Dame, 11-24)
1971	Nebraska	Bob Devaney (10-15)	13-0-0	Orange (beat Alabama, 38-6)
1972	Southern Cal	John McKay (13-13)	12-0-0	Rose (beat Ohio St., 42-17)
1973	Alabama	Paul "Bear" Bryant (16-29)	11-1-0	Sugar (lost to Notre Dame, 23-24)
	Notre Dame	Ara Parseghian (10-23)	11-0-0	Sugar (beat Alabama, 24-23)
1974	Oklahoma	Barry Switzer (2-2)	11-0-0	None
	Southern Cal	John McKay (15-15)	10-1-1	Rose (beat Ohio St., 18-17)
1975	Oklahoma	Barry Switzer (3-3)	11-1-0	Orange (beat Michigan, 14-6)
1976	Pittsburgh	Johnny Majors (4-9)	12-0-0	Sugar (beat Georgia, 27-3)
1977	Notre Dame	Dan Devine (3-19)	11-1-0	Cotton (beat Texas, 38-10)
1978	Alabama	Paul "Bear" Bryant (21-34)	11-1-0	Sugar (beat Penn St., 14-7)
	Southern Cal	John Robinson (3-3)	12-1-0	Rose (beat Michigan, 17-10)
1979	Alabama	Paul "Bear" Bryant (22-35)	12-0-0	Sugar (beat Arkansas, 24-9)
1980	Georgia	Vince Dooley (17-17)	12-0-0	Sugar (beat Notre Dame, 17-10)
1981	Clemson	Danny Ford (4-4#)	12-0-0	Orange (beat Nebraska, 22-15)
1982	Penn St.	Joe Paterno (17-17)	11-1-0	Sugar (beat Georgia, 27-23)
1983	Miami (Fla.)	Howard Schnellenberger (5-5)	11-1-0	Orange (beat Nebraska, 31-30)
1984	Brigham Young	LaVell Edwards (13-13)	13-0-0	Holiday (beat Michigan, 24-17)
1985	Oklahoma	Barry Switzer (13-13)	11-1-0	Orange (beat Penn St., 25-10)
1986	Penn St.	Joe Paterno (21-21)	12-0-0	Fiesta (beat Miami, Fla., 14-10)
1987	Miami (Fla.)	Jimmy Johnson (3-9)	12-0-0	Orange (beat Oklahoma, 20-14)
1988	Notre Dame	Lou Holtz (3-19)	12-0-0	Fiesta (beat West Va., 34-21)
1989	Miami (Fla.)	Dennis Erickson (1-8)	11-1-0	Sugar (beat Alabama, 33-25)
1990	Colorado	Bill McCartney (9-9)	11-1-0	Orange (beat Notre Dame, 10-9)
	Georgia Tech	Bobby Ross (4-14)	11-0-1	Fla. Citrus (beat Nebraska, 45-21)
1991	Miami (Fla.)	Dennis Erickson (3-10)	12-0-0	Orange (beat Nebraska, 22-0)
	Washington	Don James (17-23)	12-0-0	Rose (beat Michigan, 34-14)
1992	Alabama	Gene Stallings (3-10)	13-0-0	Sugar (beat Miami, Fla., 34-13)
1993	Florida St.	Bobby Bowden (18-28)	12-1-0	Orange (beat Nebraska, 18-16)

†Years head coach at that college and total years at four-year colleges. #Includes last game of 1978 season.

Herschel Walker turned in the first of his three all-American seasons to help Georgia capture the mythical national championship in 1980.

Associated Press Weekly Leaders

The weekly dates are for Tuesday, the most frequent release date of the poll, except when the final poll was taken after January 1-2 bowl games. A team's record includes its last game before the weekly poll. A new weekly leader's rank the previous week is indicated in parentheses after its record. Final poll leaders (annual champions) are in bold face. (Note: Only 10 teams were ranked in the weekly polls during 1962, 1963, 1964, 1965, 1966 and 1967; 20 were ranked in all other seasons until 1989, when 25 were ranked.)

1936

10-20	Minnesota	(3-0-0)
10-27	Minnesota	(4-0-0)
11-3	Northwestern	(5-0-0) (3)
11-10	Northwestern	(6-0-0)
11-17	Northwestern	(7-0-0)
11-24	Minnesota	(7-1-0) (2)
12-1	**Minnesota**	**(7-1-0)**

1937

10-20	California	(5-0-0)
10-27	California	(6-0-0)
11-2	California	(7-0-0)
11-9	Pittsburgh	(6-0-1) (3)
11-16	Pittsburgh	(7-0-1)
11-23	Pittsburgh	(8-0-1)
11-30	**Pittsburgh**	**(9-0-1)**

1938

10-18	Pittsburgh	(4-0-0)
10-25	Pittsburgh	(5-0-0)
11-1	Pittsburgh	(6-0-0)
11-8	Texas Christian	(7-0-0) (2)
11-15	Notre Dame	(7-0-0) (2)
11-22	Notre Dame	(8-0-0)
11-29	Notre Dame	(8-0-0)
12-6	**Texas Christian**	**(10-0-0) (2)**

1939

10-17	Pittsburgh	(3-0-0)

10-24	Tennessee	(4-0-0) (5)
10-31	Tennessee	(5-0-0)
11-7	Tennessee	(6-0-0)
11-14	Tennessee	(7-0-0)
11-21	Texas A&M	(9-0-0) (2)
11-28	(tie) Texas A&M	(9-0-0)
	(tie) Southern Cal	(6-0-1) (4)
12-5	Texas A&M	(10-0-0)
12-12	**Texas A&M.**	**(10-0-0)**

1940

10-15	Cornell	(2-0-0)
10-22	Cornell	(3-0-0)
10-29	Cornell	(4-0-0)
11-5	Cornell	(5-0-0)
11-12	Minnesota	(6-0-0) (2)
11-19	Minnesota	(7-0-0)
11-26	Minnesota	(8-0-0)
12-3	**Minnesota**	**(8-0-0)**

1941

10-14	Minnesota	(2-0-0)
10-21	Minnesota	(3-0-0)
10-28	(tie) Minnesota	(4-0-0)
	(tie) Texas	(5-0-0) (2)
11-4	Texas	(6-0-0)
11-11	Minnesota	(6-0-0) (2)
11-18	Minnesota	(7-0-0)
11-25	Minnesota	(8-0-0)
12-2	**Minnesota**	**(8-0-0)**

1942

10-13	Ohio St.	(3-0-0)
10-20	Ohio St.	(4-0-0)
10-27	Ohio St.	(5-0-0)
11-3	Georgia	(7-0-0) (2)
11-10	Georgia	(8-0-0)
11-17	Georgia	(9-0-0)
11-24	Boston College	(8-0-0) (3)
12-1	**Ohio St.**	**(9-1-0) (3)**

1943

10-5	Notre Dame	(2-0-0)
10-12	Notre Dame	(3-0-0)
10-19	Notre Dame	(4-0-0)
10-26	Notre Dame	(5-0-0)
11-2	Notre Dame	(6-0-0)
11-9	Notre Dame	(7-0-0)
11-16	Notre Dame	(8-0-0)
11-23	Notre Dame	(9-0-0)
11-30	**Notre Dame**	**(9-1-0)**

1944

10-10	Notre Dame	(2-0-0)
10-17	Notre Dame	(3-0-0)
10-24	Notre Dame	(4-0-0)
10-31	Army	(5-0-0) (2)
11-7	Army	(6-0-0)
11-14	Army	(7-0-0)
11-21	Army	(8-0-0)
11-28	Army	(8-0-0)
12-5	**Army**	**(9-0-0)**

1945

10-9	Army	(2-0-0)
10-16	Army	(3-0-0)
10-23	Army	(4-0-0)
10-30	Army	(5-0-0)
11-6	Army	(6-0-0)
11-13	Army	(7-0-0)
11-20	Army	(8-0-0)
11-27	Army	(8-0-0)
12-4	**Army**	**(9-0-0)**

1946

10-8	Texas	(3-0-0)
10-15	Army	(4-0-0) (2)
10-22	Army	(5-0-0)
10-29	Army	(6-0-0)
11-5	Army	(7-0-0)
11-12	Army	(7-0-1)
11-19	Army	(8-0-1)
11-26	Army	(8-0-1)
12-3	**Notre Dame**	**(8-0-1) (2)**

1947*

10-7	Notre Dame	(1-0-0)
10-14	Michigan	(3-0-0) (2)
10-21	Michigan	(4-0-0)
10-28	Notre Dame	(4-0-0) (2)
11-4	Notre Dame	(5-0-0)
11-11	Notre Dame	(6-0-0)
11-18	Michigan	(8-0-0) (2)
11-25	Notre Dame	(8-0-0) (2)
12-2	Notre Dame	(8-0-0)
12-9	**Notre Dame**	**(9-0-0)**

1948

10-5	Notre Dame	(2-0-0)
10-12	North Caro.	(3-0-0) (2)
10-19	Michigan	(4-0-0) (4)
10-26	Michigan	(5-0-0)
11-2	Notre Dame	(6-0-0) (2)
11-9	Michigan	(7-0-0) (2)
11-16	Michigan	(8-0-0)
11-23	Michigan	(9-0-0)
11-30	**Michigan**	**(9-0-0)**

1949

10-4	Michigan	(2-0-0)
10-11	Notre Dame	(3-0-0) (2)
10-18	Notre Dame	(4-0-0)
10-25	Notre Dame	(4-0-0)
11-1	Notre Dame	(5-0-0)
11-8	Notre Dame	(6-0-0)
11-15	Notre Dame	(7-0-0)
11-22	Notre Dame	(8-0-0)
11-29	**Notre Dame**	**(9-0-0)**

1950

10-3	Notre Dame	(1-0-0)
10-10	Army	(2-0-0) (4)
10-17	Army	(3-0-0)
10-24	Southern Methodist	(5-0-0) (3)
10-31	Southern Methodist	(5-0-0)
11-7	Army	(6-0-0) (2)
11-14	Ohio St.	(6-1-0) (2)
11-21	Oklahoma	(8-0-0) (2)
11-28	**Oklahoma**	**(9-0-0)**

1951

10-2	Michigan St.	(2-0-0)
10-9	Michigan St.	(3-0-0)
10-16	California	(4-0-0) (2)
10-23	Tennessee	(4-0-0) (2)
10-30	Tennessee	(5-0-0)
11-6	Tennessee	(6-0-0)
11-13	Michigan St.	(7-0-0)(5)
11-20	Tennessee	(8-0-0) (2)
11-27	Tennessee	(9-0-0)
12-4	**Tennessee**	**(10-0-0)**

1952

9-30	Michigan St.	(1-0-0)
10-7	Wisconsin	(2-0-0) (8)
10-14	Michigan St.	(3-0-0)(2)
10-21	Michigan St.	(4-0-0)
10-28	Michigan St.	(5-0-0)
11-4	Michigan St.	(6-0-0)
11-11	Michigan St.	(7-0-0)
11-18	Michigan St.	(8-0-0)
11-25	Michigan St.	(9-0-0)
12-1	**Michigan St.**	**(9-0-0)**

1953

9-29	Notre Dame	(1-0-0)
10-6	Notre Dame	(2-0-0)
10-13	Notre Dame	(2-0-0)
10-20	Notre Dame	(3-0-0)
10-27	Notre Dame	(4-0-0)
11-3	Notre Dame	(5-0-0)
11-10	Notre Dame	(6-0-0)
11-17	Notre Dame	(7-0-0)
11-24	Maryland	(10-0-0) (2)
12-1	**Maryland**	**(10-0-0)**

1954

9-21	Oklahoma	(1-0-0)
9-28	Notre Dame	(1-0-0) (2)
10-5	Oklahoma	(2-0-0) (2)
10-12	Oklahoma	(3-0-0)
10-19	Oklahoma	(4-0-0)
10-26	Ohio St.	(5-0-0) (4)
11-2	UCLA	(7-0-0) (3)
11-9	UCLA	(8-0-0)
11-16	Ohio St.	(8-0-0) (2)
11-23	Ohio St.	(9-0-0)
11-30	**Ohio St.**	**(9-0-0)**

1955

9-20	UCLA	(1-0-0)
9-27	Maryland	(2-0-0) (5)
10-4	Maryland	(3-0-0)
10-11	Michigan	(3-0-0) (2)
10-18	Michigan	(4-0-0)
10-25	Maryland	(6-0-0) (2)
11-1	Maryland	(7-0-0)
11-8	Oklahoma	(7-0-0) (2)
11-15	Oklahoma	(8-0-0)
11-22	Oklahoma	(9-0-0)
11-29	**Oklahoma**	**(10-0-0)**

1956

9-25	Oklahoma	(0-0-0)
10-2	Oklahoma	(1-0-0)
10-9	Oklahoma	(2-0-0)
10-16	Oklahoma	(3-0-0)
10-23	Michigan St.	(4-0-0) (2)
10-30	Oklahoma	(5-0-0) (2)
11-6	Oklahoma	(6-0-0)
11-13	Tennessee	(7-0-0) (3)
11-20	Oklahoma	(8-0-0) (2)
11-27	Oklahoma	(9-0-0)
12-4	**Oklahoma**	**(10-0-0)**

1957

9-24	Oklahoma	(1-0-0)
10-1	Oklahoma	(1-0-0)
10-8	Oklahoma	(2-0-0)
10-15	Michigan St.	(3-0-0) (2)
10-22	Oklahoma	(4-0-0) (2)
10-29	Texas A&M	(6-0-0) (2)
11-5	Texas A&M	(7-0-0)
11-12	Texas A&M	(8-0-0)
11-19	Michigan St.	(7-1-0)(4)
11-26	Auburn	(9-0-0) (2)
12-3	**Auburn**	**(10-0-0)**

1958

9-23	Ohio St.	(0-0-0)
9-30	Oklahoma	(1-0-0) (2)
10-7	Auburn	(2-0-0) (2)
10-14	Army	(3-0-0) (3)
10-21	Army	(4-0-0)
10-28	Louisiana St.	(6-0-0) (3)
11-4	Louisiana St.	(7-0-0)
11-11	Louisiana St.	(8-0-0)
11-18	Louisiana St.	(9-0-0)
11-25	Louisiana St.	(10-0-0)
12-2	**Louisiana St.**	**(10-0-0)**

1959

9-22	Louisiana St.	(1-0-0)
9-29	Louisiana St.	(2-0-0)
10-6	Louisiana St.	(3-0-0)
10-13	Louisiana St.	(4-0-0)
10-20	Louisiana St.	(5-0-0)
10-27	Louisiana St.	(6-0-0)
11-3	Louisiana St.	(7-0-0)
11-10	Syracuse	(7-0-0) (4)
11-17	Syracuse	(8-0-0)
11-24	Syracuse	(9-0-0)
12-1	Syracuse	(9-0-0)
12-8	**Syracuse**	**(10-0-0)**

1960

9-20	Mississippi	(1-0-0)
9-27	Mississippi	(2-0-0)
10-4	Syracuse	(2-0-0) (2)
10-11	Mississippi	(4-0-0) (2)
10-18	Iowa	(4-0-0) (2)
10-25	Iowa	(5-0-0)
11-1	Iowa	(6-0-0)
11-8	Minnesota	(7-0-0) (3)
11-15	Missouri	(9-0-0) (2)
11-22	Minnesota	(8-1-0) (4)
11-29	**Minnesota**	**(8-1-0)**

1961

9-26	Iowa	(0-0-0)
10-3	Iowa	(1-0-0)
10-10	Mississippi	(3-0-0) (2)
10-17	Michigan St.	(3-0-0) (5)
10-24	Michigan St.	(4-0-0)
10-31	Michigan St.	(5-0-0)
11-7	Texas	(7-0-0) (3)
11-14	Texas	(8-0-0)
11-21	Alabama	(9-0-0) (2)

11-28	Alabama	(9-0-0)
12-5	**Alabama**	**(10-0-0)**

1962

9-25	Alabama	(1-0-0)
10-2	Ohio St.	(1-0-0) (2)
10-9	Alabama	(3-0-0) (2)
10-16	Texas	(4-0-0) (2)
10-23	Texas	(5-0-0)
10-30	Northwestern	(5-0-0) (3)
11-6	Northwestern	(6-0-0)
11-13	Alabama	(8-0-0) (3)
11-20	Southern Cal	(8-0-0) (2)
11-27	Southern Cal	(9-0-0)
12-4	**Southern Cal**	**(10-0-0)**

1963

9-24	Southern Cal	(1-0-0)
10-1	Oklahoma	(1-0-0) (3)
10-8	Oklahoma	(2-0-0)
10-15	Texas	(4-0-0) (3)
10-22	Texas	(5-0-0)
10-29	Texas	(6-0-0)
11-5	Texas	(7-0-0)
11-12	Texas	(8-0-0)
11-19	Texas	(9-0-0)
11-26	Texas	(9-0-0)
12-3	Texas	(10-0-0)
12-10	**Texas**	**(10-0-0)**

1964

9-29	Texas	(2-0-0)
10-6	Texas	(3-0-0)
10-13	Texas	(4-0-0)
10-20	Ohio St.	(4-0-0)(2)
10-27	Ohio St.	(5-0-0)
11-3	Notre Dame	(6-0-0)(2)
11-10	Notre Dame	(7-0-0)
11-17	Notre Dame	(8-0-0)
11-24	Notre Dame	(9-0-0)
12-1	**Alabama**	**(10-0-0) (2)**

1965

9-21	Notre Dame	(1-0-0)
9-28	Texas	(2-0-0) (3)
10-5	Texas	(3-0-0)
10-12	Texas	(4-0-0)
10-19	Arkansas	(5-0-0) (3)
10-26	Michigan St.	(6-0-0) (2)
11-2	Michigan St.	(7-0-0)
11-9	Michigan St.	(8-0-0)
11-16	Michigan St.	(9-0-0)
11-23	Michigan St.	(10-0-0)
11-30	Michigan St.	(10-0-0)
1-4	**Alabama**	**(9-1-1) (4)**

1966

9-20	Michigan St.	(1-0-0)
9-27	Michigan St.	(2-0-0)
10-4	Michigan St.	(3-0-0)
10-11	Michigan St.	(4-0-0)
10-18	Notre Dame	(4-0-0) (2)
10-25	Notre Dame	(5-0-0)
11-1	Notre Dame	(6-0-0)
11-8	Notre Dame	(7-0-0)
11-15	Notre Dame	(8-0-0)
11-22	Notre Dame	(8-0-1)
11-29	Notre Dame	(9-0-1)
12-5	**Notre Dame**	**(9-0-1)**

1967

9-19	Notre Dame	(0-0-0)
9-26	Notre Dame	(1-0-0)
10-3	Southern Cal	(3-0-0) (2)
10-10	Southern Cal	(4-0-0)
10-17	Southern Cal	(5-0-0)
10-24	Southern Cal	(6-0-0)
10-31	Southern Cal	(7-0-0)
11-7	Southern Cal	(8-0-0)
11-14	UCLA	(7-0-1) (2)
11-21	Southern Cal	(9-1-0) (4)
11-28	**Southern Cal**	**(9-1-0)**

1968

9-17	Purdue	(0-0-0)
9-24	Purdue	(1-0-0)
10-1	Purdue	(2-0-0)
10-8	Purdue	(3-0-0)
10-15	Southern Cal	(4-0-0) (2)
10-22	Southern Cal	(5-0-0)

10-29	Southern Cal	(5-0-0)
11-5	Southern Cal	(6-0-0)
11-12	Southern Cal	(7-0-0)
11-19	Southern Cal	(8-0-0)
11-26	Ohio St.	(9-0-0) (2)
12-2	Ohio St.	(9-0-0)
12-9	**Ohio St.**	**(10-0-0)**

1969

9-23	Ohio St.	(0-0-0)
9-30	Ohio St.	(1-0-0)
10-7	Ohio St.	(2-0-0)
10-14	Ohio St.	(3-0-0)
10-21	Ohio St.	(4-0-0)
10-28	Ohio St.	(5-0-0)
11-4	Ohio St.	(6-0-0)
11-11	Ohio St.	(7-0-0)
11-18	Ohio St.	(8-0-0)
11-25	Texas	(8-0-0) (2)
12-2	Texas	(9-0-0)
12-9	Texas	(10-0-0)
1-4	**Texas**	**(11-0-0)**

1970

9-15	Ohio St.	(0-0-0)
9-22	Ohio St.	(0-0-0)
9-29	Ohio St.	(1-0-0)
10-6	Ohio St.	(2-0-0)
10-13	Ohio St.	(3-0-0)
10-20	Ohio St.	(4-0-0)
10-27	Texas	(5-0-0) (2)
11-3	Texas	(6-0-0)
11-10	Texas	(7-0-0)
11-17	Texas	(8-0-0)
11-24	Texas	(8-0-0)
12-1	Texas	(9-0-0)
12-8	Texas	(10-0-0)
1-6	**Nebraska**	**(11-0-1) (3)**

1971

9-14	Nebraska	(1-0-0)
9-21	Nebraska	(2-0-0)
9-28	Nebraska	(3-0-0)
10-5	Nebraska	(4-0-0)
10-12	Nebraska	(5-0-0)
10-19	Nebraska	(6-0-0)
10-26	Nebraska	(7-0-0)
11-2	Nebraska	(8-0-0)
11-9	Nebraska	(9-0-0)
11-16	Nebraska	(10-0-0)
11-23	Nebraska	(10-0-0)
11-30	Nebraska	(11-0-0)
12-7	Nebraska	(12-0-0)
1-4	**Nebraska**	**(13-0-0)**

1972

9-12	Southern Cal	(1-0-0)
9-19	Southern Cal	(2-0-0)
9-26	Southern Cal	(3-0-0)
10-3	Southern Cal	(4-0-0)
10-10	Southern Cal	(5-0-0)
10-17	Southern Cal	(6-0-0)
10-24	Southern Cal	(7-0-0)
10-31	Southern Cal	(8-0-0)
11-7	Southern Cal	(9-0-0)
11-14	Southern Cal	(9-0-0)
11-21	Southern Cal	(10-0-0)
11-28	Southern Cal	(10-0-0)
12-5	Southern Cal	(11-0-0)
1-3	**Southern Cal**	**(12-0-0)**

1973

9-11	Southern Cal	(0-0-0)
9-18	Southern Cal	(1-0-0)
9-25	Southern Cal	(2-0-0)
10-2	Ohio St.	(2-0-0) (3)
10-9	Ohio St.	(3-0-0)
10-16	Ohio St.	(4-0-0)
10-23	Ohio St.	(5-0-0)
10-30	Ohio St.	(6-0-0)
11-6	Ohio St.	(7-0-0)
11-13	Ohio St.	(8-0-0)
11-20	Ohio St.	(9-0-0)
11-27	Alabama	(10-0-0) (2)
12-4	Alabama	(11-0-0)
1-3	**Notre Dame**	**(11-0-0) (3)**

1974

9-10	Oklahoma	(0-0-0)
9-17	Notre Dame	(1-0-0) (2)
9-24	Ohio St.	(2-0-0) (2)

10-1	Ohio St.	(3-0-0)
10-8	Ohio St.	(4-0-0)
10-15	Ohio St.	(5-0-0)
10-22	Ohio St.	(6-0-0)
10-29	Ohio St.	(7-0-0)
11-5	Ohio St.	(8-0-0)
11-12	Oklahoma	(8-0-0) (2)
11-19	Oklahoma	(9-0-0)
11-26	Oklahoma	(10-0-0)
12-3	Oklahoma	(11-0-0)
1-3	**Oklahoma**	**(11-0-0)**

1975

9-9	Oklahoma	(0-0-0)
9-16	Oklahoma	(1-0-0)
9-23	Oklahoma	(2-0-0)
9-30	Oklahoma	(3-0-0)
10-7	Ohio St.	(4-0-0) (2)
10-14	Ohio St.	(5-0-0)
10-21	Ohio St.	(6-0-0)
10-28	Ohio St.	(7-0-0)
11-4	Ohio St.	(8-0-0)
11-11	Ohio St.	(9-0-0)
11-18	Ohio St.	(10-0-0)
11-25	Ohio St.	(11-0-0)
12-2	Ohio St.	(11-0-0)
1-3	**Oklahoma**	**(11-1-0) (3)**

1976

9-14	Michigan	(1-0-0)
9-21	Michigan	(2-0-0)
9-28	Michigan	(3-0-0)
10-5	Michigan	(4-0-0)
10-12	Michigan	(5-0-0)
10-19	Michigan	(6-0-0)
10-26	Michigan	(7-0-0)
11-2	Michigan	(8-0-0)
11-9	Pittsburgh	(9-0-0) (2)
11-16	Pittsburgh	(10-0-0)
11-23	Pittsburgh	(10-0-0)
11-30	Pittsburgh	(11-0-0)
1-5	**Pittsburgh**	**(12-0-0)**

1977

9-13	Michigan	(1-0-0)
9-20	Michigan	(2-0-0)
9-27	Oklahoma	(3-0-0) (3)
10-4	Southern Cal	(4-0-0) (2)
10-11	Michigan	(5-0-0) (3)
10-18	Michigan	(6-0-0)
10-25	Texas	(6-0-0) (2)
11-1	Texas	(7-0-0)
11-8	Texas	(8-0-0)
11-15	Texas	(9-0-0)
11-22	Texas	(10-0-0)
11-29	Texas	(11-0-0)
1-4	**Notre Dame**	**(11-1-0) (5)**

1978

9-12	Alabama	(1-0-0)
9-19	Alabama	(2-0-0)
9-26	Oklahoma	(3-0-0) (tie 3)
10-3	Oklahoma	(4-0-0)
10-10	Oklahoma	(5-0-0)
10-17	Oklahoma	(6-0-0)
10-24	Oklahoma	(7-0-0)
10-31	Oklahoma	(8-0-0)
11-7	Oklahoma	(9-0-0)
11-14	Penn St.	(10-0-0) (2)
11-21	Penn St.	(10-0-0)
11-28	Penn St.	(11-0-0)
12-5	Penn St.	(11-0-0)
1-4	**Alabama**	**(11-1-0) (2)**

1979

9-11	Southern Cal	(1-0-0)
9-18	Southern Cal	(2-0-0)
9-25	Southern Cal	(3-0-0)
10-2	Southern Cal	(4-0-0)
10-9	Southern Cal	(5-0-0)
10-16	Alabama	(5-0-0) (2)
10-23	Alabama	(6-0-0)
10-30	Alabama	(7-0-0)
11-6	Alabama	(8-0-0)
11-13	Alabama	(9-0-0)
11-20	Alabama	(10-0-0)
11-27	Alabama	(10-0-0)
12-4	Ohio St.	(11-0-0) (3)
1-3	**Alabama**	**(12-0-0) (2)**

1980
Date	Team	Record
9-9	Ohio St.	(0-0-0)
9-16	Alabama	(1-0-0) (2)
9-23	Alabama	(2-0-0)
9-30	Alabama	(3-0-0)
10-7	Alabama	(4-0-0)
10-14	Alabama	(5-0-0)
10-21	Alabama	(6-0-0)
10-28	Alabama	(7-0-0)
11-4	Notre Dame	(7-0-0) (3)
11-11	Georgia	(9-0-0) (2)
11-18	Georgia	(10-0-0)
11-25	Georgia	(10-0-0)
12-2	Georgia	(11-0-0)
12-9	Georgia	(11-0-0)
1-4	**Georgia**	**(12-0-0)**

1981
Date	Team	Record
9-8	Michigan	(0-0-0)
9-15	Notre Dame	(1-0-0) (4)
9-22	Southern Cal	(2-0-0) (2)
9-29	Southern Cal	(3-0-0)
10-6	Southern Cal	(4-0-0)
10-13	Texas	(4-0-0) (3)
10-20	Penn St.	(5-0-0) (2)
10-27	Penn St.	(6-0-0)
11-3	Pittsburgh	(7-0-0) (2)
11-10	Pittsburgh	(8-0-0)
11-17	Pittsburgh	(9-0-0)
11-24	Pittsburgh	(10-0-0)
12-1	Clemson	(11-0-0) (2)
1-3	**Clemson**	**(12-0-0)**

1982
Date	Team	Record
9-7	Pittsburgh	(0-0-0)
9-14	Washington	(1-0-0) (2)
9-21	Washington	(2-0-0)
9-28	Washington	(3-0-0)
10-5	Washington	(4-0-0)
10-12	Washington	(5-0-0)
10-19	Washington	(6-0-0)
10-26	Pittsburgh	(6-0-0) (2)
11-2	Pittsburgh	(7-0-0)
11-9	Georgia	(9-0-0) (3)
11-16	Georgia	(10-0-0)
11-23	Georgia	(10-0-0)
11-30	Georgia	(11-0-0)
12-7	Georgia	(11-0-0)
1-3	**Penn St.**	**(11-1-0) (2)**

1983
Date	Team	Record
9-6	Nebraska	(1-0-0)
9-13	Nebraska	(2-0-0)
9-20	Nebraska	(3-0-0)
9-27	Nebraska	(4-0-0)
10-4	Nebraska	(5-0-0)
10-11	Nebraska	(6-0-0)
10-18	Nebraska	(7-0-0)
10-25	Nebraska	(8-0-0)
11-1	Nebraska	(9-0-0)
11-8	Nebraska	(10-0-0)
11-15	Nebraska	(11-0-0)
11-22	Nebraska	(11-0-0)
11-29	Nebraska	(12-0-0)
12-6	Nebraska	(12-0-0)
1-3	**Miami (Fla.)**	**(11-1-0) (5)**

1984
Date	Team	Record
9-4	Miami (Fla.)	(2-0-0)
9-11	Nebraska	(1-0-0) (2)
9-18	Nebraska	(2-0-0)
9-25	Nebraska	(3-0-0)
10-2	Texas	(2-0-0) (2)
10-9	Texas	(3-0-0)
10-16	Washington	(6-0-0) (2)
10-23	Washington	(7-0-0)
10-30	Washington	(8-0-0)
11-6	Washington	(9-0-0)
11-13	Nebraska	(9-1-0) (2)
11-20	Brigham Young	(11-0-0) (3)
11-27	Brigham Young	(12-0-0)

Date	Team	Record
12-4	Brigham Young	(12-0-0)
1-3	**Brigham Young**	**(13-0-0)**

1985
Date	Team	Record
9-3	Oklahoma	(0-0-0)
9-10	Auburn	(1-0-0) (2)
9-17	Auburn	(2-0-0)
9-24	Auburn	(2-0-0)
10-1	Iowa	(3-0-0) (3)
10-8	Iowa	(4-0-0)
10-15	Iowa	(5-0-0)
10-22	Iowa	(6-0-0)
10-29	Iowa	(7-0-0)
11-5	Florida	(7-0-1) (2)
11-12	Penn St.	(9-0-0) (2)
11-19	Penn St.	(10-0-0)
11-26	Penn St.	(11-0-0)
12-3	Penn St.	(11-0-0)
1-3	**Oklahoma**	**(11-1-0) (4)**

1986
Date	Team	Record
9-9	Oklahoma	(1-0-0)
9-16	Oklahoma	(1-0-0)
9-23	Oklahoma	(2-0-0)
9-30	Miami (Fla.)	(4-0-0) (2)
10-7	Miami (Fla.)	(5-0-0)
10-14	Miami (Fla.)	(6-0-0)
10-21	Miami (Fla.)	(7-0-0)
10-28	Miami (Fla.)	(7-0-0)
11-4	Miami (Fla.)	(8-0-0)
11-11	Miami (Fla.)	(9-0-0)
11-18	Miami (Fla.)	(10-0-0)
11-25	Miami (Fla.)	(10-0-0)
12-2	Miami (Fla.)	(11-0-0)
1-4	**Penn St.**	**(12-0-0) (2)**

1987
Date	Team	Record
9-8	Oklahoma	(1-0-0)
9-15	Oklahoma	(2-0-0)
9-22	Oklahoma	(2-0-0)
9-29	Oklahoma	(3-0-0)
10-6	Oklahoma	(4-0-0)
10-13	Oklahoma	(5-0-0)
10-20	Oklahoma	(6-0-0)
10-27	Oklahoma	(7-0-0)
11-3	Oklahoma	(8-0-0)
11-10	Oklahoma	(9-0-0)
11-17	Nebraska	(9-0-0) (2)
11-24	Oklahoma	(11-0-0) (2)
12-1	Oklahoma	(11-0-0)
12-8	Oklahoma	(11-0-0)
1-3	**Miami (Fla.)**	**(12-0-0) (2)**

1988
Date	Team	Record
9-6	Miami (Fla.)	(1-0-0)
9-13	Miami (Fla.)	(1-0-0)
9-20	Miami (Fla.)	(2-0-0)
9-27	Miami (Fla.)	(3-0-0)
10-4	Miami (Fla.)	(4-0-0)
10-11	Miami (Fla.)	(4-0-0)
10-18	UCLA	(6-0-0) (2)
10-25	UCLA	(7-0-0)
11-1	Notre Dame	(8-0-0) (2)
11-8	Notre Dame	(9-0-0)
11-15	Notre Dame	(9-0-0)
11-22	Notre Dame	(10-0-0)
11-29	Notre Dame	(11-0-0)
12-6	Notre Dame	(11-0-0)
1-3	**Notre Dame**	**(12-0-0)**

1989
Date	Team	Record
9-5	Notre Dame	(1-0-0)
9-12	Notre Dame	(1-0-0)
9-19	Notre Dame	(2-0-0)
9-26	Notre Dame	(3-0-0)
10-3	Notre Dame	(4-0-0)
10-10	Notre Dame	(5-0-0)
10-17	Notre Dame	(6-0-0)
10-24	Notre Dame	(7-0-0)
10-31	Notre Dame	(8-0-0)
11-7	Notre Dame	(9-0-0)
11-14	Notre Dame	(10-0-0)

Date	Team	Record
11-21	Notre Dame	(11-0-0)
11-28	Colorado	(11-0-0) (2)
12-5	Colorado	(11-0-0)
1-2	**Miami (Fla.)**	**(11-1-0) (2)**

1990
Date	Team	Record
9-4	Miami (Fla.)	(0-0-0)
9-11	Notre Dame	(0-0-0) (2)
9-18	Notre Dame	(1-0-0)
9-25	Notre Dame	(2-0-0)
10-2	Notre Dame	(3-0-0)
10-9	Michigan	(3-1-0) (3)
10-16	Virginia	(6-0-0) (2)
10-23	Virginia	(7-0-0)
10-30	Virginia	(7-0-0)
11-6	Notre Dame	(7-1-0) (2)
11-13	Notre Dame	(8-1-0)
11-20	Colorado	(10-1-1) (2)
11-27	Colorado	(10-1-1)
12-4	Colorado	(10-1-1)
1-2	**Colorado**	**(11-1-1)**

1991
Date	Team	Record
9-3	Florida St.	(1-0-0)
9-10	Florida St.	(2-0-0)
9-17	Florida St.	(3-0-0)
9-23	Florida St.	(3-0-0)
9-30	Florida St.	(4-0-0)
10-7	Florida St.	(5-0-0)
10-14	Florida St.	(6-0-0)
10-21	Florida St.	(7-0-0)
10-28	Florida St.	(8-0-0)
11-4	Florida St.	(9-0-0)
11-11	Florida St.	(10-0-0)
11-18	Miami (Fla.)	(9-0-0) (2)
11-25	Miami (Fla.)	(10-0-0)
12-2	Miami (Fla.)	(11-0-0)
1-2	**Miami (Fla.)**	**(12-0-0)**

1992
Date	Team	Record
9-8	Miami (Fla.)	(1-0-0)
9-15	Miami (Fla.)	(1-0-0)
9-22	Miami (Fla.)	(2-0-0)
9-29	Washington	(3-0-0) (2)
10-6	Washington	(4-0-0)
10-13	Washington	(5-0-0)
10-20	Miami (Fla.)†	(6-0-0) (2)
10-27	Miami (Fla.)	(7-0-0)
11-3	Washington	(8-0-0) (2)
11-10	Miami (Fla.)	(8-0-0) (2)
11-17	Miami (Fla.)	(9-0-0)
11-24	Miami (Fla.)	(10-0-0)
12-1	Miami (Fla.)	(11-0-0)
12-8	Miami (Fla.)	(11-0-0)
1-2	**Alabama**	**(13-0-0) (2)**

1993
Date	Team	Record
8-31	Florida St.	(1-0-0)
9-7	Florida St.	(2-0-0)
9-14	Florida St.	(3-0-0)
9-21	Florida St.	(4-0-0)
9-28	Florida St.	(4-0-0)
10-5	Florida St.	(5-0-0)
10-12	Florida St.	(6-0-0)
10-19	Florida St.	(7-0-0)
10-26	Florida St.	(7-0-0)
11-2	Florida St.	(8-0-0)
11-9	Florida St.	(9-0-0)
11-16	Notre Dame	(10-0-0) (2)
11-23	Florida St.	(10-1-0) (2)
11-30	Florida St.	(11-1-0)
12-7	Florida St.	(11-1-0)
1-3	**Florida St.**	**(12-1-0)**

*On January 6, 1948, in a special postseason poll after the Rose Bowl, The Associated Press voted Michigan No. 1 and Notre Dame No. 2. However, the postseason poll did not supersede the final regular-season poll of December 9, 1947. †Miami (Fla.) and Washington actually tied for first place in The Associated Press poll for the first time in 51 years, but Miami (Fla.) had one more first-place vote, 31-30, than Washington.

DIVISION I-A

1993 Associated Press Week-By-Week Polls

Rank	Team	Preseason (8-23)	8-31	9-7	9-14	9-21	9-28	10-5	10-12	10-19	10-26	11-2	11-9	11-16	11-23	11-30	12-7	1-3
1.	Florida St.	1	1	1	1	1	1	1	1	1	1	1	1	2	1	1	1	1
2.	Alabama	2	2	2	2	2	2	2	2	4	5	5	12	11	17	16	18	14
3.	Michigan	3	3	3	10	8	8	9	18	13	24	NR	NR	NR	23	23	23	21
4.	Texas A&M	5	5	5	16	14	14	14	13	11	11	10	11	10	8	7	7	9
5.	Miami (Fla.)	4	4	3	3	3	3	8	6	4	4	4	3	4	9	8	10	15
6.	Syracuse	6	6	6	12	13	23	24	23	NR	NR	NR	NR	NR	NR	NR	NR	NR
7.	Notre Dame	7	11	4	4	4	4	3	2	2	2	2	2	1	4	5	4	2
8.	Nebraska	9	9	8	6	6	7	6	5	6	6	4	4	3	2	2	2	3
9.	Florida	8	7	9	5	5	5	4	9	10	9	8	8	7	9	8	8	5
10.	Tennessee	10	8	5	11	11	11	10	8	8	7	6	7	6	6	6	6	12
11.	Colorado	11	10	10	7	13	19	20	20	16	20	23	21	18	18	18	17	16
12.	Washington	12	12	18	16	15	13	12	22	19	NR	25	NR	NR	NR	NR	NR	NR
13.	Georgia	14	22	NR	NR	NR	NR	NR	NR	NR	NR	NR	NR	NR	NR	NR	NR	NR
14.	Arizona	13	13	15	15	12	12	11	7	7	14	13	19	19	17	16	16	10
15.	Stanford	15	23	20	17	NR	NR	NR	NR	NR	NR	NR	NR	NR	NR	NR	NR	NR
16.	Penn St.	17	15	14	9	9	8	7	14	12	19	16	14	14	14	13	13	8
17.	Ohio St.	18	16	11	7	7	6	5	3	3	3	5	5	12	11	11	11	11
18.	Southern Cal	NR	NR	NR	NR	NR	NR	NR	NR	NR	NR	NR	NR	22	NR	NR	NR	NR
19.	Brigham Young	19	20	19	21	20	19	14	12	18	16	15	NR	NR	NR	NR	NR	NR
20.	North Caro.	16	14	13	18	16	15	14	12	18	16	15	13	13	12	12	12	19
21.	Boston College	20	25	22	NR	NR	NR	NR	NR	NR	NR	NR	22	17	11	15	15	13
22.	Oklahoma	21	17	12	10	10	10	9	17	14	20	17	15	16	19	19	19	17
23.	Clemson	22	21	NR	NR	NR	NR	NR	NR	NR	NR	NR	NR	24	24	24	24	23
24.	Mississippi St.	23	NR	NR	NR	NR	NR	NR	NR	NR	NR	NR	NR	NR	NR	NR	NR	NR
25.	North Caro. St.	24	18	17	19	24	NR	NR	NR	NR	NR	22	NR	NR	NR	NR	NR	NR
NR	Fresno St.	25	25	NR	NR	NR	NR	NR	NR	NR	NR	NR	NR	NR	NR	NR	25T	NR
NR	South Caro.	NR	NR	19	NR	NR	NR	NR	NR	NR	NR	NR	NR	NR	NR	NR	NR	NR
NR	Baylor	NR	NR	24	NR	NR	NR	NR	NR	NR	NR	NR	NR	NR	NR	NR	NR	NR
NR	California	NR	NR	NR	21	20	17	16	21	NR	NR	NR	NR	NR	NR	NR	NR	25
NR	Arizona St.	NR	NR	NR	23	NR	NR	NR	NR	NR	NR	NR	NR	NR	NR	NR	NR	NR
NR	Wisconsin	NR	NR	NR	24	23	22	21	16	15	21	15	14	12	10	10	9	6
NR	Virginia	NR	NR	25	22	21	18	15	21	16	21	18	23	NR	NR	NR	NR	NR
NR	Louisville	NR	NR	NR	NR	24	18	17	23	20	17	13	20	NR	NR	NR	25T	24
NR	Auburn	NR	NR	NR	NR	25	23	22	19	10	9	8	7	6	3	4	5	4
NR	West Va.	NR	NR	NR	NR	25	24	17	18	13	11	9	9	5	3	3	3	7
NR	UCLA	NR	NR	NR	NR	NR	NR	25	22	19	15	12	10	16	15	14	14	18
NR	Michigan St.	NR	NR	NR	NR	NR	NR	NR	25	24	22	NR	NR	NR	25	25	NR	NR
NR	Washington St.	NR	NR	NR	NR	NR	NR	NR	NR	25	NR	NR	NR	NR	NR	NR	NR	NR
NR	Indiana	NR	NR	NR	NR	NR	NR	NR	NR	NR	23	17	19	21	21	21	21	NR
NR	Kansas St.	NR	NR	NR	NR	NR	NR	NR	NR	NR	25	18	24	20	20	20	20	20
NR	Wyoming	NR	NR	NR	NR	NR	NR	NR	NR	NR	NR	24	23	NR	NR	NR	NR	NR
NR	Virginia Tech	NR	NR	NR	NR	NR	NR	NR	NR	NR	NR	25	NR	25	22	22	22	22

No. 1 vs. No. 2

The No. 1 and No. 2 teams in The Associated Press poll (begun in 1936) have faced each other 29 times (19 in regular-season games and 10 in bowl games). The No. 1 team has won 17, with two games ending in ties.

Date	Score	Stadium (Site)
10-9-43	No. 1 Notre Dame 35, No. 2 Michigan 12	Michigan Stadium (Ann Arbor)
11-20-43	No. 1 Notre Dame 14, No. 2 Iowa Pre-Flight 13	Notre Dame (South Bend)
12-2-44	No. 1 Army 23, No. 2 Navy 7	Municipal (Baltimore)
11-10-45	No. 1 Army 48, No. 2 Notre Dame 0	Yankee (New York)
12-1-45	No. 1 Army 32, No. 2 Navy 13	Municipal (Philadelphia)
11-9-46	No. 1 Army 0, No. 2 Notre Dame 0 (tie)	Yankee (New York)
1-1-63	No. 1 Southern Cal 42, No. 2 Wisconsin 37 (Rose Bowl)	Rose Bowl (Pasadena)
10-12-63	No. 2 Texas 28, No. 1 Oklahoma 7	Cotton Bowl (Dallas)
1-1-64	No. 1 Texas 28, No. 2 Navy 6 (Cotton Bowl)	Cotton Bowl (Dallas)
11-19-66	No. 1 Notre Dame 10, No. 2 Michigan St. 10 (tie)	Spartan (East Lansing)
9-28-68	No. 1 Purdue 37, No. 2 Notre Dame 22	Notre Dame (South Bend)
1-1-69	No. 1 Ohio St. 27, No. 2 Southern Cal 16 (Rose Bowl)	Rose Bowl (Pasadena)
12-6-69	No. 1 Texas 15, No. 2 Arkansas 14	Razorback (Fayetteville)
11-25-71	No. 1 Nebraska 35, No. 2 Oklahoma 31	Owen Field (Norman)
1-1-72	No. 1 Nebraska 38, No. 2 Alabama 6 (Orange Bowl)	Orange Bowl (Miami)
1-1-79	No. 2 Alabama 14, No. 1 Penn St. 7 (Sugar Bowl)	Sugar Bowl (New Orleans)
9-26-81	No. 1 Southern Cal 28, No. 2 Oklahoma 24	Coliseum (Los Angeles)
1-1-83	No. 2 Penn St. 27, No. 1 Georgia 23 (Sugar Bowl)	Sugar Bowl (New Orleans)
10-19-85	No. 1 Iowa 12, No. 2 Michigan 10	Kinnick (Iowa City)
9-27-86	No. 2 Miami (Fla.) 28, No. 1 Oklahoma 16	Orange Bowl (Miami)
1-2-87	No. 2 Penn St. 14, No. 1 Miami (Fla.) 10 (Fiesta Bowl)	Sun Devil (Tempe)
11-21-87	No. 2 Oklahoma 17, No. 1 Nebraska 7	Memorial (Lincoln)
1-1-88	No. 2 Miami (Fla.) 20, No. 1 Oklahoma 14 (Orange Bowl)	Orange Bowl (Miami)
11-26-88	No. 1 Notre Dame 27, No. 2 Southern Cal 10	Coliseum (Los Angeles)
9-16-89	No. 1 Notre Dame 24, No. 2 Michigan 19	Michigan (Ann Arbor)
11-16-91	No. 2 Miami (Fla.) 17, No. 1 Florida St. 16	Doak Campbell (Tallahassee)
1-1-93	No. 2 Alabama 34, No. 1 Miami (Fla.) 13 (Sugar Bowl)	Superdome (New Orleans)
11-13-93	No. 2 Notre Dame 31, No. 1 Florida St. 24	Notre Dame (South Bend)
1-1-94	No. 1 Florida St. 18, No. 2 Nebraska 16 (Orange Bowl)	Orange Bowl (Miami)

The 1994 Orange Bowl matchup between Nebraska and Florida State marked the 29th time that the top two teams in The Associated Press poll have squared off. When Florida State claimed an 18-16 victory, it was the 17th win for the top-ranked team.

Games in Which a No. 1-Ranked Team Was Defeated or Tied

Listed here are 105 games in which the No. 1-ranked team in The Associated Press poll was defeated or tied. An asterisk (*) indicates the home team, an (N) a neutral site. In parentheses after the winning or tying team is its rank in the previous week's poll (NR indicates it was not ranked), its won-lost record entering the game and its score. The defeated or tied No. 1-ranked team follows with its score, and in parentheses is its rank in the poll the following week. Before 1965, the polls were final before bowl games. (Note: Only 10 teams were ranked in the weekly polls during 1962, 1963, 1964, 1965, 1966 and 1967; 20 teams all other seasons until 1989, when 25 teams were ranked.)

10-31-36	*Northwestern (3, 4-0-0) 6, Minnesota 0 (2)
11-21-36	*Notre Dame (11, 5-2-0) 26, Northwestern 6 (7)
10-30-37	(Tie) Washington (NR, 3-2-1) 0, *California 0 (2)
10-29-38	Carnegie Mellon (T19, 4-1-0) 20, *Pittsburgh 10 (3)
12-2-38	*Southern Cal (8, 7-2-0) 13, Notre Dame 0 (5)
10-14-39	Duquesne (NR, 3-0-0) 21, *Pittsburgh 13 (18)
11-8-41	(Tie) Baylor (NR, 3-4-0) 7, *Texas 7 (2)
10-31-42	*Wisconsin (6, 5-0-1) 17, Ohio St. 7 (6)
11-21-42	(N) Auburn (NR, 4-4-1) 27, Georgia 13 (5)
11-28-42	Holy Cross (NR, 4-4-1) 55, *Boston College 12 (8)
11-27-43	*Great Lakes NTS (NR, 9-2-0) 19, Notre Dame 14 (1)
11-9-46	(Tie) (N) Notre Dame (2, 5-0-0) 0, Army 0 (1)
10-8-49	Army (7, 2-0-0) 21, *Michigan 7 (7)
10-7-50	Purdue (NR, 0-1-0) 28, *Notre Dame 14 (10)
11-4-50	*Texas (7, 4-1-0) 23, Southern Methodist 20 (7)
11-18-50	*Illinois (10, 6-1-0) 14, Ohio St. 7 (8)
1-1-51	(Sugar Bowl) Kentucky (7, 10-1-0) 13, Oklahoma 7 (1)
10-20-51	Southern Cal (11, 4-1-0) 21, *California 14 (9)
1-1-52	(Sugar Bowl) Maryland (3, 9-0-0) 28, Tennessee 13 (1)
10-11-52	*Ohio St. (NR, 1-1-0) 23, Wisconsin 14 (12)
11-21-53	(Tie) Iowa (20, 5-3-0) 14, *Notre Dame 14 (2)
1-1-54	(Orange Bowl) Oklahoma (4, 8-1-1) 7, Maryland 0 (1)
10-2-54	Purdue (19, 1-0-0) 27, *Notre Dame 14 (8)
9-24-55	*Maryland (5, 1-0-0) 7, UCLA 0 (7)
10-27-56	*Illinois (NR, 1-3-0) 20, Michigan St. 13 (4)
10-19-57	Purdue (NR, 0-3-0) 20, *Michigan St. 13 (8)
11-16-57	*Rice (20, 4-3-0) 7, Texas A&M 6 (4)
10-25-58	(Tie) *Pittsburgh (NR, 4-1-0) 14, Army 14 (3)
11-7-59	*Tennessee (13, 4-1-1) 14, Louisiana St. 13 (3)
11-5-60	*Minnesota (3, 6-0-0) 27, Iowa 10 (5)
11-12-60	Purdue (NR, 2-4-1) 23, *Minnesota 14 (4)
11-19-60	Kansas (NR, 6-2-1) 23, *Missouri 7 (5)
1-1-61	(Rose Bowl) Washington (6, 9-1-0) 17, Minnesota 7 (1)
11-4-61	*Minnesota (NR, 4-1-0) 13, Michigan St. 0 (6)
11-18-61	Texas Christian (NR, 2-4-1) 6, *Texas 0 (5)
10-6-62	*UCLA (NR, 0-0-0) 9, Ohio St. 7 (10)
10-27-62	(Tie) *Rice (NR, 0-3-1) 14, Texas 14 (5)
11-10-62	*Wisconsin (8, 5-1-0) 37, Northwestern 6 (9)
11-17-62	*Georgia Tech (NR, 5-2-1) 7, Alabama 6 (6)
9-28-63	Oklahoma (3, 1-0-0) 17, *Southern Cal 12 (8)
10-12-63	(N)Texas (2, 3-0-0) 28, Oklahoma 7 (6)
10-17-64	Arkansas (8, 4-0-0) 14, *Texas 13 (6)
11-28-64	*Southern Cal (NR, 6-3-0) 20, Notre Dame 17 (3)
1-1-65	(Orange Bowl) Texas (5, 9-1-0) 21, Alabama 17 (1)
9-25-65	*Purdue (6, 1-0-0) 25, Notre Dame 21 (8)
10-16-65	*Arkansas (3, 4-0-0) 27, Texas 24 (5)
1-1-66	(Rose Bowl) UCLA (5, 7-2-1) 14, Michigan St. 12 (2)
11-19-66	(Tie) *Michigan St. (2, 9-0-0) 10, Notre Dame 10 (1)
9-30-67	*Purdue (10, 1-0-0) 28, Notre Dame 21 (6)
11-11-67	*Oregon St. (NR, 5-2-1) 3, Southern Cal 0 (4)
11-18-67	*Southern Cal (4, 8-1-0) 21, UCLA 20 (4)
10-12-68	*Ohio St. (4, 2-0-0) 13, Purdue 0 (5)
11-22-69	*Michigan (12, 7-2-0) 24, Ohio St. 12 (4)
1-1-71	(Cotton Bowl) Notre Dame (6, 8-1-1) 24, Texas 11 (3)
9-29-73	(Tie) Oklahoma (8, 1-0-0) 7, *Southern Cal 7 (4)
11-24-73	(Tie) *Michigan (4, 10-0-0) 10, Ohio St. 10 (3)
12-31-73	(Sugar Bowl) Notre Dame (3, 10-0-0) 24, Alabama 23 (4)
11-9-74	*Michigan St. (NR, 4-3-1) 16, Ohio St. 13 (4)
1-1-76	(Rose Bowl) UCLA (11, 8-2-1) 23, Ohio St. 10 (4)
11-6-76	*Purdue (NR, 3-5-0) 16, Michigan 14 (4)
10-8-77	Alabama (T7, 3-1-0) 21, *Southern Cal 20 (6)
10-22-77	*Minnesota (NR, 4-2-0) 16, Michigan 0 (6)
1-2-78	(Cotton Bowl) Notre Dame (5, 10-1-0) 38, Texas 10 (4)
9-23-78	(N) Southern Cal (7, 2-0-0) 24, Alabama 14 (3)
11-11-78	*Nebraska (4, 8-1-0) 17, Oklahoma 14 (4)
1-1-79	(Sugar Bowl) Alabama (2, 10-1-0) 14, Penn St. 7 (4)
10-13-79	(Tie) Stanford (NR, 3-2-0) 21, *Southern Cal 21 (4)
1-1-80	(Rose Bowl) Southern Cal (3, 10-0-1) 17, Ohio St. 16 (4)
11-1-80	(N) Mississippi St. (NR, 6-2-0) 6, Alabama 3 (6)
11-8-80	(Tie) *Georgia Tech (NR, 1-7-0) 3, Notre Dame 3 (6)
9-12-81	*Wisconsin (NR, 0-0-0) 21, Michigan 14 (11)
9-19-81	*Michigan (11, 0-1-0) 25, Notre Dame 7 (13)
10-10-81	Arizona (NR, 2-2-0) 13, *Southern Cal 10 (7)
10-17-81	*Arkansas (NR, 4-1-0) 42, Texas 11 (10)
10-31-81	*Miami (Fla.) (NR, 4-2-0) 17, Penn St. 14 (5)
11-28-81	Penn St. (11, 8-2-0) 48, *Pittsburgh 14 (10)
11-6-82	Notre Dame (NR, 5-1-1) 31, *Pittsburgh 16 (8)
1-1-83	(Sugar Bowl) Penn St. (2, 10-1-0) 27, Georgia 23 (4)
1-2-84	(Orange Bowl) Miami (Fla.) (5, 10-1-0) 31, Nebraska 30 (4)
9-8-84	*Michigan (14, 0-0-0) 22, Miami (Fla.) 14 (5)
9-29-84	*Syracuse (NR, 2-1-0) 17, Nebraska 9 (8)
10-13-84	(N) (Tie) Oklahoma (3, 4-0-0) 15, Texas 15 (3)
11-10-84	*Southern Cal (12, 7-1-0) 16, Washington 7 (5)
11-17-84	Oklahoma (6, 7-1-1) 17, *Nebraska 7 (7)
9-28-85	*Tennessee (NR, 0-0-1) 38, Auburn 20 (14)
11-2-85	*Ohio St. (7, 6-1-0) 22, Iowa 13 (6)
11-9-85	(N) Georgia (17, 6-1-1) 24, Florida 3 (11)
1-1-86	(Orange Bowl) Oklahoma (4, 9-1-0) 25, Penn St. 10 (3)
9-27-86	*Miami (Fla.) (2, 3-0-0) 28, Oklahoma 16 (6)
1-2-87	(Fiesta Bowl) Penn St. (2, 11-0-0) 14, Miami (Fla.) 10 (2)
11-21-87	Oklahoma (2, 11-0-0) 17, *Nebraska 7 (5)
1-1-88	(Orange Bowl) Miami (Fla.) (2, 11-1-0) 20, Oklahoma 14 (3)
10-15-88	*Notre Dame (4, 5-0-0) 31, Miami (Fla.) 30 (4)
10-29-88	Washington St. (NR, 4-3-0) 34, *UCLA 30 (6)
11-25-89	*Miami (Fla.) (7, 9-1-0) 27, Notre Dame 10 (5)
1-1-90	(Orange Bowl) Notre Dame (4, 11-1-0) 21, Colorado 6 (4)
9-8-90	*Brigham Young (16, 1-0-0) 28, Miami (Fla.) 21 (10)
10-6-90	Stanford (NR, 1-3-0) 36, *Notre Dame 31 (8)
10-13-90	Michigan St. (NR, 1-2-1) 28, *Michigan 27 (10)
11-3-90	Georgia Tech (16, 6-0-1) 41, *Virginia 38 (11)
11-17-90	Penn St. (18, 7-2-0) 24, *Notre Dame 21 (7)
11-16-91	Miami (Fla.) (2, 8-0-0) 17, *Florida St. 16 (3)
11-7-92	*Arizona (12, 5-2-1) 16, Washington 3 (6)
1-1-93	(Sugar Bowl) Alabama (2, 12-0) 34, Miami (Fla.) 13 (3)
11-13-93	*Notre Dame (2, 9-0-0) 31, Florida St. 24 (2)

Associated Press (Writers and Broadcasters) Final Polls

1936
Team
1. Minnesota
2. Louisiana St.
3. Pittsburgh
4. Alabama
5. Washington
6. Santa Clara
7. Northwestern
8. Notre Dame
9. Nebraska
10. Pennsylvania
11. Duke
12. Yale
13. Dartmouth
14. Duquesne
15. Fordham
16. Texas Christian
17. Tennessee
18. Arkansas
    Navy
20. Marquette

1937
Team
1. Pittsburgh
2. California
3. Fordham
4. Alabama
5. Minnesota
6. Villanova
7. Dartmouth
8. Louisiana St.
9. Notre Dame
   Santa Clara
11. Nebraska
12. Yale
13. Ohio St.
14. Holy Cross
    Arkansas
16. Texas Christian
17. Colorado
18. Rice
19. North Caro.
20. Duke

1938
Team
1. Texas Christian
2. Tennessee
3. Duke
4. Oklahoma
5. Notre Dame
6. Carnegie Mellon
7. Southern Cal
8. Pittsburgh
9. Holy Cross
10. Minnesota
11. Texas Tech
12. Cornell
13. Alabama
14. California
15. Fordham
16. Michigan
17. Northwestern
18. Villanova
19. Tulane
20. Dartmouth

1939
Team
1. Texas A&M
2. Tennessee
3. Southern Cal
4. Cornell
5. Tulane
6. Missouri
7. UCLA
8. Duke
9. Iowa
10. Duquesne
11. Boston College
12. Clemson
13. Notre Dame
14. Santa Clara
15. Ohio St.
16. Georgia Tech
17. Fordham
18. Nebraska
19. Oklahoma
20. Michigan

1940
Team
1. Minnesota
2. Stanford
3. Michigan
4. Tennessee
5. Boston College
6. Texas A&M
7. Nebraska
8. Northwestern
9. Mississippi St.
10. Washington
11. Santa Clara
12. Fordham
13. Georgetown
14. Pennsylvania
15. Cornell
16. Southern Methodist
17. Hardin-Simmons
18. Duke
19. Lafayette

1941
Team
1. Minnesota
2. Duke
3. Notre Dame
4. Texas
5. Michigan
6. Fordham
7. Missouri
8. Duquesne
9. Texas A&M
10. Navy
11. Northwestern
12. Oregon St.
13. Ohio St.
14. Georgia
15. Pennsylvania
16. Mississippi St.
17. Mississippi
18. Tennessee
19. Washington St.
20. Alabama

1942
Team
1. Ohio St.
2. Georgia
3. Wisconsin
4. Tulsa
5. Georgia Tech
6. Notre Dame
7. Tennessee
8. Boston College
9. Michigan
10. Alabama
11. Texas
12. Stanford
13. UCLA
14. William & Mary
15. Santa Clara
16. Auburn
17. Washington St.
18. Mississippi St.
19. Minnesota
    Holy Cross
    Penn St.

1943
Team
1. Notre Dame
2. Iowa Pre-Flight
3. Michigan
4. Navy
5. Purdue
6. Great Lakes
7. Duke
8. Del Monte P-F
9. Northwestern
10. March Field
11. Army
12. Washington
13. Georgia Tech
14. Texas
15. Tulsa
16. Dartmouth
17. Bainbridge NTS
18. Colorado Col.
19. Pacific (Cal.)
20. Pennsylvania

1944
Team
1. Army
2. Ohio St.
3. Randolph Field
4. Navy
5. Bainbridge NTS
6. Iowa Pre-Flight
7. Southern Cal
8. Michigan
9. Notre Dame
10. March Field
11. Duke
12. Tennessee
13. Georgia Tech
    Norman P-F
15. Illinois
16. El Toro Marines
17. Great Lakes
18. Fort Pierce
19. St. Mary's P-F
20. Second Air Force

1945
Team
1. Army
2. Alabama
3. Navy
4. Indiana
5. Oklahoma St.
6. Michigan
7. St. Mary's (Cal.)
8. Pennsylvania
9. Notre Dame
10. Texas
11. Southern Cal
12. Ohio St.
13. Duke
14. Tennessee
15. Louisiana St.
16. Holy Cross
17. Tulsa
18. Georgia
19. Wake Forest
20. Columbia

1946
Team
1. Notre Dame
2. Army
3. Georgia
4. UCLA
5. Illinois
6. Michigan
7. Tennessee
8. Louisiana St.
9. North Caro.
10. Rice
11. Georgia Tech
12. Yale
13. Pennsylvania
14. Oklahoma
15. Texas
16. Arkansas
17. Tulsa
18. North Caro. St.
19. Delaware
20. Indiana

*1947
Team
1. Notre Dame
2. Michigan
3. Southern Methodist
4. Penn St.
5. Texas
6. Alabama
7. Pennsylvania
8. Southern Cal
9. North Caro.
10. Georgia Tech
11. Army
12. Kansas
13. Mississippi
14. William & Mary
15. California
16. Oklahoma
17. North Caro. St.
18. Rice
19. Duke
20. Columbia

1948
Team
1. Michigan
2. Notre Dame
3. North Caro.
4. California
5. Oklahoma
6. Army
7. Northwestern
8. Georgia
9. Oregon
10. Southern Methodist
11. Clemson
12. Vanderbilt
13. Tulane
14. Michigan St.
15. Mississippi
16. Minnesota
17. William & Mary
18. Penn St.
19. Cornell
20. Wake Forest

1949
Team
1. Notre Dame
2. Oklahoma
3. California
4. Army
5. Rice
6. Ohio St.
7. Michigan
8. Minnesota
9. Louisiana St.
10. Pacific (Cal.)
11. Kentucky
12. Cornell
13. Villanova
14. Maryland
15. Santa Clara
16. North Caro.
17. Tennessee
18. Princeton
19. Michigan St.
20. Missouri
    Baylor

1950
Team
1. Oklahoma
2. Army
3. Texas
4. Tennessee
5. California
6. Princeton
7. Kentucky
8. Michigan St.
9. Michigan
10. Clemson
11. Washington
12. Wyoming
13. Illinois
14. Ohio St.
15. Miami (Fla.)
16. Alabama
17. Nebraska
18. Wash. & Lee
19. Tulsa
20. Tulane

1951
Team
1. Tennessee
2. Michigan St.
3. Maryland
4. Illinois
5. Georgia Tech
6. Princeton
7. Stanford
8. Wisconsin
9. Baylor
10. Oklahoma
11. Texas Christian
12. California
13. Virginia
14. San Francisco
15. Kentucky
16. Boston U.
17. UCLA
18. Washington St.
19. Holy Cross
20. Clemson

1952
Team
1. Michigan St.
2. Georgia Tech
3. Notre Dame
4. Oklahoma
5. Southern Cal
6. UCLA
7. Mississippi
8. Tennessee
9. Alabama
10. Texas
11. Wisconsin
12. Tulsa
13. Maryland
14. Syracuse
15. Florida
16. Duke
17. Ohio St.
18. Purdue
19. Princeton
20. Kentucky

1953
Team
1. Maryland
2. Notre Dame
3. Michigan St.
4. Oklahoma
5. UCLA
6. Rice
7. Illinois
8. Georgia Tech
9. Iowa
10. West Va.
11. Texas
12. Texas Tech
13. Alabama
14. Army
15. Wisconsin
16. Kentucky
17. Auburn
18. Duke
19. Stanford
20. Michigan

1954
Team
1. Ohio St.
2. UCLA
3. Oklahoma
4. Notre Dame
5. Navy
6. Mississippi
7. Army
8. Maryland
9. Wisconsin
10. Arkansas
11. Miami (Fla.)
12. West Va.
13. Auburn
14. Duke
15. Michigan
16. Virginia Tech
17. Southern Cal
18. Baylor
19. Rice
20. Penn St.

1955
Team
1. Oklahoma
2. Michigan St.
3. Maryland
4. UCLA
5. Ohio St.
6. Texas Christian
7. Georgia Tech
8. Auburn
9. Notre Dame
10. Mississippi
11. Pittsburgh
12. Michigan
13. Southern Cal
14. Miami (Fla.)
15. Miami (Ohio)
16. Stanford
17. Texas A&M
18. Navy
19. West Va.
20. Army

1956
Team
1. Oklahoma
2. Tennessee
3. Iowa
4. Georgia Tech
5. Texas A&M
6. Miami (Fla.)
7. Michigan
8. Syracuse
9. Michigan St.
10. Oregon St.
11. Baylor
12. Minnesota
13. Pittsburgh
14. Texas Christian
15. Ohio St.
16. Navy
17. Geo. Washington
18. Southern Cal
19. Clemson
20. Colorado

1957
Team
1. Auburn
2. Ohio St.
3. Michigan St.
4. Oklahoma
5. Navy
6. Iowa
7. Mississippi
8. Rice
9. Texas A&M
10. Notre Dame
11. Texas
12. Arizona St.
13. Tennessee
14. Mississippi St.
15. North Caro. St.
16. Duke
17. Florida
18. Army
19. Wisconsin
20. Va. Military

1958
Team
1. Louisiana St.
2. Iowa
3. Army
4. Auburn
5. Oklahoma
6. Air Force
7. Wisconsin
8. Ohio St.
9. Syracuse
10. Texas Christian
11. Mississippi
12. Clemson
13. Purdue
14. Florida
15. South Caro.
16. California
17. Notre Dame
18. Southern Methodist
19. Oklahoma St.
20. Rutgers

1959
Team
1. Syracuse
2. Mississippi
3. Louisiana St.
4. Texas
5. Georgia
6. Wisconsin
7. Texas Christian
8. Washington
9. Arkansas
10. Alabama
11. Clemson
12. Penn St.
13. Illinois
14. Southern Cal
15. Oklahoma
16. Wyoming
17. Notre Dame
18. Missouri
19. Florida
20. Pittsburgh

1960
Team
1. Minnesota
2. Mississippi
3. Iowa
4. Navy
5. Missouri
6. Washington
7. Arkansas
8. Ohio St.
9. Alabama
10. Duke
11. Kansas
12. Baylor
13. Auburn
14. Yale
15. Michigan St.
16. Penn St.
17. New Mexico St.
18. Florida
19. Syracuse
    Purdue

1961
Team
1. Alabama
2. Ohio St.
3. Texas
4. Louisiana St.
5. Mississippi
6. Minnesota
7. Colorado
8. Michigan St.
9. Arkansas
10. Utah St.
11. Missouri
12. Purdue
13. Georgia Tech
14. Syracuse
15. Rutgers
16. UCLA
17. Rice
    Penn St.
    Arizona
20. Duke

1962
Team
1. Southern Cal
2. Wisconsin
3. Mississippi
4. Texas
5. Alabama
6. Arkansas
7. Louisiana St.
8. Oklahoma
9. Penn St.
10. Minnesota
Only 10 ranked

1963
Team
1. Texas
2. Navy
3. Illinois
4. Pittsburgh
5. Auburn
6. Nebraska
7. Mississippi
8. Alabama
9. Oklahoma
10. Michigan St.
Only 10 ranked

1964
Team
1. Alabama
2. Arkansas
3. Notre Dame
4. Michigan
5. Texas
6. Nebraska
7. Louisiana St.
8. Oregon St.
9. Ohio St.
10. Southern Cal
Only 10 ranked

1965
Team
1. Alabama
2. Michigan St.
3. Arkansas
4. UCLA
5. Nebraska
6. Missouri
7. Tennessee
8. Louisiana St.
9. Notre Dame
10. Southern Cal
Only 10 ranked

1966
Team
1. Notre Dame
2. Michigan St.
3. Alabama
4. Georgia
5. UCLA
6. Nebraska
7. Purdue
8. Georgia Tech
9. Miami (Fla.)
10. Southern Methodist
Only 10 ranked

1967
Team
1. Southern Cal
2. Tennessee
3. Oklahoma
4. Indiana
5. Notre Dame
6. Wyoming
7. Oregon St.
8. Alabama
9. Purdue
10. Penn St.
Only 10 ranked

1968
Team
1. Ohio St.
2. Penn St.
3. Texas
4. Southern Cal
5. Notre Dame
6. Arkansas
7. Kansas
8. Georgia
9. Missouri
10. Purdue
11. Oklahoma
12. Michigan
13. Tennessee
14. Southern Methodist
15. Oregon St.
16. Auburn
17. Alabama
18. Houston
19. Louisiana St.
20. Ohio

1969
Team
1. Texas
2. Penn St.
3. Southern Cal
4. Ohio St.
5. Notre Dame
6. Missouri
7. Arkansas
8. Mississippi
9. Michigan
10. Louisiana St.
11. Nebraska
12. Houston
13. UCLA
14. Florida
15. Tennessee
16. Colorado
17. West Va.
18. Purdue
19. Stanford
20. Auburn

1970
Team
1. Nebraska
2. Notre Dame
3. Texas
4. Tennessee
5. Ohio St.
6. Arizona St.
7. Louisiana St.
8. Stanford
9. Michigan
10. Auburn
11. Arkansas
12. Toledo
13. Georgia Tech
14. Dartmouth
15. Southern Cal
16. Air Force
17. Tulane
18. Penn St.
19. Houston
20. Oklahoma
    Mississippi

1971
Team
1. Nebraska
2. Oklahoma
3. Colorado
4. Alabama
5. Penn St.
6. Michigan
7. Georgia
8. Arizona St.
9. Tennessee
10. Stanford
11. Louisiana St.
12. Auburn
13. Notre Dame
14. Toledo
15. Mississippi
16. Arkansas
17. Houston
18. Texas
19. Washington
20. Southern Cal

1972
Team
1. Southern Cal
2. Oklahoma
3. Texas
4. Nebraska
5. Auburn
6. Michigan
7. Alabama
8. Tennessee
9. Ohio St.
10. Penn St.
11. Louisiana St.
12. North Caro.
13. Arizona St.
14. Notre Dame
15. UCLA
16. Colorado
17. North Caro. St.
18. Louisville
19. Washington St.
20. Georgia Tech

1973
Team
1. Notre Dame
2. Ohio St.
3. Oklahoma
4. Alabama
5. Penn St.
6. Michigan
7. Nebraska
8. Southern Cal
9. Arizona St.
   Houston
11. Texas Tech
12. UCLA
13. Louisiana St.
14. Texas
15. Miami (Ohio)
16. North Caro. St.
17. Missouri
18. Kansas
19. Tennessee
20. Maryland
    Tulane

1974
Team
1. Oklahoma
2. Southern Cal
3. Michigan
4. Ohio St.
5. Alabama
6. Notre Dame
7. Penn St.
8. Auburn
9. Nebraska
10. Miami (Ohio)
11. North Caro. St.
12. Michigan St.
13. Maryland
14. Baylor
15. Florida
16. Texas A&M
17. Mississippi St.
    Texas
19. Houston
20. Tennessee

1975
Team
1. Oklahoma
2. Arizona St.
3. Alabama
4. Ohio St.
5. UCLA
6. Texas
7. Arkansas
8. Michigan
9. Nebraska
10. Penn St.
11. Texas A&M
12. Miami (Ohio)
13. Maryland
14. California
15. Pittsburgh
16. Colorado
17. Southern Cal
18. Arizona
19. Georgia
20. West Va.

1976
Team
1. Pittsburgh
2. Southern Cal
3. Michigan
4. Houston
5. Oklahoma
6. Ohio St.
7. Texas A&M
8. Maryland
9. Nebraska
10. Georgia
11. Alabama
12. Notre Dame
13. Texas Tech
14. Oklahoma St.
15. UCLA
16. Colorado
17. Rutgers
18. Kentucky
19. Iowa St.
20. Mississippi St.

1977
Team
1. Notre Dame
2. Alabama
3. Arkansas
4. Texas
5. Penn St.
6. Kentucky
7. Oklahoma
8. Pittsburgh
9. Michigan
10. Washington
11. Ohio St.
12. Nebraska
13. Southern Cal
14. Florida St.
15. Stanford
16. San Diego St.
17. North Caro.
18. Arizona St.
19. Clemson
20. Brigham Young

1978
Team
1. Alabama
2. Southern Cal
3. Oklahoma
4. Penn St.
5. Michigan
6. Clemson
7. Notre Dame
8. Nebraska
9. Texas
10. Houston
11. Arkansas
12. Michigan St.
13. Purdue
14. UCLA
15. Missouri
16. Georgia
17. Stanford
18. North Caro. St.
19. Texas A&M
20. Maryland

1979
Team
1. Alabama
2. Southern Cal
3. Oklahoma
4. Ohio St.
5. Houston
6. Florida St.
7. Pittsburgh
8. Arkansas
9. Nebraska
10. Purdue
11. Washington
12. Texas
13. Brigham Young
14. Baylor
15. North Caro.
16. Auburn
17. Temple
18. Michigan
19. Indiana
20. Penn St.

1980
Team
1. Georgia
2. Pittsburgh
3. Oklahoma
4. Michigan
5. Florida St.
6. Alabama
7. Nebraska
8. Penn St.
9. Notre Dame
10. North Caro.
11. Southern Cal
12. Brigham Young
13. UCLA
14. Baylor
15. Ohio St.
16. Washington
17. Purdue
18. Miami (Fla.)
19. Mississippi St.
20. Southern Methodist

1981
Team
1. Clemson
2. Texas
3. Penn St.
4. Pittsburgh
5. Southern Methodist
6. Georgia
7. Alabama
8. Miami (Fla.)
9. North Caro.
10. Washington
11. Nebraska
12. Michigan
13. Brigham Young
14. Southern Cal
15. Ohio St.
16. Arizona St.
17. West Va.
18. Iowa
19. Missouri
20. Oklahoma

1982
Team
1. Penn St.
2. Southern Methodist
3. Nebraska
4. Georgia
5. UCLA
6. Arizona St.
7. Washington
8. Clemson
9. Arkansas
10. Pittsburgh
11. Louisiana St.
12. Ohio St.
13. Florida St.
14. Auburn
15. Southern Cal
16. Oklahoma
17. Texas
18. North Caro.
19. West Va.
20. Maryland

1983
Team
1. Miami (Fla.)
2. Nebraska
3. Auburn
4. Georgia
5. Texas
6. Florida
7. Brigham Young
8. Michigan
9. Ohio St.
10. Illinois
11. Clemson
12. Southern Methodist
13. Air Force
14. Iowa
15. Alabama
16. West Va.
17. UCLA
18. Pittsburgh
19. Boston College
20. East Caro.

1984
Team
1. Brigham Young
2. Washington
3. Florida
4. Nebraska
5. Boston College
6. Oklahoma
7. Oklahoma St.
8. Southern Methodist
9. UCLA
10. Southern Cal
11. South Caro.
12. Maryland
13. Ohio St.
14. Auburn
15. Louisiana St.
16. Iowa
17. Florida St.
18. Miami (Fla.)
19. Kentucky
20. Virginia

1985
Team
1. Oklahoma
2. Michigan
3. Penn St.
4. Tennessee
5. Florida
6. Texas A&M
7. UCLA
8. Air Force
9. Miami (Fla.)
10. Iowa
11. Nebraska
12. Arkansas
13. Alabama
14. Ohio St.
15. Florida St.
16. Brigham Young
17. Baylor
18. Maryland
19. Georgia Tech
20. Louisiana St.

1986
Team
1. Penn St.
2. Miami (Fla.)
3. Oklahoma
4. Arizona St.
5. Nebraska
6. Auburn
7. Ohio St.
8. Michigan
9. Alabama
10. Louisiana St.
11. Arizona
12. Baylor
13. Texas A&M
14. UCLA
15. Arkansas
16. Iowa
17. Clemson
18. Washington
19. Boston College
20. Virginia Tech

1987
Team
1. Miami (Fla.)
2. Florida St.
3. Oklahoma
4. Syracuse
5. Louisiana St.
6. Nebraska
7. Auburn
8. Michigan St.
9. UCLA
10. Texas A&M
11. Oklahoma St.
12. Clemson
13. Georgia
14. Tennessee
15. South Caro.
16. Iowa
17. Notre Dame
18. Southern Cal
19. Michigan
20. Arizona St.

1988
Team
1. Notre Dame
2. Miami (Fla.)
3. Florida St.
4. Michigan
5. West Va.
6. UCLA
7. Southern Cal
8. Auburn
9. Clemson
10. Nebraska
11. Oklahoma St.
12. Arkansas
13. Syracuse
14. Oklahoma
15. Georgia
16. Washington St.
17. Alabama
18. Houston
19. Louisiana St.
20. Indiana

†1989
Team
1. Miami (Fla.)
2. Notre Dame
3. Florida St.
4. Colorado
5. Tennessee
6. Auburn
7. Michigan
8. Southern Cal
9. Alabama
10. Illinois
11. Nebraska
12. Clemson
13. Arkansas
14. Houston
15. Penn St.
16. Michigan St.
17. Pittsburgh
18. Virginia
19. Texas Tech
20. Texas A&M
21. West Va.
22. Brigham Young
23. Washington
24. Ohio St.
25. Arizona

1990
Team
1. Colorado
2. Georgia Tech
3. Miami (Fla.)
4. Florida St.
5. Washington
6. Notre Dame
7. Michigan
8. Tennessee
9. Clemson
10. Houston
11. Penn St.
12. Texas
13. Florida
14. Louisville
15. Texas A&M
16. Michigan St.
17. Oklahoma
18. Iowa
19. Auburn
20. Southern Cal
21. Mississippi
22. Brigham Young
23. Virginia
24. Nebraska
25. Illinois

1991
Team
1. Miami (Fla.)
2. Washington
3. Penn St.
4. Florida St.
5. Alabama
6. Michigan
7. Florida
8. California
9. East Caro.
10. Iowa
11. Syracuse
12. Texas A&M
13. Notre Dame
14. Tennessee
15. Nebraska
16. Oklahoma
17. Georgia
18. Clemson
19. UCLA
20. Colorado
21. Tulsa
22. Stanford
23. Brigham Young
24. North Caro. St.
25. Air Force

1992
Team
1. Alabama
2. Florida St.
3. Miami (Fla.)
4. Notre Dame
5. Michigan
6. Syracuse
7. Texas A&M
8. Georgia
9. Stanford
10. Florida
11. Washington
12. Tennessee
13. Colorado
14. Nebraska
15. Washington St.
16. Mississippi
17. North Caro. St.
18. Ohio St.
19. North Caro.
20. Hawaii
21. Boston College
22. Kansas
23. Mississippi St.
24. Fresno St.
25. Wake Forest

1993
Team
1. Florida St.
2. Notre Dame
3. Nebraska
4. Auburn
5. Florida
6. Wisconsin
7. West Va.
8. Penn St.
9. Texas A&M
10. Arizona
11. Ohio St.
12. Tennessee
13. Boston College
14. Alabama
15. Miami (Fla.)
16. Colorado
17. Oklahoma
18. UCLA
19. North Caro.
20. Kansas St.
21. Michigan
22. Virginia Tech
23. Clemson
24. Louisville
25. California

*On January 6, 1948, in a special postseason poll after the Rose Bowl, the Associated Press voted Michigan No. 1 and Notre Dame No. 2. However, the postseason poll did not supersede the final regular-season poll of December 6, 1947. †Beginning in 1989 season, AP selected top 25 teams instead of 20.

United Press International/National Football Foundation Final Polls

United Press (UP), 1950-57; United Press International (UPI) from 1958 after merger with International News Service (INS). Served as the coaches' poll until 1991, when it was taken over by USA Today/Cable News Network (CNN) poll.

1950
Team
1. Oklahoma
2. Texas
3. Tennessee
4. California
5. Army
6. Michigan
7. Kentucky
8. Princeton
9. Michigan St.
10. Ohio St.
11. Illinois
12. Clemson
13. Miami (Fla.)
14. Wyoming
15. Washington
    Baylor
17. Alabama
18. Wash. & Lee
19. Navy
20. Nebraska
    Wisconsin
    Cornell

1951
Team
1. Tennessee
2. Michigan St.
3. Illinois
4. Maryland
5. Georgia Tech
6. Princeton
7. Stanford
8. Wisconsin
9. Baylor
10. Texas Christian
11. Oklahoma
12. California
13. Notre Dame
14. San Francisco
    Purdue
    Washington St.
17. Holy Cross
    UCLA
    Kentucky
20. Kansas

1952
Team
1. Michigan St.
2. Georgia Tech
3. Notre Dame
4. Oklahoma
    Southern Cal
6. UCLA
7. Mississippi
8. Tennessee
9. Alabama
10. Wisconsin
11. Texas
12. Purdue
13. Maryland
14. Princeton
15. Ohio St.
    Pittsburgh
17. Navy
18. Duke
19. Houston
    Kentucky

1953
Team
1. Maryland
2. Notre Dame
3. Michigan St.
4. UCLA
5. Oklahoma
6. Rice
7. Illinois
8. Texas
9. Georgia Tech
10. Iowa
11. Alabama
12. Texas Tech
13. West Va.
14. Wisconsin
15. Kentucky
16. Army
17. Stanford
18. Duke
19. Michigan
20. Ohio St.

1954
Team
1. UCLA
2. Ohio St.
3. Oklahoma
4. Notre Dame
5. Navy
6. Mississippi
7. Army
8. Arkansas
9. Miami (Fla.)
10. Wisconsin
11. Southern Cal
    Maryland
    Georgia Tech
14. Duke
15. Michigan
16. Penn St.
17. Southern Methodist
18. Denver
19. Rice
20. Minnesota

1955
Team
1. Oklahoma
2. Michigan St.
3. Maryland
4. UCLA
5. Ohio St.
6. Texas Christian
7. Georgia Tech
8. Auburn
9. Mississippi
10. Notre Dame
11. Pittsburgh
12. Southern Cal
13. Michigan
14. Texas A&M
15. Army
16. Duke
17. West Va.
18. Miami (Fla.)
19. Iowa
20. Navy
    Stanford
    Miami (Ohio)

1956
Team
1. Oklahoma
2. Tennessee
3. Iowa
4. Georgia Tech
5. Texas A&M
6. Miami (Fla.)
7. Michigan
8. Syracuse
9. Minnesota
10. Michigan St.
11. Baylor
12. Pittsburgh
13. Oregon St.
14. Texas Christian
15. Southern Cal
16. Wyoming
17. Yale
18. Colorado
19. Navy
20. Duke

1957
Team
1. Ohio St.
2. Auburn
3. Michigan St.
4. Oklahoma
5. Iowa
6. Navy
7. Rice
8. Mississippi
9. Notre Dame
10. Texas A&M
11. Texas
12. Arizona St.
13. Army
14. Duke
    Wisconsin
16. Tennessee
17. Oregon
18. Clemson
    UCLA
20. North Caro. St.

1958
Team
1. Louisiana St.
2. Iowa
3. Army
4. Auburn
5. Oklahoma
6. Wisconsin
7. Ohio St.
8. Air Force
9. Texas Christian
10. Syracuse
11. Purdue
12. Mississippi
13. Clemson
14. Notre Dame
15. Florida
16. California
17. Northwestern
18. Southern Methodist

1959
Team
1. Syracuse
2. Mississippi
3. Louisiana St.
4. Texas
5. Georgia
6. Wisconsin
7. Washington
8. Texas Christian
9. Arkansas
10. Penn St.
11. Illinois
12. Southern Cal
13. Alabama
14. Penn St.
15. Oklahoma
16. Northwestern
    Michigan St.
18. Wyoming
19. Auburn
    Missouri

1960
Team
1. Minnesota
2. Iowa
3. Mississippi
4. Missouri
5. Wisconsin
6. Navy
7. Arkansas
8. Ohio St.
9. Kansas
10. Alabama
11. Duke
    Baylor
    Michigan St.
14. Auburn
15. Purdue
16. Florida
17. Texas
18. Yale
19. New Mexico St.
    Tennessee

1961
Team
1. Alabama
2. Ohio St.
3. Louisiana St.
4. Texas
5. Mississippi
6. Minnesota
7. Colorado
8. Arkansas
9. Michigan St.
10. Utah St.
11. Purdue
    Missouri
13. Georgia Tech
14. Duke
15. Kansas
16. Syracuse
17. Wyoming
18. Wisconsin
19. Miami (Fla.)
    Penn St.

1962
Team
1. Southern Cal
2. Wisconsin
3. Mississippi
4. Texas
5. Alabama
6. Arkansas
7. Oklahoma
8. Louisiana St.
9. Penn St.
10. Minnesota
11. Georgia Tech
12. Missouri
13. Ohio St.
14. Duke
    Washington
16. Northwestern
    Oregon St.
18. Arizona St.
    Illinois
    Miami (Fla.)

1963
Team
1. Texas
2. Navy
3. Pittsburgh
4. Illinois
5. Nebraska
6. Auburn
7. Mississippi
8. Oklahoma
9. Alabama
10. Michigan St.
11. Mississippi St.
12. Syracuse
13. Arizona St.
14. Memphis
15. Washington
16. Penn St.
    Southern Cal
    Missouri
19. North Caro.
20. Baylor

1964
Team
1. Alabama
2. Arkansas
3. Notre Dame
4. Michigan
5. Texas
6. Nebraska
7. Louisiana St.
8. Oregon St.
9. Ohio St.
10. Southern Cal
11. Florida St.
12. Syracuse
13. Princeton
14. Penn St.
    Utah
16. Illinois
    New Mexico
18. Tulsa
    Missouri
20. Mississippi
    Michigan St.

1965
Team
1. Michigan St.
2. Arkansas
3. Nebraska
4. Alabama
5. UCLA
6. Missouri
7. Tennessee
8. Notre Dame
9. Southern Cal
10. Texas Tech
11. Ohio St.
12. Florida
13. Purdue
14. Louisiana St.
15. Georgia
16. Tulsa
17. Mississippi
18. Kentucky
19. Syracuse
20. Colorado

1966
Team
1. Notre Dame
2. Michigan St.
3. Alabama
4. Georgia
5. UCLA
6. Purdue
7. Nebraska
8. Georgia Tech
9. Southern Methodist
10. Miami (Fla.)
11. Florida
12. Mississippi
13. Arkansas
14. Tennessee
15. Wyoming
16. Syracuse
17. Houston
18. Southern Cal
19. Oregon St.
20. Virginia Tech

1967
Team
1. Southern Cal
2. Tennessee
3. Oklahoma
4. Notre Dame
5. Wyoming
6. Indiana
7. Alabama
8. Oregon St.
9. Purdue
10. UCLA
11. Penn St.
12. Syracuse
13. Colorado
14. Minnesota
15. Florida St.
16. Miami (Fla.)
17. North Caro. St.
18. Georgia
19. Houston
20. Arizona St.

1968
Team
1. Ohio St.
2. Southern Cal
3. Penn St.
4. Georgia
5. Texas
6. Kansas
7. Tennessee
8. Notre Dame
9. Arkansas
10. Oklahoma
11. Purdue
12. Alabama
13. Oregon St.
14. Florida St.
15. Michigan
16. Southern Methodist
17. Missouri
18. Ohio
    Minnesota
20. Houston
    Stanford

1969
Team
1. Texas
2. Penn St.
3. Arkansas
4. Southern Cal
5. Ohio St.
6. Missouri
7. Louisiana St.
8. Michigan
9. Notre Dame
10. UCLA
11. Tennessee
12. Nebraska
13. Mississippi
14. Stanford
15. Auburn
16. Houston
17. Florida
18. Purdue
    San Diego St.
    West Va.

1970
Team
1. Texas
2. Ohio St.
3. Nebraska
4. Tennessee
5. Notre Dame
6. Louisiana St.
7. Michigan
8. Arizona St.
9. Auburn
10. Stanford
11. Air Force
12. Arkansas
13. Houston
    Dartmouth
15. Oklahoma
16. Colorado
17. Georgia Tech
    Toledo
19. Penn St.
    Southern Cal

1971
Team
1. Nebraska
2. Alabama
3. Oklahoma
4. Michigan
5. Auburn
6. Arizona St.
7. Colorado
8. Georgia
9. Tennessee
10. Louisiana St.
11. Penn St.
12. Texas
13. Toledo
14. Houston
15. Notre Dame
16. Stanford
17. Iowa St.
18. North Caro.
19. Florida St.
20. Arkansas
    Mississippi

1972
Team
1. Southern Cal
2. Oklahoma
3. Ohio St.
4. Alabama
5. Texas
6. Michigan
7. Auburn
8. Penn St.
9. Nebraska
10. Louisiana St.
11. Tennessee
12. Notre Dame
13. Arizona St.
14. Colorado
    North Caro.
16. Louisville
17. UCLA
    Washington St.
19. Utah St.
20. San Diego St.

1973
Team
1. Alabama
2. Oklahoma
3. Ohio St.
4. Notre Dame
5. Penn St.
6. Michigan
7. Southern Cal
8. Texas
9. UCLA
10. Arizona St.
11. Nebraska
    Texas Tech
13. Houston
14. Louisiana St.
15. Kansas
    Tulane
17. Miami (Ohio)
18. Maryland
19. San Diego St.
    Florida

*1974
Team
1. Southern Cal
2. Alabama
3. Ohio St.
4. Notre Dame
5. Michigan
6. Auburn
7. Penn St.
8. Nebraska
9. North Caro. St.
10. Miami (Ohio)
11. Houston
12. Florida
13. Maryland
14. Baylor
15. Texas A&M
    Tennessee
17. Mississippi St.
18. Michigan St.
19. Tulsa

1975
Team
1. Oklahoma
2. Arizona St.
3. Alabama
4. Ohio St.
5. UCLA
6. Arkansas
7. Texas
8. Michigan
9. Nebraska
10. Penn St.
11. Maryland
12. Texas A&M
13. Arizona
    Pittsburgh
15. California
16. Miami (Ohio)
17. Notre Dame
    West Va.
19. Georgia
    Southern Cal

1976
Team
1. Pittsburgh
2. Southern Cal
3. Michigan
4. Houston
5. Ohio St.
6. Oklahoma
7. Nebraska
8. Texas A&M
9. Alabama
10. Georgia
11. Maryland
12. Notre Dame
13. Texas Tech
14. Oklahoma St.
15. UCLA
16. Colorado
17. Rutgers
18. Iowa St.
19. Baylor
    Kentucky

1977
Team
1. Notre Dame
2. Alabama
3. Arkansas
4. Penn St.
5. Texas
6. Oklahoma
7. Pittsburgh
8. Michigan
9. Washington
10. Nebraska
11. Florida St.
12. Ohio St.
    Southern Cal
14. North Caro.
15. Stanford
16. North Texas
    Brigham Young
18. Arizona St.
19. San Diego St.
    North Caro. St.

1978
Team
1. Southern Cal
2. Alabama
3. Oklahoma
4. Penn St.
5. Michigan
6. Notre Dame
7. Clemson
8. Nebraska
9. Texas
10. Arkansas
11. Houston
12. UCLA
13. Purdue
14. Missouri
15. Georgia
16. Stanford
17. Navy
18. Texas A&M
19. Arizona St.
    North Caro. St.

1979
Team
1. Alabama
2. Southern Cal
3. Oklahoma
4. Ohio St.
5. Houston
6. Pittsburgh
7. Nebraska
8. Florida St.
9. Arkansas
10. Purdue
11. Washington
12. Brigham Young
13. Texas
14. North Caro.
15. Baylor
16. Indiana
17. Temple
18. Penn St.
19. Michigan
20. Missouri

1980

Team
1. Georgia
2. Pittsburgh
3. Oklahoma
4. Michigan
5. Florida St.
6. Alabama
7. Nebraska
8. Penn St.
9. North Caro.
10. Notre Dame
11. Brigham Young
12. Southern Cal
13. Baylor
14. UCLA
15. Ohio St.
16. Purdue
17. Washington
18. Miami (Fla.)
19. Florida
20. Southern Methodist

1981

Team
1. Clemson
2. Pittsburgh
3. Penn St.
4. Texas
5. Georgia
6. Alabama
7. Washington
8. North Caro.
9. Nebraska
10. Michigan
11. Brigham Young
12. Ohio St.
13. Southern Cal
14. Oklahoma
15. Iowa
16. Arkansas
17. Mississippi St.
18. West Va.
19. Southern Miss.
20. Missouri

1982

Team
1. Penn St.
2. Southern Methodist
3. Nebraska
4. Georgia
5. UCLA
6. Arizona St.
7. Washington
8. Arkansas
9. Pittsburgh
10. Florida St.
11. Louisiana St.
12. Ohio St.
13. North Caro.
14. Auburn
15. Michigan
16. Oklahoma
17. Alabama
18. Texas
19. West Va.
20. Maryland

1983

Team
1. Miami (Fla.)
2. Nebraska
3. Auburn
4. Georgia
5. Texas
6. Florida
7. Brigham Young
8. Ohio St.
9. Michigan
10. Illinois
11. Southern Methodist
12. Alabama
13. UCLA
14. Iowa
15. Air Force
16. West Va.
17. Penn St.
18. Oklahoma St.
19. Pittsburgh
20. Boston College

1984

Team
1. Brigham Young
2. Washington
3. Nebraska
4. Boston College
5. Oklahoma St.
6. Oklahoma
7. Florida
8. Southern Methodist
9. Southern Cal
10. UCLA
11. Maryland
12. Ohio St.
13. South Caro.
14. Auburn
15. Iowa
16. Louisiana St.
17. Virginia
18. West Va.
19. Kentucky
    Florida St.

1985

Team
1. Oklahoma
2. Michigan
3. Penn St.
4. Tennessee
5. Air Force
6. UCLA
7. Texas A&M
8. Miami (Fla.)
9. Iowa
10. Nebraska
11. Ohio St.
12. Arkansas
13. Florida St.
14. Alabama
15. Baylor
16. Fresno St.
17. Brigham Young
18. Georgia Tech
19. Maryland
20. Louisiana St.

1986

Team
1. Penn St.
2. Miami (Fla.)
3. Oklahoma
4. Nebraska
5. Arizona St.
6. Ohio St.
7. Michigan
8. Auburn
9. Alabama
10. Arizona
11. Louisiana St.
12. Texas A&M
13. Baylor
14. UCLA
15. Iowa
16. Arkansas
17. Washington
18. Boston College
19. Clemson
20. Florida St.

1987

Team
1. Miami (Fla.)
2. Florida St.
3. Oklahoma
4. Syracuse
5. Louisiana St.
6. Nebraska
7. Auburn
8. Michigan St.
9. Texas A&M
10. Clemson
11. UCLA
12. Oklahoma St.
13. Tennessee
14. Georgia
15. South Caro.
16. Iowa
17. Southern Cal
18. Michigan
19. Texas
20. Indiana

1988

Team
1. Notre Dame
2. Miami (Fla.)
3. Florida St.
4. Michigan
5. West Va.
6. UCLA
7. Auburn
8. Clemson
9. Southern Cal
10. Nebraska
11. Oklahoma St.
12. Syracuse
13. Arkansas
14. Oklahoma
15. Georgia
16. Washington St.
17. North Caro. St.
    Alabama
19. Indiana
20. Wyoming

1989

Team
1. Miami (Fla.)
2. Florida St.
3. Notre Dame
4. Colorado
5. Tennessee
6. Auburn
7. Alabama
8. Michigan
9. Southern Cal
10. Illinois
11. Clemson
12. Nebraska
13. Arkansas
14. Penn St.
15. Virginia
16. Texas Tech
    Michigan St.
18. Brigham Young
19. Pittsburgh
20. Washington

#1990

Team
1. Georgia Tech
2. Colorado
3. Miami (Fla.)
4. Florida St.
5. Washington
6. Notre Dame
7. Tennessee
8. Michigan
9. Clemson
10. Penn St.
11. Texas
12. Louisville
13. Texas A&M
14. Michigan St.
15. Virginia
16. Iowa
17. Brigham Young
    Nebraska
19. Auburn
20. San Jose St.
21. Syracuse
22. Southern Cal
23. Mississippi
24. Illinois
25. Virginia Tech

¢1991

Team
1. Washington
2. Miami (Fla.)
3. Penn St.
4. Florida St.
5. Alabama
6. Michigan
7. Florida
8. California
9. East Caro.
10. Iowa
11. Syracuse
12. Notre Dame
13. Texas A&M
14. Tennessee
15. Nebraska
16. Oklahoma
17. Clemson
18. Colorado
19. UCLA
20. Georgia
21. Tulsa
22. Stanford
23. North Caro. St.
24. Brigham Young
25. Ohio St.

1992

Team
1. Alabama
2. Florida St.
3. Miami (Fla.)
4. Notre Dame
5. Michigan
6. Syracuse
7. Texas A&M
8. Georgia
9. Stanford
10. Florida
11. Washington
12. Tennessee
13. Colorado
14. Nebraska
15. Washington St.
16. Mississippi
17. North Caro. St.
18. North Caro.
19. Ohio St.
20. Hawaii
21. Boston College
22. Kansas
23. Fresno St.
24. Penn St.
25. Mississippi St.

Beginning in 1974, by agreement with the American Football Coaches Association, teams on probation by the NCAA were ineligible for ranking and national championship consideration by the UPI Board of Coaches. #Beginning in 1990 season, UPI selected top 25 teams instead of 20. ¢In 1991-92, the No. 1 team in the final UPI/NFF poll received the MacArthur Bowl, awarded by the NFF since 1959 to recognize its national champion. Beginning in 1993, the No. 1 team in the USA Today/Hall of Fame poll was awarded the MacArthur Bowl. The National Football Foundation and Hall of Fame MacArthur Bowl national champions before 1991 are listed in national polls section.

DIVISION I-A

USA Today/Cable News Network (Coaches) Poll Weekly Leaders

1992

Date	Team	Record
9-8	Miami (Fla.)	(1-0-0)
9-15	Miami (Fla.)	(1-0-0)
9-22	Miami (Fla.)	(2-0-0)
9-29	Washington	(3-0-0) (2)
10-6	Washington	(4-0-0)
10-13	Miami (Fla.)	(5-0-0) (2)
10-20	Miami (Fla.)	(6-0-0)
10-27	Miami (Fla.)	(7-0-0)
11-3	Miami (Fla.)	(8-0-0)
11-10	Miami (Fla.)	(8-0-0)
11-17	Miami (Fla.)	(9-0-0)
11-24	Miami (Fla.)	(10-0-0)
12-1	Miami (Fla.)	(11-0-0)
12-8	Miami (Fla.)	(11-0-0)
1-2	**Alabama**	**(13-0-0) (2)**

1993

Date	Team	Record
8-31	Florida St.	(1-0-0)
9-7	Florida St.	(2-0-0)
9-14	Florida St.	(3-0-0)
9-21	Florida St.	(4-0-0)
9-28	Florida St.	(4-0-0)
10-5	Florida St.	(5-0-0)
10-12	Florida St.	(6-0-0)
10-19	Florida St.	(7-0-0)
10-26	Florida St.	(7-0-0)
11-2	Florida St.	(8-0-0)
11-9	Florida St.	(9-0-0)
11-16	Notre Dame	(10-0-0) (2)
11-23	Nebraska	(10-0-0) (2)
11-30	Nebraska	(11-0-0)
12-7	Nebraska	(11-0-0)
1-3	**Florida St.**	**(12-1-0) (3)**

1993 USA Today/CNN Week-by-Week Polls

#	Team	First Week (8-31)	9-7	9-14	9-21	9-28	10-5	10-12	10-19	10-26	11-2	11-9	11-16	11-23	11-30	12-7	1-3
1	Florida St.	1	1	1	1	1	1	1	1	1	1	1	3	2	3	3	1
2	Alabama	3	2	2	2	2	2	5	5	5	11	10	17	15	18	18	13
3	Michigan	2	10	9	10	10	17	14	23	NR	NR	NR	NR	22	22	22	19
4	Miami (Fla.)	4	3	3	3	3	9	6	6	6	4	4	9	8	9	9	15
5	Texas A&M	5	16	15	14	13	12	9	8	8	8	8	6T	6	6	6	8
6	Notre Dame	10	5	4	4	4	3	2	2	2	2	1	4	4	4	4	2
7	Syracuse	6	4	11	13	22	19	21	NR	NR	NR	NR	NR	NR	NR	NR	NR
8	Nebraska	7	6	5	5	5	5	3	4	4	3	2	1	1	1	1	3
9	Florida	8	9	6	6	6	4	10	10	10	9	9	6T	9	8	8	4
10	Colorado	9	8	12	21	21	18	16	18	24	22	18	18	18	18	17	16
11	Tennessee	11	7	13	12	12	11	8	9	7	6	7	5	5	5	5	11
12	Penn St.	12	12	8	8	8	7	13	12	16	14	12	11	12	12	12	7
13	Georgia	21	NR	NR	NR	NR	NR	NR	NR	NR	NR	NR	NR	NR	NR	NR	NR
14	Stanford	22	19	20	NR	NR	NR	NR	NR	NR	NR	NR	NR	NR	NR	NR	NR
15	Arizona	13	15	14	11	11	10	7	7	12	12	17	16	14	14	14	9
16	Ohio St.	14	11	7	7	7	6	4	3	3	5	5	10	10	10	10	10
17	Southern Cal	23	NR	NR	NR	NR	NR	NR	NR	NR	24	19	25	NR	NR	NR	25
18	North Caro.	15	14	19	16	15	13	11	19	18	15	13	13	11	11	11	21
19	Oklahoma	16	13	10	9	9	8	17	13	20	17	14	15	17	16	16	14
20	Brigham Young	19	18	17	17	18	NR	NR	NR	NR	NR	NR	NR	NR	NR	NR	NR
21	Clemson	17	NR	NR	NR	24	NR	NR	NR	NR	NR	25	23	23	23	23	22
22	North Caro. St.	17	17	16	23	NR	NR	NR	NR	22	NR	NR	NR	NR	NR	NR	NR
23	Boston College	NR	24	NR	NR	NR	NR	NR	NR	NR	25	21	16	12	16	15	12
24	Texas	NR	NR	NR	NR	NR	NR	NR	NR	NR	NR	NR	NR	NR	NR	NR	NR
25	Mississippi St.	NR	NR	NR	NR	NR	NR	NR	NR	NR	NR	NR	NR	NR	NR	NR	NR
NR	South Caro.	20	NR	NR	NR	NR	NR	NR	NR	NR	NR	NR	NR	NR	NR	NR	NR
NR	Arizona St.	24	20	NR	NR	NR	NR	NR	NR	NR	NR	NR	NR	NR	NR	NR	NR
NR	Baylor	25	NR	NR	NR	NR	NR	NR	NR	NR	NR	NR	NR	NR	NR	NR	NR
NR	California	NR	21	18	15	14	20	NR	NR	NR	NR	NR	NR	NR	NR	NR	24
NR	Iowa	NR	22	NR	NR	NR	NR	NR	NR	NR	NR	NR	NR	NR	NR	NR	NR
NR	Virginia	NR	23	21	18	16	14	20	14	19	16	22	NR	NR	NR	NR	NR
NR	Wisconsin	NR	25	22	20	19	16	12	20	14	13	11	8	7	7	7	5
NR	Louisville	NR	NR	23	19	17	21	19	16	15	20	NR	NR	25	25	25	23
NR	West Va.	NR	NR	NR	24	22	20	15	15	11	9	7	6	3	2	2	6
NR	Fresno St.	NR	NR	25	24	23	NR	NR	NR	NR	NR	NR	NR	NR	NR	24	NR
NR	Mississippi	NR	NR	NR	25	NR	NR	NR	NR	NR	NR	NR	NR	NR	NR	NR	NR
NR	Indiana	NR	NR	NR	NR	25	22	22	17	13	18	21	21	21	21	20T	NR
NR	UCLA	NR	NR	NR	NR	NR	23	18	15	11	10	15	14	13	13	13	17
NR	Kansas St.	NR	NR	NR	NR	NR	NR	NR	NR	24	25	22	17	23	20	19	18
NR	Michigan St.	NR	NR	NR	NR	NR	NR	25	23	21	NR	25	24	24	NR	NR	NR
NR	Washington St.	NR	NR	NR	NR	NR	NR	24	NR	NR	NR	NR	NR	NR	NR	NR	NR
NR	Virginia Tech	NR	NR	NR	NR	NR	NR	NR	24	23	NR	23	20	20	20T	20T	20
NR	Wyoming	NR	NR	NR	NR	NR	NR	NR	25	21	19	NR	NR	NR	NR	NR	NR

USA Today/Cable News Network Final Polls (Coaches)

Took over as coaches poll in 1991.

1982
Team
1. Penn St.
2. Southern Methodist
3. Nebraska
4. Georgia
5. UCLA
6. Arizona St.
7. Pittsburgh
8. Arkansas
9. Clemson
10. Washington
11. Louisiana St.
12. Florida St.
13. Ohio St.
14. Southern Cal
15. Oklahoma
16. Auburn
17. West Va.
18. Maryland
19. North Caro.
20. Texas
21. Michigan
22. Alabama
23. Tulsa
24. Iowa
25. Florida

1983
Team
1. Miami (Fla.)
2. Auburn
3. Nebraska
4. Georgia
5. Texas
6. Brigham Young
7. Michigan
8. Ohio St.
9. Florida
10. Clemson
11. Illinois
12. Southern Methodist
13. Alabama
14. Air Force
15. West Va.
16. Iowa
17. Tennessee
18. UCLA
19. Pittsburgh
20. Penn St.
21. Oklahoma
22. Boston College
23. Oklahoma St.
24. Maryland
25. East Caro.

1984
Team
1. Brigham Young
2. Washington
3. Florida
4. Nebraska
5. Oklahoma
6. Boston College
7. Oklahoma St.
8. Southern Methodist
9. Maryland
10. South Caro.
11. Southern Cal
12. UCLA
13. Louisiana St.
14. Ohio St.
15. Auburn
16. Miami (Fla.)
17. Florida St.
18. Virginia
19. Kentucky
20. Iowa
21. West Va.
22. Army
23. Georgia
24. Air Force
25. Notre Dame

1985
Team
1. Oklahoma
2. Penn St.
3. Michigan
4. Tennessee
5. Florida
6. Miami (Fla.)
7. Air Force
8. Texas A&M
9. UCLA
10. Iowa
11. Nebraska
12. Alabama
13. Ohio St.
14. Florida St.
15. Arkansas
16. Brigham Young
17. Maryland
18. Georgia Tech
19. Baylor
20. Auburn
21. Louisiana St.
22. Army
23. Fresno St.
24. Georgia
25. Oklahoma St.

1986
Team
1. Penn St.
2. Miami (Fla.)
3. Oklahoma
4. Nebraska
5. Arizona St.
6. Ohio St.
7. Auburn
8. Michigan
9. Alabama
10. Louisiana St.
11. Arizona
12. Texas A&M
13. UCLA
14. Baylor
15. Boston College
16. Iowa
17. Arkansas
18. Clemson
19. Washington
20. Virginia Tech
21. Florida St.
22. Stanford
23. Georgia
24. North Caro. St.
25. San Diego St.

1987
Team
1. Miami (Fla.)
2. Florida St.
3. Oklahoma
4. Syracuse
5. Nebraska
6. Louisiana St.
7. Auburn
8. Michigan St.
9. Texas A&M
10. UCLA
11. Clemson
12. Oklahoma St.
13. Georgia
14. Tennessee
15. Iowa
16. Notre Dame
17. Southern Cal
18. South Caro.
19. Michigan
20. Texas
21. Pittsburgh
22. Indiana
23. Penn St.
24. Ohio St.
25. Alabama

1988
Team
1. Notre Dame
2. Miami (Fla.)
3. Florida St.
4. UCLA
5. Michigan
6. West Va.
7. Southern Cal
8. Nebraska
9. Auburn
10. Clemson
11. Oklahoma St.
12. Syracuse
13. Oklahoma
14. Arkansas
15. Washington St.
16. Georgia
17. Alabama
18. North Caro. St.
19. Houston
20. Indiana
21. Wyoming
22. Louisiana St.
23. Colorado
24. Southern Miss.
25. Brigham Young

1989
Team
1. Miami (Fla.)
2. Notre Dame
3. Florida St.
4. Colorado
5. Tennessee
6. Auburn
7. Southern Cal
8. Michigan
9. Alabama
10. Illinois
11. Nebraska
12. Clemson
13. Arkansas
14. Houston
15. Penn St.
16. Virginia
17. Michigan St.
18. Texas Tech
19. Pittsburgh
20. Texas A&M
21. West Va.
22. Brigham Young
23. Syracuse
24. Ohio St.
25. Washington

1990
Team
1. Colorado
2. Georgia Tech
3. Miami (Fla.)
4. Florida St.
5. Washington
6. Notre Dame
7. Tennessee
8. Michigan
9. Clemson
10. Texas
11. Penn St.
12. Houston
13. Florida
14. Louisville
15. Michigan St.
16. Texas A&M
17. Oklahoma
18. Iowa
19. Auburn
20. Brigham Young
21. Mississippi
22. Southern Cal
23. Nebraska
24. Illinois
25. Virginia

1991
Team
1. Washington
2. Miami (Fla.)
3. Penn St.
4. Florida St.
5. Alabama
6. Michigan
7. California
8. Florida
9. East Caro.
10. Iowa
11. Syracuse
12. Notre Dame
13. Texas A&M
14. Oklahoma
15. Tennessee
16. Nebraska
17. Clemson
18. UCLA
19. Georgia
20. Colorado
21. Tulsa
22. Stanford
23. Brigham Young
24. Air Force
25. North Caro. St.

1992
Team
1. Alabama
2. Florida St.
3. Miami (Fla.)
4. Notre Dame
5. Michigan
6. Texas A&M
7. Syracuse
8. Georgia
9. Stanford
10. Washington
11. Florida
12. Tennessee
13. Colorado
14. Nebraska
15. North Caro. St.
16. Mississippi
17. Washington St.
18. North Caro.
19. Ohio St.
20. Hawaii
21. Boston College
22. Fresno St.
23. Kansas
24. Penn St.
25. Wake Forest

1993
Team
1. Florida St.
2. Notre Dame
3. Nebraska
4. Florida
5. Wisconsin
6. West Va.
7. Penn St.
8. Texas A&M
9. Arizona
10. Ohio St.
11. Tennessee
12. Boston College
13. Alabama
14. Oklahoma
15. Miami (Fla.)
16. Colorado
17. UCLA
18. Kansas St.
19. Michigan
20. Virginia Tech
21. North Caro.
22. Clemson
23. Louisville
24. California
25. Southern Cal

USA Today/National Football Foundation and College Hall of Fame Poll Weekly Leaders

1993

9-7	Florida St.	(2-0-0)
9-14	Florida St.	(3-0-0)
9-21	Florida St.	(4-0-0)
9-28	Florida St.	(4-0-0)
10-5	Florida St.	(5-0-0)
10-12	Florida St.	(6-0-0)
10-19	Florida St.	(7-0-0)
10-26	Florida St.	(7-0-0)
11-2	Florida St.	(8-0-0)
11-9	Florida St.	(9-0-0)
11-16	Notre Dame	(10-0-0) (2)
11-23	Nebraska	(10-0-0) (3)
11-30	Nebraska	(11-0-0)
12-7	Nebraska	(11-0-0)
1-3	**Florida St.**	**(12-1-0) (2)**

USA Today/National Football Foundation and College Hall of Fame Poll (MacArthur Bowl)

Voters are members of the National Football Foundation and College Hall of Fame, Inc. They include former players and coaches as well as current athletics administrators and sports journalists. Beginning in 1993, the winner of the poll's national championship receives the MacArthur Bowl, given by the National Football Foundation since 1959 and sponsored by Sears.

1993

Team

1. Florida St.
2. Notre Dame
3. Nebraska
4. Florida
5. Wisconsin
6. Penn St.
7. West Va.
8. Arizona
9. Texas A&M
10. Ohio St.
11. Tennessee
12. Boston College
13. Alabama
14. Miami (Fla.)
15. Oklahoma
16. UCLA
17. Colorado
18. Michigan
19. Kansas St.
20. North Caro.
21. Virginia Tech
22. Louisville
23. Clemson
24. California
25. Southern Cal

College Football Bowl Coalition Poll

The College Football Bowl Coalition adopted a Bowl Coalition Poll for the 1993 season, combining The Associated Press (media) and USA Today/CNN (coaches) polls. The final regular-season Bowl Coalition Poll was used to determine the picking order for the Mobil Cotton, Federal Express Orange, USF&G Sugar and IBM O/S2 Fiesta Bowls. The Bowl Coalition Poll is determined by combining the point totals of the coaches and media polls.

1993

Team

1. Nebraska
2. Florida St.
3. West Va.
4. Notre Dame
5. Auburn*
6. Tennessee
7. Texas A&M
8. Florida
9. Wisconsin
10. Miami (Fla.)
11. Ohio St.
12. North Caro.
13. Penn St.
14. UCLA
15. Boston College
16. Arizona
17. Colorado
18. Alabama
19. Oklahoma
20. Kansas St.
21. Indiana
22. Virginia Tech
23. Michigan
24. Clemson
25. Fresno St.

Auburn was ineligible for bowl participation because of NCAA sanctions.

Undefeated, Untied Teams

(Regular-Season Games Only)

Minimum of five games played against opponents above the high-school level. Subsequent bowl win is indicated by (†), loss (‡) and tie ($). Unscored-on teams are indicated by (•).

Year	College	Wins
1878	Princeton	6
1882	Yale	8
1883	Yale	8
1885	Princeton	9
1887	Yale	9
1888	Yale	•13
1889	Princeton	10
1890	Harvard	11
1891	Yale	•13
1892	Minnesota	5
	Purdue	8
	Yale	•13
1893	Minnesota	6
	Princeton	11
1894	Pennsylvania	12
	Va. Military	5
	Yale	16
1895	Pennsylvania	14
1896	Louisiana St.	6
1897	Pennsylvania	15
1898	Harvard	11
	Kentucky	•7
	Michigan	10
	North Caro.	9
1899	Kansas	10
	Sewanee	12
1900	Clemson	6
	Texas	6
	Tulane	•5
	Yale	12
1901	Harvard	12
	Michigan	†•10
	Wisconsin	9
1902	Arizona	•5
	California	8
	Michigan	11
	Nebraska	•9
1903	Nebraska	10
	Princeton	11
1904	Auburn	5
	Michigan	10
	Minnesota	13
	Pennsylvania	12
	Pittsburgh	10
	Vanderbilt	9
1905	Chicago	10
	Stanford	8
	Yale	10
1906	New Mexico St.	5
	Washington St.	•6
	Wisconsin	5
1907	Oregon St.	•6
1908	Kansas	9
	Louisiana St.	10
1909	Arkansas	7
	Colorado	•6
	Washington	7
	Yale	•10
1910	Colorado	6
	Illinois	•7
	Pittsburgh	•9
	Washington	6
1911	Colorado	6
	Oklahoma	8
	Utah St.	•5
	Washington	7
1912	Harvard	9
	Notre Dame	7
	Penn St.	8
	Washington	6
	Wisconsin	7
1913	Auburn	8
	Chicago	7
	Harvard	9
	Michigan St.	7
	Nebraska	8
	Notre Dame	7
	Washington	7
1914	Army	9
	Illinois	7
	Tennessee	9
	Texas	8

Year	College	Wins
	Wash. & Lee	9
1915	Colorado St.	7
	Columbia	5
	Cornell	9
	Nebraska	8
	Oklahoma	10
	Pittsburgh	8
	Washington	7
	Washington St.	†6
1916	Army	9
	Ohio St.	7
	Pittsburgh	8
	Tulsa	10
1917	Denver	9
	Georgia Tech	9
	Pittsburgh	9
	Texas A&M	•8
	Washington St.	6
1918	Michigan	5
	Oklahoma	6
	Texas	9
	Virginia Tech	7
	Washington (Mo.)	6
1919	Notre Dame	9
	Texas A&M	•10
1920	Boston College	8
	California	†8
	Notre Dame	9
	Ohio St.	‡7
	Southern Cal	6
	Texas	9
	Va. Military	9
1921	California	$9
	Cornell	8
	Iowa	7
1922	California	9
	Cornell	8
	Drake	7
	Iowa	7
	Princeton	8
	Tulsa	7
1923	Colorado	9
	Cornell	8
	Illinois	8
	Michigan	8
	Southern Methodist	9
	Yale	8
1924	Notre Dame	†9
1925	Alabama	†9
	Dartmouth	8
1926	Alabama	$9
	Stanford	$10
	Utah	7
1927	(None)	
1928	Boston College	9
	Detroit Mercy	9
	Georgia Tech	†9
1929	Notre Dame	9
	Pittsburgh	‡9
	Purdue	8
	Tulane	9
	Utah	7
1930	Alabama	†9
	Notre Dame	10
	Utah	8
	Washington St.	‡9
1931	Tulane	‡11
1932	Colgate	•9
	Michigan	8
	Southern Cal	†9
1933	Princeton	9
1934	Alabama	†9
	Minnesota	8
1935	Minnesota	8
	Princeton	9
	Southern Methodist	‡12
1936	(None)	
1937	Alabama	‡9
	Colorado	‡8
	Santa Clara	†8
1938	Duke	‡•9
	Georgetown	8
	Oklahoma	‡10
	Tennessee	†10
	Texas Christian	†10
	Texas Tech	‡10
1939	Cornell	8
	Tennessee	‡•10
	Texas A&M	†10
1940	Boston College	†10
	Lafayette	9

Year	College	Wins	Year	College	Wins	Year	College	Wins
	Minnesota	8	1956	Oklahoma	10		Miami (Ohio)	†10
	Stanford	†9		Tennessee	‡10		Notre Dame	†10
	Tennessee	‡10		Wyoming	10		Penn St.	†11
1941	Duke	‡9	1957	Arizona St.	10	1974	Alabama	‡11
	Duquesne	8		Auburn	10		Oklahoma	11
	Minnesota	8	1958	Louisiana St.	†10	1975	Arizona St.	†11
1942	Tulsa	‡10	1959	Syracuse	†10		Arkansas St.	11
1943	Purdue	9	1960	New Mexico St.	†10		Ohio St.	‡11
1944	Army	9		Yale	9	1976	Maryland	†11
	Ohio St.	9	1961	Alabama	†10		Pittsburgh	†11
1945	Alabama	†9		Rutgers	9		Rutgers	11
	Army	9	1962	Dartmouth	9	1977	Texas	‡11
	Oklahoma St.	†8		Mississippi	†9	1978	Penn St.	‡11
1946	Georgia	†10		Southern Cal	†10	1979	Alabama	‡11
	Hardin-Simmons	†10	1963	Texas	†10		Brigham Young	‡11
	UCLA	‡10	1964	Alabama	‡10		Florida St.	‡11
1947	Michigan	†9		Arkansas	†10		McNeese St.	‡11
	Notre Dame	9		Princeton	9		Ohio St.	‡11
	Penn St.	$9	1965	Arkansas	‡10	1980	Georgia	†11
1948	California	‡10		Dartmouth	9	1981	Clemson	†11
	Clemson	†10		Michigan St.	‡10	1982	Georgia	†11
	Michigan	9		Nebraska	†10	1983	Nebraska	‡12
1949	Army	9	1966	Alabama	†10		Texas	‡11
	California	‡10	1967	Wyoming	‡10	1984	Brigham Young	†12
	Notre Dame	10	1968	Ohio	†10	1985	Bowling Green	‡11
	Oklahoma	†		Ohio St.	†9		Penn St.	†11
1950	Oklahoma	‡10		Penn St.	†10	1986	Miami (Fla.)	‡11
	Princeton	9	1969	Penn St.	†10		Penn St.	†11
	Wyoming	†9		San Diego St.	†10	1987	Miami (Fla.)	†11
1951	Maryland	†9		Texas	†10		Oklahoma	‡11
	Michigan St.	9		Toledo	†10		Syracuse	$11
	Princeton	9	1970	Arizona St.	†10	1988	Notre Dame	†11
	San Francisco	9		Dartmouth	9		West Va.	†11
	Tennessee	‡10		Ohio St.	‡9	1989	Colorado	‡11
1952	Georgia Tech	†11		Texas	†10	1990	(None)	
	Michigan St.	9		Toledo	†11	1991	Miami (Fla.)	†11
1953	Maryland	†10	1971	Alabama	‡11		Washington	†11
1954	Ohio St.	†9		Michigan	†11	1992	Alabama	†12
	Oklahoma	10		Nebraska	†12	1993	Auburn	11
	UCLA	9		Toledo	†11			
1955	Maryland	‡10	1972	Southern Cal	†11			
	Oklahoma	†10	1973	Alabama	‡11			

The Spoilers

(From 1937 Season)

Following is a list of the spoilers of major-college teams that lost their perfect (undefeat-ed, untied) record in their **final** game of the season, including a bowl game (in paren-theses). Confrontations of two undefeated, untied teams at the time are in bold face. An asterisk (*) indicates the home team in a regular-season game, a dagger (†) indicates a neutral site.

Date	Spoiler	Victim	Score
1-1-38	California	Alabama (Rose)	13-0
1-1-38	Rice	Colorado (Cotton)	28-14
12-3-38	*Southern Cal	Notre Dame	13-0
1-2-39	Southern Cal	Duke (Rose)	7-3
1-2-39	**Tennessee**	**Oklahoma (Orange)**	17-0
1-2-39	St. Mary's (Cal.)	Texas Tech (Cotton)	20-13
12-2-39	*Duquesne	Detroit Mercy	tie 10-10
1-1-40	Southern Cal	Tennessee (Rose)	14-0
1-1-41	**Boston College**	**Tennessee (Sugar)**	19-13
1-1-42	Oregon St.	Duke (Rose)	20-16
11-27-43	*Great Lakes	Notre Dame	19-14
1-1-44	Southern Cal	Washington (Rose)	29-0
11-25-44	*Virginia	Yale	tie 6-6
1-1-47	Illinois	UCLA (Rose)	45-14
1-1-48	Southern Methodist	Penn St. (Cotton)	tie 13-13
11-27-48	†Navy	Army	tie 21-21
12-2-48	*Southern Cal	Notre Dame	tie 14-14
1-1-49	Northwestern	California (Rose)	20-14
1-2-50	Ohio St.	California (Rose)	17-14
12-2-50	†Navy	Army	14-2
1-1-51	Kentucky	Oklahoma (Sugar)	13-7
1-1-52	**Maryland**	**Tennessee (Sugar)**	28-13
11-22-52	Southern Cal	*UCLA	14-12
1-1-54	Oklahoma	Maryland (Orange)	7-0
1-2-56	**Oklahoma**	**Maryland (Orange)**	20-6
1-1-57	Baylor	Tennessee (Sugar)	13-7
11-28-64	*Southern Cal	Notre Dame	20-17
1-1-65	Texas	Alabama (Orange)	21-17
11-20-65	**Dartmouth**	*Princeton	28-14
1-1-66	UCLA	Michigan St. (Rose)	14-12
1-1-66	Alabama	Nebraska (Orange)	39-28
1-1-66	Louisiana St.	Arkansas (Cotton)	14-7
11-19-66	**Notre Dame**	* **Michigan St.**	tie 10-10
1-1-68	Louisiana St.	Wyoming (Sugar)	20-13
11-23-68	*Harvard	Yale	tie 29-29
12-27-68	Richmond	Ohio (Tangerine)	49-42
11-22-69	*Michigan	Ohio St.	24-12
11-22-69	*Princeton	Dartmouth	35-7
11-21-70	* **Ohio St.**	**Michigan**	20-9
1-1-71	Stanford	Ohio St. (Rose)	27-17
1-1-71	Notre Dame	Texas (Cotton)	24-11
1-1-72	Stanford	Michigan (Rose)	13-12
1-1-72	**Nebraska**	**Alabama (Orange)**	38-6
11-25-72	*Ohio St.	Michigan	14-11
11-24-73	**Ohio St.**	* **Michigan**	tie 10-10
12-31-73	**Notre Dame**	**Alabama (Sugar)**	24-23
11-23-74	*Ohio St.	Michigan	12-10
11-23-74	*Harvard	Yale	21-16
1-1-75	Notre Dame	Alabama (Orange)	13-11
1-1-76	UCLA	Ohio St. (Rose)	23-10
1-1-77	Houston	Maryland (Cotton)	30-21
11-19-77	*Delaware	Colgate	21-3
1-2-78	Notre Dame	Texas (Cotton)	38-10
1-1-79	Alabama	Penn St. (Sugar)	14-7
11-17-79	Harvard	*Yale	22-7
12-15-79	Syracuse	McNeese St. (Independence)	31-7
12-21-79	Indiana	Brigham Young (Holiday)	38-37
1-1-80	Southern Cal	Ohio St. (Rose)	17-16
1-1-80	Oklahoma	Florida St. (Orange)	24-7
1-1-83	Penn St.	Georgia (Sugar)	27-23
1-2-84	Georgia	Texas (Cotton)	10-9
1-2-84	Miami (Fla.)	Nebraska (Orange)	31-30
12-14-85	Fresno St.	Bowling Green (California)	51-7
1-1-86	Oklahoma	Penn St. (Orange)	25-10
1-2-87	**Penn St.**	**Miami (Fla.) (Fiesta)**	14-10
1-1-88	Auburn	Syracuse (Sugar)	tie 16-16
1-1-88	**Miami (Fla.)**	**Oklahoma (Orange)**	20-14
1-2-89	**Notre Dame**	**West Va. (Fiesta)**	34-21
1-1-90	Notre Dame	Colorado (Orange)	21-6
1-1-93	Notre Dame	Texas A&M (Cotton)	28-3
1-1-93	**Alabama**	**Miami (Fla.) (Sugar)**	34-13
1-1-94	Florida St.	Nebraska (Orange)	18-16
1-1-94	Florida	West Va. (Sugar)	41-7

Streaks and Rivalries

Longest Winning Streaks

(Includes Bowl Games)

Wins	Team	Years	Ended by	Score
47	Oklahoma	1953-57	Notre Dame	7-0
39	Washington	1908-14	Oregon St.	0-0
37	Yale	1890-93	Princeton	6-0
37	Yale	1887-89	Princeton	10-0
35	Toledo	1969-71	Tampa	21-0
34	Pennsylvania	1894-96	Lafayette	6-4
31	Oklahoma	1948-50	Kentucky	*13-7
31	Pittsburgh	1914-18	Cleveland Naval Reserve	10-9
31	Pennsylvania	1896-98	Harvard	10-0
30	Texas	1968-70	Notre Dame	*24-11
29	Miami (Fla.)	1990-93	Alabama	*34-13
29	Michigan	1901-03	Minnesota	6-6
28	Alabama	1991-93	Tennessee	17-17
28	Alabama	1978-80	Mississippi St.	6-3
28	Oklahoma	1973-75	Kansas	23-3
28	Michigan St.	1950-53	Purdue	6-0
26	Cornell	1921-24	Williams	14-7
26	Michigan	1903-05	Chicago	2-0
25	Brigham Young	1983-85	UCLA	27-24
25	Michigan	1946-49	Army	21-7
25	Army	1944-46	Notre Dame	0-0
25	Southern Cal	1931-33	Oregon St.	0-0
24	Princeton	1949-52	Pennsylvania	13-7
24	Minnesota	1903-05	Wisconsin	16-12
24	Nebraska	1901-04	Colorado	6-0
24	Yale	1894-95	Boston AC	0-0
24	Harvard	1890-91	Yale	10-0
24	Yale	1882-84	Princeton	0-0
23	Notre Dame	1988-89	Miami (Fla.)	27-10
23	Nebraska	1970-71	UCLA	20-17
23	Penn St.	1968-70	Colorado	41-13
23	Tennessee	1937-39	Southern Cal	*14-0
23	Harvard	1901-02	Yale	23-0
22	Washington	1990-92	Arizona	16-3
22	Nebraska	1982-83	Miami (Fla.)	*31-30
22	Ohio St.	1967-69	Michigan	24-12
22	Arkansas	1963-65	Louisiana St.	*14-7
22	Harvard	1912-14	Penn St.	13-13
22	Yale	1904-06	Princeton	0-0
21	Arizona St.	1969-71	Oregon St.	24-18
21	San Diego St.	1968-70	Long Beach St.	27-11
21	Notre Dame	1946-48	Southern Cal	14-14
21	Minnesota	1933-36	Northwestern	6-0
21	Colorado	1908-12	Colorado St.	21-0
21	Pennsylvania	1903-05	Lafayette	6-6
21	Yale	1900-01	Army	5-5
21	Harvard	1898-99	Yale	0-0
20	Oklahoma	1986-87	Miami (Fla.)	*20-14
20	Tennessee	1950-51	Maryland	*28-13
20	Notre Dame	1929-31	Northwestern	0-0
20	Alabama	1924-26	Stanford	*7-7
20	Iowa	1920-23	Illinois	9-6
20	Notre Dame	1919-21	Iowa	10-7

Streak ended in bowl game.

Longest Unbeaten Streaks

(Includes Bowl Games; May Include Ties)

No.	Wins	Ties	Team	Years	Ended by	Score
63	59	4	Washington	1907-17	California	27-0
56	55	1	Michigan	1901-05	Chicago	2-0
50	46	4	California	1920-25	Olympic Club	15-0
48	47	1	Oklahoma	1953-57	Notre Dame	7-0
48	47	1	Yale	1885-89	Princeton	10-0
47	42	5	Yale	1879-85	Princeton	6-5
44	42	2	Yale	1894-96	Princeton	24-6
42	39	3	Yale	1904-08	Harvard	4-0
39	37	2	Notre Dame	1946-50	Purdue	28-14
37	36	1	Oklahoma	1972-75	Kansas	23-3
37	37	0	Yale	1890-93	Princeton	6-0
35	35	0	Toledo	1969-71	Tampa	21-0
35	34	1	Minnesota	1903-05	Wisconsin	16-12
34	33	1	Nebraska	1912-16	Kansas	7-3
34	34	0	Pennsylvania	1894-96	Lafayette	6-4

No.	Wins	Ties	Team	Years	Ended by	Score
34	32	2	Princeton	1884-87	Harvard	12-0
34	29	5	Princeton	1877-82	Harvard	1-0
33	30	3	Tennessee	1926-30	Alabama	18-6
33	31	2	Georgia Tech	1914-18	Pittsburgh	32-0
33	30	3	Harvard	1911-15	Cornell	10-0
32	31	1	Nebraska	1969-71	UCLA	20-17
32	30	2	Army	1944-47	Columbia	21-20
32	31	1	Harvard	1898-00	Yale	28-0
31	30	1	Alabama	1991-93	Louisiana St.	17-13
31	30	1	Penn St.	1967-70	Colorado	41-13
31	30	1	San Diego St.	1967-70	Long Beach St.	27-11
31	29	2	Georgia Tech	1950-53	Notre Dame	27-14
31	31	0	Oklahoma	1948-50	Kentucky	13-7
31	31	0	Pittsburgh	1914-18	Cleveland Naval.	10-9
31	31	0	Pennsylvania	1896-98	Harvard	10-0
30	30	0	Texas	1968-70	Notre Dame	24-11
30	25	5	Penn St.	1919-22	Navy	14-0
30	28	2	Pennsylvania	1903-06	Swarthmore	4-0
29	29	0	Miami (Fla.)	1990-93	Alabama	34-13
28	28	0	Alabama	1978-80	Mississippi St.	6-3
28	26	2	Southern Cal	1978-80	Washington	20-10
28	28	0	Michigan St.	1950-53	Purdue	6-0
28	26	2	Army	1947-50	Navy	14-2
28	24	4	Minnesota	1933-36	Northwestern	6-0
28	26	2	Tennessee	1930-33	Duke	10-2
27	26	1	Southern Cal	1931-33	Stanford	13-7
27	24	3	Notre Dame	1910-14	Yale	28-0

Longest Home Winning Streaks

(Includes Bowl Games)

Wins	Team	Years	Ended by	Score
57	Miami (Fla.)	1985-93	Current	
57	Alabama	1963-82	Southern Miss.	38-29
50	Michigan	1901-07	Pennsylvania	6-0
42	Texas	1968-76	Houston	30-0
40	Notre Dame	1907-18	Great Lakes	7-7
33	Nebraska	1901-06	Iowa St.	14-2
30	Auburn	1952-61	Kentucky	14-12
28	Michigan	1969-73	Ohio St.	0-0
27	Vanderbilt	1903-07	Michigan	8-0
26	California	1919-23	Nevada	0-0
25	Ohio St.	1972-76	Missouri	22-21
25	Wisconsin	1900-03	Chicago	15-6
24	Georgia	1980-83	Auburn	13-7
24	Georgia Tech	1916-19	Wash. & Lee	3-0
24	Virginia	1899-04	Navy	5-0
23	Florida	1990-93	Florida St.	33-21
23	Tulane	1929-32	Vanderbilt	6-6
23	Michigan St.	1904-08	Michigan	0-0
23	Michigan	1897-00	Ohio St.	0-0
22	Wyoming	1965-70	Air Force	41-17
22	Minnesota	1933-37	Notre Dame	7-6
21	Arizona St.	1969-72	Air Force	39-31
21	Mississippi	1952-59	Louisiana St.	10-10
21	North Caro.	1893-00	Virginia Tech	0-0
20	Fresno St.	1987-90	Utah St.	24-24
20	Rutgers	1974-78	Colgate	14-9
20	Mississippi St.	1939-45	Mississippi	7-6
20	Missouri	1938-43	Oklahoma	20-13
20	Southern Cal	1927-29	California	15-7
20	Southern Cal	1919-23	California	13-7

Longest Losing Streaks

Losses	Team	Years	Ended by	Score
34	Northwestern	1979-82	Northern Ill.	31-6
28	Virginia	1958-61	William & Mary	21-6
28	Kansas St.	1944-48	Arkansas St.	37-6
27	New Mexico St.	1988-90	Cal St. Fullerton	43-9
27	Eastern Mich.	1980-82	Kent	9-7
26	Colorado St.	1960-62	Pacific (Cal.)	20-0
21	Kent	1981-83	Eastern Mich.	37-13
20	Florida St.	1972-74	Miami (Fla.)	21-14
18	Wake Forest	1962-63	South Caro.	20-19
17	Memphis	1981-82	Arkansas St.	12-0
17	Tulane	1961-63	South Caro.	20-7
17	Kansas	1953-55	Washington St.	13-0
16	Kent	1992-93	Current	
16	Indiana	1983-85	Louisville	41-28
16	Vanderbilt	1961-62	Tulane	20-0

Most-Played Rivalries

(Ongoing Unless Indicated)

Games	Opponents (Series leader listed first)	Rivalry Record	First Game
103	Minnesota-Wisconsin	56-39-8	1890
102	Missouri-Kansas	48-45-9	1891
100	Nebraska-Kansas	76-21-3	1892
100	Texas Christian-Baylor	47-46-7	1899
100	Texas-Texas A&M	64-31-5	1894
98	North Caro.-Virginia	53-41-4	1892
98	Miami (Ohio)-Cincinnati	53-39-6	1888
97	Auburn-Georgia	46-44-7	1892
97	Oregon-Oregon St.	47-40-10	1894
96	Purdue-Indiana	58-32-6	1891
96	Stanford-California	47-38-11	1892
94	Army-Navy	44-43-7	1890
92	$Penn St.-Pittsburgh	47-41-4	1893
91	Louisiana St.-Tulane	*62-22-7	1893
91	Clemson-South Caro.	54-33-4	1896
91	Kansas-Kansas St.	61-25-5	1902
91	Oklahoma-Kansas	61-24-6	1903
91	Utah-Utah St.	60-27-4	1892
90	#Auburn-Georgia Tech	47-39-4	1892
90	North Caro.-Wake Forest	59-29-2	1888
90	Michigan-Ohio St.	51-33-6	1897
90	Mississippi-Mississippi St.	52-32-6	1901
89	Tennessee-Kentucky	57-23-9	1893
88	Nebraska-Iowa St.	72-14-2	1896
88	Texas-Oklahoma	51-33-4	1900
88	Oklahoma-Oklahoma St.	70-11-7	1904
88	Georgia-Georgia Tech	48-35-5	1893
87	North Caro. St.-Wake Forest	52-29-6	1895
87	Nebraska-Missouri	52-32-3	1892
87	Tennessee-Vanderbilt	56-26-5	1892
87	Illinois-Northwestern	46-36-5	1892
86	Michigan-Michigan St.	56-25-5	1898
86	Pittsburgh-West Va.	55-28-3	1895
86	Washington-Washington St.	55-25-6	1900

$ Did not meet in 1993. *Disputed series record: Tulane claims 23-60-7 record. #Have not met since 1989.

Additional Records

Longest Uninterrupted Series (Must have played every year)
- 91 games—Kansas-Oklahoma (from 1903)
- 88 games—Kansas-Nebraska (from 1906)
- 87 games—Minnesota-Wisconsin (from 1907)
- 85 games—Clemson-South Caro. (from 1909)
- 84 games—Wake Forest-North Caro. St. (from 1910)
- 84 games—North Caro.-Virginia (from 1910)

- 83 games—Kansas-Kansas St. (from 1911)
- 80 games—Illinois-Ohio St. (from 1914)
- 78 games—Southern Methodist-Baylor (from 1916)
- 76 games—Michigan-Ohio St. (from 1918)
- 75 games—Kansas-Missouri (from 1919)
- 75 games—Missouri-Iowa St. (from 1919)
- 75 games—Missouri-Oklahoma (from 1919)
- 75 games—North Caro.-Virginia (from 1919)
- 75 games—Tulane-Louisiana St. (from 1919)
- 74 games—Indiana-Purdue (from 1920)
- 74 games—Southern Methodist-Texas A&M (from 1920)
- 73 games—Southern Methodist-Texas Christian (from 1921)
- 72 games—Missouri-Nebraska (from 1922)
- 72 games—North Caro.-Duke (from 1922)
- 70 games—Michigan-Illinois (from 1924)
- 70 games—Southern Methodist-Texas (from 1924)

Most Consecutive Wins Over a Major Opponent in an Uninterrupted Series (Must have played in consecutive years)
- 32—Oklahoma over Kansas St., 1937-68
- 30—Notre Dame over Navy, 1964-93 (current)
- 28—Texas over Rice, 1966-93 (current)
- 25—Nebraska over Kansas, 1969-93 (current)
- 25—Nebraska over Kansas St., 1969-93 (current)
- 25—Syracuse over Hobart, 1906-31
- 22—Arkansas over Texas Christian, 1959-80
- 22—Alabama over Mississippi St., 1958-79
- 20—Purdue over Iowa, 1961-80
- 17—New Mexico over UTEP, 1970-86
- 17—Arizona St. over UTEP, 1957-73
- 17—Louisiana St. over Tulane, 1956-72
- 16—Michigan over Illinois, 1967-82
- 15—Southern Methodist over Texas Christian, 1972-86

Most Consecutive Wins Over a Major Opponent in a Series (Did not have to play in consecutive years)
- 29—Clemson over Virginia, 1955-90 (over 36-year period)
- 20—Southern Cal over Oregon St., 1968-93 (26-year period)
- 19—Vanderbilt over Mississippi, 1894-1938 (45-year period)
- 17—Tulsa over Drake, 1939-85 (47-year period)

Most Consecutive Current Wins Over a Major Opponent in a Series (Must have played every year)
- 30—Notre Dame over Navy, 1964-93 (57-9-1 in rivalry)
- 28—Texas over Rice, 1966-93 (59-20-1 in rivalry)
- 25—Nebraska over Kansas, 1969-93 (76-21-3 in rivalry)
- 25—Nebraska over Kansas St., 1969-93 (66-10-2 in rivalry)

Most Consecutive Games Without a Loss Against a Major Opponent
- 34—Oklahoma over Kansas St., 1935-68 (1 tie)

Chris Brantley (above) caught a 15-yard pass from Bryan Fortay on the game's final play to give Rutgers a 50-49 victory over Virginia Tech in 1992.

Cliffhangers

Regular-season Division I-A games won on the final play (since 1971, when first recorded). The extra point is listed when it provided the margin of victory after the winning touchdown on the game's final play.

Date	Opponents, Score	Game-Winning Play
9-25-71	Marshall 15, Xavier (Ohio) 13	Terry Gardner 13 pass from Reggie Oliver
10-9-71	California 30, Oregon St. 27	Steve Sweeney 7 pass from Jay Cruze
10-23-71	Washington St. 24, Stanford 23	Don Sweet 27 FG
11-6-71	Kentucky 14, Vanderbilt 7	Darryl Bishop 43 interception return
11-4-72	Louisiana St. 17, Mississippi 16	Brad Davis 10 pass from Bert Jones (Rusty Jackson kick)
11-18-72	California 24, Stanford 21	Steve Sweeney 7 pass from Vince Ferragamo
9-15-73	Lamar 21, Howard Payne 17	Larry Spears 14 pass from Jabo Leonard
9-22-73	Hawaii 13, Fresno St. 10	Reinhold Stuprich 29 FG
11-17-73	New Mexico 23, Wyoming 21	Bob Berg 43 FG
11-23-74	Stanford 22, California 20	Mike Langford 50 FG
9-20-75	Indiana St. 23, Southern Ill. 21	Dave Vandercook 50 FG
10-18-75	Cal St. Fullerton 32, UC Riverside 31	John Choukair 52 FG
11-8-75	West Va. 17, Pittsburgh 14	Bill McKenzie 38 FG
11-8-75	Stanford 13, Southern Cal 10	Mike Langford 37 FG
11-15-75	North Caro. 17, Tulane 15	Tom Biddle 40 FG
11-6-76	Eastern Mich. 30, Central Mich. 27	Ken Dudal 38 FG
9-30-78	Virginia Tech 22, William & Mary 19	Ron Zollicoffer 50 pass from David Lamie
10-21-78	Arkansas St. 6, McNeese St. 3	Doug Dobbs 42 FG
11-9-78	San Jose St. 33, Pacific (Cal.) 31	Rick Parma 5 pass from Ed Luther
10-6-79	Stanford 27, UCLA 24	Ken Naber 56 FG

Date	Opponents, Score	Game-Winning Play
10-20-79	Nevada-Las Vegas 43, Utah 41	Todd Peterson 49 FG
10-27-79	Michigan 27, Indiana 21	Anthony Carter 45 pass from John Wangler
11-10-79	Penn St. 9, North Caro. St. 7	Herb Menhardt 54 FG
11-17-79	Air Force 30, Vanderbilt 29	Andy Bark 14 pass from Dave Ziebart
11-24-79	Arizona 27, Arizona St. 24	Brett Weber 27 FG
9-13-80	Southern Cal 20, Tennessee 17	Eric Hipp 47 FG
9-13-80	Illinois 20, Michigan St. 17	Mike Bass 38 FG
9-20-80	Notre Dame 29, Michigan 27	Harry Oliver 51 FG
9-27-80	Tulane 26, Mississippi 24	Vince Manalla 29 FG
10-18-80	Connecticut 18, Holy Cross 17	Ken Miller 4 pass from Ken Sweitzer (Keith Hugger pass from Sweitzer)
10-18-80	Washington 27, Stanford 24	Chuck Nelson 25 FG
11-1-80	Tulane 24, Kentucky 22	Vince Manalla 22 FG
11-15-80	Florida 17, Kentucky 15	Brian Clark 34 FG
10-16-82	Arizona 16, Notre Dame 13	Max Zendejas 48 FG
10-23-82	Illinois 29, Wisconsin 28	Mike Bass 46 FG
11-20-82	California 25, Stanford 20	57 (5 laterals) kickoff return involving, in order: Kevin Moen, Richard Rodgers, Dwight Garner, Rodgers, Mariet Ford and Moen
10-8-83	Iowa St. 38, Kansas 35	Marc Bachrodt 47 FG
10-29-83	Bowling Green 15, Central Mich. 14	Stan Hunter 8 pass from Brian McClure
11-5-83	Baylor 24, Arkansas 21	Marty Jimmerson 24 FG
11-12-83	Pacific (Cal.) 30, San Jose St. 26	Ron Woods 85 pass from Mike Pitz
11-12-83	Miami (Fla.) 17, Florida St. 16	Jeff Davis 19 FG
11-26-83	Arizona 17, Arizona St. 15	Max Zendejas 45 FG
9-8-84	Southwestern La. 17, Louisiana Tech 16	Patrick Broussard 21 FG
9-15-84	Syracuse 13, Northwestern 12	Jim Tait 2 pass from Todd Norley (Don McAulay kick)
10-13-84	UCLA 27, Washington St. 24	John Lee 47 FG
11-17-84	Southwestern La. 18, Tulsa 17	Patrick Broussard 45 FG
11-17-84	Temple 19, West Va. 17	Jim Cooper 36 FG
11-23-84	Boston College 47, Miami (Fla.) 45	Gerard Phelan 48 pass from Doug Flutie
9-14-85	Clemson 20, Virginia Tech 17	David Treadwell 36 FG
9-14-85	Oregon St. 23, California 20	Jim Nielsen 20 FG
9-14-85	Utah 29, Hawaii 27	Andre Guardi 19 FG
9-21-85	New Mexico St. 22, UTEP 20	Andy Weiler 32 FG
10-5-85	Mississippi St. 31, Memphis 28	Artie Cosby 54 FG
10-5-85	Illinois 31, Ohio St. 28	Chris White 38 FG
10-12-85	Tulsa 37, Long Beach St. 35	Jason Staurovsky 46 FG
10-19-85	Northwestern 17, Wisconsin 14	John Duvic 42 FG
10-19-85	Iowa 12, Michigan 10	Rob Houghtlin 29 FG
10-19-85	Utah 39, San Diego St. 37	Andre Guardi 42 FG
11-30-85	Alabama 25, Auburn 23	Van Tiffin 52 FG
9-13-86	Oregon 32, Colorado 30	Matt MacLeod 35 FG
9-13-86	Wyoming 23, Pacific (Cal.) 20	Greg Worker 38 FG
9-20-86	Clemson 31, Georgia 28	David Treadwell 46 FG
9-20-86	Southern Cal 17, Baylor 14	Don Shafer 32 FG
10-18-86	Michigan 20, Iowa 17	Mike Gillette 34 FG
10-25-86	Syracuse 27, Temple 24	Tim Vesling 32 FG
11-1-86	North Caro. St. 23, South Caro. 22	Danny Peebles 33 pass from Erik Kramer
11-1-86	North Caro. 32, Maryland 30	Lee Gliarmis 28 FG
11-8-86	Southern Miss. 23, East Caro. 21	Rex Banks 31 FG
11-15-86	Minnesota 20, Michigan 17	Chip Lohmiller 30 FG
11-29-86	Notre Dame 38, Southern Cal 37	John Carney 19 FG
9-12-87	Youngstown St. 20, Bowling Green 17	John Dowling 36 FG
9-19-87	Utah 31, Wisconsin 28	Scott Lieber 39 FG
10-10-87	Marshall 34, Louisville 31	Keith Baxter 31 pass from Tony Petersen
10-17-87	Texas 16, Arkansas 14	Tony Jones 18 pass from Bret Stafford
11-12-88	New Mexico 24, Colorado St. 23	Tony Jones 28 pass from Jeremy Leach
9-16-89	Southern Methodist 31, Connecticut 30	Mike Bowen 4 pass from Mike Romo
9-30-89	Kansas St. 20, North Texas 17	Frank Hernandez 12 pass from Carl Straw
10-7-89	Florida 16, Louisiana St. 13	Arden Czyzewski 41 FG
10-14-89	Southern Miss. 16, Louisville 10	Darryl Tillman 79 pass from Brett Favre
10-28-89	Virginia 16, Louisville 15	Jake McInerney 37 FG
11-4-89	Toledo 19, Western Mich. 18	Romauldo Brown 9 pass from Kevin Meger
11-4-89	Northern Ill. 23, Southwestern La. 20	Stacey Robinson 7 run
9-8-90	Utah 35, Minnesota 29	Lavon Edwards 91 run of blocked FG
9-29-90	North Caro. St. 12, North Caro. 9	Damon Hartman 56 FG
10-6-90	Colorado 33, Missouri 31	Charles S. Johnson 1 run
10-20-90	Alabama 9, Tennessee 6	Philip Doyle 47 FG
11-3-90	Southern Miss. 14, Southwestern La. 13	Michael Welch 11 pass from Brett Favre (Jim Taylor kick)
11-17-90	Stanford 27, California 25	John Hopkins 39 FG
11-24-90	Michigan 16, Ohio St. 13	J. D. Carlson 37 FG
9-7-91	Central Mich. 27, Southwestern La. 24	L. J. Muddy 2 pass from Jeff Bender
9-21-91	California 23, Arizona 21	Doug Brien 33 FG
9-21-91	Georgia Tech 24, Virginia 21	Scott Sisson 33 FG
9-21-91	Louisiana Tech 17, Eastern Mich. 14	Chris Bonoil 54 FG
10-12-91	Ball St. 10, Eastern Mich. 8	Kenny Stucker 41 FG
11-2-91	Kentucky 20, Cincinnati 17	Doug Pelphrey 53 FG
11-2-91	Tulsa 13, Southern Miss. 10	Eric Lange 24 FG
9-5-92	Louisiana Tech 10, Baylor 9	Chris Bonoil 30 FG
9-19-92	Southern Miss. 16, Louisiana Tech 13	Johnny Lomoro 46 FG
10-3-92	Texas A&M 19, Texas Tech 17	Terry Venetoulias 21 FG
10-3-92	Georgia Tech 16, North Caro. St. 13	Scott Sisson 29 FG

Anthony Carter caught a 45-yard touchdown pass from John Wangler on the game's final play to give Michigan a 27-21 victory over Indiana on October 27, 1979.

Div. I-A Games Won by Field Goal on Last Play, Per Year	
1971-75	1.8
1976-80	2.6
1981-85	4.2
1986-90	3.6
1991-93	5.0

Date	Opponents, Score	Game-Winning Play
10-3-92	San Jose St. 26, Wyoming 24	Joe Nedney 60 FG
10-24-92	Maryland 27, Duke 25	Marcus Badgett 38 pass from John Kaleo
10-31-92	Rutgers 50, Virginia Tech 49	Chris Brantley 15 pass from Bryan Fortay
11-14-92	UCLA 9, Oregon 6	Louis Perez 40 FG
10-2-93	Tulane 27, Navy 25	Bart Baldwin 43 FG
10-9-93	Ball St. 31, Toledo 30	Eric McCray 6 pass from Mike Neu (Matt Swart kick)
10-9-93	North Caro. St. 36, Texas Tech 34	Gary Downs 11 pass from Robert Hinton
10-16-93	Arizona 27, Stanford 24	Steve McLaughlin 27 FG
11-20-93	Maryland 33, Wake Forest 32	Russ Weaver 8 pass from Scott Milanovich (John Milligan kick)
11-20-93	Boston College 41, Notre Dame 39	David Gordon 41 FG

"CARDIAC SEASONS"

(From 1937; Won-Lost Record in Parentheses)

Games Decided by Two Points or Less

6—Kansas, 1973 (3-2-1): Tennessee 27-28, Nebraska 9-10, Iowa St. 22-20, Oklahoma St. 10-10, Colorado 17-15, Missouri 14-13 (season record: 7-3-1)

5—Illinois, 1992 (2-2-1): Minnesota 17-18, Ohio St. 18-16, Northwestern 26-27, Wisconsin 13-12, Michigan 22-22 (season record: 6-4-1)

5—Columbia, 1971 (4-1-0): Princeton 22-20, Harvard 19-21, Yale 15-14, Rutgers 17-16, Dartmouth 31-29 (season record: 6-3-0)

5—Missouri, 1957 (2-2-1): Vanderbilt 7-7, Southern Methodist 7-6, Nebraska 14-13, Kansas St. 21-23, Kansas 7-9 (season record: 5-4-1)

Games Decided by Three Points or Less

7—Bowling Green, 1980 (2-5-0): Ohio 20-21, Ball St. 24-21, Western Mich. 17-14, Kentucky 20-21, Long Beach St. 21-23, Eastern Mich. 16-18, Richmond 17-20 (season record: 4-7-0)

7—Columbia, 1971 (4-3-0): Lafayette 0-3, Princeton 22-20, Harvard 19-21, Yale 15-14, Rutgers 17-16, Cornell 21-24, Dartmouth 31-29 (season record: 6-3-0)

6—Illinois, 1992 (3-2-1): Minnesota 17-18, Ohio St. 18-16, Northwestern 26-27, Wisconsin 13-12, Purdue 20-17, Michigan 22-22 (season record: 6-4-1)

6—Central Mich., 1991 (2-0-4): Ohio 17-17, Southwestern La. 27-24, Akron 31-29, Toledo 16-16, Miami (Ohio) 10-10, Eastern Mich. 14-14 (season record: 6-1-4)

6—Air Force, 1967 (2-2-2): Oklahoma St. 0-0, California 12-14, North Caro. 10-8, Tulane 13-10, Colorado St. 17-17, Army 7-10 (season record: 2-6-2)

6—Missouri, 1957 (3-2-1): Vanderbilt 7-7, Southern Methodist 7-6, Nebraska 14-13, Colorado 9-6, Kansas St. 21-23, Kansas 7-9 (season record: 5-4-1)

Division I-A Stadiums

STADIUMS LISTED ALPHABETICALLY

School	Stadium	Conference	Year Built	Cap.	Surface* (Year)
Air Force	Falcon	Western Athletic	1962	50,049	Grass
Akron	√ Rubber Bowl	Mid-American	1940	35,202	AstroTurf (83)
Alabama	√ Legion Field	Southeastern	1927	83,091	AstroTurf
	Bryant-Denny	Southeastern	1929	70,123	PAT (S91)
Arizona	Arizona	Pacific-10	1928	56,167	Grass
Arizona St.	Sun Devil	Pacific-10	1959	73,656	Grass
Arkansas	√ War Memorial	Southeastern	1948	53,727	Grass (S94)
	Razorback	Southeastern	1938	50,019	AstroTurf
Arkansas St.	Indian	Big West	1974	33,410	Grass
Army	Michie	Independent	1924	39,929	AstroTurf (92)
Auburn	Jordan-Hare	Southeastern	1939	85,214	Grass
Ball St.	Ball St.	Mid-American	1967	16,319	Grass
Baylor	Floyd Casey	Southwest	1950	48,500	All-Pro Turf (90)
Boston College	Alumni	Big East	1957	44,500	PolyknitTurf
Bowling Green	Doyt Perry	Mid-American	1966	30,599	Grass
Brigham Young	Cougar	Western Athletic	1964	65,000	Grass
California	Memorial	Pacific-10	1923	75,662	AstroTurf (90)
Central Mich.	Kelly/Shorts	Mid-American	1972	20,086	AstroTurf (83)
Cincinnati	Nippert	Mid-American	1916	35,000	AstroTurf-8 (92)
Clemson	Memorial/Howard	Atlantic Coast	1942	81,473	Grass
Colorado	Folsom Field	Big Eight	1924	51,748	AstroTurf-8 (89)
Colorado St.	Hughes	Western Athletic	1968	30,000	Grass
Duke	Wallace Wade	Atlantic Coast	1929	33,941	Grass
East Caro.	Ficklen Memorial	Independent	1963	35,000	Grass
Eastern Mich.	Rynearson	Mid-American	1969	30,200	StadiaTurf (91)
Florida	Florida Field	Southeastern	1929	83,000	Grass (S90)
Florida St.	Doak Campbell	Atlantic Coast	1950	75,000	PAT (88)
Fresno St.	Bulldog	Western Athletic	1980	41,031	Grass
Georgia	Sanford	Southeastern	1929	86,117	Grass
Georgia Tech	Dodd/Grant	Atlantic Coast	1913	46,000	All-Pro Turf (88)
Hawaii	√ Aloha	Western Athletic	1975	50,000	AstroTurf (85)
Houston	√ Astrodome@	Southwest	1965	60,000	AstroTurf
Illinois	Memorial	Big Ten	1923	70,904	AstroTurf (89)
Indiana	Memorial	Big Ten	1960	52,354	AstroTurf (86)
Iowa	Kinnick	Big Ten	1929	70,397	PAT (S89)
Iowa St.	Jack Trice Field	Big Eight	1975	50,000	All-ProTurf (85)
Kansas	Memorial	Big Eight	1921	50,250	AstroTurf (90)

School	Stadium	Conference	Year Built	Cap.	Surface* (Year)
Kansas St.	KSU	Big Eight	1968	42,000	AstroTurf (91)
Kent	Dix	Mid-American	1969	30,520	Grass
Kentucky	Commonwealth	Southeastern	1973	57,800	Grass
Louisiana St.	Tiger	Southeastern	1924	80,150	Grass
Louisiana Tech	Joe Aillet	Big West	1968	30,200	Grass
Louisville	√ Cardinal	Independent	1956	35,500	AstroTurf (89)
Maryland	Byrd	Atlantic Coast	1950	45,000	Grass
Memphis	√ Liberty Bowl	Independent	1965	62,380	PAT (87)
Miami (Fla.)	√ Orange Bowl	Big East	1935	74,712	PAT (S77)
Miami (Ohio)	Fred Yager	Mid-American	1983	25,183	Grass
Michigan	Michigan	Big Ten	1927	102,501	PAT (S91)
Michigan St.	Spartan	Big Ten	1957	76,000	AstroTurf (83)
Minnesota	Metrodome@	Big Ten	1982	62,345	Turf
Mississippi	√ Mississippi Mem.	Southeastern	1953	62,500	Grass
	Vaught-Hemingway	Southeastern	1941	42,577	Grass
Mississippi St.	Scott Field	Southeastern	1915	40,656	PAT (86)
Missouri	Faurot Field	Big Eight	1926	62,000	Omni-Turf (85)
Navy	Navy-MC	Independent	1959	30,000	Grass
Nebraska	Memorial	Big Eight	1923	72,700	AstroTurf-8 (92)
Nevada	Mackay	Big West	1965	31,545	Grass
Nevada-Las Vegas	√ Silver Bowl	Big West	1971	32,000	MonsantoTurf (85)
New Mexico	University	Western Athletic	1960	30,646	Grass
New Mexico St.	Aggie Memorial	Big West	1978	30,343	Grass
North Caro.	Kenan Memorial	Atlantic Coast	1927	52,000	Grass
North Caro. St.	Carter-Finley	Atlantic Coast	1966	†50,000	Grass
Northeast La.	Malone	Independent	$1978	30,427	Grass
Northern Ill.	Huskie	Big West	1965	30,998	AstroTurf (89)
Northwestern	Dyche	Big Ten	1926	49,256	SuperTurf (84)
Notre Dame	Notre Dame	Independent	1930	59,075	Grass
Ohio	Peden	Mid-American	1929	20,000	Grass
Ohio St.	Ohio	Big Ten	1922	91,470	PAT (S90)
Oklahoma	Memorial	Big Eight	1924	75,004	Grass (S94)
Oklahoma St.	Lewis	Big Eight	1920	50,614	AstroTurf (87)
Oregon	Autzen	Pacific-10	1967	41,678	Omni-Turf (84)
Oregon St.	Parker	Pacific-10	1953	35,547	All-Pro Turf (84)
Pacific (Cal.)	Stagg Memorial	Big West	1950	30,000	Grass
Penn St.	Beaver	Big Ten	1960	93,967	Grass
Pittsburgh	Pitt	Big East	1925	56,500	AstroTurf (90)
Purdue	Ross-Ade	Big Ten	1924	67,861	PAT (75)
Rice	Rice	Southwest	1950	70,000	All-Pro Turf (84)
Rutgers	Rutgers	Big East	1994	41,500	Grass
San Diego St.	√ Jack Murphy	Western Athletic	1967	60,049	Grass
San Jose St.	Spartan	Big West	1933	31,218	Grass
South Caro.	Williams-Brice	Southeastern	1934	72,400	Grass
Southern Cal	√ LA Mem. Coliseum	Pacific-10	1923	&68,000	Grass
Southern Methodist	Ownby	Southwest	1926	23,783	AstroTurf (89)
	√ Cotton Bowl	Southwest	1930	71,456	Grass (S93)
Southern Miss.	Roberts	Independent	1976	33,000	Grass
Southwestern La.	Cajun Field	Big West	1971	31,000	Grass
Stanford	Stanford	Pacific-10	1921	85,500	Grass
Syracuse	Carrier Dome@	Big East	1980	50,000	AstroTurf
Temple	Veterans	Big East	1971	66,592	AstroTurf-8
Tennessee	Neyland	Southeastern	1921	91,902	Grass (S94)
Texas	Memorial	Southwest	1924	77,809	AstroTurf (93)
Texas A&M	Kyle Field	Southwest	1925	70,210	AstroTurf (87)
Texas Christian	Amon Carter	Southwest	1929	46,000	Grass
Texas Tech	Jones	Southwest	1947	50,500	AstroTurf-8 (88)
Toledo	Glass Bowl	Mid-American	1937	26,248	AstroTurf (90)
Tulane	√ Superdome@	Independent	1975	69,065	AstroTurf
Tulsa	Skelly	Independent	1930	40,385	Stadia Turf (91)
UCLA	√ Rose Bowl	Pacific-10	1922	98,101	Grass
Utah	Robert Rice	Western Athletic	1927	32,500	AstroTurf (82)
Utah St.	E. L. Romney	Big West	1968	30,257	Grass
UTEP	√ Sun Bowl	Western Athletic	1963	51,270	AstroTurf (83)
Vanderbilt	Vanderbilt	Southeastern	11922	41,000	AstroTurf (81)
Virginia	Scott	Atlantic Coast	1931	40,000	AstroTurf (81)
Virginia Tech	Lane	Big East	1965	51,000	Grass
Wake Forest	Groves	Atlantic Coast	1968	31,500	Grass
Washington	Husky	Pacific-10	1920	72,500	AstroTurf (87)
Washington St.	Martin	Pacific-10	1972	40,000	Omni-Turf (90)
West Va.	Mountaineer	Big East	1980	63,500	Omni-Turf (88)
Western Mich.	Waldo	Mid-American	1939	30,000	PAT (92)
Wisconsin	Camp Randall	Big Ten	1917	77,745	AstroTurf (90)
Wyoming	War Memorial	Western Athletic	1950	33,500	Grass

STADIUMS LISTED BY CAPACITY (Top 29)

School	Stadium	Surface* (Year)	Capacity
Michigan	Michigan	PAT(S91)	102,501
UCLA	√ Rose Bowl	Grass	98,101
Penn St.	Beaver	Grass	93,967
Tennessee	Neyland	Grass (S94)	91,902
Ohio St.	Ohio	PAT (S90)	91,470
Georgia	Sanford	Grass	86,117
Stanford	Stanford	Grass	85,500
Auburn	Jordan-Hare	Grass	85,214
Alabama	√ Legion Field	AstroTurf	83,091
Florida	Florida Field	Grass (S90)	83,000
Clemson	Memorial/Howard	Grass	81,473
Louisiana St.	Tiger	Grass	80,150
Texas	Memorial	AstroTurf (93)	77,809
Wisconsin	Camp Randall	AstroTurf (90)	77,745
Michigan St.	Spartan	AstroTurf (83)	76,000
California	Memorial	AstroTurf (90)	75,662
Oklahoma	Memorial	Grass (S94)	75,004
Florida St.	Doak Campbell	PAT (88)	75,000
Miami (Fla.)	√ Orange Bowl	PAT (S77)	74,712
Arizona St.	Sun Devil	Grass	73,656
Nebraska	Memorial	AstroTurf-8 (92)	72,700
Washington	Husky	AstroTurf (87)	72,500
South Caro.	Williams-Brice	Grass	72,400
Southern Methodist	√ Cotton Bowl	Grass (S93)	71,456
Illinois	Memorial	AstroTurf (89)	70,904
Iowa	Kinnick	PAT (S89)	70,397
Texas A&M	Kyle Field	AstroTurf (87)	70,210
Alabama	Bryant-Denny	PAT (S91)	70,123
Rice	Rice	All-Pro Turf (84)	70,000

√Not located on campus. @ Indoor facility. †Grass bank holds additional 10,000. & Reconfiguration of Los Angeles Memorial Coliseum undertaken before 1993 season changed full capacity from 94,159 seats to 68,000 for some Southern Cal home games, and capacity could change again as a result of 1994 earthquake damage. $ Built in 1978, additions in 1979, 1983 and 1993 !Renovated almost completely in 1981.

Surface Notes: *This column indicates the type of surface (either artificial or natural grass) present this year in the stadium. The brand name of the artificial turf, if known, is listed as well as the year the last installation occurred. The "S" preceding the year indicates that the school has switched either from natural grass to artificial turf or vice-versa. Legend: Turf—Any of several types of artificial turfs (name brands include AstroTurf, All-Pro, Omniturf, SuperTurf, etc.); Grass—Natural grass surface; PAT—Prescription Athletic Turf (a "natural-artificial" surface featuring a network of pipes connected to pumps capable of sucking water from the natural turf or watering it. The pipes are located 18 inches from the surface and covered with a mixture of sand and filler. The turf also is lined with heating coils to keep it from freezing in temperatures below 32 degrees).

Division I-A Stadium Facts: Houston and Tulsa claim to be the first college football teams to play in an indoor stadium (the Astrodome on September 11, 1964). But actually, Utah and West Virginia met in the 1964 Liberty Bowl in the Atlantic City Convention Hall. Technically, the Astrodome was the first indoor stadium built specially for football and baseball. The first major-college football game ever played on artificial turf was between Houston and Washington State on September 23, 1966.

Famous Major-College Dynasties

The following are singled out because of their historical significance, and all represent an outstanding record as well as more than one national championship.

NOTRE DAME (1919-30)

Under Knute Rockne, the Fighting Irish posted an overall record of 101-11-3 (.891 winning percentage) and captured three national titles during this 12-year period. Rockne, who died in an airplane crash in 1931, did not accomplish this by himself, with athletes like George Gipp and the legendary Four Horsemen (Harry Stuhldreher, Elmer Layden, Jim Crowley and Don Miller) around. The longest winning streak was 22 games, which began in 1918 under Gipp, but the South Benders had three other streaks of at least 15 games in the period.

MINNESOTA (1933-41)

Bernie Bierman, known as "The Silver Fox" for his prematurely gray hair, led the Golden Gophers through their best era. In the nine-year span, Minnesota posted a 58-9-5 (.840) record and won five national titles (1934, 1936, 1940 and 1941 outright and 1935 shared). Bierman oversaw five undefeated teams in the span, and the longest winning streak was 28 games. Defense was a trademark of the Gophers, who notched 23 shutouts in the 72 games. The top offensive player was 1941 Heisman Trophy winner Bruce Smith.

NOTRE DAME (1946-53)

Under head coach Frank Leahy, Notre Dame began another streak almost as successful as the Rockne era. Leahy led the Irish to a national title in 1943, and beginning in 1946, Notre Dame set off on a 63-8-6 (.857) journey that yielded three more national championships (1946, 1947 and 1949) in four years. The longest unbeaten streak stretched to 39 games. The top players were Heisman Trophy winners Johnny Lujack (1947), Leon Hart (1949) and John Lattner (1953).

OKLAHOMA (1948-58)

Many felt this particular span featured the greatest accomplishment in modern-day collegiate football—Oklahoma's Bud Wilkinson-led 47-game winning streak from 1953-57. The Sooners posted a 107-8-2 (.923) mark during the 11-year stretch that included three consensus national titles (1950, 1955 and 1956). Halfback Billy Vessels, the 1952 Heisman winner, was the outstanding individual player in the streak, but Wilkinson's teams were typified by overall speed and quickness.

ALABAMA (1959-67)

Paul "Bear" Bryant's return to his alma mater started a chain of events that eventually yielded one of the greatest dynasties in history. During the nine-year span, Bryant's teams fashioned an 83-10-6 (.869) record and captured three national prizes (1961, 1964 and 1965). His players included Joe Namath, Ken Stabler, Pat Trammell, Ray Perkins, Steve Sloan and Lee Roy Jordan, an eclectic group that featured no Heisman winners. All his players knew how to do was win football games, and the 1963-67 teams never lost a home game.

SOUTHERN CAL (1967-79)

Two coaches—John McKay and John Robinson—shared this dynasty, which posted a 122-23-7 (.826) record and four national titles (1967, 1972 and 1974 under McKay and 1978 under Robinson). The longest unbeaten streak was 28 games. Southern Cal had two Heisman winners—O. J. Simpson (1968) and Charles White (1979)—and 18 consensus all-Americans in the 13-year period.

ALABAMA (1971-80)

This was the second great run for the Crimson Tide under Bryant. Alabama reeled off a 28-game unbeaten streak and posted a 107-13-0 (.892) record during the 10-year span, including national championships in 1973, 1978 and 1979. Again, there were no Heisman winners for Bryant, but he had a list of players like John Hannah, Steadman Shealy, Jeff Rutledge, Tony Nathan and Major Ogilvie. Bryant died in 1983 as the winningest college coach.

OKLAHOMA (1971-80)

Barry Switzer led the Sooner dynasty to a 102-14-2 (.873) record that included a 37-game unbeaten string and 10 Big Eight championships. Back-to-back national titles in 1974 and 1975 were the result of enormous talent and Switzer's coaching. Some of the Sooner all-Americans during the 10-year period included Jack Mildren, Greg Pruitt, Lucious Selmon, Rod Shoate, Tinker Owens, Dewey Selmon, Lee Roy Selmon, Joe Washington, Billy Brooks and George Cumby. Heisman Trophy winner Billy Sims (1978) was the biggest name in a Sooner rushing attack that was virtually unstoppable.

MIAMI (FLA.) (1983-92)

The loss to Alabama in the 1993 Sugar Bowl ended a real streak for the Hurricanes, going for a fifth national title since 1983. Few would argue that during the 1980s under three different coaches—Howard Schnellenberger, Jimmy Johnson and Dennis Erickson—the Hurricanes were the most successful team in America. With a 107-13-0 (.892) record that included national titles in 1983, 1987, 1989 and 1991, the Hurricanes served notice that an undefeated season was a possibility every year.

Other College Football Dynasties

(Listed Because of Their Historical Significance)

School (Years)	W-L-T	Pct.	Duration	Titles*
Yale (1876-1909)	315-14-18	.934	34 years	19
Princeton (1877-1903)	233-21-11	.900	27 years	12
Pennsylvania (1894-1908)	168-21-7	.875	15 years	4
Harvard (1908-15)	64-4-5	.911	8 years	5
Pittsburgh (1913-20)	55-5-4	.891	8 years	3
Southern Cal (1919-33)	129-18-3	.870	15 years	2
Army (1943-50)	64-5-5	.899	8 years	3
Michigan St. (1950-66)	117-37-4	.753	17 years	4
Ohio St. (1954-61)	56-14-4	.784	8 years	3
Nebraska (1969-76)	79-14-4	.835	8 years	2
Penn St. (1980-87)	76-19-1	.797	8 years	2

*Some titles were shared.
(Special thanks to Bob Kirlin of Spokane, Wash., for his compilations.)

Major-College Statistics Trends†

(Average Per Game, Both Teams)

Year	Rushing Plays	Rushing Yds.	Rushing Avg.	Passing Att.	Passing Cmp.	Passing Pct.	Passing Yds.	Passing Av. Att.	Total Offense Plays	Total Offense Yds.	Total Offense Avg.	Scoring TD	Scoring FG	Scoring Pts.
1937	—	267.6	—	26.0	9.9	.381	129.0	4.96	—	396.8	—	—	—	20.2
1938	81.6	280.2	3.43	28.0	10.4	.371	140.2	5.01	109.6	420.4	3.85	3.50	0.12	23.5
1939	81.6	271.8	3.33	27.6	10.3	.374	132.8	4.81	109.2	404.6	3.70	3.32	0.18	22.7
1940	83.8	281.0	3.35	29.6	11.5	.386	156.0	5.26	113.4	437.0	3.85	3.94	0.16	26.6
1941	84.4	282.4	3.35	30.0	11.7	.392	161.2	5.38	114.4	443.6	3.88	4.06	0.12	27.5
1946	84.6	304.8	3.60	31.0	12.1	.389	176.6	5.69	115.6	481.4	4.16	4.78	0.08	32.1
1947	84.6	317.4	3.75	30.5	12.6	.414	180.2	5.91	115.1	497.6	4.32	4.73	0.07	31.8
1948	87.4	324.4	3.71	31.7	13.4	.423	188.4	5.95	119.0	513.0	4.31	5.04	0.09	34.2
1949	94.4	361.2	3.83	35.3	15.1	.431	220.1	6.24	129.7	581.3	4.48	5.71	0.08	38.8
1950	94.0	360.3	3.83	35.0	15.3	.438	216.9	6.19	129.0	577.2	4.47	5.58	0.07	37.8
1951	97.1	365.0	3.76	37.7	16.8	.446	227.1	6.02	134.9	592.1	4.39	5.72	0.09	38.8
1952	96.6	352.7	3.65	36.7	16.2	.441	223.6	6.09	133.4	576.3	4.32	5.36	0.14	36.7
1953	90.1	353.1	3.92	30.4	13.0	.428	183.4	6.03	120.5	536.4	4.45	5.07	0.09	34.2
1954	90.9	368.1	*4.05	29.7	13.0	.437	182.2	6.14	120.6	550.2	4.56	5.17	0.09	34.7
1955	92.1	353.3	3.83	27.1	11.8	.435	169.3	6.24	119.2	522.6	4.38	4.74	0.10	32.1
1956	98.3	386.2	3.93	28.2	12.3	.437	171.8	6.09	126.5	558.0	4.41	4.90	0.09	33.0
1957	98.5	355.0	3.60	28.8	12.8	.444	171.0	5.94	127.2	526.0	4.14	4.61	0.11	31.1
1958	94.2	341.4	3.62	32.2	14.7	.458	195.3	6.06	126.4	536.7	4.24	4.61	0.18	32.0
1959	92.4	332.0	3.59	33.0	14.9	.451	197.0	5.96	125.4	529.0	4.21	4.50	0.34	31.7
1960	90.6	339.7	3.75	31.5	14.3	.454	187.1	5.94	122.1	526.8	4.31	4.37	0.38	31.1
1961	91.1	333.3	3.66	31.8	14.3	.448	189.4	5.95	122.9	522.7	4.25	4.46	0.47	32.0
1962	90.5	328.0	3.63	34.4	15.9	.463	209.9	6.10	124.9	537.9	4.31	4.59	0.42	32.7
1963	88.2	320.0	3.63	35.2	16.2	.461	210.5	5.98	123.4	530.6	4.30	4.38	0.53	31.6
1964	87.4	299.3	3.43	35.8	16.9	.472	219.9	6.14	123.2	519.2	4.21	4.13	0.59	30.1
1965	90.2	298.7	3.31	41.5	19.3	.464	246.4	5.93	131.7	545.0	4.14	4.51	0.83	33.3
1966	88.5	297.3	3.36	43.9	20.6	.470	266.3	6.07	132.3	563.6	4.26	4.70	0.84	34.9
1967	94.6	309.3	3.27	45.8	21.4	.467	279.6	6.10	140.4	588.9	4.19	4.95	0.91	36.8
1968	99.4	341.5	3.44	50.7	24.1	.474	315.4	6.22	*150.1	657.0	4.38	5.77	0.92	42.4
1969	98.9	343.6	3.47	50.9	24.0	.471	314.1	6.17	149.8	657.7	4.39	5.80	1.08	43.2
1970	98.5	351.3	3.57	49.9	23.3	.467	305.3	6.12	148.4	656.6	4.42	5.66	1.13	42.6
1971	99.3	364.3	3.67	43.4	20.1	.463	264.6	6.10	142.6	628.9	4.41	5.38	1.08	40.4
1972	99.6	369.0	3.70	43.9	20.3	.462	273.7	6.24	143.5	642.7	4.48	5.42	1.22	41.1
1973	100.2	385.5	3.85	40.8	19.2	.472	261.7	6.41	141.0	647.2	4.59	5.50	1.29	41.9
1974	103.7	403.6	3.89	37.6	17.8	.474	244.6	6.50	141.3	648.2	4.59	5.27	1.26	40.3
1975	*103.8	*408.9	3.94	36.7	17.3	.473	239.2	6.52	140.5	648.1	4.61	5.14	1.48	40.1
1976	102.7	397.5	3.87	38.1	18.1	.474	246.9	6.49	140.8	644.4	4.58	5.13	1.49	40.0
1977	102.5	389.2	3.80	40.3	19.5	.483	269.0	6.67	142.9	658.2	4.61	5.34	1.46	41.5
1978	101.7	385.2	3.79	42.4	20.6	.486	277.7	6.55	144.1	662.9	4.60	5.28	1.51	41.1
1979	98.1	375.8	3.83	43.1	21.2	.491	278.6	6.47	141.2	654.4	4.63	5.09	1.53	39.9
1980	95.3	356.6	3.74	46.6	23.3	.500	303.7	6.52	141.9	660.3	4.65	5.22	1.61	41.0
1981	92.6	338.8	3.66	50.6	25.4	.502	329.4	6.51	143.2	668.2	4.67	5.14	1.73	41.0
1982	90.2	338.5	3.75	55.2	28.9	.522	364.8	6.61	145.4	703.3	4.84	5.42	2.04	43.8
1983	89.2	338.9	3.80	53.9	28.8	.536	365.5	6.79	143.1	704.5	4.92	5.45	2.11	44.2
1984	89.4	336.2	3.76	53.5	28.2	.527	362.2	6.77	142.9	698.4	4.89	5.32	2.30	44.1
1985	89.1	338.3	3.80	54.5	29.3	.537	372.2	6.82	143.6	710.5	4.95	5.48	2.18	44.7
1986	88.4	335.8	3.80	54.4	29.2	.537	370.2	6.81	142.8	706.0	4.95	5.59	2.14	45.4
1987	88.8	348.4	3.92	54.1	28.5	.526	367.1	6.78	142.9	715.5	5.01	5.65	2.25	46.1
1988	88.0	349.1	3.97	54.1	28.6	.529	371.5	6.87	142.1	720.6	5.07	5.82	*2.31	47.5
1989	85.4	332.8	3.90	57.0	30.8	.540	401.8	7.05	142.4	734.6	5.16	5.94	2.26	48.2
1990	86.1	335.3	3.90	56.6	30.2	.534	394.3	6.96	142.7	729.6	5.11	6.07	2.16	*48.8
1991	86.6	339.4	3.91	54.4	29.1	.535	379.2	6.98	141.0	718.7	5.10	5.90	1.77	46.2
1992	85.3	331.2	3.89	56.2	29.8	.530	380.9	6.77	141.5	712.1	5.03	5.67	2.08	45.8
1993	83.5	332.6	3.98	*57.4	*31.7	*.551	*409.7	*7.13	141.0	*742.3	*5.27	*6.18	1.93	48.8

*Record. †Records not compiled in 1942-45 except for Scoring Points Per Game: 1942 (31.3); 1943 (31.3); 1944 (32.6); 1945 (32.2).

Additional Major-College Statistics Trends†

Rules changes and statistics changes affecting trends: PUNTING—Beginning in 1965, 20 yards not deducted from a punt into the end zone for a touchback. INTERCEPTIONS—Interception yards not compiled, 1958-65. KICKOFF RETURNS—During 1937-45, if a kickoff went out of bounds, the receiving team put the ball in play on its 35-yard line instead of a second kickoff; in 1984 (rescinded in 1985), a 30-yard-line touchback for kickoffs crossing the goal line in flight and first touching the ground out of the end zone; in 1986, kickoffs from the 35-yard line. PUNT RETURNS—In 1967, interior linemen restricted from leaving until the ball is kicked.

(Average Per Game, Both Teams)

Year	Punting No.	Punting Avg.	Punting Net Avg.	Interceptions No.	Interceptions Avg. Ret.	Interceptions Yds.	Punt Returns No.	Punt Returns Avg. Ret.	Punt Returns Yds.	Kickoff Returns No.	Kickoff Returns Avg. Ret.	Kickoff Returns Yds.	Kickoff Returns Pct. Ret'd
1937	18.4	36.3	—	3.36	—	—	—	—	—	—	—	—	—
1938	18.6	37.2	—	3.40	9.19	31.6	—	—	—	—	—	—	—
1939	*18.7	36.7	—	3.34	9.84	33.0	*8.84	9.40	83.2	4.28	19.3	82.6	.764
1940	18.1	36.6	—	3.58	10.05	36.0	8.41	10.58	89.0	4.64	*20.4	95.0	.753
1941	17.7	36.1	—	*3.62	11.28	40.8	8.54	11.10	*94.8	4.82	20.2	97.2	.768
1946	14.6	35.7	—	3.50	11.79	41.2	7.40	11.32	83.8	6.02	18.9	113.8	.870
1947	13.4	36.4	30.3	3.21	11.93	38.3	6.94	11.73	81.4	6.07	18.9	114.5	.884
1948	12.6	36.3	30.2	3.20	12.59	40.3	6.18	*12.16	75.1	6.34	18.5	117.2	.873
1949	12.5	36.6	30.3	3.37	*13.23	*44.6	6.41	12.13	77.7	7.02	17.9	125.5	.885
1950	12.0	36.3	30.8	3.21	11.99	38.5	6.07	10.72	65.1	6.92	16.6	114.8	.889

(Average Per Game, Both Teams) Year	Punting No.	Avg.	Net Avg.	Interceptions No.	Avg. Ret.	Yds.	Punt Returns No.	Avg. Ret.	Yds.	Kickoff Returns No.	Avg. Ret.	Yds.	Pct. Ret'd
1951	12.8	35.9	30.7	3.34	12.00	40.1	6.20	10.58	65.6	7.06	17.0	119.7	.884
1952	12.5	36.4	31.6	3.19	11.60	37.0	6.13	9.95	61.0	6.89	17.6	121.4	.908
1953	10.4	34.9	29.7	2.74	12.12	33.2	5.13	10.66	54.7	6.54	17.8	116.4	.903
1954	9.7	34.9	29.4	2.71	12.48	33.8	4.84	11.16	54.0	6.64	18.4	122.0	*.910
1955	9.8	34.9	29.8	2.52	12.96	33.5	4.78	10.54	50.4	6.17	18.5	114.4	.892
1956	10.1	35.1	30.1	2.57	12.86	33.1	4.97	10.07	50.1	6.37	18.0	114.8	.906
1957	10.6	34.8	30.2	2.52	11.95	30.1	5.06	9.57	48.4	6.09	18.7	114.1	.897
1958	11.1	35.4	30.9	2.65	—	—	5.13	9.70	49.8	6.03	18.9	113.9	.880
1959	11.0	35.9	31.5	2.66	—	—	5.34	9.06	48.4	6.18	18.7	115.6	.892
1960	10.2	36.0	31.4	2.48	—	—	4.78	9.73	46.5	6.09	18.8	114.6	.890
1961	10.3	35.5	31.1	2.44	—	—	4.85	9.44	45.8	6.12	18.3	112.2	.873
1962	10.4	35.7	31.3	2.50	—	—	4.72	9.66	45.6	6.20	19.6	121.4	.876
1963	10.3	36.3	32.5	2.38	—	—	4.68	9.71	45.4	6.15	20.1	123.7	.880
1964	10.6	36.4	32.5	2.39	—	—	4.65	8.99	41.8	5.86	19.6	114.6	.862
1965	11.7	38.5	33.9	2.84	—	—	5.46	9.99	54.5	6.30	18.8	118.6	.849
1966	11.8	37.5	33.5	3.00	12.07	36.2	5.26	8.82	46.4	6.48	18.7	121.6	.849
1967	12.9	36.8	31.6	3.04	11.39	34.6	6.83	9.92	67.7	6.61	18.7	123.3	.831
1968	13.3	37.4	33.3	3.22	11.51	37.1	6.01	8.95	53.8	7.27	19.1	139.1	.829
1969	13.1	37.5	33.4	3.39	11.07	37.5	6.00	9.00	54.0	7.34	18.9	138.7	.818
1970	12.6	37.4	33.2	3.32	11.65	38.7	5.78	9.28	53.7	7.37	19.0	140.2	.828
1971	12.3	37.6	33.4	2.97	11.75	34.9	5.78	9.04	52.3	7.14	19.2	137.2	.834
1972	12.1	37.2	33.4	3.07	11.54	35.4	5.44	8.61	46.8	6.99	19.0	132.8	.803
1973	11.6	37.8	34.1	2.72	11.30	30.8	5.03	8.65	43.5	7.08	19.6	138.4	.797
1974	11.2	37.6	34.2	2.46	11.30	27.8	4.80	7.92	38.0	6.75	19.1	128.5	.784
1975	10.8	38.1	35.0	2.42	11.26	27.2	4.77	7.19	34.3	6.39	19.3	123.3	.733
1976	11.3	38.0	35.1	2.45	11.44	28.0	4.83	6.83	33.0	6.28	18.3	114.7	.722
1977	11.5	38.0	35.0	2.51	11.05	27.8	4.89	7.10	34.6	6.32	18.4	116.1	.711
1978	12.0	38.0	34.9	2.68	10.83	29.0	5.02	7.39	37.1	6.36	18.7	119.1	.665
1979	11.6	37.7	34.8	2.62	10.66	27.9	4.76	7.09	33.8	6.03	18.8	113.7	.637
1980	11.6	38.3	35.4	2.74	10.85	29.7	4.88	7.01	34.2	5.81	19.0	110.2	.651
1981	11.9	38.9	35.9	2.76	10.22	28.2	4.90	7.22	35.4	5.72	18.8	107.8	.636
1982	11.7	*39.8	*36.5	2.78	10.70	29.7	4.79	8.00	38.3	5.37	19.3	103.7	.561
1983	11.0	39.5	35.9	2.74	10.43	28.6	4.94	7.95	39.3	5.29	19.2	101.6	.549
1984	11.1	39.7	36.3	2.61	10.07	26.3	4.94	7.61	37.6	6.05	18.6	112.3	.621
1985	11.0	39.6	36.1	2.59	10.47	27.1	4.89	7.92	38.8	5.88	19.4	114.0	.603
1986	10.7	39.2	35.4	2.59	10.99	28.5	5.01	8.23	41.3	7.55	19.8	149.2	.770
1987	10.7	38.6	34.7	2.64	10.82	28.6	4.95	8.31	41.1	7.78	19.1	149.0	.780
1988	10.4	38.4	34.7	2.47	11.17	28.0	4.78	7.96	38.1	*7.94	19.4	154.2	.778
1989	10.4	38.5	34.3	2.56	10.75	27.6	4.72	8.46	39.9	7.83	19.7	*154.3	.776
1990	10.6	38.6	34.3	2.46	11.40	28.0	4.89	9.33	45.7	7.58	19.6	148.9	.738
1991	10.5	38.4	34.3	2.35	11.30	26.6	5.00	8.74	43.7	6.86	19.4	133.1	.741
1992	11.2	39.0	34.9	2.39	11.00	26.3	5.25	9.04	47.5	6.60	20.1	132.7	.732
1993	10.3	38.8	35.1	2.27	11.00	24.9	4.56	8.28	37.7	6.86	20.0	137.3	.679

*Record. †Records not compiled in 1942-45.

Field Goal Trends (1938-1968)

Year	Made	Year	Made	Year	Made	Atts.	Pct.
1938	47	1951	53	1961	277		
1939	80	1952	83	1962	261		
1940	84	1953	50	1963	314		
1941	59	1954	48	1964	368		
1942-45	*	1955	57	1965	484	1,035	.468
1946	44	1956	53	1966	522	1,125	.464
1947	38	1957	64	1967	555	1,266	.438
1948	53	1958	103	1968	566	1,287	.440
1949	46	1959	†199				
1950	46	1960	224				

*Records not compiled. †Goal posts widened from 18 feet, 6 inches to 23 feet, 4 inches in 1959.

Field Goal Trends (From 1969)

(Includes Field Goal Attempts by Divisions I-AA, II and III Opponents)

Year	Totals Made	Atts.	Pct.	16-39	Pct.	Breakdown by Distances 16-49	Pct.	40-49	Pct.	50 Plus	Pct.	60 Plus
1969	669	1,402	.477	538-872	.617	654-1,267	.516	116-395	.294	15-135	.111	0-8
1970	754	1,548	.487	614-990	.620	740-1,380	.536	126-390	.323	14-168	.083	1-9
1971	780	1,625	.480	607-1,022	.594	760-1,466	.518	153-444	.345	20-159	.126	0-11
1972	876	1,828	.479	705-1,150	.613	855-1,641	.521	150-491	.305	21-187	.112	1-12
1973	958	1,920	.499	728-1,139	.639	914-1,670	.547	186-531	.350	44-250	.176	1-21
1974	947	1,905	.497	706-1,096	.644	906-1,655	.547	200-559	.358	41-250	.164	1-17
1975	1,164	2,237	.520	849-1,255	.676	1,088-1,896	.574	239-641	.373	76-341	.223	4-32
1976	1,187	2,330	.509	854-1,301	.656	1,131-1,997	.566	277-696	.398	56-333	.168	3-24
1977	1,238	2,514	.492	882-1,315	.671	1,160-2,088	.556	278-773	.360	78-426	.183	6-40
1978	1,229	2,113	.582	938-1,361	.689	1,193-1,982	.602	255-621	.411	36-131	.275	1-4

Year	Made	Totals Atts.	Pct.	Under 20	Pct.	20-29	Pct.	Breakdown by Distances 30-39	Pct.	40-49	Pct.	50-59	Pct.	60 Plus	Pct.
1979	1,241	2,129	.583	34-43	.791	455-601	.757	425-706	.602	286-600	.477	41-173	.237	0-6	.000
1980	1,302	2,241	.581	31-39	.795	408-529	.771	452-696	.649	317-682	.465	37-175	.211	0-7	.000
1981	1,360	2,254	.603	42-48	.875	471-598	.788	461-731	.631	335-698	.480	58-169	.343	1-10	.100
1982	1,224	1,915	.639	31-34	.912	384-475	.808	415-597	.695	319-604	.528	73-190	.384	2-15	.133
1983	1,329	2,025	.656	34-37	.919	417-508	.821	477-636	.750	329-628	.524	72-201	.358	0-15	.000
1984	1,442	2,112	.683	44-49	.898	450-532	.846	503-681	.739	363-630	.576	80-206	.388	2-14	.143
1985	1,360	2,106	.646	40-47	.851	416-511	.814	478-657	.728	341-647	.527	84-227	.370	1-17	.059
1986	1,326	2,034	.652	45-48	.938	445-525	.848	448-641	.699	340-629	.541	44-182	.242	4-9	.444
1987	1,381	2,058	.671	45-48	.938	484-559	.866	469-638	.735	311-604	.515	72-200	.360	0-9	.000
1988	1,421	2,110	.673	33-35	.943	487-573	.850	495-664	.745	337-610	.552	68-217	.313	1-11	.091
1989#	1,389	2,006	*.692	50-53	.943	497-565	.880	471-655	.719	319-573	.557	52-154	.338	0-6	.000
1990	1,348	2,011	.670	39-42	.929	477-546	.874	454-626	.725	319-625	.510	59-167	.353	0-5	.000
1991$	1,092	1,831	.596	31-32	.969	395-519	.761	366-612	.598	254-531	.478	45-132	.341	1-5	.200
1992	1,288	1,986	.649	32-38	.842	464-569	.815	447-673	.664	294-577	.510	49-126	.389	2-3	.667
1993§	1,182	1,832	.645	23-25	.920	490-599	.818	407-617	.660	224-488	.459	38-98	.388	0-5	.000

*Record. #First year after kicking tee became illegal. $First year after goal-post width narrowed back to 18'6'' from 23'4''. §First year after hash marks narrowed to 60 feet from each sideline.

Field-Goal Trends By Soccer-Style and Conventional Kickers

(Division I-A Kickers Only)

(Pete Gogolak of Cornell was documented as the first soccer-style kicker in college football history. The Hungarian-born kicker played at Cornell from 1961 through 1963. He set a national major-college record of 44 consecutive extra-point conversions and finished 54 of 55 for his career. His younger brother, Charley, also a soccer-styler, kicked at Princeton from 1963 through 1965.)

SOCCER-STYLE

Year	†No.	Totals Made	Atts.	Pct.	16-39	Pct.	Breakdown by Distances 16-49	Pct.	40-49	Pct.	50 Plus	Pct.	60 Plus
1975	70	528	1,012	.522	370-540	.685	479-816	.587	109-276	.395	49-196	.250	1-17
1976	84	517	1,019	.507	350-517	.677	477-831	.574	127-314	.404	40-188	.213	3-16
1977	96	665	1,317	.505	450-649	.693	615-1,047	.587	165-398	.415	50-270	.185	2-27
1978	98	731	1,244	.588	540-768	.703	703-1,148	.612	163-380	.429	28-96	.292	1-3

Year	†No.	Totals Made	Atts.	Pct.	Under 20	20-29	30-39	Breakdown by Distances 40-49	50-59	60 Plus
1979	116	839	1,413	.594	23-28	288-380	282-455	214-419	32-126	0-5
1980	121	988	1,657	.596	26-32	327-416	342-522	261-540	32-147	0-5
1981	138	1,108	1,787	.620	32-36	377-476	376-576	279-551	43-142	1-6
1982	105	1,026	1,548	.663	26-27	317-375	346-482	273-495	62-156	2-13
1983	110	1,139	1,724	.661	29-31	345-416	403-541	294-543	68-179	0-14
1984	127	1,316	1,898	*.694	43-47	414-480	438-589	341-572	78-197	2-13
1985	133	1,198	1,838	.652	35-41	369-452	415-578	306-560	72-191	1-16
1986	128	1,201	1,829	.657	37-40	398-467	410-575	313-576	39-162	4-9
1987	122	1,275	1,892	.674	40-43	458-523	424-574	290-566	63-177	0-9
1988	140	1,317	1,947	.676	31-33	445-521	468-630	311-562	61-201	1-11
1989	138	1,313	1,897	.692	49-52	462-526	441-612	310-551	51-150	0-6
1990	135	1,282	1,890	.678	36-38	450-515	432-589	308-590	56-154	0-4
1991	132	1,048	1,763	.594	30-31	381-500	349-589	243-512	44-130	1-1
1992	135	1,244	1,926	.646	31-37	447-554	429-647	288-561	47-124	2-3
1993	132	1,153	1,776	.649	23-25	475-578	398-600	219-475	38-93	0-5

CONVENTIONAL

Year	†No.	Totals Made	Atts.	Pct.	16-39	Pct.	Breakdown by Distances 16-49	Pct.	40-49	Pct.	50 Plus	Pct.	60 Plus
1975	116	564	1,085	.520	427-640	.667	541-959	.564	114-319	.357	23-126	.183	3-13
1976	101	608	1,192	.510	460-720	.639	594-1,065	.558	134-345	.388	14-127	.110	0-7
1977	98	513	1,054	.487	384-586	.655	487-916	.532	103-330	.312	26-138	.188	4-14
1978	86	440	761	.578	352-516	.682	434-729	.595	82-213	.385	6-32	.188	0-0

Year	†No.	Totals Made	Atts.	Pct.	Under 20	20-29	30-39	Breakdown by Distances 40-49	50-59	60 Plus
1979	70	333	585	.569	10-14	140-185	111-198	63-150	9-37	0-1
1980	62	258	471	.548	5-7	81-113	110-174	56-142	6-33	0-2
1981	50	195	367	.531	8-9	70-97	69-126	41-112	7-22	0-1
1982	25	103	195	.528	3-4	36-50	34-62	25-59	5-18	0-2
1983	23	112	181	.619	4-5	40-55	46-58	22-50	0-12	0-1
1984	10	44	76	.579	0-1	17-26	20-33	7-15	0-1	0-0
1985	12	81	138	.587	3-4	22-29	29-40	19-44	8-20	0-1
1986	8	58	89	.652	4-4	21-28	17-27	14-24	2-6	0-0
1987	4	35	50	.700	4-4	10-14	14-16	6-9	1-7	0-0
1988	5	26	40	.650	0-0	17-21	5-7	4-10	0-2	0-0
1989	2	37	47	*.787	1-1	19-20	12-16	5-9	0-1	0-0
1990	2	23	38	.605	1-1	8-10	8-9	4-13	2-5	0-0
1991	2	16	24	.667	0-0	5-9	6-7	5-7	0-1	0-0
1992	1	12	18	.667	0-0	5-6	6-8	1-4	0-0	0-0
1993	1	6	11	.545	0-0	4-5	2-3	0-3	0-0	0-0

*Record. †Number of kickers attempting at least one field goal.

Average Yardage of Field Goals

(Division I-A Kickers Only)

	Soccer-Style			Conventional			Nation		
Year	Made	Missed	Total	Made	Missed	Total	Made	Missed	Total
1975	35.1	43.2	39.0	33.1	41.3	37.0	34.1	42.2	37.9
1976	35.0	43.1	39.0	33.2	40.7	36.9	34.0	41.8	37.9
1977	34.7	44.3	39.5	33.3	41.9	37.7	34.1	43.2	38.7
1978	34.0	39.9	36.4	31.9	38.3	34.6	33.2	39.3	35.7
1979	33.7	39.9	36.2	31.9	38.0	34.5	33.2	39.3	35.7
1980	34.0	40.7	36.7	33.4	39.6	36.2	33.8	40.4	36.6
1981	33.9	40.1	36.2	33.2	38.6	35.7	33.8	39.8	36.1
1982	34.8	41.8	37.2	34.0	39.8	36.7	34.7	41.5	37.1
1983	34.7	42.1	37.2	32.3	40.5	35.5	34.5	41.9	37.0
1984	34.4	41.8	36.7	32.3	34.9	33.4	34.3	41.5	36.5
1985	34.5	41.3	36.8	35.4	41.7	38.0	34.5	41.3	36.9
1986	33.9	41.6	36.6	32.5	38.6	34.7	33.9	41.4	36.5
1987	33.5	41.8	36.2	32.3	41.4	35.1	33.5	41.8	36.2
1988	33.9	41.7	36.4	30.0	37.6	32.7	32.0	39.3	34.4
1989	33.5	41.2	35.9	30.5	39.6	32.4	33.4	41.2	35.8
1990	33.4	41.3	36.0	33.4	42.0	36.7	33.4	41.3	36.0
1991	33.2	40.7	35.8	28.6	31.9	40.7	35.9	40.4	36.1
1992	34.1	41.2	36.7	30.1	37.8	32.7	37.2	41.3	37.8
1993	32.4	38.9	34.7	26.8	38.0	31.9	32.3	38.9	34.6

Division I-A Extra-Point Trends

(From Start of Two-Point Attempts)

		Percent Total Tries		Kick Attempts			Two-Point Attempts		
Year	Games	Kick	2-Pt.	Atts.	Made	Pct.	Atts.	Made	Pct.
1958	578	#.486	*.514	1,295	889	.686	*1,371	*613	.447
1959	578	.598	.402	1,552	1,170	.754	1,045	421	.403
1960	596	.701	.299	1,849	1,448	.783	790	345	.437
1961	574	.723	.277	1,842	1,473	.800	706	312	.442
1962	602	.724	.276	1,987	1,549	.780	757	341	.450
1963	605	.776	.224	2,057	1,659	.807	595	256	.430
1964	613	.814	.186	2,053	1,704	.830	469	189	.403
1965	619	.881	.119	2,460	2,083	.847	331	134	.405
1966	626	.861	.139	2,530	2,167	.857	410	165	.402
1967	611	.869	.131	2,629	2,252	.857	397	160	.403
1968	615	.871	.129	3,090	2,629	.851	456	181	.397
1969	621	.880	.120	3,168	2,781	.878	432	170	.394
1970	667	.862	.138	3,255	2,875	.883	522	246	*.471
1971	726	.889	.111	3,466	3,081	.889	433	173	.400
1972	720	.872	.128	3,390	3,018	.890	497	219	.441
1973	741	.893	.107	3,637	3,258	.896	435	180	.414
1974	749	.885	.115	3,490	3,146	.901	455	211	.464
1975	785	.891	.109	3,598	3,266	.908	440	171	.389
1976	796	.877	.123	3,579	3,241	.906	502	203	.404
1977	849	.891	.109	*4,041	*3,668	.908	495	209	.422
1978	816	.884	.116	3,808	3,490	.916	498	208	.418
1979	811	.897	.103	3,702	3,418	.923	424	176	.415
1980	810	.895	.105	3,785	3,480	.919	442	170	.384
1981	788	.901	.099	3,655	3,387	.927	403	172	.427
1982	599	.901	.099	2,920	2,761	.946	320	120	.375
1983	631	.896	.104	3,080	2,886	.937	356	151	.424
1984	626	.889	.111	2,962	2,789	.942	370	173	.468
1985	623	.899	.101	3,068	2,911	.949	345	121	.351
1986	619	.905	.095	3,132	2,999	.958	330	131	.397
1987	615	.892	.108	3,094	2,935	.949	375	163	.435
1988	616	.899	.101	3,215	3,074	.956	363	156	.430
1989	614	.888	.112	3,233	3,090	.956	409	179	.438
1990	623	.911	.089	3,429	3,291	*.960	335	138	.412
1991	617	.906	.094	3,279	3,016	.920	342	128	.374
1992	619	.899	.101	3,156	2,967	.940	353	159	.450
1993	613	*.912	#.088	3,455	3,251	.941	333	143	.429

*Record high. #Record low.

Division I-A Extra-Point Kick Attempts (1938-1957)

Year	Pct. Made	Year	Pct. Made	Year	Pct. Made	Year	Pct. Made
1938	.608	1946	.657	1951	.711	1956	.666
1939	.625	1947	.657	1952	.744	1957	.653
1940	.607	1948	.708	1953	.650		
1941	.638	1949	.738	1954	.656		
1942-45	*	1950	.713	1955	.669		

*Not compiled.

All-Divisions Defensive Extra-Point Trends

In 1988, the NCAA Football Rules Committee adopted a rule that gave defensive teams an opportunity to score two points on point-after-touchdown tries. The two points were awarded for returning an interception or advancing a blocked kick for a touchdown on point-after tries.

DIVISION I-A

Year	Games	Kick Ret./TDs	Int. Ret./TDs	Total Ret./TDs
1988	616	8/2	6/0	14/2
1989	614	12/3	9/2	21/5
1990	623	9/3	5/2	14/5
1991	617	9/3	10/3	19/6
1992	619	8/5	1/0	9/5
1993	613	5/2	6/1	11/3

DIVISION I-AA

Year	Games	Kick Ret./TDs	Int. Ret./TDs	Total Ret./TDs
1988	553	4/1	7/1	11/2
1989	554	11/4	4/2	15/6
1990	548	7/3	4/2	11/5
1991	560	12/3	9/2	21/5
1992	553	9/5	8/5	17/10
1993	725	11/5	19/3	30/8

DIVISION II

Year	Games	Kick Ret./TDs	Int. Ret./TDs	Total Ret./TDs
1988	580	19/4	9/0	28/4
1989	590	18/8	11/3	29/11
1990	596	9/3	2/2	11/5
1991	575	10/3	8/2	18/5
1992	580	9/4	7/3	16/7
1993	694	16/6	9/5	25/11

DIVISION III

Year	Games	Kick Ret./TDs	Int. Ret./TDs	Total Ret./TDs
1988	994	29/8	25/3	54/11
1989	1,012	16/5	13/4	29/9
1990	1,020	25/10	16/6	41/16
1991	1,006	18/7	14/5	32/12
1992	1,028	14/6	17/7	31/13
1993	997	17/5	18/6	35/11

ALL DIVISIONS—NATIONWIDE

Year	Games	Kick Ret./TDs	Int. Ret./TDs	Total Ret./TDs
1988	2,743	60/15	47/4	107/19
1989	2,770	57/20	37/11	94/31
1990	2,787	50/19	27/12	77/31
1991	2,758	49/16	41/12	90/28
1992	2,780	40/20	33/15	73/35
1993	3,029	49/18	52/15	101/33

All-Divisions Fumble-Recovery Returns

In 1990, the NCAA Football Rules Committee adopted a rule that gave the defense an opportunity to advance fumbles that occur beyond the neutral zone (or line of scrimmage). In 1992, the rule was changed to allow defenses to advance any fumble regardless of position behind or beyond the line of scrimmage. Here are the number of fumble recoveries by division that were advanced, and the number that resulted in a score.

DIVISION I-A

Year	Games	Fumble Rec./TDs
1990	623	51/17
1991	617	60/16
1992	619	126/34
1993	613	117/24

DIVISION I-AA

Year	Games	Fumble Rec./TDs
1990	548	34/16
1991	560	42/13
1992	553	96/42
1993	725	86/25

DIVISION II

Year	Games	Fumble Rec./TDs
1990	596	46/25
1991	575	43/19
1992	580	77/39
1993	694	110/41

DIVISION III

Year	Games	Fumble Rec./TDs
1990	1,020	55/19
1991	1,006	62/22
1992	1,028	94/47
1993	997	88/33

ALL DIVISIONS—NATIONWIDE

Year	Games	Fumble Rec./TDs
1990	2,787	186/77
1991	2,758	207/70
1992	2,780	393/162
1993	3,029	401/123

Major-College Tie Games

The record for most tie games in a single week is six—on October 27, 1962; September 28, 1963, and October 9, 1982.

Year	No.	Games	Pct.	Scoreless
1954	15	551	2.72	2
1955	22	536	4.10	1
1956	28	558	5.02	2
1957	24	570	4.21	4
1958*	19	578	3.29	2
1959	13	578	2.25	4
1960	23	596	3.86	4
1961	11	574	1.92	1
1962	20	602	3.32	2
1963	25	605	4.13	4
1964	19	613	3.10	2
1965	19	619	3.07	4
1966	13	626	2.08	0
1967	14	611	2.29	1
1968	17	615	2.76	1
1969	9	621	1.45	0
1970	7	667	1.05	0
1971	12	726	1.65	1
1972	14	720	1.94	1
1973	18	741	2.43	2
1974	18	749	2.40	0
1975	16	785	2.04	0
1976	13	796	1.63	1
1977	16	849	1.88	1
1978	16	816	1.96	1
1979	17	811	2.10	1
1980	12	810	1.48	0
1981	17	788	2.16	0
1982	14	599	2.34	0
1983	13	631	2.06	†1
1984	15	626	2.40	0
1985	13	623	2.09	0
1986	10	619	1.62	0
1987	13	615	2.11	0
1988	12	616	1.95	0
1989	15	614	2.44	0
1990	15	623	2.41	0
1991	14	617	2.27	0
1992	13	619	2.10	0
1993	11	613	1.79	0

*First year of two-point conversion rule. †Last scoreless tie game: Nov. 19, 1983, Oregon vs. Oregon St.

Highest-Scoring Tie Games

(Home Team Listed First)

Score	Date	Opponents
52-52	11-16-91	San Diego St.-Brigham Young
48-48	9-8-79	San Jose St.-Utah St.
43-43	11-12-88	Duke-North Caro. St.
41-41	9-23-89	San Diego St.-Cal St. Fullerton
40-40	11-8-75	Idaho-Weber St.
39-39	11-7-82	Texas Tech-Texas Christian
37-37	9-23-67	*Alabama-Florida St.
36-36	9-30-72	Georgia Tech-Rice
35-35	11-16-91	San Jose St.-Hawaii
35-35	12-9-89	Hawaii-Air Force
35-35	9-23-89	Colorado St.-Eastern Mich.
35-35	10-7-78	Ohio St.-Southern Methodist
35-35	10-19-74	Idaho-Montana
35-35	10-9-71	New Mexico-New Mexico St.
35-35	9-27-69	Minnesota-Ohio
35-35	9-21-68	Washington-Rice
35-35	11-18-67	Navy-Vanderbilt
35-35	12-11-48	†Pacific (Cal.)—Hardin-Simmons
34-34	10-6-90	Iowa St.-Kansas
33-33	10-1-83	California-Arizona
33-33	9-24-49	Texas Christian-Oklahoma St.
33-33	10-31-31	Yale-Dartmouth

*At Birmingham. †Grape Bowl, Lodi, Calif.

Home-Field Records

(Includes Host Teams at Neutral-Site Games)

Year	Games	Home Team			Pct.
		Won	Lost	Tied	
1966	626	365	248	13	.594
1967	611	333	264	14	.557
1968	615	348	250	17	.580
1969	621	366	246	9	.596
1970	667	399	261	7	.603
1971	726	416	298	12	.581
1972	720	441	265	14	.622
1973	741	439	284	18	.605
1974	749	457	274	18	.622
1975	785	434	335	16	.563
1976	796	463	320	13	.590
1977	849	501	332	16	.600
1978	816	482	318	16	.601
1979	811	460	334	17	.578
1980	809	471	327	12	.589
1981	788	457	314	17	.591
1982	599	368	217	14	.626
1983	631	364	254	13	.587
1984	626	371	240	15	.605
1985	623	371	239	13	.606
1986	619	363	246	10	.595
1987	615	387	215	13	*.640
1988	616	370	234	12	.610
1989	614	365	234	15	.607
1990	623	373	235	15	.611
1991	617	362	241	14	.598
1992	619	388	218	13	.637
1993	613	375	227	11	.621

* Record.

College Football Rules Changes

The Ball

1869—Round, rubber Association ball.
1875—Egg-shaped, leather-covered Rugby ball.
1896—Prolate spheroid, without specific measurements.
1912—28-28½ inches around ends, 22½-23 inches around middle, weight 14-15 ounces.
1929—28-28½ inches around ends, 22-22½ inches around middle, weight 14-15 ounces.
1934—28-28½ inches around ends, 21¼-21½ inches around middle, weight 14-15 ounces.
1952—Ball may be inclined no more than 45 degrees by snapper.
1956—Rubber-covered ball permitted.
1973—Teams allowed to use ball of their choice while in possession.
1978—Ball may not be altered, and new or nearly new balls added.
1982—10⅞ to 11⁷/₁₆ inches long, 20¾ to 21¼ inches around middle, and 27¾ to 28½ inches long-axis circumference.
1993—Rubber or composition ball ruled illegal.

The Field

1869—120 yards by 75 yards; uprights 24 feet apart.
1871—166⅔ yards by 100 yards.
1872—133⅓ yards by 83⅓ yards.
1873—Uprights 25 feet apart.
1876—110 yards by 53⅓ yards. Uprights 18½ feet apart; crossbar 10 feet high.
1882—Field marked with transverse lines every five yards. This distance to be gained in three downs to retain possession.
1912—Field 120 yards by 53⅓ yards, including two 10-yard end zones.
1927—Goal posts moved back 10 yards, to end line.
1957—Team area at 35-yard lines.
1959—Uprights widened to 23 feet, 4 inches.
1966—Pylons placed in corners of end zone and at goal lines.
1991—Uprights moved back to 18 feet, 6 inches.
1993—Hash marks moved six feet, eight inches closer to center of field to 60 feet from each sideline.

Points

1869—All goals count 1 each.
1883—Safety 1, touchdown 2, goal after TD 4, goal from field 5.
1884—Safety 2, touchdown 4, goal after TD 2.
1898—Touchdown 5, goal after TD 1.
1904—Goal from field 4.
1909—Goal from field 3.
1912—Touchdown 6.
1922—Try-for-point by scrimmage play from 5-yard line.
1929—Try-for-point by scrimmage play from 2-yard line.
1958—One-point & two-point conversion (from 3-yard line).
1958—One-point safety added.
1974—Ball must go between the uprights for a successful field goal, over the uprights previously scored.
1976—Forfeit score changed from 1-0 to score at time of forfeit if the offended team is ahead at time of forfeit.
1984—Try may be eliminated at end of game if both captains agree.

Players

1869—Each team consisted of 25 players.
1873—Each team consisted of 20 players.
1876—Each team consisted of 15 players.
1880—Each team consisted of 11 players.
1895—Only one man in motion forward before the snap. No more than three players behind the line. One player permitted in motion toward own goal line.
1910—Seven players required on line.
1911—Illegal to conceal ball beneath a player's clothing.
1915—Numbering of players recommended.
1937—Number front and back mandatory with 6-inch Arabic in front and 10-inch in the rear.
1939—All players must wear head protectors.
1951—Face masks legal.
1966—Mandatory numbering of five players on the line 50-79.
1982—Tearaway jersey eliminated by charging a time-out.
1983—Mandatory white jersey for visiting teams.
1994—Jerseys that extend below the top of the pants must be tucked into the pants.
1994—Standards to limit glove stickiness adopted.

Substitutions

1876—Fifteen players to a team and few if any substitutions.
1882—Replacements for disqualified or injured players.
1897—Substitutions may enter the game any time at discretion of captains.
1922—Players withdrawn during the first half may be returned during the second half. A player withdrawn in the second half may not return.
1941—A player may substitute any time but may not be withdrawn or the outgoing player returned to the game until one play had intervened. Platoon football made possible.
1948—Unlimited substitution on change of team possession.
1953—Two-platoon abolished and players allowed to enter the game only once in each quarter.

1954-64—Changes each year toward more liberalized substitution rule and platoon football.
1965—Platoon football returns. Unlimited substitutions between periods, after a score or try.
1974—Substitutes must be in for one play and replaced players out for one play.
1993—Players who are bleeding or whose uniforms are saturated with blood must come out of the game until their return has been approved by medical personnel.

Passing Game

1906—One forward pass legalized behind the line if made five yards right or left of center. Ball went to opponents if it failed to touch a player of either side before touching the ground. Either team could recover a pass touched by an opponent. One pass each scrimmage down.
1910—Pass interference does not apply 20 yards beyond the line of scrimmage. Passer must be five yards behind the line of scrimmage. One forward pass permitted during each down.
1914—Roughing the passer added.
1923—Handing the ball forward is an illegal forward pass and receivers going out of bounds and returning prohibited.
1934—Three changes encourage use of pass. (1) First forward pass in series of downs can be incomplete in the end zone without loss of ball except on fourth down. (2) Circumference of ball reduced, making it easier to throw. (3) Five-yard penalty for more than one incomplete pass in same series of downs eliminated.
1941—Fourth-down forward pass incomplete in end zone no longer a touchback. Ball goes to opponent at spot where put in play.
1945—Forward pass may be thrown from anywhere behind the line, encouraging use of modern T formation.
1968—Compulsory numbering system makes only players numbered other than 50-79 eligible forward-pass receivers.
1976—Offensive blocking changed to provide half extension of arms to assist pass blocking.
1980—Retreat blocking added with full arm extension to assist pass blocking, and illegal use of hands reduced to five yards.
1982—Pass interference only on a catchable forward pass. Forward pass intentionally grounded to conserve time permitted.
1983—First down added to roughing the passer.
1985—Retreat block deleted and open hands and extended arms permitted anywhere on the field.
1994—Ball must be catchable for offensive player to be charged with pass interference.

General Changes

1876—Holding and carrying the ball permitted.
1880—Eleven players on a side and a scrimmage line established.
1882—Downs and yards to gain enter the rules.
1883—Scoring system established.
1906—Forward passes permitted. Ten yards for first down.
1920—Clipping defined.
1922—Try-for-point introduced. Ball brought out five yards from goal line for scrimmage, allowing try for extra point by place kick, drop kick, run or forward pass.
1925—Kickoff returned to 40-yard line. Clipping made a violation, with penalty of 25 yards.
1927—One-second pause imposed on shift. Thirty seconds allowed for putting ball in play. Huddle limited to 15 seconds. To encourage use of lateral pass, missed backward pass other than from center declared dead ball when it hits the ground and cannot be recovered by opponents.
1929—All fumbles ruled dead at point of recovery.
1932—Most far-reaching changes in nearly a quarter of a century set up safeguards against hazards of game. (1) Ball declared dead when any portion of player in possession, except his hands or feet, touches ground. (2) Use of flying block and flying tackle barred under penalty of five yards. (3) Players on defense forbidden to strike opponents on head, neck or face. (4) Hard and dangerous equipment must be covered with padding.
1937—Numerals on front and back of jerseys required.
1941—Legal to hand ball forward behind the neutral zone.
1948—One-inch kicking tees permitted.

1949—Blockers required to keep hands against their chest.
1951—Fair catch restored.
1952—Penalty for striking with forearm, elbow or locked hands, or for flagrantly rough play or unsportsmanlike conduct, changed from 15 yards to mandatory suspension.
1957—Penalty for grabbing face mask.
1959—Distance penalties limited to one-half distance to offending team's goal line.
1965—Two-inch kicking tees permitted.
1967—Coaching from sideline permitted.
1971—Crack-back block (blocking below waist) illegal.
1972—Freshman eligibility restored.
1977—Clock started on snap after a penalty.
1978—Unsuccessful field goal returned to the previous spot.
1983—Offensive encroachment changed...no offensive player permitted in or beyond the neutral zone after snapper touches ball.
1985—One or both feet on ground required for blocking below waist foul.
1986—Kickoff from the 35-yard line.
1988—Defensive team allowed to score two points on return of blocked extra-point kick attempt or interception of extra-point pass attempt.
1989—Kicking tees eliminated for field goals and extra-point attempts.
1990—Defense allowed to advance fumbles that occur beyond the neutral zone.
1991—Width between goal-post uprights reduced from 23 feet, 4 inches to 18 feet, 6 inches. Kickoffs out of bounds allow receiving team to elect to take ball 30 yards beyond yard line where kickoff occurred.
1992—Defense allowed to advance fumbles regardless of where they occur. Changes ruling of 1990 fumble advancement.
1993—Guard-around or "fumblerooski" play ruled illegal.
1994—Players involved in a fight after half time disqualified for first half of next game; substitutes and coaches who participate in a fight in their team area or leave the team area to join a fight disqualified for entire next game; squad members and coaches involved in a fight during half time disqualified for first half of next game.

Division I-AA Records

Individual Records

Total Offense

(Rushing Plus Passing)

MOST PLAYS
Quarter
31—Mike Hanlin, Morehead St. vs. Austin Peay, Oct. 10, 1981 (4th)
Half
48—John Witkowski, Columbia vs. Dartmouth, Nov. 6, 1982 (2nd)
Game
89—Thomas Leonard, Mississippi Val. vs. Texas Southern, Oct. 25, 1986 (440 yards)
Season
611—Neil Lomax, Portland St., 1979 (3,966 yards)
Career
1,901—Neil Lomax, Portland St., 1977-80 (13,345 yards)

MOST PLAYS PER GAME
Season
56.4—Willie Totten, Mississippi Val., 1984 (564 in 10)
Career
45.3—Willie Totten, Mississippi Val., 1982-85 (1,812 in 40)

MOST PLAYS BY A FRESHMAN
Game
79—Adrian Breen, Morehead St. vs. Austin Peay, Oct. 8, 1983 (206 yards)
Season
462—Greg Wyatt, Northern Ariz., 1986 (2,695 yards)
Per-game record—44.7, Jason Whitmer, Idaho St., 1987 (402 in 9)

MOST YARDS GAINED
Quarter
278—Willie Totten, Mississippi Val. vs. Kentucky St., Sept. 1, 1984 (2nd)
Half
404—Todd Hammel, Stephen F. Austin vs. Northeast La., Nov. 11, 1989 (1st)
Game
643—Jamie Martin, Weber St. vs. Idaho St., Nov. 23, 1991 (624 passing, 19 rushing)
Season
4,572—Willie Totten, Mississippi Val., 1984 (4,557 passing, 15 rushing)
2 Yrs
8,314—Willie Totten, Mississippi Val., 1984-85 (8,255 passing, 59 rushing)
3 Yrs
11,647—Neil Lomax, Portland St., 1978-80 (11,550 passing, 97 rushing)
Career
(4 yrs.) 13,345—Neil Lomax, Portland St., 1977-80 (13,220 passing, 125 rushing)

MOST YARDS GAINED PER GAME
Season
457.2—Willie Totten, Mississippi Val., 1984 (4,572 in 10)
Career
325.2—Willie Totten, Mississippi Val., 1982-85 (13,007 in 40)

MOST SEASONS GAINING 3,000 YARDS OR MORE
3—Steve McNair, Alcorn St., 1991-93; Doug Nussmeier, Idaho, 1991-93; Jamie Martin, Weber St., 1990-92; Sean Payton, Eastern Ill., 1984-86; Neil Lomax, Portland St., 1978-80

MOST YARDS GAINED BY A FRESHMAN
Game
536—Brad Otton, Weber St. vs. Northern Ariz., Nov. 6, 1993 (48 plays)
Season
3,137—Steve McNair, Alcorn St., 1991
Also holds per-game record at 313.7

MOST YARDS GAINED IN TWO, THREE AND FOUR CONSECUTIVE GAMES
2 Games
1,088—Willie Totten, Mississippi Val., 1984 (561 vs. Southern-B.R., Sept. 29; 527 vs. Grambling, Oct. 13)
3 Games
1,576—Willie Totten, Mississippi Val., 1984 (488 vs. Jackson St., Sept. 22; 561 vs. Southern-B.R., Sept. 29; 527 vs. Grambling, Oct. 13)
4 Games
2,068—Willie Totten, Mississippi Val., 1984 (561 vs. Southern-B.R., Sept. 29; 527 vs. Grambling, Oct. 13; 359 vs. Texas Southern, Oct. 20; 621 vs. Prairie View, Oct. 27)

MOST GAMES GAINING 300 YARDS OR MORE
Season
10—Willie Totten, Mississippi Val., 1984; Neil Lomax, Portland St., 1980
Career
28—Neil Lomax, Portland St., 1977-80

MOST CONSECUTIVE GAMES GAINING 300 YARDS OR MORE
Season
10—Willie Totten, Mississippi Val., 1984
Career
13—Neil Lomax, Portland St., 1979-80

MOST GAMES GAINING 400 YARDS OR MORE
Season
7—Willie Totten, Mississippi Val., 1984
Career
13—Willie Totten, Mississippi Val., 1982-85

MOST CONSECUTIVE GAMES GAINING 400 YARDS OR MORE
Season
5—Willie Totten, Mississippi Val., 1984

MOST GAMES GAINING 500 YARDS OR MORE
Season
4—Willie Totten, Mississippi Val., 1984
Also holds career record at 4 (1982-85)

MOST YARDS GAINED AGAINST ONE OPPONENT
Career
1,713—Willie Totten, Mississippi Val. vs. Prairie View, 1982-85
Also holds per-game record at 428.3 (1,713 in 4)

GAINING 1,000 YARDS RUSHING AND 1,000 YARDS PASSING
Season
Tracy Ham (QB), Ga. Southern, 1986 (1,048 rushing, 1,772 passing)

GAINING 2,000 YARDS RUSHING AND 4,000 YARDS PASSING
Career
Bill Vergantino (QB), Delaware, 1989-92 (2,287 rushing, 6,177 passing); Tracy Ham (QB), Ga. Southern, 1984-86 (2,506 rushing, 4,871 passing)

HIGHEST AVERAGE GAIN PER PLAY
Game
(Min. 39-49 plays) 12.2—Todd Hammel, Stephen F. Austin vs. Northeast La., Nov. 11, 1989 (46 for 562)
(Min. 50-59 plays) 9.98—Dave Dickenson, Montana vs. Idaho, Nov. 6, 1993 (54 for 539)
(Min. 60 plays) 9.70—Willie Totten, Mississippi Val. vs. Prairie View, Oct. 27, 1984 (64 for 621)
Season
(Min. 2,500-3,299 yards) 9.57—Frank Baur, Lafayette, 1988 (285 for 2,727)
(Min. 3,300 yards) 8.79—Doug Nussmeier, Idaho, 1993 (400 for 3,514)
Career
(Min. 4,000-4,999 yards) 7.55—Reggie Lewis, Sam Houston St., 1986-87 (653 for 4,929)
(Min. 5,000 yards) 7.75—Doug Nussmeier, Idaho, 1990-93 (1,556 for 12,054)

MOST TOUCHDOWNS RESPONSIBLE FOR
(TDs Scored and Passed For)
Game
9—Willie Totten, Mississippi Val. vs. Prairie View, Oct. 27, 1984 (passed for 8, scored 1) & vs. Kentucky

St., Sept. 1, 1984 (passed for 9); Neil Lomax, Portland St. vs. Delaware St., Nov. 8, 1980 (passed for 8, scored 1)
Season
61—Willie Totten, Mississippi Val., 1984 (passed for 56, scored 5)
Also holds per-game record at 6.1 (61 in 10)
Career
157—Willie Totten, Mississippi Val., 1982-85 (passed for 139, scored 18)
Also holds per-game record at 3.93 (157 in 40)

MOST POINTS RESPONSIBLE FOR
(Points Scored and Passed For)
Game
56—Willie Totten, Mississippi Val. vs. Kentucky St., Sept. 1, 1984 (passed for 9 TDs and 1 two-point conversion)
Season
368—Willie Totten, Mississippi Val., 1984 (passed for 56 TDs, scored 5 TDs and passed for 1 two-point conversion)
Also holds per-game record at 36.8 (368 in 10)
Career
946—Willie Totten, Mississippi Val., 1982-85 (passed for 139 TDs, scored 18 TDs and passed for 1 two-point conversion)
Also holds per-game record at 23.7 (946 in 40)

Rushing

MOST RUSHES
Quarter
19—Mal Najarian, Boston U. vs. Northeastern, Sept. 30, 1978 (4th)
Half
32—David Clark, Dartmouth vs. Pennsylvania, Nov. 18, 1989 (2nd)
Game
52—James Black, Akron vs. Austin Peay, Nov. 19, 1983 (295 yards)
Season
351—James Black, Akron, 1983 (1,568 yards)
Career
963—Kenny Gamble, Colgate, 1984-87 (5,220 yards)

MOST RUSHES PER GAME
Season
34.0—James Black, Akron, 1982 (306 in 9)
Career
24.5—Keith Elias, Princeton, 1991-93 (736 in 30)

MOST CONSECUTIVE CARRIES BY SAME PLAYER
Game
14—Dave Mixon, Tennessee Tech vs. Morehead St., Oct. 22, 1983 (during 4 series)

MOST YARDS GAINED
Quarter
194—Otto Kelly, Nevada vs. Idaho, Nov. 12, 1983 (3rd, 8 rushes)
Half
263—Joe Delaney, Northwestern St. vs. Nicholls St., Oct. 28, 1978 (2nd, 19 rushes)
Game
364—Tony Vinson, Towson St. vs. Bucknell, Nov. 13, 1993 (33 rushes)
Season
2,016—Tony Vinson, Towson St., 1993 (293 rushes)
Career
5,333—Frank Hawkins, Nevada, 1977-80 (945 rushes)

MOST YARDS GAINED PER GAME
Season
201.6—Tony Vinson, Towson St., 1993 (2,016 in 10)
Career
(2 yrs.) 124.7—Rich Erenberg, Colgate, 1982-83 (2,618 in 21 games)
(3 yrs.) 140.3—Keith Elias, Princeton, 1991-93 (4,208 in 30)
(4 yrs.) 124.3—Kenny Gamble, Colgate, 1984-87 (5,220 in 42)

MOST YARDS GAINED BY A FRESHMAN
Game
304—Tony Citizen, McNeese St. vs. Prairie View,

Sept. 6, 1986 (30 rushes)

Season

1,620—Markus Thomas, Eastern Ky., 1989 (232 rushes)

MOST YARDS GAINED PER GAME BY A FRESHMAN
Season

147.3—Markus Thomas, Eastern Ky., 1989 (1,620 in 11)

MOST YARDS GAINED BY A QUARTERBACK
Game

309—Eddie Thompson, Western Ky. vs. Southern Ill., Oct. 31, 1992 (28 rushes)

Season

1,159—Alfredo Anderson, Idaho St., 1993 (161 rushes)

Also holds per-game record at 105.4

Career

3,674—Jack Douglas, Citadel, 1989-92 (832 rushes)

MOST GAMES GAINING 100 YARDS OR MORE
Season

11—Frank Hawkins, Nevada, 1980

Career

29—Kenny Gamble, Colgate, 1984-87 (42 games); Frank Hawkins, Nevada, 1977-80 (43 games)

MOST CONSECUTIVE GAMES GAINING 100 YARDS OR MORE
Season

11—Frank Hawkins, Nevada, 1980

Career

20—Frank Hawkins, Nevada, 1979-80

MOST GAMES GAINING 100 YARDS OR MORE BY A FRESHMAN

8—David Wright, Indiana St., 1992; Markus Thomas, Eastern Ky., 1989

MOST GAMES GAINING 200 YARDS OR MORE
Season

4—Tony Vinson, Towson St., 1993; Kenny Gamble, Colgate, 1986; Rich Erenberg, Colgate, 1983

Career

7—Keith Elias, Princeton, 1991-93

MOST CONSECUTIVE GAMES GAINING 200 YARDS OR MORE
Season

4—Rich Erenberg, Colgate, 1983

MOST YARDS GAINED IN TWO, THREE AND FOUR CONSECUTIVE GAMES
2 Games

572—Keith Elias, Princeton, 1992 (299 vs. Lafayette, Sept. 26; 273 vs. Lehigh, Oct. 3)

3 Games

711—Keith Elias, Princeton, 1992 (299 vs. Lafayette, Sept. 26; 273 vs. Lehigh, Oct. 3; 139 vs. Brown, Oct. 10); Gene Lake, Delaware St., 1984 (143 vs. Central St., Ohio, Oct. 27; 232 vs. Howard, Nov. 3; 336 vs. Liberty, Nov. 10)

4 Games

874—Gene Lake, Delaware St., 1984 (163 vs. Towson St., Oct. 20; 143 vs. Central St., Ohio, Oct. 27; 232 vs. Howard, Nov. 3; 336 vs. Liberty, Nov. 10)

MOST SEASONS GAINING 1,000 YARDS OR MORE
Career

3—By 16 players. Most recent: Eric Gant, Grambling, 1991-93; Markus Thomas, Eastern Ky., 1989, 1991-92; Joe Segreti, Holy Cross, 1988-90; Elroy Harris, Eastern Ky., 1985, 1987-88

TWO PLAYERS, SAME TEAM, EACH GAINING 1,000 YARDS OR MORE

Eastern Ky., 1993—Mike Penman (1,139) & Leon Brown (1,046); Northeast La., 1992—Greg Robinson (1,011) & Roosevelt Potts (1,004); Yale, 1991—Chris Kouri (1,101) & Nick Crawford (1,024); William & Mary, 1990—Robert Green (1,185) & Tyrone Shelton (1,020); Citadel, 1988—Adrian Johnson (1,091) & Gene Brown (1,006); Eastern Ky., 1986—Elroy Harris (1,152) & James Crawford (1,070); Eastern Ky., 1985—James Crawford (1,282) & Elroy Harris (1,134); Nevada, 1983—Otto Kelly (1,090) & Tony Corley (1,006);

Jackson St., 1978—Perry Harrington (1,105) & Jeffrey Moore (1,094)

MOST YARDS GAINED BY TWO PLAYERS, SAME TEAM
Game

445—Joe Delaney (299) & Brett Knecht (146), Northwestern St. vs. Nicholls St., Oct. 28, 1978

Season

2,429—Frank Hawkins (1,683) & John Vicari (746), Nevada, 1979

MOST YARDS GAINED IN OPENING GAME OF SEASON

304—Tony Citizen, McNeese St. vs. Prairie View, Sept. 6, 1986 (30 rushes)

MOST YARDS GAINED IN FIRST GAME OF CAREER

304—Tony Citizen, McNeese St. vs. Prairie View, Sept. 6, 1986 (30 rushes)

HIGHEST AVERAGE GAIN PER RUSH
Game

(Min. 15-19 rushes) 19.1—Gene Brown, Citadel vs. Va. Military, Nov. 12, 1988 (15 for 286)

(Min. 20 rushes) 17.3—Russell Davis, Idaho vs. Portland St., Oct. 3, 1981 (20 for 345)

Season

(Min. 150-199 rushes) 7.74—Harvey Reed, Howard, 1986 (179 for 1,386)

(Min. 200 rushes) 7.29—Mike Clark, Akron, 1986 (245 for 1,786)

Career

(Min. 350-599 rushes) 7.30—Keith Williams, Southwest Mo. St., 1982-85 (369 for 2,694)

(Min. 600 rushes) 6.57—Markus Thomas, Eastern Ky., 1989-92 (784 for 5,149)

MOST TOUCHDOWNS SCORED BY RUSHING
Game

6—Gene Lake, Delaware St. vs. Howard, Nov. 3, 1984; Gill Fenerty, Holy Cross vs. Columbia, Oct. 29, 1983; Henry Odom, South Caro. St. vs. Morgan St., Oct. 18, 1980

Season

24—Geoff Mitchell, Weber St., 1991

Career

55—Kenny Gamble, Colgate, 1984-87

MOST TOUCHDOWNS SCORED PER GAME BY RUSHING
Season

2.3—Tony Vinson, Towson St., 1993 (23 in 10)

Career

1.63—Keith Elias, Princeton, 1991-93 (49 in 30)

MOST TOUCHDOWNS SCORED BY RUSHING BY A QUARTERBACK
Season

18—Tracy Ham, Ga. Southern, 1986

Career

48—Jack Douglas, Citadel, 1989-92

Also holds per-game record at 1.09 (48 in 44)

LONGEST PLAY

99—Phillip Collins, Southwest Mo. St. vs. Western Ill., Sept. 16, 1989; Pedro Bacon, Western Ky. vs. Livingston, Sept. 13, 1986 (only rush of the game); Hubert Owens, Mississippi Val. vs. Ark.-Pine Bluff, Sept. 20, 1980

Passing

HIGHEST PASSING EFFICIENCY RATING POINTS
Game

(Min. 15-24 atts.) 368.5—Rich Green, New Hampshire vs. Rhode Island, Nov. 13, 1993 (15 attempts, 12 completions, 0 interceptions, 358 yards, 4 TD passes)

(Min. 25-44 atts.) 283.3—Mike Smith, Northern Iowa vs. McNeese St., Nov. 8, 1986 (27 attempts, 22 completions, 0 interceptions, 413 yards, 6 TD passes)

(Min. 45 atts.) 220.8—Todd Hammel, Stephen F. Austin vs. Northeast La., Nov. 11, 1989 (45 attempts, 31 completions, 3 interceptions, 571 yards, 8 TD passes)

Season

(Min. 15 atts. per game) 204.6—Shawn Knight, William & Mary, 1993 (177 attempts, 125 completions, 4 interceptions, 2,055 yards, 22 TD passes)

Career

(Min. 300-399 comps.) 148.9—Jay Johnson, Northern Iowa, 1989-92 (744 attempts, 397 completions, 25 interceptions, 7,049 yards, 51 TD passes)

(Min. 400 comps.) 154.4—Doug Nussmeier, Idaho, 1990-93 (1,225 attempts, 746 completions, 32 interceptions, 10,824 yards, 91 TD passes)

MOST PASSES ATTEMPTED
Quarter

28—Paul Peterson, Idaho St. vs. Cal Poly SLO, Oct. 22, 1983 (4th)

Half

42—Doug Pederson, Northeast La. vs. Stephen F. Austin, Nov. 11, 1989 (1st, completed 27); Mike Machurek, Idaho St. vs. Weber St., Sept. 20, 1980 (2nd, completed 18)

Game

77—Neil Lomax, Portland St. vs. Northern Colo., Oct. 20, 1979 (completed 44)

Season

518—Willie Totten, Mississippi Val., 1984 (completed 324)

Also holds per-game record at 51.8

Career

1,606—Neil Lomax, Portland St., 1977-80 (completed 938)

Per-game record—42.9, Stan Greene, Boston U., 1989-90 (944 in 22)

MOST PASSES ATTEMPTED BY A FRESHMAN
Game

66—Chris Swartz, Morehead St. vs. Tennessee Tech, Oct. 17, 1987 (completed 35)

Season

392—Greg Wyatt, Northern Ariz., 1986 (completed 250)

Per-game record—37.8, Jason Whitmer, Idaho St., 1987 (340 in 9)

MOST PASSES COMPLETED
Quarter

18—Kirk Schulz, Villanova vs. Central Conn. St., Oct. 10, 1987 (3rd); Willie Totten, Mississippi Val. vs. Grambling, Oct. 31, 1984 (2nd) & vs. Kentucky St., Sept. 1, 1984 (2nd)

Half

27—Doug Pederson, Northeast La. vs. Stephen F. Austin, Nov. 11, 1989 (1st, attempted 42)

Game

47—Jamie Martin, Weber St. vs. Idaho St., Nov. 23, 1991 (attempted 62)

Season

324—Willie Totten, Mississippi Val., 1984 (attempted 518)

Also holds per-game record at 32.4

Career

938—Neil Lomax, Portland St., 1977-80 (attempted 1,606)

Per-game record—23.8, Stan Greene, Boston U., 1989-90 (524 in 22)

MOST PASSES COMPLETED BY A FRESHMAN
Game

35—Chris Swartz, Morehead St. vs. Tennessee Tech, Oct. 17, 1987 (attempted 66)

Season

250—Greg Wyatt, Northern Ariz., 1986 (attempted 392)

Also holds per-game record at 22.7 (250 in 11)

MOST PASSES COMPLETED IN FRESHMAN AND SOPHOMORE SEASONS

518—Greg Wyatt, Northern Ariz., 1986-87 (attempted 804)

MOST CONSECUTIVE PASSES COMPLETED
Game

19—Kirk Schulz, Villanova vs. Central Conn. St., Oct. 10, 1987

MOST CONSECUTIVE PASS COMPLETIONS TO START GAME

18—Scott Auchenbach, Bucknell vs. Colgate, Nov. 11, 1989

HIGHEST PERCENTAGE OF PASSES COMPLETED
Game

(Min. 20-29 comps.) 95.7%—Butch Mosby, Murray St. vs. Tenn.-Martin, Oct. 2, 1993 (22 of 23)

(Min. 30 comps.) 81.6%—Eric Beavers, Nevada vs. Idaho St., Nov. 17, 1984 (31 of 38)

Season

(Min. 200 atts.) 68.2%—Jason Garrett, Princeton, 1988 (204 of 299)

Career

(Min. 500-749 atts.) 66.9%—Jason Garrett, Princeton, 1987-88 (366 of 550)

(Min. 750 atts.) 61.9%—Michael Payton, Marshall, 1989-92 (542 of 876)

MOST PASSES HAD INTERCEPTED
Game

7—Dan Crowley, Towson St. vs. Maine, Nov. 16, 1991 (53 attempts); Carlton Jenkins, Mississippi Val. vs. Prairie View, Oct. 31, 1987 (34 attempts); Charles Hebert, Southeastern La. vs. Northwestern St., Nov. 12, 1983 (23 attempts); Mick Spoon, Idaho St. vs. Montana, Oct. 21, 1978 (attempted 35)

Season

29—Willie Totten, Mississippi Val., 1985 (492 attempts)

Also holds per-game record at 2.64 (29 in 11)

Career

75—Willie Totten, Mississippi Val., 1982-85

Per-game record—2.0, John Witkowski, Columbia, 1981-83 (60 in 30)

LOWEST PERCENTAGE OF PASSES HAD INTERCEPTED
Season

(Min. 175-324 atts.) 0.84%—Jeff Mladenich, Boise St., 1991 (2 of 239)

(Min. 325 atts.) 1.22%—Bill Lazor, Cornell, 1992 (4 of 328)

Career

(Min. 500-749 atts.) 1.82%—Jason Garrett, Princeton, 1987-88 (10 of 550)

(Min. 750 atts.) 2.67%—Brad Lebo, Montana, 1989-92 (25 of 938)

MOST PASSES ATTEMPTED WITHOUT INTERCEPTION
Game

68—Tony Petersen, Marshall vs. Western Caro., Nov. 14, 1987 (completed 34)

MOST CONSECUTIVE PASSES ATTEMPTED WITHOUT INTERCEPTION
Season

176—Jason Garrett, Princeton, 1988 (in 7 games, from Sept. 17 through Oct. 29)

Career

199—Thomas Debow, Tennessee Tech, began Sept. 17, 1988, ended Oct. 14, 1989

MOST YARDS GAINED
Quarter

278—Willie Totten, Mississippi Val. vs. Kentucky St., Sept. 1, 1984 (2nd)

Half

383—Michael Payton, Marshall vs. Va. Military, Nov. 16, 1991 (1st)

Game

624—Jamie Martin, Weber St. vs. Idaho St., Nov. 23, 1991

Season

4,557—Willie Totten, Mississippi Val., 1984

Career

13,220—Neil Lomax, Portland St., 1977-80

MOST YARDS GAINED PER GAME
Season

455.7—Willie Totten, Mississippi Val., 1984 (4,557 in 10)

Career

320.1—Tom Ehrhardt, Rhode Island, 1984-85 (6,722 in 21)

MOST YARDS GAINED BY A FRESHMAN
Game

540—Brad Otton, Weber St. vs. Northern Ariz., Nov. 6, 1993

Season

2,895—Steve McNair, Alcorn St., 1991

Also holds per-game record at 289.5 (2,895 in 10)

MOST YARDS GAINED IN FRESHMAN AND SOPHOMORE SEASONS

6,436—Steve McNair, Alcorn St., 1991-92

MOST YARDS GAINED IN TWO, THREE AND FOUR CONSECUTIVE GAMES
2 Games

1,105—Todd Hammel, Stephen F. Austin, 1989 (534 vs. Sam Houston St., Nov. 4; 571 vs. Northeast La., Nov. 11)

3 Games

1,624—Willie Totten, Mississippi Val., 1984 (526 vs. Jackson St., Sept. 22; 553 vs. Southern-B.R., Sept. 29; 545 vs. Grambling, Oct. 13)

4 Games

2,065—Willie Totten, Mississippi Val., 1984 (553 vs. Southern-B.R., Sept. 29; 545 vs. Grambling, Oct. 13; 368 vs. Texas Southern, Oct. 20; 599 vs. Prairie View, Oct. 27)

MOST GAMES GAINING 200 YARDS OR MORE
Season

11—By 12 players. Most recent: Chris Hakel, William & Mary, 1991; Jamie Martin, Weber St., 1991; John Friesz, Idaho, 1989; Todd Hammel, Stephen F. Austin, 1989

Career

36—Neil Lomax, Portland St., 1977-80 (42 games)

MOST CONSECUTIVE GAMES GAINING 200 YARDS OR MORE
Season

11—By 10 players. Most recent: Chris Hakel, William & Mary, 1991; Jamie Martin, Weber St., 1991; Jeff Wiley, Holy Cross, 1987; Tony Petersen, Marshall, 1987

Career

28—Neil Lomax, Portland St., 1978-80

MOST GAMES GAINING 300 YARDS OR MORE
Season

10—John Friesz, Idaho, 1989; Willie Totten, Mississippi Val., 1984

Career

28—Neil Lomax, Portland St., 1977-80

MOST CONSECUTIVE GAMES GAINING 300 YARDS OR MORE
Season

10—John Friesz, Idaho, 1989; Willie Totten, Mississippi Val., 1984

Career

13—Neil Lomax, Portland St., 1979-80

MOST YARDS GAINED AGAINST ONE OPPONENT
Career

1,675—Willie Totten, Mississippi Val. vs. Prairie View, 1982-85

Also holds per-game record at 418.8 (1,675 in 4)

MOST YARDS PER ATTEMPT
Game

(Min. 30-44 atts.) 16.1—Gilbert Renfroe, Tennessee St. vs. Dist. Columbia, Nov. 5, 1983 (30 for 484)

(Min. 45 atts.) 12.69—Todd Hammel, Stephen F. Austin vs. Northeast La., Nov. 11, 1989 (45 for 571)

Season

(Min. 250-324 atts.) 10.31—Mike Smith, Northern Iowa, 1986 (303 for 3,125)

(Min. 325 atts.) 9.51—John Friesz, Idaho, 1989 (425 for 4,041)

Career

(Min. 500-999 atts.) 9.47—Jay Johnson, Northern Iowa, 1989-92 (744 for 7,049)

(Min. 1,000 atts.) 8.34—Doug Nussmeier, Idaho, 1990-93 (1,225 for 10,824)

MOST YARDS GAINED PER COMPLETION
Game

(Min. 15-19 comps.) 22.79—Matt Griffin, New Hampshire vs. Hofstra, Sept. 21, 1991 (19 for 433)

(Min. 20 comps.) 22.55—Michael Payton, Marshall vs. Va. Military, Nov. 16, 1991 (22 for 496)

Season

(Min. 200 comps.) 16.4—Todd Hammel, Stephen F. Austin, 1989 (238 for 3,914)

Career

(Min. 350-399 comps.) 17.76—Jay Johnson, Northern Iowa, 1989-92 (397 for 7,049)

(Min. 400 comps.) 15.31—Todd Hammel, Stephen F Austin, 1986-89 (443 for 6,784)

MOST TOUCHDOWN PASSES
Quarter

7—Neil Lomax, Portland St. vs. Delaware St., Nov. 8, 1980 (1st)

Half

7—Neil Lomax, Portland St. vs. Delaware St., Nov. 8, 1980 (1st)

Game

9—Willie Totten, Mississippi Val. vs. Kentucky St., Sept. 1, 1984

Season

56—Willie Totten, Mississippi Val., 1984

Also holds per-game record at 5.6 (56 in 10)

Career

139—Willie Totten, Mississippi Val., 1982-85

Also holds per-game record at 3.48 (139 in 40)

MOST CONSECUTIVE GAMES THROWING A TOUCHDOWN PASS
Career

27—Willie Totten, Mississippi Val., 1983-85

MOST TOUCHDOWN PASSES, SAME PASSER AND RECEIVER
Season

27—Willie Totten to Jerry Rice, Mississippi Val., 1984

Career

47—Willie Totten to Jerry Rice, Mississippi Val., 1982-84

HIGHEST PERCENTAGE OF PASSES FOR TOUCHDOWNS
Season

(Min. 200-299 atts.) 11.7%—Mike Williams, Grambling, 1980 (28 of 239)

(Min. 300 atts.) 10.86%—Doug Nussmeier, Idaho, 1993 (33 of 304)

Career

(Min. 500-749 atts.) 8.46%—Mike Williams, Grambling, 1977-80 (44 of 520)

(Min. 750 atts.) 7.43%—Doug Nussmeier, Idaho, 1990-93 (91 of 1,225)

Receiving

MOST PASSES CAUGHT
Game

24—Jerry Rice, Mississippi Val. vs. Southern-B.R., Oct. 1, 1983 (219 yards)

Season

115—Brian Forster, Rhode Island, 1985 (1,617 yards)

Career

301—Jerry Rice, Mississippi Val., 1981-84 (4,693 yards)

MOST PASSES CAUGHT PER GAME
Season

11.5—Brian Forster, Rhode Island, 1985 (115 in 10)

Career

7.3—Jerry Rice, Mississippi Val., 1981-84 (301 in 41)

MOST PASSES CAUGHT BY A TIGHT END
Game

18—Brian Forster, Rhode Island vs. Brown, Sept. 28, 1985 (327 yards)

Season

115—Brian Forster, Rhode Island, 1985 (1,617 yards)

Also holds per-game record at 11.5 (115 in 10)

Career

245—Brian Forster, Rhode Island, 1983-85, 1987 (3,410 yards)

MOST PASSES CAUGHT BY A RUNNING BACK
Game

21—David Pandt, Montana St. vs. Eastern Wash., Sept. 21, 1985 (169 yards)

Season

78—Gordie Lockbaum, Holy Cross, 1987 (1,152 yards)

2 Yrs
135—Gordie Lockbaum, Holy Cross, 1986-87 (2,012 yards)
Also holds per-game record at 6.1 (135 in 22)
Career
182—Merril Hoge, Idaho St., 1983-86 (1,734 yards)

MOST PASSES CAUGHT BY TWO PLAYERS, SAME TEAM
Season
183—Jerry Rice (103 for 1,682 yards and 27 TDs) & Joe Thomas (80 for 1,119 yards and 11 TDs), Mississippi Val., 1984
Career
420—Darrell Colbert (217 for 3,177 yards and 33 TDs) & Donald Narcisse (203 for 2,429 yards and 26 TDs), Texas Southern, 1983-86

MOST YARDS GAINED
Game
370—Michael Lerch, Princeton vs. Brown, Oct. 12, 1991 (caught 9)
Season
1,682—Jerry Rice, Mississippi Val., 1984 (caught 103)
Career
4,693—Jerry Rice, Mississippi Val., 1981-84 (caught 301)

MOST YARDS GAINED PER GAME
Season
168.2—Jerry Rice, Mississippi Val., 1984 (1,682 in 10)
Career
114.5—Jerry Rice, Mississippi Val., 1981-84 (4,693 in 41)

MOST YARDS GAINED BY A TIGHT END
Game
327—Brian Forster, Rhode Island vs. Brown, Sept. 28, 1985 (caught 18)
Season
1,617—Brian Forster, Rhode Island, 1985 (caught 115)
Also holds per-game record at 161.7 (1,617 in 10)
Career
3,410—Brian Forster, Rhode Island, 1983-85, 87 (caught 245)

MOST YARDS GAINED BY A RUNNING BACK
Game
220—Alvin Atkinson, Davidson vs. Furman, Nov. 3, 1979 (caught 9)
Season
1,152—Gordie Lockbaum, Holy Cross, 1987 (caught 78)
Also holds per-game record at 104.7 (1,152 in 11)

MOST YARDS GAINED BY TWO PLAYERS, SAME TEAM
Season
2,801—Jerry Rice (1,682, 103 caught and 27 TDs) & Joe Thomas (1,119, 80 caught and 11 TDs), Mississippi Val., 1984
Career
5,806—Roy Banks (3,177, 184 caught and 38 TDs) & Cal Pierce (2,629, 163 caught and 13 TDs), Eastern Ill., 1983-86

HIGHEST AVERAGE GAIN PER RECEPTION
Game
(Min. 5-9 receps.) 44.6—John Taylor, Delaware St. vs. St. Paul's, Sept. 21, 1985 (5 for 223)
(Min. 10 receps.) 29.0—Jason Cristino, Lehigh vs. Lafayette, Nov. 21, 1992 (11 for 319)
Season
(Min. 30-39 receps.) 26.3—Brian Allen, Idaho, 1983 (31 for 814)
(Min. 40-59 receps.) 25.0—Mark Stock, Va. Military, 1986 (45 for 1,123)
(Min. 60 receps.) 20.7—Golden Tate, Tennessee St., 1983 (63 for 1,307)
Career
(Min. 90-124 receps.) 24.3—John Taylor, Delaware St., 1982-85 (100 for 2,426)
(Min. 125 receps.) 20.0—Tracy Singleton, Howard, 1979-82 (159 for 3,187)

MOST GAMES GAINING 100 YARDS OR MORE
Career
23—Jerry Rice, Mississippi Val., 1981-84 (in 41 games played)

MOST TOUCHDOWN PASSES CAUGHT
Game
5—Rennie Benn, Lehigh vs. Indiana (Pa.), Sept. 14, 1985 (266 yards); Jerry Rice, Mississippi Val. vs. Prairie View, Oct. 27, 1984 & vs. Kentucky St., Sept. 1, 1984
Season
27—Jerry Rice, Mississippi Val., 1984
Career
50—Jerry Rice, Mississippi Val., 1981-84

MOST TOUCHDOWN PASSES CAUGHT PER GAME
Season
2.7—Jerry Rice, Mississippi Val., 1984 (27 in 10)
Career
1.22—Jerry Rice, Mississippi Val., 1981-84 (50 in 41)

MOST GAMES CATCHING A TOUCHDOWN PASS
Season
10—Jerry Rice, Mississippi Val., 1984
Also holds consecutive record at 10 (1984)
Career
26—Jerry Rice, Mississippi Val., 1981-84
Also holds consecutive record at 17 (1983-84)

Punting

MOST PUNTS
Game
16—Matt Stover, Louisiana Tech vs. Northeast La., Nov. 18, 1988 (567 yards)
Season
98—Barry Hickingbotham, Louisiana Tech, 1987 (3,821 yards)
Career
301—Barry Bowman, Louisiana Tech, 1983-86 (11,441 yards)

HIGHEST AVERAGE PER PUNT
Game
(Min. 5-9 punts) 55.7—Harold Alexander, Appalachian St. vs. Citadel, Oct. 3, 1992 (6 for 334); Jody Farmer, Montana vs. Nevada, Oct. 1, 1988 (9 for 501)
(Min. 10 punts) 52.2—Stuart Dodds, Montana St. vs. Northern Ariz., Oct. 20, 1979 (10 for 522)
Season
(Min. 60 punts) 47.0—Harold Alexander, Appalachian St., 1991 (64 for 3,009)
Career
(Min. 150 punts) 44.4—Pumpy Tudors, Tenn.-Chatt., 1989-91 (181 for 8,041)

LONGEST PUNT
91—Bart Helsley, North Texas vs. Northeast La., Nov. 17, 1990

Interceptions

MOST PASSES INTERCEPTED
Game
5—Mark Cordes, Eastern Wash. vs. Boise St., Sept. 6, 1986 (48 yards); Michael Richardson, Northwestern St. vs. Southeastern La., Nov. 12, 1983 (128 yards); Karl Johnson, Jackson St. vs. Grambling, Oct. 23, 1982 (29 yards)
Season
12—Dean Cain, Princeton, 1987 (98 yards)
Also holds per-game record at 1.2 (12 in 10)
Career
28—Dave Murphy, Holy Cross, 1986-89 (309 yards)
Per-game record—0.73, Dean Cain, Princeton, 1985-87 (22 in 30)

MOST YARDS ON INTERCEPTION RETURNS
Game
216—Keiron Bigby, Brown vs. Yale, Sept. 29, 1984 (3 interceptions) (first career game)

Season
251—Zack Bronson, McNeese St., 1993 (9 interceptions)
Career
452—Rick Harris, East Tenn. St., 1986-88 (20 interceptions)

MOST TOUCHDOWNS SCORED ON INTERCEPTION RETURNS
Game
2—By five players. Most recent: Lance Guidry, McNeese St. vs. Stephen F. Austin, Nov. 7, 1992; Bill Curry, Maine vs. Liberty, Oct. 10, 1992
Season
4—Robert Turner, Jackson St., 1990 (9 interceptions, 212 yards)
Career
4—Robert Turner (DB), Jackson St., 1990 (9 interceptions); Ken Braden (LB), Southwest Mo. St., 1984-87 (8 interceptions); Roger Robinson (DB), Tennessee St., 1981-84 (12 interceptions)

HIGHEST AVERAGE GAIN PER INTERCEPTION
Game
(Min. 3 ints.) 72.0—Keiron Bigby, Brown vs. Yale, Sept. 29, 1984 (3 for 216)
Season
(Min. 3 ints.) 72.0—Keiron Bigby, Brown, 1984 (3 for 216)
Career
(Min. 12 ints.) 24.9—Roger Robinson, Tennessee St., 1981-84 (12 for 299)

Punt Returns

MOST PUNT RETURNS
Game
9—By 13 players. Most recent: Dexter Dawson, Ga. Southern vs. Va. Military, Oct. 23, 1993 (130 yards)
Season
55—Tommy Houk, Murray St., 1980 (442 yards)
Also holds per-game record at 5.0 (55 in 11)
Career
117—David McCrary, Tenn.-Chatt., 1982-85 (1,230 yards)
Per-game record—3.8, Tommy Houk, Murray St., 1979-80 (84 in 22)

MOST YARDS ON PUNT RETURNS
Game
216—Gary Harrell, Howard vs. Morgan St., Nov. 3, 1990 (7 returns); Willie Ware, Mississippi Val. vs. Washburn, Sept. 15, 1984 (7 returns)
Season
561—Willie Ware, Mississippi Val., 1985 (31 returns)
Also holds per-game record at 51.0 (561 in 11)
Career
1,230—David McCrary, Tenn.-Chatt., 1982-85 (117 returns)

HIGHEST AVERAGE GAIN PER RETURN
Game
(Min. 5 rets.) 30.9—Gary Harrell, Howard vs. Morgan St., Nov. 3, 1990 (7 for 216); Willie Ware, Mississippi Val. vs. Washburn, Sept. 15, 1984 (7 for 216)
Season
(Min. 1.2 rets. per game) 23.0—Tim Egerton, Delaware St., 1988 (16 for 368)
Career
(Min. 1.2 rets. per game) 16.4—Willie Ware, Mississippi Val., 1982-85 (61 for 1,003)

MOST TOUCHDOWNS SCORED ON PUNT RETURNS
Game
2—By four players. Most recent: Sebron Spivey, Southern Ill. vs. Southeast Mo. St., Oct. 19, 1985
Season
4—Kenny Shedd, Northern Iowa, 1992 (27 returns); Howard Huckaby, Florida A&M, 1988 (26 returns)
Career
7—Kenny Shedd, Northern Iowa, 1989-92

LONGEST PUNT RETURN
98—Barney Bussey, South Caro. St. vs. Johnson Smith, Oct. 10, 1981

DIVISION I-AA

MOST CONSECUTIVE GAMES RETURNING PUNT FOR TOUCHDOWN

3—Troy Jones, McNeese St., 1989 (vs. Mississippi Col., Sept. 2; vs. Samford, Sept. 9; vs. Northeast La., Sept. 16)

Kickoff Returns

MOST KICKOFF RETURNS
Game

10—Merril Hoge, Idaho St. vs. Weber St., Oct. 25, 1986 (179 yards)

Season

50—David Primus, Samford, 1989 (1,411 yards)

Career

118—Clarence Alexander, Mississippi Val., 1986-89 (2,439 yards)

MOST KICKOFF RETURNS PER GAME
Season

4.55—David Primus, Samford, 1989 (50 in 11)

Career

2.95—Clarence Alexander, Mississippi Val., 1986-89 (118 in 40); Lorenza Rivers, Tennessee Tech, 1985, 1987 (62 in 21)

MOST YARDS ON KICKOFF RETURNS
Game

262—Herman Hunter, Tennessee St. vs. Mississippi Val., Nov. 13, 1982 (6 returns)

Season

1,411—David Primus, Samford, 1989 (50 returns)

Career

2,439—Clarence Alexander, Mississippi Val., 1986-89 (118 returns)

MOST YARDS PER GAME ON KICKOFF RETURNS
Season

128.3—David Primus, Samford, 1989 (1,411 in 11)

Career

60.98—Clarence Alexander, Mississippi Val., 1986-89 (2,439 in 40)

HIGHEST AVERAGE GAIN PER RETURN
Game

(Min. 5 rets.) 45.6—Jerome Stelly, Western Ill. vs. Youngstown St., Nov. 7, 1981 (5 for 228)

Season

(Min. 1.2 rets. per game) 37.3—David Fraterrigo, Canisius, 1993 (13 for 485)

Career
(Min. 1.2 Returns Per Game)

(Min. 30-44 rets.) 29.7—Troy Brown, Marshall, 1991-92 (32 for 950)

(Min. 45 rets.) 29.3—Charles Swann, Indiana St., 1989-91 (45 for 1,319)

MOST TOUCHDOWNS SCORED ON KICKOFF RETURNS
Game

2—Rory Lee, Western Ill. vs. St. Ambrose, Nov. 13, 1993; Kerry Hayes, Western Caro. vs. Va. Military, Oct. 10, 1992 (90 & 94 yards); Paul Ashby, Alabama St. vs. Grambling, Nov. 9, 1991 (97 & 94 yards); David Lucas, Florida A&M vs. North Caro. A&T, Oct. 12, 1991 (99 & 93 yards); Jerome Stelly, Western Ill. vs. Youngstown St., Nov. 7, 1981 (99 & 97 yards)

Season

3—Kerry Hayes, Western Caro., 1993; Troy Brown, Marshall, 1991; David Lucas, Florida A&M, 1991

Career

3—By 10 players. Most recent: Jerry Ellison, Tenn.-Chatt., 1993

Total Kick Returns

(Combined Punt and Kickoff Returns)

MOST KICK RETURNS
Game

12—Craig Hodge, Tennessee St. vs. Morgan St., Oct. 24, 1987 (8 punts, 4 kickoffs, 319 yards)

Season

64—Joe Markus, Connecticut, 1981 (34 punts, 30 kickoffs, 939 yards)

Career

199—Herman Hunter, Tennessee St., 1981-84 (103 punts, 96 kickoffs, 3,232 yards)

MOST YARDS ON KICK RETURNS
Game

319—Craig Hodge, Tennessee St. vs. Morgan St., Oct. 24, 1987 (12 returns, 206 on punts, 113 on kickoffs)

Season

1,469—David Primus, Samford, 1989 (1,411 on kickoffs, 58 on punts)
Also holds per-game record at 133.5 (1,469 in 11)

Career

3,232—Herman Hunter, Tennessee St., 1981-84 (974 on punts, 2,258 on kickoffs)
Also holds per-game record at 75.2 (3,232 in 43)

GAINING 1,000 YARDS ON PUNT RETURNS AND 1,000 YARDS ON KICKOFF RETURNS
Career

Kenny Shedd, Northern Iowa, 1989-92 (1,081 on punts and 1,359 on kickoffs); Joe Markus, Connecticut, 1979-82 (1,012 on punts and 1,185 on kickoffs)

HIGHEST AVERAGE PER KICK RETURN
Game

(Min. 6 rets.) 42.3—Herman Hunter, Tennessee St. vs. Mississippi Val., Nov. 13, 1982 (7 for 296)

Season

(Min. 40 rets.) 26.7—David Primus, Samford, 1989 (55 for 1,469)

Career

(Min. 60 rets.) 20.9—Bill LaFreniere, Northeastern, 1978-81 (112 for 2,336)

MOST TOUCHDOWNS SCORED ON KICK RETURNS
Season

4—Troy Brown, Marshall, 1991 (3 kickoffs and 1 punt); Howard Huckaby, Florida A&M, 1988 (4 punts); Willie Ware, Mississippi Val., 1985 (2 punts and 2 kickoffs)

Career

7—Kenny Shedd, Northern Iowa, 1989-92 (7 punts); Willie Ware, Mississippi Val., 1982-85 (5 punts and 2 kickoffs)

All-Purpose Yards

(Yardage Gained From Rushing, Receiving and All Runbacks)

MOST PLAYS
Game

54—Ron Darby, Marshall vs. Western Caro., Nov. 12, 1988 (47 rushes, 4 receptions, 3 kickoff returns; 329 yards)

Season

364—Toby Davis, Illinois St., 1992 (341 rushes, 17 receptions, 6 kickoff returns; 1,762 yards)

Career

1,096—Kenny Gamble, Colgate, 1984-87 (963 rushes, 43 receptions, 10 punt returns, 80 kickoff returns; 7,623 yards)

MOST YARDS GAINED
Game

463—Michael Lerch, Princeton vs. Brown, Oct. 12, 1991 (15 rushing, 370 receiving, 78 kickoff returns; 16 plays)

Season

2,425—Kenny Gamble, Colgate, 1986 (1,816 rushing, 178 receiving, 40 punt returns, 391 kickoff returns; 343 plays)

Career

7,623—Kenny Gamble, Colgate, 1984-87 (5,220 rushing, 53 receiving, 104 punt returns, 1,763 kickoff returns; 1,096 plays)

MOST YARDS GAINED PER GAME
Season

220.5—Kenny Gamble, Colgate, 1986 (2,425 in 11)

Career

189.1—David Meggett, Towson St., 1987-88 (3,403 in 18)

MOST YARDS GAINED BY A FRESHMAN
Season

2,014—David Wright, Indiana St., 1992 (1,313 rushing, 108 receiving, 593 kickoff returns; 254 plays)

HIGHEST AVERAGE GAIN PER PLAY
Game

(Min. 20 plays) 20.6—Herman Hunter, Tennessee St. vs. Mississippi Val., Nov. 13, 1982 (453 on 22)

Season

(Min. 1,000 yards, 100 plays) 19.68—Otis Washington, Western Caro., 1988 (2,086 on 106)

Career

(Min. 4,000 yards, 350 plays) 14.8—Pete Mandley, Northern Ariz., 1979-80, 1982-83 (5,925 on 401)

Scoring

MOST POINTS SCORED
Game

36—By five players. Most recent: Erwin Matthews, Richmond vs. Massachusetts, Sept. 19, 1987 (6 TDs, including 1 TD and 6 points in OT)

Season

170—Geoff Mitchell, Weber St., 1991 (28 TDs, 2 PATs)

Career

385—Marty Zendejas, Nevada, 1984-87 (72 FGs, 169 PATs)

MOST POINTS SCORED PER GAME
Season

16.2—Jerry Rice, Mississippi Val., 1984 (162 in 10)

Career

10.7—Keith Elias, Princeton, 1991-93 (320 in 30)

MOST TOUCHDOWNS SCORED
Game

6—By five players. Most recent: Erwin Matthews, Richmond vs. Massachusetts, Sept. 19, 1987 (1 TD in OT)

Season

28—Geoff Mitchell, Weber St., 1991

Career

60—Charvez Foger, Nevada, 1985-88

MOST TOUCHDOWNS SCORED PER GAME
Season

2.7—Jerry Rice, Mississippi Val., 1984 (27 in 10)

Career

1.73—Keith Elias, Princeton, 1991-93 (52 in 30)

MOST TOUCHDOWNS SCORED BY A FRESHMAN
Season

18—Charvez Foger, Nevada, 1985
Also holds per-game record at 1.8 (18 in 10)

MOST EXTRA POINTS ATTEMPTED BY KICKING
Game

15—John Kincheloe, Portland St. vs. Delaware St., Nov. 8, 1980 (15 made)

Season

74—John Kincheloe, Portland St., 1980 (70 made)
Per-game record—7.2, Jonathan Stokes, Mississippi Val., 1984 (72 in 10)

Career

175—Thayne Doyle, Idaho, 1988-91 (160 made); Marty Zendejas, Nevada, 1984-87 (169 made)

MOST EXTRA POINTS MADE BY KICKING
Game

15—John Kincheloe, Portland St. vs. Delaware St., Nov. 8, 1980 (15 attempts)

Season

70—John Kincheloe, Portland St., 1980 (74 attempts)
Per-game record—6.8, Jonathan Stokes, Mississippi Val., 1984 (68 in 10)

Career

169—Marty Zendejas, Nevada, 1984-87 (175 attempts)
Also holds per-game record at 3.84 (169 in 44)

BEST PERFECT RECORD OF EXTRA POINTS MADE
Season

68 of 68—Mike Hollis, Idaho, 1993

HIGHEST PERCENTAGE OF EXTRA POINTS MADE
Career
(Min. 100-119 atts.) 100%—Anders Larsson, Montana St., 1985-88 (101 of 101)
(Min. 120 atts.) 99.2%—Brian Mitchell, Marshall/ Northern Iowa, 1987, 1989-91 (130 of 131)

MOST CONSECUTIVE EXTRA POINTS MADE
Game
15—John Kincheloe, Portland St. vs. Delaware St., Nov. 8, 1980
Season
68—Mike Hollis, Idaho, 1993
Career
121—Brian Mitchell, Marshall/Northern Iowa, 1987, 1989-91

MOST POINTS SCORED BY KICKING
Game
24—Goran Lingmerth, Northern Ariz. vs. Idaho, Oct. 25, 1986 (8 FGs)
Season
109—Brian Mitchell, Northern Iowa, 1990 (26 FGs, 31 PATs)
Career
385—Marty Zendejas, Nevada, 1984-87 (72 FGs, 169 PATs)

MOST POINTS SCORED BY KICKING PER GAME
Season
9.9—Brian Mitchell, Northern Iowa, 1990 (109 in 11)
Career
9.09—Tony Zendejas, Nevada, 1981-83 (300 in 33)

MOST DEFENSIVE EXTRA-POINT RETURNS, ONE GAME, SINGLE PLAYER
2—Joe Lee Johnson, Western Ky. vs. Indiana St., Nov. 10, 1990 (both kick returns, scored on neither)

MOST DEFENSIVE EXTRA POINTS SCORED
Game
1—By many players
Season
2—Jackie Kellogg, Eastern Wash. vs. Weber St., Oct. 6, 1990 (90-yard interception return) & vs. Portland St., Oct. 27, 1990 (94-yard interception return)

LONGEST RETURN OF A DEFENSIVE EXTRA POINT
100—Rich Kinsman (DB), William & Mary vs. Lehigh, Nov. 14, 1992; Morgan Ryan (DB), Montana St. vs. Sam Houston St., Sept. 7, 1991 (interception return)

FIRST DEFENSIVE EXTRA-POINT ATTEMPTS
Mike Rogers (DB), Davidson vs. Lehigh, Sept. 10, 1988 (30-yard interception return); Dave Benna (LB), Towson St. vs. Northeastern, Sept. 10, 1988 (35-yard interception return)

MOST TWO-POINT ATTEMPTS
Season
11—Jamie Martin, Weber St., 1990; Brent Woods, Princeton, 1982

Northern Iowa's Brian Mitchell made 26 consecutive field goals during his career.

MOST SUCCESSFUL TWO-POINT PASSES
Game
3—Brent Woods, Princeton vs. Lafayette, Nov. 6, 1982 (attempted 3)
Season
7—Jamie Martin, Weber St., 1992 (attempted 7)
Career
15—Jamie Martin, Weber St., 1989-92 (attempted 28)

Kick Blocks

MOST KICKS BLOCKED
Game
3—Adrian Hardy, Northwestern St. vs. Arkansas St., Oct. 3, 1992 (2 PATs, 1 FG)
Career
9—Adrian Hardy, Northwestern St., 1989-92 (3 PATs, 6 FGs)

Field Goals

MOST FIELD GOALS ATTEMPTED
Game
8—Goran Lingmerth, Northern Ariz. vs. Idaho, Oct. 25, 1986 (made 8)
Season
33—Tony Zendejas, Nevada, 1982 (made 26)
Career
102—Kirk Roach, Western Caro., 1984-87 (made 71)

MOST FIELD GOALS MADE
Quarter
4—Ryan Weeks, Tennessee Tech vs. Tenn.-Chatt., Sept. 9, 1989 (3rd); Tony Zendejas, Nevada vs. Northern Ariz., Oct. 16, 1982 (4th)
Half
5—Ryan Weeks, Tennessee Tech vs. Tenn.-Chatt., Sept. 9, 1989 (2nd); Tony Zendejas, Nevada vs. Northern Ariz., Oct. 16, 1982 (2nd); Dean Biasucci, Western Caro. vs. Mars Hill, Sept. 18, 1982 (1st)
Game
8—Goran Lingmerth, Northern Ariz. vs. Idaho, Oct. 25, 1986 (39, 18, 20, 33, 46, 27, 22, 35 yards; by quarters—1, 3, 2, 2), 8 attempts
Season
26—Brian Mitchell, Northern Iowa, 1990 (27 attempts); Tony Zendejas, Nevada, 1982 (33 attempts)
Career
72—Marty Zendejas, Nevada, 1984-87 (90 attempts)

MOST FIELD GOALS MADE PER GAME
Season
2.36—Brian Mitchell, Northern Iowa, 1990 (26 in 11); Tony Zendejas, Nevada, 1982 (26 in 11)
Career
2.12—Tony Zendejas, Nevada, 1981-83 (70 in 33)

HIGHEST PERCENTAGE OF FIELD GOALS MADE
Season
(Min. 20 atts.) 96.3%—Brian Mitchell, Northern Iowa, 1990 (26 of 27)
Career
(Min. 50 atts.) 81.4%—Tony Zendejas, Nevada, 1981-83 (70 of 86)

MOST CONSECUTIVE FIELD GOALS MADE
Game
8—Goran Lingmerth, Northern Ariz. vs. Idaho, Oct. 25, 1986
Season
21—Brian Mitchell, Northern Iowa, 1990
Career
26—Brian Mitchell, Northern Iowa, 1990-91

MOST CONSECUTIVE GAMES KICKING A FIELD GOAL
Career
33—Tony Zendejas, Nevada, 1981-83 (at least one in every game played)

MOST FIELD GOALS MADE, 50 YARDS OR MORE
Game
3—Jesse Garcia, Northeast La. vs. McNeese St., Oct. 29, 1983 (52, 56, 53 yards)

Season
7—Kirk Roach, Western Caro., 1987 (12 attempts); Jesse Garcia, Northeast La., 1983 (12 attempts)
Career
11—Kirk Roach, Western Caro., 1984-87 (26 attempts)

HIGHEST PERCENTAGE OF FIELD GOALS MADE, 50 YARDS OR MORE
Season
(Min. 6 atts.) 83.3%—Tim Foley, Ga. Southern, 1987 (5 of 6)
Career
(Min. 10 atts.) 90.9%—Tim Foley, Ga. Southern, 1984-87 (10 of 11)

MOST FIELD GOALS MADE, 40 YARDS OR MORE
Season
12—Marty Zendejas, Nevada, 1985 (15 attempts)
Career
30—Marty Zendejas, Nevada, 1984-87 (45 attempts)

HIGHEST PERCENTAGE OF FIELD GOALS MADE, 40 YARDS OR MORE
Season
(Min. 8 made) 100.0%—Tim Foley, Ga. Southern, 1985 (8 of 8)
Career
(Min. 15 made) 72.0%—Tim Foley, Ga. Southern, 1984-87 (18 of 25)

HIGHEST PERCENTAGE OF FIELD GOALS MADE, 40-49 YARDS
Season
(Min. 8 made) 90.0%—Marty Zendejas, Nevada, 1985 (9 of 10)
Career
(Min. 12 made) 72.0%—Tony Zendejas, Nevada, 1981-83 (18 of 25)

HIGHEST PERCENTAGE OF FIELD GOALS MADE, UNDER 40 YARDS
Season
(Min. 15 made) 100.0%—Brian Mitchell, Northern Iowa, 1990 (23 of 23); Kirk Roach, Western Caro., 1986 (17 of 17); Matt Stover, Louisiana Tech, 1986 (15 of 15)
Career
(Min. 25 made) 93.3%—Marty Zendejas, Nevada, 1984-87 (42 of 45)

MOST TIMES KICKING TWO OR MORE FIELD GOALS IN A GAME
Season
10—Brian Mitchell, Northern Iowa, 1991
Career
25—Kirk Roach, Western Caro., 1984-87

MOST TIMES KICKING THREE OR MORE FIELD GOALS IN A GAME
Season
7—Brian Mitchell, Northern Iowa, 1991
Career
11—Brian Mitchell, Marshall/Northern Iowa, 1987, 1989-91

MOST CONSECUTIVE QUARTERS KICKING A FIELD GOAL
Season
7—Scott Roper, Arkansas St., 1986 (last 3 vs. McNeese St., Oct. 25; all 4 vs. North Texas, Nov. 1)

LONGEST AVERAGE DISTANCE FIELD GOALS MADE
Game
(Min. 3 made) 53.7—Jesse Garcia, Northeast La. vs. McNeese St., Oct. 29, 1983 (52, 56, 53 yards)
Season
(Min. 14 made) 45.0—Jesse Garcia, Northeast La., 1983 (15 made)
Career
(Min. 35 made) 37.5—Roger Ruzek, Weber St., 1979-82 (46 made)

LONGEST AVERAGE DISTANCE FIELD GOALS ATTEMPTED
Season
(Min. 20 atts.) 45.9—Jesse Garcia, Northeast La., 1983 (26 attempts)

Career
(Min. 60 atts.) 40.5—Kirk Roach, Western Caro., 1984-87 (102 attempts)

LONGEST FIELD GOAL MADE
63—Scott Roper, Arkansas St. vs. North Texas, Nov. 7, 1987; Tim Foley, Ga. Southern vs. James Madison, Nov. 7, 1987

LONGEST FIELD GOAL MADE BY A FRESHMAN
60—David Cool, Ga. Southern vs. James Madison, Nov. 5, 1988

MOST FIELD GOALS MADE BY A FRESHMAN
Game
5—Chuck Rawlinson, Stephen F. Austin vs. Prairie View, Sept. 10, 1988 (5 attempts); Marty Zendejas, Nevada vs. Idaho St., Nov. 17, 1984 (5 attempts); Mike Powers, Colgate vs. Army, Sept. 10, 1983 (6 attempts)
Season
22—Marty Zendejas, Nevada, 1984 (27 attempts)

MOST FIELD GOALS MADE IN FIRST GAME OF CAREER
5—Mike Powers, Colgate vs. Army, Sept. 10, 1983 (6 attempts)

MOST GAMES IN WHICH FIELD GOAL(S) PROVIDED WINNING MARGIN
Career
11—John Dowling, Youngstown St., 1984-87

LONGEST RETURN OF A MISSED FIELD GOAL
89—Pat Bayers, Western Ill. vs. Youngstown St., Nov. 6, 1982 (TD)

Team Records

SINGLE GAME—Offense

Total Offense

MOST PLAYS
113—Villanova vs. Connecticut, Oct. 7, 1989 (553 yards)

MOST PLAYS, BOTH TEAMS
196—Villanova (113) & Connecticut (83), Oct. 7, 1989 (904 yards)

MOST YARDS GAINED
876—Weber St. vs. Idaho St., Nov. 23, 1991 (252 rushing, 624 passing)

MOST YARDS GAINED, BOTH TEAMS
1,418—Howard (740) & Bethune-Cookman (678), Sept. 19, 1987 (161 plays)

MOST YARDS GAINED BY A LOSING TEAM
678—Bethune-Cookman vs. Howard, Sept. 19, 1987 (lost 51-58)

FEWEST YARDS GAINED BY A WINNING TEAM
31—Middle Tenn. St. vs. Murray St., Oct. 17, 1981 (won 14-9)

HIGHEST AVERAGE GAIN PER PLAY
(Min. 55 Plays)
12.7—Marshall vs. Va. Military, Nov. 16, 1991 (62 for 789)

MOST TOUCHDOWNS SCORED BY RUSHING AND PASSING
14—Portland St. vs. Delaware St., Nov. 8, 1980 (10 passing, 4 rushing)

Rushing

MOST RUSHES
90—Va. Military vs. East Tenn. St., Nov. 17, 1990 (311 yards)

MOST RUSHES, BOTH TEAMS
125—Austin Peay (81) & Murray St. (44), Nov. 17, 1990 (443 yards); Southwest Mo. St. (71) & Northern Ill. (54), Oct. 17, 1987 (375 yards)

FEWEST RUSHES
11—Western Ill. vs. Northern Iowa, Oct. 24, 1987 (-11 yards); Mississippi Val. vs. Kentucky St., Sept. 1, 1984 (17 yards)

MOST YARDS GAINED
681—Southwest Mo. St. vs. Mo. Southern St., Sept. 10, 1988 (83 rushes)

MOST YARDS GAINED, BOTH TEAMS
762—Arkansas St. (604) & East Tex. St. (158), Sept. 26, 1987 (102 rushes)

MOST YARDS GAINED BY A LOSING TEAM
429—Nevada vs. Weber St., Nov. 6, 1982 (lost 43-46, 3 OT)

HIGHEST AVERAGE GAIN PER RUSH
(Min. 45 Rushes)
11.2—Southwest Mo. St. vs. Northeast Mo. St., Oct. 5, 1985 (45 for 505)

MOST TOUCHDOWNS SCORED BY RUSHING
10—Arkansas St. vs. East Tex. St., Sept. 26, 1987

Passing

MOST PASSES ATTEMPTED
77—Portland St. vs. Northern Colo., Oct. 20, 1979 (completed 44 for 499 yards)

MOST PASSES ATTEMPTED, BOTH TEAMS
122—Idaho (62) & Idaho St. (60), Sept. 24, 1983 (completed 48 for 639 yards)

FEWEST PASSES ATTEMPTED
1—By many teams. Most recent: Northeastern vs. Towson St., Sept. 9, 1989 (completed 1)

FEWEST PASSES ATTEMPTED, BOTH TEAMS
11—Western Ky. (6) & North Caro. A&T (5), Nov. 19, 1988 (completed 2); Arkansas St. (8) & Memphis (3), Nov. 27, 1982 (completed 6)

MOST PASSES ATTEMPTED WITHOUT INTERCEPTION
72—Marshall vs. Western Caro., Nov. 14, 1987 (completed 35)

MOST PASSES COMPLETED
50—Mississippi Val. vs. Prairie View, Oct. 27, 1984 (attempted 66 for 642 yards); Mississippi Val. vs. Southern-B.R., Sept. 29, 1984 (attempted 70 for 633 yards)

MOST PASSES COMPLETED, BOTH TEAMS I-AA
77—Northeast La. (46) & Stephen F. Austin (31), Nov. 11, 1989 (attempted 116 for 1,190 yards)

MOST PASSES COMPLETED, BOTH TEAMS
80—Hofstra (50) & Fordham (30), Oct. 19, 1991 (attempted 120 for 987 yards)

FEWEST PASSES COMPLETED
0—By many teams. Most recent: Citadel vs. East Tenn. St., Sept. 19, 1992; Delaware St. vs. North Caro. A&T, Nov. 9, 1991

FEWEST PASSES COMPLETED, BOTH TEAMS
2—North Caro. A&T (0) & Western Ky. (2), Nov. 19, 1988 (attempted 11)

HIGHEST PERCENTAGE COMPLETED
(Min. 30-44 atts.) 81.6%—Nevada vs. Idaho St., Nov. 17, 1984 (31 of 38)
(Min. 45 atts.) 75.7%—Mississippi Val. vs. Prairie View, Oct. 27, 1984 (50 of 66)

LOWEST PERCENTAGE COMPLETED
(Min. 20 Attempts)
9.5%—Florida A&M vs. Central St. (Ohio), Oct. 11, 1986 (2 of 21)

MOST PASSES HAD INTERCEPTED
10—Boise St. vs. Montana, Oct. 28, 1989 (55 attempts); Mississippi Val. vs. Grambling, Oct. 17, 1987 (47 attempts)

MOST YARDS GAINED
699—Mississippi Val. vs. Kentucky St., Sept. 1, 1984

MOST YARDS GAINED, BOTH TEAMS
1,190—Northeast La. (619) & Stephen F. Austin (571), Nov. 11, 1989

MOST YARDS GAINED PER ATTEMPT
(Min. 25 Attempts)
17.4—Marshall vs. Va. Military, Nov. 16, 1991 (37 for 642)

MOST YARDS GAINED PER COMPLETION
(Min. 10-24 comps.) 33.0—Jackson St. vs. Southern-B.R., Oct. 13, 1990 (14 for 462)
(Min. 25 comps.) 22.9—Marshall vs. Va. Military, Nov. 16, 1991 (28 for 642)

MOST TOUCHDOWN PASSES
11—Mississippi Val. vs. Kentucky St., Sept. 1, 1984

MOST TOUCHDOWN PASSES, BOTH TEAMS
14—Mississippi Val. (8) & Texas Southern (6), Oct. 26, 1985

Punting

MOST PUNTS
16—Louisiana Tech vs. Northeast La., Nov. 19, 1988 (567 yards)

HIGHEST AVERAGE PER PUNT
(Min. 5 punts) 55.7—Appalachian St. vs. Citadel, Oct. 3, 1992 (6 for 334); Montana vs. Nevada, Oct. 1, 1988 (9 for 501)
(Min. 10 punts) 52.2—Montana St. vs. Northern Ariz., Oct. 20, 1979 (10 for 522)

FEWEST PUNTS
0—By many teams. Most recent: Southwest Mo. St. vs. Southern Ill., Nov. 7, 1992; Dartmouth vs. Brown, Nov. 16, 1991

FEWEST PUNTS, BOTH TEAMS
0—Ga. Southern & James Madison, Nov. 15, 1986

MOST OPPONENT'S PUNTS BLOCKED BY
4—Middle Tenn. St. vs. Mississippi Val., Oct. 8, 1988 (7 punts); Montana vs. Montana St., Oct. 31, 1987 (13 punts)

Punt Returns

MOST PUNT RETURNS
12—Northern Iowa vs. Youngstown St., Oct. 20, 1984 (83 yards)

MOST YARDS ON PUNT RETURNS
221—Howard vs. Morgan St., Nov. 3, 1990 (8 returns)

HIGHEST AVERAGE GAIN PER RETURN
(Min. 6 Returns)
30.9—Mississippi Val. vs. Washburn, Sept. 15, 1984 (7 for 216, 2 TDs)

MOST TOUCHDOWNS SCORED ON PUNT RETURNS
2—By nine teams. Most recent: Lehigh vs. Davidson, Sept. 10, 1988 (includes a blocked punt return)

Kickoff Returns

MOST KICKOFF RETURNS
15—Delaware St. vs. Portland St., Nov. 8, 1980 (209 yards)

MOST YARDS ON KICKOFF RETURNS
277—Idaho St. vs. Tex. A&M-Kingsville, Sept. 12, 1987 (10 returns)

HIGHEST AVERAGE GAIN PER RETURN
(Min. 3-5 rets.) 50.5—Eastern Ky. vs. Murray St., Oct. 28, 1978 (4 for 202)
(Min. 6 rets.) 46.3—Western Caro. vs. Va. Military, Oct. 10, 1992 (6 for 278)

MOST TOUCHDOWNS SCORED ON KICKOFF RETURNS
2—Western Ill. vs. St. Ambrose, Nov. 13, 1993; Western Caro. vs. Va. Military, Oct. 10, 1992; Western Ill. vs. Youngstown St., Nov. 7, 1981

Total Kick Returns

(Combined Punt and Kickoff Returns)

MOST YARDS ON KICK RETURNS
318—Tennessee St. vs. Morgan St., Oct. 24, 1987 (12 returns)

HIGHEST AVERAGE GAIN PER RETURN (Min. 6 Returns)
46.8—Connecticut vs. Yale, Sept. 24, 1983 (6 for 281)

Scoring

MOST POINTS SCORED
105—Portland St. vs. Delaware St., Nov. 8, 1980 (15 TDs, 15 PATs)

MOST POINTS SCORED, BOTH TEAMS
122—Weber St. (63) & Eastern Wash. (59), Sept. 28, 1991 (17 TDs, 14 PATs, 2 FGs)

MOST POINTS SCORED BY A LOSING TEAM
59—Eastern Wash. vs. Weber St. (63), Sept. 28, 1991

MOST POINTS SCORED EACH QUARTER
1st: 49—Portland St. vs. Delaware St., Nov. 8, 1980
2nd: 50—Alabama St. vs. Prairie View, Oct. 26, 1991
3rd: 35—Northeast La. vs. Arkansas St., Nov. 6, 1993; Portland St. vs. Delaware St., Nov. 8, 1980
4th: 39—Montana vs. South Dak. St., Sept. 4, 1993

MOST POINTS SCORED EACH HALF
1st: 73—Montana St. vs. Eastern Ore., Sept. 14, 1985
2nd: 49—Northern Iowa vs. Wis.-Whitewater, Oct. 13, 1984; Southeastern La. vs. Delta St., Nov. 8, 1980

MOST TOUCHDOWNS SCORED
15—Portland St. vs. Delaware St., Nov. 8, 1980

MOST TOUCHDOWNS SCORED, BOTH TEAMS
17—Weber St. (9) & Eastern Wash. (8), Sept. 28, 1991; Furman (9) & Davidson (8), Nov. 3, 1979

MOST EXTRA POINTS MADE BY KICKING
15—Portland St. vs. Delaware St., Nov. 8, 1980 (15 attempts)

MOST TWO-POINT ATTEMPTS MADE
5—Weber St. vs. Eastern Wash., Oct. 6, 1990 (5 passes attempted)

MOST FIELD GOALS MADE
8—Northern Ariz. vs. Idaho, Oct. 25, 1986 (8 attempts)

MOST FIELD GOALS ATTEMPTED
8—Northern Ariz. vs. Idaho, Oct. 25, 1986 (made 8)

MOST FIELD GOALS MADE, BOTH TEAMS
9—Nevada (5) & Weber St. (4), Nov. 6, 1982 (11 attempts, 3 OT); Nevada (5) & Northern Ariz. (4), Oct. 9, 1982 (12 attempts)

MOST SAFETIES SCORED
3—Alabama St. vs. Albany St. (Ga.), Oct. 15, 1988

MOST DEFENSIVE EXTRA POINTS SCORED
2—Va. Military vs. Davidson, Nov. 4, 1989 (Jeff Barnes, 95-yard interception return, and Wayne Purcell, 90-yard interception return)

MOST DEFENSIVE EXTRA-POINT ATTEMPTS
2—Western Ky. vs. Indiana St., Nov. 10, 1990 (2 interception returns); Va. Military vs. Davidson, Nov. 4, 1989 (2 interception returns)

First Downs

MOST FIRST DOWNS
46—Weber St. vs. Idaho St., Nov. 23, 1991 (12 rushing, 31 passing, 3 penalty)

MOST FIRST DOWNS, BOTH TEAMS
72—Bethune-Cookman (40) & Howard (32), Sept. 19, 1987

MOST FIRST DOWNS BY RUSHING
29—By six teams. Most recent: Arkansas St. vs. Southern Ill., Nov. 5, 1988; Southwest Mo. St. vs. Mo. Southern St., Sept. 10, 1988

MOST FIRST DOWNS BY PASSING
31—Weber St. vs. Idaho St., Nov. 23, 1991

MOST FIRST DOWNS BY PENALTY
11—Towson St. vs. Liberty, Oct. 21, 1990

Fumbles

MOST FUMBLES
16—Delaware St. vs. Portland St., Nov. 8, 1980 (lost 6)

MOST FUMBLES, BOTH TEAMS
20—Prairie View (11) & Southern-B.R. (9), Sept. 24, 1983 (lost 7); Morgan St. (11) & South Caro. St. (9), Oct. 14, 1978 (lost 9)

MOST FUMBLES LOST
8—By four teams. Most recent: Morgan St. vs. North Caro. A&T, Sept. 22, 1990 (12 fumbles)

MOST FUMBLES LOST, BOTH TEAMS
12—Austin Peay (8) & Mars Hill (4), Nov. 17, 1979 (18 fumbles); Virginia St. (7) & Howard (5), Oct. 13, 1979 (16 fumbles)

Penalties

MOST PENALTIES AGAINST
23—Idaho vs. Idaho St., Oct. 10, 1992 (204 yards)

MOST PENALTIES, BOTH TEAMS
39—In four games. Most recent: Jackson St. (22) & Grambling (17), Oct. 24, 1987 (370 yards)

MOST YARDS PENALIZED
260—Southern-B.R. vs. Howard, Nov. 4, 1978 (22 penalties)

MOST YARDS PENALIZED, BOTH TEAMS
423—Southern-B.R. (260) & Howard (163), Nov. 4, 1978 (37 penalties)

Turnovers

(Passes Had Intercepted and Fumbles Lost)

MOST TURNOVERS
12—Texas Southern vs. Lamar, Sept. 6, 1980 (4 interceptions, 8 fumbles lost)

MOST TURNOVERS, BOTH TEAMS
15—Stephen F. Austin (8) & Nicholls St. (7), Sept. 22, 1990 (8 interceptions, 7 fumbles lost); Bucknell (8) & Hofstra (7), Sept. 8, 1990 (10 interceptions, 5 fumbles lost)

SINGLE GAME—Defense

Total Defense

FEWEST PLAYS ALLOWED
31—Howard vs. Dist. Columbia, Sept. 2, 1989 (32 yards)

FEWEST YARDS ALLOWED
Minus 12—Eastern Ill. vs. Kentucky St., Nov. 13, 1982 (-67 rushing, 55 passing)

Rushing Defense

FEWEST RUSHES ALLOWED
10—Ga. Southern vs. Valdosta St., Sept. 12, 1992 (21 yards)

FEWEST RUSHING YARDS ALLOWED
Minus 88—Austin Peay vs. Morehead St., Oct. 8, 1983 (31 rushes)

Pass Defense

FEWEST ATTEMPTS ALLOWED
1—By five teams. Most recent: Towson St. vs. Northeastern, Sept. 9, 1989 (1 completed)

FEWEST COMPLETIONS ALLOWED
0—By many teams. Most recent: Colgate vs. Army, Nov. 18, 1989 (2 attempts); Illinois St. vs. Arkansas St., Nov. 11, 1989 (3 attempts); Marshall vs. Va. Military, Oct. 28, 1989 (4 attempts)

LOWEST COMPLETION PERCENTAGE ALLOWED (Min. 30 Attempts)
11.8%—Southern-B.R. vs. Nicholls St., Oct. 11, 1980 (4 of 34)

FEWEST YARDS ALLOWED
Minus 2—Florida A&M vs. Albany St. (Ga.), Oct. 16, 1982

MOST PASSES INTERCEPTED BY
10—Montana vs. Boise St., Oct. 28, 1989 (55 attempts); Grambling vs. Mississippi Val., Oct. 17, 1987 (47 attempts)

MOST TIMES OPPONENT TACKLED FOR LOSS ATTEMPTING TO PASS
13—Austin Peay vs. Morehead St., Oct. 8, 1983 (110 yards)

MOST INTERCEPTIONS RETURNED FOR TOUCHDOWNS
3—Delaware St. vs. Akron, Oct. 17, 1987 (5 for 124 yards); Montana vs. Eastern Wash., Nov. 12, 1983 (4 for 134 yards); Tenn.-Chatt. vs. Southwestern La., Sept. 17, 1983 (4 for 122 yards)

Kick Blocks

MOST KICKS BLOCKED
3—Northwestern St. vs. Arkansas St., Oct. 3, 1992 (2 PATs, 1 FG)

MOST PUNTS BLOCKED
4—Middle Tenn. St. vs. Mississippi Val., Oct. 8, 1988 (7 punts); Montana vs. Montana St., Oct. 31, 1987 (13 punts)

Fumble Returns

(Since 1992)

MOST FUMBLES RETURNED FOR TOUCHDOWNS
2—Marshall vs. Va. Military, Oct. 9, 1993 (30 & 22 yards)

SEASON—Offense

Total Offense

MOST YARDS GAINED PER GAME
640.1—Mississippi Val., 1984 (6,401 in 10)

HIGHEST AVERAGE GAIN PER PLAY
7.40—Idaho, 1993 (791 for 5,852)

MOST PLAYS PER GAME
89.6—Weber St., 1991 (986 in 11)

MOST TOUCHDOWNS BY RUSHING AND PASSING PER GAME
8.4—Mississippi Val., 1984 (84 in 10)

Rushing

MOST YARDS GAINED PER GAME
381.6—Howard, 1987 (3,816 in 10)

HIGHEST AVERAGE GAIN PER RUSH
6.60—Howard, 1987 (578 for 3,816)

MOST RUSHES PER GAME
69.8—Northeastern, 1986 (698 in 10)

MOST TOUCHDOWNS BY RUSHING PER GAME
4.5—Howard, 1987 (45 in 10)

DIVISION I-AA

Passing

MOST YARDS GAINED PER GAME
496.8—Mississippi Val., 1984 (4,968 in 10)

HIGHEST AVERAGE GAIN PER ATTEMPT
(Min. 250-399 atts.) 10.17—Marshall, 1991 (298 for 3,032)
(Min. 400 atts.) 9.25—Idaho, 1989 (445 for 4,117)

HIGHEST AVERAGE GAIN PER COMPLETION
(Min. 125-199 comps.) 19.27—Jackson St., 1990 (156 for 3,006)
(Min. 200 comps.) 16.6—Stephen F. Austin, 1989 (240 for 3,985)

MOST PASSES ATTEMPTED PER GAME
55.8—Mississippi Val., 1984 (558 in 10)

MOST PASSES COMPLETED PER GAME
35.1—Mississippi Val., 1984 (351 in 10)

HIGHEST PERCENTAGE COMPLETED
(Min. 200-449 atts.) 69.4%—William & Mary, 1993 (161 of 232)
(Min. 450 atts.) 62.9%—Mississippi Val., 1984 (351 of 558)

LOWEST PERCENTAGE HAD INTERCEPTED
(Min. 200-399 atts.) 1.00%—Princeton, 1988 (3 of 301)
(Min. 400 atts.) 1.22%—Lamar, 1988 (5 of 411)

MOST CONSECUTIVE PASSES ATTEMPTED WITHOUT AN INTERCEPTION
275—Lamar, 1988 (during 8 games, Sept. 3 to Oct. 29)

MOST TOUCHDOWN PASSES PER GAME
6.4—Mississippi Val., 1984 (64 in 10)

HIGHEST PASSING EFFICIENCY RATING POINTS
190.6—William & Mary, 1993 (232 attempts, 161 completions, 4 interceptions, 2,499 yards, 24 TDs)

Punting

MOST PUNTS PER GAME
9.64—Louisiana Tech, 1987 (106 in 11)

FEWEST PUNTS PER GAME
2.4—Howard, 1987 (24 in 10)

HIGHEST PUNTING AVERAGE
47.0—Appalachian St., 1991 (64 for 3,009)

HIGHEST NET PUNTING AVERAGE
42.8—Western Caro., 1984 (49 for 2,127 yards; 32 yards returned)

MOST PUNTS HAD BLOCKED
8—Western Ky., 1982

Punt Returns

MOST PUNT RETURNS PER GAME
5.4—Murray St., 1980 (59 in 11)

FEWEST PUNT RETURNS PER GAME
0.64—Southern Ill., 1991 (7 in 11); Prairie View, 1991 (7 in 11); Youngstown St., 1990 (7 in 11)

MOST PUNT-RETURN YARDS PER GAME
56.1—South Caro. St., 1981 (617 in 11)

HIGHEST AVERAGE GAIN PER PUNT RETURN
(Min. 20-29 rets.) 18.6—Richmond, 1985 (23 for 427)
(Min. 30 rets.) 18.1—Mississippi Val., 1985 (31 for 561)

MOST TOUCHDOWNS SCORED ON PUNT RETURNS
5—Southern Ill., 1985

Kickoff Returns

MOST KICKOFF RETURNS PER GAME
7.0—Prairie View, 1991 (77 in 11; 1,128 yards); Idaho St., 1987 (77 in 11; 1,577 yards); Davidson, 1986 (63 in 9; 1,104 yards)

FEWEST KICKOFF RETURNS PER GAME
1.4—North Texas, 1983 (15 in 11)

MOST KICKOFF-RETURN YARDS PER GAME
143.4—Idaho St., 1987 (1,577 in 11; 77 returns)

HIGHEST AVERAGE GAIN PER KICKOFF RETURN (Min. 20 Returns)
29.5—Eastern Ky., 1986 (34 for 1,022)

Combined Returns

(Interceptions, Punt Returns and Kickoff Returns)

MOST TOUCHDOWNS SCORED
9—Delaware St., 1987 (5 interceptions, 3 punt returns, 1 kickoff return)

Scoring

MOST POINTS PER GAME
60.9—Mississippi Val., 1984 (609 in 10)

MOST TOUCHDOWNS PER GAME
8.7—Mississippi Val., 1984 (87 in 10)

MOST EXTRA POINTS MADE BY KICKING PER GAME
7.7—Mississippi Val., 1984 (77 in 10)

MOST CONSECUTIVE EXTRA POINTS MADE BY KICKING
51—Lafayette, 1988

MOST TWO-POINT ATTEMPTS MADE
9—Weber St., 1992 (11 attempts)

MOST DEFENSIVE EXTRA-POINT ATTEMPTS
2—Western Ky., 1990; Eastern Wash., 1990; Va. Military, 1989

MOST DEFENSIVE EXTRA POINTS SCORED
2—Eastern Wash., 1990 (2 interception returns); Va. Military, 1989 (2 interception returns)

MOST FIELD GOALS MADE PER GAME
2.4—Northern Iowa, 1990 (26 in 11); Nevada, 1982 (26 in 11)

MOST SAFETIES SCORED
5—Jackson St., 1986

First Downs

MOST FIRST DOWNS PER GAME
31.7—Mississippi Val., 1984 (317 in 10)

MOST RUSHING FIRST DOWNS PER GAME
17.9—Howard, 1987 (179 in 10)

MOST PASSING FIRST DOWNS PER GAME
21.4—Mississippi Val., 1984 (214 in 10)

MOST FIRST DOWNS BY PENALTY PER GAME
3.7—Texas Southern, 1987 (41 in 11; 134 penalties by opponents); Alabama St., 1984 (41 in 11; 109 penalties by opponents)

Fumbles

MOST FUMBLES PER GAME
5.3—Prairie View, 1984 (58 in 11)

MOST FUMBLES LOST PER GAME
3.1—Delaware St., 1980 (31 in 10); Idaho, 1978 (31 in 10)

FEWEST OWN FUMBLES LOST
3—By four teams. Most recent: Tennessee St., 1987 (10 fumbles)

Penalties

MOST PENALTIES PER GAME
13.7—Grambling, 1984 (151 in 11; 1,206 yards)

MOST YARDS PENALIZED PER GAME
125.5—Tennessee St., 1982 (1,255 in 10; 132 penalties)

Turnovers

FEWEST TURNOVERS
10—Appalachian St., 1985 (3 fumbles, 7 interceptions)

MOST TURNOVERS
59—Texas Southern, 1980 (27 fumbles, 32 interceptions)

HIGHEST TURNOVER MARGIN PER GAME OVER OPPONENTS
2.5—Appalachian St., 1985; Florida A&M, 1981

SEASON—Defense

Total Defense

FEWEST YARDS ALLOWED PER GAME
149.9—Florida A&M, 1978 (1,649 in 11)

FEWEST RUSHING AND PASSING TOUCHDOWNS ALLOWED PER GAME
0.7—Western Mich., 1982 (8 in 11)

LOWEST AVERAGE YARDS ALLOWED PER PLAY
2.4—South Caro. St., 1978 (719 for 1,736)

Rushing Defense

FEWEST YARDS ALLOWED PER GAME
44.5—Grambling, 1984 (489 in 11)

LOWEST AVERAGE YARDS ALLOWED PER RUSH
1.3—Florida A&M, 1978 (419 for 535)

FEWEST RUSHING TOUCHDOWNS ALLOWED PER GAME
0.3—Florida A&M, 1978 (3 in 11)

Pass Defense

FEWEST YARDS ALLOWED PER GAME
59.9—Bethune-Cookman, 1981 (659 in 11)

FEWEST YARDS ALLOWED PER ATTEMPT (Min. 200 Attempts)
3.98—Middle Tenn. St., 1988 (251 for 999)

FEWEST YARDS ALLOWED PER COMPLETION (Min. 100 Completions)
9.08—Middle Tenn. St., 1988 (110 for 999)

LOWEST COMPLETION PERCENTAGE ALLOWED
(Min. 200-299 atts.) 32.3%—Alcorn St., 1979 (76 of 235)
(Min. 300 atts.) 34.2%—Tennessee St., 1986 (107 of 313)

FEWEST TOUCHDOWNS ALLOWED BY PASSING
1—Middle Tenn. St., 1990; Nevada, 1978

LOWEST PASSING EFFICIENCY DEFENSE RATING (Since 1990)
70.01—South Caro. St., 1991 (278 attempts, 97 completions, 21 interceptions, 1,360 yards, 8 TDs)

MOST PASSES INTERCEPTED BY, PER GAME
3.2—Florida A&M, 1981 (35 in 11)

HIGHEST PERCENTAGE INTERCEPTED BY
13.4—Florida A&M, 1981 (35 of 262)

MOST YARDS GAINED ON INTERCEPTIONS
498—Jackson St., 1985 (28 interceptions)

MOST YARDS GAINED PER GAME ON INTERCEPTIONS
49.8—Jackson St., 1985 (498 in 10)

HIGHEST AVERAGE PER INTERCEPTION RETURN (Min. 15 Returns)
21.6—Jackson St., 1986 (23 for 497)

MOST TOUCHDOWNS ON INTERCEPTION RETURNS
7—Jackson St., 1985

Punting

MOST OPPONENT'S PUNTS BLOCKED BY
9—Middle Tenn. St., 1988 (73 punts)

Punt Returns

LOWEST AVERAGE YARDS ALLOWED PER PUNT RETURN
0.96—Yale, 1988 (24 for 23)

FEWEST RETURNS ALLOWED
7—Furman, 1984 (11 games, 8 yards)

Kickoff Returns

LOWEST AVERAGE YARDS ALLOWED PER KICKOFF RETURN
11.0—Lafayette, 1980 (20 for 220)

Scoring

FEWEST POINTS ALLOWED PER GAME
6.5—South Caro. St., 1978 (72 in 11)

Fumbles

MOST OPPONENT'S FUMBLES RECOVERED
29—Western Ky., 1982 (43 fumbles)

Fumble Returns

(Since 1992)

MOST FUMBLES RETURNED FOR TOUCHDOWNS
2—Marshall, 1993 (both vs. Va. Military, Oct. 9); Citadel, 1992 (vs. Arkansas, Sept. 5 & vs. Western Caro., Oct. 24)

Turnovers

MOST OPPONENT'S TURNOVERS PER GAME
4.8—Grambling, 1985 (53 in 11)

Additional Records

MOST CONSECUTIVE VICTORIES
20—Holy Cross, 1990-91

MOST CONSECUTIVE HOME VICTORIES
38—Ga. Southern, from Oct. 5, 1985, through Sept. 22, 1990 (includes 10 I-AA playoff games)

MOST CONSECUTIVE LOSSES
44—Columbia, from Nov. 12, 1983, through Oct. 1, 1988 (ended Oct. 8, 1988, with 16-13 win over Princeton)

MOST CONSECUTIVE GAMES WITHOUT A WIN
47—Columbia, from Oct. 22, 1983, through Oct. 1, 1988, including two ties (ended Oct. 8, 1988, with 16-13 win over Princeton)

MOST CONSECUTIVE GAMES WITHOUT BEING SHUT OUT
193—Boise St., from Sept. 21, 1968, through Nov. 10, 1984

MOST SHUTOUTS IN A SEASON
5—South Caro. St., 1978

MOST CONSECUTIVE QUARTERS HOLDING OPPONENTS SCORELESS
14—McNeese St., 1985; Bucknell, 1979

MOST CONSECUTIVE GAMES WITHOUT A TIE
326—Richmond (current)

LAST SCORELESS-TIE GAME
Oct. 26, 1985—McNeese St. & North Texas

HIGHEST-SCORING TIE GAME
51-51—William & Mary & Villanova, Oct. 23, 1993

MOST CONSECUTIVE PASSES ATTEMPTED WITHOUT AN INTERCEPTION
297—Lamar (in 9 games from Nov. 21, 1987, to Oct. 29, 1988)

MOST POINTS OVERCOME IN SECOND HALF TO WIN A GAME
35—Nevada (55) vs. Weber St. (49), Nov. 2, 1991 (trailed 14-49 with 12:16 remaining in 3rd quarter)
32—Morehead St. (36) vs. Wichita St. (35), Sept. 20, 1986 (trailed 3-35 with 9:03 remaining in 3rd quarter)
31—Montana (52) vs. South Dak. St. (48), Sept. 4, 1993 (trailed 7-38 with 8:12 remaining in 3rd quarter)

MOST POINTS OVERCOME IN FOURTH QUARTER TO WIN A GAME
28—Delaware St. (38) vs. Liberty (37), Oct. 6, 1990 (trailed 9-37 with 13:00 remaining in 4th quarter)

MOST POINTS SCORED IN FOURTH QUARTER TO WIN A GAME
39—Montana (52) vs. South Dak. St. (48), Sept. 4, 1993 (trailed 13-38 to begin 4th quarter)
33—Southwest Mo. St. (40) vs. Illinois St. (28), Oct. 9, 1993 (trailed 7-21 with 11:30 remaining in 4th quarter)

MOST OVERTIME PERIODS IN A GAME
6—Villanova vs. Connecticut, Oct. 7, 1989 (score after regulation time was 21-21; Villanova won, 41-35)

Score by Periods

				Regulation
Connecticut	0	14	0	7—21
Villanova	0	0	14	7—21
				Overtime
Connecticut	0	0	7	0—35
Villanova	0	0	7	6—41

There were 11 TDs, 10 PATs. Game time was 3:40. Villanova's Jeff Johnson scored the winning TD on a 3-yard run (his third TD of the game).

6—Rhode Island vs. Maine, Sept. 18, 1982 (score after regulation time was 21-21; Rhode Island won, 58-55)

Score by Periods

				Regulation
Rhode Island	7	7	0	7—21
Maine	0	7	0	14—21
				Overtime
Rhode Island	7	7	3	7 6—58
Maine	7	7	3	7 3—55

There were 15 TDs, 14 PATs, 3 FGs. Game time was 3:46, including 51 minutes of overtime. Rhode Island's T. J. Del Santo scored the winning TD on a 2-yard run (his fourth TD of the game) after Maine kicked a field goal in the sixth overtime.

MOST CONSECUTIVE OVERTIME GAMES PLAYED
2—Connecticut, 1989 (Connecticut 35, Villanova 41, 6 OT, Oct. 7; and Connecticut 39, Massachusetts 33, 1 OT, Oct. 14); Maine, 1982 (Maine 55, Rhode Island 58, 6 OT, Sept. 18; and Maine 45, Boston U. 48, 4 OT, Sept. 25)

MOST CONSECUTIVE EXTRA-POINT KICKS MADE
134—Boise St. (began Oct. 27, 1984; ended Nov. 12, 1988)

MOST CONSECUTIVE WINNING SEASONS
27—Grambling (1960-86)

MOST IMPROVED WON-LOST RECORD
9 1/2 games—Montana St., 1984 (12-2-0, including 3 Division I-AA playoff games) from 1983 (1-10-0)

DIVISION I-AA

Southwest Missouri State quarterback Phil Johnson threw three touchdown passes in less than four minutes to spur a 33-point fourth-quarter scoring burst in a 40-28 victory against Illinois State.

Annual Champions, All-Time Leaders

Total Offense

CAREER YARDS PER GAME

Player, Team	Years	G	Plays	Yards	TDR‡	Yd. PG
Willie Totten, Mississippi Val.	1982-85	40	1,812	13,007	*157	*325.2
Neil Lomax, Portland St.............	1977-80	42	*1,901	*13,345	120	317.7
Tom Ehrhardt, Rhode Island........	#1984-85	21	1,010	6,492	66	309.1
Doug Nussmeier, Idaho	1990-93	39	1,556	12,054	109	309.1
Tod Mayfield, West Tex. A&M ...	¢1984-86	24	1,165	7,316	58	304.8
Jamie Martin, Weber St.	1989-92	41	1,838	12,287	93	299.7
Stan Greene, Boston U..............	1989-90	22	1,167	6,408	49	291.3
John Friesz, Idaho....................	1986-89	35	1,459	10,187	79	291.1
Vern Harris, Idaho St...............	1984-85	19	813	5,302	36	279.1
Grady Bennett, Montana	1988-90	31	1,389	8,304	69	267.9
Sean Payton, Eastern Ill.	1983-86	39	1,690	10,298	91	264.1
John Witkowski, Columbia	1981-83	30	1,330	7,748	58	258.3
Dave Stireman, Weber St..........	1984-85	21	762	5,396	43	257.0
Ken Hobart, Idaho...................	1980-83	44	1,847	11,127	105	252.9
Mike Machurek, Idaho St.	1980-81	20	805	4,974	43	248.7
Tony Petersen, Marshall..............	1986-87	20	756	4,940	31	247.0
Jeff Wiley, Holy Cross	1985-88	40	1,428	9,877	76	246.9
Doug Butler, Princeton	1983-85	29	1,137	7,157	52	246.8
Tom Ciaccio, Holy Cross............	1988-91	37	1,283	9,066	87	245.0
Greg Wyatt, Northern Ariz.	1986-89	42	1,753	10,277	75	244.7
Jay Fiedler, Dartmouth..............	1991-93	30	1,063	7,249	73	241.6
Chris Hakel, William & Mary	1988-91	28	915	6,458	56	239.2
Bob Jean, New Hampshire........	1985-88	32	1,287	7,621	59	238.2
Michael Proctor, Murray St.......	1986-89	43	1,577	9,886	66	230.0
Jason Garrett, Princeton	1987-88	20	731	4,555	24	227.8
Paul Peterson, Idaho St..............	1982-83	22	1,057	4,967	36	225.8
Frank Baur, Lafayette	1985, 87-89	38	1,312	8,579	72	225.8
Eric Beavers, Nevada	1983-86	40	1,307	9,025	85	225.6

*Record. ‡Touchdowns-responsible-for are player's TDs scored and passed for. ¢Two years in Division I-AA and two years in Division II (LIU-C. W. Post). Four-year totals: 9,793 yards and 232.2 average.

SEASON YARDS PER GAME

Player, Team	Year	G	Plays	Yards	TDR‡	Yd. PG
Willie Totten, Mississippi Val.	†1984	10	564	*4,572	*61	*457.2
Steve McNair, Alcorn St...............	†1992	10	519	4,057	39	405.7
Jamie Martin, Weber St.	†1991	11	591	4,337	37	394.3
Neil Lomax, Portland St.	†1980	11	550	4,157	42	377.9
Dave Dickenson, Montana	†1993	11	530	3,978	46	361.6
Neil Lomax, Portland St.	†1979	11	*611	3,966	31	360.5
John Friesz, Idaho	†1989	11	464	3,853	31	350.3
Steve McNair, Alcorn St..............	1993	11	493	3,830	30	348.2
Todd Hammel, Stephen F. Austin	1989	11	487	3,822	38	347.5
Tom Ehrhardt, Rhode Island.................	†1985	10	529	3,460	35	346.0
Ken Hobart, Idaho.................	†1983	11	578	3,800	37	345.5
Dave Stireman, Weber St.	1985	11	502	3,759	33	341.7
Willie Totten, Mississippi Val.	1985	11	561	3,742	43	340.2
Jeff Wiley, Holy Cross	†1987	11	445	3,722	34	338.4
Jamie Martin, Weber St.	†1990	11	508	3,713	25	337.6
Sean Payton, Eastern Ill...............	1984	11	584	3,661	31	332.8
Tod Mayfield, West Tex. A&M...........	1985	10	526	3,328	21	332.8
Tom Proudian, Iona	1993	10	521	3,322	30	332.2

*Record. †National champion. ‡Touchdowns-responsible-for are player's TDs scored and passed for.

CAREER YARDS

Player, Team	Years	Plays	Yards	Avg.
Neil Lomax, Portland St.................	1977-80	*1,901	*13,345	7.02
Willie Totten, Mississippi Val.	1982-85	1,812	13,007	7.18
Jamie Martin, Weber St.	1989-92	1,838	12,287	6.68
Doug Nussmeier, Idaho	1990-93	1,556	12,054	*7.75
Ken Hobart, Idaho......................	1980-83	1,847	11,127	6.02
¢Steve McNair, Alcorn St.	1991-93	1,406	11,024	7.84
Sean Payton, Eastern Ill.	1983-86	1,690	10,298	6.09
Greg Wyatt, Northern Ariz.	1986-89	1,753	10,277	5.86
John Friesz, Idaho	1986-89	1,459	10,187	6.98
Michael Proctor, Murray St..........	1986-89	1,577	9,886	6.27
Jeff Wiley, Holy Cross...............	1985-88	1,428	9,877	6.92
Matt DeGennaro, Connecticut	1987-90	1,619	9,269	5.73
Tom Ciaccio, Holy Cross.............	1988-91	1,283	9,066	7.07
Eric Beavers, Nevada	1983-86	1,307	9,025	6.91
Marty Horn, Lehigh	1982-85	1,612	8,956	5.56
Kirk Schulz, Villanova	1986-89	1,534	8,900	5.80
Robbie Justino, Liberty	1989-92	1,469	8,803	5.99
Chris Swartz, Morehead St.	1987-90	1,559	8,648	5.55
Frank Baur, Lafayette	1985, 87-89	1,312	8,579	6.54
Fred Gatlin, Nevada	%1989-92	1,330	8,568	6.44
Steve Calabria, Colgate.............	1981-84	1,342	8,532	6.36
Mike Buck, Maine	1986-89	1,288	8,457	6.57
Jason Whitmer, Idaho St..............	1987-90	1,618	8,449	5.22
Scott Davis, North Texas	1987-90	1,548	8,436	5.45
Grady Bennett, Montana	1988-90	1,389	8,304	5.98
Bill Vergantino, Delaware............	1989-92	1,459	8,225	5.64
Stan Yagiello, William & Mary	$1981-85	1,492	8,168	5.47
Mike Smith, Northern Iowa	1984-87	1,163	8,145	7.00
Bob Bleier, Richmond...............	1983-86	1,313	7,991	6.09
Alan Hooker, North Caro. A&T	1984-87	1,476	7,787	5.28
John Witkowski, Columbia	1981-83	1,330	7,748	5.83
Michael Payton, Marshall.............	1989-92	1,106	7,744	7.00
Kelly Bradley, Montana St.............	1983-86	1,547	7,740	5.00
Jeff Cesarone, Western Ky.	1984-87	1,502	7,694	5.12

*Record. $See page 6 for explanation. ¢Active player. %Played 1992 season in Division I-A.

SEASON YARDS

Player, Team	Year	G	Plays	Yards	Avg.
Willie Totten, Mississippi Val.	†1984	10	564	*4,572	8.11
Jamie Martin, Weber St.	†1991	11	591	4,337	7.34
Neil Lomax, Portland St.	†1980	11	550	4,157	7.56
Steve McNair, Alcorn St....................	†1992	10	519	4,057	7.82
Dave Dickenson, Montana	†1993	11	530	3,978	7.51
Neil Lomax, Portland St.	†1979	11	*611	3,966	6.49
John Friesz, Idaho.........................	†1989	11	464	3,853	8.30
Steve McNair, Alcorn St....................	1993	11	493	3,830	7.77
Todd Hammel, Stephen F. Austin	1989	11	487	3,822	7.85
Ken Hobart, Idaho.........................	†1983	11	578	3,800	6.57
Dave Stireman, Weber St.	1985	11	502	3,759	7.49
Willie Totten, Mississippi Val.	1985	11	561	3,742	6.67
Jeff Wiley, Holy Cross	†1987	11	445	3,722	8.36
Jamie Martin, Weber St.	†1990	11	508	3,713	7.31
Sean Payton, Eastern Ill..................	1984	11	584	3,661	6.27
Todd Brunner, Lehigh	1989	11	504	3,639	7.22
Scott Semptimphelter, Lehigh	1993	11	515	3,528	6.85
Neil Lomax, Portland St.	†1978	11	519	3,524	6.79
Doug Nussmeier, Idaho	1993	11	400	3,514	*8.79
Glenn Kempa, Lehigh	1991	11	513	3,511	6.84
John Friesz, Idaho........................	1987	11	543	3,489	6.43
Jay Walker, Howard	1993	11	466	3,469	7.44
Doug Nussmeier, Idaho	1991	11	472	3,460	7.33
Tom Ehrhardt, Rhode Island...............	†1985	10	529	3,460	6.54

*Record. †National champion.

SINGLE-GAME YARDS

Yds.	Player, Team (Opponent)	Date
643	Jamie Martin, Weber St. (Idaho St.)	Nov. 23, 1991
621	Willie Totten, Mississippi Val. (Prairie View)	Oct. 27, 1984
604	Steve McNair, Alcorn St. (Jackson St.)	Nov. 21, 1992
595	Doug Pederson, Northeast La. (Stephen F. Austin)	Nov. 11, 1989
587	Vern Harris, Idaho St. (Montana)	Oct. 12, 1985
570	Steve McNair, Alcorn St. (Texas Southern)	Sept. 11, 1993
566	Tom Ehrhardt, Rhode Island (Connecticut)	Nov. 16, 1985
562	Todd Hammel, Stephen F. Austin (Northeast La.)	Nov. 11, 1989
561	Willie Totten, Mississippi Val. (Southern-B.R.)	Sept. 29, 1984
549	Steve McNair, Alcorn St. (Jacksonville St.)	Oct. 31, 1992
547	Tod Mayfield, West Tex. A&M (New Mexico St.)	Nov. 16, 1985
546	Dave Stireman, Weber St. (Montana)	Nov. 2, 1985
543	Ken Hobart, Idaho (Southern Colo.)	Sept. 10, 1983
539	Dave Dickenson, Montana (Idaho)	Nov. 6, 1993
539	Jamie Martin, Weber St. (Montana St.)	Sept. 26, 1992
536	Brad Otten, Weber St. (Northern Ariz.)	Nov. 6, 1993
536	Willie Totten, Mississippi Val. (Kentucky St.)	Sept. 1, 1984
527	Willie Totten, Mississippi Val. (Grambling)	Oct. 13, 1984
519	Bernard Hawk, Bethune-Cookman (Ga. Southern)	Oct. 6, 1984

ANNUAL CHAMPIONS

Year	Player, Team	Class	G	Plays	Yards	Avg.
1978	Neil Lomax, Portland St.	So.	11	519	3,524	320.4
1979	Neil Lomax, Portland St.	Jr.	11	*611	3,966	360.5
1980	Neil Lomax, Portland St.	Sr.	11	550	4,157	377.9
1981	Mike Machurek, Idaho St.	Sr.	9	363	2,645	293.9
1982	Brent Woods, Princeton	Sr.	10	577	3,079	307.9
1983	Ken Hobart, Idaho	Sr.	11	578	3,800	345.5
1984	Willie Totten, Mississippi Val.	Jr.	10	564	*4,572	*457.2
1985	Tom Ehrhardt, Rhode Island	Sr.	10	529	3,460	346.0
1986	Brent Pease, Montana	Sr.	10	499	3,094	309.4
1987	Jeff Wiley, Holy Cross	Jr.	11	445	3,722	338.4
1988	John Friesz, Idaho	Jr.	10	424	2,751	275.1
1989	John Friesz, Idaho	Sr.	11	464	3,853	350.3
1990	Jamie Martin, Weber St.	So.	11	508	3,713	337.6
1991	Jamie Martin, Weber St.	Jr.	11	591	4,337	394.3
1992	Steve McNair, Alcorn St.	So.	10	519	4,057	405.7
1993	Dave Dickenson, Montana	So.	11	530	3,978	361.6

*Record.

Rushing

CAREER YARDS PER GAME†
(Minimum 2,500 Yards)

Player, Team	Years	G	Plays	Yards	TD	Yd. PG
Keith Elias, Princeton	1991-93	30	736	4,208	49	*140.3
Mike Clark, Akron	1984-86	32	804	4,257	24	133.0
Rich Erenberg, Colgate	1982-83	21	464	2,618	22	124.7
Kenny Gamble, Colgate	1984-87	42	*963	5,220	*55	124.3
Frank Hawkins, Nevada	1977-80	43	945	*5,333	39	124.0
Elroy Harris, Eastern Ky.	1985, 87-88	31	648	3,829	47	123.5
Gill Fenerty, Holy Cross	1983-85	30	622	3,618	26	120.6
Markus Thomas, Eastern Ky.	1989-92	42	784	5,149	51	119.7
Derrick Harmon, Cornell	1981-83	28	545	3,074	26	109.8
Paul Lewis, Boston U.	1982-84	37	878	3,995	50	108.0
Eric Gant, Grambling	1990-93	34	617	3,667	32	107.9
Derrick Franklin, Indiana St.	1989-91	30	710	3,231	23	107.7
Charvez Foger, Nevada	1985-88	42	864	4,484	52	106.8
James Crawford, Eastern Ky.	1985-87	32	661	3,404	22	106.4
Bryan Keys, Pennsylvania	1987-89	30	609	3,137	34	104.6
Judd Garrett, Princeton	1987-89	30	687	3,109	32	103.6

*Record. †The following players competed two years in Division I-AA and two years in Division I-A: Rich Erenberg, Colgate (four years: 3,689 yards and 94.6 average); Buford Jordan, McNeese St. (four years: 4,106 yards and 100.1 average), and Stanford Jennings, Furman (four years: 3,868 yards and 90.0 average).

SEASON YARDS PER GAME

Player, Team	Year	G	Plays	Yards	TD	Yd. PG
Tony Vinson, Towson St.	†1993	10	293	*2,016	23	*201.6
Keith Elias, Princeton	1993	10	305	1,731	19	173.1
Gene Lake, Delaware St.	†1984	10	238	1,722	20	172.2
Rich Erenberg, Colgate	†1983	11	302	1,883	20	171.2
Kenny Gamble, Colgate	†1986	11	307	1,816	21	165.1
Mike Clark, Akron	1986	11	245	1,786	8	162.4
Keith Elias, Princeton	†1992	10	245	1,575	18	157.5
Frank Hawkins, Nevada	†1980	11	307	1,719	9	156.3
Brad Baxter, Alabama St.	1986	11	302	1,705	13	155.0
Elroy Harris, Eastern Ky.	1988	10	277	1,543	21	154.3
Richard Johnson, Butler	1993	10	322	1,535	10	153.5
Frank Hawkins, Nevada	†1979	11	293	1,683	13	153.0
Carl Smith, Maine	†1989	11	305	1,680	20	152.7
Harvey Reed, Howard	†1987	10	211	1,512	20	151.2
John Settle, Appalachian St.	1986	11	317	1,661	20	151.0
Garry Pearson, Massachusetts	†1982	11	312	1,631	13	148.3
Lorenzo Bouier, Maine	1980	11	349	1,622	9	147.5

*Record. †National champion.

CAREER YARDS@

Player, Team	Years	Plays	Yards	Avg.	Long
Frank Hawkins, Nevada	1977-80	945	*5,333	5.64	50
Kenny Gamble, Colgate	1984-87	*963	5,220	5.42	91
Markus Thomas, Eastern Ky.	1989-92	784	5,149	*6.57	90
Cedric Minter, Boise St.	1977-80	752	4,475	5.95	77
John Settle, Appalachian St.	1983-86	891	4,409	4.95	88
Mike Clark, Akron	1984-86	804	4,257	5.29	†65
Keith Elias, Princeton	1991-93	736	4,208	5.72	69
Warren Marshall, James Madison	$1982-86	737	4,168	5.66	59
Carl Tremble, Furman	1989-92	696	4,149	5.96	65
Harvey Reed, Howard	1984-87	635	4,142	6.52	85
Paul Lewis, Boston U.	1981-84	878	3,995	4.55	80
Joe Ross, Ga. Southern	1987-90	687	3,876	5.64	75
Garry Pearson, Massachusetts	1979-82	808	3,859	4.78	71
Elroy Harris, Eastern Ky.	1985, 87-88	648	3,829	5.91	64
Lorenzo Bouier, Maine	1979-82	879	3,827	4.35	77
Lewis Tillman, Jackson St.	$1984-88	779	3,824	4.91	39
Joe Campbell, Middle Tenn. St.	1988-91	638	3,823	5.99	81
Carl Smith, Maine	1988-91	759	3,815	5.03	89
Brad Baxter, Alabama St.	1985-88	773	3,732	4.83	71
Toby Davis, Illinois St.	1989-92	825	3,702	4.49	34
Eric Gant, Grambling	1990-93	617	3,667	5.94	49
Gill Fenerty, Holy Cross	1983-85	622	3,618	5.82	76

*Record. †Did not score. $See page 6 for explanation. @ The following players competed two years in Division I-AA and two years in Division I-A: Rich Erenberg, Colgate (four years: 3,689 yards); Buford Jordan, McNeese St. (four years: 4,106 yards), and Stanford Jennings, Furman (four years: 3,868 yards).

SEASON YARDS

Player, Team	Year	G	Plays	Yards	Avg.
Tony Vinson, Towson St.	†1993	10	293	*2,016	6.89
Rich Erenberg, Colgate	†1983	11	302	1,883	6.24
Kenny Gamble, Colgate	†1986	11	307	1,816	5.92
Mike Clark, Akron	1986	11	245	1,786	‡7.29
Keith Elias, Princeton	1993	10	305	1,731	5.68
Gene Lake, Delaware St.	†1984	10	238	1,722	7.24
Frank Hawkins, Nevada	†1980	11	307	1,719	5.60
Brad Baxter, Alabama St.	1986	11	302	1,705	5.65
Frank Hawkins, Nevada	†1979	11	293	1,683	5.74
Carl Smith, Maine	†1989	11	305	1,680	5.51
John Settle, Appalachian St.	1986	11	317	1,661	5.24
Garry Pearson, Massachusetts	†1982	11	312	1,631	5.23
Lorenzo Bouier, Maine	1980	11	349	1,622	4.65
Markus Thomas, Eastern Ky.	1989	11	232	1,620	6.98
Keith Elias, Princeton	†1992	10	245	1,575	6.43
James Black, Akron	1983	11	*351	1,568	4.47
Irving Spikes, Northeast La.	1993	11	246	1,563	6.35
Toby Davis, Illinois St.	1992	11	341	1,561	4.58
Anthony Russo, St. John's (N.Y.)	1993	11	311	1,558	5.01
Carl Tremble, Furman	1992	11	228	1,555	6.82
Burton Murchison, Lamar	†1985	11	265	1,547	5.84
Jerome Bledsoe, Massachusetts	†1991	11	264	1,545	5.85

*Record. †National champion. ‡Record for minimum of 200 carries.

DIVISION I-AA

SINGLE-GAME YARDS

Yds.	Player, Team (Opponent)	Date
364	Tony Vinson, Towson St. (Bucknell)	Nov. 13, 1993
346	William Arnold, Jackson St. (Texas Southern)	Nov. 6, 1993
345	Russell Davis, Idaho (Portland St.)	Oct. 3, 1981
337	Gill Fenerty, Holy Cross (Columbia)	Oct. 29, 1983
336	Gene Lake, Delaware St. (Liberty)	Nov. 10, 1984
327	Tony Vinson, Towson St. (Morgan St.)	Nov. 20, 1993
323	Matt Johnson, Harvard (Brown)	Nov. 9, 1991
312	Surkano Edwards, Samford (Tenn.-Martin)	Nov. 14, 1992
309	Eddie Thompson, Western Ky. (Southern Ill.)	Oct. 29, 1992
305	Lucius Floyd, Nevada (Montana St.)	Sept. 27, 1986
304	Tony Citizen, McNeese St. (Prairie View)	Sept. 6, 1986
302	Lorenzo Bouier, Maine (Northeastern)	Nov. 1, 1980
300	Markus Thomas, Eastern Ky. (Marshall)	Oct. 21, 1989
299	Keith Elias, Princeton (Lafayette)	Sept. 26, 1992
299	Joe Delaney, Northwestern St. (Nicholls St.)	Oct. 28, 1978
293	Terence Thompson, Eastern Ky. (Akron)	Sept. 26, 1981
293	Frank Hawkins, Nevada (San Fran. St.)	Sept. 30, 1978

ANNUAL CHAMPIONS

Year	Player, Team	Class	G	Plays	Yards	Avg.
1978	Frank Hawkins, Nevada	So.	10	259	1,445	144.5
1979	Frank Hawkins, Nevada	Jr.	11	293	1,683	153.0
1980	Frank Hawkins, Nevada	Sr.	11	307	1,719	156.3
1981	Gregg Drew, Boston U.	Jr.	10	309	1,257	125.7
1982	Garry Pearson, Massachusetts	Sr.	11	312	1,631	148.3
1983	Rich Erenberg, Colgate	Sr.	11	302	1,883	171.2
1984	Gene Lake, Delaware St.	Jr.	10	238	1,722	172.2
1985	Burton Murchison, Lamar	So.	11	265	1,547	140.6
1986	Kenny Gamble, Colgate	Jr.	11	307	1,816	165.1
1987	Harvey Reed, Howard	Sr.	10	211	1,512	151.2
1988	Elroy Harris, Eastern Ky.	Jr.	10	277	1,543	154.3
1989	Carl Smith, Maine	So.	11	305	1,680	152.7
1990	Walter Dean, Grambling	Sr.	11	221	1,401	127.4
1991	Al Rosier, Dartmouth	Sr.	10	258	1,432	143.2
1992	Keith Elias, Princeton	Jr.	10	245	1,575	157.5
1993	Tony Vinson, Towson St.	Sr.	10	293	*2,016	*201.6

*Record.

Quarterback Rushing

CAREER YARDS
(Since 1978)

Player, Team	Years	G	Plays	Yards	TD	Yd.PG
Jack Douglas, Citadel	1989-92	44	*832	*3,674	*48	83.5
Tracy Ham, Ga. Southern	1984-86	33	511	2,506	32	75.9
Tony Scales, Va. Military	1989-92	44	561	2,475	19	56.3
Eddie Thompson, Western Ky.	1991-93	27	387	2,349	19	*87.0
Eriq Williams, James Madison	1989-92	43	642	2,321	32	54.0
Raymond Gross, Ga. Southern	1987-90	42	695	2,290	20	54.5
Bill Vergantino, Delaware	1989-92	44	656	2,287	34	52.0
Dwane Brown, Arkansas St.	1984-87	42	595	2,192	33	52.2
Roy Johnson, Arkansas St.	1988-91	43	558	2,182	22	50.7
DeAndre Smith, Southwest Mo. St.	1987-90	42	558	2,140	36	50.9
Ken Hobart, Idaho	1980-83	44	628	1,827	26	41.5
Darin Kehler, Yale	1987-90	28	402	1,643	13	58.7

*Record.

SEASON YARDS
(Since 1978)

Player, Team	Year	G	Plays	Yards	TD	Avg.
Alfredo Anderson, Idaho St.	1993	11	161	*1,159	5	7.20
Jack Douglas, Citadel	1991	11	*266	1,152	13	4.33
Tony Scales, Va. Military	1991	11	185	1,105	8	5.97
Tracy Ham, Ga. Southern	1986	11	207	1,048	*18	5.06
Nick Crawford, Yale	1991	10	210	1,024	8	4.98
Gene Brown, Citadel	1988	9	152	1,006	13	6.62
Jack Douglas, Citadel	1992	11	178	926	13	5.20
Roy Johnson, Arkansas St.	1989	11	193	925	6	4.79
Darin Kehler, Yale	1989	10	210	903	6	4.30
Jim O'Leary, Northeastern	1986	10	195	884	10	4.53
Earl Easley, Arkansas St.	1988	11	196	861	11	4.39
Brad Brown, Northwestern St.	1990	11	192	843	8	4.39
DeAndre Smith, Southwest Mo. St.	1989	11	176	841	12	4.78
Eddie Thompson, Western Ky.	1992	9	113	837	9	*7.41
Gilbert Price, Southwest Tex. St.	1991	11	244	837	8	3.43
Jack Douglas, Citadel	1990	11	211	836	13	3.96

*Record.

Joe Ryan photo

Scott Semptimphelter connected on 59.9 percent of his passes during his career at Lehigh to lead career passing efficiency leaders with a minimum of 300 completions.

Passing

CAREER PASSING EFFICIENCY
(Minimum 300 Completions)

Player, Team	Years	Att.	Cmp.	Int.	Pct.	Yards	TD	Pts.
Doug Nussmeier, Idaho	1990-93	1,225	746	32	.609	10,824	91	*154.4
Jay Johnson, Northern Iowa	1989-92	744	397	25	.534	7,049	51	148.9
Willie Totten, Mississippi Val.	1982-85	1,555	907	*75	.583	12,711	*139	146.8
Kenneth Biggles, Tennessee St.	1981-84	701	397	28	.566	5,933	57	146.6
Mike Smith, Northern Iowa	1984-87	943	557	43	.591	8,219	58	143.5
Neil Lomax, Portland St.	1977-80	*1,606	*938	55	.584	*13,220	106	142.5
Tom Ciaccio, Holy Cross	1988-91	1,073	658	46	.613	8,603	72	142.2
Jim Zaccheo, Nevada	1987-88	554	326	27	.588	4,750	35	142.0
Eric Beavers, Nevada	1983-86	1,094	646	37	.591	8,626	77	141.8
Scott Semptimphelter, Lehigh	1990-93	823	493	27	.599	6,668	50	141.5
Jason Garrett, Princeton	1987-88	550	368	10	*.669	4,274	20	140.6
Connell Maynor, Winston-Salem/ North Caro. A&T	1987, 89-91	661	365	31	.552	5,390	50	139.3
Jamie Martin, Weber St.	1989-92	1,544	934	56	.605	12,207	87	138.2
Ricky Jones, Alabama St.	1988-91	644	324	30	.503	5,472	49	137.5
Jeff Carlson, Weber St.	1984, 86-88	723	384	33	.531	6,147	47	136.9
Chris Hakel, William & Mary	1988-91	812	489	26	.602	6,447	40	136.7
Jeff Wiley, Holy Cross	1985-88	1,208	723	63	.599	9,698	71	136.3
Tom Ehrhardt, Rhode Island	††1984-85	919	526	35	.572	6,722	66	134.8
Mike Buck, Maine	1986-89	1,134	637	41	.562	8,721	68	133.4
Frankie DeBusk, Furman	1987-90	634	333	29	.525	5,414	35	133.3
Frank Novak, Lafayette	1981-83	834	478	36	.573	6,378	51	133.1
Robbie Justino, Liberty	1989-92	1,267	769	51	.607	9,548	64	132.6
Rick Worman, Eastern Wash.	**1982, 84-85	673	382	23	.568	5,013	41	132.6
Glenn Kempa, Lehigh	1989-91	901	520	27	.577	6,722	49	132.3
Gilbert Renfroe, Tennessee St.	1982-85	721	370	23	.513	5,556	48	131.6

Player, Team	Years	Att.	Cmp.	Int.	Pct.	Yards	TD	Pts.
Tod Mayfield, West Tex. A&M	##1984-86	1,035	630	38	.609	7,424	55	131.3
Jay Walker, Long Beach St./Howard	••1991-93	722	378	24	.524	5,691	42	131.1
Tracy Ham, Ga. Southern	1984-86	568	301	31	.530	4,881	29	131.1
Matt DeGennaro, Connecticut	1987-90	1,319	803	49	.609	9,288	73	130.9
Lonnie Galloway, Western Caro.	1990-93	639	355	43	.556	5,545	30	130.5
Ken Hobart, Idaho	1980-83	1,219	629	42	.516	9,300	79	130.2

*Record. $See page 6 for explanation. **At Fresno St. in 1982. ##Two years in Division I-AA (1984-85) and one year in Division II (1986). ††Two years in Division I-AA and two years in Division II (LIU-C. W. Post). ••Played one season at Long Beach St. (1991).

SEASON PASSING EFFICIENCY
(Minimum 15 Attempts Per Game)

Player, Team	Year	G	Att.	Cmp.	Int.	Pct.	Yards	TD	Pts.
Shawn Knight, William & Mary	†1993	10	177	125	4	.706	2,055	22	*204.6
Michael Payton, Marshall	†1991	9	216	143	5	.622	2,333	19	181.3
Doug Nussmeier, Idaho	1993	11	304	185	5	.609	2,960	33	175.2
Kelvin Simmons, Troy St.	1993	11	224	143	6	.638	2,144	23	172.8
Frank Baur, Lafayette	†1988	10	256	164	11	.641	2,621	23	171.1
Bobby Lamb, Furman	†1985	11	181	106	6	.586	1,856	18	170.9
Jay Fiedler, Dartmouth	†1992	10	273	175	13	.641	2,748	25	169.4
Mike Smith, Northern Iowa	†1986	11	303	190	16	.627	3,125	27	168.2
Dave Dickenson, Montana	1993	11	390	262	9	.672	3,640	32	168.0
Willie Totten, Mississippi Val.	†1983	9	279	174	9	.624	2,566	29	167.5
Lonnie Galloway, Western Caro.	1992	11	211	128	12	.607	2,181	20	167.4
Eriq Williams, James Madison	1991	11	192	107	7	.557	1,914	19	164.8
Willie Totten, Mississippi Val.	†1984	10	*518	*324	22	.626	*4,557	*56	163.6
Jeff Wiley, Holy Cross	†1987	11	400	265	17	.663	3,677	34	163.0
Todd Hammel, Stephen F. Austin	†1989	11	401	238	13	.594	3,914	34	162.8
Mike Williams, Grambling	†1980	11	239	127	5	.531	2,116	28	162.0
Dan Crowley, Towson St.	1993	10	217	125	4	.576	1,882	23	161.7
John Friesz, Idaho	1989	11	425	260	8	.612	4,041	31	161.4
Wendal Lowrey, Northeast La.	1992	11	227	147	9	.648	2,190	16	161.1
Donny Simmons, Western Ill.	1992	11	281	182	11	.648	2,496	25	160.9
David Charpia, Furman	1983	9	155	99	4	.635	1,419	12	160.1
Joe Aliotti, Boise St.	†1979	11	219	144	7	.658	1,870	19	159.9
Gilbert Renfroe, Tennessee St.	1984	11	165	95	5	.576	1,458	17	159.7
Mike Buck, Maine	1989	11	264	170	3	.644	2,315	19	159.5
Bobby Lamb, Furman	1984	11	191	106	7	.555	1,781	19	159.3
Kenneth Biggles, Tennessee St.	1984	11	258	157	7	.609	2,242	24	159.1
Michael Payton, Marshall	1992	11	313	200	11	.639	2,788	26	159.1

*Record. †National champion.

CAREER YARDS

Player, Team	Years	Att.	Cmp.	Int.	Pct.	Yards	TD
Neil Lomax, Portland St.	1977-80	*1,606	*938	55	.584	*13,220	106
Willie Totten, Mississippi Val.	1982-85	1,555	907	*75	.583	12,711	*139
Jamie Martin, Weber St.	1989-92	1,544	934	56	.605	12,207	87
Doug Nussmeier, Idaho	1990-93	1,225	746	32	.609	10,824	91
John Friesz, Idaho	1986-89	1,350	801	40	.593	10,697	77
Greg Wyatt, Northern Ariz.	1986-89	1,510	926	49	.613	10,697	70
Sean Payton, Eastern Ill.	1983-86	1,408	756	55	.537	10,655	87
Jeff Wiley, Holy Cross	1985-88	1,208	723	63	.599	9,698	71
¢Steve McNair, Alcorn St.	1991-93	1,150	625	41	.543	9,633	75
Robbie Justino, Liberty	1989-92	1,267	769	51	.607	9,548	64
Kirk Schulz, Villanova	1986-89	1,297	774	70	.597	9,305	70
Ken Hobart, Idaho	1980-83	1,219	629	42	.516	9,300	79
Matt DeGennaro, Connecticut	1987-90	1,319	803	49	.609	9,288	73
Marty Horn, Lehigh	1982-85	1,390	744	64	.535	9,120	62
Jason Whitmer, Idaho St.	1987-90	1,349	721	53	.534	9,081	55
Chris Swartz, Morehead St.	1987-90	1,408	774	47	.550	9,027	56
Michael Proctor, Murray St.	1986-89	1,148	578	45	.503	8,682	52
Eric Beavers, Nevada	1983-86	1,094	646	37	.590	8,626	77
Tom Ciaccio, Holy Cross	1988-91	1,073	658	46	.613	8,603	72
Steve Calabria, Colgate	1981-84	1,143	626	68	.548	8,555	54
Mike Buck, Maine	1986-89	1,102	619	39	.562	8,491	67
Jeff Cesarone, Western Ky.	1984-87	1,339	714	39	.533	8,404	45
Frank Baur, Lafayette	1985, 87-89	1,103	636	46	.577	8,399	62
Fred Gatlin, Nevada	%1989-92	1,116	613	46	.549	8,312	63
Stan Yagiello, William & Mary	$1981-85	1,247	737	36	.591	8,249	51
Mike Smith, Northern Iowa	1984-87	943	557	43	.591	8,219	58
Kelly Bradley, Montana St.	1983-86	1,238	714	45	.577	8,152	60
Bob Bleier, Richmond	1983-86	1,169	672	56	.575	8,057	54
John Gregory, Marshall	$#1985, 86-89	1,074	552	45	.513	7,896	59
Chris Goetz, Towson St.	1987-90	1,172	648	51	.553	7,882	42
Paul Singer, Western Ill.	1985-88	1,171	646	43	.552	7,850	61
John Witkowski, Columbia	1981-83	1,176	613	60	.521	7,849	56
Grady Bennett, Montana	1987-90	1,097	641	42	.584	7,778	55
Bernard Hawk, Bethune-Cookman	1982-85	1,120	554	51	.495	7,737	56
Bob Jean, New Hampshire	1985-88	1,126	567	49	.504	7,704	51

*Record. $See page 6 for explanation. #At Southeastern La. in 1985. ¢Active player. %Played 1992 season in Division I-A.

Alcorn State's Steve McNair has passed for 9,633 yards and 75 touchdowns during his career with the Braves.

Weber State's Jamie Martin set the division's single-game passing record with 624 yards against Idaho State in 1991.

CAREER YARDS PER GAME
(Minimum 5,000 Yards)

Player, Team	Years	G	Att.	Cmp.	Yards	TD	Yd.PG
Willie Totten, Mississippi Val.	1982-85	40	1,555	907	12,711	*139	*317.8
Neil Lomax, Portland St.	1977-80	42	*1,606	*938	*13,220	106	314.8
John Friesz, Idaho	1986-89	35	1,350	801	10,697	77	305.6
Jamie Martin, Weber St.	1989-92	41	1,544	934	12,207	87	297.7
Sean Payton, Eastern Ill.	1983-86	37	1,408	756	10,655	75	288.0
Doug Nussmeier, Idaho	1990-93	39	1,225	746	10,824	91	277.5
Scott Semptimphelter, Lehigh	1990-93	26	823	493	6,668	50	256.5
Greg Wyatt, Northern Ariz.	1986-89	42	1,510	926	10,697	70	254.7

*Record.

CAREER TOUCHDOWN PASSES

Player, Team	Years	G	TD Passes
Willie Totten, Mississippi Val.	1982-85	40	*139
Neil Lomax, Portland St.	1977-80	42	106
Doug Nussmeier, Idaho	1990-93	39	91
Jamie Martin, Weber St.	1989-92	41	87
Ken Hobart, Idaho	1980-83	44	79
John Friesz, Idaho	1986-89	35	77
Eric Beavers, Nevada	1983-86	40	77
¢Steve McNair, Alcorn St.	1991-93	31	75
Sean Payton, Eastern Ill.	1983-86	39	75
Matt DeGennaro, Connecticut	1987-90	43	73
Tom Ciaccio, Holy Cross	1988-91	37	72
Jeff Wiley, Holy Cross	1985-88	41	71
Kirk Schulz, Villanova	1986-89	42	70
Greg Wyatt, Northern Ariz.	1986-89	42	70

*Record. ¢Active player.

Special Note: *Tom Ehrhardt played two years at LIU-C. W. Post (Division II) and two years at Rhode Island (Division I-AA) and totaled 92 career touchdown passes. For I-AA, he totaled 66.*

SEASON YARDS

Player, Team	Year	G	Att.	Cmp.	Int.	Pct.	Yards	TD
Willie Totten, Mississippi Val.	†1984	10	*518	*324	22	.626	*4,557	*56
Jamie Martin, Weber St.	1991	11	500	310	17	.620	4,125	35
Neil Lomax, Portland St.	1980	11	473	296	12	.626	4,094	37
John Friesz, Idaho	1989	11	425	260	8	.612	4,041	31
Neil Lomax, Portland St.	1979	11	516	299	16	.579	3,950	26
Todd Hammel, Stephen F. Austin	†1989	11	401	238	13	.594	3,914	34
Sean Payton, Eastern Ill.	1984	11	473	270	15	.571	3,843	28
Jamie Martin, Weber St.	1990	11	428	256	15	.598	3,700	23
Willie Totten, Mississippi Val.	1985	11	492	295	29	.600	3,698	39
Jeff Wiley, Holy Cross	†1987	11	400	265	17	.663	3,677	34
John Friesz, Idaho	1987	11	502	311	14	.620	3,677	28
Dave Dickenson, Montana	1993	11	390	262	9	.672	3,640	32
Ken Hobart, Idaho	1983	11	477	268	19	.562	3,618	32
Glenn Kempa, Lehigh	1991	11	474	286	15	.603	3,565	31
Tom Ehrhardt, Rhode Island	1985	10	497	283	19	.569	3,542	35
Steve McNair, Alcorn St.	1992	10	427	231	11	.541	3,541	29
Tony Petersen, Marshall	1987	11	466	251	25	.539	3,529	22
Todd Brunner, Lehigh	1989	11	450	273	19	.607	3,516	26
Kelly Bradley, Montana St.	1984	11	499	289	20	.579	3,508	30
Neil Lomax, Portland St.	†1978	11	436	241	22	.553	3,506	25

*Record. †National pass-efficiency champion.

SEASON YARDS PER GAME

Player, Team	Year	G	Att.	Cmp.	Int.	Pct.	Yards	TD	Yd.PG
Willie Totten, Mississippi Val.	†1984	10	*518	*324	22	.626	*4,557	*56	*455.7
Jamie Martin, Weber St.	1991	11	500	310	17	.620	4,125	35	375.0
Neil Lomax, Portland St.	1980	11	473	296	12	.626	4,094	37	372.2
John Friesz, Idaho	1989	11	425	260	8	.612	4,041	31	367.4
Neil Lomax, Portland St.	1979	11	516	299	16	.579	3,950	26	359.1
Todd Hammel, Stephen F. Austin	†1989	11	401	238	13	.594	3,914	34	355.8
Tom Ehrhardt, Rhode Island	1985	10	497	283	19	.569	3,542	35	354.2
Steve McNair, Alcorn St.	1992	10	427	231	11	.541	3,541	29	354.1
Sean Payton, Eastern Ill.	1984	11	473	270	15	.571	3,843	28	349.4
Tom Proudian, Iona	1993	10	440	262	13	.595	3,368	29	336.8
Jamie Martin, Weber St.	1990	11	428	256	15	.598	3,700	23	336.4
Willie Totten, Mississippi Val.	1985	11	492	295	29	.600	3,698	39	336.2

*Record. †National pass-efficiency champion.

SEASON TOUCHDOWN PASSES

Player, Team	Year	G	TD Passes
Willie Totten, Mississippi Val.	1984	10	*56
Willie Totten, Mississippi Val.	1985	11	39
Neil Lomax, Portland St.	1980	11	37
Jamie Martin, Weber St.	1991	11	35
Tom Ehrhardt, Rhode Island	1985	10	35

Player, Team	Year	G	TD Passes
Todd Hammel, Stephen F. Austin	1989	11	34
Jeff Wiley, Holy Cross	1987	11	34
Doug Nussmeier, Idaho	1993	11	33
Dave Dickenson, Montana	1993	11	32
Doug Hudson, Nicholls St.	1986	11	32
Ken Hobart, Idaho	1983	11	32
Glenn Kempa, Lehigh	1991	11	31
John Friesz, Idaho	1989	11	31
Scott Semptimphelter, Lehigh	1993	11	30
Brent Pease, Montana	1986	11	30
Kelly Bradley, Montana St.	1984	11	30

*Record.

Rick Haye photo

Marshall's Michael Payton finished the 1991 season as the division's top-rated quarterback in passing efficiency.

SINGLE-GAME YARDS

Yds.	Player, Team (Opponent)	Date
624	Jamie Martin, Weber St. (Idaho St.)	Nov. 23, 1991
619	Doug Pederson, Northeast La. (Stephen F. Austin)	Nov. 11, 1989
599	Willie Totten, Mississippi Val. (Prairie View)	Oct. 27, 1984
589	Vern Harris, Idaho St. (Montana)	Oct. 12, 1985
571	Todd Hammel, Stephen F. Austin (Northeast La.)	Nov. 11, 1989
566	Tom Ehrhardt, Rhode Island (Connecticut)	Nov. 16, 1985
553	Willie Totten, Mississippi Val. (Southern-B.R.)	Sept. 29, 1984
547	Jamie Martin, Weber St. (Montana St.)	Sept. 26, 1992
545	Willie Totten, Mississippi Val. (Grambling)	Oct. 13, 1984
540	Brad Otten, Weber St. (Northern Ariz.)	Nov. 6, 1993
537	Tod Mayfield, West Tex. A&M (New Mexico St.)	Nov. 16, 1985
536	Willie Totten, Mississippi Val. (Kentucky St.)	Sept. 1, 1984
534	Todd Hammel, Stephen F. Austin (Sam Houston St.)	Nov. 4, 1989
527	Bernard Hawk, Bethune-Cookman (Ga. Southern)	Oct. 6, 1984
527	Ken Hobart, Idaho (Southern Colo.)	Sept. 1, 1983
526	Willie Totten, Mississippi Val. (Jackson St.)	Sept. 22, 1984

SINGLE-GAME ATTEMPTS

No.	Player, Team (Opponent)	Date
77	Neil Lomax, Portland St. (Northern Colo.)	Oct. 20, 1979
74	Paul Peterson, Idaho St. (Nevada)	Oct. 1, 1983
71	Doug Pederson, Northeast La. (Stephen F. Austin)	Nov. 11, 1989
70	Greg Farland, Rhode Island (Boston U.)	Oct. 18, 1986
69	Steve McNair, Alcorn St. (Jacksonville St.)	Oct. 31, 1992
68	Tony Petersen, Marshall (Western Caro.)	Nov. 14, 1987
67	Michael Payton, Marshall (Western Caro.)	Oct. 31, 1992
67	Vern Harris, Idaho St. (Montana)	Oct. 12, 1985
67	Rick Worman, Eastern Wash. (Nevada)	Oct. 12, 1985
67	Tod Mayfield, West Tex. A&M (Indiana St.)	Oct. 5, 1985
67	Tom Ehrhardt, Rhode Island (Brown)	Sept. 28, 1985
66	Chris Swartz, Morehead St. (Tennessee Tech)	Oct. 17, 1987
66	Sean Cook, Texas Southern (Tex. A&M-Kingsville)	Sept. 6, 1986
66	Kelly Bradley, Montana St. (Eastern Wash.)	Sept. 21, 1985
66	Bernard Hawk, Bethune-Cookman (Ga. Southern)	Oct. 6, 1984
66	Willie Totten, Mississippi Val. (Southern-B.R.)	Sept. 29, 1984
66	Paul Peterson, Idaho St. (Cal Poly SLO)	Oct. 22, 1983

SINGLE-GAME COMPLETIONS

No.	Player, Team (Opponent)	Date
47	Jamie Martin, Weber St. (Idaho St.)	Nov. 23, 1991
46	Doug Pederson, Northeast La. (Stephen F. Austin)	Nov. 11, 1989
46	Willie Totten, Mississippi Val. (Southern-B.R.)	Sept. 29, 1984
45	Willie Totten, Mississippi Val. (Prairie View)	Oct. 27, 1984
44	Neil Lomax, Portland St. (Northern Colo.)	Oct. 20, 1979
42	Tod Mayfield, West Tex. A&M (Indiana St.)	Oct. 5, 1985
42	Kelly Bradley, Montana St. (Eastern Wash.)	Sept. 21, 1985
42	Rusty Hill, North Texas (Tulsa)	Nov. 20, 1982

ANNUAL CHAMPIONS

Year	Player, Team	Class	G	Att.	Cmp.	Avg.	Int.	Pct.	Yds.	TD
1978	Neil Lomax, Portland St.	So.	11	436	241	21.9	22	.553	3,506	25

Beginning in 1979, ranked on passing efficiency rating points (instead of per-game completions)

Year	Player, Team	Class	G	Att.	Cmp.	Int.	Pct.	Yds.	TD	Pts.
1979	Joe Aliotti, Boise St.	Jr.	11	219	144	7	.658	1,870	19	159.7
1980	Mike Williams, Grambling	Sr.	11	239	127	5	.531	2,116	28	162.0
1981	Mike Machurek, Idaho St.	Sr.	9	313	188	11	.601	2,752	22	150.1
1982	Frank Novak, Lafayette	Jr.	10	257	154	12	.599	2,257	20	150.0
1983	Willie Totten, Mississippi Val.	So.	9	279	174	9	.624	2,566	29	167.5
1984	Willie Totten, Mississippi Val.	Jr.	10	*518	*324	22	.626	*4,557	*56	163.6
1985	Bobby Lamb, Furman	Sr.	11	181	106	6	.586	1,856	18	170.9
1986	Mike Smith, Northern Iowa	Jr.	11	303	190	16	.627	3,125	27	168.2
1987	Jeff Wiley, Holy Cross	Jr.	11	400	265	17	.663	3,677	34	163.0
1988	Frank Baur, Lafayette	Jr.	10	256	164	11	.641	2,621	23	171.1
1989	Todd Hammel, Stephen F. Austin	Sr.	11	401	238	13	.594	3,914	34	162.8
1990	Connell Maynor, North Caro. A&T	Jr.	11	191	123	10	.644	1,699	16	156.3
1991	Michael Payton, Marshall	Jr.	9	216	143	5	.662	2,333	19	181.3
1992	Jay Fiedler, Dartmouth	Jr.	10	273	175	13	.641	2,748	25	169.4
1993	Shawn Knight, William & Mary	Jr.	10	177	125	4	.706	2,055	22	*204.6

*Record.

DIVISION I-AA

Receiving

CAREER CATCHES PER GAME
(Minimum 20 Games)

Player, Team	Years	G	Rec.	Yards	TD	Rec.PG
Jerry Rice, Mississippi Val.	1981-84	41	*301	*4,693	*50	*7.3
Kevin Guthrie, Princeton	1981-83	28	193	2,645	16	6.9
Eric Yarber, Idaho	1984-85	19	129	1,920	17	6.8
Brian Forster, Rhode Island (TE)	1983-85, 87	38	245	3,410	31	6.5
Kasey Dunn, Idaho	1988-91	42	268	3,847	25	6.4
Gordie Lockbaum, Holy Cross (RB)	‡1986-87	22	135	2,012	17	6.1
Derek Graham, Princeton	1981, 83-84	29	176	2,819	19	6.1
Stuart Gaussoin, Portland St.	1978-80	23	135	1,909	14	5.9
Don Lewis, Columbia	1981-83	30	176	2,207	11	5.9
Mike Barber, Marshall	1985-88	36	209	3,250	20	5.8
Sebastian Brown, Bethune-Cookman	1984-85	20	116	1,830	17	5.8
Rennie Benn, Lehigh	1982-85	41	237	3,662	44	5.8
Daren Altieri, Boston U.	1987-90	39	225	2,518	15	5.8
Bill Reggio, Columbia	1981-83	30	170	2,384	26	5.7

*Record. ‡Defensive back in 1984-85.

SEASON CATCHES PER GAME

Player, Team	Year	G	Rec.	Yards	TD	Rec.PG
Brian Forster, Rhode Island (TE)	†1985	10	*115	1,617	12	*11.5
Jerry Rice, Mississippi Val.	1984	10	103	*1,682	*27	10.3
Jerry Rice, Mississippi Val.	1983	10	102	1,450	14	10.2
Stuart Gaussoin, Portland St.	†1979	9	90	1,132	8	10.0
Kevin Guthrie, Princeton	1983	10	88	1,259	9	8.8
Alfred Pupunu, Weber St. (TE)	†1991	11	93	1,204	12	8.5
Derek Graham, Princeton	1983	10	84	1,363	11	8.4
Don Lewis, Columbia	†1982	10	84	1,000	6	8.4
Peter Macon, Weber St.	†1989	11	92	1,047	6	8.4
Marvin Walker, North Texas	1982	11	91	934	11	8.3

*Record. †National champion.

CAREER CATCHES

Player, Team	Years	Rec.	Yards	Avg.	TD
Jerry Rice, Mississippi Val.	1981-84	*301	*4,693	15.6	*50
Kasey Dunn, Idaho	1988-91	268	3,847	14.4	25
Brian Forster, Rhode Island	1983-85, 87	245	3,410	13.9	31
Mark Didio, Connecticut	1988-91	239	3,535	14.8	21
Rennie Benn, Lehigh	1982-85	237	3,662	15.5	44
Daren Altieri, Boston U.	1987-90	225	2,518	11.2	15
Darrell Colbert, Texas Southern	1983-86	217	3,177	14.6	33
Mike Barber, Marshall	1985-88	209	3,520	16.8	20
Trevor Shaw, Weber St.	1989-90, 92-93	206	2,383	11.6	17
William Brooks, Boston U.	1982-85	204	3,154	15.5	26
Donald Narcisse, Texas Southern	1983-86	203	2,429	12.0	26
Alex Davis, Connecticut	1989-92	202	2,567	12.7	24
Shawn Collins, Northern Ariz.	1985-88	201	2,764	13.8	24
Leland Melvin, Richmond	1982-85	198	2,669	13.5	16
Mike Wilson, Boise St.	1990-93	196	3,017	15.4	13
Curtis Olds, New Hampshire	1985-88	193	3,028	15.7	23
Kevin Guthrie, Princeton	1981-83	193	2,645	13.7	16
Sergio Hebra, Maine	1984-87	189	2,612	13.8	17
John Perry, New Hampshire	1989-92	186	2,798	15.0	19
Glenn Antrum, Connecticut	1985-88	186	2,552	13.7	14
Joe Thomas, Mississippi Val.	1982-85	186	2,816	15.1	36
Gary Harrell, Howard	1990-93	184	2,619	14.2	19
Roy Banks, Eastern Ill.	1983-86	184	3,177	17.3	38
Merril Hoge, Idaho St. (RB)	1983-86	182	1,734	9.5	13
George Delaney, Colgate	1988-91	181	2,938	16.2	25
Robert Brady, Villanova	1986-89	180	2,725	15.1	28
Cisco Richard, Northeast La.	1987-90	179	1,874	10.5	12
David Gamble, New Hampshire	1990-93	178	2,990	16.8	23

*Record.

SEASON CATCHES

Player, Team	Year	G	Rec.	Yards	TD
Brian Forster, Rhode Island (TE)	†1985	10	*115	1,617	12
Jerry Rice, Mississippi Val.	†1984	10	103	*1,682	*27
Jerry Rice, Mississippi Val.	†1983	10	102	1,450	14
Alfred Pupunu, Weber St. (TE)	†1991	11	93	1,204	12
Peter Macon, Weber St.	†1989	11	92	1,047	6
Marvin Walker, North Texas	1982	11	91	934	11
Stuart Gaussoin, Portland St.	†1979	9	90	1,132	8
Dave Cecchini, Lehigh	†1993	11	88	1,318	16
Mark Didio, Connecticut	1991	11	88	1,354	8
Kasey Dunn, Idaho	†1990	11	88	1,164	7
Donald Narcisse, Texas Southern	†1986	11	88	1,074	15
Kevin Guthrie, Princeton	1983	10	88	1,259	9
Kasey Dunn, Idaho	1991	11	85	1,263	6
Derek Graham, Princeton	1983	10	84	1,363	11
Don Lewis, Columbia	†1982	10	84	1,000	6

*Record. †National champion.

SINGLE-GAME CATCHES

No.	Player, Team (Opponent)	Date
24	Jerry Rice, Mississippi Val. (Southern-B.R.)	Oct. 1, 1983
22	Marvin Walker, North Texas (Tulsa)	Nov. 20, 1982
21	David Pandt, Montana St. (Eastern Wash.)	Sept. 21, 1985
18	Jerome Williams, Morehead St. (Eastern Ky.)	Nov. 18, 1989
18	Brian Forster, Rhode Island (Brown)	Sept. 28, 1985
17	Elliot Miller, St. Francis, Pa. (Central Conn. St.)	Oct. 2, 1993
17	Lifford Jackson, Louisiana Tech (Kansas St.)	Oct. 1, 1988
17	Brian Forster, Rhode Island (Lehigh)	Oct. 12, 1985
17	Jerry Rice, Mississippi Val. (Southern-B.R.)	Sept. 29, 1984
17	Jerry Rice, Mississippi Val. (Kentucky St.)	Sept. 1, 1984

CAREER YARDS

Player, Team	Years	Rec.	Yards	Avg.	TD
Jerry Rice, Mississippi Val.	1981-84	*301	*4,693	15.6	*50
Kasey Dunn, Idaho	1988-91	268	3,847	14.4	25
Rennie Benn, Lehigh	1982-85	237	3,662	15.5	44
Mark Didio, Connecticut	1988-91	239	3,535	14.8	21
Mike Barber, Marshall	1985-88	209	3,520	16.8	20
Brian Forster, Rhode Island (TE)	1983-85, 87	245	3,410	13.9	31
Tracy Singleton, Howard	1979-82	159	3,187	‡20.0	16
Roy Banks, Eastern Ill.	1983-86	184	3,177	17.3	38
Darrell Colbert, Texas Southern	1983-86	217	3,177	14.6	33
William Brooks, Boston U.	1982-85	204	3,154	15.5	26

*Record. ‡Record for minimum of 125 catches.

CAREER YARDS PER GAME
(Minimum 20 Games)

Player, Team	Years	G	Yards	Yds.PG
Jerry Rice, Mississippi Val.	1981-84	41	*4,693	*114.5
Derek Graham, Princeton	1981, 83-84	29	2,819	97.2
Kevin Guthrie, Princeton	1981-83	28	2,645	94.5
Tracy Singleton, Howard	1979-82	34	3,187	93.7
Kasey Dunn, Idaho	1988-91	42	3,847	91.6
Sebastian Brown, Bethune-Cookman	1984-85	20	1,830	91.5
Gordie Lockbaum, Holy Cross	‡1986-87	22	2,012	91.5
Bryan Calder, Nevada	1984-86	28	2,559	91.4
Mike Barber, Marshall	1985-88	36	3,250	90.3
Brian Forster, Rhode Island	1983-85, 87	38	3,410	89.7

*Record. ‡Defensive back in 1984-85.

SEASON YARDS

Player, Team	Year	Rec.	Yards	Avg.	TD
Jerry Rice, Mississippi Val.	†1984	103	*1,682	16.3	*27
Brian Forster, Rhode Island	†1985	*115	1,617	14.1	12
Jerry Rice, Mississippi Val.	†1983	102	1,450	14.2	14
Derek Graham, Princeton	1983	84	1,363	16.2	11
Mark Didio, Connecticut	†1991	88	1,354	15.4	8
Dave Cecchini, Lehigh	†1993	88	1,318	15.0	16
Golden Tate, Tennessee St.	1983	63	1,307	20.7	13

*Record. †National champion.

SINGLE-GAME YARDS

Yds.	Player, Team (Opponent)	Date
370	Michael Lerch, Princeton (Brown)	Oct. 12, 1991
330	Nate Singleton, Grambling (Virginia Union)	Sept. 14, 1991
327	Brian Forster, Rhode Island (Brown)	Sept. 28, 1985
319	Jason Cristino, Lehigh (Lafayette)	Nov. 21, 1992
299	Treamelle Taylor, Nevada (Montana)	Oct. 14, 1989
299	Brian Forster, Rhode Island (Lehigh)	Oct. 12, 1985
294	Jerry Rice, Mississippi Val. (Kentucky St.)	Sept. 1, 1984
285	Jerry Rice, Mississippi Val. (Jackson St.)	Sept. 22, 1984
279	Jerry Rice, Mississippi Val. (Southern-B.R.)	Oct. 1, 1983
266	Rennie Benn, Lehigh (Indiana, Pa.)	Sept. 14, 1985
263	Mark Stock, Va. Military (East Tenn. St.)	Nov. 22, 1986
262	Andre Motley, Marshall (Tenn.-Chatt.)	Oct. 20, 1990
262	Kenneth Gilstrap, Tennessee Tech (Morehead St.)	Oct. 17, 1987
253	Chris Johnson, Indiana St. (Illinois St.)	Oct. 18, 1986
252	Jeff Sanders, William & Mary (Miami, Ohio)	Sept. 11, 1982
251	Lifford Jackson, Louisiana Tech (Kansas St.)	Oct. 1, 1988

ANNUAL CHAMPIONS

Year	Player, Team	Class	G	Rec.	Avg.	Yards	TD
1978	Dan Ross, Northeastern	Sr.	11	68	6.2	988	7
1979	Stuart Gaussoin, Portland St.	Jr.	9	90	10.0	1,132	8
1980	Kenny Johnson, Portland St.	So.	11	72	6.5	1,011	11
1981	Ken Harvey, Northern Iowa	Sr.	11	78	7.1	1,161	15
1982	Don Lewis, Columbia	Jr.	10	84	8.4	1,000	6
1983	Jerry Rice, Mississippi Val.	Jr.	10	102	10.2	1,450	14
1984	Jerry Rice, Mississippi Val.	Sr.	10	103	10.3	*1,682	*27
1985	Brian Forster, Rhode Island (TE)	Jr.	10	*115	*11.5	1,617	12
1986	Donald Narcisse, Texas Southern	Sr.	11	88	8.0	1,074	15
1987	Mike Barber, Marshall	Jr.	11	78	7.1	1,237	7
	Gordie Lockbaum, Holy Cross (RB)	Sr.	11	78	7.1	1,152	9
1988	Glenn Antrum, Connecticut	Sr.	11	77	7.0	1,130	7
1989	Peter Macon, Weber St.	Sr.	11	92	8.4	1,047	6

Beginning in 1990, ranked on both per-game catches and yards per game.

PER-GAME CATCHES

Year	Player, Team	Class	G	Rec.	Avg.	Yards	TD
1990	Kasey Dunn, Idaho	Jr.	11	88	8.0	1,164	7
1991	Alfred Pupunu, Weber St. (TE)	Sr.	11	93	8.5	1,204	12
1992	Glenn Krupa, Southeast Mo. St.	Sr.	11	77	7.0	773	4
1993	Dave Cecchini, Lehigh	Sr.	11	88	8.0	1,318	16

YARDS PER GAME

Year	Player, Team	Class	G	Rec.	Yards	Avg.	TD
1990	Kasey Dunn, Idaho	Jr.	11	88	1,164	105.8	7
1991	Mark Didio, Connecticut	Sr.	11	88	1,354	123.1	8
1992	Jason Cristino, Lehigh	Sr.	11	65	1,282	116.5	9
1993	Dave Cecchini, Lehigh	Sr.	11	88	1,318	119.8	16

*Record.

Scoring

CAREER POINTS PER GAME§
(Minimum 19 Games)

Player, Team	Years	G	TD	XPt.	FG	Pts.	Pt.PG
Keith Elias, Princeton	1991-93	30	52	8	0	320	*10.7
Elroy Harris, Eastern Ky.	1985, 87-88	31	47	6	0	288	9.3
Tony Zendejas, Nevada	1981-83	33	0	90	70	300	9.1
Gerald Harris, Ga. Southern	1984-86	31	45	2	0	272	8.8
Marty Zendejas, Nevada	1984-87	44	0	*169	*72	*385	8.8
Charvez Foger, Nevada	1985-88	42	*60	2	0	362	8.6
Paul Lewis, Boston U.	1981-84	37	51	2	0	308	8.3
Judd Garrett, Princeton	1987-89	30	41	1	0	248	8.3
Andre Garron, New Hampshire	1982-85	30	41	0	0	246	8.2
Micky Penaflor, Northern Ariz.	1986-88	22	0	66	38	180	8.2
Kenny Gamble, Colgate	1984-87	42	57	0	0	342	8.1
Barry Bourassa, New Hampshire	1989-92	39	51	0	0	306	7.8
Markus Thomas, Eastern Ky.	1989-92	43	53	4	0	322	7.5
Jerry Rice, Mississippi Val.	1981-84	41	50	2	0	302	7.4
Joel Sigel, Portland St.	1977-80	41	50	2	0	302	7.4
Brian Mitchell, Marshall/ Northern Iowa	1987, 89-91	44	0	130	64	322	7.3
George Benyola, Louisiana Tech	1984-85	22	0	40	40	160	7.3
Roberto Moran, Boise St.	1985-86	22	0	57	34	159	7.2
Harvey Reed, Howard	1984-87	41	48	6	0	294	7.2
Thayne Doyle, Idaho	1988-91	43	0	160	49	307	7.1
Dwight Stone, Middle Tenn. St.	1985-86	22	26	0	0	156	7.1
Stanford Jennings, Furman	1982-83	22	26	0	0	156	7.1
Rich Erenberg, Colgate	1982-83	21	23	10	0	148	7.0

*Record. §The following players competed two years in Division I-AA and two years in Division I-A: Stanford Jennings, Furman (four years: 262 points and 6.1 average); Rich Erenberg, Colgate (four years: 202 points and 5.2 average), and Buford Jordan, McNeese St. (four years: 266 points and 6.5 average).

SEASON POINTS PER GAME

Player, Team	Year	G	TD	XPt.	FG	Pts.	Pt.PG
Jerry Rice, Mississippi Val.	†1984	10	27	0	0	162	*16.2
Geoff Mitchell, Weber St.	†1991	11	*28	1	0	*170	15.5
Tony Vinson, Towson St.	†1993	10	24	0	0	144	14.4
Sherriden May, Idaho	†1992	11	25	0	0	150	13.6
Keith Elias, Princeton	1993	10	21	4	0	130	13.0
Elroy Harris, Eastern Ky.	†1988	10	21	2	0	128	12.8
Sean Sanders, Weber St.	†1987	10	21	0	0	126	12.6
Rich Erenberg, Colgate	†1983	11	21	10	0	136	12.4
Harvey Reed, Howard	1987	10	20	2	0	122	12.2
Paul Lewis, Boston U.	1983	10	20	2	0	122	12.2
Sherriden May, Idaho	1993	11	22	0	0	132	12.0
Gordie Lockbaum, Holy Cross	1987	11	22	0	0	132	12.0
Gordie Lockbaum, Holy Cross	†1986	11	22	0	0	132	12.0
Gene Lake, Delaware St.	1984	10	20	0	0	120	12.0
Ernest Thompson, Ga. Southern	1988	10	19	2	0	116	11.6
Barry Bourassa, New Hampshire	1991	11	21	0	0	126	11.5
Kenny Gamble, Colgate	1986	11	21	0	0	126	11.5
Gerald Harris, Ga. Southern	1984	9	17	0	0	102	11.3
Richard Howell, Davidson	1993	10	18	2	0	110	11.0
Keith Elias, Princeton	1992	10	18	2	0	110	11.0
Harvey Reed, Howard	1986	10	18	2	0	110	11.0
Rupert Grant, Howard	1993	11	20	0	0	120	10.9
Toby Davis, Illinois St.	1992	11	20	0	0	120	10.9
Carl Smith, Maine	†1989	11	20	0	0	120	10.9
Joe Segreti, Holy Cross	1988	11	20	0	0	120	10.9
Luther Turner, Sam Houston St.	1987	11	20	0	0	120	10.9
John Settle, Appalachian St.	1986	11	20	0	0	120	10.9

*Record. †National champion.

CAREER POINTS
(Non-Kickers)

Player, Team	Years	TD	XPt.	Pts.
Charvez Foger, Nevada	1985-88	*60	2	362
Kenny Gamble, Colgate	1984-87	57	0	342
Markus Thomas, Eastern Ky.	1989-92	53	4	322
Keith Elias, Princeton	1991-93	52	8	320
Paul Lewis, Boston U.	1981-84	51	2	308
Barry Bourassa, New Hampshire	1989-92	51	0	306
Erick Torain, Lehigh	1987-90	50	6	306
Jerry Rice, Mississippi Val.	1981-84	50	2	302
Joel Sigel, Portland St.	1977-80	50	2	302
¢Sherriden May, Idaho	1991-93	49	0	294
Harvey Reed, Howard	1984-87	48	6	294
Jack Douglas, Citadel (QB)	1989-92	48	0	288
Elroy Harris, Eastern Ky.	1985, 87-88	47	6	288
Joe Campbell, Middle Tenn. St.	1988-91	45	2	272
Gerald Harris, Ga. Southern	1984-86	45	2	272
Carl Tremble, Furman	1989-92	45	0	270
Norm Ford, New Hampshire	1986-89	45	0	270
John Settle, Appalachian St.	1983-86	44	4	268
Ernest Thompson, Ga. Southern	1985, 87-89	44	2	266
Rennie Benn, Lehigh	1982-85	44	2	266
Joe Segreti, Holy Cross	1987-90	44	0	264
Gordie Lockbaum, Holy Cross	1984-87	44	0	264
Frank Hawkins, Nevada	1977-80	44	0	264

*Record. ¢Active player.

CAREER POINTS
(Kickers)

Player, Team	Years	PAT	PAT Att.	FG	FG Att.	Pts.
Marty Zendejas, Nevada	1984-87	*169	*175	*72	90	*385
Brian Mitchell, Marshall/ Northern Iowa	1987, 89-91	130	131	64	81	322
Thayne Doyle, Idaho	1988-91	160	174	49	75	307
Kirk Roach, Western Caro.	1984-87	89	91	71	*102	302
Tim Foley, Ga. Southern	1984-87	151	156	50	62	301
Dewey Klein, Marshall	1988-91	156	165	48	66	300
Tony Zendejas, Nevada	1981-83	90	96	70	86	300
Jeff Wilkins, Youngstown St.	1990-93	134	136	50	73	286
Steve Christie, William & Mary	1986-89	108	116	57	83	279
Franco Grilla, Central Fla.	1989-92	141	147	45	69	278
Mike Black, Boise St.	1988-91	122	127	51	75	275
Kirk Duce, Montana	1988-91	131	141	47	78	272
Paul Hickert, Murray St.	1984-87	116	121	49	79	263
Dean Biasucci, Western Caro.	1980-83	101	106	54	80	263
Matt Stover, Louisiana Tech	#1986-89	70	72	64	88	262
Kelly Potter, Middle Tenn. St.	1981-84	105	109	52	78	261
Billy Hayes, Sam Houston St.	1985-88	117	120	47	71	258
Michael O'Neal, Samford	1989-92	142	152	38	60	256
Jim Hodson, Lafayette	1987-90	134	140	40	66	254
Dave Parkinson, Delaware St.	1985-88	134	143	40	77	254

Player, Team	Years	PAT	PAT Att.	FG	FG Att.	Pts.
Chuck Rawlinson, Stephen F. Austin.....	1988-91	106	110	49	69	253
Paul Politi, Illinois St.	1983-86	101	103	50	78	251
Teddy Garcia, Northeast La.	1984-87	78	81	56	88	246
Paul McFadden, Youngstown St.	1980-83	87	90	52	90	243

Record. #Member of Division I-A 1989 only.

SEASON POINTS

Player, Team	Year	TD	XPt.	FG	Pts.
Geoff Mitchell, Weber St.	†1991	*28	2	0	*170
Jerry Rice, Mississippi Val.	†1984	27	0	0	162
Sherriden May, Idaho	†1992	25	0	0	150
Tony Vinson, Towson St.	†1993	24	0	0	144
Rich Erenberg, Colgate	†1983	21	10	0	136
Sherriden May, Idaho	1993	22	0	0	132
Gordie Lockbaum, Holy Cross.....	1987	22	0	0	132
Gordie Lockbaum, Holy Cross.....	†1986	22	0	0	132
Keith Elias, Princeton	1993	21	4	0	130
Elroy Harris, Eastern Ky.	†1988	21	1	0	128
Barry Bourassa, New Hampshire	1991	21	0	0	126
Sean Sanders, Weber St.	†1987	21	0	0	126
Kenny Gamble, Colgate	1986	21	0	0	126
Harvey Reed, Howard	1987	20	2	0	122
Paul Lewis, Boston U.	1983	20	2	0	122
Rupert Grant, Howard	1993	20	0	0	120
Toby Davis, Illinois St.	1992	20	0	0	120
Carl Smith, Maine	†1989	20	0	0	120
Joe Segreti, Holy Cross	1988	20	0	0	120
Luther Turner, Sam Houston St.	1987	20	0	0	120
John Settle, Appalachian St.....	1986	20	0	0	120
Gene Lake, Delaware St.	1984	20	0	0	120

Record. †National champion.

ANNUAL CHAMPIONS

Year	Player, Team	Class	G	TD	XPt.	FG	Pts.	Avg.
1978	Frank Hawkins, Nevada.....	So.	10	17	0	0	102	10.2
1979	Joel Sigel, Portland St.	Jr.	10	16	0	0	96	9.6
1980	Ken Jenkins, Bucknell.....	Jr.	10	16	0	0	96	9.6
1981	Paris Wicks, Youngstown St.	Jr.	11	17	2	0	104	9.5
1982	Paul Lewis, Boston U.	So.	10	18	0	0	108	10.8
1983	Rich Erenberg, Colgate	Sr.	11	21	10	0	136	12.4
1984	Jerry Rice, Mississippi Val.	Sr.	10	27	0	0	162	*16.2
1985	Charvez Foger, Nevada.....	Fr.	10	18	0	0	108	10.8
1986	Gordie Lockbaum, Holy Cross	Jr.	11	22	0	0	132	12.0
1987	Sean Sanders, Weber St.	Sr.	10	21	0	0	126	12.6
1988	Elroy Harris, Eastern Ky.	Jr.	10	21	1	0	128	12.8
1989	Carl Smith, Maine	So.	11	20	0	0	120	10.9
1990	Barry Bourassa, New Hampshire	So.	9	16	0	0	96	10.7
1991	Geoff Mitchell, Weber St.	Sr.	11	*28	1	0	*170	15.5
1992	Sherriden May, Idaho	So.	11	25	0	0	150	13.6
1993	Tony Vinson, Towson St.	Sr.	10	24	0	0	144	14.4

Record.

Interceptions

CAREER INTERCEPTIONS

Player, Team	Years	No.	Yards	Avg.
Dave Murphy, Holy Cross	1986-89	*28	309	11.0
Cedric Walker, Stephen F. Austin	1990-93	25	230	9.2
Issiac Holt, Alcorn St.	1981-84	24	319	13.3
Bill McGovern, Holy Cross	1981-84	24	168	7.0
Adrion Smith, Southwest Mo. St.	1990-93	23	219	9.5
William Carroll, Florida A&M	1989-92	23	328	14.3
Kevin Smith, Rhode Island	1987-90	23	287	12.5
Mike Prior, Illinois St.	1981-84	23	211	9.2
Morgan Ryan, Montana St.	1990-93	22	245	11.1
Dave Roberts, Youngstown St.	1989-92	22	131	6.0
Frank Robinson, Boise St.	1988-91	22	203	9.2
Dean Cain, Princeton	1985-87	22	203	9.2
Kevin Dent, Jackson St.	1985-88	21	280	13.3
Mark Seals, Boston U.	1985-88	21	169	8.0
Jeff Smith, Illinois St.	1985-88	21	152	7.2
Chris Demarest, Northeastern	1984-87	21	255	12.1
Greg Greely, Nicholls St.	1981-84	21	218	10.4
George Floyd, Eastern Ky.	1978-81	21	318	15.1
Rick Harris, East Tenn. St.	1986-88	20	*452	22.6
Mark Kelso, William & Mary	1981-84	20	171	8.6

Player, Team	Years	No.	Yards	Avg.
Leslie Frazier, Alcorn St.	1977-80	20	269	13.5
Bob Jordan, New Hampshire	1990-93	19	96	5.1
Ricky Thomas, South Caro. St.	1988-91	19	374	19.7
Dwayne Harper, South Caro. St.	1984-87	19	163	8.6
Joe Burton, Delaware St.	1983-86	19	248	13.1
Michael Richardson, Northwestern St.	1981-84	19	344	18.1
Mike Genetti, Northeastern	1980-83	19	296	15.6
George Schmitt, Delaware	1980-82	19	280	14.7

Record.

SEASON INTERCEPTIONS

Player, Team	Year	No.	Yards
Dean Cain, Princeton	†1987	*12	98
Aeneas Williams, Southern-B.R.	‡1990	11	173
Claude Pettaway, Maine	†1990	11	161
Bill McGovern, Holy Cross	†1984	11	102
Everson Walls, Grambling	†1980	11	145
Anthony Young, Jackson St.	†1978	11	108
Chris Helon, Boston U.	†1993	10	42
Cedric Walker, Stephen F. Austin	1990	10	11
Chris Demarest, Northeastern	1987	10	129
Kevin Dent, Jackson St.	‡1986	10	192
Eric Thompson, New Hampshire	†1986	10	94
Anthony Anderson, Grambling	†1986	10	37
Mike Armentrout, Southwest Mo. St.	†1983	10	42
George Schmitt, Delaware	†1982	10	186
Mike Genetti, Northeastern	†1981	10	144
Bob Mahr, Lafayette	1981	10	48
Neale Henderson, Southern-B.R.	†1979	10	151

Record. †National champion. ‡National championship shared.

ANNUAL CHAMPIONS
(Ranked on Per-Game Average)

Year	Player, Team	Class	G	No.	Avg.	Yards
1978	Anthony Young, Jackson St.	Sr.	11	11	1.00	108
1979	Neale Henderson, Southern-B.R.	Sr.	11	10	0.91	151
1980	Everson Walls, Grambling	Sr.	11	11	1.00	145
1981	Mike Genetti, Northeastern	So.	10	10	1.00	144
1982	George Schmitt, Delaware	Sr.	11	10	0.91	186
1983	Mike Armentrout, Southwest Mo. St.	Jr.	11	10	0.91	42
1984	Bill McGovern, Holy Cross	Sr.	11	11	1.00	102
1985	Mike Cassidy, Rhode Island	Sr.	10	9	0.90	169
	George Duarte, Northern Ariz.	Jr.	10	9	0.90	150
1986	Kevin Dent, Jackson St.	So.	11	10	0.91	192
	Eric Thompson, New Hampshire	Sr.	11	10	0.91	94
	Anthony Anderson, Grambling	Sr.	11	10	0.91	37
1987	Dean Cain, Princeton	Sr.	10	*12	*1.20	98
1988	Kevin Smith, Rhode Island	So.	10	9	0.90	94
1989	Mike Babb, Weber St.	Sr.	11	9	0.82	90
1990	Aeneas Williams, Southern-B.R.	Sr.	11	11	1.00	173
	Claude Pettaway, Maine	Sr.	11	11	1.00	161
1991	Warren McIntire, Delaware	Jr.	11	9	0.82	208
1992	Dave Roberts, Youngstown St.	Sr.	11	9	0.82	39
1993	Chris Helon, Boston U.	Jr.	11	10	0.91	42

Record.

Punting

CAREER AVERAGE
(Minimum 150 Punts)

Player, Team	Years	No.	Yards	Long	Avg.
Pumpy Tudors, Tenn.-Chatt.	1989-91	181	8,041	79	*44.4
Case de Bruijn, Idaho St.	1978-81	256	11,184	76	43.7
Terry Belden, Northern Ariz.	1990-93	225	9,760	76	43.4
George Cimadevilla, East Tenn. St.	1983-86	225	9,676	72	43.0
Harold Alexander, Appalachian St.	1989-92	259	11,100	78	42.9
John Christopher, Morehead St.	1979-82	298	12,633	62	42.4
Colin Godfrey, Tennessee St.	1989-92	213	9,012	69	42.3
Russell Griffith, Utah St./Weber St.	1983, 85-86	187	7,908	67	42.3
Bret Wright, Southeastern La.	1981-83	165	6,963	66	42.2
Jeff Kaiser, Idaho St.	1982-84	156	6,571	88	42.1
Greg Davis, Citadel	1983-86	263	11,076	81	42.1
Mark Royals, Appalachian St.	1983-85	223	9,372	67	42.0

Record.

SEASON AVERAGE
(Qualifiers for Championship)

Player, Team	Year	No.	Yards	Avg.
Harold Alexander, Appalachian St.	†1991	64	3,009	*47.0
Terry Belden, Northern Ariz.	†1993	59	2,712	46.0
Case de Bruijn, Idaho St.	†1981	42	1,928	45.9
Colin Godfrey, Tennessee St.	†1990	57	2,614	45.9
Stuart Dodds, Montana St.	†1979	59	2,689	45.6
Pumpy Tudors, Tenn.-Chatt.	1991	53	2,414	45.5
Paul Asbury, Southwest Tex. St.	1990	39	1,749	44.9
Tom Sugg, Idaho	1991	53	2,371	44.7
Mike Rice, Montana	†1985	62	2,771	44.7
Case de Bruijn, Idaho St.	1979	73	3,261	44.7
George Cimadevilla, East Tenn. St.	1985	66	2,948	44.7
Greg Davis, Citadel	†1986	61	2,723	44.6
Pumpy Tudors, Tenn.-Chatt.	1990	63	2,810	44.6
Pat Velarde, Marshall	†1983	64	2,852	44.6
Bart Bradley, Sam Houston St.	1986	44	1,957	44.5
Harold Alexander, Appalachian St.	†1992	55	2,445	44.5
Curtis Moody, Texas Southern	1985	64	2,844	44.4
Terry Belden, Northern Ariz.	1991	43	1,908	44.4
Terry Belden, Northern Ariz.	1992	59	2,614	44.3
Bret Wright, Southeastern La.	1983	66	2,923	44.3
George Cimadevilla, East Tenn. St.	1986	65	2,876	44.2
Case de Bruijn, Idaho St.	†1980	67	2,945	44.0

*Record. †National champion.

ANNUAL CHAMPIONS

Year	Player, Team	Class	No.	Yards	Avg.
1978	Nick Pavich, Nevada	So.	47	1,939	41.3
1979	Stuart Dodds, Montana St.	Sr.	59	2,689	45.6
1980	Case de Bruijn, Idaho St.	Jr.	67	2,945	44.0
1981	Case de Bruijn, Idaho St.	Sr.	42	1,928	45.9
1982	John Christopher, Morehead St.	Sr.	93	4,084	43.9
1983	Pat Velarde, Marshall	Sr.	64	2,852	44.6
1984	Steve Kornegay, Western Caro.	Jr.	49	2,127	43.4
1985	Mike Rice, Montana	Jr.	62	2,771	44.7
1986	Greg Davis, Citadel	Sr.	61	2,723	44.6
1987	Eric Stein, Eastern Wash.	Sr.	74	3,193	43.2
1988	Mike McCabe, Illinois St.	Sr.	69	3,042	44.1
1989	Pumpy Tudors, Tenn.-Chatt.	So.	65	2,817	43.3
1990	Colin Godfrey, Tennessee St.	So.	57	2,614	45.9
1991	Harold Alexander, Appalachian St.	Jr.	64	3,009	*47.0
1992	Harold Alexander, Appalachian St.	Sr.	55	2,445	44.5
1993	Terry Belden, Northern Ariz.	Sr.	59	2,712	46.0

*Record.

Punt Returns

CAREER AVERAGE
(Minimum 1.2 Returns Per Game)

Player, Team	Years	No.	Yards	Avg.
Willie Ware, Mississippi Val.	1982-85	61	1,003	*16.4
Tim Egerton, Delaware St.	1986-89	59	951	16.1
Chris Darrington, Weber St.	1984-86	26	415	16.0
John Armstrong, Richmond	1984-85	31	449	14.5
Kenny Shedd, Northern Iowa	1989-92	79	1,081	13.7
Joe Fuller, Northern Iowa	1982-85	69	888	12.9
Eric Yarber, Idaho	1984-85	32	406	12.7
Troy Brown, Marshall	1991-92	36	455	12.6
Trumaine Johnson, Grambling	1979-82	53	662	12.5
Tony Merriwether, North Texas	1982-83	41	507	12.4
Eric Alden, Idaho St.	1992-93	31	383	12.4
Thaylen Armstead, Grambling	1989-91	44	540	12.3
Barney Bussey, South Caro. St.	1980-83	47	573	12.2
Cornell Johnson, Southern-B.R.	1990-92	40	482	12.1
John Taylor, Delaware St.	1982-85	48	576	12.0

*Record.

SEASON AVERAGE
(Minimum 1.2 Returns Per Game and Qualifiers for Championship)

Player, Team	Year	No.	Yards	Avg.
Tim Egerton, Delaware St.	†1988	16	368	*23.0
Ryan Priest, Lafayette	†1982	12	271	22.6
Craig Hodge, Tennessee St.	†1987	19	398	21.0
John Armstrong, Richmond	†1985	19	391	20.6
Willie Ware, Mississippi Val.	†1984	19	374	19.7
Mark Hurt, Alabama St.	1988	10	185	18.5
Howard Huckaby, Florida A&M	1988	26	478	18.4
Ashley Ambrose, Mississippi Val.	†1991	28	514	18.4
Quincy Miller, South Caro. St.	†1992	17	311	18.3
Barney Bussey, South Caro. St.	†1981	14	255	18.2
Chris Darrington, Weber St.	†1986	16	290	18.1
Willie Ware, Mississippi Val.	1985	31	*561	18.1
Kerry Lawyer, Boise St.	1992	18	325	18.1
Kenny Shedd, Northern Iowa	1992	27	477	17.7
Clarence Alexander, Mississippi Val.	1986	22	380	17.3
Henry Richard, Northeast La.	1989	15	258	17.2
Ray Marshall, St. Peter's	†1993	10	171	17.1
Carl Williams, Texas Southern	1981	16	269	16.8
Jerome Bledsoe, Massachusetts	1988	17	285	16.8

*Record. †National champion.

ANNUAL CHAMPIONS

Year	Player, Team	Class	No.	Yards	Avg.
1978	Ray Smith, Northern Ariz.	Sr.	13	181	13.9
1979	Joseph Markus, Connecticut	Fr.	17	219	12.9
1980	Trumaine Johnson, Grambling	So.	††13	226	17.4
1981	Barney Bussey, South Caro. St.	So.	14	255	18.2
1982	Ryan Priest, Lafayette	Fr.	12	271	22.6
1983	Joe Fuller, Northern Iowa	So.	22	344	15.6
1984	Willie Ware, Mississippi Val.	Jr.	19	374	19.7
1985	John Armstrong, Richmond	Sr.	19	391	20.6
1986	Chris Darrington, Weber St.	Sr.	16	290	18.1
1987	Craig Hodge, Tennessee St.	Sr.	19	398	21.0
1988	Tim Egerton, Delaware St.	Jr.	16	368	*23.0
1989	Henry Richard, Northeast La.	Jr.	15	258	17.2
1990	Gary Harrell, Howard	Fr.	26	417	16.0
1991	Ashley Ambrose, Mississippi Val.	Sr.	28	514	18.4
1992	Quincy Miller, South Caro. St.	Jr.	17	311	18.3
1993	Ray Marshall, St. Peter's	Jr.	10	171	17.1

*Record. ††Declared champion; with one more return (making 1.3 per game) for zero yards, still would have highest average.

Kickoff Returns

CAREER AVERAGE
(Minimum 1.2 Returns Per Game)

Player, Team	Years	No.	Yards	Avg.
Troy Brown, Marshall	1991-92	32	950	*29.7
Charles Swann, Indiana St.	1989-91	45	1,319	29.3
Craig Richardson, Eastern Wash.	1983-86	71	2,021	28.5
Daryl Holcombe, Eastern Ill.	1986-89	49	1,379	28.1
Curtis Chappell, Howard	1984-87	42	1,177	28.0
Leon Brown, Eastern Ky.	1990-93	44	1,230	28.0
Marcus Durgin, Samford	1990-93	44	1,218	27.7
Jerry Parrish, Eastern Ky.	1978-81	61	1,668	27.3
Tony James, Eastern Ky.	1982-84	57	1,552	27.2
Frank Selto, Idaho St.	1986-87	30	803	26.8
Chris Hickman, Northeast La.	1991-92	30	798	26.6
Chris Pollard, Dartmouth	1986-88	52	1,376	26.5
John Jarvis, Howard	1986-88	39	1,031	26.4
Ronald Scott, Southern-B.R.	1982-85	38	1,003	26.4
Rob Tesch, Montana St.	1989-92	50	1,317	26.3
Vernon Williams, Eastern Wash.	1986-88	40	1,052	26.3
Steve Ortman, Pennsylvania	1982-84	31	808	26.1
John Armstrong, Richmond	1984-85	32	826	25.8
Renard Coleman, Montana	1985-88	57	1,465	25.7
Michael Haynes, Northern Ariz.	1986-87	36	925	25.7
Kevin Gainer, Bethune-Cookman	1988-90	42	1,070	25.5
Archie Herring, Youngstown St.	1987-90	79	2,005	25.4
Kenny Shedd, Northern Iowa	1989-92	54	1,359	25.2
Michael High, North Texas	1991-93	47	1,171	24.9
Jerome Stelly, Western Ill.	1981-82	42	1,024	24.4
Chris Pierce, Rhode Island	1989-92	63	1,521	24.1
Albert Brown, Western Ill.	1985-86	30	723	24.1
Sylvester Stamps, Jackson St.	1980, 82-83	42	1,012	24.1
Sean Hill, Montana St.	1991-93	44	1,060	24.1

*Record.

Special Note: Leader in number and yardage: Herman Hunter, Tennessee St., 1981-84, with 96 returns for 2,258 yards.

SEASON AVERAGE
(Minimum 1.2 Returns Per Game)

Player, Team	Year	No.	Yards	Avg.
David Fraterrigo, Canisius	†1993	13	485	*37.3
Kerry Hayes, Western Caro.	1993	16	584	36.5
Craig Richardson, Eastern Wash.	†1984	21	729	34.7
Marcus Durgin, Samford	†1992	15	499	33.3
Rory Lee, Western Ill.	1993	16	527	32.9
Dave Meggett, Towson St.	†1988	13	418	32.2
Charles Swann, Indiana St.	†1990	20	642	32.1
Archie Herring, Youngstown St.	1990	18	575	31.9
Davlin Mullen, Western Ky.	†1982	18	574	31.9
Naylon Albritton, South Caro. St.	1993	15	475	31.7
Danny Copeland, Eastern Ky.	†1986	26	812	31.2
Chris Chappell, Howard	1986	17	528	31.1
Dave Loehle, New Hampshire	†1978	15	460	30.7
Paul Ashby, Alabama St.	†1991	17	520	30.6
Juan Jackson, North Caro. A&T	1986	16	487	30.4
Kevin Gainer, Bethune-Cookman	1990	21	635	30.2
Howard Huckaby, Florida A&M	†1987	20	602	30.1
Tony James, Eastern Ky.	†1983	17	511	30.1
Robert Johnson, Idaho St.	1992	14	416	29.7
Jerry Parrish, Eastern Ky.	†1981	18	534	29.7
John Armstrong, Richmond	1984	18	531	29.5
Renard Coleman, Montana	1987	20	588	29.4

*Record. †National champion.

ANNUAL CHAMPIONS

Year	Player, Team	Class	No.	Yards	Avg.
1978	Dave Loehle, New Hampshire	Jr.	15	460	30.7
1979	Garry Pearson, Massachusetts	Fr.	12	348	29.0
1980	Danny Thomas, North Caro. A&T	Fr.	15	381	25.4
1981	Jerry Parrish, Eastern Ky.	Sr.	18	534	29.7
1982	Davlin Mullen, Western Ky.	Sr.	18	574	31.9
1983	Tony James, Eastern Ky.	Jr.	17	511	30.1
1984	Craig Richardson, Eastern Wash.	So.	21	729	34.7
1985	Rodney Payne, Murray St.	Fr.	16	464	29.0
1986	Danny Copeland, Eastern Ky.	Jr.	26	812	31.2
1987	Howard Huckaby, Florida A&M	So.	20	602	30.1
1988	Dave Meggett, Towson St.	Sr.	13	418	32.2
1989	Scott Thomas, Liberty	Fr.	13	373	28.7
1990	Charles Swann, Indiana St.	Jr.	20	642	32.1
1991	Paul Ashby, Alabama St.	Jr.	17	520	30.6
1992	Marcus Durgin, Samford	Jr.	15	499	33.3
1993	David Fraterrigo, Canisius	Sr.	13	485	*37.3

*Record.

Princeton's Keith Elias averaged 193.9 all-purpose yards a game last season.

All-Purpose Yards

CAREER YARDS PER GAME

Player, Team	Years	Rush	Rcv.	Int.	PR	KOR	Yds.	Yd.PG
Dave Meggett, Towson St.	1987-88	1,658	788	0	212	745	3,403	*189.1
Kenny Gamble, Colgate	1984-87	5,220	536	0	104	1,763	*7,623	181.5
Rich Erenberg, Colgate	#1982-83	2,618	423	0	268	315	3,624	172.6
Fine Unga, Weber St.	1987-88	2,298	391	0	7	967	3,663	166.5
Gill Fenerty, Holy Cross	1983-85	3,618	477	0	1	731	4,827	160.9
Keith Elias, Princeton	1991-93	4,208	508	0	0	25	4,741	158.0
Barry Bourassa, New Hampshire	1989-92	2,960	1,307	0	306	1,370	5,943	152.4
Judd Garrett, Princeton	1987-89	3,109	1,385	0	0	10	4,510	150.3
Treamelle Taylor, Nevada	1987-90	0	1,926	0	662	687	3,275	148.9
Troy Brown, Marshall	1991-92	138	1,716	0	455	950	3,259	148.1
Andre Garron, New Hampshire	1982-85	2,901	809	0	8	651	4,369	145.6
Carl Boyd, Northern Iowa	1983, 85-87	2,735	1,987	0	0	183	4,905	144.3
Merril Hoge, Idaho St.	1983-86	2,713	1,734	0	1	1,005	5,453	139.8
Pete Mandley, Northern Ariz.	1979-80, 82-83	436	2,598	11	901	1,979	5,925	137.8
Frank Hawkins, Nevada	1977-80	*5,333	519	0	0	0	5,852	136.1
Derrick Harmon, Cornell	1981-83	3,074	679	0	5	42	3,800	135.7
Dorron Hunter, Morehead St.	1977-80	1,336	1,320	0	510	1,970	5,136	135.2

*Record. #Two years in Division I-AA and two years in Division I-A. Four-year totals: 5,695 yards and 146.0 average.

SEASON YARDS PER GAME

Player, Team	Years	Rush	Rcv.	Int.	PR	KOR	Yds.	Yd.PG
Kenny Gamble, Colgate	†1986	1,816	178	0	40	391	*2,425	*220.5
Michael Clemons, William & Mary	1986	1,065	516	0	330	423	2,334	212.2
Tony Vinson, Towson St.	†1993	*2,016	57	0	0	0	2,073	207.3
Rich Erenberg, Colgate	†1983	1,883	214	0	126	18	2,241	203.7
Dave Meggett, Towson St.	†1987	814	572	0	78	327	1,791	199.0
Gordie Lockbaum, Holy Cross	1986	827	860	34	0	452	2,173	197.6
Gill Fenerty, Holy Cross	†1985	1,368	187	0	1	414	1,970	197.0
Barry Bourassa, New Hampshire	†1991	1,130	426	0	0	596	2,152	195.6
Keith Elias, Princeton	1993	1,731	193	0	0	15	1,939	193.9
Barry Bourassa, New Hampshire	†1990	957	276	0	133	368	1,734	192.7
Merril Hoge, Idaho St.	1985	1,041	708	0	0	364	2,113	192.1
Andre Garron, New Hampshire	1983	1,009	539	0	0	359	1,907	190.7
Kenny Gamble, Colgate	1987	1,411	151	0	64	471	2,097	190.6
Otis Washington, Western Caro.	†1988	64	907	0	0	1,113	2,086	189.6
Ken Jenkins, Bucknell	†1980	1,270	293	0	65	256	1,884	188.4
Kenny Gamble, Colgate	1985	1,361	162	0	0	520	2,043	185.7
Gordie Lockbaum, Holy Cross	1987	403	1,152	0	209	277	2,041	185.6
Dominic Corr, Eastern Wash.	†1989	796	52	0	0	807	1,655	183.9
Al Rosier, Dartmouth	1991	1,432	113	0	0	290	1,835	183.5
Jerome Bledsoe, Massachusetts	1991	1,545	178	0	0	293	2,016	183.3

Player, Team	Years	Rush	Rcv.	Int.	PR	KOR	Yds.	Yd.PG
David Wright, Indiana St.	†1992	1,313	108	0	0	593	2,014	183.1
Mark Stock, Va. Military	1988	90	1,161	0	260	500	2,011	182.8
Jamie Jones, Eastern Ill.	1991	1,403	299	0	0	305	2,007	182.5
Pete Mandley, Northern Ariz.	†1982	36	1,067	0	344	532	1,979	179.9
Kelvin Anderson, Southeast Mo. St.	1992	1,371	171	0	0	253	1,795	179.5
Dave Meggett, Towson St.	1988	844	216	0	134	418	1,612	179.1
Carl Smith, Maine	1989	1,680	169	0	0	120	1,969	179.0

*Record. †National champion.

CAREER YARDS†

Player, Team	Years	Rush	Rcv.	Int.	PR	KOR	Yds.	Yd.PP
Kenny Gamble, Colgate	1984-87	5,220	536	0	104	1,763	*7,623	7.0
Barry Bourassa, New Hampshire	1989-92	2,960	1,307	0	306	1,370	5,943	7.5
Pete Mandley, Northern Ariz.	1979-80, 82-83	436	2,598	11	901	1,979	5,925	*14.8
Frank Hawkins, Nevada	1977-80	*5,333	519	0	0	0	5,852	5.8
Jamie Jones, Eastern Ill.	1988-91	3,466	816	0	66	1,235	5,583	6.2
Merril Hoge, Idaho St.	1983-86	2,713	1,734	0	1	1,005	5,453	6.6
Herman Hunter, Tennessee St.	1981-84	1,049	1,129	0	974	*2,258	5,410	10.5
Cedric Minter, Boise St.	1977-80	4,475	525	0	49	267	5,316	6.5
Charvez Foger, Nevada	1985-88	4,484	821	0	0	0	5,305	5.7
Garry Pearson, Massachusetts	1979-82	3,859	466	0	0	952	5,277	5.9
John Settle, Appalachian St.	1983-86	4,409	526	0	0	319	5,254	5.3
Dorron Hunter, Morehead St.	1977-80	1,336	1,320	0	510	1,970	5,136	9.6

*Record. †Rich Erenberg, Colgate, competed two years in Division I-AA and two years in Division I-A (four-year total: 5,695 yards), and Dwight Walker, Nicholls St., competed two years in Division I-AA and two years in Division II (four-year total: 5,200 yards).

Colgate tailback Kenny Gamble's record of 7,623 career all-purpose yardage has stood as the mark to beat in Division I-AA since 1987.

SEASON YARDS

Player, Team	Year	Rush	Rcv.	Int.	PR	KOR	Yds.	Yd.PP
Kenny Gamble, Colgate	†1986	1,816	178	0	40	391	*2,425	7.1
Michael Clemons, William & Mary	1986	1,065	516	0	330	423	2,334	6.7
Rich Erenberg, Colgate	†1983	1,883	214	0	126	18	2,241	6.7
Gordie Lockbaum, Holy Cross	1986	827	860	34	0	452	2,173	9.7
Barry Bourassa, New Hampshire	†1991	1,130	426	0	0	596	2,152	7.5
Merril Hoge, Idaho St.	1985	1,041	708	0	0	364	2,113	7.4
Kenny Gamble, Colgate	1987	1,411	151	0	64	471	2,097	6.5
Otis Washington, Western Caro.	†1988	66	907	0	0	1,113	2,086	*19.7
Tony Vinson, Towson St.	†1993	*2,016	57	0	0	0	2,073	6.8
Kenny Gamble, Colgate	1985	1,361	162	0	0	520	2,043	7.3
Gordie Lockbaum, Holy Cross	1987	403	1,152	0	209	277	2,041	10.4
Jerome Bledsoe, Massachusetts	1991	1,545	178	0	0	293	2,016	6.7
David Wright, Indiana St.	†1992	1,313	108	0	0	593	2,014	7.9
Mark Stock, Va. Military	1988	90	1,161	0	260	500	2,011	14.0
Jamie Jones, Eastern Ill.	1991	1,403	299	0	0	305	2,007	7.2
Pete Mandley, Northern Ariz.	†1982	36	1,067	0	344	532	1,979	18.7
Gill Fenerty, Holy Cross	†1985	1,368	187	0	1	414	1,970	6.8

*Record. †National champion.

ALL-PURPOSE SINGLE-GAME HIGHS

Yds.	Player, Team (Opponent)	Date
463	Michael Lerch, Princeton (Brown)	Oct. 12, 1991
453	Herman Hunter, Tennessee St. (Mississippi Val.)	Nov. 13, 1982
395	Scott Oliaro, Cornell (Yale)	Nov. 3, 1990
386	Gill Fenerty, Holy Cross (Columbia)	Oct. 29, 1983
378	Joe Delaney, Northwestern St. (Nicholls St.)	Oct. 28, 1978
373	William Arnold, Jackson St. (Texas Southern)	Nov. 6, 1993
372	Gary Harrell, Howard (Morgan St.)	Nov. 3, 1990
372	Treamelle Taylor, Nevada (Montana)	Oct. 14, 1989
369	Flip Johnson, McNeese St. (Southwestern La.)	Nov. 15, 1986
367	Chris Darrington, Weber St. (Idaho St.)	Oct. 25, 1986
365	Erwin Matthews, Richmond (Delaware)	Sept. 26, 1987
361	Patrick Robinson, Tennessee St. (Jackson St.)	Sept. 12, 1992
357	Tony Vinson, Towson St. (Bucknell)	Nov. 13, 1993
352	Andre Garron, New Hampshire (Lehigh)	Oct. 15, 1983
347	Tony Vinson, Towson St. (Morgan St.)	Nov. 20, 1993
345	Russell Davis, Idaho (Weber St.)	Oct. 2, 1982
341	Barry Bourassa, New Hampshire (Delaware)	Oct. 5, 1991
340	Gene Lake, Delaware St. (Liberty)	Nov. 10, 1984
335	Judd Garrett, Princeton (Harvard)	Oct. 22, 1988

ANNUAL CHAMPIONS

Year	Player, Team	Class	Rush	Rcv.	Int.	PR	KOR	Yds.	Yd.PG
1978	Frank Hawkins, Nevada	So.	1,445	211	0	0	0	1,656	165.6
1979	Frank Hawkins, Nevada	Jr.	1,683	123	0	0	0	1,806	164.2
1980	Ken Jenkins, Bucknell	Jr.	1,270	293	0	65	256	1,884	188.4
1981	Garry Pearson, Massachusetts	Jr.	1,026	105	0	0	450	1,581	175.7
1982	Pete Mandley, Northern Ariz.	Jr.	36	1,067	0	344	532	1,979	179.9
1983	Rich Erenberg, Colgate	Sr.	1,883	214	0	126	18	2,241	203.7
1984	Gene Lake, Delaware St.	Jr.	1,722	37	0	0	0	1,759	175.9
1985	Gill Fenerty, Holy Cross	Sr.	1,368	187	0	1	414	1,970	197.0
1986	Kenny Gamble, Colgate	Jr.	1,816	178	0	40	391	*2,425	*220.5
1987	Dave Meggett, Towson St.	Jr.	814	572	0	78	327	1,791	199.0

DIVISION I-AA

Year	Player, Team	Class	Rush	Rcv.	Int.	PR	KOR	Yds.	Yd.PG
1988	Otis Washington, Western Caro.	Sr.	66	907	0	0	1,113	2,086	189.6
1989	Dominic Corr, Eastern Wash.	Sr.	796	52	0	0	807	1,655	183.9
1990	Barry Bourassa, New Hampshire	So.	957	276	0	133	368	1,734	192.7
1991	Barry Bourassa, New Hampshire	Jr.	1,130	426	0	0	596	2,152	195.6
1992	David Wright, Indiana St.	Fr.	1,313	108	0	0	593	2,014	183.1
1993	Tony Vinson, Towson St.	Sr.	*2,016	57	0	0	0	2,073	207.3

*Record.

Field Goals

CAREER FIELD GOALS

Player, Team	Years	Total	Pct.	Under 40 Yds.	40 Plus	Long
Marty Zendejas, Nevada (S)	1984-87	*72-90	.800	42-45	30-45	54
Kirk Roach, Western Caro. (S)	1984-87	71-*102	.696	45-49	26-53	57
Tony Zendejas, Nevada (S)	1981-83	70-86	*.814	45-49	25-37	58
Brian Mitchell, Marshall/Northern Iowa (S)	1987, 89-91	64-81	.790	48-55	16-26	57
Matt Stover, Louisiana Tech (S)	1986-89	64-88	.727	36-42	28-46	57
Steve Christie, William & Mary (S)	1986-89	57-83	.686	39-49	18-34	53
Teddy Garcia, Northeast La. (S)	1984-87	56-88	.636	35-43	21-45	55
Bjorn Nittmo, Appalachian St. (S)	1985-88	55-74	.743	35-40	20-34	54
Kelly Potter, Middle Tenn. St. (S)	1981-84	52-78	.667	37-49	15-29	57
Paul McFadden, Youngstown St. (S)	1980-83	52-90	.578	28-42	24-48	54
Mike Black, Boise St. (S)	1988-91	51-75	.680	35-43	16-32	48
Jeff Wilkins, Youngstown St. (S)	1990-93	50-73	.685	33-38	17-35	54
Tim Foley, Ga. Southern (S)	1984-87	50-62	.806	32-37	18-25	**63
Paul Politi, Illinois St. (S)	1983-86	50-78	.641	34-48	16-30	50
Chuck Rawlinson, Stephen F. Austin (S)	1988-91	49-69	.710	34-43	15-26	58
Thayne Doyle, Idaho (S)	1988-91	49-75	.653	35-51	14-24	52
Scott Roper, Texas-Arlington/Arkansas St. (S)	1985, 86-87	49-75	.653	35-43	14-32	**63
Paul Hickert, Murray St. (S)	1984-87	49-79	.620	34-48	15-31	62
Dewey Klein, Marshall (S)	1988-91	48-66	.727	37-47	11-19	54
John Dowling, Youngstown St. (S)	1984-87	48-76	.632	36-44	12-32	49
Kirk Duce, Montana (S)	1988-91	47-78	.603	37-51	10-27	51
Billy Hayes, Sam Houston St. (S)	1985-88	47-71	.662	37-55	10-16	54
Roger Ruzek, Weber St. (S)	1979-82	46-78	.590	28-37	18-41	51

*Record. **Record tied. (S) Soccer-style kicker.

SEASON FIELD GOALS

Player, Team	Year	Total	Pct.	Under 40 Yds.	40 Plus	Long
Brian Mitchell, Northern Iowa (S)	†1990	**26-27	*.963	23-23	3-4	45
Tony Zendejas, Nevada (S)	†1982	**26-*33	.788	18-20	8-13	52
Kirk Roach, Western Caro. (S)	†1986	24-28	.857	17-17	7-11	52
George Benyola, Louisiana Tech (S)	†1985	24-31	.774	15-18	9-13	53
Goran Lingmerth, Northern Ariz. (S)	1986	23-29	.793	16-19	7-10	55
Tony Zendejas, Nevada (S)	†1983	23-29	.793	14-15	9-14	58
Jose Larios, McNeese St. (S)	†1993	22-28	.786	19-21	3-7	47
Mike Dodd, Boise St. (S)	†1992	22-31	.710	16-21	6-10	50
Marty Zendejas, Nevada (S)	†1984	22-27	.815	12-13	10-14	52
Kevin McKelvie, Nevada (S)	1990	21-24	.875	16-17	5-7	52
Matt Stover, Louisiana Tech (S)	1986	21-25	.840	15-15	6-10	53
Scott Roper, Arkansas St. (S)	1986	21-28	.750	15-17	6-11	50
Tony Zendejas, Nevada (S)	†1981	21-24	.875	13-14	8-10	55
Darren Goodman, Idaho St. (S)	1990	20-28	.714	12-14	8-14	53
Steve Christie, William & Mary (S)	†1989	20-29	.690	16-17	4-12	53
Teddy Garcia, Northeast La. (S)	1987	20-28	.714	10-11	10-17	55

*Record. **Record tied. †National champion. (S) Soccer-style kicker.

Nevada got its kicks for six straight years from the Zendejas brothers. Tony (No. 11) set the division's career accuracy mark of .814 from 1981 to 1983. Marty (No. 7) took over in 1984 and made 80 percent of his field-goal attempts over the next four years.

ANNUAL CHAMPIONS
(Ranked on Per-Game Average)

Year	Player, Team	Total	PG	Pct.	Under 40 Yds.	40 Plus	Long
1978	Tom Sarette, Boise St. (S)	12-20	1.2	.600	8-10	4-10	47
1979	Wilfredo Rosales, Alcorn St. (S)	13-20	1.3	.650	10-11	3-9	45
	Sandro Vitiello, Massachusetts (S)	13-22	1.3	.591	10-12	3-10	47
1980	Scott Norwood, James Madison (S)	15-21	1.5	.714	10-11	5-10	48
1981	Tony Zendejas, Nevada (S)	21-24	1.9	.875	13-14	8-10	55
1982	Tony Zendejas, Nevada (S)	**26-*33	**2.4	.788	18-20	8-13	52
1983	Tony Zendejas, Nevada (S)	23-29	2.1	.793	14-15	9-14	58
1984	Marty Zendejas, Nevada (S)	22-27	2.0	.815	12-13	10-14	52
1985	George Benyola, Louisiana Tech (S)	24-31	2.2	.774	15-18	9-13	53
1986	Kirk Roach, Western Caro. (S)	24-28	2.2	.857	17-17	7-11	52
1987	Micky Penaflor, Northern Ariz. (S)	19-27	1.9	.704	12-16	7-11	51
1988	Chris Lutz, Princeton (S)	19-24	1.9	.792	19-21	0-3	39
1989	Steve Christie, William & Mary (S)	20-29	1.8	.690	16-17	4-12	53
1990	Brian Mitchell, Northern Iowa (S)	**26-27	**2.4	*.963	23-23	3-4	45
1991	Brian Mitchell, Northern Iowa (S)	19-24	1.7	.792	15-16	4-8	57
1992	Mike Dodd, Boise St. (S)	22-31	2.0	.710	16-21	6-10	50
1993	Jose Larios, McNeese St. (S)	22-28	2.0	.786	19-21	3-7	47

*Record. **Record tied. (S) Soccer-style kicker.

All-Time Longest Plays

Since 1941, official maximum length of all plays fixed at 100 yards.

RUSHING

Yds.	Player, Team (Opponent)	Year
99	Phillip Collins, Southwest Mo. St. (Western Ill.)	1989
99	Pedro Bacon, Western Ky. (Livingston)	1986
99	Hubert Owens, Mississippi Val. (Ark.-Pine Bluff)	1980
98	Johnny Gordon, Nevada (Montana St.)	1984
97	Norman Bradford, Grambling (Prairie View)	1992
97	David Clark, Dartmouth (Harvard)	1989
97	David Clark, Dartmouth (Princeton)	1988
96	Kelvin Anderson, Southeast Mo. St. (Murray St.)	1992
96	Andre Lockhart, Tenn.-Chatt. (East Tenn. St.)	1986
95	Jeff Sawulski, Siena (Iona)	1993
95	Jerry Ellison, Tenn.-Chatt. (Boise St.)	1992
95	Joe Sparksman, James Madison (William & Mary)	1990
94	Mark Vigil, Idaho (Simon Fraser)	1980

PASSING

Yds.	Passer-Receiver, Team (Opponent)	Year
99	Aaron Garcia-Greg Ochoa, Cal St. Sacramento (Cal Poly SLO)	1993
99	Todd Donnan-Troy Brown, Marshall (East Tenn. St.)	1991
99	Antoine Ezell-Tyrone Davis, Florida A&M (Bethune-Cookman)	1991
99	Jay Johnson-Kenny Shedd, Northern Iowa (Oklahoma St.)	1990
99	John Bonds-Hendricks Johnson, Northern Ariz. (Boise St.)	1990
99	Scott Stoker-Victor Robinson, Northwestern St. (Northeast La.)	1989
98	Antoine Ezell-Tim Daniel, Florida A&M (Delaware St.)	1991
98	John Friesz-Lee Allen, Idaho (Northern Ariz.)	1989
98	Fred Gatlin-Treamelle Taylor, Nevada (Montana)	1989
98	Steve Monaco-Emerson Foster, Rhode Island (Holy Cross)	1988
98	Frank Baur-Maurice Caldwell, Lafayette (Columbia)	1988
98	David Gabianelli-Craig Morton, Dartmouth (Columbia)	1986
98	Joe Pizzo-Bryan Calder, Nevada (Eastern Wash.)	1984
98	Bobby Hebert-Randy Liles, Northwestern St. (Southeastern La.)	1980
97	Lester Anderson-Kevin Glenn, Illinois St. (Ball St.)	1993
97	Nate Harrison-Brian Thomas, Southern-B.R. (Dist. Columbia)	1989
97	Jerome Baker-John Taylor, Delaware St. (St. Paul's)	1985
97	John McKenzie-Chris Burkett, Jackson St. (Mississippi Val.)	1983
96	Greg Wyatt-Shawn Collins, Northern Ariz. (Montana St.)	1988
96	Rick Fahnestock-Albert Brown, Western Ill. (Northern Iowa)	1986
96	Jeff Cesarone-Keith Paskett, Western Ky. (Akron)	1985
96	Mike Williams-Trumaine Johnson, Grambling (Jackson St.)	1980

INTERCEPTION RETURNS

Yds.	Player, Team (Opponent)	Year
100	Derek Grier, Marshall (East Tenn. St.)	1991
100	Ricky Fields, Samford (Concord, W. Va.)	1990
100	Warren Smith, Stephen F. Austin (Nicholls St.)	1990
100	Rob Pouliot, Montana St. (Boise St.)	1988
100	Rick Harris, East Tenn. St. (Davidson)	1986
100	Bruce Alexander, Stephen F. Austin (Lamar)	1986
100	Guy Carbone, Rhode Island (Lafayette)	1985
100	Moses Aimable, Northern Iowa (Western Ill.)	1985
100	Kervin Fontennette, Southeastern La. (Nicholls St.)	1985
100	Jim Anderson, Princeton (Cornell)	1984
100	Keiron Bigby, Brown (Yale)	1984
100	Vencie Glenn, Indiana St. (Wayne St., Mich.)	1984
100	George Floyd, Eastern Ky. (Youngstown St.)	1980

PUNT RETURNS

Yds.	Player, Team (Opponent)	Year
98	Willie Ware, Mississippi Val. (Bishop)	1985
98	Barney Bussey, South Caro. St. (Johnson Smith)	1981
96	Carl Williams, Texas Southern (Grambling)	1981
95	Clarence Weathers, Delaware St. (Salisbury St.)	1980
93	Joe Fuller, Northern Iowa (Wis.-Whitewater)	1984

KICKOFF RETURNS

Twenty-nine players have returned kickoffs 100 yards. The most recent:

Yds.	Player, Team (Opponent)	Year
100	Leon Brown, Eastern Ky. (Western Ky.)	1992
100	Eddie Godfrey, Western Ky. (Louisville)	1990
100	Roman Carter, Idaho (Cal St. Chico)	1990
100	Dominic Corr, Eastern Wash. (Weber St.)	1989
100	Leon Brown, Eastern Ky. (Austin Peay)	1989
100	Dave Meggett, Towson St. (Northeastern)	1988
100	Dominic Corr, Eastern Wash. (Illinois St.)	1987
100	Barry Chubb, Colgate (Lafayette)	1986
100	Marco Kornegay, Morgan St. (Norfolk St.)	1986

PUNTS

Yds.	Player, Team (Opponent)	Year
91	Bart Helsley, North Texas (Northeast La.)	1990
89	Jim Carriere, Connecticut (Maine)	1987
88	Jeff Kaiser, Idaho St. (UTEP)	1983
87	John Starnes, North Texas (Texas-Arlington)	1983
85	Don Alonzo, Nicholls St. (Northwestern St.)	1980
84	Billy Smith, Tenn.-Chatt. (Appalachian St.)	1988
83	Jason Harkins, Appalachian St. (Citadel)	1986
82	Tim Healy, Delaware (Boston U.)	1987
82	John Howell, Tenn.-Chatt. (Vanderbilt)	1982

FIELD GOALS

Yds.	Player, Team (Opponent)	Year
63	Scott Roper, Arkansas St. (North Texas)	1987
63	Tim Foley, Ga. Southern (James Madison)	1987
62	Paul Hickert, Murray St. (Eastern Ky.)	1986
60	Terry Belden, Northern Ariz. (Cal St. Northridge)	1993
58	Rich Emke, Eastern Ill. (Northern Iowa)	1986
58	Tony Zendejas, Nevada (Boise St.)	1983

DIVISION I-AA

Team Champions

Annual Offense Champions

TOTAL OFFENSE

Year	Team	Avg.
1978	Portland St.	477.4
1979	Portland St.	460.7
1980	Portland St.	504.3
1981	Idaho	438.8
1982	Drake	444.8
1983	Idaho	479.5
1984	Mississippi Val.	*640.1
1985	Weber St.	516.1
1986	Nevada	492.0
1987	Holy Cross	552.2
1988	Lehigh	485.6
1989	Idaho	495.9
1990	William & Mary	498.7
1991	Weber St.	581.4
1992	Alcorn St.	502.9
1993	Idaho	532.0

*Record.

RUSHING OFFENSE

Year	Team	Avg.
1978	Jackson St.	314.5
1979	Jackson St.	288.4
1980	North Caro. A&T	322.1
1981	Idaho	266.3
1982	Delaware	258.4
1983	Furman	287.1
1984	Delaware St.	377.3
1985	Southwest Mo. St.	298.7
1986	Northeastern	336.0
1987	Howard	*381.6
1988	Eastern Ky.	303.0
1989	Ga. Southern	329.2
1990	Delaware St.	298.7
1991	Va. Military	316.9
1992	Citadel	345.5
1993	Western Ky.	300.1

*Record.

PASSING OFFENSE

Year	Team	Avg.
1978	Portland St.	367.1
1979	Portland St.	368.9
1980	Portland St.	434.9

Year	Team	Avg.
1981	Idaho St.	325.7
1982	West Tex. A&M	313.7
1983	Idaho	336.1
1984	Mississippi Val.	*496.8
1985	Rhode Island	384.3
1986	Eastern Ill.	326.1
1987	Holy Cross	358.4
1988	Lehigh	330.1
1989	Idaho	374.3
1990	Weber St.	342.2
1991	Weber St.	389.1
1992	Alcorn St.	360.5
1993	Montana	359.0

*Record.

SCORING OFFENSE

Year	Team	Avg.
1978	Nevada	35.6
1979	Portland St.	34.3
1980	Portland St.	49.2
1981	Delaware	34.1
1982	Delaware	34.1
1983	Mississippi Val.	39.2
1984	Mississippi Val.	*60.9
1985	Mississippi Val.	41.5
1986	Nevada	39.4
1987	Holy Cross	46.5
1988	Lafayette	38.2
1989	Grambling	37.1
1990	Jackson St.	38.0
1991	Nevada	45.1
1992	Marshall	42.4
1993	Idaho	47.5

*Record.

Annual Defense Champions

TOTAL DEFENSE

Year	Team	Avg.
1978	Florida A&M	*149.9
1979	Alcorn St.	166.3
1980	Massachusetts	193.5
1981	South Caro. St.	204.0
1982	South Caro. St.	191.4
1983	Grambling	206.0
1984	Tennessee St.	187.0
1985	Arkansas St.	258.8
1986	Tennessee St.	178.5
1987	Southern-B.R.	202.8
1988	Alcorn St.	215.4
1989	Howard	220.0
1990	Middle Tenn. St.	244.8
1991	South Caro. St.	208.9
1992	South Caro. St.	250.9
1993	McNeese St.	249.5

*Record.

RUSHING DEFENSE

Year	Team	Avg.
1978	Florida A&M	48.6
1979	Alcorn St.	56.7
1980	South Caro. St.	61.8
1981	South Caro. St.	60.8
1982	South Caro. St.	59.4
1983	Jackson St.	79.2
1984	Grambling	*44.5
1985	Jackson St.	63.0
1986	Eastern Ky.	62.8
1987	Southern-B.R.	64.5
1988	Stephen F. Austin	83.5
1989	Montana	70.2
1990	Delaware St.	77.2
1991	Boise St.	84.4
1992	Villanova	77.8
1993	Wagner	87.0

*Record.

PASSING DEFENSE

Year	Team	$Avg.
1978	Southern-B.R.	85.6
1979	Mississippi Val.	64.2
1980	Howard	93.8
1981	Bethune-Cookman	*59.9
1982	Northeastern	98.8
1983	Louisiana Tech	111.4
1984	Louisiana Tech	105.5
1985	Dartmouth	110.3
1986	Bethune-Cookman	99.8
1987	Alcorn St.	101.3
1988	Middle Tenn. St.	90.8
1989	Tenn.-Chatt.	104.4
1990	Middle Tenn. St.	78.83
1991	South Caro. St.	*70.01
1992	Middle Tenn. St.	76.93
1993	Georgetown	76.92

*Record. $Beginning in 1990, ranked on passing-efficiency defense rating points instead of per-game yardage allowed.

SCORING DEFENSE

Year	Team	Avg.
1978	South Caro. St.	*6.5
1979	Lehigh	7.2
1980	Murray St.	9.1
1981	Jackson St.	9.4
1982	Western Mich.	7.1
1983	Grambling	8.6
1984	Northwestern St.	9.0
1985	Appalachian St.	9.9
1986	Tennessee St.	8.3
1987	Holy Cross	10.0
1988	Furman	9.7
1989	Howard	10.5
1990	Middle Tenn. St.	9.2
1991	Villanova	12.0
1992	Citadel	13.0
1993	Marshall	11.2

*Record.

Toughest-Schedule Annual Leaders

The Division I-AA toughest-schedule program, which began in 1982, is based on what all Division I-AA opponents did against other Division I-AA and Division I-A teams when *not* playing the team in question. Games against non-I-AA and I-A teams are deleted. (Playoff or postseason games are not included.) The top two leaders by year:

Year	Team (Record†)	‹Opponents' Record		
		W	L	T	Pct.
1982	Massachusetts (5-6-0)	50	30	1	.623
	Lehigh (4-6-0)	44	31	0	.587
1983	Florida A&M (7-4-0)	42	23	3	.640
	Grambling (8-1-2)	49	31	0	.613
1984	North Texas (2-9-0)	55	35	2	.609
	Va. Military (1-9-0)	53	37	2	.587
1985	South Caro. St. (5-6-0)	43	20	1	.680
	Lehigh (5-6-0)	47	33	1	.586
1986	James Madison (5-5-1)	46	28	1	.620
	Bucknell (3-7-0)	43	27	0	.614
1987	Ga. Southern (8-3-0)	47	31	0	.603
	Northeastern (6-5-0)	50	37	0	.575
1988	Northwestern St. (9-2-0)	54	36	2	.598
	Ga. Southern (9-2-0)	43	31	1	.580
1989	Liberty (7-3-0)	39	22	2	.635
	Western Caro. (3-7-1)	46	34	2	.573

Year	Team (Record†)	‹Opponents' Record		
		W	L	T	Pct.
1990	Ga. Southern (8-3-0)	53	25	1	.677
	Western Ky. (2-8-0)	55	36	1	.603
1991	Bucknell (1-9-0)	53	29	1	.645
	William & Mary (5-6-0)	62	43	0	.590
1992	Va. Military (3-8-0)	46	36	0	.561
	Harvard (3-7-0)	51	40	0	.560
1993	Samford (5-6-0)	55	26	0	.679
	Delaware St. (6-5-0)	44	30	0	.595

†Not including playoff or postseason games. ¢When not playing the team listed.

Top 10 Toughest-Schedule Leaders for 1989-93†

1989

Team	‹Opp. Record	Pct.
1. Liberty	39-22-2	.635
2. Western Caro.	46-34-2	.573
3. Northwestern St.	54-41-0	.568
4. Western Ky.	57-44-2	.563
5. Boston U.	52-41-2	.558
6. Villanova	57-45-2	.558
7. Southern Ill.	49-39-1	.556
8. Tennessee St.	50-40-1	.555
9. Northeastern	50-41-1	.549
10. Western Ill.	40-33-0	.548

1990

Team	‹Opp. Record	Pct.
1. Ga. Southern	53-25-1	.677
2. Western Ky.	55-36-1	.603
3. Liberty	47-35-1	.572
4. Eastern Wash.	47-36-0	.566
5. Arkansas St.	60-48-0	.556
6. Holy Cross	55-44-1	.555
7. William & Mary	57-46-0	.553
8. Tenn.-Chatt.	54-44-1	.551
9. Tennessee St.	47-40-0	.540
10. Austin Peay	48-41-1	.539

1991

Team	‹Opp. Record	Pct.
1. Bucknell	53-29-1	.645
2. William & Mary	62-43-0	.590
3. North Texas	51-36-5	.582
4. Liberty	45-33-0	.577
5. Morgan St.	41-30-1	.576
6. Massachusetts	60-47-0	.561
7. Fordham	46-36-1	.560
8. Connecticut	59-47-0	.557
9. Idaho	48-39-0	.552
10. Ga. Southern	43-35-1	.551

1992

Team	‹Opp. Record	Pct.
1. Va. Military	46-36-0	.561
2. Harvard	51-40-0	.560
3. Florida A&M	47-37-0	.560
4. Appalachian St.	53-43-1	.552
5. McNeese St.	52-42-4	.551
6. Maine	50-41-2	.548
7. Massachusetts	51-42-2	.547
8. James Madison	45-37-3	.547
9. New Hampshire	56-47-0	.544
10. Delaware St.	40-34-1	.540

1993

Team	‹Opp. Record	Pct.
1. Samford	55-26-0	.679
2. Delaware St.	44-30-0	.595
3. Troy St.	47-32-1	.594
4. Eastern Wash.	46-32-0	.590
5. James Madison	52-37-0	.584
6. Illinois St.	58-42-2	.578
7. Nicholls St.	53-39-0	.575
8. Alcorn St.	44-32-4	.575
9. North Texas	53-41-0	.564
10. Idaho	56-44-0	.560

†Not including playoff or postseason games. ¢When not playing the team listed.

Annual Most-Improved Teams

Year	Team	$Games Improved	From		To		Coach
1978	Western Ky.	6½	1977	1-8-1	1978	8-2-0	Jimmy Feix
1979	Murray St.	5	1978	4-7-0	1979	*9-2-1	Mike Gottfried
1980	Idaho St.	6	1979	0-11-0	1980	6-5-0	#Dave Kragthorpe
1981	Lafayette	5½	1980	3-7-0	1981	9-2-0	#Bill Russo
1982	Pennsylvania	6	1981	1-9-0	1982	7-3-0	Jerry Berndt
1983	North Texas	5½	1982	2-9-0	1983	*8-4-0	Corky Nelson
	Southern Ill.	5½	1982	6-5-0	1983	*13-1-0	Rey Dempsey
1984	Montana St.	9½	1983	1-10-0	1984	*12-2-0	Dave Arnold
1985	Appalachian St.	4	1984	4-7-0	1985	8-3-0	Sparky Woods
	Massachusetts	4	1984	3-8-0	1985	7-4-0	Bob Stull
	West Tex. A&M	4	1984	3-8-0	1985	6-3-1	#Bill Kelly
1986	Morehead St.	6	1985	1-10-0	1986	7-4-0	Bill Baldridge
1987	Weber St.	6	1986	3-8-0	1987	*10-3-0	Mike Price
1988	Stephen F. Austin	5½	1987	3-7-1	1988	*10-3-0	Jim Hess
1989	Yale	4½	1988	3-6-1	1989	8-2-0	Carmen Cozza
1990	Nevada	4	1989	7-4-0	1990	*13-2-0	Chris Ault
	North Caro. A&T	4	1989	5-6-0	1990	9-2-0	Bill Hayes
1991	Alcorn St.	5	1990	2-7-0	1991	7-2-1	#Cardell Jones
	Austin Peay	5	1990	0-11-0	1991	5-6-0	#Roy Gregory
	Princeton	5	1990	3-7-0	1991	8-2-0	Steve Tosches
	Southern Ill.	5	1990	2-9-0	1991	7-4-0	Bob Smith
1992	Howard	5	1991	2-9-0	1992	7-4-0	Steve Wilson
	Pennsylvania	5	1991	2-8-0	1992	7-3-0	#Al Bagnoli
	Richmond	5	1991	2-9-0	1992	7-4-0	Jim Marshall
	Tennessee Tech	5	1991	2-9-0	1992	7-4-0	Jim Ragland
	Western Caro.	5	1991	2-9-0	1992	7-4-0	Steve Hodgin
1993	Boston U.	8	1992	3-8-0	1993	12-1-0	Dan Allen

$To determine games improved, add the difference in victories between the two seasons to the difference in losses, then divide by two; ties not counted. *I-AA playoff included. #First year as head coach at that college.

Boston University Photo Services photo

Quarterback Robert Dougherty was a catalyst in Boston University's turnaround in the 1993 season.

ALL-TIME MOST-IMPROVED TEAMS

Games	Team (Year)
9½	Montana St. (1984)
8	Boston U. (1993)
6½	Western Ky. (1978)
6	Weber St. (1987)
6	Morehead St. (1986)
6	Pennsylvania (1982)
6	Idaho St. (1980)
5½	Southern-B.R. (1993)
5½	Stephen F. Austin (1988)
5½	East Tenn. St. (1986)
5½	Holy Cross (1986)
5½	North Texas (1983)
5½	Southern Ill. (1983)
5½	Lafayette (1981)

1993 MOST-IMPROVED TEAMS
(Includes Playoff Games)

College (Coach)	1993	1992	$Games Improved
Boston U. (Dan Allen)	12-1-0	3-8-0	8
Southern-B.R. (Pete Richardson)	11-1-0	5-6-0	5½
Stephen F. Austin (John Pearce)	8-4-0	3-8-0	4½
Brown (Mickey Kwiatkowski)	4-6-0	0-10-0	4
Lehigh (Hank Small)	7-4-0	3-8-0	4
Central Conn. St. (Sal Cintorino)#	5-5-0	1-8-0	3½
Howard (Steve Wilson)	11-1-0	7-4-0	3½
Iona (Harold Crocker)#	9-2-0	5-5-0	3½
Montana (Don Read)	10-2-0	6-5-0	3½
Western Ky. (Jack Harbaugh)	8-3-0	4-6-0	3½
Montana St. (Cliff Hysell)	7-4-0	4-7-0	3
Northern Ariz. (Stephen Axman)	7-4-0	4-7-0	3
Pennsylvania (Al Bagnoli)	10-0-0	7-3-0	3
Tenn.-Martin (Don McLeary)	6-5-0	3-8-0	3
Towson St. (Gordy Combs)	8-2-0	5-5-0	3
Hofstra (Joe Gardi)#	6-3-1	4-6-0	2½
St. John's (N.Y.) (Bob Ricca)#	8-3-0	5-5-0	2½
Valparaiso (Tom Horne)#	5-5-0	3-8-0	2½

$To determine games improved, add the difference in victories between the two seasons to the difference in losses, then divide by two; ties not counted. #First year in Division I-AA.

All-Time Team Won-Lost Records

Includes records as a senior college only, minimum of 20 seasons of competition. Bowl and playoff games are included, and each tie game is computed as half won and half lost.

PERCENTAGE (TOP 29)

Team	Yrs.	Won	Lost	Tied	Pct.†	*Playoffs W-L-T	Total Games
Yale	121	773	264	55	.733	0-0-0	1,092
Grambling	51	388	140	15	.728	9-6-0	543
Tennessee St.@	66	423	151	30	.725	8-2-1	604
Florida A&M	61	420	168	18	.708	2-1-1	606
Princeton	124	706	289	49	.700	0-0-0	1,044
Harvard	119	701	322	50	.677	1-0-0	1,073
Boise St.	26	199	96	2	.673	7-6-0	297
Fordham	95	671	338	52	.657	2-3-0	1,061
Jackson St.	48	304	168	13	.640	1-8-0	485
Dartmouth	112	591	324	45	.639	0-0-0	960
Eastern Ky.	70	418	241	27	.629	16-14-0	686
Pennsylvania	117	694	409	42	.624	0-1-0	1,145
South Caro. St.	67	360	214	27	.621	5-5-0	601
Southern-B.R.	72	414	248	25	.621	5-0-0	687
Ga. Southern	25	163	100	7	.617	21-3-0	270
Hofstra#	53	296	191	10	.606	2-7-0	497
Dayton#	86	476	306	26	.605	16-11-0	808
Alcorn St.	70	344	220	37	.603	1-3-0	601
Appalachian St.	64	384	248	29	.603	3-9-0	661
Middle Tenn. St.	77	428	278	27	.602	8-8-0	733
Bethune-Cookman	55	295	194	22	.599	6-2-0	511
McNeese St.	43	264	175	14	.598	5-6-0	453
Western Ky.	75	403	267	31	.597	7-4-0	701
Butler#	104	473	315	35	.596	0-3-0	823
Delaware	102	507	347	42	.589	19-11-0	896
Cornell	106	548	377	34	.589	0-0-0	959
Georgetown#	82	389	267	31	.589	0-2-0	687
Northern Iowa	95	463	318	47	.588	5-7-0	828
Holy Cross	98	522	360	55	.586	0-2-0	937

ALPHABETICAL LISTING

Team	Yrs.	Won	Lost	Tied	Pct.†	*Playoffs W-L-T	Total Games
Alabama St.	88	354	336	42	.512	1-0-0	732
Alcorn St.	70	344	220	37	.603	1-3-0	601
Appalachian St.	64	384	248	29	.603	3-9-0	661
Austin Peay	57	216	336	16	.394	0-0-0	568
Bethune-Cookman	55	295	194	22	.599	6-2-0	511
Boise St.	26	199	96	2	.673	7-6-0	297
Boston U.	74	301	340	28	.471	2-5-0	669
Brown	108	475	475	40	.500	0-1-0	990
Bucknell	108	476	443	51	.517	1-0-0	970
Buffalo#	80	284	330	29	.464	0-0-0	643
Butler#	104	473	315	35	.596	0-3-0	823
Cal Poly SLO√	53	282	215	9	.566	4-3-0	506
Cal St. Northridge#	32	145	181	4	.445	0-2-0	330
Cal St. Sacramento#	40	181	213	7	.460	2-3-0	401
Canisius#	48	207	164	24	.554	0-1-0	395
Central Conn. St.#	55	205	233	22	.470	0-0-0	460
Citadel	86	389	399	32	.494	2-3-0	820
Colgate	103	480	373	50	.559	1-2-0	903
Columbia	103	313	505	41	.388	1-0-0	859
Connecticut	95	373	409	38	.478	0-0-0	820
Cornell	106	548	377	34	.589	0-0-0	959
Dartmouth	112	591	324	45	.639	0-0-0	960
Davidson#	96	328	466	44	.418	0-1-0	838
Dayton#	86	476	306	26	.605	16-11-0	808
Delaware	102	507	347	42	.589	19-11-0	896
Delaware St.	48	212	233	8	.477	1-0-0	453
Drake#	100	444	421	28	.513	2-3-0	893
Duquesne#	46	189	198	18	.489	1-0-0	405
East Tenn. St.	70	284	342	27	.456	1-0-0	653
Eastern Ill.	93	356	399	44	.473	8-6-0	799
Eastern Ky.	70	418	241	27	.629	16-14-0	686
Eastern Wash.	83	355	296	23	.544	2-3-0	674
Evansville#	68	249	345	22	.422	1-1-0	616
Florida A&M	61	420	168	18	.708	2-1-1	606
Fordham	95	671	338	52	.657	2-3-0	1,061
Furman	80	434	337	37	.560	10-6-0	808
Ga. Southern	25	163	100	7	.617	21-3-0	270
Georgetown#	82	389	267	31	.589	0-2-0	687
Grambling	51	388	140	15	.728	9-6-0	543
Harvard	119	701	322	50	.677	1-0-0	1,073
Hofstra#	53	296	191	10	.606	2-7-0	497
Holy Cross	98	522	360	55	.586	0-2-0	937
Howard	97	389	308	42	.555	0-1-0	739
Idaho	96	360	427	25	.459	6-9-0	812
Idaho St.	89	377	336	20	.528	3-1-0	733
Illinois St.	94	351	409	64	.465	0-0-0	824
Indiana St.	77	294	331	20	.471	1-2-0	645
Jackson St.	48	304	168	13	.640	1-8-0	485
James Madison	21	120	102	3	.540	1-2-0	225
Lafayette	112	564	450	38	.554	0-0-0	1,052
Lehigh	109	509	500	44	.504	4-4-0	1,053
Liberty	21	101	106	4	.488	0-0-0	211
Maine	102	394	366	38	.518	0-3-0	798
Marshall	90	375	434	44	.465	15-4-0	853
Massachusetts	111	428	441	51	.493	2-5-0	920
McNeese St.	43	264	175	14	.598	5-6-0	453
Middle Tenn. St.	77	428	278	27	.602	8-8-0	733
Mississippi Val.	41	170	203	11	.457	0-1-0	384
Montana	94	348	422	26	.454	2-6-0	796
Montana St.	90	346	356	34	.493	7-1-2	736
Morehead St.	64	221	335	22	.401	0-0-0	578
Morgan St.	73	352	250	30	.581	1-2-0	632
Murray St.	69	351	287	34	.548	0-2-1	672
New Hampshire	97	397	350	54	.518	1-3-0	801
Nicholls St.	22	109	130	4	.457	1-1-0	243
North Caro. A&T	70	341	278	39	.548	1-6-0	658
North Texas	78	402	321	32	.554	1-4-0	755
Northeastern	58	215	259	17	.455	0-1-0	491
Northern Ariz.	69	292	310	22	.486	1-2-0	624
Northern Iowa	95	463	318	47	.588	5-7-0	828
Northwestern St.	85	395	319	33	.550	2-1-0	747
Pennsylvania	117	694	409	42	.598	0-1-0	1,145
Prairie View	67	327	307	31	.515	1-3-0	665
Princeton	124	706	289	49	.700	0-0-0	1,044
Rhode Island	93	317	410	41	.439	2-4-0	768
Richmond	110	386	515	52	.432	2-3-0	953
Sam Houston St.	78	348	347	34	.501	4-3-1	729
Samford	77	310	310	46	.500	2-2-0	666
San Diego#	26	118	118	8	.500	0-0-0	244
South Caro. St.	67	360	214	27	.621	5-5-0	601
Southeast Mo. St.	81	343	337	37	.504	0-0-0	717
Southern-B.R.	72	414	248	25	.621	5-0-0	687
Southern Ill.	78	308	377	33	.452	3-0-0	718
Southern Utah#	31	153	140	6	.522	0-0-0	299
Southwest Mo. St.	82	361	341	40	.513	1-5-0	742
Southwest Tex. St.	79	393	290	27	.573	6-1-0	710
St. Francis (Pa.)#	45	143	199	12	.421	0-0-0	354
St. John's (N.Y.)#	25	127	97	7	.565	0-0-0	231
St. Mary's (Cal.)#	65	318	227	20	.581	1-2-0	565
St. Peter's#	22	47	123	1	.278	0-0-0	171
Stephen F. Austin$	67	260	376	28	.413	5-3-0	664
Tenn.-Chatt.	86	416	370	33	.528	0-1-0	819
Tenn.-Martin	37	168	206	5	.450	1-0-0	379
Tennessee St.@	66	423	151	30	.725	8-2-1	604
Tennessee Tech	72	306	353	31	.466	0-3-0	690
Texas Southern	48	229	241	27	.488	1-0-0	497
Towson St.	25	141	112	4	.556	3-4-0	257
Troy St.#	63	317	263	15	.545	11-2-0	595
Va. Military	103	418	480	43	.467	0-0-0	941
Valparaiso#	73	288	329	24	.468	0-1-0	641
Villanova	96	442	369	41	.543	2-5-1	852
Wagner#	63	277	235	17	.540	6-3-0	529
Weber St.	32	163	171	3	.488	1-2-0	337
Western Caro.	60	248	321	23	.438	3-2-0	592
Western Ill.	90	370	333	37	.525	1-4-0	740
Western Ky.	75	403	267	31	.597	7-4-0	701
William & Mary	98	424	439	37	.492	2-6-0	900
Yale	121	773	264	55	.733	0-0-0	1,092
Youngstown St.	53	296	211	16	.581	15-7-0	523

I-AA teams lacking 20 seasons:

Team	Yrs.	Won	Lost	Tied	Pct.†	*Playoffs W-L-T	Total Games
Ala.-Birmingham#	3	20	8	2	.700	0-0-0	30
Central Fla.	15	82	77	1	.516	2-2-0	160
Charleston So.#	3	8	21	0	.276	0-0-0	29
Iona#	16	74	82	3	.475	0-1-0	159
Marist#	16	53	88	3	.378	0-0-0	144
Monmouth (N. J.)√!	0	0	0	0	.000	0-0-0	0
Siena#	6	11	44	0	.200	0-0-0	55

VICTORIES

Team	Wins	Team	Wins
Yale	773	Appalachian St.	384
Princeton	706	Idaho St.	377
Harvard	701	Marshall	375
Pennsylvania	694	Connecticut	373
Fordham	671	Western Ill.	370
Dartmouth	591	Southwest Mo. St.	361
Lafayette	564	Idaho	360
Cornell	548	South Caro. St.	360
Holy Cross	522	Eastern Ill.	356
Lehigh	509	Eastern Wash.	355
Delaware	507	Alabama St.	354
Colgate	480	Morgan St.	352
Bucknell	476	Illinois St.	351
Dayton#	476	Murray St.	351
Brown	475	Montana	348
Butler#	473	Sam Houston St.	348
Northern Iowa	463	Montana St.	346
Drake#	444	Alcorn St.	344
Villanova	442	Southeast Mo. St.	343
Furman	434	North Caro. A&T	341
Massachusetts	428	Davidson#	328
Middle Tenn. St.	428	Prairie View	327
William & Mary	424	St. Mary's (Cal.)#	318
Tennessee St.@	423	Rhode Island	317
Florida A&M	420	Troy St.#	317
Eastern Ky.	418	Columbia	313
Va. Military	418	Samford	310
Tenn.-Chatt.	416	Southern Ill.	308
Southern-B.R.	414	Tennessee Tech	306
Western Ky.	403	Jackson St.	304
North Texas	402	Boston U.	301
New Hampshire	397	Hofstra#	296
Northwestern St.	395	Youngstown St.	296
Maine	394	Bethune-Cookman	295
Southwest Tex. St.	393	Indiana St.	294
Citadel	389	Northern Ariz.	292
Georgetown#	389	Valparaiso#	288
Howard	389	Buffalo#	284
Grambling	388	East Tenn. St.	284
Richmond	386	Cal Poly SLO√	282

Team	Wins	Team	Wins
Wagner#	277	Cal St. Northridge#	145
McNeese St.	264	St. Francis (Pa.)#	143
Stephen F. Austin$	260	Towson St.	141
Evansville#	249	St. John's (N.Y.)#	127
Western Caro.	248	James Madison	120
Texas Southern	229	San Diego#	118
Morehead St.	221	Nicholls St.	109
Austin Peay	216	Liberty	101
Northeastern	215	Central Fla.	82
Delaware St.	212	Iona#	74
Canisius#	207	Marist#	53
Central Conn. St.#	205	St. Peter's#	47
Boise St.	199	Ala.-Birmingham#	20
Duquesne#	189	Siena#	11
Cal St. Sacramento#	181	Charleston So.#	8
Mississippi Val.	170	Monmouth (N.J.)√	0
Tenn.-Martin	168		
Ga. Southern	163		
Weber St.	163		
Southern Utah#	153		

*Also includes any participation in major bowl games. †Ties computed as half won and half lost. #Joined I-AA in 1993. √Joined I-AA in 1994. @Tennessee State's participation in 1981 and 1982 Division I-AA championships (1-2 record) voided. $Stephen F. Austin's participation in 1989 Division I-AA championship (3-1 record) voided. !Began varsity program in 1994.

Records in the 1990s

(1990-91-92-93, Includes Playoffs)

PERCENTAGE

Team	W-L-T	Pct.†	Team	W-L-T	Pct.†
Dayton#	43-4-0	.915	Lafayette	23-19-2	.545
Youngstown St.	47-9-1	.833	Liberty	24-20-0	.545
Eastern Ky.	39-11-0	.780	Appalachian St.	25-21-0	.543
Northern Iowa	39-12-0	.765	Davidson#	20-17-0	.541
North Caro. A&T	35-11-0	.761	Evansville#	21-18-0	.538
Dartmouth	29-9-2	.750	Southern-B.R.	24-21-0	.533
Delaware	36-14-0	.720	Boise St.	25-22-0	.532
Ga. Southern	36-14-0	.720	St. Francis (Pa.)#	20-18-1	.526
Ala.-Birmingham*#	14-5-2	.714	Mississippi Val.	20-18-3	.524
Marshall	40-16-0	.714	Northwestern#	23-21-0	.523
Hofstra#	30-12-1	.709	Southern Utah	22-20-2	.523
Troy St.#	32-13-1	.707	Tennessee Tech	23-21-0	.523
San Diego#	27-11-1	.705	Boston U.	24-22-0	.522
William & Mary	33-14-0	.702	James Madison	24-22-0	.522
Idaho	35-15-0	.700	Sam Houston St.	22-20-3	.522
Middle Tenn. St.	35-15-0	.700	Illinois St.	21-22-1	.489
Alabama St.	29-12-3	.693	Georgetown#	19-20-0	.487
Samford	32-15-1	.677	Western Ill.	21-23-1	.478
Princeton	27-13-0	.675	Yale	19-21-0	.475
Holy Cross	29-14-1	.670	Southwest Tex. St.	20-23-1	.466
Grambling	30-15-0	.667	Cal St. Northridge#	19-22-0	.463
Montana	30-15-0	.667	Connecticut	20-24-0	.455
Iona#	26-13-1	.663	Northern Ariz.	19-25-0	.432
Central Fla.	31-16-0	.660	Tenn.-Chatt.	19-25-0	.432
Wagner#	26-14-0	.650	Tennessee St.	19-25-0	.432
Massachusetts	27-15-1	.640	St. Peter's#	14-19-0	.424
Citadel	30-17-0	.638	Canisius#	16-22-1	.423
Drake#	25-14-1	.638	Colgate	18-25-1	.420
Southwest Mo. St.	28-16-1	.633	Tenn.-Martin$	18-26-0	.409
McNeese St.	30-17-2	.633	Western Caro.	18-26-0	.409
Butler#	26-15-1	.631	Western Ky.	17-25-0	.405
Delaware St.	27-16-0	.628	Eastern Ill.	17-26-1	.398
New Hampshire	27-16-2	.622	North Texas	17-26-1	.398
St. Mary's (Cal.)#	24-15-1	.613	Harvard	15-24-1	.388
Villanova	28-18-0	.609	Indiana St.	17-27-0	.386
Furman	27-18-1	.598	Montana St.	17-27-0	.386
Alcorn St.	24-16-1	.598	Towson St.	16-26-0	.381
Lehigh	26-18-0	.591	Texas Southern	16-27-1	.375
South Caro. St.	26-18-0	.591	Bucknell	16-27-0	.372
St. John's (N.Y.)#	24-17-0	.585	Bethune-Cookman	15-27-0	.357
Cal Poly SLO√	24-17-1	.583	Southeast Mo. St.	15-28-0	.349
Jackson St.	25-18-1	.580	Stephen F. Austin	15-29-1	.344
Howard	26-19-0	.578	Maine	15-29-0	.341
Weber St.	26-19-0	.578	Morehead St.	15-29-0	.341
Cal St. Sacramento#	23-17-0	.575	Rhode Island	15-29-0	.341
Cornell	23-17-0	.575	Richmond	15-29-0	.341
Marist#	22-16-2	.575	Southern Ill.	15-29-0	.341
Eastern Wash.	24-19-0	.558	East Tenn. St.	13-31-0	.295
Florida A&M	25-20-0	.556	Nicholls St.	12-31-1	.284
Pennsylvania	22-18-0	.556	Northeastern	12-31-1	.284

Team	W-L-T	Pct.†	Team	W-L-T	Pct.†
Duquesne#	10-27-1	.276	Columbia	7-33-0	.175
Charleston So.*#	8-21-0	.276	Siena#	6-30-0	.167
Va. Military	12-32-0	.273	Morgan St.	6-37-0	.140
Idaho St.	11-32-1	.261	Fordham	5-36-0	.122
Valparaiso#	10-30-1	.256	Prairie View@	0-33-0	.000
Central Conn. St.#	9-28-1	.250	Monmouth (N.J.)√&	0-0-0	.000
Murray St.	11-33-0	.250			
Buffalo#	10-31-0	.244			
Austin Peay	9-35-0	.205			
Brown	7-33-0	.175			

VICTORIES

(Minimum 28 Wins)

Team	Wins	Team	Wins
Youngstown St.	47	Grambling	30
Dayton#	43	Hofstra#	30
Marshall	40	Montana	30
Eastern Ky.	39	Alabama St.	29
Northern Iowa	39	Dartmouth	29
Delaware	36	Holy Cross	29
Ga. Southern	36	Villanova	28
Idaho	35		
Middle Tenn. St.	35		
North Caro. A&T	35		
William & Mary	33		
Samford	32		
Troy St.#	32		
Central Fla.	31		
Citadel	30		

†Ties counted as half won and half lost. * Began varsity program in 1991. # Joined I-AA in 1993. √Joined I-AA in 1994. &Began varsity program in 1994. @ Did not play in 1990. $ Joined I-AA in 1991.

Records in the 1980s

(Playoffs Included)

PERCENTAGE

Rank	Team	W-L-T	Pct.†	Rank	Team	W-L-T	Pct.†
1	Eastern Ky.	88-24-2	.781	11	Delaware	68-36-0	.654
2	Furman	83-23-4	.773	12	Middle Tenn. St.	65-36-0	.644
3	Ga. Southern	68-22-1	*.753	13	Boise St.	66-38-0	.635
4	Jackson St.	71-25-5	.728	14	Southwest Tex. St.	66-39-0	.629
5	Grambling	68-30-3	.688	15	Murray St.	61-36-2	.626
6	Nevada	71-35-1	.668	16	Northern Iowa	64-38-2	.625
7	Holy Cross	67-33-2	.667	17	Towson St.	60-36-2	.622
8	Tennessee St.	64-32-4	.660	18	Alcorn St.	56-34-0	.622
9	Eastern Ill.	70-36-1	.659	19	Northeast La.	64-39-0	.621
10	Idaho	69-36-0	.657	20	South Caro. St.	55-34-1	.617

†Ties counted as half won and half lost. *Includes two nonvarsity seasons and five varsity seasons; varsity record, 55-14-0 for .797.

National Poll Rankings

Final Poll Leaders

(Released Before Division Championship Playoffs)

Year	Team, Record*	Coach	Record in Championship†
1978	Nevada (10-0-0)	Chris Ault	0-1 Lost in semifinals
1979	Grambling (8-2-0)	Eddie Robinson	Did not compete
1980	South Caro. St. (10-0-0)	Bill Davis	Did not compete
1981	Eastern Ky. (9-1-0)	Roy Kidd	2-1 Runner-up
1982	Eastern Ky. (10-0-0)	Roy Kidd	3-0 Champion
1983	Southern Ill. (10-1-0)	Rey Dempsey	3-0 Champion
1984	Alcorn St. (9-0-0)	Marino Casem	0-1 Lost in quarterfinals
1985	Middle Tenn. St. (11-0-0)	James Donnelly	0-1 Lost in quarterfinals
1986	Nevada (11-0-0)	Chris Ault	2-1 Lost in semifinals
1987	Holy Cross (11-0-0)	Mark Duffner	Did not compete
1988	Idaho (9-1-0)	Keith Gilbertson	2-1 Lost in semifinals
1989	Ga. Southern (11-0-0)	Erk Russell	4-0 Champion
1990	Middle Tenn. St. (10-1-0)	James Donnelly	1-1 Lost in quarterfinals
1991	Nevada (11-0-0)	Chris Ault	1-1 Lost in quarterfinals
1992	tie Citadel (10-1-0)	Charlie Taaffe	1-1 Lost in quarterfinals
	Northeast La. (9-2-0)	Dave Roberts	1-1 Lost in quarterfinals
1993	Troy St. (10-0-1)	Larry Blakeney	2-1 Lost in semifinals

*Final poll record; in some cases, a team had one or two games remaining before the championship playoffs. †Number of teams in the championship: 4 (1978-80); 8 (1981); 12 (1982-85); 16 (1986-present).

Final Regular-Season Top 20 Polls

1982
Team
1. Eastern Ky.
2. Louisiana Tech
3. Delaware
4. Tennessee St.
5. Eastern Ill.
6. Furman
7. South Caro. St.
8. Jackson St.
9. Colgate
10. Grambling
11. Idaho
12. Northern Ill.
13. Holy Cross
14. Bowling Green
15. Boise St.
16. Western Mich.
17. Tenn.-Chatt.
18. Northwestern St.
19. Montana
20. Lafayette

1983
Team
1. Southern Ill.
2. Furman
3. Holy Cross
4. North Texas
5. Indiana St.
6. Eastern Ill.
7. Colgate
8. Eastern Ky.
9. Western Caro.
10. Grambling
11. Nevada
12. Idaho St.
13. Boston U.
    Northeast La.
15. Jackson St.
16. Middle Tenn. St.
17. Tennessee St.
18. South Caro. St.
19. Mississippi Val.
20. New Hampshire

1984
Team
1. Alcorn St.
2. Montana St.
   Rhode Island
4. Boston U.
5. Indiana St.
6. Middle Tenn. St.
   Mississippi Val.
8. Eastern Ky.
9. Louisiana Tech
10. Arkansas St.
11. New Hampshire
12. Richmond
13. Murray St.
14. Western Caro.
15. Holy Cross
16. Furman
17. Tenn.-Chatt.
18. Northern Iowa
19. Delaware
20. McNeese St.

1985
Team
1. Middle Tenn. St.
2. Furman
   Nevada
4. Northern Iowa
5. Idaho
6. Arkansas St.
7. Rhode Island
8. Grambling
9. Ga. Southern
10. Akron
11. Eastern Wash.
12. Appalachian St.
    Delaware St.
14. Louisiana Tech
15. Jackson St.
16. William & Mary
17. Murray St.
18. Richmond
19. Eastern Ky.
20. Alcorn St.

1986
Team
1. Nevada
2. Arkansas St.
3. Eastern Ill.
4. Ga. Southern
5. Holy Cross
6. Appalachian St.
7. Pennsylvania
8. William & Mary
9. Jackson St.
10. Eastern Ky.
11. Sam Houston St.
12. Nicholls St.
13. Delaware
14. Tennessee St.
15. Furman
16. Idaho
17. Southern Ill.
18. Murray St.
19. Connecticut
20. North Caro. A&T

1987
Team
1. Holy Cross
2. Appalachian St.
3. Northeast La.
4. Northern Iowa
5. Idaho
6. Ga. Southern
7. Eastern Ky.
8. James Madison
9. Jackson St.
10. Weber St.
11. Western Ky.
12. Arkansas St.
13. Maine
14. Marshall
15. Youngstown St.
16. North Texas
17. Richmond
18. Howard
19. Sam Houston St.
20. Delaware St.

1988
Team
1. Stephen F. Austin
2. Idaho
3. Ga. Southern
4. Western Ill.
5. Furman
6. Jackson St.
7. Marshall
8. Eastern Ky.
9. Citadel
10. Northwestern St.
11. Massachusetts
12. North Texas
13. Boise St.
14. Florida A&M
    Pennsylvania
16. Western Ky.
17. Connecticut
18. Grambling
19. Montana
20. New Hampshire

1989
Team
1. Ga. Southern
2. Furman
3. Stephen F. Austin
4. Holy Cross
   Idaho
6. Montana
7. Appalachian St.
8. Maine
9. Southwest Mo. St.
10. Middle Tenn. St.
    William & Mary
12. Eastern Ky.
13. Grambling
14. Youngstown St.
15. Eastern Ill.
16. Villanova
17. Jackson St.
18. Connecticut
19. Nevada
20. Northern Iowa

1990
Team
1. Middle Tenn. St.
2. Youngstown St.
3. Ga. Southern
4. Nevada
5. Eastern Ky.
6. Southwest Mo. St.
7. William & Mary
8. Holy Cross
9. Massachusetts
10. Boise St.
11. Northern Iowa
12. Furman
13. Idaho
14. Northeast La.
15. Citadel
16. Jackson St.
17. Dartmouth
18. Central Fla.
19. New Hampshire
    North Caro. A&T

1991
Team
1. Nevada
2. Eastern Ky.
3. Holy Cross
4. Northern Iowa
5. Alabama St.
6. Delaware
7. Villanova
8. Marshall
9. Middle Tenn. St.
10. Samford
11. New Hampshire
12. Sam Houston St.
13. Youngstown St.
14. Western Ill.
15. Weber St.
16. James Madison
17. Appalachian St.
18. Northeast La.
19. McNeese St.
20. Citadel
    Furman

1992
Team
1. Citadel
   Northeast La.
3. Northern Iowa
4. Middle Tenn. St.
5. Idaho
6. Marshall
7. Youngstown St.
8. Delaware
9. Samford
10. Villanova
11. McNeese St.
12. Eastern Ky.
13. William & Mary
14. Eastern Wash.
15. Florida A&M
16. Appalachian St.
17. North Caro. A&T
18. Alcorn St.
19. Liberty
20. Western Ill.

1993

Team (First-Place Votes)	Record*	Total Pts.	How Season Ended†
1. Troy St. (27)	10-0-1	1,516	Lost in I-AA semifinals
2. Ga. Southern (16)	9-2-0	1,470	Lost in I-AA quarterfinals
3. Montana (7)	10-1-0	1,450	Lost in I-AA first round
4. Northeast La. (3)	9-2-0	1,390	Lost in I-AA first round
5. McNeese St. (2)	9-2-0	1,322	Lost in I-AA quarterfinals
6. Boston U. (3)	11-0-0	1,250	Lost in I-AA quarterfinals
7. Youngstown St. (1)	9-2-0	1,210	I-AA national champion
8. Howard (3)	11-0-0	1,099	Lost in I-AA first round
9. Marshall	8-3-0	1,070	Lost in I-AA championship
10. William & Mary	9-2-0	1,034	Lost in I-AA first round
11. Idaho	9-2-0	991	Lost in I-AA semifinals
12. Central Fla.	9-2-0	937	Lost in I-AA first round
13. Northern Iowa	8-3-0	816	Lost in I-AA first round
14. Stephen F. Austin	8-3-0	720	Lost in I-AA first round
15. Southern-B.R.	9-1-0	630	Won Heritage Bowl
16. Pennsylvania	10-0-0	600	Not in postseason play
17. Eastern Ky.	8-3-0	587	Lost in I-AA first round
18. Delaware	8-3-0	529	Lost in I-AA quarterfinals
19. Western Ky.	8-3-0	423	Not in postseason play
20. Eastern Wash.	7-3-0	303	Not in postseason play
21. North Caro. A&T	8-3-0	250	Not in postseason play
22. Tennessee Tech	8-3-0	245	Not in postseason play
23. Alcorn St.	8-3-0	225	Not in postseason play
24. Towson St.	8-2-0	208	Not in postseason play
25. Massachusetts	8-3-0	103	Not in postseason play

*Regular-season record does not include postseason results. †Vote taken before Division I-AA playoffs.

Troy State quarterback Kelvin Simmons led the Trojans to a No.-1 ranking in the final Division I-AA regular-season poll.

1993 Week-by-Week Polls

Final Poll—11-23	11-16	11-9	11-2	10-27	10-20	10-13	10-6	9-28	9-21	9-14	9-7
1. Troy St.	1	4	4	5	2	2	3	5	5	8	9
2. Ga. Southern	2	3	3	3	6	6	8	7	8	7	8
3. Montana	3	5	5	4	8	8	12	12	16	19	21
4. Northeast La.	4	6	7	8	12	12	4	6	6	5	6
5. McNeese St.	5	7	8	9	13	13	18	19	10	2	4
6. Boston U.	6	8	9	10	15	18	23	NR	NR	NR	NR
7. Youngstown St.	7	1	1	1	3	4	6	8	7	10	2
8. Howard	8	9	10	11	19	22	25	NR	NR	NR	NR
9. Marshall	9	2	2	2	4	3	5	1	1	1	1
10. William & Mary	10	10	11	13	17	17	17	18	20	17	11
11. Idaho	11	11	6	7	1	1	1	2	2	4	5
12. Central Fla.	12	12	13	6	11	11	16	16	22	20	23
13. Northern Iowa	13	13	15	17	9	9	11	11	14	14	10
14. Stephen F. Austin	17	19	22	16	10	10	13	13	18	22	NR
15. Southern-B.R.	14	14	17	12	16	16	19	21	25	NR	NR
16. Pennsylvania	15	17	21	23	25	NR	NR	NR	NR	NR	NR
17. Eastern Ky.	18	20	23	25	NR	NR	NR	NR	NR	NR	18
18. Delaware	19	22	14	15	7	7	2	3	3	3	3
19. Western Ky.	20	25	24	NR	18	21	21	25	NR	NR	NR
20. Eastern Wash.	22	NR	NR	NR	NR	NR	NR	NR	NR	NR	NR
21. North Caro. A&T	16	18	12	13	5	5	7	9	12	13	17
22. Tennessee Tech	24	NR	NR	NR	NR	NR	NR	NR	NR	NR	NR
23. Alcorn St.	23	15	18	20	14	15	15	17	9	11	15
24. Towson St.	25	NR	NR	NR	NR	NR	NR	NR	NR	NR	NR
25. Massachusetts	NR	NR	25	NR	NR	NR	NR	NR	NR	25	NR
Other Teams	**11-16**	**11-9**	**11-2**	**10-27**	**10-20**	**10-13**	**10-6**	**9-28**	**9-21**	**9-14**	**9-7**
Princeton	21	24	16	18	21	24	NR	NR	NR	NR	NR
Middle Tenn. St.	NR	23	NR	19	20	23	10	4	4	6	7
Western Caro.	NR	16	24	22	24	25	20	22	11	12	13
Montana St.	NR	NR	19	24	NR	NR	NR	NR	NR	NR	NR
Richmond	NR	NR	NR	21	22	14	14	15	19	9	14
Northern Ariz.	NR	NR	NR	NR	23	20	24	NR	NR	NR	NR
Samford	NR	NR	NR	NR	NR	19	9	10	13	15	12
Florida A&M	NR	NR	NR	NR	NR	NR	22	14	17	23	NR
Liberty	NR	NR	NR	NR	NR	NR	NR	24	15	18	25
Furman	NR	NR	NR	NR	NR	NR	23	NR	24	NR	22
Illinois St.	NR	NR	NR	NR	NR	NR	20	24	NR	NR	NR
Villanova	NR	NR	NR	NR	NR	NR	NR	NR	23	NR	19
Jackson St.	NR	NR	NR	NR	NR	NR	NR	NR	21	16	20
Southwest Mo. St.	NR	NR	NR	NR	NR	NR	NR	NR	NR	21	16
Citadel	NR	NR	NR	NR	NR	NR	NR	NR	NR	NR	24

NR = Not Ranked.

Undefeated, Untied Teams

Regular-season games only, from 1978. Subsequent loss in Division I-AA championship is indicated by (††).

Year	Team	Wins	Year	Team	Wins
1978	Nevada	††11	1988	(None)	
1979	(None)		1989	*Ga. Southern	11
1980	(None)		1990	Youngstown St.	††11
1981	(None)		1991	Holy Cross	11
1982	*Eastern Ky.	10		Nevada	††11
1983	(None)		1992	(None)	
1984	Tennessee St.	11	1993	Boston U.	††11
	Alcorn St.	††9		Howard	††11
1985	Middle Tenn. St.	††11		Pennsylvania	10
1986	Nevada	††11			
	Pennsylvania	10			
1987	Holy Cross	11			

*Won Division I-AA championship.

The Spoilers

(From 1978 Season)

Following is a list of the spoilers of Division I-AA teams that lost their perfect (undefeated, untied) record in their **season-ending** game, including the Division I-AA championship playoffs. An asterisk (*) indicates a championship playoff game and a dagger (†) indicates the home team in a regular-season game.

Date	Spoiler	Victim	Score
12-9-78	*Massachusetts	Nevada	44-21
11-15-80	†Grambling	South Caro. St.	26-3
11-22-80	†Murray St.	Western Ky.	49-0
12-1-84	*Louisiana Tech	Alcorn St.	44-21
12-7-85	*Ga. Southern	Middle Tenn. St.	28-21
11-22-86	Boston College	†Holy Cross	56-26
12-19-86	*Ga. Southern	Nevada	48-38
11-19-88	*Cornell	Pennsylvania	19-6
11-24-90	*Central Fla.	Youngstown St.	20-17
12-7-91	*Youngstown St.	Nevada	30-28
11-27-93	*Marshall	Howard	28-14
12-4-93	*Idaho	Boston U.	21-14

DIVISION I-AA

Streaks and Rivalries

Because Division I-AA began in 1978, only those streaks from the period (1978-present) are listed. Only schools that have been I-AA members for five years are eligible for inclusion.

Longest Winning Streaks

(From 1978; Includes Playoff Games)

Wins	Team	Years	Ended by	Score
20	Holy Cross	1990-92	Army	7-17
18	Eastern Ky.	1982-83	Western Ky.	10-10
16	Ga. Southern	1989-90	Middle Tenn. St.	13-16
14	Delaware	1979-80	Lehigh	20-27
13	Holy Cross	1988-89	Army	9-45
13	Nevada	1986	Ga. Southern	38-48
13	Tennessee St.	1983-85	Western Ky.	17-22
12	Pennsylvania	1992-93	Current	
12	Nevada	1989-90	Boise St.	14-30
12	Furman	1989	Stephen F. Austin	19-21
12	Holy Cross	1987-88	Army	3-23
12	Southern Ill.	1982-83	Wichita St.	6-28
12	Florida A&M	1978-79	Tennessee St.	3-20

Longest Unbeaten Streaks

(From 1978; Includes Playoff Games and Ties)

No.	Wins	Ties	Team	Years	Ended by
20	20	0	Holy Cross	1990-92	Army
19	18	1	Eastern Ky.	1982-83	Murray St.
17	16	1	Alabama St.	1990-92	Alcorn St.
17	16	1	Grambling	1977-78	Florida A&M
16	16	0	Ga. Southern	1989-90	Middle Tenn. St.
14	14	0	Delaware	1979-80	Lehigh
13	13	0	Holy Cross	1988-89	Army
13	13	0	Nevada	1986	Ga. Southern
13	13	0	Tennessee St.	1983-85	Western Ky.
13	12	1	Mississippi Val.	1983-84	Alcorn St.
13	12	1	Eastern Ill.	1981-82	Tennessee St.
12	12	0	Pennsylvania	1992-93	Current
12	12	0	Nevada	1989-90	Boise St.
12	12	0	Furman	1989	Stephen F. Austin
12	12	0	Holy Cross	1987-88	Army
12	11	1	Tennessee St.	1985-86	Alabama St.
12	12	0	Southern Ill.	1982-83	Wichita St.
12	11	1	Tennessee St.	1981-83	Jackson St.
12	12	0	Florida A&M	1978-79	Tennessee St.
11	11	0	Pennsylvania	1985-87	Cornell
10	9	1	Stephen F. Austin	1989	Ga. Southern
10	9	1	Holy Cross	1983	Boston College
10	9	1	Jackson St.	1980	Grambling

Longest Home Winning Streaks

(From 1978; Includes Playoff Games)

Wins	Team	Years	Ended by
38	Ga. Southern	1985-90	Eastern Ky.
31	Middle Tenn. St.	1987-93	Current
30	Eastern Ky.	1978-83	Western Ky.
25	Northern Iowa	1989-92	Youngstown St.
23	Northern Iowa	1983-87	Montana
22	Nevada	1989-91	Youngstown St.
20	Arkansas St.	1984-87	Northwestern St.
16	Southwest Tex. St.	1981-83	Central St. (Ohio)
16	Citadel	1980-82	East Tenn. St.
15	Holy Cross	1987-89	Massachusetts
13	William & Mary	1988-91	Delaware
12	Idaho	1988-89	Eastern Ill.
12	Delaware St.	1983-86	Northeastern
12	Eastern Ill.	1981-83	Indiana St.

Longest Losing Streaks

(From 1978; Can Include Playoff Games)

Losses	Team	Years	Ended by
19	Idaho St.	1978-80	Portland St.
16	Middle Tenn. St.	1978-79	Tennessee Tech
12	Fordham	1991-92	Bucknell

Most-Played Rivalries

(Ongoing Unless Indicated)

Games	Opponents (Series leader listed first)	Rivalry Record	First Game
129	Lafayette-Lehigh	70-54-5	1884
116	Yale-Princeton	63-43-10	1873
110	Yale-Harvard	60-42-8	1875
103	William & Mary-Richmond	51-47-5	1898
100	Pennsylvania-Cornell	56-39-5	1893
98	Yale-Brown	69-24-5	1880
97	Harvard-Dartmouth	50-42-5	1882
93	Montana-Montana St.	56-32-5	1897
93	Harvard-Brown	68-23-2	1893
86	Princeton-Harvard	47-32-7	1877
85	Princeton-Pennsylvania	59-25-1	1876
84	Connecticut-Rhode Island	44-32-8	1897
82	Illinois St.-Eastern Ill.	40-33-9	1901
81	Maine-New Hampshire	37-36-8	1903
81	Cornell-Columbia	52-26-3	1889
79	Cornell-Colgate	46-30-3	1896

Additional Records

LONGEST UNINTERRUPTED SERIES
(Must have played every year)
104 games—Lafayette-Lehigh (from 1897)$
100 games—Cornell-Pennsylvania (from 1893)
76 games—Dartmouth-Cornell (from 1919)
70 games—Dartmouth-Yale (from 1924)
61 games—Dartmouth-Princeton (from 1933)
52 games—Dartmouth-Columbia (from 1942)
51 games—Dartmouth-Holy Cross (from 1942)
50 games—William & Mary-Richmond (from 1944)
50 games—William & Mary-Va. Military (from 1944)
50 games—Eastern Ky.-Western Ky. (from 1946)
49 games—Princeton-Yale (from 1945)
48 games—Southwest Tex. St.-Sam Houston St. (from 1946)
48 games—Southwest Tex. St.-Stephen F. Austin (from 1946)
47 games—Southwest Tex. St.-Tex. A&M-Kingsville (from 1946)√

$Played twice in 1897-1901 and 1943-44. √Played twice in 1983.

MOST CONSECUTIVE WINS OVER AN OPPONENT IN AN UNINTERRUPTED SERIES
(Must have played in consecutive years)
21—Eastern Ky. over Morehead St., 1972-93 (current)
18—Eastern Ky. over Tennessee Tech, 1976-93 (current)
17—Grambling over Prairie View, 1977-93 (current)
17—Princeton over Columbia, 1954-70
16—Middle Tenn. St. over Morehead St., 1951-66
15—Delaware over West Chester, 1968-82
15—Dartmouth over Brown, 1960-74
12—Idaho over Boise St., 1982-93 (current)
12—Cornell over Columbia, 1977-88
11—Evansville over Ky. Wesleyan, 1983-93 (current)
11—Marshall over Va. Military, 1983-93 (current)
11—Tennessee Tech over Morehead St., 1951-61
11—William & Mary over Richmond, 1944-54

MOST CONSECUTIVE WINS OVER AN OPPONENT IN A SERIES
(Did not have to play in consecutive years)
21—Grambling over Mississippi Val., 1957-77
12—Idaho over Ricks College, 1919-33

MOST CONSECUTIVE CURRENT WINS OVER AN OPPONENT IN AN UNINTERRUPTED SERIES
(Must have played every year)
21—Eastern Ky. over Morehead St., 1972-93
18—Eastern Ky. over Tennessee Tech, 1976-93
17—Grambling over Prairie View, 1977-93
12—Idaho over Boise St., 1982-93
11—Evansville over Ky. Wesleyan, 1983-93
11—Marshall over Va. Military, 1983-93
10—Dartmouth over Columbia, 1984-93

Cliffhangers

Regular-season Division I-AA games won on the final play in regulation time. The extra point is listed when it provided the margin of victory after the winning touchdown on the game's final play.

Date	Opponents, Score	Game-Winning Play
10-21-78	Western Ky. 17, Eastern Ky. 16	Kevin McGrath 25 FG
9-8-79	Northern Ariz. 22, Portland St. 21	Ken Fraser 15 pass from Brian Potter (Mike Jenkins pass from Potter)
10-18-80	Connecticut 18, Holy Cross 17	Ken Miller 4 pass from Ken Sweitzer (Keith Hugger pass from Sweitzer)
11-15-80	Morris Brown 19, Bethune-Cookman 18	Ray Mills 1 run (Carlton Johnson kick)
9-26-81	Abilene Christian 41, Northwestern St. 38	David Russell 17 pass from Loyal Proffitt
10-10-81	LIU-C.W. Post 37, James Madison 36	Tom DeBona 10 pass from Tom Ehrhardt
11-13-82	Pennsylvania 23, Harvard 21	Dave Shulman 27 FG
10-1-83	Connecticut 9, New Hampshire 7	Larry Corn 7 run
9-8-84	Southwestern La. 17, Louisiana Tech 16	Patrick Broussard 21 FG
9-15-84	Lehigh 10, Connecticut 7	Dave Melick 45 FG
9-15-84	William & Mary 23, Delaware 21	Jeff Sanders 18 pass from Stan Yagiello
10-13-84	Lafayette 20, Connecticut 13	Ryan Priest 2 run
10-20-84	Central Fla. 28, Illinois St. 24	Jeff Farmer 30 punt return
10-27-84	Western Ky. 33, Morehead St. 31	Arnold Grier 50 pass from Jeff Cesarone
9-7-85	Central Fla. 39, Bethune-Cookman 37	Ed O'Brien 55 FG
10-26-85	Va. Military 39, William & Mary 38	Al Comer 3 run (James Wright run)
8-30-86	Texas Southern 38, Prairie View 35	Don Espinoza 23 FG
9-20-86	Delaware 33, West Chester 31	Fred Singleton 3 run
10-4-86	Northwestern St. 17, Northeast La. 14	Keith Hodnett 27 FG
10-11-86	Eastern Ill. 31, Northern Iowa 30	Rich Ehmke 58 FG
9-12-87	Youngstown St. 20, Bowling Green 17	John Dowling 36 FG
10-3-87	Northeast La. 33, Northwestern St. 31	Jackie Harris 48 pass from Stan Humphries
10-10-87	Marshall 34, Louisville 31	Keith Baxter 31 pass from Tony Petersen
10-17-87	Princeton 16, Lehigh 15	Rob Goodwin 38 FG
11-12-87	South Caro. St. 15, Grambling 13	William Wrighten 23 FG
9-24-88	Holy Cross 30, Princeton 26	70 kickoff return; Tim Donovan 55 on lateral from Darin Cromwell (15)
10-15-88	Weber St. 37, Nevada 31	Todd Beightol 57 pass from Jeff Carlson
10-29-88	Nicholls St. 13, Southwest Tex. St. 10	Jim Windham 33 FG
9-2-89	Alabama St. 16, Troy St. 13	Reggie Brown 28 pass from Antonius Smith
9-16-89	Western Caro. 26, Tenn.-Chatt. 20	Terrell Wagner 68 interception return
9-23-89	Northwestern St. 18, McNeese St. 17	Chris Hamler 25 FG
10-14-89	East Tenn. St. 24, Tenn.-Chatt. 23	George Searcy 1 run
9-29-90	Southwest Tex. St. 33, Nicholls St. 30	Robbie Roberson 32 FG
10-6-90	Grambling 27, Alabama A&M 20	Dexter Butcher 28 pass from Shawn Burras
11-2-91	Grambling 30, Texas Southern 27	Gilad Landau 37 FG
9-19-92	Eastern Ky. 26, Northeast La. 21	Sean Little recovered fumble in end zone
10-10-92	Appalachian St. 27, James Madison 21	Craig Styron 44 pass from D. J. Campbell
11-14-92	Towson St. 33, Northeastern 32	Mark Orlando 10 pass from Dan Crowley
9-4-93	Delaware St. 31, Fayetteville St. 28	Jon Jensen 17 FG
9-11-93	Connecticut 24, New Hampshire 23	Wilbur Gilliard 14 run (Nick Sosik kick)
10-16-93	Howard 44, Towson St. 41	Germaine Kohn 9 pass from Jay Walker
11-20-93	Arkansas St. 23, Nevada 21	Reginald Murphy 30 pass from Johnny Covington

Elsburgh Clarke photo

Delaware State's Jon Jensen kicked a 17-yard field goal on the game's final play to give the Hornets a 31-28 win over Fayetteville State on September 4, 1993.

DIVISION I-AA

Regular-Season Overtime Games

In 1981, the NCAA Football Rules Committee approved an overtime tie-breaker system to decide a tie game for the purpose of determining a conference champion. The following conferences have used the tie-breaker system to decide conference-only tie games. In an overtime period, one end of the field is used and each team gets an offensive series beginning at the 25-yard line. Each team shall have possession until it has scored, failed to gain a first down or lost possession. The team scoring the greater number of points after completion of both possessions is declared the winner. The periods continue until a winner is determined.

BIG SKY CONFERENCE

Date	Opponents, Score	No. OTs	Score, Reg.
10-31-81	‡Weber St. 24, Northern Ariz. 23	1	17-17
11-21-81	‡Idaho St. 33, Weber St. 30	3	23-23
10-2-82	‡Montana St. 30, Idaho St. 27	3	17-17
11-6-82	Nevada 46, ‡Weber St. 43	3	30-30
10-13-84	‡Montana St. 44, Nevada 41	4	21-21
9-17-88	Boise St. 24, ‡Northern Ariz. 21	2	14-14
10-15-88	‡Montana 33, Northern Ariz. 26	2	26-26
9-15-90	‡Weber St. 45, Idaho St. 38	2	31-31
9-29-90	‡Nevada 31, Idaho 28	1	28-28
11-3-90	Eastern Wash. 33, ‡Idaho St. 26	1	26-26
11-10-90	Montana St. 28, ‡Eastern Wash. 25	1	25-25
10-26-91	Eastern Wash. 34, ‡Idaho 31	2	24-24
11-16-91	Montana 35, ‡Idaho 34	1	28-28

MID-EASTERN ATHLETIC CONFERENCE

Date	Opponents, Score	No. OTs	Score, Reg.
11-1-86	‡North Caro. A&T 30, Bethune-Cookman 24	1	24-24
10-22-93	Howard 41, ‡North Caro. A&T 35	1	35-35
11-20-93	‡South Caro. St. 58, North Caro. A&T 52	1	52-52

OHIO VALLEY CONFERENCE

Date	Opponents, Score	No. OTs	Score, Reg.
10-13-84	Youngstown St. 17, ‡Austin Peay 13	1	10-10
11-3-84	‡Murray St. 20, Austin Peay 13	2	10-10
10-19-85	‡Middle Tenn. St. 31, Murray St. 24	2	17-17
11-2-85	‡Middle Tenn. St. 28, Youngstown St. 21	2	14-14
10-4-86	‡Austin Peay 7, Middle Tenn. St. 0	1	0-0
10-10-87	‡Austin Peay 20, Morehead St. 13	1	13-13
11-7-87	‡Youngstown St. 20, Murray St. 13	1	13-13
10-1-88	Tennessee Tech 16, ‡Murray St. 13	1	10-10
10-29-88	Eastern Ky. 31, ‡Murray St. 24	1	24-24
11-18-89	Eastern Ky. 38, ‡Morehead St. 31	3	24-24
11-10-90	‡Tennessee Tech 20, Austin Peay 14	1	14-14
11-17-90	Murray St. 31, ‡Austin Peay 24	3	24-24
11-7-92	‡Eastern Ky. 21, Murray St. 18	1	18-18
10-2-93	Murray St. 28, ‡Tenn.-Martin 21	1	21-21
11-20-93	Tenn.-Martin 39, ‡Austin Peay 33	2	26-26

YANKEE CONFERENCE

Date	Opponents, Score	No. OTs	Score, Reg.
9-18-82	Rhode Island 58, ‡Maine 55	6	21-21
9-25-82	‡Boston U. 48, Maine 45	4	24-24
10-27-84	Maine 13, ‡Connecticut 10	1	10-10
9-13-86	New Hampshire 28, ‡Delaware 21	1	21-21
11-15-86	‡Connecticut 21, Rhode Island 14	1	14-14
9-19-87	‡Richmond 52, Massachusetts 51	4	28-28
9-19-87	New Hampshire 27, ‡Boston U. 20	3	17-17
10-31-87	Maine 59, ‡Delaware 56	2	49-49
11-21-87	‡Delaware 17, Boston U. 10	1	10-10
9-24-88	Villanova 31, ‡Boston U. 24	1	24-24
10-8-88	‡Richmond 23, New Hampshire 17	1	17-17
10-7-89	‡Villanova 41, Connecticut 35	6	21-21
11-16-91	Boston U. 29, ‡Connecticut 26	2	23-23
9-11-93	‡Connecticut 24, New Hampshire 23	1	17-17
10-16-93	Maine 26, ‡Rhode Island 23	2	17-17

‡Home team.

Division I-AA Stadiums

STADIUMS LISTED ALPHABETICALLY

School	Stadium	Conference	Year Built	Cap.	Surface*
Ala.-Birmingham	√ Legion Field	Independent	1927	83,091	AstroTurf
Alabama St.	√ Cramton Bowl	SWAC	1922	24,600	Grass
Alcorn St.	Jack Spinks	SWAC	1992	25,000	Grass
Appalachian St.	Kidd Brewer	Southern	1962	18,000	AstroTurf
Austin Peay	Governors	Ohio Valley	1946	10,000	Stadia Turf
Bethune-Cookman	Municipal	MEAC	NA	10,000	Grass
Boise St.	Bronco	Big Sky	1970	22,600	Blue AstroTurf
Boston U.	Nickerson Field	Yankee	1930	17,369	AstroTurf
Brown	Brown	Ivy	1925	20,000	Grass
Bucknell	Christy Mathewson	Patriot	1924	13,100	Grass
Buffalo	UB Stadium	Independent	1992	16,500	Grass
Butler	Butler Bowl	Pioneer	1927	19,000	Grass
Cal Poly SLO	Mustang	AWC	1935	8,500	Grass
Cal St. Northridge	North Campus	AWC	#1944	6,000	Grass
Cal St. Sacramento	Hornet Field	AWC	%1969	21,418	Grass
Canisius	Demske	MAAC	1990	1,000	AstroTurf
Central Conn. St.	Arute Field	Independent	1969	5,000	Grass
Central Fla.	†√ Florida Citrus	Independent	1989	70,349	Grass
Charleston So.	CSU	Independent	1991	3,000	Grass
Citadel	Johnson Hagood	Southern	1948	22,500	Grass
Colgate	Andy Kerr	Patriot	1932	10,221	Grass
Columbia	Lawrence Wien	Ivy	1984	17,000	Grass
Connecticut	Memorial	Yankee	1953	16,200	Grass
Cornell	Schoellkopf Field	Ivy	1915	27,000	All-Pro Turf
Dartmouth	Memorial Field	Ivy	1923	20,416	Grass
Davidson	Richardson	Independent	1924	6,000	Grass
Dayton	Welcome	Pioneer	1949	11,000	AstroTurf
Delaware	Delaware	Yankee	1952	23,000	Grass
Delaware St.	Alumni Field	MEAC	1957	5,000	Grass
Drake	Drake	Pioneer	1925	18,000	Grass
Duquesne	Arthur Rooney Field	Independent	1993	2,500	Artificial
East Tenn. St.	@ Memorial	Southern	1977	12,000	AstroTurf
Eastern Ill.	O'Brien	Gateway	1970	10,000	Grass
Eastern Ky.	Roy Kidd	Ohio Valley	1969	20,000	Grass
Eastern Wash.	Woodward	Big Sky	1967	6,000	Grass
Evansville	Arad McCutchan	Pioneer	1984	3,000	Grass
Florida A&M	Bragg Memorial	MEAC	1957	25,500	Grass
Fordham	Jack Coffey Field	Patriot	1930	7,000	Grass
Furman	Paladin	Southern	1981	16,000	Grass
Ga. Southern	Paulson	Southern	1984	18,000	PAT
Georgetown	Kehoe Field	MAAC	NA	2,400	AstroTurf
Grambling	Robinson	SWAC	1983	19,600	Grass
Harvard	Harvard	Ivy	1903	37,289	Grass
Hofstra	Hofstra	Independent	1963	7,000	AstroTurf
Holy Cross	Fitton Field	Patriot	1924	23,500	Grass
Howard	William H. Greene	MEAC	1986	12,500	AstroTurf
Idaho	@ Kibbie Dome	Big Sky	$1971	16,000	AstroTurf
Idaho St.	@ Holt Arena	Big Sky	1970	12,000	AstroTurf
Illinois St.	Hancock	Gateway	1967	15,000	AstroTurf
Indiana St.	Memorial	Gateway	!1924	20,500	All-Pro Turf
Iona	Mazzella Field	MAAC	1989	1,200	AstroTurf
Jackson St.	√ Miss. Veterans	SWAC	1949	62,512	Grass
James Madison	Bridgeforth	Yankee	1974	12,800	Poly-Turf
Lafayette	Fisher Field	Patriot	1926	13,750	Grass
Lehigh	Goodman	Patriot	1988	16,000	Grass
Liberty	Liberty University	Independent	1989	12,000	AstroTurf
Maine	Alumni	Yankee	1942	10,000	Grass
Marist	Leonidoff	MAAC	1972	2,500	Grass
Marshall	Marshall University	Southern	1991	28,000	AstroTurf
Massachusetts	McGuirk	Yankee	1965	16,000	Grass
McNeese St.	Cowboy	Southland	1965	17,500	AstroTurf
Middle Tenn. St.	Johnny Floyd	Ohio Valley	!!1933	15,000	AstroTurf
Mississippi Val.	Magnolia	SWAC	1958	10,500	Grass
Monmouth (N. J.)	Kessler	Independent	1993	3,000	Grass
Montana	Wash.-Grizzly	Big Sky	1986	14,000	Grass

School	Stadium	Conference	Year Built	Cap.	Surface*
Montana St.	Reno Sales	Big Sky	1973	15,197	Grass
Morehead St.	Jayne	Ohio Valley	1964	10,000	OmniTurf
Morgan St.	Hughes	MEAC	NA	10,000	Grass
Murray St.	Roy Stewart	Ohio Valley	1973	16,800	AstroTurf
New Hampshire	Cowell	Yankee	1936	9,571	Grass
Nicholls St.	John L. Guidry	Southland	1972	12,800	Grass
North Caro. A&T	Aggie	MEAC	1981	17,500	Grass
North Texas	Fouts Field	Southland	1952	30,500	AstroTurf
Northeastern	E. S. Parson	Yankee	1933	7,000	AstroTurf
Northern Ariz.	@ Walkup Skydome	Big Sky	1978	15,300	AstroTurf
Northern Iowa	@ UNI-Dome	Gateway	1976	16,324	AstroTurf
Northwestern St.	Turpin	Southland	1976	15,971	AstroTurf
Pennsylvania	Franklin Field	Ivy	1895	60,546	AstroTurf
Prairie View	Blackshear	SWAC	1960	6,000	Grass
Princeton	Palmer	Ivy	1914	45,725	Grass
Rhode Island	Meade	Yankee	1928	7,600	Grass
Richmond	Richmond	Yankee	1929	22,611	SuperTurf
Sam Houston St.	Bowers	Southland	1986	14,885	All-Pro Turf
Samford	Siebert	Independent	NA	6,700	Grass
San Diego	USD Torero	Pioneer	1955	4,000	Grass
Siena	Siena Field	MAAC	NA	500	Grass
South Caro. St.	Dawson Bulldog	MEAC	1955	22,000	Grass
Southeast Mo. St.	Houck	Ohio Valley	1930	10,000	Grass
Southern-B.R.	Mumford	SWAC	1928	24,000	Grass
Southern Ill.	McAndrew	Gateway	1975	17,324	OmniTurf
Southern Utah	Coliseum	AWC	1967	6,500	Grass
Southwest Mo. St.	Plaster Field	Gateway	1941	16,300	OmniTurf
Southwest Tex. St.	Bobcat	Southland	1981	14,104	Grass
St. Francis (Pa.)	Pine Bowl	Independent	1979	1,500	Grass
St. John's (N.Y.)	Redmen Field	MAAC	1961	3,000	OmniTurf
St. Mary's (Cal.)	St. Mary's	Independent	1973	5,000	Grass
St. Peter's	JFK	MAAC	1990	4,000	Grass
Stephen F. Austin	Homer Bryce	Southland	1973	14,575	All-Pro Turf
Tenn.-Chatt.	Chamberlain	Southern	1947	10,501	Grass
Tenn.-Martin	Pacer	Ohio Valley	1964	7,500	Grass
Tennessee St.	W. J. Hale	Ohio Valley	1953	16,000	Grass
Tennessee Tech.	Tucker	Ohio Valley	1966	16,500	AstroTurf
Texas Southern	√ Robertson	SWAC	1965	25,000	Grass
Towson St.	Minnegan	Independent	1978	5,000	Grass
Troy St.	Memorial	Independent	1950	12,000	Grass
Va. Military	Alumni Field	Southern	1962	10,000	Grass
Valparaiso	Brown Field	Pioneer	1947	5,000	Grass
Villanova	Villanova	Yankee	1927	12,000	AstroTurf-8
Wagner	Fischer Memorial	Independent	1967	5,000	Grass
Weber St.	Wildcat	Big Sky	1966	17,500	Grass
Western Caro.	E. J. Whitmire	Southern	1974	12,000	AstroTurf
Western Ill.	Hanson Field	Gateway	1948	15,000	Grass
Western Ky.	L. T. Smith	Independent	1968	17,500	Grass
William & Mary	Walter Zable	Yankee	1935	15,000	Grass
Yale	Yale Bowl	Ivy	1914	70,896	Grass
Youngstown St.	Stambaugh	Independent	1982	16,000	Artificial

STADIUMS LISTED BY CAPACITY (TOP 26)

School	Stadium	Surface	Capacity
Ala.-Birmingham	√ Legion Field	AstroTurf	83,091
Yale	Yale Bowl	Grass	70,896
Central Fla.	√ Florida Citrus	Grass	70,349
Jackson St.	√ Miss. Veterans	Grass	62,512
Pennsylvania	Franklin Field	AstroTurf	60,546
Princeton	Palmer	Grass	45,725
Harvard	Harvard	Grass	37,289
North Texas	Fouts Field	AstroTurf	30,500
Marshall	Marshall University	AstroTurf	28,000
Cornell	Schoellkopf Field	All-Pro Turf	27,000
Florida A&M	Bragg Memorial	Grass	25,500
Alcorn St.	Jack Spinks	Grass	25,000
Texas Southern	√ Robertson	Grass	25,000
Alabama St.	√ Cramton Bowl	Grass	24,600
Southern-B.R.	Mumford	Grass	24,000
Holy Cross	Fitton Field	Grass	23,500
Delaware	Delaware	Grass	23,000
Richmond	Richmond	SuperTurf	22,611
Boise St.	Bronco	Blue AstroTurf	22,600
Citadel	Johnson Hagood	Grass	22,500
South Caro. St.	Dawson Bulldog	Grass	22,000
Cal St. Sacramento	Hornet Field	Grass	21,418
Indiana St.	Memorial	All-Pro Turf	20,500
Dartmouth	Memorial Field	Grass	20,416
Brown	Brown	Grass	20,000
Eastern Ky.	Roy Kidd	Grass	20,000

√Not located on campus. @ Indoor facility. *This column indicates the type of surface (either artificial or natural grass) present this year in the stadium. The brand name of the artificial turf, if known, is listed. #Built in 1944 as Devonshire Downs Race Track, refurbished in 1971 for football. %Originally built in 1969 with 6,000 capacity, renovated 1992 and increased to 21,418. †Florida Citrus: Renovated by adding 19,000 seats in 1989. $Built in 1971, roof added in 1975. !Built in 1924 as minor league baseball field, acquired by school in 1967 and renovated for football in 1967. !!Built in 1933, remodeled and expanded in 1950 and 1968.

Division I-AA Statistics Trends

(Average Per Game, Both Teams)

Year	Rushing					Passing				Total Offense			Scoring		
	Plays	Yds.	Avg.	Att.	Cmp.	Pct.	Yds.	Av. Att.		Plays	Yds.	Avg.	TD	FG	Pts.
1978	*96.7	*343.5	3.55	41.4	19.1	46.2	258.6	6.24		138.1	602.1	4.36	5.20	1.03	39.0
1979	94.1	329.3	3.50	40.9	18.4	45.0	250.4	6.13		135.0	579.7	4.30	4.79	1.23	36.9
1980	90.3	329.6	3.65	44.8	20.8	46.5	288.8	6.45		135.1	618.4	4.58	5.15	1.18	39.2
1981	88.5	309.9	3.50	49.7	23.7	47.7	322.9	6.49		138.2	632.8	4.58	5.42	1.38	41.7
1982	88.8	313.1	3.53	52.2	25.6	48.9	332.0	6.35		141.0	645.1	4.57	5.24	1.59	41.0
1983	87.8	310.3	3.54	52.4	25.9	49.4	334.5	6.38		140.2	644.8	4.60	5.38	1.58	42.1
1984	85.7	305.1	3.56	55.7	27.9	50.0	361.9	6.49		141.4	666.9	4.72	5.59	1.60	43.6
1985	84.7	315.2	3.72	*57.7	*29.1	50.4	*374.6	6.49		*142.4	689.8	4.84	5.67	1.61	44.2
1986	84.8	315.8	3.72	56.5	28.1	49.7	372.8	6.60		141.3	688.6	4.87	5.80	1.72	45.4
1987	86.2	317.2	3.68	54.2	27.1	50.1	351.1	6.48		140.4	668.3	4.76	5.55	1.81	44.0
1988	86.3	322.5	3.74	52.9	26.5	50.2	345.4	6.53		139.2	667.9	4.80	5.59	*1.81	44.2
1989	84.9	320.4	3.77	55.4	28.4	51.3	372.0	6.71		140.3	692.4	4.93	5.43	1.49	45.5
1990	85.3	323.0	3.79	55.6	28.1	50.6	374.0	6.73		140.9	697.0	4.95	5.96	1.67	46.4
1991	86.4	341.2	3.95	53.7	27.9	*51.9	369.3	6.87		140.1	*710.5	5.07	6.38	1.33	48.1
1992	86.0	342.8	*3.99	52.0	26.9	51.7	358.8	6.89		138.0	701.6	5.08	6.32	1.36	47.7
1993	84.7	336.6	3.97	54.0	28.0	51.8	372.8	*6.90		138.7	709.3	*5.11	*6.40	1.40	*48.4

*Record.

Additional Division I-AA Statistics Trends

(Average Per Game, Both Teams)

Year	Punting		Net Avg.	Interceptions	Avg. Ret.	Yds.	Punt Returns	Avg. Ret.	Yds.	Kickoff Returns	Avg. Ret.	Yds.
	No.	Avg.		No.			No.			No.		
1978	*12.2	36.5	33.6	2.84	11.92	33.9	4.78	7.49	35.8	6.45	18.4	118.4
1979	11.9	36.5	33.4	2.88	11.39	32.8	4.82	7.46	35.9	6.11	18.4	112.3
1980	11.6	37.0	33.7	2.74	10.06	27.6	4.87	7.94	38.7	6.17	17.4	107.4
1981	11.8	37.2	33.9	*3.19	10.63	*33.9	4.99	7.77	38.8	6.54	18.4	120.1
1982	12.0	37.1	34.0	2.99	10.15	30.3	4.88	7.63	37.2	6.15	19.0	116.8
1983	11.9	37.3	34.1	3.03	9.99	30.2	*5.17	7.58	39.2	6.11	18.6	113.8
1984	11.6	37.3	33.9	3.05	10.40	31.7	5.10	7.84	40.0	6.46	18.6	120.0
1985	11.4	37.6	*34.2	3.02	10.56	31.9	5.09	7.52	38.3	6.39	18.1	115.7
1986	11.2	*37.6	34.0	3.01	10.90	32.8	5.09	7.92	40.3	*8.04	19.4	*155.7
1987	11.2	36.8	33.4	2.80	10.57	29.7	4.96	7.51	37.3	7.91	19.0	149.1
1988	10.9	36.3	32.8	2.68	10.61	28.4	4.80	7.96	38.3	7.90	18.8	148.6
1989	11.0	36.1	32.8	2.62	10.40	27.3	4.63	7.93	36.7	7.92	18.9	149.4
1990	10.8	36.7	32.7	2.76	*11.94	32.9	4.97	8.46	42.0	8.03	18.9	151.7
1991	10.6	36.6	32.6	2.70	10.81	29.1	4.92	8.57	42.2	7.68	19.1	146.7
1992	10.6	36.6	32.2	2.41	10.24	24.6	5.05	*9.35	*47.2	7.63	*19.5	148.7
1993	10.4	36.0	32.3	2.45	10.79	26.4	4.70	8.26	38.9	7.44	19.3	143.4

*Record.

Black College National Champions

Sheridan Poll

Selected by the Pittsburgh Courier, 1920-1980, and compiled by Collie Nicholson, former Grambling sports information director; William Nunn Jr., Pittsburgh Courier sports editor, and Eric "Ric" Roberts, Pittsburgh Courier sports writer and noted black college sports historian. Selected from 1981 by the Sheridan Broadcasting Network, 411 Seventh Ave., Suite 1500, Pittsburgh, Pa. 15219-1905. Records include postseason games.

Year	Team	Won	Lost	Tied	Coach
1920	Howard	7	0	0	Edward Morrison
	Talladega	5	0	1	Jubie Bragg
1921	Talladega	6	0	1	Jubie Bragg
	Wiley	7	0	1	Jason Grant
1922	Hampton	6	1	0	Gideon Smith
1923	Virginia Union	6	0	1	Harold Martin
1924	Tuskegee	9	0	1	Cleve Abbott
	Wiley	8	0	1	Fred Long
1925	Tuskegee	8	0	1	Cleve Abbott
	Howard	6	0	2	Louis Watson
1926	Tuskegee	10	0	0	Cleve Abbott
	Howard	7	0	0	Louis Watson
1927	Tuskegee	9	0	1	Cleve Abbott
	Bluefield St. (Va.)	8	0	1	Harry Jefferson
1928	Bluefield St. (Va.)	8	0	1	Harry Jefferson
	Wiley	8	0	1	Fred Long
1929	Tuskegee	10	0	0	Cleve Abbott

Year	Team	Won	Lost	Tied	Coach
1930	Tuskegee	11	0	1	Cleve Abbott
1931	Wilberforce	9	0	0	Harry Graves
1932	Wiley	9	0	0	Fred Long
1933	Morgan St.	9	0	0	Edward Hurt
1934	Kentucky St.	9	0	0	Henry Kean
1935	Texas College	9	0	0	Arnett Mumford
1936	West Va. St.	8	0	0	Adolph Hamblin
	Virginia St.	7	0	2	Harry Jefferson
1937	Morgan St.	7	0	0	Edward Hurt
1938	Florida A&M	8	0	0	Bill Bell
1939	Langston	9	0	0	Felton "Zip" Gayles
1940	Morris Brown	9	1	0	Artis Graves
1941	Morris Brown	8	1	0	William Nicks
1942	Florida A&M	9	0	0	Bill Bell
1943	Morgan St.	5	0	0	Edward Hurt
1944	Morgan St.	6	1	0	Edward Hurt
1945	Wiley	10	0	0	Fred Long
1946	Tennessee St.	10	1	0	Henry Kean
	Morgan St.	8	0	0	Edward Hurt
1947	Tennessee St.	10	0	0	Henry Kean
	Shaw	10	0	0	Brutus Wilson
1948	Southern-B.R.	12	0	0	Arnett Mumford
1949	Southern-B.R.	10	0	1	Arnett Mumford
	Morgan St.	8	0	0	Edward Hurt

DIVISION I-AA

Year	Team	Won	Lost	Tied	Coach
1950	Southern-B.R.	10	0	1	Arnett Mumford
	Florida A&M	8	1	1	Alonzo "Jake" Gaither
1951	Morris Brown	10	1	0	Edward "Ox" Clemons
1952	Florida A&M	8	2	0	Alonzo "Jake" Gaither
	Texas Southern	10	0	1	Alexander Durley
	Lincoln (Mo.)	8	0	1	Dwight Reed
	Virginia St.	8	1	0	Sylvester "Sal" Hall
1953	Prairie View	12	0	0	William Nicks
1954	Tennessee St.	10	1	0	Henry Kean
	Southern-B.R.	10	1	0	Arnett Mumford
	Florida A&M	8	1	0	Alonzo "Jake" Gaither
	Prairie View	10	1	0	William Nicks
1955	Grambling	10	0	0	Eddie Robinson
1956	Tennessee St.	10	0	0	Howard Gentry
1957	Florida A&M	9	0	0	Alonzo "Jake" Gaither
1958	Prairie View	10	0	1	William Nicks
1959	Florida A&M	10	0	0	Alonzo "Jake" Gaither
1960	Southern-B.R.	9	1	0	Arnett Mumford
1961	Florida A&M	10	0	0	Alonzo "Jake" Gaither
1962	Jackson St.	10	1	0	John Merritt
1963	Prairie View	10	1	0	William Nicks
1964	Prairie View	9	0	0	William Nicks
1965	Tennessee St.	9	0	1	John Merritt
1966	Tennessee St.	10	0	0	John Merritt
1967	Morgan St.	8	0	0	Earl Banks
	Grambling	9	1	0	Eddie Robinson
1968	Alcorn St.	9	1	0	Marino Casem
	North Caro. A&T	8	1	0	Hornsby Howell
1969	Alcorn St.	8	0	1	Marino Casem
1970	Tennessee St.	11	0	0	John Merritt
1971	Tennessee St.	9	1	0	John Merritt
1972	Grambling	11	2	0	Eddie Robinson
1973	Tennessee St.	10	0	0	John Merritt
1974	Grambling	11	1	0	Eddie Robinson
	Alcorn St.	9	2	0	Marino Casem
1975	Grambling	10	2	0	Eddie Robinson
1976	South Caro. St.	10	1	0	Willie Jeffries
1977	South Caro. St.	9	1	1	Willie Jeffries
	Grambling	10	1	0	Eddie Robinson
	Florida A&M	11	0	0	Rudy Hubbard
1978	Florida A&M	12	1	0	Rudy Hubbard
1979	Tennessee St.	8	3	0	John Merritt
1980	Grambling	10	2	0	Eddie Robinson
1981	South Caro. St.	10	3	0	Bill Davis
1982	* Tennessee St.	9	0	1	John Merritt
1983	Grambling	8	1	2	Eddie Robinson
1984	Alcorn St.	9	1	0	Marino Casem
1985	Jackson St.	8	3	0	W. C. Gorden
1986	Central St. (Ohio)	10	1	1	Billy Joe
1987	Central St. (Ohio)	10	1	1	Billy Joe
1988	Central St. (Ohio)	11	2	0	Billy Joe
1989	Central St. (Ohio)	10	2	0	Billy Joe
1990	# Central St. (Ohio)	11	1	0	Billy Joe
1991	Alabama St.	11	0	1	Houston Markham
1992	Grambling	10	2	0	Eddie Robinson
1993	Southern-B.R.	11	1	0	Pete Richardson

*Tennessee State's participation in the 1982 Division I-AA championship (1-1 record) voided. #NAIA Division I national champion.

American Sports Wire

Selected by American Sports Wire and compiled by Dick Simpson, CEO. Selected from 1991 by the American Sports Wire, Shadow Hills, 28770 Kathleen Avenue, Sangus, Calif. 91350. Record includes postseason games.

Year	Team	Won	Lost	Tied	Coach
1991	Alabama St.	11	0	1	Houston Markham
1992	Grambling	10	2	0	Eddie Robinson
1993	Southern-B.R.	11	1	0	Pete Richardson

Heritage Bowl

The first bowl game matching historically black schools in Division I-AA . The champion of the Southwestern Athletic Conference meets the champion of the Mid-Eastern Athletic Conference.

Date	Score (Attendance)	Site
12-21-91	Alabama St. 36, North Caro. A&T 13 (7,724)	Miami, Fla.
1-2-93	Grambling 45, Florida A&M 15 (11,273)	Tallahassee, Fla.
1-1-94	Southern-B.R. 11, South Caro. St. 0 (36,128)	Atlanta, Ga.

Division II Records

Individual Records

Official national statistics for all nonmajor four-year colleges began in 1946 with a limited postseason survey. In 1948, the service was expanded to include weekly individual and team statistics rankings in all categories except interceptions, field goals, punt returns and kickoff returns; these categories were added to official individual rankings and records in 1970. In 1992, statistics compilations for individual all-purpose yards and team net punting, punt returns, kickoff returns and turnover margin were begun.

From 1946, individual rankings were by totals. Beginning in 1970, most season individual rankings were by per-game averages. In total offense, receiving yards, all-purpose yards, rushing and scoring, yards or points per game determine rankings; in receiving and interceptions, catches per game; in punt and kickoff returns, yards per return; and in field goals, number made per game. Punting always has been by average, and all team rankings have been per game.

Beginning in 1979, passers were ranked in all divisions on efficiency rating points (see page 6 for explanation).

Before 1967, rankings and records included all four-year colleges that reported their statistics to the NCAA. Beginning with the 1967 season, rankings and records included only members of the NCAA.

In 1973, College Division teams were divided into Division II and Division III under a three-division reorganization plan adopted by the special NCAA Convention on August 1, 1973. Career records of players who played in both Divisions II and III will be found where they played the majority of their careers (i.e., two of the last three or three of the last four years).

Collegiate records for all NCAA divisions can be determined by comparing records for all four divisions.

All individual and team statistics rankings include regular-season games only.

Total Offense

(Rushing Plus Passing)

MOST PLAYS
Game
85—Dave Walter, Michigan Tech vs. Ferris St., Oct. 18, 1986 (457 yards)
Season
594—Chris Hegg, Northeast Mo. St., 1985 (3,782 yards)
Per-game record—58.3, Dave Walter, Michigan Tech, 1986 (525 in 9)
Career
2,045—Earl Harvey, N.C. Central, 1985-88 (10,667 yards)
Also holds per-game record at 52.4 (2,045 in 39)

MOST PLAYS BY A FRESHMAN
Season
538—Earl Harvey, N.C. Central, 1985 (3,008 yards)
Also holds per-game record at 53.8 (538 in 10)

MOST YARDS GAINED
Game
623—Perry Klein, LIU-C.W. Post vs. Salisbury St., Nov. 6, 1993 (9 rushing, 614 passing)

Season
4,052—Perry Klein, LIU-C.W. Post, 1993 (295 rushing, 3,757 passing)
Also holds per-game record at 405.2 (4,052 in 10)
Career
10,667—Earl Harvey, N.C. Central, 1985-88 (46 rushing, 10,621 passing)
Per-game record—306.6, Marty Washington, Livingston, 1992-93 (5,212 in 17)

MOST SEASONS GAINING 3,000 YARDS OR MORE
2—Pat Brennan, Franklin, 1983 (3,239) & 1984 (3,248)

MOST SEASONS GAINING 2,500 YARDS OR MORE
3—Jim Lindsey, Abilene Christian, 1968 (2,740), 1969 (2,646) & 1970 (2,654)

GAINING 2,500 YARDS RUSHING AND 3,000 YARDS PASSING
Career
Jeff Bentrim, North Dak. St., 1983-86 (2,946 rushing, 3,453 passing)

MOST YARDS GAINED BY A FRESHMAN
Game
482—Matthew Montgomery, Hampton vs. Tuskegee, Oct. 26, 1991
Season
3,008—Earl Harvey, N.C. Central, 1985 (538 plays)
Per-game record—318.1, Shawn Dupris, Southwest St., 1993 (2,863 in 9)

MOST GAMES GAINING 300 YARDS OR MORE
Season
8—Chris Hegg, Northeast Mo. St., 1985
Career
15—June Jones, Portland St., 1975-76; Jim Lindsey, Abilene Christian, 1967-70

HIGHEST AVERAGE GAIN PER PLAY
Season
(Min. 350 plays) 8.8—Brett Salisbury, Wayne St. (Neb.), 1993 (424 for 3,732)
Career
(Min. 950 plays) 7.6—Doug Williams, Grambling, 1974-77 (1,072 for 8,195)

MOST TOUCHDOWNS RESPONSIBLE FOR
(TDs Scored and Passed For)
Game
10—Bruce Swanson, North Park vs. North Central, Oct. 12, 1968 (passed for 10)
Also holds Most Points Responsible For record at 60
Season
46—Bob Toledo, San Fran. St., 1967 (scored 1, passed for 45)
Also holds per-game record at 4.6 (46 in 10) and Most Points Responsible For record at 276
Career
106—Earl Harvey, N.C. Central, 1985-88 (scored 20, passed for 86)
Also holds Most Points Responsible For record at 636

Rushing

MOST RUSHES
Game
62—Nelson Edmonds, Northern Mich. vs. Wayne St. (Mich.), Oct. 26, 1991 (291 yards)
Season
350—Leon Burns, Long Beach St., 1969 (1,659 yards)
Per-game record—38.6, Mark Perkins, Hobart, 1968 (309 in 8)
Career
1,072—Bernie Peeters, Luther, 1968-71 (4,435 yards)
Also holds per-game record at 29.8 (1,072 in 36)

MOST CONSECUTIVE RUSHES BY SAME PLAYER
Game
13—Michael Mann, Indiana (Pa.) vs. Edinboro, Nov. 7, 1992; Randy Walker, Wheaton (Ill.) vs. North Park, Nov. 4, 1972 (during one ball possession)

MOST RUSHES BY A QUARTERBACK
Career
730—Shawn Graves, Wofford, 1989-92

MOST YARDS GAINED
Half
213—Chad Guthrie, Northeast Mo. St. vs. Southwest Baptist, Oct. 3, 1992 (16 rushes)
Game
382—Kelly Ellis, Northern Iowa vs. Western Ill., Oct. 13, 1979 (40 rushes)
Season
2,011—Johnny Bailey, Tex. A&M-Kingsville, 1986 (271 rushes)
Also holds per-game record at 182.8 (2,011 in 11)
Career
6,320—Johnny Bailey, Tex. A&M-Kingsville, 1986-89 (885 rushes)
Also holds per-game record (min. 3,000 yds.) at 162.1 (6,320 in 39)

MOST YARDS GAINED BY A FRESHMAN
Game
370—Jim Hissam, Marietta vs. Bethany (W. Va.), Nov. 15, 1958 (22 rushes)
Season
2,011—Johnny Bailey, Tex. A&M-Kingsville, 1986 (271 rushes)
Also holds per-game record at 182.8 (2,011 in 11)

MOST YARDS GAINED IN FIRST GAME OF CAREER
238—Johnny Bailey, Tex. A&M-Kingsville vs. Texas Southern, Sept. 6, 1986

MOST YARDS GAINED BY TWO PLAYERS, SAME TEAM
Game
514—Thelbert Withers (333) & Derrick Ray (181), N.M. Highlands vs. Fort Lewis, Oct. 17, 1992
Season
3,526—Johnny Bailey (2,011) & Heath Sherman (1,515), Tex. A&M-Kingsville, 1986
Also hold per-game record at 320.5 (3,526 in 11)
Career
8,594—Johnny Bailey (5,051) & Heath Sherman (3,543), Tex. A&M-Kingsville, 1986-88 (1,317 rushes)

TWO PLAYERS, SAME TEAM, EACH GAINING 200 YARDS OR MORE
Game
Ed Tillison (272) & Jeremy Wilson (204), Northwest Mo. St. vs. Neb.-Kearney, Nov. 11, 1990; Jeremy Monroe (220) & Mark Kieliszewski (212), Michigan Tech vs. Trinity (Ill.), Nov. 3, 1990; Johnny Bailey (207) & Heath Sherman (206), Tex. A&M-Kingsville vs. East Central Okla., Sept. 20, 1986; Johnny Bailey (244) & Heath Sherman (216), Tex. A&M-Kingsville vs. North Dak., Sept. 13, 1986 (consecutive games)

TWO PLAYERS, SAME TEAM, EACH GAINING 1,000 YARDS OR MORE
Season
11 times. Most recent: Pittsburg St., 1991—Darren Dawson (1,176) & Ronald Moore (1,040); Pittsburg St., 1990—Darren Dawson (1,170) & Ronald Moore (1,013)

MOST GAMES GAINING 100 YARDS OR MORE
Season
11—Ronald Moore, Pittsburg St., 1992; Johnny Bailey, Tex. A&M-Kingsville, 1986
Bailey also holds freshman record at 11
Career
33—Johnny Bailey, Tex. A&M-Kingsville, 1986-89 (39 games)

MOST CONSECUTIVE GAMES GAINING 100 YARDS OR MORE
Season
11—Ronald Moore, Pittsburg St., 1992; Johnny Bailey, Tex. A&M-Kingsville, 1986
Bailey also holds freshman record at 11
Career
24—Peter Gorniewicz, Colby, 1971-73

MOST GAMES GAINING 200 YARDS OR MORE
Season
5—Johnny Bailey, Tex. A&M-Kingsville, 1986
Also holds freshman record at 5

Career

11—Johnny Bailey, Tex. A&M-Kingsville, 1986-89 (39 games)

MOST CONSECUTIVE GAMES GAINING 200 YARDS OR MORE
Season

4—Johnny Bailey, Tex. A&M-Kingsville, 1986 (first games of his career)

MOST YARDS GAINED BY A QUARTERBACK
Game

323—Shawn Graves, Wofford vs. Lenoir-Rhyne, Sept. 15, 1990 (23 rushes)

Season

1,483—Shawn Graves, Wofford, 1989 (241 rushes)

Career

5,128—Shawn Graves, Wofford, 1989-92 (730 rushes)

MOST YARDS GAINED BY A FRESHMAN IN FIRST GAME OF CAREER

238—Johnny Bailey, Tex. A&M-Kingsville vs. Texas Southern, Sept. 6, 1986

MOST SEASONS GAINING 1,000 YARDS OR MORE
Career

4—Jeremy Monroe, Michigan Tech, 1990-93; Johnny Bailey, Tex. A&M-Kingsville, 1986-89; Vincent Allen, Indiana St., 1973-75, 77

HIGHEST AVERAGE GAIN PER RUSH
Game

(Min. 20 rushes) 17.5—Don Polkinghorne, Washington (Mo.) vs. Wash. & Lee, Nov. 23, 1957 (21 for 367)

Season

(Min. 140 rushes) 10.5—Billy Johnson, Widener, 1972 (148 for 1,556)

(Min. 200 rushes) 8.6—Roger Graham, New Haven, 1992 (200 for 1,717)

(Min. 250 rushes) 7.4—Johnny Bailey, Tex. A&M-Kingsville, 1986 (271 for 2,011)

Career

(Min. 300 rushes) 9.1—Billy Johnson, Widener, 1971-73 (411 for 3,735)

(Min. 500 rushes) 8.5—Bill Rhodes, Western St., 1953-56 (506 for 4,294)

MOST RUSHING TOUCHDOWNS SCORED
Game

8—Junior Wolf, Panhandle St. vs. St. Mary (Kan.), Nov. 8, 1958

Season

28—Terry Metcalf, Long Beach St., 1971

Career

72—Shawn Graves, Wofford, 1989-92

Per-game record—1.8, Jeff Bentrim, North Dak. St., 1983-86 (64 in 35)

MOST RUSHING TOUCHDOWNS SCORED BY A FRESHMAN
Season

24—Shawn Graves, Wofford, 1989

Also holds per-game record at 2.2 (24 in 11)

MOST RUSHING TOUCHDOWNS SCORED BY A QUARTERBACK
Season

24—Shawn Graves, Wofford, 1989

Per-game record—2.3, Jeff Bentrim, North Dak. St. (23 in 10)

Career

72—Shawn Graves, Wofford, 1989-92

Per-game record—1.8, Jeff Bentrim, North Dak. St., 1983-86 (64 in 35)

MOST RUSHING TOUCHDOWNS SCORED BY TWO PLAYERS, SAME TEAM
Season

41—Roger Graham (22) & A. J. Livingston (19), New Haven, 1992; Heath Sherman (23) & Johnny Bailey (18), Tex. A&M-Kingsville, 1986

Per-game record—4.1, Roger Graham & A. J. Livingston, New Haven, 1992 (41 in 10)

Career

106—Heath Sherman (55) & Johnny Bailey (51), Tex. A&M-Kingsville, 1985-88

LONGEST PLAY

99 yards—20 times. Most recent: Thelbert Withers, N.M. Highlands vs. Fort Lewis, Oct. 17, 1992

Passing

HIGHEST PASSING EFFICIENCY RATING POINTS
Season

(Min. 15 atts. per game) 210.1—Boyd Crawford, Col. of Idaho, 1953 (120 attempts, 72 completions, 6 interceptions, 1,462 yards, 21 TD passes)

(Min. 100 comps.) 189.0—Chuck Green, Wittenberg, 1963 (182 attempts, 114 completions, 8 interceptions, 2,181 yards, 19 TD passes)

(Min. 200 comps.) 166.3—Brett Salisbury, Wayne St. (Neb.), 1993 (395 attempts, 276 completions, 14 interceptions, 3,729 yards, 29 TD passes)

Career

(Min. 375 comps.) 164.0—Chris Petersen, UC Davis, 1985-86 (553 attempts, 385 completions, 13 interceptions, 4,988 yards, 39 TD passes)

MOST PASSES ATTEMPTED
Game

72—Kurt Otto, North Dak. vs. Tex. A&M-Kingsville, Sept. 13, 1986 (completed 41); Kaipo Spencer, Santa Clara vs. Portland St., Oct. 11, 1975 (completed 37); Joe Stetser, Cal St. Chico vs. Oregon Tech, Sept. 23, 1967 (completed 38)

Season

515—Tod Mayfield, West Tex. A&M, 1986 (completed 317)

Per-game record—50.5, Marty Washington, Livingston, 1993 (404 in 8)

Career

1,442—Earl Harvey, N.C. Central, 1985-88 (completed 690)

Per-game record—46.2, Tim Von Dulm, Portland St., 1969-70 (924 in 20)

MOST PASSES COMPLETED
Game

45—Chris Hatcher, Valdosta St. vs. Mississippi Col., Oct. 23, 1993 (attempted 56), and vs. West Ga., Oct. 16, 1993 (attempted 61)

Season

335—Chris Hatcher, Valdosta St., 1993 (attempted 471)

Also holds per-game record at 30.5 (335 in 11)

Career

748—Rob Tomlinson, Cal St. Chico, 1988-91 (attempted 1,328)

Per-game record—25.0, Tim Von Dulm, Portland St., 1969-70 (500 in 20)

MOST PASSES COMPLETED BY A FRESHMAN
Game

41—Neil Lomax, Portland St. vs. Montana St., Nov. 19, 1977 (attempted 59)

MOST CONSECUTIVE PASSES COMPLETED
Game

20—Rod Bockwoldt, Weber St. vs. South Dak. St., Nov. 6, 1976

Season

23—Mike Ganey, Allegheny, 1967 (completed last 16 attempts vs. Carnegie Mellon, Oct. 9, and first 7 vs. Oberlin, Oct. 16)

HIGHEST PERCENTAGE OF PASSES COMPLETED
Game

(Min. 20 comps.) 90.9%—Rod Bockwoldt, Weber St. vs. South Dak. St., Nov. 6, 1976 (20 of 22)

(Min. 35 comps.) 80.4%—Chris Hatcher, Valdosta St. vs. Mississippi Col., Oct. 23, 1993 (45 of 56)

Season

(Min. 225 atts.) 71.1%—Chris Hatcher, Valdosta St., 1993 (335 of 471)

Career

(Min. 500 atts.) 69.6%—Chris Petersen, UC Davis, 1985-86 (385 of 553)

MOST PASSES HAD INTERCEPTED
Game

9—Pat Brennan, Franklin vs. Saginaw Valley, Sept. 24, 1983; Henry Schafer, Johns Hopkins vs. Haverford, Oct. 16, 1965

Season

32—Joe Stetser, Cal St. Chico, 1967 (attempted 464)

Career

83—Mike Houston, St. Joseph's (Ind.), 1978-81 (attempted 1,031)

LOWEST PERCENTAGE OF PASSES HAD INTERCEPTED
Season

(Min. 200 atts.) 0.4%—James Weir, New Haven, 1993 (1 of 266)

(Min. 300 atts.) 1.9%—Scott Jones, South Dak., 1985 (6 of 311)

Career

(Min. 500 atts.) 2.4%—Chris Petersen, UC Davis, 1985-86 (13 of 553)

(Min. 700 atts.) 2.6%—Jack Hull, Grand Valley St., 1988-91 (22 of 835)

MOST PASSES ATTEMPTED WITHOUT INTERCEPTION
Game

70—Tim Von Dulm, Portland St. vs. Eastern Wash., Nov. 21, 1970

Season

113—Jeff Allen, New Hampshire, 1975

MOST CONSECUTIVE PASSES ATTEMPTED WITHOUT INTERCEPTION

211—Ken Suhl, New Haven, during 10 games from Sept. 5 to Nov. 14, 1992

MOST YARDS GAINED
Game

614—Perry Klein, LIU-C.W. Post vs. Salisbury St., Nov. 6, 1993

Season

3,757—Perry Klein, LIU-C.W. Post, 1993

Per-game record—382.8, Marty Washington, Livingston, 1993 (3,062 in 8)

Career

10,621—Earl Harvey, N.C. Central, 1985-88

Per-game record—298.4, Tim Von Dulm, Portland St., 1969-70 (5,967 in 20)

MOST YARDS GAINED BY A FRESHMAN
Game

469—Neil Lomax, Portland St. vs. Montana St., Nov. 19, 1977

Season

3,190—Earl Harvey, N.C. Central, 1985

MOST GAMES GAINING 200 YARDS OR MORE
Season

11—Chris Hatcher, Valdosta St., 1993; Tod Mayfield, West Tex. A&M, 1986; Chris Hegg, Northeast Mo. St., 1985

Career

29—Dave DenBraber, Ferris St., 1984-87

MOST CONSECUTIVE GAMES GAINING 200 YARDS OR MORE
Career

17—Chris Hatcher, Valdosta St., during last six games of 1992 and all 11 games of 1993

MOST GAMES GAINING 300 YARDS OR MORE
Season

10—Brett Salisbury, Wayne St. (Neb.), 1993

Career

15—Earl Harvey, N.C. Central, 1987-88

MOST CONSECUTIVE GAMES GAINING 300 YARDS OR MORE
Season

10—Brett Salisbury, Wayne St. (Neb.), 1993

MOST YARDS GAINED PER ATTEMPT
Season

(Min. 300 atts.) 11.3—Jayson Merrill, Western St., 1991 (309 for 3,484)

Career

(Min. 500 atts.) 10.6—John Charles, Portland St., 1991-92 (510 for 5,389)

(Min. 700 atts.) 9.0—Bruce Upstill, Col. of Emporia, 1960-63 (769 for 6,935)

MOST YARDS GAINED PER COMPLETION
Season

(Min. 125 comps.) 18.7—Matt Cook, Mo. Southern St., 1991 (141 for 2,637)

DIVISION II

(Min. 175 comps.) 17.9—Jayson Merrill, Western St., 1991 (195 for 3,484)

Career
(Min. 300 comps.) 17.8—Jayson Merrill, Western St., 1990-91 (328 for 5,830)
(Min. 450 comps.) 17.4—Doug Williams, Grambling, 1974-77 (484 for 8,411)

MOST TOUCHDOWN PASSES
Quarter
5—Kevin Russell, Calif. (Pa.) vs. Frostburg St., Nov. 5, 1983 (2nd quarter)
Game
10—Bruce Swanson, North Park vs. North Central, Oct. 12, 1968
Season
45—Bob Toledo, San Fran. St., 1967
Also holds per-game record at 4.5 (45 in 10)
Career
93—Doug Williams, Grambling, 1974-77
Per-game record—2.7, Bob Toledo, San Fran. St., 1966-67 (53 in 20)

MOST TOUCHDOWN PASSES BY A FRESHMAN
Game
6—Earl Harvey, N.C. Central vs. Johnson Smith, Nov. 9, 1985
Season
28—Shawn Dupris, Southwest St., 1993

HIGHEST PERCENTAGE OF PASSES FOR TOUCHDOWNS
Season
(Min. 150 atts.) 16.0%—John Ford, Hardin-Simmons, 1949 (26 of 163)
(Min. 300 atts.) 11.4%—Bob Toledo, San Fran. St., 1967 (45 of 396)
Career
(Min. 500 atts.) 12.2%—Al Niemela, West Chester, 1985-88 (73 of 600)

MOST CONSECUTIVE GAMES THROWING A TOUCHDOWN PASS
Career
24—Matt Cook, Mo. Southern St., 1990-93 (last 2 in 1990, all 11 in 1991, 1 in 1992, all 10 in 1993)

MOST GAMES THROWING A TOUCHDOWN PASS
Career
38—Doug Williams, Grambling, 1974-77 (played in 40 games)

LONGEST COMPLETION
99 yards—11 times. Most recent: Ray Morrow to Jeff Williamson, Cal St. Hayward vs. Redlands, Sept. 25, 1993; Bob McLaughlin to Eric Muldowney, Lock Haven vs. Mansfield, Sept. 25, 1993

Receiving

MOST PASSES CAUGHT
Game
23—Barry Wagner, Alabama A&M vs. Clark Atlanta, Nov. 4, 1989 (370 yards)
Season
117—Chris George, Glenville St., 1993 (1,876 yards)
Also holds per-game record at 11.7 (117 in 10)
Career
253—Chris Myers, Kenyon, 1967-70 (3,897 yards)
Per-game record—8.6, Ed Bell, Idaho St., 1968-69 (163 in 19)

MOST CONSECUTIVE GAMES CATCHING A PASS
Career
42—Gary Compton, East Tex. St., 1987-90 (42 of 42 games played)

MOST PASSES CAUGHT BY A TIGHT END
Game
15—By six players. Most recent: Mark Martin, Cal St. Chico vs. San Fran. St., Oct. 21, 1989 (223 yards)
Season
77—Bob Tucker, Bloomsburg, 1967 (1,325 yards)

Career
199—Barry Naone, Portland St., 1985-88 (2,237 yards)

MOST PASSES CAUGHT BY A RUNNING BACK
Season
94—Billy Joe Masters, Evansville, 1987 (960 yards)
Also holds per-game record at 9.4 (94 in 10)
Career
200—Mark Steinmeyer, Kutztown, 1988-91 (2,118 yards)
Per-game record—5.4, Mark Marana, Northern Mich., 1979-80 (107 in 20)

MOST PASSES CAUGHT BY A FRESHMAN
Season
66—Don Hutt, Boise St., 1971 (928 yards)

MOST PASSES CAUGHT BY TWO PLAYERS, SAME TEAM
Career
363—Robert Clark (210) & Robert Green (153), N.C. Central, 1983-86 (6,528 yards)

MOST YARDS GAINED
Game
370—Barry Wagner, Alabama A&M vs. Clark Atlanta, Nov. 4, 1989 (caught 23)
Season
1,876—Chris George, Glenville St., 1993 (caught 117)
Also holds per-game record at 187.6 (1,876 in 10)
Career
4,354—Bruce Cerone, Yankton/Emporia St., 1966-67, 68-69 (caught 241)
Per-game record—137.3, Ed Bell, Idaho St., 1968-69 (2,608 in 19)

MOST YARDS GAINED BY A TIGHT END
Game
290—Bob Tucker, Bloomsburg vs. Susquehanna, Oct. 7, 1967 (caught 15)
Season
1,325—Bob Tucker, Bloomsburg, 1967 (caught 77)
Career
2,494—Dan Anderson, Northwest Mo. St., 1982-85 (caught 186)

MOST YARDS GAINED BY A RUNNING BACK
Game
209—Don Lenhard, Bucknell vs. Delaware, Nov. 19, 1966 (caught 11)
Season
960—Billy Joe Masters, Evansville, 1987 (caught 94)
Also holds per-game record at 96.0 (960 in 10)
Career
2,118—Mark Steinmeyer, Kutztown, 1988-91 (caught 200)

MOST YARDS GAINED BY TWO PLAYERS, SAME TEAM
Career
6,528—Robert Clark (4,231) & Robert Green (2,297), N.C. Central, 1983-86 (caught 363)

HIGHEST AVERAGE GAIN PER RECEPTION
Season
(Min. 30 receps.) 32.5—Tyrone Johnson, Western St., 1991 (32 for 1,039)
(Min. 40 receps.) 27.6—Chris Harkness, Ashland, 1987 (41 for 1,131)
(Min. 55 receps.) 24.0—Rod Smith, Mo. Southern St., 1991 (60 for 1,439)
Career
(Min. 135 receps.) 22.8—Tyrone Johnson, Western St., 1990-93 (163 for 3,717)
(Min. 180 receps.) 20.1—Robert Clark, N.C. Central, 1983-86 (210 for 4,231)

HIGHEST AVERAGE GAIN PER RECEPTION BY A RUNNING BACK
Season
(Min. 40 receps.) 19.4—John Smith, Boise St., 1975 (45 for 854)
Career
(Min. 80 receps.) 18.1—John Smith, Boise St., 1972-75 (89 for 1,608)

MOST TOUCHDOWN PASSES CAUGHT
Game
8—Paul Zaeske, North Park vs. North Central, Oct. 12,

1968 (11 receptions)
Season
20—Ed Bell, Idaho St., 1969 (96 receptions)
Per-game record—2.0, Shannon Sharpe, Savannah St., 1989 (18 in 9); Ed Bell, Idaho St., 1969 (20 in 10)
Career
49—Bruce Cerone, Yankton/Emporia St., 1966-67, 68-69 (241 receptions)
Per-game record—1.6, Ed Bell, Idaho St., 1968-69 (30 in 19)

MOST TOUCHDOWN PASSES CAUGHT BY A TIGHT END
Game
5—Mike Palomino, Portland St. vs. Cal Poly SLO, Nov. 16, 1991; Alex Preuss, Grand Valley St. vs. Winona St., Sept. 17, 1988
Season
13—Bob Tucker, Bloomsburg, 1967

MOST TOUCHDOWN PASSES CAUGHT BY A RUNNING BACK
Season
11—John Smith, Boise St., 1975
Career
24—John Smith, Boise St., 1972-75

MOST TOUCHDOWN PASSES CAUGHT BY A FRESHMAN
Season
11—Charles Davis, Saginaw Valley, 1993; Douglas Grant, Savannah St., 1990; Harold "Red" Roberts, Austin Peay, 1967

HIGHEST PERCENTAGE OF PASSES CAUGHT FOR TOUCHDOWNS
Season
(Min. 10 TDs) 68.8%—Jim Callahan, Temple, 1966 (11 of 16)
Career
(Min. 20 TDs) 30.0%—Bob Cherry, Wittenberg, 1960-63 (27 of 90)

MOST CONSECUTIVE PASSES CAUGHT FOR TOUCHDOWNS
Season
10—Jim Callahan, Temple, 1966 (first 5 games, first games of career)

MOST CONSECUTIVE GAMES CATCHING A TOUCHDOWN PASS
Career
14—Jeff Tiefenthaler, South Dak. St., from Oct. 27, 1984, through Nov. 9, 1985

MOST GAMES CATCHING A TOUCHDOWN PASS
Career
25—Jeff Tiefenthaler, South Dak. St., 1983-86 (in 36 games)

LONGEST RECEPTION
99 yards—11 times. Most recent: Jeff Williamson from Ray Morrow, Cal St. Hayward vs. Redlands, Sept. 25, 1993; Eric Muldowney from Bob McLaughlin, Lock Haven vs. Mansfield, Sept. 25, 1993

Punting

MOST PUNTS
Game
32—Jan Jones, Sam Houston St. vs. East Tex. St., Nov. 2, 1946 (1,203 yards)
Season
98—John Tassi, Lincoln (Mo.), 1981 (3,163 yards)
Career
328—Dan Brown, Nicholls St., 1976-79 (12,883 yards)

HIGHEST AVERAGE PER PUNT
Game
(Min. 5 punts) 57.5—Tim Baer, Colorado Mines vs. Fort Lewis, Oct. 25, 1986 (8 for 460)
Season
(Min. 20 punts) 49.1—Steve Ecker, Shippensburg, 1965 (32 for 1,570)
(Min. 40 punts) 46.3—Mark Bounds, West Tex. A&M, 1990 (69 for 3,198)

Career
(Min. 100 punts) 44.3—Steve Lewis, Jacksonville St., 1989-92 (100 for 4,434)

LONGEST PUNT
97 yards—Earl Hurst, Emporia St. vs. Central Mo. St., Oct. 3, 1964

Interceptions

(From 1970)

MOST PASSES INTERCEPTED
Quarter
3—Anthony Devine, Millersville vs. Cheyney, Oct. 13, 1990 (3rd quarter; 90 yards); Mike McDonald, Southwestern La. vs. Lamar, Oct. 24, 1970 (4th quarter; 25 yards)
Game
5—By five players. Most recent: Gary Evans, Northeast Mo. St. vs. Missouri-Rolla, Oct. 18, 1975
Season
14—By five players. Most recent: Luther Howard, Delaware St., 1972 (99 yards); Eugene Hunter, Fort Valley St., 1972 (211 yards)
Per-game record—1.56, Luther Howard, Delaware St., 1972 (14 in 9); Eugene Hunter, Fort Valley St., 1972 (14 in 9); Tom Rezzuti, Northeastern, 1971 (14 in 9)
Career
37—Tom Collins, Indianapolis, 1982-85 (390 yards)

MOST YARDS ON INTERCEPTION RETURNS
Game
152—Desmond Brown, Tuskegee vs. Morris Brown, Sept. 15, 1990 (2 interceptions)
Season
300—Mike Brim, Virginia Union, 1986 (8 interceptions)
Career
504—Anthony Leonard, Virginia Union, 1973-76 (17 interceptions)

HIGHEST AVERAGE GAIN PER INTERCEPTION
Season
(Min. 6 ints.) 40.0—Steve Smith, Bowie St., 1992 (6 for 240)
Career
(Min. 10 ints.) 37.4—Greg Anderson, Montana, 1974-76 (11 for 411)
(Min. 15 ints.) 29.6—Anthony Leonard, Virginia Union, 1973-76 (17 for 504)

MOST TOUCHDOWNS SCORED ON INTERCEPTIONS
Season
4—Clay Blalack, Tenn.-Martin, 1976 (8 interceptions)

LONGEST INTERCEPTION RETURN
100 yards—Many times. Most recent: Neely Lovett, Savannah St. vs. Tuskegee, Sept. 11, 1993

Punt Returns

(From 1970)

MOST PUNT RETURNS
Game
12—David Nelson, Ferris St. vs. Northern Mich., Oct. 2, 1993 (240 yards)
Season
61—Armin Anderson, UC Davis, 1984 (516 yards)
Career
153—Armin Anderson, UC Davis, 1983-85 (1,207 yards)

MOST YARDS ON PUNT RETURNS
Game
265—Billy Johnson, Widener vs. St. John's (N.Y.), Sept. 23, 1972 (4 returns)
Season
604—David Nelson, Ferris St., 1993 (50 returns)
Career
1,207—Armin Anderson, UC Davis, 1983-85 (153 returns)

HIGHEST AVERAGE GAIN PER RETURN
Game
(Min. 4 rets.) 66.3—Billy Johnson, Widener vs. St. John's (N.Y.), Sept. 23, 1972 (4 for 265)
Season
(Min. 1.2 rets. per game) 34.1—Billy Johnson, Widener, 1972 (15 for 511)
Career
(Min. 1.2 rets. per game) 24.7—Billy Johnson, Widener, 1971-73 (40 for 989)

MOST TOUCHDOWNS SCORED ON PUNT RETURNS
Game
3—By four players. Most recent: Virgil Seay, Troy St. vs. Livingston, Sept. 29, 1979
Season
4—Michael Fields, Mississippi Col., 1984; Billy Johnson, Widener, 1972
Career
7—Billy Johnson, Widener, 1971-73

Kickoff Returns

(From 1970)

MOST KICKOFF RETURNS
Game
9—Darron Turner, Tenn.-Martin vs. Jacksonville St., Oct. 21, 1989; Thad Kuehnl, Michigan Tech vs. Northern Mich., Sept. 5, 1987; Matthew Williams, Northeast La. vs. Jacksonville St., Nov. 3, 1973
Season
47—Sean Tarrant, Lincoln (Mo.), 1986 (729 yards) Also holds per-game record at 4.3 (47 in 11)
Career
116—Johnny Cox, Fort Lewis, 1990-93 (2,476 yards)

MOST YARDS ON KICKOFF RETURNS
Game
276—Matt Pericolosi, Central Conn. St. vs. Hofstra, Sept. 14, 1991 (6 returns); Tom Dufresne, Hamline vs. Minn.-Duluth, Sept. 30, 1972 (7 returns)
Season
983—Doug Parrish, San Fran. St., 1990 (34 returns)
Career
2,476—Johnny Cox, Fort Lewis, 1990-93 (116 returns)

HIGHEST AVERAGE GAIN PER RETURN
Game
(Min. 3 rets.) 71.7—Clarence Martin, Cal Poly SLO vs. Cal Poly Pomona, Nov. 20, 1982 (3 for 215)
Season
(Min. 1.2 rets. per game) 39.4—LaVon Reis, Western St., 1993 (14 for 552)
Career
(Min. 1.2 rets. per game) 34.0—Glen Printers, Southern Colo., 1973-74 (25 for 851)

MOST TOUCHDOWNS SCORED ON KICKOFF RETURNS
Game
2—Clarence Martin, Cal Poly SLO vs. Cal Poly Pomona, Nov. 20, 1982 (successive); Tom Dufresne, Hamline vs. Minn.-Duluth, Sept. 30, 1972
Season
3—Danny Lee, Jacksonville St., 1992; Dave Ludy, Winona St., 1992; Otha Hill, Central St. (Ohio), 1979
Career
7—Dave Ludy, Winona St., 1991-93

LONGEST KICKOFF RETURN
100 yards—Many times. Most recent: Wilson Hookfin, Wayne St. (Neb.) vs. Neb.-Kearney, Oct. 9, 1993

Total Kick Returns

(Combined Punt and Kickoff Returns)

MOST KICK RETURNS
Season
63—Bobby Yates, Central Mo. St., 1990 (31 kickoffs, 32 punts, 840 yards)

MOST KICK-RETURN YARDS
Career
2,971—Johnny Cox, Fort Lewis, 1990-93 (157 returns, 495 on punt returns, 2,476 on kickoff returns)

MOST TOUCHDOWNS
Career
10—Anthony Leonard, Virginia Union, 1973-76 (6 punt returns, 4 kickoff returns)

MOST CONSECUTIVE TOUCHDOWNS ON KICK RETURNS
Game
2—Victor Barnes, Nebraska-Omaha vs. Neb.-Kearney, Sept. 8, 1990 (94-yard kickoff return & 79-yard punt return)

All Runbacks

(Combined Interceptions, Punt Returns and Kickoff Returns)

MOST TOUCHDOWNS
Season
6—Anthony Leonard, Virginia Union, 1974 (2 interceptions, 2 punt returns, 2 kickoff returns)
Career
13—Anthony Leonard, Virginia Union, 1973-76 (3 interceptions, 6 punt returns, 4 kickoff returns)

LONGEST RETURN OF A MISSED FIELD GOAL
100—Kalvin Simmons, Clark Atlanta vs. Morris Brown, Sept. 5, 1987 (actually from 6 yards in end zone)

Opponent's Punts Blocked

Career
13—Bernard Ford, Central Fla., 1985-87

All-Purpose Yards

(Yardage Gained From Rushing, Receiving and All Runbacks)

MOST PLAYS
Season
415—Steve Roberts, Butler, 1989 (325 rushes, 49 receptions, 21 punt returns, 20 kickoff returns; 2,669 yards)
Career
1,195—Steve Roberts, Butler, 1986-89 (1,026 rushes, 120 receptions, 21 punt returns, 28 kickoff returns)

MOST YARDS GAINED
Game
525—Andre Johnson, Ferris St. vs. Clarion, Sept. 16, 1989 (19 rushing, 235 receiving, 10 punt returns, 261 kickoff returns; 17 plays)
Season
2,669—Steve Roberts, Butler, 1989 (1,450 rushing, 532 receiving, 272 punt returns, 415 kickoff returns; 415 plays)
Also holds per-game record at 266.9 (2,669 in 10)
Career
7,803—Johnny Bailey, Tex. A&M-Kingsville, 1986-89 (6,302 rushing, 452 receiving, 20 punt returns, 1,011 kickoff returns)
Per-game record—205.1, Howard Stevens, Randolph-Macon, 1968-69 (3,691 in 18)

MOST YARDS GAINED BY A FRESHMAN
Season
2,425—Johnny Bailey, Tex. A&M-Kingsville, 1986 (2,011 rushing, 54 receiving, 20 punt returns, 340 kickoff returns; 296 plays)
Also holds per-game record at 220.5 (2,425 in 11)

MOST YARDS GAINED BY TWO PLAYERS, SAME TEAM
Season
4,076—Johnny Bailey (2,425) & Heath Sherman (1,651), Tex. A&M-Kingsville, 1986
Also hold per-game record at 370.5 (4,076 in 11)

HIGHEST AVERAGE GAIN PER PLAY
Game
(Min. 15 plays) 30.9—Andre Johnson, Ferris St. vs. Clarion, Sept. 16, 1989 (17 for 525)
Season
(Min. 1,500 yards, 150 plays) 12.9—Billy Johnson, Widener, 1972 (175 for 2,265)

DIVISION II

Career
(Min. 4,000 yards, 300 plays) 11.3—Billy Johnson, Widener, 1971-73 (479 for 5,404)

Scoring

MOST POINTS SCORED
Game
48—Paul Zaeske, North Park vs. North Central, Oct. 12, 1968 (8 TDs); Junior Wolf, Panhandle St. vs. St. Mary (Kan.), Nov. 8, 1958 (8 TDs)
Season
178—Terry Metcalf, Long Beach St., 1971 (29 TDs, 4 PATs)
Per-game record—21.0, Carl Herakovich, Rose-Hulman, 1958 (168 in 8)
Career
464—Walter Payton, Jackson St., 1971-74 (66 TDs, 53 PATs, 5 FGs)
Per-game record—13.4, Ole Gunderson, St. Olaf, 1969-71 (362 in 27)

MOST POINTS SCORED BY A FRESHMAN
Season
144—Shawn Graves, Wofford, 1989
Also holds per-game record at 13.1 (144 in 11)

MOST POINTS SCORED BY A QUARTERBACK
Season
144—Shawn Graves, Wofford, 1989
Per-game record—13.8, Jeff Bentrim, North Dak. St., 1986 (138 in 10)
Career
438—Shawn Graves, Wofford, 1989-92
Per-game record—11.0, Jeff Bentrim, North Dak. St., 1983-86 (386 in 35)

MOST POINTS SCORED BY TWO PLAYERS, SAME TEAM
Season
254—Heath Sherman (138) & Johnny Bailey (116), Tex. A&M-Kingsville, 1986
Also hold per-game record at 23.1 (254 in 11)
Career
666—Heath Sherman (336) & Johnny Bailey (330), Tex. A&M-Kingsville, 1986-88

MOST TOUCHDOWNS SCORED
Game
8—Paul Zaeske, North Park vs. North Central, Oct. 12, 1968 (all on pass receptions); Junior Wolf, Panhandle St. vs. St. Mary (Kan.), Nov. 8, 1958 (all by rushing)
Season
29—Terry Metcalf, Long Beach St., 1971
Per-game record—3.1, Carl Herakovich, Rose-Hulman, 1958 (25 in 8)
Career
72—Shawn Graves, Wofford, 1989-92
Per-game record—2.2, Billy Johnson, Widener, 1971-73 (62 in 28)

MOST TOUCHDOWNS SCORED BY A FRESHMAN
Season
24—Shawn Graves, Wofford, 1989
Also holds per-game record at 2.2 (24 in 11)

MOST TOUCHDOWNS SCORED BY A QUARTERBACK
Season
24—Shawn Graves, Wofford, 1989
Per-game record—2.3, Jeff Bentrim, North Dak. St., 1986 (23 in 10)
Career
72—Shawn Graves, Wofford, 1989-92
Per-game record—1.8, Jeff Bentrim, North Dak. St., 1983-86 (64 in 35)

MOST TOUCHDOWNS SCORED BY TWO PLAYERS, SAME TEAM
Season
42—Heath Sherman (23) & Johnny Bailey (19), Tex. A&M-Kingsville, 1986
Also hold per-game record at 3.8 (42 in 11)
Career
110—Heath Sherman (56) & Johnny Bailey (54), Tex. A&M-Kingsville, 1986-88

MOST CONSECUTIVE GAMES SCORING A TOUCHDOWN
Career
25—Billy Johnson, Widener, 1971-73

MOST EXTRA POINTS MADE BY KICKING
Game
14—Art Anderson, North Park vs. North Central, Oct. 12, 1968 (attempted 15); Matt Johnson, Connecticut vs. Newport Naval Training, Oct. 22, 1949 (attempted 17)
Season
71—John O'Riordan, New Haven, 1993 (attempted 78)
Career
163—Miguel Sagaro, Grand Valley St., 1989-92 (attempted 179)

MOST EXTRA POINTS ATTEMPTED BY KICKING
Game
17—Matt Johnson, Connecticut vs. Newport Naval Training, Oct. 22, 1949 (made 14)
Season
78—John O'Riordan, New Haven, 1993 (made 71)
Career
179—Miguel Sagaro, Grand Valley St., 1989-92 (made 163); James Jenkins, Pittsburg St., 1988-91 (made 156)

HIGHEST PERCENTAGE OF EXTRA POINTS MADE BY KICKING
Season
(Best perfect season) 100.0%—Bryan Thompson, Angelo St., 1989 (51 of 51)
Career
(Min. 90 atts.) 98.9%—Mark DeMoss, Liberty, 1980-83 (92 of 93)
(Min. 130 atts.) 93.7%—Billy Watkins, East Tex. St., 1990-93 (134 of 143)

MOST CONSECUTIVE EXTRA POINTS MADE BY KICKING
Season
51—Bryan Thompson, Angelo St., 1989 (entire season)
Career
82—Mark DeMoss, Liberty (from Sept. 13, 1980, to Oct. 1, 1983; ended with missed PAT vs. Central St., Ohio, Oct. 1, 1983)

MOST POINTS SCORED BY KICKING
Game
20—Clarence Joseph, Central St. (Ohio) vs. Kentucky St., Oct. 16, 1982 (5 FGs, 5 PATs)
Season
92—Tom Jurich, Northern Ariz., 1977 (20 FGs, 32 PATs)
Per-game record—8.8, Jay Masek, Chadron St., 1990 (88 in 10)
Career
281—Billy Watkins, East Tex. St., 1990-93 (49 FGs, 134 PATs)
Per-game record (min. 145 pts.)—8.3, Dave Austinson, Northeast Mo. St., 1981-82 (149 in 18)
Per-game record (min. 200 pts.)—6.7, Eddie Loretto, UC Davis, 1985-88 (266 in 40)

Defensive Extra Points

MOST DEFENSIVE EXTRA POINTS SCORED
Game and Season
1—Many times

LONGEST DEFENSIVE EXTRA POINT BLOCKED-KICK RETURN
97—Dominic Kurtyan (DB), West Chester vs. Kutztown, Oct. 7, 1988 (scored)

LONGEST DEFENSIVE EXTRA POINT FUMBLE RETURN
87—Rod Beauchamp (DB), Colorado Mines vs. Hastings, Sept. 3, 1988

LONGEST DEFENSIVE EXTRA POINT INTERCEPTION RETURN
90—Jermal Pulliam (DE), Jacksonville St. vs. Kentucky St., Nov. 14, 1992

Field Goals

MOST FIELD GOALS MADE
Game
6—Steve Huff, Central Mo. St. vs. Southeast Mo. St., Nov. 2, 1985 (37, 45, 37, 24, 32, 27 yards; 6 attempts)
Season
20—Raul De la Flor, Humboldt St., 1993 (26 attempts); Pat Beaty, North Dak., 1988 (26 attempts); Tom Jurich, Northern Ariz., 1977 (29 attempts)
Per-game record—1.9, Dennis Hochman, Sonoma St., 1986 (19 in 10); Jaime Nunez, Weber St., 1971 (19 in 10)
Career
64—Mike Wood, Southeast Mo. St., 1974-77 (109 attempts)
Also holds per-game record at 1.5 (64 in 44)

MOST CONSECUTIVE FIELD GOALS MADE
Career
14—Keith Kasnic, Tenn.-Martin, 1982-83; Kurt Seibel, South Dak., 1982-83

MOST FIELD GOALS ATTEMPTED
Game
7—Jim Turcotte, Mississippi Col. vs. Troy St., Oct. 3, 1981 (made 2)
Season
35—Mike Wood, Southeast Mo. St., 1977 (made 16)
Per-game record—3.3, Skipper Butler, Texas-Arlington, 1968 (33 in 10)
Career
109—Mike Wood, Southeast Mo. St., 1974-77 (made 64)
Per-game record—2.7, Jaime Nunez, Weber St., 1969-71 (83 in 31)

HIGHEST PERCENTAGE OF FIELD GOALS MADE
Season
(Min. 15 atts.) 88.2%—Howie Guarini, Shippensburg, 1990 (15 of 17); Kurt Seibel, South Dak., 1983 (15 of 17)
(Min. 20 atts.) 86.4%—Dennis Hochman, Sonoma St., 1986 (19 of 22)
Career
(Min. 35 made) 80.0%—Billy May, Clarion, 1977-80 (48 of 60)

LONGEST FIELD GOAL
67 yards—Tom Odle, Fort Hays St. vs. Washburn, Nov. 5, 1988
Special reference: Ove Johannson, Abilene Christian (not an NCAA-member institution at the time), kicked a 69-yard field goal against East Tex. St., Oct. 16, 1976

Team Records

SINGLE GAME—Offense

Total Offense

MOST YARDS GAINED
910—Hanover vs. Franklin, Oct. 30, 1948 (426 rushing, 484 passing; 75 plays)

MOST PLAYS
117—Tex. A&M-Kingsville vs. Angelo St., Oct. 30, 1982 (96 rushes, 21 passes; 546 yards)

HIGHEST AVERAGE GAIN PER PLAY
12.1—Hanover vs. Franklin, Oct. 30, 1948 (75 for 910)

MOST TOUCHDOWNS SCORED BY RUSHING AND PASSING
15—North Park vs. North Central, Oct. 12, 1968 (4 by rushing, 11 by passing)

MOST TOUCHDOWNS SCORED BY RUSHING AND PASSING, BOTH TEAMS
20—North Park (15) & North Central (5), Oct. 12, 1968

MOST YARDS GAINED BY A LOSING TEAM
645—Tex. A&M-Kingsville vs. West Tex. A&M, Nov. 1, 1986 (lost 54-49)

Rushing

MOST YARDS GAINED
719—Coe vs. Beloit, Oct. 16, 1971 (73 rushes)

MOST RUSHES
97—Hobart vs. Union (N.Y.), Oct. 23, 1971 (444 yards)

HIGHEST AVERAGE GAIN PER RUSH (Min. 50 Rushes)
10.5—St. Olaf vs. Beloit, Nov. 8, 1969 (51 for 537)

MOST TOUCHDOWNS SCORED BY RUSHING
12—Coe vs. Beloit, Oct. 16, 1971

MOST PLAYERS, ONE TEAM, EACH GAINING 100 YARDS OR MORE
5—South Dak. vs. St. Cloud St., Nov. 1, 1986 (James Hambrick 125, Darryl Colvin 123, Tony Higgins 118, Dave Elle 109, Joe Longueville [QB] 106; team gained 581)

Passing

MOST PASSES ATTEMPTED
84—Livingston vs. Jacksonville St., Nov. 7, 1992 (completed 49)

MOST PASSES ATTEMPTED, BOTH TEAMS
121—Franklin (68) & Saginaw Valley (53), Sept. 22, 1984 (completed 63)

MOST PASSES COMPLETED
49—Livingston vs. Jacksonville St., Nov. 7, 1992 (attempted 84)

MOST PASSES COMPLETED, BOTH TEAMS
67—Indiana (Pa.) (34) & Lehigh (33), Sept. 14, 1985 (attempted 92)

MOST PASSES HAD INTERCEPTED
11—Hamline vs. Concordia-M'head, Nov. 5, 1955; Rhode Island vs. Brown, Oct. 8, 1949

MOST PASSES ATTEMPTED WITHOUT INTERCEPTION
63—Hamline vs. St. John's (Minn.), Oct. 8, 1955 (completed 34)

HIGHEST PERCENTAGE OF PASSES COMPLETED (Min. 20 Attempts)
90.0%—Northwestern St. vs. Southwestern La., Nov. 12, 1966 (20 of 22)

MOST YARDS GAINED
678—Portland St. vs. Eastern Mont., Nov. 20, 1976

MOST YARDS GAINED, BOTH TEAMS
904—New Haven (455) & West Chester (449), Oct. 5, 1990

MOST TOUCHDOWN PASSES
11—North Park vs. North Central, Oct. 12, 1968

MOST TOUCHDOWN PASSES, BOTH TEAMS
14—North Park (11) & North Central (3), Oct. 12, 1968

Punting

MOST PUNTS
32—Sam Houston St. vs. East Tex. St., Nov. 2, 1946 (1,203 yards)

MOST PUNTS, BOTH TEAMS
63—Sam Houston St. (32) & East Tex. St. (31), Nov. 2, 1946

HIGHEST AVERAGE PER PUNT (Min. 5 Punts)
57.5—Colorado Mines vs. Fort Lewis, Oct. 21, 1989 (8 for 460)

Punt Returns

MOST YARDS ON PUNT RETURNS
265—Widener vs. St. John's (N.Y.), Sept. 23, 1972 (4 returns)

MOST TOUCHDOWNS SCORED ON PUNT RETURNS
3—Troy St. vs. Livingston, Sept. 29, 1979; Widener vs. St. John's (N.Y.), Sept. 23, 1972

Scoring

MOST POINTS SCORED
125—Connecticut vs. Newport Naval Training, Oct. 22, 1949

MOST POINTS SCORED AGAINST A COLLEGE OPPONENT
106—Fort Valley St. vs. Knoxville, Oct. 11, 1969 (14 TDs, 2 PATs, 9 two-point conversions, 1 safety)

MOST POINTS SCORED BY A LOSING TEAM
60—New Haven vs. Southern Conn. St. (64), Oct. 25, 1991

MOST POINTS SCORED, BOTH TEAMS
136—North Park (104) & North Central (32), Oct. 12, 1968

MOST POINTS SCORED IN TWO CONSECUTIVE GAMES
172—Tuskegee, 1966 (93-0 vs. Morehouse, Oct. 14; 79-0 vs. Lane, Oct. 22)

MOST POINTS OVERCOME TO WIN A GAME
27—New Haven (58) vs. West Chester (57), Oct. 5, 1990 (trailed 24-51 with 5:51 remaining in 3rd quarter)

MOST POINTS SCORED IN A BRIEF PERIOD OF TIME
21 in 1:30—Colorado Mines vs. Chadron St., Oct. 16, 1993 (turned 14-13 game into 35-13 in second quarter; won 51-28)

MOST TOUCHDOWNS SCORED
17—Connecticut vs. Newport Naval Training, Oct. 22, 1949

MOST TOUCHDOWNS SCORED AGAINST A COLLEGE OPPONENT
15—North Park vs. North Central, Oct. 12, 1968; Alcorn St. vs. Paul Quinn, Sept. 9, 1967; Iowa Wesleyan vs. William Penn, Oct. 31, 1953

MOST SAFETIES SCORED
3—Fort Valley St. vs. Miles, Oct. 16, 1993

MOST POINTS AFTER TOUCHDOWN MADE BY KICKING
14—North Park vs. North Central, Oct. 12, 1968 (attempted 15); Connecticut vs. Newport Naval Training, Oct. 22, 1949 (attempted 17)

MOST TWO-POINT ATTEMPTS
11—Fort Valley St. vs. Knoxville, Oct. 11, 1969 (made 9)

MOST TWO-POINT ATTEMPTS MADE
9—Fort Valley St. vs. Knoxville, Oct. 11, 1969 (attempted 11)

MOST FIELD GOALS MADE
6—Central Mo. St. vs. Southeast Mo. St., Nov. 2, 1985 (6 attempts)

MOST DEFENSIVE EXTRA POINTS SCORED
1—By many teams

MOST DEFENSIVE EXTRA-POINT OPPORTUNITIES
2—North Dak. St. vs. Augustana (S.D.), Sept. 24, 1988 (2 interceptions; none scored)

First Downs

MOST TOTAL FIRST DOWNS
42—Delaware vs. Baldwin-Wallace, Oct. 6, 1973

MOST FIRST DOWNS BY PENALTY
14—La Verne vs. Northern Ariz., Oct. 11, 1958

MOST TOTAL FIRST DOWNS, BOTH TEAMS
66—North Dak. (36) & Tex. A&M-Kingsville (30), Sept. 13, 1986; Ferris St. (33) & Northwood (33), Oct. 26, 1985

Penalties

MOST PENALTIES
28—Northern Ariz. vs. La Verne, Oct. 11, 1958 (155 yards)

MOST PENALTIES, BOTH TEAMS
42—N.C. Central (23) & St. Paul's (19), Sept. 13, 1986 (453 yards)

MOST YARDS PENALIZED
293—Cal Poly SLO vs. Portland St., Oct. 31, 1981 (26 penalties)

MOST YARDS PENALIZED, BOTH TEAMS
453—N.C. Central (256) & St. Paul's (197), Sept. 13, 1986 (42 penalties)

Fumbles

MOST FUMBLES
16—Carthage vs. North Park, Nov. 14, 1970 (lost 7)

SINGLE GAME—Defense

Total Defense

FEWEST TOTAL OFFENSE PLAYS ALLOWED
29—North Park vs. Concordia (Ill.), Sept. 26, 1964

FEWEST TOTAL OFFENSE YARDS ALLOWED
Minus 69—Fort Valley St. vs. Miles, Oct. 16, 1993 (39 plays)

FEWEST RUSHES ALLOWED
7—Indianapolis vs. Valparaiso, Oct. 30, 1982 (-57 yards)

FEWEST RUSHING YARDS ALLOWED
Minus 95—San Diego St. vs. U.S. Int'l, Nov. 27, 1965 (35 plays)

FEWEST PASS COMPLETIONS ALLOWED
0—By many teams. Most recent: Fort Valley St. vs. Miles, Oct. 16, 1993 (attempted 2)

FEWEST PASSING YARDS ALLOWED
Minus 19—Ashland vs. Heidelberg, Sept. 25, 1948 (completed 4)

MOST QUARTERBACK SACKS
19—Southern Conn. St. vs. Albany (N.Y.), Oct. 6, 1984

Punting

MOST OPPONENT'S PUNTS BLOCKED BY
5—Winston-Salem vs. N.C. Central, Oct. 4, 1986; Southeastern La. vs. Troy St., Oct. 7, 1978 (holds record for most consecutive punts blocked with 4)

Interceptions

MOST PASSES INTERCEPTED BY
11—St. Cloud St. vs. Bemidji St., Oct. 31, 1970 (45 attempts); Concordia-M'head vs. Hamline, Nov. 5, 1955 (37 attempts)

DIVISION II

MOST TOUCHDOWNS ON INTERCEPTION RETURNS
3—By many teams. Most recent: Fort Valley St. vs. North Ala., Oct. 12, 1991

SEASON—Offense

Total Offense

MOST YARDS GAINED
5,969—Tex. A&M-Kingsville, 1986 (899 plays, 11 games)
Per-game record—624.1, Hanover, 1948 (4,993 in 8)

HIGHEST AVERAGE GAIN PER PLAY
(Min. 500 plays) 9.2—Hanover, 1948 (543 for 4,993)
(Min. 800 plays) 6.6—Tex. A&M-Kingsville, 1986 (899 for 5,969)

MOST PLAYS PER GAME
88.7—Cal St. Chico, 1967 (887 in 10)

Rushing

MOST YARDS GAINED
4,347—Tex. A&M-Kingsville, 1986 (689 rushes, 11 games)
Per-game record—404.7, Col. of Emporia, 1954 (3,643 in 9)

HIGHEST AVERAGE GAIN PER RUSH
(Min. 300 rushes) 8.4—Hanover, 1948 (382 for 3,203)
(Min. 600 rushes) 6.3—Tex. A&M-Kingsville, 1986 (689 for 4,347)

MOST RUSHES PER GAME
78.9—Panhandle St., 1963 (789 in 10)

Passing

MOST YARDS GAINED
4,445—Portland St., 1976 (308 completions, 11 games)
Per-game record—409.0, LIU-C.W. Post, 1993 (4,090 in 10)

HIGHEST AVERAGE GAIN PER ATTEMPT
(Min. 175 Attempts)
10.8—Western St., 1991 (330 for 3,574)

HIGHEST AVERAGE GAIN PER COMPLETION
(Min. 100 comps.) 19.4—Calif. (Pa.), 1966 (116 for 2,255)
(Min. 200 comps.) 17.6—Western St., 1991 (203 for 3,574)

MOST PASSES ATTEMPTED PER GAME
53.8—Livingston, 1993 (538 in 10)

MOST PASSES COMPLETED
363—Valdosta St., 1993 (attempted 513)
Also holds per-game record at 33.0 (363 in 11)

FEWEST PASSES COMPLETED PER GAME
0.4—Hobart, 1971 (4 in 9)

HIGHEST PERCENTAGE COMPLETED
(Min. 200 Attempts)
70.8%—Valdosta St., 1993 (363 of 513)

LOWEST PERCENTAGE OF PASSES HAD INTERCEPTED
(Min. 275 Attempts)
0.7%—New Haven, 1993 (2 of 296)

MOST TOUCHDOWN PASSES PER GAME
4.9—San Fran. St., 1967 (49 in 10)

HIGHEST PASSING EFFICIENCY RATING POINTS
(Min. 200 atts.) 183.8—Wittenberg, 1963 (216 attempts, 138 completions, 10 interceptions, 2,457 yards, 22 TDs)

(Min. 300 atts.) 180.2—Western St., 1991 (330 attempts, 203 completions, 12 interceptions, 3,574 yards, 35 TDs)

Punting

MOST PUNTS PER GAME
10.0—Wash. & Lee, 1968 (90 in 9)

FEWEST PUNTS PER GAME
1.9—Kent, 1954 (17 in 9)

HIGHEST PUNTING AVERAGE
48.0—Adams St., 1966 (36 for 1,728)

Punt Returns

MOST PUNT RETURNS
64—UC Davis, 1984 (557 yards)

MOST TOUCHDOWNS SCORED ON PUNT RETURNS
4—Central Ark., 1992; Norfolk St., 1992; Tex. A&M-Kingsville, 1992; Eastern N. Mex., 1991; Mississippi Col., 1984; Widener, 1972

Kickoff Returns

MOST KICKOFF RETURNS
73—Lock Haven, 1993 (1,257 yards)

Scoring

MOST POINTS PER GAME
54.7—New Haven, 1993 (547 in 10)

MOST TOUCHDOWNS PER GAME
7.8—New Haven, 1993 (78 in 10)

MOST CONSECUTIVE EXTRA POINTS MADE BY KICKING
51—Angelo St., 1989

MOST CONSECUTIVE FIELD GOALS MADE
13—UC Davis, 1976

MOST TWO-POINT ATTEMPTS PER GAME
6.8—Florida A&M, 1961 (61 in 9, made 32)

MOST TWO-POINT ATTEMPTS MADE PER GAME
3.6—Florida A&M, 1961 (32 in 9, attempted 61)

MOST FIELD GOALS MADE
20—Humboldt St., 1993 (attempted 26); North Dak., 1988 (attempted 26); Northern Ariz., 1977 (attempted 29)

MOST DEFENSIVE EXTRA POINTS SCORED
1—By many teams

MOST DEFENSIVE EXTRA-POINT OPPORTUNITIES
3—Central Okla., 1989 (2 blocked kick returns, 1 interception; one scored); Northern Colo., 1988 (2 blocked kick returns, 1 interception; none scored)

Penalties

MOST PENALTIES AGAINST
146—Gardner-Webb, 1992 (1,344 yards)
Per-game record—14.3, N.C. Central, 1986 (143 in 10)

MOST YARDS PENALIZED
1,356—Hampton, 1977 (124 penalties, 11 games)

Turnovers (Giveaways)

(Passes Had Intercepted and Fumbles Lost; From 1985)

FEWEST TURNOVERS
9—North Dak. St., 1991 (1 interception, 8 fumbles lost)

Per-game record—1.0, Hillsdale, 1993 (11 in 11); North Dak. St., 1991 (9 in 9)

MOST TURNOVERS
61—Cheyney, 1990 (36 interceptions, 25 fumbles lost)
Per-game record—5.8, Livingstone, 1986 (58 in 10)

SEASON—Defense

Total Defense

FEWEST YARDS ALLOWED PER GAME
44.4—John Carroll, 1962 (311 in 7)

LOWEST AVERAGE YARDS ALLOWED PER PLAY
(Min. 300 plays) 1.0—John Carroll, 1962 (310 for 311 yards)
(Min. 600 plays) 1.8—Alcorn St., 1976 (603 for 1,089)

FEWEST RUSHING AND PASSING TOUCHDOWNS ALLOWED PER GAME
0.0—Albany St. (Ga.), 1960 (0 in 9)

Rushing Defense

FEWEST YARDS ALLOWED PER GAME
Minus 16.7—Tennessee St., 1967 (-150 in 9)

LOWEST AVERAGE YARDS ALLOWED PER RUSH
(Min. 250 rushes) Minus 0.5—Tennessee St., 1967 (296 for -150 yards)
(Min. 400 rushes) 1.3—Luther, 1971 (414 for 518)

Pass Defense

FEWEST YARDS ALLOWED PER GAME
10.1—Ashland, 1948 (91 in 9)

FEWEST YARDS ALLOWED PER ATTEMPT
(Min. 200 atts.) 3.1—Virginia St., 1971 (205 for 630)
(Min. 300 atts.) 3.2—Southwest Mo. St., 1966 (315 for 996)

FEWEST YARDS ALLOWED PER COMPLETION
(Min. 100 Completions)
8.8—Long Beach St., 1965 (144 for 1,264)

LOWEST COMPLETION PERCENTAGE ALLOWED
(Min. 250 Attempts)
24.1%—Southwest Mo. St., 1966 (76 of 315)

MOST PASSES INTERCEPTED BY PER GAME
3.9—Whitworth, 1959 (35 in 9); Delaware, 1946 (35 in 9)

FEWEST PASSES INTERCEPTED BY
(Min. 150 Attempts)
1—Gettysburg, 1972 (175 attempts; 0 yards returned)

HIGHEST PERCENTAGE INTERCEPTED BY
(Min. 150 atts.) 21.7%—Stephen F. Austin, 1949 (35 of 161)
(Min. 275 atts.) 11.8%—Missouri-Rolla, 1978 (35 of 297)

MOST TOUCHDOWNS ON INTERCEPTION RETURNS
7—Gardner-Webb, 1992 (35 interceptions); Fort Valley St., 1991 (15 interceptions); Virginia Union, 1986 (31 interceptions)

LOWEST PASSING EFFICIENCY RATING ALLOWED
(Min. 250 Attempts)
41.7—Fort Valley St., 1985 (allowed 283 attempts, 90 completions, 1,039 yards, 2 TDs and intercepted 33)

Blocked Kicks

MOST BLOCKED KICKS
27—Winston-Salem, 1986 (16 punts, 7 field goal attempts, 4 point-after-touchdown kicks)

Scoring

FEWEST POINTS ALLOWED PER GAME
0.0—Albany St. (Ga.), 1960 (0 in 9 games)

MOST POINTS ALLOWED PER GAME
64.5—Rose-Hulman, 1961 (516 in 8)

Turnovers (Takeaways)

(Opponent's Passes Intercepted and Fumbles Recovered; From 1985)

HIGHEST TURNOVER MARGIN PER GAME
2.7—Hillsdale, 1993 (plus 30 in 11; 11 giveaways vs. 41 takeaways)

MOST TAKEAWAYS
56—Gardner-Webb, 1992 (35 interceptions, 21 fumble recoveries)
Per-game record—5.1, Gardner-Webb, 1992 (56 in 11)

Additional Records

MOST CONSECUTIVE VICTORIES
34—Hillsdale (from Oct. 2, 1954, to Nov. 16, 1957; ended with 27-26 loss to Pittsburg St., Dec. 21, 1957)
Special reference: Tex. A&M-Kingsville, from Nov. 17, 1973, to Oct. 1, 1977, a period during which it was not an NCAA-member institution, won 42 consecutive games. The streak ended Oct. 8, 1977, with a 25-25 tie vs. Abilene Christian

MOST CONSECUTIVE GAMES UNBEATEN
54—Morgan St. (from Nov. 5, 1931, to Nov. 18, 1938; ended with 15-0 loss to Virginia St., Nov. 30, 1938)

MOST CONSECUTIVE GAMES WITHOUT BEING SHUT OUT
178—North Dak. (from Oct. 7, 1967, to Nov. 10, 1984; ended with 41-0 loss to Northern Ariz., Aug. 31, 1985)

MOST CONSECUTIVE LOSSES
39—St. Paul's (from Oct. 23, 1948, to Oct. 24, 1953; ended with 7-6 win over Delaware St., Oct. 31, 1953)

MOST CONSECUTIVE GAMES WITHOUT A VICTORY
49—Paine (1954-61, includes 1 tie)

MOST CONSECUTIVE GAMES WITHOUT A TIE
329—West Chester (from Oct. 26, 1945, to Oct. 31, 1980; ended with 24-24 tie vs. Cheyney, Nov. 8, 1980)

MOST TIE GAMES IN A SEASON
5—Wofford, 1948 (Sept. 25 to Oct. 23, consecutive)

HIGHEST-SCORING TIE GAME
54-54—Norfolk St. vs. Winston-Salem, Oct. 9, 1993

MOST CONSECUTIVE QUARTERS WITHOUT YIELDING A RUSHING TOUCHDOWN
51—Butler (from Sept. 25, 1982, to Oct. 15, 1983)

MOST CONSECUTIVE POINT-AFTER-TOUCHDOWN KICKS MADE
123—Liberty (from 1976 to Sept. 10, 1983; ended with missed PAT vs. Saginaw Valley, Sept. 10, 1983)

MOST IMPROVED WON-LOST RECORD
11 games—Northern Mich., 1975 (13-1, including three Division II playoff victories, from 0-10 in 1974)

Annual Champions, All-Time Leaders

Total Offense

CAREER YARDS PER GAME

Player, Team	Years	G	Plays	Yards	Yd. PG
Marty Washington, Livingston	1992-93	17	773	5,212	*306.6
Jayson Merrill, Western St.	1990-91	20	641	5,619	281.0
Chris Petersen, UC Davis	1985-86	20	735	5,532	276.6
Tim Von Dulm, Portland St.	1969-70	20	989	5,501	275.1
Troy Mott, Wayne St. (Neb.)	1991-92	20	943	5,212	260.6
Earl Harvey, N.C. Central	1985-88	41	*2,045	*10,667	260.2
Chris Hegg, Northern Iowa/ Northeast Mo. St.	1982, 84-85	21	932	5,412	257.7
Jim Zorn, Cal Poly Pomona	1973-74	21	946	5,364	255.4
Rob Tomlinson, Cal St. Chico	1988-91	40	1,656	9,921	248.0
Pat Brennan, Franklin	1981-84	30	1,286	7,316	243.9
June Jones, Hawaii/Portland St.	1974, 75-76	23	760	5,601	243.5
Carl Wright, Virginia Union	1989-91	31	1,104	7,517	242.5
Steve Wray, Franklin	1978-79, 81-82	32	1,370	7,606	237.7
Jim Lindsey, Abilene Christian	1967-70	36	1,510	8,385	232.9

*Record.

SEASON YARDS PER GAME

Player, Team	Year	G	Plays	Yards	Yd. PG
Perry Klein, LIU-C.W. Post	†1993	10	499	*4,052	*405.2
Marty Washington, Livingston	1993	8	453	3,146	393.3
Brett Salisbury, Wayne St. (Neb.)	1993	10	424	3,732	373.2
Jed Drenning, Glenville St.	1993	10	473	3,593	359.3
Rob Tomlinson, Cal St. Chico	†1989	10	534	3,525	352.5
Chris Hegg, Northeast Mo. St.	†1985	11	*594	3,782	343.8
Bob Toledo, San Fran. St.	†1967	10	409	3,407	340.7
Jayson Merrill, Western St.	†1991	10	337	3,400	340.0
John Charles, Portland St.	†1992	8	303	2,708	338.5
George Bork, Northern Ill.	†1963	9	413	2,945	327.2
Richard Strasser, San Fran. St.	1985	10	536	3,259	325.9
Pat Brennan, Franklin	†1984	10	583	3,248	324.8
Pat Brennan, Franklin	†1983	10	524	3,239	323.9
Jamie Pass, Mankato St.	1993	11	543	3,537	321.5
Tod Mayfield, West Tex. St.	†1986	11	555	3,533	321.2
Chris Hatcher, Valdosta St.	1993	11	495	3,532	321.1
Shawn Dupris, Southwest St.	1993	9	408	2,863	318.1
June Jones, Portland St.	†1976	11	465	3,463	314.8
Jim McMillan, Boise St.	†1974	10	403	3,101	310.1

*Record. †National champion.

CAREER YARDS

Player, Team	Years	Plays	Yards
Earl Harvey, N.C. Central	1985-88	*2,045	*10,667
Rob Tomlinson, Cal St. Chico	1988-91	1,656	9,921
Sam Mannery, Calif. (Pa.)	1987-90	1,669	9,125
Andy Breault, Kutztown	1989-92	1,459	8,975
Steward Perez, Chadron St.	1988-91	1,072	8,443
Jim Lindsey, Abilene Christian	1967-70	1,510	8,385
Dave Walter, Michigan Tech	1983-86	1,660	8,345
Maurice Heard, Tuskegee	1988-91	1,289	8,321
Jack Hull, Grand Valley St.	1988-91	1,196	8,221
Doug Williams, Grambling	1974-77	1,072	8,195
Dave DenBraber, Ferris St.	1984-87	1,522	8,115
Tracy Kendall, Alabama A&M	1988-91	1,480	8,112
Bill Bair, Mansfield	1989-92	1,352	8,101
Ned Cox, Angelo St.	1983-86	1,831	8,097
¢Thad Trujillo, Fort Lewis	1991-93	1,363	7,674
Steve Wray, Franklin	1978-82	1,370	7,606
Rex Lamberti, Abilene Christian	1984-86, 93	1,223	7,546
Carl Wright, Virginia Union	1989-91	1,104	7,517
John St. Jacques, Santa Clara	1988-89, 91-92	1,219	7,505
John Schultz, Augustana (S.D.)	1982-85	1,328	7,474
Tom Nelson, St. Cloud St.	1980-83	1,421	7,430
Donald Smith, Langston	1958-61	998	7,376
Tom Bonds, Cal Lutheran	1984-87	1,439	7,374
Al Niemela, West Chester	1985-88	1,259	7,359
Loyal Proffitt, Abilene Christian	1981-84	1,418	7,337

*Record. ¢Active player.

SEASON YARDS

Player, Team	Year	G	Plays	Yards
Perry Klein, LIU-C.W. Post	†1993	10	499	*4,052
Chris Hegg, Northeast Mo. St.	†1985	11	*594	3,782
Brett Salisbury, Wayne St. (Neb.)	1993	10	424	3,732
Jed Drenning, Glenville St.	1993	10	473	3,593
Jamie Pass, Mankato St.	1993	11	543	3,537
Tod Mayfield, West Tex. A&M	†1986	11	555	3,533
Chris Hatcher, Valdosta St.	1993	11	495	3,532
Rob Tomlinson, Cal St. Chico	†1989	10	534	3,525
June Jones, Portland St.	†1976	11	465	3,463
Bob Toledo, San Fran. St.	†1967	10	409	3,407
Jayson Merrill, Western St.	†1991	10	337	3,400
Gregory Clark, Virginia St.	1993	11	425	3,386
Vernon Buck, Wingate	1993	11	463	3,307
Richard Strasser, San Fran. St.	1985	10	536	3,259
Pat Brennan, Franklin	†1984	10	583	3,248
Pat Brennan, Franklin	†1983	10	524	3,239
Phil Basso, Liberty	1984	11	456	3,227
John Craven, Gardner-Webb	1992	11	453	3,216
Andy Breault, Kutztown	†1990	11	562	3,173
Marty Washington, Livingston	1993	8	453	3,146

*Record. †National champion.

DIVISION II

SINGLE-GAME YARDS

Yds.	Player, Team (Opponent)	Date
623	Perry Klein, LIU-C.W. Post (Salisbury St.)	Nov. 6, 1993
591	Marty Washington, Livingston (Nicholls St.)	Sept. 11, 1993
584	Tracy Kendall, Alabama A&M (Clark Atlanta)	Nov. 4, 1989
571	John Charles, Portland St. (Cal Poly SLO)	Nov. 16, 1991
562	Bob Toledo, San Fran. St. (Cal St. Hayward)	Oct. 21, 1967
555	A. J. Vaughn, Wayne St., Mich. (Wis.-Milwaukee)	Sept. 30, 1967
542	Perry Klein, LIU-C.W. Post (Gannon)	Oct. 9, 1993
536	Earl Harvey, N.C. Central (Jackson St.)	Aug. 30, 1986
528	Rob Tomlinson, Cal St. Chico (Southern Conn. St.)	Oct. 7, 1989
526	Dwayne Butler, Dist. Columbia (Central St., Ohio)	Nov. 20, 1982
526	Dennis Shaw, San Diego St. (Southern Miss.)	Nov. 9, 1968
519	Maurice Heard, Tuskegee (Alabama A&M)	Nov. 10, 1990
517	Jeff Petrucci, Calif., Pa. (Edinboro)	Nov. 9, 1968
506	Kurt Otto, North Dak. (Tex. A&M-Kingsville)	Sept. 13, 1986
505	Jim Zorn, Cal Poly Pomona (Southern Utah)	Sept. 14, 1974

ANNUAL CHAMPIONS

Year	Player, Team	Class	Plays	Yards
1946	Buster Dixon, Abilene Christian	Sr.	170	960
1947	Jim Peterson, Hanover	So.	108	1,449
1948	Jim Peterson, Hanover	Jr.	130	1,589
1949	Connie Callahan, Morningside	Sr.	311	2,006
1950	Bob Heimerdinger, Northern Ill.	Jr.	286	1,782
1951	Bob Heimerdinger, Northern Ill.	Sr.	292	1,775
1952	Don Gottlob, Sam Houston St.	Sr.	303	2,470
1953	Ralph Capitani, Northern Iowa	Jr.	317	1,755
1954	Bill Engelhardt, Nebraska-Omaha	So.	243	1,645
1955	Jim Stehlin, Brandeis	Sr.	222	1,455
1956	Dick Jamieson, Bradley	So.	240	1,925
1957	Stan Jackson, Cal Poly Pomona	Jr.	301	2,145
1958	Stan Jackson, Cal Poly Pomona	Sr.	334	2,478
1959	Gary Campbell, Whittier	Sr.	309	2,383
1960	Charles Miller, Austin	Sr.	287	1,966
1961	Denny Spurlock, Whitworth	Sr.	224	1,684
1962	George Bork, Northern Ill.	Jr.	397	2,398
1963	George Bork, Northern Ill.	Sr.	413	2,945
1964	Jerry Bishop, Austin	Jr.	332	2,152
1965	Ron Christian, Northern Ill.	Sr.	377	2,307
1966	Joe Stetser, Cal St. Chico	Jr.	406	2,382
1967	Bob Toledo, San Fran. St.	Sr.	409	3,407
1968	Terry Bradshaw, Louisiana Tech	Jr.	426	2,987
1969	Tim Von Dulm, Portland St.	Jr.	462	2,736

Beginning in 1970, ranked on per-game (instead of total) yards

Year	Player, Team	Class	G	Plays	Yards	Avg.
1970	Jim Lindsey, Abilene Christian	Sr.	9	440	2,654	294.9
1971	Randy Mattingly, Evansville	Jr.	9	402	2,234	248.2
1972	Bob Biggs, UC Davis	Sr.	9	381	2,356	261.8
1973	Jim Zorn, Cal Poly Pomona	Jr.	11	499	3,000	272.7
1974	Jim McMillan, Boise St.	Sr.	10	403	3,101	310.1
1975	Lynn Hieber, Indiana (Pa.)	Sr.	10	402	2,503	250.3
1976	June Jones, Portland St.	Sr.	11	465	3,463	314.8
1977	Steve Mariucci, Northern Mich.	Sr.	8	270	1,780	222.5
1978	Charlie Thompson, Western St.	Jr.	9	304	2,138	237.6
1979	Phil Kessel, Northern Mich.	Jr.	9	368	2,164	240.4
1980	Curt Strasheim, Southwest St.	Jr.	10	501	2,565	256.5
1981	Steve Wray, Franklin	Jr.	10	488	2,726	272.6
1982	Steve Wray, Franklin	Sr.	8	382	2,114	264.3
1983	Pat Brennan, Franklin	Jr.	10	524	3,239	323.9
1984	Pat Brennan, Franklin	Sr.	10	583	3,248	324.8
1985	Chris Hegg, Northeast Mo. St.	Sr.	11	*594	3,782	343.8
1986	Tod Mayfield, West Tex. A&M	Sr.	11	555	3,533	312.2
1987	Randy Hobson, Evansville	Sr.	10	457	2,964	296.4
1988	Mark Sedinger, Northern Colo.	Sr.	10	413	2,828	282.8
1989	Rob Tomlinson, Cal St. Chico	So.	10	534	3,525	352.5
1990	Andy Breault, Kutztown	Jr.	10	562	3,173	288.5
1991	Jayson Merrill, Western St.	Sr.	10	337	3,400	340.0
1992	John Charles, Portland St.	Sr.	8	303	2,708	338.5
1993	Perry Klein, LIU-C.W. Post	Sr.	10	499	*4,052	*405.2

*Record.

Rushing

CAREER YARDS PER GAME

Player, Team	Years	G	Plays	Yards	Yd. PG
Johnny Bailey, Tex. A&M-Kingsville	1986-89	39	885	*6,320	*162.1
Ole Gunderson, St. Olaf	1969-71	27	639	4,060	150.4
Brad Hustad, Luther	1957-59	27	655	3,943	146.0
Joe Iacone, West Chester	1960-62	27	565	3,767	139.5
Billy Johnson, Widener	1971-73	28	411	3,737	133.5
Don Aleksiewicz, Hobart	1969-72	34	819	4,525	133.1
Jim VanWagner, Michigan Tech	1973-76	36	958	4,788	133.0
Steve Roberts, Butler	1986-89	35	1,026	4,623	132.1

*Record.

SEASON YARDS PER GAME

Player, Team	Year	G	Plays	Yards	TD	Yd. PG
Johnny Bailey, Tex. A&M-Kingsville	†1986	11	271	*2,011	18	*182.8
Bob White, Western N. Mex.	†1951	9	202	1,643	20	182.6
Kevin Mitchell, Saginaw Valley	†1989	8	236	1,460	6	182.5
Don Aleksiewicz, Hobart	†1971	9	276	1,616	19	179.6
Jim Holder, Panhandle St.	†1963	10	275	1,775	9	177.5
Jim Baier, Wis.-River Falls	†1966	9	240	1,587	17	176.3
Billy Johnson, Widener	†1972	9	148	1,556	23	172.9
Hank Treesh, Hanover	†1948	8	100	1,383	17	172.9
Dave Kiarsis, Trinity (Conn.)	†1970	8	201	1,374	10	171.8
Roger Graham, New Haven	†1992	10	200	1,717	22	171.7

*Record. †National champion.

CAREER YARDS

Player, Team	Years	Plays	Yards	Avg.
Johnny Bailey, Tex. A&M-Kingsville	1986-89	885	*6,320	7.14
Shawn Graves, Wofford	1989-92	730	5,128	7.02
Chris Cobb, Eastern Ill.	1976-79	930	5,042	5.42
Harry Jackson, St. Cloud St.	1986-89	915	4,890	5.34
Jerry Linton, Panhandle St.	1959-62	648	4,839	7.47
Jim VanWagner, Michigan Tech	1973-76	958	4,788	5.00
Jeremy Monroe, Michigan Tech	1990-93	666	4,661	7.00
Heath Sherman, Tex. A&M-Kingsville	1985-88	804	4,654	5.79
Steve Roberts, Butler	1986-89	1,026	4,623	4.51
Don Aleksiewicz, Hobart	1969-72	819	4,525	5.53
Dale Mills, Northeast Mo. St.	1957-60	751	4,502	5.99
Scott Schulte, Hillsdale	1990-93	879	4,495	5.11
Leo Lewis, Lincoln (Mo.)	1951-54	623	4,458	7.16
Bernie Peeters, Luther	1968-71	*1,072	4,435	4.14
Larry Schreiber, Tennessee Tech	1966-69	878	4,421	5.04
Brad Rowland, McMurry	1947-50	683	4,347	6.36
Vincent Allen, Indiana St.	1973-75, 77	832	4,335	5.21
Ronald Moore, Pittsburg St.	1989-92	619	4,299	6.95
Bill Rhodes, Western St.	1953-56	506	4,294	‡8.49
Lem Harkey, Col. of Emporia	1951-54	502	4,232	8.43
Shannon Burnell, North Dak.	1990-93	828	4,218	5.09
Curtis Delgardo, Portland St.	1987-90	703	4,178	5.94
Ricke Stonewall, Millersville	1981-84	648	4,169	6.43

*Record. ‡Record for minimum 500 rushes.

SEASON YARDS

Player, Team	Year	G	Plays	Yards	Avg.
Johnny Bailey, Tex. A&M-Kingsville	†1986	11	271	*2,011	‡7.42
Ronald Moore, Pittsburg St.	1992	11	239	1,864	7.80
Zed Robinson, Southern Utah	1991	11	254	1,828	7.20
Jim Holder, Panhandle St.	†1963	10	275	1,775	6.45
Keith Higdon, Cheyney	†1993	10	330	1,742	5.28
Mike Thomas, Nevada-Las Vegas	†1973	11	274	1,741	6.35
Roger Graham, New Haven	†1992	10	200	1,717	+8.59
Joe Simmons, N.C. Central	1993	11	249	1,699	6.82
Roger Graham, New Haven	1993	10	182	1,687	9.27
Terry Metcalf, Long Beach St.	1971	11	273	1,673	6.13
Troy Mills, Cal St. Sacramento	1991	10	223	1,668	7.48
Leon Burns, Long Beach St.	†1969	11	*350	1,659	4.74
Chad Guthrie, Northeast Mo. St.	1991	11	302	1,649	5.46
Bob White, Western N. Mex.	†1951	9	202	1,643	8.13
Thelbert Withers, N.M. Highlands	1992	11	240	1,621	6.75
Don Aleksiewicz, Hobart	†1971	9	276	1,616	5.86

*Record. †National champion. ‡Record for minimum 250 rushes. +Record for minimum 200 rushes.

SINGLE-GAME YARDS

Yds.	Player, Team (Opponent)	Date
382	Kelly Ellis, Northern Iowa (Western Ill.)	Oct. 13, 1979
373	Dallas Garber, Marietta (Wash. & Jeff.)	Nov. 7, 1959
370	Jim Baier, Wis.-River Falls (Wis.-Stevens Point)	Nov. 5, 1966
370	Jim Hissam, Marietta (Bethany, W. Va.)	Nov. 15, 1958
367	Don Polkinghorne, Washington, Mo. (Wash. & Lee)	Nov. 23, 1957
363	Richie Weaver, Widener (Moravian)	Oct. 17, 1970
356	Ole Gunderson, St. Olaf (Monmouth, Ill.)	Oct. 11, 1969
350	Ricke Stonewall, Millersville (New Haven)	Nov. 13, 1982
343	Zed Robinson, Southern Utah (Santa Clara)	Oct. 12, 1991
343	Jesse Lakes, Central Mich. (Wis.-Milwaukee)	Sept. 27, 1969
342	Leonard Davis, Lenoir-Rhyne (Gardner-Webb)	Oct. 9, 1993
337	Harry Jackson, St. Cloud St. (South Dak.)	Nov. 4, 1989
333	Thelbert Withers, N.M. Highlands (Fort Lewis)	Oct. 17, 1992
327	Bill Rhodes, Western St. (Adams St.)	Oct. 20, 1956
323	Shawn Graves, Wofford (Lenoir-Rhyne)	Sept. 15, 1990
323	Gary Nelson, Wartburg (Buena Vista)	Oct. 26, 1968

ANNUAL CHAMPIONS

Year	Player, Team	Class	Plays	Yards
1946	V. T. Smith, Abilene Christian	So.	99	733
1947	John Williams, Jacksonville St.	Jr.	150	931
1948	Hank Treesh, Hanover	Jr.	100	1,383
1949	Odie Posey, Southern-B.R.	Jr.	121	1,399
1950	Meriel Michelson, Eastern Wash.	Sr.	180	1,234
1951	Bob White, Western N. Mex.	Jr.	202	1,643
1952	Al Conway, William Jewell	Sr.	134	1,325
1953	Elroy Payne, McMurry	So.	183	1,274
1954	Lem Harkey, Col. of Emporia	Sr.	121	1,146
1955	Gene Scott, Centre	Sr.	107	1,138
1956	Bill Rhodes, Western St.	Sr.	130	1,200
1957	Brad Hustad, Luther	So.	219	1,401
1958	Dale Mills, Northeast Mo. St.	So.	186	1,358
1959	Dale Mills, Northeast Mo. St.	Jr.	248	1,385
1960	Joe Iacone, West Chester	So.	199	1,438
1961	Bobby Lisa, St. Mary (Kan.)	Jr.	156	1,082
1962	Jerry Linton, Panhandle St.	Sr.	272	1,483
1963	Jim Holder, Panhandle St.	Sr.	275	1,775
1964	Jim Allison, San Diego St.	Sr.	174	1,186
1965	Allen Smith, Findlay	Jr.	207	1,240

Year	Player, Team	Class	Plays	Yards
1966	Jim Baier, Wis.-River Falls	Sr.	240	1,587
1967	Dickie Moore, Western Ky.	Jr.	208	1,444
1968	Howard Stevens, Randolph-Macon	Fr.	191	1,468
1969	Leon Burns, Long Beach St.	Jr.	*350	1,659

Beginning in 1970, ranked on per-game (instead of total) yards

Year	Player, Team	Class	G	Plays	Yards	Avg.
1970	Dave Kiarsis, Trinity (Conn.)	Sr.	8	201	1,374	171.8
1971	Don Aleksiewicz, Hobart	Jr.	9	276	1,616	179.6
1972	Billy Johnson, Widener	So.	9	148	1,556	172.9
1973	Mike Thomas, Nevada-Las Vegas	Jr.	11	274	1,741	158.3
1974	Jim VanWagner, Michigan Tech	So.	9	246	1,453	161.4
1975	Jim VanWagner, Michigan Tech	Jr.	9	289	1,331	147.9
1976	Ted McKnight, Minn.-Duluth	Sr.	10	220	1,482	148.2
1977	Bill Burnham, New Hampshire	Sr.	10	281	1,422	142.2
1978	Mike Harris, Northeast Mo. St.	Sr.	11	329	1,598	145.3
1979	Chris Cobb, Eastern Ill.	Sr.	11	293	1,609	146.3
1980	Louis Jackson, Cal Poly SLO	Sr.	10	287	1,424	142.4
1981	Rick Porter, Slippery Rock	Sr.	9	208	1,179	131.0
1982	Ricke Stonewall, Millersville	So.	10	191	1,387	138.7
1983	Mark Corbin, Central St. (Ohio)	So.	10	208	1,502	150.2
1984	Charles Sanders, Slippery Rock	Jr.	10	269	1,280	128.0
1985	Dan Sonnek, South Dak. St.	So.	11	303	1,518	138.0
1986	Johnny Bailey, Tex. A&M-Kingsville	Fr.	11	271	*2,011	*182.8
1987	Johnny Bailey, Tex. A&M-Kingsville	So.	10	217	1,598	159.8
1988	Johnny Bailey, Tex. A&M-Kingsville	Jr.	10	229	1,442	144.2
1989	Kevin Mitchell, Saginaw Valley	Jr.	8	236	1,460	182.5
1990	David Jones, Chadron St.	Sr.	10	225	1,570	157.0
1991	Quincy Tillmon, Emporia St.	So.	9	259	1,544	171.6
1992	Roger Graham, New Haven	So.	10	200	1,717	171.7
1993	Keith Higdon, Cheyney	Sr.	10	330	1,742	174.2

*Record.

Passing

CAREER PASSING EFFICIENCY
(Minimum 375 Completions)

Player, Team	Years	Att.	Cmp.	Int.	Pct.	Yards	TD	Pts.
Chris Petersen, UC Davis	1985-86	553	385	13	*.696	4,988	39	*164.0
Jim McMillan, Boise St.	1971-74	640	382	29	.597	5,508	58	152.8
Jack Hull, Grand Valley St.	1988-91	835	485	22	.581	7,120	64	149.7
Bruce Upstill, Col. of Emporia	1960-63	769	438	36	.570	6,935	48	144.0
George Bork, Northern Ill.	1960-63	902	577	33	.640	6,782	60	141.8
Steve Mariucci, Northern Mich.	1974-77	678	380	33	.561	6,022	41	140.9
Scott Barry, UC Davis	1982-84	588	377	16	.641	4,421	33	140.4
June Jones, Hawaii/Portland St.	1974, 75-76	666	376	35	.565	5,809	41	139.5
Doug Williams, Grambling	1974-77	1,009	484	52	.480	8,411	*93	138.1
Matt Cook, Mo. Southern St.	$1989-93	816	411	29	.504	6,715	63	137.9
Chris Crawford, Portland St.	1985-88	954	588	35	.616	7,543	48	137.3
Trevor Spradley, Southwest Baptist	1990-92	712	441	27	.619	6,851	29	137.2
Dan Miles, Southern Ore.	1964-67	871	577	56	.662	6,531	52	136.1
Al Niemela, West Chester	1985-88	1,063	600	36	.564	7,853	73	134.4
Steward Perez, Chadron St.	1988-91	1,015	565	60	.557	8,186	69	134.0
Denny Spurlock, Whitworth	1958-61	723	388	48	.537	5,526	63	133.4
Jeff Tisdel, Nevada	1974-77	776	394	34	.508	6,098	59	133.1

*Record. $See page 6 for explanation.

Missouri Southern State quarterback Matt Cook ranks 10th among Division II career passing efficiency leaders with a minimum of 375 completions.

Long Island-C.W. Post quarterback Perry Klein threw for 3,757 yards last year to set the division's record for passing yardage in a season. Klein also set the division's single-game passing yardage record in 1993 with 614 yards against Salisbury State.

SEASON PASSING EFFICIENCY
(Minimum 15 Attempts Per Game)

Player, Team	Year	G	Att.	Cmp.	Int.	Pct.	Yards	TD	Pts.
Boyd Crawford, Col. of Idaho	†1953	8	120	72	6	.600	1,462	21	*210.1
Chuck Green, Wittenberg	†1963	9	182	114	8	.626	2,181	19	189.0
Jayson Merrill, Western St.	†1991	10	309	195	11	.631	3,484	35	188.1
Jim Feely, Johns Hopkins	†1967	7	110	69	5	.627	1,264	12	186.2
John Charles, Portland St.	1991	11	247	147	7	.595	2,619	32	185.7
Steve Smith, Western St.	†1992	10	271	180	5	.664	2,719	30	183.5
Jim Peterson, Hanover	†1948	8	125	81	12	.648	1,571	12	182.9
John Wristen, Southern Colo.	†1982	8	121	68	2	.562	1,358	13	182.6
John Charles, Portland St.	1992	8	263	179	7	.681	2,770	24	181.3
Richard Basil, Savannah St.	†1989	9	211	120	7	.569	2,148	29	181.1
Jim Cahoon, Ripon	†1964	8	127	74	7	.583	1,206	19	176.4
Ken Suhl, New Haven	1992	10	239	148	5	.619	2,336	26	175.7
Tony Aliucci, Indiana (Pa.)	†1990	10	181	111	10	.613	1,801	21	172.2
James Weir, New Haven	†1993	10	266	161	1	.605	2,336	31	172.0
John Costello, Widener	†1956	9	149	74	10	.497	1,702	17	169.8
Kurt Coduti, Michigan Tech	1992	9	155	92	3	.594	1,518	15	169.7
Chris Petersen, UC Davis	†1985	10	242	167	6	.690	2,366	17	169.4
Mike Rieker, Lehigh	†1977	11	230	137	14	.596	2,431	23	169.2
Steve Michuta, Grand Valley St.	†1981	8	173	114	11	.659	1,702	17	168.3
James Armendariz, Southern Utah	1991	11	184	109	5	.592	1,839	17	168.2

Record. †National champion.

CAREER YARDS

Player, Team	Years	Att.	Cmp.	Int.	Pct.	Yards	TD
Earl Harvey, N.C. Central	1985-88	*1,442	690	81	.479	*10,621	86
Rob Tomlinson, Cal St. Chico	1988-91	1,328	*748	43	.563	9,434	52
Andy Breault, Kutztown	1989-92	1,259	733	63	.582	9,086	86
Sam Mannery, Calif. (Pa.)	1987-90	1,283	649	68	.506	8,680	64
Dave DenBraber, Ferris St.	1984-87	1,254	661	45	.527	8,536	52
Jim Lindsey, Abilene Christian	1967-70	1,237	642	69	.519	8,521	61
Maurice Heard, Tuskegee	1988-91	1,134	556	54	.490	8,434	87
Doug Williams, Grambling	1974-77	1,009	484	52	.480	8,411	*93
Steward Perez, Chadron St.	1988-91	1,015	565	60	.557	8,186	69
Steve Wray, Franklin	1978-82	1,230	592	48	.481	8,123	62
John St. Jacques, Santa Clara	1988-89, 91-92	1,060	543	36	.512	7,968	68
Rex Lamberti, Abilene Christian	1984-86, 93	1,133	595	44	.525	7,934	84
Al Niemela, West Chester	1985-88	1,063	600	36	.564	7,853	73
Ned Cox, Angelo St.	1983-86	1,205	589	58	.489	7,843	56
Loyal Proffitt, Abilene Christian	1981-84	1,157	550	80	.475	7,824	54
Tom Bonds, Cal Lutheran	1984-87	1,137	625	52	.550	7,773	57
Pat Brennan, Franklin	1981-84	1,123	535	62	.476	7,717	53
¢Thad Trujillo, Fort Lewis	1991-93	1,127	586	44	.520	7,639	59
Chris Crawford, Portland St.	1985-88	954	588	35	.616	7,543	48
Bill Bair, Mansfield	1989-92	1,041	617	44	.593	7,531	56
Chris Fagan, Millersville	1989-92	1,098	556	52	.506	7,362	48
Tom Bertoldi, Northern Mich.	1980-83	987	524	50	.531	7,330	45
¢Chris Hatcher, Valdosta St.	1991-93	1,021	680	29	.666	7,287	66
Chris Teal, West Ga.	1990-93	1,039	572	39	.551	7,258	59
Tracy Kendall, Alabama A&M	1988-91	1,117	564	54	.505	7,205	49

Record. ¢Active player.

CAREER YARDS PER GAME

Player, Team	Years	G	Att.	Cmp.	Int.	Pct.	Yards	TD	Avg.
Tim Von Dulm, Portland St.	1969-70	20	924	500	41	.541	5,967	51	*298.4
Marty Washington, Livingston	1992-93	17	690	379	25	.549	5,018	40	295.2
Jayson Merrill, Western St.	1990-91	20	580	328	25	.566	5,830	56	291.5
John Charles, Portland St.	1991-92	19	510	326	14	.639	5,389	56	283.6
Earl Harvey, N.C. Central	1985-88	40	*1,442	690	81	.479	*10,621	86	265.5
Pat Brennan, Franklin	1981-84	30	1,123	535	62	.476	7,717	53	257.2
Jay McLucas, New Haven	1989-90	20	699	370	30	.529	5,139	37	257.0
Steve Wray, Franklin	1978-79, 81-82	32	1,230	592	48	.481	8,123	62	253.8
Chris Hegg, Northern Iowa/ Northeast Mo. St.	1982, 84-85	21	772	410	33	.531	5,306	44	252.7
Troy Mott, Wayne St. (Neb.)	1991-92	20	757	437	37	.577	5,003	25	250.2
Chris Petersen, UC Davis	1985-86	20	553	385	13	*.696	4,988	39	249.4
Jeff Phillips, Central Mo. St.	1986-88	26	892	496	54	.556	6,294	46	242.1
June Jones, Hawaii/Portland St.	1974, 75-76	24	666	376	35	.565	5,809	41	242.0
Rich Ingold, South Caro./Indiana (Pa.)	1981, 83-85	27	862	503	36	.584	6,494	50	240.5
Joe Stetser, Cal St. Chico	1966-67	20	813	394	48	.485	4,803	40	240.2
Leonard Williams, Tenn.-Martin	1990-91	19	594	305	21	.513	4,518	40	237.8
Jim Lindsey, Abilene Christian	1967-70	36	1,237	642	69	.519	8,521	61	236.7

*Record.

SEASON YARDS

Player, Team	Year	G	Att.	Cmp.	Int.	Pct.	Yards	TD
Perry Klein, LIU-C.W. Post	1993	10	407	248	18	.609	*3,757	38
Chris Hegg, Northeast Mo. St.	1985	11	503	284	20	.565	3,741	32
Brett Salisbury, Wayne St. (Neb.)	1993	10	395	276	14	.699	3,729	29
Tod Mayfield, West Tex. A&M	1986	11	*515	317	20	.616	3,664	31
Chris Hatcher, Valdosta St.	1993	11	471	*335	11	*.711	3,651	37

Player, Team	Year	G	Att.	Cmp.	Int.	Pct.	Yards	TD
June Jones, Portland St.	†1976	11	423	238	24	.563	3,518	25
Bob Toledo, San Fran. St.	1967	10	396	211	24	.533	3,513	*45
Pat Brennan, Franklin	1983	10	458	226	30	.493	3,491	25
Jayson Merrill, Western St.	†1991	10	309	195	11	.631	3,484	35
Gregory Clark, Virginia St.	1993	11	380	227	11	.597	3,437	38
Jed Drenning, Glenville St.	1993	10	390	244	12	.626	3,391	25
Pat Brennan, Franklin	1984	10	502	238	20	.474	3,340	18
Phil Basso, Liberty	1984	11	426	250	15	.587	3,326	24
John Craven, Gardner-Webb	1992	11	423	240	16	.567	3,320	32
Richard Strasser, San Fran. St.	1985	10	452	250	19	.553	3,317	20
Rob Tomlinson, Cal St. Chico	1989	10	438	255	16	.582	3,258	19
Earl Harvey, N.C. Central	1985	10	392	188	19	.480	3,190	22
Andy Breault, Kutztown	1990	11	474	269	19	.568	3,143	23
Jamie Pass, Mankato St.	1993	11	396	219	13	.553	3,142	25
Jay McLucas, New Haven	1990	10	402	209	18	.520	3,114	23

*Record. †National champion.

SEASON YARDS PER GAME

Player, Team	Year	G	Att.	Cmp.	Int.	Pct.	Yards	TD	Avg.
Marty Washington, Livingston	1993	8	404	221	13	.547	3,062	26	*382.8
Perry Klein, LIU-C.W. Post	1993	10	407	248	18	.609	*3,757	38	375.7
Brett Salisbury, Wayne St. (Neb.)	1993	10	395	276	14	.699	3,729	29	372.9
Bob Toledo, San Fran. St.	1967	10	396	211	24	.533	3,513	*45	351.3
Pat Brennan, Franklin	1983	10	458	226	30	.493	3,491	25	349.1
Jayson Merrill, Western St.	†1991	10	309	195	11	.631	3,484	35	348.4
John Charles, Portland St.	1992	8	263	179	7	.681	2,770	24	346.3
George Bork, Northern Ill.	†1963	9	374	244	12	.652	3,077	32	341.9
Chris Hegg, Northeast Mo. St.	†1985	11	503	284	20	.565	3,741	32	340.1
Jed Drenning, Glenville St.	1993	10	390	244	12	.626	3,391	25	339.1
Pat Brennan, Franklin	1984	10	502	238	20	.474	3,340	18	334.0
Tod Mayfield, West Tex. A&M	1986	11	*515	317	20	.615	3,664	31	333.1
Chris Hatcher, Valdosta St.	1993	11	471	*335	11	*.711	3,651	37	331.9
Richard Strasser, San Fran. St.	1985	10	452	250	19	.553	3,317	20	331.7
Shawn Dupris, Southwest St.	1993	9	373	220	14	.590	2,955	28	328.3
Rob Tomlinson, Cal St. Chico	1989	10	438	255	16	.582	3,258	19	325.8
June Jones, Portland St.	†1976	11	423	238	24	.563	3,518	25	319.8
Earl Harvey, N.C. Central	1985	10	392	188	19	.480	3,190	22	319.0
Gregory Clark, Virginia St.	1993	11	380	227	11	.597	3,437	38	312.5
Jay McLucas, New Haven	1990	10	402	209	18	.520	3,114	23	311.4

*Record. †National champion.

Livingston quarterback Marty Washington (12) holds Division II's record for passing yards per game in a season.

SINGLE-GAME YARDS

Yds.	Player, Team (Opponent)	Date
614	Perry Klein, LIU-C.W. Post (Salisbury St.)	Nov. 6, 1993
592	John Charles, Portland St. (Cal Poly SLO)	Nov. 16, 1991
568	Bob Toledo, San Fran. St. (Cal St. Hayward)	Oct. 21, 1967
550	Earl Harvey, N.C. Central (Jackson St.)	Aug. 30, 1986
539	Maurice Heard, Tuskegee (Alabama A&M)	Nov. 10, 1990
525	Rob Tomlinson, Cal St. Chico (Southern Conn. St.)	Oct. 7, 1989
524	Dennis Shaw, San Diego St. (Southern Miss.)	Nov. 9, 1968
523	Marty Washington, Livingston (Nicholls St.)	Sept. 11, 1993
520	Perry Klein, LIU-C.W. Post (Gannon)	Oct. 9, 1993
514	Tracy Kendall, Alabama A&M (Clark Atlanta)	Nov. 4, 1989
506	Jeff King, Bloomsburg (Lock Haven)	Sept. 19, 1992
506	Tod Mayfield, West Tex. A&M (Tex. A&M-Kingsville)	Nov. 1, 1986
502	Marty Washington, Livingston (Delta St.)	Oct. 23, 1993
502	John Linhart, Slippery Rock (Clarion)	Nov. 7, 1992
502	Mike Packer, Lock Haven (Delaware Valley)	Oct. 24, 1970

SINGLE-GAME ATTEMPTS

No.	Player, Team (Opponent)	Date
72	Kurt Otto, North Dak. (Tex. A&M-Kingsville)	Sept. 13, 1986
72	Kaipo Spencer, Santa Clara (Portland St.)	Oct. 11, 1975
72	Joe Stetser, Cal St. Chico (Oregon Tech)	Sept. 23, 1967
71	Pat Brennan, Franklin (Ashland)	Nov. 3, 1984

SINGLE-GAME COMPLETIONS

No.	Player, Team (Opponent)	Date
45	Chris Hatcher, Valdosta St. (Mississippi Col.)	Oct. 23, 1993
45	Chris Hatcher, Valdosta St. (West Ga.)	Oct. 16, 1993
44	Tom Bonds, Cal Lutheran (St. Mary's, Cal.)	Nov. 22, 1986
43	George Bork, Northern Ill. (Central Mich.)	Nov. 9, 1963
42	Marty Washington, Livingston (Jacksonville St.)	Nov. 7, 1992
42	Chris Teal, West Ga. (Valdosta St.)	Oct. 19, 1991
42	Tim Von Dulm, Portland St. (Eastern Wash.)	Nov. 21, 1970
41	Kurt Otto, North Dak. (Tex. A&M-Kingsville)	Sept. 13, 1986
41	Neil Lomax, Portland St. (Montana St.)	Nov. 19, 1977
40	Kurt Beathard, Towson St. (Lafayette)	Nov. 2, 1985
39	Jeff King, Bloomsburg (Lock Haven)	Sept. 19, 1992
39	Pat Brennan, Franklin (Saginaw Valley)	Sept. 22, 1984
39	Mark Beans, Shippensburg (Edinboro)	Sept. 24, 1983
39	Curt Strasheim, Southwest St. (Moorhead St.)	Nov. 14, 1981
39	Craig Blackford, Evansville (Ball St.)	Oct. 17, 1970

DIVISION II

George Bork led Division II in passing in 1962 and 1963 during his career at Northern Illinois.

ANNUAL CHAMPIONS

Year	Player, Team	Class	Att.	Cmp.	Int.	Pct.	Yds.	TD
1946	Hank Caver, Presbyterian	Sr.	128	59	13	.461	790	7
1947	James Batchelor, East Tex. St.	Sr.	184	94	10	.511	1,114	9
1948	Sam Gary, Swarthmore	Jr.	153	93	11	.608	1,218	16
1949	Sam McGowan, New Mexico St.	Sr.	219	112	22	.511	1,712	12
1950	Andy MacDonald, Central Mich.	Jr.	200	109	12	.545	1,577	15
1951	Andy MacDonald, Central Mich.	Sr.	183	114	7	.623	1,560	12
1952	Wes Bair, Illinois St.	So.	242	135	18	.558	1,375	14
1953	Pence Dacus, Southwest Tex. St.	Sr.	207	113	10	.546	1,654	11
1954	Tommy Egan, Brandeis	Sr.	144	87	8	.604	1,050	11
1955	Jerry Foley, Hamline	Fr.	167	87	8	.521	1,034	6
1956	James Stehlin, Brandeis	Sr.	206	116	11	.563	1,155	6
1957	Jay Roelen, Pepperdine	Sr.	214	106	16	.495	1,428	13
1958	Stan Jackson, Cal Poly Pomona	Sr.	256	123	14	.480	1,994	16
1959	Gary Campbell, Whittier	Sr.	183	111	4	.607	1,717	12
1960	Denny Spurlock, Whitworth	Jr.	257	135	16	.525	1,892	14
1961	Tom Gryzwinski, Defiance	Jr.	258	127	17	.492	1,684	14
1962	George Bork, Northern Ill.	Jr.	356	232	11	.652	2,506	22
1963	George Bork, Northern Ill.	Sr.	374	244	12	.652	3,077	32
1964	Jerry Bishop, Austin	Jr.	300	182	16	.607	2,246	17
1965	Bob Caress, Bradley	Sr.	393	210	21	.534	2,167	24
1966	Paul Krause, Dubuque	Sr.	318	179	22	.563	2,210	16
1967	Joe Stetser, Cal St. Chico	Sr.	464	220	*32	.474	2,446	14
1968	Jim Lindsey, Abilene Christian	So.	396	204	19	.515	2,717	18
1969	Tim Von Dulm, Portland St.	Jr.	434	241	18	.555	2,926	26

Beginning in 1970, ranked on per-game (instead of total) completions

Year	Player, Team	Class	G	Att.	Cmp.	Avg.	Int.	Pct.	Yds.	TD
1970	Tim Von Dulm, Portland St.	Sr.	10	490	259	25.9	23	.529	3,041	25
1971	Bob Baron, Rensselaer	Sr.	9	302	168	18.7	13	.556	2,105	15
1972	Bob Biggs, UC Davis	Sr.	9	327	186	20.7	16	.569	2,291	15
1973	Kim McQuilken, Lehigh	Sr.	11	326	196	17.8	13	.601	2,603	19
1974	Jim McMillan, Boise St.	Sr.	10	313	192	19.2	15	.613	2,900	13
1975	Dan Hayes, UC Riverside	Sr.	10	316	171	17.1	20	.541	2,215	21
1976	June Jones, Portland St.	Sr.	11	423	238	21.6	24	.563	3,518	25
1977	Ed Schultz, Moorhead St.	Sr.	10	304	187	18.7	16	.615	1,943	21
1978	Jeff Knapple, Northern Colo.	Sr.	10	349	178	17.8	21	.510	2,191	16

Beginning in 1979, ranked on passing efficiency rating points (instead of per-game completions)

Year	Player, Team	Class	G	Att.	Cmp.	Int.	Pct.	Yds.	TD	Pts.
1979	Dave Alfaro, Santa Clara	Jr.	9	168	110	9	.655	1,721	13	166.3
1980	Willie Tullis, Troy St.	Sr.	10	203	108	8	.532	1,880	15	147.5
1981	Steve Michuta, Grand Valley St.	Sr.	8	173	114	11	.659	1,702	17	168.3
1982	John Wristen, Southern Colo.	Jr.	8	121	68	2	.562	1,358	13	182.6
1983	Kevin Parker, Fort Valley St.	Jr.	9	168	87	8	.518	1,539	18	154.6
1984	Brian Quinn, Northwest Mo. St.	Sr.	10	178	96	2	.539	1,561	14	151.3
1985	Chris Petersen, UC Davis	Jr.	10	242	167	6	.690	2,366	17	169.4
1986	Chris Petersen, UC Davis	Sr.	10	311	218	7	.701	2,622	22	159.7
1987	Dave Biondo, Ashland	Jr.	10	177	95	11	.537	1,828	14	154.1
1988	Al Niemela, West Chester	Sr.	10	217	138	9	.636	1,932	21	162.0
1989	Richard Basil, Savannah St.	Sr.	9	211	120	7	.569	2,148	29	181.1
1990	Tony Aliucci, Indiana (Pa.)	Jr.	10	181	111	10	.613	1,801	21	172.2
1991	Jayson Merrill, Western St.	Sr.	10	309	195	11	.631	3,484	35	188.1
1992	Steve Smith, Western St.	Sr.	10	271	180	5	.664	2,719	30	183.5
1993	James Weir, New Haven	Jr.	10	266	161	1	.605	2,336	31	172.0

*Record.

ANNUAL PASSING EFFICIENCY LEADERS BEFORE 1979
(Minimum 11 Attempts Per Game)

1948—Jim Peterson, Hanover, 182.9; **1949**—John Ford, Hardin-Simmons, 179.6; **1950**—Edward Ludorf, Trinity (Conn.), 167.8; **1951**—Vic Lesch, Western Ill., 182.4; **1952**—Jim Gray, East Tex. St., 205.5; **1953**—Boyd Crawford, Col. of Idaho, *210.1; **1954**—Bill Englehardt, Nebraska-Omaha, 170.7; **1955**—Robert Alexander, Trinity (Conn.), 208.7; **1956**—John Costello, Widener, 169.8; **1957**—Doug Maison, Hillsdale, 200.0; **1958**—Kurt Duecker, Ripon, 161.7; **1959**—Fred Whitmire, Humboldt St., 188.7; **1960**—Larry Cline, Otterbein, 195.2.

(Minimum 15 Attempts Per Game)

Year	Player, Team	G	Att.	Cmp.	Int.	Pct.	Yds.	TD	Pts.
1961	Denny Spurlock, Whitworth	10	189	115	16	.608	1,708	26	165.2
1962	Roy Curry, Jackson St.	10	194	104	8	.536	1,862	15	151.5
1963	Chuck Green, Wittenberg	9	182	114	8	.626	2,181	19	189.0
1964	Jim Cahoon, Ripon	8	127	74	7	.583	1,206	19	176.4
1965	Ed Buzzell, Ottawa	9	238	118	5	.496	2,170	31	165.0
1966	Jim Alcorn, Clarion	9	199	107	4	.538	1,714	24	161.9
1967	Jim Feely, Johns Hopkins	7	110	69	5	.627	1,264	12	186.2
1968	Larry Green, Doane	9	182	97	7	.533	1,592	22	159.0
1969	George Kaplan, Northern Colo.	9	155	92	5	.594	1,396	16	162.6
1970	Gary Wichard, LIU-C. W. Post	9	186	100	5	.538	1,527	12	138.6
1971	Peter Mackey, Middlebury	8	180	101	4	.561	1,597	19	161.0
1972	David Hamilton, Fort Valley St.	9	180	99	9	.550	1,571	24	162.3
1973	Jim McMillan, Boise St.	11	179	110	5	.615	1,525	17	158.8
1974	Jim McMillan, Boise St.	10	313	192	15	.613	2,900	13	164.4
1975	Joe Sterrett, Lehigh	11	228	135	13	.592	2,114	22	157.5
1976	Mike Makings, Western St.	10	179	90	6	.503	1,617	14	145.3
1977	Mike Rieker, Lehigh	11	230	137	14	.596	2,431	23	169.2
1978	Mike Moroski, UC Davis	10	205	119	9	.580	1,689	17	145.9

*Record.

(See above for annual leaders beginning in 1979.)

Receiving

CAREER CATCHES PER GAME

Player, Team	Years	G	Rec.	Yards	TD	Rec.PG
Ed Bell, Idaho St.	1968-69	19	163	2,608	30	*8.6
Jerry Hendren, Idaho	1967-69	30	230	3,435	27	7.7
Gary Garrison, San Diego St.	1964-65	20	148	2,188	26	7.4
Chris Myers, Kenyon	1967-70	35	*253	3,897	33	7.2

*Record.

SEASON CATCHES PER GAME

Player, Team	Year	G	Rec.	Yards	TD	Rec.PG
Chris George, Glenville St.	†1993	10	*117	*1,876	15	*11.7
Bruce Cerone, Emporia St.	1968	9	91	1,479	15	10.1
Mike Healey, Valparaiso	†1985	10	101	1,279	11	10.1
Barry Wagner, Alabama A&M	†1989	11	106	1,812	17	9.6
Ed Bell, Idaho St.	†1969	10	96	1,522	*20	9.6
Jerry Hendren, Idaho	1968	9	86	1,457	14	9.6
Dick Hewins, Drake	†1968	10	95	1,316	13	9.5
Billy Joe Masters, Evansville	†1987	10	‡94	‡960	4	‡9.4
Joe Dittrich, Southwest St.	†1980	9	83	974	7	9.2
Manley Sarnowsky, Drake	†1966	10	92	1,114	7	9.2

*Record. †National champion. ‡Record for a running back.

CAREER CATCHES

Player, Team	Years	Rec.	Yards	TD
Chris Myers, Kenyon	1967-70	*253	3,897	33
Bruce Cerone, Yankton/Emporia St.	1966-67, 68-69	241	*4,354	*49
Harold "Red" Roberts, Austin Peay	1967-70	232	3,005	31
Jerry Hendren, Idaho	1967-69	230	3,435	27
Mike Healey, Valparaiso	1982-85	228	3,212	26
William Mackall, Tenn.-Martin	1985-88	224	2,488	16
Johnny Cox, Fort Lewis	1990-93	220	3,611	33
Robert Clark, N.C. Central	1983-86	210	4,231	38
Terry Fredenberg, Wis.-Milwaukee	1965-68	206	2,789	24
Dan Bogar, Valparaiso	1981-84	204	2,816	26
Rich Otte, Northeast Mo. St.	1980-83	202	2,821	16
Mark Steinmeyer, Kutztown (RB)	1988-91	200	2,118	23
Barry Naone, Portland St. (TE)	1985-88	199	2,237	8
Tony Willis, New Haven	1990-93	194	3,420	38
Jon Braff, St. Mary's (Cal.) (TE)	1985-88	193	2,461	20
Shannon Sharpe, Savannah St.	1986-89	192	3,744	40
Bill Wick, Carroll (Wis.)	1966-69	190	2,967	20
Don Hutt, Boise St.	1971-73	187	2,716	30
Steve Hansley, Northwest Mo. St.	1983-85	186	2,898	24
Dan Anderson, Northwest Mo. St. (TE)	1982-85	186	2,494	16

*Record.

SEASON CATCHES

Player, Team	Year	G	Rec.	Yards	TD
Chris George, Glenville St.	†1993	10	*117	*1,876	15
Barry Wagner, Alabama A&M	†1989	11	106	1,812	17
Mike Healey, Valparaiso	†1985	10	101	1,279	11
Ed Bell, Idaho St.	†1969	10	96	1,522	*20
Dick Hewins, Drake	†1968	10	95	1,316	13
Billy Joe Masters, Evansville	†1987	10	‡94	‡960	4
Stan Carraway, West Tex. A&M	†1986	11	94	1,175	9
Manley Sarnowsky, Drake	†1966	10	92	1,114	7
Rus Bailey, N.M. Highlands	1993	10	91	1,192	12
Bruce Cerone, Emporia St.	1968	9	91	1,479	15
Rodney Robinson, Gardner-Webb	1992	11	89	1,496	16
Matt Carman, Livingston	1993	10	88	1,085	14
Harvey Tanner, Murray St.	†1967	10	88	1,019	3

*Record. †National champion. ‡Record for a running back.

SINGLE-GAME CATCHES

No.	Player, Team (Opponent)	Date
23	Barry Wagner, Alabama A&M (Clark Atlanta)	Nov. 4, 1989
20	Harold "Red" Roberts, Austin Peay (Murray St.)	Nov. 8, 1969
19	Matt Carman, Livingston (Jacksonville St.)	Nov. 7, 1992
19	Aaron Marsh, Eastern Ky. (Northwood)	Oct. 14, 1967
19	George LaPorte, Union, N.Y. (Rensselaer)	Oct. 16, 1965
18	Chris Pelczarski, Millersville (Bloomsburg)	Nov. 9, 1991
18	Carl Bruere, N.M. Highlands (Western St.)	Oct. 12, 1991
18	Billy Joe Masters, Evansville (Ashland)	Oct. 31, 1987
18	Bruce Cerone, Emporia St. (Washburn)	Nov. 9, 1968
18	Dick Donlin, Hamline (St. John's, Minn.)	Oct. 8, 1955

CAREER YARDS

Player, Team	Years	Rec.	Yards	Avg.	TD
Bruce Cerone, Yankton/Emporia St.	1966-67, 68-69	241	*4,345	18.1	*49
Robert Clark, N.C. Central	1983-86	210	4,231	‡20.1	38
Chris Myers, Kenyon	1967-70	*253	3,897	15.4	33
Shannon Sharpe, Savannah St.	1986-89	192	3,744	19.5	40
Tyrone Johnson, Western St.	1990-93	163	3,717	††22.8	35
Jeff Tiefenthaler, South Dak. St.	1983-86	173	3,621	20.9	31
Willie Richardson, Jackson St.	1959-62	166	3,616	21.8	36
Johnny Cox, Fort Lewis	1990-93	220	3,611	16.4	33

*Record. ‡Record for minimum 180 catches. ††Record for minimum 135 catches.

SEASON YARDS

Player, Team	Year	Rec.	Yards	Avg.	TD
Chris George, Glenville St.	†1993	*117	*1,876	16.0	15
Barry Wagner, Alabama A&M	†1989	106	1,812	17.1	17
Dan Fulton, Nebraska-Omaha	1976	67	1,581	23.6	16
Jeff Tiefenthaler, South Dak. St.	1986	73	1,534	21.0	11
Ed Bell, Idaho St.	†1969	96	1,522	15.9	*20
Rodney Robinson, Gardner-Webb	†1992	89	1,496	16.8	16
Bruce Cerone, Emporia St.	1968	91	1,479	16.3	15
Jerry Hendren, Idaho	1968	86	1,457	16.9	14

*Record. †National champion.

ANNUAL CHAMPIONS

Year	Player, Team	Class	Rec.	Yards	TD
1946	Hugh Taylor, Oklahoma City	Jr.	23	457	8
1947	Bill Klein, Hanover	So.	52	648	12
1948	Bill Klein, Hanover	Jr.	43	812	6
1949	Cliff Coggin, Southern Miss.	Sr.	53	1,087	9
1950	Jack Bighead, Pepperdine	Jr.	38	551	6
1951	Jim Stefoff, Kalamazoo	Jr.	45	680	5
1952	Jim McKinzie, Northern Ill.	Sr.	44	703	6
1953	Dick Beetsch, Northern Iowa	So.	54	837	9
1954	R. C. Owens, Col. of Idaho	Sr.	48	905	7
1955	Dick Donlin, Hamline	Sr.	41	480	2
1956	Tom Rychlec, American Int'l	Sr.	40	353	3
1957	Tom Whitaker, Nevada	Jr.	40	527	4
1958	Bruce Shenk, West Chester	Sr.	39	580	9
1959	Fred Tunnicliffe, UC Santa Barb.	So.	48	1,087	11
1960	Ken Gregory, Whittier	Sr.	74	1,018	4
1961	Marty Baumhower, Defiance	Jr.	57	708	4
1962	Hugh Rohrschneider, Northern Ill.	Jr.	76	795	5
1963	Hugh Rohrschneider, Northern Ill.	Sr.	75	1,036	14
1964	Steve Gilliatt, Parsons	So.	81	984	12
1965	George LaPorte, Union (N.Y.)	Sr.	74	724	5
1966	Manley Sarnowsky, Drake	Sr.	92	1,114	7
1967	Harvey Tanner, Murray St.	Jr.	88	1,019	3
1968	Dick Hewins, Drake	Sr.	95	1,316	13
1969	Ed Bell, Idaho St.	Sr.	96	1,522	*20

Beginning in 1970, ranked on per-game (instead of total) catches

Year	Player, Team	Class	G	Rec.	Avg.	Yards	TD
1970	Steve Mahaffey, Wash. & Lee	Sr.	9	74	8.2	897	2
1971	Kalle Kontson, Rensselaer	Sr.	9	69	7.7	1,031	7
1972	Freddie Scott, Amherst	Jr.	8	66	8.3	936	12
1973	Ron Gustafson, North Dak.	Jr.	10	67	6.7	1,210	10
1974	Andy Sanchez, Cal Poly Pomona	Sr.	10	62	6.2	903	0
1975	Butch Johnson, UC Riverside	Sr.	8	67	8.4	1,027	8
1976	Bo Darden, Shaw	So.	9	57	6.3	863	4
1977	Jeff Tesch, Moorhead St.	Sr.	10	67	6.7	760	9
1978	Mike Chrobot, Butler	Sr.	10	55	5.5	628	5
	Tom Ferguson, Cal St. Hayward	Jr.	10	55	5.5	698	6
	Mark McDaniel, Northern Colo.	Sr.	10	55	5.5	761	6
1979	Robbie Ray, Franklin	Sr.	10	63	6.3	987	3
1980	Joe Dittrich, Southwest St.	Sr.	9	83	9.2	974	7
1981	Paul Choudek, Southwest St.	Sr.	10	70	7.0	747	5
1982	Jay Barnett, Evansville	Sr.	10	81	8.1	1,181	12
1983	Perry Kemp, Calif. (Pa.)	Sr.	10	74	7.4	1,101	9
1984	Dan Bogar, Valparaiso	Sr.	10	73	7.3	861	11
1985	Mike Healey, Valparaiso	Sr.	10	101	10.1	1,279	11
1986	Stan Carraway, West Tex. A&M	Sr.	11	94	8.5	1,175	9
1987	Billy Joe Masters, Evansville	Sr.	10	‡94	‡9.4	‡960	4
1988	Todd Smith, Morningside	Sr.	11	86	7.8	1,006	8
1989	Barry Wagner, Alabama A&M	Sr.	11	106	9.6	1,812	17

Beginning in 1990, ranked on both per-game catches and yards per game

PER-GAME CATCHES

Year	Player, Team	Class	G	Rec.	Avg.	Yards	TD
1990	Mark Steinmeyer, Kutztown	Jr.	11	86	7.8	940	5
1991	Jesse Lopez, Cal St. Hayward	Sr.	10	86	8.6	861	4
1992	Randy Bartosh, Southwest Baptist	Sr.	8	65	8.1	860	2
1993	Chris George, Glenville St.	Jr.	10	*117	*11.7	*1,876	15

DIVISION II

YARDS PER GAME

Year	Player, Team	Class	G	Rec.	Yards	Avg.	TD
1990	Ernest Priester, Edinboro	Sr.	8	45	1,060	132.5	14
1991	Rod Smith, Mo. Southern St.	Jr.	11	60	1,439	130.8	15
1992	Rodney Robinson, Gardner-Webb	Sr.	11	89	1,496	136.0	16
1993	Chris George, Glenville St.	Jr.	10	*117	*1,876	*187.6	15

*Record. ‡Record for a running back.

Scoring

CAREER POINTS PER GAME

Player, Team	Years	G	TD	XPt.	FG	Pts.	Pt.PG
Ole Gunderson, St. Olaf	1969-71	27	60	2	0	362	*13.4
Billy Johnson, Widener	1971-73	28	62	0	0	372	13.3
Leon Burns, Long Beach St.	1969-70	22	47	2	0	284	12.9
Dale Mills, Northeast Mo. St.	1957-60	36	64	23	0	407	11.3
Walter Payton, Jackson St.	1971-74	42	66	53	5	*464	11.0
Steve Roberts, Butler	1986-89	35	63	4	0	386	11.0
Jeff Bentrim, North Dak. St.	1983-86	35	64	2	0	386	11.0
Shawn Graves, Wofford	1989-92	40	*72	3	0	438	11.0
Johnny Bailey, Tex. A&M-Kingsville	1986-89	39	70	3	0	426	10.9
Garney Henley, Huron	1956-59	37	63	16	0	394	10.6

*Record.

SEASON POINTS PER GAME

Player, Team	Year	G	TD	XPt.	FG	Pts.	Pt.PG
Carl Herakovich, Rose-Hulman	†1958	8	25	18	0	168	*21.0
Jim Switzer, Col. of Emporia	†1963	9	28	0	0	168	18.7
Billy Johnson, Widener	†1972	9	27	0	0	162	18.0
Carl Garrett, N. M. Highlands	†1966	9	26	2	0	158	17.6
Ted Scown, Sul Ross St.	†1948	10	28	0	0	168	16.8

*Record. †National champion.

CAREER POINTS

Player, Team	Year	TD	XPt.	FG	Pts.
Walter Payton, Jackson St.	1971-74	66	53	5	*464
Shawn Graves, Wofford	1989-92	*72	3	0	438
Johnny Bailey, Tex. A&M-Kingsville	1986-89	70	3	0	426
Dale Mills, Northeast Mo. St.	1957-60	64	23	0	407
Jeremy Monroe, Michigan Tech	1990-93	67	0	0	402
Garney Henley, Huron	1956-59	63	16	0	394
Steve Roberts, Butler	1986-89	63	4	0	386
Jeff Bentrim, North Dak. St.	1983-86	64	2	0	386
Leo Lewis, Lincoln (Mo.)	1951-54	64	0	0	384
Heath Sherman, Tex. A&M-Kingsville	1985-88	63	0	0	378
Billy Johnson, Widener	1971-73	62	0	0	372
Tank Younger, Grambling	1945-48	60	9	0	369
Bill Cooper, Muskingum	1957-60	54	37	1	364

*Record.

SEASON POINTS

Player, Team	Year	TD	XPt.	FG	Pts.
Terry Metcalf, Long Beach St.	1971	*29	4	0	*178
Jim Switzer, Col. of Emporia	†1963	28	0	0	168
Carl Herakovich, Rose-Hulman	†1958	25	18	0	168
Ted Scown, Sul Ross St.	†1948	28	0	0	168
Ronald Moore, Pittsburg St.	1992	27	4	0	166
Leon Burns, Long Beach St.	†1969	27	2	0	164
Mike Deutsch, North Dak.	1972	27	0	0	162
Billy Johnson, Widener	†1972	27	0	0	162

*Record. †National champion.

ANNUAL CHAMPIONS

Year	Player, Team	Class	TD	XPt.	FG	Pts.
1946	Joe Carter, Florida N&I	So.	21	26	0	152
1947	Darwin Horn, Pepperdine	Jr.	19	1	0	115
	Chuck Schoenherr, Wheaton (Ill.)	So.	19	1	0	115
1948	Ted Scown, Sul Ross St.	So.	28	0	0	168
1949	Sylvester Polk, Md.-East. Shore	Jr.	19	15	0	129
1950	Carl Taseff, John Carroll	Sr.	23	0	0	138
1951	Paul Yackey, Heidelberg	Jr.	22	0	0	132
1952	Al Conway, William Jewell	Sr.	22	1	0	133
1953	Leo Lewis, Lincoln (Mo.)	Jr.	22	0	0	132
1954	Jim Podoley, Central Mich.	Jr.	18	1	0	109
	Dick Nyers, Indianapolis	Sr.	16	13	0	109
1955	Nate Clark, Hillsdale	Jr.	24	0	0	144
1956	Larry Houdek, Kan. Wesleyan	Sr.	19	0	0	114
1957	Lenny Lyles, Louisville	Sr.	21	6	0	132
1958	Carl Herakovich, Rose-Hulman	Sr.	25	18	0	168
1959	Garney Henley, Huron	Sr.	22	9	0	141
1960	Bill Cooper, Muskingum	Sr.	23	14	0	152

Year	Player, Team	Class	TD	XPt.	FG	Pts.
1961	John Murio, Whitworth	Jr.	15	33	2	129
1962	Mike Goings, Bluffton	So.	22	0	0	132
1963	Jim Switzer, Col. of Emporia	Sr.	28	0	0	168
1964	Henry Dyer, Grambling	Jr.	17	2	0	104
	Dunn Marteen, Cal St. Los Angeles	Sr.	11	38	0	104
1965	Allen Smith, Findlay	Jr.	24	2	0	146
1966	Carl Garrett, N. M. Highlands	So.	26	2	0	158
1967	Bert Nye, West Chester	Jr.	19	13	0	127
1968	Howard Stevens, Randolph-Macon	Fr.	23	4	0	142
1969	Leon Burns, Long Beach St.	Jr.	27	2	0	164

Beginning in 1970, ranked on per-game (instead of total) points

Year	Player, Team	Class	G	TD	XPt.	FG	Pts.	Avg.
1970	Mike DiBlasi, Mount Union	Sr.	9	22	0	0	132	14.7
1971	Larry Ras, Michigan Tech	Sr.	9	24	0	0	144	16.0
1972	Billy Johnson, Widener	Jr.	9	27	0	0	162	18.0
1973	Walter Payton, Jackson St.	Jr.	11	24	13	1	160	14.5
1974	Walter Payton, Jackson St.	Sr.	10	19	6	1	123	12.3
1975	Dale Kasowski, North Dak.	Sr.	7	16	4	0	100	14.3
1976	Ted McKnight, Minn.-Duluth	Sr.	10	24	0	0	144	14.4
1977	Bill Burnham, New Hampshire	Sr.	10	22	0	0	132	13.2
1978	Marschell Brunfield, Youngstown St.	Sr.	9	14	0	0	84	9.3
	Charlie Thompson, Western St.	Sr.	9	14	0	0	84	9.3
1979	Robby Robson, Youngstown St.	Jr.	10	20	0	0	120	12.0
1980	Amory Bodin, Minn.-Duluth	Sr.	10	19	2	0	116	11.6
1981	George Works, Northern Mich.	Jr.	10	21	0	0	126	12.6
1982	George Works, Northern Mich.	Sr.	10	23	0	0	138	13.8
1983	Clarence Johnson, North Ala.	Jr.	10	16	0	0	96	9.6
1984	Jeff Bentrim, North Dak. St.	So.	9	14	0	0	84	9.3
1985	Jeff Bentrim, North Dak. St.	Jr.	8	18	2	0	110	††13.8
1986	Jeff Bentrim, North Dak. St.	Sr.	10	23	0	0	138	13.8
1987	Johnny Bailey, Tex. A&M-Kingsville	So.	10	20	0	0	120	12.0
1988	Steve Roberts, Butler	Jr.	10	23	4	0	142	14.2
1989	Jimmy Allen, St. Joseph's (Ind.)	Jr.	10	23	0	0	138	13.8
1990	Ernest Priester, Edinboro	Sr.	8	16	0	0	96	12.0
1991	Quincy Tillmon, Emporia St.	So.	9	19	0	0	114	12.7
1992	David McCartney, Chadron St.	Jr.	10	25	4	0	154	15.4
1993	Roger Graham, New Haven	Jr.	10	23	0	0	138	13.8

††Declared champion; with one more game (to meet 75 percent of games played minimum) for zero points, still would have highest per-game average.

Interceptions

CAREER INTERCEPTIONS

Player, Team	Years	No.	Yards	Avg.
Tom Collins, Indianapolis	1982-85	*37	390	10.5
Scott Wiedeman, Adams St.	1988-91	31	289	9.3
Dean Diaz, Humboldt St.	1980-83	31	328	10.6
Bill Grantham, Missouri-Rolla	1977-80	29	263	9.1
Tony Woods, Bloomsburg	1982-85	26	105	4.0
Buster West, Gust. Adolphus	1967-70	26	192	7.4
Gary Rubeling, Towson St.	1980-83	25	122	4.9
Greg Mercier, Ripon	1968-70	25	243	9.7

*Record.

SEASON INTERCEPTIONS

Player, Team	Year	No.	Yards
Eugene Hunter, Fort Valley St.	†1972	**14	211
Luther Howard, Delaware St.	†1972	**14	99
Tom Rezzuti, Northeastern	†1971	**14	153
Jim Blackwell, Southern-B.R.	†1970	**14	196
Carl Ray Harris, Fresno St.	1970	**14	98

**Record tied. †National champion.

ANNUAL CHAMPIONS

Year	Player, Team	Class	G	No.	Avg.	Yards
1970	Jim Blackwell, Southern-B.R.	Sr.	11	**14	1.27	196
1971	Tom Rezzuti, Northeastern	Jr.	9	**14	**1.56	153
1972	Eugene Hunter, Fort Valley St.	So.	9	**14	**1.56	211
	Luther Howard, Delaware St.	Sr.	9	**14	**1.56	99
1973	Mike Pierce, Northern Colo.	Sr.	7	7	1.00	158
	James Smith, Shaw	So.	8	8	1.00	94
1974	Terry Rusin, Wayne St. (Mich.)	Fr.	10	10	1.00	62
1975	Jim Poettgen, Cal Poly Pomona	Jr.	11	12	1.09	156
1976	Johnny Tucker, Tennessee Tech	Sr.	11	10	0.91	74
1977	Mike Ellis, Norfolk St.	So.	11	12	1.09	257
	Cornelius Washington, Winston-Salem	Sr.	11	12	1.09	128
1978	Bill Grantham, Missouri-Rolla	So.	11	11	1.00	109
1979	Jeff Huffman, Michigan Tech	Sr.	10	11	1.10	97

Year	Player, Team	Class	G	No.	Avg.	Yards
1980	Mike Lush, East Stroudsburg	Sr.	10	12	1.20	208
1981	Bobby Futrell, Elizabeth City St.	So.	9	11	1.22	159
1982	Greg Maack, Central Mo. St.	Sr.	10	11	1.10	192
1983	Matt Didio, Wayne St. (Mich.)	Sr.	10	13	1.30	131
1984	Bob Jahelka, LIU-C.W. Post	Sr.	8	9	1.13	83
1985	Duvaal Callaway, Fort Valley St.	Sr.	11	10	0.91	175
	Tony Woods, Bloomsburg	Sr.	11	10	0.91	10
1986	Doug Smart, Winona St.	Jr.	8	10	1.25	56
1987	Mike Petrich, Minn.-Duluth	Jr.	11	9	0.82	151
1988	Pete Jaros, Augustana (S.D.)	Jr.	11	13	1.18	120
1989	Jacque DeMatteo, Clarion	Jr.	8	6	0.75	21
1990	Eric Turner, East Tex. St.	So.	11	10	0.91	105
1991	Jeff Fickes, Shippensburg	Sr.	11	12	1.09	154
1992	Pat Williams, East Tex. St.	Sr.	11	13	1.18	145
1993	Troy Crissman, Ky. Wesleyan	So.	10	9	0.90	39

**Record tied.

Punting

CAREER AVERAGE
(Minimum 100 Punts)

Player, Team	Years	No.	Yards	Avg.
Steve Lewis, Jacksonville St.	1989-92	100	4,434	*44.34
Tim Baer, Colorado Mines	1986-89	235	10,406	44.28
Jeff Guy, Western St.	1983-85	113	4,967	44.0
Russ Pilcher, Carroll (Mont.)	1964-66	124	5,424	43.7
Russell Gonzales, Morris Brown	1976-77	111	4,833	43.5
Gerald Circo, Cal St. Chico	1964-65	103	4,470	43.4
Trent Morgan, Cal St. Northridge	1987-88	128	5,531	43.2
Bryan Wagner, Cal St. Northridge	1981-84	203	8,762	43.2
Tom Kolesar, Nevada	1973-74	140	6,032	43.1
Jimmy Morris, Angelo St.	1991-92	101	4,326	42.8
Don Geist, Northern Colo.	1981-84	263	11,247	42.8
Jan Chapman, San Diego	1958-60	106	4,533	42.8
Eric Fadness, Fort Lewis	1989-92	209	8,905	42.6
Warner Robertson, Md.-East. Shore	1968-70	131	5,578	42.6

*Record.

SEASON AVERAGE
(Qualifiers for Championship)

Player, Team	Year	No.	Yards	Avg.
Steve Ecker, Shippensburg	†1965	32	1,570	*49.1
Don Cockroft, Adams St.	†1966	36	1,728	48.0
Jack Patterson, William Jewell	1965	29	1,377	47.5
Art Calandrelli, Canisius	†1949	25	1,177	47.1
Grover Perkins, Southern-B.R.	†1961	22	1,034	47.0
Erskine Valrie, Alabama A&M	1966	36	1,673	46.5
Mark Bounds, West Tex. A&M	†1990	69	3,198	46.3
Bruce Swanson, North Park	†1967	53	2,455	46.3
Lyle Johnston, Weber St.	1965	29	1,340	46.2

*Record. †National champion.

ANNUAL CHAMPIONS

Year	Player, Team	Class	No.	Yards	Avg.
1948	Arthur Teixeira, Central Mich.	Sr.	42	1,867	44.5
1949	Art Calandrelli, Canisius	Jr.	25	1,177	47.1
1950	Flavian Weidekamp, Butler	Sr.	41	1,762	43.0
1951	Curtiss Harris, Savannah St.	Sr.	42	1,854	44.1
1952	Virgil Stan, Western St.	Sr.	37	1,622	43.8
1953	Bill Bradshaw, Bowling Green	Jr.	50	2,199	44.0
1954	Bill Bradshaw, Bowling Green	Sr.	28	1,228	43.9
1955	Don Baker, North Texas	Sr.	30	1,349	45.0
1956	Marion Zody, Ashland	Jr.	34	1,475	43.4
1957	Lawson Persley, Mississippi Val.	Sr.	36	1,659	46.1
1958	Tom Lewis, Lake Forest	Jr.	24	1,089	45.4
1959	Buck Grover, Salem-Teikyo	Fr.	27	1,203	44.6
1960	Joe Roy, N. M. Highlands	So.	40	1,744	43.6
1961	Grover Perkins, Southern-B.R.	Fr.	22	1,034	47.0
1962	Ron Crouse, Catawba	Jr.	37	1,653	44.7
1963	Steve Bailey, Kentucky St.	Sr.	39	1,747	44.8
1964	Russ Pilcher, Carroll (Mont.)	So.	34	1,545	45.4
1965	Steve Ecker, Shippensburg	Sr.	32	1,570	*49.1
1966	Don Cockroft, Adams St.	Sr.	36	1,728	48.0
1967	Bruce Swanson, North Park	Jr.	53	2,455	46.3
1968	Warner Robertson, Md.-East. Shore	Fr.	61	2,699	44.2
1969	Warner Robertson, Md.-East. Shore	So.	37	1,629	44.0
1970	John Bonner, Tenn.-Chatt.	Sr.	73	3,243	44.4
1971	Ken Gamble, Fayetteville St.	Sr.	47	2,092	44.5
1972	Raymond Key, Jackson St.	Jr.	44	1,883	42.8

Year	Player, Team	Class	No.	Yards	Avg.
1973	Jerry Pope, Louisiana Tech	Fr.	48	2,064	43.0
1974	Mike Shawen, Middle Tenn. St.	Sr.	62	2,720	43.9
1975	Mike Wood, Southeast Mo. St.	Jr.	40	1,729	43.2
1976	Russell Gonzales, Morris Brown	So.	54	2,474	45.8
1977	Jeff Gossett, Eastern Ill.	Jr.	62	2,668	43.0
1978	Bill Moats, South Dak.	Sr.	77	3,377	43.9
1979	Bob Fletcher, Northeast Mo. St.	Sr.	79	3,409	43.2
1980	Sean Landeta, Towson St.	So.	47	2,038	43.4
1981	Gregg Lowery, Jacksonville St.	Jr.	64	2,787	43.5
1982	Don Geist, Northern Colo.	So.	66	2,966	44.4
1983	Jeff Guy, Western St.	So.	39	1,734	44.5
1984	Jeff Guy, Western St.	Jr.	46	2,012	43.7
1985	Jeff Williams, Slippery Rock	Sr.	46	1,977	43.0
1986	Tim Baer, Colorado Mines	Fr.	62	2,797	45.1
1987	Jeff McComb, Southern Utah	Sr.	42	1,863	44.4
1988	Tim Baer, Colorado Mines	Jr.	65	2,880	43.9
1989	Tim Baer, Colorado Mines	Sr.	55	2,382	43.3
1990	Mark Bounds, West Tex. A&M	Jr.	69	3,198	46.3
1991	Doug O'Neill, Cal Poly SLO	Sr.	42	1,895	45.1
1992	Jimmy Morris, Angelo St.	So.	45	2,001	44.5
1993	Chris Carter, Henderson St.	Sr.	53	2,305	43.5

*Record.

Punt Returns

CAREER AVERAGE
(Minimum 1.2 Returns Per Game)

Player, Team	Years	No.	Yards	Avg.
Billy Johnson, Widener	1971-73	40	989	*24.7
Chuck Goehl, Monmouth (Ill.)	1970-72	48	911	19.0
Robbie Martin, Cal Poly SLO	1978-80	69	1,168	16.9
Roscoe Word, Jackson St.	1970-73	35	554	15.8
Darryl Skinner, Hampton	1983-86	53	835	15.8
Michael Fields, Mississippi Col.	1984-85	50	695	13.9

*Record.

SEASON AVERAGE
(Minimum 1.2 Returns Per Game)

Player, Team	Year	No.	Yards	Avg.
Billy Johnson, Widener	†1972	15	511	*34.1
William Williams, Livingstone	†1976	16	453	28.3
Terry Egerdahl, Minn.-Duluth	†1975	13	360	27.7
Ennis Thomas, Bishop	†1971	18	450	25.0
Chuck Goehl, Monmouth (Ill.)	1972	17	416	24.5

*Record. †National champion.

ANNUAL CHAMPIONS

Year	Player, Team	Class	No.	Yards	Avg.
1970	Kevin Downs, Ill. Benedictine	Jr.	11	255	23.2
1971	Ennis Thomas, Bishop	So.	18	450	25.0
1972	Billy Johnson, Widener	Jr.	15	511	*34.1
1973	Roscoe Word, Jackson St.	Sr.	19	316	16.6
1974	Greg Anderson, Montana	So.	13	263	20.2
1975	Terry Egerdahl, Minn.-Duluth	Sr.	13	360	27.7
1976	William Williams, Livingstone	So.	16	453	28.3
1977	Armando Olivieri, New York Tech	So.	14	270	19.3
1978	Dwight Walker, Nicholls St.	Fr.	16	284	17.8
1979	Ricky Eberhart, Morris Brown	Fr.	18	401	22.3
1980	Ron Bagby, Puget Sound	So.	16	242	15.1
1981	Ron Trammell, East Tex. St.	Jr.	29	467	16.1
1982	Darrel Green, Tex. A&M-Kingsville	Sr.	19	392	20.6
1983	Steve Carter, Albany St. (Ga.)	Sr.	27	511	18.9
1984	Michael Fields, Mississippi Col.	Jr.	23	487	21.2
1985	Darryl Skinner, Hampton	Jr.	19	426	22.4
1986	Ben Frazier, Cheyney	So.	14	246	17.6
1987	Ronald Day, Savannah St.	Sr.	12	229	19.1
1988	Donnie Morris, Norfolk St.	Jr.	12	283	23.6
1989	Dennis Mailhot, East Stroudsburg	Jr.	16	284	17.8
1990	Ron West, Pittsburg St.	Jr.	23	388	16.9
1991	Doug Grant, Savannah St.	So.	19	331	17.4
1992	Doug Grant, Savannah St.	Jr.	15	366	24.4
1993	Jerry Garrett, Wayne St. (Neb.)	Jr.	26	498	19.2

*Record.

DIVISION II

Kickoff Returns

CAREER AVERAGE
(Minimum 1.2 Returns Per Game)

Player, Team	Years	No.	Yards	Avg.
Glen Printers, Southern Colo.	1973-74	25	851	*34.0
Karl Evans, Mo. Southern St.	1991-92	32	959	30.0
Clarence Chapman, Eastern Mich.	1973-75	45	1,278	28.4
Greg Wilson, East Tenn. St.	1975-78	37	1,032	27.9
Bernie Rose, Samford/North Ala.	1973, 74-76	64	1,715	26.8
Roscoe Word, Jackson St.	1970-73	74	1,980	26.8

*Record.

SEASON AVERAGE
(Minimum 1.2 Returns Per Game)

Player, Team	Year	No.	Yards	Avg.
LaVon Reis, Western St.	†1993	14	552	*39.43
Danny Lee, Jacksonville St.	†1992	12	473	39.42
Fran DeFalco, Assumption	1993	12	461	38.4
Kendall James, Carson-Newman	1993	15	549	36.6
Roscoe Word, Jackson St.	†1973	18	650	36.1
Steve Levenseller, Puget Sound	†1978	17	610	35.9
Winston Horshaw, Shippensburg	†1991	15	536	35.7
Anthony Rivera, Western St.	1991	18	635	35.3
Dave Ludy, Winona St.	1992	25	881	35.2
Mike Scullin, Baldwin-Wallace	†1970	14	492	35.1
Rufus Smith, Eastern N. Mex.	†1985	11	386	35.1
Greg Anderson, Montana	†1974	10	335	33.5
Kevin McDevitt, Butler	†1975	12	395	32.9

*Record. †National champion.

ANNUAL CHAMPIONS

Year	Player, Team	Class	No.	Yards	Avg.
1970	Mike Scullin, Baldwin-Wallace	So.	14	492	35.1
1971	Joe Brockmeyer, Western Md.	Jr.	16	500	31.3
1972	Rick Murphy, Indiana St.	Jr.	22	707	32.1
1973	Roscoe Word, Jackson St.	Sr.	18	650	36.1
1974	Greg Anderson, Montana	So.	10	335	33.5
1975	Kevin McDevitt, Butler	Jr.	12	395	32.9
1976	Henry Vereen, Nevada-Las Vegas	So.	20	628	31.4
1977	Dickie Johnson, Southern Colo.	Jr.	13	385	29.6
1978	Steve Levenseller, Puget Sound	Sr.	17	610	35.9
1979	Otha Hill, Central St. (Ohio)	Sr.	18	526	29.2
1980	Charlie Taylor, Southeast Mo. St.	Sr.	13	396	30.5
1981	Willie Canady, Fort Valley St.	Jr.	13	415	31.9
1982	Clarence Martin, Cal Poly SLO	So.	11	360	32.7
1983	David Anthony, Southern Ore.	Jr.	14	436	31.1
1984	Larry Winters, St. Paul's	Sr.	20	644	32.2
1985	Rufus Smith, Eastern N. Mex.	Fr.	11	386	35.1
1986	John Barron, Butler	So.	21	653	31.1
1987	Albert Fann, Cal St. Northridge	Fr.	16	468	29.3
1988	Pierre Fils, New Haven	So.	12	378	31.5
1989	Dennis Mailhot, East Stroudsburg	Jr.	11	359	32.6
1990	Alfred Banks, Livingston	Sr.	17	529	31.1
1991	Winston Horshaw, Shippensburg	Jr.	15	536	35.7
1992	Danny Lee, Jacksonville St.	Sr.	12	473	39.4
1993	LaVon Reis, Western St.	Sr.	14	552	*39.4

*Record.

All-Purpose Yards

ANNUAL CHAMPIONS

Year	Player, Team	Cl.	Rush	Rcv.	Int.	PR	KOR	Yds.	Yd.PG
1992	Johnny Cox, Fort Lewis	Jr.	95	1,331	0	80	679	2,185	218.5
1993	Chris George, Glenville St.	Jr.	23	1,876	0	157	562	2,618	261.8

Field Goals

CAREER FIELD GOALS

Player, Team	Year	Made	Atts.	Pct.
Mike Wood, Southeast Mo. St. (S)	1974-77	*64	*109	.587
Pat Beaty, North Dak. (S)	1985-88	52	82	.634
Bob Gilbreath, Eastern N. Mex. (S)	1986-89	50	77	.649
Ed O'Brien, Central Fla. (S)	1984-87	50	77	.649
Billy Watkins, East Tex. St. (S)	1990-93	49	84	.583
Bill May, Clarion (C)	1977-80	48	60	*.800
Ed Detwiler, East Stroudsburg	1989-92	48	87	.552
Mike Thomas, Angelo St. (S)	1980-83	47	68	.691
Steve Huff, Central Mo. St. (C)	1982-85	47	80	.588
Phil Brandt, Central Mo. St. (S)	1987-90	46	66	.697
Howie Guarini, Shippensburg (S)	1988-91	45	62	.726
James Knowles, North Ala. (C)	1982-85	45	77	.584
Ed Hotz, Southeast Mo. St. (S)	1978-81	45	77	.584
Kurt Seibel, South Dak. (C)	1980-83	44	62	.710
Jason Monday, Lenoir-Rhyne	1989-92	44	64	.688
Pat Bolton, Montana St. (C)	1972-75	44	76	.579
Skipper Butler, Texas-Arlington (C)	1966-69	44	101	.436

*Record. (C) Conventional kicker. (S) Soccer-style kicker.

SEASON FIELD GOALS

Player, Team	Year	Made	Atts.	Pct.
Raul De la Flor, Humboldt St. (S)	†1993	**20	26	.769
Pat Beaty, North Dak. (S)	†1988	**20	26	.769
Tom Jurich, Northern Ariz. (C)	†1977	**20	29	.690
Dennis Hochman, Sonoma St. (S)	†1986	19	22	.864
Cory Solberg, North Dak. (S)	†1989	19	27	.704
Jaime Nunez, Weber St. (S)	†1971	19	32	.594
Bernard Henderson, Albany St. (Ga.) (S)	†1985	18	26	.692
Ki Tok Chu, Tenn.-Martin (S)	1988	17	22	.773
Jack McTyre, Valdosta St. (S)	1990	17	23	.739
Dino Beligrinis, Winston-Salem (S)	1988	17	23	.739
Ed O'Brien, Central Fla. (S)	†1987	17	26	.654
Mike Wood, Southeast Mo. St. (S)	1976	17	33	.515

**Record tied. (C) Conventional kicker. (S) Soccer-style kicker.

ANNUAL CHAMPIONS

Year	Player, Team	Class	Made	Atts.	Pct.	PG
1970	Chris Guerrieri, Alfred (S)	Sr.	11	21	.524	*.800
1971	Jaime Nunez, Weber St. (S)	Sr.	19	32	.594	**1.90
1972	Randy Walker, Northwestern St. (C)	Jr.	13	19	.684	1.30
1973	Reinhold Struprich, Hawaii (S)	Jr.	15	23	.652	1.36
1974	Mike Wood, Southeast Mo. St. (S)	Fr.	16	23	.696	1.45
1975	Wolfgang Taylor, Western St. (S)	Sr.	14	21	.667	1.56
1976	Rolf Benirschke, UC Davis (S)	Sr.	14	19	.737	1.56
1977	Tom Jurich, Northern Ariz. (C)	Sr.	**20	29	.690	1.81
1978	Frank Friedman, Cal St. Northridge (S)	Jr.	15	22	.682	1.50
1979	Bill May, Clarion (S)	Jr.	16	21	.762	1.60
1980	Nelson McMurain, North Ala. (S)	Jr.	14	22	.636	1.40
	Sean Landeta, Towson St. (S)	So.	14	28	.500	1.40
1981	Russ Meier, South Dak. St. (S)	Fr.	16	21	.762	1.60
1982	Joey Malone, Alabama A&M (C)	Fr.	15	21	.714	1.36
	Rick Ruszkiewicz, Edinboro (S)	Sr.	15	24	.625	1.36
1983	Mike Thomas, Angelo St. (S)	Sr.	16	22	.727	1.45
1984	Terry Godfrey, South Dak. (S)	Jr.	16	26	.615	1.60
1985	Bernard Henderson, Albany St. (Ga.) (S)	Sr.	18	26	.692	1.64
1986	Dennis Hochman, Sonoma St. (S)	Sr.	19	22	.864	**1.90
1987	Ed O'Brien, Central Fla. (S)	Sr.	17	26	.654	1.70
1988	Pat Beaty, North Dak. (S)	Sr.	**20	26	.769	1.82
1989	Cory Solberg, North Dak. (S)	Jr.	19	27	.704	1.73
1990	Jack McTyre, Valdosta St. (S)	Sr.	17	23	.739	1.70
1991	Billy Watkins, East Tex. St. (S)	So.	15	24	.625	1.36
1992	Mike Estrella, St. Mary's (Cal.) (S)	Jr.	15	27	.556	1.67
1993	Raul De la Flor, Humboldt St. (S)	Sr.	**20	26	.769	1.82

**Record tied. (C) Conventional kicker. (S) Soccer-style kicker.

All-Time Longest Plays

Since 1941, official maximum length of all plays fixed at 100 yards.

RUSHING

Yds.	Player, Team (Opponent)	Year
99	Thelbert Withers, N.M. Highlands (Fort Lewis)	1992
99	Lester Frye, Edinboro (Calif., Pa.)	1991
99	Kelvin Minefee, Southern Utah (Mesa St.)	1988
99	Fred Deutsch, Springfield (Wagner)	1977
99	Sammy Croom, San Diego (Azusa Pacific)	1972
99	John Stenger, Swarthmore (Widener)	1970
99	Jed Knuttila, Hamline (St. Thomas, Minn.)	1968
99	Dave Lanoha, Colorado Col. (Texas Lutheran)	1967
99	Tom Pabst, UC Riverside (Cal Tech)	1965
99	George Phillips, Concord (Davis & Elkins)	1961
99	Gerry White, Connecticut (Rhode Island)	1960
99	Leo Williams, St. Augustine's (Morris)	1960
99	George Phelps, Cornell College (Monmouth, Ill.)	1959
99	Mark Lydon, Tufts (Bowdoin)	1958
99	David Wells, Tufts (Williams)	1956
99	Jack Moskal, Case Reserve (Case Tech)	1956
99	Lou Mariano, Kent (Case Reserve)	1954
99	Ron Temple, Cal St. Chico (Southern Ore.)	1953
99	Ellis Horton, Eureka (Rose-Hulman)	1952
99	Pat Abbruzzi, Rhode Island (New Hampshire)	1951

PASSING

Pass plays have resulted in 99-yard completions 15 times. The most recent:

Yds.	Passer-Receiver, Team (Opponent)	Year
99	Ray Morrow-Jeff Williamson, Cal St. Hayward (Redlands)	1993
99	Bob McLaughlin-Eric Muldowney, Lock Haven (Mansfield)	1993
99	Rob Rayl-John Unger, Valparaiso (Hillsdale)	1992
99	Bret Comp-Ken Kopetchny, East Stroudsburg (Mansfield)	1990
99	Mike Turk-Titus Dixon, Troy St. (Nicholls St.)	1986

Yds.	Passer-Receiver, Team (Opponent)	Year
99	Keith Young-John Ragin, Dist. Columbia (Fayetteville St.)	1985
99	Nick Pannunzo-Herman Heard, Southern Colo. (Adams St.)	1982
99	Tim Ebersole-Ed Noon, Shippensburg (Indiana, Pa.)	1982
99	John Guercio-Tom Bennett, LIU-C.W. Post (Juniata)	1980
99	Mike Moroski-Calvin Ellison, UC Davis (Puget Sound)	1978
99	Gary Duesenberg-Harvey King, North Park (Ill. Wesleyan)	1970

PUNTS

Yds.	Player, Team (Opponent)	Year
97	Earl Hurst, Emporia St. (Central Mo. St.)	1964
96	Gary Frens, Hope (Olivet)	1966
96	Jim Jarrett, North Dak. (South Dak.)	1957
93	Elliot Mills, Carleton (Monmouth, Ill.)	1970
93	Kaspar Fitins, Taylor (Georgetown, Ky.)	1966
93	Leeroy Sweeney, Pomona-Pitzer (UC Riverside)	1960

FIELD GOALS

Yds.	Player, Team (Opponent)	Year
67	Tom Odle, Fort Hays St. (Washburn)	1988
63	Joe Duren, Arkansas St. (McNeese St.)	1974
62	Mike Flater, Colorado Mines (Western St.)	1973
61	Duane Christian, Cameron (Southwestern Okla.)	1976
61	Mike Wood, Southeast Mo. St. (Lincoln, Mo.)	1975
61	Bill Shear, Cortland St. (Hobart)	1966
60	Mike Panasuk, Ferris St. (St. Joseph's, Ind.)	1990
60	Ed Beaulac, Sonoma St. (St. Mary's, Cal.)	1989
60	Roger McCoy, Grand Valley St. (Grand Rapids)	1976
60	Skipper Butler, Texas-Arlington (East Tex. St.)	1968

Since 1941, many players have returned interceptions, punts and kickoffs 100 yards. For the 1993 season leaders, see page 387.

Team Champions

Annual Offense Champions

TOTAL OFFENSE

Year	Team	Avg.
1948	Hanover	*624.1
1949	Pacific (Cal.)	505.3
1950	West Tex. A&M	465.3
1951	Western Ill.	473.6
1952	Sam Houston St.	448.2
1953	Col. of Idaho	476.3
1954	Col. of Emporia	469.7
1955	Centre	431.0
1956	Florida A&M	475.0
1957	Denison	430.8
1958	Mo. Valley	449.6
1959	Whittier	461.3
1960	Muskingum	456.4
1961	Florida A&M	413.6
1962	Baker	438.4
1963	Col. of Emporia	517.1
1964	San Diego St.	422.6
1965	Long Beach St.	439.5
1966	Weber St.	460.1
1967	San Fran. St.	490.0
1968	Louisiana Tech	459.1
1969	Delaware	488.9
1970	Grambling	457.7
1971	Delaware	515.6
1972	Hobart	457.3
1973	Boise St.	466.5
1974	Boise St.	516.9
1975	Portland St.	472.4
1976	Portland St.	497.5
1977	Portland St.	506.7
1978	Western St.	487.0
1979	Delaware	450.5
1980	Southwest Tex. St.	423.0
1981	Southwest Tex. St.	482.3

Year	Team	Avg.
1982	Northern Mich.	450.4
1983	Central St. (Ohio)	491.1
1984	North Dak. St.	455.3
1985	Northeast Mo. St.	471.4
1986	Tex. A&M-Kingsville	542.6
1987	Tex. A&M-Kingsville	486.4
1988	Cal St. Sacramento	486.0
1989	Grand Valley St.	480.8
1990	Chadron St.	479.6
1991	Western St.	549.8
1992	New Haven	587.7
1993	Wayne St. (Neb.)	581.5

*Record.

RUSHING OFFENSE

Year	Team	Avg.
1948	Hanover	400.4
1949	Southern-B.R.	382.9
1950	St. Lawrence	356.1
1951	Western N. Mex.	379.2
1952	William Jewell	345.0
1953	McPherson	375.9
1954	Col. of Emporia	*404.8
1955	Centre	373.4
1956	Tufts	359.9
1957	Denison	372.1
1958	Huron	353.3
1959	Bemidji St.	326.6
1960	Muskingum	355.2
1961	Huron	313.1
1962	Northern St.	355.3
1963	Luther	356.0
1964	Cal St. Los Angeles	325.9
1965	Huron	303.3
1966	Neb.-Kearney	370.1
1967	North Dak. St.	299.6
1968	Delaware	315.8
1969	St. Olaf	369.1
1970	Delaware	385.9
1971	Delaware	371.2
1972	Hobart	380.7
1973	Bethune-Cookman	308.8
1974	Central Mich.	324.6

Year	Team	Avg.
1975	North Dak.	344.4
1976	Montana St.	287.5
1977	South Caro. St.	321.5
1978	Western St.	320.2
1979	Mississippi Col.	314.5
1980	Minn.-Duluth	307.3
1981	Millersville	322.9
1982	Mississippi Col.	297.0
1983	Jamestown	297.7
1984	North Dak. St.	334.7
1985	Saginaw Valley	300.4
1986	Tex. A&M-Kingsville	395.2
1987	Tex. A&M-Kingsville	330.5
1988	North Dak. St.	373.1
1989	Wofford	373.7
1990	North Dak. St.	364.2
1991	Wofford	347.9
1992	Pittsburg St.	353.8
1993	North Ala.	371.5

*Record.

PASSING OFFENSE

Year	Team	Avg.
1948	Hanover	223.8
1949	Baldwin-Wallace	196.9
1950	Northern Ill.	187.0
1951	Central Mich.	213.8
1952	Sam Houston St.	263.0
1953	Southern Conn. St.	193.5
1954	Northern Iowa	206.1
1955	Hamline	210.7
1956	Widener	207.7
1957	Cal Poly Pomona	236.0
1958	Cal Poly Pomona	217.6
1959	Whittier	199.3
1960	Whitworth	213.6
1961	Cal Poly Pomona	244.1
1962	Northern Ill.	285.6
1963	Northern Ill.	349.3
1964	Parsons	301.3
1965	Southern Ore.	268.9
1966	San Diego St.	268.1
1967	San Fran. St.	387.0

Year	Team	Avg.
1968	Louisiana Tech	316.4
1969	Portland St.	308.6
1970	Portland St.	313.8
1971	LIU-C.W. Post	262.5
1972	Maryville (Tenn.)	277.8
1973	Lehigh	275.0
1974	Boise St.	334.5
1975	Portland St.	361.7
1976	Portland St.	404.1
1977	Portland St.	378.5
1978	Northern Mich.	242.3
1979	Northern Mich.	284.2
1980	Northern Mich.	269.6
1981	Franklin	306.5
1982	Evansville	313.0
1983	Franklin	358.0
1984	Franklin	334.0
1985	Northeast Mo. St.	345.1
1986	West Tex. A&M	345.5
1987	Evansville	306.6
1988	Central Fla.	292.2
1989	Cal St. Chico	328.8
1990	New Haven	335.4
1991	Western St.	357.4
1992	Gardner-Webb	367.8
1993	LIU-C.W. Post	*409.0

*Record.

SCORING OFFENSE

Year	Team	Avg.
1948	Sul Ross St.	43.1
1949	Pacific (Cal.)	50.0
1950	West Tex. A&M	37.2
1951	Western Ill.	42.1
1952	East Tex. St.	49.6
1953	Col. of Idaho	42.4
1954	Col. of Emporia	43.2
1955	Central Mich.	36.3
1956	Florida A&M	45.9
1957	Denison	38.6
1958	Wheaton (Ill.)	44.6
1959	Florida A&M	42.6
1960	Florida A&M	52.8
1961	Florida A&M	54.7
1962	Florida A&M	42.0
1963	Col. of Emporia	42.4
1964	San Diego St.	42.3
1965	Ottawa	43.2
1966	N. M. Highlands	48.1
1967	Waynesburg	53.7
1968	Doane	52.9
1969	St. Olaf	45.2
1970	Wittenberg	40.0
1971	Michigan Tech	42.4
1972	Fort Valley St.	45.0
1973	Western Ky.	37.7
1974	Boise St.	44.6
1975	Bethune-Cookman	37.9
1976	Northern Mich.	43.0
1977	South Caro. St.	38.4
1978	Western St.	45.2
1979	Delaware	35.5
1980	Minn.-Duluth	35.4
1981	Southwest Tex. St.	37.5
1982	Northeast Mo. St.	40.0
1983	Central St. (Ohio)	43.6
1984	North Dak. St.	39.0
1985	UC Davis	37.6
1986	Tex. A&M-Kingsville	43.1
1987	Central Fla.	34.5
	West Chester	34.5
1988	North Dak. St.	39.6
	Tex. A&M-Kingsville	39.6
1989	Grand Valley St.	44.5
1990	Indiana (Pa.)	44.2
1991	Western St.	46.1
1992	New Haven	50.5
1993	New Haven	*54.7

*Record.

Annual Defense Champions

TOTAL DEFENSE

Year	Team	Avg.
1948	Morgan St.	104.4
1949	Southern Conn. St.	95.6
1950	Southern Conn. St.	93.6
1951	Southern Conn. St.	84.3
1952	West Chester	128.4
1953	Shippensburg	81.9
1954	Geneva	106.3
1955	Col. of Emporia	102.0
1956	Tennessee St.	118.9
1957	West Chester	90.2
1958	Rose-Hulman	95.8
1959	Maryland St.	75.3
1960	Maryland St.	104.8
1961	Florida A&M	85.3
1962	John Carroll	*44.4
1963	West Chester	100.8
1964	Morgan St.	126.4
1965	Morgan St.	91.5
1966	Tennessee St.	85.7
1967	Tennessee St.	61.6
1968	Alcorn St.	103.4
1969	Livingstone	148.5
1970	Delaware St.	103.5
1971	Hampden-Sydney	115.6
1972	Wis.-Whitewater	143.8
1973	Livingstone	114.9
1974	Livingstone	120.5
1975	South Caro. St.	100.6
1976	Alcorn St.	108.9
1977	Virginia Union	160.3
1978	East Stroudsburg	153.8
1979	Virginia Union	138.2
1980	Concordia-M'head	191.7
1981	Fort Valley St.	148.3
1982	Jamestown	187.9
1983	Virginia Union	143.7
1984	Virginia St.	180.6
1985	Fort Valley St.	162.2
1986	Virginia Union	163.5
1987	Alabama A&M	167.1
1988	Alabama A&M	175.8
1989	Winston-Salem	185.7
1990	Sonoma St.	218.5
1991	Ashland	195.5
1992	Ashland	211.5
1993	Bentley	188.3

*Record.

RUSHING DEFENSE

Year	Team	Avg.
1948	Morgan St.	44.8
1949	Hanover	43.5
1950	Lewis & Clark	50.3
1951	Southern Conn. St.	17.1
1952	East Tex. St.	48.5
1953	Shippensburg	53.6
1954	Tennessee St.	29.2
1955	Muskingum	52.5
1956	Hillsdale	51.1
1957	West Chester	27.9
1958	Ithaca	48.4
1959	Maryland St.	36.3
1960	West Chester	41.4
1961	Florida A&M	20.1
1962	John Carroll	-1.0
1963	St. John's (Minn.)	12.9
1964	Fort Valley St.	39.7
1965	Morgan St.	15.0
1966	Tennessee St.	13.9
1967	Tennessee St.	*-16.7
1968	Alcorn St.	8.8
1969	Merchant Marine	16.2
1970	Delaware St.	-4.9
1971	Northern Colo.	27.5
1972	Alcorn St.	49.8
1973	Alcorn St.	45.9
1974	Livingstone	53.0
1975	Alcorn St.	15.9
1976	Alcorn St.	32.5
1977	Virginia Union	63.6
1978	East Stroudsburg	52.2
1979	Virginia Union	41.0
1980	Missouri-Rolla	34.6
1981	Fort Valley St.	46.9
1982	Butler	71.1
1983	Butler	38.2
1984	Norfolk St.	53.8
1985	Norfolk St.	50.9
1986	Central St. (Ohio)	44.5
1987	West Chester	67.2
1988	Cal Poly SLO	56.4
1989	Tex. A&M-Kingsville	60.7
1990	Sonoma St.	58.3
1991	Sonoma St.	63.6
1992	Ashland	64.4
1993	Albany St. (Ga.)	59.1

*Record.

PASSING DEFENSE

Year	Team	Avg.
1948	Ashland	*10.1
1949	Wilmington (Ohio)	39.8
1950	Vermont	34.4
1951	Alfred	52.0
1952	Cortland St.	45.9
1953	Shippensburg	28.3
1954	St. Augustine's	26.5
1955	Ithaca	15.5
1956	West Va. Tech	29.1
1957	Lake Forest	25.0
1958	Coast Guard	25.4
1959	Huron	21.9
1960	Susquehanna	27.3
1961	Westminster (Utah)	24.8
1962	Principia	27.8
1963	Western Caro.	39.3
1964	Eastern Mont.	44.1
1965	Minot St.	44.5
1966	Manchester	54.7
1967	Mount Union	61.4
1968	Bridgeport	47.6
1969	Wabash	72.0
1970	Hampden-Sydney	62.9
1971	Western Ky.	57.7
1972	Howard	48.8
1973	East Stroudsburg	37.6
1974	Tennessee St.	52.6
1975	N.C. Central	60.2
1976	Morris Brown	60.8
1977	Delaware St.	64.3
1978	Concordia-M'head	55.8
1979	Kentucky St.	62.3
1980	Norfolk St.	71.5
1981	Bowie St.	75.7
1982	Elizabeth City St.	49.0
1983	Elizabeth City St.	65.0

Texas A&M-Kingsville built its prolific offense around running backs Johnny Bailey (left) and Heath Sherman during the 1986 and 1987 seasons.

Year	Team	Avg.
1984	Virginia St.	80.4
1985	Fort Valley St.	94.5
1986	Virginia Union	84.7
1987	Alabama A&M	72.5
1988	Alabama A&M	84.3
1989	Mo. Southern St.	93.0
1990	Angelo St.	65.4
1991	Carson-Newman	64.9
1992	East Tex. St.	61.8
1993	Alabama A&M	71.5

*Record.

SCORING DEFENSE

Year	Team	Avg.
1959	Huron	2.1
1960	Albany St. (Ga.)	*0.0
1961	Florida A&M	2.8
1962	John Carroll	2.9
1963	Massachusetts	1.3
1964	Central (Iowa)	4.8
1965	St. John's (Minn.)	2.2
1966	Morgan St.	3.6
1967	Waynesburg	4.3
1968	Central Conn. St.	4.4
1969	Carthage	6.0
1970	Hampden-Sydney	2.8
1971	Hampden-Sydney	3.4
1972	Ashland	5.6
1973	Virginia Union	3.8
1974	Minn.-Duluth	5.5
1975	South Caro. St.	2.9
1976	South Caro. St.	3.4
1977	Minn.-Duluth	7.8
1978	Southwestern La.	7.1
1979	Virginia Union	6.1
1980	Minn.-Duluth	7.6
1981	Moorhead St.	5.0
1982	Jamestown	5.9
1983	Towson St.	5.8
1984	Cal Poly SLO	9.0
1985	Fort Valley St.	6.3
1986	North Dak. St.	6.8
1987	Tuskegee	9.1
1988	Alabama A&M	7.5
1989	Jacksonville St.	7.0
1990	Cal Poly SLO	11.3
1991	Butler	7.1
1992	Ferris St.	10.5
1993	Albany St. (Ga.)	8.7

*Record.

Other Annual Team Champions

NET PUNTING

Year	Team	Avg.
1992	Fort Lewis	37.9
1993	North Ala.	39.5

PUNT RETURNS

Year	Team	Avg.
1992	Savannah St.	21.2
1993	Wayne St. (Neb.)	19.1

KICKOFF RETURNS

Year	Team	Avg.
1992	Jacksonville St.	34.0
1993	Adams St.	27.5

TURNOVER MARGIN

Year	Team	Avg.
1992	Hillsdale	2.2
1993	Hillsdale	2.7

All-Time Team Won-Lost Records

Includes records as a senior college only, minimum 20 seasons of competition since 1937. Postseason games are included, and each tie game is computed as half won and half lost.

PERCENTAGE (TOP 25)

Team	Yrs.	Won	Lost	Tied	Pct.
West Chester	65	419	171	16	.705
Tex. A&M-Kingsville	65	439	199	16	.683
Indiana (Pa.)	64	360	196	23	.642
Central Okla.	88	483	269	46	.634
Neb.-Kearney	70	390	220	26	.634
Grand Valley St.	23	145	85	3	.629
Pittsburg St.	86	482	279	46	.626
Northern St.	88	434	256	33	.623
Minn.-Duluth	61	315	186	23	.623
Northeast Mo. St.	86	441	270	35	.615
Carson-Newman	70	395	243	30	.614
Virginia Union	93	428	261	45	.614
Hillsdale	101	491	301	46	.613
East Stroudsburg	66	340	212	19	.612
Tuskegee	98	480	296	50	.611
Angelo St.	30	193	122	6	.611
North Dak. St.	97	481	301	34	.610
Fort Valley St.	48	265	169	21	.605
Virginia St.	82	408	260	48	.603
Jacksonville St.	61	328	218	27	.596
North Dak.	97	457	311	29	.592
LIU-C.W. Post	37	207	143	5	.590
Central Ark.	82	402	286	42	.579
North Ala.	45	259	186	16	.579
East Tex. St.	76	398	293	31	.573

ALPHABETICAL LISTING
(No Minimum Seasons of Competition)

Team	Yrs.	Won	Lost	Tied	Pct.
Abilene Christian	72	362	294	32	.549
Adams St.	59	259	227	16	.532
Alabama A&M	56	253	229	26	.524
Albany St. (Ga.)	48	221	204	21	.519
American Int'l	57	229	239	20	.490
Angelo St.	30	193	122	6	.611
Ashland	71	329	266	29	.550
Assumption	6	19	33	1	.368
Augustana (S.D.)	73	284	333	13	.461
Bemidji St.	68	218	318	23	.411
Bentley	6	38	13	1	.740
Bloomsburg	66	252	278	20	.476
Bowie St.	22	72	133	6	.355
Cal St. Chico	70	285	322	22	.471
Calif. (Pa.)	64	239	272	19	.469
Carson-Newman	70	395	243	30	.614
Catawba	74	351	338	26	.509
Central Ark.	82	402	286	42	.579
Central Mo. St.	97	374	419	51	.473
Central Okla.	88	483	269	46	.634
Chadron St.	79	338	290	15	.537
Cheyney	40	82	266	4	.239
Clarion	65	299	229	17	.564
Clark Atlanta	55	174	260	23	.406
Colorado Mines	104	310	433	31	.421
Concord	69	309	279	27	.524
Delta St.	64	292	293	21	.499
East Stroudsburg	66	340	212	19	.612
East Tex. St.	76	398	293	31	.573
Eastern N. Mex.	50	247	237	13	.510
Edinboro	65	235	276	24	.462
Elizabeth City St.	52	224	224	18	.500
Elon	72	386	291	18	.568
Emporia St.	96	374	409	44	.479
Fairmont St.	80	342	280	44	.547
Fayetteville St.	48	162	257	23	.393
Ferris St.	65	226	286	34	.445
Fort Hays St.	72	321	336	46	.489
Fort Lewis	30	102	172	3	.374
Fort Valley St.	48	265	169	21	.605
Gannon	6	35	19	1	.645
Gardner-Webb	24	116	136	2	.461
Glenville St.	81	240	315	37	.437
Grand Valley St.	23	145	85	3	.629
Hampton	92	397	317	34	.553
Hardin-Simmons	57	268	205	35	.562
Henderson St.	86	371	315	43	.538
Hillsdale	101	491	301	46	.613
Humboldt St.	66	294	258	19	.532
Indiana (Pa.)	64	360	196	23	.642
Indianapolis	56	234	253	22	.481
Jacksonville St.	61	328	218	27	.596
Johnson Smith	66	266	290	34	.480
Kentucky St.	65	274	324	25	.460
Kutztown	63	206	295	21	.415
Ky. Wesleyan	33	95	135	16	.419
Lane	70	178	326	26	.360
Lenoir-Rhyne	74	381	301	34	.556
LIU-C.W. Post	37	207	143	5	.590
Livingston	52	204	256	15	.445

Team	Yrs.	Won	Lost	Tied	Pct.
Livingstone	45	171	230	14	.429
Lock Haven	65	244	315	25	.439
Mankato St.	68	294	267	27	.523
Mansfield	64	202	303	30	.406
Mars Hill	30	131	159	10	.453
Mass.-Lowell	14	70	59	2	.542
Mercyhurst	13	65	49	3	.568
Mesa St.	18	114	71	5	.613
Michigan Tech	71	249	238	17	.511
Miles	24	43	165	6	.215
Millersville	62	270	234	20	.534
Minn.-Duluth	61	315	186	23	.623
Minn.-Morris	32	163	137	10	.542
Mississippi Col.	81	387	293	35	.566
Missouri-Rolla	88	333	388	35	.464
Mo. Southern St.	26	142	115	7	.551
Mo. Western St.	24	106	136	8	.440
Moorhead St.	76	327	277	29	.539
Morehouse	94	325	335	49	.493
Morningside	92	328	410	35	.447
Morris Brown	68	306	276	37	.524
N.C. Central	63	317	241	24	.565
Neb.-Kearney	70	390	220	26	.634
Nebraska-Omaha	77	317	319	30	.498
New Haven	21	110	93	4	.541
Newberry	80	293	430	33	.409
N.M. Highlands	67	231	293	26	.444
Norfolk St.	33	161	149	7	.519
North Ala.	45	259	186	16	.579
North Dak.	97	457	311	29	.592
North Dak. St.	97	481	301	34	.610
Northeast Mo. St.	86	441	270	35	.615
Northern Colo.	81	308	323	24	.489
Northern Mich.	80	327	247	26	.567
Northern St.	88	434	256	33	.623
Northwest Mo. St.	76	307	344	32	.473
Northwood	32	126	155	7	.450
Pace	16	56	93	2	.377
Pittsburg St.	86	482	279	46	.626
Portland St.	39	201	196	7	.506
Presbyterian	81	381	362	35	.512
Quincy	8	40	33	1	.547
Sacred Heart	3	7	20	0	.259
Saginaw Valley	19	96	99	3	.492
San Fran. St.	61	239	297	21	.448
Savannah St.	41	155	207	15	.431
Shepherd	70	293	262	26	.527
Shippensburg	64	304	251	21	.546
Slippery Rock	66	316	238	28	.567
Sonoma St.	15	59	91	1	.394
South Dak.	98	413	387	34	.516
South Dak. St.	96	423	352	38	.544
Southern Conn. St.	46	238	177	11	.572
Southwest Baptist	11	39	67	1	.369
Southwest St.	26	101	150	5	.404
Springfield	100	410	370	55	.524
St. Cloud St.	66	304	247	21	.550
St. Francis (Ill.)	8	48	33	0	.593
St. Joseph's (Ind.)	74	229	289	24	.445
Stonehill	6	30	19	3	.606
Tarleton St.	33	139	187	2	.427
Tex. A&M-Kingsville	65	439	199	16	.683
Tuskegee	98	480	296	50	.611
UC Davis	75	357	290	32	.549
Valdosta St.	12	70	51	3	.577
Virginia St.	82	408	260	48	.603
Virginia Union	93	428	261	45	.614
Washburn	102	416	448	40	.482
Wayne St. (Mich.)	76	267	332	29	.448
Wayne St. (Neb.)	68	289	327	38	.471
West Chester	65	419	171	16	.705
West Ga.	15	63	90	0	.412
West Liberty St.	67	323	260	35	.551
West Tex. A&M	82	357	385	22	.482
West Va. Tech	74	262	308	35	.462
West Va. Wesleyan	88	319	382	30	.457
Western N. Mex.	57	213	265	15	.447
Western St.	71	289	301	13	.490
Wingate	8	34	45	0	.430
Winona St.	93	254	404	31	.391
Winston-Salem	50	259	203	20	.558
Wofford	85	361	388	36	.483

VICTORIES

Team	Wins
Hillsdale	491
Central Okla.	483
Pittsburg St.	482
North Dak. St.	481
Tuskegee	480
North Dak.	457
Northeast Mo. St.	441
Tex. A&M-Kingsville	439
Northern St.	434
Virginia Union	428
South Dak. St.	423
West Chester	419
Washburn	416

Team	Wins
South Dak.	413
Springfield	410
Virginia St.	408
Central Ark.	402
East Tex. St.	398
Hampton	397
Carson-Newman	395
Neb.-Kearney	390
Mississippi Col.	387
Elon	386
Lenoir-Rhyne	381
Presbyterian	381

National Poll Rankings

Wire Service National Champions

(1958-74)

(For what was then known as College Division teams. Selections by United Press International from 1958 and Associated Press from 1960.)

Year	Team	Coach	Record*
1958	Southern Miss.	Thad "Pie" Vann	9-0-0
1959	Bowling Green	Doyt Perry	9-0-0
1960	Ohio	Bill Hess	10-0-0
1961	Pittsburg St.	Carnie Smith	9-0-0
1962	Southern Miss. (UPI)	Thad "Pie" Vann	9-1-0
	Florida A&M (AP)	Jake Gaither	9-0-0
1963	Delaware (UPI)	Dave Nelson	8-0-0
	Northern Ill. (AP)	Howard Fletcher	9-0-0
1964	Cal St. Los Angeles (UPI)	Homer Beatty	9-0-0
	Wittenberg (AP)	Bill Edwards	8-0-0
1965	North Dak. St.	Darrell Mudra	10-0-0
1966	San Diego St.	Don Coryell	10-0-0
1967	San Diego St.	Don Coryell	9-1-0
1968	San Diego St. (UPI)	Don Coryell	9-0-1
	North Dak. St. (AP)	Ron Erhardt	9-0-0
1969	North Dak. St.	Ron Erhardt	9-0-0
1970	Arkansas St.	Bennie Ellender	10-0-0
1971	Delaware	Harold "Tubby" Raymond	9-1-0
1972	Delaware	Harold "Tubby" Raymond	10-0-0
1973	Tennessee St.	John Merritt	10-0-0
1974	Louisiana Tech (UPI)	Maxie Lambright	10-0-0
	Central Mich. (AP)	Roy Kramer	9-1-0

*Regular season.

Final Poll Leaders

(Released Before Division Championship Playoffs)

Year	Team (Record*)	Coach	Record in Championship†
1975	North Dak. (9-0-0)	Jerry Olson	0-1 Lost in first round
1976	Northern Mich. (10-0-0)	Gil Krueger	1-1 Lost in semifinals
1977	North Dak. St. (8-1-1)	Jim Wacker	1-1 Lost in semifinals
1978	Winston-Salem (10-0-0)	Bill Hayes	Did not compete
1979	Delaware (9-1-0)	Harold "Tubby" Raymond	3-0 Champion
1980	Eastern Ill. (8-2-0)	Darrell Mudra	2-1 Runner-up
1981	Southwest Tex. St. (9-0-0)	Jim Wacker	3-0 Champion
1982	Southwest Tex. St. (11-0-0)	Jim Wacker	3-0 Champion
1983	UC Davis (9-0-0)	Jim Sochor	1-1 Lost in semifinals
1984	North Dak. St. (9-1-0)	Don Morton	2-1 Runner-up
1985	UC Davis (9-1-0)	Jim Sochor	0-1 Lost in first round
1986	North Dak. St. (10-0-0)	Earle Solomonson	3-0 Champion
1987	Tex. A&M-Kingsville (9-1-0)	Ron Harms	Did not compete
1988	North Dak. St. (10-0-0)	Rocky Hager	4-0 Champion
1989	Tex. A&M-Kingsville (10-0-0)	Ron Harms	0-1 Lost in first round
1990	North Dak. St. (10-0-0)	Rocky Hager	4-0 Champion
1991	Indiana (Pa.) (10-0-0)	Frank Cignetti	2-1 Lost in semifinals
1992	Pittsburg St. (11-0-0)	Chuck Broyles	3-1 Runner-up
1993	North Ala. (10-0-0)	Bobby Wallace	4-0 Champion

*Final poll record; in some cases, a team had one game remaining before the championship playoffs. †Number of teams in the championship: 8 (1975-87); 16 (1988-present).

Undefeated, Untied Teams

(Regular-Season Games Only)

In 1948, official national statistics rankings began to include all nonmajor four-year colleges. Until the 1967 season, rankings and records included all four-year colleges that reported their statistics to the NCAA. Beginning with the 1967 season, statistics (and won-lost records) included only members of the NCAA.

Since 1981, conference playoff games have been included in a team's regular-season statistics and won-lost record (previously, such games were considered postseason contests).

The regular-season list includes games in which a home team served as a predetermined, preseason host of a "bowl game" regardless of its record and games scheduled before the season, thus eliminating postseason designation for the Orange Blossom Classic, annually hosted by Florida A&M, and the Prairie View Bowl, annually hosted by Prairie View, for example.

Figures are regular-season wins only. A subsequent postseason win(s) is indicated by (*), a loss by (†) and a tie by (‡).

Year	College	Wins
1948	Alma	8
	Bloomsburg	9
	Denison	8
	Heidelberg	9
	Michigan Tech	7
	Missouri Valley	†‡9
	Occidental	*8
	Southern-B.R.	*11
	Sul Ross St.	‡10
	Wesleyan	8
1949	Ball St.	8
	Emory & Henry	*†10
	Gannon	8
	Hanover	†8
	Lewis	8
	Md.-East. Shore	8
	Morgan St.	8
	Pacific (Cal.)	11
	St. Ambrose	8
	St. Vincent	*9
	Trinity (Conn.)	8
	Wayne St. (Neb.)	9
	Wofford	11
1950	Abilene Christian	*10
	Canterbury	8
	Florida St.	8
	Frank. & Marsh.	9
	Lehigh	9
	Lewis & Clark	*8
	Md.-East. Shore	8
	Mission House	6
	New Hampshire	8
	St. Lawrence	8
	St. Norbert	7
	Thiel	7
	Valparaiso	†9
	West Liberty St.	*8
	Wis.-La Crosse	*9
	Wis.-Whitewater	6
1951	Bloomsburg	8
	Bucknell	9
	Col. of Emporia	8
	Ill. Wesleyan	8
	Lawrence	7
	Northern Ill.	9
	Principia	6
	South Dak. Tech	8
	St. Michael's	6
	Susquehanna	6
	Trenton St.	6
	Valparaiso	9
	Western Md.	8
1952	Beloit	8
	Clarion	*8
	East Tex. St.	*10
	Fairmont St.	6
	Idaho St.	8
	Lenoir-Rhyne	†8
	Northeastern Okla.	†9
	Peru St.	10
	Rochester	8

Year	College	Wins
	Shippensburg	7
	St. Norbert	6
	West Chester	7
1953	Cal Poly SLO	9
	Col. of Emporia	8
	Col. of Idaho	†8
	Defiance	8
	East Tex. St.	‡10
	Florida A&M	10
	Indianapolis	8
	Iowa Wesleyan	†9
	Juniata	7
	Northern St.	8
	N'western (Wis.)	6
	Peru St.	8
	Prairie View	10
	Shippensburg	8
	St. Olaf	8
	Westminster (Pa.)	8
	Wis.-La Crosse	‡9
	Wis.-Platteville	6
1954	Ashland	7
	Carleton	8
	Central Conn. St.	6
	Col. of Emporia	†9
	Delta St.	8
	Hastings	*8
	Hobart	8
	Juniata	8
	Luther	9
	Miles	8
	Nebraska-Omaha	*9
	N'western (Wis.)	6
	Pomona-Pitzer	8
	Principia	7
	Southeastern La.	9
	Tennessee St.	†10
	Trinity (Conn.)	7
	Trinity (Tex.)	9
	Whitworth	8
	Widener	7
	Worcester Tech	6
1955	Alfred	8
	Centre	8
	Coe	8
	Col. of Emporia	9
	Drexel	8
	Grambling	10
	Heidelberg	9
	Hillsdale	9
	Juniata	‡8
	Md.-East. Shore	9
	Miami (Ohio)	9
	Muskingum	8
	Northern St.	†9
	Parsons	8
	Shepherd	8
	Southeast Mo. St.	9
	Trinity (Conn.)	7
	Whitworth	9
	Wis.-Stevens Point	8
1956	Alfred	7
	Central Mich.	9
	Hillsdale	9
	Lenoir-Rhyne	10
	Milton	6
	Montana St.	‡9
	Neb.-Kearney	9
	Redlands	9
	Sam Houston St.	*9
	Southern Conn. St.	9
	St. Thomas (Minn.)	8
	Tennessee St.	10
	Westminster (Pa.)	8
1957	Elon	6
	Fairmont St.	7
	Florida A&M	9
	Hillsdale	†9
	Hobart	6
	Idaho St.	9
	Jamestown	7
	Juniata	7
	Lock Haven	8
	Middle Tenn. St.	10
	Pittsburg St.	*10
	Ripon	8
	St. Norbert	8
	West Chester	9
1958	Calif. (Pa.)	8
	Chadron St.	8
	Gust. Adolphus	†8

Year	College	Wins
	Missouri Valley	†8
	N'eastern Okla.	**9
	Neb.-Kearney	9
	Northern Ariz.	*†10
	Rochester	8
	Rose-Hulman	8
	Sewanee	8
	Southern Miss.	9
	St. Benedict's	†10
	Wheaton (Ill.)	8
1959	Bowling Green	9
	Butler	9
	Coe	8
	Fairmont St.	9
	Florida A&M	10
	Hofstra	9
	John Carroll	7
	Lenoir-Rhyne	*†9
	San Fran. St.	10
	Western Ill.	9
1960	Albright	9
	Arkansas Tech	†10
	Humboldt St.	*†10
	Langston	9
	Lenoir-Rhyne	*‡10
	Montclair St.	8
	Muskingum	9
	Northern Iowa	†9
	Ohio	10
	Ottawa	9
	Wagner	9
	West Chester	9
	Whitworth	9
	Willamette	8
1961	Albion	8
	Baldwin-Wallace	9
	Butler	9
	Central Okla.	9
	Florida A&M	10
	Fresno St.	*9
	Linfield	*†10
	Mayville St.	8
	Millikin	9
	Northern St.	9
	Ottawa	9
	Pittsburg St.	**9
	Wash. & Lee	9
	Wheaton (Ill.)	8
	Whittier	†9
1962	Carthage	8
	Central Okla.	**9
	Col. of Emporia	†10
	Earlham	8
	East Stroudsburg	†8
	John Carroll	7
	Kalamazoo	8
	Lenoir-Rhyne	*†10
	Northern St.	†9
	Parsons	9
	St. John's (Minn.)	9
	Susquehanna	9
	Wittenberg	9
1963	Alabama A&M	8
	Central Wash.	9
	Coast Guard	†8
	Col. of Emporia	10
	Delaware	8
	John Carroll	7
	Lewis & Clark	8
	Luther	9
	McNeese St.	8
	N'eastern Okla.	*10
	Neb.-Kearney	†9
	Northeastern	†8
	Northern Ill.	*9
	Prairie View	*†9
	Ripon	8
	Sewanee	8
	Southwest Mo. St.	†9
	Southwest Tex. St.	10
	St. John's (Minn.)	**8
	Wis.-Eau Claire	7
1964	Albion	8
	Amherst	8
	Cal St. Los Angeles	9
	Concordia-M'head	*†9
	Frank. & Marsh.	8
	Montclair St.	7
	Prairie View	9
	Wagner	10
	Western St.	†9

Year	College	Wins	Year	College	Wins	Year	College	Wins
	Westminster (Pa.)	8		East Stroudsburg	‡8		Winston-Salem	†11
	Wittenberg	8		Indiana (Pa.)	†9	1978	Western St	*†9
1965	Ball St.	‡9		North Dak. St.	*9		Winston-Salem	*†10
	East Stroudsburg	*9		Randolph-Macon	9	1979	(None)	
	Fairmont St.	†8	1969	Albion	8	1980	Minn.-Duluth	10
	Georgetown (Ky.)	9		Carthage	9		Missouri-Rolla	10
	Ill. Wesleyan	8		Defiance	9	1981	Northern Mich.	*†10
	Ithaca	8		Doane	8		Shippensburg	*†11
	Middle Tenn. St.	10		Montana	†10		Virginia Union	†11
	Morgan St.	9		North Dak. St.	*9	1982	North Dak. St.	*†11
	North Dak. St.	*10		Northern Colo.	10		Southwest Tex. St.	***11
	Northern Ill.	†9		Wesleyan (Conn.)	8		UC Davis	**†10
	Ottawa	9		Wittenberg	*9	1983	Central St. (Ohio)	***†10
	Springfield	9	1970	Arkansas St.	*10		UC Davis	*†10
	St. John's (Minn.)	**9		Jacksonville St.	10	1984	(None)	
	Sul Ross St.	†10		Montana	†10	1985	Bloomsburg	*†11
	Tennessee St.	‡9		St. Olaf	9	1986	North Dak. St.	***†10
1966	Central (Iowa)	*9		Tennessee St.	*10		UC Davis	†10
	Clarion	*9		Westminster (Pa.)	**8		Virginia Union	†11
	Defiance	9		Wittenberg#	9	1987	(None)	
	Morgan St.	*8	1971	Alfred	8	1988	North Dak. St.	****10
	Muskingum	†9		Hampden-Sydney	†10		St. Mary's (Cal.)	10
	Northwestern St.	9		Westminster (Pa.)	†‡8	1989	Grand Valley St.	†11
	San Diego St.	*10	1972	Ashland	11		Jacksonville St.	***†10
	Tennessee St.	*9		Bridgeport	*10		Pittsburg St.	*†11
	Waynesburg	**9		Delaware	10		Tex. A&M-Kingsville	†10
	Wilkes	8		Doane	†10	1990	North Dak. St.	****†10
	Wis.-Whitewater	*†9		Frank. & Marsh.	9		Pittsburg St.	**†10
				Heidelberg	**9	1991	Carson-Newman	†10
Beginning in 1967, NCAA members only.				Louisiana Tech	*11		Indiana (Pa.)	**†10
1967	Alma	8		Middlebury	8		Jacksonville St.	***†9
	Central (Iowa)	9		Monmouth (Ill.)	9	1992	New Haven	**†10
	Doane	‡8	1973	Tennessee St.	10		Pittsburg St.	***†11
	Lawrence	8		Western Ky.	**†10	1993	Albany St. (Ga.)	†11
	Morgan St.	8	1974	Louisiana Tech	*†10		Bentley	10
	North Dak. St.	†9		Michigan Tech	9		Hampton	*†11
	Northern Mich.	†9		Nevada-Las Vegas	*†11		Indiana (Pa.)	***†10
	Wagner	9	1975	East Stroudsburg	*9		New Haven	*†10
	West Chester	*†9		North Dak.	†9		North Ala.	****10
	Wilkes	8	1976	East Stroudsburg	‡9		Quincy	9
1968	Alma	8	1977	Florida A&M	11			
	Doane	*9		UC Davis	*†10	#Later forfeited all games.		

The Spoilers

Compiled since 1973, when the three-division reorganization plan was adopted by the special NCAA Convention. Following is a list of the spoilers of Division II teams that lost their perfect (undefeated, untied) record in their **season-ending** game, including the Division II championship playoffs. An asterisk (*) indicates an NCAA championship play-off game, a pound sign (#) indicates an NAIA championship playoff game, a dagger (†) indicates the home team in a regular-season game, and (@) indicates a neutral-site game. A game involving two undefeated, untied teams is in bold face.

Date	Spoiler	Victim	Score
12-15-73	*Louisiana Tech	Western Ky.	34-0
11-30-74	*Louisiana Tech	Western Caro.	10-7
11-15-75	†LIU-C.W. Post	American Int'l	21-0
11-15-75	Eastern N. Mex.	†Northern Colo.	16-14
11-29-75	*Livingston	North Dak.	34-14
11-20-76	†Shippensburg	East Stroudsburg	tie 14-14
12-3-77	‡South Caro. St.	Winston-Salem	10-7
12-3-77	*Lehigh	UC Davis	39-30
12-2-78	*Delaware	Winston-Salem	41-0
11-28-81	*Shippensburg	Virginia Union	40-27
12-5-81	*North Dak. St.	Shippensburg	18-6
12-5-81	*Southwest Tex. St.	Northern Mich.	62-0
12-4-82	*UC Davis	North Dak. St.	19-14
12-11-82	**Southwest Tex. St.**	**UC Davis**	34-9
12-3-83	*North Dak. St.	UC Davis	26-17
12-10-83	*North Dak. St.	Central St. (Ohio)	41-21
12-7-85	*North Ala.	Bloomsburg	34-0
11-15-86	West Chester	†Millersville	7-3
11-29-86	*Troy St.	Virginia Union	31-7
11-29-86	*South Dak.	UC Davis	26-23
12-10-88	#Adams St.	Pittsburg St.	13-10
11-18-89	*Mississippi Col.	Tex. A&M-Kingsville	34-19
11-18-89	*Indiana (Pa.)	Grand Valley St.	34-24
11-25-89	*Angelo St.	Pittsburg St.	24-21
12-9-89	*Mississippi Col.	Jacksonville St.	3-0

Date	Spoiler	Victim	Score
12-1-90	**North Dak. St.**	**Pittsburg St.**	39-29
11-23-91	#Western St.	Carson-Newman	38-21
12-7-91	**Jacksonville St.**	**Indiana (Pa.)**	27-20
12-14-91	*Pittsburg St.	Jacksonville St.	23-6
11-14-92	@ Moorhead St.	Michigan Tech	36-35
12-5-92	*Jacksonville St.	New Haven	46-35
12-12-92	*Jacksonville St.	Pittsburg St.	17-13
11-13-93	@ Minn.-Duluth	Wayne St. (Neb.)	29-28
11-20-93	**Hampton**	**Albany St. (Ga.)**	33-7
11-27-93	**Indiana (Pa.)**	**New Haven**	38-35
11-27-93	**North Ala.**	**Hampton**	45-20
12-11-93	**North Ala.**	**Indiana (Pa.)**	41-34

‡Gold Bowl.

Streaks and Rivalries

Longest Winning Streaks

(From 1931; Includes Postseason Games)

Wins	Team	Years
34	Hillsdale	1954-57
32	Wilkes	1965-69
31	Morgan St.	1965-68
31	Missouri Valley	1946-48
29	East Tex. St.	1951-53
25	Pittsburg St.	1991-92
25	San Diego St.	1965-67
25	Peru St.	1951-54
25	Maryland St.	1948-51
24	North Dak. St.	1964-66
24	Wesleyan (Conn.)	1945-48

Note: During 1973-77 (a period when it was not an NCAA-member institution), Tex. A&M-Kingsville won 42 consecutive games.

Longest Unbeaten Streaks

(From 1931; Includes Postseason Games)

No.	Wins	Ties	Team	Years
54	47	7	Morgan St.	1931-38
38	36	2	Doane	1965-70
37	35	2	Southern-B.R.	1947-51
35	34	1	North Dak. St.	1968-71
34	34	0	Hillsdale	1954-57
32	32	0	Wilkes	1965-69
31	31	0	Morgan St.	1965-68
31	31	0	Missouri Valley	1946-48
31	29	2	St. Ambrose	1935-38
30	29	1	Wittenberg	1961-65
30	29	1	East Tex. St.	1951-53
28	27	1	Wesleyan (Conn.)	†1942-48
28	27	1	Case Reserve	1934-37
27	26	1	Pittsburg St.	1991-92
27	26	1	Juniata	1956-59

†Did not field teams in 1943-44. Note: During 1973-77 (a period when it was not an NCAA-member institution), Tex. A&M-Kingsville was unbeaten during 46 consecutive games (including one tie).

Most-Played Rivalries

Games	Opponents (Series leader listed first)	Series Record	First Game
98	North Dak.-North Dak. St.	53-42-3	1894
94	South Dak.-South Dak. St.	48-39-7	1889
88	Colorado Mines-Colorado Col.	46-37-5	1889
84	South Dak.-Morningside	51-28-5	1898
83	Tuskegee-Morehouse	51-26-6	1902
82	Virginia Union-Hampton	41-38-3	1906
80	North Dak. St.-South Dak. St.	41-34-5	1903

Cliffhangers

Regular-season Division II games won on the final play of the game (from 1973). The extra point is listed when it provided the margin of victory after the winning touchdown.

Date	Opponents, Score	Game-Winning Play
9-22-73	South Dak. 9, North Dak. St. 7	Kelly Higgins 5 pass from Mark Jenkins
10-12-74	Westminster (Pa.) 23, Indiana (Pa.) 20	Rick Voltz 20 FG
11-23-74	Arkansas St. 22, McNeese St. 20	Joe Duren 56 FG
10-11-75	Indiana (Pa.) 16, Westminster (Pa.) 14	Tom Alper 37 FG
10-18-75	Cal St. Fullerton 32, UC Riverside 31	John Choukair 52 FG
9-25-76	Portland St. 50, Montana 49	Dave Stief 2 pass from June Jones
10-30-76	South Dak. St. 16, Northern Iowa 13	Monte Mosiman 53 pass from Dick Weikert
10-27-77	Albany (N.Y.) 42, Maine 39	Larry Leibowitz 19 FG
10-6-79	Indiana (Pa.) 31, Shippensburg 24	Jeff Heath 4 run
10-20-79	North Dak. 23, South Dak. 22	Tom Biolo 6 run
9-6-80	Ferris St. 20, St. Joseph's (Ind.) 15	Greg Washington 17 pass from (holder) John Gibson (after bad snap on 34 FG attempt)
11-15-80	Morris Brown 19, Bethune-Cookman 18	Ray Mills 1 run (Carlton Jackson kick)
11-15-80	Tuskegee 23, Alabama A&M 21	Korda Joseph 45 FG
9-26-81	Abilene Christian 41, Northwestern St. 38	David Russell 17 pass from Loyal Proffitt
9-26-81	Cal St. Chico 10, Santa Clara 7	Mike Sullivan 46 FG
10-10-81	LIU-C.W. Post 37, James Madison 36	Tom DeBona 10 pass from Tom Ehrhardt (Ehrhardt run)
10-9-82	Grand Valley St. 38, Ferris St. 35	Randy Spangler 20 FG
10-9-82	Westminster (Pa.) 3, Indiana (Pa.) 0	Ron Bauer 35 FG
11-6-82	South Dak. 30, Augustana (S.D.) 28	Kurt Seibel 47 FG
9-17-83	Central Mo. St. 13, Sam Houston St. 10	Steve Huff 27 FG
9-22-84	Clarion 16, Shippensburg 13	Eric Fairbanks 26 FG
9-29-84	Angelo St. 18, Eastern N. Mex. 17	Ned Cox 3 run
10-13-84	Northwest Mo. St. 35, Central Mo. St. 34	Pat Johnson 20 FG
10-13-84	UC Davis 16, Cal St. Chico 13	Ray Sullivan 48 FG
11-3-84	Bloomsburg 34, West Chester 31	Curtis Still 50 pass from Jay Dedea
11-20-84	Central Fla. 28, Illinois St. 24	Jeff Farmer 30 punt return
9-7-85	Central Fla. 39, Bethune-Cookman 37	Ed O'Brien 55 FG
10-12-85	South Dak. 40, Morningside 38	Scott Jones 2 run
9-13-86	Michigan Tech 34, St. Norbert 30	Jim Wallace 41 pass from Dave Walter
9-20-86	Delaware 33, West Chester 31	Fred Singleton 3 run
10-18-86	Indianapolis 25, Evansville 24	Ken Bruce 18 FG
10-24-87	Indianapolis 27, Evansville 24	Doug Sabotin 2 pass from Tom Crowell
11-7-87	Central Mo. St. 35, Northeast Mo. St. 33	Phil Brandt 25 FG
9-3-88	Alabama A&M 17, North Ala. 16	Edmond Allen 30 FG
9-17-89	Morehouse 22, Fort Valley St. 21	David Boone 18 pass from Jimmie Davis
11-11-89	East Stroudsburg 22, Central Conn. St. 19	Frank Magolon 4 pass from Tom Taylor
10-13-90	East Stroudsburg 23, Bloomsburg 21	Ken Kopetchny 3 pass from Bret Comp
11-10-90	Southern Conn. St. 12, Central Conn. St. 10	Paul Boulanger 48 FG
9-21-91	Livingston 22, Albany St. (Ga.) 21	Matt Carman 24 pass from Deon Timmons (Anthony Armstrong kick)
10-26-91	Central Mo. St. 38, Northeast Mo. St. 37	Chris Pyatt 45 FG
10-26-91	Eastern N. Mex. 17, East Tex. St. 14	Jodie Peterson 35 FG
10-9-93	Delta St. 20, Henderson St. 19	Greg Walker 3 run (Stephen Coker kick)
11-6-93	Henderson St. 46, Livingston 44	Craig Moses 44 FG

Craig Moses kicked a 44-yard field goal on the final play of the game to give Henderson State a 46-44 victory over Livingston last season.

DIVISION II

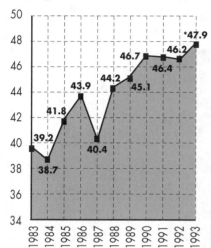

Division II Scoring, 1983-1993

(Avg. Per Game, Both Teams)

* Record

Division II Statistics Trends

For valid comparisons from 1973, when College Division teams were divided into Division II and Division III.

(Average Per Game, Both Teams)

Year	Rushing Plays	Yds.	Avg.	Passing Att.	Cmp.	Pct.	Yds.	Av.Att.	Total Offense Plays	Yds.	Avg.	Scoring TD	FG	Pts.
1973	95.1	339.1	3.57	40.0	17.6	.442	243.0	6.08	135.1	582.1	4.31	5.06	0.83	36.4
1974	95.1	312.6	3.29	38.9	17.3	.445	244.8	6.28	134.0	557.3	4.16	5.10	0.86	37.9
1975	94.6	337.1	3.56	38.9	17.4	.448	241.2	6.21	133.5	578.3	4.33	4.98	0.89	37.1
1976	94.7	331.4	3.50	39.8	18.2	.457	251.8	6.32	134.5	583.2	4.34	5.03	0.93	37.4
1977	*96.7	*347.6	3.59	40.6	18.4	.453	252.4	6.21	137.3	599.9	4.37	5.16	0.91	38.2
1978	95.9	338.5	3.52	41.1	18.4	.448	248.5	6.05	137.0	587.0	4.29	5.11	0.98	38.6
1979	91.6	309.4	3.38	41.9	18.9	.450	251.6	6.00	133.4	560.9	4.20	4.73	1.03	35.8
1980	90.5	307.5	3.40	44.7	20.7	.463	275.2	6.16	135.2	582.6	4.31	5.02	1.04	37.8
1981	89.1	293.2	3.29	47.9	21.9	.457	291.7	6.09	137.0	584.9	4.27	4.95	1.08	37.4
1982	86.5	288.2	3.32	52.2	24.5	.469	322.0	6.17	138.6	610.2	4.40	5.25	1.24	39.6
1983	86.3	290.7	3.37	52.1	25.0	.479	329.0	6.31	138.4	619.7	4.48	5.27	1.23	39.2
1984	83.8	284.3	3.39	52.0	25.0	.481	329.5	6.33	135.8	613.8	4.52	5.25	1.23	38.7
1985	83.3	288.0	3.46	54.8	26.4	.483	341.2	6.23	138.1	629.2	4.56	5.46	1.30	41.8
1986	83.6	297.7	3.56	53.7	26.0	.484	336.8	6.27	137.3	634.5	4.62	5.78	1.27	43.9
1987	85.6	303.7	3.55	49.2	23.8	.483	311.0	6.31	134.9	614.7	4.56	5.29	1.28	40.4
1988	87.7	318.8	3.64	49.2	23.8	.484	319.5	6.49	136.9	638.3	4.66	5.83	1.29	44.2
1989	87.3	332.0	3.80	50.1	24.3	.485	323.0	6.45	137.4	655.0	4.77	5.94	1.24	45.1
1990	87.3	336.6	3.86	52.8	25.6	.485	346.6	6.57	140.0	683.2	4.88	6.19	1.29	46.7
1991	87.4	335.5	3.84	52.7	25.5	.484	344.8	6.54	140.0	680.3	4.86	6.09	*1.31	46.4
1992	88.1	335.1	3.80	51.2	24.8	.484	342.8	*6.70	139.3	677.9	4.87	6.01	1.30	46.2
1993	85.4	334.5	*3.92	*54.8	*27.1	*.495	*360.3	6.11	*140.2	*694.8	*4.96	*6.55	1.06	*47.9

*Record.

Additional Division II Statistics Trends

(Average Per Game, Both Teams)

Year	Teams†	Games	Punting No.	Avg.	PAT Kick Attempts Pct. Made	Pct. of Total Tries	Two-Point Attempts Pct. Made	Pct. of Total Tries	Field Goals Pct. Made
1973	131	1,326	11.5	36.0	.833	.876	.419	.124	.439
1974	136	1,388	11.4	*36.8	.830	.859	.432	.141	.472
1975	126	1,282	11.0	36.3	.837	.874	.464	.126	.476
1976	122	1,244	11.6	36.2	.841	.878	.419	.122	.461
1977	124	1,267	11.7	36.1	.832	.874	.436	.126	.442
1978	91	921	11.9	35.9	.830	.880	.452	.120	.519
1979	99	1,016	12.1	35.2	.854	.861	.459	.139	.543
1980	103	1,040	11.7	35.6	.852	.864	.438	.136	.512
1981	113	1,138	*12.2	35.6	.856	.861	.440	.139	.531
1982	118	1,196	12.2	36.4	.862	.877	.431	.123	.560
1983	115	1,175	11.9	36.1	.866	.847	.428	.153	.564
1984	112	1,150	11.8	36.4	.876	.875	.448	.125	.567
1985	107	1,098	11.5	35.9	*.905	.864	.414	.136	.549
1986	109	1,124	11.1	36.5	.870	.865	.466	.135	*.576
1987	105	1,100	11.4	35.7	.857	.865	.435	.135	.547
1988	111	1,114	11.2	35.6	.886	.868	.399	.132	.555
1989	106	1,084	10.9	36.7	.873	.845	.376	*.155	.567
1990	105	1,065	11.3	35.7	.876	*.885	*.474	.115	.568
1991	114	1,150	10.9	36.1	.882	.880	.426	.120	.572
1992	115	1,145	11.0	35.9	.888	.870	.442	.130	.575
1993	136	1,354	10.6	35.2	.839	.853	.438	.147	.528

*Record. †Teams reporting statistics, not the total number of teams in the division.

Division III Records

Individual Records

Division III football records are based on the performances of Division III teams since the three-division reorganization plan was adopted by the special NCAA Convention in August 1973.

Total Offense

(Rushing Plus Passing)

MOST PLAYS
Quarter
33—Aaron Keen, Washington (Mo.) vs. Trinity (Tex.), Oct. 3, 1992 (4th)
Half
59—Mike Wallace, Ohio Wesleyan vs. Denison, Oct. 3, 1981 (2nd)
Game
91—Jordan Poznick, Principia vs. Blackburn, Oct. 10, 1992 (81 passes, 10 rushes; 538 yards)
Season
614—Tim Peterson, Wis.-Stout, 1989 (3,244 yards)
Per-game record—64.9, Jordan Poznick, Principia, 1992 (519 in 8)
Career
2,007—Kirk Baumgartner, Wis.-Stevens Point, 1986-89 (12,767 yards)
Also holds per-game record at 49.0 (2,007 in 41)

MOST PLAYS BY A FRESHMAN
Season
479—Jason Cooperider, Denison, 1989 (2,301 yards)
Also holds per-game record at 47.9 (479 in 10)

MOST YARDS GAINED
Game
596—John Love, North Park vs. Elmhurst, Oct. 13, 1990 (533 passing, 63 rushing)
Season
3,790—Kirk Baumgartner, Wis.-Stevens Point, 1988 (-38 rushing, 3,828 passing)
Per-game record—354.8, Keith Bishop, Wheaton (Ill.), 1983 (3,193 in 9)
Career
12,767—Kirk Baumgartner, Wis.-Stevens Point, 1986-89 (-261 rushing, 13,028 passing)
Also holds per-game record at 311.4 (12,767 in 41)

MOST YARDS GAINED BY A FRESHMAN
Season
2,554—Brad Hensley, Kenyon, 1991 (441 plays)
Per-game record—271.8, Chris Ings, Wabash, 1992 (2,446 in 9)

MOST GAMES GAINING 300 YARDS OR MORE
Season
8—Kirk Baumgartner, Wis.-Stevens Point, 1989
Career
26—Kirk Baumgartner, Wis.-Stevens Point, 1986-89

MOST CONSECUTIVE GAMES GAINING 300 YARDS OR MORE
Season
6—Kirk Baumgartner, Wis.-Stevens Point, 1987

GAINING 4,000 YARDS RUSHING AND 2,000 YARDS PASSING
Career
Chris Spriggs, Denison, 1983-86 (4,248 rushing & 2,799 passing)
Also holds record for yards gained by a running back at 7,047

GAINING 3,000 YARDS RUSHING AND 3,000 YARDS PASSING
Career
Clay Sampson (TB), Denison, 1977-80 (3,726 rushing & 3,194 passing)

HIGHEST AVERAGE GAIN PER PLAY
Season
(Min. 2,500 yards) 10.1—Willie Seiler, St. John's (Minn.), 1993 (263 for 2,648)
Career
(Min. 6,000 yards) 7.9—Jim Ballard, Wilmington

(Ohio)/Mount Union, 1990, 91-93 (1,328 for 10,545)

MOST TOUCHDOWNS RESPONSIBLE FOR
(TDs Scored and Passed For)
Career
123—Kirk Baumgartner, Wis.-Stevens Point, 1986-89 (110 passing, 13 rushing)
Per-game record—3.1, Jim Ballard, Wilmington (Ohio)/Mount Union, 1990, 91-93 (122 in 40)

Rushing

MOST RUSHES
Game
58—Bill Kaiser, Wabash vs. DePauw, Nov. 9, 1985 (211 yards)
Season
380—Mike Birosak, Dickinson, 1989 (1,798 yards)
Also holds per-game record at 38.0 (380 in 10)
Career
1,152—Anthony Russo, St. John's (N.Y.), 1990-93 (5,834 yards)
Per-game record—32.7, Chris Sizemore, Bridgewater (Va.), 1972-74 (851 in 26)

MOST RUSHES BY A QUARTERBACK
Season
231—Jeff Sauevessig, Wis.-River Falls, 1988 (1,095 yards)
Also holds per-game record at 25.7 (231 in 9)

MOST CONSECUTIVE RUSHES BY THE SAME PLAYER
Game
46—Dan Walsh, Montclair St. vs. Ramapo, Sept. 30, 1989 (during 13 ball possessions)
Season
51—Dan Walsh, Montclair St., 1989 (Sept. 23 to Sept. 30)

MOST YARDS GAINED
Half
310—Leroy Horn, Montclair St. vs. Jersey City St., Nov. 9, 1985 (21 rushes)
Game
417—Carey Bender, Coe vs. Grinnell, Oct. 9, 1993 (33 rushes)
Season
2,035—Ricky Gales, Simpson, 1989 (297 rushes)
Also holds per-game record at 203.5 (2,035 in 10)
Career
5,834—Anthony Russo, St. John's (N.Y.), 1990-93 (1,152 rushes)
Per-game record—151.8, Terry Underwood, Wagner, 1985-88 (5,010 in 33)

MOST YARDS GAINED BY A FRESHMAN
Season
1,283—Jason Wooley, Worcester Tech, 1990 (209 rushes)
Per-game record—148.4, Chris Harper, Carthage, 1990 (1,187 in 8)

MOST RUSHING YARDS GAINED BY A QUARTERBACK
Game
235—Mark Cota, Wis.-River Falls vs. Minn.-Morris, Sept. 13, 1986 (27 rushes)
Season
1,279—Mark Cota, Wis.-River Falls, 1986 (227 rushes)
Also holds per-game record at 127.9 (1,279 in 10)
Career
2,171—Sam Juarascio, DePauw, 1972-75 (407 rushes)

LONGEST GAIN BY A QUARTERBACK
Game
98 yards—Jon Hinds, Principia vs. Illinois Col., Sept. 20, 1986 (TD)

MOST GAMES GAINING 100 YARDS OR MORE
Career
30—Joe Dudek, Plymouth St., 1982-85 (41 games)

MOST CONSECUTIVE GAMES GAINING 100 YARDS OR MORE
Career
18—Hank Wineman, Albion, 1990-91

MOST GAMES GAINING 200 YARDS OR MORE
Season
8—Ricky Gales, Simpson, 1989 (consecutive)
Career
11—Ricky Gales, Simpson, 1988-89

MOST SEASONS GAINING 1,000 YARDS OR MORE
Career
4—Anthony Russo, St. John's (N.Y.), 1990-93; Steve Dixon, Beloit, 1990-93; Joe Dudek, Plymouth St., 1982-85; Rich Kowalski, Hobart, 1972-75

TWO PLAYERS, SAME TEAM, EACH GAINING 1,000 YARDS OR MORE
Season
By seven teams. Most recent: Thomas More, 1992—Ryan Reynolds (TB) 1,042 & Derrick Jett (FB) 1,021

MOST YARDS GAINED RUSHING BY TWO PLAYERS, SAME TEAM
Game
519—Carey Bender 417 & Jason Whitaker 102, Coe vs. Grinnell, Oct. 9, 1993
Season
2,590—Jon Warga (TB) 1,836 & Jeff Stockdale (FB) 727, Wittenberg, 1990 (10 games)

HIGHEST AVERAGE GAIN PER RUSH
Game
(Min. 15 rushes) 19.1—Billy Johnson, Widener vs. Swarthmore, Nov. 10, 1973 (15 for 286)
(Min. 24 rushes) 15.9—Pete Baranek, Carthage vs. North Central, Oct. 5, 1985 (24 for 382)
Season
(Min. 140 rushes) 8.9—Billy Johnson, Widener, 1973 (168 for 1,494)
(Min. 195 rushes) 7.5—Sandy Rogers, Emory & Henry, 1986 (231 for 1,730)
Career
(Min. 500 rushes) 7.1—Joe Dudek, Plymouth St., 1982-85 (785 for 5,570)

MOST TOUCHDOWNS SCORED BY RUSHING
Game
6—Eric Leiser, Eureka vs. Concordia (Wis.), Nov. 2, 1991; Rob Sinclair, Simpson vs. Upper Iowa, Nov. 10, 1990; Scott Bailey, Buena Vista vs. Dubuque, Nov. 11, 1989
Season
27—Matt Malmberg, St. John's (Minn.), 1993; Stanley Drayton, Allegheny, 1991
Per-game record—3.0, Stanley Drayton, Allegheny, 1991 (27 in 9)
Career
76—Joe Dudek, Plymouth St., 1982-85
Also holds per-game record at 1.9 (76 in 41)

MOST RUSHING TOUCHDOWNS SCORED BY A QUARTERBACK
Season
17—Mark Reed, Monmouth (Ill.), 1987
Also holds per-game record at 1.7 (17 in 10)

Passing

HIGHEST PASSING EFFICIENCY RATING POINTS
Season
(Min. 15 atts. per game) 224.6—Willie Seiler, St. John's (Minn.), 1993 (205 attempts, 141 completions, 6 interceptions, 2,648 yards, 33 TDs)
(Min. 25 atts. per game) 193.2—Jim Ballard, Mount Union, 1993 (314 attempts, 229 completions, 11 interceptions, 3,304 yards, 37 TDs)
Career
(Min. 325 comps.) 159.5—Jim Ballard, Wilmington (Ohio)/Mount Union, 1990, 91-93 (1,199 attempts, 743 completions, 41 interceptions, 10,379 yards, 115 TDs)

MOST PASSES ATTEMPTED
Quarter
31—Mike Wallace, Ohio Wesleyan vs. Denison, Oct. 3, 1981 (4th)

Half

57—Mike Wallace, Ohio Wesleyan vs. Denison, Oct. 3, 1981 (2nd)

Game

81—Jordan Poznick, Principia vs. Blackburn, Oct. 10, 1992 (completed 48)

Season

527—Kirk Baumgartner, Wis.-Stevens Point, 1988 (completed 276)

Per-game record—56.4, Jordan Poznick, Principia, 1992 (451 in 8)

Career

1,696—Kirk Baumgartner, Wis.-Stevens Point, 1986-89 (completed 883)

Per-game record—42.3, Keith Bishop, Ill. Wesleyan/Wheaton (Ill.), 1981, 83-85 (1,311 in 31)

MOST PASSES ATTEMPTED BY A FRESHMAN
Season

384—Brad Hensley, Kenyon, 1991 (completed 198)

Per-game record—46.3, Jordan Poznick, Principia, 1990 (278 in 6)

MOST PASSES COMPLETED
Quarter

21—Rob Bristow, Pomona-Pitzer vs. Whittier, Oct. 19, 1985 (4th)

Half

36—Mike Wallace, Ohio Wesleyan vs. Denison, Oct. 3, 1981 (2nd)

Game

50—Tim Lynch, Hofstra vs. Fordham, Oct. 19, 1991 (attempted 69)

Season

276—Kirk Baumgartner, Wis.-Stevens Point, 1988 (attempted 527)

Per-game record—30.1, Jordan Poznick, Principia, 1992 (241 in 8)

Career

883—Kirk Baumgartner, Wis.-Stevens Point, 1986-89 (attempted 1,696)

Per-game record—24.9, Keith Bishop, Ill. Wesleyan/Wheaton (Ill.), 1981, 83-85 (772 in 31)

MOST PASSES COMPLETED BY A FRESHMAN
Season

199—Luke Hanks, Otterbein, 1990 (attempted 370)

Per-game record—21.8, Jordan Poznick, Principia, 1990 (131 in 6)

HIGHEST PERCENTAGE OF PASSES COMPLETED
Game

(Min. 20 comps.) 84.6%—Bob Krepfle, Wis.-La Crosse vs. Anderson, Oct. 6, 1984 (22 of 26)

(Min. 25 comps.) 83.3%—Scott Driggers, Colorado Col. vs. Neb. Wesleyan, Sept. 10, 1983 (35 of 42)

Season

(Min. 250 atts.) 72.9%—Jim Ballard, Mount Union, 1993 (229 of 314)

Career

(Min. 550 atts.) 62.2%—Brian Moore, Baldwin-Wallace, 1981-84 (437 of 703)

(Min. 750 atts.) 62.0%—Jim Ballard, Wilmington (Ohio)/Mount Union, 1990, 91-93 (743 of 1,199)

MOST CONSECUTIVE PASSES COMPLETED
Game

17—Jim Ballard, Mount Union vs. Ill. Wesleyan, Nov. 28, 1992; William Snyder, Carnegie Mellon vs. Wooster, Oct. 20, 1990

Season

20—Dick Puccio, Cortland St. vs. Brockport St., Oct. 12, and Albany (N.Y.), Oct. 19, 1991

MOST PASSES HAD INTERCEPTED
Game

8—Jason Clark, Ohio Northern vs. John Carroll, Nov. 9, 1991; Jim Higgins, Brockport St. vs. Buffalo St., Sept. 29, 1990; Dennis Bogacz, Wis.-Oshkosh vs. Wis.-Stevens Point, Oct. 29, 1988; Kevin Karwath, Canisius vs. Liberty, Nov. 19, 1979

Season

43—Steve Hendry, Wis.-Superior, 1982 (attempted 480)

Also holds per-game record at 3.9 (43 in 11)

Career

117—Steve Hendry, Wis.-Superior, 1980-83 (attempted 1,343)

Per-game record—3.2, Willie Martinez, Oberlin,

1973-74 (58 in 18)

LOWEST PERCENTAGE OF PASSES HAD INTERCEPTED
Season

(Min. 150 atts.) 0.9%—Brett Russ, Union (N.Y.), 1991 (2 of 224)

Career

(Min. 600 atts.) 1.9%—Mark Casale, Montclair St., 1980-83 (16 of 828)

MOST PASSES ATTEMPTED WITHOUT INTERCEPTION
Game

61—Mark Krajnik, Occidental vs. La Verne, Oct. 18, 1986 (32 completions); Brion Demski, Wis.-Stevens Point vs. Wis.-Superior, Oct. 16, 1981 (31 completions)

Season

124—Tim Tenhet, Sewanee, 1982

MOST CONSECUTIVE PASSES ATTEMPTED WITHOUT AN INTERCEPTION
Season

205—Kirk Baumgartner, Wis.-Stevens Point, 1989 (during 6 games; began Sept. 16 vs. Wis.-Platteville, ended Oct. 21 vs. Wis.-Whitewater)

MOST YARDS GAINED
Game

602—Tom Stallings, St. Thomas (Minn.) vs. Bethel (Minn.), Nov. 13, 1993

Season

3,828—Kirk Baumgartner, Wis.-Stevens Point, 1988

Also holds per-game record at 369.2 (3,692 in 10, 1989)

Career

13,028—Kirk Baumgartner, Wis.-Stevens Point, 1986-89

Also holds per-game record at 317.8 (13, 028 in 41)

MOST YARDS GAINED BY A FRESHMAN
Season

2,520—Brad Hensley, Kenyon, 1991

Per-game record—268.8, Dennis Bogacz, Wis.-Oshkosh, 1988 (2,150 in 8)

MOST GAMES PASSING FOR 200 YARDS OR MORE
Season

10—Kirk Baumgartner, Wis.-Stevens Point, 1989, 1988, 1987

Career

32—Kirk Baumgartner, Wis.-Stevens Point, 1986-89

MOST CONSECUTIVE GAMES PASSING FOR 200 YARDS OR MORE
Season

10—Kirk Baumgartner, Wis.-Stevens Point, 1989 (entire season)

Career

27—Keith Bishop, Ill. Wesleyan/Wheaton (Ill.), 1981, 83-85

MOST GAMES PASSING FOR 300 YARDS OR MORE
Season

9—Kirk Baumgartner, Wis.-Stevens Point, 1989

Career

24—Kirk Baumgartner, Wis.-Stevens Point, 1986-89

MOST CONSECUTIVE GAMES PASSING FOR 300 YARDS OR MORE
Season

9—Kirk Baumgartner, Wis.-Stevens Point, 1989 (began Sept. 9 vs. St. Norbert, through Nov. 4 vs. Wis.-Superior)

Career

13—Kirk Baumgartner, Wis.-Stevens Point, 1988-89 (began Oct. 22, 1988, vs. Wis.-Stout, through Nov. 4, 1989, vs. Wis.-Superior)

MOST YARDS GAINED BY TWO OPPOSING PLAYERS
Game

928—Brion Demski, Wis.-Stevens Point (477) & Steve Hendry, Wis.-Superior (451), Oct. 17, 1981 (completed 70 of 123)

MOST YARDS GAINED PER ATTEMPT
Season

(Min. 175 atts.) 12.9—Willie Seiler, St. John's (Minn.),

1993 (205 for 2,648)

(Min. 275 atts.) 10.5—Jim Ballard, Mount Union, 1993 (314 for 3,304)

Career

(Min. 600 atts.) 9.2—Joe Blake, Simpson, 1987-90 (672 for 6,183)

(Min. 950 atts.) 8.7—Jim Ballard, Wilmington (Ohio)/Mount Union, 1990, 91-93 (1,199 for 10,379)

MOST YARDS GAINED PER COMPLETION
Season

(Min. 100 comps.) 19.7—David Parker, Bishop, 1981 (114 for 2,242)

(Min. 200 comps.) 15.5—Kirk Baumgartner, Wis.-Stevens Point, 1987 (243 for 3,755)

Career

(Min. 300 comps.) 18.3—David Parker, Bishop, 1981-84 (378 for 6,934)

(Min. 425 comps.) 15.1—Rob Light, Moravian, 1986-89 (438 for 6,624)

MOST TOUCHDOWN PASSES
Quarter

5—David Sullivan, Williams vs. Hamilton, Oct. 30, 1993 (2nd)

Game

8—Steve Austin, Mass.-Boston vs. Framingham St., Nov. 14, 1992; Kirk Baumgartner, Wis.-Stevens Point vs. Wis.-Superior, Nov. 4, 1989

Season

39—Kirk Baumgartner, Wis.-Stevens Point, 1989

Also holds per-game record at 3.9 (39 in 10)

Career

115—Jim Ballard, Wilmington (Ohio)/Mount Union, 1990, 91-93

Also holds per-game record at 2.9 (115 in 40)

HIGHEST PERCENTAGE OF PASSES FOR TOUCHDOWNS
Season

(Min. 200 atts.) 16.1%—Willie Seiler, St. John's (Minn.), 1993 (33 of 205)

(Min. 300 atts.) 11.8%—Jim Ballard, Mount Union, 1993 (37 of 314)

Career

(Min. 625 atts.) 10.8%—Gary Collier, Emory & Henry, 1984-87 (80 of 738)

(Min. 800 atts.) 9.6%—Jim Ballard, Wilmington (Ohio)/Mount Union, 1990, 91-93 (115 of 1,199)

MOST TOUCHDOWN PASSES BY A FRESHMAN
Season

25—David Parker, Bishop, 1981

Per-game record—2.4, Jim Ballard, Wilmington (Ohio), 1990 (22 in 9)

MOST CONSECUTIVE GAMES THROWING A TOUCHDOWN PASS
Career

27—Dan Stewart, Union (N.Y.) (from Nov. 14, 1981, through Nov. 10, 1984)

Receiving

MOST PASSES CAUGHT
Game

23—Sean Munroe, Mass.-Boston vs. Mass. Maritime, Oct. 10, 1992 (332 yards)

Season

106—Theo Blanco (RB), Wis.-Stevens Point, 1987 (1,616 yards)

Per-game record—12.3, Matt Newton, Principia, 1992 (98 in 8)

Career

287—Matt Newton, Principia, 1990-93 (3,646 yards)

Also holds per-game record at 8.7 (287 in 33)

MOST PASSES CAUGHT BY A TIGHT END
Game

16—Shawn Graham, St. Thomas (Minn.) vs. Hamline, Nov. 13, 1982

Season

72—Don Moehling, Wis.-Stevens Point, 1988 (1,290 yards)

Career

185—Hanz Hoag, Evansville, 1991-93 (2,173 yards)

DIVISION III

MOST PASSES CAUGHT BY A RUNNING BACK
Game
17—Theo Blanco, Wis.-Stevens Point vs. Wis.-Oshkosh, Oct. 31, 1987 (271 yards); Tim Mowery, Wis.-Superior vs. Wis.-Stevens Point, Oct. 17, 1981 (154 yards)
Season
106—Theo Blanco, Wis.-Stevens Point, 1987 (1,616 yards)
Career
169—Mike Christman, Wis.-Stevens Point, 1983-86 (2,190 yards)

MOST PASSES CAUGHT BY A FRESHMAN
Season
67—Bill Stromberg, Johns Hopkins, 1978 (1,027 yards)

MOST PASSES CAUGHT BY TWO PLAYERS, SAME TEAM
Season
158—Theo Blanco (RB) 106 & Aatron Kenney (WR) 52, Wis.-Stevens Point, 1987 (2,713 yards, 24 TDs)

MOST PASSES CAUGHT BY THREE PLAYERS, SAME TEAM
Season
217—Theo Blanco (WR) 80, Don Moehling (TE) 72 & Jim Mares (RB) 65, Wis.-Stevens Point, 1988. Totaled 2,959 yards and 19 TDs (team totals: 285-3,924-26)

MOST CONSECUTIVE GAMES CATCHING A PASS
Career
37—Kendall Griffin, Loras, 1990-93

MOST YARDS GAINED
Game
332—Sean Munroe, Mass.-Boston vs. Mass. Maritime, Oct. 10, 1992 (caught 23)
Season
1,693—Sean Munroe, Mass.-Boston, 1992 (caught 95)
Also holds per-game record at 188.1 (1,693 in 9)
Career
3,846—Dale Amos, Frank. & Marsh., 1986-89 (caught 233)
Per-game record—110.5, Matt Newton, Principia, 1990-93 (3,646 in 33)

MOST YARDS GAINED BY A TIGHT END
Game
267—Tom Mullady, Rhodes vs. Rose-Hulman, Nov. 11, 1978 (caught 13)
Season
1,290—Don Moehling, Wis.-Stevens Point, 1988 (caught 72)
Career
2,663—Don Moehling, Wis.-Stevens Point, 1986-89 (caught 152)

MOST YARDS GAINED BY A RUNNING BACK
Game
271—Theo Blanco, Wis.-Stevens Point vs. Wis.-Oshkosh, Oct. 31, 1987 (caught 17)
Season
1,616—Theo Blanco, Wis.-Stevens Point, 1987 (caught 106)
Career
2,190—Mike Christman, Wis.-Stevens Point, 1983-86 (caught 169)

MOST YARDS GAINED BY TWO PLAYERS, SAME TEAM
Season
2,713—Theo Blanco (RB) 1,616 & Aatron Kenney (WR) 1,097, Wis.-Stevens Point, 1987 (158 receptions, 24 TDs)

HIGHEST AVERAGE GAIN PER RECEPTION
Game
(Min. 3 receps.) 68.3—Paul Jaeckel, Elmhurst vs. Ill. Wesleyan, Oct. 8, 1983 (3 for 205)
(Min. 5 receps.) 56.8—Tom Casperson, Trenton St. vs. Ramapo, Nov. 15, 1980 (5 for 284)
Season
(Min. 35 receps.) 26.9—Marty Redlawsk, Concordia (Ill.), 1985 (38 for 1,022)
(Min. 50 receps.) 23.5—Evan Elkington, Worcester Tech, 1989 (52 for 1,220)

Career
(Min. 125 receps.) 20.6—Rodd Patten, Framingham St., 1990-93 (154 for 3,170)

HIGHEST AVERAGE GAIN PER RECEPTION BY A RUNNING BACK
Season
(Min. 50 receps.) 17.5—Barry Rose, Wis.-Stevens Point, 1989 (67 for 1,171)

MOST TOUCHDOWN PASSES CAUGHT
Game
5—By 10 players. Most recent: Sean Munroe, Mass.-Boston vs. Framingham St., Nov. 14, 1992
Season
20—John Aromando, Trenton St., 1983
Also holds per-game record at 2.0 (20 in 10)
Career
55—Chris Bisaillon, Ill. Wesleyan, 1989-92 (223 receptions)
Also holds per-game record at 1.5 (55 in 36)

MOST TOUCHDOWN PASSES CAUGHT BY A FRESHMAN
Season
12—Chris Bisaillon, Ill. Wesleyan, 1989

HIGHEST PERCENTAGE OF PASSES CAUGHT FOR TOUCHDOWNS
Season
(Min. 12 TDs) 54.3%—Keith Gilliam, Randolph-Macon, 1984 (19 of 35)
Career
(Min. 20 TDs) 28.0%—Pat Schwanke, Lawrence, 1979-82 (28 of 100)

MOST CONSECUTIVE PASSES CAUGHT FOR TOUCHDOWNS
9—Keith Gilliam, Randolph-Macon, 1984 (during four games)

Punting

MOST PUNTS
Game
17—Jerry Williams, Frostburg St. vs. Salisbury St., Sept. 30, 1978
Season
106—Bob Blake, Wis.-Superior, 1977 (3,404 yards)
Per-game record—11.0, Mark Roedelbronn, FDU-Madison, 1990 (99 in 9)
Career
263—Chris Gardner, Loras, 1987-90 (9,394 yards)

HIGHEST AVERAGE PER PUNT
Season
(Min. 40 punts) 44.9—Bob Burwell, Rose-Hulman, 1978 (61 for 2,740)
Career
(Min. 110 punts) 42.1—Mike Manson, Ill. Benedictine, 1975-78 (120 for 5,056)

Interceptions

MOST PASSES INTERCEPTED
Game
5—By eight players. Most recent: Chris Butts, Worcester St. vs. Fitchburg St., Oct. 10, 1992
Season
15—Mark Dorner, Juniata, 1987 (202 yards)
Also holds per-game record at 1.5 (15 in 10)
Career
34—Ralph Gebhardt, Rochester, 1972-75 (406 yards)

MOST CONSECUTIVE GAMES INTERCEPTING A PASS
Season
9—Brent Sands, Cornell College, 1992
Also holds career record at 9

MOST YARDS ON INTERCEPTION RETURNS
Game
164—Rick Conner, Western Md. vs. Dickinson, Oct. 15, 1983 (89-yard interception and 75-yard lateral after an interception)
Season
358—Rod Pesek, Whittier, 1987 (10 interceptions)

Career
479—Eugene Hunter, Fort Valley St., 1972-74 (29 interceptions)

HIGHEST AVERAGE GAIN PER INTERCEPTION
Season
(Min. 7 ints.) 35.8—Rod Pesek, Whittier, 1987 (10 for 358)
Career
(Min. 20 ints.) 20.4—Todd Schoelzel, Wis.-Oshkosh, 1985-88 (22 for 448)

MOST TOUCHDOWNS SCORED ON INTERCEPTIONS
Game
2—By many players. Most recent: Aaron Brown, Capital vs. Bethany (W.Va.), Sept. 14, 1991
Season
3—By eight players. Most recent: Will Hall, Millsaps, 1992 (6 interceptions); Michael Sikma, Carroll (Wis.), 1992 (4 interceptions)

Punt Returns

MOST PUNT RETURNS
Game
10—Ellis Wangelin, Wis.-River Falls vs. Wis.-Platteville, Oct. 12, 1985 (87 yards)
Season
48—Rick Bealer, Lycoming, 1989 (492 yards)
Career
126—Mike Caterbone, Frank. & Marsh., 1980-83 (1,141 yards)

MOST YARDS ON PUNT RETURNS
Game
212—Melvin Dillard, Ferrum vs. Newport News App., Oct. 13, 1990 (6 returns)
Season
688—Melvin Dillard, Ferrum, 1990 (25 returns)
Career
1,198—Chuck Downey, Stony Brook, 1984-87 (59 returns)

HIGHEST AVERAGE GAIN PER RETURN
Season
(Min. 1.2 rets. per game) 31.2—Chuck Downey, Stony Brook, 1986 (17 for 530)
Career
(Min. 1.2 rets. per game) 22.9—Keith Winston, Knoxville, 1986-87 (30 for 686)
(Min. 50 rets.) 20.3—Chuck Downey, Stony Brook, 1984-87 (59 for 1,198)

MOST TOUCHDOWNS SCORED ON PUNT RETURNS
Game
2—By seven players. Most recent: Charles Jordan, Occidental vs. Cal Lutheran, Nov. 6, 1993 (50 & 56 yards)
Season
4—Chris Warren, Ferrum, 1989 (18 returns); Keith Winston, Knoxville, 1986 (14 returns); Chuck Downey, Stony Brook, 1986 (17 returns); Matt Pekarske, Wis.-La Crosse, 1986 (37 returns)
Career
7—Chuck Downey, Stony Brook, 1984-87 (59 returns)

Kickoff Returns

MOST KICKOFF RETURNS
Game
9—Larry Schurder, North Park vs. Elmhurst, Sept. 17, 1983 (229 yards)
Season
42—Phil Puryear, Wooster, 1990 (834 yards); Dirk Blood, Ohio Northern, 1987 (973 yards)
Career
85—Tom Southall, Colorado Col., 1981-84 (1,876 yards)

MOST YARDS ON KICKOFF RETURNS
Game
279—Chuck Downey, Stony Brook vs. Trenton St., Oct. 5, 1984 (7 returns)

Season
973—Dirk Blood, Ohio Northern, 1987 (42 returns)

Career
1,876—Tom Southall, Colorado Col., 1981-84 (85 returns)

HIGHEST AVERAGE GAIN PER RETURN
Game
(Min. 3 rets.) 68.0—Victor Johnson, Elmhurst vs. Wheaton (Ill.), Sept. 15, 1979 (3 for 204)

Season
(Min. 1.2 rets. per game) 39.8—Jason Martin, Coe, 1992 (11 for 438)

Career
(Min. 1.2 rets. per game) 29.2—Daryl Brown, Tufts, 1974-76 (38 for 1,111)

MOST TOUCHDOWNS SCORED ON KICKOFF RETURNS
Game
2—By many players. Most recent: Bill Nashwinter, Buffalo St. vs. Alfred, Oct. 27, 1990

Season
4—Byron Womack, Iona, 1989

Career
6—Byron Womack, Iona, 1988-91

Total Kick Returns

(Combined Punt and Kickoff Returns)

MOST YARDS ON KICK RETURNS
Game
354—Chuck Downey, Stony Brook vs. Trenton St., Oct. 5, 1984 (7 kickoff returns for 279 yards, 1 punt return for 75 yards)

GAINING 1,000 YARDS ON PUNT RETURNS AND 1,000 YARDS ON KICKOFF RETURNS
Career
Chuck Downey, Stony Brook, 1984-87 (1,281 on kickoff returns, 1,198 on punt returns)

MOST TOUCHDOWNS ON KICK RETURNS
Game
3—Chuck Downey, Stony Brook vs. Trenton St., Oct. 5, 1984 (2 kickoff returns 98 & 95 yards, 1 punt return 75 yards)

Season
5—Charles Jordan, Occidental, 1993 (2 punt returns, 3 kickoff returns); Chris Warren, Ferrum, 1989 (4 punt returns, 1 kickoff return); Chuck Downey, Stony Brook, 1986 (4 punt returns, 1 kickoff return)

Career
10—Chuck Downey, Stony Brook, 1984-87 (7 punt returns, 3 kickoff returns)

HIGHEST AVERAGE PER KICK RETURN
(Min. 1.2 Returns Per Game Each)
Career
23.6—Chuck Downey, Stony Brook, 1984-87 (59 for 1,198 on punt returns, 46 for 1,281 on kickoff returns)

AVERAGING 20 YARDS EACH ON PUNT RETURNS AND KICKOFF RETURNS
(Min. 1.2 Returns Per Game Each)
Career
Chuck Downey, Stony Brook, 1984-87 (20.3 on punt returns, 59 for 1,198; 27.8 on kickoff returns, 46 for 1,281)

All Runbacks

(Combined Interceptions, Punt Returns and Kickoff Returns)

MOST TOUCHDOWNS ON INTERCEPTIONS, PUNT RETURNS AND KICKOFF RETURNS
Season
6—Chuck Downey, Stony Brook, 1986 (4 punt returns, 1 kickoff return, 1 interception return)

Career
11—Chuck Downey, Stony Brook, 1984-87 (7 punt returns, 3 kickoff returns, 1 interception return)

Punts Blocked By

MOST PUNTS BLOCKED BY
Game
3—Jim Perryman, Millikin vs. Carroll (Wis.), Nov. 1, 1980

Season
9—Jim Perryman, Millikin, 1980

Career
13—Frank Lyle, Millsaps, 1979-82
(Daryl Hobson, Ill. Benedictine DB, blocked 9 punts during 17 games in 1987-88)

All-Purpose Yards

(Yardage Gained From Rushing, Receiving and All Runbacks)

MOST PLAYS
Season
383—Mike Birosak, Dickinson, 1989 (380 rushes, 3 receptions)

Career
1,158—Eric Frees, Western Md., 1988-91 (1,059 rushes, 34 receptions, 58 kickoff returns, 7 punt returns)

MOST YARDS GAINED
Game
509—Carey Bender, Coe vs. Grinnell, Oct. 9, 1993 (417 rushing, 92 receiving)

Season
2,418—Theo Blanco, Wis.-Stevens Point, 1987 (454 rushing, 1,616 receiving, 245 punt returns, 103 kickoff returns; 271 plays)
Per-game record—243.1, Kirk Matthieu, Maine Maritime, 1992 (2,188 in 9)

Career
6,878—Eric Frees, Western Md., 1988-91 (5,281 rushing, 392 receiving, 47 punt returns, 1,158 kickoff returns; 1,158 plays)
Per-game record—197.4, Gary Trettel, St. Thomas (Minn.), 1988-90 (5,724 in 29)

HIGHEST AVERAGE GAIN PER PLAY
Season
(Min. 1,500 yards, 125 plays) 10.2—Billy Johnson, Widener, 1973 (1,868 in 183)

Career
(Min. 4,000 yards, 300 plays) 16.0—Chris Wiesehan, Wabash, 1990-93 (4,825 yards on 301)

Scoring

MOST POINTS SCORED
Season
168—Stanley Drayton, Allegheny, 1991 (28 TDs)
Also holds per-game record at 16.8 (168 in 10)

Career
474—Joe Dudek, Plymouth St., 1982-85 (79 TDs)
Also holds per-game record at 11.6 (474 in 41)

TWO PLAYERS, SAME TEAM, EACH SCORING 100 POINTS OR MORE
Season
Denis McDermott (126) & Manny Tsantes (102), St. John's (N.Y.), 1989; Theo Blanco (102) & Aatron Kenney (102), Wis.-Stevens Point, 1987

MOST TOUCHDOWNS SCORED
Season
28—Stanley Drayton, Allegheny, 1991
Also holds per-game record at 2.8 (28 in 10)

Career
79—Joe Dudek, Plymouth St., 1982-85
Also holds per-game record at 1.9 (79 in 41)

MOST GAMES SCORING A TOUCHDOWN
Career
33—Joe Dudek, Plymouth St., 1982-85 (41 games)

MOST GAMES SCORING TWO OR MORE TOUCHDOWNS
Career
24—Joe Dudek, Plymouth St., 1982-85 (41 games)

MOST EXTRA POINTS ATTEMPTED BY KICKING
Game
14—Kurt Christenson, Concordia-M'head vs. Macalester, Sept. 24, 1977 (made 13)

Season
70—Greg Poulin, St. John's (Minn.), 1993 (made 63)

Career
194—Tim Mercer, Ferrum, 1987-90 (made 183)

MOST EXTRA POINTS MADE BY KICKING
Game
13—Kurt Christenson, Concordia-M'head vs. Macalester, Sept. 24, 1977 (attempted 14)

Season
63—Greg Poulin, St. John's (Minn.), 1993 (attempted 70)

Career
183—Tim Mercer, Ferrum, 1987-90 (attempted 194)

HIGHEST PERCENTAGE OF EXTRA POINTS MADE
(Best Perfect Season)
100.0%—Mike Duvic, Dayton, 1989 (46 of 46)

HIGHEST PERCENTAGE OF EXTRA POINTS MADE
Career
(Min. 80 atts.) 100.0%—Mike Farrell, Adrian, 1983-85 (84 of 84)
(Min. 100 atts.) 98.5%—Rims Roof, Coe, 1982-85 (135 of 137)

MOST CONSECUTIVE EXTRA POINTS MADE BY KICKING
Game
13—Kurt Christenson, Concordia-M'head vs. Macalester, Sept. 24, 1977

Career
102—Rims Roof, Coe (from Sept. 24, 1983, through Nov. 9, 1985)

MOST POINTS SCORED BY KICKING
Game
20—Jim Hever, Rhodes vs. Millsaps, Sept. 22, 1984 (6 FGs, 2 PATs)

Season
102—Ken Edelman, Mount Union, 1990 (20 FGs, 42 PATs)
Also holds per-game record at 10.2 (102 in 10)

Career
274—Ken Edelman, Mount Union, 1987-90 (52 FGs, 118 PATs)
Also holds per-game record at 6.9 (274 in 40)

MOST SUCCESSFUL TWO-POINT PASS ATTEMPTS
Game
4—Rob Bristow, Pomona-Pitzer vs. Whittier, Oct. 19, 1985 (all in 4th quarter); Dave Geissler, Wis.-Stevens Point vs. Wis.-La Crosse, Sept. 21, 1985 (all in 4th quarter)

Season
7—Kirk Baumgartner, Wis.-Stevens Point, 1988 (8 attempts); Gary Collier, Emory & Henry, 1987 (11 attempts); Dave Geissler, Wis.-Stevens Point, 1985 (8 attempts)

Career
11—Dave Geissler, Wis.-Stevens Point, 1982-85 (14 attempts)
Rob Bristow, Pomona-Pitzer, 1983-86, holds record for highest percentage of successful two-point pass attempts (best perfect record) at 9 of 9

MOST TWO-POINT PASSES CAUGHT
Season
4—Rob Brooks, Albright, 1992; Don Moehling, Wis.-Stevens Point, 1988; Mike Christman, Wis.-Stevens Point, 1985

Defensive Extra Points

MOST DEFENSIVE EXTRA POINTS SCORED
Game
1—By many players

Season
2—Dan Fichter, Brockport St., 1990 (2 blocked kick returns)

DIVISION III

LONGEST DEFENSIVE EXTRA POINT BLOCKED KICK RETURN

97—Keith Mottram (CB), Colorado Col. vs. Austin, Oct. 10, 1992 (scored)

LONGEST DEFENSIVE EXTRA POINT INTERCEPTION

100—By four players. Most recent: Chris Schleeper (FS), Quincy vs. Ill. Wesleyan, Sept. 29, 1990 (scored)

FIRST DEFENSIVE EXTRA POINT SCORED

Steve Nieves (DB), St. John's (N.Y.) vs. Iona, Sept. 10, 1988 (83-yard blocked kick return)

Field Goals

MOST FIELD GOALS MADE
Game
6—Jim Hever, Rhodes vs. Millsaps, Sept. 22, 1984 (30, 24, 42, 44, 46, 30 yards; attempted 8)
Season
20—Ken Edelman, Mount Union, 1990 (attempted 27) Also holds per-game record at 2.0 (20 in 10)
Career
52—Ken Edelman, Mount Union, 1987-90 (attempted 71) Also holds per-game record (Min. 30) at 1.3 (52 in 40)

MOST FIELD GOALS ATTEMPTED
Game
8—Jim Hever, Rhodes vs. Millsaps, Sept. 22, 1984 (made 6)
Season
29—Scott Ryerson, Central Fla., 1981 (made 18)
Career
71—Ken Edelman, Mount Union, 1987-90 (made 52); Doug Hart, Grove City, 1985-88 (made 40)

HIGHEST PERCENTAGE OF FIELD GOALS MADE
Season
(Min. 15 atts.) 93.8%—Steve Graeca, John Carroll, 1988 (15 of 16)
Career
(Min. 50 atts.) *77.6%—Mike Duvic, Dayton, 1986-89 (38 of 49)

*Declared champion; with one more attempt (making 50), failed, still would have highest percentage (76.0).

LONGEST FIELD GOAL MADE
62—Dom Antonini, Rowan vs. Salisbury St., Sept. 18, 1976

MOST FIELD GOALS ATTEMPTED WITHOUT SUCCESS
Season
11—Scott Perry, Moravian, 1986

Team Records

SINGLE GAME—Offense

Total Offense

MOST PLAYS
112—Gust. Adolphus vs. Bethel (Minn.), Nov. 2, 1985 (65 passes, 47 rushes; 493 yards)

MOST PLAYS, BOTH TEAMS
214—Gust. Adolphus (112) & Bethel (Minn.) (102), Nov. 2, 1985 (143 passes, 71 rushes; 930 yards)

MOST YARDS GAINED
771—Coe vs. Grinnell, Oct. 9, 1993

MOST YARDS GAINED, BOTH TEAMS
1,395—Occidental (753) & Claremont-M-S (642), Oct. 30, 1993 (136 plays)

MOST TOUCHDOWNS SCORED BY RUSHING AND PASSING
14—Concordia-M'head vs. Macalester, Sept. 24, 1977 (12 rushing, 2 passing)

Rushing

MOST RUSHES
92—Wis.-River Falls vs. Wis.-Platteville, Oct. 21, 1989 (464 yards)

MOST YARDS GAINED RUSHING
642—Wis.-River Falls vs. Wis.-Superior, Oct. 14, 1989 (88 rushes)

MOST TOUCHDOWNS SCORED BY RUSHING
12—Concordia-M'head vs. Macalester, Sept. 24, 1977

Passing

MOST PASSES ATTEMPTED
81—Principia vs. Blackburn, Oct. 10, 1992 (completed 48)

MOST PASSES ATTEMPTED, BOTH TEAMS
143—Bethel (Minn.) (78) & Gust. Adolphus (65), Nov. 2, 1985 (completed 65)

MOST PASSES ATTEMPTED WITHOUT AN INTERCEPTION
61—Occidental vs. La Verne, Oct. 18, 1986 (completed 32); Wis.-Stevens Point vs. Wis.-Superior, Oct. 16, 1981 (completed 31)

MOST PASSES COMPLETED
50—Hofstra vs. Fordham, Oct. 19, 1991 (attempted 69)

MOST PASSES COMPLETED, BOTH TEAMS
72—Wis.-Superior (41) & Wis.-Stevens Point (31), Oct. 17, 1981 (attempted 131)

HIGHEST PERCENTAGE OF PASSES COMPLETED (Min. 35 Attempts)
78.9%—Wheaton (Ill.) vs. North Park, Oct. 8, 1983 (30 of 38)

MOST YARDS GAINED
602—St. Thomas (Minn.) vs. Bethel (Minn.), Nov. 13, 1993

MOST YARDS GAINED, BOTH TEAMS
1,100—St. Thomas (Minn.) (602) & Bethel (Minn.) (498), Nov. 13, 1993 (attempted 113, completed 69)

MOST TOUCHDOWN PASSES
8—Mass.-Boston vs. Framingham St., Nov. 14, 1992; Wis.-Stevens Point vs. Wis.-Superior, Nov. 4, 1989

MOST TOUCHDOWN PASSES, BOTH TEAMS
12—St. Thomas (Minn.) (6) & Bethel (Minn.) (6), Nov. 13, 1993

Punt Returns

MOST TOUCHDOWNS SCORED ON PUNT RETURNS
2—By many teams. Most recent: Widener vs. Susquehanna, Oct. 20, 1990; Widener vs. Albright, Oct. 13, 1990 (consecutive games, 3 returns on blocked punts)

Kickoff Returns

MOST YARDS ON KICKOFF RETURNS
283—Oberlin vs. Wittenberg, Oct. 30, 1993

Scoring

MOST POINTS SCORED
97—Concordia-M'head vs. Macalester, Sept. 24, 1977

MOST POINTS SCORED, BOTH TEAMS
111—Carroll (Wis.) (58) & Ill. Wesleyan (53), Nov. 11, 1989

MOST POINTS SCORED BY A LOSING TEAM
53—Ill. Wesleyan vs. Carroll (Wis.) (58), Nov. 11, 1989

MOST POINTS OVERCOME TO WIN A GAME
33—Salisbury St. vs. Randolph-Macon, Sept. 15, 1984 (trailed 33-0 with 14:18 left in 2nd quarter; won 34-33); Wis.-Platteville vs. Wis.-Eau Claire, Nov. 8, 1980 (trailed 33-0 with 7:00 left in 2nd quarter; won 52-43)

MOST POINTS SCORED IN A BRIEF PERIOD OF TIME
21 in 1:58—Occidental vs. Claremont-M-S, Oct. 30, 1993 (turned 14-14 game into 35-20 in 2nd quarter; won 68-42)
32 in 4:04—Wis.-Stevens Point vs. Wis.-La Crosse, Sept. 21, 1985 (trailed 3-27 and 11-35 in 4th quarter; ended in 35-35 tie)

MOST POINTS SCORED IN FIRST VARSITY GAME
63—Bentley vs. Brooklyn (26), Sept. 24, 1988

MOST TOUCHDOWNS SCORED
14—Concordia-M'head vs. Macalester, Sept. 24, 1977

MOST EXTRA POINTS MADE BY KICKING
13—Concordia-M'head vs. Macalester, Sept. 24, 1977 (attempted 14)

MOST FIELD GOALS MADE
6—Rhodes vs. Millsaps, Sept. 22, 1984 (attempted 8)

MOST FIELD GOALS ATTEMPTED
8—Rhodes vs. Millsaps, Sept. 22, 1984 (made 6)

MOST DEFENSIVE EXTRA-POINT RETURNS SCORED
1—By many teams

MOST DEFENSIVE EXTRA-POINT OPPORTUNITIES
2—Frank. & Marsh. vs. Johns Hopkins, Nov. 7, 1992 (1 interception & 1 kick return; none scored); Wis.-River Falls vs. Wis.-La Crosse, Nov. 11, 1989 (2 kick returns; 1 scored); Wis.-Platteville vs. Wis.-Oshkosh, Oct. 15, 1988 (2 interceptions; none scored); Buffalo St. vs. Brockport St., Oct. 1, 1988 (1 interception & 1 kick return; none scored)

Turnovers

(Most Times Losing the Ball on Interceptions and Fumbles)

MOST TURNOVERS
13—St. Olaf vs. St. Thomas (Minn.), Oct. 12, 1985 (10 interceptions, 3 fumbles); Mercyhurst vs. Buffalo St., Oct. 23, 1982 (12 fumbles, 1 interception); Albany (N.Y.) vs. Rochester Inst., Oct. 1, 1977

MOST TURNOVERS, BOTH TEAMS
24—Albany (N.Y.) (13) & Rochester Inst. (11), Oct. 1, 1977

First Downs

MOST TOTAL FIRST DOWNS
40—Upper Iowa vs. Loras, Nov. 7, 1992 (19 rushing, 17 passing, 4 by penalty)

Penalties

MOST PENALTIES AGAINST
25—Norwich vs. Coast Guard, Sept. 29, 1985 (192 yards)

SINGLE GAME—Defense

Total Defense

FEWEST YARDS ALLOWED
Minus 50—Ithaca vs. Springfield, Oct. 11, 1975 (-94 rushing, 44 passing)

Rushing Defense

FEWEST RUSHES ALLOWED
10—Augustana (Ill.) vs. Ill. Wesleyan, Oct. 11, 1983 (28 yards); Wis.-Superior vs. Wis.-Stevens Point, Oct. 17, 1981 (-3 yards)

FEWEST YARDS ALLOWED
Minus 112—Coast Guard vs. Wesleyan, Oct. 7, 1989 (23 plays)

Pass Defense

FEWEST ATTEMPTS ALLOWED
0—By many teams. Most recent: Concordia-M'head vs. Macalester, Oct. 12, 1991

FEWEST COMPLETIONS ALLOWED
0—By many teams. Most recent: Frank. & Marsh. vs. Gettysburg, Nov. 14, 1992 (2 attempts)

FEWEST YARDS ALLOWED
Minus 6—Central (Iowa) vs. Simpson, Oct. 19, 1985 (1 completion)

MOST PASSES INTERCEPTED BY
10—St. Thomas (Minn.) vs. St. Olaf, Oct. 12, 1985 (91 yards; 50 attempts)

MOST PLAYERS INTERCEPTING A PASS
8—Samford vs. Anderson, Oct. 11, 1986 (8 interceptions in the game)

Punts Blocked By

MOST OPPONENT'S PUNTS BLOCKED BY
4—Ill. Benedictine vs. Olivet Nazarene, Oct. 22, & vs. Aurora, Oct. 29, 1988 (consecutive games, resulting in 4 TDs and 1 safety). Blocked 9 punts in three consecutive games, vs. MacMurray, Oct. 15, Olivet Nazarene and Aurora, resulting in 4 TDs and 2 safeties

First Downs

FEWEST FIRST DOWNS ALLOWED
0—Case Reserve vs. Wooster, Sept. 21, 1985

SEASON—Offense

Total Offense

MOST YARDS GAINED PER GAME
549.7—St. John's (Minn.), 1993 (5,497 in 10)

HIGHEST AVERAGE GAIN PER PLAY
8.1—Ferrum, 1990 (534 for 4,350)

MOST PLAYS PER GAME
85.6—Hampden-Sydney, 1978 (856 in 10)

MOST TOUCHDOWNS SCORED PER GAME BY RUSHING AND PASSING
8.4—St. John's (Minn.), 1993 (84 in 10; 44 rushing, 40 passing)

Rushing

MOST YARDS GAINED PER GAME
434.7—Ferrum, 1990 (3,912 in 9)

HIGHEST AVERAGE GAIN PER RUSH
8.3—Ferrum, 1990 (470 for 3,912)

MOST RUSHES PER GAME
71.4—Wis.-River Falls, 1988 (714 in 10)

MOST TOUCHDOWNS SCORED PER GAME BY RUSHING
5.4—Ferrum, 1990 (49 in 9)

Passing

MOST YARDS GAINED PER GAME
403.5—Hofstra, 1991 (4,035 in 10)

FEWEST YARDS GAINED PER GAME
18.4—Wis.-River Falls, 1983 (184 in 10)

HIGHEST AVERAGE GAIN PER ATTEMPT
(Min. 250 atts.) 11.1—St. John's (Minn.), 1993 (299 for 3,308)
(Min. 350 atts.) 8.7—Wheaton (Ill.), 1983 (393 for 3,424)

HIGHEST AVERAGE GAIN PER COMPLETION (Min. 200 Completions)
15.4—Wis.-Stevens Point, 1987 (249 for 3,836)

MOST PASSES ATTEMPTED PER GAME
58.5—Hofstra, 1991 (585 in 10)

FEWEST PASSES ATTEMPTED PER GAME
4.0—Wis.-River Falls, 1988 (40 in 10)

MOST PASSES COMPLETED PER GAME
34.4—Hofstra, 1991 (344 in 10)

FEWEST PASSES COMPLETED PER GAME
1.3—Wis.-River Falls, 1983 (13 in 10)

HIGHEST PERCENTAGE COMPLETED (Min. 200 Attempts)
70.7%—Mount Union, 1993 (244 of 345)

LOWEST PERCENTAGE OF PASSES HAD INTERCEPTED (Min. 150 Attempts)
0.7%—San Diego, 1990 (1 of 153)

MOST TOUCHDOWN PASSES PER GAME
4.0—St. John's (Minn.), 1993 (40 in 10); Samford, 1987 (40 in 10)

HIGHEST PASSING EFFICIENCY RATING POINTS
(Min. 15 atts. per game) 192.9—St. John's (Minn.), 1993 (299 attempts, 189 completions, 11 interceptions, 3,308 yards, 40 TDs)
(Min. 300 atts.) 186.0—Mount Union, 1993 (345 attempts, 244 completions, 12 interceptions, 3,528 yards, 38 TDs)

Punting

MOST PUNTS PER GAME
11.0—FDU-Madison, 1990 (99 in 9)

FEWEST PUNTS PER GAME
2.4—Frostburg St., 1990 (24 in 10)

HIGHEST PUNTING AVERAGE
44.6—Occidental, 1982 (55 for 2,454)

Scoring

MOST POINTS PER GAME
61.5—St. John's (Minn.), 1993 (615 in 10)

MOST TOUCHDOWNS PER GAME
8.9—St. John's (Minn.), 1993 (89 in 10)

BEST PERFECT RECORD ON EXTRA POINTS MADE BY KICKING
49 of 49—Dayton, 1989

MOST TWO-POINT ATTEMPTS PER GAME
2.8—N'western (Wis.), 1990 (17 in 6)

MOST FIELD GOALS MADE PER GAME
2.0—Mount Union, 1990 (20 in 10)

HIGHEST SCORING MARGIN
51.8—St. John's (Minn.), 1993 (averaged 61.5 and allowed 9.7 in 10 games)

MOST TOUCHDOWNS ON BLOCKED PUNT RETURNS
5—Widener, 1990

MOST SAFETIES
4—Alfred, 1992; Central (Iowa), 1992; Westfield St., 1992; Wis.-Stevens Point, 1990

MOST DEFENSIVE EXTRA-POINT RETURNS SCORED
2—Eureka, 1991; Brockport St., 1990

MOST DEFENSIVE EXTRA POINT BLOCKED KICK RETURNS
3—Assumption, 1992 (1 scored); Ohio Wesleyan, 1991 (0 scored); Brockport St., 1990 (2 scored)

MOST DEFENSIVE EXTRA POINT INTERCEPTIONS
2—Swarthmore, 1989 (1 scored); Wis.-Platteville, 1988 (none scored)

Penalties

MOST PENALTIES PER GAME
13.3—Kean, 1990 (133 in 10, 1,155 yards)

MOST YARDS PENALIZED PER GAME
121.9—Hofstra, 1991 (1,219 in 10, 124 penalties)

Turnovers (Giveaways)

(Passes Had Intercepted and Fumbles Lost, From 1985)

FEWEST TURNOVERS
8—North Central, 1989 (7 interceptions, 1 fumble lost); Occidental, 1988 (2 interceptions, 6 fumbles lost)
Per-game record—0.9, North Central, 1989 (8 in 9); Occidental, 1988 (8 in 9)

MOST TURNOVERS
52—William Penn, 1985 (19 interceptions, 33 fumbles lost)
Per-game record—5.2, William Penn, 1985 (52 in 10)

SEASON—Defense

Total Defense

FEWEST YARDS ALLOWED PER GAME
94.0—Knoxville, 1977 (940 in 10)

LOWEST AVERAGE YARDS ALLOWED PER PLAY
(Min. 500 plays) 1.8—Bowie St., 1978 (576 for 1,011)
(Min. 650 plays) 2.0—Plymouth St., 1987 (733 for 1,488)

FEWEST RUSHING AND PASSING TOUCHDOWNS ALLOWED PER GAME
0.3—Montclair St., 1984 (3 in 10)

Rushing Defense

FEWEST YARDS ALLOWED PER GAME
Minus 2.3—Knoxville, 1977 (-23 in 10 games)

LOWEST AVERAGE YARDS ALLOWED PER RUSH
(Min. 275 rushes) Minus 0.1—Knoxville, 1977 (333 for -23)
(Min. 400 rushes) 1.0—Lycoming, 1976 (400 for 399)

FEWEST TOUCHDOWNS BY RUSHING ALLOWED
0—Union (N.Y.), 1983 (9 games); New Haven, 1978 (9 games)

Pass Defense

FEWEST YARDS ALLOWED PER GAME
48.5—Mass. Maritime, 1976 (388 in 8)

FEWEST YARDS ALLOWED PER ATTEMPT
(Min. 150 atts.) 2.9—Plymouth St., 1982 (170 for 488)
(Min. 225 atts.) 3.3—Plymouth St., 1987 (281 for 919)

DIVISION III

FEWEST YARDS ALLOWED PER COMPLETION (Min. 100 Completions)
8.6—Baldwin-Wallace, 1990 (151 for 1,305)

LOWEST COMPLETION PERCENTAGE ALLOWED
(Min. 150 atts.) 24.3%—Doane, 1973 (41 of 169)
(Min. 250 atts.) 33.5%—Plymouth St., 1987 (94 of 281)

HIGHEST PERCENTAGE INTERCEPTED BY (Min. 200 Attempts)
15.2%—Rose-Hulman, 1977 (32 of 210)

MOST PASSES INTERCEPTED BY
35—Plymouth St., 1987 (12 games, 281 attempts against, 348 yards returned)
Per-game record—3.4, Montclair St., 1981 (34 in 10)

FEWEST PASSES INTERCEPTED BY (Min. 125 Attempts)
1—Bates, 1987 (134 attempts against in 8 games, 0 yards returned)

MOST YARDS ON INTERCEPTION RETURNS
576—Emory & Henry, 1987 (31 interceptions)

MOST TOUCHDOWNS SCORED ON INTERCEPTIONS
6—Coe, 1992 (22 interceptions, 272 passes against); Augustana (Ill.), 1987 (23 interceptions, 229 passes against)

FEWEST TOUCHDOWN PASSES ALLOWED
0—By many teams. Most recent: Dayton, 1980 (11 games)

LOWEST PASSING EFFICIENCY RATING POINTS ALLOWED OPPONENTS
(Min. 150 atts.) 27.8—Plymouth St., 1982 (allowed 170 attempts, 53 completions, 488 yards, 1 TD & intercepted 25 passes)
(Min. 275 atts.) 43.1—Plymouth St., 1987 (allowed 281 attempts, 94 completions, 919 yards, 6 TDs & intercepted 35 passes)

Punting

MOST OPPONENT'S PUNTS BLOCKED BY
11—Ill. Benedictine, 1987 (78 punts against in 10 games). Blocked 17 punts in 18 games during 1987-88, resulting in 5 TDs and 3 safeties

Scoring

FEWEST POINTS ALLOWED PER GAME
3.4—Millsaps, 1980 (31 in 9)

FEWEST TOUCHDOWNS ALLOWED
4—Baldwin-Wallace, 1981 (10 games); Millsaps, 1980 (9 games); Bentley, 1990 (8 games)

MOST SHUTOUTS
6—Cortland St., 1989; Plymouth St., 1982 (consecutive)

MOST CONSECUTIVE SHUTOUTS
6—Plymouth St., 1982

MOST POINTS ALLOWED PER GAME
59.1—Macalester, 1977 (532 in 9; 76 TDs, 64 PATs, 4 FGs)

MOST DEFENSIVE EXTRA-POINT ATTEMPTS BY OPPONENTS
5—Norwich, 1992 (4 blocked kick returns, 1 interception; none scored)

Turnovers (Takeaways)

(Opponent's Passes Intercepted and Fumbles Recovered, From 1985)

HIGHEST MARGIN OF TURNOVERS PER GAME OVER OPPONENTS
2.9—Macalester, 1986 (29 in 10; 29 giveaways vs. 58 takeaways)

MOST TAKEAWAYS
58—Macalester, 1986 (28 interceptions, 30 fumbles gained)
Also holds per-game record at 5.8 (58 in 10)

Additional Records

MOST CONSECUTIVE VICTORIES
37—Augustana (Ill.) (from Sept. 17, 1983, through 1985 Division III playoffs; ended with 0-0 tie vs. Elmhurst, Sept. 13, 1986)

MOST CONSECUTIVE REGULAR-SEASON VICTORIES
49—Augustana (Ill.) (from Oct. 25, 1980, through 1985; ended with 0-0 tie vs. Elmhurst, Sept. 13, 1986)

MOST CONSECUTIVE GAMES WITHOUT DEFEAT
60—Augustana (Ill.), (from Sept. 17, 1983, through Nov. 22, 1987; ended with 38-36 loss to Dayton, Nov. 29, 1987, in Division III playoffs and included one tie)

MOST CONSECUTIVE REGULAR-SEASON GAMES WITHOUT DEFEAT
70—Augustana (Ill.) (from Oct. 25, 1980, through Oct. 1, 1988; ended with 24-21 loss to Carroll, Wis., Oct. 8, 1988)

MOST CONSECUTIVE WINNING SEASONS
34—Wittenberg (from 1955 through 1988; ended with 4-5 record in 1989)

MOST CONSECUTIVE GAMES WITHOUT BEING SHUT OUT
205—Carnegie Mellon (current from Sept. 30, 1972)

MOST CONSECUTIVE LOSSES
50—Macalester (from Oct. 5, 1974, to Nov. 10, 1979; ended with 17-14 win over Mount Senario, Sept. 6, 1980)

MOST CONSECUTIVE GAMES WITHOUT A TIE
371—Widener (from Oct. 29, 1949, to Nov. 11, 1989; ended with 14-14 tie against Gettysburg, Sept. 8, 1990)

HIGHEST-SCORING TIE GAME
40-40—Wagner & Montclair St., Sept. 11, 1982

LAST SCORELESS TIE GAME
Oct. 4, 1986—Delaware Valley & Moravian

MOST CONSECUTIVE QUARTERS WITHOUT YIELDING A TOUCHDOWN BY RUSHING
61—Augustana (Ill.) (in 16 games from Sept. 27, 1986, to Nov. 7, 1987; 77 including four 1986 Division III playoff games); Union (N.Y.) (in 16 games from Oct. 23, 1982, to Sept. 29, 1984)

MOST CONSECUTIVE QUARTERS WITHOUT YIELDING A TOUCHDOWN BY PASSING
44—Swarthmore (from Oct. 31, 1981, to Nov. 13, 1982)

MOST IMPROVED WON-LOST RECORD (Including Postseason Games)
7 games—Susquehanna, 1986 (11-1-0) from 1985 (3-7-0); Maryville (Tenn.), 1976 (7-2-0) from 1975 (0-9-0)

Carnegie Mellon fullback Brian Horton (32) rushed for 13 touchdowns in 1993, helping the Tartans extend to 205 their record for consecutive games without being shut out.

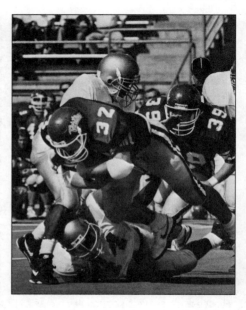

Annual Champions, All-Time Leaders

Total Offense

CAREER YARDS PER GAME

Player, Team	Years	G	Plays	Yards	Yd. PG
Kirk Baumgartner, Wis.-Stevens Point .	1986-89	41	*2,007	*12,767	*311.4
Willie Reyna, La Verne	1991-92	17	551	4,996	293.9
Keith Bishop, Ill. Wesleyan/ Wheaton (Ill.)................................	1981, 83-85	31	1,467	9,052	292.0
Jordan Poznick, Principia	1990-93	32	1,757	8,983	280.7
John Rooney, Ill. Wesleyan	1982-84	27	1,260	7,393	273.8
Tim Peterson, Wis.-Stout...................	1986-89	36	1,558	9,701	269.5
Jim Ballard, Wilmington (Ohio)/ Mount Union	1990, 91-93	40	1,328	10,545	263.6
Robert Farra, Claremont-M-S	1978-79	16	690	4,179	261.2
Dennis Bogacz, Wis.-Oshkosh/ Wis.-Whitewater	1988-89, 90-91	38	1,394	8,850	232.9
John Clark, Wis.-Eau Claire	1987-90	38	1,354	8,838	232.6
Tom Stallings, St. Thomas (Minn.)	1990-93	24	819	5,460	227.5
Mark Peterson, Neb. Wesleyan.........	1982-84	28	1,151	6,367	227.4
Scott Scesney, St. John's (N.Y.).........	1986-89	32	1,048	7,196	224.9
Rob Bristow, Pomona-Pitzer	1983-86	29	1,290	6,465	222.9
Dave Geissler, Wis.-Stevens Point	1982-85	42	1,695	8,990	214.0
Jeff Beer, Bethany (W.Va.)	1978-80	25	878	5,228	209.1
John Love, North Park......................	1988-90	27	1,182	5,613	207.9
Seamus Crotty, Hamilton..................	1982-85	31	1,225	6,402	206.5
Jeff Voris, DePauw.........................	1986-89	28	993	5,754	205.5
Matt Jozokos, Plymouth St	1987-90	40	1,234	8,188	204.7
Steve Osterberger, Drake.................	1987-90	37	1,263	7,520	203.2
Tim Tully, Wheaton (Ill.)	1989-92	33	1,064	6,669	202.1
Marty Barrett, Buffalo......................	1980-82	32	1,280	6,466	202.1

*Record.

SEASON YARDS PER GAME

Player, Team	Year	G	Plays	Yards	Yd. PG
Keith Bishop, Wheaton (Ill.)	†1983	9	421	3,193	*354.8
Kirk Baumgartner, Wis.-Stevens Point	†1989	10	530	3,540	354.0
Kirk Baumgartner, Wis.-Stevens Point	†1988	11	604	*3,790	344.5
Jordan Poznick, Principia	†1992	8	519	2,747	343.4
Jordan Poznick, Principia	†1993	8	488	2,705	338.1
Kirk Baumgartner, Wis.-Stevens Point	1987	11	561	3,712	337.5
Jim Ballard, Mount Union	1993	10	372	3,371	337.1
Steve Austin, Mass.-Boston	1992	9	466	3,003	333.7
Willie Reyna, La Verne	†1991	8	220	2,633	329.1
Keith Bishop, Wheaton (Ill.)	†1985	9	521	2,951	327.9
Tim Peterson, Wis.-Stout	1989	10	*614	3,244	324.4
Tom Stallings, St. Thomas (Minn.)	1993	10	438	3,158	315.8
Scott Isphording, Hanover	1992	10	484	3,150	315.0
Keith Bishop, Wheaton (Ill.)	†1984	9	479	2,777	308.6
Rhory Moss, Hofstra	†1990	9	372	2,775	308.3
Bill Lech, Coe	1989	9	404	2,743	304.8
Robert Farra, Claremont-M-S........................	†1978	9	427	2,685	298.3
Rob Shippy, Concordia (Ill.)	1985	9	370	2,682	298.0
Brett Butler, Wabash	1989	9	449	2,666	296.2
Dennis Bogacz, Wis.-Oshkosh	1989	10	417	2,939	293.9

*Record. †National champion.

CAREER YARDS

Player, Team	Years	Plays	Yards
Kirk Baumgartner, Wis.-Stevens Point....................	1986-89	*2,007	*12,767
Jim Ballard, Wilmington (Ohio)/Mount Union	1990, 91-93	1,328	10,545
Tim Peterson, Wis.-Stout	1986-89	1,558	9,701
Keith Bishop, Ill. Wesleyan/Wheaton (Ill.).............	1981, 83-85	1,467	9,052
Dave Geissler, Wis.-Stevens Point.........................	1982-85	1,695	8,990
Jordan Poznick, Principia...................................	1990-93	1,757	8,983
Dennis Bogacz, Wis.-Oshkosh/Wis.-Whitewater ...	1988-89, 90-91	1,394	8,850
John Clark, Wis.-Eau Claire.................................	1987-90	1,354	8,838
Matt Jozokos, Plymouth St.................................	1987-90	1,234	8,188
Darryl Kosut, William Penn	1983-86	1,583	7,817
Luke Hanks, Otterbein......................................	1990-93	1,503	7,686
Steve Osterberger, Drake..................................	1987-90	1,263	7,520
David Parker, Bishop..	1981-84	1,257	7,516
John Koz, Baldwin-Wallace	1990-93	1,171	7,511
John Rooney, Ill. Wesleyan................................	1982-84	1,260	7,393
Larry Barretta, Lycoming	1983-86	1,205	7,320
John Wortham, Earlham....................................	1989-92	1,574	7,296
Shane Fulton, Heidelberg	1983-86	1,344	7,203
Scott Scesney, St. John's (N.Y.)	1986-89	1,048	7,196
Ron Devorsky, Hiram	1984-87	1,178	7,059
Ed Dougherty, Lycoming	1988-91	1,320	7,055
Craig Solomon, Rhodes.....................................	1975-78	1,261	7,055
Chris Spriggs, Denison	1983-86	1,219	7,047
Bill Hyland, Iona...	1989-92	1,240	7,041
Gary Collier, Emory & Henry..............................	1984-87	1,089	7,036
Clay Sampson, Denison	1977-80	1,225	6,920

*Record.

SEASON YARDS

Player, Team	Year	G	Plays	Yards
Kirk Baumgartner, Wis.-Stevens Point..........................	†1988	11	604	*3,790
Kirk Baumgartner, Wis.-Stevens Point..........................	1987	11	561	3,712
Kirk Baumgartner, Wis.-Stevens Point..........................	†1989	10	530	3,540
Jim Ballard, Mount Union	1993	10	372	3,371
Tim Peterson, Wis.-Stout......................................	1989	10	*614	3,244
Keith Bishop, Wheaton (Ill.)	†1983	9	421	3,193
Tom Stallings, St. Thomas (Minn.).............................	1993	10	438	3,158
Scott Isphording, Hanover	1992	10	484	3,150
Tim Peterson, Wis.-Stout......................................	1987	11	393	3,052
Steve Austin, Mass.-Boston	1992	9	466	3,003
Keith Bishop, Wheaton (Ill.)	†1985	9	521	2,951
Dennis Bogacz, Wis.-Oshkosh	1989	10	417	2,939
Brion Demski, Wis.-Stevens Point	†1981	10	503	2,895
Larry Barretta, Lycoming	†1986	10	453	2,875
Shane Fulton, Heidelberg	1985	10	485	2,858
Mark Peterson, Neb. Wesleyan...............................	1983	10	425	2,846
Leroy Williams, Upsala	1992	10	476	2,822
Keith Bishop, Wheaton (Ill.)	†1984	9	479	2,777
Rhory Moss, Hofstra	†1990	9	372	2,775
Dave Geissler, Wis.-Stevens Point............................	1985	11	456	2,756

*Record. †National champion.

SINGLE-GAME YARDS

Yds.	Player, Team (Opponent)	Date
596	John Love, North Park (Elmhurst) ....Oct. 13, 1990	
590	Tom Stallings, St. Thomas, Minn. (Bethel, Minn.) ......Nov. 13, 1993	
564	Tim Lynch, Hofstra (Fordham)...........................Oct. 19, 1991	
538	Jordan Poznick, Principia (Blackburn) ....Oct. 10, 1992	
534	Cliff Scott, Buffalo (New Haven) ....Sept. 12, 1992	
528	Steve Austin, Mass.-Boston (Mass. Maritime) ....Oct. 10, 1992	
527	Rob Shippy, Concordia, Ill. (Concordia, Wis.) ....Oct. 5, 1985	
515	Seamus Crotty, Hamilton (Middlebury) ....Oct. 27, 1984	
512	Bob Monroe, Knox (Cornell College) ....Oct. 11, 1986	
511	Kirk Baumgartner, Wis.-Stevens Point (Wis.-Superior) ....Nov. 4, 1989	
511	Kirk Baumgartner, Wis.-Stevens Point (Wis.-Stout) ....Oct. 24, 1987	
509	Michael Ferraro, LIU-C. W. Post (Alfred) ....Nov. 14, 1992	
509	Craig Solomon, Rhodes (Rose-Hulman) ....Nov. 11, 1978	
507	George Beisel, Hofstra (LIU-C. W. Post) ....Sept. 28, 1991	
506	Todd Coolidge, Susquehanna (Muhlenberg) ....Sept. 12, 1987	
504	Jeff Hagan, Coast Guard (Trinity, Conn.)...............Oct. 26, 1985	

ANNUAL CHAMPIONS

Year	Player, Team	Class	G	Plays	Yards	Avg.
1973	Bob Dulich, San Diego	Jr.	11	340	2,543	231.2
1974	Larry Cenotto, Pomona-Pitzer	Sr.	9	436	2,127	236.3
1975	Ricky Haygood, Millsaps	Jr.	9	332	2,176	241.8
1976	Rollie Wiebers, Buena Vista	So.	9	353	2,198	244.2
1977	Tom Hamilton, Occidental.....................	Sr.	9	358	2,050	227.8
1978	Robert Farra, Claremont-M-S	Jr.	9	427	2,685	298.3
1979	Clay Sampson, Denison	Jr.	9	412	2,255	250.6
1980	Jeff Beer, Bethany (W.Va.)	Sr.	9	372	2,331	259.0
1981	Brion Demski, Wis.-Stevens Point	Sr.	10	503	2,895	289.5
1982	Dave McCarrell, Wheaton (Ill.)..............	Sr.	9	387	2,503	278.1
1983	Keith Bishop, Wheaton (Ill.)	So.	9	421	3,193	*354.8
1984	Keith Bishop, Wheaton (Ill.)	Jr.	9	479	2,777	308.6
1985	Keith Bishop, Wheaton (Ill.)	Sr.	9	521	2,951	327.9
1986	Larry Barretta, Lycoming	Sr.	10	453	2,875	287.5
1987	Todde Greenough, Willamette	Jr.	9	436	2,567	285.2
1988	Kirk Baumgartner, Wis.-Stevens Point	Jr.	11	604	*3,790	344.5
1989	Kirk Baumgartner, Wis.-Stevens Point	Sr.	10	530	3,540	354.0
1990	Rhory Moss, Hofstra	Jr.	9	372	2,775	308.3
1991	Willie Reyna, La Verne	Jr.	8	220	2,633	329.1
1992	Jordan Poznick, Principia	Jr.	8	519	2,747	343.4
1993	Jordan Poznick, Principia	Sr.	8	488	2,705	338.1

*Record.

DIVISION III

Rushing

CAREER YARDS PER GAME

Player, Team	Years	G	Plays	Yards	Yd. PG
Kirk Matthieu, Maine Maritime	$1989-93	33	964	5,107	*154.8
Terry Underwood, Wagner	1985-88	33	742	5,010	151.8
Anthony Russo, St. John's (N.Y.)	1990-93	41	*1,152	*5,834	142.3
Joe Dudek, Plymouth St.	1982-85	41	785	5,570	135.9
Eric Frees, Western Md.	1988-91	40	1,059	5,281	132.0
Heath Butler, N'western (Wis.)	1990-93	31	767	4,000	129.0
Rich Kowalski, Hobart	1972-75	36	907	4,631	128.6
Peter Gorniewicz, Colby	1971-74	32	1,024	4,113	128.5
Scott Reppert, Lawrence	1979-82	33	757	4,211	127.6
Chris Babirad, Wash. & Jeff.	1989-92	35	683	4,419	126.3
Steve Dixon, Beloit	1990-93	38	986	4,792	126.1
Tim Barrett, John Carroll	1972-74	29	662	3,621	124.9

*Record. $See page 6 for explanation.

SEASON YARDS PER GAME

Player, Team	Years	G	Plays	Yards	TD	Yd. PG
Ricky Gales, Simpson	†1989	10	297	*2,035	26	*203.5
Terry Underwood, Wagner	†1988	9	245	1,809	21	201.0
Kirk Matthieu, Maine Maritime	†1992	9	327	1,733	16	192.6
Jon Warga, Wittenberg	†1990	10	254	1,836	15	183.6
Hank Wineman, Albion	†1991	9	307	1,629	14	181.0
Eric Grey, Hamilton	1991	8	217	1,439	13	179.9
Mike Birosak, Dickinson	1989	10	*380	1,798	18	179.8
Chris Babirad, Wash. & Jeff.	1992	9	243	1,589	22	176.6
Carey Bender, Coe	†1993	10	261	1,718	15	171.8
Heath Butler, N'western (Wis.)	1993	8	236	1,371	15	171.4
Clay Sampson, Denison	†1979	9	323	1,517	13	168.6
Anthony Russo, St. John's (N.Y.)	1991	10	287	1,685	18	168.5
Chris Babirad, Wash. & Jeff.	1991	9	224	1,508	18	167.6
John Bernatavitz, Dickinson	1990	10	266	1,666	15	166.6
Billy Johnson, Widener	†1973	9	168	1,494	21	166.0
Scott Reppert, Lawrence	†1982	8	254	1,323	14	165.4
Chris Dabrow, Claremont-M-S	†1987	9	265	1,486	13	165.1
Don Dawson, Ripon	1993	9	214	1,482	16	164.7
Wes Stearns, Merchant Marine	1992	9	247	1,477	12	164.1

*Record. †National champion.

CAREER YARDS

Player, Team	Years	Plays	Yards	Avg.
Anthony Russo, St. John's (N.Y.)	1990-93	*1,152	*5,834	5.06
Joe Dudek, Plymouth St.	1982-85	785	5,570	‡7.10
Eric Frees, Western Md.	1988-91	1,059	5,281	4.99
Kirk Matthieu, Maine Maritime	$1989-93	964	5,107	5.30
Terry Underwood, Wagner	1985-88	742	5,010	6.75
Steve Dixon, Beloit	1990-93	986	4,792	4.86
Mike Birosak, Dickinson	1986-89	1,112	4,662	4.19
Rich Kowalski, Hobart	1972-75	907	4,631	5.11
Jim Romagna, Loras	1989-92	983	4,493	4.57
Chris Babirad, Wash. & Jeff.	1989-92	683	4,419	6.47
Willie Beers, John Carroll	1989-92	848	4,332	5.11
Frank Baker, Chicago	1990-93	855	4,283	5.01
Remon Smith, Randolph-Macon	1984-87	737	4,249	5.77
Chris Spriggs, Denison	1983-86	787	4,248	5.40
Scott Reppert, Lawrence	1979-82	757	4,211	5.56
Alonzo Patterson, Wagner	1979-82	816	4,177	5.12
Von Cummings, Defiance	1989-92	810	4,131	5.10
Peter Gorniewicz, Colby	1971-74	1,024	4,113	4.02
Bryce Tuohy, Heidelberg	1986-89	905	4,067	4.49
Ricky Gales, Nebraska-Omaha/Simpson	1986-87, 88-89	701	4,061	5.79
Brian Grandison, Wooster	1988-91	899	4,042	4.50
Jay Wessler, Illinois Col.	1977-80	807	4,016	4.98
Sandy Rogers, Emory & Henry	1983-86	641	4,005	6.25
Heath Butler, N'western (Wis.)	1990-93	767	4,000	5.22
Jody Stoldt, Muskingum	1990-93	902	3,969	4.40

*Record. $See page 6 for explanation. ‡Record for minimum 500 carries.

SEASON YARDS

Player, Team	Year	G	Plays	Yards	Avg.
Ricky Gales, Simpson	†1989	10	297	*2,035	6.85
Jon Warga, Wittenberg	†1990	10	254	1,836	7.23
Terry Underwood, Wagner	†1988	9	245	1,809	6.75
Mike Birosak, Dickinson	1989	10	*380	1,798	4.73
Kirk Matthieu, Maine Maritime	†1992	9	327	1,733	5.30
Sandy Rogers, Emory & Henry	†1986	11	231	1,730	+7.49
Carey Bender, Coe	†1993	10	261	1,718	6.58
Anthony Russo, St. John's (N.Y.)	†1991	10	287	1,685	5.87
John Bernatavitz, Dickinson	1990	10	266	1,666	6.26
Hank Wineman, Albion	1991	9	307	1,629	5.31
Gary Trettel, St. Thomas (Minn.)	1990	10	293	1,620	5.53
Joe Dudek, Plymouth St.	†1985	11	216	1,615	7.48
Ronnie Howard, Bridgewater (Va.)	1993	10	281	1,610	5.73
Frank Baker, Chicago	1993	10	281	1,606	5.72
Eric Frees, Western Md.	1990	10	295	1,594	5.40
Chris Babirad, Wash. & Jeff.	1992	9	243	1,589	6.54
George Rainey, Wis.-Whitewater	1987	11	279	1,567	5.62
Rob Johnson, Western Md.	1992	10	330	1,560	4.73
Jimmy Henderson, Wis.-Stevens Point	1993	10	261	1,556	5.96
Eric Frees, Western Md.	1991	10	304	1,545	5.08

*Record. †National champion. +Record for minimum 195 carries.

SINGLE-GAME YARDS

Yds.	Player, Team (Opponent)	Date
417	Carey Bender, Coe (Grinnell)	Oct. 9, 1993
382	Pete Baranek, Carthage (North Central)	Oct. 5, 1985
363	Terry Underwood, Wagner (Hofstra)	Oct. 15, 1988
354	Terry Underwood, Wagner (Western Conn. St.)	Oct. 3, 1986
347	Chuck Wotkowicz, Johns Hopkins (Georgetown)	Oct. 22, 1993
342	Dave Bednarek, Wis.-River Falls (Wis.-Stevens Point)	Oct. 29, 1983
337	Kirk Matthieu, Maine Maritime (Curry)	Oct. 27, 1990
337	Ted Helsel, St. Francis, Pa. (Gallaudet)	Nov. 3, 1979
334	Oliver Bridges, Stony Brook (Pace)	Nov. 16, 1991
329	Don Williams, Lowell (Colby)	Oct. 4, 1985
326	Mike Krueger, Tufts (Amherst)	Oct. 25, 1980
321	Jack Davis, Hobart (Brockport St.)	Nov. 5, 1977
317	Greg Novarro, Bentley (St. John's, N.Y.)	Nov. 14, 1992
314	Anthony Russo, St. John's, N.Y. (Georgetown)	Nov. 7, 1992
313	Pedro Arruza, Wheaton, Ill. (North Central)	Oct. 30, 1993
312	Don Taylor, Central, Iowa (Dubuque)	Oct. 9, 1976
311	Jason Wooley, Worcester Tech (MIT)	Nov. 10, 1990
311	Mike Birosak, Dickinson (Gettysburg)	Nov. 4, 1989
311	Roy Heffernan, Middlebury (Worcester Tech)	Oct. 4, 1975

ANNUAL CHAMPIONS

Year	Player, Team	Class	G	Plays	Yards	Avg.
1973	Billy Johnson, Widener	Sr.	9	168	1,494	166.0
1974	Tim Barrett, John Carroll	Sr.	9	256	1,409	156.6
1975	Ron Baker, Monmouth (Ill.)	Sr.	8	200	1,116	139.5
1976	Chuck Evans, Ferris St.	Jr.	10	224	1,509	150.9
1977	Don Taylor, Central (Iowa)	Sr.	9	267	1,329	147.7
1978	Dino Hall, Rowan	Sr.	10	239	1,330	133.0
1979	Clay Sampson, Denison	Jr.	9	323	1,517	168.6
1980	Scott Reppert, Lawrence	So.	8	223	1,223	152.9
1981	Scott Reppert, Lawrence	Jr.	9	250	1,410	156.7
1982	Scott Reppert, Lawrence	Sr.	8	254	1,323	165.4
1983	John Franco, Wagner	Sr.	8	175	1,166	145.8
1984	Gary Errico, Mass.-Lowell	Sr.	9	165	1,404	156.0
1985	Bruce Montella, Chicago	Sr.	9	265	1,372	152.4
1986	Sandy Rogers, Emory & Henry	Sr.	11	231	1,730	157.3
1987	Chris Dabrow, Claremont-M-S	Sr.	9	265	1,486	165.1
1988	Terry Underwood, Wagner	Sr.	9	245	1,809	201.0
1989	Ricky Gales, Simpson	Sr.	10	297	*2,035	*203.5
1990	Jon Warga, Wittenberg	Sr.	10	254	1,836	183.6
1991	Hank Wineman, Albion	Sr.	9	307	1,629	181.0
1992	Kirk Matthieu, Maine Maritime	Jr.	9	327	1,733	192.6
1993	Carey Bender, Coe	Sr.	10	261	1,718	171.8

*Record.

Passing

CAREER PASSING EFFICIENCY
(Minimum 325 Completions)

Player, Team	Years	Att.	Cmp.	Int.	Pct.	Yards	TD	Pts.
Jim Ballard, Wilmington (Ohio)/Mount Union	1990, 91-93	1,199	743	41	.620	10,379	*115	*159.5
Joe Blake, Simpson	1987-90	672	399	15	.594	6,183	43	153.3
Willie Reyna, La Verne	1991-92	542	346	19	.638	4,712	37	152.4
Gary Collier, Emory & Henry	1984-87	738	386	33	.523	6,103	80	148.6
John Koz, Baldwin-Wallace	1990-93	981	609	28	.621	7,724	71	146.4
Greg Heeres, Hope	1981-84	630	347	21	.537	5,120	53	144.4
Ed Hesson, Rowan	1990-93	895	504	26	.563	7,035	67	141.2
Bruce Crosthwaite, Adrian	1984-87	618	368	31	.596	4,959	45	141.0
Matt Jozokos, Plymouth St.	1987-90	1,003	527	39	.525	7,658	95	140.2
Joe Coviello, Frank. & Marsh.	1973-76	591	334	36	.565	4,651	52	139.5
John Clark, Wis.-Eau Claire	1987-90	1,119	645	42	.576	9,196	63	137.7
Joe Shield, Trinity (Conn.)	1981-84	845	476	39	.563	6,646	52	133.5
David Broecker, Wabash	1979-82	633	369	45	.583	4,895	45	132.5
Dick Puccio, Cortland St.	1988-91	727	451	34	.501	5,301	40	131.9
Mike Culver, Juniata	1983-86	756	406	41	.537	5,799	56	131.7
Robb Disbennett, Salisbury St.	1982-85	633	359	40	.567	5,023	40	131.6
Kirk Baumgartner, Wis.-Stevens Point	1986-89	*1,696	*883	57	.521	*13,028	110	131.3
Walter Briggs, Montclair St.	1983-86	832	417	36	.501	6,489	59	130.4
Brian Cox, Beloit	1988-91	620	337	43	.544	4,641	50	130.0
Randy Muetzel, St. Thomas (Minn.)	1979-82	613	339	20	.553	4,462	36	129.3
Larry Barretta, Lycoming	1983-86	732	361	26	.493	5,345	57	129.3
Ed Dougherty, Lycoming	1988-91	1,025	589	47	.575	7,108	69	128.7
Keith Bishop, Ill. Wesleyan/Wheaton (Ill.)	1981, 83-85	1,311	772	65	.589	9,579	71	128.2
Kevin King, Ripon	1978-81	635	348	43	.548	5,029	39	128.1

*Record.

Jim Ballard finished his collegiate career at Mount Union last season with the Division III record for career passing efficiency (159.5). His 1993 rating of 193.2 is a single-season record for passers with a minimum of 25 attempts per game.

SEASON PASSING EFFICIENCY
(Minimum 15 Attempts Per Game)

Player, Team	Year	G	Att.	Cmp.	Int.	Pct.	Yards	TD	Pts.
Willie Seiler, St. John's (Minn.)	†1993	10	205	141	6	.687	2,648	33	*224.6
Jim Ballard, Mount Union	1993	10	314	229	11	*.729	3,304	37	‡193.2
Mitch Sanders, Bridgeport	1973	10	151	84	7	.556	1,551	23	182.9
Pat Mayew, St. John's (Minn.)	†1991	9	247	154	4	.623	2,408	30	181.0
Guy Simons, Coe	1993	10	185	110	9	.594	1,979	21	177.1
Jimbo Fisher, Samford	†1987	10	252	139	5	.551	2,394	34	175.4
Gary Collier, Emory & Henry	1987	11	249	152	10	.610	2,317	33	174.8
James Grant, Ramapo	1989	9	147	91	7	.619	1,441	17	172.7
Gary Urwiler, Eureka	1991	10	171	103	5	.602	1,656	18	170.3
Steve Keller, Dayton	†1992	10	153	99	5	.647	1,350	17	168.9
Robb Disbennett, Salisbury St.	†1985	10	153	94	6	.614	1,462	16	168.4
Chris Conkling, Anderson	1993	10	185	127	3	.686	1,788	12	168.0
Scott Scesney, St. John's (N.Y.)	1989	10	244	131	9	.536	2,314	31	167.8
Jim Ballard, Mount Union	1992	10	292	186	8	.637	2,656	29	167.4
Chuck Hooker, Cornell College	1985	9	186	108	10	.581	1,818	21	166.7
Steve Varley, St. John's (Minn.)	1989	9	162	106	8	.654	1,476	16	164.6
Brad Forsyth, Ill. Wesleyan	1989	9	159	100	4	.628	1,380	16	163.9
Cody Dearing, Randolph-Macon	†1984	10	226	125	12	.553	2,139	27	163.4
Paul Foye, Amherst	1985	8	133	87	7	.654	1,161	14	163.0
Matt Dillon, Cornell College	1978	9	166	98	7	.590	1,567	16	161.7

*Record. †National champion. ‡Record for minimum 25 attempts per game.

CAREER YARDS

Player, Team	Years	Att.	Cmp.	Int.	Pct.	Yards	TD
Kirk Baumgartner, Wis.-Stevens Point	1986-89	*1,696	*883	57	.521	*13,028	110
Jim Ballard, Wilmington (Ohio)/Mount Union	1990, 91-93	1,199	743	41	.620	10,379	*115
Keith Bishop, Ill. Wesleyan/Wheaton (Ill.)	1981, 83-85	1,311	772	65	.589	9,579	71
Dennis Bogacz, Wis.-Oshkosh/Wis.-Whitewater	1988-89, 90-91	1,275	654	59	.513	9,536	66
Dave Geissler, Wis.-Stevens Point	1982-85	1,346	789	57	.586	9,518	65
John Clark, Wis.-Eau Claire	1987-90	1,119	645	42	.576	9,196	63
Tim Peterson, Wis.-Stout	1986-89	1,185	653	62	.551	8,881	59
Jordan Poznick, Principia	1990-93	1,480	765	68	.517	8,485	55
John Koz, Baldwin-Wallace	1990-93	981	609	28	.621	7,724	71
Luke Hanks, Otterbein	1990-93	1,267	715	62	.564	7,718	47
Matt Jozokos, Plymouth St.	1987-90	1,003	527	39	.525	7,658	95
Bill Hyland, Iona	1989-92	1,017	511	55	.502	7,382	57
Shane Fulton, Heidelberg	1983-86	1,024	587	55	.573	7,372	50
Paul Brandenburg, Ripon	1984-87	1,181	607	66	.514	7,320	39
Craig Solomon, Rhodes	1975-78	1,022	542	70	.530	7,314	71
Rob Bristow, Pomona-Pitzer	1983-86	1,155	628	60	.544	7,120	27
Ed Dougherty, Lycoming	1988-91	1,025	589	47	.575	7,108	69
Ed Hesson, Rowan	1990-93	895	504	26	.563	7,035	67
Steve Osterberger, Drake	1987-90	981	536	33	.546	7,021	53
Ron Devorsky, Hiram	1984-87	1,028	542	59	.527	7,012	50

Kirk Baumgartner set numerous collegiate passing marks during his career at Wisconsin-Stevens Point, including career yards (13,028), career yards per game (317.8), season yards (3,828 in 1988) and season yards per game (369.2 in 1989).

Player, Team	Years	Att.	Cmp.	Int.	Pct.	Yards	TD
Gary Walljasper, Wartburg	1981-84	974	521	50	.535	6,992	49
Marty Barrett, Buffalo	1980-83	956	513	53	.537	6,945	44
David Parker, Bishop	1981-84	938	378	63	.403	6,934	69
Scott Scesney, St. John's (N.Y.)	1986-89	945	463	44	.490	6,914	72
John Wortham, Earlham	1989-92	1,189	615	74	.517	6,812	38

*Record.

CAREER YARDS PER GAME

Player, Team	Years	G	Att.	Cmp.	Int.	Pct.	Yards	TD	Avg.
Kirk Baumgartner, Wis.-Stevens Point	1986-89	41	*1,696	*883	57	.521	*13,028	110	*317.8
Keith Bishop, Ill. Wesleyan/Wheaton (Ill.).	1981, 83-85	31	1,311	772	65	.589	9,579	71	309.0
Willie Reyna, La Verne	1991-92	17	542	346	19	.638	4,712	37	277.2
Robert Farra, Claremont-M-S	1978-79	16	579	313	24	.541	4,360	31	272.5
Jordan Poznick, Principia	1990-93	32	1,480	765	68	.517	8,485	55	265.2
Jim Ballard, Wilmington (Ohio)/ Mount Union	1990, 91-93	40	1,199	743	41	.620	10,379	*115	259.5
Dennis Bogacz, Wis.-Oshkosh/ Wis.-Whitewater	1988-89, 90-91	38	1,275	654	59	.513	9,536	66	250.9
Tim Peterson, Wis.-Stout	1986-89	36	1,185	653	62	.551	8,881	59	246.7
Rob Bristow, Pomona-Pitzer	1983-86	29	1,155	628	60	.544	7,120	27	245.5
John Rooney, Ill. Wesleyan	1982-84	27	986	489	47	.496	6,576	55	243.6
John Clark, Wis.-Eau Claire	1987-90	38	1,119	645	42	.576	9,196	63	242.0
Tom Stallings, St. Thomas (Minn.)	1990-93	24	726	387	40	.533	5,608	44	233.7
Ed Smith, Ill. Benedictine	1991-93	29	862	456	41	.529	6,734	47	232.2
Dave Geissler, Wis.-Stevens Point	1982-85	42	1,346	789	57	.586	9,518	65	226.6
Scott Scesney, St. John's (N.Y.)	1986-89	32	945	463	44	.490	6,914	72	216.1
Jeff Voris, DePauw	1986-89	28	910	504	25	.554	6,035	56	215.5
Paul Brandenburg, Ripon	1984-87	34	1,181	607	66	.514	7,320	39	215.3

*Record.

SEASON YARDS

Player, Team	Year	G	Att.	Cmp.	Int.	Pct.	Yards	TD
Kirk Baumgartner, Wis.-Stevens Point	1988	11	*527	*276	16	.524	*3,828	25
Kirk Baumgartner, Wis.-Stevens Point	1987	11	466	243	22	.521	3,755	31
Kirk Baumgartner, Wis.-Stevens Point	1989	10	455	247	9	.542	3,692	*39
Jim Ballard, Mount Union	1993	10	314	229	11	*.729	3,304	37
Keith Bishop, Wheaton (Ill.)	1983	9	375	236	19	.629	3,274	24
Tom Stallings, St. Thomas (Minn.)	1993	10	395	219	20	.554	3,210	22
Keith Bishop, Wheaton (Ill.)	1985	9	457	262	22	.573	3,171	25
Scott Isphording, Hanover	1992	10	359	207	19	.576	3,098	24
Dennis Bogacz, Wis.-Oshkosh	1989	10	378	219	18	.579	3,051	18
Steve Austin, Mass.-Boston	1992	9	396	181	25	.457	2,991	29
Keith Bishop, Wheaton (Ill.)	1984	9	440	259	21	.589	2,968	21
Tim Peterson, Wis.-Stout	1989	10	445	256	15	.575	2,956	20
Brion Demski, Wis.-Stevens Point	1981	10	452	222	20	.491	2,889	16
Shane Fulton, Heidelberg	1985	10	393	222	14	.565	2,876	19
Tim Peterson, Wis.-Stout	1987	11	302	180	19	.596	2,871	18
Chris Creighton, Kenyon	1990	10	398	231	18	.580	2,843	29
Kevin Enterlein, Pace	1986	10	427	205	28	.480	2,829	20
John Clark, Wis.-Eau Claire	1989	10	344	199	14	.578	2,785	22
Ed Smith, Ill. Benedictine	1992	10	320	184	16	.575	2,770	25
Robert Farra, Claremont-M-S	†1978	9	359	196	15	.546	2,770	20

*Record. †National champion.

SEASON YARDS PER GAME

Player, Team	Year	G	Att.	Cmp.	Int.	Pct.	Yards	TD	Avg.
Kirk Baumgartner, Wis.-Stevens Point	1989	10	455	247	9	.543	3,692	*39	*369.2
Keith Bishop, Wheaton (Ill.)	1983	9	375	236	19	.629	3,274	24	363.8
Keith Bishop, Wheaton (Ill.)	1985	9	457	262	22	.573	3,171	25	352.3
Kirk Baumgartner, Wis.-Stevens Point	1988	11	*527	*276	16	.524	*3,828	25	348.0
Kirk Baumgartner, Wis.-Stevens Point	1987	11	466	243	22	.521	3,755	31	341.4
Steve Austin, Mass.-Boston	1992	9	396	181	25	.457	2,991	29	332.3
Jim Ballard, Mount Union	1993	10	314	229	11	*.729	3,304	37	330.4
Keith Bishop, Wheaton (Ill.)	1984	9	440	259	21	.589	2,968	21	329.8
Jordan Poznick, Principia	1992	8	451	241	13	.534	2,618	21	327.3
Tom Stallings, St. Thomas (Minn.)	1993	10	395	219	20	.554	3,210	22	321.0
Willie Reyna, La Verne	1991	8	267	170	6	.636	2,543	16	317.9
Scott Isphording, Hanover	1992	10	359	207	19	.576	3,098	24	309.8
Robert Farra, Claremont-M-S	†1978	9	359	196	15	.546	2,770	20	307.8
Dennis Bogacz, Wis.-Oshkosh	1989	10	378	219	18	.580	3,051	18	305.1

*Record. †National champion.

SINGLE-GAME YARDS

Yds.	Player, Team (Opponent)	Date
602	Tom Stallings, St. Thomas, Minn. (Bethel, Minn.)	Nov. 13, 1993
585	Tim Lynch, Hofstra (Fordham)	Oct. 19, 1991
533	John Love, North Park (Elmhurst)	Oct. 13, 1990
532	Bob Monroe, Knox (Cornell College)	Oct. 11, 1986
523	Kirk Baumgartner, Wis.-Stevens Point (Wis.-Stout)	Oct. 24, 1987
513	Craig Solomon, Rhodes (Rose-Hulman)	Nov.11, 1978
509	Bob Krepfle, Wis.-La Crosse (Wis.-River Falls)	Nov. 12, 1983
507	George Beisel, Hofstra (LIU-C. W. Post)	Sept. 28, 1991
506	Keith Bishop, Wheaton, Ill. (Ill. Wesleyan)	Oct. 29, 1983
505	Kirk Baumgartner, Wis.-Stevens Point (Wis.-Superior)	Nov. 4, 1989
504	Jordan Poznick, Principia (Blackburn)	Oct. 10, 1992
504	Rob Shippy, Concordia, Ill. (Concordia, Wis.)	Oct. 5, 1985
503	Dave Detrick, Wis.-Superior (Wis.-Oshkosh)	Sept. 16, 1989
501	Keith Bishop, Wheaton, Ill. (North Park)	Oct. 12, 1985

SINGLE-GAME COMPLETIONS

Cmp.	Player, Team (Opponent)	Date
50	Tim Lynch, Hofstra (Fordham)	Oct. 19, 1991
48	Jordan Poznick, Principia (Blackburn)	Oct. 10, 1992
47	Mike Wallace, Ohio Wesleyan (Denison)	Oct. 3, 1981
42	Tim Lynch, Hofstra (Towson St.)	Nov. 2, 1991
42	Keith Bishop, Wheaton, Ill. (Millikin)	Sept. 14, 1985
41	Michael Doto, Hofstra (Central Conn. St.)	Sept. 14, 1991
41	Todd Monken, Knox (Cornell College)	Oct. 8, 1988
40	Dave Geissler, Wis.-Stevens Point (Wis.-Eau Claire)	Nov. 12, 1983
39	Rob Bristow, Pomona-Pitzer (La Verne)	Oct. 12, 1985
39	Steve Hendry, Wis.-Superior (Wis.-Stevens Point)	Oct. 17, 1981
38	George Beisel, Hofstra vs. Southern Conn. St.	Oct. 9, 1992
38	Jeff Voris, DePauw (Findlay)	Oct. 31, 1987
38	Todde Greenough, Willamette (Southern Ore.)	Sept. 26, 1987
38	Pat Moyer, Maryville, Tenn. (Cumberland)	Oct. 5, 1985

St. John's (Minnesota) quarterback Willie Seiler led Division III in passing in 1993 with an efficiency rating of 224.6, a collegiate record for passers with a minimum of 15 attempts per game.

ANNUAL CHAMPIONS

Year	Player, Team	Class	G	Att.	Cmp.	Avg.	Int.	Pct.	Yds.	TD
1973	Pat Clements, Kenyon	Jr.	9	239	133	14.8	17	.556	1,738	12
1974	Larry Cenotto, Pomona-Pitzer	Sr.	9	294	147	16.3	23	.500	2,024	15
1975	Ron Miller, Elmhurst	Sr.	8	205	118	14.8	15	.576	1,398	7
1976	Tom Hamilton, Occidental	Jr.	8	235	131	16.4	10	.557	1,988	10
1977	Tom Hamilton, Occidental	Sr.	9	323	171	19.0	17	.529	2,132	13
1978	Robert Farra, Claremont-M-S	Jr.	9	359	196	21.8	15	.546	2,770	20

Beginning in 1979, ranked on passing efficiency rating points, minimum 15 attempts per game (instead of per-game completions)

Year	Player, Team	Class	G	Att.	Cmp.	Int.	Pct.	Yds.	TD	Pts.
1979	David Broecker, Wabash	Fr.	9	145	81	9	.559	1,311	13	149.0
1980	George Muller, Hofstra	Sr.	10	189	115	14	.608	1,983	15	160.4
1981	Larry Atwater, Coe	Sr.	9	172	92	10	.535	1,615	15	147.2
1982	Mike Bennett, Cornell College	Sr.	9	154	83	8	.539	1,436	17	158.3
1983	Joe Shield, Trinity (Conn.)	Jr.	8	238	135	13	.567	2,185	19	149.1
1984	Cody Dearing, Randolph-Macon	Sr.	10	226	125	12	.553	2,139	27	163.4
1985	Robb Disbennett, Salisbury St.	Sr.	10	153	94	6	.614	1,462	16	168.4
1986	Gary Collier, Emory & Henry	Jr.	11	171	88	6	.514	1,509	21	158.9
1987	Jimbo Fisher, Samford	Sr.	10	252	139	5	.551	2,394	34	175.4
1988	Steve Flynn, Central (Iowa)	Jr.	8	133	82	6	.616	1,190	10	152.5
1989	Joe Blake, Simpson	††Jr.	10	144	93	3	.645	1,705	19	203.3
1990	Dan Sharley, Dayton	†††Sr.	10	149	95	2	.637	1,377	12	165.1
1991	Pat Mayew, St. John's (Minn.)	Sr.	9	247	154	4	.623	2,408	30	181.0
1992	Steve Keller, Dayton	Sr.	10	153	99	5	.647	1,350	17	168.9
1993	Willie Seiler, St. John's (Minn.)	Sr.	10	205	141	6	.687	2,648	33	*224.6

*Record. ††Declared champion; with six more pass attempts (making 15 per game), all interceptions, still would have highest efficiency (187.3). †††Declared champion; with one more attempt (making 15 per game), an interception, still would have highest efficiency (162.8).

ANNUAL PASSING EFFICIENCY LEADERS BEFORE 1979
(Minimum 15 Attempts Per Game)

Year	Player, Team	G	Att.	Cmp.	Int.	Pct.	Yds.	TD	Pts.
1973	Mitch Sanders, Bridgeport	10	151	84	7	.556	1,551	23	182.9
1974	Tom McGuire, Ill. Benedictine	10	221	142	16	.643	2,206	16	157.5
1975	Jim Morrow, Wash. & Jeff.	9	137	82	7	.599	1,283	11	154.8
1976	Aaron Van Dyke, Cornell College	9	154	91	12	.591	1,611	14	161.4
1977	Matt Winslow, Middlebury	8	130	79	5	.608	919	17	155.6
1978	Matt Dillon, Cornell College	9	166	98	7	.590	1,567	16	161.7

DIVISION III

Receiving

CAREER CATCHES PER GAME

Player, Team	Years	G	Rec.	Yards	TD	Rec.PG
Matt Newton, Principia	1990-93	33	*287	3,646	32	*8.7
Bill Stromberg, Johns Hopkins	1978-81	36	258	3,776	39	7.2
Tim McNamara, Trinity (Conn.)	1981-84	21	146	2,313	19	7.0
Ron Severance, Otterbein	1989-91	30	207	2,378	17	6.9
Chuck Braun, Wis.-Stevens Point	1980-81	18	124	1,914	19	6.9
Jim Jorden, Wheaton (Ill.)	1982-85	33	225	3,022	22	6.8
Mike Whitehouse, St. Norbert	1986-89	35	230	3,480	37	6.6
Dan Daley, Pomona-Pitzer	1985-88	35	227	2,598	10	6.5
Rich Johnson, Pace	1985-87	29	188	2,614	8	6.5
Chris Bisaillon, Ill. Wesleyan	1989-92	36	223	3,670	*55	6.2
Rick Fry, Occidental	1974-77	33	200	3,073	18	6.1
Mike Funk, Wabash	1985, 87-89	38	228	2,858	33	6.0
Scott Faessler, Framingham St.	1989-92	34	201	2,121	8	5.9
Ted Taggart, Kenyon	1988-90	28	165	2,034	20	5.9
Pat McNamara, Trinity (Conn.)	1977-79	24	141	2,280	20	5.9
Theo Blanco, Wis.-Stevens Point	1985-88	38	223	3,139	18	5.9
Dale Amos, Frank. & Marsh.	1986-89	40	233	*3,846	35	5.8
Scott Fredrickson, Wis.-Stout	1986-89	40	233	3,390	23	5.8

*Record.

SEASON CATCHES PER GAME

Player, Team	Year	G	Rec.	Yards	TD	Rec.PG
Matt Newton, Principia	†1992	8	98	1,487	14	*12.3
Matt Newton, Principia	†1993	8	96	1,080	11	12.0
Sean Munroe, Mass.-Boston	1992	9	95	*1,693	17	10.6
Scott Faessler, Framingham St.	†1990	9	92	916	5	10.2
Mike Funk, Wabash	†1989	9	87	1,169	12	9.7
Jim Jorden, Wheaton (Ill.)	†1985	9	87	1,011	8	9.7
Theo Blanco, Wis.-Stevens Point	1987	11	*106	1,616	8	9.6
Rick Fry, Occidental	†1976	8	74	1,214	8	9.3
Ron Severance, Otterbein	1990	10	92	1,049	8	9.2
Rick Fry, Occidental	†1977	9	82	1,222	5	9.1
Jim Myers, Kenyon	†1974	9	82	1,483	12	9.1
Bob Glanville, Lewis & Clark	1985	9	80	1,054	9	8.9
Ed Brady, Ill. Wesleyan	†1983	9	80	873	7	8.9
John Tucci, Amherst	†1986	8	70	1,025	8	8.8
Greg Lehrer, Heidelberg	1993	10	87	1,202	8	8.7
Ted Taggart, Kenyon	1989	10	87	1,004	7	8.7

*Record. †National champion.

CAREER CATCHES

Player, Team	Years	Rec.	Yards	TD
Matt Newton, Principia	1990-93	*287	3,646	32
Bill Stromberg, Johns Hopkins	1978-81	258	3,776	39
Dale Amos, Frank. & Marsh.	1986-89	233	*3,846	35
Scott Fredrickson, Wis.-Stout	1986-89	233	3,390	23
Mike Whitehouse, St. Norbert	1986-89	230	3,480	37
Mike Funk, Wabash	1985, 87-89	228	2,858	33
Dan Daley, Pomona-Pitzer	1985-88	227	2,598	10
Jim Jorden, Wheaton (Ill.)	1982-85	225	3,022	22
Chris Bisaillon, Ill. Wesleyan	1989-92	223	3,670	*55
Theo Blanco, Wis.-Stevens Point	1985-88	223	3,139	18
Ed Brady, Ill. Wesleyan	1981-84	220	2,907	22
Walter Kalinowski, Catholic	1983-86	219	2,430	16
Jim Bradford, Carleton	1988-91	212	3,719	32
Mike Cottle, Juniata	1985-88	212	2,607	36
John Ward, Cornell College	1979-82	211	3,085	30
Kendall Griffin, Loras	1990-93	208	3,036	26
Ron Severance, Otterbein	1989-91	207	2,378	17
Vince Dortch, Jersey City St.	1983-86	206	3,037	28
Chris Murphy, Georgetown	1989-92	205	2,817	26
Scott Faessler, Framingham St.	1989-92	201	2,121	8
Rick Fry, Occidental	1974-77	200	3,073	18
Steve Endres, Wilkes	1990-93	198	2,901	11
Ted Brockman, Kenyon	1990-93	198	2,180	21
Todd Stoner, Kenyon	1981-84	197	3,191	31
Steve Feyrer, Ripon	1983-86	196	2,852	19

*Record.

SEASON CATCHES

Player, Team	Year	G	Rec.	Yards	TD
Theo Blanco, Wis.-Stevens Point	1987	11	*106	1,616	8
Matt Newton, Principia	†1992	8	98	1,487	14
Matt Newton, Principia	†1993	8	96	1,080	11
Sean Munroe, Mass.-Boston	1992	9	95	*1,693	17
Ron Severance, Otterbein	1990	10	92	1,049	8

Player, Team	Year	G	Rec.	Yards	TD
Scott Faessler, Framingham St.	†1990	9	92	916	5
Greg Lehrer, Heidelberg	1993	10	87	1,202	8
Mike Funk, Wabash	†1989	9	87	1,169	12
Ted Taggart, Kenyon	1989	10	87	1,004	7
Jim Jorden, Wheaton (Ill.)	†1985	9	87	1,011	8
Ron Severance, Otterbein	†1991	10	85	929	4
Sam Williams, Defiance	1993	10	84	1,209	14
Scott Fredrickson, Wis.-Stout	1989	10	83	1,102	7
Rick Fry, Occidental	†1977	9	82	1,222	5
Jim Myers, Kenyon	†1974	9	82	1,483	12
Wayne Morris, Hofstra	1991	10	80	890	7
Theo Blanco, Wis.-Stevens Point	†1988	10	80	1,009	7
Bob Glanville, Lewis & Clark	1985	9	80	1,054	9
Ed Brady, Ill. Wesleyan	†1983	9	80	873	7
Vincent Hooper, Bethel (Minn.)	1993	10	79	1,000	12
Roger Little, Dubuque	1988	10	79	1,025	7
Walt Kalinowski, Catholic	1985	11	79	875	4

*Record. †National champion.

SINGLE-GAME CATCHES

No.	Player, Team (Opponent)	Date
23	Sean Munroe, Mass.-Boston (Mass. Maritime)	Oct. 10, 1992
20	Rich Johnson, Pace (Fordham)	Nov. 7, 1987
20	Pete Thompson, Carroll, Wis. (Augustana, Ill.)	Nov. 4, 1978
18	Craig Antonio, Waynesburg (Bethany, W.Va.)	Oct. 16, 1993
18	Ed Sullivan, Catholic (Carnegie Mellon)	Nov. 7, 1992
17	Chris Garrity, Wilmington, Ohio (Defiance)	Oct. 16, 1993
17	Matt Newton, Principia (Concordia, Ill.)	Nov. 7, 1992
17	Danny Cole, Lake Forest (Monmouth, Ill.)	Sept. 29, 1990
17	Dan Daley, Pomona-Pitzer (Occidental)	Oct. 15, 1988
17	Theo Blanco, Wis.-Stevens Point (Wis.-Oshkosh)	Oct. 31, 1987
17	Tim Mowery, Wis.-Superior (Wis.-Stevens Point)	Oct. 17, 1971
16	Ken Morton, Dubuque (Wis.-Whitewater)	Sept. 6, 1986
16	Shawn Graham, St. Thomas, Minn. (Hamline)	Nov. 13, 1982
16	Steve Forsythe, Frostburg St. (Allegheny)	Sept. 18, 1982
16	John Dettmann, Wis.-Oshkosh (Wis.-River Falls)	Oct. 10, 1981
16	Jay True, DePauw (Butler)	Nov. 4, 1978
16	Rick Fry, Occidental (Azusa Pacific)	Sept. 24, 1977
16	Pete Bylsma, Wheaton, Ill. (Millikin)	Oct. 19, 1974

CAREER YARDS

Player, Team	Years	Rec.	Yards	Avg.	TD
Dale Amos, Frank. & Marsh.	1986-89	233	*3,846	16.5	35
Bill Stromberg, Johns Hopkins	1978-81	258	3,776	14.6	39
Jim Bradford, Carleton	1988-91	212	3,719	17.5	32
Chris Bisaillon, Ill. Wesleyan	1989-92	223	3,670	16.5	*55
Matt Newton, Principia	1990-93	*287	3,646	12.7	32
Mike Whitehouse, St. Norbert	1986-89	230	3,480	15.1	37
Scott Fredrickson, Wis.-Stout	1986-89	233	3,390	14.5	23
John Aromando, Trenton St.	1981-84	165	3,197	19.4	39
Todd Stoner, Kenyon	1981-84	197	3,191	16.2	31
Rodd Patten, Framingham St.	1990-93	154	3,170	*20.6	38
Theo Blanco, Wis.-Stevens Point	1985-88	223	3,139	14.1	18
John Ward, Cornell College	1979-82	211	3,085	14.6	30
Rick Fry, Occidental	1974-77	200	3,073	15.4	18

*Record.

SEASON YARDS

Player, Team	Year	Rec.	Yards	Avg.	TD
Sean Munroe, Mass.-Boston	†1992	95	*1,693	17.8	17
Theo Blanco, Wis.-Stevens Point	1987	*106	1,616	15.2	8
Matt Newton, Principia	1992	98	1,487	15.2	14
Jim Myers, Kenyon	†1974	82	1,483	18.1	12
Beau Almodobar, Norwich	1984	71	1,375	19.4	10
Chris Vogel, Knox	†1987	78	1,326	17.0	15
Dale Amos, Frank. & Marsh.	1989	72	1,302	18.1	15
Don Moehling, Wis.-Stevens Point	1988	72	1,290	17.9	7
Ed Bubonics, Mount Union	1993	74	1,286	17.4	10
Tom Buslee, St. Olaf	1993	75	1,281	17.1	10
Rob Lokerson, Muhlenberg	1993	76	1,275	16.8	6
Jim Bradford, Carleton	1989	69	1,238	17.9	6
Rick Fry, Occidental	†1977	82	1,222	14.9	5
Evan Elkington, Worcester Tech	1989	52	1,220	+23.5	16
Vic Moncato, FDU-Madison	1993	64	1,217	19.0	11
Rick Fry, Occidental	†1976	74	1,214	16.4	8
Sam Williams, Defiance	1993	84	1,209	14.4	14
Mike Howey, Moravian	1989	61	1,203	19.7	7
Greg Lehrer, Heidelberg	1993	87	1,202	13.8	8
Scott Fredrickson, Wis.-Stout	1987	70	1,185	16.9	7

*Record. †National champion. +Record for minimum 50 receptions.

SINGLE-GAME YARDS

Yds.	Player, Team (Opponent)	Date
332	Sean Munroe, Mass.-Boston (Mass. Maritime)	Oct. 10, 1992
309	Dale Amos, Frank. & Marsh. (Western Md.)	Oct. 24, 1987
303	Chuck Braun, Wis.-Stevens Point (Wis.-Superior)	Oct. 17, 1981
303	Rick Fry, Occidental (Claremont-M-S)	Oct. 30, 1976
301	Greg Holmes, Carroll, Wis. (North Central)	Nov. 7, 1981
296	Joe Richards, Johns Hopkins (Georgetown)	Oct. 26, 1991
296	Vince Hull, Minn.-Morris (Bemidji St.)	Oct. 10, 1981
295	Aatron Kenney, Wis.-Stevens Point (Wis.-Stout)	Oct. 24, 1987
293	Mike Stotz, Catholic (Bridgewater, Va.)	Nov. 15, 1980
292	Andy Steckel, Western Md. (Gettysburg)	Sept. 15, 1990
287	Matt Newton, Principia (Concordia, Wis.)	Nov. 7, 1992
287	Chris Bisaillon, Ill. Wesleyan (Carroll, Wis.)	Sept. 15, 1990
285	Jim Bradford, Carleton (Gust. Adolphus)	Oct. 20, 1990
284	Tom Casperson, Trenton St. (Ramapo)	Nov. 15, 1980
280	Chris Vogel, Knox (Ripon)	Oct. 3, 1987

ANNUAL CHAMPIONS

CATCHES PER GAME

Year	Player, Team	Class	G	Rec.	Avg.	Yards	TD
1973	Ron Duckett, Trinity (Conn.)	Sr.	8	57	7.1	834	7
1974	Jim Myers, Kenyon	Sr.	9	82	9.1	1,483	12
1975	C. J. DeWitt, Bridgewater (Va.)	Sr.	9	64	7.1	836	2
1976	Rick Fry, Occidental	Jr.	8	74	9.3	1,214	8
1977	Rick Fry, Occidental	Sr.	9	82	9.1	1,222	5
1978	Pat McNamara, Trinity (Conn.)	Jr.	8	67	8.4	1,024	11
1979	Theodore Anderson, Fisk	Jr.	7	49	7.0	699	2
1980	Bill Stromberg, Johns Hopkins	Jr.	9	66	7.3	907	11
1981	Bill Stromberg, Johns Hopkins	Sr.	9	78	8.7	924	10
1982	Jim Gustafson, St. Thomas (Minn.)	Jr.	10	72	7.2	990	5
1983	Ed Brady, Ill. Wesleyan	Jr.	9	80	8.9	873	7
1984	Tim McNamara, Trinity (Conn.)	Sr.	8	67	8.4	1,004	10
1985	Jim Jorden, Wheaton (Ill.)	Sr.	9	87	9.7	1,011	8
1986	John Tucci, Amherst	Sr.	8	70	8.8	1,025	8
1987	Chris Vogel, Knox	So.	9	78	8.7	1,326	15
1988	Theo Blanco, Wis.-Stevens Point	Sr.	10	80	8.0	1,009	7
1989	Mike Funk, Wabash	Sr.	9	87	9.7	1,169	12
1990	Scott Faessler, Framingham St.	So.	9	92	10.2	916	5
1991	Ron Severance, Otterbein	Sr.	10	85	8.5	929	4
1992	Matt Newton, Principia	Jr.	8	98	*12.3	1,487	14
1993	Matt Newton, Principia	Sr.	8	96	12.0	1,080	11

*Record.

YARDS PER GAME

Year	Player, Team	Class	G	Rec.	Yards	TD	Avg.
1990	Ray Shelley, Juniata	Sr.	10	54	1,147	12	114.7
1991	Rodd Patten, Framingham St.	So.	8	49	956	13	119.5
1992	Sean Munroe, Mass.-Boston	Sr.	9	95	*1,693	17	*188.1
1993	Rob Lokerson, Muhlenberg	Jr.	9	76	1,275	6	141.7

Scoring

CAREER POINTS PER GAME

Player, Team	Years	G	TD	XPt.	FG	Pts.	Pt.PG
Joe Dudek, Plymouth St.	1982-85	41	*79	0	0	*474	*11.6
Chris Babirad, Wash. & Jeff.	1989-92	35	62	2	0	374	10.7
Terry Underwood, Wagner	1985-88	33	58	0	0	348	10.5
Chris Bisaillon, Ill. Wesleyan	1989-92	36	61	12	0	378	10.5
Stanley Drayton, Allegheny	1989-92	32	56	0	0	336	10.5
Greg Novarro, Bentley	1990-93	24	42	0	0	252	10.5
Ryan Kolpin, Coe	1987-90	28	48	0	0	288	10.3
Trent Nauholz, Simpson	1990-93	31	49	4	0	298	9.6
Jason Wooley, Worcester Tech	1990-93	37	55	8	0	338	9.1
A. J. Pagano, Wash. & Jeff.	1984-87	36	53	5	0	323	9.0
Heath Butler, N'western (Wis.)	1990-93	31	44	14	0	278	9.0
Gary Trettel, St. Thomas (Minn.)	1988-90	29	43	0	0	258	8.9
Vance Mueller, Occidental	1982-85	36	51	8	0	314	8.7
Jeff Norman, St. John's (Minn.)	1974-77	34	25	119	8	293	8.6
Denis McDermott, St. John's (N.Y.)	1987-89	30	43	0	0	258	8.6
Joe Thompson, Augustana (Ill.)	1973-76	34	48	4	0	292	8.6
Kirk Matthieu, Maine Maritime	$1989-93	33	47	0	0	282	8.5
Tim McDaniel, Centre	1988-91	38	54	0	0	324	8.5
Jeff Wittman, Ithaca	1989-92	32	45	0	0	270	8.4
Jay Wessler, Illinois Col.	1977-80	34	46	6	0	282	8.3
Scott Reppert, Lawrence	1979-82	33	45	0	0	270	8.2
Pedro Bowman, Duquesne	1981-84	34	46	2	0	278	8.2

*Record. $See page 6 for explanation.

SEASON POINTS PER GAME

Player, Team	Year	G	TD	XPt.	FG	Pts.	Pt.PG
Stanley Drayton, Allegheny	†1991	10	*28	0	0	*168	*16.8
Ricky Gales, Simpson	†1989	10	26	10	0	166	16.6
Matt Malmberg, St. John's (Minn.)	†1993	10	27	2	0	164	16.4
Chris Babirad, Wash. & Jeff.	†1992	9	24	0	0	144	16.0
Trent Nauholz, Simpson	†1992	8	21	2	0	128	16.0
Billy Johnson, Widener	†1973	9	23	0	0	138	15.3
Greg Novarro, Bentley	1992	10	25	0	0	150	15.0
Bruce Naszimento, Jersey City St.	1973	10	25	0	0	150	15.0
Chris Babirad, Wash. & Jeff.	1991	9	22	2	0	134	14.9
Chris Hipsley, Cornell College	†1976	9	14	42	2	132	14.7
Carey Bender, Coe	1992	9	21	4	0	130	14.4
Michael Waithe, Curry	†1987	8	19	0	0	114	14.3
Kelvin Gladney, Millsaps	1993	9	21	2	0	128	14.2
Rick Bell, St. John's (Minn.)	†1982	9	21	2	0	128	14.2
Terry Underwood, Wagner	†1988	9	21	0	0	126	14.0
Scott Barnyak, Carnegie Mellon	†1990	10	22	6	0	138	13.8
Ryan Kolpin, Coe	†1990	10	23	0	0	138	13.8
Kelvin Weaver, Wash. & Lee.	†1985	8	17	8	0	110	13.8
Joe Dudek, Plymouth St.	1985	11	25	0	0	150	13.6

* Record. †National champion.

CAREER POINTS

Player, Team	Year	TD	XPt.	FG	Pts.
Joe Dudek, Plymouth St.	1982-85	*79	0	0	*474
Chris Bisaillon, Ill. Wesleyan	1989-92	61	12	0	378
Chris Babirad, Wash. & Jeff.	1989-92	62	2	0	374
Terry Underwood, Wagner	1985-88	58	0	0	348
Jim Romagna, Loras	1989-92	57	2	0	344
Jason Wooley, Worcester Tech	1990-93	55	8	0	338
Stanley Drayton, Allegheny	1989-92	56	0	0	336
Cary Osborn, Wis.-Eau Claire	1987-90	55	0	0	330
Tim McDaniel, Centre	1988-91	54	0	0	324
A. J. Pagano, Wash. & Jeff.	1984-87	53	5	0	323
Ricky Gales, Nebraska-Omaha/Simpson	1986-87, 88-89	51	10	0	316
Greg Corning, Wis.-River Falls	1984-87	52	2	0	314
Vance Mueller, Occidental	1982-85	51	8	0	314
Scott Barnyak, Carnegie Mellon	1987-90	49	14	0	308
Prentes Wilson, Ill. Benedictine	1987-90	50	0	0	300
Trent Nauholz, Simpson	1990-93	49	4	0	298
Eric Frees, Western Md.	1988-91	49	4	0	298
Michael Waithe, Curry	1984-87	49	0	0	294
Jeff Norman, St. John's (Minn.)	1974-77	25	119	8	293
Joe Thompson, Augustana (Ill.)	1973-76	48	4	0	292
Mark Kelly, Wartburg	1989-92	48	0	0	288
Ryan Kolpin, Coe	1987-90	48	0	0	288

*Record.

SEASON POINTS

Player, Team	Year	TD	XPt.	FG	Pts.
Stanley Drayton, Allegheny	†1991	*28	0	0	*168
Ricky Gales, Simpson	†1989	26	10	0	166
Matt Malmberg, St. John's (Minn.)	†1993	27	2	0	164
Greg Novarro, Bentley	1992	25	0	0	150
Joe Dudek, Plymouth St.	1985	25	0	0	150
Bruce Naszimento, Jersey City St.	1973	25	0	0	150
Chris Babirad, Wash. & Jeff.	†1992	24	0	0	144
Scott Barnyak, Carnegie Mellon	1990	22	6	0	138
Ryan Kolpin, Coe	†1990	23	0	0	138
Ron Corbett, Cornell College	1982	23	0	0	138
Billy Johnson, Widener	†1973	23	0	0	138
Chris Babirad, Wash. & Jeff.	1991	22	2	0	134
Thomas Lee, Anderson	1992	22	0	0	132
Tim McDaniel, Centre	1990	22	0	0	132
Chris Hipsley, Cornell College	†1976	14	42	2	132
Carey Bender, Coe	1993	21	4	0	130
Carey Bender, Coe	1992	21	4	0	130
Kelvin Gladney, Millsaps	1993	21	2	0	128
Trent Nauholz, Simpson	†1992	21	2	0	128
Karl Kohl, Catholic	1989	21	2	0	128

* Record. †National champion.

ANNUAL CHAMPIONS

Year	Player, Team	Class	G	TD	XPt.	FG	Pts.	Avg.
1973	Billy Johnson, Widener	Sr.	9	23	0	0	138	15.3
1974	Joe Thompson, Augustana (Ill.)	So.	9	17	0	0	102	11.3
1975	Ron Baker, Monmouth (Ill.)	Sr.	8	15	2	0	92	11.5
1976	Chris Hipsley, Cornell College	So.	9	14	42	2	132	14.7
1977	Chip Zawoiski, Widener	Sr.	9	18	0	0	108	12.0

DIVISION III

Year	Player, Team	Class	G	TD	XPt.	FG	Pts.	Avg.
1978	Roger Andrachik, Baldwin-Wallace ..	Sr.	8	16	0	0	96	12.0
1979	Jay Wessler, Illinois Col.	Jr.	8	16	4	0	100	12.5
1980	Daryl Johnson, Wabash	Jr.	9	20	0	0	120	13.3
1981	Scott Reppert, Lawrence	Jr.	9	15	0	0	90	10.0
	Daryl Johnson, Wabash	Sr.	9	15	0	0	90	10.0
1982	Rick Bell, St. John's (Minn.)	Sr.	9	21	2	0	128	14.2
1983	John Aromando, Trenton St.	Jr.	10	20	0	0	120	12.0
1984	Joe Dudek, Plymouth St.	Jr.	10	21	0	0	126	12.6
1985	Kevin Weaver, Wash. & Lee	Jr.	8	17	8	0	110	13.8
1986	Jim Korfonta, Hamilton	Sr.	8	16	0	0	96	12.0
	Russ Kring, Mount Union	Jr.	10	20	0	0	120	12.0
1987	Michael Waithe, Curry	Sr.	8	19	0	0	114	14.3
1988	Terry Underwood, Wagner	Sr.	9	21	0	0	126	14.0
1989	Ricky Gales, Simpson	Sr.	10	26	10	0	166	16.6
1990	Scott Barnyak, Carnegie Mellon	Sr.	10	22	6	0	138	13.8
	Ryan Kolpin, Coe	Sr.	10	23	0	0	138	13.8
1991	Stanley Drayton, Allegheny	Jr.	10	*28	0	0	*168	*16.8
1992	Chris Babirad, Wash. & Jeff.	Sr.	9	24	0	0	144	16.0
	Trent Nauholz, Simpson	Jr.	8	21	2	0	128	16.0
1993	Matt Malmberg, St. John's (Minn.)....	Jr.	10	27	2	0	164	16.4

*Record.

Interceptions

CAREER INTERCEPTIONS

Player, Team	Years	No.	Yards	Avg.
Ralph Gebhardt, Rochester	1972-75	*34	406	11.9
Eugene Hunter, Fort Valley St.	1972-74	29	*479	16.5
Rick Bealer, Lycoming	1987-90	28	279	10.0
Brian Fetterolf, Aurora	1986-89	28	390	13.9
Tim Lennon, Curry	1986-89	27	190	7.0
Mike Hintz, Wis.-Platteville	1983-86	27	183	6.8
Cory Mabry, Susquehanna	1988-91	26	400	15.4
Mark Dorner, Juniata	1984-87	26	443	17.0
Jeff Hughes, Ripon	1975-78	26	333	12.8
Dave Adams, Carleton	1984-87	25	327	13.1
Will Hill, Bishop	1983-86	25	261	10.4
Neal Guggemos, St. Thomas (Minn.)	1982-85	25	377	15.1
Tom Devine, Juniata	1979-82	25	248	9.9
Gary Ellis, Rose-Hulman	1974-77	25	226	9.1

* Record.

SEASON INTERCEPTIONS

Player, Team	Year	No.	Yards
Mark Dorner, Juniata	†1987	*15	202
Steve Nappo, Buffalo	†1986	13	155
Chris McMahon, Catholic	†1984	13	105
Ralph Gebhardt, Rochester	†1973	13	105
Chris Butts, Worcester St.	†1992	12	109
Brian Barr, Gettysburg	†1985	12	144
John Bernard, Buffalo	†1983	12	143
Mick McConkey, Neb. Wesleyan	†1982	12	111
Tom Devine, Juniata	†1981	12	91

* Record. †National champion.

ANNUAL CHAMPIONS
(Ranked on Average Per Game)

Year	Player, Team	Class	G	No.	Avg.	Yards
1973	Ralph Gebhardt, Rochester	So.	9	13	1.44	105
1974	Kevin Birkholz, Carleton	Jr.	9	11	1.22	137
1975	Mark Persichetti, Wash. & Jeff.	So.	9	10	1.11	97
1976	Gary Jantzer, Southern Ore.	Sr.	9	10	1.11	63
1977	Greg Jones, FDU-Madison	So.	9	10	1.11	106
	Mike Jones, Norwich	So.	9	10	1.11	98
1978	Don Sutton, San Fran. St.	Fr.	8	10	1.25	43
1979	Greg Holland, Simpson	Fr.	9	11	1.22	150
1980	Tim White, Lawrence	Sr.	8	10	1.25	131
1981	Tom Devine, Juniata	Sr.	9	12	1.33	91
1982	Mick McConkey, Neb. Wesleyan	Sr.	9	12	1.33	111
1983	John Bernard, Buffalo	Sr.	10	12	1.20	143
1984	Chris McMahon, Catholic	Sr.	9	13	1.44	140
1985	Kim McManis, Lane	Sr.	9	11	1.22	165
1986	Steve Nappo, Buffalo	Sr.	11	13	1.18	155
1987	Mark Dorner, Juniata	Sr.	10	*15	*1.50	202

Year	Player, Team	Class	G	No.	Avg.	Yards
1988	Tim Lennon, Curry	Jr.	9	11	1.22	86
1989	Ron Davies, Coast Guard	So.	9	11	1.22	90
1990	Craig Garritano, FDU-Madison	Jr.	9	10	1.11	158
	Brad Bohn, Neb. Wesleyan	So.	9	10	1.11	90
	Frank Greer, Sewanee	So.	9	10	1.11	67
	Harold Krebs, Merchant Marine	Sr.	9	10	1.11	19
1991	Murray Meadows, Millsaps	Sr.	9	11	1.22	46
1992	Chris Butts, Worcester St.	Jr.	9	12	1.33	109
1993	Ricky Webb, Emory & Henry	Sr.	8	8	1.0	56

* Record.

Punting

CAREER AVERAGE
(Minimum 100 Punts)

Player, Team	Years	No.	Yards	Avg.
Mike Manson, Ill. Benedictine	1975-78	120	5,056	*42.13
Kirk Seufert, Memphis/Rhodes	1981, 83-84	109	4,587	42.08
Dan Osborn, Occidental	1981-83	157	6,528	41.6
Thomas Murray, Catholic	1983-84	122	5,028	41.2
Scott Lanz, Bethany (W.Va.)	1975-78	235	9,592	40.8
Mitch Holloway, Millsaps	1992-93	105	4,283	40.8
Jim Allshouse, Adrian	1972-75	210	8,525	40.6

* Record.

SEASON AVERAGE
(Qualifiers for Championship)

Player, Team	Year	No.	Yards	Avg.
Bob Burwell, Rose-Hulman	†1978	61	2,740	*44.9
Charles McPherson, Clark Atlanta	1978	50	2,237	44.7
Dan Osborn, Occidental	†1982	55	2,454	44.6
Mike Manson, Ill. Benedictine	†1976	36	1,587	44.1
Linc Welles, Bloomsburg	†1973	39	1,708	43.8
Kirk Seufert, Rhodes	†1983	44	1,921	43.7
Kelvin Albert, Knoxville	†1987	30	1,308	43.6

*Record. †National champion.

ANNUAL CHAMPIONS

Year	Player, Team	Class	No.	Yards	Avg.
1973	Linc Welles, Bloomsburg	Sr.	39	1,708	43.8
1974	Sylvester Cunningham, Fort Valley St.	So.	40	1,703	42.6
1975	Larry Hersh, Shepherd	Jr.	58	2,519	43.4
1976	Mike Manson, Ill. Benedictine	So.	36	1,587	44.1
1977	Scott Lanz, Bethany (W.Va.)	Jr.	78	3,349	42.9
1978	Bob Burwell, Rose-Hulman	Sr.	61	2,740	*44.9
1979	Jay Lenstrom, Neb. Wesleyan	Sr.	64	2,641	41.3
1980	Duane Harrison, Bridgewater (Va.)	Sr.	43	1,792	41.7
1981	Dan Paro, Denison	Jr.	54	2,223	41.2
1982	Dan Osborn, Occidental	Jr.	55	2,454	44.6
1983	Kirk Seufert, Rhodes	Jr.	44	1,921	43.7
1984	Thomas Murray, Catholic	Sr.	59	2,550	43.2
1985	Dave Lewis, Muhlenberg	So.	55	2,290	41.6
	Mike Matzen, Coe	Sr.	55	2,290	41.6
1986	Darren Estes, Millsaps	Jr.	45	1,940	43.1
1987	Kelvin Albert, Knoxville	So.	30	1,308	43.6
1988	Bobby Graves, Sewanee	So.	57	2,445	42.9
1989	Paul Becker, Kenyon	Sr.	57	2,307	40.5
1990	Bill Nolan, Carroll (Wis.)	Sr.	33	1,322	40.1
1991	Jeff Stolte, Chicago	So.	54	2,295	42.5
1992	Robert Ray, San Diego	So.	44	1,860	42.3
1993	Mitch Holloway, Millsaps	Sr.	45	1,910	42.4

*Record.

Punt Returns

CAREER AVERAGE
(Minimum 1.2 Returns Per Game)

Player, Team	Years	No.	Yards	Avg.
Keith Winston, Knoxville	1986-87	30	686	*22.9
Robert Middlebrook, Knoxville	1984-85	21	473	22.5
Kevin Doherty, Mass. Maritime	1976-78, 80	45	939	20.9
Chuck Downey, Stony Brook	1984-87	59	*1,198	+20.3
Mike Askew, Kean	1980-81	28	555	19.8
Willie Canady, Fort Valley St.	1979-82	41	772	18.8

* Record. +Record for minimum of 50 returns.

SEASON AVERAGE
(Minimum 1.2 Returns Per Game)

Player, Team	Year	No.	Yards	Avg.
Chuck Downey, Stony Brook	†1986	17	530	*31.2
Kevin Doherty, Mass. Maritime	†1976	11	332	30.2
Robert Middlebrook, Knoxville	†1984	9	260	28.9
Joe Troise, Kean	†1974	12	342	28.5
Melvin Dillard, Ferrum	†1990	25	*688	27.5
Eric Green, Ill. Benedictine	†1993	13	346	26.6
Chris Warren, Ferrum	†1989	18	421	23.4
Kevin Doherty, Mass. Maritime	1978	11	246	22.4

Record. †National champion.

ANNUAL CHAMPIONS

Year	Player, Team	Class	No.	Yards	‡Avg.
1973	Al Shepherd, Monmouth (Ill.)	Sr.	18	347	19.3
1974	Joe Troise, Kean	Fr.	12	342	28.5
1975	Mitch Brown, St. Lawrence	So.	25	430	17.2
1976	Kevin Doherty, Mass. Maritime	Fr.	11	332	30.2
1977	Charles Watkins, Knoxville	Sr.	15	278	18.5
1978	Dennis Robinson, Wesleyan	Sr.	†† 9	263	29.2
1979	Steve Moffett, Maryville (Tenn.)	Jr.	19	357	18.8
1980	Mike Askew, Kean	Jr.	16	304	19.0
1981	Mike Askew, Kean	Sr.	12	251	20.9
1982	Tom Southall, Colorado Col.	So.	13	281	21.6
1983	Edmond Donald, Millsaps	Jr.	15	320	21.3
1984	Robert Middlebrook, Knoxville	So.	9	260	28.9
1985	Dan Schone, Illinois Col.	Fr.	11	231	21.0
1986	Chuck Downey, Stony Brook	Jr.	17	530	*31.2
1987	Keith Winston, Knoxville	Sr.	16	343	21.4
1988	Dennis Tarr, Framingham St.	Jr.	9	178	19.8
1989	Chris Warren, Ferrum	Sr.	18	421	23.4
1990	Melvin Dillard, Ferrum	Sr.	25	*688	27.5
1991	Jordan Nixon, Augustana (Ill.)	Sr.	27	473	17.5
1992	Vic Moncato, FDU-Madison	So.	†††10	243	24.3
1993	Eric Green, Ill. Benedictine	Sr.	13	346	26.6

*Record. ‡Ranked on minimum of 1.5 returns per game in 1973; 1.2 from 1974.
††Declared champion; with one more return (making 1.25 per game) for zero yards,
still would have highest average (26.3). †††Declared champion; with one more return
(making 1.22 per game) for zero yards, still would have highest average (22.1).*

Kickoff Returns

CAREER AVERAGE
(Minimum 1.2 Returns Per Game)

Player, Team	Years	No.	Yards	Avg.
Daryl Brown, Tufts	1974-76	38	1,111	*29.2
Mike Askew, Kean	1980-81	33	938	28.4
Chuck Downey, Stony Brook	1984-87	46	1,281	27.8
Scott Reppert, Lawrence	1979-82	44	1,134	25.8
Rick Rosenfeld, Western Md.	1973-76	69	1,732	25.1

Record.

SEASON AVERAGE
(Minimum 1.2 Returns Per Game)

Player, Team	Year	No.	Yards	Avg.
Jason Martin, Coe	†1992	11	438	*39.8
Nate Kirtman, Pomona-Pitzer	†1990	14	515	36.8
Tom Myers, Coe	†1983	11	401	36.5
Ron Scott, Occidental	1983	10	363	36.3
Alan Hill, DePauw	1980	12	434	36.2
Al White, Wm. Paterson	1990	12	427	35.6
Byron Womack, Iona	†1989	15	531	35.4
Darnell Marshall, Carroll (Wis.)	1989	17	586	34.5
Daryl Brown, Tufts	†1976	11	377	34.3
Rich Jinnette, Methodist	1992	15	514	34.3
Sean Healy, Coe	1989	11	372	33.8
Anthony Drakeford, Ferrum	†1987	15	507	33.8
Ryan Reynolds, Thomas More	1992	14	473	33.8
Glenn Koch, Tufts	†1986	14	472	33.7

Record. †National champion.

ANNUAL CHAMPIONS

Year	Player, Team	Class	No.	Yards	‡Avg.
1973	Greg Montgomery, Wis.-Whitewater	So.	17	518	30.5
1974	Tom Oleksa, Muhlenberg	Sr.	15	467	31.1
1975	Jeff Levant, Beloit	Jr.	15	434	28.9
1976	Daryl Brown, Tufts	Sr.	11	377	34.3
1977	Charlie Black, Marietta	Jr.	14	465	33.2

Year	Player, Team	Class	No.	Yards	‡Avg.
1978	Russ Atchison, Centre	So.	11	284	25.8
1979	Jim Iannone, Rochester	Jr.	13	411	31.6
1980	Mike Askew, Kean	So.††10	415	41.5
1981	Gene Cote, Wesleyan	Sr.	16	521	32.6
1982	Jim Hachey, Bri'water (Mass.)	Jr.	16	477	29.8
1983	Tom Myers, Coe	So.	11	401	36.5
1984	Mike Doetsch, Trinity (Conn.)	Jr.	13	434	33.4
1985	Gary Newsom, Lane	So.	10	319	31.9
1986	Glenn Koch, Tufts	Sr.	14	472	33.7
1987	Anthony Drakeford, Ferrum	Sr.	15	507	33.8
1988	Harold Owens, Wis.-La Crosse	Jr.	10	508	29.9
1989	Byron Womack, Iona	Sr.	15	531	35.4
1990	Nate Kirtman, Pomona-Pitzer	Jr.	14	515	36.8
1991	Tom Reason, Albion	So.	13	423	32.5
1992	Jason Martin, Coe	So.	11	438	*39.8
1993	Eric Green, Ill. Benedictine	Sr.	19	628	33.1

*Record. ‡Ranked on minimum of 1.5 returns per game in 1973; 1.2 from 1974.
††Declared champion; with one more return (making 1.2 per game) for zero yards, still
would have highest average (37.7).*

All-Purpose Yards

ANNUAL CHAMPIONS

Year	Player, Team	Cl.	Rush	Rcv.	Int.	PR	KOR	Yds.	Yd.PG
1992	Kirk Matthieu, Maine Maritime	Jr.	1,733	91	0	56	308	2,188	243.1
1993	Carey Bender, Coe	Sr.	1,718	601	0	0	0	2,319	231.9

Field Goals

CAREER FIELD GOALS

Player, Team	Year	Made	Atts.	Pct.
Ken Edelman, Mount Union (S)	1987-90	*52	**71	.732
Ted Swan, Colorado Col. (S)	1973-76	43	57	.754
Jim Hever, Rhodes (S)	1982-85	42	66	.636
Manny Matsakis, Capital (C)	1980-83	40	66	.606
Doug Hart, Grove City (S)	1985-88	40	**71	.563
Mike Duvic, Dayton (S)	1986-89	38	49	$.776
Jeff Reitz, Lawrence (C)	1974-77	37	60	.617
Dan Deneher, Montclair St. (S)	1978-79, 81-82	37	65	.569
Jim Flynn, Gettysburg (S)	1982-85	37	68	.544

*Record. **Record tied. $Declared record; with one more attempt (making 50), failed,
still would have highest percentage (.760). (C) Conventional kicker. (S) Soccer-style kicker.*

SEASON FIELD GOALS

Player, Team	Year	Made	Atts.	Pct.
Ken Edelman, Mount Union (S)	†1990	*20	27	.741
Scott Ryerson, Central Fla. (S)	†1981	18	*29	.621
Steve Graeca, John Carroll (S)	†1988	15	16	*.938
Ken Edelman, Mount Union (S)	1988	15	17	.882
Gary Potter, Hamline (C)	†1984	15	21	.714
Jeff Reitz, Lawrence (C)	†1975	15	26	.577

Record. (C) Conventional kicker. (S) Soccer-style kicker. †National champion.

ANNUAL CHAMPIONS

Year	Player, Team	Class	Made	Atts.	Pct.	PG
1973	Chuck Smeltz, Susquehanna (C)	Jr.	10	14	.714	1.11
1974	Ted Swan, Colorado Col. (S)	So.	13	15	.867	1.44
1975	Jeff Reitz, Lawrence (C)	So.	15	26	.577	1.67
1976	Mark Sniegocki, Bethany (W.Va.) (C)	So.	11	14	.786	1.22
1977	Bob Unruh, Wheaton (Ill.) (S)	Jr.	11	14	.786	1.22
1978	Craig Walker, Western Md. (C)	So.	13	24	.542	1.44
1979	Jeff Holter, Concordia-M'head (S)	Jr.	12	15	.800	1.33
1980	Jeff Holter, Concordia-M'head (S)	Sr.	13	19	.684	1.30
1981	Scott Ryerson, Central Fla. (S)	So.	18	*29	.621	1.80
1982	Manny Matsakis, Capital (C)	Jr.	13	20	.650	1.44
1983	Mike Farrell, Adrian (S)	So.	12	21	.571	1.33
1984	Gary Potter, Hamline (C)	Jr.	15	21	.714	1.50
1985	Joe Bevelhimer, Wabash (C)	Sr.	14	22	.636	1.40
	Jim Hever, Rhodes (S)	Sr.	14	23	.609	1.40
1986	Tim Dewberry, Occidental (C)	Sr.	13	21	.619	1.44
1987	Doug Dickason, John Carroll (S)	Sr.	13	21	.619	1.44

DIVISION III

Year	Player, Team	Class	Made	Atts.	Pct.	PG
1988	Steve Graeca, John Carroll (S)	Fr.	15	16	*.938	1.67
1989	Dave Bergmann, San Diego (S)	So.	14	18	.778	1.56
	Rich Egal, Merchant Marine (S)	Fr.	14	22	.636	1.56
1990	Ken Edelman, Mount Union (S)	Sr.	*20	27	.741	*2.00
1991	Greg Harrison, Union (N.Y.) (S)	So.	12	16	.750	1.33
1992	Todd Holthaus, Rose-Hulman (S)	Jr.	13	19	.684	1.30
1993	Steve Milne, Brockport St. (S)	Sr.	13	16	81.3	1.30

*Record. (C) Conventional kicker. (S) Soccer-style kicker.

All-Time Longest Plays

Since 1941, official maximum length of all plays fixed at 100 yards.

RUSHING

Yds.	Player, Team (Opponent)	Year
99	Arnie Boigner, Ohio Northern (Muskingum)	1992
99	Reese Wilson, MacMurray (Eureka)	1986
99	Don Patria, Rensselaer (Mass.-Lowell)	1981
99	Kevin Doherty, Mass. Maritime (New Haven)	1980
99	Sam Halliston, Albany, N.Y. (Norwich)	1977
98	Rich Vargas, Wis.-Stout (Wis.-Oshkosh)	1992
98	Ted Pretasky, Wis.-La Crosse (Wis.-River Falls)	1987
98	Jon Hinds, Principia (Illinois Col.)	1986
98	Alex Schmidt, Muhlenberg (Lebanon Valley)	1984
98	Eric Batt, Ohio Northern (Ohio Wesleyan)	1982
98	Mike Shannon, Centre (Sewanee)	1978

PASSING

Yds.	Passer-Receiver, Team (Opponent)	Year
99	Jim Connolley-Duane Martin, Wesley (FDU-Madison)	1993
99	Marc Klausner-Eric Frink, Pace (Hobart)	1992
99	Carlos Nazario-Ray Marshall, St. Peter's (Georgetown)	1991
99	Mike Jones-Warren Tweedy, Frostburg St. (Waynesburg)	1990
99	Chris Etzler-Andy Nowlin, Bluffton (Urbana)	1990
99	John Clark-Pete Balistrieri, Wis.-Eau Claire (Minn.-Duluth)	1989
99	Kelly Sandidge-Mark Green, Centre (Sewanee)	1988
99	Mike Francis-John Winter, Carleton (Trinity, Tex.)	1983
99	Rich Boling-Lewis Borsellino, DePauw (Valparaiso)	1976
99	John Wicinski-Donnell Lipford, John Carroll (Allegheny)	1975
99	Jack Berry-Mercer West, Wash. & Lee (Hampden-Sydney)	1974
99	Gary Shope-Rick Rudolph, Juniata (Moravian)	1973

INTERCEPTION RETURNS

Eighteen players have returned interceptions 100 yards. The most recent:

Yds.	Player, Team (Opponent)	Year
100	Russell Williams, Frostburg St. (Wesley)	1993
100	Scott Schuster, Stony Brook (Pace)	1992
100	Randy Ashe, Loras (Quincy)	1991
100	Bill Zagger, Stony Brook (Merchant Marine)	1990
100	Dana Cruickshank, Dubuque (Upper Iowa)	1987
100	Todd Schoelzel, Wis.-Oshkosh (Wis.-Platteville)	1987

PUNT RETURNS

Yds.	Player, Team (Opponent)	Year
99	Robert Middlebrook, Knoxville (Miles)	1985
98	Mark Griggs, Wooster (Oberlin)	1980
98	Ron Mabry, Emory & Henry (Maryville, Tenn.)	1973
97	Rob Allard, Nichols (Curry)	1991
96	Marvin Robbins, Salisbury St. (Wesley)	1987
96	Gary Martin, Muskingum (Wooster)	1976
95	Tyrone Croom, Susquehanna (Delaware Valley)	1993
95	Brian Sarver, William Penn (Dubuque)	1992
95	Stan Thompson, Knoxville (Livingstone)	1982

KICKOFF RETURNS

Forty players have returned kickoffs 100 yards. The most recent:

Yds.	Player, Team (Opponent)	Year
100	Eric Green, Ill. Benedictine (Carthage)	1992
100	Nate Kirtman, Pomona-Pitzer (Redlands)	1990
100	Phil Bryant, Wilmington, Ohio (Tiffin)	1990
100	Steve Burns, Mass.-Boston (Curry)	1989
100	Wayne Morris, Hofstra (Pace)	1989

PUNTS

Yds.	Player, Team (Opponent)	Year
90	Dan Heeren, Coe (Lawrence)	1974
86	David Anastasi, Buffalo (John Carroll)	1989
86	Dana Loucks, Buffalo (Frostburg St.)	1987
86	John Pavlik, Wabash (Centre)	1978
83	Geoff Hansen, Gust. Adolphus (Augustana, S.D.)	1992
82	John Massab, Albion (Adrian)	1982
82	Mike Manson, Ill. Benedictine (Monmouth, Ill.)	1976
81	Jason Berg, Mass. Maritime (Mass.-Lowell)	1990
81	Tom Illig, Ohio Wesleyan (Wittenberg)	1975

FIELD GOALS

Yds.	Player, Team (Opponent)	Year
62	Dom Antonini, Rowan (Salisbury St.)	1976
59	Chris Gustafson, Carroll, Wis. (North Park)	1985
59	Hartmut Strecker, Dayton (Iowa St.)	1977
57	Scott Fritz, Wartburg (Simpson)	1982
57	Kevin Shea, St. Mary's, Cal. (Oregon Tech)	1976

Team Champions

Annual Offense Champions

TOTAL OFFENSE

Year	Team	Avg.
1973	San Diego	441.0
1974	Ithaca	487.9
1975	Frank. & Marsh.	439.4
1976	St. John's (Minn.)	451.8
1977	St. John's (Minn.)	437.5
1978	Lawrence	432.6
1979	Norwich	465.2
1980	Widener	459.0
1981	Middlebury	446.5
1982	West Ga.	470.6
1983	Elmhurst	483.3
1984	Alma	465.1
1985	St. Thomas (Minn.)	446.9
1986	Mount Union	452.8
1987	Samford	523.1
1988	Wagner	465.9
1989	Simpson	514.0
1990	Hofstra	505.7
1991	St. John's (Minn.)	503.8
1992	Mount Union	463.7
1993	St. John's (Minn.)	*549.7

*Record.

RUSHING OFFENSE

Year	Team	Avg.
1973	Widener	361.7
1974	Albany (N.Y.)	361.6
1975	Widener	345.8
1976	St. John's (Minn.)	348.9
1977	St. John's (Minn.)	315.3
1978	Ithaca	320.1
1979	Norwich	383.1
1980	Widener	317.5
1981	Augustana (Ill.)	313.6
1982	West Ga.	319.6
1983	Augustana (Ill.)	345.7
1984	Augustana (Ill.)	338.4
1985	Denison	351.0
1986	Wis.-River Falls	361.4
1987	Augustana (Ill.)	369.1
1988	Tufts	369.0
1989	Wis.-River Falls	388.5
1990	Ferrum	*434.7
1991	Ferrum	361.4
1992	Wis.-River Falls	315.6
1993	Chicago	324.8

*Record.

PASSING OFFENSE

Year	Team	Avg.
1973	San Diego	231.7
1974	Ill. Benedictine	255.4
1975	St. Norbert	227.7
1976	Occidental	255.4
1977	Southwestern	257.8
1978	Claremont-M-S	331.7
1979	Claremont-M-S	250.1
1980	Occidental	255.9
1981	Wis.-Stevens Point	288.9
1982	Wheaton (Ill.)	308.7
1983	Wheaton (Ill.)	*380.4

Year	Team	Avg.
1984	Wheaton (Ill.)	351.6
1985	Wheaton (Ill.)	371.6
1986	Pace	286.9
1987	Wis.-Stout	314.6
1988	Wis.-Stevens Point	356.7
1989	Wis.-Stevens Point	380.4
1990	Hofstra	342.2
1991	St. John's (Minn.)	302.8
1992	Mass.-Boston	337.0
1993	Mount Union	352.8

*Record.

SCORING OFFENSE

Year	Team	Avg.
1973	San Diego	40.1
1974	Frank. & Marsh.	45.1
1975	Frank. & Marsh.	38.2
1976	St. John's (Minn.)	42.5
1977	Lawrence	38.2
1978	Georgetown	36.5
1979	Wittenberg	39.7
1980	Widener	43.3
1981	Lawrence	35.3
1982	West Ga.	42.1
1983	Elmhurst	38.1
1984	Hope	40.3
1985	Salisbury St.	39.5
1986	Dayton	40.8
1987	Samford	51.7
1988	Central (Iowa)	37.6
1989	Ferrum	46.7
1990	Ferrum	47.3
1991	Union (N.Y.)	46.1
1992	Coe	46.4
1993	St. John's (Minn.)	*61.5

*Record.

Annual Defense Champions

TOTAL DEFENSE

Year	Team	Avg.
1973	Doane	144.3
1974	Alfred	153.6
1975	Lycoming	133.1
1976	Albion	129.9
1977	Knoxville	*94.0
1978	Bowie St.	112.3
1979	Catholic	116.9
1980	Maine Maritime	127.2
1981	Millsaps	147.6
1982	Plymouth St.	122.2
1983	Lycoming	154.5
1984	Swarthmore	159.2
1985	Augustana (Ill.)	149.1
1986	Augustana (Ill.)	136.2
1987	Plymouth St.	135.3

Year	Team	Avg.
1988	Plymouth St.	143.6
1989	Frostburg St.	119.7
1990	Bentley	139.8
1991	Wash. & Jeff.	143.0
1992	Bentley	184.5
1993	Wash. & Jeff.	142.4

*Record.

RUSHING DEFENSE

Year	Team	Avg.
1973	Oregon Col.	61.2
1974	Millersville	57.2
1975	Cal Lutheran	62.4
1976	Lycoming	44.3
1977	Knoxville	*-2.3
1978	Western Md.	43.4
1979	Catholic	46.4
1980	Maine Maritime	3.2
1981	Augustana (Ill.)	30.7
1982	Lycoming	34.2
1983	DePauw	41.6
1984	Swarthmore	40.0
1985	Augustana (Ill.)	35.1
1986	Dayton	13.5
1987	Lycoming	35.4
1988	Worcester St.	43.9
1989	Frostburg St.	49.7
1990	Ohio Wesleyan	18.9
1991	Wash. & Jeff.	64.6
1992	Bri'water (Mass.)	43.2
1993	Wash. & Jeff.	19.1

*Record.

PASSING DEFENSE

Year	Team	$Avg.
1973	Nichols	53.0
1974	Findlay	49.2
1975	Wash. & Jeff.	56.0
1976	Mass. Maritime	*48.5
1977	Hofstra	49.4
1978	Bowie St.	64.7
1979	Wagner	59.5
1980	Williams	63.8
1981	Plymouth St.	66.9
1982	Plymouth St.	48.8
1983	Muhlenberg	76.4
1984	Bri'water (Mass.)	68.7
1985	Bri'water (Mass.)	77.3
1986	Knoxville	83.2
1987	Jersey City St.	67.0
1988	Colorado Col.	78.9
1989	Frostburg St.	70.0
1990	Bentley	47.4
1991	Wash. & Jeff.	50.3
1992	St. Peter's	51.7
1993	Worcester St.	50.0

*Record. $Beginning in 1990, ranked on passing effi-
ciency defense rating points instead of per-game yardage
allowed.

SCORING DEFENSE

Year	Team	Avg.
1973	Fisk	6.4
	Slippery Rock	6.4
1974	Central (Iowa)	6.9
	Rhodes	6.9
1975	Millsaps	5.0
1976	Albion	5.4
1977	Central (Iowa)	5.0
1978	Minn.-Morris	5.9
1979	Carnegie Mellon	4.9
1980	Millsaps	*3.4
1981	Baldwin-Wallace	3.9
1982	West Ga.	4.6
1983	Carnegie Mellon	5.3
1984	Union (N.Y.)	4.6
1985	Augustana (Ill.)	4.7
1986	Augustana (Ill.)	5.1
1987	Plymouth St.	6.2
1988	Plymouth St.	6.5
1989	Millikin	4.8
1990	Bentley	4.5
1991	Mass.-Lowell	5.4
1992	Dayton	6.7
1993	Wash. & Jeff.	6.1

*Record.

Other Annual Team Champions

NET PUNTING

Year	Team	Avg.
1992	San Diego	39.2
1993	Ill. Benedictine	38.9

PUNT RETURNS

Year	Team	Avg.
1992	Occidental	18.7
1993	Curry	17.9
	Wheaton (Ill.)	17.9

KICKOFF RETURNS

Year	Team	Avg.
1992	Thomas More	27.7
1993	St. John's (Minn.)	28.9

TURNOVER MARGIN

Year	Team	Avg.
1992	Illinois Col.	2.44
1993	Trinity (Conn.)	2.87

All-Time Team Won-Lost Records

Includes records as a senior college only, minimum 20 seasons of competition since 1937. Postseason games are included, and each tie game is computed as half won and half lost.

PERCENTAGE (TOP 26)

Team	Yrs.	Won	Lost	Tied	Pct.
Plymouth St.	24	155	64	7	.701
Wis.-La Crosse	69	412	177	40	.687
St. John's (Minn.)	83	402	195	23	.667
Ithaca	61	314	171	11	.644
Cal Lutheran	32	200	110	6	.642
Wittenberg	100	545	312	32	.631
Montclair St.	63	316	181	20	.631
Augustana (Ill.)	81	406	234	28	.629
Wis.-Whitewater	69	351	203	21	.629
Concordia-M'head	74	371	214	37	.626
Baldwin-Wallace	89	434	258	30	.622
Gust. Adolphus	78	380	232	21	.617
Millikin	88	431	271	28	.610
Central (Iowa)	85	416	268	26	.604
Williams	108	508	325	46	.604
St. Thomas (Minn.)	88	417	271	32	.601
Wash. & Jeff.	102	518	338	40	.600
Albany (N.Y.)	21	123	82	0	.600
Widener	113	518	340	38	.599
Lawrence	100	443	293	29	.598
Wis.-River Falls	68	322	215	32	.594
Albion	107	461	318	43	.588
Wabash	107	479	330	59	.586
Whittier	84	405	289	36	.579
Frank. & Marsh.	106	507	362	47	.579
Coe	101	442	316	38	.579

ALPHABETICAL LISTING
(No Minimum Seasons of Competition)

Team	Yrs.	Won	Lost	Tied	Pct.
Adrian	91	287	370	17	.438
Albany (N.Y.)	21	123	82	0	.600
Albion	107	461	318	43	.588
Albright	81	322	378	21	.461
Alfred	95	369	285	44	.560
Allegheny	99	375	335	44	.527
Alma	97	382	331	27	.534
Amherst	114	493	369	53	.568
Anderson	47	207	202	12	.506
Augsburg	62	137	347	18	.291
Augustana (Ill.)	81	406	234	28	.629
Aurora	8	43	25	1	.630
Baldwin-Wallace	89	434	258	30	.622
Bates	98	277	403	46	.413
Beloit	103	344	414	47	.457
Bethany (W.Va.)	93	282	435	34	.398
Bethel (Minn.)	41	118	237	8	.336
Blackburn	5	9	33	0	.214
Bluffton	71	225	316	23	.419
Bowdoin	100	342	384	44	.473
Bri'water (Mass.)	34	139	145	6	.490
Bridgewater (Va.)	49	119	267	10	.313
Brockport St.	47	121	247	2	.330
Buena Vista	89	343	316	28	.520
Buffalo St.	13	53	66	0	.445
Cal Lutheran	32	200	110	6	.642
Capital	70	276	266	27	.509
Carleton	99	413	299	25	.577
Carnegie Mellon	84	385	297	29	.562
Carroll (Wis.)	90	352	268	38	.564
Carthage	97	350	334	41	.511
Case Reserve	24	89	126	4	.416
Catholic	48	184	202	12	.477
Central (Iowa)	85	416	268	26	.604
Centre	101	449	336	37	.569
Chicago	74	317	303	33	.511
Claremont-M-S	36	119	193	5	.383
Coast Guard	70	237	312	49	.437
Coe	101	442	316	38	.579
Colby	100	286	398	33	.422

Team	Yrs.	Won	Lost	Tied	Pct.
Colorado Col.	108	423	374	34	.529
Concordia (Ill.)	55	165	248	18	.404
Concordia-M'head	74	371	214	37	.626
Cornell College	103	422	345	33	.548
Cortland St.	67	272	235	27	.535
Curry	29	95	144	5	.400
Defiance	71	283	292	20	.492
Delaware Valley	46	173	208	10	.455
Denison	104	458	357	56	.558
DePauw	106	430	402	41	.516
Dickinson	105	374	457	54	.453
Dubuque	71	260	301	25	.465
Earlham	103	303	445	23	.408
Elmhurst	74	230	353	24	.399
Emory & Henry	78	400	321	19	.553
Eureka	60	128	316	26	.300
FDU-Madison	20	53	120	1	.307
Ferrum	9	63	31	1	.668
Fitchburg St.	10	7	80	1	.085
Framingham St.	20	75	101	1	.427
Frank. & Marsh.	106	507	362	47	.579
Franklin	93	333	393	31	.460
Frostburg St.	33	145	158	7	.479
Gallaudet	94	201	414	19	.332
Gettysburg	101	463	390	41	.541
Grinnell	103	328	454	33	.423
Grove City	99	386	380	60	.504
Guilford	88	227	464	25	.334
Gust. Adolphus	78	380	232	21	.617
Hamilton	100	319	382	47	.458
Hamline	102	350	344	30	.504
Hampden-Sydney	99	412	356	28	.535
Hanover	101	339	346	29	.495
Hartwick	22	45	108	11	.308
Heidelberg	98	392	380	41	.507
Hiram	95	231	461	32	.341
Hobart	100	350	403	40	.467
Hope	84	325	256	37	.556
Howard Payne	88	374	364	41	.506
Ill. Benedictine	72	237	271	24	.468
Ill. Wesleyan	102	420	328	41	.558
Illinois Col.	97	337	375	36	.475
Ithaca	61	314	171	11	.644
Jersey City St.	26	86	153	3	.362
John Carroll	71	320	255	35	.553
Johns Hopkins	109	349	413	56	.461
Juniata	71	301	262	21	.533
Kalamazoo	99	328	381	41	.465
Kean	22	90	118	6	.435
Kenyon	104	296	471	46	.392
King's (Pa.)	1	1	9	0	.100
Knox	100	341	429	43	.446
La Verne	68	255	292	18	.467
Lake Forest	101	340	367	55	.482
Lawrence	100	443	293	29	.598
Lebanon Valley	93	336	413	36	.451
Loras	65	276	221	31	.552
Luther	80	348	274	21	.558
Lycoming	44	212	162	11	.565
Macalester	91	224	411	29	.359
MacMurray	9	36	48	1	.429
Maine Maritime	48	198	172	9	.534
Manchester	68	210	324	20	.397
Marietta	99	334	435	35	.437
Maryville (Tenn.)	96	369	390	35	.487
Mass. Maritime	21	105	81	1	.564
Mass.-Boston	6	19	34	1	.361
Mass.-Dartmouth	6	24	30	0	.444
Menlo	8	31	39	2	.444
Merchant Marine	49	209	226	13	.481
Methodist	5	6	44	0	.120
Middlebury	97	327	336	42	.494
Millikin	88	431	271	28	.610
Millsaps	71	299	272	36	.522
MIT	6	16	28	1	.367
Monmouth (Ill.)	101	414	379	39	.521
Montclair St.	63	316	181	20	.631
Moravian	60	253	239	20	.514
Mount Union	97	451	378	34	.542
Muhlenberg	94	384	405	41	.487

Team	Yrs.	Won	Lost	Tied	Pct.
Muskingum	99	439	325	38	.571
Neb. Wesleyan	85	375	323	42	.535
Nichols	35	145	129	6	.529
North Central	89	308	350	35	.470
North Park	36	75	234	7	.248
Norwich	95	279	400	31	.415
N'western (Wis.)	95	293	302	30	.493
Oberlin	103	351	441	39	.446
Occidental	92	382	316	26	.546
Ohio Northern	95	352	386	35	.478
Ohio Wesleyan	103	465	393	44	.540
Olivet	93	260	417	33	.389
Otterbein	104	334	474	43	.418
Plymouth St.	24	155	64	7	.701
Pomona-Pitzer	96	323	359	31	.475
Principia	60	177	275	16	.395
Randolph-Macon	106	386	377	56	.505
Redlands	84	366	342	27	.516
Rensselaer	104	278	473	46	.378
Rhodes	82	295	304	37	.493
Ripon	100	399	291	46	.573
Rochester	105	429	373	38	.533
Rose-Hulman	98	326	414	29	.443
Rowan	34	162	143	7	.530
Salisbury St.	22	119	91	4	.565
Salve Regina	1	3	3	0	.500
Sewanee	99	413	363	39	.531
Simpson	88	348	408	37	.462
St. John Fisher	6	22	34	0	.393
St. John's (Minn.)	83	402	195	23	.667
St. Lawrence	99	338	343	29	.496
St. Norbert	60	268	223	20	.544
St. Olaf	76	344	254	20	.573
St. Thomas (Minn.)	88	417	271	32	.601
Stony Brook	11	46	51	2	.475
Susquehanna	95	334	381	38	.469
Swarthmore	113	429	408	36	.512
Thiel	89	293	349	36	.459
Thomas More	4	30	10	0	.750
Trenton St.	69	243	257	31	.487
Trinity (Conn.)	109	431	311	42	.577
Trinity (Tex.)	89	310	402	49	.440
Tufts	112	430	424	46	.503
Union (N.Y.)	106	385	382	62	.502
Upper Iowa	91	275	357	25	.438
Upsala	68	234	313	18	.430
Ursinus	101	298	476	54	.393
Wabash	107	479	330	59	.586
Wartburg	58	228	254	12	.474
Wash. & Jeff.	102	518	338	40	.600
Wash. & Lee	100	383	423	38	.476
Washington (Mo.)	96	373	392	28	.488
Waynesburg	90	337	313	37	.517
Wesley	8	31	43	1	.420
Wesleyan (Conn.)	112	430	415	42	.508
Western Conn. St.	22	69	136	2	.338
Western Md.	99	409	378	47	.519
Western New Eng.	13	46	69	1	.401
Westfield St.	12	52	60	1	.465
Wheaton (Ill.)	81	329	295	29	.526
Whittier	84	405	289	36	.579
Widener	113	518	340	38	.599
Wilkes	48	181	219	8	.453
William Penn	93	257	437	35	.377
Williams	108	508	325	46	.604
Wilmington (Ohio)	61	239	260	13	.479
Wis.-Eau Claire	75	280	288	34	.493
Wis.-La Crosse	69	412	177	40	.687
Wis.-Oshkosh	67	213	296	30	.423
Wis.-Platteville	85	288	282	31	.505
Wis.-River Falls	68	322	215	32	.594
Wis.-Stevens Point	94	357	304	43	.538
Wis.-Stout	74	198	373	33	.355
Wis.-Whitewater	69	351	203	21	.629
Wittenberg	100	545	312	32	.631
Wm. Paterson	22	97	116	4	.456
Wooster	95	395	354	41	.526
Worcester St.	9	37	41	0	.474
Worcester Tech	104	245	394	30	.389

VICTORIES

Team	Wins	Team	Wins
Wittenberg	545	Lawrence	443
Wash. & Jeff.	518	Coe	442
Widener	518		
Williams	508	Muskingum	439
Frank. & Marsh.	507	Baldwin-Wallace	434
		Millikin	431
Amherst	493	Trinity (Conn.)	431
Wabash	479	DePauw	430
Ohio Wesleyan	465		
Gettysburg	463	Tufts	430
Albion	461	Wesleyan (Conn.)	430
		Rochester	429
Denison	458	Swarthmore	429
Mount Union	451	Colorado Col.	423
Centre	449		

National Poll Rankings

Final Poll Leaders

(Released Before Division Championship Playoffs)

Year	Team, Record*	Coach	Record in Championship†
1975	Ithaca (8-0-0)	Jim Butterfield	2-1 Runner-up
1976	St. John's (Minn.) (7-0-1)	John Gagliardi	3-0 Champion
1977	Wittenberg (8-0-0)	Dave Maurer	Did not compete
1978	Minn.-Morris (9-0-0)	Al Molde	1-1 Lost in semifinals
1979	Wittenberg (8-0-0)	Dave Maurer	2-1 Runner-up
1980	Ithaca (10-0-0)	Jim Butterfield	2-1 Runner-up
1981	Widener (9-0-0)	Bill Manlove	3-0 Champion
1982	Baldwin-Wallace (10-0-0)	Bob Packard	0-1 Lost in first round
1983	Augustana (Ill.) (9-0-0)	Bob Reade	3-0 Champion
1984	Augustana (Ill.) (9-0-0)	Bob Reade	3-0 Champion
1985	Augustana (Ill.) (9-0-0)	Bob Reade	4-0 Champion
1986	Dayton (10-0-0)	Mike Kelly	0-1 Lost in first round
1987	Augustana (Ill.) (9-0-0)	Bob Reade	1-1 Lost in quarterfinals
1988	**East Region**		
	Cortland St. (9-0-0)	Dennis Kayser	1-1 Lost in quarterfinals
	North Region		
	Dayton (9-1-0)	Mike Kelly	0-1 Lost in first round
	South Region		
	Ferrum (9-0-0)	Hank Norton	2-1 Lost in semifinals
	West Region		
	Central (Iowa) (8-0-0)	Ron Schipper	3-1 Runner-up
1989	**East Region**		
	Union (N.Y.) (9-0-0)	Al Bagnoli	3-1 Runner-up
	North Region		
	Dayton (8-0-1)	Mike Kelly	4-0 Champion
	South Region		
	Rhodes (7-0-0)	Mike Clary	Did not compete
	West Region		
	Central (Iowa) (8-0-0)	Ron Schipper	1-1 Lost in quarterfinals
1990	**East Region**		
	Hofstra (9-0-0)	Joe Gardi	2-1 Lost in semifinals
	North Region		
	Dayton (9-0-0)	Mike Kelly	1-1 Lost in quarterfinals
	South Region		
	Ferrum (8-0-0)	Hank Norton	0-1 Lost in first round
	West Region		
	Wis.-Whitewater (9-0-0)	Bob Berezowitz	0-1 Lost in first round
1991	**East Region**		
	Ithaca (7-1-0)	Jim Butterfield	4-0 Champion
	North Region		
	Allegheny (10-0-0)	Ken O'Keefe	1-1 Lost in quarterfinals
	South Region		
	Lycoming (8-0-0)	Frank Girardi	1-1 Lost in quarterfinals
	West Region		
	St. John's (Minn.) (9-0-0)	John Gagliardi	2-1 Lost in semifinals
1992	**East Region**		
	Rowan (9-0-0)	John Bunting	2-1 Lost in semifinals
	North Region		
	Dayton (9-0-0)	Mike Kelly	0-1 Lost in first round
	South Region		
	Wash. & Jeff. (8-0-0)	John Luckhardt	3-1 Runner-up
	West Region		
	Central (Iowa) (9-0-0)	Ron Schipper	1-1 Lost in quarterfinals
1993	**East Region**		
	Rowan (7-1-0)	K.C. Keeler	3-1 Runner-up
	North Region		
	Mount Union (9-0-0)	Larry Kehres	4-0 Champion
	South Region		
	Wash. & Jeff. (8-0-0)	John Luckhardt	2-1 Lost in semifinals
	West Region		
	Wis.-La Crosse (9-0-0)	Roger Harring	1-1 Lost in quarterfinals

*Final poll record. †Number of teams in the championship: 8 (1975-84); 16 (1985-present).

DIVISION III

Undefeated, Untied Teams

(Regular-Season Games Only)

Following is a list of undefeated and untied teams since 1973, when College Division teams were divided into Division II and Division III under a three-division reorganization plan adopted by the special NCAA Convention on August 1, 1973. Since 1981, conference play-off games have been included in a team's won-lost record (previously, such games were considered postseason contests). Figures indicate the regular-season wins (minimum seven games against four-year varsity opponents). A subsequent postseason win(s) in the Division III championship or a conference playoff game (before 1981) is indicated by (*), a loss by (†) and a tie by (‡).

Year	College	Wins
1973	Fisk	9
	Wittenberg	***9
1974	Albany (N.Y.)	9
	Central (Iowa)	**9
	Frank. & Marsh.	9
	Ithaca	*†9
	Towson St.	10
1975	Cal Lutheran	*†9
	Ithaca	**†8
	Widener	*†9
	Wittenberg	***†9
1976	Albion	9
1977	Central (Iowa)	†9
	Cornell College	†8
	Wittenberg	†9
1978	Baldwin-Wallace	‡***8
	Illinois Col.	9
	Minn.-Morris	*†10
	Wittenberg	‡**†8
1979	Carnegie Mellon	*†9

Year	College	Wins
	Dubuque	†9
	Jamestown	7
	Tufts	8
	Widener	*†9
	Wittenberg	***†8
1980	Adrian	9
	Baldwin-Wallace	†9
	Bethany (W.Va.)	†9
	Dayton	***11
	Ithaca	**†10
	Millsaps	9
	Widener	*†10
1981	Alfred	†10
	Augustana (Ill.)	†9
	Lawrence	*†9
	West Ga.	†9
	Widener	***†10
1982	Augustana (Ill.)	**†9
	Baldwin-Wallace	†10
	Plymouth St.	10
	St. John's (Minn.)	†9
	St. Lawrence	*†9
	Wabash	10
	West Ga.	***9
1983	Augustana (Ill.)	***9
	Carnegie Mellon	†9
	Hofstra	†10
	Worcester Tech	8
1984	Amherst	8
	Augustana (Ill.)	***9
	Case Reserve	9
	Central (Iowa)	**†9
	Dayton	†10
	Hope	9
	Occidental	†10
	Plymouth St.	†10
1985	Augustana (Ill.)	****9
	Carnegie Mellon	†8
	Central (Iowa)	**†9
	Denison	†10
	Lycoming	†10
	Mount Union	*†10
	Union (N.Y.)	†9
1986	Central (Iowa)	*†10
	Dayton	†10
	Ithaca	**†9
	Mount Union	*†10
	Salisbury St.	***†10

Year	College	Wins
	Susquehanna	*†10
	Union (N.Y.)	†9
1987	Augustana (Ill.)	*†9
	Gust. Adolphus	†10
	Wash. & Jeff.	*†9
1988	Cortland St.	*†10
	Ferrum	**†9
1989	Central (Iowa)	*†9
	Millikin	*†9
	Union (N.Y.)	***†10
	Williams	8
1990	Carnegie Mellon	†10
	Dayton	*†10
	Hofstra	**†10
	Lycoming	****†9
	Mount Union	†10
	Wash. & Jeff.	*†9
	Williams	8
	Wis.-Whitewater	†10
1991	Allegheny	*†10
	Baldwin-Wallace	†10
	Dayton	****†10
	Dickinson	†10
	Eureka	*†9
	Lycoming	*†9
	Mass.-Lowell	†10
	Simpson	†10
	St. John's (Minn.)	**†9
	Thomas More	10
	Union (N.Y.)	*†9
1992	Aurora	†9
	Central (Iowa)	*†9
	Cornell College	10
	Dayton	†10
	Emory & Henry	*†10
	Ill. Wesleyan	*†9
	Mount Union	**†10
	Rowan	**†10
1993	Albion	*†9
	Anderson	†10
	Coe	†10
	Mount Union	****10
	St. John's (Minn.)	**†10
	Trinity (Conn.)	8
	Union (N.Y.)	†9
	Wash. & Jeff.	**†9
	Wilkes	†10
	Wis.-La Crosse	*†10

The Spoilers

(Since 1973, when the three-division reorganization plan was adopted by the special NCAA Convention, creating Divisions II and III.)

Following is a list of the spoilers of Division III teams that lost their perfect (undefeated, untied) record in their **season-ending** game, including the Division III championship playoffs. An asterisk (*) indicates a Division III championship playoff game and a dagger (†) indicates the home team in a regular-season game. A game involving two undefeated, untied teams is in bold face.

Date	Spoiler	Victim	Score
11-17-73	†Williams	Amherst	30-14
12-7-74	*Central (Iowa)	Ithaca	10-8
11-8-75	Cornell College	†Lawrence	17-16
11-22-75	*Ithaca	Widener	23-14
12-6-75	*Wittenberg	Ithaca	28-0
11-12-77	Norwich	†Middlebury	34-20
11-12-77	Ripon	†Cornell College	10-7
11-19-77	†Baldwin-Wallace	Wittenberg	14-7
11-19-77	*Widener	Central (Iowa)	19-0
11-25-78	*Wittenberg	Minn.-Morris	35-14
11-17-79	*Ithaca	Dubuque	27-7
11-17-79	‡Findlay	Jamestown	41-15
11-24-79	*Wittenberg	Widener	17-14
11-24-79	*Ithaca	Carnegie Mellon	15-6
12-1-79	*Ithaca	Wittenberg	14-10
11-8-80	DePauw	†Wabash	tie 22-22
11-22-80	*Widener	Bethany (W.Va.)	43-12
11-22-80	*Dayton	Baldwin-Wallace	34-0
11-29-80	*Dayton	Widener	28-24
12-6-80	#*Dayton	Ithaca	63-0

Date	Spoiler	Victim	Score
11-14-81	†DePauw	Wabash	21-14
11-14-81	†St. Mary's (Cal.)	San Diego	31-14
11-21-81	*Widener	West Ga.	10-3
11-21-81	*Dayton	Augustana (Ill.)	19-7
11-21-81	*Montclair St.	Alfred	13-12
11-28-81	*Dayton	Lawrence	38-0
11-13-82	†Widener	Swarthmore	24-7
11-20-82	‡N'western (Iowa)	St. John's (Minn.)	33-28
11-20-82	*Augustana (Ill.)	Baldwin-Wallace	28-22
11-27-82	*Augustana (Ill.)	St. Lawrence	14-0
12-4-82	**West Ga.**	**Augustana (Ill.)**	14-0
11-19-83	*Salisbury St.	Carnegie Mellon	16-14
11-19-83	*Union (N.Y.)	Hofstra	51-19
11-10-84	St. John's (N.Y.)	†Hofstra	19-16
11-10-84	†St. Olaf	Hamline	tie 7-7
11-17-84	*Union (N.Y.)	Plymouth St.	26-14
11-17-84	*Central (Iowa)	Occidental	23-22
11-17-84	*Augustana (Ill.)	Dayton	14-13
12-8-84	**Augustana (Ill.)**	**Central (Iowa)**	21-12
11-23-85	*Gettysburg	Lycoming	14-10
11-23-85	**Mount Union**	**Denison**	35-3
11-23-85	*Salisbury St.	Carnegie Mellon	35-22
11-23-85	*Ithaca	Union (N.Y.)	13-12
12-7-85	**Augustana (Ill.)**	**Central (Iowa)**	14-7
11-15-86	†Lawrence	Coe	14-10
11-22-86	**Mount Union**	**Dayton**	42-36
11-22-86	*Ithaca	Union (N.Y.)	OT 24-17
11-29-86	*Concordia-M'head	Central (Iowa)	17-14
11-29-86	*Salisbury St.	Susquehanna	31-17
11-29-86	*Augustana (Ill.)	Mount Union	16-7

Date	Spoiler	Victim	Score
12-6-86	*Salisbury St.	Ithaca	44-40
12-13-86	***Augustana (Ill.)**	**Salisbury St.**	31-3
11-11-87	St. Norbert	†Monmouth (Ill.)	20-15
11-21-87	*St. John's (Minn.)	Gust. Adolphus	7-3
11-28-87	*Emory & Henry	Wash. & Jeff.	23-16
11-28-87	$*Dayton	Augustana (Ill.)	38-36
11-12-88	†St. Norbert	Monmouth (Ill.)	12-0
11-19-88	Coast Guard	†Plymouth St.	28-19
11-26-88	*Ithaca	Cortland St.	24-17
12-3-88	*Ithaca	Ferrum	62-28
11-11-89	†Baldwin-Wallace	John Carroll	25-19
11-11-89	**†Bri'water (Mass.)**	**Mass.-Lowell**	14-10
11-11-89	†Centre	Rhodes	13-10
11-18-89	†Alfred	Bri'water (Mass.)	30-27
11-25-89	*St. John's (Minn.)	Central (Iowa)	27-24
11-25-89	*Dayton	Millikin	28-16
12-9-89	*Dayton	Union (N.Y.)	17-7
11-10-90	Trenton St.	†Ramapo	9-0
11-10-90	†Waynesburg	Frostburg St.	28-18
11-17-90	*Allegheny	Mount Union	26-15
11-17-90	***Lycoming**	**Carnegie Mellon**	17-7
11-17-90	*St. Thomas (Minn.)	Wis.-Whitewater	24-23
11-24-90	*Allegheny	Dayton	31-23
11-24-90	***Lycoming**	**Wash. & Jeff.**	24-0
12-1-90	***Lycoming**	**Hofstra**	20-10
12-8-90	*Allegheny	Lycoming	OT 21-14
11-9-91	†Coe	Beloit	26-10
11-23-91	*Union (N.Y.)	Mass.-Lowell	55-16
11-23-91	*Dayton	Baldwin-Wallace	27-10
11-30-91	*Dayton	Allegheny	OT 28-25
11-30-91	*Ithaca	Union (N.Y.)	35-23
11-30-91	*Susquehanna	Lycoming	31-24
12-7-91	*Dayton	St. John's (Minn.)	19-7
12-14-91	*Ithaca	Dayton	34-20
11-7-92	Cornell College	†Coe	37-20
11-7-92	Union (N.Y.)	†Rochester	14-10
11-21-92	***Ill. Wesleyan**	**Aurora**	21-12
11-21-92	***Mount Union**	**Dayton**	27-10
11-28-92	***Mount Union**	**Ill. Wesleyan**	49-27
11-28-92	*Wash. & Jeff.	Emory & Henry	51-15
11-28-92	*Wis.-La Crosse	Central (Iowa)	34-9
12-5-92	*Wash. & Jeff.	Rowan	18-13
12-5-92	*Wis.-La Crosse	Mount Union	29-24
10-30-93	Mount Senario	†N'western (Wis.)	21-20
11-13-93	Hastings	†Colorado Col.	22-21
11-20-93	***Albion**	**Anderson**	41-21
11-20-93	***St. John's (Minn.)**	**Coe**	32-14
11-20-93	*Frostburg St.	Wilkes	26-25
11-20-93	*Wm. Paterson	Union (N.Y.)	17-7
11-27-93	***Mount Union**	**Albion**	30-16
11-27-93	***St. John's (Minn.)**	**Wis.-La Crosse**	47-25
12-5-93	***Mount Union**	**St. John's (Minn.)**	56-8
12-5-93	*Rowan	Wash. & Jeff.	23-16

‡NAIA championship playoff game. #Defeated three consecutive perfect-record teams in the Division III championship playoffs. $Ended Augustana's (Ill.) 60-game undefeated streak.

Streaks and Rivalries

Longest Winning Streaks

(Minimum Two Seasons in Division III; Includes Postseason Games)

Wins	Team	Years
37	Augustana (Ill.)	1983-85
24	Allegheny	1990-91
23	Williams	1988-91
22	Dayton	1989-90
22	Augustana (Ill.)	1986-87
21	Dayton	1979-81
20	Plymouth St.	1987-88
19	Plymouth St.	1981-82
18	Lawrence	1980-81
18	Ithaca	1979-80

Longest Unbeaten Streaks

(Minimum Two Seasons in Division III; Includes Postseason Games)

No.	Wins	Ties	Team	Years
60	59	1	Augustana (Ill.)	1983-87
25	24	1	Dayton	1989-90
24	24	0	Allegheny	1990-91
24	23	1	Wabash	1979-81
23	23	0	Williams	1988-91
22	21	1	Dayton	1979-81
21	20	1	Baldwin-Wallace	1977-79
20	20	0	Plymouth St.	1987-88
20	18	2	St. John's (Minn.)	1975-76

Longest Division III Series

Games	Opponents (Series leader listed first)	Series Record	First Game
108	Williams-Amherst	59-45-4	1884
107	Albion-Kalamazoo	69-34-4	1896
105	Bowdoin-Colby	59-37-9	1892
104	Monmouth (Ill.)-Knox	48-46-10	1891
103	Coe-Cornell College	55-44-4	1891
100	Wabash-DePauw	46-45-9	1890
99	Amherst-Wesleyan	50-40-9	1882
99	Williams-Wesleyan	59-35-5	1881
98	Hampden-Sydney—Randolph-Macon	50-37-11	1893
96	Colby-Bates	51-37-8	1893
96	Union (N.Y.)-Hamilton	46-38-12	1890

Cliffhangers

Greg Harrison kicked a 38-yard field goal on the game's final play to give Union (New York) a 16-13 victory over Rensselaer on October 16, 1993.

Regular-season Division III games won on the final play of the game in regulation time (from 1973). The extra point is listed when it provided the margin of victory after the winning touchdown.

Date	Opponents, Score	Game-Winning Play
9-22-73	Hofstra 21, Seton Hall 20	Tom Calder 15 pass from Steve Zimmer (Jim Hogan kick)
9-18-76	Ohio Wesleyan 23, DePauw 20	Tom Scurfield 48 pass from Bob Mauck
10-27-77	Albany (N.Y.) 42, Maine 39	Larry Leibowitz 19 FG
9-22-79	Augustana (Ill.) 19, Carthage 18	John Stockton 14 pass from Mark Schick
10-6-79	Carleton 17, Lake Forest 14	Tim Schoonmaker 46 FG
11-10-79	Dayton 24, St. Norbert 22	Jim Fullenkamp 21 FG
9-13-80	Cornell College 14, Lawrence 13	John Bryant 8 pass from Matt Dillon (Keith Koehler kick)
9-27-80	Muhlenberg 41, Johns Hopkins 38	Mickey Mottola 1 run
10-25-80	Mass.-Lowell 15, Marist 13	Ed Kulis 3 run
10-17-81	Carleton 22, Ripon 21	John Winter 23 pass from Billy Ford (Dave Grein kick)
10-2-82	Frostburg St. 10, Mercyhurst 7	Mike Lippold 34 FG
11-6-82	Williams 27, Wesleyan 24	Marc Hummon 33 pass from Robert Connolly
10-7-83	Johns Hopkins 18, Ursinus 17	John Tucker 10 pass from Mark Campbell
10-8-83	Susquehanna 17, Widener 14	Todd McCarthy 20 FG
10-29-83	Frank. & Marsh. 16, Swarthmore 15	Billy McLean 51 pass from Niall Rosenzweig
9-24-84	Muhlenberg 3, Frank. & Marsh. 0	Tom Mulroy 26 FG
10-26-85	Buffalo 13, Brockport St. 11	Dan Friedman 37 FG
11-9-85	Frank. & Marsh. 29, Johns Hopkins 28	Brad Ramsey 1 run (Ken Scalet pass from John Travagline)
9-18-86	Beloit 16, Lakeland 13	Sean Saturnio 38 pass from Ed Limon
9-20-86	Susquehanna 43, Lycoming 42	Rob Sochovka 40 pass from Todd Coolidge (Randy Pozsar kick)
10-18-86	Ill. Wesleyan 25, Elmhurst 23	Dave Anderson 11 pass from Doug Moews
9-5-87	Wash. & Jeff. 17, Ohio Wesleyan 16	John Ivory 28 FG
9-26-87	Gust. Adolphus 19, Macalester 17	Dave Fuecker 8 pass from Dean Kraus
10-3-87	Wis.-Whitewater 10, Wis.-Platteville 7	Dave Emond 25 FG
10-24-87	Geneva 9, St. Francis (Pa.) 7	John Moores 19 FG
10-1-88	Canisius 17, Rochester 14	Jim Ehrig 34 FG
10-1-88	Cortland St. 24, Western Conn. St. 21	Ted Nagengast 35 FG
10-8-88	UC Santa Barb. 20, Sonoma St. 18	Harry Konstantinopoulos 52 FG
10-8-88	Hamilton 13, Bowdoin 10	Nate O'Steen 19 FG
11-5-88	Colby 20, Middlebury 18	Eric Aulenback 1 run
11-12-88	Wis.-River Falls 24, Wis.-Stout 23	Andy Feil 45 FG
10-7-89	Moravian 13, Juniata 10	Mike Howey 75 pass from Rob Light
10-21-89	Western New Eng. 17, Bentley 14	Leo Coughlin 17 FG
10-21-89	Thiel 19, Carnegie Mellon 14	Bill Barber 4 pass from Jeff Sorenson
9-8-90	Emory & Henry 22, Wash. & Lee 21	Todd Woodall 26 pass from Pat Walker
9-15-90	Otterbein 20, Capital 17	Korey Brown 39 FG
10-27-90	Hamline 26, Gust. Adolphus 24	Mike Sunnarborg 2 pass from Bob Hackney
11-10-90	Colby 23, Bowdoin 20	Paul Baisley 10 pass from Bob Ward
9-7-91	Central (Iowa) 26, Gust. Adolphus 25	Brian Krob 1 pass from Shad Flynn
9-13-91	St. John's (N.Y.) 30, Iona 27	John Ledwith 42 FG
10-5-91	Trinity (Conn.) 30, Williams 27	John Mullaney 5 pass from James Lane
10-26-91	DePauw 12, Anderson 7	Steve Broderick 65 pass from Brian Goodman
10-17-92	Elmhurst 30, North Central 28	Eric Ekstrom 2 pass from Jack Lamb
10-16-93	Union (N.Y.) 16, Rensselaer 13	Greg Harrison 38 FG
10-23-93	Stony Brook 21, Merchant Marine 20	Brian Hughes 44 FG
10-30-93	Thomas More 24, Defiance 18	Greg Stofko 6 blocked field goal return

Regular-Season Overtime Games

In 1981, the NCAA Football Rules Committee approved an overtime tie-breaker system to decide a tie game for the purpose of determining a conference champion. The following conferences are currently using the tie-breaker system to decide conference-only tie games. The number of overtimes is indicated in parentheses.

IOWA INTERCOLLEGIATE ATHLETIC CONFERENCE

Date	Opponents, Score
9-26-81	William Penn 24, Wartburg 21 (1 OT)
9-25-82	Dubuque 16, Buena Vista 13 (1 OT)
10-2-82	Luther 25, Dubuque 22 (1 OT)
10-30-82	Wartburg 27, Dubuque 24 (3 OT)
10-4-86	Luther 28, Wartburg 21 (1 OT)
9-26-87	William Penn 19, Upper Iowa 13 (2 OT)
11-7-87	William Penn 17, Loras 10 (1 OT)
10-10-92	Simpson 20, Loras 14 (1 OT)
11-14-92	Luther 17, Buena Vista 10 (1 OT)

MIDWEST COLLEGIATE ATHLETIC CONFERENCE

Date	Opponents, Score
10-25-86	Lake Forest 30, Chicago 23 (1 OT)
10-26-86	Lawrence 7, Beloit 0 (1 OT)
9-30-89	Illinois Col. 26, Ripon 20 (3 OT)
10-27-90	Beloit 16, St. Norbert 10 (1 OT)
11-2-91	Monmouth (Ill.) 13, Knox 7 (1 OT)

NEW ENGLAND FOOTBALL CONFERENCE
(From 1987)

Date	Opponents, Score
10-31-87	Nichols 21, Mass.-Lowell 20 (1 OT)
9-17-88	Mass.-Lowell 22, Worcester St. 19 (2 OT)
9-30-89	Worcester St. 23, Mass.-Dartmouth 20 (1 OT)
10-28-89	Worcester St. 27, Nichols 20 (1 OT)
11-7-92	Mass.-Dartmouth 21, Westfield St. 14 (3 OT)

SOUTHERN CALIFORNIA INTERCOLLEGIATE ATHLETIC CONFERENCE

Date	Opponents, Score
10-18-86	La Verne 53, Occidental 52 (1 OT)
9-26-87	Claremont-M-S 33, Occidental 30 (1 OT)
10-27-90	Occidental 47, Claremont-M-S 41 (1 OT)
10-17-92	Cal Lutheran 17, Occidental 14 (1 OT)

Individual Collegiate Records

Dean Hendrickson photo

Idaho quarterback Doug Nussmeier finished his collegiate career in 1993 with an average of 309.1 yards per game in total offense, the sixth-best per-game average in history.

Individual Collegiate Records

Individual collegiate records are determined by comparing the best records in all four divisions (I-A, I-AA, II and III) in comparable categories. Included are career records of players who played half their careers in two divisions (e.g., Dennis Shaw of San Diego St., Howard Stevens of Randolph-Macon and Louisville, and Tom Ehrhardt of LIU-C.W. Post and Rhode Island).

Total Offense

CAREER YARDS PER GAME
(Minimum 20 Games)

Player, Team (Division[s])	Years	G	Plays	Yards	TDR‡	Yd. PG
Willie Totten, Mississippi Val. (I-AA)	1982-85	40	1,812	13,007	*157	*325.2
Ty Detmer, Brigham Young (I-A)	1988-91	46	1,795	*14,665	135	318.8
Neil Lomax, Portland St. (II; I-AA)	1977; 78-80	42	1,901	13,345	120	317.7
Kirk Baumgartner, Wis.-Stevens Point (III)	1986-89	41	2,007	12,767	110	311.4
Mike Perez, San Jose St. (I-A)	1986-87	20	875	6,182	37	309.1
Doug Nussmeier, Idaho (I-AA)	1990-93	39	1,556	12,054	109	309.1
Doug Gaynor, Long Beach St. (I-A)	1984-85	22	1,067	6,710	45	305.0
Tod Mayfield, West Tex. A&M (I-AA; II)	1984-85; 86	24	1,165	7,316	58	304.8
Jamie Martin, Weber St. (I-AA)	1989-92	41	1,838	12,287	93	299.7
Tony Eason, Illinois (I-A)	1981-82	22	1,016	6,589	43	299.5
Keith Bishop, Ill. Wesleyan/Wheaton (Ill.) (III)	1981, 83-85	31	1,467	9,052	77	292.0
David Klingler, Houston (I-A)	1988-91	32	1,431	9,327	93	291.5
Stan Greene, Boston U. (I-AA)	1989-90	22	1,167	6,408	49	291.3
John Friesz, Idaho (I-AA)	1986-89	35	1,459	10,187	79	291.1
Steve Young, Brigham Young (I-A)	1981-83	31	1,177	8,817	74	284.4
Jayson Merrill, Western St. (II)	1990-91	20	641	5,619	57	281.0
Jordan Poznick, Principia (III)	1990-93	32	1,757	8,983	71	280.7
Andre Ware, Houston (I-A)	1987-89	29	1,194	8,058	81	277.9
Chris Petersen, UC Davis (II)	1985-86	20	735	5,532	52	276.6
Tim Von Dulm, Portland St. (II)	1969-70	20	989	5,501	51	275.1
John Rooney, Ill. Wesleyan (III)	1982-84	27	1,260	7,363	71	273.8
Tim Peterson, Wis.-Stout (III)	1986-89	36	1,558	9,701	59	269.5
Doug Flutie, Boston College (I-A)	1981-84	42	1,558	11,317	74	269.5
Bret Snyder, Utah St. (I-A)	1987-88	22	1,040	5,916	43	268.9
Dennis Shaw, San Diego St. (II; I-A)	1968; 69	20	682	5,371	72	268.6

*Record. ‡Touchdowns-responsible-for are player's TDs scored and passed for.

SEASON YARDS PER GAME

Player, Team (Division)	Year	G	Plays	Yards	TDR‡	Yd. PG
David Klingler, Houston (I-A)	†1990	11	*704	*5,221	55	*474.6
Willie Totten, Mississippi Val. (I-AA)	†1984	10	564	4,572	*61	457.2
Andre Ware, Houston (I-A)	†1989	11	628	4,661	49	423.7
Ty Detmer, Brigham Young (I-A)	1990	12	635	5,022	45	418.5
Steve McNair, Alcorn St. (I-AA)	†1992	10	519	4,057	39	405.7
Perry Klein, LIU-C.W. Post (II)	†1993	10	499	4,052	41	405.2
Steve Young, Brigham Young (I-A)	†1983	11	531	4,346	41	395.1
Jamie Martin, Weber St. (I-AA)	†1991	11	591	4,337	37	394.3
Chris Vargas, Nevada (I-A)	†1993	11	535	4,332	35	393.8
Marty Washington, Livingston (II)	1993	8	453	3,146	29	393.8
Scott Mitchell, Utah (I-A)	†1988	11	589	4,299	29	390.8
Jim McMahon, Brigham Young (I-A)	†1980	12	540	4,627	53	385.6
Neil Lomax, Portland St. (I-AA)	†1980	11	550	4,157	42	377.9
Brett Salisbury, Wayne St. (Neb.) (II)	1993	10	424	3,732	32	373.2
Ty Detmer, Brigham Young (I-A)	1989	12	497	4,433	38	369.4
Troy Kopp, Pacific (Cal.) (I-A)	1990	9	485	3,276	32	364.0
Dave Dickenson, Montana (I-AA)	†1993	11	530	3,978	46	361.6
Neil Lomax, Portland St. (I-AA)	†1979	11	611	3,966	31	360.5
Jed Drenning, Glenville St. (II)	1993	10	473	3,593	32	359.3
Keith Bishop, Wheaton (Ill.) (III)	†1983	9	421	3,193	24	354.8
Kirk Baumgartner, Wis.-Stevens Point (III)	†1989	10	530	3,540	39	354.0
Rob Tomlinson, Cal St. Chico (II)	†1989	10	534	3,525	26	352.5
John Friesz, Idaho (I-AA)	†1989	11	464	3,853	31	350.3
Steve McNair, Alcorn St. (I-AA)	1993	11	493	3,830	30	348.2
Todd Hammel, Stephen F. Austin (I-AA)	1989	11	487	3,822	38	347.5
Tom Ehrhardt, Rhode Island (I-AA)	†1985	10	529	3,460	35	346.0
Jim McMahon, Brigham Young (I-A)	†1981	10	487	3,458	30	345.8
Ken Hobart, Idaho (I-AA)	†1983	11	578	3,800	37	345.5
Kirk Baumgartner, Wis.-Stevens Point (III)	†1988	11	604	3,790	27	344.5
Chris Hegg, Northeast Mo. St. (II)	†1985	11	594	3,782	35	343.8
Jordan Poznick, Principia (III)	†1992	8	519	2,747	25	343.4
Jimmy Klingler, Houston (I-A)	†1992	11	544	3,768	34	342.5
Dave Stireman, Weber St. (I-AA)	1985	11	502	3,759	33	341.7
Bob Toledo, San Fran. St. (II)	†1967	10	409	3,407	46	340.7
Willie Totten, Mississippi Val. (I-AA)	1985	11	561	3,742	43	340.2

*Record. †National total-offense champion. ‡Touchdowns-responsible-for are player's TDs scored and passed for.

CAREER YARDS

Player, Team (Division[s])	Years	Plays	Yards	Avg.
Ty Detmer, Brigham Young (I-A)	1988-91	1,795	*14,665	*8.17
Neil Lomax, Portland St. (II; I-AA)	1977; 78-80	1,901	13,345	7.02
Willie Totten, Mississippi Val. (I-AA)	1982-85	1,812	13,007	7.18
Kirk Baumgartner, Wis.-Stevens Point (III)	1986-89	2,007	12,767	6.36
Jamie Martin, Weber St. (I-AA)	1989-92	1,838	12,287	6.68
Doug Nussmeier, Idaho (I-AA)	1990-93	1,556	12,054	7.75
Doug Flutie, Boston College (I-A)	1981-84	1,558	11,317	7.26
Ken Hobart, Idaho (I-AA)	1980-83	1,847	11,127	6.02
¢Steve McNair, Alcorn St. (I-AA)	1991-93	1,406	11,024	7.84
Alex Van Pelt, Pittsburgh (I-A)	1989-92	1,570	10,814	6.89
Earl Harvey, N.C. Central (II)	1985-88	*2,045	10,667	5.22
Jim Ballard, Wilmington (Ohio)/ Mount Union (III)	1990, 91-93	1,328	10,545	7.94
Todd Santos, San Diego St. (I-A)	1984-87	1,722	10,513	6.11
Sean Payton, Eastern Ill. (I-AA)	1983-86	1,690	10,298	6.09
Greg Wyatt, Northern Ariz. (I-AA)	1986-89	1,753	10,277	5.86
Kevin Sweeney, Fresno St. (I-A)	$1982-86	1,700	10,252	6.03
John Friesz, Idaho (I-AA)	1986-89	1,459	10,187	6.98
Troy Kopp, Pacific (Cal.) (I-A)	1989-92	1,595	10,037	6.29
Rob Tomlinson, Cal St. Chico (II)	1988-91	1,656	9,921	5.99
Michael Proctor, Murray St. (I-AA)	1986-89	1,577	9,886	6.27
Jeff Wiley, Holy Cross (I-AA)	1985-88	1,428	9,877	6.92
Tom Ehrhardt, LIU-C.W. Post (II); Rhode Island (I-AA)	1981-82; 84-85	1,674	9,793	5.85
Brian McClure, Bowling Green (I-A)	1982-85	1,630	9,774	6.00
Jim McMahon, Brigham Young (I-A)	1977-78, 80-81	1,325	9,723	7.34
Glenn Foley, Boston College (I-A)	1990-93	1,440	9,702	6.74
Tim Peterson, Wis.-Stout (III)	1986-89	1,558	9,701	6.23
Terrence Jones, Tulane (I-A)	1985-88	1,620	9,445	5.83
David Klingler, Houston (I-A)	1988-91	1,431	9,327	6.52
Shawn Jones, Georgia Tech (I-A)	1989-92	1,609	9,296	5.78
Matt DeGennaro, Connecticut (I-AA)	1987-90	1,619	9,269	5.73
Shane Matthews, Florida (I-A)	1989-92	1,397	9,241	6.61
Sam Mannery, Calif. (Pa.) (II)	1987-90	1,669	9,125	5.47
T. J. Rubley, Tulsa (I-A)	1987-89, 91	1,541	9,080	5.89
Brad Tayles, Western Mich. (I-A)	1989-92	1,675	9,071	5.42
John Elway, Stanford (I-A)	1979-82	1,505	9,070	6.03
Tom Ciaccio, Holy Cross (I-AA)	1988-91	1,283	9,066	7.07
Erik Wilhelm, Oregon St. (I-A)	1985-88	1,689	9,062	5.37
Ben Bennett, Duke (I-A)	1980-83	1,582	9,061	5.73
Keith Bishop, Ill. Wesleyan/ Wheaton (Ill.) (III)	1981, 83-85	1,467	9,052	6.17
Chuck Long, Iowa (I-A)	$1981-85	1,411	9,034	6.40

*Record. $See page 6 for explanation. ¢Active player.

SEASON YARDS

Player, Team (Division)	Year	G	Plays	Yards	Avg.
David Klingler, Houston (I-A)	†1990	11	*704	*5,221	7.42
Ty Detmer, Brigham Young (I-A)	1990	12	635	5,022	7.91
Andre Ware, Houston (I-A)	†1989	11	628	4,661	7.42
Jim McMahon, Brigham Young (I-A)	†1980	12	540	4,627	8.57
Willie Totten, Mississippi Val. (I-AA)	†1984	10	564	4,572	8.11
Ty Detmer, Brigham Young (I-A)	1989	12	497	4,433	@8.92
Steve Young, Brigham Young (I-A)	†1983	11	531	4,346	8.18
Jamie Martin, Weber St. (I-AA)	†1991	11	591	4,337	7.34
Chris Vargas, Nevada (I-AA)	†1993	11	535	4,332	8.10
Scott Mitchell, Utah (I-A)	†1988	11	589	4,299	7.30
Neil Lomax, Portland St. (I-AA)	†1980	11	550	4,157	7.56
Robbie Bosco, Brigham Young (I-A)	1985	13	578	4,141	7.16
Steve McNair, Alcorn St. (I-AA)	†1992	10	519	4,057	7.82
Perry Klein, LIU-C.W. Post (II)	†1993	10	499	4,052	8.12
Ty Detmer, Brigham Young (I-A)	†1991	12	478	4,001	8.37
Dave Dickenson, Montana (I-AA)	†1993	11	530	3,978	7.51
Neil Lomax, Portland St. (I-AA)	†1979	11	611	3,966	6.49
Robbie Bosco, Brigham Young (I-A)	†1984	12	543	3,932	7.24
Mike McCoy, Utah (I-A)	1993	12	529	3,860	7.50
John Friesz, Idaho (I-AA)	†1989	11	464	3,853	8.30
Steve McNair, Alcorn St. (I-AA)	1993	11	493	3,830	7.77
Todd Hammel, Stephen F. Austin (I-AA)	1989	11	487	3,822	7.85
Ken Hobart, Idaho (I-AA)	1983	11	578	3,800	6.57
Kirk Baumgartner, Wis.-Stevens Point (III)	†1988	11	604	3,790	6.27
Chris Hegg, Northeast Mo. St. (II)	1985	11	594	3,782	6.36
Jimmy Klingler, Houston (I-A)	†1992	11	544	3,768	6.93
Dave Stireman, Weber St. (I-AA)	1985	11	502	3,759	7.49
Willie Totten, Mississippi Val. (I-AA)	1985	11	561	3,742	6.67
Brett Salisbury, Wayne St. (Neb.) (II)	1993	10	424	3,732	8.80
Jeff Wiley, Holy Cross (I-AA)	†1987	11	445	3,722	8.36
Jamie Martin, Weber St. (I-AA)	1990	11	508	3,713	7.31
Anthony Dilweg, Duke (I-A)	1988	11	539	3,713	6.89
Kirk Baumgartner, Wis.-Stevens Point (III)	1987	11	561	3,712	6.62

*Record. †National total-offense champion. @ Record for minimum of 3,000 yards.

SINGLE-GAME YARDS

Yds.	Div.	Player, Team (Opponent)	Date
732	I-A	David Klingler, Houston (Arizona St.)	Dec. 2, 1990
696	I-A	Matt Vogler, Texas Christian (Houston)	Nov. 3, 1990
643	I-AA	Jamie Martin, Weber St. (Idaho St.)	Nov. 23, 1991
625	I-A	David Klingler, Houston (Texas Christian)	Nov. 3, 1990
625	I-A	Scott Mitchell, Utah (Air Force)	Oct. 15, 1988
623	II	Perry Klein, LIU-C.W. Post (Salisbury St.)	Nov. 6, 1993
621	I-AA	Willie Totten, Mississippi Val. (Prairie View)	Oct. 27, 1984
612	I-A	Jimmy Klingler, Houston (Rice)	Nov. 28, 1992
604	I-A	Steve McNair, Alcorn St. (Jackson St.)	Nov. 21, 1992
603	I-A	Ty Detmer, Brigham Young (San Diego St.)	Nov. 16, 1991
601	I-A	Troy Kopp, Pacific, Cal. (New Mexico St.)	Oct. 20, 1990
599	I-A	Virgil Carter, Brigham Young (UTEP)	Nov. 5, 1966
597	I-A	John Walsh, Brigham Young (Utah St.)	Oct. 30, 1993
596	III	John Love, North Park (Elmhurst)	Oct. 13, 1990
595	I-AA	Doug Pederson, Northeast La. (Stephen F. Austin)	Nov. 11, 1989
594	I-A	Jeremy Leach, New Mexico (Utah)	Nov. 11, 1989
591	II	Marty Washington, Livingston (Nicholls St.)	Sept. 11, 1993
590	III	Tom Stallings, St. Thomas, Minn. (Bethel, Minn.)	Nov. 13, 1993
587	I-AA	Vern Harris, Idaho St. (Montana)	Oct. 12, 1985
585	I-A	Dave Wilson, Illinois (Ohio St.)	Nov. 8, 1980
584	II	Tracy Kendall, Alabama A&M (Clark Atlanta)	Nov. 4, 1989
582	I-A	Marc Wilson, Brigham Young (Utah)	Nov. 5, 1977
578	I-A	David Klingler, Houston (Eastern Wash.)	Nov. 17, 1990
571	II	John Charles, Portland St. (Cal Poly SLO)	Nov. 16, 1991
570	I-AA	Steve McNair, Alcorn St. (Texas Southern)	Sept. 11, 1993
566	I-AA	Tom Ehrhardt, Rhode Island (Connecticut)	Nov. 16, 1985
564	III	Tim Lynch, Hofstra (Fordham)	Oct. 19, 1991
562	I-AA	Todd Hammel, Stephen F. Austin (Northeast La.)	Nov. 11, 1989
562	I-A	Ty Detmer, Brigham Young (Washington St.)	Sept. 7, 1989
562	II	Bob Toledo, San Fran. St. (Cal St. Hayward)	Oct. 21, 1967
561	I-AA	Willie Totten, Mississippi Val. (Southern-B.R.)	Sept. 29, 1984
555	II	A. J. Vaughn, Wayne St., Mich. (Wis.-Milwaukee)	Sept. 30, 1967

Rushing

CAREER YARDS PER GAME
(Minimum 18 Games)

Player, Team (Division[s])	Years	G	Plays	Yards	TD	Yd. PG
Ed Marinaro, Cornell (I-A)	1969-71	27	918	4,715	50	*174.6
O. J. Simpson, Southern Cal (I-A)	1967-68	19	621	3,214	33	164.4
Johnny Bailey, Tex. A&M-Kingsville (II)	1986-89	39	885	*6,320	66	162.1
Herschel Walker, Georgia (I-A)	1980-82	33	994	5,259	49	159.4
Kirk Matthieu, Maine Maritime (III)	$1989-93	33	964	5,107	41	154.8
Terry Underwood, Wagner (III)	1985-88	33	742	5,010	52	151.8
LeShon Johnson, Northern Ill. (I-A)	1992-93	22	592	3,314	18	150.6
Ole Gunderson, St. Olaf (II)	1969-71	27	639	4,060	56	150.4
Marshall Faulk, San Diego St. (I-A)	1991-93	31	766	4,589	57	148.0
Brad Hustad, Luther (II)	1957-59	27	655	3,943	25	146.0
Anthony Russo, St. John's (N.Y.) (III)	1990-93	41	1,152	5,834	57	142.3
Tony Dorsett, Pittsburgh (I-A)	1973-76	43	1,074	6,082	55	141.4
Keith Elias, Princeton (I-AA)	1991-93	30	736	4,208	49	140.3
Joe Iacone, West Chester (II)	1960-62	27	565	3,767	40	139.5
Howard Stevens, Rand.-Macon (II); Louisville (I-A)	1968-69; 71-72	38	891	5,297	58	139.4
Mike Rozier, Nebraska (I-A)	1981-83	35	668	4,780	50	136.6
Joe Dudek, Plymouth St. (III)	1982-85	41	785	5,570	*76	135.9
Jerome Persell, Western Mich. (I-A)	1976-78	31	842	4,190	39	135.2

*Record. $See page 6 for explanation.

SEASON YARDS PER GAME

Player, Team (Division)	Year	G	Plays	Yards	TD	Yd. PG
Barry Sanders, Oklahoma St. (I-A)	†1988	11	344	*2,628	*37	*238.9
Marcus Allen, Southern Cal (I-A)	†1981	11	*403	2,342	22	212.9
Ed Marinaro, Cornell (I-A)	†1971	9	356	1,881	24	209.0
Ricky Gales, Simpson (III)	†1989	10	297	2,035	26	203.5
Tony Vinson, Towson St. (I-AA)	†1993	10	293	2,016	23	201.6
Terry Underwood, Wagner (III)	†1988	9	245	1,809	21	201.0
Kirk Matthieu, Maine Maritime (III)	†1992	9	327	1,733	16	192.6
Jon Warga, Wittenberg (III)	†1990	10	254	1,836	15	183.6
Johnny Bailey, Tex. A&M-Kingsville (II)	†1986	11	271	2,011	18	182.8
Bob White, Western N. Mex. (II)	†1951	9	202	1,643	20	182.6
Kevin Mitchell, Saginaw Valley (II)	1989	8	236	1,460	6	182.5
Hank Wineman, Albion (III)	†1991	9	307	1,629	14	181.0
Charles White, Southern Cal (I-A)	†1979	10	293	1,803	18	180.3
Eric Grey, Hamilton (III)	1991	8	217	1,439	13	179.9
Mike Birosak, Dickinson (III)	1989	10	380	1,798	18	179.8

Player, Team (Division)	Year	G	Plays	Yards	TD	Yd. PG
LeShon Johnson, Northern Ill. (I-A)	†1993	11	327	1,976	12	179.6
Don Aleksiewicz, Hobart (II)	†1971	9	276	1,616	19	179.6
Mike Rozier, Nebraska (I-A)	†1983	12	275	2,148	29	179.0
Jim Holder, Panhandle St. (II)	†1963	10	275	1,775	9	177.5
Tony Dorsett, Pittsburgh (I-A)	†1976	11	338	1,948	21	177.1
Chris Babirad, Wash. & Jeff. (III)	1992	9	243	1,589	22	176.6
Jim Baier, Wis.-River Falls (II)	†1966	9	240	1,587	17	176.3
Ollie Matson, San Francisco (I-A)	†1951	9	245	1,566	20	174.0

*Record. †National champion.

CAREER YARDS

Player, Team (Division[s])	Years	Plays	Yards	Avg.
Johnny Bailey, Tex. A&M-Kingsville (II)	1986-89	885	*6,320	7.14
Tony Dorsett, Pittsburgh (I-A)	1973-76	1,074	6,082	5.66
Anthony Russo, St. John's (N.Y.) (III)	1990-93	1,152	5,834	5.06
Charles White, Southern Cal (I-A)	1976-79	1,023	5,598	5.47
Joe Dudek, Plymouth St. (III)	1982-85	785	5,570	7.10
Frank Hawkins, Nevada (I-AA)	1977-80	945	5,333	5.64
Howard Stevens, Randolph-Macon (II); Louisville (I-A)	1968-69; 71-72	891	5,297	5.95
Eric Frees, Western Md. (III)	1988-91	1,059	5,281	4.99
Herschel Walker, Georgia (I-A)	1980-82	994	5,259	5.29
Kenny Gamble, Colgate (I-AA)	1984-87	963	5,220	5.42
Archie Griffin, Ohio St. (I-A)	1972-75	845	5,177	6.13
Markus Thomas, Eastern Ky. (I-AA)	1989-92	784	5,149	6.57
Shawn Graves, Wofford (QB) (II)	1989-92	730	5,128	7.02
Kirk Matthieu, Maine Maritime (III)	$1989-93	964	5,107	5.30
Chris Cobb, Eastern Ill. (II)	1976-79	930	5,042	5.42
Darren Lewis, Texas A&M (I-A)	1987-90	909	5,012	5.51
Terry Underwood, Wagner (III)	1985-88	742	5,010	6.75
Anthony Thompson, Indiana (I-A)	1986-89	1,089	4,965	4.56
George Rogers, South Caro. (I-A)	1977-80	902	4,958	5.50
Trevor Cobb, Rice (I-A)	1989-92	1,091	4,948	4.54
Paul Palmer, Temple (I-A)	1983-86	948	4,895	5.16
Harry Jackson, St. Cloud St. (II)	1986-89	915	4,890	5.34
Jerry Linton, Panhandle St. (II)	1959-62	648	4,839	‡7.47
Steve Bartalo, Colorado St. (I-A)	1983-86	*1,215	4,813	3.96

*Record. ‡Record for minimum of 600 carries. $See page 6 for explanation.

SEASON YARDS

Player, Team (Division)	Year	G	Plays	Yards	Avg.
Barry Sanders, Oklahoma St. (I-A)	†1988	11	344	*2,628	@7.64
Marcus Allen, Southern Cal (I-A)	†1981	11	*403	2,342	5.81
Mike Rozier, Nebraska (I-A)	†1983	12	275	2,148	††7.81
Ricky Gales, Simpson (III)	1989	10	297	2,035	6.85
Tony Vinson, Towson St. (I-AA)	†1993	10	293	2,016	6.89
Johnny Bailey, Tex. A&M-Kingsville (II)	†1986	11	271	2,011	7.42
LeShon Johnson, Northern Ill. (I-A)	†1993	11	327	1,976	6.04
Tony Dorsett, Pittsburgh (I-A)	†1976	11	338	1,948	5.76
Lorenzo White, Michigan St. (I-A)	†1985	11	386	1,908	4.94
Herschel Walker, Georgia (I-A)	†1981	11	385	1,891	4.91
Rich Erenberg, Colgate (I-AA)	†1983	11	302	1,883	6.24
Ed Marinaro, Cornell (I-A)	†1971	9	356	1,881	5.28
Ernest Anderson, Oklahoma St. (I-A)	†1982	11	353	1,877	5.32
Ricky Bell, Southern Cal (I-A)	†1975	11	357	1,875	5.25
Paul Palmer, Temple (I-A)	†1986	11	346	1,866	5.39
Ronald Moore, Pittsburg St. (II)	1992	11	239	1,864	7.80
Jon Warga, Wittenberg (III)	†1990	10	254	1,836	7.23
Zed Robinson, Southern Utah (II)	1991	11	254	1,828	7.20
Kenny Gamble, Colgate (I-AA)	†1986	11	307	1,816	5.92
Terry Underwood, Wagner (III)	†1988	9	245	1,809	6.75
Charles White, Southern Cal (I-A)	†1979	10	293	1,803	6.15

*Record. †National champion. ††Record for minimum of 214 carries. @ Record for minimum of 282 carries.

SINGLE-GAME YARDS

Yds.	Div.	Player, Team (Opponent)	Date
417	III	Carey Bender, Coe (Grinnell)	Oct. 9, 1993
396	I-A	Tony Sands, Kansas (Missouri)	Nov. 23, 1991
386	I-A	Marshall Faulk, San Diego St. (Pacific, Cal.)	Sept. 14, 1991
382	III	Pete Baranek, Carthage (North Central)	Oct. 5, 1985
382	II	Kelly Ellis, Northern Iowa (Western Ill.)	Oct. 13, 1979
377	I-A	Anthony Thompson, Indiana (Wisconsin)	Nov. 11, 1989
373	II	Dallas Garber, Marietta (Wash. & Jeff.)	Nov. 7, 1959
370	II	Jim Baier, Wis.-River Falls (Wis.-Stevens Point)	Nov. 5, 1966
370	II	Jim Hissam, Marietta (Bethany, W.Va.)	Nov. 15, 1958
367	II	Don Polkinghorne, Washington, Mo. (Wash. & Lee)	Nov. 23, 1957
364	I-AA	Tony Vinson, Towson St. (Bucknell)	Nov. 13, 1993
363	III	Terry Underwood, Wagner (Hofstra)	Oct. 15, 1988
363	II	Richie Weaver, Widener (Moravian)	Oct. 17, 1970
357	I-A	Mike Pringle, Cal St. Fullerton (New Mexico St.)	Nov. 4, 1989
357	I-A	Rueben Mayes, Washington St. (Oregon)	Oct. 27, 1984
356	I-A	Eddie Lee Ivery, Georgia Tech (Air Force)	Nov. 11, 1978
356	II	Ole Gunderson, St. Olaf (Monmouth, Ill.)	Oct. 11, 1969
354	III	Terry Underwood, Wagner (Western Conn. St.)	Oct. 3, 1986
350	II	Ricke Stonewall, Millersville (New Haven)	Nov. 13, 1982
350	I-A	Eric Allen, Michigan St. (Purdue)	Oct. 30, 1971

Ty Detmer of Brigham Young has the highest career passing efficiency rating (162.7) of any collegiate quarterback with 475 or more completions.

Passing

CAREER PASSING EFFICIENCY
(Minimum 475 Completions)

Player, Team (Division[s])	Years	Att.	Cmp.	Int.	Pct.	Yds.	TD	Pts.
Ty Detmer, Brigham Young (I-A)	1988-91	1,530	*958	65	.626	*15,031	121	*162.7
Jim Ballard, Wilmington (Ohio)/ Mount Union (III)	1990, 91-93	1,199	743	41	.620	10,379	115	159.5
Jim McMahon, Brigham Young (I-A)	1977-78, 80-81	1,060	653	34	.616	9,536	84	156.9
Doug Nussmeier, Idaho (I-AA)	1990-93	1,225	746	32	.609	10,824	91	154.4
Steve Young, Brigham Young (I-A)	1981-83	908	592	33	.652	7,733	56	149.8
Jack Hull, Grand Valley St. (II)	1988-91	835	485	22	.581	7,120	64	149.7
Robbie Bosco, Brigham Young (I-A)	1983-85	997	638	36	.640	8,400	66	149.4
Elvis Grbac, Michigan (I-A)	1989-92	754	477	29	.633	5,859	64	148.9
Chuck Long, Iowa (I-A)	$1981-85	1,072	692	46	.646	9,210	64	147.8
Willie Totten, Mississippi Val. (I-AA)	1982-85	1,555	907	*75	.583	12,711	*139	146.8
John Koz, Baldwin-Wallace (III)	1990-93	981	609	28	.621	7,724	71	146.4
Mike Smith, Northern Iowa (I-AA)	1984-87	943	557	43	.591	8,219	58	143.5
Neil Lomax, Portland St. (II; I-AA)	1977; 78-80	1,606	938	55	.584	13,220	106	142.5
Marvin Graves, Syracuse (I-A)	1990-93	943	563	45	.597	8,466	48	142.4
Tom Ciaccio, Holy Cross (I-AA)	1988-91	1,073	658	46	.613	8,603	72	142.2
George Bork, Northern Ill. (II)	1960-63	902	577	33	.640	6,782	60	141.8
Eric Beavers, Nevada (I-AA)	1983-86	1,094	646	37	.591	8,626	77	141.8
Doug Gaynor, Long Beach St. (I-A)	1984-85	837	569	35	.680	6,793	35	141.6
Scott Semptimphelter, Lehigh (I-AA)	1990-93	823	493	27	.599	6,668	50	141.5
Ed Hesson, Rowan (III)	1990-93	895	504	26	.563	7,053	67	141.2

Player, Team (Division[s])	Years	Att.	Cmp.	Int.	Pct.	Yds.	TD	Pts.
Steve Stenstrom, Stanford (I-A)	1991-93	987	616	30	.624	7,709	56	140.7
Matt Jozokos, Plymouth St. (III)	1987-90	1,003	527	39	.525	7,658	95	140.2
Dan McGwire, Iowa/San Diego St. (I-A)	1986-87, 89-90	973	575	30	.591	8,164	49	140.0
Chris Vargas, Nevada (I-AA; I-A)	1990-91; 92-93	1,017	625	42	.615	8,130	60	139.8
John Elway, Stanford (I-A)	1979-82	1,246	774	39	.621	9,349	77	139.3
Jamie Martin, Weber St. (I-AA)	1989-92	1,544	934	56	.605	12,207	87	138.2
David Klingler, Houston (I-A)	1988-91	1,261	726	38	.576	9,430	91	138.2
Doug Williams, Grambling (II; I-A)	1974-76; 77	1,009	484	52	.480	8,411	93	138.1

*Record. $See page 6 for explanation.

CAREER PASSING EFFICIENCY
(Minimum 325-474 Completions)

Player, Team (Division[s])	Years	Att.	Cmp.	Int.	Pct.	Yds.	TD	Pts.
John Charles, Portland St. (II)	1991-92	510	326	14	.639	5,389	56	*183.4
Tony Aliucci, Indiana (Pa.) (II)	1988-91	579	350	24	.604	5,655	53	164.4
Jayson Merrill, Western St. (II)	1990-91	580	328	25	.566	5,830	56	164.2
Chris Petersen, UC Davis (II)	1985-86	553	385	13	*.696	4,988	39	164.0
Dennis Shaw, San Diego St. (II; I-A)	1968; 69	575	333	41	.579	5,324	58	154.7
Joe Blake, Simpson (III)	1987-90	672	399	15	.594	6,183	43	153.3
Vinny Testaverde, Miami (Fla.) (I-A)	1982, 84-86	674	413	25	.613	6,058	48	152.9
Jim McMillan, Boise St. (II)	1971-74	640	382	29	.597	5,508	58	152.8
Willie Reyna, La Verne (III)	1991-92	542	346	19	.638	4,712	37	152.4
Trent Dilfer, Fresno St. (I-A)	1991-93	774	461	21	.596	6,944	51	151.2
Troy Aikman, Oklahoma/UCLA (I-A)	1984-85, 87-88	637	401	18	.630	5,436	40	149.7
Jim Harbaugh, Michigan (I-A)	1983-86	582	368	19	.632	5,215	31	149.6
Chuck Hartlieb, Iowa (I-A)	1985-88	716	461	17	.643	6,269	34	148.9
Jay Johnson, Northern Iowa (I-AA)	1989-92	744	397	25	.534	7,049	51	148.9
Danny White, Arizona St. (I-A)	1971-73	649	345	36	.532	5,932	59	148.9
Gary Collier, Emory & Henry (III)	1984-87	738	386	33	.523	6,103	80	148.6
Kenneth Biggles, Tennessee St. (I-AA)	1981-84	701	397	28	.566	5,933	57	146.6
Gifford Nielsen, Brigham Young (I-A)	1975-77	708	415	29	.586	5,833	55	145.3
Greg Heeres, Hope (III)	1981-84	630	347	21	.537	5,120	53	144.4
Bruce Upstill, Col. of Emporia (II)	1960-63	769	438	36	.570	6,935	48	144.0
Tom Ramsey, UCLA (I-A)	1979-82	691	411	33	.595	5,844	48	143.9
Shawn Moore, Virginia (I-A)	1987-90	762	421	32	.552	6,629	55	143.8
Jerry Rhome, Southern Methodist/Tulsa (I-A)	1961, 63-64	713	448	23	.628	5,472	47	142.6
Jim Zaccheo, Nevada (I-AA)	1987-88	554	326	27	.588	4,750	35	142.0
Charlie Ward, Florida St. (I-A)	1989, 91-93	759	474	21	.625	5,747	49	141.8
Bruce Crosthwaite, Adrian (III)	1984-87	618	368	31	.596	4,959	45	141.0
Steve Mariucci, Northern Mich. (II)	1974-77	678	380	33	.561	6,022	41	140.9
Jim Karsatos, Ohio St. (I-A)	1983-86	573	330	19	.576	4,698	36	140.6
Jason Garrett, Princeton (I-AA)	1987-88	550	368	10	.669	4,274	20	140.6
Scott Barry, UC Davis (II)	1982-84	588	377	16	.641	4,421	33	140.4
Jerry Tagge, Nebraska (I-A)	1969-71	581	348	19	.599	4,704	33	140.1

*Record.

SEASON PASSING EFFICIENCY
(Minimum 30 Attempts Per Game)

Player, Team (Division)	Year	G	Att.	Cmp.	Int.	Pct.	Yds.	TD	Pts.
Jim Ballard, Mount Union (III)	1993	10	314	229	11	*.729	3,304	37	*193.2
Jayson Merrill, Western St. (II)	†1991	10	309	195	11	.631	3,484	35	188.1
John Charles, Portland St. (II)	1992	8	263	179	7	.681	2,770	24	181.3
Jim McMahon, Brigham Young (I-A)	†1980	12	445	284	18	.638	4,571	47	176.9
Ty Detmer, Brigham Young (I-A)	†1989	12	412	265	15	.643	4,560	32	175.6
Trent Dilfer, Fresno St. (I-A)	†1993	11	333	217	4	.652	3,276	28	173.1
Jerry Rhome, Tulsa (I-A)	†1964	10	326	224	4	.687	2,870	32	172.6
Ty Detmer, Brigham Young (I-A)	1991	12	403	249	12	.618	4,031	35	168.5
Steve Young, Brigham Young (I-A)	†1983	11	429	306	10	.713	3,902	33	168.5
Willie Totten, Mississippi Val. (I-AA)	†1983	9	279	174	19	.624	2,566	29	167.5
Jim McMillan, Boise St. (II)	†1974	10	313	192	15	.613	2,900	33	164.4
Willie Totten, Mississippi Val. (I-AA)	†1984	10	518	324	22	.626	4,557	*56	163.6
Jeff Wiley, Holy Cross (I-AA)	†1987	11	400	265	17	.663	3,677	34	163.0
Todd Hammel, Stephen F. Austin (I-AA)	†1989	11	401	238	13	.594	3,914	34	162.8
Dennis Shaw, San Diego St. (I-A)	†1969	10	335	199	26	.594	3,185	39	162.2
John Friesz, Idaho (I-AA)	1989	11	425	260	8	.612	4,041	31	161.4
Willie Reyna, La Verne (III)	1991	8	267	170	6	.636	2,543	16	158.8
Charlie Ward, Florida St. (I-A)	1993	11	380	264	4	.695	3,032	27	157.8
Glenn Foley, Boston College (I-A)	1993	11	363	222	10	.612	3,395	25	157.0
Chris Vargas, Nevada (I-A)	1993	11	490	331	18	.676	4,265	34	156.2
George Bork, Northern Ill. (II)	1963	9	374	244	12	.652	2,824	32	156.2
John Walsh, Brigham Young (I-A)	1993	11	397	244	15	.615	3,727	28	156.0
Neil Lomax, Portland St. (I-AA)	1980	11	473	296	12	.626	4,094	37	156.0
Ty Detmer, Brigham Young (I-A)	1990	12	562	361	28	.642	*5,188	41	155.9
Rob Johnson, Southern Cal (I-A)	1993	12	405	278	5	.686	3,285	26	155.5
Doug Williams, Grambling (I-A)	1977	11	352	181	18	.514	3,286	38	155.2
Jim McMahon, Brigham Young (I-A)	†1981	10	423	272	7	.643	3,555	30	155.0
Andy Breault, Kutztown (II)	1991	10	360	225	20	.625	2,927	37	153.4
Chuck Long, Iowa (I-A)	1985	11	351	231	15	.658	2,978	26	153.0
Doug Flutie, Boston College (I-A)	1984	11	386	233	11	.604	3,454	27	152.9

*Record. †National pass-efficiency champion.

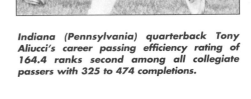

Indiana (Pennsylvania) quarterback Tony Aliucci's career passing efficiency rating of 164.4 ranks second among all collegiate passers with 325 to 474 completions.

Neil Lomax passed for 13,220 yards, the second-best total in collegiate history, during his four seasons at Portland State.

SEASON PASSING EFFICIENCY
(Minimum 15 Attempts Per Game)

Player, Team (Division)	Year	G	Att.	Cmp.	Int.	Pct.	Yds.	TD	Pts.
Willie Seiler, St. John's (Minn.) (III)	†1993	10	205	141	6	.687	2,648	33	*224.6
Boyd Crawford, Col. of Idaho (II)	†1953	8	120	72	6	.600	1,462	21	210.1
Shawn Knight, William & Mary (I-AA)	†1993	10	177	125	4	.706	2,055	22	204.6
Chuck Green, Wittenberg (III)	†1963	9	182	114	8	.626	2,181	19	189.0
Jim Feeley, Johns Hopkins (II)	†1967	7	110	69	5	.627	1,264	12	186.2
John Charles, Portland St. (II)	1991	11	247	147	7	.595	2,619	32	185.7
Steve Smith, Western St. (II)	†1992	10	271	180	5	.664	2,719	30	183.5
Mitch Sanders, Bridgeport (III)	†1973	10	151	84	7	.556	1,551	23	182.9
Jim Peterson, Hanover (II)	†1948	8	125	81	12	.648	1,571	12	182.9
John Wristen, Southern Colo. (II)	†1982	8	121	68	2	.562	1,358	13	182.6
Michael Payton, Marshall (I-AA)	†1991	9	216	143	5	.622	2,333	19	181.3
Richard Basil, Savannah St. (II)	†1989	9	211	120	7	.568	2,148	29	181.1
Pat Mayew, St. John's (Minn.) (III)	†1991	9	247	154	4	.623	2,408	30	181.0
Guy Simons, Coe (III)	1993	10	185	110	9	.594	1,979	21	177.1
Jim Cahoon, Ripon (II)	†1964	8	127	74	7	.583	1,206	19	176.4
Ken Suhl, New Haven (II)	1992	10	239	148	5	.619	2,336	26	175.7
Jimbo Fisher, Samford (III)	†1987	10	252	139	5	.551	2,394	34	175.4
Doug Nussmeier, Idaho (I-AA)	1993	11	304	185	5	.609	2,960	33	175.2
Gary Collier, Emory & Henry (III)	1987	11	249	152	10	.610	2,317	33	174.8
Kelvin Simmons, Troy St. (I-AA)	1993	11	224	143	6	.638	2,144	23	172.8
James Grant, Ramapo (III)	1989	9	147	91	7	.619	1,441	17	172.7
Tony Aliucci, Indiana (Pa.) (II)	†1990	10	181	111	10	.613	1,801	21	172.7
James Weir, New Haven (II)	†1993	10	266	161	1	.605	2,336	31	172.0
Frank Baur, Lafayette (I-AA)	†1988	10	256	164	11	.641	2,621	23	171.1
Bobby Lamb, Furman (I-AA)	†1985	11	181	106	6	.586	1,856	18	170.9
Gary Urwiler, Eureka (III)	1991	10	171	103	5	.602	1,656	18	170.3
John Costello, Widener (II)	†1956	9	149	74	10	.497	1,702	17	169.8
Kurt Coduti, Michigan Tech (II)	1992	9	155	92	3	.594	1,518	15	169.7
Chris Petersen, UC Davis (II)	†1985	10	242	167	6	.690	2,366	17	169.4
Jay Fiedler, Dartmouth (I-AA)	†1992	10	273	175	13	.641	2,748	25	169.4

Record. †National pass-efficiency champion.

CAREER YARDS

Player, Team (Division[s])	Years	Att.	Cmp.	Int.	Pct.	Yds.	TD
Ty Detmer, Brigham Young (I-A)	1988-91	1,530	*958	65	.626	*15,031	121
Neil Lomax, Portland St. (II; I-AA)	1977; 78-80	1,606	938	55	.584	13,220	106
Kirk Baumgartner, Wis.-Stevens Point (III)	1986-89	*1,696	883	57	.521	13,028	110
Willie Totten, Mississippi Val. (I-AA)	1982-85	1,555	907	*75	.583	12,711	*139
Jamie Martin, Weber St. (I-AA)	1989-92	1,544	934	56	.605	12,207	87
Todd Santos, San Diego St. (I-A)	1984-87	1,484	910	57	.613	11,425	70
Alex Van Pelt, Pittsburgh (I-A)	1989-92	1,463	845	59	.578	10,913	64
Doug Nussmeier, Idaho (I-AA)	1990-93	1,225	746	32	.609	10,824	91
John Friesz, Idaho (I-AA)	1986-89	1,350	801	40	.593	10,697	77
Greg Wyatt, Northern Ariz. (I-AA)	1986-89	1,510	926	49	.613	10,697	70
Sean Payton, Eastern Ill. (I-AA)	1983-86	1,408	756	55	.537	10,655	75
Kevin Sweeney, Fresno St. (I-A)	$1982-86	1,336	731	48	.547	10,623	66
Earl Harvey, N.C. Central (II)	1985-88	1,442	690	81	.479	10,621	86
Doug Flutie, Boston College (I-A)	1981-84	1,270	677	54	.533	10,579	67
Jim Ballard, Wilmington (Ohio)/Mount Union (III)	1990, 91-93	1,199	743	41	.620	10,379	115
Tom Ehrhardt, LIU-C.W. Post (II); Rhode Island (I-AA)	1981-82; 84-85	1,489	833	63	.559	10,325	92
Brian McClure, Bowling Green (I-A)	1982-85	1,427	900	58	.631	10,280	63
Troy Kopp, Pacific (Cal.) (I-A)	1989-92	1,374	798	47	.581	10,258	87
Glenn Foley, Boston College (I-A)	1990-93	1,275	703	60	.551	10,042	72
Jeff Wiley, Holy Cross (I-AA)	1985-88	1,208	723	63	.599	9,698	71
¢Steve McNair, Alcorn St. (I-AA)	1991-93	1,150	625	41	.543	9,633	75
Ben Bennett, Duke (I-A)	1980-83	1,375	820	57	.596	9,614	53
Keith Bishop, Ill. Wesleyan/Wheaton (Ill.) (III)	1981, 83-85	1,311	772	65	.589	9,579	71
Robbie Justino, Liberty (I-AA)	1989-92	1,267	769	51	.607	9,548	64
Dennis Bogacz, Wis.-Oshkosh/Wis.-Whitewater (III)	1988-89, 90-91	1,275	654	59	.513	9,536	66
Jim McMahon, Brigham Young (I-A)	1977-78, 80-81	1,060	653	34	.616	9,536	84
Todd Ellis, South Caro. (I-A)	1986-89	1,266	704	66	.556	9,519	97
Dave Geissler, Wis.-Stevens Point (III)	1982-85	1,346	789	57	.586	9,518	65
Rob Tomlinson, Cal St. Chico (II)	1988-91	1,328	748	43	.563	9,434	52
David Klingler, Houston (I-A)	1988-91	1,261	726	38	.576	9,430	91
Erik Wilhelm, Oregon St. (I-A)	1985-88	1,480	870	61	.588	9,393	52
Jeremy Leach, New Mexico (I-A)	1988-91	1,432	735	62	.513	9,382	50
John Elway, Stanford (I-A)	1979-82	1,246	774	39	.621	9,349	77
T. J. Rubley, Tulsa (I-A)	1987-89, 91	1,336	682	54	.510	9,324	73
Kirk Schulz, Villanova (I-AA)	1986-89	1,297	774	70	.597	9,305	70
Ken Hobart, Idaho (I-AA)	1980-83	1,219	629	42	.516	9,300	79

Record. $See page 6 for explanation. ¢Active player.

CAREER YARDS PER GAME
(Minimum 20 Games)

Player, Team (Division[s])	Years	G	Att.	Cmp.	Int.	Pct.	Yds.	TD	Yd.PG
Ty Detmer, Brigham Young (I-A)	1988-91	46	1,530	*958	65	.626	*15,031	121	*326.8
Willie Totten, Mississippi Val. (I-AA)	1982-85	40	1,555	907	*75	.583	12,711	*139	317.8
Kirk Baumgartner, Wis.-Stevens Point (III)	1986-89	41	*1,696	883	57	.521	13,028	110	317.8
Neil Lomax, Portland St. (II; I-AA)	1977; 78-80	42	1,606	938	55	.584	13,220	106	314.8
Mike Perez, San Jose St. (I-A)	1986-87	20	792	471	30	.595	6,194	36	309.7
Keith Bishop, Ill. Wes./Wheaton (Ill.) (III)	1981, 83-85	31	1,311	772	65	.589	9,579	71	309.0
Doug Gaynor, Long Beach St. (I-A)	1984-85	22	837	569	35	.680	6,793	35	308.8
John Friesz, Idaho (I-AA)	1986-89	35	1,350	801	40	.593	10,697	77	305.6
Tony Eason, Illinois (I-A)	1981-82	22	856	526	29	.615	6,608	37	300.4

*Record.

CAREER TOUCHDOWN PASSES

Player, Team (Division[s])	Years	Att.	Cmp.	Int.	Pct.	Yds.	TD
Willie Totten, Mississippi Val. (I-AA)	1982-85	1,555	907	*75	.583	12,711	*139
Ty Detmer, Brigham Young (I-A)	1988-91	1,530	*958	65	.626	*15,031	121
Jim Ballard, Wilmington (Ohio)/Mount Union (III)	1990, 91-93	1,199	743	41	.620	10,379	115
Kirk Baumgartner, Wis.-Stevens Point (III)	1986-89	*1,696	883	57	.521	13,028	110
Neil Lomax, Portland St. (II; I-AA)	1977; 78-80	1,606	938	55	.584	13,220	106
Matt Jozokos, Plymouth St. (III)	1987-90	1,003	527	39	.525	7,658	95
Doug Williams, Grambling (II; I-A)	1974-76; 77	1,009	484	52	.480	8,411	93
Tom Ehrhardt, LIU-C.W. Post (II); Rhode Island (I-AA)	1981-82; 84-85	1,489	833	63	.559	10,325	92
Doug Nussmeier, Idaho (I-AA)	1990-93	1,225	746	32	.609	10,824	91
David Klingler, Houston (I-A)	1988-91	1,261	726	38	.576	9,430	91
Troy Kopp, Pacific (Cal.) (I-A)	1989-92	1,374	798	47	.581	10,258	87
Jamie Martin, Weber St. (I-AA)	1989-92	1,544	934	56	.605	12,207	87
Andy Breault, Kutztown (II)	1989-92	1,259	733	63	.582	9,086	86
Earl Harvey, N.C. Central (II)	1985-88	1,442	690	81	.479	10,621	86
Rex Lamberti, Abilene Christian (II)	1984-86, 93	1,133	595	44	.525	7,934	84
Jim McMahon, Brigham Young (I-A)	1977-78, 80-81	1,060	653	34	.616	9,536	84
Joe Adams, Tennessee St. (I-A)	1977-80	1,100	604	60	.549	8,649	81
Gary Collier, Emory & Henry (III)	1984-87	738	386	33	.523	6,103	80
Ken Hobart, Idaho (I-AA)	1980-83	1,219	629	42	.516	9,300	79

*Record.

SEASON YARDS

Player, Team (Division)	Year	G	Att.	Cmp.	Int.	Pct.	Yds.	TD
Ty Detmer, Brigham Young (I-A)	†1990	12	562	361	28	.642	*5,188	41
David Klingler, Houston (I-A)	1990	11	*643	*374	20	.582	5,140	54
Andre Ware, Houston (I-A)	†1989	11	578	365	15	.631	4,699	46
Jim McMahon, Brigham Young (I-A)	†1980	12	445	284	18	.638	4,571	47
Ty Detmer, Brigham Young (I-A)	1989	12	412	265	15	.643	4,560	32
Willie Totten, Mississippi Val. (I-AA)	†1984	10	518	324	22	.626	4,557	*56
Scott Mitchell, Utah (I-A)	1988	11	533	323	15	.606	4,322	29
Chris Vargas, Nevada (I-A)	1993	11	490	331	18	.676	4,265	34
Robbie Bosco, Brigham Young (I-A)	1985	13	511	338	24	.661	4,257	30
Jamie Martin, Weber St. (I-AA)	1991	11	500	310	17	.620	4,125	35
Neil Lomax, Portland St. (I-AA)	1980	11	473	296	12	.626	4,094	37
John Friesz, Idaho (I-AA)	†1989	11	425	260	8	.612	4,041	31
Ty Detmer, Brigham Young (I-A)	1991	12	403	249	12	.618	4,031	35
Neil Lomax, Portland St. (I-AA)	1979	11	516	299	16	.579	3,950	26
Todd Santos, San Diego St. (I-A)	1987	12	492	306	15	.622	3,932	26
Todd Hammel, Stephen F. Austin (I-AA)	1989	11	401	238	13	.594	3,914	34
Steve Young, Brigham Young (I-A)	†1983	11	429	306	10	*.713	3,902	33
Robbie Bosco, Brigham Young (I-A)	1984	12	458	283	11	.618	3,875	33
Mike McCoy, Utah (I-A)	1993	12	430	276	10	.642	3,860	21
Sean Payton, Eastern Ill. (I-AA)	1984	11	473	270	15	.571	3,843	28
Dan McGwire, San Diego St. (I-A)	1990	11	449	270	7	.601	3,833	27
Kirk Baumgartner, Wis.-Stevens Point (III)	1988	11	527	276	16	.524	3,828	25
Anthony Dilweg, Duke (I-A)	1988	11	484	287	18	.593	3,824	24
Jimmy Klingler, Houston (I-A)	1992	11	504	303	18	.601	3,818	32
Sam King, Nevada-Las Vegas (I-A)	1981	12	433	255	19	.589	3,778	18
Troy Kopp, Pacific (Cal.) (I-A)	1991	12	449	275	16	.612	3,767	37
Perry Klein, LIU-C.W. Post (II)	1993	10	407	248	18	.609	3,757	38
Kirk Baumgartner, Wis.-Stevens Point (III)	1987	11	466	243	22	.521	3,755	31
Chris Hegg, Northeast Mo. St. (II)	1985	11	503	284	20	.565	3,741	32
Brett Salisbury, Wayne St. (Neb.) (II)	1993	10	395	276	14	.699	3,729	29
John Walsh, Brigham Young (I-A)	1993	11	397	244	15	.615	3,727	28
Marc Wilson, Brigham Young (I-A)	1979	12	427	250	15	.585	3,720	29

*Record. †National pass-efficiency champion.

SEASON YARDS PER GAME

Player, Team (Division)	Year	G	Att.	Cmp.	Int.	Pct.	Yds.	TD	Yd.PG
David Klingler, Houston (I-A)	1990	11	*643	*374	20	.582	5,140	54	*467.3
Willie Totten, Mississippi Val. (I-AA)	1984	10	518	324	22	.626	4,557	*56	455.7
Ty Detmer, Brigham Young (I-A)	1990	12	562	361	28	.642	*5,188	41	432.3
Andre Ware, Houston (I-A)	1989	11	578	365	15	.631	4,699	46	427.2
Scott Mitchell, Utah (I-A)	1988	11	533	323	15	.606	4,322	29	392.9
Chris Vargas, Nevada (I-A)	1993	11	490	331	18	.676	4,265	34	387.7
Marty Washington, Livingston (II)	1993	8	404	221	13	.547	3,062	26	382.8
Jim McMahon, Brigham Young (I-A)	1980	12	445	284	18	.638	4,571	47	380.9
Ty Detmer, Brigham Young (I-A)	1989	12	412	265	15	.643	4,560	32	380.0

*Record.

In 1990, Houston's David Klingler passed for a collegiate record 467.3 yards per game. He also set records for single-season attempts (643) and completions (374).

SEASON TOUCHDOWN PASSES

Player, Team (Division)	Year	Att.	Cmp.	Int.	Pct.	Yds.	TD
Willie Totten, Mississippi Val. (I-AA)	1984	518	324	22	.626	4,557	*56
David Klingler, Houston (I-A)	1990	*643	*374	20	.582	5,140	54
Jim McMahon, Brigham Young (I-A)	1980	445	284	18	.638	4,571	47
Andre Ware, Houston (I-A)	1989	578	365	15	.631	4,699	46
Bob Toledo, San Fran. St. (II)	1967	396	211	24	.533	3,513	45
Ty Detmer, Brigham Young (I-A)	1990	562	361	28	.642	*5,188	41
Kirk Baumgartner, Wis.-Stevens Point (III)	1989	455	247	9	.542	3,692	39
Willie Totten, Mississippi Val. (I-AA)	1985	492	295	29	.600	3,698	39
Dennis Shaw, San Diego St. (I-A)	1969	335	199	26	.594	3,185	39
Perry Klein, LIU-C.W. Post (II)	1993	407	248	18	.609	3,757	38
Doug Williams, Grambling (I-A)	1977	352	181	18	.514	3,286	38
Jim Ballard, Mount Union (III)	1993	314	229	11	.729	3,304	37
Chris Hatcher, Valdosta St. (II)	1993	471	335	11	.711	3,651	37
Andy Breault, Kutztown (II)	1991	360	225	20	.625	2,927	37
Troy Kopp, Pacific (Cal.) (I-A)	1991	449	275	16	.613	3,767	37
Neil Lomax, Portland St. (I-AA)	1980	473	296	12	.626	4,094	37
Jayson Merrill, Western St. (II)	1991	309	195	11	.631	3,484	35
Ty Detmer, Brigham Young (I-A)	1991	403	249	12	.618	4,031	35
Jamie Martin, Weber St. (I-AA)	1991	500	310	17	.620	4,125	35
Tom Ehrhardt, Rhode Island (I-AA)	1985	497	283	19	.569	3,542	35

*Record.

SINGLE-GAME YARDS

Yds.	Div.	Player, Team (Opponent)	Date
716	I-A	David Klingler, Houston (Arizona St.)	Dec. 2, 1990
690	I-A	Matt Vogler, Texas Christian (Houston)	Nov. 3, 1990
631	I-A	Scott Mitchell, Utah (Air Force)	Oct. 15, 1988
624	I-AA	Jamie Martin, Weber St. (Idaho St.)	Nov. 23, 1991
622	I-A	Jeremy Leach, New Mexico (Utah)	Nov. 11, 1989
621	I-A	Dave Wilson, Illinois (Ohio St.)	Nov. 8, 1980
619	I-A	John Walsh, Brigham Young (Utah St.)	Oct. 30, 1993
619	I-AA	Doug Pederson, Northeast La. (Stephen F. Austin)	Nov. 11, 1989
614	II	Perry Klein, LIU-C.W. Post (Salisbury St.)	Nov. 6, 1993
613	I-A	Jimmy Klingler, Houston (Rice)	Nov. 28, 1992
602	III	Tom Stallings, St. Thomas, Minn. (Bethel, Minn.)	Nov. 13, 1993
599	I-A	Ty Detmer, Brigham Young (San Diego St.)	Nov. 16, 1991
599	I-AA	Willie Totten, Mississippi Val. (Prairie View)	Oct. 27, 1984
592	II	John Charles, Portland St. (Cal Poly SLO)	Nov. 16, 1991
589	I-AA	Vern Harris, Idaho St. (Montana)	Oct. 12, 1985
585	III	Tim Lynch, Hofstra (Fordham)	Oct. 19, 1991
585	I-A	Robbie Bosco, Brigham Young (New Mexico)	Oct. 19, 1985
572	I-A	David Klingler, Houston (Eastern Wash.)	Nov. 17, 1990
571	I-AA	Todd Hammel, Stephen F. Austin (Northeast La.)	Nov. 11, 1989
571	I-A	Marc Wilson, Brigham Young (Utah)	Nov. 5, 1977
568	I-A	David Lowery, San Diego St. (Brigham Young)	Nov. 16, 1991
568	II	Bob Toledo, San Fran. St. (Cal St. Hayward)	Oct. 21, 1967
566	I-AA	Tom Ehrhardt, Rhode Island (Connecticut)	Nov. 16, 1985
565	I-A	Jim McMahon, Brigham Young (Utah)	Nov. 21, 1981
564	I-A	Troy Kopp, Pacific, Cal. (New Mexico St.)	Oct. 20, 1990
563	I-A	David Klingler, Houston (Texas Christian)	Nov. 3, 1990
561	I-A	Tony Adams, Utah St. (Utah)	Nov. 11, 1972

SINGLE-GAME ATTEMPTS

Atts.	Div.	Player, Team (Opponent)	Date
81	III	Jordan Poznick, Principia (Blackburn)	Oct. 10, 1992
79	I-A	Matt Vogler, Texas Christian (Houston)	Nov. 3, 1990
79	III	Mike Wallace, Ohio Wesleyan (Denison)	Oct. 3, 1981
77	I-AA	Neil Lomax, Portland St. (Northern Colo.)	Oct. 20, 1979
76	I-A	David Klingler, Houston (Southern Methodist)	Oct. 20, 1990
75	I-A	Chris Vargas, Nevada (McNeese St.)	Sept. 19, 1992
74	I-AA	Paul Peterson, Idaho St. (Nevada)	Oct. 1, 1983
73	I-A	Jeff Handy, Missouri (Oklahoma St.)	Oct. 17, 1992
73	I-A	Troy Kopp, Pacific, Cal. (Hawaii)	Oct. 27, 1990
73	I-A	Shane Montgomery, North Caro. St. (Duke)	Nov. 11, 1989
72	I-A	Matt Vogler, Texas Christian (Texas Tech)	Nov. 10, 1990
72	II	Kurt Otto, North Dak. (Tex. A&M-Kingsville)	Sept. 13, 1986
72	III	Bob Lockhart, Millikin (Franklin)	Nov. 12, 1977
72	II	Kaipo Spencer, Santa Clara (Portland St.)	Oct. 11, 1975
72	II	Joe Stetser, Cal St. Chico (Oregon Tech)	Sept. 23, 1967

SINGLE-GAME COMPLETIONS

Cmp.	Div.	Player, Team (Opponent)	Date
50	III	Tim Lynch, Hofstra (Fordham)	Oct. 19, 1991
48	III	Jordan Poznick, Principia (Blackburn)	Oct. 10, 1992
48	I-A	David Klingler, Houston (Southern Methodist)	Oct. 20, 1990
47	I-AA	Jamie Martin, Weber St. (Idaho St.)	Nov. 23, 1991
47	III	Mike Wallace, Ohio Wesleyan (Denison)	Oct. 3, 1981
46	I-A	Jimmy Klingler, Houston (Rice)	Nov. 28, 1992
46	I-AA	Doug Pederson, Northeast La. (Stephen F. Austin)	Nov. 11, 1989
46	I-AA	Willie Totten, Mississippi Val. (Southern-B.R.)	Sept. 23, 1984
45	II	Chris Hatcher, Valdosta St. (Mississippi Col.)	Oct. 23, 1993
45	II	Chris Hatcher, Valdosta St. (West Ga.)	Oct. 16, 1993
45	I-AA	Willie Totten, Mississippi Val. (Prairie View)	Oct. 27, 1984
45	I-A	Sandy Schwab, Northwestern (Michigan)	Oct. 23, 1982
44	I-A	Matt Vogler, Texas Christian (Houston)	Nov. 3, 1990
44	I-A	Chuck Hartlieb, Iowa (Indiana)	Oct. 29, 1988
44	II	Tom Bonds, Cal Lutheran (St. Mary's, Cal.)	Nov. 22, 1986
44	I-A	Jim McMahon, Brigham Young (Colorado St.)	Nov. 7, 1981
44	I-AA	Neil Lomax, Portland St. (Northern Colo.)	Oct. 20, 1979
43	I-A	Jeff Handy, Missouri (Oklahoma St.)	Oct. 17, 1992
43	I-A	Chris Vargas, Nevada (McNeese St.)	Sept. 19, 1992
43	I-A	Gary Schofield, Wake Forest (Maryland)	Oct. 17, 1981
43	I-A	Dave Wilson, Illinois (Ohio St.)	Nov. 8, 1980
43	I-A	Rich Campbell, California (Florida)	Sept. 13, 1980
43	II	George Bork, Northern Ill. (Central Mich.)	Nov. 9, 1963

Receiving

CAREER CATCHES

Player, Team (Division[s])	Years	Rec.	Yards	Avg.	TD
Jerry Rice, Mississippi Val. (I-AA)	1981-84	*301	*4,693	15.6	50
Matt Newton, Principia (III)	1990-93	287	3,646	12.7	32
Kasey Dunn, Idaho (I-AA)	1988-91	268	3,847	14.4	25
Aaron Turner, Pacific (Cal.) (I-A)	1989-92	266	4,345	16.3	43
Terance Mathis, New Mexico (I-A)	1985-87, 89	263	4,254	16.2	36
Mark Templeton, Long Beach St. (I-A) (RB)	1983-86	¢262	1,969	7.5	11
Howard Twilley, Tulsa (I-A)	1963-65	261	3,343	12.8	32
Bill Stromberg, Johns Hopkins (III)	1978-81	258	3,776	14.6	39
Chris Myers, Kenyon (II)	1967-70	253	3,897	15.4	33
Brian Forster, Rhode Island (I-AA) (TE)	1983-85, 87	#245	#3,410	13.9	31
David Williams, Illinois (I-A)	1983-85	245	3,195	13.0	22
Bruce Cerone, Yankton/Emporia St. (II)	1966-67, 68-69	241	4,354	18.1	49
Mark Didio, Connecticut (I-AA)	1988-91	239	3,535	14.8	21
Rennie Benn, Lehigh (I-AA)	1982-85	237	3,662	15.5	44
Marc Zeno, Tulane (I-A)	1984-87	236	3,725	15.8	25
Jason Wolf, Southern Methodist (I-A)	1989-92	235	2,232	9.5	17
Bryan Reeves, Nevada (I-AA; I-A)	1991; 92-93	234	3,407	14.6	32
Dale Amos, Frank. & Marsh. (III)	1986-89	233	3,846	16.5	35
Scott Fredrickson, Wis.-Stout (III)	1986-89	233	3,390	14.5	23
Harold "Red" Roberts, Austin Peay (II)	1967-70	232	3,005	13.0	31
Mike Whitehouse, St. Norbert (III)	1986-89	230	3,480	15.1	37
Jerry Hendren, Idaho (II; I-A)	1967-68; 69	230	3,435	14.9	27

*Record. ¢Record for a running back. #Record for a tight end.

CAREER CATCHES PER GAME
(Minimum 20 Games)

Player, Team (Division[s])	Years	G	Rec.	Yards	TD	Rec.PG
Manny Hazard, Houston (I-A)	1989-90	21	220	2,635	31	*10.5
Howard Twilley, Tulsa (I-A)	1963-65	26	261	3,343	32	10.0
Jason Phillips, Houston (I-A)	1987-88	22	207	2,319	18	9.4
Matt Newton, Principia (III)	1990-93	33	287	3,646	32	8.7
Jerry Hendren, Idaho (II)	1967-69	30	230	3,435	27	7.7
Bryan Reeves, Nevada (I-AA; I-A)	1991-93	31	234	3,407	32	7.6
David Williams, Illinois (I-A)	1983-85	33	245	3,195	22	7.4
Gary Garrison, San Diego St. (II)	1964-65	20	148	2,188	26	7.4
Jerry Rice, Mississippi Val. (I-AA)	1981-84	41	*301	*4,693	50	7.3
James Dixon, Houston (I-A)	1987-88	22	161	1,762	14	7.3

*Record.

CAREER TOUCHDOWN RECEPTIONS

Player, Team (Division[s])	Years	G	TD
Chris Bisaillon, Ill. Wesleyan (III)	1989-92	36	*55
Jerry Rice, Mississippi Val. (I-AA)	1981-84	41	50
Bruce Cerone, Yankton/Emporia St. (II)	1966-67, 68-69	42	49
Rennie Benn, Lehigh (I-AA)	1982-85	41	44
Aaron Turner, Pacific (Cal.) (I-A)	1989-92	44	43
Ryan Yarborough, Wyoming (I-A)	1990-93	46	42
Shannon Sharpe, Savannah St. (II)	1986-89	42	40
John Aromando, Trenton St. (III)	1981-84	40	39
Bill Stromberg, Johns Hopkins (III)	1978-81	40	39
Tony Willis, New Haven (II)	1990-93	40	38
Clarkston Hines, Duke (I-A)	1986-89	44	38
Roy Banks, Eastern Ill. (I-AA)	1983-86	38	38
Robert Clark, N.C. Central (II)	1983-86	40	38
Mike Jones, Tennessee St. (I-AA)	1979-82	42	38
Chris Holder, Tuskegee (II)	1988-91	40	37
Mike Whitehouse, St. Norbert (III)	1986-89	38	37
Terance Mathis, New Mexico (I-A)	1985-87, 89	44	36
Mike Cottle, Juniata (III)	1985-88	37	36
Joe Thomas, Mississippi Val. (I-AA)	1982-85	41	36
Willie Richardson, Jackson St. (II)	1959-62	38	36

*Record.

SEASON CATCHES

Player, Team (Division)	Year	G	Rec.	Yards	TD
Manny Hazard, Houston (I-A)	†1989	11	*142	1,689	22
Howard Twilley, Tulsa (I-A)	†1965	10	134	1,779	16
Brian Forster, Rhode Island (I-AA) (TE)	†1985	10	115	1,617	12
Chris George, Glenville St. (II)	†1993	10	117	*1,876	15
Fred Gilbert, Houston (I-A)	†1991	11	106	957	7
Barry Wagner, Alabama A&M (II)	†1989	11	106	1,812	17
Theo Blanco, Wis.-Stevens Point (III) (RB)	1987	11	#106	#1,616	8
Chris Penn, Tulsa (I-A)	†1993	11	105	1,578	12
Sherman Smith, Houston (I-A)	†1992	11	103	923	6
Jerry Rice, Mississippi Val. (I-AA)	†1984	10	103	1,682	*27
Jerry Rice, Mississippi Val. (I-AA)	†1983	10	102	1,450	14
Mike Healey, Valparaiso (II)	†1985	10	101	1,279	11
David Williams, Illinois (I-A)	†1984	11	101	1,278	8
Jay Miller, Brigham Young (I-A)	†1973	11	100	1,181	8
Jason Phillips, Houston (I-A)	†1987	11	99	875	3
Mark Templeton, Long Beach St. (I-A) (RB)	1986	11	99	688	2
Matt Newton, Principia (III)	†1992	8	98	1,487	14
Rodney Carter, Purdue (I-A)	†1985	11	98	1,099	4
Keith Edwards, Vanderbilt (I-A)	†1983	11	97	909	0

*Record. †National champion. #Record for a running back.

SEASON CATCHES PER GAME

Player, Team (Division)	Year	G	Rec.	Yards	TD	Rec.PG
Howard Twilley, Tulsa (I-A)	†1965	10	134	1,779	16	*13.4
Manny Hazard, Houston (I-A)	†1989	11	*142	1,689	22	12.9
Matt Newton, Principia (III)	†1992	8	98	1,487	14	12.3
Matt Newton, Principia (III)	†1993	8	96	1,080	11	12.0
Chris George, Glenville St. (II)	†1993	10	117	*1,876	15	11.7
Brian Forster, Rhode Island (I-AA) (TE)	†1985	10	115	1,617	12	11.5
Sean Munroe, Mass.-Boston (III)	1992	9	95	1,693	17	10.6
Jerry Rice, Mississippi Val. (I-AA)	†1984	10	103	1,682	*27	10.3
Scott Faessler, Framingham St. (III)	†1990	9	92	916	5	10.2
Jerry Rice, Mississippi Val. (I-AA)	†1983	10	102	1,450	14	10.2
Bruce Cerone, Emporia St. (II)	†1968	9	91	1,479	15	10.1
Mike Healy, Valparaiso (II)	†1985	10	101	1,279	11	10.1
Stuart Gaussoin, Portland St. (I-AA)	†1979	9	90	1,132	8	10.0

*Record. †National champion.

SINGLE-GAME CATCHES

No.	Div.	Player, Team (Opponent)	Date
24	I-AA	Jerry Rice, Mississippi Val. (Southern-B.R.)	Oct. 1, 1983
23	III	Sean Munroe, Mass.-Boston (Mass. Maritime)	Oct. 10, 1992
23	II	Barry Wagner, Alabama A&M (Clark Atlanta)	Nov. 4, 1989
22	I-AA	Marvin Walker, North Texas (Tulsa)	Nov. 20, 1982
22	I-A	Jay Miller, Brigham Young (New Mexico)	Nov. 3, 1973
21#	I-AA	David Pandt, Montana St. (Eastern Wash.)	Sept. 21, 1985
20	III	Rich Johnson, Pace (Fordham)	Nov. 7, 1987
20	III	Pete Thompson, Carroll, Wis. (Augustana, Ill.)	Nov. 4, 1978
20	II	Harold "Red" Roberts, Austin Peay (Murray St.)	Nov. 8, 1969
20	I-A	Rick Eber, Tulsa (Idaho St.)	Oct. 7, 1967

#Record for a running back.

CAREER YARDS

Player, Team (Division[s])	Years	Rec.	Yards	Avg.	TD
Jerry Rice, Mississippi Val. (I-AA)	1981-84	*301	*4,693	15.6	50
Ryan Yarborough, Wyoming (I-A)	1990-93	229	4,357	19.0	42
Bruce Cerone, Yankton/Emporia St. (II)	1966-67, 68-69	241	4,354	18.1	49
Aaron Turner, Pacific (Cal.) (I-A)	1989-92	266	4,345	16.3	43
Terance Mathis, New Mexico (I-A)	1985-87, 89	263	4,254	16.2	36
Robert Clark, N.C. Central (II)	1983-86	210	4,231	‡20.1	38
Chris Myers, Kenyon (II)	1967-70	253	3,897	15.4	33
Kasey Dunn, Idaho (I-AA)	1988-91	268	3,847	14.4	25
Dale Amos, Frank. & Marsh. (III)	1986-89	233	3,846	16.5	35
Bill Stromberg, Johns Hopkins (III)	1978-81	258	3,776	14.6	39
Shannon Sharpe, Savannah St. (II)	1986-89	192	3,744	19.5	40
Marc Zeno, Tulane (I-A)	1984-87	236	3,725	15.8	25
Jim Bradford, Carleton (III)	1988-91	212	3,719	17.5	32
Tyrone Johnson, Western St. (II)	1990-93	163	3,717	22.8	35
Chris Bisaillon, Ill. Wesleyan (III)	1989-92	223	3,670	16.5	*55
Rennie Benn, Lehigh (I-AA)	1982-85	237	3,662	15.5	44
Matt Newton, Principia (III)	1990-93	287	3,646	12.7	32
Jeff Tiefenthaler, South Dak. St. (II)	1983-86	173	3,621	20.9	31
Willie Richardson, Jackson St. (II)	1959-62	166	3,616	21.8	36
Johnny Cox, Fort Lewis (II)	1990-93	220	3,611	16.4	33
Ron Sellers, Florida St. (I-A)	1966-68	212	3,598	17.0	23

*Record. ‡Record for minimum of 180 catches.

SEASON YARDS

Player, Team (Division)	Year	Rec.	Yards	Avg.	TD
Chris George, Glenville St. (II)	†1993	117	*1,876	16.0	15
Barry Wagner, Alabama A&M (II)	†1989	106	1,812	17.1	17
Howard Twilley, Tulsa (I-A)	†1965	134	1,779	13.3	16
Sean Munroe, Mass.-Boston (III)	†1992	95	1,693	17.8	17
Manny Hazard, Houston (I-A)	†1989	*142	1,689	11.9	22
Jerry Rice, Mississippi Val. (I-AA)	†1984	103	1,682	16.3	*27
Brian Forster, Rhode Island (I-AA) (TE)	†1985	115	1,617	14.1	12
Theo Blanco, Wis.-Stevens Point (III) (RB)	1987	#106	#1,616	15.2	8
Aaron Turner, Pacific (Cal.) (I-A)	†1991	92	1,604	17.4	18
Dan Fulton, Nebraska-Omaha (II)	1976	67	1,581	23.6	16
Chris Penn, Tulsa (I-A)	†1993	105	1,578	15.0	12
Jeff Tiefenthaler, South Dak. St. (II)	1986	73	1,534	21.0	11
Ed Bell, Idaho St. (II)	†1969	96	1,522	15.9	20
Chuck Hughes, UTEP (I-A)	1965	80	1,519	19.0	12
Ryan Yarborough, Wyoming (I-A)	1993	67	1,512	22.6	16
Henry Ellard, Fresno St. (I-A)	1982	62	1,510	††24.4	15
Rodney Richardson, Gardner-Webb (II)	†1992	89	1,496	16.8	16
Ron Sellers, Florida St. (I-A)	†1968	86	1,496	17.4	12

*Record. †National champion. ††Record for minimum of 55 catches. #Record for a running back.

SEASON TOUCHDOWN RECEPTIONS

Player, Team (Division)	Year	G	TD
Jerry Rice, Mississippi Val. (I-AA)	1984	10	*27
Manny Hazard, Houston (I-A)	1989	11	22
John Aromando, Trenton St. (III)	1983	10	20
Ed Bell, Idaho St. (II)	1969	10	20
Desmond Howard, Michigan (I-A)	1991	11	19
Aaron Turner, Pacific (Cal.) (I-A)	1991	11	18
Dennis Smith, Utah (I-A)	1989	12	18
Tom Reynolds, San Diego St. (I-A)	1971	10	18
Bryan Reeves, Nevada (I-A)	1993	10	17
J. J. Stokes, UCLA (I-A)	1993	11	17
Sean Munroe, Mass.-Boston (III)	1992	9	17
Chris Bisaillon, Ill. Wesleyan (III)	1991	9	17
Mario Bailey, Washington (I-A)	1991	11	17
Clarkston Hines, Duke (I-A)	1989	11	17
Barry Wagner, Alabama A&M (II)	1989	11	17
Dameon Reilly, Rhode Island (I-AA)	1985	11	17
Dave Cecchini, Lehigh (I-AA)	1993	11	16
Ryan Yarborough, Wyoming (I-A)	1993	11	16
Rodney Richardson, Gardner-Webb (II)	1992	11	16
Evan Elkington, Worcester Tech (III)	1989	10	16
Dan Bitson, Tulsa (I-A)	1989	11	16
Dan Fulton, Nebraska-Omaha (II)	1976	10	16
Howard Twilley, Tulsa (I-A)	1965	10	16

*Record.

SINGLE-GAME YARDS

Yds.	Div.	Player, Team (Opponent)	Date
370	I-AA	Michael Lerch, Princeton (Brown)	Oct. 12, 1991
370	II	Barry Wagner, Alabama A&M (Clark Atlanta)	Nov. 4, 1989
363	II	Tom Nettles, San Diego St. (Southern Miss.)	Nov. 9, 1968
354	II	Robert Clark, N.C. Central (Jackson St.)	Aug. 30, 1986
349	I-A	Chuck Hughes, UTEP (North Texas)	Sept. 18, 1965
332	III	Sean Munroe, Mass.-Boston (Mass. Maritime)	Oct. 10, 1992
330	I-AA	Nate Singleton, Grambling (Virginia Union)	Sept. 14, 1991
327@	I-AA	Brian Forster, Rhode Island (Brown)	Sept. 28, 1985
325	II	Paul Zaeske, North Park (North Central)	Oct. 12, 1968
322	I-A	Rick Eber, Tulsa (Idaho St.)	Oct. 7, 1967
319	I-AA	Jason Cristino, Lehigh (Lafayette)	Nov. 21, 1992
318	I-A	Harry Wood, Tulsa (Idaho St.)	Oct. 7, 1967
317	II	Dan Fulton, Nebraska-Omaha (South Dak.)	Sept. 4, 1976
316	I-A	Jeff Evans, New Mexico St. (Southern Ill.)	Sept. 30, 1978
310	II	Mike Collodi, Colorado Mines (Westminster, Utah)	Oct. 3, 1970
309	III	Dale Amos, Frank. & Marsh. (Western Md.)	Oct. 24, 1987

@Record for a tight end.

Interceptions

CAREER INTERCEPTIONS

Player, Team (Division[s])	Years	No.	Yards	Avg.
Tom Collins, Indianapolis (II)	1982-85	*37	390	10.5
Ralph Gebhardt, Rochester (III)	1972-75	34	406	11.9
Scott Wiedeman, Adams St. (II)	1988-91	31	289	9.3
Dean Diaz, Humboldt St. (II)	1980-83	31	328	10.6
Bill Grantham, Missouri-Rolla (II)	1977-80	29	263	9.1
Eugene Hunter, Fort Valley St. (II)	1972-74	29	479	16.5
Al Brosky, Illinois (I-A)	1950-52	29	356	12.3
Rick Bealer, Lycoming (III)	1987-90	28	279	10.0
Brian Fetterolf, Aurora (III)	1986-89	28	390	13.9
Dave Murphy, Holy Cross (I-AA)	1986-89	28	309	11.0
Tim Lennon, Curry (III)	1986-89	27	190	7.0
Mike Hintz, Wis.-Platteville (III)	1983-86	27	183	6.8
Martin Bayless, Bowling Green (I-A)	1980-83	27	266	9.9
John Provost, Holy Cross (I-AA)	1972-74	27	470	17.4
Cory Mabry, Susquehanna (III)	1988-91	26	400	15.4
Tony Woods, Bloomsburg (II)	1982-85	26	105	4.0
Jeff Hughes, Ripon (III)	1975-78	26	333	12.8
Buster West, Gust. Adolphus (II)	1967-70	26	192	7.4

*Record.

SEASON INTERCEPTIONS

Player, Team (Division)	Year	No.	Yards
Mark Dorner, Juniata (III)	†1987	*15	202
Eugene Hunter, Fort Valley St. (II)	†1972	14	211
Luther Howard, Delaware St. (II)	†1972	14	99
Tom Rezzuti, Northeastern (II)	†1971	14	153
Jim Blackwell, Southern-B.R. (II)	†1970	14	196
Carl Ray Harris, Fresno St. (II)	†1970	14	98
Al Worley, Washington (I-A)	†1968	14	130

*Record. †National champion.

Punt Returns

CAREER AVERAGE
(Minimum 1.2 Returns Per Game)

Player, Team (Division[s])	Years	No.	Yards	Avg.
Billy Johnson, Widener (II; III)	1971-72; 73	40	989	*24.7
Jack Mitchell, Oklahoma (I-A)	1946-48	39	922	23.6
Keith Winston, Knoxville (III)	1986-87	30	686	22.9
Robert Middlebrook, Knoxville (III)	1984-85	21	473	22.5
Kevin Doherty, Mass. Maritime (III)	1976-78, 80	45	939	20.9
Chuck Downey, Stony Brook (III)	1984-87	59	1,198	**20.3
Mike Askew, Kean (III)	1980-81	28	555	19.8
Chuck Goehl, Monmouth (Ill.) (II)	1970-72	48	911	19.0
Eddie Macon, Pacific (Cal.) (I-A)	1949-51	48	907	18.9
Willie Canady, Fort Valley St. (III)	1979-82	41	772	18.8
Jackie Robinson, UCLA (I-A)	1939-40	37	694	18.8

*Record. **Record for minimum of 50 returns.

SEASON AVERAGE
(Minimum 1.2 Returns Per Game)

Player, Team (Division)	Year	No.	Yards	Avg.
Billy Johnson, Widener (II)	†1972	15	511	*34.1
Chuck Downey, Stony Brook (III)	†1986	17	530	31.2
Kevin Doherty, Mass. Maritime (III)	†1976	11	332	30.2
Dennis Robinson, Wesleyan (III)	†1978	9	263	29.2
Robert Middlebrook, Knoxville (III)	†1984	9	260	28.9
Joe Troise, Kean (III)	†1974	12	342	28.5
William Williams, Livingstone (II)	†1976	16	453	28.3
Terry Egerdahl, Minn.-Duluth (II)	†1975	13	360	27.7
Melvin Dillard, Ferrum (III)	†1990	25	688	27.5
Eric Green, Ill. Benedictine (III)	†1993	13	346	26.6
Bill Blackstock, Tennessee (I-A)	1951	12	311	25.9
Ennis Thomas, Bishop (II)	†1971	18	450	25.0
George Sims, Baylor (I-A)	1948	15	375	25.0

*Record. †National champion.

Kickoff Returns

CAREER AVERAGE
(Minimum 1.2 Returns Per Game)

Player, Team (Division[s])	Years	No.	Yards	Avg.
Forrest Hall, San Francisco (I-A)	1946-47	22	796	*36.2
Anthony Davis, Southern Cal (I-A)	1972-74	37	1,299	35.1
Glen Printers, Southern Colo. (II)	1973-74	25	851	34.0
Overton Curtis, Utah St. (I-A)	1957-58	32	991	31.0
Fred Montgomery, New Mexico St. (I-A)	1991-92	39	1,191	30.5
Karl Evans, Mo. Southern St. (II)	1991-92	32	959	30.0
Troy Brown, Marshall (I-AA)	1991-92	32	950	29.7
Charles Swann, Indiana St. (I-AA)	1989-91	45	1,319	29.3
Altie Taylor, Utah St. (I-A)	1966-68	40	1,170	29.3
Daryl Brown, Tufts (III)	1974-76	38	1,111	29.2
Stan Brown, Purdue (I-A)	1968-70	49	1,412	28.8
Henry White, Colgate (I-A)	1974-77	41	1,180	28.8
Donald Dennis, West Tex. A&M (I-A)	1964-65	27	777	28.8
Bobby Ward, Memphis (I-A)	1973-74	27	770	28.5
Craig Richardson, Eastern Wash. (I-AA)	1983-86	71	2,021	28.5

*Record.

SEASON AVERAGE
(Minimum 1.2 Returns Per Game)

Player, Team (Division)	Year	No.	Yards	Avg.
Paul Allen, Brigham Young (I-A)	1961	12	481	*40.1
Jason Martin, Coe (III)	†1992	11	438	39.8
LaVon Reis, Western St. (II)	†1993	14	552	39.4
Danny Lee, Jacksonville St. (II)	†1992	12	473	39.4
Leeland McElroy, Texas A&M (I-A)	†1993	15	590	39.3
Fran DeFalco, Assumption (II)	1993	12	461	38.4
Forrest Hall, San Francisco (I-A)	1946	15	573	@38.2
David Fraterrigo, Canisius (II)	†1993	13	485	37.3
Nate Kirtman, Pomona-Pitzer (III)	†1990	14	515	36.8
Kendall James, Carson-Newman (II)	1993	15	549	36.6
Kerry Hayes, Western Caro. (I-AA)	1993	16	584	36.5
Tom Myers, Coe (III)	†1983	11	401	36.5
Tony Ball, Tenn.-Chatt. (I-A)	†1977	13	473	36.4
Ron Scott, Occidental (III)	1983	10	363	36.3
Alan Hill, DePauw (III)	1980	12	434	36.2
Roscoe Word, Jackson St. (II)	†1973	18	650	36.1
Steve Levenseller, Puget Sound (II)	†1978	17	610	35.9
George Marinkov, North Caro. St. (I-A)	1954	13	465	35.8

*Record. †National champion. @ Record for minimum of 1.5 returns per game.

Field Goals

(One-inch tees were permitted in 1949, two-inch tees were permitted in 1965, and use of tees was eliminated before the 1989 season. The goal posts were widened from 18 feet, 6 inches to 23 feet, 4 inches in 1959 and were narrowed back to 18 feet, 6 inches before the 1991 season. The hash marks were moved six feet, eight inches closer to the center of the field to 60 feet from each sideline in 1993.)

CAREER FIELD GOALS

Player, Team (Division[s])	Years	FGM	FGA	Pct.
Jeff Jaeger, Washington (S) (I-A)	1983-86	*80	99	.808
John Lee, UCLA (S) (I-A)	1982-85	79	92	*.859
Philip Doyle, Alabama (S) (I-A)	1987-90	78	**105	.743
Luis Zendejas, Arizona St. (S) (I-A)	1981-84	78	**105	.743
Max Zendejas, Arizona (S) (I-A)	1982-85	77	104	.740
Kevin Butler, Georgia (S) (I-A)	1981-84	77	98	.786
Carlos Huerta, Miami (Fla.) (S) (I-A)	1988-91	73	91	.802
Derek Schmidt, Florida St. (S) (I-A)	1984-87	73	104	.702
Marty Zendejas, Nevada (S) (I-AA)	1984-87	72	90	.800
Kirk Roach, Western Caro. (S) (I-AA)	1984-87	71	102	.696
Fuad Reveiz, Tennessee (S) (I-A)	1981-84	71	95	.747
Roman Anderson, Houston (S) (I-A)	1988-91	70	101	.693
Barry Belli, Fresno St. (S) (I-A)	1984-87	70	99	.707
Tony Zendejas, Nevada (S) (I-A)	1981-83	70	86	.814
Collin Mackie, South Caro. (S) (I-A)	1987-90	69	95	.726
Gary Gussman, Miami (Ohio) (S) (I-A)	1984-87	68	94	.723
Larry Roach, Oklahoma St. (S) (I-A)	1981-84	68	101	.673
Paul Woodside, West Va. (S) (I-A)	1981-84	65	81	.802

*Record. **Record tied. (S) Soccer-style kicker.

SEASON FIELD GOALS

Player, Team (Division)	Year	FGM	FGA	Pct.
John Lee, UCLA (S) (I-A)	1984	*29	33	.879
Luis Zendejas, Arizona St. (S) (I-A)	1983	28	37	.757
Paul Woodside, West Va. (S) (I-A)	1982	28	31	.903
Fuad Reveiz, Tennessee (S) (I-A)	1982	27	31	.871
Brian Mitchell, Northern Iowa (S) (I-AA)	1990	26	27	*.963
Tony Zendejas, Nevada (S) (I-AA)	1982	26	33	.788
Chris Jacke, UTEP (S) (I-A)	1988	25	27	.926
John Diettrich, Ball St. (S) (I-A)	1985	25	29	.862
Chuck Nelson, Washington (S) (I-A)	1982	25	26	.962
Philip Doyle, Alabama (S) (I-A)	1990	24	29	.828
Kendall Trainor, Arkansas (S) (I-A)	1988	24	27	.889
Kirk Roach, Western Caro. (S) (I-AA)	1986	24	28	.857
Carlos Reveiz, Tennessee (S) (I-A)	1985	24	28	.857
George Benyola, Louisiana Tech (S) (I-AA)	1985	24	31	.774
Chris White, Illinois (S) (I-A)	1984	24	28	.857
Mike Prindle, Western Mich. (S) (I-A)	1984	24	30	.800
Bruce Kallmeyer, Kansas (S) (I-A)	1983	24	29	.828

*Record. (S) Soccer-style kicker.
(Record for attempts is 38)

LONGEST FIELD GOALS

Yds.	Div.	Player, Team (Opponent)	Year
67	II	Tom Odle, Fort Hays St. (Washburn)	1988
67	I-A	Joe Williams, Wichita St. (Southern Ill.)	1978
67	I-A	Steve Little, Arkansas (Texas)	1977
67	I-A	Russell Erxleben, Texas (Rice)	1977
65	I-A	Tony Franklin, Texas A&M (Baylor)	1976
64	I-A	Russell Erxleben, Texas (Oklahoma)	1977
64	I-A	Tony Franklin, Texas A&M (Baylor)	1976
63	I-AA	Scott Roper, Arkansas St. (North Texas)	1987
63	I-AA	Tim Foley, Ga. Southern (James Madison)	1987
63	I-A	Morten Andersen, Michigan St. (Ohio St.)	1981
63	I-A	Clark Kemble, Colorado St. (Arizona)	1975
63	II	Joe Duren, Arkansas St. (McNeese St.)	1974
62*	I-A	Jason Hanson, Washington St. (Nevada-Las Vegas)	1991
62	I-A	John Diettrich, Ball St. (Ohio)	1986
62	I-AA	Paul Hickert, Murray St. (Eastern Ky.)	1986
62	I-A	Chip Lohmiller, Minnesota (Iowa)	1986
62	I-A	Tom Whelihan, Missouri (Colorado)	1986
62	I-A	Dan Christopulos, Wyoming (Colorado St.)	1977
62	I-A	Iseed Khoury, North Texas (Richmond)	1977
62	III	Dom Antonini, Rowan (Salisbury St.)	1976
62	I-A	Dave Lawson, Air Force (Iowa St.)	1975
62	II	Mike Flater, Colorado Mines (Western St.)	1973

*Longest collegiate field goal without use of a tee.

Special Reference: Ove Johannson, Abilene Christian (not an NCAA-member college at the time), kicked a 69-yard field goal against East Tex. St., Oct. 16, 1976.

Punting

CAREER PUNTING AVERAGE
(Minimum 150 Punts)

Player, Team (Division[s])	Years	No.	Yards	Avg.
Reggie Roby, Iowa (I-A)	1979-82	172	7,849	*45.6
Greg Montgomery, Michigan St. (I-A)	1985-87	170	7,721	45.4
Tom Tupa, Ohio St. (I-A)	1984-87	196	8,854	45.2
Barry Helton, Colorado (I-A)	1984-87	153	6,873	44.9
Ray Guy, Southern Miss. (I-A)	1970-72	200	8,934	44.7
Bucky Scribner, Kansas (I-A)	1980-82	217	9,670	44.6
Greg Horne, Arkansas (I-A)	1983-86	180	8,002	44.5
Ray Criswell, Florida (I-A)	1982-85	161	7,153	44.4
Pumpy Tudors, Tenn.-Chatt. (I-AA)	1988-91	181	8,041	44.4
Bill Smith, Mississippi (I-A)	1983-86	254	11,260	44.3
Tim Baer, Colorado Mines (II)	1986-89	235	10,406	44.3
Russell Erxleben, Texas (I-A)	1975-78	214	9,467	44.2
Mark Simon, Air Force (I-A)	1984-86	156	6,898	44.2
Johnny Evans, North Caro. St. (I-A)	1974-77	185	8,143	44.0
Chuck Ramsey, Wake Forest (I-A)	1971-73	205	9,010	44.0

*Record.

SEASON PUNTING AVERAGE
(Qualifiers for Championship)

Player, Team (Division)	Year	No.	Yards	Avg.
Reggie Roby, Iowa (I-A)	†1981	44	2,193	*49.8
Kirk Wilson, UCLA (I-A)	†1956	30	1,479	49.3
Steve Ecker, Shippensburg (II)	†1965	32	1,570	49.1
Zack Jordan, Colorado (I-A)	†1950	38	1,830	48.2
Ricky Anderson, Vanderbilt (I-A)	†1984	58	2,793	48.2
Reggie Roby, Iowa (I-A)	†1982	52	2,501	48.1
Marv Bateman, Utah (I-A)	†1971	68	3,269	48.1
Don Cockroft, Adams St. (II)	†1966	36	1,728	48.0
Owen Price, UTEP (I-A)	†1940	30	1,440	48.0
Jack Jacobs, Oklahoma (I-A)	1940	31	1,483	47.8
Bill Smith, Mississippi (I-A)	1984	44	2,099	47.7

*Record. †National champion.

LONGEST PUNTS

Yds.	Div.	Player, Team (Opponent)	Year
99	I-A	Pat Brady, Nevada (Loyola, Cal.)	1950
97	II	Earl Hurst, Emporia St. (Central Mo. St.)	1964
96	II	Gary Frens, Hope (Olivet)	1966
96	II	Jim Jarrett, North Dak. (South Dak.)	1957
96	I-A	George O'Brien, Wisconsin (Iowa)	1952
94	I-A	John Hadl, Kansas (Oklahoma)	1959
94	I-A	Carl Knox, Texas Christian (Oklahoma St.)	1947
94	I-A	Preston Johnson, Southern Methodist (Pittsburgh)	1940
93	II	Elliot Mills, Carleton (Monmouth, Ill.)	1970
93	II	Kasper Fitins, Taylor (Georgetown, Ky.)	1966
93	II	Leeroy Sweeney, Pomona-Pitzer (UC Riverside)	1960
93	I-A	Bob Handke, Drake (Wichita St.)	1949

Maine Maritime running back Kirk Matthieu finished his collegiate career last season with an average of 210.8 all-purpose yards per game, the second-best average in collegiate history. His career total of 6,955 yards ranks sixth.

All-Purpose Yards

CAREER YARDS

Player, Team (Division[s])	Years	Rush	Rcv.	Int.	PR	KO	Yds.
Johnny Bailey, Tex. A&M-Kingsville (II)	1986-89	*6,320	452	0	20	1,011	*7,803
Kenny Gamble, Colgate (I-AA)	1984-87	5,220	536	0	104	1,763	7,623
Howard Stevens, Randolph-Macon (II); Louisville (I-A)	1968-69; 71-72	5,297	738	0	781	748	7,564
Napoleon McCallum, Navy (I-A)	$1981-85	4,179	796	0	858	1,339	7,172
Albert Fann, Cal St. Northridge (II)	1987-90	4,090	803	0	0	2,141	7,032
Kirk Matthieu, Maine Maritime (III)	$1989-93	5,107	315	0	254	1,279	6,955
Curtis Delgardo, Portland St. (II)	$1986-90	4,178	1,258	0	318	1,188	6,942
Darrin Nelson, Stanford (I-A)	1977-78, 80-81	4,033	2,368	0	471	13	6,885
Eric Frees, Western Md. (III)	1988-91	5,281	392	0	47	1,158	6,878
Steve Roberts, Butler (II)	1986-89	4,623	1,201	0	272	578	6,674
Anthony Russo, St. John's (N.Y.) (III; I-AA)	1990-92; 93	5,834	405	0	25	379	6,643
Tony Dorsett, Pittsburgh (I-A)	1973-76	6,082	406	0	0	127	6,615
Paul Palmer, Temple (I-A)	1983-86	4,895	705	0	0	997	6,609
Charles White, Southern Cal (I-A)	1976-79	5,598	507	0	0	440	6,545
Trevor Cobb, Rice (I-A)	1989-92	4,948	892	0	21	651	6,512
Joe Dudek, Plymouth St. (III)	1982-85	5,570	348	0	0	243	6,509
Glyn Milburn, Oklahoma/Stanford (I-A)	1988, 90-92	2,302	1,495	0	1,145	1,246	6,188
Chris Cobb, Eastern Ill. (II)	1976-79	5,042	520	0	37	478	6,077
Don Aleksiewicz, Hobart (II)	1969-72	4,525	470	0	320	748	6,063
Gary Trettel, St. Thomas (Minn.) (III)	1988-90	3,724	853	0	0	1,467	6,044
Archie Griffin, Ohio St. (I-A)	1972-75	5,177	286	0	0	540	6,003
Ron "Po" James, New Mexico St. (I-A)	1968-71	3,884	217	0	8	1,870	5,979
Eric Wilkerson, Kent (I-A)	1985-88	3,830	506	0	0	1,638	5,974

*Record. $See page 6 for explanation.

CAREER YARDS PER GAME
(Minimum 18 Games)

Player, Team (Division[s])	Years	G	Rush	Rcv.	Int.	PR	KO	Yds.	Yd.PG
Ryan Benjamin, Pacific (Cal.) (I-A)	1990-92	24	3,119	1,063	0	100	1,424	5,706	*237.8
Kirk Matthieu, Maine Maritime (III)	$1989-93	33	5,107	315	0	254	1,279	6,955	210.8
Sheldon Canley, San Jose St. (I-A)	1988-90	25	2,513	828	0	5	1,800	5,146	205.8
Johnny Bailey, Tex. A&M-Kingsville (II)	1986-89	39	*6,320	452	0	20	1,011	*7,803	200.1
Howard Stevens, Randolph-Macon (II); Louisville (I-A)	1968-69; 71-72	38	5,297	738	0	781	748	7,564	199.1
Gary Trettel, St. Thomas (Minn.) (III)	1988-90	29	3,483	834	0	0	1,407	5,724	197.4
Billy Johnson, Widener (II; III)	1971-72; 73	28	3,737	27	0	43	989	5,404	193.0
O. J. Simpson, Southern Cal (I-A)	1967-68	19	3,124	235	0	0	307	3,666	192.9
Dave Meggett, Towson St. (I-AA)	1987-88	18	1,658	788	0	212	745	3,403	189.1

*Record. $See page 6 for explanation.

SEASON YARDS

Player, Team (Division)	Year	Rush	Rcv.	Int.	PR	KO	Yds.
Barry Sanders, Oklahoma St. (I-A)	†1988	*2,628	106	0	95	421	*3,250
Ryan Benjamin, Pacific (Cal.) (I-A)	†1991	1,581	612	0	4	798	2,995
Mike Pringle, Cal St. Fullerton (I-A)	†1989	1,727	249	0	0	714	2,690
Steve Roberts, Butler (II)	†1989	1,450	532	0	272	415	2,669
Paul Palmer, Temple (I-A)	†1986	1,866	110	0	0	657	2,633
Chris George, Glenville St. (II)	†1993	23	1,876	0	157	562	2,618
Ryan Benjamin, Pacific (Cal.) (I-A)	†1992	1,441	434	0	96	626	2,597
Marcus Allen, Southern Cal (I-A)	†1981	2,342	217	0	0	0	2,559
Sheldon Canley, San Jose St. (I-A)	1989	1,201	353	0	0	959	2,513
Mike Rozier, Nebraska (I-A)	1983	2,148	106	0	0	232	2,486
Johnny Bailey, Tex. A&M-Kingsville (II)	†1986	2,011	54	0	20	340	2,425
Kenny Gamble, Colgate (I-AA)	†1986	1,816	198	0	40	391	2,425
Theo Blanco, Wis.-Stevens Point (III)	1987	454	1,616	0	245	103	2,418
Rick Wegher, South Dak. St. (II)	1984	1,317	264	0	0	824	2,405
Ronald Moore, Pittsburg St. (II)	1992	1,864	141	0	0	388	2,393
Chuck Weatherspoon, Houston (I-A)	1989	1,146	735	0	415	95	2,391
Anthony Thompson, Indiana (I-A)	1989	1,793	201	0	0	394	2,388
Ricky Gales, Simpson (III)	†1989	2,035	102	0	0	248	2,385
Napoleon McCallum, Navy (I-A)	†1983	1,587	166	0	272	360	2,385
Gary Trettel, St. Thomas (Minn.) (III)	1989	1,502	337	0	0	496	2,335
Michael Clemons, William & Mary (I-AA)	1986	1,065	516	0	330	423	2,334
Napoleon McCallum, Navy (I-A)	†1985	1,327	358	0	157	488	2,330
Gary Trettel, St. Thomas (Minn.) (III)	1990	1,620	388	0	0	319	2,327
Roger Graham, New Haven (II)	1993	1,687	116	0	0	516	2,319
Keith Byars, Ohio St. (I-A)	†1984	1,655	453	0	0	176	2,284

*Record. †National champion.

185

SEASON YARDS PER GAME

Player, Team (Division)	Year	G	Rush	Rcv.	Int.	PR	KO	Yds.	Yd.PG
Barry Sanders, Oklahoma St. (I-A)	†1988	11	*2,628	106	0	0	95	*3,250	*295.5
Steve Roberts, Butler (II)	†1989	10	1,450	532	0	272	415	2,669	266.9
Chris George, Glenville St. (II)	†1993	10	23	1,876	0	157	562	2,618	261.8
Billy Johnson, Widener (II)	†1972	9	1,556	40	43	511	115	2,265	251.7
Ryan Benjamin, Pacific (Cal.) (I-A)	†1991	12	1,581	612	0	4	798	2,995	249.6
Byron "Whizzer" White, Colorado (I-A)	†1937	8	1,121	0	103	587	159	1,970	246.3
Mike Pringle, Cal St. Fullerton (I-A)	†1989	11	1,727	249	0	0	714	2,690	244.6
Kirk Matthieu, Maine Maritime (III)	†1992	9	1,733	91	0	56	308	2,188	243.1
Paul Palmer, Temple (I-A)	†1986	11	1,866	110	0	0	657	2,633	239.4
Ricky Gales, Simpson (III)	†1989	10	2,035	102	0	0	248	2,385	238.5
Ryan Benjamin, Pacific (Cal.) (I-A)	†1992	11	1,441	434	0	96	626	2,597	236.1
Gary Trettel, St. Thomas (Minn.) (III)	1989	10	1,502	337	0	0	496	2,335	233.5
Kirk Matthieu, Maine Maritime (III)	1990	9	1,428	77	0	99	495	2,099	233.2
Gary Trettel, St. Thomas (Minn.) (III)	1990	10	1,620	388	0	0	319	2,327	232.7

*Record. †National champion.

Scoring

CAREER POINTS

Player, Team (Division[s])	Years	TD	XPt.	FG	Pts.
Joe Dudek, Plymouth St. (III)	1982-85	*79	0	0	*474
Walter Payton, Jackson St. (II)	1971-74	66	53	5	464
Shawn Graves, Wofford (QB) (II)	1989-92	72	3	0	438
Johnny Bailey, Tex. A&M-Kingsville (II)	1986-89	70	3	0	426
Roman Anderson, Houston (I-A)	1988-91	0	213	70	423
Howard Stevens, Randolph-Macon (II); Louisville (I-A)	1968-69; 71-72	69	4	0	418
Dale Mills, Northeast Mo. St. (II)	1957-60	64	23	0	407
Jeremy Monroe, Michigan Tech (II)	1990-93	67	0	0	402
Carlos Huerta, Miami (Fla.) (I-A)	1988-91	0	178	73	397
Jason Elam, Hawaii (I-A)	$1988-92	0	158	79	395
Anthony Thompson, Indiana (I-A)	1986-89	65	4	0	394
Garney Henley, Huron (II)	1956-59	63	16	0	394
Derek Schmidt, Florida St. (I-A)	1984-87	0	174	73	393
Steve Roberts, Butler (II)	1986-89	63	4	0	386
Jeff Bentrim, North Dak. St. (QB) (II)	1983-86	64	2	0	386
Marty Zendejas, Nevada (I-AA)	1984-87	0	169	72	385
Leo Lewis, Lincoln (Mo.) (II)	1951-54	64	0	0	384
Chris Bisaillon, Ill. Wesleyan (III)	1989-92	61	12	0	378
Heath Sherman, Tex. A&M-Kingsville (II)	1985-88	63	0	0	378
Marshall Faulk, San Diego St. (I-A)	1991-93	62	4	0	376
Chris Babirad, Wash. & Jeff. (III)	1989-92	62	2	0	374
Billy Johnson, Widener (II; III)	1971-72; 73	62	0	0	372
Tank Younger, Grambling (II)	1945-48	60	9	0	369
Luis Zendejas, Arizona St. (I-A)	1981-84	0	134	78	368
Bill Cooper, Muskingum (II)	1957-60	54	37	1	364
Charvez Foger, Nevada (I-AA)	1985-88	60	2	0	362
Ole Gunderson, St. Olaf (II)	1969-71	60	2	0	362
Jeff Jaeger, Washington (I-A)	1983-86	0	118	*80	358
Tony Dorsett, Pittsburgh (I-A)	1973-76	59	2	0	356
Glenn Davis, Army (I-A)	1943-46	59	0	0	354

*Record. $See page 6 for explanation.

CAREER POINTS PER GAME
(Minimum 18 Games)

Player, Team (Division[s])	Years	G	TD	XPt.	FG	Pts.	Pt.PG
Ole Gunderson, St. Olaf (II)	1969-71	27	60	2	0	362	*13.4
Billy Johnson, Widener (II; III)	1971-72; 73	28	62	0	0	372	13.3
Leon Burns, Long Beach St. (II)	1969-70	22	47	2	0	284	12.9
Marshall Faulk, San Diego St. (I-A)	1991-93	31	62	4	0	376	12.1
Ed Marinaro, Cornell (I-A)	1969-71	27	52	6	0	318	11.8
Joe Dudek, Plymouth St. (III)	1982-85	41	*79	0	0	*474	11.6
Bill Burnett, Arkansas (I-A)	1968-70	26	49	0	0	294	11.3
Dale Mills, Northeast Mo. St. (II)	1957-60	36	64	23	0	407	11.3
Steve Owens, Oklahoma (I-A)	1967-69	30	56	0	0	336	11.2
Walter Payton, Jackson St. (II)	1971-74	42	66	53	5	464	11.0
Steve Roberts, Butler (II)	1986-89	35	63	4	0	386	11.0
Jeff Bentrim, North Dak. St. (II)	1983-86	35	64	2	0	386	11.0
Shawn Graves, Wofford (II)	1989-92	40	72	3	0	438	11.0
Johnny Bailey, Tex. A&M-Kingsville (II)	1986-89	39	70	3	0	426	10.9
Eddie Talboom, Wyoming (I-A)	1948-50	28	34	99	0	303	10.8
Chris Babirad, Wash. & Jeff. (III)	1989-92	35	62	2	0	374	10.7
Keith Elias, Princeton (I-AA)	1991-93	30	52	8	0	320	10.7

*Record.

SEASON POINTS

Player, Team (Division)	Year	TD	XPt.	FG	Pts.
Barry Sanders, Oklahoma St. (I-A)	†1988	*39	0	0	*234
Terry Metcalf, Long Beach St. (II)	1971	29	4	0	178
Mike Rozier, Nebraska (I-A)	†1983	29	0	0	174
Lydell Mitchell, Penn St. (I-A)	1971	29	0	0	174
Geoff Mitchell, Weber St. (I-AA)	†1991	28	2	0	170
Stanley Drayton, Allegheny (III)	†1991	28	0	0	168
Jim Switzer, Col. of Emporia (II)	†1963	28	0	0	168
Carl Herakovich, Rose-Hulman (II)	†1958	25	18	0	168
Ted Scown, Sul Ross St. (II)	†1948	28	0	0	168
Ronald Moore, Pittsburg St. (II)	1992	27	4	0	166
Ricky Gales, Simpson (III)	†1989	26	10	0	166
Art Luppino, Arizona (I-A)	†1954	24	22	0	166
Matt Malmberg, St. John's (Minn.) (III)	†1993	27	2	0	164
Leon Burns, Long Beach St. (II)	†1969	27	2	0	164
Jerry Rice, Mississippi Val. (I-AA)	†1984	27	0	0	162
Mike Deutsch, North Dak. (II)	1972	27	0	0	162
Billy Johnson, Widener (II)	†1972	27	0	0	162
Bobby Reynolds, Nebraska (I-A)	†1950	22	25	0	157

*Record. †National champion.

SEASON POINTS PER GAME

Player, Team (Division)	Year	G	TD	XPt.	FG	Pts.	Pt.PG
Barry Sanders, Oklahoma St. (I-A)	†1988	11	*39	0	0	*234	21.3
Carl Herakovich, Rose-Hulman (II)	†1958	8	25	18	0	168	21.0
Jim Switzer, Col. of Emporia (II)	†1963	9	28	0	0	168	18.7
Billy Johnson, Widener (II)	†1972	9	27	0	0	162	18.0
Carl Garrett, N.M. Highlands (II)	†1966	9	26	2	0	158	17.6
Bobby Reynolds, Nebraska (I-A)	†1950	9	22	25	0	157	17.4
Stanley Drayton, Allegheny (III)	†1991	10	28	0	0	168	16.8
Ted Scown, Sul Ross St. (II)	†1948	10	28	0	0	168	16.8
Ricky Gales, Simpson (III)	†1989	10	26	10	0	166	16.6
Art Luppino, Arizona (I-A)	†1954	10	24	22	0	166	16.6
Ed Marinaro, Cornell (I-A)	†1971	9	24	4	0	148	16.4
Matt Malmberg, St. John's (Minn.) (III)	†1993	10	27	2	0	164	16.4
Jerry Rice, Mississippi Val. (I-AA)	†1984	10	27	0	0	162	16.2
Chris Babirad, Wash. & Jeff. (III)	†1992	9	24	0	0	144	16.0
Larry Ras, Michigan Tech (II)	†1971	9	24	0	0	144	16.0
Trent Nauholz, Simpson (III)	†1992	8	21	2	0	128	16.0
Lydell Mitchell, Penn St. (I-A)	1971	11	29	0	0	174	15.8
Marshall Faulk, San Diego St. (I-A)	†1991	9	23	2	0	140	15.6

*Record. †National champion.

SINGLE-GAME POINTS

Pts.	Div.	Player, Team (Opponent)	Date
48	I-A	Howard Griffith, Illinois (Southern Ill.)	Sept. 22, 1990
48	II	Paul Zaeske, North Park (North Central)	Oct. 12, 1968
48	II	Junior Wolf, Panhandle St. (St. Mary, Kan.)	Nov. 8, 1958
44	I-A	Marshall Faulk, San Diego St. (Pacific, Cal.)	Sept. 14, 1991
43	I-A	Jim Brown, Syracuse (Colgate)	Nov. 17, 1956
42	I-A	Arnold "Showboat" Boykin, Mississippi (Mississippi St.)	Dec. 1, 1951
42	I-A	Fred Wendt, UTEP (New Mexico St.)	Nov. 25, 1948

Award Winners

Consensus All-America Selections, 1889-1993

In 1950, the National Collegiate Athletic Bureau (the NCAA's service bureau) compiled the first official comprehensive roster of all-time all-Americans. The compilation of the all-American roster was supervised by a panel of analysts working in large part with the historical records contained in the files of the Dr. Baker Football Information Service.

The roster consists of only those players who were first-team selections on one or more of the all-America teams that were selected for the national audience and received nationwide circulation. Not included are the thousands of players who received mention on all-America second or third teams, nor the numerous others who were selected by newspapers or agencies with circulations that were not primarily national and with viewpoints, therefore, that were not normally nationwide in scope.

The following chart indicates, by year (in left column), which national media and organizations selected all-America teams. The headings at the top of each column refer to the selector (see legend after chart).

All-America Selectors

Year	AA	AP	C	COL	CP	FBW	FC	FN	FW	INS	L	LIB	M	N	NA	NEA	NM	SN	UP	UPI	W	WCF
1889	-	-	-	-	-	-	-	-	-	-	-	-	-	-	-	-	-	-	-	-	√	-
1890	-	-	-	-	-	-	-	-	-	-	-	-	-	-	-	-	-	-	-	-	√	-
1891	-	-	-	-	-	-	-	-	-	-	-	-	-	-	-	-	-	-	-	-	√	-
1892	-	-	-	-	-	-	-	-	-	-	-	-	-	-	-	-	-	-	-	-	√	-
1893	-	-	-	-	-	-	-	-	-	-	-	-	-	-	-	-	-	-	-	-	√	-
1894	-	-	-	-	-	-	-	-	-	-	-	-	-	-	-	-	-	-	-	-	√	-
1895	-	-	-	-	-	-	-	-	-	-	-	-	-	-	-	-	-	-	-	-	√	-
1896	-	-	-	-	-	-	-	-	-	-	-	-	-	-	-	-	-	-	-	-	√	-
1897	-	-	-	-	-	-	-	-	-	-	-	-	-	-	-	-	-	-	-	-	√	-
1898	-	-	√	-	-	-	-	-	-	-	-	-	-	-	-	-	-	-	-	-	√	-
1899	-	-	√	-	-	-	-	-	-	-	-	-	-	-	-	-	-	-	-	-	√	-
1900	-	-	√	-	-	-	-	-	-	-	-	-	-	-	-	-	-	-	-	-	√	-
1901	-	-	√	-	-	-	-	-	-	-	-	-	-	-	-	-	-	-	-	-	√	-
1902	-	-	√	-	-	-	-	-	-	-	-	-	-	-	-	-	-	-	-	-	√	-
1903	-	-	√	-	-	-	-	-	-	-	-	-	-	-	-	-	-	-	-	-	√	-
1904	-	-	√	-	-	-	-	-	-	-	-	-	-	-	-	-	-	-	-	-	√	-
1905	-	-	√	-	-	-	-	-	-	-	-	-	-	-	-	-	-	-	-	-	√	-
1906	-	-	√	-	-	-	-	-	-	-	-	-	-	-	-	-	-	-	-	-	√	-
1907	-	-	√	-	-	-	-	-	-	-	-	-	-	-	-	-	-	-	-	-	√	-
1908	-	-	√	-	-	-	-	-	-	-	-	-	-	-	-	-	-	-	-	-	√	-
1909	-	-	√	-	-	-	-	-	-	-	-	-	-	-	-	-	-	-	-	-	-	-
1910	-	-	√	-	-	-	-	-	-	-	-	-	-	-	-	-	-	-	-	-	-	-
1911	-	-	√	-	-	-	-	-	-	-	-	-	-	-	-	-	-	-	-	-	-	-
1912	-	-	√	-	-	-	-	-	-	-	-	-	-	-	-	-	-	-	-	-	-	-
1913	-	-	√	-	-	-	-	-	-	√	-	-	-	-	-	-	-	-	-	-	-	-
1914	-	-	√	-	-	-	-	-	-	√	-	-	-	-	-	-	-	-	-	-	-	-
1915	-	-	√	-	-	-	-	-	-	√	-	-	-	-	-	-	-	-	-	-	-	-
1916	-	-	(√)	-	-	-	-	-	-	√	-	-	-	-	-	-	-	-	-	-	-	-
1917	-	-	(*)	-	-	-	-	-	-	√	-	-	√	-	-	√	-	-	-	-	-	-
1918	-	-	√	-	-	-	-	-	-	-	-	-	√	-	-	-	-	-	-	-	-	-
1919	-	-	√	-	-	-	-	-	-	-	-	-	√	-	-	-	-	-	-	-	-	-
1920	-	-	√	-	-	√	-	-	-	√	-	-	√	-	-	-	-	-	-	-	-	-
1921	-	-	√	-	-	-	-	-	-	-	-	-	-	-	-	-	-	-	-	-	-	-
1922	-	-	√	-	-	-	-	-	-	-	-	-	-	-	-	-	-	-	-	-	-	-
1923	-	-	√	-	-	√	-	-	-	-	-	-	-	-	-	-	-	-	-	-	-	-
1924	√	-	√	-	-	√	-	-	-	√	-	√	-	-	√	-	-	-	-	-	-	-
1925	√	√	-	√	-	√	-	-	-	√	-	-	-	-	-	-	-	-	√	-	-	-
1926	√	√	-	√	-	-	-	-	-	√	-	-	-	-	-	-	-	-	-	-	-	-
1927	√	√	-	√	-	-	-	-	-	√	-	-	-	-	-	√	-	-	√	-	-	-
1928	√	√	-	√	-	-	-	-	-	√	-	-	-	-	-	√	-	-	√	-	-	-
1929	√	√	-	√	-	-	-	-	-	√	-	-	-	√	-	√	-	-	√	-	-	-
1930	√	√	-	√	-	-	-	-	-	√	-	-	-	√	-	√	-	-	√	-	-	-
1931	√	√	-	√	-	-	-	-	-	√	-	√	-	√	-	√	-	-	√	-	-	-
1932	√	√	-	√	-	-	-	-	-	√	-	-	-	√	-	√	-	-	√	-	-	-
1933	√	√	-	√	-	-	-	-	-	√	-	-	-	√	-	√	-	-	√	-	-	-
1934	√	√	-	√	-	-	-	-	-	√	-	-	-	√	-	√	-	√	√	-	-	-
1935	√	√	-	√	-	-	-	-	-	√	-	-	-	√	-	√	-	√	√	-	-	-
1936	√	√	-	√	-	-	-	-	-	√	-	-	√	√	-	√	-	√	√	-	-	-
1937	√	√	-	√	-	-	-	-	-	√	-	-	√	√	-	√	-	√	√	-	-	-
1938	√	√	-	√	-	-	-	-	-	√	-	-	√	√	√	√	-	√	√	-	-	-
1939	√	√	-	√	-	-	-	-	-	√	-	-	√	√	√	√	-	√	√	-	-	-
1940	√	√	-	√	-	-	-	-	-	√	-	-	√	√	√	√	-	√	√	-	-	-
1941	√	√	-	√	-	-	-	-	-	√	-	-	√	√	√	√	-	√	√	-	-	-
1942	√	√	-	√	-	-	-	-	-	√	√	-	√	√	√	√	-	√	√	-	-	-
1943	√	√	-	√	-	-	-	√	-	√	√	-	-	√	√	√	-	√	√	-	-	-
1944	√	√	-	√	-	-	√	√	√	√	√	-	-	√	-	√	-	√	√	-	-	-
1945	-	√	-	√	-	-	-	√	√	√	-	-	-	√	-	-	-	√	√	-	-	-
1946	-	√	-	-	-	-	√	√	√	√ (†)	-	-	-	√	-	-	-	√	√	-	-	-
1947	-	√	-	(§)	-	-	-	√	√	√	-	-	-	-	-	-	-	√	√	-	-	-
1948	-	√	-	(§)	-	-	√	-	√	(#)√	-	-	-	-	-	-	√	√	√	-	-	-

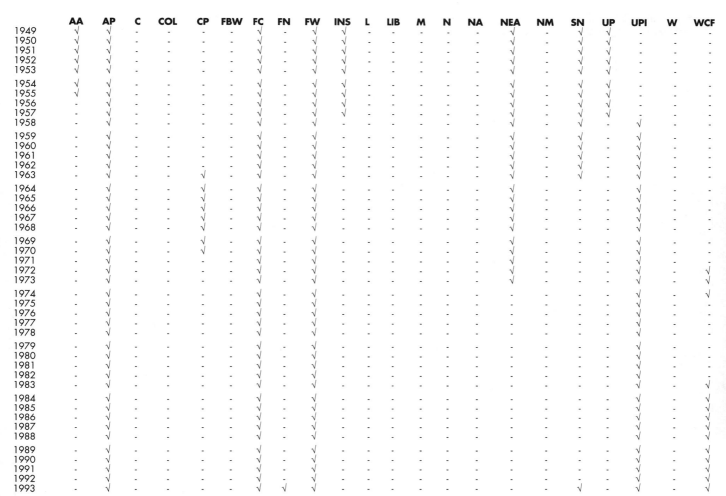

	AA	AP	C	COL	CP	FBW	FC	FN	FW	INS	L	LIB	M	N	NA	NEA	NM	SN	UP	UPI	W	WCF
1949	√	√	-	-	-	-	√	-	√	√	-	-	-	-	-	√	-	√	√	-	-	-
1950	√	√	-	-	-	-	√	-	√	√	-	-	-	-	-	√	-	√	√	-	-	-
1951	√	√	-	-	-	-	√	-	√	√	-	-	-	-	-	√	-	√	√	-	-	-
1952	√	√	-	-	-	-	√	-	√	√	-	-	-	-	-	√	-	√	√	-	-	-
1953	√	√	-	-	-	-	√	-	√	√	-	-	-	-	-	√	-	√	√	-	-	-
1954	-	√	-	-	-	-	√	-	√	√	-	-	-	-	-	√	-	√	√	-	-	-
1955	√	√	-	-	-	-	√	-	√	√	-	-	-	-	-	√	-	√	√	-	-	-
1956	-	√	-	-	-	-	√	-	√	√	-	-	-	-	-	√	-	√	√	-	-	-
1957	-	√	-	-	-	-	√	-	√	√	-	-	-	-	-	√	-	√	√	-	-	-
1958	-	√	-	-	-	-	√	-	√	-	-	-	-	-	-	√	-	√	-	√	-	-
1959	-	√	-	-	-	-	√	-	√	-	-	-	-	-	-	√	-	√	-	√	-	-
1960	-	√	-	-	-	-	√	-	√	-	-	-	-	-	-	√	-	√	-	√	-	-
1961	-	√	-	-	-	-	√	-	√	-	-	-	-	-	-	√	-	√	-	√	-	-
1962	-	√	-	-	-	-	√	-	√	-	-	-	-	-	-	√	-	√	-	√	-	-
1963	-	√	-	-	√	-	√	-	√	-	-	-	-	-	-	√	-	√	-	√	-	-
1964	-	√	-	-	-	-	√	-	√	-	-	-	-	-	-	√	-	√	-	√	-	-
1965	-	√	-	-	-	-	√	-	√	-	-	-	-	-	-	√	-	√	-	√	-	-
1966	-	√	-	-	-	-	√	-	√	-	-	-	-	-	-	√	-	√	-	√	-	-
1967	-	√	-	-	-	-	√	-	√	-	-	-	-	-	-	√	-	√	-	√	-	-
1968	-	√	-	-	-	-	√	-	√	-	-	-	-	-	-	√	-	√	-	√	-	-
1969	-	√	-	-	-	-	√	-	√	-	-	-	-	-	-	√	-	√	-	√	-	-
1970	-	√	-	-	√	-	√	-	√	-	-	-	-	-	-	√	-	√	-	√	-	-
1971	-	√	-	-	-	-	√	-	√	-	-	-	-	-	-	√	-	√	-	√	-	-
1972	-	√	-	-	-	-	√	-	√	-	-	-	-	-	-	√	-	√	-	√	-	-
1973	-	√	-	-	-	-	√	-	√	-	-	-	-	-	-	√	-	√	-	√	-	√
1974	-	√	-	-	-	-	√	-	√	-	-	-	-	-	-	-	-	-	-	√	-	√
1975	-	√	-	-	-	-	√	-	√	-	-	-	-	-	-	-	-	-	-	√	-	-
1976	-	√	-	-	-	-	√	-	√	-	-	-	-	-	-	-	-	-	-	√	-	-
1977	-	√	-	-	-	-	√	-	√	-	-	-	-	-	-	-	-	-	-	√	-	-
1978	-	√	-	-	-	-	√	-	√	-	-	-	-	-	-	-	-	-	-	√	-	-
1979	-	√	-	-	-	-	√	-	√	-	-	-	-	-	-	-	-	-	-	√	-	-
1980	-	√	-	-	-	-	√	-	√	-	-	-	-	-	-	-	-	-	-	√	-	-
1981	-	√	-	-	-	-	√	-	√	-	-	-	-	-	-	-	-	-	-	√	-	-
1982	-	√	-	-	-	-	√	-	√	-	-	-	-	-	-	-	-	-	-	√	-	-
1983	-	√	-	-	-	-	√	-	√	-	-	-	-	-	-	-	-	-	-	√	-	√
1984	-	√	-	-	-	-	√	-	√	-	-	-	-	-	-	-	-	-	-	√	-	√
1985	-	√	-	-	-	-	√	-	√	-	-	-	-	-	-	-	-	-	-	√	-	√
1986	-	√	-	-	-	-	√	-	√	-	-	-	-	-	-	-	-	-	-	√	-	√
1987	-	√	-	-	-	-	√	-	√	-	-	-	-	-	-	-	-	-	-	√	-	√
1988	-	√	-	-	-	-	√	-	√	-	-	-	-	-	-	-	-	-	-	√	-	√
1989	-	√	-	-	-	-	√	-	√	-	-	-	-	-	-	-	-	-	-	√	-	√
1990	-	√	-	-	-	-	√	-	√	-	-	-	-	-	-	-	-	-	-	√	-	√
1991	-	√	-	-	-	-	√	-	√	-	-	-	-	-	-	-	-	-	-	√	-	√
1992	-	√	-	-	-	-	√	√	√	-	-	-	-	-	-	-	-	-	-	√	-	√
1993	-	√	-	-	-	√	√	√	√	-	-	-	-	-	-	-	-	√	-	√	-	√

*In 1917, Walter Camp selected an all-Service, all-America team composed of military personnel. †During 1946-70, Look Magazine published the Football Writers Association of America's selections, listed under FW. §During 1948-56, Collier's Magazine published the American Football Coaches Association's selections, listed under FC. #International News Service was the first to select offensive and defensive teams.

LEGEND FOR SELECTORS
AA—All-America Board
AP—Associated Press
C—Walter Camp (published in Harper's Weekly, 1897; in Collier's Magazine, 1898-1924)
COL—Collier's Magazine (selections by Grantland Rice, 1925-47; published American Football Coaches Association teams, 1948-56, listed under FC)
CP—Central Press
FBW—Football World Magazine
FC—American Football Coaches Association (published in Saturday Evening Post Magazine, 1945-47; in Collier's Magazine, 1948-56; sponsored by General Mills in 1957-59 and by Eastman Kodak from 1960)
FN—Football News
FW—Football Writers Association of America (published in Look Magazine, 1946-70)
INS—International News Service (merged with United Press in 1958 to form UPI)
L—Look Magazine (published Football Writers Association of America teams, 1946-70, listed under FW)
LIB—Liberty Magazine
M—Frank Menke Syndicate
N—Newsweek
NA—North American Newspaper Alliance
NEA—Newspaper Enterprise Association
SN—Sporting News
UP—United Press (merged with International News Service in 1958 to form UPI)
UPI—United Press International
W—Caspar Whitney (published in The Week's Sport in association with Walter Camp, 1889-90; published in Harper's Weekly, 1891-96, and in Outing Magazine, which he owned, 1898-1908; Walter Camp substituted for Whitney, who was on a world sports tour, and selected Harper's Weekly's team for 1897)
WCF—Walter Camp Foundation

All-America Selections

Listed on the following pages are the consensus all-Americans (i.e., the players who were accorded a majority of votes at their positions by the selectors). Included are the selections of 1889-97, 1909-12 and 1922 when there was only one selector.

1889
E—Amos Alonzo Stagg, Yale; Arthur Cumnock, Harvard; T—Hector Cowan, Princeton; Charles Gill, Yale; G—Pudge Heffelfinger, Yale; John Cranston, Harvard; C—William George, Princeton; B—Edgar Allan Poe, Princeton; Roscoe Channing, Princeton; Knowlton Ames, Princeton; James Lee, Harvard.

1890
E—Frank Hallowell, Harvard; Ralph Warren, Princeton; T—Marshall Newell, Harvard; William Rhodes, Yale; G—Pudge Heffelfinger, Yale; Jesse Riggs, Princeton; C—John Cranston, Harvard; B—Thomas McClung, Yale; Sheppard Homans, Princeton; Dudley Dean, Harvard; John Corbett, Harvard.

1891
E—Frank Hinkey, Yale; John Hartwell, Yale; T—Wallace Winter, Yale; Marshall Newell, Harvard; G—Pudge Heffelfinger, Yale; Jesse Riggs, Princeton; C—John Adams, Pennsylvania; B—Philip King, Princeton; Everett Lake, Harvard; Thomas McClung, Yale; Sheppard Homans, Princeton.

1892
E—Frank Hinkey, Yale; Frank Hallowell, Harvard; T—Marshall Newell, Harvard; A. Hamilton Wallis, Yale; G—Arthur Wheeler, Princeton; Bertram Waters, Harvard; C—William Lewis, Harvard; B—Charles Brewer, Harvard; Vance McCormick, Yale; Philip King, Princeton; Harry Thayer, Pennsylvania.

1893
E—Frank Hinkey, Yale; Thomas Trenchard, Princeton; T—Langdon Lea, Princeton; Marshall Newell, Harvard; G—Arthur Wheeler, Princeton; William Hickok, Yale; C—William Lewis, Harvard; B—Philip King, Princeton; Charles Brewer, Harvard; Franklin Morse, Princeton; Frank Butterworth, Yale.

1894
E—Frank Hinkey, Yale; Charles Gelbert, Pennsylvania; T—Bertram Waters, Harvard; Langdon Lea, Princeton; G—Arthur Wheeler, Princeton; William Hickok, Yale; C—Philip Stillman, Yale; B—George Adee, Yale; Arthur Knipe, Pennsylvania; George Brooke, Pennsylvania; Frank Butterworth, Yale.

1895
E—Norman Cabot, Harvard; Charles Gelbert, Pennsylvania; T—Langdon Lea, Princeton; Fred Murphy, Yale; G—Charles Wharton, Pennsylvania; Dudley Riggs, Princeton; C—Alfred Bull, Pennsylvania; B—Clinton Wyckoff, Cornell; Samuel Thorne, Yale; Charles Brewer, Harvard; George Brooke, Pennsylvania.

1896
E—Norman Cabot, Harvard; Charles Gelbert, Pennsylvania; T—William Church, Princeton; Fred Murphy, Yale; G—Charles Wharton, Pennsylvania; Wylie Woodruff, Pennsylvania; C—Robert Gailey, Princeton; B—Clarence Fincke, Yale; Edgar Wrightington, Harvard; Addison Kelly, Princeton; John Baird, Princeton.

1897
E—Garrett Cochran, Princeton; John Hall, Yale; T—Burr Chamberlain, Yale; John Outland, Pennsylvania; G—T. Truxton Hare, Pennsylvania; Gordon Brown, Yale; C—Alan Doucette, Harvard; B—Charles DeSaulles, Yale; Benjamin Dibblee, Harvard; Addison Kelly, Princeton; John Minds, Pennsylvania.

1898
E—Lew Palmer, Princeton; John Hallowell, Harvard; T—Arthur Hillebrand, Princeton; Burr Chamberlain, Yale; G—T. Truxton Hare, Pennsylvania; Gordon Brown, Yale; Walter Boal, Harvard; C—Pete Overfield, Pennsylvania; William Cunningham, Michigan; B—Charles Daly, Harvard; Benjamin Dibblee, Harvard; John Outland, Pennsylvania; Clarence Herschberger, Chicago; Malcolm McBride, Yale; Charles Romeyn, Army.

1899
E—David Campbell, Harvard; Arthur Poe, Princeton; T—Arthur Hillebrand, Princeton; George Stillman, Yale; G—T. Truxton Hare, Pennsylvania; Gordon Brown, Yale; C—Pete Overfield, Pennsylvania; B—Charles Daly, Harvard; Josiah McCracken, Pennsylvania; Malcolm McBride, Yale; Isaac Seneca, Carlisle; Albert Sharpe, Yale; Howard Reiter, Princeton.

1900
E—John Hallowell, Harvard; David Campbell, Harvard; William Smith, Army; T—George Stillman, Yale; James Bloomer, Yale; G—Gordon Brown, Yale; T. Truxton Hare, Pennsylvania; C—Herman Olcott, Yale; Walter Bachman, Lafayette; B—Bill Morley, Columbia; George Chadwick, Yale; Perry Hale, Yale; William Fincke, Yale; Charles Daly, Harvard; Raymond Starbuck, Cornell.

1901
E—David Campbell, Harvard; Ralph Davis, Princeton; Edward Bowditch, Harvard; Neil Snow, Michigan; T—Oliver Cutts, Harvard; Paul Bunker, Army; Crawford Blagden, Harvard; G—William Warner, Cornell; William Lee, Harvard; Charles Barnard, Harvard; Sanford Hunt, Cornell; C—Henry Holt, Yale; Walter Bachman, Lafayette; B—Robert Kernan, Harvard; Charles Daly, Army; Thomas Graydon, Harvard; Harold Weekes, Columbia; Bill Morley, Columbia.

1902
E—Thomas Shevlin, Yale; Edward Bowditch, Harvard; T—Ralph Kinney, Yale; James Hogan, Yale; Paul Bunker, Army; G—Edgar Glass, Yale; John DeWitt, Princeton; William Warner, Cornell; C—Henry Holt, Yale; Robert Boyers, Army; B—Foster Rockwell, Yale; George Chadwick, Yale; Thomas Graydon, Harvard; Thomas Barry, Brown.

1903
E—Howard Henry, Princeton; Charles Rafferty, Yale; T—Daniel Knowlton, Harvard; James Hogan, Yale; Fred Schacht, Minnesota; G—John DeWitt, Princeton; Andrew Marshall, Harvard; James Bloomer, Yale; C—Henry Hooper, Dartmouth; B—Willie Heston, Michigan; J. Dana Kafer, Princeton; James Johnson, Carlisle; Richard Smith, Columbia; Myron Witham, Dartmouth; W. Ledyard Mitchell, Yale.

1904
E—Thomas Shevlin, Yale; Fred Speik, Chicago; T—James Hogan, Yale; James Cooney, Princeton; G—Frank Piekarski, Pennsylvania; Joseph Gilman, Dartmouth; Ralph Kinney, Yale; C—Arthur Tipton, Army; B—Daniel Hurley, Harvard; Walter Eckersall, Chicago; Vincent Stevenson, Pennsylvania; Willie Heston, Michigan; Andrew Smith, Pennsylvania; Foster Rockwell, Yale; Henry Torney, Army.

1905
E—Thomas Shevlin, Yale; Ralph Glaze, Dartmouth; Mark Catlin, Chicago; T—Otis Lamson, Pennsylvania; Beaton Squires, Harvard; Karl Brill, Harvard; G—Roswell Tripp, Yale; Francis Burr, Harvard; C—Robert Torrey, Pennsylvania; B—Walter Eckersall, Chicago; Howard Roome, Yale; John Hubbard, Amherst; James McCormick, Princeton; Guy Hutchinson, Yale; Daniel Hurley, Harvard; Henry Torney, Army.

1906
E—Robert Forbes, Yale; L. Casper Wister, Princeton; T—L. Horatio Biglow, Yale; James Cooney, Princeton; Charles Osborne, Harvard; G—Francis Burr, Harvard; Elmer Thompson, Cornell; August Ziegler, Pennsylvania; C—William Dunn, Penn St.; William Newman, Cornell; B—Walter Eckersall, Chicago; Hugh Knox, Yale; Edward Dillon, Princeton; John Mayhew, Brown; William Hollenback, Pennsylvania; Paul Veeder, Yale.

1907
E—Bill Dague, Navy; Clarence Alcott, Yale; Albert Exendine, Carlisle; L. Casper Wister, Princeton; T—Dexter Draper, Pennsylvania; L. Horatio Biglow, Yale; G—August Ziegler, Pennsylvania; William Erwin, Army; C—Adolph Schulz, Michigan; Patrick Grant, Harvard; B—John Wendell, Harvard; Thomas A. D. Jones, Yale; Edwin Harlan, Princeton; James McCormick, Princeton; Edward Coy, Yale; Peter Hauser, Carlisle.

1908
E—Hunter Scarlett, Pennsylvania; George Schildmiller, Dartmouth; T—Hamilton Fish, Harvard; Frank Horr, Syracuse; Percy Northcroft, Navy; G—Clark Tobin, Dartmouth; William Goebel, Yale; Hamlin Andrus, Yale; Bernard O'Rourke, Cornell; C—Charles Nourse, Harvard; B—Edward Coy, Yale; Frederick Tibbott, Princeton; William Hollenback, Pennsylvania; Walter Steffen, Chicago; Ed Lange, Navy; Hamilton Corbett, Harvard.

1909
E—Adrian Regnier, Brown; John Kilpatrick, Yale; T—Hamilton Fish, Harvard; Henry Hobbs, Yale; G—Albert Benbrook, Michigan; Hamlin Andrus, Yale; C—Carroll Cooney, Yale; B—Edward Coy, Yale; John McGovern, Minnesota; Stephen Philbin, Yale; Wayland Minot, Harvard.

1910
E—John Kilpatrick, Yale; Stanfield Wells, Michigan; T—Robert McKay, Harvard; James Walker, Minnesota; G—Robert Fisher, Harvard; Albert Benbrook, Michigan; C—Ernest Cozens, Pennsylvania; B—E. LeRoy Mercer, Pennsylvania; Percy Wendell, Harvard; Earl Sprackling, Brown; Talbot Pendleton, Princeton.

1911
E—Douglass Bomeisler, Yale; Sanford White, Princeton; T—Edward Hart, Princeton; Leland Devore, Army; G—Robert Fisher, Harvard; Joseph Duff, Princeton; C—Henry Ketcham, Yale; B—Jim Thorpe, Carlisle; Percy Wendell, Harvard; Arthur Howe, Yale; Jack Dalton, Navy.

1912
E—Samuel Felton, Harvard; Douglass Bomeisler, Yale; T—Wesley Englehorn, Dartmouth; Robert Butler, Wisconsin; G—Stanley Pennock, Harvard; John Logan, Princeton; C—Henry Ketcham, Yale; B—Charles Brickley, Harvard; Jim Thorpe, Carlisle; George Crowther, Brown; E. LeRoy Mercer, Pennsylvania.

1913
E—Robert Hogsett, Dartmouth; Louis Merrillat, Army; T—Harold Ballin, Princeton; Nelson Talbott, Yale; Miller Pontius, Michigan; Harvey Hitchcock, Harvard; G—John Brown, Navy; Stanley Pennock, Harvard; Ray Keeler, Wisconsin; C—Paul Des Jardien, Chicago; B—Charles Brickley, Harvard; Edward Mahan, Harvard; Jim Craig, Michigan; Ellery Huntington, Colgate; Gus Dorais, Notre Dame.

1914
E—Huntington Hardwick, Harvard; John O'Hearn, Cornell; Perry Graves, Illinois; T—Harold Ballin, Princeton; Walter Trumbull, Harvard; G—Stanley Pennock, Harvard; Ralph Chapman, Illinois; Clarence Spears, Dartmouth; C—John McEwan, Army; B—John Maulbetsch, Michigan; Edward Mahan, Harvard; Charles Barrett, Cornell; John Spiegel, Wash. & Jeff.; Harry LeGore, Yale.

1915
E—Murray Shelton, Cornell; Guy Chamberlin, Nebraska; T—Joseph Gilman, Harvard; Howard Buck, Wisconsin; G—Clarence Spears, Dartmouth; Harold White, Syracuse; C—Robert Peck, Pittsburgh; B—Charles Barrett, Cornell; Edward Mahan, Harvard; Richard King, Harvard; Bart Macomber, Illinois; Eugene Mayer, Virginia; Neno Jerry DaPrato, Michigan St.

1916
E—Bert Baston, Minnesota; James Herron, Pittsburgh; T—Clarence Horning, Colgate; D. Belford West, Colgate; G—Clinton Black, Yale; Harrie Dadmun, Harvard; Frank Hogg, Princeton; C—Robert Peck, Pittsburgh; B—Elmer Oliphant, Army; Oscar Anderson, Colgate; Fritz Pollard, Brown; Charles Harley, Ohio St.

1917
E—Charles Bolen, Ohio St.; Paul Robeson, Rutgers; Henry Miller, Pennsylvania; T—Alfred Cobb, Syracuse; George Hauser, Minnesota; G—Dale Seis, Pittsburgh; John Sutherland, Pittsburgh; Eugene Neely, Dartmouth; C—Frank Rydzewski, Notre Dame; B—Elmer Oliphant, Army; Ben Boynton, Williams; Everett Strupper, Georgia Tech; Charles Harley, Ohio St.

1918
E—Paul Robeson, Rutgers; Bill Fincher, Georgia Tech; T—

Wilbur Henry, Wash. & Jeff.; Leonard Hilty, Pittsburgh; Lou Usher, Syracuse; Joe Guyon, Georgia Tech; G—Joe Alexander, Syracuse; Lyman Perry, Navy; C—Ashel Day, Georgia Tech; John Depler, Illinois; B—Frank Murrey, Princeton; Tom Davies, Pittsburgh; Wolcott Roberts, Navy; George McLaren, Pittsburgh.

1919
E—Bob Higgins, Penn St.; Henry Miller, Pennsylvania; Lester Belding, Iowa; T—Wilbur Henry, Wash. & Jeff.; D. Belford West, Colgate; G—Joe Alexander, Syracuse; Adolph Youngstrom, Dartmouth; C—James Weaver, Centre; Charles Carpenter, Wisconsin; B—Charles Harley, Ohio St.; Ira Rodgers, West Va.; Edward Casey, Harvard; Bo McMillin, Centre; Ben Boynton, Williams.

1920
E—Luke Urban, Boston College; Charles Carney, Illinois; Bill Fincher, Georgia Tech; T—Stan Keck, Princeton; Ralph Scott, Wisconsin; G—Tim Callahan, Yale; Tom Woods, Harvard; Iolas Huffman, Ohio St.; C—Herb Stein, Pittsburgh; B—George Gipp, Notre Dame; Donald Lourie, Princeton; Gaylord Stinchcomb, Ohio St.; Charles Way, Penn St.

1921
E—Brick Muller, California; Eddie Anderson, Notre Dame; T—Dan McMillan, California; Iolas Huffman, Ohio St.; G—Frank Schwab, Lafayette; John Brown, Harvard; Stan Keck, Princeton; C—Herb Stein, Pittsburgh; B—Aubrey Devine, Iowa; Glenn Killinger, Penn St.; Bo McMillin, Centre; Malcolm Aldrich, Yale; Edgar Kaw, Cornell.

1922
E—Brick Muller, California; Wendell Taylor, Navy; T—C. Herbert Treat, Princeton; John Thurman, Pennsylvania; G—Frank Schwab, Lafayette; Charles Hubbard, Harvard; C—Ed Garbisch, Army; B—Harry Kipke, Michigan; Gordon Locke, Iowa; John Thomas, Chicago; Edgar Kaw, Cornell.

1923
E—Pete McRae, Syracuse; Ray Ecklund, Minnesota; Lynn Bomar, Vanderbilt; T—Century Milstead, Yale; Marty Below, Wisconsin; G—Charles Hubbard, Harvard; James McMillen, Illinois; C—Jack Blott, Michigan; B—George Pfann, Cornell; Red Grange, Illinois; William Mallory, Yale; Harry Wilson, Penn St.

Beginning in 1924, unanimous selections are indicated by (*).

1924
E—Jim Lawson, Stanford, 5-11, 190, Long Beach, Calif.; (tie) E—Dick Luman, Yale, 6-1, 176, Pinedale, Wyo.; E—Henry Wakefield, Vanderbilt, 5-10, 160, Petersburg, Tenn.; T—Ed McGinley, Pennsylvania, 5-11, 185, Swarthmore, Pa.; T—Ed Weir, Nebraska, 6-1, 194, Superior, Neb.; G—Joe Pondelik, Chicago, 5-11, 215, Cicero, Ill.; G—Carl Diehl, Dartmouth, 6-1, 205, Chicago, Ill.; C—Edwin Horrell, California, 5-11, 185, Pasadena, Calif.; B—*Red Grange, Illinois, 5-10, 170, Wheaton, Ill.; B—Harry Stuhldreher, Notre Dame, 5-7, 151, Massillon, Ohio; B—Jimmy Crowley, Notre Dame, 5-11, 162, Green Bay, Wis.; B—Elmer Layden, Notre Dame, 6-0, 162, Davenport, Iowa.

1925
E—Bennie Oosterbaan, Michigan, 6-0, 180, Muskegon, Mich.; E—George Tully, Dartmouth, 5-10, 175, Orange, N.J.; T—*Ed Weir, Nebraska, 6-1, 194, Superior, Neb.; T—Ralph Chase, Pittsburgh, 6-3, 202, Easton, Pa.; G—Carl Diehl, Dartmouth, 6-1, 205, Chicago, Ill.; G—Ed Hess, Ohio St., 6-1, 190, Cincinnati, Ohio; C—Ed McMillan, Princeton, 6-0, 208, Pittsburgh, Pa.; B—*Andy Oberlander, Dartmouth, 6-0, 197, Everett, Mass.; B—Red Grange, Illinois, 5-10, 170, Wheaton, Ill.; B—Ernie Nevers, Stanford, 6-0, 200, Superior, Wis.; (tie) B—Benny Friedman, Michigan, 5-8, 170, Cleveland, Ohio; B—George Wilson, Washington, 5-11, 190, Everett, Wash.

1926
E—Bennie Oosterbaan, Michigan, 6-0, 186, Muskegon, Mich.; E—Vic Hanson, Syracuse, 5-10, 174, Syracuse, N.Y.; T—*Frank Wickhorst, Navy, 6-0, 218, Oak Park, Ill.; T—Bud Sprague, Army, 6-2, 210, Dallas, Texas; G—Harry Connaughton, Georgetown, 6-2, 275, Philadelphia, Pa.; G—Bernie Shively, Illinois, 6-4, 208, Oliver, Ill.; C—Bud Boeringer, Notre Dame, 6-1, 186, St.

Paul, Minn.; B—Benny Friedman, Michigan, 5-8, 172, Cleveland, Ohio; B—Mort Kaer, Southern Cal, 5-11, 167, Red Bluff, Calif.; B—Ralph Baker, Northwestern, 5-10, 172, Rockford, Ill.; B—Herb Joesting, Minnesota, 6-1, 192, Owatonna, Minn.

1927
E—*Bennie Oosterbaan, Michigan, 6-0, 186, Muskegon, Mich.; E—Tom Nash, Georgia, 6-3, 200, Washington, Ga.; T—Jesse Hibbs, Southern Cal, 5-11, 185, Glendale, Calif.; T—Ed Hake, Pennsylvania, 6-0, 190, Philadelphia, Pa.; G—Bill Webster, Yale, 6-0, 200, Shelton, Conn.; G—John Smith, Notre Dame, 5-9, 164, Hartford, Conn.; (tie) C—Larry Bettencourt, St. Mary's (Cal.), 5-10, 187, Centerville, Calif.; C—John Charlesworth, Yale, 5-11, 198, North Adams, Mass.; B—*Gibby Welch, Pittsburgh, 5-11, 170, Parkersburg, W. Va.; B—Morley Drury, Southern Cal, 6-0, 185, Long Beach, Calif.; B—Red Cagle, Army, 5-9, 167, Merryville, La.; B—Herb Joesting, Minnesota, 6-1, 192, Owatonna, Minn.

1928
E—Irv Phillips, California, 6-1, 188, Salinas, Calif.; E—Wes Fesler, Ohio St., 6-0, 173, Youngstown, Ohio; T—Otto Pommerening, Michigan, 6-0, 178, Ann Arbor, Mich.; T—Mike Getto, Pittsburgh, 6-2, 198, Jeannette, Pa.; G—Seraphim Post, Stanford, 6-0, 190, Berkeley, Calif.; (tie) Don Robesky, Stanford, 5-11, 198, Bakersfield, Calif.; G—Edward Burke, Navy, 6-0, 180, Larksville, Pa.; C—Pete Pund, Georgia Tech, 6-0, 195, Augusta, Ga.; B—*Red Cagle, Army, 5-9, 167, Merryville, La.; B—Paul Scull, Pennsylvania, 5-8, 187, Bala, Pa.; B—(tie) Ken Strong, New York U., 6-0, 201, West Haven, Conn.; Howard Harpster, Carnegie Mellon, 6-1, 160, Akron, Ohio; B—Charles Carroll, Washington, 6-0, 190, Seattle, Wash.

1929
E—*Joe Donchess, Pittsburgh, 6-0, 175, Youngstown, Ohio; E—Wes Fesler, Ohio St., 6-0, 183, Youngstown, Ohio; T—Bronko Nagurski, Minnesota, 6-2, 217, International Falls, Minn.; T—Elmer Sleight, Purdue, 6-2, 193, Morris, Ill.; G—Jack Cannon, Notre Dame, 5-11, 193, Columbus, Ohio; G—Ray Montgomery, Pittsburgh, 6-1, 189, Wheeling, W. Va.; C—Ben Ticknor, Harvard, 6-2, 193, New York, N.Y.; B—*Frank Carideo, Notre Dame, 5-7, 175, Mount Vernon, N.Y.; B—Ralph Welch, Purdue, 6-1, 189, Whitesboro, Texas; B—Red Cagle, Army, 5-9, 167, Merryville, La.; B—Gene McEver, Tennessee, 5-10, 185, Bristol, Va.

1930
E—*Wes Fesler, Ohio St., 6-0, 185, Youngstown, Ohio; E—Frank Baker, Northwestern, 6-2, 175, Cedar Rapids, Iowa; T—*Fred Sington, Alabama, 6-2, 215, Birmingham, Ala.; T—Milo Lubratovich, Wisconsin, 6-2, 216, Duluth, Minn.; G—Ted Beckett, California, 6-1, 190, Oroville, Calif.; G—Barton Koch, Baylor, 5-10, 195, Temple, Texas; C—*Ben Ticknor, Harvard, 6-2, 193, New York, N.Y.; B—*Frank Carideo, Notre Dame, 5-7, 175, Mount Vernon, N.Y.; B—Marchy Schwartz, Notre Dame, 5-11, 172, Bay St. Louis, Miss.; B—Erny Pinckert, Southern Cal, 6-0, 189, San Bernardino, Calif.; B—Leonard Macaluso, Colgate, 6-2, 210, East Aurora, N.Y.

1931
E—*Jerry Dalrymple, Tulane, 5-10, 175, Arkadelphia, Ark.; E—Vernon Smith, Georgia, 6-2, 190, Macon, Ga.; T—Jesse Quatse, Pittsburgh, 5-8, 198, Greensburg, Pa.; (tie) T—Jack Riley, Northwestern, 6-2, 218, Wilmette, Ill.; T—Dallas Marvil, Northwestern, 6-3, 227, Laurel, Del.; G—Biggie Munn, Minnesota, 5-10, 217, Minneapolis, Minn.; G—John Baker, Southern Cal, 5-10, 185, Kingsburg, Calif.; C—Tommy Yarr, Notre Dame, 5-11, 197, Chimacum, Wash.; B—Gus Shaver, Southern Cal, 5-11, 185, Covina, Calif.; B—Marchy Schwartz, Notre Dame, 5-11, 178, Bay St. Louis, Miss.; B—Pug Rentner, Northwestern, 6-1, 185, Joliet, Ill.; B—Barry Wood, Harvard, 6-1, 173, Milton, Mass.

1932
E—*Paul Moss, Purdue, 6-2, 185, Terre Haute, Ind.; E—Joe Skladany, Pittsburgh, 5-10, 185, Larksville, Pa.; T—*Joe Kurth, Notre Dame, 6-2, 204, Madison, Wis.; T—*Ernie Smith, Southern Cal, 6-2, 215, Los Angeles, Calif.; G—Milt Summerley, Army, 6-0, 181, Benton Harbor, Mich.; G—Bill Corbus, Stanford, 5-11, 188, Vallejo, Calif.; C—Pete Gracey, Vanderbilt, 6-0, 188, Franklin, Tenn.; B—*Harry Newman, Michigan, 5-7, 175, Detroit,

Mich.; B—*Warren Heller, Pittsburgh, 6-0, 170, Steelton, Pa.; B—Don Zimmerman, Tulane, 5-10, 190, Lake Charles, La.; B—Jimmy Hitchcock, Auburn, 5-11, 172, Union Springs, Ala.

1933
E—Joe Skladany, Pittsburgh, 5-10, 190, Larksville, Pa.; E—Paul Geisler, Centenary (La.), 6-2, 189, Berwick, La.; T—Fred Crawford, Duke, 6-2, 195, Waynesville, N.C.; T—Francis Wistert, Michigan, 6-3, 212, Chicago, Ill.; G—Bill Corbus, Stanford, 5-11, 195, Vallejo, Calif.; G—Aaron Rosenberg, Southern Cal, 6-0, 210, Los Angeles, Calif.; C—*Chuck Bernard, Michigan, 6-2, 215, Benton Harbor, Mich.; B—*Cotton Warburton, Southern Cal, 5-7, 147, San Diego, Calif.; B—George Sauer, Nebraska, 6-2, 195, Lincoln, Neb.; B—Beattie Feathers, Tennessee, 5-10, 180, Bristol, Va.; B—Duane Purvis, Purdue, 6-1, 190, Mattoon, Ill.

1934
E—Don Hutson, Alabama, 6-1, 185, Pine Bluff, Ark.; E—Frank Larson, Minnesota, 6-3, 190, Duluth, Minn.; T—Bill Lee, Alabama, 6-2, 225, Eutaw, Ala.; T—Bob Reynolds, Stanford, 6-4, 220, Okmulgee, Okla.; G—Chuck Hartwig, Pittsburgh, 6-0, 190, Benwood, W. Va.; G—Bill Bevan, Minnesota, 5-11, 194, St. Paul, Minn.; C—Jack Robinson, Notre Dame, 6-3, 195, Huntington, N.Y.; B—Bobby Grayson, Stanford, 5-11, 186, Portland, Ore.; B—Pug Lund, Minnesota, 5-11, 185, Rice Lake, Wis.; B—Dixie Howell, Alabama, 5-10, 164, Hartford, Ala.; B—Fred Borries, Navy, 6-0, 175, Louisville, Ky.

1935
E—Wayne Millner, Notre Dame, 6-0, 184, Salem, Mass.; (tie) E—James Moscrip, Stanford, 6-0, 186, Adena, Ohio; E—Gaynell Tinsley, Louisiana St., 6-0, 188, Homer, La.; T—Ed Widseth, Minnesota, 6-2, 220, McIntosh, Minn.; T—Larry Lutz, California, 6-0, 201, Santa Ana, Calif.; G—John Weller, Princeton, 6-0, 195, Wynnewood, Pa.; (tie) G—Sidney Wagner, Michigan St., 5-11, 186, Lansing, Mich.; G—J. C. Wetsel, Southern Methodist, 5-10, 185, Dallas, Texas; (tie) C—Gomer Jones, Ohio St., 5-8, 210, Cleveland, Ohio; C—Darrell Lester, Texas Christian, 6-4, 218, Jacksboro, Texas; B—*Jay Berwanger, Chicago, 6-0, 195, Dubuque, Iowa; B—*Bobby Grayson, Stanford, 5-11, 190, Portland, Ore.; B—Bobby Wilson, Southern Methodist, 5-10, 147, Corsicana, Texas; B—Riley Smith, Alabama, 6-1, 195, Columbus, Miss.

1936
E—*Larry Kelley, Yale, 6-1, 190, Williamsport, Pa.; E—*Gaynell Tinsley, Louisiana St., 6-0, 196, Homer, La.; T—*Ed Widseth, Minnesota, 6-2, 220, McIntosh, Minn.; T—Averell Daniell, Pittsburgh, 6-3, 200, Mt. Lebanon, Pa.; G—Steve Reid, Northwestern, 5-9, 192, Chicago, Ill.; G—Max Starcevich, Washington, 5-10, 198, Duluth, Minn.; (tie) C—Alex Wojciechowicz, Fordham, 6-0, 192, South River, N.J.; C—Mike Basrak, Duquesne, 6-1, 210, Bellaire, Ohio; B—Sammy Baugh, Texas Christian, 6-2, 180, Sweetwater, Texas; B—Ace Parker, Duke, 5-11, 175, Portsmouth, Va.; B—Ray Buivid, Marquette, 6-1, 193, Port Washington, Wis.; B—Sam Francis, Nebraska, 6-1, 207, Oberlin, Kan.

1937
E—Chuck Sweeney, Notre Dame, 6-0, 190, Bloomington, Ill.; E—Andy Bershak, North Caro., 6-0, 190, Clairton, Pa.; T—Ed Franco, Fordham, 5-8, 196, Jersey City, N.J.; T—Tony Matisi, Pittsburgh, 6-0, 224, Endicott, N.Y.; G—Joe Routt, Texas A&M, 6-0, 193, Chappel Hill, Texas; G—Leroy Monsky, Alabama, 6-0, 198, Montgomery, Ala.; C—Alex Wojciechowicz, Fordham, 6-0, 196, South River, N.J.; B—*Clint Frank, Yale, 5-10, 190, Evanston, Ill.; B—Marshall Goldberg, Pittsburgh, 5-11, 185, Elkins, W.Va.; B—Byron ``Whizzer'' White, Colorado, 6-1, 185, Wellington, Colo.; B—Sam Chapman, California, 6-0, 190, Tiburon, Calif.

1938
E—Waddy Young, Oklahoma, 6-2, 203, Ponca City, Okla.; (tie) E—Brud Holland, Cornell, 6-1, 205, Auburn, N.Y.; E—Bowden Wyatt, Tennessee, 6-1, 190, Kingston, Tenn.; T—*Ed Beinor, Notre Dame, 6-2, 207, Harvey, Ill.; T—Alvord Wolff, Santa Clara, 6-2, 220, San Francisco, Calif.; G—*Ralph Heikkinen, Michigan, 5-10, 185, Ramsey, Mich.; G—Ed Bock, Iowa St., 6-0, 202, Fort Dodge, Iowa; C—Ki Aldrich, Texas Christian, 5-11, 195, Temple, Texas; B—*Davey O'Brien, Texas Christian, 5-7, 150, Dallas, Texas; B—*Marshall

Goldberg, Pittsburgh, 6-0, 190, Elkins, W. Va.; B—Bob MacLeod, Dartmouth, 6-0, 190, Glen Ellyn, Ill.; B—Vic Bottari, California, 5-9, 182, Vallejo, Calif.

1939

E—Esco Sarkkinen, Ohio St., 6-0, 192, Fairport Harbor, Ohio; E—Ken Kavanaugh, Louisiana St., 6-3, 203, Little Rock, Ark.; T—Nick Drahos, Cornell, 6-3, 200, Cedarhurst, N.Y.; T—Harley McCollum, Tulane, 6-4, 235, Wagoner, Okla.; G—*Harry Smith, Southern Cal, 5-11, 218, Ontario, Calif.; G—Ed Molinski, Tennessee, 5-10, 190, Massillon, Ohio; C—John Schiechl, Santa Clara, 6-2, 220, San Francisco, Calif.; B—Nile Kinnick, Iowa, 5-8, 167, Omaha, Neb.; B—Tom Harmon, Michigan, 6-0, 195, Gary, Ind.; B—John Kimbrough, Texas A&M, 6-2, 210, Haskell, Texas; B—George Cafego, Tennessee, 6-0, 174, Scarbro, W. Va.

1940

E—Gene Goodreault, Boston College, 5-10, 184, Haverhill, Mass.; E—Dave Rankin, Purdue, 6-1, 190, Warsaw, Ind.; T—Nick Drahos, Cornell, 6-3, 212, Cedarhurst, N.Y.; (tie) T—Alf Bauman, Northwestern, 6-1, 210, Chicago, Ill.; T—Urban Odson, Minnesota, 6-3, 247, Clark, S.D.; G—*Bob Suffridge, Tennessee, 6-0, 190, Knoxville, Tenn.; G—Marshall Robnett, Texas A&M, 6-1, 205, Klondike, Texas; C—Rudy Mucha, Washington, 6-2, 210, Chicago, Ill.; B—*Tom Harmon, Michigan, 6-0, 195, Gary, Ind.; B—*John Kimbrough, Texas A&M, 6-2, 221, Haskell, Texas; B—Frank Albert, Stanford, 5-9, 170, Glendale, Calif.; B—George Franck, Minnesota, 6-0, 175, Davenport, Iowa.

1941

E—Holt Rast, Alabama, 6-1, 185, Birmingham, Ala.; E—Bob Dove, Notre Dame, 6-2, 195, Youngstown, Ohio; T—Dick Wildung, Minnesota, 6-0, 210, Luverne, Minn.; T—Ernie Blandin, Tulane, 6-3, 245, Keighley, Kan.; G—*Endicott Peabody, Harvard, 6-0, 181, Syracuse, N.Y.; G—Ray Frankowski, Washington, 5-10, 210, Hammond, Ind.; C—Darold Jenkins, Missouri, 6-0, 195, Higginsville, Mo.; B—Bob Westfall, Michigan, 5-8, 190, Ann Arbor, Mich.; B—Bruce Smith, Minnesota, 6-0, 193, Faribault, Minn.; B—Frank Albert, Stanford, 5-9, 173, Glendale, Calif.; (tie) B—Bill Dudley, Virginia, 5-10, 175, Bluefield, Va.; B—Frank Sinkwich, Georgia, 5-8, 180, Youngstown, Ohio.

1942

E—*Dave Schreiner, Wisconsin, 6-2, 198, Lancaster, Wis.; E—Bob Dove, Notre Dame, 6-2, 195, Youngstown, Ohio; T—Dick Wildung, Minnesota, 6-0, 215, Luverne, Minn.; T—Albert Wistert, Michigan, 6-2, 205, Chicago, Ill.; G—Chuck Taylor, Stanford, 5-11, 200, San Jose, Calif.; (tie) G—Harvey Hardy, Georgia Tech, 5-10, 185, Thomaston, Ga.; G—Julie Franks, Michigan, 6-0, 187, Hamtramck, Mich.; C—Joe Domnanovich, Alabama, 6-1, 200, South Bend, Ind.; B—*Frank Sinkwich, Georgia, 5-8, 185, Youngstown, Ohio; B—Paul Governali, Columbia, 5-11, 186, New York, N.Y.; B—Mike Holovak, Boston College, 6-2, 214, Lansford, Pa.; B—Billy Hillenbrand, Indiana, 6-0, 195, Evansville, Ind.

1943

E—Ralph Heywood, Southern Cal, 6-2, 195, Huntington Park, Calif.; E—John Yonakor, Notre Dame, 6-4, 220, Dorchester, Mass.; T—Jim White, Notre Dame, 6-2, 210, Edgewater, N.J.; T—Don Whitmire, Navy, 5-11, 215, Decatur, Ala.; G—Alex Agase, Purdue, 5-10, 190, Evanston, Ill.; G—Pat Filley, Notre Dame, 5-8, 175, South Bend, Ind.; C—*Casimir Myslinski, Army, 5-11, 186, Steubenville, Ohio; B—*Bill Daley, Michigan, 6-2, 206, St. Cloud, Minn.; B—Angelo Bertelli, Notre Dame, 6-1, 173, West Springfield, Mass.; B—Creighton Miller, Notre Dame, 6-0, 185, Wilmington, Del.; B—Bob Odell, Pennsylvania, 5-11, 182, Sioux City, Iowa.

1944

E—Phil Tinsley, Georgia Tech, 6-1, 188, Bessemer, Ala.; (tie) E—Paul Walker, Yale, 6-3, 203, Oak Park, Ill.; E—Jack Dugger, Ohio St., 6-3, 210, Canton, Ohio; T—*Don Whitmire, Navy, 5-11, 215, Decatur, Ala.; T—John Ferraro, Southern Cal, 6-4, 235, Maywood, Calif.; G—Bill Hackett, Ohio St., 5-9, 191, London, Ohio; G—Ben Chase, Navy, 6-1, 195, San Diego, Calif.; C—John Tavener, Indiana, 6-0, 220, Granville, Ohio; B—*Les Horvath, Ohio St., 5-10, 167, Parma, Ohio; B—*Glenn Davis, Army, 5-9, 170, Claremont, Calif.; B—Doc Blanchard, Army, 6-0, 205, Bishopville, S.C.; B—Bob Jenkins, Navy, 6-1, 195, Talladega, Ala.

1945

E—Dick Duden, Navy, 6-2, 203, New York, N.Y.; E—(tie) Hubert Bechtol, Texas, 6-2, 190, Lubbock, Texas; E—Bob Ravensberg, Indiana, 6-1, 180, Bellevue, Ky.; E—Max Morris, Northwestern, 6-2, 195, West Frankfort, Ill.; T—Tex Coulter, Army, 6-3, 220, Fort Worth, Texas; T—George Savitsky, Pennsylvania, 6-3, 250, Camden, N.J.; G—*Warren Amling, Ohio St., 6-0, 197, Pana, Ill.; G—John Green, Army, 5-11, 190, Shelbyville, Ky.; C—Vaughn Mancha, Alabama, 6-0, 235, Birmingham, Ala.; B—*Glenn Davis, Army, 5-9, 170, Claremont, Calif.; B—*Doc Blanchard, Army, 6-0, 205, Bishopville, S.C.; B—*Herman Wedemeyer, St. Mary's (Cal.), 5-10, 173, Honolulu, Hawaii; B—Bob Fenimore, Oklahoma St., 6-2, 188, Woodward, Okla.

1946

E—*Burr Baldwin, UCLA, 6-1, 196, Bakersfield, Calif.; E—(tie) Hubert Bechtol, Texas, 6-2, 201, Lubbock, Texas; Hank Foldberg, Army, 6-1, 200, Dallas, Texas; T—George Connor, Notre Dame, 6-3, 225, Chicago, Ill.; (tie) T—Warren Amling, Ohio St., 6-0, 197, Pana, Ill.; T—Dick Huffman, Tennessee, 6-2, 230, Charleston, W.Va.; G—Alex Agase, Illinois, 5-10, 191, Evanston, Ill.; G—Weldon Humble, Rice, 6-1, 214, San Antonio, Texas; C—Paul Duke, Georgia Tech, 6-1, 210, Atlanta, Ga.; B—*John Lujack, Notre Dame, 6-0, 180, Connellsville, Pa.; B—*Charley Trippi, Georgia, 5-11, 185, Pittston, Pa.; B—*Glenn Davis, Army, 5-9, 170, Claremont, Calif.; B—*Doc Blanchard, Army, 6-0, 205, Bishopville, S.C.

1947

E—Paul Cleary, Southern Cal, 6-1, 195, Santa Ana, Calif.; E—Bill Swiacki, Columbia, 6-2, 198, Southbridge, Mass.; T—Bob Davis, Georgia Tech, 6-4, 220, Columbus, Ga.; T—George Connor, Notre Dame, 6-3, 225, Chicago, Ill.; G—Joe Steffy, Army, 5-11, 190, Chattanooga, Tenn.; G—Bill Fischer, Notre Dame, 6-2, 230, Chicago, Ill.; C—Chuck Bednarik, Pennsylvania, 6-3, 220, Bethlehem, Pa.; B—*John Lujack, Notre Dame, 6-0, 180, Connellsville, Pa.; B—*Bob Chappuis, Michigan, 6-0, 180, Toledo, Ohio; B—Doak Walker, Southern Methodist, 5-11, 170, Dallas, Texas; (tie) B—Charley Conerly, Mississippi, 6-0, 184, Clarksdale, Miss.; B—Bobby Layne, Texas, 6-0, 191, Dallas, Texas.

1948

E—Dick Rifenburg, Michigan, 6-3, 197, Saginaw, Mich.; E—Leon Hart, Notre Dame, 6-4, 225, Turtle Creek, Pa.; T—Leo Nomellini, Minnesota, 6-2, 248, Chicago, Ill.; T—Alvin Wistert, Michigan, 6-3, 218, Chicago, Ill.; G—Buddy Burris, Oklahoma, 5-11, 214, Muskogee, Okla.; G—Bill Fischer, Notre Dame, 6-2, 230, Chicago, Ill.; C—Chuck Bednarik, Pennsylvania, 6-3, 220, Bethlehem, Pa.; B—*Doak Walker, Southern Methodist, 5-11, 168, Dallas, Texas; B—Charlie Justice, North Caro., 5-10, 165, Asheville, N.C.; B—Jackie Jensen, California, 5-11, 195, Oakland, Calif.; (tie) B—Emil Sitko, Notre Dame, 5-8, 180, Fort Wayne, Ind.; B—Clyde Scott, Arkansas, 6-0, 175, Smackover, Ark.

1949

E—*Leon Hart, Notre Dame, 6-5, 260, Turtle Creek, Pa.; E—James Williams, Rice, 6-0, 197, Waco, Texas; T—Leo Nomellini, Minnesota, 6-2, 255, Chicago, Ill.; T—Alvin Wistert, Michigan, 6-3, 223, Chicago, Ill.; G—*Rod Franz, California, 6-1, 198, San Francisco, Calif.; G—Ed Bagdon, Michigan St., 5-10, 200, Dearborn, Mich.; C—*Clayton Tonnemaker, Minnesota, 6-3, 240, Minneapolis, Minn.; B—*Emil Sitko, Notre Dame, 5-8, 180, Fort Wayne, Ind.; B—Doak Walker, Southern Methodist, 5-11, 170, Dallas, Texas; B—Arnold Galiffa, Army, 6-2, 190, Donora, Pa.; B—Bob Williams, Notre Dame, 6-1, 180, Baltimore, Md.

1950

E—*Dan Foldberg, Army, 6-1, 185, Dallas, Texas; E—Bill McColl, Stanford, 6-4, 225, San Diego, Calif.; T—Bob Gain, Kentucky, 6-3, 230, Weirton, W.Va.; T—*Jim Weatherall, Oklahoma, 6-4, 220, White Deer, Texas; G—Bud McFadin, Texas, 6-3, 225, Iraan, Texas; G—Les Richter, California, 6-2, 220, Fresno, Calif.; C—Jerry Groom, Notre Dame, 6-3, 215, Des Moines, Iowa; B—*Vic Janowicz, Ohio St., 5-9, 189, Elyria, Ohio; B—Kyle Rote, Southern Methodist, 6-0, 190, San Antonio, Texas; B—Babe Parilli, Kentucky, 6-1, 183, Rochester, Pa.; B—Leon Heath, Oklahoma, 6-1, 195, Hollis, Okla.

1951

E—*Bill McColl, Stanford, 6-4, 225, San Diego, Calif.; E—Bob Carey, Michigan St., 6-5, 215, Charlevoix, Mich.; T—*Don Coleman, Michigan St., 5-10, 185, Flint, Mich.; T—*Jim Weatherall, Oklahoma, 6-4, 230, White Deer, Texas; G—*Bob Ward, Maryland, 5-10, 185, Elizabeth, N.J.; G—Les Richter, California, 6-2, 230, Fresno, Calif.; C—Dick Hightower, Southern Methodist, 6-1, 215, Tyler, Texas; B—*Dick Kazmaier, Princeton, 5-11, 171, Maumee, Ohio; B—*Hank Lauricella, Tennessee, 5-10, 169, New Orleans, La.; B—Babe Parilli, Kentucky, 6-1, 188, Rochester, Pa.; B—Johnny Karras, Illinois, 5-11, 171, Argo, Ill.

1952

E—Frank McPhee, Princeton, 6-3, 203, Youngstown, Ohio; E—Bernie Flowers, Purdue, 6-1, 189, Erie, Pa.; T—Dick Modzelewski, Maryland, 6-0, 235, West Natrona, Pa.; T—Hal Miller, Georgia Tech, 6-4, 235, Kingsport, Tenn.; G—John Michels, Tennessee, 5-10, 195, Philadelphia, Pa.; G—Elmer Wilhoite, Southern Cal, 6-2, 216, Winton, Calif.; C—Donn Moomaw, UCLA, 6-4, 220, Santa Ana, Calif.; B—*Jack Scarbath, Maryland, 6-1, 190, Baltimore, Md.; B—*Johnny Lattner, Notre Dame, 6-1, 190, Chicago, Ill.; B—Billy Vessels, Oklahoma, 6-0, 185, Cleveland, Okla.; B—Jim Sears, Southern Cal, 5-9, 167, Inglewood, Calif.

1953

E—Don Dohoney, Michigan St., 6-1, 193, Ann Arbor, Mich.; E—Carlton Massey, Texas, 6-4, 210, Rockwall, Texas; T—*Stan Jones, Maryland, 6-0, 235, Lemoyne, Pa.; T—Art Hunter, Notre Dame, 6-2, 226, Akron, Ohio; G—J. D. Roberts, Oklahoma, 5-10, 210, Dallas, Texas; G—Crawford Mims, Mississippi, 5-10, 200, Greenwood, Miss.; C—Larry Morris, Georgia Tech, 6-0, 205, Decatur, Ga.; B—*Johnny Lattner, Notre Dame, 6-1, 190, Chicago, Ill.; B—*Paul Giel, Minnesota, 5-11, 185, Winona, Minn.; B—Paul Cameron, UCLA, 6-0, 185, Burbank, Calif.; B—J. C. Caroline, Illinois, 6-0, 184, Columbia, S.C.

1954

E—Max Boydston, Oklahoma, 6-2, 207, Muskogee, Okla.; E—Ron Beagle, Navy, 6-0, 185, Covington, Ky.; T—Jack Ellena, UCLA, 6-3, 214, Susanville, Calif.; T—Sid Fournet, Louisiana St., 5-11, 225, Baton Rouge, La.; G—*Bud Brooks, Arkansas, 5-11, 200, Wynne, Ark.; G—Calvin Jones, Iowa, 6-0, 200, Steubenville, Ohio; C—Kurt Burris, Oklahoma, 6-1, 209, Muskogee, Okla.; B—*Ralph Guglielmi, Notre Dame, 6-0, 185, Columbus, Ohio; B—*Howard Cassady, Ohio St., 5-10, 177, Columbus, Ohio; B—*Alan Ameche, Wisconsin, 6-0, 215, Kenosha, Wis.; B—Dicky Maegle, Rice, 6-0, 175, Taylor, Texas.

1955

E—*Ron Beagle, Navy, 6-0, 186, Covington, Ky.; E—Ron Kramer, Michigan, 6-3, 218, East Detroit, Mich.; T—Norman Masters, Michigan St., 6-2, 225, Detroit, Mich.; T—Bruce Bosley, West Va., 6-2, 225, Green Bank, W.Va.; T—Bo Bolinger, Oklahoma, 5-10, 206, Muskogee, Okla.; (tie) G—Calvin Jones, Iowa, 6-0, 220, Steubenville, Ohio; G—Hardiman Cureton, UCLA, 6-0, 213, Duarte, Calif.; C—*Bob Pellegrini, Maryland, 6-2, 225, Yatesboro, Pa.; B—*Howard Cassady, Ohio St., 5-10, 172, Columbus, Ohio; B—*Jim Swink, Texas Christian, 6-1, 180, Rusk, Texas; B—Earl Morrall, Michigan St., 6-1, 180, Muskegon, Mich.; B—Paul Hornung, Notre Dame, 6-2, 205, Louisville, Ky.

1956

E—*Joe Walton, Pittsburgh, 5-11, 205, Beaver Falls, Pa.; E—*Ron Kramer, Michigan, 6-3, 220, East Detroit, Mich.; T—John Witte, Oregon St., 6-2, 232, Klamath Falls, Ore.; T—Lou Michaels, Kentucky, 6-2, 229, Swoyersville, Pa.; G—*Jim Parker, Ohio St., 6-2, 251, Toledo, Ohio; G—*Bill Glass, Baylor, 6-4, 220, Corpus Christi, Texas; C—*Jerry Tubbs, Oklahoma, 6-2, 205, Breckenridge, Texas; B—*Jim Brown, Syracuse, 6-2, 212, Manhasset, N.Y.; B—*John Majors, Tennessee, 5-10, 162, Huntland, Tenn.; B—Tommy McDonald, Oklahoma, 5-9, 169, Albuquerque, N.M.; B—John Brodie, Stanford, 6-1, 190, Oakland, Calif.

1957

E—*Jimmy Phillips, Auburn, 6-2, 205, Alexander City, Ala.; E—Dick Wallen, UCLA, 6-0, 185, Alhambra, Calif.; T—Lou Michaels, Kentucky, 6-2, 235, Swoyersville, Pa.; T—Alex Karras, Iowa, 6-2, 233, Gary, Ind.; G—Bill

Krisher, Oklahoma, 6-1, 213, Midwest City, Okla.; G—Al Ecuyer, Notre Dame, 5-10, 190, New Orleans, La.; C—Dan Currie, Michigan St., 6-3, 225, Detroit, Mich.; B—*John David Crow, Texas A&M, 6-2, 214, Springhill, La.; B—Walt Kowalczyk, Michigan St., 6-0, 205, Westfield, Mass.; B—Bob Anderson, Army, 6-2, 200, Cocoa, Fla.; B—Clendon Thomas, Oklahoma, 6-2, 188, Oklahoma City, Okla.

1958

E—Buddy Dial, Rice, 6-1, 185, Magnolia, Texas; E—Sam Williams, Michigan St., 6-5, 225, Dansville, Mich.; T—Ted Bates, Oregon St., 6-2, 215, Los Angeles, Calif.; T—Brock Strom, Air Force, 6-0, 217, Ironwood, Mich.; G—John Guzik, Pittsburgh, 6-3, 223, Lawrence, Pa.; (tie) G—Zeke Smith, Auburn, 6-2, 210, Uniontown, Ala.; G—George Deiderich, Vanderbilt, 6-1, 198, Toronto, Ohio; C—Bob Harrison, Oklahoma, 6-2, 206, Stamford, Texas; B—*Randy Duncan, Iowa, 6-0, 180, Des Moines, Iowa; B—*Pete Dawkins, Army, 6-1, 197, Royal Oak, Mich.; B—*Billy Cannon, Louisiana St., 6-1, 200, Baton Rouge, La.; B—Bob White, Ohio St., 6-2, 212, Covington, Ky.

1959

E—Bill Carpenter, Army, 6-2, 210, Springfield, Pa.; E—Monty Stickles, Notre Dame, 6-4, 225, Poughkeepsie, N.Y.; T—*Dan Lanphear, Wisconsin, 6-2, 214, Madison, Wis.; T—Don Floyd, Texas Christian, 6-3, 215, Midlothian, Texas; G—*Roger Davis, Syracuse, 6-2, 228, Solon, Ohio; G—Bill Burrell, Illinois, 6-0, 210, Chebanse, Ill.; C—Maxie Baughan, Georgia Tech, 6-1, 212, Bessemer, Ala.; B—Richie Lucas, Penn St., 6-1, 185, Glassport, Pa.; B—Billy Cannon, Louisiana St., 6-1, 208, Baton Rouge, La.; B—Charlie Flowers, Mississippi, 6-0, 198, Marianna, Ark.; B—Ron Burton, Northwestern, 5-9, 185, Springfield, Ohio.

1960

E—*Mike Ditka, Pittsburgh, 6-3, 215, Aliquippa, Pa.; E—*Danny LaRose, Missouri, 6-4, 220, Crystal City, Mo.; T—*Bob Lilly, Texas Christian, 6-5, 250, Throckmorton, Texas; T—Ken Rice, Auburn, 6-3, 250, Bainbridge, Ga.; G—*Tom Brown, Minnesota, 6-0, 225, Minneapolis, Minn.; G—Joe Romig, Colorado, 5-10, 197, Lakewood, Colo.; C—E. J. Holub, Texas Tech, 6-4, 215, Lubbock, Texas; B—*Jake Gibbs, Mississippi, 6-0, 185, Grenada, Miss.; B—*Joe Bellino, Navy, 5-9, 181, Winchester, Mass.; B—*Bob Ferguson, Ohio St., 6-0, 217, Troy, Ohio; B—Ernie Davis, Syracuse, 6-2, 205, Elmira, N.Y.

1961

E—Gary Collins, Maryland, 6-3, 205, Williamstown, Pa.; E—Bill Miller, Miami (Fla.), 6-0, 188, McKeesport, Pa.; T—*Billy Neighbors, Alabama, 5-11, 229, Tuscaloosa, Ala.; T—Merlin Olsen, Utah St., 6-5, 265, Logan, Utah; G—*Roy Winston, Louisiana St., 6-1, 225, Baton Rouge, La.; G—Joe Romig, Colorado, 5-10, 199, Lakewood, Colo.; C—Alex Kroll, Rutgers, 6-2, 228, Leechburg, Pa.; B—*Ernie Davis, Syracuse, 6-2, 210, Elmira, N.Y.; B—*Bob Ferguson, Ohio St., 6-0, 217, Troy, Ohio; B—*Jimmy Saxton, Texas, 5-11, 160, Palestine, Texas; B—Sandy Stephens, Minnesota, 6-0, 215, Uniontown, Pa.

1962

E—Hal Bedsole, Southern Cal, 6-5, 225, Northridge, Calif.; E—Pat Richter, Wisconsin, 6-5, 229, Madison, Wis.; T—*Bobby Bell, Minnesota, 6-4, 214, Shelby, N.C.; T—Jim Dunaway, Mississippi, 6-4, 260, Columbia, Miss.; G—*Johnny Treadwell, Texas, 6-1, 194, Austin, Texas; G—Jack Cvercko, Northwestern, 6-0, 230, Campbell, Ohio; C—*Lee Roy Jordan, Alabama, 6-2, 207, Monroeville, Ala.; B—*Terry Baker, Oregon St., 6-3, 191, Portland, Ore.; B—*Jerry Stovall, Louisiana St., 6-2, 195, West Monroe, La.; B—Mel Renfro, Oregon, 5-11, 190, Portland, Ore.; B—George Saimes, Michigan St., 5-10, 186, Canton, Ohio.

1963

E—Vern Burke, Oregon St., 6-4, 195, Bakersfield, Calif.; E—Lawrence Elkins, Baylor, 6-1, 187, Brownwood, Texas; T—*Scott Appleton, Texas, 6-3, 235, Brady, Texas; T—Carl Eller, Minnesota, 6-6, 241, Winston-Salem, N.C.; G—*Bob Brown, Nebraska, 6-5, 259, Cleveland, Ohio; G—Rick Redman, Washington, 5-11, 210, Seattle, Wash.; C—*Dick Butkus, Illinois, 6-3, 234, Chicago, Ill.; B—*Roger Staubach, Navy, 6-2, 190, Cincinnati, Ohio; B—Sherman Lewis, Michigan St., 5-8, 154, Louisville, Ky.; B—Jim Grisham, Oklahoma, 6-2, 205, Olney, Texas; (tie) B—Gale Sayers, Kansas, 6-0, 196, Omaha, Neb.; B—Paul Martha, Pittsburgh, 6-1, 180, Wilkinsburg, Pa.

1964

E—Jack Snow, Notre Dame, 6-2, 210, Long Beach, Calif.; E—Fred Biletnikoff, Florida St., 6-1, 186, Erie, Pa.; T—*Larry Kramer, Nebraska, 6-2, 240, Austin, Minn.; T—Ralph Neely, Oklahoma, 6-5, 243, Farmington, N.M.; G—Rick Redman, Washington, 5-11, 215, Seattle, Wash.; G—Glenn Ressler, Penn St., 6-2, 230, Dornsife, Pa.; C—Dick Butkus, Illinois, 6-3, 237, Chicago, Ill.; B—John Huarte, Notre Dame, 6-0, 180, Anaheim, Calif.; B—Gale Sayers, Kansas, 6-0, 194, Omaha, Neb.; B—Lawrence Elkins, Baylor, 6-1, 187, Brownwood, Texas; B—Tucker Frederickson, Auburn, 6-2, 210, Hollywood, Fla.

Beginning in 1965, offense and defense selected.

1965

Offense E—*Howard Twilley, Tulsa, 5-10, 180, Galena Park, Texas; E—Freeman White, Nebraska, 6-5, 220, Detroit, Mich.; T—Sam Ball, Kentucky, 6-4, 241, Henderson, Ky.; T—Glen Ray Hines, Arkansas, 6-5, 235, El Dorado, Ark.; G—*Dick Arrington, Notre Dame, 5-11, 232, Erie, Pa.; G—Stas Maliszewski, Princeton, 6-1, 215, Davenport, Iowa; C—Paul Crane, Alabama, 6-2, 188, Prichard, Ala.; B—*Mike Garrett, Southern Cal, 5-9, 185, Los Angeles, Calif.; B—*Jim Grabowski, Illinois, 6-2, 211, Chicago, Ill.; B—Bob Griese, Purdue, 6-1, 185, Evansville, Ind.; B—Donny Anderson, Texas Tech, 6-3, 210, Stinnett, Texas.

Defense E—Aaron Brown, Minnesota, 6-4, 230, Port Arthur, Texas; E—Bubba Smith, Michigan St., 6-7, 268, Beaumont, Texas; T—Walt Barnes, Nebraska, 6-3, 235, Chicago, Ill.; T—Loyd Phillips, Arkansas, 6-3, 221, Longview, Texas; T—Bill Yearby, Michigan, 6-3, 222, Detroit, Mich.; LB—Carl McAdams, Oklahoma, 6-3, 215, White Deer, Texas; LB—Tommy Nobis, Texas, 6-2, 230, San Antonio, Texas; LB—Frank Emanuel, Tennessee, 6-3, 228, Newport News, Va.; B—George Webster, Michigan St., 6-4, 204, Anderson, S.C.; B—Johnny Roland, Missouri, 6-2, 198, Corpus Christi, Texas; B—Nick Rassas, Notre Dame, 6-0, 185, Winnetka, Ill.

1966

Offense E—*Jack Clancy, Michigan, 6-1, 192, Detroit, Mich.; E—Ray Perkins, Alabama, 6-0, 184, Petal, Miss.; T—*Cecil Dowdy, Alabama, 6-0, 206, Cherokee, Ala.; T—Ron Yary, Southern Cal, 6-6, 265, Bellflower, Calif.; G—Tom Regner, Notre Dame, 6-1, 245, Kenosha, Wis.; G—LaVerne Allers, Nebraska, 6-0, 209, Davenport, Iowa; C—Jim Breland, Georgia Tech, 6-2, 223, Blacksburg, Va.; B—*Steve Spurrier, Florida, 6-2, 203, Johnson City, Tenn.; B—*Nick Eddy, Notre Dame, 6-0, 195, Lafayette, Calif.; B—Mel Farr, UCLA, 6-2, 208, Beaumont, Texas; B—Clint Jones, Michigan St., 6-0, 206, Cleveland, Ohio.

Defense E—*Bubba Smith, Michigan St., 6-7, 283, Beaumont, Texas; E—Alan Page, Notre Dame, 6-5, 238, Canton, Ohio; T—*Loyd Phillips, Arkansas, 6-3, 230, Longview, Texas; T—Tom Greenlee, Washington, 6-0, 195, Seattle, Wash.; MG—Wayne Meylan, Nebraska, 6-0, 239, Bay City, Mich.; MG—John LaGrone, Southern Methodist, 5-10, 232, Borger, Texas; LB—*Jim Lynch, Notre Dame, 6-1, 225, Lima, Ohio; LB—Paul Naumoff, Tennessee, 6-1, 209, Columbus, Ohio; B—*George Webster, Michigan St., 6-4, 218, Anderson, S.C.; B—Tom Beier, Miami (Fla.), 5-11, 197, Fremont, Ohio; B—Nate Shaw, Southern Cal, 6-2, 205, San Diego, Calif.

1967

Offense E—Dennis Homan, Alabama, 6-0, 182, Muscle Shoals, Ala.; E—Ron Sellers, Florida St., 6-4, 187, Jacksonville, Fla.; T—*Ron Yary, Southern Cal, 6-6, 245, Bellflower, Calif.; T—Ed Chandler, Georgia, 6-2, 222, Cedartown, Ga.; G—Harry Olszewski, Clemson, 5-11, 237, Baltimore, Md.; G—Rich Stotter, Houston, 5-11, 225, Shaker Heights, Ohio; C—*Bob Johnson, Tennessee, 6-4, 232, Cleveland, Tenn.; B—Gary Beban, UCLA, 6-0, 191, Redwood City, Calif.; B—*Leroy Keyes, Purdue, 6-3, 199, Newport News, Va.; B—*O. J. Simpson, Southern Cal, 6-2, 205, San Francisco, Calif.; B—*Larry Csonka, Syracuse, 6-3, 230, Stow, Ohio.

Defense E—*Ted Hendricks, Miami (Fla.), 6-8, 222, Miami Springs, Fla.; E—Tim Rossovich, Southern Cal, 6-5, 235, Mountain View, Calif.; T—Dennis Byrd, North Caro. St., 6-4, 250, Lincolnton, N.C.; MG—*Granville Liggins, Oklahoma, 5-11, 216, Tulsa, Okla.; MG—Wayne Meylan, Nebraska, 6-0, 231, Bay City, Mich.; LB—Adrian Young, Southern Cal, 6-1, 210, La Puente, Calif.; LB—Don Manning, UCLA, 6-2, 204, Culver City, Calif.; B—Tom Schoen, Notre Dame, 5-11, 178, Euclid, Ohio; B—Frank Loria, Virginia Tech, 5-9, 174, Clarksburg, W. Va.; B—Bobby Johns, Alabama, 6-1, 180, Birmingham, Ala.; B—Dick Anderson, Colorado, 6-2, 204, Boulder, Colo.

1968

Offense E—*Ted Kwalick, Penn St., 6-4, 230, McKees Rocks, Pa.; E—Jerry LeVias, Southern Methodist, 5-10, 170, Beaumont, Texas; T—*Dave Foley, Ohio St., 6-5, 246, Cincinnati, Ohio; T—George Kunz, Notre Dame, 6-5, 240, Arcadia, Calif.; G—*Charles Rosenfelder, Tennessee, 6-1, 220, Humboldt, Tenn.; (tie) G—Jim Barnes, Arkansas, 6-4, 227, Pine Bluff, Ark.; G—Mike Montler, Colorado, 6-4, 235, Columbus, Ohio; C—*John Didion, Oregon St., 6-4, 242, Woodland, Calif.; B—*O. J. Simpson, Southern Cal, 6-2, 205, San Francisco, Calif.; B—*Leroy Keyes, Purdue, 6-3, 205, Newport News, Va.; B—Terry Hanratty, Notre Dame, 6-1, 200, Butler, Pa.; B—Chris Gilbert, Texas, 5-11, 176, Spring, Texas.

Defense E—*Ted Hendricks, Miami (Fla.), 6-8, 222, Miami Springs, Fla.; E—John Zook, Kansas, 6-4, 230, Larned, Kan.; T—Bill Stanfill, Georgia, 6-5, 245, Cairo, Ga.; T—Joe Greene, North Texas, 6-4, 274, Temple, Texas; MG—Ed White, California, 6-3, 245, Palm Desert, Calif.; MG—Chuck Kyle, Purdue, 6-1, 225, Fort Thomas, Ky.; LB—Steve Kiner, Tennessee, 6-1, 205, Tampa, Fla.; LB—Dennis Onkotz, Penn St., 6-2, 205, Northampton, Pa.; B—Jake Scott, Georgia, 6-1, 188, Arlington, Va.; B—Roger Wehrli, Missouri, 6-0, 184, King City, Mo.; B—Al Worley, Washington, 6-0, 175, Wenatchee, Wash.

1969

Offense E—Jim Mandich, Michigan, 6-3, 222, Solon, Ohio; (tie) E—Walker Gillette, Richmond, 6-5, 200, Capron, Va.; E—Carlos Alvarez, Florida, 5-11, 180, Miami, Fla.; T—Bob McKay, Texas, 6-6, 245, Crane, Texas; T—John Ward, Oklahoma St., 6-5, 248, Tulsa, Okla.; G—Chip Kell, Tennessee, 6-0, 255, Decatur, Ga.; G—Bill Bridges, Houston, 6-2, 230, Carrollton, Texas; C—Rodney Brand, Arkansas, 6-2, 218, Newport, Ark.; B—*Mike Phipps, Purdue, 6-3, 206, Columbus, Ind.; B—*Steve Owens, Oklahoma, 6-2, 215, Miami, Okla.; B—Jim Otis, Ohio St., 6-0, 214, Celina, Ohio; B—Bob Anderson, Colorado, 6-0, 208, Boulder, Colo.

Defense E—Jim Gunn, Southern Cal, 6-1, 210, San Diego, Calif.; E—Phil Olsen, Utah St., 6-5, 255, Logan, Utah; T—*Mike Reid, Penn St., 6-3, 240, Altoona, Pa.; T—*Mike McCoy, Notre Dame, 6-5, 274, Erie, Pa.; MG—Jim Stillwagon, Ohio St., 6-0, 216, Mount Vernon, Ohio; LB—*Steve Kiner, Tennessee, 6-1, 215, Tampa, Fla.; LB—Dennis Onkotz, Penn St., 6-2, 212, Northampton, Pa.; LB—Mike Ballou, UCLA, 6-3, 230, Los Angeles, Calif.; B—Jack Tatum, Ohio St., 6-0, 204, Passaic, N.J.; B—Buddy McClinton, Auburn, 5-11, 190, Montgomery, Ala.; B—Tom Curtis, Michigan, 6-1, 190, Aurora, Ohio.

1970

Offense E—Tom Gatewood, Notre Dame, 6-2, 208, Baltimore, Md.; E—Ernie Jennings, Air Force, 6-0, 172, Kansas City, Mo.; E—Elmo Wright, Houston, 6-0, 195, Brazoria, Texas; T—Dan Dierdorf, Michigan, 6-4, 250, Canton, Ohio; (tie) T—Bobby Wuensch, Texas, 6-3, 230, Houston, Texas; T—Bob Newton, Nebraska, 6-4, 248, LaMirada, Calif.; G—*Chip Kell, Tennessee, 6-0, 240, Decatur, Ga.; G—Larry DiNardo, Notre Dame, 6-1, 235, New York, N.Y.; C—Don Popplewell, Colorado, 6-2, 240, Raytown, Mo.; QB—Jim Plunkett, Stanford, 6-3, 204, San Jose, Calif.; RB—Steve Worster, Texas, 6-0, 210, Bridge City, Texas; RB—Don McCauley, North Caro., 6-0, 211, Garden City, N.Y.

Defense E—Bill Atessis, Texas, 6-3, 255, Houston, Texas; E—Charlie Weaver, Southern Cal, 6-2, 214, Richmond, Calif.; T—Rock Perdoni, Georgia Tech, 5-11, 236, Wellesley, Mass.; T—Dick Bumpas, Arkansas, 6-1, 225, Fort Smith, Ark.; MG—*Jim Stillwagon, Ohio St., 6-0, 220, Mount Vernon, Ohio; LB—Jack Ham, Penn St., 6-3, 212, Johnstown, Pa.; LB—Mike Anderson, Louisiana St., 6-3, 225, Baton Rouge, La.; B—*Jack Tatum, Ohio St., 6-0, 208, Passaic, N.J.; B—Larry Willingham, Auburn, 6-1, 185, Birmingham, Ala.; B—Dave

Elmendorf, Texas A&M, 6-1, 190, Houston, Texas; B—Tommy Casanova, Louisiana St., 6-1, 191, Crowley, La.

1971

Offense E—*Terry Beasley, Auburn, 5-11, 184, Montgomery, Ala.; E—Johnny Rodgers, Nebraska, 5-10, 171, Omaha, Neb.; T—*Jerry Sisemore, Texas, 6-4, 255, Plainview, Texas; T—Dave Joyner, Penn St., 6-0, 235, State College, Pa.; G—*Royce Smith, Georgia, 6-3, 240, Savannah, Ga.; G—Reggie McKenzie, Michigan, 6-4, 232, Highland Park, Mich.; C—Tom Brahaney, Oklahoma, 6-2, 231, Midland, Texas; QB—*Pat Sullivan, Auburn, 6-0, 191, Birmingham, Ala.; RB—*Ed Marinaro, Cornell, 6-3, 210, New Milford, N.J.; RB—*Greg Pruitt, Oklahoma, 5-9, 176, Houston, Texas; RB—Johnny Musso, Alabama, 5-11, 194, Birmingham, Ala.

Defense E—*Walt Patulski, Notre Dame, 6-5, 235, Liverpool, N.Y.; E—Willie Harper, Nebraska, 6-3, 207, Toledo, Ohio; T—Larry Jacobson, Nebraska, 6-6, 250, Sioux Falls, S.D.; T—Mel Long, Toledo, 6-1, 230, Toledo, Ohio; T—Sherman White, California, 6-5, 250, Portsmouth, N.H.; LB—*Mike Taylor, Michigan, 6-2, 224, Detroit, Mich.; LB—Jeff Siemon, Stanford, 6-2, 225, Bakersfield, Calif.; B—*Bobby Majors, Tennessee, 6-1, 197, Sewanee, Tenn.; B—Clarence Ellis, Notre Dame, 6-0, 178, Grand Rapids, Mich.; B—Ernie Jackson, Duke, 5-10, 170, Hopkins, S.C.; B—Tommy Casanova, Louisiana St., 6-2, 195, Crowley, La.

1972

Offense WR—*Johnny Rodgers, Nebraska, 5-9, 173, Omaha, Neb.; TE—*Charles Young, Southern Cal, 6-4, 228, Fresno, Calif.; T—*Jerry Sisemore, Texas, 6-4, 260, Plainview, Texas; T—Paul Seymour, Michigan, 6-5, 250, Berkley, Mich.; G—*John Hannah, Alabama, 6-3, 282, Albertville, Ala.; G—Ron Rusnak, North Caro., 6-1, 223, Prince George, Va.; C—Tom Brahaney, Oklahoma, 6-2, 227, Midland, Texas; QB—Bert Jones, Louisiana St., 6-3, 205, Ruston, La.; RB—*Greg Pruitt, Oklahoma, 5-9, 177, Houston, Texas; RB—Otis Armstrong, Purdue, 5-11, 197, Chicago, Ill.; RB—Woody Green, Arizona St., 6-1, 190, Portland, Ore.

Defense E—Willie Harper, Nebraska, 6-2, 207, Toledo, Ohio; E—Bruce Bannon, Penn St., 6-3, 224, Rockaway, N.J.; T—*Greg Marx, Notre Dame, 6-5, 265, Redford, Mich.; T—Dave Butz, Purdue, 6-7, 279, Park Ridge, Ill.; MG—*Rich Glover, Nebraska, 6-1, 234, Jersey City, N.J.; LB—Randy Gradishar, Ohio St., 6-3, 232, Champion, Ohio; LB—John Skorupan, Penn St., 6-2, 208, Beaver, Pa.; B—*Brad VanPelt, Michigan St., 6-5, 221, Owosso, Mich.; B—Cullen Bryant, Colorado, 6-2, 215, Colorado Springs, Colo.; B—Robert Popelka, Southern Methodist, 6-1, 190, Temple, Texas; B—Randy Logan, Michigan, 6-2, 192, Detroit, Mich.

1973

Offense WR—Lynn Swann, Southern Cal, 6-0, 180, Foster City, Calif.; TE—Dave Casper, Notre Dame, 6-3, 252, Chilton, Wis.; T—*John Hicks, Ohio St., 6-3, 258, Cleveland, Ohio; T—Booker Brown, Southern Cal, 6-3, 270, Santa Barbara, Calif.; G—Buddy Brown, Alabama, 6-2, 242, Tallahassee, Fla.; G—Bill Yoest, North Caro. St., 6-0, 235, Pittsburgh, Pa.; C—Bill Wyman, Texas, 6-2, 235, Spring, Texas; QB—Dave Jaynes, Kansas, 6-2, 212, Bonner Springs, Kan.; RB—*John Cappelletti, Penn St., 6-1, 206, Upper Darby, Pa.; RB—Roosevelt Leaks, Texas, 5-11, 209, Brenham, Texas; RB—Woody Green, Arizona St., 6-1, 202, Portland, Ore.; RB—Kermit Johnson, UCLA, 6-0, 185, Los Angeles, Calif.

Defense L—*John Dutton, Nebraska, 6-7, 248, Rapid City, S.D.; L—Dave Gallagher, Michigan, 6-4, 245, Piqua, Ohio; L—*Lucious Selmon, Oklahoma, 5-11, 236, Eufaula, Okla.; L—Tony Cristiani, Miami (Fla.), 5-10, 215, Brandon, Fla.; LB—*Randy Gradishar, Ohio St., 6-3, 236, Champion, Ohio; LB—Rod Shoate, Oklahoma, 6-1, 214, Spiro, Okla.; LB—Richard Wood, Southern Cal, 6-2, 217, Elizabeth, N.J.; B—Mike Townsend, Notre Dame, 6-3, 183, Hamilton, Ohio; B—Artimus Parker, Southern Cal, 6-3, 215, Sacramento, Calif.; B—Dave Brown, Michigan, 6-1, 188, Akron, Ohio; B—Randy Rhino, Georgia Tech, 5-10, 179, Charlotte, N.C.

1974

Offense WR—Pete Demmerle, Notre Dame, 6-1, 190, New Canaan, Conn.; TE—Bennie Cunningham, Clemson, 6-5, 252, Seneca, S.C.; T—Kurt Schumacher, Ohio St., 6-4, 250, Lorain, Ohio; T—Marvin Crenshaw, Nebraska, 6-6, 240, Toledo, Ohio; G—Ken Huff, North Caro., 6-4, 261, Coronado, Calif.; G—John Roush, Oklahoma, 6-0, 252, Arvada, Colo.; G—Gerry DiNardo, Notre Dame, 6-1, 237, New York, N.Y.; C—Steve Myers, Ohio St., 6-2, 244, Kent, Ohio; QB—Steve Bartkowski, California, 6-4, 215, Santa Clara, Calif.; RB—*Archie Griffin, Ohio St., 5-9, 184, Columbus, Ohio; RB—*Joe Washington, Oklahoma, 5-10, 178, Port Arthur, Texas; RB—*Anthony Davis, Southern Cal, 5-9, 183, San Fernando, Calif.

Defense L—*Randy White, Maryland, 6-4, 238, Wilmington, Del.; L—Mike Hartenstine, Penn St., 6-4, 233, Bethlehem, Pa.; L—Pat Donovan, Stanford, 6-5, 240, Helena, Mont.; L—Jimmy Webb, Mississippi St., 6-5, 245, Florence, Miss.; L—Leroy Cook, Alabama, 6-4, 205, Abbeville, Ala.; MG—Louie Kelcher, Southern Methodist, 6-5, 275, Beaumont, Texas; MG—Rubin Carter, Miami (Fla.), 6-3, 260, Ft. Lauderdale, Fla.; LB—*Rod Shoate, Oklahoma, 6-1, 213, Spiro, Okla.; LB—Richard Wood, Southern Cal, 6-2, 213, Elizabeth, N.J.; LB—Ken Bernich, Auburn, 6-2, 240, Gretna, La.; LB—Woodrow Lowe, Alabama, 6-0, 211, Phenix City, Ala.; B—*Dave Brown, Michigan, 6-1, 188, Akron, Ohio; B—Pat Thomas, Texas A&M, 5-9, 180, Plano, Texas; B—John Provost, Holy Cross, 5-10, 180, Quincy, Mass.

1975

Offense E—Steve Rivera, California, 6-0, 185, Wilmington, Calif.; E—Larry Seivers, Tennessee, 6-4, 198, Clinton, Tenn.; T—Bob Simmons, Texas, 6-5, 245, Temple, Texas; T—Dennis Lick, Wisconsin, 6-3, 262, Chicago, Ill.; G—Randy Johnson, Georgia, 6-2, 250, Rome, Ga.; G—Ted Smith, Ohio St., 6-1, 242, Gibsonburg, Ohio; C—*Rik Bonness, Nebraska, 6-4, 223, Bellevue, Neb.; QB—John Sciarra, UCLA, 5-10, 178, Alhambra, Calif.; RB—*Archie Griffin, Ohio St., 5-9, 182, Columbus, Ohio; RB—*Ricky Bell, Southern Cal, 6-2, 215, Los Angeles, Calif.; RB—Chuck Muncie, California, 6-3, 220, Uniontown, Pa.

Defense E—*Leroy Cook, Alabama, 6-4, 205, Abbeville, Ala.; E—Jimbo Elrod, Oklahoma, 6-0, 210, Tulsa, Okla.; T—*Lee Roy Selmon, Oklahoma, 6-2, 256, Eufaula, Okla.; T—*Steve Niehaus, Notre Dame, 6-5, 260, Cincinnati, Ohio; MG—Dewey Selmon, Oklahoma, 6-1, 257, Eufaula, Okla.; LB—*Ed Simonini, Texas A&M, 6-0, 215, Las Vegas, Nev.; LB—Greg Buttle, Penn St., 6-3, 220, Linwood, N.J.; LB—Sammy Green, Florida, 6-2, 228, Ft. Meade, Fla.; B—*Chet Moeller, Navy, 6-0, 189, Kettering, Ohio; B—Tim Fox, Ohio St., 6-0, 186, Canton, Ohio; B—Pat Thomas, Texas A&M, 5-10, 180, Plano, Texas.

1976

Offense TE—Ken MacAfee, Notre Dame, 6-4, 251, Brockton, Mass.; SE—Larry Seivers, Tennessee, 6-4, 200, Clinton, Tenn.; T—Mike Vaughan, Oklahoma, 6-5, 275, Ada, Okla.; T—Chris Ward, Ohio St., 6-4, 274, Dayton, Ohio; G—Joel Parrish, Georgia, 6-3, 232, Douglas, Ga.; G—Mark Donahue, Michigan, 6-3, 245, Oak Lawn, Ill.; C—Derrel Gofourth, Oklahoma St., 6-2, 250, Parsons, Kan.; QB—Tommy Kramer, Rice, 6-2, 190, San Antonio, Texas; RB—*Tony Dorsett, Pittsburgh, 5-11, 192, Aliquippa, Pa.; RB—*Ricky Bell, Southern Cal, 6-2, 218, Los Angeles, Calif.; RB—Rob Lytle, Michigan, 6-1, 195, Fremont, Ohio; PK—Tony Franklin, Texas A&M, 5-10, 170, Fort Worth, Texas.

Defense E—*Ross Browner, Notre Dame, 6-3, 248, Warren, Ohio; E—Bob Brudzinski, Ohio St., 6-4, 228, Fremont, Ohio; T—Wilson Whitley, Houston, 6-3, 268, Brenham, Texas; T—Gary Jeter, Southern Cal, 6-5, 255, Cleveland, Ohio; T—Joe Campbell, Maryland, 6-6, 255, Wilmington, Del.; MG—Al Romano, Pittsburgh, 6-3, 230, Solvay, N.Y.; LB—*Robert Jackson, Texas A&M, 6-2, 228, Houston, Texas; LB—Jerry Robinson, UCLA, 6-3, 208, Santa Rosa, Calif.; B—*Bill Armstrong, Wake Forest, 6-4, 205, Randolph, N.J.; B—Gary Green, Baylor, 5-11, 182, San Antonio, Texas; B—Dennis Thurman, Southern Cal, 5-11, 170, Santa Monica, Calif.; B—Dave Butterfield, Nebraska, 5-10, 182, Kersey, Colo.

1977

Offense TE—*Ken MacAfee, Notre Dame, 6-4, 250, Brockton, Mass.; WR—John Jefferson, Arizona St., 6-1, 184, Dallas, Texas; WR—Ozzie Newsome, Alabama, 6-4, 210, Leighton, Ala.; T—*Chris Ward, Ohio St., 6-4, 272, Dayton, Ohio; T—Dan Irons, Texas Tech, 6-7, 260, Lubbock, Texas; G—*Mark Donahue, Michigan, 6-3, 245, Oak Lawn, Ill.; G—Leotis Harris, Arkansas, 6-1, 254, Little Rock, Ark.; C—Tom Brzoza, Pittsburgh, 6-3, 240, New Castle, Pa.; QB—Guy Benjamin, Stanford, 6-4, 202, Sepulveda, Calif.; RB—*Earl Campbell, Texas, 6-1, 220, Tyler, Texas; RB—*Terry Miller, Oklahoma St., 6-0, 196, Colorado Springs, Colo.; RB—Charles Alexander, Louisiana St., 6-1, 215, Galveston, Texas; K—Steve Little, Arkansas, 6-0, 179, Overland Park, Kan.

Defense L—*Ross Browner, Notre Dame, 6-3, 247, Warren, Ohio; L—*Art Still, Kentucky, 6-8, 247, Camden, N.J.; L—*Brad Shearer, Texas, 6-4, 255, Austin, Texas; L—Randy Holloway, Pittsburgh, 6-6, 228, Sharon, Pa.; L—Dee Hardison, North Caro., 6-4, 252, Newton Grove, N.C.; LB—*Jerry Robinson, UCLA, 6-3, 208, Santa Rosa, Calif.; LB—Tom Cousineau, Ohio St., 6-3, 228, Fairview Park, Ohio; LB—Gary Spani, Kansas St., 6-2, 222, Manhattan, Kan.; B—*Dennis Thurman, Southern Cal, 5-11, 173, Santa Monica, Calif.; B—*Zac Henderson, Oklahoma, 6-1, 184, Burkburnett, Texas; B—Luther Bradley, Notre Dame, 6-2, 204, Muncie, Ind.; B—Bob Jury, Pittsburgh, 6-0, 190, Library, Pa.

1978

Offense TE—Kellen Winslow, Missouri, 6-6, 235, East St. Louis, Ill.; WR—Emanuel Tolbert, Southern Methodist, 5-10, 180, Little Rock, Ark.; T—*Keith Dorney, Penn St., 6-5, 257, Allentown, Pa.; T—Kelvin Clark, Nebraska, 6-4, 275, Odessa, Texas; G—*Pat Howell, Southern Cal, 6-6, 255, Fresno, Calif.; G—*Greg Roberts, Oklahoma, 6-3, 238, Nacogdoches, Texas; C—Dave Huffman, Notre Dame, 6-5, 245, Dallas, Texas; C—Jim Ritcher, North Caro. St., 6-3, 242, Hinckley, Ohio; QB—*Chuck Fusina, Penn St., 6-1, 195, McKees Rocks, Pa.; RB—*Billy Sims, Oklahoma, 6-0, 205, Hooks, Texas; RB—*Charles White, Southern Cal, 5-11, 183, San Fernando, Calif.; RB—Ted Brown, North Caro. St., 5-10, 195, High Point, N.C.; RB—Charles Alexander, Louisiana St., 6-1, 214, Galveston, Texas.

Defense L—*Al Harris, Arizona St., 6-5, 240, Wheeler AFB, Hawaii; L—*Bruce Clark, Penn St., 6-3, 246, New Castle, Pa.; L—Hugh Green, Pittsburgh, 6-2, 215, Natchez, Miss.; L—Mike Bell, Colorado St., 6-5, 265, Wichita, Kan.; L—Marty Lyons, Alabama, 6-6, 250, St. Petersburg, Fla.; LB—*Bob Golic, Notre Dame, 6-3, 244, Willowick, Ohio; LB—*Jerry Robinson, UCLA, 6-3, 209, Santa Rosa, Calif.; LB—Tom Cousineau, Ohio St., 6-3, 227, Fairview Park, Ohio; B—*Johnnie Johnson, Texas, 6-2, 183, LaGrange, Texas; B—Kenny Easley, UCLA, 6-2, 202, Chesapeake, Va.; B—Jeff Nixon, Richmond, 6-4, 195, Glendale, Ariz.

1979

Offense TE—*Junior Miller, Nebraska, 6-4, 222, Midland, Texas; WR—Ken Margerum, Stanford, 6-1, 175, Fountain Valley, Calif.; T—*Greg Kolenda, Arkansas, 6-1, 258, Kansas City, Kan.; T—Jim Bunch, Alabama, 6-2, 240, Mechanicsville, Va.; G—*Brad Budde, Southern Cal, 6-5, 253, Kansas City, Mo.; G—Ken Fritz, Ohio St., 6-3, 238, Ironton, Ohio; C—*Jim Ritcher, North Caro. St., 6-3, 245, Hinckley, Ohio; QB—*Marc Wilson, Brigham Young, 6-5, 204, Seattle, Wash.; RB—*Charles White, Southern Cal, 6-0, 185, San Fernando, Calif.; RB—*Billy Sims, Oklahoma, 6-0, 205, Hooks, Texas; RB—Vagas Ferguson, Notre Dame, 6-1, 194, Richmond, Ind.; PK—Dale Castro, Maryland, 6-1, 170, Shady Side, Md.

Defense L—*Hugh Green, Pittsburgh, 6-2, 220, Natchez, Miss.; L—*Steve McMichael, Texas, 6-2, 250, Freer, Texas; L—Bruce Clark, Penn St., 6-3, 255, New Castle, Pa.; L—Jim Stuckey, Clemson, 6-5, 241, Cayce, S.C.; MG—Ron Simmons, Florida St., 6-1, 235, Warner Robins, Ga.; LB—*George Cumby, Oklahoma, 6-0, 205, Tyler, Texas; LB—Ron Simpkins, Michigan, 6-2, 220, Detroit, Mich.; LB—Mike Singletary, Baylor, 6-1, 224, Houston, Texas; B—*Kenny Easley, UCLA, 6-3, 204, Chesapeake, Va.; B—*Johnnie Johnson, Texas, 6-2, 190, LaGrange, Texas; B—Roland James, Tennessee, 6-2, 182, Jamestown, Ohio; P—Jim Miller, Mississippi, 5-11, 183, Ripley, Miss.

1980

Offense WR—*Ken Margerum, Stanford, 6-1, 175, Fountain Valley, Calif.; TE—*Dave Young, Purdue, 6-6, 242, Akron, Ohio; L—*Mark May, Pittsburgh, 6-6, 282, Oneonta, N.Y.; L—Keith Van Horne, Southern Cal, 6-7, 265, Fullerton, Calif.; L—Nick Eyre, Brigham Young, 6-5, 276, Las Vegas, Nev.; L—Louis Oubre, Oklahoma, 6-4, 262, New Orleans, La.; L—Randy Schleusener,

Nebraska, 6-7, 242, Rapid City, S.D.; C—*John Scully, Notre Dame, 6-5, 255, Huntington, N.Y.; QB—*Mark Herrmann, Purdue, 6-4, 187, Carmel, Ind.; RB—*George Rogers, South Caro., 6-2, 220, Duluth, Ga.; RB—*Herschel Walker, Georgia, 6-2, 220, Wrightsville, Ga.; RB—Jarvis Redwine, Nebraska, 5-11, 204, Inglewood, Calif.

Defense L—*Hugh Green, Pittsburgh, 6-2, 222, Natchez, Miss.; L—*E. J. Junior, Alabama, 6-3, 227, Nashville, Tenn.; L—Kenneth Sims, Texas, 6-6, 265, Groesbeck, Texas; L—Leonard Mitchell, Houston, 6-7, 270, Houston, Texas; MG—Ron Simmons, Florida St., 6-1, 230, Warner Robins, Ga.; LB—*Mike Singletary, Baylor, 6-1, 232, Houston, Texas; LB—*Lawrence Taylor, North Caro., 6-3, 237, Williamsburg, Va.; LB—David Little, Florida, 6-1, 228, Miami, Fla.; LB—Bob Crable, Notre Dame, 6-3, 222, Cincinnati, Ohio; B—*Kenny Easley, UCLA, 6-3, 206, Chesapeake, Va.; B—*Ronnie Lott, Southern Cal, 6-2, 200, Rialto, Calif.; B—John Simmons, Southern Methodist, 5-11, 188, Little Rock, Ark.

1981

Offense WR—*Anthony Carter, Michigan, 5-11, 161, Riviera Beach, Fla.; TE—*Tim Wrightman, UCLA, 6-3, 237, San Pedro, Calif.; L—*Sean Farrell, Penn St., 6-3, 266, Westhampton Beach, N.Y.; L—Roy Foster, Southern Cal, 6-4, 265, Overland Park, Kan.; L—Terry Crouch, Oklahoma, 6-1, 275, Dallas, Texas; L—Ed Muransky, Michigan, 6-7, 275, Youngstown, Ohio; L—Terry Tausch, Texas, 6-4, 265, New Braunfels, Texas; L—Kurt Becker, Michigan, 6-6, 260, Aurora, Ill.; C—*Dave Rimington, Nebraska, 6-3, 275, Omaha, Neb.; QB—*Jim McMahon, Brigham Young, 6-0, 185, Roy, Utah; RB—*Marcus Allen, Southern Cal, 6-2, 202, San Diego, Calif.; RB—*Herschel Walker, Georgia, 6-2, 222, Wrightsville, Ga.

Defense L—*Billy Ray Smith, Arkansas, 6-4, 228, Plano, Texas; L—*Kenneth Sims, Texas, 6-6, 265, Groesbeck, Texas; L—Andre Tippett, Iowa, 6-4, 235, Newark, N.J.; L—Tim Krumrie, Wisconsin, 6-3, 237, Mondovi, Wis.; LB—Bob Crable, Notre Dame, 6-3, 225, Cincinnati, Ohio; LB—Jeff Davis, Clemson, 6-0, 223, Greensboro, N.C.; LB—Sal Sunseri, Pittsburgh, 6-0, 220, Pittsburgh, Pa.; DB—Tommy Wilcox, Alabama, 5-11, 187, Harahan, La.; DB—Mike Richardson, Arizona St., 6-1, 192, Compton, Calif.; DB—Terry Kinard, Clemson, 6-1, 183, Sumter, S.C.; DB—Fred Marion, Miami (Fla.), 6-3, 194, Gainesville, Fla.; P—Reggie Roby, Iowa, 6-3, 215, Waterloo, Iowa.

1982

Offense WR—*Anthony Carter, Michigan, 5-11, 161, Riviera Beach, Fla.; TE—*Gordon Hudson, Brigham Young, 6-4, 224, Salt Lake City, Utah; L—*Don Mosebar, Southern Cal, 6-7, 270, Visalia, Calif.; L—*Steve Korte, Arkansas, 6-2, 270, Littleton, Colo.; L—Jimbo Covert, Pittsburgh, 6-5, 279, Conway, Pa.; L—Bruce Matthews, Southern Cal, 6-5, 265, Arcadia, Calif.; C—*Dave Rimington, Nebraska, 6-3, 290, Omaha, Neb.; QB—*John Elway, Stanford, 6-4, 202, Northridge, Calif.; RB—*Herschel Walker, Georgia, 6-2, 222, Wrightsville, Ga.; RB—*Eric Dickerson, Southern Methodist, 6-2, 215, Sealy, Texas; RB—Mike Rozier, Nebraska, 5-11, 210, Camden, N.J.; PK—*Chuck Nelson, Washington, 5-11, 178, Everett, Wash.

Defense L—*Billy Ray Smith, Arkansas, 6-3, 228, Plano, Texas; L—Vernon Maxwell, Arizona St., 6-2, 225, Carson, Calif.; L—Mike Pitts, Alabama, 6-5, 255, Baltimore, Md.; L—Wilber Marshall, Florida, 6-1, 230, Titusville, Fla.; L—Gabriel Rivera, Texas Tech, 6-3, 270, San Antonio, Texas; L—Rick Bryan, Oklahoma, 6-4, 260, Coweta, Okla.; MG—George Achica, Southern Cal, 6-5, 260, San Jose, Calif.; LB—*Darryl Talley, West Va., 6-4, 210, East Cleveland, Ohio; LB—Ricky Hunley, Arizona, 6-1, 230, Petersburg, Va.; LB—Marcus Marek, Ohio St., 6-2, 224, Masury, Ohio; DB—*Terry Kinard, Clemson, 6-1, 189, Sumter, S.C.; DB—Mike Richardson, Arizona St., 6-0, 190, Compton, Calif.; DB—Terry Hoage, Georgia, 6-3, 196, Huntsville, Texas; P—*Jim Arnold, Vanderbilt, 6-3, 205, Dalton, Ga.

1983

Offense WR—*Irving Fryar, Nebraska, 6-0, 200, Mount Holly, N.J.; TE—*Gordon Hudson, Brigham Young, 6-4, 231, Salt Lake City, Utah; L—*Bill Fralic, Pittsburgh, 6-5, 270, Penn Hills, Pa.; L—Terry Long, East Caro., 6-0, 280, Columbia, S.C.; L—Dean Steinkuhler, Nebraska, 6-3, 270, Burr, Neb.; L—Doug Dawson, Texas, 6-3, 263, Houston, Texas; C—Tony Slaton, Southern Cal, 6-4, 260, Merced, Calif.; QB—*Steve Young, Brigham Young, 6-1, 198, Greenwich, Conn.; RB—*Mike Rozier, Nebraska, 5-11, 210, Camden, N.J.; RB—Bo Jackson, Auburn, 6-1, 222, Bessemer, Ala.; RB—Greg Allen, Florida St., 6-0, 200, Milton, Fla.; RB—Napoleon McCallum, Navy, 6-2, 208, Milford, Ohio; PK—Luis Zendejas, Arizona St., 5-9, 186, Chino, Calif.

Defense L—*Rick Bryan, Oklahoma, 6-4, 260, Coweta, Okla.; L—*Reggie White, Tennessee, 6-5, 264, Chattanooga, Tenn.; L—William Perry, Clemson, 6-3, 320, Aiken, S.C.; L—William Fuller, North Caro., 6-4, 250, Chesapeake, Va.; LB—*Ricky Hunley, Arizona, 6-2, 230, Petersburg, Va.; LB—Wilber Marshall, Florida, 6-1, 230, Titusville, Fla.; LB—Ron Rivera, California, 6-3, 225, Monterey, Calif.; LB—Jeff Leiding, Texas, 6-4, 240, Tulsa, Okla.; DB—*Russell Carter, Southern Methodist, 6-3, 193, Ardmore, Pa.; DB—Jerry Gray, Texas, 6-1, 183, Lubbock, Texas; DB—Terry Hoage, Georgia, 6-3, 196, Huntsville, Texas; DB—Don Rogers, UCLA, 6-2, 208, Sacramento, Calif.; P—Jack Weil, Wyoming, 5-11, 171, Northglenn, Colo.

1984

Offense WR—*David Williams, Illinois, 6-3, 195, Los Angeles, Calif.; WR—Eddie Brown, Miami (Fla.), 6-0, 185, Miami, Fla.; TE—Jay Novacek, Wyoming, 6-4, 211, Gothenburg, Neb.; T—*Bill Fralic, Pittsburgh, 6-5, 285, Penn Hills, Pa.; T—Lomas Brown, Florida, 6-5, 277, Miami, Fla.; G—Del Wilkes, South Caro., 6-3, 255, Columbia, S.C.; G—Jim Lachey, Ohio St., 6-6, 274, St. Henry, Ohio; G—Bill Mayo, Tennessee, 6-3, 280, Dalton, Ga.; C—*Mark Traynowicz, Nebraska, 6-6, 265, Bellevue, Neb.; QB—*Doug Flutie, Boston College, 5-9, 177, Natick, Mass.; RB—*Keith Byars, Ohio St., 6-2, 233, Dayton, Ohio; RB—*Kenneth Davis, Texas Christian, 5-11, 205, Temple, Texas; RB—Rueben Mayes, Washington St., 6-0, 200, North Battleford, Saskatchewan, Canada; PK—Kevin Butler, Georgia, 6-1, 190, Stone Mountain, Ga.

Defense DL—Bruce Smith, Virginia Tech, 6-4, 275, Norfolk, Va.; DL—Tony Degrate, Texas, 6-4, 280, Snyder, Texas; DL—Ron Holmes, Washington, 6-4, 255, Lacey, Wash.; DL—Tony Casillas, Oklahoma, 6-3, 272, Tulsa, Okla.; LB—Gregg Carr, Auburn, 6-2, 215, Birmingham, Ala.; LB—Jack Del Rio, Southern Cal, 6-4, 235, Hayward, Calif.; LB—Larry Station, Iowa, 5-11, 233, Omaha, Neb.; DB—*Jerry Gray, Texas, 6-1, 183, Lubbock, Texas; DB—Tony Thurman, Boston College, 6-0, 179, Lynn, Mass.; DB—Jeff Sanchez, Georgia, 6-0, 183, Yorba Linda, Calif.; DB—David Fulcher, Arizona St., 6-3, 220, Los Angeles, Calif.; DB—Rod Brown, Oklahoma St., 6-3, 188, Gainesville, Texas; P—*Ricky Anderson, Vanderbilt, 6-2, 190, St. Petersburg, Fla.

1985

Offense WR—*David Williams, Illinois, 6-3, 195, Los Angeles, Calif.; WR—Tim McGee, Tennessee, 5-10, 181, Cleveland, Ohio; TE—Willie Smith, Miami (Fla.), 6-2, 230, Jacksonville, Fla.; L—*Jim Dombrowski, Virginia, 6-5, 290, Williamsville, N.Y.; L—Jeff Bregel, Southern Cal, 6-4, 280, Granada Hills, Calif.; L—Brian Jozwiak, West Va., 6-6, 290, Catonsville, Md.; L—John Rienstra, Temple, 6-4, 280, Colorado Springs, Colo.; L—J. D. Maarleveld, Maryland, 6-5, 300, Rutherford, N.J.; L—Jamie Dukes, Florida St., 6-0, 272, Orlando, Fla.; C—Pete Anderson, Georgia, 6-3, 264, Glen Ridge, N.J.; QB—*Chuck Long, Iowa, 6-4, 213, Wheaton, Ill.; RB—*Bo Jackson, Auburn, 6-1, 222, Bessemer, Ala.; RB—*Lorenzo White, Michigan St., 5-11, 205, Fort Lauderdale, Fla.; RB—Thurman Thomas, Oklahoma St., 5-11, 186, Missouri City, Texas; RB—Reggie Dupard, Southern Methodist, 6-0, 201, New Orleans, La.; RB—Napoleon McCallum, Navy, 6-2, 214, Milford, Ohio; PK—*John Lee, UCLA, 5-11, 187, Downey, Calif.

Defense L—*Tim Green, Syracuse, 6-2, 246, Liverpool, N.Y.; L—*Leslie O'Neal, Oklahoma St., 6-3, 245, Little Rock, Ark.; L—Tony Casillas, Oklahoma, 6-3, 280, Tulsa, Okla.; L—Mike Ruth, Boston College, 6-2, 250, Norristown, Pa.; L—Mike Hammerstein, Michigan, 6-4, 240, Wapakoneta, Ohio; LB—*Brian Bosworth, Oklahoma, 6-2, 234, Irving, Texas; LB—*Larry Station, Iowa, 5-11, 227, Omaha, Neb.; LB—Johnny Holland, Texas A&M, 6-2, 219, Hempstead, Texas; DB—David Fulcher, Arizona St., 6-3, 228, Los Angeles, Calif.; DB—Brad Cochran, Michigan, 6-3, 219, Royal Oak, Mich.; DB—Scott Thomas, Air Force, 6-0, 185, San Antonio, Texas; P—Barry Helton, Colorado, 6-3, 195, Simla, Colo.

1986

Offense WR—Cris Carter, Ohio St., 6-3, 194, Middletown, Ohio; TE—*Keith Jackson, Oklahoma, 6-3, 241, Little Rock, Ark.; L—Jeff Bregel, Southern Cal, 6-4, 280, Granada Hills, Calif.; L—Randy Dixon, Pittsburgh, 6-4, 286, Clewiston, Fla.; L—Danny Villa, Arizona St., 6-5, 284, Nogales, Ariz.; L—John Clay, Missouri, 6-5, 285, St. Louis, Mo.; C—*Ben Tamburello, Auburn, 6-3, 268, Birmingham, Ala.; QB—*Vinny Testaverde, Miami (Fla.), 6-5, 218, Elmont, N.Y.; RB—*Brent Fullwood, Auburn, 5-11, 209, St. Cloud, Fla.; RB—*Paul Palmer, Temple, 5-10, 180, Potomac, Md.; RB—Terrence Flagler, Clemson, 6-1, 200, Fernandina Beach, Fla.; RB—Brad Muster, Stanford, 6-3, 226, Novato, Calif.; RB—D. J. Dozier, Penn St., 6-1, 204, Virginia Beach, Va.; PK—Jeff Jaeger, Washington, 5-11, 191, Kent, Wash.

Defense L—*Jerome Brown, Miami (Fla.), 6-2, 285, Brooksville, Fla.; L—*Danny Noonan, Nebraska, 6-4, 280, Lincoln, Neb.; L—Tony Woods, Pittsburgh, 6-4, 240, Newark, N.J.; L—Jason Buck, Brigham Young, 6-6, 270, St. Anthony, Idaho; L—Reggie Rogers, Washington, 6-6, 260, Sacramento, Calif.; LB—*Cornelius Bennett, Alabama, 6-4, 235, Birmingham, Ala.; LB—Shane Conlan, Penn St., 6-3, 225, Frewsburg, N.Y.; LB—Brian Bosworth, Oklahoma, 6-2, 240, Irving, Texas; LB—Chris Spielman, Ohio St., 6-2, 227, Massillon, Ohio; DB—*Thomas Everett, Baylor, 5-9, 180, Daingerfield, Texas; DB—Tim McDonald, Southern Cal, 6-3, 205, Fresno, Calif.; DB—Bennie Blades, Miami (Fla.), 6-0, 207, Ft. Lauderdale, Fla.; DB—Rod Woodson, Purdue, 6-0, 195, Fort Wayne, Ind.; DB—Garland Rivers, Michigan, 6-1, 187, Canton, Ohio; P—Barry Helton, Colorado, 6-4, 200, Simla, Colo.

1987

Offense WR—*Tim Brown, Notre Dame, 6-0, 195, Dallas, Texas; WR—Wendell Davis, Louisiana St., 6-0, 186, Shreveport, La.; TE—*Keith Jackson, Oklahoma, 6-3, 248, Little Rock, Ark.; L—*Mark Hutson, Oklahoma, 6-4, 282, Fort Smith, Ark.; L—Dave Cadigan, Southern Cal, 6-5, 280, Newport Beach, Calif.; L—John Elliott, Michigan, 6-7, 306, Lake Ronkonkoma, N.Y.; L—Randall McDaniel, Arizona St., 6-5, 261, Avondale, Ariz.; C—*Nacho Albergamo, Louisiana St., 6-2, 257, Marrera, La.; QB—*Don McPherson, Syracuse, 6-0, 182, West Hempstead, N.Y.; RB—Lorenzo White, Michigan St., 5-11, 211, Fort Lauderdale, Fla.; RB—Craig Heyward, Pittsburgh, 6-0, 260, Passaic, N.J.; PK—David Treadwell, Clemson, 6-1, 165, Jacksonville, Fla.

Defense L—*Daniel Stubbs, Miami (Fla.), 6-4, 250, Red Bank, N.J.; L—*Chad Hennings, Air Force, 6-5, 260, Elboron, Iowa; L—Tracy Rocker, Auburn, 6-3, 258, Atlanta, Ga.; L—Ted Gregory, Syracuse, 6-1, 260, East Islip, N.Y.; L—John Roper, Texas A&M, 6-2, 215, Houston, Texas; LB—*Chris Spielman, Ohio St., 6-2, 236, Massillon, Ohio; LB—Aundray Bruce, Auburn, 6-6, 236, Montgomery, Ala.; LB—Dante Jones, Oklahoma, 6-2, 235, Dallas, Texas; DB—*Bennie Blades, Miami (Fla.), 6-0, 215, Fort Lauderdale, Fla.; DB—*Deion Sanders, Florida St., 6-0, 192, Fort Myers, Fla.; DB—Rickey Dixon, Oklahoma, 5-10, 184, Dallas, Texas; DB—Chuck Cecil, Arizona, 6-0, 185, Red Bluff, Calif.; P—*Tom Tupa, Ohio St., 6-5, 215, Brecksville, Ohio.

1988

Offense WR—Jason Phillips, Houston, 5-9, 175, Houston, Texas; WR—Hart Lee Dykes, Oklahoma St., 6-4, 220, Bay City, Texas; TE—Marv Cook, Iowa, 6-4, 243, West Branch, Iowa; L—*Tony Mandarich, Michigan St., 6-6, 315, Oakville, Ontario, Canada; L—*Anthony Phillips, Oklahoma, 6-3, 286, Tulsa, Okla.; L—Mike Utley, Washington St., 6-6, 302, Seattle, Wash.; L—Mark Stepnoski, Pittsburgh, 6-3, 265, Erie, Pa.; C—Jake Young, Nebraska, 6-5, 260, Midland, Texas; C—John Vitale, Michigan, 6-1, 273, Detroit, Mich.; QB—Steve Walsh, Miami (Fla.), 6-3, 195, St. Paul, Minn.; QB—Troy Aikman, UCLA, 6-4, 217, Henryetta, Okla.; RB—*Barry Sanders, Oklahoma St., 5-8, 197, Wichita, Kan.; RB—Anthony Thompson, Indiana, 6-0, 205, Terre Haute, Ind.; RB—Tim Worley, Georgia, 6-2, 216, Lumberton, N.C.; PK—Kendall Trainor, Arkansas, 6-2, 205, Fredonia, Kan.

Defense L—*Mark Messner, Michigan, 6-3, 244, Hartland, Mich.; L—*Tracy Rocker, Auburn, 6-3, 278, Atlanta, Ga.; L—Wayne Martin, Arkansas, 6-5, 263, Cherry Valley, Ark.; L—Frank Stams, Notre Dame, 6-4, 237, Akron, Ohio; L—Bill Hawkins, Miami (Fla.), 6-6, 260, Hollywood, Fla.; LB—*Derrick Thomas, Alabama, 6-4, 230, Miami, Fla.; LB—*Broderick Thomas,

Nebraska, 6-3, 235, Houston, Texas; LB—Michael Stonebreaker, Notre Dame, 6-1, 228, River Ridge, La.; DB—*Deion Sanders, Florida St., 6-0, 195, Fort Myers, Fla.; DB—Donnell Woolford, Clemson, 5-10, 195, Fayetteville, N.C.; DB—Louis Oliver, Florida, 6-2, 222, Bell Glade, Fla.; DB—Darryl Henley, UCLA, 5-10, 165, Ontario, Calif.; P—Keith English, Colorado, 6-3, 215, Greeley, Colo.

1989

Offense WR—*Clarkston Hines, Duke, 6-1, 170, Chapel Hill, N.C.; WR—Terance Mathis, New Mexico, 5-9, 167, Stone Mountain, Ga.; TE—Mike Busch, Iowa St., 6-5, 252, Donahue, Iowa; L—Jim Mabry, Arkansas, 6-4, 262, Memphis, Tenn.; L—Bob Kula, Michigan St., 6-4, 282, West Bloomfield, Mich.; L—Mohammed Elewonibi, Brigham Young, 6-5, 290, Kamloops, British Columbia, Canada; L—Joe Garten, Colorado, 6-3, 280, Placentia, Calif.; L—*Eric Still, Tennessee, 6-3, 283, Germantown, Tenn.; C—Jake Young, Nebraska, 6-4, 270, Midland, Texas; QB—Andre Ware, Houston, 6-2, 205, Dickinson, Texas; RB—*Anthony Thompson, Indiana, 6-0, 209, Terre Haute, Ind.; RB—*Emmitt Smith, Florida, 5-10, 201, Pensacola, Fla.; PK—*Jason Hanson, Washington St., 6-0, 164, Spokane, Wash.

Defense L—Chris Zorich, Notre Dame, 6-1, 268, Chicago, Ill.; L—Greg Mark, Miami (Fla.), 6-4, 255, Pennsauken, N.J.; L—Tim Ryan, Southern Cal, 6-5, 260, San Jose, Calif.; L—*Moe Gardner, Illinois, 6-2, 250, Indianapolis, Ind.; LB—*Percy Snow, Michigan St., 6-3, 240, Canton, Ohio; LB—*Keith McCants, Alabama, 6-5, 256, Mobile, Ala.; LB—Alfred Williams, Colorado, 6-6, 230, Houston, Texas; DB—*Todd Lyght, Notre Dame, 6-1, 181, Flint, Mich.; DB—*Mark Carrier, Southern Cal, 6-1, 185, Long Beach, Calif.; DB—*Tripp Welborne, Michigan, 6-1, 193, Greensboro, N.C.; DB—LeRoy Butler, Florida St., 6-0, 194, Jacksonville, Fla.; P—Tom Rouen, Colorado, 6-3, 220, Littleton, Colo.

1990

Offense WR—*Raghib Ismail, Notre Dame, 5-10, 175, Wilkes-Barre, Pa.; WR—Herman Moore, Virginia, 6-5, 197, Danville, Va.; TE—*Chris Smith, Brigham Young, 6-4, 230, La Canada, Calif.; OL—*Antone Davis, Tennessee, 6-4, 310, Fort Valley, Ga.; OL—*Joe Garten, Colorado, 6-3, 280, Placentia, Calif.; OL—*Ed King, Auburn, 6-4, 284, Phenix City, Ala.; OL—Stacy Long, Clemson, 6-2, 275, Griffin, Ga.; C—John Flannery, Syracuse, 6-4, 301, Pottsville, Pa.; QB—Ty Detmer, Brigham Young, 6-0, 175, San Antonio, Texas; RB—*Eric Bieniemy, Colorado, 5-7, 195, West Covina, Calif.; RB—Darren Lewis, Texas A&M, 6-0, 220, Dallas, Texas; PK—*Philip Doyle, Alabama, 6-1, 190, Birmingham, Ala.

Defense DL—*Russell Maryland, Miami (Fla.), 6-2, 273, Chicago, Ill.; DL—*Chris Zorich, Notre Dame, 6-1, 266, Chicago, Ill.; DL—*Moe Gardner, Illinois, 6-2, 258, Indianapolis, Ind.; DL—David Rocker, Auburn, 6-4, 264, Atlanta, Ga.; LB—*Alfred Williams, Colorado, 6-6, 236, Houston, Texas; LB—*Michael Stonebreaker, Notre Dame, 6-1, 228, River Ridge, La.; LB—Maurice Crum, Miami (Fla.), 6-0, 222, Tampa, Fla.; DB—*Tripp Welborne, Michigan, 6-1, 201, Greensboro, N.C.; DB—*Darryll Lewis, Arizona, 5-9, 186, West Covina, Calif.; DB—*Ken Swilling, Georgia Tech, 6-3, 230, Toccoa, Ga.; DB—Todd Lyght, Notre Dame, 6-1, 184, Flint, Mich.; P—Brian Greenfield, Pittsburgh, 6-1, 210, Sherman Oaks, Calif.

1991

Offense WR—*Desmond Howard, Michigan, 5-9, 176, Cleveland, Ohio; WR—Mario Bailey, Washington, 5-9, 167, Seattle, Wash.; TE—Kelly Blackwell, Texas Christian, 6-2, 242, Fort Worth, Texas; OL—*Greg Skrepenak, Michigan, 6-8, 322, Wilkes-Barre, Pa.; OL—Bob Whitfield, Stanford, 6-7, 300, Carson, Calif.; OL—Jeb Flesch, Clemson, 6-3, 266, Morrow, Ga.; OL—(tie) Jerry Ostroski, Tulsa, 6-4, 305, Collegeville, Pa.; Mirko Jurkovic, Notre Dame, 6-4, 289, Calumet City, Ill.; C—*Jay Leeuwenburg, Colorado, 6-3, 265, Kirkwood, Mo.; QB—Ty Detmer, Brigham Young, 6-0, 175, San Antonio, Texas; RB—*Vaughn Dunbar, Indiana, 6-0, 207, Fort Wayne, Ind.; RB—(tie) Trevor Cobb, Rice, 5-9, 180, Houston, Texas; Russell White, California, 6-0, 210, Van Nuys, Calif.; PK—Carlos Huerta, Miami (Fla.), 5-9, 186, Miami, Fla.

Defense DL—*Steve Emtman, Washington, 6-4, 280, Cheney, Wash.; DL—*Santana Dotson, Baylor, 6-5, 264, Houston, Texas; DL—Brad Culpepper, Florida, 6-2, 263, Tallahassee, Fla.; DL—Leroy Smith, Iowa, 6-2,

214, Sicklerville, N. J.; LB—*Robert Jones, East Caro., 6-3, 234, Blackstone, Va.; LB—Marvin Jones, Florida St., 6-2, 220, Miami, Fla.; LB—Levon Kirkland, Clemson, 6-2, 245, Lamar, S.C.; DB—*Terrell Buckley, Florida St., 5-10, 175, Pascagoula, Miss.; DB—Dale Carter, Tennessee, 6-2, 182, Oxford, Ga.; DB—Kevin Smith, Texas A&M, 6-0, 180, Orange, Texas; DB—Darryl Williams, Miami (Fla.), 6-2, 190, Miami, Fla.; P—*Mark Bounds, Texas Tech, 5-11, 185, Stamford, Texas.

1992

Offense WR—O. J. McDuffie, Penn St., 5-11, 185, Warrensville Heights, Ohio; WR—Sean Dawkins, California, 6-4, 205, Sunnyvale, Calif.; TE—*Chris Gedney, Syracuse, 6-5, 256, Liverpool, N.Y.; OL—*Lincoln Kennedy, Washington, 6-7, 325, San Diego, Calif.; OL—*Will Shields, Nebraska, 6-1, 305, Lawton, Okla.; OL—Aaron Taylor, Notre Dame, 6-4, 294, Concord, Calif.; OL—(tie) Willie Roaf, Louisiana Tech, 6-5, 300, Pine Bluff, Ark.; Everett Lindsay, Mississippi, 6-5, 290, Raleigh, N.C.; C—Mike Compton, West Va., 6-7, 289, Richlands, Va.; QB—*Gino Torretta, Miami (Fla.), 6-3, 205, Pinole, Calif.; RB—*Marshall Faulk, San Diego St., 5-10, 200, New Orleans, La.; RB—*Garrison Hearst, Georgia, 5-11, 202, Lincolnton, Ga.; PK—Joe Allison, Memphis, 6-0, 184, Atlanta, Ga.

Defense DL—Eric Curry, Alabama, 6-6, 265, Thomasville, Ga.; DL—John Copeland, Alabama, 6-3, 261, Lanett, Ala.; DL—Chris Slade, Virginia, 6-5, 235, Tabb, Va.; DL—Rob Waldrop, Arizona, 6-2, 265, Phoenix, Ariz.; LB—*Marcus Buckley, Texas A&M, 6-4, 230, Fort Worth, Texas; LB—*Marvin Jones, Florida St., 6-2, 235, Miami, Fla.; LB—Micheal Barrow, Miami (Fla.), 6-2, 230, Homestead, Fla.; DB—*Carlton McDonald, Air Force, 6-0, 185, Jacksonville, Fla.; DB—Carlton Gray, UCLA, 6-0, 194, Cincinnati, Ohio; DB—Deon Figures, Colorado, 6-1, 195, Compton, Calif.; DB—Ryan McNeil, Miami (Fla.), 6-2, 185, Fort Pierce, Fla.; P—Sean Snyder, Kansas St., 6-1, 190, Greenville, Texas.

1993

Offense WR—*J. J. Stokes, UCLA, 6-5, 214, San Diego, Calif.; WR—Johnnie Morton, Southern Cal, 6-0, 190, Torrance, Calif.; OL—Mark Dixon, Virginia, 6-4, 283, Jamestown, N.C.; OL—Stacy Seegars, Clemson, 6-4, 320, Kershaw, S.C.; OL—*Aaron Taylor, Notre Dame, 6-4, 299, Concord, Calif.; OL—Wayne Gandy, Auburn, 6-5, 275, Haines City, Fla.; C—*Jim Pyne, Virginia Tech, 6-2, 280, Milford, Mass.; QB—*Charlie Ward, Florida St., 6-2, 190, Thomasville, Ga.; RB—*Marshall Faulk, San Diego St., 5-10, 200, New Orleans, La.; RB—*LeShon Johnson, Northern Ill., 6-0, 201, Haskell, Okla.; RB—Bjorn Merten, UCLA, 6-0, 203, Centreville, Va.; KR—David Palmer, Alabama, 5-9, 170, Birmingham, Ala.

Defense DL—*Rob Waldrop, Arizona, 6-2, 275, Phoenix, Ariz.; DL—Dan Wilkinson, Ohio St., 6-5, 300, Dayton, Ohio; DL—Sam Adams, Texas A&M, 6-4, 269, Cypress, Texas; LB—*Trev Alberts, Nebraska, 6-4, 240, Cedar Falls, Iowa; LB—*Derrick Brooks, Florida St., 6-1, 225, Pensacola, Fla.; LB—Jamir Miller, UCLA, 6-4, 233, El Cerrito, Calif.; DB—*Antonio Langham, Alabama, 6-1, 170, Town Creek, Ala.; DB—Aaron Glenn, Texas A&M, 5-10, 182, Aldine, Texas; DB—Jeff Burris, Notre Dame, 6-0, 204, Rock Hill, S.C.; DB—Corey Sawyer, Florida St., 5-11, 171, Key West, Fla.; P—Terry Daniel, Auburn, 6-1, 226, Valley, Ala.

1993 Selectors: Associated Press, United Press International, Football Writers Association of America, American Football Coaches Association (Kodak), Walter Camp Foundation, The Football News and The Sporting News.

*Indicates unanimous selection.

Consensus All-Americans by College

Beginning in 1924, unanimous selections are indicated by (*).

AIR FORCE
58— Brock Strom, T
70— Ernie Jennings, E
85— Scott Thomas, DB
87— *Chad Hennings, DL
92— *Carlton McDonald, DB

ALABAMA
30— *Fred Sington, T
34— Don Hutson, E
     Bill Lee, T
     Dixie Howell, B
35— Riley Smith, B
37— Leroy Monsky, G
41— Holt Rast, E
42— Joe Domnanovich, C
45— Vaughn Mancha, C
61— *Billy Neighbors, T
62— *Lee Roy Jordan, C
65— Paul Crane, C
66— Ray Perkins, E
     *Cecil Dowdy, T
67— Dennis Homan, E
     Bobby Johns, DB
71— Johnny Musso, B
72— *John Hannah, G
73— Buddy Brown, G
74— Leroy Cook, DL
     Woodrow Lowe, LB
75— *Leroy Cook, DE
77— Ozzie Newsome, WR
78— Marty Lyons, DL
79— Jim Bunch, T
80— *E. J. Junior, DL
81— Tommy Wilcox, DB
82— Mike Pitts, DL
86— *Cornelius Bennett, LB
88— *Derrick Thomas, LB
89— *Keith McCants, LB
90— *Philip Doyle, PK
92— John Copeland, DL
     Eric Curry, DL
93— David Palmer, KR
     *Antonio Langham, DB

AMHERST
05— John Hubbard, B

ARIZONA
82— Ricky Hunley, LB
83— *Ricky Hunley, LB
87— Chuck Cecil, DB
90— *Darryll Lewis, DB
92— Rob Waldrop, DL
93— *Rob Waldrop, DL

ARIZONA ST.
72— Woody Green, B
73— Woody Green, B
77— John Jefferson, WR
78— Al Harris, DL
81— Mike Richardson, DB
82— Mike Richardson, DB
     Vernon Maxwell, DL
83— Luis Zendejas, PK
84— David Fulcher, DB
85— David Fulcher, DB
86— Danny Villa, OL
87— Randall McDaniel, OL

ARKANSAS
48— Clyde Scott, B
54— *Bud Brooks, G
65— Glen Ray Hines, T
     Loyd Phillips, DT
66— *Loyd Phillips, DT
68— Jim Barnes, G
69— Rodney Brand, C
70— Dick Bumpas, DT
77— Leotis Harris, G
     Steve Little, K
79— *Greg Kolenda, T
81— *Billy Ray Smith, DL
82— *Billy Ray Smith, DL
     *Steve Korte, OL
88— Kendall Trainor, PK
     Wayne Martin, DL
89— Jim Mabry, OL

ARMY
98— Charles Romeyn, B
00— William Smith, E
01— Paul Bunker, T
     Charles Daly, B
02— Paul Bunker, T-B
     Robert Boyers, C
04— Arthur Tipton, C
     Henry Torney, B
05— Henry Torney, B
07— William Erwin, G
11— Leland Devore, T
13— Louis Merillat, E

14— John McEwan, C
16— Elmer Oliphant, B
17— Elmer Oliphant, B
22— Ed Garbisch, C
26— Bud Sprague, T
27— Red Cagle, B
28— *Red Cagle, B
29— Red Cagle, B
32— Milt Summerfelt, G
43— *Casimir Myslinski, C
44— Glenn Davis, B
    Doc Blanchard, B
45— Tex Coulter, T
    John Green, G
    *Glenn Davis, B
    *Doc Blanchard, B
46— Hank Foldberg, E
    *Glenn Davis, B
    *Doc Blanchard, B
47— Joe Steffy, G
49— Arnold Galiffa, B
50— *Dan Foldberg, E
57— Bob Anderson, B
58— *Pete Dawkins, B
59— Bill Carpenter, E

AUBURN
32— Jimmy Hitchcock, B
57— *Jimmy Phillips, E
58— Zeke Smith, G
60— Ken Rice, T
64— Tucker Frederickson, B
69— Buddy McClinton, DB
70— Larry Willingham, DB
71— *Pat Sullivan, QB
    *Terry Beasley, E
74— Ken Bernich, LB
83— Bo Jackson, RB
84— Gregg Carr, LB
85— Bo Jackson, RB
86— *Ben Tamburello, C
    *Brent Fullwood, RB
87— Tracy Rocker, DL
    Aundray Bruce, LB
88— *Tracy Rocker, DL
90— *Ed King, OL
    David Rocker, DL
93— Wayne Gandy, OL
    Terry Daniel, P

BAYLOR
30— Barton Koch, G
56— *Bill Glass, G
63— Lawrence Elkins, E
64— Lawrence Elkins, B
76— Gary Green, DB
79— Mike Singletary, LB
80— *Mike Singletary, LB
86— *Thomas Everett, DB
91— *Santana Dotson, DL

BOSTON COLLEGE
20— Luke Urban, E
40— Gene Goodreault, E
42— Mike Holovak, B
84— *Doug Flutie, QB
    Tony Thurman, DB
85— Mike Ruth, DL

BRIGHAM YOUNG
79— *Marc Wilson, QB
80— Nick Eyre, OL
81— *Jim McMahon, QB
82— *Gordon Hudson, TE
83— *Gordon Hudson, TE
    *Steve Young, QB
86— Jason Buck, DL
89— Mohammed Elewonibi, OL
90— Ty Detmer, QB
    *Chris Smith, TE
91— Ty Detmer, QB

BROWN
02— Thomas Barry, B
06— John Mayhew, B
09— Adrian Regnier, E
10— Earl Sprackling, B
12— George Crowther, B
16— Fritz Pollard, B

CALIFORNIA
21— Brick Muller, E
    Dan McMillan, T
22— Brick Muller, E
24— Edwin Horrell, C

28— Irv Phillips, E
30— Ted Beckett, G
35— Larry Lutz, T
37— Sam Chapman, B
38— Vic Bottari, B
48— Jackie Jensen, B
49— *Rod Franz, G
50— Les Richter, G
51— Les Richter, G
68— Ed White, MG
71— Sherman White, DT
74— Steve Bartkowski, QB
75— Chuck Muncie, RB
    Steve Rivera, E
83— Ron Rivera, LB
91— Russell White, RB
92— Sean Dawkins, WR

CARLISLE
99— Isaac Seneca, B
03— James Johnson, B
07— Albert Exendine, E
    Peter Hauser, B
11— Jim Thorpe, B
12— Jim Thorpe, B

CARNEGIE MELLON
28— Howard Harpster, B

CENTENARY (LA.)
33— Paul Geisler, E

CENTRE
19— James Weaver, C
    Bo McMillin, B
21— Bo McMillin, B

CHICAGO
98— Clarence Herschberger, B
04— Fred Speik, E
    Walter Eckersall, B
05— Mark Catlin, E
    Walter Eckersall, B
06— Walter Eckersall, B
08— Walter Steffen, B
13— Paul Des Jardien, C
22— John Thomas, B
24— Joe Pondelik, G
35— *Jay Berwanger, B

CLEMSON
67— Harry Olszewski, G
74— Bennie Cunningham, TE
79— Jim Stuckey, DL
81— Jeff Davis, LB
    Terry Kinard, DB
82— *Terry Kinard, DB
83— William Perry, DL
86— Terrence Flagler, RB
87— David Treadwell, PK
88— Donnell Woolford, DB
90— Stacy Long, OL
91— Jeb Flesch, OL
    Levon Kirkland, LB
93— Stacy Seegars, OL

COLGATE
13— Ellery Huntington, B
16— Clarence Horning, T
    D. Belford West, T
    Oscar Anderson, B
19— D. Belford West, T
30— Leonard Macaluso, B

COLORADO
37— Byron White, B
60— Joe Romig, G
61— Joe Romig, G
67— Dick Anderson, DB
68— Mike Montler, G
69— Bob Anderson, B
70— Don Popplewell, C
72— Cullen Bryant, DB
85— Barry Helton, P
86— Barry Helton, P
88— Keith English, P
89— Joe Garten, OL
    Alfred Williams, LB
    Tom Rouen, P
90— *Eric Bieniemy, RB
    *Joe Garten, OL
    *Alfred Williams, LB
91— *Jay Leeuwenburg, OL
92— Deon Figures, DB

COLORADO ST.
78— Mike Bell, DL

COLUMBIA
00— Bill Morley, B
01— Harold Weekes, B
    Bill Morley, B
03— Richard Smith, B
42— Paul Governali, B
47— Bill Swiacki, E

CORNELL
95— Clinton Wyckoff, B
00— Raymond Starbuck, B
01— William Warner, G
    Sanford Hunt, G
02— William Warner, G
06— Elmer Thompson, G
    William Newman, C
08— Bernard O'Rourke, G
14— John O'Hearn, E
    Charles Barrett, B
15— Murray Shelton, E
    Charles Barrett, B
21— Edgar Kaw, B
22— Edgar Kaw, B
23— George Pfann, B
38— Brud Holland, E
39— Nick Drahos, T
40— Nick Drahos, T
71— *Ed Marinaro, B

DARTMOUTH
03— Henry Hooper, C
    Myron Witham, B
04— Joseph Gilman, G
05— Ralph Glaze, E
08— George Schildmiller, E
    Clark Tobin, G
12— Wesley Englehorn, T
13— Robert Hogsett, E
14— Clarence Spears, G
15— Clarence Spears, G
17— Eugene Neely, G
19— Adolph Youngstrom, G
24— Carl Diehl, G
25— Carl Diehl, G
    George Tully, E
    *Andy Oberlander, B
38— Bob MacLeod, B

DUKE
33— Fred Crawford, T
36— Ace Parker, B
71— Ernie Jackson, DB
89— *Clarkston Hines, WR

DUQUESNE
36— Mike Basrak, C

EAST CARO.
83— Terry Long, OL
91— *Robert Jones, LB

The legendary Jim Thorpe was a consensus all-American back for Carlisle in 1911 and 1912.

FLORIDA
66— *Steve Spurrier, B
69— Carlos Alvarez, E
75— Sammy Green, LB
80— David Little, LB
82— Wilber Marshall, DL
83— Wilber Marshall, LB
84— Lomas Brown, OT
88— Louis Oliver, DB
89— *Emmitt Smith, RB
91— Brad Culpepper, DL

FLORIDA ST.
64— Fred Biletnikoff, E
67— Ron Sellers, E
79— Ron Simmons, MG
80— Ron Simmons, MG
83— Greg Allen, RB
85— Jamie Dukes, OL
87— *Deion Sanders, DB
88— *Deion Sanders, DB
89— LeRoy Butler, DB
91— *Terrell Buckley, DB
      Marvin Jones, LB
92— *Marvin Jones, LB
93— *Charlie Ward, QB
      *Derrick Brooks, LB
      Corey Sawyer, DB

FORDHAM
36— Alex Wojciechowicz, C
37— Ed Franco, T
      Alex Wojciechowicz, C

GEORGETOWN
26— Harry Connaughton, G

GEORGIA
27— Tom Nash, E
31— Vernon Smith, E
41— Frank Sinkwich, B
42— *Frank Sinkwich, B
46— *Charley Trippi, B
67— Ed Chandler, T
68— Bill Stanfill, DT
      Jake Scott, DB
71— *Royce Smith, G
75— Randy Johnson, G
76— Joel Parrish, G
80— *Herschel Walker, RB
81— *Herschel Walker, RB
82— *Herschel Walker, RB
      Terry Hoage, DB
83— Terry Hoage, DB
84— Kevin Butler, PK
      Jeff Sanchez, DB
85— Pete Anderson, C
88— Tim Worley, RB
92— *Garrison Hearst, RB

GEORGIA TECH
17— Everett Strupper, B
18— Bill Fincher, E
      Joe Guyon, T
      Ashel Day, C
20— Bill Fincher, E
28— Pete Pund, C
42— Harvey Hardy, G
44— Phil Tinsley, E
46— Paul Duke, C
47— Bob Davis, T
52— Hal Miller, T
53— Larry Morris, C
59— Maxie Baughan, C
66— Jim Breland, C
70— Rock Perdoni, DT
73— Randy Rhino, DB
90— *Ken Swilling, DB

HARVARD
89— Arthur Cumnock, E
      John Cranston, G
      James Lee, B
90— Frank Hallowell, E
      Marshall Newell, T
      John Cranston, C
      Dudley Dean, B
      John Corbett, B
91— Marshall Newell, T
      Everett Lake, B
92— Frank Hallowell, E
      Marshall Newell, T
      Bertram Waters, G
      William Lewis, C
      Charles Brewer, B

93— Marshall Newell, T
      William Lewis, C
      Charles Brewer, B
94— Bertram Waters, T
95— Norman Cabot, E
      Charles Brewer, B
96— Norman Cabot, E
      Edgar Wrightington, B
97— Alan Doucette, C
      Benjamin Dibblee, B
98— John Hallowell, E
      Walter Boal, G
      Charles Daly, B
      Benjamin Dibblee, B
99— David Campbell, E
      Charles Daly, B
00— John Hallowell, E
      David Campbell, E
      Charles Daly, B
01— David Campbell, E
      Edward Bowditch, E
      Oliver Cutts, T
      Crawford Blagden, T
      William Lee, G
      Charles Barnard, G
      Robert Kernan, B
      Thomas Graydon, B
02— Edward Bowditch, E
      Thomas Graydon, B
03— Daniel Knowlton, T
      Andrew Marshall, G
04— Daniel Hurley, B
05— Beaton Squires, T
      Karl Brill, T
      Francis Burr, G
      Daniel Hurley, B
06— Charles Osborne, T
      Francis Burr, G
07— Patrick Grant, C
      John Wendell, B
08— Hamilton Fish, T
      Charles Nourse, C
      Hamilton Corbett, B
09— Hamilton Fish, T
      Wayland Minot, B
10— Robert McKay, T
      Robert Fisher, G
      Percy Wendell, B
11— Robert Fisher, G
      Percy Wendell, B
12— Samuel Felton, E
      Stanley Pennock, G
      Charles Brickley, B
13— Harvey Hitchcock, T
      Stanley Pennock, G
      Charles Brickley, B
      Edward Mahan, B
14— Huntington Hardwick, E
      Walter Trumbull, T
      Stanley Pennock, G
      Edward Mahan, B
15— Joseph Gilman, T
      Edward Mahan, B
      Richard King, B
16— Harrie Dadmun, G
19— Edward Casey, B
20— Tom Woods, G
21— John Brown, G
22— Charles Hubbard, G
23— Charles Hubbard, G
29— Ben Ticknor, C
30— *Ben Ticknor, C
31— Barry Wood, B
41— *Endicott Peabody, G

HOLY CROSS
74— John Provost, DB

HOUSTON
67— Rich Stotter, G
69— Bill Bridges, G
70— Elmo Wright, E
76— Wilson Whitley, DT
80— Leonard Mitchell, DL
88— Jason Phillips, WR
89— Andre Ware, QB

ILLINOIS
14— Perry Graves, E
      Ralph Chapman, G
15— Bart Macomber, B
18— John Depler, C
20— Charles Carney, E
23— James McMillen, G

      Red Grange, B
24— *Red Grange, B
25— Red Grange, B
26— Bernie Shively, G
46— Alex Agase, G
51— Johnny Karras, B
53— J. C. Caroline, B
59— Bill Burrell, G
63— *Dick Butkus, C
64— Dick Butkus, C
65— *Jim Grabowski, B
84— *David Williams, WR
85— *David Williams, WR
89— *Moe Gardner, DL
90— Moe Gardner, DL

INDIANA
42— Billy Hillenbrand, B
44— John Tavener, C
45— Bob Ravensberg, E
88— Anthony Thompson, RB
89— *Anthony Thompson, RB
91— *Vaughn Dunbar, RB

IOWA
19— Lester Belding, E
21— Aubrey Devine, B
22— Gordon Locke, B
39— Nile Kinnick, B
54— Calvin Jones, G
55— Calvin Jones, G
57— Alex Karras, T
58— *Randy Duncan, B
81— Andre Tippett, DL
      Reggie Roby, P
84— *Larry Station, LB
85— *Chuck Long, QB
      *Larry Station, LB
88— Marv Cook, TE
91— Leroy Smith, DL

IOWA ST.
38— Ed Bock, G
89— Mike Busch, TE

KANSAS
63— Gale Sayers, B
64— Gale Sayers, B
68— John Zook, DE
73— David Jaynes, QB

KANSAS ST.
77— Gary Spani, LB
92— Sean Snyder, P

KENTUCKY
50— Bob Gain, T
      Babe Parilli, B
51— Babe Parilli, B
56— Lou Michaels, T
57— Lou Michaels, T
65— Sam Ball, T
77— *Art Still, DL

LAFAYETTE
00— Walter Bachman, C
01— Walter Bachman, C
21— Frank Schwab, G
22— Frank Schwab, G

LOUISIANA ST.
35— Gaynell Tinsley, E
36— *Gaynell Tinsley, E
39— Ken Kavanaugh, E
54— Sid Fournet, T
58— *Billy Cannon, B
59— Billy Cannon, B
61— *Roy Winston, G
62— *Jerry Stovall, B
70— Mike Anderson, LB
      Tommy Casanova, DB
71— Tommy Casanova, DB
72— Bert Jones, QB
77— Charles Alexander, RB
78— Charles Alexander, RB
87— Wendell Davis, WR
      *Nacho Albergamo, C

LOUISIANA TECH
92— Willie Roaf, OL

MARQUETTE
36— Ray Buivid, B

MARYLAND
51— *Bob Ward, G
52— Dick Modzelewski, T
      *Jack Scarbath, B

53— *Stan Jones, T
55— *Bob Pellegrini, C
61— Gary Collins, E
74— *Randy White, DL
76— Joe Campbell, DT
79— Dale Castro, PK
85— J. D. Maarleveld, OL

MEMPHIS
92— Joe Allison, PK

MIAMI (FLA.)
61— Bill Miller, E
66— Tom Beier, DB
67— *Ted Hendricks, DE
68— *Ted Hendricks, DE
73— Tony Cristiani, DL
74— Rubin Carter, MG
81— Fred Marion, DB
84— Eddie Brown, WR
85— Willie Smith, TE
86— *Vinny Testaverde, QB
    *Jerome Brown, DL
    Bennie Blades, DB
87— *Daniel Stubbs, DL
    *Bennie Blades, DB
88— Steve Walsh, QB
    Bill Hawkins, DL
89— Greg Mark, DL
90— Maurice Crum, LB
    *Russell Maryland, DL
91— Carlos Huerta, PK
    Darryl Williams, DB
92— *Gino Torretta, QB
    Micheal Barrow, LB
    Ryan McNeil, DB

MICHIGAN
98— William Cunningham, C
01— Neil Snow, E
03— Willie Heston, B
04— Willie Heston, B
07— Adolph Schulz, C
09— Albert Benbrook, G
10— Stanfield Wells, E
    Albert Benbrook, G
13— Miller Pontius, T
    Jim Craig, B
14— John Maulbetsch, B
22— Harry Kipke, B
23— Jack Blott, C
25— Bennie Oosterbaan, E
    Benny Friedman, B
26— Bennie Oosterbaan, E
    Benny Friedman, B
27— *Bennie Oosterbaan, E
28— Otto Pommerening, T
32— *Harry Newman, B
33— Francis Wistert, T
    *Chuck Bernard, C
38— *Ralph Heikkinen, G
39— Tom Harmon, B
40— *Tom Harmon, B
41— Bob Westfall, B
42— Albert Wistert, T
    Julie Franks, G
43— *Bill Daley, B
47— *Bob Chappuis, B
48— Dick Rifenburg, E
    Alvin Wistert, T
49— Alvin Wistert, T
55— Ron Kramer, E
56— *Ron Kramer, E
65— Bill Yearby, DT
66— *Jack Clancy, E
69— *Jim Mandich, E
    Tom Curtis, DB
70— Dan Dierdorf, T
71— Reggie McKenzie, G
    *Mike Taylor, LB
72— Paul Seymour, T
    Randy Logan, DB
73— Dave Gallagher, DL
    Dave Brown, DB
74— *Dave Brown, DB
76— Rob Lytle, RB
    Mark Donahue, G
77— *Mark Donahue, G
79— Ron Simpkins, LB
81— *Anthony Carter, WR
    Ed Muransky, OL
    Kurt Becker, OL
82— *Anthony Carter, WR
85— Mike Hammerstein, DL

Brad Cochran, DB
86— Garland Rivers, DB
87— John Elliott, OL
88— John Vitale, C
    *Mark Messner, DL
89— *Tripp Welborne, DB
90— *Tripp Welborne, DB
91— *Desmond Howard, WR
    *Greg Skrepenak, OL

MICHIGAN ST.
15— Neno Jerry DaPrato, B
35— Sidney Wagner, G
49— Ed Bagdon, G
51— Bob Carey, E
    *Don Coleman, T
53— Don Dohoney, E
55— Norman Masters, T
    Earl Morrall, B
57— Dan Currie, C
    Walt Kowalczyk, B
58— Sam Williams, E
62— George Saimes, B
63— Sherman Lewis, B
65— Bubba Smith, DE
    *George Webster, DB
66— Clint Jones, B
    *Bubba Smith, DE
    *George Webster, DB
72— *Brad VanPelt, DB
85— *Lorenzo White, RB
87— Lorenzo White, RB
88— Tony Mandarich, OL
89— *Percy Snow, LB
    Bob Kula, OL

MINNESOTA
03— Fred Schacht, T
09— John McGovern, B
10— James Walker, T
16— Bert Baston, E
17— George Hauser, T
23— Ray Ecklund, E
26— Herb Joesting, B
27— Herb Joesting, B
29— Bronko Nagurski, T
31— Biggie Munn, G
34— Frank Larson, E
    Bill Bevan, G
    Pug Lund, B
35— Ed Widseth, T
36— *Ed Widseth, T
40— Urban Odson, T
    George Franck, B
41— Dick Wildung, T
    Bruce Smith, B
42— Dick Wildung, T
48— Leo Nomellini, T
49— Leo Nomellini, T
    *Clayton Tonnemaker, C
53— *Paul Giel, B
60— *Tom Brown, G
61— Sandy Stephens, B
62— *Bobby Bell, T
63— Carl Eller, T
65— Aaron Brown, DE

MISSISSIPPI
47— Charley Conerly, B
53— Crawford Mims, G
59— Charlie Flowers, B
60— *Jake Gibbs, B
62— Jim Dunaway, T
79— Jim Miller, P
92— Everett Lindsay, OL

MISSISSIPPI ST.
74— Jimmy Webb, DL

MISSOURI
41— Darold Jenkins, C
60— *Danny LaRose, E
65— Johnny Roland, DB
68— Roger Wehrli, DB
78— Kellen Winslow, TE
86— John Clay, OL

NAVY
07— Bill Dague, E
08— Percy Northcroft, T
    Ed Lange, T
11— Jack Dalton, B
13— John Brown, G
18— Lyman Perry, G
    Wolcott Roberts, B

22— Wendell Taylor, T
26— *Frank Wickhorst, T
28— Edward Burke, G
34— Fred Borries, B
43— Don Whitmire, T
44— *Don Whitmire, T
    Ben Chase, G
    Bob Jenkins, B
45— Dick Duden, E
54— Ron Beagle, E
55— *Ron Beagle, E
60— *Joe Bellino, B
63— *Roger Staubach, B
75— *Chet Moeller, DB
83— Napoleon McCallum, RB
85— Napoleon McCallum, RB

NEBRASKA
15— Guy Chamberlin, E
24— Ed Weir, T
25— *Ed Weir, T
33— George Sauer, B
36— Sam Francis, B
63— *Bob Brown, G
64— *Larry Kramer, T
65— Freeman White, E
    Walt Barnes, DT
66— LaVerne Allers, G
    Wayne Meylan, MG
67— Wayne Meylan, MG
70— Bob Newton, T
71— Johnny Rodgers, FL
    Willie Harper, DE
    Larry Jacobson, DT
72— *Johnny Rodgers, FL
    Willie Harper, DE
    *Rich Glover, MG
73— *John Dutton, DL
74— Marvin Crenshaw, OT
75— *Rik Bonness, C
76— Dave Butterfield, DB
78— Kelvin Clark, OT
79— *Junior Miller, TE
80— Randy Schleusener, OL
    Jarvis Redwine, RB
81— *Dave Rimington, C
82— *Dave Rimington, C
    Mike Rozier, RB
83— *Irving Fryar, WR
    Dean Steinkuhler, OL
    *Mike Rozier, RB
84— *Mark Traynowicz, C
86— Danny Noonan, DL
88— Jake Young, C
    *Broderick Thomas, LB
89— Jake Young, C
92— *Will Shields, OL
93— *Trev Alberts, LB

NEW MEXICO
89— Terance Mathis, WR

NEW YORK U.
28— Ken Strong, B

NORTH CARO.
37— Andy Bershak, E
48— Charlie Justice, B
70— Don McCauley, B
72— Ron Rusnak, G
74— Ken Huff, G
77— Dee Hardison, DL
80— *Lawrence Taylor, LB
83— William Fuller, DL

NORTH CARO. ST.
67— Dennis Byrd, DT
73— Bill Yoest, G
78— Jim Ritcher, C
    Ted Brown, RB
79— *Jim Ritcher, C .

NORTH TEXAS
68— Joe Greene, DT

NORTHERN ILL.
93— *LeShon Johnson, RB

NORTHWESTERN
26— Ralph Baker, B
30— Frank Baker, E
31— Jack Riley, T
    Dallas Marvil, T
    Pug Rentner, B
36— Steve Reid, G
40— Alf Bauman, T
45— Max Morris, E

59— Ron Burton, B
62— Jack Cvercko, G

NOTRE DAME
13— Gus Dorais, B
17— Frank Rydzewski, C
20— George Gipp, B
21— Eddie Anderson, E
24— Harry Stuhldreher, B
     Jimmy Crowley, B
     Elmer Layden, B
26— Bud Boeringer, C
27— John Smith, G
29— Jack Cannon, G
    *Frank Carideo, B
30— *Frank Carideo, B
     Marchy Schwartz, B
31— Tommy Yarr, C
     Marchy Schwartz, B
32— *Joe Kurth, T
34— Jack Robinson, C
35— Wayne Millner, E
37— Chuck Sweeney, E
38— *Ed Beinor, T
41— Bob Dove, E
42— Bob Dove, E
43— John Yonakor, E
     Jim White, T
     Pat Filley, G
     Angelo Bertelli, B
     Creighton Miller, B
46— George Connor, T
    *John Lujack, B
47— George Connor, T
     Bill Fischer, G
    *John Lujack, B
48— Leon Hart, E
     Bill Fischer, G
     Emil Sitko, B
49— *Leon Hart, E
    *Emil Sitko, B
     Bob Williams, B
50— Jerry Groom, C
52— *Johnny Lattner, B
53— Art Hunter, T
    *Johnny Lattner, B
54— *Ralph Guglielmi, B
55— Paul Hornung, B
57— Al Ecuyer, G
59— Monty Stickles, E
64— Jack Snow, E
     John Huarte, B
65— *Dick Arrington, G
     Nick Rassas, B
66— Tom Regner, G
    *Nick Eddy, B
     Alan Page, DE
    *Jim Lynch, LB
67— Tom Schoen, DB
68— George Kunz, T
     Terry Hanratty, QB
69— *Mike McCoy, DT
70— Tom Gatewood, E
     Larry DiNardo, G
71— *Walt Patulski, DE
     Clarence Ellis, DB
72— *Greg Marx, DT
73— Dave Casper, TE
     Mike Townsend, DB
74— Pete Demmerle, WR
     Gerry DiNardo, G
75— *Steve Niehaus, DT
76— Ken MacAfee, TE
    *Ross Browner, DE
77— *Ken MacAfee, TE
    *Ross Browner, DL
     Luther Bradley, DB
78— Dave Huffman, C
    *Bob Golic, LB
79— Vagas Ferguson, RB
80— *John Scully, C
     Bob Crable, LB
81— Bob Crable, LB
87— *Tim Brown, WR
88— Frank Stams, DL
     Michael Stonebreaker, LB
89— *Todd Lyght, DB
     Chris Zorich, DL
90— *Raghib Ismail, WR/RB
     Todd Lyght, DB
    *Michael Stonebreaker, LB
    *Chris Zorich, DL

91— Mirko Jurkovic, OL
92— Aaron Taylor, OL
93— *Aaron Taylor, OL
     Jeff Burris, DB

OHIO ST.
16— Charles Harley, B
17— Charles Bolen, E
     Charles Harley, B
19— Charles Harley, B
20— Iolas Huffman, G
     Gaylord Stinchcomb, B
21— Iolas Huffman, T
25— Ed Hess, G
28— Wes Fesler, E
29— Wes Fesler, E
30— *Wes Fesler, E
35— Gomer Jones, C
39— Esco Sarkkinen, E
44— Jack Dugger, E
     Bill Hackett, G
    *Les Horvath, B
45— *Warren Amling, G
46— Warren Amling, T
50— *Vic Janowicz, B
54— *Howard Cassady, B
55— *Howard Cassady, B
56— *Jim Parker, OL
58— Bob White, B
60— *Bob Ferguson, B
61— *Bob Ferguson, B
68— *Dave Foley, T
69— Jim Otis, B
     Jim Stillwagon, MG
     Jack Tatum, DB
70— *Jim Stillwagon, MG
    *Jack Tatum, DB
72— Randy Gradishar, LB
73— *John Hicks, OT
    *Randy Gradishar, LB
74— Kurt Schumacher, OT
     Steve Myers, C
    *Archie Griffin, RB
75— *Archie Griffin, RB
     Ted Smith, G
     Tim Fox, DB
76— Chris Ward, T
     Bob Brudzinski, DE
77— *Chris Ward, T
     Tom Cousineau, LB
78— Tom Cousineau, LB
79— Ken Fritz, G
82— Marcus Marek, LB
84— Jim Lachey, OG
    *Keith Byars, RB
86— Cris Carter, WR
     Chris Spielman, LB
87— *Chris Spielman, LB
    *Tom Tupa, P
93— Dan Wilkinson, DL

OKLAHOMA
38— Waddy Young, E
48— Buddy Burris, G
50— Jim Weatherall, T
     Leon Heath, B
51— *Jim Weatherall, T
52— Billy Vessels, B
53— J. D. Roberts, G
54— Max Boydston, E
     Kurt Burris, C
55— Bo Bolinger, G
56— *Jerry Tubbs, C
     Tommy McDonald, B
57— Bill Krisher, G
     Clendon Thomas, B
58— Bob Harrison, C
63— Jim Grisham, B
64— Ralph Neely, T
65— Carl McAdams, LB
67— *Granville Liggins, MG
69— *Steve Owens, B
71— *Greg Pruitt, B
     Tom Brahaney, C
72— *Greg Pruitt, B
     Tom Brahaney, C
73— *Lucious Selmon, DL
     Rod Shoate, LB
74— John Roush, G
    *Joe Washington, RB
    *Rod Shoate, LB
75— *Lee Roy Selmon, DT
     Dewey Selmon, MG

     Jimbo Elrod, DE
76— *Mike Vaughan, OT
77— *Zac Henderson, DB
78— *Greg Roberts, G
    *Billy Sims, RB
79— *Billy Sims, RB
    *George Cumby, LB
80— Louis Oubre, OL
81— Terry Crouch, OL
82— Rick Bryan, DL
83— *Rick Bryan, DL
84— Tony Casillas, DL
85— Tony Casillas, DL
    *Brian Bosworth, LB
86— *Keith Jackson, TE
    *Brian Bosworth, LB
87— *Keith Jackson, TE
    *Mark Hutson, OL
     Dante Jones, LB
     Rickey Dixon, DB
88— *Anthony Phillips, OL

OKLAHOMA ST.
45— Bob Fenimore, B
69— John Ward, T
76— Derrel Gofourth, C
77— *Terry Miller, RB
84— Rod Brown, DB
85— Thurman Thomas, RB
    *Leslie O'Neal, DL
88— Hart Lee Dykes, WR
    *Barry Sanders, RB

OREGON
62— Mel Renfro, B

OREGON ST.
56— John Witte, T
58— Ted Bates, T
62— *Terry Baker, B
63— Vern Burke, E
68— John Didion, C

PENN ST.
06— William Dunn, C
19— Bob Higgins, E
20— Charles Way, B
21— Glenn Killinger, B
23— Harry Wilson, B
59— Richie Lucas, B
64— Glenn Ressler, G
68— *Ted Kwalick, E
     Dennis Onkotz, LB
69— *Mike Reid, DT
     Dennis Onkotz, LB
70— Jack Ham, LB
71— Dave Joyner, T
72— Bruce Bannon, DE
     John Skorupan, LB
73— *John Cappelletti, B
74— Mike Hartenstine, DL
75— Greg Buttle, LB
78— *Keith Dorney, OT
    *Chuck Fusina, QB
    *Bruce Clark, DL
79— Bruce Clark, DL
81— *Sean Farrell, OL
86— D. J. Dozier, RB
     Shane Conlan, LB
92— O. J. McDuffie, WR

PENNSYLVANIA
91— John Adams, C
92— Harry Thayer, B
94— Charles Gelbert, E
     Arthur Knipe, B
     George Brooke, B
95— Charles Gelbert, E
     Charles Wharton, G
     Alfred Bull, C
     George Brooke, B
96— Charles Gelbert, E
     Charles Wharton, G
     Wylie Woodruff, G
97— John Outland, T
     T. Truxton Hare, G
     John Minds, B
98— T. Truxton Hare, G
     Pete Overfield, C
     John Outland, B
99— T. Truxton Hare, G
     Pete Overfield, C
     Josiah McCracken, B
00— T. Truxton Hare, G
04— Frank Piekarski, G

Vincent Stevenson, B
Andrew Smith, B
05— Otis Lamson, T
Robert Torrey, C
06— August Ziegler, G
William Hollenback, B
07— Dexter Draper, T
August Ziegler, G
08— Hunter Scarlett, E
William Hollenback, B
10— Ernest Cozens, C
E. LeRoy Mercer, B
12— E. LeRoy Mercer, B
17— Henry Miller, E
19— Henry Miller, E
22— John Thurman, T
24— Ed McGinley, T
27— Ed Hake, T
28— Paul Scull, B
43— Bob Odell, B
45— George Savitsky, T
47— Chuck Bednarik, C
48— Chuck Bednarik, C

PITTSBURGH
15— Robert Peck, C
16— James Herron, E
Robert Peck, C
17— Dale Seis, G
John Sutherland, G
18— Leonard Hilty, T
Tom Davies, B
George McLaren, B
20— Herb Stein, C
21— Herb Stein, C
25— Ralph Chase, T
27— *Gibby Welch, B
28— Mike Getto, T
29— *Joe Donchess, E
Ray Montgomery, G
31— Jesse Quatse, T
32— Joe Skladany, E
*Warren Heller, B
33— Joe Skladany, E
34— Chuck Hartwig, G
36— Averell Daniell, T
37— Tony Matisi, T
Marshall Goldberg, B
38— *Marshall Goldberg, B
56— *Joe Walton, E
58— John Guzik, G
60— *Mike Ditka, E
63— Paul Martha, B
76— *Tony Dorsett, RB
Al Romano, MG
77— Tom Brzoza, C
Randy Holloway, DL
Bob Jury, DB
78— Hugh Green, DL
79— *Hugh Green, DL
80— *Hugh Green, DL
*Mark May, OL
81— Sal Sunseri, LB
82— Jimbo Covert, OL
83— *Bill Fralic, OL
84— *Bill Fralic, OT
86— Randy Dixon, OL
Tony Woods, DL
87— Craig Heyward, RB
88— Mark Stepnoski, OL
90— Brian Greenfield, P

PRINCETON
89— Hector Cowan, T
William George, C
Edgar Allan Poe, B
Roscoe Channing, B
Knowlton Ames, B
90— Ralph Warren, E
Jesse Riggs, G
Sheppard Homans, B
91— Jesse Riggs, G
Philip King, B
Sheppard Homans, B
92— Arthur Wheeler, G
Philip King, B
93— Thomas Trenchard, E
Langdon Lea, T
Arthur Wheeler, G
Philip King, B
Franklin Morse, B
94— Langdon Lea, T
Arthur Wheeler, G

95— Langdon Lea, T
Dudley Riggs, G
96— William Church, T
Robert Gailey, C
Addison Kelly, B
John Baird, B
97— Garrett Cochran, E
Addison Kelly, B
98— Lew Palmer, E
Arthur Hillebrand, T
99— Arthur Hillebrand, T
Arthur Poe, E
Howard Reiter, B
01— Ralph Davis, E
02— John DeWitt, G
03— Howard Henry, E
John DeWitt, G
J. Dana Kafer, B
04— James Cooney, T
05— James McCormick, B
06— L. Casper Wister, E
James Cooney, T
Edward Dillon, B
07— L. Casper Wister, E
Edwin Harlan, B
James McCormick, B
08— Frederick Tibbott, B
10— Talbot Pendleton, B
11— Sanford White, E
Edward Hart, T
Joseph Duff, G
12— John Logan, G
13— Harold Ballin, T
14— Harold Ballin, T
16— Frank Hogg, G
18— Frank Murrey, B
20— Stan Keck, T
Donold Lourie, B
21— Stan Keck, G
22— C. Herbert Treat, T
25— Ed McMillan, C
35— John Weller, G
51— *Dick Kazmaier, B
52— Frank McPhee, E
65— Stas Maliszewski, G

PURDUE
29— Elmer Sleight, T
Ralph Welch, B
32— *Paul Moss, E
33— Duane Purvis, B
40— Dave Rankin, E
43— Alex Agase, G
52— Bernie Flowers, E
65— Bob Griese, QB
67— *Leroy Keyes, B
68— *Leroy Keyes, B
Chuck Kyle, MG
69— *Mike Phipps, QB
72— Otis Armstrong, B
Dave Butz, DT
80— *Dave Young, TE
*Mark Herrmann, QB
86— Rod Woodson, DB

RICE
46— Weldon Humble, G
49— James Williams, E
54— Dicky Maegle, B
58— Buddy Dial, E
76— Tommy Kramer, QB
91— Trevor Cobb, RB

RICHMOND
69— Walker Gillette, E
78— Jeff Nixon, DB

RUTGERS
17— Paul Robeson, E
18— Paul Robeson, E
61— Alex Kroll, C

SAN DIEGO ST.
92— *Marshall Faulk, RB
93— *Marshall Faulk, RB

SANTA CLARA
38— Alvord Wolff, T
39— John Schiechl, C

SOUTH CARO.
80— *George Rogers, RB
84— Del Wilkes, OG

SOUTHERN CAL
26— Mort Kaer, B
27— Jesse Hibbs, T

Morley Drury, B
30— Erny Pinckert, B
31— John Baker, G
Gus Shaver, B
32— *Ernie Smith, T
33— Aaron Rosenberg, G
*Cotton Warburton, B
39— *Harry Smith, G
43— Ralph Heywood, E
44— John Ferraro, T
47— Paul Cleary, E
52— Elmer Willhoite, G
Jim Sears, B
62— Hal Bedsole, E
65— *Mike Garrett, B
66— Ron Yary, T
Nate Shaw, DB
67— *Ron Yary, T
*O. J. Simpson, B
Tim Rossovich, DE
Adrian Young, LB
68— *O. J. Simpson, B
69— Jim Gunn, DE
70— Charlie Weaver, DE
72— *Charles Young, TE
73— Lynn Swann, WR
Booker Brown, OT
Richard Wood, LB
Artimus Parker, DB
74— *Anthony Davis, RB
Richard Wood, LB
75— *Ricky Bell, RB
76— *Ricky Bell, RB
Gary Jeter, DT
Dennis Thurman, DB
77— *Dennis Thurman, DB
78— *Pat Howell, G
*Charles White, RB
79— *Brad Budde, G
*Charles White, RB
80— Keith Van Horne, OL
*Ronnie Lott, DB
81— Roy Foster, OL
*Marcus Allen, RB
82— *Don Mosebar, OL
Bruce Matthews, OL
George Achica, MG
83— Tony Slaton, C
84— Jack Del Rio, LB
85— Jeff Bregel, OL
86— Jeff Bregel, OL
Tim McDonald, DB
87— Dave Cadigan, OL
89— *Mark Carrier, DB
Tim Ryan, DL
93— Johnnie Morton, WR

SOUTHERN METHODIST
35— J. C. Wetsel, G
Bobby Wilson, B
47— Doak Walker, B
48— *Doak Walker, B
49— Doak Walker, B
50— Kyle Rote, B
51— Dick Hightower, C
66— John LaGrone, MG
68— Jerry LeVias, E
72— Robert Popelka, DB
74— Louie Kelcher, G
78— Emanuel Tolbert, WR
80— John Simmons, DB
82— *Eric Dickerson, RB
83— *Russell Carter, DB
85— Reggie Dupard, RB

ST. MARY'S (CAL.)
27— Larry Bettencourt, C
45— *Herman Wedemeyer, B

STANFORD
24— Jim Lawson, E
25— Ernie Nevers, B
28— Seraphim Post, G
Don Robesky, G
32— Bill Corbus, G
33— Bill Corbus, G
34— Bob Reynolds, T
Bobby Grayson, B
35— James Moscrip, E
*Bobby Grayson, B
40— Frank Albert, B
41— Frank Albert, B
42— Chuck Taylor, G
50— Bill McColl, E

51— *Bill McColl, E
56— John Brodie, QB
70— Jim Plunkett, QB
71— Jeff Siemon, LB
74— Pat Donovan, DL
77— Guy Benjamin, QB
79— Ken Margerum, WR
80— *Ken Margerum, WR
82— *John Elway, QB
86— Brad Muster, RB
91— Bob Whitfield, OL

SYRACUSE
08— Frank Horr, T
15— Harold White, G
17— Alfred Cobb, T
18— Lou Usher, T
      Joe Alexander, G
19— Joe Alexander, G
23— Pete McRae, E
26— Vic Hanson, E
56— *Jim Brown, B
59— *Roger Davis, G
60— Ernie Davis, B
61— *Ernie Davis, B
67— *Larry Csonka, B
85— *Tim Green, DL
87— *Don McPherson, QB
      Ted Gregory, DL
90— John Flannery, C
92— *Chris Gedney, TE

TEMPLE
85— John Rienstra, OL
86— *Paul Palmer, RB

TENNESSEE
29— Gene McEver, B
33— Beattie Feathers, B
38— Bowden Wyatt, E
39— Ed Molinski, G
      George Cafego, B
40— *Bob Suffridge, G
46— Dick Huffman, T
51— *Hank Lauricella, B
52— John Michels, G
56— *John Majors, B
65— Frank Emanuel, LB
66— Paul Naumoff, LB
67— *Bob Johnson, C
68— *Charles Rosenfelder, G
      Steve Kiner, LB
69— Chip Kell, G
      *Steve Kiner, LB
70— *Chip Kell, G
71— *Bobby Majors, DB
75— Larry Seivers, E
76— Larry Seivers, SE
79— Roland James, DB
83— *Reggie White, DL
84— Bill Mayo, OG
85— Tim McGee, WR
89— *Eric Still, OL
90— *Antone Davis, OL
91— Dale Carter, DB

TEXAS
45— Hubert Bechtol, E
46— Hubert Bechtol, E
47— Bobby Layne, B
50— *Bud McFadin, G
53— Carlton Massey, E
61— *Jimmy Saxton, B
62— *Johnny Treadwell, G
63— *Scott Appleton, T
65— Tommy Nobis, LB
68— Chris Gilbert, B
69— Bob McKay, T
70— Bobby Wuensch, T
      Steve Worster, B
      Bill Atessis, DE
71— *Jerry Sisemore, T
72— *Jerry Sisemore, T
73— *Bill Wyman, C
      Roosevelt Leaks, B
75— Bob Simmons, T
77— *Earl Campbell, RB
      *Brad Shearer, DL
78— *Johnnie Johnson, DB
79— *Steve McMichael, DL
      *Johnnie Johnson, DB
80— Kenneth Sims, DL
81— Terry Tausch, OL
      *Kenneth Sims, DL

83— Doug Dawson, OL
      Jeff Leiding, LB
      Jerry Gray, DB
84— Tony Degrate, DL
      *Jerry Gray, DB

TEXAS A&M
37— Joe Routt, G
39— John Kimbrough, B
40— Marshall Robnett, G
      *John Kimbrough, B
57— *John David Crow, B
70— Dave Elmendorf, DB
74— Pat Thomas, DB
75— *Ed Simonini, LB
      Pat Thomas, DB
76— Tony Franklin, PK
      *Robert Jackson, LB
85— Johnny Holland, LB
87— John Roper, DL
90— Darren Lewis, RB
91— Kevin Smith, DB
92— *Marcus Buckley, LB
93— Aaron Glenn, DB
      Sam Adams, DL

TEXAS CHRISTIAN
35— Darrell Lester, C
36— Sammy Baugh, B
38— Ki Aldrich, C
      *Davey O'Brien, B
55— *Jim Swink, B
59— Don Floyd, T
60— *Bob Lilly, T
84— *Kenneth Davis, RB
91— Kelly Blackwell, TE

TEXAS TECH
60— E. J. Holub, C
65— Donny Anderson, B
77— Dan Irons, T
82— Gabriel Rivera, DL
91— *Mark Bounds, P

TOLEDO
71— Mel Long, DT

TULANE
31— *Jerry Dalrymple, E
32— Don Zimmerman, B
39— Harley McCollum, T
41— Ernie Blandin, T

TULSA
65— *Howard Twilley, E
91— Jerry Ostroski, OL

UCLA
46— *Burr Baldwin, E
52— Donn Moomaw, C
53— Paul Cameron, B
54— Jack Ellena, T
55— Hardiman Cureton, G
57— Dick Wallen, E
66— Mel Farr, B
67— *Gary Beban, B
      Don Manning, LB
69— Mike Ballou, LB
73— Kermit Johnson, B
75— John Sciarra, QB
76— Jerry Robinson, LB
77— *Jerry Robinson, LB
78— *Jerry Robinson, LB
      Kenny Easley, DB
79— *Kenny Easley, DB
80— *Kenny Easley, DB
81— *Tim Wrightman, TE
83— Don Rogers, DB
85— *John Lee, PK
88— Troy Aikman, QB
      Darryl Henley, DB
92— Carlton Gray, DB
93— *J. J. Stokes, WR
      Bjorn Merten, PK
      Jamir Miller, LB

UTAH ST.
61— Merlin Olsen, T
69— Phil Olsen, DE

VANDERBILT
23— Lynn Bomar, E
24— Henry Wakefield, E
32— Pete Gracey, C
58— George Deiderich, G
82— *Jim Arnold, P
84— *Ricky Anderson, P

VIRGINIA
15— Eugene Mayer, B
41— Bill Dudley, B
85— *Jim Dombrowski, OL
90— Herman Moore, WR
92— Chris Slade, DL
93— Mark Dixon, OL

VIRGINIA TECH
67— Frank Loria, DB
84— Bruce Smith, DL
93— *Jim Pyne, C

WAKE FOREST
76— *Bill Armstrong, DB

WASH. & JEFF.
14— John Spiegel, B
18— Wilbur Henry, T
19— Wilbur Henry, T

WASHINGTON
25— George Wilson, B
28— Charles Carroll, B
36— Max Starcevich, G
40— Rudy Mucha, C
41— Ray Frankowski, G
63— Rick Redman, G
64— Rick Redman, G
66— Tom Greenlee, DT
68— Al Worley, DB
82— *Chuck Nelson, PK
84— Ron Holmes, DL
86— Jeff Jaeger, PK
      Reggie Rogers, DL
91— *Steve Emtman, DL
      Mario Bailey, WR
92— *Lincoln Kennedy, OL

WASHINGTON ST.
84— Rueben Mayes, RB
88— Mike Utley, OL
89— *Jason Hanson, PK

WEST VA.
19— Ira Rodgers, B
55— Bruce Bosley, T
82— *Darryl Talley, LB
85— Brian Jozwiak, OL
92— Mike Compton, C

WILLIAMS
17— Ben Boynton, B
19— Ben Boynton, B

WISCONSIN
12— Robert Butler, T
13— Ray Keeler, G
15— Howard Buck, T
19— Charles Carpenter, C
20— Ralph Scott, T
23— Marty Below, T
30— Milo Lubratovich, T
42— *Dave Schreiner, E
54— *Alan Ameche, B
59— *Dan Lanphear, T
62— Pat Richter, E
75— Dennis Lick, T
81— Tim Krumrie, DL

WYOMING
83— Jack Weil, P
84— Jay Novacek, TE

YALE
89— Amos Alonzo Stagg, E
      Charles Gill, T
      Pudge Heffelfinger, G
90— William Rhodes, T
      Pudge Heffelfinger, G
      Thomas McClung, B
91— Frank Hinkey, E
      John Hartwell, E
      Wallace Winter, T
      Pudge Heffelfinger, G
      Thomas McClung, B
92— Frank Hinkey, E
      A. Hamilton Wallis, T
      Vance McCormick, B
93— Frank Hinkey, E
      William Hickok, G
      Frank Butterworth, B
94— Frank Hinkey, E
      William Hickok, G
      Philip Stillman, C
      George Adee, B
      Frank Butterworth, B
95— Fred Murphy, T

	Samuel Thorne, B
96—	Fred Murphy, T
	Clarence Fincke, B
97—	John Hall, E
	Burr Chamberlin, T
	Gordon Brown, G
	Charles DeSaulles, B
98—	Burr Chamberlin, T
	Gordon Brown, G
	Malcolm McBride, B
99—	George Stillman, T
	Gordon Brown, G
	Malcolm McBride, B
	Albert Sharpe, B
00—	George Stillman, T
	James Bloomer, T
	Gordon Brown, G
	Herman Olcott, C
	George Chadwick, B
	Perry Hale, B
	William Fincke, B
01—	Henry Holt, C
02—	Thomas Shevlin, E
	Ralph Kinney, T
	James Hogan, T
	Edgar Glass, G
	Henry Holt, C
	Foster Rockwell, B
	George Chadwick, B
03—	Charles Rafferty, E
	James Hogan, T
	James Bloomer, G
	W. Ledyard Mitchell, B
04—	Thomas Shevlin, E
	James Hogan, T
	Ralph Kinney, G
	Foster Rockwell, B
05—	Thomas Shevlin, E
	Roswell Tripp, G
	Howard Roome, B
	Guy Hutchinson, B
06—	Robert Forbes, E
	L. Horatio Biglow, T
	Hugh Knox, B
	Paul Veeder, B
07—	Clarence Alcott, E
	L. Horatio Biglow, T
	Thomas A. D. Jones, B
	Edward Coy, B
08—	William Goebel, G
	Hamlin Andrus, G
	Edward Coy, B
09—	John Kilpatrick, E
	Henry Hobbs, T
	Hamlin Andrus, G
	Carroll Cooney, C
	Edward Coy, B
	Stephen Philbin, B
10—	John Kilpatrick, E
11—	Douglass Bomeisler, E
	Henry Ketcham, C
	Arthur Howe, B
12—	Douglass Bomeisler, E
	Henry Ketcham, C
13—	Nelson Talbott, T
14—	Harry LeGore, B
16—	Clinton Black, G
20—	Tim Callahan, G
21—	Malcolm Aldrich, B
23—	Century Milstead, T
	William Mallory, B
24—	Dick Luman, E
27—	Bill Webster, G
	John Charlesworth, C
36—	Larry Kelley, E
37—	*Clint Frank, B
44—	Paul Walker, E

Team Leaders in Consensus All-Americans

(Ranked on Total Number of Selections)

Team	No.	Players
Yale	100	69
Notre Dame	92	76
Harvard	89	59
Michigan	65	53
Princeton	65	49
Southern Cal	58	51

Team	No.	Players
Ohio St.	54	39
Oklahoma	52	43
Pittsburgh	46	39
Pennsylvania	46	32
Nebraska	39	32
Army	37	28
Alabama	36	35
Texas	32	28
Minnesota	29	25
Tennessee	28	25
UCLA	27	23
Penn St.	26	24
Stanford	25	20
Miami (Fla.)	24	22
Michigan St.	24	21
Navy	23	20
Auburn	22	20
California	21	19
Georgia	21	17
Illinois	21	16
Colorado	19	15
Cornell	19	15
Syracuse	18	16
Texas A&M	18	16
Georgia Tech	17	16
Purdue	17	16
Arkansas	17	15
Dartmouth	17	15
Washington	16	15
Southern Methodist	16	14
Louisiana St.	16	12
Iowa	15	13
Florida St.	15	12
Clemson	14	13
Wisconsin	13	13
Arizona St.	12	9
Brigham Young	11	9
Chicago	11	9
Maryland	10	10
Northwestern	10	10
Florida	10	9
Oklahoma St.	9	9
Texas Christian	9	9
Baylor	9	7
North Caro.	8	8
Houston	7	7
Mississippi	7	7
Kentucky	7	5
Boston College	6	6
Brown	6	6
Missouri	6	6
Rice	6	6
Vanderbilt	6	6
Virginia	6	6
Carlisle	6	5
Colgate	6	5
Columbia	6	5
Indiana	6	5
Arizona	6	4
Air Force	5	5
Oregon St.	5	5
Texas Tech	5	5
West Va.	5	5
North Caro. St.	5	4

1993 First-Team All-America Teams

ASSOCIATED PRESS

Offense QB—Charlie Ward, Florida St.; RB—LeShon Johnson, Northern Ill.; RB—Marshall Faulk, San Diego St.; WR—J. J. Stokes, UCLA; WR—Johnnie Morton, Southern Cal; WR—Ryan Yarborough, Wyoming; OC—Jim Pyne, Virginia Tech; OG—Mark Dixon, Virginia; OG—Stacy Seegars, Clemson; OT—Aaron Taylor, Notre Dame; OT—Wayne Gandy, Auburn; AP*—David Palmer, Alabama; PK—Bjorn Merten, UCLA.

Defense DL—Rob Waldrop, Arizona; DL—Dan Wilkinson, Ohio St.; DL—Sam Adams, Texas A&M; DL—Kevin Patric, Miami (Fla.); LB—Trev Alberts, Nebraska; LB—Derrick Brooks, Florida St.; LB—Dana Howard, Illinois; DB—Antonio Langham, Alabama; DB—Aaron Glenn, Texas A&M; DB—Jeff Burris, Notre Dame; DB—Jaime Mendez, Kansas St.; P—Terry Daniel, Auburn.

*All-purpose.

FOOTBALL WRITERS ASSOCIATION OF AMERICA

Offense QB—Charlie Ward, Florida St.; RB—LeShon Johnson, Northern Ill.; RB—Marshall Faulk, San Diego St.; WR—J. J. Stokes, UCLA; WR—Johnnie Morton, Southern Cal; WR—Ryan Yarborough, Wyoming; OL—Aaron Taylor, Notre Dame; OL—Wayne Gandy, Auburn; OL—Marcus Spears, Northwestern St.; OL—Mark Dixon, Virginia; OL—Jim Pyne, Virginia Tech; KR—David Palmer, Alabama; PK—John Becksvoort, Tennessee.

Defense DL—Rob Waldrop, Arizona; DL—Dan Wilkinson, Ohio St.; DL—Derrick Alexander, Florida St.; DL—Shante Carver, Arizona St.; LB—Trev Alberts, Nebraska; LB—Derrick Brooks, Florida St.; LB—Barron Wortham, UTEP; DB—Antonio Langham, Alabama; DB—Aaron Glenn, Texas A&M; DB—Bobby Taylor, Notre Dame; DB—Bracey Walker, North Caro.; P—Terry Daniel, Auburn.

UNITED PRESS INTERNATIONAL

Offense QB—Charlie Ward, Florida St.; RB—LeShon Johnson, Northern Ill.; RB—Marshall Faulk, San Diego St.; WR—J. J. Stokes, UCLA; WR—David Palmer, Alabama; TE—Pete Mitchell, Boston College; OL—Rich Braham, West Va.; OL—Mark Dixon, Virginia; OL—Wayne Gandy, Auburn; OL—Jim Pyne, Virginia Tech; OL—Aaron Taylor, Notre Dame; PK—Judd Davis, Florida.

Defense DL—Sam Adams, Texas A&M; DL—Kevin Patric, Miami (Fla.); DL—Rob Waldrop, Arizona; DL—Dan Wilkinson, Ohio St.; LB—Trev Alberts, Nebraska; LB—Derrick Brooks, Florida St.; LB—Jamir Miller, UCLA; DB—Jeff Burris, Notre Dame; DB—Aaron Glenn, Texas A&M; DB—Antonio Langham, Alabama; DB—Corey Sawyer, Florida St.; P—Chris MacInnis, Air Force.

THE SPORTING NEWS

Offense QB—Charlie Ward, Florida St.; RB—LeShon Johnson, Northern Ill.; RB—Marshall Faulk, San Diego St.; WR—J. J. Stokes UCLA; WR—Johnnie Morton, Southern Cal; TE—Pete Mitchell, Boston College; OL—Aaron Taylor, Notre Dame; OL—Jim Pyne, Virginia Tech; OL—Mark Dixon, Virginia; OL—Stacy Seegars, Clemson; OL—Wayne Gandy, Auburn; KR—David Palmer, Alabama; K—Bjorn Merten, UCLA.

Defense DL—Rob Waldrop, Arizona; DL—Sam Adams, Texas A&M; DL—Dan Wilkinson, Ohio St.; DL—Shante Carver, Arizona St.; LB—Trev Alberts, Nebraska; LB—Derrick Brooks, Florida St.; LB—Jamir Miller, UCLA; DB—Antonio Langham, Alabama; DB—Aaron Glenn, Texas A&M; DB—Bobby Taylor, Notre Dame; DB—Corey Sawyer, Florida St.; P—Terry Daniel, Auburn.

WALTER CAMP

Offense QB—Charlie Ward, Florida St.; RB—LeShon Johnson, Northern Ill.; RB—Marshall Faulk, San Diego St.; WR—J. J. Stokes, UCLA; WR—David Palmer, Alabama; TE—Carlester Crumpler, East Caro.; OC—Jim Pyne, Virginia Tech; OG—Mark Dixon, Virginia; OG—Stacy Seegars, Clemson; OT—Korey Stringer, Ohio St.; OT—Aaron Taylor, Notre Dame; PK—Bjorn Merten, UCLA.

Defense DL—Sam Adams, Texas A&M; DL—Lou Benfatti, Penn St.; DL—Rob Waldrop, Arizona; DL—Dan Wilkinson, Ohio St.; LB—Trev Alberts, Nebraska; LB—Derrick Brooks, Florida St.; LB—Jamir Miller, UCLA; DB—Jeff Burris, Notre Dame; DB—Aaron Glenn, Texas A&M; DB—Antonio Langham, Alabama; DB—Corey Sawyer, Florida St.; P—Terry Daniel, Auburn.

AWARD WINNERS

KODAK
(American Football Coaches Association)

Offense QB—Charlie Ward, Florida St.; RB—LeShon Johnson, Northern Ill.; RB—Marshall Faulk, San Diego St.; WR—J. J. Stokes, UCLA; WR—Johnnie Morton, Southern Cal; WR—David Palmer, Alabama; OL—Rich Braham, West Va.; OL—Todd Steussie, California; OL—Korey Stringer, Ohio St.; OL—Aaron Taylor, Notre Dame; OL—Jim Pyne, Virginia Tech; PK—John Stewart, Southern Methodist.

Defense DL—Sam Adams, Texas A&M; DL—Trev Alberts, Nebraska; DL—Kevin Patric, Miami (Fla.); DL—Rob Waldrop, Arizona; DL—Bryant Young, Notre Dame; LB—Derrick Brooks, Florida St.; LB—Dana Howard, Illinois; DB—Aaron Glenn, Texas A&M; DB—Antonio Langham, Alabama; DB—Jaime Mendez, Kansas St.; DB—Bracey Walker, North Caro.; P—Terry Daniel, Auburn.

FOOTBALL NEWS

Offense QB—Charlie Ward, Florida St.; RB—LeShon Johnson, Northern Ill.; RB—Errict Rhett, Florida; WR—J. J. Stokes, UCLA; WR—Johnnie Morton, Southern Cal; OC—Jim Pyne, Virginia Tech; OG—Stacy Seegars, Clemson; OG—Mark Dixon, Virginia; OT—Aaron Taylor, Notre Dame; OT—Bernard Williams, Georgia; PK—Michael Proctor, Alabama.

Defense DL—Rob Waldrop, Arizona; DL—Dan Wilkinson, Ohio St.; DL—Sam Adams, Texas A&M; LB—Trev Alberts, Nebraska; LB—Derrick Brooks, Florida St.; LB—Jamir Miller, UCLA; LB—Dana Howard, Illinois; DB—Antonio Langham, Alabama; DB—Corey Sawyer, Florida St.; DB—Jeff Burris, Notre Dame; DB—Jamie Mendez, Kansas St.; P—Terry Daniel, Auburn.

Special Awards

HEISMAN MEMORIAL TROPHY

Originally presented in 1935 as the DAC Trophy by the Downtown Athletic Club of New York City to the best college player east of the Mississippi River. In 1936, players across the country were eligible and the award was renamed the Heisman Memorial Trophy to honor former college coach and DAC athletics director John W. Heisman. The award now goes to the outstanding college football player in the United States.

Year	Player, College, Position
1935	Jay Berwanger, Chicago, HB
1936	Larry Kelley, Yale, E
1937	Clint Frank, Yale, HB
1938	Davey O'Brien, Texas Christian, QB
1939	Nile Kinnick, Iowa, HB
1940	Tom Harmon, Michigan, HB
1941	Bruce Smith, Minnesota, HB
1942	Frank Sinkwich, Georgia, HB
1943	Angelo Bertelli, Notre Dame, QB
1944	Les Horvath, Ohio St., QB
1945	*Doc Blanchard, Army, FB
1946	Glenn Davis, Army, HB
1947	John Lujack, Notre Dame, QB
1948	*Doak Walker, Southern Methodist, HB
1949	Leon Hart, Notre Dame, E
1950	*Vic Janowicz, Ohio St., HB
1951	Dick Kazmaier, Princeton, HB
1952	Billy Vessels, Oklahoma, HB
1953	Johnny Lattner, Notre Dame, HB
1954	Alan Ameche, Wisconsin, FB
1955	Howard Cassady, Ohio St., HB
1956	Paul Hornung, Notre Dame, QB
1957	John David Crow, Texas A&M, HB
1958	Pete Dawkins, Army, HB
1959	Billy Cannon, Louisiana St., HB
1960	Joe Bellino, Navy, HB
1961	Ernie Davis, Syracuse, HB
1962	Terry Baker, Oregon St., QB
1963	*Roger Staubach, Navy, QB

Year	Player, College, Position
1964	John Huarte, Notre Dame, QB
1965	Mike Garrett, Southern Cal, HB
1966	Steve Spurrier, Florida, QB
1967	Gary Beban, UCLA, QB
1968	O. J. Simpson, Southern Cal, HB
1969	Steve Owens, Oklahoma, HB
1970	Jim Plunkett, Stanford, QB
1971	Pat Sullivan, Auburn, QB
1972	Johnny Rodgers, Nebraska, FL
1973	John Cappelletti, Penn St., HB
1974	*Archie Griffin, Ohio St., HB
1975	Archie Griffin, Ohio St., HB
1976	Tony Dorsett, Pittsburgh, HB
1977	Earl Campbell, Texas, HB
1978	*Billy Sims, Oklahoma, HB
1979	Charles White, Southern Cal, HB
1980	George Rogers, South Caro., HB
1981	Marcus Allen, Southern Cal, HB
1982	*Herschel Walker, Georgia, HB
1983	Mike Rozier, Nebraska, HB
1984	Doug Flutie, Boston College, QB
1985	Bo Jackson, Auburn, HB
1986	Vinny Testaverde, Miami (Fla.), QB
1987	Tim Brown, Notre Dame, WR
1988	*Barry Sanders, Oklahoma St., RB
1989	*Andre Ware, Houston, QB
1990	*Ty Detmer, Brigham Young, QB
1991	#Desmond Howard, Michigan, WR
1992	Gino Torretta, Miami (Fla.), QB
1993	Charlie Ward, Florida St., QB

*Juniors (all others seniors). #Had one year of eligibility remaining.

1993 HEISMAN VOTING

(Voting on a 3-2-1 basis)	1st	2nd	3rd	Total
1. Charlie Ward, QB, Florida St.	740	39	12	2,310
2. *Heath Shuler, QB, Tennessee	10	274	110	688
3. *David Palmer, WR, Alabama	16	78	88	292
4. *Marshall Faulk, RB, San Diego St.	7	74	81	250
5. Glenn Foley, QB, Boston College	5	47	71	180
6. LeShon Johnson, RB, Northern Ill.	5	51	59	176
7. *J. J. Stokes, WR, UCLA	3	37	48	131
8. *Tyrone Wheatley, RB, Michigan	2	31	32	100
9. *Trent Dilfer, QB, Fresno St.	2	28	29	91
10. *Eric Zeier, QB, Georgia	0	24	37	85

*Junior (all others seniors).

OUTLAND TROPHY

Honoring the outstanding interior lineman in the nation, first presented in 1946 by the Football Writers Association of America. The award is named for its benefactor, Dr. John H. Outland.

Year	Player, College, Position
1946	George Connor, Notre Dame, T
1947	Joe Steffy, Army, G
1948	Bill Fischer, Notre Dame, G
1949	Ed Bagdon, Michigan St., G
1950	Bob Gain, Kentucky, T
1951	Jim Weatherall, Oklahoma, T
1952	Dick Modzelewski, Maryland, T
1953	J. D. Roberts, Oklahoma, G
1954	Bill Brooks, Arkansas, G
1955	Calvin Jones, Iowa, G
1956	Jim Parker, Ohio St., G
1957	Alex Karras, Iowa, T
1958	Zeke Smith, Auburn, G
1959	Mike McGee, Duke, T
1960	Tom Brown, Minnesota, G
1961	Merlin Olsen, Utah St., T
1962	Bobby Bell, Minnesota, T
1963	Scott Appleton, Texas, T
1964	Steve DeLong, Tennessee, T
1965	Tommy Nobis, Texas, G
1966	Loyd Phillips, Arkansas, T

Year	Player, College, Position
1967	Ron Yary, Southern Cal, T
1968	Bill Stanfill, Georgia, T
1969	Mike Reid, Penn St., DT
1970	Jim Stillwagon, Ohio St., MG
1971	Larry Jacobson, Nebraska, DT
1972	Rich Glover, Nebraska, MG
1973	John Hicks, Ohio St., OT
1974	Randy White, Maryland, DE
1975	Lee Roy Selmon, Oklahoma, DT
1976	*Ross Browner, Notre Dame, DE
1977	Brad Shearer, Texas, DT
1978	Greg Roberts, Oklahoma, G
1979	Jim Ritcher, North Caro. St., C
1980	Mark May, Pittsburgh, OT
1981	*Dave Rimington, Nebraska, C
1982	Dave Rimington, Nebraska, C
1983	Dean Steinkuhler, Nebraska, G
1984	Bruce Smith, Virginia Tech, DT
1985	Mike Ruth, Boston College, NG
1986	Jason Buck, Brigham Young, DT
1987	Chad Hennings, Air Force, DT
1988	Tracy Rocker, Auburn, DT
1989	Mohammed Elewonibi, Brigham Young, G
1990	Russell Maryland, Miami (Fla.), DT
1991	*Steve Emtman, Washington, DT
1992	Will Shields, Nebraska, G
1993	Rob Waldrop, Arizona, NG

*Juniors (all others seniors).

VINCE LOMBARDI/ROTARY AWARD

Honoring the outstanding college lineman of the year, first presented in 1970 by the Rotary Club of Houston, Texas. The award is named after professional football coach Vince Lombardi, a member of the legendary "Seven Blocks of Granite" at Fordham in the 1930s.

Year	Player, College, Position
1970	Jim Stillwagon, Ohio St., MG
1971	Walt Patulski, Notre Dame, DE
1972	Rich Glover, Nebraska, MG
1973	John Hicks, Ohio St., OT
1974	Randy White, Maryland, DT
1975	Lee Roy Selmon, Oklahoma, DT
1976	Wilson Whitley, Houston, DT
1977	Ross Browner, Notre Dame, DE
1978	Bruce Clark, Penn St., DT
1979	Brad Budde, Southern Cal, G
1980	Hugh Green, Pittsburgh, DE
1981	Kenneth Sims, Texas, DT
1982	Dave Rimington, Nebraska, C
1983	Dean Steinkuhler, Nebraska, G
1984	Tony Degrate, Texas, DT
1985	Tony Casillas, Oklahoma, NG
1986	Cornelius Bennett, Alabama, LB
1987	Chris Spielman, Ohio St., LB
1988	Tracy Rocker, Auburn, DT
1989	Percy Snow, Michigan St., LB
1990	Chris Zorich, Notre Dame, NT
1991	Steve Emtman, Washington, DT
1992	Marvin Jones, Florida St., LB
1993	Aaron Taylor, Notre Dame, OT

MAXWELL AWARD

Honoring the nation's outstanding college football player, first presented in 1937 by the Maxwell Memorial Football Club of Philadelphia. The award is named after Robert "Tiny" Maxwell, a Philadelphia native who played at the University of Chicago as a lineman near the turn of the century.

Year	Player, College, Position
1937	Clint Frank, Yale, HB
1938	Davey O'Brien, Texas Christian, QB
1939	Nile Kinnick, Iowa, HB
1940	Tom Harmon, Michigan, HB
1941	Bill Dudley, Virginia, HB
1942	Paul Governali, Columbia, QB
1943	Bob Odell, Pennsylvania, HB
1944	Glenn Davis, Army, HB
1945	Doc Blanchard, Army, FB
1946	Charley Trippi, Georgia, HB
1947	Doak Walker, Southern Methodist, HB
1948	Chuck Bednarik, Pennsylvania, C
1949	Leon Hart, Notre Dame, E

Year	Player, College, Position
1950	Reds Bagnell, Pennsylvania, HB
1951	Dick Kazmaier, Princeton, HB
1952	Johnny Lattner, Notre Dame, HB
1953	Johnny Lattner, Notre Dame, HB
1954	Ron Beagle, Navy, E
1955	Howard Cassady, Ohio St., HB
1956	Tommy McDonald, Oklahoma, HB
1957	Bob Reifsnyder, Navy, T
1958	Pete Dawkins, Army, HB
1959	Rich Lucas, Penn St., QB
1960	Joe Bellino, Navy, HB
1961	Bob Ferguson, Ohio St., FB
1962	Terry Baker, Oregon St., QB
1963	Roger Staubach, Navy, QB
1964	Glenn Ressler, Penn St., C
1965	Tommy Nobis, Texas, LB
1966	Jim Lynch, Notre Dame, LB
1967	Gary Beban, UCLA, QB
1968	O. J. Simpson, Southern Cal, RB
1969	Mike Reid, Penn St., DT
1970	Jim Plunkett, Stanford, QB
1971	Ed Marinaro, Cornell, RB
1972	Brad VanPelt, Michigan St., DB
1973	John Cappelletti, Penn St., RB
1974	Steve Joachim, Temple, QB
1975	Archie Griffin, Ohio St., RB
1976	Tony Dorsett, Pittsburgh, RB
1977	Ross Browner, Notre Dame, DE
1978	Chuck Fusina, Penn St., QB
1979	Charles White, Southern Cal, RB
1980	Hugh Green, Pittsburgh, DE
1981	Marcus Allen, Southern Cal, RB
1982	Herschel Walker, Georgia, RB
1983	Mike Rozier, Nebraska, RB
1984	Doug Flutie, Boston College, QB
1985	Chuck Long, Iowa, QB
1986	Vinny Testaverde, Miami (Fla.), QB
1987	Don McPherson, Syracuse, QB
1988	Barry Sanders, Oklahoma St., RB
1989	Anthony Thompson, Indiana, RB
1990	Ty Detmer, Brigham Young, QB
1991	Desmond Howard, Michigan, WR
1992	Gino Torretta, Miami (Fla.), QB
1993	Charlie Ward, Florida St., QB

BUTKUS AWARD

First presented in 1985 to honor the nation's best collegiate linebacker by the Downtown Athletic Club of Orlando, Fla. The award is named after Dick Butkus, two-time consensus all-American at Illinois and six-time all-pro linebacker with the Chicago Bears.

Year	Player, College
1985	Brian Bosworth, Oklahoma
1986	Brian Bosworth, Oklahoma
1987	Paul McGowan, Florida St.
1988	Derrick Thomas, Alabama
1989	Percy Snow, Michigan St.
1990	Alfred Williams, Colorado
1991	Erick Anderson, Michigan
1992	Marvin Jones, Florida St.
1993	Trev Alberts, Nebraska

JIM THORPE AWARD

First presented in 1986 to honor the nation's best defensive back by the Jim Thorpe Athletic Club of Oklahoma City. The award is named after Jim Thorpe, Olympic champion, two-time consensus all-American halfback at Carlisle and professional football player.

Year	Player, College
1986	Thomas Everett, Baylor
1987	(tie) Bennie Blades, Miami (Fla.)
	Rickey Dixon, Oklahoma
1988	Deion Sanders, Florida St.
1989	Mark Carrier, Southern Cal
1990	Darryll Lewis, Arizona
1991	Terrell Buckley, Florida St.
1992	Deon Figures, Colorado
1993	Antonio Langham, Alabama

DAVEY O'BRIEN NATIONAL QUARTERBACK AWARD

First presented in 1977 as the O'Brien Memorial Trophy to the outstanding player in the Southwest. In 1981, the Davey O'Brien Educational and Charitable Trust of Fort Worth, Texas, renamed the award the Davey O'Brien National Quarterback Award, and it now honors the nation's best quarterback.

MEMORIAL TROPHY

Year	Player, College, Position
1977	Earl Campbell, Texas, RB
1978	Billy Sims, Oklahoma, RB
1979	Mike Singletary, Baylor, LB
1980	Mike Singletary, Baylor, LB

NATIONAL QB AWARD

Year	Player, College
1981	Jim McMahon, Brigham Young
1982	Todd Blackledge, Penn St.
1983	Steve Young, Brigham Young
1984	Doug Flutie, Boston College
1985	Chuck Long, Iowa
1986	Vinny Testaverde, Miami (Fla.)
1987	Don McPherson, Syracuse
1988	Troy Aikman, UCLA
1989	Andre Ware, Houston
1990	Ty Detmer, Brigham Young
1991	Ty Detmer, Brigham Young
1992	Gino Torretta, Miami (Fla.)
1993	Charlie Ward, Florida St.

DOAK WALKER NATIONAL RUNNING BACK AWARD

Presented for the first time in 1990 to honor the nation's best running back among Division I-A juniors or seniors who combine outstanding achievements on the field, in the classroom and in the community. Sponsored by the GTE/Southern Methodist Athletic Forum in Dallas, Texas, a $10,000 scholarship is donated to the recipient's university in his name. It is voted on by a 16-member panel of media and former college football standouts. The award is named after Doak Walker, Southern Methodist's three-time consensus all-American halfback and 1948 Heisman Trophy winner.

Year	Player, College
1990	Greg Lewis, Washington
1991	Trevor Cobb, Rice
1992	Garrison Hearst, Georgia
1993	Byron Morris, Texas Tech

LOU GROZA COLLEGIATE PLACE-KICKER AWARD

Presented for the first time in 1992 to honor the nation's top collegiate place-kicker. Sponsored by the Palm Beach County Sports Authority in conjunction with the Orange Bowl Committee. The award is named after NFL Hall of Fame kicker Lou Groza.

Year	Player, College
1992	Joe Allison, Memphis
1993	Judd Davis, Florida

WALTER PAYTON PLAYER OF THE YEAR AWARD

First presented in 1987 to honor the top Division I-AA football player by the Sports Network and voted on by Division I-AA sports information directors. The award is named after Walter Payton, former Jackson St. player and the National Football League's all-time leading rusher.

Year	Player, College, Position
1987	Kenny Gamble, Colgate, RB
1988	Dave Meggett, Towson St., RB
1989	John Friesz, Idaho, QB
1990	Walter Dean, Grambling, RB
1991	Jamie Martin, Weber St., QB
1992	Michael Payton, Marshall, QB
1993	Doug Nussmeier, Idaho, QB

ERNIE DAVIS AWARD

First presented in 1992 to honor a Division I-AA college football player who has overcome personal, athletic or academic adversity and performs in an exemplary manner. The annual award is presented by the American Sports Wire of Saugus, Calif., and is named after the late Ernie Davis, Syracuse halfback who won the Heisman Trophy in 1961.

Year	Player, College, Position
1992	Gilad Landau, Grambling, PK
1993	Jay Walker, Howard, QB

HARLON HILL TROPHY

First presented in 1986 to honor the best Division II player by Division II sports information directors. The award is named after Harlon Hill, former receiver at North Alabama and the National Football League's most valuable player for the Chicago Bears in 1955.

Year	Player, College, Position
1986	Jeff Bentrim, North Dak. St., QB
1987	Johnny Bailey, Tex. A&M-Kingsville, RB
1988	Johnny Bailey, Tex. A&M-Kingsville, RB
1989	Johnny Bailey, Tex. A&M-Kingsville, RB
1990	Chris Simdorn, North Dak. St., QB
1991	Ronnie West, Pittsburg St., WR
1992	Ronald Moore, Pittsburg St., RB
1993	Roger Graham, New Haven, RB

COLLEGE FOOTBALL HALL OF FAME

Established: In 1947, by the National Football Foundation and College Hall of Fame, Inc. The first class of enshrinees was inducted in 1951. **Eligibility:** A nominated player must be out of college at least 10 years and a first-team all-America selection during his career. Coaches must be retired three years. The voting is done by a 12-member panel made up of athletics directors, conference and bowl officials, and media representatives.

Class of 1994 (to be inducted at the National Football Foundation and College Hall of Fame awards dinner December 6 in New York, N.Y.): Players—LB Bob Babich, Miami, Ohio (1966-68); RB Tony Dorsett, Pittsburgh (1973-76); G Steve Eisenhauer, Navy (1952-53); SE Lawrence Elkins, Baylor (1962-64); B Pete Elliott, Michigan (1945-48); B Tucker Frederickson, Auburn (1962-64); LB Jerry Groom, Notre Dame (1948-50); QB-HB John Hadl, Kansas (1959-61); QB Gifford Nielsen, Brigham Young (1975-77); SE Ozzie Newsome, Alabama (1974-77); OT Marvin Powell, Southern Cal (1974-76); DT Randy White, Maryland (1972-74). Coaches—Vince Dooley, Georgia (1964-88); John Merritt, Jackson St. (1953-62) and Tennessee St. (1963-83).

Member players are listed with the final year they played in college, and member coaches are listed with their year of induction. (†) Indicates deceased members.

Hall Facts: Only two individuals are enshrined in the College Football Hall of Fame as both a player and a coach. Amos Alonzo Stagg was an all-American at Yale (1889) and was inducted as a coach in 1951. The other two-way inductee is Bobby Dodd, who played at Tennessee (1930) and was inducted as a coach in 1993.

PLAYERS

Player, College	Year
†Earl Abell, Colgate	1915
Alex Agase, Purdue/Illinois	1946
†Harry Agganis, Boston U.	1952
Frank Albert, Stanford	1941
†Ki Aldrich, Texas Christian	1938
†Malcolm Aldrich, Yale	1921
†Joe Alexander, Syracuse	1920
Lance Alworth, Arkansas	1961
†Alan Ameche, Wisconsin	1954
†Knowlton Ames, Princeton	1889
Warren Amling, Ohio St.	1946
Dick Anderson, Colorado	1967
Donny Anderson, Texas Tech	1966
†Hunk Anderson, Notre Dame	1921
Doug Atkins, Tennessee	1952
†Everett Bacon, Wesleyan	1912
Reds Bagnell, Pennsylvania	1950
†Hobey Baker, Princeton	1913
†John Baker, Southern Cal	1931
†Moon Baker, Northwestern	1926
Terry Baker, Oregon St.	1962
†Harold Ballin, Princeton	1914
†Bill Banker, Tulane	1929
Vince Banonis, Detroit Mercy	1941
†Stan Barnes, California	1921

Player, College	Year
†Charles Barrett, Cornell	1915
†Bert Baston, Minnesota	1916
†Cliff Battles, West Va. Wesleyan	1931
Sammy Baugh, Texas Christian	1936
Maxie Baughan, Georgia Tech	1959
†James Bausch, Kansas	1930
Ron Beagle, Navy	1955
Gary Beban, UCLA	1967
Hub Bechtol, Texas	1946
†John Beckett, Oregon	1916
Chuck Bednarik, Pennsylvania	1948
Forrest Behm, Nebraska	1940
Bobby Bell, Minnesota	1962
Joe Bellino, Navy	1960
†Marty Below, Wisconsin	1923
†Al Benbrook, Michigan	1910
†Charlie Berry, Lafayette	1924
Angelo Bertelli, Notre Dame	1943
Jay Berwanger, Chicago	1935
†Lawrence Bettencourt, St. Mary's (Cal.)	1927
Fred Biletnikoff, Florida St.	1964
Doc Blanchard, Army	1946
†Al Blozis, Georgetown	1942
Ed Bock, Iowa St.	1938
†Lynn Bomar, Vanderbilt	1924
†Douglass Bomeisler, Yale	1913
†Albie Booth, Yale	1931
†Fred Borries, Navy	1934
Bruce Bosely, West Va.	1955
Don Bosseler, Miami (Fla.)	1956
Vic Bottari, California	1938
†Ben Boynton, Williams	1920
†Charles Brewer, Harvard	1895
†Johnny Bright, Drake	1951
John Brodie, Stanford	1956
†George Brooke, Pennsylvania	1895
Bob Brown, Nebraska	1963
George Brown, Navy/San Diego St.	1947
†Gordon Brown, Yale	1900
†John Brown Jr., Navy	1913
†Johnny Mack Brown, Alabama	1925
Tay Brown, Southern Cal	1932
†Paul Bunker, Army	1902
Ron Burton, Northwestern	1959
Dick Butkus, Illinois	1964
†Robert Butler, Wisconsin	1912
George Cafego, Tennessee	1939
†Red Cagle, Southwestern La./Army	1929
†John Cain, Alabama	1932
Ed Cameron, Wash. & Lee	1924
†David Campbell, Harvard	1901
Earl Campbell, Texas	1977
†Jack Cannon, Notre Dame	1929
John Cappelletti, Penn St.	1973
†Frank Carideo, Notre Dame	1930
†Charles Carney, Illinois	1921
J. C. Caroline, Illinois	1954
Bill Carpenter, Army	1959
†Hunter Carpenter, Virginia Tech	1905
Charles Carroll, Washington	1928
†Edward Casey, Harvard	1919
Howard Cassady, Ohio St.	1955
†Guy Chamberlin, Nebraska	1915
Sam Chapman, California	1938
Bob Chappuis, Michigan	1947
†Paul Christman, Missouri	1940
†Dutch Clark, Colorado Col.	1929
Paul Cleary, Southern Cal	1947
†Zora Clevenger, Indiana	1903
Jack Cloud, William & Mary	1948
†Gary Cochran, Princeton	1897
†Josh Cody, Vanderbilt	1919
Don Coleman, Michigan St.	1951
Charlie Conerly, Mississippi	1947
George Connor, Holy Cross/Notre Dame	1947
†William Corbin, Yale	1888
William Corbus, Stanford	1933
†Hector Cowan, Princeton	1889
†Edward Coy, Yale	1909
†Fred Crawford, Duke	1933
John David Crow, Texas A&M	1957
†Jim Crowley, Notre Dame	1924
Larry Csonka, Syracuse	1967
Slade Cutter, Navy	1934

Player, College	Year
†Ziggie Czarobski, Notre Dame	1947
Carroll Dale, Virginia Tech	1959
†Gerald Dalrymple, Tulane	1931
†John Dalton, Navy	1911
†Charles Daly, Harvard/Army	1902
Averell Daniell, Pittsburgh	1936
†James Daniell, Ohio St.	1941
†Tom Davies, Pittsburgh	1921
†Ernie Davis, Syracuse	1961
Glenn Davis, Army	1946
Robert Davis, Georgia Tech	1947
Pete Dawkins, Army	1958
Steve DeLong, Tennessee	1964
Al DeRogatis, Duke	1948
†Paul DesJardien, Chicago	1914
†Aubrey Devine, Iowa	1921
†John DeWitt, Princeton	1903
Buddy Dial, Rice	1958
Mike Ditka, Pittsburgh	1960
Glenn Dobbs, Tulsa	1942
†Bobby Dodd, Tennessee	1930
Holland Donan, Princeton	1950
†Joseph Donchess, Pittsburgh	1929
†Nathan Dougherty, Tennessee	1909
Nick Drahos, Cornell	1940
†Paddy Driscoll, Northwestern	1917
†Morley Drury, Southern Cal	1927
Bill Dudley, Virginia	1941
Kenny Easley, UCLA	1980
†Walter Eckersall, Chicago	1906
†Turk Edwards, Washington St.	1931
†William Edwards, Princeton	1899
†Ray Eichenlaub, Notre Dame	1914
Bump Elliott, Michigan/Purdue	1947
Ray Evans, Kansas	1947
†Albert Exendine, Carlisle	1907
†Nello Falaschi, Santa Clara	1936
Tom Fears, Santa Clara/UCLA	1947
†Beattie Feathers, Tennessee	1933
Bob Fenimore, Oklahoma St.	1946
†Doc Fenton, Louisiana St.	1909
John Ferraro, Southern Cal	1944
†Wes Fesler, Ohio St.	1930
†Bill Fincher, Georgia Tech	1920
Bill Fischer, Notre Dame	1948
†Hamilton Fish, Harvard	1909
†Robert Fisher, Harvard	1911
†Allen Flowers, Georgia Tech	1920
Danny Fortmann, Colgate	1935
Sam Francis, Nebraska	1936
Ed Franco, Fordham	1937
†Clint Frank, Yale	1937
Rodney Franz, California	1949
†Benny Friedman, Michigan	1926
Roman Gabriel, North Caro. St.	1961
Bob Gain, Kentucky	1950
†Arnold Galiffa, Army	1949
Hugh Gallarneau, Stanford	1940
†Edgar Garbisch, Wash. & Jeff./Army	1924
Mike Garrett, Southern Cal	1965
†Charles Gelbert, Pennsylvania	1896
†Forest Geyer, Oklahoma	1915
Paul Giel, Minnesota	1953
Frank Gifford, Southern Cal	1951
†Walter Gilbert, Auburn	1936
Harry Gilmer, Alabama	1947
†George Gipp, Notre Dame	1920
†Chet Gladchuk, Boston College	1940
Bill Glass, Baylor	1956
Marshall Goldberg, Pittsburgh	1938
Gene Goodreault, Boston College	1940
†Walter Gordon, California	1918
†Paul Governali, Columbia	1942
Otto Graham, Northwestern	1943
†Red Grange, Illinois	1925
†Bobby Grayson, Stanford	1935
†Jack Green, Tulane/Army	1945
Joe Greene, North Texas	1968
Bob Griese, Purdue	1966
Archie Griffin, Ohio St.	1975
†Merle Gulick, Toledo/Hobart	1929
†Joe Guyon, Georgia Tech	1918
†Edwin Hale, Mississippi Col.	1921
L. Parker Hall, Mississippi	1938

Player, College	Year
Jack Ham, Penn St.	1970
Bob Hamilton, Stanford	1935
Tom Hamilton, Navy	1926
†Vic Hanson, Syracuse	1926
†Pat Harder, Wisconsin	1942
†Tack Hardwick, Harvard	1914
†T. Truxton Hare, Pennsylvania	1900
†Chick Harley, Ohio St.	1919
†Tom Harmon, Michigan	1940
†Howard Harpster, Carnegie Mellon	1928
†Edward Hart, Princeton	1911
Leon Hart, Notre Dame	1949
Bill Hartman, Georgia	1937
†Homer Hazel, Rutgers	1924
†Matt Hazeltine, California	1954
†Ed Healey, Dartmouth	1916
†Pudge Heffelfinger, Yale	1891
†Mel Hein, Washington St.	1930
†Don Heinrich, Washington	1952
Ted Hendricks, Miami (Fla.)	1968
†Wilbur Henry, Wash. & Jeff.	1919
†Clarence Herschberger, Chicago	1898
†Robert Herwig, California	1937
†Willie Heston, Michigan	1904
†Herman Hickman, Tennessee	1931
†William Hickok, Yale	1894
†Dan Hill, Duke	1938
†Art Hillebrand, Princeton	1899
†Frank Hinkey, Yale	1894
†Carl Hinkle, Vanderbilt	1937
Clarke Hinkle, Bucknell	1931
Elroy Hirsch, Wisconsin/Michigan	1943
†James Hitchcock, Auburn	1932
Frank Hoffmann, Notre Dame	1931
†James J. Hogan, Yale	1904
†Brud Holland, Cornell	1938
†Don Holleder, Army	1955
†Bill Hollenback, Pennsylvania	1908
Mike Holovak, Boston College	1942
E. J. Holub, Texas Tech	1960
Paul Hornung, Notre Dame	1956
Edwin Horrell, California	1924
Les Horvath, Ohio St.	1944
†Arthur Howe, Yale	1911
†Dixie Howell, Alabama	1934
†Cal Hubbard, Centenary	1926
†John Hubbard, Amherst	1906
†Pooley Hubert, Alabama	1925
Sam Huff, West Va.	1955
Weldon Humble, Rice	1946
†Joel Hunt, Texas A&M	1927
†Ellery Huntington, Colgate	1914
Don Hutson, Alabama	1934
†Jonas Ingram, Navy	1906
†Cecil Isbell, Purdue	1937
†Harvey Jablonsky, Army/Washington	1933
Vic Janowicz, Ohio St.	1951
†Darold Jenkins, Missouri	1941
†Jackie Jensen, California	1948
†Herbert Joesting, Minnesota	1927
Bob Johnson, Tennessee	1967
†Jimmie Johnson, Carlisle/Northwestern	1903
Ron Johnson, Michigan	1968
†Calvin Jones, Iowa	1955
†Gomer Jones, Ohio St.	1935
Lee Roy Jordan, Alabama	1962
†Frank Juhan, Sewanee	1910
Charlie Justice, North Caro.	1949
†Mort Kaer, Southern Cal	1926
Alex Karras, Iowa	1957
Ken Kavanaugh, Louisiana St.	1939
†Edgar Kaw, Cornell	1922
Dick Kazmaier, Princeton	1951
†Stan Keck, Princeton	1921
Larry Kelley, Yale	1936
†Wild Bill Kelly, Montana	1926
Doug Kenna, Army	1944
†George Kerr, Boston College	1941
†Henry Ketcham, Yale	1913
Leroy Keyes, Purdue	1968
†Glenn Killinger, Penn St.	1921
†John Kilpatrick, Yale	1910
John Kimbrough, Texas A&M	1940
†Frank Kinard, Mississippi	1937

Player, College	Year
†Phillip King, Princeton	1893
†Nile Kinnick, Iowa	1939
†Harry Kipke, Michigan	1923
†John Kitzmiller, Oregon	1930
†Barton Koch, Baylor	1931
†Walt Koppisch, Columbia	1924
Ron Kramer, Michigan	1956
Charlie Krueger, Texas A&M	1957
Malcolm Kutner, Texas	1941
Ted Kwalick, Penn St.	1968
†Steve Lach, Duke	1941
†Myles Lane, Dartmouth	1927
Johnny Lattner, Notre Dame	1953
Hank Lauricella, Tennessee	1952
†Lester Lautenschlaeger, Tulane	1925
†Elmer Layden, Notre Dame	1924
†Bobby Layne, Texas	1947
†Langdon Lea, Princeton	1895
Eddie LeBaron, Pacific (Cal.)	1949
†James Leech, Va. Military	1920
Darrell Lester, Texas Christian	1935
Bob Lilly, Texas Christian	1960
†Augie Lio, Georgetown	1940
Floyd Little, Syracuse	1966
†Gordon Locke, Iowa	1922
Don Lourie, Princeton	1921
Richie Lucas, Penn St.	1959
Sid Luckman, Columbia	1938
Johnny Lujack, Notre Dame	1947
Pug Lund, Minnesota	1934
Jim Lynch, Notre Dame	1966
Robert MacLeod, Dartmouth	1938
†Bart Macomber, Illinois	1915
Dicky Maegle, Rice	1954
†Ned Mahon, Harvard	1915
Johnny Majors, Tennessee	1956
†William Mallory, Yale	1923
Vaughn Mancha, Alabama	1947
†Gerald Mann, Southern Methodist	1927
Archie Manning, Mississippi	1970
Edgar Manske, Northwestern	1933
Ed Marinaro, Cornell	1971
Vic Markov, Washington	1937
†Bobby Marshall, Minnesota	1906
Ollie Matson, San Francisco	1952
Ray Matthews, Texas Christian	1927
†John Maulbetsch, Michigan	1914
†Pete Mauthe, Penn St.	1912
†Robert Maxwell, Chicago/Swarthmore	1906
George McAfee, Duke	1939
†Thomas McClung, Yale	1891
Bill McColl, Stanford	1951
†Jim McCormick, Princeton	1907
Tommy McDonald, Oklahoma	1956
†Jack McDowall, North Caro. St.	1927
Hugh McElhenny, Washington	1951
†Gene McEver, Tennessee	1931
†John McEwan, Army	1916
Banks McFadden, Clemson	1939
Bud McFadin, Texas	1950
Mike McGee, Duke	1959
†Edward McGinley, Pennsylvania	1924
†John McGovern, Minnesota	1910
Thurman McGraw, Colorado St.	1949
†Mike McKeever, Southern Cal	1960
†George McLaren, Pittsburgh	1918
†Dan McMillan, Southern Cal/California	1922
†Bo McMillin, Centre	1921
†Bob McWhorter, Georgia	1913
†LeRoy Mercer, Pennsylvania	1912
Don Meredith, Southern Methodist	1959
†Bert Metzger, Notre Dame	1930
†Wayne Meylan, Nebraska	1967
Lou Michaels, Kentucky	1957
Abe Mickal, Louisiana St.	1935
Creighton Miller, Notre Dame	1943
†Don Miller, Notre Dame	1924
†Eugene Miller, Penn St.	1913
†Fred Miller, Notre Dame	1928
†Rip Miller, Notre Dame	1924
†Wayne Millner, Notre Dame	1935
†Century Milstead, Wabash/Yale	1923
†John Minds, Pennsylvania	1897
Skip Minisi, Pennsylvania/Navy	1947

Player, College	Year
Dick Modzelewski, Maryland	1952
†Alex Moffat, Princeton	1883
†Ed Molinski, Tennessee	1940
Cliff Montgomery, Columbia	1933
Donn Moomaw, UCLA	1952
†William Morley, Columbia	1902
George Morris, Georgia Tech	1952
Larry Morris, Georgia Tech	1954
†Bill Morton, Dartmouth	1931
Craig Morton, California	1964
†Monk Moscrip, Stanford	1935
†Brick Muller, California	1922
†Bronko Nagurski, Minnesota	1929
†Ernie Nevers, Stanford	1925
†Marshall Newell, Harvard	1893
Harry Newman, Michigan	1932
Tommy Nobis, Texas	1965
Leo Nomellini, Minnesota	1949
†Andrew Oberlander, Dartmouth	1925
†Davey O'Brien, Texas Christian	1938
†Pat O'Dea, Wisconsin	1899
Bob Odell, Pennsylvania	1943
†Jack O'Hearn, Cornell	1915
Robin Olds, Army	1942
†Elmer Oliphant, Army/Purdue	1917
Merlin Olsen, Utah St.	1961
†Bennie Oosterbaan, Michigan	1927
Charles O'Rourke, Boston College	1940
†John Orsi, Colgate	1931
†Win Osgood, Cornell/Pennsylvania	1894
Bill Osmanski, Holy Cross	1938
†George Owen, Harvard	1922
Jim Owens, Oklahoma	1949
Steve Owens, Oklahoma	1969
Alan Page, Notre Dame	1966
Jack Pardee, Texas A&M	1956
Babe Parilli, Kentucky	1951
Ace Parker, Duke	1936
Jackie Parker, Mississippi St.	1953
Jim Parker, Ohio St.	1956
†Vince Pazzetti, Lehigh	1912
Chub Peabody, Harvard	1941
†Robert Peck, Pittsburgh	1916
†Stan Pennock, Harvard	1914
George Pfann, Cornell	1923
†H. D. Phillips, Sewanee	1904
Loyd Phillips, Arkansas	1966
Pete Pihos, Indiana	1946
†Erny Pinckert, Southern Cal	1931
John Pingel, Michigan St.	1938
Jim Plunkett, Stanford	1970
†Arthur Poe, Princeton	1899

Player, College	Year
†Fritz Pollard, Brown	1916
George Poole, Mississippi/North Caro./Army	1947
Merv Pregulman, Michigan	1943
†Eddie Price, Tulane	1949
†Peter Pund, Georgia Tech	1928
Garrard Ramsey, William & Mary	1942
†Claude Reeds, Oklahoma	1913
Mike Reid, Penn St.	1969
Steve Reid, Northwestern	1936
†William Reid, Harvard	1899
Mel Renfro, Oregon	1963
†Pug Rentner, Northwestern	1932
Bob Reynolds, Stanford	1935
†Bobby Reynolds, Nebraska	1952
Les Richter, California	1951
†Jack Riley, Northwestern	1931
†Charles Rinehart, Lafayette	1897
J. D. Roberts, Oklahoma	1953
†Ira Rodgers, West Va.	1919
†Edward Rogers, Carlisle/Minnesota	1903
Joe Romig, Colorado	1961
†Aaron Rosenberg, Southern Cal	1933
Kyle Rote, Southern Methodist	1950
†Joe Routt, Texas A&M	1937
†Red Salmon, Notre Dame	1903
George Sauer, Nebraska	1933
George Savitsky, Pennsylvania	1947
Gale Sayers, Kansas	1964
Jack Scarbath, Maryland	1952
†Hunter Scarlett, Pennsylvania	1908
Bob Schloredt, Washington	1960
†Wear Schoonover, Arkansas	1929
†Dave Schreiner, Wisconsin	1942
†Germany Schultz, Michigan	1908
†Dutch Schwab, Lafayette	1922
†Marchy Schwartz, Notre Dame	1931
†Paul Schwegler, Washington	1931
Clyde Scott, Navy/Arkansas	1948
Richard Scott, Navy	1947
Tom Scott, Virginia	1953
†Henry Seibels, Sewanee	1899
Ron Sellers, Florida St.	1968
Lee Roy Selmon, Oklahoma	1975
†Bill Shakespeare, Notre Dame	1935
†Murray Shelton, Cornell	1915
†Tom Shevlin, Yale	1905
†Bernie Shively, Illinois	1926
†Monk Simons, Tulane	1934
O. J. Simpson, Southern Cal	1968
Fred Sington, Alabama	1930
†Frank Sinkwich, Georgia	1942
†Emil Sitko, Notre Dame	1949

Notre Dame halfback Johnny Lattner won the 1953 Heisman Trophy and is a member of the College Football Hall of Fame.

Player, College	Year
†Joe Skladany, Pittsburgh	1933
†Duke Slater, Iowa	1921
†Bruce Smith, Minnesota	1941
Bubba Smith, Michigan St.	1966
†Clipper Smith, Notre Dame	1927
†Ernie Smith, Southern Cal	1932
Harry Smith, Southern Cal	1939
Jim Ray Smith, Baylor	1954
Riley Smith, Alabama	1935
†Vernon Smith, Georgia	1931
†Neil Snow, Michigan	1901
Al Sparlis, UCLA	1945
†Clarence Spears, Dartmouth	1915
W. D. Spears, Vanderbilt	1927
†William Sprackling, Brown	1911
†Bud Sprague, Army/Texas	1928
Steve Spurrier, Florida	1966
Harrison Stafford, Texas	1932
†Amos Alonzo Stagg, Yale	1889
†Max Starcevich, Washington	1936
Roger Staubach, Navy	1964
†Walter Steffen, Chicago	1908
Joe Steffy, Tennessee/Army	1947
†Herbert Stein, Pittsburgh	1921
Bob Steuber, Missouri	1943
†Mal Stevens, Yale	1923
†Vincent Stevenson, Pennsylvania	1905
Jim Stillwagon, Ohio St.	1970
†Pete Stinchcomb, Ohio St.	1920
Brock Strom, Air Force	1959
†Ken Strong, New York U.	1928
†George Strupper, Georgia Tech	1917
†Harry Stuhldreher, Notre Dame	1924
†Herb Sturhan, Yale	1926
†Joe Stydahar, West Va.	1935
†Bob Suffridge, Tennessee	1940
Steve Suhey, Penn St.	1947
Pat Sullivan, Auburn	1971
†Frank Sundstrom, Cornell	1923
Lynn Swann, Southern Cal	1973
†Clarence Swanson, Nebraska	1921
†Bill Swiacki, Columbia	1947
Jim Swink, Texas Christian	1956
George Taliaferro, Indiana	1948
Fran Tarkenton, Georgia	1960
John Tavener, Indiana	1944
†Chuck Taylor, Stanford	1942
Aurelius Thomas, Ohio St.	1957
†Joe Thompson, Pittsburgh	1907
†Samuel Thorne, Yale	1895
†Jim Thorpe, Carlisle	1912
†Ben Ticknor, Harvard	1930
†John Tigert, Vanderbilt	1904
Gaynell Tinsley, Louisiana St.	1936
Eric Tipton, Duke	1938
Clayton Tonnemaker, Minnesota	1949
†Bob Torrey, Pennsylvania	1905
†Brick Travis, Missouri	1920
Charley Trippi, Georgia	1946
†Edward Tryon, Colgate	1925
Bulldog Turner, Hardin-Simmons	1939
Howard Twilley, Tulsa	1965
†Joe Utay, Texas A&M	1907
†Norm Van Brocklin, Oregon	1948
†Dale Van Sickel, Florida	1929
†H. Van Surdam, Wesleyan	1905
†Dexter Very, Penn St.	1912
Billy Vessels, Oklahoma	1952
Ernie Vick, Michigan	1921
†Hube Wagner, Pittsburgh	1913
Doak Walker, Southern Methodist	1949
†Bill Wallace, Rice	1935
†Adam Walsh, Notre Dame	1924
†Cotton Warburton, Southern Cal	1934
Bob Ward, Maryland	1951
†William Warner, Cornell	1904
†Kenny Washington, UCLA	1939
†Jim Weatherall, Oklahoma	1951
George Webster, Michigan St.	1966
Herman Wedemeyer, St. Mary's (Cal.)	1947

Player, College	Year
†Harold Weekes, Columbia	1902
Art Weiner, North Caro.	1949
†Ed Weir, Nebraska	1925
†Gus Welch, Carlisle	1914
†John Weller, Princeton	1935
†Percy Wendell, Harvard	1912
†Belford West, Colgate	1919
†Bob Westfall, Michigan	1941
†Babe Weyand, Army	1915
†Buck Wharton, Pennsylvania	1896
†Arthur Wheeler, Princeton	1894
Byron White, Colorado	1938
†Don Whitmire, Navy/Alabama	1944
†Frank Wickhorst, Navy	1926
Ed Widseth, Minnesota	1936
†Dick Wildung, Minnesota	1942
Bob Williams, Notre Dame	1950
Froggie Williams, Rice	1949
Bill Willis, Ohio St.	1944
Bobby Wilson, Southern Methodist	1935
†George Wilson, Washington	1925
†Harry Wilson, Army/Penn St.	1926
Mike Wilson, Lafayette	1928
Albert Wistert, Michigan	1942
Alvin Wistert, Michigan	1949
†Whitey Wistert, Michigan	1933
†Alex Wojciechowicz, Fordham	1937
†Barry Wood, Harvard	1931
†Andy Wyant, Chicago	1894
†Bowden Wyatt, Tennessee	1938
†Clint Wyckoff, Cornell	1895
†Tommy Yarr, Notre Dame	1931
Ron Yary, Southern Cal	1967
†Lloyd Yoder, Carnegie Mellon	1926
†Buddy Young, Illinois	1946
†Harry Young, Wash. & Lee	1916
†Waddy Young, Oklahoma	1938
Jack Youngblood, Florida	1970
Gust Zarnas, Ohio St.	1937

COACHES

Coach	Year
†Joe Aillet	1989
†Bill Alexander	1951
†Ed Anderson	1971
†Ike Armstrong	1957
†Charlie Bachman	1978
Earl Banks	1992
†Harry Baujan	1990
†Matty Bell	1955
†Hugo Bezdek	1954
†Dana X. Bible	1951
†Bernie Bierman	1955
Bob Blackman	1987
†Earl (Red) Blaik	1965
Frank Broyles	1983
†Paul (Bear) Bryant	1986
†Charlie Caldwell	1961
†Walter Camp	1951
Len Casanova	1977
†Frank Cavanaugh	1954
†Dick Colman	1990
†Fritz Crisler	1954
†Duffy Daugherty	1984
Bob Devaney	1981
Dan Devine	1985
†Gil Dobie	1951
†Bobby Dodd	1993
†Michael Donohue	1951
†Gus Dorais	1954
†Bill Edwards	1986
†Rip Engle	1973
Don Faurot	1961
†Jake Gaither	1973
Sid Gillman	1989
†Ernest Godfrey	1972
Ray Graves	1990
†Andy Gustafson	1985
†Edward Hall	1951
†Jack Harding	1980

Coach	Year
†Richard Harlow	1954
†Harvey Harman	1981
†Jesse Harper	1971
†Percy Haughton	1951
†Woody Hayes	1983
†John W. Heisman	1954
†Robert Higgins	1954
†Babe Hollingbery	1979
Frank Howard	1989
†Bill Ingram	1973
†Morley Jennings	1973
†Biff Jones	1954
†Howard Jones	1951
†Tad Jones	1958
†Lloyd Jordan	1978
†Ralph (Shug) Jordan	1982
†Andy Kerr	1951
†Frank Leahy	1970
†George Little	1955
†Lou Little	1960
†Slip Madigan	1974
Dave Maurer	1991
Charlie McClendon	1986
Herb McCracken	1973
†Dan McGugin	1951
John McKay	1988
Allyn McKeen	1991
†Tuss McLaughry	1962
†Dutch Meyer	1956
†Jack Mollenkopf	1988
†Bernie Moore	1954
†Scrappy Moore	1980
†Ray Morrison	1954
†George Munger	1976
†Clarence (Biggie) Munn	1959
†Bill Murray	1974
†Frank Murray	1983
†Ed (Hooks) Mylin	1974
†Earle (Greasy) Neale	1967
†Jess Neely	1971
†David Nelson	1987
†Robert Neyland	1956
†Homer Norton	1971
†Frank (Buck) O'Neill	1951
†Bennie Owen	1951
Ara Parseghian	1980
†Doyt Perry	1988
†Jimmy Phelan	1973
Tommy Prothro	1991
John Ralston	1992
†E. N. Robinson	1955
†Knute Rockne	1951
†Dick Romney	1954
†Bill Roper	1951
Darrell Royal	1983
†George Sanford	1971
Glenn (Bo) Schembechler	1993
†Francis Schmidt	1971
†Ben Schwartzwalder	1982
†Clark Shaughnessy	1968
†Buck Shaw	1972
†Andy Smith	1951
†Carl Snavely	1965
†Amos Alonzo Stagg	1951
†Jock Sutherland	1951
†Jim Tatum	1984
†Frank Thomas	1951
†Thad Vann	1987
Johnny Vaught	1979
†Wallace Wade	1955
†Lynn (Pappy) Waldorf	1966
†Glenn (Pop) Warner	1951
†E. E. (Tad) Wieman	1956
†John Wilce	1954
†Bud Wilkinson	1969
†Henry Williams	1951
†George Woodruff	1963
Warren Woodson	1989
†Fielding (Hurry Up) Yost	1951
†Bob Zuppke	1951

First-Team All-Americans Below Division I-A

(Selected by The Associated Press and the American Football Coaches Association)

Selection of Associated Press Little All-America Teams began in 1934. Early AP selectors were not bound by NCAA membership classifications; therefore, 30 current Division I-A teams are included in this list.

The American Football Coaches Association began selecting all-America teams below Division I-A in 1967 for two College-Division classifications. Its College-Division I team includes NCAA Division II and National Association of Intercollegiate Athletics (NAIA) Division I players. The AFCA College-Division II team includes NCAA Division III and NAIA Division II players. The AFCA added a Division I-AA team in 1979; AP began selecting a Division I-AA team in 1982, and these players are included. In 1990, the Champion USA Division III team was added, selected by a panel of 25 sports information directors. In 1993, Football Gazette's team was added for Divisions II and III.

Nonmembers of the NCAA are included in this list, as are colleges that no longer play varsity football.

Players selected to a Division I-AA all-America team are indicated by (†). Current members of Division I-A are indicated by (*).

All-Americans are listed by college, year selected and position.

ABILENE CHRISTIAN (16)
48— V. T. Smith, B
51— Lester Wheeler, OT
52— Wallace Bullington, DB
65— Larry Cox, OT
69— Chip Bennett, LB
70— Jim Lindsey, QB
73— Wilbert Montgomery, RB
74— Chip Martin, DL
77— Chuck Sitton, DB
82— Grant Feasel, C
83— Mark Wilson, DB
84— Dan Remsberg, OT
87— Richard Van Druten, OT
89— John Layfield, OG
90— Dennis Brown, PK
91— Jay Jones, LB

ADAMS ST. (3)
79— Ronald Johnson, DB
84— Bill Stone, RB
87— Dave Humann, DB

AKRON* (9)
69— John Travis, OG
71— Michael Hatch, DB
76— Mark Van Horn, OG
       Steve Cockerham, LB
77— Steve Cockerham, LB
80— †Brad Reece, LB
81— †Brad Reece, LB
85— †Wayne Grant, DL
86— †Mike Clark, RB

ALABAMA A&M (3)
87— Howard Ballard, OL
88— Fred Garner, DB
89— Barry Wagner, WR

ALABAMA ST. (3)
90— †Eddie Robinson, LB

91— †Patrick Johnson, OL
       †Eddie Robinson, LB

ALBANY (N.Y.) (1)
92— Scott Turrin, OL

ALBANY ST. (GA.) (1)
72— Harold Little, DE

ALBION (8)
40— Walter Ptak, G
58— Tom Taylor, E
76— Steve Spencer, DL
86— Joe Felton, OG
       Mike Grant, DB
91— Hank Wineman, RB
93— Ron Dawson, OL
       Jeff Brooks, OL

ALBRIGHT (3)
36— Richard Riffle, B
37— Richard Riffle, B
75— Chris Simcic, OL

ALCORN ST. (12)
69— David Hadley, DB
70— Fred Carter, DT
71— Harry Gooden, LB
72— Alex Price, DT
73— Leonard Fairley, DB
74— Jerry Dismuke, OG
75— Lawrence Pillers, DE
76— Augusta Lee, RB
       Larry Warren, DT
79— †Leslie Frazier, DB
84— †Issiac Holt, DB
93— †Goree White, KR

ALFRED (7)
51— Ralph DiMicco, B
52— Ralph DiMicco, B
55— Charles Schultz, E
56— Charles Schultz, E
75— Joseph Van Cura, DE
82— Brian O'Neil, DB
92— Mark Obuszewski, DB

ALLEGHENY (11)
75— Charles Slater, OL
87— Mike Mates, OL
88— Mike Parker, DL
90— Jeff Filkovski, QB
       David LaCarte, DB
       John Marzca, C
91— Ron Bendekovic, OT
       Stanley Drayton, RB
       Tony Bifulco, DB
92— Ron Bendekovic, OT
       Stanley Drayton, RB

AMERICAN INT'L (10)
71— Bruce Laird, RB
80— Ed Cebula, C
82— Paul Thompson, DT
85— Keith Barry, OL
86— Jon Provost, OL
87— Jon Provost, OL
88— Greg Doherty, OL
89— Lamont Cato, DB
90— George Patterson, DL
91— Gabe Mokwuah, DL

AMHERST (3)
42— Adrian Hasse, E
72— Richard Murphy, QB
73— Fred Scott, FL

ANGELO ST. (12)
75— James Cross, DB
78— Jerry Aldridge, RB
       Kelvin Smith, LB
81— Clay Weishuhn, LB
82— Mike Elarms, WR
83— Mike Thomas, K
85— Henry Jackson, LB
86— Pierce Holt, DL
87— Pierce Holt, DL
88— Henry Alsbrooks, LB
92— Jimmy Morris, P
93— Anthony Hooper, DB

APPALACHIAN ST. (10)
48— John Caskey, E
63— Greg Van Orden, G
85— †Dino Hackett, LB
87— †Anthony Downs, DE
88— †Bjorn Nittmo, PK
89— †Derrick Graham, OL

†Keith Collins, DB
91— †Harold Alexander, P
92— †Avery Hall, DL
       †Harold Alexander, P

ARIZONA* (1)
41— Henry Stanton, E

ARKANSAS ST.* (17)
53— Richard Woit, B
64— Dan Summers, OG
65— Dan Summers, OG
68— Bill Bergey, LB
69— Dan Buckley, C
       Clovis Swinney, DT
70— Bill Phillips, OG
       Calvin Harrell, HB
71— Calvin Harrell, RB
       Dennis Meyer, DB
       Wayne Dorton, OG
73— Doug Lowrey, OG
84— †Carter Crawford, DL
85— †Carter Crawford, DL
86— †Randy Barnhill, OG
87— †Jim Wiseman, C
       †Charlie Fredrick, DT

ARKANSAS TECH (2)
58— Edward Meador, B
61— Powell McClellan, E

ASHLAND (8)
70— Len Pettigrew, LB
78— Keith Dare, DL
85— Jeff Penko, OL
86— Vince Mazza, PK
89— Douglas Powell, DB
90— Morris Furman, LB
91— Ron Greer, LB
93— Bill Royce, DL

AUGUSTANA (ILL.) (10)
72— Willie Van, DT
73— Robert Martin, OT
83— Kurt Kapischke, OL
84— Greg King, C
86— Lynn Thomsen, DL
87— Carlton Beasley, DL
88— John Bothe, OL
90— Barry Reade, PK
91— Mike Hesler, DB
92— George Annang, DL

AUGUSTANA (S.D.) (3)
60— John Simko, E
87— Tony Adkins, DL
88— Pete Jaros, DB

AUSTIN (9)
37— Wallace Johnson, C
79— Price Clifford, LB
80— Chris Luper, DB
81— Larry Shillings, QB
83— Ed Holt, DL
84— Jeff Timmons, PK
87— Otis Amy, WR
88— Otis Amy, WR
90— Jeff Cordell, DB

AUSTIN PEAY (8)
65— Tim Chilcutt, DB
66— John Ogles, FB
70— Harold Roberts, OE
77— Bob Bible, LB
78— Mike Betts, DB
80— Brett Williams, DE
82— Charlie Tucker, OL
92— †Richard Darden, DL

AZUSA PACIFIC (1)
86— Christian Okoye, RB

BAKER (3)
83— Chris Brown, LB
85— Kevin Alewine, RB
90— John Campbell, OL

BALDWIN-WALLACE (9)
50— Norbert Hecker, E
68— Bob Quackenbush, DT
78— Jeff Jenkins, OL
80— Dan Delfino, DE
82— Pete Primeau, DL
83— Steve Varga, K
89— Doug Halbert, DL
91— John Koz, QB
       Jim Clardy, LB

BALL ST.* (4)
67— Oscar Lubke, OT
68— Amos Van Pelt, HB
72— Douglas Bell, C
73— Terry Schmidt, DB

BATES (1)
81— Larry DiGammarino, WR

BEMIDJI ST. (1)
83— Bruce Ecklund, TE

BENEDICTINE (1)
36— Leo Deutsch, E

BETHANY (W. VA.) (2)
77— Scott Lanz, P
93— Brian Darden, PK

BETHEL (KAN.) (1)
80— David Morford, C

BETHUNE-COOKMAN (2)
75— Willie Lee, DE
81— Booker Reese, DE

BIRMINGHAM-SOUTHERN (1)
37— Walter Riddle, T

BISHOP (1)
81— Carlton Nelson, DL

BLOOMSBURG (7)
79— Mike Morucci, RB
82— Mike Blake, TE
83— Frank Sheptock, LB
84— Frank Sheptock, LB
85— Frank Sheptock, LB
      Tony Woods, DB
91— Eric Jonassen, OL

BOISE ST. (21)
72— Al Marshall, OE
73— Don Hutt, WR
74— Jim McMillan, QB
75— John Smith, FL
77— Chris Malmgren, DT
      Terry Hutt, WR
      Harold Cotton, OT
79— †Joe Aliotti, QB
      †Doug Scott, DT
80— †Randy Trautman, DT
81— †Randy Trautman, DT
      †Rick Woods, DB
82— †John Rade, DL
      †Carl Keever, LB
84— †Carl Keever, LB
85— †Marcus Koch, DL
87— †Tom DeWitz, OG
      †Pete Kwiatkowski, DT
90— †Erik Helgeson, DL
91— †Frank Robinson, DB
92— †Michael Dodd, PK

BOSTON U. (16)
67— Dick Farley, DB
68— Bruce Taylor, DB
69— Bruce Taylor, DB
79— †Mal Najarian, RB
      †Tom Pierzga, DL
81— †Bob Speight, OT
      †Gregg Drew, RB
82— †Mike Mastrogiacomo, OG
83— †Paul Lewis, RB
84— †Paul Lewis, RB
86— †Kevin Murphy, DT
87— †Mark Seals, DB
88— †Mark Seals, DB
89— †Daren Altieri, WR
93— †Chris Helon, DB
      †Andre Maksimov, C

BOWDOIN (1)
77— Steve McCabe, OL

BOWIE ST. (2)
80— Victor Jackson, CB
81— Marco Tongue, DB

BOWLING GREEN* (2)
59— Bob Zimpfer, T
82— †Andre Young, DL

BRADLEY (1)
38— Ted Panish, B

BRANDEIS (2)
54— William McKenna, E
56— James Stehlin, B

BRIDGEPORT (1)
72— Dennis Paldin, DB

BRIDGEWATER (VA.) (1)
75— C. J. DeWitt, SE

BRI'WATER (MASS.) (1)
92— Erik Arthur, DL

BROCKPORT ST. (2)
90— Ed Smart, TE
93— Steve Milne, PK

BUCKNELL (7)
51— George Young, DT
60— Paul Terhes, B
64— Tom Mitchell, OE
65— Tom Mitchell, OE
74— Larry Schoenberger, LB
80— Mike McDonald, OT
90— †Mike Augsberger, DB

BUENA VISTA (4)
72— Joe Kotval, OG
73— Joe Kotval, OG
76— Keith Kerkhoff, DL
87— Jim Higley, LB

BUFFALO (2)
84— Gerry Quinlivan, LB
87— Steve Wojciechowski, LB

BUFFALO ST. (1)
93— John Mattey, OL

BUTLER (1)
88— Steve Roberts, RB

CAL LUTHERAN (2)
72— Brian Kelley, LB
79— Mike Hagen, SE

CAL POLY SLO (13)
53— Stan Sheriff, C
58— Charles Gonzales, G
66— David Edmondson, C
72— Mike Amos, DB
73— Fred Stewart, OG
78— Louis Jackson, RB
80— Louis Jackson, RB
      Robbie Martin, FL
81— Charles Daum, OL
84— Nick Frost, DB
89— Robert Morris, DL
90— Pat Moore, DL
91— Doug O'Neill, P

CAL ST. CHICO (1)
87— Chris Verhulst, TE

CAL ST. HAYWARD (4)
75— Greg Blankenship, LB
84— Ed Lively, DT
86— Fred Williams, OL
93— Jeff Williamson, TE

CAL ST. NORTHRIDGE (5)
75— Mel Wilson, DB
82— Pat Hauser, OT
83— Pat Hauser, OT
87— Kip Dukes, DB
91— Don Goodman, OL

CAL ST. SACRAMENTO (4)
64— William Fuller, OT
91— Troy Mills, RB
      Jim Crouch, PK
92— Jon Kirksey, DL

CALIF. (PA.) (1)
83— Perry Kemp, WR

CANISIUS (2)
87— Tom Doctor, LB
88— Marty Hurley, DB

CAPITAL (3)
74— Greg Arnold, OG
80— John Phillips, DL
      Steve Wigton, C

CARLETON (1)
90— Jim Bradford, WR

CARNEGIE MELLON (4)
81— Ken Murawski, LB
85— Robert Butts, OL
91— Chuck Jackson, OT
93— Chad Wilson, LB

CARROLL (MONT.) (5)
76— Richard Dale, DB
79— Don Diggins, DL
87— Jeff Beaudry, DB
88— Paul Petrino, QB
89— Suitoa Keleti, OL

CARROLL (WIS.) (3)
74— Robert Helf, TE
90— Bill Nolan, P
93— Andy Ostrand, DB

CARSON-NEWMAN (6)
78— Tank Black, FL
80— Brad Payne, S
83— Dwight Wilson, OL
90— Robert Hardy, RB
92— Darryl Gooden, LB
93— Kendall James, KR

CASE RESERVE (4)
41— Mike Yurcheshen, E
52— Al Feeny, DE
84— Fred Manley, DE
85— Mark Raiff, OL

CATAWBA (5)
34— Charles Garland, T
35— Charles Garland, T
45— Carroll Bowen, B
72— David Taylor, OT
74— Mike McDonald, LB

CATHOLIC (1)
84— Chris McMahon, DB

CENTRAL ARK. (3)
80— Otis Chandler, MG
84— David Burnette, DT
91— David Henson, DL

CENTRAL CONN. ST. (4)
74— Mike Walton, C
84— Sal Cintorino, LB
88— Doug Magazu, DL
89— Doug Magazu, DL

CENTRAL FLA. (3)
87— Bernard Ford, WR
      Ed O'Brien, PK
93— †David Rhodes, WR

CENTRAL (IOWA) (10)
70— Vernon Den Herder, DT
74— Al Dorenkamp, LB
77— Donald Taylor, RB
84— Scott Froehle, DB
85— Rich Thomas, DL
88— Mike Stumberg, DL
89— Mike Estes, DL
      Kris Reis, LB
92— Bill Maulder, LB
93— Jeff Helle, OL

CENTRAL MICH.* (4)
42— Warren Schmakel, G
59— Walter Beach, B
62— Ralph Soffredine, G
74— Rick Newsome, DL

CENTRAL MO. ST. (5)
68— Jim Urczyk, OT
85— Steve Huff, PK
88— Jeff Wright, DL
92— Bart Woods, DL
93— Bart Woods, DL

CENTRAL OKLA. (2)
65— Jerome Bell, OE
78— Gary Smith, TE

CENTRAL ST. (OHIO) (8)
83— Mark Corbin, RB
84— Dave Dunham, OT
85— Mark Corbin, RB
86— Terry Morrow, RB
89— Kenneth Vines, OG
90— Eric Williams, OL
92— Marvin Coleman, DB
93— Marvin Coleman, DB

CENTRAL WASH. (4)
48— Robert Osgood, G
50— Jack Hawkins, G
88— Mike Estes, DL
91— Eric Lamphere, OL

CENTRE (6)
55— Gene Scott, B
84— Teel Bruner, DB
85— Teel Bruner, DB
86— Jeff Leonard, OL
88— John Gohmann, LB
89— Jeff Bezold, LB

CHADRON ST. (3)
74— Dennis Fitzgerald, DB

78— Rick Mastey, OL
90— David Jones, RB

CHICAGO (3)
91— Neal Cawi, DE
        Jeff Stolte, P
93— Frank Baker, FB

CITADEL (8)
82— Jim Ettari, DL
84— Jim Gabrish, OL
85— Jim Gabrish, OL
86— Scott Thompson, DT
88— †Carlos Avalos, OL
90— †DeRhon Robinson, OL
92— †Corey Cash, OL
        †Lester Smith, DB

CLARION (8)
78— Jeff Langhans, OL
80— Steve Scillitani, MG
        Gary McCauley, TE
81— Gary McCauley, TE
83— Elton Brown, RB
85— Chuck Duffy, OL
87— Lou Weiers, DL
93— Tim Brown, TE

CLARK ATLANTA (1)
79— Curtis Smith, OL

COAST GUARD (2)
90— Ron Davies, DB
91— Ron Davies, DB

COE (6)
74— Dan Schmidt, OG
76— Paul Wagner, OT
85— Mike Matzen, P
90— Richard Matthews, DB
93— Carey Bender, RB
        Craig Chmelicek, OL

COLGATE (7)
82— †Dave Wolf, LB
83— †Rich Erenberg, RB
84— †Tom Stenglein, WR
85— †Tom Stenglein, WR
86— †Kenny Gamble, RB
87— †Kenny Gamble, RB
        †Greg Manusky, LB

COL. OF EMPORIA (1)
51— William Chai, OG

COL. OF IDAHO (2)
53— Norman Hayes, T
54— R. C. Owens, E

COLORADO COL. (4)
72— Ed Smith, DE
73— Darryl Crawford, DB
82— Ray Bridges, DL
93— Todd Mays, DL

COLORADO MINES (5)
39— Lloyd Madden, B
41— Dick Moe, T
59— Vince Tesone, B
72— Roger Cirimotich, DB
86— Tim Baer, P

CONCORD (2)
86— Kevin Johnson, LB
92— Chris Hairston, RB

CONCORDIA-M'HEAD (3)
77— Barry Bennett, DT
90— Mike Gindorff, DT
        Shayne Lindsay, NG

CONNECTICUT (7)
45— Walter Trojanowski, B
73— Richard Foye, C
80— †Reggie Eccleston, WR
83— †John Dorsey, LB
88— †Glenn Antrum, WR
89— †Troy Ashley, LB
91— †Mark Didio, WR

CORNELL (3)
82— †Dan Suren, TE
86— †Tom McHale, DE
93— †Chris Zingo, LB

CORNELL COLLEGE (2)
82— John Ward, WR
92— Brent Sands, DB

CORTLAND ST. (5)
67— Rodney Verkey, DE
89— Jim Cook, OL

90— Chris Lafferty, OG
        Vinny Swanda, LB
91— Vinny Swanda, LB

CUMBERLAND (KY.) (3)
87— David Carmichael, DB
89— Ralph McWilliams, OL
93— Doug Binkley, DB

DAKOTA WESLEYAN (1)
45— Robert Kirkman, T

DARTMOUTH (2)
91— †Al Rosier, RB
92— †Dennis Durkin, PK

DAVIDSON (1)
34— John Mackorell, B

DAYTON (9)
36— Ralph Niehaus, T
78— Rick Chamberlin, LB
81— Chris Chaney, DB
84— David Kemp, LB
86— Gerry Meyer, OL
89— Mike Duvic, PK
90— Steve Harder, OL
91— Brian Olson, OG
92— Andy Pellegrino, OL

DEFIANCE (1)
93— Sammy Williams, WR

DELAWARE (29)
42— Hugh Bogovich, G
46— Tony Stalloni, T
54— Don Miller, B
63— Mike Brown, B
66— Herb Slattery, OT
69— John Favero, LB
70— Conway Hayman, OG
71— Gardy Kahoe, RB
72— Joe Carbone, DE
        Dennis Johnson, DT
73— Jeff Cannon, DT
74— Ed Clark, LB
        Ray Sweeney, OG
75— Sam Miller, DE
76— Robert Pietuszka, DB
78— Jeff Komlo, QB
79— †Herb Beck, OG
        †Scott Brunner, QB
80— †Gary Kuhlman, OT
81— †Gary Kuhlman, OL
82— †George Schmitt, DB
85— †Jeff Rosen, OL
86— †Darrell Booker, LB
87— †James Anderson, WR
88— †Mike Renna, DL
89— †Mike Renna, DL
91— †Warren McIntire, DB
92— †Matt Morrill, DL
93— †Matt Morrill, DL

DELAWARE ST. (4)
84— Gene Lake, RB
86— Joe Burton, DB
91— †Rod Milstead, OL
92— †LeRoy Thompson, DL

DELTA ST. (1)
67— Leland Hughes, OG

DENISON (5)
47— William Hart, E
48— William Wehr, C
75— Dennis Thome, DL
79— Clay Sampson, RB
86— Dan Holland, DL

DePAUW (1)
63— Richard Dean, C

DETROIT TECH (1)
39— Mike Kostiuk, T

DICKINSON (1)
92— Brian Ridgway, DL

DICKINSON ST. (3)
81— Tony Moore, DL
91— Shaughn White, DB
92— Rory Farstveet, OL

DOANE (1)
66— Fred Davis, OT

DRAKE (3)
72— Mike Samples, DT
82— Pat Dunsmore, TE
        Craig Wederquist, OT

DREXEL (2)
55— Vincent Vidas, T
56— Vincent Vidas, T

EAST CARO.* (1)
64— Bill Cline, HB

EAST CENTRAL (1)
84— Don Wilson, C

EAST STROUDSBURG (6)
65— Barry Roach, DB
75— William Stem, DB
79— Ronald Yakavonis, DL
83— Mike Reichenbach, LB
84— Andy Baranek, QB
91— Curtis Bunch, DB

EAST TENN. ST. (5)
53— Hal Morrison, E
68— Ron Overbay, DB
70— William Casey, DB
85— George Cimadevilla, P
86— George Cimadevilla, P

EAST TEX. ST. (17)
38— Darrell Tully, B
53— Bruno Ashley, G
58— Sam McCord, B
59— Sam McCord, B
68— Chad Brown, OT
70— William Lewis, C
72— Curtis Wester, OG
73— Autry Beamon, DB
84— Alan Veingrad, OG
88— Kim Morton, DL
90— Terry Bagsby, DL
91— Eric Turner, DB
        Dwayne Phorne, OL
92— Eric Turner, DB
        Pat Williams, DB
93— Fred Woods, LB
        Billy Watkins, PK

EASTERN ILL. (16)
72— Nate Anderson, RB
76— Ted Petersen, C
78— James Warring, WR
79— Chris Cobb, RB
        Pete Catan, DE
80— Pete Catan, DE
81— †Kevin Grey, DB
82— †Robert Williams, DB
        †Bob Norris, OG
83— †Robert Williams, DB
        †Chris Nicholson, DT
84— †Jerry Wright, WR
86— †Roy Banks, WR
88— †John Jurkovic, DL
89— †John Jurkovic, DL
90— †Tim Lance, DB

EASTERN KY. (23)
69— Teddy Taylor, MG
74— Everett Talbert, RB
75— Junior Hardin, MG
76— Roosevelt Kelly, OL
79— †Bob McIntyre, LB
80— †George Floyd, DB
81— †George Floyd, DB
        †Kevin Greve, OG
82— †Steve Bird, WR
83— †Chris Sullivan, OL
84— †Chris Sullivan, C
85— †Joe Spadafino, OL
86— †Fred Harvey, LB
87— †Aaron Jones, DL
88— †Elroy Harris, RB
        †Jessie Small, DL
89— †Al Jacevicius, OL
90— †Kelly Blount, LB
        †Al Jacevicius, OL
91— †Carl Satterly, OL
        †Ernest Thompson, DL
92— †Markus Thomas, RB
93— †Chad Bratzke, DL

EASTERN MICH.* (5)
68— John Schmidt, C
69— Robert Lints, MG
70— Dave Pureifory, DT
71— Dave Pureifory, DT
73— Jim Pietrzak, OT

EASTERN N. MEX. (5)
81— Brad Beck, RB
83— Kevin Kott, QB

87— Earl Jones, OL
89— Murray Garrett, DL
90— Anthony Pertile, DB

EASTERN WASH. (7)
57— Richard Huston, C
65— Mel Stanton, HB
73— Scott Garske, TE
81— John Tighe, OL
86— Ed Simmons, OT
87— †Eric Stein, P
91— †Kevin Sargent, OL

EDINBORO (4)
82— Rick Ruszkiewicz, K
89— Elbert Cole, RB
90— Ernest Priester, WR
93— Mike Kegarise, OL

ELMHURST (1)
82— Lindsay Barich, OL

ELON (9)
50— Sal Gero, T
68— Richard McGeorge, OE
69— Richard McGeorge, OE
73— Glenn Ellis, DT
76— Ricky Locklear, DT
       Dan Bass, OL
77— Dan Bass, OL
80— Bobby Hedrick, RB
86— Ricky Sigmon, OL

EMORY & HENRY (14)
50— Robert Miller, B
51— Robert Miller, B
56— William Earp, C
68— Sonny Wade, B
85— Keith Furr, DB
       Rob McMillen, DL
86— Sandy Rogers, RB
87— Gary Collier, QB
88— Steve Bowman, DL
89— Doug Reavis, DB
90— Billy Salyers, OL
91— Jason Grooms, DL
92— Pat Buchanan, OL
       Scott Pruner, DL

EMPORIA ST. (5)
35— James Fraley, B
37— Harry Klein, E
68— Bruce Cerone, OE
69— Bruce Cerone, OE
91— Quincy Tillmon, RB

EVANSVILLE (2)
46— Robert Hawkins, T
93— †Hanz Hoag, TE

FAIRMONT ST. (3)
67— Dave Williams, DT
84— Ed Coleman, WR
88— Lou Mabin, DB

FAYETTEVILLE ST. (1)
90— Terrence Smith, LB

FDU-MADISON (4)
84— Ira Epstein, DL
86— Eric Brey, DB
87— Frank Illidge, DL
93— Vic Moncato, P

FERRIS ST. (3)
76— Charles Evans, RB
92— Monty Brown, LB
93— Ed Phillion, DL

FERRUM (5)
87— Dave Harper, LB
88— Dave Harper, LB
89— Chris Warren, RB
90— Melvin Dillard, DB/KR
91— John Sheets, OG

FINDLAY (4)
65— Allen Smith, HB
80— Nelson Bolden, FB
85— Dana Wright, RB
90— Tim Russ, OL

FLORIDA A&M (12)
61— Curtis Miranda, C
62— Robert Paremore, B
67— Major Hazelton, DB
       John Eason, OE
73— Henry Lawrence, OT
75— Frank Poole, LB
77— Tyrone McGriff, OG

78— Tyrone McGriff, OG
79— †Tyrone McGriff, OG
       †Kiser Lewis, C
80— †Gifford Ramsey, DB
83— †Ray Alexander, WR

FLORIDA ST.* (1)
51— William Dawkins, OG

FORT LEWIS (3)
89— Eric Fadness, P
92— Johnny Cox, WR
93— Johnny Cox, AP

FORT VALLEY ST. (6)
74— Fred Harris, OT
80— Willie Canady, DB
81— Willie Canady, DB
83— Tugwan Taylor, DB
92— Joseph Best, DB
93— Joseph Best, DB

FRANK. & MARSH. (8)
35— Woodrow Sponaugle, C
38— Sam Roeder, B
40— Alex Schibanoff, T
47— William Iannicelli, E
50— Charles Cope, C
81— Vin Carioscia, OL
82— Vin Carioscia, OL
89— Dale Amos, WR

FRANKLIN (1)
82— Joe Chester, WR

FRESNO ST.* (5)
39— Jack Mulkey, E
40— Jack Mulkey, E
60— Douglas Brown, G
68— Tom McCall, LB
       Erv Hunt, DB

FROSTBURG ST. (8)
80— Terry Beamer, LB
82— Steve Forsythe, WR
83— Kevin Walsh, DL
85— Bill Bagley, WR
86— Marcus Wooley, LB
88— Ken Boyd, DB
89— Ken Boyd, DB
93— Russell Williams, DB

FURMAN (10)
82— †Ernest Gibson, DB
83— †Ernest Gibson, DB
84— †Rock Hurst, LB
85— †Gene Reeder, C
88— †Jeff Blankenship, LB
89— †Kelly Fletcher, DL
90— †Steve Duggan, C
       †Kevin Kendrick, DL
91— †Eric Walter, OL
92— †Kota Suttle, LB

GA. SOUTHERN (16)
85— †Vance Pike, OL
       †Tim Foley, PK
86— †Fred Stokes, OT
       †Tracy Ham, QB
87— †Flint Matthews, LB
       †Dennis Franklin, C
       †Tim Foley, PK
88— †Dennis Franklin, C
       †Darren Alford, DL
89— †Joe Ross, RB
       †Giff Smith, DL
90— †Giff Smith, DL
91— †Rodney Oglesby, DB
92— †Alex Mash, DL
93— †Alex Mash, DL
       †Franklin Stephens, OL

GA. SOUTHWESTERN (2)
85— Roger Glover, LB
86— Roger Glover, LB

GALLAUDET (1)
87— Shannon Simon, OL

GARDNER-WEBB (4)
73— Richard Grissom, LB
87— Jeff Parker, PK
92— Rodney Robinson, WR
93— Gabe Wilkins, DL

GEORGETOWN (3)
73— Robert Morris, DE
74— Robert Morris, DE
91— Chris Murphy, DE

GEORGETOWN (KY.) (8)
74— Charles Pierson, DL
78— John Martinelli, OL
85— Rob McCrary, RB
87— Chris Reed, C
88— Chris Reed, OL
89— Steve Blankenbaker, DL
91— Chris Hogan, DL
92— Chris Hogan, DL

GETTYSBURG (4)
66— Joseph Egresitz, DE
83— Ray Condren, RB
84— Ray Condren, RB
85— Brian Barr, DB

GLENVILLE ST. (4)
73— Scotty Hamilton, DB
83— Byron Brooks, RB
84— Mike Payne, DB
93— Chris George, WR

GONZAGA (2)
34— Ike Peterson, B
39— Tony Canadeo, B

GRAMBLING (27)
62— Junious Buchanan, T
64— Alphonse Dotson, OT
65— Willie Young, OG
       Frank Cornish, DT
69— Billy Manning, C
70— Richard Harris, DE
       Charles Roundtree, DT
71— Solomon Freelon, OG
       John Mendenhall, DE
72— Steve Dennis, DB
       Gary Johnson, DT
73— Gary Johnson, DT
       Willie Bryant, DB
74— Gary Johnson, DT
75— Sammie White, WR
       James Hunter, DB
79— †Joe Gordon, DT
       †Aldrich Allen, LB
       †Robert Salters, DB
80— †Trumaine Johnson, WR
       †Mike Barker, DT
81— †Andre Robinson, LB
82— †Trumaine Johnson, WR
83— †Robert Smith, DL
85— †James Harris, LB
90— †Walter Dean, RB
       †Jake Reed, WR

GRAND VALLEY ST. (3)
79— Ronald Essink, OL
89— Todd Tracey, DL
91— Chris Tiede, C

GROVE CITY (1)
87— Doug Hart, PK

GUILFORD (2)
75— Steve Musulin, OT
91— Rodney Alexander, DE

GUST. ADOLPHUS (7)
37— Wendell Butcher, B
50— Calvin Roberts, T
51— Haldo Norman, OE
52— Calvin Roberts, DT
54— Gene Nei, G
67— Richard Jaeger, LB
84— Kurt Ploeger, DL

HAMILTON (2)
86— Joe Gilbert, OL
91— Eric Grey, RB

HAMLINE (4)
55— Dick Donlin, E
84— Kevin Graslewicz, WR
85— Ed Hitchcock, OL
89— Jon Voss, TE

HAMPDEN-SYDNEY (8)
48— Lynn Chewning, B
54— Stokeley Fulton, C
72— Michael Leidy, LB
74— Ed Kelley, DE
75— Ed Kelley, DE
77— Robert Wilson, OL
78— Tim Smith, DL
86— Jimmy Hondroulis, PK

HAMPTON (3)
84— Ike Readon, MG

85— Ike Readon, DL
93— Emerson Martin, OL

HANOVER (2)
86— Jon Pinnick, QB
88— Mike Luker, WR

HARDIN-SIMMONS (5)
37— Burns McKinney, B
39— Clyde Turner, C
40— Owen Goodnight, B
42— Rudy Mobley, B
46— Rudy Mobley, B

HARDING (2)
74— Barney Crawford, DL
91— Pat Gill, LB

HARVARD (2)
82— †Mike Corbat, OL
84— †Roger Caron, OL

HASTINGS (1)
84— Dennis Sullivan, OL

HAWAII* (2)
41— Nolle Smith, B
68— Tim Buchanan, LB

HENDERSON ST. (2)
90— Todd Jones, OL
93— Chris Carter, P

HILLSDALE (9)
49— William Young, B
55— Nate Clark, B
56— Nate Clark, B
75— Mark Law, OG
81— Mike Broome, OG
82— Ron Gladnick, DE
86— Al Huge, DL
87— Al Huge, DL
88— Rodney Patterson, LB

HOBART (4)
72— Don Aleksiewicz, RB
75— Rich Kowalski, RB
86— Brian Verdon, DB
93— Bill Palmer, DB

HOFSTRA (4)
83— Chuck Choinski, DL
86— Tom Salamone, P
88— Tom Salamone, DB
90— George Tischler, LB

HOLY CROSS (13)
83— †Bruce Kozerski, OT
     †Steve Raquet, DL
84— †Bill McGovern, DB
     †Kevin Garvey, OG
85— †Gill Fenerty, RB
86— †Gordie Lockbaum, RB-DB
87— †Jeff Wiley, QB
     †Gordie Lockbaum, WR-SP
88— †Dennis Golden, OL
89— †Dave Murphy, DB
90— †Craig Callahan, LB
91— †Jerome Fuller, RB
93— †Rob Milanette, LB

HOPE (2)
79— Craig Groendyk, OL
82— Kurt Brinks, C

HOWARD (2)
75— Ben Harris, DL
87— †Harvey Reed, RB

HOWARD PAYNE (4)
61— Ray Jacobs, T
72— Robert Woods, LB
73— Robert Woods, LB
92— Scott Lichner, QB

HUMBOLDT ST. (5)
61— Drew Roberts, E
62— Drew Roberts, E
76— Michael Gooing, OL
82— David Rush, MG
83— Dean Diaz, DB

HURON (1)
76— John Aldridge, OL

IDAHO (11)
83— †Ken Hobart, QB
85— †Eric Yarber, WR
88— †John Friesz, QB
89— †John Friesz, QB
     †Lee Allen, WR
90— †Kasey Dunn, WR

91— †Kasey Dunn, WR
92— †Yo Murphy, WR
     †Jeff Robinson, DL
93— †Doug Nussmeier, QB
     †Mat Groshong, C

IDAHO ST. (6)
69— Ed Bell, OE
77— Ray Allred, MG
81— †Case de Bruijn, P
     †Mike Machurek, QB
83— †Jeff Kaiser, P
84— †Steve Anderson, DL

ILL. BENEDICTINE (3)
72— Mike Rogowski, LB
92— Bob McMillen, TE
93— Eric Green, KR

ILL. WESLEYAN (4)
34— Tony Blazine, T
74— Caesar Douglas, OT
91— Chris Bisaillon, WR
92— Chris Bisaillon, WR

ILLINOIS COLL. (1)
81— Joe Aiello, DL

ILLINOIS ST. (5)
68— Denny Nelson, OT
85— †Jim Meyer, OL
86— †Brian Gant, LB
88— †Mike McCabe, P
93— †Todd Kurz, PK

INDIANA (PA.) (14)
75— Lynn Hieber, QB
76— Jim Haslett, DE
77— Jim Haslett, DE
78— Jim Haslett, DE
79— Terrence Skelley, OE
80— Joe Cuigari, DT
84— Gregg Brenner, WR
86— Jim Angelo, OL
87— Troy Jackson, LB
88— Dean Cottrill, LB
90— Andrew Hill, WR
91— Tony Aliucci, QB
93— Mike Geary, PK
     Michael Mann, RB

INDIANA ST. (8)
69— Jeff Keller, DE
75— Chris Hicks, OL
     Vince Allen, RB
83— †Ed Martin, DE
84— †Wayne Davis, DB
85— †Vencie Glenn, DB
86— †Mike Simmonds, OL
93— †Shawn Moore, OL

INDIANAPOLIS (6)
83— Mark Bless, DL
84— Paul Loggan, DB
85— Tom Collins, DB
86— Dan Jester, TE
87— Thurman Montgomery, DL
91— Greg Matheis, DL

IOWA WESLEYAN (1)
87— Mike Wiggins, P

ITHACA (11)
72— Robert Wojnar, OT
74— David Remick, RB
75— Larry Czarnecki, DT
79— John Laper, LB
80— Bob Ferrigno, HB
84— Bill Sheerin, DL
85— Tim Torrey, LB
90— Jeff Wittman, FB
91— Jeff Wittman, FB
92— Jeff Wittman, FB
     Dave Brumfield, OL

JACKSON ST. (17)
62— Willie Richardson, E
69— Joe Stephens, OG
71— Jerome Barkum, OE
74— Walter Payton, RB
     Robert Brazile, LB
78— Robert Hardy, DT
80— †Larry Werts, LB
81— †Mike Fields, OT
85— †Jackie Walker, LB
86— †Kevin Dent, DB
87— †Kevin Dent, DB
88— †Lewis Tillman, RB

     †Kevin Dent, DB
89— †Darion Conner, LB
90— †Robert Turner, DB
91— †Deltrich Lockridge, OL
92— †Lester Holmes, OL

JACKSONVILLE ST. (8)
52— Jodie Connell, OG
66— Ray Vinson, DB
70— Jimmy Champion, C
77— Jesse Baker, DT
78— Jesse Baker, DT
82— Ed Lett, QB
86— Joe Billingsley, OT
88— Joe Billingsley, OT

JAMES MADISON (7)
77— Woody Bergeria, DT
78— Rick Booth, OL
85— †Charles Haley, LB
86— †Carlo Bianchini, OG
89— †Steve Bates, DL
90— †Eupton Jackson, DB
93— †David McLeod, WR

JAMESTOWN (2)
76— Brent Tischer, OL
81— Ron Hausauer, OL

JOHN CARROLL (2)
50— Carl Taseff, B
74— Tim Barrett, RB

JOHNS HOPKINS (2)
80— Bill Stromberg, WR
81— Bill Stromberg, WR

JOHNSON SMITH (2)
82— Dan Beauford, DE
88— Ronald Capers, LB

JUNIATA (3)
54— Joe Veto, T
86— Steve Yerger, OL
87— Mark Dorner, DB

KANSAS WESLEYAN (2)
35— Virgil Baker, G
56— Larry Houdek, B

KEAN (1)
87— Kevin McGuirl, TE

KENTUCKY ST. (1)
72— Wiley Epps, LB

KENYON (1)
74— Jim Myers, WR

KNOX (2)
86— Rich Schiele, TE
87— Chris Vogel, WR

KNOXVILLE (1)
77— Dwight Treadwell, OL

KUTZTOWN (1)
77— Steve Head, OG

LA SALLE (2)
38— George Somers, T
39— Frank Loughney, G

LA VERNE (2)
72— Dana Coleman, DT
91— Willie Reyna, QB

LAFAYETTE (5)
79— †Rich Smith, TE
81— †Joe Skladany, LB
82— †Tony Green, DL
88— †Frank Baur, QB
92— †Edward Hudak, OL

LAKELAND (1)
89— Jeff Ogiego, P

LAMAR (5)
57— Dudley Meredith, T
61— Bobby Jancik, B
67— Spergon Wynn, OG
83— †Eugene Seale, LB
85— †Burton Murchison, RB

LAMBUTH (1)
93— Jo Jo Jones, RB

LANE (1)
73— Edward Taylor, DT

LANGSTON (1)
73— Thomas Henderson, DE

LAWRENCE (9)
49— Claude Radtke, E
67— Charles McKee, QB

77— Frank Bouressa, C
78— Frank Bouressa, C
80— Scott Reppert, HB
81— Scott Reppert, HB
82— Scott Reppert, RB
83— Murray McDonough, DB
86— Dan Galante, DL

LEHIGH (17)
49— Robert Numbers, C
50— Dick Doyne, B
57— Dan Nolan, B
59— Walter Meincke, T
69— Thad Jamula, OT
71— John Hill, C
73— Kim McQuilken, QB
75— Joe Sterrett, QB
77— Steve Kreider, WR
      Mike Reiker, QB
79— †Dave Melone, OT
      †Jim McCormick, DL
80— †Bruce Rarig, LB
83— †John Shigo, LB
85— †Rennie Benn, WR
90— †Keith Petzold, OL
93— †Dave Cecchini, WR

LENOIR-RHYNE (4)
52— Steve Trudnak, B
62— Richard Kemp, B
67— Eddie Joyner, OT
92— Jason Monday, PK

LEWIS & CLARK (2)
68— Bill Bailey, DT
91— Dan Ruhl, RB

LIBERTY (2)
82— John Sanders, LB
86— Mark Mathis, DB

LINCOLN (MO.) (2)
53— Leo Lewis, B
54— Leo Lewis, B

LINFIELD (8)
57— Howard Morris, G
64— Norman Musser, C
72— Bernard Peterson, OE
75— Ken Cutcher, OL
78— Paul Dombroski, DB
80— Alan Schmidlin, QB
83— Steve Lopes, OL
84— Steve Boyea, OL

LIU-C. W. POST (5)
71— Gary Wichard, QB
77— John Mohring, DE
78— John Mohring, DE
81— Tom DeBona, WR
89— John Levelis, DL

LIVINGSTON (4)
82— Charles Martin, DT
84— Andrew Fields, WR
87— Ronnie Glanton, DL
93— Matt Carman, WR

LIVINGSTONE (1)
84— Jo Jo White, RB

LOCK HAVEN (1)
45— Robert Eyer, E

LONG BEACH ST. (4)
68— Bill Parks, OE
69— Leon Burns, FB
70— Leon Burns, RB
71— Terry Metcalf, RB

LORAS (2)
47— Robert Hanlon, B
84— James Drew, P

LOS ANGELES ST. (1)
64— Walter Johnson, OG

LOUISIANA COLLEGE (1)
50— Bernard Calendar, E

LOUISIANA TECH* (15)
41— Garland Gregory, G
46— Mike Reed, G
68— Terry Bradshaw, QB
69— Terry Bradshaw, QB
72— Roger Carr, WR
73— Roger Carr, FL
74— Mike Barber, TE
      Fred Dean, DT
82— †Matt Dunigan, QB
84— †Doug Landry, LB

      †Walter Johnson, DE
85— †Doug Landry, LB
86— †Walter Johnson, LB-DE
87— †Glenell Sanders, LB
88— †Glenell Sanders, LB

LOUISVILLE* (1)
57— Leonard Lyles, B

LOYOLA (ILL.) (2)
35— Billy Roy, B
37— Clay Calhoun, B

LOYOLA MARYMOUNT (1)
42— Vince Pacewic, B

LUTHER (1)
57— Bruce Hartman, T

LYCOMING (7)
83— John Whalen, OL
85— Walt Zataveski, OL
89— Rick Bealer, DB
90— Rick Bealer, DB
91— Darrin Kenney, OT
      Don Kinney, DL
      Bill Small, LB

MAINE (6)
65— John Huard, LB
66— John Huard, LB
80— †Lorenzo Bouier, RB
89— †Carl Smith, RB
      †Scott Hough, OL
90— †Claude Pettaway, DB

MAINE MARITIME (1)
92— Kirk Matthieu, RB

MANKATO ST. (3)
73— Marty Kranz, DB
87— Duane Goldammer, OG
91— John Kelling, DB

MARS HILL (3)
78— Alan Rice, OL
79— Steven Campbell, DB
87— Lee Marchman, LB

MARSHALL (15)
37— William Smith, E
40— Jackie Hunt, B
41— Jackie Hunt, B
87— †Mike Barber, WR
      †Sean Doctor, TE
88— †Mike Barber, WR
      †Sean Doctor, TE
90— †Eric Ihnat, TE
91— †Phil Ratliff, OL
92— †Michael Payton, QB
      †Troy Brown, WR
      †Phil Ratliff, OL
93— †Chris Deaton, OL
      †William King, LB
      †Roger Johnson, DB

MARYVILLE (TENN.) (5)
67— Steve Dockery, DB
73— Earl McMahon, OG
77— Wayne Dunn, LB
92— Tom Smith, OL
93— Tom Smith, OL

MASS.-BOSTON (1)
92— Sean Munroe, WR

MASSACHUSETTS (20)
52— Tony Chambers, OE
63— Paul Graham, T
64— Milt Morin, DE
67— Greg Landry, QB
71— William DeFlavio, MG
72— Steve Schubert, OE
73— Tim Berra, OE
75— Ned Deane, OL
76— Ron Harris, DB
77— Kevin Cummings, TE
      Bruce Kimball, OL
78— Bruce Kimball, OG
80— †Bob Manning, DB
81— †Garry Pearson, RB
82— †Garry Pearson, RB
85— †Mike Dwyer, DL
88— †John McKeown, LB
90— †Paul Mayberry, OL
92— †Don Caparotti, DB
93— †Bill Durkin, OL

McMURRY (6)
49— Brad Rowland, B

50— Brad Rowland, B
58— Charles Davis, G
68— Telly Windham, DE
74— Randy Roemisch, OT
80— Rick Nolly, OL

McNEESE ST. (8)
52— Charles Kuehn, DE
69— Glenn Kidder, OG
72— James Moore, TE
74— James Files, OT
82— †Leonard Smith, DB
92— †Terry Irving, LB
93— †Jose Larios, PK
      †Terry Irving, LB

MD.-EAST. SHORE (2)
64— John Smith, DT
68— Bill Thompson, DB

MEMPHIS* (1)
54— Robert Patterson, G

MERCHANT MARINE (3)
52— Robert Wiechard, LB
69— Harvey Adams, DE
90— Harold Krebs, DB

MESA ST. (8)
82— Dean Haugum, DT
83— Dean Haugum, DL
84— Don Holmes, DB
85— Mike Berk, OL
86— Mike Berk, OL
88— Tracy Bennett, PK
89— Jeff Russell, OT
90— Brian Johnson, LB

MIAMI (FLA.)* (2)
45— Ed Cameron, G
      William Levitt, C

MIAMI (OHIO)* (1)
82— †Brian Pillman, MG

MICHIGAN TECH (1)
76— Jim VanWagner, RB

MIDDLE TENN. ST. (11)
64— Jimbo Pearson, S
65— Keith Atchley, LB
83— †Robert Carroll, OL
84— †Kelly Potter, PK
85— †Don Griffin, DB
88— †Don Thomas, LB
90— †Joe Campbell, RB
91— †Steve McAdoo, OL
      †Joe Campbell, RB
92— †Steve McAdoo, OL
93— †Pat Hicks, OL

MIDDLEBURY (2)
36— George Anderson, G
83— Jonathan Good, DL

MIDLAND LUTHERAN (2)
76— Dave Marreel, DE
79— Scott Englehardt, OL

MILLERSVILLE (6)
76— Robert Parr, DB
80— Rob Riddick, RB
81— Mark Udovich, C
86— Jeff Hannis, DL
93— Scott Martin, DL
      Greg Faulkner, OL

MILLIKIN (2)
42— Virgil Wagner, B
92— Mike Hall, KR

MILLSAPS (11)
72— Rowan Torrey, DB
73— Michael Reams, LB
76— Rickie Haygood, QB
78— David Culpepper, LB
79— David Culpepper, LB
83— Edmond Donald, RB
85— Tommy Powell, LB
90— Sean Brewer, DL
91— Sean Brewer, DL
92— Sean Brewer, DL
93— Mitch Holloway, P

MINN.-DULUTH (4)
74— Mark Johnson, DB
75— Terry Egerdahl, RB
76— Ted McKnight, RB
82— Gary Birkholz, OG

MISSISSIPPI COL. (11)
72— Ricky Herzog, FL
79— Calvin Howard, RB
80— Bert Lyles, DE
82— Major Everett, RB
83— Wayne Frazier, OL
85— Earl Conway, DL
88— Terry Fleming, DL
89— Terry Fleming, DL
90— Fred McAfee, RB
92— Johnny Poole, OL
93— Kelly Ray, C

MISSISSIPPI VAL. (6)
79— †Carl White, OG
83— †Jerry Rice, WR
84— †Jerry Rice, WR
      †Willie Totten, QB
87— †Vincent Brown, LB
91— †Ashley Ambrose, DB

MISSOURI-ROLLA (5)
41— Ed Kromka, T
69— Frank Winfield, OG
74— Merle Dillow, TE
80— Bill Grantham, S
93— Elvind Listerud, PK

MISSOURI VALLEY (3)
47— James Nelson, G
48— James Nelson, G
49— Herbert McKinney, T

MO. SOUTHERN ST. (1)
93— Rod Smith, WR

MONMOUTH (ILL.) (1)
75— Ron Baker, RB

MONTANA (12)
67— Bob Beers, LB
70— Ron Stein, DB
76— Greg Anderson, DB
79— †Jim Hard, FL
83— †Brian Salonen, TE
85— †Mike Rice, P
87— †Larry Clarkson, OL
88— †Tim Hauck, DB
89— †Kirk Scafford, OL
      †Tim Hauck, DB
93— †Dave Dickenson, QB
      †Todd Ericson, DB

MONTANA ST. (11)
66— Don Hass, HB
67— Don Hass, HB
70— Gary Gustafson, LB
73— Bill Kollar, DT
75— Steve Kracher, RB
76— Lester Leininger, DL
78— Jon Borchardt, OT
81— †Larry Rubens, OL
84— †Mark Fellows, LB
      †Dirk Nelson, P
93— †Sean Hill, DB

MONTANA TECH (3)
73— James Persons, OT
80— Steve Hossler, HB
81— Craig Opatz, OL

MONTCLAIR ST. (12)
75— Barry Giblin, DB
77— Mario Benimeo, DT
79— Tom Morton, OL
80— Sam Mills, LB
81— Terrance Porter, WR
82— Mark Casale, QB
84— Jim Rennae, OL
85— Dan Zakashefski, DL
86— Dan Zakashefski, DL
89— Paul Cioffi, LB
90— Paul Cioffi, LB
93— Jeff Bargiel, DL

MOORHEAD ST. (2)
76— Rocky Gullickson, OG
84— Randy Sullivan, DB

MOREHEAD ST. (5)
38— John Horton, C
42— Vincent Zachem, C
69— Dave Haverdick, DT
82— †John Christopher, P
86— †Randy Poe, OG

MORGAN ST. (8)
65— Willie Lanier, LB
67— Jeff Queen, DE

70— Willie Germany, DB
72— Stan Cherry, LB
73— Eugene Simms, LB
78— Joe Fowlkes, DB
80— Mike Holston, WR
93— †Matthew Steeple, DL

MORNINGSIDE (2)
49— Connie Callahan, B
91— Jorge Diaz, PK

MOUNT UNION (11)
84— Troy Starr, LB
87— Russ Kring, RB
90— Ken Edelman, PK
      Dave Lasecki, LB
92— Mike Elder, OL
      Jim Ballard, QB
      Chris Dattilio, LB
93— Rob Atwood, TE
      Jim Ballard, QB
      Ed Bubonics, WR
      Mike Hallet, DL

MUHLENBERG (3)
46— George Bibighaus, E
47— Harold Bell, B
93— Rob Lokerson, WR

MURRAY ST. (4)
37— Elmer Cochran, G
73— Don Clayton, RB
79— †Terry Love, DB
86— †Charley Wiles, OL

MUSKINGUM (4)
40— Dave Evans, T
60— Bill Cooper, B
66— Mark DeVilling, DT
75— Jeff Heacock, DB

N.C. CENTRAL (4)
68— Doug Wilkerson, MG
69— Doug Wilkerson, OT
74— Charles Smith, DE
88— Earl Harvey, QB

N'EASTERN OKLA. ST. (4)
69— Manuel Britto, HB
71— Roosevelt Manning, DT
74— Kevin Goodlet, DB
82— Cedric Mack, WR

NEB.-KEARNEY (2)
76— Dale Mitchell Johnson, DB
78— Doug Peterson, DL

NEB. WESLEYAN (3)
90— Brad Bohn, DB
91— Darren Stohlmann, TE
92— Darren Stohlmann, TE

NEBRASKA-OMAHA (9)
64— Gerald Allen, HB
68— Dan Klepper, OG
76— Dan Fulton, WR
77— Dan Fulton, OE
80— Tom Sutko, LB
82— John Walker, DT
83— Tim Carlson, LB
84— Ron Petersen, OT
86— Keith Coleman, LB

NEVADA* (23)
52— Neil Garrett, DB
74— Greg Grouwinkel, DB
78— James Curry, MG
      Frank Hawkins, RB
79— †Frank Hawkins, RB
      †Lee Fobbs, DB
80— †Frank Hawkins, RB
      †Bubba Puha, DL
81— †John Ramatici, LB
      †Tony Zendejas, K
82— †Tony Zendejas, K
      †Charles Mann, DT
83— †Tony Zendejas, K
      †Jim Werbeckes, OG
      †Tony Shaw, DB
85— †Greg Rea, OL
      †Marty Zendejas, PK
      †Pat Hunter, DB
86— †Henry Rolling, DE-LB
88— †Bernard Ellison, DB
90— †Bernard Ellison, DB
      †Treamelle Taylor, KR
91— †Matt Clafton, LB

NEVADA-LAS VEGAS* (3)
73— Mike Thomas, RB
74— Mike Thomas, RB
75— Joseph Ingersoll, DL

NEW HAMPSHIRE (10)
50— Ed Douglas, G
68— Al Whittman, DT
75— Kevin Martell, C
76— Bill Burnham, RB
77— Bill Burnham, RB
      Grady Vigneau, OT
85— †Paul Dufault, OL
87— †John Driscoll, OL
91— †Barry Bourassa, RB
      †Dwayne Sabb, LB

NEW HAVEN (9)
85— David Haubner, OL
87— Erik Lesinski, LB
88— Rob Thompson, OL
90— Jay McLucas, QB
92— Scott Emmert, OL
      Roger Graham, RB
93— Roger Graham, RB
      George Byrd, DB
      Tony Willis, WR

NEWBERRY (2)
40— Dominic Collangelo, B
81— Stan Stanton, DL

NICHOLLS ST. (6)
76— Gerald Butler, OE
77— Rusty Rebowe, LB
81— †Dwight Walker, WR
82— †Clint Conque, LB
84— †Dewayne Harrison, TE
86— †Mark Carrier, WR

NICHOLS (1)
81— Ed Zywien, LB

N.M. HIGHLANDS (6)
66— Carl Garrett, HB
67— Carl Garrett, HB
68— Carl Garrett, HB
81— Jay Lewis, DL
85— Neil Windham, LB
86— Tim Salz, PK

NORFOLK ST. (2)
79— Mike Ellis, DB
89— Arthur Jimmerson, LB

NORTH ALA. (10)
82— Don Smith, C
84— Daryl Smith, DB
85— Bruce Jones, DB
90— James Davis, RB
      Mike Nord, OL
92— Harvey Summerhill, DB
93— Jeff Redcross, DL
      Tyrone Rush, RB
      Jeff Surbaugh, OL
      Ronald McKinnon, LB

NORTH CARO. A&T (6)
69— Merl Code, DB
70— Melvin Holmes, OT
81— †Mike West, OL
86— †Ernest Riddick, NG
88— †Demetrius Harrison, LB
93— †Ronald Edwards, OL

NORTH DAK. (16)
55— Steve Myhra, G
56— Steve Myhra, G
63— Neil Reuter, T
65— Dave Lince, DE
66— Roger Bonk, LB
71— Jim LeClair, LB
      Dan Martinsen, DB
72— Mike Deutsch, RB
75— Bill Deutsch, RB
79— Paul Muckenhirn, TE
80— Todd Thomas, OT
81— Milson Jones, RB
89— Cory Solberg, PK
91— Shannon Burnell, RB
93— Shannon Burnell, RB
      Kevin Robson, OL

NORTH DAK. ST. (27)
34— Melvin Hanson, B
46— Cliff Rothrock, C
66— Walt Odegaard, MG
67— Jim Ferge, LB

68— Jim Ferge, DT
Paul Hatchett, B
69— Paul Hatchett, HB
Joe Cichy, DB
70— Joe Cichy, DB
74— Jerry Dahl, DE
76— Rick Budde, LB
77— Lew Curry, OL
81— Wayne Schluchter, DB
82— Cliff Carmody, OG
Steve Garske, LB
83— Mike Whetstone, OG
84— Greg Hagfors, C
86— Jeff Bentrim, QB
Jim Dick, LB
87— Mike Favor, C
88— Matt Tracy, OL
Mike Favor, C
Yorrick Byers, LB
90— Phil Hansen, DL
Chris Simdorn, QB
93— Scott Fuchs, OL
T. R. McDonald, WR

NORTH PARK (2)
72— Greg Nugent, OE
90— John Love, QB

NORTH TEXAS (6)
47— Frank Whitlow, T
51— Ray Renfro, DB
83— †Ronnie Hickman, DE
†Rayford Cooks, DL
88— †Rex Johnson, DL
90— †Mike Davis, DL

NORTHEAST LA. (19)
67— Vic Bender, C
70— Joe Profit, RB
72— Jimmy Edwards, RB
73— Glenn Fleming, MG
74— Glenn Fleming, MG
82— †Arthur Christophe, C
†Bruce Daigle, DB
83— †Mike Grantham, OG
84— †Mike Grantham, OG
85— †Mike Turner, DB
87— †John Clement, OT
†Claude Brumfield, DT
88— †Cyril Crutchfield, DB
89— †Jackie Harris, E
92— †Jeff Blackshear, OL
†Vic Zordan, OL
†Roosevelt Potts, RB
93— †Raymond Batiste, OL
†James Folston, DL

NORTHEAST MO. ST. (4)
60— Dale Mills, B
65— Richard Rhodes, OT
85— Chris Hegg, QB
93— Mike Roos, DL

NORTHEASTERN (2)
72— Tom Rezzuti, DB
78— Dan Ross, TE

NORTHERN ARIZ. (13)
66— Rick Ries, LB
67— Bill Hanna, DE
68— Larry Small, OG
77— Larry Friedrichs, OL
Tom Jurich, K
78— Jerry Lumpkin, LB
79— †Ed Judie, LB
82— †Pete Mandley, WR
83— †Pete Mandley, WR
†James Gee, DT
86— †Goran Lingmerth, PK
89— †Darrell Jordan, LB
93— †Terry Belden, P

NORTHERN COLO. (9)
68— Jack O'Brien, DB
80— Todd Volkart, DT
81— Brad Wimmer, OL
82— Mark Mostek, OG
Kevin Jelden, PK
89— Vance Lechman, DB
90— Frank Wainwright, TE
92— David Oliver, OL
93— Jeff Pease, LB

NORTHERN ILL.* (2)
62— George Bork, B
63— George Bork, B

NORTHERN IOWA (13)
52— Lou Bohnsack, C
60— George Asleson, G
61— Wendell Williams, G
64— Randy Schultz, FB
65— Randy Schultz, FB
67— Ray Pedersen, MG
75— Mike Timmermans, OT
85— Joe Fuller, DB
87— †Carl Boyd, RB
90— †Brian Mitchell, PK
91— †Brian Mitchell, PK
92— †Kenny Shedd, WR
†William Freeney, LB

NORTHERN MICH. (6)
75— Daniel Stencil, OL
76— Maurice Mitchell, FL
77— Joseph Stemo, DB
82— George Works, RB
87— Jerry Woods, DB
88— Jerry Woods, DB

NORTHERN ST. (1)
76— Larry Kolbo, DL

NORTHWEST MO. ST. (3)
39— Marion Rogers, G
84— Steve Hansley, WR
89— Jason Agee, DB

NORTHWESTERN ST. (12)
66— Al Dodd, DB
80— †Warren Griffith, C
†Joe Delaney, RB
81— †Gary Reasons, LB
82— †Gary Reasons, LB
83— †Gary Reasons, LB
84— †Arthur Berry, DT
87— †John Kulakowski, DE
91— †Andre Carron, LB
92— †Adrian Hardy, DB
†Marcus Spears, OL
93— †Marcus Spears, OL

NORTHWOOD (2)
73— Bill Chandler, DT
74— Bill Chandler, DT

NORWICH (3)
79— Milt Williams, RB
84— Beau Almodobar, WR
85— Mike Norman, OL

N'WESTERN (IOWA) (1)
71— Kevin Korvor, DE

OBERLIN (1)
45— James Boswell, B

OCCIDENTAL (6)
76— Rick Fry, FL
77— Rick Fry, SE
82— Dan Osborn, P
83— Ron Scott, DB
89— David Hodges, LB
90— Peter Tucker, OL

OHIO* (2)
35— Art Lewis, T
60— Dick Grecni, C

OHIO WESLEYAN (7)
34— John Turley, B
51— Dale Bruce, OE
71— Steve Dutton, DE
83— Eric DiMartino, LB
90— Jeff Court, OG
Neil Ringers, DL
91— Kevin Rucker, DL

OTTERBEIN (3)
82— Jim Hoyle, K
90— Ron Severance, WR
91— Ron Severance, WR

OUACHITA BAPTIST (1)
79— Ezekiel Vaughn, LB

PACIFIC (CAL.)* (4)
34— Cris Kjeldsen, G
47— Eddie LeBaron, B
48— Eddie LeBaron, B
49— Eddie LeBaron, B

PACIFIC LUTHERAN (9)
40— Marv Tommervik, B
41— Marv Tommervik, B
47— Dan D'Andrea, C
52— Ron Billings, DB
65— Marvin Peterson, C

78— John Zamberlin, LB
85— Mark Foege, PK
Tim Shannon, DL
88— Jon Kral, DL

PANHANDLE ST. (2)
82— Tom Rollison, DB
83— Tom Rollison, DB

PENNSYLVANIA (4)
86— †Marty Peterson, OL
88— †John Zinser, OL
90— †Joe Valerio, OL
93— †Miles Macik, WR

PEPPERDINE (2)
47— Darwin Horn, B
55— Wixie Robinson, G

PERU ST. (4)
52— Robert Lade, OT
53— Robert Lade, T
81— Alvin Holder, RB
91— Tim Herman, DL

PILLSBURY (1)
85— Calvin Addison, RB

PITTSBURG ST. (9)
61— Gary Snadon, B
70— Mike Potchard, OT
78— Brian Byers, OL
88— Jesse Wall, OL
89— John Roderique, LB
90— Ron West, WR
91— Ron West, WR
92— Ronald Moore, RB
93— Doug Bullard, OL

PLYMOUTH ST. (6)
74— Robert Gibson, DB
82— Mark Barrows, LB
83— Joe Dudek, RB
84— Joe Dudek, RB
85— Joe Dudek, RB
91— Scott Allen, LB

POMONA-PITZER (1)
74— Larry Cenotto, QB

PORTLAND ST. (12)
76— June Jones, QB
77— Dave Stief, OE
79— †Stuart Gaussoin, SE
†Kurt Ijanoff, OT
80— †Neil Lomax, QB
84— Doug Mikolas, DL
88— Bary Naone, TE
Chris Crawford, QB
89— Darren Del'Andrae, QB
91— James Fuller, DB
92— John Charles, QB
93— Rick Cruz, LB

PRAIRIE VIEW (2)
64— Otis Taylor, OE
70— Bivian Lee, DB

PRESBYTERIAN (8)
45— Andy Kavounis, G
46— Hank Caver, B
52— Joe Kirven, OE
68— Dan Eckstein, DB
71— Robert Norris, LB
78— Roy Walker, OL
79— Roy Walker, OL
83— Jimmie Turner, LB

PRINCETON (4)
87— †Dean Cain, DB
89— †Judd Garrett, RB
92— †Keith Elias, RB
93— †Keith Elias, RB

PRINCIPIA (1)
93— Matt Newton, WR

PUGET SOUND (9)
56— Robert Mitchell, G
63— Ralph Bauman, G
66— Joseph Peyton, OE
75— Bill Linnenkohl, LB
76— Dan Kuehl, DL
81— Bob Jackson, MG
82— Mike Bos, WR
83— Larry Smith, DB
87— Mike Oliphant, RB

RANDOLPH-MACON (6)
47— Albert Oley, G
57— Dave Young, G

79— Rick Eades, DL
80— Rick Eades, DL
84— Cody Dearing, QB
88— Aaron Boston, OL

REDLANDS (2)
77— Randy Van Horn, OL
92— James Shields, DL

RHODE ISLAND (8)
55— Charles Gibbons, T
82— †Richard Pelzer, OL
83— †Tony DeLuca, DL
84— †Brian Forster, TE
85— †Brian Forster, TE
    †Tom Ehrhardt, QB
90— †Kevin Smith, DB
92— †Darren Rizzi, TE

RHODES (5)
36— Henry Hammond, E
38— Gaylon Smith, B
76— Conrad Bradburn, DB
85— Jim Hever, PK
88— Larry Hayes, OL

RICHMOND (1)
84— †Eddie Martin, OL

RIPON (5)
57— Peter Kasson, E
75— Dick Rehbein, C
76— Dick Rehbein, OL
79— Art Peters, TE
82— Bob Wallner, OL

ROANOKE (1)
38— Kenneth Moore, E

ROCHESTER (7)
51— Jack Wilson, DE
52— Donald Bardell, DG
67— Dave Ragusa, LB
75— Ralph Gebhardt, DB
90— Craig Chodak, P
92— Brian Laudadio, DL
93— Geoff Long, DL

ROCKHURST (1)
41— Joe Kiernan, T

ROLLINS (1)
40— Charles Lingerfelt, E

ROSE-HULMAN (2)
77— Gary Ellis, DB
92— Todd Holthaus, PK

ROWAN (2)
78— Dino Hall, RB
93— Bill Fisher, DL

SAGINAW VALLEY (4)
81— Eugene Marve, LB
84— Joe Rice, DL
90— David Cook, DB
92— Bill Schafer, TE

SALISBURY ST. (4)
82— Mark Lagowski, LB
84— Joe Mammano, OL
85— Robb Disbennett, QB
86— Tom Kress, DL

SAM HOUSTON ST. (3)
49— Charles Williams, E
52— Don Gottlob, B
91— †Michael Bankston, DL

SAMFORD (1)
36— Norman Cooper, C

SAN DIEGO (3)
73— Bob Dulich, QB
81— Dan Herbert, DB
92— Robert Ray, P

SAN DIEGO ST.* (6)
35— John Butler, G
66— Don Horn, QB
67— Steve Duich, OT
    Haven Moses, OE
68— Fred Dryer, DE
    Lloyd Edwards, B

SAN FRAN. ST. (7)
51— Robert Williamson, OT
60— Charles Fuller, B
67— Joe Koontz, OE
76— Forest Hancock, LB
78— Frank Duncan, DB
82— Poncho James, RB
84— Jim Jones, TE

SAN FRANCISCO (1)
42— John Sanchez, T

SAN JOSE ST.* (2)
38— Lloyd Thomas, E
39— LeRoy Zimmerman, B

SANTA CLARA (8)
64— Lou Pastorini, LB
71— Ronald Sani, C
79— Jim Leonard, C
80— Brian Sullivan, K
82— Gary Hoffman, OT
83— Alex Vlahos, C
    Mike Rosselli, LB
85— Brent Jones, TE

SAVANNAH ST. (2)
79— Timothy Walker, DL
89— Shannon Sharpe, TE

SEWANEE (8)
63— Martin Agnew, B
73— Mike Lumpkin, DE
77— Nino Austin, DB
79— John Hill, DB
80— Mallory Nimocs, TE
81— Greg Worsowicz, DB
86— Mark Kent, WR
90— Ray McGowan, DL

SHIPPENSBURG (2)
53— Robert Adams, G
91— Jeff Fickes, DB

SIMON FRASER (1)
90— Nick Mazzoli, WR

SIMPSON (1)
89— Ricky Gales, RB

SLIPPERY ROCK (6)
74— Ed O'Reilly, RB
75— Jerry Skocik, TE
76— Chris Thull, LB
77— Bob Schrantz, TE
78— Bob Schrantz, TE
85— Jeff Williams, P

SONOMA ST. (3)
86— Mike Henry, LB
92— Larry Allen, OL
93— Larry Allen, OL

SOUTH CARO. ST. (19)
67— Tyrone Caldwell, DE
71— James Evans, LB
72— Barney Chavous, DE
73— Donnie Shell, DB
75— Harry Carson, DE
76— Robert Sims, DL
77— Ricky Anderson, RB
79— †Phillip Murphy, DL
80— †Edwin Bailey, OG
81— †Anthony Reed, FB
    †Dwayne Jackson, DL
82— †Dwayne Jackson, DE
    †Anthony Reed, RB
    †Ralph Green, OT
    †John Courtney, DT
83— †Ralph Green, OT
89— †Eric Douglas, OL
91— †Robert Porcher, DL
93— †Anthony Cook, DE

SOUTH DAK. (10)
68— John Kohler, OT
69— John Kohler, OT
71— Gene Macken, OG
72— Gary Kipling, OG
78— Bill Moats, DB
79— Benjamin Long, LB
83— Kurt Seibel, K
86— Jerry Glinsky, C
    Todd Salat, DB
88— Doug VanderEsch, LB

SOUTH DAK. ST. (10)
67— Darwin Gonnerman, HB
68— Darwin Gonnerman, FB
74— Lynn Boden, OT
77— Bill Matthews, DE
79— Charles Loewen, OL
84— Rick Wegher, RB
85— Jeff Tiefenthaler, WR
86— Jeff Tiefenthaler, WR
91— Kevin Tetzlaff, DL
92— Doug Miller, LB

Sonoma State offensive tackle Larry Allen earned Division II all-American honors in 1992 and 1993.

SOUTH DAK. TECH (1)
73— Charles Waite, DB

SOUTHEAST MO. ST. (1)
37— Wayne Goddard, T

SOUTHEASTERN LA. (3)
70— Ronnie Hornsby, LB
83— †Bret Wright, P
85— †Willie Shepherd, DL

SOUTHERN ARK. (2)
84— Greg Stuman, LB
85— Greg Stuman, LB

SOUTHERN-B.R. (6)
70— Isiah Robertson, LB
72— James Wright, OG
73— Godwin Turk, LB
79— †Ken Times, DL
87— †Gerald Perry, OT
93— †Sean Wallace, DB

SOUTHERN CONN. ST. (6)
82— Mike Marshall, DB
83— Kevin Gray, OL
84— William Sixsmith, LB
86— Rick Atkinson, DB
91— Ron Lecointe, OL
92— Steve Lawrence, LB

SOUTHERN ILL. (4)
70— Lionel Antoine, OE
71— Lionel Antoine, OE
83— †Donnell Daniel, DB
    †Terry Taylor, DB

SOUTHERN MISS.* (4)
53— Hugh Pepper, B
56— Don Owens, T
58— Robert Yencho, E
59— Hugh McInnis, E

SOUTHERN ORE. ST. (1)
75— Dennis Webber, LB

SOUTHERN UTAH (4)
79— Lane Martino, DL
87— Jeff McComb, P
89— Randy Bostic, C
90— Randy Bostic, C

SOUTHWEST MO. ST. (6)
66— William Stringer, OG
87— †Matt Soraghan, LB
89— †Mark Christenson, OL
90— †DeAndre Smith, QB
91— †Bill Walter, DL
93— †Adrion Smith, DB

SOUTHWEST ST. (2)
87— James Ashley, WR
91— Wayne Hawkins, DE

SOUTHWEST TEX. ST. (10)
53— Pence Dacus, B
63— Jerry Cole, E
64— Jerry Cole, DB
72— Bob Daigle, C
75— Bobby Kotzur, DT
82— Tim Staskus, LB
83— Tim Staskus, LB
84— †Scott Forester, C
90— †Reggie Rivers, RB
91— †Ervin Thomas, C

SOUTHWESTERN LA.* (1)
69— Glenn LaFleur, LB

SPRINGFIELD (11)
68— Dick Dobbert, C
70— John Curtis, OE
76— Roy Samuelsen, MG
78— Jack Quinn, DB
79— Jack Quinn, DB
80— Steve Foster, OT
81— Jon Richardson, LB
83— Wally Case, DT
      Ed Meachum, TE
85— Jim Anderson, LB
91— Fran Papasedero, DL

ST. AMBROSE (4)
40— Nick Kerasiotis, G
51— Robert Flanagan, B
58— Robert Webb, B
87— Jerry Klosterman, DL

ST. BONAVENTURE (2)
46— Phil Colella, B
48— Frank LoVuola, E

ST. CLOUD ST. (1)
85— Mike Lambrecht, DL

ST. JOHN'S (MINN.) (7)
65— Pat Whalin, DB
79— Ernie England, MG
82— Rick Bell, RB
83— Chris Biggins, TE
91— Pat Mayew, QB
93— Burt Chamberlin, OL
      Jim Wagner, DL

ST. JOHN'S (N.Y.) (1)
83— Todd Jamison, QB

ST. LAWRENCE (2)
51— Ken Spencer, LB
77— Mitch Brown, DB

ST. MARY (KAN.) (1)
86— Joe Brinson, RB

ST. MARY'S (CAL.) (4)
79— Fran McDermott, DB
80— Fran McDermott, DB
88— Jon Braff, TE
92— Mike Estrella, PK

ST. MARY'S (TEX.) (1)
36— Douglas Locke, B

ST. NORBERT (2)
57— Norm Jarock, B
64— Dave Jauquet, DE

ST. OLAF (3)
53— John Gustafson, E
78— John Nahorniak, LB
80— Jon Anderson, DL

ST. THOMAS (MINN.) (6)
45— Theodore Molitor, E
48— Jack Salscheider, B
84— Neal Guggemos, DB
85— Neal Guggemos, DB
90— Gary Trettel, RB
91— Kevin DeVore, OL

STEPHEN F. AUSTIN (7)
51— James Terry, DE
79— Ronald Haynes, DL
85— James Noble, WR
86— †Darrell Harkless, DB
88— †Eric Lokey, LB
89— †David Whitmore, DB
93— †Cedric Walker, DB

STONY BROOK (2)
87— Chuck Downey, B
88— David Lewis, P

SUL ROSS ST. (2)
65— Tom Nelson, DE
88— Francis Jones, DB

SUSQUEHANNA (3)
51— James Hazlett, C
90— Keith Henry, DL
92— Andy Watkins, LB

SWARTHMORE (1)
89— Marshall Happer, OL

S'WESTERN (KAN.) (2)
82— Tom Audley, DL
84— Jackie Jenson, RB

S'WESTERN OKLA. ST. (2)
77— Louis Blanton, DB
82— Richard Lockman, LB

TAMPA (5)
65— John Perry, DB
68— Ron Brown, MG
70— Leon McQuay, RB
71— Ron Mikolajczyk, OT
      Sammy Gellerstedt, MG

TENN.-CHATT. (22)
35— Robert Klein, E
38— Robert Sutton, G
39— Jack Gregory, T
45— Thomas Stewart, T
46— Gene Roberts, B
48— Ralph Hutchinson, T
49— Vincent Sarratore, G
51— Chester LaGod, DT
52— Chester LaGod, DT
54— Richard Young, B
57— Howard Clark, E
58— John Green, B
60— Charles Long, T
64— Jerry Harris, S
66— Harry Sorrell, OG
76— Tim Collins, LB
86— †Mike Makins, DL
89— †Pumpy Tudors, P
      †Junior Jackson, LB
90— †Troy Boeck, DL
      †Tony Hill, DL
      †Pumpy Tudors, P

TENN.-MARTIN (3)
68— Julian Nunnamaker, OG
88— Emanuel McNeil, DL
91— Oscar Bunch, TE

TENN. WESLEYAN (1)
92— Derrick Scott, PK

TENNESSEE ST. (17)
67— Claude Humphrey, DT
68— Jim Marsalis, DB
69— Joe Jones, DE
70— Vernon Holland, OT
71— Cliff Brooks, DB
      Joe Gilliam, QB
72— Robert Woods, OT
      Waymond Bryant, LB
73— Waymond Bryant, LB
      Ed Jones, DE
74— Cleveland Elam, DE
81— †Mike Jones, WR
      †Malcolm Taylor, DT
82— †Walter Tate, OL
86— †Onzy Elam, LB
90— †Colin Godfrey, P
93— †Brent Alexander, DB

TENNESSEE TECH (10)
52— Tom Fann, OT
59— Tom Hackler, E
60— Tom Hackler, E
61— David Baxter, T
69— Larry Schreiber, HB
71— Jim Youngblood, LB
72— Jim Youngblood, LB
74— Elois Grooms, DE
76— Ed Burns, OT
89— †Ryan Weeks, PK

TEX. A&M-KINGSVILLE (43)
40— Stuart Clarkson, C
41— Stuart Clarkson, C
59— Gerald Lambert, G
60— William Crafts, T
62— Douglas Harvey, C
63— Sid Banks, B
65— Randy Johnson, QB
66— Dwayne Nix, OE
67— Dwayne Nix, OE
68— Dwayne Nix, OE
      Ray Hickl, OG

70— Dwight Harrison, DB
      Margarito Guerrero, MG
71— Eldridge Small, OE
      Levi Johnson, DB
72— Ernest Price, DE
74— Don Hardeman, RB
75— David Hill, TE
76— Richard Ritchie, QB
      Larry Grunewald, LB
77— Larry Collins, RB
      John Barefield, DE
78— Billy John, OT
79— Andy Hawkins, LB
80— Don Washington, CB
81— Durwood Roquemore, DB
82— Darrell Green, DB
83— Loyd Lewis, OG
84— Neal Lattue, PK
85— Charles Smith, C
86— Johnny Bailey, RB
      Moses Horn, OG
87— Johnny Bailey, RB
      Moses Horn, OG
88— Rod Mounts, OL
      Johnny Bailey, RB
      John Randle, DL
89— Johnny Bailey, RB
90— Keithen DeGrate, OL
91— Brian Nielsen, OL
92— Earl Dotson, OL
93— Anthony Phillips, DB
      Moke Simon, DL

TEXAS-ARLINGTON (5)
66— Ken Ozee, DT
67— Robert Diem, OG
      Robert Willbanks, S
83— †Mark Cannon, C
84— †Bruce Collie, OL

TEXAS LUTHERAN (3)
73— David Wehmeyer, RB
74— D. W. Rutledge, LB
75— Jerry Ellis, OL

TEXAS SOUTHERN (3)
70— Nathaniel Allen, DB
76— Freddie Dean, OL
92— †Michael Strahan, DL

TEXAS TECH* (2)
35— Herschel Ramsey, E
45— Walter Schlinkman, B

THOMAS MORE (1)
93— Mike Flesch, OL

TIFFIN (1)
93— Brian Diliberto, RB

TOLEDO* (1)
38— Dan Buckwick, G

TOWSON ST. (10)
75— Dan Dullea, QB
76— Skip Chase, OE
77— Randy Bielski, DB
78— Ken Snoots, SE
82— Sean Landeta, P
83— Gary Rubeling, DB
84— Terry Brooks, OG
85— Stan Eisentooth, OL
86— David Haden, LB
93— †Tony Vinson, RB

TRENTON ST. (3)
74— Eric Hamilton, C
83— John Aromando, WR
91— Chris Shaw, C

TRINITY (CONN.) (7)
35— Mickey Kobrosky, B
36— Mickey Kobrosky, B
55— Charles Sticka, B
59— Roger LeClerc, C
70— David Kiarsis, HB
78— Pat McNamara, FL
93— Eric Mudry, DB

TRINITY (TEX.) (4)
54— Alvin Beal, B
55— Hubert Cook, C
56— Milton Robichaux, E
67— Marvin Upshaw, DT

TROY ST. (10)
39— Sherrill Busby, E
73— Mark King, C
74— Mark King, C

76— Perry Griggs, OE
78— Tim Tucker, LB
80— Willie Tullis, QB
84— Mitch Geier, OG
86— Freddie Thomas, DB
87— Mike Turk, QB
   Freddie Thomas, DB

TUFTS (6)
34— William Grinnell, E
76— Tim Whelan, RB
78— Mark Buben, DL
79— Chris Connors, QB
80— Mike Brown, OL
86— Bob Patz, DL

TULSA* (1)
34— Rudy Prochaska, C

UC DAVIS (10)
72— Bob Biggs, QB
   David Roberts, OT
76— Andrew Gagnon, OL
77— Chuck Fomasi, DT
78— Casey Merrill, DL
79— Jeffrey Allen, DB
82— Ken O'Brien, QB
83— Bo Eason, DB
84— Scott Barry, QB
85— Mike Wise, DL

UC RIVERSIDE (1)
75— Michael Johnson, SE

UC SANTA BARB. (3)
36— Douglas Oldershaw, G
37— Douglas Oldershaw, G
67— Paul Vallerga, DB

UNION (N.Y.) (9)
39— Sam Hammerstrom, B
82— Steve Bodmer, DL
83— Tim Howell, LB
84— Brian Cox, DE
85— Anthony Valente, DL
86— Rich Romer, DL
87— Rich Romer, DL
91— Greg Harrison, PK
93— Marco Lainez, LB

UNION (TENN.) (2)
41— James Jones, B
42— James Jones, B

UPSALA (1)
64— Dick Giessuebel, LB

U.S. INT'L (2)
72— Jerry Robinson, DB
75— Steve Matson, FL

VA. MILITARY (1)
88— †Mark Stock, WR

VALDOSTA ST. (5)
82— Mark Catano, OL
86— Jessie Tuggle, LB
89— Randy Fisher, WR
90— Deon Searcy, DB
93— Chris Hatcher, QB

VALPARAISO (5)
51— Joe Pahr, B
71— Gary Puetz, OT
72— Gary Puetz, OT
76— John Belskis, DB
85— Mike Healey, WR

VILLANOVA (4)
88— †Paul Berardelli, OL
89— †Bryan Russo, OL
91— †Curtis Eller, LB
92— †Curtis Eller, LB

VIRGINIA ST. (3)
71— Larry Brooks, DT
84— John Greene, LB
85— James Ward, DL

VIRGINIA UNION (12)
73— Herb Scott, OG
74— Herb Scott, OG
75— Anthony Leonard, DB
77— Frank Dark, DB
79— Plummer Bullock, DE
80— William Dillon, DB
81— William Dillon, DB
82— William Dillon, DB
83— Larry Curtis, DT
88— Leroy Gause, LB

91— Paul DeBerry, DB
   Kevin Williams, LB

WABASH (5)
76— Jimmy Parker, DB
77— David Harvey, QB
81— Pete Metzelaars, TE
88— Tim Pliske, PK
89— Mike Funk, WR

WAGNER (9)
67— John Gloistein, OT
80— Phil Theis, OL
81— Alonzo Patterson, RB
82— Alonzo Patterson, RB
83— Selwyn Davis, OT
86— Charles Stinson, DL
87— Rich Negrin, OT
88— Terry Underwood, RB
91— Walter Lopez, PK

WASH. & JEFF. (9)
84— Ed Kusko, OL
87— A. J. Pagano, RB
91— Chris Babirad, RB
   Gilbert Floyd, DB
92— Chris Babirad, RB
   Todd Pivnick, OL
   Kevin Pintar, OL
93— Jason Moore, OL
   Shawn Prendergast, LB

WASH. & LEE (4)
76— Tony Perry, OE
81— Mike Pressler, G
83— Glenn Kirschner, OL
86— John Packett, OL

WASHBURN (2)
64— Robert Hardy, DB
88— Troy Slusser, WR

WASHINGTON (MO.) (4)
72— Shelby Jordan, LB
73— Stu Watkins, OE
74— Marion Stallings, DB
88— Paul Matthews, TE

WAYNE ST. (NEB.) (2)
84— Herve Roussel, PK
85— Ruben Mendoza, OL

WAYNESBURG (1)
41— Nick George, G

WEBER ST. (14)
66— Ronald McCall, DE
67— Lee White, FB
   Jim Schmedding, OG
69— Carter Campbell, DE
70— Henry Reed, DE
71— David Taylor, OT
77— Dennis Duncanson, DB
78— Dennis Duncanson, DB
   Randy Jordan, WR
80— †Mike Humiston, LB
89— †Peter Macon, WR
91— †Jamie Martin, QB
   †Alfred Pupunu, WR
93— †Pat McNarney, TE

WESLEY (1)
91— Fran Naselli, KR

WESLEYAN (6)
46— Bert VanderClute, G
48— Jack Geary, T
72— Robert Heller, C
73— Robert Heller, C
76— John McVicar, DL
77— John McVicar, DL

WEST CHESTER (9)
52— Charles Weber, DG
58— Richard Emerich, T
61— Joe Iacone, B
62— Joe Iacone, B
72— Tim Pierantozzi, QB
76— William Blystone, RB
87— Ralph Tamm, OL
88— Bill Hess, WR
92— Lee Woodall, DL

WEST TEX. A&M (2)
86— Stan Carraway, WR
90— Mark Bounds, P

WEST VA.* (1)
34— Tod Goodwin, E

WEST VA. TECH (3)
82— Elliott Washington, DB
86— Calvin Wallace, DL
89— Phil Hudson, WR

WEST VA. WESLEYAN (2)
36— George Mike, T
82— Jerry Free, T

WESTERN CARO. (13)
49— Arthur Byrd, G
71— Steve Williams, DT
73— Mark Ferguson, OT
74— Jerry Gaines, SE
   Steve Yates, LB
84— †Louis Cooper, DL
   †Kirk Roach, PK
   †Steve Kornegay, P
85— †Clyde Simmons, DL
86— †Alonzo Carmichael, TE
   †Kirk Roach, PK
87— †Kirk Roach, PK
93— †Kerry Hayes, KR/WR

WESTERN ILL. (15)
59— Bill Larson, B
61— Leroy Jackson, B
74— John Passananti, OT
76— Scott Levenhagen, TE
   Greg Lee, DB
77— Craig Phalen, DT
78— Bill Huskisson, DL
80— Mike Maher, TE
   Don Greco, OG
83— †Chris Gunderson, MG
84— †Chris Gunderson, T
86— †Frank Winters, C
   †Todd Auer, DL
88— †Marlin Williams, DL
93— †Rodney Harrison, DB

WESTERN KY. (15)
64— Dale Lindsey, LB
70— Lawrence Brame, DE
73— Mike McKoy, DB
74— John Bushong, DL
   Virgil Livers, DB
75— Rick Green, LB
77— Chip Carpenter, OL
80— †Pete Walters, OG
   †Tim Ford, DL
81— †Donnie Evans, DE
82— †Paul Gray, LB
83— †Paul Gray, LB
87— †James Edwards, DB
88— †Dean Tiebout, OL
   †Joe Arnold, RB

WESTERN MD. (3)
51— Victor Makovitch, DG
78— Ricci Bonaccorsy, DL
79— Ricci Bonaccorsy, DL

WESTERN MICH.* (1)
82— †Matt Meares, OL

WESTERN NEW MEX. (2)
83— Jay Ogle, WR
88— Pat Maxwell, P

WESTERN ST. (5)
56— Bill Rhodes, B
78— Bill Campbell, DB
80— Justin Cross, OT
84— Jeff Guy, P
92— Reggie Alexander, WR

WESTERN WASH. (2)
51— Norman Hash, DB
79— Patrick Locker, RB

WESTMINSTER (PA.) (10)
73— Robert Pontius, DB
77— Rex Macey, FL
82— Gary DeGruttola, LB
83— Scott Higgins, DB
86— Joe Keaney, LB
88— Kevin Myers, LB
89— Joe Micchia, QB
90— Brad Tokar, RB
91— Brian DeLorenzo, DL
92— Matt Raich, LB

WHEATON (ILL.) (5)
55— Dave Burnham, B
58— Robert Bakke, T
77— Larry Wagner, LB

78— Scott Hall, QB
83— Keith Bishop, QB

WHITTIER (3)
38— Myron Claxton, T
62— Richard Peter, T
77— Michael Ciacci, DB

WHITWORTH (4)
52— Pete Swanson, OG
54— Larry Paradis, T
85— Wayne Ralph, WR
86— Wayne Ralph, WR

WIDENER (10)
72— Billy Johnson, RB
73— Billy Johnson, RB
75— John Warrington, DB
76— Al Senni, OL
77— Chip Zawoiski, RB
79— Tom Deery, DB
80— Tom Deery, DB
81— Tom Deery, DB
82— Tony Stefanoni, DL
88— Dave Duffy, DL

WILKES (2)
73— Jeff Grandinetti, DT
93— Jason Feese, DL

WILLAMETTE (11)
34— Loren Grannis, G
35— John Oravec, B
36— Richard Weisgerber, B
46— Marvin Goodman, E
58— William Long, C
59— Marvin Cisneros, G
64— Robert Burles, DT
65— Robert Burles, DT
69— Calvin Lee, LB
75— Gary Johnson, DL
82— Richard Milroy, DB

WILLIAM & MARY (5)
83— †Mario Shaffer, OL
86— †Michael Clemons, RB
89— †Steve Christie, P
90— †Pat Crowley, DL
93— †Craig Staub, DL

WILLIAM JEWELL (4)
52— Al Conway, B
73— John Strada, OE
81— Guy Weber, DL
83— Mark Mundel, OL

WILLIAM PENN (1)
72— Bruce Polen, DB

WILLIAMS (5)
51— Charles Salmon, DG
69— Jack Maitland, HB
74— John Chandler, LB
78— Greg McAleenan, DB
90— George Rogers, DL

WILMINGTON (OHIO) (1)
72— William Roll, OG

WINGATE (1)
89— Jimmy Sutton, OT

WINONA ST. (1)
92— Dave Ludy, AP

WINSTON-SALEM (4)
77— Cornelius Washington, DB
78— Tim Newsome, RB
84— Danny Moore, OG
87— Barry Turner, G

WIS.-EAU CLAIRE (1)
81— Roger Vann, RB

WIS.-LA CROSSE (11)
52— Ted Levanhagen, LB
72— Bryon Buelow, DB
78— Joel Williams, LB
83— Jim Byrne, DL
85— Tom Newberry, OL
88— Ted Pretasky, RB
89— Terry Strouf, OL
91— Jon Lauscher, LB
92— Norris Thomas, DB
       Mike Breit, LB
93— Rick Schaaf, DL

WIS.-MILWAUKEE (1)
70— Pete Papara, LB

WIS.-PLATTEVILLE (2)
73— William Vander Velden, DE
86— Mike Hintz, DB

WIS.-RIVER FALLS (3)
80— Gerald Sonsalla, OG
82— Roland Hall, LB
87— Greg Corning, RB

WIS.-STEVENS POINT (4)
77— Reed Giordana, QB
81— Chuck Braun, WR
92— Randy Simpson, DB
93— Jimmy Henderson, RB

WIS.-STOUT (1)
79— Joseph Bullis, DL

WIS.-SUPERIOR (3)
66— Mel Thake, DB
83— Larry Banks, MG
85— Phil Eiting, LB

WIS.-WHITEWATER (4)
75— William Barwick, OL
79— Jerry Young, WR
82— Daryl Schleim, DE
90— Reggie White, OL

WITTENBERG (20)
62— Donald Hunt, G
63— Bob Cherry, E
64— Chuck Green, QB
68— Jim Felts, DE
73— Steve Drongowski, OT
74— Arthur Thomas, LB
75— Robert Foster, LB
76— Dean Caven, DL
78— Dave Merritt, RB
79— Joe Govern, DL
80— Mike Dowds, DE
81— Bill Beach, DB
83— Bryant Lemon, DL
87— Eric Horstman, OL
88— Ken Bonner, OT
       Eric Horstman, OL
90— Jon Warga, RB
92— Taver Johnson, LB
93— Taver Johnson, LB
       Greg Brame, PK

WM. PATERSON (2)
92— Craig Paskas, DB
93— Craig Paskas, DB

WOFFORD (10)
42— Aubrey Faust, E
47— Ken Dubard, T
49— Elbert Hammett, T
51— Jack Beeler, DB
57— Charles Bradshaw, B
61— Dan Lewis, G
70— Sterling Allen, OG
79— Keith Kinard, OL
90— David Wiley, OL
91— Tom Cotter, OL

WOOSTER (1)
79— Blake Moore, C

WORCESTER ST. (2)
92— Chris Butts, DB
93— Chris Butts, DB

XAVIER (OHIO) (1)
51— Tito Carinci, LB

YALE (1)
84— †John Zanieski, DL

YOUNGSTOWN ST. (16)
74— Don Calloway, DB
75— Don Calloway, DB
78— Ed McGlasson, OL
79— James Ferranti, OE
       Jeff Lear, OT
80— Jeff Gergel, LB
81— †Paris Wicks, RB
82— †Paris Wicks, RB
88— †Jim Zdelar, OL
89— †Paul Soltis, LB
90— †Tony Bowens, DL
91— †Pat Danko, DL
92— †Dave Roberts, DB
93— †Drew Garber, OL
       †Tamron Smith, RB
       †Jeff Wilkins, PK

NCAA Postgraduate Scholarship Winners

Following are football players who are NCAA postgraduate scholarship winners, whether or not they were able to accept the grant, plus all alternates (indicated by *) who accepted grants. The program began with the 1964 season. (Those who played in 1964 are listed as 1965 winners, those who played in 1965 as 1966 winners, etc.) To qualify, student-athletes must maintain a 3.000 grade-point average (on a 4.000 scale) during their collegiate careers and perform with distinction in varsity football.

ABILENE CHRISTIAN
71— James Lindsey
83— *Grant Feasel
85— Daniel Remsberg
86— *James Embry
       Craig Huff
90— William Clayton

ADRIAN
94— Jeffrey Toner

AIR FORCE
65— Edward Fausti
67— James Hogarty
68— Kenneth Zagzebski
69— *Richard Rivers Jr.
70— Charles Longnecker
       *Alfred Wurglitz
71— Ernest Jennings
       Robert Parker Jr.
72— Darryl Haas
73— Mark Prill
75— *Joseph Debes
84— Jeffrey Kubiak
86— Derek Brown
88— Chad Hennings
89— David Hlatky
90— Steven Wilson
91— Christopher Howard
92— Ronald James
93— Scott Hufford

ALABAMA
69— Donald Sutton
72— John Musso Jr.
75— Randy Hall
80— Steadman Shealy

ALABAMA ST.
92— Edward Robinson Jr.

ALBANY (N.Y.)
88— *Thomas Higgins

ALBION
81— Joel Manby
94— Michael Montico

ALBRIGHT
67— *Paul Chaiet

ALLEGHENY
65— David Wion
92— Darren Hadlock

ALMA
67— Keith Bird Jr.
79— Todd Friesner

AMHERST
66— David Greenblatt
76— Geoffrey Miller
85— Raymond Nurme

APPALACHIAN ST.
78— Gill Beck
93— D. J. Campbell

ARIZONA
69— William Michael Moody
78— Jon Abbott

80— Jeffrey Whitton
88— Charles Cecil

ARIZONA ST.
78— John Harris
90— Mark Tingstad

ARKANSAS
70— Terry Stewart
71— William Burnett
79— William Bradford Shoup
85— *Mark Lee

ARKANSAS ST.
72— John Meyer
77— Thomas Humphreys

ARMY
66— Samuel Champi Jr.
68— Bohdan Neswiacheny
69— James McCall Jr.
        Thomas Wheelock
70— Theodore Shadid Jr.
78— Curtis Downs
81— *Stanley March
86— Donald Smith
        Douglas Black
88— William Conner
90— Michael Thorson
93— Michael McElrath

ASHLAND
78— Daniel Bogden
88— David Biondo
90— Douglas Powell

AUBURN
66— John Cochran
69— *Roger Giffin
85— Gregg Carr
90— James Lyle IV

AUGSBURG
90— Terry Mackenthun

AUGUSTANA (ILL.)
69— *Jeffrey Maurus
71— Kenneth Anderson
77— Joe Thompson
86— Steven Sanders

AUGUSTANA (S.D.)
72— Michael Olson
75— David Zelinsky
77— James Clemens
78— Dee Donlin
        Roger Goebel
90— *David Gubbrud
91— Scott Boyens

BALL ST.
67— *John Hostrawser
73— Gregory Mack
77— Arthur Yaroch
84— Richard Chitwood
88— Ronald Duncan
90— Theodore Ashburn
93— Troy Hoffer

BATES
79— Christopher Howard

BAYLOR
65— Michael Kennedy
66— Edward Whiddon
94— John Eric Joe

BOISE ST.
72— Brent McIver
76— *Glenn Sparks
79— Samuel Miller
82— Kip Bedard
92— Larry Stayner
93— David Tingstad

BOSTON COLLEGE
66— *Lawrence Marzetti
67— Michael O'Neill
69— Gary Andrachik
70— Robert Bouley
78— Richard Scudellari
87— Michael Degnan

BOSTON U.
69— Suren Donabedian Jr.
81— David Bengtson

BOWDOIN
65— Steven Ingram
67— Thomas Allen

BOWIE ST.
92— Mark Fitzgerald

BOWLING GREEN
77— Richard Preston
78— Mark Miller
91— Patrick Jackson

BRIDGEPORT
70— Terry Sparker

BRIGHAM YOUNG
67— Virgil Carter
76— Orrin Olsen
77— *Stephen Miller
78— Gifford Nielsen
80— Marc Wilson
82— Daniel Plater
83— Bart Oates
84— Steve Young
85— Marvin Allen
89— Charles Cutler
94— Eric Drage

BROWN
65— John Kelly Jr.
70— James Lukens
74— Douglas Jost
75— William Taylor
77— Scott Nelson
78— Louis Cole
79— Robert Forster
82— Travis Holcombe

BUCKNELL
71— *Kenneth Donahue
74— John Dailey
75— Steve Leskinen
77— Lawrence Brunt
85— David Kucera
93— David Berardinelli

BUENA VISTA
77— Steven Trost
87— Michael Habben
94— Cary Murphy

BUFFALO ST.
87— James Dunbar

BUTLER
72— George Yearsich
78— William Ginn
85— Stephen Kollias

CAL LUTHERAN
90— *Gregory Maw

CAL POLY SLO
69— William Creighton

CAL TECH
67— William Mitchell
68— John Frazzini
74— Frank Hobbs Jr.

CALIFORNIA
66— William Krum
67— John Schmidt
68— Robert Crittenden
70— James Calkins
71— Robert Richards
83— Harvey Salem
94— Douglas Brien

CANISIUS
84— Thomas Schott

CAPITAL
84— *Michael Linton

CARLETON
67— Robert Paarlberg
73— Mark Williams
83— Paul Vaaler
93— Arthur Gilliland

CARNEGIE MELLON
80— Gusty Sunseri
91— Robert O'Toole

CARROLL (WIS.)
77— Stephen Thompson

CARTHAGE
70— William Radakovitz

CASE RESERVE
89— Christopher Nutter
91— James Meek

CENTRAL (IOWA)
71— Vernon Den Herder
87— Scott Lindell

89— Eric Perry
92— Richard Kacmarynski

CENTRAL MICH.
77— John Wunderlich
80— *Michael Ball
85— Kevin Egnatuk
88— Robert Stebbins
92— Jeffrey Bender

CENTRAL WASH.
70— Danny Collins

CENTRE
69— Glenn Shearer
86— Casteel "Teel" Bruner II
88— *Robert Clark
90— James Ellington

CHEYNEY
76— Steven Anderson

CHICAGO
86— *Bruce Montella
89— Paul Haar
94— Frank Baker

CINCINNATI
71— *Earl Willson

CITADEL
74— Thomas Leitner
79— Kenneth Caldwell
84— *William West IV

CLAREMONT-M-S
68— Craig Dodel
70— *Gregory Long
71— Stephen Endemano
73— Christopher Stecher
74— Samuel Reece

CLEMSON
65— James Bell Jr.
68— James Addison
73— Benjamin Anderson
79— Stephen Fuller

COAST GUARD
73— Rodney Leis
74— Leonard Kelly
81— Bruce Hensel
89— *Ty Rinoski
        *Jeffery Peters
90— Richard Schachner
91— John Freda

COE
67— Lynn Harris

COLBY
71— Ronald Lupton
        Frank Apantaku

COLGATE
73— Kenneth Nelson
80— Angelo Colosimo
89— Donald Charney

COLORADO
93— James Hansen

COLORADO COL.
69— Steven Ehrhart
72— Randy Bobier
75— Bruce Kolbezen
84— Herman Motz III

COLORADO MINES
66— Stuart Bennett
67— Michael Greensburg
        Charles Kirby
75— David Chambers

COLORADO ST.
65— Russel Mowrer
76— Mark Driscoll
87— Stephan Bartalo
88— Joseph Brookhart
93— Gregory Primus

COLUMBIA
72— John Sefcik
80— Mario Biaggi Jr.

CONNECTICUT
77— *Bernard Palmer

CORNELL
68— Ronald Kipicki
72— Thomas Albright
84— Derrick Harmon

CORNELL COLLEGE
65— Steven Miller
72— David Hilmers
73— Robert Ash
79— Brian Farrell
      Thomas Zinkula
81— *Timothy Garry
83— John Ward
93— Brent Sands
94— Matthew Miller

DARTMOUTH
66— Anthony Yezer
68— Henry Paulson Jr.
69— Randolph Wallick
71— Willie Bogan
73— Frederick Radke
74— Thomas Csatari
      *Robert Funk
77— Patrick Sullivan
89— Paul Sorensen

DAVIDSON
66— Stephen Smith
71— Rick Lyon
72— Robert Norris
86— *Louis Krempel

DAYTON
73— Timothy Quinn
76— Roy Gordon III
83— *Michael Pignatiello
91— Daniel Sharley

DELAWARE
86— Brian Farrell

DELAWARE VALLEY
85— Daniel Glowatski

DELTA ST.
76— William Hood

DENISON
70— Richard Trumball
73— Steven Smiljanich
76— *Dennis Thome
78— David Holcombe
86— Brian Gearinger
88— Grant Jones
92— Jonathan Fortkamp

DePAUW
68— Bruce Montgomerie
78— Mark Frazer
81— Jay True
85— Richard Bonaccorsi
86— Anthony deNicola
92— Thomas Beaulieu

DICKINSON
66— Robert Averback
71— *John West
75— *Gerald Urich

DOANE
68— John Lothrop
70— Richard Held

DRAKE
73— Joseph Worobec

DREXEL
72— Blake Lynn Ferguson

DUBUQUE
82— Timothy Finn

DUKE
68— Robert Lasky
71— *Curt Rawley

EAST CARO.
92— Keith Arnold

EAST TENN. ST.
82— Jay Patterson

EASTERN KY.
78— Steven Frommeyer

EASTERN N. MEX.
66— Richard James

ELIZABETH CITY ST.
73— Darnell Johnson
80— David Nickelson

ELMHURST
80— Richard Green

EMORY & HENRY
82— Thomas Browder Jr.

EVANSVILLE
75— David Mattingly
76— Charles Uhde Jr.
79— *Neil Saunders

FERRIS ST.
79— Robert Williams
93— Monty Brown

FLORIDA
72— Carlos Alvarez
77— Darrell Carpenter
85— Garrison Rolle
87— Bret Wiechmann
90— *Cedric Smith
91— Huey Richardson

FLORIDA ST.
88— David Palmer
91— David Roberts
94— Kenneth Alexander

FORDHAM
91— Eric Schweiker

FORT HAYS ST.
94— David Foster

FRANK. & MARSH.
69— Frank deGenova
83— *Robert Shepardson

FRESNO ST.
70— *Henry Corda
74— Dwayne Westphal
83— William Griever Jr.

FURMAN
77— Thomas Holcomb III
82— Charles Anderson
84— Ernest Gibson
86— *David Jager
87— Stephen Squire
90— Christopher Roper
92— Paul Siffri
      Eric Von Walter

GEORGETOWN
75— James Chesley Jr.

GEORGIA
68— Thomas Lawhorne Jr.
69— William Payne
71— Thomas Lyons
72— Thomas Nash Jr.
      Raleigh Mixon Robinson
78— Jeffrey Lewis
80— Jeffrey Pyburn
81— Christopher Welton
84— Terrell Hoage
88— Kim Stephens
89— Richard Tardits

GEORGIA TECH
68— William Eastman
75— James Robinson
81— Sheldon Fox
83— Ellis Gardner
86— John Ivemeyer

GETTYSBURG
70— *Herbert Ruby III
80— Richard Swartz

GRAMBLING
73— Stephen Dennis

GRINNELL
72— Edward Hirsch
80— *Derek Muehrcke

GUST. ADOLPHUS
74— James Goodwin
81— *David Najarian

HAMLINE
85— Kyle Aug
91— Robert Hackney

HAMPDEN-SYDNEY
78— *Wilson Newell
80— Timothy Maxa

HARVARD
68— Alan Bersin
71— *Richard Frisbie
75— Patrick McInally
76— William Emper
81— Charles Durst
85— Brian Bergstrom
87— Scott Collins

HAWAII
68— James Roberts
73— *Don Satterlee

HIRAM
68— Sherman Riemenschneider
74— Donald Brunetti

HOLY CROSS
84— *Bruce Kozerski
89— Jeffrey Wiley
91— John Lavalette

HOPE
74— Ronald Posthuma
80— Craig Groendyk
83— Kurt Brinks
85— *Scott Jecmen

HOUSTON
86— Gary Schoppe
87— Robert Brezina

IDAHO
67— Michael Lavens
      Joseph McCollum Jr.
84— Boyce Bailey

IDAHO ST.
76— Richard Rodgers
92— Steven Boyenger

ILL. BENEDICTINE
70— David Cyr
71— Thomas Danaher

ILL. WESLEYAN
93— Christopher Bisaillon

ILLINOIS
72— Robert Bucklin
73— Laurence McCarren Jr.
91— Curtis Lovelace
92— Michael Hopkins
93— John Wright

INDIANA
73— Glenn Scolnik
79— David Abrams
81— Kevin Speer

INDIANA (PA.)
78— *John Mihota
84— Kenneth Moore

INDIANA ST.
86— Jeffrey Miller

INDIANAPOLIS
76— Rodney Pawlik

IONA
81— Neal Kurtti
82— *Paul Rupp

IOWA
69— Michael Miller
76— Robert Elliott
78— Rodney Sears
86— Larry Station Jr.
88— Michael Flagg
89— Charles Hartlieb

IOWA ST.
70— William Bliss

JACKSON ST.
80— *Lester Walls

JACKSONVILLE ST.
79— Dewey Barker

JAMES MADISON
79— Warren Coleman
90— Mark Kiefer

JOHNS HOPKINS
73— Joseph Ouslander
74— Gunter Glocker
94— Steuart Markley

JUNIATA
72— Maurice Taylor
87— Robert Crossey

KANSAS
65— Ronald Oelschlager
69— David Morgan
72— Michael McCoy
73— John Schroll
78— Tom Fitch
87— Mark Henderson

KANSAS ST.
66— *Larry Anderson

83— James Gale
88— Matthew Garver
KENTUCKY
76— Thomas Ranieri
79— James Kovach
84— *Keith Martin
KENTUCKY ST.
68— James Jackson
KENYON
75— Patrick Clements
KNOX
88— Robert Monroe
LAFAYETTE
71— William Sprecher
76— Michael Kline
78— Victor Angeline III
LAMAR
73— *Richard Kubiak
LAWRENCE
68— Charles McKee
83— Christopher Matheus
LEBANON VALLEY
74— *Alan Shortell
LEHIGH
66— Robert Adelaar
68— Richard Miller
73— *Thomas Benfield
75— James Addonizio
76— *Robert Liptak
77— *Michael Yaszemski
80— David Melone
LIU-C. W. POST
79— John Luchsinger
LONG BEACH ST.
84— Joseph Donohue
LOUISIANA ST.
79— Robert Dugas
83— James Britt
88— Ignazio Albergamo
91— Solomon Graves
94— Chad Loup
LUTHER
67— Thomas Altemeier
78— *Mark Larson
85— Larry Bonney
MANKATO ST.
70— Bernard Maczuga
MARYLAND
78— Jonathan Claiborne
MARYVILLE (TENN.)
67— Frank Eggers II
McNEESE ST.
81— Daryl Burckel
86— Ross Leger
MEMPHIS
77— *James Mincey Jr.
MERCHANT MARINE
70— Robert Lavinia
76— *John Castagna
MIAMI (FLA.)
90— Robert Chudzinski
91— Michael Sullivan
MICHIGAN
67— David Fisher
74— David Gallagher
81— *John Wangler
82— Norm Betts
84— Stefan Humphries
　　Thomas Dixon
86— Clayton Miller
87— Kenneth Higgins
93— Christopher Hutchinson
94— Marc Milia
MICHIGAN ST.
69— Allen Brenner
70— Donald Baird
94— Steven Wasylk
MICHIGAN TECH
72— Larry Ras
74— Bruce Trusock
75— Daniel Rhude

MIDDLE TENN. ST.
73— *Edwin Zaunbrecher
MIDDLEBURY
79— Franklin Kettle
MIDLAND LUTHERAN
76— Thomas Hale
MILLERSVILLE
92— Thomas Burns III
MILLIKIN
90— *Charles Martin
MILLSAPS
67— Edward Weller
73— *Russell Gill
92— David Harrison Jr.
MINNESOTA
69— Robert Stein
71— Barry Mayer
73— Douglas Kingsriter
78— Robert Weber
MISSISSIPPI
66— Stanley Hindman
69— Steve Hindman
81— Kenneth Toler Jr.
86— Richard Austin
87— Jeffrey Noblin
88— Daniel Hoskins
89— Charles Walls
91— Todd Sandroni
MISSISSIPPI COL.
80— Stephen Johnson
MISSISSIPPI ST.
69— William Nelson
73— Frank Dowsing Jr.
75— James Webb
77— William Coltharp
93— Daniel Boyd
MISSOURI
66— Thomas Lynn
67— James Whitaker
69— *Charles Weber
71— John Weisenfels
79— Christopher Garlich
82— Van Darkow
MISSOURI-ROLLA
69— Robert Nicodemus
73— Kim Colter
81— Paul Janke
MIT
91— Darcy Prather
92— Rodrigo Rubiano
93— Roderick Tranum
MONMOUTH (ILL.)
72— Dale Brooks
90— Brent Thurness
MONTANA
75— Rock Svennungsen
79— Steven Fisher
84— Brian Salonen
91— Michael McGowan
MONTANA ST.
65— Gene Carlson
68— Russell Dodge
71— Jay Groepper
77— Bert Markovich
79— Jon Borchardt
　　James Mickelson
90— Derrick Isackson
92— Travis Annette
MORAVIAN
73— Daniel Joseph
94— Judson Frank
MOREHEAD ST.
92— James Appel
MORNINGSIDE
65— Larry White
MORRIS BROWN
83— Arthur Knight Jr.
MOUNT UNION
89— Paul Hrics
MUHLENBERG
73— Edward Salo
76— Eric Butler
78— Mark Stull

81— Arthur Scavone
91— Michael Hoffman
MURRAY ST.
71— Matthew Haug
78— Edward McFarland
81— *Kris Robbins
90— Eric Crigler
NAVY
65— William Donnelly
69— William Newton
70— Daniel Pike
75— *Timothy Harden
76— Chester Moeller II
81— Theodore Dumbauld
N.C. CENTRAL
91— Anthony Cooley
NEBRASKA
70— Randall Reeves
71— *John Decker
72— Larry Jacobson
73— David Mason
74— Daniel Anderson
76— Thomas Heiser
77— Vince Ferragamo
78— Ted Harvey
79— James Pillen
80— Timothy Smith
81— Randy Schleusener
　　Jeffrey Finn
82— Eric Lindquist
85— Scott Strasburger
88— Jeffrey Jamrog
89— Mark Blazek
90— Gerald Gdowski
　　Jacob Young III
91— David Edeal
　　Patrick Tyrance Jr.
92— Patrick Engelbert
93— Michael Stigge
94— Trev Alberts
NEBRASKA-OMAHA
84— Kirk Hutton
　　Clark Toner
NEW HAMPSHIRE
85— Richard Leclerc
NEW MEXICO
72— Roderick Long
76— Robert Berg
79— Robert Rumbaugh
83— George Parks
NEW MEXICO ST.
76— Ralph Jackson
77— *Joseph Fox
NORTH ALA.
82— *Warren Moore
NORTH CARO.
75— Christopher Kupec
81— William Donnalley
83— David Drechsler
91— Kevin Donnalley
NORTH CARO. ST.
75— Justus Everett
82— *Calvin Warren Jr.
NORTH DAK.
79— Dale Lian
81— Douglas Moen
82— Paul Franzmeier
85— Glen Kucera
88— Kurt Otto
89— Matthew Gulseth
93— Timothy Gelinske
NORTH DAK. ST.
66— James Schindler
69— *Stephen Stephens
71— Joseph Cichy
75— Paul Cichy
84— Doug Hushka
89— Charles Stock
94— Arden Beachy
NORTH TEXAS
68— Ruben Draper
77— Peter Morris
NORTHEAST LA.
93— Darren Rimmer
94— Robert Cobb
　　Michael Young

AWARD WINNERS

NORTHEAST MO. ST.
83— Roy Pettibone

NORTHERN ARIZ.
78— Larry Friedrichs

NORTHERN COLO.
76— Robert Bliss
91— Thomas Langer

NORTHERN IOWA
81— Owen Dockter

NORTHERN MICH.
73— Guy Falkenhagen
81— Phil Kessel
86— Keith Nelsen

NORTHWEST MO. ST.
82— Robert Gregory

NORTHWESTERN
70— *Bruce Hubbard
74— Steven Craig
77— Randolph Dean
81— Charles Kern

NORWICH
68— Richard Starbuck
74— Matthew Hincks

NOTRE DAME
67— Frederick Schnurr
68— James Smithberger
69— George Kunz
70— Michael Oriard
71— Lawrence DiNardo
72— Thomas Gatewood
73— Gregory Marx
74— David Casper
75— Peter Demmerle
      Reggie Barnett
79— Joseph Restic
81— Thomas Gibbons
82— John Krimm Jr.
86— Gregory Dingens
89— Reginald Ho
94— Timothy Ruddy

OCCIDENTAL
66— James Wanless
67— Richard Verry
69— John St. John
78— Richard Fry
80— *Timothy Bond
89— *Curtis Page

OHIO
78— *Robert Weidaw
80— Mark Geisler

OHIO NORTHERN
79— Mark Palmer
82— Larry Egbert

OHIO ST.
65— Arnold Chonko
66— Donald Unverferth
67— Ray Pryor
69— David Foley
71— Rex Kern
74— Randolph Gradishar
76— Brian Baschnagel
77— William Lukens
80— James Laughlin
84— John Frank
85— David Crecelius
86— Michael Lanese

OKLAHOMA
72— Larry Jack Mildren Jr.
73— Joe Wylie
81— Jay Jimerson
89— Anthony Phillips
91— Michael Sawatzky

OKLAHOMA ST.
83— *Doug Freeman

OLIVET
75— William Ziem

OREGON
79— *Willie Blasher Jr.
91— William Musgrave

OREGON ST.
69— William Enyart
69— *Jerry Belcher

PACIFIC (CAL.)
72— *Byron Cosgrove

78— Brian Peets
80— Bruce Filarsky

PENN ST.
66— Joseph Bellas
67— John Runnells III
71— Robert Holuba
72— David Joyner
73— Bruce Bannon
74— Mark Markovich
75— John Baiorunos
79— *Charles Correal
80— *Michael Guman
81— John Walsh
84— Harry Hamilton
85— Douglas Strange
87— Brian Silverling
90— Roger Thomas Duffy
94— Craig Fayak

PENNSYLVANIA
68— Ben Mortensen

PITTSBURGH
79— Jeff Delaney
86— Robert Schilken
89— Mark Stepnoski

POMONA-PITZER
69— *Lee Piatek
77— Scott Borg
83— *Calvin Oishi
85— *Derek Watanabe
88— Edward Irick
93— Torin Cunningham

PORTLAND ST.
79— John Urness

PRINCETON
67— Charles Peters
69— Richard Sandler
70— Keith Mauney
76— Ronald Beible
81— Mark Bailey
83— Brent Woods
86— James Petrucci
87— John Hammond

PUGET SOUND
68— Stephen Doolittle
79— *Patrick O'Loughlin
83— *Anthony Threlkeld

PURDUE
70— Michael Phipps
74— Robert Hoftiezer
75— Lawrence Burton

REDLANDS
65— Robert Jones

RENSSELAER
67— Robert Darnall
69— John Contento

RHODES
71— John Churchill
79— *Philip Mischke
81— Jeffrey Lane
83— *Russell Ashford
85— *John Foropoulos
89— James Augustine

RICE
81— *Lamont Jefferson
91— Donald Hollas

RICHMOND
86— Leland Melvin

RIPON
65— Phillip Steans
69— Steven Thompson
80— Thomas Klofta

RUTGERS
90— Steven Tardy

SANTA CLARA
72— Ronald Sani
77— Mark Tiernan
81— *David Alfaro
85— Alexis Vlahos
87— Patrick Sende

SEWANEE
65— Frank Stubblefield
66— Douglas Paschall
69— James Beene
71— John Popham IV
77— Dudley West

82— Gregory Worsowicz
      Domenick Reina
83— Michael York
84— Michael Jordan
93— Jason Forrester
94— Frederick Cravens

SHIPPENSBURG
77— Anthony Winter

SIMPSON
71— Richard Clogg
74— Hugh Lickiss
90— Roger Grover
94— Chad Earwood

SOUTH CARO.
67— Steven Stanley Juk Jr.

SOUTH DAK.
79— Michael Schurrer
87— Todd Salat
93— Jason Seurer

SOUTH DAK. ST.
80— Charles Loewen
81— Paul Kippley
88— Daniel Sonnek

SOUTHEASTERN LA.
74— William Percy Jr.

SOUTHERN-B.R.
70— Alden Roche

SOUTHERN CAL
66— Charles Arrobio
69— Steven Sogge
70— Harry Khasigian
      Steve Lehmer
74— Monte Doris
75— Patrick Haden
76— Kevin Bruce
78— Gary Bethel
80— Brad Budde
      Paul McDonald
81— Gordon Adams
      *Jeffrey Fisher
85— Duane Bickett
86— Anthony Colorito
      *Matthew Koart
87— Jeffrey Bregel
90— John Jackson

SOUTHERN COLO.
70— Gregory Smith
73— Collon Kennedy III

SOUTHERN METHODIST
83— *Brian O'Meara
85— *Monte Goen
87— David Adamson
93— Cary Brabham

SOUTHERN MISS.
83— Richard Thompson
84— Stephen Carmody

SOUTHERN UTAH
92— Stephen McDowell

SOUTHWEST MO. ST.
80— Richard Suchenski
      Mitchel Ware
85— Michael Armentrout

SOUTHWEST TEX. ST.
82— Michael Miller

SOUTHWESTERN LA.
71— *George Coussa

ST. CLOUD ST.
90— Richard Rodgers

ST. FRANCIS (PA.)
87— Christopher Tantlinger

ST. JOHN'S (MINN.)
92— Denis McDonough

ST. JOSEPH'S (IND.)
80— Michael Bettinger

ST. NORBERT
66— Michael Ryan
88— Matthew Lang

ST. PAUL'S
80— Gerald Hicks

ST. THOMAS (MINN.)
75— Mark Dienhart

STANFORD
65— *Joe Neal

66— *Terry DeSylvia
68— John Root
71— John Sande III
72— Jackie Brown
74— Randall Poltl
75— *Keith Rowen
76— Gerald Wilson
77— Duncan McColl
81— Milton McColl
84— John Bergren
85— Scott Carpenter
86— Matthew Soderlund
87— Brian Morris
88— Douglas Robison

STONEHILL
93— Kevin Broderick

SUSQUEHANNA
77— Gerald Huesken
82— Daniel Distasio

SWARTHMORE
72— Christopher Leinberger
83— *John Walsh

SYRACUSE
78— *Robert Avery
86— Timothy Green
94— Patrick O'Neill

TEMPLE
74— Dwight Fulton

TENN.-CHATT.
67— Harvey Ouzts
72— *Frank Webb
74— John McBrayer
76— Russell Gardner

TENNESSEE
71— Donald Denbo
Timothy Priest
77— Michael Mauck
81— Timothy Irwin

TEXAS
69— Corbin Robertson Jr.
71— Willie Zapalac Jr.
73— *Michael Bayer
74— Patrick Kelly
75— Wade Johnston
76— Robert Simmons
77— William Hamilton

TEXAS A&M
69— Edward Hargett
71— David Elmendorf
72— Stephen Luebbehusen
88— Kip Corrington

TEXAS-ARLINGTON
69— Michael Baylor

TEXAS CHRISTIAN
67— John Richards
68— Eldon Gresham Jr.
73— Scott Walker
75— Terry Drennan
88— J. Clinton Hailey

TEXAS SOUTHERN
65— Leon Hardy

TEXAS TECH
65— James Ellis Jr.
68— John Scovell
75— Jeffrey Jobe
78— *Richard Arledge
85— *Bradford White
90— Thomas Mathiasmeier

TOLEDO
82— Tad Wampfler
89— Kenneth Moyer

TRINITY (CONN.)
67— *Howard Wrzosek
68— Keith Miles

TRINITY (TEX.)
84— *Peter Broderick

TROY ST.
75— Mark King

TUFTS
65— Peter Smith
70— Robert Bass
79— Don Leach
80— *James Ford
82— *Brian Gallagher

87— Robert Patz
92— Paulo Oliveira

TULSA
67— *Larry Williams
75— James Mack Lancaster II

TUSKEGEE
68— James Greene

UC DAVIS
76— Daniel Carmazzi
David Gellerman
77— Rolf Benirschke
79— Mark Markel
86— Robert Hagenau
90— *James Tomasin
92— Robert Kincade
Michael Shepard
93— Brian Andersen

UC RIVERSIDE
72— Tyrone Hooks
74— Gary Van Jandegian

UCLA
67— *Raymond Armstrong
Dallas Grider
70— Gregory Jones
74— Steven Klosterman
76— John Sciarra
77— Jeffrey Dankworth
78— John Fowler Jr.
83— Cormac Carney
84— Richard Neuheisel
86— Michael Hartmeier
90— Richard Meyer
93— Carlton Gray

UNION (N.Y.)
88— Richard Romer

UTAH
81— James Baldwin
93— Steven Young

UTAH ST.
67— Ronnie Edwards
68— Garth Hall
70— Gary Anderson
76— Randall Stockham

UTEP
80— Eddie Forkerway
89— Patrick Hegarty
92— Robert Sesich

VA. MILITARY
79— Robert Bookmiller
80— Richard Craig Jones

VALPARAISO
75— *Richard Seall

VANDERBILT
73— Barrett Sutton Jr.
75— Douglas Martin

VILLANOVA
77— David Graziano
89— Richard Spugnardi

VIRGINIA
67— Frederick Jones
83— Patrick Chester
94— Thomas Burns Jr.

VIRGINIA TECH
73— Thomas Carpenito

WABASH
74— *Mark Nicolini
81— *Melvin Gore
83— David Broecker
87— James Herrmann
92— William Padgett

WAKE FOREST
70— Joseph Dobner
74— *Daniel Stroup
76— Thomas Fehring
78— *Michael McGlamry
83— Philip Denfeld
87— Toby Cole Jr.

WARTBURG
75— Conrad Mandsager
76— James Charles Peterson
82— *Rod Feddersen
94— Koby Kreinbring

WASH. & JEFF.
70— Edward Guna

82— Max Regula
91— David Conn
93— Raymond Cross Jr.

WASH. & LEE
70— Michael Thornton
74— William Wallace Jr.
78— Jeffrey Slatcoff
79— Richard Wiles
80— *Scott Smith
81— Lonnie Nunley III
89— Michael Magoline

WASHINGTON
65— William Douglas
67— Michael Ryan
72— *James Krieg
73— John Brady
77— Scott Phillips
78— Blair Bush
80— Bruce Harrell
82— Mark Jerue
83— Charles Nelson
Mark Stewart
88— David Rill
92— Edward Cunningham

WASHINGTON (MO.)
94— Aaron Keen

WASHINGTON ST.
67— Richard Sheron
68— A. Douglas Flansburg
83— Gregory Porter
84— Patrick Lynch Jr.
85— Daniel Lynch

WAYNE ST. (MICH.)
76— Edward Skowneski Jr.
81— Phillip Emery

WEBER ST.
68— Phillip Tuckett
74— *Douglas Smith
92— David Hall
94— Deric Gurley

WESLEYAN
67— John Dwyer
69— Stuart Blackburn
71— James Lynch
78— John McVicar

WEST TEX. A&M
75— *Ben Bentley
82— Kevin Dennis

WEST VA.
74— Ade Dillion
*Daniel Larcamp
82— Oliver Luck

WESTERN CARO.
94— Thomas Jackson III

WESTERN ILL.
89— Paul Singer

WESTERN KY.
72— Jimmy Barber
80— Charles DeLacey

WESTERN MICH.
68— Martin Barski
71— Jonathan Bull

WESTERN N. MEX.
68— Richard Mahoney

WHEATON (ILL.)
89— David Lauber
93— Bart Moseman

WHITTIER
76— John Getz
79— Mark Deven
87— *Timothy Younger

WILLAMETTE
87— *Gerry Preston

WILLIAM & MARY
78— G. Kenneth Smith
80— Clarence Gaines
85— Mark Kelso

WILLIAM JEWELL
66— Charles Scrogin
70— Thomas Dunn
John Johnston

WILLIAMS
65— Jerry Jones
72— John Murray

WINSTON-SALEM
84— Eddie Sauls

WIS.-PLATTEVILLE
87— Michael Hintz

WISCONSIN
66— David Fronek
80— Thomas Stauss
82— *David Mohapp
83— Mathew Vanden Boom

WITTENBERG
82— William Beach

WOOSTER
80— Edward Blake Moore

WYOMING
74— Steven Cockreham
85— Bob Gustafson
89— Randall Welniak

XAVIER (OHIO)
65— William Eastlake

YALE
66— *James Groninger
67— Howard Hilgendorf Jr.
69— Frederick Morris
71— Thomas Neville
72— David Bliss
75— John Burkus
77— *Stone Phillips
79— William Crowley
82— Richard Diana
91— Vincent Mooney

Academic All-America Hall of Fame

Since its inception in 1988, 24 former NCAA football players have been inducted into the GTE Academic All-America Hall of Fame. They were selected from among nominees by the College Sports Information Directors of America from past academic all-Americans of the 1950s, '60s and '70s. Following are the selections by the year selected and each player's team, position and last year played:

1988
Pete Dawkins, Army, HB, 1958
Pat Haden, Southern Cal, QB, 1974
Rev. Donn Moomaw, UCLA, LB, 1953
Merlin Olsen, Utah St., T, 1961

1989
Carlos Alvarez, Florida, WR, 1971
Willie Bogan, Dartmouth, DB, 1970
Steve Bramwell, Washington, DB, 1965
Joe Romig, Colorado, G, 1961
Jim Swink, Texas Christian, B, 1956
John Wilson, Michigan St., DB, 1952

1990
Joe Theismann, Notre Dame, QB, 1970
Howard Twilley, Tulsa, TE, 1965

1991
Terry Baker, Oregon St., QB, 1962
Joe Holland, Cornell, RB, 1978
David Joyner, Penn St., OT, 1971
Brock Strom, Air Force, T, 1958

1992
Alan Ameche, Wisconsin, RB, 1954
Stephen Eisenhauer, Navy, G, 1953
Randy Gradishar, Ohio St., LB, 1973

1993
Raymond Berry, Southern Methodist, E, 1954
Dave Casper, Notre Dame, E, 1973
Jim Grabowski, Illinois, FB, 1965

1994
Richard Mayo, Air Force, QB, 1961
Lee Roy Selmon, Oklahoma, DT, 1975

Academic All-Americans by School

Since 1952, academic all-America teams have been selected by the College Sports Information Directors of America. To be eligible, student-athletes must be regular performers and have at least a 3.200 grade-point average (on a 4.000 scale) during their college careers. University division teams (I-A and I-AA) are complete in this list, but college division teams (II, III, NAIA) before 1970 are missing from CoSIDA archives, with few exceptions. Following are all known first-team selections:

ABILENE CHRISTIAN
63— Jack Griggs, LB
70— Jim Lindsey, QB
74— Greg Stirman, E
76— Bill Curbo, T
77— Bill Curbo, T
87— Bill Clayton, DL
88— Bill Clayton, DL
89— Bill Clayton, DL
90— Sean Grady, WR

ADRIAN
84— Steve Dembowski, QB

AIR FORCE
58— Brock Strom, T
59— Rich Mayo, B
60— Rich Mayo, B
70— Ernie Jennings, E
71— Darryl Haas, LB/K
72— Bob Homburg, DE
       Mark Prill, LB
73— Joe Debes, OT
74— Joe Debes, OT
78— Steve Hoog, WR
81— Mike France, LB
83— Jeff Kubiak, P
86— Chad Hennings, DL
87— Chad Hennings, DL
88— David Hlatky, OL
90— Chris Howard, RB
92— Grant Johnson, LB

AKRON
80— Andy Graham, PK

ALABAMA
61— Tommy Brooker, E
       Pat Trammell, B
64— Gaylon McCollough, C
65— Steve Sloan, QB
       Dennis Homan, HB
67— Steve Davis, K
       Bob Childs, LB
70— Johnny Musso, HB
71— Johnny Musso, HB
73— Randy Hall, DT
74— Randy Hall, DT
75— Danny Ridgeway, KS
79— Major Ogilvie, RB

ALABAMA A&M
89— Tracy Kendall, QB
90— Tracy Kendall, QB

ALBANY (N.Y.)
86— Thomas Higgins, OT
87— Thomas Higgins, OT

ALBION
82— Bruce Drogosch, LB
86— Michael Grant, DB
90— Scott Bissell, DB

ALFRED
93— Eric Baxmann, LB
       Jeffrey Shooks, P
89— Mark Szynkowski, OL

ALLEGHENY
81— Kevin Baird, P
91— Adam Lechman, OL
       Darren Hadlock, LB

ALMA
86— Greg Luczak, TE

AMERICAN INT'L
81— Todd Scyocurka, LB

APPALACHIAN ST.
77— Gill Beck, C
92— D. J. Campbell, QB

ARIZONA
68— Mike Moody, OG
75— Jon Abbott, LB
76— Jon Abbott, T/LB
77— Jon Abbott, T/LB
79— Jeffrey Whitton, DL
87— Charles Cecil, DB

ARIZONA ST.
66— Ken Dyer, OE
88— Mark Tingstad, LB

ARKANSAS
57— Gerald Nesbitt, FB
61— Lance Alworth, B
64— Ken Hatfield, B
65— Randy Stewart, C
       Jim Lindsey, HB
       Jack Brasuell, DB
68— Bob White, K
69— Bill Burnett, HB
       Terry Stewart, DB
78— Brad Shoup, DB

ARKANSAS-MONTICELLO
85— Ray Howard, OG
88— Sean Rochelle, QB

ARKANSAS ST.
59— Larry Zabrowski, OT
61— Jim McMurray, QB

ARKANSAS TECH
90— Karl Kuhn, TE
91— Karl Kuhn, TE

ARMY
55— Ralph Chesnauskas, E
57— James Kernan, C
       Pete Dawkins, HB
58— Pete Dawkins, HB
59— Don Usry, E
65— Sam Champi, DE
67— Bud Neswiacheny, DE
69— Theodore Shadid, C
89— Michael Thorson, DB
92— Mike McElrath, DB

ASHLAND
73— Mark Gulling, DB
74— Ron Brown, LB
76— Dan Bogden, E
77— Bruce Niehm, LB
81— Mark Braun, C
91— Thomas Shiban, RB
93— Jerry Spatny, DL

AUBURN
57— Jimmy Phillips, E
59— Jackie Burkett, C
60— Ed Dyas, B
65— Bill Cody, LB
69— Buddy McClinton, DB
74— Bobby Davis, LB
75— Chuck Fletcher, DT
76— Chris Vacarella, RB
84— Gregg Carr, LB

AUGSBURG
81— Paul Elliott, DL

AUGUSTANA (ILL.)
75— George Wesbey, T
80— Bill Dannehl, WR
84— Steve Sanders, OT
85— Steve Sanders, OT

AUGUSTANA (S.D.)
72— Pat McNerney, T
73— Pat McNerney, T
74— Jim Clemens, G

75—Jim Clemens, C
77—Stan Biondi, K
86—David Gubbrud, DL
87—David Gubbrud, DL
88—David Gubbrud, LB
89—David Gubbrud, LB

AUSTIN
81—Gene Branum, PK

AUSTIN PEAY
74—Gregory Johnson, G

BAKER
61—John Jacobs, B

BALDWIN-WALLACE
70—Earl Stolberg, DB
72—John Yezerski, G
78—Roger Andrachik, RB
      Greg Monda, LB
81—Chuck Krajacic, OG
88—Shawn Gorman, P
91—Tom Serdinak, P
93—Adrian Allison, DL
      David Coverdale, DL

BALL ST.
83—Rich Chitwood, C
85—Ron Duncan, TE
86—Ron Duncan, TE
87—Ron Duncan, TE
88—Ted Ashburn, OL
      Greg Shackelford, DL
89—Ted Ashburn, OL
      David Haugh, DB
91—Troy Hoffer, DB
92—Troy Hoffer, DB

BATES
82—Neal Davidson, DB

BAYLOR
61—Ronnie Bull, RB
62—Don Trull, QB
63—Don Trull, QB
76—Cris Quinn, DE
89—Mike Welch, DB
90—Mike Welch, DB

BELOIT
90—Shane Stadler, RB

BETHANY (KAN.)
86—Wade Gaeddert, DB

BLOOMSBURG
83—Dave Pepper, DL

BOISE ST.
71—Brent McIver, IL
73—Glenn Sparks, G
78—Sam Miller, DB

BOSTON COLLEGE
77—Richard Scudellari, LB
86—Michael Degnan, DL

BOSTON U.
83—Steve Shapiro, K
85—Brad Hokin, DB
93—Andre Maksimov, OL

BOWDOIN
84—Mike Siegel, P
93—Michael Turmelle, DB

BOWLING GREEN
75—John Boles, DE
89—Pat Jackson, LB
90—Pat Jackson, TE

BRIGHAM YOUNG
73—Steve Stratton, RB
80—Scott Phillips, RB
81—Dan Plater, WR
87—Chuck Cutler, WR
88—Chuck Cutler, WR
      Tim Clark, DL
89—Fred Whittingham, RB
90—Andy Boyce, WR
93—Eric Drage, WR

BROWN
81—Travis Holcombe, OG
82—Dave Folsom, DB
86—Marty Edwards, C
87—John Cuozzo, C

BUCKNELL
72—Douglas Nauman, T
      John Ondrasik, DB
73—John Dailey, LB

74—Steve Leskinen, T
75—Larry Brunt, E
76—Larry Brunt, E
84—Rob Masonis, RB
      Jim Reilly, TE
86—Mike Morrow, WR
91—David Berardinelli, WR
92—David Berardinelli, WR

BUFFALO
63—Gerry Philbin, T
84—Gerry Quinlivan, LB
85—James Dunbar, C
86—James Dunbar, C

BUFFALO ST.
87—Clint Morano, OT

BUTLER
84—Steve Kollias, L

CAL LUTHERAN
81—John Walsh, OT

CALIFORNIA
67—Bob Crittenden, DG
70—Robert Richards, OT
82—Harvey Salem, OT

CANISIUS
82—Tom Schott, WR
83—Tom Schott, TE
86—Mike Panepinto, RB

CAPITAL
70—Ed Coy, E
83—Mike Linton, G
85—Kevin Sheets, WR

CARLETON
92—Scott Hanks, TE

CARNEGIE MELLON
76—Rick Lackner, LB
      Dave Nackoul, E
84—Roger Roble, WR
87—Bryan Roessler, DL
      Chris Haupt, LB
89—Robert O'Toole, LB
90—Frank Bellante, RB
      Robert O'Toole, LB

CARROLL (WIS.)
76—Stephen Thompson, QB

CARSON-NEWMAN
61—David Dale, E
93—Chris Horton, OL

CARTHAGE
61—Bob Halsey, B
77—Mark Phelps, QB

CASE RESERVE
75—John Kosko, T
82—Jim Donnelly, RB
83—Jim Donnelly, RB
84—Jim Donnelly, RB
88—Chris Hutter, TE
90—Michael Bissler, DB

CENTRAL (IOWA)
79—Chris Adkins, LB
85—Scott Lindrell, LB
86—Scott Lindrell, LB
91—Rich Kacmarynski, RB

CENTRAL MICH.
70—Ralph Burde, DL
74—Mike Franckowiak, QB
      John Wunderlich, T
79—Mike Ball, WR
84—John DeBoer, WR
91—Jeff Bender, QB

CENTRE
84—Teel Bruner, DB
85—Teel Bruner, DB
89—Bryan Ellington, DB
91—Eric Horstmeyer, WR

CHADRON ST.
73—Jerry Sutton, LB
75—Bob Lacey, KS
79—Jerry Carder, TE

CHEYNEY
75—Steve Anderson, G

CHICAGO
87—Paul Haar, OG
88—Paul Haar, OL
93—Frank Baker, RB

CINCINNATI
81—Kari Yli-Renko, OT
90—Kyle Stroh, DL
91—Kris Bjorson, TE

CITADEL
63—Vince Petno, E
76—Kenny Caldwell, LB
77—Kenny Caldwell, LB
78—Kenny Caldwell, LB
87—Thomas Frooman, RB
89—Thomas Frooman, RB

CLEMSON
59—Lou Cordileone, T
78—Steve Fuller, QB

COAST GUARD
70—Charles Pike, LB
71—Bruce Melnick, DB
81—Mark Butt, DB

COE
93—Marcus Adkins, DL

COLGATE
78—Angelo Colosimo, RB
79—Angelo Colosimo, RB
85—Tom Stenglein, WR
89—Jeremy Garvey, TE

COLORADO
60—Joe Romig, G
61—Joe Romig, G
67—Kirk Tracy, OG
70—Jim Cooch, DB
73—Rick Stearns, LB
74—Rick Stearns, LB
75—Steve Young, DT
87—Eric McCarty, LB
90—Jim Hansen, OL
91—Jim Hansen, OL
92—Jim Hansen, OL

COLORADO MINES
72—Dave Chambers, RB
83—Charles Lane, T

COLORADO ST.
55—Gary Glick, B
69—Tom French, OT
86—Steve Bartalo, RB

COLUMBIA
52—Mitch Price, B
53—John Gasella, T
56—Claude Benham, B
71—John Sefcik, HB

CORNELL
77—Joseph Holland, RB
78—Joseph Holland, RB

Chicago fullback Frank Baker was honored in 1993 for his work both on the field (first team Division III all-American) and in the classroom (academic all-American).

82— Derrick Harmon, RB
83— Derrick Harmon, RB
85— Dave Van Metre, DL

CORNELL COLLEGE
72— Rob Ash, QB
   Dewey Birkhofer, S
76— Joe Lauterbach, G
   Tom Zinkula, DT
77— Tom Zinkula, DT
78— Tom Zinkula, DL
82— John Ward, WR
91— Bruce Feldmann, QB
92— Brent Sands, DB
93— Mark McDermott, DB

DARTMOUTH
70— Willie Bogan, DB
83— Michael Patsis, DB
87— Paul Sorensen, LB
88— Paul Sorensen, LB
90— Brad Preble, DB
91— Mike Bobo, WR
   Tom Morrow, LB
92— Russ Torres, RB

DAYTON
71— Tim Quinn, LB
72— Tim Quinn, DT
79— Scott Terry, QB
84— Greg French, K
   David Kemp, LB
   Jeff Slayback, L
85— Greg French, K
86— Gerry Meyer, OT
91— Brett Cuthbert, DB
   Dan Rosenbaum, DB
92— Steve Lochow, DL
   Dan Rosenbaum, DB
93— Steve Lochow, DL
   Brad Mager, DB

DEFIANCE
80— Jill Bailey, OT
   Mark Bockelman, TE

DELAWARE
70— Yancey Phillips, T
71— Robert Depew, DE
72— Robert Depew, DE

DELAWARE VALLEY
84— Dan Glowatski, WR

DELTA ST.
70— Hal Posey, RB
74— Billy Hood, E
   Ricky Lewis, LB
   Larry Miller, RB
75— Billy Hood, E
78— Terry Moody, DB
79— Charles Stavley, G

DENISON
75— Dennis Thome, LB
87— Grant Jones, DB

DePAUW
70— Jim Ceaser, LB
71— Jim Ceaser, LB
73— Neil Oslos, RB
80— Jay True, WR
85— Tony deNicola, QB
87— Michael Sherman, DB
90— Tom Beaulieu, DL
91— Tom Beaulieu, DL
   Matt Nelson, LB

DICKINSON
74— Gerald Urich, RB
79— Scott Mumma, RB

DRAKE
74— Todd Gaffney, KS
83— Tom Holt, RB

DREXEL
70— Lynn Ferguson, S

DUBUQUE
80— Tim Finn, RB

DUKE
66— Roger Hayes, DE
67— Bob Lasky, DT
70— Curt Rawley, DT
86— Mike Diminick, DB
87— Mike Diminick, DB
88— Mike Diminick, DB

89— Doug Key, DL
93— Travis Pearson, DL

EAST STROUDSBURG
84— Ernie Siegrist, TE

EAST TENN. ST.
71— Ken Oster, DB

EAST TEX. ST.
77— Mike Hall, OT

EASTERN KY.
77— Steve Frommeyer, S

EASTERN N. MEX.
80— Tom Sager, DL
81— Tom Sager, DL

ELON
73— John Rascoe, E
79— Bryan Burney, DB

EMORY & HENRY
71— Tom Wilson, LB

EMPORIA ST.
79— Tom Lingg, DL

EVANSVILLE
74— David Mattingly, S
76— Michael Pociask, C
87— Jeffery Willman, TE

FERRIS ST.
81— Vic Trecha, OT
92— Monty Brown, LB

FLORIDA
65— Charles Casey, E
69— Carlos Alvarez, WR
71— Carlos Alvarez, WR
76— David Posey, KS
77— Wes Chandler, RB
80— Cris Collinsworth, WR
91— Brad Culpepper, DL
93— Michael Gilmore, DB

FLORIDA A&M
90— Irvin Clark, DL

FLORIDA ST.
72— Gary Huff, QB
79— William Jones, DB
   Phil Williams, WR
80— William Jones, DB
81— Rohn Stark, P

FORDHAM
90— Eric Schweiker, OL

FORT HAYS ST.
75— Greg Custer, RB
82— Ron Johnson, P
85— Paul Nelson, DL
86— Paul Nelson, DL
89— Dean Gengler, OL

FORT LEWIS
72— Dee Tennison, E

FRANK. & MARSH.
77— Joe Fry, DB
78— Joe Fry, DB

FURMAN
76— Jeff Holcomb, T
85— Brian Jager, RB
88— Kelly Fletcher, DL
89— Kelly Fletcher, DL
   Chris Roper, LB
91— Eric Walter, OL

GA. SOUTHWESTERN
87— Gregory Slappery, RB

GEORGETOWN
71— Gerry O'Dowd, HB
86— Andrew Phelan, OG

GEORGETOWN (KY.)
89— Eric Chumbley, OL
92— Bobby Wasson, PK

GEORGIA
60— Francis Tarkenton, QB
65— Bob Etter, K
66— Bob Etter, K
   Lynn Hughes, DB
68— Bill Stanfill, DT
71— Tom Nash, OT
   Mixon Robinson, DE
77— Jeff Lewis, LB
82— Terry Hoage, DB

83— Terry Hoage, DB
92— Todd Peterson, PK

GEORGIA TECH
52— Ed Gossage, T
   Cecil Trainer, DE
   Larry Morris, LB
55— Wade Mitchell, B
56— Allen Ecker, G
66— Jim Breland, C
   W. J. Blaine, LB
   Bill Eastman, DB
67— Bill Eastman, DB
80— Sheldon Fox, LB
90— Stefen Scotton, RB

GETTYSBURG
79— Richard Swartz, LB

GRAMBLING
72— Floyd Harvey, RB
93— Gilad Landau, PK

GRAND VALLEY ST.
91— Mark Smith, OL
   Todd Wood, DB

GRINNELL
71— Edward Hirsch, E
81— David Smiley, TE

GROVE CITY
74— Pat McCoy, LB
89— Travis Croll, P

GUST. ADOLPHUS
80— Dave Najarian, DL
81— Dave Najarian, LB

HAMLINE
73— Thomas Dufresne, E
89— Jon Voss, TE

HAMPDEN-SYDNEY
82— John Dickinson, OG
90— W. R. Jones, OL
91— David Brickhill, PK

HAMPTON
93— Tim Benson, WR

HARVARD
84— Brian Bergstrom, DB

HEIDELBERG
82— Jeff Kurtzman, DL

HILLSDALE
61— James Richendollar, T
72— John Cervini, G
81— Mark Kellogg, LB
93— Jason Ahee, DB

HOLY CROSS
83— Bruce Kozerski, T
85— Kevin Reilly, OT
87— Jeff Wiley, QB
91— Pete Dankert, DL

HOPE
73— Ronald Posthuma, T
79— Craig Groendyk, T
80— Greg Bekius, PK
82— Kurt Brinks, C
84— Scott Jecmen, DB
86— Timothy Chase, OG

HOUSTON
64— Horst Paul, E
76— Mark Mohr, DB
   Kevin Rollwage, OT
77— Kevin Rollwage, OT

IDAHO
70— Bruce Langmeade, T

IDAHO ST.
84— Brent Koetter, DB
91— Steve Boyenger, DB

ILL. WESLEYAN
71— Keith Ihlanfeldt, DE
80— Jim Eaton, DL
   Rick Hanna, DL
   Mike Watson, DB
81— Mike Watson, DB
91— Chris Bisaillon, WR
92— Chris Udovich, DL

ILLINOIS
52— Bob Lenzini, DT
64— Jim Grabowski, FB
65— Jim Grabowski, FB
66— John Wright, E

70—Jim Rucks, DE
71—Bob Bucklin, DE
80—Dan Gregus, DL
81—Dan Gregus, DL
82—Dan Gregus, DL
91—Mike Hopkins, DB
92—John Wright Jr., WR

ILLINOIS COL.
80—Jay Wessler, RB

ILLINOIS ST.
76—Tony Barnes, C
80—Jeff Hembrough, DL
89—Dan Hackman, OL

INDIANA
67—Harry Gonso, HB
72—Glenn Scolnik, RB
80—Kevin Speer, C

INDIANA (PA.)
82—Kenny Moore, DB
83—Kenny Moore, DB

INDIANA ST.
71—Gary Brown, E
72—Michael Eads, E

INDIANAPOLIS
76—William Willan, E

IONA
80—Neal Kurtti, DL

IOWA
52—Bill Fenton, DE
53—Bill Fenton, DE
75—Bob Elliott, DB
85—Larry Station, LB

IOWA ST.
52—Max Burkett, DB
82—Mark Carlson, LB

ITHACA
72—Dana Hallenbeck, LB
85—Brian Dougherty, DB
89—Peter Burns, OL

JACKSONVILLE ST.
77—Dewey Barker, E
78—Dewey Barker, TE

JAMES MADISON
78—Warren Coleman, OT

JOHN CARROLL
83—Nick D'Angelo, LB
Jim Sferra, DL
85—Joe Burrello, LB
86—Joe Burrello, LB

JOHNS HOPKINS
77—Charles Hauck, DT
93—Michael House, DL

JUNIATA
70—Ray Grabiak, DL
71—Ray Grabiak, DE
Maurice Taylor, IL

KALAMAZOO
92—Sean Mullendore, LB

KANSAS
64—Fred Elder, T
67—Mike Sweatman, LB
68—Dave Morgan, LB
71—Mike McCoy, C
76—Tom Fitch, S

KANSAS ST.
74—Don Lareau, LB
77—Floyd Dorsey, OG
81—Darren Gale, DB
82—Darren Gale, DB
Mark Hundley, RB
85—Troy Faunce, P

KENT
72—Mark Reiheld, DB
91—Brad Smith, RB

KENTUCKY
74—Tom Ranieri, LB
78—Mark Keene, C
Jim Kovach, LB
85—Ken Pietrowiak, C

KENYON
77—Robert Jennings, RB
85—Dan Waldeck, TE

LA VERNE
82—Scott Shier, OT

LAFAYETTE
70—William Sprecher, T
74—Mike Kline, DB
79—Ed Rogusky, RB
80—Ed Rogusky, RB

LAWRENCE
81—Chris Matheus, DL
Scott Reppert, RB
82—Chris Matheus, DL

LEHIGH
90—Shon Harker, DB

LEWIS & CLARK
61—Pat Clock, G
81—Dan Jones, WR

LIU-C.W. POST
70—Art Canario, T
75—Frank Prochilo, RB
84—Bob Jahelka, DB
93—Jim Byrne, WR

LONG BEACH ST.
83—Joe Donohue, LB

LORAS
84—John Coyle, DL
Pete Kovatisis, DB
85—John Coyle, DL
91—Mark Goedken, DL
93—Travis Michaels, LB

LOUISIANA ST.
59—Mickey Mangham, E
60—Charles Strange, C
61—Billy Booth, T
71—Jay Michaelson, KS
73—Tyler Lafauci, OG
Joe Winkler, DB
74—Brad Davis, RB
77—Robert Dugas, OT
84—Juan Carlos Betanzos, PK

LUTHER
83—Larry Bonney, DL
84—Larry Bonney, DL
89—Larry Anderson, RB
90—Joel Nerem, DL
91—Joel Nerem, DL

LYCOMING
74—Thomas Vanaskie, DB
85—Mike Kern, DL

MACALESTER
82—Lee Schaefer, OG

MANKATO ST.
74—Dan Miller, C

MANSFIELD
83—John Delate, DB

MARIETTA
83—Matt Wurtzbacher, DL

MARS HILL
92—Brent Taylor, DL

MARYLAND
53—Bernie Faloney, B
75—Kim Hoover, DE
78—Joe Muffler, DL

MASS.-LOWELL
85—Don Williams, RB

McGILL
87—Bruno Pietrobon, WR

McNEESE ST.
78—Jim Downing, OT
79—Jim Downing, OT
90—David Easterling, DB

MEMPHIS
92—Pat Jansen, DL

MIAMI (FLA.)
59—Fran Curci, B
84—Bernie Kosar, QB

MIAMI (OHIO)
73—Andy Pederzolli, DB

MICHIGAN
52—Dick Balzhiser, B
55—Jim Orwig, T
57—Jim Orwig, T
64—Bob Timberlake, QB
66—Dave Fisher, FB

Dick Vidmer, FB
69—Jim Mandich, OE
70—Phil Seymour, DE
71—Bruce Elliott, DB
72—Bill Hart, OG
74—Kirk Lewis, OG
75—Dan Jilek, DE
81—Norm Betts, TE
82—Stefan Humphries, OG
Robert Thompson, LB
83—Stefan Humphries, OG
85—Clay Miller, OT
86—Kenneth Higgins, WR

MICHIGAN ST.
52—John Wilson, DB
53—Don Dohoney, E
55—Buck Nystrom, G
57—Blanche Martin, HB
65—Don Bierowicz, DT
Don Japinga, DB
66—Pat Gallinagh, DT
68—Al Brenner, E/DB
69—Ron Saul, OG
Rich Saul, DE
73—John Shinsky, DT
79—Alan Davis, DB
85—Dean Altobelli, DB
86—Dean Altobelli, DB
86—Shane Bullough, LB
92—Steve Wasylk, DB
93—Steve Wasylk, DB

MICHIGAN TECH
71—Larry Ras, HB
73—Bruce Trusock, C
76—Jim Van Wagner, RB
92—Kurt Coduti, QB

MILLERSVILLE
91—Tom Burns, OL

MILLIKIN
61—Gerald Domesick, B
75—Frank Stone, G
78—Charlie Sammis, K
79—Eric Stevens, WR
83—Marc Knowles, WR
84—Tom Kreller, RB
85—Cary Bottorff, LB
Tom Kreller, RB
90—Tim Eimermann, PK

MINNESOTA
56—Bob Hobert, T
60—Frank Brixius, T
68—Bob Stein, DE
70—Barry Mayer, RB
89—Brent Herbel, P

MISSISSIPPI
54—Harold Easterwood, C
59—Robert Khayat, T
Charlie Flowers, B
61—Doug Elmore, B
65—Stan Hindman, G
68—Steve Hindman, HB
69—Julius Fagan, K
74—Greg Markow, DE
77—Robert Fabris, OE
George Plasketes, DE
80—Ken Toler, WR
86—Danny Hoskins, OG
87—Danny Hoskins, OG
88—Wesley Walls, TE
89—Todd Sandroni, DB

MISSISSIPPI COL.
75—Anthony Saway, S
78—Steve Johnson, OT
79—Steve Johnson, OT
83—Wayne Frazier, C

MISSISSIPPI ST.
53—Jackie Parker, B
56—Ron Bennett, E
72—Frank Dowsing, DB
73—Jimmy Webb, DE
76—Will Coltharp, DE
89—Stacy Russell, DB

MISSOURI
62—Tom Hertz, G
66—Dan Schuppan, DE
Bill Powell, DT
68—Carl Garber, MG
70—John Weisenfels, LB

72— Greg Hill, KS
81— Van Darkow, LB
93— Matt Burgess, OL

MISSOURI-ROLLA
72— Kim Colter, DB
80— Paul Janke, OG
86— Tom Reed, RB
87— Jim Pfeiffer, OT
88— Jim Pfeiffer, OL
91— Don Huff, DB
92— Don Huff, DB

MIT
89— Anthony Lapes, WR
90— Darcy Prather, LB
91— Rodrigo Rubiano, DL
92— Roderick Tranum, WR
93— Corey Foster, OL

MO. SOUTHERN ST.
85— Mike Testman, DB
93— Chris Tedford, OL

MONMOUTH (ILL.)
83— Robb Long, QB

MONTANA
77— Steve Fisher, DE
79— Ed Cerkovnik, DB
88— Michael McGowan, LB
89— Michael McGowan, LB
90— Michael McGowan, LB
93— Dave Dickenson, QB

MONTANA ST.
84— Dirk Nelson, P
88— Anders Larsson, PK

MONTCLAIR ST.
70— Bill Trimmer, DL
82— Daniel Deneher, KS

MOORHEAD ST.
88— Brad Shamla, DL

MORAVIAN
87— Jeff Pollock, WR

MOREHEAD ST.
74— Don Russell, KS
90— James Appel, OL
91— James Appel, OL

MOUNT UNION
71— Dennis Montgomery, QB
84— Rick Marabito, L
86— Scott Gindlesberger, QB
87— Paul Hrics, C

MUHLENBERG
70— Edward Salo, G
71— Edward Salo, IL
72— Edward Salo, C
75— Keith Ordemann, LB
80— Arthur Scavone, OT
89— Joe Zeszotarski, DL
90— Mike Hoffman, DB

MURRAY ST.
76— Eddie McFarland, DB

MUSKINGUM
78— Dan Radalia, DL
79— Dan Radalia, DL

NAVY
53— Steve Eisenhauer, G
57— Tom Forrestal, QB
58— Joe Tranchini, B
69— Dan Pike, RB
80— Ted Dumbauld, LB

NEB.-KEARNEY
70— John Makovicka, RB
75— Tim Brodahl, E

NEB. WESLEYAN
87— Pat Sweeney, DB
88— Pat Sweeney, DB
     Mike Surls, LB
89— Scott Shaffer, RB
     Scott Shipman, DB

NEBRASKA
62— James Huge, E
63— Dennis Calridge, B
66— Marv Mueller, DB
69— Randy Reeves, DB
71— Larry Jacobson, DT
     Jeff Kinney, HB
73— Frosty Anderson, E
75— Rik Bonness, C

Tom Heiser, RB
76— Vince Ferragamo, QB
     Ted Harvey, DB
77— Ted Harvey, DB
78— George Andrews, DL
     James Pillen, DB
79— Rod Horn, DL
     Kelly Saalfeld, C
     Randy Schleusener, OG
80— Jeff Finn, TE
     Randy Schleusener, OG
81— Eric Lindquist, DB
     David Rimington, C
     Randy Theiss, OT
82— David Rimington, C
83— Scott Strasburger, DL
     Rob Stuckey, DL
84— Scott Strasburger, DL
     Rob Stuckey, DL
     Mark Traynowicz, C
86— Dale Klein, K
     Thomas Welter, OT
87— Jeffrey Jamrog, DL
     Mark Blazek, DB
88— Mark Blazek, DB
     John Kroeker, P
89— Gerry Gdowski, QB
     Jake Young, OL
90— David Edeal, OL
     Pat Tyrance, LB
     Jim Wanek, OL
91— Pat Engelbert, DL
     Mike Stigge, P
92— Mike Stigge, P
93— Rob Zatechka, OL
     Terry Connealy, DL
     Trev Alberts, LB

NEBRASKA-OMAHA
82— Kirk Hutton, DB
     Clark Toner, LB
83— Kirk Hutton, DB
84— Jerry Kripal, QB

NEVADA
82— David Heppe, P

NEW HAMPSHIRE
52— John Driscoll, T
84— Dave Morton, OL

NEW MEXICO
75— Bob Johnson, S
77— Robert Rumbaugh, DT
78— Robert Rumbaugh, DL
93— Justin Hall, OL

NEW MEXICO ST.
66— Jim Bohl, B
74— Ralph Jackson, OG
75— Ralph Jackson, OG
85— Andy Weiler, KS
92— Todd Cutler, TE
     Shane Hackney, OL
     Tim Mauck, LB
93— Tim Mauck, LB

NICHOLS
89— David Kane, DB

NORTH CARO.
64— Ken Willard, QB
85— Kevin Anthony, QB

NORTH CARO. ST.
60— Roman Gabriel, QB
63— Joe Scarpati, B
67— Steve Warren, OT
71— Craig John, OG
73— Justus Everett, C
     Stan Fritts, RB
74— Justus Everett, C
80— Calvin Warren, P

NORTH DAK.
87— Kurt Otto, QB
88— Chuck Clairmont, OL
     Matt Gulseth, DB
92— Tim Gelinske, WR
     Mark Ewen, LB

NORTH DAK. ST.
71— Tomm Smail, DT
93— T. R. McDonald, WR

NORTH PARK
83— Mike Lilgegren, DB
85— Scott Love, WR

86— Todd Love, WR
87— Todd Love, WR

NORTH TEXAS
75— Pete Morris, LB
76— Pete Morris, LB

NORTHEAST LA.
70— Tom Miller, KS
74— Mike Bialas, T

NORTHEAST MO. ST.
73— Tom Roberts, T
78— Keith Driscoll, LB
79— Keith Driscoll, LB
92— K. C. Conaway, P

NORTHEASTERN
85— Shawn O'Malley, LB

NORTHERN ARIZ.
89— Chris Baniszewski, WR

NORTHERN COLO.
71— Charles Putnik, OG
81— Duane Hirsch, DL
     Ray Sperger, DB
82— Jim Bright, RB
89— Mike Yonkovich, DL
     Tom Langer, LB
90— Tom Langer, LB

NORTHERN MICH.
83— Bob Stefanski, WR

NORTHWEST MO. ST.
81— Robert "Chip" Gregory, LB

NORTHWESTERN
56— Al Viola, G
58— Andy Cvercko, T
61— Larry Onesti, C
62— Paul Flatley, B
63— George Burman, E
70— Joe Zigulich, OG
76— Randolph Dean, E
80— Jim Ford, OT
86— Michael Baum, OT
     Bob Dirkes, DL
     Todd Krehbiel, DB
87— Mike Baum, OL
88— Mike Baum, OL
90— Ira Adler, PK

NORTHWESTERN ST.
92— Guy Hedrick, RB

NORWICH
70— Gary Fry, RB

NOTRE DAME
52— Joe Heap, B
53— Joe Heap, B
54— Joe Heap, B
55— Don Schaefer, B
58— Bob Wetoska, E
63— Bob Lehmann, G
66— Tom Regner, OG
     Jim Lynch, LB
67— Jim Smithberger, DB
68— George Kunz, OT
69— Jim Reilly, OT
70— Tom Gatewood, E
     Larry DiNardo, OG
     Joe Theismann, QB
71— Greg Marx, DT
     Tom Gatewood, E
72— Michael Creaney, E
     Greg Marx, DT
73— David Casper, E
     Gary Potempa, LB
     Robert Thomas, KS
74— Reggie Barnett, DB
     Pete Demmerle, E
77— Ken MacAfee, E
     Joe Restic, S
     Dave Vinson, OG
78— Joe Restic, DB
80— Bob Burger, OG
     Tom Gibbons, DB
81— John Krimm, DB
85— Greg Dingens, DL
87— Ted Gradel, PK
     Vince Phelan, P
92— Tim Ruddy, OL
93— Tim Ruddy, OL

N'WESTERN (IOWA)
83— Mark Muilenberg, RB
92— Joel Bundt, OL

N'WESTERN (OKLA.)
61—Stewart Arthurs, B

OCCIDENTAL
88—Curtis Page, DL

OHIO
71—John Rousch, HB

OHIO NORTHERN
76—Jeff McFarlin, S
79—Robert Coll, WR
86—David Myers, DL
90—Chad Hummell, OL

OHIO ST.
52—John Borton, B
54—Dick Hilinski, T
58—Bob White, B
61—Tom Perdue, E
65—Bill Ridder, MG
66—Dave Foley, OT
68—Dave Foley, OT
    Mark Stier, LB
69—Bill Urbanik, DT
71—Rick Simon, OG
73—Randy Gradishar, LB
74—Brian Baschnagel, RB
75—Brian Baschnagel, RB
76—Pete Johnson, RB
    Bill Lukens, OG
77—Jeff Logan, RB
80—Marcus Marek, LB
82—John Frank, TE
    Joseph Smith, OT
83—John Frank, TE
84—David Crecelius, DL
    Michael Lanese, WR
85—Michael Lanese, WR
89—Joseph Staysniak, OL
92—Leonard Hartman, OL
    Gregory Smith, DL

OHIO WESLEYAN
70—Tony Heald, LB
    Tom Liller, E
81—Ric Kinnan, WR
85—Kevin Connell, OG

OKLAHOMA
52—Tom Catlin, C
54—Carl Allison, E
56—Jerry Tubbs, C
57—Doyle Jenning, T
58—Ross Coyle, E
62—Wayne Lee, C
63—Newt Burton, G
64—Newt Burton, G
66—Ron Shotts, HB
67—Ron Shotts, HB
68—Eddie Hinton, DB
70—Joe Wylie, RB
71—Jack Mildren, QB
72—Joe Wylie, RB
74—Randy Hughes, S
75—Dewey Selmon, LB
    Lee Roy Selmon, DT
80—Jay Jimerson, DB
86—Brian Bosworth, LB

OKLAHOMA ST.
54—Dale Meinert, G
72—Tom Wolf, OT
73—Doug Tarrant, LB
74—Tom Wolf, OT
77—Joe Avanzini, DE

OREGON
62—Steve Barnett, T
65—Tim Casey, LB
86—Mike Preacher, P
90—Bill Musgrave, QB

OREGON ST.
62—Terry Baker, B
67—Bill Enyart, FB
68—Bill Enyart, FB
93—Chad Paulson, RB

OUACHITA BAPTIST
78—David Cowling, OG

PACIFIC (CAL.)
78—Bruce Filarsky, OG
79—Bruce Filarsky, DL

PACIFIC LUTHERAN
82—Curt Rodin, TE

PANHANDLE ST.
76—Larry Johnson, G

PENN ST.
65—Joe Bellas, T
    John Runnells, LB
66—John Runnells, LB
67—Rich Buzin, OT
69—Charlie Pittman, HB
    Dennis Onkotz, LB
71—Dave Joyner, OT
72—Bruce Bannon, DE
73—Mark Markovich, OG
76—Chuck Benjamin, OT
78—Keith Dorney, OT
82—Todd Blackledge, QB
    Harry Hamilton, DB
    Scott Radicec, LB
83—Harry Hamilton, LB
84—Lance Hamilton, DB
    Carmen Masciantonio, LB
85—Lance Hamilton, DB
86—John Shaffer, QB

PENNSYLVANIA
86—Rich Comizio, RB

PITTSBURG ST.
72—Jay Sperry, RB
89—Brett Potts, DL
91—Mike Brockel, OL
92—Mike Brockel, OL

PITTSBURGH
52—Dick Deitrick, DT
54—Lou Palatella, T
56—Joe Walton, E
58—John Guzik, G
76—Jeff Delaney, LB
80—Greg Meisner, DL
81—Rob Fada, OG
82—Rob Fada, OG
    J. C. Pelusi, DL
88—Mark Stepnoski, OL

PORTLAND ST.
72—Bill Dials, T
77—John Urness, WR
78—John Urness, WR

PRINCETON
68—Dick Sandler, DT
76—Kevin Fox, OG
82—Kevin Guthrie, WR
83—Kevin Guthrie, WR

PUGET SOUND
82—Buster Crook, DB

PURDUE
56—Len Dawson, QB
60—Jerry Beabout, T
65—Sal Ciampi, G
67—Jim Beirne, E
    Lance Olssen, DT
68—Tim Foley, DB
69—Tim Foley, DB
    Mike Phipps, QB
    Bill Yanchar, DT
73—Bob Hoftiezer, DE
79—Ken Loushin, DL
80—Tim Seneff, DB
81—Tim Seneff, DB
89—Bruce Brineman, OL

RHODE ISLAND
76—Richard Moser, RB
77—Richard Moser, RB

RHODES
90—Robert Heck, DL

RICE
52—Richard Chapman, DG
53—Richard Chapman, DG
54—Dicky Maegle, B
69—Steve Bradshaw, DG
79—LaMont Jefferson, LB
83—Brian Patterson, DB

ROCHESTER
82—Bob Cordaro, LB
92—Jeremy Hurd, RB
93—Jeremy Hurd, RB

ROSE-HULMAN
78—Rick Matovich, DL
79—Scott Lindner, DL
80—Scott Lindner, DL
    Jim Novacek, P

PANHANDLE ST.
83—Jack Grote, LB
84—Jack Grote, LB
88—Greg Kremer, LB
    Shawn Ferron, PK
89—Shawn Ferron, PK
90—Ed Huonden, WR
92—Greg Hubbard, OL
93—Greg Hubbard, OL

SAGINAW VALLEY
93—Troy Hendrickson, PK

SAM HOUSTON ST.
72—Walter Anderson, KS
73—Walter Anderson, KS
93—Kevin Riley, DB

SAN DIEGO
87—Bryan Day, DB
88—Bryan Day, DB

SAN JOSE ST.
75—Tim Toews, OG

SANTA CLARA
71—Ron Sani, IL
73—Alex Damascus, RB
74—Steve Lagorio, LB
75—Mark Tiernen, LB
76—Lou Marengo, KS
    Mark Tiernan, LB
80—Dave Alfaro, QB

SHIPPENSBURG
76—Tony Winter, LB
82—Dave Butler, DL

SOUTH CARO.
87—Mark Fryer, OL
88—Mark Fryer, OL
91—Joe Reeves, LB

SOUTH DAK.
78—Scott Pollock, QB
82—Jerus Campbell, DL
83—Jeff Sime, T
87—Dan Sonnek, RB

SOUTH DAK. ST.
74—Bob Gissler, E
75—Bill Matthews, T
77—Bill Matthews, DE
79—Tony Harris, PK
    Paul Kippley, DB

SOUTHERN CAL
52—Dick Nunis, DB
59—Mike McKeever, G
60—Mike McKeever, G
    Marlin McKeever, E
65—Charles Arrobio, T
67—Steve Sogge, QB
68—Steve Sogge, QB
69—Harry Khasigian, OG
73—Pat Haden, QB
74—Pat Haden, QB
78—Rich Dimler, DL
79—Brad Budde, OG
    Paul McDonald, QB
    Keith Van Horne, T
84—Duane Bickett, LB
85—Matt Koart, DL
86—Jeffrey Bregel, OG
88—John Jackson, WR
89—John Jackson, WR

SOUTHERN COLO.
83—Dan DeRose, LB

SOUTHERN CONN. ST.
84—Gerald Carbonaro, OL

SOUTHERN ILL.
70—Sam Finocchio, G
88—Charles Harmke, RB
91—Dwayne Summers, DL
    Jon Manley, LB

SOUTHERN METHODIST
52—Dave Powell, E
53—Darrell Lafitte, G
54—Raymond Berry, E
55—David Hawk, G
57—Tom Koenig, G
58—Tom Koenig, G
62—Raymond Schoenke, T
66—John LaGrone, MG
    Lynn Thornhill, OG
68—Jerry LeVias, OE

72—Cleve Whitener, LB
83—Brian O'Meara, T

SOUTHERN MISS.
92—James Singleton, DL

SOUTHERN UTAH
88—Jim Andrus, RB
90—Steve McDowell, P

SOUTHWEST MO. ST.
73—Kent Stringer, QB
75—Kent Stringer, QB
78—Steve Newbold, WR

SOUTHWEST ST.
88—Bruce Saugstad, DB

SOUTHWEST TEX. ST.
72—Jimmy Jowers, LB
73—Jimmy Jowers, LB
78—Mike Ferris, OG
79—Mike Ferris, G
    Allen Kiesling, DL
81—Mike Miller, QB

SPRINGFIELD
71—Bruce Rupert, LB
84—Sean Flanders, DL
85—Sean Flanders, DL

ST. CLOUD ST.
88—Rick Rodgers, DB
89—Rick Rodgers, DB

ST. FRANCIS (PA.)
93—Todd Eckenroad, WR

ST. JOHN'S (MINN.)
72—Jim Kruzich, E
79—Terry Geraghty, DB

ST. JOHN'S (N.Y.)
93—Anthony Russo, RB

ST. JOSEPH'S (IND.)
77—Mike Bettinger, DB
78—Mike Bettinger, DB
79—Mike Bettinger, DB
85—Ralph Laura, OT
88—Keith Woodason, OL
89—Jeff Fairchild, P

ST. NORBERT
86—Matthew Lang, LB
    Karl Zacharias, P
87—Karl Zacharias, PK
    Matthew Lang, LB
88—Mike Whitehouse, WR
89—Mike Whitehouse, WR

ST. OLAF
61—Dave Hindermann, T

ST. THOMAS (MINN.)
73—Mark Dienhart, T
74—Mark Dienhart, T
77—Tom Kelly, OG
80—Doug Groebner, C

STANFORD
70—John Sande, C
    Terry Ewing, DB
75—Don Stevenson, RB
76—Don Stevenson, RB
77—Guy Benjamin, QB
78—Vince Mulroy, WR
    Jim Stephens, OG
79—Pat Bowe, TE
    Milt McColl, LB
    Joe St. Geme, DB
81—John Bergren, DL
    Darrin Nelson, RB
82—John Bergren, DL
83—John Bergren, DL
85—Matt Soderlund, LB
87—Brad Muster, RB
90—Ed McCaffrey, WR
91—Tommy Vardell, RB

SUL ROSS ST.
73—Archie Nexon, RB

SUSQUEHANNA
75—Gerry Huesken, T
76—Gerry Huesken, T
80—Dan Distasio, LB

SYRACUSE
60—Fred Mautino, E
71—Howard Goodman, LB
83—Tony Romano, LB

84—Tim Green, DL
85—Tim Green, DL

TARLETON ST.
81—Ricky Bush, RB
90—Mike Loveless, OL

TENN.-MARTIN
74—Randy West, E

TENNESSEE
56—Charles Rader, T
57—Bill Johnson, G
65—Mack Gentry, DT
67—Bob Johnson, C
70—Tim Priest, DB
80—Timothy Irwin, OT
82—Mike Terry, DL

TENNESSEE TECH
87—Andy Rittenhouse, DL

TEXAS
59—Maurice Doke, G
61—Johnny Treadwell, G
62—Johnny Treadwell, G
    Pat Culpepper, B
63—Duke Carlisle, B
66—Gene Bledsoe, OT
67—Mike Perrin, DE
    Corby Robertson, LB
68—Corby Robertson, LB
    Scott Henderson, LB
69—Scott Henderson, LB
    Bill Zapalac, DE
70—Scott Henderson, LB
    Bill Zapalac, LB
72—Mike Bayer, DB
    Tommy Keel, S
    Steve Oxley, T
73—Tommy Keel, S
83—Doug Dawson, G
88—Lee Brockman, DL

TEX. A&M-KINGSVILLE
72—Floyd Goodwin, T
73—Johnny Jackson, E
76—Wade Whitmer, DL
77—Joe Henke, LB
    Wade Whitmer, DL
78—Wade Whitmer, DL

TEXAS A&M
56—Jack Pardee, B
71—Steve Luebbehusen, LB
76—Kevin Monk, LB
77—Kevin Monk, LB
85—Kip Corrington, DB
86—Kip Corrington, DB
87—Kip Corrington, DB

TEXAS CHRISTIAN
52—Marshall Harris, T
55—Hugh Pitts, C
    Jim Swink, B
56—Jim Swink, B
57—John Nikkel, E
68—Jim Ray, G
72—Scott Walker, C
74—Terry Drennan, DB
80—John McClean, DL

TEXAS TECH
72—Jeff Jobe, E
79—Maury Buford, P
83—Chuck Alexander, DB
93—Robert King, P

TOLEDO
83—Michael Matz, DL

TRINITY (TEX.)
92—Jeff Bryan, OL

TUFTS
70—Bruce Zinsmeister, DL
81—Brian Gallagher, OG
83—Richard Guiunta, G

TULANE
71—David Hebert, DB

TULSA
64—Howard Twilley, E
65—Howard Twilley, E
74—Mack Lancaster, T

UC DAVIS
72—Steve Algeo, LB
75—Dave Gellerman, LB
90—Mike Shepard, DL

UC RIVERSIDE
71—Tyrone Hooks, HB

UCLA
52—Ed Flynn, G
    Donn Moomaw, LB
53—Ira Pauly, C
54—Sam Boghosian, G
66—Ray Armstrong, E
75—John Sciarra, QB
77—John Fowler, LB
81—Cormac Carney, WR
    Tim Wrightman, TE
82—Cormac Carney, WR
85—Mike Hartmeier, OG
92—Carlton Gray, DB

UNION (N.Y.)
71—Tom Anacher, LB
73—Dave Ricks, DB
87—Richard Romer, DL
93—Greg Oswitt, OL

URSINUS
86—Chuck Odgers, DB
87—Chuck Odgers, LB

UTAH
64—Mel Carpenter, T
71—Scott Robbins, DB
73—Steve Odom, RB
76—Dick Graham, E

UTAH ST.
61—Merlin Olsen, T
69—Gary Anderson, LB
74—Randy Stockham, DE
75—Randy Stockham, DE

UTEP
88—Pat Hegarty, QB

VA. MILITARY
78—Craig Jones, PK
79—Craig Jones, PK
84—David Twillie, OL
86—Dan Young, DL
88—Anthony McIntosh, DB

VALDOSTA ST.
93—Chris Hatcher, QB

VANDERBILT
58—Don Donnell, C
68—Jim Burns, DB
74—Doug Martin, E
75—Damon Regen, LB
77—Greg Martin, K
83—Phil Roach, WR

VILLANOVA
86—Ron Sency, RB
88—Peter Lombardi, RB
92—Tim Matas, DL

VIRGINIA
72—Tom Kennedy, OG
75—Bob Meade, DT
92—Tom Burns, LB
93—Tom Burns, LB

VIRGINIA TECH
67—Frank Loria, DB
72—Tommy Carpenito, LB

WABASH
70—Roscoe Fouts, DB
71—Kendrick Shelburne, DT
82—Dave Broecker, QB

WARTBURG
75—James Charles Peterson, DB
76—Randy Groth, DB
77—Neil Mandsager, LB
90—Jerrod Staack, OL
93—Koby Kreinbring, LB

WASH. & JEFF.
92—Raymond Cross, DL
93—Michael Jones, OL

WASH. & LEE
75—John Cocklereece, DB
78—George Ballantyne, LB
92—Evans Edwards, OL

WASHINGTON
55—Jim Houston, E
63—Mike Briggs, T
64—Rick Redman, G
65—Steve Bramwell, DB
79—Bruce Harrell, LB

81— Mark Jerue, LB
    Chuck Nelson, PK
82— Chuck Nelson, PK
86— David Rill, LB
87— David Rill, LB
91— Ed Cunningham, OL

WASHINGTON ST.
89— Jason Hanson, PK
90— Lee Tilleman, DL
    Jason Hanson, PK
91— Jason Hanson, PK

WAYNE ST. (MICH.)
71— Gary Schultz, DB
72— Walt Stasinski, DB

WAYNESBURG
77— John Culp, RB
78— John Culp, RB
89— Andrew Barrish, OL
90— Andrew Barrish, OL
91— Karl Petrof, OL

WEST CHESTER
83— Eric Wentling, K
86— Gerald Desmond, K

WEST VA.
52— Paul Bischoff, E
54— Fred Wyant, B
55— Sam Huff, T
70— Kim West, K
80— Oliver Luck, QB
81— Oliver Luck, QB
83— Jeff Hostetler, QB
92— Mike Compton, OL

WESTERN CARO.
75— Mike Wade, E
76— Mike Wade, LB
84— Eddie Maddox, RB

WESTERN ILL.
61— Jerry Blew, G
85— Jeff McKinney, RB
91— David Fierke, OL

WESTERN KY.
71— James Barber, LB
81— Tim Ford, DL
84— Mark Fatkin, OL
85— Mark Fatkin, OG

WESTERN MD.
73— Chip Chaney, S

WESTERN MICH.
70— Jon Bull, OT

WESTERN OREGON
61— Francis Tresler, C

WESTERN ST.
78— Bill Campbell, DB
88— Damon Lockhart, RB

WESTMINSTER (PA.)
73— Bob Clark, G
77— Scott McLuckey, LB
93— Brian Wilson, OL

WHEATON (ILL.)
73— Bill Hyer, E
75— Eugene Campbell, RB
76— Eugene Campbell, RB
88— Paul Sternenberg, DL
92— Bart Moseman, DB

WHITTIER
86— Brent Kane, DL

WILKES
70— Al Kenney, C

WILLAMETTE
61— Stuart Hall

WILLIAM & MARY
74— John Gerdelman, RB
75— Ken Smith, DB
77— Ken Smith, DB
78— Robert Muscalus, TE
84— Mark Kelso, DB
88— Chris Gessner, DB
90— Jeff Nielsen, LB
93— Craig Staub, DL

WINONA ST.
93— Nathan Gruber, DB

WIS.-EAU CLAIRE
74— Mark Anderson, RB
80— Mike Zeihen, DB

WIS.-PLATTEVILLE
85— Mark Hintz, DB
    Mark Rae, P
86— Mike Hintz, QB
87— Mark Rae, P

WIS.-RIVER FALLS
91— Mike Olson, LB

WISCONSIN
52— Bob Kennedy, DG
53— Alan Ameche, B
54— Alan Ameche, B
58— Jon Hobbs, B
59— Dale Hackbart, B
62— Pat Richter, E
63— Ken Bowman, C
72— Rufus Ferguson, RB
82— Kyle Borland, LB
87— Don Davey, DL
88— Don Davey, DL
89— Don Davey, DL
90— Don Davey, DL

WITTENBERG
80— Bill Beach, DB
81— Bill Beach, DB
82— Tom Jones, OT
88— Paul Kungl, WR
90— Victor Terebuh, DB

WM. PATERSON
92— John Trust, RB

WOOSTER
73— Dave Foy, LB
77— Blake Moore, C
78— Blake Moore, C
79— Blake Moore, C
80— Dale Fortner, DB
    John Weisensell, OG

WYOMING
65— Bob Dinges, DE
67— George Mills, OG
73— Mike Lopiccolo, OT
84— Bob Gustafson, OT
87— Patrick Arndt, OG

YALE
68— Fred Morris, C
70— Tom Neville, DT
78— William Crowley, LB
81— Rich Diana, RB
    Frederick Leone, DL
89— Glover Lawrence, DL
91— Scott Wagner, DB

YOUNGSTOWN ST.
93— John Quintana, TE

AWARD WINNERS

Bowl/All-Star Game Results

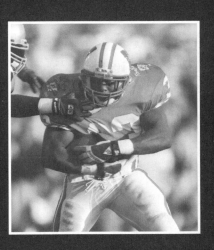

1994-95 Bowl Schedule

(All Starting Times Eastern)

BUILDERS SQUARE ALAMO BOWL
December 31, 1994—8 p.m.
Alamodome (cap. 65,000)
San Antonio, Texas
Televising Network: ESPN

CARQUEST BOWL
January 2, 1995—1:30 p.m.
Joe Robbie Stadium (cap. 73,000)
Miami, Florida
Televising Network: CBS Network

CompUSA FLORIDA CITRUS BOWL
January 2, 1995—1 p.m.
Florida Citrus Bowl Stadium (cap. 70,349)
Orlando, Florida
Televising Network: ABC

FEDERAL EXPRESS ORANGE BOWL
January 1, 1995—8 p.m.
Orange Bowl Stadium (cap. 74,712)
Miami, Florida
Televising Network: NBC

FREEDOM BOWL
December 29, 1994—9 p.m.
Anaheim Stadium (cap. 70,962)
Anaheim, California
Televising Network: Raycom

HALL OF FAME BOWL
January 2, 1995—11 a.m.
Tampa Stadium (cap. 74,350)
Tampa, Florida
Televising Network: ESPN

IBM OS/2 FIESTA BOWL
January 2, 1995—4:30 p.m.
Sun Devil Stadium (cap. 73,656)
Tempe, Arizona
Televising Network: NBC

JEEP EAGLE ALOHA BOWL
December 25, 1994—3:30 p.m.
Aloha Stadium (cap. 50,000)
Honolulu, Hawaii
Televising Network: ABC

JOHN HANCOCK BOWL
December 30, 1994—2:30 p.m.
Sun Bowl Stadium (cap. 51,270)
El Paso, Texas
Televising Network: CBS

LAS VEGAS BOWL
December 15, 1994—9 p.m.
Sam Boyd Silver Bowl (cap. 32,000)
Las Vegas, Nevada
Televising Network: ESPN

MOBIL COTTON BOWL CLASSIC
January 2, 1995—1 p.m.
Cotton Bowl (cap. 68,245)
Dallas, Texas
Televising Network: NBC

OUTBACK STEAKHOUSE GATOR BOWL
January 1, 1995—7:30 p.m.
Ben Hill Griffin Stadium/Florida Field (cap. 83,000)
Gainesville, Florida (for 1995 only)
Televising Network: TBS

PEACH BOWL
January 1, 1995—8 p.m.
Georgia Dome (cap. 71,596)
Atlanta, Georgia
Televising Network: ESPN

POULAN/WEED EATER INDEPENDENCE BOWL
December 28, 1994—8 p.m.
Independence Stadium (cap. 60,128)
Shreveport, Louisiana
Televising Network: ESPN

ROSE BOWL
January 2, 1995—5 p.m.
Rose Bowl (cap. 98,101)
Pasadena, California
Televising Network: ABC

ST. JUDE LIBERTY BOWL
December 31, 1994—3 p.m.
Liberty Bowl Stadium (under renovation)
Memphis, Tennessee
Televising Network: To be determined

THRIFTY CAR RENTAL HOLIDAY BOWL
December 30, 1994—8 p.m.
San Diego Jack Murphy Stadium (cap. 61,124)
San Diego, California
Televising Network: ESPN

USF&G SUGAR BOWL
January 2, 1995—8:30 p.m.
Louisiana Superdome (cap. 72,704)
New Orleans, Louisiana
Televising Network: ABC

WEISER LOCK COPPER BOWL
December 29, 1994—8 p.m.
Arizona Stadium (cap. 56,167)
Tucson, Arizona
Televising Network: ESPN

1993-94 Bowl Results

Game-by-Game Scores

Las Vegas Bowl (Dec. 17)
Utah St. 42, Ball St. 33

John Hancock Bowl (Dec. 24)
Oklahoma 41, Texas Tech 10

Jeep Eagle Aloha Bowl (Dec. 25)
Colorado 41, Fresno St. 30

St. Jude Liberty Bowl (Dec. 28)
Louisville 18, Michigan St. 7

Weiser Lock Copper Bowl (Dec. 29)
Kansas St. 52, Wyoming 17

Thrifty Car Rental Holiday Bowl (Dec. 30)
Ohio St. 28, Brigham Young 21

Freedom Bowl (Dec. 30)
Southern Cal 28, Utah 21

Poulan/Weed Eater Independence Bowl (Dec. 31)
Virginia Tech 45, Indiana 20

Peach Bowl (Dec. 31)
Clemson 14, Kentucky 13

Outback Steakhouse Gator Bowl (Dec. 31)
Alabama 24, North Caro. 10

Builders Square Alamo Bowl (Dec. 31)
California 37, Iowa 3

Hall of Fame Bowl (Jan. 1)
Michigan 42, North Caro. St. 7

CompUSA Florida Citrus Bowl (Jan. 1)
Penn St. 31, Tennessee 13

IBM OS/2 Fiesta Bowl (Jan. 1)
Arizona 29, Miami (Fla.) 0

Carquest Bowl (Jan. 1)
Boston College 31, Virginia 13

Mobil Cotton Bowl (Jan. 1)
Notre Dame 24, Texas A&M 21

Rose Bowl (Jan. 1)
Wisconsin 21, UCLA 16

Federal Express Orange Bowl (Jan. 1)
Florida St. 18, Nebraska 16

USF&G Sugar Bowl (Jan. 1)
Florida 41, West Va. 7

Other Postseason Games:

Kelly Tire Blue-Gray All-Star Game (Dec. 25)
Gray 17, Blue 10

Heritage Bowl (I-AA) (Jan. 1)
Southern-B.R. 11, South Caro. St. 0

East-West Shrine Game (Jan. 15)
West 29, East 28

Senior Bowl (Jan. 22)
South 35, North 32

Kodak Hula Bowl (Jan. 22)
College All-Stars 28, Hawaii All-Stars 15

Game-by-Game Summaries

LAS VEGAS BOWL
December 17, 1993
Las Vegas, Nevada

Synopsis: Quarterback Anthony Calvillo threw for three touchdowns and Profall Grier ran for two more to lead Utah State to a 42-33 win over Ball State in the second Las Vegas Bowl.

Ball St.	0	0	17	16 —	33
Utah St.	14	7	14	7 —	42

US—McMahon 22 pass from Calvillo (Morreale kick)
US—Grier 3 rush (Morreale kick)
US—Thompson 3 pass from Calvillo (Morreale kick)
BS—McCray 7 pass from Neu (Swart kick)
BS—Swart 31 field goal
US—Grier 15 rush (Morreale kick)
US—Lee 16 pass from Calvillo (Morreale kick)
BS—Blair 2 pass from Neu (Swart kick)
BS—Safety (Calvillo tackled in end zone)
US—Toomer 32 interception return (Morreale kick)
BS—Nibbs 2 rush (Oliver pass from Neu)
BS—Oliver 2 pass from Neu (pass failed)

Game Statistics

	BS	US
First Downs	14	27
Rushes-Yards	26-73	45-205
Passing Yards	241	288
Comp.-Att.-Int.	21-38-2	25-39-2
Punts-Avg.	5-41	3-39
Fumbles-Lost	1-1	2-1
Penalties-Yards	5-30	15-150
Time of Possession	24:49	35:11

Weather: Cloudy, 49 degrees
Attendance: 15,508

JOHN HANCOCK BOWL
December 24, 1993
El Paso, Texas

Synopsis: Oklahoma freshman Jerald Moore rushed for two touchdowns to lead the Sooners to a 41-10 victory over Texas Tech in the John Hancock Bowl.

Texas Tech	0	3	7	0 —	10
Oklahoma	14	14	0	13 —	41

O—Chandler 2 rush (Blanton kick)
O—Brady 9 pass from Gundy (Blanton kick)
T—Davis 22 field goal
O—Warren 34 pass from Gundy (Blanton kick)
O—Brady 15 pass from Gundy (Blanton kick)
T—Morris 2 rush (Davis kick)
O—Moore 32 rush (Blanton kick)
O—Moore 6 rush (no attempt)

Game Statistics

	TT	OU
First Downs	18	21
Rushes-Yards	33-116	49-177
Passing Yards	199	215
Comp.-Att.-Int.	19-37-4	15-26-1
Punts-Avg.	7-43	7-48
Fumbles-Lost	0-0	4-2
Penalties-Yards	6-65	9-65

	TT	OU
Time of Possession	24:38	35:22

Weather: Sunny, 55 degrees
Attendance: 43,848

JEEP EAGLE ALOHA BOWL

December 25, 1993
Honolulu, Hawaii

Synopsis: Rashaan Salaam scored three touchdowns and Colorado turned four fumbles into 24 points as Colorado downed Fresno State, 41-30, in the Jeep Eagle Aloha Bowl.

Fresno St.	0	10	14	6	— 30
Colorado	10	10	14	7	— 41

CO—Salaam 2 rush (Berger kick)
CO—Berger 44 field goal
CO—Hill 7 rush (Berger kick)
FS—Mahoney 27 field goal
CO—Berger 49 field goal
FS—Seabron 68 kickoff return (Mahoney kick)
CO—Salaam 40 rush (Berger kick)
FS—Daigle 1 rush (kick failed)
CO—Leomiti 28 fumble return (Berger kick)
FS—Winans 8 pass from Dilfer (Daigle pass from Dilfer)
CO—Salaam 4 rush (Berger kick)
FS—Winans 11 pass from Dilfer (pass failed)

Game Statistics

	FS	CO
First Downs	34	19
Rushes-Yards	25-3	46-271
Passing Yards	523	124
Comp.-Att.-Int.	37-63-1	8-15-0
Punts-Avg.	3-31	4-43
Fumbles-Lost	5-4	1-1
Penalties-Yards	9-88	7-84
Time of Possession	31:09	28:51

Weather: Sunny, 76 degrees
Attendance: 44,009

ST. JUDE LIBERTY BOWL

December 28, 1993
Memphis, Tennessee

Synopsis: Jeff Brohm hit Reggie Ferguson with a 25-yard touchdown pass with 12:05 left, helping lift Louisville over Michigan State, 18-7, in the St. Jude Liberty Bowl.

Michigan St.	7	0	0	0	— 7
Louisville	3	0	0	15	— 18

MS—Goulborne 1 rush (Stoyanovich kick)
LO—Akers 31 field goal
LO—Ferguson 25 pass from Brohm (Akers kick)
LO—Safety, Thomas tackled in end zone
LO—Dawkins 11 rush (kick failed)

Game Statistics

	MS	LO
First Downs	18	20
Rushes-Yards	31-114	40-172
Passing Yards	193	197
Comp.-Att.-Int.	15-28-1	19-31-0
Punts-Avg.	5-29	5-36
Fumbles-Yards	0-0	1-0
Penalties-Yards	5-60	6-45
Time of Possession	26:25	33:35

Weather: Freezing rain, 28 degrees
Attendance: 21,097

WEISER LOCK COPPER BOWL

December 29, 1993
Tucson, Arizona

Synopsis: Kansas State piled up 502 total yards en route to an easy 52-17 victory over Wyoming in the Weiser Lock Copper Bowl.

Kansas St.	9	15	14	14	— 52
Wyoming	3	7	0	7	— 17

WY—Sorenson 35 field goal
KS—Smith 2 rush (kick failed)
KS—Wright 22 field goal
KS—May 2 rush (Wright kick)
WY—Christopherson 3 rush (Sorenson kick)
KS—Coleman 68 punt return (May run)
KS—Coleman 61 pass from May (Wright kick)
KS—Lockett 30 pass from May (Wright kick)
WY—Pratt 14 pass from Gustin (Sorenson kick)
KS—Edwards 13 rush (Claassen kick)
KS—McEntyre 37 interception return (Wright kick)

Game Statistics

	KS	WY
First Downs	22	20
Rushes-Yards	39-227	23-36

	KS	WY
Passing Yards	275	266
Comp.-Att.-Int.	19-28-0	31-51-2
Punts-Avg.	3-23	5-44
Fumbles-Lost	0-0	2-1
Penalties-Yards	5-40	8-70
Time of Possession	30:01	29:59

Weather: Clear, 64 degrees
Attendance: 49,075

THRIFTY CAR RENTAL HOLIDAY BOWL

December 30, 1993
San Diego, California

Synopsis: Raymont Harris set Thrifty Car Rental Holiday Bowl records with 235 yards rushing on 39 carries and scored on three short runs, lifting Ohio State to a 28-21 victory over Brigham Young.

Ohio St.	14	7	7	0	— 28
Brigham Young	7	14	0	0	— 21

OS—Patillo 20 punt return (Williams kick)
BY—Willis 27 pass from Walsh (Herrick kick)
OS—Harris 2 rush (Williams kick)
OS—Harris 2 rush (Williams kick)
BY—Lewis 8 pass from Walsh (Herrick kick)
BY—Dorman 27 pass from Walsh (Herrick kick)
OS—Harris 1 rush (Williams kick)

Game Statistics

	OS	BY
First Downs	21	24
Rushes-Yards	56-330	26-50
Passing Yards	61	389
Comp.-Att.-Int.	6-13-0	25-44-1
Punts-Avg.	6-36	2-21
Fumbles-Lost	0-0	2-1
Penalties-Yards	7-45	5-25
Time of Possession	32:23	27:37

Weather: Fair, 66 degrees
Attendance: 52,108

FREEDOM BOWL

December 30, 1993
Anaheim, California

Synopsis: Rob Johnson threw for 345 yards and three touchdown passes, stifling Utah's second-half comeback and leading Southern California past the Utes, 28-21, in the Freedom Bowl.

Utah	0	0	13	8	— 21
Southern Cal	20	8	0	0	— 28

SC—Morton 31 pass from Johnson (Ford kick)
SC—Morton 9 pass from Johnson (Ford kick)
SC—Dotson 2 rush (kick failed)
SC—McWilliams 5 pass from Johnson (Banta pass from Johnson)
UT—Lusk 59 pass from McCoy (Yergensen kick)
UT—Anderson 34 rush (kick failed)
UT—Williams 1 rush (Anderson pass from McCoy)

Game Statistics

	UT	SC
First Downs	17	20
Rushes-Yards	25-106	38-91
Passing Yards	286	345
Comp.-Att.-Int.	23-40-3	30-44-1
Punts-Avg.	8-34	6-37
Fumbles-Lost	2-0	2-1
Penalties-Yards	5-51	10-96
Time of Possession	27:46	32:14

Weather: High clouds, 64 degrees
Attendance: 37,203

POULAN/WEED EATER INDEPENDENCE BOWL

December 31, 1993
Shreveport, Louisiana

Synopsis: Virginia Tech safety Antonio Banks recovered a fumble, intercepted a pass and returned a blocked field goal 80 yards for a touchdown to lead the Hokies over Indiana, 45-20, in the Poulan/Weed Eater Independence Bowl.

Virginia Tech	7	21	0	17	— 45
Indiana	7	6	0	7	— 20

IN—T. Lewis 75 pass from Paci (Manolopoulos kick)
VT—Thomas 13 pass from DeShazo (Williams kick)
VT—Swarm 6 rush (Williams kick)
IN—Manolopoulos 26 field goal
IN—Manolopoulos 40 field goal
VT—L. Lewis 20 fumble return (Williams kick)

VT—Banks 80 blocked field goal return (Williams kick)
VT—Freeman 42 pass from DeShazo (Williams kick)
VT—Edwards 5 rush (Williams kick)
VT—Williams 42 field goal
IN—T. Lewis 42 pass from Dittoe (Manolopoulos kick)

Game Statistics

	VT	IN
First Downs	17	11
Rushes-Yards	48-125	31-20
Passing Yards	193	276
Comp.-Att.-Int.	19-33-2	17-37-2
Punts-Avg.	8-39	7-38
Fumbles-Lost	2-1	2-2
Penalties-Yards	8-84	7-55
Time of Possession	32:48	27:12

Weather: Clear, 49 degrees
Attendance: 33,819

PEACH BOWL

December 31, 1993
Atlanta, Georgia

Synopsis: Patrick Sapp's 21-yard touchdown pass to Terry Smith and Nelson Welch's extra point with 20 seconds remaining gave Clemson a 14-13 victory over Kentucky in the Peach Bowl.

Kentucky	0	3	0	10	— 13
Clemson	7	0	0	7	— 14

CL—E. Smith 2 rush (Welch kick)
KY—Nickels 34 field goal
KY—Chatmon 5 pass from Jones (Nickels kick)
KY—Nickels 26 field goal
CL—T. Smith 21 pass from Sapp (Welch kick)

Game Statistics

	KY	CL
First Downs	20	14
Rushes-Yards	34-139	46-119
Passing Yards	154	129
Comp.-Att.-Int.	16-32-0	8-16-3
Punts-Avg.	5-41	6-39
Fumbles-Lost	2-2	1-0
Penalties-Yards	3-25	10-75
Time of Possession	28:51	31:09

Weather: Perfect, indoors
Attendance: 63,416

OUTBACK STEAKHOUSE GATOR BOWL

December 31, 1993
Jacksonville, Florida

Synopsis: Alabama's stingy defense held North Carolina's vaunted rushing offense to only 42 yards to post a 24-10 victory in the Outback Steakhouse Gator Bowl.

North Caro.	0	10	0	0	— 10
Alabama	0	10	7	7	— 24

AL—Proctor 22 field goal
NC—Henderson 1 rush (Pignetti kick)
AL—Burgdorf 33 rush (Proctor kick)
NC—Pignetti 23 field goal
AL—Lynch 8 pass from Burgdorf (Proctor kick)
AL—Key 10 pass from Burgdorf (Proctor kick)

Game Statistics

	NC	AL
First Downs	14	21
Rushes-Yards	25-42	46-164
Passing Yards	225	166
Comp.-Att.-Int.	19-35-0	15-23-0
Punts-Avg.	7-30	6-40
Fumbles-Lost	1-1	3-0
Penalties-Yards	1-15	4-34
Time of Possession	25:23	34:37

Weather: Cloudy, 51 degrees
Attendance: 67,205

BUILDERS SQUARE ALAMO BOWL

December 31, 1993
San Antonio, Texas

Synopsis: California scored on four of its first five possessions and coasted to an easy 37-3 victory over Iowa in the inaugural Builders Square Alamo Bowl.

California	6	17	7	7	— 37
Iowa	0	3	0	0	— 3

CA—Brien 27 field goal
CA—Brien 20 field goal
CA—Brien 30 field goal
CA—Caldwell 6 pass from Barr (Brien kick)
CA—Willard 61 interception return (Brien kick)

BOWL/ALL-STAR RESULTS

IA—Hurley 42 field goal
CA—Uwaezucke 34 pass from Barr (Brien kick)
CA—Remington 12 pass from Barr (Brien kick)

Game Statistics

	CA	IA
First Downs	29	5
Rushes-Yards	55-168	21-20
Passing Yards	266	70
Comp.-Att.-Int.	21-28-0	6-17-1
Punts-Avg.	2-33	8-43
Fumbles-Lost	3-1	1-0
Penalties-Yards	5-35	10-74
Time of Possession	43:14	16:46

Weather: Perfect, indoors
Attendance: 45,716

HALL OF FAME BOWL

January 1, 1994
Tampa, Florida

Synopsis: Tyrone Wheatley rushed for 124 yards and two touchdowns to lead Michigan to a 42-7 pounding of North Carolina State in the Hall of Fame Bowl.

North Caro. St.	0	0	7	0	— 7
Michigan	0	21	21	0	— 42

MI—Wheatley 26 rush (Elezovic kick)
MI—Alexander 79 punt return (Elezovic kick)
MI—Toomer 31 pass from Collins (Elezovic kick)
MI—Thompson 43 interception return (Elezovic kick)
MI—Wheatley 18 rush (Elezovic kick)
NCS—Fitzgerald 12 pass from Bender (Videtich kick)
MI—Powers 16 rush (Elezovic kick)

Game Statistics

	NCS	MI
First Downs	18	21
Rushes-Yards	36-117	44-265
Passing Yards	195	201
Comp.-Att.-Int.	19-38-4	12-23-0
Punts-Avg.	6-42	6-47
Fumbles-Lost	4-2	1-0
Penalties-Yards	3-15	5-35
Time of Possession	32:31	27:29

Weather: Light rain, 64 degrees
Attendance: 52,649

CompUSA FLORIDA CITRUS BOWL

January 1, 1994
Orlando, Florida

Synopsis: Penn State dominated Tennessee with its stout defense as the Nittany Lions cruised to a 31-13 win in the CompUSA Florida Citrus Bowl.

Penn St.	7	10	7	7	— 31
Tennessee	10	3	0	0	— 13

TN—Becksvoort 46 field goal
TN—Fleming 19 pass from Shuler (Becksvoort kick)
PS—Carter 3 rush (Fayak kick)
PS—Fayak 19 field goal
TN—Becksvoort 50 field goal
PS—Carter 14 rush (Fayak kick)
PS—Brady 7 pass from Collins (Fayak kick)
PS—Engram 15 pass from Collins (Fayak kick)

Game Statistics

	PS	TN
First Downs	20	16
Rushes-Yards	42-209	29-135
Passing Yards	162	213
Comp.-Att.-Int.	15-24-1	23-44-1
Punts-Avg.	6-32	6-44
Fumbles-Lost	0-0	0-0
Penalties-Yards	4-30	10-79
Time of Possession	30:13	29:47

Weather: Overcast, 67 degrees
Attendance: 72,456

IBM OS/2 FIESTA BOWL

January 1, 1994
Tempe, Arizona

Synopsis: Arizona's "Desert Storm" defense kept Miami's (Florida) high-powered offense bottled up and blanked the surprised Hurricanes, 29-0, before a stunned IBM OS/2 Fiesta Bowl crowd.

Miami (Fla.)	0	0	0	0	— 0
Arizona	9	7	6	7	— 29

AR—Dickey 13 pass from White (kick failed)
AR—McLaughlin 39 field goal
AR—Levy 68 rush (McLaughlin kick)
AR—McLaughlin 31 field goal
AR—McLaughlin 21 field goal
AR—Dickey 14 pass from White (McLaughlin kick)

Game Statistics

	MI	AR
First Downs	13	24
Rushes-Yards	20-35	50-257
Passing Yards	147	152
Comp.-Att.-Int.	15-44-3	12-24-2
Punts-Avg.	10-37	5-36
Fumbles-Lost	2-1	2-0
Penalties-Yards	6-40	2-25
Time of Possession	22:40	37:20

Weather: Clear, 58 degrees
Attendance: 72,260

CARQUEST BOWL

January 1, 1994
Miami, Florida

Synopsis: Boston College quarterback Glenn Foley broke most of the Carquest Bowl's passing records as he led the Eagles to a 31-13 victory over Virginia.

Boston College	3	14	7	7	— 31
Virginia	7	6	0	0	— 13

VA—Washington 8 rush (Kirkeide kick)
BC—Gordon 19 field goal
BC—Cannon 78 pass from Foley (Gordon kick)
VA—Way 7 rush (kick failed)
BC—Cannon 5 pass from Foley (Gordon kick)
BC—Miller 46 pass from Foley (Gordon kick)
BC—Campbell 12 rush (Gordon kick)

Game Statistics

	BC	VA
First Downs	27	16
Rushes-Yards	44-166	28-85
Passing Yards	391	213
Comp.-Att.-Int.	25-36-2	21-36-0
Punts-Avg.	2-40	6-41
Fumbles-Lost	2-1	1-0
Penalties-Yards	4-33	3-35
Time of Possession	32:54	27:06

Weather: Cloudy, 74 degrees
Attendance: 38,516

MOBIL COTTON BOWL

January 1, 1994
Dallas, Texas

Synopsis: Kevin Pendergast's 31-yard field goal with 2:17 remaining helped Notre Dame ease by Texas A&M, 24-21, in the Mobil Cotton Bowl.

Notre Dame	7	0	14	3	— 24
Texas A&M	7	7	7	0	— 21

ND—McDougal 19 rush (Pendergast kick)
TAM—Hill 8 rush (Venetoulias kick)
TAM—D. Smith 15 pass from Pullig (Venetoulias kick)
ND—Zellars 2 rush (Pendergast kick)
TAM—Thomas 1 rush (Venetoulias kick)
ND—Edwards 2 rush (Pendergast kick)
ND—Pendergast 31 field goal

Game Statistics

	ND	TAM
First Downs	19	20
Rushes-Yards	51-206	37-103
Passing Yards	105	238
Comp.-Att.-Int.	7-15-0	17-31-1
Punts-Avg.	7-38	4-37
Fumbles-Lost	1-0	4-2
Penalties-Yards	5-34	3-15
Time of Possession	33:02	26:58

Weather: Sunny, 62 degrees
Attendance: 69,855

ROSE BOWL

January 1, 1994
Pasadena, California

Synopsis: Wisconsin took advantage of six UCLA turnovers to post a 21-16 Rose Bowl victory in the Badgers' first trip to Pasadena since 1963.

UCLA	3	0	0	13	— 16
Wisconsin	7	7	0	7	— 21

UC—Merten 27 field goal
WI—Moss 3 rush (Schnetzky kick)
WI—Moss 1 rush (Schnetzky kick)
UC—Davis 12 rush (Merten kick)
WI—Bevell 21 rush (Schnetzky kick)
UC—Nguyen 5 pass from Cook (pass failed)

Game Statistics

	UC	WI
First Downs	31	21
Rushes-Yards	40-212	46-250
Passing Yards	288	96
Comp.-Att.-Int.	28-43-1	10-20-1
Punts-Avg.	2-35	6-38
Fumbles-Lost	5-5	2-0
Penalties-Yards	9-95	12-89
Time of Possession	29:03	30:57

Weather: Sunny, 68 degrees
Attendance: 101,237

FEDERAL EXPRESS ORANGE BOWL

January 1, 1994
Miami, Florida

Synopsis: Freshman Scott Bentley hit four field goals including the 22-yard game-winner with 21 seconds left to help Florida State post an 18-16 win over Nebraska in the Federal Express Orange Bowl and claim the national championship.

Nebraska	0	7	0	9	— 16
Florida St.	0	6	9	3	— 18

FS—Bentley 34 field goal
NE—Baul 34 pass from Frazier (Bennett kick)
FS—Bentley 25 field goal
FS—Floyd 1 rush (pass failed)
FS—Bentley 39 field goal
NE—Phillips 13 rush (run failed)
NE—Bennett 27 field goal
FS—Bentley 22 field goal

Game Statistics

	NE	FS
First Downs	20	22
Rushes-Yards	44-183	24-47
Passing Yards	206	286
Comp.-Att.-Int.	13-25-2	24-43-0
Punts-Avg.	7-38	6-45
Fumbles-Lost	2-0	0-0
Penalties-Yards	11-115	10-69
Time of Possession	32:57	27:03

Weather: Cloudy, 75 degrees
Attendance: 81,536

USF&G SUGAR BOWL

January 1, 1994
New Orleans, Louisiana

Synopsis: Florida used its quick-strike offense and overwhelmed previously unbeaten West Virginia, 41-7, in the USF&G Sugar Bowl.

Florida	7	14	14	6	— 41
West Va.	7	0	0	0	— 7

WV—Kearney 32 pass from Kelchner (Mazzone kick)
FL—Rhett 3 rush (Davis kick)
FL—Wright 52 interception return (Davis kick)
FL—Jackson 39 pass from Dean (Davis kick)
FL—Rhett 2 rush (Davis kick)
FL—Rhett 1 rush (Davis kick)
FL—Davis 43 field goal
FL—Davis 26 field goal

Game Statistics

	FL	WV
First Downs	30	16
Rushes-Yards	48-201	31-122
Passing Yards	281	143
Comp.-Att.-Int.	24-39-1	16-40-1
Punts-Avg.	3-53	8-43
Fumbles-Lost	2-1	2-1
Penalties-Yards	5-43	8-71
Time of Possession	33:22	26:38

Weather: Perfect, indoors
Attendance: 75,437

All-Time Bowl-Game Results

Major Bowl Games

ROSE BOWL

Present Site: Pasadena, Calif.
Stadium (Capacity): Rose Bowl (98,101)
Playing Surface: Grass

Playing Sites: Tournament Park, Pasadena (1902, 1916-22); Rose Bowl, Pasadena (1923-41); Duke Stadium, Durham, N.C. (1942); Rose Bowl (since 1943)

1-1-02—Michigan 49, Stanford 0
1-1-16—Washington St. 14, Brown 0
1-1-17—Oregon 14, Pennsylvania 0
1-1-18—Mare Island 19, Camp Lewis 7
1-1-19—Great Lakes 17, Mare Island 0

1-1-20—Harvard 7, Oregon 6
1-1-21—California 28, Ohio St. 0
1-2-22—California 0, Wash. & Jeff. 0
1-1-23—Southern Cal 14, Penn St. 3
1-1-24—Navy 14, Washington 14

1-1-25—Notre Dame 27, Stanford 10
1-1-26—Alabama 20, Washington 19
1-1-27—Alabama 7, Stanford 7
1-2-28—Stanford 7, Pittsburgh 6
1-1-29—Georgia Tech 8, California 7

1-1-30—Southern Cal 47, Pittsburgh 14
1-1-31—Alabama 24, Washington St. 0
1-1-32—Southern Cal 21, Tulane 12
1-2-33—Southern Cal 35, Pittsburgh 0
1-1-34—Columbia 7, Stanford 0

1-1-35—Alabama 29, Stanford 13
1-1-36—Stanford 7, Southern Methodist 0
1-1-37—Pittsburgh 21, Washington 0
1-1-38—California 13, Alabama 0
1-2-39—Southern Cal 7, Duke 3

1-1-40—Southern Cal 14, Tennessee 0
1-1-41—Stanford 21, Nebraska 13
1-1-42—Oregon St. 20, Duke 16 (at Durham)
1-1-43—Georgia 9, UCLA 0
1-1-44—Southern Cal 29, Washington 0

1-1-45—Southern Cal 25, Tennessee 0
1-1-46—Alabama 34, Southern Cal 14
1-1-47—Illinois 45, UCLA 14
1-1-48—Michigan 49, Southern Cal 0
1-1-49—Northwestern 20, California 14

1-2-50—Ohio St. 17, California 14
1-1-51—Michigan 14, California 6
1-1-52—Illinois 40, Stanford 7
1-1-53—Southern Cal 7, Wisconsin 0
1-1-54—Michigan St. 28, UCLA 20

1-1-55—Ohio St. 20, Southern Cal 7
1-2-56—Michigan St. 17, UCLA 14
1-1-57—Iowa 35, Oregon St. 19
1-1-58—Ohio St. 10, Oregon 7
1-1-59—Iowa 38, California 12

1-1-60—Washington 44, Wisconsin 8
1-2-61—Washington 17, Minnesota 7
1-1-62—Minnesota 21, UCLA 3
1-1-63—Southern Cal 42, Wisconsin 37
1-1-64—Illinois 17, Washington 7

1-1-65—Michigan 34, Oregon St. 7
1-1-66—UCLA 14, Michigan St. 12
1-2-67—Purdue 14, Southern Cal 13
1-1-68—Southern Cal 14, Indiana 3
1-1-69—Ohio St. 27, Southern Cal 16

1-1-70—Southern Cal 10, Michigan 3
1-1-71—Stanford 27, Ohio St. 17
1-1-72—Stanford 13, Michigan 12
1-1-73—Southern Cal 42, Ohio St. 17
1-1-74—Ohio St. 42, Southern Cal 21

1-1-75—Southern Cal 18, Ohio St. 17
1-1-76—UCLA 23, Ohio St. 10
1-1-77—Southern Cal 14, Michigan 6
1-2-78—Washington 27, Michigan 20
1-1-79—Southern Cal 17, Michigan 10

1-1-80—Southern Cal 17, Ohio St. 16
1-1-81—Michigan 23, Washington 6
1-1-82—Washington 28, Iowa 0
1-1-83—UCLA 24, Michigan 14
1-2-84—UCLA 45, Illinois 9

1-1-85—Southern Cal 20, Ohio St. 17
1-1-86—UCLA 45, Iowa 28
1-1-87—Arizona St. 22, Michigan 15
1-1-88—Michigan St. 20, Southern Cal 17
1-2-89—Michigan 22, Southern Cal 14

1-1-90—Southern Cal 17, Michigan 10
1-1-91—Washington 46, Iowa 34
1-1-92—Washington 34, Michigan 14
1-1-93—Michigan 38, Washington 31
1-1-94—Wisconsin 21, UCLA 16

ORANGE BOWL

Present Site: Miami, Fla.
Stadium (Capacity): Orange Bowl (74,712)
Playing Surface: Prescription Athletic Turf
Name Changes: Orange Bowl (1935-88); Federal Express Orange Bowl (since 1989)
Playing Sites: Miami Field Stadium (1935-37); Orange Bowl (since 1938)

1-1-35—Bucknell 26, Miami (Fla.) 0
1-1-36—Catholic 20, Mississippi 19
1-1-37—Duquesne 13, Mississippi St. 12
1-1-38—Auburn 6, Michigan St. 0
1-2-39—Tennessee 17, Oklahoma 0

1-1-40—Georgia Tech 21, Missouri 7
1-1-41—Mississippi St. 14, Georgetown 7
1-1-42—Georgia 40, Texas Christian 26
1-1-43—Alabama 37, Boston College 21
1-1-44—Louisiana St. 19, Texas A&M 14

1-1-45—Tulsa 26, Georgia Tech 12
1-1-46—Miami (Fla.) 13, Holy Cross 6
1-1-47—Rice 8, Tennessee 0
1-1-48—Georgia Tech 20, Kansas 14
1-1-49—Texas 41, Georgia 28

1-2-50—Santa Clara 21, Kentucky 13
1-1-51—Clemson 15, Miami (Fla.) 14
1-1-52—Georgia Tech 17, Baylor 14
1-1-53—Alabama 61, Syracuse 6
1-1-54—Oklahoma 7, Maryland 0

1-1-55—Duke 34, Nebraska 7
1-2-56—Oklahoma 20, Maryland 6
1-1-57—Colorado 27, Clemson 21
1-1-58—Oklahoma 48, Duke 21
1-1-59—Oklahoma 21, Syracuse 6

1-1-60—Georgia 14, Missouri 0
1-2-61—Missouri 21, Navy 14
1-1-62—Louisiana St. 25, Colorado 7
1-1-63—Alabama 17, Oklahoma 0
1-1-64—Nebraska 13, Auburn 7

1-1-65—Texas 21, Alabama 17
1-1-66—Alabama 39, Nebraska 28
1-2-67—Florida 27, Georgia Tech 12
1-1-68—Oklahoma 26, Tennessee 24
1-1-69—Penn St. 15, Kansas 14

1-1-70—Penn St. 10, Missouri 3
1-1-71—Nebraska 17, Louisiana St. 12
1-1-72—Nebraska 38, Alabama 6
1-1-73—Nebraska 40, Notre Dame 6
1-1-74—Penn St. 16, Louisiana St. 9

1-1-75—Notre Dame 13, Alabama 11
1-1-76—Oklahoma 14, Michigan 6
1-1-77—Ohio St. 27, Colorado 10
1-2-78—Arkansas 31, Oklahoma 6
1-1-79—Oklahoma 31, Nebraska 24

1-1-80—Oklahoma 24, Florida St. 7
1-1-81—Oklahoma 18, Florida St. 17
1-1-82—Clemson 22, Nebraska 15
1-1-83—Nebraska 21, Louisiana St. 20
1-2-84—Miami (Fla.) 31, Nebraska 30

1-1-85—Washington 28, Oklahoma 17
1-1-86—Oklahoma 25, Penn St. 10
1-1-87—Oklahoma 42, Arkansas 8
1-1-88—Miami (Fla.) 20, Oklahoma 14
1-2-89—Miami (Fla.) 23, Nebraska 3

1-1-90—Notre Dame 21, Colorado 6
1-1-91—Colorado 10, Notre Dame 9
1-1-92—Miami (Fla.) 22, Nebraska 0
1-1-93—Florida St. 27, Nebraska 14
1-1-94—Florida St. 18, Nebraska 16

SUGAR BOWL

Present Site: New Orleans, La.
Stadium (Capacity): Louisiana Superdome (72,704)
Playing Surface: AstroTurf
Name Changes: Sugar Bowl (1935-87); USF&G Sugar Bowl (since 1988)
Playing Sites: Tulane Stadium, New Orleans (1935-74); Louisiana Superdome (since 1975)

1-1-35—Tulane 20, Temple 14
1-1-36—Texas Christian 3, Louisiana St. 2
1-1-37—Santa Clara 21, Louisiana St. 14
1-1-38—Santa Clara 6, Louisiana St. 0
1-2-39—Texas Christian 15, Carnegie Mellon 7

1-1-40—Texas A&M 14, Tulane 13
1-1-41—Boston College 19, Tennessee 13

1-1-42—Fordham 2, Missouri 0
1-1-43—Tennessee 14, Tulsa 7
1-1-44—Georgia Tech 20, Tulsa 18
1-1-45—Duke 29, Alabama 26
1-1-46—Oklahoma St. 33, St. Mary's (Cal.) 13
1-1-47—Georgia 20, North Caro. 10
1-1-48—Texas 27, Alabama 7
1-1-49—Oklahoma 14, North Caro. 6

1-2-50—Oklahoma 35, Louisiana St. 0
1-1-51—Kentucky 13, Oklahoma 7
1-1-52—Maryland 28, Tennessee 13
1-1-53—Georgia Tech 24, Mississippi 7
1-1-54—Georgia Tech 42, West Va. 19

1-1-55—Navy 21, Mississippi 0
1-2-56—Georgia Tech 7, Pittsburgh 0
1-1-57—Baylor 13, Tennessee 7
1-1-58—Mississippi 39, Texas 7
1-1-59—Louisiana St. 7, Clemson 0

1-1-60—Mississippi 21, Louisiana St. 0
1-2-61—Mississippi 14, Rice 6
1-1-62—Alabama 10, Arkansas 3
1-1-63—Mississippi 17, Arkansas 13
1-1-64—Alabama 12, Mississippi 7

1-1-65—Louisiana St. 13, Syracuse 10
1-1-66—Missouri 20, Florida 18
1-2-67—Alabama 34, Nebraska 7
1-1-68—Louisiana St. 20, Wyoming 13
1-1-69—Arkansas 16, Georgia 2

1-1-70—Mississippi 27, Arkansas 22
1-1-71—Tennessee 34, Air Force 13
1-1-72—Oklahoma 40, Auburn 22
12-31-72—Oklahoma 14, Penn St. 0
12-31-73—Notre Dame 24, Alabama 23

12-31-74—Nebraska 13, Florida 10
12-31-75—Alabama 13, Penn St. 6
1-1-77—Pittsburgh 27, Georgia 3
1-2-78—Alabama 35, Ohio St. 6
1-1-79—Alabama 14, Penn St. 7

1-1-80—Alabama 24, Arkansas 9
1-1-81—Georgia 17, Notre Dame 10
1-1-82—Pittsburgh 24, Georgia 20
1-1-83—Penn St. 27, Georgia 23
1-2-84—Auburn 9, Michigan 7

1-1-85—Nebraska 28, Louisiana St. 10
1-1-86—Tennessee 35, Miami (Fla.) 7
1-1-87—Nebraska 30, Louisiana St. 15
1-1-88—Auburn 16, Syracuse 16
1-2-89—Florida St. 13, Auburn 7

1-1-90—Miami (Fla.) 33, Alabama 25
1-1-91—Tennessee 23, Virginia 22
1-1-92—Notre Dame 39, Florida 28
1-1-93—Alabama 34, Miami (Fla.) 13
1-1-94—Florida 41, West Va. 7

COTTON BOWL

Present Site: Dallas, Texas
Stadium (Capacity): Cotton Bowl (68,245)
Playing Surface: Grass
Name Changes: Cotton Bowl (1937-88); Mobil Cotton Bowl (since 1989)
Playing Sites: Fair Park Stadium, Dallas (1937); Cotton Bowl (since 1938)

1-1-37—Texas Christian 16, Marquette 6
1-1-38—Rice 28, Colorado 14
1-2-39—St. Mary's (Cal.) 20, Texas Tech 13
1-1-40—Clemson 6, Boston College 3
1-1-41—Texas A&M 13, Fordham 12

1-1-42—Alabama 29, Texas A&M 21
1-1-43—Texas 14, Georgia Tech 7
1-1-44—Texas 7, Randolph Field 7
1-1-45—Oklahoma St. 34, Texas Christian 0
1-1-46—Texas 40, Missouri 27

1-1-47—Arkansas 0, Louisiana St. 0
1-1-48—Penn St. 13, Southern Methodist 13
1-1-49—Southern Methodist 21, Oregon 13
1-2-50—Rice 27, North Caro. 13
1-1-51—Tennessee 20, Texas 14

1-1-52—Kentucky 20, Texas Christian 7
1-1-53—Texas 16, Tennessee 0
1-1-54—Rice 28, Alabama 6
1-1-55—Georgia Tech 14, Arkansas 6
1-2-56—Mississippi 14, Texas Christian 13

1-1-57—Texas Christian 28, Syracuse 27
1-1-58—Navy 20, Rice 7
1-1-59—Air Force 0, Texas Christian 0

1-1-60—Syracuse 23, Texas 14
1-2-61—Duke 7, Arkansas 6

1-1-62—Texas 12, Mississippi 7
1-1-63—Louisiana St. 13, Texas 0
1-1-64—Texas 28, Navy 6
1-1-65—Arkansas 10, Nebraska 7
1-1-66—Louisiana St. 14, Arkansas 7

12-31-66—Georgia 24, Southern Methodist 9
1-1-68—Texas A&M 20, Alabama 16
1-1-69—Texas 36, Tennessee 13
1-1-70—Texas 21, Notre Dame 17
1-1-71—Notre Dame 24, Texas 11

1-1-72—Penn St. 30, Texas 6
1-1-73—Texas 17, Alabama 13
1-1-74—Nebraska 19, Texas 3
1-1-75—Penn St. 41, Baylor 20
1-1-76—Arkansas 31, Georgia 10

1-1-77—Houston 30, Maryland 21
1-2-78—Notre Dame 38, Texas 10
1-1-79—Notre Dame 35, Houston 34
1-1-80—Houston 17, Nebraska 14
1-1-81—Alabama 30, Baylor 2

1-1-82—Texas 14, Alabama 12
1-1-83—Southern Methodist 7, Pittsburgh 3
1-2-84—Georgia 10, Texas 9
1-1-85—Boston College 45, Houston 28
1-1-86—Texas A&M 36, Auburn 16

1-1-87—Ohio St. 28, Texas A&M 12
1-1-88—Texas A&M 35, Notre Dame 10
1-2-89—UCLA 17, Arkansas 3
1-1-90—Tennessee 31, Arkansas 27
1-1-91—Miami (Fla.) 46, Texas 3

1-1-92—Florida St. 10, Texas A&M 2
1-1-93—Notre Dame 28, Texas A&M 3
1-1-94—Notre Dame 24, Texas A&M 21

JOHN HANCOCK BOWL

Present Site: El Paso, Texas
Stadium (Capacity): Sun Bowl (51,270)
Playing Surface: AstroTurf
Name Changes: Sun Bowl (1936-86); John Hancock Sun Bowl (1987-88); John Hancock Bowl (since 1989)
Playing Sites: Kidd Field, UTEP, El Paso (1936-62); Sun Bowl Stadium (since 1963)

1-1-36—Hardin-Simmons 14, New Mexico St. 14
1-1-37—Hardin-Simmons 34, UTEP 6
1-1-38—West Va. 7, Texas Tech 6
1-2-39—Utah 26, New Mexico 0
1-1-40—Arizona St. 0, Catholic 0

1-1-41—Case Reserve 26, Arizona St. 13
1-1-42—Tulsa 6, Texas Tech 0
1-1-43—Second Air Force 13, Hardin-Simmons 7
1-1-44—Southwestern (Tex.) 7, New Mexico 0
1-1-45—Southwestern (Tex.) 35, U. of Mexico 0

1-1-46—New Mexico 34, Denver 24
1-1-47—Cincinnati 18, Virginia Tech 6
1-1-48—Miami (Ohio) 13, Texas Tech 12
1-1-49—West Va. 21, UTEP 12
1-2-50—UTEP 33, Georgetown 20

1-1-51—West Tex. A&M 14, Cincinnati 13
1-1-52—Texas Tech 25, Pacific (Cal.) 14
1-1-53—Pacific (Cal.) 26, Southern Miss. 7
1-1-54—UTEP 37, Southern Miss. 14
1-1-55—UTEP 47, Florida St. 20

1-2-56—Wyoming 21, Texas Tech 14
1-1-57—Geo. Washington 13, UTEP 0
1-1-58—Louisville 34, Drake 20
12-31-58—Wyoming 14, Hardin-Simmons 6
12-31-59—New Mexico St. 28, North Texas 8

12-31-60—New Mexico St. 20, Utah St. 13
12-30-61—Villanova 17, Wichita St. 9
12-31-62—West Tex. A&M 15, Ohio 14
12-31-63—Oregon 21, Southern Methodist 14
12-26-64—Georgia 7, Texas Tech 0

12-31-65—UTEP 13, Texas Christian 12
12-24-66—Wyoming 28, Florida St. 20
12-30-67—UTEP 14, Mississippi 7
12-28-68—Auburn 34, Arizona 10
12-20-69—Nebraska 45, Georgia 6

12-19-70—Georgia Tech 17, Texas Tech 9
12-18-71—Louisiana 33, Iowa St. 15
12-30-72—North Caro. 32, Texas Tech 28
12-29-73—Missouri 34, Auburn 17
12-28-74—Mississippi St. 26, North Caro. 24

12-26-75—Pittsburgh 33, Kansas 19
1-2-77—Texas A&M 37, Florida 14
12-31-77—Stanford 24, Louisiana St. 14
12-23-78—Texas 42, Maryland 0
12-22-79—Washington 14, Texas 7

12-27-80—Nebraska 31, Mississippi St. 17
12-26-81—Oklahoma 40, Houston 14
12-25-82—North Caro. 26, Texas 10
12-24-83—Alabama 28, Southern Methodist 7
12-22-84—Maryland 28, Tennessee 27

12-28-85—Arizona 13, Georgia 13
12-25-86—Alabama 28, Washington 6
12-25-87—Oklahoma St. 35, West Va. 33
12-24-88—Alabama 29, Army 28
12-30-89—Pittsburgh 31, Texas A&M 28

12-31-90—Michigan St. 17, Southern Cal 16
12-31-91—UCLA 6, Illinois 3
12-31-92—Baylor 20, Arizona 15
12-24-93—Oklahoma 41, Texas Tech 10

GATOR BOWL

Present Site: Jacksonville, Fla.
Stadium (Capacity): Gator Bowl (80,129); Ben Hill Griffin Stadium (83,000)
Playing Surface: Grass
Name Changes: Gator Bowl (1946-85); Mazda Gator Bowl (1986-91); Outback Steakhouse Gator Bowl (since 1992)
Playing Sites: Gator Bowl (1946-93); Ben Hill Griffin Stadium, Gainesville, Fla. (1994)

1-1-46—Wake Forest 26, South Caro. 14
1-1-47—Oklahoma 34, North Caro. St. 13
1-1-48—Georgia 20, Maryland 20
1-1-49—Clemson 24, Missouri 23
1-2-50—Maryland 20, Missouri 7

1-1-51—Wyoming 20, Wash. & Lee 7
1-1-52—Miami (Fla.) 14, Clemson 0
1-1-53—Florida 14, Tulsa 13
1-1-54—Texas Tech 35, Auburn 13
12-31-54—Auburn 33, Baylor 13

12-31-55—Vanderbilt 25, Auburn 13
12-29-56—Georgia Tech 21, Pittsburgh 14
12-28-57—Tennessee 3, Texas A&M 0
12-27-58—Mississippi 7, Florida 3
1-2-60—Arkansas 14, Georgia Tech 7

12-31-60—Florida 13, Baylor 12
12-30-61—Penn St. 30, Georgia Tech 15
12-29-62—Florida 17, Penn St. 7
12-28-63—North Caro. 35, Air Force 0
1-2-65—Florida St. 36, Oklahoma 19

12-31-65—Georgia Tech 31, Texas Tech 21
12-31-66—Tennessee 18, Syracuse 12
12-30-67—Florida St. 17, Penn St. 17
12-28-68—Missouri 35, Alabama 10
12-27-69—Florida 14, Tennessee 13

1-2-71—Auburn 35, Mississippi 28
12-31-71—Georgia 7, North Caro. 3
12-30-72—Auburn 24, Colorado 3
12-29-73—Texas Tech 28, Tennessee 19
12-30-74—Auburn 27, Texas 3

12-29-75—Maryland 13, Florida 0
12-27-76—Notre Dame 20, Penn St. 9
12-30-77—Pittsburgh 34, Clemson 3
12-29-78—Clemson 17, Ohio St. 15
12-28-79—North Caro. 17, Michigan 15

12-29-80—Pittsburgh 37, South Caro. 9
12-28-81—North Caro. 31, Arkansas 27
12-30-82—Florida St. 31, West Va. 12
12-30-83—Florida 14, Iowa 6
12-28-84—Oklahoma St. 21, South Caro. 14

12-30-85—Florida St. 34, Oklahoma St. 23
12-27-86—Clemson 27, Stanford 21
12-31-87—Louisiana St. 30, South Caro. 13
1-1-89—Georgia 34, Michigan St. 27
12-30-89—Clemson 27, West Va. 7

1-1-91—Michigan 35, Mississippi 3
12-29-91—Oklahoma 48, Virginia 14
12-31-92—Florida 27, North Caro. St. 10
12-31-93—Alabama 24, North Caro. 10

FLORIDA CITRUS BOWL

Present Site: Orlando, Fla.
Stadium (Capacity): Florida Citrus Bowl-Orange County (70,349)
Playing Surface: Grass

Name Changes: Tangerine Bowl (1947-82); Florida Citrus Bowl (1983-93); CompUSA Florida Citrus Bowl (since 1994)
Playing Sites: Tangerine Bowl, Orlando (1947-72); Florida Field, Gainesville (1973); Tangerine Bowl (now Florida Citrus Bowl-Orange County) (1974-82); Orlando Stadium (now Florida Citrus Bowl-Orange County) (1983-85); Florida Citrus Bowl-Orange County (since 1986)

1-1-47—Catawba 31, Maryville (Tenn.) 6
1-1-48—Catawba 7, Marshall 0
1-1-49—Murray St. 21, Sul Ross St. 21
1-2-50—St. Vincent 7, Emory & Henry 6
1-1-51—Morris Harvey 35, Emory & Henry 14

1-1-52—Stetson 35, Arkansas St. 20
1-1-53—East Tex. St. 33, Tennessee Tech 0
1-1-54—Arkansas St. 7, East Tex. St. 7
1-1-55—Nebraska-Omaha 7, Eastern Ky. 6
1-2-56—Juniata 6, Missouri Valley 6

1-1-57—West Tex. A&M 20, Southern Miss. 13
1-1-58—East Tex. St. 10, Southern Miss. 9
12-27-58—East Tex. St. 26, Missouri Valley 7
1-1-60—Middle Tenn. St. 21, Presbyterian 12
12-30-60—Citadel 27, Tennessee Tech 0

12-29-61—Lamar 21, Middle Tenn. St. 14
12-22-62—Houston 49, Miami (Ohio) 21
12-28-63—Western Ky. 27, Coast Guard 0
12-12-64—East Caro. 14, Massachusetts 13
12-11-65—East Caro. 31, Maine 0

12-10-66—Morgan St. 14, West Chester 6
12-16-67—Tenn.-Martin 25, West Chester 8
12-27-68—Richmond 49, Ohio 42
12-26-69—Toledo 56, Davidson 33
12-28-70—Toledo 40, William & Mary 12

12-28-71—Toledo 28, Richmond 3
12-29-72—Tampa 21, Kent 18
12-22-73—Miami (Ohio) 16, Florida 7
12-21-74—Miami (Ohio) 21, Georgia 10
12-20-75—Miami (Ohio) 20, South Caro. 7

12-18-76—Oklahoma St. 49, Brigham Young 21
12-23-77—Florida St. 40, Texas Tech 17
12-23-78—North Caro. St. 30, Pittsburgh 17
12-22-79—Louisiana St. 34, Wake Forest 10
12-20-80—Florida 35, Maryland 20

12-19-81—Missouri 19, Southern Miss. 17
12-18-82—Auburn 33, Boston College 26
12-17-83—Tennessee 30, Maryland 23
12-22-84—Florida St. 17, Georgia 17
12-28-85—Ohio St. 10, Brigham Young 7

1-1-87—Auburn 16, Southern Cal 7
1-1-88—Clemson 35, Penn St. 10
1-2-89—Clemson 13, Oklahoma 6
1-1-90—Illinois 31, Virginia 21
1-1-91—Georgia Tech 45, Nebraska 21

1-1-92—California 37, Clemson 13
1-1-93—Georgia 21, Ohio St. 14
1-1-94—Penn St. 31, Tennessee 13

Note: No classified major teams participated in games from January 1, 1947, through December 30, 1960, or in 1961 and 1963 through 1967.

LIBERTY BOWL

Present Site: Memphis, Tenn.
Stadium (Capacity): Liberty Bowl Memorial (under renovation)
Playing Surface: Prescription Athletic Turf
Name Changes: Liberty Bowl (1959-92); St. Jude Liberty Bowl (since 1993)
Playing Sites: Municipal Stadium, Philadelphia (1959-63); Convention Hall, Atlantic City, N.J. (1964); Liberty Bowl Memorial (since 1965)

12-19-59—Penn St. 7, Alabama 0
12-17-60—Penn St. 41, Oregon 12
12-16-61—Syracuse 15, Miami (Fla.) 14
12-15-62—Oregon St. 6, Villanova 0
12-21-63—Mississippi St. 16, North Caro. St. 12

12-19-64—Utah 32, West Va. 6
12-18-65—Mississippi 13, Auburn 7
12-10-66—Miami (Fla.) 14, Virginia Tech 7
12-16-67—North Caro. St. 14, Georgia 7
12-14-68—Mississippi 34, Virginia Tech 17

12-13-69—Colorado 47, Alabama 33
12-12-70—Tulane 17, Colorado 3
12-20-71—Tennessee 14, Arkansas 13
12-18-72—Georgia Tech 31, Iowa St. 30
12-17-73—North Caro. St. 31, Kansas 18

12-16-74—Tennessee 7, Maryland 3
12-22-75—Southern Cal 20, Texas A&M 0
12-20-76—Alabama 36, UCLA 6
12-19-77—Nebraska 21, North Caro. 17
12-23-78—Missouri 20, Louisiana St. 15

12-22-79—Penn St. 9, Tulane 6
12-27-80—Purdue 28, Missouri 25
12-30-81—Ohio St. 31, Navy 28
12-29-82—Alabama 21, Illinois 15
12-29-83—Notre Dame 19, Boston College 18

12-27-84—Auburn 21, Arkansas 15
12-27-85—Baylor 21, Louisiana St. 7
12-29-86—Tennessee 21, Minnesota 14
12-29-87—Georgia 20, Arkansas 17
12-28-88—Indiana 34, South Caro. 10

12-28-89—Mississippi 42, Air Force 29
12-27-90—Air Force 23, Ohio St. 11
12-29-91—Air Force 38, Mississippi St. 15
12-31-92—Mississippi 13, Air Force 0
12-28-93—Louisville 18, Michigan St. 7

PEACH BOWL

Present Site: Atlanta, Ga.
Stadium (Capacity): Georgia Dome (71,596)
Playing Surface: AstroTurf
Playing Sites: Grant Field, Atlanta (1968-70); Atlanta/Fulton County (1971-92); Georgia Dome (since 1993)

12-30-68—Louisiana St. 31, Florida St. 27
12-30-69—West Va. 14, South Caro. 3
12-30-70—Arizona St. 48, North Caro. 26
12-30-71—Mississippi 41, Georgia Tech 18
12-29-72—North Caro. St. 49, West Va. 13

12-28-73—Georgia 17, Maryland 16
12-28-74—Texas Tech 6, Vanderbilt 6
12-31-75—West Va. 13, North Caro. St. 10
12-31-76—Kentucky 21, North Caro. 0
12-31-77—North Caro. St. 24, Iowa St. 14

12-25-78—Purdue 41, Georgia Tech 21
12-31-79—Baylor 24, Clemson 18
1-2-81—Miami (Fla.) 20, Virginia Tech 10
12-31-81—West Va. 26, Florida 6
12-31-82—Iowa 28, Tennessee 22

12-30-83—Florida St. 28, North Caro. 3
12-31-84—Virginia 27, Purdue 24
12-31-85—Army 31, Illinois 29
12-31-86—Virginia Tech 25, North Caro. St. 24
1-2-88—Tennessee 27, Indiana 22

12-31-88—North Caro. St. 28, Iowa 23
12-30-89—Syracuse 19, Georgia 18
12-29-90—Auburn 27, Indiana 23
1-1-92—East Caro. 37, North Caro. St. 34
1-2-93—North Caro. 21, Mississippi St. 17

12-31-93—Clemson 14, Kentucky 13

FIESTA BOWL

Present Site: Tempe, Ariz.
Stadium (Capacity): Sun Devil (73,656)
Playing Surface: Grass
Name Changes: Fiesta Bowl (1971-85); Sunkist Fiesta Bowl (1986-90); Fiesta Bowl (1991-92); IBM OS/2 Fiesta Bowl (since 1993)
Playing Sites: Sun Devil Stadium (since 1971)

12-27-71—Arizona St. 45, Florida St. 38
12-23-72—Arizona St. 49, Missouri 35
12-21-73—Arizona St. 28, Pittsburgh 7
12-28-74—Oklahoma St. 16, Brigham Young 6
12-26-75—Arizona St. 17, Nebraska 14

12-25-76—Oklahoma 41, Wyoming 7
12-25-77—Penn St. 42, Arizona St. 30
12-25-78—Arkansas 10, UCLA 10
12-25-79—Pittsburgh 16, Arizona 10
12-26-80—Penn St. 31, Ohio St. 19

1-1-82—Penn St. 26, Southern Cal 10
1-1-83—Arizona St. 32, Oklahoma 21
1-2-84—Ohio St. 28, Pittsburgh 23
1-1-85—UCLA 39, Miami (Fla.) 37
1-1-86—Michigan 27, Nebraska 23

1-2-87—Penn St. 14, Miami (Fla.) 10

1-1-88—Florida St. 31, Nebraska 28
1-2-89—Notre Dame 34, West Va. 21
1-1-90—Florida St. 41, Nebraska 17
1-1-91—Louisville 34, Alabama 7

1-1-92—Penn St. 42, Tennessee 17
1-1-93—Syracuse 26, Colorado 22
1-1-94—Arizona 29, Miami (Fla.) 0

INDEPENDENCE BOWL

Present Site: Shreveport, La.
Stadium (Capacity): Independence (60,128)
Playing Surface: Grass
Name Changes: Independence Bowl (1976-89); Poulan Independence Bowl (1990); Poulan/Weed Eater Independence Bowl (since 1991)
Playing Sites: Independence Stadium (since 1976)

12-13-76—McNeese St. 20, Tulsa 16
12-17-77—Louisiana Tech 24, Louisville 14
12-16-78—East Caro. 35, Louisiana Tech 13
12-15-79—Syracuse 31, McNeese St. 7
12-13-80—Southern Miss. 16, McNeese St. 14

12-12-81—Texas A&M 33, Oklahoma St. 16
12-11-82—Wisconsin 14, Kansas St. 3
12-10-83—Air Force 9, Mississippi 3
12-15-84—Air Force 23, Virginia Tech 7
12-21-85—Minnesota 20, Clemson 13

12-20-86—Mississippi 20, Texas Tech 17
12-19-87—Washington 24, Tulane 12
12-23-88—Southern Miss. 38, UTEP 18
12-16-89—Oregon 27, Tulsa 24
12-15-90—Louisiana Tech 34, Maryland 34

12-29-91—Georgia 24, Arkansas 15
12-31-92—Wake Forest 39, Oregon 35
12-31-93—Virginia Tech 45, Indiana 20

HOLIDAY BOWL

Present Site: San Diego, Calif.
Stadium (Capacity): San Diego Jack Murphy (61,124)
Playing Surface: Grass
Name Changes: Holiday Bowl (1978-85); Sea World Holiday Bowl (1986-90); Thrifty Car Rental Holiday Bowl (since 1991)
Playing Sites: San Diego Jack Murphy Stadium (since 1978)

12-22-78—Navy 23, Brigham Young 16
12-21-79—Indiana 38, Brigham Young 37
12-19-80—Brigham Young 46, Southern Methodist 45
12-18-81—Brigham Young 38, Washington St. 36
12-17-82—Ohio St. 47, Brigham Young 17

12-23-83—Brigham Young 21, Missouri 17
12-21-84—Brigham Young 24, Michigan 17
12-22-85—Arkansas 18, Arizona St. 17
12-30-86—Iowa 39, San Diego St. 38
12-30-87—Iowa 20, Wyoming 19

12-30-88—Oklahoma St. 62, Wyoming 14
12-29-89—Penn St. 50, Brigham Young 39
12-29-90—Texas A&M 65, Brigham Young 14
12-30-91—Brigham Young 13, Iowa 13
12-30-92—Hawaii 27, Illinois 17

12-30-93—Ohio St. 28, Brigham Young 21

ALOHA BOWL

Present Site: Honolulu, Hawaii
Stadium (Capacity): Aloha (50,000)
Playing Surface: AstroTurf
Name Changes: Aloha Bowl (1982-84); Eagle Aloha Bowl (1985-88); Jeep Eagle Aloha Bowl (since 1989)
Playing Sites: Aloha Stadium (since 1982)

12-25-82—Washington 21, Maryland 20
12-26-83—Penn St. 13, Washington 10
12-29-84—Southern Methodist 27, Notre Dame 20
12-28-85—Alabama 24, Southern Cal 3
12-27-86—Arizona 30, North Caro. 21

12-25-87—UCLA 20, Florida 16
12-25-88—Washington St. 24, Houston 22
12-25-89—Michigan St. 33, Hawaii 13
12-25-90—Syracuse 28, Arizona 0
12-25-91—Georgia Tech 18, Stanford 17

12-25-92—Kansas 23, Brigham Young 20
12-25-93—Colorado 41, Fresno St. 30

FREEDOM BOWL

Present Site: Anaheim, Calif.
Stadium (Capacity): Anaheim (70,962)
Playing Surface: Grass
Name Changes: Anaheim Freedom Bowl (1984-90); Freedom Bowl (since 1991)
Playing Sites: Anaheim Stadium (since 1984)

12-26-84—Iowa 55, Texas 17
12-30-85—Washington 20, Colorado 17
12-30-86—UCLA 31, Brigham Young 10
12-30-87—Arizona St. 33, Air Force 28
12-29-88—Brigham Young 20, Colorado 17

12-30-89—Washington 34, Florida 7
12-29-90—Colorado St. 32, Oregon 31
12-30-91—Tulsa 28, San Diego St. 17
12-29-92—Fresno St. 24, Southern Cal 7
12-30-93—Southern Cal 28, Utah 21

HALL OF FAME BOWL

Present Site: Tampa, Fla.
Stadium (Capacity): Tampa (74,350)
Playing Surface: Grass
Playing Sites: Tampa Stadium (since 1986)

12-23-86—Boston College 27, Georgia 24
1-2-88—Michigan 28, Alabama 24
1-2-89—Syracuse 23, Louisiana St. 10
1-1-90—Auburn 31, Ohio St. 14
1-1-91—Clemson 30, Illinois 0

1-1-92—Syracuse 24, Ohio St. 17
1-1-93—Tennessee 38, Boston College 23
1-1-94—Michigan 42, North Caro. St. 7

COPPER BOWL

Present Site: Tucson, Ariz.
Stadium (Capacity): Arizona (56,167)
Playing Surface: Grass
Name Changes: Copper Bowl (1989); Domino's Pizza Copper Bowl (1990-91); Weiser Lock Copper Bowl (since 1992)
Playing Sites: Arizona Wildcats Stadium (since 1989)

12-31-89—Arizona 17, North Caro. St. 10
12-31-90—California 17, Wyoming 15
12-31-91—Indiana 24, Baylor 0
12-29-92—Washington St. 31, Utah 28
12-29-93—Kansas St. 52, Wyoming 17

CARQUEST BOWL

Present Site: Miami, Fla.
Stadium (Capacity): Joe Robbie (73,000)
Playing Surface: Grass
Name Changes: Blockbuster Bowl (1990-93); Carquest Bowl (since 1994)
Playing Sites: Joe Robbie Stadium (since 1990)

12-28-90—Florida St. 24, Penn St. 17
12-28-91—Alabama 30, Colorado 25
1-1-93—Stanford 24, Penn St. 3
1-1-94—Boston College 31, Virginia 13

LAS VEGAS BOWL

Present Site: Las Vegas, Nev.
Stadium (Capacity): Sam Boyd (32,000)
Playing Surface: Monsanto Turf (retractable)
Playing Sites: Sam Boyd (since 1992)

12-18-92—Bowling Green 35, Nevada 34
12-17-93—Utah St. 42, Ball St. 33

ALAMO BOWL

Present Site: San Antonio, Texas
Stadium (Capacity): Alamodome (65,000)
Playing Surface: AstroTurf
Name Changes: Builders Square Alamo Bowl (since 1993)
Playing Sites: Alamodome (since 1993)

12-31-93—California 37, Iowa 3

BOWL/ALL-STAR RESULTS

Bowl-Game Title Sponsors

Bowl	Title Sponsor (Year Began)	Bowl Name (Years)
Alamo	Builders Square (since 1993)	Builders Square Alamo (1993)
Aloha	Jeep Eagle (since 1985)	Aloha (1982-84) Eagle Aloha (1985-88) Jeep Eagle Aloha (1989-93)
Carquest	Blockbuster (1990-93) Carquest Auto Parts (since 1994)	Blockbuster (1990-93) Sunshine Football Classic (brief) Carquest (1994)
Copper	Domino's Pizza (1990-91) Weiser Lock (since 1992)	Copper (1989) Domino's Pizza Copper (1990-91) Weiser Lock Copper (1992-93)
Cotton	Mobil (since 1989)	Cotton (1937-88) Mobil Cotton (1989-94)
Fiesta	Sunkist (1986-90) IBM (since 1993)	Fiesta (1971-85; 1991-92) Sunkist Fiesta (1986-90) IBM OS/2 Fiesta (1993-94)
Florida Citrus	CompUSA (since 1994)	Tangerine (1947-82) Florida Citrus (1983-93) CompUSA Florida Citrus (1994)
Freedom	None	Anaheim Freedom (1984-90) Freedom (1991-93)
Gator	Mazda (1986) Outback Steakhouse (since 1992)	Gator (1946-85) Mazda Gator (1986-91) Outback Steakhouse Gator (1992-93)
Hall of Fame	None	Hall of Fame (1986-94)
Holiday	Sea World (1986-90) Thrifty Car Rental (since 1991)	Holiday (1976-85) Sea World Holiday (1986-90) Thrifty Car Rental Holiday (1991-93)
John Hancock	John Hancock (since 1989)	Sun (1936-86) John Hancock Sun (1987-88) John Hancock (1989-93)

Bowl	Title Sponsor (Year Began)	Bowl Name (Years)
Independence	Poulan (since 1990)	Independence (1976-89) Poulan Independence (1990) Poulan/Weed Eater Independence (1991-93)
Las Vegas	None (since 1992)	Las Vegas (1992-93)
Liberty	St. Jude (since 1993)	Liberty (1959-92) St. Jude Liberty (1993)
Orange	Federal Express (since 1989)	Orange (1935-88) Federal Express Orange (1989-94)
Peach	None (since 1968)	Peach (1968-93)
Rose	None (1902, 1916-94)	Rose (since 1902)
Sugar	USF&G Sugar (since 1988)	Sugar (1935-87) USF&G Sugar (1988-94)

Bowl Financial Analysis, 1976-94

Year	No. Bowls	No. Teams	Total Payout	Per-Game Payout	Per-Team Payout
1976-77	11	22	$11,345,851	$515,714	$257,857
1977-78	12	24	13,323,638	1,110,303	555,152
1978-79	13	26	15,506,516	1,192,809	596,405
1979-80	13	26	17,219,624	1,324,586	662,293
1980-81	13	26	19,517,938	1,501,380	750,690
1981-82	14	28	21,791,222	1,556,516	778,258
1982-83	15	30	26,682,486	1,778,832	889,416
1983-84	15	30	32,535,788	2,169,052	1,084,526
1984-85	16	32	36,666,738	2,291,671	1,145,836
1985-86	16	32	36,995,864	2,312,242	1,156,121
1986-87	17	34	45,830,906	2,695,936	1,347,968
1987-88	17	34	48,251,516	2,838,324	1,419,162
1988-89	17	34	52,905,426	3,112,084	1,556,042
1989-90	18	36	58,208,058	3,233,781	1,616,891
1990-91	19	38	60,378,362	3,177,809	1,588,904
1991-92	18	36	63,494,554	3,527,475	1,763,738
1992-93	18	36	67,950,000	3,775,000	1,887,500
1993-94	19	38	71,006,000	3,737,158	1,868,579

26 Former Major Bowl Games

(Games in which at least one team was classified major that season)

ALAMO
(San Antonio, Texas)

1-4-47—Hardin-Simmons 20, Denver 0

ALL-AMERICAN
(Birmingham, Ala.)

12-22-77—Maryland 17, Minnesota 7
12-20-78—Texas A&M 28, Iowa St. 12
12-29-79—Missouri 24, South Caro. 14
12-27-80—Arkansas 34, Tulane 15
12-31-81—Mississippi St. 10, Kansas 0

12-31-82—Air Force 36, Vanderbilt 28
12-22-83—West Va. 20, Kentucky 16
12-29-84—Kentucky 20, Wisconsin 19
12-31-85—Georgia Tech 17, Michigan St. 14
12-31-86—Florida St. 27, Indiana 13

12-22-87—Virginia 22, Brigham Young 16
12-29-88—Florida 14, Illinois 10
12-28-89—Texas Tech 49, Duke 21
12-28-90—North Caro. St. 31, Southern Miss. 27

AVIATION
(Dayton, Ohio)

12-9-61—New Mexico 28, Western Mich. 12

BACARDI
(Cuban National Sports Festival at Havana)

1-1-37—Auburn 7, Villanova 7

BLUEBONNET
(Houston, Texas)

12-19-59—Clemson 23, Texas Christian 7
12-17-60—Alabama 3, Texas 3
12-16-61—Kansas 33, Rice 7
12-22-62—Missouri 14, Georgia Tech 10
12-21-63—Baylor 14, Louisiana St. 7

12-19-64—Tulsa 14, Mississippi 7
12-18-65—Tennessee 27, Tulsa 6
12-17-66—Texas 19, Mississippi 0
12-23-67—Colorado 31, Miami (Fla.) 21
12-31-68—Southern Methodist 28, Oklahoma 27

12-31-69—Houston 36, Auburn 7
12-31-70—Alabama 24, Oklahoma 24
12-31-71—Colorado 29, Houston 17
12-30-72—Tennessee 24, Louisiana St. 17
12-29-73—Houston 47, Tulane 7

12-23-74—Houston 31, North Caro. St. 31
12-27-75—Texas 38, Colorado 21
12-31-76—Nebraska 27, Texas Tech 24
12-31-77—Southern Cal 47, Texas A&M 28
12-31-78—Stanford 25, Georgia 22

12-31-79—Purdue 27, Tennessee 22
12-31-80—North Caro. 16, Texas 7
12-31-81—Michigan 33, UCLA 14
12-31-82—Arkansas 28, Florida 24
12-31-83—Oklahoma St. 24, Baylor 14

12-31-84—West Va. 31, Texas Christian 14
12-31-85—Air Force 24, Texas 16

12-31-86—Baylor 21, Colorado 9
12-31-87—Texas 32, Pittsburgh 27

BLUEGRASS
(Louisville, Ky.)

12-13-58—Oklahoma St. 15, Florida St. 6

CALIFORNIA
(Fresno, Calif.)

12-19-81—Toledo 27, San Jose St. 25
12-18-82—Fresno St. 29, Bowling Green 28
12-17-83—Northern Ill. 20, Cal St. Fullerton 13
12-15-84—Nevada-Las Vegas 30, *Toledo 13
12-14-85—Fresno St. 51, Bowling Green 7

12-13-86—San Jose St. 37, Miami (Ohio) 7
12-12-87—Eastern Mich. 30, San Jose St. 27
12-10-88—Fresno St. 35, Western Mich. 30
12-9-89—Fresno St. 27, Ball St. 6
12-8-90—San Jose St. 48, Central Mich. 24

12-14-91—Bowling Green 28, Fresno St. 21

*Won by forfeit.

CAMELLIA
(Lafayette, La.)

12-30-48—Hardin-Simmons 49, Wichita St. 12

CHERRY
(Pontiac, Mich.)

12-22-84—Army 10, Michigan St. 6
12-21-85—Maryland 35, Syracuse 18

DELTA
(Memphis, Tenn.)

1-1-48—Mississippi 13, Texas Christian 9
1-1-49—William & Mary 20, Oklahoma St. 0

DIXIE
(Birmingham, Ala.)

1-1-48—Arkansas 21, William & Mary 19
1-1-49—Baylor 20, Wake Forest 7

DIXIE CLASSIC
(Dallas, Texas)

1-2-22—Texas A&M 22, Centre 14
1-1-25—West Va. Wesleyan 9, Southern Methodist 7
1-1-34—Arkansas 7, Centenary (La.) 7

FORT WORTH CLASSIC
(Fort Worth, Texas)

1-1-21—Centre 63, Texas Christian 7

GARDEN STATE
(East Rutherford, N.J.)

12-16-78—Arizona St. 34, Rutgers 18
12-15-79—Temple 28, California 17
12-14-80—Houston 35, Navy 0
12-13-81—Tennessee 28, Wisconsin 21

GOTHAM
(New York, N.Y.)

12-9-61—Baylor 24, Utah St. 9
12-15-62—Nebraska 36, Miami (Fla.) 34

GREAT LAKES
(Cleveland, Ohio)

12-6-47—Kentucky 24, Villanova 14

HARBOR
(San Diego, Calif.)

1-1-47—Montana St. 13, New Mexico 13
1-1-48—Hardin-Simmons 53, San Diego St. 0
1-1-49—Villanova 27, Nevada 7

LOS ANGELES CHRISTMAS FESTIVAL
(Los Angeles, Calif.)

12-25-24—Southern Cal 20, Missouri 7

MERCY
(Los Angeles, Calif.)

11-23-61—Fresno St. 36, Bowling Green 6

OIL
(Houston, Texas)

1-1-46—Georgia 20, Tulsa 6
1-1-47—Georgia Tech 41, St. Mary's (Calif.) 19

PASADENA
(Called Junior Rose in 1967)
(Pasadena, Calif.)

12-2-67—West Tex. A&M 35, Cal St. Northridge 13
12-6-69—San Diego St. 28, Boston U. 7
12-19-70—Long Beach St. 24, Louisville 24
12-18-71—Memphis 28, San Jose St. 9

PRESIDENTIAL CUP
(College Park, Md.)

12-9-50—Texas A&M 40, Georgia 20

RAISIN
(Fresno, Calif.)

1-1-46—Drake 13, Fresno St. 12
1-1-47—San Jose St. 20, Utah St. 0
1-1-48—Pacific (Cal.) 26, Wichita St. 14
1-1-49—Occidental 21, Colorado St. 20
12-31-49— San Jose St. 20, Texas Tech 13

SALAD
(Phoenix, Ariz.)

1-1-48—Nevada 13, North Texas 6
1-1-49—Drake 14, Arizona 13
1-1-50—Xavier (Ohio) 33, Arizona St. 21
1-1-51—Miami (Ohio) 34, Arizona St. 21
1-1-52—Houston 26, Dayton 21

SAN DIEGO EAST-WEST CHRISTMAS CLASSIC
(San Diego, Calif.)

12-26-21—Centre 38, Arizona 0
12-25-22—West Va. 21, Gonzaga 13

SHRINE
(Little Rock, Ark.)

12-18-48—Hardin-Simmons 40, Ouachita Baptist 12

Other Major Postseason Games

There was a proliferation of postseason benefit games specially scheduled at the conclusion of the regular season during the Great Depression (principally in 1931) to raise money for relief of the unemployed in response to the President's Committee on Mobilization of Relief Resources and for other charitable causes.

The exact number of these games is unknown, but it is estimated that more than 100 college games were played nationwide during this period, often irrespective of the competing teams' records. Proceeds went to the benefit of the emergency relief for unemployment and numerous charities.

Most notable among these postseason games were the Tennessee-New York University game of 1931 and the Army-Navy contests of 1930 and 1931 (the two academies had severed athletics relations during 1928-31 and did not meet in regular-season play). All three games were played before huge crowds in New York City's Yankee Stadium.

Following is a list of the principal postseason benefit and charity games involving at least one major college. Not included (nor included in all-time team won-lost records) are several special feature, same-day double-header tournaments in 1931 in which four participating teams were paired to play halves or modified quarters.

Date	Site	Opposing Teams
12-6-30	New York	Colgate 7, New York U. 0
12-13-30	New York	Army 6, Navy 0
11-28-31	Kansas City	Temple 38, Missouri 6
11-28-31	Chicago	Purdue 7, Northwestern 0
11-28-31	Minneapolis	Minnesota 19, Ohio St. 7
11-28-31	Ann Arbor	Michigan 16, Wisconsin 0
11-28-31	Philadelphia	Penn St. 31, Lehigh 0
12-2-31	Chattanooga	Alabama 49, Tenn.-Chatt. 0
12-3-31	Brooklyn	Manhattan 7, Rutgers 6
12-5-31	Denver	Nebraska 20, Colorado St. 7
12-5-31	Pittsburgh	Carnegie Mellon 0, Duquesne 0
12-5-31	New York	Tennessee 13, New York U. 0
12-5-31	St. Louis	St. Louis 31, Missouri 0
12-5-31	Topeka	Kansas 6, Washburn 0
12-5-31	Wichita	Kansas St. 20, Wichita St. 6
12-5-31	Columbia	Centre 9, South Caro. 7
12-5-31	Norman	Oklahoma City 6, Oklahoma 0
12-12-31	New York	Army 17, Navy 7
12-12-31	Tulsa	Oklahoma 20, Tulsa 7
1-2-33	El Paso	Southern Methodist 26, UTEP 0
12-8-34	St. Louis	Southern Methodist 7, Washington (Mo.) 0

Team-by-Team Bowl Results

All-Time Bowl-Game Records

This list includes all bowls played by a current major team, providing its opponent was classified major that season or it was a major team then. The list excludes games in which a home team served as a predetermined, preseason host regardless of its record and/or games scheduled before the season, thus eliminating the old Pineapple, Glass and Palm Festival. Following is the alphabetical list showing the record of each current major team in all major bowls.

Team	W	L	T	Team	W	L	T
Air Force	6	5	1	Houston	7	5	1
Alabama	26	17	3	Illinois	4	7	0
Arizona	3	6	1	Indiana	3	5	0
Arizona St.	9	5	1				
Arkansas	9	15	3	Iowa	6	6	1
				Iowa St.	0	4	0
Army	2	1	0	Kansas	2	5	0
Auburn	12	9	2	Kansas St.	1	1	0
Ball St.	0	2	0	Kent	0	1	0
Baylor	8	7	0				
Boston College	4	5	0	Kentucky	5	3	0
Bowling Green	2	3	0	Louisiana St.	11	16	1
Brigham Young	5	12	1	Louisiana Tech	1	1	1
California	5	6	1	Louisville	3	1	1
Central Mich.	0	1	0	Maryland	6	9	2
Cincinnati	1	1	0				
				Memphis	1	0	0
Clemson	12	7	0	Miami (Fla.)	10	10	0
Colorado	6	12	0	Miami (Ohio)	5	2	0
Colorado St.	1	1	0	Michigan	12	13	0
Duke	3	4	0	Michigan St.	5	6	0
East Caro.	2	0	0	Minnesota	2	3	0
				Mississippi	14	11	0
Eastern Mich.	1	0	0	Mississippi St.	4	4	0
Florida	10	11	0	Missouri	8	11	0
Florida St.	13	7	2	Navy	3	4	1
Fresno St.	6	3	0	Nebraska	14	18	0
Georgia	15	13	3	Nevada	1	2	0
Georgia Tech	17	8	0	Nevada-Las Vegas	#1	0	0
Hawaii	1	1	0	New Mexico	2	2	1

Team	W	L	T
New Mexico St.	2	0	1
North Caro.	7	11	0
North Caro. St.	7	8	1
Northern Ill.	1	0	0
Northwestern	1	0	0
Notre Dame	13	6	0
Ohio	0	2	0
Ohio St.	12	14	0
Oklahoma	20	10	1
Oklahoma St.	9	3	0
Oregon	3	6	0
Oregon St.	2	2	0
Pacific (Cal.)	2	1	0
Penn St.	18	10	2
Pittsburgh	8	10	0
Purdue	4	1	0
Rice	4	3	0
Rutgers	0	1	0
San Diego St.	1	3	0
San Jose St.	4	3	0
South Caro.	0	8	0
Southern Cal.	23	13	0
Southern Methodist	4	6	1
Southern Miss.	2	4	0
Stanford	8	7	1

Team	W	L	T
Syracuse	8	6	1
Temple	1	1	0
Tennessee	18	16	0
Texas	16	16	2
Texas A&M	11	10	0
Texas Christian	4	9	1
Texas Tech	4	14	1
Toledo	4	1	0
Tulane	2	6	0
Tulsa	4	7	0
UCLA	10	8	1
Utah	2	2	0
Utah St.	1	3	0
UTEP	5	4	0
Vanderbilt	1	1	1
Virginia	2	4	0
Virginia Tech	2	5	0
Wake Forest	2	2	0
Washington	12	8	1
Washington St.	3	2	0
West Va.	8	8	0
Western Mich.	0	2	0
Wisconsin	2	5	0
Wyoming	4	6	0

#Later lost game by forfeit.

The following current Division I-A teams have not played in a major bowl game: Akron, Arkansas St., Northeast La. and Southwestern La.

Major Bowl Records of Non-Division I-A Teams

Boston U. 0-1-0; Brown 0-1-0; Bucknell 1-0-0; Cal St. Fullerton 0-1-0; Cal St. Northridge 0-1-0; Carnegie Mellon 0-1-0; Case Reserve 1-0-0; Catholic 1-0-1; Centenary (La.) 0-0-1; Centre 2-1-0; Citadel 1-0-0; Columbia 1-0-0; Davidson 0-1-0; Dayton 0-1-0; Denver 0-2-0; Drake 2-1-0; Duquesne 1-0-0; Fordham 1-1-0; Geo. Washington 1-0-0; Georgetown 0-2-0; Gonzaga 0-1-0; Hardin-Simmons 5-2-1; Harvard 1-0-0; Holy Cross 0-1-0; Long Beach St. 0-0-1; Marquette 0-1-0; McNeese St. 1-2-0; Montana St. 0-0-1; North Texas 0-2-0; Occidental 1-0-0; Ouachita Baptist 0-1-0; Pennsylvania 0-1-0; Randolph Field 0-0-1; Richmond 1-1-0; Santa Clara 3-0-0; Second Air Force 1-0-0; Southwestern (Tex.) 2-0-0; St. Mary's (Cal.) 1-2-0; Tampa 1-2-0; Tennessee Tech 0-1-0; U. of Mexico 0-1-0; Villanova 2-2-1; Wash. & Jeff. 0-0-1; Wash. & Lee 0-1-0; West Tex. A&M 3-0-0; West Va. Wesleyan 1-0-0; Wichita St. 0-3-0; William & Mary 1-2-0; Xavier (Ohio) 1-0-0. **TOTALS: 37-38-8**

All-Time Bowl Appearances

(Must be classified as a major bowl game where one team was considered a major college at the time.)

Team	Appearances
Alabama	46
Southern Cal	36
Tennessee	34
Texas	34
Nebraska	32
Georgia	31
Oklahoma	31
Penn St.	30
Louisiana St.	28
Arkansas	27
Ohio St.	26
Georgia Tech	25
Michigan	25
Mississippi	25
Auburn	23

Team	Appearances
Florida St.	22
Florida	21
Texas A&M	21
Washington	21
Miami (Fla.)	20
Clemson	19
Missouri	19
Notre Dame	19
Texas Tech	19
UCLA	19
Brigham Young	18
Colorado	18
North Caro.	18
Pittsburgh	18
Maryland	17

All-Time Bowl Victories

(Includes bowls where at least one team was classified a major college at the time.)

Team	Victories
Alabama	26
Southern Cal	23
Oklahoma	20
Penn St.	18
Tennessee	18
Georgia Tech	17
Texas	16
Georgia	15
Mississippi	14
Nebraska	14
Florida St.	13
Notre Dame	13
Auburn	12
Clemson	12
Michigan	12
Ohio St.	12

Team	Victories
Washington	12
Louisiana St.	11
Texas A&M	11
Florida	10
Miami (Fla.)	10
UCLA	10
Arizona St.	9
Arkansas	9
Oklahoma St.	9
Baylor	8
Missouri	8
Pittsburgh	8
Stanford	8
Syracuse	8
West Va.	8

Team-by-Team Major Bowl Scores With Coach of Each Bowl Team

Listed below are the 103 I-A teams that have participated in history's 653 major bowl games (the term "major bowl" is defined above the alphabetical list of team bowl records). The teams are listed alphabetically, with each coach listed along with the bowl participated in, date played, opponent, score and team's all-time bowl-game record. Following the I-A list is a group of 49 teams that played in a major bowl game or games but are no longer classified as I-A.

School/Coach	Bowl/Date	Opponent/Score
AIR FORCE		
Ben Martin	Cotton 1-1-59	Texas Christian 0-0
Ben Martin	Gator 12-28-63	North Caro. 0-35
Ben Martin	Sugar 1-1-71	Tennessee 13-34
Ken Hatfield	All-American 12-31-82	Vanderbilt 36-28
Ken Hatfield	Independence 12-10-83	Mississippi 9-3
Fisher DeBerry	Independence 12-15-84	Virginia Tech 23-7
Fisher DeBerry	Bluebonnet 12-31-85	Texas 24-16
Fisher DeBerry	Freedom 12-30-87	Arizona St. 28-33
Fisher DeBerry	Liberty 12-28-89	Mississippi 29-42
Fisher DeBerry	Liberty 12-27-90	Ohio St. 23-11
Fisher DeBerry	Liberty 12-29-91	Mississippi St. 38-15
Fisher DeBerry	Liberty 12-31-92	Mississippi 0-13
All bowls 6-5-1		
ALABAMA		
Wallace Wade	Rose 1-1-26	Washington 20-19
Wallace Wade	Rose 1-1-27	Stanford 7-7
Wallace Wade	Rose 1-1-31	Washington St. 24-0
Frank Thomas	Rose 1-1-35	Stanford 29-13
Frank Thomas	Rose 1-1-38	California 0-13
Frank Thomas	Cotton 1-1-42	Texas A&M 29-21
Frank Thomas	Orange 1-1-43	Boston College 37-21
Frank Thomas	Sugar 1-1-45	Duke 26-29
Frank Thomas	Rose 1-1-46	Southern Cal 34-14
Harold "Red" Drew	Sugar 1-1-48	Texas 7-27
Harold "Red" Drew	Orange 1-1-53	Syracuse 61-6
Harold "Red" Drew	Cotton 1-1-54	Rice 6-28
Paul "Bear" Bryant	Liberty 12-19-59	Penn St. 0-7
Paul "Bear" Bryant	Bluebonnet 12-17-60	Texas 3-3
Paul "Bear" Bryant	Sugar 1-1-62	Arkansas 10-3
Paul "Bear" Bryant	Orange 1-1-63	Oklahoma 17-0
Paul "Bear" Bryant	Sugar 1-1-64	Mississippi 12-7
Paul "Bear" Bryant	Orange 1-1-65	Texas 17-21
Paul "Bear" Bryant	Orange 1-1-66	Nebraska 39-28
Paul "Bear" Bryant	Sugar 1-2-67	Nebraska 34-7
Paul "Bear" Bryant	Cotton 1-1-68	Texas A&M 16-20
Paul "Bear" Bryant	Gator 12-28-68	Missouri 10-35
Paul "Bear" Bryant	Liberty 12-13-69	Colorado 33-47
Paul "Bear" Bryant	Bluebonnet 12-31-70	Oklahoma 24-24
Paul "Bear" Bryant	Orange 1-1-72	Nebraska 6-38
Paul "Bear" Bryant	Cotton 1-1-73	Texas 13-17
Paul "Bear" Bryant	Sugar 12-31-73	Notre Dame 23-24
Paul "Bear" Bryant	Orange 1-1-75	Notre Dame 11-13
Paul "Bear" Bryant	Sugar 12-31-75	Penn St. 13-6
Paul "Bear" Bryant	Liberty 12-20-76	UCLA 36-6

School/Coach	Bowl/Date	Opponent/Score
Paul "Bear" Bryant	Sugar 1-2-78	Ohio St. 35-6
Paul "Bear" Bryant	Sugar 1-1-79	Penn St. 14-7
Paul "Bear" Bryant	Sugar 1-1-80	Arkansas 24-9
Paul "Bear" Bryant	Cotton 1-1-81	Baylor 30-2
Paul "Bear" Bryant	Cotton 1-1-82	Texas 12-14
Paul "Bear" Bryant	Liberty 12-29-82	Illinois 21-15
Ray Perkins	Sun 12-24-83	Southern Methodist 28-7
Ray Perkins	Aloha 12-28-85	Southern Cal 24-3
Ray Perkins	Sun 12-25-86	Washington 28-6
Bill Curry	Hall of Fame 1-2-88	Michigan 24-28
Bill Curry	Sun 12-24-88	Army 29-28
Bill Curry	Sugar 1-1-90	Miami (Fla.) 25-33
Gene Stallings	Fiesta 1-1-91	Louisville 7-34
Gene Stallings	Blockbuster 12-28-91	Colorado 30-25
Gene Stallings	Sugar 1-1-93	Miami (Fla.) 34-13
Gene Stallings	Gator 12-31-93	North Caro. 24-10

All bowls 26-17-3

ARIZONA

School/Coach	Bowl/Date	Opponent/Score
J. F. "Pop" McKale	San Diego East-West Christmas Classic 12-26-21	Centre 0-38
Miles Casteel	Salad 1-1-49	Drake 13-14
Darrell Mudra	Sun 12-28-68	Auburn 10-34
Tony Mason	Fiesta 12-25-79	Pittsburgh 10-16
Larry Smith	Sun 12-28-85	Georgia 13-13
Larry Smith	Aloha 12-27-86	North Caro. 30-21
Dick Tomey	Copper 12-31-89	North Caro. St. 17-10
Dick Tomey	Aloha 12-25-90	Syracuse 0-28
Dick Tomey	John Hancock 12-31-92	Baylor 15-20
Dick Tomey	Fiesta 1-1-94	Miami (Fla.) 29-0

All bowls 3-6-1.

ARIZONA ST.

School/Coach	Bowl/Date	Opponent/Score
Millard "Dixie" Howell	Sun 1-1-40	Catholic 0-0
Millard "Dixie" Howell	Sun 1-1-41	Case Reserve 13-26
Ed Doherty	Salad 1-1-50	Xavier (Ohio) 21-33
Ed Doherty	Salad 1-1-51	Miami (Ohio) 21-34
Frank Kush	Peach 12-30-70	North Caro. 48-26
Frank Kush	Fiesta 12-27-71	Florida St. 45-38
Frank Kush	Fiesta 12-23-72	Missouri 49-35
Frank Kush	Fiesta 12-21-73	Pittsburgh 28-7
Frank Kush	Fiesta 12-26-75	Nebraska 17-14
Frank Kush	Fiesta 12-25-77	Penn St. 30-42
Frank Kush	Garden State 12-16-78	Rutgers 34-18
Darryl Rogers	Fiesta 1-1-83	Oklahoma 32-21
John Cooper	Holiday 12-22-85	Arkansas 17-18
John Cooper	Rose 1-1-87	Michigan 22-15
John Cooper	Freedom 12-30-87	Air Force 33-28

All bowls 9-5-1

ARKANSAS

School/Coach	Bowl/Date	Opponent/Score
Fred Thomsen	Dixie Classic 1-1-34	Centenary (La.) 7-7
John Barnhill	Cotton 1-1-47	Louisiana St. 0-0
John Barnhill	Dixie 1-1-48	William & Mary 21-19
Bowden Wyatt	Cotton 1-1-55	Georgia Tech 6-14
Frank Broyles	Gator 1-2-60	Georgia Tech 14-7
Frank Broyles	Cotton 1-2-61	Duke 6-7
Frank Broyles	Sugar 1-1-62	Alabama 3-10
Frank Broyles	Sugar 1-1-63	Mississippi 13-17
Frank Broyles	Cotton 1-1-65	Nebraska 10-7
Frank Broyles	Cotton 1-1-66	Louisiana St. 7-14
Frank Broyles	Sugar 1-1-69	Georgia 16-2
Frank Broyles	Sugar 1-1-70	Mississippi 22-27
Frank Broyles	Liberty 12-20-71	Tennessee 13-14
Frank Broyles	Cotton 1-1-76	Georgia 31-10
Lou Holtz	Orange 1-2-78	Oklahoma 31-6
Lou Holtz	Fiesta 12-25-78	UCLA 10-10
Lou Holtz	Sugar 1-1-80	Alabama 9-24
Lou Holtz	All-American 12-27-80	Tulane 34-15
Lou Holtz	Gator 12-28-81	North Caro. 27-31
Lou Holtz	Bluebonnet 12-31-82	Florida 28-24
Ken Hatfield	Liberty 12-27-84	Auburn 15-21
Ken Hatfield	Holiday 12-22-85	Arizona St. 18-17
Ken Hatfield	Orange 1-1-87	Oklahoma 8-42
Ken Hatfield	Liberty 12-29-87	Georgia 17-20
Ken Hatfield	Cotton 1-2-89	UCLA 3-17
Ken Hatfield	Cotton 1-1-90	Tennessee 27-31
Jack Crowe	Independence 12-29-91	Georgia 15-24

All bowls 9-15-3

ARMY

School/Coach	Bowl/Date	Opponent/Score
Jim Young	Cherry 12-22-84	Michigan St. 10-6
Jim Young	Peach 12-31-85	Illinois 31-29
Jim Young	Sun 12-24-88	Alabama 28-29

All bowls 2-1-0

AUBURN

School/Coach	Bowl/Date	Opponent/Score
Jack Meagher	Bacardi, Cuba 1-1-37	Villanova 7-7
Jack Meagher	Orange 1-1-38	Michigan St. 6-0
Ralph "Shug" Jordan	Gator 1-1-54	Texas Tech 13-35
Ralph "Shug" Jordan	Gator 12-31-54	Baylor 33-13
Ralph "Shug" Jordan	Gator 12-31-55	Vanderbilt 13-25
Ralph "Shug" Jordan	Orange 1-1-64	Nebraska 7-13
Ralph "Shug" Jordan	Liberty 12-18-65	Mississippi 7-13
Ralph "Shug" Jordan	Sun 12-28-68	Arizona 34-10
Ralph "Shug" Jordan	Bluebonnet 12-31-69	Houston 7-36
Ralph "Shug" Jordan	Gator 1-2-71	Mississippi 35-28
Ralph "Shug" Jordan	Sugar 1-1-72	Oklahoma 22-40
Ralph "Shug" Jordan	Gator 12-30-72	Colorado 24-3
Ralph "Shug" Jordan	Sun 12-29-73	Missouri 17-34
Ralph "Shug" Jordan	Gator 12-30-74	Texas 27-3
Pat Dye	Tangerine 12-18-82	Boston College 33-26
Pat Dye	Sugar 1-2-84	Michigan 9-7
Pat Dye	Liberty 12-27-84	Arkansas 21-15
Pat Dye	Cotton 1-1-86	Texas A&M 16-36
Pat Dye	Florida Citrus 1-1-87	Southern Cal 16-7
Pat Dye	Sugar 1-1-88	Syracuse 16-16
Pat Dye	Sugar 1-2-89	Florida St. 7-13
Pat Dye	Hall of Fame 1-1-90	Ohio St. 31-24
Pat Dye	Peach 12-29-90	Indiana 27-23

All bowls 12-9-2

BALL ST.

School/Coach	Bowl/Date	Opponent/Score
Paul Schudel	California 12-9-89	Fresno St. 6-27
Paul Schudel	Las Vegas 12-17-93	Utah St. 33-42

All bowls 0-2-0

BAYLOR

School/Coach	Bowl/Date	Opponent/Score
Bob Woodruff	Dixie 1-1-49	Wake Forest 20-7
George Sauer	Orange 1-1-52	Georgia Tech 14-17
George Sauer	Gator 12-31-54	Auburn 13-33
Sam Boyd	Sugar 1-1-57	Tennessee 13-7
John Bridgers	Gator 12-31-60	Florida 12-13
John Bridgers	Gotham 12-9-61	Utah St. 24-9
John Bridgers	Bluebonnet 12-21-63	Louisiana St. 14-7
Grant Teaff	Cotton 1-1-75	Penn St. 20-41
Grant Teaff	Peach 12-31-79	Clemson 24-18
Grant Teaff	Cotton 1-1-81	Alabama 2-30
Grant Teaff	Bluebonnet 12-31-83	Oklahoma St. 14-24
Grant Teaff	Liberty 12-27-85	Louisiana St. 21-7
Grant Teaff	Bluebonnet 12-31-86	Colorado 21-9
Grant Teaff	Copper 12-31-91	Indiana 0-24
Grant Teaff	John Hancock 12-31-92	Arizona 20-15

All bowls 8-7-0

BOSTON COLLEGE

School/Coach	Bowl/Date	Opponent/Score
Frank Leahy	Cotton 1-1-40	Clemson 3-6
Frank Leahy	Sugar 1-1-41	Tennessee 19-13
Denny Myers	Orange 1-1-43	Alabama 21-37
Jack Bicknell	Tangerine 12-18-82	Auburn 26-33
Jack Bicknell	Liberty 12-29-83	Notre Dame 18-19

Arizona defensive end Tedy Bruschi led the Wildcats' "Desert Swarm" defense to a 29-0 shutout of Miami (Florida) in the Fiesta Bowl. Bruschi was named most valuable defensive player of the game.

BOWL/ALL-STAR RESULTS

School/Coach	Bowl/Date	Opponent/Score
Jack Bicknell	Cotton 1-1-85	Houston 45-28
Jack Bicknell	Hall of Fame 12-23-86	Georgia 27-24
Tom Coughlin	Hall of Fame 1-1-93	Tennessee 23-38
Tom Coughlin	Carquest 1-1-94	Virginia 31-13

All bowls 4-5-0

BOWLING GREEN

Doyt Perry	Mercy 11-23-61	Fresno St. 6-36
Denny Stolz	California 12-18-82	Fresno St. 28-29
Denny Stolz	California 12-14-85	Fresno St. 7-51
Gary Blackney	California 12-14-91	Fresno St. 28-21
Gary Blackney	Las Vegas 12-18-92	Nevada 35-34

All bowls 2-3-0

BRIGHAM YOUNG

LaVell Edwards	Fiesta 12-28-74	Oklahoma St. 6-16
LaVell Edwards	Tangerine 12-18-76	Oklahoma St. 21-49
LaVell Edwards	Holiday 12-22-78	Navy 16-23
LaVell Edwards	Holiday 12-21-79	Indiana 37-38
LaVell Edwards	Holiday 12-19-80	Southern Methodist 46-45
LaVell Edwards	Holiday 12-18-81	Washington St. 38-36
LaVell Edwards	Holiday 12-17-82	Ohio St. 17-47
LaVell Edwards	Holiday 12-23-83	Missouri 21-17
LaVell Edwards	Holiday 12-21-84	Michigan 24-17
LaVell Edwards	Florida Citrus 12-28-85	Ohio St. 7-10
LaVell Edwards	Freedom 12-30-86	UCLA 10-31
LaVell Edwards	All-American 12-22-87	Virginia 16-22
LaVell Edwards	Freedom 12-29-88	Colorado 20-17
LaVell Edwards	Holiday 12-29-89	Penn St. 39-50
LaVell Edwards	Holiday 12-29-90	Texas A&M 14-65
LaVell Edwards	Holiday 12-30-91	Iowa 13-13
LaVell Edwards	Aloha 12-25-92	Kansas 20-23
LaVell Edwards	Holiday 12-30-93	Ohio St. 21-28

All bowls 5-12-1

CALIFORNIA

Andy Smith	Rose 1-1-21	Ohio St. 28-0
Andy Smith	Rose 1-2-22	Wash. & Jeff. 0-0
Clarence "Nibs" Price	Rose 1-1-29	Georgia Tech 7-8
Leonard "Stub" Allison	Rose 1-1-38	Alabama 13-0
Lynn "Pappy" Waldorf	Rose 1-1-49	Northwestern 14-20
Lynn "Pappy" Waldorf	Rose 1-2-50	Ohio St. 14-17
Lynn "Pappy" Waldorf	Rose 1-1-51	Michigan 6-14
Pete Elliott	Rose 1-1-59	Iowa 12-38
Roger Theder	Garden State 12-15-79	Temple 17-28
Bruce Snyder	Copper 12-31-90	Wyoming 17-15
Bruce Snyder	Florida Citrus 1-1-92	Clemson 37-13
Keith Gilbertson	Alamo 12-31-93	Iowa 37-3

All bowls 5-6-1

CENTRAL MICH.

Herb Deromedi	California 12-8-90	San Jose St. 24-48

All bowls 0-1-0

CINCINNATI

Ray Nolting	Sun 1-1-47	Virginia Tech 18-6
Sid Gillman	Sun 1-1-51	West Tex. A&M 13-14

All bowls 1-1-0

CLEMSON

Jess Neely	Cotton 1-1-40	Boston College 6-3
Frank Howard	Gator 1-1-49	Missouri 24-23
Frank Howard	Orange 1-1-51	Miami (Fla.) 15-14
Frank Howard	Gator 1-1-52	Miami (Fla.) 0-14
Frank Howard	Orange 1-1-57	Colorado 21-27
Frank Howard	Sugar 1-1-59	Louisiana St. 0-7
Frank Howard	Bluebonnet 12-19-59	Texas Christian 23-7
Charley Pell	Gator 12-30-77	Pittsburgh 3-34
Danny Ford	Gator 12-29-78	Ohio St. 17-15
Danny Ford	Peach 12-31-79	Baylor 18-24
Danny Ford	Orange 1-1-82	Nebraska 22-15
Danny Ford	Independence 12-21-85	Minnesota 13-20
Danny Ford	Gator 12-27-86	Stanford 27-21
Danny Ford	Florida Citrus 1-1-88	Penn St. 35-10
Danny Ford	Florida Citrus 1-2-89	Oklahoma 23-6
Danny Ford	Gator 12-30-89	West Va. 27-7
Ken Hatfield	Hall of Fame 1-1-91	Illinois 30-0
Ken Hatfield	Florida Citrus 1-1-92	California 13-37
Tommy West	Peach 12-31-93	Kentucky 14-13

All bowls 12-7-0

COLORADO

Bernard "Bunnie" Oaks	Cotton 1-1-38	Rice 14-28
Dallas Ward	Orange 1-1-57	Clemson 27-21
Sonny Grandelius	Orange 1-1-62	Louisiana St. 7-25
Eddie Crowder	Bluebonnet 12-23-67	Miami (Fla.) 31-21
Eddie Crowder	Liberty 12-13-69	Alabama 47-33
Eddie Crowder	Liberty 12-12-70	Tulane 3-17
Eddie Crowder	Bluebonnet 12-31-71	Houston 29-17
Eddie Crowder	Gator 12-30-72	Auburn 3-24
Bill Mallory	Bluebonnet 12-27-75	Texas 21-38
Bill Mallory	Orange 1-1-77	Ohio St. 10-27
Bill McCartney	Freedom 12-30-85	Washington 17-20
Bill McCartney	Bluebonnet 12-31-86	Baylor 9-21
Bill McCartney	Freedom 12-29-88	Brigham Young 17-20
Bill McCartney	Orange 1-1-90	Notre Dame 6-21
Bill McCartney	Orange 1-1-91	Notre Dame 10-9
Bill McCartney	Blockbuster 12-28-91	Alabama 25-30
Bill McCartney	Fiesta 1-1-93	Syracuse 22-26
Bill McCartney	Aloha 12-25-93	Fresno St. 41-30

All bowls 6-12-0

COLORADO ST.

Bob Davis	Raisin 1-1-49	Occidental 20-21
Earle Bruce	Freedom 12-24-90	Oregon 32-31

All bowls 1-1-0

DUKE

Wallace Wade	Rose 1-2-39	Southern Cal 3-7
Wallace Wade	Rose 1-1-42	Oregon St. 16-20
Eddie Cameron	Sugar 1-1-45	Alabama 29-26
Bill Murray	Orange 1-1-55	Nebraska 34-7
Bill Murray	Orange 1-1-58	Oklahoma 21-48
Bill Murray	Cotton 1-2-61	Arkansas 7-6
Steve Spurrier	All-American 12-28-89	Texas Tech 21-49

All bowls 3-4-0

EAST CARO.

Pat Dye	Independence 12-16-78	Louisiana Tech 35-13
Bill Lewis	Peach 1-1-92	North Caro. St. 37-34

All bowls 2-0-0

EASTERN MICH.

Jim Harkema	California 12-12-87	San Jose St. 30-27

All bowls 1-0-0

FLORIDA

Bob Woodruff	Gator 1-1-53	Tulsa 14-13
Bob Woodruff	Gator 12-27-58	Mississippi 3-7
Ray Graves	Gator 12-31-60	Baylor 13-12
Ray Graves	Gator 12-29-62	Penn St. 17-7
Ray Graves	Sugar 1-1-66	Missouri 18-20
Ray Graves	Orange 1-2-67	Georgia Tech 27-12
Ray Graves	Gator 12-27-69	Tennessee 14-13
Doug Dickey	Tangerine 12-22-73	Miami (Ohio) 7-16
Doug Dickey	Sugar 12-31-74	Nebraska 10-13
Doug Dickey	Gator 12-29-75	Maryland 0-13
Doug Dickey	Sun 1-2-77	Texas A&M 14-37
Charley Pell	Tangerine 12-20-80	Maryland 35-20
Charley Pell	Peach 12-31-81	West Va. 6-26
Charley Pell	Bluebonnet 12-31-82	Arkansas 24-28
Charley Pell	Gator 12-30-83	Iowa 14-6
Galen Hall	Aloha 12-25-87	UCLA 16-20
Galen Hall	All-American 12-29-88	Illinois 14-10
Gary Darnell	Freedom 12-30-89	Washington 7-34
Steve Spurrier	Sugar 1-1-92	Notre Dame 28-39
Steve Spurrier	Gator 12-31-92	North Caro. St. 27-10
Steve Spurrier	Sugar 1-1-94	West Va. 41-7

All bowls 10-11-0

FLORIDA ST.

Tom Nugent	Sun 1-1-55	UTEP 20-47
Tom Nugent	Bluegrass 12-13-58	Oklahoma St. 6-15
Bill Peterson	Gator 1-2-65	Oklahoma 36-19
Bill Peterson	Sun 12-24-66	Wyoming 20-28
Bill Peterson	Gator 12-30-67	Penn St. 17-17
Bill Peterson	Peach 12-30-68	Louisiana St. 27-31
Larry Jones	Fiesta 12-27-71	Arizona St. 38-45
Bobby Bowden	Tangerine 12-23-77	Texas Tech 40-17
Bobby Bowden	Orange 1-1-80	Oklahoma 7-24
Bobby Bowden	Orange 1-1-81	Oklahoma 17-18
Bobby Bowden	Gator 12-30-82	West Va. 31-12
Bobby Bowden	Peach 12-30-83	North Caro. 28-3
Bobby Bowden	Florida Citrus 12-22-84	Georgia 17-17
Bobby Bowden	Gator 12-30-85	Oklahoma St. 34-23
Bobby Bowden	All-American 12-31-86	Indiana 27-13
Bobby Bowden	Fiesta 1-1-88	Nebraska 31-28
Bobby Bowden	Sugar 1-2-89	Auburn 13-7
Bobby Bowden	Fiesta 1-1-90	Nebraska 41-17
Bobby Bowden	Blockbuster 12-28-90	Penn St. 24-17
Bobby Bowden	Cotton 1-1-92	Texas A&M 10-2

School/Coach	Bowl/Date	Opponent/Score
Bobby Bowden	Orange 1-1-93	Nebraska 27-14
Bobby Bowden	Orange 1-1-94	Nebraska 18-16

All bowls 13-7-2

FRESNO ST.

School/Coach	Bowl/Date	Opponent/Score
Alvin "Pix" Pierson	Raisin 1-1-46	Drake 12-13
Cecil Coleman	Mercy 11-23-61	Bowling Green 36-6
Jim Sweeney	California 12-18-82	Bowling Green 29-28
Jim Sweeney	California 12-14-85	Bowling Green 51-7
Jim Sweeney	California 12-10-88	Western Mich. 35-30
Jim Sweeney	California 12-9-89	Ball St. 27-6
Jim Sweeney	California 12-14-91	Bowling Green 21-28
Jim Sweeney	Freedom 12-29-92	Southern Cal 24-7
Jim Sweeney	Aloha 12-25-93	Colorado 30-41

All bowls 6-3-0

GEORGIA

School/Coach	Bowl/Date	Opponent/Score
Wally Butts	Orange 1-1-42	Texas Christian 40-26
Wally Butts	Rose 1-1-43	UCLA 9-0
Wally Butts	Oil 1-1-46	Tulsa 20-6
Wally Butts	Sugar 1-1-47	North Caro. 20-10
Wally Butts	Gator 1-1-48	Maryland 20-20
Wally Butts	Orange 1-1-49	Texas 28-41
Wally Butts	Presidential 12-9-50	Texas A&M 20-40
Wally Butts	Orange 1-1-60	Missouri 14-0
Vince Dooley	Sun 12-26-64	Texas Tech 7-0
Vince Dooley	Cotton 12-31-66	Southern Methodist 24-9
Vince Dooley	Liberty 12-16-67	North Caro. St. 7-14
Vince Dooley	Sugar 1-1-69	Arkansas 2-16
Vince Dooley	Sun 12-20-69	Nebraska 6-45
Vince Dooley	Gator 12-31-71	North Caro. 7-3
Vince Dooley	Peach 12-28-73	Maryland 17-16
Vince Dooley	Tangerine 12-21-74	Miami (Ohio) 10-21
Vince Dooley	Cotton 1-1-76	Arkansas 10-31
Vince Dooley	Sugar 1-1-77	Pittsburgh 3-27
Vince Dooley	Bluebonnet 12-31-78	Stanford 22-25
Vince Dooley	Sugar 1-1-81	Notre Dame 17-10
Vince Dooley	Sugar 1-1-82	Pittsburgh 20-24
Vince Dooley	Sugar 1-1-83	Penn St. 23-27
Vince Dooley	Cotton 1-2-84	Texas 10-9
Vince Dooley	Florida Citrus 12-22-84	Florida St. 17-17
Vince Dooley	Sun 12-28-85	Arizona 13-13
Vince Dooley	Hall of Fame 12-23-86	Boston College 24-27
Vince Dooley	Liberty 12-29-87	Arkansas 20-17
Vince Dooley	Gator 1-1-89	Michigan St. 34-27
Ray Goff	Peach 12-30-89	Syracuse 18-19
Ray Goff	Independence 12-29-91	Arkansas 24-15
Ray Goff	Florida Citrus 1-1-93	Ohio St. 21-14

All bowls 15-13-3

GEORGIA TECH

School/Coach	Bowl/Date	Opponent/Score
Bill Alexander	Rose 1-1-29	California 8-7
Bill Alexander	Orange 1-1-40	Missouri 21-7
Bill Alexander	Cotton 1-1-43	Texas 7-14
Bill Alexander	Sugar 1-1-44	Tulsa 20-18
Bill Alexander	Orange 1-1-45	Tulsa 12-26
Bobby Dodd	Oil 1-1-47	St. Mary's (Cal.) 41-19
Bobby Dodd	Orange 1-1-48	Kansas 20-14
Bobby Dodd	Orange 1-1-52	Baylor 17-14
Bobby Dodd	Sugar 1-1-53	Mississippi 24-7
Bobby Dodd	Sugar 1-1-54	West Va. 42-19
Bobby Dodd	Cotton 1-1-55	Arkansas 14-6
Bobby Dodd	Sugar 1-2-56	Pittsburgh 7-0
Bobby Dodd	Gator 12-29-56	Pittsburgh 21-14
Bobby Dodd	Gator 1-2-60	Arkansas 7-14
Bobby Dodd	Gator 12-30-61	Penn St. 15-30
Bobby Dodd	Bluebonnet 12-22-62	Missouri 10-14
Bobby Dodd	Gator 12-31-65	Texas Tech 31-21
Bobby Dodd	Orange 1-2-67	Florida 12-27
Bud Carson	Sun 12-19-70	Texas Tech 17-9
Bud Carson	Peach 12-30-71	Mississippi 18-41
Bill Fulcher	Liberty 12-18-72	Iowa St. 31-30
Pepper Rodgers	Peach 12-25-78	Purdue 21-41
Bill Curry	All-American 12-31-85	Michigan St. 17-14
Bobby Ross	Florida Citrus 1-1-91	Nebraska 45-21
Bobby Ross	Aloha 12-25-91	Stanford 18-17

All bowls 17-8-0

HAWAII

School/Coach	Bowl/Date	Opponent/Score
Bob Wagner	Aloha 12-25-89	Michigan St. 13-33
Bob Wagner	Holiday 12-30-92	Illinois 27-17

All bowls 1-1-0

HOUSTON

School/Coach	Bowl/Date	Opponent/Score
Clyde Lee	Salad 1-1-52	Dayton 26-21
Bill Yeoman	Tangerine 12-22-62	Miami (Ohio) 49-21
Bill Yeoman	Bluebonnet 12-31-69	Auburn 36-7
Bill Yeoman	Bluebonnet 12-31-71	Colorado 17-29
Bill Yeoman	Bluebonnet 12-29-73	Tulane 47-7
Bill Yeoman	Bluebonnet 12-23-74	North Caro. St. 31-31
Bill Yeoman	Cotton 1-1-77	Maryland 30-21
Bill Yeoman	Cotton 1-1-79	Notre Dame 34-35
Bill Yeoman	Cotton 1-1-80	Nebraska 17-14
Bill Yeoman	Garden State 12-14-80	Navy 35-0
Bill Yeoman	Sun 12-26-81	Oklahoma 14-40
Bill Yeoman	Cotton 1-1-85	Boston College 28-45
Jack Pardee	Aloha 12-25-88	Washington St. 22-24

All bowls 7-5-1

ILLINOIS

School/Coach	Bowl/Date	Opponent/Score
Ray Eliot	Rose 1-1-47	UCLA 45-14
Ray Eliot	Rose 1-1-52	Stanford 40-7
Pete Elliott	Rose 1-1-64	Washington 17-7
Mike White	Liberty 12-29-82	Alabama 15-21
Mike White	Rose 1-2-84	UCLA 9-45
Mike White	Peach 12-31-85	Army 29-31
John Mackovic	All-American 12-29-88	Florida 10-14
John Mackovic	Florida Citrus 1-1-90	Virginia 31-21
John Mackovic	Hall of Fame 1-1-91	Clemson 0-30
Lou Tepper	John Hancock 12-31-91	UCLA 3-6
Lou Tepper	Holiday 12-30-92	Hawaii 17-27

All bowls 4-7-0

INDIANA

School/Coach	Bowl/Date	Opponent/Score
John Pont	Rose 1-1-68	Southern Cal 3-14
Lee Corso	Holiday 12-21-79	Brigham Young 38-37
Bill Mallory	All-American 12-31-86	Florida St. 13-27
Bill Mallory	Peach 1-2-88	Tennessee 22-27
Bill Mallory	Liberty 12-28-88	South Caro. 34-10
Bill Mallory	Peach 12-29-90	Auburn 23-27
Bill Mallory	Copper 12-31-91	Baylor 24-0
Bill Mallory	Independence 12-31-93	Virginia Tech 20-45

All bowls 3-5-0

IOWA

School/Coach	Bowl/Date	Opponent/Score
Forest Evashevski	Rose 1-1-57	Oregon St. 35-19
Forest Evashevski	Rose 1-1-59	California 38-12
Hayden Fry	Rose 1-1-82	Washington 0-28
Hayden Fry	Peach 12-31-82	Tennessee 28-22
Hayden Fry	Gator 12-30-83	Florida 6-14
Hayden Fry	Freedom 12-26-84	Texas 55-17
Hayden Fry	Rose 1-1-86	UCLA 28-45
Hayden Fry	Holiday 12-30-86	San Diego St. 39-38
Hayden Fry	Holiday 12-30-87	Wyoming 20-19
Hayden Fry	Peach 12-31-88	North Caro. St. 23-28
Hayden Fry	Rose 1-1-91	Washington 34-46
Hayden Fry	Holiday 12-30-91	Brigham Young 13-13
Hayden Fry	Alamo 12-31-93	California 3-37

All bowls 6-6-1

IOWA ST.

School/Coach	Bowl/Date	Opponent/Score
Johnny Majors	Sun 12-18-71	Louisiana St. 15-33
Johnny Majors	Liberty 12-18-72	Georgia Tech 30-31
Earle Bruce	Peach 12-31-77	North Caro. St. 14-24
Earle Bruce	All-American 12-20-78	Texas A&M 12-28

All bowls 0-4-0

KANSAS

School/Coach	Bowl/Date	Opponent/Score
George Sauer	Orange 1-1-48	Georgia Tech 14-20
Jack Mitchell	Bluebonnet 12-16-61	Rice 33-7
Pepper Rodgers	Orange 1-1-69	Penn St. 14-15
Don Fambrough	Liberty 12-17-73	North Caro. St. 18-31
Bud Moore	Sun 12-26-75	Pittsburgh 19-33
Don Fambrough	All-American 12-31-81	Mississippi St. 0-10
Glen Mason	Aloha 12-25-92	Brigham Young 23-20

All bowls 2-5-0

KANSAS ST.

School/Coach	Bowl/Date	Opponent/Score
Jim Dickey	Independence 12-11-82	Wisconsin 3-14
Bill Snyder	Copper 12-29-93	Wyoming 52-17

All bowls 1-1-0

KENT

School/Coach	Bowl/Date	Opponent/Score
Don James	Tangerine 12-29-72	Tampa 18-21

All bowls 0-1-0

BOWL/ALL-STAR RESULTS

School/Coach	Bowl/Date	Opponent/Score
KENTUCKY		
Paul "Bear" Bryant	Great Lakes 12-6-47	Villanova 24-14
Paul "Bear" Bryant	Orange 1-2-50	Santa Clara 13-21
Paul "Bear" Bryant	Sugar 1-1-51	Oklahoma 13-7
Paul "Bear" Bryant	Cotton 1-1-52	Texas Christian 20-7
Fran Curci	Peach 12-31-76	North Caro. 21-0
Jerry Claiborne	All-American 12-22-83	West Va. 16-20
Jerry Claiborne	All-American 12-29-84	Wisconsin 20-19
Bill Curry	Peach 12-31-93	Clemson 13-14
All bowls 5-3-0		
LOUISIANA ST.		
Bernie Moore	Sugar 1-1-36	Texas Christian 2-3
Bernie Moore	Sugar 1-1-37	Santa Clara 14-21
Bernie Moore	Sugar 1-1-38	Santa Clara 0-6
Bernie Moore	Orange 1-1-44	Texas A&M 19-14
Bernie Moore	Cotton 1-1-47	Arkansas 0-0
Gaynell Tinsley	Sugar 1-2-50	Oklahoma 0-35
Paul Dietzel	Sugar 1-1-59	Clemson 7-0
Paul Dietzel	Sugar 1-1-60	Mississippi 0-21
Paul Dietzel	Orange 1-1-62	Colorado 25-7
Charlie McClendon	Cotton 1-1-63	Texas 13-0
Charlie McClendon	Bluebonnet 12-21-63	Baylor 7-14
Charlie McClendon	Sugar 1-1-65	Syracuse 13-10
Charlie McClendon	Cotton 1-1-66	Arkansas 14-7
Charlie McClendon	Sugar 1-1-68	Wyoming 20-13
Charlie McClendon	Peach 12-30-68	Florida St. 31-27
Charlie McClendon	Orange 1-1-71	Nebraska 12-17
Charlie McClendon	Sun 12-18-71	Iowa St. 33-15
Charlie McClendon	Bluebonnet 12-30-72	Tennessee 17-24
Charlie McClendon	Orange 1-1-74	Penn St. 9-16
Charlie McClendon	Sun 12-31-77	Stanford 14-24
Charlie McClendon	Liberty 12-23-78	Missouri 15-20
Charlie McClendon	Tangerine 12-22-79	Wake Forest 34-10
Jerry Stovall	Orange 1-1-83	Nebraska 20-21
Bill Arnsparger	Sugar 1-1-85	Nebraska 10-28
Bill Arnsparger	Liberty 12-27-85	Baylor 7-21
Bill Arnsparger	Sugar 1-1-87	Nebraska 15-30
Mike Archer	Gator 12-31-87	South Caro. 30-13
Mike Archer	Hall of Fame 1-2-89	Syracuse 10-23
All bowls 11-16-1		
LOUISIANA TECH		
Maxie Lambright	Independence 12-17-77	Louisville 24-14
Maxie Lambright	Independence 12-16-78	East Caro. 13-35
Joe Raymond Peace	Independence 12-15-90	Maryland 34-34
All bowls 1-1-1		
LOUISVILLE		
Frank Camp	Sun 1-1-58	Drake 34-20
Lee Corso	Pasadena 12-19-70	Long Beach St. 24-24
Vince Gibson	Independence 12-17-77	Louisiana Tech 14-24
Howard Schnellenberger	Fiesta 1-1-91	Alabama 34-7
Howard Schnellenberger	Liberty 12-28-93	Michigan St. 18-7
All bowls 3-1-1		
MARYLAND		
Jim Tatum	Gator 1-1-48	Georgia 20-20
Jim Tatum	Gator 1-2-50	Missouri 20-7
Jim Tatum	Sugar 1-1-52	Tennessee 28-13
Jim Tatum	Orange 1-1-54	Oklahoma 0-7
Jim Tatum	Orange 1-2-56	Oklahoma 6-20
Jerry Claiborne	Peach 12-28-73	Georgia 16-17
Jerry Claiborne	Liberty 12-16-74	Tennessee 3-7
Jerry Claiborne	Gator 12-29-75	Florida 13-0
Jerry Claiborne	Cotton 1-1-77	Houston 21-30
Jerry Claiborne	All-American 12-22-77	Minnesota 17-7
Jerry Claiborne	Sun 12-23-78	Texas 0-42
Jerry Claiborne	Tangerine 12-20-80	Florida 20-35
Bobby Ross	Aloha 12-25-82	Washington 20-21
Bobby Ross	Florida Citrus 12-17-83	Tennessee 23-30
Bobby Ross	Sun 12-22-84	Tennessee 27-26
Bobby Ross	Cherry 12-21-85	Syracuse 35-18
Joe Krivak	Independence 12-15-90	Louisiana Tech 34-34
All bowls 6-9-2		
MEMPHIS		
Billy Murphy	Pasadena 12-18-71	San Jose St. 28-9
All bowls 1-0-0		
MIAMI (FLA.)		
Tom McCann	Orange 1-1-35	Bucknell 0-26
Jack Harding	Orange 1-1-46	Holy Cross 13-6
Andy Gustafson	Orange 1-1-51	Clemson 14-15
Andy Gustafson	Gator 1-1-52	Clemson 14-0
Andy Gustafson	Liberty 12-16-61	Syracuse 14-15
Andy Gustafson	Gotham 12-15-62	Nebraska 34-36
Charlie Tate	Liberty 12-10-66	Virginia Tech 14-7
Charlie Tate	Bluebonnet 12-31-67	Colorado 21-31
Howard Schnellenberger	Peach 1-2-81	Virginia Tech 20-10
Howard Schnellenberger	Orange 1-2-84	Nebraska 31-30
Jimmy Johnson	Fiesta 1-1-85	UCLA 37-39
Jimmy Johnson	Sugar 1-1-86	Tennessee 7-35
Jimmy Johnson	Fiesta 1-2-87	Penn St. 10-14
Jimmy Johnson	Orange 1-1-88	Oklahoma 20-14
Jimmy Johnson	Orange 1-2-89	Nebraska 23-3
Dennis Erickson	Sugar 1-1-90	Alabama 33-25
Dennis Erickson	Cotton 1-1-91	Texas 46-3
Dennis Erickson	Orange 1-1-92	Nebraska 22-0
Dennis Erickson	Sugar 1-1-93	Alabama 13-34
Dennis Erickson	Fiesta 1-1-94	Arizona 0-29
All bowls 10-10-0		
MIAMI (OHIO)		
Sid Gillman	Sun 1-1-48	Texas Tech 13-12
Woody Hayes	Salad 1-1-51	Arizona St. 34-21
John Pont	Tangerine 12-22-62	Houston 21-49
Bill Mallory	Tangerine 12-22-73	Florida 16-7
Dick Crum	Tangerine 12-21-74	Georgia 21-10
Dick Crum	Tangerine 12-20-75	South Caro. 20-7
Tim Rose	California 12-13-86	San Jose St. 7-37
All bowls 5-2-0		
MICHIGAN		
Fielding "Hurry Up" Yost	Rose 1-1-02	Stanford 49-0
H. O. "Fritz" Crisler	Rose 1-1-48	Southern Cal 49-0
Bennie Oosterbaan	Rose 1-1-51	California 14-6
Chalmers "Bump" Elliott	Rose 1-1-65	Oregon St. 34-7
Glenn "Bo" Schembechler	Rose 1-1-70	Southern Cal 3-10
Glenn "Bo" Schembechler	Rose 1-1-72	Stanford 12-13
Glenn "Bo" Schembechler	Orange 1-1-76	Oklahoma 6-14
Glenn "Bo" Schembechler	Rose 1-1-77	Southern Cal 6-14
Glenn "Bo" Schembechler	Rose 1-2-78	Washington 20-27
Glenn "Bo" Schembechler	Rose 1-1-79	Southern Cal 10-17
Glenn "Bo" Schembechler	Gator 12-28-79	North Caro. 15-17
Glenn "Bo" Schembechler	Rose 1-1-81	Washington 23-6
Glenn "Bo" Schembechler	Bluebonnet 12-31-81	UCLA 33-14
Glenn "Bo" Schembechler	Rose 1-1-83	UCLA 14-24
Glenn "Bo" Schembechler	Sugar 1-2-84	Auburn 7-9
Glenn "Bo" Schembechler	Holiday 12-21-84	Brigham Young 17-24
Glenn "Bo" Schembechler	Fiesta 1-1-86	Nebraska 27-23
Glenn "Bo" Schembechler	Rose 1-1-87	Arizona St. 15-22
Glenn "Bo" Schembechler	Hall of Fame 1-2-88	Alabama 28-24
Glenn "Bo" Schembechler	Rose 1-2-89	Southern Cal 22-14
Glenn "Bo" Schembechler	Rose 1-1-90	Southern Cal 10-17
Gary Moeller	Gator 1-1-91	Mississippi 35-3
Gary Moeller	Rose 1-1-92	Washington 14-34
Gary Moeller	Rose 1-1-93	Washington 38-31
Gary Moeller	Hall of Fame 1-1-94	North Caro. St. 42-7
All bowls 12-13-0		
MICHIGAN ST.		
Charlie Bachman	Orange 1-1-38	Auburn 0-6
Clarence "Biggie" Munn	Rose 1-1-54	UCLA 28-20
Duffy Daugherty	Rose 1-2-56	UCLA 17-14
Duffy Daugherty	Rose 1-1-66	UCLA 12-14
George Perles	Cherry 12-22-84	Army 6-10
George Perles	All-American 12-31-85	Georgia Tech 14-17
George Perles	Rose 1-1-88	Southern Cal 20-17
George Perles	Gator 1-1-89	Georgia 27-34
George Perles	Aloha 12-25-89	Hawaii 33-13
George Perles	John Hancock 12-31-90	Southern Cal 17-6
George Perles	Liberty 12-28-93	Louisville 7-18
All bowls 5-6-0		
MINNESOTA		
Murray Warmath	Rose 1-2-61	Washington 7-17
Murray Warmath	Rose 1-1-62	UCLA 21-3
Cal Stoll	All-American 12-22-77	Maryland 7-17
John Gutekunst	Independence 12-21-85	Clemson 20-13
John Gutekunst	Liberty 12-29-86	Tennessee 14-21
All bowls 2-3-0		
MISSISSIPPI		
Ed Walker	Orange 1-1-36	Catholic 19-20
John Vaught	Delta 1-1-48	Texas Christian 13-9
John Vaught	Sugar 1-1-53	Georgia Tech 7-24
John Vaught	Sugar 1-1-55	Navy 0-21
John Vaught	Cotton 1-2-56	Texas Christian 14-13

School/Coach	Bowl/Date	Opponent/Score
John Vaught	Sugar 1-1-58	Texas 39-7
John Vaught	Gator 12-27-58	Florida 7-3
John Vaught	Sugar 1-1-60	Louisiana St. 21-0
John Vaught	Sugar 1-2-61	Rice 14-6
John Vaught	Cotton 1-1-62	Texas 7-12
John Vaught	Sugar 1-1-63	Arkansas 17-13
John Vaught	Sugar 1-1-64	Alabama 7-12
John Vaught	Bluebonnet 12-19-64	Tulsa 7-14
John Vaught	Liberty 12-18-65	Auburn 13-7
John Vaught	Bluebonnet 12-17-66	Texas 0-19
John Vaught	Sun 12-30-67	UTEP 7-14
John Vaught	Liberty 12-14-68	Virginia Tech 34-17
John Vaught	Sugar 1-1-70	Arkansas 27-22
John Vaught	Gator 1-2-71	Auburn 28-35
Billy Kinard	Peach 12-30-71	Georgia Tech 41-18
Billy Brewer	Independence 12-10-83	Air Force 3-9
Billy Brewer	Independence 12-20-86	Texas Tech 20-17
Billy Brewer	Liberty 12-28-89	Air Force 42-29
Billy Brewer	Gator 1-1-91	Michigan 3-35
Billy Brewer	Liberty 12-31-92	Air Force 13-0

All bowls 14-11-0

MISSISSIPPI ST.

School/Coach	Bowl/Date	Opponent/Score
Ralph Sasse	Orange 1-1-37	Duquesne 12-13
Allyn McKeen	Orange 1-1-41	Georgetown 14-7
Paul Davis	Liberty 12-21-63	North Caro. St. 16-12
Bob Tyler	Sun 12-28-74	North Caro. 26-24
Emory Bellard	Sun 12-27-80	Nebraska 17-31
Emory Bellard	All-American 12-31-81	Kansas 10-0
Jackie Sherrill	Liberty 12-29-91	Air Force 15-38
Jackie Sherrill	Peach 1-2-93	North Caro. 17-21

All bowls 4-4-0

MISSOURI

School/Coach	Bowl/Date	Opponent/Score
Gwinn Henry	Los Angeles Christmas Festival 12-25-24	Southern Cal 7-20
Don Faurot	Orange 1-1-40	Georgia Tech 7-21
Don Faurot	Sugar 1-1-42	Fordham 0-2
Chauncey Simpson	Cotton 1-1-46	Texas 27-40
Don Faurot	Gator 1-1-49	Clemson 23-24
Don Faurot	Gator 1-2-50	Maryland 7-20
Dan Devine	Orange 1-1-60	Georgia 0-40
Dan Devine	Orange 1-2-61	Navy 21-14
Dan Devine	Bluebonnet 12-22-62	Georgia Tech 14-10
Dan Devine	Sugar 1-1-66	Florida 20-18
Dan Devine	Gator 12-28-68	Alabama 35-10
Dan Devine	Orange 1-1-70	Penn St. 3-10
Al Onofrio	Fiesta 12-23-72	Arizona St. 35-49
Al Onofrio	Sun 12-29-73	Auburn 34-17
Warren Powers	Liberty 12-23-78	Louisiana St. 20-15
Warren Powers	All-American 12-29-79	South Caro. 24-14
Warren Powers	Liberty 12-27-80	Purdue 25-28
Warren Powers	Tangerine 12-19-81	Southern Miss. 19-17
Warren Powers	Holiday 12-23-83	Brigham Young 17-21

All bowls 8-11-0

NAVY

School/Coach	Bowl/Date	Opponent/Score
Bob Folwell	Rose 1-1-24	Washington 14-14
Eddie Erdelatz	Sugar 1-1-55	Mississippi 21-0
Eddie Erdelatz	Cotton 1-1-58	Rice 20-7
Wayne Hardin	Orange 1-1-61	Missouri 14-21
Wayne Hardin	Cotton 1-1-64	Texas 6-28
George Welsh	Holiday 12-22-78	Brigham Young 23-16
George Welsh	Garden State 12-14-80	Houston 0-35
George Welsh	Liberty 12-30-81	Ohio St. 28-31

All bowls 3-4-1

NEBRASKA

School/Coach	Bowl/Date	Opponent/Score
Lawrence McC. "Biff" Jones	Rose 1-1-41	Stanford 13-21
Bill Glassford	Orange 1-1-55	Duke 7-34
Bob Devaney	Gotham 12-15-62	Miami (Fla.) 36-34
Bob Devaney	Orange 1-1-64	Auburn 13-7
Bob Devaney	Cotton 1-1-65	Arkansas 7-10
Bob Devaney	Orange 1-1-66	Alabama 28-39
Bob Devaney	Sugar 1-2-67	Alabama 7-34
Bob Devaney	Sun 12-20-69	Georgia 45-6
Bob Devaney	Orange 1-1-71	Louisiana St. 17-12
Bob Devaney	Orange 1-1-72	Alabama 38-6
Bob Devaney	Orange 1-1-73	Notre Dame 40-6
Tom Osborne	Cotton 1-1-74	Texas 19-3
Tom Osborne	Sugar 12-31-74	Florida 13-10
Tom Osborne	Fiesta 12-26-75	Arizona St. 14-17
Tom Osborne	Bluebonnet 12-31-76	Texas Tech 27-24

School/Coach	Bowl/Date	Opponent/Score
Tom Osborne	Liberty 12-19-77	North Caro. 21-17
Tom Osborne	Orange 1-1-79	Oklahoma 24-31
Tom Osborne	Cotton 1-1-80	Houston 14-17
Tom Osborne	Sun 12-27-80	Mississippi St. 31-17
Tom Osborne	Orange 1-1-82	Clemson 15-22
Tom Osborne	Orange 1-1-83	Louisiana St. 21-20
Tom Osborne	Orange 1-2-84	Miami (Fla.) 30-31
Tom Osborne	Sugar 1-1-85	Louisiana St. 28-10
Tom Osborne	Fiesta 1-1-86	Michigan 23-27
Tom Osborne	Sugar 1-1-87	Louisiana St. 30-15
Tom Osborne	Fiesta 1-1-88	Florida St. 28-31
Tom Osborne	Orange 1-2-89	Miami (Fla.) 3-23
Tom Osborne	Fiesta 1-1-90	Florida St. 17-41
Tom Osborne	Florida Citrus 1-1-91	Georgia Tech 21-45
Tom Osborne	Orange 1-1-92	Miami (Fla.) 0-22
Tom Osborne	Orange 1-1-93	Florida St. 14-27
Tom Osborne	Orange 1-1-94	Florida St. 16-18

All bowls 14-18-0

NEVADA

School/Coach	Bowl/Date	Opponent/Score
Joe Sheeketski	Salad 1-1-48	North Texas 13-6
Joe Sheeketski	Harbor 1-1-49	Villanova 7-27
Chris Ault	Las Vegas 12-18-92	Bowling Green 34-35

All bowls 1-2-0

NEVADA-LAS VEGAS

School/Coach	Bowl/Date	Opponent/Score
Harvey Hyde	California 12-15-84	Toledo 30-13

All bowls 1-0-0

NEW MEXICO

School/Coach	Bowl/Date	Opponent/Score
Ted Shipkey	Sun 1-2-39	Utah 0-26
Willis Barnes	Sun 1-1-44	Southwestern (Tex.) 0-7
Willis Barnes	Sun 1-1-46	Denver 34-24
Willis Barnes	Harbor 1-1-47	Montana St. 13-13
Bill Weeks	Aviation 12-9-61	Western Mich. 28-12

All bowls 2-2-1

NEW MEXICO ST.

School/Coach	Bowl/Date	Opponent/Score
Jerry Hines	Sun 1-1-36	Hardin-Simmons 14-14
Warren Woodson	Sun 12-31-59	North Texas 28-8
Warren Woodson	Sun 12-31-60	Utah St. 20-13

All bowls 2-0-1

NORTH CARO.

School/Coach	Bowl/Date	Opponent/Score
Carl Snavely	Sugar 1-1-47	Georgia 10-20
Carl Snavely	Sugar 1-1-49	Oklahoma 6-14
Carl Snavely	Cotton 1-2-50	Rice 13-27
Jim Hickey	Gator 12-28-63	Air Force 35-0
Bill Dooley	Peach 12-30-70	Arizona St. 26-48
Bill Dooley	Gator 12-31-71	Georgia 3-7
Bill Dooley	Sun 12-30-72	Texas Tech 32-28
Bill Dooley	Sun 12-28-74	Mississippi St. 24-26
Bill Dooley	Peach 12-31-76	Kentucky 0-21
Bill Dooley	Liberty 12-19-77	Nebraska 17-21
Dick Crum	Gator 12-28-79	Michigan 17-15
Dick Crum	Bluebonnet 12-31-80	Texas 16-7
Dick Crum	Gator 12-28-81	Arkansas 31-27
Dick Crum	Sun 12-25-82	Texas 26-10
Dick Crum	Peach 12-30-83	Florida St. 3-28
Dick Crum	Aloha 12-27-86	Arizona 21-30
Mack Brown	Peach 1-2-93	Mississippi St. 21-17
Mack Brown	Gator 12-31-93	Alabama 10-24

All bowls 7-11-0

NORTH CARO. ST.

School/Coach	Bowl/Date	Opponent/Score
Beattie Feathers	Gator 1-1-47	Oklahoma 13-34
Earle Edwards	Liberty 12-21-63	Mississippi St. 12-16
Earle Edwards	Liberty 12-16-67	Georgia 14-7
Lou Holtz	Peach 12-29-72	West Va. 49-13
Lou Holtz	Liberty 12-17-73	Kansas 31-18
Lou Holtz	Bluebonnet 12-23-74	Houston 31-31
Lou Holtz	Peach 12-31-75	West Va. 10-13
Bo Rein	Peach 12-31-77	Iowa St. 24-14
Bo Rein	Tangerine 12-23-78	Pittsburgh 30-17
Dick Sheridan	Peach 12-31-86	Virginia Tech 24-25
Dick Sheridan	Peach 12-31-88	Iowa 28-23
Dick Sheridan	Copper 12-31-89	Arizona 10-17
Dick Sheridan	All-American 12-28-90	Southern Miss. 31-27
Dick Sheridan	Peach 1-1-92	East Caro. 34-37
Dick Sheridan	Gator 12-31-92	Florida 10-27
Mike O'Cain	Hall of Fame 1-1-94	Michigan 7-42

All bowls 7-8-1

NORTHERN ILL.

School/Coach	Bowl/Date	Opponent/Score
Bill Mallory	California 12-17-83	Cal St. Fullerton 20-13

All bowls 1-0-0

NORTHWESTERN

School/Coach	Bowl/Date	Opponent/Score
Bob Voigts	Rose 1-1-49	California 20-14

All bowls 1-0-0

NOTRE DAME

School/Coach	Bowl/Date	Opponent/Score
Knute Rockne	Rose 1-1-25	Stanford 27-10
Ara Parseghian	Cotton 1-1-70	Texas 17-21
Ara Parseghian	Cotton 1-1-71	Texas 24-11
Ara Parseghian	Orange 1-1-73	Nebraska 6-40
Ara Parseghian	Sugar 12-31-73	Alabama 24-23
Ara Parseghian	Orange 1-1-75	Alabama 13-11
Dan Devine	Gator 12-27-76	Penn St. 20-9
Dan Devine	Cotton 1-2-78	Texas 38-10
Dan Devine	Cotton 1-1-79	Houston 35-34
Dan Devine	Sugar 1-1-81	Georgia 10-17
Gerry Faust	Liberty 12-29-83	Boston College 19-18
Gerry Faust	Aloha 12-29-84	Southern Methodist 20-27
Lou Holtz	Cotton 1-1-88	Texas A&M 10-35
Lou Holtz	Fiesta 1-2-89	West Va. 34-21
Lou Holtz	Orange 1-1-90	Colorado 21-6
Lou Holtz	Orange 1-1-91	Colorado 9-10
Lou Holtz	Sugar 1-1-92	Florida 39-28
Lou Holtz	Cotton 1-1-93	Texas A&M 28-3
Lou Holtz	Cotton 1-1-94	Texas A&M 24-21

All bowls 13-6-0

OHIO

School/Coach	Bowl/Date	Opponent/Score
Bill Hess	Sun 12-31-62	West Tex. A&M 14-15
Bill Hess	Tangerine 12-27-68	Richmond 42-49

All bowls 0-2-0

OHIO ST.

School/Coach	Bowl/Date	Opponent/Score
John Wilce	Rose 1-1-21	California 0-28
Wes Fesler	Rose 1-2-50	California 17-14
Woody Hayes	Rose 1-1-55	Southern Cal 20-7
Woody Hayes	Rose 1-1-58	Oregon 10-7
Woody Hayes	Rose 1-1-69	Southern Cal 27-16
Woody Hayes	Rose 1-1-71	Stanford 17-27
Woody Hayes	Rose 1-1-73	Southern Cal 17-42
Woody Hayes	Rose 1-1-74	Southern Cal 42-21
Woody Hayes	Rose 1-1-75	Southern Cal 17-18
Woody Hayes	Rose 1-1-76	UCLA 10-23
Woody Hayes	Orange 1-1-77	Colorado 27-10
Woody Hayes	Sugar 1-2-78	Alabama 6-35
Woody Hayes	Gator 12-29-78	Clemson 15-17
Earle Bruce	Rose 1-1-80	Southern Cal 16-17
Earle Bruce	Fiesta 12-26-80	Penn St. 19-31
Earle Bruce	Liberty 12-30-81	Navy 31-28
Earle Bruce	Holiday 12-17-82	Brigham Young 47-17
Earle Bruce	Fiesta 1-2-84	Pittsburgh 28-23
Earle Bruce	Rose 1-1-85	Southern Cal 17-20
Earle Bruce	Florida Citrus 12-28-85	Brigham Young 10-7
Earle Bruce	Cotton 1-1-87	Texas A&M 28-12
John Cooper	Hall of Fame 1-1-90	Auburn 14-31
John Cooper	Liberty 12-27-90	Air Force 11-23
John Cooper	Hall of Fame 1-1-92	Syracuse 17-24
John Cooper	Florida Citrus 1-1-93	Georgia 14-21
John Cooper	Holiday 12-30-93	Brigham Young 28-21

All bowls 12-14-0

OKLAHOMA

School/Coach	Bowl/Date	Opponent/Score
Tom Stidham	Orange 1-2-39	Tennessee 0-17
Jim Tatum	Gator 1-1-47	North Caro. St. 34-13
Bud Wilkinson	Sugar 1-1-49	North Caro. 14-6
Bud Wilkinson	Sugar 1-1-50	Louisiana St. 35-0
Bud Wilkinson	Sugar 1-1-51	Kentucky 7-13
Bud Wilkinson	Orange 1-1-54	Maryland 7-0
Bud Wilkinson	Orange 1-2-56	Maryland 20-6
Bud Wilkinson	Orange 1-1-58	Duke 48-21
Bud Wilkinson	Orange 1-1-59	Syracuse 21-6
Bud Wilkinson	Orange 1-1-63	Alabama 0-17
Gomer Jones	Gator 1-2-65	Florida St. 19-36
Chuck Fairbanks	Orange 1-1-68	Tennessee 26-24
Chuck Fairbanks	Bluebonnet 12-31-68	Southern Methodist 27-28
Chuck Fairbanks	Bluebonnet 12-31-70	Alabama 24-24
Chuck Fairbanks	Sugar 1-1-72	Auburn 40-22
Chuck Fairbanks	Sugar 12-31-72	Penn St. 14-0
Barry Switzer	Orange 1-1-76	Michigan 14-6
Barry Switzer	Fiesta 12-25-76	Wyoming 41-7
Barry Switzer	Orange 1-2-78	Arkansas 6-31
Barry Switzer	Orange 1-1-79	Nebraska 31-24
Barry Switzer	Orange 1-1-80	Florida St. 24-7
Barry Switzer	Orange 1-1-81	Florida St. 18-17
Barry Switzer	Sun 12-26-81	Houston 40-14
Barry Switzer	Fiesta 1-1-83	Arizona St. 21-32
Barry Switzer	Orange 1-1-85	Washington 17-28
Barry Switzer	Orange 1-1-86	Penn St. 25-10
Barry Switzer	Orange 1-1-87	Arkansas 42-8
Barry Switzer	Orange 1-1-88	Miami (Fla.) 14-20
Barry Switzer	Florida Citrus 1-2-89	Clemson 6-13
Gary Gibbs	Gator 12-29-91	Virginia 48-14
Gary Gibbs	John Hancock 12-24-93	Texas Tech 41-10

All bowls 20-10-1

OKLAHOMA ST.

School/Coach	Bowl/Date	Opponent/Score
Jim Lookabaugh	Cotton 1-1-45	Texas Christian 34-0
Jim Lookabaugh	Sugar 1-1-46	St. Mary's (Cal.) 33-13
Jim Lookabaugh	Delta 1-1-49	William & Mary 0-20
Cliff Speegle	Bluegrass 12-13-58	Florida St. 15-6
Jim Stanley	Fiesta 12-28-74	Brigham Young 16-6
Jim Stanley	Tangerine 12-18-76	Brigham Young 49-12
Jimmy Johnson	Independence 12-12-81	Texas A&M 16-33
Jimmy Johnson	Bluebonnet 12-31-83	Baylor 24-14
Pat Jones	Gator 12-28-84	South Caro. 21-14
Pat Jones	Gator 12-30-85	Florida St. 23-34
Pat Jones	Sun 12-25-87	West Va. 35-33
Pat Jones	Holiday 12-30-88	Wyoming 62-14

All bowls 9-3-0

OREGON

School/Coach	Bowl/Date	Opponent/Score
Hugo Bezdek	Rose 1-1-17	Pennsylvania 14-0
Charles "Shy" Huntington	Rose 1-1-20	Harvard 6-7
Jim Aiken	Cotton 1-1-49	Southern Methodist 13-21
Len Casanova	Rose 1-1-58	Ohio St. 7-10
Len Casanova	Liberty 12-17-60	Penn St. 12-41
Len Casanova	Sun 12-31-63	Southern Methodist 21-14
Rich Brooks	Independence 12-16-89	Tulsa 27-24
Rich Brooks	Freedom 12-29-90	Colorado St. 31-32
Rich Brooks	Independence 12-31-92	Wake Forest 35-39

All bowls 3-6-0

OREGON ST.

School/Coach	Bowl/Date	Opponent/Score
Lon Stiner	Rose 1-1-42	Duke 20-16
Tommy Prothro	Rose 1-1-57	Iowa 19-35
Tommy Prothro	Liberty 12-15-62	Villanova 6-0
Tommy Prothro	Rose 1-1-65	Michigan 7-34

All bowls 2-2-0

PACIFIC (CAL.)

School/Coach	Bowl/Date	Opponent/Score
Larry Siemering	Raisin 1-1-48	Wichita St. 26-14
Ernie Jorge	Sun 1-1-52	Texas Tech 14-25
Ernie Jorge	Sun 1-1-53	Southern Miss. 26-7

All bowls 2-1-0

PENN ST.

School/Coach	Bowl/Date	Opponent/Score
Hugo Bezdek	Rose 1-1-23	Southern Cal 3-14
Bob Higgins	Cotton 1-1-48	Southern Methodist 13-13
Charles "Rip" Engle	Liberty 12-19-59	Alabama 7-0
Charles "Rip" Engle	Liberty 12-17-60	Oregon 41-12
Charles "Rip" Engle	Gator 12-30-61	Georgia Tech 30-15
Charles "Rip" Engle	Gator 12-29-62	Florida 7-17
Joe Paterno	Gator 12-30-67	Florida St. 17-17
Joe Paterno	Orange 1-1-69	Kansas 15-14
Joe Paterno	Orange 1-1-70	Missouri 10-3
Joe Paterno	Cotton 1-1-72	Texas 30-6
Joe Paterno	Sugar 12-31-72	Oklahoma 0-14
Joe Paterno	Orange 1-1-74	Louisiana St. 16-9
Joe Paterno	Cotton 1-1-75	Baylor 41-20
Joe Paterno	Sugar 12-31-75	Alabama 6-13
Joe Paterno	Gator 12-27-76	Notre Dame 9-20
Joe Paterno	Fiesta 12-25-77	Arizona 42-30
Joe Paterno	Sugar 1-1-79	Alabama 7-14
Joe Paterno	Liberty 12-22-79	Tulane 9-6
Joe Paterno	Fiesta 12-26-80	Ohio St. 31-19
Joe Paterno	Fiesta 1-1-82	Southern Cal 26-10
Joe Paterno	Sugar 1-1-83	Georgia 27-23
Joe Paterno	Aloha 12-26-83	Washington 13-10
Joe Paterno	Orange 1-1-86	Oklahoma 10-25
Joe Paterno	Fiesta 1-2-87	Miami (Fla.) 14-10
Joe Paterno	Florida Citrus 1-1-88	Clemson 10-35
Joe Paterno	Holiday 12-29-89	Brigham Young 50-39
Joe Paterno	Blockbuster 12-28-90	Florida St. 17-24
Joe Paterno	Fiesta 1-1-92	Tennessee 42-17
Joe Paterno	Blockbuster 1-1-93	Stanford 3-24
Joe Paterno	Florida Citrus 1-1-94	Tennessee 31-13

All bowls 18-10-2

PITTSBURGH

School/Coach	Bowl/Date	Opponent/Score
Jock Sutherland	Rose 1-2-28	Stanford 6-7
Jock Sutherland	Rose 1-1-30	Southern Cal 14-47
Jock Sutherland	Rose 1-2-33	Southern Cal 0-35
Jock Sutherland	Rose 1-1-37	Washington 21-0
John Michelosen	Sugar 1-2-56	Georgia Tech 0-7

School/Coach	Bowl/Date	Opponent/Score
John Michelosen	Gator 12-29-56	Georgia Tech 14-21
Johnny Majors	Fiesta 12-21-73	Arizona St. 7-28
Johnny Majors	Sun 12-26-75	Kansas 33-19
Johnny Majors	Sugar 1-1-77	Georgia 27-3
Jackie Sherrill	Gator 12-30-77	Clemson 34-3
Jackie Sherrill	Tangerine 12-23-78	North Caro. St. 17-30
Jackie Sherrill	Fiesta 12-25-79	Arizona 16-10
Jackie Sherrill	Gator 12-29-80	South Caro. 37-9
Jackie Sherrill	Sugar 1-1-82	Georgia 24-20
Foge Fazio	Cotton 1-1-83	Southern Methodist 3-7
Foge Fazio	Fiesta 1-2-84	Ohio St. 23-28
Mike Gottfried	Bluebonnet 12-31-87	Texas 27-32
Paul Hackett	John Hancock 12-30-89	Texas A&M 31-28

All bowls 8-10-0

PURDUE

Jack Mollenkopf	Rose 1-2-67	Southern Cal 14-13
Jim Young	Peach 12-25-78	Georgia Tech 41-21
Jim Young	Bluebonnet 12-31-79	Tennessee 27-22
Jim Young	Liberty 12-27-80	Missouri 28-25
Leon Burtnett	Peach 12-31-84	Virginia 24-27

All bowls 4-1-0

RICE

Jimmy Kitts	Cotton 1-1-38	Colorado 28-14
Jess Neely	Orange 1-1-47	Tennessee 8-0
Jess Neely	Cotton 1-2-50	North Caro. 27-13
Jess Neely	Cotton 1-1-54	Alabama 28-6
Jess Neely	Cotton 1-1-58	Navy 7-20
Jess Neely	Sugar 1-2-61	Mississippi 6-14
Jess Neely	Bluebonnet 12-16-61	Kansas 7-33

All bowls 4-3-0

RUTGERS

Frank Burns	Garden State 12-16-78	Arizona St. 18-34

All bowls 0-1-0

SAN DIEGO ST.

Bill Schutte	Harbor 1-1-48	Hardin-Simmons 0-53
Don Coryell	Pasadena 12-6-69	Boston U. 28-7
Denny Stolz	Holiday 12-30-86	Iowa 38-39
Al Luginbill	Freedom 12-30-91	Tulsa 17-28

All bowls 1-3-0

SAN JOSE ST.

Bill Hubbard	Raisin 1-1-47	Utah St. 20-0
Bill Hubbard	Raisin 12-31-49	Texas Tech 20-13
Dewey King	Pasadena 12-18-71	Memphis 9-28
Jack Elway	California 12-19-81	Toledo 25-27
Claude Gilbert	California 12-31-86	Miami (Ohio) 37-7
Claude Gilbert	California 12-12-87	Eastern Mich. 27-30
Terry Shea	California 12-8-90	Central Mich. 48-24

All bowls 4-3-0

SOUTH CARO.

Johnny McMillan	Gator 1-1-46	Wake Forest 14-26
Paul Dietzel	Peach 12-30-69	West Va. 3-14
Jim Carlen	Tangerine 12-20-75	Miami (Ohio) 7-20
Jim Carlen	All-American 12-29-79	Missouri 14-24
Jim Carlen	Gator 12-29-80	Pittsburgh 9-37
Joe Morrison	Gator 12-28-84	Oklahoma St. 14-21
Joe Morrison	Gator 12-31-87	Louisiana St. 13-30
Joe Morrison	Liberty 12-28-88	Indiana 10-34

All bowls 0-8-0

SOUTHERN CAL

Elmer "Gus" Henderson	Rose 1-1-23	Penn St. 14-3
Elmer "Gus" Henderson	Los Angeles Christmas Festival 12-25-24	Missouri 20-7
Howard Jones	Rose 1-1-30	Pittsburgh 47-14
Howard Jones	Rose 1-1-32	Tulane 21-12
Howard Jones	Rose 1-2-33	Pittsburgh 35-0
Howard Jones	Rose 1-2-39	Duke 7-3
Howard Jones	Rose 1-1-40	Tennessee 14-0
Jeff Cravath	Rose 1-1-44	Washington 29-0
Jeff Cravath	Rose 1-1-45	Tennessee 25-0
Jeff Cravath	Rose 1-1-46	Alabama 14-34
Jeff Cravath	Rose 1-1-48	Michigan 0-49
Jess Hill	Rose 1-1-53	Wisconsin 7-0
Jess Hill	Rose 1-1-55	Ohio St. 7-20
John McKay	Rose 1-1-63	Wisconsin 42-37
John McKay	Rose 1-2-67	Purdue 13-14
John McKay	Rose 1-1-68	Indiana 14-3
John McKay	Rose 1-1-69	Ohio St. 16-27
John McKay	Rose 1-1-70	Michigan 10-3
John McKay	Rose 1-1-73	Ohio St. 42-17
John McKay	Rose 1-1-74	Ohio St. 21-42

School/Coach	Bowl/Date	Opponent/Score
John McKay	Rose 1-1-75	Ohio St. 18-17
John McKay	Liberty 12-22-75	Texas A&M 20-0
John Robinson	Rose 1-1-77	Michigan 14-6
John Robinson	Bluebonnet 12-31-77	Texas A&M 47-28
John Robinson	Rose 1-1-79	Michigan 17-10
John Robinson	Rose 1-1-80	Ohio St. 17-16
John Robinson	Fiesta 1-1-82	Penn St. 10-26
Ted Tollner	Rose 1-1-85	Ohio St. 20-17
Ted Tollner	Aloha 12-28-85	Alabama 3-24
Ted Tollner	Florida Citrus 1-1-87	Auburn 7-16
Larry Smith	Rose 1-1-88	Michigan St. 17-20
Larry Smith	Rose 1-2-89	Michigan 14-22
Larry Smith	Rose 1-1-90	Michigan 17-10
Larry Smith	John Hancock 12-31-90	Michigan St. 16-17
Larry Smith	Freedom 12-29-92	Fresno St. 7-24
John Robinson	Freedom 12-30-93	Utah 28-21

All bowls 23-13-0

SOUTHERN METHODIST

Ray Morrison	Dixie Classic 1-1-25	West Va. Wesleyan 7-9
Matty Bell	Rose 1-1-36	Stanford 0-7
Matty Bell	Cotton 1-1-48	Penn St. 13-13
Matty Bell	Cotton 1-1-49	Oregon 21-13
Hayden Fry	Sun 12-31-63	Oregon 14-21
Hayden Fry	Cotton 12-31-66	Georgia 9-24
Hayden Fry	Bluebonnet 12-31-68	Oklahoma 28-27
Ron Meyer	Holiday 12-19-80	Brigham Young 45-46
Bobby Collins	Cotton 1-1-83	Pittsburgh 7-3
Bobby Collins	Sun 12-24-83	Alabama 7-28
Bobby Collins	Aloha 12-29-84	Notre Dame 27-20

All bowls 4-6-1

SOUTHERN MISS.

Thad "Pie" Vann	Sun 1-1-53	Pacific (Cal.) 7-26
Thad "Pie" Vann	Sun 1-1-54	UTEP 14-37
Bobby Collins	Independence 12-13-80	McNeese St. 16-14
Bobby Collins	Tangerine 12-19-81	Missouri 17-19
Curley Hallman	Independence 12-23-88	UTEP 38-18
Jeff Bower	All-American 12-28-90	North Caro. St. 27-31

All bowls 2-4-0

STANFORD

Charlie Fickert	Rose 1-1-02	Michigan 0-49
Glenn "Pop" Warner	Rose 1-1-25	Notre Dame 10-27
Glenn "Pop" Warner	Rose 1-1-27	Alabama 7-7
Glenn "Pop" Warner	Rose 1-2-28	Pittsburgh 7-6
Claude "Tiny" Thornhill	Rose 1-1-34	Columbia 0-7
Claude "Tiny" Thornhill	Rose 1-1-35	Alabama 13-29
Claude "Tiny" Thornhill	Rose 1-1-36	Southern Methodist 7-0
Clark Shaughnessy	Rose 1-1-41	Nebraska 21-13
Chuck Taylor	Rose 1-1-52	Illinois 7-40
John Ralston	Rose 1-1-71	Ohio St. 27-17
John Ralston	Rose 1-1-72	Michigan 13-12
Bill Walsh	Sun 12-31-77	Louisiana St. 24-14
Bill Walsh	Bluebonnet 12-31-78	Georgia 25-22
Jack Elway	Gator 12-27-86	Clemson 21-27
Dennis Green	Aloha 12-25-91	Georgia Tech 17-18
Bill Walsh	Blockbuster 1-1-93	Penn St. 24-3

All bowls 8-7-1

SYRACUSE

Ben Schwartzwalder	Orange 1-1-53	Alabama 6-61
Ben Schwartzwalder	Cotton 1-1-57	Texas Christian 27-28
Ben Schwartzwalder	Orange 1-1-59	Oklahoma 6-21
Ben Schwartzwalder	Cotton 1-1-60	Texas 23-14
Ben Schwartzwalder	Liberty 12-16-61	Miami (Fla.) 15-14
Ben Schwartzwalder	Sugar 1-1-65	Louisiana St. 10-13
Ben Schwartzwalder	Gator 12-31-66	Tennessee 12-18
Frank Maloney	Independence 12-15-79	McNeese St. 31-7
Dick MacPherson	Cherry 12-21-85	Maryland 18-35
Dick MacPherson	Sugar 1-1-88	Auburn 16-16
Dick MacPherson	Hall of Fame 1-2-89	Louisiana St. 23-10
Dick MacPherson	Peach 12-30-89	Georgia 19-18
Dick MacPherson	Aloha 12-25-90	Arizona 28-0
Paul Pasqualoni	Hall of Fame 1-1-92	Ohio St. 24-17
Paul Pasqualoni	Fiesta 1-1-93	Colorado 26-22

All bowls 8-6-1

TEMPLE

Glenn "Pop" Warner	Sugar 1-1-35	Tulane 14-20
Wayne Hardin	Garden State 12-15-79	California 28-17

All bowls 1-1-0

School/Coach	Bowl/Date	Opponent/Score
TENNESSEE		
Bob Neyland	Orange 1-2-39	Oklahoma 17-0
Bob Neyland	Rose 1-1-40	Southern Cal 0-14
Bob Neyland	Sugar 1-1-41	Boston College 13-19
John Barnhill	Sugar 1-1-43	Tulsa 14-7
John Barnhill	Rose 1-1-45	Southern Cal 0-25
Bob Neyland	Orange 1-1-47	Rice 0-8
Bob Neyland	Cotton 1-1-51	Texas 20-14
Bob Neyland	Sugar 1-1-52	Maryland 13-28
Bob Neyland	Cotton 1-1-53	Texas 0-16
Bowden Wyatt	Sugar 1-1-57	Baylor 7-13
Bowden Wyatt	Gator 12-28-57	Texas A&M 3-0
Doug Dickey	Bluebonnet 12-18-65	Tulsa 27-6
Doug Dickey	Gator 12-31-66	Syracuse 18-12
Doug Dickey	Orange 1-1-68	Oklahoma 24-26
Doug Dickey	Cotton 1-1-69	Texas 13-36
Doug Dickey	Gator 12-27-69	Florida 13-14
Bill Battle	Sugar 1-1-71	Air Force 34-13
Bill Battle	Liberty 12-20-71	Arkansas 14-13
Bill Battle	Bluebonnet 12-30-72	Louisiana St. 24-17
Bill Battle	Gator 12-29-73	Texas Tech 19-28
Bill Battle	Liberty 12-16-74	Maryland 7-3
Johnny Majors	Bluebonnet 12-31-79	Purdue 22-27
Johnny Majors	Garden State 12-13-81	Wisconsin 28-21
Johnny Majors	Peach 12-31-82	Iowa 22-28
Johnny Majors	Florida Citrus 12-17-83	Maryland 30-23
Johnny Majors	Sun 12-24-84	Maryland 26-27
Johnny Majors	Sugar 1-1-86	Miami (Fla.) 35-7
Johnny Majors	Liberty 12-29-86	Minnesota 21-14
Johnny Majors	Peach 1-2-88	Indiana 27-22
Johnny Majors	Cotton 1-1-90	Arkansas 31-27
Johnny Majors	Sugar 1-1-91	Virginia 23-22
Johnny Majors	Fiesta 1-1-92	Penn St. 17-42
Phillip Fulmer	Hall of Fame 1-1-93	Boston College 38-23
Phillip Fulmer	Florida Citrus 1-1-94	Penn St. 13-31
All bowls 18-16-0		
TEXAS		
Dana Bible	Cotton 1-1-43	Georgia Tech 14-7
Dana Bible	Cotton 1-1-44	Randolph Field 7-7
Dana Bible	Cotton 1-1-46	Missouri 40-27
Blair Cherry	Sugar 1-1-48	Alabama 27-7
Blair Cherry	Orange 1-1-49	Georgia 41-28
Blair Cherry	Cotton 1-1-51	Tennessee 14-20
Ed Price	Cotton 1-1-53	Tennessee 16-0
Darrell Royal	Sugar 1-1-58	Mississippi 7-39
Darrell Royal	Cotton 1-1-60	Syracuse 14-23
Darrell Royal	Bluebonnet 12-17-60	Alabama 3-3
Darrell Royal	Cotton 1-1-62	Mississippi 12-7
Darrell Royal	Cotton 1-1-63	Louisiana St. 0-13
Darrell Royal	Cotton 1-1-64	Navy 28-6
Darrell Royal	Orange 1-1-65	Alabama 21-17
Darrell Royal	Bluebonnet 12-17-66	Mississippi 19-0
Darrell Royal	Cotton 1-1-69	Tennessee 36-13
Darrell Royal	Cotton 1-1-70	Notre Dame 21-17
Darrell Royal	Cotton 1-1-71	Notre Dame 11-24
Darrell Royal	Cotton 1-1-72	Penn St. 6-30
Darrell Royal	Cotton 1-1-73	Alabama 17-13
Darrell Royal	Cotton 1-1-74	Nebraska 3-19
Darrell Royal	Gator 12-30-74	Auburn 3-27
Darrell Royal	Bluebonnet 12-27-75	Colorado 38-21
Fred Akers	Cotton 1-2-78	Notre Dame 10-38
Fred Akers	Sun 12-23-78	Maryland 42-0
Fred Akers	Sun 12-22-79	Washington 7-14
Fred Akers	Bluebonnet 12-31-80	North Caro. 7-16
Fred Akers	Cotton 1-1-82	Alabama 14-12
Fred Akers	Sun 12-25-82	North Caro. 10-26
Fred Akers	Cotton 1-2-84	Georgia 9-10
Fred Akers	Freedom 12-26-84	Iowa 17-55
Fred Akers	Bluebonnet 12-31-85	Air Force 16-24
David McWilliams	Bluebonnet 12-31-87	Pittsburgh 32-27
David McWilliams	Cotton 1-1-91	Miami (Fla.) 3-46
All bowls 16-16-2		
TEXAS A&M		
Dana Bible	Dixie Classic 1-2-22	Centre 22-14
Homer Norton	Sugar 1-1-40	Tulane 14-13
Homer Norton	Cotton 1-1-41	Fordham 13-12
Homer Norton	Cotton 1-1-42	Alabama 21-29
Homer Norton	Orange 1-1-44	Louisiana St. 14-19
Harry Stiteler	Presidential 12-9-50	Georgia 40-20
Paul "Bear" Bryant	Gator 12-28-57	Tennessee 0-3
Gene Stallings	Cotton 1-1-68	Alabama 20-16
Emory Bellard	Liberty 12-22-75	Southern Cal 0-20
Emory Bellard	Sun 1-2-77	Florida 37-14

School/Coach	Bowl/Date	Opponent/Score
Emory Bellard	Bluebonnet 12-31-77	Southern Cal 28-47
Tom Wilson	All-American 12-20-78	Iowa St. 28-12
Tom Wilson	Independence 12-12-81	Oklahoma St. 33-16
Jackie Sherrill	Cotton 1-1-86	Auburn 36-16
Jackie Sherrill	Cotton 1-1-87	Ohio St. 12-28
Jackie Sherrill	Cotton 1-1-88	Notre Dame 35-10
R. C. Slocum	John Hancock 12-30-89	Pittsburgh 28-31
R. C. Slocum	Holiday 12-29-90	Brigham Young 65-14
R. C. Slocum	Cotton 1-1-92	Florida St. 2-10
R. C. Slocum	Cotton 1-1-93	Notre Dame 3-28
R. C. Slocum	Cotton 1-1-94	Notre Dame 21-24
All bowls 11-10-0		
TEXAS CHRISTIAN		
Bill Driver	Fort Worth Classic 1-1-21	Centre 7-63
Leo "Dutch" Meyer	Sugar 1-1-36	Louisiana St. 3-2
Leo "Dutch" Meyer	Cotton 1-1-37	Marquette 16-6
Leo "Dutch" Meyer	Sugar 1-2-39	Carnegie Mellon 15-7
Leo "Dutch" Meyer	Orange 1-1-42	Georgia 26-40
Leo "Dutch" Meyer	Cotton 1-1-45	Oklahoma St. 0-34
Leo "Dutch" Meyer	Delta 1-1-48	Mississippi 9-13
Leo "Dutch" Meyer	Cotton 1-1-52	Kentucky 7-20
Abe Martin	Cotton 1-2-56	Mississippi 13-14
Abe Martin	Cotton 1-1-57	Syracuse 28-27
Abe Martin	Cotton 1-1-59	Air Force 0-0
Abe Martin	Bluebonnet 12-19-59	Clemson 7-23
Abe Martin	Sun 12-31-65	UTEP 12-13
Jim Wacker	Bluebonnet 12-31-84	West Va. 14-31
All bowls 4-9-1		
TEXAS TECH		
Pete Cawthon	Sun 1-1-38	West Va. 6-7
Pete Cawthon	Cotton 1-2-39	St. Mary's (Cal.) 13-20
Dell Morgan	Sun 1-1-42	Tulsa 0-6
Dell Morgan	Sun 1-1-48	Miami (Ohio) 12-13
Dell Morgan	Raisin 12-31-49	San Jose St. 13-20
DeWitt Weaver	Sun 1-1-52	Pacific (Cal.) 25-14
DeWitt Weaver	Gator 1-1-54	Auburn 35-13
DeWitt Weaver	Sun 1-2-56	Wyoming 14-21
J. T. King	Sun 12-26-64	Georgia 0-7
J. T. King	Gator 12-31-65	Georgia Tech 21-31
Jim Carlen	Sun 12-19-70	Georgia Tech 9-17
Jim Carlen	Sun 12-30-72	North Caro. 28-32
Jim Carlen	Gator 12-29-73	Tennessee 28-19
Jim Carlen	Peach 12-28-74	Vanderbilt 6-6
Steve Sloan	Bluebonnet 12-31-76	Nebraska 24-27
Steve Sloan	Tangerine 12-23-77	Florida St. 17-40
Spike Dykes	Independence 12-20-86	Mississippi 17-20
Spike Dykes	All-American 12-28-89	Duke 49-21
Spike Dykes	John Hancock 12-24-93	Oklahoma 10-41
All bowls 4-14-1		
TOLEDO		
Frank Lauterbur	Tangerine 12-26-69	Davidson 56-33
Frank Lauterbur	Tangerine 12-28-70	William & Mary 40-12
Jack Murphy	Tangerine 12-28-71	Richmond 28-3
Chuck Stobart	California 12-19-81	San Jose St. 27-25
Dan Simrell	California 12-15-84	Nevada-Las Vegas 13-30
All bowls 4-1-0		
TULANE		
Bernie Bierman	Rose 1-1-32	Southern Cal 12-21
Ted Cox	Sugar 1-1-35	Temple 20-14
Lowell "Red" Dawson	Sugar 1-1-40	Texas A&M 13-14
Jim Pittman	Liberty 12-12-70	Colorado 17-3
Bennie Ellender	Bluebonnet 12-29-73	Houston 7-47
Larry Smith	Liberty 12-22-79	Penn St. 6-9
Vince Gibson	All-American 12-27-80	Arkansas 15-34
Mack Brown	Independence 12-19-87	Washington 12-24
All bowls 2-6-0		
TULSA		
Henry Frnka	Sun 1-1-42	Texas Tech 6-0
Henry Frnka	Sugar 1-1-43	Tennessee 7-14
Henry Frnka	Sugar 1-1-44	Georgia Tech 18-20
Henry Frnka	Orange 1-1-45	Georgia Tech 26-12
Henry Frnka	Oil 1-1-46	Georgia 6-20
J. O. "Buddy" Brothers	Gator 1-1-53	Florida 13-14
Glenn Dobbs	Bluebonnet 12-19-64	Mississippi 14-7
Glenn Dobbs	Bluebonnet 12-18-65	Tennessee 6-27
F. A. Dry	Independence 12-13-76	McNeese St. 16-20
Dave Rader	Independence 12-16-89	Oregon 24-27
Dave Rader	Freedom 12-30-91	San Diego St. 28-17
All bowls 4-7-0		

School/Coach	Bowl/Date	Opponent/Score
UCLA		
Edwin "Babe" Horrell	Rose 1-1-43	Georgia 0-9
Bert LaBrucherie	Rose 1-1-47	Illinois 14-45
Henry "Red" Sanders	Rose 1-1-54	Michigan St. 20-28
Henry "Red" Sanders	Rose 1-2-56	Michigan 14-17
Bill Barnes	Rose 1-1-62	Minnesota 3-21
Tommy Prothro	Rose 1-1-66	Michigan St. 14-12
Dick Vermeil	Rose 1-1-76	Ohio St. 23-10
Terry Donahue	Liberty 12-20-76	Alabama 6-36
Terry Donahue	Fiesta 12-25-78	Arkansas 10-10
Terry Donahue	Bluebonnet 12-31-81	Michigan 14-33
Terry Donahue	Rose 1-1-83	Michigan 24-14
Terry Donahue	Rose 1-2-84	Illinois 45-9
Terry Donahue	Fiesta 1-1-85	Miami (Fla.) 39-37
Terry Donahue	Rose 1-1-86	Iowa 45-28
Terry Donahue	Freedom 12-30-86	Brigham Young 31-10
Terry Donahue	Aloha 12-25-87	Florida 20-16
Terry Donahue	Cotton 1-1-89	Arkansas 17-3
Terry Donahue	John Hancock 12-31-91	Illinois 6-3
Terry Donahue	Rose 1-1-94	Wisconsin 16-21
All bowls 10-8-1		
UTAH		
Ike Armstrong	Sun 1-2-39	New Mexico 26-0
Ray Nagel	Liberty 12-19-64	West Va. 32-6
Ron McBride	Copper 12-29-92	Washington St. 28-31
Ron McBride	Freedom 12-30-93	Southern Cal 21-28
All bowls 2-2-0		
UTAH ST.		
E. L. "Dick" Romney	Raisin 1-1-47	San Jose St. 0-20
John Ralston	Sun 12-31-60	New Mexico St. 13-20
John Ralston	Gotham 12-9-61	Baylor 9-24
Charlie Weatherbie	Las Vegas 12-17-93	Ball St. 42-33
All bowls 1-3-0		
UTEP		
Mack Saxon	Sun 1-1-37	Hardin-Simmons 6-34
Jack "Cactus Jack" Curtice	Sun 1-1-49	West Va. 12-21
Jack "Cactus Jack" Curtice	Sun 1-2-50	Georgetown 33-20
Mike Brumbelow	Sun 1-1-54	Southern Miss. 37-14
Mike Brumbelow	Sun 1-1-55	Florida St. 47-20
Mike Brumbelow	Sun 1-1-57	Geo. Washington 0-13
Bobby Dobbs	Sun 12-31-65	Texas Christian 13-12
Bobby Dobbs	Sun 12-30-67	Mississippi 14-7
Bob Stull	Independence 12-23-88	Southern Miss. 18-38
All bowls 5-4-0		
VANDERBILT		
Art Guepe	Gator 12-31-55	Auburn 25-13
Steve Sloan	Peach 12-28-74	Texas Tech 6-6
George MacIntyre	All-American 12-31-82	Air Force 28-36
All bowls 1-1-1		
VIRGINIA		
George Welsh	Peach 12-31-84	Purdue 27-24
George Welsh	All-American 12-22-87	Brigham Young 22-16
George Welsh	Florida Citrus 1-1-90	Illinois 21-31
George Welsh	Sugar 1-1-91	Tennessee 22-23
George Welsh	Gator 12-29-91	Oklahoma 14-48
George Welsh	Carquest 1-1-94	Boston College 13-31
All bowls 2-4-0		
VIRGINIA TECH		
Jimmy Kitts	Sun 1-1-47	Cincinnati 6-18
Jerry Claiborne	Liberty 12-10-66	Miami (Fla.) 7-14
Jerry Claiborne	Liberty 12-14-68	Mississippi 17-34
Bill Dooley	Peach 1-2-81	Miami (Fla.) 10-20
Bill Dooley	Independence 12-15-84	Air Force 7-23
Bill Dooley	Peach 12-31-86	North Caro. St. 25-24
Frank Beamer	Independence 12-31-93	Indiana 45-20
All bowls 2-5-0		
WAKE FOREST		
D. C. "Peahead" Walker	Gator 1-1-46	South Caro. 26-14
D. C. "Peahead" Walker	Dixie 1-1-49	Baylor 7-20
John Mackovic	Tangerine 12-22-79	Louisiana St. 10-34
Bill Dooley	Independence 12-31-92	Oregon 39-35
All bowls 2-2-0		

School/Coach	Bowl/Date	Opponent/Score
WASHINGTON		
Enoch Bagshaw	Rose 1-1-24	Navy 14-14
Enoch Bagshaw	Rose 1-1-26	Alabama 19-20
Jimmy Phelan	Rose 1-1-37	Pittsburgh 0-21
Ralph "Pest" Welch	Rose 1-1-44	Southern Cal 0-29
Jim Owens	Rose 1-1-60	Wisconsin 44-8
Jim Owens	Rose 1-2-61	Minnesota 17-7
Jim Owens	Rose 1-1-64	Illinois 7-17
Don James	Rose 1-2-78	Michigan 27-20
Don James	Sun 12-22-79	Texas 14-7
Don James	Rose 1-1-81	Michigan 6-23
Don James	Rose 1-1-82	Iowa 28-0
Don James	Aloha 12-25-82	Maryland 21-20
Don James	Aloha 12-26-83	Penn St. 10-13
Don James	Orange 1-1-85	Oklahoma 28-17
Don James	Freedom 12-30-85	Colorado 20-17
Don James	Sun 12-25-86	Alabama 6-28
Don James	Independence 12-19-87	Tulane 24-12
Don James	Freedom 12-30-89	Florida 34-7
Don James	Rose 1-1-91	Iowa 46-34
Don James	Rose 1-1-92	Michigan 34-14
Don James	Rose 1-1-93	Michigan 31-38
All bowls 12-8-1		
WASHINGTON ST.		
Bill "Lone Star" Dietz	Rose 1-1-16	Brown 14-0
Orin "Babe" Hollingbery	Rose 1-1-31	Alabama 0-24
Jim Walden	Holiday 12-18-81	Brigham Young 36-38
Dennis Erickson	Aloha 12-25-88	Houston 24-22
Mike Price	Copper 12-29-92	Utah 31-28
All bowls 3-2-0		
WEST VA.		
Clarence "Doc" Spears	San Diego East-West Christmas Classic 12-25-22	Gonzaga 21-13
Marshall "Little Sleepy" Glenn	Sun 1-1-38	Texas Tech 7-6
Dud DeGroot	Sun 1-1-49	UTEP 21-12
Art Lewis	Sugar 1-1-54	Georgia Tech 19-42
Gene Corum	Liberty 12-19-64	Utah 6-32
Jim Carlen	Peach 12-30-69	South Caro. 14-3
Bobby Bowden	Peach 12-29-72	North Caro. St. 13-49
Bobby Bowden	Peach 12-31-75	North Caro. St. 13-10
Don Nehlen	Peach 12-31-81	Florida 26-6
Don Nehlen	Gator 12-30-82	Florida St. 12-31
Don Nehlen	All-American 12-22-83	Kentucky 20-16
Don Nehlen	Bluebonnet 12-31-84	Texas Christian 31-14
Don Nehlen	Sun 12-25-87	Oklahoma St. 33-35
Don Nehlen	Fiesta 1-2-89	Notre Dame 21-34
Don Nehlen	Gator 12-30-89	Clemson 7-27
Don Nehlen	Sugar 1-1-94	Florida 7-41
All bowls 8-8-0		
WESTERN MICH.		
Merle Schlosser	Aviation 12-9-61	New Mexico 12-28
Al Molde	California 12-10-88	Fresno St. 30-35
All bowls 0-2-0		
WISCONSIN		
Ivy Williamson	Rose 1-1-53	Southern Cal 0-7
Milt Bruhn	Rose 1-1-60	Washington 8-44
Milt Bruhn	Rose 1-2-63	Southern Cal 37-42
Dave McClain	Garden State 12-13-81	Tennessee 21-28
Dave McClain	Independence 12-11-82	Kansas St. 14-3
Dave McClain	All-American 12-29-84	Kentucky 19-20
Barry Alvarez	Rose 1-1-94	UCLA 21-16
All bowls 2-5-0		
WYOMING		
Bowden Wyatt	Gator 1-1-51	Wash. & Lee 20-7
Phil Dickens	Sun 1-2-56	Texas Tech 21-14
Bob Devaney	Sun 12-31-58	Hardin-Simmons 14-6
Lloyd Eaton	Sun 12-24-66	Florida St. 28-20
Lloyd Eaton	Sugar 1-1-68	Louisiana St. 13-20
Fred Akers	Fiesta 12-25-76	Oklahoma 7-41
Paul Roach	Holiday 12-30-87	Iowa 19-20
Paul Roach	Holiday 12-30-88	Oklahoma St. 14-62
Paul Roach	Copper 12-31-90	California 15-17
Joe Tiller	Copper 12-29-93	Kansas St. 17-52
All bowls 4-6-0		

Played in Major Bowl—No Longer I-A

School/Coach	Bowl/Date	Opponent/Score
BOSTON U.		
Larry Naviaux	Pasadena 12-6-69	San Diego St. 7-28
All bowls 0-1-0		
BROWN		
Ed Robinson	Rose 1-1-16	Washington St. 0-14
All bowls 0-1-0		
BUCKNELL		
Edward "Hook" Mylin	Orange 1-1-35	Miami (Fla.) 26-0
All bowls 1-0-0		
CAL ST. FULLERTON		
Gene Murphy	California 12-17-83	Northern Ill. 13-20
All bowls 0-1-0		
CAL ST. NORTHRIDGE		
Sam Winningham	Pasadena 12-2-67	West Tex. A&M 13-35
All bowls 0-1-0		
CARNEGIE MELLON		
Bill Kern	Sugar 1-2-39	Texas Christian 7-15
All bowls 0-1-0		
CASE RESERVE		
Bill Edwards	Sun 1-1-41	Arizona St. 26-13
All bowls 1-0-0		
CATHOLIC		
Arthur "Dutch" Bergman	Orange 1-1-36	Mississippi 20-19
Arthur "Dutch" Bergman	Sun 1-1-40	Arizona St. 0-0
All bowls 1-0-1		
CENTENARY (LA.)		
Homer Norton	Dixie Classic 1-1-34	Arkansas 7-7
All bowls 0-0-1		
CENTRE		
Charley Moran	Fort Worth Classic 1-1-21	Texas Christian 63-7
Charley Moran	San Diego East-West Christmas Classic 12-26-21	Arizona 38-0
Charley Moran	Dixie Classic 1-2-22	Texas A&M 14-22
All bowls 2-1-0		
CITADEL		
Eddie Teague	Tangerine 12-30-60	Tennessee Tech 27-0
All bowls 1-0-0		
COLUMBIA		
Lou Little	Rose 1-1-34	Stanford 7-0
All bowls 1-0-0		
DAVIDSON		
Homer Smith	Tangerine 12-26-69	Toledo 33-56
All bowls 0-1-0		
DAYTON		
Joe Gavin	Salad 1-1-52	Houston 21-26
All bowls 0-1-0		
DENVER		
Clyde "Cac" Hubbard	Sun 1-1-46	New Mexico 24-34
Clyde "Cac" Hubbard	Alamo 1-4-47	Hardin-Simmons 0-20
All bowls 0-2-0		
DRAKE		
Vee Green	Raisin 1-1-46	Fresno St. 13-12
Al Kawal	Salad 1-1-49	Arizona 14-13
Warren Gaer	Sun 1-1-58	Louisville 20-34
All bowls 2-1-0		
DUQUESNE		
John "Little Clipper" Smith	Orange 1-1-37	Mississippi St. 13-12
All bowls 1-0-0		
FORDHAM		
Jim Crowley	Cotton 1-1-41	Texas A&M 12-13
Jim Crowley	Sugar 1-1-42	Missouri 2-0
All bowls 1-1-0		
GEO. WASHINGTON		
Eugene "Bo" Sherman	Sun 1-1-57	UTEP 13-0
All bowls 1-0-0		
GEORGETOWN		
Jack Hagerty	Orange 1-1-41	Mississippi St. 7-14
Bob Margarita	Sun 1-2-50	UTEP 20-33
All bowls 0-2-0		
GONZAGA		
Charles "Gus" Dorais	San Diego East-West Christmas Classic 12-15-22	West Va. 13-21
All bowls 0-1-0		
HARDIN-SIMMONS		
Frank Kimbrough	Sun 1-1-36	New Mexico St. 14-14
Frank Kimbrough	Sun 1-1-37	UTEP 34-6
Warren Woodson	Sun 1-1-43	Second Air Force 7-13
Warren Woodson	Alamo 1-4-47	Denver 20-6
Warren Woodson	Harbor 1-1-48	San Diego St. 53-0
Warren Woodson	Shrine 12-18-48	Ouachita Baptist 40-12
Warren Woodson	Camellia 12-30-48	Wichita St. 29-12
Sammy Baugh	Sun 12-31-58	Wyoming 6-14
All bowls 5-2-1		
HARVARD		
Robert Fisher	Rose 1-1-20	Oregon 7-6
All bowls 1-0-0		
HOLY CROSS		
John "Ox" Da Grosa	Orange 1-1-46	Miami (Fla.) 6-13
All bowls 0-1-0		
LONG BEACH ST.		
Jim Stangeland	Pasadena 12-19-70	Louisville 24-24
All bowls 0-0-1		
MARQUETTE		
Frank Murray	Cotton 1-1-37	Texas Christian 6-16
All bowls 0-1-0		
McNEESE ST.		
Jack Doland	Independence 12-13-76	Tulsa 20-16
Ernie Duplechin	Independence 12-15-79	Syracuse 7-31
Ernie Duplechin	Independence 12-13-80	Southern Miss. 14-16
All bowls 1-2-0		
MONTANA ST.		
Clyde Carpenter	Harbor 1-1-47	New Mexico 13-13
All bowls 0-0-1		
NORTH TEXAS		
Odus Mitchell	Salad 1-1-48	Nevada 6-13
Odus Mitchell	Sun 12-31-59	New Mexico St. 8-28
All bowls 0-2-0		
OCCIDENTAL		
Roy Dennis	Raisin 1-1-49	Colorado St. 21-20
All bowls 1-0-0		
OUACHITA BAPTIST		
Wesley Bradshaw	Shrine 12-18-48	Hardin-Simmons 12-40
All bowls 0-1-0		
PENNSYLVANIA		
Bob Folwell	Rose 1-1-17	Oregon 0-14
All bowls 0-1-0		
RANDOLPH FIELD		
Frank Tritico	Cotton 1-1-44	Texas 7-7
All bowls 0-0-1		
RICHMOND		
Frank Jones	Tangerine 12-27-68	Ohio 49-42
Frank Jones	Tangerine 12-28-71	Toledo 3-28
All bowls 1-1-0		
SANTA CLARA		
Lawrence "Buck" Shaw	Sugar 1-1-37	Louisiana St. 21-14
Lawrence "Buck" Shaw	Sugar 1-1-38	Louisiana St. 6-0
Len Casanova	Orange 1-2-50	Kentucky 21-13
All bowls 3-0-0		
SECOND AIR FORCE		
Red Reese	Sun 1-1-43	Hardin-Simmons 13-7
All bowls 1-0-0		
SOUTHWESTERN (TEX.)		
Randolph R. M. Medley	Sun 1-1-44	New Mexico 7-0
Randolph R. M. Medley	Sun 1-1-45	U. of Mexico 35-0
All bowls 2-0-0		

School/Coach	Bowl/Date	Opponent/Score
ST. MARY'S (CAL.)		
Edward "Slip" Madigan	Cotton 1-2-39	Texas Tech 20-13
Jimmy Phelan	Sugar 1-1-46	Oklahoma St. 13-33
Jimmy Phelan	Oil 1-1-47	Georgia Tech 19-41
All bowls 1-2-0		
TAMPA		
Earle Bruce	Tangerine 12-29-72	Kent 21-18
All bowls 1-0-0		
TENNESSEE TECH		
Wilburn Tucker	Tangerine 12-30-60	Citadel 0-27
All bowls 0-1-0		
U. OF MEXICO		
Bernard A. Hoban	Sun 1-1-45	Southwestern (Tex.) 0-35
All bowls 0-1-0		
VILLANOVA		
Maurice "Clipper" Smith	Bacardi, Cuba 1-1-37	Auburn 7-7
Jordan Olivar	Great Lakes 12-6-47	Kentucky 14-24
Jordan Olivar	Harbor 1-1-49	Nevada 27-7
Alex Bell	Sun 12-30-61	Wichita St. 17-9
Alex Bell	Liberty 12-15-62	Oregon St. 0-6
All bowls 2-2-1		
WASH. & JEFF.		
Earle "Greasy" Neale	Rose 1-2-22	California 0-0
All bowls 0-0-1		

School/Coach	Bowl/Date	Opponent/Score
WASH. & LEE		
George Barclay	Gator 1-1-51	Wyoming 7-20
All bowls 0-1-0		
WEST TEX. A&M		
Frank Kimbrough	Sun 1-1-51	Cincinnati 14-13
Joe Kerbel	Sun 12-31-62	Ohio 15-14
Joe Kerbel	Pasadena 12-2-67	Cal St. Northridge 35-13
All bowls 3-0-0		
WEST VA. WESLEYAN		
Bob Higgins	Dixie Classic 1-1-25	Southern Methodist 9-7
All bowls 1-0-0		
WICHITA ST.		
Ralph Graham	Raisin 1-1-48	Pacific (Cal.) 14-26
Jim Trimble	Camellia 12-30-48	Hardin-Simmons 12-49
Hank Foldberg	Sun 12-30-61	Villanova 9-17
All bowls 0-3-0		
WILLIAM & MARY		
Rube McCray	Dixie 1-1-48	Arkansas 19-21
Rube McCray	Delta 1-1-49	Oklahoma St. 20-0
Lou Holtz	Tangerine 12-28-70	Toledo 12-40
All bowls 1-2-0		
XAVIER (OHIO)		
Ed Kluska	Salad 1-1-50	Arizona St. 33-21
All bowls 1-0-0		

Major Bowl-Game Attendance

(Current site and stadium capacity in parentheses. For participating teams, refer to pages 238-243.)

ROSE BOWL

(Rose Bowl Stadium, Pasadena, Calif.; Capacity: 98,101)

Date	Attendance
1-1-02	8,000
1-1-16	7,000
1-1-17	26,000
1-1-20	30,000
1-1-21	42,000
1-2-22	40,000
1-1-23	43,000
1-1-24	40,000
1-1-25	53,000
1-1-26	50,000
1-1-27	57,417
1-2-28	65,000
1-1-29	66,604
1-1-30	72,000
1-1-31	60,000
1-1-32	75,562
1-2-33	78,874
1-1-34	35,000
1-1-35	84,474
1-1-36	84,474
1-1-37	87,196
1-1-38	90,000
1-2-39	89,452
1-1-40	92,200
1-1-41	91,500
1-1-42#	56,000
1-1-43	93,000
1-1-44	68,000
1-1-45	91,000
1-1-46	93,000
1-1-47	90,000
1-1-48	93,000
1-1-49	93,000
1-2-50	100,963
1-1-51	98,939
1-1-52	96,825
1-1-53	101,500
1-1-54	101,000
1-1-55	89,191
1-2-56	100,809
1-1-57	97,126
1-1-58	98,202
1-1-59	98,297
1-1-60	100,809
1-2-61	97,314
1-1-62	98,214
1-1-63	98,698
1-1-64	96,957
1-1-65	100,423
1-1-66	100,087
1-2-67	100,807
1-1-68	102,946
1-1-69	102,063
1-1-70	103,878
1-1-71	103,839
1-1-72	103,154
1-1-73	*106,869
1-1-74	105,267
1-1-75	106,721
1-1-76	105,464
1-1-77	106,182
1-2-78	105,312
1-1-79	105,629
1-1-80	105,526
1-1-81	104,863
1-1-82	105,611
1-1-83	104,991
1-2-84	103,217
1-1-85	102,594
1-1-86	103,292
1-1-87	103,168
1-1-88	103,847
1-2-89	101,688
1-1-90	103,450
1-1-91	101,273
1-1-92	103,566
1-1-93	94,236
1-1-94	101,237

*Record attendance. #Game held at Duke, Durham, N.C., due to war-time West Coast restrictions.

ORANGE BOWL

(Orange Bowl Stadium, Miami, Fla.; Capacity: 74,712)

Date	Attendance
1-1-35	5,134
1-1-36	6,568
1-1-37	9,210
1-1-38	18,972
1-2-39	32,191
1-1-40	29,278
1-1-41	29,554
1-1-42	35,786
1-1-43	25,166
1-1-44	25,203
1-1-45	23,279
1-1-46	35,709
1-1-47	36,152
1-1-48	59,578
1-1-49	60,523
1-2-50	64,816
1-1-51	65,181
1-1-52	65,839
1-1-53	66,280
1-1-54	68,640
1-1-55	68,750
1-2-56	76,561
1-1-57	73,280
1-1-58	76,561
1-1-59	75,281
1-1-60	72,186

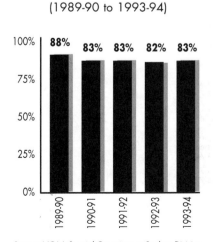

Bowl-Game Attendance as Percent of Capacity
(1989-90 to 1993-94)

1989-90	1990-91	1991-92	1992-93	1993-94
88%	83%	83%	82%	83%

Source: NCAA Special Committee to Study a Division I-A Football Championship.

BOWL/ALL-STAR RESULTS

Date	Attendance
1-2-61	72,212
1-1-62	68,150
1-1-63	72,880
1-1-64	72,647
1-1-65	72,647
1-1-66	72,214
1-2-67	72,426
1-1-68	77,993
1-1-69	77,719
1-1-70	77,282
1-1-71	80,699
1-1-72	78,151
1-1-73	80,010
1-1-74	60,477
1-1-75	71,801
1-1-76	76,799
1-1-77	65,537
1-2-78	60,987
1-1-79	66,365
1-1-80	66,714
1-1-81	71,043
1-1-82	72,748
1-1-83	68,713
1-2-84	72,549
1-1-85	56,294
1-1-86	74,178
1-1-87	52,717
1-1-88	74,760
1-2-89	79,480
1-1-90	81,190
1-1-91	77,062
1-1-92	77,747
1-1-93	57,324
1-1-94	*81,536

*Record attendance.

SUGAR BOWL

(Louisiana Superdome, New Orleans, La.; Capacity: 72,704)

Date	Attendance
1-1-35	22,026
1-1-36	35,000
1-1-37	41,000
1-1-38	45,000
1-2-39	50,000
1-1-40	73,000
1-1-41	73,181
1-1-42	72,000
1-1-43	70,000
1-1-44	69,000
1-1-45	72,000
1-1-46	75,000
1-1-47	73,300
1-1-48	72,000
1-1-49	82,000
1-2-50	82,470
1-1-51	82,000
1-1-52	82,000
1-1-53	82,000
1-1-54	76,000
1-1-55	82,000
1-2-56	80,175
1-1-57	81,000
1-1-58	82,000
1-1-59	82,000
1-1-60	83,000
1-2-61	82,851
1-1-62	82,910
1-1-63	82,900
1-1-64	80,785
1-1-65	65,000
1-1-66	67,421
1-2-67	82,000
1-1-68	78,963
1-1-69	82,113
1-1-70	82,500
1-1-71	78,655
1-1-72	84,031
12-31-72	80,123
12-31-73	*85,161
12-31-74	67,890
12-31-75	75,212
1-1-77	76,117
1-2-78	76,811
1-1-79	76,824

Date	Attendance
1-1-80	77,486
1-1-81	77,895
1-1-82	77,224
1-1-83	78,124
1-2-84	77,893
1-1-85	75,608
1-1-86	77,432
1-1-87	76,234
1-1-88	75,495
1-2-89	61,934
1-1-90	77,452
1-1-91	75,132
1-1-92	76,447
1-1-93	76,789
1-1-94	75,437

*Record attendance.

COTTON BOWL

(Cotton Bowl Stadium, Dallas, Texas; Capacity: 68,245)

Date	Attendance
1-1-37	17,000
1-1-38	37,000
1-2-39	40,000
1-1-40	20,000
1-1-41	45,500
1-1-42	38,000
1-1-43	36,000
1-1-44	15,000
1-1-45	37,000
1-1-46	45,000
1-1-47	38,000
1-1-48	43,000
1-1-49	69,000
1-2-50	75,347
1-1-51	75,349
1-1-52	75,347
1-1-53	75,504
1-1-54	75,504
1-1-55	75,504
1-2-56	75,504
1-1-57	68,000
1-1-58	75,504
1-1-59	75,504
1-1-60	75,504
1-2-61	74,000
1-1-62	75,504
1-1-63	75,504
1-1-64	75,504
1-1-65	75,504
1-1-66	76,200
12-31-66	75,400
1-1-68	75,504
1-1-69	72,000
1-1-70	73,000
1-1-71	72,000
1-1-72	72,000
1-1-73	72,000
1-1-74	67,500
1-1-75	67,500
1-1-76	74,500
1-1-77	54,500
1-2-78	*76,601
1-1-79	32,500
1-1-80	72,032
1-1-81	74,281
1-1-82	73,243
1-1-83	60,359
1-2-84	67,891
1-1-85	56,522
1-1-86	73,137
1-1-87	74,188
1-1-88	73,006
1-2-89	74,304
1-1-90	74,358
1-1-91	73,521
1-1-92	73,728
1-1-93	71,615
1-1-94	69,855

*Record attendance.

JOHN HANCOCK BOWL#

(Sun Bowl Stadium, El Paso, Texas; Capacity: 51,270)

Date	Attendance
1-1-36	11,000
1-1-37	10,000
1-1-38	12,000
1-2-39	13,000
1-1-40	12,000
1-1-41	14,000
1-1-42	14,000
1-1-43	16,000
1-1-44	18,000
1-1-45	13,000
1-1-46	15,000
1-1-47	10,000
1-1-48	18,000
1-1-49	13,000
1-2-50	15,000
1-1-51	16,000
1-1-52	17,000
1-1-53	11,000
1-1-54	9,500
1-1-55	14,000
1-2-56	14,500
1-1-57	13,500
1-1-58	12,000
12-31-58	13,000
12-31-59	14,000
12-31-60	16,000
12-30-61	15,000
12-31-62	16,000
12-31-63	26,500
12-26-64	28,500
12-31-65	27,450
12-24-66	24,381
12-30-67	34,685
12-28-68	32,307
12-20-69	29,723
12-19-70	30,512
12-18-71	33,503
12-30-72	31,312
12-29-73	30,127
12-28-74	30,131
12-26-75	33,240
1-2-77	33,252
12-31-77	31,318
12-23-78	33,122
12-22-79	33,412
12-27-80	34,723
12-26-81	33,816
12-25-82	31,359
12-24-83	41,412
12-22-84	50,126
12-28-85	*52,203
12-25-86	48,722
12-25-87	43,240
12-24-88	48,719
12-30-89	44,887
12-31-90	50,562
12-31-91	42,821
12-31-92	41,622
12-24-93	43,848

*Record attendance. #Named Sun Bowl before 1989.

GATOR BOWL

(Ben Hill Griffin Stadium, Gainesville, Fla.; Capacity: 83,000)

Date	Attendance
1-2-46	7,362
1-1-47	10,134
1-1-48	16,666
1-1-49	32,939
1-2-50	18,409
1-1-51	19,834
1-1-52	34,577
1-1-53	30,015
1-1-54	28,641
12-31-54	28,426
12-31-55	32,174
12-29-56	36,256
12-28-57	41,160
12-27-58	41,312
1-2-60	45,104
12-31-60	50,112
12-30-61	50,202
12-29-62	50,026
12-28-63	50,018
1-2-65	50,408

12-31-65	60,127
12-31-66	60,312
12-30-67	68,019
12-28-68	68,011
12-27-69	72,248
1-2-71	71,136
12-31-71	71,208
12-30-72	71,114
12-29-73	62,109
12-30-74	63,811
12-29-75	64,012
12-27-76	67,827
12-30-77	72,289
12-29-78	72,011
12-28-79	70,407
12-29-80	72,297
12-28-81	71,009
12-30-82	80,913
12-30-83	81,293
12-28-84	82,138
12-30-85	79,417
12-27-86	80,104
12-31-87	82,119
1-1-89	76,236
12-30-89	*82,911
1-1-91	68,927
12-29-91	62,003
12-31-92	71,233
12-31-93	67,205

*Record attendance.

LIBERTY BOWL†

(Liberty Bowl Memorial Stadium, Memphis, Tenn.; under renovation)

Date	Attendance
12-19-59	36,211
12-17-60	16,624
12-16-61	15,712
12-15-62	17,048
12-31-63	8,309
12-19-64	6,059
12-18-65	38,607
12-10-66	39,101
12-16-67	35,045
12-14-68	46,206
12-13-69	50,042
12-12-70	44,640
12-20-71	51,410
12-18-72	50,021
12-17-73	50,011
12-16-74	51,284
12-22-75	52,129
12-20-76	52,736
12-19-77	49,456
12-23-78	53,064
12-22-79	50,021
12-27-80	53,667
12-30-81	43,216
12-29-82	54,123
12-29-83	38,229
12-27-84	50,108
12-27-85	40,186
12-29-86	51,327
12-29-87	53,249
12-28-88	39,210
12-28-89	60,128
12-27-90	13,144
12-29-91	*61,497
12-31-92	32,107
12-28-93	21,097

*Record attendance. †Played at Philadelphia, 1959-63; Atlantic City, 1964; Memphis, from 1965.

FLORIDA CITRUS BOWL#

(Florida Citrus Bowl—Orange County Stadium, Orlando, Fla.; Capacity: 70,349)

Date	Attendance
12-30-60	13,000
12-22-62	7,500
12-27-68	16,114
12-26-69	16,311
12-28-70	15,164
12-28-71	16,750
12-29-72	20,062

12-22-73@	37,234
12-21-74	20,246
12-20-75	20,247
12-18-76	37,812
12-23-77	44,502
12-23-78	31,356
12-22-79	38,666
12-20-80	52,541
12-19-81	50,045
12-18-82	51,296
12-17-83	50,183
12-22-84	51,821
12-28-85	50,920
1-1-87	51,113
1-1-88	53,152
1-2-89	53,571
1-1-90	60,016
1-1-91	72,328
1-1-92	64,192
1-1-93	65,861
1-1-94	*72,456

*Record attendance. #Named Tangerine Bowl before 1982. The first 14 games in the Tangerine Bowl, through 1-1-60, are not listed because no major teams were involved. The same is true for those games played in December 1961, 1963, 1964, 1965, 1966 and 1967. @ Played at Gainesville, Fla.

PEACH BOWL

(Georgia Dome, Atlanta, Ga.; Capacity: 71,596)

Date	Attendance
12-30-68	35,545
12-30-69	48,452
12-30-70	52,126
12-30-71	36,771
12-29-72	52,671
12-28-73	38,107
12-28-74	31,695
12-31-75	45,134
12-31-76	54,132
12-31-77	36,733
12-25-78	20,277
12-31-79	57,371
1-2-81	45,384
12-31-81	37,582
12-31-82	50,134
12-30-83	25,648
12-31-84	41,107
12-31-85	29,857
12-31-86	53,668
1-2-88	58,737
12-31-88	44,635
12-30-89	44,991
12-29-90	38,912
1-1-92	59,322
1-2-93	*69,125
12-31-93	63,416

*Record attendance.

FIESTA BOWL

(Sun Devil Stadium, Tempe, Ariz.; Capacity: 73,656)

Date	Attendance
12-27-71	51,089
12-23-72	51,318
12-21-73	50,878
12-28-74	50,834
12-26-75	51,396
12-25-76	48,174
12-25-77	57,727
12-25-78	55,227
12-25-79	55,347
12-26-80	66,738
1-1-82	71,053
1-1-83	70,533
1-2-84	66,484
1-1-85	60,310
1-1-86	72,454
1-2-87	73,098
1-1-88	72,112
1-2-89	*74,911
1-1-90	73,953
1-1-91	69,098
1-1-92	71,133
1-1-93	70,224

1-1-94	72,260

*Record attendance.

INDEPENDENCE BOWL

(Independence Stadium, Shreveport, La.; Capacity: 60,128)

Date	Attendance
12-13-76	15,542
12-17-77	18,500
12-16-78	18,200
12-15-79	27,234
12-13-80	45,000
12-12-81	47,300
12-11-82	*49,503
12-10-83	41,274
12-15-84	41,000
12-21-85	42,800
12-20-86	46,369
12-19-87	41,683
12-23-88	20,242
12-16-89	30,333
12-15-90	48,325
12-29-91	46,932
12-31-92	31,337
12-31-93	33,819

*Record attendance.

HOLIDAY BOWL

(San Diego Jack Murphy Stadium, San Diego, Calif.; Capacity: 61,124)

Date	Attendance
12-28-78	52,500
12-21-79	52,200
12-19-80	50,214
12-18-81	52,419
12-17-82	52,533
12-23-83	51,480
12-21-84	61,243
12-22-85	42,324
12-30-86	59,473
12-30-87	*61,892
12-30-88	60,718
12-29-89	61,113
12-29-90	61,441
12-30-91	60,646
12-30-92	44,457
12-30-93	52,108

*Record attendance.

ALOHA BOWL

(Aloha Stadium, Honolulu, Hawaii; Capacity: 50,000)

Date	Attendance
12-25-82	30,055
12-26-83	37,212
12-29-84	41,777
12-28-85	35,183
12-27-86	26,743
12-25-87	24,839
12-25-88	35,132
12-25-89	*50,000
12-25-90	14,185
12-25-91	34,433
12-25-92	42,933
12-25-93	44,009

*Record attendance.

FREEDOM BOWL

(Anaheim Stadium, Anaheim, Calif.; Capacity: 70,962)

Date	Attendance
12-26-84	24,093
12-30-85	30,961
12-30-86	*55,422
12-30-87	33,261
12-29-88	35,941
12-30-89	33,858
12-29-90	41,450
12-30-91	34,217
12-29-92	50,745
12-30-93	37,203

*Record attendance.

BOWL/ALL-STAR RESULTS

HALL OF FAME BOWL
(Tampa Stadium, Tampa, Fla.; Capacity: 74,350)

Date	Attendance
12-23-86	25,368
1-2-88	60,156
1-2-89	51,112
1-1-90	52,535
1-1-91	*63,154
1-1-92	57,789
1-1-93	52,056
1-1-94	52,649

*Record attendance.

COPPER BOWL
(Arizona Stadium, Tucson, Ariz.; Capacity: 56,167)

Date	Attendance
12-31-89	37,237
12-31-90	36,340
12-31-91	35,752
12-29-92	40,876
12-29-93	*49,075

*Record attendance.

CARQUEST BOWL#
(Joe Robbie Stadium, Miami, Fla.; Capacity: 73,000)

Date	Attendance
12-28-90	*74,021
12-28-91	52,644
1-1-93	45,554
1-1-94	38,516

*Record attendance. #Named Blockbuster Bowl before 1993.

LAS VEGAS BOWL
(Sam Boyd Silver Bowl, Las Vegas, Nev.; Capacity: 32,000)

Date	Attendance
12-18-92	15,476
12-17-93	*15,508

*Record attendance.

ALAMO BOWL
(Alamodome, San Antonio, Texas; Capacity: 65,000)

Date	Attendance
12-31-93	45,716

Former Major Bowl Games

ALAMO
(San Antonio, Texas)

Date	Attendance
1-4-47	3,730

ALL-AMERICAN
(Birmingham, Ala.)

Date	Attendance
12-22-77	47,000
12-20-78	41,500
12-29-79	62,785
12-27-80	30,000
12-31-81	41,672
12-31-82	75,000
12-22-83	42,000
12-29-84	47,300
12-31-85	45,000
12-31-86	30,000
12-22-87	37,000
12-29-88	48,218
12-28-89	47,750
12-28-90	44,000

(Named Hall of Fame Classic until 1985 and then discontinued after 1990 game; played at Legion Field, capacity 75,952)

AVIATION
(Dayton, Ohio)

Date	Attendance
12-9-61	3,694

BACARDI
(Havana, Cuba)

Date	Attendance
1-1-37	12,000

BLUEBONNET
(Houston, Texas)

Date	Attendance
12-19-59	55,000
12-17-60	68,000
12-16-61	52,000
12-22-62	55,000
12-21-63	50,000
12-19-64	50,000
12-18-65	40,000
12-17-66	67,000
12-23-67	30,156
12-31-68	53,543
12-31-69	55,203
12-31-70	53,829
12-31-71	54,720
12-30-72	52,961
12-29-73	44,358
12-23-74	35,122
12-27-75	52,748
12-31-76	48,618
12-31-77	52,842
12-31-78	34,084
12-31-79	40,542
12-31-80	36,667
12-31-81	40,309
12-31-82	31,557
12-31-83	50,090
12-31-84	43,260
12-31-85	42,000
12-31-86	40,476
12-31-87	23,282

(Played at Rice Stadium 1959-67 and 1985, Astrodome 1968-84 and from 1986; Astrodome capacity 60,000)

BLUEGRASS
(Louisville, Ky.)

Date	Attendance
12-13-58	7,000

CALIFORNIA
(Fresno, Calif.)

Date	Attendance
12-19-81	15,565
12-18-82	30,000
12-17-83	20,464
12-15-84	21,741
12-14-85	32,554
12-13-86	10,743
12-12-87	24,000
12-10-88	31,272
12-9-89	31,610
12-8-90	25,431
12-14-91	34,825

CAMELLIA
(Lafayette, La.)

Date	Attendance
12-30-48	4,500

CHERRY
(Pontiac, Mich.)

Date	Attendance
12-22-84	70,332
12-21-85	51,858

DELTA
(Memphis, Tenn.)

Date	Attendance
1-1-48	28,120
1-1-49	15,069

DIXIE BOWL
(Birmingham, Ala.)

Date	Attendance
1-1-48	22,000
1-1-49	20,000

DIXIE CLASSIC
(Dallas, Texas)

Date	Attendance
1-2-22	12,000
1-1-25	7,000
1-1-34	12,000

FORT WORTH CLASSIC
(Fort Worth, Texas)

Date	Attendance
1-1-21	9,000

GARDEN STATE
(East Rutherford, N.J.)

Date	Attendance
12-16-78	33,402
12-15-79	55,493
12-14-80	41,417
12-13-81	38,782

GOTHAM
(New York, N.Y.)

Date	Attendance
12-9-61	15,123
12-15-62	6,166

GREAT LAKES
(Cleveland, Ohio)

Date	Attendance
12-6-47	14,908

HARBOR
(San Diego, Calif.)

Date	Attendance
1-1-47	7,000
1-1-48	12,000
1-1-49	20,000

LOS ANGELES CHRISTMAS FESTIVAL
(Los Angeles, Calif.)

Date	Attendance
12-25-24	47,000

MERCY
(Los Angeles, Calif.)

Date	Attendance
11-23-61	33,145

OIL
(Houston, Texas)

Date	Attendance
1-1-46	27,000
1-1-47	23,000

PASADENA
(Pasadena, Calif.)

Date	Attendance
12-2-67	28,802
12-6-69	41,276
12-19-70	20,472
12-18-71	15,244

PRESIDENTIAL CUP
(College Park, Md.)

Date	Attendance
12-9-50	12,245

RAISIN
(Fresno, Calif.)

Date	Attendance
1-1-46	10,000
1-1-47	13,000
1-1-48	13,000

1-1-49...10,000
12-31-49...9,000

SALAD
(Phoenix, Ariz.)

Date	Attendance
1-1-48	12,500
1-1-49	17,500
1-1-50	18,500
1-1-51	23,000
1-1-52	17,000

SAN DIEGO EAST-WEST CHRISTMAS CLASSIC
(San Diego, Calif.)

Date	Attendance
12-26-21	5,000
12-25-22	5,000

SHRINE
(Little Rock, Ark.)

Date	Attendance
12-18-48	5,000

Individual Records

Only official records after 1937 are included. Prior records are included if able to be substantiated. Each team's score is in parentheses after the team name. The year listed is the actual (calendar) year the game was played; the date is included if the bowl was played twice (i.e., January and December) during one calendar year. The list also includes discontinued bowls, marked with (D). Bowls are listed by the name of the bowl at the time it was played: The Florida Citrus Bowl was the Tangerine Bowl in 1947-82; the first Hall of Fame Bowl (1977-85) was called the All-American Bowl in 1986-90; the current Hall of Fame Bowl is played in Tampa, Fla., and started in 1986; the John Hancock Bowl was called the Sun Bowl in 1936-86 and the John Hancock Sun Bowl in 1987-88; and the Blockbuster Bowl changed its name to Carquest Bowl in 1993. The NCAA Statistics Service thanks former staff member Steve Boda for his valuable assistance in compiling these records.

Total Offense

MOST TOTAL PLAYS
74—(D) Tony Kimbrough, Western Mich. (30) vs. Fresno St. (35) (California, 1988) (431 yards)

MOST TOTAL YARDS
594—Ty Detmer, Brigham Young (39) vs. Penn St. (50) (Holiday, 1989) (576 passing yards, 67 plays)

HIGHEST AVERAGE PER PLAY
(Min. 10 Plays)
24.1—Dicky Maegle, Rice (28) vs. Alabama (6) (Cotton, 1954) (11 for 265)

MOST TOUCHDOWNS RESPONSIBLE FOR
(TDs Scored & Passed For)
6—Chuck Long, Iowa (55) vs. Texas (17) (Freedom, 1984) (6 pass); Bobby Layne, Texas (40) vs. Missouri (27) (Cotton, 1946) (3 rush, 2 pass, 1 catch)

Rushing

MOST RUSHING ATTEMPTS
46—Ron Jackson, Tulsa (28) vs. San Diego St. (17) (Freedom, 1991) (211 yards)

MOST NET RUSHING YARDS
280—(D) James Gray, Texas Tech (49) vs. Duke (21) (All-American, 1989) (33 carries)

MOST NET RUSHING YARDS BY A QUARTERBACK
180—(D) Mike Mosley, Texas A&M (28) vs. Southern Cal (47) (Bluebonnet, 1977) (20 carries)

HIGHEST AVERAGE PER RUSH
(Min. 9 Carries)
24.1—Dicky Maegle, Rice (28) vs. Alabama (6) (Cotton, 1954) (11 for 265)

MOST NET RUSHING YARDS BY TWO RUSHERS, SAME TEAM, OVER 100 YARDS RUSHING EACH
373—Woody Green (202) & Brent McClanahan (171), Arizona St. (49) vs. Missouri (35) (Fiesta, 1972)

MOST RUSHING TOUCHDOWNS
5—Barry Sanders, Oklahoma St. (62) vs. Wyoming (14) (Holiday, 1988) (runs of 33, 2, 67, 1, 10 yards); Neil Snow, Michigan (49) vs. Stanford (0) (Rose, 1902) (touchdowns counted as five-point scores)

Passing

MOST PASS ATTEMPTS
62—(D) Steve Clarkson, San Jose St. (25) vs. Toledo (27) (California, 1981) (completed 43)

MOST PASS COMPLETIONS
43—(D) Steve Clarkson, San Jose St. (25) vs. Toledo (27) (California, 1981) (attempted 62)

MOST CONSECUTIVE PASS COMPLETIONS
10—Rick Neuheisel, UCLA (45) vs. Illinois (9) (Rose, 1984) (22 of 31 for 298 yards and 4 touchdowns)

MOST NET PASSING YARDS
576—Ty Detmer, Brigham Young (39) vs. Penn St. (50) (Holiday, 1989) (42 of 59 with 2 interceptions)

MOST NET PASSING YARDS, ONE QUARTER
223—Browning Nagle, Louisville (34) vs. Alabama (7) (Fiesta, 1991) (1st quarter, 9 of 16)

MOST TOUCHDOWN PASSES THROWN
6—Chuck Long, Iowa (55) vs. Texas (17) (Freedom, 1984) (29 of 39 with no interceptions) (touchdown passes of 6, 11, 33, 49, 4, 15 yards)

MOST PASSES HAD INTERCEPTED
6—Bruce Lee, Arizona (10) vs. Auburn (34) (Sun, 1968) (6 of 24)

HIGHEST COMPLETION PERCENTAGE
(Min. 10 Attempts)
.917—Bobby Layne, Texas (40) vs. Missouri (27) (Cotton, 1946) (11 of 12 with no interceptions)

MOST YARDS PER PASS ATTEMPT
(Min. 10 Attempts)
19.4—Tony Rice, Notre Dame (34) vs. West Va. (21) (Fiesta, 1989) (11 for 213 yards)

MOST YARDS PER PASS COMPLETION
(Min. 7 Completions)
30.4—Tony Rice, Notre Dame (34) vs. West Va. (21) (Fiesta, 1989) (7 for 213 yards); Duke Carlisle, Texas (28) vs. Navy (6) (Cotton, 1964) (7 for 213 yards)

Receiving

MOST PASS RECEPTIONS
20—(D) Norman Jordan, Vanderbilt (28) vs. Air Force (36) (Hall of Fame, 1982) (173 yards); Walker Gillette, Richmond (49) vs. Ohio (42) (Tangerine, 1968) (242 yards)

MOST PASS RECEIVING YARDS
252—Andre Rison, Michigan St. (27) vs. Georgia (34) (Gator, Jan. 1, 1989) (9 catches)

HIGHEST AVERAGE PER CATCH
(Min. 3 Receptions)
52.3—Phil Harris, Texas (28) vs. Navy (6) (Cotton, 1964) (3 for 157 yards)

MOST TOUCHDOWNS RECEIVING
4—Fred Biletnikoff, Florida St. (36) vs. Oklahoma (19) (Gator, Jan. 2, 1965) (13 catches); (D) Bob McChesney, Hardin-Simmons (49) vs. Wichita St. (12) (Camellia, 1948) (8 catches)

Scoring

MOST POINTS SCORED
30—(D) Sheldon Canley, San Jose St. (48) vs. Central Mich. (24) (California, 1990) (5 touchdowns); Barry Sanders, Oklahoma St. (62) vs. Wyoming (14) (Holiday, 1988) (5 touchdowns)

MOST POINTS RESPONSIBLE FOR (TDS SCORED & PASSED FOR, EXTRA POINTS AND FGS)
40—Bobby Layne, Texas (40) vs. Missouri (27) (Cotton, 1946) (18 rushing, 12 passing, 6 receiving and 4 PATs)

MOST TOUCHDOWNS SCORED
5—(D) Sheldon Canley, San Jose St. (48) vs. Central Mich. (24) (California, 1990) (4 rushing, 1 receiving); Barry Sanders, Oklahoma St. (62) vs. Wyoming (14) (Holiday, 1988) (5 rushing); Neil Snow, Michigan (49) vs. Stanford (0) (Rose, 1902) (5 rushing five-point TDs)

MOST TWO-POINT CONVERSIONS
2—Ernie Davis, Syracuse (23) vs. Texas (14) (Cotton, 1960) (2 receptions)

Kicking

MOST FIELD GOALS ATTEMPTED
5—Arden Czyzewski, Florida (28) vs. Notre Dame (39) (Sugar, 1992) (5 made); Jess Atkinson, Maryland (23) vs. Tennessee (30) (Florida Citrus, 1983) (5 made); Bob White, Arkansas (16) vs. Georgia (2) (Sugar, 1969) (3 made); Tim Davis, Alabama (12) vs. Mississippi (7) (Sugar, 1964) (4 made)

MOST FIELD GOALS MADE
5—Arden Czyzewski, Florida (28) vs. Notre Dame (39) (Sugar, 1992) (26, 24, 36, 37, 24 yards); Jess Atkinson, Maryland (23) vs. Tennessee (30) (Florida Citrus, 1983) (18, 48, 31, 22, 26 yards)

MOST EXTRA-POINT KICK ATTEMPTS
9—Layne Talbot, Texas A&M (65) vs. Brigham Young (14) (Holiday, 1990) (9 made); Bobby Luna, Alabama (61) vs. Syracuse (6) (Orange, 1953) (7 made); (D) James Weaver, Centre (63) vs. Texas Christian (7) (Fort Worth Classic, 1921) (9 made)

MOST EXTRA-POINT KICKS MADE
9—Layne Talbot, Texas A&M (65) vs. Brigham Young (14) (Holiday, 1990) (9 attempts); (D) James Weaver, Centre (63) vs. Texas Christian (7) (Fort Worth Classic, 1921) (9 attempts)

MOST POINTS BY A KICKER
16—Arden Czyzewski, Florida (28) vs. Notre Dame (39) (Sugar, 1992) (5 FGs, 1 PAT)

Punting

MOST PUNTS
21—Everett Sweeney, Michigan (49) vs. Stanford (0) (Rose, 1902)

HIGHEST AVERAGE PER PUNT
(Min. 5 Punts)
52.7—Des Koch, Southern Cal (7) vs. Wisconsin (0) (Rose, 1953) (7 for 369 yards)

Punt Returns

MOST PUNT RETURNS
9—Buzy Rosenberg, Georgia (7) vs. North Caro. (3) (Gator, Dec. 31, 1971) (54 yards); Paddy Driscoll, Great Lakes (17) vs. Mare Island (0) (Rose, 1919) (115 yards)

MOST PUNT RETURN YARDS
136—Johnny Rodgers, Nebraska (38) vs. Alabama (6) (Orange, 1972) (6 returns)

HIGHEST PUNT RETURN AVERAGE
(Min. 3 Returns)
40.7—George Fleming, Washington (44) vs. Wisconsin (8) (Rose, 1960) (3 for 122 yards)

MOST TOUCHDOWNS ON PUNT RETURNS
2—James Henry, Southern Miss. (38) vs. UTEP (18) (Independence, 1988) (65 and 45 yards)

Kickoff Returns

MOST KICKOFF RETURNS
7—Dale Carter, Tennessee (17) vs. Penn St. (42) (Fiesta, 1992) (132 yards); Jeff Sydner, Hawaii (13) vs. Michigan St. (33) (Aloha, 1989) (174 yards); Homer Jones, Brigham Young (37) vs. Indiana (38) (Holiday, 1979) (126 yards)

MOST KICKOFF RETURN YARDS
203—Mike Fink, Missouri (35) vs. Arizona St. (49) (Fiesta, 1972) (6 returns)

HIGHEST KICKOFF RETURN AVERAGE
(Min. 2 Returns)
60.5—(D) Bob Smith, Texas A&M (40) vs. Georgia (20) (Presidential Cup, 1950) (2 for 121 yards)

MOST TOUCHDOWNS ON KICKOFF RETURNS
1—Many players tied

Interceptions

MOST INTERCEPTIONS MADE
4—Jim Dooley, Miami (Fla.) (14) vs. Clemson (0) (Gator, 1952); (D) Manuel Aja, Arizona St. (21) vs. Xavier (Ohio) (33) (Salad, 1950)

MOST INTERCEPTION RETURN YARDAGE
148—Elmer Layden, Notre Dame (27) vs. Stanford (10) (Rose, 1925) (2 interceptions)

All-Purpose Yards

(Includes All Runs From Scrimmage, Pass Receptions and All Returns)

MOST ALL-PURPOSE PLAYS
(Must Have at Least One Reception or Return)
47—Ron Jackson, Tulsa (28) vs. San Diego St. (17) (Freedom, 1991) (46 rushes, 1 reception)

MOST ALL-PURPOSE YARDS GAINED
(Must Have at Least One Reception or Return)
303—(D) Bob Smith, Texas A&M (40) vs. Georgia (20) (Presidential Cup, 1950) (160 rushing, 22 receiving, 121 kickoff returns)

Defensive Statistics

MOST TOTAL TACKLES MADE (INCLUDES ASSISTS)
31—Lee Roy Jordan, Alabama (17) vs. Oklahoma (0) (Orange, 1963)

MOST UNASSISTED TACKLES
18—Rod Smith, Notre Dame (39) vs. Florida (28) (Sugar, 1992)

MOST TACKLES MADE FOR LOSSES
5—Michael Jones, Colorado (17) vs. Brigham Young (20) (Freedom, 1988) (20 yards in losses); Jimmy Walker, Arkansas (10) vs. UCLA (10) (Fiesta, 1978)

MOST QUARTERBACK SACKS
4—Rusty Medearis, Miami (Fla.) (22) vs. Nebraska (0) (Orange, 1992); Bobby Bell, Missouri (17) vs. Brigham Young (21) (Holiday, 1983)

FUMBLE RECOVERIES
2—(D) Michael Stewart, Fresno St. (51) vs. Bowling Green (7) (California, 1985); Rod Kirby, Pittsburgh (7) vs. Arizona St. (28) (Fiesta, 1973)

BLOCKED KICKS
2—Carlton Williams, Pittsburgh (7) vs. Arizona St. (28) (Fiesta, 1973)

PASSES BROKEN UP
3—Tyrone Williams, Nebraska (16) vs. Florida St. (18) (Orange, 1994); John Herpin, Southern Cal (28) vs. Utah (21) (Freedom, 1993); Demouy Williams, Washington (24) vs. Tulane (12) (Independence, 1987)

Team Records

Totals for each team in both-team records are in brackets after the team's score.

Total Offense

MOST TOTAL PLAYS
96—North Caro. St. (10) vs. Arizona (17) (Copper, 1989) (310 yards)

MOST TOTAL PLAYS, BOTH TEAMS
171—Auburn (34) [82] & Arizona (10) [89] (Sun, 1968) (537 yards)

MOST YARDS GAINED
718—Arizona St. (49) vs. Missouri (35) (Fiesta, 1972) (452 rush, 266 pass)

MOST YARDS GAINED, BOTH TEAMS
1,143—(D) Southern Cal (47) [624] & Texas A&M (28) [519] (Bluebonnet, 1977) (148 plays)

HIGHEST AVERAGE GAINED PER PLAY
9.5—Louisville (34) vs. Alabama (7) (Fiesta, 1991) (60 plays for 571 yards)

FEWEST PLAYS
35—Tennessee (0) vs. Texas (16) (Cotton, 1953) (29 rush, 6 pass)

FEWEST PLAYS, BOTH TEAMS
107—Texas Christian (16) [54] & Marquette (6) [53] (Cotton, 1937)

FEWEST YARDS
Minus 21—U. of Mexico (0) vs. Southwestern (Tex.) (35) (Sun, 1945) (29 rush, -50 pass)

FEWEST YARDS, BOTH TEAMS
260—Randolph Field (7) [150] & Texas (7) [110] (Cotton, 1944)

LOWEST AVERAGE PER PLAY
0.9—Tennessee (0) vs. Texas (16) (Cotton, 1953) (35 plays for 32 yards)

Rushing

MOST RUSHING ATTEMPTS
87—Oklahoma (40) vs. Auburn (22) (Sugar, Jan. 1, 1972) (439 yards)

MOST RUSHING ATTEMPTS, BOTH TEAMS
122—(D) Southern Cal (47) [50] & Texas A&M (28) [72] (Bluebonnet, 1977) (864 yards); Mississippi St. (26) [68] & North Caro. (24) [54] (Sun, 1974) (732 yards)

MOST NET RUSHING YARDS
486—(D) Texas A&M (28) vs. Southern Cal (47) (Bluebonnet, 1977) (72 attempts)

MOST NET RUSHING YARDS, BOTH TEAMS
864—(D) Southern Cal (47) [378] & Texas A&M (28) [486] (Bluebonnet, 1977) (122 attempts)

HIGHEST RUSHING AVERAGE
(Min. 30 Attempts)
8.6—UCLA (31) vs. Brigham Young (10) (Freedom, 1986) (49 for 423 yards)

FEWEST RUSHING ATTEMPTS
12—(D) Vanderbilt (28) vs. Air Force (36) (Hall of Fame, 1982) (35 yards)

FEWEST RUSHING ATTEMPTS, BOTH TEAMS
57—Iowa (20) [36] & Wyoming (19) [21] (Holiday, 1987)

FEWEST RUSHING YARDS
Minus 45—Alabama (10) vs. Missouri (35) (Gator, 1968) (29 attempts)

FEWEST RUSHING YARDS, BOTH TEAMS
74—Tennessee (34) [86] & Air Force (13) [-12] (Sugar, 1971)

LOWEST RUSHING AVERAGE
(Min. 20 Attempts)
Minus 1.6—Alabama (10) vs. Missouri (35) (Gator, 1968) (29 for -45 yards)

RUSHING DEFENSE, FEWEST YARDS ALLOWED
Minus 45—Missouri (35) vs. Alabama (10) (Gator, 1968) (29 attempts)

Passing

MOST PASS ATTEMPTS
63—(D) San Jose St. (25) vs. Toledo (27) (California, 1981) (43 completions, 5 interceptions, 467 yards)

MOST PASS ATTEMPTS, BOTH TEAMS
92—Air Force (13) [46] & Tennessee (34) [46] (Sugar, 1971) (47 completions)

MOST PASS COMPLETIONS
43—(D) San Jose St. (25) vs. Toledo (27) (California, 1981) (63 attempts, 5 interceptions, 467 yards)

MOST PASS COMPLETIONS, BOTH TEAMS
56—Richmond (49) [39] & Ohio (42) [17] (Tangerine, 1968) (91 attempts)

MOST PASSING YARDS
576—Brigham Young (39) vs. Penn St. (50) (Holiday, 1989) (42 completions, 59 attempts, 2 interceptions)

MOST PASSING YARDS, BOTH TEAMS
808—Washington St. (31) [492] & Utah (28) [316] (Copper, 1992) (88 attempts)

MOST PASSES HAD INTERCEPTED
8—Arizona (10) vs. Auburn (34) (Sun, 1968)

MOST PASSES HAD INTERCEPTED, BOTH TEAMS
12—Arizona (10) [8] & Auburn (34) [4] (Sun, 1968)

MOST PASSES ATTEMPTED WITHOUT AN INTERCEPTION
57—(D) Western Mich. (30) vs. Fresno St. (35) (California, 1988) (24 completions)

MOST PASSES ATTEMPTED BY BOTH TEAMS WITHOUT AN INTERCEPTION
90—Bowling Green (35) [49] & Nevada (34) [41] (Las Vegas, 1992) (54 completions)

HIGHEST COMPLETION PERCENTAGE
(Min. 10 Attempts)
.929—Texas (40) vs. Missouri (27) (Cotton, 1946) (13 of 14, no interceptions, 234 yards)

MOST YARDS PER ATTEMPT
(Min. 10 Attempts)
21.7—Southern Cal (47) vs. Pittsburgh (14) (Rose, 1930) (13 for 282 yards)

MOST YARDS PER COMPLETION
(Min. 8 Completions)
35.2—Southern Cal (47) vs. Pittsburgh (14) (Rose, 1930) (8 for 282 yards)

FEWEST PASS ATTEMPTS
2—Air Force (38) vs. Mississippi St. (15) (Liberty, 1991) (1 completion); (D) Army (10) vs. Michigan St.

(6) (Cherry, 1984) (1 completion); West Va. (14) vs. South Caro. (3) (Peach, 1969) (1 completion)

FEWEST PASS ATTEMPTS, BOTH TEAMS
9—Fordham (2) [4] & Missouri (0) [5] (Sugar, 1942)

FEWEST PASS COMPLETIONS
0—13 teams tied (see Team Record Lists)

FEWEST PASS COMPLETIONS, BOTH TEAMS
3—Arizona St. (0) [0] & Catholic (0) [3] (Sun, 1940)

FEWEST PASSING YARDS
Minus 50—U. of Mexico (0) vs. Southwestern (Tex.) (35) (Sun, 1945) (2 completions, 9 attempts, 3 interceptions)

FEWEST PASSING YARDS, BOTH TEAMS
15—Rice (8) [-17] & Tennessee (0) [32] (Orange, 1947)

LOWEST COMPLETION PERCENTAGE
.000—13 teams tied (see Team Record Lists)

FEWEST YARDS PER PASS ATTEMPT
Minus 5.6—U. of Mexico (0) vs. Southwestern (Tex.) (35) (Sun, 1945) (9 for -50 yards)

FEWEST YARDS PER PASS COMPLETION (Min. 1 Completion)
Minus 25.0—U. of Mexico (0) vs. Southwestern (Tex.) (35) (Sun, 1945) (2 for -50 yards)

Scoring

MOST TOUCHDOWNS
9—Texas A&M (65) vs. Brigham Young (14) (Holiday, 1990) (5 rush, 4 pass); Alabama (61) vs. Syracuse (6) (Orange, 1953) (4 rush, 3 pass, 1 punt return, 1 interception return); (D) Centre (63) vs. Texas Christian (7) (Fort Worth Classic, 1921) (8 rush, 1 blocked punt recovery in end zone)

MOST TOUCHDOWNS, BOTH TEAMS
13—Richmond (49) [7] & Ohio (42) [6] (Tangerine, 1968)

MOST TOUCHDOWNS RUSHING
8—(D) Centre (63) vs. Texas Christian (7) (Fort Worth Classic, 1921)

MOST TOUCHDOWNS RUSHING, BOTH TEAMS
9—Arizona St. (48) [6] & North Caro. (26) [3] (Peach, 1970)

MOST TOUCHDOWNS PASSING
6—Iowa (55) vs. Texas (17) (Freedom, 1984)

MOST TOUCHDOWNS PASSING, BOTH TEAMS
8—Iowa (55) [6] & Texas (17) [2] (Freedom, 1984); Richmond (49) [4] & Ohio (42) [4] (Tangerine, 1968)

MOST FIELD GOALS MADE
5—Florida (28) vs. Notre Dame (39) (Sugar, 1992) (26, 24, 36, 37, 24 yards); Maryland (23) vs. Tennessee (30) (Florida Citrus, 1983) (18, 48, 31, 22, 26 yards)

MOST FIELD GOALS MADE, BOTH TEAMS
6—Notre Dame (39) [1] & Florida (28) [5] (Sugar, 1992); Syracuse (16) [3] & Auburn (16) [3] (Sugar, 1988); Maryland (23) [5] & Tennessee (30) [1] (Florida Citrus, 1983)

MOST POINTS, WINNING TEAM
65—Texas A&M vs. Brigham Young (14) (Holiday, 1990)

MOST POINTS, LOSING TEAM
45—Southern Methodist vs. Brigham Young (46) (Holiday, 1980)

MOST POINTS, BOTH TEAMS
91—Brigham Young (46) & Southern Methodist (45) (Holiday, 1980); Richmond (49) & Ohio (42) (Tangerine, 1968)

LARGEST MARGIN OF VICTORY
55—Alabama (61) vs. Syracuse (6) (Orange, 1953)

FEWEST POINTS, WINNING TEAM
2—Fordham vs. Missouri (0) (Sugar, 1942)

FEWEST POINTS, LOSING TEAM
0—By many teams

FEWEST POINTS, BOTH TEAMS
0—Texas Christian (0) & Air Force (0) (Cotton, 1959); Arkansas (0) & Louisiana St. (0) (Cotton, 1947); Arizona St. (0) & Catholic (0) (Sun, 1940); California (0) & Wash. & Jeff. (0) (Rose, 1922)

MOST POINTS SCORED IN FIRST HALF
42—Toledo (56) vs. Davidson (33) (Tangerine, 1969)

MOST POINTS SCORED IN SECOND HALF
45—Oklahoma St. (62) vs. Wyoming (14) (Holiday, 1988)

MOST POINTS SCORED IN FIRST HALF, BOTH TEAMS
49—Arizona St. (45) [21] & Florida St. (38) [28] (Fiesta, 1971); Toledo (56) [42] & Davidson (33) [7] (Tangerine, 1969)

MOST POINTS SCORED IN SECOND HALF, BOTH TEAMS
64—Penn St. (50) [38] & Brigham Young (39) [26] (Holiday, 1989)

MOST POINTS SCORED EACH QUARTER
1st: 25—Louisville (34) vs. Alabama (7) (Fiesta, 1991)
2nd: 28—Missouri (34) vs. Auburn (17) (Sun, 1973); Mississippi (41) vs. Georgia Tech (18) (Peach, 1971); Toledo (56) vs. Davidson (33) (Tangerine, 1969); Houston (49) vs. Miami (Ohio) (21) (Tangerine, 1962)
3rd: 31—Iowa (55) vs. Texas (17) (Freedom, 1984)
4th: 30—Oklahoma (40) vs. Houston (14) (Sun, 1981)

MOST POINTS SCORED EACH QUARTER, BOTH TEAMS
1st: 28—Indiana (38) [14] & Brigham Young (37) [14] (Holiday, 1979); Louisiana Tech (24) [21] & Louisville (14) [7] (Independence, 1977)
2nd: 40—Arizona St. (48) [14] & North Caro. (26) [26] (Peach, 1970)
3rd: 35—Oklahoma St. (62) [28] & Wyoming (14) [7] (Holiday, 1988)
4th: 37—Oklahoma (40) [30] & Houston (14) [7] (Sun, 1981)

First Downs

MOST FIRST DOWNS
36—Oklahoma (48) vs. Virginia (14) (Gator, Dec. 29, 1991) (16 rush, 18 pass, 2 penalty)

MOST FIRST DOWNS, BOTH TEAMS
61—Penn St. (50) [26] & Brigham Young (39) [35] (Holiday, 1989)

MOST FIRST DOWNS RUSHING
26—Oklahoma (40) vs. Auburn (22) (Sugar, Jan. 1, 1972)

MOST FIRST DOWNS RUSHING, BOTH TEAMS
36—Miami (Fla.) (46) [16] & Texas (3) [20] (Cotton, 1991); Colorado (47) [24] & Alabama (33) [12] (Liberty, 1969)

MOST FIRST DOWNS PASSING
27—Brigham Young (39) vs. Penn St. (50) (Holiday, 1989)

MOST FIRST DOWNS PASSING, BOTH TEAMS
30—(D) Fresno St. (29) [21] & Bowling Green (28) [9] (California, 1982); Richmond (49) [24] & Ohio (42) [6] (Tangerine, 1968)

MOST FIRST DOWNS BY PENALTY
6—Texas (3) vs. Miami (Fla.) (46) (Cotton, 1991)

MOST FIRST DOWNS BY PENALTY, BOTH TEAMS
8—Miami (Fla.) (46) [2] & Texas (3) [6] (Cotton, 1991)

FEWEST FIRST DOWNS
1—Alabama (29) vs. Texas A&M (21) (Cotton, 1942)

(1 pass); Arkansas (0) vs. Louisiana St. (0) (Cotton, 1947) (1 rush)

FEWEST FIRST DOWNS, BOTH TEAMS
10—Randolph Field (7) [7] & Texas (7) [3] (Cotton, 1944)

FEWEST FIRST DOWNS RUSHING
0—Florida (18) vs. Missouri (20) (Sugar, 1966); Navy (6) vs. Texas (28) (Cotton, 1964); Alabama (29) vs. Texas A&M (21) (Cotton, 1942)

FEWEST FIRST DOWNS RUSHING, BOTH TEAMS
3—Texas A&M (21) [3] & Alabama (29) [0] (Cotton, 1942)

FEWEST FIRST DOWNS PASSING
0—By 13 teams (see Team Record Lists)

FEWEST FIRST DOWNS PASSING, BOTH TEAMS
1—Alabama (10) [0] & Arkansas (3) [1] (Sugar, 1962)

Punting

MOST PUNTS
17—Duke (3) vs. Southern Cal (7) (Rose, 1939)

MOST PUNTS, BOTH TEAMS
28—Rice (8) [13] & Tennessee (0) [15] (Orange, 1947); Santa Clara (6) [14] & Louisiana St. (0) [14] (Sugar, 1938)

HIGHEST PUNTING AVERAGE (Min. 5 Punts)
53.9—Southern Cal (7) vs. Wisconsin (0) (Rose, 1953) (8 for 431)

FEWEST PUNTS
0—Oklahoma St. (62) vs. Wyoming (14) (Holiday, 1988); Oklahoma (41) vs. Wyoming (7) (Fiesta, 1976)

LOWEST PUNTING AVERAGE (Min. 3 Punts)
17.0—Nevada (34) vs. Bowling Green (35) (Las Vegas, 1992) (4 for 68 yards)

MOST PUNTS BLOCKED BY ONE TEAM
2—North Caro. St. (14) vs. Georgia (7) (Liberty, 1967)

Punt Returns

MOST PUNT RETURNS
9—Georgia (7) vs. North Caro. (3) (Gator, Dec. 31, 1971) (6.8 average)

MOST PUNT RETURN YARDS
136—Nebraska (38) vs. Alabama (6) (Orange, 1972) (6 returns)

HIGHEST PUNT RETURN AVERAGE (Min. 3 Returns)
33.0—Kent (18) vs. Tampa (21) (Tangerine, 1972) (3 for 99 yards)

Kickoff Returns

MOST KICKOFF RETURNS
10—Wyoming (14) vs. Oklahoma St. (62) (Holiday, 1988) (20.5 average)

MOST KICKOFF RETURN YARDS
259—UCLA (14) vs. Illinois (45) (Rose, 1947) (8 returns)

HIGHEST KICKOFF RETURN AVERAGE (Min. 3 Returns)
42.5—Tennessee (27) vs. Maryland (28) (Sun, 1984) (4 for 170 yards)

Fumbles

MOST FUMBLES
11—Mississippi (7) vs. Alabama (12) (Sugar, 1964) (lost 6)

BOWL/ALL-STAR RESULTS

MOST FUMBLES, BOTH TEAMS
17—Mississippi (7) [11] & Alabama (12) [6] (Sugar, 1964) (lost 9)

MOST FUMBLES LOST
6—By five teams (see Team Record Lists)

MOST FUMBLES LOST, BOTH TEAMS
9—Mississippi (7) [6] & Alabama (12) [3] (Sugar, 1964) (17 fumbles)

Penalties

MOST PENALTIES
20—(D) Fresno St. (35) vs. Western Mich. (30) (California, 1988) (166 yards)

MOST PENALTIES, BOTH TEAMS
29—McNeese St. (20) [13] & Tulsa (16) [16]

(Independence, 1976) (205 yards)

MOST YARDS PENALIZED
202—Miami (Fla.) (46) vs. Texas (3) (Cotton, 1991) (16 penalties)

MOST YARDS PENALIZED, BOTH TEAMS
270—Miami (Fla.) (46) [202] & Texas (3) [68] (Cotton, 1991)

FEWEST PENALTIES
0—By eight teams (see Team Record Lists)

FEWEST PENALTIES, BOTH TEAMS
3—In five games (see Team Record Lists)

FEWEST YARDS PENALIZED
0—By eight teams (see Team Record Lists)

FEWEST YARDS PENALIZED, BOTH TEAMS
10—Mississippi St. (12) [5] & Duquesne (13) [5] (Orange, 1937)

Wisconsin running back Brent Moss ran for 158 yards on 36 carries in the Badgers' 21-16 victory over UCLA in the Rose Bowl.

Individual Record Lists

Only official records after 1937 are included. Prior records are included if able to be substantiated. Each team's score is in parentheses after the team name. The year listed is the actual (calendar) year the game was played; the date is included if the bowl was played twice (i.e., January and December) during one calendar year. The list also includes discontinued bowls, marked with (D). Bowls are listed by the name of the bowl at the time it was played: The Florida Citrus Bowl was the Tangerine Bowl in 1947-82; the first Hall of Fame Bowl (1977-85) was called the All-American Bowl in 1986-90; the current Hall of Fame Bowl is played in Tampa, Fla., and started in 1986; the John Hancock Bowl was called the Sun Bowl in 1936-86 and the John Hancock Sun Bowl in 1987-88; and the Blockbuster Bowl changed its name to Carquest Bowl in 1993.

Total Offense

MOST PLAYS
74—(D) Tony Kimbrough, Western Mich. (30) vs. Fresno St. (35) (California, 1988)
67—Ty Detmer, Brigham Young (39) vs. Penn St. (50) (Holiday, 1989)
65—Shane Matthews, Florida (28) vs. Notre Dame (39) (Sugar, 1992)
65—Tony Eason, Illinois (15) vs. Alabama (21) (Liberty, 1982)
65—Buster O'Brien, Richmond (49) vs. Ohio (42) (Tangerine, 1968)
63—(D) Steve Clarkson, San Jose St. (25) vs. Toledo (27) (California, 1981)
62—Mark Young, Mississippi (20) vs. Texas Tech (17) (Independence, 1986)
62—Jack Trudeau, Illinois (29) vs. Army (31) (Peach, 1985)
62—Dennis Sproul, Arizona St. (30) vs. Penn St. (42) (Fiesta, 1977)
61—Jeff Blake, East Caro. (37) vs. North Caro. St. (34) (Peach, 1992)
61—Shawn Halloran, Boston College (27) vs. Georgia (24) (Hall of Fame, 1986)
61—Kim Hammond, Florida St. (17) vs. Penn St. (17) (Gator, 1967)
59—Vinny Testaverde, Miami (Fla.) (10) vs. Penn St. (14) (Fiesta, 1987)
59—Jim McMahon, Brigham Young (46) vs. Southern Methodist (45) (Holiday, 1980)
58—Terrence Jones, Tulane (12) vs. Washington (24) (Independence, 1987)
58—(D) Jerry Rhome, Tulsa (14) vs. Mississippi (7) (Bluebonnet, 1964)

MOST TOTAL YARDS
594—Ty Detmer, Brigham Young (39) vs. Penn St. (50) (Holiday, 1989) (576 pass)
486—Buster O'Brien, Richmond (49) vs. Ohio (42) (Tangerine, 1968) (447 pass)
481—Chuck Long, Iowa (55) vs. Texas (17) (Freedom, 1984) (461 pass)
474—Trent Dilfer, Fresno St. (30) vs. Colorado (41) (Aloha, 1993) (523 pass)
464—(D) Steve Clarkson, San Jose St. (25) vs. Toledo (27) (California, 1981) (467 pass)
446—(D) Whit Taylor, Vanderbilt (28) vs. Air Force (36) (Hall of Fame, 1982) (452 pass)
446—Jim McMahon, Brigham Young (46) vs. Southern Methodist (45) (Holiday, 1980) (446 pass)
431—Browning Nagle, Louisville (34) vs. Alabama (7) (Fiesta, 1991) (451 pass)
431—(D) Tony Kimbrough, Western Mich. (30) vs. Fresno St. (35) (California, 1988) (366 pass)
420—(D) Ralph Martini, San Jose St. (48) vs. Central Mich. (24) (California, 1990) (404 pass)
414—Peter Tom Willis, Florida St. (41) vs. Nebraska (17) (Fiesta, 1990) (422 pass)
413—Tony Eason, Illinois (15) vs. Alabama (21) (Liberty, 1982) (423 pass)
412—David Smith, Alabama (29) vs. Army (28) (John Hancock Sun, 1988) (412 pass)
410—Chuck Hartlieb, Iowa (23) vs. North Caro. St. (28) (Peach, Dec. 31, 1988) (428 pass)

408—Marc Wilson, Brigham Young (37) vs. Indiana (38) (Holiday, 1979) (380 pass)
407—Jack Trudeau, Illinois (29) vs. Army (31) (Peach, 1985) (401 pass)

HIGHEST AVERAGE PER PLAY (Minimum 10 Plays)
24.1—Dicky Maegle, Rice (28) vs. Alabama (6) (Cotton, 1954) (11 for 265 yards)
14.1—Marcus Dupree, Oklahoma (21) vs. Arizona St. (32) (Fiesta, 1983) (17 for 239 yards)
14.0—Bucky Richardson, Texas A&M (65) vs. Brigham Young (14) (Holiday, 1990) (23 for 322 yards)
12.2—Ger Schwedes, Syracuse (23) vs. Texas (14) (Cotton, 1960) (10 for 122 yards)
12.0—Tony Rice, Notre Dame (34) vs. West Va. (21) (Fiesta, 1989) (24 for 288 yards)
11.2—(D) Dwight Ford, Southern Cal (47) vs. Texas A&M (28) (Bluebonnet, 1977) (14 for 157 yards)
11.1—Browning Nagle, Louisville (34) vs. Alabama (7) (Fiesta, 1991) (39 for 431 yards)
10.8—Danny White, Arizona St. (49) vs. Missouri (35) (Fiesta, 1972) (27 for 291 yards)
10.8—(D) Ralph Martini, San Jose St. (48) vs. Central Mich. (24) (California, 1990) (39 for 420 yards)
10.5—Chuck Long, Iowa (55) vs. Texas (17) (Freedom, 1984) (46 for 481 yards)
10.4—Frank Sinkwich, Georgia (40) vs. Texas Christian (26) (Orange, 1942) (35 for 365 yards)
10.3—Chuck Curtis, Texas Christian (28) vs. Syracuse (27) (Cotton, 1957) (18 for 185 yards)

MOST TOUCHDOWNS RESPONSIBLE FOR (TDS SCORED & PASSED FOR)
6—Chuck Long, Iowa (55) vs. Texas (17) (Freedom, 1984) (6 pass)
6—Bobby Layne, Texas (40) vs. Missouri (27) (Cotton, 1946) (3 rush, 2 pass, 1 catch)
5—Jeff Blake, East Caro. (37) vs. North Caro. St. (34) (Peach, 1992) (4 pass, 1 rush)
5—Peter Tom Willis, Florida St. (41) vs. Nebraska (17) (Fiesta, 1990) (5 pass)
5—(D) Sheldon Canley, San Jose St. (48) vs. Central Mich. (24) (California, 1990) (4 rush, 1 pass)
5—Buster O'Brien, Richmond (49) vs. Ohio (42) (Tangerine, 1968) (4 pass, 1 rush)
5—Steve Tensi, Florida St. (36) vs. Oklahoma (19) (Gator, Jan. 2, 1965) (5 pass)
5—Neil Snow, Michigan (49) vs. Stanford (0) (Rose, 1902) (5 rush)

Rushing

MOST RUSHING ATTEMPTS
46—Ron Jackson, Tulsa (28) vs. San Diego St. (17) (Freedom, 1991) (211 yards)
41—Blake Ezor, Michigan St. (33) vs. Hawaii (13) (Aloha, 1989) (179 yards)
39—Raymont Harris, Ohio St. (28) vs. Brigham Young (21) (Holiday, 1993) (235 yards)
39—Errict Rhett, Florida (27) vs. North Caro. St. (10) (Gator, 1992) (182 yards)
39—Charlie Wysocki, Maryland (20) vs. Florida (35) (Tangerine, 1980) (159 yards)
39—Charles White, Southern Cal (17) vs. Ohio St. (16) (Rose, 1980) (247 yards)
37—(D) Charles Davis, Colorado (29) vs. Houston (17) (Bluebonnet, 1971) (202 yards)
36—Brent Moss, Wisconsin (21) vs. UCLA (16) (Rose, 1994) (158 yards)
36—Herschel Walker, Georgia (17) vs. Notre Dame (10) (Sugar, 1981) (150 yards)
36—Don McCauley, North Caro. (26) vs. Arizona St. (48) (Peach, 1970) (143 yards)
35—Blair Thomas, Penn St. (50) vs. Brigham Young (39) (Holiday, 1989) (186 yards)
35—Lorenzo White, Michigan St. (20) vs. Southern Cal (17) (Rose, 1988) (113 yards)
35—(D) Robert Newhouse, Houston (17) vs. Colorado (29) (Bluebonnet, 1971) (168 yards)
35—Ed Williams, West Va. (14) vs. South Caro. (3) (Peach, 1969) (208 yards)
35—Bob Anderson, Colorado (47) vs. Alabama (33) (Liberty, 1969) (254 yards)

34—Curtis Dickey, Texas A&M (28) vs. Iowa St. (12) (Hall of Fame, 1978) (276 yards)

34—Vic Bottari, California (13) vs. Alabama (0) (Rose, 1938) (137 yards)

34—Ernie Nevers, Stanford (10) vs. Notre Dame (27) (Rose, 1925) (114 yards)

MOST NET RUSHING YARDS

280—(D) James Gray, Texas Tech (49) vs. Duke (21) (All-American, 1989) (33 carries)

276—Curtis Dickey, Texas A&M (28) vs. Iowa St. (12) (Hall of Fame, 1978) (34 carries)

266—Gaston Green, UCLA (31) vs. Brigham Young (10) (Freedom, 1986) (33 carries)

265—Dicky Maegle, Rice (28) vs. Alabama (6) (Cotton, 1954) (11 carries)

254—Bob Anderson, Colorado (47) vs. Alabama (33) (Liberty, 1969) (35 carries)

250—Chuck Webb, Tennessee (31) vs. Arkansas (27) (Cotton, 1990) (26 carries)

247—Charles White, Southern Cal (17) vs. Ohio St. (16) (Rose, 1980) (39 carries)

239—Marcus Dupree, Oklahoma (21) vs. Arizona St. (32) (Fiesta, 1983) (17 carries)

235—Raymont Harris, Ohio St. (28) vs. Brigham Young (21) (Holiday, 1993) (39 carries)

235—Tyrone Wheatley, Michigan (38) vs. Washington (31) (Rose, 1993) (15 carries)

234—Jamie Morris, Michigan (28) vs. Alabama (24) (Hall of Fame, 1988) (23 carries)

227—Eric Ball, UCLA (45) vs. Iowa (28) (Rose, 1986) (22 carries)

225—Craig James, Southern Methodist (45) vs. Brigham Young (46) (Holiday, 1980) (23 carries)

222—Barry Sanders, Oklahoma St. (62) vs. Wyoming (14) (Holiday, 1988) (29 carries)

216—Floyd Little, Syracuse (12) vs. Tennessee (18) (Gator, 1966) (29 carries)

211—Ron Jackson, Tulsa (28) vs. San Diego St. (17) (Freedom, 1991) (46 carries)

208—Ed Williams, West Va. (14) vs. South Caro. (3) (Peach, 1969) (35 carries)

205—(D) Sammie Smith, Florida St. (27) vs. Indiana (13) (All-American, 1986) (25 carries)

205—Roland Sales, Arkansas (31) vs. Oklahoma (6) (Orange, 1978) (22 carries)

202—Tony Dorsett, Pittsburgh (27) vs. Georgia (3) (Sugar, 1979) (32 carries)

202—Woody Green, Arizona St. (49) vs. Missouri (35) (Fiesta, 1972) (25 carries)

202—(D) Charles Davis, Colorado (29) vs. Houston (17) (Bluebonnet, 1971) (37 carries)

MOST NET RUSHING YARDS BY A QUARTERBACK

180—(D) Mike Mosley, Texas A&M (28) vs. Southern Cal (47) (Bluebonnet, 1977) (20 carries)

164—Eddie Phillips, Texas (11) vs. Notre Dame (24) (Cotton, 1971) (23 carries)

136—(D) Nate Sassaman, Army (10) vs. Michigan St. (6) (Cherry, 1984) (28 carries)

133—(D) Eddie Wolgast, Arizona (13) vs. Drake (14) (Salad, 1949) (22 carries) (listed in newspaper accounts as halfback but also attempted 15 passes in game)

129—Rex Kern, Ohio St. (17) vs. Stanford (27) (Rose, 1971) (20 carries)

127—J. C. Watts, Oklahoma (24) vs. Florida St. (7) (Orange, 1980) (12 carries)

119—Bucky Richardson, Texas A&M (65) vs. Brigham Young (14) (Holiday, 1990) (12 carries)

113—Harry Gilmer, Alabama (34) vs. Southern Cal (14) (Rose, 1946)

107—Darrell Shepard, Oklahoma (40) vs. Houston (14) (Sun, 1981) (12 carries)

103—Major Harris, West Va. (33) vs. Oklahoma St. (35) (John Hancock Sun, 1987)

HIGHEST AVERAGE PER RUSH
(Minimum 9 Carries)

24.1—Dicky Maegle, Rice (28) vs. Alabama (6) (Cotton, 1954) (11 for 265 yards)

21.6—Bob Jeter, Iowa (38) vs. California (12) (Rose, 1959) (9 for 194 yards)

15.7—Tyrone Wheatley, Michigan (38) vs. Washington (31) (Rose, 1993) (15 for 235 yards)

14.2—(D) Gary Anderson, Arkansas (34) vs. Tulane (15) (Hall of Fame, 1980) (11 for 156 yards)

14.1—Mike Holovak, Boston College (21) vs. Alabama (37) (Orange, 1943) (10 for 141 yards)

14.1—Marcus Dupree, Oklahoma (21) vs. Arizona St. (32) (Fiesta, 1983) (17 for 239 yards)

12.6—Randy Baldwin, Mississippi (42) vs. Air Force (29) (Liberty, 1989) (14 for 177 yards)

12.6—Ben Barnett, Army (28) vs. Alabama (29) (John Hancock Sun, 1988) (14 for 177 yards)

12.3—George Smith, Texas Tech (28) vs. North Caro. (32) (Sun, 1972) (14 for 172 yards)

11.2—(D) Dwight Ford, Southern Cal (47) vs. Texas A&M (28) (Bluebonnet, 1977) (14 for 157 yards)

11.2—Elliott Walker, Pittsburgh (33) vs. Kansas (19) (Sun, 1975) (11 for 123 yards)

10.9—Rodney Hampton, Georgia (34) vs. Michigan St. (27) (Gator, Jan. 1, 1989) (10 for 109 yards)

10.8—Bobby Cavazos, Texas Tech (35) vs. Auburn (13) (Gator, Jan. 1, 1954) (13 for 141 yards)

10.6—J. C. Watts, Oklahoma (24) vs. Florida St. (7) (Orange, 1980) (12 for 127 yards)

10.5—Ray Brown, Mississippi (39) vs. Texas (7) (Sugar, 1958) (15 for 157 yards)

10.3—Eric Ball, UCLA (45) vs. Iowa (28) (Rose, 1986) (22 for 227 yards)

10.2—(D) Bill Tobin, Missouri (14) vs. Georgia Tech (10) (Bluebonnet, 1962) (11 for 112 yards)

10.2—Jamie Morris, Michigan (28) vs. Alabama (24) (Hall of Fame, 1988) (23 for 234 yards)

THREE RUSHERS, SAME TEAM, OVER 100 YARDS

366—Tony Dorsett (142), Elliott Walker (123) & Robert Haygood (QB) (101), Pittsburgh (33) vs. Kansas (19) (Sun, 1975)

TWO RUSHERS, SAME TEAM, OVER 100 YARDS

373—Woody Green (202) & Brent McClanahan (171), Arizona St. (49) vs. Missouri (35) (Fiesta, 1972)

365—(D) George Woodard (185) & Mike Mosley (QB) (180), Texas A&M (28) vs. Southern Cal (47) (Bluebonnet, 1977)

365—Bob Anderson (254) & Jim Bratten (111), Colorado (47) vs. Alabama (33) (Liberty, 1969)

347—Walter Packer (183) & Terry Vitrano (164), Mississippi St. (26) vs. North Caro. (24) (Sun, 1974)

343—(D) Charles White (186) & Dwight Ford (157), Southern Cal (47) vs. Texas A&M (28) (Bluebonnet, 1977)

330—Floyd Little (216) & Larry Csonka (114), Syracuse (12) vs. Tennessee (18) (Gator, 1966)

297—Monroe Eley (173) & Bob Thomas (124), Arizona St. (48) vs. North Caro. (26) (Peach, 1970)

292—Kelvin Bryant (148) & Ethan Horton (144), North Caro. (31) vs. Arkansas (27) (Gator, 1981)

291—Billy Sims (164) & J. C. Watts (QB) (127), Oklahoma (24) vs. Florida St. (7) (Orange, 1980)

288—Billy Sims (181) & Darrell Shepard (QB) (107), Oklahoma (40) vs. Houston (14) (Sun, 1981)

277—Willie Heston (170) & Neil Snow (107), Michigan (49) vs. Stanford (0) (Rose, 1902)

270—Anthony Brown (167) & Major Harris (QB) (103), West Va. (33) vs. Oklahoma St. (35) (John Hancock Sun, 1987)

253—Alois Blackwell (149) & Dyral Thomas (104), Houston (30) vs. Maryland (21) (Cotton, 1977)

246—T. Robert Hopkins (125) & Leonard Brown (121), Missouri (27) vs. Texas (40) (Cotton, 1946)

240—Jon Vaughn (128) & Ricky Powers (112), Michigan (35) vs. Mississippi (3) (Gator, Jan. 1, 1991)

237—James Rouse (134) & Barry Foster (103), Arkansas (27) vs. Tennessee (31) (Cotton, 1990)

237—Raymond Bybee (127) & Thomas Reamon (110), Missouri (34) vs. Auburn (17) (Sun, 1973)

230—Rex Kern (QB) (129) & John Brockington (101), Ohio St. (17) vs. Stanford (27) (Rose, 1971)

223—Bucky Richardson (QB) (119) & Darren Lewis (104), Texas A&M (65) vs. Brigham Young (14) (Holiday, 1990)

222—(D) Marshall Johnson (114) & Donnie McGraw (108), Houston (47) vs. Tulane (7) (Bluebonnet, 1973)

218—Travis Sims (113) & Michael Carter (105), Hawaii (27) vs. Illinois (17) (Holiday, 1992)

218—Steve Giese (111) & Bob Torrey (107), Penn St. (42) vs. Arizona St. (30) (Fiesta, 1977)

215—Jeff Atkins (112) & Reggie Dupard (103), Southern Methodist (27) vs. Notre Dame (20) (Aloha, 1984)

215—Allen Pinkett (111) & Chris Smith (104), Notre Dame (19) vs. Boston College (18) (Liberty, 1983)

204—Johnny "Ham" Jones (104) & Johnny "Jam" Jones (100), Texas (42) vs. Maryland (0) (Sun, 1978)

201—Jerome Heavens (101) & Vagas Ferguson (100), Notre Dame (38) vs. Texas (10) (Cotton, 1978)

MOST RUSHING TOUCHDOWNS

5—Barry Sanders, Oklahoma St. (62) vs. Wyoming (14) (Holiday, 1988) (runs of 33, 2, 67, 1, 10)

5—Neil Snow, Michigan (49) vs. Stanford (0) (Rose, 1902) (five-point scores)

4—Ron Jackson, Tulsa (28) vs. San Diego St. (17) (Freedom, 1991) (runs of 10, 6, 3, 4)

4—(D) Sheldon Canley, San Jose St. (48) vs. Central Mich. (24) (California, 1990) (runs of 5, 22, 59, 5)

4—(D) James Gray, Texas Tech (49) vs. Duke (21) (All-American, 1989) (runs of 2, 54, 18, 32)

4—Thurman Thomas, Oklahoma St. (35) vs. West Va. (33) (John Hancock Sun, 1987) (runs of 5, 9, 4, 4)

4—Eric Ball, UCLA (45) vs. Iowa (28) (Rose, 1986) (runs of 30, 40, 6, 32)

4—Terry Miller, Oklahoma St. (49) vs. Brigham Young (21) (Tangerine, 1976) (runs of 3, 78, 6, 1)

4—Sam Cunningham, Southern Cal (42) vs. Ohio St. (17) (Rose, 1973) (runs of 2, 1, 1, 1)

4—Woody Green, Arizona St. (49) vs. Missouri (35) (Fiesta, 1972) (runs of 2, 12, 17, 21)

4—Charles Cole, Toledo (56) vs. Davidson (33) (Tangerine, 1969) (runs of 1, 11, 16, 1)

4—(D) Gene Shannon, Houston (26) vs. Dayton (21) (Salad, 1952) (runs of 15, 19, 1, 10)

Passing

MOST PASS ATTEMPTS

63—Trent Dilfer, Fresno St. (30) vs. Colorado (41) (Aloha, 1993)

62—(D) Steve Clarkson, San Jose St. (25) vs. Toledo (27) (California, 1981)
61—(D) Sean Covey, Brigham Young (16) vs. Virginia (22) (All-American, 1987)
59—Ty Detmer, Brigham Young (39) vs. Penn St. (50) (Holiday, 1989)
58—Shane Matthews, Florida (28) vs. Notre Dame (39) (Sugar, 1992)
58—Buster O'Brien, Richmond (49) vs. Ohio (42) (Tangerine, 1968)
57—(D) Tony Kimbrough, Western Mich. (30) vs. Fresno St. (35) (California, 1988)
56—Gino Torretta, Miami (Fla.) (13) vs. Alabama (34) (Sugar, 1993)
55—Jack Trudeau, Illinois (29) vs. Army (31) (Peach, 1985)
55—Tony Eason, Illinois (15) vs. Alabama (21) (Liberty, 1982)
53—Tim Cowan, Washington (21) vs. Maryland (20) (Aloha, 1982)
53—Kim Hammond, Florida St. (17) vs. Penn St. (17) (Gator, 1967)
52—David Smith, Alabama (29) vs. Army (28) (John Hancock Sun, 1988)
52—Shawn Halloran, Boston College (27) vs. Georgia (24) (Hall of Fame, 1986)
51—Jeff Blake, East Caro. (37) vs. North Caro. St. (34) (Peach, 1992)
51—Danny McManus, Florida St. (31) vs. Nebraska (28) (Fiesta, 1988)
51—Chuck Hartlieb, Iowa (23) vs. North Caro. St. (28) (Peach, Dec. 31, 1988)
51—Craig Burnett, Wyoming (19) vs. Iowa (20) (Holiday, 1987)
51—Whit Taylor, Vanderbilt (28) vs. Air Force (36) (Hall of Fame, 1982)

MOST PASS COMPLETIONS
43—(D) Steve Clarkson, San Jose St. (25) vs. Toledo (27) (California, 1981)
42—Ty Detmer, Brigham Young (39) vs. Penn St. (50) (Holiday, 1989)
39—Buster O'Brien, Richmond (49) vs. Ohio (42) (Tangerine, 1968)
38—Jack Trudeau, Illinois (29) vs. Army (31) (Peach, 1985)
38—(D) Whit Taylor, Vanderbilt (28) vs. Air Force (36) (Hall of Fame, 1982)
37—Trent Dilfer, Fresno St. (30) vs. Colorado (41) (Aloha, 1993)
37—(D) Sean Covey, Brigham Young (16) vs. Virginia (22) (All-American, 1987)
37—Kim Hammond, Florida St. (17) vs. Penn St. (17) (Gator, 1967)
35—Tony Eason, Illinois (15) vs. Alabama (21) (Liberty, 1982)
33—David Smith, Alabama (29) vs. Army (28) (John Hancock Sun, 1988)
33—Tim Cowan, Washington (21) vs. Maryland (20) (Aloha, 1982)
33—Ron VanderKelen, Wisconsin (37) vs. Southern Cal (42) (Rose, 1963)
32—Jim McMahon, Brigham Young (46) vs. Southern Methodist (45) (Holiday, 1980)
31—Jeff Blake, East Caro. (37) vs. North Caro. St. (34) (Peach, 1992)
31—Stan White, Auburn (27) vs. Indiana (23) (Peach, 1990)
31—Shawn Halloran, Boston College (27) vs. Georgia (24) (Hall of Fame, 1986)
31—Mark Young, Mississippi (20) vs. Texas Tech (17) (Independence, 1986)
31—Bernie Kosar, Miami (Fla.) (37) vs. UCLA (39) (Fiesta, 1985)
31—John Congemi, Pittsburgh (23) vs. Ohio St. (28) (Fiesta, 1984)
31—(D) Jeff Tedford, Fresno St. (29) vs. Bowling Green (28) (California, 1982)

MOST CONSECUTIVE PASS COMPLETIONS
10—Rick Neuheisel, UCLA (45) vs. Illinois (9) (Rose, 1984)
9—Rob Johnson, Southern Cal (28) vs. Utah (21) (Freedom, 1993)
9—Bill Montgomery, Arkansas (16) vs. Georgia (2) (Sugar, 1969)
9—Glenn Dobbs, Tulsa (7) vs. Tennessee (14) (Sugar, 1943)
8—Billy Roland, Houston (49) vs. Miami (Ohio) (21) (Tangerine, 1962)
8—Bobby Layne, Texas (40) vs. Missouri (27) (Cotton, 1946)
8—Harry Gilmer, Alabama (26) vs. Duke (29) (Sugar, 1945)
7—Daniel Ford, Arizona St. (33) vs. Air Force (28) (Freedom, 1987)

MOST NET PASSING YARDS
(Followed by Comp.-Att.-Int.)
576—Ty Detmer, Brigham Young (39) vs. Penn St. (50) (Holiday, 1989) (42-59-2)
523—Trent Dilfer, Fresno St. (30) vs. Colorado (41) (Aloha, 1993) (37-63-1)
476—Drew Bledsoe, Washington St. (31) vs. Utah (28) (Copper, 1992) (30-46-1)
467—(D) Steve Clarkson, San Jose St. (25) vs. Toledo (27) (California, 1981) (43-62-5)
461—Chuck Long, Iowa (55) vs. Texas (17) (Freedom, 1984) (29-39-0)
452—(D) Whit Taylor, Vanderbilt (28) vs. Air Force (36) (Hall of Fame, 1982) (38-51-3)
451—Browning Nagle, Louisville (34) vs. Alabama (7) (Fiesta, 1991) (20-33-1)
447—Buster O'Brien, Richmond (49) vs. Ohio (42) (Tangerine, 1968) (39-58-2)
446—Jim McMahon, Brigham Young (46) vs. Southern Methodist (45) (Holiday, 1980) (32-49-1)
428—Chuck Hartlieb, Iowa (23) vs. North Caro. St. (28) (Peach, Dec. 31, 1988) (30-51-4)
423—Tony Eason, Illinois (15) vs. Alabama (21) (Liberty, 1982) (35-55-4)
422—Peter Tom Willis, Florida St. (41) vs. Nebraska (17) (Fiesta, 1990) (25-40-0)
412—David Smith, Alabama (29) vs. Army (28) (John Hancock Sun, 1988) (33-52-1)
404—(D) Ralph Martini, San Jose St. (48) vs. Central Mich. (24) (California, 1990) (27-36-1)
401—Jack Trudeau, Illinois (29) vs. Army (31) (Peach, 1985) (38-55-2)
401—Ron VanderKelen, Wisconsin (37) vs. Southern Cal (42) (Rose, 1963) (33-48-3)

MOST NET PASSING YARDS, ONE QUARTER
223—Browning Nagle, Louisville (34) vs. Alabama (7) (Fiesta, 1991) (1st, 9 of 16)
202—(D) Bret Stafford, Texas (32) vs. Pittsburgh (27) (Bluebonnet, 1987) (1st)

MOST TOUCHDOWN PASSES THROWN
6—Chuck Long, Iowa (55) vs. Texas (17) (Freedom, 1984) (29-39-0) (6, 11, 33, 49, 4, 15 yards)
5—Peter Tom Willis, Florida St. (41) vs. Nebraska (17) (Fiesta, 1990)
5—Steve Tensi, Florida St. (36) vs. Oklahoma (19) (Gator, Jan. 2, 1965)
4—Tony Sacca, Penn St. (42) vs. Tennessee (17) (Fiesta, 1992)
4—Jeff Blake, East Caro. (37) vs. North Caro. St. (34) (Peach, 1992)
4—Elvis Grbac, Michigan (35) vs. Mississippi (3) (Gator, Jan. 1, 1991)

4—Rick Neuheisel, UCLA (45) vs. Illinois (9) (Rose, 1984)
4—Jim McMahon, Brigham Young (46) vs. Southern Methodist (45) (Holiday, 1980)
4—Mark Hermann, Purdue (28) vs. Missouri (25) (Liberty, 1980)
4—(D) Rob Hertel, Southern Cal (47) vs. Texas A&M (28) (Bluebonnet, 1977)
4—Matt Cavanaugh, Pittsburgh (34) vs. Clemson (3) (Gator, 1977)
4—Gordon Slade, Davidson (33) vs. Toledo (55) (Tangerine, 1969)
4—Buster O'Brien, Richmond (49) vs. Ohio (42) (Tangerine, 1968)
4—Cleve Bryant, Ohio (42) vs. Richmond (49) (Tangerine, 1968)
4—Pete Beathard, Southern Cal (42) vs. Wisconsin (37) (Rose, 1963)

MOST PASSES HAD INTERCEPTED
(Followed by Comp.-Att.-Int.)
6—Bruce Lee, Arizona (10) vs. Auburn (34) (Sun, 1968) (6-24-6)
5—Wade Hill, Arkansas (15) vs. Georgia (24) (Independence, 1991) (12-31-5)
5—Kevin Murray, Texas A&M (12) vs. Ohio St. (28) (Cotton, 1987) (12-31-5)
5—Vinny Testaverde, Miami (Fla.) (10) vs. Penn St. (14) (Fiesta, 1987) (26-50-5)
5—Jeff Wickersham, Louisiana St. (10) vs. Nebraska (28) (Sugar, 1985) (20-38-5)
5—(D) Steve Clarkson, San Jose St. (25) vs. Toledo (27) (California, 1981) (43-62-5)
5—Terry McMillan, Missouri (3) vs. Penn St. (10) (Orange, 1970) (6-28-5)
5—Paul Gilbert, Georgia (6) vs. Nebraska (45) (Sun, 1969) (10-30-5)

HIGHEST COMPLETION PERCENTAGE
(Minimum 10 Attempts) (Followed by Comp.-Att.-Int.)
.917—Bobby Layne, Texas (40) vs. Missouri (27) (Cotton, 1946) (11-12-0)
.900—Ken Ploen, Iowa (35) vs. Oregon St. (19) (Rose, 1957) (9-10-0)
.846—Tom Sorley, Nebraska (21) vs. North Caro. (17) (Liberty, 1977) (11-13-0)
.833—Mike Gundy, Oklahoma St. (62) vs. Wyoming (14) (Holiday, 1988) (20-24-0)
.833—Richard Todd, Alabama (13) vs. Penn St. (6) (Sugar, 1975) (10-12-0)
.818—Bucky Richardson, Texas A&M (65) vs. Brigham Young (14) (Holiday, 1990) (9-11-0)
.806—Cale Gundy, Oklahoma (48) vs. Virginia (14) (Gator, Dec. 29, 1991) (25-31-0)
.800—Art Schlichter, Ohio St. (15) vs. Clemson (17) (Gator, 1978) (16-20-1)
.800—Jim Stevens, Georgia Tech (31) vs. Iowa St. (30) (Liberty, 1972) (12-15-0)
.800—Don Altman, Duke (7) vs. Arkansas (6) (Cotton, 1961) (12-15-0)
.800—Chuck Curtis, Texas Christian (28) vs. Syracuse (27) (Cotton, 1957) (12-15-0)
.789—Charles Ortmann, Michigan (14) vs. California (6) (Rose, 1951) (15-19-0)
.786—Mark Hermann, Purdue (28) vs. Missouri (25) (Liberty, 1980) (22-28-0)

MOST YARDS PER PASS ATTEMPT
(Minimum 10 Attempts)
19.4—Tony Rice, Notre Dame (34) vs. West Va. (21) (Fiesta, 1989) (11 for 213)
18.7—Frank Sinkwich, Georgia (40) vs. Texas Christian (26) (Orange, 1942) (13 for 243)
18.5—Bucky Richardson, Texas A&M (65) vs. Brigham Young (14) (Holiday, 1990) (11 for 203)
17.3—Don Rumley, New Mexico (34) vs. Denver (24) (Sun, 1946) (12 for 207)
16.4—(D) Rob Hertel, Southern Cal (47) vs. Texas A&M (28) (Bluebonnet, 1977) (15 for 246)
15.4—James Street, Texas (36) vs. Tennessee (13) (Cotton, 1969) (13 for 200)
14.2—Danny White, Arizona St. (28) vs. Pittsburgh (7) (Fiesta, 1973) (19 for 269)
13.7—Browning Nagle, Louisville (34) vs. Alabama (7) (Fiesta, 1991) (33 for 451)
13.6—Bob Churchich, Nebraska (28) vs. Alabama (39) (Orange, 1966) (17 for 232)
13.2—Bobby Layne, Texas (40) vs. Missouri (27) (Cotton, 1946) (12 for 158)

MOST YARDS PER PASS COMPLETION
(Minimum 7 Completions)
30.4—Tony Rice, Notre Dame (34) vs. West Va. (21) (Fiesta, 1989) (7 for 213)
30.4—Duke Carlisle, Texas (28) vs. Navy (6) (Cotton, 1964) (7 for 213)
28.6—James Street, Texas (36) vs. Tennessee (13) (Cotton, 1969) (7 for 200)
27.0—Frank Sinkwich, Georgia (40) vs. Texas Christian (26) (Orange, 1942) (9 for 243)

Receiving

MOST PASS RECEPTIONS
20—(D) Norman Jordan, Vanderbilt (28) vs. Air Force (36) (Hall of Fame, 1982) (173 yards)
20—Walker Gillette, Richmond (49) vs. Ohio (42) (Tangerine, 1968) (242 yards)
18—(D) Gerald Willhite, San Jose St. (25) vs. Toledo (27) (California, 1981) (124 yards)
15—(D) Stephone Paige, Fresno St. (29) vs. Bowling Green (28) (California, 1982) (246 yards)
14—J. J. Stokes, UCLA (16) vs. Wisconsin (21) (Rose, 1994) (176 yards)
14—Ron Sellers, Florida St. (17) vs. Penn St. (17) (Gator, 1967) (145 yards)
13—Fred Biletnikoff, Florida St. (36) vs. Oklahoma (19) (Gator, Jan. 2, 1965) (192 yards)
12—Luke Fisher, East Caro. (37) vs. North Caro. St. (34) (Peach, 1992) (144 yards)
12—Chuck Dicus, Arkansas (16) vs. Georgia (2) (Sugar, 1969) (169 yards)
12—Bill Moremen, Florida St. (17) vs. Penn St. (17) (Gator, 1967) (106 yards)
11—(D) Mark Szlachcic, Bowling Green (28) vs. Fresno St. (21) (California, 1991) (189 yards)
11—Ronnie Harmon, Iowa (28) vs. UCLA (45) (Rose, 1986) (102 yards)
11—David Mills, Brigham Young (24) vs. Michigan (17) (Holiday, 1984) (103 yards)

11—(D) Chip Otten, Bowling Green (28) vs. Fresno St. (29) (California, 1982) (76 yards)

11—(D) Anthony Hancock, Tennessee (28) vs. Wisconsin (21) (Garden State, 1981) (196 yards)

11—(D) James Ingram, Baylor (14) vs. Louisiana St. (7) (Bluebonnet, 1963) (163 yards)

11—Pat Richter, Wisconsin (37) vs. Southern Cal (42) (Rose, 1963) (163 yards)

10—Johnnie Morton, Southern Cal (28) vs. Utah (21) (Freedom, 1993) (147 yards)

10—Mike Blair, Ball St. (33) vs. Utah St. (42) (Las Vegas, 1993) (66 yards)

10—Matt Bellini, Brigham Young (39) vs. Penn St. (50) (Holiday, 1989) (124 yards)

10—Hart Lee Dykes, Oklahoma St. (62) vs. Wyoming (14) (Holiday, 1988) (163 yards)

10—(D) David Miles, Brigham Young (16) vs. Virginia (22) (All-American, 1987) (188 yards)

10—Lakei Heimuli, Brigham Young (7) vs. Ohio St. (10) (Florida Citrus, 1985)

10—Bobby Joe Edmonds, Arkansas (15) vs. Auburn (21) (Liberty, 1984)

10—David Williams, Illinois (9) vs. UCLA (45) (Rose, 1984)

10—Kelly Smith, Brigham Young (24) vs. Michigan (17) (Holiday, 1984) (88 yards)

10—Paul Skansi, Washington (21) vs. Maryland (20) (Aloha, 1982) (87 yards)

10—(D) Tim Kearse, San Jose St. (25) vs. Toledo (27) (California, 1981) (104 yards)

10—Scott Phillips, Brigham Young (46) vs. Southern Methodist (45) (Holiday, 1980) (81 yards)

10—Gordon Jones, Pittsburgh (34) vs. Clemson (3) (Gator, 1977) (163 yards)

10—Bobby Crockett, Arkansas (7) vs. Louisiana St. (14) (Cotton, 1966)

10—Ron Stover, Oregon (7) vs. Ohio St. (10) (Rose, 1958) (144 yards)

MOST PASS RECEIVING YARDS

252—Andre Rison, Michigan St. (27) vs. Georgia (34) (Gator, Jan. 1, 1989) (9 catches)

246—(D) Stephone Paige, Fresno St. (29) vs. Bowling Green (28) (California, 1982) (15 catches)

242—(D) Tony Jones, Texas (32) vs. Pittsburgh (27) (Bluebonnet, 1987) (8 catches)

242—Walker Gillette, Richmond (49) vs. Ohio (42) (Tangerine, 1968) (20 catches)

212—Phillip Bobo, Washington St. (31) vs. Utah (28) (Copper, 1992) (7 catches)

201—(D) Bob McChesney, Hardin-Simmons (49) vs. Wichita St. (12) (Camellia, 1948) (8 catches)

196—(D) Anthony Hancock, Tennessee (28) vs. Wisconsin (21) (Garden State, 1981) (11 catches)

192—Fred Biletnikoff, Florida St. (36) vs. Oklahoma (19) (Gator, Jan. 2, 1965) (13 catches)

189—(D) Mark Szlachcic, Bowling Green (28) vs. Fresno St. (21) (California, 1991) (11 catches)

188—(D) David Miles, Brigham Young (16) vs. Virginia (22) (All-American, 1987) (10 catches)

186—Greg Hudson, Arizona St. (28) vs. Pittsburgh (7) (Fiesta, 1973) (8 catches)

182—Rob Turner, Indiana (34) vs. South Caro. (10) (Liberty, 1988) (5 catches)

178—Ray Perkins, Alabama (34) vs. Nebraska (25) (Sugar, 1967) (7 catches)

177—Thomas Lewis, Indiana (20) vs. Virginia Tech (45) (Independence, 1993) (6 catches)

176—J. J. Stokes, UCLA (16) vs. Wisconsin (21) (Rose, 1994) (14 catches)

173—(D) Norman Jordan, Vanderbilt (28) vs. Air Force (36) (Hall of Fame, 1982) (20 catches)

172—Cris Carter, Ohio St. (17) vs. Southern Cal (20) (Rose, 1985) (9 catches)

HIGHEST AVERAGE PER CATCH
(Minimum 3 Receptions)

52.3—Phil Harris, Texas (28) vs. Navy (6) (Cotton, 1964) (3 for 157 yards)

36.4—Rob Turner, Indiana (34) vs. South Caro. (10) (Liberty, 1988) (5 for 182 yards)

36.3—Clarence Cannon, Boston College (31) vs. Virginia (13) (Carquest, 1994) (3 for 109 yards)

35.5—Rodney Harris, Kansas (23) vs. Brigham Young (20) (Aloha, 1992) (4 for 142 yards)

35.3—Anthony Carter, Michigan (15) vs. North Caro. (17) (Gator, 1979) (4 for 141 yards)

34.3—(D) Andre Alexander, Fresno St. (35) vs. Western Mich. (30) (California, 1988) (3 for 103 yards)

34.3—Ron Beverly, Arizona St. (49) vs. Missouri (35) (Fiesta, 1972) (3 for 103 yards)

34.0—Jimmy Cefalo, Penn St. (41) vs. Baylor (20) (Cotton, 1975) (3 for 102 yards)

33.7—J. D. Hill, Arizona St. (48) vs. North Caro. (26) (Peach, 1970) (3 for 101 yards)

33.3—Tony Buford, Indiana (34) vs. South Caro. (10) (Liberty, 1988) (3 for 100 yards)

33.2—Melvin Bonner, Baylor (20) vs. Arizona (15) (John Hancock, 1992) (5 for 166 yards)

33.2—Todd Dixon, Wake Forest (39) vs. Oregon (35) (Independence, 1992) (5 for 166 yards)

32.2—Cotton Speyrer, Texas (36) vs. Tennessee (13) (Cotton, 1969) (5 for 161 yards)

31.0—Olanda Truitt, Pittsburgh (31) vs. Texas A&M (28) (John Hancock, 1989) (4 for 124 yards)

31.0—Clay Brown, Brigham Young (46) vs. Southern Methodist (45) (Holiday, 1980) (5 for 155 yards)

MOST TOUCHDOWNS RECEIVING

4—Fred Biletnikoff, Florida St. (36) vs. Oklahoma (19) (Gator, Jan. 2, 1965) (13 catches)

4—(D) Bob McChesney, Hardin-Simmons (49) vs. Wichita St. (12) (Camellia, 1948) (8 catches)

3—(D) Ken Ealy, Central Mich. (24) vs. San Jose St. (48) (California, 1990) (7 catches)

3—Wendell Davis, Louisiana St. (30) vs. South Caro. (13) (Gator, 1987) (9 catches)

3—Anthony Allen, Washington (21) vs. Maryland (20) (Aloha, 1982) (8 catches)

3—(D) Norman Jordan, Vanderbilt (28) vs. Air Force (36) (Hall of Fame, 1982) (20 catches)

3—(D) Dwayne Dixon, Florida (24) vs. Arkansas (28) (Bluebonnet, 1982) (8 catches)

3—(D) Mervyn Fernandez, San Jose St. (25) vs. Toledo (27) (California, 1981) (9 catches)

3—Clay Brown, Brigham Young (46) vs. Southern Methodist (45) (Holiday, 1980) (5 catches)

3—Elliott Walker, Pittsburgh (34) vs. Clemson (3) (Gator, 1977) (6 catches)

3—Rhett Dawson, Florida St. (38) vs. Arizona St. (45) (Fiesta, 1971) (8 catches)

3—George Hannen, Davidson (33) vs. Toledo (56) (Tangerine, 1969)

3—Todd Snyder, Richmond (49) vs. Ohio (42) (Tangerine, 1968)

Scoring

MOST POINTS SCORED

30—(D) Sheldon Canley, San Jose St. (48) vs. Central Mich. (24) (California, 1990) (5 TDs)

30—Barry Sanders, Oklahoma St. (62) vs. Wyoming (14) (Holiday, 1988) (5 TDs)

28—Bobby Layne, Texas (40) vs. Missouri (27) (Cotton, 1946) (4 TDs, 4 PATs)

25—Neil Snow, Michigan (49) vs. Stanford (0) (Rose, 1902) (5 five-point TDs)

24—Ron Jackson, Tulsa (28) vs. San Diego St. (17) (Freedom, 1991) (4 TDs)

24—(D) James Gray, Texas Tech (49) vs. Duke (21) (All-American, 1989) (4 TDs)

24—Thurman Thomas, Oklahoma St. (35) vs. West Va. (33) (John Hancock Sun, 1987) (4 TDs)

24—Eric Ball, UCLA (45) vs. Iowa (28) (Rose, 1986) (4 TDs)

24—Terry Miller, Oklahoma St. (49) vs. Brigham Young (21) (Tangerine, 1976) (4 TDs)

24—Sam Cunningham, Southern Cal (42) vs. Ohio St. (17) (Rose, 1973) (4 TDs)

24—Johnny Rodgers, Nebraska (40) vs. Notre Dame (6) (Orange, 1973) (4 TDs)

24—Woody Green, Arizona St. (49) vs. Missouri (35) (Fiesta, 1972) (4 TDs)

24—Charles Cole, Toledo (56) vs. Davidson (33) (Tangerine, 1969) (4 TDs)

24—Fred Biletnikoff, Florida St. (36) vs. Oklahoma (19) (Gator, Jan. 2, 1965) (4 TDs)

24—Joe Lopasky, Houston (49) vs. Miami (Ohio) (21) (Tangerine, 1962) (4 TDs)

24—(D) Gene Shannon, Houston (26) vs. Dayton (21) (Salad, 1952) (4 TDs)

24—(D) Bob McChesney, Hardin-Simmons (49) vs. Wichita St. (12) (Camellia, 1948) (4 TDs)

MOST POINTS RESPONSIBLE FOR
(TDs Scored & Passed For, Extra Points and FGs)

40—Bobby Layne, Texas (40) vs. Missouri (27) (Cotton, 1946) (18 rush, 12 pass, 6 receiving and 4 PATs)

36—Chuck Long, Iowa (55) vs. Texas (17) (Freedom, 1984) (36 pass)

30—Jeff Blake, East Caro. (37) vs. North Caro. St. (34) (Peach, 1992) (24 pass, 6 rush)

30—(D) Sheldon Canley, San Jose St. (48) vs. Central Mich. (24) (California, 1990) (24 rush, 6 receiving)

30—Peter Tom Willis, Florida St. (41) vs. Nebraska (17) (Fiesta, 1990) (30 pass)

30—Barry Sanders, Oklahoma St. (62) vs. Wyoming (14) (Holiday, 1988) (30 rush)

30—Johnny Rodgers, Nebraska (40) vs. Notre Dame (6) (Orange, 1973) (18 rush, 6 pass, 6 receiving)

30—Steve Tensi, Florida St. (36) vs. Oklahoma (19) (Gator, Jan. 2, 1965) (30 pass)

MOST TOUCHDOWNS

5—(D) Sheldon Canley, San Jose St. (48) vs. Central Mich. (24) (California, 1990) (4 rush, 1 catch)

5—Barry Sanders, Oklahoma St. (62) vs. Wyoming (14) (Holiday, 1988) (5 rush)

5—Neil Snow, Michigan (49) vs. Stanford (0) (Rose, 1902) (5 rush five-point TDs)

4—Ron Jackson, Tulsa (28) vs. San Diego St. (17) (Freedom, 1991) (4 rush)

4—(D) James Gray, Texas Tech (49) vs. Duke (21) (All-American, 1989) (4 rush)

4—Thurman Thomas, Oklahoma St. (35) vs. West Va. (33) (John Hancock Sun, 1987) (4 rush)

4—Eric Ball, UCLA (45) vs. Iowa (28) (Rose, 1986) (4 rush)

4—Terry Miller, Oklahoma St. (49) vs. Brigham Young (21) (Tangerine, 1976) (4 rush)

4—Sam Cunningham, Southern Cal (42) vs. Ohio St. (17) (Rose, 1973) (4 rush)

4—Johnny Rodgers, Nebraska (40) vs. Notre Dame (6) (Orange, 1973) (3 rush, 1 catch)

4—Woody Green, Arizona St. (49) vs. Missouri (35) (Fiesta, 1972) (4 rush)

4—Charles Cole, Toledo (56) vs. Davidson (33) (Tangerine, 1969) (4 rush)

4—Fred Biletnikoff, Florida St. (36) vs. Oklahoma (19) (Gator, Jan. 2, 1965) (4 catch)

4—Joe Lopasky, Houston (49) vs. Miami (Ohio) (21) (Tangerine, 1962) (2 rush, 1 catch, 1 punt return)

4—(D) Gene Shannon, Houston (26) vs. Dayton (21) (Salad, 1952) (4 rush)

4—(D) Bob McChesney, Hardin-Simmons (49) vs. Wichita St. (12) (Camellia, 1948) (4 catch)

4—Bobby Layne, Texas (40) vs. Missouri (27) (Cotton, 1946) (3 rush, 1 catch)

4—(D) Alvin McMillin, Centre (63) vs. Texas Christian (7) (Fort Worth Classic, 1921) (4 rush)

MOST TWO-POINT CONVERSIONS

2—Ernie Davis, Syracuse (23) vs. Texas (14) (Cotton, 1960) (2 pass receptions)

BOWL/ALL-STAR RESULTS

Kicking

MOST FIELD GOALS ATTEMPTED

5—Scott Bentley, Florida St. (18) vs. Nebraska (16) (Orange, 1994) (4 made)
5—Arden Czyzewski, Florida (28) vs. Notre Dame (39) (Sugar, 1992) (5 made)
5—Jess Atkinson, Maryland (23) vs. Tennessee (30) (Florida Citrus, 1983) (5 made)
5—Bob White, Arkansas (16) vs. Georgia (2) (Sugar, 1969) (3 made)
5—Tim Davis, Alabama (12) vs. Mississippi (7) (Sugar, 1964) (4 made)
4—Carlos Huerta, Miami (Fla.) (22) vs. Nebraska (0) (Orange, 1992) (3 made)
4—Greg Worker, Wyoming (19) vs. Iowa (20) (Holiday, 1987) (2 made)
4—Tim Lashar, Oklahoma (25) vs. Penn St. (10) (Orange, 1986) (4 made)
4—Kent Bostrom, Arizona St. (17) vs. Arkansas (18) (Holiday, 1985) (3 made)
4—(D) Todd Gregoire, Wisconsin (19) vs. Kentucky (20) (Hall of Fame, 1984) (4 made)
4—Bill Capece, Florida St. (17) vs. Oklahoma (18) (Orange, 1981) (1 made)
4—David Hardy, Texas A&M (33) vs. Oklahoma St. (16) (Independence, 1981)(4 made)
4—Bob Lucchesi, Missouri (19) vs. Southern Miss. (17) (Tangerine, 1981) (4 made)
4—Paul Woodside, West Va. (26) vs. Florida (6) (Peach, Dec. 31, 1981) (4 made)
4—(D) Fuad Reveiz, Tennessee (28) vs. Wisconsin (21) (Garden State, 1981) (2 made)
4—Dale Castro, Maryland (20) vs. Florida (35) (Tangerine, 1980) (4 made)
4—Brent Johnson, Brigham Young (37) vs. Indiana (38) (Holiday, 1979) (3 made)
4—Ricky Townsend, Tennessee (19) vs. Texas Tech (28) (Gator, 1973) (2 made)
4—Paul Rogers, Nebraska (45) vs. Georgia (6) (Sun, 1969) (4 made)

MOST FIELD GOALS MADE

5—Arden Czyzewski, Florida (28) vs. Notre Dame (39) (Sugar, 1992) (26, 24, 36, 37, 24 yards)
5—Jess Atkinson, Maryland (23) vs. Tennessee (30) (Florida Citrus, 1983) (18, 48, 31, 22, 26 yards)
4—Scott Bentley, Florida St. (18) vs. Nebraska (16) (Orange, 1994) (34, 25, 39, 22 yards)
4—Tim Lashar, Oklahoma (25) vs. Penn St. (10) (Orange, 1986) (26, 31, 21, 22 yards)
4—(D) Todd Gregoire, Wisconsin (19) vs. Kentucky (20) (Hall of Fame, 1984) (40, 27, 20, 40 yards)
4—David Hardy, Texas A&M (33) vs. Oklahoma St. (16) (Independence, 1981) (33, 32, 50, 18 yards)
4—Paul Woodside, West Va. (26) vs. Florida (6) (Peach, Dec. 31, 1981) (35, 42, 49, 24 yards)
4—Bob Lucchesi, Missouri (19) vs. Southern Miss. (17) (Tangerine, 1981) (45, 41, 30, 28 yards)
4—Dale Castro, Maryland (20) vs. Florida (35) (Tangerine, 1980) (35, 27, 27, 43 yards)
4—Paul Rogers, Nebraska (45) vs. Georgia (6) (Sun, 1969) (50, 32, 42, 37 yards, all in 1st quarter)
4—Tim Davis, Alabama (12) vs. Mississippi (7) (Sugar, 1964) (31, 46, 22, 48 yards)

MOST EXTRA-POINT KICK ATTEMPTS

9—Layne Talbot, Texas A&M (65) vs. Brigham Young (14) (Holiday, 1990) (9 made)
9—Bobby Luna, Alabama (61) vs. Syracuse (6) (Orange, 1953) (7 made)
9—(D) James Weaver, Centre (63) vs. Texas Christian (7) (Fort Worth Classic, 1921) (9 made)
8—Cary Blanchard, Oklahoma St. (62) vs. Wyoming (14) (Holiday, 1988) (8 made)
8—Ken Crots, Toledo (56) vs. Davidson (33) (Tangerine, 1969) (8 made)
7—Scott Blanton, Oklahoma (48) vs. Virginia (14) (Gator, Dec. 29, 1991) (6 made)
7—(D) Barry Belli, Fresno St. (51) vs. Bowling Green (7) (California, 1985) (7 made)
7—Tom Nichol, Iowa (55) vs. Texas (17) (Freedom, 1984) (7 made)
7—Juan Cruz, Arizona St. (49) vs. Missouri (35) (Fiesta, 1972) (7 made)
7—Ron Sewell, North Caro. St. (49) vs. West Va. (13) (Peach, 1972) (7 made)
7—Don Ekstrand, Arizona St. (48) vs. North Caro. (26) (Peach, 1970) (6 made)
7—Bill McMillan, Houston (49) vs. Miami (Ohio) (21) (Tangerine, 1962) (7 made)
7—Jesse Whittenton, UTEP (47) vs. Florida St. (20) (Sun, 1955) (5 made)
7—Jim Brieske, Michigan (49) vs. UCLA (0) (Rose, 1948) (7 made)
7—(D) Pat Bailey, Hardin-Simmons (49) vs. Wichita St. (12) (Camellia, 1948) (7 made)

MOST EXTRA-POINT KICKS MADE

9—Layne Talbot, Texas A&M (65) vs. Brigham Young (14) (Holiday, 1990) (9 attempts)
9—(D) James Weaver, Centre (63) vs. Texas Christian (7) (Fort Worth Classic, 1921) (9 attempts)
8—Cary Blanchard, Oklahoma St. (62) vs. Wyoming (14) (Holiday, 1988) (8 attempts)
8—Ken Crots, Toledo (56) vs. Davidson (33) (Tangerine, 1969) (8 attempts)
7—(D) Barry Belli, Fresno St. (51) vs. Bowling Green (7) (California, 1985) (7 attempts)
7—Tom Nichol, Iowa (55) vs. Texas (17) (Freedom, 1984) (7 attempts)
7—Juan Cruz, Arizona St. (49) vs. Missouri (35) (Fiesta, 1972) (7 attempts)
7—Ron Sewell, North Caro. St. (49) vs. West Va. (13) (Peach, 1972) (7 attempts)
7—Bill McMillan, Houston (49) vs. Miami (Ohio) (21) (Tangerine, 1962) (7 attempts)
7—Bobby Luna, Alabama (61) vs. Syracuse (6) (Orange, 1953) (9 attempts)
7—Jim Brieske, Michigan (49) vs. UCLA (0) (Rose, 1948) (7 attempts)
7—(D) Pat Bailey, Hardin-Simmons (49) vs. Wichita St. (12) (Camellia, 1948) (7 attempts)

MOST POINTS BY A KICKER

16—Arden Czyzewski, Florida (28) vs. Notre Dame (39) (Sugar, 1992) (5 FGs, 1 PAT)
15—Jess Atkinson, Maryland (23) vs. Tennessee (30) (Florida Citrus, 1983) (5 FGs)
15—David Hardy, Texas A&M (33) vs. Oklahoma St. (16) (Independence, 1981) (4 FGs, 3 PATs)
15—Paul Rogers, Nebraska (45) vs. Georgia (6) (John Hancock, 1969) (4 FGs, 3 PATs)
14—Cary Blanchard, Oklahoma St. (62) vs. Wyoming (14) (Holiday, 1988) (2 FGs, 8 PATs)
14—Paul Woodside, West Va. (26) vs. Florida (6) (Peach, Dec. 31, 1981) (4 FGs, 2 PATs)
13—Tim Lashar, Oklahoma (25) vs. Penn. St. (10) (Orange, 1986) (4 FGs, 1 PAT)
13—John Lee, UCLA (39) vs. Miami (Fla.) (37) (Fiesta, 1985) (3 FGs, 4 PATs)
13—Tom Nichol, Iowa (55) vs. Texas (17) (Freedom, 1984) (2 FGs, 7 PATs)
13—(D) Todd Gregoire, Wisconsin (19) vs. Kentucky (20) (Hall of Fame, 1984) (4 FGs, 1 PAT)
13—Bob Lucchesi, Missouri (19) vs. Southern Miss. (17) (Tangerine, 1981) (4 FGs, 1 PAT)
13—Dave Johnson, Brigham Young (37) vs. Indiana (38) (Holiday, 1979) (3 FGs, 4 PATs)
12—Scott Bentley, Florida St. (18) vs. Nebraska (16) (Orange, 1994) (4 FGs)
12—Chris Gardocki, Clemson (30) vs. Illinois (0) (Hall of Fame, 1991) (3 FGs, 3 PATs)
12—Ray Tarasi, Penn St. (50) vs. Brigham Young (39) (Holiday, 1989) (3 FGs, 3 PATs)
12—Luis Zendejas, Arizona St. (32) vs. Oklahoma (21) (Fiesta, 1983) (3 FGs, 3 PATs)
12—Dale Castro, Maryland (20) vs. Florida (35) (Tangerine, 1980) (4 FGs)
12—Nathan Ritter, North Caro. St. (30) vs. Pittsburgh (17) (Tangerine, 1978) (3 FGs, 3 PATs)
12—Buckey Berrey, Alabama (36) vs. UCLA (6) (Liberty, 1976) (3 FGs, 3 PATs)
12—Al Vitiello, Penn St. (30) vs. Texas (6) (Cotton, 1972) (3 FGs, 3 PATs)
12—Frank Fontes, Florida St. (38) vs. Arizona St. (45) (Fiesta, 1971) (3 FGs, 3 PATs)

Punting

MOST PUNTS

21—Everett Sweeney, Michigan (49) vs. Stanford (0) (Rose, 1902)
16—Lem Pratt, New Mexico St. (14) vs. Hardin-Simmons (14) (Sun, 1936) (38.4 average)
14—Sammy Baugh, Texas Christian (3) vs. Louisiana St. (2) (Sugar, 1936)
13—Hugh Keeney, Rice (8) vs. Tennessee (0) (Orange, 1947)
13—N. A. Keithley, Tulsa (6) vs. Texas Tech (0) (Sun, 1942) (37.0 average)
13—Hugh McCullough, Oklahoma (0) vs. Tennessee (17) (Orange, 1939) (40.6 average)
13—Tyler, Hardin-Simmons (14) vs. New Mexico St. (14) (Sun, 1936) (45.2 average)
13—(D) Tom Murphy, Arkansas (7) vs. Centenary (7) (Dixie Classic, 1934) (44.0 average)
12—Mitch Berger, Colorado (25) vs. Alabama (30) (Blockbuster, 1991) (41.0 average)
12—Bob Parsons, Penn St. (10) vs. Missouri (3) (Orange, 1970) (42.6 average)
12—Jim Callahan, Texas Tech (0) vs. Tulsa (6) (Sun, 1942) (43.0 average)
12—Mike Palm, Penn St. (3) vs. Southern Cal (14) (Rose, 1923)

HIGHEST AVERAGE PER PUNT
(Minimum 5 Punts)

52.7—Des Koch, Southern Cal (7) vs. Wisconsin (0) (Rose, 1953) (7 for 369 yards) (adjusted to current statistical rules)
52.4—Mike Sochko, Maryland (21) vs. Houston (30) (Cotton, 1977) (5 for 262 yards)
51.0—Chris Clauss, Penn St. (10) vs. Clemson (35) (Florida Citrus, 1988) (5 for 255 yards)
50.0—Dana Moore, Mississippi St. (17) vs. Nebraska (31) (Sun, 1980) (5 for 250 yards)
49.2—(D) Mark Simon, Air Force (24) vs. Texas (16) (Bluebonnet, 1985) (11 for 541 yards)
49.2—Allen Meacham, Arkansas (3) vs. UCLA (17) (Cotton, 1989) (6 for 295 yards)
49.0—Jim DiGuilio, Indiana (24) vs. Baylor (0) (Copper, 1991) (6 for 294 yards)
49.0—(D) Dana Moore, Mississippi St. (10) vs. Kansas (0) (Hall of Fame, 1981) (9 for 441 yards)
48.0—Dan Eichloff, Kansas (23) vs. Brigham Young (20) (Aloha, 1992) (8 for 384 yards)
47.9—Doug Helkowski, Penn St. (42) vs. Tennessee (17) (Fiesta, 1992) (9 for 431 yards)
47.8—(D) Kevin Buenafe, UCLA (14) vs. Michigan (33) (Bluebonnet, 1981) (8 for 382 yards)
47.6—Todd Thomsen, Oklahoma (42) vs. Arkansas (8) (Orange, 1987) (5 for 238 yards)
47.5—Jerry Dowd, St. Mary's (Cal.) (20) vs. Texas Tech (13) (Cotton, 1939) (11 for 523 yards)
47.4—Jason Bender, Georgia Tech (18) vs. Stanford (17) (Aloha, 1991) (7 for 332 yards)
47.4—(D) Mike Mancini, Fresno St. (51) vs. Bowling Green (7) (California, 1985) (7 for 332 yards)

47.4—(D) Jimmy Colquitt, Tennessee (28) vs. Wisconsin (21) (Garden State, 1981) (5 for 237 yards)

Punt Returns

MOST PUNT RETURNS
9—Buzy Rosenberg, Georgia (7) vs. North Caro. (3) (Gator, Dec. 31, 1971) (54 yards)
9—Paddy Driscoll, Great Lakes (17) vs. Mare Island (0) (Rose, 1919) (115 yards)
8—Thomas Lewis, Indiana (20) vs. Virginia Tech (45) (Independence, 1993) (58 yards)
6—Dale Carter, Tennessee (17) vs. Penn St. (42) (Fiesta, 1992)
6—Joey Smith, Louisville (34) vs. Alabama (7) (Fiesta, 1991) (35 yards)
6—David Palmer, Alabama (30) vs. Colorado (25) (Blockbuster, 1991) (74 yards)
6—(D) Hesh Colar, San Jose St. (48) vs. Central Mich. (24) (California, 1990)
6—David Kintigh, Miami (Fla.) (10) vs. Penn St. (14) (Fiesta, 1987) (32 yards)
6—(D) Eric Metcalf, Texas (16) vs. Air Force (24) (Bluebonnet, 1985) (49 yards)
6—Vai Sikahema, Brigham Young (7) vs. Ohio St. (10) (Florida Citrus, 1985)
6—Ray Horton, Washington (21) vs. Maryland (20) (Aloha, 1982) (28 yards)
6—Bill Gribble, Washington St. (36) vs. Brigham Young (38) (Holiday, 1981) (39 yards)
6—Johnny Rodgers, Nebraska (38) vs. Alabama (6) (Orange, 1972) (136 yards)
6—Rick Sygar, Michigan (34) vs. Oregon St. (7) (Rose, 1965) (50 yards)
6—Billy Hair, Clemson (0) vs. Miami (Fla.) (14) (Gator, 1952) (73 yards)
6—Don Zimmerman, Tulane (12) vs. Southern Cal (21) (Rose, 1932)

MOST PUNT RETURN YARDS
136—Johnny Rodgers, Nebraska (38) vs. Alabama (6) (Orange, 1972) (6 returns)
122—George Fleming, Washington (44) vs. Wisconsin (8) (Rose, 1960) (3 returns)
122—Bobby Kellogg, Tulane (13) vs. Texas A&M (14) (Sugar, 1940) (5 returns)
115—Paddy Driscoll, Great Lakes (17) vs. Mare Island (0) (Rose, 1919) (9 returns)
110—James Henry, Southern Miss. (38) vs. UTEP (18) (Independence, 1988) (2 returns, touchdowns of 65 and 45 yards)
106—Kevin Baugh, Penn St. (27) vs. Georgia (23) (Sugar, 1983) (5 returns)
106—Steve Holden, Arizona St. (45) vs. Florida St. (38) (Fiesta, 1971) (3 returns)
104—Leo Daniels, Texas A&M (21) vs. Alabama (29) (Cotton, 1942) (5 returns)
103—Jon Staggers, Missouri (3) vs. Penn St. (10) (Orange, 1970)
89—Lawrence Williams, Texas Tech (28) vs. North Caro. (32) (Sun, 1972) (5 returns)
87—Vai Sikahema, Brigham Young (46) vs. Southern Methodist (45) (Holiday, 1980) (2 returns)
86—Bobby Majors, Tennessee (34) vs. Air Force (13) (Sugar, 1971) (4 returns)
86—Aramis Dandoy, Southern Cal (7) vs. Ohio St. (20) (Rose, 1955) (1 return)
82—Willie Drewrey, West Va. (12) vs. Florida St. (31) (Gator, 1982) (1 return)
80—(D) Gary Anderson, Arkansas (34) vs. Tulane (15) (Hall of Fame, 1980) (2 returns)
80—Cecil Ingram, Alabama (61) vs. Syracuse (6) (Orange, 1953) (1 return)

HIGHEST PUNT RETURN AVERAGE
(Minimum 3 Returns)
40.7—George Fleming, Washington (44) vs. Wisconsin (8) (Rose, 1960) (3 for 122 yards)
35.3—Steve Holden, Arizona St. (45) vs. Florida St. (38) (Fiesta, 1971) (3 for 106 yards)
24.4—Bobby Kellogg, Tulane (13) vs. Texas A&M (14) (Sugar, 1940) (5 for 122 yards)
24.0—Shayne Wasden, Auburn (31) vs. Ohio St. (14) (Hall of Fame, 1990) (3 for 72 yards)
22.7—Johnny Rodgers, Nebraska (38) vs. Alabama (6) (Orange, 1972) (6 for 136 yards)
21.5—Bobby Majors, Tennessee (34) vs. Air Force (13) (Sugar, 1971) (4 for 86 yards)
21.0—(D) Brian Williams, Kentucky (16) vs. West Va. (20) (Hall of Fame, 1983) (3 for 63 yards)
20.8—Leo Daniels, Texas A&M (21) vs. Alabama (29) (Cotton, 1942) (5 for 104 yards)
19.5—(D) Zippy Morocco, Georgia (20) vs. Texas A&M (40) (Presidential Cup, 1950) (4 for 78 yards)
19.3—Dave Liegi, Nebraska (14) vs. Houston (17) (Cotton, 1980) (3 for 58 yards)
19.0—Gary Moss, Georgia (10) vs. Texas (9) (Cotton, 1984) (3 for 57 yards)

Kickoff Returns

MOST KICKOFF RETURNS
7—Dale Carter, Tennessee (17) vs. Penn St. (42) (Fiesta, 1992) (132 yards)
7—Jeff Sydner, Hawaii (13) vs. Michigan St. (33) (Aloha, 1989) (174 yards)
7—Homer Jones, Brigham Young (37) vs. Indiana (38) (Holiday, 1979) (126 yards)
6—Eugene Napoleon, West Va. (21) vs. Notre Dame (34) (Fiesta, 1989) (107 yards)
6—Tim Brown, Notre Dame (10) vs. Texas A&M (35) (Cotton, 1988) (129 yards)
6—Leroy Thompson, Penn St. (10) vs. Clemson (35) (Florida Citrus, 1988)
6—Anthony Roberson, Air Force (28) vs. Arizona St. (33) (Freedom, 1987) (109 yards)
6—Casey Tiumalu, Brigham Young (17) vs. Ohio St. (47) (Holiday, 1982) (116 yards)

6—Brian Nelson, Texas Tech (17) vs. Florida St. (40) (Tangerine, 1977) (143 yards)
6—Wally Henry, UCLA (6) vs. Alabama (36) (Liberty, 1976)
6—Steve Williams, Alabama (6) vs. Nebraska (38) (Orange, 1972)
6—Mike Fink, Missouri (35) vs. Arizona St. (49) (Fiesta, 1972) (203 yards)

MOST KICKOFF RETURN YARDS
203—Mike Fink, Missouri (35) vs. Arizona St. (49) (Fiesta, 1972) (6 returns)
178—Al Hoisch, UCLA (14) vs. Illinois (45) (Rose, 1947) (4 returns)
174—Jeff Sydner, Hawaii (13) vs. Michigan St. (33) (Aloha, 1989) (7 returns)
166—Willie Jones, Iowa St. (30) vs. Georgia Tech (31) (Liberty, 1972) (4 returns)
154—Dave Lowery, Brigham Young (21) vs. Oklahoma St. (49) (Tangerine, 1976) (4 returns)
154—(D) Martin Mitchell, Tulane (7) vs. Houston (47) (Bluebonnet, 1973) (5 returns)
148—Earl Allen, Houston (28) vs. Boston College (45) (Cotton, 1985) (4 returns)
147—Carlos Snow, Ohio St. (17) vs. Syracuse (24) (Hall of Fame, 1992) (4 returns)
144—Clint Johnson, Notre Dame (39) vs. Florida (28) (Sugar, 1992) (5 returns)
143—Barry Smith, Florida St. (38) vs. Arizona St. (45) (Fiesta, 1971) (5 returns)
143—Brian Nelson, Texas Tech (17) vs. Florida St. (40) (Tangerine, 1977) (6 returns)

HIGHEST KICKOFF RETURN AVERAGE
(Minimum 2 Returns)
60.5—(D) Bob Smith, Texas A&M (40) vs. Georgia (20) (Presidential Cup, 1950) (2 for 121 yards)
57.5—Pete Panuska, Tennessee (27) vs. Maryland (28) (Sun, 1984) (2 for 115 yards)
55.5—Todd Snyder, Ohio (42) vs. Richmond (49) (Tangerine, 1968) (2 for 111 yards)
44.5—Al Hoisch, UCLA (14) vs. Illinois (45) (Rose, 1947) (4 for 178 yards)
43.7—Larry Key, Florida St. (40) vs. Texas Tech (17) (Tangerine, 1977) (3 for 131 yards)
41.5—Willie Jones, Iowa St. (30) vs. Georgia Tech (31) (Liberty, 1972) (4 for 166 yards)
41.0—Kevin Williams, Miami (Fla.) (46) vs. Texas (3) (Cotton, 1991) (2 for 82 yards)
40.3—(D) Willie Gault, Tennessee (28) vs. Wisconsin (21) (Garden State, 1981) (3 for 121 yards)
37.0—Earl Allen, Houston (28) vs. Boston College (45) (Cotton, 1985) (4 for 148 yards)
36.8—Carlos Snow, Ohio St. (17) vs. Syracuse (24) (Hall of Fame, 1992) (4 for 147 yards)
33.8—Mike Fink, Missouri (35) vs. Arizona St. (49) (Fiesta, 1972) (6 for 203 yards)
32.0—Eric Alozie, Washington (34) vs. Florida (7) (Freedom, 1989) (2 for 64 yards)
32.0—Harry Jones, Kentucky (20) vs. Texas Christian (7) (Cotton, 1952) (2 for 64 yards)
32.0—Jim Brown, Syracuse (27) vs. Texas Christian (28) (Cotton, 1957) (3 for 96 yards)

Interceptions

MOST INTERCEPTIONS MADE
4—Jim Dooley, Miami (Fla.) (14) vs. Clemson (0) (Gator, 1952)
4—(D) Manuel Aja, Arizona St. (21) vs. Xavier (Ohio) (33) (Salad, 1950)
3—Michael Brooks, North Caro. St. (28) vs. Iowa (23) (Peach, Dec. 31, 1988)
3—Bud Hebert, Oklahoma (24) vs. Florida St. (7) (Orange, 1980)
3—Louis Campbell, Arkansas (13) vs. Tennessee (14) (Liberty, 1971)
3—Bud McClinton, Auburn (34) vs. Arizona (10) (Sun, 1968)
3—(D) Les Derrick, Texas (19) vs. Mississippi (0) (Bluebonnet, 1966)
3—(D) Tommy Luke, Mississippi (0) vs. Texas (19) (Bluebonnet, 1966)
3—Jerry Cook, Texas (12) vs. Mississippi (7) (Cotton, 1962)
3—Ray Brown, Mississippi (39) vs. Texas (7) (Sugar, 1958)
3—Bill Paulman, Stanford (7) vs. Southern Methodist (0) (Rose, 1936)
3—Shy Huntington, Oregon (14) vs. Pennsylvania (0) (Rose, 1917)

MOST INTERCEPTION RETURN YARDAGE
148—Elmer Layden, Notre Dame (27) vs. Stanford (10) (Rose, 1925) (2 interceptions)
94—David Baker, Oklahoma (48) vs. Duke (21) (Orange, 1958) (1 interception)
90—Norm Beal, Missouri (21) vs. Navy (14) (Orange, 1961) (1 interception)
90—Charlie Brembs, South Caro. (14) vs. Wake Forest (26) (Gator, 1946) (1 interception)
89—Al Hudson, Miami (Fla.) (13) vs. Holy Cross (6) (Orange, 1946) (1 interception)
81—Gary Moss, Georgia (24) vs. Boston College (27) (Hall of Fame, 1986) (1 interception)
80—(D) Russ Meredith, West Va. (21) vs. Gonzaga (13) (San Diego East-West Christmas Classic, 1922) (1 interception)
77—George Halas, Great Lakes (17) vs. Mare Island (0) (Rose, 1919) (1 interception)
75—Hugh Morrow, Alabama (26) vs. Duke (29) (Sugar, 1945) (1 interception)
72—Alton Montgomery, Houston (22) vs. Washington St. (24) (Aloha, 1988) (1 interception)
70—Robert Bailey, Mississippi (34) vs. Virginia Tech (17) (Liberty, 1968) (1 interception)
70—(D) Mel McGaha, Arkansas (21) vs. William & Mary (19) (Dixie, 1948) (1 interception)
69—Howard Ehler, Florida St. (36) vs. Oklahoma (19) (Gator, Jan. 2, 1965) (1 interception)
67—John Matsock, Michigan St. (28) vs. UCLA (20) (Rose, 1954) (2 interceptions)

All-Purpose Yards

(Includes All Runs From Scrimmage, Pass Receptions and All Returns)

MOST ALL-PURPOSE PLAYS
(Must Have at Least One Reception or Return)

47—Ron Jackson, Tulsa (28) vs. San Diego St. (17) (Freedom, 1991) (46 rush, 1 reception)

46—Errict Rhett, Florida (27) vs. North Caro. St. (10) (Gator, 1992) (39 rush, 7 receptions)

42—Blake Ezor, Michigan St. (33) vs. Hawaii (13) (Aloha, 1989) (41 rush, 1 reception)

39—Marshall Faulk, San Diego St. (17) vs. Tulsa (28) (Freedom, 1991) (30 rush, 9 receptions)

37—O. J. Simpson, Southern Cal (16) vs. Ohio St. (27) (Rose, 1969) (28 rush, 8 receptions, 1 kickoff return)

36—Thurman Thomas, Oklahoma St. (35) vs. West Va. (33) (John Hancock Sun, 1987)

36—Bob Anderson, Colorado (47) vs. Alabama (33) (Liberty, 1969) (35 rush, 1 kickoff return)

35—Ricky Ervins, Southern Cal (17) vs. Michigan (10) (Rose, 1990) (30 rush, 5 receptions)

35—Eric Bieniemy, Colorado (17) vs. Brigham Young (20) (Freedom, 1988) (33 rush, 2 receptions)

33—Shaumbe Wright-Fair, Washington St. (31) vs. Utah (28) (Copper, 1992) (27 rush, 6 receptions)

33—Greg Lewis, Washington (34) vs. Florida (7) (Freedom, 1989) (27 rush, 6 receptions)

33—Bo Jackson, Auburn (16) vs. Texas A&M (36) (Cotton, 1986) (31 rush, 2 receptions)

MOST ALL-PURPOSE YARDS GAINED
(Must Have at Least One Reception or Return)

303—(D) Bob Smith, Texas A&M (40) vs. Georgia (20) (Presidential Cup, 1950) (160 rush, 22 receptions, 121 kickoff returns)

277—Bob Anderson, Colorado (47) vs. Alabama (33) (Liberty, 1969) (254 rush, 23 kickoff returns)

276—O. J. Simpson, Southern Cal (16) vs. Ohio St. (27) (Rose, 1969) (171 rush, 85 receptions, 20 kickoff returns)

247—(D) Wilford White, Arizona St. (21) vs. Miami (Ohio) (34) (Salad, 1951) (106 rush, 87 receptions, 54 kickoff returns)

246—Ernie Jones, Indiana (22) vs. Tennessee (27) (Peach, 1987) (15 rush, 150 receiving, 81 kickoff returns)

242—Errict Rhett, Florida (27) vs. North Caro. St. (10) (Gator, 1992) (182 rush, 60 receptions)

239—Tyrone Wheatley, Michigan (38) vs. Washington (31) (Rose, 1993) (235 rush, 4 receptions)

236—(D) Gary Anderson, Arkansas (34) vs. Tulane (15) (Hall of Fame, 1980) (156 rush, 80 punt returns)

230—Jamie Morris, Michigan (28) vs. Alabama (24) (Hall of Fame, 1987) (234 rush, -4 receptions)

228—Phillip Bobo, Washington St. (31) vs. Utah (28) (Copper, 1992) (16 rush, 212 receptions)

225—Ron Jackson, Tulsa (28) vs. San Diego St. (17) (Freedom, 1991) (211 rush, 14 receptions)

223—Donny Anderson, Texas Tech (21) vs. Georgia Tech (31) (Gator, 1966) (85 rush, 138 receptions)

212—Troy Stradford, Boston College (45) vs. Houston (28) (Cotton, 1985) (196 rush, 16 receptions)

211—(D) Charles White, Southern Cal (47) vs. Texas A&M (28) (Bluebonnet, 1977) (186 rush, 25 receptions)

208—(D) Sheldon Canley, San Jose St. (48) vs. Central Mich. (24) (California, 1990) (164 rush, 44 receptions)

Defensive Statistics

MOST TOTAL TACKLES MADE
(Includes Assists)

31—Lee Roy Jordan, Alabama (17) vs. Oklahoma (0) (Orange, 1963)

22—Bubba Brown, Clemson (17) vs. Ohio St. (15) (Gator, 1978)

22—Gordy Ceresino, Stanford (24) vs. Louisiana St. (14) (Sun, 1977)

20—Vada Murray, Michigan (10) vs. Southern Cal (17) (Rose, 1990)

20—(D) Gordy Ceresino, Stanford (25) vs. Georgia (22) (Bluebonnet, 1978)

18—Rod Smith, Notre Dame (39) vs. Florida (28) (Sugar, 1992)

18—Erick Anderson, Michigan (10) vs. Southern Cal (17) (Rose, 1990)

18—(D) Yepi Pauu, San Jose St. (27) vs. Eastern Mich. (30) (California, 1987)

18—Garland Rivers, Michigan (17) vs. Brigham Young (24) (Holiday, 1984)

18—(D) Terry Hubbard, Cal St. Fullerton (13) vs. Northern Ill. (20) (California, 1983)

18—(D) Don Turner, Fresno St. (29) vs. Bowling Green (28) (California, 1982)

18—Matt Millen, Penn St. (42) vs. Arizona St. (30) (Fiesta, 1977)

MOST UNASSISTED TACKLES

18—Rod Smith, Notre Dame (39) vs. Florida (28) (Sugar, 1992)

17—Garland Rivers, Michigan (17) vs. Brigham Young (24) (Holiday, 1984)

15—Ken Norton Jr., UCLA (31) vs. Brigham Young (10) (Freedom, 1986)

15—Lynn Evans, Missouri (35) vs. Arizona St. (49) (Fiesta, 1972)

MOST TACKLES MADE FOR LOSSES

5—Michael Jones, Colorado (17) vs. Brigham Young (20) (Freedom, 1988) (20 yards)

5—Jimmy Walker, Arkansas (10) vs. UCLA (10) (Fiesta, 1978)

4—Ken Norton Jr., UCLA (31) vs. Brigham Young (10) (Freedom, 1986) (6 yards)

3—(D) Guy Boliaux, Wisconsin (21) vs. Tennessee (28) (Garden State, 1981)

MOST QUARTERBACK SACKS

4—Rusty Medearis, Miami (Fla.) (22) vs. Nebraska (0) (Orange, 1992)

4—Bobby Bell, Missouri (17) vs. Brigham Young (21) (Holiday, 1983)

3—Trev Alberts, Nebraska (16) vs. Florida St. (18) (Orange, 1994)

3—Alfred Williams, Colorado (17) vs. Brigham Young (20) (Freedom, 1988)

3—Jim Wahler, UCLA (31) vs. Brigham Young (10) (Freedom, 1986)

3—James Mosley, Texas Tech (17) vs. Mississippi (20) (Independence, 1986)

3—(D) Ernie Barnes, Mississippi St. (10) vs. Kansas (0) (Hall of Fame, 1981)

FUMBLE RECOVERIES

2—(D) Michael Stewart, Fresno St. (51) vs. Bowling Green (7) (California, 1985)

2—Rod Kirby, Pittsburgh (7) vs. Arizona St. (28) (Fiesta, 1973)

BLOCKED KICKS

2—Bracey Walker, North Caro. (21) vs. Mississippi St. (17) (Peach, Jan. 2, 1993)

2—Carlton Williams, Pittsburgh (7) vs. Arizona St. (28) (Fiesta, 1973)

PASSES BROKEN UP

3—Tyrone Williams, Nebraska (16) vs. Florida St. (18) (Orange, 1994)

3—John Herpin, Southern Cal (28) vs. Utah (21) (Freedom, 1993)

3—Demouy Williams, Washington (24) vs. Tulane (12) (Independence, 1987)

Team Record Lists

Only official records after 1937 are included. Prior records are included if able to be substantiated. Each team's score is in parentheses after the team name. Totals for each team in both-team records are in brackets after the team's score. The year listed is the actual (calendar) year the game was played; the date is included if the bowl was played twice (i.e., January and December) during one calendar year. The list also includes discontinued bowls, marked with (D). Bowls are listed by the name of the bowl at the time it was played: The Florida Citrus Bowl was the Tangerine Bowl in 1947-82; the first Hall of Fame Bowl (1977-85) was called the All-American Bowl in 1986-90; the current Hall of Fame Bowl is played in Tampa, Fla., and started in 1986; the John Hancock Bowl was called the Sun Bowl in 1936-86 and the John Hancock Sun Bowl in 1987-88; and the Blockbuster Bowl changed its name to Carquest Bowl in 1993.

Total Offense

MOST TOTAL PLAYS

96—North Caro. St. (10) vs. Arizona (17) (Copper, 1989) (310 yards)

95—North Caro. St. (28) vs. Iowa (23) (Peach, Dec. 31, 1988) (431 yards)

94—Arkansas (27) vs. Tennessee (31) (Cotton, 1990) (568 yards)

93—Miami (Fla.) (10) vs. Penn St. (14) (Fiesta, 1987) (445 yards)

92—Washington St. (24) vs. Houston (22) (Aloha, 1988) (460 yards)

92—(D) Western Mich. (30) vs. Fresno St. (35) (California, 1988) (503 yards)

92—(D) Purdue (27) vs. Tennessee (22) (Bluebonnet, 1979) (483 yards)

92—Arizona St. (30) vs. Penn St. (42) (Fiesta, 1977) (426 yards)

91—Florida (28) vs. Notre Dame (39) (Sugar, 1992) (511 yards)

91—Baylor (21) vs. Louisiana St. (7) (Liberty, 1985) (489 yards)

90—Virginia Tech (25) vs. North Caro. St. (24) (Peach, 1986) (487 yards)

90—Maryland (0) vs. Texas (42) (Sun, 1978) (248 yards)

90—Nebraska (40) vs. Notre Dame (6) (Orange, 1973) (560 yards)

90—(D) Oklahoma (27) vs. Southern Methodist (28) (Bluebonnet, 1968)

90—Richmond (49) vs. Ohio (42) (Tangerine, 1968) (556 yards)

MOST TOTAL PLAYS, BOTH TEAMS

171—Auburn (34) [82] & Arizona (10) [89] (Sun, 1968) (537 yards)

167—(D) Fresno St. (35) [75] & Western Mich. (30) [92] (California, 1988) (943 yards)

167—Arizona St. (45) [86] & Florida St. (38) [81] (Fiesta, 1971) (863 yards)

166—Colorado (47) [86] & Alabama (33) [80] (Liberty, 1969) (930 yards)

165—North Caro. St. (28) [95] & Iowa (23) [70] (Peach, Dec. 31, 1988)

165—East Caro. (35) [80] & Louisiana Tech (13) [85] (Independence, 1978) (607 yards)

165—Penn St. (42) [73] & Arizona St. (30) [92] (Fiesta, 1977) (777 yards)

163—Nebraska (45) [88] & Georgia (6) [75] (Sun, 1969) (540 yards)

161—Ohio St. (28) [78] & Pittsburgh (23) [83] (Fiesta, 1984) (897 yards)

161—Auburn (35) [84] & Mississippi (28) [77] (Gator, Jan. 2, 1971) (1,024 yards)

160—Mississippi (42) [78] & Air Force (29) [82] (Liberty, 1989) (1,047 yards)

159—Notre Dame (39) [68] & Florida (28) [91] (Sugar, 1992) (944 yards)
159—Notre Dame (38) [85] & Texas (10) [74] (Cotton, 1978) (690 yards)
159—Texas (42) [69] & Maryland (0) [90] (Sun, 1978) (517 yards)

MOST YARDS GAINED

718—Arizona St. (49) vs. Missouri (35) (Fiesta, 1972) (452 rush, 266 pass)
715—Michigan (35) vs. Mississippi (3) (Gator, Jan. 1, 1991) (324 rush, 391 pass)
698—Oklahoma St. (62) vs. Wyoming (14) (Holiday, 1988) (320 rush, 378 pass)
680—Texas A&M (65) vs. Brigham Young (14) (Holiday, 1989) (356 rush, 324 pass)
655—(D) Houston (47) vs. Tulane (7) (Bluebonnet, 1973) (402 rush, 253 pass)
651—Brigham Young (39) vs. Penn St. (50) (Holiday, 1989) (75 rush, 576 pass)
642—(D) San Jose St. (48) vs. Central Mich. (24) (California, 1990) (200 rush, 442 pass)
624—(D) Southern Cal (47) vs. Texas A&M (28) (Bluebonnet, 1977) (378 rush, 246 pass)
618—Oklahoma (48) vs. Virginia (14) (Gator, Dec. 29, 1991) (261 rush, 357 pass)
596—Alabama (61) vs. Syracuse (6) (Orange, 1953) (296 rush, 300 pass)
575—Indiana (34) vs. South Caro. (10) (Liberty, 1988) (185 rush, 390 pass)
571—Louisville (34) vs. Alabama (7) (Fiesta, 1991) (113 rush, 458 pass)
569—Florida St. (34) vs. Oklahoma St. (23) (Gator, 1985) (231 rush, 338 pass)
568—Arkansas (27) vs. Tennessee (31) (Cotton, 1990) (361 rush, 207 pass)
566—Pittsburgh (34) vs. Clemson (3) (Gator, 1977) (179 rush, 387 pass)

MOST YARDS GAINED, BOTH TEAMS

1,143—(D) Southern Cal (47) [624] & Texas A&M (28) [519] (Bluebonnet, 1977) (148 plays)
1,129—Arizona St. (49) [718] & Missouri (35) [411] (Fiesta, 1972) (134 plays)
1,115—Penn St. (50) [464] & Brigham Young (39) [651] (Holiday, 1989) (157 plays)
1,048—Michigan (35) [715] & Mississippi (3) [333] (Gator, Jan. 1, 1991) (153 plays)
1,047—Mississippi (42) [533] & Air Force (29) [514] (Liberty, 1989) (160 plays)
1,038—Tennessee (31) [470] & Arkansas (27) [568] (Cotton, 1990) (155 plays)
1,024—Auburn (35) [559] & Mississippi (28) [465] (Gator, Jan. 2, 1971) (161 plays)
1,007—(D) Toledo (27) [486] & San Jose St. (25) [521] (California, 1981) (158 plays)
978—Pittsburgh (31) [530] & Texas A&M (28) [448] (John Hancock, 1989) (158 plays)
954—Mississippi (27) [427] & Arkansas (22) [527] (Sugar, 1970)
950—Texas (40) [436] & Missouri (27) [514] (Cotton, 1946)
944—Notre Dame (39) [433] & Florida (28) [511] (Sugar, 1992) (159 plays)
943—(D) Fresno St. (35) [440] & Western Mich. (30) [503] (California, 1988) (167 plays)
939—(D) Texas Tech (49) [523] & Duke (21) [416] (All-American, 1989) (141 plays)

HIGHEST AVERAGE GAINED PER PLAY

9.5—Louisville (34) vs. Alabama (7) (Fiesta, 1991) (60 for 571 yards)
8.7—Oklahoma St. (62) vs. Wyoming (14) (Holiday, 1988) (80 for 698 yards)
8.4—Michigan (35) vs. Mississippi (3) (Gator, Jan. 1, 1991) (85 for 715 yards)
8.3—Texas A&M (65) vs. Brigham Young (14) (Holiday, 1990) (82 for 680 yards)
8.1—Arizona St. (49) vs. Missouri (35) (Fiesta, 1972) (89 for 718 yards)
7.9—Brigham Young (39) vs. Penn St. (50) (Holiday, 1989) (82 for 651 yards)
7.7—Alabama (61) vs. Syracuse (6) (Orange, 1953) (77 for 596 yards)
7.7—(D) Vanderbilt (28) vs. Air Force (36) (Hall of Fame, 1982) (63 for 487 yards)
7.7—Tennessee (31) vs. Arkansas (27) (Cotton, 1990) (61 for 470 yards)
7.6—Florida St. (41) vs. Nebraska (17) (Fiesta, 1990) (65 for 494 yards)
7.5—(D) Houston (47) vs. Tulane (7) (Bluebonnet, 1973) (87 for 655 yards)
7.5—Iowa (38) vs. California (12) (Rose, 1959) (69 for 516 yards)
7.4—UCLA (31) vs. Brigham Young (10) (Freedom, 1986) (70 for 518 yards)
7.3—(D) Nevada-Las Vegas (30) vs. Toledo (13) (California, 1984) (56 for 409 yards)
7.3—(D) San Jose St. (48) vs. Central Mich. (24) (California, 1990) (88 for 642 yards)

FEWEST PLAYS

35—Tennessee (0) vs. Texas (16) (Cotton, 1953) (29 rush, 6 pass)
36—Arkansas (3) vs. UCLA (17) (Cotton, 1989) (22 rush, 14 pass)
37—Texas Christian (0) vs. Oklahoma St. (34) (Cotton, 1945) (27 rush, 10 pass)
38—Iowa (3) vs. California (37) (Alamo, 1993) (21 rush, 17 pass)

FEWEST PLAYS, BOTH TEAMS

107—Texas Christian (16) [54] & Marquette (6) [53] (Cotton, 1937)

FEWEST YARDS

-21—U. of Mexico (0) vs. Southwestern (Tex.) (35) (Sun, 1945) (29 rush, -50 pass)
23—Alabama (10) vs. Missouri (35) (Gator, 1968) (-45 rush, 68 pass)
28—Miami (Fla.) (0) vs. Bucknell (26) (Orange, 1935) (15 rush, 13 pass)
32—Tennessee (0) vs. Texas (16) (Cotton, 1953) (-14 rush, 46 pass)
41—Southern Cal (14) vs. Alabama (34) (Rose, 1946) (6 rush, 35 pass)
42—Arkansas (3) vs. UCLA (17) (Cotton, 1989) (21 rush, 21 pass)
48—New Mexico (0) vs. Southwestern (Tex.) (7) (Sun, 1944) (38 rush, 10 pass)
54—Arkansas (0) vs. Louisiana St. (0) (Cotton, 1947) (54 rush, 0 pass)
57—Michigan St. (0) vs. Auburn (6) (Orange, 1938) (32 rush, 25 pass)

FEWEST YARDS, BOTH TEAMS

260—Randolph Field (7) [150] & Texas (7) [110] (Cotton, 1944)
263—Louisiana St. (19) [92] & Texas A&M (14) [171] (Orange, 1944)

LOWEST AVERAGE PER PLAY

0.9—Tennessee (0) vs. Texas (16) (Cotton, 1953) (35 for 32 yards)
1.2—Arkansas (3) vs. UCLA (17) (Cotton, 1989) (36 for 42 yards)

Rushing

MOST RUSHING ATTEMPTS

87—Oklahoma (40) vs. Auburn (22) (Sugar, Jan. 1, 1972) (439 yards)
82—Missouri (35) vs. Alabama (10) (Gator, 1968) (402 yards)
79—West Va. (14) vs. South Caro. (3) (Peach, 1969) (356 yards)
79—Georgia Tech (31) vs. Texas Tech (21) (Gator, Dec. 31, 1965) (364 yards)
78—(D) Houston (35) vs. Navy (0) (Garden State, 1980) (405 yards)
78—Texas (16) vs. Tennessee (0) (Cotton, 1953) (296 yards)
76—Oklahoma (14) vs. Penn St. (0) (Sugar, Dec. 31, 1972) (278 yards)
74—Oklahoma (41) vs. Wyoming (7) (Fiesta, 1976) (415 yards)
74—Michigan (12) vs. Stanford (13) (Rose, 1972) (264 yards)
74—Ohio St. (20) vs. Southern Cal (7) (Rose, 1955) (305 yards)
73—Syracuse (31) vs. McNeese St. (7) (Independence, 1979) (276 yards)
73—Penn St. (41) vs. Oregon (12) (Liberty, 1960) (301 yards)
72—Arkansas (27) vs. Tennessee (31) (Cotton, 1990) (361 yards)
72—North Caro. St. (28) vs. Iowa (23) (Peach, Dec. 31, 1988) (236 yards)
72—(D) Texas A&M (28) vs. Southern Cal (47) (Bluebonnet, 1977) (486 yards)

MOST RUSHING ATTEMPTS, BOTH TEAMS

122—(D) Southern Cal (47) [50] & Texas A&M (28) [72] (Bluebonnet, 1977) (864 yards)
122—Mississippi St. (26) [68] & North Caro. (24) [54] (Sun, 1974) (732 yards)
120—Pittsburgh (33) [53] & Kansas (19) [67] (Sun, 1975) (714 yards)
117—Oklahoma (14) [65] & Michigan (6) [52] (Orange, 1976) (451 yards)
117—West Va. (14) [79] & South Caro. (3) [38] (Peach, 1969) (420 yards)
116—Oklahoma (41) [74] & Wyoming (7) [42] (Fiesta, 1976) (568 yards)
116—Colorado (47) [70] & Alabama (33) [46] (Liberty, 1969) (628 yards)
115—Southern Cal (7) [47] & Wisconsin (0) [68] (Rose, 1953) (259 yards)
113—Oklahoma (40) [54] & Houston (14) [59] (Sun, 1981) (566 yards)
113—(D) Houston (35) [78] & Navy (0) [35] (Garden State, 1980) (540 yards)
113—Missouri (34) [71] & Auburn (17) [42] (Sun, 1973) (408 yards)
112—Arkansas (31) [65] & Georgia (10) [47] (Cotton, 1976) (426 yards)
112—(D) Colorado (29) [62] & Houston (17) [50] (Bluebonnet, 1971) (552 yards)

MOST NET RUSHING YARDS

486—(D) Texas A&M (28) vs. Southern Cal (47) (Bluebonnet, 1977) (72 attempts)
473—Colorado (47) vs. Alabama (33) (Liberty, 1969) (70 attempts)
455—Mississippi St. (26) vs. North Caro. (24) (Sun, 1974) (68 attempts)
452—Arizona St. (49) vs. Missouri (35) (Fiesta, 1972) (65 attempts)
439—Oklahoma (40) vs. Auburn (22) (Sugar, Jan. 1, 1972) (87 attempts)
434—Oklahoma (41) vs. Wyoming (7) (Fiesta, 1976) (74 attempts)
429—Iowa (38) vs. California (12) (Rose, 1959) (55 attempts)
423—UCLA (31) vs. Brigham Young (10) (Freedom, 1986) (49 attempts)
423—Auburn (33) vs. Baylor (13) (Gator, Dec. 31, 1954) (48 attempts)
417—Oklahoma (21) vs. Arizona St. (32) (Fiesta, 1983) (63 attempts)
411—Oklahoma (24) vs. Florida St. (7) (Orange, 1980) (62 attempts)
409—Oklahoma (40) vs. Houston (14) (Sun, 1981) (54 attempts)
408—Missouri (27) vs. Texas (40) (Cotton, 1946)
405—(D) Houston (35) vs. Navy (0) (Garden State, 1980) (78 attempts)
402—(D) Houston (47) vs. Tulane (7) (Bluebonnet, 1973) (58 attempts)

MOST NET RUSHING YARDS, BOTH TEAMS

864—(D) Southern Cal (47) [378] & Texas A&M (28) [486] (Bluebonnet, 1977) (122 attempts)
732—Mississippi St. (26) [455] & North Caro. (24) [277] (Sun, 1974) (122 attempts)
714—Pittsburgh (33) [372] & Kansas (19) [342] (Sun, 1975) (120 attempts)
701—Arizona St. (49) [453] & Missouri (35) [248] (Fiesta, 1972) (109 attempts)
681—Tennessee (31) [320] & Arkansas (27) [361] (Cotton, 1990) (110 attempts)
643—Iowa (38) [429] & California (12) [214] (Rose, 1959) (108 attempts)
628—Colorado (47) [473] & Alabama (33) [155] (Liberty, 1969) (116 attempts)
616—Oklahoma (41) [434] & Wyoming (7) [182] (Fiesta, 1976) (116 attempts)
610—Texas (40) [202] & Missouri (27) [408] (Cotton, 1946)

HIGHEST RUSHING AVERAGE
(Minimum 30 Attempts)

8.6—UCLA (31) vs. Brigham Young (10) (Freedom, 1986) (49 for 423 yards)
8.6—Michigan (38) vs. Washington (31) (Rose, 1993) (36 for 308 yards)
8.4—Tennessee (31) vs. Arkansas (27) (Cotton, 1990) (38 for 320 yards)
8.0—Toledo (56) vs. Davidson (33) (Tangerine, 1969) (42 for 334 yards)
7.8—Iowa (38) vs. California (12) (Rose, 1959) (55 for 429 yards)
7.7—Texas Tech (28) vs. North Caro. (32) (Sun, 1972) (38 for 293 yards)
7.6—Oklahoma (42) vs. Arkansas (8) (Orange, 1987) (48 for 366 yards)
7.6—Oklahoma (40) vs. Houston (14) (Sun, 1981) (54 for 409 yards)
7.6—(D) Southern Cal (47) vs. Texas A&M (28) (Bluebonnet, 1977) (50 for 378 yards)
7.4—Michigan (35) vs. Mississippi (3) (Gator, Jan. 1, 1991) (53 for 391 yards)
7.1—Boston College (45) vs. Houston (28) (Cotton, 1985) (50 for 353 yards)
7.0—Pittsburgh (33) vs. Kansas (19) (Sun, 1975) (53 for 372 yards)
7.0—Arizona St. (49) vs. Missouri (35) (Fiesta, 1972) (65 for 453 yards)

FEWEST RUSHING ATTEMPTS

12—(D) Vanderbilt (28) vs. Air Force (36) (Hall of Fame, 1982) (35 yards)

BOWL/ALL-STAR RESULTS

16—Florida (18) vs. Missouri (20) (Sugar, 1966) (-2 yards)
16—Colorado (7) vs. Louisiana St. (25) (Orange, 1962) (24 yards)
17—(D) Duke (21) vs. Texas Tech (49) (All-American, 1989) (67 yards)
17—Illinois (9) vs. UCLA (45) (Rose, 1984) (0 yards)
18—Brigham Young (46) vs. Southern Methodist (45) (Holiday, 1980) (-2 yards)
19—Iowa (23) vs. North Caro. (28) (Peach, Dec. 31, 1988) (46 yards)
19—Baylor (13) vs. Auburn (33) (Gator, Dec. 31, 1954) (108 yards)
20—(D) San Jose St. (27) vs. Eastern Mich. (30) (California, 1987) (81 yards)
20—Tulane (6) vs. Penn St. (9) (Liberty, 1979) (-8 yards)
21—Iowa (3) vs. California (37) (Alamo, 1993) (20 yards)
21—Brigham Young (14) vs. Texas A&M (65) (Holiday, 1990) (-12 yards)
21—Houston (22) vs. Washington St. (24) (Aloha, 1988) (68 yards)
21—Wyoming (19) vs. Iowa (20) (Holiday, 1987) (43 yards)
21—(D) San Jose St. (25) vs. Toledo (27) (California, 1981) (54 yards)

FEWEST RUSHING ATTEMPTS, BOTH TEAMS
57—Iowa (20) [36] & Wyoming (19) [21] (Holiday, 1987)
63—Southern Cal (28) [38] & Utah (21) [25] (Freedom, 1993)
66—Brigham Young (13) [33] & Iowa (13) [33] (Holiday, 1991)
66—Miami (Fla.) (23) [28] & Nebraska (3) [38] (Orange, 1989)
66—Texas Christian (16) [34] & Marquette (6) [32] (Cotton, 1937)
67—UCLA (6) [41] & Illinois (3) [26] (John Hancock, 1991)
67—Southern Cal (7) [39] & Duke (3) [28] (Rose, 1939)
68—(D) Fresno St. (29) [24] & Bowling Green (28) [44] (California, 1982)
70—Arizona (29) [50] & Miami (Fla.) (0) [20] (Fiesta, 1994)
70—Florida St. (41) [24] & Nebraska (17) [46] (Fiesta, 1990)
70—Florida St. (24) [39] & Penn St. (17) [31] (Blockbuster, 1990)

FEWEST RUSHING YARDS
-45—Alabama (10) vs. Missouri (35) (Gator, 1968) (29 attempts)
-30—Florida (6) vs. West Va. (26) (Peach, Dec. 31, 1981) (34 attempts)
-21—Florida St. (20) vs. Wyoming (28) (Sun, 1966) (31 attempts)
-15—Louisiana St. (0) vs. Mississippi (20) (Sugar, 1960)
-14—Navy (6) vs. Texas (28) (Cotton, 1964) (29 attempts)
-14—Tennessee (0) vs. Texas (16) (Cotton, 1953) (29 attempts)
-12—Brigham Young (14) vs. Texas A&M (65) (Holiday, 1990) (21 attempts)
-12—Air Force (13) vs. Tennessee (34) (Sugar, 1971)
-11—Colorado (25) vs. Alabama (30) (Blockbuster, 1991) (30 attempts)
-8—Tulane (6) vs. Penn St. (9) (Liberty, 1979) (20 attempts)
-8—Navy (14) vs. Missouri (21) (Orange, 1961) (24 attempts)
-2—Brigham Young (46) vs. Southern Methodist (45) (Holiday, 1980) (24 attempts)
-2—Florida (18) vs. Missouri (20) (Sugar, 1966) (16 attempts)

FEWEST RUSHING YARDS, BOTH TEAMS
74—Tennessee (34) [86] & Air Force (13) [-12] (Sugar, 1971)
137—Iowa (20) [94] & Wyoming (19) [43] (Holiday, 1987)
145—Arkansas (10) [45] & Nebraska (7) [100] (Cotton, 1965)
147—(D) San Jose St. (37) [123] & Miami (Ohio) (7) [24] (California, 1986)

LOWEST RUSHING AVERAGE
(Minimum 20 Attempts)
-1.6—Alabama (10) vs. Missouri (35) (Gator, 1968) (29 for -45 yards)
-0.9—Florida (6) vs. West Va. (26) (Peach, Dec. 31, 1981) (32 for -30 yards)
-0.7—Florida St. (20) vs. Wyoming (28) (Sun, 1966) (31 for -21 yards)
-0.6—Brigham Young (14) vs. Texas A&M (65) (Holiday, 1990) (21 for -12 yards)
-0.5—Navy (6) vs. Texas (28) (Cotton, 1964) (29 for -14 yards)
-0.5—Tennessee (0) vs. Texas (16) (Cotton, 1953) (29 for -14 yards)
-0.4—Colorado (25) vs. Alabama (30) (Blockbuster, 1991) (30 for -11 yards)
-0.3—Navy (14) vs. Missouri (21) (Orange, 1961) (24 for -8 yards)

RUSHING DEFENSE, FEWEST YARDS ALLOWED
-45—Missouri (35) vs. Alabama (10) (Gator, 1968) (29 attempts)
-30—West Va. (26) vs. Florida (6) (Peach, Dec. 31, 1981) (32 attempts)
-21—Wyoming (28) vs. Florida St. (20) (Sun, 1966) (31 attempts)
-15—Mississippi (20) vs. Louisiana St. (0) (Sugar, 1960)
-14—Texas (28) vs. Navy (6) (Cotton, 1964) (29 attempts)
-14—Texas (16) vs. Tennessee (0) (Cotton, 1953) (29 attempts)
-12—Texas A&M (65) vs. Brigham Young (14) (Holiday, 1990) (21 attempts)
-12—Tennessee (34) vs. Air Force (13) (Sugar, 1971)
-11—Alabama (30) vs. Colorado (25) (Blockbuster, 1991) (30 attempts)
-8—Penn St. (9) vs. Tulane (6) (Liberty, 1979) (20 attempts)
-8—Missouri (21) vs. Navy (14) (Orange, 1961) (24 attempts)
-2—Southern Methodist (45) vs. Brigham Young (46) (Holiday, 1980) (24 attempts)
-2—Missouri (20) vs. Florida (18) (Sugar, 1966) (16 attempts)

Passing

MOST PASS ATTEMPTS
(Followed by Comp.-Att.-Int. and Yardage)
63—Fresno St. (30) vs. Colorado (41) (Aloha, 1993) (37-63-1, 523 yards)
63—(D) San Jose St. (25) vs. Toledo (27) (California, 1981) (43-63-5, 467 yards)
61—(D) Brigham Young (16) vs. Virginia (22) (All-American, 1987) (37-61-1, 394 yards)
59—Brigham Young (39) vs. Penn St. (50) (Holiday, 1989) (42-59-2, 576 yards)
58—Florida (28) vs. Notre Dame (39) (Sugar, 1992) (28-58-2, 370 yards)
58—Illinois (15) vs. Alabama (21) (Liberty, 1982) (35-58-7, 423 yards)
58—Richmond (49) vs. Ohio (42) (Tangerine, 1968) (39-58-2, 447 yards)

57—(D) Western Mich. (30) vs. Fresno St. (35) (California, 1988) (24-57-0, 366 yards)
56—Miami (Fla.) (13) vs. Alabama (34) (Sugar, 1993) (24-56-3, 278 yards)
56—Washington (21) vs. Maryland (20) (Aloha, 1982) (35-56-0, 369 yards)
55—Illinois (29) vs. Army (31) (Peach, 1985) (38-55-2, 401 yards)
55—Florida St. (17) vs. Penn St. (17) (Gator, 1967) (38-55-4, 363 yards)
52—Alabama (29) vs. Army (28) (John Hancock Sun, 1988) (33-52-1, 412 yards)
52—Louisiana Tech (13) vs. East Caro. (35) (Independence, 1978) (18-52-3, 263 yards)

MOST PASS ATTEMPTS, BOTH TEAMS
92—Tennessee (34) [46] & Air Force (13) [46] (Sugar, 1971) (47 completed)
91—Richmond (49) [58] & Ohio (42) [33] (Tangerine, 1968) (56 completed)
90—Bowling Green (35) [41] & Nevada (34) [49] (Las Vegas, 1992) (54 completed)
90—Mississippi (20) [50] & Texas Tech (17) [40] (Independence, 1986) (48 completed)
88—Washington St. (31) [48] & Utah (28) [40] (Copper, 1992) (53 completed)
88—Washington (21) [56] & Maryland (20) [32] (Aloha, 1982) (54 completed)
86—(D) Fresno St. (35) [29] & Western Mich. (30) [57] (California, 1988) (39 completed)
86—Iowa (20) [35] & Wyoming (19) [51] (Holiday, 1987) (49 completed)
85—Ohio St. (10) [35] & Brigham Young (7) [50] (Florida Citrus, 1985) (45 completed)
85—(D) Toledo (27) [22] & San Jose St. (25) [63] (California, 1981) (54 completed)
84—Southern Cal (28) [44] & Utah (21) [40] (Freedom, 1993) (53 completed)
83—Auburn (35) [44] & Mississippi (28) [39] (Gator, Jan. 2, 1971) (50 completed)
82—(D) Fresno St. (29) [50] & Bowling Green (28) [32] (California, 1982) (53 completed)
80—Penn St. (50) [21] & Brigham Young (39) [59] (Holiday, 1989) (53 completed)
80—(D) Virginia (22) [19] & Brigham Young (16) [61] (All-American, 1987) (47 completed)
80—(D) San Jose St. (37) [39] & Miami (Ohio) (7) [41] (California, 1986) (40 completed)

MOST PASS COMPLETIONS
(Followed by Comp.-Att.-Int. and Yardage)
43—(D) San Jose St. (25) vs. Toledo (27) (California, 1981) (43-63-5, 467 yards)
42—Brigham Young (39) vs. Penn St. (50) (Holiday, 1989) (42-59-2, 576 yards)
39—Richmond (49) vs. Ohio (42) (Tangerine, 1968) (39-58-2, 447 yards)
38—Illinois (29) vs. Army (31) (Peach, 1985) (38-55-2, 401 yards)
38—Vanderbilt (28) vs. Air Force (36) (Hall of Fame, 1982) (38-51-3, 452 yards)
38—Florida St. (17) vs. Penn St. (17) (Gator, 1967) (38-55-4, 363 yards)
37—Fresno St. (30) vs. Colorado (41) (Aloha, 1993) (37-63-1, 523 yards)
37—(D) Brigham Young (16) vs. Virginia (22) (All-American, 1987) (37-61-1, 394 yards)
35—Brigham Young (24) vs. Michigan (17) (Holiday, 1984) (35-49-3, 371 yards)
35—Illinois (15) vs. Alabama (21) (Liberty, 1982) (35-58-7, 423 yards)
35—Washington (21) vs. Maryland (20) (Aloha, 1982) (35-56-0, 369 yards)
34—Wisconsin (37) vs. Southern Cal (42) (Rose, 1963) (34-49-3, 419 yards)
33—Alabama (29) vs. Army (28) (John Hancock Sun, 1988) (33-52-1, 412 yards)

MOST PASS COMPLETIONS, BOTH TEAMS
56—Richmond (49) [39] & Ohio (42) [17] (Tangerine, 1968) (91 attempted)
54—Bowling Green (35) [25] & Nevada (34) [29] (Las Vegas, 1992) (90 attempted)
54—Washington (21) [35] & Maryland (20) [19] (Aloha, 1982) (88 attempted)
54—(D) Toledo (27) [11] & San Jose St. (25) [43] (California, 1981) (85 attempted)
53—Southern Cal (28) [30] & Utah (21) [23] (Freedom, 1993) (84 attempted)
53—Washington St. (31) [32] & Utah (28) [21] (Copper, 1992) (88 attempted)
53—Penn St. (50) [11] & Brigham Young (39) [42] (Holiday, 1989) (80 attempted)
53—(D) Fresno St. (29) [31] & Bowling Green (28) [22] (California, 1982) (82 attempted)
50—Auburn (35) [27] & Mississippi (28) [23] (Gator, Jan. 2, 1971) (83 attempted)
49—Iowa (20) [21] & Wyoming (19) [28] (Holiday, 1987) (86 attempted)
49—UCLA (39) [18] & Miami (Fla.) (37) [31] (Fiesta, 1985) (71 attempted)
49—Air Force (36) [11] & Vanderbilt (28) [38] (Hall of Fame, 1982) (68 attempted)
48—Brigham Young (13) [29] & Iowa (13) [19] (Holiday, 1991) (72 attempted)
48—Louisiana St. (30) [20] & South Caro. (13) [28] (Gator, 1987) (79 attempted)
48—Mississippi (20) [31] & Texas Tech (17) [17] (Independence, 1986) (90 attempted)

MOST PASSING YARDS
(Followed by Comp.-Att.-Int.)
576—Brigham Young (39) vs. Penn St. (50) (Holiday, 1989) (42-59-2)
523—Fresno St. (30) vs. Colorado (41) (Aloha, 1993) (37-63-1)
492—Washington St. (31) vs. Utah (28) (Copper, 1992) (32-48-1)
469—Iowa (55) vs. Texas (17) (Freedom, 1984) (30-40-0)
467—(D) San Jose St. (25) vs. Toledo (27) (California, 1981) (43-63-5)
458—Louisville (34) vs. Alabama (7) (Fiesta, 1991) (21-39-3)
455—Florida St. (40) vs. Texas Tech (17) (Tangerine, 1977) (25-35-0)
452—Vanderbilt (28) vs. Air Force (36) (Hall of Fame, 1982) (38-51-3)
447—Richmond (49) vs. Ohio (42) (Tangerine, 1968) (39-58-2)
446—Brigham Young (46) vs. Southern Methodist (45) (Holiday, 1980) (32-49-1)
442—(D) San Jose St. (48) vs. Central Mich. (24) (California, 1990) (32-43-1)
428—Iowa (23) vs. North Caro. (28) (Peach, Dec. 31, 1988) (30-51-4)
423—Illinois (15) vs. Alabama (21) (Liberty, 1982) (35-58-7)
422—Florida St. (41) vs. Nebraska (17) (Fiesta, 1990) (25-41-0)

419—Wisconsin (37) vs. Southern Cal (42) (Rose, 1963) (34-49-3)
412—Alabama (29) vs. Army (28) (John Hancock Sun, 1988) (33-52-1)

MOST PASSING YARDS, BOTH TEAMS

808—Washington St. (31) [492] & Utah (28) [316] (Copper, 1992) (88 attempted)
791—Penn St. (50) [215] & Brigham Young (39) [576] (Holiday, 1989) (80 attempted)
734—Florida St. (40) [455] & Texas Tech (17) [279] (Tangerine, 1977) (63 attempted)
732—(D) Toledo (27) [265] & San Jose St. (25) [467] (California, 1981) (85 attempted)
672—Southern Cal (42) [253] & Wisconsin (37) [419] (Rose, 1963) (69 attempted)
662—(D) San Jose St. (48) [442] & Central Mich. (24) [220] (California, 1990) (68 attempted)
654—Iowa (55) [469] & Texas (17) [185] (Freedom, 1984) (74 attempted)
647—Colorado (41) [124] & Fresno St. (30) [523] (Aloha, 1993) (78 attempted)
631—Southern Cal (28) [345] & Utah (21) [286] (Freedom, 1993) (84 attempted)
629—Florida St. (41) [422] & Nebraska (17) [207] (Fiesta, 1990) (67 attempted)
623—North Caro. St. (28) [195] & Iowa (23) [428] (Peach, Dec. 31, 1988) (74 attempted)
620—Washington (21) [369] & Maryland (20) [251] (Aloha, 1982) (88 attempted)
619—(D) Fresno St. (29) [373] & Bowling Green (28) [246] (California, 1982) (82 attempted)
611—Arizona St. (45) [250] & Florida St. (38) [361] (Fiesta, 1971) (77 attempted)
611—Mississippi (27) [273] & Arkansas (22) [338] (Sugar, 1970) (70 attempted)
607—Auburn (35) [351] & Mississippi (28) [256] (Gator, Jan. 2, 1971) (83 attempted)
606—(D) Fresno St. (35) [240] & Western Mich. (30) [366] (California, 1988) (86 attempted)

MOST PASSES HAD INTERCEPTED

8—Arizona (10) vs. Auburn (34) (Sun, 1968)
7—Illinois (15) vs. Alabama (21) (Liberty, 1982)
7—Missouri (3) vs. Penn St. (10) (Orange, 1970)
7—Texas A&M (21) vs. Alabama (29) (Cotton, 1942)
6—Georgia (6) vs. Nebraska (45) (Sun, 1969)
6—Texas Christian (26) vs. Georgia (40) (Orange, 1942)
6—Southern Methodist (0) vs. Stanford (7) (Rose, 1936)

MOST PASSES HAD INTERCEPTED, BOTH TEAMS

12—Auburn (34) [4] & Arizona (10) [8] (Sun, 1968)
10—Georgia (40) [6] & Texas Christian (26) [4] (Orange, 1942)
9—Alabama (21) [2] & Illinois (15) [7] (Liberty, 1982)
8—Ohio St. (28) [3] & Texas A&M (12) [5] (Cotton, 1987)
8—Nebraska (28) [3] & Louisiana St. (10) [5] (Sugar, 1985)
8—Penn St. (10) [1] & Missouri (3) [7] (Orange, 1970)
8—Nebraska (45) [2] & Georgia (6) [6] (Sun, 1969)
8—Texas (12) [3] & Mississippi (7) [5] (Cotton, 1962)

MOST PASSES ATTEMPTED WITHOUT AN INTERCEPTION
(Followed by Comp.-Att.-Int. and Yardage)

57—(D) Western Mich. (30) vs. Fresno St. (35) (California, 1988) (24-57-0, 366 yards)

MOST PASSES ATTEMPTED BY BOTH TEAMS WITHOUT AN INTERCEPTION
(Followed by Comp.-Att.-Int. and Yardage)

90—Bowling Green (35) [49] & Nevada (34) [41] (Las Vegas, 1992) (54-90-0, 597 yards)

HIGHEST COMPLETION PERCENTAGE
(Minimum 10 Attempts) (Followed by Comp.-Att.-Int. and Yardage)

.929—Texas (40) vs. Missouri (27) (Cotton, 1946) (13-14-0, 234 yards)
.900—Mississippi (13) vs. Air Force (0) (Liberty, 1992) (9-10-0, 163 yards)
.889—Texas A&M (65) vs. Brigham Young (14) (Holiday, 1990) (16-18-0, 324 yards)
.833—Alabama (13) vs. Penn St. (6) (Sugar, 1975) (10-12-0, 210 yards)
.828—Oklahoma St. (62) vs. Wyoming (14) (Holiday, 1988) (24-29-0, 378 yards)
.824—Nebraska (21) vs. North Caro. (17) (Liberty, 1977) (14-17-2, 161 yards)
.813—Texas Christian (28) vs. Syracuse (27) (Cotton, 1957) (13-16-0, 202 yards)
.800—Ohio St. (15) vs. Clemson (17) (Gator, 1978) (16-20-1, 205 yards)
.800—Georgia Tech (31) vs. Iowa St. (30) (Liberty, 1972) (12-15-1, 157 yards)
.778—Tennessee (27) vs. Indiana (22) (Peach, 1987) (21-27-0, 230 yards)
.765—Illinois (17) vs. Hawaii (27) (Holiday, 1992) (26-34-1, 248 yards)
.765—Duke (7) vs. Arkansas (6) (Cotton, 1961) (13-17-1, 93 yards)
.763—Iowa (28) vs. UCLA (45) (Rose, 1986) (29-38-1, 319 yards)
.750—Oklahoma (48) vs. Virginia (14) (Gator, Dec. 29, 1991) (27-36-0, 357 yards)
.750—Iowa (55) vs. Texas (17) (Freedom, 1984) (30-40-0, 469 yards)

MOST YARDS PER ATTEMPT
(Minimum 10 Attempts)

21.7—Southern Cal (47) vs. Pittsburgh (14) (Rose, 1930) (13 for 282 yards)
18.0—Texas A&M (65) vs. Brigham Young (14) (Holiday, 1990) (18 for 324 yards)
17.5—Alabama (13) vs. Penn St. (6) (Sugar, 1975) (12 for 210 yards)
16.7—Texas (36) vs. Tennessee (13) (Cotton, 1969) (14 for 234 yards)
16.7—Texas (40) vs. Missouri (27) (Cotton, 1946) (14 for 234 yards)

MOST YARDS PER COMPLETION
(Minimum 8 Completions)

35.2—Southern Cal (47) vs. Pittsburgh (14) (Rose, 1930) (8 for 282 yards)
29.3—Texas (36) vs. Tennessee (13) (Cotton, 1969) (8 for 234 yards)

29.3—Texas (28) vs. Navy (6) (Cotton, 1964) (8 for 234 yards)

FEWEST PASS ATTEMPTS

2—Air Force (38) vs. Mississippi St. (15) (Liberty, 1991) (completed 1)
2—(D) Army (10) vs. Michigan St. (6) (Cherry, 1984) (completed 1)
2—West Va. (14) vs. South Caro. (3) (Peach, 1969) (completed 1)
3—Air Force (23) vs. Ohio St. (11) (Liberty, 1990) (completed 1)
3—Oklahoma (31) vs. Nebraska (24) (Orange, 1979) (completed 2)
3—Georgia Tech (21) vs. Pittsburgh (14) (Gator, 1956) (completed 3)
3—Georgia Tech (7) vs. Pittsburgh (0) (Sugar, 1956) (completed 0)
3—Miami (Fla.) (14) vs. Clemson (0) (Gator, 1952) (completed 2)
3—Hardin-Simmons (7) vs. Second Air Force (13) (Sun, 1943) (completed 1)
3—Catholic (20) vs. Mississippi (19) (Orange, 1936) (completed 1)

FEWEST PASS ATTEMPTS, BOTH TEAMS

9—Fordham (2) [4] & Missouri (0) [5] (Sugar, 1942)
13—Colorado (27) [9] & Clemson (21) [4] (Orange, 1957)
14—Texas (16) [8] & Tennessee (0) [6] (Cotton, 1953)
15—Louisiana St. (7) [11] & Clemson (0) [4] (Sugar, 1959)
15—Utah (26) [4] & New Mexico (0) [11] (Sun, 1939)

FEWEST PASS COMPLETIONS
(Followed by Comp.-Att.-Int.)

0—Army (28) vs. Alabama (29) (John Hancock Sun, 1988) (0-6-1)
0—Missouri (35) vs. Alabama (10) (Gator, 1968) (0-6-2)
0—(D) Missouri (14) vs. Georgia Tech (10) (Bluebonnet, 1962) (0-7-2)
0—(D) New Mexico (28) vs. Western Mich. (12) (Aviation, 1961) (0-4-0)
0—Utah St. (13) vs. New Mexico St. (20) (Sun, 1960) (0-4-0)
0—Georgia Tech (7) vs. Pittsburgh (0) (Sugar, 1956) (0-3-1)
0—Arkansas (0) vs. Louisiana St. (0) (Cotton, 1947) (0-4-1)
0—Rice (8) vs. Tennessee (0) (Orange, 1947) (0-6-2)
0—Miami (Fla.) (13) vs. Holy Cross (6) (Orange, 1946) (0-10-3)
0—Fordham (2) vs. Missouri (0) (Sugar, 1942) (0-4-0)
0—Arizona St. (0) vs. Catholic (0) (Sun, 1940) (0-7-2)
0—Tulane (13) vs. Texas A&M (14) (Sugar, 1940) (0-4-0)
0—West Va. (7) vs. Texas Tech (6) (Sun, 1938) (0-7-0)

FEWEST PASS COMPLETIONS, BOTH TEAMS

3—Arizona St. (0) [0] & Catholic (0) [3] (Sun, 1940)
4—Penn St. (7) [2] & Alabama (0) [2] (Liberty, 1959)
5—Oklahoma (14) [3] & Michigan (6) [2] (Orange, 1976)
5—Kentucky (21) [2] & North Caro. (0) [3] (Peach, 1976)
5—Texas (16) [2] & Tennessee (0) [3] (Cotton, 1953)
5—Louisiana St. (0) [5] & Arkansas (0) [0] (Cotton, 1947)
5—Wake Forest (26) [1] & South Caro. (14) [4] (Gator, 1946)
5—Utah (26) [1] & New Mexico (0) [4] (Sun, 1939)

FEWEST PASSING YARDS
(Followed by Comp.-Att.-Int.)

-50—U. of Mexico (0) vs. Southwestern (Tex.) (35) (Sun, 1945) (2-9-3)
-17—Rice (8) vs. Tennessee (0) (Orange, 1947) (0-6-2)
-2—Oklahoma (40) vs. Houston (14) (Sun, 1981) (1-5-1)
0—Army (28) vs. Alabama (29) (John Hancock Sun, 1988) (0-6-1)
0—Missouri (35) vs. Alabama (10) (Gator, 1968) (0-6-2)
0—(D) Missouri (14) vs. Georgia Tech (10) (Bluebonnet, 1962) (0-7-2)
0—(D) New Mexico (28) vs. Western Mich. (12) (Aviation, 1961) (0-4-0)
0—Georgia Tech (7) vs. Pittsburgh (0) (Sugar, 1956) (0-3-1)
0—Arkansas (0) vs. Louisiana St. (0) (Cotton, 1947) (0-4-1)
0—Miami (Fla.) (13) vs. Holy Cross (6) (Orange, 1946) (0-10-3)
0—Fordham (2) vs. Missouri (0) (Sugar, 1942) (0-4-0)
0—Arizona St. (0) vs. Catholic (0) (Sun, 1940) (0-7-2)
0—West Va. (7) vs. Texas Tech (6) (Sun, 1938) (0-7-0)
0—California (0) vs. Wash. & Jeff. (0) (Rose, 1922)
0—Oregon (6) vs. Harvard (7) (Rose, 1920)

FEWEST PASSING YARDS, BOTH TEAMS

15—Rice (8) [-17] & Tennessee (0) [32] (Orange, 1947)
16—Louisiana St. (0) [16] & Arkansas (0) [0] (Cotton, 1947)
16—Arizona St. (0) [0] & Catholic (0) [16] (Sun, 1940)
21—Fordham (2) [0] & Missouri (0) [21] (Sugar, 1942)
52—Colorado (27) [25] & Clemson (21) [27] (Orange, 1957)
59—Miami (Fla.) (13) [0] & Holy Cross (6) [59] (Orange, 1946)
68—Missouri (35) [0] & Alabama (10) [68] (Gator, 1968)
68—Penn St. (7) [41] & Alabama (0) [27] (Liberty, 1959)
74—Oklahoma (41) [23] & Wyoming (7) [51] (Fiesta, 1976)
75—Southwestern (Tex.) (7) [65] & New Mexico (0) [10] (Sun, 1944)
77—Utah (26) [18] & New Mexico (0) [59] (Sun, 1939)
78—Texas (16) [32] & Tennessee (0) [46] (Cotton, 1953)

LOWEST COMPLETION PERCENTAGE
(Followed by Comp.-Att.-Int.)

.000—Army (28) vs. Alabama (29) (John Hancock Sun, 1988) (0-6-1)
.000—Missouri (35) vs. Alabama (10) (Gator, 1968) (0-6-2)
.000—(D) Missouri (14) vs. Georgia Tech (10) (Bluebonnet, 1962) (0-7-2)
.000—(D) New Mexico (28) vs. Western Mich. (12) (Aviation, 1961) (0-4-0)
.000—Utah St. (13) vs. New Mexico St. (20) (Sun, 1960) (0-4-0)
.000—Georgia Tech (7) vs. Pittsburgh (0) (Sugar, 1956) (0-3-1)
.000—Arkansas (0) vs. Louisiana St. (0) (Cotton, 1947) (0-4-1)
.000—Rice (8) vs. Tennessee (0) (Orange, 1947) (0-6-2)
.000—Miami (Fla.) (13) vs. Holy Cross (6) (Orange, 1946) (0-10-3)

.000—Fordham (2) vs. Missouri (0) (Sugar, 1942) (0-4-0)
.000—Arizona St. (0) vs. Catholic (0) (Sun, 1940) (0-7-2)
.000—Tulane (13) vs. Texas A&M (14) (Sugar, 1940) (0-4-0)
.000—West Va. (7) vs. Texas Tech (6) (Sun, 1938) (0-7-0)

FEWEST YARDS PER PASS ATTEMPT
-5.6—U. of Mexico (0) vs. Southwestern (Tex.) (35) (Sun, 1945) (9 for -50 yards)
-2.8—Rice (8) vs. Tennessee (0) (Orange, 1947) (6 for -17 yards)
-0.4—Oklahoma (40) vs. Houston (14) (Sun, 1981) (5 for -2 yards)
0.0—Army (28) vs. Alabama (29) (John Hancock Sun, 1988) (6 for 0 yards)
0.0—Missouri (35) vs. Alabama (10) (Gator, 1968) (6 for 0 yards)
0.0—(D) Missouri (14) vs. Georgia Tech (10) (Bluebonnet, 1962) (7 for 0 yards)
0.0—(D) New Mexico (28) vs. Western Mich. (12) (Aviation, 1961) (4 for 0 yards)
0.0—Utah St. (13) vs. New Mexico St. (20) (Sun, 1960) (4 for 0 yards)
0.0—Georgia Tech (7) vs. Pittsburgh (0) (Sugar, 1956) (3 for 0 yards)
0.0—Arkansas (0) vs. Louisiana St. (0) (Cotton, 1947) (4 for 0 yards)
0.0—Miami (Fla.) (13) vs. Holy Cross (6) (Orange, 1946) (10 for 0 yards)
0.0—Fordham (2) vs. Missouri (0) (Sugar, 1942) (4 for 0 yards)
0.0—Arizona St. (0) vs. Catholic (0) (Sun, 1940) (7 for 0 yards)
0.0—Tulane (13) vs. Texas A&M (14) (Sugar, 1940) (4 for 0 yards)
0.0—West Va. (7) vs. Texas Tech (6) (Sun, 1938) (7 for 0 yards)

FEWEST YARDS PER PASS COMPLETION
(Minimum 1 completion)
-25.0—U. of Mexico (0) vs. Southwestern (Tex.) (35) (Sun, 1945) (2 for -50 yards)
-2.0—Oklahoma (40) vs. Houston (14) (Sun, 1981) (1 for -2 yards)
3.0—West Va. (14) vs. South Caro. (3) (Peach, 1969) (1 for 3 yards)
3.2—Louisiana St. (0) vs. Arkansas (0) (Cotton, 1947) (5 for 16 yards)
3.3—New Mexico (7) vs. Southwestern (Tex.) (7) (Sun, 1944) (3 for 10 yards)
4.5—Alabama (34) vs. Miami (Fla.) (13) (Sugar, 1993) (4 for 18 yards)
4.6—Texas (14) vs. Georgia Tech (7) (Cotton, 1943) (5 for 23 yards)
4.8—UTEP (33) vs. Georgetown (20) (Sun, 1950) (5 for 24 yards)
5.3—Case Reserve (26) vs. Arizona St. (13) (Sun, 1941) (3 for 16 yards)
5.3—Arkansas (3) vs. UCLA (17) (Cotton, 1989) (4 for 21 yards)

Scoring

MOST TOUCHDOWNS
9—Texas A&M (65) vs. Brigham Young (14) (Holiday, 1990) (5 rush, 4 pass)
9—Alabama (61) vs. Syracuse (6) (Orange, 1953) (4 rush, 3 pass, 1 punt return, 1 interception return)
9—(D) Centre (63) vs. Texas Christian (7) (Fort Worth Classic, 1921) (8 rush, 1 blocked punt recovery in end zone)
8—Oklahoma St. (62) vs. Wyoming (14) (Holiday, 1988) (6 rush, 2 pass)
8—Toledo (56) vs. Davidson (33) (Tangerine, 1969) (4 rush, 3 pass, 1 fumble return)
7—Kansas St. (52) vs. Wyoming (17) (Copper, 1993) (3 rush, 2 pass, 1 punt return, 1 interception return)
7—Oklahoma (48) vs. Virginia (14) (Gator, Dec. 29, 1991) (4 rush, 2 pass, 1 blocked punt return)
7—(D) Texas Tech (49) vs. Duke (21) (All-American, 1989) (6 rush, 1 pass)
7—(D) Fresno St. (51) vs. Bowling Green (7) (California, 1985) (4 rush, 3 pass)
7—Iowa (55) vs. Texas (17) (Freedom, 1984) (1 rush, 6 pass)
7—(D) Houston (47) vs. Tulane (7) (Bluebonnet, 1973) (7 rush)
7—Arizona St. (49) vs. Missouri (35) (Fiesta, 1972) (5 rush, 2 pass)
7—North Caro. St. (49) vs. West Va. (13) (Peach, 1972) (4 rush, 3 pass)

Florida place-kicker Arden Czyzewski booted five field goals in five attempts against Notre Dame in the 1992 Sugar Bowl.

7—Arizona St. (48) vs. North Caro. (26) (Peach, 1970) (6 rush, 1 pass)
7—Houston (49) vs. Miami (Ohio) (21) (Tangerine, 1962) (4 rush, 2 pass, 1 punt return)
7—Oklahoma (48) vs. Duke (21) (Orange, 1958) (3 rush, 2 pass, 1 pass interception return, 1 intercepted lateral return)
7—UTEP (47) vs. Florida St. (20) (Sun, 1955) (4 rush, 3 pass)
7—Michigan (49) vs. Southern Cal (0) (Rose, 1948) (3 rush, 4 pass)
7—Illinois (45) vs. UCLA (14) (Rose, 1947) (5 rush, 2 pass interception returns)

MOST TOUCHDOWNS, BOTH TEAMS
13—Richmond (49) [7] & Ohio (42) [6] (Tangerine, 1968)
11—Washington (46) [6] & Iowa (34) [5] (Rose, 1991)
11—Texas A&M (65) [9] & Brigham Young (14) [2] (Holiday, 1990)
11—Penn St. (50) [6] & Brigham Young (39) [5] (Holiday, 1989)
11—Arizona St. (49) [7] & Missouri (35) [4] (Fiesta, 1971)
11—Arizona St. (48) [7] & North Caro. (26) [4] (Peach, 1970)
11—Southern Cal (42) [6] & Wisconsin (37) [5] (Rose, 1963)
10—Utah St. (42) [6] & Ball St. (33) [4] (Las Vegas, 1993)
10—East Caro. (37) [5] & North Caro. St. (34) [5] (Peach, 1992)
10—(D) Texas Tech (49) [7] & Duke (21) [3] (All-American, 1989)
10—Mississippi (42) [6] & Air Force (29) [4] (Liberty, 1989)
10—Oklahoma St. (62) [8] & Wyoming (14) [2] (Holiday, 1988)
10—Boston College (45) [6] & Houston (28) [4] (Cotton, 1985)
10—Colorado (47) [6] & Alabama (33) [4] (Liberty, 1969)
10—(D) Nebraska (36) [5] & Miami (Fla.) (34) [5] (Gotham, 1962)
10—UTEP (47) [7] & Florida St. (20) [3] (Sun, 1955)
10—Alabama (61) [9] & Syracuse (6) [1] (Orange, 1953)

MOST TOUCHDOWNS RUSHING
8—(D) Centre (63) vs. Texas Christian (7) (Fort Worth Classic, 1921)
7—(D) Houston (47) vs. Tulane (7) (Bluebonnet, 1973)
6—(D) Texas Tech (49) vs. Duke (21) (All-American, 1989)
6—Oklahoma St. (62) vs. Wyoming (14) (Holiday, 1988)
6—Oklahoma (42) vs. Arkansas (8) (Orange, 1987)
6—Ohio St. (47) vs. Brigham Young (17) (Holiday, 1982)
6—Oklahoma St. (49) vs. Brigham Young (21) (Tangerine, 1976)
6—Arizona St. (48) vs. North Caro. (26) (Peach, 1970)
6—Michigan (49) vs. Stanford (0) (Rose, 1902)

MOST TOUCHDOWNS RUSHING, BOTH TEAMS
9—Arizona St. (48) [6] & North Caro. (26) [3] (Peach, 1970)
8—Oklahoma St. (62) [6] & Wyoming (14) [2] (Holiday, 1988)
8—Colorado (47) [5] & Alabama (33) [3] (Liberty, 1969)
7—Oklahoma (42) [6] & Arkansas (8) [1] (Orange, 1987)
7—Oklahoma (35) [4] & West Va. (33) [3] (John Hancock Sun, 1987)
7—UCLA (45) [5] & Iowa (28) [2] (Rose, 1986)
7—Oklahoma St. (49) [6] & Brigham Young (21) [1] (Tangerine, 1976)
7—Arizona St. (49) [5] & Missouri (35) [2] (Fiesta, 1972)
7—Penn St. (41) [5] & Oregon (12) [2] (Liberty, 1960)

MOST TOUCHDOWNS PASSING
6—Iowa (55) vs. Texas (17) (Freedom, 1984)
5—Florida St. (41) vs. Nebraska (17) (Fiesta, 1990)
5—Florida St. (36) vs. Oklahoma (19) (Gator, Jan. 2, 1965)
4—East Caro. (37) vs. North Caro. St. (34) (Peach, 1992)
4—Miami (Fla.) (46) vs. Texas (3) (Cotton, 1991)
4—Michigan (35) vs. Mississippi (3) (Gator, Jan. 1, 1991)
4—Texas A&M (65) vs. Brigham Young (14) (Holiday, 1990)
4—UCLA (45) vs. Illinois (9) (Rose, 1984)
4—Purdue (28) vs. Missouri (25) (Liberty, 1980)
4—Pittsburgh (34) vs. Clemson (3) (Gator, 1977)
4—Florida St. (40) vs. Texas Tech (17) (Tangerine, 1977)
4—Davidson (33) vs. Toledo (56) (Tangerine, 1969)
4—Richmond (49) vs. Ohio (42) (Tangerine, 1968)
4—Ohio (42) vs. Richmond (49) (Tangerine, 1968)
4—Southern Cal (42) vs. Wisconsin (37) (Rose, 1963)
4—Michigan (49) vs. Southern Cal (0) (Rose, 1948)
4—Georgia (40) vs. Texas Christian (26) (Orange, 1942)
4—Southern Cal (47) vs. Pittsburgh (14) (Rose, 1930)

MOST TOUCHDOWNS PASSING, BOTH TEAMS
8—Iowa (55) [6] & Texas (17) [2] (Freedom, 1984)
8—Richmond (49) [4] & Ohio (42) [4] (Tangerine, 1968)
7—East Caro. (37) [4] & North Caro. St. (34) [3] (Peach, 1992)
7—Toledo (56) [3] & Davidson (33) [4] (Tangerine, 1969)
7—Georgia (40) [4] & Texas Christian (26) [3] (Orange, 1942)
6—Utah St. (42) [3] & Ball St. (33) [3] (Las Vegas, 1993)
6—Miami (Fla.) (33) [3] & Alabama (25) [3] (Sugar, 1990)
6—Florida St. (41) [5] & Nebraska (17) [1] (Fiesta, 1990)
6—Texas A&M (65) [4] & Brigham Young (14) [2] (Holiday, 1990)
6—Florida St. (36) [5] & Oklahoma (19) [1] (Gator, Jan. 2, 1965)
6—Southern Cal (42) [4] & Wisconsin (37) [2] (Rose, 1963)

MOST FIELD GOALS MADE
5—Florida (28) vs. Notre Dame (39) (Sugar, 1992) (26, 24, 36, 37, 24 yards)
5—Maryland (23) vs. Tennessee (30) (Florida Citrus, 1983) (18, 48, 31, 22, 26 yards)
4—Oklahoma (25) vs. Penn St. (10) (Orange, 1986) (26, 31, 21, 22 yards)
4—North Caro. (26) vs. Texas (10) (Sun, 1982) (53, 47, 24, 42 yards)

4—Texas A&M (33) vs. Oklahoma St. (16) (Independence, 1981) (33, 32, 50, 18 yards)
4—West Va. (26) vs. Florida (6) (Peach, Dec. 31, 1981) (35, 42, 49, 24 yards)
4—Missouri (19) vs. Southern Miss. (17) (Tangerine, 1981) (45, 41, 30, 28 yards)
4—Nebraska (45) vs. Georgia (6) (Sun, 1969) (50, 32, 42, 37 yards)
4—Alabama (12) vs. Mississippi (7) (Sugar, 1964) (46, 31, 34, 48 yards)

MOST FIELD GOALS MADE, BOTH TEAMS
6—Notre Dame (39) [1] & Florida (28) [5] (Sugar, 1992)
6—Syracuse (16) [3] & Auburn (16) [3] (Sugar, 1988)
6—Tennessee (30) [1] & Maryland (23) [5] (Florida Citrus, 1983)
5—Penn St. (50) [3] & Brigham Young (39) [2] (Holiday, 1989)
5—Oklahoma (25) [4] & Penn St. (10) [1] (Orange, 1986)
5—North Caro. (26) [4] & Texas (10) [1] (Sun, 1982)
5—Texas A&M (33) [4] & Oklahoma St. (16) [1] (Independence, 1981)
5—Missouri (19) [4] & Southern Miss. (17) [1] (Tangerine, 1981)
5—Penn St. (9) [3] & Tulane (6) [2] (Liberty, 1979)
5—Penn St. (30) [3] & Texas (6) [2] (Cotton, 1972)

MOST POINTS, WINNING TEAM
65—Texas A&M vs. Brigham Young (14) (Holiday, 1990)
62—Oklahoma St. vs. Wyoming (14) (Holiday, 1988)
61—Alabama vs. Syracuse (6) (Orange, 1953)
56—Toledo vs. Davidson (33) (Tangerine, 1969)
55—Iowa vs. Texas (17) (Freedom, 1984)
52—Kansas St. vs. Wyoming (17) (Copper, 1993)
51—(D) Fresno St. vs. Bowling Green (7) (California, 1985)
50—Penn St. vs. Brigham Young (39) (Holiday, 1989)
49—(D) Texas Tech vs. Duke (21) (All-American, 1989)
49—Oklahoma St. vs. Brigham Young (21) (Tangerine, 1976)
49—North Caro. St. vs. West Va. (13) (Peach, 1972)
49—Arizona St. vs. Missouri (35) (Fiesta, 1972)
49—Richmond vs. Ohio (42) (Tangerine, 1968)
49—Michigan vs. Southern Cal (0) (Rose, 1948)

MOST POINTS, LOSING TEAM
45—Southern Methodist vs. Brigham Young (46) (Holiday, 1980)
42—Ohio vs. Richmond (49) (Tangerine, 1968)
39—Brigham Young vs. Penn St. (50) (Holiday, 1989)
38—San Diego St. vs. Iowa (39) (Holiday, 1986)
38—Florida St. vs. Arizona St. (45) (Fiesta, 1971)
37—Miami (Fla.) vs. UCLA (39) (Fiesta, 1985)
37—Brigham Young vs. Indiana (38) (Holiday, 1979)
37—Wisconsin vs. Southern Cal (42) (Rose, 1963)
36—Washington St. vs. Brigham Young (38) (Holiday, 1981)
35—Oregon vs. Wake Forest (39) (Independence, 1992)
35—Missouri vs. Arizona St. (49) (Fiesta, 1972)
34—Nevada vs. Bowling Green (35) (Las Vegas, 1992)
34—North Caro. St. vs. East Caro. (37) (Peach, 1992)
34—Iowa vs. Washington (46) (Rose, 1991)
34—Houston vs. Notre Dame (35) (Cotton, 1979)
34—(D) Miami (Fla.) vs. Nebraska (36) (Gotham, 1962)

MOST POINTS, BOTH TEAMS
91—Brigham Young (46) & Southern Methodist (45) (Holiday, 1980)
91—Richmond (49) & Ohio (42) (Tangerine, 1968)
89—Penn St. (50) & Brigham Young (39) (Holiday, 1989)
89—Toledo (56) & Davidson (33) (Tangerine, 1969)
84—Arizona St. (49) & Missouri (35) (Fiesta, 1972)
83—Arizona St. (45) & Florida St. (38) (Fiesta, 1971)
80—Washington (46) & Iowa (34) (Rose, 1991)
80—Colorado (47) & Alabama (33) (Liberty, 1969)
79—Texas A&M (65) & Brigham Young (14) (Holiday, 1990)
79—Southern Cal (42) & Wisconsin (37) (Rose, 1963)
77—Iowa (39) & San Diego St. (38) (Holiday, 1986)
76—Oklahoma St. (62) & Wyoming (14) (Holiday, 1988)
76—UCLA (39) & Miami (Fla.) (37) (Fiesta, 1985)
75—Utah St. (42) & Ball St. (33) (Las Vegas, 1993)
75—Indiana (38) & Brigham Young (37) (Holiday, 1979)
75—Houston (47) & Miami (Ohio) (28) (Tangerine, 1962)

LARGEST MARGIN OF VICTORY
55—Alabama (61) vs. Syracuse (6) (Orange, 1953)
51—Texas A&M (65) vs. Brigham Young (14) (Holiday, 1990)
48—Oklahoma St. (62) vs. Wyoming (14) (Holiday, 1988)
44—(D) Fresno St. (51) vs. Bowling Green (7) (California, 1985)
43—Miami (Fla.) (46) vs. Texas (3) (Cotton, 1991)
42—Texas (42) vs. Maryland (0) (Sun, 1978)
40—(D) Houston (47) vs. Tulane (7) (Bluebonnet, 1973)
39—Nebraska (45) vs. Georgia (6) (Sun, 1969)
38—Iowa (55) vs. Texas (17) (Freedom, 1984)
36—North Caro. St. (49) vs. West Va. (13) (Peach, 1972)
35—Michigan (42) vs. North Caro. St. (7) (Hall of Fame, 1994)
35—Kansas St. (52) vs. Wyoming (17) (Copper, 1993)
35—(D) Houston (35) vs. Navy (0) (Garden State, 1980)
35—North Caro. (35) vs. Air Force (0) (Gator, 1963)
35—Oklahoma (35) vs. Louisiana St. (0) (Sugar, 1950)
35—Southwestern (Tex.) (35) vs. U. of Mexico (0) (Sun, 1945)

FEWEST POINTS, WINNING TEAM
2—Fordham vs. Missouri (0) (Sugar, 1942)
3—Tennessee vs. Texas A&M (0) (Gator, 1957)
3—Texas Christian vs. Louisiana St. (2) (Sugar, 1936)
6—UCLA vs. Illinois (3) (John Hancock, 1991)
6—Oregon St. vs. Villanova (0) (Liberty, 1962)
6—Tulsa vs. Texas Tech (0) (Sun, 1942)
6—Clemson vs. Boston College (3) (Cotton, 1940)
6—Auburn vs. Michigan St. (0) (Orange, 1938)
6—Santa Clara vs. Louisiana St. (0) (Sugar, 1938)

FEWEST POINTS, LOSING TEAM
0—By many teams

FEWEST POINTS, BOTH TEAMS
0—Air Force (0) & Texas Christian (0) (Cotton, 1959)
0—Arkansas (0) & Louisiana St. (0) (Cotton, 1947)
0—Arizona St. (0) & Catholic (0) (Sun, 1940)
0—California (0) & Wash. & Jeff. (0) (Rose, 1922)

MOST POINTS SCORED IN ONE HALF
45—Oklahoma St. (62) vs. Wyoming (14) (Holiday, 1988) (2nd half)
42—Toledo (56) vs. Davidson (33) (Tangerine, 1969) (1st half)
40—Alabama (61) vs. Syracuse (6) (Orange, 1953) (2nd half)
38—Penn St. (50) vs. Brigham Young (39) (Holiday, 1989) (2nd half)
38—Penn St. (41) vs. Baylor (20) (Cotton, 1975) (2nd half)
38—Mississippi (41) vs. Georgia Tech (18) (Peach, 1971) (2nd half)
37—Texas A&M (65) vs. Brigham Young (14) (Holiday, 1990) (1st half)
35—Penn St. (42) vs. Tennessee (17) (Fiesta, 1992) (2nd half)
35—Southern Cal (42) vs. Ohio St. (17) (Rose, 1973) (2nd half)
35—North Caro. St. (49) vs. West Va. (13) (Peach, 1972) (2nd half)
35—Houston (49) vs. Miami (Ohio) (21) (Tangerine, 1962) (1st half)
34—Oklahoma (48) vs. Virginia (14) (Gator, Dec. 29, 1991) (1st half)
34—Purdue (41) vs. Georgia Tech (21) (Peach, 1978) (1st half)
34—Oklahoma (48) vs. Duke (21) (Orange, 1958) (2nd half)
34—UTEP (47) vs. Florida St. (20) (Sun, 1955) (1st half)

MOST POINTS SCORED IN ONE HALF, BOTH TEAMS
64—Penn St. (50) [38] & Brigham Young (39) [26] (Holiday, 1989) (2nd half)
54—Utah St. (42) [21] & Ball St. (33) [33] (Las Vegas, 1993) (2nd half)
52—Oklahoma St. (62) [45] & Wyoming (14) [7] (Holiday, 1988) (2nd half)
51—Penn St. (41) [38] & Baylor (20) [13] (Cotton, 1975) (2nd half)
49—Brigham Young (46) [33] & Southern Methodist (45) [16] (Holiday, 1980) (2nd half)
49—(D) Houston (31) [28] & North Caro. St. (31) [21] (Bluebonnet, 1974) (2nd half)
49—Arizona St. (49) [21] & Missouri (35) [28] (Fiesta, 1972) (2nd half)
49—Arizona St. (45) [21] & Florida St. (38) [28] (Fiesta, 1971) (1st half)
49—Toledo (56) [42] & Davidson (33) [7] (Tangerine, 1969) (1st half)
49—Richmond (49) [28] & Ohio (42) [21] (Tangerine, 1968) (1st half)
48—Oklahoma (48) [34] & Duke (21) [14] (Orange, 1958) (2nd half)
47—Arizona St. (48) [21] & North Caro. (26) [26] (Peach, 1970) (1st half)
45—Boston College (45) [31] & Houston (28) [14] (Cotton, 1985) (1st half)
45—Southern Cal (42) [35] & Ohio St. (17) [10] (Rose, 1973) (2nd half)

MOST POINTS SCORED IN ONE QUARTER
31—Iowa (55) vs. Texas (17) (Freedom, 1984) (3rd quarter)
30—Oklahoma (40) vs. Houston (14) (Sun, 1981) (4th quarter)
28—Oklahoma St. (62) vs. Wyoming (14) (Holiday, 1988) (3rd quarter)
28—Missouri (34) vs. Auburn (17) (Sun, 1973) (2nd quarter)
28—Mississippi (41) vs. Georgia Tech (18) (Peach, 1971) (2nd quarter)
28—Toledo (56) vs. Davidson (33) (Tangerine, 1969) (2nd quarter)
28—Houston (49) vs. Miami (Ohio) (21) (Tangerine, 1962) (2nd quarter)
27—Oklahoma (48) vs. Virginia (14) (Gator, Dec. 29, 1991) (2nd quarter)
27—Brigham Young (46) vs. Southern Methodist (45) (Holiday, 1980) (4th quarter)
27—Oklahoma (48) vs. Duke (21) (Orange, 1958) (4th quarter)
27—UTEP (47) vs. Florida St. (20) (Sun, 1955) (2nd quarter)
27—Illinois (40) vs. Stanford (7) (Rose, 1952) (4th quarter)
26—North Caro. (26) vs. Arizona St. (48) (Peach, 1970) (2nd quarter)
25—Louisville (34) vs. Alabama (7) (Fiesta, 1991) (1st quarter)

MOST POINTS SCORED IN ONE QUARTER, BOTH TEAMS
40—Arizona St. (48) [14] & North Caro. (26) [26] (Peach, 1970) (2nd quarter)
38—Missouri (34) [28] & Auburn (17) [10] (Sun, 1973) (2nd quarter)
37—Oklahoma (40) [30] & Houston (14) [7] (Sun, 1981) (4th quarter)
35—Oklahoma St. (62) [28] & Wyoming (14) [7] (Holiday, 1988) (3rd quarter)
35—Oklahoma St. (49) [21] & Brigham Young (21) [14] (Tangerine, 1976) (2nd quarter)
35—(D) Houston (31) [21] & North Caro. St. (31) [14] (Bluebonnet, 1974) (4th quarter)
35—Arizona St. (49) [21] & Missouri (35) [14] (Fiesta, 1972) (4th quarter)
35—Richmond (49) [21] & Ohio (42) [14] (Tangerine, 1968) (2nd quarter)
34—Oklahoma (48) [27] & Virginia (14) [7] (Gator, Dec. 29, 1991) (2nd quarter)
34—Penn St. (50) [21] & Brigham Young (39) [13] (Holiday, 1989) (4th quarter)
34—Brigham Young (46) [27] & Southern Methodist (45) [7] (Holiday, 1980) (4th quarter)
34—Penn St. (42) [18] & Arizona St. (30) [16] (Fiesta, 1977) (4th quarter)
34—Mississippi (41) [28] & Georgia Tech (18) [6] (Peach, 1971) (2nd quarter)
34—Oklahoma (48) [27] & Duke (21) [7] (Orange, 1958) (4th quarter)

First Downs

MOST FIRST DOWNS
36—Oklahoma (48) vs. Virginia (14) (Gator, Dec. 29, 1991) (16 rush, 18 pass, 2 penalty)
35—Michigan (35) vs. Mississippi (3) (Gator, Jan. 1, 1991) (20 rush, 14 pass, 1 penalty)
35—Brigham Young (39) vs. Penn St. (50) (Holiday, 1989) (8 rush, 27 pass, 0 penalty)
34—Fresno St. (30) vs. Colorado (41) (Aloha, 1993) (4 rush, 25 pass, 5 penalty)
34—Oklahoma St. (62) vs. Wyoming (14) (Holiday, 1988) (15 rush, 17 pass, 2 penalty)
34—(D) Miami (Fla.) (34) vs. Nebraska (36) (Gotham, 1962)
33—Arizona St. (49) vs. Missouri (35) (Fiesta, 1972) (22 rush, 11 pass, 0 penalty)
32—Brigham Young (24) vs. Michigan (17) (Holiday, 1984)
32—Richmond (49) vs. Ohio (42) (Tangerine, 1968) (8 rush, 24 pass, 0 penalty)
32—Wisconsin (37) vs. Southern Cal (42) (Rose, 1963) (7 rush, 23 pass, 2 penalty)
31—UCLA (16) vs. Wisconsin (21) (Rose, 1994)
31—Arkansas (27) vs. Tennessee (31) (Cotton, 1990) (21 rush, 10 pass, 0 penalty)
31—Florida St. (34) vs. Oklahoma St. (23) (Gator, 1985) (10 rush, 21 pass, 0 penalty)
31—Brigham Young (37) vs. Indiana (38) (Holiday, 1979) (9 rush, 21 pass, 1 penalty)
31—(D) Purdue (27) vs. Tennessee (22) (Bluebonnet, 1979)
31—(D) Houston (26) vs. Dayton (21) (Salad, 1952) (25 rush, 6 pass, 0 penalty)

MOST FIRST DOWNS, BOTH TEAMS
61—Penn St. (50) [26] & Brigham Young (39) [35] (Holiday, 1989)
56—Mississippi (42) [30] & Air Force (29) [26] (Liberty, 1989)
55—Michigan (35) [35] & Mississippi (3) [20] (Gator, Jan. 1, 1991)
54—UCLA (45) [29] & Iowa (28) [25] (Rose, 1986)
54—Florida St. (34) [31] & Oklahoma St. (23) [23] (Gator, 1985)
53—Colorado (41) [19] & Fresno St. (30) [34] (Aloha, 1993)
53—Tennessee (23) [28] & Virginia (22) [25] (Sugar, 1991)
53—Colorado (47) [29] & Alabama (33) [24] (Liberty, 1969)
52—Wisconsin (21) [21] & UCLA (16) [31] (Rose, 1994)
52—Notre Dame (39) [23] & Florida (28) [29] (Sugar, 1992)
52—Indiana (38) [21] & Brigham Young (37) [31] (Holiday, 1979)
51—(D) Arkansas (28) [28] & Florida (24) [23] (Bluebonnet, 1982)
50—(D) Toledo (27) [21] & San Jose St. (25) [29] (California, 1981)
50—Texas (21) [25] & Notre Dame (17) [25] (Cotton, 1970)

MOST FIRST DOWNS RUSHING
26—Oklahoma (40) vs. Auburn (22) (Sugar, Jan. 1, 1972)
25—(D) Houston (26) vs. Dayton (21) (Salad, 1952)
24—Colorado (47) vs. Alabama (33) (Liberty, 1969)
23—Georgia Tech (31) vs. Texas Tech (21) (Gator, Dec. 31, 1965)
22—(D) Arkansas (28) vs. Florida (24) (Bluebonnet, 1982)
22—Oklahoma (41) vs. Wyoming (7) (Fiesta, 1976)
22—Arizona St. (49) vs. Missouri (35) (Fiesta, 1972)
21—Arkansas (27) vs. Tennessee (31) (Cotton, 1990)
21—Florida St. (7) vs. Oklahoma (24) (Orange, 1980)
21—(D) Houston (35) vs. Navy (0) (Garden State, 1980)
21—Mississippi St. (26) vs. North Caro. (24) (Sun, 1974)
21—Missouri (35) vs. Alabama (10) (Gator, 1968)

MOST FIRST DOWNS RUSHING, BOTH TEAMS
36—Miami (Fla.) (46) [16] & Texas (3) [20] (Cotton, 1991)
36—Colorado (47) [24] & Alabama (33) [12] (Liberty, 1969)
32—Oklahoma (41) [22] & Wyoming (7) [10] (Fiesta, 1976)
32—Arizona St. (49) [22] & Missouri (35) [10] (Fiesta, 1972)
32—Texas (21) [19] & Notre Dame (17) [13] (Cotton, 1970)
32—Tennessee (31) [11] & Arkansas (27) [21] (Cotton, 1990)
31—Air Force (38) [18] & Mississippi St. (15) [13] (Liberty, 1991)

MOST FIRST DOWNS PASSING
27—Brigham Young (39) vs. Penn St. (50) (Holiday, 1989)
25—Fresno St. (30) vs. Colorado (41) (Aloha, 1993)
24—Richmond (49) vs. Ohio (42) (Tangerine, 1968)
23—(D) San Jose St. (25) vs. Toledo (27) (California, 1981)
23—Wisconsin (37) vs. Southern Cal (42) (Rose, 1963)
21—(D) Fresno St. (29) vs. Bowling Green (28) (California, 1982)
21—Brigham Young (46) vs. Southern Methodist (45) (Holiday, 1980)
21—Brigham Young (37) vs. Indiana (38) (Holiday, 1979)
20—Mississippi (20) vs. Texas Tech (17) (Independence, 1986)
20—Brigham Young (24) vs. Michigan (17) (Holiday, 1984)
20—(D) Vanderbilt (28) vs. Air Force (36) (Hall of Fame, 1982)
19—Brigham Young (21) vs. Ohio St. (28) (Holiday, 1993)
19—Oregon (31) vs. Colorado (32) (Freedom, 1990)
19—Florida St. (31) vs. Nebraska (28) (Fiesta, 1988)
19—Florida St. (34) vs. Oklahoma (23) (Gator, 1985)
19—Illinois (29) vs. Army (31) (Peach, 1985)

MOST FIRST DOWNS PASSING, BOTH TEAMS
30—Colorado (41) [5] & Fresno St. (30) [25] (Aloha, 1993)
30—(D) Fresno St. (29) [21] & Bowling Green (28) [9] (California, 1982)
30—Richmond (49) [24] & Ohio (42) [6] (Tangerine, 1968)

29—Mississippi (42) [17] & Air Force (29) [12] (Liberty, 1989)
29—Indiana (38) [8] & Brigham Young (37) [21] (Holiday, 1979)
28—Ohio St. (28) [12] & Pittsburgh (23) [16] (Fiesta, 1984)
27—Arizona St. (45) [13] & Florida St. (38) [14] (Fiesta, 1971)
26—Boston College (31) [16] & Virginia (13) [10] (Carquest, 1994)
26—Southern Cal (28) [15] & Utah (21) [11] (Freedom, 1993)
26—Brigham Young (24) [20] & Michigan (17) [6] (Holiday, 1984)
26—Washington (21) [15] & Maryland (20) [11] (Aloha, 1982)
26—(D) Air Force (36) [6] & Vanderbilt (28) [20] (Hall of Fame, 1982)
25—Oklahoma St. (62) [17] & Wyoming (14) [8] (Holiday, 1988)
25—Florida St. (31) [19] & Nebraska (28) [6] (Fiesta, 1988)
25—Miami (Fla.) (31) [15] & Nebraska (30) [10] (Orange, 1984)
25—Brigham Young (46) [21] & Southern Methodist (45) [4] (Holiday, 1980)

MOST FIRST DOWNS BY PENALTY
6—Texas (3) vs. Miami (Fla.) (46) (Cotton, 1991)
5—Fresno St. (30) vs. Colorado (41) (Aloha, 1993)
5—West Va. (21) vs. Notre Dame (34) (Fiesta, 1989)
5—Washington (34) vs. Florida (7) (Freedom, 1989)
5—(D) Western Mich. (30) vs. Fresno St. (35) (California, 1988)
5—Miami (Fla.) (7) vs. Tennessee (35) (Sugar, 1986)
5—(D) Miami (Ohio) (7) vs. San Jose St. (37) (California, 1986)
4—Alabama (25) vs. Miami (Fla.) (33) (Sugar, 1990)
4—Brigham Young (14) vs. Texas A&M (65) (Holiday, 1990)
4—Georgia (10) vs. Texas (9) (Cotton, 1984)
4—Iowa (55) vs. Texas (17) (Freedom, 1984)
4—(D) Vanderbilt (28) vs. Air Force (36) (Hall of Fame, 1982)
4—Maryland (20) vs. Florida (35) (Tangerine, 1980)
4—Baylor (20) vs. Penn St. (41) (Cotton, 1975)
4—Arkansas (13) vs. Tennessee (14) (Liberty, 1971)
4—Arizona St. (45) vs. Florida St. (38) (Fiesta, 1971)
4—Alabama (33) vs. Colorado (47) (Liberty, 1969)
4—Texas A&M (21) vs. Alabama (29) (Cotton, 1942)

MOST FIRST DOWNS BY PENALTY, BOTH TEAMS
8—Miami (Fla.) (46) [2] & Texas (3) [6] (Cotton, 1991)
7—Washington (34) [5] & Florida (7) [2] (Freedom, 1989)
7—Tennessee (35) [2] & Miami (Fla.) (7) [5] (Sugar, 1986)
6—Colorado (41) [1] & Fresno St. (30) [5] (Aloha, 1993)
6—Miami (Fla.) (33) [2] & Alabama (25) [4] (Sugar, 1990)
5—Florida (41) [3] & West Va. (7) [2] (Sugar, 1994)
5—Texas A&M (65) [1] & Brigham Young (14) [4] (Holiday, 1990)
5—Notre Dame (34) [0] & West Va. (21) [5] (Fiesta, 1989)
5—Georgia (10) [4] & Texas (9) [1] (Cotton, 1984)
5—Southern Methodist (7) [3] & Pittsburgh (3) [2] (Cotton, 1983)
5—Pittsburgh (16) [3] & Arizona (10) [2] (Fiesta, 1979)
5—Penn St. (41) [1] & Baylor (20) [4] (Cotton, 1975)

FEWEST FIRST DOWNS
1—Arkansas (0) vs. Louisiana St. (0) (Cotton, 1947) (rushing)
1—Alabama (29) vs. Texas A&M (21) (Cotton, 1942) (passing)
2—Michigan St. (0) vs. Auburn (6) (Orange, 1938) (1 rushing, 1 passing)

FEWEST FIRST DOWNS, BOTH TEAMS
10—Texas (7) [3] & Randolph Field (7) [7] (Cotton, 1944)
12—Louisiana St. (19) [4] & Texas A&M (14) [8] (Orange, 1944)

FEWEST FIRST DOWNS RUSHING
0—Florida (18) vs. Missouri (20) (Sugar, 1966)
0—Navy (6) vs. Texas (28) (Cotton, 1964)
0—Alabama (29) vs. Texas A&M (21) (Cotton, 1942)

FEWEST FIRST DOWNS RUSHING, BOTH TEAMS
3—Alabama (29) [0] & Texas A&M (21) [3] (Cotton, 1942)
8—Southern Cal (28) [4] & Utah (21) [4] (Freedom, 1993)
9—Florida St. (41) [2] & Nebraska (17) [7] (Fiesta, 1990)
9—Texas (28) [9] & Navy (6) [0] (Cotton, 1964)

FEWEST FIRST DOWNS PASSING
0—Army (28) vs. Alabama (29) (John Hancock Sun, 1988)
0—Oklahoma (40) vs. Houston (10) (Sun, 1981)
0—West Va. (14) vs. South Caro. (3) (Peach, 1969)
0—Missouri (35) vs. Alabama (10) (Gator, 1968)
0—Virginia Tech (7) vs. Miami (Fla.) (14) (Liberty, 1966)
0—Auburn (7) vs. Mississippi (13) (Liberty, 1965)
0—Alabama (10) vs. Arkansas (3) (Sugar, 1962)
0—(D) Missouri (14) vs. Georgia Tech (10) (Bluebonnet, 1962)
0—Utah St. (13) vs. New Mexico St. (20) (Sun, 1960)
0—Arkansas (0) vs. Louisiana St. (0) (Cotton, 1947)
0—Fordham (2) vs. Missouri (0) (Sugar, 1942)
0—Arizona St. (0) vs. Catholic (0) (Sun, 1940)
0—West Va. (7) vs. Texas Tech (6) (Sun, 1938)

FEWEST FIRST DOWNS PASSING, BOTH TEAMS
1—Alabama (10) [0] & Arkansas (3) [1] (Sugar, 1962)
4—Oklahoma (41) [1] & Wyoming (7) [3] (Fiesta, 1976)
4—Texas (16) [2] & Tennessee (0) [2] (Cotton, 1953)
4—Rice (28) [3] & Colorado (14) [1] (Cotton, 1938)

Punting

MOST PUNTS
17—Duke (3) vs. Southern Cal (7) (Rose, 1939)
16—Alabama (29) vs. Texas A&M (21) (Cotton, 1942)
16—New Mexico St. (14) vs. Hardin-Simmons (14) (Sun, 1936)
15—Tennessee (0) vs. Rice (8) (Orange, 1947)
14—Tulsa (7) vs. Tennessee (14) (Sugar, 1943)
14—Santa Clara (6) vs. Louisiana St. (0) (Sugar, 1938)
14—Louisiana St. (0) vs. Santa Clara (6) (Sugar, 1938)
14—Texas Christian (3) vs. Louisiana St. (2) (Sugar, 1936)
13—Rice (8) vs. Tennessee (0) (Orange, 1947)
13—Tennessee (0) vs. Southern Cal (25) (Rose, 1945)
13—Oklahoma (0) vs. Tennessee (17) (Orange, 1939)
13—Catholic (20) vs. Mississippi (19) (Orange, 1936)
13—Louisiana St. (2) vs. Texas Christian (3) (Sugar, 1936)
13—Miami (Fla.) (0) vs. Bucknell (26) (Orange, 1935)

MOST PUNTS, BOTH TEAMS
28—Rice (8) [13] & Tennessee (0) [15] (Orange, 1947)
28—Santa Clara (6) [14] & Louisiana St. (0) [14] (Sugar, 1938)
27—Texas Christian (3) [14] & Louisiana St. (2) [13] (Sugar, 1936)
25—Tennessee (17) [12] & Oklahoma (0) [13] (Orange, 1939)
24—Catholic (20) [13] & Mississippi (19) [11] (Orange, 1936)
23—UTEP (14) [12] & Mississippi (7) [11] (Sun, 1967)
22—Auburn (6) [10] & Michigan St. (0) [12] (Orange, 1938)

HIGHEST PUNTING AVERAGE
(Minimum 5 Punts)
53.9—Southern Cal (7) vs. Wisconsin (0) (Rose, 1953) (8 for 431 yards)
51.0—Penn St. (10) vs. Clemson (35) (Florida Citrus, 1988) (5 for 255 yards)
50.0—Mississippi St. (17) vs. Nebraska (31) (Sun, 1980) (5 for 250 yards)
49.2—(D) Air Force (24) vs. Texas (16) (Bluebonnet, 1985) (11 for 541 yards)
49.2—Arkansas (3) vs. UCLA (17) (Cotton, 1989) (6 for 295 yards)
49.0—Indiana (24) vs. Baylor (0) (Copper, 1991) (6 for 294 yards)
49.0—(D) Mississippi St. (10) vs. Kansas (0) (Hall of Fame, 1981) (9 for 441 yards)
48.0—Oklahoma (41) vs. Texas Tech (10) (John Hancock, 1993) (7 for 336 yards)
48.0—Kansas (23) vs. Brigham Young (20) (Aloha, 1992) (8 for 384 yards)
47.9—Penn St. (42) vs. Tennessee (17) (Fiesta, 1992) (9 for 431 yards)
47.9—Oregon St. (20) vs. Duke (16) (Rose, 1942) (7 for 335 yards)
47.6—Oklahoma (42) vs. Arkansas (8) (Orange, 1987) (5 for 238 yards)
47.5—St. Mary's (Cal.) (20) vs. Texas Tech (13) (Cotton, 1939) (11 for 523 yards)
47.4—Georgia Tech (18) vs. Stanford (17) (Aloha, 1991) (7 for 332 yards)
47.4—(D) Fresno St. (51) vs. Bowling Green (7) (California, 1985) (7 for 332 yards)
47.4—(D) Tennessee (28) vs. Wisconsin (21) (Garden State, 1981) (5 for 237 yards)

FEWEST PUNTS
0—Oklahoma St. (62) vs. Wyoming (14) (Holiday, 1988)
0—Oklahoma (41) vs. Wyoming (7) (Fiesta, 1976)
1—Brigham Young (39) vs. Penn St. (50) (Holiday, 1989)
1—Nebraska (21) vs. Louisiana (20) (Orange, 1983)
1—North Caro. St. (31) vs. Kansas (18) (Liberty, 1973)
1—Utah (32) vs. West Va. (6) (Liberty, 1964)
1—(D) Miami (Fla.) (34) vs. Nebraska (36) (Gotham, 1962)
1—Georgia Tech (42) vs. West Va. (19) (Sugar, 1954)
1—West Va. (19) vs. Georgia Tech (42) (Sugar, 1954)
1—Missouri (23) vs. Clemson (24) (Gator, 1949)

LOWEST PUNTING AVERAGE
(Minimum 3 Punts)
17.0—Nevada (34) vs. Bowling Green (35) (Las Vegas, 1992) (4 for 68 yards)
19.0—Cincinnati (18) vs. Virginia Tech (6) (Sun, 1947) (6 for 114 yards)
22.0—Mississippi St. (16) vs. North Caro. St. (12) (Liberty, 1963) (3 for 66 yards)
23.0—Bowling Green (35) vs. Nevada (34) (Las Vegas, 1992) (5 for 115 yards)
25.5—Houston (34) vs. Notre Dame (35) (Cotton, 1979) (10 for 255 yards)
26.3—Oklahoma St. (34) vs. Texas Christian (0) (Cotton, 1945) (6 for 158 yards)
26.3—Notre Dame (35) vs. Houston (34) (Cotton, 1979) (7 for 184 yards)
26.3—Rice (28) vs. Alabama (6) (Cotton, 1954) (8 for 210 yards)

MOST PUNTS BLOCKED BY ONE TEAM
2—North Caro. (21) vs. Mississippi St. (17) (Peach, Jan. 2, 1993)
2—North Caro. St. (14) vs. Georgia (7) (Liberty, 1967)

Punt Returns

MOST PUNT RETURNS
9—Georgia (7) vs. North Caro. (3) (Gator, Dec. 31, 1971) (6.8 average)
8—Indiana (20) vs. Virginia Tech (45) (Independence, 1993) (7.3 average)
8—Tennessee (34) vs. Air Force (13) (Sugar, 1971) (10.8 average)
8—Mississippi (7) vs. UTEP (14) (Sun, 1967) (9.4 average)
8—Michigan (34) vs. Oregon St. (7) (Rose, 1965) (10.6 average)
7—Louisville (34) vs. Alabama (7) (Fiesta, 1991) (7.3 average)
6—Tennessee (17) vs. Penn St. (42) (Fiesta, 1992) (8.2 average)
6—Clemson (30) vs. Illinois (0) (Hall of Fame, 1991)
6—(D) San Jose St. (48) vs. Central Mich. (24) (California, 1990)
6—Brigham Young (7) vs. Ohio St. (10) (Florida Citrus, 1985)

6—Texas (9) vs. Georgia (10) (Cotton, 1984) (2.5 average)
6—Washington (21) vs. Maryland (20) (Aloha, 1982) (4.7 average)
6—(D) Vanderbilt (28) vs. Air Force (36) (Hall of Fame, 1982)
6—Washington St. (36) vs. Brigham Young (38) (Holiday, 1981)
6—Nebraska (38) vs. Alabama (6) (Orange, 1972) (22.7 average)
6—Miami (Fla.) (14) vs. Syracuse (15) (Liberty, 1961) (13.0 average)
6—Air Force (0) vs. Texas Christian (0) (Cotton, 1959) (5.8 average)
6—Tulane (13) vs. Texas A&M (14) (Sugar, 1940) (21.0 average)
6—Tulane (20) vs. Temple (14) (Sugar, 1935)
6—Tulane (12) vs. Southern Cal (21) (Rose, 1932)

MOST PUNT RETURN YARDS
136—Nebraska (38) vs. Alabama (6) (Orange, 1972) (6 returns)
128—Oklahoma (48) vs. Duke (21) (Orange, 1958)
126—Tulane (13) vs. Texas A&M (14) (Sugar, 1940) (6 returns)
124—California (37) vs. Clemson (13) (Florida Citrus, 1992) (5 returns)
124—Washington (44) vs. Wisconsin (8) (Rose, 1960) (4 returns)
108—Southern Miss. (38) vs. UTEP (18) (Independence, 1988) (2 returns)
107—Arizona St. (45) vs. Florida St. (38) (Fiesta, 1971) (5 returns)
104—Texas A&M (21) vs. Alabama (29) (Cotton, 1942) (5 returns)
99—Kent (18) vs. Tampa (21) (Tangerine, 1972) (3 returns)
98—Brigham Young (46) vs. Southern Methodist (45) (Holiday, 1980) (3 returns)
94—Denver (24) vs. New Mexico (34) (Sun, 1946)
93—Auburn (35) vs. Mississippi (28) (Gator, Jan. 2, 1971) (4 returns)
92—Southern Cal (7) vs. Ohio St. (20) (Rose, 1955) (2 returns)
89—Nebraska (28) vs. Florida St. (31) (Fiesta, 1988) (3 returns)
88—Penn St. (42) vs. Arizona St. (30) (Fiesta, 1977) (2 returns)

HIGHEST PUNT RETURN AVERAGE
(Minimum 3 Returns)
33.0—Kent (18) vs. Tampa (21) (Tangerine, 1972) (3 for 99 yards)
32.7—Brigham Young (46) vs. Southern Methodist (45) (Holiday, 1980) (3 for 98 yards)
31.0—Washington (44) vs. Wisconsin (8) (Rose, 1960) (4 for 124 yards)
30.7—Michigan (42) vs. North Caro. St. (7) (Hall of Fame, 1994) (3 for 92 yards)
29.7—Nebraska (28) vs. Florida St. (31) (Fiesta, 1988) (3 for 89 yards)
27.6—Kansas (52) vs. Wyoming (17) (Copper, 1993) (3 for 83 yards)
24.8—California (37) vs. Clemson (13) (Florida Citrus, 1992) (5 for 124 yards)
24.0—Auburn (31) vs. Ohio St. (14) (Hall of Fame, 1990) (3 for 72 yards)
23.3—Auburn (35) vs. Mississippi (28) (Gator, Jan. 2, 1971) (4 for 93 yards)
22.7—Nebraska (38) vs. Alabama (6) (Orange, 1972) (6 for 136 yards)
21.4—Arizona St. (45) vs. Florida St. (38) (Fiesta, 1971) (5 for 107 yards)
21.0—Arkansas (6) vs. Duke (7) (Cotton, 1961) (3 for 63 yards)
21.0—Tulane (13) vs. Texas A&M (14) (Sugar, 1940) (6 for 126 yards)
20.8—Texas A&M (21) vs. Alabama (29) (Cotton, 1942) (5 for 104 yards)
19.5—(D) Georgia (20) vs. Texas A&M (40) (Presidential Cup, 1950) (4 for 78 yards)
19.3—Nebraska (14) vs. Houston (17) (Cotton, 1980) (3 for 58 yards)

Kickoff Returns

MOST KICKOFF RETURNS
10—Wyoming (14) vs. Oklahoma St. (62) (Holiday, 1988) (20.5 average)
9—Brigham Young (14) vs. Texas A&M (65) (Holiday, 1990) (18.2 average)
9—Colorado (47) vs. Alabama (33) (Liberty, 1969)
8—Nebraska (21) vs. Georgia Tech (45) (Florida Citrus, 1991) (23.6 average)
8—Notre Dame (10) vs. Texas A&M (35) (Cotton, 1988) (18.9 average)
8—Texas Tech (17) vs. Florida St. (40) (Tangerine, 1977)
8—UCLA (6) vs. Alabama (36) (Liberty, 1976) (17.6 average)
8—Brigham Young (21) vs. Oklahoma St. (49) (Tangerine, 1976)
8—(D) Tulane (7) vs. Houston (47) (Bluebonnet, 1973) (28.1 average)
8—Missouri (35) vs. Arizona St. (49) (Fiesta, 1972) (32.3 average)
8—Arizona St. (45) vs. Florida St. (38) (Fiesta, 1971)
8—Florida St. (38) vs. Arizona St. (45) (Fiesta, 1971) (23.0 average)
8—Colorado (47) vs. Alabama (33) (Liberty, 1969) (27.8 average)
8—Ohio (42) vs. Richmond (49) (Tangerine, 1968)
8—Florida St. (20) vs. UTEP (47) (Sun, 1955)
8—UCLA (14) vs. Illinois (45) (Rose, 1947) (32.4 average)

MOST KICKOFF RETURN YARDS
259—UCLA (14) vs. Illinois (45) (Rose, 1947) (8 returns)
258—Missouri (35) vs. Arizona St. (49) (Fiesta, 1972) (8 returns)
225—(D) Tulane (7) vs. Houston (47) (Bluebonnet, 1973) (8 returns)
222—Colorado (47) vs. Alabama (33) (Liberty, 1969) (8 returns)
205—Wyoming (14) vs. Oklahoma (62) (Holiday, 1988) (10 returns)
204—Brigham Young (21) vs. Oklahoma St. (49) (Tangerine, 1976) (8 returns)
191—Houston (22) vs. Washington St. (24) (Aloha, 1988) (5 returns)
189—Nebraska (21) vs. Georgia Tech (45) (Florida Citrus, 1991) (8 returns)
187—Houston (28) vs. Boston College (45) (Cotton, 1985) (7 returns)
184—Florida St. (38) vs. Arizona St. (45) (Fiesta, 1971) (8 returns)
174—Hawaii (13) vs. Michigan St. (33) (Aloha, 1989) (7 returns)
170—Tennessee (27) vs. Maryland (28) (John Hancock, 1984) (4 returns)
169—Oregon St. (19) vs. Iowa (35) (Rose, 1957) (5 returns)
164—Brigham Young (14) vs. Texas A&M (65) (Holiday, 1990) (9 returns)

HIGHEST KICKOFF RETURN AVERAGE
(Minimum 3 Returns)
42.5—Tennessee (27) vs. Maryland (28) (John Hancock, 1984) (4 for 170 yards)
38.3—Fresno St. (30) vs. Colorado (41) (Aloha, 1993) (3 for 115 yards)
38.3—Ohio St. (28) vs. Pittsburgh (23) (Fiesta, 1984) (4 for 153 yards)
38.2—Houston (22) vs. Washington St. (24) (Aloha, 1988) (5 for 191 yards)
37.5—Notre Dame (24) vs. Alabama (23) (Sugar, 1973) (4 for 150 yards)
36.8—Ohio St. (17) vs. Syracuse (24) (Hall of Fame, 1992) (4 for 147 yards)
36.7—Indiana (20) vs. Virginia Tech (45) (Independence, 1993) (3 for 110)
33.8—Oregon (19) vs. Iowa (35) (Rose, 1957) (5 for 169 yards)
32.8—Florida St. (40) vs. Texas Tech (17) (Tangerine, 1977) (4 for 131 yards)
32.4—UCLA (14) vs. Illinois (45) (Rose, 1947) (8 for 259 yards)
32.3—Missouri (35) vs. Arizona St. (49) (Fiesta, 1972) (8 for 258 yards)
31.7—Penn St. (41) vs. Baylor (20) (Cotton, 1975) (3 for 95 yards)
29.0—Mississippi St. (17) vs. Nebraska (31) (Sun, 1980) (4 for 116 yards)
27.8—Brigham Young (21) vs. Ohio St. (28) (Holiday, 1993) (5 for 139)
27.0—Arizona St. (17) vs. Arkansas (18) (Holiday, 1985) (3 for 81 yards)
26.7—Houston (28) vs. Boston College (45) (Cotton, 1985) (7 for 187 yards)

Fumbles

MOST FUMBLES
11—Mississippi (7) vs. Alabama (12) (Sugar, 1964) (lost 6)
9—Texas (11) vs. Notre Dame (24) (Cotton, 1971) (lost 5)
8—North Caro. St. (28) vs. Iowa (23) (Peach, Dec. 31, 1988) (lost 5)
8—(D) Houston (35) vs. Navy (0) (Garden State, 1980) (lost 3)
8—Louisville (14) vs. Louisiana Tech (24) (Independence, 1977) (lost 3)
8—North Texas (8) vs. New Mexico St. (28) (Sun, 1959) (lost 6)
8—Texas Christian (0) vs. Air Force (13) (Cotton, 1959) (lost 3)
8—Colorado (27) vs. Clemson (21) (Orange, 1957) (lost 3)
7—Florida (7) vs. Washington (34) (Freedom, 1989) (lost 3)
7—Hawaii (13) vs. Michigan St. (33) (Aloha, 1989) (lost 4)
7—(D) Toledo (27) vs. San Jose St. (25) (California, 1981) (lost 2)
7—(D) Texas A&M (28) vs. Southern Cal (47) (Bluebonnet, 1977) (lost 5)
7—Auburn (27) vs. Texas (3) (Gator, 1974) (lost 5)
7—Tennessee (34) vs. Air Force (13) (Sugar, 1971) (lost 4)
7—Air Force (13) vs. Tennessee (34) (Sugar, 1971) (lost 3)
7—Georgia (2) vs. Arkansas (16) (Sugar, 1969) (lost 5)
7—Alabama (0) vs. Penn St. (7) (Liberty, 1959) (lost 4)
7—Southern Cal (7) vs. Ohio St. (20) (Rose, 1955) (lost 3)
7—Wash. & Lee (7) vs. Wyoming (20) (Gator, 1951) (lost 2)
7—Missouri (7) vs. Maryland (20) (Gator, 1950) (lost 5)
7—(D) Georgia (20) vs. Texas A&M (40) (Presidential Cup, 1950)
7—(D) Arizona St. (21) vs. Xavier (Ohio) (33) (Salad, 1950) (lost 6)

MOST FUMBLES, BOTH TEAMS
17—Alabama (12) [6] & Mississippi (7) [11] (Sugar, 1964) (lost 9)
14—Louisiana Tech (24) [6] & Louisville (14) [8] (Independence, 1977) (lost 6)
14—Tennessee (34) [7] & Air Force (13) [7] (Sugar, 1971) (lost 7)
13—Texas Christian (0) [8] & Air Force (13) [7] (Cotton, 1959) (lost 6)
12—North Caro. St. (28) [8] & Iowa (23) [4] (Peach, Dec. 31, 1988) (lost 8)
12—(D) Houston (35) [8] & Navy (0) [4] (Garden State, 1980) (lost 6)
12—New Mexico St. (28) [4] & North Texas (8) [8] (Sun, 1959) (lost 8)
11—(D) Toledo (27) [7] & San Jose St. (25) [4] (California, 1981) (lost 3)
11—Oklahoma (41) [6] & Wyoming (7) [5] (Fiesta, 1976)
10—Alabama (30) [5] & Baylor (2) [5] (Cotton, 1981) (lost 5)
10—(D) Houston (31) [5] & North Caro. St. (31) [5] (Bluebonnet, 1974) (lost 4)
10—Notre Dame (24) [1] & Texas (11) [9] (Cotton, 1971) (lost 6)
10—Illinois (17) [5] & Washington (7) [5] (Rose, 1964) (lost 6)
10—Navy (20) [5] & Rice (7) [5] (Cotton, 1958) (lost 8)
10—Mississippi (7) [5] & Florida (3) [5] (Gator, 1958) (lost 5)
10—Texas (16) [5] & Tennessee (0) [5] (Cotton, 1953) (lost 6)

MOST FUMBLES LOST
6—Texas A&M (2) vs. Florida St. (10) (Cotton, 1992) (6 fumbles)
6—East Caro. (31) vs. Maine (0) (Tangerine, 1965) (6 fumbles)
6—Mississippi (7) vs. Alabama (12) (Sugar, 1964) (11 fumbles)
6—North Texas (8) vs. New Mexico St. (28) (Sun, 1959) (8 fumbles)
6—(D) Arizona St. (21) vs. Xavier (Ohio) (33) (Salad, 1950) (7 fumbles)
5—UCLA (16) vs. Wisconsin (21) (Rose, 1994) (5 fumbles)
5—North Caro. St. (28) vs. Iowa (23) (Peach, Dec. 31, 1988) (8 fumbles)
5—North Caro. (21) vs. Arizona (30) (Aloha, 1986) (5 fumbles)
5—(D) Bowling Green (7) vs. Fresno St. (51) (California, 1985) (6 fumbles)
5—(D) Georgia (22) vs. Stanford (25) (Bluebonnet, 1978) (6 fumbles)
5—(D) Texas A&M (28) vs. Southern Cal (47) (Bluebonnet, 1977) (7 fumbles)
5—Auburn (27) vs. Texas (3) (Gator, 1974) (7 fumbles)
5—Texas (11) vs. Notre Dame (24) (Cotton, 1971) (9 fumbles)
5—Georgia (2) vs. Arkansas (16) (Sugar, 1969) (7 fumbles)
5—(D) Utah St. (9) vs. Baylor (24) (Gotham, 1961) (5 fumbles)
5—Rice (7) vs. Navy (20) (Cotton, 1958) (5 fumbles)
5—Auburn (13) vs. Vanderbilt (25) (Gator, 1955) (5 fumbles)
5—Oklahoma (7) vs. Kentucky (13) (Sugar, 1951)
5—Missouri (7) vs. Maryland (20) (Gator, 1950) (7 fumbles)
5—Texas A&M (21) vs. Alabama (29) (Cotton, 1942) (6 fumbles)

MOST FUMBLES LOST, BOTH TEAMS
9—Alabama (12) [3] & Mississippi (7) [6] (Sugar, 1964) (17 fumbles)
8—North Caro. St. (28) [5] & Iowa (23) [3] (Peach, Dec. 31, 1988) (12 fumbles)
8—New Mexico St. (28) [2] & North Texas (8) [6] (Sun, 1959) (12 fumbles)
8—Navy (20) [3] & Rice (7) [5] (Cotton, 1958) (10 fumbles)
7—Florida St. (10) [1] & Texas A&M (2) [6] (Cotton, 1992) (7 fumbles)
7—Texas A&M (37) [3] & Florida (14) [4] (Sun, 1977) (8 fumbles)
7—Arizona St. (28) [3] & Pittsburgh (7) [4] (Fiesta, 1973) (9 fumbles)
7—Tennessee (34) [4] & Air Force (13) [3] (Sugar, 1971) (14 fumbles)
7—Michigan St. (28) [4] & UCLA (20) [3] (Rose, 1954) (8 fumbles)

Penalties

MOST PENALTIES
20—(D) Fresno St. (35) vs. Western Mich. (30) (California, 1988) (166 yards)
18—Washington St. (31) vs. Utah (28) (Copper, 1992) (136 yards)
17—Tennessee (17) vs. Oklahoma (0) (Orange, 1939) (157 yards)
16—Miami (Fla.) (46) vs. Texas (3) (Cotton, 1991) (202 yards)
16—Tulsa (16) vs. McNeese St. (20) (Independence, 1976) (100 yards)
15—Utah St. (42) vs. Ball St. (33) (Las Vegas, 1993) (150 yards)
15—Miami (Fla.) (7) vs. Tennessee (35) (Sugar, 1986) (120 yards)
15—(D) Michigan (33) vs. UCLA (14) (Bluebonnet, 1981) (148 yards)
14—(D) San Jose St. (37) vs. Miami (Ohio) (7) (California, 1986) (163 yards)
13—Florida St. (41) vs. Nebraska (17) (Fiesta, 1990) (135 yards)
13—(D) San Jose St. (27) vs. Eastern Mich. (30) (California, 1987) (103 yards)
13—Washington (20) vs. Colorado (17) (Freedom, 1985) (88 yards)
13—Miami (Fla.) (31) vs. Nebraska (30) (Orange, 1984) (101 yards)
13—McNeese St. (20) vs. Tulsa (16) (Independence, 1976) (105 yards)
13—Lamar (21) vs. Middle Tenn. St. (14) (Tangerine, 1961) (140 yards)

MOST PENALTIES, BOTH TEAMS
29—McNeese St. (20) [13] & Tulsa (16) [16] (Independence, 1976) (205 yards)
28—(D) Fresno St. (35) [20] & Western Mich. (30) [8] (California, 1988) (231 yards)
26—Tennessee (35) [11] & Miami (Fla.) (7) [15] (Sugar, 1986) (245 yards)
26—Tennessee (17) [17] & Oklahoma (0) [9] (Orange, 1939) (221 yards)
25—Washington St. (31) [18] & Utah (28) [7] (Copper, 1992) (191 yards)
24—Miami (Fla.) (46) [16] & Texas (3) [8] (Cotton, 1991) (270 yards)
24—(D) San Jose St. (37) [14] & Miami (Ohio) (7) [10] (California, 1986) (264 yards)
24—(D) Michigan (33) [15] & UCLA (14) [9] (Bluebonnet, 1981) (242 yards)
23—(D) Fresno St. (51) [12] & Bowling Green (7) [11] (California, 1985) (183 yards)
22—(D) Eastern Mich. (30) [9] & San Jose St. (27) [13] (California, 1987) (162 yards)
21—Florida St. (18) [10] & Nebraska (16) [11] (Orange, 1994) (184 yards)
21—Ohio St. (47) [12] & Brigham Young (17) [9] (Holiday, 1982) (184 yards)
21—Oklahoma St. (16) [12] & Brigham Young (6) [9] (Fiesta, 1974) (150 yards)
20—Utah St. (42) [15] & Ball St. (33) [5] (Las Vegas, 1993) (180 yards)
20—Penn St. (50) [10] & Brigham Young (39) [10] (Holiday, 1989) (181 yards)
20—Washington St. (24) [11] & Houston (22) [9] (Aloha, 1988) (153 yards)
20—Brigham Young (24) [9] & Michigan (17) [11] (Holiday, 1984) (194 yards)

MOST YARDS PENALIZED
202—Miami (Fla.) (46) vs. Texas (3) (Cotton, 1991) (16 penalties)
166—(D) Fresno St. (35) vs. Western Mich. (30) (California, 1988) (20 penalties)
163—(D) San Jose St. (37) vs. Miami (Ohio) (7) (California, 1986) (14 penalties)
150—Utah St. (42) vs. Ball St. (33) (Las Vegas, 1993) (15 penalties)
150—Oklahoma (48) vs. Duke (21) (Orange, 1958) (12 penalties)
148—(D) Michigan (33) vs. UCLA (14) (Bluebonnet, 1981) (15 penalties)
143—Miami (Fla.) (22) vs. Nebraska (0) (Orange, 1992) (12 penalties)
140—Lamar (21) vs. Middle Tenn. St. (14) (Tangerine, 1961) (13 penalties)
136—Washington St. (31) vs. Utah (28) (Copper, 1992) (18 penalties)
135—Florida St. (41) vs. Nebraska (17) (Fiesta, 1990) (13 penalties)
130—Louisiana St. (15) vs. Nebraska (30) (Sugar, 1987) (12 penalties)
130—Tennessee (17) vs. Oklahoma (0) (Orange, 1939)
128—Oklahoma (48) vs. Virginia (14) (Gator, Dec. 29, 1991) (12 penalties)
126—Penn St. (42) vs. Arizona St. (30) (Fiesta, 1977) (12 penalties)
125—Tennessee (35) vs. Miami (Fla.) (7) (Sugar, 1986) (11 penalties)
122—Mississippi St. (16) vs. North Caro. St. (12) (Liberty, 1963) (11 penalties)

MOST YARDS PENALIZED, BOTH TEAMS
270—Miami (Fla.) (46) [202] & Texas (3) [68] (Cotton, 1991)
264—(D) San Jose St. (37) [163] & Miami (Ohio) (7) [101] (California, 1986)
245—Tennessee (35) [125] & Miami (Fla.) (7) [120] (Sugar, 1986)
242—(D) Michigan (33) [148] & UCLA (14) [94] (Bluebonnet, 1981)
231—(D) Fresno St. (35) [166] & Western Mich. (30) [65] (California, 1988)
221—Tennessee (17) [130] & Oklahoma (0) [91] (Orange, 1939)
205—McNeese St. (20) [105] & Tulsa (16) [100] (Independence, 1976)
194—Brigham Young (24) [82] & Michigan (17) [112] (Holiday, 1984)
191—Washington St. (31) [136] & Utah (28) [55] (Copper, 1992)
184—Florida St. (18) [69] & Nebraska (16) [115] (Orange, 1994)
183—Florida St. (41) [135] & Nebraska (17) [48] (Fiesta, 1990)
183—(D) Fresno St. (51) [112] & Bowling Green (7) [71] (California, 1985)
181—Penn St. (50) [93] & Brigham Young (39) [88] (Holiday, 1989)
180—Utah St. (42) [150] & Ball St. (33) [30] (Las Vegas, 1993)
179—Miami (Fla.) (22) [143] & Neb. (0) [36] (Orange, 1992)

176—Oklahoma (48) [128] & Virginia (14) [48] (Gator, Dec. 29, 1991)
175—Oklahoma (48) [150] & Duke (21) [25] (Orange, 1958)

FEWEST PENALTIES
0—Southern Methodist (7) vs. Alabama (28) (Sun, 1983)
0—Louisiana Tech (13) vs. East Caro. (35) (Independence, 1978)
0—Texas (17) vs. Alabama (13) (Cotton, 1973)
0—(D) Rice (7) vs. Kansas (33) (Bluebonnet, 1961)
0—Pittsburgh (14) vs. Georgia Tech (21) (Gator, 1956)
0—Clemson (0) vs. Miami (Fla.) (14) (Gator, 1952)
0—Texas (7) vs. Randolph Field (7) (Cotton, 1944)
0—Alabama (20) vs. Washington (19) (Rose, 1926)

FEWEST PENALTIES, BOTH TEAMS
3—Alabama (28) [3] & Southern Methodist (7) [0] (Sun, 1983)
3—Penn St. (30) [2] & Texas (6) [1] (Cotton, 1972)
3—Texas (21) [1] & Notre Dame (17) [2] (Cotton, 1970)
3—Penn St. (15) [1] & Kansas (14) [2] (Orange, 1969)
3—(D) Kansas (33) [3] & Rice (7) [0] (Bluebonnet, 1961)

FEWEST YARDS PENALIZED
0—Southern Methodist (7) vs. Alabama (28) (Sun, 1983)
0—Louisiana Tech (13) vs. East Caro. (35) (Independence, 1978)
0—Texas (17) vs. Alabama (13) (Cotton, 1973)
0—(D) Rice (7) vs. Kansas (33) (Bluebonnet, 1961)
0—Pittsburgh (14) vs. Georgia Tech (21) (Gator, 1956)
0—Clemson (0) vs. Miami (Fla.) (14) (Gator, 1952)
0—Texas (7) vs. Randolph Field (7) (Cotton, 1944)
0—Alabama (20) vs. Washington (19) (Rose, 1926)

FEWEST YARDS PENALIZED, BOTH TEAMS
10—Duquesne (13) [5] & Mississippi St. (12) [5] (Orange, 1937)
15—Texas (21) [5] & Notre Dame (17) [10] (Cotton, 1970)
15—(D) Kansas (33) [15] vs. Rice (7) [0] (Bluebonnet, 1961)

Miscellaneous Records

SCORELESS TIES
1959—Air Force 0, Texas Christian 0 (Cotton)
1947—Arkansas 0, Louisiana St. 0 (Cotton)
1940—Arizona St. 0, Catholic 0 (Sun)
1922—California 0, Wash. & Jeff. 0 (Rose)

TIE GAMES
(Not Scoreless)
1991—Brigham Young 13, Iowa 13 (Holiday)
1990—Louisiana Tech 34, Maryland 34 (Independence)
1988—Auburn 16, Syracuse 16 (Sugar)
1985—Arizona 13, Georgia 13 (Sun)
1984—Florida St. 17, Georgia 17 (Florida Citrus)
1978—Arkansas 10, UCLA 10 (Fiesta)
1977—(D) Maryland 17, Minnesota 17 (Hall of Fame)
1974—Texas Tech 6, Vanderbilt 6 (Peach)
1974—(D) Houston 31, North Caro. St. 31 (Bluebonnet)
1970—(D) Alabama 24, Oklahoma 24 (Bluebonnet)
1970—(D) Long Beach St. 24, Louisville 24 (Pasadena)
1967—Florida St. 17, Penn St. 17 (Gator)
1960—(D) Alabama 3, Texas 3 (Bluebonnet)
1948—Georgia 20, Maryland 20 (Gator)
1948—Penn St. 13, Southern Methodist 13 (Cotton)
1947—(D) Montana St. 13, New Mexico 13 (Harbor)
1944—Randolph Field 7, Texas 7 (Cotton)
1937—(D) Auburn 7, Villanova 7 (Bacardi)
1936—Hardin-Simmons 14, New Mexico St. 14 (Sun)
1934—Arkansas 7, Centenary (La.) 7 (Dixie Classic)
1927—Alabama 7, Stanford 7 (Rose)
1924—Navy 14, Washington 14 (Rose)

LARGEST DEFICIT OVERCOME TO WIN
22—Brigham Young (46) vs. Southern Methodist (45) (Holiday, 1980) (trailed 35-13 in 3rd quarter and then trailed 45-25 with four minutes remaining in the game)
22—Notre Dame (35) vs. Houston (34) (Cotton, 1979) (trailed 34-12 in 4th quarter)
21—(D) Fresno St. (29) vs. Bowling Green (28) (California, 1982) (trailed 21-0 in 2nd quarter)
19—Wake Forest (39) vs. Oregon (35) (Independence, 1992) (trailed 29-10 in 3rd quarter)
14—Rice (28) vs. Colorado (14) (Cotton, 1938) (trailed 14-0 in 2nd quarter)
13—Mississippi (14) vs. Texas Christian (13) (Cotton, 1956) (trailed 13-0 in 2nd quarter)
11—Michigan (27) vs. Nebraska (23) (Fiesta, 1986) (trailed 14-3 in 3rd quarter)

Longest Plays

(D) Denotes discontinued bowl. Year listed is actual year bowl was played.

LONGEST RUNS FROM SCRIMMAGE

Yds.	Player, Team (Score) vs. Opponent (Score)	Bowl, Year
99*	Terry Baker (QB), Oregon St. (6) vs. Villanova (0)	Liberty, 1962
95*#	Dicky Maegle, Rice (28) vs. Alabama (6)	Cotton, 1954
94*(D)	Dwight Ford, Southern Cal (47) vs. Texas A&M (28)	Bluebonnet, 1977
94*	Larry Smith, Florida (27) vs. Georgia Tech (12)	Orange, 1967
94*	Hascall Henshaw, Arizona St. (13) vs. Case Reserve (26)	Sun, 1941

#Famous bench-tackle play; Maegle tackled on Alabama 40-yard line by Tommy Lewis, awarded touchdown. *Scored touchdown on play.

LONGEST PASS PLAYS

Yds.	Players, Team (Score) vs. Opponent (Score)	Bowl, Year
95*	Ronnie Fletcher to Ben Hart, Oklahoma (19) vs. Florida St. (36)	Gator, 1965
93*(D)	Stan Heath to Tommy Kalminir, Nevada (13) vs. North Texas (6)	Salad, 1948
91*(D)	Mark Barsotti to Stephen Shelley, Fresno St. (27) vs. Ball St. (6)	California, 1989
88*	Dave Schnell to Rob Turner, Indiana (34) vs. South Caro. (10)	Liberty, 1988
87*	Drew Bledsoe to Phillip Bobo, Washington St. (31) vs. Utah (28)	Copper, 1992
87*	Randy Wright to Tim Stracka, Wisconsin (14) vs. Kansas St. (3)	Independence, 1982
87*	Ger Schwedes to Ernie Davis, Syracuse (23) vs. Texas (14)	Cotton, 1960

*Scored touchdown on play.

LONGEST FIELD GOALS

Yds.	Player, Team (Score) vs. Opponent (Score)	Bowl, Year
62	Tony Franklin, Texas A&M (37) vs. Florida (14)	Sun, 1977
56	Greg Cox, Miami (Fla.) (20) vs. Oklahoma (14)	Orange, 1988
55(D)	Russell Erxleben, Texas (38) vs. Colorado (21)	Bluebonnet, 1975
54	Carlos Huerta, Miami (Fla.) (22) vs. Nebraska (0)	Orange, 1992
54	Quin Rodriguez, Southern Cal (16) vs. Michigan St. (17)	John Hancock, 1990
54	Luis Zendejas, Arizona St. (32) vs. Oklahoma (21)	Fiesta, 1983

LONGEST PUNTS

Yds.	Player, Team (Score) vs. Opponent (Score)	Bowl, Year
84$	Kyle Rote, Southern Methodist (21) vs. Oregon (13)	Cotton, 1949
82	Ike Pickle, Mississippi St. (12) vs. Duquesne (13)	Orange, 1937
80	Elmer Layden, Notre Dame (27) vs. Stanford (10)	Rose, 1925
79$	Doak Walker, Southern Methodist (21) vs. Oregon (13)	Cotton, 1949
77	Mike Sochko, Maryland (21) vs. Houston (30)	Cotton, 1977

$Quick kick.

LONGEST PUNT RETURNS

Yds.	Player, Team (Score) vs. Opponent (Score)	Bowl, Year
86*	Aramis Dandoy, Southern Cal (7) vs. Ohio St. (20)	Rose, 1955
83*	Vai Sikahema, Brigham Young (46) vs. Southern Methodist (45)	Holiday, 1980
82	Willie Drewrey, West Va. (12) vs. Florida St. (31)	Gator, 1982
80*(D)	Gary Anderson, Arkansas (34) vs. Tulane (15)	All-American, 1980
80*	Cecil Ingram, Alabama (61) vs. Syracuse (6)	Orange, 1953

*Scored touchdown on play.

LONGEST KICKOFF RETURNS

Yds.	Player, Team (Score) vs. Opponent (Score)	Bowl, Year
100*	Kirby Dar Dar, Syracuse (26) vs. Colorado (22)	Fiesta, 1993
100*	Pete Panuska, Tennessee (27) vs. Maryland (28)	Sun, 1984
100*	Dave Lowery, Brigham Young (21) vs. Oklahoma St. (49)	Tangerine, 1976
100*	Mike Fink, Missouri (35) vs. Arizona St. (49)	Fiesta, 1972
100*(D)	Bob Smith, Texas A&M (40) vs. Georgia (20)	Presidential Cup, 1950
100*!	Al Hoisch, UCLA (14) vs. Illinois (45)	Rose, 1947

!Rose Bowl records carry as 103-yard return. *Scored touchdown on play.

LONGEST INTERCEPTION RETURNS

Yds.	Player, Team (Score) vs. Opponent (Score)	Bowl, Year
94*	David Baker, Oklahoma (48) vs. Duke (21)	Orange, 1958
91*	Don Hoover, Ohio (14) vs. West Tex. A&M (15)	Sun, 1962
90*	Norm Beal, Missouri (21) vs. Navy (14)	Orange, 1961
90*	Charlie Brembs, South Caro. (14) vs. Wake Forest (26)	Gator, 1946
90*(D)	G. P. Jackson, Texas Christian (7) vs. Centre (63)	Fort Worth Classic, 1921

*Scored touchdown on play.

LONGEST MISCELLANEOUS RETURNS

Yds.	Player, Team (Score) vs. Opponent (Score)	Bowl, Year
98	Greg Mather, Navy (14) vs. Missouri (21) (Int. Lat.)	Orange, 1961
80	Antonio Banks, Virginia Tech (45) vs. Indiana (20) (Blocked field goal return)	Independence, 1993
73	Dick Carpenter, Oklahoma (48) vs. Duke (21) (Int. Lat.)	Orange, 1958
65	Steve Manstedt, Nebraska (19) vs. Texas (3) (Live Fum.)	Cotton, 1974

Bowl Coaching Records

All-Time Bowl Appearances

(Ranked by Most Bowl Games Coached)

Coach (Teams Taken to Bowl)	G	W-L-T	Pct.
Paul "Bear" Bryant, Alabama, Texas A&M, Kentucky	29	15-12-2	.552
*Joe Paterno, Penn St.	24	15-8-1	.646
*Tom Osborne, Nebraska	21	8-13-0	.381
Vince Dooley, Georgia	20	8-10-2	.450
*Lou Holtz, William & Mary, North Caro. St., Arkansas, Notre Dame	18	10-6-2	.611
John Vaught, Mississippi	18	10-8-0	.556
*LaVell Edwards, Brigham Young	18	5-12-1	.306
*Bobby Bowden, West Va., Florida St.	17	13-3-1	.794
"Bo" Schembechler, Michigan	17	5-12-0	.294
*Johnny Majors, Iowa St., Pittsburgh, Tennessee	16	9-7-0	.563
Darrell Royal, Texas	16	8-7-1	.531
Don James, Kent, Washington	15	10-5-0	.667
*Hayden Fry, Southern Methodist, Iowa	14	5-8-1	.393
Bobby Dodd, Georgia Tech	13	9-4-0	.692
Barry Switzer, Oklahoma	13	8-5-0	.615
Charlie McClendon, Louisiana St.	13	7-6-0	.538
*Terry Donahue, UCLA	12	8-3-1	.708
Earle Bruce, Ohio St., Colorado St.	12	7-5-0	.583
"Woody" Hayes, Miami (Ohio), Ohio St.	12	6-6-0	.500
Ralph "Shug" Jordan, Auburn	12	5-7-0	.417
Bill Yeoman, Houston	11	6-4-1	.591
Jerry Claiborne, Virginia Tech, Maryland, Kentucky	11	3-8-0	.273

*Active coach.

All-Time Bowl Victories

Coach	Wins	Record	Coach	Wins	Record
Paul "Bear" Bryant	15	15-12-2	Barry Switzer	8	8-5-0
*Joe Paterno	15	15-8-1	Darrell Royal	8	8-7-1
*Bobby Bowden	13	13-3-1	Vince Dooley	8	8-10-2
Don James	10	10-5-0	*Tom Osborne	8	8-13-0
*Lou Holtz	10	10-6-2	Bob Devaney	7	7-3-0
John Vaught	10	10-8-0	Dan Devine	7	7-3-0
Bobby Dodd	9	9-4-0	Earle Bruce	7	7-5-0
*Johnny Majors	9	9-7-0	Charlie McClendon	7	7-6-0
*Terry Donahue	8	8-3-1			

*Active coach.

All-Time Bowl Winning Percentage

(Minimum 11 Games)

Coach, Last Team Coached	G	W-L-T	Pct.
*Bobby Bowden, Florida St.	17	13-3-1	.794
*Terry Donahue, UCLA	12	8-3-1	.708
Bobby Dodd, Georgia Tech	13	9-4-0	.692
Don James, Washington	15	10-5-0	.667
*Joe Paterno, Penn St.	24	15-8-1	.646
Barry Switzer, Oklahoma	13	8-5-0	.615
Bill Yeoman, Houston	11	6-4-1	.591
*Lou Holtz, Notre Dame	18	10-6-2	.611
Earle Bruce, Colorado St.	12	7-5-0	.583
*Johnny Majors, Pittsburgh	16	9-7-0	.563
John Vaught, Mississippi	18	10-8-0	.556
Paul "Bear" Bryant, Alabama	29	15-12-2	.552
Charlie McClendon, Louisiana St.	13	7-6-0	.538
Darrell Royal, Texas	16	8-7-1	.531
"Woody" Hayes, Ohio St.	12	6-6-0	.500
Vince Dooley, Georgia	20	8-10-2	.450
*Hayden Fry, Iowa	14	5-8-1	.393
Ralph "Shug" Jordan, Auburn	12	5-7-0	.417
*Tom Osborne, Nebraska	21	8-13-0	.381
*LaVell Edwards, Brigham Young	18	5-12-1	.306
"Bo" Schembechler, Michigan	17	5-12-0	.294
Jerry Claiborne, Kentucky	11	3-8-0	.273

*Active coach.

All-Time Bowl Coaching History

A total of 404 coaches have head-coached in history's 653 major bowl games (the term "major bowl" is defined above the alphabetical list of team bowl records). Below is an alphabetical list of all 404 bowl coaches, with their alma mater and year, their birth date, and their game-by-game bowl records, with name and date of each bowl, opponent, final score (own score first) and opposing coach (in parentheses). A handful coached service teams or colleges never in the major category but are included because they coached against a major team in a major bowl.

Coach/School	Bowl/Date	Opponent/Score (Coach)
JIM AIKEN, 0-1-0	(Wash. & Jeff. '22)	Born 5-26-99
Oregon	Cotton 1-1-49	Southern Methodist 12-21 (Matty Bell)
FRED AKERS, 2-8-0	(Arkansas '60)	Born 3-17-38
Wyoming	Fiesta 12-19-76	Oklahoma 7-41 (Barry Switzer)
Texas	Cotton 1-2-78	Notre Dame 10-38 (Dan Devine)
Texas	Sun 12-23-78	Maryland 42-0 (Jerry Claiborne)
Texas	Sun 12-22-79	Washington 7-14 (Don James)
Texas	Bluebonnet 12-31-80	North Caro. 7-16 (Dick Crum)
Texas	Cotton 1-1-82	Alabama 14-12 (Paul "Bear" Bryant)
Texas	Sun 12-25-82	North Caro. 10-26 (Dick Crum)
Texas	Cotton 1-2-84	Georgia 9-10 (Vince Dooley)
Texas	Freedom 12-26-84	Iowa 17-55 (Hayden Fry)
Texas	Bluebonnet 12-31-85	Air Force 16-24 (Fisher DeBerry)
BILL ALEXANDER, 3-2-0	(Georgia Tech '12)	Born 6-6-89
Georgia Tech	Rose 1-1-29	California 8-7 (Clarence "Nibs" Price)
Georgia Tech	Orange 1-1-40	Missouri 21-7 (Don Faurot)
Georgia Tech	Cotton 1-1-43	Texas 7-14 (Dana Bible)
Georgia Tech	Sugar 1-1-44	Tulsa 20-18 (Henry Frnka)
Georgia Tech	Orange 1-1-45	Tulsa 12-26 (Henry Frnka)
LEONARD "STUB" ALLISON, 1-0-0	(Carleton '17)	Born 1892
California	Rose 1-1-38	Alabama 13-0 (Frank Thomas)
BARRY ALVAREZ, 1-0-0	(Nebraska '69)	Born 12-30-46
Wisconsin	Rose 1-1-94	UCLA 21-16 (Terry Donahue)
MIKE ARCHER, 1-1-0	(Miami, Fla. '75)	Born 7-26-53
Louisiana St.	Gator 12-31-87	South Caro. 30-13 (Joe Morrison)
Louisiana St.	Hall of Fame 1-2-89	Syracuse 10-23 (Dick MacPherson)
IKE ARMSTRONG, 1-0-0	(Drake '23)	Born 6-8-95
Utah	Sun 1-2-39	New Mexico 16-0 (Ted Shipkey)
BILL ARNSPARGER, 0-3-0	(Miami, Ohio '50)	Born 12-16-26
Louisiana St.	Sugar 1-1-85	Nebraska 10-28 (Tom Osborne)
Louisiana St.	Liberty 12-27-85	Baylor 7-21 (Grant Teaff)
Louisiana St.	Sugar 1-1-87	Nebraska 15-30 (Tom Osborne)
CHRIS AULT, 0-1-0	(Nevada '68)	Born 11-8-47
Nevada	Las Vegas 12-18-92	Bowling Green 34-35 (Gary Blackney)
CHARLEY BACHMAN, 0-1-0	(Notre Dame '17)	Born 12-1-92
Michigan St.	Orange 1-1-38	Auburn 0-6 (Jack Meagher)
ENOCH BAGSHAW, 0-1-1	(Washington '08)	Born 1884
Washington	Rose 1-1-24	Navy 14-14 (Bob Folwell)
Washington	Rose 1-1-26	Alabama 19-20 (Wallace Wade)
GEORGE BARCLAY, 0-1-0	(North Caro. '35)	Born 5-14-11
Wash. & Lee	Gator 1-1-51	Wyoming 7-20 (Bowden Wyatt)

Coach/School	Bowl/Date	Opponent/Score (Coach)
BILL BARNES, 0-1-0 (Tennessee '41) Born 10-20-17		
UCLA	Rose 1-1-62	Minnesota 3-21 (Murray Warmath)
WILLIS BARNES, 1-1-1 (Nebraska) Born 10-22-00		
New Mexico	Sun 1-1-44	Southwestern (Tex.) 0-7 (R. M. Medley)
New Mexico	Sun 1-1-46	Denver 34-24 (Clyde "Cac" Hubbard)
New Mexico	Harbor 1-1-47	Montana St. 13-13 (Clyde Carpenter)
JOHN BARNHILL, 2-1-1 (Tennessee '28) Born 2-21-03		
Tennessee	Sugar 1-1-43	Tulsa 14-7 (Henry Frnka)
Tennessee	Rose 1-1-45	Southern Cal 0-25 (Jeff Cravath)
Arkansas	Cotton 1-1-47	Louisiana St. 0-0 (Bernie Moore)
Arkansas	Dixie 1-1-48	William & Mary 21-19 (Rube McCray)
BILL BATTLE, 4-1-0 (Alabama '63) Born 12-8-41		
Tennessee	Sugar 1-1-71	Air Force 34-13 (Ben Martin)
Tennessee	Liberty 12-20-71	Arkansas 14-13 (Frank Broyles)
Tennessee	Bluebonnet 12-30-72	Louisiana St. 24-17 (Charlie McClendon)
Tennessee	Gator 12-29-73	Texas Tech 19-28 (Jim Carlen)
Tennessee	Liberty 12-16-74	Maryland 7-3 (Jerry Claiborne)
SAMMY BAUGH, 0-1-0 (Texas Christian '37) Born 3-17-14		
Hardin-Simmons	Sun 12-31-58	Wyoming 6-14 (Bob Devaney)
FRANK BEAMER, 1-0-0 (Virginia Tech '69) Born 10-18-46		
Virginia Tech	Independence 12-31-93	Indiana 45-20 (Bill Mallory)
ALEX BELL, 1-1-0 (Villanova '38) Born 8-12-15		
Villanova	Sun 12-20-61	Wichita St. 17-9 (Hank Foldberg)
Villanova	Liberty 12-15-62	Oregon St. 0-6 (Tommy Prothro)
MATTY BELL, 1-1-1 (Centre '20) Born 2-22-99		
Southern Methodist	Rose 1-1-36	Stanford 0-7 (Claude "Tiny" Thornhill)
Southern Methodist	Cotton 1-1-48	Penn St. 13-13 (Bob Higgins)
Southern Methodist	Cotton 1-1-49	Oregon 21-13 (Jim Aiken)
EMORY BELLARD, 2-3-0 (Southwest Tex. St. '49) Born 12-17-27		
Texas A&M	Liberty 12-22-75	Southern Cal 0-20 (John McKay)
Texas A&M	Sun 1-2-77	Florida 37-14 (Doug Dickey)
Texas A&M	Bluebonnet 12-31-77	Southern Cal 28-47 (John Robinson)
Mississippi St.	Sun 12-27-80	Nebraska 17-31 (Tom Osborne)
Mississippi St.	All-American 12-31-81	Kansas 10-0 (Don Fambrough)
ARTHUR "DUTCH" BERGMAN, 1-0-1 (Notre Dame '20) Born 2-23-95		
Catholic	Orange 1-1-36	Mississippi 20-19 (Ed Walker)
Catholic	Sun 1-1-40	Arizona St. 0-0 (Millard "Dixie" Howell)
HUGO BEZDEK, 1-1-0 (Chicago '06) Born 4-1-84		
Oregon	Rose 1-1-17	Pennsylvania 14-0 (Bob Folwell)
Penn St.	Rose 1-1-23	Southern Cal 3-14 (Elmer "Gus" Henderson)
DANA BIBLE, 3-0-1 (Carson-Newman '12) Born 10-8-91		
Texas A&M	Dixie Classic 1-2-22	Centre 22-14 (Charley Moran)
Texas	Cotton 1-1-43	Georgia Tech 14-7 (Bill Alexander)
Texas	Cotton 1-1-44	Randolph Field 7-7 (Frank Tritico)
Texas	Cotton 1-1-46	Missouri 40-27 (Chauncey Simpson)
JACK BICKNELL, 2-2-0 (Montclair St. '60) Born 2-20-38		
Boston College	Tangerine 12-18-82	Auburn 26-33 (Pat Dye)
Boston College	Liberty 12-29-83	Notre Dame 18-19 (Gerry Faust)
Boston College	Cotton 1-1-85	Houston 45-28 (Bill Yeoman)
Boston College	Hall of Fame 12-23-86	Georgia 27-24 (Vince Dooley)
BERNIE BIERMAN, 0-1-0 (Minnesota '16) Born 3-11-94		
Tulane	Rose 1-1-32	Southern Cal 12-21 (Howard Jones)
GARY BLACKNEY, 2-0-0 (Connecticut '67) Born 12-10-55		
Bowling Green	California 12-14-91	Fresno St. 28-21 (Jim Sweeney)
Bowling Green	Las Vegas 12-18-92	Nevada 35-34 (Chris Ault)
BOBBY BOWDEN, 13-3-1 (Samford '53) Born 11-8-29		
West Va.	Peach 12-29-72	North Caro. St. 13-49 (Lou Holtz)
West Va.	Peach 12-31-75	North Caro. St. 13-10 (Lou Holtz)
Florida St.	Tangerine 12-23-77	Texas Tech 40-17 (Steve Sloan)
Florida St.	Orange 1-1-80	Oklahoma 7-24 (Barry Switzer)
Florida St.	Orange 1-1-81	Oklahoma 17-18 (Barry Switzer)
Florida St.	Gator 12-30-82	West Va. 31-12 (Don Nehlen)
Florida St.	Peach 12-30-83	North Caro. 28-3 (Dick Crum)
Florida St.	Fla. Citrus 12-22-84	Georgia 17-17 (Vince Dooley)
Florida St.	Gator 12-30-85	Oklahoma St. 34-23 (Pat Jones)
Florida St.	All-American 12-31-86	Indiana 27-13 (Bill Mallory)
Florida St.	Fiesta 1-1-88	Nebraska 31-28 (Tom Osborne)
Florida St.	Sugar 1-2-89	Auburn 13-7 (Pat Dye)
Florida St.	Fiesta 1-1-90	Nebraska 41-17 (Tom Osborne)
Florida St.	Blockbuster 12-28-90	Penn St. 24-17 (Joe Paterno)
Florida St.	Cotton 1-1-92	Texas A&M 10-2 (R. C. Slocum)
Florida St.	Orange 1-1-93	Nebraska 27-14 (Tom Osborne)
Florida St.	Orange 1-1-94	Nebraska 18-16 (Tom Osborne)
JEFF BOWER, 0-1-0 (Southern Miss. '76) Born 5-28-53		
Southern Miss.	All-American 12-28-90	North Caro. St. 27-31 (Dick Sheridan)
SAM BOYD, 1-0-0 (Baylor '38) Born 8-12-15		
Baylor	Sugar 1-1-57	Tennessee 13-7 (Bowden Wyatt)
WESLEY BRADSHAW, 0-1-0 (Baylor '23) Born 11-26-98		
Ouachita Baptist	Shrine 12-18-48	Hardin-Simmons 12-40 (Warren Woodson)

Coach/School	Bowl/Date	Opponent/Score (Coach)
BILLY BREWER, 3-2-0 (Mississippi '61) Born 10-8-35		
Mississippi	Independence 12-10-83	Air Force 3-9 (Ken Hatfield)
Mississippi	Independence 12-20-86	Texas Tech 20-17 (Spike Dykes)
Mississippi	All-American 12-29-89	Air Force 42-29 (Fisher DeBerry)
Mississippi	Gator 1-1-91	Michigan 3-35 (Gary Moeller)
Mississippi	Liberty 12-31-92	Air Force 13-0 (Fisher DeBerry)
JOHN BRIDGERS, 2-1-0 (Auburn '47) Born 1-13-22		
Baylor	Gator 12-31-60	Florida 12-13 (Ray Graves)
Baylor	Gotham 12-9-61	Utah St. 24-9 (John Ralston)
Baylor	Bluebonnet 12-21-63	Louisiana St. 14-7 (Charlie McClendon)
RICH BROOKS, 1-2-0 (Oregon St. '63) Born 8-20-41		
Oregon	Independence 12-16-89	Tulsa 27-24 (Dave Rader)
Oregon	Freedom 12-29-90	Colorado St. 31-32 (Earle Bruce)
Oregon	Independence 12-31-92	Wake Forest 35-39 (Bill Dooley)
J. O. "BUDDY" BROTHERS, 0-1-0 (Texas Tech '31) Born 5-29-09		
Tulsa	Sun 1-1-53	Florida 13-14 (Bob Woodruff)
MACK BROWN, 1-2-0 (Florida St. '74) Born 8-27-51		
Tulane	Independence 12-19-87	Washington 12-24 (Don James)
North Caro.	Peach 1-2-93	Mississippi St. 21-17 (Jackie Sherrill)
North Caro.	Gator 12-31-93	Alabama 10-24 (Gene Stallings)
FRANK BROYLES, 4-6-0 (Georgia Tech '47) Born 12-26-24		
Arkansas	Gator 1-2-60	Georgia Tech 14-7 (Bobby Dodd)
Arkansas	Cotton 1-2-61	Duke 6-7 (Bill Murray)
Arkansas	Sugar 1-1-62	Alabama 3-10 (Paul "Bear" Bryant)
Arkansas	Sugar 1-1-63	Mississippi 13-17 (John Vaught)
Arkansas	Cotton 1-1-65	Nebraska 10-7 (Bob Devaney)
Arkansas	Cotton 1-1-66	Louisiana St. 7-14 (Charlie McClendon)
Arkansas	Sugar 1-1-69	Georgia 16-2 (Vince Dooley)
Arkansas	Sugar 1-1-70	Mississippi 22-27 (John Vaught)
Arkansas	Liberty 12-20-71	Tennessee 13-14 (Bill Battle)
Arkansas	Cotton 1-1-76	Georgia 31-10 (Vince Dooley)
EARLE BRUCE, 7-5-0 (Ohio St. '53) Born 3-8-31		
Tampa	Tangerine 12-29-72	Kent 21-18 (Don James)
Iowa St.	Peach 12-31-77	North Caro. St. 14-24 (Bo Rein)
Iowa St.	All-American 12-20-78	Texas A&M 12-28 (Tom Wilson)
Ohio St.	Rose 1-1-80	Southern Cal 16-17 (John Robinson)
Ohio St.	Fiesta 12-26-80	Penn St. 19-31 (Joe Paterno)
Ohio St.	Liberty 12-30-81	Navy 31-28 (George Welsh)
Ohio St.	Holiday 12-17-82	Brigham Young 47-17 (LaVell Edwards)
Ohio St.	Fiesta 1-2-84	Pittsburgh 28-23 (Foge Fazio)
Ohio St.	Rose 1-1-85	Southern Cal 17-20 (Ted Tollner)
Ohio St.	Fla. Citrus 12-28-85	Brigham Young 10-7 (LaVell Edwards)
Ohio St.	Cotton 1-1-87	Texas A&M 28-12 (Jackie Sherrill)
Colorado St.	Freedom 12-29-90	Oregon 32-31 (Rich Brooks)
MILT BRUHN, 0-2-0 (Minnesota '35) Born 7-28-12		
Wisconsin	Rose 1-1-60	Washington 8-44 (Jim Owens)
Wisconsin	Rose 1-2-63	Southern Cal 37-42 (John McKay)
MIKE BRUMBELOW, 2-1-0 (Texas Christian '30) Born 7-13-06		
UTEP	Sun 1-1-54	Southern Miss. 37-14 (Thad "Pie" Vann)
UTEP	Sun 1-1-55	Florida St. 47-20 (Tom Nugent)
UTEP	Sun 1-1-57	Geo. Washington 0-13 (Eugene "Bo" Sherman)
PAUL "BEAR" BRYANT, 15-12-2 (Alabama '36) Born 9-11-13		
Kentucky	Great Lakes 12-6-47	Villanova 24-14 (Jordan Oliver)
Kentucky	Orange 1-2-50	Santa Clara 13-21 (Len Casanova)
Kentucky	Sugar 1-1-51	Oklahoma 13-7 (Bud Wilkinson)
Kentucky	Cotton 1-1-52	Texas Christian 20-7 (Leo "Dutch" Meyer)
Texas A&M	Gator 12-28-57	Tennessee 0-3 (Bowden Wyatt)
Alabama	Liberty 12-19-59	Penn St. 0-7 (Charles "Rip" Engle)
Alabama	Bluebonnet 12-17-60	Texas 3-3 (Darrell Royal)
Alabama	Sugar 1-1-62	Arkansas 10-3 (Frank Broyles)
Alabama	Orange 1-1-63	Oklahoma 17-0 (Bud Wilkinson)
Alabama	Sugar 1-1-64	Mississippi 12-7 (John Vaught)
Alabama	Orange 1-1-65	Texas 17-21 (Darrell Royal)
Alabama	Orange 1-1-66	Nebraska 39-28 (Bob Devaney)
Alabama	Sugar 1-2-67	Nebraska 34-7 (Bob Devaney)
Alabama	Cotton 1-1-68	Texas A&M 16-20 (Gene Stallings)
Alabama	Gator 12-28-68	Missouri 10-35 (Dan Devine)
Alabama	Liberty 12-13-69	Colorado 33-47 (Eddie Crowder)
Alabama	Bluebonnet 12-31-70	Oklahoma 24-24 (Chuck Fairbanks)
Alabama	Orange 1-1-72	Nebraska 6-38 (Bob Devaney)
Alabama	Cotton 1-1-73	Texas 13-17 (Darrell Royal)
Alabama	Sugar 12-31-73	Notre Dame 23-24 (Ara Parseghian)
Alabama	Orange 1-1-75	Notre Dame 11-13 (Ara Parseghian)
Alabama	Sugar 12-31-75	Penn St. 13-6 (Joe Paterno)
Alabama	Liberty 12-20-76	UCLA 36-6 (Terry Donahue)
Alabama	Sugar 1-2-78	Ohio St. 35-6 (Woody Hayes)
Alabama	Sugar 1-1-79	Penn St. 14-7 (Joe Paterno)
Alabama	Sugar 1-1-80	Arkansas 24-9 (Lou Holtz)
Alabama	Cotton 1-1-81	Baylor 30-2 (Grant Teaff)
Alabama	Cotton 1-1-82	Texas 12-14 (Fred Akers)
Alabama	Liberty 12-29-82	Illinois 21-15 (Mike White)
FRANK BURNS, 0-1-0 (Rutgers '49) Born 3-16-28		
Rutgers	Garden State 12-16-78	Arizona St. 18-34 (Frank Kush)

Coach/School	Bowl/Date	Opponent/Score (Coach)
LEON BURTNETT, 0-1-0 (Southwestern, Kan. '65) Born 5-30-43		
Purdue	Peach 12-31-84	Virginia 24-27 (George Welsh)
WALLY BUTTS, 5-2-1 (Mercer '28) Born 2-7-05		
Georgia	Orange 1-1-42	Texas Christian 40-26 (Leo "Dutch" Meyer)
Georgia	Rose 1-1-43	UCLA 9-0 (Edwin "Babe" Horrell)
Georgia	Oil 1-1-46	Tulsa 20-6 (Henry Frnka)
Georgia	Sugar 1-1-47	North Caro. 20-10 (Carl Snavely)
Georgia	Gator 1-1-48	Maryland 20-20 (Jim Tatum)
Georgia	Orange 1-1-49	Texas 28-41 (Blair Cherry)
Georgia	Presidential Cup 12-9-50	Texas A&M 20-40 (Harry Stiteler)
Georgia	Orange 1-1-60	Missouri 14-0 (Dan Devine)
EDDIE CAMERON, 1-0-0 (Wash. & Lee '24) Born 4-22-02		
Duke	Sugar 1-1-45	Alabama 29-26 (Frank Thomas)
FRANK CAMP, 1-0-0 (Transylvania '30) Born 12-23-05		
Louisville	Sun 1-1-58	Drake 34-20 (Warren Gaer)
JIM CARLEN, 2-5-1 (Georgia Tech '55) Born 7-11-33		
West Va.	Peach 12-30-69	South Caro. 14-3 (Paul Dietzel)
Texas Tech	Sun 12-19-70	Georgia Tech 9-17 (Bud Carson)
Texas Tech	Sun 12-30-72	North Caro. 28-32 (Bill Dooley)
Texas Tech	Gator 12-29-73	Tennessee 28-19 (Bill Battle)
Texas Tech	Peach 12-28-74	Vanderbilt 6-6 (Steve Sloan)
South Caro.	Tangerine 12-20-75	Miami (Ohio) 7-20 (Dick Crum)
South Caro.	All-American 12-29-79	Missouri 14-24 (Warren Powers)
South Caro.	Gator 12-29-80	Pittsburgh 8-37 (Jackie Sherrill)
CLYDE CARPENTER, 0-0-1 (Montana '32) Born 4-17-08		
Montana St.	Harbor 1-1-47	New Mexico 13-13 (Willis Barnes)
BUD CARSON, 1-1-0 (North Caro. '52) Born 4-28-30		
Georgia Tech	Sun 12-19-70	Texas Tech 17-9 (Jim Carlen)
Georgia Tech	Peach 12-30-71	Mississippi 18-41 (Billy Kinard)
LEN CASANOVA, 2-2-0 (Santa Clara '27) Born 6-12-05		
Santa Clara	Orange 1-2-50	Kentucky 21-13 (Paul "Bear" Bryant)
Oregon	Rose 1-1-58	Ohio St. 7-10 (Woody Hayes)
Oregon	Liberty 12-17-60	Penn St. 12-41 (Charles "Rip" Engle)
Oregon	Sun 12-31-63	Southern Methodist 21-14 (Hayden Fry)
MILES CASTEEL, 0-1-0 (Kalamazoo '25) Born 12-30-96		
Arizona	Salad 1-1-49	Drake 13-14 (Al Kawal)
PETE CAWTHON, 0-2-0 (Southwestern, Tex. '20) Born 8-24-98		
Texas Tech	Sun 1-1-38	West Va. 6-7 (Marshall "Little Sleepy" Glenn)
Texas Tech	Cotton 1-2-39	St. Mary's (Cal.) 13-20 (Edward "Slip" Madigan)
BLAIR CHERRY, 2-1-0 (Texas Christian '24) Born 9-7-01		
Texas	Sugar 1-1-48	Alabama 27-7 (Harold "Red" Drew)
Texas	Orange 1-1-49	Georgia 41-28 (Wally Butts)
Texas	Cotton 1-1-51	Tennessee 14-20 (Bob Neyland)
JERRY CLAIBORNE, 3-8-0 (Kentucky '50) Born 8-26-28		
Virginia Tech	Liberty 12-10-66	Miami (Fla.) 7-14 (Charlie Tate)
Virginia Tech	Liberty 12-14-68	Mississippi 17-34 (John Vaught)
Maryland	Peach 12-28-73	Georgia 16-17 (Vince Dooley)
Maryland	Liberty 12-16-74	Tennessee 3-7 (Bill Battle)
Maryland	Gator 12-29-75	Florida 13-0 (Doug Dickey)
Maryland	Cotton 1-1-77	Houston 21-30 (Bill Yeoman)
Maryland	All-American 12-22-77	Minnesota 17-3 (Cal Stoll)
Maryland	Sun 12-23-78	Texas 0-42 (Fred Akers)
Maryland	Tangerine 12-20-80	Florida 20-35 (Charley Pell)
Kentucky	All-American 12-22-83	West Va. 16-20 (Don Nehlen)
Kentucky	All-American 12-29-84	Wisconsin 20-19 (Dave McClain)
CECIL COLEMAN, 1-0-0 (Arizona St. '50) Born 4-12-26		
Fresno St.	Mercy 11-23-61	Bowling Green 36-6 (Doyt Perry)
BOBBY COLLINS, 3-2-0 (Mississippi St. '55) Born 10-25-33		
Southern Miss.	Independence 12-13-70	McNeese St. 16-14 (Ernie Duplechin)
Southern Miss.	Tangerine 12-19-81	Missouri 19-17 (Warren Powers)
Southern Methodist	Cotton 1-1-83	Pittsburgh 7-3 (Foge Fazio)
Southern Methodist	Sun 12-24-83	Alabama 7-28 (Ray Perkins)
Southern Methodist	Aloha 12-29-84	Notre Dame 27-20 (Gerry Faust)
JOHN COOPER, 3-5-0 (Iowa St. '62) Born 7-2-37		
Arizona St.	Holiday 12-22-85	Arkansas 17-18 (Ken Hatfield)
Arizona St.	Rose 1-1-87	Michigan 22-15 (Glenn "Bo" Schembechler)
Arizona St.	Freedom 12-30-87	Air Force 33-28 (Fisher DeBerry)
Ohio St.	Hall of Fame 1-1-90	Auburn 14-31 (Pat Dye)
Ohio St.	Liberty 12-27-90	Air Force 11-23 (Fisher DeBerry)
Ohio St.	Hall of Fame 1-1-92	Syracuse 24-17 (Paul Pasqualoni)
Ohio St.	Fla. Citrus 1-1-93	Georgia 14-21 (Ray Goff)
Ohio St.	Holiday 12-30-93	Brigham Young 28-21 (LaVell Edwards)
LEE CORSO, 1-0-1 (Florida St. '57) Born 8-7-35		
Louisville	Pasadena 12-19-70	Long Beach St. 24-24 (Jim Stangeland)
Indiana	Holiday 12-21-79	Brigham Young 38-37 (LaVell Edwards)
GENE CORUM, 0-1-0 (West Va. '48) Born 5-29-21		
West Va.	Liberty 12-19-64	Utah 6-32 (Ray Nagel)
DON CORYELL, 1-0-0 (Washington '50) Born 10-17-24		
San Diego St.	Pasadena 12-6-69	Boston U. 28-7 (Larry Naviaux)
TOM COUGHLIN, 1-1-0 (Syracuse '68) Born 8-31-46		
Boston College	Hall of Fame 1-1-93	Tennessee 23-38 (Phillip Fulmer)
Boston College	Carquest 1-1-94	Virginia 31-13 (George Welsh)
TED COX, 1-0-0 (Minnesota '26) Born 6-30-03		
Tulane	Sugar 1-1-35	Temple 20-14 (Glenn "Pop" Warner)
JEFF CRAVATH, 2-2-0 (Southern Cal '27) Born 2-5-05		
Southern Cal	Rose 1-1-44	Washington 29-0 (Ralph "Pest" Welch)
Southern Cal	Rose 1-1-45	Tennessee 25-0 (John Barnhill)
Southern Cal	Rose 1-1-46	Alabama 14-34 (Frank Thomas)
Southern Cal	Rose 1-1-48	Michigan 0-49 (H. O. "Fritz" Crisler)
H. O. "FRITZ" CRISLER, 1-0-0 (Chicago '22) Born 1-2-99		
Michigan	Rose 1-1-48	Southern Cal 49-0 (Jeff Cravath)
EDDIE CROWDER, 3-2-0 (Oklahoma '55) Born 8-26-31		
Colorado	Bluebonnet 12-23-67	Miami (Fla.) 31-21 (Charlie Tate)
Colorado	Liberty 12-13-69	Alabama 47-33 (Paul "Bear" Bryant)
Colorado	Liberty 12-12-70	Tulane 3-17 (Jim Pittman)
Colorado	Bluebonnet 12-31-71	Houston 29-17 (Bill Yeoman)
Colorado	Gator 12-30-72	Auburn 3-24 (Ralph "Shug" Jordan)
JACK CROWE, 0-1-0 (Ala.-Birmingham '70) Born 4-6-48		
Arkansas	Independence 12-29-91	Georgia 15-24 (Ray Goff)
JIM CROWLEY, 1-1-0 (Notre Dame '25) Born 9-10-02		
Fordham	Cotton 1-1-41	Texas A&M 12-13 (Homer Norton)
Fordham	Sugar 1-1-42	Missouri 2-0 (Don Faurot)
DICK CRUM, 6-2-0 (Mount Union '57) Born 4-29-34		
Miami (Ohio)	Tangerine 12-21-74	Georgia 21-10 (Vince Dooley)
Miami (Ohio)	Tangerine 12-20-75	South Caro. 20-7 (Jim Carlen)
North Caro.	Gator 12-29-79	Michigan 17-15 (Glenn "Bo" Schembechler)
North Caro.	Bluebonnet 12-31-80	Texas 16-7 (Fred Akers)
North Caro.	Gator 12-28-81	Arkansas 31-27 (Lou Holtz)
North Caro.	Sun 12-25-82	Texas 26-10 (Fred Akers)
North Caro.	Peach 12-30-83	Florida St. 3-28 (Bobby Bowden)
North Caro.	Aloha 12-27-86	Arizona 21-30 (Larry Smith)
FRAN CURCI, 1-0-0 (Miami, Fla. '60) Born 6-11-38		
Kentucky	Peach 12-31-76	North Caro. 21-0 (Bill Dooley)
BILL CURRY, 2-3-0 (Georgia Tech '65) Born 10-21-42		
Georgia Tech	All-American 12-31-85	Michigan St. 17-14 (George Perles)
Alabama	Hall of Fame 1-2-88	Michigan 24-28 (Glenn "Bo" Schembechler)
Alabama	Sun 12-24-88	Army 29-28 (Jim Young)
Alabama	Sugar 1-1-90	Miami (Fla.) 25-33 (Dennis Erickson)
Kentucky	Peach 12-31-93	Clemson 13-14 (Tommy West)
JACK "CACTUS JACK" CURTICE, 1-1-0 (Transylvania '30) Born 5-24-07		
UTEP	Sun 1-1-49	West Va. 12-21 (Dud DeGroot)
UTEP	Sun 1-2-50	Georgetown 33-20 (Bob Margarita)
JOHN "OX" Da GROSA, 0-1-0 (Colgate '26) Born 2-17-02		
Holy Cross	Orange 1-1-46	Miami (Fla.) 6-13 (Jack Harding)
GARY DARNELL, 0-1-0 (Oklahoma St. '71) Born 10-15-48		
Florida	Freedom 12-29-89	Washington 7-34 (Don James)
DUFFY DAUGHERTY, 1-1-0 (Syracuse '40) Born 9-8-15		
Michigan St.	Rose 1-2-56	UCLA 17-14 (Henry "Red" Sanders)
Michigan St.	Rose 1-1-66	UCLA 12-14 (Tommy Prothro)
BOB DAVIS, 0-1-0 (Utah '30) Born 2-13-08		
Colorado St.	Raisin 1-1-49	Occidental 20-21 (Roy Dennis)
PAUL DAVIS, 1-0-0 (Mississippi '47) Born 2-3-22		
Mississippi St.	Liberty 12-21-63	North Caro. St. 16-12 (Earle Edwards)
LOWELL "RED" DAWSON, 0-1-0 (Tulane '30) Born 12-26-06		
Tulane	Sugar 1-1-40	Texas A&M 13-14 (Homer Norton)
FISHER DeBERRY, 4-3-0 (Wofford '60) Born 9-9-38		
Air Force	Independence 12-15-84	Virginia Tech 23-7 (Bill Dooley)
Air Force	Bluebonnet 12-31-85	Texas 24-16 (Fred Akers)
Air Force	Freedom 12-30-87	Arizona St. 28-33 (John Cooper)
Air Force	Liberty 12-29-89	Mississippi 29-42 (Billy Brewer)
Air Force	Liberty 12-27-90	Ohio St. 23-11 (John Cooper)
Air Force	Liberty 12-29-91	Mississippi St. 38-15 (Jackie Sherrill)
Air Force	Liberty 12-31-92	Mississippi 0-13 (Billy Brewer)
DUD DeGROOT, 1-0-0 (Stanford '24) Born 11-20-95		
West Va.	Sun 1-1-49	UTEP 21-12 (Jack "Cactus Jack" Curtice)
ROY DENNIS, 1-0-0 (Occidental '33) Born 5-13-05		
Occidental	Raisin 1-1-49	Colorado St. 21-20 (Bob Davis)
HERB DeROMEDI, 0-1-0 (Michigan '60) Born 5-26-39		
Central Mich.	California 12-8-90	San Jose St. 24-48 (Terry Shea)
BOB DEVANEY, 7-3-0 (Alma '39) Born 4-2-15		
Wyoming	Sun 12-31-58	Hardin-Simmons 14-6 (Sammy Baugh)
Nebraska	Gotham 12-15-62	Miami (Fla.) 36-34 (Andy Gustafson)
Nebraska	Orange 1-1-64	Auburn 13-7 (Ralph "Shug" Jordan)

Coach/School	Bowl/Date	Opponent/Score (Coach)
Nebraska	Cotton 1-1-65	Arkansas 7-10 (Frank Broyles)
Nebraska	Orange 1-1-66	Alabama 28-39 (Paul "Bear" Bryant)
Nebraska	Sugar 1-2-67	Alabama 7-34 (Paul "Bear" Bryant)
Nebraska	Sun 12-20-69	Georgia 45-6 (Vince Dooley)
Nebraska	Orange 1-1-71	Louisiana St. 17-12 (Charlie McClendon)
Nebraska	Orange 1-1-72	Alabama 38-6 (Paul "Bear" Bryant)
Nebraska	Orange 1-1-73	Notre Dame 40-6 (Ara Parseghian)

DAN DEVINE, 7-3-0 (Minn.-Duluth '48) Born 12-23-24

Missouri	Orange 1-1-60	Georgia 0-14 (Wally Butts)
Missouri	Orange 1-2-61	Navy 21-14 (Wayne Hardin)
Missouri	Bluebonnet 12-22-62	Georgia Tech 14-10 (Bobby Dodd)
Missouri	Sugar 1-1-66	Florida 20-18 (Ray Graves)
Missouri	Gator 12-28-68	Alabama 35-10 (Paul "Bear" Bryant)
Missouri	Orange 1-1-70	Penn St. 3-10 (Joe Paterno)
Notre Dame	Gator 12-27-76	Penn St. 20-9 (Joe Paterno)
Notre Dame	Cotton 1-2-78	Texas 38-10 (Fred Akers)
Notre Dame	Cotton 1-1-79	Houston 35-34 (Bill Yeoman)
Notre Dame	Sugar 1-1-81	Georgia 10-17 (Vince Dooley)

PHIL DICKENS, 1-0-0 (Tennessee '37) Born 6-29-14

Wyoming	Sun 1-2-56	Texas Tech 21-14 (DeWitt Weaver)

DOUG DICKEY, 2-7-0 (Florida '54) Born 6-24-32

Tennessee	Bluebonnet 12-18-65	Tulsa 27-6 (Glenn Dobbs)
Tennessee	Gator 12-31-66	Syracuse 18-12 (Ben Schwartzwalder)
Tennessee	Orange 1-1-68	Oklahoma 24-26 (Chuck Fairbanks)
Tennessee	Cotton 1-1-69	Texas 13-35 (Darrell Royal)
Tennessee	Gator 12-27-69	Florida 13-14 (Ray Graves)
Florida	Tangerine 12-22-73	Miami (Ohio) 7-16 (Bill Mallory)
Florida	Sugar 12-31-74	Nebraska 10-13 (Tom Osborne)
Florida	Gator 12-29-75	Maryland 0-13 (Jerry Claiborne)
Florida	Sun 1-2-77	Texas A&M 14-37 (Emory Bellard)

JIM DICKEY, 0-1-0 (Houston '56) Born 3-22-34

Kansas St.	Independence 12-11-82	Wisconsin 3-14 (Dave McClain)

BILL "LONE STAR" DIETZ, 1-0-0 (Carlisle '12) Born 8-15-85

Washington St.	Rose 1-1-16	Brown 14-0 (Ed Robinson)

PAUL DIETZEL, 2-2-0 (Miami, Ohio '48) Born 9-5-24

Louisiana St.	Sugar 1-1-59	Clemson 7-0 (Frank Howard)
Louisiana St.	Sugar 1-1-60	Mississippi 0-21 (John Vaught)
Louisiana St.	Orange 1-1-62	Colorado 25-7 (Sonny Grandelius)
South Caro.	Peach 12-20-69	West Va. 3-14 (Jim Carlen)

BOBBY DOBBS, 2-0-0 (Army '46) Born 10-13-22

UTEP	Sun 12-31-65	Texas Christian 13-12 (Abe Martin)
UTEP	Sun 12-30-67	Mississippi 14-7 (John Vaught)

GLENN DOBBS, 1-1-0 (Tulsa '43) Born 7-12-20

Tulsa	Bluebonnet 12-19-64	Mississippi 14-7 (John Vaught)
Tulsa	Bluebonnet 12-18-65	Tennessee 6-27 (Doug Dickey)

BOBBY DODD, 9-4-0 (Tennessee '31) Born 11-11-08

Georgia Tech	Oil 1-1-47	St. Mary's (Cal.) 41-19 (Jimmy Phelan)
Georgia Tech	Orange 1-1-48	Kansas 20-14 (George Sauer)
Georgia Tech	Orange 1-1-52	Baylor 17-14 (George Sauer)
Georgia Tech	Sugar 1-1-53	Mississippi 24-7 (John Vaught)
Georgia Tech	Sugar 1-1-54	West Va. 42-19 (Art Lewis)
Georgia Tech	Cotton 1-1-55	Arkansas 14-6 (Bowden Wyatt)
Georgia Tech	Sugar 1-2-56	Pittsburgh 7-0 (John Michelosen)
Georgia Tech	Gator 12-29-56	Pittsburgh 21-14 (John Michelosen)
Georgia Tech	Gator 1-2-60	Arkansas 7-14 (Frank Broyles)
Georgia Tech	Gator 12-30-61	Penn St. 15-30 (Charles "Rip" Engle)
Georgia Tech	Bluebonnet 12-22-62	Missouri 10-14 (Dan Devine)
Georgia Tech	Gator 12-31-65	Texas Tech 31-21 (J. T. King)
Georgia Tech	Orange 1-2-67	Florida 12-27 (Ray Graves)

ED DOHERTY, 0-2-0 (Boston College '44) Born 7-25-18

Arizona St.	Salad 1-1-50	Xavier (Ohio) 21-33 (Ed Kluska)
Arizona St.	Salad 1-1-51	Miami (Ohio) 21-34 (Woody Hayes)

JACK DOLAND, 1-0-0 (Tulane '50) Born 3-3-28

McNeese St.	Independence 12-13-76	Tulsa 20-16 (F. A. Dry)

TERRY DONAHUE, 8-3-1 (UCLA '67) Born 6-24-44

UCLA	Liberty 12-30-76	Alabama 6-36 (Paul "Bear" Bryant)
UCLA	Fiesta 12-25-78	Arkansas 10-10 (Lou Holtz)
UCLA	Bluebonnet 12-31-81	Michigan 14-33 (Glenn "Bo" Schembechler)
UCLA	Rose 1-1-83	Michigan 24-14 (Glenn "Bo" Schembechler)
UCLA	Rose 1-2-84	Illinois 45-9 (Mike White)
UCLA	Fiesta 1-1-85	Miami (Fla.) 39-37 (Jimmy Johnson)
UCLA	Rose 1-1-86	Iowa 45-28 (Hayden Fry)
UCLA	Freedom 12-30-86	Brigham Young 31-10 (LaVell Edwards)
UCLA	Aloha 12-25-87	Florida 20-16 (Galen Hall)
UCLA	Cotton 1-2-89	Arkansas 17-3 (Ken Hatfield)
UCLA	John Hancock 12-31-91	Illinois 6-3 (Lou Tepper)
UCLA	Rose 1-1-94	Wisconsin 16-21 (Barry Alvarez)

BILL DOOLEY, 3-7-0 (Mississippi St. '56) Born 5-19-34

North Caro.	Peach 12-30-70	Arizona St. 26-48 (Frank Kush)
North Caro.	Gator 12-31-71	Georgia 3-7 (Vince Dooley)
North Caro.	Sun 12-30-72	Texas Tech 32-28 (Jim Carlen)
North Caro.	Sun 12-28-74	Mississippi St. 24-26 (Bob Tyler)
North Caro.	Peach 12-31-76	Kentucky 0-21 (Fran Curci)
North Caro.	Liberty 12-19-77	Nebraska 17-21 (Tom Osborne)
Virginia Tech	Peach 1-2-81	Miami (Fla.) 10-20 (Howard Schnellenberger)
Virginia Tech	Independence 12-15-84	Air Force 7-23 (Fisher DeBerry)
Virginia Tech	Peach 12-31-86	North Caro. St. 25-24 (Dick Sheridan)
Wake Forest	Independence 12-31-92	Oregon 39-35 (Rich Brooks)

VINCE DOOLEY, 8-10-2 (Auburn '54) Born 9-4-32

Georgia	Sun 12-26-64	Texas Tech 7-0 (J. T. King)
Georgia	Cotton 12-31-66	Southern Methodist 24-9 (Hayden Fry)
Georgia	Liberty 12-16-67	North Caro. St. 7-14 (Earle Edwards)
Georgia	Sugar 1-1-69	Arkansas 2-16 (Frank Broyles)
Georgia	Sun 12-20-69	Nebraska 6-45 (Bob Devaney)
Georgia	Gator 12-31-71	North Caro. 7-3 (Bill Dooley)
Georgia	Peach 12-28-73	Maryland 17-16 (Jerry Claiborne)
Georgia	Tangerine 12-21-74	Miami (Ohio) 10-21 (Dick Crum)
Georgia	Cotton 1-1-76	Arkansas 10-31 (Frank Broyles)
Georgia	Sugar 1-1-77	Pittsburgh 3-27 (Johnny Majors)
Georgia	Bluebonnet 12-31-78	Stanford 22-25 (Bill Walsh)
Georgia	Sugar 1-1-81	Notre Dame 17-10 (Dan Devine)
Georgia	Sugar 1-1-82	Pittsburgh 20-24 (Jackie Sherrill)
Georgia	Sugar 1-1-83	Penn St. 23-27 (Joe Paterno)
Georgia	Cotton 1-2-84	Texas 10-9 (Fred Akers)
Georgia	Fla. Citrus 12-22-84	Florida St. 17-17 (Bobby Bowden)
Georgia	Sun 12-28-85	Arizona 13-13 (Larry Smith)
Georgia	Hall of Fame 12-23-86	Boston College 24-27 (Jack Bicknell)
Georgia	Liberty 12-29-87	Arkansas 20-17 (Ken Hatfield)
Georgia	Gator 1-1-89	Michigan St. 34-27 (George Perles)

CHARLES "GUS" DORAIS, 0-1-0 (Notre Dame '14) Born 7-21-91

Gonzaga	San Diego East-West Christmas Classic 12-25-22	West Va. 13-21 (Clarence "Doc" Spears)

HAROLD "RED" DREW, 1-2-0 (Bates '16) Born 11-9-94

Alabama	Sugar 1-1-48	Texas 7-27 (Blair Cherry)
Alabama	Orange 1-1-53	Syracuse 61-6 (Ben Schwartzwalder)
Alabama	Cotton 1-1-54	Rice 6-28 (Jess Neely)

BILL DRIVER, 0-1-0 (Missouri '09) Born 11-7-83

Texas Christian	Fort Worth Classic 1-1-21	Centre 7-63 (Charley Moran)

F. A. DRY, 0-1-0 (Oklahoma St. '53) Born 9-2-31

Tulsa	Independence 12-13-76	McNeese St. 16-20 (Jack Doland)

ERNIE DUPLECHIN, 0-2-0 (Louisiana Col. '55) Born 7-19-32

McNeese St.	Independence 12-15-79	Syracuse 7-31 (Frank Maloney)
McNeese St.	Independence 12-13-80	Southern Miss. 14-16 (Bobby Collins)

PAT DYE, 7-2-1 (Georgia '62) Born 11-6-39

East Caro.	Independence 12-16-78	Louisiana Tech 35-13 (Maxie Lambright)
Auburn	Tangerine 12-18-82	Boston College 33-26 (Jack Bicknell)
Auburn	Sugar 1-2-84	Michigan 9-7 (Glenn "Bo" Schembechler)
Auburn	Liberty 12-27-84	Arkansas 21-15 (Ken Hatfield)
Auburn	Cotton 1-1-86	Texas A&M 16-36 (Jackie Sherrill)
Auburn	Fla. Citrus 1-1-87	Southern Cal 16-7 (Ted Tollner)
Auburn	Sugar 1-1-88	Syracuse 16-16 (Dick MacPherson)
Auburn	Sugar 1-2-89	Florida St. 7-13 (Bobby Bowden)
Auburn	Hall of Fame 1-1-90	Ohio St. 31-14 (John Cooper)
Auburn	Peach 12-29-90	Indiana 27-23 (Bill Mallory)

SPIKE DYKES, 1-2-0 (Stephen F. Austin '59) Born 4-15-38

Texas Tech	Independence 12-20-86	Mississippi 17-20 (Billy Brewer)
Texas Tech	All-American 12-28-89	Duke 49-21 (Steve Spurrier)
Texas Tech	John Hancock 12-24-93	Oklahoma 10-41 (Gary Gibbs)

LLOYD EATON, 1-1-0 (Black Hills St. '40) Born 3-23-18

Wyoming	Sun 12-24-66	Florida St. 28-20 (Bill Peterson)
Wyoming	Sugar 1-1-68	Louisiana St. 13-20 (Charlie McClendon)

BILL EDWARDS, 1-0-0 (Wittenberg '31) Born 6-21-05

Case Reserve	Sun 1-1-41	Arizona St. 26-13 (Millard "Dixie" Howell)

EARLE EDWARDS, 1-1-0 (Penn St. '31) Born 11-10-08

North Caro. St.	Liberty 12-21-63	Mississippi St. 12-16 (Paul Davis)
North Caro. St.	Liberty 12-16-67	Georgia 14-7 (Vince Dooley)

LaVELL EDWARDS, 5-12-1 (Utah St. '52) Born 10-11-30

Brigham Young	Fiesta 12-28-74	Oklahoma St. 6-16 (Jim Stanley)
Brigham Young	Tangerine 12-20-76	Oklahoma St. 21-49 (Jim Stanley)
Brigham Young	Holiday 12-22-78	Navy 16-23 (George Welsh)
Brigham Young	Holiday 12-21-79	Indiana 37-38 (Lee Corso)
Brigham Young	Holiday 12-19-80	Southern Methodist 46-45 (Ron Meyer)
Brigham Young	Holiday 12-18-81	Washington St. 38-36 (Jim Walden)
Brigham Young	Holiday 12-17-82	Ohio St. 17-47 (Earle Bruce)
Brigham Young	Holiday 12-23-83	Missouri 21-17 (Warren Powers)
Brigham Young	Holiday 12-21-84	Michigan 24-17 (Glenn "Bo" Schembechler)
Brigham Young	Fla. Citrus 12-28-85	Ohio St. 7-10 (Earle Bruce)
Brigham Young	Freedom 12-30-86	UCLA 10-31 (Terry Donahue)

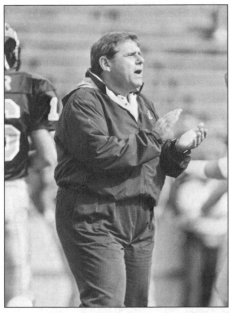

California coach Keith Gilbertson had a successful debut in post-season play against Iowa in last year's Alamo Bowl. The Golden Bears defeated the Hawkeyes, 37-3.

Coach/School	Bowl/Date	Opponent/Score (Coach)
Brigham Young	All-American 12-22-87	Virginia 16-22 (George Welsh)
Brigham Young	Freedom 12-29-88	Colorado 20-17 (Bill McCartney)
Brigham Young	Holiday 12-29-89	Penn St. 39-50 (Joe Paterno)
Brigham Young	Holiday 12-29-90	Texas A&M 14-65 (R. C. Slocum)
Brigham Young	Holiday 12-30-91	Iowa 13-13 (Hayden Fry)
Brigham Young	Aloha 12-25-92	Kansas 20-23 (Glen Mason)
Brigham Young	Holiday 12-30-93	Ohio St. 21-28 (John Cooper)

RAY ELIOT, 2-0-0 (Illinois '32) Born 6-13-05
Illinois	Rose 1-1-47	UCLA 45-14 (Bert LaBrucherie)
Illinois	Rose 1-1-52	Stanford 40-7 (Chuck Taylor)

BENNIE ELLENDER, 0-1-0 (Tulane '48) Born 3-2-25
Tulane	Bluebonnet 12-29-73	Houston 7-47 (Bill Yeoman)

CHALMERS "BUMP" ELLIOTT, 1-0-0 (Michigan '48) Born 1-30-25
Michigan	Rose 1-1-65	Oregon St. 34-7 (Tommy Prothro)

PETE ELLIOTT, 1-1-0 (Michigan '49) Born 9-29-26
California	Rose 1-1-59	Iowa 12-38 (Forest Evashevski)
Illinois	Rose 1-1-64	Washington 17-7 (Jim Owens)

JACK ELWAY, 0-2-0 (Washington St. '53) Born 5-30-31
San Jose St.	California 12-19-81	Toledo 25-27 (Chuck Stobart)
Stanford	Gator 12-27-86	Clemson 21-27 (Danny Ford)

CHARLES "RIP" ENGLE, 3-1-0 (Western Md. '30) Born 3-26-06
Penn St.	Liberty 12-19-53	Alabama 7-0 (Paul "Bear" Bryant)
Penn St.	Liberty 12-17-60	Oregon 41-12 (Len Casanova)
Penn St.	Gator 12-30-61	Georgia Tech 30-15 (Bobby Dodd)
Penn St.	Gator 12-29-62	Florida 7-17 (Ray Graves)

EDDIE ERDELATZ, 2-0-0 (St. Mary's, Cal. '36) Born 4-21-13
Navy	Sugar 1-1-55	Mississippi 21-0 (John Vaught)
Navy	Cotton 1-1-58	Rice 20-7 (Jess Neely)

DENNIS ERICKSON, 4-2-0 (Montana St. '70) Born 3-24-47
Washington St.	Aloha 12-25-88	Houston 24-22 (Jack Pardee)
Miami (Fla.)	Sugar 1-1-90	Alabama 33-25 (Bill Curry)
Miami (Fla.)	Cotton 1-1-91	Texas 46-3 (David McWilliams)
Miami (Fla.)	Orange 1-1-92	Nebraska 22-0 (Tom Osborne)
Miami (Fla.)	Sugar 1-1-93	Alabama 13-34 (Gene Stallings)
Miami (Fla.)	Fiesta 1-1-94	Arizona 0-24 (Dick Tomey)

FOREST EVASHEVSKI, 2-0-0 (Michigan '41) Born 2-19-18
Iowa	Rose 1-1-57	Oregon St. 35-19 (Tommy Prothro)
Iowa	Rose 1-1-59	California 38-12 (Pete Elliott)

CHUCK FAIRBANKS, 3-1-1 (Michigan St. '55) Born 6-10-33
Oklahoma	Orange 1-1-68	Tennessee 26-24 (Doug Dickey)
Oklahoma	Bluebonnet 12-31-68	Southern Methodist 27-28 (Hayden Fry)
Oklahoma	Bluebonnet 12-31-70	Alabama 24-24 (Paul "Bear" Bryant)
Oklahoma	Sugar 1-1-72	Auburn 40-22 (Ralph "Shug" Jordan)
Oklahoma	Sugar 12-31-72	Penn St. 14-0 (Joe Paterno)

DON FAMBROUGH, 0-2-0 (Kansas '48) Born 10-19-22
Kansas	Liberty 12-17-73	North Caro. St. 18-31 (Lou Holtz)
Kansas	All-American 12-31-81	Mississippi St. 0-10 (Emory Bellard)

DON FAUROT, 0-4-0 (Missouri '25) Born 6-23-02
Missouri	Orange 1-1-40	Georgia Tech 7-21 (Bill Alexander)
Missouri	Sugar 1-1-42	Fordham 0-2 (Jim Crowley)
Missouri	Gator 1-1-49	Clemson 23-24 (Frank Howard)
Missouri	Gator 1-2-50	Maryland 7-21 (Jim Tatum)

Coach/School	Bowl/Date	Opponent/Score (Coach)
GERRY FAUST, 1-1-0 (Dayton '58) Born 5-21-35		
Notre Dame	Liberty 12-29-83	Boston College 19-18 (Jack Bicknell)
Notre Dame	Aloha 12-29-84	Southern Methodist 20-27 (Bobby Collins)

FOGE FAZIO, 0-2-0 (Pittsburgh '60) Born 2-28-39
Pittsburgh	Cotton 1-1-83	Southern Methodist 3-7 (Bobby Collins)
Pittsburgh	Fiesta 1-2-84	Ohio St. 23-28 (Earle Bruce)

BEATTIE FEATHERS, 0-1-0 (Tennessee '34) Born 6-1-12
North Caro. St.	Gator 1-1-47	Oklahoma 13-34 (Jim Tatum)

WES FESLER, 1-0-0 (Ohio St. '32) Born 6-29-08
Ohio St.	Rose 1-2-50	California 17-14 (Lynn "Pappy" Waldorf)

CHARLIE FICKERT, 0-1-0 (Stanford '98) Born 2-23-73
Stanford	Rose 1-1-02	Michigan 0-49 (Fielding "Hurry Up" Yost)

ROBERT FISHER, 1-0-0 (Harvard '12) Born 12-3-88
Harvard	Rose 1-1-20	Oregon 7-6 (Charles "Shy" Huntington)

HANK FOLDBERG, 0-1-0 (Army '48) Born 3-12-23
Wichita St.	Sun 12-30-61	Villanova 9-17 (Alex Bell)

BOB FOLWELL, 0-1-1 (Pennsylvania '08) Born 1885
Pennsylvania	Rose 1-1-17	Oregon 0-14 (Hugo Bezdek)
Navy	Rose 1-1-24	Washington 14-14 (Enoch Bagshaw)

DANNY FORD, 6-2-0 (Alabama '70) Born 4-2-48
Clemson	Gator 12-29-78	Ohio St. 17-15 (Woody Hayes)
Clemson	Peach 12-31-79	Baylor 18-24 (Grant Teaff)
Clemson	Orange 1-1-82	Nebraska 22-15 (Tom Osborne)
Clemson	Independence 12-21-85	Minnesota 13-20 (John Gutekunst)
Clemson	Gator 12-27-86	Stanford 27-21 (Jack Elway)
Clemson	Fla. Citrus 1-1-88	Penn St. 35-10 (Joe Paterno)
Clemson	Fla. Citrus 1-2-89	Oklahoma 23-6 (Barry Switzer)
Clemson	Gator 12-30-89	West Va. 27-7 (Don Nehlen)

HENRY FRNKA, 2-3-0 (Austin '26) Born 3-16-03
Tulsa	Sun 1-1-42	Texas Tech 6-0 (Dell Morgan)
Tulsa	Sugar 1-1-43	Tennessee 7-14 (John Barnhill)
Tulsa	Sugar 1-1-44	Georgia Tech 18-20 (Bill Alexander)
Tulsa	Orange 1-1-45	Georgia Tech 26-12 (Bill Alexander)
Tulsa	Oil 1-1-46	Georgia 6-20 (Wally Butts)

HAYDEN FRY, 5-8-1 (Baylor '51) Born 2-28-29
Southern Methodist	Sun 12-31-63	Oregon 13-21 (Len Casanova)
Southern Methodist	Cotton 12-31-66	Georgia 9-24 (Vince Dooley)
Southern Methodist	Bluebonnet 12-31-68	Oklahoma 28-27 (Chuck Fairbanks)
Iowa	Rose 1-1-82	Washington 0-28 (Don James)
Iowa	Peach 12-31-82	Tennessee 28-22 (Johnny Majors)
Iowa	Gator 12-30-83	Florida 6-14 (Charley Pell)
Iowa	Freedom 12-26-84	Texas 55-17 (Fred Akers)
Iowa	Rose 1-1-86	UCLA 28-45 (Terry Donahue)
Iowa	Holiday 12-30-86	San Diego St. 39-38 (Denny Stolz)
Iowa	Holiday 12-30-87	Wyoming 20-19 (Paul Roach)
Iowa	Peach 12-31-88	North Caro. St. 23-29 (Dick Sheridan)
Iowa	Rose 1-1-91	Washington 34-46 (Don James)
Iowa	Holiday 12-30-91	Brigham Young 13-13 (LaVell Edwards)
Iowa	Alamo 12-31-93	California 3-37 (Keith Gilbertson)

BILL FULCHER, 1-0-0 (Georgia Tech '57) Born 2-9-34
Georgia Tech	Liberty 12-18-72	Iowa St. 31-30 (Johnny Majors)

PHILLIP FULMER, 1-1-0 (Tennessee '72) Born 9-1-50
Tennessee	Hall of Fame 1-1-93	Boston College 38-23 (Tom Coughlin)
Tennessee	Fla. Citrus 1-1-94	Penn St. 13-31 (Joe Paterno)

WARREN GAER, 0-1-0 (Drake '35) Born 2-7-12
Drake	Sun 1-1-58	Louisville 20-34 (Frank Camp)

JOE GAVIN, 0-1-0 (Notre Dame '31) Born 3-20-08
Dayton	Salad 1-1-52	Houston 21-26 (Clyde Lee)

GARY GIBBS, 2-0-0 (Oklahoma '75) Born 8-13-52
Oklahoma	Gator 12-29-91	Virginia 48-14 (George Welsh)
Oklahoma	John Hancock 12-24-93	Texas Tech 41-10 (Spike Dykes)

VINCE GIBSON, 0-2-0 (Florida St. '55) Born 3-27-33
Louisville	Independence 12-17-77	Louisiana Tech 14-24 (Maxie Lambright)
Tulane	All-American 12-27-80	Arkansas 15-34 (Lou Holtz)

CLAUDE GILBERT, 1-1-0 (San Jose St. '59) Born 7-10-32
San Jose St.	California 12-13-86	Miami (Ohio) 37-7 (Tim Rose)
San Jose St.	California 12-12-87	Eastern Mich. 27-30 (Jim Harkema)

KEITH GILBERTSON, 1-0-0 (Central Wash. '71) Born 5-15-48
California	Alamo 12-31-93	Iowa 37-3 (Hayden Fry)

SID GILLMAN, 1-1-0 (Ohio St. '34) Born 10-26-11
Miami (Ohio)	Sun 1-1-48	Texas Tech 13-12 (Dell Morgan)
Cincinnati	Sun 1-1-51	West Tex. A&M 13-14 (Frank Kimbrough)

BILL GLASSFORD, 0-1-0 (Pittsburgh '37) Born 3-8-14
Nebraska	Orange 1-1-55	Duke 7-34 (Bill Murray)

MARSHALL "LITTLE SLEEPY" GLENN, 1-0-0 (West Va. '31) Born 4-22-08
West Va.	Sun 1-1-38	Texas Tech 7-6 (Pete Cawthon)

Coach/School	Bowl/Date	Opponent/Score (Coach)
RAY GOFF, 2-1-0 (Georgia '78) Born 7-10-55		
Georgia	Peach 12-30-89	Syracuse 18-19 (Dick MacPherson)
Georgia	Independence 12-29-91	Arkansas 24-15 (Jack Crowe)
Georgia	Fla. Citrus 1-1-93	Ohio St. 21-14 (John Cooper)
MIKE GOTTFRIED, 0-1-0 (Morehead St. '66) Born 12-17-44		
Pittsburgh	Bluebonnet 12-31-87	Texas 27-32 (David McWilliams)
RALPH GRAHAM, 0-1-0 (Kansas St. '34) Born 8-16-10		
Wichita St.	Raisin 1-1-48	Pacific (Cal.) 14-26 (Larry Siemering)
SONNY GRANDELIUS, 0-1-0 (Michigan St. '51) Born 4-16-29		
Colorado	Orange 1-1-62	Louisiana St. 7-25 (Paul Dietzel)
RAY GRAVES, 4-1-0 (Tennessee '43) Born 12-31-18		
Florida	Gator 12-31-60	Baylor 13-12 (John Bridgers)
Florida	Gator 12-29-62	Penn St. 17-7 (Charles "Rip" Engle)
Florida	Sugar 1-1-66	Missouri 18-20 (Dan Devine)
Florida	Orange 1-2-67	Georgia Tech 27-12 (Bobby Dodd)
Florida	Gator 12-27-69	Tennessee 14-13 (Doug Dickey)
DENNIS GREEN, 0-1-0 (Iowa '71) Born 2-17-49		
Stanford	Aloha 12-25-91	Georgia Tech 17-18 (Bobby Ross)
VEE GREEN, 1-0-0 (Illinois '24) Born 10-9-00		
Drake	Raisin 1-1-46	Fresno St. 13-12 (Alvin "Pix" Pierson)
ART GUEPE, 1-0-0 (Marquette '37) Born 1-28-15		
Vanderbilt	Gator 12-31-55	Auburn 25-13 (Ralph "Shug" Jordan)
ANDY GUSTAFSON, 1-3-0 (Pittsburgh '26) Born 4-3-03		
Miami (Fla.)	Orange 1-1-51	Clemson 14-15 (Frank Howard)
Miami (Fla.)	Gator 1-1-52	Clemson 14-0 (Frank Howard)
Miami (Fla.)	Liberty 12-16-61	Syracuse 14-15 (Ben Schwartzwalder)
Miami (Fla.)	Gotham 12-15-62	Nebraska 34-36 (Bob Devaney)
JOHN GUTEKUNST, 1-1-0 (Duke '66) Born 4-13-44		
Minnesota	Independence 12-21-85	Clemson 20-13 (Danny Ford)
Minnesota	Liberty 12-29-86	Tennessee 14-21 (Johnny Majors)
PAUL HACKETT, 1-0-0 (UC Davis '69) Born 6-5-47		
Pittsburgh	John Hancock 12-30-89	Texas A&M 31-28 (R. C. Slocum)
JACK HAGERTY, 0-1-0 (Georgetown '26) Born 7-3-03		
Georgetown	Orange 1-1-41	Mississippi St. 7-14 (Alvin McKeen)
GALEN HALL, 1-1-0 (Penn St. '62) Born 8-14-40		
Florida	Aloha 12-25-87	UCLA 16-20 (Terry Donahue)
Florida	All-American 12-29-88	Illinois 14-10 (John Mackovic)
CURLEY HALLMAN, 1-0-0 (Texas A&M '70) Born 9-3-47		
Southern Miss.	Independence 12-23-88	UTEP 38-18 (Bob Stull)
WAYNE HARDIN, 1-2-0 (Pacific, Cal. '50) Born 3-23-27		
Navy	Orange 1-2-61	Missouri 14-21 (Dan Devine)
Navy	Cotton 1-1-64	Texas 6-28 (Darrell Royal)
Temple	Garden State 12-15-79	California 28-17 (Roger Theder)
JACK HARDING, 1-0-0 (Pittsburgh '26) Born 1-5-98		
Miami (Fla.)	Orange 1-1-48	Holy Cross 13-6 (John "Ox" Da Grosa)
JIM HARKEMA, 1-0-0 (Kalamazoo '64) Born 6-25-42		
Eastern Mich.	California 12-12-87	San Jose St. 30-27 (Claude Gilbert)
KEN HATFIELD, 4-6-0 (Arkansas '65) Born 6-8-43		
Air Force	All-American 12-31-82	Vanderbilt 36-28 (George MacIntyre)
Air Force	Independence 12-10-83	Mississippi 9-3 (Billy Brewer)
Arkansas	Liberty 12-27-84	Auburn 15-21 (Pat Dye)
Arkansas	Holiday 12-22-85	Arizona St. 18-17 (John Cooper)
Arkansas	Orange 1-1-87	Oklahoma 8-42 (Barry Switzer)
Arkansas	Liberty 12-29-87	Georgia 17-20 (Vince Dooley)
Arkansas	Cotton 1-2-89	UCLA 3-17 (Terry Donahue)
Arkansas	Cotton 1-1-90	Tennessee 27-31 (Johnny Majors)
Clemson	Hall of Fame 1-1-91	Illinois 30-0 (John Mackovic)
Clemson	Fla. Citrus 1-1-92	California 13-37 (Bruce Snyder)
WOODY HAYES, 6-6-0 (Denison '35) Born 2-14-13		
Miami (Ohio)	Salad 1-1-51	Arizona St. 34-21 (Ed Doherty)
Ohio St.	Rose 1-1-55	Southern Cal 20-7 (Jess Hill)
Ohio St.	Rose 1-1-58	Oregon 10-7 (Len Casanova)
Ohio St.	Rose 1-1-69	Southern Cal 27-16 (John McKay)
Ohio St.	Rose 1-1-71	Stanford 17-27 (John Ralston)
Ohio St.	Rose 1-1-73	Southern Cal 17-42 (John McKay)
Ohio St.	Rose 1-1-74	Southern Cal 42-21 (John McKay)
Ohio St.	Rose 1-1-75	Southern Cal 17-18 (John McKay)
Ohio St.	Rose 1-1-76	UCLA 10-23 (Dick Vermeil)
Ohio St.	Orange 1-1-77	Colorado 27-10 (Bill Mallory)
Ohio St.	Sugar 1-2-78	Alabama 6-35 (Paul "Bear" Bryant)
Ohio St.	Gator 12-29-78	Clemson 15-17 (Danny Ford)
ELMER "GUS" HENDERSON, 2-0-0 (Oberlin '12) Born 3-10-89		
Southern Cal	Rose 1-1-23	Penn St. 14-3 (Hugo Bezdek)
Southern Cal	L.A. Christmas Festival 12-25-24	Missouri 20-7 (Gwinn Henry)
GWINN HENRY, 0-1-0 (Howard Payne '17) Born 8-5-87		
Missouri	L.A. Christmas Festival 12-25-24	Southern Cal 7-20 (Elmer "Gus" Henderson)

Coach/School	Bowl/Date	Opponent/Score (Coach)
BILL HESS, 0-2-0 (Ohio '47) Born 2-5-23		
Ohio	Sun 12-31-62	West Tex. A&M 14-15 (Joe Kerbel)
Ohio	Tangerine 12-27-68	Richmond 42-49 (Frank Jones)
JIM HICKEY, 1-0-0 (William & Mary '42) Born 1-22-20		
North Caro.	Gator 12-28-63	Air Force 35-0 (Ben Martin)
BOB HIGGINS, 1-0-1 (Penn St. '20) Born 12-24-93		
West Va. Wesleyan	Dixie Classic 1-1-25	Southern Methodist 9-7 (Ray Morrison)
Penn St.	Cotton 1-1-48	Southern Methodist 13-13 (Matty Bell)
JESS HILL, 1-1-0 (Southern Cal '30) Born 1-20-07		
Southern Cal	Rose 1-1-53	Wisconsin 7-0 (Ivy Williamson)
Southern Cal	Rose 1-1-55	Ohio St. 7-20 (Woody Hayes)
JERRY HINES, 0-0-1 (New Mexico St. '26) Born 10-11-03		
New Mexico St.	Sun 1-1-36	Hardin-Simmons 14-14 (Frank Kimbrough)
BERNARD A. HOBAN, 0-1-0 (Dartmouth '12) Born 4-21-90		
U. of Mexico	Sun 1-1-45	Southwestern (Tex.) 0-35 (Randolph R. M. Medley)
ORIN "BABE" HOLLINGBERY, 0-1-0 (No college) Born 7-15-93		
Washington St.	Rose 1-1-31	Alabama 0-24 (Wallace Wade)
LOU HOLTZ, 10-6-2 (Kent '59) Born 1-6-37		
William & Mary	Tangerine 12-28-70	Toledo 12-40 (Frank Lauterbur)
North Caro. St.	Peach 12-29-72	West Va. 49-13 (Bobby Bowden)
North Caro. St.	Liberty 12-17-73	Kansas 31-18 (Don Fambrough)
North Caro. St.	Bluebonnet 12-23-74	Houston 31-31 (Bill Yeoman)
North Caro. St.	Peach 12-31-75	West Va. 10-13 (Bobby Bowden)
Arkansas	Orange 1-2-78	Oklahoma 31-6 (Barry Switzer)
Arkansas	Fiesta 12-25-78	UCLA 10-10 (Terry Donahue)
Arkansas	Sugar 1-1-80	Alabama 9-24 (Paul "Bear" Bryant)
Arkansas	All-American 12-27-80	Tulane 34-15 (Vince Gibson)
Arkansas	Gator 12-28-81	North Caro. 27-31 (Dick Crum)
Arkansas	Bluebonnet 12-31-82	Florida 28-24 (Charley Pell)
Notre Dame	Cotton 1-1-88	Texas A&M 10-35 (Jackie Sherrill)
Notre Dame	Fiesta 1-2-89	West Va. 34-21 (Don Nehlen)
Notre Dame	Orange 1-1-90	Colorado 21-6 (Bill McCartney)
Notre Dame	Orange 1-1-91	Colorado 9-10 (Bill McCartney)
Notre Dame	Sugar 1-1-92	Florida 39-28 (Steve Spurrier)
Notre Dame	Cotton 1-1-93	Texas A&M 28-3 (R. C. Slocum)
Notre Dame	Cotton 1-1-94	Texas A&M 24-21 (R. C. Slocum)
EDWIN "BABE" HORRELL, 0-1-0 (California '26) Born 9-29-02		
UCLA	Rose 1-1-43	Georgia 0-9 (Wally Butts)
FRANK HOWARD, 3-3-0 (Alabama '31) Born 3-25-09		
Clemson	Gator 1-1-49	Missouri 24-23 (Don Faurot)
Clemson	Orange 1-1-51	Miami (Fla.) 15-14 (Andy Gustafson)
Clemson	Gator 1-1-52	Miami (Fla.) 0-14 (Andy Gustafson)
Clemson	Orange 1-1-57	Colorado 21-27 (Dallas Ward)
Clemson	Sugar 1-1-59	Louisiana St. 0-7 (Paul Dietzel)
Clemson	Bluebonnet 12-19-59	Texas Christian 23-7 (Abe Martin)
MILLARD "DIXIE" HOWELL, 0-1-1 (Alabama '35) Born 11-24-12		
Arizona St.	Sun 1-1-40	Catholic 0-0 (Arthur "Dutch" Bergman)
Arizona St.	Sun 1-1-41	Case Reserve 13-26 (Bill Edwards)
BILL HUBBARD, 2-0-0 (Stanford '30) Born 2-5-07		
San Jose St.	Raisin 1-1-47	Utah St. 20-0 (E. L. "Dick" Romney)
San Jose St.	Raisin 12-31-49	Texas Tech 20-13 (Dell Morgan)
CLYDE "CAC" HUBBARD, 0-2-0 (Oregon St. '21) Born 9-13-97		
Denver	Sun 1-1-46	New Mexico 24-34 (Willis Barnes)
Denver	Alamo 1-4-47	Hardin-Simmons 0-20 (Warren Woodson)
CHARLES "SHY" HUNTINGTON, 0-1-0 (Oregon) Born 7-7-91		
Oregon	Rose 1-1-20	Harvard 6-7 (Robert Fisher)
HARVEY HYDE, 1-0-0 (Redlands '62) Born 7-13-39		
Nevada-Las Vegas	California 12-15-84	Toledo 30-13 (Dan Simrell)
DON JAMES, 10-5-0 (Miami, Fla. '54) Born 12-31-32		
Kent	Tangerine 12-29-72	Tampa 18-21 (Earle Bruce)
Washington	Rose 1-2-78	Michigan 27-20 (Glenn "Bo" Schembechler)
Washington	Sun 12-22-79	Texas 14-7 (Fred Akers)
Washington	Rose 1-1-81	Michigan 6-23 (Glenn "Bo" Schembechler)
Washington	Rose 1-1-82	Iowa 28-0 (Hayden Fry)
Washington	Aloha 12-25-82	Maryland 21-20 (Bobby Ross)
Washington	Aloha 12-26-83	Penn St. 10-13 (Joe Paterno)
Washington	Orange 1-1-85	Oklahoma 28-17 (Barry Switzer)
Washington	Freedom 12-30-85	Colorado 20-17 (Bill McCartney)
Washington	Sun 12-25-86	Alabama 6-28 (Ray Perkins)
Washington	Independence 12-18-87	Tulane 24-12 (Mack Brown)
Washington	Freedom 12-29-89	Florida 34-7 (Gary Darnell)
Washington	Rose 1-1-91	Iowa 46-34 (Hayden Fry)
Washington	Rose 1-1-92	Michigan 34-14 (Gary Moeller)
Washington	Rose 1-1-93	Michigan 31-38 (Gary Moeller)

Coach/School	Bowl/Date	Opponent/Score (Coach)
JIMMY JOHNSON, 3-4-0	(Arkansas '65)	Born 7-16-43
Oklahoma St............	Independence 12-12-81	Texas A&M 16-33 (Tom Wilson)
Oklahoma St............	Bluebonnet 12-31-83	Baylor 24-14 (Grant Teaff)
Miami (Fla.).............	Fiesta 1-1-85	UCLA 37-39 (Terry Donahue)
Miami (Fla.).............	Sugar 1-1-86	Tennessee 7-35 (Johnny Majors)
Miami (Fla.).............	Fiesta 1-2-87	Penn St. 10-14 (Joe Paterno)
Miami (Fla.).............	Orange 1-1-88	Oklahoma 20-14 (Barry Switzer)
Miami (Fla.).............	Orange 1-2-89	Nebraska 23-3 (Tom Osborne)
FRANK JONES, 1-1-0	(North Caro. '48)	Born 8-30-21
Richmond	Tangerine 12-27-68	Ohio 49-42 (Bill Hess)
Richmond	Tangerine 12-28-71	Toledo 3-28 (John Murphy)
GOMER JONES, 0-1-0	(Ohio St. '36)	Born 2-26-14
Oklahoma	Gator 1-2-65	Florida St. 19-36 (Bill Peterson)
HOWARD JONES, 5-0-0	(Yale '08)	Born 8-23-85
Southern Cal............	Rose 1-1-30	Pittsburgh 47-14 (Jock Sutherland)
Southern Cal............	Rose 1-1-32	Tulane 21-12 (Bernie Bierman)
Southern Cal............	Rose 1-2-33	Pittsburgh 35-0 (Jock Sutherland)
Southern Cal............	Rose 1-2-39	Duke 7-3 (Wallace Wade)
Southern Cal............	Rose 1-1-40	Tennessee 14-0 (Bob Neyland)
LARRY JONES, 0-1-0	(Louisiana St. '54)	Born 12-18-33
Florida St.	Fiesta 12-27-71	Arizona St. 38-45 (Frank Kush)
LAWRENCE McC. "BIFF" JONES, 0-1-0	(Army '17)	Born 10-8-95
Nebraska	Rose 1-1-41	Stanford 13-21 (Clark Shaughnessy)
PAT JONES, 3-1-0	(Arkansas '69)	Born 11-4-47
Oklahoma St............	Gator 12-28-84	South Caro. 21-14 (Joe Morrison)
Oklahoma St............	Gator 12-30-85	Florida St. 23-34 (Bobby Bowden)
Oklahoma St............	Sun 12-25-87	West Va. 35-33 (Don Nehlen)
Oklahoma St............	Holiday 12-30-88	Wyoming 62-14 (Paul Roach)
RALPH "SHUG" JORDAN, 5-7-0	(Auburn '32)	Born 9-25-10
Auburn	Gator 1-1-54	Texas Tech 13-35 (DeWitt Weaver)
Auburn	Gator 12-31-54	Baylor 33-13 (George Sauer)
Auburn	Gator 12-31-55	Vanderbilt 13-25 (Art Gueppe)
Auburn	Orange 1-1-64	Nebraska 7-13 (Bob Devaney)
Auburn	Liberty 12-18-65	Mississippi 7-13 (John Vaught)
Auburn	Sun 12-28-68	Arizona 34-10 (Darrell Mudra)
Auburn	Bluebonnet 12-31-69	Houston 7-36 (Bill Yeoman)
Auburn	Gator 1-2-71	Mississippi 35-28 (John Vaught)
Auburn	Sugar 1-1-72	Oklahoma 22-40 (Chuck Fairbanks)
Auburn	Gator 12-30-72	Colorado 24-3 (Eddie Crowder)
Auburn	Sun 12-29-73	Missouri 17-34 (Al Onofrio)
Auburn	Gator 12-30-74	Texas 27-3 (Darrell Royal)
ERNIE JORGE, 1-1-0	(St. Mary's, Cal. '36)	Born 10-7-14
Pacific (Cal.)	Sun 1-1-52	Texas Tech 14-25 (DeWitt Weaver)
Pacific (Cal.)	Sun 1-1-53	Southern Miss. 26-7 (Thad "Pie" Vann)
AL KAWAL, 1-0-0	(Northwestern '35)	Born 7-4-12
Drake	Salad 1-1-49	Arizona 14-13 (Miles Casteel)
JOE KERBEL, 2-0-0	(Oklahoma '47)	Born 5-3-21
West Tex. A&M	Sun 12-21-62	Ohio 15-14 (Bill Hess)
West Tex. A&M	Pasadena 12-2-67	Cal St. Northridge 35-13 (Sam Winningham)
BILL KERN, 0-1-0	(Pittsburgh '28)	Born 9-2-06
Carnegie Mellon	Sugar 1-2-39	Texas Christian 7-15 (Leo "Dutch" Meyer)
FRANK KIMBROUGH, 2-0-1	(Hardin-Simmons '26)	Born 6-24-04
Hardin-Simmons	Sun 1-1-36	New Mexico St. 14-14 (Jerry Hines)
Hardin-Simmons	Sun 1-1-37	UTEP 34-6 (Max Saxon)
West Tex. A&M	Sun 1-1-51	Cincinnati 14-13 (Sid Gillman)
BILLY KINARD, 1-0-0	(Mississippi '56)	Born 12-16-33
Mississippi	Peach 12-30-71	Georgia Tech 41-18 (Bud Carson)
DEWEY KING, 0-1-0	(North Dak. '50)	Born 10-1-25
San Jose St.	Pasadena 12-18-71	Memphis 9-28 (Billy Murphy)
J. T. KING, 0-2-0	(Texas '38)	Born 10-22-12
Texas Tech.............	Sun 12-26-64	Georgia 0-7 (Vince Dooley)
Texas Tech.............	Gator 12-31-65	Georgia Tech 21-31 (Bobby Dodd)
JIMMY KITTS, 1-1-0	(Southern Methodist)	Born 6-14-00
Rice	Cotton 1-1-38	Colorado 28-14 (Bernard "Bunnie" Oakes)
Virginia Tech...........	Sun 1-1-47	Cincinnati 6-18 (Ray Nolting)
ED KLUSKA, 1-0-0	(Xavier, Ohio '40)	Born 5-21-18
Xavier (Ohio)	Salad 1-1-50	Arizona St. 33-21 (Ed Doherty)
JOE KRIVAK, 0-0-1	(Syracuse '57)	Born 3-20-35
Maryland................	Independence 12-15-90	Louisiana Tech 34-34 (Joe Raymond Peace)
FRANK KUSH, 6-1-0	(Michigan St. '53)	Born 1-20-29
Arizona St.	Peach 12-30-70	North Caro. 48-26 (Bill Dooley)
Arizona St.	Fiesta 12-27-71	Florida St. 45-38 (Larry Jones)
Arizona St.	Fiesta 12-23-72	Missouri 49-35 (Al Onofrio)
Arizona St.	Fiesta 12-21-73	Pittsburgh 28-7 (Johnny Majors)
Arizona St.	Fiesta 12-26-75	Nebraska 17-14 (Tom Osborne)
Arizona St.	Fiesta 12-25-77	Penn St. 30-42 (Joe Paterno)
Arizona St.	Garden State 12-16-78	Rutgers 34-18 (Frank Burns)

Coach/School	Bowl/Date	Opponent/Score (Coach)
BERT LaBRUCHERIE, 0-1-0	(UCLA '29)	Born 1-19-05
UCLA	Rose 1-1-47	Illinois 14-45 (Ray Eliot)
MAXIE LAMBRIGHT, 1-1-0	(Southern Miss. '49)	Born 6-3-24
Louisiana Tech	Independence 12-17-77	Louisville 24-14 (Vince Gibson)
Louisiana Tech	Independence 12-16-78	East Caro. 13-35 (Pat Dye)
FRANK LAUTERBUR, 2-0-0	(Mount Union '49)	Born 8-8-25
Toledo	Tangerine 12-26-69	Davidson 56-33 (Homer Smith)
Toledo	Tangerine 12-28-70	William & Mary 40-12 (Lou Holtz)
FRANK LEAHY, 1-1-0	(Notre Dame '31)	Born 8-27-08
Boston College.........	Cotton 1-1-40	Clemson 3-6 (Jess Neely)
Boston College.........	Sugar 1-1-41	Tennessee 19-13 (Bob Neyland)
CLYDE LEE, 1-0-0	(Centenary '32)	Born 2-11-08
Houston	Salad 1-1-52	Dayton 26-21 (Joe Gavin)
ART LEWIS, 0-1-0	(Ohio '36)	Born 2-18-11
West Va.	Sugar 1-1-54	Georgia Tech 19-42 (Bobby Dodd)
BILL LEWIS, 1-0-0	(East Stroudsburg '63)	Born 8-5-41
East Caro.	Peach 1-1-92	North Caro. St. 37-34 (Dick Sheridan)
LOU LITTLE, 1-0-0	(Pennsylvania '20)	Born 12-6-93
Columbia................	Rose 1-1-34	Stanford 7-0 (Claude "Tiny" Thornhill)
JIM LOOKABAUGH, 2-1-0	(Oklahoma St. '25)	Born 6-15-02
Oklahoma St............	Cotton 1-1-45	Texas Christian 34-0 (Leo "Dutch" Meyer)
Oklahoma St............	Sugar 1-1-46	St. Mary's (Cal.) 33-13 (Jimmy Phelan)
Oklahoma St............	Delta 1-1-49	William & Mary 0-20 (Rube McCray)
AL LUGINBILL, 0-1-0	(Cal Poly Pomona '67)	Born 11-3-46
San Diego St............	Freedom 12-30-91	Tulsa 17-28 (Dave Rader)
GEORGE MacINTYRE, 0-1-0	(Miami, Fla. '61)	Born 4-30-39
Vanderbilt	All-American 12-31-82	Air Force 28-36 (Ken Hatfield)
JOHN MACKOVIC, 1-3-0	(Wake Forest '65)	Born 10-1-43
Wake Forest	Tangerine 12-22-79	Louisiana St. 10-34 (Charlie McClendon)
Illinois	All-American 12-29-88	Florida 10-14 (Galen Hall)
Illinois	Fla. Citrus 1-1-90	Virginia 31-21 (George Welsh)
Illinois	Hall of Fame 1-1-91	Clemson 0-30 (Ken Hatfield)
DICK MacPHERSON, 3-1-1	(Springfield '58)	Born 11-4-30
Syracuse	Cherry 12-21-85	Maryland 18-35 (Bobby Ross)
Syracuse	Sugar 1-1-88	Auburn 16-16 (Pat Dye)
Syracuse	Hall of Fame 1-2-89	Louisiana St. 23-10 (Mike Archer)
Syracuse	Peach 12-30-89	Georgia 19-18 (Ray Goff)
Syracuse	Aloha 12-25-90	Arizona 28-0 (Dick Tomey)
EDWARD "SLIP" MADIGAN, 1-0-0	(Notre Dame '20)	Born 11-18-95
St. Mary's (Cal.).......	Cotton 1-2-39	Texas Tech 20-13 (Pete Cawthon)
JOHNNY MAJORS, 9-7-0	(Tennessee '57)	Born 5-21-35
Iowa St.	Sun 12-18-71	Louisiana St. 15-33 (Charlie McClendon)
Iowa St.	Liberty 12-18-72	Georgia Tech 30-31 (Bill Fulcher)
Pittsburgh	Fiesta 12-21-73	Arizona St. 7-28 (Frank Kush)
Pittsburgh	Sun 12-26-75	Kansas 33-19 (Bud Moore)
Pittsburgh	Sugar 1-1-77	Georgia 27-3 (Vince Dooley)
Tennessee	Bluebonnet 12-31-79	Purdue 22-27 (Jim Young)
Tennessee	Garden State 12-13-81	Wisconsin 28-21 (Dave McClain)
Tennessee	Peach 12-31-82	Iowa 22-28 (Hayden Fry)
Tennessee	Fla. Citrus 12-17-83	Maryland 30-23 (Bobby Ross)
Tennessee	Sun 12-24-84	Maryland 26-27 (Bobby Ross)
Tennessee	Sugar 1-1-86	Miami (Fla.) 35-7 (Jimmy Johnson)
Tennessee	Liberty 12-29-86	Minnesota 21-14 (John Gutekunst)
Tennessee	Peach 1-2-88	Indiana 27-22 (Bill Mallory)
Tennessee	Cotton 1-1-90	Arkansas 31-27 (Ken Hatfield)
Tennessee	Sugar 1-1-91	Virginia 23-22 (George Welsh)
Tennessee	Fiesta 1-1-92	Penn St. 17-42 (Joe Paterno)
BILL MALLORY, 4-6-0	(Miami, Ohio '57)	Born 5-30-35
Miami (Ohio)	Tangerine 12-22-73	Florida 16-7 (Doug Dickey)
Colorado	Bluebonnet 12-27-75	Texas 21-38 (Darrell Royal)
Colorado	Orange 1-1-77	Ohio St. 10-27 (Woody Hayes)
Northern Ill.	California 12-17-83	Cal St. Fullerton 20-13 (Gene Murphy)
Indiana	All-American 12-31-86	Florida St. 13-27 (Bobby Bowden)
Indiana	Peach 1-2-88	Tennessee 22-27 (Johnny Majors)
Indiana	Liberty 12-28-88	South Caro. 34-10 (Joe Morrison)
Indiana	Peach 12-29-90	Auburn 23-27 (Pat Dye)
Indiana	Copper 12-31-91	Baylor 24-0 (Grant Teaff)
Indiana	Independence 12-31-93	Virginia Tech 20-45 (Frank Beamer)
FRANK MALONEY, 1-0-0	(Michigan '62)	Born 9-26-40
Syracuse................	Independence 12-15-79	McNeese St. 31-7 (Ernie Duplechin)
BOB MARGARITA, 0-1-0	(Brown '44)	Born 11-3-20
Georgetown	Sun 1-2-50	UTEP 20-33 (Jack "Cactus Jack" Curtice)
ABE MARTIN, 1-3-1	(Texas Christian '32)	Born 10-8-08
Texas Christian	Cotton 1-2-56	Mississippi 13-14 (John Vaught)
Texas Christian	Cotton 1-1-57	Syracuse 28-27 (Ben Schwartzwalder)
Texas Christian	Cotton 1-1-59	Air Force 0-0 (Ben Martin)
Texas Christian	Bluebonnet 12-19-59	Clemson 7-23 (Frank Howard)
Texas Christian	Sun 12-31-65	UTEP 12-13 (Bobby Dobbs)

Coach/School	Bowl/Date	Opponent/Score (Coach)
BEN MARTIN, 0-2-1	(Navy '46)	Born 6-28-21
Air Force	Cotton 1-1-59	Texas Christian 0-0 (Abe Martin)
Air Force	Gator 12-28-63	North Caro. 0-35 (Jim Hickey)
Air Force	Sugar 1-1-71	Tennessee 13-34 (Bill Battle)
GLEN MASON, 1-0-0	(Ohio St. '72)	Born 4-9-50
Kansas	Aloha 12-25-92	Brigham Young 23-20 (LaVell Edwards)
TONY MASON, 0-1-0	(Clarion '50)	Born 3-2-30
Arizona	Fiesta 12-25-79	Pittsburgh 10-16 (Jackie Sherrill)
RON McBRIDE, 0-2-0	(San Jose St. '63)	Born 10-14-39
Utah	Copper 12-29-92	Washington St. 28-31 (Mike Price)
Utah	Freedom 12-30-93	Southern Cal 21-28 (John Robinson)
TOM McCANN, 0-1-0	(Illinois '24)	Born 11-7-98
Miami (Fla.)	Orange 1-1-35	Bucknell 0-26 (Edward "Hook" Mylin)
BILL McCARTNEY, 2-6-0	(Missouri '62)	Born 8-22-40
Colorado	Freedom 12-30-85	Washington 17-20 (Don James)
Colorado	Bluebonnet 12-31-86	Baylor 9-21 (Grant Teaff)
Colorado	Freedom 12-29-88	Brigham Young 17-20 (LaVell Edwards)
Colorado	Orange 1-1-90	Notre Dame 6-21 (Lou Holtz)
Colorado	Orange 1-1-91	Notre Dame 10-9 (Lou Holtz)
Colorado	Blockbuster 12-28-91	Alabama 25-30 (Gene Stallings)
Colorado	Fiesta 1-1-93	Syracuse 22-26 (Paul Pasqualoni)
Colorado	Aloha 12-25-93	Fresno St. 41-30 (Jim Sweeney)
DAVE McCLAIN, 1-2-0	(Bowling Green '60)	Born 1-28-38
Wisconsin	Garden State 12-13-81	Tennessee 21-28 (Johnny Majors)
Wisconsin	Independence 12-11-82	Kansas St. 14-3 (Jim Dickey)
Wisconsin	All-American 12-29-84	Kentucky 19-20 (Jerry Claiborne)
CHARLIE McCLENDON, 7-6-0	(Kentucky '50)	Born 10-17-22
Louisiana St.	Cotton 1-1-63	Texas 13-0 (Darrell Royal)
Louisiana St.	Bluebonnet 12-21-63	Baylor 7-14 (John Bridgers)
Louisiana St.	Sugar 1-1-65	Syracuse 13-10 (Ben Schwartzwalder)
Louisiana St.	Cotton 1-1-66	Arkansas 14-7 (Frank Broyles)
Louisiana St.	Sugar 1-1-68	Wyoming 20-13 (Lloyd Eaton)
Louisiana St.	Peach 12-30-68	Florida St. 31-27 (Bill Peterson)
Louisiana St.	Orange 1-1-71	Nebraska 12-17 (Bob Devaney)
Louisiana St.	Sun 12-18-71	Iowa St. 33-15 (Johnny Majors)
Louisiana St.	Bluebonnet 12-30-72	Tennessee 17-24 (Bill Battle)
Louisiana St.	Orange 1-1-74	Penn St. 9-16 (Joe Paterno)
Louisiana St.	Sun 12-31-77	Stanford 14-24 (Bill Walsh)
Louisiana St.	Liberty 12-23-78	Missouri 15-20 (Warren Powers)
Louisiana St.	Tangerine 12-22-79	Wake Forest 34-10 (John Mackovic)
RUBE McCRAY, 1-1-0	(Ky. Wesleyan '30)	Born 6-13-05
William & Mary	Dixie 1-1-48	Arkansas 19-21 (John Barnhill)
William & Mary	Delta 1-1-49	Oklahoma St. 20-0 (Jim Lookabaugh)
J. F. "POP" McKALE, 0-1-0	(Albion '10)	Born 6-12-87
Arizona	San Diego East-West Christmas Classic 12-26-21	Centre 0-38 (Charley Moran)
JOHN McKAY, 6-3-0	(Oregon St. '50)	Born 7-5-23
Southern Cal	Rose 1-2-63	Wisconsin 42-37 (Milt Bruhn)
Southern Cal	Rose 1-2-67	Purdue 13-14 (Jack Mollenkopf)
Southern Cal	Rose 1-1-68	Indiana 14-3 (John Pont)
Southern Cal	Rose 1-1-69	Ohio St. 16-27 (Woody Hayes)
Southern Cal	Rose 1-1-70	Michigan 10-3 (Glenn "Bo" Schembechler)
Southern Cal	Rose 1-1-73	Ohio St. 42-17 (Woody Hayes)
Southern Cal	Rose 1-1-74	Ohio St. 21-42 (Woody Hayes)
Southern Cal	Rose 1-1-75	Ohio St. 18-17 (Woody Hayes)
Southern Cal	Liberty 12-22-75	Texas A&M 20-0 (Emory Bellard)
ALLYN McKEEN, 1-0-0	(Tennessee '29)	Born 1-26-05
Mississippi St.	Orange 1-1-41	Georgetown 14-7 (Jack Hagerty)
JOHNNIE McMILLAN, 0-1-0	(South Caro. '41)	Born 1-27-19
South Caro.	Gator 1-1-46	Wake Forest 14-26 (D. C. "Peahead" Walker)
DAVID McWILLIAMS, 1-1-0	(Texas '64)	Born 4-18-42
Texas	Bluebonnet 12-31-87	Pittsburgh 32-27 (Mike Gottfried)
Texas	Cotton 1-1-91	Miami (Fla.) 3-46 (Dennis Erickson)
JACK MEAGHER, 1-0-1	(Notre Dame '17)	Born 7-4-94
Auburn	Bacardi, Cuba 1-1-37	Villanova 7-7 (Maurice "Clipper" Smith)
Auburn	Orange 1-1-38	Michigan St. 6-0 (Charlie Bachman)
RANDOLPH R. M. MEDLEY, 2-0-0	(Mo. Wesleyan '21)	Born 9-22-98
Southwestern (Tex.)	Sun 1-1-44	New Mexico 7-0 (Willis Barnes)
Southwestern (Tex.)	Sun 1-1-45	U. of Mexico 35-0 (Bernard A. Hoban)
LEO "DUTCH" MEYER, 3-4-0	(Texas Christian '22)	Born 1-15-98
Texas Christian	Sugar 1-1-36	Louisiana St. 3-2 (Bernie Moore)
Texas Christian	Cotton 1-1-37	Marquette 16-6 (Frank Murray)
Texas Christian	Sugar 1-2-39	Carnegie Mellon 15-7 (Bill Kern)
Texas Christian	Orange 1-1-42	Georgia 26-40 (Wally Butts)
Texas Christian	Cotton 1-1-45	Oklahoma St. 0-34 (Jim Lookabaugh)
Texas Christian	Delta 1-1-48	Mississippi 9-13 (John Vaught)
Texas Christian	Cotton 1-1-52	Kentucky 7-20 (Paul "Bear" Bryant)

Coach/School	Bowl/Date	Opponent/Score (Coach)
RON MEYER, 0-1-0	(Purdue '63)	Born 2-17-41
Southern Methodist	Holiday 12-19-80	Brigham Young 45-46 (LaVell Edwards)
JOHN MICHELOSEN, 0-2-0	(Pittsburgh '38)	Born 2-13-16
Pittsburgh	Sugar 1-2-56	Georgia Tech 0-7 (Bobby Dodd)
Pittsburgh	Gator 12-29-56	Georgia Tech 14-21 (Bobby Dodd)
JACK MITCHELL, 1-0-0	(Oklahoma '49)	Born 12-3-24
Kansas	Bluebonnet 12-16-61	Rice 33-7 (Jess Neely)
ODUS MITCHELL, 0-2-0	(West Tex. A&M '25)	Born 6-29-99
North Texas	Salad 1-1-48	Nevada 6-13 (Joe Sheeketski)
North Texas	Sun 12-31-59	New Mexico St. 8-28 (Warren Woodson)
GARY MOELLER, 3-1-0	(Ohio St. '63)	Born 1-26-41
Michigan	Gator 1-1-91	Mississippi 35-3 (Billy Brewer)
Michigan	Rose 1-1-92	Washington 14-34 (Don James)
Michigan	Rose 1-1-93	Washington 38-31 (Don James)
Michigan	Hall of Fame 1-1-94	North Caro. St. 42-7 (Mike O'Cain)
AL MOLDE, 0-1-0	(Gust. Adolphus '66)	Born 11-15-43
Western Mich.	California 12-10-88	Fresno St. 30-35 (Jim Sweeney)
JACK MOLLENKOPF, 1-0-0	(Bowling Green '31)	Born 11-24-05
Purdue	Rose 1-2-67	Southern Cal 14-13 (John McKay)
BERNIE MOORE, 1-3-1	(Carson-Newman '17)	Born 4-30-95
Louisiana St.	Sugar 1-1-36	Texas Christian 2-3 (Leo "Dutch" Meyer)
Louisiana St.	Sugar 1-1-37	Santa Clara 14-21 (Lawrence "Buck" Shaw)
Louisiana St.	Sugar 1-1-38	Santa Clara 0-6 (Lawrence "Buck" Shaw)
Louisiana St.	Orange 1-1-44	Texas A&M 19-14 (Homer Norton)
Louisiana St.	Cotton 1-1-47	Arkansas 0-0 (John Barnhill)
BUD MOORE, 0-1-0	(Alabama '61)	Born 10-16-39
Kansas	Sun 12-26-75	Pittsburgh 19-33 (Johnny Majors)
CHARLEY MORAN, 2-1-0	(Tennessee '98)	Born 2-22-78
Centre	Fort Worth Classic 1-1-21	Texas Christian 63-7 (Bill Driver)
Centre	San Diego East-West Christmas Classic 12-26-21	Arizona 38-0 (J. F. "Pop" McKale)
Centre	Dixie Classic 1-2-22	Texas A&M 14-22 (Dana Bible)
DELL MORGAN, 0-3-0	(Austin '25)	Born 2-14-02
Texas Tech	Sun 1-1-42	Tulsa 0-6 (Henry Frnka)
Texas Tech	Sun 1-1-48	Miami (Ohio) 12-13 (Sid Gillman)
Texas Tech	Raisin 12-31-49	San Jose St. 13-20 (Bill Hubbard)
JOE MORRISON, 0-3-0	(Cincinnati '59)	Born 8-21-37
South Caro.	Gator 12-28-84	Oklahoma St. 14-21 (Pat Jones)
South Caro.	Gator 12-28-87	Louisiana St. 13-30 (Mike Archer)
South Caro.	Liberty 12-28-88	Indiana 10-34 (Bill Mallory)
RAY MORRISON, 0-1-0	(Vanderbilt '12)	Born 2-28-85
Southern Methodist	Dixie Classic 1-1-25	West Va. Wesleyan 7-9 (Bob Higgins)
DARRELL MUDRA, 0-1-0	(Peru St. '51)	Born 1-4-29
Arizona	Sun 12-28-68	Auburn 10-34 (Ralph "Shug" Jordan)
CLARENCE "BIGGIE" MUNN, 1-0-0	(Minnesota '32)	Born 9-11-08
Michigan St.	Rose 1-1-54	UCLA 28-20 (Henry "Red" Sanders)
BILLY MURPHY, 1-0-0	(Mississippi St. '47)	Born 1-13-21
Memphis	Pasadena 12-18-71	San Jose St. 28-9 (Dewey King)
GENE MURPHY, 0-1-0	(North Dak. '62)	Born 8-6-39
Cal St. Fullerton	California 12-17-83	Northern Ill. 13-20 (Bill Mallory)
JACK MURPHY, 1-0-0	(Heidelberg '54)	Born 8-6-32
Toledo	Tangerine 12-28-71	Richmond 28-3 (Frank Jones)
BILL MURRAY, 2-1-0	(Duke '31)	Born 9-9-08
Duke	Orange 1-1-55	Nebraska 34-7 (Bill Glassford)
Duke	Orange 1-1-58	Oklahoma 21-48 (Bud Wilkinson)
Duke	Cotton 1-2-61	Arkansas 7-6 (Frank Broyles)
FRANK MURRAY, 0-1-0	(Tufts '08)	Born 2-12-85
Marquette	Cotton 1-1-37	Texas Christian 6-16 (Leo "Dutch" Meyer)
DENNY MYERS, 0-1-0	(Iowa '30)	Born 11-10-05
Boston College	Orange 1-1-43	Alabama 21-37 (Frank Thomas)
EDWARD "HOOK" MYLIN, 1-0-0	(Frank. & Marsh.)	Born 10-23-97
Bucknell	Orange 1-1-35	Miami (Fla.) 26-0 (Tom McCann)
RAY NAGEL, 1-0-0	(UCLA '50)	Born 5-18-27
Utah	Liberty 12-19-64	West Va. 32-6 (Gene Corum)
LARRY NAVIAUX, 0-1-0	(Nebraska '59)	Born 12-17-36
Boston U.	Pasadena 12-6-69	San Diego St. 7-28 (Don Coryell)
EARLE "GREASY" NEALE, 0-0-1	(West Va. Wesleyan '14)	Born 11-5-91
Wash. & Jeff.	Rose 1-2-22	California 0-0 (Andy Smith)
JESS NEELY, 4-3-0	(Vanderbilt '23)	Born 1-4-98
Clemson	Cotton 1-1-40	Boston College 6-3 (Frank Leahy)
Rice	Orange 1-1-47	Tennessee 8-0 (Bob Neyland)

Coach/School	Bowl/Date	Opponent/Score (Coach)
Rice	Cotton 1-2-50	North Caro. 27-13 (Carl Snavely)
Rice	Cotton 1-1-54	Alabama 28-6 (Harold "Red" Drew)
Rice	Cotton 1-1-58	Navy 7-20 (Eddie Erdelatz)
Rice	Sugar 1-2-61	Mississippi 6-14 (John Vaught)
Rice	Bluebonnet 12-16-61	Kansas 7-33 (Jack Mitchell)

DON NEHLEN, 3-5-0 (Bowling Green '58) Born 1-1-36

West Va.	Peach 12-31-81	Florida 26-6 (Charley Pell)
West Va.	Gator 12-30-82	Florida St. 12-31 (Bobby Bowden)
West Va.	All-American 12-22-83	Kentucky 20-16 (Jerry Claiborne)
West Va.	Bluebonnet 12-31-84	Texas Christian 31-14 (Jim Wacker)
West Va.	Sun 12-25-87	Oklahoma St. 33-35 (Pat Jones)
West Va.	Fiesta 1-2-89	Notre Dame 21-34 (Lou Holtz)
West Va.	Gator 12-30-89	Clemson 7-27 (Danny Ford)
West Va.	Sugar 1-1-94	Florida 7-41 (Steve Spurrier)

BOB NEYLAND, 2-5-0 (Army '16) Born 2-17-92

Tennessee	Orange 1-2-39	Oklahoma 17-0 (Tom Stidham)
Tennessee	Rose 1-1-40	Southern Cal 0-14 (Howard Jones)
Tennessee	Sugar 1-1-41	Boston College 13-19 (Frank Leahy)
Tennessee	Orange 1-1-47	Rice 0-8 (Jess Neely)
Tennessee	Cotton 1-1-51	Texas 20-14 (Blair Cherry)
Tennessee	Sugar 1-1-52	Maryland 13-28 (Jim Tatum)
Tennessee	Cotton 1-1-53	Texas 0-16 (Ed Price)

RAY NOLTING, 1-0-0 (Cincinnati '36) Born 11-8-13

Cincinnati	Sun 1-1-47	Virginia Tech 18-6 (Jimmy Kitts)

HOMER NORTON, 2-2-1 (Birmingham Southern '16) Born 12-30-96

Centenary (La.)	Dixie Classic 1-1-34	Arkansas 7-7 (Fred Thomsen)
Texas A&M	Sugar 1-1-40	Tulane 14-13 (Lowell "Red" Dawson)
Texas A&M	Cotton 1-1-41	Fordham 13-12 (Jim Crowley)
Texas A&M	Cotton 1-1-42	Alabama 21-29 (Frank Thomas)
Texas A&M	Orange 1-1-44	Louisiana St. 14-19 (Bernie Moore)

TOM NUGENT, 0-2-0 (Ithaca '36) Born 2-24-16

Florida St.	Sun 1-1-55	UTEP 20-47 (Mike Brumbelow)
Florida St.	Bluegrass 12-13-58	Oklahoma St. 6-15 (Cliff Speegle)

BERNARD "BUNNIE" OAKES, 0-1-0 (Illinois '24) Born 9-15-98

Colorado	Cotton 1-1-38	Rice 14-28 (Jimmy Kitts)

MIKE O'CAIN, 0-1-0 (Clemson '77) Born 7-20-54

North Caro. St.	Hall of Fame 1-1-94	Michigan 7-42 (Gary Moeller)

JORDAN OLIVAR, 1-1-0 (Villanova '38) Born 1-30-15

Villanova	Great Lakes 12-6-47	Kentucky 14-24 (Paul "Bear" Bryant)
Villanova	Harbor 1-1-49	Nevada 27-7 (Joe Sheeketski)

AL ONOFRIO, 1-1-0 (Arizona St. '43) Born 3-15-21

Missouri	Fiesta 12-23-72	Arizona St. 35-49 (Frank Kush)
Missouri	Sun 12-29-73	Auburn 34-17 (Ralph "Shug" Jordan)

BENNIE OOSTERBAAN, 1-0-0 (Michigan '28) Born 2-24-06

Michigan	Rose 1-1-51	California 14-6 (Lynn "Pappy" Waldorf)

TOM OSBORNE, 8-13-0 (Hastings '59) Born 2-23-37

Nebraska	Cotton 1-1-74	Texas 19-3 (Darrell Royal)
Nebraska	Sugar 12-31-74	Florida 13-10 (Doug Dickey)
Nebraska	Fiesta 12-26-75	Arizona St. 14-17 (Frank Kush)
Nebraska	Bluebonnet 12-31-76	Texas Tech 27-24 (Steve Sloan)
Nebraska	Liberty 12-19-77	North Caro. 21-17 (Bill Dooley)
Nebraska	Orange 1-1-79	Oklahoma 24-31 (Barry Switzer)
Nebraska	Cotton 1-1-80	Houston 14-17 (Bill Yeoman)
Nebraska	Sun 12-27-80	Mississippi St. 31-17 (Emory Bellard)
Nebraska	Orange 1-1-82	Clemson 15-22 (Danny Ford)
Nebraska	Orange 1-1-83	Louisiana St. 21-20 (Jerry Stovall)
Nebraska	Orange 1-2-84	Miami (Fla.) 30-31 (Howard Schnellenberger)
Nebraska	Sugar 1-1-85	Louisiana St. 28-10 (Bill Arnsparger)
Nebraska	Fiesta 1-1-86	Michigan 23-27 (Glenn "Bo" Schembechler)
Nebraska	Sugar 1-1-87	Louisiana St. 30-15 (Bill Arnsparger)
Nebraska	Fiesta 1-1-88	Florida St. 28-31 (Bobby Bowden)
Nebraska	Orange 1-2-89	Miami (Fla.) 3-23 (Jimmy Johnson)
Nebraska	Fiesta 1-1-90	Florida St. 17-41 (Bobby Bowden)
Nebraska	Fla. Citrus 1-1-91	Georgia Tech 21-45 (Bobby Ross)
Nebraska	Orange 1-1-92	Miami (Fla.) 0-22 (Dennis Erickson)
Nebraska	Orange 1-1-93	Florida St. 14-27 (Bobby Bowden)
Nebraska	Orange 1-1-94	Florida St. 16-18 (Bobby Bowden)

JIM OWENS, 2-1-0 (Oklahoma '50) Born 3-6-27

Washington	Rose 1-1-60	Wisconsin 44-8 (Milt Bruhn)
Washington	Rose 1-2-61	Minnesota 17-7 (Murray Warmath)
Washington	Rose 1-1-64	Illinois 7-17 (Pete Elliott)

JACK PARDEE, 0-1-0 (Texas A&M '57) Born 4-9-36

Houston	Aloha 12-25-88	Washington St. 22-24 (Dennis Erickson)

ARA PARSEGHIAN, 3-2-0 (Miami, Ohio '49) Born 5-21-23

Notre Dame	Cotton 1-1-70	Texas 17-21 (Darrell Royal)
Notre Dame	Cotton 1-1-71	Texas 24-11 (Darrell Royal)
Notre Dame	Orange 1-1-73	Nebraska 6-40 (Bob Devaney)
Notre Dame	Sugar 12-31-73	Alabama 24-23 (Paul "Bear" Bryant)
Notre Dame	Orange 1-1-75	Alabama 13-11 (Paul "Bear" Bryant)

PAUL PASQUALONI, 2-0-0 (Penn St. '72) Born 8-16-49

Syracuse	Hall of Fame 1-1-92	Ohio St. 24-17 (John Cooper)
Syracuse	Fiesta 1-1-93	Colorado 26-22 (Bill McCartney)

JOE PATERNO, 15-8-1 (Brown '50) Born 12-21-26

Penn St.	Gator 12-30-67	Florida St. 17-17 (Bill Peterson)
Penn St.	Orange 1-1-69	Kansas 15-14 (Pepper Rodgers)
Penn St.	Orange 1-1-70	Missouri 10-3 (Dan Devine)
Penn St.	Cotton 1-1-72	Texas 30-6 (Darrell Royal)
Penn St.	Sugar 12-31-72	Oklahoma 0-14 (Chuck Fairbanks)
Penn St.	Orange 1-1-74	Louisiana St. 16-9 (Charlie McClendon)
Penn St.	Cotton 1-1-75	Baylor 41-20 (Grant Teaff)
Penn St.	Sugar 12-31-75	Alabama 6-13 (Paul "Bear" Bryant)
Penn St.	Gator 12-27-76	Notre Dame 9-20 (Dan Devine)
Penn St.	Fiesta 12-25-77	Arizona St. 42-30 (Frank Kush)
Penn St.	Sugar 1-1-79	Alabama 7-14 (Paul "Bear" Bryant)
Penn St.	Liberty 12-22-79	Tulane 9-6 (Larry Smith)
Penn St.	Fiesta 12-26-80	Ohio St. 31-19 (Earle Bruce)
Penn St.	Fiesta 1-1-82	Southern Cal 26-10 (John Robinson)
Penn St.	Sugar 1-1-83	Georgia 27-23 (Vince Dooley)
Penn St.	Aloha 12-26-83	Washington 13-10 (Don James)
Penn St.	Orange 1-1-86	Oklahoma 10-25 (Barry Switzer)
Penn St.	Fiesta 1-1-87	Miami (Fla.) 14-10 (Jimmy Johnson)
Penn St.	Fla. Citrus 1-1-88	Clemson 10-35 (Danny Ford)
Penn St.	Holiday 12-29-89	Brigham Young 50-39 (LaVell Edwards)
Penn St.	Blockbuster 12-28-90	Florida St. 17-24 (Bobby Bowden)
Penn St.	Fiesta 1-1-92	Tennessee 42-17 (Johnny Majors)
Penn St.	Blockbuster 1-1-93	Stanford 3-24 (Bill Walsh)
Penn St.	Fla. Citrus 1-1-94	Tennessee 31-13 (Phillip Fulmer)

JOE RAYMOND PEACE, 0-0-1 (Louisiana Tech '68) Born 6-5-45

Louisiana Tech	Independence 12-15-90	Maryland 34-34 (Joe Krivak)

CHARLEY PELL, 2-3-0 (Alabama '64) Born 2-27-41

Clemson	Gator 12-30-77	Pittsburgh 3-34 (Jackie Sherrill)
Florida	Tangerine 12-20-80	Maryland 35-20 (Jerry Claiborne)
Florida	Peach 12-31-81	West Va. 6-26 (Don Nehlen)
Florida	Bluebonnet 12-31-82	Arkansas 24-28 (Lou Holtz)
Florida	Gator 12-30-83	Iowa 14-6 (Hayden Fry)

RAY PERKINS, 3-0-0 (Alabama '67) Born 11-6-41

Alabama	Sun 12-24-83	Southern Methodist 28-7 (Bobby Collins)
Alabama	Aloha 12-28-85	Southern Cal 24-3 (Ted Tollner)
Alabama	Sun 12-26-86	Washington 28-6 (Don James)

GEORGE PERLES, 3-4-0 (Michigan St. '60) Born 7-16-34

Michigan St.	Cherry 12-22-84	Army 6-10 (Jim Young)
Michigan St.	All-American 12-31-85	Georgia Tech 14-17 (Bill Curry)
Michigan St.	Rose 1-1-88	Southern Cal 20-17 (Larry Smith)
Michigan St.	Gator 1-1-89	Georgia 27-34 (Vince Dooley)
Michigan St.	Aloha 12-25-89	Hawaii 33-13 (Bob Wagner)
Michigan St.	John Hancock 12-31-90	Southern Cal 17-16 (Larry Smith)
Michigan St.	Liberty 12-28-93	Louisville 7-18 (Howard Schnellenberger)

DOYT PERRY, 0-1-0 (Bowling Green '32) Born 1-6-10

Bowling Green	Mercy 11-23-61	Fresno St. 6-36 (Cecil Coleman)

BILL PETERSON, 1-2-1 (Ohio Northern '46) Born 5-14-20

Florida St.	Gator 1-2-65	Oklahoma 36-19 (Gomer Jones)
Florida St.	Sun 12-24-66	Wyoming 20-28 (Lloyd Eaton)
Florida St.	Gator 12-30-67	Penn St. 17-17 (Joe Paterno)
Florida St.	Peach 12-30-68	Louisiana St. 27-31 (Charlie McClendon)

JIMMY PHELAN, 0-3-0 (Notre Dame '19) Born 12-5-92

Washington	Rose 1-1-37	Pittsburgh 0-21 (Jock Sutherland)
St. Mary's (Cal.)	Sugar 1-1-46	Oklahoma 13-33 (Jim Lookabaugh)
St. Mary's (Cal.)	Oil 1-1-47	Georgia Tech 19-41 (Bobby Dodd)

ALVIN "PIX" PIERSON, 0-1-0 (Nevada '22) Born 7-25-98

Fresno St.	Raisin 1-1-46	Drake 12-13 (Vee Green)

JIM PITTMAN, 1-0-0 (Mississippi St. '50) Born 8-28-25

Tulane	Liberty 12-12-70	Colorado 17-3 (Eddie Crowder)

JOHN PONT, 0-2-0 (Miami, Ohio '52) Born 11-13-27

Miami (Ohio)	Tangerine 12-22-52	Houston 21-49 (Bill Yeoman)
Indiana	Rose 1-1-68	Southern Cal 3-14 (John McKay)

WARREN POWERS, 3-2-0 (Nebraska '63) Born 2-19-41

Missouri	Liberty 12-23-78	Louisiana St. 20-15 (Charlie McClendon)
Missouri	All-American 12-29-79	South Caro. 24-14 (Jim Carlen)
Missouri	Liberty 12-27-80	Purdue 25-28 (Jim Young)
Missouri	Tangerine 12-19-81	Southern Miss. 19-17 (Bobby Collins)
Missouri	Holiday 12-23-83	Brigham Young 17-21 (LaVell Edwards)

CLARENCE "NIBS" PRICE, 0-1-0 (California '14) Born 1889

California	Rose 1-1-29	Georgia Tech 7-8 (Bill Alexander)

ED PRICE, 1-0-0 (Texas '33) Born 1-12-09

Texas	Cotton 1-1-53	Tennessee 16-0 (Bob Neyland)

MIKE PRICE, 1-0-0 (Puget Sound '69) Born 4-6-46

Washington St.	Copper 12-29-92	Utah 31-28 (Ron McBride)

Coach/School	Bowl/Date	Opponent/Score (Coach)

TOMMY PROTHRO, 2-2-0 (Duke '42) Born 7-20-20
Oregon St. .... Rose 1-1-57 Iowa 19-35 (Forest Evashevski)
Oregon St. .... Liberty 12-15-62 Villanova 6-0 (Alex Bell)
Oregon St. .... Rose 1-1-65 Michigan 7-34 (Chalmers "Bump" Elliott)
UCLA .... Rose 1-1-66 Michigan St. 14-12 (Duffy Daugherty)

DAVE RADER, 1-1-0 (Tulsa '80) Born 3-9-57
Tulsa .... Independence 12-16-89 Oregon 24-27 (Rich Brooks)
Tulsa .... Freedom 12-30-91 San Diego St. 28-17 (Al Luginbill)

JOHN RALSTON, 2-2-0 (California '54) Born 4-25-27
Utah St. .... Sun 12-31-60 New Mexico St. 13-20 (Warren Woodson)
Utah St. .... Gotham 12-9-61 Baylor 9-24 (John Bridgers)
Stanford .... Rose 1-1-71 Ohio St. 27-17 (Woody Hayes)
Stanford .... Rose 1-1-72 Michigan 13-12 (Glenn "Bo" Schembechler)

RED REESE, 1-0-0 (Washington St. '25) Born 3-2-99
Second Air Force ..... Sun 1-1-43 Hardin-Simmons 13-7 (Warren Woodson)

BO REIN, 2-0-0 (Ohio St. '58) Born 7-20-45
North Caro. St. .... Peach 12-31-77 Iowa St. 24-14 (Earle Bruce)
North Caro. St. .... Tangerine 12-23-78 Pittsburgh 30-17 (Jackie Sherrill)

PAUL ROACH, 0-3-0 (Black Hills St. '52) Born 10-24-27
Wyoming .... Holiday 12-30-87 Iowa 19-20 (Hayden Fry)
Wyoming .... Holiday 12-30-88 Oklahoma St. 14-62 (Pat Jones)
Wyoming .... Copper 12-31-90 California 15-17 (Bruce Snyder)

ED ROBINSON, 0-1-0 (Brown '96) Born 10-15-73
Brown .... Rose 1-1-16 Washington St. 0-14 (Bill "Lone Star" Dietz)

JOHN ROBINSON, 5-1-0 (Oregon '58) Born 7-25-35
Southern Cal .... Rose 1-1-77 Michigan 14-6 (Glenn "Bo" Schembechler)
Southern Cal .... Bluebonnet 12-31-77 Texas A&M 47-28 (Emory Bellard)
Southern Cal .... Rose 1-1-79 Michigan 17-10 (Glenn "Bo" Schembechler)
Southern Cal .... Rose 1-1-80 Ohio St. 17-16 (Earle Bruce)
Southern Cal .... Fiesta 1-1-82 Penn St. 10-26 (Joe Paterno)
Southern Cal .... Freedom 12-30-93 Utah 28-21 (Ron McBride)

KNUTE ROCKNE, 1-0-0 (Notre Dame '14) Born 3-4-88
Notre Dame .... Rose 1-1-25 Stanford 27-10 (Glenn "Pop" Warner)

PEPPER RODGERS, 0-2-0 (Georgia Tech '55) Born 10-8-31
Kansas .... Orange 1-1-69 Penn St. 14-15 (Joe Paterno)
Georgia Tech .... Peach 12-25-78 Purdue 21-41 (Jim Young)

DARRYL ROGERS, 1-0-0 (Fresno St. '57) Born 5-28-34
Arizona St. .... Fiesta 1-1-83 Oklahoma 32-21 (Barry Switzer)

E. L. "DICK" ROMNEY, 0-1-0 (Utah '17) Born 2-12-95
Utah St. .... Raisin 1-1-47 San Jose St. 0-20 (Bill Hubbard)

TIM ROSE, 0-1-0 (Xavier, Ohio '62) Born 10-14-41
Miami (Ohio) .... California 12-13-86 San Jose St. 7-37 (Claude Gilbert)

BOBBY ROSS, 4-2-0 (Va. Military '59) Born 12-23-36
Maryland .... Aloha 12-25-82 Washington 20-21 (Don James)
Maryland .... Fla. Citrus 12-17-83 Tennessee 23-30 (Johnny Majors)
Maryland .... Sun 12-22-84 Tennessee 27-26 (Johnny Majors)
Maryland .... Cherry 12-21-85 Syracuse 35-18 (Dick MacPherson)
Georgia Tech .... Fla. Citrus 1-1-91 Nebraska 45-21 (Tom Osborne)
Georgia Tech .... Aloha 12-25-91 Stanford 18-17 (Dennis Green)

DARRELL ROYAL, 8-7-1 (Oklahoma '50) Born 7-6-24
Texas .... Sugar 1-1-58 Mississippi 7-39 (John Vaught)
Texas .... Cotton 1-1-60 Syracuse 14-23 (Ben Schwartzwalder)
Texas .... Bluebonnet 12-17-60 Alabama 3-3 (Paul "Bear" Bryant)
Texas .... Cotton 1-1-62 Mississippi 12-7 (John Vaught)
Texas .... Cotton 1-1-63 Louisiana St. 0-13 (Charlie McClendon)
Texas .... Cotton 1-1-64 Navy 28-6 (Wayne Hardin)
Texas .... Orange 1-1-65 Alabama 21-17 (Paul "Bear" Bryant)
Texas .... Bluebonnet 12-17-66 Mississippi 19-0 (John Vaught)
Texas .... Cotton 1-1-69 Tennessee 36-13 (Doug Dickey)
Texas .... Cotton 1-1-70 Notre Dame 21-17 (Ara Parseghian)
Texas .... Cotton 1-1-71 Notre Dame 11-24 (Ara Parseghian)
Texas .... Cotton 1-1-72 Penn St. 6-30 (Joe Paterno)
Texas .... Cotton 1-1-73 Alabama 17-13 (Paul "Bear" Bryant)
Texas .... Cotton 1-1-74 Nebraska 3-19 (Tom Osborne)
Texas .... Gator 12-30-74 Auburn 3-27 (Ralph "Shug" Jordan)
Texas .... Bluebonnet 12-27-75 Colorado 38-21 (Bill Mallory)

HENRY "RED" SANDERS, 0-2-0 (Vanderbilt '27) Born 3-7-05
UCLA .... Rose 1-1-54 Michigan St. 20-28 (Clarence "Biggie" Munn)
UCLA .... Rose 1-2-56 Michigan St. 14-17 (Duffy Daugherty)

RALPH SASSE, 0-1-0 (Army '10) Born 7-19-89
Mississippi St. .... Orange 1-1-37 Duquesne 12-13 (John Smith)

GEORGE SAUER, 0-3-0 (Nebraska '34) Born 12-11-10
Kansas .... Orange 1-1-48 Georgia Tech 14-20 (Bobby Dodd)
Baylor .... Orange 1-1-52 Georgia Tech 14-17 (Bobby Dodd)
Baylor .... Gator 12-31-54 Auburn 13-33 (Ralph "Shug" Jordan)

MACK SAXON, 0-1-0 (Texas) Born 1901
UTEP .... Sun 1-1-37 Hardin-Simmons 6-34 (Frank Kimbrough)

GLENN "BO" SCHEMBECHLER, 5-12-0 (Miami, Ohio '51) Born 4-1-29
Michigan .... Rose 1-1-70 Southern Cal 3-10 (John McKay)
Michigan .... Rose 1-1-72 Stanford 12-13 (John Ralston)
Michigan .... Orange 1-1-76 Oklahoma 6-14 (Barry Switzer)
Michigan .... Rose 1-1-77 Southern Cal 6-14 (John Robinson)
Michigan .... Rose 1-2-78 Washington 20-27 (Don James)
Michigan .... Rose 1-1-79 Southern Cal 10-17 (John Robinson)
Michigan .... Gator 12-28-79 North Caro. 15-17 (Dick Crum)
Michigan .... Rose 1-1-81 Washington 23-6 (Don James)
Michigan .... Bluebonnet 12-31-81 UCLA 33-14 (Terry Donahue)
Michigan .... Rose 1-1-83 UCLA 14-24 (Terry Donahue)
Michigan .... Sugar 1-2-84 Auburn 7-9 (Pat Dye)
Michigan .... Holiday 12-21-84 Brigham Young 17-24 (LaVell Edwards)
Michigan .... Fiesta 1-1-86 Nebraska 27-23 (Tom Osborne)
Michigan .... Rose 1-1-87 Arizona St. 15-22 (John Cooper)
Michigan .... Hall of Fame 1-2-88 Alabama 28-24 (Bill Curry)
Michigan .... Rose 1-2-89 Southern Cal 22-14 (Larry Smith)
Michigan .... Rose 1-1-90 Southern Cal 10-17 (Larry Smith)

MERLE SCHLOSSER, 0-1-0 (Illinois '50) Born 10-14-27
Western Mich. .... Aviation 12-9-61 New Mexico 12-28 (Bill Weeks)

HOWARD SCHNELLENBERGER, 4-0-0 (Kentucky '56) Born 3-16-34
Miami (Fla.) .... Peach 1-2-81 Virginia Tech 20-10 (Bill Dooley)
Miami (Fla.) .... Orange 1-2-84 Nebraska 31-30 (Tom Osborne)
Louisville .... Fiesta 1-1-91 Alabama 34-7 (Gene Stallings)
Louisville .... Liberty 12-28-93 Michigan St. 18-7 (George Perles)

PAUL SCHUDEL, 0-2-0 (Miami, Ohio '66) Born 7-2-44
Ball St. .... California 12-9-89 Fresno St. 6-27 (Jim Sweeney)
Ball St. .... Las Vegas 12-17-93 Utah St. 33-42 (Charlie Weatherbie)

BILL SCHUTTE, 0-1-0 (Idaho '33) Born 5-7-10
San Diego St. .... Harbor 1-1-48 Hardin-Simmons 0-53 (Warren Woodson)

BEN SCHWARTZWALDER, 2-5-0 (West Va. '35) Born 6-2-09
Syracuse .... Orange 1-1-53 Alabama 6-61 (Harold "Red" Drew)
Syracuse .... Cotton 1-1-57 Texas Christian 27-28 (Abe Martin)
Syracuse .... Orange 1-1-59 Oklahoma 6-21 (Bud Wilkinson)
Syracuse .... Cotton 1-1-60 Texas 23-14 (Darrell Royal)
Syracuse .... Liberty 12-16-61 Miami (Fla.) 15-14 (Andy Gustafson)
Syracuse .... Sugar 1-1-65 Louisiana St. 10-13 (Charlie McClendon)
Syracuse .... Gator 12-31-66 Tennessee 12-18 (Doug Dickey)

CLARK SHAUGHNESSY, 1-0-0 (Minnesota '14) Born 3-6-92
Stanford .... Rose 1-1-41 Nebraska 21-13 (Lawrence McC. "Biff" Jones)

LAWRENCE "BUCK" SHAW, 2-0-0 (Notre Dame '22) Born 3-28-99
Santa Clara .... Sugar 1-1-37 Louisiana St. 21-14 (Bernie Moore)
Santa Clara .... Sugar 1-1-38 Louisiana St. 6-0 (Bernie Moore)

TERRY SHEA, 1-0-0 (Oregon '68) Born 6-12-46
San Jose St. .... California 12-8-90 Central Mich. 48-24 (Herb Deromedi)

JOE SHEEKETSKI, 1-1-0 (Notre Dame '33) Born 4-15-09
Nevada .... Salad 1-1-48 North Texas 13-6 (Odus Mitchell)
Nevada .... Harbor 1-1-49 Villanova 7-27 (Jordan Olivar)

DICK SHERIDAN, 2-4-0 (South Caro. '64) Born 8-9-41
North Caro. St. .... Peach 12-31-86 Virginia Tech 24-25 (Bill Dooley)
North Caro. St. .... Peach 12-31-88 Iowa 28-23 (Hayden Fry)
North Caro. St. .... Copper 12-31-89 Arizona 10-17 (Dick Tomey)
North Caro. St. .... All-American 12-28-90 Southern Miss. 31-27 (Jeff Bower)
North Caro. St. .... Peach 1-1-92 East Caro. 34-37 (Bill Lewis)
North Caro. St. .... Gator 12-31-92 Florida 10-27 (Steve Spurrier)

EUGENE "BO" SHERMAN, 1-0-0 (Henderson St. '30) Born 7-5-08
Geo. Washington .... Sun 1-1-57 UTEP 13-0 (Mike Brumbelow)

JACKIE SHERRILL, 6-4-0 (Alabama '66) Born 11-28-43
Pittsburgh .... Gator 12-30-77 Clemson 34-3 (Charley Pell)
Pittsburgh .... Tangerine 12-23-78 North Caro. St. 17-30 (Bo Rein)
Pittsburgh .... Fiesta 12-25-79 Arizona 16-10 (Tony Mason)
Pittsburgh .... Gator 12-29-80 South Caro. 37-9 (Jim Carlen)
Pittsburgh .... Sugar 1-1-82 Georgia 24-20 (Vince Dooley)
Texas A&M .... Cotton 1-1-86 Auburn 36-16 (Pat Dye)
Texas A&M .... Cotton 1-1-87 Ohio St. 12-28 (Earle Bruce)
Texas A&M .... Cotton 1-1-88 Notre Dame 35-10 (Lou Holtz)
Mississippi St. .... Liberty 12-29-91 Air Force 15-38 (Fisher DeBerry)
Mississippi St. .... Peach 1-2-93 North Caro. 17-21 (Mack Brown)

TED SHIPKEY, 0-1-0 (Stanford '27) Born 9-28-04
New Mexico .... Sun 1-2-39 Utah 0-28 (Ike Armstrong)

LARRY SIEMERING, 1-0-0 (San Francisco '35) Born 11-24-10
Pacific (Cal.) .... Raisin 1-1-48 Wichita St. 26-14 (Ralph Graham)

Coach/School	Bowl/Date	Opponent/Score (Coach)
CHAUNCEY SIMPSON, 0-1-0 (Missouri '25) Born 12-21-02		
Missouri	Cotton 1-1-46	Texas 27-40 (Dana Bible)
DAN SIMRELL, 0-1-0 (Toledo '65) Born 4-9-43		
Toledo	California 12-15-84	Nevada-Las Vegas 13-30 (Harvey Hyde)
STEVE SLOAN, 0-2-1 (Alabama '66) Born 8-19-44		
Vanderbilt	Peach 12-28-74	Texas Tech 6-6 (Jim Carlen)
Texas Tech	Bluebonnet 12-31-76	Nebraska 24-27 (Tom Osborne)
Texas Tech	Tangerine 12-23-77	Florida St. 17-40 (Bobby Bowden)
R. C. SLOCUM, 1-4-0 (McNeese St. '67) Born 11-7-44		
Texas A&M	John Hancock 12-30-89	Pittsburgh 28-31 (Paul Hackett)
Texas A&M	Holiday 12-29-90	Brigham Young 65-14 (LaVell Edwards)
Texas A&M	Cotton 1-1-92	Florida St. 2-10 (Bobby Bowden)
Texas A&M	Cotton 1-1-93	Notre Dame 3-28 (Lou Holtz)
Texas A&M	Cotton 1-1-94	Notre Dame 21-24 (Lou Holtz)
ANDY SMITH, 1-0-1 (Pennsylvania '06) Born 9-10-83		
California	Rose 1-1-21	Ohio St. 28-0 (John Wilce)
California	Rose 1-2-22	Wash. & Jeff. 0-0 (Earle "Greasy" Neale)
HOMER SMITH, 0-1-0 (Princeton '54) Born 10-9-31		
Davidson	Tangerine 12-26-69	Toledo 33-56 (Frank Lauterbur)
JOHN "LITTLE CLIPPER" SMITH, 1-0-0 (Notre Dame '29) Born 12-12-04		
Duquesne	Orange 1-1-37	Mississippi St. 13-12 (Ralph Sasse)
LARRY SMITH, 2-5-1 (Bowling Green '62) Born 9-12-39		
Tulane	Liberty 12-22-79	Penn St. 6-9 (Joe Paterno)
Arizona	Sun 12-28-85	Georgia 13-13 (Vince Dooley)
Arizona	Aloha 12-27-86	North Caro. 30-21 (Dick Crum)
Southern Cal	Rose 1-1-88	Michigan 17-20 (George Perles)
Southern Cal	Rose 1-2-89	Michigan 14-22 (Glenn "Bo" Schembechler)
Southern Cal	Rose 1-1-90	Michigan 17-10 (Glenn "Bo" Schembechler)
Southern Cal	John Hancock 12-31-90	Michigan St. 16-17 (George Perles)
Southern Cal	Freedom 12-29-92	Fresno St. 7-24 (Jim Sweeney)
MAURICE "CLIPPER" SMITH, 0-0-1 (Notre Dame '21) Born 10-15-98		
Villanova	Bacardi, Cuba 1-1-37	Auburn 7-7 (Jack Meagher)
CARL SNAVELY, 0-3-0 (Lebanon Valley '15) Born 7-30-94		
North Caro.	Sugar 1-1-47	Georgia 10-20 (Wally Butts)
North Caro.	Sugar 1-1-49	Oklahoma 6-14 (Bud Wilkinson)
North Caro.	Cotton 1-2-50	Rice 13-27 (Jess Neely)
BILL SNYDER, 1-0-0 (William Jewell '63) Born 10-7-41		
Kansas St.	Copper 12-29-93	Wyoming 52-17 (Joe Tiller)
BRUCE SNYDER, 2-0-0 (Oregon '62) Born 3-14-40		
California	Copper 12-31-90	Wyoming 17-15 (Paul Roach)
California	Fla. Citrus 1-1-92	Clemson 37-13 (Ken Hatfield)
CLARENCE "DOC" SPEARS, 1-0-0 (Dartmouth '16) Born 7-24-94		
West Va.	San Diego East-West Christmas Classic 12-25-22	Gonzaga 21-13 (Charles "Gus" Dorais)
CLIFF SPEEGLE, 1-0-0 (Oklahoma '41) Born 11-4-17		
Oklahoma St.	Bluegrass 12-13-58	Florida St. 15-6 (Tom Nugent)
STEVE SPURRIER, 2-2-0 (Florida '67) Born 4-20-45		
Duke	All-American 12-28-89	Texas Tech 21-49 (Spike Dykes)
Florida	Sugar 1-1-92	Notre Dame 28-39 (Lou Holtz)
Florida	Gator 12-31-92	North Caro. St. 27-10 (Dick Sheridan)
Florida	Sugar 1-1-94	West Va. 41-7 (Don Nehlen)
GENE STALLINGS, 4-1-0 (Texas A&M '57) Born 3-2-35		
Texas A&M	Cotton 1-1-68	Alabama 20-16 (Paul "Bear" Bryant)
Alabama	Fiesta 1-1-91	Louisville 7-34 (Howard Schnellenberger)
Alabama	Blockbuster 12-28-91	Colorado 30-25 (Bill McCartney)
Alabama	Sugar 1-1-93	Miami (Fla.) 34-13 (Dennis Erickson)
Alabama	Gator 12-31-93	North Caro. 24-10 (Mack Brown)
JIM STANGELAND, 0-0-1 (Arizona St. '48) Born 12-21-21		
Long Beach St.	Pasadena 12-19-70	Louisville 24-24 (Lee Corso)
JIM STANLEY, 2-0-0 (Texas A&M '59) Born 5-22-35		
Oklahoma St.	Fiesta 12-28-74	Brigham Young 16-6 (LaVell Edwards)
Oklahoma St.	Tangerine 12-18-76	Brigham Young 49-12 (LaVell Edwards)
TOM STIDHAM, 0-1-0 (Haskell '27) Born 3-27-04		
Oklahoma	Orange 1-2-39	Tennessee 0-17 (Bob Neyland)
LON STINER, 1-0-0 (Nebraska '27) Born 6-20-03		
Oregon St.	Rose 1-1-42	Duke 20-16 (Wallace Wade)
HARRY STITELER, 1-0-0 (Texas A&M '31) Born 9-17-09		
Texas A&M	Presidential Cup 12-9-50	Georgia 40-20 (Wally Butts)
CHUCK STOBART, 1-0-0 (Ohio '59) Born 10-27-34		
Toledo	California 12-19-81	San Jose St. 27-25 (Jack Elway)
CAL STOLL, 0-1-0 (Minnesota '50) Born 12-12-23		
Minnesota	All-American 12-22-77	Maryland 7-17 (Jerry Claiborne)
DENNY STOLZ, 0-3-0 (Alma '55) Born 9-12-34		
Bowling Green	California 12-18-82	Fresno St. 28-29 (Jim Sweeney)
Bowling Green	California 12-14-85	Fresno St. 7-51 (Jim Sweeney)
San Diego St.	Holiday 12-30-86	Iowa 38-39 (Hayden Fry)
JERRY STOVALL, 0-1-0 (Louisiana St. '63) Born 4-30-41		
Louisiana St.	Orange 1-1-83	Nebraska 20-21 (Tom Osborne)
BOB STULL, 0-1-0 (Kansas St. '68) Born 11-21-45		
UTEP	Independence 12-23-88	Southern Miss. 18-38 (Curley Hallman)
JOCK SUTHERLAND, 1-3-0 (Pittsburgh '18) Born 3-21-89		
Pittsburgh	Rose 1-1-28	Stanford 6-7 (Glenn "Pop" Warner)
Pittsburgh	Rose 1-1-30	Southern Cal 14-47 (Howard Jones)
Pittsburgh	Rose 1-2-33	Southern Cal 0-35 (Howard Jones)
Pittsburgh	Rose 1-1-37	Washington 21-0 (Jimmy Phelan)
JIM SWEENEY, 5-2-0 (Portland '51) Born 9-1-29		
Fresno St.	California 12-18-82	Bowling Green 29-28 (Denny Stolz)
Fresno St.	California 12-14-85	Bowling Green 51-7 (Denny Stolz)
Fresno St.	California 12-10-88	Western Mich. 35-30 (Al Molde)
Fresno St.	California 12-9-89	Ball St. 27-8 (Paul Schudel)
Fresno St.	California 12-13-91	Bowling Green 21-28 (Gary Blackney)
Fresno St.	Freedom 12-29-92	Southern Cal 24-7 (Larry Smith)
Fresno St.	Aloha 12-25-93	Colorado 30-41 (Bill McCartney)
BARRY SWITZER, 8-5-0 (Arkansas '60) Born 10-5-37		
Oklahoma	Orange 1-1-76	Michigan 14-6 (Glenn "Bo" Schembechler)
Oklahoma	Fiesta 12-25-76	Wyoming 41-7 (Fred Akers)
Oklahoma	Orange 1-2-78	Arkansas 6-31 (Lou Holtz)
Oklahoma	Orange 1-1-79	Nebraska 31-24 (Tom Osborne)
Oklahoma	Orange 1-1-80	Florida St. 24-7 (Bobby Bowden)
Oklahoma	Orange 1-1-81	Florida St. 18-17 (Bobby Bowden)
Oklahoma	Sun 12-26-81	Houston 40-14 (Bill Yeoman)
Oklahoma	Fiesta 1-1-83	Arizona St. 21-32 (Darryl Rogers)
Oklahoma	Orange 1-1-85	Washington 17-28 (Don James)
Oklahoma	Orange 1-1-86	Penn St. 25-10 (Joe Paterno)
Oklahoma	Orange 1-1-87	Arkansas 42-8 (Ken Hatfield)
Oklahoma	Orange 1-1-88	Miami (Fla.) 14-20 (Jimmy Johnson)
Oklahoma	Fla. Citrus 1-2-89	Clemson 6-13 (Danny Ford)
CHARLIE TATE, 1-1-0 (Florida '42) Born 2-20-21		
Miami (Fla.)	Liberty 12-10-66	Virginia Tech 14-7 (Jerry Claiborne)
Miami (Fla.)	Bluebonnet 12-23-67	Colorado 21-31 (Eddie Crowder)
JIM TATUM, 3-2-1 (North Caro. '35) Born 7-22-13		
Oklahoma	Gator 1-1-47	North Caro. St. 34-13 (Beattie Feathers)
Maryland	Gator 1-1-48	Georgia 20-20 (Wally Butts)
Maryland	Gator 1-2-50	Missouri 20-7 (Don Faurot)
Maryland	Sugar 1-1-52	Tennessee 28-13 (Bob Neyland)
Maryland	Orange 1-1-54	Oklahoma 0-7 (Bud Wilkinson)
Maryland	Orange 1-2-56	Oklahoma 6-20 (Bud Wilkinson)
CHUCK TAYLOR, 0-1-0 (Stanford '43) Born 1-24-20		
Stanford	Rose 1-1-52	Illinois 7-40 (Ray Eliot)
GRANT TEAFF, 4-4-0 (McMurry '56) Born 11-12-33		
Baylor	Cotton 1-1-75	Penn St. 20-41 (Joe Paterno)
Baylor	Peach 12-31-79	Clemson 24-18 (Danny Ford)
Baylor	Cotton 1-1-81	Alabama 2-30 (Paul "Bear" Bryant)
Baylor	Bluebonnet 12-31-83	Oklahoma St. 14-24 (Jimmy Johnson)
Baylor	Liberty 12-27-85	Louisiana St. 21-7 (Bill Arnsparger)
Baylor	Bluebonnet 12-31-86	Colorado 21-9 (Bill McCartney)
Baylor	Copper 12-31-91	Indiana 0-24 (Bill Mallory)
Baylor	John Hancock 12-31-92	Arizona 20-15 (Dick Tomey)
EDDIE TEAGUE, 1-0-0 (North Caro. '44) Born 12-14-21		
Citadel	Tangerine 12-30-60	Tennessee Tech 27-0 (Wilburn Tucker)
LOU TEPPER, 0-2-0 (Rutgers '67) Born 7-21-45		
Illinois	John Hancock 12-31-91	UCLA 3-6 (Terry Donahue)
Illinois	Holiday 12-30-92	Hawaii 17-27 (Bob Wagner)
ROBERT THEDER, 0-1-0 (Western Mich. '63) Born 9-22-39		
California	Garden State 12-15-79	Temple 17-28 (Wayne Hardin)
FRANK THOMAS, 4-2-0 (Notre Dame '23) Born 11-14-98		
Alabama	Rose 1-1-35	Stanford 29-13 (Claude "Tiny" Thornhill)
Alabama	Rose 1-1-38	California 0-13 (Leonard "Stub" Allison)
Alabama	Cotton 1-1-42	Texas A&M 29-21 (Homer Norton)
Alabama	Orange 1-1-43	Boston College 37-21 (Denny Myers)
Alabama	Sugar 1-1-45	Duke 26-29 (Eddie Cameron)
Alabama	Rose 1-1-46	Southern Cal 34-14 (Jeff Cravath)
FRED THOMSEN, 0-0-1 (Nebraska '25) Born 4-25-97		
Arkansas	Dixie Classic 1-1-34	Centenary (La.) 7-7 (Homer Norton)
CLAUDE "TINY" THORNHILL, 1-2-0 (Pittsburgh '17) Born 4-14-93		
Stanford	Rose 1-1-34	Columbia 0-7 (Lou Little)
Stanford	Rose 1-1-35	Alabama 13-29 (Frank Thomas)
Stanford	Rose 1-1-36	Southern Methodist 7-0 (Matty Bell)
JOE TILLER, 0-1-0 (Montana St. '64) Born 12-7-42		
Wyoming	Copper 12-29-93	Kansas St. 17-52 (Bill Snyder)
GAYNELL TINSLEY, 0-1-0 (Louisiana St. '37) Born 2-1-15		
Louisiana St.	Sugar 1-2-50	Oklahoma 0-35 (Bud Wilkinson)

Coach/School	Bowl/Date	Opponent/Score (Coach)
TED TOLLNER, 1-2-0	(Cal Poly SLO '62)	Born 5-29-40
Southern Cal............	Rose 1-1-85	Ohio St. 20-17 (Earle Bruce)
Southern Cal............	Aloha 12-28-85	Alabama 3-24 (Ray Perkins)
Southern Cal............	Fla. Citrus 1-1-87	Auburn 7-16 (Pat Dye)
DICK TOMEY, 2-2-0	(DePauw '61)	Born 6-20-38
Arizona...................	Copper 12-30-89	North Caro. St. 17-10 (Dick Sheridan)
Arizona...................	Aloha 12-28-90	Syracuse 0-28 (Dick MacPherson)
Arizona...................	John Hancock 12-31-92	Baylor 15-20 (Grant Teaff)
Arizona...................	Fiesta 1-1-94	Miami (Fla.) 29-0 (Dennis Erickson)
JIM TRIMBLE, 0-1-0	(Indiana '42)	Born 5-29-18
Wichita St.	Camellia 12-30-48	Hardin-Simmons 12-49 (Warren Woodson)
FRANK TRITICO, 0-0-1	(Southwestern La. '34)	Born 3-25-09
Randolph Field.........	Cotton 1-1-44	Texas 7-7 (Dana Bible)
WILBURN TUCKER, 0-1-0	(Tennessee Tech '43)	Born 8-11-20
Tennessee Tech.........	Tangerine 12-30-60	Citadel 0-27 (Eddie Teague)
BOB TYLER, 1-0-0	(Mississippi '58)	Born 7-4-32
Mississippi St.	Sun 12-28-74	North Caro. 26-24 (Bill Dooley)
THAD "PIE" VANN, 0-2-0	(Mississippi '28)	Born 9-22-07
Southern Miss.	Sun 1-1-53	Pacific (Cal.) 7-26 (Ernie Jorge)
Southern Miss.	Sun 1-1-54	UTEP 14-37 (Mike Brumbelow)
JOHN VAUGHT, 10-8-0	(Texas Christian '33)	Born 5-6-08
Mississippi	Delta 1-1-48	Texas Christian 13-9 (Leo "Dutch" Meyer)
Mississippi	Sugar 1-1-53	Georgia Tech 7-24 (Bobby Dodd)
Mississippi	Sugar 1-1-55	Navy 0-21 (Eddie Erdelatz)
Mississippi	Cotton 1-2-56	Texas Christian 14-13 (Abe Martin)
Mississippi	Sugar 1-1-58	Texas 39-7 (Darrell Royal)
Mississippi	Gator 12-27-58	Florida 7-3 (Bob Woodruff)
Mississippi	Sugar 1-1-60	Louisiana St. 21-0 (Paul Dietzel)
Mississippi	Sugar 1-2-61	Rice 14-6 (Jess Neely)
Mississippi	Cotton 1-1-62	Texas 7-12 (Darrell Royal)
Mississippi	Sugar 1-1-63	Arkansas 17-13 (Frank Broyles)
Mississippi	Sugar 1-1-64	Alabama 7-12 (Paul "Bear" Bryant)
Mississippi	Bluebonnet 12-19-64	Tulsa 7-14 (Glenn Dobbs)
Mississippi	Liberty 12-18-65	Auburn 13-7 (Ralph "Shug" Jordan)
Mississippi	Bluebonnet 12-17-66	Texas 0-19 (Darrell Royal)
Mississippi	Sun 12-30-67	UTEP 7-14 (Bobby Dobbs)
Mississippi	Liberty 12-14-68	Virginia Tech 34-17 (Jerry Claiborne)
Mississippi	Sugar 1-1-70	Arkansas 27-22 (Frank Broyles)
Mississippi	Gator 1-2-71	Auburn 28-35 (Ralph "Shug" Jordan)
DICK VERMEIL, 1-0-0	(San Jose St. '58)	Born 10-30-36
UCLA	Rose 1-1-76	Ohio St. 23-10 (Woody Hayes)
BOB VOIGTS, 1-0-0	(Northwestern '39)	Born 3-29-16
Northwestern	Rose 1-1-49	California 20-14 (Lynn "Pappy" Waldorf)
JIM WACKER, 0-1-0	(Valparaiso '60)	Born 4-28-37
Texas Christian.........	Bluebonnet 12-31-84	West Va. 14-31 (Don Nehlen)
WALLACE WADE, 2-2-1	(Brown '17)	Born 6-15-92
Alabama	Rose 1-1-26	Washington 20-19 (Enoch Bagshaw)
Alabama	Rose 1-1-27	Stanford 7-7 (Glenn "Pop" Warner)
Alabama	Rose 1-1-31	Washington St. 24-0 (Orin "Babe" Hollingbery)
Duke	Rose 1-2-39	Southern Cal 3-7 (Howard Jones)
Duke	Rose 1-1-42	Oregon St. 16-20 (Lon Stiner)
BOB WAGNER, 1-1-0	(Wittenberg '69)	Born 5-16-47
Hawaii	Aloha 12-25-89	Michigan St. 13-33 (George Perles)
Hawaii	Holiday 12-30-92	Illinois 27-17 (Lou Tepper)
JIM WALDEN, 0-1-0	(Wyoming '60)	Born 4-10-38
Washington St.	Holiday 12-18-81	Brigham Young 36-38 (LaVell Edwards)
LYNN "PAPPY" WALDORF, 0-3-0	(Syracuse '25)	Born 10-3-02
California	Rose 1-1-49	Northwestern 14-20 (Bob Voigts)
California	Rose 1-2-50	Ohio St. 14-17 (Wes Fesler)
California	Rose 1-1-51	Michigan 6-14 (Bennie Oosterbaan)
D. C. "PEAHEAD" WALKER, 1-1-0	(Samford '22)	Born 2-17-00
Wake Forest	Gator 1-1-46	South Caro. 26-14 (Johnnie McMillan)
Wake Forest	Dixie 1-1-49	Baylor 7-20 (Bob Woodruff)
ED WALKER, 0-1-0	(Stanford '27)	Born 3-25-01
Mississippi	Orange 1-1-36	Catholic 19-20 (Arthur "Dutch" Bergman)
BILL WALSH, 3-0-0	(San Jose St. '54)	Born 11-30-31
Stanford	Sun 12-31-77	Louisiana St. 24-14 (Charlie McClendon)
Stanford	Bluebonnet 12-31-78	Georgia 25-22 (Vince Dooley)
Stanford	Blockbuster 1-1-93	Penn St. 24-3 (Joe Paterno)
DALLAS WARD, 1-0-0	(Oregon St. '27)	Born 8-11-06
Colorado	Orange 1-1-57	Clemson 27-21 (Frank Howard)
MURRAY WARMATH, 1-1-0	(Tennessee '35)	Born 12-26-13
Minnesota	Rose 1-2-61	Washington 7-17 (Jim Owens)
Minnesota	Rose 1-1-62	UCLA 21-3 (Bill Barnes)

Coach/School	Bowl/Date	Opponent/Score (Coach)
GLENN "POP" WARNER, 1-2-1	(Cornell '95)	Born 4-5-71
Stanford	Rose 1-1-25	Notre Dame 10-27 (Knute Rockne)
Stanford	Rose 1-1-27	Alabama 7-7 (Wallace Wade)
Stanford	Rose 1-2-28	Pittsburgh 7-6 (Jock Sutherland)
Temple	Sugar 1-1-35	Tulane 14-20 (Ted Cox)
CHARLIE WEATHERBIE, 1-0-0	(Oklahoma St. '77)	Born 1-17-55
Utah St.	Las Vegas 12-17-93	Ball St. 42-33 (Paul Schudel)
DeWITT WEAVER, 2-1-0	(Tennessee '37)	Born 5-11-12
Texas Tech..............	Sun 1-1-52	Pacific (Cal.) 25-14 (Ernie Jorge)
Texas Tech..............	Gator 1-1-54	Auburn 35-13 (Ralph "Shug" Jordan)
Texas Tech..............	Sun 1-2-56	Wyoming 14-21 (Phil Dickens)
BILL WEEKS, 1-0-0	(Iowa St. '51)	Born 10-20-29
New Mexico.............	Aviation 12-9-61	Western Mich. 28-12 (Merle Schlosser)
RALPH "PEST" WELCH, 0-1-0	(Purdue '30)	Born 8-11-07
Washington	Rose 1-1-44	Southern Cal 0-29 (Jeff Cravath)
GEORGE WELSH, 3-6-0	(Navy '56)	Born 8-26-33
Navy.......................	Holiday 12-22-78	Brigham Young 23-16 (LaVell Edwards)
Navy.......................	Garden State 12-14-80	Houston 0-35 (Bill Yeoman)
Navy.......................	Liberty 12-30-81	Ohio St. 28-31 (Earle Bruce)
Virginia	Peach 12-31-84	Purdue 27-24 (Leon Burtnett)
Virginia	All-American 12-22-87	Brigham Young 22-16 (LaVell Edwards)
Virginia	Fla. Citrus 1-1-90	Illinois 21-31 (John Mackovic)
Virginia	Sugar 1-1-91	Tennessee 22-23 (Johnny Majors)
Virginia	Gator 12-29-91	Oklahoma 44-48 (Gary Gibbs)
Virginia	Carquest 1-1-94	Boston College 13-31 (Tom Coughlin)
TOMMY WEST, 1-0-0	(Tennessee '75)	Born 7-31-54
Clemson	Peach 12-31-93	Kentucky 14-13 (Bill Curry)
MIKE WHITE, 0-3-0	(California '58)	Born 1-3-36
Illinois....................	Liberty 12-29-82	Alabama 15-21 (Paul "Bear" Bryant)
Illinois....................	Rose 1-2-84	UCLA 9-45 (Terry Donahue)
Illinois....................	Peach 12-31-85	Army 29-31 (Jim Young)
JOHN WILCE, 0-1-0	(Wisconsin '10)	Born 5-12-88
Ohio St.	Rose 1-1-21	California 0-28 (Andy Smith)
BUD WILKINSON, 6-2-0	(Minnesota '37)	Born 4-12-16
Oklahoma	Sugar 1-1-49	North Caro. 14-6 (Carl Snavely)
Oklahoma	Sugar 1-2-50	Louisiana St. 35-0 (Gaynell Tinsley)
Oklahoma	Sugar 1-1-51	Kentucky 7-13 (Paul "Bear" Bryant)
Oklahoma	Orange 1-1-54	Maryland 7-0 (Jim Tatum)
Oklahoma	Orange 1-2-56	Maryland 20-6 (Jim Tatum)
Oklahoma	Orange 1-1-58	Duke 48-21 (Bill Murray)
Oklahoma	Orange 1-1-59	Syracuse 21-6 (Ben Schwartzwalder)
Oklahoma	Orange 1-1-63	Alabama 0-17 (Paul "Bear" Bryant)
IVY WILLIAMSON, 0-1-0	(Michigan '33)	Born 2-4-11
Wisconsin................	Rose 1-1-53	Southern Cal 0-7 (Jess Hill)
TOM WILSON, 2-0-0	(Texas Tech '66)	Born 2-24-44
Texas A&M..............	All-American 12-20-78	Iowa St. 28-12 (Earle Bruce)
Texas A&M..............	Independence 12-12-81	Oklahoma St. 33-16 (Jimmy Johnson)
SAM WINNINGHAM, 0-1-0	(Colorado '50)	Born 10-11-26
Cal St. Northridge....	Pasadena 12-2-67	West Tex. A&M 13-35 (Joe Kerbel)
BOB WOODRUFF, 2-1-0	(Tennessee '39)	Born 3-14-16
Baylor	Dixie 1-1-49	Wake Forest 20-7 (D. C. "Peahead" Walker)
Florida....................	Gator 1-1-53	Tulsa 14-13 (J. O. "Buddy" Brothers)
Florida....................	Gator 12-27-58	Mississippi 3-7 (John Vaught)
WARREN WOODSON, 6-1-0	(Baylor '24)	Born 2-24-03
Hardin-Simmons	Sun 1-1-43	Second Air Force 7-13 (Red Reese)
Hardin-Simmons	Alamo 1-4-47	Denver 20-6 (Clyde "Cac" Hubbard)
Hardin-Simmons	Harbor 1-1-48	San Diego St. 53-0 (Bill Schutte)
Hardin-Simmons	Shrine 12-18-48	Ouachita Baptist 40-12 (Wesley Bradshaw)
Hardin-Simmons	Camellia 12-30-48	Wichita St. 49-12 (Jim Trimble)
New Mexico St.	Sun 12-31-59	North Texas 28-8 (Odus Mitchell)
New Mexico St.	Sun 12-31-60	Utah St. 20-13 (John Ralston)
BOWDEN WYATT, 2-2-0	(Tennessee '39)	Born 11-3-17
Wyoming	Gator 1-1-51	Wash. & Lee 20-7 (George Barclay)
Arkansas	Cotton 1-1-55	Georgia Tech 6-14 (Bobby Dodd)
Tennessee	Sugar 1-1-57	Baylor 7-13 (Sam Boyd)
Tennessee	Gator 12-26-57	Texas A&M 3-0 (Paul "Bear" Bryant)
BILL YEOMAN, 6-4-1	(Army '50)	Born 12-26-27
Houston	Tangerine 12-22-62	Miami (Ohio) 49-21 (John Pont)
Houston	Bluebonnet 12-31-69	Auburn 36-7 (Ralph "Shug" Jordan)
Houston	Bluebonnet 12-31-71	Colorado 17-29 (Eddie Crowder)
Houston	Bluebonnet 12-29-73	Tulane 47-7 (Bennie Ellender)
Houston	Bluebonnet 12-23-74	North Caro. St. 31-31 (Lou Holtz)
Houston	Cotton 1-1-77	Maryland 30-21 (Jerry Claiborne)
Houston	Cotton 1-1-79	Notre Dame 34-35 (Dan Devine)
Houston	Cotton 1-1-80	Nebraska 17-14 (Tom Osborne)
Houston	Garden State 12-14-80	Navy 35-0 (George Welsh)
Houston	Sun 12-26-81	Oklahoma 14-40 (Barry Switzer)
Houston	Cotton 1-1-85	Boston College 28-45 (Jack Bicknell)

BOWL/ALL-STAR RESULTS

Coach/School	Bowl/Date	Opponent/Score (Coach)
FIELDING "HURRY UP" YOST, 1-0-0	(Lafayette '97)	Born 4-30-71
Michigan	Rose 1-1-02	Stanford 49-0 (Charlie Fickert)
JIM YOUNG, 5-1-0	(Bowling Green '57)	Born 4-21-35
Purdue	Peach 12-25-78	Georgia Tech 41-21 (Pepper Rodgers)
Purdue	Bluebonnet 12-31-79	Tennessee 27-22 (Johnny Majors)
Purdue	Liberty 12-27-80	Missouri 28-25 (Warren Powers)
Army	Cherry 12-22-84	Michigan St. 10-6 (George Perles)
Army	Peach 12-31-85	Illinois 31-29 (Mike White)
Army	Sun 12-24-88	Alabama 28-29 (Bill Curry)

Coaches Who Have Taken More Than One Team to a Bowl Game

FOUR TEAMS (3)
Earle Bruce: Tampa, Iowa St., Ohio St. & Colorado St.
* Lou Holtz: William & Mary, North Caro. St., Arkansas & Notre Dame
* Bill Mallory: Miami (Ohio), Colorado, Northern Ill. & Indiana

THREE TEAMS (10)
Paul "Bear" Bryant: Kentucky, Texas A&M & Alabama
Jim Carlen: West Va., Texas Tech & South Caro.
Jerry Claiborne: Virginia Tech, Maryland & Kentucky
* Bill Curry: Georgia Tech, Alabama & Kentucky
Bill Dooley: North Caro., Virginia Tech & Wake Forest

* Ken Hatfield: Air Force, Arkansas & Clemson
* Johnny Majors: Iowa St., Pittsburgh & Tennessee
* Jackie Sherrill: Pittsburgh, Texas A&M & Mississippi St.
* Larry Smith: Tulane, Arizona & Southern Cal
Bowden Wyatt: Wyoming, Arkansas & Tennessee

TWO TEAMS (54)
Fred Akers: Wyoming & Texas
John Barnhill: Tennessee & Arkansas
Emory Bellard: Texas A&M & Mississippi St.
Hugo Bezdek: Oregon & Penn St.
Dana X. Bible: Texas A&M & Texas

* Bobby Bowden: West Va. & Florida St.
* Mack Brown: Tulane & North Caro.
Len Casanova: Santa Clara & Oregon
Bobby Collins: Southern Miss. & Southern Methodist
* John Cooper: Arizona St. & Ohio St.

Lee Corso: Louisville & Indiana
Dick Crum: Miami (Ohio) & North Caro.
Bob Devaney: Wyoming & Nebraska
Dan Devine: Missouri & Notre Dame
Doug Dickey: Tennessee & Florida

Paul Dietzel: Louisiana St. & South Caro.
Pat Dye: East Caro. & Auburn
Pete Elliott: California & Illinois
Jack Elway: San Jose St. & Stanford
* Dennis Erickson: Washington St. & Miami (Fla.)

Bob Folwell: Pennsylvania & Navy
* Hayden Fry: Southern Methodist & Iowa
Vince Gibson: Louisville & Tulane
Sid Gillman: Miami (Ohio) & Cincinnati
Wayne Hardin: Navy & Temple

Woody Hayes: Miami (Ohio) & Ohio St.
Bob Higgins: West Va. Wesleyan & Penn St.
Don James: Kent & Washington
Jimmy Johnson: Oklahoma St. & Miami (Fla.)
Frank Kimbrough: Hardin-Simmons & West Tex. A&M

Jimmy Kitts: Rice & Virginia Tech
* John Mackovic: Wake Forest & Illinois
Jess Neely: Clemson & Rice
Homer Norton: Centenary & Texas A&M
Charley Pell: Clemson & Florida

Jimmy Phelan: Washington & St. Mary's (Cal.)
John Pont: Miami (Ohio) & Indiana
Tommy Prothro: Oregon St. & UCLA
* John Ralston: Utah St. & Stanford
Pepper Rodgers: Kansas & Georgia Tech

Bobby Ross: Maryland & Georgia Tech
George Sauer: Kansas & Baylor
* Howard Schnellenberger: Miami (Fla.) & Louisville
Steve Sloan: Vanderbilt & Texas Tech
* Steve Spurrier: Duke & Florida

* Gene Stallings: Texas A&M & Alabama
Denny Stolz: Bowling Green & San Diego St.
Jim Tatum: Oklahoma & Maryland
Wallace Wade: Alabama & Duke
Glenn "Pop" Warner: Stanford & Temple

* George Welsh: Navy & Virginia

Bob Woodruff: Baylor & Florida
Warren Woodson: Hardin-Simmons & New Mexico St.
Jim Young: Purdue & Army

*Active coach.

Coaches With the Most Years Taking One College to a Bowl Game

Coach, Team Taken	Bowls	Consecutive Years
Paul "Bear" Bryant, Alabama	24	24 (1959-82)
* Joe Paterno, Penn St.	24	13 (1971-83)
* Tom Osborne, Nebraska	21	21 (1973-93)
Vince Dooley, Georgia	20	9 (1980-88)
* LaVell Edwards, Brigham Young	18	16 (1978-93)
John Vaught, Mississippi	18	14 (1957-70)
"Bo" Schembechler, Michigan	17	15 (1975-89)
Darrell Royal, Texas	16	8 (1968-75)
* Bobby Bowden, Florida St.	14	12 (1982-93)
Don James, Washington	14	9 (1979-87)
Bobby Dodd, Georgia Tech	13	6 (1951-56)
Charlie McClendon, Louisiana St.	13	4 (1970-73)
Barry Switzer, Oklahoma	13	8 (1975-82)
* Terry Donahue, UCLA	12	8 (1981-88)
Ralph Jordan, Auburn	12	7 (1968-74)
* Hayden Fry, Iowa	11	8 (1981-88)
* Johnny Majors, Tennessee	11	7 (1981-87)
"Woody" Hayes, Ohio St.	11	7 (1972-78)
Bill Yeoman, Houston	11	4 (1978-81)
Frank Broyles, Arkansas	10	4 (1959-62)
Fred Akers, Texas	9	9 (1977-85)
Bob Devaney, Nebraska	9	5 (1962-66)
Pat Dye, Auburn	9	9 (1982-90)
John McKay, Southern Cal	9	4 (1966-69, 1972-75)
Earle Bruce, Ohio St.	8	8 (1979-86)
Wally Butts, Georgia	8	4 (1945-48)
* Danny Ford, Clemson	8	5 (1985-89)
Grant Teaff, Baylor	8	2 (1979-80; 1985-86; 1991-92)
Bud Wilkinson, Oklahoma	8	3 (1948-50)

*Active coach.

Conference Bowl Records

1993-94 Bowl Records by Conference

Conference	W-L-T	Pct.
Independents	2-0-0	1.000
Big West Conference	1-0-0	1.000
Big Eight Conference	3-1-0	.750
Pacific-10 Conference	3-1-0	.750
Big Ten Conference	4-3-0	.571
Big East Conference	2-2-0	.500
Southeastern Conference	2-2-0	.500
Atlantic Coast Conference	2-3-0	.400
Mid-American Athletic Conference	0-1-0	.000
Southwest Conference	0-2-0	.000
Western Athletic Conference	0-4-0	.000

All-Time Conference Bowl Records

(Through 1993-94 Bowls, Using Present Conference Alignments)

ATLANTIC COAST CONFERENCE

Institution	Bowls	W-L-T	Pct.	Last Appearance
Clemson	19	12-7-0	.632	12-31-93 Peach
Duke	7	3-4-0	.429	1989 All-American
Florida St.	22	13-7-2	.636	1994 Orange
Georgia Tech	25	17-8-0	.680	1991 Aloha
Maryland	17	6-9-2	.412	1990 Independence
North Caro.	18	7-11-0	.389	1-2-93 Peach
North Caro. St.	16	7-8-1	.469	1994 Hall of Fame
Virginia	6	2-4-0	.333	1994 Carquest
Wake Forest	4	2-2-0	.500	1992 Independence
Current Members	**134**	**69-60-5**	**.534**	

BIG EAST CONFERENCE

Institution	Bowls	W-L-T	Pct.	Last Appearance
Boston College	9	4-5-0	.444	1994 Carquest
Miami (Fla.)	20	10-10-0	.500	1994 Fiesta
Pittsburgh	18	8-10-0	.444	1989 John Hancock
Rutgers	1	0-1-0	.000	1978 Garden State
Syracuse	15	8-6-1	.567	1993 Fiesta
Temple	2	1-1-0	.500	1979 Garden State
Virginia Tech	7	2-5-0	.286	1993 Independence
West Va.	16	8-8-0	.500	1994 Sugar
Current Members	**88**	**41-46-1**	**.472**	

BIG EIGHT CONFERENCE

Institution	Bowls	W-L-T	Pct.	Last Appearance
Colorado	17	6-11-0	.353	1993 Aloha
Iowa St.	4	0-4-0	.000	1978 Hall of Fame
Kansas	7	2-5-0	.286	1992 Aloha
Kansas St.	2	1-1-0	.500	1993 Copper
Missouri	18	8-10-0	.444	1983 Holiday
Nebraska	32	14-18-0	.438	1994 Orange
Oklahoma	31	20-10-1	.661	1993 John Hancock
Oklahoma St.	12	9-3-0	.750	1988 Holiday
Current Members	**123**	**60-62-1**	**.492**	

BIG TEN CONFERENCE

Institution	Bowls	W-L-T	Pct.	Last Appearance
Illinois	11	4-7-0	.364	1992 Holiday
Indiana	8	3-5-0	.375	1993 Independence
Iowa	13	6-6-1	.500	1993 Alamo
Michigan	25	12-13-0	.480	1994 Hall of Fame
Michigan St.	11	5-6-0	.455	1993 Liberty
Minnesota	5	2-3-0	.400	1986 Liberty
Northwestern	1	1-0-0	1.000	1948 Rose
Ohio St.	26	12-14-0	.462	1993 Holiday
Penn St.	30	18-10-2	.633	1994 Fla. Citrus
Purdue	5	4-1-0	.800	1984 Peach
Wisconsin	7	2-5-0	.286	1994 Rose
Current Members	**142**	**69-70-3**	**.496**	

BIG WEST CONFERENCE

Institution	Bowls	W-L-T	Pct.	Last Appearance
Arkansas St.	0	0-0-0	.000	Has never appeared
Louisiana Tech	3	1-1-1	.500	1990 Independence
Nevada	3	1-2-0	.333	1992 Las Vegas
Nevada-Las Vegas	1	1-0-0	1.000	1984 California
New Mexico St.	3	2-0-1	.833	1960 Sun
Northern Ill.	1	1-0-0	1.000	1983 California
Pacific (Cal.)	3	2-1-0	.667	1953 Sun
San Jose St.	7	4-3-0	.571	1990 California
Southwestern La.	0	0-0-0	.000	Has never appeared
Utah St.	4	1-3-0	.250	1993 Las Vegas
Current Members	**25**	**13-10-2**	**.560**	

MID-AMERICAN CONFERENCE

Institution	Bowls	W-L-T	Pct.	Last Appearance
Akron	0	0-0-0	.000	Has never appeared
Ball St.	2	0-2-0	.000	1993 Las Vegas
Bowling Green	5	2-3-0	.400	1992 Las Vegas
Central Mich.	1	0-1-0	.000	1990 California
Eastern Mich.	1	1-0-0	1.000	1987 California
Kent	1	0-1-0	.000	1972 Tangerine
Miami (Ohio)	7	5-2-0	.714	1986 California
Ohio	2	0-2-0	.000	1968 Tangerine
Toledo	5	4-1-0	.800	1984 California
Western Mich.	2	0-2-0	.000	1988 California
Current Members	**26**	**12-14-0**	**.462**	

PACIFIC-10 CONFERENCE

Institution	Bowls	W-L-T	Pct.	Last Appearance
Arizona	10	3-6-1	.350	1994 Fiesta
Arizona St.	15	9-5-1	.633	1987 Freedom
California	12	5-6-1	.458	1993 Alamo
Oregon	9	3-6-0	.333	1992 Independence
Oregon St.	4	2-2-0	.500	1965 Rose
Southern Cal	36	23-13-0	.639	1993 Freedom
Stanford	16	8-7-1	.531	1993 Blockbuster
UCLA	19	10-8-1	.553	1994 Rose
Washington	21	12-8-1	.595	1993 Rose
Washington St.	5	3-2-0	.600	1992 Copper
Current Members	**147**	**78-63-6**	**.551**	

SOUTHEASTERN CONFERENCE

Institution	Bowls	W-L-T	Pct.	Last Appearance
Alabama	46	26-17-3	.598	1993 Gator
Arkansas	27	9-15-3	.389	1991 Independence
Auburn	23	12-9-2	.565	1990 Peach
Florida	21	10-11-0	.476	1994 Sugar
Georgia	31	15-13-3	.532	1993 Florida Citrus
Kentucky	8	5-3-0	.625	12-31-93 Peach
Louisiana St.	28	11-16-1	.411	1989 Hall of Fame
Mississippi	25	14-11-0	.560	1992 Liberty
Mississippi St.	8	4-4-0	.500	1-2-93 Peach
South Caro.	8	0-8-0	.000	1988 Liberty
Tennessee	34	18-16-0	.529	1994 Fla. Citrus
Vanderbilt	3	1-1-1	.500	1982 Hall of Fame
Current Members	**262**	**125-124-13**	**.502**	

SOUTHWEST CONFERENCE

Institution	Bowls	W-L-T	Pct.	Last Appearance
Baylor	15	8-7-0	.533	1992 John Hancock
Houston	13	7-5-1	.577	1988 Aloha
Rice	7	4-3-0	.571	1961 Bluebonnet
Southern Methodist	11	4-6-1	.409	1984 Aloha
Texas	34	16-16-2	.500	1991 Cotton
Texas A&M	21	11-10-0	.524	1994 Cotton
Texas Christian	14	4-9-1	.321	1984 Bluebonnet
Texas Tech	19	4-14-1	.237	1993 John Hancock
Current Members	**134**	**58-70-6**	**.455**	

WESTERN ATHLETIC CONFERENCE

Institution	Bowls	W-L-T	Pct.	Last Appearance
Air Force	12	6-5-1	.542	1992 Liberty
Brigham Young	18	5-12-1	.306	1993 Holiday
Colorado St.	2	1-1-0	.500	1990 Freedom
Fresno St.	9	6-3-0	.667	1993 Aloha
Hawaii	2	1-1-0	.500	1992 Holiday
New Mexico	5	2-2-1	.500	1961 Aviation
San Diego St.	4	1-3-0	.250	1991 Freedom
Utah	4	2-2-0	.500	1993 Freedom
UTEP	9	5-4-0	.556	1988 Independence
Wyoming	10	4-6-0	.400	1993 Copper
Current Members	**75**	**33-39-3**	**.460**	

INDEPENDENTS

Institution	Bowls	W-L-T	Pct.	Last Appearance
Army	3	2-1-0	.667	1988 Sun
Cincinnati	2	1-1-0	.500	1951 Sun
East Caro.	2	2-0-0	1.000	1992 Peach
Louisville	5	3-1-1	.700	1993 Liberty
Memphis	1	1-0-0	1.000	1971 Pasadena
Navy	8	3-4-1	.438	1981 Liberty
Notre Dame	19	13-6-0	.684	1994 Cotton
Southern Miss.	6	2-4-0	.333	1990 All-American
Tulane	8	2-6-0	.250	1987 Independence
Tulsa	11	4-7-0	.364	1991 Freedom
Current Independents	**65**	**33-30-2**	**.523**	

BOWL/ALL-STAR RESULTS

Award Winners in Bowl Games

Most Valuable Players in Major Bowls

ALAMO BOWL

Year Player, Team, Position
1993 Dave Barr, California, quarterback
Jerrott Willard, California, linebacker
Larry Blue, Iowa, defensive tackle (sportsmanship award)

ALOHA BOWL

Year Player, Team, Position
1982 Offense—Tim Cowan, Washington, quarterback
Defense—Tony Caldwell, Washington, linebacker
1983 Offense—Danny Greene, Washington, wide receiver
Defense—George Reynolds, Penn St., punter
1984 Offense—Jeff Atkins, Southern Methodist, running back
Defense—Jerry Ball, Southern Methodist, nose guard
1985 Offense—Gene Jelks, Alabama, running back
Defense—Cornelius Bennett, Alabama, linebacker
1986 Offense—Alfred Jenkins, Arizona, quarterback
Defense—Chuck Cecil, Arizona, safety
1987* Troy Aikman, UCLA, quarterback
Emmitt Smith, Florida, running back
1988 David Dacus, Houston, quarterback
Victor Wood, Washington St., wide receiver
1989 Blake Ezor, Michigan St., tailback
Chris Roscoe, Hawaii, wide receiver
1990 Todd Burden, Arizona, cornerback
Marvin Graves, Syracuse, quarterback
1991 Tommy Vardell, Stanford, running back
Shawn Jones, Georgia Tech, quarterback
1992 Tom Young, Brigham Young, quarterback
Dana Stubblefield, Kansas, defensive tackle
1993 Rashaan Salaam, Colorado, tailback
Trent Dilfer, Fresno St., quarterback

*Began selecting one MVP for each team.

CARQUEST BOWL

(Named Blockbuster Bowl, 1990-92)

Brian Piccolo Most Valuable Player Award
Year Player, Team, Position
1990 Amp Lee, Florida St., running back

Kansas State wide receiver Andre Coleman scored on a 68-yard punt return and 61-yard pass to earn the most valuable offensive player award in the Wildcats' 52-17 victory over Wyoming in the Copper Bowl.

1991 David Palmer, Alabama, wide receiver
1992 Darrien Gordon, Stanford, cornerback
1993 Glenn Foley, Boston College, quarterback

COPPER BOWL

Year Player, Team, Position
1989 Shane Montgomery, North Caro. St., quarterback
Scott Geyer, Arizona, defensive back
1990 Mike Pawlawski, California, quarterback
Robert Midgett, Wyoming, linebacker
1991 Vaughn Dunbar, Indiana, tailback
Mark Hagen, Indiana, linebacker
1992 Drew Bledsoe, Washington St., quarterback (overall)
Phillip Bobo, Washington St., wide receiver (offense)
Kareem Leary, Utah, defensive back (defense)
1993 Andre Coleman, Kansas St., wide receiver (offense)
Kenny McEntyre, Kansas St., cornerback (defense)

COTTON BOWL

Year Player, Team, Position
1937 Ki Aldrich, Texas Christian, center
Sammy Baugh, Texas Christian, quarterback
L. D. Meyer, Texas Christian, end
1938 Ernie Lain, Rice, back
Byron "Whizzer" White, Colorado, quarterback
1939 Jerry Dowd, St. Mary's (Tex.), center
Elmer Tarbox, Texas Tech, back
1940 Banks McFadden, Clemson, back
1941 Charles Henke, Texas A&M, guard
John Kimbrough, Texas A&M, fullback
Chip Routt, Texas A&M, tackle
Lou De Filippo, Fordham, center
Joe Ungerer, Fordham, tackle
1942 Martin Ruby, Texas A&M, tackle
Jimmy Nelson, Alabama, halfback
Holt Rast, Alabama, end
Don Whitmire, Alabama, tackle
1943 Jack Freeman, Texas, guard
Roy McKay, Texas, fullback
Stanley Mauldin, Texas, tackle
Harvey Hardy, Georgia Tech, guard
Jack Marshall, Georgia Tech, end
1944 Joe Parker, Texas, end
Martin Ruby, Randolph Field, tackle
Glenn Dobbs, Randolph Field, quarterback
1945 Neil Armstrong, Oklahoma St., end
Bob Fenimore, Oklahoma St., back
Ralph Foster, Oklahoma St., tackle
1946 Hub Bechtol, Texas, end
Bobby Layne, Texas, back
Jim Kekeris, Missouri, tackle
1947 Alton Baldwin, Arkansas, end
Y. A. Tittle, Louisiana St., quarterback
1948 Doak Walker, Southern Methodist, back
Steve Suhey, Penn St., guard
1949 Kyle Rote, Southern Methodist, back
Doak Walker, Southern Methodist, back
Brad Ecklund, Oregon, center
Norm Van Brocklin, Oregon, quarterback
1950 Billy Burkhalter, Rice, halfback
Joe Watson, Rice, center
James "Froggie" Williams, Rice, end
1951 Bud McFadin, Texas, guard
Andy Kozar, Tennessee, fullback
Hank Lauricella, Tennessee, halfback
Horace "Bud" Sherrod, Tennessee, defensive end
1952 Keith Flowers, Texas Christian, fullback
Emery Clark, Kentucky, halfback
Ray Correll, Kentucky, guard
Vito "Babe" Parilli, Kentucky, quarterback
1953 Richard Ochoa, Texas, fullback
Harley Sewell, Texas, guard
Bob Griesbach, Tennessee, linebacker
1954 Richard Chapman, Rice, tackle
Dan Hart, Rice, end
Dicky Maegle, Rice, halfback
1955 Bud Brooks, Arkansas, guard
George Humphreys, Georgia Tech, fullback
1956 Buddy Alliston, Mississippi, guard
Eagle Day, Mississippi, quarterback
1957 Norman Hamilton, Texas Christian, tackle
Jim Brown, Syracuse, halfback
1958 Tom Forrestal, Navy, quarterback
Tony Stremic, Navy, guard

1959 Jack Spikes, Texas Christian, fullback
Dave Phillips, Air Force, tackle
1960 Maurice Doke, Texas, guard
Ernie Davis, Syracuse, halfback
1961 Lance Alworth, Arkansas, halfback
Dwight Bumgarner, Duke, tackle
1962 Mike Cotten, Texas, quarterback
Bob Moser, Texas, end
1963 Johnny Treadwell, Texas, guard
Lynn Amedee, Louisiana St., quarterback
1964 Scott Appleton, Texas, tackle
Duke Carlisle, Texas, quarterback
1965 Ronnie Caveness, Arkansas, linebacker
Fred Marshall, Arkansas, quarterback
1966 Joe Labruzzo, Louisiana St., tailback
David McCormick, Louisiana St., tackle
1966 Kent Lawrence, Georgia, tailback
George Patton, Georgia, tackle
1968 Grady Allen, Texas A&M, defensive end
Edd Hargett, Texas A&M, quarterback
Bill Hobbs, Texas A&M, linebacker
1969 Tom Campbell, Texas, linebacker
Charles "Cotton" Speyrer, Texas, wide receiver
James Street, Texas, quarterback
1970 Steve Worster, Texas, fullback
Bob Olson, Notre Dame, linebacker
1971 Eddie Phillips, Texas, quarterback
Clarence Ellis, Notre Dame, cornerback
1972 Bruce Bannon, Penn St., defensive end
Lydell Mitchell, Penn St., running back
1973 Randy Braband, Texas, linebacker
Alan Lowry, Texas, quarterback
1974 Wade Johnston, Texas, linebacker
Tony Davis, Nebraska, tailback
1975 Ken Quesenberry, Baylor, safety
Tom Shuman, Penn St., quarterback
1976 Ike Forte, Arkansas, running back
Hal McAfee, Arkansas, linebacker
1977 Alois Blackwell, Houston, running back
Mark Mohr, Houston, cornerback
1978 Vagas Ferguson, Notre Dame, running back
Bob Golic, Notre Dame, linebacker
1979 David Hodge, Houston, linebacker
Joe Montana, Notre Dame, quarterback
1980 Terry Elston, Houston, quarterback
David Hodge, Houston, linebacker
1981 Warren Lyles, Alabama, nose guard
Major Ogilvie, Alabama, running back
1982 Robert Brewer, Texas, quarterback
Robbie Jones, Alabama, linebacker
1983 Wes Hopkins, Southern Methodist, strong safety
Lance McIlhenny, Southern Methodist, quarterback
1984 Jeff Leiding, Texas, linebacker
John Lastinger, Georgia, quarterback
1985 Bill Romanowski, Boston College, linebacker
Steve Strachan, Boston College, fullback
1986 Domingo Bryant, Texas A&M, strong safety
Bo Jackson, Auburn, tailback
1987 Chris Spielman, Ohio St., linebacker
Roger Vick, Texas A&M, fullback
1988 Adam Bob, Texas A&M, linebacker
Bucky Richardson, Texas A&M, quarterback
1989 LaSalle Harper, Arkansas, linebacker
Troy Aikman, UCLA, quarterback
1990 Carl Pickens, Tennessee, free safety
Chuck Webb, Tennessee, tailback
1991 Craig Erickson, Miami (Fla.), quarterback
Russell Maryland, Miami (Fla.), defensive lineman
1992 Sean Jackson, Florida St., running back
Chris Crooms, Texas A&M, safety
1993 Rick Mirer, Notre Dame, quarterback
Devon McDonald, Notre Dame, defensive end
1994 Lee Becton, Notre Dame, running back
Antonio Shorter, Texas A&M, linebacker

FIESTA BOWL

Year Player, Team, Position
1971 Gary Huff, Florida St., quarterback
Junior Ah You, Arizona St., defensive end
1972 Woody Green, Arizona St., halfback
Mike Fink, Missouri, defensive back
1973 Greg Hudson, Arizona St., split end
Mike Haynes, Arizona St., cornerback
1974 Kenny Walker, Oklahoma St., running back
Phillip Dokes, Oklahoma St., defensive tackle
1975 John Jefferson, Arizona St., split end
Larry Gordon, Arizona St., linebacker
1976 Thomas Lott, Oklahoma, quarterback
Terry Peters, Oklahoma, cornerback

1977 Dennis Sproul, Arizona St., quarterback (sportsmanship award)
Matt Millen, Penn St., linebacker
1978 James Owens, UCLA, running back
Jimmy Walker, Arkansas, defensive tackle
Kenny Easley, UCLA, safety (sportsmanship award)
1979 Mark Schubert, Pittsburgh, kicker
Dave Liggins, Arizona, safety
Dan Fidler, Pittsburgh, offensive guard (sportsmanship award)
1980 Curt Warner, Penn St., running back
Frank Case, Penn St., defensive end (sportsmanship award)
1982 Curt Warner, Penn St., running back
Leo Wisniewski, Penn St., nose tackle
George Achica, Southern Cal, nose guard (sportsmanship award)
1983 Marcus Dupree, Oklahoma, running back
Jim Jeffcoat, Arizona St., defensive lineman
Paul Ferrer, Oklahoma, center (sportsmanship award)
1984 John Congemi, Pittsburgh, quarterback
Rowland Tatum, Ohio St., linebacker (sportsmanship award)
1985 Gaston Green, UCLA, tailback
James Washington, UCLA, defensive back
Bruce Fleming, Miami (Fla.), linebacker (sportsmanship award)
1986 Jamie Morris, Michigan, running back
Mark Messner, Michigan, defensive tackle
Mike Mallory, Michigan, linebacker (sportsmanship award)
1987 D. J. Dozier, Penn St., running back
Shane Conlan, Penn St., linebacker
Paul O'Connor, Miami (Fla.), offensive guard (sportsmanship award)
1988 Danny McManus, Florida St., quarterback
Neil Smith, Nebraska, defensive lineman
Steve Forch, Nebraska, linebacker (sportsmanship award)
1989 Tony Rice, Notre Dame, quarterback
Frank Stams, Notre Dame, defensive end
Chris Parker, West Va., defensive lineman (sportsmanship award)
1990 Peter Tom Willis, Florida St., quarterback
Odell Haggins, Florida St., nose guard
Jake Young, Nebraska, center (sportsmanship award)
1991 Browning Nagle, Louisville, quarterback
Ray Buchanan, Louisville, free safety
1992 O. J. McDuffie, Penn St., wide receiver
Reggie Givens, Penn St., outside linebacker
1993 Marvin Graves, Syracuse, quarterback
Kevin Mitchell, Syracuse, nose guard
1994 Chuck Levy, Arizona, running back
Tedy Bruschi, Arizona, defensive end
Paul White, Miami (Fla.), cornerback (sportsmanship award)

FLORIDA CITRUS BOWL
(Named Tangerine Bowl, 1947-82)
Players of the Game (Pre-1977)

Year	Player, Team, Position
1949	Dale McDaniels, Murray St.
	Ted Scown, Sul Ross St.
1950	Don Henigan, St. Vincent
	Chick Davis, Emory & Henry
1951	Pete Anania, Morris Harvey
	Charles Hubbard, Morris Harvey
1952	Bill Johnson, Stetson
	Dave Laude, Stetson
1953	Marvin Brown, East Tex. St.
1954	Billy Ray Norris, East Tex. St.
	Bobby Spann, Arkansas St.
1955	Bill Englehardt, Nebraska-Omaha
1956	Pat Tarquinio, Juniata
1957	Ron Mills, West Tex. A&M
1958	Garry Berry, East Tex. St.
	Neal Hinson, East Tex. St.
1958	Sam McCord, East Tex. St.
1960	Bucky Pitts, Middle Tenn. St.
	Bob Waters, Presbyterian
1960	Jerry Nettles, Citadel
1961	Win Herbert, Lamar
1962	Joe Lopasky, Houston
	Billy Roland, Houston
1963	Sharon Miller, Western Ky.
1964	Bill Cline, East Caro.
	Jerry Whelchel, Massachusetts
1965	Dave Alexander, East Caro.

1966 Willie Lanier, Morgan St.
1967 Errol Hook, Tenn.-Martin
Gordon Lambert, Tenn.-Martin
1968 Buster O'Brien, Richmond, back
Walker Gillette, Richmond, lineman
1969 Chuck Ealy, Toledo, back
Dan Crockett, Toledo, lineman
1970 Chuck Ealy, Toledo, back
Vince Hubler, William & Mary, lineman
1971 Chuck Ealy, Toledo, back
Mel Long, Toledo, lineman
1972 Freddie Solomon, Tampa, back
Jack Lambert, Kent, lineman
1973 Chuck Varner, Miami (Ohio), back
Brad Cousino, Miami (Ohio), lineman
1974 Sherman Smith, Miami (Ohio), back
Brad Cousino, Miami (Ohio), lineman (tie)
John Roudebush, Miami (Ohio), lineman (tie)
1975 Rob Carpenter, Miami (Ohio), back
Jeff Kelly, Miami (Ohio), lineman
1976 Terry Miller, Oklahoma St., back
Phillip Dokes, Oklahoma St., lineman

Most Valuable Player (1977-Present)

Year	Player, Team, Position
1977	Jimmy Jordan, Florida St., quarterback
1978	Ted Brown, North Caro. St., running back
1979	David Woodley, Louisiana St., quarterback
1980	Cris Collinsworth, Florida, wide receiver
1981	Jeff Gaylord, Missouri, linebacker
1982	Randy Campbell, Auburn, quarterback
1983	Johnnie Jones, Tennessee, running back
1984	James Jackson, Georgia, quarterback
1985	Larry Kolic, Ohio St., middle guard
1987	Aundray Bruce, Auburn, linebacker
1988	Rodney Williams, Clemson, quarterback
1989	Terry Allen, Clemson, tailback
1990	Jeff George, Illinois, quarterback
1991	Shawn Jones, Georgia Tech, quarterback
1992	Mike Pawlawski, California, quarterback
1993	Garrison Hearst, Georgia, running back
1994	Bobby Engram, Penn St., wide receiver (overall)
	Charlie Garner, Tennessee, tailback (offense)
	Lee Rubin, Penn St., free safety (defense)
	Raymond Austin, Tennessee, strong safety (defense)

FREEDOM BOWL

Year	Player, Team, Position
1984	Chuck Long, Iowa, quarterback
	William Harris, Texas, tight end
1985	Chris Chandler, Washington, quarterback
	Barry Helton, Colorado, punter
1986	Gaston Green, UCLA, tailback
	Shane Shumway, Brigham Young, defensive back
1987	Daniel Ford, Arizona St., quarterback
	Chad Hennings, Air Force, defensive tackle
1988	Ty Detmer, Brigham Young, quarterback
	Eric Bieniemy, Colorado, halfback
1989	Cary Conklin, Washington, quarterback
	Huey Richardson, Florida, linebacker
1990	Todd Yert, Colorado St., running back
	Bill Musgrave, Oregon, quarterback
1991	Marshall Faulk, San Diego St., running back
	Ron Jackson, Tulsa, running back
1992	Lorenzo Neal, Fresno St., fullback
	Estrus Crayton, Southern Cal, tailback
1993	Johnnie Morton, Southern Cal, wide receiver
	Henry Lusk, Utah, wide receiver

GATOR BOWL

Year	Player, Team
1946	Nick Sacrinty, Wake Forest
1947	Joe Golding, Oklahoma
1948	Lu Gambino, Maryland
1949	Bobby Gage, Clemson
1950	Bob Ward, Maryland
1951	Eddie Talboom, Wyoming
1952	Jim Dooley, Miami (Fla.)
1953	Marv Matuszak, Tulsa
	John Hall, Florida
1954	Vince Dooley, Auburn
	Bobby Cavazos, Texas Tech
1954	Billy Hooper, Baylor
	Joe Childress, Auburn
1955	Joe Childress, Auburn
	Don Orr, Vanderbilt
1956	Corny Salvaterra, Pittsburgh
	Wade Mitchell, Georgia Tech

1957 John David Crow, Texas A&M
Bobby Gordon, Tennessee
1958 Dave Hudson, Florida
Bobby Franklin, Mississippi
1960 Maxie Baughan, Georgia Tech
Jim Mooty, Arkansas
1960 Bobby Ply, Baylor
Larry Libertore, Florida
1961 Joe Auer, Georgia Tech
Galen Hall, Penn St.
1962 Dave Robinson, Penn St.
Tom Shannon, Florida
1963 David Sicks, Air Force
Ken Willard, North Caro.
1965 Carl McAdams, Oklahoma
Fred Biletnikoff, Florida St.
Steve Tensi, Florida
1965 Donny Anderson, Texas Tech
Lenny Snow, Georgia Tech
1966 Floyd Little, Syracuse
Dewey Warren, Tennessee
1967 Tom Sherman, Penn St.
Kim Hammond, Florida St.
1968 Mike Hall, Alabama
Terry McMillan, Missouri
1969 Curt Watson, Tennessee
Mike Kelley, Florida
1971 Archie Manning, Mississippi
Pat Sullivan, Auburn
1971 James Webster, North Caro.
Jimmy Poulos, Georgia
1972 Mark Cooney, Colorado
Wade Whatley, Auburn
1973 Haskell Stanback, Tennessee
Joe Barnes, Texas Tech
1974 Earl Campbell, Texas
Phil Gargis, Auburn
1975 Sammy Green, Florida
Steve Atkins, Maryland
1976 Jim Cefalo, Penn St.
Al Hunter, Notre Dame
1977 Jerry Butler, Clemson
Matt Cavanaugh, Pittsburgh
1978 Art Schlichter, Ohio St.
Steve Fuller, Clemson
1979 John Wangler, Michigan
Anthony Carter, Michigan
Matt Kupec, North Caro.
Amos Lawrence, North Caro.
1980 George Rogers, South Caro.
Rick Trocano, Pittsburgh
1981 Gary Anderson, Arkansas
Kelvin Bryant, North Caro.
Ethan Horton, North Caro.
1982 Paul Woodside, West Va.
Greg Allen, Florida St.
1983 Owen Gill, Iowa
Tony Lilly, Florida
1984 Mike Hold, South Caro.
Thurman Thomas, Oklahoma St.
1985 Thurman Thomas, Oklahoma St.
Chip Ferguson, Florida St.
1986 Brad Muster, Stanford
Rodney Williams, Clemson
1987 Harold Green, South Caro.
Wendell Davis, Louisiana St.
1989 Andre Rison, Michigan St.
Wayne Johnson, Georgia
1989 Mike Fox, West Va.
Levon Kirkland, Clemson
1991 Tyrone Ashley, Mississippi
Michigan offensive line: Tom Dohring, Matt Elliott, Steve Everitt, Dean Dingman, Greg Skrepenak
1991 Cale Gundy, Oklahoma
Tyrone Lewis, Virginia
1992 Errict Rhett, Florida
Reggie Lawrence, North Caro. St.
1993 Brian Burgdorf, Alabama
Corey Hamilton, North Caro.

HALL OF FAME BOWL
(Tampa Bay)

Year	Player, Team, Position
1987	Shawn Halloran, Boston College, quarterback
	James Jackson, Georgia, quarterback
1988	Jamie Morris, Michigan, tailback
	Bobby Humphrey, Alabama, tailback
1989	Robert Drummond, Syracuse, running back
1990	Reggie Slack, Alabama, quarterback
	Derek Isaman, Ohio St., linebacker

1991 DeChane Cameron, Clemson, quarterback
1992 Marvin Graves, Syracuse, quarterback
1993 Heath Shuler, Tennessee, quarterback
1994 Tyrone Wheatley, Michigan, running back

HOLIDAY BOWL

Year	Player, Team, Position
1978	Phil McConkey, Navy, wide receiver
1979	Marc Wilson, Brigham Young, quarterback
	Tim Wilbur, Indiana, cornerback
1980	Jim McMahon, Brigham Young, quarterback
	Craig James, Southern Methodist, running back
1981	Jim McMahon, Brigham Young, quarterback
	Kyle Whittingham, Brigham Young, linebacker
1982	Tim Spencer, Ohio St., running back
	Garcia Lane, Ohio St., cornerback
1983	Steve Young, Brigham Young, quarterback
	Bobby Bell, Missouri, defensive end
1984	Robbie Bosco, Brigham Young, quarterback
	Leon White, Brigham Young, linebacker
1985	Bobby Joe Edmonds, Arkansas, running back
	Greg Battle, Arizona St., linebacker
1986	Todd Santos, San Diego St., quarterback (co-offensive)
	Mark Vlasic, Iowa, quarterback (co-offensive)
	Richard Brown, San Diego St., linebacker
1987	Craig Burnett, Wyoming, quarterback
	Anthony Wright, Iowa, cornerback
1988	Barry Sanders, Oklahoma St., running back
	Sim Drain, Oklahoma St., linebacker
1989	Blair Thomas, Penn St., running back
	Ty Detmer, Brigham Young, quarterback
1990	Bucky Richardson, Texas A&M, quarterback
	William Thomas, Texas A&M, linebacker
1991	Ty Detmer, Brigham Young, quarterback
	Josh Arnold, Brigham Young, defensive back (co-defensive)
	Carlos James, Iowa, defensive back (co-defensive)
1992	Michael Carter, Hawaii, quarterback
	Junior Tagoai, Hawaii, defensive tackle
1993	John Walsh, Brigham Young, quarterback (co-offensive)
	Raymont Harris, Ohio St., running back (co-offensive)
	Lorenzo Styles, Ohio St., linebacker

INDEPENDENCE BOWL

Year	Player, Team, Position
1976	Terry McFarland, McNeese St., quarterback
	Terry Clark, Tulsa, cornerback
1977	Keith Thibodeaux, Louisiana Tech, quarterback
	Otis Wilson, Louisville, linebacker
1978	Theodore Sutton, East Caro., fullback
	Zack Valentine, East Caro., defensive end
1979	Joe Morris, Syracuse, running back
	Clay Carroll, McNeese St., defensive tackle
1980	Stephan Starring, McNeese St., quarterback
	Jerald Baylis, Southern Miss., nose guard
1981	Gary Kubiak, Texas A&M, quarterback
	Mike Green, Oklahoma St., linebacker
1982	Randy Wright, Wisconsin, quarterback
	Tim Krumrie, Wisconsin, nose guard
1983	Marty Louthan, Air Force, quarterback
	Andre Townsend, Mississippi, defensive tackle
1984	Bart Weiss, Air Force, quarterback
	Scott Thomas, Air Force, safety
1985	Rickey Foggie, Minnesota, quarterback
	Bruce Holmes, Minnesota, linebacker
1986	Mark Young, Mississippi, quarterback
	James Mosley, Texas Tech, defensive end
1987	Chris Chandler, Washington, quarterback
	David Rill, Washington, linebacker
1988	James Henry, Southern Miss., punt returner/cornerback
1989	Bill Musgrave, Oregon, quarterback
	Chris Oldham, Oregon, defensive back
1990	Mike Richardson, Louisiana Tech, running back
	Lorenzo Baker, Louisiana Tech, linebacker
1991	Andre Hastings, Georgia, flanker
	Torrey Evans, Georgia, linebacker
1992	Todd Dixon, Wake Forest, split end
1993	Maurice DeShazo, Virginia Tech, quarterback
	Antonio Banks, Virginia Tech, safety

JOHN HANCOCK BOWL

(Named Sun Bowl, 1936-86; John Hancock Sun Bowl, 1987-88)

C. M. Hendricks Most Valuable Player Trophy (1954-Present)
Jimmy Rogers Jr. Most Valuable Lineman Trophy (1961-Present)

Year	Player, Team, Position
1950	Harvey Gabriel, UTEP, halfback
1951	Bill Cross, West Tex. A&M, end
1952	Junior Arteburn, Texas Tech, quarterback
1953	Tom McCormick, Pacific (Cal.), halfback
1954	Dick Shinaut, UTEP, quarterback
1955	Jesse Whittenton, UTEP, quarterback
1956	Jim Crawford, Wyoming, halfback
1957	Claude Austin, Geo. Washington
1958	Leonard Kucewski, Wyoming, guard
1959	Charley Johnson, New Mexico St., quarterback
1960	Charley Johnson, New Mexico St., quarterback
1961	Billy Joe, Villanova, fullback
	Richie Ross, Villanova, guard
1962	Jerry Logan, West Tex. A&M, halfback
	Don Hoovler, Ohio, guard
1963	Bob Berry, Oregon, quarterback
	John Hughes, Southern Methodist, guard
1964	Preston Ridlehuber, Georgia, quarterback
	Jim Wilson, Georgia, tackle
1965	Billy Stevens, UTEP, quarterback
	Ronny Nixon, Texas Christian, tackle
1966	Jim Kiick, Wyoming, tailback
	Jerry Durling, Wyoming, middle guard
1967	Billy Stevens, UTEP, quarterback
	Fred Carr, UTEP, linebacker
1968	Buddy McClintock, Auburn, defensive back
	David Campbell, Auburn, tackle
1969	Paul Rogers, Nebraska, halfback
	Jerry Murtaugh, Nebraska, linebacker
1970	Rock Perdoni, Georgia Tech, defensive tackle
	Bill Flowers, Georgia Tech, linebacker
1971	Bert Jones, Louisiana St., quarterback
	Matt Blair, Iowa St., linebacker
1972	George Smith, Texas Tech, halfback
	Ecomet Burley, Texas Tech, defensive tackle
1973	Ray Bybee, Missouri, fullback
	John Kelsey, Missouri, tight end
1974	Terry Vitrano, Mississippi St., fullback
	Jimmy Webb, Mississippi St., defensive tackle
1975	Robert Haygood, Pittsburgh, quarterback
	Al Romano, Pittsburgh, middle guard
1977	Tony Franklin, Texas A&M, kicker
	Edgar Fields, Texas A&M, defensive tackle
1977	Charles Alexander, Louisiana St., tailback
	Gordon Ceresino, Stanford, linebacker
1978	Johnny "Ham" Jones, Texas, running back
	Dwight Jefferson, Texas, defensive end
1979	Paul Skansi, Washington, flanker
	Doug Martin, Washington, defensive tackle
1980	Jeff Quinn, Nebraska, quarterback
	Jimmy Williams, Nebraska, defensive end
1981	Darrell Shepard, Oklahoma, quarterback
	Rick Bryan, Oklahoma, defensive tackle
1982	Ethan Horton, North Caro., tailback
	Ronnie Mullins, Texas, defensive end
1983	Walter Lewis, Alabama, quarterback
	Wes Neighbors, Alabama, center
1984	Rick Badanjek, Maryland, fullback
	Carl Zander, Tennessee, linebacker
1985	Max Zendejas, Arizona, kicker
	Peter Anderson, Georgia, center
1986	Cornelius Bennett, Alabama, defensive end
	Steve Alvord, Washington, middle guard
1987	Thurman Thomas, Oklahoma St., running back
	Darnell Warren, West Va., linebacker
1988	David Smith, Alabama, quarterback
	Derrick Thomas, Alabama, linebacker
1989	Alex Van Pelt, Pittsburgh, quarterback
	Anthony Williams, Texas A&M, linebacker
1990	Courtney Hawkins, Michigan St., wide receiver
	Craig Hartsuyker, Southern Cal, linebacker
1991	Arnold Ale, UCLA, inside linebacker
	Jimmy Rogers Jr., Illinois, lineman
1992	Melvin Bonner, Baylor, flanker
1993	Jerald Moore, Oklahoma, running back

LAS VEGAS BOWL

Year	Player, Team, Position
1992	Chris Vargas, Nevada, quarterback
1993	Anthony Calvillo, Utah St., quarterback
	Mike Neu, Ball St., quarterback

LIBERTY BOWL

Year	Player, Team
1959	Jay Huffman, Penn St.

Year	Player, Team, Position
1960	Dick Hoak, Penn St.
1961	Ernie Davis, Syracuse
1962	Terry Baker, Oregon St.
1963	Ode Burrell, Mississippi St.
1964	Ernest Adler, Utah
1965	Tom Bryan, Auburn
1966	Jimmy Cox, Miami (Fla.)
1967	Jim Donnan, North Caro. St.
1968	Steve Hindman, Mississippi
1969	Bob Anderson, Colorado
1970	Dave Abercrombie, Tulane
1971	Joe Ferguson, Arkansas
1972	Jim Stevens, Georgia Tech
1973	Stan Fritts, North Caro. St.
1974	Randy White, Maryland
1975	Ricky Bell, Southern Cal
1976	Barry Krauss, Alabama
1977	Matt Kupec, North Caro.
1978	James Wilder, Missouri
1979	Roch Hontas, Tulane
1980	Mark Herrmann, Purdue
1981	Eddie Meyers, Navy
1982	Jeremiah Castille, Alabama
1983	Doug Flutie, Boston College
1984	Bo Jackson, Auburn
1985	Cody Carlson, Baylor
1986	Jeff Francis, Tennessee
1987	Greg Thomas, Arkansas
1988	Dave Schnell, Indiana
1989	Randy Baldwin, Mississippi
1990	Rob Perez, Air Force
1991	Rob Perez, Air Force
1992	Cassius Ware, Mississippi
1993	Jeff Brohm, Louisville

ORANGE BOWL

Year	Player, Team, Position
1965	Joe Namath, Alabama, quarterback
1966	Steve Sloan, Alabama, quarterback
1967	Larry Smith, Florida, tailback
1968	Bob Warmack, Oklahoma, quarterback
1969	Donnie Shanklin, Kansas, halfback
1970	Chuck Burkhart, Penn St., quarterback
	Mike Reid, Penn St., defensive tackle
1971	Jerry Tagge, Nebraska, quarterback
	Willie Harper, Nebraska, defensive end
1972	Jerry Tagge, Nebraska, quarterback
	Rich Glover, Nebraska, defensive guard
1973	Johnny Rodgers, Nebraska, wingback
	Rich Glover, Nebraska, defensive guard
1974	Tom Shuman, Penn St., quarterback
	Randy Crowder, Penn St., defensive tackle
1975	Wayne Bullock, Notre Dame, fullback
	Leroy Cook, Alabama, defensive end
1976	Steve Davis, Oklahoma, quarterback
	Lee Roy Selmon, Oklahoma, defensive tackle
1977	Rod Gerald, Ohio St., quarterback
	Tom Cousineau, Ohio St., linebacker
1978	Roland Sales, Arkansas, running back
	Reggie Freeman, Arkansas, nose guard
1979	Billy Sims, Oklahoma, running back
	Reggie Kinlaw, Oklahoma, nose guard
1980	J. C. Watts, Oklahoma, quarterback
	Bud Hebert, Oklahoma, free safety
1981	J. C. Watts, Oklahoma, quarterback
	Jarvis Coursey, Florida St., defensive end
1982	Homer Jordan, Clemson, quarterback
	Jeff Davis, Clemson, linebacker
1983	Turner Gill, Nebraska, quarterback
	Dave Rimington, Nebraska, center
1984	Bernie Kosar, Miami (Fla.), quarterback
	Jack Fernandez, Miami (Fla.), linebacker
1985	Jacque Robinson, Washington, tailback
	Ron Holmes, Washington, defensive tackle
1986	Sonny Brown, Oklahoma, defensive back
	Tim Lashar, Oklahoma, kicker
1987	Dante Jones, Oklahoma, linebacker
	Spencer Tillman, Oklahoma, halfback
1988	Bernard Clark, Miami (Fla.), linebacker
	Darrell Reed, Oklahoma, defensive end
1989	Steve Walsh, Miami (Fla.), quarterback
	Charles Fryar, Nebraska, cornerback
1990	Raghib Ismail, Notre Dame, tailback/wide receiver
	Darian Hagan, Colorado, quarterback
1991	Charles Johnson, Colorado, quarterback
	Chris Zorich, Notre Dame, nose guard
1992	Larry Jones, Miami (Fla.), running back
1993	Charlie Ward, Florida St., quarterback
	Corey Dixon, Nebraska, split end
1994	Charlie Ward, Florida St., quarterback

PEACH BOWL

Year	Player, Team, Position
1968	Mike Hillman, Louisiana St. (offense)
	Buddy Millican, Florida St. (defense)
1969	Ed Williams, West Va. (offense)
	Carl Crennel, West Va. (defense)
1970	Monroe Eley, Arizona St. (offense)
	Junior Ah You, Arizona St. (defense)
1971	Norris Weese, Mississippi (offense)
	Crowell Armstrong, Mississippi (defense)
1972	Dave Buckey, North Caro. St. (offense)
	George Bell, North Caro. St. (defense)
1973	Louis Carter, Maryland (offense)
	Sylvester Boler, Georgia (defense)
1974	Larry Isaac, Texas Tech (offense)
	Dennis Harrison, Vanderbilt (defense)
1975	Dan Kendra, West Va. (offense)
	Ray Marshall, West Va. (defense)
1976	Rod Stewart, Kentucky (offense)
	Mike Martin, Kentucky (defense)
1977	Johnny Evans, North Caro. St. (offense)
	Richard Carter, North Caro. St. (defense)
1978	Mark Herrmann, Purdue (offense)
	Calvin Clark, Purdue (defense)
1979	Mike Brannan, Baylor (offense)
	Andrew Melontree, Baylor (defense)
1980	Jim Kelly, Miami (Fla.) (offense)
	Jim Burt, Miami (Fla.) (defense)
1981	Mickey Walczak, West Va. (offense)
	Don Stemple, West Va. (defense)
1982	Chuck Long, Iowa (offense)
	Clay Uhlenhake, Iowa (defense)
1983	Eric Thomas, Florida St. (offense)
	Alphonso Carreker, Florida St. (defense)
1984	Howard Petty, Virginia (offense)
	Ray Daly, Virginia (defense)
1985	Rob Healy, Army (offense)
	Peel Chronister, Army (defense)
1986	Erik Kramer, North Caro. St. (offense)
	Derrick Taylor, North Caro. St. (defense)
1987	Reggie Cobb, Tennessee (offense)
	Van Waiters, Indiana (defense)
1988	Shane Montgomery, North Caro. St. (offense)
	Michael Brooks, North Caro. St. (defense)
1989	Michael Owens, Syracuse (offense)
	Rodney Hampton, Georgia (offense)
	Terry Wooden, Syracuse (defense)
	Morris Lewis, Georgia (defense)
1990	Stan White, Auburn (offense)
	Vaughn Dunbar, Indiana (offense)
	Darrel Crawford, Auburn (defense)
	Mike Dumas, Indiana (defense)
1991	Jeff Blake, East Caro. (offense)
	Terry Jordan, North Caro. St. (offense)
	Robert Jones, East Caro. (defense)
	Billy Ray Haynes, North Caro. St. (defense)
1993	Natrone Means, North Caro., running back (offense)
	Greg Plump, Mississippi St., quarterback (offense)
	Bracey Walker, North Caro., strong safety (defense)
	Marc Woodard, Mississippi St., linebacker (defense)
1993	Emory Smith, Clemson, fullback (offense)
	Pookie Jones, Kentucky, quarterback (offense)
	Brentson Buckner, Clemson, tackle (defense)
	Zane Beehn, Kentucky, end (defense)

ROSE BOWL

Year	Player, Team, Position
1902	Neil Snow, Michigan, fullback
1916	Carl Dietz, Washington St., fullback
1917	John Beckett, Oregon, tackle
1918	Hollis Huntington, Mare Island, fullback
1919	George Halas, Great Lakes, end
1920	Edward Casey, Harvard, halfback
1921	Harold "Brick" Muller, California, end
1922	Russell Stein, Wash. & Jeff., tackle
1923	Leo Calland, Southern Cal, guard
1924	Ira McKee, Navy, quarterback
1925	Elmer Layden, Notre Dame, fullback
	Ernie Nevers, Stanford, fullback
1926	Johnny Mack Brown, Alabama, halfback
	George Wilson, Washington, halfback
1927	Fred Pickhard, Alabama, tackle
1928	Clifford Hoffman, Stanford, fullback
1929	Benjamin Lom, California, fullback
1930	Russell Saunders, Southern Cal, quarterback
1931	John "Monk" Campbell, Alabama, quarterback

Year	Player, Team, Position
1932	Ernie Pinckert, Southern Cal, halfback
1933	Homer Griffith, Southern Cal, quarterback
1934	Cliff Montgomery, Columbia, quarterback
1935	Millard "Dixie" Howell, Alabama, halfback
1936	James "Monk" Moscrip, Stanford, end
	Keith Topping, Stanford, end
1937	William Daddio, Pittsburgh, end
1938	Victor Bottari, California, halfback
1939	Doyle Nave, Southern Cal, quarterback
	Alvin Krueger, Southern Cal, end
1940	Ambrose Schindler, Southern Cal, quarterback
1941	Peter Kmetovic, Stanford, halfback
1942	Donald Durdan, Oregon St., halfback
1943	Charles Trippi, Georgia, halfback
1944	Norman Verry, Southern Cal, guard
1945	James Hardy, Southern Cal, quarterback
1946	Harry Gilmer, Alabama, halfback
1947	Claude "Buddy" Young, Illinois, halfback
	Julius Rykovich, Illinois, halfback
1948	Robert Chappius, Michigan, halfback
1949	Frank Aschenbrenner, Northwestern, halfback
1950	Fred Morrison, Ohio St., fullback
1951	Donald Dufek, Michigan, fullback
1952	William Tate, Illinois, halfback
1953	Rudy Bukich, Southern Cal, quarterback
1954	Billy Wells, Michigan St., halfback
1955	Dave Leggett, Ohio St., quarterback
1956	Walter Kowalczyk, Michigan St., halfback
1957	Kenneth Ploen, Iowa, quarterback
1958	Jack Crabtree, Oregon, quarterback
1959	Bob Jeter, Iowa, halfback
1960	Bob Schloredt, Washington, quarterback
	George Fleming, Washington, halfback
1961	Bob Schloredt, Washington, quarterback
1962	Sandy Stephens, Minnesota, quarterback
1963	Pete Beathard, Southern Cal, quarterback
	Ron VanderKelen, Wisconsin, quarterback
1964	Jim Grabowski, Illinois, fullback
1965	Mel Anthony, Michigan, fullback
1966	Bob Stiles, UCLA, defensive back
1967	John Charles, Purdue, halfback
1968	O. J. Simpson, Southern Cal, tailback
1969	Rex Kern, Ohio St., quarterback
1970	Bob Chandler, Southern Cal, flanker
1971	Jim Plunkett, Stanford, quarterback
1972	Don Bunce, Stanford, quarterback
1973	Sam Cunningham, Southern Cal, fullback
1974	Cornelius Greene, Ohio St., quarterback
1975	Pat Haden, Southern Cal, quarterback
	John McKay Jr., Southern Cal, split end
1976	John Sciarra, UCLA, quarterback
1977	Vince Evans, Southern Cal, quarterback
1978	Warren Moon, Washington, quarterback
1979	Charles White, Southern Cal, tailback
	Rick Leach, Michigan, quarterback
1980	Charles White, Southern Cal, tailback
1981	Butch Woolfolk, Michigan, running back
1982	Jacque Robinson, Washington, running back
1983	Don Rogers, UCLA, free safety
	Tom Ramsey, UCLA, quarterback
1984	Rick Neuheisel, UCLA, quarterback
1985	Tim Green, Southern Cal, quarterback
	Jack Del Rio, Southern Cal, linebacker
1986	Eric Ball, UCLA, tailback
1987	Jeff Van Raaphorst, Arizona St., quarterback
1988	Percy Snow, Michigan St., linebacker
1989	Leroy Hoard, Michigan, fullback
1990	Ricky Ervins, Southern Cal, tailback
1991	Mark Brunell, Washington, quarterback
1992	Steve Emtman, Washington, defensive tackle
	Billy Joe Hobert, Washington, quarterback
1993	Tyrone Wheatley, Michigan, running back
1994	Brent Moss, Wisconsin, tailback

SUGAR BOWL

Miller-Digby Memorial Trophy

Year	Player, Team, Position
1948	Bobby Layne, Texas, quarterback
1949	Jack Mitchell, Oklahoma, quarterback
1950	Leon Heath, Oklahoma, fullback
1951	Walt Yowarsky, Kentucky, tackle
1952	Ed Modzelewski, Maryland, fullback
1953	Leon Hardemann, Georgia Tech, halfback
1954	"Pepper" Rodgers, Georgia Tech, quarterback
1955	Joe Gattuso, Navy, fullback
1956	Franklin Brooks, Georgia Tech, guard
1957	Del Shofner, Baylor, halfback
1958	Raymond Brown, Mississippi, quarterback
1959	Billy Cannon, Louisiana St., halfback
1960	Bobby Franklin, Mississippi, quarterback
1961	Jake Gibbs, Mississippi, quarterback

Year	Player, Team, Position
1962	Mike Fracchia, Alabama, fullback
1963	Glynn Griffing, Mississippi, quarterback
1964	Tim Davis, Alabama, kicker
1965	Doug Moreau, Louisiana St., flanker
1966	Steve Spurrier, Florida, quarterback
1967	Kenny Stabler, Alabama, quarterback
1968	Glenn Smith, Louisiana St., halfback
1969	Chuck Dicus, Arkansas, flanker
1970	Archie Manning, Mississippi, quarterback
1971	Bobby Scott, Tennessee, quarterback
1972	Jack Mildren, Oklahoma, quarterback
1972	Tinker Owens, Oklahoma, flanker
1973	Tom Clements, Notre Dame, quarterback
1974	Tony Davis, Nebraska, fullback
1975	Richard Todd, Alabama, quarterback
1977	Matt Cavanaugh, Pittsburgh, quarterback
1978	Jeff Rutledge, Alabama, quarterback
1979	Barry Krauss, Alabama, linebacker
1980	Major Ogilvie, Alabama, running back
1981	Herschel Walker, Georgia, running back
1982	Dan Marino, Pittsburgh, quarterback
1983	Todd Blackledge, Penn St., quarterback
1984	Bo Jackson, Auburn, running back
1985	Craig Sundberg, Nebraska, quarterback
1986	Daryl Dickey, Tennessee, quarterback
1987	Steve Taylor, Nebraska, quarterback
1988	Don McPherson, Syracuse, quarterback
1989	Sammie Smith, Florida St., running back
1990	Craig Erickson, Miami (Fla.), quarterback
1991	Andy Kelly, Tennessee, quarterback
1992	Jerome Bettis, Notre Dame, fullback
1993	Derrick Lassic, Alabama, running back
1994	Errict Rhett, Florida, running back

Most Valuable Players in Former Major Bowls

ALL-AMERICAN BOWL
(Birmingham, Ala.; Known as Hall of Fame Classic, 1977-84)

Year	Player, Team, Position
1977	Chuck White, Maryland, split end
	Charles Johnson, Maryland, defensive tackle
1978	Curtis Dickey, Texas A&M, running back
1979	Phil Bradley, Missouri, quarterback
1980	Gary Anderson, Arkansas, running back
	Billy Ray Smith, Arkansas, linebacker
1981	John Bond, Mississippi St., quarterback
	Johnie Cooks, Mississippi St., linebacker
1982	Whit Taylor, Vanderbilt, quarterback
	Carl Dieudonne, Air Force, defensive end
1983	Jeff Hostetler, West Va., quarterback
1984	Mark Logan, Kentucky, running back
	Todd Gregoire, Wisconsin, placekicker
1985	Mark Ingram, Michigan St., wide receiver
1986	Sammie Smith, Florida St., running back
1987	Scott Secules, Virginia, quarterback
1988	Emmitt Smith, Florida, running back
1989	Jerry Gray, Texas Tech, running back
1990	Brett Favre, Southern Miss., quarterback

AVIATION BOWL
(Dayton, Ohio)

Year	Player, Team, Position
1961	Bobby Santiago, New Mexico, running back
	Chuck Cummings, New Mexico, guard

BLUEBONNET BOWL
(Houston, Texas)

Year	Player, Team
1959	Lowndes Shingles, Clemson
	Bob Lilly, Texas Christian
1960	James Saxton, Texas
	Lee Roy Jordan, Alabama
1961	Ken Coleman, Kansas
	Elvin Basham, Kansas
1962	Bill Tobin, Missouri
	Conrad Hitchler, Missouri
1963	Don Trull, Baylor
	James Ingram, Baylor
1964	Jerry Rhome, Tulsa
	Willy Townes, Tulsa
1965	Dewey Warren, Tennessee
	Frank Emanuel, Tennessee
1966	Chris Gilbert, Texas
	Fred Edwards, Texas

1967	Bob Anderson, Colorado
	Ted Hendricks, Miami (Fla.)
1968	Joe Pearce, Oklahoma
	Rufus Cormier, Southern Methodist
1969	Jim Strong, Houston
	Jerry Drones, Houston
1970	Greg Pruitt, Oklahoma
	Jeff Rouzie, Alabama
1971	Charlie Davis, Colorado
	Butch Brezina, Houston
1972	Condredge Holloway, Tennessee
	Carl Johnson, Tennessee
1973	D. C. Nobles, Houston
	Deryl McGallion, Houston
1974	John Housmann, Houston
	Mack Mitchell, Houston
1975	Earl Campbell, Texas
	Tim Campbell, Texas
1976	Chuck Malito, Nebraska
	Rodney Allison, Texas Tech
1977	Rob Hertel, Southern Cal
	Walt Underwood, Southern Cal
1978	Steve Dils, Stanford
	Gordy Ceresino, Stanford
1979	Mark Herrmann, Purdue
	Roland James, Tennessee
1980	Amos Lawrence, North Caro.
	Steve Streater, North Caro.
1981	Butch Woolfolk, Michigan
	Ben Needham, Michigan
1982	Gary Anderson, Arkansas
	Dwayne Dixon, Florida
1983	Rusty Hilger, Oklahoma St.
	Alfred Anderson, Baylor
1984	Willie Drewrey, West Va.
1985	Pat Evans, Air Force
	James McKinney, Texas
1986	Ray Berry, Baylor
	Mark Hatcher, Colorado
1987	Tony Jones, Texas
	Zeke Gadson, Pittsburgh

BLUEGRASS BOWL

(Louisville, Ky.)

Year	Player, Team
1958	Forrest Campbell, Oklahoma St.

CALIFORNIA RAISIN BOWL

(Beginning in 1992, Mid-American Conference

and Big West Conference winners met in Las Vegas Bowl)

Year	Player, Team, Position
1981	Arnold Smiley, Toledo, running back
	Marlin Russell, Toledo, linebacker
1982	Chip Otten, Bowling Green, tailback
	Jac Tomasello, Bowling Green, defensive back
1983	Lou Wicks, Northern Ill., fullback
	James Pruitt, Cal St. Fullerton, wide receiver
1984	Randall Cunningham, Nevada-Las Vegas, quarterback
	Steve Morgan, Toledo, tailback
1985	Mike Mancini, Fresno St., punter
	Greg Meehan, Bowling Green, flanker
1986	Mike Perez, San Jose St., quarterback
	Andrew Marlatt, Miami (Ohio), defensive tackle
1987	Gary Patton, Eastern Mich., tailback
	Mike Perez, San Jose St., quarterback
1988	Darrell Rosette, Fresno St., running back
	Tony Kimbrough, Western Mich., quarterback
1989	Ron Cox, Fresno St., linebacker
	Sean Jones, Ball St., wide receiver
1990	Sheldon Canley, San Jose St., tailback
	Ken Ealy, Central Mich., wide receiver
1991	Mark Szlachcic, Bowling Green, wide receiver
	Mark Barsotti, Fresno St., quarterback

CHERRY BOWL

(Pontiac, Mich.)

Year	Player, Team
1984	Nate Sassaman, Army
1985	Stan Gelbaugh, Maryland
	Scott Shankweiler, Maryland

DELTA BOWL

(Memphis, Tenn.)

Year	Player, Team
1948	Charlie Conerly, Mississippi

GARDEN STATE BOWL

(East Rutherford, N. J.)

Year	Player, Team
1978	John Mistler, Arizona St.
1979	Mark Bright, Temple
1980	Terald Clark, Houston
1981	Steve Alatorre, Tennessee
	Anthony Hancock, Tennessee
	Randy Wright, Wisconsin

GOTHAM BOWL

(New York, N.Y.)

Year	Player, Team
1961	Don Trull, Baylor
1962	Willie Ross, Nebraska
	George Mira, Miami (Fla.)

HARBOR BOWL

(San Diego, Calif.)

Year	Player, Team
1947	Bryan Brock, New Mexico
	Bill Nelson, Montana St.

MERCY BOWL

(Los Angeles, Calif.)

Year	Player, Team
1961	Beau Carter, Fresno St.

PASADENA BOWL

(Pasadena, Calif.; called Junior Rose Bowl in 1967)

Year	Player, Team
1967	Eugene "Mercury" Morris, West Tex. A&M
	Albie Owens, West Tex. A&M
1969	John Featherstone, San Diego St.
1970	Leon Burns, Long Beach St.
	Paul Mattingly, Louisville
1971	Tom Carlsen, Memphis
	Dornell Harris, Memphis

PRESIDENTIAL CUP

(College Park, Md.)

Year	Player, Team
1950	Bob Smith, Texas A&M
	Zippy Morocco, Georgia

SALAD BOWL

(Phoenix, Ariz.)

Year	Player, Team
1950	Bob McQuade, Xavier (Ohio)
	Wilford "Whizzer" White, Arizona St.
1951	Jim Bailey, Miami (Ohio)
1952	Gene Shannon, Houston

Heisman Trophy Winners in Bowl Games

YEAR-BY-YEAR BOWL RESULTS FOR HEISMAN WINNERS
(Includes bowl games immediately after award of Heisman Trophy)

Of the 58 winners of the 59 Heisman Trophies (Archie Griffin won twice), 34 played in bowl games after they received their prize. Of those 34 players, only 15 were on the winning team in the bowl.

Houston's Andre Ware is the only Heisman recipient to miss a bowl date since 1969. The Cougars were on probation during the 1989 season and were ineligible for selection to a bowl. Before that lapse, Oklahoma's Steve Owens in 1969 was the last Heisman awardee not to participate in a bowl game.

Only three of the first 22 Heisman Trophy winners played in bowl games after receiving the award—Texas Christian's Davey O'Brien in 1938, Georgia's Frank Sinkwich in 1942 and Southern Methodist's Doak Walker in 1948.

Year	Heisman Winner, Team, Position	Bowl (Opponent, Result)
1935	Jay Berwanger, Chicago, HB	Did not play in bowl
1936	Larry Kelley, Yale, E	Did not play in bowl
1937	Clint Frank, Yale, HB	Did not play in bowl
1938	Davey O'Brien, Texas Christian, QB	Sugar (Carnegie Mellon, W 15-7)
1939	Nile Kinnick, Iowa, HB	Did not play in bowl
1940	Tom Harmon, Michigan, HB	Did not play in bowl
1941	Bruce Smith, Minnesota, HB	Did not play in bowl
1942	Frank Sinkwich, Georgia, HB	Rose (UCLA, W 9-0)
1943	Angelo Bertelli, Notre Dame, QB	Did not play in bowl
1944	Les Horvath, Ohio St., QB	Did not play in bowl

Year	Heisman Winner, Team, Position	Bowl (Opponent, Result)
1945	Doc Blanchard, Army, FB	Did not play in bowl
1946	Glenn Davis, Army, HB	Did not play in bowl
1947	Johnny Lujack, Notre Dame, QB	Did not play in bowl
1948	Doak Walker, Southern Methodist, HB	Cotton (Oregon, W 21-13)
1949	Leon Hart, Notre Dame, E	Did not play in bowl
1950	Vic Janowicz, Ohio St., HB	Did not play in bowl
1951	Dick Kazmeier, Princeton, HB	Did not play in bowl
1952	Billy Vessels, Oklahoma, HB	Did not play in bowl
1953	John Lattner, Notre Dame, HB	Did not play in bowl
1954	Alan Ameche, Wisconsin, FB	Did not play in bowl
1955	Howard Cassady, Ohio St., HB	Did not play in bowl
1956	Paul Hornung, Notre Dame, QB	Did not play in bowl
1957	John David Crow, Texas A&M, HB	Gator (Tennessee, L 0-3)
1958	Pete Dawkins, Army, HB	Did not play in bowl
1959	Billy Cannon, Louisiana St., HB	Sugar (Mississippi, L 0-21)
1960	Joe Bellino, Navy, HB	Orange (Missouri, L 14-21)
1961	Ernie Davis, Syracuse, HB	Liberty (Miami, Fla., W 15-14)
1962	Terry Baker, Oregon St., QB	Liberty (Villanova, W 6-0)
1963	Roger Staubach, Navy, QB	Cotton (Texas, L 6-28)
1964	John Huarte, Notre Dame, QB	Did not play in bowl
1965	Mike Garrett, Southern Cal, HB	Did not play in bowl
1966	Steve Spurrier, Florida, QB	Orange (Georgia Tech, W 27-12)
1967	Gary Beban, UCLA, QB	Did not play in bowl
1968	O. J. Simpson, Southern Cal, HB	Rose (Ohio St., L 16-27)
1969	Steve Owens, Oklahoma, HB	Did not play in bowl
1970	Jim Plunkett, Stanford, QB	Rose (Ohio St., W 27-17)
1971	Pat Sullivan, Auburn, QB	Sugar (Oklahoma, L 22-40)
1972	Johnny Rodgers, Nebraska, FL	Orange (Notre Dame, W 40-6)
1973	John Cappelletti, Penn St., HB	Orange (Louisiana St., W 16-9)
1974	Archie Griffin, Ohio St., HB	Rose (Southern Cal, L 17-18)

Year	Heisman Winner, Team, Position	Bowl (Opponent, Result)
1975	Archie Griffin, Ohio St., HB	Rose (UCLA, L 10-23)
1976	Tony Dorsett, Pittsburgh, HB	Sugar (Georgia, W 27-3)
1977	Earl Campbell, Texas, HB	Cotton (Notre Dame, L 10-38)
1978	Billy Sims, Oklahoma, HB	Orange (Nebraska, W 31-24)
1979	Charles White, Southern Cal, HB	Rose (Ohio St., W 17-16)
1980	George Rogers, South Caro., HB	Gator (Pittsburgh, L 9-37)
1981	Marcus Allen, Southern Cal, HB	Fiesta (Penn St., L 10-26)
1982	Herschel Walker, Georgia, HB	Sugar (Penn St., L 23-27)
1983	Mike Rozier, Nebraska, HB	Orange (Miami, Fla., L 30-31)
1984	Doug Flutie, Boston College, QB	Cotton (Houston, W 45-28)
1985	Bo Jackson, Auburn, HB	Cotton (Texas A&M, L 16-36)
1986	Vinny Testaverde, Miami (Fla.), QB	Fiesta (Penn St., L 10-14)
1987	Tim Brown, Notre Dame, WR	Cotton (Texas A&M, L 10-35)
1988	Barry Sanders, Oklahoma St., RB	Holiday (Wyoming, W 62-14)
1989	Andre Ware, Houston, QB	Did not play in bowl
1990	Ty Detmer, Brigham Young, QB	Holiday (Texas A&M, L 14-65)
1991	Desmond Howard, Michigan, WR	Rose (Washington, L 14-34)
1992	Gino Torretta, Miami (Fla.), QB	Sugar (Alabama, L 13-34)
1993	Charlie Ward, Florida St., QB	Orange (Nebraska, W 18-16)

TOP BOWLS FOR HEISMAN WINNERS

Bowl	Heisman Winner Year	Heisman Winners
Orange	1960, 1966, 1972, 1973, 1978, 1983, 1993	7
Rose	1942, 1968, 1970, 1974, 1975, 1979, 1991	7
Cotton	1948, 1963, 1977, 1984, 1985, 1987	6
Sugar	1938, 1959, 1971, 1976, 1982, 1992	6
Fiesta	1981, 1986	2
Gator	1957, 1980	2
Liberty	1961, 1962	2
Holiday	1988, 1990	2

HEISMAN TROPHY WINNERS WHO WERE BOWL-GAME MVPs

Heisman Winner, Team (Year Won)	Bowl, Year Played
Doak Walker, Southern Methodist (1948)	Cotton, 1948
Doak Walker, Southern Methodist (1948)	Cotton, 1949
John David Crow, Texas A&M (1957)	Gator, 1957
Billy Cannon, Louisiana St. (1959)	Sugar, 1959
Ernie Davis, Syracuse (1961)	Cotton, 1960
Ernie Davis, Syracuse (1961)	Liberty, 1961
Terry Baker, Oregon St. (1962)	Liberty, 1962
Steve Spurrier, Florida (1966)	Sugar, 1966
O. J. Simpson, Southern Cal (1968)	Rose, 1968
Jim Plunkett, Stanford (1970)	Rose, 1971
Pat Sullivan, Auburn (1971)	Gator, 1971
Johnny Rodgers, Nebraska (1972)	Orange, 1973
Earl Campbell, Texas (1977)	Gator, 1974
Earl Campbell, Texas (1977)	Bluebonnet, 1975*
Billy Sims, Oklahoma (1978)	Orange, 1979
Charles White, Southern Cal (1979)	Rose, 1979
Charles White, Southern Cal (1979)	Rose, 1980
George Rogers, South Caro. (1980)	Gator, 1980
Herschel Walker, Georgia (1982)	Sugar, 1981
Doug Flutie, Boston College (1984)	Liberty, 1983
Bo Jackson, Auburn (1985)	Liberty, 1984
Bo Jackson, Auburn (1985)	Sugar, 1984
Bo Jackson, Auburn (1985)	Cotton, 1986
Barry Sanders, Oklahoma St. (1988)	Holiday, 1988
Ty Detmer, Brigham Young (1990)	Freedom, 1988
Ty Detmer, Brigham Young (1990)	Holiday, 1989
Ty Detmer, Brigham Young (1990)	Holiday, 1991
Charlie Ward, Florida St. (1993)	Orange, 1994

*Discontinued bowl.

Bowls and Polls

Associated Press No. 1 Teams Defeated in Bowl Games

Date	Bowl	Teams Involved	Score	New No. 1
1-1-51	Sugar	No. 7 Kentucky beat No. 1 Oklahoma	13-7	Same
1-1-52	Sugar	No. 3 Maryland beat No. 1 Tennessee	28-13	Same
1-1-54	Orange	No. 4 Oklahoma beat No. 1 Maryland	7-0	Same
1-1-61	Rose	No. 6 Washington beat No. 1 Minnesota	17-7	Same
1-1-65	Orange	No. 5 Texas beat No. 1 Alabama	21-17	Same

Date	Bowl	Teams Involved	Score	New No. 1
1-1-71	Cotton	No. 6 Notre Dame beat No. 1 Texas	24-11	Nebraska
12-31-73	Sugar	No. 3 Notre Dame beat No. 1 Alabama	24-23	Notre Dame
1-1-76	Rose	No. 11 UCLA beat No. 1 Ohio St.	23-10	Oklahoma
1-2-78	Cotton	No. 5 Notre Dame beat No. 1 Texas	38-10	Notre Dame
1-1-79	Sugar	No. 2 Alabama beat No. 1 Penn St.	14-7	Alabama
1-1-83	Sugar	No. 2 Penn St. beat No. 1 Georgia	27-23	Penn St.
1-2-84	Orange	No. 5 Miami (Fla.) beat No. 1 Nebraska	31-30	Miami (Fla.)
1-1-86	Orange	No. 3 Oklahoma beat No. 1 Penn St.	25-10	Oklahoma
1-2-87	Fiesta	No. 2 Penn St. beat No. 1 Miami (Fla.)	14-10	Penn St.
1-1-88	Orange	No. 2 Miami (Fla.) beat No. 1 Oklahoma	20-14	Miami (Fla.)
1-1-90	Orange	No. 4 Notre Dame beat No. 1 Colorado	21-6	Miami (Fla.)
1-1-93	Sugar	No. 2 Alabama beat No. 1 Miami (Fla.)	34-13	Alabama

Associated Press No. 1 Vs. No. 2 in Bowl Games

Date	Bowl	Teams, Score
1-1-63	Rose	No. 1 Southern Cal 42, No. 2 Wisconsin 37
1-1-64	Cotton	No. 1 Texas 28, No. 2 Navy 6
1-1-69	Rose	No. 1 Ohio St. 27, No. 2 Southern Cal 16
1-1-72	Orange	No. 1 Nebraska 28, No. 2 Alabama 6
1-1-79	Sugar	No. 2 Alabama 14, No. 1 Penn St. 7
1-1-83	Sugar	No. 2 Penn St. 27, No. 1 Georgia 23
1-2-87	Fiesta	No. 2 Penn St. 14, No. 1 Miami (Fla.) 10
1-1-88	Orange	No. 2 Miami (Fla.) 20, No. 1 Oklahoma 14
1-1-93	Sugar*	No. 2 Alabama 34, No. 1 Miami (Fla.) 13
1-1-94	Orange*	No. 1 Florida St. 18, No. 2 Nebraska 16

*Bowl alliance matched the No. 1 and No. 2 teams.

Bowl Games and the National Championship

(How the bowl games determined the national champion from 1965 to present. Year listed is the football season before the bowl games.)

Note: The national champion was selected before the bowl games as follows: Associated Press (1936-64 and 1966-67); United Press International (1950-73); Football Writers Association of America (1954), and National Football Foundation and Hall of Fame (1959-70).

1965 The Associated Press (AP) selected Alabama as national champion after it defeated Nebraska, 39-28, in the Orange Bowl on January 1, 1966.

1968 AP selected Ohio St. as national champion after it defeated Southern Cal, 27-16, in the Rose Bowl on January 1, 1969.

1969 AP selected Texas as national champion after it defeated Notre Dame, 21-17, in the Cotton Bowl on January 1, 1970.

1970 AP selected Nebraska as national champion after it defeated Louisiana St., 17-12, in the Orange Bowl on January 1, 1971.

1971 AP selected Nebraska as national champion after it defeated Alabama, 38-6, in the Orange Bowl on January 1, 1972.

1972 AP selected Southern Cal as national champion after it defeated Ohio St., 42-17, in the Rose Bowl on January 1, 1973.

1973 AP selected Notre Dame as national champion after it defeated Alabama, 24-23, in the Sugar Bowl on December 31, 1973.

Beginning in 1974, all four of the national polls waited until after the bowl-game results before selecting a national champion. The following list shows how the bowl games figured in the final national championship polls for AP and UPI:

1974 First year of the agreement between the American Football Coaches Association (AFCA) and the UPI Board of Coaches to declare any teams on NCAA probation ineligible for the poll. AP—Oklahoma (11-0-0) did not participate in a bowl game because of NCAA probation. UPI—Southern Cal (10-1-1) defeated Ohio St., 18-17, in the Rose Bowl on January 1, 1975.

1975 AP and UPI both selected Oklahoma (11-1-0). Coach Barry Switzer's Sooners defeated Michigan, 14-6, in the Orange Bowl on January 1, 1976. Ohio St. had led the AP poll for nine consecutive weeks until a 23-10 loss to UCLA in the Rose Bowl on January 1, 1976. Oklahoma had led the AP poll for the first four weeks of the year.

1976 AP and UPI both selected Tony Dorsett-led Pittsburgh (12-0-0). Pittsburgh whipped Georgia, 27-3, in the Sugar Bowl on January 1, 1977. Pittsburgh took over the No. 1 position from Michigan in the ninth week of the season en route to an undefeated year.

1977 AP and UPI were in agreement again, picking Notre Dame as national titlist. The Irish crushed previously undefeated and top-ranked Texas, 38-10, in the Cotton Bowl on January 2, 1978. Notre Dame was the sixth team to be ranked No. 1 during the 1977 season in the AP poll.

1978 This was the last time until the 1991 season that the two polls split on a national champion, with AP selecting Alabama (11-1-0) and UPI going for Southern Cal (12-1-0). Alabama, ranked No. 2 in the AP poll, upset No. 1 Penn St., 14-7, in the Sugar Bowl on January 1, 1979. Alabama had been ranked No. 1 in the first two weeks of the season until a 24-14 loss to Southern Cal.

BOWL/ALL-STAR RESULTS

1979 Unbeaten Alabama (12-0-0) was the unanimous choice of both polls. Bear Bryant's Tide whipped Arkansas easily, 24-9, in the Sugar Bowl on January 1, 1980, to claim the title.

1980 Georgia made it three No. 1s in a row for the Southeastern Conference with an undefeated season (12-0-0) to take the top spot in both polls. Vince Dooley's Bulldogs downed Notre Dame, 17-10, behind freshman phenom Herschel Walker in the Sugar Bowl on January 1, 1981.

1981 Both polls selected unbeaten Clemson (12-0-0). The Tigers gave coach Danny Ford the first Clemson national football championship with a 22-15 victory over Nebraska in the Orange Bowl on January 1, 1982. Clemson did not take over the AP No. 1 slot until the next-to-last poll of the year.

1982 AP and UPI both selected Penn St. (11-1-0). The Nittany Lions were No. 2 in the AP poll but knocked off No. 1 Georgia, 27-23, in the Sugar Bowl on January 1, 1983. Georgia had led the AP poll for the final five weeks of the season.

1983 AP and UPI had no choice but to select Miami (Fla.) as the unanimous champion after the No. 2 Hurricanes downed No. 1 Nebraska, 31-30, in the Orange Bowl on January 2, 1984. Many observers felt this may have been the most exciting Orange Bowl ever played as the Cornhuskers failed on a two-point conversion attempt with 48 seconds remaining. Nebraska had led the AP poll since the first week of the season.

1984 Unknown and a victim of the Mountain time zone, Brigham Young (13-0-0) overcame many obstacles to ascend to No. 1 in both polls. Coach LaVell Edwards' Cougars downed Michigan, 24-17, in the Holiday Bowl on December 21, 1984. BYU took over the top spot in the AP poll with three weeks left in the season after four other teams came and went as the top-rated team.

1985 Oklahoma (11-1-0) returned as the unanimous choice of both polls. Barry Switzer's Sooners knocked off top-rated Penn St., 25-10, in the Orange Bowl on January 1, 1986, to claim the national title.

1986 Penn St. (12-0-0) had to battle top-rated Miami (Fla.) in the Fiesta Bowl to take the top slot in both polls. Joe Paterno's No. 2 Nittany Lions upset the Hurricanes, 14-10, on January 2, 1987, to claim the championship. Miami (Fla.) had been ranked No. 1 for the final 10 weeks of the season.

1987 Miami (Fla.) (12-0-0) bounced back to a similar scenario as Jimmy Johnson's Hurricanes played underdog and finished ranked first in both polls. The No. 2 Hurricanes beat No. 1-ranked Oklahoma, 20-14, in the Orange Bowl on January 1, 1988. The Sooners had been the top-rated AP team for 13 of the season's 15 polls.

1988 Notre Dame (12-0-0) finished as the top team in both polls and gave the Fiesta Bowl its second national title game in three seasons. Lou Holtz's Irish whipped West Va., 34-21, on January 2, 1989, to claim their eighth AP title. Notre Dame took over the top spot in the poll from UCLA in the ninth week of the season.

1989 Miami (Fla.) (11-1-0) claimed its second national title in three years in both polls. The Hurricanes downed Alabama, 33-25, in the Sugar Bowl on January 1, 1990, while No. 1-ranked Colorado lost to Notre Dame, 21-6, in the Orange Bowl to clear the way. Notre Dame led the AP poll for 12 of the 15 weeks.

1990 Colorado (11-1-1) and Georgia Tech (11-0-1) split the polls for the first time since 1978 with the Buffs taking the AP vote and the Jackets the UPI. Colorado bounced back from a disappointing 1989 title march to edge Notre Dame, 10-9, in the Orange Bowl on January 1, 1991. Georgia Tech had little trouble with Nebraska, 45-21, in the Florida Citrus Bowl on January 1, 1991, to finish as Division I-A's only undefeated team.

1991 Miami (Fla.) (12-0-0) and Washington (12-0-0) kept Division I-A playoff talk alive with a split in the national polls for the second consecutive year. The Hurricanes took the AP vote, while the Huskies took both the USA Today/CNN and UPI polls. If either had stumbled in a bowl, the other would have been a unanimous selection. However, Washington drubbed Michigan, 34-14, in the Rose Bowl, and Miami had little trouble shutting out Nebraska, 22-0, in the Orange Bowl later that evening.

1992 No. 2 Alabama (13-0-0) turned in a magnificent performance in the Sugar Bowl by upsetting No. 1 Miami (Fla.), 34-13, in a game dominated by the Crimson Tide. It marked the first year of the bowl coalition, and the bowlmeisters managed to match the top two teams for the national championship. It also marked the 17th time that a No. 1 team in the AP poll was knocked off in a bowl game since 1951. Alabama was named No. 1 in all polls after the January 1, 1993, matchup.

1993 No. 1 Florida St. downed No. 2 Nebraska, 18-16, in the Orange Bowl to become a unanimous national champion. Notre Dame, winner over Texas A&M (24-21) in the Cotton Bowl, wanted to claim the title after beating the Seminoles in the regular season. But a late-season loss to Boston College cost the Irish in the polls. Florida St. was No. 1 in all polls after the bowls.

Bowl Results of Teams Ranked in The Associated Press Poll

The bowls and national polls have been perpetually linked since 1936, when The Associated Press introduced its weekly college football poll. The final AP poll was released at the end of the regular season until 1965, when bowl results were included for one year, dropped for two more and then added again in 1968 until the present. This is a list of the key bowl games as they related to the AP poll since 1936 (with pertinent references made to other polls where applicable).

(Key to polls: AP, Associated Press; UPI, United Press International; FW, Football Writers; NFF, National Football Foundation and Hall of Fame; USA/CNN, USA Today/Cable News Network; USA/NFF, USA Today/National Football Foundation and Hall of Fame; UPI/NFF, United Press International/National Football Foundation and Hall of Fame.)

1936 SUGAR—No. 6 Santa Clara beat No. 2 Louisiana St., 21-14; ROSE—No. 3 Pittsburgh beat No. 5 Washington, 21-0; ORANGE—No. 14 Duquesne beat unranked Mississippi St., 13-12; COTTON—No. 16 Texas Christian beat No. 20 Marquette, 16-6. (Minnesota selected No. 1 but did not play in a bowl)

1937 ROSE—No. 2 California beat No. 4 Alabama, 13-0; SUGAR—No. 9 Santa Clara beat No. 8 Louisiana St., 6-0; COTTON—No. 18 Rice beat No. 17 Colorado, 28-14. (Pittsburgh selected No. 1 but did not play in a bowl)

1938 SUGAR—No. 1 Texas Christian beat No. 6 Carnegie Mellon, 15-7; ORANGE—No. 2 Tennessee beat No. 4 Oklahoma, 17-0; ROSE—No. 7 Southern Cal beat No. 3 Duke, 7-3; COTTON—Unranked St. Mary's (Cal.) beat No. 11 Texas Tech, 20-13. (Texas Christian selected No. 1)

1939 SUGAR—No. 1 Texas A&M beat No. 5 Tulane, 14-13; ROSE—No. 3 Southern Cal beat No. 2 Tennessee, 14-0; ORANGE—No. 16 Georgia Tech beat No. 6 Missouri, 21-7; COTTON—No. 12 Clemson beat No. 11 Boston College, 6-3. (Texas A&M selected No. 1)

1940 ROSE—No. 2 Stanford beat No. 7 Nebraska, 21-13; SUGAR—No. 5 Boston College beat No. 4 Tennessee, 19-13; COTTON—No. 6 Texas A&M beat No. 12 Fordham, 13-12; ORANGE—No. 9 Mississippi St. beat No. 13 Georgetown, 14-7. (Minnesota selected No. 1 but did not play in a bowl)

1941 ROSE—No. 12 Oregon St. beat No. 2 Duke, 20-16 (played at Durham, N.C., because of World War II); SUGAR—No. 6 Fordham beat No. 7 Missouri, 2-0; COTTON—No. 20 Alabama beat No. 9 Texas A&M, 29-21; ORANGE—No. 14 Georgia beat unranked Texas Christian, 40-26. (Minnesota selected No. 1 but did not play in a bowl)

1942 ROSE—No. 2 Georgia beat No. 13 UCLA, 9-0; SUGAR—No. 7 Tennessee beat No. 4 Tulsa, 14-7; COTTON—No. 11 Texas beat No. 5 Georgia Tech, 14-7; ORANGE—No. 10 Alabama beat No. 8 Boston College, 37-21. (Ohio St. selected No. 1 but did not play in a bowl)

1943 ROSE—Unranked Southern Cal beat No. 12 Washington, 29-0; COTTON—No. 14 Texas tied unranked Randolph Field, 7-7; SUGAR—No. 13 Georgia Tech beat No. 15 Tulsa, 20-18. (Notre Dame selected No. 1 but did not play in a bowl)

1944 ROSE—No. 7 Southern Cal beat No. 12 Tennessee, 25-0; ORANGE—Unranked Tulsa beat No. 13 Georgia Tech, 26-12; No. 3 Randolph Field beat No. 20 Second Air Force, 13-6, in a battle of military powers. (Army selected No. 1 but did not play in a bowl)

1945 ROSE—No. 2 Alabama beat No. 11 Southern Cal, 34-14; COTTON—No. 10 Texas beat unranked Missouri, 40-27; ORANGE—Unranked Miami (Fla.) beat No. 16 Holy Cross, 13-6; SUGAR—No. 5 Oklahoma St. beat No. 7 St. Mary's (Cal.), 33-13. (Army selected No. 1 but did not play in a bowl)

1946 COTTON—No. 8 Louisiana St. tied No. 16 Arkansas, 0-0; ROSE—No. 5 Illinois beat No. 4 UCLA, 45-14; SUGAR—No. 3 Georgia beat No. 9 North Caro., 20-10; ORANGE—No. 10 Rice beat No. 7 Tennessee, 8-0. (Notre Dame selected No. 1 but did not play in a bowl)

1947 ORANGE—No. 10 Georgia Tech beat No. 12 Kansas, 20-14; ROSE—No. 2 Michigan beat No. 8 Southern Cal, 49-0; SUGAR—No. 6 Alabama, 27-7; COTTON—No. 3 Southern Methodist tied No. 4 Penn St., 13-13. (Notre Dame selected No. 1 but did not play in a bowl; Michigan also declared champion in vote after Rose Bowl victory but AP kept Notre Dame as vote of record)

1948 ROSE—No. 7 Northwestern beat No. 4 California, 20-14; COTTON—No. 10 Southern Methodist beat No. 9 Oregon, 21-13; SUGAR—No. 5 Oklahoma beat No. 3 North Caro., 14-6; ORANGE—Unranked Texas beat No. 8 Georgia, 41-28. (Michigan selected No. 1 but did not play in a bowl)

1949 ORANGE—No. 15 Santa Clara beat No. 11 Kentucky, 21-13; COTTON—No. 5 Rice beat No. 16 North Caro., 27-13; ROSE—No. 6 Ohio St. beat No. 3 California, 17-14; SUGAR—No. 2 Oklahoma beat No. 9 Louisiana St., 35-0. (Notre Dame selected No. 1 but did not play in a bowl)

1950 ROSE—No. 9 Michigan beat No. 5 California, 14-6; SUGAR—No. 7 Kentucky beat No. 1 Oklahoma, 13-7; ORANGE—No. 10 Clemson beat No. 15 Miami (Fla.), 15-14; COTTON—No. 4 Tennessee beat No. 3 Texas, 20-14. (Oklahoma selected No. 1 in vote before losing in Sugar Bowl)

1951 COTTON—No. 15 Kentucky beat No. 11 Texas Christian, 20-7; ORANGE—No. 5 Georgia Tech beat No. 9 Baylor, 17-14; ROSE—No. 4 Illinois beat No. 7 Stanford, 40-7; SUGAR—No. 3 Maryland beat No. 1 Tennessee, 28-13. (Tennessee selected No. 1 in vote before losing in Sugar Bowl)

1952 ROSE—No. 5 Southern Cal beat No. 11 Wisconsin, 7-0; SUGAR—No. 2 Georgia Tech beat No. 7 Mississippi, 24-7; ORANGE—No. 9 Alabama beat No. 14 Syracuse, 61-6; COTTON—No. 10 Texas beat No. 8 Tennessee, 16-0. (Michigan St. selected No. 1 but did not play in bowl)

1953 SUGAR—No. 8 Georgia Tech beat No. 10 West Va., 42-19; ORANGE—No. 4 Oklahoma beat No. 1 Maryland, 7-0; COTTON—No. 5 Rice beat No. 13 Alabama, 28-6; ROSE—No. 3 Michigan St. beat No. 5 UCLA, 28-20. (Maryland selected No. 1 before losing in Orange Bowl)

1954 ROSE—No. 1 Ohio St. beat No. 17 Southern Cal, 20-7; ORANGE—No. 14 Duke beat unranked Nebraska, 34-7; SUGAR—No. 5 Navy beat No. 6 Mississippi, 21-0; COTTON—Unranked Georgia Tech beat No. 10 Arkansas, 14-6. (Ohio St. remained No. 1 but UCLA named in UPI and FW polls)

1955 GATOR—Unranked Vanderbilt beat No. 8 Auburn, 25-13; ROSE—No. 2 Michigan St. beat No. 4 UCLA, 17-14; ORANGE—No. 8 Oklahoma beat No. 3 Maryland, 20-6; COTTON—No. 10 Mississippi beat No. 6 Texas Christian, 14-13; SUGAR—No. 7 Georgia Tech beat No. 11 Pittsburgh, 7-0. (Oklahoma remained No. 1)

1956 SUGAR—No. 11 Baylor beat No. 2 Tennessee, 13-7; ORANGE—No. 20 Colorado beat No. 19 Clemson, 27-21; GATOR—No. 4 Georgia Tech beat No. 13 Pittsburgh, 21-14; ROSE—No. 3 Iowa beat No. 10 Oregon St., 35-19; COTTON—No. 14 Texas Christian beat No. 8 Syracuse, 28-27. (Oklahoma selected No. 1 but did not play in a bowl)

1957 GATOR—No. 13 Tennessee beat No. 9 Texas A&M, 3-0; ROSE—No. 2 Ohio St. beat unranked Oregon, 10-7; COTTON—No. 5 Navy beat No. 8 Rice, 20-7; ORANGE—No. 4 Oklahoma beat No. 16 Duke, 48-21; SUGAR—No. 7 Mississippi beat No. 11 Texas, 39-7. (Auburn selected No. 1 but did not play in a bowl; Ohio St. selected No. 1 in both UPI and FW polls)

1958 SUGAR—No. 1 Louisiana St. beat No. 12 Clemson, 7-0; COTTON—No. 6 Air Force tied No. 10 Texas Christian, 0-0; ROSE—No. 2 Iowa beat No. 16 California, 38-12; ORANGE—No. 5 Oklahoma beat No. 9 Syracuse, 21-6. (Louisiana St. remained No. 1 in AP and UPI but Iowa selected in FW poll)

1959 COTTON—No. 1 Syracuse beat No. 4 Texas, 23-14; ROSE—No. 8 Washington beat No. 6 Wisconsin, 44-8; ORANGE—No. 5 Georgia beat No. 18 Missouri, 14-0; SUGAR—No. 2 Mississippi beat No. 3 Louisiana St., 21-0; BLUEBON-NET—No. 11 Clemson beat No. 7 Texas Christian, 23-7; LIBERTY—No. 12 Penn St. beat No. 10 Alabama, 7-0; GATOR—No. 9 Arkansas beat unranked Georgia Tech, 14-7. (Syracuse selected No. 1 by all four polls)

1960 ROSE—No. 6 Washington beat No. 1 Minnesota, 17-7; COTTON—No. 10 Duke beat No. 7 Arkansas, 7-6; SUGAR—No. 2 Mississippi beat unranked Rice, 14-6; ORANGE—No. 5 Missouri beat No. 4 Navy, 21-14; BLUEBONNET—No. 9 Alabama tied unranked Texas, 3-3. (Minnesota selected No. 1 by AP, UPI and NFF before losing in Rose Bowl; Mississippi named No. 1 in FW poll)

1961 COTTON—No. 3 Texas beat No. 5 Mississippi, 12-7; SUGAR—No. 1 Alabama beat No. 9 Arkansas, 10-3; ORANGE—No. 4 Louisiana St. beat No. 7 Colorado, 25-7; GOTHAM—Unranked Baylor beat No. 10 Utah St., 24-9; ROSE—No. 6 Minnesota beat No. 16 UCLA, 21-3. (Alabama selected No. 1 in AP, UPI and NFF but Ohio St. picked by FW poll)

1962 ROSE—No. 1 Southern Cal beat No. 2 Wisconsin, 42-37; SUGAR—No. 3 Mississippi beat No. 6 Arkansas, 17-13; COTTON—No. 7 Louisiana St. beat No. 4 Texas, 13-0; GATOR—Unranked Florida beat No. 9 Penn St., 17-7; ORANGE—No. 5 Alabama beat No. 8 Oklahoma, 17-0. (Southern Cal selected No. 1 by all four polls)

1963 COTTON—No. 1 Texas beat No. 2 Navy, 28-6; ORANGE—No. 6 Nebraska beat No. 5 Auburn, 13-7; ROSE—No. 3 Illinois beat unranked Washington, 17-7; SUGAR—No. 8 Alabama beat No. 7 Mississippi, 12-7. (Texas selected No. 1 by all four polls)

1964 ORANGE—No. 5 Texas beat No. 1 Alabama, 21-17; ROSE—No. 4 Michigan beat No. 8 Oregon St., 34-7; COTTON—No. 2 Arkansas beat No. 6 Nebraska, 10-7; SUGAR—No. 7 Louisiana St. beat unranked Syracuse, 13-10. (Alabama selected No. 1 by AP and UPI before losing in the Orange Bowl, while Arkansas No. 1 in FW poll and Notre Dame No. 1 in NFF poll)

1965 *(First year final poll taken after bowl games)* ROSE—No. 5 UCLA beat No. 1 Michigan St., 14-12; COTTON—Unranked Louisiana St. beat No. 2 Arkansas, 14-7; SUGAR—No. 6 Missouri beat unranked Florida, 20-18; ORANGE—No. 4 Alabama beat No. 3 Nebraska, 39-28; BLUEBONNET—No. 7 Tennessee beat unranked Tulsa, 27-6; GATOR—Unranked Georgia Tech beat No. 10 Texas Tech, 31-21. (Alabama selected No. 1 in final poll but Michigan St. named by UPI and NFF polls and they tied in FW poll)

1966 *(Returned to final poll taken before bowls)* SUGAR—No. 3 Alabama beat No. 6 Nebraska, 34-7; ROSE—No. 7 Purdue beat unranked Southern Cal, 14-13; COTTON—No. 4 Georgia beat No. 10 Southern Methodist, 24-9; ORANGE—Unranked Florida beat No. 8 Georgia Tech, 27-12; LIBERTY—No. 9 Miami (Fla.) beat unranked Virginia Tech, 14-7. (Notre Dame selected No. 1 by AP, UPI and FW polls and tied with Michigan St. in NFF poll; neither team played in a bowl game and they tied in a regular-season game)

1967 ROSE—No. 1 Southern Cal beat No. 4 Indiana, 14-3; SUGAR—Unranked Louisiana St. beat No. 6 Wyoming, 20-13; ORANGE—No. 3 Oklahoma beat No. 2 Tennessee, 26-24; COTTON—Unranked Texas A&M beat No. 8 Alabama, 20-16; GATOR—No. 10 Penn St. tied unranked Florida St., 17-17. (Southern Cal selected No. 1 in all four polls)

1968 *(Returned to final poll taken after bowl games)* ROSE—No. 1 Ohio St. beat No. 2 Southern Cal, 27-16; SUGAR—No. 9 Arkansas beat No. 4 Georgia, 16-2; ORANGE—No. 3 Penn St. beat No. 6 Kansas, 15-14; COTTON—No. 5 Texas beat No. 8 Tennessee, 36-13; BLUEBONNET—No. 20 Southern Methodist beat No. 10 Oklahoma, 28-27; GATOR—No. 16 Missouri beat No. 12 Alabama, 35-10. (Ohio St. remained No. 1)

1969 COTTON—No. 1 Texas beat No. 9 Notre Dame, 21-17; SUGAR—No. 13 Mississippi beat No. 3 Arkansas, 27-22; ORANGE—No. 2 Penn St. beat No. 6 Missouri, 10-3; ROSE—No. 5 Southern Cal beat No. 7 Michigan, 10-3. (Texas remained No. 1)

1970 ROSE—No. 12 Stanford beat No. 2 Ohio St., 27-17; COTTON—No. 6 Notre Dame beat No. 1 Texas, 24-11; ROSE—No. 12 Stanford beat No. 2 Ohio St., 27-17; SUGAR—No. 5 Tennessee beat No. 11 Air Force, 34-13; ORANGE—No. 3 Nebraska beat No. 8 Louisiana St., 17-12; PEACH—No. 9 Arizona St. beat unranked North Caro., 48-26. (Nebraska selected No. 1 in AP and FW polls while Texas was No. 1 in UPI and tied with Ohio St. in NFF poll)

1971 ORANGE—No. 1 Nebraska beat No. 2 Alabama, 38-6; SUGAR—No. 3 Oklahoma beat No. 5 Auburn, 40-22; ROSE—No. 16 Stanford beat No. 4 Michigan, 13-12; GATOR—No. 12 Georgia beat unranked North Caro., 7-3; COTTON—No. 10 Penn St. beat No. 12 Texas, 30-6; FIESTA—No. 8 Arizona St. beat unranked Florida St., 45-38; BLUEBONNET—No. 7 Colorado beat No. 15 Houston, 29-17. (Nebraska remained No. 1 in all four polls)

1972 ROSE—No. 1 Southern Cal beat No. 3 Ohio St., 42-17; COTTON—No. 7 Texas beat No. 4 Alabama, 17-13; SUGAR—No. 2 Oklahoma beat No. 5 Penn St., 14-0; ORANGE—No. 9 Nebraska beat No. 12 Notre Dame, 40-6; GATOR—No. 6 Auburn beat No. 13 Colorado, 24-3; BLUEBONNET—No. 11 Tennessee beat No. 10 Louisiana St., 24-17. (Southern Cal remained No. 1 in all four polls)

1973 SUGAR—No. 3 Notre Dame beat No. 1 Alabama, 24-23; ROSE—No. 4 Ohio St. beat No. 7 Southern Cal, 42-21; ORANGE—No. 6 Penn St. beat No. 13 Louisiana St., 16-9; COTTON—No. 12 Nebraska beat No. 8 Texas, 19-3; FIESTA—No. 10 Arizona St. beat unranked Pittsburgh, 28-7; BLUEBONNET—No. 14 Houston beat No. 17 Tulane, 47-7. (Notre Dame selected No. 1 in AP, FW and NFF polls, Alabama named No. 1 by UPI but No. 2 Oklahoma was on probation and could not go to a bowl game)

1974 ROSE—No. 5 Southern Cal beat No. 3 Ohio St., 18-17; ORANGE—No. 9 Notre Dame beat No. 2 Alabama, 13-11; GATOR—No. 6 Auburn beat No. 11 Texas, 27-3; COTTON—No. 7 Penn St. beat No. 12 Baylor, 41-20; SUGAR—No. 8 Nebraska beat No. 18 Florida, 13-10; LIBERTY—Unranked Tennessee beat No. 10 Maryland, 7-3. (Oklahoma selected No. 1 in AP poll despite being on probation and not able to participate in bowl game; Southern Cal named No. 1 by UPI, FW and NFF polls)

1975 ROSE—No. 11 UCLA beat No. 1 Ohio St., 23-10; ORANGE—No. 3 Oklahoma beat No. 5 Michigan, 14-6; LIBERTY—No. 17 Southern Cal beat No. 2 Texas A&M, 20-0; SUGAR—No. 4 Alabama beat No. 8 Penn St., 13-6; FIESTA—No. 7 Arizona St. beat No. 6 Nebraska, 17-14; COTTON—No. 18 Arkansas beat No. 12 Georgia, 31-10; BLUEBONNET—No. 9 Texas beat No. 10 Colorado, 38-21. (Oklahoma selected No. 1 in all four polls)

1976 SUGAR—No. 1 Pittsburgh beat No. 5 Georgia, 27-3; ROSE—No. 3 Southern Cal beat No. 2 Michigan, 14-6; COTTON—No. 6 Houston beat No. 4 Maryland, 30-21; LIBERTY—No. 16 Alabama beat No. 7 UCLA, 36-6; ORANGE—No. 11 Ohio St. beat No. 12 Colorado, 27-10; FIESTA—No. 8 Oklahoma beat unranked Wyoming, 41-7; SUN—No. 10 Texas A&M beat unranked Florida, 37-14; BLUEBONNET—No. 13 Nebraska beat No. 9 Texas Tech, 27-24. (Pittsburgh remained No. 1 in all four polls)

1977 COTTON—No. 5 Notre Dame beat No. 1 Texas, 38-10; ORANGE—No. 6 Arkansas beat No. 2 Oklahoma, 31-6; SUGAR—No. 3 Alabama beat No. 9 Ohio St., 35-6; ROSE—No. 13 Washington beat No. 4 Michigan, 27-20; FIESTA—No. 8 Penn St. beat No. 15 Arizona St., 42-30; GATOR—No. 10 Pittsburgh beat No. 11 Clemson, 34-3. (Notre Dame selected No. 1 in all four polls)

1978 SUGAR—No. 2 Alabama beat No. 1 Penn St., 14-7; ROSE—No. 3 Southern Cal beat No. 5 Michigan, 17-10; ORANGE—No. 4 Oklahoma beat No. 6 Nebraska, 31-24; COTTON—No. 10 Notre Dame beat No. 9 Houston, 35-34; GATOR—No. 7 Clemson beat No. 20 Ohio St., 17-15; FIESTA—No. 8 Arkansas tied No. 15 UCLA, 10-10. (Alabama selected No. 1 in AP, FW and NFF polls while Southern Cal named in UPI)

1979 ROSE—No. 3 Southern Cal beat No. 1 Ohio St., 17-16; SUGAR—No. 2 Alabama beat No. 6 Arkansas, 24-9; ORANGE—No. 5 Oklahoma beat No. 4 Florida St., 24-7; COTTON—No. 8 Houston beat No. 7 Nebraska, 17-14; SUN—No. 13 Washington beat No. 11 Texas, 14-7; FIESTA—No. 10 Pittsburgh beat unranked Arizona, 16-10. (Alabama selected No. 1 in all four polls)

1980 SUGAR—No. 1 Georgia beat No. 7 Notre Dame, 17-10; ORANGE—No. 4 Oklahoma beat No. 2 Florida St., 18-17; ROSE—No. 5 Michigan beat No. 16 Washington, 23-6; COTTON—No. 9 Alabama beat No. 6 Baylor, 30-2; GATOR—No. 3 Pittsburgh beat No. 18 South Caro., 37-9; SUN—No. 8 Nebraska beat No. 17 Mississippi St., 31-17; FIESTA—No. 10 Penn St. beat No. 11 Ohio St., 31-19; BLUEBONNET—No. 13 North Caro. beat unranked Texas, 16-7. (Georgia remained No. 1 in all four polls)

1981 ORANGE—No. 1 Clemson beat No. 4 Nebraska, 22-15; SUGAR—No. 10 Pittsburgh beat No. 2 Georgia, 24-20; COTTON—No. 6 Texas beat No. 3 Alabama, 14-12; GATOR—No. 11 North Caro. beat unranked Arkansas, 31-27; ROSE—No. 12 Washington beat No. 13 Iowa, 28-0; FIESTA—No. 7 Penn St. beat No. 8 Southern Cal, 26-10. (Clemson remained No. 1 in all four polls)

1982 SUGAR—No. 2 Penn St. beat No. 1 Georgia, 27-23; ORANGE—No. 3 Nebraska beat No. 13 Louisiana St., 21-20; COTTON—No. 4 Southern Methodist beat No. 6 Pittsburgh, 7-3; ROSE—No. 5 UCLA beat No. 19 Michigan, 24-14; ALOHA—No. 9 Washington beat No. 16 Maryland, 21-20; FIESTA—No. 11 Arizona St. beat No. 12 Oklahoma, 32-21; BLUEBONNET—No. 14 Arkansas beat unranked Florida, 28-24. (Penn St. selected No. 1 in all four polls)

1983 ORANGE—No. 5 Miami (Fla.) beat No. 1 Nebraska, 31-30; COTTON—No. 7 Georgia beat No. 2 Texas, 10-9; SUGAR—No. 3 Auburn beat No. 8 Michigan, 9-7; ROSE—Unranked UCLA beat No. 4 Illinois, 45-9; HOLIDAY—No. 9 Brigham Young beat unranked Missouri, 21-17; GATOR—No. 11 Florida beat No. 10 Iowa, 14-6; FIESTA—No. 14 Ohio St. beat No. 15 Pittsburgh, 28-23. (Miami, Fla., selected No. 1 in all four polls)

1984 HOLIDAY—No. 1 Brigham Young beat unranked Michigan, 24-17; ORANGE—No. 4 Washington beat No. 2 Oklahoma, 28-17; SUGAR—No. 5 Nebraska beat No. 11 Louisiana St., 28-10; ROSE—No. 18 Southern Cal beat No. 6 Ohio St., 20-17; COTTON—No. 8 Boston College beat unranked Houston, 45-28; GATOR—No. 9 Oklahoma beat No. 7 South Caro., 21-14; ALOHA—No. 10 Southern Methodist beat No. 17 Notre Dame, 27-20. (Brigham Young remained No. 1 in all four polls)

1985 ORANGE—No. 3 Oklahoma beat No. 1 Penn St., 25-10; SUGAR—No. 8 Tennessee beat No. 2 Miami (Fla.), 35-7; ROSE—No. 13 UCLA beat No. 4 Iowa, 45-28; COTTON—No. 11 Texas A&M beat No. 16 Auburn, 36-16; FIESTA—No. 5 Michigan beat No. 7 Nebraska, 27-23; BLUEBONNET—No. 10 Air Force beat unranked Texas, 24-16. (Oklahoma selected No. 1 in all four polls)

1986 FIESTA—No. 2 Penn St. beat No. 1 Miami (Fla.), 14-10; ORANGE—No. 3 Oklahoma beat No. 9 Arkansas, 42-8; ROSE—No. 7 Arizona St. beat No. 4 Michigan, 22-15; SUGAR—No. 6 Nebraska beat No. 5 Louisiana St., 30-15; COTTON—No. 11 Ohio St. beat No. 8 Texas A&M, 28-12; CITRUS—No. 10 Auburn beat unranked Southern Cal, 16-7; SUN—No. 13 Alabama beat No. 12 Washington, 28-6. (Penn St. selected No. 1 in all four polls)

BOWL/ALL-STAR RESULTS

1987 ORANGE—No. 2 Miami (Fla.) beat No. 1 Oklahoma, 20-14; FIESTA—No. 3 Florida St. beat No. 5 Nebraska, 31-28; SUGAR—No. 4 Syracuse tied No. 6 Auburn, 16-16; ROSE—No. 8 Michigan St. beat No. 16 Southern Cal, 20-17; COTTON—No. 13 Texas A&M beat No. 12 Notre Dame, 35-10; GATOR—No. 7 Louisiana St. beat No. 9 South Caro., 30-13; ALOHA—No. 10 UCLA beat unranked Florida, 20-16. (Miami, Fla., selected No. 1 in all four polls)

1988 FIESTA—No. 1 Notre Dame beat No. 3 West Va., 34-21; ORANGE—No. 2 Miami (Fla.) beat No. 6 Nebraska, 23-3; SUGAR—No. 4 Florida St. beat No. 7 Auburn, 13-7; ROSE—No. 11 Michigan beat No. 5 Southern Cal, 22-14; COTTON—No. 9 UCLA beat No. 8 Arkansas, 17-3; CITRUS—No. 13 Clemson beat No. 10 Oklahoma, 13-6. (Notre Dame selected No. 1 in all four polls)

1989 ORANGE—No. 4 Notre Dame beat No. 1 Colorado, 21-6; SUGAR—No. 2 Miami (Fla.) beat No. 7 Alabama, 33-25; ROSE—No. 12 Southern Cal beat No. 3 Michigan, 17-10; COTTON—No. 8 Tennessee beat No. 10 Arkansas, 31-27; FIESTA—No. 5 Florida St. beat No. 6 Nebraska, 41-17; HALL OF FAME—No. 9 Auburn beat No. 21 Ohio St., 31-14; CITRUS—No. 11 Illinois beat No. 15 Virginia, 31-21. (Miami, Fla., selected No. 1 in all four polls)

1990 ORANGE—No. 1 Colorado beat No. 5 Notre Dame, 10-9; CITRUS—No. 2 Georgia Tech beat No. 19 Nebraska, 45-21; COTTON—No. 4 Miami (Fla.) beat No. 3 Texas, 46-3; BLOCKBUSTER—No. 6 Florida St. beat No. 7 Penn St., 24-17; ROSE—No. 8 Washington beat No. 17 Iowa, 46-34; GATOR—No. 12 Michigan beat No. 15 Mississippi, 35-3; SUGAR—No. 10 Tennessee beat unranked Virginia, 23-22. (Colorado selected No. 1 in AP, FW and NFF polls but Georgia Tech picked in UPI poll)

1991 ORANGE—No. 1 Miami (Fla.) beat No. 11 Nebraska, 22-0; ROSE—No. 2 Washington beat No. 4 Michigan, 34-14; COTTON—No. 5 Florida St. beat No. 9 Texas A&M, 10-3; BLOCKBUSTER—No. 8 Alabama beat No. 15 Colorado, 30-25; SUGAR—No. 18 Notre Dame beat No. 3 Florida, 39-28; FIESTA—No. 6 Penn St. beat No. 10 Tennessee, 42-17; CITRUS—No. 14 California beat No. 13 Clemson, 37-13; PEACH—No. 12 East Caro. beat No. 21 North Caro. St., 37-34; HOLIDAY—No. 7 Iowa tied unranked Brigham Young, 13-13. (Miami, Fla., selected No. 1 in AP poll while Washington named in USA/CNN, NFF and FW polls)

1992 SUGAR—No. 2 Alabama beat No. 1 Miami (Fla.), 34-13; GATOR—No. 14 Florida beat No. 12 North Caro. St., 27-10; COTTON—No. 5 Notre Dame beat No. 4 Texas A&M, 28-3; HALL OF FAME—No. 17 Tennessee beat No. 16 Boston College, 38-23; CITRUS—No. 8 Georgia beat No. 15 Ohio St., 21-14; ROSE—No. 7 Michigan beat No. 9 Washington, 38-31; ORANGE—No. 3 Florida St. beat No. 11 Nebraska, 27-14; FIESTA—No. 6 Syracuse beat No. 10 Colorado, 26-22; BLOCKBUSTER—No. 13 Stanford beat No. 21 Penn St., 24-3; PEACH—No. 19 North Caro. beat No. 24 Mississippi St., 21-17; COPPER—No. 18 Washington St. beat unranked Utah, 31-28. (Alabama selected No. 1 in all four polls)

1993 ORANGE—No. 1 Florida St. beat No. 2 Nebraska, 18-16; SUGAR—No. 8 Florida beat No. 3 West Va., 41-7; ROSE—No. 9 Wisconsin beat No. 14 UCLA, 21-16; COTTON—No. 4 Notre Dame beat No. 7 Texas A&M, 24-21; CARQUEST—No. 15 Boston College beat unranked Virginia, 31-13; FIESTA—No. 16 Arizona beat No. 10 Miami (Fla.), 29-0; FLORIDA CITRUS—No. 3 Penn St. beat No. 6 Tennessee, 31-13; HALL OF FAME—No. 23 Michigan beat unranked North Caro. St., 42-7; GATOR—No. 18 Alabama beat No. 12 North Caro., 24-10; PEACH—No. 24 Clemson beat unranked Kentucky, 14-13; INDEPENDENCE—No. 22 Virginia Tech beat unranked Indiana, 45-20; HOLIDAY—No. 11 Ohio St. beat unranked Brigham Young, 28-21; COPPER—No. 20 Kansas St. beat unranked Wyoming, 52-17; LIBERTY—No. 25 Louisville beat unranked Michigan St., 18-7; ALOHA—No. 17 Colorado beat No. 25 Fresno St., 41-30; JOHN HANCOCK—No. 19 Oklahoma beat unranked Texas Tech, 41-10. (Florida St. selected in all four major polls—AP, FW, USA/CNN and USA/NFF)

Most Consecutive Bowl-Game Victories

(Bowls do not have to be in consecutive years)

College	Victories (Years)
Florida St.	9 (1985-86-88-89-90-90-92-93-94)
Southern Cal	9 (1923-24-30-32-33-39-40-44-45)
UCLA	8 (1983-84-85-86-86-87-89-91)
Georgia Tech	8 (1947-48-52-53-54-55-56-56)
Alabama	6 (1975-76-78-79-80-81)
Syracuse	5 (1989-89-90-92-93)
Notre Dame	5 (1973-75-76-78-79)
Arizona St.	5 (1970-71-72-73-75)
Alabama	4 (1982-83-85-86)
Air Force	4 (1982-83-84-85)
Notre Dame	3 (1992-93-94)
Alabama	3 (1991-91-93)
California	3 (1990-92-93)

Most Consecutive Seasons With Bowl-Game Victories

*9 **Florida St.**—85 Gator, Oklahoma St. 34-23; 86 All-American, Indiana 27-13; 87 Fiesta, Nebraska 31-28; 88 Sugar, Auburn 13-7; 89 Fiesta, Nebraska 41-17; 90 Blockbuster, Penn St. 24-17; 92 Cotton, Texas A&M 10-2; 93 Orange, Nebraska 27-14; 94 Orange, Nebraska 18-16. Coach: Bobby Bowden.

7 **UCLA**—83 Rose, Michigan 24-14; 84 Rose, Illinois 45-9; 85 Fiesta, Miami (Fla.) 39-37; 86 Rose, Iowa 45-28; 86 Freedom, Brigham Young 31-10; 87 Aloha, Florida 20-16; 89 Cotton, Arkansas, 17-3. Coach: Terry Donahue.

6 **Alabama**—75 Sugar, Penn St. 13-6; 76 Liberty, UCLA 36-6; 78 Sugar, Ohio St. 35-6; 79 Sugar, Penn St. 14-7; 80 Sugar, Arkansas 24-9; 81 Cotton, Baylor 30-2. Coach: Paul "Bear" Bryant.

6 **Nebraska**—69 Sun, Georgia 45-6; 71 Orange, Louisiana St. 17-12; 72 Orange, Alabama 38-6; 73 Orange, Notre Dame 40-6; 74 Cotton, Texas 19-3; 74 Sugar, Florida 13-10. Coaches: Bob Devaney first 4 games, Tom Osborne last 2.

6 **Georgia Tech**—52 Orange, Baylor 17-14; 53 Sugar, Mississippi 24-7; 54 Sugar, West Va. 42-19; 55 Cotton, Arkansas 14-6; 56 Sugar, Pittsburgh 7-0; 56 Gator, Pittsburgh 21-14. Coach: Bobby Dodd.

*Active streak.

Active Consecutive Appearances in Bowl Games

(Must have appeared in 1993-94 bowls)

Team	Appearances	Team	Appearances
Nebraska	25	Notre Dame	7
Michigan	19	Alabama	5
Brigham Young	16	Tennessee	5
Florida St.	12	Texas A&M	5
Miami (Fla.)	11		

Most Bowl Teams Faced in 1993

(Teams that faced the most 1993-94 bowl teams during their 1993 regular-season schedule)

Team	No. Faced	Team	No. Faced
Maryland	8	Louisiana St.	6
Northwestern	8	Michigan	6
Purdue	8	Minnesota	6
Florida St.	7	Missouri	6
Kansas	7	Notre Dame	6
Michigan St.	7	Penn St.	6
Pittsburgh	7	San Diego St.	6
Duke	6	Southern Cal	6
Illinois	6	Stanford	6
Indiana	6	UTEP	6
Iowa St.	6		

Undefeated, Untied Team Matchups in Bowl Games

Bowl	Date	Winner (Record Going In, Coach)	Loser (Record Going In, Coach)
Rose	1-1-21	California 28 (8-0, Andy Smith)	Ohio St. 0 (7-0, John Wilce)
Rose	1-2-22	0-0 tie: California (9-0, Andy Smith)	
		Wash. & Jeff. (10-0, Earle "Greasy" Neale)	
Rose	1-1-27	7-7 tie: Alabama (9-0, Wallace Wade)	
		Stanford (10-0, Glenn "Pop" Warner)	
Rose	1-1-31	Alabama 24 (9-0, Wallace Wade)	Washington St. 0 (9-0, Orin "Babe" Hollingbery)
Orange	1-2-39	Tennessee 17 (10-0, Bob Neyland)	Oklahoma 0 (10-0, Tom Stidham)
Sugar	1-1-41	Boston College 19 (10-0, Frank Leahy)	Tennessee 13 (10-0, Bob Neyland)
Sugar	1-1-52	Maryland 28 (9-0, Jim Tatum)	Tennessee 13 (10-0, Bob Neyland)
Orange	1-2-56	Oklahoma 20 (10-0, Bud Wilkinson)	Maryland 6 (10-0, Jim Tatum)
Orange	1-1-72	Nebraska 38 (12-0, Bob Devaney)	Alabama 6 (11-0, Paul "Bear" Bryant)
Sugar	12-31-73	Notre Dame 24 (10-0, Ara Parseghian)	Alabama 23 (11-0, Paul "Bear" Bryant)
Fiesta	1-2-87	Penn St. 14 (11-0, Joe Paterno)	Miami (Fla.) 10 (11-0, Jimmy Johnson)
Orange	1-1-88	Miami (Fla.) 20 (11-0, Jimmy Johnson)	Oklahoma 14 (11-0, Barry Switzer)
Fiesta	1-2-89	Notre Dame 34 (11-0, Lou Holtz)	West Va. 21 (11-0, Don Nehlen)
Sugar	1-1-93	Alabama 34 (12-0, Gene Stallings)	Miami (Fla.) 13 (11-0, Dennis Erickson)

Undefeated Team Matchups in Bowl Games

(Both teams were undefeated but one or both was tied one or more times)

Bowl	Date	Winner (Record Going In, Coach)	Loser (Record Going In, Coach)
Rose	1-1-25	Notre Dame 27 (9-0, Knute Rockne)	Stanford 10 (7-0-1, Glenn "Pop" Warner)
Rose	1-1-26	Alabama 20 (9-0, Wallace Wade)	Washington 19 (10-0-1, Enoch Bagshaw)
Rose	1-2-33	Southern Cal 35 (9-0, Howard Jones)	Pittsburgh 0 (8-0-2, Jock Sutherland)
Rose	1-1-35	Alabama 29 (9-0, Frank Thomas)	Stanford 13 (9-0-1, Claude "Tiny" Thornhill)
Rose	1-1-38	California 13 (9-0-1, Leonard "Stub" Allison)	Alabama 0 (9-0, Frank Thomas)
Rose	1-1-40	Southern Cal 14 (7-0-2, Howard Jones)	Tennessee 0 (10-0, Bob Neyland)
Sugar	1-1-40	Texas A&M 14 (10-0, Homer Norton)	Tulane 13 (8-0-1, Lowell "Red" Dawson)
Rose	1-1-45	Southern Cal 25 (7-0-2, Jeff Cravath)	Tennessee 0 (7-0-1, John Barnhill)
Cotton	1-1-48	13-13 tie: Penn St. (9-0, Bob Higgins)	
		Southern Methodist (9-0-1, Matty Bell)	
Orange	1-1-51	Clemson 15 (8-0-1, Frank Howard)	Miami (Fla.) 14 (9-0-1, Andy Gustafson)
Sugar	1-1-53	Georgia Tech 24 (11-0, Bobby Dodd)	Mississippi 7 (8-0-2, John Vaught)
Rose	1-1-69	Ohio St. 27 (9-0, Woody Hayes)	Southern Cal 16 (9-0-1, John McKay)
Rose	1-1-80	Southern Cal 17 (10-0-1, John Robinson)	Ohio St. 16 (11-0, Earle Bruce)
California	12-14-85	Fresno St. 51 (10-0-1, Jim Sweeney)	Bowling Green 7 (11-0, Denny Stolz)

Major-Bowl Rematches of Regular-Season Opponents

Date	Regular Season	Date	Bowl-Game Rematch
10-9-43	Texas A&M 28, Louisiana St. 13	1-1-44	(Orange) Louisiana St. 19, Texas A&M 14
10-6-56	Iowa 14, Oregon St. 13	1-1-57	(Rose) Iowa 35, Oregon St. 19
10-31-59	Louisiana St. 7, Mississippi 3	1-1-60	(Sugar) Mississippi 21, Louisiana St. 0
9-18-65	Michigan St. 13, UCLA 3	1-1-66	(Rose) UCLA 14, Michigan St. 12
10-4-75	Ohio St. 41, UCLA 20	1-1-76	(Rose) UCLA 23, Ohio St. 10
11-11-78	Nebraska 17, Oklahoma 14	1-1-79	(Orange) Oklahoma 31, Nebraska 24
9-25-82	UCLA 31, Michigan 27	1-1-83	(Rose) UCLA 24, Michigan 14
9-7-87	Michigan St. 27, Southern Cal 13	1-1-88	(Rose) Michigan St. 20, Southern Cal 17

Alabama's Gene Stallings (left) and Dennis Erickson of Miami (Florida) chat before their teams square off in the 1993 Sugar Bowl. The game, won by Alabama, 34-13, was the last matchup of undefeated, untied teams in a bowl game.

Bowl-Game Facts

The Bowl/Basketball Connection

Nine times in history, a football bowl winner also won the NCAA basketball championship during the same academic year. They are as follows:

Year	School	Bowl	Date of Bowl
1992-93	North Caro.	Peach	1-2-93
1988-89	Michigan	Rose	1-2-89
1981-82	North Caro.	Gator	12-28-81
1973-74	North Caro. St.	Liberty	12-17-73
1965-66	UTEP	Sun	12-31-65
1950-51	Kentucky	Sugar	1-1-51
1947-48	Kentucky	Great Lakes	12-6-47
1945-46	Oklahoma St.	Sugar	1-1-46
1944-45	Oklahoma St.	Cotton	1-1-45

One-Time Wonders

Ten major-college teams have played in only one bowl game in their football history, and only five of those have posted victories. The winners were Eastern Mich., Memphis, Nevada-Las Vegas, Northern Ill. and Northwestern. The one-time bowlers are as follows:

School	Date	Bowl	Opponent (Score)
Cal St. Fullerton	12-17-83	California	Northern Ill. (13-20)
Central Mich.	12-8-90	California	San Jose St. (24-48)
Eastern Mich.	12-12-87	California	San Jose St. (30-27)
Kent	12-29-72	Tangerine	Tampa (18-21)
Long Beach St.	12-19-70	Pasadena	Louisville (24-24)
Memphis	12-18-71	Pasadena	San Jose St. (28-9)
Nevada-Las Vegas	12-15-84	California	Toledo (30-13)
Northern Ill.	12-17-83	California	Cal St. Fullerton (20-13)
Northwestern	1-1-49	Rose	California (20-14)
Rutgers	12-16-78	Garden State	Arizona St. (18-34)

Year-by-Year Bowl Facts

(A note about bowl-game dates: Traditionally, bowl games have been played on January 1, but as more bowl games joined the holiday lineup, schedule adjustments were made whereby some bowl games are now played as early as mid-December. In the interest of avoiding confusion, all years referred to in bowl records are the actual calendar year in which the bowl game was played.)

1917 Coach Hugo Bezdek led the first of three teams to the Rose Bowl from 1917 to 1923. His Oregon team beat Pennsylvania, 14-0, in 1917; his Mare Island squad defeated Camp Lewis, 19-7, in 1918; and his Penn St. team lost to Southern Cal, 14-3, in 1923. In his 1923 trip with the Nittany Lions, Bezdek almost came to blows with Southern Cal coach Elmer "Gloomy Gus" Henderson because Penn St. did not arrive for the game until an hour after the scheduled kickoff time. Henderson accused Bezdek of not taking the field until the hot California sun had gone down to give his winterized Easterners an advantage.

1919 George Halas (yes, "Papa Bear") was the player of the game for Great Lakes Naval Training Station in Chicago as the Sailors shut out Mare Island, 17-0, in another of the wartime Rose Bowls.

1923 The first Rose Bowl game actually played in the stadium in Pasadena saw Southern Cal defeat Penn St., 14-3.

1926 Johnny Mack Brown, one of Hollywood's most famous movie cowboys, also was one of college football's most exciting players at Alabama. He was selected player of the game for the Rose Bowl in the Crimson Tide's 20-19 victory over Washington.

1927 The Rose Bowl becomes the first coast-to-coast radio broadcast of a sporting event.

1929 The Rose Bowl game became one of the most famous in bowl history because of California player Roy Riegels' now-legendary wrong-way run. Early in the second quarter, with each team just changing directions, Georgia Tech was on its own 20. Tech halfback Stumpy Thompson broke for a seven-yard run, fumbled, and Riegels picked up the ball, momentarily headed for the Tech goal, then reversed his field and started running the wrong way. Teammate Benny Lom tried to stop him and finally did on the California one-yard line, where the dazed Riegels was pounced on by a group of Tech tacklers. Lom went back to punt on the next play and the kick was blocked out of the end zone for a safety, which decided the contest, eventually won by Tech, 8-7.

1938 The first Orange Bowl played in Miami's new stadium, which sat 22,000 at the time, saw Auburn edge Michigan St., 6-0. Also, in the second annual Cotton Bowl, Colorado's do-it-all standout Byron "Whizzer" White, the Rhodes Scholar and future U.S. Supreme Court justice, passed for one score and returned a pass interception for another, but the Buffs lost to Rice, 28-14.

1941 On December 6, 1941, Hawaii defeated Willamette, 20-6, but a second post-season game, scheduled with San Jose St. for the next week, was cancelled after the attack on Pearl Harbor.

1942 You would think a team making only one first down and gaining only 75 yards to its opponent's 309 yards could not come out of a game a 29-21 victor, but it happened in the Cotton Bowl as Alabama downed Texas A&M. The Tide intercepted seven of A&M's 42 passes and recovered five Aggie fumbles. Also, the Rose Bowl was moved for one year to Durham, N.C., because of wartime considerations that precluded large gatherings on the West Coast, and Oregon St. downed Duke, 20-16.

1946 The first and only game decided after time expired was the Orange Bowl when Miami (Fla.) downed Holy Cross, 13-6. Time expired as Miami (Fla.) halfback Al Hudson returned an 89-yard intercepted pass for the deciding score.

1949 A Pacific Coast team had never been allowed to play in a major bowl other than the Rose Bowl, but the conference fathers let Oregon play in the Cotton Bowl against Southern Methodist. Doak Walker and Kyle Rote led Southern Methodist to a 20-13 victory over the Ducks and quarterback Norm Van Brocklin. John McKay, later the head coach at Southern Cal, also was on the Oregon roster.

1953 The Rose, Cotton, Sugar and Orange Bowls were televised nationally for the first time.

1954 Dicky Maegle of Rice may be the best-remembered bowl player, not because of his 265 yards rushing and three touchdowns vs. Alabama in 1954, but because of what happened off the bench to tackle Maegle in the Cotton Bowl, won by Rice, 28-6.

1960 In one of those pupil-vs.-teacher battles, former Georgia Tech player and assistant coach Frank Broyles led his Arkansas Razorbacks to a 14-7 Gator Bowl victory over his former coach, Bobby Dodd, and the Yellow Jackets.

1962 Oregon St. quarterback Terry Baker turned in the longest run in bowl history with a 99-yard scamper to down Villanova, 6-0, in the Liberty Bowl. Baker, an outstanding athlete, became the only Heisman Trophy winner to play in an NCAA Final Four basketball game later that academic year (1963).

1964 Utah and West Va. became the first teams to play a major bowl game indoors when they met in the Atlantic City Convention Hall. Utah won, 32-6, beneath the bright indoor lights.

1965 The first Orange Bowl played under the lights in Miami saw Texas stun national champion Alabama and quarterback Joe Namath, 21-17.

1968 It was the student beating the teacher in the Cotton Bowl as Texas A&M head coach Gene Stallings saw his Aggies hold on for a 20-16 victory over Alabama and legendary head coach Paul "Bear" Bryant. Stallings had played (at Texas A&M) and coached (at Alabama) under Bryant. The "Bear" met Stallings at midfield after the contest and lifted the 6-foot-3 Aggie coach up in admiration. Also, the Astro-Bluebonnet Bowl (also known as the Bluebonnet Bowl) became the first bowl game to be played in a domed stadium as the Astrodome served as the site of the December 31, 1968, game between Southern Methodist (28) and Oklahoma (27).

1970 Three of the four legendary Four Horsemen of Notre Dame came to Dallas to watch the Fighting Irish drop a 21-17 Cotton Bowl game to Texas. The only other time Notre Dame had played in a bowl game was the 1925 Rose Bowl, when the Four Horsemen led the Irish to a 27-10 victory over Stanford.

1971 Notre Dame snapped the second-longest winning streak going into a bowl game by halting Texas' 30-game string, 24-11, in the Cotton Bowl. In 1951, Kentucky had stopped Oklahoma's 31-game streak in the Sugar Bowl, 13-7.

1976 Archie Griffin started his fourth straight Rose Bowl for Ohio St. (1973-76), totaling 412 yards on 79 carries in the four games. The Buckeyes, under legendary head coach Woody Hayes, won only the 1974 contest, but Griffin is the only player to win two Heisman Trophies (1974-75).

Special Regular- and Postseason Games

Postseason Games

UNSANCTIONED OR OTHER BOWLS

The following bowl games were unsanctioned by the NCAA or otherwise had no team classified as major college at the time of the bowl. Most are postseason games; in many cases, complete dates and/or statistics are not available and the scores are listed only to provide a historical reference. Attendance of the game, if known, is listed in parentheses after the score.

ALL-SPORTS BOWL
(Oklahoma City, Okla.)
12-9-62—Panhandle St. 28, Langston 14 (8,000)
12-8-63—Nebraska-Omaha 34, East Central (Okla.) 21 (2,500)
12-64—Northeastern Okla. 59, Slippery Rock 12
12-65—Sul Ross St. 21, East Central (Okla.) 13

ALOHA BOWL
(Honolulu, Hawaii)
12-6-47—Hawaii 27, Fresno St. 13 (25,000)

ALUMINUM BOWL
12-56—Montana St. 0, St. Joseph's (Ind.) 0

ANGEL BOWL
(Los Angeles, Calif.)
12-28-46—Florida A&M 6, Wiley 6 (12,000)

AZALEA BOWL
(Orlando, Fla.)
1-1-46—Knoxville 18, Florida Normal 0 (4,000)

AZALEA CLASSIC
(Mobile, Ala.)
12-4-71—Jackson St. 40, Alabama A&M 21
12-7-74—Bethune-Cookman 19, Langston 3 (1,000)

AZTEC BOWL
(Mexico City, Mexico)
12-50—Whittier 27, Mexico All-Stars 14
12-53—Mexico City 45, Eastern N. Mex. 26

BAYOU CITY BOWL
(Houston, Texas)
1-1-45—Wiley 20, Prairie View 0 (4,000)

BEAN BOWL
(Scottsbluff, Neb.)
1-1-50—Idaho St. 20, Chadron St. 2
1-1-51—Doane 14, Colorado St. 6

BEAVER BOWL
(Corry, Pa.)
11-15-58—Slippery Rock 6, Edinboro 0 (3,000)

BICENTENNIAL BOWL
(Little Rock, Ark.)
11-29-76—Henderson St. 27, East Central (Okla.) 14 (2,000)

BICENTENNIAL BOWL
(Richmond, Va.)
12-11-76—South Caro. St. 26, Norfolk St. 10 (7,500)

BOOT HILL BOWL
(Dodge City, Kan.)
12-4-71—Dakota St. 23, Northwestern Okla. 20 (2,000)
12-2-72—William Penn 17, Emporia St. 14 (2,000)
12-1-73—Millikin 51, Bethany (Kan.) 7 (1,600)
11-30-74—Washburn 21, Millikin 7 (2,500)
11-22-75—Buena Vista 24, St. Mary's (Kan.) 21 (2,700)
11-20-76—Benedictine 29, Washburn 14 (3,000)
11-19-77—Mo. Western St. 35, Benedictine 30 (1,000)
11-18-78—Chadron St. 30, Baker (Kan.) 19 (3,000)
11-17-79—Pittsburg St. 43, Peru St. 14 (2,800)

BOTANY BOWL
12-55—Neb.-Kearney 34, Northern St. 13

BOY'S RANCH BOWL
(Abilene, Texas)
12-13-47—Missouri Valley 20, McMurry (Tex.) 13 (2,500)

BURLEY BOWL
(Johnson City, Tenn.)
1-1-46—High Point 7, Milligan 7 (3,500)
1-1-47—Southeastern La. 21, Milligan 13 (7,500)
11-47—West Chester 20, Carson-Newman 6 (10,000)
11-24-49—Emory & Henry 32, Hanover 0 (12,000)
11-25-49—West Chester 7, Appalachian St. 2 (12,000)
11-23-50—Emory & Henry 26, Appalachian St. 6 (12,000)
11-22-51—Morris Harvey (now Charleston) 27, Lebanon Valley 20 (9,000)
12-52—East Tenn. St. 34, Emory & Henry 16
12-53—East Tenn. St. 48, Emory & Henry 12
11-14-54—Appalachian St. 28, East Tenn. St. 13
11-16-55—East Tenn. St. 7, Appalachian St. 0
11-22-56—Memphis 32, East Tenn. St. 12

CAJUN BOWL
12-47—McNeese St. 0, Southern Ark. 0

CATTLE BOWL
(Fort Worth, Texas)
1-1-47—Ark.-Pine Bluff 7, Lane 0 (1,000)
1-1-48—Samuel Huston 7, Philander Smith 0 (800)

CEMENT BOWL
(Allentown, Pa.)
12-8-62—West Chester 46, Hofstra 12

CHARITY BOWL
(Los Angeles, Calif.)
12-25-37—Fresno St. 27, Central Ark. 26 (5,000)

CHRISTMAS BOWL
(Natchitoches, La.)
12-25-58—Northwestern St. 18, Sam Houston St. 11
12-25-59—Delta St. 19, East Central (Okla.) 0

CIGAR BOWL
(Tampa, Fla.)
1-1-47—Delaware 21, Rollins 7 (9,500)
1-1-48—Missouri Valley 26, West Chester 7 (10,000)
1-1-49—Missouri Valley 13, St. Thomas (Minn.) 13 (11,000)
1-2-50—Florida St. 19, Wofford 6 (14,000)
1-1-51—Wis.-La Crosse 47, Valparaiso 14 (12,000)
12-29-51—Brooke Army Medical 20, Camp Lejeune Marines 0 (7,500) (see Cigar Bowl in Service Games)
12-13-52—Tampa 21, Lenoir-Rhyne 12 (7,500)
1-1-54—Missouri Valley 12, Wis.-La Crosse 12 (5,000)
12-54—Tampa 21, Morris Harvey (now Charleston) 0

CITRACADO BOWL
(see Citracado Bowl in Service Games)

COCONUT BOWL
(Miami, Fla.)
1-1-42—Florida Normal 0, Miami All-Stars 0 (9,000)
1-1-46—Bethune-Cookman 32, Albany St. (Ga.) 0 (5,000)
1-1-47—Bethune-Cookman 13, Columbia (S.C.) Sporting Club 0 (5,000)

CORN BOWL
(Bloomington, Ill.)
1-1-47—Southern Ill. 21, North Central 0 (5,500)
11-25-48—Ill. Wesleyan 6, Eastern Ill. 0 (8,500)
11-24-49—Western Ill. 13, Wheaton (Ill.) 0 (4,567)
11-23-50—Missouri-Rolla 7, Illinois St. 6 (2,500)
11-22-51—Lewis (Ill.) 21, William Jewell 12 (2,000)
12-53—Western Ill. 32, Iowa Wesleyan 0
11-24-55—Luther 24, Western Ill. 20 (3,100)

COSMOPOLITAN BOWL
(Alexandria, La.)
12-51—McNeese St. 13, Louisiana Col. 6

COTTON-TOBACCO BOWL
(Greensboro, N.C.)
1-1-46—Johnson Smith 18, Allen 6
1-1-47—Norfolk St. 0, Richmond 0 (10,000)

COWBOY BOWL
(Lawton, Okla.)
12-11-71—Howard Payne 16, Cameron 13
12-9-72—Harding 30, Langston 27

DOLL AND TOY CHARITY GAME
(Gulfport, Miss.)
12-3-37—Southern Miss. 7, Appalachian St. 0 (2,000)

EASTERN BOWL
(Allentown, Pa.)
12-14-63—East Caro. 27, Northeastern 6 (2,700)

ELKS BOWL
1-2-54—Morris-Harvey (now Charleston) 12, East Caro. 0 (4,500) (at Greenville, N.C.)

FISH BOWL
(Corpus Christi, Texas)
11-48—Southwestern (Tex.) 7, Corpus Christi 0

FISH BOWL
(Norfolk, Va.)
12-48—Hampton 20, Central St. (Ohio) 19

FLOWER BOWL
(Jacksonville, Fla.)
1-1-42—Johnson Smith 13, Lane 0 (4,500)
1-1-43—North Caro. A&T 14, Southern-B.R. 6 (2,000)
1-1-44—Allen 33, Winston-Salem 0 (2,000)
1-1-45—Texas College 18, North Caro. A&T 0 (5,000)
1-1-46—Grambling 19, Lane 6 (6,000)
1-1-47—Delaware St. 7, Florida Normal 6 (3,000)
1-1-48—Bethune-Cookman 6, Lane 0 (3,000)

FRUIT BOWL
(San Francisco, Calif.)
12-14-47—Central St. (Ohio) 26, Prairie View 0 (9,000)
12-48—Southern-B.R. 30, San Fran. St. 0 (5,000)

GATE CITY BOWL
(Atlanta, Ga.)
12-21-74—Tuskegee 15, Norfolk St. 14 (6,252)

GLASS BOWL
(Toledo, Ohio)
12-46—Toledo 21, Bates 12 (12,000)
12-47—Toledo 20, New Hampshire 14 (13,500)
12-48—Toledo 27, Oklahoma City 14 (8,500)
1-1-50—Cincinnati 33, Toledo 13

GOLD BOWL
(Richmond, Va.)
12-3-77—South Caro. St. 10, Winston-Salem 7 (14,000)
12-2-78—Virginia Union 21, North Caro. A&T 6 (7,500)
12-1-79—South Caro. St. 39, Norfolk St. 7 (8,000)
12-6-80—North Caro. A&T 37, N.C. Central 0 (3,374)

GOLDEN ISLES BOWL
(Brunswick, Ga.)
12-1-62—McNeese St. 21, Samford 14

GRAPE BOWL
(Lodi, Calif.)
12-13-47—Pacific (Cal.) 35, Utah St. 21 (12,000)
12-11-48—Hardin-Simmons 35, Pacific (Cal.) 35 (10,000)

GREAT LAKES BOWL
(Cleveland, Ohio)
12-48—John Carroll 14, Canisius 13 (18,000)

GREAT SOUTHWEST BOWL
(Grand Prairie, Texas)
12-31-60—Tex. A&M-Kingsville 45, Arkansas Tech 14 (3,900)

HOLIDAY BOWL
(St. Petersburg, Fla.)
12-57—Pittsburg St. 27, Hillsdale 26
12-58—Northeastern Okla. 19, Northern Ariz. 13
12-19-59—Tex. A&M-Kingsville 20, Lenoir-Rhyne 7 (9,500)
12-10-60—Lenoir-Rhyne 15, Humboldt St. 14 (also served as NAIA national title game)

HOOSIER BOWL
(Evansville, Ind.)
11-28-46—Evansville 19, DeKalb St. (now Northern Ill.) 7 (12,000) (see Turkey Bowl)

INTERNATIONAL BOWL
12-52—Tex. A&M-Kingsville 49, Hereico Colegio Military 0

IODINE BOWL
(Charleston, S.C.)
1-1-50—Johnson Smith 20, Allen 12
12-9-50—Allen 20, Bethune-Cookman 0 (1,000)
12-1-51—Allen 33, Morris Harvey (now Charleston) 14 (3,000)
12-53—Allen 33, Paul Quinn 6

KICKAPOO BOWL
(Wichita Falls, Texas)
12-47—Hardin (Tex.) 39, Arkansas St. (Conway) 20 (5,000)

LIONS BOWL
(Ruston, La.)
12-49—Grambling 21, Texas College 18

12-50—Bishop 38, Grambling 0

LIONS BOWL
(Salisbury, N.C.)
12-13-52—Clarion 13, East Caro. 6 (3,000)

MERCY BOWL II
(Anaheim, Calif.)
12-11-71—Cal St. Fullerton 17, Fresno St. 14 (16,854)

MINERAL WATER BOWL
(Excelsior Springs, Mo.)
11-25-54—Hastings 20, Col. of Emporia 14 (4,000)
11-24-55—Missouri Valley 31, Hastings 7
11-22-56—St. Benedict's 14, Northeastern Okla. 13 (2,000)
11-30-57—William Jewell 33, Hastings 14 (2,000)
11-22-58—Lincoln (Mo.) 21, Emporia St. 0 (2,500)
11-59—Col. of Emporia 21, Austin (Tex.) 20 (3,000)
11-26-60—Hillsdale 17, Northern Iowa 6 (6,000)
11-25-61—Northeast Mo. St. 22, Parsons 8 (8,000)
11-62—Adams St. 23, Northern Ill. 20
11-28-64—North Dak. St. 14, Western St. 13 (4,500)
11-26-66—Adams St. 14, Southwest Mo. St. 8 (5,500)
11-25-67—Doane 14, William Jewell 14 (6,500)
11-30-68—Doane 10, Central Mo. St. 0 (6,000)
11-29-69—St. John's (Minn.) 21, Simpson 0 (5,000)
11-28-70—Franklin 40, Wayne St. (Neb.) 12 (2,500)
12-4-71—Bethany (Kan.) 17, Missouri Valley 14 (2,500)
11-18-72—Ottawa 27, Friends 20 (4,500)
11-73—William Jewell 20, St. Mary's (Kan.) 9
11-23-74—Midland 32, Friends 6 (1,500)
11-22-75—Mo. Western St. 44, Graceland (Ia.) 0 (3,300)

MIRZA SHRINE BOWL
12-50—Central Mo. St. 32, Pittsburg St. 21

MISSOURI-KANSAS BOWL
12-48—Emporia St. 34, Southwest Mo. St. 20

MOILA SHRINE CLASSIC
(St. Joseph, Mo.)
11-24-79—Mo. Western St. 72, William Jewell 44 (1,600)
11-22-80—Northeast Mo. St. 17, Pittsburg St. 14 (500)

NATIONAL CLASSIC
12-54—N.C. Central 19, Tennessee St. 6

NEW YEAR'S CLASSIC
(Honolulu, Hawaii)
1-1-34—Santa Clara 26, Hawaii 7
1-1-35—Hawaii 14, California 0 (later called Poi Bowl)

OIL BOWL
(Houston, Texas)
1-1-44—Southwestern La. 24, Ark.-Pine Bluff 7 (12,000)

OLEANDER BOWL
(Galveston, Texas)
1-2-50—McMurry (Tex.) 19, Missouri Valley 13 (7,500)

OLIVE BOWL
12-53—College of the Sequoias 26, La Verne 12

OLYMPIAN BOWL
(see Pythian Bowl)

OPTIMIST BOWL
(Houston, Texas)
12-21-46—North Texas 14, Pacific (Cal.) 13 (5,000)

ORANGE BLOSSOM CLASSIC
(Miami, Fla.)
12-33—Florida A&M 9, Howard 6
12-34—Florida A&M 13, Virginia St. 12
12-35—Kentucky St. 19, Florida A&M 10
12-36—Prairie View 25, Florida A&M 0
12-37—Florida A&M 25, Hampton 20
12-38—Florida A&M 9, Kentucky St. 7
12-39—Florida A&M 42, Wiley 0
12-40—Central St. (Ohio) 0, Florida A&M 0
12-41—Florida A&M 15, Tuskegee 7
12-42—Florida A&M 12, Texas College 6
12-43—Hampton 39, Florida A&M 0
12-44—Virginia St. 19, Florida A&M 6
12-45—Wiley 32, Florida A&M 6
12-46—Lincoln (Pa.) 20, Florida A&M 0 (at Tampa)
12-47—Florida A&M 7, Hampton 0
12-48—Virginia Union 10, Florida A&M 6 (16,000)
1-1-50—North Caro. A&T 20, Florida A&M 6
12-50—Central St. (Ohio) 13, Florida A&M 6
12-51—Florida A&M 67, N.C. Central 6
12-52—Florida A&M 29, Virginia St. 8
12-53—Prairie View 33, Florida A&M 27
12-54—Florida A&M 67, Md.-East. Shore 19

12-55—Grambling 28, Florida A&M 21
12-56—Tennessee St. 41, Florida A&M 39
12-57—Florida A&M 27, Md.-East. Shore 21
12-58—Prairie View 26, Florida A&M 8
12-59—Florida A&M 28, Prairie View 7
12-60—Florida A&M 40, Langston 26
12-9-61—Florida A&M 14, Jackson St. 8 (47,791)
12-62—Jackson St. 22, Florida A&M 6
12-63—Morgan St. 30, Florida A&M 7
12-64—Florida A&M 42, Grambling 15
12-65—Morgan St. 36, Florida A&M 7
12-66—Florida A&M 43, Alabama A&M 26
12-67—Grambling 28, Florida A&M 25
12-7-68—Alcorn St. 36, Florida A&M 9 (37,398)
12-6-69—Florida A&M 23, Grambling 19 (36,784) (at Tallahassee, Fla.)
12-12-70—Jacksonville St. 21, Florida A&M 7 (31,184)
12-11-71—Florida A&M 27, Kentucky St. 9 (26,161)
12-2-72—Florida A&M 41, Md.-East. Shore 21 (21,606)
12-8-73—Florida A&M 23, South Caro. St. 12 (18,996)
12-7-74—Florida A&M 17, Howard 13 (20,166)
12-6-75—Florida A&M 40, Kentucky St. 13 (27,875)
12-4-76—Florida A&M 26, Central St. (Ohio) 21 (18,000)
12-3-77—Florida A&M 37, Delaware St. 15 (29,493)

ORCHID BOWL
(Mexico City, Mexico)
1-1-42—Louisiana College 10, U. of Mexico 0 (8,000)
12-46—Mississippi Col. 43, U. of Mexico 7 (7,500)

PALMETTO SHRINE
(Columbia, S.C.)
12-10-55—Lenoir-Rhyne 14, Newberry 13 (6,000)

PALM FESTIVAL
(Miami, Fla.)
1-2-33—Miami (Fla.) 7, Manhattan 0 (6,000)
1-1-34—Duquesne 33, Miami (Fla.) 7 (3,500) (forerunner to Orange Bowl)

PAPER BOWL
(Pensacola, Fla.)
12-18-48—Jacksonville St. 19, Troy St. 0
12-16-49—Jacksonville St. 12, Livingston 7 (3,000)
Pensacola Alumni Cardinals 7, Jacksonville St. 6 (3,660)

PEACH BLOSSOM CLASSIC
(Atlanta, Ga.)
12-9-39—Morris Brown 13, Virginia St. 7
12-6-40—Morris Brown 28, Kentucky St. 6 (1,500)
12-6-41—Morris Brown 7, N.C. Central 6 (6,000) (at Columbus, Ga.)
12-4-42—Morris Brown 20, Lane 0 (3,000)

PEACH BOWL
(Macon, Ga.)
12-46—Tenn. Wesleyan 14, Ga. Military 13 (5,000)
1-1-50—Morris Brown 33, Texas College 28

PEANUT BOWL
(Dothan, Ala.)
12-21-68—Ouachita Baptist 39, Livingston 6

PEAR BOWL
(Medford, Ore.)
11-28-46—Southern Ore. 13, Central Wash. 8 (3,000) (at Ashland, Ore.)
11-25-48—Col. of Idaho 27, Southern Ore. 20 (2,500)
11-24-49—Pacific (Ore.) 33, UC Davis 15 (4,000)
11-23-50—Lewis & Clark 61, San Fran. St. 7 (4,000)
11-24-51—Pacific (Ore.) 25, UC Davis 7 (4,000)

PECAN BOWL
(Orangeburg, S.C.)
12-14-46—South Caro. St. 13, Johnson Smith 6
12-13-47—South Caro. St. 7, Allen 0 (3,000)

PELICAN BOWL
(New Orleans, La.)
12-2-72—Grambling 56, N.C. Central 6 (22,500) (at Durham, N.C.)
12-7-74—Grambling 28, South Caro. St. 7 (30,120)
12-27-75—Southern-B.R. 15, South Caro. St. 12 (6,748)

PENINSULA BOWL
(Charleston, S.C.)
12-2-50—Allen 47, South Caro. St. 13 (7,500)

PHILLIPS FIELD BOWL
(Tampa, Fla.)
12-51—Tampa 7, Brandeis 0

PIEDMONT TOBACCO BOWL
(Fayetteville, N.C.)
12-7-46—Allen 40, Fayetteville St. 6 (900)

PINEAPPLE BOWL
(Honolulu, Hawaii)
1-1-40—Oregon St. 39, Hawaii 6
1-1-41—Fresno St. 3, Hawaii 0
1-1-47—Hawaii 19, Utah 16 (20,000)
1-1-48—Hawaii 33, Redlands 32 (12,000)
1-1-49—Oregon St. 47, Hawaii 27 (15,000)
1-2-50—Stanford 74, Hawaii 20
1-1-51—Hawaii 28, Denver 27
1-1-52—San Diego St. 34, Hawaii 13

PITTSBURGH CHARITY GAME
(Pittsburgh, Pa.)
12-5-31—Carnegie Mellon 0, Duquesne 0 (42,539) (see Other Postseason Games)

POI BOWL
(Honolulu, Hawaii)
1-1-36—Southern Cal 38, Hawaii 6
1-2-37—Hawaii 18, Honolulu All-Stars 12
1-1-38—Washington 53, Hawaii 13
1-2-39—UCLA 32, Hawaii 7 (later called Pineapple Bowl)

POTATO BOWL
(Belfast, Ireland)
1-1-44—Galloping Gaels 0, Wolverines 0

POULTRY BOWL
(Gainesville, Fla.)
12-7-73—Stephen F. Austin 31, Gardner-Webb 10 (2,500)
12-7-74—Guilford 7, William Penn 7 (1,000) (at Greensboro, N.C.) (Guilford awarded win on 10-8 edge in first downs)

PRAIRIE VIEW BOWL
(Houston, Texas)
1-1-37—Tuskegee 6, Prairie View 0 (3,000)
1-1-43—Prairie View 6, Wiley 0 (5,000)
1-1-46—Prairie View 12, Tuskegee 0 (10,000)
1-1-47—Prairie View 14, Lincoln (Mo.) 0 (1,500) (called Houston Bowl)
1-1-48—Central St. (Ohio) 13, Prairie View 0
1-1-49—Central St. (Ohio) 6, Prairie View 0 (9,000)
1-2-50—Prairie View 27, Fisk 6 (4,718)
1-1-51—Prairie View 6, Bishop 0
1-1-52—Prairie View 27, Ark.-Pine Bluff 26
1-1-53—Texas Southern 13, Prairie View 12 (13,000)
1-1-54—Prairie View 33, Texas Southern 8
1-1-55—Prairie View 14, Texas Southern 12 (10,000)
1-2-56—Prairie View 59, Fisk 0 (7,500)
1-1-57—Prairie View 27, Texas Southern 6
1-1-58—Prairie View 6, Texas Southern 6 (3,500)
1-1-59—Prairie View 34, Langston 8
1-1-60—Prairie View 47, Wiley 10 (1,200)
12-31-60—Prairie View 19, Ark.-Pine Bluff 8 (1,400)
1-1-63—Prairie View 37, Central St. (Ohio) 16

PRETZEL BOWL
(Reading, Pa.)
11-24-51—West Chester 32, Albright 9 (7,500)
12-52—Albright 20, Penn. Military 0

PYTHIAN BOWL
(Salisbury, N.C.)
11-26-49—Appalachian St. 21, Catawba 7
12-9-50—West Liberty St. 28, Appalachian St. 26
12-8-51—Lenoir-Rhyne 13, Calif. (Pa.) 7 (4,500)

REFRIGERATOR BOWL
(Evansville Ind.)
12-4-48—Evansville 13, Missouri Valley 7 (7,500)
12-49—Evansville 22, Hillsdale 7
12-2-50—Abilene Christian 13, Gust. Adolphus 7 (8,000)
12-2-51—Arkansas St. 46, Camp Breckinridge 12 (10,000)
12-7-52—Western Ky. 34, Arkansas St. 19 (9,500)
12-6-53—Sam Houston St. 14, Col. of Idaho 12 (7,500)
12-5-54—Delaware 19, Kent 7 (4,500)
12-4-55—Jacksonville St. 12, Rhode Island 10 (7,000)
12-1-56—Sam Houston St. 27, Middle Tenn. St. 13 (3,000)

RICE BOWL
(Stuggart, Ark.)
12-57—Arkansas Tech 19, Ark.-Pine Bluff 7
12-58—Louisiana College 39, Arkansas Tech 12
12-2-60—East Central (Okla.) 25, Henderson St. 7

ROCKET BOWL
12-60—Maryville (Tenn.) 19, Millsaps 0

SAN JACINTO SHRINE BOWL
(Pasadena, Texas)
12-4-76—Abilene Christian 22, Harding 12 (8,000)

SHARE BOWL
(Knoxville, Tenn.)
12-11-71—Carson-Newman 54, Fairmont St. 3 (1,200)

SHRIMP BOWL
(Galveston, Texas)
12-27-52—Sam Houston St. 41, Northeastern Okla. 20 (3,500)

SHRINE BOWL
(Ardmore, Okla.)
12-9-72—Southwestern Okla. 28, Angelo St. 6

SILVER BOWL
(Mexico City, Mexico)
12-47—Mexico All-Stars 24, Randolph Field 19

SMOKY MOUNTAIN BOWL
(Bristol, Tenn.)
11-24-49—West Liberty St. 20, Western Caro. 0 (1,000)

SPACE CITY BOWL
12-66—Jacksonville St. 41, Ark.-Pine Bluff 30

SPUD BOWL
(Pocatello, Idaho)
1-1-51—Idaho St. 39, Montana St. 13

STEEL BOWL
(Birmingham, Ala.)
1-1-41—Morris Brown 19, Central St. (Ohio) 3 (8,000)
1-1-42—Southern College All-Stars 26, Nashville Pros 13
1-1-52—Bethune-Cookman 27, Texas College 13 (1,500) (see Vulcan Bowl)

SUGAR CUP CLASSIC
12-64—Grambling 42, Bishop 6

TANGERINE BOWL#
(Orlando, Fla.)
1-1-47—Catawba 31, Maryville (Tenn.) 6
1-1-48—Catawba 7, Marshall 0
1-1-49—Murray St. 21, Sul Ross St. 21
1-2-50—St. Vincent (Pa.) 7, Emory & Henry 6
1-1-51—Morris Harvey (now Charleston) 35, Emory & Henry 14
1-1-52—Stetson 35, Arkansas St. 20 (12,500)
1-1-53—East Tex. St. 33, Tennessee Tech 0 (12,340)
1-1-54—Arkansas St. 7, East Tex. St. 7
1-1-55—Nebraska-Omaha 7, Eastern Ky. 6
1-2-56—Juniata 6, Missouri Valley 6 (10,000)
1-1-57—West Tex. A&M 20, Southern Miss. 13 (11,000)
1-1-58—East Tex. St. 10, Southern Miss. 9
12-27-58—East Tex. St. 26, Missouri Valley 7 (4,000)
1-1-60—Middle Tenn. St. 21, Presbyterian 12 (12,500)
12-29-61—Lamar 21, Middle Tenn. St. 14
12-28-63—Western Ky. 27, Coast Guard 0 (7,500)
12-12-64—East Caro. 14, Massachusetts 13
12-11-65—East Caro. 31, Maine 0 (8,350)
12-10-66—Morgan St. 14, West Chester 6
12-16-67—Tenn.-Martin 25, West Chester 8

TEXHOMA BOWL
(Denison, Texas)
12-48—Ouachita Baptist 7, Southeastern Okla. 0
12-49—Austin (Tex.) 27, East Central (Okla.) 6

TEXTILE BOWL
(Spartanburg, S.C.)
11-30-74—Wofford 20, South Caro. St. 0 (3,000)

TOBACCO BOWL
(Lexington, Ky.)
12-14-46—Muhlenberg 26, St. Bonaventure 25 (3,000)

TROPICAL BOWL
12-51—Morris Brown 21, Alcorn St. 0
12-52—Bethune-Cookman 54, Albany St. (Ga.) 0
12-53—Virginia Union 13, Bethune-Cookman 0

TURKEY BOWL
11-28-46—Evansville 19, DeKalb St. (now Northern Ill.) 7 (12,000) (also called Hoosier Bowl)

VULCAN BOWL
(Birmingham, Ala.)
1-1-42—Langston 13, Morris Brown 0 (7,000)
1-1-43—Texas College 13, Tuskegee 10 (6,000)
1-1-44—Tuskegee 12, Clark (Ga.) 7 (6,000)
1-1-45—Tennessee St. 13, Tuskegee 0 (5,000)

1-1-46—Tennessee St. 33, Texas College 6 (9,000)
1-1-47—Tennessee St. 32, Louisville Municipal 0 (4,000)
1-2-48—Central St. (Ohio) 27, Grambling 21 (8,000)
1-1-49—Kentucky St. 23, North Caro. A&T 13 (5,000)
1-1-52—Bethune-Cookman 27, Texas College 13 (1,500) (see Steel Bowl)

WEST VIRGINIA BOWL
(Clarksburg, W.Va.)
12-60—Fairmont St. 13, Salem (Va.) 7
11-23-61—West Va. Wesleyan 12, Salem (W.Va.) 0 (1,100)

WILL ROGERS BOWL
(Oklahoma City, Okla.)
1-1-47—Pepperdine 38, Neb. Wesleyan 13 (800)

YAM BOWL
(Dallas, Texas)
12-25-46—Texas Southern 64, Tuskegee 7 (5,000)
12-25-47—Southern-B.R. 46, Fort Valley St. 0 (1,200)

#Became Florida Citrus Bowl (no classified major teams participated in games from January 1, 1947, through December 30, 1960, or in 1961 and 1963 through 1967.

SERVICE GAMES

AIRBORNE BOWL
12-57—101st Airborne 20, 82nd Airborne 14

ARAB BOWL
(Oran, Africa)
1-1-44—Army 10, Navy 7 (15,000)

ARMY PACIFIC OLYMPICS
(Tokyo, Japan)
1-27-46—11th Airborne Division Angels 18, Honolulu All-Stars 0

ATOM BOWL
(Nagasaki, Japan)
12-45—Nishahaya Tigers 14, Bertelli's Bears 13 (2,000)

BAMBINO BOWL
(Bari, Italy)
11-23-44—Technical School 13, Playboys 0 (5,000)

BAMBOO BOWL
(Manila, Philippines)
1-1-46—Clark Field Acpacs 14, Leyte Base 12 (40,000)
12-46—Manila Raiders 13, Scofield Barracks 6 (12,000)
12-47—Ryukgus Command Sea Horses 21, Hawaiian Mid-Pacific Commandos 0
1-1-50—All-Navy Guam 19, Clark Air Force Base 7

CHERRY BOWL
(Yokohama, Japan)
1-1-52—Camp Drake 26, Yoksuka Naval Base 12

CHIGGER BOWL
(Dutch Guiana)
1-1-45—Army Air Base Bonecrushers 6, Army Airway Rams 0 (1,200)

CHINA BOWL
(Shanghai)
1-27-46—Navy All-Stars 12, Army All-Stars 0
12-46—11th Airborne 12, Army-Navy All-Stars 6
12-47—Marines (Guam) 45, China All-Stars 0

CIGAR BOWL
12-29-51—Brooke Army Medical 20, Camp Lejeune 0 (7,500)

CITRICADO BOWL
12-56—San Diego Marines 25, UC Santa Barb. 14

COCONUT BOWL
(New Guinea)
1-6-45—Bulldogs 18, Crimson Tide 7 (3,000)

COFFEE BOWL
(London, England)
3-19-44—United States 18, Canada 0

CONCH BOWL
12-57—Keesler Air Force Base 27, Maxwell Air Force Base 7

COSMOPOLITAN BOWL
(Alexandria, La.)
12-50—Camp Polk 26, Louisiana Col. 7
12-52—Louisiana Col. 14, Alexander Air Base 0

ELECTRONICS BOWL
12-53—Eglin Air Force Base 19, Keesler Air Force Base 8
12-54—Shaw Air Force Base 20, Keesler Air Force Base 19

EUROPEAN "ORANGE BOWL"
(Heidelberg, Germany)
12-46—1st Division Artillery 27, 60th Infantry 13

EUROPEAN "ROSE BOWL"
(Augsburg, Germany)
12-46—9th Division 20, 16th Infantry 7 (3,000)

EUROPEAN "SUGAR BOWL"
(Nuremberg, Germany)
12-46—Grafenwohr Military 0, 39th Infantry 0

G. I. BOWL
(London, England)
11-12-44—Army G.I.'s 20, Navy Bluejackets 0 (60,000)

ICE BOWL
(Fairbanks, Alaska)
1-1-49—Ladd Air Force Base 0, University of Alaska 0 (500)
1-1-50—University of Alaska 3, Ladd Air Force Base 0

IRANIAN BOWL
(Teheran, Iran)
12-12-44—Camp Amirabad 20, Camp Khorramsahr 0 (9,000)

JUNGLE BOWL
(Southwest Pacific)
1-1-45—American All-Stars 49, Marines 0 (6,400)

LILY BOWL
(Hamilton, Bermuda)
1-7-45—Navy 39, Army 6 (11,000)
12-46—Army 7, Navy 7 (9,000)
12-47—Air Force 12, Navy 12
1-1-49—Navy All-Stars 25, Kindley Fliers 6

MARINE BOWL
(Pritchard Field, Southwest Pacific)
12-24-44—4th Marines 0, 29th Marines 0 (7,000)

MISSILE BOWL
(Orlando, Fla.)
12-61—Fort Eustis 25, Quantico Marines 24
12-63—Quantico Marines 13, San Diego Marines 10
12-64—Fort Benning 9, Fort Eustis 3

PALMETTO SHRINE
(Charleston, S.C.)
1-1-55—Fort Jackson 26, Shaw Air Force Base 21

PARC DES PRINCES BOWL
(Paris, France)
12-19-44—9th Air Force 6, 1st General Hospital 0 (20,000)

POI BOWL
(Honolulu, Hawaii)
(Pacific Ocean Areas Service Championship)
1-8-45—Navy 14, Army Air Force 0 (29,000)

POINSETTIA BOWL
12-53—Fort Ord 55, Quantico Marines 19
12-54—Fort Sill 27, Bolling Air Force Base 6

RICE BOWL
(Tokyo, Japan)
1-1-46—11th Airborne Division Angels 25, 41st Division 12 (15,000)
12-46—Yokota Air Base 13, 1st AD 8 (7,000)
1-1-49—Army Ground Forces 13, Air Force 7 (20,000)
1-1-50—Air Force All-Stars 18, Army All-Stars 14
1-1-53—Camp Drake 25, Yokosuka Naval Base 6
1-1-54—Camp Fisher 19, Nagoya Air Base 13
1-1-55—Air Force 21, Marines 14
1-1-56—Air Force 33, Army 14 (40,000)
12-56—Army 21, Air Force 6
12-57—Johnson Air Base Vanguards 6, Marine Corps Sukiran Streaks 0
12-58—Air Force 20, Army 0

RIVIERA BOWL
(Marseille, France)
1-1-45—Railway Shop Battalion Unit 37, Army All-Stars 0 (18,000)

SALAD BOWL
(Phoenix, Ariz.)
1-1-53—San Diego Navy 81, 101st Airborne 20
1-1-54—Fort Ord 67, Great Lakes 12

SATELLITE BOWL
12-57—Fort Carson 12, Fort Dix 6

SHRIMP BOWL
12-54—Fort Ord 36, Fort Hood 0
12-55—Fort Hood 33, Little Creek 13
12-56—Bolling Air Force Base 29, Fort Hood 14
12-57—Bolling Air Force Base 28, San Diego Marines 7
12-58—Eglin Air Force Base 15, Brooke Medics 7
12-59—Quantico Marines 90, McClellan Air Force Base 0

SHURI BOWL
12-58—Air Force 60, Marine Corps 0

SPAGHETTI BOWL
(Florence, Italy)
1-1-45—5th Army 20, 12th Air Force 0 (20,000)
1-1-53—Salzburg Army 12, Wiesbaden AFC 7 (at Leghorn, Italy)

SUKIYAKI BOWL
12-56—Air Force 29, Marines 7

TEA BOWL
(London, England)
2-13-44—Canada 16, United States 6 (30,000)
12-31-44—Air Service Command Warriors 13, 8th Air Force Shuttle Raiders 0 (12,000)

TREASURY BOWL
(New York, N.Y.)
12-16-44—Randolph Field 13, 2nd Air Force 6 (8,356)

TYPHOON BOWL
12-56—Army 13, Marines 0

VALOR BOWL
12-57—Hamilton Air Force Base 12, Quantico Marines 6

POSTSEASON BOWL INVOLVING NON-I-A TEAMS

HERITAGE BOWL
Site: Atlanta, Ga.
Stadium (Capacity): Georgia Dome (71,596)
Name Changes: Alamo Heritage Bowl (1991); Heritage Bowl (1993)
Playing Surface: AstroTurf
Playing Sites: Joe Robbie Stadium, Miami (1991); Bragg Memorial Stadium, Tallahassee (1993); Georgia Dome, Atlanta (since 1994)

Date	Score (Attendance)
12-21-91	Alabama St. 36, North Caro. A&T 13 (7,724)
1-2-93	Grambling 45, Florida A&M 15 (11,273)
1-1-94	Southern-B.R. 11, South Caro. St. 0 (36,128)

NCAA-CERTIFIED ALL-STAR GAMES

EAST-WEST SHRINE CLASSIC
Present Site: Palo Alto, Calif.
Stadium (Capacity): Stanford (85,500)
Playing Surface: Grass
Playing Sites: Ewing Field, San Francisco (1925); Kezar Stadium, San Francisco (1927-41); Sugar Bowl, New Orleans (1942); Kezar Stadium, San Francisco (1943-66); Candlestick Park, San Francisco (1967-68); Stanford Stadium, Palo Alto (1969); Oakland Coliseum (1971); Candlestick Park, San Francisco (1971-73); Stanford Stadium, Palo Alto (since 1974)

Date	Score (Attendance)
12-26-25	West 7-0 (20,000)
1-1-27	West 7-3 (15,000)
12-26-27	West 16-6 (27,500)
12-29-28	East 20-0 (55,000)
1-1-30	East 19-7 (58,000)
12-27-30	West 3-0 (40,000)
1-1-32	East 6-0 (45,000)
1-2-33	West 21-13 (45,000)
1-1-34	West 12-0 (35,000)
1-1-35	West 19-13 (52,000)
1-1-36	East 19-3 (55,000)
1-1-37	East 3-0 (38,000)
1-1-38	Tie 0-0 (55,000)
1-2-39	West 14-0 (60,000)
1-1-40	West 28-11 (50,000)
1-1-41	West 20-14 (60,000)
1-3-42	Tie 6-6 (35,000)
1-1-43	East 13-12 (57,000)
1-1-44	Tie 13-13 (55,000)
1-1-45	West 13-7 (60,000)

Date	Score (Attendance)
1-1-46	Tie 7-7 (60,000)
1-1-47	West 13-9 (60,000)
1-1-48	East 40-9 (60,000)
1-1-49	East 14-12 (59,000)
12-31-49	East 28-6 (60,000)
12-30-50	West 16-7 (60,000)
12-29-51	East 15-14 (60,000)
12-27-52	East 21-20 (60,000)
1-2-54	West 31-7 (60,000)
1-1-55	East 13-12 (60,000)
12-31-55	East 29-6 (60,000)
12-29-56	West 7-6 (60,000)
12-28-57	West 27-13 (60,000)
12-27-58	East 26-14 (60,000)
1-2-60	West 21-14 (60,000)
12-31-60	East 7-0 (60,000)
12-30-61	West 21-8 (60,000)
12-29-62	East 25-19 (60,000)
12-28-63	Tie 6-6 (60,000)
1-2-65	West 11-7 (60,000)
12-31-65	West 22-7 (47,000)
12-31-66	East 45-22 (46,000)
12-30-67	East 16-14 (29,000)
12-28-68	West 18-7 (29,000)
12-27-69	West 15-0 (70,000)
1-2-71	West 17-13 (50,000)
12-31-71	West 17-13 (35,000)
12-30-72	East 9-3 (37,000)
12-29-73	East 35-7 (30,000)
12-28-74	East 16-14 (35,000)
1-3-76	West 21-14 (75,000)
1-2-77	West 30-14 (45,000)
12-31-77	West 23-3 (65,000)
1-6-79	East 56-17 (72,000)
1-5-80	West 20-10 (75,000)
1-10-81	East 21-3 (76,000)
1-9-82	West 20-13 (75,000)
1-15-83	East 26-25 (72,999)
1-7-84	East 27-19 (77,000)
1-5-85	West 21-10 (72,000)
1-11-86	East 18-7 (77,000)
1-10-87	West 24-21 (74,000)
1-16-88	West 16-13 (62,000)
1-16-89	East 24-6 (76,000)
1-21-90	West 22-21 (78,000)
1-24-91	West 24-21 (70,000)
1-19-92	West 14-6 (83,000)
1-24-93	East 31-17 (84,000)
1-15-94	West 29-28 (60,000)

Series record: West won 36, East 28, 5 ties.

BLUE-GRAY ALL-STAR CLASSIC
Present Site: Montgomery, Ala.
Stadium (Capacity): Cramton Bowl (24,600)
Playing Surface: Grass
Playing Sites: Cramton Bowl, Montgomery (since 1939)

Date	Score (Attendance)
1-2-39	Blue 7-0 (8,000)
12-30-39	Gray 33-20 (10,000)
12-28-40	Blue 14-12 (14,000)
12-27-41	Gray 16-0 (15,571)
12-26-42	Gray 24-0 (16,000)
1943	No Game
12-30-44	Gray 24-7 (16,000)
12-29-45	Blue 26-0 (20,000)
12-28-46	Gray 20-13 (22,500)
12-27-47	Gray 33-6 (22,500)
12-25-48	Blue 19-13 (15,000)
12-31-49	Gray 27-13 (21,500)
12-30-50	Gray 31-6 (21,000)
12-29-51	Gray 20-14 (22,000)
12-27-52	Gray 28-7 (22,000)
12-26-53	Gray 40-20 (18,500)
12-25-54	Blue 14-7 (18,000)
12-31-55	Gray 20-19 (19,000)
12-29-56	Blue 14-0 (21,000)
12-28-57	Gray 21-20 (16,000)
12-27-58	Blue 16-0 (16,000)
12-26-59	Blue 20-8 (20,000)
12-31-60	Blue 35-7 (18,000)
12-30-61	Gray 9-7 (18,000)
12-29-62	Blue 10-6 (20,000)
12-28-63	Gray 21-14 (20,000)
12-26-64	Blue 10-6 (16,000)
12-25-65	Gray 23-19 (18,000)

Date	Score (Attendance)
12-24-66	Blue 14-9 (18,000)
12-30-67	Blue 22-16 (23,350)
12-28-68	Gray 28-7 (18,000)
12-27-69	Tie 6-6 (21,500)
12-28-70	Gray 38-7 (23,000)
12-28-71	Gray 9-0 (24,000)
12-27-72	Gray 27-15 (20,000)
12-18-73	Blue 20-14 (21,000)
12-17-74	Blue 29-24 (12,000)
12-19-75	Blue 14-13 (10,000)
12-24-76	Gray 31-10 (16,000)
12-30-77	Blue 20-16 (5,000)
12-29-78	Gray 28-24 (18,380)
12-25-79	Blue 22-13 (18,312)
12-25-80	Blue 24-23 (25,000)
12-25-81	Blue 21-9 (19,000)
12-25-82	Gray 20-10 (21,000)
12-25-83	Gray 17-13 (2,000)
12-25-84	Gray 33-6 (24,080)
12-25-85	Blue 27-20 (18,500)
12-25-86	Blue 31-7 (18,500)
12-25-87	Gray 12-10 (20,300)
12-25-88	Blue 22-21 (20,000)
12-25-89	Gray 28-10 (16,000)
12-25-90	Blue 17-14 (17,500)
12-25-91	Gray 20-12 (21,000)
12-25-92	Gray 27-17 (20,500)
12-25-93	Gray 17-10 (18,500)

Series record: Gray won 30, Blue 24, 1 tie.

HULA BOWL
Present Site: Honolulu, Hawaii
Stadium (Capacity): Aloha (50,000)
Playing Surface: AstroTurf
Format: From 1947 through 1950, the College All-Stars played the Hawaii All-Stars. Beginning in 1951, the Hawaiian team was augmented by players from the National Football League. This format, however, was changed to an all-collegiate contest—first between the East and West, then between North and South (in 1963), and then back to East and West in 1974. In 1994, the format reverted to a collection of collegiate all-stars versus a collection of Hawaiian former collegiate players.
Playing Sites: Honolulu Stadium (1960-74); Aloha Stadium (since 1975)

Date	Score (Attendance)
1-10-60	East 34-8 (23,000)
1-8-61	East 14-7 (17,017)
1-7-62	Tie 7-7 (20,598)
1-6-63	North 20-13 (20,000)
1-4-64	North 23-13 (18,177)
1-9-65	South 16-14 (22,100)
1-8-66	North 27-26 (25,000)
1-7-67	North 28-27 (23,500)
1-6-68	North 50-6 (23,000)
1-4-69	North 13-7 (23,000)
1-10-70	South 35-13 (25,000)
1-9-71	North 42-32 (23,500)
1-8-72	North 24-7 (23,000)
1-6-73	South 17-3 (23,000)
1-5-74	East 24-14 (23,000)
1-4-75	East 34-25 (22,000)
1-10-76	East 16-0 (45,458)
1-8-77	West 20-17 (45,579)
1-7-78	West 42-22 (48,197)
1-6-79	East 29-24 (49,132)
1-5-80	East 17-10 (47,096)
1-10-81	West 24-17 (39,010)
1-9-82	West 26-23 (43,002)
1-15-83	East 30-14 (39,456)
1-7-84	West 21-16 (34,216)
1-5-85	East 34-14 (30,767)
1-11-86	West 23-10 (29,564)
1-10-87	West 16-14 (17,775)
1-16-88	West 20-18 (26,737)
1-7-89	East 21-10 (25,000)
1-13-90	West 21-13 (28,742)
1-19-91	East 23-10 (21,926)
1-11-92	West 27-20 (23,112)
1-16-93	West 13-10 (25,479)
1-22-94	College All-Stars 28-15 (33,947)

Series records: North-South (1963-73)—North won 8, South 3; East-West (1960-62 and 1974-93)—East won 11, West 11, 1 tie; College All-Stars vs. Hawaiian All-Stars (1994)—College All-Stars won 1, Hawaiian All-Stars 0.

JAPAN BOWL
Present Site: Yokohama, Japan
Stadium (Capacity): Yokohama (30,000)
Playing Surface: Grass
Playing Sites: Tokyo National Olympic Stadium (1976-79); Yokohama Stadium (since 1980)

Date	Score (Attendance)
1-18-76	West 27-18 (68,000)
1-16-77	West 21-10 (58,000)
1-15-78	East 26-10 (32,500)
1-14-79	East 33-14 (55,000)
1-13-80	West 28-17 (27,000)
1-17-81	West 25-13 (30,000)
1-16-82	West 28-17 (28,000)
1-23-83	West 30-21 (30,000)
1-15-84	West 26-21 (26,000)
1-13-85	West 28-14 (30,000)
1-11-86	East 31-14 (30,000)
1-11-87	West 24-17 (30,000)
1-10-88	West 17-3 (30,000)
1-15-89	East 30-7 (29,000)
1-13-90	West 24-10 (27,000)
1-12-91	West 20-14 (30,000)
1-11-92	East 14-13 (50,000)
1-9-93	East 27-13 (46,000)

Series record: West won 11, East 7.

CHICAGO COLLEGE ALL-STAR FOOTBALL GAME
(Discontinued after 1976 game)

An all-star team composed of the top senior collegiate players met the National Football League champions (1933-66) or the Super Bowl champions (1967-75) from the previous season, beginning in 1934. The only times the all-stars did not play the league champions were in 1935 and 1946. All games were played at Soldier Field, Chicago, Ill.

Date	Score (Attendance)
8-31-34	(Tie) Chicago Bears 0-0 (79,432)
8-29-35	Chicago Bears 5, All-Stars 0 (77,450)
9-3-36	(Tie) Detroit 7-7 (76,000)
9-1-37	All-Stars 6, Green Bay 0 (84,560)
8-31-38	All-Stars 28, Washington 16 (74,250)
8-30-39	New York Giants 9, All-Stars 0 (81,456)
8-29-40	Green Bay 45, All-Stars 28 (84,567)
8-28-41	Chicago Bears 37, All-Stars 13 (98,203)
8-28-42	Chicago Bears 21, All-Stars 0 (101,100)
8-25-43	All-Stars 27, Washington 7 (48,471)
8-30-44	Chicago Bears 24, All-Stars 21 (48,769)
8-30-45	Green Bay 19, All-Stars 7 (92,753)
8-23-46	All-Stars 16, Los Angeles 0 (97,380)
8-22-47	All-Stars 16, Chicago Bears 0 (105,840)
8-20-48	Chicago Cardinals 28, All-Stars 0 (101,220)
8-12-49	Philadelphia 38, All-Stars 0 (93,780)
8-11-50	All-Stars 17, Philadelphia 7 (88,885)
8-17-51	Cleveland 33, All-Stars 0 (92,180)
8-15-52	Los Angeles 10, All-Stars 7 (88,316)
8-14-53	Detroit 24, All-Stars 10 (93,818)
8-13-54	Detroit 31, All-Stars 6 (93,470)
8-12-55	All-Stars 30, Cleveland 27 (75,000)
8-10-56	Cleveland 26, All-Stars 0 (75,000)
8-9-57	New York Giants 22, All-Stars 12 (75,000)
8-15-58	All-Stars 35, Detroit 19 (70,000)
8-14-59	Baltimore 29, All-Stars 0 (70,000)
8-12-60	Baltimore 32, All-Stars 7 (70,000)
8-4-61	Philadelphia 28, All-Stars 14 (66,000)
8-3-62	Green Bay 42, All-Stars 20 (65,000)
8-2-63	All-Stars 20, Green Bay 17 (65,000)
8-7-64	Chicago Bears 28, All-Stars 17 (65,000)
8-6-65	Cleveland 24, All-Stars 16 (68,000)
8-5-66	Green Bay 38, All-Stars 0 (72,000)
8-4-67	Green Bay 27, All-Stars 0 (70,934)
8-2-68	Green Bay 34, All-Stars 17 (69,917)
8-1-69	New York Jets 26, All-Stars 24 (74,208)
7-31-70	Kansas City 24, All-Stars 3 (69,940)
7-30-71	Baltimore 24, All-Stars 17 (52,289)
7-28-72	Dallas 20, All-Stars 7 (54,162)
7-27-73	Miami 14, All-Stars 3 (54,103)
1974	No game played
8-1-75	Pittsburgh 21, All-Stars 14 (54,103)
7-23-76	*Pittsburgh 24, All-Stars 0 (52,895)

*Game was not completed due to thunderstorms.

DISCONTINUED ALL-STAR FOOTBALL GAMES

Many of these games were identified without complete

information such as scores, teams, sites or dates. Please send any updates or additional information to: NCAA Statistics Service, 6201 College Boulevard, Overland Park, Kansas 66211-2422.

ALL-AMERICAN BOWL (1969-77)
Tampa, Fla.

Date	Score (Attendance)
1-4-69	North 21, South 15 (16,380)
1-3-70	South 24, North 23 (17,642)
1-10-71	North 39, South 2 (12,000)
1-9-72	North 27, South 8 (20,137)
1-7-73	North 10, South 6 (23,416)
1-6-74	North 28, South 7 (24,536)
1-5-75	South 28, North 22 (19,246)
1-10-76	North 14, South 14 (15,321)
1-2-77	North 21, South 20 (14,207)

AMERICAN COLLEGE ALL-STAR GAME (1948)
Los Angeles, Calif.

Date	Score
12-48	American All-Stars 43, Canadian All-Stars 0
12-48	American All-Stars 14, Hawaiian All-Stars 0

BLACK COLLEGE ALL-STAR BOWL (1980-81)

Date	Score (Location, Attendance)
1-5-80	West 27, East 21 (at New Orleans, La.)
1-17-81	West 19, East 10 (at Jackson, Miss., 7,500)

CAMP FOOTBALL FOUNDATION BOWL (1974)

CANADIAN-AMERICAN BOWL (1978-79)
Tampa, Fla.

Date	Score (Attendance)
1-8-78	U.S. All-Stars 22, Canadian All-Stars 7 (11,328)
1-6-79	U.S. All-Stars 34, Canadian All-Stars 14 (11,033)

CHALLENGE BOWL (1978-79)
Seattle, Wash.

Date	Score (Attendance)
1-14-78	Pacific-8 27, Big Ten 20 (20,578)
1-13-79	Pacific-10 36, Big Eight 23 (23,961)

CHRISTIAN BOWL (1955)
Murfreesboro, Tenn.

Date	Score (Attendance)
12-26-55	East 21, West 10 (4,000)

COACHES ALL-AMERICAN GAME (1961-75)

Date	Score (Attendance)
at Buffalo, N.Y.	
6-23-61	West 30, East 20 (12,913)
6-29-62	East 13, West 8 (22,759)
6-29-63	West 22, East 21 (20,840)
6-27-64	East 18, West 15 (21,112)
6-26-65	East 34, West 14 (25,501)
at Atlanta, Ga.	
7-9-66	West 24, East 7 (38,236)
7-9-67	East 12, West 9 (29,145)
6-28-68	West 34, East 20 (21,120)
6-28-69	West 14, East 10 (17,008)
at Lubbock, Texas	
6-28-70	East 34, West 27 (42,150)
6-26-71	West 33, East 28 (43,320)
6-24-72	East 42, West 20 (42,314)
6-23-73	West 20, East 6 (43,272)
6-22-74	West 36, East 6 (42,368)
6-21-75	East 23, West 21 (36,108)
6-19-76	West 35, East 17 (36,504)

COCANUT BOWL (1942)
Miami, Fla.

Date	Score (Attendance)
1-1-42	Florida Normal 0, Miami All-Stars 0 (9,000)

COLLEGE ALL-STAR GAME (1940-41)
New York, N.Y.

COPPER BOWL (1958-60)
Tempe, Ariz. (Sun Devil Stadium)

Date	Score (Attendance)
12-20-58	Southwest All-Stars 22, National All-Stars 13 (12,000)
12-26-59	National All-Stars 21, Southwest All-Stars 6 (16,000)
12-31-60	National All-Stars 27, South-West All-Stars 8 (8,000)

CRUSADE BOWL (1963)
Baltimore, Md.

Date	Score
1-6-63	East 38, West 10 (2,400)

DALLAS ALL-STAR GAME (1938-39)
Dallas, Texas

DIXIE CLASSIC (1929-31)
Dallas, Texas

Date	Score (Attendance)
1-1-29	Big Six Conference 14, Southwest Conference 6 (10,000)
1-1-30	Big Ten Conference 25, Southwest Conference 12 (15,000)
1-1-31	Southwest Conference 18, Big Ten Conference 0 (14,000)

EAST-WEST BLACK ALL-STAR GAME (1971)
Houston, Texas

Date	Score (Attendance)
12-11-71	East 19, West 10 (5,156)

EAST-WEST COLLEGE ALL-STAR GAME (1932)
(Demonstrated at Tenth Olympiad, Los Angeles, Calif.; East team composed of players from Harvard and Yale, West team composed of players from California, Southern Cal and Stanford)

Date	Score (Attendance)
8-8-32	West 7, East 6 (50,000)

EASTERN COLLEGE ALL-STAR BENEFIT GAME (1949)
(A group of Eastern college all-stars played the New York Giants for the Fresh Air Fund at the Polo Grounds, New York City)

Date	Score
9-1-49	Eastern All-Stars 28, New York Giants 13

FREEDOM BOWL ALL-STAR CLASSIC (1984-86)
Southwestern Athletic Conference vs. Mid-Eastern Athletic Conference, Atlanta, Ga.

Date	Score (Attendance)
1-14-84	SWAC 36, MEAC 22 (16,097)
1-12-85	SWAC 14, MEAC 0 (18,352)
1-11-86	SWAC 16, MEAC 14 (10,200)

FREEDOM BOWL ALL-STAR CLASSIC (1990)
Houston, Texas

Date	Score
1-13-90	North 14, South 13 (at Houston Astrodome)

FREEDOM CLASSIC (1976)

Year	Score (Attendance)
1976	West 12, East 9 (6,654)

MARTIN LUTHER KING ALL-AMERICA CLASSIC (1990-91)
(Division I-A vs. all other divisions)

Date	Score (Attendance)
1-15-90	All Div. All-Stars 35, I-A All-Stars 24 (350) (at San Jose, Calif.)
1-14-91	I-A All-Stars 21, All Div. All-Stars 14 (6,272) (at St. Petersburg, Fla.)

NORTH-SOUTH ALL-STAR SHRINE GAME (1932-76)

Date	Score (Attendance)
1-1-30	North 21, South 12 (20,000) (at Atlanta, Ga.)
1-1-30	Midwest 25, Southwest 12 (15,000) (at Dallas, Texas)
12-28-30	South 7, North 0 (2,000) (at New York, N.Y.)
12-10-32	South 7, North 6 (500) (at Baltimore, Md.)
12-24-33	North 3, South 0 (5,000) (at New York, N.Y.)
1-1-34	North 7, South 0 (12,000) (at Knoxville, Tenn.)
1-2-39	North 7, South 0 (8,000) (Jan. 2)
12-30-39	South 33, North 20 (Dec.30)
1940	North 14, South 12
1941	South 16, North 0
1942	South 24, North 0
1944	South 24, North 7
1945	North 26, South 0
1946	South 20, North 13
1947	South 33, North 6
1948	North 19, South 13
at Miami, Fla.	
12-25-48	South 24, North 14 (33,056)
12-25-49	North 20, South 14 (37,378)

12-25-50   South 14, North 9 (39,132)
12-25-51   South 35, North 7 (39,995)
12-25-52   North 21, South 21 (42,866)

12-25-53   South 20, North 0 (44,715)
12-25-54   South 20, North 17 (37,847)
12-25-55   South 20, North 7 (42,179)
12-26-56   North 17, South 7 (39,181)
12-25-57   North 23, South 20 (28,303)

12-27-58   South 49, North 20 (35,519)
12-26-59   North 27, South 17 (35,185)
12-26-60   North 41, South 14 (26,146)
12-25-61   South 35, North 16 (18,892)
12-25-62   South 15, North 14 (16,952)

12-21-63   South 23, North 14 (19,120)
12-25-64   South 37, North 30 (29,124)
12-25-65   South 21, North 14 (25,640)
12-26-66   North 27, South 14 (28,569)
12-25-67   North 24, South 0 (17,400)

12-25-68   North 3, South 0 (18,063)
12-25-69   North 31, South 10 (23,527)
12-25-70   North 28, South 7 (15,402)
12-27-71   South 7, North 6 (18,640)
12-25-72   North 17, South 10 (18,013)

12-25-73   South 27, North 6 (10,672)

at Pontiac, Mich.
12-17-76   South 24, North 0 (41,627)

OHIO SHRINE BOWL (1972-75)
Columbus, Ohio

Date	Score
12-10-72	East 20, West 7
1973	East 8, West 6
12-7-74	East 27, West 6
1975	West 17, East 7

OLYMPIA GOLD BOWL (1982)
San Diego, Calif.

Date	Score
1-16-82	National All-Stars 30, American All-Stars 21 (22,316)

OLYMPIC GAME (1933)
Chicago, Ill.

Date	Score (Attendance)
8-24-33	East 13, West 7 (50,000)

OPTIMIST ALL-AMERICA BOWL (1959-62)
Tucson, Ariz. (Varsity Stadium)

Date	Score (Attendance)
1-3-59	Major-College 14, Small-College 12 (10,000)
1-2-60	Major-College 53, Small-College 0 (14,500)
12-26-60	Major-College 25, Small-College 12
12-30-61	Major-College 31, Small-College 0 (14,000)
12-29-62	Small-College 14, Major-College 13

POTATO BOWL (1967)
Bakersfield, Calif.

Date	Score (Attendance)
12-23-67	North 23, South 7 (5,600)

ROCKY MOUNTAIN CONFERENCE-NORTH CENTRAL CONFERENCE GAME (1930)
Denver, Colo.

Date	Score
1-1-30	North Central 13, Rocky Mountain 6

SALAD BOWL ALL-STAR GAME (1955)
Phoenix, Ariz.

Date	Score (Attendance)
1-1-55	Skyline Conference 20, Border Conference 13 (8,000)
12-31-55	Border Conference 13, Skyline Conference 10

SMOKE BOWL (1941)
Richmond, Va.

Date	Score (Attendance)
1-1-41	Norfolk All-Stars 16, Richmond All-Stars 2 (5,000)

SOUTHWEST CHALLENGE BOWL (1963-64)
Corpus Christi, Texas

Date	Score
1-5-63	National 33, Southwest 13
1-4-64	National 66, Southwest 14 (10,200)

STEEL BOWL (1942)
Birmingham, Ala.

Date	Score
1-1-42	Southern All-Stars 26, Nashville Pros 13

U.S. BOWL (1962)
Washington, D. C.
(Teams were composed of players selected in the recent NFL draft)

Date	Score
1-5-62	West 33, East 19

Special Regular-Season Games

REGULAR-SEASON GAMES PLAYED IN USA

KICKOFF CLASSIC
Present Site: East Rutherford, N.J.
Stadium (Capacity): Giants (76,000)
Playing Surface: AstroTurf
Sponsor: National Association of Collegiate Directors of Athletics (NACDA). It is a permitted 12th regular-season game.
Playing Sites: Giants Stadium (since 1983)

Date	Teams, Score (Attendance)
8-29-83	Nebraska 44, Penn St. 6 (71,123)
8-27-84	Miami (Fla.) 20, Auburn 18 (51,131)
8-29-85	Brigham Young 28, Boston College 14 (51,227)
8-27-86	Alabama 16, Ohio St. 10 (68,296)
8-30-87	Tennessee 23, Iowa 22 (54,681)
8-27-88	Nebraska 23, Texas A&M 14 (58,172)
8-31-89	Notre Dame 36, Virginia 13 (77,323)
8-31-90	Southern Cal 34, Syracuse 16 (57,293)
8-28-91	Penn St. 34, Georgia Tech 22 (77,409)
8-29-92	North Caro. St. 24, Iowa 14 (46,251)
8-28-93	Florida St. 42, Kansas 0 (51,734)
8-28-94	Nebraska vs. West Va.

PIGSKIN CLASSIC
Present Site: Anaheim, Calif.
Stadium (Capacity): Anaheim (70,962)
Playing Surface: Grass
Sponsor: Disneyland. It is a permitted 12th regular-season game.
Playing Sites: Anaheim Stadium (since 1990)

Date	Teams, Score (Attendance)
8-26-90	Colorado 31, Tennessee 31 (33,458)
8-29-91	Florida St. 44, Brigham Young 28 (38,363)
8-26-92	Texas A&M 10, Stanford 7 (35,240)
8-29-93	North Caro. 31, Southern Cal 9 (49,309)
8-29-94	Fresno St. vs. Ohio St.

SOUTHEASTERN CONFERENCE CHAMPIONSHIP
Present Site: Birmingham, Ala.
Stadium (Capacity): Legion Field (83,091)
Playing Surface: AstroTurf
Playing Sites: Legion Field (since 1992)

Date	Teams, Score (Attendance)
12-5-92	Alabama (Western Div.) 28, Florida (Eastern Div.) 21 (83,091)
12-4-93	Florida (Eastern Div.) 28, Alabama (Western Div.) 13 (76,345)

REGULAR-SEASON GAMES PLAYED IN FOREIGN COUNTRIES

TOKYO, JAPAN
(Called Mirage Bowl 1976-85, Coca-Cola Classic from 1986. Played at Tokyo Olympic Memorial Stadium 1976-87, Tokyo Dome from 1988.)

Date	Teams, Score (Attendance)
9-4-76	Grambling 42, Morgan St. 16 (50,000)
12-11-77	Grambling 35, Temple 8 (50,000)
12-10-78	Temple 28, Boston College 24 (55,000)
11-24-79	Notre Dame 40, Miami (Fla.) 15 (62,574)
11-30-80	UCLA 34, Oregon St. 3 (86,000)
11-28-81	Air Force 21, San Diego St. 16 (80,000)
11-27-82	Clemson 21, Wake Forest 17 (64,700)
11-26-83	Southern Methodist 34, Houston 12 (70,000)
11-17-84	Army 45, Montana 31 (60,000)
11-30-85	Southern Cal 20, Oregon 6 (65,000)
11-30-86	Stanford 29, Arizona 24 (55,000)
11-28-87	California 17, Washington St. 17 (45,000)
12-3-88	Oklahoma St. 45, Texas Tech 42 (56,000)
12-4-89	Syracuse 24, Louisville 13 (50,000)
12-2-90	Houston 62, Arizona St. 45 (50,000)
11-30-91	Clemson 33, Duke 21 (50,000)
12-6-92	Nebraska 38, Kansas St. 24 (50,000)
12-5-93	Wisconsin 41, Michigan St. 20 (51,500)

MELBOURNE, AUSTRALIA

Date	Teams, Score (Attendance)
12-6-85*	Wyoming 24, UTEP 21 (22,000)
12-4-87†	Brigham Young 30, Colorado St. 26 (76,652)

*Played at V.F.L. Park. †Played at Princes Park.

YOKOHAMA, JAPAN

Date	Teams, Score (Attendance)
12-2-78	Brigham Young 28, Nevada-Las Vegas 24 (27,500)

OSAKA, JAPAN

Date	Teams, Score (Attendance)
9-3-78	Utah St. 10, Idaho St. 0 (15,000)

DUBLIN, IRELAND
(Called Emerald Isle Classic. Played at Lansdowne Road Stadium.)

Date	Teams, Score (Attendance)
11-19-88	Boston College 38, Army 24 (45,525)
12-2-89	Pittsburgh 46, Rutgers 29 (19,800)

LONDON, ENGLAND

Date	Teams, Score (Attendance)
10-16-88	Richmond 20, Boston U. 17 (6,000)

MILAN, ITALY
(Played at The Arena.)

Date	Teams, Score (Attendance)
10-28-89	Villanova 28, Rhode Island 25 (5,000)

LIMERICK, IRELAND
(Wild Geese Classic. Played at Limerick Gaelic Grounds.)

Date	Teams, Score (Attendance)
11-16-91	Holy Cross 24, Fordham 19 (17,411)

FRANKFURT, GERMANY
(Played at Wald Stadium.)

Date	Teams, Score (Attendance)
9-19-92	Heidelberg 7, Otterbein 7 (4,351)

GALWAY, IRELAND
(Called Christopher Columbus Classic.)

Date	Teams, Score (Attendance)
11-29-92	Bowdoin 7, Tufts 6 (2,500)

HAMILTON, BERMUDA
(Played at Bermuda National Soccer Stadium.)

Date	Teams, Score (Attendance)
11-20-93	Georgetown 17, Wash. & Lee 14 (3,218)

COLLEGE FOOTBALL TROPHY GAMES

Following is a list of the current college football trophy games. The games are listed alphabetically by the trophy-object name. The date refers to the season the trophy was first exchanged and is not necessarily the start of competition between the participants. A game involving interdivision teams is listed in the higher-division classification.

DIVISION I-A

Trophy	Date	Colleges
Anniversary Award	1985	Bowling Green-Kent
Apple Cup	1962	Washington-Washington St.
Axe	1933	California-Stanford
Bayou Bucket	1974	Houston-Rice
Beehive Boot	1971	Brigham Young, Utah, Weber St.
Beer Barrel	1925	Kentucky-Tennessee
Bell	1927	Missouri-Nebraska
Bell Clapper	1931	Oklahoma-Oklahoma St.
Big Game	1953	Arizona-Arizona St.
Blue Key Victory Bell	1940	Ball St.-Indiana St.
Bourbon Barrel	1967	Indiana-Kentucky
Brass Spittoon	1950	Indiana-Michigan St.
Brass Spittoon	1981	New Mexico St.-UTEP
Bronze Boot	1968	Colorado St.-Wyoming
Cannon	1943	Illinois-Purdue
Commander in Chief's	1972	Air Force, Army, Navy
Cy-Hawk	1977	Iowa-Iowa St.
Floyd of Rosedale	1935	Iowa-Minnesota
Foy-O.D.K.	1948	Alabama-Auburn
Fremont Cannon	1970	Nevada—Nevada-Las Vegas
Golden Egg	1927	Mississippi-Mississippi St.
Golden Hat	1941	Oklahoma-Texas
Governor's	1969	Kansas-Kansas St.
Governor's Cup	1958	Florida-Florida St.
Governor's Cup	1983	Colorado-Colorado St.
Illibuck	1925	Illinois-Ohio St.
Indian War Drum	1935	Kansas-Missouri
Iron Bowl	1983	Alabama-Auburn
Keg of Nails	1950	Cincinnati-Louisville
Kit Carson Rifle	1938	Arizona-New Mexico
Little Brown Jug	1909	Michigan-Minnesota
Megaphone	1949	Michigan St.-Notre Dame
Old Oaken Bucket	1925	Indiana-Purdue
Old Wagon Wheel	1948	Brigham Young-Utah St.
Paniolo Trophy	1979	Hawaii-Wyoming
Paul Bunyan Axe	1948	Minnesota-Wisconsin
Paul Bunyan-Governor of Michigan	1953	Michigan-Michigan St.
Peace Pipe	1929	Missouri-Oklahoma
Peace Pipe	1955	Miami (Ohio)-Western Mich.
Peace Pipe	1980	Bowling Green-Toledo
Ram-Falcon	1980	Air Force-Colorado St.
Sabine Shoe	1937	Lamar-Southwestern La.
Shillelagh	1952	Notre Dame-Southern Cal
Shillelagh	1958	Notre Dame-Purdue
Silver Spade	1955	New Mexico St.-UTEP
Steel Tire	1976	Akron-Youngstown St.
Telephone	1960	Iowa St.-Missouri
Textile Bowl	1981	Clemson-North Caro. St.
Tomahawk	1945	Illinois-Northwestern
Victory Bell	1942	Southern Cal-UCLA
Victory Bell	1948	Cincinnati-Miami (Ohio)
Victory Bell	1948	Duke-North Caro.
Wagon Wheel	1946	Akron-Kent

DIVISION I-AA

Trophy	Date	Colleges
Bill Knight	1986	Massachusetts-New Hampshire
Brice-Colwell Musket	1946	Maine-New Hampshire
Chief Caddo	1962	Northwestern St.-Stephen F. Austin
Gem State	1978	Boise St., Idaho, Idaho St.
Governor's Cup	1972	Brown-Rhode Island
Governor's Cup	1975	Dartmouth-Princeton
Governor's Cup	1984	Eastern Wash.-Idaho
Harvey—Shin-A-Ninny Totem Pole	1961	Middle Tenn. St.-Tennessee Tech
Little Brown Stein	1938	Idaho-Montana
Mare's	1987	Murray St.—Tenn.-Martin
Mayor's Cup	1981	Bethune-Cookman—Central Fla.
Ol' Mountain Jug	1937	Appalachian St.-Western Caro.
Painting Grizzly-Bobcat	1984	Montana-Montana St.
Red Belt	1978	Murray St.-Western Ky.
Ron Rogerson Memorial	1988	Maine-Rhode Island
Silver Shako	1976	Citadel-Va. Military
Team of Game's MVP	1960	Lafayette-Lehigh

DIVISION II

Trophy	Date	Colleges
Axe	1946	Cal St. Chico-Humboldt St.
Axe Bowl	1975	Northwood-Saginaw Valley
Backyard Bowl	1987	Cheyney-West Chester
Battle Axe	1948	Bemidji St.-Moorhead St.
Battle of the Ravine	1976	Henderson St.-Ouachita Baptist
Bell (Little Big Game)	1947	Santa Clara-St. Mary's (Cal.)
Bishop's	1970	Lenoir-Rhyne—Newberry
Board of Trustees	1987	Central Conn. St.-Western Conn. St.
Bronze Derby	1946	Newberry-Presbyterian
Eagle-Rock	1980	Black Hills St.-Chadron St.
East Meets West	1987	Chadron St.-Peru St.
Elm City	1983	New Haven-Southern Conn. St.
Governor's	1979	Central Conn. St.-Southern Conn. St.
Heritage Bell	1979	Delta St.-Mississippi Col.
Miner's Bowl	1986	Mo. Southern St.-Pittsburg St.
Nickel	1938	North Dak.-North Dak. St.
Ol' School Bell	1988	Jacksonville St.-Troy St.
Old Hickory Stick	1931	Northeast Mo. St.-Northwest Mo. St.
Old Settler's Musket	1975	Adams St.-Fort Lewis St.
Sitting Bull	1953	North Dak.-South Dak.
Springfield Mayor's	1941	American Int'l-Springfield
Textile	1960	Clark Atlanta-Fort Valley St.
Top Dog	1971	Butler-Indianapolis
Traveling	1976	Ashland-Hillsdale
Victory Carriage	1960	Cal St. Sacramento-UC Davis
Wagon Wheel	1986	Eastern N. Mex.-West Tex. A&M
Wooden Shoes	1977	Grand Valley St.-Wayne St. (Mich.)

DIVISION III

Trophy	Date	Colleges
Academic Bowl	1986	Carnegie Mellon-Case Reserve
Admiral's Cup	1980	Maine Maritime-Mass. Maritime
Baird Bros. Golden Stringer	1984	Case Reserve-Wooster
Bell	*1931	Franklin-Hanover
Bill Edwards Trophy	1989	Case Reserve-Wittenberg
Bridge Bowl	1990	Mt. St. Joseph-Thomas More
Bronze Turkey	1929	Knox-Monmouth (Ill.)
CBB	1966	Bates, Bowdoin, Colby
Conestoga Wagon	1963	Dickinson-Frank. & Marsh.
Cortaca Jug	1959	Cortland St.-Ithaca
Cranberry Bowl	1979	Bri'water (Mass.)-Mass. Maritime
Doehling-Heselton Helmet	1988	Lawrence-Ripon
Drum	1940	Occidental—Pomona-Pitzer
Dutchman's Shoes	1950	Rensselaer-Union (N.Y.)
Edmund Orgill	1954	Rhodes-Sewanee
Field Cup	1983	Evansville-Ky. Wesleyan
Founder's	1987	Chicago-Washington (Mo.)
Goal Post	1953	Juniata-Susquehanna
Goat	1931	Carleton-St. Olaf
Golden Circle	1988	Drake-Simpson
John Wesley	1984	Ky. Wesleyan-Union (Ky.)
Keystone Cup	1981	Delaware Valley-Widener
Little Brass Bell	1947	North Central-Wheaton (Ill.)
Little Brown Bucket	1938	Dickinson-Gettysburg
Little Three	1971	Amherst, Wesleyan, Williams
Mercer County Cup	1984	Grove City-Thiel
Monon Bell	1932	DePauw-Wabash
Mug	1931	Coast Guard-Norwich
Old Goal Post	1953	Juniata-Susquehanna
Old Musket	1964	Carroll (Wis.)-Carthage
Old Rocking Chair	1980	Hamilton-Middlebury
Old Tin Cup	1954	Gettysburg-Muhlenberg
Old Water Bucket	1989	Maranatha-N'western (Wis.)
Paint Bucket	1965	Hamline-Macalester
Pella Corporation Classic	1988	Central (Iowa)-William Penn
President's Cup	1971	Case Reserve-John Carroll
Secretary's Cup	1981	Coast Guard-Merchant Marine
Shoes	1946	Occidental-Whittier
Shot Glass	1938	Coast Guard-Rensselaer
Steve Dean Memorial	1976	Catholic-Georgetown
Transit	1980	Rensselaer-Worcester Tech
Victory Bell	1946	Loras-St. Thomas (Minn.)
Victory Bell	1949	Upper Iowa-Wartburg
Wadsworth	1977	Middlebury-Norwich
Wilson Brothers Cup	1986	Hamline-St. Thomas (Minn.)
Wooden Shoes	1946	Hope-Kalamazoo

NON-NCAA MEMBERS

Trophy	Date	Colleges
Baptist Bible Bowl	1982	Maranatha-Pillsbury
Home Stake-Gold Mine	1950	Black Hills St.-South Dak. Tech
KTEN Savage-Tiger	1979	East Central Okla.-Southeastern Okla.
Paint Bucket	1961	Jamestown-Valley City St.
Wagon Wheel	1957	Lewis & Clark-Willamette

*Was reinstated in 1988 after a 17-year lapse.

BOWL/ALL-STAR RESULTS

Coaching Records

All-Division Coaching Records

Coaches With Career Winning Percentage of .800 or Better

This list includes all coaches in history with a winning percentage of at least .800 over a career of at least 10 seasons at four-year colleges (regardless of division or association). Bowl and playoff games included.

Coach (Alma Mater) (Colleges Coached, Tenure)	Years	Won	Lost	Tied	Pct.
Knute Rockne (Notre Dame '14) (Notre Dame 1918-30)	13	105	12	5	.881
#Bob Reade (Cornell College '54) (Augustana, Ill. 1979—)	†15	138	21	1	.866
Frank Leahy (Notre Dame '31) (Boston College 1939-40; Notre Dame 1941-43, 1946-53)	13	107	13	9	.864
Doyt Perry (Bowling Green '32) (Bowling Green 1955-64)	†10	77	11	5	.855
George Woodruff (Yale '89) (Pennsylvania 1892-1901; Illinois 1903; Carlisle 1905)	12	142	25	2	.846
#Mike Kelly (Manchester '70) (Dayton 1981—)	†13	128	23	1	.845
Jake Gaither (Knoxville '27) (Florida A&M 1945-69)	†25	203	36	4	.844
Dave Maurer (Denison '54) (Wittenberg 1969-83)	†15	129	23	3	.842
Paul Hoereman (Heidelberg '38) (Heidelberg 1946-59)	†14	102	18	4	.839
Barry Switzer (Arkansas '60) (Oklahoma 1973-88)	16	157	29	4	.837
Don Coryell (Washington '50) (Whittier 1957-59; San Diego St. 1961-72)	†15	127	24	3	.834
Percy Haughton (Harvard '99) (Cornell 1899-1900; Harvard 1908-16; Columbia 1923-24)	13	96	17	6	.832
Bob Neyland (Army '16) (Tennessee 1926-34, 1936-40, 1946-52)	21	173	31	12	.829
"Hurry Up" Yost (Lafayette '97) (Ohio Wesleyan 1897; Nebraska 1898; Kansas 1899; Stanford 1900; Michigan 1901-23, 1925-26)	29	196	36	12	.828
"Bud" Wilkinson (Minnesota '37) (Oklahoma 1947-63)	17	145	29	4	.826
#Al Bagnoli (Central Conn. St. '74) (Union, N.Y. 1982-91; Pennsylvania 1992—)	†12	103	22	0	.824
Chuck Klausing (Slippery Rock '48) (Indiana, Pa. 1964-69; Carnegie Mellon 1976-85)	†16	123	26	2	.821
Vernon McCain (Langston '31) (Md.-East. Shore 1948-63)	†16	102	21	5	.816
"Jock" Sutherland (Pittsburgh '18) (Lafayette 1919-23; Pittsburgh 1924-38)	20	144	28	14	.812
#Tom Osborne (Hastings '59) (Nebraska 1973—)	21	206	47	3	.811
Bob Devaney (Alma '39) (Wyoming 1957-61; Nebraska 1962-72)	16	136	30	7	.806
"Biggie" Munn (Minnesota '32) (Albright 1935-36; Syracuse 1946; Michigan St. 1947-53)	10	71	16	3	.805
#Ron Schipper (Hope '52) (Central, Iowa 1961—)	†33	260	62	3	.805
Sid Gillman (Ohio St. '34) (Miami, Ohio 1944-47; Cincinnati 1949-54)	†10	81	19	2	.804

†Zero to nine years in Division I-A. #Active coach.

Coaches With 200 or More Career Victories

This list includes all coaches in NCAA history who have won at least 200 games at four-year colleges (regardless of whether the college was an NCAA member at the time). Bowl and playoff games included.

Coach (Alma Mater) (Colleges Coached, Tenure)	Years	Won	Lost	Tied	Pct.
#Eddie Robinson (Leland '41) (Grambling 1941-42, 1945—)	†51	388	140	15	.728
"Bear" Bryant (Alabama '36) (Maryland 1945; Kentucky 1946-53; Texas A&M 1954-57; Alabama 1958-82)	38	323	85	17	.780
"Pop" Warner (Cornell '95) (Georgia 1895-96; Cornell 1897-98; Carlisle 1899-1903; Cornell 1904-06; Carlisle 1907-14; Pittsburgh 1915-23; Stanford 1924-32; Temple 1933-38)	44	319	106	32	.733
Amos Alonzo Stagg (Yale '88) (Springfield 1890-91; Chicago 1892-1932; Pacific, Cal. 1933-46)	57	314	199	35	.605
#John Gagliardi (Colorado Col. '49) (Carroll, Mont. 1949-52; St. John's, Minn. 1953—)	†45	306	96	10	.755
#Ron Schipper (Hope '52) (Central, Iowa 1961—)	†33	260	62	3	.805
Joe Paterno (Brown '50) (Penn St. 1966—)	28	257	69	3	.786
#Roy Kidd (Eastern Ky. '54) (Eastern Ky. 1964—)	†30	247	88	8	.732
#Bobby Bowden (Samford '53) (Samford 1959-62; West Va. 1970-75; Florida St. 1976—)	28	239	78	3	.752
"Woody" Hayes (Denison '35) (Denison 1946-48; Miami, Ohio 1949-50; Ohio St. 1951-78)	33	238	72	10	.759
"Bo" Schembechler (Miami, Ohio '51) (Miami, Ohio 1963-68; Michigan 1969-89)	27	234	65	8	.775
Arnett Mumford (Wilberforce '24) (Jarvis 1924-26; Bishop 1927-29; Texas College 1931-35; Southern-B.R. 1936-42, 1944-61)	†36	233	85	23	.717
††John Merritt (Kentucky St. '50) (Jackson St. 1953-62; Tennessee St. 1963-83)	†31	232	65	11	.771
#"Tubby" Raymond (Michigan '50) (Delaware 1966—)	†28	232	92	2	.715
#Jim Malosky (Minnesota '51) (Minn.-Duluth 1958—)	†36	231	107	12	.677
Fred Long (Millikin '18) (Paul Quinn 1921-22; Wiley 1923-47; Prairie View 1948; Texas College 1949-55; Wiley 1956-65)	†45	227	151	31	.593
Fred Martinelli (Otterbein '51) (Ashland 1959-93)	†35	217	119	12	.641
#Roger Harring (Wis.-La Crosse '58) (Wis.-La Crosse 1969—)	†25	210	60	7	.771
Jess Neely (Vanderbilt '24) (Southwestern, Tenn. 1924-27; Clemson 1931-39; Rice 1940-66)	40	207	176	19	.539
#Tom Osborne (Hastings '59) (Nebraska 1973—)	21	206	47	3	.811
Jim Butterfield (Maine '53) (Ithaca 1967-93)	†27	206	71	1	.743
Jake Gaither (Knoxville '27) (Florida A&M 1945-69)	†25	203	36	4	.844
Warren Woodson (Baylor '24) (Conway St. 1935-40; Hardin-Simmons 1941-42, 1946-51; Arizona 1952-56; New Mexico St. 1958-67; Trinity, Tex. 1972-73)	31	203	95	14	.673
Vince Dooley (Auburn '54) (Georgia 1964-88)	25	201	77	10	.715
Eddie Anderson (Notre Dame '22) (Loras 1922-24; DePaul 1925-31; Holy Cross 1933-38; Iowa 1939-42, 1946-49; Holy Cross 1950-64)	39	201	128	15	.606
Darrell Mudra (Peru St. '51) (Adams St. 1959-62; North Dak. St. 1963-65; Arizona 1967-68; Western Ill. 1969-73; Florida St. 1974-75; Eastern Ill. 1978-82; Northern Iowa 1983-87)	†26	200	81	4	.709
#Hayden Fry (Baylor '51) (Southern Methodist 1962-72; North Texas 1973-78; Iowa 1979—)	32	200	153	9	.565

†Zero to nine years in Division I-A. ††Tennessee State's participation in 1981 and 1982 Division I-AA championships (1-2 record) voided. #Active coach.

Matchups of Coaches Each With 200 Victories

Date	Coaches, Teams (Victories Going In)	Winner (Score)
11-11-61	Arnett Mumford, Southern-B.R. (232) Fred Long, Wiley (215)	Wiley (21-19)
1-1-78 Sugar Bowl	"Bear" Bryant, Alabama (272) "Woody" Hayes, Ohio St. (231)	Alabama (35-6)
10-11-80	Eddie Robinson, Grambling (284) John Merritt, Tennessee St. (200)	Grambling (52-27)
10-10-81	Eddie Robinson, Grambling (294) John Merritt, Tennessee St. (209)	Tennessee St. (14-10)
10-9-82	Eddie Robinson, Grambling (301) John Merritt, Tennessee St. (218)	Tennessee St. (22-8)
10-8-83	Eddie Robinson, Grambling (308) John Merritt, Tennessee St. (228)	Tie (7-7)
11-28-87	John Gagliardi, St. John's (Minn.) (251) Ron Schipper, Central (Iowa) (202)	Central (Iowa) (13-3)
11-25-89	John Gagliardi, St. John's (Minn.) (268) Ron Schipper, Central (Iowa) (224)	St. John's (Minn.) (27-24)
12-28-90 Blockbuster Bowl	Joe Paterno, Penn St. (229) Bobby Bowden, Florida St. (204)	Florida St. (24-17)
11-27-93	John Gagliardi, St. John's (Minn.) (305) Roger Harring, Wis.-La Crosse (210)	St. John's (Minn.) (47-25)
1-1-94 Orange Bowl	Bobby Bowden, Florida St. (238) Tom Osborne, Nebraska (206)	Florida St. (18-16)

Coaches With 200 or More Victories at One College

(Bowl and Playoff Games Included)

Coach (College, Tenure)	Years	Won	Lost	Tied	Pct.
#Eddie Robinson (Grambling 1941-42, 1945—)	†51	388	140	15	.728
#John Gagliardi (St. John's, Minn. 1953—)	†41	281	90	9	.751
#Ron Schipper (Central, Iowa 1961—)	†33	260	62	3	.805
#Joe Paterno (Penn St. 1966—)	28	257	69	3	.786
#Roy Kidd (Eastern Ky. 1964—)	†30	247	88	8	.732
Amos Alonzo Stagg (Chicago 1892-1932)	41	244	111	27	.674
"Bear" Bryant (Alabama 1958-82)	25	232	46	9	.824
#"Tubby" Raymond (Delaware 1966—)	†28	232	92	2	.715
#Jim Malosky (Minn.-Duluth 1958—)	†36	231	107	12	.677
Fred Martinelli (Ashland 1959-93)	†35	217	119	12	.641
#Roger Harring (Wis.-La Crosse 1969—)	†25	210	60	7	.771
#Tom Osborne (Nebraska 1973—)	21	206	47	3	.811
Jim Butterfield (Ithaca 1967-93)	†27	206	71	1	.743
"Woody" Hayes (Ohio St. 1951-78)	28	205	61	10	.761
Jake Gaither (Florida A&M 1945-69)	†25	203	36	4	.844
Vince Dooley (Georgia 1964-88)	25	201	77	10	.715

†Zero to nine years in Division I-A. #Active coach.

Division I-A Coaching Records

Winningest Active Division I-A Coaches

(Minimum Five Years as Division I-A Head Coach; Record at Four-Year Colleges Only)

BY PERCENTAGE

Coach, College	Years	Won	Lost	Tied	*Pct.	Bowls W	L	T
Tom Osborne, Nebraska	21	206	47	3	.811	8	13	0
R. C. Slocum, Texas A&M	5	49	12	1	.798	1	4	0
John Robinson, Southern Cal	8	75	19	2	.792	5	1	0
Joe Paterno, Penn St.	28	257	69	3	.786	15	8	1
Bobby Bowden, Florida St.	28	239	78	3	.752	13	3	1
Danny Ford, Arkansas@	13	101	34	5	.739	6	2	0
Dennis Erickson, Miami (Fla.)	12	103	38	1	.729	%5	4	0
LaVell Edwards, Brigham Young	22	197	73	3	.727	5	12	1
Steve Spurrier, Florida	7	59	23	1	.717	2	2	0
Lou Holtz, Notre Dame	24	193	84	6	.693	10	6	2

Coach, College	Years	Won	Lost	Tied	*Pct.	Bowls W	L	T
Gary Gibbs, Oklahoma	5	38	17	2	.684	2	0	0
Terry Donahue, UCLA	18	139	63	8	.681	8	3	1
Jackie Sherrill, Mississippi St.	16	122	61	4	.663	6	4	0
John Cooper, Ohio St.	17	126	63	6	.662	3	5	0
Ken Hatfield, Rice	15	113	62	3	.643	4	6	0
Al Molde, Western Mich.	23	152	87	8	.632	%3	6	0
Don Nehlen, West Va.	23	156	91	8	.627	3	5	0
Fisher DeBerry, Air Force	10	76	46	1	.622	4	3	0
John Ralston, San Jose St.	14	88	56	4	.608	2	2	0
Johnny Majors, Pittsburgh	26	176	113	10	.605	9	7	0
Bob Wagner, Hawaii	7	51	33	2	.605	1	1	0
Bill McCartney, Colorado	12	82	54	5	.599	2	6	0
Bill Mallory, Indiana	24	156	108	4	.590	4	6	0
Ray Goff, Georgia	5	34	24	0	.586	2	1	0
Jim Wacker, Minnesota	23	150	107	3	.583	%13	2	0
Jim Sweeney, Fresno St.	29	186	133	3	.582	5	2	0
Larry Smith, Missouri	17	110	80	6	.577	2	5	1
Howard Schnellenberger, Louisville	14	89	67	2	.570	4	0	0
George Welsh, Virginia	21	135	102	4	.568	3	6	0
Hayden Fry, Iowa	32	200	153	9	.565	5	8	1
Billy Brewer, Mississippi	20	124	95	6	.564	%4	3	0
Paul Schudel, Ball St.	9	55	43	3	.559	0	2	0
Gary Moeller, Michigan	7	42	33	6	.556	3	1	0
Dick Tomey, Arizona	17	109	77	7	.554	2	2	0
George Perles, Michigan St.	11	68	56	4	.547	3	4	0
John Mackovic, Texas	9	55	46	2	.544	1	3	0
Gene Stallings, Alabama	10	58	51	1	.532	3	1	0
Frank Beamer, Virginia Tech	13	75	66	4	.531	%1	1	0
Pat Jones, Oklahoma St.	10	59	53	2	.526	3	1	0
Curley Hallman, Louisiana St.	6	35	32	0	.522	1	0	0
Bruce Snyder, Arizona St.	14	78	72	6	.519	2	0	0
Spike Dykes, Texas Tech#	8	41	38	1	.519	1	2	0
Joe Raymond Peace, Louisiana Tech	6	32	30	4	.515	0	0	1
Gerry Faust, Akron	13	72	69	4	.510	1	1	0
Mike Price, Washington St.	13	73	73	0	.500	%2	1	0
Bill Lewis, Georgia Tech	8	44	45	2	.495	1	0	0
Bill Snyder, Kansas St.	5	27	28	1	.491	1	0	0
Nelson Stokley, Southwestern La.	8	42	45	1	.483	0	0	0
Bill Curry, Kentucky	14	74	81	4	.478	2	3	0
Dave Rader, Tulsa	6	31	36	1	.463	1	1	0
Mack Brown, North Caro.	10	51	62	1	.452	1	2	0
Chuck Stobart, Memphis	13	63	79	3	.445	1	0	0
Rich Brooks, Oregon	17	82	105	4	.440	1	2	0
Glen Mason, Kansas	8	39	50	1	.439	1	0	0
Jim Walden, Iowa St.	16	69	102	6	.407	0	1	0
Jerry Pettibone, Oregon St.	9	39	58	2	.404	0	0	0
Fred Goldsmith, Duke	6	25	38	1	.398	0	0	0
Chuck Shelton, Pacific (Cal.)	17	72	114	1	.388	0	0	0
Jim Colletto, Purdue	8	26	62	1	.298	0	0	0

Less Than 5 Years in Division I-A (school followed by years in I-A, includes record at all four-year colleges):

Coach, College	Years	Won	Lost	Tied	Pct.	Bowls W	L	T
Mark Duffner, Maryland (2)	8	65	22	1	.744	0	0	0
Dennis Franchione, New Mexico (2)	11	89	32	2	.732	%6	5	0
Chris Ault, Nevada (1)	17	145	58	1	.713	%9	8	0
Paul Pasqualoni, Syracuse (3)	8	60	25	1	.703	%2	1	0
Terry Bowden, Auburn (1)	10	75	36	1	.674	%2	4	0
Keith Gilbertson, California (2)	5	41	20	0	.672	%3	3	0
Jim Hess, New Mexico St. (4)	19	126	83	5	.600	%5	3	0
Sonny Lubick, Colorado St. (1)	5	26	25	0	.510	0	0	0
George Chaump, Navy (4)	12	67	66	2	.504	%4	2	0
Buddy Teevens, Tulane (2)	9	44	49	2	.474	0	0	0
Doug Graber, Rutgers (4)	5	26	29	0	.473	0	0	0
Tom Lichtenberg, Ohio (4)	7	26	48	3	.357	%0	1	0

*Ties computed as half won and half lost. Overall record includes bowl and playoff games. %Includes record in NCAA and/or NAIA championships. @ Win in Gator Bowl in first game. #Loss in Independence Bowl in first game.

BY VICTORIES
(Minimum 100 Victories)

Coach, College, Winning Percentage	Won
Joe Paterno, Penn St. .786	257
Bobby Bowden, Florida St. .752	239
Tom Osborne, Nebraska .811	206
Hayden Fry, Iowa .565	200
LaVell Edwards, Brigham Young .727	197
Lou Holtz, Notre Dame .693	193
Jim Sweeney, Fresno St. .582	186
Johnny Majors, Pittsburgh .605	176
Bill Mallory, Indiana .590	156
Don Nehlen, West Va. .627	156
Al Molde, Western Mich. .632	152
Jim Wacker, Minnesota .583	150

Coach, College, Winning Percentage	Won
Terry Donahue, UCLA .681	139
George Welsh, Virginia .568	135
John Cooper, Ohio St. .662	126
Billy Brewer, Mississippi .564	124
Jackie Sherrill, Mississippi St. .663	122
Ken Hatfield, Rice .643	113
Larry Smith, Missouri .577	110
Dick Tomey, Arizona .554	109
Dennis Erickson, Miami (Fla.) .729	103
Danny Ford, Arkansas .739	101

Less Than 5 Years in Division I-A (includes record at all four-year colleges):

Coach, College		Won
Chris Ault, Nevada .713		145
Jim Hess, New Mexico St. .600		126

Winningest All-Time Division I-A Coaches

Minimum 10 years as head coach at Division I institutions; record at four-year colleges only; bowl games included; ties computed as half won, half lost. Active coaches indicated by (*). Hall of Fame members indicated by (†).

BY PERCENTAGE

Coach (Alma Mater) (Colleges Coached, Tenure)	Years	Won	Lost	Tied	Pct.
Knute Rockne (Notre Dame '14)† (Notre Dame 1918-30)	13	105	12	5	.881
Frank Leahy (Notre Dame '31)† (Boston College 1939-40; Notre Dame 1941-43, 1946-53)	13	107	13	9	.864
George Woodruff (Yale '89)† (Pennsylvania 1892-01; Illinois 1903; Carlisle 1905)	12	142	25	2	.846
Barry Switzer (Arkansas '60) (Oklahoma 1973-88)	16	157	29	4	.837
Percy Haughton (Harvard '99)† (Cornell 1899-00; Harvard 1908-16; Columbia 1923-24)	13	96	17	6	.832
Bob Neyland (Army '16)† (Tennessee 1926-34, 1936-40, 1946-52)	21	173	31	12	.829
Fielding "Hurry Up" Yost (West Va. '95)† (Ohio Wesleyan 1897; Nebraska 1898; Kansas 1899; Stanford 1900; Michigan 1901-23, 1925-26)	29	196	36	12	.828
"Bud" Wilkinson (Minnesota '37)† (Oklahoma 1947-63)	17	145	29	4	.826
"Jock" Sutherland (Pittsburgh '18)† (Lafayette 1919-23; Pittsburgh 1924-38)	20	144	28	14	.812
*Tom Osborne (Hastings '59) (Nebraska 1973—)	21	206	47	3	.811
Bob Devaney (Alma '39)† (Wyoming 1957-61; Nebraska 1962-72)	16	136	30	7	.806
Frank Thomas (Notre Dame '23)† (Chattanooga 1925-28; Alabama 1931-42, 1944-46)	19	141	33	9	.795
Henry Williams (Yale '91)† (Army 1891; Minnesota 1900-21)	23	141	34	12	.786
*Joe Paterno (Brown '50)† (Penn St. 1966—)	28	257	69	3	.786
"Gloomy Gil" Dobie (Minnesota '02)† (North Dak. St. 1906-07; Washington 1908-16; Navy 1917-19; Cornell 1920-35; Boston College 1936-38)	33	180	45	15	.781
"Bear" Bryant (Alabama '36)† (Maryland 1945; Kentucky 1946-53; Texas A&M 1954-57; Alabama 1958-82)	38	323	85	17	.780
Fred Folsom (Dartmouth '95) (Colorado 1895-99, 1901-02; Dartmouth 1903-06; Colorado 1908-15)	19	106	28	6	.779
"Bo" Schembechler (Miami, Ohio '51)† (Miami, Ohio 1963-68; Michigan 1969-89)	27	234	65	8	.775
"Fritz" Crisler (Chicago '22)† (Minnesota 1930-31; Princeton 1932-37; Michigan 1938-47)	18	116	32	9	.768
Charley Moran (Tennessee '98) (Texas A&M 1909-14; Centre 1919-23; Bucknell 1924-26; Catawba 1930-33)	18	122	33	12	.766
Wallace Wade (Brown '17)† (Alabama 1923-30; Duke 1931-41, 1946-50)	24	171	49	10	.765
Frank Kush (Michigan St. '53) (Arizona St. 1958-79)	22	176	54	1	.764
Dan McGugin (Michigan '04)† (Vanderbilt 1904-17, 1919-34)	30	197	55	19	.762
Jimmy Crowley (Notre Dame '25)# (Michigan St. 1929-32; Fordham 1933-41)	13	78	21	10	.761
Andy Smith (Penn St., Pennsylvania '05)† (Pennsylvania 1909-12; Purdue 1913-15; California 1916-25)	17	116	32	13	.761
"Woody" Hayes (Denison '35)† (Denison 1946-48; Miami, Ohio 1949-50; Ohio St. 1951-78)	33	238	72	10	.759
"Red" Blaik (Miami, Ohio '18; Army '20)† (Dartmouth 1934-40; Army 1941-58)	25	166	48	14	.759
*Bobby Bowden (Samford '53)√ (Samford 1959-62; West Va. 1970-75; Florida St. 1976—)	28	239	78	3	.752
Darrell Royal (Oklahoma '50)† (Mississippi St. 1954-55; Washington 1956; Texas 1957-76)	23	184	60	5	.749
John McKay (Oregon '50)† (Southern Cal 1960-75)	16	127	40	8	.749

Coach (Alma Mater) (Colleges Coached, Tenure)	Years	Won	Lost	Tied	Pct.
John Vaught (Texas Christian '33)† (Mississippi 1947-70, 1973)	25	190	61	12	.745
Dan Devine (Minn.-Duluth '48)† (Arizona St. 1955-57; Missouri 1958-70; Notre Dame 1975-80)	22	172	57	9	.742
"Gus" Henderson (Oberlin '12) (Southern Cal 1919-24; Tulsa 1925-35; Occidental 1940-42)	20	126	42	7	.740
Ara Parseghian (Miami, Ohio '49)† (Miami, Ohio 1951-55; Northwestern 1956-63; Notre Dame 1964-74)	24	170	58	6	.739
*Danny Ford (Alabama '70) (Clemson 1978-89; Arkansas 1993—)	‡13	101	34	5	.739
Elmer Layden (Notre Dame '25)# (Loras 1925-26; Duquesne 1927-33; Notre Dame 1934-40)	16	103	34	11	.733
"Pop" Warner (Cornell '95)† (Georgia 1895-96; Cornell 1897-98; Carlisle 1899-1903; Cornell 1904-06; Carlisle 1907-14; Pittsburgh 1915-23; Stanford 1924-32; Temple 1933-38)	44	319	106	32	.733
Howard Jones (Yale '08)† (Syracuse 1908; Yale 1909; Ohio St. 1910; Yale 1913; Iowa 1916-23; Duke 1924; Southern Cal 1925-40)	29	194	64	21	.733
Frank Cavanaugh (Dartmouth '97)† (Cincinnati 1898; Holy Cross 1903-05; Dartmouth 1911-16; Boston College 1919-26; Fordham 1927-32)	24	145	48	17	.731
Jim Tatum (North Caro. '35)† (North Caro. 1942; Oklahoma 1946; Maryland 1947-55; North Caro. 1956-58)	14	100	35	7	.729
*LaVell Edwards (Utah St. '52) (Brigham Young 1972—)	22	197	73	3	.727
Francis Schmidt (Nebraska '14)† (Tulsa 1919-21; Arkansas 1922-28; Texas Christian 1929-33; Ohio St. 1934-40; Idaho 1941-42)	24	158	57	11	.723
Bill Roper (Princeton '03)† (Va. Military 1903-04; Princeton 1906-08; Missouri 1909; Princeton 1910-11; Swarthmore 1915-16; Princeton 1919-30)	22	112	37	19	.723
"Doc" Kennedy (Kansas & Pennsylvania '03) (Kansas 1904-10; Haskell 1911-16)	13	85	31	7	.720
"Tad" Jones (Yale '08)† (Syracuse 1909-10; Yale 1916, 1920-27)	11	66	24	6	.719
Vince Dooley (Auburn '54)† (Georgia 1964-88)	25	201	77	10	.715
Dana Bible (Carson-Newman '12)† (Mississippi Col. 1913-15; Louisiana St. 1916; Texas A&M 1917, 1919-28; Nebraska 1929-36; Texas 1937-46)	33	198	72	23	.715
Bobby Dodd (Tennessee '31)†# (Georgia Tech 1945-66)	22	165	64	8	.713
John Heisman (Brown '90, Pennsylvania '92)† (Oberlin 1892; Akron 1893; Oberlin 1894; Auburn 1895-99; Clemson 1900-03; Georgia Tech 1904-19; Pennsylvania 1920-22; Wash. & Jeff. 1923; Rice 1924-27)	36	185	70	17	.711
"Jumbo" Stiehm (Wisconsin '09) (Ripon 1910; Nebraska 1911-15; Indiana 1916-21)	12	59	23	4	.709
"Red" Sanders (Vanderbilt '27) (Vanderbilt 1940-42, 1946-48; UCLA 1949-57)	15	102	41	3	.709
Pat Dye (Georgia '62) (East Caro. 1974-79; Wyoming 1980; Auburn 1981-92)	19	153	62	5	.707
"Chick" Meehan (Syracuse '18) (Syracuse 1920-24; New York U. 1925-31; Manhattan 1932-37)	18	115	44	14	.705
John McEwan (Army '17) (Army 1923-25; Oregon 1926-29; Holy Cross 1930-32)	10	59	23	6	.705
Bennie Owen (Kansas '00)† (Washburn 1900; Bethany, Kan. 1901-04; Oklahoma 1905-26)	27	155	60	19	.703
Ike Armstrong (Drake '23)† (Utah 1925-49)	25	140	55	15	.702
Frank Broyles (Georgia Tech '47)† (Missouri 1957; Arkansas 1958-76)	20	149	62	6	.700
"Biff" Jones (Army '17)† (Army 1926-29; Louisiana St. 1932-34; Oklahoma 1935-36; Nebraska 1937-41)	14	87	33	15	.700

#Member of College Football Hall of Fame as a player. ‡Last game of 1978 season counted as full season. √Includes games forfeited, team and/or individual statistics abrogated, and coaching records changed by action of the NCAA Council under the restitution provisions of Bylaw 19.6 of the Official Procedure Governing the NCAA Enforcement Program (adopted by the NCAA membership at the 69th annual Convention in January 1975). The restitution provisions may be applied by the Council when a student-athlete has been permitted to participate while ineligible as a result of a court order against his institution or the NCAA, if the court order subsequently is overturned.

All-Time Division I-A Coaching Victories

Minimum 10 years as head coach at Division I institutions; record at four-year colleges only; bowl games included. After each coach's name is his alma mater, year graduated, total years coached, won-lost record and percentage, tenure at each college coached, and won-lost record there. Active coaches are denoted by an asterisk (*).

(Minimum 150 Victories)

323 "Bear" Bryant (Born 9-11-13 Moro Bottoms, Ark.; Died 1-26-83)
Alabama 1936 (38: 323-85-17 .780)
Maryland 1945 (6-2-1); Kentucky 1946-53 (60-23-5); Texas A&M 1954-57 (25-14-2); Alabama 1958-82 (232-46-9)

319 "Pop" Warner (Born 4-5-1871 Springville, N.Y.; Died 9-7-54)
Cornell 1895 (44: 319-106-32 .733)
Georgia 1895-96 (7-4-0); Cornell 1897-98, 1904-06 (36-13-3); Carlisle 1899-1903, 1907-14 (114-42-8); Pittsburgh 1915-23 (60-12-4); Stanford 1924-32 (71-17-8); Temple 1933-38 (31-18-9)

314 Amos Alonzo Stagg (Born 8-16-1862 West Orange, N.J.; Died 3-17-65)
Yale 1888 (57: 314-199-35 .605)
Springfield 1890-91 (10-11-1); Chicago 1892-1932 (244-111-27); Pacific (Cal.) 1933-46 (60-77-7)

257 *Joe Paterno (Born 12-21-26 Brooklyn, N.Y.)
Brown 1951 (28: 257-69-3 .786)
Penn St. 1966-93 (257-69-3)

239 *Bobby Bowden (Born 11-8-29 Birmingham, Ala.)
Samford 1953 (√28: 239-78-3 .752)
Samford 1959-62 (31-6-0); West Va. 1970-75 (√42-26-0); Florida St. 1976-93 (166-46-3)

238 "Woody" Hayes (Born 2-13-14 Clifton, Ohio; Died 3-12-87)
Denison 1935 (33: 238-72-10 .759)
Denison 1946-48 (19-6-0); Miami (Ohio) 1949-50 (14-5-0); Ohio St. 1951-78 (205-61-10)

234 "Bo" Schembechler (Born 9-1-29 Barberton, Ohio)
Miami (Ohio) 1951 (27: 234-65-8 .775)
Miami (Ohio) 1963-68 (40-17-3); Michigan 1969-89 (194-48-5)

207 Jess Neely (Born 1-4-1898 Smyrna, Tenn.; Died 4-9-83)
Vanderbilt 1924 (40: 207-176-19 .539)
Rhodes 1924-27 (20-17-2); Clemson 1931-39 (43-35-7); Rice 1940-66 (144-124-10)

206 *Tom Osborne (Born 2-23-37 Hastings, Neb.)
Hastings 1959 (21: 206-47-3 .811)
Nebraska 1973-93 (206-47-3)

203 Warren Woodson (Born 2-24-03 Fort Worth, Texas)
Baylor 1924 (31: 203-95-14 .673)
Central Ark. 1935-39 (40-8-3); Hardin-Simmons 1941-42, 1946-51 (58-24-6); Arizona 1952-56 (26-22-2); New Mexico St. 1958-67 (63-36-3); Trinity (Tex.) 1972-73 (16-5-0)

201 Vince Dooley (Born 9-4-32 Mobile, Ala.)
Auburn 1954 (25: 201-77-10 .715)
Georgia 1964-88 (201-77-10)

201 Eddie Anderson (Born 11-13-1900 Mason City, Iowa; Died 4-26-74)
Notre Dame 1922 (39: 201-128-15 .606)
Loras 1922-24 (16-6-2); DePaul 1925-31 (21-22-3); Holy Cross 1933-38, 1950-64 (129-67-8); Iowa 1939-42, 1946-49 (35-33-2)

200 *Hayden Fry (Born 2-28-29 Odessa, Texas)
Baylor 1951 (√32: 200-153-9 .565)
Southern Methodist 1962-72 (49-66-1); North Texas 1973-78 (√40-23-3); Iowa 1979-93 (111-64-5)

198 Dana Bible (Born 10-8-1891 Jefferson City, Tenn.; Died 1-19-80)
Carson-Newman 1912 (33: 198-72-23 .715)
Mississippi Col. 1913-15 (12-7-2); Louisiana St. 1916 (1-0-2); Texas A&M 1917, 1919-28 (72-19-9); Nebraska 1929-36 (50-15-7); Texas 1937-46 (63-31-3)

197 Dan McGugin (Born 7-29-1879 Tingley, Iowa; Died 1-19-36)
Michigan 1904 (30: 197-55-19 .762)
Vanderbilt 1904-17, 1919-34 (197-55-19)

197 *LaVell Edwards (Born 10-11-30 Provo, Utah)
Utah St. 1952 (22: 197-73-3 .727)
Brigham Young 1972-93 (197-73-3)

196 "Hurry Up" Yost (Born 4-30-1871 Fairview, W.Va.; Died 8-20-46)
West Va. '95 (29: 196-36-12 .828)
Ohio Wesleyan 1897 (7-1-1); Nebraska 1898 (7-4-0); Kansas 1899 (10-0-0); Stanford 1900 (7-2-1); Michigan 1901-23, 1925-26 (165-29-10)

194 Howard Jones (Born 8-23-1885 Excello, Ohio; Died 7-27-41)
Yale 1908 (29: 194-64-21 .733)
Syracuse 1908 (6-3-1); Yale 1909, 1913 (15-2-3); Ohio St. 1910 (6-1-3); Iowa 1916-23 (42-17-1); Duke 1924 (4-5-0); Southern Cal 1925-40 (121-36-13)

193 *Lou Holtz (Born 1-6-37 Follansbee, W.Va.)
Kent 1959 (24: 193-84-6 .693)
William & Mary 1969-71 (13-20-0); North Caro. St. 1972-75 (33-12-3); Arkansas 1977-83 (60-21-2); Minnesota 1984-85 (10-12-0); Notre Dame 1986-93 (77-19-1)

190 John Vaught (Born 5-6-08 Olney, Texas)
Texas Christian 1933 (25: 190-61-12 .745)
Mississippi 1947-70, 1973 (190-61-12)

186 *Jim Sweeney (Born 9-1-29 Butte, Mont.)
Portland 1951 (29: 186-133-3 .582)
Montana St. 1963-67 (31-20-0); Washington St. 1968-75 (26-59-1); Fresno St. 1976-77, 1980-93 (129-54-2)

185 John Heisman (Born 10-23-1869 Cleveland, Ohio; Died 10-3-36)
Brown 1890 (36: 185-70-17 .711)
Oberlin 1892, 1894 (11-3-1); Akron 1893 (5-2-0); Auburn 1895-99 (12-4-2); Clemson 1900-03 (19-3-2); Georgia Tech 1904-19 (102-29-6); Pennsylvania 1920-22 (16-10-2); Wash. & Jeff. 1923 (6-1-1); Rice 1924-27 (14-18-3)

184 Darrell Royal (Born 7-6-24 Hollis, Okla.)
Oklahoma 1950 (23: 184-60-5 .749)
Mississippi St. 1954-55 (12-8-0); Washington 1956 (5-5-0); Texas 1957-76 (167-47-5)

180 Gil Dobie (Born 1-31-1879 Hastings, Minn.; Died 12-24-48)
Minnesota 1902 (33: 180-45-15 .781)
North Dak. St. 1906-07 (7-0-0); Washington 1908-16 (58-0-3); Navy 1917-19 (17-3-0); Cornell 1920-35 (82-36-7); Boston College 1936-38 (16-6-5)

180 Carl Snavely (Born 7-30-1894 Omaha, Neb.; Died 7-12-75)
Lebanon Valley 1915 (32: 180-96-16 .644)
Bucknell 1927-33 (42-16-8); North Caro. 1934-35, 1945-52 (59-35-5); Cornell 1936-44 (46-26-3); Washington (Mo.) 1953-58 (33-19-0)

179 Jerry Claiborne (Born 8-26-28 Hopkinsville, Ky.)
Kentucky 1950 (28: 179-122-8 .592)
Virginia Tech 1961-70 (61-39-2); Maryland 1972-81 (77-37-3); Kentucky 1982-89 (41-46-3)

178 Ben Schwartzwalder (Born 6-2-09 Point Pleasant, W.Va.; Died 4-28-93)
West Va. 1933 (28: 178-96-3 .648)
Muhlenberg 1946-48 (25-5-0); Syracuse 1949-73 (153-91-3)

176 Frank Kush (Born 1-20-29 Windber, Pa.)
Michigan St. 1953 (22: 176-54-1 .764)
Arizona St. 1958-79 (176-54-1)

176 Don James (Born 12-31-32 Massillon, Ohio)
Miami (Fla.) 1954 (22: 176-78-3 .691)
Kent 1971-74 (25-19-1); Washington 1975-92 (151-59-2)

176 Ralph Jordan (Born 9-25-10 Selma, Ala.; Died 7-17-80)
Auburn 1932 (√25: 176-83-6 .675)
Auburn 1951-75 (√176-83-6)

176 *Johnny Majors (Born 5-21-35 Lynchburg, Tenn.)
Tennessee 1957 (26: 176-113-10 .605)
Iowa St. 1968-72 (24-30-1); Pittsburgh 1973-76, 1993 (36-21-1); Tennessee 1977-92 (116-62-8)

174 "Pappy" Waldorf (Born 10-3-02 Clifton Springs, N.Y.; Died 8-15-81)
Syracuse 1925 (31: 174-100-22 .625)
Oklahoma City 1925-27 (17-11-3); Oklahoma St. 1929-33 (34-10-7); Kansas St. 1934 (7-2-1); Northwestern 1935-46 (49-45-7); California 1947-56 (67-32-4)

173 Bob Neyland (Born 2-17-92 Greenville, Texas; Died 3-28-62)
Army 1916 (21: 173-31-12 .829)
Tennessee 1926-34, 1936-40, 1946-52 (173-31-12)

172 Dan Devine (Born 12-23-24 Augusta, Wis.)
Minn.-Duluth 1948 (22: 172-57-9 .742)
Arizona St. 1955-57 (27-3-1); Missouri 1958-70 (92-38-7); Notre Dame 1975-80 (53-16-1)

171 Wallace Wade (Born 6-15-1892 Trenton, Tenn.; Died 10-7-86)
Brown 1917 (24: 171-49-10 .765)
Alabama 1923-30 (61-13-3); Duke 1931-41, 1946-50 (110-36-7)

170 Ara Parseghian (Born 5-21-23 Akron, Ohio)
Miami (Ohio) 1949 (24: 170-58-6 .739)
Miami (Ohio) 1951-55 (39-6-1); Northwestern 1956-63 (36-35-1); Notre Dame 1964-74 (95-17-4)

170 Grant Teaff (Born 11-12-33 Hermleigh, Texas)
McMurry 1956 (30: 170-151-8 .529)
McMurry 1960-65 (23-35-2); Angelo St. 1969-71 (19-11-0); Baylor 1972-92 (128-105-6)

168 Bob Blackman (Born 7-7-18 De Soto, Iowa)
Southern Cal 1941 (30: 168-112-7 .598)
Denver 1953-54 (12-6-2); Dartmouth 1955-70 (104-37-3); Illinois 1971-76 (29-36-1); Cornell 1977-82 (23-33-1)

166 "Red" Blaik (Born 2-17-1897 Detroit, Mich.; Died 5-6-89)
Miami (Ohio) 1918; Army 1920 (25: 166-48-14 .759)
Dartmouth 1934-40 (45-15-4); Army 1941-58 (121-33-10)

165 Bobby Dodd (Born 11-11-08 Galax, Va.; Died 6-21-88)
Tennessee 1931 (22: 165-64-8 .713)
Georgia Tech 1945-66 (165-64-8)

165 Frank Howard (Born 3-25-09 Barlow Bend, Ala.)
Alabama 1931 (30: 165-118-12 .580)
Clemson 1940-69 (165-118-12)

163 Don Faurot (Born 6-23-02 Mountain Grove, Mo.)
Missouri 1925 (28: 163-93-13 .630)
Northeast Mo. St. 1926-34 (63-13-3); Missouri 1935-42, 1946-56 (100-80-10)

162 Ossie Solem (Born 12-13-1891 Minneapolis, Minn.; Died 10-26-70)
Minnesota 1915 (37: 162-117-20 .575)
Luther 1920 (5-1-1); Drake 1921-31 (54-35-2); Iowa 1932-36 (15-21-4); Syracuse 1937-45 (30-27-6); Springfield 1946-57 (58-33-7)

161 Bill Dooley (Born 5-19-34 Mobile, Ala.)
Mississippi St. 1956 (26: 161-127-5 .558)
North Caro. 1967-77 (69-53-2); Virginia Tech 1978-86 (64-37-1); Wake Forest 1987-92 (29-36-2)

160 Bill Yeoman (Born 12-26-27 Elnora, Ind.)
Army 1949 (25: 160-108-8 .595)
Houston 1962-86 (160-108-8)

158   Francis Schmidt (Born 12-3-1885 Downs, Kan.; Died 9-19-44)
           Nebraska 1914 (24: 158-57-11 .723)
           Tulsa 1919-21 (24-3-2); Arkansas 1922-28 (42-20-3); Texas Christian 1929-
           33 (46-6-5); Ohio St. 1934-40 (39-16-1); Idaho 1941-42 (7-12-0)
157   Barry Switzer (Born 10-5-37 Crossett, Ark.)
           Arkansas 1960 (16: 157-29-4 .837)
           Oklahoma 1973-88 (157-29-4)
157   Edward Robinson (Born 10-15-1873 Lynn, Miss.; Died 3-10-45)
           Brown 1896 (27: 157-88-13 .632)
           Nebraska 1896-97 (11-4-1); Brown 1898-1901, 1904-07, 1910-1925 (140-
           82-12); Maine 1902 (6-2-0)
156   *Don Nehlen (Born 1-1-36 Canton, Ohio)
           Bowling Green 1958 (23: 156-91-8 .628)
           Bowling Green 1968-76 (53-35-4); West Va. 1980-93 (103-56-4)
156   *Bill Mallory (Born 5-30-35 Sandusky, Ohio)
           Miami (Ohio) 1957 (24: 156-108-4 .590)
           Miami (Ohio) 1969-73 (39-12-0); Colorado 1974-78 (35-21-1); Northern Ill.
           1980-83 (25-19-0); Indiana 1984-93 (57-56-3)
155   Bennie Owen (Born 7-24-1875 Chicago, Ill.; Died 2-9-70)
           Kansas 1900 (27: 155-60-19 .703)
           Washburn 1900 (6-2-0); Bethany (Kan.) 1901-04 (27-4-3); Oklahoma 1905-
           26 (122-54-16)
155   Ray Morrison (Born 2-28-1885 Switzerland Co., Ind.; Died 11-19-82)
           Vanderbilt 1912 (34: 155-130-33 .539)
           Southern Methodist 1915-16, 1922-34 (84-44-22); Vanderbilt 1918, 1935-
           39 (29-22-2); Temple 1940-48 (31-38-9); Austin 1949-52 (11-26-0)
154   Earle Bruce (Born 3-8-31 Massillon, Ohio)
           Ohio St. 1953 (21: 154-90-2 .630)
           Tampa 1972 (10-2-0); Iowa St. 1973-78 (36-32-0); Ohio St. 1979-87 (81-26-
           1); Northern Iowa 1988 (5-6-0); Colorado St. 1989-92 (22-24-1)
153   Pat Dye (Born 11-6-39 Augusta, Ga.)
           Georgia 1962 (19: 153-62-5 .707)
           East Caro. 1974-79 (48-18-1); Wyoming 1980 (6-5-0); Auburn 1981-92 (99-
           39-4)
153   Morley Jennings (Born 1-23-1885 Holland, Mich.; Died 5-13-85)
           Mississippi St. 1912 (29: 153-75-18 .658)
           Ouachita Baptist 1912-25 (70-15-12); Baylor 1926-40 (83-60-6)

153   Matty Bell (Born 2-22-1899 Baylor Co., Texas; Died 6-30-83)
           Centre 1920 (26: 153-87-16 .630)
           Haskell 1920-21 (13-6-0); Carroll (Wis.) 1922 (4-3-0); Texas Christian 1923-
           28 (33-17-5); Texas A&M 1929-33 (24-21-3); Southern Methodist 1935-41,
           1945-49 (79-40-8)
151   Lou Little (Born 12-6-1893 Leominster, Pa.; Died 5-28-79)
           Pennsylvania 1920 (33: 151-128-13 .539)
           Georgetown 1924-29 (41-12-3); Columbia 1930-56 (110-116-10)
150   *Jim Wacker (Born 4-28-37 Detroit, Mich.)
           Valparaiso 1960 (23: 150-107-3 .583)
           Texas Lutheran 1971-75 (38-16-0); North Dak. St. 1976-78 (24-9-1);
           Southwest Tex. St. 1979-82 (42-8-0); Texas Christian 1983-91 (40-58-2);
           Minnesota 1992-93 (6-16-0)

√Includes games forfeited, team and/or individual statistics abrogated, and coaching
records changed by action of the NCAA Council under the restitution provisions of Bylaw
19.6 of the Official Procedure Governing the NCAA Enforcement Program (adopted by
the NCAA membership at the 69th annual Convention in January 1975). The restitution
provisions may be applied by the Council when a student-athlete has been permitted to
participate while ineligible as a result of a court order against his institution or the
NCAA, if the court order subsequently is overturned.

*Florida State's Bobby Bowden ranks second
among active coaches in all-time Division I-A
coaching victories with 239.*

Coaches to Reach 100, 200 and 300 Victories

(Must have five years or 50 victories at a school that was classified as a major college at the time)

100 VICTORIES

Coach (Date Reached Milestone) (Schools Coached and Years)	Age in Yrs.-Days	WHEN MILESTONE REACHED	
		Career Game (Record)	Career Yr.-Game
FRED AKERS (9-17-88) (Wyoming 1975-76, Texas 1977-86, Purdue 1987-90)	50-184	155th (100-52-3)	14-2
WILLIAM ALEXANDER (11-18-39) (Georgia Tech 1920-44)	49-233	189th (100-74-15)	20-7
EDDIE ANDERSON (10-12-46) (Loras 1922-24, DePaul 1925-31, Holy Cross 1933-38, Iowa 1939- 42, 1946-49, Holy Cross 1950-64)	45-333	160th (100-50-10)	21-4
IKE ARMSTRONG (10-17-42) (Utah 1925-49)	47-131	141st (100-30-11)	18-4
MATTY BELL (11-5-38) (Haskell 1920-21, Carroll, Wis. 1922, Texas Christian 1923-28, Texas A&M 1929-33, Southern Methodist 1935-41, 1945-49)	39-256	169th (100-60-9)	18-6
HUGO BEZDEK (11-22-24) (Oregon 1906, Arkansas 1908-12, Oregon 1913-17, Penn St. 1918-29, Delaware Valley 1949)	40-120	147th (100-34-13)	18-9
DANA X. BIBLE (11-21-31) (Mississippi Col. 1913-15, Louisiana St. 1916, Texas A&M 1917, 1919-28, Nebraska 1929-36, Texas 1937-46)	40-44	149th (100-31-18)	18-8
BERNIE BIERMAN (11-11-39) (Montana St. 1919-21, Mississippi St. 1925-26, Tulane 1927-31, Minnesota 1932-41, 1945-50)	45-245	149th (100-38-11)	18-6
BOB BLACKMAN (9-27-69) (Denver 1953-54, Dartmouth 1955-70, Illinois 1971-76, Cornell 1977-82)	51-82	147th (100-42-5)	17-1
"RED" BLAIK (10-23-48) (Dartmouth 1934-40, Army 1941-58)	51-249	134th (100-25-9)	15-5
#BOBBY BOWDEN (10-7-78) (Samford 1959-62, West Va. 1970-75, Florida St. 1976-93)	48-333	144th (100-44-0)	14-5
#BILLY BREWER (10-6-90) (Southeast La. 1974-79, Louisiana Tech 1980-82, Mississippi 1983- 93)	54-363	184th (100-78-6)	17-5
FRANK BROYLES (11-27-69) (Missouri 1957, Arkansas 1958-76)	44-336	138th (100-36-2)	13-9
EARLE BRUCE (11-3-84) (Tampa 1972, Iowa 1973-78, Ohio St. 1979-87, Northern Iowa 1988, Colorado St. 1989-92)	53-240	149th (100-49-0)	13-9
"BEAR" BRYANT (11-7-59) (Maryland 1945, Kentucky 1946-53, Texas A&M 1954-57, Alabama 1958-82)	46-57	154th (100-44-10)	15-7

Coach (Date Reached Milestone) (Schools Coached and Years)	WHEN MILESTONE REACHED		
	Age in Yrs.-Days	Career Game (Record)	Career Yr.-Game
WALLY BUTTS (11-15-52) (Georgia 1939-60)	47-281	151st (100-44-7)	14-9
CHARLIE CALDWELL (10-21-50) (Williams 1928-42, Princeton 1945-56)	48-80	163rd (100-55-8)	21-4
FRANK CAMP (10-23-65) (Louisville 1946-68)	60-39	182nd (100-80-2)	20-6
JIM CARLEN (11-8-80) (West Va. 1966-69, Texas Tech 1970-74, South Caro. 1975-81)	47-120	167th (100-61-6)	15-9
LEN CASANOVA (10-2-65) (Santa Clara 1946-49, Pittsburgh 1950, Oregon 1951-66)	59-263	192nd (100-82-10)	20-3
FRANK CAVANAUGH (10-3-25) (Cincinnati 1898, Holy Cross 1903-05, Dartmouth 1911-16, Boston College 1919-26, Fordham 1927-32)	49-158	143rd (100-32-11)	17-1
JERRY CLAIBORNE (11-6-76) (Virginia Tech 1961-70, Maryland 1972-81, Kentucky 1982-89)	48-72	158th (100-54-4)	15-9
#JOHN COOPER (11-17-90) (Tulsa 1977-84, Arizona St. 1985-87, Ohio St. 1988-93)	53-137	162nd (100-57-5)	14-10
FRITZ CRISLER (11-24-45) (Minnesota 1930-31, Princeton 1932-37, Michigan 1938-47)	46-316	138th (100-30-8)	16-10
DICK CRUM (11-15-86) (Miami, Ohio 1974-77, North Caro. 1978-87, Kent 1988-90)	52-200	148th (100-44-4)	13-10
JACK CURTICE (10-3-64) (West Tex. A&M 1940-41, UTEP 1946-49, Utah 1950-57, Stanford 1958-61, UC Santa Barb. 1962-69)	56-118	202nd (100-95-7)	21-1
DUFFY DAUGHERTY (9-25-71) (Michigan St. 1954-72)	56-17	164th (100-60-4)	18-3
DUDLEY DeGROOT (9-17-49) (UC Santa Barb. 1926-28, 1931, San Jose St. 1932-39, Rochester 1940-43, West Va. 1948-49, New Mexico 1950-52)	49-302	152nd (100-44-8)	17-1
HERB DEROMEDI (11-16-91) (Central Mich. 1978-93)	52-171	153rd (100-43-10)	14-11
BOB DEVANEY (11-8-69) (Wyoming 1957-61, Nebraska 1962-72)	54-209	133rd (100-28-5)	13-8
DAN DEVINE (10-12-68) (Arizona St. 1955-57, Missouri 1958-70, Notre Dame 1975-80)	43-293	139th (100-31-8)	14-4
DOUG DICKEY (11-27-77) (Tennessee 1964-69, Florida 1970-78)	45-202	156th (100-50-6)	14-10
PAUL DIETZEL (10-6-73) (Louisiana St. 1955-61, Army 1962-65, South Caro. 1966-74)	47-188	191st (100-86-5)	19-4
GIL DOBIE (10-20-22) (North Dak. St. 1906-07, Washington 1908-16, Navy 1917-19, Cornell 1920-35, Boston College 1936-38)	43-262	108th (100-5-3)	17-4
BOBBY DODD (12-1-56) (Georgia Tech 1945-66)	48-20	131st (100-28-3)	12-10
MIKE DONAHUE (9-29-23) (Auburn 1904-06, 1908-22, Louisiana St. 1923-27)	42-111	140th (100-35-5)	19-1
#TERRY DONAHUE (9-10-88) (UCLA 1976-93)	44-78	143rd (100-36-7)	13-2
ALDO DONELLI (10-16-65) (Duquesne 1939-42, Boston U. 1947-56, Columbia 1957-67)	58-86	197th (100-89-8)	23-4
BILL DOOLEY (11-27-82) (North Caro. 1967-77, Virginia Tech 1978-86, Wake Forest 1987-92)	48-192	180th (100-78-2)	16-11
VINCE DOOLEY (9-24-77) (Georgia 1964-88)	45-20	149th (100-44-5)	14-3
FRED DUNLAP (10-29-83) (Lehigh 1965-75, Colgate 1976-87)	55-194	195th (100-91-4)	19-8
PAT DYE (10-4-86) (East Caro. 1974-79, Wyoming 1980, Auburn 1981-92)	46-332	142nd (100-41-1)	13-4
LLOYD EATON (10-4-69) (Alma 1949-55, Northern Mich. 1956, Wyoming 1962-70)	51-101	145th (100-40-5)	16-3
#LaVELL EDWARDS (10-22-83) (Brigham Young 1972-93)	53-11	138th (100-37-1)	12-7
RAY ELIOT (10-10-59) (Illinois Col. 1933-36, Illinois 1942-59)	54-119	191st (100-79-12)	22-3
RIP ENGLE (10-21-61) (Brown 1944-49, Penn St. 1950-65)	55-209	161st (100-53-8)	18-5
#DENNIS ERICKSON (10-30-93) (Idaho 1982-85, Wyoming 1986, Washington St. 1987-88, Miami, Fla. 1989-93)	46-334	137th (100-36-1)	12-7
DON FAUROT (11-1-41) (Northeast Mo. St. 1926-34, Missouri 1935-42, 1946-56)	39-131	171st (100-63-8)	16-6
FRED FOLSOM (11-1-13) (Colorado 1895-1902, Dartmouth 1903-06, Colorado 1908-15)	41-357	126th (100-20-6)	17-6
#DANNY FORD (11-13-93) (Clemson 1978-89, Arkansas 1993)	45-225	139th (100-34-5)	13-9
#HAYDEN FRY (9-26-81) (Southern Methodist 1962-72, North Texas 1973-78, Iowa 1979-93)	52-185	207th (100-103-4)	20-3
ANDY GUSTAFSON (9-29-61) (Virginia Tech 1926-29, Miami, Fla. 1948-63)	58-179	168th (100-64-4)	18-3
WAYNE HARDIN (10-13-79) (Navy 1959-64, Temple 1970-82)	52-204	159th (100-54-5)	16-6
JIM HARKEMA (9-16-89) (Grand Valley St. 1973-82, Eastern Mich. 1983-92)	47-83	167th (100-63-4)	17-3
DICK HARLOW (11-3-34) (Penn St. 1915-17, Colgate 1922-25, Western Md. 1926-34, Harvard 1935-42, 1945-47)	44-67	142nd (100-31-11)	16-5

Miami (Florida) coach Dennis Erickson garnered his 100th victory in the 12th year of his coaching career.

COACHES' RECORDS

Ohio State University photo

Woody Hayes reached the 100-victory plateau in 140 games.

Coach (Date Reached Milestone) (Schools Coached and Years)	WHEN MILESTONE REACHED		
	Age in Yrs.-Days	Career Game (Record)	Career Yr.-Game
HARVEY HARMAN (10-4-47) (Haverford 1922-29, Sewanee 1930, Pennsylvania 1931-37, Rutgers 1938-55)	46-334	177th (100-70-7)	22-2
#KEN HATFIELD (11-20-91) (Air Force 1979-83, Arkansas 1984-89, Clemson 1990-93)	48-174	155th (100-52-3)	13-11
"WOODY" HAYES (10-21-61) (Denison 1946-48, Miami, Ohio 1949-50, Ohio St. 1951-78)	48-249	140th (100-34-6)	16-4
JOHN HEISMAN (9-27-13) (Oberlin 1892, Akron 1893, Oberlin 1894, Auburn 1895-99, Clemson 1900-03, Georgia Tech 1904-19, Pennsylvania 1920-22, Wash. & Jeff. 1923, Rice 1924-27)	43-339	142nd (100-33-9)	22-1
"GUS" HENDERSON (11-24-32) (Southern Cal 1919-24, Tulsa 1925-35, Occidental 1940-42)	43-259	126th (100-23-3)	14-8
BILL HESS (9-4-76) (Ohio 1958-77)	51-106	182nd (100-78-4)	19-1
#LOU HOLTZ (12-31-82) (William & Mary 1969-71, North Caro. St. 1972-75, Arkansas 1977-83, Minnesota 1984-85, Notre Dame 1986-93)	45-359	153rd (100-48-5)	13-12
FRANK HOWARD (9-27-58) (Clemson 1940-69)	49-186	175th (100-65-10)	19-2
DON JAMES (9-15-84) (Kent 1971-74, Washington 1975-92)	51-258	153rd (100-52-1)	14-2
MORLEY JENNINGS (10-3-31) (Ouachita Baptist 1912-25, Baylor 1926-40)	46-253	136th (100-33-3)	20-1
HOWARD JONES (12-3-27) (Syracuse 1908, Yale 1909, Ohio St. 1910, Yale 1913, Iowa 1916-23, Duke 1924, Southern Cal 1925-40)	42-102	142nd (100-33-9)	16-10
LLOYD JORDAN (10-27-56) (Amherst 1932-49, Harvard 1950-56)	55-317	172nd (100-65-7)	22-4
"SHUG" JORDAN (10-9-65) (Auburn 1951-75)	55-14	148th (100-43-5)	15-4
FRANK KIMBROUGH (9-29-56) (Hardin-Simmons 1935-40, Baylor 1941-42, 1945-46, West Tex. A&M 1947-57)	52-97	181st (100-73-8)	20-3
TONY KNAP (10-2-76) (Utah St. 1963-66, Boise St. 1968-75, Nevada-Las Vegas 1976-81)	61-298	135th (100-33-2)	13-4
FRANK KUSH (12-30-70) (Arizona St. 1958-79)	41-344	131st (100-30-1)	13-11
ELMER LAYDEN (10-26-40) (Loras 1925-26, Duquesne 1927-33, Notre Dame 1934-40)	37-175	143rd (100-32-11)	16-4
FRANK LEAHY (10-3-53) (Boston College 1939-40, Notre Dame 1941-53)	45-37	121st (100-13-8)	13-2
LOU LITTLE (9-26-42) (Georgetown 1924-29, Columbia 1930-56)	48-294	161st (100-49-12)	19-1
DICK MacPHERSON (10-28-89) (Massachusetts 1971-77, Syracuse 1981-90)	58-358	171st (100-68-3)	16-7
#JOHNNY MAJORS (11-19-83) (Iowa St. 1968-72, Pittsburgh 1973-76, Tennessee 1977-92, Pittsburgh 1993)	48-181	185th (100-81-4)	16-10
#BILL MALLORY (9-14-85) (Miami, Ohio 1969-73, Colorado 1974-78, Northern Ill. 1980-83, Indiana 1984-93)	50-107	164th (100-63-1)	16-1
BEN MARTIN (11-20-76) (Virginia 1956-57, Air Force 1958-77)	55-145	217th (100-108-9)	21-11
CHARLEY McCLENDON (11-2-74) (Louisiana St. 1962-79)	46-222	141st (100-35-6)	13-7
DAN McGUGIN (11-15-19) (Vanderbilt 1904-34)	40-78	132nd (100-25-7)	15-7
JOHN McKAY (1-1-73) (Southern Cal 1960-75)	49-209	139th (100-33-6)	13-12
"TUSS" McLAUGHRY (10-25-41) (Westminster 1916-18, 1921, Amherst 1922-25, Brown 1926-40, Dartmouth 1941-42, 1945-54)	48-109	196th (100-86-10)	23-5
"CHICK" MEEHAN (9-28-35) (Syracuse 1920-24, New York U. 1925-31, Manhattan 1932-37)	42-23	146th (100-34-12)	16-2
DUTCH MEYER (9-29-51) (Texas Christian 1934-52)	53-204	182nd (100-71-11)	18-2
ODUS MITCHELL (11-25-61) (North Texas 1946-66)	59-116	167th (100-59-8)	16-10
#AL MOLDE (10-11-86) (Sioux Falls 1971-72, Minn.-Morris 1973-79, Central Mo. St. 1980-82, Eastern Ill. 1983-86, Western Mich. 1987-93)	42-330	162nd (100-56-6)	16-6
CHARLEY MORAN (9-27-30) (Texas A&M 1909-14, Centre 1919-23, Bucknell 1924-26, Catawba 1930-33)	52-217	131st (100-24-7)	15-1
JOE MORRISON (10-29-88) (Tenn.-Chatt. 1973-79, New Mexico 1980-82, South Caro. 1983-88)	51-69	176th (100-69-7)	16-8
RAY MORRISON (10-2-37) (Southern Methodist 1915-16, Vanderbilt 1918, Southern Methodist 1922-34, Vanderbilt 1935-39, Temple 1940-48, Austin College 1949-52)	52-216	177th (100-54-3)	19-2
DARRELL MUDRA (9-22-73) (Adams St. 1959-62, North Dak. St. 1963-65, Arizona 1967-68, Western Ill. 1969-73, Florida St. 1974-75, Eastern Ill. 1978-82, Northern Iowa 1983-87)	44-261	131st (100-29-2)	14-2

Coach (Date Reached Milestone) (Schools Coached and Years)	WHEN MILESTONE REACHED		
	Age in Yrs.-Days	Career Game (Record)	Career Yr.-Game
BILL MURRAY (11-22-58) .... (Delaware 1940-42, 1946-50, Duke 1951-65)	50-74	149th (100-40-9)	16-10
JESS NEELY (10-19-46) .... (Rhodes 1924-27, Clemson 1931-39, Rice 1940-66)	48-288	190th (100-79-11)	20-4
#DON NEHLEN (11-16-85) .... (Bowling Green 1968-76, West Va. 1980-93)	48-319	162nd (100-57-5)	15-10
BOB NEYLAND (9-29-39) .... (Tennessee 1926-34, 1936-52)	47-224	120th (100-12-8)	13-1
BOB ODELL (9-24-77) .... (Bucknell 1958-64, Pennsylvania 1965-70, Williams 1971-86)	55-203	166th (100-64-2)	20-1
JORDAN OLIVAR (10-15-60) .... (Villanova 1943-48, Loyola Marymount 1949-51, Yale 1952-60)	45-258	159th (100-53-6)	18-4
#TOM OSBORNE (9-24-83) .... (Nebraska 1973-93)	46-211	126th (100-24-2)	10-4
BENNIE OWEN (10-4-15) .... (Washburn 1900, Bethany, Kan. 1901-04, Oklahoma 1905-26)	40-72	136th (100-28-8)	16-5
ARA PARSEGHIAN (11-26-66) .... (Miami, Ohio 1951-55, Northwestern 1956-63, Notre Dame 1964-74)	43-189	147th (100-43-4)	16-10
#JOE PATERNO (11-6-76) .... (Penn St. 1966-93)	49-320	122nd (100-21-1)	11-9
TOMMY PROTHRO (9-19-70) .... (Oregon St. 1955-64, UCLA 1965-70)	50-38	155th (100-50-5)	16-2
EDWARD ROBINSON (11-6-15) .... (Nebraska 1896-97, Brown 1898-1901, Maine 1902, Brown 1904-07, 1910-25)	41-344	165th (100-56-9)	17-7
KNUTE ROCKNE (11-1-30) .... (Notre Dame 1918-30)	42-242	117th (100-12-5)	13-5
DARRYL ROGERS (9-12-81) .... (Cal St. Hayward 1965, Fresno St. 1966-72, San Jose St. 1973-75, Michigan St. 1976-79, Arizona St. 1980-84)	47-106	176th (100-70-6)	17-1
BILL ROPER (10-8-27) .... (Va. Military 1903-04, Princeton 1906-08, Missouri 1909, Princeton 1910-11, Swarthmore 1915-16, Princeton 1919-30)	47-47	141st (100-26-15)	19-2
DARRELL ROYAL (10-7-67) .... (Mississippi St. 1954-55, Washington 1956, Texas 1957-76)	43-93	141st (100-38-3)	14-3
"RED" SANDERS (11-9-57) .... (Vanderbilt 1940-48, UCLA 1949-57)	52-216	144th (100-41-3)	15-8
PHILIP SARBOE (12-1-60) .... (Central Wash. 1941-42, Washington St. 1945-49, Humboldt St. 1951-65, Hawaii 1966)	48-233	160th (100-53-7)	17-11
"BO" SCHEMBECHLER (10-4-75) .... (Miami, Ohio 1963-68, Michigan 1969-89)	46-33	130th (100-24-6)	13-4
FRANCIS SCHMIDT (11-5-32) .... (Tulsa 1919-21, Arkansas 1922-28, Texas Christian 1929-33, Ohio St. 1934-40, Idaho 1941-42)	46-336	136th (100-27-9)	14-8
BEN SCHWARTZWALDER (9-30-65) .... (Muhlenberg 1946-48, Syracuse 1949-73)	52-120	143rd (100-41-2)	16-2
CLARK SHAUGHNESSY (10-20-34) .... (Tulane 1915-20, 1922-26, Loyola, Ill. 1927-32, Chicago 1933-39, Stanford 1940-41, Maryland 1942, Pittsburgh 1943-45, Maryland 1946, Hawaii 1965)	42-228	164th (100-50-14)	19-3
DICK SHERIDAN (10-6-90) .... (Furman 1978-85, North Caro. St. 1986-92)	49-58	147th (100-43-4)	13-6
#JACKIE SHERRILL (10-8-88) .... (Washington St. 1976, Pittsburgh 1977-81, Texas A&M 1982-88, Mississippi St. 1991-93)	44-314	145th (100-43-2)	13-5
ANDY SMITH (11-10-23) .... (Pennsylvania 1909-12, Purdue 1913-15, California 1916-25)	40-71	140th (100-29-11)	15-8
"CLIPPER" SMITH (11-6-42) .... (Gonzaga 1925-28, Santa Clara 1929-35, Villanova 1936-42, San Francisco 1946, Lafayette 1949-51)	44-81	159th (100-47-12)	18-5
#LARRY SMITH (11-10-90) .... (Tulane 1976-79, Arizona 1980-86, Southern Cal 1987-92)	51-59	170th (100-65-5)	15-10
CARL SNAVELY (9-30-44) .... (Bucknell 1927-33, North Caro. 1934-35, Cornell 1936-44, North Caro. 1945-52, Washington, Mo. 1953-58)	50-60	152nd (100-40-12)	18-2
OSSIE SOLEM (10-24-42) .... (Luther 1920, Drake 1921-31, Iowa 1932-36, Syracuse 1937-45, Springfield 1946-57)	50-315	183rd (100-71-12)	23-5
AMOS ALONZO STAGG (10-6-1900) .... (Springfield 1890-91, Chicago 1892-1932, Pacific, Cal. 1933-46)	38-51	143rd (100-34-9)	11-6
DENNY STOLZ (9-14-85) .... (Alma 1965-70, Michigan St. 1973-75, Bowling Green 1977-85, San Diego St. 1986-88)	51-2	175th (100-73-2)	18-2
"ABE" STUBER (10-16-48) .... (Westminster, Mo. 1929-31, Southeast Mo. St. 1932-44, 1946, Iowa St. 1947-52)	43-338	162nd (100-54-8)	19-5
JOCK SUTHERLAND (10-14-33) .... (Lafayette 1919-23, Pittsburgh 1924-38)	44-207	132nd (100-22-10)	15-4
#JIM SWEENEY (9-8-84) .... (Montana St. 1963-67, Washington St. 1968-75, Fresno St. 1976-77, 1980-93)	55-7	206th (100-105-1)	20-2
BARRY SWITZER (9-24-83) .... (Oklahoma 1973-88)	45-353	122nd (100-18-4)	11-3

Darrell Royal got his 100th career victory at Texas in the 14th year of his coaching career. He recorded 84 more victories in the next nine years.

Amos Alonzo Stagg ranks fourth in all-time coaching victories with 314. He was 81 years of age and in the 54th year of his coaching career when he reached the 300-victory mark.

Coach (Date Reached Milestone) (Schools Coached and Years)	WHEN MILESTONE REACHED		
	Age in Yrs.-Days	Career Game (Record)	Career Yr.-Game
JIM TATUM (11-8-58) (North Caro. 1942, Oklahoma 1946, Maryland 1947-55, North Caro. 1956-58)	45-78	140th (100-33-7)	14-8
GRANT TEAFF (9-25-82) (McMurry 1960-65, Angelo St. 1969-71, Baylor 1972-92)	48-317	206th (100-101-5)	20-3
FRANK THOMAS (11-9-40) (Tenn.-Chatt. 1925-28, Alabama 1931-46)	41-359	128th (100-21-7)	14-6
#DICK TOMEY (9-4-93) (Hawaii 1977-86, Arizona 1987-93)	55-76	182nd (100-75-7)	17-1
"PIE" VANN (10-6-62) (Southern Miss. 1949-68)	55-14	137th (100-36-1)	14-4
JOHNNY VAUGHT (11-28-59) (Mississippi 1947-73)	51-206	135th (100-29-6)	13-10
#JIM WACKER (11-14-81) (Texas Lutheran 1971-75, North Dak. St. 1976-78, Southwest Tex. St. 1979-82, Texas Christian 1983-91, Minnesota 1992-93)	44-200	134th (100-33-1)	12-10
WALLACE WADE (10-3-36) (Alabama 1923-30, Duke 1931-41, 1946-50)	44-110	129th (100-24-5)	14-3
"PAPPY" WALDORF (10-27-45) (Oklahoma City 1925-27, Oklahoma St. 1929-33, Kansas St. 1934, Northwestern 1935-46, California 1947-56)	43-24	173rd (100-56-17)	20-5
"POP" WARNER (11-26-08) (Georgia 1895-96, Cornell 1897-98, Carlisle 1899-1903, Cornell 1904-06, Carlisle 1907-14, Pittsburgh 1915-23, Stanford 1924-32, Temple 1933-38)	37-235	145th (100-38-7)	14-11
#GEORGE WELSH (10-14-89) (Navy 1973-81, Virginia 1982-93)	56-49	188th (100-85-3)	17-7
BUD WILKINSON (11-2-57) (Oklahoma 1947-63)	41-193	111th (100-8-3)	11-6
HENRY WILLIAMS (10-2-12) (Army 1891, Minnesota 1900-21)	43-98	122nd (100-13-9)	14-4
GEORGE WOODRUFF (11-11-1898) (Pennsylvania 1892-1901, Illinois 1903, Carlisle 1905)	35-261	109th (100-9-0)	8-11
WARREN WOODSON (9-27-52) (Conway 1935-40, Hardin-Simmons 1941-51, Arizona St. 1952-56, New Mexico St. 1958-67, Trinity, Tex. 1972-73)	49-215	141st (100-32-9)	15-2
BILL YEOMAN (9-12-77) (Houston 1962-86)	49-260	161st (100-56-5)	16-1
"HURRY UP" YOST (11-7-08) (Ohio Wesleyan 1897, Nebraska 1898, Kansas 1899, Stanford 1900, Michigan 1901-23, 1925-26)	37-191	114th (100-10-4)	12-6
JIM YOUNG (9-10-88) (Arizona 1973-76, Purdue 1977-81, Army 1983-90)	53-142	160th (100-58-2)	15-1
JOHN YOVICSIN (11-16-68) (Gettysburg 1952-56, Harvard 1957-70)	50-131	150th (100-45-5)	17-8
JOSEPH YUKICA (11-20-82) (New Hampshire 1966-67, Boston College 1968-77, Dartmouth 1978-86)	51-177	169th (100-68-1)	17-10
ROBERT ZUPPKE (11-12-32) (Illinois 1913-41)	53-102	152nd (100-44-8)	20-9

#Active coach.

200 VICTORIES

Coach (Date Reached Milestone)	WHEN MILESTONE REACHED		
	Age in Yrs.-Days	Career Game (Record)	Career Yr.-Game
Eddie Anderson (11-14-64)	64-1	342nd (200-127-15)	39-8
#Bobby Bowden (10-27-90)	60-353	279th (200-76-3)	25-7
"Bear" Bryant (9-10-71)	57-364	282nd (200-66-16)	27-1
Vince Dooley (11-26-88)	56-84	286th (200-76-10)	25-11
#Hayden Fry (11-20-93)	64-265	361st (200-152-9)	32-11
"Woody" Hayes (11-2-74)	61-261	268th (200-60-8)	29-8
Darrell Mudra (12-5-87)	58-335	284th (200-80-4)	26-13
Jess Neely (9-26-64)	66-265	373rd (200-155-18)	38-1
#Tom Osborne (10-7-93)	56-224	249th (200-46-3)	20-5
#Joe Paterno (9-5-87)	60-258	246th (200-44-2)	22-1
"Bo" Schembechler (10-4-86)	57-33	262nd (200-55-7)	24-4
Amos Alonzo Stagg (10-11-19)	57-56	294th (200-74-20)	30-1
"Pop" Warner (9-24-21)	50-172	276th (200-62-14)	28-1
Warren Woodson (10-13-73)	70-231	307th (200-93-14)	31-6

#Active coach.

300 VICTORIES

Coach (Date Reached Milestone)	WHEN MILESTONE REACHED		
	Age in Yrs.-Days	Career Game (Record)	Career Yr.-Game
"Bear" Bryant (10-3-80)	67-22	393rd (300-77-16)	36-4
Amos Alonzo Stagg (11-6-43)	81-82	507th (300-173-34)	54-7
"Pop" Warner (11-24-34)	63-233	415th (300-91-24)	41-8

Other Coaching Milestones

YOUNGEST COACHES TO REACH 100 VICTORIES

Coach	Age in Yrs.-Days
George Woodruff	35-261
Elmer Layden	37-175
"Hurry Up" Yost	37-191
"Pop" Warner	37-235
Amos Alonzo Stagg	38-51
Don Faurot	39-131
Matty Bell	39-256
Dana Bible	40-44
Andy Smith	40-71
Bennie Owen	40-72
Dan McGugin	40-78
Hugo Bezdek	40-120

YOUNGEST COACHES TO REACH 200 VICTORIES

Coach	Age in Yrs.-Days
"Pop" Warner	50-172
Vince Dooley	56-84
*Tom Osborne	56-224
"Bo" Schembechler	57-33
Amos Alonzo Stagg	57-56
"Bear" Bryant	57-364
Darrell Mudra	58-335

*Active coach.

YOUNGEST COACHES TO REACH 300 VICTORIES

Coach	Age in Yrs.-Days
"Pop" Warner	63-233
"Bear" Bryant	67-22
Amos Alonzo Stagg	81-82

FEWEST GAMES TO REACH 100 VICTORIES

Coach	Career Game (Record at Time)
Gil Dobie	108 (100-5-3)
George Woodruff	109 (100-9-0)
Bud Wilkinson	111 (100-8-3)
"Hurry Up" Yost	114 (100-10-4)
Knute Rockne	117 (100-12-5)
Bob Neyland	120 (100-12-8)
Frank Leahy	121 (100-13-8)
*Joe Paterno	122 (100-21-1)
Barry Switzer	122 (100-18-4)
Henry Williams	122 (100-13-9)
Fred Folsom	126 (100-20-6)
"Gus" Henderson	126 (100-23-3)
*Tom Osborne	126 (100-24-2)
Frank Thomas	128 (100-21-7)
Wallace Wade	129 (100-24-5)
"Bo" Schembechler	130 (100-24-6)
Bobby Dodd	131 (100-28-3)
Frank Kush	131 (100-30-1)
Charley Moran	131 (100-24-7)
Darrell Mudra	131 (100-29-2)
Dan McGugin	132 (100-25-7)
Jock Sutherland	132 (100-22-10)
Bob Devaney	133 (100-28-5)
"Red" Blaik	134 (100-25-9)
*Jim Wacker	134 (100-33-1)
Tony Knap	135 (100-33-2)
Johnny Vaught	135 (100-29-6)
Morley Jennings	136 (100-33-3)
Bennie Owen	136 (100-28-8)
Francis Schmidt	136 (100-27-9)
*Dennis Erickson	137 (100-36-1)
"Pie" Vann	137 (100-36-1)
Frank Broyles	138 (100-36-2)
Fritz Crisler	138 (100-30-8)
*LaVell Edwards	138 (100-37-1)
Dan Devine	139 (100-31-8)
*Danny Ford	139 (100-34-5)
John McKay	139 (100-33-6)

*Active coach.

FEWEST GAMES TO REACH 200 VICTORIES

Coach	Career Game (Record at Time)
*Joe Paterno	246 (200-44-2)
*Tom Osborne	249 (200-46-3)
"Bo" Schembechler	262 (200-55-7)
"Woody" Hayes	268 (200-60-8)
"Pop" Warner	276 (200-62-14)
*Bobby Bowden	279 (200-76-3)
"Bear" Bryant	282 (200-66-16)
Darrell Mudra	284 (200-80-4)
Vince Dooley	286 (200-76-10)

*Active coach.

FEWEST GAMES TO REACH 300 VICTORIES

Coach	Career Game (Record at Time)
"Bear" Bryant	393 (300-77-16)
"Pop" Warner	415 (300-91-24)
Amos Alonzo Stagg	507 (300-173-34)

All-Time Division I Coaching Longevity Records

(Minimum 10 Head-Coaching Seasons in Division I; Bowl Games Included)

MOST GAMES

Games	Coach, School(s) and Years
548	Amos Alonzo Stagg, Springfield 1890-91, Chicago 1892-1932, Pacific (Cal.) 1933-46
457	"Pop" Warner, Georgia 1895-96, Cornell 1897-98 and 1904-06, Carlisle 1899-1903 and 1907-14, Pittsburgh 1915-23, Stanford 1924-32, Temple 1933-38
425	"Bear" Bryant, Maryland 1945, Kentucky 1946-53, Texas A&M 1954-57, Alabama 1958-82
402	Jess Neely, Rhodes 1924-27, Clemson 1931-39, Rice 1940-66
362	*Hayden Fry, Southern Methodist 1962-72, North Texas 1973-78, Iowa 1979-93
344	Eddie Anderson, Loras 1922-24, DePaul 1925-31, Holy Cross 1933-38 and 1950-64, Iowa 1939-42 and 1946-49
329	*Joe Paterno, Penn St. 1966-93
329	Grant Teaff, McMurry 1960-65, Angelo St. 1969-71, Baylor 1972-92
322	*Jim Sweeney, Montana St. 1963-67, Washington St. 1968-75, Fresno St. 1976-77 and 1980-93
320	*Bobby Bowden, Samford 1959-62, West Va. 1970-75, Florida St. 1976-93
320	"Woody" Hayes, Denison 1946-48, Miami (Ohio) 1949-50, Ohio St. 1951-78
318	Ray Morrison, Southern Methodist 1915-16 and 1922-34, Vanderbilt 1918 and 1935-39, Temple 1940-48, Austin 1949-52
312	Warren Woodson, Central Ark. 1935-39, Hardin-Simmons 1941-42 and 1946-51, Arizona 1952-56, New Mexico St. 1958-67, Trinity (Tex.) 1972-73
309	Jerry Claiborne, Virginia Tech 1961-70, Maryland 1972-81, Kentucky 1982-89
307	"Bo" Schembechler, Miami (Ohio) 1963-68, Michigan 1969-89
299	*Johnny Majors, Iowa St. 1968-72, Pittsburgh 1973-76 and 1993, Tennessee 1977-92
299	Ossie Solem, Luther 1920, Drake 1921-31, Iowa 1932-36, Syracuse 1937-45, Springfield 1946-57
296	"Tuss" McLaughry, Westminster 1916, 1918 and 1921, Amherst 1922-25, Brown 1926-40, Dartmouth 1941-54
296	"Pappy" Waldorf, Oklahoma City 1925-27, Oklahoma St. 1929-33, Kansas St. 1934, Northwestern 1935-46, California 1947-56
295	Frank Howard, Clemson 1940-69
293	Dana Bible, Mississippi Col. 1913-15, Louisiana St. 1916, Texas A&M 1917 and 1919-28, Nebraska 1929-36, Texas 1937-46
293	Bill Dooley, North Caro. 1967-77, Virginia Tech 1978-86, Wake Forest 1987-92
292	Lou Little, Georgetown 1924-29, Columbia 1930-56
292	Carl Snavely, Bucknell 1927-33, North Caro. 1934-35 and 1945-52, Cornell 1936-44, Washington (Mo.) 1953-58
288	Vince Dooley, Georgia 1964-88
287	Bob Blackman, Denver 1953-54, Dartmouth 1955-70, Illinois 1971-76, Cornell 1977-82
283	*Lou Holtz, William & Mary 1969-71, North Caro. St. 1972-75, Arkansas 1977-83, Minnesota 1984-85, Notre Dame 1986-93
282	Clark Shaughnessy, Tulane 1915-20 and 1922-26, Loyola (La.) 1927-32, Chicago 1933-39, Stanford 1940-41, Maryland 1942 and 1946, Pittsburgh 1943-45, Hawaii 1965
279	Howard Jones, Syracuse 1908, Yale 1909 and 1913, Ohio St. 1910, Iowa 1916-23, Duke 1924, Southern Cal 1925-40
277	Ben Schwartzwalder, Muhlenberg 1946-48, Syracuse 1949-73

COACHES' RECORDS

Games	Coach, School(s) and Years
276	Bill Yeoman, Houston 1962-86
273	*LaVell Edwards, Brigham Young 1972-93
272	John Heisman, Oberlin 1892 and 1894, Akron 1893, Auburn 1895-99, Clemson 1900-03, Georgia Tech 1904-19, Pennsylvania 1920-22, Wash. & Jeff. 1923, Rice 1924-27
271	Dan McGugin, Vanderbilt 1904-17 and 1919-34
269	Don Faurot, Northeast Mo. St. 1926-34, Missouri 1935-42 and 1946-56
268	*Bill Mallory, Miami (Ohio) 1969-73, Colorado 1974-78, Northern Ill. 1980-83, Indiana 1984-93
265	"Shug" Jordan, Auburn 1951-75
263	John Vaught, Mississippi 1947-70 and 1973
260	Jack Curtice, West Tex. A&M 1940-41, UTEP 1946-49, Utah 1950-57, Stanford 1958-61, UC Santa Barb. 1962-69
260	*Jim Wacker, Texas Lutheran 1971-75, North Dak. St. 1976-78, Southwest Tex. St. 1979-82, Texas Christian 1983-91, Minnesota 1992-93
259	Chuck Mills, Pomona-Pitzer 1959-61, Indiana (Pa.) 1962-63, Merchant Marine 1964, Utah St. 1967-72, Wake Forest 1973-77, Southern Ore. 1980-88
258	Edward Robinson, Nebraska 1896-97, Brown 1898-1901, 1904-07 and 1910-25
257	Don James, Kent 1971-74, Washington 1975-92
256	Matty Bell, Haskell 1920-21, Carroll (Wis.) 1922, Texas Christian 1923-28, Texas A&M 1929-33, Southern Methodist 1935-41 and 1945-49
256	*Tom Osborne, Nebraska 1973-93
255	*Don Nehlen, Bowling Green 1968-76, West Va. 1980-93
252	Harvey Harman, Haverford 1922-29, Sewanee 1930, Pennsylvania 1931-37, Rutgers 1938-55

*Active.

MOST YEARS

Years	Coach, School(s) and Years
57	Amos Alonzo Stagg, Springfield 1890-91, Chicago 1892-1932, Pacific (Cal.) 1933-46
44	"Pop" Warner, Georgia 1895-96, Cornell 1897-98 and 1904-06, Carlisle 1899-1903 and 1907-14, Pittsburgh 1915-23, Stanford 1924-32, Temple 1933-38
40	Jess Neely, Rhodes 1924-27, Clemson 1931-39, Rice 1940-66
39	Eddie Anderson, Loras 1922-24, DePaul 1925-31, Holy Cross 1933-38 and 1950-54, Iowa 1939-42 and 1946-49
38	"Bear" Bryant, Maryland 1945, Kentucky 1946-53, Texas A&M 1954-57, Alabama 1958-82
37	Ossie Solem, Luther 1920, Drake 1921-31, Iowa 1932-36, Syracuse 1937-45, Springfield 1946-57
36	John Heisman, Oberlin 1892 and 1894, Akron 1893, Auburn 1895-99, Clemson 1900-03, Georgia Tech 1904-19, Pennsylvania 1920-22, Wash. & Jeff. 1923, Rice 1924-27
34	"Tuss" McLaughry, Westminster 1916, 1918 and 1921, Amherst 1922-25, Brown 1926-40, Dartmouth 1941-54
34	Ray Morrison, Southern Methodist 1915-16 and 1922-34, Vanderbilt 1918 and 1935-39, Temple 1940-48, Austin 1949-52
33	Dana Bible, Mississippi Col. 1913-15, Louisiana St. 1916, Texas A&M 1917 and 1919-28, Nebraska 1929-36, Texas 1937-46
33	Gil Dobie, North Dak. St. 1906-07, Washington 1908-16, Navy 1917-19, Cornell 1920-35, Boston College 1936-38
33	"Woody" Hayes, Denison 1946-48, Miami (Ohio) 1949-50, Ohio St. 1951-78
33	Lou Little, Georgetown 1924-29, Columbia 1930-56
32	*Hayden Fry, Southern Methodist 1962-72, North Texas 1973-78, Iowa 1979-93
32	Clark Shaughnessy, Tulane 1915-20 and 1922-26, Loyola (La.) 1927-32, Chicago 1933-39, Stanford 1940-41, Maryland 1942 and 1946, Pittsburgh 1943-45, Hawaii 1965
32	Carl Snavely, Bucknell 1927-33, North Caro. 1934-35 and 1945-52, Cornell 1936-44, Washington (Mo.) 1953-58
31	"Pappy" Waldorf, Oklahoma City 1925-27, Oklahoma St. 1929-33, Kansas St. 1934, Northwestern 1935-46, California 1947-56
31	Warren Woodson, Central Ark. 1935-39, Hardin-Simmons 1941-42 and 1946-51, Arizona 1952-56, New Mexico St. 1958-67, Trinity (Tex.) 1972-73
30	Bob Blackman, Denver 1953-54, Dartmouth 1955-70, Illinois 1971-76, Cornell 1977-82
30	Harvey Harman, Haverford 1922-29, Sewanee 1930, Pennsylvania 1931-37, Rutgers 1938-55
30	Frank Howard, Clemson 1940-69
30	Dan McGugin, Vanderbilt 1904-17 and 1919-34
30	Grant Teaff, McMurry 1960-65, Angelo St. 1969-71, Baylor 1972-92

*Active.

MOST SCHOOLS
(Must Have Coached at Least One Division I or Major-College Team)

Schools	Coach, Schools and Years
8	John Heisman, Oberlin 1892 and 1894, Akron 1893, Auburn 1895-99, Clemson 1900-03, Georgia Tech 1904-19, Pennsylvania 1920-22, Wash. & Jeff. 1923, Rice 1924-27
7	Darrell Mudra, Adams St. 1959-62, North Dak. St. 1963-65, Arizona 1967-68, Western Ill. 1969-73, Florida St. 1974-75, Eastern Ill. 1978-82, Northern Iowa 1983-87
7	Lou Saban, Case Reserve 1950-52, Northwestern 1955, Western Ill. 1957-59, Maryland 1966, Miami (Fla.) 1977-78, Army 1979, Central Fla. 1983-84
7	Clark Shaughnessy, Tulane 1915-20 and 1922-26, Loyola (La.) 1927-32, Chicago 1933-39, Stanford 1940-41, Maryland 1942 and 1946, Pittsburgh 1943-45, Hawaii 1965
6	Howard Jones, Syracuse 1908, Yale 1909 and 1913, Ohio St. 1910, Iowa 1916-23, Duke 1924, Southern Cal 1925-40
6	Chuck Mills, Pomona-Pitzer 1959-61, Indiana (Pa.) 1962-63, Merchant Marine 1964, Utah St. 1967-72, Wake Forest 1973-77, Southern Ore. 1980-88
6	"Pop" Warner, Georgia 1895-96, Cornell 1897-98 and 1904-06, Carlisle 1899-1903 and 1907-14, Pittsburgh 1915-23, Stanford 1924-32, Temple 1933-38
5	Matty Bell, Haskell 1920-21, Carroll (Wis.) 1922, Texas Christian 1923-28, Texas A&M 1929-33, Southern Methodist 1935-41 and 1945-49
5	Dana Bible, Mississippi Col. 1913-15, Louisiana St. 1916, Texas A&M 1917 and 1919-28, Nebraska 1929-36, Texas 1937-46
5	Earle Bruce, Tampa 1972, Iowa St. 1973-78, Ohio St. 1979-87, Northern Iowa 1988, Colorado St. 1989-92
5	Frank Cavanaugh, Cincinnati 1898, Holy Cross 1903-05, Dartmouth 1911-16, Boston College 1919-26, Fordham 1927-32
5	Jack Curtice, West Tex. A&M 1940-41, UTEP 1946-49, Utah 1950-57, Stanford 1958-61, UC Santa Barb. 1962-69
5	Gil Dobie, North Dak. St. 1906-07, Washington 1908-16, Navy 1917-19, Cornell 1920-35, Boston College 1936-38
5	Ed Doherty, Arizona St. 1947-50, Rhode Island 1951, Arizona 1957-58, Xavier (Ohio) 1959-61, Holy Cross 1971-75
5	"Red" Drew, Trinity (Conn.) 1921-23, Birmingham So. 1924-27, Tenn.-Chatt. 1929-30, Mississippi 1946, Alabama 1947-54
5	Stuart Holcomb, Findlay 1932-35, Muskingum 1936-40, Wash. & Jeff. 1941, Miami (Ohio) 1942-43, Purdue 1947-55
5	*Lou Holtz, William & Mary 1969-71, North Caro. St. 1972-75, Arkansas 1977-83, Minnesota 1984-85, Notre Dame 1986-93
5	*Al Molde, Sioux Falls 1971-72, Minn.-Morris 1973-79, Central Mo. St. 1980-82, Eastern Ill. 1983-86, Western Ill. 1987-93
5	Darryl Rogers, Cal St. Hayward 1965, Fresno St. 1966-72, San Jose St. 1973-75, Michigan St. 1976-79, Arizona St. 1980-84
5	John Rowland, Henderson St. 1925-30, Ouachita Baptist 1931, Citadel 1940-42, Oklahoma City 1946-47, Geo. Washington 1948-51
5	Francis Schmidt, Tulsa 1919-21, Arkansas 1922-28, Texas Christian 1929-33, Ohio St. 1934-40, Idaho 1941-42
5	"Clipper" Smith, Gonzaga 1925-28, Santa Clara 1929-35, Villanova 1936-42, San Francisco 1946, Lafayette 1949-51
5	Carl Snavely, Bucknell 1927-33, North Caro. 1934-35 and 1945-52, Cornell 1936-44, Washington (Mo.) 1953-58
5	Ossie Solem, Luther 1920, Drake 1921-31, Iowa 1932-36, Syracuse 1937-45, Springfield 1946-57
5	"Skip" Stahley, Delaware 1934, Brown 1941-43, Geo. Washington 1946-47, Toledo 1948-49, Idaho 1954-60
5	*Jim Wacker, Texas Lutheran 1971-75, North Dak. St. 1976-78, Southwest Tex. St. 1979-82, Texas Christian 1983-91, Minnesota 1992-93
5	"Pappy" Waldorf, Oklahoma City 1925-27, Oklahoma St. 1929-33, Kansas St. 1934, Northwestern 1935-46, California 1947-56
5	Warren Woodson, Central Ark. 1935-39, Hardin-Simmons 1941-42, Arizona 1952-56, New Mexico St. 1958-67, Trinity (Tex.) 1972-73
5	"Hurry Up" Yost, Ohio Wesleyan 1897, Nebraska 1898, Kansas 1899, Stanford 1900, Michigan 1901-23 and 1925-26
4	Eddie Anderson, Loras 1922-24, DePaul 1925-31, Holy Cross 1933-38 and 1950-64, Iowa 1939-42 and 1946-49
4	Jerry Berndt, DePauw 1979-80, Pennsylvania 1981-85, Rice 1986-88, Temple 1989-92
4	Bob Blackman, Denver 1953-54, Dartmouth 1955-70, Illinois 1971-76, Cornell 1977-82
4	Watson Brown, Austin Peay 1979-80, Cincinnati 1983, Rice 1984-85, Vanderbilt 1986-90
4	"Bear" Bryant, Maryland 1945, Kentucky 1946-53, Texas A&M 1954-57, Alabama 1958-82
4	Dudley DeGroot, UC Santa Barb. 1926-31, San Jose St. 1932-43, West Va. 1948-49, New Mexico 1950-52
4	Pete Elliott, Nebraska 1956, California 1957-59, Illinois 1960-66, Miami (Fla.) 1973-74
4	*Dennis Erickson, Idaho 1982-85, Wyoming 1986, Washington St. 1987-88, Miami (Fla.) 1989-93
4	Wesley Fesler, Wesleyan 1941-42, Pittsburgh 1946, Ohio St. 1947-50, Minnesota 1951-53
4	*Dennis Franchione, S'western (Kan.) 1981-82, Pittsburg St. 1985-89, Southwest Tex. St. 1990-91, New Mexico 1992-93
4	Mike Gottfried, Murray St. 1978-80, Cincinnati 1981-82, Kansas 1983-85, Pittsburgh 1986-89

Schools	Coach, Schools and Years
4	Harvey Harman, Haverford 1922-29, Sewanee 1930, Pennsylvania 1931-37, Rutgers 1938-55
4	*Ken Hatfield, Air Force 1979-83, Arkansas 1984-89, Clemson 1990-93, Rice 1994
4	*Bill Mallory, Miami (Ohio) 1969-73, Colorado 1974-78, Northern Ill. 1980-83, Indiana 1984-93
4	"Tuss" McLaughry, Westminster 1916, 1918 and 1921, Amherst 1922-25, Brown 1926-40, Dartmouth 1941-54
4	Joe McMullen, Stetson 1950-51, Wash. & Jeff. 1952-53, Akron 1954-60, San Jose St. 1969-70
4	Bill Meek, Kansas St. 1951-54, Houston 1955-56, Southern Methodist 1957-61, Utah 1968-73
4	Charley Moran, Texas A&M 1909-14, Centre 1919-23, Bucknell 1924-26, Catawba 1930-31
4	Ray Morrison, Southern Methodist 1915-16 and 1922-34, Vanderbilt 1918 and 1935-39, Temple 1940-48, Austin 1949-52
4	Frank Navarro, Williams 1963-67, Columbia 1968-73, Wabash 1974-77, Princeton 1978-84
4	John Pont, Miami (Ohio) 1956-62, Yale 1963-64, Indiana 1965-72, Northwestern 1973-77
4	Bill Roper, Va. Military 1903-04, Princeton 1906-08, 1910-11 and 1919-30, Missouri 1909, Swarthmore 1915-16
4	Philip Sarboe, Central Wash. 1941-42, Washington St. 1945-49, Humboldt St. 1951-65, Hawaii 1966
4	George Sauer, New Hampshire 1937-41, Kansas 1946-47, Navy 1948-49, Baylor 1950-55
4	*Jackie Sherrill, Washington St. 1976, Pittsburgh 1977-81, Texas A&M 1982-88, Mississippi St. 1991-93
4	Steve Sloan, Vanderbilt 1973-74, Texas Tech 1975-77, Mississippi 1978-82, Duke 1983-86
4	*Larry Smith, Tulane 1976-79, Arizona 1980-86, Southern Cal 1987-92, Missouri 1994
4	Denny Stolz, Alma 1965-70, Michigan St. 1973-75, Bowling Green 1977-85, San Diego St. 1986-88

*Active.

MOST YEARS COACHED AT ONE COLLEGE

(Minimum 15 Years)

Coach, College (Years)	Years	School W-L-T	Overall W-L-T
Amos Alonzo Stagg, Chicago (1892-1932)	41	244-111-27	314-199-35
Frank Howard, Clemson (1940-69)	30 #	165-118-12	165-118-12
Dan McGugin, Vanderbilt (1904-17, 1919-34)	30 #	197-55-19	197-55-19
Robert Zuppke, Illinois (1913-41)	29 #	131-81-13	131-81-13
"Woody" Hayes, Ohio St. (1951-78)	28	205-61-10	238-72-10
*Joe Paterno, Penn St. (1966-93)	28 #	257-69-3	257-69-3
Lou Little, Columbia (1930-56)	27	110-116-10	151-128-13
Jess Neely, Rice (1940-66)	27	144-124-10	207-176-19
Ike Armstrong, Utah (1925-49)	25 #	140-55-15	140-55-15
"Bear" Bryant, Alabama (1958-82)	25	232-46-9	323-85-17
Vince Dooley, Georgia (1964-88)	25 #	201-77-10	201-77-10
Ralph Jordan, Auburn (1951-75)	25 #	176-83-6	176-83-6
Ben Schwartzwalder, Syracuse (1949-73)	25	153-91-3	178-96-3
John Vaught, Mississippi (1947-70, 1973)	25 #	190-61-12	190-61-12
Bill Yeoman, Houston (1962-86)	25 #	160-108-8	160-108-8
"Hurry Up" Yost, Michigan (1901-23, 1925-26)	25	165-29-10	196-36-12
Frank Camp, Louisville (1946-68)	23 #	118-96-2	118-96-2
Edward Robinson, Brown (1898-1901, 1904-07, 1910-25)	23	140-82-12	157-88-13
Wally Butts, Georgia (1939-60)	22 #	140-86-9	140-86-9
Bobby Dodd, Georgia Tech (1945-66)	22 #	165-64-8	165-64-8
*LaVell Edwards, Brigham Young (1972-93)	22 #	197-73-3	197-73-3
Frank Kush, Arizona St. (1958-79)	22 #	176-54-1	176-54-1
Bennie Owen, Oklahoma (1905-26)	22	122-54-16	155-60-19
Henry Williams, Minnesota (1900-21)	22	140-33-11	141-34-12
Eddie Anderson, Holy Cross (1933-38, 1950-64)	21	129-67-8	201-128-15
Bob Neyland, Tennessee (1926-34, 1936-40, 1946-50)	21 #	173-31-12	173-31-12
*Tom Osborne, Nebraska (1973-93)	21 #	206-47-3	206-47-3
"Bo" Schembechler, Michigan (1969-89)	21	194-48-5	234-65-8
Grant Teaff, Baylor (1972-92)	21	128-105-6	170-151-8
Bill Hess, Ohio (1958-77)	20 #	107-92-4	107-92-4
Ben Martin, Air Force (1958-77)	20	96-103-9	102-116-10
Darrell Royal, Texas (1957-76)	20	167-47-5	184-60-5
"Pie" Vann, Southern Miss. (1949-68)	20 #	139-59-2	139-59-2
Frank Broyles, Arkansas (1958-76)	19	144-58-5	149-62-6
"Red" Blaik, Army (1941-58)	18	121-33-10	166-48-14
*Bobby Bowden, Florida St. (1976-93)	18	166-46-3	239-78-3
*Terry Donahue, UCLA (1976-93)	18	139-63-8	139-63-8
Ray Eliot, Illinois (1942-59)	18	83-73-11	102-82-13
Don James, Washington (1975-92)	18	151-59-2	176-78-3
Charles McClendon, Louisiana St. (1962-79)	18 #	137-59-7	137-59-7

Coach, College (Years)	Years	School W-L-T	Overall W-L-T
Jim Owens, Washington (1957-74)	18 #	99-82-6	99-82-6
Murray Warmath, Minnesota (1954-71)	18	87-78-7	97-84-10
*Chris Ault, Nevada (1976-92)	17 #	145-58-1	145-58-1
*Rich Brooks, Oregon (1977-93)	17 #	82-105-4	82-105-4
Earle Edwards, North Caro. St. (1954-70)	17 #	77-88-8	77-88-8
Bud Wilkinson, Oklahoma (1947-63)	17 #	145-29-4	145-29-4
Bob Blackman, Dartmouth (1955-70)	16	104-37-3	168-112-7
Len Casanova, Oregon (1951-66)	16	82-73-8	104-94-11
Herb Deromedi, Central Mich. (1978-93)	16 #	110-55-10	110-55-10
Gil Dobie, Cornell (1920-35)	16	82-36-7	180-45-15
Rip Engle, Penn St. (1950-65)	16	104-48-4	132-68-8
Andy Gustafson, Miami (Fla.) (1948-63)	16	93-65-3	115-78-4
John Heisman, Georgia Tech (1904-19)	16	102-29-6	185-70-17
Howard Jones, Southern Cal (1925-40)	16	121-36-13	194-64-21
*Johnny Majors, Tennessee (1977-92)	16	116-62-8	176-113-10
John McKay, Southern Cal (1960-75)	16 #	127-40-8	127-40-8
*Jim Sweeney, Fresno St. (1976-77, 1980-93)	16	129-54-2	186-133-3
Barry Switzer, Oklahoma (1973-88)	16 #	157-29-4	157-29-4
Wallace Wade, Duke (1931-41, 1946-50)	16	110-36-7	171-49-10
Rex Enright, South Caro. (1938-42, 1946-55)	15 #	64-69-7	64-69-7
*Hayden Fry, Iowa (1979-93)	15	111-64-5	200-153-9
Morley Jennings, Baylor (1926-40)	15	83-60-6	153-75-18
Ray Morrison, Southern Methodist (1915-16, 1922-34)	15	84-44-22	155-130-33
Bill Murray, Duke (1951-65)	15	83-51-9	142-67-11
Jock Sutherland, Pittsburgh (1924-38)	15	111-20-12	144-28-14
Frank Thomas, Alabama (1931-42, 1944-46)	15	115-24-7	141-33-9

*Active coach. #Never coached at any other college.

Active Coaching Longevity Records

(Minimum Five Years as a Division I-A Head Coach; Includes Bowl Games)

MOST GAMES

Games	Coach, School(s) and Years
362	Hayden Fry, Southern Methodist 1962-72, North Texas 1973-78, Iowa 1979-93
329	Joe Paterno, Penn St., 1966-93
322	Jim Sweeney, Montana St. 1963-67, Washington St. 1968-75, Fresno St. 1976-77 and 1980-93
320	Bobby Bowden, Samford 1959-62, West Va. 1970-75, Florida St. 1976-93
299	Johnny Majors, Iowa St. 1968-72, Pittsburgh 1973-76 and 1993, Tennessee 1977-92
283	Lou Holtz, William & Mary 1969-71, North Caro. St. 1972-75, Arkansas 1977-83, Minnesota 1984-85, Notre Dame 1986-93
273	LaVell Edwards, Brigham Young 1972-93
268	Bill Mallory, Miami (Ohio) 1969-73, Colorado 1974-78, Northern Ill. 1980-83, Indiana 1984-93
260	Jim Wacker, Texas Lutheran 1971-75, North Dak. St. 1976-78, Southwest Tex. St. 1979-82, Texas Christian 1983-91, Minnesota 1992-93
256	Tom Osborne, Nebraska 1973-93
255	Don Nehlen, Bowling Green 1968-76, West Va. 1980-93
247	Al Molde, Sioux Falls 1971-72, Minn.-Morris 1973-79, Central Mo. St. 1980-82, Eastern Ill. 1983-86, Western Mich. 1987-93
241	George Welsh, Navy 1973-81, Virginia 1982-93
225	Billy Brewer, Southeastern La. 1974-79, Louisiana Tech 1980-82, Mississippi 1983-93

MOST YEARS

Years	Coach, School(s) and Years
32	Hayden Fry, Southern Methodist 1962-72, North Texas 1973-78, Iowa 1979-93
29	Jim Sweeney, Montana St. 1963-67, Washington St. 1968-75, Fresno St. 1976-77 and 1980-93
28	Bobby Bowden, Samford 1959-62, West Va. 1970-75, Florida St. 1976-93
28	Joe Paterno, Penn St. 1966-93
26	Johnny Majors, Iowa St. 1968-72, Pittsburgh 1973-76 and 1993, Tennessee 1977-92
24	Lou Holtz, William & Mary 1969-71, North Caro. St. 1972-75, Arkansas 1977-83, Minnesota 1984-85, Notre Dame 1986-93
24	Bill Mallory, Miami (Ohio) 1969-73, Colorado 1974-78, Northern Ill. 1980-83, Indiana 1984-93
23	Al Molde, Sioux Falls 1971-72, Minn.-Morris 1973-79, Central Mo. St. 1980-82, Eastern Ill. 1983-86, Western Mich. 1987-93
23	Don Nehlen, Bowling Green 1968-76, West Va. 1980-93
23	Jim Wacker, Texas Lutheran 1971-75, North Dak. St. 1976-78, Southwest Tex. St. 1979-82, Texas Christian 1983-91, Minnesota 1992-93

Years	Coach, School(s) and Years
22	LaVell Edwards, Brigham Young 1972-93
21	Tom Osborne, Nebraska 1973-93
21	George Welsh, Navy 1973-81, Virginia 1982-93
20	Billy Brewer, Southeastern La. 1974-79, Louisiana Tech 1980-82, Mississippi 1983-93
18	Terry Donahue, UCLA 1976-93
17	Rich Brooks, Oregon 1977-93
17	John Cooper, Tulsa 1977-84, Arizona 1985-87, Ohio St. 1988-93
17	Chuck Shelton, Drake 1977-85, Utah St. 1986-91, Pacific (Cal.) 1992-93
17	Larry Smith, Tulane 1976-79, Arizona 1980-86, Southern Cal 1987-92
17	Dick Tomey, Hawaii 1977-86, Arizona 1987-93
16	Jackie Sherrill, Washington St. 1976, Pittsburgh 1977-81, Texas A&M 1982-88, Mississippi St. 1991-93
16	Jim Walden, Washington St. 1978-86, Iowa St. 1987-93
15	Ken Hatfield, Air Force 1979-83, Arkansas 1984-89, Clemson 1990-93

Less Than 5 Years as Division I-A Head Coach:

19	Jim Hess, Angelo St. 1974-81, Stephen F. Austin 1982-88, New Mexico St. 1990-93
17	Chris Ault, Nevada 1976-92

MOST YEARS AT CURRENT SCHOOL

Years	Coach, School and Years
28	Joe Paterno, Penn St. 1966-93
22	LaVell Edwards, Brigham Young 1972-93
21	Tom Osborne, Nebraska 1973-93
18	Bobby Bowden, Florida St. 1976-93
18	Terry Donahue, UCLA 1976-93
17	Rich Brooks, Oregon 1977-93
16	Jim Sweeney, Fresno St. 1976-77, 1980-93
15	Hayden Fry, Iowa 1979-93
14	Don Nehlen, West Va. 1980-93
12	Bill McCartney, Colorado 1982-93
12	George Welsh, Virginia 1982-93
11	Billy Brewer, Mississippi 1983-93
11	George Perles, Michigan St. 1983-93
10	Pat Jones, Oklahoma St. 1984-93

Less Than 5 Years as Division I-A Head Coach:

17	Chris Ault, Nevada 1976-92

MOST SCHOOLS

Schools	Coach, Schools and Years
5	Lou Holtz, William & Mary 1969-71, North Caro. St. 1972-75, Arkansas 1977-83, Minnesota 1984-85, Notre Dame 1986-93
5	Al Molde, Sioux Falls 1971-72, Minn.-Morris 1973-79, Central Mo. St. 1980-82, Eastern Ill. 1983-86, Western Mich. 1987-93
5	Jim Wacker, Texas Lutheran 1971-75, North Dak. St. 1976-78, Southwest Tex. St. 1979-82, Texas Christian 1983-91, Minnesota 1992-93
4	Dennis Erickson, Idaho 1982-85, Wyoming 1986, Washington St. 1987-88, Miami (Fla.) 1989-93
4	Ken Hatfield, Air Force 1979-83, Arkansas 1984-89, Clemson 1990-93, Rice 1994
4	Bill Mallory, Miami (Ohio) 1969-73, Colorado 1974-78, Northern Ill. 1980-83, Indiana 1984-93
4	Jackie Sherrill, Washington St. 1976, Pittsburgh 1977-81, Texas A&M 1982-88, Mississippi St. 1991-93
4	Larry Smith, Tulane 1976-79, Arizona 1980-86, Southern Cal 1987-92, Missouri 1994
3	Bobby Bowden, Samford 1959-62, West Va. 1970-75, Florida St. 1976-93
3	Billy Brewer, Southeastern La. 1974-79, Louisiana Tech 1980-82, Mississippi 1983-93
3	Mack Brown, Appalachian St. 1983, Tulane 1985-87, North Caro. 1988-93
3	George Chaump, Indiana (Pa.) 1982-85, Marshall 1986-89, Navy 1990-93
3	John Cooper, Tulsa 1977-84, Arizona St. 1985-87, Ohio St. 1988-93
3	Bill Curry, Georgia Tech 1980-86, Alabama 1987-89, Kentucky 1990-93
3	Hayden Fry, Southern Methodist 1962-72, North Texas 1973-78, Iowa 1979-93
3	Fred Goldsmith, Slippery Rock 1981, Rice 1989-93, Duke 1994
3	Bill Lewis, Wyoming 1977-79, East Caro. 1989-91, Georgia Tech 1992-93
3	John Mackovic, Wake Forest 1978-80, Illinois 1988-91, Texas 1992-93
3	Johnny Majors, Iowa St. 1968-72, Pittsburgh 1973-76 and 1993, Tennessee 1977-92
3	John Ralston, Utah St. 1959-62, Stanford 1963-71, San Jose St. 1993
3	Chuck Shelton, Drake 1977-85, Utah St. 1986-91, Pacific (Cal.) 1992-93
3	Bruce Snyder, Utah St. 1976-82, California 1987-91, Arizona St. 1992-93
3	Chuck Stobart, Toledo 1977-81, Utah 1982-84, Memphis 1989-93
3	Jim Sweeney, Montana St. 1963-67, Washington St. 1968-75, Fresno St. 1976-77 and 1980-93

Less Than 5 Years as Division I-A Head Coach:

4	Dennis Franchione, S'western (Kan.) 1981-82, Pittsburg St. 1985-89, Southwest Tex. St. 1990-91, New Mexico 1992-93
3	Terry Bowden, Salem (W. Va.) 1984-86, Samford 1987-92, Auburn 1993
3	Jim Hess, Angelo St. 1974-81, Stephen F. Austin 1982-88, New Mexico St. 1990-93
3	Tom Lichtenberg, Morehead St. 1979-80, Maine 1989, Ohio 1990-93
3	Buddy Teevens, Maine 1985-86, Dartmouth 1987-91, Tulane 1992-93

Major-College Brother vs. Brother Coaching Matchups

(Each brother's victories in parentheses)

Bump Elliott, Michigan (6), vs. Pete, Illinois (1), 1960-66
Howard Jones, Yale 1909 and Iowa 1922 (2), vs. Tad, Syracuse 1909 and Yale 1922 (0)
Mack Brown, Tulane (2), vs. Watson, Vanderbilt (0), 1986-87
Vince Dooley, Georgia (1), vs. Bill, North Caro. (0), 1971 Gator Bowl

Annual Division I-A Head-Coaching Changes

Year	Changes	Teams	Pct.
1947	27	125	.216
1948	24	121	.198
1949	22	114	.193
1950	23	119	.193
1951	23	115	.200
1952	15	113	.133
1953	18	111	.162
1954	14	103	.136
1955	23	103	.223
1956	19	105	.181
1957	22	108	.204
1958	18	109	.165
1959	18	110	.164
1960	18	114	.158
1961	11	112	.098
1962	20	119	.168
1963	12	118	.102
1964	14	116	.121
1965	16	114	.140
1966	16	116	.138
1967	21	114	.184
1968	14	114	.123
1969	22	118	.186
1970	13	118	.110
1971	27	119	.227
1972	17	121	.140
1973	36	126	†.286
1974	28	128	.219
1975	18	134	.134
1976	23	137	.168
1977	27	144	.188
1978	27	139	.194
1979	26	139	.187
1980	27	139	.194
1981	17	137	.123
1982	17	97	.175
1983	22	105	.210
1984	16	105	.152
1985	15	105	.143
1986	22	105	.210
1987	24	104	.231
1988	9	104	*.087
1989	19	106	.179
1990	20	106	.189
1991	16	106	.151
1992	16	107	.150
1993	15	106	.142
1994	12	107	.112

*Record low. †Record high.

Records of Division I-A First-Year Head Coaches

(Coaches with no previous head-coaching experience at a four-year college.)

					Bowl	Team's Previous Season Record				Bowl
Year	No.	Won	Lost	Tied	Pct. Record	Won	Lost	Tied	Pct.	Record
1948	14	56	68	7	.454 0-1	76	52	8	.588	2-1
1949	8	26	49	3	.353 0-1	35	41	4	.463	0-0
1950	10	37	56	4	.402 0-0	49	42	6	.536	2-0
1951	13	60	67	4	.473 1-2	39	88	7	.317	1-1
1952	8	31	42	3	.428 0-0	38	40	0	.487	0-0
1953	8	29	45	5	.399 0-0	48	28	7	.620	1-2
1954	8	31	43	4	.423 0-0	40	33	7	.543	1-0
1955	9	36	50	4	.422 0-1	36	52	1	.410	0-0
1956	14	47	80	11	.380 1-0	61	68	6	.474	0-1
1957	9	32	50	6	.398 0-0	44	42	2	.511	0-0
1958	7	26	44	0	.371 0-0	37	31	2	.543	0-0
1959	8	34	43	2	.443 0-0	41	35	2	.538	0-1
1960	14	54	80	5	.406 1-0	57	78	2	.423	0-0
1961	8	26	50	1	.342 0-0	38	38	2	.500	0-0
1962	12	40	74	4	.356 2-0	52	66	2	.442	1-1
1963	8	23	49	6	.333 0-0	32	46	1	.411	0-1
1964	12	45	67	7	.408 1-1	42	71	4	.376	0-0
1965	8	28	47	2	.377 0-0	36	42	1	.462	0-0
1966	10	46	50	3	.480 0-0	38	56	5	.409	0-0
1967	18	58	114	5	.342 1-0	60	116	4	.344	0-1
1968	6	19	40	1	.325 0-0	20	38	2	.350	0-0
1969	15	49	90	1	.353 0-0	62	85	3	.423	0-1
1970	10	45	61	1	.425 1-0	46	54	0	.460	0-2
1971	12	57	72	0	.442 1-1	64	61	0	.512	0-1
1972	11	57	64	1	.471 1-0	53	64	2	.454	1-0
1973	14	84	63	8	.568 1-0	83	71	2	.538	3-0
1974	17	63	116	5	.356 1-0	78	105	1	.427	1-0
1975	10	38	72	0	.345 0-1	43	67	0	.391	0-0
1976	15	57	109	2	.345 3-1	72	91	5	.443	3-1
1977	14	55	94	1	.373 1-0	66	88	1	.430	0-2
1978	16	68	104	3	.397 0-0	77	96	3	.446	0-1
1979	11	53	66	3	.447 0-0	66	57	1	.536	2-2
1980	12	54	75	2	.420 0-0	60	68	3	.469	1-0
1981	6	25	40	0	.385 0-0	31	35	1	.470	0-1
1982	10	51	59	1	.464 0-1	58	57	2	.504	2-2
1983	12	51	82	2	.385 1-0	60	73	1	.451	1-1
1984	7	47	28	1*	.625 2-1	45	35	1	.562	3-0
1985	5	19	37	0	.339 0-0	20	32	4	.393	0-0
1986	12	53	81	0	.396 0-1	56	76	3	.426	1-1
1987	9	51	49	3	.510 1-1	52	50	1	.510	0-2
1988	4	25	20	0	.556 1-0	22	23	1	.489	1-1
1989	7	32	49	1	.396 0-2	39	43	0	.476	1-2
1990	9	46	42	2	.522 1-1	41	48	1	.461	0-1
1991	10	38	72	1	.347 1-0	46	64	2	.420	0-2
1992	4	15	20	1	.431 0-0	32	14	0	.696	1-1
1993	8	29	58	2	.337 0-1	41	51	1	.446	2-2

*Record percentage for first-year coaches. 1984 coaches and their records, with bowl game indicated by an asterisk (*): Pat Jones, Oklahoma St. (*10-2-0); Galen Hall, Florida (8-0-0, took over from Charley Pell after three games); Bill Arnsparger, Louisiana St. (8-*3-1); Fisher DeBerry, Air Force (*8-4-0); Dick Anderson, Rutgers (7-3-0); Mike Sheppard, Long Beach St. (4-7-0); Ron Chismar, Wichita St. (2-9-0).

Most Victories by First-Year Head Coaches

Coach, College, Year	W	L	T
Gary Blackney, Bowling Green, 1991	*11	1	0
John Robinson, Southern Cal, 1976	*11	1	0
Bill Battle, Tennessee, 1970	*11	1	0
Dick Crum, Miami (Ohio), 1974	*10	0	1
Barry Switzer, Oklahoma, 1973	10	0	1
John Jenkins, Houston, 1990	10	1	0
Dwight Wallace, Ball St., 1978	10	1	0
Chuck Fairbanks, Oklahoma, 1967	*10	1	0
Mike Archer, Louisiana St., 1987	*10	1	1
Curley Hallman, Southern Miss., 1988	*10	2	0
Pat Jones, Oklahoma St., 1984	*10	2	0
Earle Bruce, Tampa, 1972	*10	2	0
Billy Kinard, Mississippi, 1971	*10	2	0

*Bowl game victory included.
Only first-year coach to win a national championship: Bennie Oosterbaan, Michigan, 1948 (9-0-0).

Division I-AA Coaching Records

Winningest Active Division I-AA Coaches

(Minimum Five Years as a Division I-A and/or Division I-AA Head Coach; Record at Four-Year Colleges Only)

BY PERCENTAGE

Coach, College	Years	Won	Lost	Tied	*Pct.	Playoffs# W	L	T
Terry Allen, Northern Iowa	5	47	15	0	.758	3	4	0
Roy Kidd, Eastern Ky.	30	247	88	8	.732	16	13	0
Eddie Robinson, Grambling	51	388	140	15	.728	10	7	0
Tubby Raymond, Delaware	28	232	92	2	.715	17	11	0
John L. Smith, Idaho	5	44	18	0	.710	3	3	0
Jim Tressel, Youngstown St.	8	70	33	1	.678	12	4	0
Houston Markham, Alabama St.	7	49	23	4	.671	1	0	0
Steve Tosches, Princeton	7	46	23	1	.664	0	0	0
Bill Hayes, North Caro. A&T	18	131	66	2	.663	1	5	0
William Collick, Delaware St.	9	62	34	0	.646	0	0	0
Bill Davis, Tennessee St.	15	104	58	1	.641	3	3	0
James Donnelly, Middle Tenn. St.	17	124	71	0	.636	6	6	0
Andy Talley, Villanova	14	87	50	2	.633	1	4	0
Bill Bowes, New Hampshire	22	142	83	5	.628	1	3	0
Carmen Cozza, Yale	29	169	99	5	.628	0	0	0
Bill Thomas, Texas Southern	5	34	20	3	.623	1	1	0
Jack McClairen, Bethune-Cookman	12	61	37	3	.619	0	1	0
Steve Wilson, Howard	5	34	22	0	.607	0	1	0
Ron Randleman, Sam Houston St.	25	155	105	6	.594	3	5	1
Willie Jeffries, South Caro. St.	21	132	92	6	.587	2	3	0
Charlie Taaffe, Citadel	7	47	33	1	.586	1	3	0
Jesse Branch, Southwest Mo. St.	8	51	37	1	.579	1	2	0
Sam Rutigliano, Liberty	5	31	23	0	.574	0	0	0
Jimmye Laycock, William & Mary.	14	90	67	2	.572	1	4	0
Bill Russo, Lafayette	16	94	73	3	.562	0	1	0
Jim Hofher, Cornell	5	27	23	0	.540	0	1	0
Dave Arslanian, Weber St.	5	29	27	0	.518	0	1	0
Don Read, Montana	24	130	122	1	.516	2	3	0
Floyd Keith, Rhode Island	5	26	25	2	.509	0	0	0
Sam Goodwin, Northwestern St.	13	71	69	4	.507	1	1	0
Dennis Raetz, Indiana St.	14	72	83	1	.465	1	2	0
Bob Spoo, Eastern Ill.	7	36	42	1	.462	1	1	0
Jerry Moore, Appalachian St.	12	61	72	2	.459	0	3	0
Jack Harbaugh, Western Ky.	10	48	57	3	.458	0	0	0
Tim Murphy, Harvard	7	32	45	1	.417	0	1	0
Jim Heacock, Illinois St.	6	27	38	1	.417	0	0	0
Lou Maranzana, Bucknell	5	21	32	0	.396	0	0	0
Jim Ragland, Tennessee Tech	8	33	53	0	.384	0	0	0
Ray Tellier, Columbia	10	29	68	1	.301	0	1	0
Jim Marshall, Richmond	5	16	39	0	.291	0	0	0

Less Than 5 Years as Division I-A and/or Division I-AA Head Coach (school followed by years in I-A or I-AA, includes record at all four-year colleges):

Coach, College	Years	Won	Lost	Tied	*Pct.	W	L	T
Mike Kelly, Dayton (1)	13	128	23	1	.845	13	8	0
Al Bagnoli, Pennsylvania (2)	12	103	22	0	.824	7	6	0
Pete Richardson, Southern-B.R. (1)	6	52	15	1	.772	0	3	0
Walt Hameline, Wagner (1)	13	103	32	2	.759	6	2	0
Billy Joe, Florida A&M (0)	20	169	54	4	.753	7	5	0
Mark Whipple, Brown (0)	6	48	17	0	.738	3	2	0
Robin Cooper, Evansville (1)	6	37	18	0	.673	0	0	0
Ed Sweeney, Colgate (1)	9	59	30	4	.656	0	2	0
Pokey Allen, Boise St. (1)	8	65	34	2	.653	10	5	0
Bob Ricca, St. John's (N.Y.) (1)	16	99	62	1	.614	0	0	0
Rick Rhoades, Nicholls St. (2)	5	35	22	1	.612	4	1	0
Gene McDowell, Central Fla. (4).	9	63	40	0	.612	3	3	0
Peter Vaas, Holy Cross (2)	6	38	24	1	.611	0	1	0
Rob Ash, Drake (1)	14	83	53	4	.607	0	0	0
Matt Ballard, Morehead St. (0)	6	35	25	1	.582	0	0	0
Mike Cavan, East Tenn. St. (2)	8	47	34	2	.578	0	1	0
Jack Bishop, Southern Utah (1)	13	74	58	4	.559	0	0	0
Brian Fogarty, San Diego (1)	11	56	45	3	.553	0	0	0
Bob Burt, Cal St. Northridge (1).	9	52	43	0	.547	0	1	0
Barry Mynter, Canisius (1)	18	83	89	3	.483	0	0	0
Harold Crocker, Iona (1)	9	42	48	1	.472	0	0	0
Frank Pergolizzi, St. Francis (Pa.) (1)	5	22	26	1	.459	0	1	0
Don McLeary, Tenn.-Martin (2)	10	49	59	0	.454	1	1	0
Tom Horne, Valparaiso (1)	8	27	53	2	.341	0	0	0
Jack Dubois, Siena (1)	7	13	49	0	.210	0	0	0

*Ties computed as half won and half lost. Overall record includes bowl and playoff games. #Playoffs includes all divisional championships as well as bowl games and NAIA playoffs.

BY VICTORIES
(Minimum 100 Victories)

Coach, College, Winning Percentage	Won
Eddie Robinson, Grambling .728	388
Roy Kidd, Eastern Ky. .732	247
Tubby Raymond, Delaware .715	232
Carmen Cozza, Yale .628	169
Ron Randleman, Sam Houston St. .594	155
Bill Bowes, New Hampshire .628	142
Willie Jeffries, South Caro. St. .587	132
Bill Hayes, North Caro. A&T .663	131
Don Read, Montana .516	130
James Donnelly, Middle Tenn. St. .636	124
Bill Davis, Tennessee St. .641	104

Less Than 5 Yrs. as a I-A/I-AA Head Coach:

Billy Joe, Florida A&M .753	169
Mike Kelly, Dayton .845	128
Al Bagnoli, Pennsylvania .824	103
Walt Hameline, Wagner .759	103

Annual Division I-AA Head-Coaching Changes

(From the 1982 reorganization of the division for parallel comparisons)

Year	Changes	Teams	Pct.
1982	7	92	.076
1983	17	84	.202
1984	14	87	.161
1985	11	87	.126
1986	18	86	.209
1987	13	87	.149
1988	12	88	.136
1989	21	89	†.236
1990	16	89	.180
1991	6	87	*.069
1992	14	89	.157
1993	13	#115	.113
1994	17	116	.147

*Record low. †Record high. #Twenty-seven teams switched from Divisions II & III to I-AA.

Division I-AA Championship Coaches

All coaches who have coached teams in the Division I-AA championship playoffs since 1978 are listed here with their playoff record, alma mater and year graduated, team, year coached, opponent, and score.

Dan Allen (1-1) (Hanover '78)
Boston U.	93	Northern Iowa 27-21 (2 OT)
Boston U.	93	Idaho 14-21

Terry Allen (3-4) (Northern Iowa '79)
Northern Iowa	90	Boise St. 3-20
Northern Iowa	91	Weber St. 38-21
Northern Iowa	91	Marshall 13-41
Northern Iowa	92	Eastern Wash. 17-14
Northern Iowa	92	McNeese St. 29-7
Northern Iowa	92	Youngstown St. 7-19
Northern Iowa	93	Boston U. 21-27 (2 OT)

Dave Arnold (3-0) (Drake '67)
Montana St.	84	Arkansas St. 31-24
Montana St.	84	Rhode Island 32-20
Montana St.	84*	Louisiana Tech 19-6

Dave Arslanian (0-1) (Weber St. '72)
Weber St.	91	Northern Iowa 21-38

Chris Ault (9-7) (Nevada '68)
Nevada	78	Massachusetts 21-44
Nevada	79	Eastern Ky. 30-33
Nevada	83	Idaho St. 27-20
Nevada	83	North Texas 20-17 (OT)
Nevada	83	Southern Ill. 7-23
Nevada	85	Arkansas St. 24-23
Nevada	85	Furman 12-35
Nevada	86	Idaho 27-7
Nevada	86	Tennessee St. 33-6
Nevada	86	Ga. Southern 38-48
Nevada	90	Northeast La. 27-14
Nevada	90	Furman 42-35 (3 OT)
Nevada	90	Boise St. 59-52 (3 OT)
Nevada	90	Ga. Southern 13-36
Nevada	91	McNeese St. 22-16
Nevada	91	Youngstown St. 28-30

Randy Ball (0-1) (Northeast Mo. St. '73)
Western Ill.	91	Marshall 17-20 (OT)

Frank Beamer (0-1) (Virginia Tech '69)
Murray St.	86	Eastern Ill. 21-28

Larry Blakeney (2-1) (Auburn '70)
Troy St.	93	Stephen F. Austin 42-20
Troy St.	93	McNeese St. 35-28
Troy St.	93	Marshall 21-24

Terry Bowden (2-2) (West Va. '78)
Samford	91	New Hampshire 29-13
Samford	91	James Madison 24-21
Samford	91	Youngstown St. 0-10
Samford	92	Delaware 21-56

Bill Bowes (0-1) (Penn St. '65)
New Hampshire	91	Samford 13-29

Jesse Branch (1-2) (Arkansas '64)
Southwest Mo. St.	89	Maine 38-35
Southwest Mo. St.	89	Stephen F. Austin 25-55
Southwest Mo. St.	90	Idaho 35-41

Billy Brewer (1-1) (Mississippi '61)
Louisiana Tech	82	South Caro. St. 38-3
Louisiana Tech	82	Delaware 0-17

Rick Carter (0-1) (Earlham '65)
Holy Cross	83	Western Caro. 21-28

Marino Casem (0-1) (Xavier, La. '56)
Alcorn St.	84	Louisiana Tech 21-44

George Chaump (4-2) (Bloomsburg '58)
Marshall	87	James Madison 41-12
Marshall	87	Weber St. 51-23
Marshall	87	Appalachian St. 24-10
Marshall	87	Northeast La. 42-43
Marshall	88	North Texas 7-0
Marshall	88	Furman 9-13

Pat Collins (4-0) (Louisiana Tech '63)
Northeast La.	87	North Texas 30-9
Northeast La.	87	Eastern Ky. 33-32
Northeast La.	87	Northern Iowa 44-41 (OT)
Northeast La.	87*	Marshall 43-42

Archie Cooley Jr. (0-1) (Jackson St. '62)
Mississippi Val.	84	Louisiana Tech 19-66

Bruce Craddock (0-1) (Northeast Mo. St. '66)
Western Ill.	88	Western Ky. 32-35

Jim Criner (3-1) (Cal Poly Pomona '61)
Boise St.	80	Grambling 14-9
Boise St.	80*	Eastern Ky. 31-29
Boise St.	81	Jackson St. 19-7
Boise St.	81	Eastern Ky. 17-23

Bill Davis (2-2) (Johnson Smith '65)
South Caro. St.	81	Tennessee St. 26-25
South Caro. St.	81	Idaho St. 12-41
South Caro. St.	82	Furman 17-0
South Caro. St.	82	Louisiana Tech 3-38

Rey Dempsey (3-0) (Geneva '58)
Southern Ill.	83	Indiana St. 23-7
Southern Ill.	83	Nevada 23-7
Southern Ill.	83*	Western Caro. 43-7

Jim Dennison (0-1) (Wooster '60)
Akron	85	Rhode Island 27-35

Jim Donnan (10-2) (North Caro. St. '67)
Marshall	91	Western Ill. 20-17 (OT)
Marshall	91	Northern Iowa 41-13
Marshall	91	Eastern Ky. 14-7
Marshall	91	Youngstown St. 17-25
Marshall	92	Eastern Ky. 44-0
Marshall	92	Middle Tenn. St. 35-21
Marshall	92	Delaware 28-7
Marshall	92*	Youngstown St. 31-28
Marshall	93	Howard 28-14
Marshall	93	Delaware 34-31
Marshall	93	Troy St. 24-21
Marshall	93	Youngstown St. 5-17

James "Boots" Donnelly (6-6) (Middle Tenn. St. '65)
Middle Tenn. St.	84	Eastern Ky. 27-10
Middle Tenn. St.	84	Indiana St. 42-41 (3 OT)
Middle Tenn. St.	84	Louisiana Tech 13-21
Middle Tenn. St.	85	Ga. Southern 13-28
Middle Tenn. St.	89	Appalachian St. 24-21
Middle Tenn. St.	89	Ga. Southern 3-45
Middle Tenn. St.	90	Jackson St. 28-7
Middle Tenn. St.	90	Boise St. 13-20
Middle Tenn. St.	91	Sam Houston St. 20-19 (OT)
Middle Tenn. St.	91	Eastern Ky. 13-23
Middle Tenn. St.	92	Appalachian St. 35-10
Middle Tenn. St.	92	Marshall 21-35

Larry Donovan (0-1) (Nebraska '64)
Montana	82	Idaho 7-21

Fred Dunlap (1-2) (Colgate '50)
Colgate	82	Boston U. 21-7
Colgate	82	Delaware 13-20
Colgate	83	Western Caro. 23-24

Dennis Erickson (1-2) (Montana St. '70)
Idaho	82	Montana 21-7
Idaho	82	Eastern Ky. 30-38
Idaho	85	Eastern Wash. 38-42

Maurice "Mo" Forte (0-1) (Minnesota '71)
North Caro. A&T	86	Ga. Southern 21-52

Keith Gilbertson (2-3) (Central Wash. '71)
Idaho	86	Nevada 7-27
Idaho	87	Weber St. 30-59
Idaho	88	Montana 38-19
Idaho	88	Northwestern St. 38-30
Idaho	88	Furman 7-38

Sam Goodwin (1-1) (Henderson St. '66)
Northwestern St.	88	Boise St. 22-13
Northwestern St.	88	Idaho 30-38

W. C. Gorden (0-9) (Tennessee St. '52)
Jackson St.	78	Florida A&M 10-15
Jackson St.	81	Boise St. 7-19
Jackson St.	82	Eastern Ill. 13-16 (OT)
Jackson St.	85	Ga. Southern 0-27
Jackson St.	86	Tennessee St. 23-32
Jackson St.	87	Arkansas St. 32-35
Jackson St.	88	Stephen F. Austin 0-24
Jackson St.	89	Montana 7-48
Jackson St.	90	Middle Tenn. St. 7-28

Mike Gottfried (0-1) (Morehead St. '66)
Murray St.	79	Lehigh 9-28

Lynn Graves (%3-1) (Stephen F. Austin '65)
Stephen F. Austin	89%	Grambling 59-56
Stephen F. Austin	89%	Southwest Mo. St. 55-25
Stephen F. Austin	89%	Furman 21-19
Stephen F. Austin	89%	Ga. Southern 34-37

Bob Griffin (2-3) (Southern Conn. St. '63)
Rhode Island	81	Idaho St. 0-51
Rhode Island	84	Richmond 23-17
Rhode Island	84	Montana St. 20-32
Rhode Island	85	Akron 35-27
Rhode Island	85	Furman 15-59

Skip Hall (2-2) (Concordia-M'head '66)
Boise St.	88	Northwestern St. 13-22
Boise St.	90	Northern Iowa 20-3
Boise St.	90	Middle Tenn. St. 20-13
Boise St.	90	Nevada 52-59 (3 OT)

Bill Hayes (0-1) (N.C. Central '64)
North Caro. A&T	92	Citadel 0-44

Jim Hess (1-1) (Southeastern Okla. '59)
Stephen F. Austin	88	Jackson St. 24-0
Stephen F. Austin	88	Ga. Southern 6-27

Rudy Hubbard (2-0) (Ohio St. '68)
Florida A&M	78	Jackson St. 15-10
Florida A&M	78*	Massachusetts 35-28

Sonny Jackson (1-1) (Nicholls St. '63)
Nicholls St.	86	Appalachian 28-26
Nicholls St.	86	Ga. Southern 31-55

Cardell Jones (0-1) (Alcorn St. '65)
Alcorn St.	92	Northeast La. 27-78

Bobby Keasler (2-3) (Northeast La. '70)
McNeese St.	91	Nevada 16-22
McNeese St.	92	Idaho 23-20
McNeese St.	92	Northern Iowa 7-29
McNeese St.	93	William & Mary 34-28
McNeese St.	93	Troy St. 28-35

Roy Kidd (15-12) (Eastern Ky. '54)
Eastern Ky.	79	Nevada 33-30
Eastern Ky.	79*	Lehigh 30-7
Eastern Ky.	80	Lehigh 23-20
Eastern Ky.	80	Boise St. 29-31
Eastern Ky.	81	Delaware 35-28
Eastern Ky.	81	Boise St. 23-17
Eastern Ky.	81	Idaho St. 23-34
Eastern Ky.	82	Idaho St. 38-30
Eastern Ky.	82	Tennessee St. 13-7
Eastern Ky.	82*	Delaware 17-14
Eastern Ky.	83	Boston U. 20-24

Eastern Ky.	84	Middle Tenn. St. 10-27	
Eastern Ky.	86	Furman 23-10	
Eastern Ky.	86	Eastern Ill. 24-22	
Eastern Ky.	86	Arkansas St. 10-24	
Eastern Ky.	87	Western Ky. 40-17	
Eastern Ky.	87	Northeast La. 32-33	
Eastern Ky.	88	Massachusetts 28-17	
Eastern Ky.	88	Western Ky. 41-24	
Eastern Ky.	88	Ga. Southern 17-21	
Eastern Ky.	89	Youngstown St. 24-28	
Eastern Ky.	90	Furman 17-45	
Eastern Ky.	91	Appalachian St. 14-3	
Eastern Ky.	91	Middle Tenn. St. 23-13	
Eastern Ky.	91	Marshall 7-14	
Eastern Ky.	92	Marshall 0-44	
Eastern Ky.	93	Ga. Southern 12-14	

Jim Koetter (0-1) (Idaho St. '61)
Idaho St. ... 83 Nevada 20-27

Dave Kragthorpe (3-0) (Utah St. '55)
Idaho St. ... 81 Rhode Island 51-0
Idaho St. ... 81 South Caro. St. 41-12
Idaho St. ... 81* Eastern Ky. 34-23

Larry Lacewell (6-4) (Ark.-Monticello '59)
Arkansas St. ... 84 Tenn.-Chatt. 37-10
Arkansas St. ... 84 Montana St. 14-31
Arkansas St. ... 85 Grambling 10-7
Arkansas St. ... 85 Nevada 23-24
Arkansas St. ... 86 Sam Houston St. 48-7
Arkansas St. ... 86 Delaware 55-14
Arkansas St. ... 86 Eastern Ky. 24-10
Arkansas St. ... 86 Ga. Southern 21-48
Arkansas St. ... 87 Jackson St. 35-32
Arkansas St. ... 87 Northern Iowa 28-49

Jimmye Laycock (1-4) (William & Mary '70)
William & Mary ... 86 Delaware 17-51
William & Mary ... 89 Furman 10-24
William & Mary ... 90 Massachusetts 38-0
William & Mary ... 90 Central Fla. 38-52
William & Mary ... 93 McNeese St. 28-34

Tom Lichtenberg (0-1) (Louisville '62)
Maine ... 89 Southwest Mo. St. 35-38

Gene McDowell (2-2) (Florida St. '63)
Central Fla. ... 90 Youngstown St. 20-17
Central Fla. ... 90 William & Mary 52-38
Central Fla. ... 90 Ga. Southern 7-44
Central Fla. ... 93 Youngstown St. 30-56

John Merritt (†1-2) (Kentucky St. '50)
Tennessee St. ... 81† South Caro. St. 25-26 (OT)
Tennessee St. ... 82† Eastern Ill. 20-19
Tennessee St. ... 82† Eastern Ky. 7-13

Al Molde (1-2) (Gust. Adolphus '66)
Eastern Ill. ... 83 Indiana St. 13-16 (2 OT)
Eastern Ill. ... 86 Murray St. 28-21
Eastern Ill. ... 86 Eastern Ky. 22-24

Jerry Moore (0-3) (Baylor '61)
Appalachian St. ... 89 Middle Tenn. St. 21-24
Appalachian St. ... 91 Eastern Ky. 3-14
Appalachian St. ... 92 Middle Tenn. St. 10-35

Darrell Mudra (4-3) (Peru St. '51)
Eastern Ill. ... 82 Jackson St. 16-13 (OT)
Eastern Ill. ... 82 Tennessee St. 19-20
Northern Iowa ... 85 Eastern Wash. 17-14
Northern Iowa ... 85 Ga. Southern 33-40
Northern Iowa ... 87 Youngstown St. 31-28
Northern Iowa ... 87 Arkansas St. 49-28
Northern Iowa ... 87 Northeast La. 41-44 (OT)

Tim Murphy (0-1) (Springfield '78)
Maine ... 87 Ga. Southern 28-31 (OT)

Corky Nelson (0-3) (Southwest Tex. St. '64)
North Texas ... 83 Nevada 17-20 (OT)
North Texas ... 87 Northeast La. 9-30
North Texas ... 88 Marshall 0-7

Buddy Nix (0-1) (Livingston '61)
Tenn.-Chatt. ... 84 Arkansas St. 10-37

John Pearce (0-1) (East Tex. St. '70)
Stephen F. Austin ... 93 Troy St. 20-42

Bob Pickett (1-1) (Maine '59)
Massachusetts ... 78 Nevada 44-21
Massachusetts ... 78 Florida A&M 28-35

Mike Price (1-1) (Puget Sound '69)
Weber St. ... 87 Idaho 59-30
Weber St. ... 87 Marshall 23-51

Joe Purzycki (0-1) (Delaware '71)
James Madison ... 87 Marshall 12-41

Dennis Raetz (1-2) (Nebraska '68)
Indiana St. ... 83 Eastern Ill. 16-13 (2 OT)
Indiana St. ... 83 Southern Ill. 7-23
Indiana St. ... 84 Middle Tenn. St. 41-42 (3 OT)

Ron Randleman (0-2) (William Penn '64)
Sam Houston St. ... 86 Arkansas St. 7-48
Sam Houston St. ... 91 Middle Tenn. St. 19-20 (OT)

Harold "Tubby" Raymond (6-7) (Michigan '50)
Delaware ... 81 Eastern Ky. 28-35
Delaware ... 82 Colgate 20-13
Delaware ... 82 Louisiana Tech 17-0
Delaware ... 82 Eastern Ky. 14-17
Delaware ... 86 William & Mary 51-17
Delaware ... 86 Arkansas St. 14-55
Delaware ... 88 Furman 7-21
Delaware ... 91 James Madison 35-42 (2 OT)
Delaware ... 92 Samford 56-21
Delaware ... 92 Northeast La. 41-18
Delaware ... 92 Marshall 7-28
Delaware ... 93 Montana 49-48
Delaware ... 93 Marshall 31-34

Don Read (2-3) (Cal St. Sacramento '59)
Montana ... 88 Idaho 19-38
Montana ... 89 Jackson St. 48-7
Montana ... 89 Eastern Ill. 25-19
Montana ... 89 Ga. Southern 15-45
Montana ... 93 Delaware 48-49

Jim Reid (0-2) (Maine '73)
Massachusetts ... 88 Eastern Ky. 17-28
Massachusetts ... 90 William & Mary 0-38

Dave Roberts (2-5) (Western Caro. '68)
Western Ky. ... 87 Eastern Ky. 17-40
Western Ky. ... 88 Western Ill. 35-32
Western Ky. ... 88 Eastern Ky. 24-41
Northeast La. ... 90 Nevada 14-27
Northeast La. ... 92 Alcorn St. 78-27
Northeast La. ... 92 Delaware 18-41
Northeast La. ... 93 Idaho 31-34

Eddie Robinson (0-3) (Leland '41)
Grambling ... 80 Boise St. 9-14
Grambling ... 85 Arkansas St. 7-10
Grambling ... 89 Stephen F. Austin 56-59

Erk Russell (16-2) (Auburn '49)
Ga. Southern ... 85 Jackson St. 27-0
Ga. Southern ... 85 Middle Tenn. St. 28-21
Ga. Southern ... 85 Northern Iowa 40-33
Ga. Southern ... 85* Furman 44-42
Ga. Southern ... 86 North Caro. A&T 52-21
Ga. Southern ... 86 Nicholls St. 55-31
Ga. Southern ... 86 Nevada 48-38
Ga. Southern ... 86* Arkansas St. 48-21
Ga. Southern ... 87 Maine 31-28 (OT)
Ga. Southern ... 87 Appalachian St. 0-19
Ga. Southern ... 88 Citadel 38-20
Ga. Southern ... 88 Stephen F. Austin 27-6
Ga. Southern ... 88 Eastern Ky. 21-17
Ga. Southern ... 88 Furman 12-17
Ga. Southern ... 89 Villanova 52-36
Ga. Southern ... 89 Middle Tenn. St. 45-3
Ga. Southern ... 89 Montana 45-15
Ga. Southern ... 89* Stephen F. Austin 37-34

Jimmy Satterfield (7-3) (South Caro. '62)
Furman ... 86 Eastern Ky. 10-23
Furman ... 88 Delaware 21-7
Furman ... 88 Marshall 13-9
Furman ... 88 Idaho 38-7
Furman ... 88* Ga. Southern 17-12
Furman ... 89 William & Mary 24-10
Furman ... 89 Youngstown St. 42-23
Furman ... 89 Stephen F. Austin 19-21
Furman ... 90 Eastern Ky. 45-17
Furman ... 90 Nevada 35-42 (3 OT)

Rip Scherer (1-1) (William & Mary '74)
James Madison ... 91 Delaware 42-35 (2 OT)
James Madison ... 91 Samford 21-24

Dal Shealy (1-2) (Carson-Newman '60)
Richmond ... 84 Boston U. 35-33
Richmond ... 84 Rhode Island 17-23
Richmond ... 87 Appalachian St. 3-20

Dick Sheridan (3-3) (South Caro. '64)
Furman ... 82 South Caro. St. 0-17
Furman ... 83 Boston U. 35-16
Furman ... 83 Western Caro. 7-14

Furman ... 85 Rhode Island 59-15
Furman ... 85 Nevada 35-12
Furman ... 85 Ga. Southern 42-44

John L. Smith (3-4) (Weber St. '71)
Idaho ... 89 Eastern Ill. 21-38
Idaho ... 90 Southwest Mo. St. 41-35
Idaho ... 90 Ga. Southern 27-28
Idaho ... 92 McNeese St. 20-23
Idaho ... 93 Northeast La. 34-31
Idaho ... 93 Boston U. 21-14
Idaho ... 93 Youngstown St. 16-35

Bob Spoo (1-1) (Purdue '60)
Eastern Ill. ... 89 Idaho 38-21
Eastern Ill. ... 89 Montana 19-25

Tim Stowers (5-1) (Auburn '79)
Ga. Southern ... 90 Citadel 31-0
Ga. Southern ... 90 Idaho 28-27
Ga. Southern ... 90 Central Fla. 44-7
Ga. Southern ... 90* Nevada 36-13
Ga. Southern ... 93 Eastern Ky. 14-12
Ga. Southern ... 93 Youngstown St. 14-34

Charlie Taaffe (1-3) (Siena '73)
Citadel ... 88 Ga. Southern 20-38
Citadel ... 90 Ga. Southern 0-31
Citadel ... 92 North Caro. A&T 44-0
Citadel ... 92 Youngstown St. 17-42

Andy Talley (0-3) (Southern Conn. St. '67)
Villanova ... 89 Ga. Southern 36-52
Villanova ... 91 Youngstown St. 16-17
Villanova ... 92 Youngstown St. 20-23

Rick Taylor (1-3) (Gettysburg '64)
Boston U. ... 82 Colgate 7-21
Boston U. ... 83 Eastern Ky. 24-20
Boston U. ... 83 Furman 16-35
Boston U. ... 84 Richmond 33-35

Bill Thomas (1-1) (Tennessee St. '71)
Tennessee St. ... 86 Jackson St. 32-23
Tennessee St. ... 86 Nevada 6-33

Jim Tressel (12-4) (Baldwin-Wallace '75)
Youngstown St. ... 87 Northern Iowa 28-31
Youngstown St. ... 89 Eastern Ky. 28-24
Youngstown St. ... 89 Furman 23-42
Youngstown St. ... 90 Central Fla. 17-20
Youngstown St. ... 91 Villanova 17-16
Youngstown St. ... 91 Nevada 30-28
Youngstown St. ... 91 Samford 10-0
Youngstown St. ... 91* Marshall 25-17
Youngstown St. ... 92 Villanova 23-20
Youngstown St. ... 92 Citadel 42-17
Youngstown St. ... 92 Northern Iowa 19-7
Youngstown St. ... 92 Marshall 28-31
Youngstown St. ... 93 Central Fla. 56-30
Youngstown St. ... 93 Ga. Southern 34-14
Youngstown St. ... 93 Idaho 35-16
Youngstown St. ... 93* Marshall 17-5

Bob Waters (3-1) (Presbyterian '60)
Western Caro. ... 83 Colgate 24-23
Western Caro. ... 83 Holy Cross 28-21
Western Caro. ... 83 Furman 14-7
Western Caro. ... 83 Southern Ill. 7-43

John Whitehead (1-2) (East Stroudsburg '50)
Lehigh ... 79 Murray St. 28-9
Lehigh ... 79 Eastern Ky. 7-30
Lehigh ... 80 Eastern Ky. 20-23

A. L. Williams (3-1) (Louisiana Tech '57)
Louisiana Tech ... 84 Mississippi Val. 66-19
Louisiana Tech ... 84 Alcorn St. 44-21
Louisiana Tech ... 84 Middle Tenn. St. 21-13
Louisiana Tech ... 84 Montana St. 6-19

Steve Wilson (0-1) (Howard '79)
Howard ... 93 Marshall 14-28

Sparky Woods (2-2) (Carson-Newman '76)
Appalachian St. ... 86 Nicholls St. 26-28
Appalachian St. ... 87 Richmond 20-3
Appalachian St. ... 87 Ga. Southern 19-0
Appalachian St. ... 87 Marshall 10-24

Dick Zornes (1-2) (Eastern Wash. '68)
Eastern Wash. ... 85 Idaho 42-38
Eastern Wash. ... 91 Northern Iowa 14-17
Eastern Wash. ... 92 Northern Iowa 14-17

*National championship. †Tennessee State's participation voided. %Stephen F. Austin's participation voided.

Division II Coaching Records

Winningest Active Division II Coaches

(Minimum Five Years as a College Head Coach; Record at Four-Year Colleges Only)

BY PERCENTAGE

Coach, College	Years	Won	Lost	Tied	*Pct.	Playoffs# W	L	T
Rocky Hager, North Dak. St.	7	66	15	1	.811	10	3	0
Ken Sparks, Carson-Newman	14	132	34	2	.792	0	1	0
Bob Cortese, Fort Hays St.	14	114	38	3	.745	0	1	0
Peter Yetten, Bentley	6	38	13	1	.740	0	0	0
Joe Taylor, Hampton	11	82	32	4	.712	1	5	0
Dick Lowry, Hillsdale	20	152	62	3	.707	0	0	0
Ron Taylor, Quincy	5	35	14	2	.706	0	0	0
Bill Burgess, Jacksonville St.	9	72	29	4	.705	12	4	0
Danny Hale, Bloomsburg	6	45	19	0	.703	0	1	0
Frank Cignetti, Indiana (Pa.)	12	99	42	1	.701	10	6	0
Gene Carpenter, Millersville	25	167	71	5	.698	1	1	0
Tom Hollman, Edinboro	10	69	30	3	.691	1	4	0
Jim Malosky, Minn.-Duluth	36	231	107	12	.677	0	0	0
Tim Walsh, Portland St.	5	35	17	0	.673	0	1	0
Hal Mumme, Valdosta St.	5	37	18	1	.670	0	0	0
Tony DeMeo, Washburn	11	63	31	4	.663	0	0	0
Jerry Vandergriff, Angelo St.	12	84	45	1	.650	2	2	0
Rick Daniels, West Chester	5	35	19	0	.648	0	2	0
Dennis Miller, Northern St.	8	57	31	0	.648	0	0	0
Bob Mullett, Concord (W.Va.)	5	32	17	2	.647	0	0	0
Carl Iverson, Western St.	11	70	38	4	.645	0	1	0
Jon Lantz, Mo. Southern St.	8	52	28	3	.645	0	1	0
Kevin Donley, Calif. (Pa.)	16	107	59	1	.644	0	0	0
Malen Luke, Clarion	6	37	21	0	.638	0	0	0
Ron Harms, Tex. A&M-Kingsville	25	163	94	4	.632	5	4	0
Rocky Rees, Shippensburg	9	60	36	2	.622	1	1	0
Dennis Douds, East Stroudsburg	20	124	76	3	.618	2	1	1
Claire Boroff, Neb.-Kearney	22	132	81	4	.618	0	0	0
Stan McGarvey, Mo. Western St.	9	57	37	3	.603	0	0	0
Joe Glenn, Northern Colo.	9	56	37	1	.601	0	2	0
Douglas Porter, Fort Valley St.	24	141	93	5	.600	0	1	0
Mel Tjeerdsma, Northwest Mo. St.	10	59	39	4	.598	0	0	0
Bobby Wallace, North Ala.	6	40	27	1	.596	5	2	0
Hampton Smith, Albany St. (Ga.)	18	104	75	4	.579	0	1	0
Dick Mannini, San Fran. St.	9	51	37	1	.579	0	0	0

Coach, College	Years	Won	Lost	Tied	*Pct.	Playoffs# W	L	T
Brad Smith, Chadron St.	7	40	31	1	.579	0	0	0
Jeff Geiser, Adams St.	10	57	43	1	.569	0	0	0
George Mihalik, Slippery Rock	6	33	25	4	.565	0	0	0
Gary Howard, Central Okla.	17	95	73	5	.564	0	0	0
Monte Cater, Shepherd	13	71	55	2	.563	0	0	0
Keith Otterbein, Ferris St.	8	49	38	3	.561	1	2	0
Denny Creehan, South Dak.	9	51	41	1	.554	0	0	0
Tom Marshall, LIU-C.W. Post	11	58	47	2	.551	0	0	0
George Ihler, Saginaw Valley	11	62	51	1	.548	0	0	0
Dennis Wagner, Wayne St. (Neb.)	5	28	23	1	.548	0	0	0
Terry Noland, Central Mo. St.	11	63	52	2	.547	0	0	0
Noel Martin, St. Cloud St.	11	65	54	0	.546	1	1	0
Mike Ayers, Wofford	9	53	45	2	.540	0	2	0
Henry Lattimore, Virginia Union	15	83	72	5	.534	1	1	0
Charlie Cowdrey, Morningside	14	78	68	2	.534	0	0	0
Woody Fish, Gardner-Webb	10	59	52	1	.531	0	0	0
Leon Hart, Elon	5	28	25	0	.528	0	0	0
Larry Kramer, Emporia St.	23	119	108	6	.524	0	0	0
Bernie Anderson, Michigan Tech.	7	35	32	0	.522	0	0	0
Eddie Vowell, East Tex. St.	8	47	43	1	.522	2	2	0
Bud Elliott, Eastern N. Mex.	26	137	130	7	.513	0	0	0
Charles Forbes, Lenoir-Rhyne	18	86	86	3	.500	0	0	0
Dan Runkle, Mankato St.	13	72	72	2	.500	2	3	0
Joe Kimball, Mercyhurst	9	42	42	1	.500	0	0	0
Mike DeLong, Springfield	12	55	58	2	.487	0	0	0
Roger Thomas, North Dak.	10	48	53	2	.476	1	2	0
George Moody, Elizabeth City St.	11	51	58	3	.469	0	0	0
Tom Herman, Gannon	5	21	24	1	.467	0	0	0
Larry Little, N.C. Central	10	48	55	1	.466	0	0	0
Rich Rodriquez, Glenville St.	5	23	27	0	.462	0	0	0
Greg Thompson, Morris Brown	13	53	67	4	.444	0	0	0
John Perry, Presbyterian	10	48	62	0	.436	0	0	0
Bill Struble, West Va. Wesleyan	11	47	62	0	.431	0	0	0
Maurice Hunt, Kentucky St.	15	63	86	3	.424	0	0	0
Richard Cavanaugh, Southern Conn. St.	9	35	53	1	.399	0	0	0
Gary Houser, Cal St. Chico	5	19	29	1	.398	0	0	0
Tom Elsasser, Mansfield St.	11	42	66	6	.395	0	0	0
Tom Hosier, Winona St.	20	75	118	3	.390	0	0	0
Bernie Gaughan, Assumption	6	19	33	1	.368	0	0	0
Bill Reagan, St. Joseph's (Ind.)	9	30	57	3	.350	0	0	0
Marvin Kay, Colorado Mines	25	80	152	5	.348	0	0	0
Ralph Micheli, Colorado St.	11	35	67	0	.343	0	0	0
Bob Gobel, West Va. Tech	5	17	33	1	.343	0	0	0
Kris Diaz, Bemidji St.	5	9	40	0	.184	0	0	0

*Ties computed as half won and half lost; bowl and postseason games included.
#NCAA Division II playoff games.

BY VICTORIES
(Minimum 80 Victories)

Coach, College, Winning Percentage	Won
Jim Malosky, Minn.-Duluth .677	231
Gene Carpenter, Millersville .698	167
Ron Harms, Tex. A&M-Kingsville .632	163
Dick Lowry, Hillsdale .707	152
Douglas Porter, Fort Valley St. .600	141
Bud Elliott, Eastern N. Mex. .513	137
Claire Boroff, Neb.-Kearney .618	132
Ken Sparks, Carson-Newman .792	132
Dennis Douds, East Stroudsburg .618	124
Larry Kramer, Emporia St. .524	119
Bob Cortese, Fort Hays St. .745	114
Kevin Donley, Calif. (Pa.) .644	107
Hampton Smith, Albany St. (Ga.) .579	104
Frank Cignetti, Indiana (Pa.) .701	99
Gary Howard, Central Okla. .564	95
Charles Forbes, Lenoir-Rhyne .500	86
Jerry Vandergriff, Angelo St. .650	84
Henry Lattimore, Virginia Union .534	83
Joe Taylor, Hampton .712	82
Marvin Kay, Colorado Mines .348	80

Division II Championship Coaches

All coaches who have coached teams in the Division II championship playoffs since 1973 are listed here with their playoff record, alma mater and year graduated, team, year coached, opponent, and score.

Phil Albert (1-3) (Arizona '66)
Towson St.	83	North Dak. St.	17-24
Towson St.	84	Norfolk St.	31-21
Towson St.	84	Troy 3-45	
Towson St.	86	Central St. (Ohio)	0-31

Pokey Allen (10-5) (Utah '65)
Portland St.	87	Mankato St.	27-21
Portland St.	87	Northern Mich.	13-7
Portland St.	87	Troy St.	17-31
Portland St.	88	Bowie St.	34-17
Portland St.	88	Jacksonville St.	20-13
Portland St.	88	Tex. A&M-Kingsville	35-27
Portland St.	88	North Dak. St.	21-35
Portland St.	89	West Chester	56-50 (3 OT)
Portland St.	89	Indiana (Pa.)	0-17
Portland St.	91	Northern Colo.	28-24
Portland St.	91	Mankato St.	37-27
Portland St.	91	Pittsburg St.	21-53
Portland St.	92	UC Davis	42-28
Portland St.	92	Tex. A&M-Kingsville	35-30
Portland St.	92	Pittsburg St.	38-41

Mike Ayers (0-2) (Georgetown, Ky. '74)
Wofford	90	Mississippi Col.	19-70
Wofford	91	Mississippi Col.	15-28

Willard Bailey (0-6) (Norfolk St. '62)
Virginia Union	79	Delaware	28-58
Virginia Union	80	North Ala.	8-17
Virginia Union	81	Shippensburg	27-40
Virginia Union	82	North Dak. St.	20-21
Virginia Union	83	North Ala.	14-16
Norfolk St.	84	Towson St.	21-31

Bob Bartolomeo (0-1) (Butler '77)
Butler	91	Pittsburg St.	16-26

Tom Beck (0-2) (Northern Ill. '61)
Grand Valley St.	89	Indiana (Pa.)	24-34
Grand Valley St.	90	East Tex. St.	14-20

Bob Biggs (1-1) (UC Davis '73)
UC Davis	93	Fort Hays St.	37-34
UC Davis	93	Tex. A&M-Kingsville	28-51

Bob Blasi (0-1) (Colorado St. '53)
Northern Colo.	80	Eastern Ill.	14-21

Bill Bowes (1-2) (Penn St. '65)
New Hampshire	75	Lehigh	35-21
New Hampshire	75	Western Ky.	3-14
New Hampshire	76	Montana St.	16-17

Chuck Broyles (9-3) (Pittsburg St. '70)
Pittsburg St.	90	Northeast Mo.	59-3
Pittsburg St.	90	East Tex. St.	60-28
Pittsburg St.	90	North Dak. St.	29-39
Pittsburg St.	91	Butler	26-16
Pittsburg St.	91	East Tex. St.	38-28
Pittsburg St.	91	Portland St.	53-21
Pittsburg St.	91*	Jacksonville St.	23-6
Pittsburg St.	92	North Dak.	26-21
Pittsburg St.	92	North Dak. St.	38-37 (OT)
Pittsburg St.	92	Portland St.	41-38
Pittsburg St.	92	Jacksonville St.	13-17
Pittsburg St.	93	North Dak.	14-17

Sandy Buda (1-2) (Kansas '67)
Nebraska-Omaha	78	Youngstown St.	14-21
Nebraska-Omaha	84	Northwest Mo. St.	28-15
Nebraska-Omaha	84	North Dak. St.	14-25

Bill Burgess (12-4) (Auburn '63)
Jacksonville St......... 88   West Chester 63-24
Jacksonville St......... 88   Portland St. 13-20
Jacksonville St......... 89   Alabama A&M 33-9
Jacksonville St......... 89   North Dak. St. 21-17
Jacksonville St......... 89   Angelo St. 34-16

Jacksonville St......... 89   Mississippi Col. 0-3
Jacksonville St......... 90   North Ala. 38-14
Jacksonville St......... 90   Mississippi Col. 7-14
Jacksonville St......... 91   Winston-Salem 49-24
Jacksonville St......... 91   Mississippi Col. 35-7

Jacksonville St......... 91   Indiana (Pa.) 27-20
Jacksonville St......... 91   Pittsburg St. 6-23
Jacksonville St......... 92   Savannah St. 41-16
Jacksonville St......... 92   North Ala. 14-12
Jacksonville St......... 92   New Haven 46-35

Jacksonville St......... 92* Pittsburg St. 17-13

Bob Burt (0-1) (Cal St. Los Angeles '62)
Cal St. Northridge .. 90   Cal Poly SLO 7-14

Gene Carpenter (1-1) (Huron '63)
Millersville 88   Indiana (Pa.) 27-24
Millersville 88   North Dak. St. 26-36

Marino Casem (0-1) (Xavier, La. '56)
Alcorn St. 74   Nevada-Las Vegas 22-35

Frank Cignetti (10-6) (Indiana, Pa. '60)
Indiana (Pa.)........... 87   Central Fla. 10-12
Indiana (Pa.)........... 88   Millersville 24-27
Indiana (Pa.)........... 89   Grand Valley St. 34-24
Indiana (Pa.)........... 89   Portland St. 17-0
Indiana (Pa.)........... 89   Mississippi Col. 14-26

Indiana (Pa.)........... 90   Winston-Salem 48-0
Indiana (Pa.)........... 90   Edinboro 14-7
Indiana (Pa.)........... 90   Mississippi Col. 27-8
Indiana (Pa.)........... 90   North Dak. St. 11-51
Indiana (Pa.)........... 91   Virginia Union 56-7

Indiana (Pa.)........... 91   Shippensburg 52-7
Indiana (Pa.)........... 91   Jacksonville St. 20-27
Indiana (Pa.)........... 93   Ferris St. 28-21
Indiana (Pa.)........... 93   New Haven 38-35
Indiana (Pa.)........... 93   North Dak. 21-6

Indiana (Pa.)........... 93   North Ala. 34-41

Bob Cortese (0-1) (Colorado '67)
Fort Hays St............ 93   UC Davis 34-37

Bruce Craddock (0-1) (Northeast Mo. St. '66)
Northeast Mo. St. ... 82   Jacksonville St. 21-34

Rick Daniels (0-2) (West Chester '75)
West Chester.......... 89   Portland St. 50-56 (3 OT)
West Chester.......... 92   New Haven 26-38

Bill Davis (0-1) (Johnson Smith '65)
Savannah St. 92   Jacksonville St. 16-41

Rey Dempsey (0-1) (Geneva '58)
Youngstown St. 74   Delaware 14-35

Jim Dennison (2-1) (Wooster '60)
Akron 76   Nevada-Las Vegas 26-6
Akron 76   Northern Mich. 29-26
Akron 76   Montana 13-24

Dennis Douds (0-1) (Slippery Rock '63)
East Stroudsburg 91   Shippensburg 33-34

Fred Dunlap (0-2) (Colgate '50)
Lehigh 73   Western Ky. 16-25
Lehigh 75   New Hampshire 21-35

Bud Elliott (0-1) (Baker '53)
Northwest Mo. St.... 89   Pittsburg St. 7-28

Jimmy Feix (4-2) (Western Ky. '53)
Western Ky. 73   Lehigh 25-16
Western Ky. 73   Grambling 28-20
Western Ky. 73   Louisiana Tech 0-34
Western Ky. 75   Northern Iowa 14-12
Western Ky. 75   New Hampshire 14-3

Western Ky. 75   Northern Mich. 14-16

Bob Foster (0-2) (UC Davis '62)
UC Davis 89   Angelo St. 23-28
UC Davis 92   Portland St. 28-42

Dennis Franchione (1-1) (Pittsburg St. '73)
Pittsburg St. 89   Northwest Mo. St. 28-7
Pittsburg St. 89   Angelo St. 21-24

Fred Freeman (0-1) (Mississippi Val. '66)
Hampton 85   Bloomsburg 28-38

Jim Fuller (3-5) (Alabama '67)
Jacksonville St......... 77   Northern Ariz. 35-0
Jacksonville St......... 77   North Dak. St. 31-7
Jacksonville St......... 77   Lehigh 0-33

Jacksonville St......... 78   Delaware 27-42
Jacksonville St......... 80   Cal Poly SLO 0-15

Jacksonville St......... 81   Southwest Tex. St. 22-38
Jacksonville St......... 82   Northeast Mo. St. 34-21
Jacksonville St......... 82   Southwest Tex. St. 14-19

Chan Gailey (3-0) (Florida '74)
Troy St. 84   Central St. (Ohio) 31-21
Troy St. 84   Towson St. 45-3
Troy St. .... 84* North Dak. St. 18-17

Joe Glenn (0-2) (South Dak. '71)
Northern Colo. 90   North Dak. St. 7-17
Northern Colo. 91   Portland St. 24-28

Ray Greene (1-1) (Akron '63)
Alabama A&M....... 79   Morgan St. 27-7
Alabama A&M....... 79   Youngstown St. 0-52

John Gregory (0-1) (Northern Iowa '61)
South Dak. 79   Youngstown St. 7-50

Herb Grenke (1-1) (Wis.-Milwaukee '63)
Northern Mich. 87   Angelo St. 23-20 (OT)
Northern Mich. 87   Portland St. 7-13

Wayne Grubb (4-3) (Tennessee '61)
North Ala............... 80   Virginia Union 17-8
North Ala............... 80   Eastern Ill. 31-56
North Ala............... 83   Virginia Union 16-14
North Ala............... 83   Central St. (Ohio) 24-27
North Ala............... 85   Fort Valley St. 14-7

North Ala............... 85   Bloomsburg 34-0
North Ala............... 85   North Dak. St. 7-35

Rocky Hager (10-3) (Minot St. '74)
North Dak. St. 88   Augustana (S.D.) 49-7
North Dak. St. 88   Millersville 36-26
North Dak. St. 88   Cal St. Sacramento 42-20
North Dak. St. .... 88* Portland St. 35-21
North Dak. St. 89   Edinboro 45-32

North Dak. St. 89   Jacksonville St. 17-21
North Dak. St. 90   Northern Colo. 17-7
North Dak. St. 90   Cal Poly SLO 47-0
North Dak. St. 90   Pittsburg St. 39-29
North Dak. St. .... 90* Indiana (Pa.) 51-11

North Dak. St. 91   Mankato St. 7-27
North Dak. St. 92   Northeast Mo. St. 42-7
North Dak. St. 92   Pittsburg St. 37-38 (OT)

Danny Hale (0-1) (West Chester '68)
West Chester.......... 88   Jacksonville St. 24-63

Ron Harms (5-4) (Valparaiso '59)
Tex. A&M-Kingsville.. 88   Mississippi Col. 39-15
Tex. A&M-Kingsville.. 88   Tenn.-Martin 34-0
Tex. A&M-Kingsville.. 88   Portland St. 27-35
Tex. A&M-Kingsville.. 89   Mississippi Col. 19-34
Tex. A&M-Kingsville.. 92   Western St. 22-13

Tex. A&M-Kingsville.. 92   Portland St. 30-35
Tex. A&M-Kingsville.. 93   Portland St. 50-15
Tex. A&M-Kingsville.. 93   UC Davis 51-28
Tex. A&M-Kingsville.. 93   North Ala. 25-27

Joe Harper (3-1) (UCLA '59)
Cal Poly SLO 78   Winston-Salem 0-17
Cal Poly SLO 80   Jacksonville St. 15-0
Cal Poly SLO 80   Santa Clara 38-14
Cal Poly SLO .... 80* Eastern Ill. 21-13

Bill Hayes (1-2) (N.C. Central '64)
Winston-Salem........ 78   Cal Poly SLO 17-0
Winston-Salem........ 78   Delaware 0-41
Winston-Salem........ 87   Troy St. 14-45

Jim Heinitz (0-2) (South Dak. '72)
Augustana (S.D.)..... 88   North Dak. St. 7-49
Augustana (S.D.)..... 89   St. Cloud St. 20-27

Andy Hinson (0-1) (Bethune-Cookman '53)
Bethune-Cookman ... 77   UC Davis 16-34

Sonny Holland (3-0) (Montana St. '60)
Montana St. 76   New Hampshire 17-16
Montana St. 76   North Dak. St. 10-3
Montana St. .... 76* Akron 24-13

Tom Hollman (1-4) (Ohio Northern '68)
Edinboro 89   North Dak. St. 32-45
Edinboro 90   Virginia Union 38-14
Edinboro 90   Indiana (Pa.) 7-14
Edinboro 92   Ferris St. 15-19
Edinboro 93   New Haven 28-48

Eric Holm (0-2) (Northeast Mo. St. '81)
Northeast Mo. St. 90   Pittsburg St. 3-59
Northeast Mo. St. 92   North Dak. St. 7-42

Carl Iverson (0-1) (Whitman '62)
Western St. 92   Tex. A&M-Kingsville 13-22

Billy Joe (3-4) (Cheyney '70)
Central St. (Ohio).... 83   Southwest Tex. St. 24-16
Central St. (Ohio).... 83   North Ala. 27-24
Central St. (Ohio).... 83   North Dak. St. 21-41
Central St. (Ohio).... 84   Troy St. 21-31
Central St. (Ohio).... 85   South Dak. 10-13 (2 OT)

Central St. (Ohio).... 86   Towson St. 31-0
Central St. (Ohio).... 86   North Dak. St. 12-35

Brian Kelly (0-1) (Assumption '83)
Grand Valley St. 91   East Tex. St. 15-36

Roy Kidd (0-1) (Eastern Ky. '54)
Eastern Ky. 76   North Dak. St. 7-10

Jim King (1-1)
Livingston 75   North Dak. 34-14
Livingston 75   Northern Mich. 26-28

Tony Knap (1-4) (Idaho '39)
Boise St. 73   South Dak. 53-10
Boise St. 73   Louisiana Tech 34-38
Boise St. 74   Central Mich. 6-20
Boise St. 75   Northern Mich. 21-24
Nevada-Las Vegas .. 76   Akron 6-26

Roy Kramer (3-0) (Maryville, Tenn. '53)
Central Mich. 74   Boise St. 20-6
Central Mich. 74   Louisiana Tech 35-14
Central Mich. .... 74* Delaware 54-14

Gil Krueger (4-2) (Marquette '52)
Northern Mich. 75   Boise St. 24-21
Northern Mich. 75   Livingston 28-26
Northern Mich. .... 75* Western Ky. 16-14
Northern Mich. 76   Delaware 28-17
Northern Mich. 76   Akron 26-29

Northern Mich. 77   North Dak. St. 6-20

Maxie Lambright (4-1) (Southern Miss. '49)
Louisiana Tech 73   Western Ill. 18-13
Louisiana Tech 73   Boise St. 38-34
Louisiana Tech .... 73* Western Ky. 34-0
Louisiana Tech 74   Western Caro. 10-7
Louisiana Tech 74   Central Mich. 14-35

George Landis (1-1) (Penn St. '71)
Bloomsburg 85   Hampton 38-28
Bloomsburg 85   North Ala. 0-34

Jon Lantz (0-1) (Panhandle St. '74)
Mo. Southern St. 93   Mankato St. 13-34

Henry Lattimore (1-1) (Jackson St. '57)
N.C. Central 88   Winston-Salem 31-16
N.C. Central 88   Cal St. Sacramento 7-56

Bill Lynch (0-1) (Butler '77)
Butler 88   Tenn.-Martin 6-23

Dick MacPherson (0-1) (Springfield '58)
Massachusetts......... 77   Lehigh 23-30

Pat Malley (1-1) (Santa Clara '53)
Santa Clara............ 80   Northern Mich. 27-26
Santa Clara............ 80   Cal Poly SLO 14-38

Noel Martin (1-1) (Nebraska '63)
St. Cloud St. 89   Augustana (S.D.) 27-20
St. Cloud St. 89   Mississippi Col. 24-55

Fred Martinelli (0-1) (Otterbein '51)
Ashland 86   North Dak. St. 0-50

Bob Mattos (2-1) (Cal St. Sacramento '64)
Cal St. Sacramento .. 88   UC Davis 35-14
Cal St. Sacramento .. 88   N.C. Central 56-7
Cal St. Sacramento .. 88   North Dak. St. 20-42

Gene McDowell (1-1) (Florida St. '65)
Central Fla. 87   Indiana (Pa.) 12-10
Central Fla. 87   Troy St. 10-31

Don McLeary (1-1) (Tennessee '70)
Tenn.-Martin 88   Butler 23-6
Tenn.-Martin 88   Tex. A&M-Kingsville 0-34

Terry McMillan (1-1) (Southern Miss. '69)
Mississippi Col. 91   Wofford 28-15
Mississippi Col. 91   Jacksonville St. 7-35

Ron Meyer (1-1) (Purdue '63)
Nevada-Las Vegas .. 74   Alcorn St. 35-22
Nevada-Las Vegas .. 74   Delaware 11-49

Don Morton (8-3) (Augustana, Ill. '69)
North Dak. St. 81   Puget Sound 24-10
North Dak. St. 81   Shippensburg 18-6
North Dak. St. 81   Southwest Tex. St. 13-42
North Dak. St. 82   Virginia Union 21-20
North Dak. St. 82   UC Davis 14-19

North Dak. St. 83   Towson St. 24-17
North Dak. St. 83   UC Davis 26-17

North Dak. St. .... 83* Central St. (Ohio) 41-21
North Dak. St. .... 84 UC Davis 31-23
North Dak. St. .... 84 Nebraska-Omaha 25-14
North Dak. St. .... 84 Troy St. 17-18

Darrell Mudra (5-2) (Peru St. '51)
Western Ill. .... 73 Louisiana Tech 13-18
Eastern Ill. .... 78 UC Davis 35-31
Eastern Ill. .... 78 Youngstown St. 26-22
Eastern Ill. .... 78* Delaware 10-9
Eastern Ill. .... 80 Northern Colo. 21-14
Eastern Ill. .... 80 North Ala. 56-31
Eastern Ill. .... 80 Cal Poly SLO 13-21

Gene Murphy (0-1) (North Dak. '62)
North Dak. .... 79 Mississippi Col. 15-35

Bill Narduzzi (3-2) (Miami, Ohio '59)
Youngstown St. .... 78 Nebraska-Omaha 21-14
Youngstown St. .... 78 Eastern Ill. 22-26
Youngstown St. .... 79 South Dak. St. 50-7
Youngstown St. .... 79 Alabama A&M 52-0
Youngstown St. .... 79 Delaware 21-38

John O'Hara (0-1) (Panhandle St. '67)
Southwest Tex. St. ... 83 Central St. (Ohio) 16-24

Jerry Olson (0-1) (Valley City St. '55)
North Dak. .... 75 Livingston 14-34

Keith Otterbein (1-2) (Ferris St. '79)
Ferris St. .... 92 Edinboro 19-15
Ferris St. .... 92 New Haven 13-35
Ferris St. .... 93 Indiana (Pa.) 21-28

Doug Porter (0-1) (Xavier, La. '52)
Fort Valley St. .... 82 Southwest Tex. St. 6-27

George Pugh (0-1) (Alabama '76)
Alabama A&M .... 89 Jacksonville St. 9-33

Bill Rademacher (1-3) (Northern Mich. '63)
Northern Mich. .... 80 Santa Clara 6-27
Northern Mich. .... 81 Elizabeth City St. 55-6
Northern Mich. .... 81 Southwest Tex. St. 0-62
Northern Mich. .... 82 UC Davis 21-42

Vito Ragazzo (1-1) (William & Mary '51)
Shippensburg .... 81 Virginia Union 40-27
Shippensburg .... 81 North Dak. St. 6-18

Harold "Tubby" Raymond (7-4) (Michigan '50)
Delaware .... 73 Grambling 8-17

"Tubby" Raymond led Delaware to the 1979 Division II championship with a 38-21 victory over Youngstown State.

Delaware .... 74 Youngstown St. 35-14
Delaware .... 74 Nevada-Las Vegas 49-11
Delaware .... 74 Central Mich. 14-54
Delaware .... 76 Northern Mich. 17-28
Delaware .... 78 Jacksonville St. 42-27
Delaware .... 78 Winston-Salem 41-0
Delaware .... 78 Eastern Ill. 9-10
Delaware .... 79 Virginia Union 58-28
Delaware .... 79 Mississippi Col. 60-10
Delaware .... 79* Youngstown St. 38-21

Rocky Rees (1-1) (West Chester '71)
Shippensburg .... 91 East Stroudsburg 34-33
Shippensburg .... 91 Indiana (Pa.) 7-52

Rick Rhodes (4-1)
Troy St. .... 86 Virginia Union 31-7
Troy St. .... 86 South Dak. 28-42
Troy St. .... 87 Winston-Salem 45-14
Troy St. .... 87 Central Fla. 31-10
Troy St. .... 87* Portland St. 31-17

Pete Richardson (0-3) (Dayton '68)
Winston-Salem........ 88 N.C. Central 16-31
Winston-Salem........ 90 Indiana (Pa.) 0-48
Winston-Salem........ 91 Jacksonville St. 24-49

Eddie Robinson (1-1) (Leland '41)
Grambling.............. 73 Delaware 17-8
Grambling.............. 73 Western Ky. 20-28

Dan Runkle (2-3) (Illinois Col. '68)
Mankato St............. 87 Portland St. 21-27
Mankato St............. 91 North Dak. St. 27-7
Mankato St............. 91 Portland St. 27-37
Mankato St............. 93 Mo. Southern St. 34-13
Mankato St............. 93 North Dak. 21-54

Joe Salem (0-2) (Minnesota '61)
South Dak. .... 73 Boise St. 10-53
Northern Ariz. .... 77 Jacksonville St. 0-35

Lyle Setencich (1-1) (Fresno St. '68)
Cal Poly SLO .... 90 Cal St. Northridge 14-7
Cal Poly SLO .... 90 North Dak. St. 0-47

Stan Sheriff (0-1) (Cal Poly SLO '54)
Northern Iowa........ 75 Western Ky. 12-14

Sanders Shiver (0-1) (Carson-Newman '76)
Bowie St. .... 88 Portland St. 17-34

Ron Simonson (0-1) (Portland St. '65)
Puget Sound .... 81 North Dak. St. 10-24

Hampton Smith (0-1) (Mississippi Val. '57)
Albany St. (Ga.) ..... 93 Hampton 7-33

Jim Sochor (4-8) (San Fran. St. '60)
UC Davis .... 77 Bethune-Cookman 34-16
UC Davis .... 77 Lehigh 30-39
UC Davis .... 78 Eastern Ill. 31-35
UC Davis .... 82 Northern Mich. 42-21
UC Davis .... 82 North Dak. St. 19-14
UC Davis .... 82 Southwest Tex. St. 9-34
UC Davis .... 83 Butler 25-6
UC Davis .... 83 North Dak. St. 17-26
UC Davis .... 84 North Dak. St. 23-31
UC Davis .... 85 North Dak. St. 12-31
UC Davis .... 86 South Dak. 23-26
UC Davis .... 88 Cal St. Sacramento 14-35

Earle Solomonson (6-0) (Augsburg '69)
North Dak. St. .... 85 UC Davis 31-12
North Dak. St. .... 85 South Dak. 16-7
North Dak. St. .... 85* North Ala. 35-7
North Dak. St. .... 86 Ashland 50-0
North Dak. St. .... 86 Central St. (Ohio) 35-12
North Dak. St. .... 86* South Dak. 27-7

Ken Sparks (0-1) (Carson-Newman '68)
Carson-Newman..... 93 North Ala. 28-38

Bill Sylvester (0-1) (Butler '50)
Butler .... 83 UC Davis 6-25

Joe Taylor (1-5) (Western Ill. '72)
Virginia Union .... 86 Troy St. 7-31
Virginia Union .... 90 Edinboro 14-38
Virginia Union .... 91 Indiana (Pa.) 7-56
Hampton .... 92 North Ala. 21-33
Hampton .... 93 Albany St. (Ga.) 33-7

Hampton .... 93 North Ala. 20-45

Clarence Thomas (0-1)
Morgan St. .... 79 Alabama A&M 7-27

Roger Thomas (2-2) (Augustana, Ill. '69)
North Dak. .... 92 Pittsburg St. 21-26
North Dak. .... 93 Pittsburg St. 17-14
North Dak. .... 93 Mankato St. 54-21
North Dak. .... 93 Indiana (Pa.) 6-21

Vern Thomsen (0-1) (Peru St. '61)
Northwest Mo. St.... 84 Nebraska-Omaha 15-28

Dave Triplett (3-2) (Iowa '72)
South Dak. .... 85 Central St. (Ohio) 13-10 (2 OT)
South Dak. .... 85 North Dak. St. 7-16
South Dak. .... 86 UC Davis 26-23
South Dak. .... 86 Troy St. 42-28
South Dak. .... 86 North Dak. St. 7-27

Jerry Vandergriff (2-2) (Corpus Christi '65)
Angelo St. .... 87 Northern Mich. 20-23 (OT)
Angelo St. .... 89 UC Davis 28-23
Angelo St. .... 89 Pittsburg St. 24-21
Angelo St. .... 89 Jacksonville St. 16-34

Eddie Vowell (2-2) (S'western Okla. '69)
East Tex. St............. 90 Grand Valley St. 20-14
East Tex. St............. 90 Pittsburg St. 28-60
East Tex. St............. 91 Grand Valley St. 36-15
East Tex. St............. 91 Pittsburg St. 28-38

Jim Wacker (8-2) (Valparaiso '60)
North Dak. St. .... 76 Eastern Ky. 10-7
North Dak. St. .... 76 Montana St. 3-10
North Dak. St. .... 77 Northern Mich. 20-6
North Dak. St. .... 77 Jacksonville St. 7-31
Southwest Tex. St. ... 81 Jacksonville St. 38-22
Southwest Tex. St. ... 81 Northern Mich. 62-0
Southwest Tex. St. ... 81* North Dak. St. 42-13
Southwest Tex. St. ... 82 Fort Valley St. 27-6
Southwest Tex. St. ... 82 Jacksonville St. 19-14
Southwest Tex. St. ... 82* UC Davis 34-9

Gerald Walker (0-1) (Lincoln, Mo. '62)
Fort Valley St. .... 85 North Ala. 7-14

Bobby Wallace (5-2) (Mississippi St. '76)
North Ala............... 90 Jacksonville St. 14-38
North Ala............... 92 Hampton 33-21
North Ala............... 92 Jacksonville St. 12-14
North Ala............... 93 Carson-Newman 38-28
North Ala............... 93 Hampton 45-20
North Ala............... 93 Tex. A&M-Kingsville 27-25
North Ala............... 93* Indiana (Pa.) 41-34

Tim Walsh (0-1) (UC Riverside '77)
Portland St............. 93 Tex. A&M-Kingsville 15-50

Johnnie Walton (0-1) (Elizabeth City St. '69)
Elizabeth City St. .... 81 Northern Mich. 6-55

Bob Waters (0-1) (Presbyterian '60)
Western Caro. .... 74 Louisiana Tech 7-10

Mark Whipple (3-2) (Brown '79)
New Haven............ 92 West Chester 38-26
New Haven............ 92 Ferris St. 35-13
New Haven............ 92 Jacksonville St. 35-46
New Haven............ 93 Edinboro 48-28
New Haven............ 93 Indiana (Pa.) 35-38

John Whitehead (3-0) (East Stroudsburg '50)
Lehigh .... 77 Massachusetts 30-23
Lehigh .... 77 UC Davis 39-30
Lehigh .... 77* Jacksonville St. 33-0

John Williams (†7-3) (Mississippi Col. '57)
Mississippi Col. ...... 79 North Dak. 35-15
Mississippi Col. ...... 79 Delaware 10-60
Mississippi Col. ...... 88 Tex. A&M-Kingsville 15-39
Mississippi Col. ...... 89† Tex. A&M-Kingsville 34-19
Mississippi Col. ...... 89† St. Cloud 55-24
Mississippi Col. ...... 89† Indiana (Pa.) 26-14
Mississippi Col. ...... 89†* Jacksonville St. 3-0
Mississippi Col. ...... 90† Wofford 70-19
Mississippi Col. ...... 90† Jacksonville St. 14-7
Mississippi Col. ...... 90† Indiana (Pa.) 8-27

National championship. †Mississippi College's participation voided.

Division III Coaching Records

Winningest Active Division III Coaches

(Minimum Five Years as a College Head Coach; Record at Four-Year Colleges Only)

BY PERCENTAGE

Coach, College	Years	Won	Lost	Tied	*Pct.	Playoffs# W	L	T
Bob Reade, Augustana (Ill.)	15	138	21	1	.866	19	5	0
Larry Kehres, Mount Union	8	74	13	3	.839	7	3	0
Dick Farley, Williams	7	45	9	2	.821	0	0	0
Ron Schipper, Central (Iowa)	33	260	62	3	.805	16	9	0
John Luckhardt, Wash. & Jeff.	12	97	25	2	.790	8	8	0
Bob Packard, Baldwin-Wallace	13	102	28	2	.780	0	2	0
Roger Harring, Wis.-La Crosse	25	210	60	7	.771	7	3	0
Rich Lackner, Carnegie Mellon	8	59	18	2	.759	0	1	0
John Gagliardi, St. John's (Minn.)	45	306	96	10	.755	23	9	0
Rick Giancola, Montclair St.	11	84	29	2	.739	3	3	0
Pete Schmidt, Albion	11	74	25	4	.738	1	3	0
Frank Girardi, Lycoming	22	156	55	5	.734	5	5	0
Bill Manlove, Delaware Valley	25	187	68	1	.732	9	5	0
Jack Siedlecki, Amherst	6	39	15	1	.718	0	1	0
Tony DeCarlo, John Carroll	7	48	19	2	.710	0	1	0
Dale Widolff, Occidental	12	79	32	2	.708	1	3	0
D. J. LeRoy, Coe	11	83	34	2	.706	0	2	0
Tom Gilburg, Frank. & Marsh.	19	128	53	2	.705	0	0	0
Carl Poelker, Millikin	12	77	32	1	.705	1	1	0
Jim Christopherson, Concordia-M'head	25	175	73	6	.701	7	2	1
Scot Dapp, Moravian	7	51	22	0	.699	1	2	0
Jim Williams, Simpson	7	49	21	1	.697	0	3	0
Don Miller, Trinity (Conn.)	27	148	63	5	.697	0	0	0
Lou Wacker, Emory & Henry	12	89	39	2	.695	3	3	0
Mike Clary, Rhodes	10	61	27	5	.683	0	1	0
Mike Maynard, Redlands	6	38	18	0	.679	0	2	0
Ray Smith, Hope	24	143	66	8	.677	0	1	0
Doug Neibhur, Wittenberg	5	32	15	1	.677	0	0	0
Greg Carlson, Wabash	11	68	32	2	.676	0	0	0
John Miech, Wis.-Stevens Point	6	40	19	2	.672	0	0	0
Nick Mourouzis, DePauw	13	81	44	4	.643	0	0	0
Mike McGlinchey, Frostburg St.	12	77	43	5	.636	6	4	0
C. Wayne Perry, Hanover	12	74	42	2	.636	0	0	0
Bob Berezowitz, Wis.-Whitewater	9	59	33	4	.635	1	2	0
Kelly Kane, Monmouth (Ill.)	10	59	34	0	.634	0	0	0
Rich Parrinello, Rochester	6	36	21	0	.632	0	0	0
Jim Scott, Aurora	8	43	25	1	.630	0	1	0
Joe King, Rensselaer	5	28	16	2	.630	0	0	0
J. R. Bishop, Wheaton (Ill.)	12	67	40	1	.625	0	0	0
Bob Bierie, Loras	14	87	53	5	.617	0	0	0
Eric Hamilton, Trenton St.	17	101	63	5	.612	1	1	0
Craig Rundle, Colorado Col.	8	47	30	0	.610	0	0	0
Norm Eash, Ill. Wesleyan	7	39	25	1	.608	1	1	0
Jim Moretti, Alfred	9	54	35	2	.604	0	0	0
Bob Nielson, Wartburg	5	29	19	1	.602	0	1	0
John O'Grady, Wis.-River Falls	5	28	18	3	.602	0	0	0
Scott Duncan, Rose-Hulman	8	47	32	1	.594	0	0	0
Dick Tressel, Hamline	16	92	63	2	.592	0	0	0
Joe Harper, Cal Lutheran	21	123	86	3	.587	0	0	0
Tommy Ranager, Millsaps	5	26	18	2	.587	0	0	0
Joe Bush, Hampden-Sydney	9	51	37	1	.579	0	0	0
Mickey Heinecken, Middlebury	21	96	70	2	.577	0	0	0
Barry Streeter, Gettysburg	16	92	67	4	.577	2	1	0
Tom Bell, Macalester	18	92	67	6	.576	0	0	0
Bob Sullivan, Carleton	15	83	62	0	.572	0	1	0

Coach, College	Years	Won	Lost	Tied	*Pct.	Playoffs# W	L	T
Mike Hollway, Ohio Wesleyan	11	61	46	2	.569	0	1	0
Don Canfield, St. Olaf	21	112	85	1	.568	0	1	0
Joe McDaniel, Centre	28	142	109	4	.565	0	3	0
Don Ruggeri, Mass. Maritime	21	105	81	1	.564	0	0	0
Bill Samko, Tufts	7	35	27	1	.563	0	0	0
Robert Ford, Albany (N.Y.)	25	132	104	1	.559	1	1	0
Steve Miller, Cornell College	15	75	60	3	.554	0	1	0
Bob Naslund, Luther	16	82	69	0	.543	0	0	0
Peter Mazzaferro, Bri'water (Mass.)	30	139	119	11	.537	0	0	0
Steve Frank, Hamilton	9	38	33	1	.535	0	0	0
Jeff Heacock, Muskingum	13	66	58	3	.532	0	0	0
Dennis Riccio, St. Lawrence	7	36	33	0	.522	0	0	0
Larry Kindbom, Washington (Mo.)	11	55	52	1	.514	0	0	0
Ed DeGeorge, Beloit	17	79	75	1	.513	0	0	0
Brien Cullen, Worcester St.	9	41	39	0	.513	0	0	0
Tim Keating, Western Md.	6	29	28	1	.509	0	0	0
Dick West, Heidelberg	10	49	49	2	.500	0	0	0
Gerry Gallagher, Wm. Paterson	8	38	38	1	.500	1	1	0
Dennis Gorsline, N'western (Wis.)	23	83	85	0	.494	0	0	0
Phil Wilks, Maryville (Tenn.)	6	29	30	0	.492	0	0	0
Roger Welsh, Capital	8	37	39	4	.488	0	1	0
Steve Johnson, Bethel (Minn.)	5	23	25	1	.480	0	0	0
Merle Masonholder, Carroll (Wis.)	12	51	56	0	.477	0	0	0
Jim Meyer, Kenyon	5	22	25	3	.470	0	0	0
Howard Vandersea, Bowdoin	17	69	78	2	.470	0	0	0
Sam Kornhauser, Stony Brook	10	43	49	2	.468	0	0	0
Gary Fallon, Wash. & Lee	16	71	81	1	.467	0	0	0
Ray Solari, Menlo	8	32	39	2	.452	0	1	0
Jim Monos, Lebanon Valley	8	35	43	2	.450	0	0	0
Steve Gilbert, Ursinus	6	26	32	0	.448	0	0	0
Jerry Boyes, Buffalo St.	8	34	42	0	.447	1	2	0
Charles Giangrosso, Thiel	5	21	26	0	.447	0	0	0
Dale Liston, Manchester	11	45	57	0	.441	0	0	0
Tom Austin, Colby	8	27	36	1	.430	0	0	0
Carlin Carpenter, Bluffton	15	58	79	1	.424	0	0	0
Mike Manley, Anderson	12	47	67	3	.415	0	1	0
Jim Braun, Concordia (Ill.)	15	54	78	3	.411	0	0	0
John Zinda, Claremont-M-S	25	88	127	4	.411	0	0	0
Rick Pardy, Bates	5	17	25	2	.409	0	0	0
Michael Hensley, MacMurray	7	28	41	1	.407	0	0	0
Ed Matejkovic, Brockport St.	8	32	47	0	.405	0	0	0
Dale Sprague, Blackburn	8	28	42	2	.403	0	0	0
Randy Oberembt, Knox	9	32	48	1	.401	0	0	0
Chris Smith, Grove City	10	35	53	2	.400	0	0	0
Ron Cardo, Wis.-Oshkosh	10	37	59	4	.390	0	0	0
Thomas Raeke, Framingham St.	9	31	49	0	.388	0	0	0
Tom Kaczkowski, Ohio Northern	8	29	48	2	.380	0	0	0
Mike McClure, Franklin	5	18	30	1	.378	0	0	0
Jim Kent, Mass.-Boston	6	19	34	1	.361	0	0	0
Maury Waugh, Lake Forest	13	41	75	2	.356	0	0	0
Gene Epley, Marietta	7	23	46	2	.338	0	0	0
Steve Stetson, Hartwick	8	23	47	2	.333	0	0	0
Bob Tucker, Wooster	9	28	57	1	.331	0	0	0
Dwight Smith, MIT	6	14	30	1	.322	0	0	0
Mike Walsh, Upsala	5	15	33	1	.316	0	0	0
Bill Klika, FDU-Madison	20	53	120	1	.307	0	0	0
Ralph Young, William Penn	8	22	51	0	.301	0	0	0
Bill Anderson, Illinois Col.	16	41	103	0	.285	0	0	0
Frank Carr, Earlham	9	18	67	0	.212	0	0	0
Greg Wallace, Grinnell	6	7	45	1	.142	0	0	0

*Ties computed as half won and half lost; bowl and postseason games included.
#NCAA Division III playoff games.

BY VICTORIES
(Minimum 100 Victories)

Coach, College, Winning Percentage	Won
John Gagliardi, St. John's (Minn.) .755	306
Ron Schipper, Central (Iowa) .805	260
Roger Harring, Wis.-La Crosse .771	210
Bill Manlove, Delaware Valley .732	187
Jim Christopherson, Concordia-M'head .701	175
Frank Girardi, Lycoming .734	156
Don Miller, Trinity (Conn.) .697	148
Ray Smith, Hope .677	143
Joe McDaniel, Centre .565	142
Peter Mazzaferro, Bri'water (Mass.) .537	139
Bob Reade, Augustana (Ill.) .866	138
Robert Ford, Albany (N.Y.) .559	132
Tom Gilburg, Frank. & Marsh. .705	128
Joe Harper, Cal Lutheran .587	123
Don Canfield, St. Olaf .568	112
Don Ruggeri, Mass. Maritime .564	105
Bob Packard, Baldwin-Wallace .780	102
Eric Hamilton, Trenton St. .612	101

Division III Championship Coaches

All coaches who have coached teams in the Division III championship playoffs since 1973 are listed here with their playoff record, alma mater and year graduated, team, year coached, opponent, and score.

Phil Albert (2-1) (Arizona '66)
Towson St.	76	LIU-C.W. Post 14-10
Towson St.	76	St. Lawrence 38-36
Towson St.	76	St. John's (Minn.) 28-31

Dom Anile (0-1) (LIU-C.W. Post '59)
| LIU-C.W. Post | 76 | Towson St. 10-14 |

John Audino (0-1) (Notre Dame '75)
| Union (N.Y.) | 93 | Wm. Paterson 7-17 |

Don Ault (0-1) (West Liberty St. '52)
| Bethany (W.Va.) | 80 | Widener 12-43 |

Al Bagnoli (7-6) (Central Conn. St. '74)
Union (N.Y.)	83	Hofstra 51-19
Union (N.Y.)	83	Salisbury St. 23-21
Union (N.Y.)	83	Augustana (Ill.) 17-21
Union (N.Y.)	84	Plymouth St. 26-14
Union (N.Y.)	84	Augustana (Ill.) 6-23
Union (N.Y.)	85	Ithaca 12-13
Union (N.Y.)	86	Ithaca 17-24 (OT)
Union (N.Y.)	89	Cortland St. 42-14
Union (N.Y.)	89	Montclair St. 45-6
Union (N.Y.)	89	Ferrum 37-21
Union (N.Y.)	89	Dayton 7-17
Union (N.Y.)	91	Mass.-Lowell 55-16
Union (N.Y.)	91	Ithaca 23-35

Bob Berezowitz (1-2) (Wis.-Whitewater '67)
Wis.-Whitewater	88	Simpson 29-27
Wis.-Whitewater	88	Central (Iowa) 13-16
Wis.-Whitewater	90	St. Thomas (Minn.) 23-24

Don Birmingham (0-2) (Westmar '62)
| Dubuque | 79 | Augustana (Ill.) 35-41 |
| Dubuque | 80 | Minn.-Morris 35-41 |

Jim Blackburn (0-1) (Virginia '71)
| Randolph-Macon | 84 | Wash. & Jeff. 21-22 |

Bill Bless (0-1) (Indianapolis '63)
| Indianapolis | 75 | Wittenberg 13-17 |

Jerry Boyes (1-2) (Ithaca '76)
Buffalo St.	92	Ithaca 28-26
Buffalo St.	92	Rowan 19-28
Buffalo St.	93	Rowan 6-29

Steve Briggs (2-1) (Springfield '84)
Susquehanna	91	Dickinson 21-20
Susquehanna	91	Lycoming 31-24
Susquehanna	91	Ithaca 13-49

John Bunting (2-2) (North Caro. '72)
Rowan	91	Ithaca 10-31
Rowan	92	Worcester Tech 41-14
Rowan	92	Buffalo St. 28-19
Rowan	92	Wash. & Jeff. 13-18

Jim Butterfield (21-8) (Maine '53)
Ithaca	74	Slippery Rock 27-14
Ithaca	74	Central (Iowa) 8-10
Ithaca	75	Fort Valley St. 41-12
Ithaca	75	Widener 23-14
Ithaca	75	Wittenberg 0-28
Ithaca	78	Wittenberg 3-6
Ithaca	79	Dubuque 27-7
Ithaca	79	Carnegie Mellon 15-6
Ithaca	79*	Wittenberg 14-10
Ithaca	80	Wagner 41-13
Ithaca	80	Minn.-Morris 36-0
Ithaca	80	Dayton 0-63
Ithaca	85	Union (N.Y.) 13-12
Ithaca	85	Montclair St. 50-28
Ithaca	85	Gettysburg 34-0
Ithaca	85	Augustana (Ill.) 7-20
Ithaca	86	Union (N.Y.) 24-17 (OT)
Ithaca	86	Montclair St. 29-15
Ithaca	86	Salisbury St. 40-44
Ithaca	88	Wagner 34-31 (OT)
Ithaca	88	Cortland St. 24-17
Ithaca	88	Ferrum 62-28
Ithaca	88*	Central (Iowa) 39-24
Ithaca	90	Trenton St. 14-24
Ithaca	91	Rowan 31-10
Ithaca	91	Union (N.Y.) 35-23
Ithaca	91	Susquehanna 49-13
Ithaca	91*	Dayton 34-20
Ithaca	92	Buffalo St. 26-28

Jim Byers (0-1) (Michigan '59)
| Evansville | 74 | Central (Iowa) 16-17 |

Don Canfield (0-1)
| Wartburg | 82 | Bishop 7-32 |

Jerry Carle (0-1) (Northwestern '48)
| Colorado Col. | 75 | Millsaps 21-28 |

Gene Carpenter (0-1) (Huron '63)
| Millersville | 79 | Wittenberg 14-21 |

Rick Carter (3-1) (Earlham '65)
Dayton	78	Carnegie Mellon 21-24
Dayton	80	Baldwin-Wallace 34-0
Dayton	80	Widener 28-24
Dayton	80*	Ithaca 63-0

Don Charlton (0-1) (Lock Haven '65)
| Hiram | 87 | Augustana (Ill.) 0-53 |

Jim Christopherson (2-2) (Concordia-M'head '60)
Concordia-M'head	86	Wis.-Stevens Point 24-15
Concordia-M'head	86	Central (Iowa) 17-14
Concordia-M'head	86	Augustana (Ill.) 7-41
Concordia-M'head	88	Central (Iowa) 0-7

Vic Clark (0-1) (Indiana St. '71)
| Thomas More | 92 | Emory & Henry 0-17 |

Mike Clary (0-1) (Rhodes '77)
| Rhodes | 88 | Ferrum 10-35 |

Jay Cottone (0-1) (Norwich '71)
| Plymouth St. | 84 | Union (N.Y.) 14-26 |

Scot Dapp (1-2) (West Chester '73)
Moravian	88	Widener 17-7
Moravian	88	Ferrum 28-49
Moravian	93	Wash. & Jeff. 7-27

Harper Davis (1-1) (Mississippi St. '49)
| Millsaps | 75 | Colorado Col. 28-21 |
| Millsaps | 75 | Wittenberg 22-55 |

Tony DeCarlo (0-1) (Kent '62)
| John Carroll | 89 | Dayton 10-35 |

Joe DeMelfi (0-1) (Delta St. '66)
| Wilkes | 93 | Frostburg St. 25-26 |

Bob Di Spirito (0-1) (Rhode Island '53)
| Slippery Rock | 74 | Ithaca 14-27 |

Norm Eash (1-1) (Ill. Wesleyan '75)
| Ill. Wesleyan | 92 | Aurora 21-12 |
| Ill. Wesleyan | 92 | Mount Union 27-49 |

Ed Farrell (0-1) (Rutgers '56)
| Bridgeport | 73 | Juniata 14-35 |

Bob Ford (1-1) (Springfield '59)
| Albany (N.Y.) | 77 | Hampden-Sydney 51-45 |
| Albany (N.Y.) | 77 | Widener 15-33 |

Stokeley Fulton (0-1) (Hampden-Sydney '55)
| Hampden-Sydney | 77 | Albany (N.Y.) 45-51 |

John Gagliardi (10-6) (Colorado Col. '49)
St. John's (Minn.)	76	Augustana (Ill.) 46-7
St. John's (Minn.)	76	Buena Vista 61-0
St. John's (Minn.)	76*	Towson St. 31-28
St. John's (Minn.)	77	Wabash 9-20
St. John's (Minn.)	85	Occidental 10-28
St. John's (Minn.)	87	Gust. Adolphus 7-3
St. John's (Minn.)	87	Central (Iowa) 3-13
St. John's (Minn.)	89	Simpson 42-35
St. John's (Minn.)	89	Central (Iowa) 27-24
St. John's (Minn.)	89	Dayton 0-28
St. John's (Minn.)	91	Coe 75-2
St. John's (Minn.)	91	Wis.-La Crosse 29-10
St. John's (Minn.)	91	Dayton 7-19
St. John's (Minn.)	93	Coe 32-14
St. John's (Minn.)	93	Wis.-La Crosse 47-25
St. John's (Minn.)	93	Mount Union 8-56

Gerry Gallagher (1-1) (Wm. Paterson '74)
| Wm. Paterson | 93 | Union (N.Y.) 17-7 |
| Wm. Paterson | 93 | Rowan 0-37 |

Joe Gardi (2-1) (Maryland '60)
Hofstra	90	Cortland St. 35-9
Hofstra	90	Trenton St. 38-3
Hofstra	90	Lycoming 10-20

Rick Giancola (3-3) (Rowan '68)
Montclair St.	85	Western Conn. St. 28-0
Montclair St.	85	Ithaca 28-50
Montclair St.	86	Hofstra 24-21
Montclair St.	86	Ithaca 15-29
Montclair St.	89	Hofstra 23-6
Montclair St.	89	Union (N.Y.) 6-45

Frank Girardi (5-5) (West Chester '61)
Lycoming	85	Gettysburg 10-14
Lycoming	89	Dickinson 21-0
Lycoming	89	Ferrum 24-49
Lycoming	90	Carnegie Mellon 17-7
Lycoming	90	Wash. & Jeff. 24-0
Lycoming	90	Hofstra 20-10
Lycoming	90	Allegheny 14-21 (OT)
Lycoming	91	Wash. & Jeff. 18-16
Lycoming	91	Susquehanna 24-31
Lycoming	92	Wash. & Jeff. 0-33

Larry Glueck (1-1) (Villanova '63)
| Fordham | 87 | Hofstra 41-6 |
| Fordham | 87 | Wagner 0-21 |

Walt Hameline (4-2) (Brockport St. '75)
Wagner	82	St. Lawrence 34-43
Wagner	87	Rochester 38-14
Wagner	87	Fordham 21-0
Wagner	87	Emory & Henry 20-15
Wagner	87*	Dayton 19-3
Wagner	88	Ithaca 31-34 (OT)

Eric Hamilton (1-1) (Trenton St. '75)
| Trenton St. | 90 | Ithaca 24-14 |
| Trenton St. | 90 | Hofstra 3-38 |

Roger Harring (7-3) (Wis.-La Crosse '58)
Wis.-La Crosse	83	Occidental 43-42
Wis.-La Crosse	83	Augustana (Ill.) 15-21
Wis.-La Crosse	91	Simpson 28-13
Wis.-La Crosse	91	St. John's (Minn.) 10-29
Wis.-La Crosse	92	Redlands 47-26
Wis.-La Crosse	92	Central (Iowa) 34-9
Wis.-La Crosse	92	Mount Union 29-24
Wis.-La Crosse	92*	Wash. & Jeff. 16-12
Wis.-La Crosse	93	Wartburg 55-26
Wis.-La Crosse	93	St. John's (Minn.) 25-47

Jim Hershberger (1-2) (Northern Iowa '57)
Buena Vista	76	Carroll (Wis.) 20-14 (OT)
Buena Vista	76	St. John's (Minn.) 0-61
Buena Vista	86	Central (Iowa) 0-37

Fred Hill (1-1) (Upsala '57)
| Montclair St. | 81 | Alfred 13-12 |
| Montclair St. | 81 | Widener 12-23 |

James Jones (1-1) (Bishop '49)
| Bishop | 82 | Wartburg 32-7 |
| Bishop | 82 | West Ga. 6-27 |

Frank Joranko (0-1) (Albion '52)
| Albion | 77 | Minn.-Morris 10-13 |

Dennis Kayser (1-2) (Ithaca '74)
Cortland St.	88	Hofstra 32-27
Cortland St.	88	Ithaca 17-24
Cortland St.	89	Union (N.Y.) 14-42

K. C. Keeler (3-1) (Delaware '81)
Rowan	93	Buffalo St. 29-6
Rowan	93	Wm. Paterson 37-0
Rowan	93	Wash. & Jeff. 23-16
Rowan	93	Mount Union 24-34

Larry Kehres (7-3) (Mount Union '71)
| Mount Union | 86 | Dayton 42-36 |

Mount Union 86   Augustana (Ill.) 7-16
Mount Union 90   Allegheny 15-26
Mount Union 92   Dayton 27-10
Mount Union 92   Ill. Wesleyan 49-27

Mount Union 92   Wis.-La Crosse 24-29
Mount Union 93   Allegheny 40-7
Mount Union 93   Albion 30-16
Mount Union 93   St. John's (Minn.) 56-8
Mount Union .... 93*   Rowan 34-24

Mike Kelly (13-8) (Manchester '70)
Dayton 81   Augustana (Ill.) 19-7
Dayton 81   Lawrence 38-0
Dayton 81   Widener 10-17
Dayton 84   Augustana (Ill.) 13-14
Dayton 86   Mount Union 36-42

Dayton 87   Capital 52-28
Dayton 87   Augustana (Ill.) 38-36
Dayton 87   Central (Iowa) 34-0
Dayton 87   Wagner 3-19
Dayton 88   Wittenberg 28-35 (2 OT)

Dayton 89   John Carroll 35-10
Dayton 89   Millikin 28-16
Dayton 89   St. John's (Minn.) 28-0
Dayton .... 89*   Union (N.Y.) 17-7
Dayton 90   Augustana (Ill.) 24-14

Dayton 90   Allegheny 23-31
Dayton 91   Baldwin-Wallace 27-10
Dayton 91   Allegheny 28-25 (OT)
Dayton 91   St. John's (Minn.) 19-7
Dayton 91   Ithaca 20-34

Dayton 92   Mount Union 10-27

Chuck Klausing (2-4) (Slippery Rock '48)
Carnegie Mellon..... 78   Dayton 24-21
Carnegie Mellon..... 78   Baldwin-Wallace 6-31
Carnegie Mellon..... 79   Minn.-Morris 31-25
Carnegie Mellon..... 79   Ithaca 6-15
Carnegie Mellon..... 83   Salisbury St. 14-16

Carnegie Mellon..... 85   Salisbury St. 22-35

Mickey Kwiatkowski (0-5) (Delaware '70)
Hofstra 83   Union (N.Y.) 19-51
Hofstra 86   Montclair St. 21-24
Hofstra 87   Fordham 6-41
Hofstra 88   Cortland St. 27-32
Hofstra 89   Montclair St. 6-23

Ron Labadie (0-2) (Adrian '71)
Adrian 83   Augustana (Ill.) 21-22
Adrian 88   Augustana (Ill.) 7-25

Rich Lackner (0-1) (Carnegie Mellon '79)
Carnegie Mellon..... 90   Lycoming 7-17

Don LaViolette (0-1) (St. Norbert '54)
St. Norbert 89   Central (Iowa) 7-55

D. J. LeRoy (0-3) (Wis.-Eau Claire '79)
Wis.-Stevens Point .. 86   Concordia-M'head 15-24
Coe 91   St. John's (Minn.) 2-75
Coe 93   St. John's (Minn.) 14-32

Leon Lomax (0-1) (Fort Valley St. '43)
Fort Valley St. 75   Ithaca 12-41

John Luckhardt (8-8) (Purdue '67)
Wash. & Jeff. 84   Randolph-Macon 22-21
Wash. & Jeff. 84   Central (Iowa) 0-20
Wash. & Jeff. 86   Susquehanna 20-28
Wash. & Jeff. 87   Allegheny 23-17 (OT)
Wash. & Jeff. 87   Emory & Henry 16-23

Wash. & Jeff. 89   Ferrum 7-41
Wash. & Jeff. 90   Ferrum 10-7
Wash. & Jeff. 90   Lycoming 0-24
Wash. & Jeff. 91   Lycoming 16-18
Wash. & Jeff. 92   Lycoming 33-0

Wash. & Jeff. 92   Emory & Henry 51-15
Wash. & Jeff. 92   Rowan 18-13
Wash. & Jeff. 92   Wis.-La Crosse 12-16
Wash. & Jeff. 93   Moravian 27-7
Wash. & Jeff. 93   Frostburg St. 28-7

Wash. & Jeff. 93   Rowan 16-23

Mike Manley (0-1) (Anderson '73)
Anderson 93   Albion 21-41

Bill Manlove (9-5) (Temple '58)
Widener 75   Albright 14-6
Widener 75   Ithaca 14-23
Widener 77   Central (Iowa) 19-0
Widener 77   Albany (N.Y.) 33-15
Widener .... 77*   Wabash 39-36

Widener 79   Baldwin-Wallace 29-8

Widener 79   Wittenberg 14-17
Widener 80   Bethany (W.Va.) 43-12
Widener 80   Dayton 24-28
Widener 81   West Ga. 10-3

Widener 81   Montclair St. 23-12
Widener .... 81*   Dayton 17-10
Widener 82   West Ga. 24-31 (3 OT)
Widener 88   Moravian 7-17

Dave Maurer (9-2) (Denison '54)
Wittenberg 73   San Diego 21-14
Wittenberg .... 73*   Juniata 41-0
Wittenberg 75   Indianapolis 17-13
Wittenberg 75   Millsaps 55-22
Wittenberg .... 75*   Ithaca 28-0

Wittenberg 78   Ithaca 6-3
Wittenberg 78   Minn.-Morris 35-14
Wittenberg 78   Baldwin-Wallace 10-24
Wittenberg 79   Millersville 21-14
Wittenberg 79   Widener 17-14

Wittenberg 79   Ithaca 10-14

Mike Maynard (0-2) (Ill. Wesleyan '80)
Redlands 90   Central (Iowa) 14-24
Redlands 92   Wis.-La Crosse 26-47

Mike McGlinchey (6-4) (Delaware '67)
Salisbury St. 83   Carnegie Mellon 16-14
Salisbury St. 83   Union (N.Y.) 21-23
Salisbury St. 85   Carnegie Mellon 35-22
Salisbury St. 85   Gettysburg 6-22
Salisbury St. 86   Emory & Henry 34-20

Salisbury St. 86   Susquehanna 31-17
Salisbury St. 86   Ithaca 44-40
Salisbury St. 86   Augustana (Ill.) 3-31
Frostburg St. 93   Wilkes 26-25
Frostburg St. 93   Wash. & Jeff. 7-28

Steve Miller (0-1) (Cornell College '65)
Carroll (Wis.) 76   Buena Vista 14-20 (OT)

Al Molde (2-3) (Gust. Adolphus '66)
Minn.-Morris........... 77   Albion 13-10
Minn.-Morris........... 77   Wabash 21-37
Minn.-Morris........... 78   St. Olaf 23-10
Minn.-Morris........... 78   Wittenberg 14-35
Minn.-Morris........... 79   Carnegie Mellon 25-31

Ron Murphy (1-1) (Wittenberg '60)
Wittenberg 88   Dayton 35-28 (2 OT)
Wittenberg 88   Augustana (Ill.) 14-28

Dave Murray (0-1) (Springfield '81)
Cortland St. 90   Hofstra 9-35

Walt Nadzak (1-1) (Denison '57)
Juniata 73   Bridgeport 35-14
Juniata 73   Wittenberg 0-41

Frank Navarro (2-1) (Maryland '53)
Wabash 77   St. John's (Minn.) 20-9
Wabash 77   Minn.-Morris 37-21
Wabash 77   Widener 36-39

Ben Newcomb (0-1) (Augustana, S.D. '57)
Augustana (Ill.)....... 76   St. John's (Minn.) 7-46

Bob Nielson (0-1) (Wartburg '81)
Wartburg 93   Wis.-La Crosse 26-55

Hank Norton (4-4) (Lynchburg '51)
Ferrum 87   Emory & Henry 7-49
Ferrum 88   Rhodes 35-10
Ferrum 88   Moravian 49-28
Ferrum 88   Ithaca 28-62
Ferrum 89   Wash. & Jeff. 41-7

Ferrum 89   Lycoming 49-24
Ferrum 89   Union (N.Y.) 21-37
Ferrum 90   Wash. & Jeff. 7-10

Ken O'Keefe (5-2) (John Carroll '75)
Allegheny 90   Mount Union 26-15
Allegheny 90   Dayton 31-23
Allegheny 90   Central (Iowa) 24-7
Allegheny .... 90*   Lycoming 21-14 (OT)
Allegheny 91   Albion 24-21 (OT)

Allegheny 91   Dayton 25-28 (OT)
Allegheny 93   Mount Union 7-40

Bob Packard (0-2) (Baldwin-Wallace '65)
Baldwin-Wallace..... 82   Augustana (Ill.) 22-28
Baldwin-Wallace..... 91   Dayton 10-27

Paul Pasqualoni (0-1) (Penn St. '72)
Western Conn. St. .. 85   Montclair St. 0-28

Bobby Pate (3-1) (Georgia '63)
West Ga. 81   Widener 3-10
West Ga. 82   Widener 31-24 (3 OT)

West Ga. 82   Bishop 27-6
West Ga. .... 82*   Augustana (Ill.) 14-0

Keith Piper (0-1) (Baldwin-Wallace '48)
Denison 85   Mount Union 3-35

Carl Poelker (1-1) (Millikin '68)
Millikin 89   Augustana (Ill.) 21-12
Millikin 89   Dayton 16-28

Tom Porter (0-1) (St. Olaf '51)
St. Olaf 78   Minn.-Morris 10-23

John Potsklan (0-2) (Penn St. '49)
Albright 75   Widener 6-14
Albright 76   St. Lawrence 7-26

Steve Raarup (0-1) (Gust. Adolphus '53)
Gust. Adolphus 87   St. John's (Minn.) 3-7

Bob Reade (19-6) (Cornell College '54)
Augustana (Ill.)....... 81   Dayton 7-19
Augustana (Ill.)....... 82   Baldwin-Wallace 28-22
Augustana (Ill.)....... 82   St. Lawrence 14-0
Augustana (Ill.)....... 82   West Ga. 0-14
Augustana (Ill.)....... 83   Adrian 22-21

Augustana (Ill.)....... 83   Wis.-La Crosse 21-15
Augustana (Ill.)....... 83*   Union (N.Y.) 21-17
Augustana (Ill.)....... 84   Dayton 14-13
Augustana (Ill.)....... 84   Union (N.Y.) 23-6
Augustana (Ill.)....... 84*   Central (Iowa) 21-12

Augustana (Ill.)....... 85   Albion 26-10
Augustana (Ill.)....... 85   Mount Union 21-14
Augustana (Ill.)....... 85   Central (Iowa) 14-7
Augustana (Ill.)....... 85*   Ithaca 20-7
Augustana (Ill.)....... 86   Hope 34-10

Augustana (Ill.)....... 86   Mount Union 16-7
Augustana (Ill.)....... 86   Concordia-M'head 41-7
Augustana (Ill.)....... 86*   Salisbury St. 31-3
Augustana (Ill.)....... 87   Hiram 53-0
Augustana (Ill.)....... 87   Dayton 36-38

Augustana (Ill.)....... 88   Adrian 25-7
Augustana (Ill.)....... 88   Wittenberg 28-14
Augustana (Ill.)....... 88   Central (Iowa) 17-23 (2 OT)
Augustana (Ill.)....... 89   Millikin 12-21
Augustana (Ill.)....... 90   Dayton 14-24

Rocky Rees (1-1) (West Chester '71)
Susquehanna 86   Wash. & Jeff. 28-20
Susquehanna 86   Salisbury St. 17-31

Ron Roberts (1-1) (Wisconsin '54)
Lawrence 81   Minn.-Morris 21-14 (OT)
Lawrence 81   Dayton 0-38

Bill Russo (0-1)
Wagner 80   Ithaca 13-41

Sam Sanders (0-1) (Buffalo '60)
Alfred 81   Montclair St. 12-13

Dennis Scannell (0-1) (Villanova '74)
Mass.-Lowell 91   Union (N.Y.) 16-55

Ron Schipper (16-9) (Hope '52)
Central (Iowa)......... 74   Evansville 17-16
Central (Iowa)......... 74*   Ithaca 10-8
Central (Iowa)......... 77   Widener 0-19
Central (Iowa)......... 84   Occidental 23-22
Central (Iowa)......... 84   Wash. & Jeff. 20-0

Central (Iowa)......... 84   Augustana (Ill.) 12-21
Central (Iowa)......... 85   Coe 27-7
Central (Iowa)......... 85   Occidental 71-0
Central (Iowa)......... 85   Augustana (Ill.) 7-14
Central (Iowa)......... 86   Buena Vista 37-0

Central (Iowa)......... 86   Concordia-M'head 14-17
Central (Iowa)......... 87   Menlo 17-0
Central (Iowa)......... 87   St. John's (Minn.) 13-3
Central (Iowa)......... 87   Dayton 0-34
Central (Iowa)......... 88   Concordia-M'head 7-0

Central (Iowa)......... 88   Wis.-Whitewater 16-13
Central (Iowa)......... 88   Augustana (Ill.) 23-17 (2 OT)
Central (Iowa)......... 88   Ithaca 34-29
Central (Iowa)......... 89   St. Norbert 55-7
Central (Iowa)......... 89   St. John's (Minn.) 24-27

Central (Iowa)......... 90   Redlands 24-14
Central (Iowa)......... 90   St. Thomas (Minn.) 33-32
Central (Iowa)......... 90   Allegheny 7-24
Central (Iowa)......... 92   Carleton 20-8
Central (Iowa)......... 92   Wis.-La Crosse 9-34

Pete Schmidt (1-3) (Alma '70)
Albion 85   Augustana (Ill.) 10-26
Albion 91   Allegheny 21-24 (OT)
Albion 93   Anderson 41-21
Albion 93   Mount Union 16-30

Jim Scott (0-1) (Luther '61)
Aurora 92   Ill. Wesleyan 12-21

Jack Siedlecki (0-1) (Union, N.Y. '73)
Worcester Tech 92   Rowan 14-41

Dick Smith (1-2) (Coe '68)
Minn.-Morris 80   Dubuque 41-35
Minn.-Morris 80   Ithaca 0-36
Minn.-Morris 81   Lawrence 14-21 (OT)

Ray Smith (0-1) (UCLA '61)
Hope 86   Augustana (Ill.) 10-34

Ray Solari (0-1) (California '51)
Menlo 87   Central (Iowa) 0-17

Ted Stratford (1-2) (St. Lawrence '57)
St. Lawrence 76   Albright 26-7
St. Lawrence 76   Towson St. 36-38
St. Lawrence 78   Baldwin-Wallace 7-71

Barry Streeter (2-1) (Lebanon Valley '71)
Gettysburg 85   Lycoming 14-10
Gettysburg 85   Salisbury St. 22-6
Gettysburg 85   Ithaca 0-34

Bob Sullivan (0-1) (St. John's, Minn. '59)
Carleton 92   Central (Iowa) 8-20

Ed Sweeney (0-2) (LIU-C.W. Post '71)
Dickinson 89   Lycoming 0-21
Dickinson 91   Susquehanna 20-21

Andy Talley (1-1) (Southern Conn. St. '67)
St. Lawrence 82   Wagner 43-34
St. Lawrence 82   Augustana (Ill.) 0-14

Ray Tellier (0-1) (Connecticut '73)
Rochester 87   Wagner 14-38

Bob Thurness (0-1) (Coe '62)
Coe 85   Central (Iowa) 7-27

Lee Tressel (3-2) (Baldwin-Wallace '48)
Baldwin-Wallace..... 78   St. Lawrence 71-7
Baldwin-Wallace..... 78   Carnegie Mellon 31-6
Baldwin-Wallace..... 78*   Wittenberg 24-10
Baldwin-Wallace..... 79   Widener 8-29
Baldwin-Wallace..... 80   Dayton 0-34

Peter Vaas (0-1) (Holy Cross '74)
Allegheny 87   Wash. & Jeff. 17-23 (OT)

Andy Vinci (0-1) (Cal St. Los Angeles '63)
San Diego.............. 73   Wittenberg 14-21

Ken Wable (1-1) (Muskingum '52)
Mount Union 85   Denison 35-3
Mount Union 85   Augustana (Ill.) 14-21

Lou Wacker (3-3) (Richmond '56)
Emory & Henry....... 86   Salisbury St. 20-34
Emory & Henry....... 87   Ferrum 49-7
Emory & Henry....... 87   Wash. & Jeff. 23-16
Emory & Henry....... 87   Wagner 15-20
Emory & Henry....... 92   Thomas More 17-0
Emory & Henry....... 92   Wash. & Jeff. 15-51

Vic Wallace (1-1) (Cornell College '65)
St. Thomas (Minn.).. 90   Wis.-Whitewater 24-23
St. Thomas (Minn.).. 90   Central (Iowa) 32-33

Roger Welsh (0-1) (Muskingum '64)
Capital.................. 87   Dayton 28-52

Dale Widolff (1-3) (Indiana Central '75)
Occidental 83   Wis.-La Crosse 42-43
Occidental 84   Central (Iowa) 22-23
Occidental 85   St. John's (Minn.) 28-10
Occidental 85   Central (Iowa) 0-71

Jim Williams (0-3) (Northern Iowa '60)
Simpson 88   Wis.-Whitewater 27-29
Simpson 89   St. John's (Minn.) 35-42
Simpson 91   Wis.-La Crosse 13-28

National championship.

Coaching Honors

Division I-A Coach-of-the-Year Award

(Selected by the American Football Coaches Association and the Football Writers Association of America)

AFCA

1935   Lynn Waldorf, Northwestern

1936	Dick Harlow, Harvard
1937	Edward Mylin, Lafayette
1938	Bill Kern, Carnegie Mellon
1939	Eddie Anderson, Iowa
1940	Clark Shaughnessy, Stanford
1941	Frank Leahy, Notre Dame
1942	Bill Alexander, Georgia Tech
1943	Amos Alonzo Stagg, Pacific (Cal.)
1944	Carroll Widdoes, Ohio St.
1945	Bo McMillin, Indiana
1946	"Red" Blaik, Army
1947	Fritz Crisler, Michigan
1948	Bennie Oosterbaan, Michigan
1949	Bud Wilkinson, Oklahoma
1950	Charlie Caldwell, Princeton
1951	Chuck Taylor, Stanford
1952	Biggie Munn, Michigan St.
1953	Jim Tatum, Maryland
1954	"Red" Sanders, UCLA
1955	Duffy Daugherty, Michigan St.
1956	Bowden Wyatt, Tennessee
1957	"Woody" Hayes, Ohio St.
1958	Paul Dietzel, Louisiana St.
1959	Ben Schwartzwalder, Syracuse
1960	Murray Warmath, Minnesota
1961	"Bear" Bryant, Alabama
1962	John McKay, Southern Cal
1963	Darrell Royal, Texas
1964	Frank Broyles, Arkansas, and Ara Parseghian, Notre Dame
1965	Tommy Prothro, UCLA
1966	Tom Cahill, Army
1967	John Pont, Indiana
1968	Joe Paterno, Penn St.
1969	"Bo" Schembechler, Michigan
1970	Charles McClendon, Louisiana St., and Darrell Royal, Texas
1971	"Bear" Bryant, Alabama
1972	John McKay, Southern Cal
1973	"Bear" Bryant, Alabama
1974	Grant Teaff, Baylor
1975	Frank Kush, Arizona St.
1976	Johnny Majors, Pittsburgh
1977	Don James, Washington
1978	Joe Paterno, Penn St.
1979	Earle Bruce, Ohio St.
1980	Vince Dooley, Georgia
1981	Danny Ford, Clemson
1982	Joe Paterno, Penn St.
1983	Ken Hatfield, Air Force
1984	LaVell Edwards, Brigham Young
1985	Fisher DeBerry, Air Force
1986	Joe Paterno, Penn St.
1987	Dick MacPherson, Syracuse
1988	Don Nehlen, West Va.
1989	Bill McCartney, Colorado
1990	Bobby Ross, Georgia Tech
1991	Bill Lewis, East Caro.
1992	Gene Stallings, Alabama
1993	Barry Alvarez, Wisconsin

FWAA

1957	"Woody" Hayes, Ohio St.
1958	Paul Dietzel, Louisiana St.
1959	Ben Schwartzwalder, Syracuse
1960	Murray Warmath, Minnesota
1961	Darrell Royal, Texas
1962	John McKay, Southern Cal
1963	Darrell Royal, Texas
1964	Ara Parseghian, Notre Dame
1965	Duffy Daugherty, Michigan St.
1966	Tom Cahill, Army
1967	John Pont, Indiana
1968	"Woody" Hayes, Ohio St.
1969	"Bo" Schembechler, Michigan
1970	Alex Agase, Northwestern
1971	Bob Devaney, Nebraska
1972	John McKay, Southern Cal
1973	Johnny Majors, Pittsburgh
1974	Grant Teaff, Baylor
1975	"Woody" Hayes, Ohio St.
1976	Johnny Majors, Pittsburgh
1977	Lou Holtz, Arkansas
1978	Joe Paterno, Penn St.
1979	Earle Bruce, Ohio St.
1980	Vince Dooley, Georgia
1981	Danny Ford, Clemson
1982	Joe Paterno, Penn St.
1983	Howard Schnellenberger, Miami (Fla.)
1984	LaVell Edwards, Brigham Young
1985	Fisher DeBerry, Air Force
1986	Joe Paterno, Penn St.

1987	Dick MacPherson, Syracuse
1988	Lou Holtz, Notre Dame
1989	Bill McCartney, Colorado
1990	Bobby Ross, Georgia Tech
1991	Don James, Washington
1992	Gene Stallings, Alabama
1993	Terry Bowden, Auburn

Division I-AA Coach-of-the-Year Award

(Selected by the American Football Coaches Association)

1983	Rey Dempsey, Southern Ill.
1984	Dave Arnold, Montana St.
1985	Dick Sheridan, Furman
1986	Erk Russell, Ga. Southern
1987	Mark Duffner, Holy Cross
1988	Jimmy Satterfield, Furman
1989	Erk Russell, Ga. Southern
1990	Tim Stowers, Ga. Southern
1991	Mark Duffner, Holy Cross
1992	Charlie Taafe, Citadel
1993	Dan Allen, Boston U.

Small College Coach-of-the-Year Awards

(Selected by the American Football Coaches Association)

COLLEGE DIVISION

1960	Warren Woodson, New Mexico St.
1961	Jake Gaither, Florida A&M
1962	Bill Edwards, Wittenberg
1963	Bill Edwards, Wittenberg
1964	Clarence Stasavich, East Caro.
1965	Jack Curtice, UC Santa Barb.
1966	Dan Jessee, Trinity (Conn.)
1967	A. C. "Scrappy" Moore, Tenn.-Chatt.
1968	Jim Root, New Hampshire
1969	Larry Naviaux, Boston U.
1970	Bennie Ellender, Arkansas St.
1971	Harold "Tubby" Raymond, Delaware
1972	Harold "Tubby" Raymond, Delaware
1973	Dave Maurer, Wittenberg
1974	Roy Kramer, Central Mich.
1975	Dave Maurer, Wittenberg
1976	Jim Dennison, Akron
1977	Bill Manlove, Widener
1978	Lee Tressel, Baldwin-Wallace
1979	Bill Narduzzi, Youngstown St.
1980	Rick Carter, Dayton
1981	Vito Ragazzo, Shippensburg
1982	Jim Wacker, Southwest Tex. St.

COLLEGE DIVISION I

(NCAA Division II and NAIA Division I)

1983	Don Morton, North Dak. St.
1984	Chan Gailey, Troy St.
1985	George Landis, Bloomsburg
1986	Earle Solomonson, North Dak. St.
1987	Rick Rhoades, Troy St.
1988	Rocky Hager, North Dak. St.
1989	John Williams, Mississippi Col.
1990	Rocky Hager, North Dak. St.
1991	Frank Cignetti, Indiana (Pa.)
1992	Bill Burgess, Jacksonville St.
1993	Bobby Wallace, North Ala.

COLLEGE DIVISION II

(NCAA Division III and NAIA Division II)

1983	Bob Reade, Augustana (Ill.)
1984	Bob Reade, Augustana (Ill.)
1985	Bob Reade, Augustana (Ill.)
1986	Bob Reade, Augustana (Ill.)
1987	Walt Hameline, Wagner
1988	Jim Butterfield, Ithaca
1989	Mike Kelly, Dayton
1990	Ken O'Keefe, Allegheny
1991	Mike Kelly, Dayton
1992	John Luckhardt, Wash. & Jeff.
1993	Larry Kehres, Mount Union

Added and Discontinued Programs

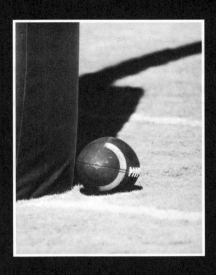

Nationally Prominent Teams That Permanently Dropped Football

Listed alphabetically at right are the all-time records of teams formerly classified as major college that permanently discontinued football. Also included are those teams that, retroactively, are considered to have been major college (before the advent of official classification in 1937) by virtue of their schedules (i.e., at least half of their games versus other major-college opponents). All schools listed were considered to have been major college or classified in either Division I-A or I-AA for a minimum of 10 consecutive seasons.

Team	Inclusive Seasons	Years	Won	Lost	Tied	Pct.†
Cal St. Fullerton	1970-1992	23	107	150	3	.417
Carlisle Indian School	1893-1917	25	167	88	13	.647
Centenary (La.)	1894-1947	36	148	100	21	.589
Creighton	1900-1942	43	183	139	27	.563
Denver	1885-1960	73	273	262	40	.510
Detroit Mercy	1896-1964	64	305	200	25	.599
Geo. Washington	1890-1966	58	209	240	34	.468
Gonzaga	1892-1941	39	130	99	20	.562
Haskell Institute	1896-1938	43	199	166	18	.543
Lamar	1951-1989	39	171	225	9	.433
Long Beach St.	1955-1991	37	199	183	4	.521
Manhattan	1923-1942	20	77	75	11	.506
Marquette	1892-1960	68	273	220	38	.550
New York U.	1873-1952	66	201	231	32	.468
San Francisco	*1924-1951; 1959-1971	38	133	169	20	.444
St. Louis	1899-1949	49	235	179	33	.563
Texas-Arlington	1959-1985	27	129	150	2	.463
Wichita St.	1897-1986	89	375	402	47	.484
Xavier (Ohio)	1900-1973	61	302	223	21	.572

†Ties computed as half won and half lost. *Discontinued football during 1952 after having been classified major college. Resumed at the Division II level during 1959-71, when it was discontinued again.

Added or Resumed Programs Since 1968

NCAA Member Colleges

1968 (4)
Boise St.; *Chicago; Jersey City St.; Nevada-Las Vegas.

1969 (2)
*Adelphi (dropped 1972); Towson St.

1970 (6)
Cal St. Fullerton (dropped 1993); *Fordham; *Georgetown; Plattsburgh St. (dropped 1979); Plymouth St.; *St. Mary's (Cal.).

1971 (6)
Boston St. (dropped 1982); D.C. Teachers (dropped 1974); Federal City (dropped 1975); *New England Col. (dropped 1973); Rochester Tech (dropped 1978); St. Peter's (suspended after one game 1984, resumed 1985, dropped 1988, resumed 1989).

1972 (6)
Kean; *Lake Forest; Nicholls St.; Salisbury St.; *San Diego; Wm. Paterson.

1973 (7)
Albany St. (N.Y.); *Benedictine; Bowie St.; James Madison; New Haven; New York Tech (dropped 1984); Seton Hall (dropped 1982).

1974 (2)
FDU-Madison; Framingham St.

1975 (2)
*Brooklyn (dropped 1991); *Canisius.

1976 (1)
Oswego St. (dropped 1977).

1977 (2)
*Catholic; *Mankato St.

1978 (7)
*Buffalo; Dist. Columbia; Iona; Marist; Pace; *St. Francis (Pa.); *St. John's (N.Y.).

1979 (2)
Central Fla.; *Duquesne.

1980 (5)
*Loras; Mass.-Lowell; *Miles (dropped 1989, resumed 1990); Ramapo (dropped 1993); *Sonoma St.

1981 (4)
Buffalo St.; Mercyhurst; *West Ga.; Western New Eng.

1982 (2)
Valdosta St.; Westfield St.

1983 (2)
*Ky. Wesleyan; Stony Brook.

1984 (3)
Fitchburg St.; *Ga. Southern; *Samford.

1985 (6)
Ferrum; MacMurray; N.Y. Maritime (dropped 1986, resumed 1987, dropped 1989); *St. Peter's (dropped 1988, resumed 1989); *Villanova; Worcester St.

1986 (4)
Menlo; *Quincy; *UC Santa Barb.; Wesley.

1987 (5)
*Aurora; *Drake; Gallaudet; *N.Y. Maritime (dropped 1989); St. John Fisher.

1988 (7)
Assumption; Bentley; Mass.-Boston; Mass.-Dartmouth; *MIT (last team was in 1901); Siena; Stonehill.

1989 (5)
*Gannon; Merrimack; Methodist; *Southern Methodist; *St. Peter's.

1990 (3)
*Hardin-Simmons; *Miles; Thomas More.

1991 (3)
Ala.-Birmingham; Charleston So.; Sacred Heart.

1992 (1)
*West Tex. A&M.

1993 (3)
King's (Pa.); Monmouth (N.J.); Salve Regina.

1994 (2)
Chapman; Robert Morris.

*Previously dropped football.

Non-NCAA Senior Colleges

1968 (2)
#Mo. Southern St.; #Southwest St.

1970 (1)
#Mo. Western St.

1971 (3)
Concordia-St. Paul (Minn.); #Gardner-Webb; #Grand Valley St.

1972 (5)
Dr. Martin Luther; #Mars Hill; N'western (Minn.); Pillsbury; #Western Conn. St.

1973 (2)
#Liberty; #Mass. Maritime.

1974 (3)
#*N.M. Highlands; #Northeastern Ill. (dropped 1988); #Saginaw Valley.

1976 (2)
Maranatha; #Mesa St.

1977 (2)
Evangel; Olivet Nazarene.

1978 (3)
*Baptist Christian (dropped 1983); *St. Ambrose; *Yankton (dropped 1984).

1979 (2)
Fort Lauderdale (dropped 1982); Lubbock Christian (dropped 1983).

1980 (1)
Mid-America Nazarene.

1983 (2)
Ga. Southwestern (dropped 1989); #Loras.

1984 (3)
#Southwest Baptist; St. Paul Bible; *Union (Ky.).

1985 (4)
*Cumberland (Ky.); *Lambuth; *Tenn. Wesleyan; Tiffin.

1986 (4)
St. Francis (Ill.); Trinity Bible (N.D.); Urbana; #Wingate.

1987 (1)
Greenville.

1988 (5)
Campbellsville; Mary; Midwestern St.; Trinity (Ill.); *Western Mont.

1990 (2)
Lindenwood; Mt. St. Joseph (Ohio).

1991 (3)
Clinch Valley; Lees-McRae (dropped 1994); Tusculum.

1993 (6)
Ark.-Pine Bluff; Bethel (Tenn.); Chowan; Malone; St. Xavier (Ill.); Sue Bennett (Ky.).

*Previously dropped football. #Now NCAA member.

Discontinued Programs Since 1950

(Includes NCAA member colleges and non-member colleges; also colleges that closed or merged with other institutions.)

1950 (9)
Alliance; Canisius (resumed 1975); Huntington; Oklahoma City; *Portland; Rio Grande; Rollins; *St. Louis; Steubenville.

1951 (38)
Arkansas Col.; Atlantic Christian; Canterbury; Catholic (resumed 1977); CCNY; Corpus Christi (resumed 1954, dropped 1967); Daniel Baker; Detroit Tech; *Duquesne (resumed 1979); East Tex. Baptist; Gannon (resumed 1989); *Georgetown (resumed 1970); Glassboro St. (resumed 1964—name changed to Rowan in 1992); Hartwick; High Point; LeMoyne-Owen; Lowell Textile; Lycoming (resumed 1954); McKendree; Milligan; Mt. St. Mary's (Md.); Nevada (resumed 1952); New Bedford Textile; New England Col. (resumed 1971, dropped 1973); Niagara; Northern Idaho; Panzer; Shurtleff (resumed 1953, dropped 1954); Southern Idaho; Southwestern (Tenn.) (resumed 1952—name changed to Rhodes in 1986); Southwestern (Tex.); St. Mary's (Cal.) (resumed 1970); St. Michael's (N.M.); Tillotson; Tusculum (resumed 1991); Washington (Md.); West Va. Wesleyan (resumed 1953); William Penn (resumed 1953).

1952 (13)
Aquinas; Clarkson; Erskine; Louisville Municipal; *Loyola Marymount; Nebraska Central; Rider; Samuel Huston; *San Francisco (resumed 1959, dropped 1972); Shaw (resumed 1953, dropped 1979); St. Bonaventure; St. Martin's; Teikyo Westmar (resumed 1953).

1953 (10)
Arnold; Aurora; Bethel (Tenn.) (resumed 1993); Cedarville; Champlain; Davis & Elkins (resumed 1955, dropped 1962); Georgetown (Ky.) (resumed 1955); *New York U.; *Santa Clara (resumed 1959, dropped 1993); Union (Tenn.).

1954 (8)
Adelphi (resumed 1969, dropped 1972); Case Tech (resumed 1955); Quincy (resumed 1986); Shurtleff; St. Francis (Pa.) (resumed 1978); St. Michael's (Vt.); *Wash. & Lee (resumed 1955); York (Neb.).

1955 (2)
*Fordham (resumed 1970); St. Mary's (Minn.).

1956 (4)
Brooklyn (resumed 1975, dropped 1991); Hendrix (resumed 1957, dropped 1961); William Carey; Wisconsin Extension.

1957 (4)
Lewis; Midwestern (Iowa) (resumed 1966); Morris Harvey; Stetson.

1959 (2)
Florida N&I; West Ga. (resumed 1981).

1960 (5)
Brandeis; Leland; Loras (resumed 1980); St. Ambrose (resumed 1978); Xavier (La.).

1961 (9)
*Denver; Hawaii (resumed 1962); Hendrix; Lincoln (Pa.); *Marquette; Paul Quinn; Scranton; Texas College; Tougaloo.

1962 (5)
Azusa Pacific (resumed 1965); Davis & Elkins; San Diego (resumed 1972); Southern Cal Col.; Westminster (Utah) (resumed 1965, dropped 1979).

1963 (3)
Benedictine (resumed 1973); *Hardin-Simmons (resumed 1990); St. Vincent (Pa.).

1964 (2)
King's (Pa.) (resumed 1993); Paine.

1965 (7)
Claflin; *Detroit Mercy; Dillard; Miss. Industrial; Morris; Philander Smith; Rust.

1966 (1)
St. Augustine's.

1967 (6)
Benedict; Corpus Christi; *Geo. Washington; Jarvis Christian; Ozarks; South Caro. Trade.

1968 (2)
Edward Waters; Frederick.

1969 (6)
Allen; Case Tech and Western Reserve merged to form Case Western Reserve; George Fox; Louisiana Col.; UC San Diego; Wiley.

1971 (5)
Bradley; *Buffalo (resumed 1978); Hiram Scott; Lake Forest (resumed 1972); Parsons.

1972 (8)
Adelphi; Haverford; North Dak.-Ellendale; Northern Mont.; Northwood (Tex.); San Francisco; Sonoma St. (resumed 1980); UC Santa Barb. (resumed 1986).

1973 (2)
New England Col.; N.M. Highlands (resumed 1974).

1974 (6)
Col. of Emporia; D.C. Teachers; Drexel; Ill.-Chicago; Samford (resumed 1984); *Xavier (Ohio).

1975 (6)
Baptist Christian (resumed 1978, dropped 1983); Bridgeport; Federal City; *Tampa; Vermont; Wis.-Milwaukee.

1976 (3)
Mankato St. (resumed 1977); Northland; UC Riverside.

1977 (4)
Cal Tech; Oswego St.; Whitman; Yankton (resumed 1978, dropped 1984).

1978 (3)
Cal St. Los Angeles; Col. of Idaho; Rochester Tech.

1979 (5)
Eastern Mont.; Miles (resumed 1980); Plattsburgh St.; Shaw; Westminster (Utah).

1980 (3)
†Gallaudet; Md.-East. Shore; U.S. Int'l.

1981 (2)
Bluefield St.; *Villanova (resumed 1985).

1982 (4)
Boston St.; Fort Lauderdale; Milton; Seton Hall.

1983 (3)
Baptist Christian; Cal Poly Pomona; Lubbock Christian.

1984 (5)
Fisk; New York Tech; So. Dak.-Springfield; St. Peter's (suspended after one game, resumed 1985, dropped 1988, resumed 1989); Yankton.

1985 (1)
Southern Colo.

1986 (4)
Drake (resumed 1987); N.Y. Maritime (resumed 1987, dropped 1989); Southeastern La.; *Texas-Arlington.

1987 (4)
Bishop; *Southern Methodist (resumed 1989); Western Mont. (resumed 1988); *Wichita St.

1988 (4)
Northeastern Ill.; St. Paul's; St. Peter's (resumed 1989); Texas Lutheran.

1989 (3)
Ga. Southwestern; Miles (resumed 1990); N.Y. Maritime.

1990 (1)
*Lamar.

1991 (3)
Brooklyn; Tarkio; West Tex. A&M (resumed 1992).

1992 (3)
*Long Beach St.; Pacific (Ore.); St. Mary of the Plains.

1993 (5)
*Cal St. Fullerton; Cameron; Ramapo; Santa Clara; Wis.-Superior.

1994 (3)
Cal St. Hayward; Lees-McRae; Oregon Tech.

*Classified major college previous year. †Did not play a 7-game varsity schedule, 1980-86.

Championship Results

Division I-AA Championship

1993 Title Game Summary

MARSHALL UNIVERSITY STADIUM, HUNTINGTON, W. VA.; DECEMBER 18, 1993

Doug Pensinger/Allsport photo

Youngstown State running back Tamron Smith celebrates his team's 17-5 victory over Marshall in the 1993 Division I-AA title game. Smith ran for 109 yards and one touchdown to help the Penguins capture their second title in three years.

	Youngstown St.	Marshall
First Downs	16	16
Rushes-Net Yardage	55-220	35-49
Passing Yardage	75	207
Return Yardage (Punts, Int. & Fum.)	33	0
Passes (Comp.-Att.-Int.)	7-8-0	19-29-2
Punts (Number-Average)	3-47.3	3-37.0
Fumbles (Number-Lost)	2-1	1-1
Penalties (Number-Yards)	9-79	3-24

Youngstown St.	17	0	0	0—17	
Marshall	0	0	3	2— 5	

Game Conditions: Temperature, 48 degrees; wind, 10 mph from southwest; weather, overcast. Attendance: 29,218.

FIRST QUARTER
Youngstown St.—Darnell Clark 50 run (Jeff Wilkins kick) (65 yards in 2 plays, 14:27 left)
Youngstown St.—Tamron Smith 5 run (Wilkins kick) (5 yards in 1 play, 12:21 left)
Youngstown St.—Wilkins 19 field goal (73 yards in 15 plays, 1:53 left)

THIRD QUARTER
Marshall—David Merrick 27 field goal (70 yards in 10 plays, 3:34 left)

FOURTH QUARTER
Marshall—Safety, Wilkins ran out of end zone (2:52 left)

INDIVIDUAL LEADERS
Rushing—Youngstown St.: Smith, 109 yards on 24 carries; Marshall: Chris Parker, 47 yards on 17 carries.
Passing—Youngstown St.: Mark Brungard, 7 of 8 for 75 yards; Marshall: Todd Donnan, 19 of 29 for 207 yards.
Receiving—Youngstown St.: Don Zwisler, 2 catches for 38 yards; Marshall: Will Brown, 7 catches for 94 yards.

NCAA I-AA Football Championship History

1978 At the 72nd NCAA Convention (January 1978) in Atlanta, Ga., the membership voted to establish the Division I-AA Football Championship and a statistics program for the division. The format for the first I-AA championship, held in Wichita Falls, Texas, was a single-elimination, four-team tournament. Florida A&M defeated Massachusetts, 35-28, in the title game. The game was televised by ABC.

1981 The championship expanded to include eight teams in a single-elimination tournament.

1982 The championship expanded to include 12 teams. Eight teams played first-round games at campus sites, and the top four teams, seeded by the Division I-AA Football Committee, received byes.

1986 The championship field expanded to its current format of 16 teams with each team playing a first-round game.

1987 Northeast Louisiana defeated Marshall, 43-42, in the closest game in championship history.

1989 A then-record 25,725 fans watched Georgia Southern down Stephen F. Austin, 37-34, in the championship game at Allen E. Paulson Stadium in Statesboro, Ga.

1990 Georgia Southern won its fourth I-AA championship, adding to its titles in 1985, 1986 and 1989.

1991 Youngstown State won its first national championship with a 25-17 victory over Marshall. Penguin head coach Jim Tressel joined his father, Lee, as the only father-son combination to win NCAA football titles. Lee Tressel won the 1978 Division III championship at Baldwin-Wallace.

1992 A championship-record crowd of 31,304 in Huntington, W.Va., saw Marshall return the favor with a 31-28 win over Youngstown State for its first I-AA title.

1993 The I-AA championship provided for a maximum field of 16 teams. Six member conferences (Big Sky, Gateway, Ohio Valley, Southern, Southland and Yankee) were granted automatic qualification for their respective winners. Youngstown State won its second I-AA title with a 17-5 victory over Marshall before a crowd of 29,218 in Huntington.

Division I-AA All-Time Championship Results

Year	Champion	Coach	Score	Runner-Up	Site
1978	Florida A&M	Rudy Hubbard	35-28	Massachusetts	Wichita Falls, Texas
1979	Eastern Ky.	Roy Kidd	30-7	Lehigh	Orlando, Fla.
1980	Boise St.	Jim Criner	31-29	Eastern Ky.	Sacramento, Calif.
1981	Idaho St.	Dave Kragthorpe	34-23	Eastern Ky.	Wichita Falls, Texas
1982	Eastern Ky.	Roy Kidd	17-14	Delaware	Wichita Falls, Texas
1983	Southern Ill.	Rey Dempsey	43-7	Western Caro.	Charleston, S.C.
1984	Montana St.	Dave Arnold	19-6	Louisiana Tech	Charleston, S.C.
1985	Ga. Southern	Erk Russell	44-42	Furman	Tacoma, Wash.
1986	Ga. Southern	Erk Russell	48-21	Arkansas St.	Tacoma, Wash.
1987	Northeast La.	Pat Collins	43-42	Marshall	Pocatello, Idaho
1988	Furman	Jimmy Satterfield	17-12	Ga. Southern	Pocatello, Idaho
1989	Ga. Southern	Erk Russell	37-34	*Stephen F. Austin	Statesboro, Ga.
1990	Ga. Southern	Tim Stowers	36-13	Nevada	Statesboro, Ga.
1991	Youngstown St.	Jim Tressel	25-17	Marshall	Statesboro, Ga.
1992	Marshall	Jim Donnan	31-28	Youngstown St.	Huntington, W.Va.
1993	Youngstown St.	Jim Tressel	17-5	Marshall	Huntington, W.Va.

*Stephen F. Austin's participation in 1989 Division I-AA championship vacated.

1993 Division I-AA Championship Results

FIRST ROUND
Ga. Southern 14, Eastern Ky. 12
Youngstown St. 56, Central Fla. 30
Boston U. 27, Northern Iowa 21 (2 OT)
Idaho 34, Northeast La. 31
Delaware 49, Montana 48
Marshall 28, Howard 14
McNeese St. 34, William & Mary 28
Troy St. 42, Stephen F. Austin 20

QUARTERFINALS
Youngstown St. 34, Ga. Southern 14
Idaho 21, Boston U. 14
Marshall 34, Delaware 31
Troy St. 35, McNeese St. 28

SEMIFINALS
Youngstown St. 35, Idaho 16
Marshall 24, Troy St. 21

CHAMPIONSHIP
Youngstown St. 17, Marshall 5

1993 Division I-AA Game Summaries

FIRST-ROUND GAMES (NOV. 27)

Ga. Southern 14, Eastern Ky. 12
at Statesboro, Ga.

Eastern Ky.	0	3	0	9—12
Ga. Southern	7	0	7	0—14

GS—Fraley 9 run (Haley kick)
EK—Collins 44 field goal
GS— Warthen 2 run (Haley kick)
EK—Collins 33 field goal
EK—Brown 27 run (run failed)
A—7,278

Youngstown St. 56, Central Fla. 30
at Youngstown, Ohio

Central Fla.	10	0	7	13—30
Youngstown St.	7	28	14	7—56

CF—Wouda 1 pass from Hinshaw (Pierce kick)
YS—Boykin 67 pass from Brungard (Wilkins kick)
CF—Pierce 33 field goal
YS—Burch 57 interception return (Wilkins kick)
YS—Clark 7 run (Wilkins kick)
YS—Brungard 1 run (Wilkins kick)
YS—Boykin 8 pass from Brungard (Wilkins kick)
YS—Smith 1 run (Wilkins kick)
YS—Vogt 21 run (Wilkins kick)
CF—Rhodes 15 pass from Hinshaw (Pierce kick)
CF—Rhodes 31 pass from Hinshaw (Pierce kick)
YS—Clark 8 run (Wilkins kick)
CF—Rhodes 7 pass from Hinshaw (pass failed)
A—7,408

Boston U. 27, Northern Iowa 21 (2 OT)
at Boston, Mass.

Northern Iowa	3	9	0	0	0—21	
Boston U.	0	6	7	8	0	6—27

NI—Obermeier 28 field goal
NI—Warner 1 run (kick failed)
BU—Dougherty 1 run (pass failed)
NI—Obermeier 36 field goal
NI—Ward 40 pass from Warner (Obermeier kick)
NI—Safety, Dougherty intentionally grounded ball in end zone
BU—Schaefer 48 fumble return (Morello kick)
BU—Dougherty 5 run (Andrade pass from Dougherty)
BU—Burwell 4 run (no kick attempt)
A—6,882

Idaho 34, Northeast La. 31
at Monroe, La.

Idaho	7	7	7	13—34
Northeast La.	7	3	0	21—31

I—May 17 pass from Nussmeier (Hollis kick)
N—Williams 7 pass from Cobb (Miller kick)
I—Nussmeier 5 run (Hollis kick)
N—Miller 22 field goal
I—Gary 64 pass from Nussmeier (Hollis kick)
N—Boyett 1 pass from Cobb (pass failed)
I—Neal 44 pass from Nussmeier (pass failed)

N—Bamburg 26 pass from Cobb (Williams pass from Cobb)
I—Gilroy 3 pass from Nussmeier (Hollis kick)
N—Williams 73 pass from Cobb (Miller kick)
A—5,500

Delaware 49, Montana 48
at Missoula, Mont.

Delaware	14	7	7	21—49
Montana	7	21	0	20—48

M—Stenstrud 3 pass from Dickenson (Larson kick)
D—Brown 6 run (Leo kick)
D—Langan 7 run (Leo kick)
D—Brown 20 run (Leo kick)
M—Dickenson 1 run (Larson kick)
M—Gurnsey 22 pass from Dickenson (Larson kick)
M—Stensrud 2 run (Larson kick)
D—Malloy 18 pass from Hamlett (Leo kick)
M—Gurnsey 13 pass from Dickenson (Larson kick)
D—Johnson 3 run (Leo kick)
M—Wells 5 pass from Dickenson (Larson kick)
D—Johnson 70 run (Leo kick)
M—Boddie 80 kickoff return (kick failed)
D—Malloy 32 pass from Hamlett (Leo kick)
A—11,271

Marshall 28, Howard 14
at Huntington, W.Va.

Howard	7	7	0	0—14
Marshall	14	7	7	0—28

M—Thomas 60 run (Merrick kick)
M—Parker 17 run (Merrick kick)
H—Grant 18 run (Decuir kick)
H—Grant 5 run (Decuir kick)
M—Parker 3 run (Merrick kick)
M— Carter 30 pass from Donnan (Merrick kick)
A—13,554

McNeese St. 34, William & Mary 28
at Lake Charles, La.

William & Mary	7	21	0	0—28
McNeese St.	14	6	11	3—34

WM—Knight 5 run (Dawson kick)
MS—Henry 61 pass from Joseph (Larios kick)
MS—Warren 4 pass from Joseph (Larios kick)
WM—Keen 1 run (Dawson kick)
MS—Owens 55 pass from Joseph (kick failed)
WM—Keen 2 run (Dawson kick)
WM—Keen 2 run (Dawson kick)
MS—Fields 6 run (Joseph run)
MS—Larios 25 field goal
MS—Larios 25 field goal
A—17,167

Troy St. 42, Stephen F. Austin 20
at Troy, Ala.

Stephen F. Austin	6	6	0	8—20
Troy St.	14	7	7	14—42

TS—Polite 4 pass from Simmons (Quass kick)
SF—Pearce 7 pass from Ritchey (kick failed)
TS—Parker 51 pass from Simmons (Quass kick)
SF—Goodwin 9 pass from Ritchey (pass failed)
TS—Godwin 2 run (Quass kick)
TS—Parker 88 kickoff return (Quass kick)
TS—Godwin 2 run (Quass kick)
TS—Kilow 25 pass from Simmons (Quass kick)
SF—Goodwin 7 pass from Goddard (Pearce pass from Goddard)
A—4,500

QUARTERFINAL GAMES (DEC. 4)

Youngstown St. 34, Ga. Southern 14
at Youngstown, Ohio

Ga. Southern	0	0	7	7—14
Youngstown St.	10	17	7	0—34

YS—Wilkins 36 field goal
YS—Mason fumble recovery in end zone (Wilkins kick)
YS—Wilkins 25 field goal
YS—Smith 1 run (Wilkins kick)
YS—Quintana 22 pass from Brungard (Wilkins kick)
GS—Bostick 2 run (Haley kick)
YS—Quintana 8 pass from Brungard (Wilkins kick)
GS— Bostick 4 run (Haley kick)
A—9,503

Idaho 21, Boston U. 14
at Moscow, Idaho

Boston U.	0	0	0	14—14
Idaho	7	0	14	0—21

I—May 1 run (Hollis kick)
I—Thomas 16 run (Hollis kick)
I—Gilroy 83 pass from Nussmeier (Hollis kick)
BU—Walker 5 run from Pincince (Morello kick)

BU—Walker 13 pass from Pincince (Morello kick)
A—8,800

Marshall 34, Delaware 31
at Huntington, W.Va.

Delaware	10	7	0	14—31
Marshall	7	7	10	10—34

M—Parker 3 run (Merrick kick)
D—Brown 31 run (Leo kick)
D—Leo 36 field goal
M—Parker 5 run (Merrick kick)
D—Brown 22 pass from Hamlett (Leo kick)
M—Parker 3 run (Merrick kick)
M—Merrick 26 field goal
M—Parker 2 run (Merrick kick)
D—Cooper 20 pass from Fry (Leo kick)
D—Malloy 11 pass from Fry (Leo kick)
M—Merrick 38 field goal
A—13,687

Troy St. 35, McNeese St. 28
at Lake Charles, La.

Troy St.	14	14	7	0—35
McNeese St.	0	21	0	7—28

TS—Parker 32 pass from Simmons (Quass kick)
TS—Simmons 16 run (Quass kick)
TS—Parker 88 pass from Simmons (Quass kick)
MS—Brown 18 run (Larios kick)
TS—Brady 31 pass from Simmons (Quass kick)
MS—Fields 7 run (Larios kick)
MS—Nunez 2 pass from Joseph (Larios kick)
TS—Simmons 7 run (Quass kick)
MS—Joseph 19 run (Larios kick)
A—20,000

SEMIFINAL GAMES (DEC. 11)

Youngstown St. 35, Idaho 16
at Youngstown, Ohio

Idaho	10	6	0	0—16
Youngstown St.	7	7	14	7—35

I—May 1 run (Hollis kick)
YS—Jones 42 fumble return (Wilkins kick)
I—Hollis 43 field goal
I—Hollis 21 field goal
YS—Smith 2 run (Wilkins kick)
I—Hollis 24 field goal
YS—Smith 8 run (Wilkins kick)
YS—Zwisler 39 pass from Brungard (Wilkins kick)
YS—Clark 15 run (Wilkins kick)
A—9,644

Marshall 24, Troy St. 21
at Huntington, W.Va.

Troy St.	0	21	0	0—21
Marshall	17	7	0	0—24

M—Parker 2 run (Merrick kick)
M—Merrick 37 field goal
M—Chapman 5 blocked punt return (Merrick kick)
TS—Davis 16 pass from Simmons (Quass kick)
TS—Godwin 1 run (Quass kick)
M—Martin 17 pass from Donnan (Merrick kick)
TS—Kilow 3 pass from Simmons (Quass kick)
A—14,472

Championship Records

INDIVIDUAL: SINGLE GAME

NET YARDS RUSHING
250—Greg Robinson, Northeast La. (78) vs. Alcorn St. (27), 11-28-92.

RUSHES ATTEMPTED
46—Tamron Smith, Youngstown St. (10) vs. Samford (0), 12-14-91.

TOUCHDOWNS BY RUSHING
6—Sean Sanders, Weber St. (59) vs. Idaho (30), 11-28-87.

NET YARDS PASSING
517—Todd Hammel, Stephen F. Austin (59) vs. Grambling (56), 11-25-89.

PASSES ATTEMPTED
78—Tom Ehrhardt, Rhode Island (15) vs. Furman (59), 12-7-85.

PASSES COMPLETED
44—Willie Totten, Mississippi Val. (19) vs. Louisiana Tech (66), 11-24-84.

PASSES HAD INTERCEPTED
7—Jeff Gilbert, Western Caro. (7) vs. Southern Ill. (43), 12-17-83.

TOUCHDOWN PASSES COMPLETED
6—Mike Smith, Northern Iowa (41) vs. Northeast La. (44), 12-12-87; Clemente Gordon, Grambling (56) vs. Stephen F. Austin (59), 11-25-89.

COMPLETION PERCENTAGE
(Min. 15 Attempts)
.841—Dave Dickenson, Montana (48) vs. Delaware (49), 11-27-93 (37 of 44).

NET YARDS RUSHING AND PASSING
539—Todd Hammel, Stephen F. Austin (59) vs. Grambling (56), 11-25-89 (517 passing, 22 rushing).

NUMBER OF RUSHING AND PASSING PLAYS
87—Steve McNair, Alcorn St. (27) vs. Northeast La. (78), 11-28-92.

PUNTING AVERAGE
(Min. 3 Punts)
50.3—Steve Rowe, Eastern Ky. (38) vs. Idaho (30), 12-4-82.

NUMBER OF PUNTS
14—Fred McRae, Jackson St. (0) vs. Stephen F. Austin (24), 11-26-88.

PASSES CAUGHT
18—Brian Forster, Rhode Island (23) vs. Richmond (17), 12-1-84.

NET YARDS RECEIVING
264—Winky White, Boise St. (52) vs. Nevada (59), 3 OT, 12-8-90 (11 catches).

TOUCHDOWN PASSES CAUGHT
4—Tony DiMaggio, Rhode Island (35) vs. Akron (27), 11-30-85.

PASSES INTERCEPTED
4—Greg Shipp, Southern Ill. (43) vs. Western Caro. (7), 12-17-83.

YARDS GAINED ON INTERCEPTION RETURNS
117—Kevin Sullivan, Massachusetts (44) vs. Nevada (21), 12-9-78.

YARDS GAINED ON PUNT RETURNS
95—Troy Brown, Marshall (44) vs. Eastern Ky. (0), 11-28-92.

YARDS GAINED ON KICKOFF RETURNS
232—Mike Cadore, Eastern Ky. (32) vs. Northeast La. (33), 12-5-87, 6 returns, 1 for 99-yard TD.

YARDS GAINED ON FUMBLE RETURNS
65—Todd Lair, Citadel (44) vs. North Caro. A&T (0), 11-28-92.

POINTS
36—Sean Sanders, Weber St. (59) vs. Idaho (30), 11-28-87.

TOUCHDOWNS
6—Sean Sanders, Weber St. (59) vs. Idaho (30), 11-28-87.

EXTRA POINTS
9—George Benyola, Louisiana Tech (66) vs. Mississippi Val. (19), 11-24-84; Rob Tallent, Northeast La. (78) vs. Alcorn St. (27), 11-28-92.

FIELD GOALS
4—Jeff Wilkins, Youngstown St. (19) vs. Northern Iowa (7), 12-12-92.

INDIVIDUAL: TOURNAMENT

NET YARDS RUSHING
661—Tracy Ham, Ga. Southern, 1986 (128 vs. North Caro. A&T, 191 vs. Nicholls St., 162 vs. Nevada, 180 vs. Arkansas St.).

RUSHES ATTEMPTED
123—Ray Whalen, Nevada, 1990 (21 vs. Northeast La., 34 vs. Furman, 44 vs. Boise St., 24 vs. Ga. Southern).

NET YARDS PASSING
1,449—Todd Hammel, Stephen F. Austin, 1989 (517

vs. Grambling, 405 vs. Southwest Mo. St., 224 vs. Furman, 303 vs. Ga. Southern).

PASSES ATTEMPTED
177—Jeff Gilbert, Western Caro., 1983 (47 vs. Colgate, 52 vs. Holy Cross, 45 vs. Furman, 33 vs. Southern Ill.).

PASSES COMPLETED
94—Stan Humphries, Northeast La., 1987 (19 vs. North Texas, 33 vs. Eastern Ky., 16 vs. Northern Iowa, 26 vs. Marshall).

TOUCHDOWN PASSES COMPLETED
14—Todd Hammel, Stephen F. Austin, 1989 (5 vs. Grambling, 4 vs. Southwest Mo. St., 2 vs. Furman, 3 vs. Ga. Southern).

COMPLETION PERCENTAGE
(Min. 2 Games)
.667—Steve Nolan, Idaho, 1990, 56 of 84 (24-41 vs. Southwest Mo. St., 32-43 vs. Ga. Southern); Michael Payton, Marshall, 1992, 68 of 102 (26-35 vs. Eastern Ky., 3-5 vs. Middle Tenn. St., 14-23 vs. Delaware, 25-39 vs. Youngstown St.).

PASSES HAD INTERCEPTED
11—Todd Hammel, Stephen F. Austin, 1989 (0 vs. Grambling, 4 vs. Southwest Mo. St., 2 vs. Furman, 5 vs. Ga. Southern).

PASSES CAUGHT
36—Ross Ortega, Nevada, 1990 (1 vs. Northeast La., 15 vs. Furman, 10 vs. Boise St., 10 vs. Ga. Southern).

NET YARDS RECEIVING
545—Troy Brown, Marshall, 1992 (188 vs. Eastern Ky., 189 vs. Middle Tenn. St., 53 vs. Delaware, 115 vs. Youngstown St.).

TOUCHDOWN PASSES CAUGHT
6—Keith Baxter, Marshall, 1987 (1 vs. James Madison, 3 vs. Weber St., 0 vs. Appalachian St., 2 vs. Northeast La.).

POINTS
66—Gerald Harris, Ga. Southern, 1986 (30 vs. North Caro. A&T, 18 vs. Nicholls St., 12 vs. Nevada, 6 vs. Arkansas St.).

TOUCHDOWNS
11—Gerald Harris, Ga. Southern, 1986 (5 vs. North Caro. A&T, 3 vs. Nicholls St., 2 vs. Nevada, 1 vs. Arkansas St.).

INDIVIDUAL: LONGEST PLAYS

LONGEST RUSH
81—Brigham Lyons, Middle Tenn. St. (21) vs. Marshall (35), 12-5-92, TD.

LONGEST PASS (INCLUDING RUN)
90—Paul Singer 22 pass to Derek Swanson and 68 fumble recovery advancement by Steve Williams, Western Ill. (32) vs. Western Ky. (35), 11-26-88.

LONGEST FIELD GOAL
56—Tony Zendejas, Nevada (27) vs. Idaho St. (20), 11-26-83.

LONGEST PUNT
88—Mike Cassidy, Rhode Island (20) vs. Montana St. (32), 12-8-84.

LONGEST PUNT RETURN
84—Rob Friese, Eastern Wash. (14) vs. Northern Iowa (17), 12-7-85, TD.

LONGEST KICKOFF RETURN
100—Chris Fontenette, McNeese St. (7) vs. Northern Iowa (29), 12-5-92, TD.

LONGEST FUMBLE RETURN
65—Todd Lair, Citadel (44) vs. North Caro. A&T (0), 11-28-92, TD.

LONGEST INTERCEPTION RETURN
99—Dwayne Hans, Montana (19) vs. Idaho (38), 11-26-88, TD.

TEAM: SINGLE GAME

FIRST DOWNS
36—Northeast La. (78) vs. Alcorn St. (27), 11-28-92.

FIRST DOWNS BY RUSHING
26—Northeast La. (78) vs. Alcorn St. (27), 11-28-92.

FIRST DOWNS BY PASSING
28—Rhode Island (35) vs. Akron (27), 11-30-85.

RUSHES ATTEMPTED
81—Youngstown St. (10) vs. Samford (0), 12-14-91.

NET YARDS RUSHING
518—Arkansas St. (55) vs. Delaware (14), 12-6-86.

NET YARDS PASSING
532—Rhode Island (15) vs. Furman (59), 12-7-85.

PASSES ATTEMPTED
90—Rhode Island (15) vs. Furman (59), 12-7-85.

PASSES COMPLETED
45—Mississippi Val. (19) vs. Louisiana Tech (66), 11-24-84; Rhode Island (15) vs. Furman (59), 12-7-85.

COMPLETION PERCENTAGE
(Min. 10 Attempts)
.841—Montana (48) vs. Delaware (49), 11-27-93 (37 of 44).

PASSES HAD INTERCEPTED
7—Western Caro. (7) vs. Southern Ill. (43), 12-17-83; Rhode Island (15) vs. Furman (59), 12-7-85; Weber St. (23) vs. Marshall (51), 12-5-87.

NET YARDS RUSHING AND PASSING
742—Northeast La. (78) vs. Alcorn St. (27), 11-28-92.

RUSHING AND PASSING PLAYS
114—Nevada (42) vs. Furman (35), 3 OT, 12-1-90 (47 rushing, 67 passing).

PUNTING AVERAGE
50.2—Montana St. (32) vs. Rhode Island (20), 12-8-84.

NUMBER OF PUNTS
14—Jackson St. (0) vs. Stephen F. Austin (24), 11-26-88.

PUNTS HAD BLOCKED
2—Florida A&M (35) vs. Massachusetts (28), 12-16-78; Boise St. (14) vs. Grambling (9), 12-13-80.

YARDS GAINED ON PUNT RETURNS
115—Youngstown St. (19) vs. Northern Iowa (7), 12-12-92.

YARDS GAINED ON KICKOFF RETURNS
232—Eastern Ky. (32) vs. Northeast La. (33), 12-5-87.

YARDS GAINED ON INTERCEPTION RETURNS
164—Marshall (51) vs. Weber St. (23), 12-5-87.

YARDS PENALIZED
172—Tennessee St. (32) vs. Jackson St. (23), 11-29-86.

FUMBLES LOST
6—South Caro. St. (12) vs. Idaho St. (41), 12-12-81; Idaho (38) vs. Eastern Wash. (42), 11-30-85.

POINTS
78—Northeast La. vs. Alcorn St. (27), 11-28-92.

TEAM: TOURNAMENT

FIRST DOWNS
105—Northeast La., 1987 (22 vs. North Texas, 31 vs. Eastern Ky., 24 vs. Northern Iowa, 28 vs. Marshall).

NET YARDS RUSHING
1,522—Ga. Southern, 1986 (442 vs. North Caro. A&T, 317 vs. Nicholls St., 466 vs. Nevada, 297 vs. Arkansas St.).

NET YARDS PASSING
1,449—Stephen F. Austin, 1989 (517 vs. Grambling, 405 vs. Southwest Mo. St., 224 vs. Furman, 303 vs. Ga. Southern).

NET YARDS RUSHING AND PASSING
2,241—Ga. Southern, 1986 (541 vs. North Caro. A&T, 484 vs. Nicholls St., 613 vs. Nevada, 603 vs. Arkansas St.).

PASSES ATTEMPTED
185—Nevada, 1990 (29 vs. Northeast La., 67 vs. Furman, 36 vs. Boise St., 53 vs. Ga. Southern).

PASSES COMPLETED
98—Nevada, 1990 (12 vs. Northeast La., 39 vs. Furman, 20 vs. Boise St., 27 vs. Ga. Southern).

PASSES HAD INTERCEPTED
11—Stephen F. Austin, 1989 (0 vs. Grambling, 4 vs. Southwest Mo. St., 2 vs. Furman, 5 vs. Ga. Southern).

NUMBER OF PUNTS
29—Northern Iowa, 1992 (11 vs. Eastern Wash., 10 vs. McNeese St., 8 vs. Youngstown St.).

YARDS PENALIZED
350—Ga. Southern, 1986 (106 vs. North Caro. A&T, 104 vs. Nicholls St., 75 vs. Nevada, 65 vs. Arkansas St.).

FUMBLES LOST
9—Nevada, 1983 (3 vs. Idaho St., 4 vs. North Texas, 2 vs. Southern Ill.); Youngstown St., 1991 (3 vs. Villanova, 1 vs. Nevada, 4 vs. Samford, 1 vs. Marshall).

POINTS
203—Ga. Southern, 1986 (52 vs. North Caro. A&T, 55 vs. Nicholls St., 48 vs. Nevada, 48 vs. Arkansas St.).

INDIVIDUAL: CHAMPIONSHIP GAME

NET YARDS RUSHING
207—Mike Solomon, Florida A&M (35) vs. Massachusetts (28), 1978 (27 carries).

RUSHES ATTEMPTED
31—Joe Ross, Ga. Southern (37) vs. Stephen F. Austin (34), 1989 (152 yards); Raymond Gross, Ga. Southern (36) vs. Nevada (13), 1990 (145 yards).

TOUCHDOWNS BY RUSHING
4—John Bagwell, Furman (42) vs. Ga. Southern (44), 1985.

NET YARDS PASSING
474—Tony Peterson, Marshall (42) vs. Northeast La. (43), 1987 (28 of 54).

PASSES ATTEMPTED
57—Kelly Bradley, Montana St. (19) vs. Louisiana Tech (6), 1984 (32 completions).

PASSES COMPLETED
32—Kelly Bradley, Montana St. (19) vs. Louisiana Tech (6), 1984 (57 attempts).

PASSES HAD INTERCEPTED
7—Jeff Gilbert, Western Caro. (7) vs. Southern Ill. (43), 1983.

TOUCHDOWN PASSES COMPLETED
4—Tracy Ham, Ga. Southern (44) vs. Furman (42), 1985; Tony Peterson, Marshall (42) vs. Northeast La. (43), 1987.

COMPLETION PERCENTAGE
(Min. 8 Attempts)
.875—Mark Brungard, Youngstown St. (17) vs. Marshall (5), 1993 (7 of 8).

NET YARDS RUSHING AND PASSING
509—Tracy Ham, Ga. Southern (44) vs. Furman (42), 1985 (56 plays).

NUMBER OF RUSHING AND PASSING PLAYS
65—Kelly Bradley, Montana St. (19) vs. Louisiana Tech (6), 1984 (309 yards).

PUNTING AVERAGE
(Min. 3 Punts)
48.3—Todd Fugate, Marshall (42) vs. Northeast La. (43), 1987 (3 punts).

NUMBER OF PUNTS
10—Rick Titus, Delaware (14) vs. Eastern Ky. (17), 1982 (41.6 average).

PASSES CAUGHT
11—David Booze, Eastern Ky. (29) vs. Boise St. (31), 1980 (212 yards).

NET YARDS RECEIVING
212—David Booze, Eastern Ky. (29) vs. Boise St. (31), 1980 (11 catches).

TOUCHDOWN PASSES CAUGHT
2—Steve Bird, Eastern Ky. (23) vs. Idaho St. (34), 1981; Joseph Bignell, Montana St. (19) vs. Louisiana Tech (6), 1984; Frank Johnson, Ga. Southern (44) vs. Furman (42), 1985; Keith Baxter, Marshall (42) vs. Northeast La. (43), 1987; Larry Centers, Stephen F. Austin (34) vs. Ga. Southern (37), 1989.

PASSES INTERCEPTED
4—Greg Shipp, Southern Ill. (43) vs. Western Caro. (7), 1983.

YARDS GAINED ON INTERCEPTION RETURNS
52—George Thomas, Marshall (31) vs. Youngstown St. (28), 1992 (1 interception).

YARDS GAINED ON PUNT RETURNS
67—Rodney Oglesby, Ga. Southern (36) vs. Nevada (13), 1990 (6 returns).

YARDS GAINED ON KICKOFF RETURNS
207—Eric Rasheed, Western Caro. (7) vs. Southern Ill. (43), 1983 (6 returns).

POINTS
24—John Bagwell, Furman (42) vs. Ga. Southern (44), 1985.

TOUCHDOWNS
4—John Bagwell, Furman (42) vs. Ga. Southern (44), 1985.

EXTRA POINTS
6—Keven Esval, Furman (42) vs. Ga. Southern (44), 1985.

FIELD GOALS
4—Tim Foley, Ga. Southern (48) vs. Arkansas St. (21), 1986.

LONGEST RUSH
58—Dale Patton, Eastern Ky. (30) vs. Lehigh (7), 1979.

LONGEST PASS COMPLETION
79—Tracy Ham to Ricky Harris, Ga. Southern (48) vs. Arkansas St. (21), 1986.

LONGEST FIELD GOAL
55—David Cool, Ga. Southern (12) vs. Furman (17), 1988.

LONGEST PUNT
72—Rick Titus, Delaware (14) vs. Eastern Ky. (17), 1982.

TEAM: CHAMPIONSHIP GAME

FIRST DOWNS
28—Furman (42) vs. Ga. Southern (44), 1985; Ga. Southern (48) vs. Arkansas St. (21), 1986; Northeast La. (43) vs. Marshall (42), 1987.

FIRST DOWNS BY RUSHING
19—Florida A&M (35) vs. Massachusetts (28), 1978.

FIRST DOWNS BY PASSING
19—Marshall (42) vs. Northeast La. (43), 1987.

FIRST DOWNS BY PENALTY
3—Eastern Ky. (23) vs. Idaho St. (34), 1981; Furman

(42) vs. Ga. Southern (44), 1985; Northeast La. (43) vs. Marshall (42), 1987.

NET YARDS RUSHING
470—Florida A&M (35) vs. Massachusetts (28), 1978 (76 attempts).

RUSHES ATTEMPTED
76—Florida A&M (35) vs. Massachusetts (28), 1978 (470 yards).

NET YARDS PASSING
474—Marshall (42) vs. Northeast La. (43), 1987 (28 of 54).

PASSES ATTEMPTED
57—Montana St. (19) vs. Louisiana Tech (6), 1984 (32 completions).

PASSES COMPLETED
32—Montana St. (19) vs. Louisiana Tech (6), 1984 (57 attempts).

COMPLETION PERCENTAGE
(Min. 10 Attempts)
.760—Southern Ill. (43) vs. Western Caro. (7), 1983 (19 of 25).

PASSES HAD INTERCEPTED
7—Western Caro. (7) vs. Southern Ill. (43), 1983.

NET YARDS RUSHING AND PASSING
640—Ga. Southern (44) vs. Furman (42), 1985 (77 plays).

RUSHING AND PASSING PLAYS
86—Boise St. (31) vs. Eastern Ky. (29), 1980 (510 yards); Nevada (13) vs. Ga. Southern (36), 1990 (321 yards).

PUNTING AVERAGE
(Min. 3 Punts)
48.3—Marshall (42) vs. Northeast La. (43), 1987 (3 punts).

NUMBER OF PUNTS
10—Delaware (14) vs. Eastern Ky. (17), 1982 (41.6 average).

YARDS GAINED ON PUNT RETURNS
67—Ga. Southern (36) vs. Nevada (13), 1990 (6 returns).

YARDS GAINED ON KICKOFF RETURNS
229—Western Caro. (7) vs. Southern Ill. (43), 1983 (8 returns).

YARDS GAINED ON INTERCEPTION RETURNS
70—Marshall (31) vs. Youngstown St. (28), 1992 (2 interceptions).

YARDS PENALIZED
162—Idaho St. (34) vs. Eastern Ky. (23), 1981 (12 penalties).

FUMBLES
5—Eastern Ky. (17) vs. Delaware (14), 1982; Western Caro. (7) vs. Southern Ill. (43), 1983; Louisiana Tech (6) vs. Montana St. (19), 1984; Northeast La. (43) vs. Marshall (42), 1987; Ga. Southern (12) vs. Furman (17), 1988; Ga. Southern (36) vs. Nevada (13), 1990.

FUMBLES LOST
4—Northeast La. (43) vs. Marshall (42), 1987; Ga. Southern (36) vs. Nevada (13), 1990.

POINTS
48—Ga. Southern vs. Arkansas St. (21), 1986.

ATTENDANCE
31,304—Marshall University Stadium, Huntington, W.Va., 1992.

Year-by-Year Division I-AA Championship Results

Year (Number of Teams)	Coach	Record	Result
1978 (4)			
Florida A&M	Rudy Hubbard	2-0	Champion
Massachusetts	Bob Pickett	1-1	Second
Jackson St.	W. C. Gorden	0-1	Lost 1st Round
Nevada	Chris Ault	0-1	Lost 1st Round
1979 (4)			
Eastern Ky.	Roy Kidd	2-0	Champion
Lehigh	John Whitehead	1-1	Second
Murray St.	Mike Gottfried	0-1	Lost 1st Round
Nevada	Chris Ault	0-1	Lost 1st Round
1980 (4)			
Boise St.	Jim Criner	2-0	Champion
Eastern Ky.	Roy Kidd	1-1	Second
Grambling	Eddie Robinson	0-1	Lost 1st Round
Lehigh	John Whitehead	0-1	Lost 1st Round
1981 (8)			
Idaho St.	Dave Kragthorpe	3-0	Champion
Eastern Ky.	Roy Kidd	2-1	Second
Boise St.	Jim Criner	1-1	Semifinalist
South Caro. St.	Bill Davis	1-1	Semifinalist
Delaware	Tubby Raymond	0-1	Lost 1st Round
Jackson St.	W. C. Gorden	0-1	Lost 1st Round
Rhode Island	Bob Griffin	0-1	Lost 1st Round
*Tennessee St.	John Merritt	0-1	Vacated
1982 (12)			
Eastern Ky.	Roy Kidd	3-0	Champion
Delaware	Tubby Raymond	2-1	Second
Louisiana Tech	Billy Brewer	1-1	Semifinalist
*Tennessee St.	John Merritt	1-1	Vacated
Colgate	Fred Dunlap	1-1	Quarterfinalist
Eastern Ill.	Darrell Mudra	1-1	Quarterfinalist
Idaho	Dennis Erickson	1-1	Quarterfinalist
South Caro. St.	Bill Davis	1-1	Quarterfinalist
Boston U.	Rick Taylor	0-1	Lost 1st Round
Furman	Dick Sheridan	0-1	Lost 1st Round
Jackson St.	W. C. Gorden	0-1	Lost 1st Round
Montana	Larry Donovan	0-1	Lost 1st Round
1983 (12)			
Southern Ill.	Rey Dempsey	3-0	Champion
Western Caro.	Bob Waters	3-1	Second
Furman	Dick Sheridan	1-1	Semifinalist
Nevada	Chris Ault	2-1	Semifinalist
Boston U.	Rick Taylor	1-1	Quarterfinalist
Holy Cross	Rick Carter	0-1	Quarterfinalist
Indiana St.	Dennis Raetz	1-1	Quarterfinalist
North Texas	Corky Nelson	0-1	Quarterfinalist
Colgate	Fred Dunlap	0-1	Lost 1st Round
Eastern Ill.	Al Molde	0-1	Lost 1st Round
Eastern Ky.	Roy Kidd	0-1	Lost 1st Round
Idaho St.	Jim Koetter	0-1	Lost 1st Round
1984 (12)			
Montana St.	Dave Arnold	3-0	Champion
Louisiana Tech	A. L. Williams	3-1	Second
Middle Tenn. St.	James Donnelly	2-1	Semifinalist
Rhode Island	Bob Griffin	1-1	Semifinalist
Alcorn St.	Marino Casem	0-1	Quarterfinalist
Arkansas St.	Larry Lacewell	1-1	Quarterfinalist
Indiana St.	Dennis Raetz	0-1	Quarterfinalist
Richmond	Dal Shealy	1-1	Quarterfinalist
Boston U.	Rick Taylor	0-1	Lost 1st Round
Eastern Ky.	Roy Kidd	0-1	Lost 1st Round
Mississippi Val.	Archie Cooley Jr.	0-1	Lost 1st Round
Tenn.-Chatt.	Buddy Nix	0-1	Lost 1st Round
1985 (12)			
Ga. Southern	Erk Russell	4-0	Champion
Furman	Dick Sheridan	2-1	Second
Nevada	Chris Ault	1-1	Semifinalist
Northern Iowa	Darrell Mudra	1-1	Semifinalist
Arkansas St.	Larry Lacewell	1-1	Quarterfinalist
Eastern Wash.	Dick Zornes	1-1	Quarterfinalist
Middle Tenn. St.	James Donnelly	0-1	Quarterfinalist
Rhode Island	Bob Griffin	1-1	Quarterfinalist
Akron	Jim Dennison	0-1	Lost 1st Round
Grambling	Eddie Robinson	0-1	Lost 1st Round
Idaho	Dennis Erickson	0-1	Lost 1st Round
Jackson St.	W. C. Gorden	0-1	Lost 1st Round
1986 (16)			
Ga. Southern	Erk Russell	4-0	Champion
Arkansas St.	Larry Lacewell	3-1	Second
Eastern Ky.	Roy Kidd	2-1	Semifinalist
Nevada	Chris Ault	2-1	Semifinalist
Delaware	Tubby Raymond	1-1	Quarterfinalist
Eastern Ill.	Al Molde	1-1	Quarterfinalist
Nicholls St.	Sonny Jackson	1-1	Quarterfinalist
Tennessee St.	William Thomas	1-1	Quarterfinalist
Appalachian St.	Sparky Woods	0-1	Lost 1st Round
Furman	Jimmy Satterfield	0-1	Lost 1st Round
Idaho	Keith Gilbertson	0-1	Lost 1st Round
Jackson St.	W. C. Gorden	0-1	Lost 1st Round
Murray St.	Frank Beamer	0-1	Lost 1st Round
North Caro. A&T	Maurice Forte	0-1	Lost 1st Round
Sam Houston St.	Ron Randleman	0-1	Lost 1st Round
William & Mary	Jimmye Laycock	0-1	Lost 1st Round
1987 (16)			
Northeast La.	Pat Collins	4-0	Champion
Marshall	George Chaump	3-1	Second
Appalachian St.	Sparky Woods	2-1	Semifinalist
Northern Iowa	Darrell Mudra	2-1	Semifinalist
Arkansas St.	Larry Lacewell	1-1	Quarterfinalist
Eastern Ky.	Roy Kidd	1-1	Quarterfinalist
Ga. Southern	Erk Russell	1-1	Quarterfinalist
Weber St.	Mike Price	1-1	Quarterfinalist
Idaho	Keith Gilbertson	0-1	Lost 1st Round
Jackson St.	W. C. Gorden	0-1	Lost 1st Round
James Madison	Joe Purzycki	0-1	Lost 1st Round
Maine	Tim Murphy	0-1	Lost 1st Round
North Texas	Corky Nelson	0-1	Lost 1st Round
Richmond	Dal Shealy	0-1	Lost 1st Round
Western Ky.	Dave Roberts	0-1	Lost 1st Round
Youngstown St.	Jim Tressel	0-1	Lost 1st Round
1988 (16)			
Furman	Jimmy Satterfield	4-0	Champion
Ga. Southern	Erk Russell	3-1	Second
Eastern Ky.	Roy Kidd	2-1	Semifinalist
Idaho	Keith Gilbertson	2-1	Semifinalist
Marshall	George Chaump	1-1	Quarterfinalist
Northwestern St.	Sam Goodwin	1-1	Quarterfinalist
Stephen F. Austin	Jim Hess	1-1	Quarterfinalist
Western Ky.	Dave Roberts	1-1	Quarterfinalist
Boise St.	Skip Hall	0-1	Lost 1st Round
Citadel	Charlie Taaffe	0-1	Lost 1st Round
Delaware	Tubby Raymond	0-1	Lost 1st Round
Jackson St.	W. C. Gorden	0-1	Lost 1st Round
Massachusetts	Jim Reid	0-1	Lost 1st Round
Montana	Don Read	0-1	Lost 1st Round
North Texas	Corky Nelson	0-1	Lost 1st Round
Western Ill.	Bruce Craddock	0-1	Lost 1st Round
1989 (16)			
Ga. Southern	Erk Russell	4-0	Champion
*Stephen F. Austin	Lynn Graves	3-1	Vacated
Furman	Jimmy Satterfield	2-1	Semifinalist
Montana	Don Read	2-1	Semifinalist
Eastern Ill.	Bob Spoo	1-1	Quarterfinalist
Middle Tenn. St.	James Donnelly	1-1	Quarterfinalist
Southwest Mo. St.	Jesse Branch	1-1	Quarterfinalist
Youngstown St.	Jim Tressel	1-1	Quarterfinalist
Appalachian St.	Jerry Moore	0-1	Lost 1st Round
Eastern Ky.	Roy Kidd	0-1	Lost 1st Round
Grambling	Eddie Robinson	0-1	Lost 1st Round
Idaho	John L. Smith	0-1	Lost 1st Round
Jackson St.	W. C. Gorden	0-1	Lost 1st Round
Maine	Tom Lichtenberg	0-1	Lost 1st Round
Villanova	Andy Talley	0-1	Lost 1st Round
William & Mary	Jimmye Laycock	0-1	Lost 1st Round
1990 (16)			
Ga. Southern	Tim Stowers	4-0	Champion
Nevada	Chris Ault	3-1	Second
Boise St.	Skip Hall	2-1	Semifinalist
Central Fla.	Gene McDowell	2-1	Semifinalist
Furman	Jimmy Satterfield	1-1	Quarterfinalist
Idaho	John L. Smith	1-1	Quarterfinalist
Middle Tenn. St.	James Donnelly	1-1	Quarterfinalist
William & Mary	Jimmye Laycock	1-1	Quarterfinalist
Citadel	Charlie Taaffe	0-1	Lost 1st Round
Eastern Ky.	Roy Kidd	0-1	Lost 1st Round

Year (Number of Teams)	Coach	Record	Result
Jackson St.	W. C. Gorden	0-1	Lost 1st Round
Massachusetts	Jim Reid	0-1	Lost 1st Round
Northeast La.	Dave Roberts	0-1	Lost 1st Round
Northern Iowa	Terry Allen	0-1	Lost 1st Round
Southwest Mo. St.	Jesse Branch	0-1	Lost 1st Round
Youngstown St.	Jim Tressel	0-1	Lost 1st Round

1991 (16)

Youngstown St.	Jim Tressel	4-0	Champion
Marshall	Jim Donnan	3-1	Second
Eastern Ky.	Roy Kidd	2-1	Semifinalist
Samford	Terry Bowden	2-1	Semifinalist
James Madison	Rip Scherer	1-1	Quarterfinalist
Middle Tenn. St.	James Donnelly	1-1	Quarterfinalist
Nevada	Chris Ault	1-1	Quarterfinalist
Northern Iowa	Terry Allen	1-1	Quarterfinalist
Appalachian St.	Jerry Moore	0-1	Lost 1st Round
Delaware	Tubby Raymond	0-1	Lost 1st Round
McNeese St.	Bobby Keasler	0-1	Lost 1st Round
New Hampshire	Bill Bowes	0-1	Lost 1st Round
Sam Houston St.	Ron Randleman	0-1	Lost 1st Round
Villanova	Andy Talley	0-1	Lost 1st Round
Weber St.	Dave Arslanian	0-1	Lost 1st Round
Western Ill.	Randy Ball	0-1	Lost 1st Round

1992 (16)

Marshall	Jim Donnan	4-0	Champion
Youngstown St.	Jim Tressel	3-1	Second
Delaware	Tubby Raymond	2-1	Semifinalist
Northern Iowa	Terry Allen	2-1	Semifinalist
Citadel	Charlie Taaffe	1-1	Quarterfinalist
McNeese St.	Bobby Keasler	1-1	Quarterfinalist
Middle Tenn. St.	James Donnelly	1-1	Quarterfinalist
Northeast La.	Dave Roberts	1-1	Quarterfinalist
Alcorn St.	Cardell Jones	0-1	Lost 1st Round
Appalachian St.	Jerry Moore	0-1	Lost 1st Round
Eastern Ky.	Roy Kidd	0-1	Lost 1st Round
Eastern Wash.	Dick Zornes	0-1	Lost 1st Round
Idaho	John L. Smith	0-1	Lost 1st Round
North Caro. A&T	Bill Hayes	0-1	Lost 1st Round
Samford	Terry Bowden	0-1	Lost 1st Round
Villanova	Andy Talley	0-1	Lost 1st Round

1993 (16)

Youngstown St.	Jim Tressel	4-0	Champion
Marshall	Jim Donnan	3-1	Second
Idaho	John L. Smith	2-1	Semifinalist
Troy St.	Larry Blakeney	2-1	Semifinalist
Boston U.	Dan Allen	1-1	Quarterfinalist
Delaware	Tubby Raymond	1-1	Quarterfinalist
Ga. Southern	Tim Stowers	1-1	Quarterfinalist
McNeese St.	Bobby Keasler	1-1	Quarterfinalist
Central Fla.	Gene McDowell	0-1	Lost 1st Round
Eastern Ky.	Roy Kidd	0-1	Lost 1st Round
Howard	Steve Wilson	0-1	Lost 1st Round
Montana	Don Read	0-1	Lost 1st Round
Northeast La.	Dave Roberts	0-1	Lost 1st Round
Northern Iowa	Terry Allen	0-1	Lost 1st Round
Stephen F. Austin	John Pearce	0-1	Lost 1st Round
William & Mary	Jimmye Laycock	0-1	Lost 1st Round

Competition in championship vacated by the NCAA.

Division I-AA Championship Record of Each College by Coach

(61 Colleges; 1978-93)

	Yrs	Won	Lost	CH	2D
AKRON					
Jim Dennison (Wooster '60) 85	1	0	1	0	0
ALCORN ST.					
Marino Casem (Xavier, La. '56) 84	1	0	1	0	0
Cardell Jones (Alcorn St. '65) 92	1	0	1	0	0
TOTAL	2	0	2	0	0
APPALACHIAN ST.					
Sparky Woods (Carson-Newman '76) 86, 87	2	2	2	0	0
Jerry Moore (Baylor '61) 89, 91, 92	3	0	3	0	0
TOTAL	5	2	5	0	0
ARKANSAS ST.					
Larry Lacewell (Ark.-Monticello '59) 84, 85, 86-2D, 87	4	6	4	0	1

	Yrs	Won	Lost	CH	2D
BOISE ST.					
Jim Criner (Cal Poly Pomona '61) 80-CH, 81	2	3	1	1	0
Skip Hall (Concordia-M'head '66) 88, 90	2	2	2	0	0
TOTAL	4	5	3	1	0
BOSTON U.					
Rick Taylor (Gettysburg '64) 82, 83, 84	3	1	3	0	0
Dan Allen (Hanover '78) 93	1	1	1	0	0
TOTAL	4	2	4	0	0
CENTRAL FLA.					
Gene McDowell (Florida St. '63) 90, 93	2	2	2	0	0
CITADEL					
Charlie Taaffe (Siena '73) 88, 90, 92	3	1	3	0	0
COLGATE					
Fred Dunlap (Colgate '50) 82, 83	2	1	2	0	0
DELAWARE					
Harold "Tubby" Raymond (Michigan '50) 81, 82-2D, 86, 87, 91, 92, 93	7	6	7	0	1
EASTERN ILL.					
Darrell Mudra (Peru St. '51) 82	1	1	1	0	0
Al Molde (Gust. Adolphus '66) 83, 86	2	1	2	0	0
Bob Spoo (Purdue '60) 89	1	1	1	0	0
TOTAL	4	3	4	0	0
EASTERN KY.					
Roy Kidd (Eastern Ky. '54) 79-CH, 80-2D, 81-2D, 82-CH, 83, 84, 86, 87, 88, 89, 90, 91, 92, 93	14	15	12	2	2
EASTERN WASH.					
Dick Zornes (Eastern Wash. '68) 85, 92	2	1	2	0	0
FLORIDA A&M					
Rudy Hubbard (Ohio St. '68) 78-CH	1	2	0	1	0
FURMAN					
Dick Sheridan (South Caro. '64) 82, 83, 85-2D	3	3	3	0	1
Jimmy Satterfield (South Caro. '62) 86, 88-CH, 89, 90	4	7	3	1	0
TOTAL	7	10	6	1	1
GA. SOUTHERN					
Erk Russell (Auburn '49) 85-CH, 86-CH, 87, 88-2D, 89-CH	5	16	2	3	1
Tim Stowers (Auburn '79) 90-CH, 93	2	5	1	1	0
TOTAL	7	21	3	4	1
GRAMBLING					
Eddie Robinson (Leland '41) 80, 85, 89	3	0	3	0	0
HOLY CROSS					
Rick Carter (Earlham '65) 83	1	0	1	0	0
HOWARD					
Steve Wilson (Howard '79) 93	1	0	1	0	0
IDAHO					
Dennis Erickson (Montana St. '70) 82, 85	2	1	2	0	0
Keith Gilbertson (Central Wash. '71) 86, 87, 88	3	2	3	0	0
John L. Smith (Weber St. '71) 89, 90, 92, 93	4	3	4	0	0
TOTAL	9	6	9	0	0
IDAHO ST.					
Dave Kragthorpe (Utah St. '55) 81-CH	1	3	0	1	0
Jim Koetter (Idaho St. '61) 83	1	0	1	0	0
TOTAL	2	3	1	1	0
INDIANA ST.					
Dennis Raetz (Nebraska '68) 83, 84	2	1	2	0	0
JACKSON ST.					
W. C. Gorden (Tennessee St. '52) 78, 81, 82, 85, 86, 87, 88, 89, 90	9	0	9	0	0
JAMES MADISON					
Joe Purzycki (Delaware '71) 87	1	0	1	0	0
Rip Scherer (William & Mary '74) 91	1	1	1	0	0
TOTAL	2	1	2	0	0
LEHIGH					
John Whitehead (East Stroudsburg '50) 79-2D, 80	2	1	2	0	1
LOUISIANA TECH					
Billy Brewer (Mississippi '61) 82	1	1	1	0	0
A. L. Williams (Louisiana Tech '57) 84-2D	1	3	1	0	1
TOTAL	2	4	2	0	1
MAINE					
Tim Murphy (Springfield '78) 87	1	0	1	0	0
Tom Lichtenberg (Louisville '62) 89	1	0	1	0	0
TOTAL	2	0	2	0	0

	Yrs	Won	Lost	CH	2D
MARSHALL					
George Chaump (Bloomsburg '58) 87-2D, 88 ..	2	4	2	0	1
Jim Donnan (North Caro. St. '67) 91-2D, 92-CH, 93-2D	3	10	2	1	2
TOTAL	5	14	4	1	3
MASSACHUSETTS					
Bob Pickett (Maine '59) 78-2D	1	1	1	0	1
Jim Reid (Maine '73) 88, 90	2	0	2	0	0
TOTAL	3	1	3	0	1
McNEESE ST.					
Bobby Keasler (Northeast La. '70) 91, 92, 93 ..	3	2	3	0	0
MIDDLE TENN. ST.					
James "Boots" Donnelly (Middle Tenn. St. '65) 84, 85, 89, 90, 91, 92	6	6	6	0	0
MISSISSIPPI VAL.					
Archie Cooley Jr. (Jackson St. '62) 84	1	0	1	0	0
MONTANA					
Larry Donovan (Nebraska '64) 82	1	0	1	0	0
Don Read (Cal St. Sacramento '59) 88, 89, 93 ..	3	2	3	0	0
TOTAL	4	2	4	0	0
MONTANA ST.					
Dave Arnold (Drake '67) 84-CH	1	3	0	1	0
MURRAY ST.					
Mike Gottfried (Morehead St. '66) 79	1	0	1	0	0
Frank Beamer (Virginia Tech '69) 86	1	0	1	0	0
TOTAL	2	0	2	0	0
NEVADA					
Chris Ault (Nevada '68) 78, 79, 83, 85, 86, 90-2D, 91	7	9	7	0	1
NEW HAMPSHIRE					
Bill Bowes (Penn St. '65) 91	1	0	1	0	0
NICHOLLS ST.					
Sonny Jackson (Nicholls St. '63) 86	1	1	1	0	0
NORTH CARO. A&T					
Maurice "Mo" Forte (Minnesota '71) 86	1	0	1	0	0
Bill Hayes (N.C. Central '64) 92	1	0	1	0	0
TOTAL	2	0	2	0	0
NORTH TEXAS					
Corky Nelson (Southwest Tex. St. '64) 83, 87, 88	3	0	3	0	0
NORTHEAST LA.					
Pat Collins (Louisiana Tech '63) 87-CH	1	4	0	1	0
Dave Roberts (Western Caro. '68) 90, 92, 93 ..	3	1	3	0	0
TOTAL	4	5	3	1	0
NORTHERN IOWA					
Darrell Mudra (Peru St. '51) 85, 87	2	3	2	0	0
Terry Allen (Northern Iowa '79) 90, 91, 92, 93 ..	4	3	4	0	0
TOTAL	6	6	6	0	0
NORTHWESTERN ST.					
Sam Goodwin (Henderson St. '66) 88	1	1	1	0	0

	Yrs	Won	Lost	CH	2D
RHODE ISLAND					
Bob Griffin (Southern Conn. St. '63) 81, 84, 85	3	2	3	0	0
RICHMOND					
Dal Shealy (Carson-Newman '60) 84, 87	2	1	2	0	0
SAM HOUSTON ST.					
Ron Randleman (William Penn '64) 86, 91	2	0	2	0	0
SAMFORD					
Terry Bowden (West Va. '78) 91, 92	2	2	2	0	0
SOUTH CARO. ST.					
Bill Davis (Johnson Smith '65) 81, 82	2	2	2	0	0
SOUTHERN ILL.					
Rey Dempsey (Geneva '58) 83-CH	1	3	0	1	0
SOUTHWEST MO. ST.					
Jesse Branch (Arkansas '64) 89, 90	2	1	2	0	0
STEPHEN F. AUSTIN¢					
Jim Hess (S'eastern Okla. '59) 88	1	1	1	0	0
Lynn Graves (Stephen F. Austin '65) 89-2D	1	3	1	0	1
John Pearce (East Tex. St. '70) 93	1	0	1	0	0
TOTAL	3	4	3	0	1
TENN.-CHATT.					
Buddy Nix (Livingston '61) 84	1	0	1	0	0
TENNESSEE ST.*					
John Merritt (Kentucky St. '50) 81, 82	2	1	2	0	0
Bill Thomas (Tennessee St. '71) 86	1	1	1	0	0
TOTAL	3	2	3	0	0
TROY ST.					
Larry Blakeney (Auburn '70) 93	1	2	1	0	0
VILLANOVA					
Andy Talley (Southern Conn. St. '67) 89, 91, 92	3	0	3	0	0
WEBER ST.					
Mike Price (Puget Sound '69) 87	1	1	1	0	0
Dave Arslanian (Weber St. '72) 91	1	0	1	0	0
TOTAL	2	1	2	0	0
WESTERN CARO.					
Bob Waters (Presbyterian '60) 83-2D	1	3	1	0	1
WESTERN ILL.					
Bruce Craddock (Northeast Mo. St. '66) 88	1	0	1	0	0
Randy Ball (Northeast Mo. St. '73) 91	1	0	1	0	0
TOTAL	2	0	2	0	0
WESTERN KY.					
Dave Roberts (Western Caro. '68) 87, 88	2	1	2	0	0
WILLIAM & MARY					
Jimmye Laycock (William & Mary '70) 86, 89, 90, 93	4	1	4	0	0
YOUNGSTOWN ST.					
Jim Tressel (Baldwin-Wallace '75) 87, 89, 90, 91-CH, 92-2D, 93-CH	6	12	4	2	1

*Tennessee State's competition in the 1981 and 1982 Division I-AA championships was vacated by the NCAA (official record is 1-1). ¢Stephen F. Austin's competition in the 1989 Division I-AA championship was vacated by the NCAA (official record is 1-2).

All-Time Results

1978 First Round: Florida A&M 15, Jackson St. 10; Massachusetts 44, Nevada 21. **Championship:** Florida A&M 35, Massachusetts 28.

1979 First Round: Lehigh 28, Murray St. 9; Eastern Ky. 33, Nevada 30 (2 OT). **Championship:** Eastern Ky. 30, Lehigh 7.

1980 First Round: Eastern Ky. 23, Lehigh 20; Boise St. 14, Grambling 9. **Championship:** Boise St. 31, Eastern Ky. 29.

1981 First Round: Eastern Ky. 35, Delaware 28; Boise St. 19, Jackson St. 7; Idaho St. 51, Rhode Island 0; South Caro. St. 26, *Tennessee St. 25 (OT). **Semifinals:** Eastern Ky. 23, Boise St. 17; Idaho St. 41, South Caro. St. 12. **Championship:** Idaho St. 34, Eastern Ky. 23.

*Tennessee State's participation in 1981 playoff vacated.

1982 First Round: Idaho 21, Montana 7; Eastern Ill. 16, Jackson St. 13 (OT); South Caro. St. 17, Furman 0; Colgate 21, Boston U. 7. **Quarterfinals:** Eastern Ky. 38, Idaho 30; *Tennessee St. 20, Eastern Ill. 19; Louisiana Tech 38, South Caro. St. 3; Delaware 20, Colgate 13. **Semifinals:** Eastern Ky. 13, *Tennessee St. 10, Delaware 17, Louisiana Tech 0. **Championship:** Eastern Ky. 17, Delaware 14.

*Tennessee State's participation in 1982 playoff vacated.

1983 First Round: Indiana St. 16, Eastern Ill. 13 (2 OT); Nevada 27, Idaho St. 20; Western Caro. 24, Colgate 23; Boston U. 24, Eastern Ky. 20. **Quarterfinals:** Southern Ill. 23, Indiana St. 7; Nevada 20, North Texas 17; Western Caro. 28, Holy Cross 21; Furman 35, Boston U. 16. **Semifinals:** Southern Ill. 23, Nevada 7; Western Caro. 14, Furman 7. **Championship:** Southern Ill. 43, Western Caro. 7.

1984 First Round: Louisiana Tech 66, Mississippi Val. 19; Middle Tenn. St. 27, Eastern Ky. 10; Richmond 35, Boston U. 33; Arkansas St. 37, Tenn.-Chatt. 10. **Quarterfinals:** Louisiana Tech 44, Middle Tenn. St. 42, Indiana St. 41 (3 OT); Rhode Island 23, Richmond 17; Montana St. 31, Arkansas St. 14. **Semifinals:** Louisiana Tech 21, Middle Tenn. St. 13; Montana St. 32, Rhode Island 20. **Championship:** Montana St. 19, Louisiana Tech 6.

1985 First Round: Ga. Southern 27, Jackson St. 0; Eastern Wash. 42, Idaho 38; Rhode Island 35, Akron 27; Arkansas St. 13, *Tennessee St. 10. **Quarterfinals:** Ga. Southern 28, Middle Tenn. St. 21; Northern Iowa 17, Eastern Wash. 14; Furman 59, Rhode Island 15; Nevada 24, Arkansas St. 23. **Semifinals:** Ga. Southern 40, Northern Iowa 33; Furman 35, Nevada 12. **Championship:** Ga. Southern 44, Furman 42.

1986 First Round: Nevada 27, Idaho 7; Tennessee St. 32, Jackson St. 23; Ga. Southern 52, North Caro. A&T 21; Nicholls St. 28, Appalachian St. 26; Arkansas St. 48, Sam Houston St. 7; Delaware 51, William & Mary 17; Eastern Ill. 28, Murray St. 21; Eastern Ky. 23, Furman 10. **Quarterfinals:** Nevada 33, Tennessee St. 6; Ga. Southern 55, Nicholls St. 31; Arkansas St. 55, Delaware 14; Eastern Ky. 24, Eastern Ill. 22. **Semifinals:** Ga. Southern 48, Nevada 38; Arkansas St. 24, Eastern Ky. 10. **Championship:** Ga. Southern 48, Arkansas St. 21.

1987 First Round: Appalachian St. 20, Richmond 3; Ga. Southern 31, Maine 28 (OT); Weber St. 59, Idaho 30; Marshall 41, James Madison 12; Northeast La. 30, North Texas 9; Eastern Ky. 40, Western Ky. 17; Northern Iowa 31, Youngstown St. 28; Arkansas St. 35, Jackson St. 32.

Quarterfinals: Appalachian St. 19, Ga. Southern 0; Marshall 51, Weber St. 23; Northeast La. 33, Eastern Ky. 32; Northern Iowa 49, Arkansas St. 28. **Semifinals:** Marshall 24, Appalachian St. 10; Northeast La. 44, Northern Iowa 41 (2 OT). **Championship:** Northeast La. 43, Marshall 42.

1988 First Round: Idaho 38, Montana 19; Northwestern St. 22, Boise St. 13; Furman 21, Delaware 7; Marshall 7, North Texas 0; Ga. Southern 38, Citadel 20; Stephen F. Austin 24, Jackson St. 0; Western Ky. 35, Western Ill. 32; Eastern Ky. 28, Massachusetts 17. **Quarterfinals:** Idaho 38, Northwestern St. 30; Furman 13, Ga. Southern 27, Stephen F. Austin 6; Eastern Ky. 41, Western Ky. 24. **Semifinals:** Furman 38, Idaho 7; Ga. Southern 21, Eastern Ky. 17. **Championship:** Furman 17, Ga. Southern 12.

1989 First Round: Ga. Southern 52, Villanova 36; Middle Tenn. 24, Appalachian St. 21; Eastern Ill. 38, Idaho 21; Montana 48, Jackson St. 7; Furman 24, William & Mary 10; Youngstown St. 28, Eastern Ky. 24; ¢Stephen F. Austin 59, Grambling 56; Southwest Mo. St. 38, Maine 35. **Quarterfinals:** Ga. Southern 45, Middle Tenn. St. 3; Montana 25, Eastern Ill. 19; Furman 42, Youngstown St. 23; ¢Stephen F. Austin 55, Southwest Mo. St. 25.

Semifinals: Ga. Southern 45, Montana 15; ¢Stephen F. Austin 21, Furman 19. **Championship:** Ga. Southern 37, ¢Stephen F. Austin 34.

¢Stephen F. Austin's participation in 1989 playoff vacated.

1990 First Round: Middle Tenn. St. 28, Jackson St. 7; Boise St. 20, Northern Iowa 3; Nevada 27, Northeast La. 14; Furman 45, Eastern Ky. 17; Central Fla. 20, Youngstown St. 17; William & Mary 38, Massachusetts 0; Ga. Southern 31, Citadel 0; Idaho 41, Southwest Mo. St. 35. **Quarterfinals:** Boise St. 20, Middle Tenn. St. 13; Nevada 42, Furman 35 (3 OT); Central Fla. 52, William & Mary 38; Ga. Southern 28, Idaho 27. **Semifinals:** Nevada 59, Boise St. 52 (3 OT); Ga. Southern 44, Central Fla. 7. **Championship:** Ga. Southern 36, Nevada 13.

1991 First Round: Nevada 22, McNeese St. 16; Youngstown St. 17, Villanova 16; James Madison 42, Delaware 35 (2 OT); Samford 29, New Hampshire 13; Eastern Ky. 14, Appalachian St. 3; Middle Tenn. St. 20, Sam Houston St. 19 (OT); Northern Iowa 38, Weber St. 21; Marshall 20, Western Ill. 17 (OT). **Quarterfinals:** Youngstown St. 30, Nevada 28; James Madison 21; Eastern Ky. 23, Middle Tenn. St. 13; Marshall 41, Northern Iowa 13. **Semifinals:**

Youngstown St. 10, Samford 0; Marshall 14, Eastern Ky. 7. **Championship:** Youngstown St. 25, Marshall 17.

1992 First Round: Northeast La. 78, Alcorn St. 27; Delaware 56, Samford 21; Middle Tenn. St. 35, Appalachian St. 10; Marshall 44, Eastern Ky. 0; Citadel 44, North Caro. A&T 0; Youngstown St. 23, Villanova 20; Northern Iowa 21, Eastern Wash. 14; McNeese St. 23, Idaho 20. **Quarterfinals:** Delaware 41, Northeast La. 18; Marshall 35, Middle Tenn. St. 21; Youngstown St. 42, Citadel 17; Northern Iowa 29, McNeese St. 7. **Semifinals:** Marshall 28, Delaware 7; Youngstown St. 19, Northern Iowa 7. **Championship:** Marshall 31, Youngstown St. 28.

1993 First Round: Ga. Southern 14, Eastern Ky. 12; Youngstown St. 56, Central Fla. 20; Boston U. 27, Northern Iowa 21 (2 OT); Idaho 34, Northeast La. 31; Delaware 49, Montana 48; Marshall 28, Howard 14; McNeese St. 34, William & Mary 28; Troy St. 42, Stephen F. Austin 20. **Quarterfinals:** Youngstown St. 34, Ga. Southern 14; Idaho 21, Boston U. 14; Marshall 34, Delaware 31; Troy St. 35, McNeese St. 28. **Semifinals:** Youngstown St. 35, Idaho 16; Marshall 24, Troy St. 21. **Championship:** Youngstown St. 17, Marshall 5.

Division II Championship

1993 Title Game Summary

BRALY MUNICIPAL STADIUM, FLORENCE, ALA.; DECEMBER 11, 1993

	Indiana (Pa.)		North Ala.	
First Downs	21		21	
Rushes-Net Yardage	36-134		56-359	
Passing Yardage	299		178	
Return Yardage (Punts, Int. & Fum.)	5		20	
Passes (Comp.-Att.-Int.)	20-37-2		8-17-0	
Punts (Number-Average)	4-31.8		4-32.3	
Fumbles (Number-Lost)	3-1		4-1	
Penalties (Number-Yards)	4-31		3-18	
Indiana (Pa.)	0	10	14	10—34
North Ala.	7	7	0	27—41

Game Conditions: Temperature, 44 degrees; wind, 14 mph from north; weather, sunny and clear. Attendance: 15,631.

FIRST QUARTER
North Ala.—Demetrea Shelton 5 run (Jamie Stoddard kick) (70 yards in 10 plays, 7:57 left)

SECOND QUARTER
Indiana (Pa.)—Michael Geary 22 field goal (48 yards in 8 plays, 13:35 left)
North Ala.—Tyrone Rush 7 run (Stoddard kick) (80 yards in 12 plays, 9:08 left)
Indiana (Pa.)—Scott McClellan 9 pass from Scott Woods (Geary kick) (71 yards in 10 plays, 5:12 left)

THIRD QUARTER
Indiana (Pa.)—Dan Glass 2 pass from Woods (Geary kick) (84 yards in 11 plays, 7:51 left)
Indiana (Pa.)—Theo Turner 24 pass from Woods (Geary kick) (28 yards in 2 plays, 0:42 left)

FOURTH QUARTER
North Ala.—Shelton 24 pass from Cody Gross (pass failed) (28 yards in 3 plays, 11:26 left)
North Ala.—Brian Satterfield 7 run (Stoddard kick) (66 yards in 5 plays, 8:22 left)
North Ala.—Satterfield 20 run (Stoddard kick) (78 yards in 7 plays, 3:17 left)
Indiana (Pa.)—Michael Mann 1 run (Geary kick) (70 yards in 9 plays, 1:54 left)
Indiana (Pa.)—Geary 34 field goal (31 yards in 6 plays, 0:45 left)
North Ala.—Gross 1 run (Stoddard kick) (69 yards in 6 plays, 0:10 left)

INDIVIDUAL LEADERS
Rushing—Indiana (Pa.): Mann, 109 yards on 25 carries; North Ala.: Satterfield, 180 yards on 23 carries.
Passing—Indiana (Pa.): Woods, 20 of 37 for 299 yards; North Ala.: Gross, 8 of 17 for 178 yards.
Receiving—Indiana (Pa.): Derrick Smith, 7 catches for 141 yards; North Ala.: Shelton, 4 catches for 98 yards.

Doug Adams/Allsport photo

Brian Satterfield capped a 180-yard performance with two fourth-quarter touchdown runs to lead North Alabama to victory over Indiana (Pennsylvania) in the 1993 Division II title game. The Lions trailed, 24-14, after three quarters but came back to win, 41-34.

Division II All-Time Championship Results

Year	Champion	Coach	Score	Runner-Up	Site
1973	Louisiana Tech	Maxie Lambright	34-0	Western Ky.	Sacramento, Calif.
1974	Central Mich.	Roy Kramer	54-14	Delaware	Sacramento, Calif.
1975	Northern Mich.	Gil Krueger	16-14	Western Ky.	Sacramento, Calif.
1976	Montana St.	Sonny Holland	24-13	Akron	Wichita Falls, Texas
1977	Lehigh	John Whitehead	33-0	Jacksonville St.	Wichita Falls, Texas

North Dakota State quarterback Chris Simdorn (10) threw for 179 yards and three touchdowns and ran for two more scores to lead the Bison to a 51-11 victory over Indiana (Pennsylvania) in the 1990 Division II title game. In four championship games, Simdorn ran for 385 yards and seven touchdowns and passed for 394 yards and four touchdowns.

Year	Champion	Coach	Score	Runner-Up	Site
1978	Eastern Ill.	Darrell Mudra	10-9	Delaware	Longview, Texas
1979	Delaware	Tubby Raymond	38-21	Youngstown St.	Albuquerque, N.M.
1980	Cal Poly SLO	Joe Harper	21-13	Eastern Ill.	Albuquerque, N.M.
1981	Southwest Tex. St.	Jim Wacker	42-13	North Dak. St.	McAllen, Texas
1982	Southwest Tex. St.	Jim Wacker	34-9	UC Davis	McAllen, Texas
1983	North Dak. St.	Don Morton	41-21	Central St. (Ohio)	McAllen, Texas
1984	Troy St.	Chan Gailey	18-17	North Dak. St.	McAllen, Texas
1985	North Dak. St.	Earle Solomonson	35-7	North Ala.	McAllen, Texas
1986	North Dak. St.	Earle Solomonson	27-7	South Dak.	Florence, Ala.
1987	Troy St.	Rick Rhoades	31-17	Portland St.	Florence, Ala.
1988	North Dak. St.	Rocky Hager	35-21	Portland St.	Florence, Ala.
1989	*Mississippi Col.	John Williams	3-0	Jacksonville St.	Florence, Ala.
1990	North Dak. St.	Rocky Hager	51-11	Indiana (Pa.)	Florence, Ala.
1991	Pittsburg St.	Chuck Broyles	23-6	Jacksonville St.	Florence, Ala.
1992	Jacksonville St.	Bill Burgess	17-13	Pittsburg St.	Florence, Ala.
1993	North Ala.	Bobby Wallace	41-34	Indiana (Pa.)	Florence, Ala.

*Mississippi College's participation in 1989 Division II championship vacated.

Regional Championship Results

Before 1973, there was no Division II Football Championship. Instead, four regional bowl games were played in order to provide postseason action for what then were called NCAA College Division member institutions. Following are the results of those bowl games:

Year	Champion	Coach	Score	Runner-Up	Site
EAST (TANGERINE BOWL)					
1964	East Caro.	Clarence Stasavich	14-13	Massachusetts	Orlando, Fla.
1965	East Caro.	Clarence Stasavich	31-0	Maine	Orlando, Fla.
1966	Morgan St.	Earl Banks	14-6	West Chester	Orlando, Fla.
1967	Tenn.-Martin	Robert Carroll	25-8	West Chester	Orlando, Fla.
EAST (BOARDWALK BOWL)					
1968	Delaware	Tubby Raymond	31-24	Indiana (Pa.)	Atlantic City, N.J.
1969	Delaware	Tubby Raymond	31-13	N.C. Central	Atlantic City, N.J.
1970	Delaware	Tubby Raymond	38-23	Morgan St.	Atlantic City, N.J.
1971	Delaware	Tubby Raymond	72-22	LIU-C.W. Post	Atlantic City, N.J.
1972	Massachusetts	Dick MacPherson	35-14	UC Davis	Atlantic City, N.J.
MIDEAST (GRANTLAND RICE BOWL)					
1964	Middle Tenn. St.	Charles Murphy	20-0	Muskingum	Murfreesboro, Tenn.
1965	Ball St.	Ray Louthen	14-14	—	Murfreesboro, Tenn.
	Tennessee St.	John Merritt			
1966	Tennessee St.	John Merritt	34-7	Muskingum	Murfreesboro, Tenn.
1967	Eastern Ky.	Roy Kidd	27-13	Ball St.	Murfreesboro, Tenn.
1968	Louisiana Tech	Maxie Lambright	33-13	Akron	Murfreesboro, Tenn.
1969	East Tenn. St.	John Bell	34-14	Louisiana Tech	Baton Rouge, La.
1970	Tennessee St.	John Merritt	26-25	Southwestern La.	Baton Rouge, La.
1971	Tennessee St.	John Merritt	26-23	McNeese St.	Baton Rouge, La.
1972	Louisiana Tech	Maxie Lambright	35-0	Tennessee Tech	Baton Rouge, La.
MIDWEST (PECAN BOWL)					
1964	Northern Iowa	Stan Sheriff	19-17	Lamar	Abilene, Texas
1965	North Dak. St.	Darrell Mudra	20-7	Grambling	Abilene, Texas
1966	North Dak.	Marv Helling	42-24	Parsons	Abilene, Texas
1967	Texas-Arlington	Burley Bearden	13-0	North Dak. St.	Abilene, Texas
1968	North Dak. St.	Ron Erhardt	23-14	Arkansas St.	Arlington, Texas
1969	Arkansas St.	Bennie Ellender	29-21	Drake	Arlington, Texas
1970	Arkansas St.	Bennie Ellender	38-21	Central Mo. St.	Arlington, Texas
MIDWEST (PIONEER BOWL)					
1971	Louisiana Tech	Maxie Lambright	14-3	Eastern Mich.	Wichita Falls, Texas
1972	Tennessee St.	John Merritt	29-7	Drake	Wichita Falls, Texas
WEST (CAMELLIA BOWL)					
1964	Montana St.	Jim Sweeney	28-7	Cal St. Sacramento	Sacramento, Calif.
1965	Cal St. Los Angeles	Homer Beatty	18-10	UC Santa Barb.	Sacramento, Calif.
1966	San Diego St.	Don Coryell	28-7	Montana St.	Sacramento, Calif.
1967	San Diego St.	Don Coryell	27-6	San Fran. St.	Sacramento, Calif.
1968	Humboldt St.	Frank VanDeren	29-14	Fresno St.	Sacramento, Calif.
1969	North Dak. St.	Ron Erhardt	30-3	Montana	Sacramento, Calif.
1970	North Dak. St.	Ron Erhardt	31-16	Montana	Sacramento, Calif.
1971	Boise St.	Tony Knap	32-28	Cal St. Chico	Sacramento, Calif.
1972	North Dak.	Jerry Olson	38-21	Cal Poly SLO	Sacramento, Calif.

1993 Division II Championship Results

FIRST ROUND
North Ala. 38, Carson-Newman 28
Hampton 33, Albany St. (Ga.) 7
Tex. A&M-Kingsville 50, Portland St. 15
UC Davis 37, Fort Hays St. 34
Mankato St. 34, Mo. Southern St. 13
North Dak. 17, Pittsburg St. 14
New Haven 48, Edinboro 28
Indiana (Pa.) 28, Ferris St. 21

QUARTERFINALS
North Ala. 45, Hampton 20
Tex. A&M-Kingsville 51, UC Davis 28
North Dak. 54, Mankato St. 21
Indiana (Pa.) 38, New Haven 35

SEMIFINALS
North Ala. 27, Tex. A&M-Kingsville 25
Indiana (Pa.) 21, North Dak. 6

CHAMPIONSHIP
North Ala. 41, Indiana (Pa.) 34

1993 Division II Game Summaries

FIRST-ROUND GAMES (NOV. 20)

North Ala. 38, Carson-Newman 28
at Florence, Ala.

Carson-Newman	0	7	14	7—28
North Ala.	14	7	10	7—38

NA—Gross 1 run (Stoddard kick)
NA—Gross 2 run (Stoddard kick)
NA—Edwards 9 run (Stoddard kick)
CN—Mathis 1 run (Standfest kick)
CN—Williams 1 run (Standfest kick)
NA—Stoddard 37 field goal
NA—Satterfield 25 run (Stoddard kick)
CN—James 85 kickoff return (Standfest kick)
NA—Hayes 20 pass from Gross (Stoddard kick)
CN—Kilgore 42 pass from Williams (Standfest kick)
A—4,748

Hampton 33, Albany St. (Ga.) 7
at Hampton, Va.

Albany St. (Ga.)	0	0	7	0— 7
Hampton	13	7	13	0—33

HU—Benson 9 pass from Montgomery (Pitts kick)
HU—Rainey 37 pass from Montgomery (kick failed)
HU—Montgomery 3 run (Pitts kick)
AS—Coneway 14 run (Allen kick)
HU—Fuller 41 fumble return (Pitts kick)
HU—Smith 13 pass from Montgomery (kick failed)
A—6,417

Tex. A&M-Kingsville 50, Portland St. 15
at Portland, Ore.

Tex. A&M-Kingsville	7	15	7	21—50
Portland St.	0	8	7	0—15

TK—Young 9 run (Cortez kick)
TK—Deese 3 run (Perkins recovery of blocked kick)
PS—Williams 25 pass from Matos (Lyons pass from Matos)
TK—Deese 2 pass from Menchaca (Cortez kick)
TK—Young 1 run (Cortez kick)
PS—Holmes 3 run (Bilic kick)
TK—Bartosh 6 pass from Menchaca (Cortez kick)
TK—Deese 64 pass from Scott (Cortez kick)
TK—Donner 5 run (Cortez kick)
A—7,925

UC Davis 37, Fort Hays St. 34
at Davis, Calif.

Fort Hays St.	21	7	6	0—34
UC Davis	9	13	0	15—37

FH—Butler 2 run (Achilles kick)
FH—Schwindt 48 pass from McEwen (Achilles kick)
UC—Fernandez 34 field goal
FH—Pritchett 66 pass from McEwen (Achilles kick)
UC—Jackson 5 run (kick blocked)
FH—Bedore 55 run (Achilles kick)
UC—Jackson 5 run (kick blocked)
UC—Hard 18 pass from Jones (Fernandez kick)
FH—Butler 1 run (pass failed)
UC—Jackson 1 run (Fernandez kick)

UC—Jackson 1 run (Jackson pass from Jones)
A—5,100

Mankato St. 34, Mo. Southern St. 13
at Joplin, Mo.

Mankato St.	10	7	0	17—34
Mo. Southern St.	0	7	6	0—13

MK—Navitsky 28 field goal
MK—Spikner 14 pass from Pass (Navitsky kick)
MO—Smith 51 pass from Cook (Crader kick)
MK—Nelson 57 pass from Pass (Navitsky kick)
MO—Cook 4 run (kick failed)
MK—Navitsky 22 field goal
MK—Erickson 24 pass from Pass (Navitsky kick)
MK—Erickson 7 run (Navitsky kick)
A—3,500

North Dak. 17, Pittsburg St. 14
at Grand Forks, N.D.

Pittsburg St.	7	0	7	0—14
North Dak.	0	0	14	3—17

PS—Sparkman 10 pass from Hutchins (Wood kick)
ND—Nagert 41 pass from Wagner (Dahlem kick)
PS—Hutchins 2 run (Wood kick)
ND—Schramm 27 pass from Wagner (Dahlem kick)
ND—Dahlem 31 field goal
A—3,759

New Haven 48, Edinboro 28
at New Haven, Conn.

Edinboro	0	14	0	14—28
New Haven	14	7	13	14—48

NH—Davis 15 pass from Weir (O'Riordan kick)
NH—Graham 3 run (O'Riordan kick)
EU—Griffin 10 pass from Dickerson (Rupert kick)
NH—Weir 4 run (O'Riordan kick)
EU—Hill 3 run (Rupert kick)
NH—Graham 2 run (O'Riordan kick)
NH—Willis 32 pass from Weir (kick failed)
EU—Hill 3 run (Rupert kick)
NH—Willis 20 pass from Weir (O'Riordan kick)
EU—Walters 5 pass from Dickerson (Rupert kick)
NH—Weir 1 run (O'Riordan kick)
A—2,286

Indiana (Pa.) 28, Ferris St. 21
at Indiana, Pa.

Ferris St.	7	0	0	14—21
Indiana (Pa.)	0	14	14	0—28

FS—Underwood 6 pass from Love (Lipke kick)
IU—Campolo 1 run (Geary kick)
IU—McClellan 3 pass from Woods (Geary kick)
IU—Campolo 1 run (Geary kick)
IU—Turner 5 pass from Woods (Geary kick)
FS—Underwood 7 pass from Love (Lipke kick)
FS—Koutsopoules 9 pass from Love (Lipke kick)
A—2,500

QUARTERFINAL GAMES (NOV. 27)

North Ala. 45, Hampton 20
at Florence, Ala.

Hampton	14	0	6	0—20
North Ala.	21	7	14	3—45

NA—Rush 1 run (Stoddard kick)
NA—Edwards 18 run (Stoddard kick)
HU—Benson 2 run (Pitts kick)
NA—Gross 42 run (Stoddard kick)
HU—Smith 5 pass from Montgomery (Pitts kick)
NA—Satterfield 4 run (Stoddard kick)
NA—Edwards 18 pass from Gross (Stoddard kick)
HU—White 80 kickoff return (kick blocked)
NA—Gross 2 run (Stoddard kick)
NA—Stoddard 23 field goal
A—5,349

Tex. A&M-Kingsville 51, UC Davis 28
at Davis, Calif.

Tex. A&M-Kingsville	7	28	13	3—51
UC Davis	0	14	7	7—28

TK—Young 11 run (Cortez kick)
TK—Deese 2 run (Cortez kick)
TK—Brown 15 pass from Menchaca (Cortez kick)
TK—Deese 1 run (Cortez kick)
UC—Jones 11 run (Fernandez kick)
UC—Hardy 35 pass from Jones (Fernandez kick)
TK—Jordan 60 pass from Menchaca (Cortez kick)
TK—Deese 1 run (Fernandez kick)
UC—Jackson 3 run (Fernandez kick)
TK—Fite 23 run (kick failed)
TK—Cortez 38 field goal
UC—Jackson 3 run (Fernandez kick)
A—6,600

North Dak. 54, Mankato St. 21
at Grand Forks, N.D.

Mankato St.	0	7	0	14—21
North Dak.	7	21	13	13—54

ND—Burnell 29 pass from Wagner (Dahlem kick)
ND—Burnell 6 run (Dahlem kick)
ND—Hagert 29 pass from Wagner (Dahlem kick)
MK—Nelson 22 pass from Pass (Navitsky kick)
ND—Hagert 40 pass from Wagner (Dahlem kick)
ND—Dahlem 29 field goal
ND—Hagert 41 pass from Wagner (Dahlem kick)
ND—Dahlem 32 field goal
MK—Erickson 5 pass from Pass (Navitsky kick)
MK—Erickson 3 run (Navitsky kick)
ND—Leingang 4 pass from Wagner (Dahlem kick)
ND—Sorenson 2 run (kick blocked)
A—3,047

Indiana (Pa.) 38, New Haven 35
at New Haven, Conn.

Indiana (Pa.)	7	7	21	3—38
New Haven	14	7	7	7—35

IU—Campolo 6 run (Geary kick)
NH—Graham 5 run (O'Riordan kick)
NH—Graham 14 run (O'Riordan kick)
NH—Graham 14 run (O'Riordan kick)
IU—Mann 3 run (Geary kick)
NH—Livingston 13 run (O'Riordan kick)
IU—Campolo 1 run (Geary kick)
IU—Smith 6 pass from Woods (Geary kick)
IU—Smith 72 pass from Woods (Geary kick)
IU—Geary 27 field goal
NH—Livingston 19 run (O'Riordan kick)
A—7,500

SEMIFINAL GAMES (DEC. 4)

North Ala. 27, Tex. A&M-Kingsville 25
at Florence, Ala.

Tex. A&M-Kingsville	0	7	6	12—25
North Ala.	7	7	7	6—27

NA—Satterfield 24 run (Stoddard kick)
TK—Runnels 31 blocked punt return (Cortez kick)
NA—Shelton 35 pass from Gross (Stoddard kick)
TK—Deese 2 run (kick failed)
NA—Jones 9 run (Stoddard kick)
TK—Deese 13 run (pass failed)
NA—Rush 3 run (kick failed)
TK—Deese 18 pass from Menchaca (pass failed)
A—4,992

Indiana (Pa.) 21, North Dak. 6
at Indiana, Pa.

North Dak.	0	0	0	6— 6
Indiana (Pa.)	7	14	0	0—21

IU—Mann 4 run (Geary kick)
IU—Smith 10 pass from Woods (Geary kick)
IU—McClellan 8 pass from Woods (Geary kick)
ND—Ostby 24 pass from Wagner (kick blocked)
A—3,000

Championship Records

INDIVIDUAL: SINGLE GAME

NET YARDS RUSHING
379—Ronald Moore, Pittsburg St. (41) vs. Portland St. (38), 12-5-92.

RUSHES ATTEMPTED
51—Terry Morrow, Central St. (Ohio) (31) vs. Towson St. (0), 11-28-86.

TOUCHDOWNS BY RUSHING
5—Ronald Moore, Pittsburg St. (38) vs. North Dak. St. (37), OT, 11-28-92; Ronald Moore, Pittsburg St. (41) vs. Portland St. (38), 12-5-92.

NET YARDS PASSING
443—Tom Bertoldi, Northern Mich. (55) vs. Elizabeth City St. (6), 11-28-81.

PASSES ATTEMPTED
59—Bob Biggs, UC Davis (14) vs. Massachusetts (35), 12-9-72.

PASSES COMPLETED
32—Darren Del'Andrae, Portland St. (56) vs. West Chester (50), 3 OT, 11-18-89.

PASSES HAD INTERCEPTED
7—George Coussan, Southwestern La. (25) vs. Tennessee St. (26), 12-12-70.

TOUCHDOWN PASSES COMPLETED
6—Darren Del'Andrae, Portland St. (56) vs. West Chester (50), 3 OT, 11-18-89.

COMPLETION PERCENTAGE
(Min. 8 Attempts)
.833—Tony Aliucci, Indiana (Pa.) (56) vs. Virginia Union (7), 11-23-91 (10 of 12).

NET YARDS RUSHING AND PASSING
444—Tom Bertoldi, Northern Mich. (55) vs. Elizabeth City St. (6), 11-28-81.

NUMBER OF RUSHING AND PASSING PLAYS
66—Jamie Pass, Mankato St. (21) vs. North Dak. (54), 11-27-93.

PUNTING AVERAGE
(Min. 3 Punts)
53.7—Chris Humes, UC Davis (23) vs. Angelo St. (28), 11-18-89.

NUMBER OF PUNTS
12—Dan Gentry, Tennessee Tech (0) vs. Louisiana Tech (35), 12-9-72.

PASSES CAUGHT
14—Don Hutt, Boise St. (34) vs. Louisiana Tech (38), 12-8-73.

NET YARDS RECEIVING
220—Steve Hansley, Northwest Mo. St. (15) vs. Nebraska-Omaha (28), 11-24-84.

TOUCHDOWN PASSES CAUGHT
4—Steve Kreider, Lehigh (30) vs. Massachusetts (23), 11-26-77; Scott Asman, West Chester (50) vs. Portland St. (56), 3 OT, 11-18-89.

PASSES INTERCEPTED
5—Don Pinson, Tennessee St. (26) vs. Southwestern La. (25), 12-12-70.

YARDS GAINED ON INTERCEPTION RETURNS
113—Darren Ryals, Millersville (27) vs. Indiana (Pa.) (24), 2 returns for 53- and 60-yard TDs, 11-19-88.

YARDS GAINED ON PUNT RETURNS
138—Rick Caswell, Western Ky. (14) vs. New Hampshire (3), 12-6-75.

YARDS GAINED ON KICKOFF RETURNS
182—Larry Anderson, LIU-C.W. Post (22) vs. Delaware (72), 12-11-71.

POINTS
32—Ronald Moore, Pittsburg St. (38) vs. North Dak. St. (37), OT, 11-28-92; Ronald Moore, Pittsburg St. (41) vs. Portland St. (38), 12-5-92.

TOUCHDOWNS
5—Ronald Moore, Pittsburg St. (38) vs. North Dak. St. (37), OT, 11-28-92; Ronald Moore, Pittsburg St. (41) vs. Portland St. (38), 12-5-92.

EXTRA POINTS
10—Larry Washington, Delaware (72) vs. LIU-C.W. Post (22), 12-11-71.

FIELD GOALS
4—Mario Ferretti, Northern Mich. (55) vs. Elizabeth City St. (6), 11-28-81; Ken Kubisz, North Dak. St. (26) vs. UC Davis (17), 12-3-83.

INDIVIDUAL: TOURNAMENT

NET YARDS RUSHING
721—Ronald Moore, Pittsburg St., 1992 (108 vs. North Dak., 151 vs. North Dak. St., 379 vs. Portland St., 83 vs. Jacksonville St.).

RUSHES ATTEMPTED
117—Ronald Moore, Pittsburg St., 1992 (29 vs. North Dak., 31 vs. North Dak. St., 37 vs. Portland St., 20 vs. Jacksonville St.).

NET YARDS PASSING
1,226—Chris Crawford, Portland St., 1988 (248 vs. Bowie St., 375 vs. Jacksonville St., 270 vs. Tex. A&M-Kingsville, 333 vs. North Dak. St.).

PASSES ATTEMPTED
139—Chris Crawford, Portland St., 1988 (31 vs. Bowie St., 41 vs. Jacksonville St., 32 vs. Tex. A&M-Kingsville, 35 vs. North Dak. St.).

PASSES COMPLETED
94—Chris Crawford, Portland St., 1988 (20 vs. Bowie St., 27 vs. Jacksonville St., 25 vs. Tex. A&M-Kingsville, 22 vs. North Dak. St.).

TOUCHDOWN PASSES COMPLETED
10—Chris Crawford, Portland St., 1988 (2 vs. Bowie St., 2 vs. Jacksonville St., 3 vs. Tex. A&M-Kingsville, 3 vs. North Dak. St.).

COMPLETION PERCENTAGE
(Min. 2 Games)
.824—Mike Turk, Troy St., 1984, 14 of 17 (4-5 vs. Central St., Ohio, 5-5 vs. Towson St., 5-7 vs. North Dak. St.).

PASSES HAD INTERCEPTED
9—Dennis Tomek, Western Ky., 1973 (0 vs. Lehigh, 6 vs. Grambling, 3 vs. Louisiana Tech).

PASSES CAUGHT
27—Don Hutt, Boise St., 1973 (13 vs. South Dak., 14 vs. Louisiana Tech).

NET YARDS RECEIVING
452—Henry Newson, Portland St., 1991 (94 vs. Northern Colo., 209 vs. Mankato St., 149 vs. Pittsburg St.).

TOUCHDOWN PASSES CAUGHT
7—Steve Kreider, Lehigh, 1977 (4 vs. Massachusetts, 1 vs. UC Davis, 2 vs. Jacksonville St.).

POINTS
88—Ronald Moore, Pittsburg St., 1992 (18 vs. North Dak., 32 vs. North Dak. St., 32 vs. Portland St., 6 vs. Jacksonville St.).

TOUCHDOWNS
14—Ronald Moore, Pittsburg St., 1992 (3 vs. North Dak., 5 vs. North Dak. St., 5 vs. Portland St., 1 vs. Jacksonville St.).

INDIVIDUAL: LONGEST PLAYS

LONGEST RUSH
93—Ronald Moore, Pittsburg St. (41) vs. Portland St. (38), 12-5-92, TD.

LONGEST PASS COMPLETION
99—Ken Suhl to Tony Willis, New Haven (35) vs. Ferris St. (13), 11-28-92, TD.

LONGEST FIELD GOAL
50—Ted Clem, Troy St. (18) vs. North Dak. St. (17), 12-8-84.

LONGEST PUNT
76—Chris Humes, UC Davis (23) vs. Angelo St. (28), 11-18-89.

LONGEST PUNT RETURN
91—Winford Wilborn, Louisiana Tech (14) vs. Eastern Mich. (3), 12-11-71, TD.

LONGEST KICKOFF RETURN
100—Ken Bowles, Nevada-Las Vegas (6) vs. Akron (26), 11-26-76, TD.

LONGEST INTERCEPTION RETURN
100—Charles Harris, Jacksonville St. (34) vs. Northeast Mo. St. (21), 11-27-82, TD.

LONGEST FUMBLE RETURN
93—Ray Neal, Middle Tenn. St. (20) vs. Muskingum (0), 12-12-64, TD.

TEAM: SINGLE GAME

FIRST DOWNS
34—Delaware (72) vs. LIU-C.W. Post (22), 12-11-71; Delaware (60) vs. Mississippi Col. (10), 12-1-79; Cal St. Sacramento (56) vs. N.C. Central (7), 11-26-88.

FIRST DOWNS BY RUSHING
27—Delaware (72) vs. LIU-C.W. Post (22), 12-11-71.

FIRST DOWNS BY PASSING
23—Central Fla. (10) vs. Troy St. (31), 12-5-87; Portland St. (56) vs. West Chester (50), 3 OT, 11-18-89.

NET YARDS RUSHING
566—Jacksonville St. (63) vs. West Chester (24), 11-19-88.

RUSHES ATTEMPTED
84—Southwest Tex. St. (34) vs. UC Davis (9), 12-11-82.

NET YARDS PASSING
464—Northern Mich. (55) vs. Elizabeth City St. (6), 11-28-81.

PASSES ATTEMPTED
60—San Fran. St. (6) vs. San Diego St. (27), 12-9-67; Central Fla. (10) vs. Troy St. (31), 12-5-87.

PASSES COMPLETED
36—Central Fla. (10) vs. Troy St. (31), 12-5-87.

COMPLETION PERCENTAGE
(Min. 10 Attempts)
.813—Delaware (60) vs. Mississippi Col. (10), 12-1-79 (13 of 16); Tex. A&M-Kingsville (51) vs. UC Davis (28), 11-27-93 (13 of 16).

PASSES HAD INTERCEPTED
8—Southwestern La. (25) vs. Tennessee St. (26), 12-12-70.

NET YARDS RUSHING AND PASSING
695—Northern Mich. (55) vs. Elizabeth City St. (6), 11-28-81.

RUSHING AND PASSING PLAYS
98—Northern Mich. (55) vs. Elizabeth City St. (6), 11-28-81.

PUNTING AVERAGE
53.7—UC Davis (23) vs. Angelo St. (28), 11-18-89.

NUMBER OF PUNTS
12—Tennessee Tech (0) vs. Louisiana Tech (35), 12-9-72; Delaware (8) vs. Grambling (17), 12-1-73; Western Ky. (0) vs. Louisiana Tech (34), 12-15-73.

PUNTS HAD BLOCKED
2—Delaware (31) vs. Indiana (Pa.) (24), 12-14-68; Humboldt St. (29) vs. Fresno St. (14), 12-14-68; Northeast Mo. St. (21) vs. Jacksonville St. (34), 11-27-82.

YARDS GAINED ON PUNT RETURNS
140—Southwest Tex. St. (62) vs. Northern Mich. (0), 12-5-81.

YARDS GAINED ON KICKOFF RETURNS
251—LIU-C.W. Post (22) vs. Delaware (72), 12-11-71.

YARDS GAINED ON INTERCEPTION RETURNS
131—Millersville (27) vs. Indiana (Pa.) (24), 11-19-88.

YARDS PENALIZED
166—San Diego St. (27) vs. San Fran. St. (6), 12-9-67.

NUMBER OF PENALTIES
21—San Diego St. (27) vs. San Fran. St. (6), 12-9-67.

FUMBLES
10—Winston-Salem (0) vs. Delaware (41), 12-2-78.

FUMBLES LOST
7—Louisiana Tech (10) vs. Western Caro. (7), 11-30-74.

POINTS
72—Delaware vs. LIU-C.W. Post (22), 12-11-72.

TEAM: TOURNAMENT

FIRST DOWNS
99—North Ala., 1993 (25 vs. Carson-Newman, 30 vs. Hampton, 23 vs. Tex. A&M-Kingsville, 21 vs. Indiana, Pa.).

NET YARDS RUSHING
1,660—North Dak. St., 1988 (474 vs. Augustana, S.D., 434 vs. Millersville, 413 vs. Cal St. Sacramento, 339 vs. Portland St.).

NET YARDS PASSING
1,226—Portland St., 1988 (248 vs. Bowie St., 375 vs. Jacksonville St., 270 vs. Tex. A&M-Kingsville, 333 vs. North Dak. St.).

NET YARDS RUSHING AND PASSING
2,032—North Ala., 1993 (455 vs. Carson-Newman, 570 vs. Hampton, 470 vs. Tex. A&M-Kingsville, 537 vs. Indiana, Pa.).

PASSES ATTEMPTED
139—Portland St., 1988 (31 vs. Bowie St., 41 vs. Jacksonville St., 32 vs. Tex. A&M-Kingsville, 35 vs. North Dak. St.).

PASSES COMPLETED
94—Portland St., 1988 (20 vs. Bowie St., 27 vs. Jacksonville St., 25 vs. Tex. A&M-Kingsville, 22 vs. North Dak. St.).

PASSES HAD INTERCEPTED
10—Western Ky., 1973 (0 vs. Lehigh, 6 vs. Grambling, 4 vs. Louisiana Tech).

NUMBER OF PUNTS
29—Western Ky., 1973 (6 vs. Lehigh, 11 vs. Grambling, 12 vs. Louisiana Tech).

YARDS PENALIZED
355—New Haven, 1992 (114 vs. West Chester, 146 vs. Ferris St., 95 vs. Jacksonville St.).

FUMBLES
16—Delaware, 1978 (8 vs. Jacksonville St., 2 vs. Winston-Salem, 6 vs. Eastern Ill.).

FUMBLES LOST
12—Delaware, 1978 (6 vs. Jacksonville St., 2 vs. Winston-Salem, 4 vs. Eastern Ill.).

POINTS
162—North Dak. St., 1988 (49 vs. Augustana, S.D., 36 vs. Millersville, 42 vs. Cal St. Sacramento, 35 vs. Portland St.).

Most Division II Championship Appearances

North Dakota State.................13
UC Davis.......................11
Jacksonville State..........10
Virginia Union.........8

CHAMPIONSHIP RESULTS

Year-by-Year Division II Championship Results

Year (Number of Teams)	Coach	Record	Result
1973 (8)			
Louisiana Tech	Maxie Lambright	3-0	Champion
Western Ky.	Jimmy Feix	2-1	Second
Boise St.	Tony Knap	1-1	Semifinalist
Grambling	Eddie Robinson	1-1	Semifinalist
Delaware	Tubby Raymond	0-1	Lost 1st Round
Lehigh	Fred Dunlap	0-1	Lost 1st Round
South Dak.	Joe Salem	0-1	Lost 1st Round
Western Ill.	Darrell Mudra	0-1	Lost 1st Round
1974 (8)			
Central Mich.	Roy Kramer	3-0	Champion
Delaware	Tubby Raymond	2-1	Second
Louisiana Tech	Maxie Lambright	1-1	Semifinalist
Nevada-Las Vegas	Ron Meyer	1-1	Semifinalist
Alcorn St.	Marino Casem	0-1	Lost 1st Round
Boise St.	Tony Knap	0-1	Lost 1st Round
Western Caro.	Bob Waters	0-1	Lost 1st Round
Youngstown St.	Rey Dempsey	0-1	Lost 1st Round
1975 (8)			
Northern Mich.	Gil Krueger	3-0	Champion
Western Ky.	Jimmy Feix	2-1	Second
Livingston	Jim King	1-1	Semifinalist
New Hampshire	Bill Bowes	1-1	Semifinalist
Boise St.	Tony Knap	0-1	Lost 1st Round
Lehigh	Fred Dunlap	0-1	Lost 1st Round
North Dak.	Jerry Olson	0-1	Lost 1st Round
Northern Iowa	Stan Sheriff	0-1	Lost 1st Round
1976 (8)			
Montana St.	Sonny Holland	3-0	Champion
Akron	Jim Dennison	2-1	Second
North Dak. St.	Jim Wacker	1-1	Semifinalist
Northern Mich.	Gil Krueger	1-1	Semifinalist
Delaware	Tubby Raymond	0-1	Lost 1st Round
Eastern Ky.	Roy Kidd	0-1	Lost 1st Round
Nevada-Las Vegas	Tony Knap	0-1	Lost 1st Round
New Hampshire	Bill Bowes	0-1	Lost 1st Round
1977 (8)			
Lehigh	John Whitehead	3-0	Champion
Jacksonville St.	Jim Fuller	2-1	Second
North Dak. St.	Jim Wacker	1-1	Semifinalist
UC Davis	Jim Sochor	1-1	Semifinalist
Bethune-Cookman	Andy Hinson	0-1	Lost 1st Round
Massachusetts	Dick MacPherson	0-1	Lost 1st Round
Northern Ariz.	Joe Salem	0-1	Lost 1st Round
Northern Mich.	Gil Krueger	0-1	Lost 1st Round
1978 (8)			
Eastern Ill.	Darrell Mudra	3-0	Champion
Delaware	Tubby Raymond	2-1	Second
Winston-Salem	Bill Hayes	1-1	Semifinalist
Youngstown St.	Bill Narduzzi	1-1	Semifinalist
Cal Poly SLO	Joe Harper	0-1	Lost 1st Round
Jacksonville St.	Jim Fuller	0-1	Lost 1st Round
Nebraska-Omaha	Sandy Buda	0-1	Lost 1st Round
UC Davis	Jim Sochor	0-1	Lost 1st Round

Year (Number of Teams)	Coach	Record	Result
1979 (8)			
Delaware	Tubby Raymond	3-0	Champion
Youngstown St.	Bill Narduzzi	2-1	Second
Alabama A&M	Ray Greene	1-1	Semifinalist
Mississippi Col.	John Williams	1-1	Semifinalist
Morgan St.	Clarence Thomas	0-1	Lost 1st Round
North Dak.	Gene Murphy	0-1	Lost 1st Round
South Dak. St.	John Gregory	0-1	Lost 1st Round
Virginia Union	Willard Bailey	0-1	Lost 1st Round
1980 (8)			
Cal Poly SLO	Joe Harper	3-0	Champion
Eastern Ill.	Darrell Mudra	2-1	Second
North Ala.	Wayne Grubb	1-1	Semifinalist
Santa Clara	Pat Malley	1-1	Semifinalist
Jacksonville St.	Jim Fuller	0-1	Lost 1st Round
Northern Colo.	Bob Blasi	0-1	Lost 1st Round
Northern Mich.	Bill Rademacher	0-1	Lost 1st Round
Virginia Union	Willard Bailey	0-1	Lost 1st Round
1981 (8)			
Southwest Tex. St.	Jim Wacker	3-0	Champion
North Dak. St.	Don Morton	2-1	Second
Northern Mich.	Bill Rademacher	1-1	Semifinalist
Shippensburg	Vito Ragazzo	1-1	Semifinalist
Elizabeth City St.	Johnnie Walton	0-1	Lost 1st Round
Jacksonville St.	Jim Fuller	0-1	Lost 1st Round
Puget Sound	Ron Simonson	0-1	Lost 1st Round
Virginia Union	Willard Bailey	0-1	Lost 1st Round
1982 (8)			
Southwest Tex. St.	Jim Wacker	3-0	Champion
UC Davis	Jim Sochor	2-1	Second
Jacksonville St.	Jim Fuller	1-1	Semifinalist
North Dak. St.	Don Morton	1-1	Semifinalist
Fort Valley St.	Doug Porter	0-1	Lost 1st Round
Northeast Mo. St.	Bruce Craddock	0-1	Lost 1st Round
Northern Mich.	Bill Rademacher	0-1	Lost 1st Round
Virginia Union	Willard Bailey	0-1	Lost 1st Round
1983 (8)			
North Dak. St.	Don Morton	3-0	Champion
Central St. (Ohio)	Billy Joe	2-1	Second
North Ala.	Wayne Grubb	1-1	Semifinalist
UC Davis	Jim Sochor	1-1	Semifinalist
Butler	Bill Sylvester	0-1	Lost 1st Round
Southwest Tex. St.	John O'Hara	0-1	Lost 1st Round
Towson St.	Phil Albert	0-1	Lost 1st Round
Virginia Union	Willard Bailey	0-1	Lost 1st Round
1984 (8)			
Troy St.	Chan Gailey	3-0	Champion
North Dak. St.	Don Morton	2-1	Second
Nebraska-Omaha	Sandy Buda	1-1	Semifinalist
Towson St.	Phil Albert	1-1	Semifinalist
Central St. (Ohio)	Billy Joe	0-1	Lost 1st Round
Norfolk St.	Willard Bailey	0-1	Lost 1st Round
Northwest Mo. St.	Vern Thomsen	0-1	Lost 1st Round
UC Davis	Jim Sochor	0-1	Lost 1st Round
1985 (8)			
North Dak. St.	Earle Solomonson	3-0	Champion
North Ala.	Wayne Grubb	2-1	Second
Bloomsburg	George Landis	1-1	Semifinalist
South Dak.	Dave Triplett	1-1	Semifinalist
Central St. (Ohio)	Billy Joe	0-1	Lost 1st Round

Year (Number of Teams)	Coach	Record	Result
Fort Valley St.	Gerald Walker	0-1	Lost 1st Round
Hampton	Fred Freeman	0-1	Lost 1st Round
UC Davis	Jim Sochor	0-1	Lost 1st Round

1986 (8)

Year (Number of Teams)	Coach	Record	Result
North Dak. St.	Earle Solomonson	3-0	Champion
South Dak.	Dave Triplett	2-1	Second
Central St. (Ohio)	Billy Joe	1-1	Semifinalist
Troy St.	Rick Rhodes	1-1	Semifinalist
Ashland	Fred Martinelli	0-1	Lost 1st Round
Towson St.	Phil Albert	0-1	Lost 1st Round
UC Davis	Jim Sochor	0-1	Lost 1st Round
Virginia Union	Joe Taylor	0-1	Lost 1st Round

1987 (8)

Year (Number of Teams)	Coach	Record	Result
Troy St.	Rick Rhodes	3-0	Champion
Portland St.	Pokey Allen	2-1	Second
Central Fla.	Gene McDowell	1-1	Semifinalist
Northern Mich.	Herb Grenke	1-1	Semifinalist
Angelo St.	Jerry Vandergriff	0-1	Lost 1st Round
Indiana (Pa.)	Frank Cignetti	0-1	Lost 1st Round
Mankato St.	Dan Runkle	0-1	Lost 1st Round
Winston-Salem	Bill Hayes	0-1	Lost 1st Round

1988 (16)

Year (Number of Teams)	Coach	Record	Result
North Dak. St.	Rocky Hager	4-0	Champion
Portland St.	Pokey Allen	3-1	Second
Cal St. Sacramento	Bob Mattos	2-1	Semifinalist
Tex. A&M-Kingsville	Ron Harms	2-1	Semifinalist
Jacksonville St.	Bill Burgess	1-1	Quarterfinalist
Millersville	Gene Carpenter	1-1	Quarterfinalist
N.C. Central	Henry Lattimore	1-1	Quarterfinalist
Tenn.-Martin	Don McLeary	1-1	Quarterfinalist
Augustana (S.D.)	Jim Heinitz	0-1	Lost 1st Round
Bowie St.	Sanders Shiver	0-1	Lost 1st Round
Butler	Bill Lynch	0-1	Lost 1st Round
Indiana (Pa.)	Frank Cignetti	0-1	Lost 1st Round
Mississippi Col.	John Williams	0-1	Lost 1st Round
UC Davis	Jim Sochor	0-1	Lost 1st Round
West Chester	Danny Hale	0-1	Lost 1st Round
Winston-Salem	Pete Richardson	0-1	Lost 1st Round

1989 (16)

Year (Number of Teams)	Coach	Record	Result
*Mississippi Col.	John Williams	4-0	Champion
Jacksonville St.	Bill Burgess	3-1	Second
Angelo St.	Jerry Vandergriff	2-1	Semifinalist
Indiana (Pa.)	Frank Cignetti	2-1	Semifinalist
North Dak. St.	Rocky Hager	1-1	Quarterfinalist
Pittsburg St.	Dennis Franchione	1-1	Quarterfinalist
Portland St.	Pokey Allen	1-1	Quarterfinalist
St. Cloud St.	Noel Martin	1-1	Quarterfinalist
Alabama A&M	George Pugh	0-1	Lost 1st Round
Augustana (S.D.)	Jim Heinitz	0-1	Lost 1st Round
Edinboro	Tom Hollman	0-1	Lost 1st Round
Grand Valley St.	Tom Beck	0-1	Lost 1st Round
Northwest Mo. St.	Bud Elliott	0-1	Lost 1st Round
Tex. A&M-Kingsville	Ron Harms	0-1	Lost 1st Round
UC Davis	Bob Foster	0-1	Lost 1st Round
West Chester	Rick Daniels	0-1	Lost 1st Round

1990 (16)

Year (Number of Teams)	Coach	Record	Result
North Dak. St.	Rocky Hager	4-0	Champion
Indiana (Pa.)	Frank Cignetti	3-1	Second
*Mississippi Col.	John Williams	2-1	Semifinalist
Pittsburg St.	Chuck Broyles	2-1	Semifinalist
Cal Poly SLO	Lyle Setencich	1-1	Quarterfinalist
East Tex. St.	Eddie Vowell	1-1	Quarterfinalist
Edinboro	Tom Hollman	1-1	Quarterfinalist
Jacksonville St.	Bill Burgess	1-1	Quarterfinalist
Cal St. Northridge	Bob Burt	0-1	Lost 1st Round
Grand Valley St.	Tom Beck	0-1	Lost 1st Round
North Ala.	Bobby Wallace	0-1	Lost 1st Round
Northeast Mo. St.	Eric Holm	0-1	Lost 1st Round
Northern Colo.	Joe Glenn	0-1	Lost 1st Round
Virginia Union	Joe Taylor	0-1	Lost 1st Round
Winston-Salem	Pete Richardson	0-1	Lost 1st Round
Wofford	Mike Ayers	0-1	Lost 1st Round

1991 (16)

Year (Number of Teams)	Coach	Record	Result
Pittsburg St.	Chuck Broyles	4-0	Champion
Jacksonville St.	Bill Burgess	3-1	Second
Indiana (Pa.)	Frank Cignetti	2-1	Semifinalist
Portland St.	Pokey Allen	2-1	Semifinalist
East Tex. St.	Eddie Vowell	1-1	Quarterfinalist
Mankato St.	Dan Runkle	1-1	Quarterfinalist
Mississippi Col.	Terry McMillan	1-1	Quarterfinalist
Shippensburg	Rocky Rees	1-1	Quarterfinalist
Butler	Bob Bartolomeo	0-1	Lost 1st Round
East Stroudsburg	Dennis Douds	0-1	Lost 1st Round
Grand Valley St.	Brian Kelly	0-1	Lost 1st Round
North Dak. St.	Rocky Hager	0-1	Lost 1st Round
Northern Colo.	Joe Glenn	0-1	Lost 1st Round
Virginia Union	Joe Taylor	0-1	Lost 1st Round
Winston-Salem	Pete Richardson	0-1	Lost 1st Round
Wofford	Mike Ayers	0-1	Lost 1st Round

1992 (16)

Year (Number of Teams)	Coach	Record	Result
Jacksonville St.	Bill Burgess	4-0	Champion
Pittsburg St.	Chuck Broyles	3-1	Second
New Haven	Mark Whipple	2-1	Semifinalist
Portland St.	Pokey Allen	2-1	Semifinalist
Ferris St.	Keith Otterbein	1-1	Quarterfinalist
North Ala.	Bobby Wallace	1-1	Quarterfinalist
North Dak. St.	Rocky Hager	1-1	Quarterfinalist
Tex. A&M-Kingsville	Ron Harms	1-1	Quarterfinalist
Edinboro	Tom Hollman	0-1	Lost 1st Round
Hampton	Joe Taylor	0-1	Lost 1st Round
North Dak.	Roger Thomas	0-1	Lost 1st Round
Northeast Mo. St.	Eric Holm	0-1	Lost 1st Round
Savannah St.	Bill Davis	0-1	Lost 1st Round
UC Davis	Bob Foster	0-1	Lost 1st Round
West Chester	Rick Daniels	0-1	Lost 1st Round
Western St.	Carl Iverson	0-1	Lost 1st Round

1993 (16)

Year (Number of Teams)	Coach	Record	Result
North Ala.	Bobby Wallace	4-0	Champion
Indiana (Pa.)	Frank Cignetti	3-1	Second
North Dak.	Roger Thomas	2-1	Semifinalist
Tex. A&M-Kingsville	Ron Harms	2-1	Semifinalist
Hampton	Joe Taylor	1-1	Quarterfinalist
Mankato St.	Dan Runkle	1-1	Quarterfinalist
New Haven	Mark Whipple	1-1	Quarterfinalist
UC Davis	Bob Biggs	1-1	Quarterfinalist
Albany St. (Ga.)	Hampton Smith	0-1	Lost 1st Round
Carson-Newman	Ken Sparks	0-1	Lost 1st Round
Edinboro	Tom Hollman	0-1	Lost 1st Round
Ferris St.	Keith Otterbein	0-1	Lost 1st Round
Fort Hays St.	Bob Cortese	0-1	Lost 1st Round
Mo. Southern St.	Jon Lantz	0-1	Lost 1st Round
Pittsburg St.	Chuck Broyles	0-1	Lost 1st Round
Portland St.	Tim Walsh	0-1	Lost 1st Round

*Competition in championship vacated by the NCAA.

Division II Championship Record of Each College by Coach

(83 Colleges; 1973-93)

	Yrs	Won	Lost	CH	2D
AKRON					
Jim Dennison (Wooster '60) 76-2D	1	2	1	0	1
ALABAMA A&M					
Ray Green (Akron '63) 79	1	1	1	0	0
George Pugh (Alabama '76) 89	1	0	1	0	0
TOTAL	2	1	2	0	0
ALBANY ST. (GA.)					
Hampton Smith (Mississippi Val. '57) 93	1	0	1	0	0
ALCORN ST.					
Marino Casem (Xavier, La. '56) 74	1	0	1	0	0
ANGELO ST.					
Jerry Vandergriff (Corpus Christi '65) 87, 89	2	2	2	0	0
ASHLAND					
Fred Martinelli (Otterbein '51) 86	1	0	1	0	0
AUGUSTANA (S.D.)					
Jim Heinitz (South Dak. St. '72) 88, 89	2	0	2	0	0
BETHUNE-COOKMAN					
Andy Hinson (Bethune-Cookman '53) 77	1	0	1	0	0
BLOOMSBURG					
George Landis (Penn St. '71) 85	1	1	1	0	0
BOISE ST.					
Tony Knap (Idaho '39) 73, 74, 75	3	1	3	0	0
BOWIE ST.					
Sanders Shiver (Carson-Newman '76) 88	1	0	1	0	0

	Yrs	Won	Lost	CH	2D
BUTLER					
Bill Sylvester (Butler '50) 83	1	0	1	0	0
Bill Lynch (Butler '77) 88	1	0	1	0	0
Bob Bartolomeo (Butler '77) 91	1	0	1	0	0
TOTAL	3	0	3	0	0
CAL POLY SLO					
Joe Harper (UCLA '59) 78, 80-CH	2	3	1	1	0
Lyle Setencich (Fresno St. '68) 90	1	1	1	0	0
TOTAL	3	4	2	1	0
CAL ST. NORTHRIDGE					
Bob Burt (Cal St. Los Angeles '62) 90	1	0	1	0	0
CAL ST. SACRAMENTO					
Bob Mattos (Cal St. Sacramento '64) 88	1	2	1	0	0
CARSON-NEWMAN					
Ken Sparks (Carson-Newman '68) 93	1	0	1	0	0
CENTRAL FLA.					
Gene McDowell (Florida St. '65) 87	1	1	1	0	0
CENTRAL MICH.					
Roy Kramer (Maryville, Tenn. '53) 74-CH	1	3	0	1	0
CENTRAL ST. (OHIO)					
Billy Joe (Cheyney '70) 83-2D, 84, 85, 86	4	3	4	0	1
DELAWARE					
Harold "Tubby" Raymond (Michigan '50) 73, 74-2D, 76, 78-2D, 79-CH	5	7	4	1	2
EAST STROUDSBURG					
Dennis Douds (Slippery Rock '63) 91	1	0	1	0	0
EAST TEX. ST.					
Eddie Vowell (S'western Okla. '69) 90, 91	2	2	2	0	0
EASTERN ILL.					
Darrell Mudra (Peru St. '51) 78-CH, 80-2D	2	5	1	1	1
EASTERN KY.					
Roy Kidd (Eastern Ky. '54) 76	1	0	1	0	0
EDINBORO					
Tom Hollman (Ohio Northern '68) 89, 90, 92, 93	4	1	4	0	0
ELIZABETH CITY ST.					
Johnnie Walton (Elizabeth City St. '69) 81	1	0	1	0	0
FERRIS ST.					
Keith Otterbein (Ferris St. '79) 92, 93	2	1	2	0	0
FORT HAYS ST.					
Bob Cortese (Colorado '67) 93	1	0	1	0	0
FORT VALLEY ST.					
Doug Porter (Xavier, La. '52) 82	1	0	1	0	0
Gerald Walker (Lincoln, Mo. '62) 85	1	0	1	0	0
TOTAL	2	0	2	0	0
GRAMBLING					
Eddie Robinson (Leland '41) 73	1	1	1	0	0
GRAND VALLEY ST.					
Tom Beck (Northern Ill. '61) 89, 90	2	0	2	0	0
Brian Kelly (Assumption '83) 91	1	0	1	0	0
TOTAL	3	0	3	0	0
HAMPTON					
Fred Freeman (Mississippi Val. '66) 85	1	0	1	0	0
Joe Taylor (Western Ill. '72) 92, 93	2	1	2	0	0
TOTAL	3	1	3	0	0
INDIANA (PA.)					
Frank Cignetti (Indiana, Pa. '60) 87, 88, 89, 90-2D, 91, 93-2D	6	10	6	0	2
JACKSONVILLE ST.					
Jim Fuller (Alabama '67) 77-2D, 78, 80, 81, 82	5	3	5	0	1
Bill Burgess (Auburn '63) 88, 89-2D, 90, 91-2D, 92-CH	5	12	4	1	2
TOTAL	10	15	9	1	3
LEHIGH					
Fred Dunlap (Colgate '50) 73, 75	2	0	2	0	0
John Whitehead (East Stroudsburg '50) 77-CH	1	3	0	1	0
TOTAL	3	3	2	1	0
LIVINGSTON					
Jim King 75	1	1	1	0	0
LOUISIANA TECH					
Maxie Lambright (Southern Miss. '49) 73-CH, 74	2	4	1	1	0
MANKATO ST.					
Dan Runkle (Illinois Col. '68) 87, 91, 93	3	2	3	0	0

	Yrs	Won	Lost	CH	2D
MASSACHUSETTS					
Dick MacPherson (Springfield '58) 77	1	0	1	0	0
MILLERSVILLE					
Gene Carpenter (Huron '63) 88	1	1	1	0	0
MISSISSIPPI COL.*					
John Williams (Mississippi Col. '57) 79, 88, 89-CH, 90	4	7	3	1	0
Terry McMillan (Southern Miss. '69) 91	1	1	1	0	0
TOTAL	5	8	4	1	0
MO. SOUTHERN ST.					
Jon Lantz (Panhandle St. '74) 93	1	0	1	0	0
MONTANA ST.					
Sonny Holland (Montana St. '60) 76-CH	1	3	0	1	0
MORGAN ST.					
Clarence Thomas 79	1	0	1	0	0
N.C. CENTRAL					
Henry Lattimore (Jackson St. '57) 88	1	1	1	0	0
NEBRASKA-OMAHA					
Sandy Buda (Kansas '67) 78, 84	2	1	2	0	0
NEVADA-LAS VEGAS					
Ron Meyer (Purdue '63) 74	1	1	1	0	0
Tony Knap (Idaho '39) 76	1	0	1	0	0
TOTAL	2	1	2	0	0
NEW HAMPSHIRE					
Bill Bowes (Penn St. '65) 75, 76	2	1	2	0	0
NEW HAVEN					
Mark Whipple (Brown '79) 92, 93	2	3	2	0	0
NORFOLK ST.					
Willard Bailey (Norfolk St. '62) 84	1	0	1	0	0
NORTH ALA.					
Wayne Grubb (Tennessee '61) 80, 83, 85-2D	3	4	3	0	1
Bobby Wallace (Mississippi St. '76) 90, 92, 93-CH	3	5	2	1	0
TOTAL	6	9	5	1	1
NORTH DAK.					
Jerry Olson (Valley City St. '55) 75	1	0	1	0	0
Gene Murphy (North Dak. '62) 79	1	0	1	0	0
Roger Thomas (Augustana, Ill. '69) 92, 93	2	2	2	0	0
TOTAL	4	2	4	0	0
NORTH DAK. ST.					
Jim Wacker (Valparaiso '60) 76, 77	2	2	2	0	0
Don Morton (Augustana, Ill. '69) 81-2D, 82, 83-CH, 84-2D	4	8	3	1	2
Earle Solomonson (Augsburg '69) 85-CH, 86-2D	2	6	0	2	0
Rocky Hager (Minot St. '74) 88-CH, 89, 90-CH, 91, 92	5	10	3	2	0
TOTAL	13	26	8	5	2
NORTHEAST MO. ST.					
Bruce Craddock (Northeast Mo. St. '66) 82	1	0	1	0	0
Eric Holm (Northeast Mo. St. '81) 90, 92	2	0	2	0	0
TOTAL	3	0	3	0	0
NORTHERN ARIZ.					
Joe Salem (Minnesota '61) 77	1	0	1	0	0
NORTHERN COLO.					
Bob Blasi (Colorado St. '53) 80	1	0	1	0	0
Joe Glenn (South Dak. '71) 90, 91	2	0	2	0	0
TOTAL	3	0	3	0	0
NORTHERN IOWA					
Stan Sheriff (Cal Poly SLO '54) 75	1	0	1	0	0
NORTHERN MICH.					
Gil Krueger (Marquette '52) 75-CH, 76, 77	3	4	2	1	0
Bill Rademacher (Northern Mich. '63) 80, 81, 82	3	1	3	0	0
Herb Grenke (Wis.-Milwaukee '63) 87	1	1	1	0	0
TOTAL	7	6	6	1	0
NORTHWEST MO. ST.					
Vern Thomsen (Peru St. '61) 84	1	0	1	0	0
Bud Elliott (Baker '53) 89	1	0	1	0	0
TOTAL	2	0	2	0	0
PITTSBURG ST.					
Dennis Franchione (Pittsburg St. '73) 89	1	1	1	0	0
Chuck Broyles (Pittsburg St. '70) 90, 91-CH, 92-2D, 93	4	9	3	1	1
TOTAL	5	10	4	1	1

	Yrs	Won	Lost	CH	2D
PORTLAND ST.					
Pokey Allen (Utah '65) 87-2D, 88-2D, 89, 91, 92	5	10	5	0	2
Tim Walsh (UC Riverside '77) 93	1	0	1	0	0
TOTAL	6	10	6	0	2
PUGET SOUND					
Ron Simonson (Portland St. '65) 81	1	0	1	0	0
SANTA CLARA					
Pat Malley (Santa Clara '53) 80	1	1	1	0	0
SAVANNAH ST.					
Bill Davis (Johnson Smith '65) 92	1	0	1	0	0
SHIPPENSBURG					
Vito Ragazzo (William & Mary '51) 81	1	1	1	0	0
Rocky Rees (West Chester '71) 91	1	1	1	0	0
TOTAL	2	2	2	0	0
SOUTH DAK.					
Joe Salem (Minnesota '61) 73	1	0	1	0	0
Dave Triplett (Iowa '72) 85, 86-2D	2	3	2	0	1
TOTAL	3	3	3	0	1
SOUTH DAK. ST.					
John Gregory (Northern Iowa '61) 79	1	0	1	0	0
SOUTHWEST TEX. ST.					
Jim Wacker (Valparaiso '60) 81-CH, 82-CH	2	6	0	2	0
John O'Hara (Panhandle St. '67) 83	1	0	1	0	0
TOTAL	3	6	1	2	0
ST. CLOUD ST.					
Noel Martin (Nebraska '63) 89	1	1	1	0	0
TEX. A&M-KINGSVILLE					
Ron Harms (Valparaiso '59) 88, 89, 92, 93	4	5	4	0	0
TENN.-MARTIN					
Don McLeary (Tennessee '70) 88	1	1	1	0	0
TOWSON ST.					
Phil Albert (Arizona '66) 83, 84, 86	3	1	3	0	0
TROY ST.					
Chan Gailey (Florida '74) 84-CH	1	3	0	1	0
Rick Rhodes 86, 87-CH	2	4	1	1	0
TOTAL	3	7	1	2	0

	Yrs	Won	Lost	CH	2D
UC DAVIS					
Jim Sochor (San Fran. St. '60) 77, 78, 82-2D, 83, 84, 85, 86, 88	8	4	8	0	1
Bob Foster (UC Davis '62) 89, 92	2	0	2	0	0
Bob Biggs (UC Davis '73) 93	1	1	1	0	0
TOTAL	11	5	11	0	1
VIRGINIA UNION					
Willard Bailey (Norfolk St. '62) 79, 80, 81, 82, 83	5	0	5	0	0
Joe Taylor (Western Ill. '72) 86, 90, 91	3	0	3	0	0
TOTAL	8	0	8	0	0
WEST CHESTER					
Danny Hale (West Chester '68) 88	1	0	1	0	0
Rick Daniels (West Chester '75) 89, 92	2	0	2	0	0
TOTAL	3	0	3	0	0
WESTERN CARO.					
Bob Waters (Presbyterian '60) 74	1	0	1	0	0
WESTERN ILL.					
Darrell Mudra (Peru St. '51) 73	1	0	1	0	0
WESTERN KY.					
Jimmy Feix (Western Ky. '53) 73-2D, 75-2D	2	4	2	0	2
WESTERN ST.					
Carl Iverson (Whitman '62) 92	1	0	1	0	0
WINSTON-SALEM					
Bill Hayes (N.C. Central '64) 78, 87	2	1	2	0	0
Pete Richardson (Dayton '68) 88, 90, 91	3	0	3	0	0
TOTAL	5	1	5	0	0
WOFFORD					
Mike Ayers (Georgetown, Ky. '74) 90, 91	2	0	2	0	0
YOUNGSTOWN ST.					
Rey Dempsey (Geneva '58) 74	1	0	1	0	0
Bill Narduzzi (Miami, Ohio '59) 78, 79-2D	2	3	2	0	1
TOTAL	3	3	3	0	1

*Mississippi College's competition in the 1989 and 1990 Division II championships was vacated by the NCAA (official record is 2-3).

All-Time Results

1973 First Round: Grambling 17, Delaware 8; Western Ky. 25, Lehigh 16; Louisiana Tech 18, Western Ill. 13; Boise St. 53, South Dak. 10. **Semifinals:** Western Ky. 28, Grambling 20; Louisiana Tech 38, Boise St. 34. **Championship:** Louisiana Tech 34, Western Ky. 0.

1974 First Round: Central Mich. 20, Boise St. 6; Louisiana Tech 10, Western Caro. 7; Nevada-Las Vegas 35, Alcorn St. 22; Delaware 35, Youngstown St. 14. **Semifinals:** Central Mich. 35, Louisiana Tech 14; Delaware 49, Nevada-Las Vegas 11. **Championship:** Central Mich. 54, Delaware 14.

1975 First Round: Northern Mich. 24, Boise St. 21; Livingston 34, North Dak. 14; Western Ky. 14, Northern Iowa 12; New Hampshire 35, Lehigh 21. **Semifinals:** Northern Mich. 28, Livingston 26; Western Ky. 14, New Hampshire 3. **Championship:** Northern Mich. 16, Western Ky. 14.

1976 First Round: Akron 26, Nevada-Las Vegas 6; Northern Mich. 28, Delaware 17; North Dak. St. 10, Eastern Ky. 7; Montana St. 17, New Hampshire 16. **Semifinals:** Akron 29, Northern Mich. 26; Montana St. 10, North Dak. St. 3. **Championship:** Montana St. 24, Akron 13.

1977 First Round: UC Davis 34, Bethune-Cookman 16; Lehigh 30, Massachusetts 23; North Dak. St. 20, Northern Mich. 6; Jacksonville St. 35, Northern Ariz. 0. **Semifinals:** Lehigh 39, UC Davis 30; Jacksonville St. 31, North Dak. St. 7. **Championship:** Lehigh 33, Jacksonville St. 0.

1978 First Round: Winston-Salem 17, Cal Poly SLO 0; Delaware 42, Jacksonville St. 27; Youngstown St. 21, Nebraska-Omaha 14; Eastern Ill. 35, UC Davis 31. **Semifinals:** Delaware 41, Winston-Salem 0; Eastern Ill. 26, Youngstown St. 22. **Championship:** Eastern Ill. 10, Delaware 9.

1979 First Round: Delaware 58, Virginia Union 28; Mississippi Col. 35, North Dak. 15; Youngstown St. 50, South Dak. St. 7; Alabama A&M 27, Morgan St. 7. **Semifinals:** Delaware 60, Mississippi Col. 10; Youngstown St. 52, Alabama A&M 0. **Championship:** Delaware 38, Youngstown St. 21.

1980 First Round: Eastern Ill. 21, Northern Colo. 14; North Ala. 17, Virginia Union 8; Santa Clara 27, Northern Mich. 26; Cal Poly SLO 15, Jacksonville St. 0. **Semifinals:** Eastern Ill. 56, North Ala. 31; Cal Poly SLO 38, Santa Clara 14. **Championship:** Cal Poly SLO 21, Eastern Ill. 13.

1981 First Round: Northern Mich. 55, Elizabeth City St. 6; Southwest Tex. St. 38, Jacksonville St. 22; North Dak. St. 24, Puget Sound 10; Shippensburg 40, Virginia Union 27. **Semifinals:** Southwest Tex. St. 62, Northern Mich. 0; North Dak. St. 18, Shippensburg 6. **Championship:** Southwest Tex. St. 42, North Dak. St. 13.

1982 First Round: Southwest Tex. St. 27, Fort Valley St. 6; Jacksonville St. 34, Northeast Mo. 21; North Dak. St. 21, Virginia Union 20; UC Davis 42, Northern Mich. 21. **Semifinals:** Southwest Tex. St. 19, Jacksonville St. 14; UC Davis 19, North Dak. St. 14. **Championship:** Southwest Tex. St. 34, UC Davis 9.

1983 First Round: UC Davis 25, Butler 6; North Dak. St. 24, Towson St. 17; North Ala. 16, Virginia Union 14; Central St. (Ohio) 24, Southwest Tex. St. 16. **Semifinals:** North Dak. St. 26, UC Davis 17; Central St. (Ohio) 27, North Ala. 24. **Championship:** North Dak. St. 41, Central St. (Ohio) 21.

1984 First Round: North Dak. St. 31, UC Davis 23; Nebraska-Omaha 28, Northwest Mo. St. 15; Troy St. 31, Central St. (Ohio) 21; Towson St. 31, Norfolk St. **Semifinals:** North Dak. St. 25, Nebraska-Omaha 14; Troy St. 45, Towson St. 3. **Championship:** Troy St. 18, North Dak. St. 17.

1985 First Round: North Dak. St. 31, UC Davis 12; South Dak. 13, Central St. (Ohio) 10 (2 OT); Bloomsburg 38, Hampton 28; North Ala. 14, Fort Valley St. 7. **Semifinals:** North Dak. St. 16, South Dak. 7; North Ala. 34, Bloomsburg 0. **Championship:** North Dak. St. 35, North Ala. 7.

1986 First Round: North Dak. St. 50, Ashland 0; Central St. (Ohio) 31, Towson St. 0; Troy St. 31, Virginia Union 7; South Dak. 26, UC Davis 23. **Semifinals:** North Dak. St. 35, Central St. (Ohio) 12; South Dak. 42, Troy St. 28. **Championship:** North Dak. St. 27, South Dak. 7.

1987 First Round: Portland St. 27, Mankato St. 21; Northern Mich. 23, Angelo St. 20 (OT); Central Fla. 12, Indiana (Pa.) 10; Troy St. 45, Winston-Salem 14. **Semifinals:** Portland St. 13, Northern Mich. 7; Troy St. 31, Central Fla. 10. **Championship:** Troy St. 31, Portland St. 17.

1988 First Round: North Dak. St. 49, Augustana (S.D.) 7; Millersville 27, Indiana (Pa.) 24; Cal St. Sacramento 35, UC Davis 14; N.C. Central 31, Winston-Salem 16; Tex. A&M-Kingsville 39, Mississippi Col. 15; Tenn.-Martin 23, Butler 6; Portland St. 34, Bowie St. 17; Jacksonville St. 63, West Chester 24. **Quarterfinals:** North Dak. St. 36, Millersville 26; Cal St. Sacramento 29, N.C. Central 7; Tex. A&M-Kingsville 34, Tenn.-Martin 0; Portland St. 20, Jacksonville St. 13. **Semifinals:** North Dak. St. 42, Cal St. Sacramento 20; Portland St. 35, Tex. A&M-Kingsville 27. **Championship:** North Dak. St. 35, Portland St. 21.

1989 First Round: *Mississippi Col. 34, Tex. A&M-Kingsville 19; St. Cloud St. 27, Augustana (S.D.) 20; Portland St. 56, West Chester 50 (3 OT); Indiana (Pa.) 34, Grand Valley St. 24; Pittsburg 28, Northwest Mo. St. 7; Angelo St. 28, UC Davis 23; North Dak. St. 45, Edinboro 32; Jacksonville St. 33, Alabama A&M 9. **Quarterfinals:** *Mississippi Col. 55, St. Cloud St. 24;

Indiana (Pa.) 17, Portland St. 0; Angelo St. 24, Pittsburg St. 21; Jacksonville St. 21, North Dak. St. 17. **Semifinals:** *Mississippi Col. 26, Indiana (Pa.) 14; Jacksonville St. 34, Angelo St. 16. **Championship:** *Mississippi Col. 3, Jacksonville St. 0.

*Mississippi College's participation in 1989 playoff vacated.

1990 First Round: *Mississippi Col. 70, Wofford 19; Jacksonville St. 38, North Ala. 14; Indiana (Pa.) 48, Winston-Salem 0; Edinboro 38, Virginia Union 14; North Dak. St. 17, Northern Colo. 7; Cal Poly SLO 14, Cal St. Northridge 7; Pittsburg St. 59, Northeast Mo. St. 3; East Tex. St. 20, Grand Valley St. 14. **Quarterfinals:** *Mississippi Col. 14, Jacksonville St. 7; Indiana (Pa.) 14, Edinboro 7; North Dak. St. 47, Cal Poly SLO 0; Pittsburg St. 60, East Tex. St. 28. **Semifinals:** Indiana (Pa.) 27, *Mississippi Col. 8; North Dak. St. 39, Pittsburg St. 29. **Championship:** North Dak. St. 51, Indiana (Pa.) 11.

*Mississippi College's participation in 1990 playoff vacated.

1991 First Round: Pittsburg St. 26, Butler 16; East Tex. St. 36, Grand Valley St. 15; Portland St. 28, Northern Colo. 24; Mankato St. 27, North Dak. St. 7; Jacksonville St. 49, Winston-Salem 24; Mississippi Col. 28, Wofford 15; Indiana (Pa.) 56, Virginia Union 7; Shippensburg 34, East Stroudsburg 33 (OT). **Quarterfinals:** Pittsburg St. 38, East Tex. St. 28; Portland St. 37, Mankato St. 27; Jacksonville St. 35, Mississippi Col. 7; Indiana (Pa.) 52, Shippensburg 7. **Semifinals:** Pittsburg St. 53, Portland St. 21; Jacksonville St. 27, Indiana (Pa.) 20. **Championship:** Pittsburg St. 23, Jacksonville St. 6.

1992 First Round: Ferris St. 19, Edinboro 15; New Haven 38, West Chester 26; Jacksonville St. 41, Savannah St. 16; North Ala. 33, Hampton 21; Tex. A&M-Kingsville 22, Western St. 13; Portland St. 42, UC Davis 28; Pittsburg St. 26, North Dak. 21; North Dak. St. 42, Northeast Mo. St. 7. **Quarterfinals:** New Haven 35, Ferris St. 13; Jacksonville St. 14, North Ala. 12; Portland St. 35, Tex. A&M-Kingsville 30; Pittsburg St. 38, North Dak. St. 37 (OT). **Semifinals:** Jacksonville St. 46, New Haven 35; Pittsburg St. 41, Portland St. 38. **Championship:** Jacksonville St. 17, Pittsburg St. 13.

1993 First Round: North Ala. 38, Carson-Newman 28; Hampton 33, Albany St. (Ga.) 7; Tex. A&M-Kingsville 50, Portland St. 15; UC Davis 37, Fort Hays St. 34; Mankato St. 34, Mo. Southern St. 13; North Dak. 17, Pittsburg St. 14; New Haven 48, Edinboro 28; Indiana (Pa.) 28, Ferris St. 21. **Quarterfinals:** North Ala. 45, Hampton 20; Tex. A&M-Kingsville 51, UC Davis 28; North Dak. 54, Mankato St. 21; Indiana (Pa.) 38, New Haven 35. **Semifinals:** North Ala. 27, Tex. A&M-Kingsville 25; Indiana (Pa.) 21, North Dak. 6. **Championship:** North Ala. 41, Indiana (Pa.) 34.

Division III Championship

1993 Title Game Summary

AMOS ALONZO STAGG BOWL, SALEM STADIUM, SALEM, VA.; DECEMBER 11, 1993

	Rowan	Mount Union
First Downs	20	25
Rushes-Net Yardage	36-130	35-75
Passing Yardage	177	387
Return Yardage (Punts, Int. & Fum.)	15	34
Passes (Comp.-Att.-Int.)	20-32-2	28-45-1
Punts (Number-Average)	4-28.8	5-27.8
Fumbles (Number-Lost)	0-0	2-0
Penalties (Number-Yards)	4-44	3-21

Rowan	0	9	15	0—24
Mount Union	7	7	7	13—34

Game Conditions: Temperature, 34 degrees; wind, 20-30 mph from northwest; weather, snow flurries. Attendance: 7,304.

FIRST QUARTER
Rowan—Jarvis Perry 13 run (kick failed) (47 yards in 7 plays, 7:25 left)
Mount Union—Rob Atwood 24 pass from Jim Ballard (Dan Ulichney kick) (82 yards in 8 plays, 4:02 left)
Rowan—Rob Juliano 37 field goal (51 yards in 11 plays, 0:23 left)

SECOND QUARTER
Mount Union—Jim Gresko 1 run (Ulichney kick) (72 yards in 8 plays, 13:43 left)

THIRD QUARTER
Mount Union—Atwood 13 pass from Ballard (Ulichney kick) (16 yards in 4 plays, 7:41 left)
Rowan—Ed Hesson 4 run (Juliano kick) (63 yards in 7 plays, 4:43 left)
Rowan—Calvin Easley 8 pass from Hesson (Joseph DiPietro pass from Hesson) (40 yards in 8 plays, 0:12 left)

FOURTH QUARTER
Mount Union—Gresko 2 pass from Ballard (Ulichney kick) (73 yards in 8 plays, 13:14 left)
Mount Union—Ballard 2 run (kick blocked) (80 yards in 12 plays, 5:04 left)

INDIVIDUAL LEADERS
Rushing—Rowan: Easley, 40 yards on 7 carries; Mount Union: Gresko, 70 yards on 24 carries.
Passing—Rowan: Hesson, 20 of 32 for 177 yards; Mount Union: Ballard, 28 of 45 for 387 yards.
Receiving—Rowan: Easley, 5 catches for 36 yards; Mount Union: Atwood, 9 catches for 160 yards.

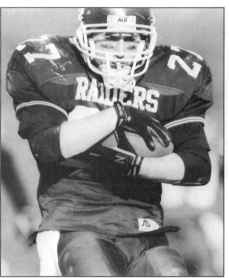

Doug Pensinger/Allsport photo

Mount Union running back Jim Gresko ran for 70 yards and one touchdown and scored another touchdown on a two-yard pass to help the Purple Raiders defeat Rowan, 34-24, in the 1993 Division III championship game.

Division III All-Time Championship Results

Year	Champion	Coach	Score	Runner-Up	Site
1973	Wittenberg	Dave Maurer	41-0	Juniata	Phenix City, Ala.
1974	Central (Iowa)	Ron Schipper	10-8	Ithaca	Phenix City, Ala.
1975	Wittenberg	Dave Maurer	28-0	Ithaca	Phenix City, Ala.
1976	St. John's (Minn.)	John Gagliardi	31-28	Towson St.	Phenix City, Ala.
1977	Widener	Bill Manlove	39-36	Wabash	Phenix City, Ala.
1978	Baldwin-Wallace	Lee Tressel	24-10	Wittenberg	Phenix City, Ala.
1979	Ithaca	Jim Butterfield	14-10	Wittenberg	Phenix City, Ala.
1980	Dayton	Rick Carter	63-0	Ithaca	Phenix City, Ala.
1981	Widener	Bill Manlove	17-10	Dayton	Phenix City, Ala.
1982	West Ga.	Bobby Pate	14-0	Augustana (Ill.)	Phenix City, Ala.
1983	Augustana (Ill.)	Bob Reade	21-17	Union (N.Y.)	Kings Island, Ohio
1984	Augustana (Ill.)	Bob Reade	21-12	Central (Iowa)	Kings Island, Ohio
1985	Augustana (Ill.)	Bob Reade	20-7	Ithaca	Phenix City, Ala.
1986	Augustana (Ill.)	Bob Reade	31-3	Salisbury St.	Phenix City, Ala.
1987	Wagner	Walt Hameline	19-3	Dayton	Phenix City, Ala.

Ithaca's Jeff Wittman scored three touchdowns and rushed for 159 yards as the Bombers defeated Dayton, 34-20, to claim the 1991 Division III championship, Ithaca's third title.

Year	Champion	Coach	Score	Runner-Up	Site
1988	Ithaca	Jim Butterfield	39-24	Central (Iowa)	Phenix City, Ala.
1989	Dayton	Mike Kelly	17-7	Union (N.Y.)	Phenix City, Ala.
1990	Allegheny	Ken O'Keefe	21-14 (OT)	Lycoming	Bradenton, Fla.
1991	Ithaca	Jim Butterfield	34-20	Dayton	Bradenton, Fla.
1992	Wis.-La Crosse	Roger Harring	16-12	Wash. & Jeff.	Bradenton, Fla.
1993	Mount Union	Larry Kehres	34-24	Rowan	Salem, Va.

Regional Championship Results

(Before Division III Championship)

Year	Champion	Coach	Score	Runner-Up	Site
EAST (KNUTE ROCKNE BOWL)					
1969	Randolph-Macon	Ted Keller	47-28	Bridgeport	Bridgeport, Conn.
1970	Montclair St.	Clary Anderson	7-6	Hampden-Sydney	Atlantic City, N.J.
1971	Bridgeport	Ed Farrell	17-12	Hampden-Sydney	Atlantic City, N.J.
1972	Bridgeport	Ed Farrell	27-22	Slippery Rock	Atlantic City, N.J.
WEST (AMOS ALONZO STAGG BOWL)					
1969	Wittenberg	Dave Maurer	27-21	William Jewell	Springfield, Ohio
1970	Capital	Gene Slaughter	34-21	Luther	Columbus, Ohio
1971	Vacated		20-10	Ohio Wesleyan	Phenix City, Ala.
1972	Heidelberg	Pete Riesen	28-16	Fort Valley St.	Phenix City, Ala.

1993 Division III Championship Results

REGIONALS
Mount Union 40, Allegheny 7
Albion 41, Anderson 21
Wis.-La Crosse 55, Wartburg 26
St. John's (Minn.) 32, Coe 14
Wash. & Jeff. 27, Moravian 7
Frostburg St. 26, Wilkes 25
Rowan 29, Buffalo St. 6
Wm. Paterson 17, Union (N.Y.) 7

QUARTERFINALS
Mount Union 30, Albion 16
St. John's (Minn.) 47, Wis.-La Crosse 25
Wash. & Jeff. 28, Frostburg St. 7
Rowan 37, Wm. Paterson 0

SEMIFINALS
Mount Union 56, St. John's (Minn.) 8
Rowan 23, Wash. & Jeff. 16

CHAMPIONSHIP
Mount Union 34, Rowan 24

1993 Division III Game Summaries

FIRST-ROUND GAMES (NOV. 20)

Mount Union 40, Allegheny 7
at Alliance, Ohio

Allegheny	7	0	0	0—7
Mount Union	12	14	7	7—40

MU—Lyons 11 pass from Ballard (kick failed)
MU—Gresko 6 pass from Ballard (run failed)
AL—McKenzie 18 pass from Bell (Merski kick)
MU—Bubonics 15 pass from Ballard (Ulichney kick)
MU—Gresko 9 pass from Ballard (Ulichney kick)
MU—Gresko 1 run (Ulichney kick)
MU—Lyons 5 pass from Ballard (Ulichney kick)
A—5,800

Albion 41, Anderson 21
at Albion, Mich.

Anderson	0	7	7	7—21
Albion	21	13	7	0—41

AL—Robinson 11 run (Zacha kick)
AL—Robinson 6 run (Zacha kick)
AL—Robinson 3 run (Zacha kick)
AL—Morris 1 run (Zacha kick)
AL—Reason 75 pass from Montico (kick blocked)
AN—Isley 2 pass from Conkling (Roberts kick)
AL—Robinson 20 run (Zacha kick)
AN—Mosgrove 55 pass from Conkling (Roberts kick)
AN—Owens 18 pass from Conkling (Roberts kick)
A—4,014

Wis.-La Crosse 55, Wartburg 26
at La Crosse, Wis.

Wartburg	0	0	14	12—26
Wis.-La Crosse	14	14	20	7—55

LC—Krause 47 run (Larson kick)
LC—Kling 27 pass from Gonnion (Larson kick)
LC—Janke 12 pass from Gonnion (Larson kick)
LC—Rogers 12 run (Larson kick)
LC—Rogers 27 run (Larson kick)
LC—Janke 1 run (kick blocked)
W—Beatty 34 run (George kick)
W—Lehman 42 pass from Elijah (George kick)
LC—Harcey 5 pass from Kusick (Larson kick)
LC—Krause 9 run (Larson kick)
W—Beatty 1 run (kick failed)
W—Briggs 16 run (pass failed)
A—1,515

St. John's (Minn.) 32, Coe 14
at Collegeville, Minn.

Coe	7	0	7	0—14
St. John's (Minn.)	7	7	12	6—32

C—Bender 1 run (Kreamer kick)
SJ—Malmberg 2 run (Poulin kick)
SJ—Malmberg 8 run (Poulin kick)
C—Peterson 20 pass from Simons (Kreamer kick)
SJ—Malmberg 5 run (kick failed)
SJ—Loretz 9 pass from Seiler (run failed)
SJ—Palmer 22 pass from Seiler (run failed)
A—4,000

Wash. & Jeff. 27, Moravian 7
at Washington, Pa.

Moravian	7	0	0	0—7
Wash. & Jeff.	14	0	7	6—27

WJ—Williams 47 run (Evan kick)
WJ—Begley 64 pass from Baer (Evan kick)
M—Frank 14 run (Kurtz kick)
WJ—Williams 1 run (Evan kick)
WJ—Miller 2 run (kick failed)
A—NA

Frostburg St. 26, Wilkes 25
at Edwardsville, Pa.

Frostburg St.	0	0	7	19—26
Wilkes	6	12	7	0—25

W—Alston 45 pass from Perry (kick failed)
W—Wade 15 run (pass failed)
W—Perry 1 run (pass failed)
FS—Telleria 1 run (Sibila kick)
W—Smith 3 run (O'Donnell kick)
FS—Telleria 1 run (kick failed)
FS—Bellamy 14 run (Sibila kick)
FS—Norman 20 blocked punt return (run failed)
A—2,500

Rowan 29, Buffalo St. 6
at Glassboro, N.J.

Buffalo St.	0	6	0	0—6
Rowan	3	7	7	12—29

R—Juliano 23 field goal
BS—Gladden 3 run (kick blocked)
R—Johnson 82 pass from Hesson (Juliano kick)
R—Easley 31 pass from Hesson (Juliano kick)
R—Easley 45 run (kick failed)
R—Easley 16 run (kick failed)
A—2,500

Wm. Paterson 17, Union (N.Y.) 7
at Schenectady, N.Y.

Wm. Paterson	0	10	0	7—17
Union (N.Y.)	0	0	0	7—7

WP—Harmon 7 pass from Smith (Moyer kick)
WP—Moyer 30 field goal
WP—Ferguson 14 pass from Smith (Moyer kick)
U—LaBonte 25 pass from Lombardo (Harrison kick)
A—3,800

QUARTERFINAL GAMES (NOV. 27)

Mount Union 30, Albion 16
at Alliance, Ohio

Albion	7	7	2	0—16
Mount Union	14	0	8	8—30

MU—Gresko 53 run (Ulichney kick)
AL—Robinson 4 run (Zacha kick)
MU—Gresko 49 run (Ulichney kick)
AL—Morris 2 run (Zacha kick)
AL—Safety, McDonald tackled Gresko in end zone
MU—Bubonics 52 pass from Ballard (Atwood pass from Ballard)
MU—Gresko 1 run (Gresko pass from Ballard)
A—4,888

St. John's (Minn.) 47, Wis.-La Crosse 25
at La Crosse, Wis.

St. John's (Minn.)	7	26	7	7—47
Wis.-La Crosse	7	12	6	0—25

LC—Janke 6 run (Larson kick)
SJ—Palmer 22 pass from Seiler (Poulin kick)
LC—Janke 1 run (kick failed)
SJ—Schroeder 43 pass from Gonnion (pass failed)
SJ—Malmberg 11 run (kick failed)
SJ—Malmberg 12 pass from Seiler (Poulin kick)
SJ—Murray 47 pass from Seiler (Poulin kick)
SJ—Murray 27 pass from Seiler (pass failed)
LC—Schroeder 40 pass from Gonnion (kick failed)
SJ—Palmer 59 pass from Seiler (Poulin kick)
SJ—O'Kane 27 pass from Seiler (Poulin kick)
A—2,671

Wash. & Jeff. 28, Frostburg St. 7
at Frostburg, Md.

Wash. & Jeff.	6	15	7	0—28
Frostburg St.	0	7	0	0—7

WJ—Jarosinski 10 pass from Baer (kick failed)

WJ—Baer 3 run (Jarosinski pass from Baer)
FS—Fuller 46 pass from Telleria (Sibila kick)
WJ—Jarosinski 37 pass from Baer (Evan kick)
WJ—Begley 36 pass from Baer (Evan kick)
A—1,500

Rowan 37, Wm. Paterson 0
at Wayne, N.J.

Rowan	14	0	17	6	37
Wm. Paterson	0	0	0	0	0

R—Anderson 33 run (Juliano kick)
R—Perry 14 run (Juliano kick)
R—Anderson 41 run (Juliano kick)
R—Juliano 33 field goal
R—Johnson 30 pass from Hesson (Juliano kick)
R—Rechner 42 interception return (kick failed)
A—4,300

SEMIFINAL GAMES (DEC. 4)

Mount Union 56, St. John's (Minn.) 8
at Alliance, Ohio

St. John's (Minn.)	0	0	8	0	8
Mount Union	21	22	13	0	56

MU—Gresko 2 pass from Ballard (Ulichney kick)
MU—Bubonics 35 pass from Ballard (Ulichney kick)
MU—Atwood 4 pass from Ballard (Ulichney kick)
MU—Safety, Seiler tackled in end zone
MU—Atwood 42 pass from Ballard (Ulichney kick)
MU—Atwood 12 pass from Ballard (Ulichney kick)
MU—Atwood 24 pass from Ballard (run failed)
MU—Bubonics 15 pass from Ballard (kick blocked)
MU—Sirianni 65 pass from Ballard (Ulichney kick)
SJ—Loretz 19 pass from Seiler (Malmberg run)
A—3,333

Rowan 23, Wash. & Jeff. 16
at Washington, Pa.

Rowan	3	13	0	7	23
Wash. & Jeff.	7	0	7	2	16

R—Juliano 27 field goal
WJ—Williams 8 run (Evan kick)
R—Easley 9 pass from Hesson (kick failed)
R—Johnson 36 pass from Hesson (Juliano kick)
WJ—Williams 1 run (Evan kick)
R—Ramsey 53 pass from Hesson (Juliano kick)
WJ—Safety, ball snapped out of end zone
A—NA

Championship Records

INDIVIDUAL: SINGLE GAME

NET YARDS RUSHING
389—Ricky Gales, Simpson (35) vs. St. John's (Minn.) (42), 11-18-89.

RUSHES ATTEMPTED
51—Ricky Gales, Simpson (35) vs. St. John's (Minn.) (42), 11-18-89.

TOUCHDOWNS BY RUSHING
5—Jeff Norman, St. John's (Minn.) (46) vs. Augustana (Ill.) (7), 11-20-76; Mike Coppa, Salisbury St. (44) vs. Ithaca (40), 12-6-86; Paul Parker, Ithaca (62) vs. Ferrum (28), 12-3-88; Kevin Hofacre, Dayton (35) vs. John Carroll (10), 11-18-89.

NET YARDS PASSING
461—Jim Ballard, Mount Union (24) vs. Wis.-La Crosse (29), 12-5-92.

PASSES ATTEMPTED
53—Walter Briggs, Montclair St. (28) vs. Ithaca (50), 11-30-85.

PASSES COMPLETED
32—Tim Lynch, Hofstra (10) vs. Lycoming (20), 12-1-90.

PASSES HAD INTERCEPTED
7—Rick Steil, Dubuque (7) vs. Ithaca (27), 11-17-79.

TOUCHDOWN PASSES COMPLETED
8—Jim Ballard, Mount Union (56) vs. St. John's (Minn.) (8), 12-4-93.

COMPLETION PERCENTAGE
(Min. 8 Attempts)
.900—Robb Disbennett, Salisbury St. (16) vs. Carnegie Mellon (14), 11-19-83 (18 of 20).

NET YARDS RUSHING AND PASSING
480—Jim Ballard, Mount Union (24) vs. Wis.-La Crosse (29), 12-5-92.

NUMBER OF RUSHING AND PASSING PLAYS
66—Steve Thompson, Carroll (Wis.) (14) vs. Buena Vista (20), 11-20-76.

PUNTING AVERAGE
(Min. 3 Punts)
48.5—Phil Macken, Minn.-Morris (25) vs. Carnegie Mellon (31), 11-17-79.

NUMBER OF PUNTS
14—Tim Flynn, Gettysburg (14) vs. Lycoming (10), 11-23-85.

PASSES CAUGHT
13—Keith Willike, Capital (28) vs. Dayton (52), 11-21-87.

NET YARDS RECEIVING
253—Eric Welgat, Augustana (Ill.) (36) vs. Dayton (38), 11-28-87.

TOUCHDOWN PASSES CAUGHT
4—Kirk Liesimer, Ill. Wesleyan (27) vs. Mount Union (49), 11-28-92; Rob Atwood, Mount Union (56) vs. St. John's (Minn.) (8), 12-4-93.

PASSES INTERCEPTED
3—By eight players. Most recent: Bill Luette, Rowan (37) vs. Wm. Paterson (0), 11-27-93.

YARDS GAINED ON INTERCEPTION RETURNS
100—Jay Zunic, Ithaca (31) vs. Rowan (10), 11-23-91 (2 interceptions, 1 for 100-yard TD).

YARDS GAINED ON PUNT RETURNS
98—Leroy Horn, Montclair St. (28) vs. Western Conn. St. (0), 11-23-85.

YARDS GAINED ON KICKOFF RETURNS
190—George Day, Susquehanna (31) vs. Lycoming (24), 11-30-91.

POINTS
36—Mike Coppa, Salisbury St. (44) vs. Ithaca (40), 12-6-86.

TOUCHDOWNS
6—Mike Coppa, Salisbury St. (44) vs. Ithaca (40), 12-6-86.

EXTRA POINTS
9—Tim Robinson, Baldwin-Wallace (71) vs. St. Lawrence (7), 11-18-78.

INDIVIDUAL: TOURNAMENT

NET YARDS RUSHING
882—Chris Babirad, Wash. & Jeff., 1992 (285 vs. Lycoming, 286 vs. Emory & Henry, 207 vs. Rowan, 104 vs. Wis.-La Crosse).

RUSHES ATTEMPTED
129—Chris Babirad, Wash. & Jeff., 1992 (37 vs. Lycoming, 31 vs. Emory & Henry, 36 vs. Rowan, 25 vs. Wis.-La Crosse).

NET YARDS PASSING
1,251—Jim Ballard, Mount Union, 1993 (347 vs. Allegheny, 192 vs. Albion, 325 vs. St. John's, Minn., 387 vs. Rowan).

PASSES ATTEMPTED
141—Brett Russ, Union (N.Y.), 1989 (23 vs. Cortland St., 37 vs. Montclair St., 38 vs. Ferrum, 43 vs. Dayton); Jim Ballard, Mount Union, 1993 (40 vs. Allegheny, 28 vs. Albion, 28 vs. St. John's, Minn., 45 vs. Rowan).

PASSES COMPLETED
90—Jim Ballard, Mount Union, 1993 (26 vs. Allegheny, 16 vs. Albion, 20 vs. St. John's, Minn., 28 vs. Rowan).

TOUCHDOWN PASSES COMPLETED
17—Jim Ballard, Mount Union, 1993 (5 vs. Allegheny, 1 vs. Albion, 8 vs. St. John's, Minn., 3 vs. Rowan).

COMPLETION PERCENTAGE
(Min. 2 Games)
.667—Greg Thomas, Central (Iowa), 1989, 10 of 15 (5-7 vs. St. Norbert, 5-8 vs. St. John's, Minn.).

PASSES HAD INTERCEPTED
9—Rollie Wiebers, Buena Vista, 1976 (4 vs. Carroll, Wis., 5 vs. St. John's, Minn.).

PASSES CAUGHT
39—Nick Ismailoff, Ithaca, 1991 (12 vs. Rowan, 6 vs. Union, N.Y., 11 vs. Susquehanna, 10 vs. Dayton).

NET YARDS RECEIVING
599—Nick Ismailoff, Ithaca, 1991 (179 vs. Rowan, 122 vs. Union, N.Y., 105 vs. Susquehanna, 193 vs. Dayton).

TOUCHDOWN PASSES CAUGHT
6—Rob Atwood, Mount Union, 1993 (0 vs. Allegheny, 0 vs. Albion, 4 vs. St. John's, Minn., 2 vs. Rowan).

POINTS
60—By four players. Most recent: Chris Babirad, Wash. & Jeff., 1992 (18 vs. Lycoming, 24 vs. Emory & Henry, 12 vs. Rowan, 6 vs. Wis.-La Crosse).

TOUCHDOWNS
10—Brad Price, Augustana (Ill.), 1986 (4 vs. Hope, 1 vs. Mount Union, 2 vs. Concordia-M'head, 3 vs. Salisbury St.); Mike Coppa, Salisbury St., 1986 (1 vs. Emory & Henry, 3 vs. Susquehanna, 6 vs. Ithaca, 0 vs. Augustana, Ill.); Chris Babirad, Wash. & Jeff., 1992 (3 vs. Lycoming, 4 vs. Emory & Henry, 2 vs. Rowan, 1 vs. Wis.-La Crosse).

INDIVIDUAL: LONGEST PLAYS

LONGEST RUSH
93—Rick Papke, Augustana (Ill.) (17) vs. Central (Iowa) (23), 12-3-88, TD.

LONGEST PASS COMPLETION
96—Mark Blom to Tom McDonald, Central (Iowa) (37) vs. Buena Vista (0), 11-22-86, TD.

LONGEST FIELD GOAL
52—Rod Vesling, St. Lawrence (43) vs. Wagner (34), 11-20-82.

LONGEST PUNT
79—Tom Hansen, Ithaca (3) vs. Wittenberg (6), 11-18-78.

LONGEST PUNT RETURN
78—Pete Minturn, Ithaca (34) vs. Gettysburg (0), 12-7-85, TD.

LONGEST KICKOFF RETURN
100—Tom Deery, Widener (23) vs. Montclair St. (12), 11-30-81, TD.

LONGEST INTERCEPTION RETURN
100—Jay Zunic, Ithaca (31) vs. Rowan (10), 11-23-91, TD.

TEAM: SINGLE GAME

FIRST DOWNS
35—Central (Iowa) (71) vs. Occidental (0), 12-7-85.

FIRST DOWNS BY RUSHING
30—Central (Iowa) (71) vs. Occidental (0), 12-7-85.

FIRST DOWNS BY PASSING
20—Rowan (10) vs. Ithaca (31), 11-23-91.

NET YARDS RUSHING
530—St. John's (Minn.) (46) vs. Augustana (Ill.) (7), 11-20-76.

RUSHES ATTEMPTED
83—Capital (34) vs. Luther (21), 11-28-70; Baldwin-Wallace (31) vs. Carnegie Mellon (6), 11-25-78.

NET YARDS PASSING
461—Mount Union (24) vs. Wis.-La Crosse (29), 12-5-92.

PASSES ATTEMPTED
59—Montclair St. (28) vs. Ithaca (50), 11-30-85.

PASSES COMPLETED
32—Hofstra (10) vs. Lycoming (20), 12-1-90.

COMPLETION PERCENTAGE
(Min. 10 Attempts)
.857—Salisbury St. (16) vs. Carnegie Mellon (14), 11-19-83 (18 of 21).

PASSES HAD INTERCEPTED
9—Dubuque (7) vs. Ithaca (27), 11-17-79.

NET YARDS RUSHING AND PASSING
607—Ferrum (49) vs. Moravian (28), 11-26-88.

RUSHING AND PASSING PLAYS
101—Union (N.Y.) (45) vs. Montclair St. (6), 11-25-89.

PUNTING AVERAGE
48.5—Minn.-Morris (25) vs. Carnegie Mellon (31), 11-17-79.

NUMBER OF PUNTS
14—Gettysburg (14) vs. Lycoming (10), 11-23-85.

YARDS GAINED ON PUNT RETURNS
100—Gettysburg (22) vs. Salisbury St. (6), 11-30-85.

YARDS GAINED ON KICKOFF RETURNS
234—Ithaca (40) vs. Salisbury St. (44), 12-6-86.

YARDS GAINED ON INTERCEPTION RETURNS
176—Augustana (Ill.) (14) vs. St. Lawrence (0), 11-27-82.

YARDS PENALIZED
166—Ferrum (49) vs. Moravian (28), 11-26-88.

FUMBLES LOST
6—Albright (7) vs. St. Lawrence (26), 11-20-76; St.

John's (Minn.) (7) vs. Dayton (19), 12-7-91.

POINTS
75—St. John's (Minn.) vs. Coe (2), 11-23-91.

TEAM: TOURNAMENT

FIRST DOWNS
94—Ithaca, 1991 (22 vs. Rowan, 15 vs. Union, N.Y., 28 vs. Susquehanna, 29 vs. Dayton).

NET YARDS RUSHING
1,377—Ithaca, 1988 (251 vs. Wagner, 293 vs. Cortland St., 425 vs. Ferrum, 408 vs. Central, Iowa).

NET YARDS PASSING
1,268—Mount Union, 1993 (347 vs. Allegheny, 192 vs. Albion, 342 vs. St. John's, Minn., 387 vs. Rowan).

NET YARDS RUSHING AND PASSING
1,867—Ithaca, 1991 (486 vs. Rowan, 350 vs. Union, N.Y., 473 vs. Susquehanna, 558 vs. Dayton).

PASSES ATTEMPTED
150—Hofstra, 1990 (51 vs. Cortland St., 50 vs. Trenton St., 49 vs. Lycoming).

PASSES COMPLETED
92—Mount Union, 1993 (26 vs. Allegheny, 16 vs. Albion, 22 vs. St. John's, Minn., 28 vs. Rowan).

PASSES HAD INTERCEPTED
11—Hofstra, 1990 (5 vs. Cortland St., 3 vs. Trenton St., 3 vs. Lycoming).

NUMBER OF PUNTS
30—Central (Iowa), 1988 (12 vs. Concordia-M'head, 8 vs. Wis.-Whitewater, 5 vs. Augustana, Ill., 5 vs. Ithaca).

YARDS PENALIZED
331—Wagner, 1987 (61 vs. Rochester, 80 vs. Fordham, 87 vs. Emory & Henry, 103 vs. Dayton).

FUMBLES LOST
10—Wittenberg, 1978 (4 vs. Ithaca, 2 vs. Minn.-Morris, 4 vs. Baldwin-Wallace).

POINTS
160—Mount Union, 1993 (40 vs. Allegheny, 30 vs. Albion, 56 vs. St. John's, Minn., 34 vs. Rowan).

Year-by-Year Division III Championship Results

Year (Number of Teams)	Coach	Record	Result
1973 (4)			
Wittenberg	Dave Maurer	2-0	Champion
Juniata	Walt Nadzak	1-1	Second
Bridgeport	Ed Farrell	0-1	Semifinalist
San Diego	Andy Vinci	0-1	Semifinalist
1974 (4)			
Central (Iowa)	Ron Schipper	2-0	Champion
Ithaca	Jim Butterfield	1-1	Second
Evansville	Jim Byers	0-1	Semifinalist
Slippery Rock	Bob Di Spirito	0-1	Semifinalist
1975 (8)			
Wittenberg	Dave Maurer	3-0	Champion
Ithaca	Jim Butterfield	2-1	Second
Millsaps	Harper Davis	1-1	Semifinalist
Widener	Bill Manlove	1-1	Semifinalist
Albright	John Potsklan	0-1	Lost 1st Round
Colorado Col.	Jerry Carle	0-1	Lost 1st Round
Fort Valley St.	Leon Lomax	0-1	Lost 1st Round
Indianapolis	Bill Bless	0-1	Lost 1st Round
1976 (8)			
St. John's (Minn.)	John Gagliardi	3-0	Champion
Towson St.	Phil Albert	2-1	Second
Buena Vista	Jim Hershberger	1-1	Semifinalist
St. Lawrence	Ted Stratford	1-1	Semifinalist
Albright	John Potsklan	0-1	Lost 1st Round
Augustana (Ill.)	Ben Newcomb	0-1	Lost 1st Round
Carroll (Wis.)	Steve Miller	0-1	Lost 1st Round
LIU-C.W. Post	Dom Anile	0-1	Lost 1st Round
1977 (8)			
Widener	Bill Manlove	3-0	Champion
Wabash	Frank Navarro	2-1	Second
Albany (N.Y.)	Bob Ford	1-1	Semifinalist
Minn.-Morris	Al Molde	1-1	Semifinalist
Albion	Frank Joranko	0-1	Lost 1st Round
Central (Iowa)	Ron Schipper	0-1	Lost 1st Round
Hampden-Sydney	Stokeley Fulton	0-1	Lost 1st Round
St. John's (Minn.)	John Gagliardi	0-1	Lost 1st Round
1978 (8)			
Baldwin-Wallace	Lee Tressel	3-0	Champion
Wittenberg	Dave Maurer	2-1	Second
Carnegie Mellon	Chuck Klausing	1-1	Semifinalist
Minn.-Morris	Al Molde	1-1	Semifinalist
Dayton	Rick Carter	0-1	Lost 1st Round
Ithaca	Jim Butterfield	0-1	Lost 1st Round
St. Lawrence	Ted Stratford	0-1	Lost 1st Round
St. Olaf	Tom Porter	0-1	Lost 1st Round
1979 (8)			
Ithaca	Jim Butterfield	3-0	Champion
Wittenberg	Dave Maurer	2-1	Second
Carnegie Mellon	Chuck Klausing	1-1	Semifinalist
Widener	Bill Manlove	1-1	Semifinalist
Baldwin-Wallace	Lee Tressel	0-1	Lost 1st Round
Dubuque	Don Birmingham	0-1	Lost 1st Round
Millersville	Gene Carpenter	0-1	Lost 1st Round
Minn.-Morris	Al Molde	0-1	Lost 1st Round
1980 (8)			
Dayton	Rick Carter	3-0	Champion
Ithaca	Jim Butterfield	2-1	Second
Minn.-Morris	Dick Smith	1-1	Semifinalist
Widener	Bill Manlove	1-1	Semifinalist
Baldwin-Wallace	Lee Tressel	0-1	Lost 1st Round
Bethany (W.Va.)	Don Ault	0-1	Lost 1st Round
Dubuque	Don Birmingham	0-1	Lost 1st Round
Wagner	Bill Russo	0-1	Lost 1st Round
1981 (8)			
Widener	Bill Manlove	3-0	Champion
Dayton	Mike Kelly	2-1	Second
Lawrence	Ron Roberts	1-1	Semifinalist
Montclair St.	Fred Hill	1-1	Semifinalist
Alfred	Sam Sanders	0-1	Lost 1st Round
Augustana (Ill.)	Bob Reade	0-1	Lost 1st Round
Minn.-Morris	Dick Smith	0-1	Lost 1st Round
West Ga.	Bobby Pate	0-1	Lost 1st Round
1982 (8)			
West Ga.	Bobby Pate	3-0	Champion
Augustana (Ill.)	Bob Reade	2-1	Second
Bishop	James Jones	1-1	Semifinalist
St. Lawrence	Andy Talley	1-1	Semifinalist
Baldwin-Wallace	Bob Packard	0-1	Lost 1st Round
Wagner	Walt Hameline	0-1	Lost 1st Round
Wartburg	Don Canfield	0-1	Lost 1st Round
Widener	Bill Manlove	0-1	Lost 1st Round
1983 (8)			
Augustana (Ill.)	Bob Reade	3-0	Champion
Union (N.Y.)	Al Bagnoli	2-1	Second
Salisbury St.	Mike McGlinchey	1-1	Semifinalist
Wis.-La Crosse	Roger Harring	1-1	Semifinalist
Adrian	Ron Labadie	0-1	Lost 1st Round
Carnegie Mellon	Chuck Klausing	0-1	Lost 1st Round
Hofstra	Mickey Kwiatkowski	0-1	Lost 1st Round
Occidental	Dale Widolff	0-1	Lost 1st Round
1984 (8)			
Augustana (Ill.)	Bob Reade	3-0	Champion
Central (Iowa)	Ron Schipper	2-1	Second
Union (N.Y.)	Al Bagnoli	1-1	Semifinalist
Wash. & Jeff.	John Luckhardt	1-1	Semifinalist
Dayton	Mike Kelly	0-1	Lost 1st Round

Year (Number of Teams)	Coach	Record	Result
Occidental	Dale Widolff	0-1	Lost 1st Round
Plymouth St.	Jay Cottone	0-1	Lost 1st Round
Randolph-Macon	Jim Blackburn	0-1	Lost 1st Round

1985 (16)

Year (Number of Teams)	Coach	Record	Result
Augustana (Ill.)	Bob Reade	4-0	Champion
Ithaca	Jim Butterfield	3-1	Second
Central (Iowa)	Ron Schipper	2-1	Semifinalist
Gettysburg	Barry Streeter	2-1	Semifinalist
Montclair St.	Rick Giancola	1-1	Quarterfinalist
Mount Union	Ken Wable	1-1	Quarterfinalist
Occidental	Dale Widolff	1-1	Quarterfinalist
Salisbury St.	Mike McGlinchey	1-1	Quarterfinalist
Albion	Pete Schmidt	0-1	Lost 1st Round
Carnegie Mellon	Chuck Klausing	0-1	Lost 1st Round
Coe	Bob Thurness	0-1	Lost 1st Round
Denison	Keith Piper	0-1	Lost 1st Round
Lycoming	Frank Girardi	0-1	Lost 1st Round
St. John's (Minn.)	John Gagliardi	0-1	Lost 1st Round
Union (N.Y.)	Al Bagnoli	0-1	Lost 1st Round
Western Conn. St.	Paul Pasqualoni	0-1	Lost 1st Round

1986 (16)

Year (Number of Teams)	Coach	Record	Result
Augustana (Ill.)	Bob Reade	4-0	Champion
Salisbury St.	Mike McGlinchey	3-1	Second
Concordia-M'head	Jim Christopherson	2-1	Semifinalist
Ithaca	Jim Butterfield	2-1	Semifinalist
Central (Iowa)	Ron Schipper	1-1	Quarterfinalist
Montclair St.	Rick Giancola	1-1	Quarterfinalist
Mount Union	Larry Kehres	1-1	Quarterfinalist
Susquehanna	Rocky Rees	1-1	Quarterfinalist
Buena Vista	Jim Hershberger	0-1	Lost 1st Round
Dayton	Mike Kelly	0-1	Lost 1st Round
Emory & Henry	Lou Wacker	0-1	Lost 1st Round
Hofstra	Mickey Kwiatkowski	0-1	Lost 1st Round
Hope	Ray Smith	0-1	Lost 1st Round
Union (N.Y.)	Al Bagnoli	0-1	Lost 1st Round
Wash. & Jeff.	John Luckhardt	0-1	Lost 1st Round
Wis.-Stevens Point	D. J. LeRoy	0-1	Lost 1st Round

1987 (16)

Year (Number of Teams)	Coach	Record	Result
Wagner	Walt Hameline	4-0	Champion
Dayton	Mike Kelly	3-1	Second
Central (Iowa)	Ron Schipper	2-1	Semifinalist
Emory & Henry	Lou Wacker	2-1	Semifinalist
Augustana (Ill.)	Bob Reade	1-1	Quarterfinalist
Fordham	Larry Glueck	1-1	Quarterfinalist
St. John's (Minn.)	John Gagliardi	1-1	Quarterfinalist
Wash. & Jeff.	John Luckhardt	1-1	Quarterfinalist
Allegheny	Peter Vaas	0-1	Lost 1st Round
Capital	Roger Welsh	0-1	Lost 1st Round
Ferrum	Hank Norton	0-1	Lost 1st Round
Gust. Adolphus	Steve Raarup	0-1	Lost 1st Round
Hiram	Don Charlton	0-1	Lost 1st Round
Hofstra	Mickey Kwiatkowski	0-1	Lost 1st Round
Menlo	Ray Solari	0-1	Lost 1st Round
Rochester	Ray Tellier	0-1	Lost 1st Round

1988 (16)

Year (Number of Teams)	Coach	Record	Result
Ithaca	Jim Butterfield	4-0	Champion
Central (Iowa)	Ron Schipper	3-1	Second
Augustana (Ill.)	Bob Reade	2-1	Semifinalist
Ferrum	Hank Norton	2-1	Semifinalist
Cortland St.	Dennis Kayser	1-1	Quarterfinalist
Moravian	Scot Dapp	1-1	Quarterfinalist
Wis.-Whitewater	Bob Berezowitz	1-1	Quarterfinalist
Wittenberg	Ron Murphy	1-1	Quarterfinalist
Adrian	Ron Labadie	0-1	Lost Regionals
Concordia-M'head	Jim Christopherson	0-1	Lost Regionals
Dayton	Mike Kelly	0-1	Lost Regionals
Hofstra	Mickey Kwiatkowski	0-1	Lost Regionals
Rhodes	Mike Clary	0-1	Lost Regionals
Simpson	Jim Williams	0-1	Lost Regionals
Wagner	Walt Hameline	0-1	Lost Regionals
Widener	Bill Manlove	0-1	Lost Regionals

1989 (16)

Year (Number of Teams)	Coach	Record	Result
Dayton	Mike Kelly	4-0	Champion
Union (N.Y.)	Al Bagnoli	3-1	Second
Ferrum	Hank Norton	2-1	Semifinalist
St. John's (Minn.)	John Gagliardi	2-1	Semifinalist
Central (Iowa)	Ron Schipper	1-1	Quarterfinalist
Lycoming	Frank Girardi	1-1	Quarterfinalist
Millikin	Carl Poelker	1-1	Quarterfinalist
Montclair St.	Rick Giancola	1-1	Quarterfinalist
Augustana (Ill.)	Bob Reade	0-1	Lost Regionals
Cortland St.	Dennis Kayser	0-1	Lost Regionals
Dickinson	Ed Sweeney	0-1	Lost Regionals
Hofstra	Mickey Kwiatkowski	0-1	Lost Regionals
John Carroll	Tony DeCarlo	0-1	Lost Regionals
Simpson	Jim Williams	0-1	Lost Regionals
St. Norbert	Don LaViolette	0-1	Lost Regionals
Wash. & Jeff.	John Luckhardt	0-1	Lost Regionals

1990 (16)

Year (Number of Teams)	Coach	Record	Result
Allegheny	Ken O'Keefe	4-0	Champion
Lycoming	Frank Girardi	3-1	Second
Central (Iowa)	Ron Schipper	2-1	Semifinalist
Hofstra	Joe Gardi	2-1	Semifinalist
Dayton	Mike Kelly	1-1	Quarterfinalist
St. Thomas (Minn.)	Vic Wallace	1-1	Quarterfinalist
Trenton St.	Eric Hamilton	1-1	Quarterfinalist
Wash. & Jeff.	John Luckhardt	1-1	Quarterfinalist
Augustana (Ill.)	Bob Reade	0-1	Lost Regionals
Carnegie Mellon	Rich Lackner	0-1	Lost Regionals
Cortland St.	Dave Murray	0-1	Lost Regionals
Ferrum	Hank Norton	0-1	Lost Regionals
Ithaca	Jim Butterfield	0-1	Lost Regionals
Mount Union	Larry Kehres	0-1	Lost Regionals
Redlands	Mike Maynard	0-1	Lost Regionals
Wis.-Whitewater	Bob Berezowitz	0-1	Lost Regionals

1991 (16)

Year (Number of Teams)	Coach	Record	Result
Ithaca	Jim Butterfield	4-0	Champion
Dayton	Mike Kelly	3-1	Second
St. John's (Minn.)	John Gagliardi	2-1	Semifinalist
Susquehanna	Steve Briggs	2-1	Semifinalist
Allegheny	Ken O'Keefe	1-1	Quarterfinalist
Lycoming	Frank Girardi	1-1	Quarterfinalist
Union (N.Y.)	Al Bagnoli	1-1	Quarterfinalist
Wis.-La Crosse	Roger Harring	1-1	Quarterfinalist
Albion	Pete Schmidt	0-1	Lost Regionals
Baldwin-Wallace	Bob Packard	0-1	Lost Regionals
Coe	D. J. LeRoy	0-1	Lost Regionals
Dickinson	Ed Sweeney	0-1	Lost Regionals
Mass.-Lowell	Dennis Scannell	0-1	Lost Regionals
Rowan	John Bunting	0-1	Lost Regionals
Simpson	Jim Williams	0-1	Lost Regionals
Wash. & Jeff.	John Luckhardt	0-1	Lost Regionals

1992 (16)

Year (Number of Teams)	Coach	Record	Result
Wis.-La Crosse	Roger Harring	4-0	Champion
Wash. & Jeff.	John Luckhardt	3-1	Second
Mount Union	Larry Kehres	2-1	Semifinalist
Rowan	John Bunting	2-1	Semifinalist
Buffalo St.	Jerry Boyes	1-1	Quarterfinalist
Central (Iowa)	Ron Schipper	1-1	Quarterfinalist
Emory & Henry	Lou Wacker	1-1	Quarterfinalist
Ill. Wesleyan	Norm Eash	1-1	Quarterfinalist
Aurora	Jim Scott	0-1	Lost Regionals
Carleton	Bob Sullivan	0-1	Lost Regionals
Dayton	Mike Kelly	0-1	Lost Regionals
Ithaca	Jim Butterfield	0-1	Lost Regionals
Lycoming	Frank Girardi	0-1	Lost Regionals
Redlands	Mike Maynard	0-1	Lost Regionals
Thomas More	Vic Clark	0-1	Lost Regionals
Worcester Tech	Jack Siedlecki	0-1	Lost Regionals

1993 (16)

Year (Number of Teams)	Coach	Record	Result
Mount Union	Larry Kehres	4-0	Champion
Rowan	K. C. Keeler	3-1	Second
St. John's (Minn.)	John Gagliardi	2-1	Semifinalist
Wash. & Jeff.	John Luckhardt	2-1	Semifinalist
Albion	Pete Schmidt	1-1	Quarterfinalist
Frostburg St.	Mike McGlinchey	1-1	Quarterfinalist
Wm. Paterson	Gerry Gallagher	1-1	Quarterfinalist
Wis.-La Crosse	Roger Harring	1-1	Quarterfinalist
Allegheny	Ken O'Keefe	0-1	Lost Regionals
Anderson	Mike Manley	0-1	Lost Regionals
Buffalo St.	Jerry Boyes	0-1	Lost Regionals
Coe	D. J. LeRoy	0-1	Lost Regionals
Moravian	Scot Dapp	0-1	Lost Regionals
Union (N.Y.)	John Audino	0-1	Lost Regionals
Wartburg	Bob Nielson	0-1	Lost Regionals
Wilkes	Joe DeMelfi	0-1	Lost Regionals

CHAMPIONSHIP RESULTS

Division III Championship Record of Each College by Coach

(92 Colleges; 1973-93)

	Yrs	Won	Lost	CH	2D
ADRIAN					
Ron Labadie (Adrian '71) 83, 88	2	0	2	0	0
ALBANY (N.Y.)					
Bob Ford (Springfield '59) 77	1	1	1	0	0
ALBION					
Frank Joranko (Albion '52) 77	1	0	1	0	0
Pete Schmidt (Alma '70) 85, 91, 93	3	1	3	0	0
TOTAL	4	1	4	0	0
ALBRIGHT					
John Potsklan (Penn St. '49) 75, 76	2	0	2	0	0
ALFRED					
Sam Sanders (Buffalo '60) 81	1	0	1	0	0
ALLEGHENY					
Peter Vaas (Holy Cross '74) 87	1	0	1	0	0
Ken O'Keefe (John Carroll '75) 90-CH, 91, 93	3	5	2	1	0
TOTAL	4	5	3	1	0
ANDERSON					
Mike Manley (Anderson '73) 93	1	0	1	0	0
AUGUSTANA (ILL.)					
Ben Newcomb 76	1	0	1	0	0
Bob Reade (Cornell College '54) 81, 82-2D, 83-CH, 84-CH, 85-CH, 86-CH, 87, 88, 89, 90	10	19	6	4	1
TOTAL	11	19	7	4	1
AURORA					
Jim Scott (Luther '61) 92	1	0	1	0	0
BALDWIN-WALLACE					
Lee Tressel (Baldwin-Wallace '48) 78-CH, 79, 80	3	3	2	1	0
Bob Packard (Baldwin-Wallace '65) 82, 91	2	0	2	0	0
TOTAL	5	3	4	1	0
BETHANY (W.VA.)					
Don Ault (West Liberty St. '52) 80	1	0	1	0	0
BISHOP					
James Jones (Bishop '49) 82	1	1	1	0	0
BRIDGEPORT					
Ed Farrell (Rutgers '56) 73	1	0	1	0	0
BUENA VISTA					
Jim Hershberger (Northern Iowa '57) 76, 86	2	1	2	0	0
BUFFALO ST.					
Jerry Boyes (Ithaca '76) 92, 93	2	1	2	0	0
CAPITAL					
Roger Welsh (Muskingum '64) 87	1	0	1	0	0
CARLETON					
Bob Sullivan (St. John's, Minn. '59) 92	1	0	1	0	0
CARNEGIE MELLON					
Chuck Klausing (Slippery Rock '48) 78, 79, 83, 85	4	2	4	0	0
Rich Lackner (Carnegie Mellon '79) 90	1	0	1	0	0
TOTAL	5	2	5	0	0
CARROLL (WIS.)					
Steve Miller (Cornell College '65) 76	1	0	1	0	0
CENTRAL (IOWA)					
Ron Schipper (Hope '52) 74-CH, 77, 84-2D, 85, 86, 87, 88-2D, 89, 90, 92	10	16	9	1	2
COE					
Bob Thurness (Coe '62) 85	1	0	1	0	0
D. J. LeRoy (Wis.-Eau Claire '79) 91, 93	2	0	2	0	0
TOTAL	3	0	3	0	0
COLORADO COL.					
Jerry Carle (Northwestern '48) 75	1	0	1	0	0
CONCORDIA-M'HEAD					
Jim Christopherson (Concordia-M'head '60) 86, 88	2	2	2	0	0
CORTLAND ST.					
Dennis Kayser (Ithaca '74) 88, 89	2	1	2	0	0
Dave Murray (Springfield '81) 90	1	0	1	0	0
TOTAL	3	1	3	0	0
DAYTON					
Rick Carter (Earlham '65) 78, 80-CH	2	3	1	1	0
Mike Kelly (Manchester '70) 81-2D, 84, 86, 87-2D, 88, 89-CH, 90, 91-2D, 92	9	13	8	1	3
TOTAL	11	16	9	2	3
DENISON					
Keith Piper (Baldwin-Wallace '48) 85	1	0	1	0	0
DICKINSON					
Ed Sweeney (LIU-C.W. Post '71) 89, 91	2	0	2	0	0
DUBUQUE					
Don Birmingham (Westmar '62) 79, 80	2	0	2	0	0
EMORY & HENRY					
Lou Wacker (Richmond '56) 86, 87, 92	3	3	3	0	0
EVANSVILLE					
Jim Byers (Michigan '59) 74	1	0	1	0	0
FERRUM					
Hank Norton (Lynchburg '51) 87, 88, 89, 90	4	4	4	0	0
FORDHAM					
Larry Glueck (Villanova '63) 87	1	1	1	0	0
FORT VALLEY ST.					
Leon Lomax (Fort Valley St. '43) 75	1	0	1	0	0
FROSTBURG ST.					
Mike McGlinchey (Delaware '67) 93	1	1	1	0	0
GETTYSBURG					
Barry Streeter (Lebanon Valley '71) 85	1	2	1	0	0
GUST. ADOLPHUS					
Steve Raarup (Gust. Adolphus '53) 87	1	0	1	0	0
HAMPDEN-SYDNEY					
Stokeley Fulton (Hampden-Sydney '55) 77	1	0	1	0	0
HIRAM					
Don Charlton (Lock Haven '65) 87	1	0	1	0	0
HOFSTRA					
Mickey Kwiatkowski (Delaware '70) 83, 86, 87, 88, 89	5	0	5	0	0
Joe Gardi (Maryland '60) 90	1	2	1	0	0
TOTAL	6	2	6	0	0
HOPE					
Ray Smith (UCLA '61) 86	1	0	1	0	0
ILL. WESLEYAN					
Norm Eash (Ill. Wesleyan '75) 92	1	1	1	0	0
INDIANAPOLIS					
Bill Bless (Indianapolis '63) 75	1	0	1	0	0
ITHACA					
Jim Butterfield (Maine '53) 74-2D, 75-2D, 78, 79-CH, 80-2D, 85-2D, 86, 88-CH, 90, 91-CH, 92	11	21	8	3	4
JOHN CARROLL					
Tony DeCarlo (Kent '62) 89	1	0	1	0	0
JUNIATA					
Walt Nadzak (Denison '57) 73-2D	1	1	1	0	1
LAWRENCE					
Ron Roberts (Wisconsin '54) 81	1	1	1	0	0
LIU-C.W. POST					
Dom Anile (LIU-C.W. Post '59) 76	1	0	1	0	0
LYCOMING					
Frank Girardi (West Chester '61) 85, 89, 90-2D, 91, 92	5	5	5	0	1
MASS.-LOWELL					
Dennis Scannell (Villanova '74) 91	1	0	1	0	0
MENLO					
Ray Solari (California '51) 87	1	0	1	0	0
MILLERSVILLE					
Gene Carpenter (Huron '63) 79	1	0	1	0	0
MILLIKIN					
Carl Poelker (Millikin '68) 89	1	1	1	0	0
MILLSAPS					
Harper Davis (Mississippi St. '49) 75	1	1	1	0	0
MINN.-MORRIS					
Al Molde (Gust. Adolphus '66) 77, 78, 79	3	2	3	0	0
Dick Smith (Coe '68) 80, 81	2	1	2	0	0
TOTAL	5	3	5	0	0
MONTCLAIR ST.					
Fred Hill (Upsala '57) 81	1	1	1	0	0
Rick Giancola (Rowan '68) 85, 86, 89	3	3	3	0	0
TOTAL	4	4	4	0	0

	Yrs	Won	Lost	CH	2D
MORAVIAN					
Scot Dapp (West Chester '73) 88, 93	2	1	2	0	0
MOUNT UNION					
Ken Wable (Muskingum '52) 85	1	1	1	0	0
Larry Kehres (Mount Union '71) 86, 90, 92, 93-CH	4	7	3	1	0
TOTAL	5	8	4	1	0
OCCIDENTAL					
Dale Widolff (Indiana Central '75) 83, 84, 85	3	1	3	0	0
PLYMOUTH ST.					
Jay Cottone (Norwich '71) 84	1	0	1	0	0
RANDOLPH-MACON					
Jim Blackburn (Virginia '71) 84	1	0	1	0	0
REDLANDS					
Mike Maynard (Ill. Wesleyan '80) 90, 92	2	0	2	0	0
RHODES					
Mike Clary (Rhodes '77) 88	1	0	1	0	0
ROCHESTER					
Ray Tellier (Connecticut '73) 87	1	0	1	0	0
ROWAN					
John Bunting (North Caro. '72) 91, 92	2	2	2	0	0
K. C. Keeler (Delaware '81) 93-2D	1	3	1	0	1
TOTAL	3	5	3	0	1
SALISBURY ST.					
Mike McGlinchey (Delaware '67) 83, 85, 86-2D ...	3	5	3	0	1
SAN DIEGO					
Andy Vinci (Cal St. Los Angeles '63) 73	1	0	1	0	0
SIMPSON					
Jim Williams (Northern Iowa '60) 88, 89, 91 ...	3	0	3	0	0
SLIPPERY ROCK					
Bob Di Spirito (Rhode Island '53) 74	1	0	1	0	0
ST. JOHN'S (MINN.)					
John Gagliardi (Colorado Col. '49) 76-CH, 77, 85, 87, 89, 91, 93 ...	7	10	6	1	0
ST. LAWRENCE					
Ted Stratford (St. Lawrence '57) 76, 78	2	1	2	0	0
Andy Talley (Southern Conn. St. '67) 82	1	1	1	0	0
TOTAL	3	2	3	0	0
ST. NORBERT					
Don LaViolette (St. Norbert '54) 89	1	0	1	0	0
ST. OLAF					
Tom Porter (St. Olaf '51) 78	1	0	1	0	0
ST. THOMAS (MINN.)					
Vic Wallace (Cornell College '65) 90.............	1	1	1	0	0
SUSQUEHANNA					
Rocky Rees (West Chester '71) 86	1	1	1	0	0
Steve Briggs (Springfield '84) 91	1	2	1	0	0
TOTAL	2	3	2	0	0

	Yrs	Won	Lost	CH	2D
THOMAS MORE					
Vic Clark (Indiana St. '71) 92	1	0	1	0	0
TOWSON ST.					
Phil Albert (Arizona '66) 76-2D	1	2	1	0	1
TRENTON ST.					
Eric Hamilton (Trenton St. '75) 90	1	1	1	0	0
UNION (N.Y.)					
Al Bagnoli (Central Conn. St. '74) 83-2D, 84, 85, 86, 89-2D, 91 ...	6	7	6	0	2
John Audino (Notre Dame '75) 93	1	0	1	0	0
TOTAL	7	7	7	0	2
WABASH					
Frank Navarro (Maryland '53) 77-2D...............	1	2	1	0	1
WAGNER					
Bill Russo 80..	1	0	1	0	0
Walt Hameline (Brockport St. '75) 82, 87-CH, 88............	3	4	2	1	0
TOTAL	4	4	3	1	0
WARTBURG					
Don Canfield 82..	1	0	1	0	0
Bob Nielson (Wartburg '81) 93	1	0	1	0	0
TOTAL	2	0	2	0	0
WASH. & JEFF.					
John Luckhardt (Purdue '67) 84, 86, 87, 89, 90, 91 92-2D, 93 ...	8	8	8	0	1
WESTERN CONN. ST.					
Paul Pasqualoni (Penn St. '72) 85...................	1	0	1	0	0
WEST GA.					
Bobby Pate (Georgia '63) 81, 82-CH.............	2	3	1	1	0
WIDENER					
Bill Manlove (Temple '58) 75, 77-CH, 79, 80, 81-CH, 82, 88............	7	9	5	2	0
WILKES					
Joe DeMelfi (Delta St. '66) 93	1	0	1	0	0
WIS.-LA CROSSE					
Roger Harring (Wis.-La Crosse '58) 83, 91, 92-CH, 93 ...	4	7	3	1	0
WIS.-STEVENS POINT					
D. J. LeRoy (Wis.-Eau Claire '79) 86	1	0	1	0	0
WIS.-WHITEWATER					
Bob Berezowitz (Wis.-Whitewater '67) 88, 90..	2	1	2	0	0
WITTENBERG					
Dave Maurer (Denison '54) 73-CH, 75-CH, 78-2D, 79-2D............	4	9	2	2	2
Ron Murphy 88	1	1	1	0	0
TOTAL	5	10	3	2	2
WM. PATERSON					
Gerry Gallagher (Wm. Paterson '74) 93	1	1	1	0	0
WORCESTER TECH					
Jack Siedlecki (Union, N.Y. '73) 92...............	1	0	1	0	0

CHAMPIONSHIP RESULTS

All-Time Results

1973 Semifinals: Juniata 35, Bridgeport 14; Wittenberg 21, San Diego 14. **Championship:** Wittenberg 41, Juniata 0.

1974 Semifinals: Central (Iowa) 17, Evansville 16; Ithaca 27, Slippery Rock 14. **Championship:** Central (Iowa) 10, Ithaca 8.

1975 First Round: Widener 14, Albright 6; Ithaca 41, Fort Valley St. 12; Wittenberg 17, Indianapolis 13; Millsaps 20, Colorado Col. 21. **Semifinals:** Ithaca 23, Widener 14; Wittenberg 55, Millsaps 22. **Championship:** Wittenberg 28, Ithaca 0.

1976 First Round: St. John's (Minn.) 46, Augustana (Ill.) 7; Buena Vista 20, Carroll (Wis.) 14 (OT); St. Lawrence 26, Albright 7; Towson St. 14, LIU-C.W. Post 10. **Semifinals:** St. John's (Minn.) 61, Buena Vista 0; Towson St. 38, St. Lawrence 36. **Championship:** St. John's (Minn.) 31, Towson St. 28.

1977 First Round: Minn.-Morris 13, Albion 10; Wabash 20, St. John's (Minn.) 9; Widener 19, Central (Iowa) 0; Albany (N.Y.) 51, Hampden-Sydney 45.

Semifinals: Wabash 37, Minn.-Morris 21; Widener 33, Albany (N.Y.) 15. **Championship:** Widener 39, Wabash 36.

1978 First Round: Minn.-Morris 23, St. Olaf 10; Wittenberg 6, Ithaca 3; Carnegie Mellon 24, Dayton 21; Baldwin-Wallace 71, St. Lawrence 7. **Semifinals:** Wittenberg 35, Minn.-Morris 14; Baldwin-Wallace 31, Carnegie Mellon 6. **Championship:** Baldwin-Wallace 24, Wittenberg 10.

1979 First Round: Wittenberg 21, Millersville 14; Widener 29, Baldwin-Wallace 8; Carnegie Mellon 31, Minn.-Morris 25; Ithaca 27, Dubuque 7. **Semifinals:** Wittenberg 17, Widener 14; Ithaca 15, Carnegie Mellon 6. **Championship:** Ithaca 14, Wittenberg 10.

1980 First Round: Ithaca 41, Wagner 13; Minn.-Morris 41, Dubuque 35; Dayton 34, Baldwin-Wallace 0; Widener 43, Bethany (W.Va.) 12. **Semifinals:** Ithaca 36, Minn.-Morris 0; Dayton 28, Widener 24. **Championship:** Dayton 63, Ithaca 0.

1981 First Round: Dayton 19, Augustana (Ill.) 7; Lawrence 21, Minn.-Morris 14 (OT); Montclair St. 13, Alfred 12; Widener 10, West Ga. 3. **Semifinals:** Dayton 38, Lawrence 0; Widener 23, Montclair St. 12. **Championship:** Widener 17, Dayton 10.

1982 First Round: Augustana (Ill.) 28, Baldwin-Wallace 22; St. Lawrence 43, Wagner 34; Bishop 32, Wartburg 7; West Ga. 31, Widener 24 (3 OT). **Semifinals:** Augustana (Ill.) 14, St. Lawrence 0; West Ga. 27, Bishop 6. **Championship:** West Ga. 14, Augustana (Ill.) 0.

1983 First Round: Union (N.Y.) 51, Hofstra 19; Salisbury St. 16, Carnegie Mellon 14; Augustana (Ill.) 22, Adrian 21; Wis.-La Crosse 43, Occidental 42. **Semifinals:** Union (N.Y.) 23, Salisbury St. 21; Augustana (Ill.) 21, Wis.-La Crosse 15. **Championship:** Augustana (Ill.) 21, Union (N.Y.) 17.

1984 First Round: Union (N.Y.) 26, Plymouth St. 14; Augustana (Ill.) 14, Dayton 13; Wash. & Jeff. 22, Randolph-Macon 21; Central (Iowa) 23, Occidental 22. **Semifinals:** Augustana (Ill.) 23, Union (N.Y.) 6; Central (Iowa) 20, Wash. & Jeff. 0. **Championship:** Augustana (Ill.) 21, Central (Iowa) 12.

1985 First Round: Ithaca 13, Union (N.Y.) 12; Montclair St. 28, Western Conn. St. 0; Salisbury St. 35, Carnegie Mellon 22; Gettysburg 14, Lycoming 10; Augustana (Ill.) 26, Albion 10; Mount Union 35, Denison 3; Central (Iowa) 27, Coe 7; Occidental 28, St. John's (Minn.) 10. **Quarterfinals:** Ithaca 50, Montclair St. 28; Gettysburg 22, Salisbury St. 6; Augustana (Ill.) 21, Mount

Union 14; Central (Iowa) 71, Occidental 0. **Semifinals:** Ithaca 34, Gettysburg 0; Augustana (Ill.) 14, Central (Iowa) 7. **Championship:** Augustana (Ill.) 20, Ithaca 7.

1986 First Round: Ithaca 24, Union (N.Y.) 17 (OT); Montclair St. 24, Hofstra 21; Susquehanna 28, Wash. & Jeff. 20; Salisbury St. 34, Emory & Henry 20; Mount Union 42, Dayton 36; Augustana (Ill.) 34, Hope 10; Central (Iowa) 37, Buena Vista 0; Concordia-M'head 24, Wis.-Stevens Point 15. **Quarterfinals:** Ithaca 29, Montclair St. 15; Salisbury St. 31, Susquehanna 17; Augustana (Ill.) 16, Mount Union 7; Concordia-M'head 17, Central (Iowa) 14. **Semifinals:** Salisbury St. 44, Ithaca 40; Augustana (Ill.) 41, Concordia-M'head 7. **Championship:** Augustana (Ill.) 31, Salisbury St. 3.

1987 First Round: Wagner 38, Rochester 14; Fordham 41, Hofstra 6; Wash. & Jeff. 23, Allegheny 17 (OT); Emory & Henry 49, Ferrum 7; Dayton 52, Capital 28; Augustana (Ill.) 53, Hiram 0; St. John's (Minn.) 7, Gust. Adolphus 3; Central (Iowa) 17, Menlo 0. **Quarterfinals:** Wagner 21, Fordham 0; Emory & Henry 23, Wash. & Jeff. 16; Dayton 38, Augustana (Ill.) 36; Central (Iowa) 13, St. John's (Minn.) 3. **Semifinals:** Wagner 20, Emory & Henry 15; Dayton 34, Central (Iowa) 0. **Championship:** Wagner 19, Dayton 3.

1988 Regionals: Cortland St. 32, Hofstra 27; Ithaca 34, Wagner 31 (OT); Ferrum 35, Rhodes 10; Moravian 17, Widener 7; Wittenberg 35, Dayton 28 (2 OT); Augustana (Ill.) 25, Adrian 7; Central (Iowa) 7, Concordia-M'head 0; Wis.-Whitewater 29, Simpson 27.

Quarterfinals: Ithaca 24, Cortland St. 17; Ferrum 49, Moravian 28; Augustana (Ill.) 28, Wittenberg 14; Central (Iowa) 16, Wis.-Whitewater 13. **Semifinals:** Ithaca 62, Ferrum 28; Central (Iowa) 23, Augustana 17 (2 OT). **Championship:** Ithaca 39, Central (Iowa) 24.

1989 Regionals: Union (N.Y.) 42, Cortland St. 14; Montclair St. 23, Hofstra 6; Lycoming 21, Dickinson 0; Ferrum 41, Wash. & Jeff. 7; Dayton 35, John Carroll 10; Millikin 21, Augustana (Ill.) 12; Central (Iowa) 55, St. Norbert 7; St. John's (Minn.) 42, Simpson 35. **Quarterfinals:** Union (N.Y.) 45, Montclair St. 6; Ferrum 49, Lycoming 24; Dayton 28, Millikin 16; St. John's (Minn.) 27, Central (Iowa) 24. **Semifinals:** Union (N.Y.) 37, Ferrum 21; Dayton 28, St. John's (Minn.) 0. **Championship:** Dayton 17, Union (N.Y.) 7.

1990 Regionals: Hofstra 35, Cortland St. 9; Trenton St. 24, Ithaca 14; Wash. & Jeff. 10, Ferrum 7; Lycoming 17, Carnegie Mellon 7; Dayton 24, Augustana (Ill.) 14; Allegheny 26, Mount Union 15; St. Thomas (Minn.) 24, Wis.-Whitewater 23; Central (Iowa) 24, Redlands 14. **Quarterfinals:** Hofstra 38, Trenton St. 3; Lycoming 24, Wash. & Jeff. 0; Allegheny 31, Dayton 23; Central (Iowa) 33, St. Thomas (Minn.) 32. **Semifinals:** Lycoming 20, Hofstra 10; Allegheny 24, Central (Iowa) 7. **Championship:** Allegheny 21, Lycoming 14 (OT).

1991 Regionals: St. John's (Minn.) 75, Coe 2; Wis.-La Crosse 28, Simpson 13; Allegheny 24, Albion 21 (OT); Dayton 27, Baldwin-Wallace 10; Ithaca 31, Rowan 10; Union (N.Y.) 55, Mass.-Lowell 16; Lycoming 18, Wash.

& Jeff. 16; Susquehanna 21, Dickinson 20. **Quarterfinals:** St. John's (Minn.) 29, Wis.-La Crosse 10; Dayton 28, Allegheny 25 (OT); Ithaca 35, Union (N.Y.) 23; Susquehanna 31, Lycoming 24. **Semifinals:** Dayton 19, St. John's (Minn.) 7; Ithaca 49, Susquehanna 13. **Championship:** Ithaca 34, Dayton 20.

1992 Regionals: Mount Union 27, Dayton 10; Ill. Wesleyan 21, Aurora 12; Central (Iowa) 20, Carleton 8; Wis.-La Crosse 47, Redlands 26; Emory & Henry 17, Thomas More 0; Wash. & Jeff. 33, Lycoming 0; Rowan 41, Worcester Tech 14; Buffalo St. 28, Ithaca 26. **Quarterfinals:** Mount Union 49, Ill. Wesleyan 27; Wis.-La Crosse 34, Central (Iowa) 9; Wash. & Jeff. 51, Emory & Henry 15; Rowan 28, Buffalo St. 6. **Semifinals:** Wis.-La Crosse 29, Mount Union 24; Wash. & Jeff. 18, Rowan 13. **Championship:** Wis.-La Crosse 16, Wash. & Jeff. 12.

1993 Regionals: Mount Union 40, Allegheny 7; Albion 41, Anderson 21; Wis.-La Crosse 55, Wartburg 26; St. John's (Minn.) 32, Coe 14; Wash. & Jeff. 27, Moravian 7; Frostburg St. 26, Wilkes 25; Rowan 29, Buffalo St. 6; Wm. Paterson 17, Union (N.Y.) 7. **Quarterfinals:** Mount Union 30, Albion 16; St. John's (Minn.) 47, Wis.-La Crosse 25; Wash. & Jeff. 28, Frostburg St. 7; Rowan 37, Wm. Paterson 0. **Semifinals:** Mount Union 56, St. John's (Minn.) 8; Rowan 23, Wash. & Jeff. 16. **Championship:** Mount Union 34, Rowan 24.

Attendance Records

All-Time NCAA Attendance

(Beginning with the formation of four separate divisions in 1978)

Annual Total NCAA Attendance

(Includes Only NCAA Teams, All Divisions)

Year	No. Teams	G	Total Attendance	P/G Avg.	Yearly Change Total	Percent
1978	484	2,422	32,369,730	13,365	—	—
1979	478	2,381	32,874,755	13,807	Up 505,025	+1.56%
1980	485	2,451	33,707,772	13,753	Up 833,017	*+2.53%
1981	497	2,505	34,230,471	13,665	Up 522,699	+1.55%
1982	510	2,569	35,176,195	13,693	*Up 945,724	+2.76%
1983	505	2,557	34,817,264	13,616	Dn 358,931	-1.02%
1984	501	2,542	35,211,076	*13,852	Up 393,812	+1.13%
1985	509	2,599	34,951,548	13,448	Dn 259,528	-0.74%
1986	510	2,605	35,030,902	13,448	Up 79,354	+2.27%
1987	507	2,589	35,007,541	13,522	Dn 23,361	-0.07%
1988	524	2,644	34,323,842	12,982	Dn 683,699	-1.95%
1989	524	2,630	35,116,188	13,352	Up 792,346	-2.31%
1990	533	2,704	35,329,946	13,066	Up 213,758	+0.61%
1991	548	2,776	*35,528,220	12,798	Up 198,274	+0.56%
1992	552	2,824	35,225,431	12,474	Dn 302,789	-0.65%
1993	*560	*2,888	34,870,634	12,074	Dn 354,797	-1.01%

*Record.

Annual Division I-A Attendance

Year	Teams	G	Attendance	Avg.
1976	137	796	23,917,522	30,047
1977	144	799	24,613,285	30,805
1978	139	772	25,017,915	32,407
1979	139	774	25,862,801	33,414
1980	139	776	26,499,022	34,148
1981	137	768	*26,588,688	34,621
1982	97	567	24,771,855	*43,689
1983	105	602	25,381,761	42,162
1984	105	606	25,783,807	42,548
1985	105	605	25,434,412	42,040
1986	105	611	25,692,095	42,049
1987	104	607	25,471,744	41,963
1988	104	605	25,079,490	41,454
1989	106	603	25,307,915	41,970
1990	106	615	25,513,098	41,485
1991	106	610	25,646,067	42,043
1992	107	617	25,402,046	41,170
1993	106	613	25,305,438	41,281

*Record.

Annual Division I-AA Attendance

Year	Teams	G	Attendance	Avg.
1978	38	201	2,032,766	10,113
1979	39	211	2,073,890	9,829
1980	46	251	2,617,932	10,430
1981	50	270	2,950,156	10,927
1982	92	483	*5,655,519	*11,709
1983	84	450	4,879,709	10,844
1984	87	465	5,061,480	10,885
1985	87	471	5,143,077	10,919
1986	86	456	5,044,992	11,064
1987	87	460	5,129,250	11,151
1988	88	465	4,801,637	10,326
1989	89	471	5,278,520	11,020
1990	87	473	5,328,477	11,265
1991	89	490	5,386,425	10,993
1992	88	485	5,057,955	10,429
1993	115	623	5,356,873	8,599

*Record.

Annual Division II Attendance

Year	Teams	G	Attendance	Avg.
1978	103	518	*2,871,683	*5,544
1979	105	526	2,775,569	5,277
1980	111	546	2,584,765	4,734
1981	121	589	2,726,537	4,629
1982	126	618	2,745,964	4,443
1983	122	611	2,705,892	4,429
1984	114	568	2,413,947	4,250
1985	114	569	2,475,325	4,350
1986	111	551	2,404,852	4,365
1987	107	541	2,424,041	4,481
1988	117	580	2,570,964	4,493
1989	116	579	2,572,496	4,428
1990	120	580	2,472,811	4,263
1991	128	622	2,490,929	4,005
1992	129	643	2,733,094	4,251
1993	142	718	2,572,053	3,582

*Record.

Annual Division III Attendance

Year	Teams	G	Attendance	Avg.
1978	204	931	*2,447,366	*2,629
1979	195	870	2,162,495	2,486
1980	189	878	2,006,053	2,285
1981	189	878	1,965,090	2,238
1982	195	901	2,002,857	2,223
1983	194	894	1,849,902	2,069
1984	195	903	1,951,842	2,162
1985	203	954	1,898,734	1,990
1986	208	987	1,888,963	1,914
1987	209	981	1,982,506	2,021
1988	215	994	1,871,751	1,883
1989	213	977	1,957,257	1,948
1990	220	1,036	2,015,560	1,946
1991	225	1,054	2,004,799	1,902
1992	228	1,079	2,032,336	1,884
1993	197	934	1,636,270	1,752

*Record.

Annual Conference Attendance Leaders

(Based on per-game average; minimum 20 games)

Division I-A

Year	Conference	Teams	Attendance	P/G Avg.
1978	Big Ten	10	3,668,926	61,149
1979	Big Ten	10	3,865,170	63,363
1980	Big Ten	10	3,781,232	64,089
1981	Big Ten	10	3,818,728	63,645
1982	Big Ten	10	3,935,722	66,707
1983	Big Ten	10	3,710,931	67,471
1984	Big Ten	10	3,943,802	*67,997
1985	Big Ten	10	4,015,693	66,928
1986	Big Ten	10	4,006,845	65,686
1987	Big Ten	10	3,990,524	65,418
1988	Southeastern	10	3,912,241	63,101
1989	Southeastern	10	4,123,005	65,445
1990	Southeastern	10	4,215,400	63,870
1991	Southeastern	10	4,063,190	66,610
1992	Southeastern	12	*4,844,014	63,737
1993	Big Ten	11	4,320,397	63,535

*Record.

Division I-AA

Year	Conference	Teams	Attendance	P/G Avg.
1978	Southwestern Athletic	5	483,159	17,895
1979	Southwestern Athletic	6	513,768	16,055
1980	Southwestern Athletic	7	611,234	16,085
1981	Southwestern Athletic	7	662,221	18,921
1982	Southwestern Athletic	7	634,505	18,129
1983	Southwestern Athletic	8	709,160	16,117
1984	Southwestern Athletic	8	702,186	17,555
1985	Southwestern Athletic	8	790,296	17,961
1986	Southwestern Athletic	8	621,584	16,357
1987	Southwestern Athletic	8	697,534	16,608
1988	Southwestern Athletic	8	541,127	14,240
1989	Southwestern Athletic	8	796,844	18,110
1990	Southwestern Athletic	7	828,169	20,704
1991	Southwestern Athletic	8	856,491	18,223
1992	Southwestern Athletic	8	*873,772	*20,804
1993	Southwestern Athletic	8	772,714	18,398

*Record.

Division II

Year	Conference	Teams	Attendance	P/G Avg.
1978	Mid-Continent	6	237,458	9,133
1979	Mid-Continent	6	313,790	*9,509
1980	Southern Intercollegiate	12	356,744	7,280
1981	Lone Star	8	340,876	7,575
1982	Lone Star	8	348,780	8,507
1983	Lone Star	8	296,350	7,228
1984	Central Intercollegiate	12	*418,075	6,743
1985	Central Intercollegiate	12	378,160	6,099
1986	Central Intercollegiate	12	380,172	6,670
1987	Lone Star	6	208,709	6,325
1988	Central Intercollegiate	12	343,070	6,473
1989	Lone Star	8	249,570	5,942
1990	Southern Intercollegiate	9	264,741	6,967
1991	Central Intercollegiate	11	349,962	6,603
1992	Southern Intercollegiate	9	344,504	7,489
1993	Southern Intercollegiate	9	342,446	8,352

*Record.

Division III

Year	Conference	Teams	Attendance	P/G Avg.
1979	Great Lakes	6	90,531	*3,482
1980	Great Lakes	7	113,307	3,333
1981	Ohio Athletic	14	*196,640	2,979
1982	New Jersey State	7	98,502	2,985
1983	Heartland	7	121,825	3,384
1984	Heartland	7	107,500	2,986
1985	Ohio Athletic	9	125,074	2,719
1986	Heartland	7	91,793	2,550
1987	Heartland	6	84,815	3,029
1988	Heartland	5	82,966	2,963
1989	Old Dominion	5	70,676	2,945
1990	Old Dominion	6	86,238	2,974
1991	Old Dominion	6	101,774	3,283
1992	Old Dominion	6	100,132	3,338
1993	Old Dominion	6	96,526	3,218

*Record.

Large Regular-Season Crowds

Largest Regular-Season Crowds*

Crowd	Date	Home	Visitor
106,867	11-20-93	Michigan 28, Ohio St. 0	
106,851	9-11-93	Michigan 23, Notre Dame 27	
106,788	10-10-92	Michigan 35, Michigan St. 10	
106,579	10-24-92	Michigan 63, Minnesota 13	
106,481	11-14-92	Michigan 22, Illinois 22	
106,385	10-23-93	Michigan 21, Illinois 24	
106,255	11-17-79	Michigan 15, Ohio St. 18	
106,208	10-8-88	Michigan 17, Michigan St. 3	
106,188	10-13-90	Michigan 27, Michigan St. 28	
106,156	11-23-91	Michigan 31, Ohio St. 3	
106,145	9-28-91	Michigan 31, Florida St. 51	
106,141	10-11-86	Michigan 27, Michigan St. 6	
106,138	9-14-91	Michigan 24, Notre Dame 14	
106,137	11-25-89	Michigan 28, Ohio St. 18	
106,132	10-3-92	Michigan 52, Iowa 28	
106,115	11-19-83	Michigan 24, Ohio St. 21	
106,113	10-9-82	Michigan 31, Michigan St. 17	

*In the 45 seasons official national attendance records have been maintained.

HIGHEST WEEKS OF THE WEEKLY TOP-10 ATTENDED GAMES

Total	Date
862,941	9-4-93
857,115	10-10-92
833,285	10-22-83
828,253	10-2-93
827,232	9-16-89
825,455	9-22-84
820,668	11-18-89
819,980	10-18-86
819,501	9-25-93
816,954	9-14-91
816,618	9-28-91
816,458	10-13-84
815,853	11-10-90
815,423	11-5-88

Largest Regular-Season Crowds for Games Not Played at Michigan

Attendance	Date	Score (Home Team in Boldface)	Site
101,799	11-30-68	Army 21, Navy 14	Philadelphia, Pa.*
100,428	12-2-67	Navy 19, Army 14	Philadelphia, Pa.*
97,731	9-28-91	**Tennessee** 30, Auburn 21	Knoxville, Tenn.
97,388	10-17-92	Alabama 17, **Tennessee** 10	Knoxville, Tenn.
97,372	11-30-85	**Tennessee** 30, Vanderbilt 0	Knoxville, Tenn.
97,137	9-19-92	**Tennessee** 31, Florida 14	Knoxville, Tenn.
97,123	11-11-90	Notre Dame 34, **Tennessee** 29	Knoxville, Tenn.
97,117	9-14-91	**Tennessee** 30, UCLA 16	Knoxville, Tenn.
96,874	10-13-90	**Tennessee** 45, Florida 3	Knoxville, Tenn.
96,748	10-18-80	Alabama 27, **Tennessee** 0	Knoxville, Tenn.
96,732	10-20-90	Alabama 9, **Tennessee** 6	Knoxville, Tenn.
96,719	10-16-93	Michigan 21, **Penn St.** 13	University Park, Pa.
96,704	10-10-92	Miami (Fla.) 17, **Penn St.** 14	University Park, Pa.
96,672	11-16-91	**Penn St.** 35, Notre Dame 13	University Park, Pa.
96,664	11-2-91	**Tennessee** 52, Memphis 24	Knoxville, Tenn.
96,597	9-26-92	**Tennessee** 40, Cincinnati 0	Knoxville, Tenn.
96,445	10-26-91	**Penn St.** 51, West Va. 6	University Park, Pa.
96,304	9-21-91	**Penn St.** 33, Brigham Young 7	University Park, Pa.
96,173	10-2-93	**Tennessee** 52, Duke 19	Knoxville, Tenn.
96,130	10-17-92	Boston College 35, **Penn St.** 32	University Park, Pa.
96,058	10-7-89	**Tennessee** 17, Georgia 14	Knoxville, Tenn.
95,974	9-21-91	**Tennessee** 26, Mississippi St. 24	Knoxville, Tenn.
95,937	11-16-91	**Tennessee** 36, Mississippi 25	Knoxville, Tenn.
95,931	9-25-93	**Tennessee** 42, Louisiana St. 20	Knoxville, Tenn.
95,927	9-28-91	**Penn St.** 28, Boston College 21	University Park, Pa.
95,891	9-26-92	**Penn St.** 49, Maryland 13	University Park, Pa.
95,824	9-3-83	Pittsburgh 13, **Tennessee** 3	Knoxville, Tenn.
95,729	10-19-91	**Penn St.** 37, Rutgers 17	University Park, Pa.
95,585	11-12-83	Mississippi 13, **Tennessee** 10	Knoxville, Tenn.
95,422	10-20-84	**Tennessee** 28, Alabama 27	Knoxville, Tenn.

*Neutral site.

Pre-1948 Regular-Season Crowds in Excess of 100,000†

Crowd	Date	Site	Opponents, Score
120,000*	11-26-27	Soldier Field, Chicago	Notre Dame 7, Southern Cal 6
120,000*	10-13-28	Soldier Field, Chicago	Notre Dame 7, Navy 0
112,912	11-16-29	Soldier Field, Chicago	Notre Dame 13, Southern Cal 12
110,000*	11-27-26	Soldier Field, Chicago	Army 21, Navy 21
110,000*	11-29-30	Soldier Field, Chicago	Notre Dame 7, Army 6
104,953	12-6-47	Los Angeles	Notre Dame 38, Southern Cal 7

*Estimated attendance; others are audited figures. †Since 1956, when Michigan Stadium's capacity was increased to 101,000, there have been 134 100,000-plus crowds at Michigan. The 17 largest crowds are listed on the previous page. Therefore, there has been a total of 142 regular-season crowds in excess of 100,000.

Additional Records

Highest Average Attendance Per Home Game: 105,867, Michigan, 1992 (635,201 in 6)

Highest Total Home Attendance: 739,620, Michigan, 1993 (7 games)

Highest Total Attendance, Home and Away: 1,035,998, Michigan, 1993 (11 games)

Highest Bowl Game Attendance: 106,869, 1973 Rose Bowl (Southern Cal 42, Ohio St. 17)

Most Consecutive Home Sellout Crowds: 194, Nebraska (current, from Nov. 3, 1962)

Most Consecutive 100,000-Plus Crowds: 116, Michigan (current, from Nov. 8, 1975)

1993 Attendance

Division I-A

	G	Attendance	Average	Change	
1. Michigan	7	739,620	105,660	Down	207
2. Tennessee	7	667,280	95,326	Down	598
3. Penn St.	6	564,190	94,032	Down	834
4. Ohio St.	6	553,489	92,248	Down	402
5. Florida	6	507,072	84,512	Up	708
6. Auburn	7	567,506	81,072	Up	8,136
7. Georgia	6	468,457	78,076	Down	5,118
8. Alabama	7	529,765	75,681	Down	1,071
9. Nebraska	7	529,521	75,646	Down	541
10. Wisconsin	5	377,537	75,507	Up	14,129
11. Florida St.	6	443,811	73,969	Up	11,172
12. Washington	6	429,401	71,567	Down	504
13. Iowa	6	410,842	68,474	Up	1,833
14. South Caro.	7	472,803	67,543	Up	3,815
15. Clemson	7	467,773	66,825	Down	9,964
16. Brigham Young	6	391,219	65,203	Up	124
17. Texas	5	312,201	62,440	Down	5,712
18. Oklahoma	5	310,620	62,124	Down	2,042
19. Michigan St.	6	368,922	61,487	Up	1,673
20. Louisiana St.	6	361,632	60,272	Down	6,756
21. Texas A&M	6	357,645	59,608	Up	4,201
22. Notre Dame	6	354,450	59,075		0
23. Southern Cal	5	295,106	59,021	Down	733
24. Stanford	7	404,600	57,800	Up	5,733
25. West Va.	7	404,500	57,786	Up	8,502
26. Kentucky	6	312,455	52,076	Down	2,070
27. Colorado	6	311,370	51,895	Up	2,203
28. Arizona St.	6	309,557	51,593	Up	2,699
29. Illinois	6	306,108	51,018	Up	815
30. Arizona	6	304,564	50,761	Up	3,740
31. North Caro.	7	340,600	48,657	Up	1,486
32. Syracuse	5	240,320	48,064	Down	1,254
33. Miami (Fla.)	6	287,319	47,887	Down	7,788
34. UCLA	6	281,478	46,913	Down	2,347
35. Arkansas	6	260,299	43,383	Down	2,650
36. Purdue	6	260,285	43,381	Up	5,152
37. Georgia Tech	6	248,127	41,355	Down	1,823
38. North Caro. St.	6	245,163	40,861	Down	6,296
39. Hawaii	8	326,454	40,807	Down	3,625
40. California	6	242,798	40,466	Down	15,566

	G	Attendance	Average	Change	
41. Minnesota	6	239,973	39,996	Up	2,088
42. Fresno St.	6	237,214	39,536	Up	4,311
43. Virginia Tech	6	236,484	39,414	Down	5,688
44. Virginia	6	234,000	39,000	Down	4,067
45. Air Force	6	233,157	38,860	Down	1,764
46. Louisville	5	188,040	37,608	Up	5,225
47. Indiana	7	262,140	37,449	Down	6,018
48. Missouri	5	186,819	37,364	Down	1,608
49. Maryland	5	186,773	37,355	Up	9,331
50. San Diego St.	7	260,832	37,262	Down	8,463
51. Oregon	5	183,445	36,689	Up	2,891
52. Iowa St.	6	213,303	35,551	Down	2,031
53. Kansas	6	210,500	35,083	Down	6,834
54. Baylor	5	171,910	34,382	Up	2,023
55. Army	6	202,812	33,802	Down	1,061
56. Boston College	6	199,188	33,198	Up	3,349
57. Mississippi St.	6	199,093	33,182	Down	6,238
58. Vanderbilt	6	198,465	33,078	Down	5,100
59. Mississippi	6	196,000	32,667	Down	3,914
60. Texas Tech	5	160,851	32,170	Down	6,812
61. Kansas St.	7	217,739	31,106	Up	3,333
62. Northwestern	6	185,791	30,965	Down	8,402
63. Rutgers	6	184,258	30,710	Up	1,574
64. Memphis	5	151,296	30,259	Down	7,149
65. Oregon St.	5	144,481	28,896	Up	779
66. Washington St.	5	135,931	27,186	Up	1,648
67. East Caro.	5	134,482	26,896	Down	5,918
68. UTEP	5	133,886	26,777	Up	5,015
69. Pittsburgh	6	155,818	25,970	Down	5,749
70. Texas Christian	6	155,342	25,890	Up	203
71. Navy	5	129,143	25,829	Down	9,280
72. New Mexico	6	151,844	25,307	Up	6,050
73. Nevada	6	150,883	25,147	Up	3,128
74. Tulsa	5	125,385	25,077	Up	2,649
75. Oklahoma St.	6	146,375	24,396	Down	14,361
76. Utah	6	143,983	23,997	Down	5,810
77. Rice	6	143,000	23,833	Down	17
78. Houston	5	117,366	23,473	Up	1,107
79. Tulane	5	116,676	23,335	Down	5,130
80. Duke	5	112,270	22,454	Down	2,551
81. Colorado St.	5	110,000	22,000	Up	3,747
82. Southwestern La.	5	109,955	21,991	Up	3,569
83. Wyoming	6	120,852	20,142	Up	2,315
84. Western Mich.	5	100,471	20,094	Up	5,129
85. Utah St.	5	99,821	19,964	Up	5,245
86. Akron	5	99,805	19,961	Up	7,713
87. Southern Methodist	5	95,223	19,045	Down	773
88. Toledo	6	113,082	18,847	Down	1,707
89. Southern Miss.	4	72,514	18,129	Up	2,631
90. Central Mich.	5	89,914	17,983	Down	1,144
91. New Mexico St.	5	83,905	16,781	Down	2,984
92. Wake Forest	6	100,528	16,755	Up	1,955
93. Temple	5	79,956	15,991	Up	4,496
94. Cincinnati	5	79,724	15,945	Down	2,357
95. Nevada-Las Vegas	5	79,258	15,852	Up	2,770
96. Miami (Ohio)	5	70,221	14,044	Down	4,777
97. Bowling Green	5	63,643	12,729	Up	1,090
98. Northern Ill.	4	50,480	12,620	Up	1,325
99. Eastern Mich.	6	74,600	12,433	Down	3,418
100. Arkansas St.	5	61,320	12,264	Up	1,139
101. San Jose St.	4	46,314	11,579	Down	2,204
102. Louisiana Tech	4	44,400	11,100	Down	6,513
103. Pacific (Cal.)	5	51,888	10,378	Down	37
104. Ball St.	5	49,922	9,984	Up	562
105. Ohio	5	46,544	9,309	Down	3,063
106. Kent	4	18,645	4,661	Down	2,176

Division I-AA

	G	Attendance	Average	Change	
1. Jackson St.	6	173,500	28,917	Up	4,167
2. Grambling	5	139,813	27,963	Up	6,372
3. Marshall	7	159,224	22,746	Down	406
4. Southern-B.R.	4	86,263	21,566	Up	7,340
5. Pennsylvania	5	101,866	20,373	Up	6,972
6. Florida A&M	5	100,571	20,114	Down	1,952
7. Alabama St.	5	100,535	20,107	Down	3,444
8. McNeese St.	5	94,216	18,843	Up	1,805
9. Northeast La.	5	89,876	17,975	Up	503
10. Boise St.	7	116,481	16,640	Down	2,495

	G	Attendance	Average	Change	
11. Delaware	7	114,526	16,361	Down	1,487
12. Yale	5	77,718	15,544	Up	3,395
13. Citadel	6	89,016	14,836	Down	4,523
14. North Caro. A&T	5	72,844	14,569	Up	234
15. Ga. Southern	6	83,160	13,860	Down	960
16. Appalachian St.	5	67,230	13,446	Down	5,192
17. Texas Southern	4	53,128	13,282	Down	593
18. South Caro. St.	5	64,306	12,861	Down	4,391
19. Northern Iowa	6	76,296	12,716	Down	1,495
20. Idaho	5	63,176	12,635	Up	2,860
21. William & Mary	5	62,379	12,476	Up	379
22. Alcorn St.	6	73,000	12,167	Down	7,762
23. Central Fla.	7	82,516	11,788	Up	2,796
24. Harvard	5	58,546	11,709	Down	2,059
25. Montana	6	69,707	11,618	Up	39
26. Howard	5	57,636	11,527	Up	4,020
27. Furman	6	67,536	11,256	Down	2,095
28 Princeton	5	51,711	10,342	Down	2,418
29. Mississippi Val.	6	61,850	10,308	Up	6,295
30. Youngstown St.	6	61,121	10,187	Down	1,091
31. Lehigh	5	50,337	10,067	Down	345
32. James Madison	6	59,060	9,843	Up	33
33. Montana St.	6	58,552	9,759	Up	2,262
34. Middle Tenn. St.	4	38,500	9,625	Down	1,075
35. Southwest Mo. St.	6	57,647	9,608	Down	2,520
36. Western Caro.	5	47,560	9,512	Up	795
37. Northern Ariz.	6	56,782	9,464	Up	2,346
38. Eastern Ky.	6	56,244	9,374	Down	3,486
39. Stephen F. Austin	6	55,888	9,315	Up	1,225
40. Connecticut	5	42,950	8,590	Up	991
41. Massachusetts	7	58,410	8,344	Up	1,404
42. Troy St.	6	48,300	8,050	Up	250
43. New Hampshire	5	38,621	7,724	Up	656
44. Va. Military	5	38,470	7,694	Up	690
45. Cornell	5	38,258	7,652	Down	261
46. Dartmouth	6	45,595	7,599	Up	426
47. Liberty	5	37,800	7,560	Up	2,345
48. Ala.-Birmingham	5	37,723	7,545	Up	1,563
49. Northwestern St.	6	43,550	7,258	Down	467
50. Boston U.	5	36,107	7,221	Up	3,179
51. Idaho St.	6	42,763	7,127	Up	127
52. Buffalo	6	41,927	6,988	Up	3,788
53. Western Ill.	5	34,824	6,965	Up	213
54. Sam Houston St.	5	34,715	6,943	Down	1,133
55. Tenn.-Chatt.	5	34,369	6,874	Up	1,974
56. Richmond	5	34,291	6,858	Down	7,373
57. Southwest Tex. St.	5	33,879	6,776	Down	1,193
58. Illinois St.	5	33,417	6,683	Down	2,256
59. Eastern Ill.	4	26,657	6,664	Up	422
60. Southern Ill.	5	31,700	6,340	Up	1,977
61. Morgan St.	5	31,532	6,306	Down	2,527
62. Lafayette	5	30,588	6,118	Down	1,544
63. Bethune-Cookman	7	42,245	6,035	Up	1,226
64. Holy Cross	5	29,461	5,892	Up	2,913
65. Bucknell	5	29,449	5,890	Up	1,711
66. Western Ky.	5	28,390	5,678	Down	4,293
67. Tennessee St.	3	16,729	5,576	Down	16,186
68. Villanova	6	32,368	5,395	Down	2,742
69. North Texas	6	32,062	5,344	Down	1,602
70. Dayton	6	31,110	5,185	Down	913
71. East Tenn. St.	6	31,055	5,176	Up	181
72. Indiana St.	5	25,380	5,076	Up	601
73. Columbia	5	24,845	4,969	Down	809
74. Southern Utah	4	19,617	4,904	Up	964
75. Delaware St.	6	29,421	4,904	Up	296
76. Southeast Mo. St.	6	28,932	4,822	Down	1,818
77. Weber St.	7	33,681	4,812	Down	3,625
78. Maine	5	23,891	4,778	Down	1,652
79. Rhode Island	5	23,578	4,716	Down	85
80. Samford	6	28,220	4,703	Down	86
81. Tenn.-Martin	6	27,774	4,629	Down	442
82. Morehead St.	5	22,400	4,480	Down	1,280
83. Cal St. Sacramento	5	22,185	4,437	Up	864
84. Tennessee Tech	6	26,458	4,410	Down	1,077
85. Prairie View	5	21,125	4,225	Down	8,508
86. Drake	5	20,803	4,161	Up	1,207
87. Austin Peay	6	24,886	4,148	Up	994
88. Northeastern	5	20,605	4,121	Up	1,054
89. Eastern Wash.	5	19,471	3,894	Down	738
90. Nicholls St.	5	19,322	3,864	Down	824

	G	Attendance	Average	Change	
91. Brown	6	22,376	3,729	Down	3,959
92. Murray St.	5	17,928	3,586	Up	1,367
93. Wagner	5	17,291	3,458	Up	597
94. Cal St. Northridge	4	13,372	3,343	Down	145
95. St. Mary's (Cal.)	5	16,508	3,302	Up	208
96. Butler	4	12,565	3,141	Down	919
97. Duquesne	5	15,635	3,127	Up	1,036
98. San Diego	6	17,776	2,963	Down	188
99. Colgate	4	11,786	2,947	Up	477
100. Fordham	5	13,960	2,792	Down	1,443
101. Hofstra	5	11,522	2,304	Down	1,382
102. Charleston So.	4	8,600	2,150	Up	1,183
103. Towson St.	5	9,504	1,901	Down	476
104. St. John's (N.Y.)	6	10,383	1,731	Up	434
105. St. Peter's	5	7,857	1,571	Up	248
106. Central Conn. St.	5	7,215	1,443	Up	18
107. Marist	5	6,817	1,363	Down	199
108. Evansville	6	7,461	1,244	Down	89
109. Davidson	5	6,083	1,217	Down	835
110. Iona	4	4,705	1,176	Up	216
111. Georgetown	4	4,382	1,096	Down	262
112. Valparaiso	5	5,280	1,056	Down	1,133
113. St. Francis (Pa.)	4	3,962	991	Up	249
114. Siena	5	4,659	932	Up	144
115. Canisius	5	2,497	499	Down	94

Division II

	G	Attendance	Average	Change	
1. Norfolk St.	6	92,075	15,346	Up	1,150
2. North Dak. St.	5	74,942	14,988	Up	3,163
3. Portland St.	6	88,321	14,720	Up	2,349
4. Jacksonville St.	4	40,839	10,210	Down	2,180
5. Winston-Salem	5	50,626	10,125	Up	1,837
6. Albany St. (Ga.)	2	20,183	10,092	Up	4,266
7. Morris Brown	4	39,089	9,772	Up	2,235
8. Clark Atlanta	3	28,500	9,500	Up	2,994
9. Morehouse	5	42,233	8,447	Down	2,146
10. Tuskegee	4	32,756	8,189	Down	5,181
11. Alabama A&M	5	38,705	7,741	Up	1,035
12. Angelo St.	5	38,300	7,660	Up	700
13. Tex. A&M-Kingsville	5	37,600	7,520	Down	2,280
14. North Dak.	6	44,984	7,497	Down	236
15. Indiana (Pa.)	5	37,000	7,400	Up	17
16. North Ala.	5	34,884	6,977	Up	2,279
17. Fort Valley St.	3	18,837	6,279	Down	327
18. Hampton	5	30,683	6,137	Down	2,488
19. Fayetteville St.	5	29,696	5,939	Up	1,254
20. Valdosta St.	6	35,559	5,927	Up	1,911

Division III

	G	Attendance	Average	Change	
1. St. John's (Minn.)	4	26,620	6,655	Up	1,764
2. Baldwin-Wallace	4	22,400	5,600	Up	960
3. Mount Union	4	21,109	5,277	Up	955
4. Trinity (Conn.)	4	20,091	5,023	Up	1,585
5. Montclair St.	4	18,348	4,587	Up	414
6. Randolph-Macon	5	22,800	4,560	Up	2,729
7. Emory & Henry	5	21,655	4,331	Down	768
8. Redlands	4	15,708	3,927	Up	766
9. Hampden-Sydney	5	19,616	3,923	Down	1,088
10. Wesleyan	4	14,750	3,688	Down	62
11. Concordia-M'head	6	21,893	3,649	Up	1,311
12. Ithaca	4	14,497	3,624	Up	845
13. Williams	4	13,588	3,397	Down	1,383
14. Union (N.Y.)	5	16,800	3,360	Up	500
15. Wis.-La Crosse	5	16,718	3,344	Up	606
16. Wabash	4	13,200	3,300	Down	460
17. Lycoming	5	16,283	3,257	Down	1,364
18. Merchant Marine	4	12,515	3,129	Up	1,576
19. Wartburg	4	12,500	3,125	Up	325
20. Wilkes	4	12,347	3,087	Up	1,804

Wisconsin drew an average of 14,129 more fans to its home games than in the 1992 season to help the Big Ten lead major conferences in attendance with a per-game average of 63,535.

Divisions I-A and I-AA Conferences and Independent Groups

	Teams	G	Attendance	Avg. PG	Change† in Avg.		Change† in Total	
1. Big Ten (I-A)#	11	68	*4,320,397	63,535	Up	359	Up	150,792
2. Southeastern (I-A)	12	78	*4,897,564	62,789	Down	948	Up	53,550
3. Pacific-10 (I-A)	10	57	2,731,361	47,919	Up	829	Down	94,040
4. Big Eight (I-A)	8	48	2,126,247	44,297	Down	3,531	Down	121,660
5. Atlantic Coast (I-A)	9	54	*2,379,045	44,056	Up	43	Up	46,371
6. Big East (I-A)	8	47	1,787,843	38,039	Down	446	Down	59,426
7. Southwest (I-A)	8	45	1,587,652	35,281	Down	829	Down	109,500
8. Western Athletic (I-A)	10	61	2,109,441	34,581	Down	612	Down	2,146
9. I-A Independents	10	51	1,554,522	30,481	Down	22	Down	303,498
10. Southwestern (I-AA)	8	42	772,714	18,398	Down	2,406	Down	101,058
11. Big West (I-A)#	10	48	*778,224	16,213	Up	929	Up	14,040
12. Mid-American (I-A)	10	51	726,847	14,252	Up	120	Up	22,614
13. Southern (I-AA)	9	51	617,620	12,110	Down	628	Down	82,993
14. Mid-Eastern (I-AA)	7	40	440,012	11,000	Down	867	Down	10,950
15. Ivy League (I-AA)	8	42	420,915	10,022	Down	28	Up	18,935
16. Big Sky (I-AA)	8	48	460,613	9,596	Up	83	Up	23,021
17. Southland (I-AA)	8	43	403,508	9,384	Down	171	Down	26,463
18. Yankee (I-AA)#	12	67	*550,245	8,213	Up	617	Down	41,355
19. Gateway (I-AA)	7	36	285,921	7,942	Down	704	Down	59,902
20. I-AA Independents#	21	107	*524,308	4,900	Up	528	Up	82,746
21. Ohio Valley (I-AA)	9	49	294,714	6,015	Down	2,052	Down	100,550
22. Patriot (I-AA)	6	29	165,581	5,710	Down	812	Down	36,606
23. Pioneer (I-AA)#	6	32	94,995	2,969	Down	572	Down	14,790
24. Metro Atlantic (I-AA)#	6	29	34,483	1,189	Up	137	Up	5,038
I-A Neutral Sites		5	306,295	61,259	—	—	—	—
I-AA Neutral Sites		8	291,244	36,406	—	—	—	—
DIVISION I-A#	106	613	25,305,438	41,281	Up	111	Down	96,608
DIVISION I-AA#	115	623	5,356,873	8,599	Down	1,830	Up	298,918
I-A & I-AA Combined	221	1,236	30,662,311	24,808	Down	2,833	Up	202,310
NCAA DIVISION II#	142	718	2,572,053	3,582	Down	669	Down	161,041
NCAA DIVISION III#	197	934	1,636,270	1,752	Down	132	Down	396,066
ALL NCAA TEAMS	**560**	**2,888**	**34,870,634**	**12,074**	**Down**	**400**	**Down**	**354,797**

By Percentage of Capacity
Div. I-A 76.69 percent—Southeastern 91.97, Atlantic Coast 86.20, Big Ten 85.94, Big Eight 78.45, Western Athletic 75.38, Big East 72.60, Pacific-10 69.81, Div. I-A Independents 68.15, Southwest 62.62, Mid-American 53.88, Big West 52.04.

Div I-AA 48.43 percent—Southern 70.06, Mid-Eastern 64.03, Big Sky 62.41, Southwestern 60.96, Yankee 56.58, Southland 55.47, Metro Atlantic 49.69, Gateway 49.54, Ohio Valley 43.10, Patriot 40.62, Pioneer 31.77, I-AA Independents 30.15, Ivy 27.36.

#Did not have same lineup in 1993 as in 1992. *Record high for this conference. †The 1993 figures used for comparison reflect changes in conference and division lineups to provide parallel, valid comparisons.

Conferences and Independent Groups Below Division I-AA

	Teams	G	Attendance	Avg. PG	Change† in Avg.		Change† in Total	
1. Southern Intercollegiate (II)	9	41	342,446	8,352	Up	863	Down	2,058
2. Central Intercollegiate (II)	11	58	327,596	5,648	Down	1,644	Down	58,869
3. North Central (II)	10	56	286,881	5,123	Up	412	Up	37,197
4. Gulf South (II)#	8	40	175,789	4,395	Up	301	Up	16,137
5. Lone Star (II)#	6	30	130,981	4,366	Down	1,082	Down	16,111
6. Pennsylvania (II)	14	70	238,058	3,401	Down	703	Down	57,396
7. Old Dominion (III)	6	30	96,526	3,218	Down	120	Down	3,606
8. Division II Independents#	25	116	362,207	3,122	Up	97	Up	11,317
9. South Atlantic (II)	8	41	121,238	2,957	Down	681	Down	24,289
10. Mid-America (II)	10	52	143,500	2,760	Down	811	Down	49,330
11. Minnesota Intercollegiate (III)	10	54	132,629	2,456	Up	65	Up	17,848
12. NESCAC (III)	10	40	95,808	2,395	Down	428	Down	17,104
13. New Jersey (III)#	6	27	63,960	2,369	Down	308	Down	16,348
14. Middle Atlantic (III)#	12	59	139,057	2,357	Up	124	Up	18,500
15. Midwest (II)#	11	59	135,805	2,302	Down	348	Down	9,952
16. Michigan Intercollegiate (III)	6	27	60,237	2,231	Down	155	Down	4,177
17. Wisconsin (III)	8	38	80,720	2,124	Down	286	Down	8,464
18. West Va. Intercollegiate (II)	8	35	73,591	2,103	Up	325	Up	7,791
19. Ohio Athletic (III)	10	49	101,190	2,065	Down	378	Down	23,417
20. Freedom Football (III)#	7	31	62,554	2,018	Up	311	Up	2,802
21. Rocky Mountain (II)	8	39	78,273	2,007	Up	115	Up	6,361
22. Indiana (III)	7	36	69,459	1,929	Down	66	Up	3,613
23. Southern California (III)	7	29	53,207	1,835	Up	388	Up	8,356
24. Northern Sun Intercollegiate (II)	7	34	57,734	1,698	Up	34	Up	4,489
25. Iowa (III)	9	42	68,369	1,628	Down	218	Down	12,834
26. Mid-East (III)	4	22	34,845	1,584	Down	57	Up	3,666
27. Illinois & Wisconsin (III)	8	36	54,725	1,520	Up	211	Up	7,577
28. Centennial (III)	8	37	56,241	1,520	Down	661	Down	26,638

#Did not have same membership in 1993 as in 1992. †The 1993 figures used for comparison reflect changes in conference and division lineups to provide parallel, valid comparisons.

Annual Team Attendance Leaders

Annual Leading Division I-A Teams in Per-Game Home Attendance

Year/Teams	G	Attendance	Avg.
1949			
Michigan	6	563,363	93,894
Ohio St.	5	382,146	76,429
Southern Methodist	8	484,000	60,500
1950			
Michigan	6	493,924	82,321
Ohio St.	5	368,021	73,604
Southern Methodist	5	309,000	61,800
1951			
Ohio St.	6	455,737	75,956
Michigan	6	445,635	74,273
Illinois	4	237,035	59,259
1952			
Ohio St.	6	453,911	75,652
Michigan	6	395,907	65,985
Texas	#5	311,160	62,232
1953			
Ohio St.	5	397,998	79,600
Southern Cal	6	413,617	68,936
Michigan	6	353,860	58,977
1954			
Ohio St.	6	479,840	79,973
Michigan	6	409,454	68,242
UCLA	5	318,371	63,674
1955			
Michigan	7	544,838	77,834
Ohio St.	7	493,178	70,454
Southern Cal	7	467,085	66,726
1956			
Ohio St.	6	494,575	82,429
Michigan	7	566,145	80,878
Minnesota	6	375,407	62,568
1957			
Michigan	6	504,954	84,159
Ohio St.	6	484,118	80,686
Minnesota	5	319,942	63,988
1958			
Ohio St.	6	499,352	82,225
Michigan	6	405,115	67,519
Louisiana St.	5	296,576	59,315
1959			
Ohio St.	6	495,536	82,589
Michigan	6	456,385	76,064
Louisiana St.	7	408,727	58,390
1960			
Ohio St.	5	413,583	82,717
Michigan St.	4	274,367	68,592
Michigan	6	374,682	62,447
1961			
Ohio St.	5	414,712	82,942
Michigan	7	514,924	73,561
Louisiana St.	6	381,409	63,651

Year/Teams	G	Attendance	Avg.
1962			
Ohio St.	6	497,644	82,941
Michigan St.	4	272,568	68,142
Louisiana St.	6	397,701	66,284
1963			
Ohio St.	5	416,023	83,205
Louisiana St.	6	396,846	66,141
Michigan St.	5	326,597	65,319
1964			
Ohio St.	7	583,740	83,391
Michigan St.	4	284,933	71,233
Michigan	6	388,829	64,805
1965			
Ohio St.	5	416,282	83,256
Michigan	6	480,487	80,081
Michigan St.	5	346,296	69,259
1966			
Ohio St.	6	488,399	81,400
Michigan St.	6	426,750	71,125
Michigan	6	413,599	68,933
1967			
Ohio St.	5	383,502	76,700
Michigan	6	447,289	74,548
Michigan St.	6	411,916	68,653
1968			
Ohio St.	6	482,564	80,427
Southern Cal	5	354,945	70,989
Michigan St.	6	414,177	69,030
1969			
Ohio St.	5	431,175	86,235
Michigan	6	428,780	71,463
Michigan St.	5	352,123	70,425
1970			
Ohio St.	5	432,451	86,490
Michigan	6	476,164	79,361
Purdue	5	340,090	68,018
1971			
Ohio St.	6	506,699	84,450
Michigan	7	564,376	80,625
Wisconsin	6	408,885	68,148
1972			
Michigan	6	513,398	85,566
Ohio St.	6	509,420	84,903
Nebraska	6	456,859	76,143
1973			
Ohio St.	6	523,369	87,228
Michigan	7	595,171	85,024
Nebraska	6	456,726	76,121
1974			
Michigan	6	562,105	93,684
Ohio St.	6	525,314	87,552
Nebraska	7	534,388	76,341
1975			
Michigan	7	689,146	98,449
Ohio St.	6	527,141	87,856
Nebraska	7	533,368	76,195
1976			
Michigan	7	722,113	103,159
Ohio St.	6	526,216	87,702
Tennessee	7	564,922	80,703
1977			
Michigan	7	729,418	104,203
Ohio St.	6	525,535	87,589
Tennessee	7	582,979	83,283
1978			
Michigan	6	629,690	104,948
Ohio St.	7	614,881	87,840
Tennessee	†8	627,381	78,422

Year/Teams	G	Attendance	Avg.
1979			
Michigan	7	730,315	104,331
Ohio St.	7	611,794	87,399
Tennessee	6	512,139	85,357
1980			
Michigan	6	625,750	104,292
Tennessee	†8	709,193	88,649
Ohio St.	7	615,476	87,925
1981			
Michigan	6	632,990	105,498
Tennessee	6	558,996	93,166
Ohio St.	6	521,760	86,960
1982			
Michigan	6	631,743	105,291
Tennessee	6	561,102	93,517
Ohio St.	7	623,152	89,022
1983			
Michigan	6	626,916	104,486
Ohio St.	6	534,110	89,018
Tennessee	†8	679,420	84,928
1984			
Michigan	7	726,734	103,819
Tennessee	7	654,602	93,515
Ohio St.	6	536,691	89,449
1985			
Michigan	6	633,530	105,588
Tennessee	7	658,690	94,099
Ohio St.	6	535,284	89,214
1986			
Michigan	6	631,261	105,210
Tennessee	7	643,317	91,902
Ohio St.	6	536,210	89,368
1987			
Michigan	7	731,281	104,469
Tennessee	‡8	705,434	88,179
Ohio St.	6	511,772	85,295
1988			
Michigan	6	628,807	104,801
Tennessee	6	551,677	91,946
Ohio St.	6	516,972	86,162
1989			
Michigan	6	632,136	105,356
Tennessee	6	563,502	93,917
Ohio St.	6	511,812	85,302
1990			
Michigan	6	627,046	104,508
Tennessee	7	666,540	95,220
Ohio St.	6	536,297	89,383
1991			
Michigan	6	632,024	105,337
Tennessee	6	578,389	96,398
Penn St.	6	575,077	95,846
1992			
Michigan	6	635,201	*105,867
Tennessee	6	575,544	95,924
Penn St.	6	569,195	94,866
1993			
Michigan	7	*739,620	105,660
Tennessee	7	667,280	95,326
Penn St.	6	564,190	94,032

*Record. #Includes neutral-site game (Oklahoma) at Dallas counted as a home game (75,500). †Includes neutral-site game at Memphis counted as a home game. Attendance: 1978 (40,879), 1980 (50,003), 1983 (20,135). ‡Includes neutral-site game at East Rutherford (54,681).

ATTENDANCE RECORDS

Jackson State has led Division I-AA in per-game home attendance in seven of the last 11 years.

Annual Leading Division I-AA Teams in Per-Game Home Attendance

Year	Team	Avg.
1978	Southern-B.R.	28,333
1979	Grambling	29,900
1980	Southern-B.R.	29,708
1981	Grambling	30,835
1982	Southern-B.R.	32,265
1983	Jackson St.	29,117
1984	Jackson St.	29,215
1985	Yale	29,347
1986	Jackson St.	25,177
1987	Jackson St.	*32,734
1988	Jackson St.	26,500
1989	Jackson St.	32,269
1990	Grambling	30,152
1991	Grambling	27,181
1992	Southern-B.R.	28,906
1993	Jackson St.	28,917

*Record.

Annual Leading Division II Teams in Per-Game Home Attendance

Year	Team	Avg.
1958	Southern Miss.	11,998
1959	Southern Miss.	13,964
1960	Florida A&M	12,083
1961	Akron	12,988
1962	Mississippi Col.	13,125
1963	San Diego St.	14,200
1964	Southern-B.R.	12,633
1965	San Diego St.	15,227
1966	San Diego St.	15,972
1967	San Diego St.	*41,030
1968	San Diego St.	36,969
1969	Grambling	27,680
1970	Tampa	24,204
1971	Grambling	29,341
1972	Grambling	22,663
1973	Morgan St.	22,371
1974	Southern-B.R.	33,563
1975	Texas Southern	22,800
1976	Southern-B.R.	25,864
1977	Florida A&M	21,376
1978	Delaware	18,981
1979	Delaware	19,644
1980	Alabama A&M	15,820
1981	Norfolk St.	19,750
1982	Norfolk St.	16,183
1983	Norfolk St.	15,417
1984	Norfolk St.	18,500
1985	Norfolk St.	18,430
1986	Norfolk St.	13,836
1987	North Dak. St.	14,120
1988	Central Fla.	21,905
1989	North Dak. St.	16,833
1990	Norfolk St.	14,904
1991	Norfolk St.	16,779
1992	Norfolk St.	14,196
1993	Norfolk St.	15,346

*Record.

Annual Leading Division III Teams in Per-Game Home Attendance

Year	Team	Avg.
1974	Albany St. (Ga.)	9,380
1975	Wittenberg	7,000
1976	Morehouse	11,600
1977	Dayton	10,315
1978	Dayton	9,827
1979	Central Fla.	11,240
1980	Central Fla.	10,450
1981	Dayton	10,025
1982	Dayton	7,906
1983	Dayton	6,542
1984	Dayton	8,332
1985	Villanova	11,740
1986	Villanova	*11,883
1987	Trinity (Conn.)	6,254
1988	St. John's (Minn.)	5,788
1989	Dayton	5,962
1990	Dayton	6,185
1991	Dayton	7,657
1992	Dayton	6,098
1993	St. John's (Minn.)	6,655

*Record.

1993 Statistical Leaders

1993 Division I-A Individual Leaders

Trent Dilfer of Fresno State was Division I-A's top-ranked quarterback in passing efficiency in 1993. Dilfer threw only four interceptions in 333 attempts.

Rushing

	1993 Class	G	Car.	Yards	Avg.	TD	Yds.PG
LeShon Johnson, Northern Ill.	Sr	11	327	1,976	6.0	12	179.64
Byron Morris, Texas Tech	Jr	11	298	1,752	5.9	22	159.27
Brent Moss, Wisconsin	Jr	11	276	1,479	5.4	14	134.45
Ron Rivers, Fresno St.	Sr	11	216	1,440	6.7	14	130.91
Marshall Faulk, San Diego St.	Jr	12	300	1,530	5.1	21	127.50
Junior Smith, East Caro.	Jr	11	278	1,352	4.9	9	122.91
Napoleon Kaufman, Washington	Jr	11	226	1,299	5.7	14	118.09
David Small, Cincinnati	Sr	10	223	1,180	5.3	17	118.00
Calvin Jones, Nebraska	Jr	9	185	1,043	5.6	12	115.89
Terrell Willis, Rutgers	Fr	11	195	1,261	6.5	13	114.64
Ki-Jana Carter, Penn St.	So	9	155	1,026	6.6	7	114.00
Tyrone Wheatley, Michigan	Jr	9	189	1,005	5.3	11	111.67
James Bostic, Auburn	Jr	11	199	1,205	6.1	12	109.55
Robert Walker, West Va.	So	11	201	1,191	5.9	11	108.27
Curtis Martin, Pittsburgh	Jr	10	210	1,075	5.1	7	107.50
Errict Rhett, Florida	Sr	12	247	1,289	5.2	11	107.42
Charlie Garner, Tennessee	Sr	11	159	1,161	7.3	8	105.55
Lee Becton, Notre Dame	Jr	10	164	1,044	6.4	6	104.40
Dwayne Thomas, Virginia Tech	So	11	214	1,130	5.3	11	102.73
Mario Bates, Arizona St.	So	11	246	1,111	4.5	8	101.00
Raymont Harris, Ohio St.	Sr	11	234	1,109	4.7	9	100.82

Passing Efficiency

(Min. 15 att. per game)	1993 Class	G	Att.	Cmp.	Cmp. Pct.	Int.	Int. Pct.	Yards	Yds./ Att.	TD	TD Pct.	Rating Points
Trent Dilfer, Fresno St.	Jr	11	333	217	65.17	4	1.20	3,276	9.84	28	8.41	173.1
Dave Barr, California	Jr	11	275	187	68.00	12	4.36	2,619	9.52	21	7.64	164.5
Darrell Bevell, Wisconsin	So	11	256	177	69.14	10	3.91	2,294	8.96	19	7.42	161.1
Charlie Ward, Florida St.	Sr	11	380	264	69.47	4	1.05	3,032	7.98	27	7.11	157.8
Maurice DeShazo, Virginia Tech	Jr	11	230	129	56.09	7	3.04	2,080	9.04	22	9.57	157.5
Heath Shuler, Tennessee	Jr	11	285	184	64.56	8	2.81	2,354	8.26	25	8.77	157.3
Glenn Foley, Boston College	Sr	11	363	222	61.16	10	2.75	3,397	9.36	25	6.89	157.0
Chris Vargas, Nevada	Sr	11	490	331	67.55	18	3.67	4,265	8.70	34	6.94	156.2
John Walsh, Brigham Young	So	11	397	244	61.46	15	3.78	3,727	9.39	28	7.05	156.0
Rob Johnson, Southern Cal	Jr	12	405	278	68.64	5	1.23	3,285	8.11	26	6.42	155.5
Tim Gutierrez, San Diego St.	Jr	10	341	208	61.00	10	2.93	3,033	8.89	24	7.04	153.1
Kevin McDougal, Notre Dame	Sr	10	159	98	61.64	5	3.14	1,541	9.69	7	4.40	151.3
Mike McCoy, Utah	Jr	12	430	276	64.19	10	2.33	3,860	8.98	21	4.88	151.1
Robert Hall, Texas Tech	Sr	11	341	216	63.34	7	2.05	2,894	8.49	21	6.16	150.8
Todd Collins, Michigan	Jr	11	274	178	64.96	7	2.55	2,320	8.47	16	5.84	150.2
Jeff Brohm, Louisville	Sr	11	304	185	60.86	9	2.96	2,626	8.64	20	6.58	149.2
Danny O'Neil, Oregon	Jr	11	360	223	61.94	15	4.17	3,224	8.96	22	6.11	149.0
Eric Zeier, Georgia	Jr	11	425	269	63.29	7	1.65	3,525	8.29	24	5.65	148.3
Marvin Graves, Syracuse	Sr	11	280	171	61.07	11	3.93	2,547	9.10	15	5.36	147.3
Terry Dean, Florida	Jr	10	200	118	59.00	10	5.00	1,651	8.25	17	8.50	146.4

Total Offense

	RUSHING				PASSING		TOTAL OFFENSE				
	Car.	Gain	Loss	Net	Att.	Yards	Plays	Yards	Avg.	TDR*	Yds.PG
Chris Vargas, Nevada	45	140	73	67	490	4,265	535	4,332	8.10	35	393.82
Mike McCoy, Utah	99	356	247	109	430	3,860	529	3,969	7.50	21	330.75
Eric Zeier, Georgia	59	161	204	-43	425	3,525	484	3,482	7.19	25	316.55
Scott Milanovich, Maryland	91	208	270	-62	431	3,499	522	3,437	6.58	29	312.45
John Walsh, Brigham Young	83	70	377	-307	397	3,727	480	3,420	7.13	31	310.91
Steve Stenstrom, Stanford	57	39	268	-229	455	3,627	512	3,398	6.64	27	308.91
Charlie Ward, Florida St.	65	452	113	339	380	3,032	445	3,371	7.58	31	306.45
Glenn Foley, Boston College	26	38	82	-44	363	3,397	389	3,353	8.62	25	304.82
Anthony Calvillo, Utah St.	89	298	186	112	469	3,148	558	3,260	5.84	23	296.36
Trent Dilfer, Fresno St.	36	74	138	-64	333	3,276	369	3,212	8.70	29	292.00
Joe Hughes, Wyoming	54	165	136	29	371	3,135	425	3,164	7.44	28	287.64
Tim Gutierrez, San Diego St.	36	2	211	-209	341	3,033	377	2,824	7.49	24	282.40
Danny O'Neil, Oregon	97	174	311	-137	360	3,224	457	3,087	6.75	23	280.64
Robert Hall, Texas Tech	101	392	247	145	341	2,894	442	3,039	6.88	25	276.27
Jeff Garcia, San Jose St.	119	559	200	359	356	2,608	475	2,967	6.25	24	269.73
Gus Frerotte, Tulsa	73	161	151	10	383	2,871	456	2,881	6.32	22	261.91
Rob Johnson, Southern Cal	76	107	284	-177	405	3,285	481	3,108	6.46	27	259.00
Kordell Stewart, Colorado	102	675	151	524	294	2,299	396	2,823	7.13	17	256.64
Stoney Case, New Mexico	126	549	220	329	304	2,490	430	2,819	6.56	22	256.27
Marvin Graves, Syracuse	102	362	213	149	280	2,547	382	2,696	7.06	21	245.09

Touchdowns responsible for are players' TDs scored and passed for.

Receptions Per Game

	1993 Class	G	Rec.	Yards	TD	Rec.PG
Chris Penn, Tulsa	Sr	11	105	1,578	12	9.55
Bryan Reeves, Nevada	Sr	10	91	1,362	17	9.10
Michael Stephens, Nevada	Sr	11	80	1,062	7	7.27
Brice Hunter, Georgia	So	11	76	970	9	6.91
Darnay Scott, San Diego St.	Jr	11	75	1,262	10	6.82
Isaac Bruce, Memphis	Sr	11	74	1,054	10	6.73
Brian Dusho, Kent	Sr	11	72	890	1	6.55
Johnnie Morton, Southern Cal	Sr	12	78	1,373	12	6.50
Mike Lee, Utah St.	Sr	11	70	715	5	6.36
Mike Jones, Wyoming	Sr	11	69	763	5	6.27
Russ Weaver, Maryland	Jr	11	69	606	2	6.27
J. J. Stokes, UCLA	Jr	11	68	1,005	17	6.18
Kez McCorvey, Florida St.	Jr	12	74	966	6	6.17
Ryan Yarborough, Wyoming	Sr	11	67	1,512	16	6.09
Pete Mitchell, Boston College	Jr	11	66	818	7	6.00
Omar Douglas, Minnesota	Sr	10	60	880	11	6.00
Lloyd Hill, Texas Tech	Sr	10	57	794	6	5.70
Justin Armour, Stanford	Jr	9	51	764	6	5.67
Demond Thompkins, Nevada-Las Vegas	Jr	11	62	1,068	8	5.64
Brian Oliver, Ball St.	Jr	11	62	1,010	10	5.64

Receiving Yards Per Game

	1993 Class	G	Rec.	Yards	TD	Yds.PG
Chris Penn, Tulsa	Sr	11	105	1,578	12	143.45
Ryan Yarborough, Wyoming	Sr	11	67	1,512	16	137.45
Bryan Reeves, Nevada	Sr	10	91	1,362	17	136.20
Darnay Scott, San Diego St.	Jr	11	75	1,262	10	114.73
Johnnie Morton, Southern Cal	Sr	12	78	1,373	12	114.42
Charles Johnson, Colorado	Sr	11	57	1,082	9	98.36
Demond Thompkins, Nevada-Las Vegas	Jr	11	62	1,068	8	97.09
Michael Stephens, Nevada	Sr	11	80	1,062	7	96.55
Isaac Bruce, Memphis	Sr	11	74	1,054	10	95.82
Brian Oliver, Ball St.	Jr	11	62	1,010	10	91.82
J. J. Stokes, UCLA	Jr	11	68	1,005	17	91.36
Deron Pointer, Washington St.	Sr	11	47	996	9	90.55
Brice Hunter, Georgia	So	11	76	970	9	88.18
Omar Douglas, Minnesota	Sr	10	60	880	11	88.00
Cotie McMahon, Utah St.	Sr	10	47	880	4	88.00
Mike Senior, Nevada	Jr	11	58	962	5	87.45
Eric Drage, Brigham Young	Sr	10	54	867	6	86.70
Shelby Hill, Syracuse	Sr	11	56	937	4	85.18
Justin Armour, Stanford	Jr	9	51	764	6	84.69
Eddie Goines, North Caro. St.	Jr	11	48	929	10	84.45

Interceptions

	1993 Class	G	Int.	Yards	TD	Int.PG
Orlanda Thomas, Southwestern La.	Jr	11	9	84	1	.82
Anthony Bridges, Louisville	Jr	11	7	184	2	.64
Alundis Brice, Mississippi	Jr	11	7	98	2	.64
Antonio Langham, Alabama	Sr	11	7	67	1	.64
Troy Jensen, San Jose St.	Sr	11	7	60	0	.64
Ernest Boyd, Utah	Jr	10	6	126	1	.60
Orlando Watters, Arkansas	Sr	11	6	185	2	.55
Marvin Goodwin, UCLA	Jr	11	6	136	0	.55
Nathan Bennett, Rice	Sr	11	6	123	1	.55
Tony Bouie, Arizona	Jr	11	6	100	0	.55
David Thomas, Miami (Ohio)	Jr	11	6	63	0	.55
Walt Harris, Mississippi St.	So	11	6	59	0	.55
Marcus Jenkins, Kentucky	Sr	11	6	45	0	.55
Jeff Messenger, Wisconsin	Jr	11	6	41	0	.55
Corey Sawyer, Florida St.	Jr	12	6	90	0	.50
Jason Sehorn, Southern Cal	Sr	12	6	45	0	.50
Tony Pittman, Penn St.	Jr	10	5	40	0	.50

Scoring

	1993 Class	G	TD	XP	FG	Pts.	Pts.PG
Byron Morris, Texas Tech	Jr	11	22	2	0	134	12.18
Marshall Faulk, San Diego St.	Jr	12	24	0	0	144	12.00
Darnell Campbell, Boston College	Sr	11	21	0	0	126	11.45
Bryan Reeves, Nevada	Sr	10	17	0	0	102	10.20
David Small, Cincinnati	Sr	10	17	0	0	102	10.20
Lindsey Chapman, California	Sr	11	17	0	0	102	9.27
J. J. Stokes, UCLA	Jr	11	17	0	0	102	9.27
Ryan Yarborough, Wyoming	Sr	11	16	2	0	98	8.91
Calvin Jones, Nebraska	Jr	9	13	0	0	78	8.67
John Becksvoort, Tennessee	Jr	11	0	59	12	95	8.64
Derek Mahoney, Fresno St.	Sr	11	0	51	14	93	8.45
Kanon Parkman, Georgia	So	11	0	35	19	92	8.36
Leon Johnson, North Caro.	Fr	12	16	4	0	100	8.33
Bjorn Merten, UCLA	Fr	11	0	31	20	91	8.27
Terry Venetoulias, Texas A&M	Sr	11	0	51	13	90	8.18
Nathan Morreale, Utah St.	Fr	11	0	33	19	90	8.18
Michael Proctor, Alabama	So	12	0	31	22	97	8.08
Judd Davis, Florida	Jr	12	0	51	15	96	8.00
Tyrone Wheatley, Michigan	Jr	9	12	0	0	72	8.00
Scott Bentley, Florida St.	Fr	12	0	56	13	95	7.92
Kevin Pendergast, Notre Dame	Sr	11	0	45	14	87	7.91
Peter Holt, San Diego St.	Fr	12	0	45	16	93	7.75

All-Purpose Yards

	1993 Class	G	Rush	Rec.	PR	KOR	Total Yards	Yds.PG
LeShon Johnson, Northern Ill.	Sr	11	1,976	106	0	0	2,082	189.27
Terrell Willis, Rutgers	Fr	11	1,261	61	0	704	2,026	184.18
Marshall Faulk, San Diego St.	Jr	12	1,530	644	0	0	2,174	181.17
Byron Morris, Texas Tech	Jr	11	1,752	150	0	0	1,902	172.91
Mike Adams, Texas	So	11	68	908	256	622	1,854	168.55
Napoleon Kaufman, Washington	Jr	11	1,299	139	25	388	1,851	168.27
David Palmer, Alabama	Jr	12	278	1,000	244	439	1,961	163.42
Tyrone Wheatley, Michigan	Jr	9	1,005	152	0	246	1,403	155.89
Chris Penn, Tulsa	Sr	11	2	1,578	134	0	1,714	155.82
John Leach, Wake Forest	Sr	11	1,089	340	9	253	1,691	153.73
Bryan Reeves, Nevada	Sr	10	3	1,362	109	25	1,499	149.90
Thomas Lewis, Indiana	Jr	11	45	881	284	429	1,639	149.00
Andre Coleman, Kansas St.	Sr	11	24	761	362	434	1,581	143.73
Darnay Scott, San Diego St.	Jr	11	98	1,262	0	220	1,580	143.64
Ron Rivers, Fresno St.	Sr	11	1,440	118	0	7	1,565	142.27
Dwayne Thomas, Virginia Tech	So	11	1,130	115	0	305	1,550	140.91
Demond Thompkins, Nevada-Las Vegas	Jr	11	0	1,068	12	442	1,522	138.36
Ryan Yarborough, Wyoming	Sr	11	0	1,512	0	0	1,512	137.45
Brent Moss, Wisconsin	Jr	11	1,479	19	0	0	1,498	136.18
Barry Boyd, Southern Miss.	Sr	11	805	74	0	587	1,466	133.27

Northern Illinois tailback LeShon Johnson averaged 189 all-purpose yards per game last season to lead Division I-A. Johnson also was the division's top rusher with 1,976 yards.

STATISTICAL LEADERS

Punt Returns

(Min. 1.2 per game)	1993 Class	No.	Yds.	TD	Avg.
Aaron Glenn, Texas A&M	Sr	17	339	2	19.94
Shawn Summers, Tennessee	So	18	255	1	14.17
Lee Gissendaner, Northwestern	Sr	16	223	0	13.94
Scott Gumina, Mississippi St.	Jr	13	180	1	13.85
Andre Coleman, Kansas St.	Sr	27	362	1	13.41
Eddie Kennison, Louisiana St.	Fr	20	266	0	13.30
Todd Dixon, Wake Forest	Sr	13	167	1	12.85
James Dye, Utah St.	So	21	256	1	12.19
Bobby Engram, Penn St.	So	33	402	0	12.18
Greg Myers, Colorado St.	So	27	325	0	12.04
Dexter McCleon, Clemson	Fr	14	168	0	12.00
L. T. Gulley, Southern Miss.	So	18	214	0	11.89
Chris Hudson, Colorado	Jr	15	175	0	11.67
Ta'Boris Fisher, Mississippi	Fr	29	330	1	11.38
Clyde McCoy, Arizona St.	Jr	23	259	0	11.26
Polee Banks, New Mexico St.	Sr	18	199	1	11.06
Ray Peterson, San Diego St.	So	30	330	0	11.00
Sorola Palmer, Florida	So	12	129	0	10.75
Paul Guidry, UCLA	Fr	27	282	0	10.44
Prentice Rhone, Wyoming	Sr	32	334	1	10.44

Kickoff Returns

(Min. 1.2 per game)	1993 Class	No.	Yds.	TD	Avg.
Leeland McElroy, Texas A&M	Fr	15	590	3	39.33
Chris Hewitt, Cincinnati	Fr	14	441	1	31.50
Tyler Anderson, Brigham Young	Sr	19	568	1	29.89
Andre Coleman, Kansas St.	Sr	15	434	0	28.93
Jack Jackson, Florida	So	17	480	1	28.24
Polee Banks, New Mexico St.	Sr	14	394	1	28.14
Demond Thompkins, Nevada-Las Vegas	Jr	16	442	0	27.63
Steve Mehl, Pacific (Cal.)	Sr	15	410	0	27.33
Mike Adams, Texas	So	23	622	0	27.04
Dondra Jolly, Army	Jr	19	510	0	26.84
Steve Christensen, Brigham Young	Sr	14	373	0	26.64
Shelly Hammonds, Penn St.	Sr	16	424	0	26.50
Sam Rogers, UTEP	So	17	450	1	26.47
Kalief Muhammad, Baylor	Fr	18	471	0	26.17
Napoleon Kaufman, Washington	Jr	15	338	0	25.87
Derrick Steagall, Georgia Tech	Fr	16	413	0	25.81
Keith Williams, Utah	Sr	21	542	1	25.81
Kenny Gunn, Tulsa	So	21	524	0	24.95
Jimmy Oliver, Texas Christian	Jr	20	492	0	24.60
Ainsworth Morgan, Toledo	Sr	29	713	1	24.59

Punting

(Min. 3.6 per game)	1993 Class	No.	Avg.
Chris MacInnis, Air Force	Sr	49	47.00
Terry Daniel, Auburn	Jr	51	46.92
Mike Nesbitt, New Mexico	Sr	53	45.04
Brad Faunce, Nevada-Las Vegas	Jr	61	45.00
Pat O'Neill, Syracuse	Sr	44	44.32
Scott Milanovich, Maryland	So	50	43.78
Bryne Diehl, Alabama	Jr	56	43.59
Scott Tyner, Oklahoma St.	Sr	75	43.32
Alan Boardman, Brigham Young	Fr	56	43.13
Stephen Wilson, Hawaii	Jr	46	42.96
Todd Jordan, Mississippi St.	Sr	56	42.91
Robert King, Texas Tech	Sr	54	42.69
Kyle Pooler, Missouri	Jr	72	42.44
Aaron Mills, Stanford	Sr	63	42.22
Gary Layton, Miami (Ohio)	Jr	65	42.22
Will Brice, Virginia	Fr	48	42.19
Darren Schager, UCLA	Jr	64	41.95
Wes Garner, Eastern Mich.	Fr	65	41.75
Dan Eichloff, Kansas	Sr	59	41.53
Nick Gallery, Iowa	Fr	50	41.42

Field Goals

	1993 Class	G	FGA	FG	Pct.	FGPG
Michael Proctor, Alabama	So	12	29	22	.759	1.83
Bjorn Merten, UCLA	Fr	11	25	20	.800	1.82
Nathan Morreale, Utah St.	Fr	11	27	19	.704	1.73
Kanon Parkman, Georgia	So	11	27	19	.704	1.73
Jon Baker, Arizona St.	Jr	11	26	18	.692	1.64
Tom Dallen, Cincinnati	Jr	11	22	17	.773	1.55
Tom Burke, Mississippi St.	Sr	11	23	17	.739	1.55
Aaron Price, Washington St.	Sr	11	31	17	.548	1.55
Tommy Thompson, Oregon	Sr	11	21	16	.762	1.45
Chris Boniol, Louisiana Tech	Sr	11	22	16	.727	1.45
Scott Szeredy, Texas	Sr	11	22	16	.727	1.45
Chris Yergensen, Utah	Sr	12	27	17	.630	1.42
Andre Lafleur, Louisiana St.	So	10	17	14	.824	1.40
Nelson Welch, Clemson	Jr	11	24	15	.625	1.36
Peter Holt, San Diego St.	Fr	12	23	16	.696	1.33
Steve McLaughlin, Arizona	Jr	10	20	13	.650	1.30
Jeff Caldwell, Arkansas	Jr	11	17	14	.824	1.27
Kevin Pendergast, Notre Dame	Sr.	11	19	14	.737	1.27
Bill Manolopoulos, Indiana	So	11	19	14	.737	1.27
Derek Mahoney, Fresno St.	Sr	11	19	14	.737	1.27
Chris Richardson, Illinois	Jr	11	20	14	.700	1.27
Travis Hanson, Washington	Sr	11	22	14	.636	1.27

1993 Division I-A Team Leaders

Total Offense

	G	Plays	Yds.	Avg.	TD*	Yds.PG
Nevada	11	955	6,260	6.6	56	569.09
Florida St.	12	939	6,576	7.0	63	548.00
Fresno St.	11	808	5,863	7.3	53	533.00
Boston College	11	827	5,570	6.7	51	506.36
Utah	12	906	5,815	6.4	43	484.58
Tennessee	11	762	5,286	6.9	58	480.55
Florida	12	888	5,719	6.4	59	476.58
Texas Tech	11	854	5,225	6.1	51	475.00
Brigham Young	11	853	5,222	6.1	51	474.73
Colorado	11	841	5,175	6.2	40	470.45
San Diego St.	12	914	5,586	6.1	51	465.50
Wisconsin	11	820	5,116	6.2	46	465.09
West Va.	11	781	5,103	6.5	49	463.91
Virginia Tech	11	830	4,885	5.9	52	444.09
Utah St.	11	879	4,863	5.5	36	442.09
Maryland	11	854	4,836	5.7	35	439.64

*Touchdowns scored by rushing or passing only.

Total Defense

	G	Plays	Yds.	Avg.	TD*	Yds.PG
Mississippi	11	727	2,580	3.5	13	234.5
Arizona	11	739	2,606	3.5	14	236.9
Texas A&M	11	740	2,724	3.7	10	247.6
Miami (Fla.)	11	723	2,814	3.9	15	255.8
Alabama	12	738	3,104	4.2	19	258.7
Florida St.	12	773	3,414	4.4	15	284.5
Bowling Green	11	715	3,285	4.6	22	298.6
Washington St.	11	773	3,287	4.3	27	298.8
Ohio St.	11	744	3,293	4.4	19	299.4
Indiana	11	747	3,336	4.5	18	303.3
Cincinnati	11	779	3,365	4.3	22	305.9
Nebraska	11	726	3,384	4.7	22	307.6
Tennessee	11	780	3,395	4.4	15	308.6
Illinois	11	746	3,402	4.6	22	309.3
Auburn	11	699	3,418	4.9	22	310.7
Memphis	11	764	3,440	4.5	23	312.7

*Touchdowns scored by rushing or passing only.

Rushing Offense

	G	Car.	Yds.	Avg.	TD	Yds.PG
Army	11	660	3,283	5.0	35	298.5
Oregon St.	11	675	3,254	4.8	25	295.8
Nebraska	11	589	3,167	5.4	39	287.9
Air Force	12	713	3,419	4.8	29	284.9
Hawaii	12	569	3,247	5.7	35	270.6
Notre Dame	11	561	2,868	5.1	37	260.7
North Caro.	12	628	3,036	4.8	39	253.0
Wisconsin	11	557	2,759	5.0	26	250.8
West Va.	11	542	2,684	5.0	28	244.0
Virginia Tech	11	582	2,671	4.6	28	242.8
Iowa St.	11	575	2,667	4.6	22	242.5
Colorado	11	522	2,640	5.1	26	240.0
Tennessee	11	442	2,621	5.9	27	238.3
Penn St.	11	532	2,597	4.9	27	236.1
Rutgers	11	479	2,588	5.4	27	235.3
Texas A&M	11	505	2,577	5.1	27	234.3

Rushing Defense

	G	Car.	Yds.	Avg.	TD	Yds.PG
Arizona	11	368	331	.9	5	30.1
Washington St.	11	438	949	2.2	11	86.3
Southwestern La.	11	378	975	2.6	12	88.6
Notre Dame	11	331	985	3.0	8	89.5
Florida St.	12	397	1,182	3.0	6	98.5
Mississippi	11	463	1,127	2.4	8	102.5
North Caro.	12	410	1,230	3.0	10	102.5
Michigan	11	379	1,179	3.1	6	107.2
Florida	12	417	1,334	3.2	9	111.2
Illinois	11	444	1,265	2.8	10	115.0
Ohio St.	11	409	1,275	3.1	6	115.9
Tennessee	11	433	1,290	3.0	8	117.3
Bowling Green	11	418	1,291	3.1	10	117.4
Miami (Fla.)	11	435	1,297	3.0	9	117.9
Penn St.	11	423	1,316	3.1	12	119.6
Memphis	11	430	1,320	3.1	9	120.0

Scoring Offense

	G	Pts.	Avg.
Florida St.	12	518	43.2
Tennessee	11	471	42.8
Fresno St.	11	437	39.7
Florida	12	472	39.3
Nebraska	11	421	38.3
Nevada	11	419	38.1
Texas Tech	11	409	37.2
Texas A&M	11	404	36.7
Notre Dame	11	403	36.6
West Va.	11	401	36.5

(Scoring Offense continued)

	G	Pts.	Avg.
Virginia Tech	11	400	36.4
Brigham Young	11	390	35.5
North Caro.	12	421	35.1
San Diego St.	12	413	34.4
Boston College	11	377	34.3
Hawaii	12	393	32.8
Penn St.	11	357	32.5
Auburn	11	353	32.1

Scoring Defense

	G	Pts.	Avg.
Florida St.	12	113	9.4
Texas A&M	11	119	10.8
Miami (Fla.)	11	138	12.5
Mississippi	11	142	12.9
Tennessee	11	144	13.1
Alabama	12	158	13.2
Indiana	11	152	13.8
Michigan	11	153	13.9
Arizona	11	161	14.6
West Va.	11	171	15.5
Ohio St.	11	172	15.6
Bowling Green	11	173	15.7
Oklahoma	11	176	16.0
Nebraska	11	176	16.0
Wisconsin	11	179	16.3
Clemson	11	179	16.3
Virginia	11	186	16.9
Western Mich.	11	187	17.0

Passing Offense

	G	Att.	Cmp.	Int.	Pct.	Yards	Yds./Att.	TD	Yds.PG
Nevada	11	516	343	19	66.5	4,373	8.5	34	397.5
Brigham Young	11	458	278	18	60.7	4,060	8.9	31	369.1
Maryland	11	473	302	21	63.8	3,823	8.1	26	347.5
Florida	12	488	284	21	58.2	4,072	8.3	41	339.3
Stanford	11	474	308	14	65.0	3,709	7.8	27	337.2
Florida St.	12	469	327	6	69.7	3,909	8.3	37	325.8
Utah	12	433	278	10	64.2	3,891	9.0	22	324.3
Georgia	11	432	272	7	63.0	3,552	8.2	24	322.9
San Diego St.	12	465	269	14	57.8	3,836	8.2	28	319.7
Fresno St.	11	350	225	5	64.3	3,425	9.8	29	311.4
Boston College	11	368	224	11	60.9	3,420	9.3	25	310.9
Minnesota	11	500	260	27	52.0	3,277	6.6	22	297.9
Oregon	11	369	228	15	61.8	3,270	8.9	25	297.3
Wyoming	11	378	212	9	56.1	3,217	8.5	25	292.5
Southern Cal	12	432	297	5	68.8	3,484	8.1	28	290.3
Tulsa	11	409	232	15	56.7	3,153	7.7	21	286.6
Utah St.	11	471	247	10	52.4	3,148	6.7	19	286.2
Duke	11	477	249	19	52.2	2,999	6.3	14	272.6
Louisville	11	343	199	11	58.0	2,923	8.5	23	265.7

Pass Efficiency Defense

	G	Att.	Cmp.	Cmp. Pct.	Int.	Int. Pct.	Yards	Yds./Att.	TD	TD Pct.	Rating Points
Texas A&M	11	292	116	39.73	13	4.45	1,339	4.59	5	1.71	74.99
Alabama	12	310	144	46.45	22	7.10	1,539	4.96	9	2.90	83.54
Mississippi	11	264	117	44.32	15	5.68	1,453	5.50	5	1.89	85.44
Miami (Fla.)	11	288	138	47.92	17	5.90	1,517	5.27	6	2.08	87.23
Tennessee	11	347	167	48.13	18	5.19	2,105	6.07	7	2.02	95.37
Iowa	11	291	143	49.14	18	6.19	1,798	6.18	6	2.06	95.47
Central Mich.	11	302	151	50.00	13	4.30	1,730	5.73	6	1.99	96.07
Florida St.	12	376	181	48.14	15	3.99	2,232	5.94	9	2.39	97.92
Auburn	11	349	153	43.84	15	4.30	2,039	5.84	15	4.30	98.50
Cincinnati	11	315	164	52.06	14	4.44	1,867	5.93	7	2.22	100.29
Kentucky	11	344	177	51.45	20	5.81	2,089	6.07	11	3.20	101.39
Nebraska	11	293	142	48.46	10	3.41	1,803	6.15	8	2.73	102.34
Virginia	11	333	189	56.76	22	6.61	2,017	6.06	9	2.70	103.34
Southern Cal	12	316	164	51.90	12	3.80	1,877	5.94	11	3.48	105.69
Southwestern La.	11	411	204	49.64	22	5.35	2,616	6.36	17	4.14	106.04
Washington	11	317	164	51.74	22	6.94	2,119	6.68	12	3.79	106.50
Louisville	11	363	202	55.65	21	5.79	2,230	6.14	12	3.31	106.59
Ohio St.	11	335	180	53.73	17	5.07	2,018	6.02	13	3.88	106.99

Texas A&M defensive back Aaron Glenn was part of an Aggie secondary that led Division I-A in pass efficiency defense.

Net Punting

	Punts	Avg.	No. Ret.	Yds. Ret.	Net Avg.
New Mexico	54	44.5	28	147	41.8
West Va.	39	45.1	20	158	41.0
Nevada-Las Vegas	61	45.0	29	310	39.9
Maryland	53	42.8	20	169	39.6
Air Force	51	46.0	31	337	39.4
Nebraska	46	41.2	17	89	39.3
Auburn	51	46.9	26	418	38.7
Wyoming	54	39.5	22	51	38.6
Florida	44	41.8	20	142	38.5
Oklahoma St.	77	42.9	41	350	38.4
Stanford	63	42.2	30	244	38.3
UCLA	64	42.0	35	231	38.3
Pittsburgh	73	43.0	47	372	37.9
Alabama	56	43.6	29	321	37.9
Mississippi St.	64	42.0	32	267	37.8
Virginia	52	40.1	16	122	37.8
Texas	47	40.3	15	121	37.7

Punt Returns

	G	No.	Yds.	TD	Avg.
Texas A&M	11	20	357	2	17.9
Pittsburgh	11	9	140	1	15.6
Penn St.	11	38	546	0	14.4
Northwestern	11	17	232	0	13.6
Kansas St.	11	27	362	1	13.4
Louisiana St.	11	20	266	0	13.3
Iowa St.	11	15	199	0	13.3
Clemson	11	27	347	0	12.9
Tennessee	11	37	453	2	12.2
Wake Forest	11	16	191	1	11.9
Arizona St.	11	26	308	1	11.8
Colorado St.	11	29	330	0	11.4
Mississippi	11	37	420	1	11.4
New Mexico St.	11	18	199	1	11.1
San Diego St.	12	30	330	0	11.0
Virginia Tech	11	35	383	1	10.9

Kickoff Returns

	G	No.	Yds.	TD	Avg.
Texas A&M	11	23	717	3	31.2
Cincinnati	11	26	720	1	27.7
Arizona	11	26	697	0	26.8
Memphis	11	40	1,071	1	26.8
New Mexico	11	26	672	0	25.8
Texas Christian	11	32	792	0	24.8
Notre Dame	11	23	566	1	24.6
West Va.	11	26	634	0	24.4
Texas	11	30	728	0	24.3
Brigham Young	11	55	1,322	1	24.0
Kansas	12	31	734	1	23.7
Tennessee	11	28	661	0	23.6
Eastern Mich.	11	33	776	2	23.5
Kansas St.	11	23	533	0	23.2
Louisville	11	31	718	0	23.2
Baylor	11	39	898	0	23.0
New Mexico St.	11	43	984	1	22.9

Turnover Margin

	TURNOVERS GAINED			TURNOVERS LOST			Margin/ Game
	Fum.	Int.	Total	Fum.	Int.	Total	
UCLA	21	18	39	13	7	20	1.73
Fresno St.	15	16	31	9	5	14	1.55
Cincinnati	13	14	27	5	7	12	1.36
Tennessee	15	18	33	11	9	20	1.18
Texas A&M	19	13	32	7	12	19	1.18
Mississippi	15	15	30	3	14	17	1.18
Penn St.	11	21	32	6	13	19	1.18
Colorado	13	13	26	6	7	13	1.18
Notre Dame	10	12	22	5	5	10	1.09
Texas Tech	16	14	30	11	7	18	1.09
Clemson	11	17	28	9	7	16	1.09

Longest Division I-A Plays of 1993

Rushing

Player, Team (Opponent)	Yards
Jerald Sowell, Tulane (Alabama)	98
LeShon Johnson, Northern Ill. (Southern Ill.)	92
Curtis Johnson, North Caro. (Maryland)	90
Robert Walker, West Va. (Syracuse)	90
Derrick Witherspoon, Clemson (Maryland)	89
Larry Jones, Miami, Fla. (Pittsburgh)	88
Frank Mandu, Washington St. (Montana St.)	85
Derek Ayers, UCLA (Brigham Young)	*83

Passing

Passer-Receiver, Team (Opponent)	Yards
John Paci -Thomas Lewis, Indiana (Penn St.)	99
Steve Stenstrom-Brian Manning, Stanford (Arizona)	91
Todd Collins-Derrick Alexander, Michigan (Illinois)	90
Dan Smith-Gordon Benning, Miami, Ohio (Bowling Green)	88
Dan O'Neil-Willy Tate, Oregon (Illinois)	87
Symmion Willis-Larry Holmes, Virginia (Ohio)	87
Joe Hughes-Ryan Yarborough, Wyoming (Air Force)	87
Marcel Weems-Jeff Blakely, Akron (Temple)	87
Mike McCoy-Henry Lusk, Utah (San Diego St.)	87

Interception Returns

Player, Team (Opponent)	Yards
Marlon Kerner, Ohio St. (Purdue)	100
Ray Jackson, Colorado St. (UTEP)	100
Marvin Goodwin, UCLA (Brigham Young)	*99
Orlando Watters, Arkansas (Louisiana St.)	99
Calvin Jackson, Auburn (Florida)	96
Charles Verner, Oklahoma St. (Texas Christian)	95
DeWayne Patterson, Washington St. (UCLA)	89

*Did not score.

Punt Returns

Player, Team (Opponent)	Yards
Ta'Boris Fisher, Mississippi (Auburn)	77
Aaron Glenn, Texas A&M (Missouri)	76
Scott Gumina, Mississippi St. (Tulane)	76
Todd Dixon, Wake Forest (Duke)	74
Prentice Rhone, Wyoming (San Diego St.)	74

Kickoff Returns

Player, Team (Opponent)	Yards
Leroy Gallman, Duke (Tennessee)	100
Jack Jackson, Florida (Mississippi St.)	100
Charles Henley, Kansas (Colorado)	100
Leeland McElroy, Texas A&M (Texas)	100
Polee Banks, New Mexico St. (Pacific, Cal.)	99
Kevin Hicks, Washington St. (Michigan)	97
Sam Rogers, UTEP (North Caro.)	96
Todd Dixon, Wake Forest (Vanderbilt)	95
Steve Clay, Eastern Mich. (Akron)	95

Field Goals

Player, Team (Opponent)	Yards
Ty Stewart, Iowa St. (Oklahoma St.)	58
Ty Stewart, Iowa St. (Missouri)	58
Scott Szeredy, Texas (Houston)	56
John Stewart, Southern Methodist (Baylor)	55
Mitch Berger, Colorado (Miami, Fla.)	54
Tommy Thompson, Oregon (Arizona)	54
Todd Romano, Iowa (Tulsa)	53
Steve Yenner, Vanderbilt (Auburn)	53
Steve McLaughlin, Arizona (Washington St.)	53
Michael Proctor, Alabama (Mississippi)	53

Punts

Player, Team (Opponent)	Yards
Robert King, Texas Tech (Texas A&M)	77
Dan Johnson, New Mexico (Hawaii)	76
Stephen Wilson, Hawaii (New Mexico)	76
Ryan Longwell, California (Southern Cal)	75
Chris MacInnis, Air Force (Colorado St.)	74
Duane Vacek, Texas (Texas Tech)	72
Josh LaRocca, Rice (Texas A&M)	72
Terry Daniel, Auburn (Florida)	71

Fumble Returns

Player, Team (Opponent)	Yards
Mike Collins, West Va. (Missouri)	97
Parrish Foster, New Mexico St. (Nevada)	93
David Thomas, Miami, Ohio (Akron)	92
Gerald Nickelberry, Northern Ill. (Arkansas St.)	92
Derrick Brooks, Florida St. (Clemson)	83

1993 Division I-AA Individual Leaders

Rushing

	1993 Class	G	Car.	Yards	Avg.	TD	Yds.PG
Tony Vinson, Towson St.	Sr	10	293	2,016	6.9	23	201.60
Keith Elias, Princeton	Sr	10	305	1,731	5.7	19	173.10
Richard Johnson, Butler	Sr	10	322	1,535	4.8	10	153.50
Irving Spikes, Northeast La.	Sr	11	246	1,563	6.4	14	142.09
Anthony Russo, St. John's (N.Y.)	Sr	11	311	1,558	5.0	16	141.64
Robert Trice, Cal St. Northridge	Sr	10	235	1,362	5.8	9	136.20
Willie High, Eastern Ill.	So	11	273	1,487	5.4	12	135.18
Erik Marsh, Lafayette	Jr	11	304	1,441	4.7	9	131.00
Michael Hicks, South Caro. St.	So	11	221	1,426	6.5	16	129.64
Rico White, Alabama St.	Sr	10	231	1,272	5.5	13	127.20
Chris Parker, Marshall	So	11	225	1,370	6.1	16	124.55
Terrance Stokes, Pennsylvania	Jr	10	256	1,211	4.7	6	121.10
James White, North Caro. A&T	Sr	11	204	1,316	6.5	14	119.64
Rene Ingoglia, Massachusetts	So	11	233	1,284	5.5	14	116.73
Leon Brown, Eastern Ky.	Sr	9	144	1,046	7.3	11	116.22
Sherriden May, Idaho	Jr	11	221	1,267	5.7	20	115.18
David Wright, Indiana St.	So	11	229	1,262	5.5	7	114.73
Eric Gant, Grambling	Sr	11	211	1,243	5.9	11	113.00
Derek Fitzgerald, William & Mary	So	9	160	1,002	6.3	10	111.33
Kippy Bayless, Middle Tenn. St.	Jr	11	198	1,214	6.1	15	110.36

William and Mary's Shawn Knight returns for the 1994 season as Division I-AA's top-rated quarterback in passing efficiency. Knight completed 71 percent of his passes last year and threw only four interceptions in 177 attempts.

Passing Efficiency

(Min. 15 att. per game)	1993 Class	G	Att.	Cmp.	Cmp. Pct.	Int.	Int. Pct.	Yards	Yds./Att.	TD	TD Pct.	Rating Points
Shawn Knight, William & Mary	Jr	10	177	125	70.62	4	2.26	2,055	11.61	22	12.43	204.6
Doug Nussmeier, Idaho	Sr	11	304	185	60.86	5	1.64	2,960	9.74	33	10.86	175.2
Kelvin Simmons, Troy St.	Sr	11	224	143	63.84	6	2.68	2,144	9.57	23	10.27	172.8
Dave Dickenson, Montana	So	11	390	262	67.18	9	2.31	3,640	9.33	32	8.21	168.0
Dan Crowley, Towson St.	Jr	10	217	125	57.60	4	1.84	1,882	8.67	23	10.60	161.7
Roy Fletcher, Drake	So	8	136	75	55.15	2	1.47	1,264	9.29	11	8.09	157.0
Robert Cobb, Northeast La.	Sr	11	345	197	57.10	8	2.32	3,008	8.72	29	8.41	153.4
Scott Semptimphelter, Lehigh	Sr	11	413	249	60.29	13	3.15	3,449	8.35	30	7.26	148.1
Kurt Warner, Northern Iowa	Sr	11	268	158	58.96	4	1.49	2,484	9.27	16	5.97	146.8
Darin Hinshaw, Central Fla.	Jr	11	322	191	59.32	12	3.73	2,645	8.21	24	7.45	145.5
Todd Bernett, Eastern Wash.	Jr	9	226	117	51.77	3	1.33	1,956	8.65	16	7.08	145.2
Rich Green, New Hampshire	Sr	9	173	92	53.18	7	4.05	1,516	8.76	12	6.94	141.6
Tom Proudian, Iona	So	10	440	262	59.55	13	2.95	3,368	7.65	29	6.59	139.7
Maseo Bolin, North Caro. A&T	So	11	235	133	56.60	5	2.13	1,832	7.80	15	6.38	138.9
Chris Hixson, Rhode Island	Fr	11	269	162	60.22	8	2.97	2,218	8.25	12	4.46	138.3
Mitch Maher, North Texas	Jr	11	324	176	54.32	13	4.01	2,595	8.01	24	7.41	138.0
John Whitcomb, Ala.-Birmingham	Jr	11	389	238	61.18	13	3.34	3,012	7.74	21	5.40	137.4
Jim McGeehan, Pennsylvania	Sr	10	318	183	57.55	5	1.57	2,197	6.91	24	7.55	137.3
Jay Walker, Howard	Sr	11	406	223	54.93	13	3.20	3,324	8.19	24	5.91	136.8
Kenyon Earl, Tenn.-Chatt.	Jr	11	264	146	55.30	15	5.68	2,233	8.46	16	6.06	135.0

Montana quarterback Dave Dickenson averaged 361 yards per game in total offense last year as a sophomore.

Total Offense

		RUSHING			PASSING			TOTAL OFFENSE			
	Car.	Gain	Loss	Net	Att.	Yards	Plays	Yards	Avg.	TDR*	Yds.PG
Dave Dickenson, Montana	140	612	274	338	390	3,640	530	3,978	7.51	46	361.64
Steve McNair, Alcorn St.	107	752	119	633	386	3,197	493	3,830	7.77	30	348.18
Tom Proudian, Iona	81	226	272	-46	440	3,368	521	3,322	6.38	30	332.20
Scott Semptimphelter, Lehigh	102	328	249	79	413	3,449	515	3,528	6.85	30	320.73
Doug Nussmeier, Idaho	96	656	102	554	304	2,960	400	3,514	8.78	41	319.45
Jay Walker, Howard	60	325	180	145	406	3,324	466	3,469	7.44	26	315.36
George Beisel, Hofstra	106	473	284	189	386	2,867	492	3,056	6.21	27	305.60
Robert Dougherty, Boston U.	123	644	209	435	318	2,435	441	2,870	6.51	27	287.00
Robert Cobb, Northeast La.	28	49	92	-43	345	3,008	373	2,965	7.95	29	269.55
Jay Fiedler, Dartmouth	92	309	166	143	321	2,542	413	2,685	6.50	24	268.50
Eric Fish, Evansville	57	178	140	38	380	2,562	437	2,600	5.95	20	260.00
John Whitcomb, Ala.-Birmingham	27	2	168	-166	389	3,012	416	2,846	6.84	21	258.73
Brad Otton, Weber St.	35	56	121	-65	314	2,307	349	2,242	6.42	16	249.11
Mitch Maher, North Texas	82	242	126	116	324	2,595	406	2,711	6.68	31	246.45
Darin Hinshaw, Central Fla.	45	73	136	-63	322	2,645	367	2,582	7.04	27	234.73
Shawn Knight, William & Mary .	71	365	83	282	177	2,055	248	2,337	9.42	26	233.70
Lonnie Galloway, Western Caro.	109	625	141	484	237	2,067	346	2,551	7.37	9	231.91
Jeff Lewis, Northern Ariz.	100	293	261	32	335	2,497	435	2,529	5.81	17	229.91
Jim McGeehan, Pennsylvania ..	67	219	123	96	318	2,197	385	2,293	5.96	26	229.30
Rob Rayl, Valparaiso	84	374	99	275	237	1,756	321	2,031	6.33	12	225.67

Receptions Per Game

	1993 Class	G	Rec.	Yards	TD	Rec.PG
Dave Cecchini, Lehigh	Sr	11	88	1,318	16	8.00
Miles Macik, Pennsylvania	So	10	72	840	13	7.20
David Rhodes, Central Fla.	Jr	11	78	1,159	12	7.09
Derrick Ingram, Ala.-Birmingham	Jr	11	76	1,115	8	6.91
Todd Eckenroad, St. Francis (Pa.) ..	Sr	9	61	678	1	6.78
Hanz Hoag, Evansville	Jr	10	66	778	6	6.60
Gary Harrell, Howard	Sr	11	72	982	8	6.55
Wayne Chrebet, Hofstra	Jr	9	57	788	9	6.33
Jeff Johnson, East Tenn. St.	Jr	11	69	915	11	6.27
John Hyland, Dartmouth	Sr	10	62	1,076	9	6.20
Chris Summers, Holy Cross	Sr	11	68	1,057	13	6.18
Blake Tuffli, St. Mary's (Cal.)	Fr	10	61	929	7	6.10
David Gamble, New Hampshire	Sr	11	67	1,138	13	6.09
Scott Gurnsey, Montana	Jr	11	67	1,079	9	6.09
Tony Brooks, Eastern Wash.	Sr	10	60	1,024	7	6.00
Eugene McGowan, Iona.................	Sr	10	60	737	4	6.00
Elliott Miller, St. Francis (Pa.)	So	9	54	454	3	6.00
Lawrence Segree, Tennessee St.	So	11	65	870	5	5.91
David McLeod, James Madison	Sr	11	64	1,207	6	5.82
Maurice Jones, Liberty..................	Sr	11	62	955	9	5.64

Receiving Yards Per Game

	1993 Class	G	Rec.	Yards	TD	Yds.PG
Dave Cecchini, Lehigh	Sr	11	88	1,318	16	119.82
David McLeod, James Madison	Sr	11	64	1,207	6	109.73
John Hyland, Dartmouth	Sr	10	62	1,076	9	107.60
David Rhodes, Central Fla.	Jr	11	78	1,159	12	105.36
David Gamble, New Hampshire	Sr	11	67	1,138	13	103.45
Tony Brooks, Eastern Wash.	Sr	10	60	1,024	7	102.40
Derrick Ingram, Ala.-Birmingham	Jr	11	76	1,115	8	101.36
Scott Gurnsey, Montana	Jr	11	67	1,079	9	98.09
Jesse Humphrey, Morgan St.	Sr	11	58	1,071	9	97.36
Chris Summers, Holy Cross	Sr	11	68	1,057	13	96.09
Blake Tuffli, St. Mary's (Cal.)	Fr	10	61	929	7	92.90
Gary Harrell, Howard	Sr	11	72	982	8	89.27
Wayne Chrebet, Hofstra	Jr	9	57	788	9	87.56
Dave Iwan, Yale.........................	Sr	10	46	873	6	87.30
Maurice Jones, Liberty..................	Sr	11	62	955	9	86.82
Tim Silo, Iona	Jr	10	54	865	13	86.50
James Cunningham, Howard..........	Jr	11	58	937	8	85.18
Stepfret Williams, Northeast La.......	So	11	40	929	10	84.45
Miles Macik, Pennsylvania	So	10	72	840	13	84.00
Jeff Johnson, East Tenn. St.	Jr	11	69	915	11	83.18

Interceptions

	1993 Class	G	Int.	Yards	TD	Int.PG
Chris Helon, Boston U.	Jr	11	10	42	0	.91
Zack Bronson, McNeese St.	Fr	11	9	251	1	.82
Shayne Snider, Valparaiso	Jr	10	8	59	0	.80
Curtis Burgins, North Caro. A&T........	Sr	11	8	174	1	.73
Brent Alexander, Tennessee St...........	Sr	11	8	121	0	.73
Bob Jordan, New Hampshire	Sr	11	8	52	1	.73
Greg Pelletier, Canisius	Sr	10	7	47	0	.70
Breon Parker, Massachusetts	So	11	7	133	1	.64
Mark Grimmer, Montana St.	So	11	7	77	0	.64
Don Blackmon, Ala.-Birmingham	Jr	11	7	33	1	.64
Donnie Abraham, East Tenn. St.	So	11	7	20	0	.64
Aaron Bates, Towson St.	Sr	10	6	77	0	.60
Scott Buccola, San Diego.................	Sr	9	5	98	1	.56
Matt Cope, Lafayette	So	11	6	130	2	.55
Matt Stevens, Appalachian St.	So	11	6	124	0	.55
Cedric Walker, Stephen F. Austin	Sr	11	6	94	0	.55
Adrion Smith, Southwest Mo. St.........	Sr	11	6	82	1	.55
Ken Forte, St. John's (N.Y.)	Fr	11	6	64	1	.55
Larry Whigham, Northeast La............	Sr	11	6	46	0	.55
Mark Miller, Bucknell	So	11	6	5	0	.55

Scoring

	1993 Class	G	TD	XP	FG	Pts.	Pts.PG
Tony Vinson, Towson St.	Sr	10	24	0	0	144	14.40
Keith Elias, Princeton	Sr	10	21	4	0	130	13.00
Sherriden May, Idaho	Jr	11	22	0	0	132	12.00
Richard Howell, Davidson	Sr	10	18	2	0	110	11.00
Rupert Grant, Howard	Jr	11	20	0	0	120	10.91
Anthony Russo, St. John's (N.Y.)	Sr	11	18	0	0	108	9.82
Kippy Bayless, Middle Tenn. St.	Jr	11	17	2	0	104	9.45
Chris Purdy, Wagner	Jr	9	13	6	0	84	9.33
Jeff Stovall, Northern Iowa	Fr	11	17	0	0	102	9.27
Wilbur Gilliard, Connecticut	So	11	17	0	0	102	9.27
Chris Parker, Marshall	So	11	17	0	0	102	9.27
Dave Cecchini, Lehigh	Sr	11	16	4	0	100	9.09
Jose Larios, McNeese St.	So	11	0	32	22	98	8.91
Kelvin Johnson, St. Peter's	Fr	9	13	2	0	80	8.89
Phil Anderson, Delaware St.	Jr	11	16	0	0	96	8.73
Michael Hicks, South Caro. St.	So	11	16	0	0	96	8.73
Mike Morello, Boston U.	Jr	11	0	48	15	93	8.45
Pat Hofacre, Dayton	Sr	10	14	0	0	84	8.40
James White, North Caro. A&T	Sr	11	15	0	0	90	8.18
Rene Ingoglia, Massachusetts	So	11	15	0	0	90	8.18
Tamron Smith, Youngstown St.	Sr	11	15	0	0	90	8.18

All-Purpose Yards

	1993 Class	G	Rush	Rec.	PR	KOR	Total Yards	Yds.PG
Tony Vinson, Towson St.	Sr	10	2,016	57	0	0	2,073	207.30
Keith Elias, Princeton	Sr	10	1,731	193	0	15	1,939	193.90
Sherriden May, Idaho	Jr	11	1,267	331	0	296	1,894	172.18
Robert Trice, Cal St. Northridge	Sr	10	1,362	157	0	139	1,658	165.80
Terrance Stokes, Pennsylvania	Jr	10	1,211	284	0	162	1,657	165.70
Daniel Harris, Southern Utah	Sr	11	1,202	86	18	493	1,799	163.55
Chris Parker, Marshall	So	11	1,370	292	0	133	1,795	163.18
Anthony Russo, St. John's (N.Y.)	Sr	11	1,558	183	0	0	1,741	158.27
Richard Johnson, Butler	Sr	10	1,535	40	0	0	1,575	157.50
Kelvin Johnson, St. Peter's	Fr	9	654	357	79	317	1,407	156.33
Irving Spikes, Northeast La.	Sr	11	1,563	150	0	0	1,713	155.73
Pete Fitzpatrick, Cornell	Sr	10	789	407	9	351	1,556	155.60
Ozzie Young, Valparaiso	So	10	446	442	162	505	1,555	155.50
Bill Sparacio, Colgate	Sr	11	1,077	151	0	443	1,671	151.91
Judd Mintz, Dayton	Sr	10	1,011	310	0	180	1,501	150.10
Leon Brown, Eastern Ky.	Sr	9	1,046	41	0	241	1,328	147.56
Tony Phillips, Morgan St.	Jr	11	644	289	50	631	1,614	146.73
Chad Briley, Drake	Sr	10	57	804	95	500	1,456	145.60
James Cunningham, Howard	Jr	11	77	937	0	556	1,570	142.73
Mike Penman, Eastern Ky.	Sr	11	1,139	144	107	149	1,539	139.91

Towson State running back Tony Vinson led Division I-AA in rushing, scoring and all-purpose yardage in 1993.

Punt Returns

(Min. 1.2 per game)	1993 Class	No.	Yds.	TD	Avg.
Ray Marshall, St. Peter's	Jr	10	171	1	17.10
Eric Harrington, Cal St. Sacramento	Sr	17	250	1	14.71
Gorrey White, Alcorn St.	Sr	17	229	1	13.47
Jackie Kellogg, Eastern Wash.	Sr	23	300	1	13.04
Kevin Washington, Northeast La.	Jr	23	291	0	12.65
Eric Alden, Idaho St.	Sr	12	150	0	12.50
Ozzie Young, Valparaiso	So	13	162	1	12.46
Mark Orlando, Towson St.	Jr	22	267	0	12.14
Shalon Baker, Montana	Jr	18	216	1	12.00
Joe Rogers, Texas Southern	Sr	14	168	0	12.00
Mike Porter, Samford	Fr	19	223	0	11.74
Reggie Barlow, Alabama St.	So	18	208	0	11.56
Dexter Dawson, Ga. Southern	So	32	366	0	11.44
Erwin Brown, McNeese St.	Sr	32	359	0	11.22
Lavelle Townsend, St. Mary's (Cal.)	Jr	29	315	0	10.86
John O'Leary, St. John's (N.Y.)	Fr	20	213	0	10.65
Curtis Luper, Stephen F. Austin	Sr	16	168	0	10.50
Barry Esposito, Dayton	Sr	19	197	0	10.37
Brian Randall, Delaware St.	Sr	14	143	0	10.21
Chuck Calhoun, Southwest Mo. St.	Sr	31	313	0	10.10

Punting

(Min. 3.6 per game)	1993 Class	No.	Avg.
Terry Belden, Northern Ariz.	Sr	59	45.97
Ronnie McCutchan, Furman	So	47	43.77
Craig Melograno, Lehigh	Sr	46	42.87
Josh Farrell, Sam Houston St.	Jr	48	42.35
Roy Hudson, Weber St.	Sr	54	41.96
Pat Neck, McNeese St.	Sr	54	41.50
Eric Colvard, Liberty	So	60	41.37
Albert Razo, Cal St. Northridge	Sr	79	41.06
Scott Holmes, Samford	So	57	41.04
Danny Meeks, Boise St.	Jr	60	40.92
Tim McNamee, Eastern Ky.	Sr	59	40.75
Randy Nate, Idaho St.	Jr	49	40.39
Josh Siefken, Tenn.-Chatt.	Jr	37	40.32
Derek Norton, Southeast Mo. St.	Sr	67	40.28
Travis Colquitt, Marshall	Jr	47	40.19
Ron White, Butler	Sr	55	40.09
Mike Neverve, Cal St. Sacramento	Jr	46	39.91
Will Burkett, Appalachian St.	So	43	39.91
Bubba Beasley, Tenn.-Martin	Sr	78	39.90
Scott Gurnsey, Montana	Jr	45	39.89

Kickoff Returns

(Min. 1.2 per game)	1993 Class	No.	Yds.	TD	Avg.
David Fraterrigo, Canisius	Sr	13	485	1	37.31
Kerry Hayes, Western Caro.	Jr	16	584	3	36.50
Rory Lee, Western Ill.	Jr	16	527	2	32.94
Naylon Albritton, South Caro. St.	So	15	475	0	31.67
Cornelius Turner, Mississippi Val.	Jr	12	349	0	29.08
Randy McKee, Fordham	Sr	21	599	1	28.52
Michael High, North Texas	Sr	27	750	2	27.78
Robert Kilow, Troy St.	Jr	14	382	0	27.29
Jon Riley, Southeast Mo. St.	Fr	23	610	0	26.52
Dwight Robinson, James Madison	Jr	18	477	2	26.50
James Cunningham, Howard	Jr	21	556	1	26.48
Chad Briley, Drake	Sr	19	500	1	26.32
Damon Boddie, Drake	Jr	24	621	1	25.88
Adam Johnson, Idaho St.	Fr	17	439	0	25.82
Brian Rodman, North Caro. A&T	Jr	22	565	2	25.68
Marcus Durgin, Samford	Sr	28	719	0	25.68
Sean Hill, Montana St.	Jr	19	487	2	25.63
Matt Pericolosi, Central Conn. St.	Sr	15	377	1	25.13
Obadiah Cooper, Eastern Ill.	Sr	25	609	0	24.36
Cory Simpson, Middle Tenn. St.	Jr	13	313	0	24.08

Field Goals

	1993 Class	G	FGA	FG	Pct.	FGPG
Jose Larios, McNeese St.	So	11	28	22	.786	2.00
Todd Kurz, Illinois St.	Fr	11	24	18	.750	1.64
Skip Thomas, Rhode Island	Fr	11	25	17	.680	1.55
Matt Ornelaz, Cal St. Northridge	Fr	8	16	11	.688	1.38
Roger Miller, Northeast La.	Jr	11	17	15	.882	1.36
David Merrick, Marshall	Jr	11	21	15	.714	1.36
Terry Belden, Northern Ariz.	Sr	11	23	15	.652	1.36
Mike Morello, Boston U.	Jr	11	26	15	.577	1.36
Mike Estrella, St. Mary's (Cal.)	Sr	10	20	13	.650	1.30
Charlie Pierce, Central Fla.	Fr	11	18	14	.778	1.27
Kevin Thomason, Ala.-Birmingham	Sr	11	18	14	.778	1.27
Jeff Stevens, Montana St.	Fr	11	20	14	.700	1.27
Eric Oke, Massachusetts	Fr	11	22	14	.636	1.27
Ray Whitehead, Southwest Tex. St.	So	11	16	13	.813	1.18
Garth Petrilli, Middle Tenn. St.	Jr	11	16	13	.813	1.18
Jim Richter, Furman	So	11	17	13	.765	1.18
Jeff Wilkins, Youngstown St.	Sr	11	20	13	.650	1.18
Derek Collins, Eastern Wash.	Fr	10	14	11	.786	1.10
Marc Horowitz, Pennsylvania	Sr	10	15	11	.733	1.10
Reed Haley, Ga. Southern	Jr	11	17	12	.706	1.09

1993 Division I-AA Team Leaders

Total Offense

	G	Plays	Yds.	Avg.	TD*	Yds.PG
Idaho	11	791	5,852	7.4	70	532.00
Towson St.	10	724	4,903	6.8	54	490.30
Northeast La.	11	758	5,201	6.9	55	472.82
Delaware	11	804	5,179	6.4	54	470.82
Montana	11	794	5,155	6.5	56	468.64
William & Mary	11	758	5,141	6.8	56	467.36
Boston U.	11	842	5,113	6.1	47	464.82
Howard	11	803	5,034	6.3	55	457.64
Alcorn St.	11	741	4,986	6.7	43	453.27
North Caro. A&T	11	829	4,969	6.0	51	451.73
Drake	10	739	4,448	6.0	39	444.80
Weber St.	11	878	4,892	5.6	39	444.73
Troy St.	11	731	4,799	6.6	54	436.27
Grambling	11	746	4,766	6.4	42	433.27
Central Fla.	11	799	4,675	5.9	45	425.00
Lehigh	11	821	4,662	5.7	42	423.82

*Touchdowns scored by rushing or passing only.

Total Defense

	G	Plays	Yds.	Avg.	TD*	Yds.PG
McNeese St.	11	724	2,744	3.8	17	249.5
Southern-B.R.	11	689	2,789	4.0	15	253.5
Grambling	11	704	3,006	4.3	24	273.3
Southwest Mo. St.	11	712	3,023	4.2	30	274.8
Pennsylvania	10	670	2,816	4.2	16	281.6
Cornell	10	691	2,854	4.1	20	285.4
Iona	10	716	2,905	4.1	24	290.5
Tennessee Tech	11	706	3,199	4.5	17	290.8
Alabama St.	10	666	2,959	4.4	23	295.9
Northern Iowa	11	792	3,264	4.1	21	296.7
Dayton	10	685	2,975	4.3	14	297.5
Marshall	11	731	3,278	4.5	13	298.0
William & Mary	11	755	3,296	4.4	27	299.6
Troy St.	11	703	3,302	4.7	17	300.2
Mississippi Val.	10	665	3,017	4.5	23	301.7
Florida A&M	11	705	3,328	4.7	32	302.5

*Touchdowns scored by rushing or passing only.

Rushing Offense

	G	Car.	Yds.	Avg.	TD	Yds.PG
Western Ky.	11	645	3,301	5.1	31	300.1
Towson St.	10	491	2,969	6.0	30	296.9
Delaware	11	610	3,263	5.3	38	296.6
Massachusetts	11	624	3,258	5.2	28	296.2
Eastern Ky.	11	543	3,189	5.9	35	289.9
North Caro. A&T	11	584	3,125	5.4	36	284.1
Citadel	11	650	3,074	4.7	30	279.5
Delaware St.	11	581	3,034	5.2	36	275.8
Ga. Southern	11	589	2,914	4.9	29	264.9
South Caro. St.	11	552	2,909	5.3	35	264.5
Stephen F. Austin	11	552	2,826	5.1	27	256.9
Idaho	11	468	2,800	6.0	37	254.5
Princeton	10	513	2,439	4.8	25	243.9
Youngstown St.	11	533	2,671	5.0	34	242.8
William & Mary	11	526	2,642	5.0	32	240.2
Drake	10	510	2,398	4.7	21	239.8

Rushing Defense

	G	Car.	Yds.	Avg.	TD	Yds.PG
Wagner	9	301	783	2.6	7	87.0
McNeese St.	11	387	996	2.6	13	90.5
Marist	10	342	952	2.8	8	95.2
Pennsylvania	10	366	967	2.6	7	96.7
Grambling	11	363	1,091	3.0	10	99.2

	G	Car.	Yds.	Avg.	TD	Yds.PG
Princeton	10	371	1,028	2.8	6	102.8
Butler	10	363	1,054	2.9	7	105.4
Central Fla.	11	415	1,181	2.8	16	107.4
Southern-B.R.	11	417	1,201	2.9	6	109.2
Cal St. Northridge	10	376	1,138	3.0	15	113.8
Troy St.	11	383	1,253	3.3	10	113.9
Iona	10	392	1,149	2.9	12	114.9
Alabama St.	10	383	1,150	3.0	11	115.0
Northern Ariz.	11	393	1,317	3.4	13	119.7
South Caro. St.	11	421	1,337	3.2	16	121.5
Cornell	10	405	1,222	3.0	9	122.2

Scoring Offense

	G	Pts.	Avg.
Idaho	11	522	47.5
Montana	11	453	41.2
Northeast La.	11	431	39.2
Howard	11	424	38.5
North Caro. A&T	11	420	38.2
Towson St.	10	381	38.1
William & Mary	11	414	37.6
Troy St.	11	407	37.0
Delaware	11	405	36.8
Boston U.	11	395	35.9
South Caro. St.	11	384	34.9
Central Fla.	11	383	34.8
James Madison	11	375	34.1
Delaware St.	11	371	33.7
Ala.-Birmingham	11	356	32.4
Middle Tenn. St.	11	354	32.2
Alcorn St.	11	347	31.5
Stephen F. Austin	11	342	31.1

Scoring Defense

	G	Pts.	Avg.
Marshall	11	123	11.2
Dayton	10	114	11.4
Southern-B.R.	11	142	12.9
Pennsylvania	10	131	13.1
Princeton	10	136	13.6
Tennessee Tech	11	154	14.0
Ga. Southern	11	154	14.0
Troy St.	11	155	14.1
Georgetown	9	136	15.1
Youngstown St.	11	167	15.2
Boston U.	11	169	15.4
McNeese St.	11	170	15.5
Cornell	10	158	15.8
Eastern Ky.	11	176	16.0
Canisius	10	165	16.5
Evansville	10	175	17.5
Iona	10	180	18.0
Mississippi Val.	10	182	18.2

Passing Offense

	G	Att.	Cmp.	Int.	Pct.	Yards	Yds./Att.	TD	Yds.PG
Montana	11	432	284	10	65.7	3,949	9.1	35	359.0
Iona	10	465	272	16	58.5	3,481	7.5	31	348.1
Lehigh	11	433	260	14	60.0	3,575	8.3	30	325.0
Howard	11	449	238	16	53.0	3,534	7.9	25	321.3
Hofstra	10	425	241	17	56.7	3,079	7.2	25	307.9
Alcorn St.	11	417	216	17	51.8	3,336	8.0	23	303.3
Ala.-Birmingham	11	418	254	16	60.8	3,215	7.7	24	292.3
St. Mary's (Cal.)	10	354	180	13	50.8	2,897	8.2	22	289.7
Boston U.	11	421	234	21	55.6	3,174	7.5	23	288.5
Northeast La.	11	356	204	8	57.3	3,114	8.7	30	283.1
Weber St.	11	466	248	17	53.2	3,075	6.6	19	279.5
Morgan St.	11	388	190	19	49.0	3,062	7.9	22	278.4
Idaho	11	323	193	6	59.8	3,052	9.4	33	277.5
Evansville	10	411	225	9	54.7	2,685	6.5	20	268.5
Northern Iowa	11	305	178	14	58.4	2,853	9.4	20	259.4
Central Fla.	11	353	203	15	57.5	2,817	8.0	25	256.1
Dartmouth	10	321	160	19	49.8	2,542	7.9	20	254.2
Eastern Wash.	10	312	168	7	53.8	2,540	8.1	24	254.0
Liberty	11	394	222	15	56.3	2,691	6.8	19	244.6
Cal St. Sacramento	10	335	187	17	55.8	2,445	7.3	20	244.5

Pass Efficiency Defense

	G	Att.	Cmp.	Cmp. Pct.	Int.	Int. Pct.	Yards	Yds./ Att.	TD	TD Pct.	Rating Points
Georgetown	9	292	127	43.49	13	4.45	1,275	4.37	5	1.71	76.92
McNeese St.	11	337	178	52.82	25	7.42	1,748	5.19	4	1.19	85.47
Southern-B.R.	11	272	113	41.54	21	7.72	1,588	5.84	9	3.31	86.06
East Tenn.	11	248	110	44.35	18	7.26	1,517	6.12	5	2.02	87.87
Ala.-Birmingham	11	295	134	45.42	23	7.80	1,677	5.68	12	4.07	91.01
Northern Iowa	11	238	108	45.38	11	4.62	1,361	5.72	5	2.10	91.10
Duquesne	10	185	81	43.78	16	8.65	1,163	6.29	7	3.78	91.78
Iona	10	324	142	43.83	14	4.32	1,756	5.42	12	3.70	92.93
Pennsylvania	10	304	136	44.74	19	6.25	1,849	6.08	9	2.96	93.10
Dayton	10	295	147	49.83	16	5.42	1,715	5.81	6	2.03	94.53
Tenn.-Martin	11	241	125	51.87	11	4.56	1,345	5.58	5	2.07	96.46
William & Mary	11	269	134	49.81	14	5.20	1,452	5.40	10	3.72	97.01
Northeast La.	11	271	125	46.13	16	5.90	1,571	5.80	12	4.43	97.63
St. Peter's	9	246	126	51.22	13	5.28	1,341	5.45	9	3.66	98.51
Davidson	10	220	98	44.55	15	6.82	1,345	6.11	11	5.00	98.76
Canisius	10	287	153	53.31	18	6.27	1,595	5.56	10	3.48	98.95
Southwest Mo. St.	11	248	110	44.35	21	8.47	1,570	6.33	14	5.65	99.23
Appalachian St.	11	235	116	49.36	14	5.96	1,454	6.19	7	2.98	99.25
Cornell	10	286	145	50.70	16	5.59	1,632	5.71	11	3.85	100.14

Defensive backs Zack Bronson (left) and Kevin Smith were part of a McNeese State secondary that intercepted 25 passes last season.

Net Punting

	Punts	Avg.	No. Ret.	Yds. Ret.	Net Avg.
Northern Ariz.	59	46.0	33	347	40.1
Furman	50	42.1	23	154	39.0
Idaho St.	52	40.2	22	101	38.3
Idaho	39	41.5	22	130	38.2
Ga. Southern	58	39.4	25	88	37.9
Marshall	48	39.7	16	106	37.5
Montana	51	40.2	21	142	37.5
Southeast Mo. St.	67	40.3	29	192	37.4
Liberty	62	40.2	21	187	37.2
Tenn.-Martin	79	39.4	38	181	37.1
Youngstown St.	46	39.2	19	112	36.8
Eastern Ky.	59	40.7	28	236	36.7
Northeast La.	38	38.9	13	91	36.6
Lehigh	46	42.9	29	291	36.5
Sam Houston St.	48	42.4	20	284	36.4
McNeese St.	56	41.3	36	289	36.1

Punt Returns

	G	No.	Yds.	TD	Avg.
Montana	11	23	336	1	14.6
Eastern Wash.	10	24	323	2	13.5
Alcorn St.	11	20	265	1	13.3
Cal St. Sacramento	10	32	407	2	12.7
Columbia	10	13	159	1	12.2
Cal St. Northridge	10	30	361	2	12.0
Texas Southern	11	14	168	0	12.0
Northern Iowa	11	35	419	2	12.0
St. Peter's	9	21	250	1	11.9
Alabama St.	10	20	235	0	11.8
Richmond	11	19	222	0	11.7
Stephen F. Austin	11	18	209	1	11.6
Northeast La.	11	40	463	0	11.6
Northern Ariz.	11	45	510	2	11.3
Idaho St.	11	27	306	0	11.3
Indiana St.	11	23	254	2	11.0
Marshall	11	33	364	2	11.0

Kickoff Returns

	G	No.	Yds.	TD	Avg.
Western Caro.	11	24	643	3	26.8
Troy St.	11	30	778	1	25.9
Northern Iowa	11	39	1,011	0	25.9
Montana	11	35	885	3	25.3
Howard	11	38	948	1	24.9

	G	No.	Yds.	TD	Avg.
Southern-B.R.	11	30	735	2	24.5
Furman	11	29	709	1	24.4
Montana	11	37	898	1	24.3
North Caro. A&T	11	30	726	2	24.2
Sam Houston St.	11	40	959	1	24.0
Eastern Ky.	11	29	687	1	23.7
South Caro. St.	11	35	828	0	23.7
Samford	11	31	733	0	23.6
Southwest Mo. St.	11	30	706	0	23.5
Southeast Mo. St.	11	40	934	0	23.4
Mississippi Val.	10	31	705	0	22.7
Canisius	10	36	808	1	22.4

Turnover Margin

	TURNOVERS GAINED			TURNOVERS LOST			Margin/ Game
	Fum.	Int.	Total	Fum.	Int.	Total	
St. John's (N.Y.)	20	19	39	6	12	18	1.91
Dayton	18	16	34	5	12	17	1.70
Montana	17	17	34	7	10	17	1.55
Mississippi Val.	14	18	32	9	9	18	1.40
Towson St.	10	20	30	12	4	16	1.40
Middle Tenn. St.	12	22	34	14	6	20	1.27
Montana St.	13	20	33	8	12	20	1.18
Colgate	18	18	36	13	10	23	1.18
Central Conn. St.	14	15	29	4	14	18	1.10

Longest Division I-AA Plays of 1993

Rushing

Player, Team (Opponent)	Yards
Jeff Sawulski, Siena (Iona)	95
Tony Phillips, Morgan St. (North Caro. A&T)	93
Charles Harris, Sam Houston St. (Rice)	90
Alfredo Anderson, Idaho St. (Chadron St.)	85
Cameron Smith, Illinois St. (Indiana St.)	84
Cameron Smith, Illinois St. (Tennessee Tech)	80
Rontae Bass, Morehead St. (Ala.-Birmingham)	80
Daniel Harris, Southern Utah (Northern Ariz.)	80
Aaron Spears, Delaware St. (Morgan St.)	80
Rich Green, New Hampshire (Villanova)	80
Tony Vinson, Towson St. (Bucknell)	80
Tony Vinson, Towson St. (Bucknell)	80
Gary Harrell, Howard (Morgan St.)	80

STATISTICAL LEADERS

Passing

Passer-Receiver, Team (Opponent)	Yards
Aaron Garcia-Greg Ochoa, Cal St. Sacramento (Cal Poly SLO)	99
Philly Jones-Rick Ford, Furman (Ga. Southern)	92
Steve Mills-David Iwan, Yale (Dartmouth)	90
Dave Dickenson-Matt Wells, Montana (Weber St.)	87
Mike Cawley-David McLeod, James Madison (New Hampshire)	86
Jason Cue-Kito Lockwood, Wagner (Marist)	86
Jason Stahl-Jon Hill, Butler (Hofstra)	85
Todd Bernett-Tony Brooks, Eastern Wash. (Cal St. Sacramento)	85
Henri Ransefore-David Johnson, Nicholls St. (Northeast La.)	85
Shawn Knight-Mike Tomlin, William & Mary (Maine)	85
George Biesel-Wayne Chreber, Hofstra (Rhode Island)	84
Jamey DeAngelo-DeShaun Diggs, Drake (Aurora)	84

Interception Returns

Player, Team (Opponent)	Yards
Tasi Autele, Boise St. (Montana)	99
Kenny Bailey, Delaware (Lehigh)	94
Matt Cope, Lafayette (Columbia)	86
Burnell Dadaux, Mississippi Val. (Prairie View)	76
Matt Stevens, Appalachian St. (Tenn.-Chatt.)	*75
Mark Paske, Colgate (Lehigh)	73
Brad Simmons, Tennessee Tech (Lock Haven)	68
Eric Dircks, Eastern Ill. (McNeese St.)	66

*Did not score.

Punt Returns

Player, Team (Opponent)	Yards
Shalon Baker, Montana (South Dak. St.)	82
Jackie Kellogg, Eastern Wash. (Northern Ariz.)	82
Ray Marshall, St. Peter's (Siena)	81
Eugene Smith, Brown (Rhode Island)	80
Brad Bernardini, Bucknell (Colgate)	71

Kickoff Returns

Player, Team (Opponent)	Yards
Damon Boddie, Montana (Idaho)	99
Jeb Dougherty, San Diego (Azusa Pacific)	98
Kerry Hayes, Western Caro. (Furman)	97
Chad Briley, Drake (Valparaiso)	97
Torrance Brooks, Prairie View (Ala.-Birmingham)	97

Player, Team (Opponent)	Yards
Kerry Hayes, Western Caro. (Appalachian St.)	95
Brian Rodman, North Caro. A&T (Delaware St.)	93
Davy Smith, Sam Houston St. (Southeast Mo. St.)	91
Dwight Robinson, James Madison (Lock Haven)	90
Kerry Hayes, Western Caro. (Citadel)	90
Brian Rodman, North Caro. A&T (Florida A&M)	90
Dwight Robinson, James Madison (William & Mary)	90
Mike Penman, Eastern Ky. (Southeast Mo. St.)	90
Randy McKee, Fordham (Hofstra)	90

Field Goals

Player, Team (Opponent)	Yards
Terry Belden, Northern Ariz. (Cal St. Northridge)	60
Andy Norrell, Idaho St. (Idaho)	56
Mike Hollis, Idaho (Northern Ariz.)	56
Gil Gutierrez, Valparaiso (Northern Ariz.)	56
Mike Hollis, Idaho (Southwest Tex. St.)	55
Terry Belden, Northern Ariz. (Cal St. Northridge)	54
Andy Norrell, Idaho St. (Idaho)	54
Terry Belden, Northern Ariz. (Eastern Wash.)	54
Reed Haley, Ga. Southern (Tenn.-Chatt.)	53
Gilad Landau, Grambling (Alcorn St.)	52
Steve Largent, Eastern Ill. (Indiana St.)	52
Jim Richter, Furman (Western Caro.)	52
Tim McDermott, Cornell (Harvard)	52
Kevin Thomason, Ala.-Birmingham (Mississippi Val.)	52

Punts

Player, Team (Opponent)	Yards
Terry Belden, Northern Ariz. (Southern Utah)	76
Jason Brower, Dayton (San Diego)	76
Tim McNamee, Eastern Ky. (Western Ky.)	72
Bubba Beasley, Tenn.-Martin (Tennessee St.)	72
Terry Belden, Northern Ariz. (Southern Utah)	70
Randy Nate, Idaho St. (Idaho)	70
Todd Kurz, Illinois St. (Indiana St.)	70
Charlie Pierce, Central Fla. (Troy St.)	70

Fumble Returns

Player, Team (Opponent)	Yards
Von Ganaway, Indiana St. (Western Ky.)	85
Shavez Hawkins, Eastern Ill. (McNeese St.)	73
Larry Whigham, Northeast La. (Southwest Tex. St.)	71
Jeff Nichol, Colgate (Cornell)	65

Northern Arizona's Terry Belden kicked the longest field goal in Division I-AA last year and one of the two longest punts.

1993 Division II Individual Leaders

Rushing

	1993 Class	G	Car.	Yards	TD	Yds.PG
Keith Higdon, Cheyney	Sr	10	330	1,742	17	174.2
Roger Graham, New Haven	Jr	10	182	1,687	19	168.7
Preston Jackson, UC Davis	Sr	10	244	1,552	18	155.2
Joe Simmons, N.C. Central	Sr	11	249	1,699	16	154.5
Michael Mann, Indiana (Pa.)	Sr	10	269	1,541	16	154.1
Thelbert Withers, N.M. Highlands	Sr	10	271	1,486	10	148.6
Clifton Davis, Fayetteville St.	Jr	11	311	1,591	17	144.6
Richard Huntley, Winston-Salem	So	11	243	1,570	11	142.7
LaMonte Coleman, Slippery Rock	Jr	10	256	1,396	15	139.6
Greg Walker, Delta St.	Sr	10	240	1,394	9	139.4
Bobby Phillips, Virginia Union	Jr	11	247	1,507	11	137.0
Scott Schulte, Hillsdale	Sr	11	300	1,499	14	136.3
Leonard Davis, Lenoir-Rhyne	Sr	10	263	1,352	21	135.2
Marc DeBellis, Millersville	Jr	10	220	1,308	10	130.8
Mason Gordon, Presbyterian	Sr	11	255	1,401	15	127.4
Joe Gough, Wayne St. (Mich.)	Jr	10	324	1,250	12	125.0
Larry Jackson, Edinboro	Jr	9	185	1,117	8	124.1
Norman White, West Tex. A&M	Fr	9	180	1,109	8	123.2
Shannon Burnell, North Dak.	Sr	10	242	1,224	11	122.4
Clint Bedore, Fort Hays St.	So	11	260	1,343	8	122.1

Passing Efficiency

(Min. 15 att. per game)	1993 Class	G	Att.	Cmp.	Pct.	Int.	Yards	TD	Rating Points
James Weir, New Haven	Jr	10	266	161	60.5	1	2,336	31	172.0
Brett Salisbury, Wayne St. (Neb.)	Sr	10	395	276	69.8	14	3,729	29	166.3
Gregory Clark, Virginia St.	Sr	11	380	227	59.7	11	3,437	38	162.9
Perry Klein, LIU-C.W. Post	Sr	10	407	248	60.9	18	3,757	38	160.4
Rob Hyland, North Dak. St.	Fr	10	151	90	59.6	6	1,434	12	157.7
Chris Hatcher, Valdosta St.	Jr	11	471	335	71.1	11	3,651	37	157.5
Mike Rymsha, Bentley	So	8	152	91	59.8	7	1,365	14	156.5
Todd McDonald, South Dak. St.	Sr	11	312	184	58.9	9	2,715	25	152.7
Jed Drenning, Glenville St.	Sr	10	390	244	62.5	12	3,391	25	150.6
Scott Woods, Indiana (Pa.)	Sr	10	210	118	56.1	6	1,920	14	149.3
Jody Dickerson, Edinboro	Jr	10	235	119	50.6	9	1,933	23	144.4
Khari Jones, UC Davis	Sr	10	334	181	54.1	8	2,686	27	143.6
Matt Cook, Mo. Southern St.	Sr	10	289	154	53.2	9	2,376	24	143.5
Shawn Dupris, Southwest St.	Fr	9	373	220	58.9	14	2,955	28	142.8
Mike Fisher, Cal Poly SLO	So	10	286	159	55.5	9	2,298	22	142.1
Ken Avent, Catawba	Sr	10	175	105	60.0	5	1,349	11	139.8
Mike Jinks, Angelo St.	Jr	9	161	78	48.4	4	1,320	13	139.0
Kip Kieso, Northern St.	Sr	11	349	206	59.0	8	2,694	20	138.2
Matt Montgomery, Hampton	Jr	11	228	132	57.8	5	1,772	13	137.6
Jamie Pass, Mankato St.	Sr	11	396	219	55.3	13	3,142	25	136.2

New Haven's Roger Graham was the 1992 Division II rushing champion and finished second in 1993.

Total Offense

	1993 Class	G	Plays	Yards	Yds.PG
Perry Klein, LIU-C.W. Post	Sr	10	499	4,052	405.2
Marty Washington, Livingston	Sr	8	453	3,146	393.3
Brett Salisbury, Wayne St. (Neb.)	Sr	10	424	3,732	373.2
Jed Drenning, Glenville St.	Sr	10	473	3,593	359.3
Jamie Pass, Mankato St.	Sr	11	543	3,537	321.5
Chris Hatcher, Valdosta St.	Jr	11	495	3,532	321.1
Shawn Dupris, Southwest St.	Fr	9	408	2,863	318.1
Gregory Clark, Virginia St.	Sr	11	425	3,386	307.8
Khari Jones, UC Davis	Sr	10	401	3,077	307.7
Vernon Buck, Wingate	Jr	11	463	3,307	300.6
John Craven, Gardner-Webb	Jr	10	473	2,946	294.6
Thad Trujillo, Fort Lewis	Jr	10	535	2,784	278.4
Todd McDonald, South Dak. St.	Sr	11	419	2,937	267.0
Bobby McLaughlin, Lock Haven	So	11	510	2,928	266.2
Jermaine Whitaker, N.M. Highlands	Jr	10	385	2,606	260.6
Brent Holsclaw, Ky. Wesleyan	Sr	10	441	2,486	248.6
Matt Cook, Mo. Southern St.	Sr	10	376	2,484	248.4
Kip Kieso, Northern St.	Sr	11	448	2,696	245.1
Bill Matos, Portland St.	Sr	10	419	2,431	243.1
James Weir, New Haven	Jr	10	303	2,372	237.2

Receptions Per Game

	1993 Class	G	Rec.	Yards	TD	Rec.PG
Chris George, Glenville St.	Jr	10	117	1,876	15	11.7
Rus Bailey, N.M. Highlands	Sr	10	91	1,192	12	9.1
Matt Carman, Livingston	Sr	10	88	1,085	14	8.8
Byron Chamberlain, Wayne St. (Neb.)	Jr	9	78	1,015	7	8.7
Damon Thomas, Wayne St. (Neb.)	Sr	10	81	1,162	12	8.1
Greg Hopkins, Slippery Rock	Jr	10	79	1,229	8	7.9
Preston Cunningham, Southwest St.	So	10	79	1,052	6	7.9
Johnny Cox, Fort Lewis	Sr	10	77	1,032	7	7.7
Calvin Walker, Valdosta St.	Sr	11	82	944	6	7.5
Tony Willis, New Haven	Sr	10	71	1,074	11	7.1

	1993 Class	G	Rec.	Yards	TD	Rec.PG
T. R. McDonald, North Dak. St.	Sr	10	69	1,181	11	6.9
Duane Joubert, West Tex. A&M	So	9	59	537	5	6.6
Nobie Gooden, Quincy	Sr	9	59	840	11	6.6
Derrick Sharpe, Mars Hill	Sr	10	64	796	4	6.4
Michael Dritlein, Washburn	So	8	51	742	4	6.4
Steve Greer, Valdosta St.	Jr	11	70	892	6	6.4
Alvin Ashley, Southwest St.	Sr	9	57	751	12	6.3
Rod Smith, Mo. Southern St.	Sr	10	63	986	13	6.3
Jerry Garrett, Wayne St. (Neb.)	Jr	10	62	813	7	6.2
Lonnie Custer, Gardner-Webb	So	10	61	898	4	6.1

Receiving Yards Per Game

	1993 Class	G	Rec.	Yards	TD	Yds.PG
Chris George, Glenville St.	Jr	10	117	1,876	15	187.6
Greg Hopkins, Slippery Rock	Jr	10	79	1,229	8	122.9
Rus Bailey, N.M. Highlands	Sr	10	91	1,192	12	119.2
T. R. McDonald, North Dak. St.	Sr	10	69	1,181	11	118.1
Damon Thomas, Wayne St. (Neb.)	Sr	10	81	1,162	12	116.2
Byron Chamberlain, Wayne St. (Neb.)	Jr	9	78	1,015	7	112.8
Matt Carman, Livingston	Sr	10	88	1,085	14	108.5
Tony Willis, New Haven	Sr	10	71	1,074	11	107.4
Preston Cunningham, Southwest St.	So	10	79	1,052	6	105.2
Tyrone Johnson, Western St.	Sr	11	65	1,141	7	103.7
Mike Ragin, Wingate	Sr	11	61	1,137	8	103.4
Johnny Cox, Fort Lewis	Sr	10	77	1,032	7	103.2
Jim Byrne, LIU-C.W. Post	Sr	10	57	1,012	13	101.2
Rod Smith, Mo. Southern St.	Sr	10	63	986	13	98.6
Stacy Graves, Virginia Union	Jr	11	53	1,073	9	97.5
Josh Nelsen, Mankato St.	Jr	11	54	1,044	10	94.9
Nobie Gooden, Quincy	Sr	9	59	840	11	93.3
Michael Dritlein, Washburn	So	8	51	742	4	92.8
Lonnie Custer, Gardner-Webb	So	10	61	898	4	89.8
Chauncey Winbush, Shepherd	Sr	8	40	715	4	89.4

STATISTICAL LEADERS

WSU Public Information photo

Winona State's Dave Ludy averaged 197 all-purpose yards a game and finished among Division II leaders in scoring with 17 touchdowns in 1993.

All-Purpose Yards

	1993 Class	G	Rush	Rec.	PR	KOR	Total Yards	Yds.PG
Chris George, Glenville St.	Jr	10	23	1,876	157	562	2,618	261.80
Roger Graham, New Haven	Jr	10	1,687	116	0	516	2,319	231.90
Johnny Cox, Fort Lewis	Sr	10	9	1,032	247	733	2,021	202.10
Keith Higdon, Cheyney	Sr	10	1,742	168	0	67	1,977	197.70
Dave Ludy, Winona St.	Jr	10	1,033	264	0	674	1,971	197.10
Fran DeFalco, Assumption	Jr	10	1,004	152	192	461	1,809	180.90
Bryce Carlson, Moorhead St.	Jr	10	1,120	27	0	651	1,798	179.80
Michael Mann, Indiana (Pa.)	Sr	10	1,541	198	0	0	1,739	173.90
Carter Eve, Morris Brown	Jr	10	805	75	0	855	1,735	173.50
Alvin Ashley, Southwest St.	Sr	9	6	751	246	537	1,540	171.11
Scott Schulte, Hillsdale	Sr	11	1,499	282	0	92	1,873	170.27
Mike Ragin, Wingate	Sr	11	14	1,137	0	720	1,871	170.09
Joe Simmons, N.C. Central	Sr	11	1,699	170	0	0	1,869	169.91
Darell Whitaker, Eastern N. Mex.	Jr	10	1,066	134	0	473	1,673	167.30
Jeremy Monroe, Michigan Tech	Sr	10	1,072	395	0	172	1,639	163.90
Tyrone Rush, North Ala.	Sr	10	1,155	25	0	428	1,608	160.80
Greg Walker, Delta St.	Sr	10	1,394	204	0	3	1,601	160.10
Willie McClelland, Livingston	Sr	10	44	767	56	730	1,597	159.70
Preston Jackson, UC Davis	Sr	10	1,552	41	0	0	1,593	159.30
Larry Jackson, Edinboro	Jr	9	1,117	151	0	161	1,429	158.78

Interceptions

	1993 Class	G	No.	Yards	Int.PG
Troy Crissman, Ky. Wesleyan	So	10	9	39	.9
Tyrone Andrews, Miles	So	10	8	86	.8
Nate Gruber, Winona St.	Jr	10	8	110	.8
Micky Reeves, N.M. Highlands	So	9	7	267	.8
Corey Bell, Morris Brown	Jr	9	7	56	.8
Robert Burnett, Elon	Jr	11	8	111	.7
Chet Henicle, Bloomsburg	Jr	11	8	84	.7
Mark Struck, South Dak. St.	So	11	8	64	.7
J. R. Allen, Ashland	Jr	11	8	90	.7
Mike Jaunich, South Dak. St.	Jr	10	7	73	.7
Ryan Davis, Ky. Wesleyan	Jr	10	7	49	.7
Jason Johnson, Shepherd	Jr	10	7	93	.7
Cedric Florence, Mo. Southern St.	Jr	10	7	94	.7
Robby Smith, Cal Poly SLO	Sr	10	7	63	.7
Cody Gamble, Chadron St.	Jr	11	7	165	.6
Rich Eash, Ferris St.	Sr	11	7	101	.6
Ken Pickhorn, Cheyney	Fr	11	7	109	.6
Chad Starks, Wofford	Sr	11	7	90	.6
Ulysses Smith, Savannah St.	Jr	8	5	91	.6

Scoring

	1993 Class	G	TD	XP	FG	Pts.	Pts.PG
Roger Graham, New Haven	Jr	10	23	0	0	138	13.8
Leonard Davis, Lenoir-Rhyne	Sr	10	21	0	0	126	12.6
Jeremy Monroe, Michigan Tech	Sr	10	19	0	0	114	11.4
Preston Jackson, UC Davis	Sr	10	18	2	0	110	11.0
Tyree Dye, Ferris St.	Jr	11	20	0	0	120	10.9
Michael Mann, Indiana (Pa.)	Sr	10	18	0	0	108	10.8
Keith Higdon, Cheyney	Sr	10	18	0	0	108	10.8
Dave Ludy, Winona St.	Jr	10	17	2	0	104	10.4
Rob Munson, Quincy	So	9	15	0	0	90	10.0
Joey Huffstetler, Wingate	Sr	11	18	0	0	108	9.8
Tyrone Rush, North Ala.	Sr	10	16	2	0	98	9.8
Alvin Ashley, Southwest St.	Sr	9	14	4	0	88	9.8
Clifton Davis, Fayetteville St.	Jr	11	17	4	0	106	9.6
Henry Caldwell, Central Mo. St.	Sr	10	16	0	0	96	9.6
LaMonte Coleman, Slippery Rock	Jr	10	16	0	0	96	9.6
Michael Geary, Indiana (Pa.)	Sr	10	0	48	15	93	9.3
Joe Simmons, N.C. Central	Sr	11	17	0	0	102	9.3
Chris George, Glenville St.	Jr	10	15	2	0	92	9.2
Oronde Gadsden, Winston-Salem	Jr	9	13	2	0	80	8.9
Matt Carman, Livingston	Sr	10	14	4	0	88	8.8
Fran DeFalco, Assumption	Jr	10	14	4	0	88	8.8

Punt Returns

(Min. 1.2 per game)	1993 Class	No.	Yds.	Avg.
Jerry Garrett, Wayne St. (Neb.)	Jr	26	498	19.2
Deon Harding, Indianapolis	Jr	15	239	15.9
Chris Banks, Bowie St.	Jr	13	207	15.9
Kasem McCullough, South Dak.	Sr	31	471	15.2
Tyrone Poole, Fort Valley St.	Jr	26	393	15.1
Nate Bush, Wayne St. (Mich.)	So	23	342	14.9
Johnny Cox, Fort Lewis	Sr	17	247	14.5
Bryan Culley, West Liberty St.	Jr	13	188	14.5
Darnell Cox, Fayetteville St.	So	30	417	13.9
Matt Wibbels, Neb.-Kearney	Jr	24	330	13.8
Dedric Smith, Savannah St.	Sr	30	393	13.1
Ryan Steen, Cal Poly SLO	Fr	18	234	13.0
Terry Beckham, Clark Atlanta	Sr	16	206	12.9
LaVon Reis, Western St.	Sr	29	361	12.4
David Nelson, Ferris St.	So	50	604	12.1
Ryan Davis, Ky. Wesleyan	Jr	12	143	11.9
Benn Sanford, Mississippi Col.	So	25	293	11.7
Cleveland Phillips, Central Okla.	Sr	26	298	11.5
Mike Carrawell, Quincy	Fr	13	148	11.4
Paul Perkins, Sonoma St.	Jr	23	260	11.3

Kickoff Returns

(Min. 1.2 per game)	1993 Class	No.	Yds.	Avg.
LaVon Reis, Western St.	Sr	14	552	39.4
Fran DeFalco, Assumption	Jr	12	461	38.4
Kendall James, Carson-Newman	So	15	549	36.6
Roger Graham, New Haven	Jr	16	516	32.3
Dean Herrboldt, South Dak. St.	Jr	19	599	31.5
Scott Warman, Sacred Heart	So	22	689	31.3
Tyrone Rush, North Ala.	Sr	14	428	30.6
Chris George, Glenville St.	Jr	19	562	29.6
Jessie Curtis, Fayetteville St.	Jr	22	650	29.5
Dave Ludy, Winona St.	Jr	23	674	29.3
David Andrews, Angelo St.	Jr	15	436	29.1
Monte Southerland, N.C. Central	Fr	18	505	28.1
Erron Bobo, Central Ark.	Jr	18	504	28.0
Kevin Cannon, Millersville	So	12	333	27.8
Dennis McWhite, East Stroudsburg	So	16	443	27.7
Albert Bland, Mo. Southern St.	So	20	544	27.2
Rod Clark, Elon	Jr	22	587	26.7
Ryan Steen, Cal Poly SLO	Fr	19	506	26.6
Frank Martin, Fort Hays St.	Jr	21	555	26.4
Keith Green, Morningside	Jr	18	475	26.4

Punting

(Min. 3.6 per game)	1993 Class	No.	Avg.
Chris Carter, Henderson St.	Sr	53	43.5
Shayne Boyd, Eastern N. Mex.	Sr	57	42.5
Bob Koning, N.M. Highlands	Jr	41	42.3
Casey Anderson, Neb.-Kearney	So	54	42.2
Carl Lyles, Johnson Smith	Jr	38	42.2
Richie Ambrose, Gardner-Webb	Sr	45	42.1
Preston Loos, Western St.	Fr	48	42.1
Chris Afarian, Cal Poly SLO	Sr	47	42.1
Barry Gillingwater, East Tex. St.	Sr	58	41.6
David Mitchell, Pittsburg St.	Jr	41	41.4
Pat Hogelin, Colorado Mines	So	56	41.4
Stan Whitlock, Wingate	So	44	40.9
Barry Reese, Abilene Christian	Jr	58	40.3
Alaric Ludgood, Alabama A&M	Fr	47	40.0
Gary Lhotsky, Edinboro	Sr	38	39.8
Mike Helmly, Savannah St.	Sr	40	39.5
Mike Nelson, Mississippi Col.	Jr	45	39.3
Lawrence Holmes, Norfolk St.	Sr	61	39.3
Jason Turner, Gannon	Sr	46	39.1
Bill Noble, Northern St.	Jr	55	39.1

Field Goals

	1993 Class	G	FGA	FG	Pct.	FGPG
Raul De la Flor, Humboldt St.	Sr	11	26	20	76.9	1.82
Michael Geary, Indiana (Pa.)	Sr	10	18	15	83.3	1.50
Ryan Achilles, Fort Hays St.	Fr	10	21	14	66.7	1.40
Eivind Listerud, Missouri-Rolla	Jr	10	13	12	92.3	1.20
Bryan Schewe, Savannah St.	Sr	10	25	12	48.0	1.20
Brad Heim, Millersville	Sr	10	23	11	47.8	1.10
Brian Porzio, Wofford	Jr	11	19	12	63.2	1.09
Jarrod Davsko, St. Francis (Ill.)	So	11	16	11	68.8	1.00
John Schwickerath, West Ga.	Fr	10	19	10	52.6	1.00
Jason Lipke, Ferris St.	So	11	22	11	50.0	1.00
Angel Ronquillo, Eastern N. Mex.	So	10	19	10	52.6	1.00
Jamie Stoddard, North Ala.	Fr	10	12	10	83.3	1.00
Richie Hahn, Mesa St.	Sr	9	14	9	64.3	1.00
Mike Driscoll, American Int'l	Fr	9	15	9	60.0	1.00
Frank Jordan, Presbyterian	Fr	11	18	11	61.1	1.00
Scott Doyle, Chadron St.	So	11	14	10	71.4	.91
Billy Watkins, East Tex. St.	Sr	11	19	10	52.6	.91
Mike Rowen, Neb.-Kearney	So	10	10	9	90.0	.90
Craig Moses, Henderson St.	Fr	10	11	9	81.8	.90
Eric Myers, West Va. Wesleyan	Fr	10	14	9	64.3	.90
Rafael Fernandez, UC Davis	Sr	10	12	9	75.0	.90
Jason Young, Winona St.	Jr	10	11	9	81.8	.90
Jason Tebeaux, Angelo St.	So	10	13	9	69.2	.90

1993 Division II Team Leaders

Total Offense

	G	Plays	Yds.	Yds.PG
Wayne St. (Neb.)	10	756	5,815	581.5
New Haven	10	760	5,666	566.6
LIU-C.W. Post	10	771	5,384	538.4
UC Davis	10	768	5,210	521.0
Glenville St.	10	761	5,026	502.6
Valdosta St.	11	785	5,259	478.1
Indiana (Pa.)	10	729	4,741	474.1
North Ala.	10	643	4,702	470.2
Livingston	10	770	4,626	462.6
Mankato St.	11	824	4,961	451.0
Wingate	11	775	4,880	443.6
Gardner-Webb	10	765	4,410	441.0
Catawba	10	703	4,290	429.0
Bentley	10	768	4,268	426.8
Hampton	11	814	4,678	425.3

	G	Plays	Yds.	Yds.PG
Slippery Rock	10	722	4,222	422.2
Southwest St.	10	713	4,205	420.5
Michigan Tech	10	692	4,201	420.1
N.M. Highlands	10	705	4,192	419.2
Edinboro	10	715	4,191	419.1

Total Defense

	G	Plays	Yds.	Yds.PG
Bentley	10	627	1,883	188.3
Albany St. (Ga.)	11	660	2,216	201.5
Ashland	11	716	2,241	203.7
Stonehill	9	597	1,868	207.6
Hampton	11	641	2,331	211.9
Abilene Christian	10	629	2,192	219.2
Glenville St.	10	613	2,237	223.7
Northern Colo.	11	770	2,685	244.1
Ferris St.	11	748	2,691	244.6
Virginia St.	11	755	2,698	245.3
Fort Valley St.	11	657	2,701	245.5
Millersville	10	637	2,486	248.6
Central Mo. St.	10	649	2,509	250.9
Quincy	9	538	2,264	251.6
Angelo St.	10	703	2,533	253.3
Wayne St. (Neb.)	10	649	2,560	256.0
Pittsburg St.	10	683	2,568	256.8
Tex. A&M-Kingsville	10	643	2,609	260.9
Alabama A&M	11	704	2,987	271.5
Mo. Western St.	11	729	3,031	275.5

Rushing Offense

	G	Car.	Yds.	Yds.PG
North Ala.	10	548	3,715	371.5
Carson-Newman	10	561	3,105	310.5
Catawba	10	526	2,941	294.1
Wofford	11	647	3,216	292.4
Pittsburg St.	10	520	2,894	289.4
New Haven	10	466	2,886	288.6
Michigan Tech	10	546	2,862	286.2
Moorhead St.	10	537	2,653	265.3
Winston-Salem	11	598	2,904	264.0
Hampton	11	584	2,887	262.5
Indiana (Pa.)	10	483	2,548	254.8
North Dak. St.	10	573	2,538	253.8
Millersville	10	523	2,508	250.8
Mass.-Lowell	10	576	2,504	250.4
Henderson St.	10	512	2,485	248.5
Elon	11	562	2,715	246.8
UC Davis	10	414	2,455	245.5
Minn.-Duluth	11	645	2,687	244.3
Jacksonville St.	10	531	2,433	243.3
Mississippi Col.	10	459	2,391	239.1

Rushing Defense

	G	Car.	Yds.	Yds.PG
Albany St. (Ga.)	11	367	650	59.1
Ashland	11	376	669	60.8
Hampton	11	353	716	65.1
Bentley	10	402	823	82.3
Central Okla.	10	345	914	91.4
Virginia St.	11	429	1,019	92.6
Angelo St.	10	404	933	93.3
Quincy	9	293	851	94.6
Abilene Christian	10	420	969	96.9
Minn.-Duluth	11	335	1,072	97.5
South Dak.	11	417	1,089	99.0
Central Mo. St.	10	410	990	99.0
Stonehill	9	390	896	99.6
Northern Colo.	11	465	1,101	100.1
Indiana (Pa.)	10	351	1,003	100.3
Ferris St.	11	434	1,107	100.6
LIU-C. W. Post	10	381	1,041	104.1
West Va. Wesleyan	10	361	1,054	105.4
Glenville St.	10	417	1,056	105.6
St. Francis (Ill.)	11	406	1,190	108.2

Scoring Offense

	G	TD	XP	2XP	DXP	FG	SAF	Pts.	Avg.
New Haven	10	78	71	0	0	2	1	547	54.7
Wayne St. (Neb.)	10	64	48	1	0	4	1	448	44.8
LIU-C.W. Post	10	59	51	2	0	6	0	427	42.7
Indiana (Pa.)	10	53	48	2	0	15	1	417	41.7
Valdosta St.	11	62	55	1	1	6	0	449	40.8
North Ala.	10	54	44	3	0	10	1	406	40.6
UC Davis	10	53	38	5	1	9	0	395	39.5
Hampton	11	61	49	0	0	4	1	429	39.0
Mankato St.	11	56	48	2	0	8	0	412	37.5
Cal Poly SLO	10	50	38	3	0	7	0	365	36.5
Quincy	9	45	29	5	0	5	1	326	36.2
South Dak. St.	11	54	47	1	0	7	0	394	35.8
Carson-Newman	10	48	41	0	0	6	1	355	35.5
Catawba	10	47	31	5	0	5	0	338	33.8
Virginia St.	11	53	34	4	0	3	1	371	33.7
Glenville St.	10	48	25	6	0	4	0	337	33.7
Edinboro	10	46	39	1	1	5	0	334	33.4
Mo. Southern St.	10	47	33	2	0	1	1	324	32.4
Bentley	10	45	26	6	0	4	0	320	32.0
Wingate	11	48	36	4	0	6	1	352	32.0

Scoring Defense

	G	TD	XP	2XP	DXP	FG	SAF	Pts.	Avg.
Albany St. (Ga.)	11	13	6	3	0	2	0	96	8.7
Hampton	11	14	5	2	0	2	0	99	9.0
Ashland	11	14	6	1	0	5	1	109	9.9
Glenville St.	10	13	12	0	0	4	0	102	10.2
Bentley	10	15	6	2	0	3	0	109	10.9
Pittsburg St.	10	16	12	1	0	3	0	119	11.9
Ferris St.	11	17	10	1	1	5	0	131	11.9
North Dak.	10	17	14	0	0	2	1	124	12.4
Millersville	10	17	14	1	0	4	0	130	13.0
Northern Colo.	11	19	16	1	0	3	1	143	13.0
Stonehill	9	18	10	1	0	0	0	120	13.3
Hillsdale	11	21	11	2	0	3	0	150	13.6
Indiana (Pa.)	10	18	14	0	0	5	0	137	13.7
Central Mo. St.	10	18	10	4	0	4	0	138	13.8
West Va. Wesleyan	10	18	9	2	0	7	0	142	14.2
East Stroudsburg	10	20	10	3	0	3	0	145	14.5
Mo. Western St.	11	21	14	2	0	6	0	162	14.7
Virginia St.	11	23	14	2	0	3	0	165	15.0
Wofford	11	20	14	1	0	10	0	166	15.1
Gannon	10	21	15	1	0	3	0	152	15.2

Passing Offense

	G	Att.	Cmp.	Pct.	Int.	Yards	Yds.PG
LIU-C.W. Post	10	437	265	60.6	20	4,090	409.0
Wayne St. (Neb.)	10	410	284	69.3	14	3,799	379.9
Livingston	10	538	294	54.6	16	3,778	377.8
Valdosta St.	11	513	362	70.6	12	3,871	351.9
Glenville St.	10	399	246	61.7	13	3,435	343.5
Mankato St.	11	431	247	57.3	15	3,577	325.2
Gardner-Webb	10	501	265	52.9	33	3,230	323.0
Virginia St.	11	391	231	59.1	12	3,479	316.3
Southwest St.	10	423	242	57.2	17	3,153	315.3
Portland St.	10	387	213	55.0	17	2,974	297.4
Fort Lewis	10	471	236	50.1	20	2,862	286.2
N.M. Highlands	10	371	200	53.9	23	2,809	280.9
Wingate	11	420	201	47.9	18	3,081	280.1
New Haven	10	296	181	61.1	2	2,780	278.0
UC Davis	10	354	189	53.4	9	2,755	275.5
Lock Haven	11	478	271	56.7	21	3,028	275.3
Ky. Wesleyan	10	397	221	55.7	21	2,683	268.3
Slippery Rock	10	333	169	50.8	19	2,641	264.1
Cal St. Hayward	9	333	178	53.5	14	2,360	262.2
Northern St.	11	370	217	58.6	8	2,842	258.4

Pass Efficiency Defense

	G	Att.	Cmp.	Pct.	Int.	Yards	TD	Rating Points
Alabama A&M	11	186	70	37.6	12	877	4	71.5
Ashland	11	340	136	40.0	21	1,572	8	74.2
Ferris St.	11	314	134	42.6	24	1,584	11	81.3
Albany St. (Ga.)	11	293	130	44.3	22	1,566	7	82.1
Bentley	10	225	95	42.2	16	1,060	10	82.2
Stonehill	9	207	83	40.1	10	972	8	82.7
Northern Colo.	11	305	133	43.6	18	1,584	7	83.0
Millersville	10	254	104	40.9	16	1,388	7	83.3
East Stroudsburg	10	301	135	44.8	24	1,571	10	83.7
Lenoir-Rhyne	10	255	117	45.8	17	1,283	8	85.2
Fort Hays St.	11	318	147	46.2	26	1,780	9	86.3
Hampton	11	288	123	42.7	16	1,615	8	87.9
Tex. A&M-Kingsville	10	280	120	42.8	13	1,524	8	88.7
Angelo St.	10	299	133	44.4	20	1,600	12	89.3
Hillsdale	11	332	148	44.5	22	1,917	11	90.7
Pittsburg St.	10	244	118	48.3	12	1,385	4	91.6
Morehouse	10	263	106	40.3	12	1,631	7	92.0
Assumption	10	224	102	45.5	13	1,208	9	92.5
Virginia St.	11	326	146	44.7	12	1,679	12	92.8
Fort Valley St.	11	211	103	48.8	15	1,239	6	93.3

Net Punting

	Punts	Avg.	No. Ret.	Yds. Ret.	Net Avg.
North Ala.	26	42.0	7	65	39.5
Western St.	48	42.1	16	141	39.2
Henderson St.	53	43.5	25	326	37.3
Eastern N. Mex.	57	42.5	30	300	37.2
Pittsburg St.	42	40.7	21	152	37.1
Indiana (Pa.)	29	38.2	9	43	36.7
East Tex. St.	58	41.6	32	304	36.4
Albany St. (Ga.)	56	37.4	23	73	36.1
Mississippi Col.	45	39.3	16	149	36.0
Neb.-Kearney	54	42.2	34	337	35.9
Abilene Christian	59	39.7	24	220	35.9
Johnson Smith	69	39.5	25	248	35.9
Minn.-Duluth	59	38.2	23	137	35.9
Mo. Western St.	46	38.7	22	134	35.7
West Ga.	43	36.3	12	25	35.7
South Dak.	63	36.4	14	46	35.7
West Liberty St.	54	36.5	27	55	35.5
Hampton	26	38.0	15	68	35.3
West Va. Wesleyan	59	36.3	15	58	35.3
Alabama A&M	60	39.7	31	264	35.3

Punt Returns

	G	No.	Yds.	TD	Avg.
Wayne St. (Neb.)	10	28	534	3	19.1
Ky. Wesleyan	10	16	267	1	16.7
Fort Lewis	10	22	339	2	15.4
Bowie St.	10	27	394	1	14.6
Wayne St. (Mich.)	11	27	393	3	14.6
Cal Poly SLO	10	25	361	0	14.4
Indianapolis	11	31	429	1	13.8
South Dak.	11	41	561	1	13.7
Fort Valley St.	11	30	406	1	13.5
Jacksonville St.	10	23	310	1	13.5
Fayetteville St.	11	32	427	1	13.3
Neb.-Kearney	10	27	336	1	12.4
Ferris St.	11	52	645	0	12.4
Western St.	11	34	411	0	12.1
Lane	9	8	94	0	11.8
Abilene Christian	10	17	198	0	11.6
Sonoma St.	9	28	323	1	11.5
Mississippi Col.	10	26	293	0	11.3
Albany St. (Ga.)	11	38	424	1	11.2
Clarion	10	17	187	1	11.0
Central Okla.	10	33	363	1	11.0

Kickoff Returns

	G	No.	Yds.	TD	Avg.
Adams St.	10	34	935	3	27.5
Western St.	11	35	934	2	26.7
North Ala.	10	23	607	0	26.4
Assumption	10	37	974	1	26.3
Angelo St.	10	29	759	1	26.2
Glenville St.	10	24	622	0	25.9
Tex. A&M-Kingsville	10	28	722	0	25.8
New Haven	10	28	715	1	25.5
Winona St.	10	31	780	2	25.2
South Dak. St.	11	44	1,107	0	25.2
Carson-Newman	10	33	806	3	24.4
Sonoma St.	9	46	1,119	1	24.3
Augustana (S.D.)	11	40	965	1	24.1
Millersville	10	25	603	0	24.1
Moorhead St.	10	37	888	0	24.0
Sacred Heart	9	33	791	1	24.0
Morehouse	10	36	850	0	23.6
Pittsburg St.	10	16	377	0	23.6
Wayne St. (Neb.)	10	32	739	2	23.1
Elon	11	33	762	1	23.1

Turnover Margin

	TURNOVERS GAINED			TURNOVERS LOST			Margin/
	Fum.	Int.	Total	Fum.	Int.	Total	Game
Hillsdale	19	22	41	7	4	11	2.72
New Haven	25	10	35	9	2	11	2.40
South Dak. St.	12	29	41	11	10	21	1.81
Quincy	18	15	33	10	7	17	1.77
Angelo St.	12	20	32	10	6	16	1.60
Mo. Southern St.	15	19	34	6	12	18	1.60
Fort Hays St.	17	26	43	13	13	26	1.54
Winona St.	21	17	38	9	14	23	1.50
Minn.-Duluth	16	21	37	10	11	21	1.45
Elon	12	19	31	7	8	15	1.45
Indiana (Pa.)	15	19	34	12	8	20	1.40
East Stroudsburg	12	24	36	9	13	22	1.40
West Liberty St.	17	20	37	11	13	24	1.30
Albany St. (Ga.)	18	22	40	15	11	26	1.27
West Va. Wesleyan	18	20	38	11	15	26	1.20
North Ala.	11	19	30	14	5	19	1.10
Cal Poly SLO	17	18	35	13	11	24	1.10
North Dak.	10	15	25	6	8	14	1.10
Ferris St.	11	24	35	8	15	23	1.09
Fairmont St.	20	12	32	8	14	22	1.00
UC Davis	15	11	26	7	9	16	1.00
Ashland	13	21	34	12	11	23	1.00
Hampton	19	16	35	19	5	24	1.00

Longest Division II Plays of 1993

Rushing

Player, Team (Opponent)	Yards
Brian Satterfield, North Ala. (Fort Valley St.)	97
Brad Widhalm, Adams St. (Northwestern Okla.)	96
Bobby Phillips, Virginia Union (Howard)	96
Marc DeBellis, Millersville (Mansfield)	93
Tim Hanson, Winona St. (Northern St.)	93
Roger Graham, New Haven (Shepherd)	91
Keith Weaver, Ashland (Slippery Rock)	90
Jason Killian, East Stroudsburg (Southern Conn. St.)	90
Ramon Leak, East Stroudsburg (American Int'l)	90
John Davis, Emporia St. (Washburn)	90
Rusty Setzer, Grand Valley St. (St. Joseph's, Ind.)	89
Norman White, West Tex. A&M (Panhandle St.)	89
Henry Caldwell, Central Mo. St. (Northwest Mo. St.)	88
Floyd Mathis, Carson-Newman (Howard Payne)	86
Joe Aska, Central Okla. (Angelo St.)	84

Passing

Passer-Receiver, Team (Opponent)	Yards
Ray Morrow-Jeff Williamson, Cal St. Hayward (Redlands)	99
Bob McLaughlin-Eric Muldowney, Lock Haven (Mansfield)	99
Todd Hirt-Freddie Temoney, Calif., Pa. (Kutztown)	97
Brian Keating-Keith Green, Morningside (Nebraska-Omaha)	95
Jeff Palladino-Darryl Forte, West Va. Wesleyan (Glenville St.)	95
Jeff Palladino-Brian Dugan, West Va. Wesleyan (Calif., Pa.)	94
Chris Hatcher-Calvin Walker, Valdosta St. (Central Fla.)	90
Brett Salisbury-Byron Chamberlain, Wayne St., Neb. (Nebraska-Omaha)	90
Gary Gaetano-Jason Miller, Mansfield (Millersville)	89
Mike Jinks-David Andrews, Angelo St. (Central Okla.)	88
Jermaine Whitaker-Michael Simms, N.M. Highlands (Chadron St.)	88
Dave Jordy-Damon Scheidt, St. Joseph's, Ind. (Indianapolis)	86
Lawrence Luster-Chris Brooks, Northwest Mo. St. (Missouri-Rolla)	85

Interception Returns

Player, Team (Opponent)	Yards
Bill Johnston, Sacred Heart (Assumption)	100
Neely Lovett, Savannah St. (Tuskegee)	100
George Byrd, New Haven (Shepherd)	98
John Fisher, Mo. Western St. (Northeast Mo. St.)	97
Darnell Jones, Mankato St. (Northern Colo.)	96
Walter Isaac, Fort Lewis (N.M. Highlands)	85
Deiago Hendrix, Ky. Wesleyan (Mt. Senario)	85
Loren Weeks, Indianapolis (Ferris St.)	84
Anthony Davis, Carson-Newman (Wingate)	80
Lloyd Atkinson, West Va. Tech (Tiffin)	80

Punt Returns

Player, Team (Opponent)	Yards
Bryan Culley, West Liberty St. (Concord)	91
Jerry Garrett, Wayne St., Neb. (Bemidji St.)	86
Kenyan Conner, Albany St., Ga. (Fort Valley St.)	85
Stewart Hackney, Presbyterian (Wingate)	85
Nate Bush, Wayne St., Mich. (St. Francis, Ill.)	80

Kickoff Returns

Player, Team (Opponent)	Yards
David Andrews, Angelo St. (Portland St.)	100
Wilson Hookfin, Wayne St., Neb. (Neb.-Kearney)	100
Anthony Phillips, Tex. A&M-Kingsville (Angelo St.)	99
Dave Ludy, Winona St. (Wis.-La Crosse)	99
Carter Eve, Morris Brown (Hampton)	98
Keith Harper, Augustana, S.D. (Neb.-Kearney)	97
Anthony Jefferson, Sonoma St. (Humboldt St.)	97
LaVon Reis, Western St. (Fort Hays St.)	97
Maurad Cave, Nebraska-Omaha (Wayne St., Neb.)	96
Tony Trisciani, Springfield (Ithaca)	96
Bryan Ruble, Adams St. (Western St.)	95
Fran DeFalco, Assumption (Nichols)	95
Scott Warman, Sacred Heart (Stony Brook)	95

Field Goals

Player, Team (Opponent)	Yards
Scott Doyle, Chadron St. (South Dak. Tech)	55
Ryan Anderson, Northern Colo. (Western St.)	54
Barry Reese, Abilene Christian (Tarleton St.)	52
Keith Loos, Grand Valley St. (St. Francis, Ill.)	49
Shannon Estrin, Cal St. Chico (UC Davis)	48
Billy Watkins, East Tex. St. (Texas Southern)	48
Ken Navitsky, Mankato St. (South Dak.)	48
Jason Arnold, Newberry (Charleston So.)	48
Ryan Achilles, Fort Hays St. (Mesa St.)	47
Brad Heim, Millersville (Shepherd)	47
Brad Heim, Millersville (Kutztown)	47
Eivind Listerud, Missouri-Rolla (Iowa Wesleyan)	47
Brian Porzio, Wofford (Newberry)	47

Punts

Player, Team (Opponent)	Yards
John Cacciatore, St. Francis, Ill. (Grand Valley St.)	80
Bob Koning, N.M. Highlands (Fort Lewis)	75
Barry Gillingwater, East Tex. St. (Texas Southern)	71

STATISTICAL LEADERS

1993 Division III Individual Leaders

Principia quarterback Jordan Poznick led Division III in total offense last year with a per-game average of 338 yards.

Rushing

	1993 Class	G	Car.	Yards	TD	Yds.PG
Carey Bender, Coe	Sr	10	261	1,718	15	171.8
Heath Butler, N'western (Wis.)	Sr	8	236	1,371	15	171.4
Don Dawson, Ripon	Sr	9	214	1,482	16	164.7
Ronnie Howard, Bridgewater (Va.)	Sr	10	281	1,610	13	161.0
Rodney Bond, Jersey City St.	Sr	9	275	1,446	11	160.7
Frank Baker, Chicago	Sr	10	281	1,606	8	160.6
Rob Marchitello, Maine Maritime	So	9	289	1,430	15	158.9
Jimmy Henderson, Wis.-Stevens Point	Sr	10	261	1,556	20	155.6
Bill Sedgwick, Ursinus	Sr	9	219	1,339	18	148.8
Dreu Beers, Merchant Marine	Sr	9	280	1,322	14	146.9
Jeff Robinson, Albion	Jr	9	204	1,305	19	145.0
Jose DeLeon, MIT	Fr	7	199	987	10	141.0
Marlon Perryman, Wittenberg	Sr	10	240	1,376	8	137.6
David Kogan, Wabash	Jr	8	222	1,084	16	135.5
Steve Dixon, Beloit	Sr	9	286	1,213	12	134.8
Pedro Arruza, Wheaton (Ill.)	So	9	227	1,209	16	134.3
John Lutz, Colorado Col.	Jr	9	244	1,205	15	133.9
Kelvin Gladney, Millsaps	Jr	9	203	1,203	17	133.7
Kevin Matarelli, Monmouth (Ill.)	Jr	9	192	1,175	6	130.6
Derrick Harris, Eureka	Sr	10	316	1,303	10	130.3

Passing Efficiency

(Min. 15 att. per game)	1993 Class	G	Att.	Cmp.	Pct.	Int.	Yards	TD	Rating Points
Willie Seiler, St. John's (Minn.)	Sr	10	205	141	68.7	6	2,648	33	224.6
Jim Ballard, Mount Union	Sr	10	314	229	72.9	11	3,304	37	193.2
Guy Simons, Coe	Sr	10	185	110	59.4	9	1,979	21	177.1
Chris Conkling, Anderson	Sr	10	185	127	68.6	3	1,788	12	168.0
Paul Bell, Allegheny	Jr	10	156	92	58.9	5	1,467	13	159.0
Eric Jencks, Whittier	So	8	125	69	55.2	3	1,130	12	158.0
Jason Baer, Wash. & Jeff.	So	9	147	84	57.1	6	1,227	17	157.3
Ed Hesson, Rowan	Sr	9	234	137	58.5	4	2,085	19	156.8
Troy Knox, Colorado Col.	Sr	9	180	113	62.7	7	1,534	16	155.9
John Smith, Defiance	Jr	10	260	164	63.0	11	2,098	22	150.3
Matt Miller, Cornell College	Sr	9	151	88	58.2	4	1,247	12	148.6
Boo Perry, Wilkes	So	10	252	147	58.3	11	2,252	18	148.3
John Koz, Baldwin-Wallace	Sr	10	320	199	62.1	10	2,453	25	146.1
Dave Sullivan, Williams	Sr	8	191	115	60.2	9	1,528	16	145.6
Roger Hauri, Wis.-Stevens Point	Sr	10	264	167	63.2	12	2,072	19	143.9
Mike Montico, Albion	Sr	9	162	94	58.0	8	1,299	12	140.0
Russ Young, Sewanee	Jr	9	192	113	58.8	7	1,552	11	138.3
Frank Plefka, FDU-Madison	Sr	10	286	148	51.7	9	2,216	24	138.2
Derek Shutz, Wis.-Eau Claire	Jr	10	191	116	60.7	8	1,508	11	137.7
Steve Stratton, St. Norbert	Jr	8	179	101	56.4	6	1,379	12	136.5

Total Offense

	1993 Class	G	Plays	Yards	Yds.PG
Jordan Poznick, Principia	Sr	8	488	2,705	338.1
Jim Ballard, Mount Union	Sr	10	372	3,371	337.1
Tom Stallings, St. Thomas (Minn.)	Sr	10	438	3,158	315.8
LeRoy Williams, Upsala	Jr	9	474	2,604	289.3
Chris Ings, Wabash	So	9	406	2,543	282.6
Jon Ebert, Bethel (Minn.)	Jr	9	455	2,531	281.2
Willie Seiler, St. John's (Minn.)	Sr	10	263	2,648	264.8
Sean McCullough, Muhlenberg	Sr	9	476	2,375	263.9
John Smith, Defiance	Jr	10	371	2,595	259.5
Keith Karpinske, St. Olaf	Sr	10	432	2,559	255.9
Brian Van Duesen, Western Md.	So	9	453	2,209	245.4
Roger Hauri, Wis.-Stevens Point	Sr	10	342	2,442	244.2
John Koz, Baldwin-Wallace	Sr	10	360	2,414	241.4
Dan Takah, Bethany (W.Va.)	Sr	9	448	2,171	241.2
John Shipp, Claremont-M-S	Jr	8	332	1,914	239.3
Jason Gonnion, Wis.-La Crosse	Sr	10	346	2,391	239.1
Len Annetta, Salisbury St.	Sr	9	365	2,079	231.0
Jay Schneider, Hamline	Jr	10	318	2,284	228.4
Ed Smith, Ill. Benedictine	Sr	10	372	2,266	226.6
Kendon Troyer, Franklin	Sr	8	330	1,808	226.0

Receptions Per Game

	1993 Class	G	Rec.	Yards	TD	Rec.PG
Matt Newton, Principia	Sr	8	96	1,080	11	12.0
Greg Lehrer, Heidelberg	Sr	10	87	1,202	8	8.7
Rob Lokerson, Muhlenberg	Jr	9	76	1,275	6	8.4
Sam Williams, Defiance	Jr	10	84	1,209	14	8.4
Vincent Hooper, Bethel (Minn.)	Sr	10	79	1,000	12	7.9
Buddy McKinley, Bethany (W.Va.)	So	9	68	690	4	7.6
Brian Vandegrift, Rhodes	Sr	10	75	1,000	8	7.5
Tom Buslee, St. Olaf	Sr	10	75	1,281	10	7.5
Joe Palumbo, Ithaca	Sr	10	74	1,119	9	7.4
Eric Green, Ill. Benedictine	Sr	10	74	1,164	7	7.4
Ed Bubonics, Mount Union	Sr	10	74	1,286	10	7.4
Kendall Griffin, Loras	Sr	9	65	932	9	7.2
Damon Klesa, Hanover	Sr	10	70	803	8	7.0
Jamey Goss, Sewanee	Sr	9	63	992	9	7.0
Tom McDavitt, Trinity (Conn.)	Jr	7	49	570	2	7.0
Ted Brockman, Kenyon	Sr	10	69	747	9	6.9
Chris Garrity, Wilmington (Ohio)	Sr	10	68	1,045	13	6.8
Tony Norton, Franklin	Sr	9	61	752	7	6.8
Andy Wenk, Knox	Sr	9	61	688	2	6.8
Pete Marine, Cal Lutheran	Jr	9	60	810	6	6.7

Receiving Yards Per Game

	1993 Class	G	Rec.	Yards	TD	Yds.PG
Rob Lokerson, Muhlenberg	Jr	9	76	1,275	6	141.7
Matt Newton, Principia	Sr	8	96	1,080	11	135.0
Ed Bubonics, Mount Union	Sr	10	74	1,286	10	128.6
Tom Buslee, St. Olaf	Sr	10	75	1,281	10	128.1
Vic Moncato, FDU-Madison	Jr	10	64	1,217	14	121.7
Sam Williams, Defiance	Jr	10	84	1,209	14	120.9
Greg Lehrer, Heidelberg	Sr	10	87	1,202	8	120.2
Eric Green, Ill. Benedictine	Sr	10	74	1,164	7	116.4
Joe Palumbo, Ithaca	Sr	10	74	1,119	9	111.9
Jamey Goss, Sewanee	Sr	9	63	992	9	110.2
Anthony Robinson, Upsala	Jr	9	56	947	8	105.2
Chris Garrity, Wilmington (Ohio)	Sr	10	68	1,045	13	104.5
Derek Moyers, Hanover	Sr	10	65	1,038	10	103.8
Kendall Griffin, Loras	Sr	9	65	932	9	103.6
Brian Vandegrift, Rhodes	Sr	10	75	1,000	8	100.0
Vincent Hooper, Bethel (Minn.)	Sr	10	79	1,000	12	100.0
Kevin Feighery, Merchant Marine	Jr	9	46	871	9	96.8
Lance Yandell, Baldwin-Wallace	Sr	10	64	964	10	96.4
Chris Palmer, St. John's (Minn.)	So	8	35	765	8	95.6
Steve Endres, Wilkes	Sr	10	66	932	3	93.2

Interceptions

	1993 Class	G	No.	Yards	Int.PG
Ricky Webb, Emory & Henry	Sr	8	8	56	1.0
Aaron Minor, Macalester	Sr	10	9	89	.9
Chris Nylund, Hamline	Sr	10	9	115	.9
Scott Miller, Lycoming	Jr	10	9	146	.9
Andy Ostrand, Carroll (Wis.)	Sr	10	9	66	.9
Bill Palmer, Hobart	Sr	10	9	83	.9
Todd Sebold, Albion	Sr	9	8	42	.9
Greg Schramm, Trinity (Conn.)	Jr	8	7	50	.9
Tim Schwartz, N'western (Wis.)	Jr	8	7	75	.9
Scott Torreso, Rensselaer	Sr	10	8	22	.8

	1993 Class	G	No.	Yards	Int.PG
Bill Connolly, Bridgewater (Va.)	Sr	10	8	82	.8
Scott Collins, Wittenberg	Sr	10	8	21	.8
Mike Malchesky, Mount Union	So	10	8	72	.8
Bill Kriesel, Augsburg	So	10	8	30	.8
Charles Warren, Dickinson	Fr	10	8	79	.8
Larry Long, St. John Fisher	Jr	9	7	66	.8
Chris Jones, Colorado Col.	So	9	7	152	.8
Brandon Benham, Buffalo St.	Sr	9	7	68	.8
Gary Giannoni, Redlands	Jr	8	6	92	.8
Eric Mudry, Trinity (Conn.)	Sr	8	6	20	.8
Calvin Newman, MIT	So	8	6	39	.8
Jason Logue, Lycoming	Jr	8	6	55	.8

Scoring

	1993 Class	G	TD	XP	FG	Pts.	Pts.PG
Matt Malmberg, St. John's (Minn.)	Jr	10	27	2	0	164	16.4
Kelvin Gladney, Millsaps	Jr	9	21	2	0	128	14.2
Jeff Robinson, Albion	Jr	9	20	0	0	120	13.3
David Kogan, Wabash	Jr	8	17	2	0	104	13.0
Carey Bender, Coe	Sr	10	21	4	0	130	13.0
Nick Mystrom, Colorado Col.	Sr	9	7	44	8	110	12.2
Bill Sedgwick, Ursinus	Sr	9	18	2	0	110	12.2
Thomas Lee, Anderson	Jr	10	20	0	0	120	12.0
Jimmy Henderson, Wis.-Stevens Point	Sr	10	20	0	0	120	12.0
Shaun Kirby, Trinity (Conn.)	Jr	8	16	0	0	96	12.0
Heath Butler, N'western (Wis.)	Sr	8	15	2	0	92	11.5
Pedro Arruza, Wheaton (Ill.)	So	9	16	4	0	100	11.1
Jim Gresko, Mount Union	Sr	10	18	0	0	108	10.8
Matt Newton, Principia	Sr	8	12	14	0	86	10.8
Mark Kacmarynski, Central (Iowa)	So	9	16	0	0	96	10.7
Dan Takah, Bethany (W.Va.)	Sr	9	16	0	0	96	10.7
Don Dawson, Ripon	Sr	9	16	0	0	96	10.7
A. J. Pittorino, Hartwick	Fr	7	12	0	0	72	10.3
Jose DeLeon, MIT	Fr	7	12	0	0	72	10.3
Kevin Hudson, Wartburg	Jr	10	17	0	0	102	10.2
Cetric Gayles, Hampden-Sydney	Sr	10	17	0	0	102	10.2

All-Purpose Yards

	1993 Class	G	Rush	Rec.	PR	KOR	Int.	Total Yards	Yds.PG
Carey Bender, Coe	Sr	10	1,718	601	0	0	0	2,319	231.90
Eric Green, Ill. Benedictine	Sr	10	12	1,164	346	628	0	2,150	215.00
Sam Williams, Defiance	Jr	10	40	1,209	459	428	0	2,136	213.60
Bill Sedgwick, Ursinus	Sr	9	1,339	77	11	367	0	1,794	199.33
Ronnie Howard, Bridgewater (Va.)	Sr	10	1,610	22	40	296	0	1,968	196.80
Scott Tumilty, Augustana (Ill.)	So	9	1,048	169	126	378	0	1,721	191.22
Rodd Patten, Framingham St.	Sr	9	62	720	391	441	43	1,657	184.11
Adam Henry, Carleton	Sr	10	859	219	91	651	0	1,820	182.00
Jamey Goss, Sewanee	Sr	9	-1	992	254	347	0	1,592	176.89
Rob Johnson, Western Md.	Sr	9	874	253	0	462	0	1,589	176.56
Jim Gresko, Mount Union	Sr	10	1,015	495	0	252	0	1,762	176.20
Heath Butler, N'western (Wis.)	Sr	8	1,371	18	0	0	0	1,389	173.63
Pete Marine, Cal Lutheran	Jr	9	30	810	267	451	0	1,558	173.11
Don Dawson, Ripon	Sr	9	1,482	42	0	33	0	1,557	173.00
Vic Moncato, FDU-Madison	Jr	10	56	1,217	106	344	0	1,723	172.30
Jose DeLeon, MIT	Fr	7	987	103	0	107	0	1,197	171.00
Greg Lehrer, Heidelberg	Sr	10	0	1,202	60	425	0	1,687	168.70
Rob Marchitello, Maine Maritime	So	9	1,430	47	0	38	0	1,515	168.33
David Kogan, Wabash	Jr	8	1,084	215	0	47	0	1,346	168.25
Rodney Bond, Jersey City St.	Sr	9	1,446	62	0	0	0	1,508	167.56

Coe running back Carey Bender led Division III in rushing as well as all-purpose yardage and finished the 1993 season among scoring leaders.

Punt Returns

(Min. 1.2 per game)	1993 Class	No.	Yds.	Avg.
Eric Green, Ill. Benedictine	Sr	13	346	26.6
Brian Lazear, Wheaton (Ill.)	Sr	14	274	19.6
LaVant King, Ohio Northern	So	17	325	19.1
Tony Lesch, St. John's (Minn.)	Sr	19	352	18.5
Mike Sikma, Carroll (Wis.)	Sr	14	241	17.2
Bryan Bown, Marietta	Sr	23	385	16.7
Nate Hilding, Ill. Wesleyan	So	29	463	16.0
Gary Furner, Hartwick	So	10	157	15.7
Charlie Jordan, Occidental	Sr	11	169	15.4
Sam Williams, Defiance	Jr	30	459	15.3
Jeramy Parsons, Augustana (Ill.)	Sr	14	206	14.7
Matt Canning, John Carroll	Jr	15	208	13.9
Shaun Clark, Wesley	So	13	180	13.8
Jeff Harrison, Otterbein	Fr	19	261	13.7
Jamey Goss, Sewanee	Sr	19	254	13.4
Ted Mason, Waynesburg	Sr	19	254	13.4
Andy McKenzie, Allegheny	Jr	16	211	13.2
Bill Schroeder, Wis.-La Crosse	Sr	22	281	12.8
Mike Gerhart, Susquehanna	Jr	19	240	12.6
Christopher Miller, Amherst	Fr	14	176	12.6

Kickoff Returns

(Min. 1.2 per game)	1993 Class	No.	Yds.	Avg.
Eric Green, Ill. Benedictine	Sr	19	628	33.1
Josh Perkins, Ohio Northern	Fr	25	784	31.4
Rob Gardner, Allegheny	Sr	12	367	30.6
Craig Stewart, La Verne	Sr	22	665	30.2
Matt Brimhall, Bethel (Minn.)	Sr	12	361	30.1
Dexter Hurt, Randolph-Macon	Sr	14	413	29.5
Petie Davis, Wesley	Jr	12	342	28.5
Greg Lehrer, Heidelberg	Sr	15	425	28.3
Brunson Parish, Wis.-Platteville	So	13	368	28.3
Charlie Jordan, Occidental	Sr	18	504	28.0
Bill Schroeder, Wis.-La Crosse	Sr	17	470	27.6
Connon Thompson, Muskingum	So	22	589	26.8
Mike Tisdale, Blackburn	Sr	11	288	26.2
Gregg Genovese, John Carroll	Sr	18	459	25.5
Fred Grant, Salisbury St.	Fr	14	354	25.3
Steve Anderson, Rowan	So	18	454	25.2
Scott Tumilty, Augustana (Ill.)	So	15	378	25.2
Sam Williams, Defiance	Jr	17	428	25.2
Pete Marine, Cal Lutheran	Jr	18	451	25.1
Bradley Hill, DePauw	Sr	16	398	24.9

Punting

(Min. 3.6 per game)	1993 Class	No.	Avg.
Mitch Holloway, Millsaps	Sr	45	42.4
Vic Moncato, FDU-Madison	Jr	59	42.3
Brett Geijer, Ill. Benedictine	Jr	45	41.8
Jon Hardy, Wesley	Sr	51	41.2
Andy Mahle, Otterbein	Jr	54	41.1
Andy Caflisch, Wis.-Stout	Sr	57	41.0
Nick Mystrom, Colorado Col.	Sr	36	40.6
Judd Sather, St. Olaf	Sr	53	40.5
Davin Lundquist, Occidental	Jr	50	40.5
Ryan Haley, John Carroll	Sr	46	40.3
Mark Middleton, Emory & Henry	Jr	61	40.2
Jason Turns, Rhodes	So	61	40.0
Chris Murray, Sewanee	Fr	62	38.9
Josh Haza, Washington (Mo.)	Fr	36	38.7
David Waddell, Ferrum	So	49	38.4
Darin Whitesel, Wash. & Jeff.	So	39	38.3
Paul McCord, Western Md.	Sr	56	38.2
Dan Leffler, Cal Lutheran	Jr	47	37.8
Tyler Laughery, Claremont-M-S	Fr	50	37.7
Dexter Hurt, Randolph-Macon	Sr	54	37.6

Field Goals

	1993 Class	G	FGA	FG	Pct.	FGPG
Steve Milne, Brockport St.	Sr	10	16	13	81.3	1.30
Greg Brame, Wittenberg	Sr	10	22	12	54.5	1.20
Alex Hernandez, Claremont-M-S	Fr	8	10	8	80.0	1.00
Jeff McDaniel, La Verne	Sr	9	11	9	81.8	1.00
Matt Carroll, Bri'water (Mass.)	Jr	10	14	10	71.4	1.00
Joe Metzka, Knox	So	9	13	9	69.2	1.00
Brian Buglewag, Whittier	Jr	9	14	9	64.3	1.00
Greg Harrison, Union (N.Y.)	Sr	9	13	9	69.2	1.00
Matt Minero, Swarthmore	So	8	11	8	72.7	1.00
Chris Merski, Allegheny	Jr	10	13	10	76.9	1.00
Vance Grant, Maryville (Tenn.)	Sr	10	17	9	52.9	.90
Brian Hughes, Stony Brook	So	10	13	9	69.2	.90
Fred Harding, Carnegie Mellon	Sr	10	17	9	52.9	.90
Tom Smith, Bethany (W.Va.)	Jr	9	13	8	61.5	.89
Alex Costa, Wabash	So	9	15	8	53.3	.89
Nick Mystrom, Colorado Col.	Sr	9	14	8	57.1	.89
Eddie Bray, Wis.-Eau Claire	Sr	10	10	8	80.0	.80
Matt Wooden, Defiance	Jr	10	14	8	57.1	.80
Joel Buseman, Central (Iowa)	Fr	9	13	7	53.8	.78
Ken Felton, Rensselaer	Jr	9	12	7	58.3	.78
Chris Gabriel, Curry	Sr	9	13	7	53.8	.78

1993 Division III Team Leaders

Total Offense

	G	Plays	Yds.	Yds.PG
St. John's (Minn.)	10	676	5,497	549.7
Coe	10	760	5,463	546.3
Mount Union	10	718	5,241	524.1
Rowan	9	575	4,350	483.3
Trinity (Conn.)	8	613	3,738	467.3
Defiance	10	751	4,541	454.1
Allegheny	10	692	4,512	451.2
Wis.-Stevens Point	10	718	4,463	446.3
Wabash	9	710	3,990	443.3
Carleton	10	776	4,426	442.6
Albion	9	636	3,899	433.2
Cornell College	9	642	3,859	428.8
St. Thomas (Minn.)	10	732	4,271	427.1
Wis.-La Crosse	10	732	4,252	425.2
Anderson	10	662	4,202	420.2
N'western (Wis.)	8	628	3,358	419.8
Carnegie Mellon	10	743	4,155	415.5
Colorado Col.	9	507	3,705	411.7
North Central	9	700	3,686	409.6
Augustana (Ill.)	9	636	3,654	406.0

Total Defense

	G	Plays	Yds.	Yds.PG
Wash. & Jeff.	9	538	1,282	142.4
Bri'water (Mass.)	10	615	1,678	167.8
Buffalo St.	9	540	1,627	180.8
Wittenberg	10	629	1,821	182.1
Union (N.Y.)	9	555	1,683	187.0
Maine Maritime	9	562	1,856	206.2
Wilkes	10	641	2,076	207.6
Central (Iowa)	9	598	1,938	215.3
MIT	8	455	1,741	217.6
Hobart	10	672	2,214	221.4
Westfield St.	10	648	2,224	222.4
Trinity (Conn.)	8	551	1,784	223.0
Mount Union	10	621	2,236	223.6
Salve Regina	8	484	1,804	225.5
Allegheny	10	645	2,286	228.6
St. John's (Minn.)	10	732	2,316	231.6
Carnegie Mellon	10	619	2,330	233.0
Coe	10	671	2,417	241.7
Rensselaer	9	635	2,186	242.9
Dickinson	10	652	2,431	243.1

Rushing Offense

	G	Car.	Yds.	Yds.PG
Chicago	10	583	3,248	324.8
N'western (Wis.)	8	495	2,581	322.6
North Central	9	538	2,765	307.2
Coe	10	517	3,018	301.8
Augustana (Ill.)	9	526	2,705	300.6
Wis.-River Falls	10	573	2,905	290.5
Occidental	9	487	2,526	280.7
Millikin	9	477	2,519	279.9
Cornell College	9	465	2,459	273.2
Allegheny	10	488	2,722	272.2
Albion	9	447	2,409	267.7
Dickinson	10	557	2,647	264.7
Trinity (Conn.)	8	386	2,103	262.9
Ohio Wesleyan	10	583	2,613	261.3
Alfred	10	559	2,610	261.0
Gettysburg	10	523	2,532	253.2
Maine Maritime	9	517	2,269	252.1
Monmouth (Ill.)	9	501	2,212	245.8
Redlands	9	410	2,207	245.2
Wabash	9	424	2,191	243.4

Rushing Defense

	G	Car.	Yds.	Yds.PG
Wash. & Jeff.	9	272	172	19.1
Mount Union	10	313	458	45.8
Central (Iowa)	9	317	414	46.0
Bri'water (Mass.)	10	371	524	52.4
Wilkes	10	371	731	73.1
Wittenberg	10	356	736	73.6
Buffalo St.	9	317	698	77.6
Union (N.Y.)	9	348	708	78.7
Trinity (Conn.)	8	296	652	81.5
Moravian	10	373	842	84.2
St. John's (Minn.)	10	433	882	88.2
Baldwin-Wallace	10	413	887	88.7
Occidental	9	284	842	93.6
Williams	8	295	749	93.6
Lycoming	10	360	956	95.6
Salve Regina	8	306	779	97.4
Wheaton (Ill.)	9	407	884	98.2
Trinity (Tex.)	10	365	987	98.7
Rensselaer	9	367	894	99.3
Middlebury	8	303	804	100.5

Scoring Offense

	G	TD	XP	2XP	DXP	FG	SAF	Pts.	Avg.
St. John's (Minn.)	10	89	68	5	0	1	0	615	61.5
Coe	10	68	50	5	0	3	1	479	47.9
Trinity (Conn.)	8	49	39	2	0	6	0	355	44.4
Defiance	10	59	51	3	0	8	2	439	43.9
Allegheny	10	59	46	1	0	10	0	432	43.2
Mount Union	10	59	53	1	0	3	2	422	42.2
Rowan	9	52	37	3	0	5	2	374	41.6
Colorado Col.	9	46	44	0	0	8	0	344	38.2
Central (Iowa)	9	46	34	3	0	7	0	337	37.4
Carnegie Mellon	10	50	39	2	0	9	0	370	37.0
Wash. & Jeff.	9	48	42	0	0	0	0	330	36.7
Occidental	9	45	33	3	0	5	1	326	36.2
Wis.-Stevens Point	10	49	42	2	0	6	0	358	35.8
Anderson	10	50	47	0	0	2	0	353	35.3
N'western (Wis.)	8	39	24	3	0	4	3	282	35.3
Augustana (Ill.)	9	46	31	2	0	1	0	314	34.9
Albion	9	44	34	0	0	5	0	313	34.8
Frostburg St.	10	48	31	1	0	3	0	330	33.0
Neb. Wesleyan	10	46	29	2	0	6	1	329	32.9
Cornell College	9	44	27	2	0	0	0	295	32.8

Scoring Defense

	G	TD	XP	2XP	DXP	FG	SAF	Pts.	Avg.
Wash. & Jeff.	9	6	4	0	0	5	0	55	6.1
Mount Union	10	9	8	0	0	1	0	65	6.5
Wilkes	10	10	3	4	0	0	1	73	7.3
Wittenberg	10	11	6	0	0	3	0	81	8.1
Williams	8	9	6	1	0	1	3	71	8.9
Allegheny	10	11	8	1	0	5	0	91	9.1
Westfield St.	10	12	6	2	0	4	0	94	9.4
Union (N.Y.)	9	10	9	0	0	6	0	87	9.7
St. John's (Minn.)	10	14	10	0	0	1	0	97	9.7
Wartburg	10	13	6	1	0	5	0	101	10.1
Central (Iowa)	9	14	5	2	0	0	0	93	10.3
Hobart	10	13	7	1	0	5	2	106	10.6
Trinity (Conn.)	8	12	6	2	0	1	0	85	10.6
Dickinson	10	15	9	1	0	2	0	107	10.7
Albion	9	13	12	1	0	2	0	98	10.9
Maine Maritime	9	14	7	2	0	1	0	98	10.9
Buffalo St.	9	13	8	1	0	4	1	102	11.3
MIT	8	12	5	1	0	4	0	91	11.4
Baldwin-Wallace	10	17	11	0	0	1	1	118	11.8
Rensselaer	9	13	9	0	1	6	0	107	11.9

Passing Offense

	G	Att.	Cmp.	Pct.	Int.	Yards	Yds.PG
Mount Union	10	345	244	70.7	12	3,528	352.8
St. Thomas (Minn.)	10	438	242	55.3	23	3,468	346.8
St. John's (Minn.)	10	299	189	63.2	11	3,308	330.8
Bethel (Minn.)	10	508	268	52.8	27	3,087	308.7
Alma	9	526	244	46.4	24	2,757	306.3
Principia	8	400	233	58.3	21	2,416	302.0
Western Md.	9	389	212	54.5	14	2,472	274.7
St. Olaf	10	397	213	53.7	20	2,708	270.8
Muhlenberg	9	390	189	48.5	19	2,416	268.4
Hanover	10	404	223	55.2	20	2,633	263.3
Rowan	9	246	146	59.3	4	2,354	261.6
Franklin	9	360	189	52.5	21	2,352	261.3
Ill. Benedictine	10	377	182	48.3	14	2,570	257.0
Salisbury St.	9	361	193	53.5	11	2,311	256.8
Neb. Wesleyan	10	342	184	53.8	18	2,553	255.3
Baldwin-Wallace	10	345	210	60.9	14	2,545	254.5
Upsala	9	345	175	50.7	22	2,252	250.2
Heidelberg	10	330	194	58.8	14	2,471	247.1
Carleton	10	229	164	71.6	21	2,466	246.6
Coe	10	243	145	59.7	10	2,445	244.5

Pass Efficiency Defense

	G	Att.	Cmp.	Pct.	Int.	Yards	TD	Rating Points
Worcester St.	9	195	69	35.3	17	706	1	50.0
Buffalo St.	9	223	77	34.5	17	929	4	60.2
Wittenberg	10	273	106	38.8	20	1,085	3	61.2
Dickinson	10	238	103	43.2	27	1,037	4	62.8
Westfield St.	10	228	84	36.8	14	993	3	65.5
MIT	8	164	53	32.3	21	846	8	66.2
Wash. & Jeff.	9	267	98	36.7	17	1,110	6	66.3
Trinity (Conn.)	8	255	111	43.5	25	1,132	4	66.4
Mass.-Boston	9	158	63	39.8	11	675	3	68.1
Framingham St.	9	182	65	35.7	15	867	5	68.3
Bri'water (Mass.)	10	244	80	32.7	18	1,154	8	68.6
Maine Maritime	9	207	69	33.3	13	907	8	70.3
Hobart	10	241	100	41.4	21	1,114	6	71.1
Mass.-Dartmouth	9	187	68	36.3	15	847	8	72.5
Union (N.Y.)	9	207	86	41.5	13	975	4	74.9
Wilkes	10	270	123	45.5	21	1,345	3	75.5
Rensselaer	9	268	112	41.7	23	1,292	9	76.2
St. John's (Minn.)	10	299	131	43.8	22	1,434	7	77.1
Frank. & Marsh.	10	291	120	41.2	11	1,393	3	77.3
Allegheny	10	275	126	45.8	16	1,230	5	77.7

Net Punting

	Punts	Avg.	No. Ret.	Yds. Ret.	Net Avg.
Ill. Benedictine	45	41.8	21	132	38.9
Wis.-Stout	57	41.0	21	197	37.6
Ferrum	49	38.4	14	74	36.9
Hope	35	38.9	13	73	36.8
Occidental	50	40.5	23	186	36.7
Wis.-La Crosse	43	38.1	16	61	36.7
Manchester	45	39.1	11	118	36.5
Colorado Col.	37	39.5	12	116	36.4
Redlands	43	38.6	14	102	36.3
Wesley	51	41.2	25	260	36.1
FDU-Madison	63	41.7	31	353	36.0
Washington (Mo.)	44	37.7	21	75	36.0
Central (Iowa)	38	36.6	13	44	35.4
Montclair St.	48	36.0	10	30	35.4
Millsaps	51	40.8	24	282	35.3
John Carroll	46	40.3	31	245	35.0
Randolph-Macon	56	36.8	23	105	35.0
Merchant Marine	43	36.4	17	70	34.8
Frostburg St.	42	36.9	18	98	34.5
Otterbein	54	41.1	32	357	34.5

Punt Returns

	G	No.	Yds.	TD	Avg.
Curry	9	9	161	0	17.9
Wheaton (Ill.)	9	18	322	3	17.9
Hope	9	7	120	0	17.1
Marietta	10	28	458	2	16.4
Ill. Benedictine	10	27	441	2	16.3
Ill. Wesleyan	9	31	501	3	16.2
Augustana (Ill.)	9	26	409	1	15.7
Olivet	9	12	186	1	15.5
Ohio Northern	10	30	463	2	15.4
St. John's (Minn.)	10	52	776	3	14.9
Carroll (Wis.)	10	21	266	2	12.7
Sewanee	9	24	303	1	12.6
Susquehanna	10	33	408	1	12.4
Amherst	8	18	220	2	12.2
Wesley	10	18	217	1	12.1
John Carroll	10	29	349	0	12.0
St. Norbert	9	23	269	0	11.7
Wabash	9	16	185	0	11.6
Mount Union	10	33	379	0	11.5
Washington (Mo.)	10	17	194	0	11.4

Kickoff Returns

	G	No.	Yds.	TD	Avg.
St. John's (Minn.)	10	23	664	0	28.9
Ohio Northern	10	39	1,020	3	26.2
La Verne	9	28	716	3	25.6
Heidelberg	10	26	637	1	24.5
Randolph-Macon	10	34	818	2	24.1
Occidental	9	29	680	3	23.4
Mount Union	10	19	441	0	23.2
Central (Iowa)	9	18	412	1	22.9
Plymouth St.	9	25	568	0	22.7
Allegheny	10	24	532	2	22.2
Wis.-La Crosse	10	28	618	1	22.1
Thomas More	10	29	635	0	21.9
Ill. Benedictine	10	48	1,048	1	21.8
Moravian	10	26	566	1	21.8
Frank. & Marsh.	10	33	714	1	21.6
Carroll (Wis.)	10	27	581	1	21.5
Augustana (Ill.)	9	34	731	0	21.5
Wartburg	10	18	387	0	21.5
Pomona-Pitzer	8	40	855	2	21.4
John Carroll	10	33	705	0	21.4

Turnover Margin

	TURNOVERS GAINED			TURNOVERS LOST			Margin/ Game
	Fum.	Int.	Total	Fum.	Int.	Total	
Trinity (Conn.)	17	25	42	7	12	19	2.87
MIT	12	21	33	8	5	13	2.50
Wilkes	24	21	45	10	12	22	2.30
Lycoming	12	30	42	5	17	22	2.00
Colorado Col.	12	22	34	8	8	16	2.00
Wittenberg	8	20	28	6	5	11	1.70
Wartburg	14	15	29	7	6	13	1.60
St. Norbert	21	13	34	13	7	20	1.55
FDU-Madison	14	17	31	7	9	16	1.50
Dickinson	10	27	37	16	6	22	1.50
Maine Maritime	15	13	28	11	4	15	1.44
Baldwin-Wallace	14	24	38	10	14	24	1.40
N'western (Wis.)	18	14	32	12	9	21	1.37
Albion	14	20	34	14	8	22	1.33
Washington (Mo.)	21	13	34	14	7	21	1.30
Adrian	8	16	24	6	7	13	1.22
Cal Lutheran	12	10	22	4	7	11	1.22
Heidelberg	14	17	31	5	14	19	1.20
Anderson	7	18	25	10	3	13	1.20
St. John's (Minn.)	14	22	36	13	11	24	1.20

Longest Division III Plays of 1993

Rushing

Player, Team (Opponent)	Yards
Arkenny Wade, Wilkes (King's, Pa.)	97
Chad Smith, Fitchburg St. (Worcester St.)	94
Chris Irving, Union, N.Y. (Coast Guard)	93
Darin Wieneke, Hamline (Carleton)	92
Charles Cole, Emory & Henry (Davidson)	92
Petie Davis, Wesley (Geneva)	91
Weyman Jones, Olivet (Taylor)	90
Ryan Smith, Wis.-River Falls (Wis.-Stout)	88
Dean Haugo, Concordia-M'head (Gust. Adolphus)	88
Kegan Franklin, William Penn (Central, Iowa)	87

Passing

Passer-Receiver, Team (Opponent)	Yards
Jim Connolley-Duane Martin, Wesley (FDU-Madison)	99
Jay Schneider-Tod Paige, Hamline (Carleton)	97
Steve Maple-Greg Lehrer, Heidelberg (Mount Union)	94
Jason Weinzierl-Craig Boen, Wis.-River Falls (Wis.-Oshkosh)	93
Eric Montgomery-Todd Woodall, Emory & Henry (Cumberland, Ky.)	90
Boo Perry-Mike Gundersdorf, Wilkes (FDU-Madison)	89
Kevin Humiston-Jason Wemer, Grinnell (St. Norbert)	88
Brian Lefond-Scott Sallack, Ursinus (FDU-Madison)	87
Ed Hesson-Priest Ramsey, Rowan (LIU-C.W. Post)	87
Pete Kutches-Jeff Kaeppe, Augsburg (Huron)	86

Interception Returns

Player, Team (Opponent)	Yards
Russell Williams, Frostburg St. (Wesley)	100
Mike Sikma, Carroll, Wis. (Ripon)	99
Dave Peabody, Millikin (Ill. Benedictine)	98
Chris Jones, Colorado Col. (Trinity, Tex.)	93
Scott Amond, Wis.-La Crosse (Wis.-Whitewater)	92
Joe Gonzalez, Mass.-Boston (Mass. Maritime)	90
Bill Linder, Baldwin-Wallace (Moravian)	90

Punt Returns

Player, Team (Opponent)	Yards
Tyrone Croom, Susquehanna (Delaware Valley)	95
Eric Green, Ill. Benedictine (Carthage)	93
Tony Lesch, St. John's, Minn. (Bethel, Minn.)	91
Ed Lowe, Upsala (Jersey City St.)	87
Ross Brady, Norwich (Worcester Tech)	84
Mark Stepansky, Adrian (Olivet)	84
Dave Peabody, Millikin (Valparaiso)	82
Garry Linn, Upper Iowa (Buena Vista)	80

Kickoff Returns

Player, Team (Opponent)	Yards
Josh Perkins, Ohio Northern (Bluffton)	99
Dexter Hurt, Randolph-Macon (Davidson)	98
Craig Stewart, La Verne (Occidental)	97
Bill Schroeder, Wis.-La Crosse (Wis.-River Falls)	96
Jim Van Dalen, Lawrence (Chicago)	96
Chris Nalley, Wesley (Trinity, Tex.)	95
Connon Thompson, Muskingum (John Carroll)	95
Rob Gardner, Allegheny (Wittenberg)	95
Tim Ott, Wis.-Stevens Point (Wis.-Whitewater)	94
Steve Rospert, Case Reserve (Allegheny)	93

Field Goals

Player, Team (Opponent)	Yards
Ed Mahoney, Ithaca (St. Lawrence)	49
Nick Mystrom, Colorado Col. (Trinity, Tex.)	49
Brian Balleweg, Whittier (Cal Lutheran)	47
Todd Passini, Wis.-Stevens Point (Wis.-Whitewater)	47
Rick Phelps, Western New Eng. (Assumption)	46
Chris Johnson, Ill. Wesleyan (Elmhurst)	46
Donnie Rossman, Bluffton (Mt. St. Joseph)	46
Eric George, Wartburg (Buena Vista)	45

Punts

Player, Team (Opponent)	Yards
Dan Leffler, Cal Lutheran (La Verne)	79
Brett Geijer, Ill. Benedictine (Quincy)	76
Mitch Holloway, Millsaps (Austin)	73
John Hlavka, Concordia, Ill. (N'western, Wis.)	73
Tom Joecken, Wartburg (Buena Vista)	71
Dexter Hurt, Randolph-Macon (Western Md.)	71
Brian Kelly, Wis.-La Crosse (Wis.-Oshkosh)	70
Daryle Pelligrino, Montclair St. (Dickinson)	70
Vic Moncato, FDU-Madison (Montclair St.)	70

STATISTICAL LEADERS

Conference
Standings and
Champions

1993 Conference Standings

(Full-Season Records Do Not Include Postseason Play)

Division I-A

ATLANTIC COAST CONFERENCE

Team	Conference				Full Season			
	W	L	T	Pct.	W	L	T	Pct.
Florida St.	8	0	0	1.000	11	1	0	.917
North Caro.	6	2	0	.750	10	2	0	.833
Clemson	5	3	0	.625	8	3	0	.727
Virginia	5	3	0	.625	7	4	0	.636
North Caro. St.	4	4	0	.500	7	4	0	.636
Georgia Tech	3	5	0	.375	5	6	0	.455
Duke	2	6	0	.250	3	8	0	.273
Maryland	2	6	0	.250	2	9	0	.182
Wake Forest	1	7	0	.125	2	9	0	.182

Bowl Games (2-3): Clemson (defeated Kentucky, 14-13, in Peach); Florida St. (defeated Nebraska, 18-16, in Orange); North Caro. (lost to Alabama, 24-10, in Gator); North Caro. St. (lost to Michigan, 42-7, in Hall of Fame); Virginia (lost to Boston College, 31-13, in Carquest)

BIG EAST CONFERENCE

Team	Conference				Full Season			
	W	L	T	Pct.	W	L	T	Pct.
West Va.	7	0	0	1.000	11	0	0	1.000
Miami (Fla.)	6	1	0	.857	9	2	0	.818
Boston College	5	2	0	.714	8	3	0	.727
Virginia Tech	4	3	0	.571	8	3	0	.727
Syracuse	3	4	0	.429	6	4	1	.591
Pittsburgh	2	5	0	.286	3	8	0	.273
Rutgers	1	6	0	.143	4	7	0	.364
Temple	0	7	0	.000	1	10	0	.091

Bowl Games (2-2): Boston College (defeated Virginia, 31-13, in Carquest); Miami (Fla.) (lost to Arizona, 29-0, in Fiesta); Virginia Tech (defeated Indiana, 45-20, in Independence); West Va. (lost to Florida, 41-7, in Sugar)

BIG EIGHT CONFERENCE

Team	Conference				Full Season			
	W	L	T	Pct.	W	L	T	Pct.
Nebraska	7	0	0	1.000	11	0	0	1.000
Colorado	5	1	1	.786	7	3	1	.682
Kansas St.	4	2	1	.643	8	2	1	.773
Oklahoma	4	3	0	.571	8	3	0	.727
Kansas	3	4	0	.429	5	7	0	.417
Missouri	2	5	0	.286	3	7	1	.318
Iowa St.	2	5	0	.286	3	8	0	.273
Oklahoma St.	0	7	0	.000	3	8	0	.273

Bowl Games (3-1): Colorado (defeated Fresno St., 41-30, in Aloha); Kansas St. (defeated Wyoming, 52-17, in Copper); Nebraska (lost to Florida St., 18-16, in Orange); Oklahoma (defeated Texas Tech, 41-10, in John Hancock)

BIG TEN CONFERENCE

Team	Conference				Full Season			
	W	L	T	Pct.	W	L	T	Pct.
Ohio St.*	6	1	1	.813	9	1	1	.864
Wisconsin*	6	1	1	.813	9	1	1	.864
Penn St.	6	2	0	.750	9	2	0	.818
Indiana	5	3	0	.625	8	3	0	.727
Michigan	5	3	0	.625	7	4	0	.636
Illinois	5	3	0	.625	5	6	0	.455
Michigan St.	4	4	0	.500	6	5	0	.545
Iowa	3	5	0	.375	6	5	0	.545
Minnesota	3	5	0	.375	4	7	0	.364
Northwestern	0	8	0	.000	2	9	0	.182
Purdue	0	8	0	.000	1	10	0	.091

*Ohio St. and Wisconsin tied, 14-14, on November 6.

Bowl Games (4-3): Indiana (lost to Virginia Tech, 45-20, in Independence); Michigan St. (lost to Louisville, 18-7, in Liberty); Iowa (lost to California, 37-3, in Alamo); Michigan (defeated North Caro. St., 42-7, in Hall of Fame); Ohio St. (defeated Brigham Young, 28-21, in Holiday); Penn St. (defeated Tennessee, 31-13, in Florida Citrus);

Wisconsin (defeated UCLA, 21-16, in Rose)

BIG WEST CONFERENCE

Team	Conference				Full Season			
	W	L	T	Pct.	W	L	T	Pct.
Southwestern La.	5	1	0	.833	8	3	0	.727
Utah St.	5	1	0	.833	6	5	0	.545
Nevada	4	2	0	.667	7	4	0	.636
New Mexico St.	4	2	0	.667	5	6	0	.455
Northern Ill.	3	3	0	.500	4	7	0	.364
Nevada-Las Vegas	2	4	0	.333	3	8	0	.273
Pacific (Cal.)	2	4	0	.333	3	8	0	.273
San Jose St.*	2	4	0	.333	2	9	0	.182
Louisiana Tech*	2	4	0	.333	2	9	0	.182
Arkansas St.	1	5	0	.167	2	8	1	.227

*San Jose St. defeated Louisiana Tech, 31-6, on October 23.

Bowl Games (1-0): Utah St. (defeated Ball St., 42-33, in Las Vegas)

MID-AMERICAN ATHLETIC CONFERENCE

Team	Conference				Full Season			
	W	L	T	Pct.	W	L	T	Pct.
Ball St.	7	0	1	.938	8	2	1	.773
Western Mich.	6	1	1	.813	7	3	1	.682
Bowling Green	5	1	2	.750	6	3	2	.636
Central Mich.	5	4	0	.556	5	6	0	.455
Akron	4	4	0	.500	5	6	0	.455
Ohio	4	5	0	.444	4	7	0	.364
Toledo*	3	5	0	.375	4	7	0	.364
Eastern Mich.*	3	5	0	.375	4	7	0	.364
Miami (Ohio)	3	6	0	.333	4	7	0	.364
Kent	0	9	0	.000	0	11	0	.000

*Toledo defeated Eastern Mich., 14-0, on November 19.

Bowl Games (0-1): Ball St. (lost Utah St., 42-33, in Las Vegas)

PACIFIC-10 CONFERENCE

Team	Conference				Full Season			
	W	L	T	Pct.	W	L	T	Pct.
Arizona*	6	2	0	.750	9	2	0	.818
UCLA*	6	2	0	.750	8	3	0	.727
Southern Cal*	6	2	0	.750	7	5	0	.583
Washington	5	3	0	.625	7	4	0	.636
California	4	4	0	.500	8	4	0	.667
Arizona St.	4	4	0	.500	6	5	0	.545
Washington St.	3	5	0	.375	5	6	0	.455
Oregon	2	6	0	.250	5	6	0	.455
Stanford#	2	6	0	.250	4	7	0	.364
Oregon St.#	2	6	0	.250	4	7	0	.364

*UCLA defeated Arizona, 37-17, on October 30 and defeated Southern Cal, 27-21, on November 20. #Stanford defeated Oregon St., 31-27, on October 30.

Bowl Games (3-1): Arizona (defeated Miami, Fla., 29-0, in Fiesta); California (defeated Iowa, 37-3, in Alamo); Southern Cal (defeated Utah, 28-21, in Freedom); UCLA (lost to Wisconsin, 21-16, in Rose)

SOUTHEASTERN CONFERENCE

Team	Conference				Full Season			
	W	L	T	Pct.	W	L	T	Pct.
East								
Florida†	7	1	0	.875	10	2	0	.833
Tennessee	6	1	1	.813	9	1	1	.864
Kentucky	4	4	0	.500	6	5	0	.545
Georgia	2	6	0	.250	5	6	0	.455
South Caro.	2	6	0	.250	4	7	0	.364
Vanderbilt	1	7	0	.125	4	7	0	.364
West								
Auburn*	8	0	0	1.000	11	0	0	1.000
Alabama†	5	2	1	.688	8	3	1	.708
Arkansas	3	4	1	.438	5	5	1	.500
Louisiana St.√	3	5	0	.375	5	6	0	.455
Mississippi√	3	5	0	.375	5	6	0	.455
Mississippi St.	2	5	1	.313	3	6	2	.364

*Auburn on NCAA probation and ineligible for conference title. †Overall record includes SEC championship game in which Florida defeated Alabama, 28-13, on December 4. √Louisiana St. defeated Mississippi, 19-17, on October 30.

Bowl Games (2-2): Alabama (defeated North Caro., 24-10, in Gator); Florida (defeated West Va., 41-7, in Sugar); Kentucky (lost to Clemson, 14-13, in Peach); Tennessee (lost to Penn St., 31-13, in Florida Citrus)

SOUTHWEST CONFERENCE

Team	Conference				Full Season			
	W	L	T	Pct.	W	L	T	Pct.
Texas A&M	7	0	0	1.000	10	1	0	.909
Texas Tech	5	2	0	.714	6	5	0	.545
Texas	5	2	0	.714	5	5	1	.500
Rice	3	4	0	.429	6	5	0	.545
Baylor	3	4	0	.429	5	6	0	.455
Texas Christian	2	5	0	.286	4	7	0	.364
Southern Methodist	1	5	1	.214	2	7	2	.273
Houston	1	5	1	.214	1	9	1	.136

Bowl Games (0-2): Texas A&M (lost to Notre Dame, 24-21, in Cotton); Texas Tech (lost to Oklahoma, 41-10, in John Hancock)

WESTERN ATHLETIC CONFERENCE

Team	Conference				Full Season			
	W	L	T	Pct.	W	L	T	Pct.
Wyoming*	6	2	0	.750	8	3	0	.727
Fresno St.*	6	2	0	.750	8	3	0	.727
Brigham Young	6	2	0	.750	6	5	0	.545
Utah	5	3	0	.625	7	5	0	.583
Colorado St.	5	3	0	.625	5	6	0	.455
New Mexico	4	4	0	.500	6	5	0	.545
San Diego St.	4	4	0	.500	6	6	0	.500
Hawaii	3	5	0	.375	6	6	0	.500
Air Force	1	7	0	.125	4	8	0	.333
UTEP	0	8	0	.000	1	11	0	.083

*Wyoming defeated Fresno St., 32-28, on October 30.

Bowl Games (0-4): Brigham Young (lost to Ohio St., 28-21, in Holiday); Fresno St. (lost to Colorado, 41-30, in Aloha); Utah (lost to Southern Cal, 28-21, in Freedom); Wyoming (lost to Kansas St., 52-17, in Copper)

DIVISION I-A INDEPENDENTS

Team	Full Season			
	W	L	T	Pct.
Notre Dame	10	1	0	.909
Cincinnati	8	3	0	.727
Louisville	8	3	0	.727
Army	6	5	0	.545
Memphis	6	5	0	.545
Tulsa	4	6	1	.409
Navy	4	7	0	.364
Tulane	3	9	0	.250
Southern Miss.	2	8	1	.227
East Caro.	2	9	0	.182

Bowl Games (2-0): Louisville (defeated Michigan St., 18-7, in Liberty); Notre Dame (defeated Texas A&M, 24-21, in Cotton)

Division I-AA

AMERICAN WEST CONFERENCE*

Team	Conference				Full Season			
	W	L	T	Pct.	W	L	T	Pct.
UC Davis#	3	1	0	.750	9	1	0	.900
Southern Utah#	3	1	0	.750	3	7	1	.318
Cal St. Sacramento	2	2	0	.500	4	6	0	.400
Cal Poly SLO	1	3	0	.250	6	4	0	.600
Cal St. Northridge	1	3	0	.250	4	6	0	.400

*Cal St. Northridge, Cal St. Sacramento and Southern Utah are Division I-AA members, others are Division II. #Southern Utah defeated UC Davis, 28-27, on September 25.

NCAA Division II Playoffs (1-1): UC Davis (1-1: defeated Fort Hays St., 37-34, in first round; lost to Tex. A&M-Kingsville, 51-28, in quarterfinals)

BIG SKY CONFERENCE

Team	Conference				Full Season			
	W	L	T	Pct.	W	L	T	Pct.
Montana	7	0	0	1.000	10	1	0	.909
Idaho	5	2	0	.714	9	2	0	.818
Eastern Wash.	5	2	0	.714	7	3	0	.700
Montana St.	4	3	0	.571	7	4	0	.636
Weber St.*	3	4	0	.429	7	4	0	.636
Northern Ariz.*	3	4	0	.429	7	4	0	.636
Boise St.	1	6	0	.143	3	8	0	.273
Idaho St.	0	7	0	.000	2	9	0	.182

*Weber St. defeated Northern Ariz., 67-28, on November 6.

NCAA Division I-AA Playoffs (2-2): Idaho (2-1: defeated Northeast La., 34-31, in first round; defeated Boston U., 21-14, in quarterfinals; lost to Youngstown St., 35-16, in semifinals); Montana (0-1: lost to Delaware, 49-48, in first round)

GATEWAY COLLEGIATE ATHLETIC CONFERENCE

	Conference				Full Season			
Team	W	L	T	Pct.	W	L	T	Pct.
Northern Iowa	5	1	0	.833	8	3	0	.727
Southwest Mo. St.	4	2	0	.667	7	4	0	.636
Western Ill.	4	2	0	.667	4	7	0	.364
Illinois St.	2	3	1	.417	6	4	1	.591
Eastern Ill.	2	3	1	.417	3	7	1	.318
Indiana St.	2	4	0	.333	4	7	0	.364
Southern Ill.	1	5	0	.167	2	9	0	.182

NCAA Division I-AA Playoffs (0-1): Northern Iowa (0-1: lost to Boston U., 27-21 in two overtimes, in first round)

IVY GROUP

	Conference				Full Season			
Team	W	L	T	Pct.	W	L	T	Pct.
Pennsylvania	7	0	0	1.000	10	0	0	1.000
Dartmouth	6	1	0	.857	7	3	0	.700
Princeton	5	2	0	.714	8	2	0	.800
Cornell*	3	4	0	.429	4	6	0	.400
Brown*	3	4	0	.429	4	6	0	.400
Yale	2	5	0	.286	3	7	0	.300
Harvard	1	6	0	.143	3	7	0	.300
Columbia	1	6	0	.143	2	8	0	.200

**Cornell defeated Brown, 21-3, on October 30.*

Ivy Group teams do not participate in postseason games.

METRO ATLANTIC ATHLETIC CONFERENCE

	Conference				Full Season			
Team	W	L	T	Pct.	W	L	T	Pct.
Iona*	5	0	0	1.000	9	1	0	.900
Canisius	4	1	0	.800	5	5	0	.500
St. John's (N.Y.)	3	2	0	.600	8	3	0	.727
Georgetown	2	3	0	.400	4	5	0	.444
St. Peter's#	1	4	0	.200	3	6	0	.333
Siena	0	5	0	.000	0	10	0	.000

**Does not include 32-0 loss to Wagner in ECAC playoff game on November 20. #Does not include game against Monmouth (N. J.).*

MID-EASTERN ATHLETIC CONFERENCE

	Conference				Full Season			
Team	W	L	T	Pct.	W	L	T	Pct.
Howard	6	0	0	1.000	11	0	0	1.000
South Caro. St.	4	2	0	.667	8	3	0	.727
Delaware St.	4	2	0	.667	6	5	0	.545
North Caro. A&T	3	3	0	.500	8	3	0	.727
Florida A&M	3	3	0	.500	5	6	0	.455
Bethune-Cookman	1	5	0	.167	3	8	0	.273
Morgan St.	0	6	0	.000	2	9	0	.182

NCAA Division I-AA Playoffs (0-1): Howard (0-1: lost to Marshall, 28-14, in first round)

Postseason Game: South Caro. St. lost to Southern-B.R., 11-0, in I-AA Heritage Bowl in Georgia Dome, Atlanta, on January 1.

OHIO VALLEY CONFERENCE

	Conference				Full Season			
Team	W	L	T	Pct.	W	L	T	Pct.
Eastern Ky.	8	0	0	1.000	8	3	0	.727
Tennessee Tech	7	1	0	.875	8	3	0	.727
Tenn.-Martin	5	3	0	.625	6	5	0	.545
Middle Tenn. St.	4	4	0	.500	5	6	0	.455
Tennessee St.*	4	4	0	.500	4	7	0	.364
Murray St.*	4	4	0	.500	4	7	0	.364
Morehead St.#	2	6	0	.250	3	8	0	.273
Southeast Mo. St.#	2	6	0	.250	3	8	0	.273
Austin Peay	0	8	0	.000	1	10	0	.091

**Tennessee St. defeated Murray St., 26-13, on November 13. #Morehead St. defeated Southeast Mo. St., 23-21, on October 2.*

NCAA Division I-AA Playoffs (0-1): Eastern Ky. (0-1: lost to Ga. Southern, 14-12, in first round)

PATRIOT LEAGUE

	Conference				Full Season			
Team	W	L	T	Pct.	W	L	T	Pct.
Lehigh	4	1	0	.800	7	4	0	.636
Lafayette	3	1	1	.700	5	4	2	.545
Bucknell	3	2	0	.600	4	7	0	.364
Holy Cross	2	3	0	.400	3	8	0	.273
Colgate	1	3	1	.300	3	7	1	.318
Fordham	1	4	0	.200	1	10	0	.091

Patriot League teams do not participate in postseason games.

PIONEER FOOTBALL LEAGUE

	Conference				Full Season			
Team	W	L	T	Pct.	W	L	T	Pct.
Dayton	5	0	0	1.000	9	1	0	.900
Drake	3	2	0	.600	8	2	0	.800
Butler	3	2	0	.600	4	6	0	.400
Evansville	2	3	0	.400	6	4	0	.600
San Diego	1	4	0	.200	6	4	0	.600
Valparaiso	1	4	0	.200	5	5	0	.500

SOUTHERN CONFERENCE

	Conference				Full Season			
Team	W	L	T	Pct.	W	L	T	Pct.
Ga. Southern	7	1	0	.875	9	2	0	.818
Marshall	6	2	0	.750	8	3	0	.727
Western Caro.	5	3	0	.625	6	5	0	.545
Furman	4	4	0	.500	5	5	1	.500
Citadel	4	4	0	.500	5	6	0	.455
Appalachian St.	4	4	0	.500	4	7	0	.364
East Tenn. St.	3	5	0	.375	5	6	0	.455
Tenn.-Chatt.	2	6	0	.250	4	7	0	.364
Va. Military	1	7	0	.125	1	10	0	.091

NCAA Division I-AA Playoffs (4-2): Ga. Southern (1-1: defeated Eastern Ky., 14-12, in first round; lost to Youngstown St., 34-14, in quarterfinals); Marshall (3-1: defeated Howard, 28-14, in first round; defeated Delaware, 34-31, in quarterfinals; defeated Troy St., 24-21, in semifinals; lost to Youngstown St., 17-5, in championship game)

SOUTHLAND CONFERENCE

	Conference				Full Season			
Team	W	L	T	Pct.	W	L	T	Pct.
McNeese St.	7	0	0	1.000	9	2	0	.818
Northeast La.	6	1	0	.857	9	2	0	.818
Stephen F. Austin	5	2	0	.714	8	3	0	.727
Northwestern St.	3	4	0	.429	5	6	0	.455
Sam Houston St.*	2	5	0	.286	4	7	0	.364
North Texas*	2	5	0	.286	4	7	0	.364
Nicholls St.	2	5	0	.286	3	8	0	.273
Southwest Tex. St.	1	6	0	.143	2	9	0	.182

**Sam Houston St. defeated North Texas, 24-24, on October 30.*

NCAA Division I-AA Playoffs (1-3): McNeese St. (1-1: defeated William & Mary, 34-28, in first round; lost to Troy St., 35-28, in quarterfinals); Northeast La. (0-1: lost to Idaho, 34-31, in first round); Stephen F. Austin (0-1: lost to Troy St., 42-20, in first round)

SOUTHWESTERN ATHLETIC CONFERENCE

	Conference				Full Season			
Team	W	L	T	Pct.	W	L	T	Pct.
Southern-B.R.	7	0	0	1.000	10	1	0	.909
Alcorn St.	6	1	0	.857	8	3	0	.727
Grambling	4	3	0	.571	7	4	0	.636
Alabama St.*	3	3	1	.500	5	4	1	.550
Jackson St.	3	3	1	.500	5	5	1	.500
Mississippi Val.	2	3	2	.429	4	4	2	.500
Texas Southern	1	6	0	.143	2	9	0	.182
Prairie View	0	7	0	.000	0	11	0	.000

**Defeated Tuskegee in Turkey Day Classic, 31-30, on November 25.*

Postseason Game: Southern-B.R. defeated South Caro. St., 11-0, in I-AA Heritage Bowl in Georgia Dome, Atlanta, on January 1.

YANKEE CONFERENCE

	Conference				Full Season			
Team	W	L	T	Pct.	W	L	T	Pct.
Mid-Atlantic								
William & Mary	7	1	0	.875	9	2	0	.818
Delaware	6	2	0	.750	8	3	0	.727
James Madison	4	5	0	.444	6	5	0	.545
Richmond	4	6	0	.400	5	6	0	.455
Villanova	2	7	0	.222	3	8	0	.273
Northeastern	2	8	0	.200	2	9	0	.182
New England								
Boston U.	9	0	0	1.000	11	0	0	1.000
Massachusetts	7	3	0	.700	8	3	0	.727
Connecticut	5	3	0	.625	6	5	0	.545
New Hampshire	5	5	0	.500	6	5	0	.545
Maine	2	7	0	.222	3	8	0	.273
Rhode Island	1	7	0	.125	3	8	0	.273

NCAA Division I-AA Playoffs (2-3): Delaware (1-1: defeated Montana, 49-48, in first round; lost to Marshall, 34-31, in quarterfinals); Boston U. (1-1: defeated Northern Iowa, 27-21 in two overtimes, in first round; lost to Idaho, 21-14, in quarterfinals); William & Mary (0-1: lost to McNeese St., 34-28, in first round)

DIVISION I-AA INDEPENDENTS

	Full Season			
Team	W	L	T	Pct.
Troy St.	10	0	1	.955
Ala.-Birmingham	9	2	0	.818
Central Fla.	9	2	0	.818
Youngstown St.	9	2	0	.818
Towson St.	8	2	0	.800
Wagner*#	7	2	0	.778
Western Ky.	8	3	0	.727
Hofstra	6	3	1	.650
St. Mary's (Cal.)	6	3	1	.650
Davidson	6	4	0	.600
Liberty	6	5	0	.545
Central Conn. St.	5	5	0	.500
Marist	5	5	0	.500
Samford	5	6	0	.455
Duquesne	4	6	0	.400
Charleston So.	3	8	0	.273
St. Francis (Pa.)#	2	7	0	.222
Buffalo	1	10	0	.091

*#Game against Monmouth (N. J.) is not included in won-lost records. *Does not include 32-0 victory over Iona in ECAC playoff game on November 20.*

NCAA Division I-AA Playoffs (6-2): Troy St. (2-1: defeated Stephen F. Austin, 42-20, in first round; defeated McNeese St., 35-23, in quarterfinals; lost to Marshall, 24-21, in semifinals); Central Fla. (0-1: lost to Youngstown St., 56-30, in first round); Youngstown St. (4-0: defeated Central Fla., 56-30, in first round; defeated Ga. Southern, 34-14, in quarterfinals; defeated Idaho, 35-16, in semifinals; defeated Marshall, 17-5, in championship game)

Division II

AMERICAN WEST CONFERENCE*

	Conference				Full Season			
Team	W	L	T	Pct.	W	L	T	Pct.
UC Davis#	3	1	0	.750	9	1	0	.900
Southern Utah#	3	1	0	.750	3	7	1	.318
Cal St. Sacramento	2	2	0	.500	4	6	0	.400
Cal Poly SLO	1	3	0	.250	6	4	0	.600
Cal St. Northridge	1	3	0	.250	4	6	0	.400

**UC Davis and Cal Poly SLO are Division II members, the others are Division I-AA members. #Southern Utah defeated UC Davis, 28-27, on September 25.*

NCAA Division II Playoffs (1-1): UC Davis (1-1: defeated Fort Hays St., 37-34, in first round; lost to Tex. A&M-Kingsville, 51-28, in quarterfinals)

CENTRAL INTERCOLLEGIATE ATHLETIC ASSOCIATION

	Conference				Full Season			
Team	W	L	T	Pct.	W	L	T	Pct.
Hampton	8	0	0	1.000	11	0	0	1.000
Virginia St.	7	1	0	.875	10	1	0	.909
Winston-Salem	5	2	1	.688	6	4	1	.591
N. C. Central	5	3	0	.625	6	5	0	.545
Fayetteville St.	4	4	0	.500	6	5	0	.545
Bowie St.	3	4	1	.438	3	6	1	.350
Johnson Smith	3	5	0	.375	3	8	0	.273
Norfolk St.	2	5	1	.313	3	7	1	.318
Virginia Union	2	5	1	.313	2	8	1	.227
Elizabeth City St.	1	7	0	.125	2	8	0	.200
Livingstone	1	7	0	.125	1	10	0	.091

NCAA Division II Playoffs (1-1): Hampton (1-1: defeated Albany St., Ga., 33-7, in first round; lost to North Ala., 45-20, in quarterfinals)

EASTERN COLLEGIATE FOOTBALL CONFERENCE*

	Conference				Full Season			
Team	W	L	T	Pct.	W	L	T	Pct.
Bentley	6	0	0	1.000	10	0	0	1.000
Stonehill	4	2	0	.667	7	2	0	.778
MIT	4	2	0	.667	5	3	0	.625
Assumption	4	2	0	.667	6	4	0	.600
Western New Eng.	2	4	0	.333	2	6	1	.278
Curry	1	5	0	.167	1	8	0	.111
Nichols	0	6	0	.000	1	7	0	.125

Assumption, Bentley and Stonehill are Division II members, others are Division III.

GULF SOUTH CONFERENCE

	Conference				Full Season			
Team	W	L	T	Pct.	W	L	T	Pct.
North Ala.	7	0	0	1.000	10	0	0	1.000
Valdosta St.	5	2	0	.714	8	3	0	.727
Central Ark.	4	3	0	.571	6	4	1	.591
West Ga.	4	3	0	.571	4	6	0	.400
Henderson St.	2	5	0	.286	4	6	0	.400
Livingston	1	5	1	.214	2	7	1	.250
Delta St.	1	6	0	.143	3	7	0	.300
Mississippi Col.*	3	3	1	.500	6	3	1	.650

**Mississippi Col. was not eligible for the conference championship. These teams played designated conference games: Central Ark. vs. East Tex. St. on September 4; Henderson St. vs. East Tex. St. on September 18; Valdosta St. vs. Fort Valley St. on September 18, and West Ga. vs. Albany St. (Ga.) on September 18.*

NCAA Division II Playoffs (4-0): North Ala. (4-0: defeated Carson-Newman, 38-28, in first round; defeated Hampton, 45-20, in quarterfinals; defeated Tex. A&M-Kingsville, 27-25, in semifinals; defeated Indiana, Pa., 41-34, in championship game)

LONE STAR CONFERENCE

	Conference				Full Season			
Team	W	L	T	Pct.	W	L	T	Pct.
Tex. A&M-Kingsville	5	0	0	1.000	5	5	0	.500
Angelo St.*	3	2	0	.600	7	3	0	.700
Abilene Christian*	3	2	0	.600	7	3	0	.700
Central Okla.	2	3	0	.400	7	3	0	.700
East Tex. St.	1	4	0	.200	5	6	0	.455
Eastern N. Mex.	1	4	0	.200	1	8	1	.150

**Angelo St. defeated Abilene Christian, 45-20, on October 16.*

NCAA Division II Playoffs (2-1): Tex. A&M-Kingsville (2-1: defeated Portland St., 50-15, in first round; defeated UC Davis, 51-28, in quarterfinals; lost to North Ala., 27-25, in semifinals)

MID-AMERICA INTERCOLLEGIATE ATHLETICS ASSOCIATION

	Conference				Full Season			
Team	W	L	T	Pct.	W	L	T	Pct.
Mo. Southern St.	9	0	0	1.000	9	1	1	.864
Pittsburg St.	8	1	0	.889	8	3	0	.727
Mo. Western St.	6	2	1	.722	8	2	1	.773
Central Mo. St.	6	2	1	.722	7	2	1	.750
Northeast Mo. St.	5	4	0	.556	6	5	0	.545
Emporia St.	3	6	0	.333	3	7	0	.300
Northwest Mo. St.	3	6	0	.333	3	8	0	.273
Missouri-Rolla	2	7	0	.222	3	7	0	.300
Southwest Baptist	2	7	0	.222	2	9	0	.182
Washburn	0	9	0	.000	0	10	0	.000

NCAA Division II Playoffs (0-2): Mo. Southern St. (0-1: lost to Mankato St., 34-13, in first round); Pittsburg St. (0-1: lost to North Dak., 17-14, in first round)

MIDWEST INTERCOLLEGIATE FOOTBALL CONFERENCE

	Conference				Full Season			
Team	W	L	T	Pct.	W	L	T	Pct.
Ferris St.	8	0	2	.900	9	0	2	.909
Ashland	8	2	0	.800	9	2	0	.818
Grand Valley St.	6	2	2	.700	6	3	2	.636
Hillsdale	6	3	1	.650	7	3	1	.682
Northern Mich.	5	4	1	.550	5	4	1	.550
Wayne St. (Mich.)	5	5	0	.500	6	5	0	.545
St. Francis (Ill.)	5	5	0	.500	5	6	0	.455
Saginaw Valley	4	6	0	.400	4	7	0	.364
Northwood	2	7	1	.250	3	7	1	.318
St. Joseph's (Ind.)	1	8	1	.150	1	8	1	.150
Indianapolis	1	9	0	.100	2	9	0	.182
Michigan Tech*	-	-	-	—	6	4	0	.600

**Michigan Tech was an affiliated member in 1993 and will become a full participating member in 1994.*

NCAA Division II Playoffs (0-1): Ferris St. (0-1: lost to Indiana, Pa., 28-21, in first round)

NORTH CENTRAL INTERCOLLEGIATE ATHLETIC CONFERENCE

	Conference				Full Season			
Team	W	L	T	Pct.	W	L	T	Pct.
Mankato St.*	7	2	0	.778	9	2	0	.818
North Dak.*	7	2	0	.778	8	2	0	.800
Northern Colo.	6	3	0	.667	8	3	0	.727
North Dak. St.	6	3	0	.667	7	3	0	.700
South Dak. St.	6	3	0	.667	7	4	0	.636
South Dak.	4	5	0	.444	6	5	0	.545
St. Cloud St.	4	5	0	.444	5	5	0	.500
Augustana (S.D.)	3	6	0	.333	4	7	0	.364
Nebraska-Omaha#	1	8	0	.111	2	9	0	.182
Morningside#	1	8	0	.111	2	9	0	.182

**North Dak. defeated Mankato St., 20-9, on October 9. #Nebraska-Omaha defeated Morningside, 31-14, on October 9.*

NCAA Division II Playoffs (3-2): Mankato St. (1-1: defeated Mo. Southern St., 34-13, in first round; lost to North Dak., 54-21, in quarterfinals); North Dak. (2-1: defeated Pittsburg St., 17-14, in first round; defeated Mankato St., 54-21, in quarterfinals; lost to Indiana, Pa., 21-6, in semifinals)

NORTHERN CALIFORNIA ATHLETIC CONFERENCE

	Conference				Full Season			
Team	W	L	T	Pct.	W	L	T	Pct.
Cal St. Chico	3	0	1	.875	4	4	1	.500
Cal St. Hayward	2	2	0	.500	3	6	0	.333
Sonoma St.	2	2	0	.500	2	7	0	.222
Humboldt St.	1	2	1	.375	4	6	1	.409
San Fran. St.	1	3	0	.250	4	7	0	.364

NORTHERN SUN INTERCOLLEGIATE CONFERENCE

	Conference				Full Season			
Team	W	L	T	Pct.	W	L	T	Pct.
Winona St.	5	1	0	.833	7	3	0	.700
Minn.-Duluth	4	2	0	.667	8	3	0	.727
Moorhead St.	4	2	0	.667	6	4	0	.600
Northern St.	4	2	0	.667	6	5	0	.545
Southwest St.	3	3	0	.500	4	6	0	.400
Minn.-Morris	1	5	0	.167	2	9	0	.182
Bemidji St.	0	6	0	.000	0	10	0	.000

NSIC Metrodome Classic (November 12-13): Neb.-Kearney 28, Bemidji St. 3; Winona St. 23, Moorhead St. 20; Northern St. 50, Minn.-Morris 14; Southwest St. 48, Michigan Tech 42; Minn.-Duluth 29, Wayne St. (Neb.) 28.

NAIA Division I Playoffs (0-1): Winona St. (0-1: lost to Central St., Ohio, 58-7, in quarterfinals)

PENNSYLVANIA STATE ATHLETIC CONFERENCE

	Conference				Full Season			
Team	W	L	T	Pct.	W	L	T	Pct.
Western Division								
Indiana (Pa.)	6	0	0	1.000	10	0	0	1.000
Edinboro	5	1	0	.833	8	2	0	.800
Slippery Rock	3	3	0	.500	6	4	0	.600
Clarion	3	3	0	.500	5	5	0	.500
Shippensburg	2	4	0	.333	6	5	0	.545
Calif. (Pa.)	2	4	0	.333	4	7	0	.364
Lock Haven	0	6	0	.000	2	9	0	.182
Eastern Division								
Millersville	6	0	0	1.000	8	2	0	.800
East Stroudsburg	4	2	0	.667	7	2	1	.750
West Chester	4	2	0	.667	6	5	0	.545
Bloomsburg	4	2	0	.667	5	6	0	.455
Mansfield	2	4	0	.333	2	8	0	.200
Cheyney	1	5	0	.167	3	8	0	.273
Kutztown	0	6	0	.000	2	9	0	.182

NCAA Division II Playoffs (3-2): Indiana (Pa.) (3-1: defeated Ferris St., 28-21, in first round; defeated New Haven, 38-28, in quarterfinals; defeated North Dak., 21-6, in semifinals; lost to North Ala., 41-34, in championship game); Edinboro (0-1: lost to New Haven, 48-28, in first round)

ROCKY MOUNTAIN ATHLETIC CONFERENCE

	Conference				Full Season			
Team	W	L	T	Pct.	W	L	T	Pct.
Fort Hays St.	6	1	0	.857	8	3	0	.727
Western St.	5	2	0	.714	8	3	0	.727
N. M. Highlands	5	2	0	.714	6	4	0	.600
Mesa St.	5	2	0	.714	5	5	0	.500
Adams St.	3	4	0	.429	4	6	0	.400
Chadron St.	2	5	0	.286	5	6	0	.455
Colorado Mines	2	5	0	.286	2	7	1	.250
Fort Lewis	0	7	0	.000	1	9	0	.100

NCAA Division II Playoffs (0-1): Fort Hays St. (0-1: lost to UC Davis, 37-34, in first round)

SOUTH ATLANTIC CONFERENCE

	Conference				Full Season			
Team	W	L	T	Pct.	W	L	T	Pct.
Carson-Newman	7	0	0	1.000	8	2	1	.773
Elon	5	2	0	.714	8	3	0	.727
Lenoir-Rhyne	4	3	0	.571	7	3	0	.700
Presbyterian	4	3	0	.571	5	6	0	.455
Wingate	3	4	0	.429	6	5	0	.545
Mars Hill	2	5	0	.286	4	6	0	.400
Gardner-Webb	0	7	0	.000	1	9	0	.100

NCAA Division II Playoffs (0-1): Carson-Newman (0-1: lost to North Ala., 38-28, in first round)

SOUTHERN INTERCOLLEGIATE ATHLETIC CONFERENCE

	Conference				Full Season			
Team	W	L	T	Pct.	W	L	T	Pct.
Albany St. (Ga.)	7	0	0	1.000	11	0	0	1.000
Fort Valley St.	5	1	1	.786	6	4	1	.591
Savannah St.	4	1	2	.714	5	3	2	.600
Morehouse	4	3	0	.571	5	5	0	.500
Alabama A&M	3	3	1	.500	4	6	1	.409
Morris Brown	3	4	0	.429	4	6	0	.400
Tuskegee	3	4	0	.429	3	8	0	.273
Clark Atlanta	1	6	0	.143	2	8	0	.200
Miles	0	7	0	.000	0	10	0	.000

NCAA Division II Playoffs (0-1): Albany St. (Ga.) (0-1: lost to Hampton, 33-7, in first round)

TEXAS INTERCOLLEGIATE CONFERENCE

	Conference				Full Season			
Team	W	L	T	Pct.	W	L	T	Pct.
Hardin-Simmons	5	0	0	1.000	8	2	0	.800
McMurry	4	1	0	.800	8	2	0	.800
Austin	2	3	0	.400	4	6	0	.400
Midwestern St.	2	3	0	.400	3	6	0	.333
Howard Payne	2	3	0	.400	3	7	0	.300
Sul Ross	0	5	0	.000	0	9	0	.000

NAIA Division II Playoffs (2-1): Hardin-Simmons (2-1: defeated Evangel, 49-21, in first round; defeated Mary, 30-20, in quarterfinals; lost to Westminster, Pa., 10-0, in semifinals)

WEST VIRGINIA INTERCOLLEGIATE ATHLETIC CONFERENCE

	Conference				Full Season			
Team	W	L	T	Pct.	W	L	T	Pct.
Glenville St.	6	1	0	.857	8	2	0	.800
West Va. Wesleyan	5	2	0	.714	7	3	0	.700
Shepherd*	5	2	0	.714	5	5	0	.500
West Liberty St.*	5	2	0	.714	5	5	0	.500
Concord	4	3	0	.571	4	6	0	.400
Fairmont St.	2	5	0	.286	3	7	0	.300
West Va. St.	1	6	0	.143	1	9	0	.100
West Va. Tech	0	7	0	.000	0	10	0	.000

**Shepherd defeated West Liberty St., 21-16, on October 2.*

NAIA Division I Playoffs (2-1): Glenville St. (2-1: defeated Carroll, Mont., 41-24, in quarterfinals; defeated Central St., Ohio, 13-12, in semifinals; lost to East Central, Okla., 49-35, in championship game)

DIVISION II INDEPENDENTS

	Full Season			
Team	W	L	T	Pct.
New Haven	10	0	0	1.000
Quincy	9	0	0	1.000
LIU-C. W. Post*	9	1	0	.900
Wayne St. (Neb.)	9	1	0	.900

Team	W	L	T	Pct.
Portland St.	8	2	0	.800
Wofford	7	3	1	.682
Gannon	6	4	0	.600
Ky. Wesleyan	6	4	0	.600
Mercyhurst*	5	4	0	.556
Mass.-Lowell	5	5	0	.500
West Tex. A&M	3	6	0	.333
Southern Conn. St.	3	7	1	.318
American Int'l.	3	7	0	.300
Jacksonville St.	3	7	0	.300
Neb.-Kearney	3	7	0	.300
Springfield	3	7	0	.300
Sacred Heart	2	7	0	.222
Newberry	2	8	0	.200
Kentucky St.	2	9	0	.182
Lane	1	8	0	.111
Pace	0	10	0	.000

*Does not include LIU-C. W. Post's 34-3 victory over Mercyhurst in ECAC playoff game on November 20.

NCAA Division II Playoffs (1-2): New Haven (1-1: defeated Edinboro, 48-28, in first round; lost to Indiana, Pa., 38-28, in quarterfinals); Portland St. (0-1: lost to Tex. A&M-Kingsville, 50-15, in first round)

Division III

ASSOCIATION OF MID-EAST COLLEGES

Team	Conference				Full Season			
	W	L	T	Pct.	W	L	T	Pct.
Thomas More	3	0	0	1.000	8	2	0	.800
Defiance	2	1	0	.667	9	1	0	.900
Wilmington (Ohio)	1	2	0	.333	6	4	0	.600
Bluffton	0	3	0	.000	3	7	0	.300

CENTENNIAL FOOTBALL CONFERENCE

Team	Conference				Full Season			
	W	L	T	Pct.	W	L	T	Pct.
Dickinson*	5	2	0	.714	7	3	0	.700
Frank. & Marsh.	5	2	0	.714	6	4	0	.600
Ursinus	4	3	0	.571	5	4	0	.556
Gettysburg	4	3	0	.571	5	5	0	.500
Muhlenberg	4	3	0	.571	4	5	0	.444
Johns Hopkins	2	5	0	.286	4	6	0	.400
Western Md.	2	5	0	.286	3	5	1	.389
Swarthmore	2	5	0	.286	3	6	0	.333

*Does not include 17-9 loss to Montclair St. on November 20 in ECAC playoff game.

COLLEGE CONFERENCE OF ILLINOIS AND WISCONSIN

Team	Conference				Full Season			
	W	L	T	Pct.	W	L	T	Pct.
Augustana (Ill.)	7	0	0	1.000	7	2	0	.778
Wheaton (Ill.)	6	1	0	.857	7	2	0	.778
Millikin	5	2	0	.714	6	3	0	.667
Ill. Wesleyan	3	4	0	.429	4	5	0	.444
North Park	2	4	1	.357	4	4	1	.500
North Central	2	5	0	.286	3	6	0	.333
Elmhurst	1	5	1	.214	1	7	1	.167
Carthage	1	6	0	.143	1	8	0	.111

EASTERN COLLEGIATE FOOTBALL CONFERENCE*

Team	Conference				Full Season			
	W	L	T	Pct.	W	L	T	Pct.
Bentley	6	0	0	1.000	10	0	0	1.000
Stonehill	4	2	0	.667	7	2	0	.778
MIT	4	2	0	.667	5	3	0	.625
Assumption	4	2	0	.667	6	4	0	.600
Western New Eng.	2	4	0	.333	2	6	1	.278
Curry	1	5	0	.167	1	8	0	.111
Nichols	0	6	0	.000	1	7	0	.125

*MIT, Western New Eng., Curry and Nichols are Division III members, others are Division II.

FREEDOM FOOTBALL CONFERENCE

Team	Conference				Full Season			
	W	L	T	Pct.	W	L	T	Pct.
Worcester Tech	5	0	0	1.000	5	4	0	.556
Plymouth St.*	5	1	0	.833	6	3	0	.667
Stony Brook	3	2	0	.600	6	3	1	.650
Coast Guard	3	3	0	.500	4	5	0	.444

Team	Conference				Full Season			
	W	L	T	Pct.	W	L	T	Pct.
Merchant Marine	2	3	0	.400	5	4	0	.556
Mass.-Lowell	2	3	0	.400	5	5	0	.500
Western Conn. St.	2	4	0	.333	4	6	0	.400
Norwich	0	6	0	.000	0	9	0	.000

*Does not include 13-10 loss to Rensselaer in ECAC play-off game on November 20.

INDIANA COLLEGIATE ATHLETIC CONFERENCE

Team	Conference				Full Season			
	W	L	T	Pct.	W	L	T	Pct.
Anderson	6	0	0	1.000	10	0	0	1.000
Franklin	5	1	0	.833	6	3	0	.667
Wabash	4	2	0	.667	5	4	0	.556
Manchester	2	4	0	.333	5	5	0	.500
Hanover	2	4	0	.333	3	7	0	.300
Rose-Hulman	1	5	0	.167	3	7	0	.300
DePauw	1	5	0	.167	2	8	0	.200

NCAA Division III Playoffs (0-1): Anderson (0-1: lost to Albion, 41-21, in first round)

IOWA INTERCOLLEGIATE ATHLETIC CONFERENCE

Team	Conference				Full Season			
	W	L	T	Pct.	W	L	T	Pct.
Wartburg	8	0	0	1.000	9	1	0	.900
Central (Iowa)	7	1	0	.875	8	1	0	.889
Loras	6	2	0	.750	7	2	1	.750
Simpson	5	3	0	.625	5	5	0	.500
Luther	3	5	0	.375	4	6	0	.400
Buena Vista	3	5	0	.375	3	6	0	.333
Upper Iowa	3	5	0	.375	3	7	0	.300
Dubuque	1	7	0	.125	2	8	0	.200
William Penn	0	8	0	.000	1	9	0	.100

NCAA Division III Playoffs (0-1): Wartburg (0-1: lost to Wis.-La Crosse, 55-26, in first round)

MICHIGAN INTERCOLLEGIATE ATHLETIC ASSOCIATION

Team	Conference				Full Season			
	W	L	T	Pct.	W	L	T	Pct.
Albion	5	0	0	1.000	10	0	0	1.000
Kalamazoo	4	1	0	.800	7	2	0	.778
Hope	3	2	0	.600	5	4	0	.556
Alma	2	3	0	.400	2	7	0	.222
Adrian	1	4	0	.200	2	7	0	.222
Olivet	0	5	0	.000	1	8	0	.111

NCAA Division III Playoffs (1-1): Albion (1-1: defeated Anderson, 41-21, in first round; lost to Mount Union, 30-16, in quarterfinals)

MIDDLE ATLANTIC STATES COLLEGIATE ATHLETIC CONFERENCE

Team	Conference				Full Season			
	W	L	T	Pct.	W	L	T	Pct.
Commonwealth League								
Moravian	7	1	0	.875	8	2	0	.800
Susquehanna	6	3	0	.667	6	4	0	.600
Widener	6	4	0	.600	6	4	0	.600
Lebanon Valley	5	4	0	.555	5	5	0	.500
Albright	3	6	0	.333	3	6	0	.333
Juniata	1	7	0	.125	1	9	0	.100
Freedom League								
Wilkes*	9	0	0	1.000	10	0	0	1.000
FDU-Madison#	6	1	0	.857	8	2	0	.800
Lycoming	6	4	0	.600	6	4	0	.600
Delaware Valley	2	8	0	.200	2	8	0	.200
Upsala	1	6	0	.143	1	8	0	.111
King's (Pa.)	1	9	0	.100	1	9	0	.100

*The league champions were determined by round-robin play and the conference champion was determined by the winning percentage of league games and crossover games. #Does not include 6-0 loss to Wesley in ECAC playoff game.

NCAA Division III Playoffs (0-2): Moravian (0-1: lost to Wash. & Jeff., 27-7, in first round); Wilkes (0-1: lost to Frostburg St., 26-25, in first round)

MIDWEST COLLEGIATE ATHLETIC CONFERENCE

Team	Conference				Full Season			
	W	L	T	Pct.	W	L	T	Pct.
North Division								
Carroll (Wis.)*	4	1	0	.800	7	3	0	.700
St. Norbert	3	2	0	.600	6	3	0	.667
Beloit	3	2	0	.600	3	6	0	.333
Ripon	2	3	0	.400	5	4	0	.556
Lawrence	2	3	0	.400	2	7	0	.222
Lake Forest	1	4	0	.200	2	7	0	.222
South Division								
Coe*	5	0	0	1.000	10	0	0	1.000
Cornell College	4	1	0	.800	7	2	0	.778
Knox	3	2	0	.600	5	4	0	.556
Monmouth (Ill.)	2	3	0	.400	4	5	0	.444
Illinois Col.	1	4	0	.200	3	6	0	.333
Grinnell	0	5	0	.000	0	9	0	.000

*Coe defeated Carroll (Wis.), 47-20, on November 13.

NCAA Division III Playoffs (0-1): Coe (0-1: lost to St. John's, Minn., 32-14, in first round)

MINNESOTA INTERCOLLEGIATE ATHLETIC CONFERENCE

Team	Conference				Full Season			
	W	L	T	Pct.	W	L	T	Pct.
St. John's (Minn.)	9	0	0	1.000	10	0	0	1.000
St. Thomas (Minn.)	8	1	0	.889	8	2	0	.800
Hamline	6	3	0	.667	7	3	0	.700
Concordia-M'head	6	3	0	.667	6	4	0	.600
Carleton	5	4	0	.556	6	4	0	.600
Augsburg	4	5	0	.444	5	5	0	.500
St. Olaf	3	6	0	.333	4	6	0	.400
Bethel (Minn.)	2	7	0	.222	2	8	0	.200
Gust. Adolphus	2	7	0	.222	2	8	0	.200
Macalester	0	9	0	.000	0	10	0	.000

NCAA Division III Playoffs (2-1): St. John's (Minn.) (2-1: defeated Coe, 32-14, in first round; defeated Wis.-La Crosse, 47-25, in quarterfinals; lost to Mount Union, 56-8, in semifinals)

NEBRASKA-IOWA CONFERENCE

Team	Conference				Full Season			
	W	L	T	Pct.	W	L	T	Pct.
Doane	6	0	0	1.000	10	1	0	.909
Hastings	5	1	0	.833	9	2	0	.818
Neb. Wesleyan	4	2	0	.667	7	3	0	.700
Midland Lutheran	3	3	0	.500	6	4	0	.600
N'western (Iowa)	2	4	0	.333	5	5	0	.500
Dana	1	5	0	.167	1	9	0	.100
Concordia (Neb.)	0	6	0	.000	2	7	0	.222

NAIA Division II Playoffs (1-2): Doane (1-1: defeated Bethany, Kan., 17-10, in first round; lost to Baker, Kan., 28-21, in quarterfinals); Hastings (0-1: lost to Baker, Kan., 39-19, in first round)

NEW ENGLAND FOOTBALL CONFERENCE

Team	Conference				Full Season			
	W	L	T	Pct.	W	L	T	Pct.
Maine Maritime*	7	1	0	.875	8	1	0	.889
Westfield St.	6	2	0	.750	7	2	1	.750
Worcester St.	5	3	0	.625	6	3	0	.667
Mass.-Dartmouth	5	3	0	.625	5	4	0	.556
Bri'water (Mass.)	5	3	0	.625	5	5	0	.500
Framingham St.	3	5	0	.375	4	5	0	.444
Mass. Maritime	3	5	0	.375	4	6	0	.400
Mass.-Boston	2	6	0	.250	2	7	0	.222
Fitchburg St.	0	8	0	.000	0	8	1	.056

*Does not include 28-20 victory over Brockport St. in ECAC playoff game.

NEW JERSEY ATHLETIC CONFERENCE

Team	Conference				Full Season			
	W	L	T	Pct.	W	L	T	Pct.
Rowan	5	0	0	1.000	8	1	0	.889
Wm. Paterson	3	2	0	.600	7	3	0	.700
Montclair St.*	3	2	0	.600	6	3	0	.667
Trenton St.#	2	3	0	.400	3	6	1	.350
Kean#	2	3	0	.400	5	4	0	.556
Jersey City St.	0	5	0	.000	1	7	1	.167

*Does not include 17-9 victory over Dickinson in ECAC playoff game. #Trenton St. defeated Kean, 28-0, on November 13.

NCAA Division III Playoffs (4-2): Rowan (3-1: defeated Buffalo St., 29-6, in first round; defeated Wm. Paterson, 37-0, in quarterfinals; defeated Wash. & Jeff., 23-16, in semifinals; lost to Mount Union, 34-24, in championship game); Wm. Paterson (1-1: defeated Union, N.Y., 17-7, in first round; lost to Rowan, 37-0, in quarterfinals)

NORTH COAST ATHLETIC CONFERENCE

Team	Conference				Full Season			
	W	L	T	Pct.	W	L	T	Pct.
Allegheny	8	0	0	1.000	9	1	0	.900
Wittenberg	7	1	0	.875	9	1	0	.900
Ohio Wesleyan	6	2	0	.750	6	4	0	.600
Earlham	3	4	0	.429	4	6	0	.400
Kenyon	3	5	0	.375	4	6	0	.400
Denison	3	5	0	.375	3	7	0	.300
Case Reserve#	2	4	0	.333	2	8	0	.200
Wooster	2	5	0	.286	2	7	0	.222
Oberlin	0	8	0	.000	0	10	0	.000

#Also member of University Athletic Association.

NCAA Division III Playoffs (0-1): Allegheny (0-1: lost to Mount Union, 40-7, in first round)

OHIO ATHLETIC CONFERENCE

Team	Conference				Full Season			
	W	L	T	Pct.	W	L	T	Pct.
Mount Union	9	0	0	1.000	10	0	0	1.000
Baldwin-Wallace	8	1	0	.889	9	1	0	.900
Heidelberg	7	2	0	.778	8	2	0	.800
John Carroll	5	4	0	.556	6	4	0	.600
Ohio Northern	4	4	1	.500	5	4	1	.550
Capital	4	5	0	.444	5	5	0	.500
Otterbein	3	6	0	.333	4	6	0	.400
Muskingum	2	6	1	.278	2	7	1	.250
Marietta	2	7	0	.222	2	8	0	.200
Hiram	0	9	0	.000	0	10	0	.000

NCAA Division III Playoffs (4-0): Mount Union (4-0: defeated Allegheny, 40-7, in first round; defeated Albion, 30-16, in quarterfinals; defeated St. John's, Minn., 56-8, in semifinals; defeated Rowan, 34-24, in championship game)

OLD DOMINION ATHLETIC CONFERENCE

Team	Conference				Full Season			
	W	L	T	Pct.	W	L	T	Pct.
Randolph-Macon	5	0	0	1.000	7	2	1	.750
Emory & Henry	4	1	0	.800	7	3	0	.700
Hampden-Sydney	3	2	0	.600	6	4	0	.600
Bridgewater (Va.)*	1	4	0	.200	2	8	0	.200
Guilford*	1	4	0	.200	2	8	0	.200
Wash. & Lee*	1	4	0	.200	2	8	0	.200

*On October 16, Bridgewater (Va.) defeated Guilford, 28-25; on October 30, Wash. & Lee defeated Bridgewater (Va.), 41-16; on November 6, Guilford defeated Wash. & Lee, 14-13.

PRESIDENTS' ATHLETIC CONFERENCE

Team	Conference				Full Season			
	W	L	T	Pct.	W	L	T	Pct.
Wash. & Jeff.	4	0	0	1.000	9	0	0	1.000
Grove City	2	2	0	.500	5	4	0	.556
Bethany (W.Va.)	2	2	0	.500	4	4	1	.500
Waynesburg	1	3	0	.250	3	6	0	.333
Thiel	1	3	0	.250	2	7	0	.222

NCAA Division III Playoffs (2-1): Wash. & Jeff. (2-1: defeated Moravian, 27-7, in first round; defeated Frostburg St., 28-7, in quarterfinals; lost to Rowan, 23-16, in semifinals)

SOUTHERN CALIFORNIA INTERCOLLEGIATE ATHLETIC CONFERENCE

Team	Conference				Full Season			
	W	L	T	Pct.	W	L	T	Pct.
La Verne	6	0	0	1.000	7	2	0	.778
Occidental	5	1	0	.833	8	1	0	.889
Redlands	3	3	0	.500	6	3	0	.667
Cal Lutheran	3	3	0	.500	5	4	0	.556
Whittier	3	3	0	.500	4	5	0	.444
Claremont-M-S.	1	5	0	.167	1	6	1	.188
Pomona-Pitzer	0	6	0	.000	1	7	0	.125

SOUTHERN COLLEGIATE ATHLETIC CONFERENCE

Team	Conference				Full Season			
	W	L	T	Pct.	W	L	T	Pct.
Trinity (Tex.)	4	0	0	1.000	6	4	0	.600
Millsaps	2	2	0	.500	5	4	0	.556
Rhodes	2	2	0	.500	3	7	0	.300

Team	Conference				Full Season			
Sewanee*	1	3	0	.250	4	5	0	.444
Centre*	1	3	0	.250	4	5	0	.444

*Sewanee defeated Centre, 27-26, on October 2.

UNIVERSITY ATHLETIC ASSOCIATION

Team	Conference				Full Season			
	W	L	T	Pct.	W	L	T	Pct.
Carnegie Mellon	4	0	0	1.000	8	2	0	.800
Rochester	3	1	0	.750	5	4	0	.556
Chicago	2	2	0	.500	5	5	0	.500
Washington (Mo.)	1	3	0	.250	6	4	0	.600
Case Reserve#	0	4	0	.000	2	8	0	.200

#Also member of North Coast Athletic Conference.

WISCONSIN STATE UNIVERSITY CONFERENCE

Team	Conference				Full Season			
	W	L	T	Pct.	W	L	T	Pct.
Wis.-La Crosse	7	0	0	1.000	11	0	0	1.000
Wis.-Stevens Point	6	1	0	.857	8	2	0	.800
Wis.-Whitewater	5	2	0	.714	6	4	0	.600
Wis.-River Falls	3	4	0	.429	6	4	0	.600
Wis.-Eau Claire	3	4	0	.429	4	6	0	.400
Wis.-Platteville	2	5	0	.286	3	7	0	.300
Wis.-Oshkosh	1	6	0	.143	3	7	0	.300
Wis.-Stout	1	6	0	.143	2	8	0	.200

NCAA Division III Playoffs (1-1): Wis.-La Crosse (1-1: defeated Wartburg, 55-26, in first round; lost to St. John's, Minn., 47-25, in quarterfinals)

DIVISION III INDEPENDENTS

Team	Full Season			
	W	L	T	Pct.
Union (N.Y.)	9	0	0	1.000
Trinity (Conn.)%	8	0	0	1.000
Frostburg St.	9	1	0	.900
Colorado Col.	8	1	0	.889
N'western (Wis.)	7	1	0	.875
Williams%	7	1	0	.875
Buffalo St.	7	2	0	.778
Rensselaer	7	2	0	.778
Wesleyan (Conn.)%	6	2	0	.750
Brockport St.	7	3	0	.700
Hobart	7	3	0	.700
Colby%	5	2	1	.688
Wesley#	6	3	1	.650
Middlebury%	5	3	0	.625
Salve Regina	5	3	0	.625
Albany (N.Y.)	6	4	0	.600
Ithaca	6	4	0	.600
MacMurray	6	4	0	.600
Maryville (Tenn.)	6	4	0	.600
Ferrum	5	4	0	.556
St. John Fisher	5	4	0	.556
Hartwick	3	3	1	.500
Principia	4	4	0	.500
Ill. Benedictine	4	5	1	.450
Aurora	4	5	0	.444
Bowdoin%	3	4	1	.438
Alfred	4	6	0	.400
Methodist	4	6	0	.400
Amherst%	3	5	0	.375
Blackburn	3	6	0	.333
Eureka	3	7	0	.300
Salisbury St.	2	7	0	.222
St. Lawrence	2	8	0	.200
Hamilton%	1	7	0	.125
Tufts%	1	7	0	.125
Catholic	1	9	0	.100
Cortland St.	1	9	0	.100
Menlo	0	8	1	.056
Gallaudet	0	7	0	.000
Bates%	0	8	0	.000
Concordia (Ill.)	0	10	0	.000

#Does not include 6-0 victory over FDU-Madison in ECAC playoff game on November 20. %Member of New England Small College Athletic Conference but league does not keep standings.

NCAA Division III Playoffs (1-3): Frostburg St. (1-1: defeated Wilkes, 26-25, in first round; lost to Wash. & Jeff., 28-7, in quarterfinals); Buffalo St. (0-1: lost to Rowan, 29-6, in first round); Union (N.Y.) (0-1: lost to Wm. Paterson, 17-7, in first round)

All-Time Conference Champions

Division I-A

ATLANTIC COAST CONFERENCE

Founded: In 1953 when charter members all left the Southern Conference to form the ACC. **Charter members** (7): Clemson, Duke, Maryland, North Caro., North Caro. St., South Caro. and Wake Forest. **Admitted later** (3): Virginia (1953), Georgia Tech (1978) and Florida St. (1992). **Withdrew later** (1): South Caro. (1971). **Current members** (9): Clemson, Duke, Florida St., Georgia Tech, Maryland, North Caro., North Caro. St., Virginia and Wake Forest.

Year	Champion (Record)
1953	Duke (4-0) & Maryland (3-0)
1954	Duke (4-0)
1955	Maryland (4-0) & Duke (4-0)
1956	Clemson (4-0-1)
1957	North Caro. St. (5-0-1)
1958	Clemson (5-1)
1959	Clemson (6-1)
1960	Duke (5-1)
1961	Duke (5-1)
1962	Duke (6-0)
1963	North Caro. (6-1) & North Caro. St. (6-1)
1964	North Caro. St. (5-2)
1965	Clemson (5-2) & North Caro. St. (5-2)
1966	Clemson (6-1)
1967	Clemson (6-0)
1968	North Caro. St. (6-1)
1969	South Caro. (6-0)
1970	Wake Forest (5-1)
1971	North Caro. (6-0)
1972	North Caro. (6-0)
1973	North Caro. St. (6-0)
1974	Maryland (6-0)
1975	Maryland (5-0)
1976	Maryland (5-0)
1977	North Caro. (5-0-1)
1978	Clemson (6-0)
1979	North Caro. St. (5-1)
1980	North Caro. (6-0)
1981	Clemson (6-0)
1982	Clemson (6-0)
1983	Maryland (5-0)
1984	Maryland (5-0)
1985	Maryland (6-0)
1986	Clemson (5-1-1)
1987	Clemson (6-1)
1988	Clemson (6-1)
1989	Virginia (6-1) & Duke (6-1)
1990	Georgia Tech (6-0-1)
1991	Clemson (6-0-1)
1992	Florida St. (8-0)
1993	Florida St. (8-0)

BIG EAST CONFERENCE

Founded: In 1991 when eight charter members all went from independent status to form the Big East. **Charter members** (8): Boston College, Miami (Fla.), Pittsburgh, Rutgers (football only), Syracuse, Temple, Virginia Tech (football only) and West Va. (football only). **Current members** (8): Boston College, Miami (Fla.), Pittsburgh, Rutgers, Syracuse, Temple, Virginia Tech and West Va. **Note:** In 1991 and 1992, the team ranked highest in the USA Today/CNN coaches poll was declared champion. Beginning in 1993, the champion was decided by a seven-game round-robin schedule.

Year	Champion (Record)
1991	Miami (Fla.) (2-0, No. 1) & Syracuse (5-0, No. 16)
1992	Miami (Fla.) (4-0, No. 1)
1993	West Va. (7-0)

BIG EIGHT CONFERENCE

Founded: Originally founded in 1907 as the Missouri Valley Intercollegiate Athletic Association. **Charter members** (5): Iowa, Kansas, Missouri, Nebraska and Washington (Mo.). **Admitted later** (6): Drake (1908),

Iowa St. (then Ames College) (1908), Kansas St. (1913), Grinnell (1919), Oklahoma (1920) and Oklahoma St. (then Oklahoma A&M) (1925). **Withdrew later** (1): Iowa (1911). **Big Six** founded in 1928 when charter members left the MVIAA. **Charter members** (6): Iowa St., Kansas, Kansas St., Missouri, Nebraska and Oklahoma. **Admitted later** (2): Colorado (1948) and Oklahoma St. (1958). Renamed **Big Seven** in 1948 and **Big Eight** in 1958. **Current members** (8): Colorado, Iowa St., Kansas, Kansas St., Missouri, Nebraska, Oklahoma and Oklahoma St.

Year	Champion (Record)
1907	Iowa (1-0) & Nebraska (1-0)
1908	Kansas (4-0)
1909	Missouri (4-0-1)
1910	Nebraska (2-0)
1911	Iowa St. (2-0-1) & Nebraska (2-0-1)
1912	Iowa St. (2-0) & Nebraska (2-0)
1913	Missouri (4-0) & Nebraska (3-0)
1914	Nebraska (3-0)
1915	Nebraska (4-0)
1916	Nebraska (3-1)
1917	Nebraska (5-0)
1918	No Champion—War
1919	Missouri (4-0-1)
1920	Oklahoma (4-0-1)
1921	Nebraska (3-0)
1922	Nebraska (5-0)
1923	Nebraska (3-0-2)
1924	Missouri (5-1)
1925	Missouri (5-1)
1926	Oklahoma St. (3-0-1)
1927	Missouri (5-1)
1928	Nebraska (4-0)
1929	Nebraska (3-0-2)
1930	Kansas (4-1)
1931	Nebraska (5-0)
1932	Nebraska (5-0)
1933	Nebraska (5-0)
1934	Kansas St. (5-0)
1935	Nebraska (4-0-1)
1936	Nebraska (5-0)
1937	Nebraska (3-0-2)
1938	Oklahoma (5-0)
1939	Missouri (5-0)
1940	Nebraska (5-0)
1941	Missouri (5-0)
1942	Missouri (4-0-1)
1943	Oklahoma (5-0)
1944	Oklahoma (4-0-1)
1945	Missouri (5-0)
1946	Oklahoma (4-1) & Kansas (4-1)
1947	Kansas (4-0-1) & Oklahoma (4-0-1)
1948	Oklahoma (5-0)
1949	Oklahoma (5-0)
1950	Oklahoma (6-0)
1951	Oklahoma (6-0)
1952	Oklahoma (5-0-1)
1953	Oklahoma (6-0)
1954	Oklahoma (6-0)
1955	Oklahoma (6-0)
1956	Oklahoma (6-0)
1957	Oklahoma (6-0)
1958	Oklahoma (6-0)
1959	Oklahoma (5-1)
1960	Missouri (7-0)
1961	Colorado (7-0)
1962	Oklahoma (7-0)
1963	Nebraska (7-0)
1964	Nebraska (6-1)
1965	Nebraska (7-0)
1966	Nebraska (6-1)
1967	Oklahoma (7-0)
1968	Kansas (6-1) & Oklahoma (6-1)
1969	Missouri (6-1) & Nebraska (6-1)
1970	Nebraska (7-0)
1971	Nebraska (7-0)
1972	Nebraska (5-1-1) & Oklahoma (5-1-1)*
1973	Oklahoma (7-0)
1974	Oklahoma (7-0)
1975	Nebraska (6-1) & Oklahoma (6-1)
1976	Colorado (5-2), Oklahoma (5-2) & Oklahoma St. (5-2)
1977	Oklahoma (7-0)
1978	Nebraska (6-1) & Oklahoma (6-1)
1979	Oklahoma (7-0)
1980	Oklahoma (7-0)
1981	Nebraska (7-0)
1982	Nebraska (7-0)
1983	Nebraska (7-0)
1984	Oklahoma (6-1) & Nebraska (6-1)
1985	Oklahoma (7-0)
1986	Oklahoma (7-0)
1987	Oklahoma (7-0)
1988	Nebraska (7-0)
1989	Colorado (7-0)
1990	Colorado (7-0)
1991	Colorado (6-0-1) & Nebraska (6-0-1)
1992	Nebraska (6-1)
1993	Nebraska (7-0)

Oklahoma forfeited title.

BIG TEN CONFERENCE

Founded: In 1895 as the Intercollegiate Conference of Faculty Representatives, better known as the Western Conference. **Charter members** (7): Chicago, Illinois, Michigan, Minnesota, Northwestern, Purdue and Wisconsin. **Admitted later** (5): Indiana (1899), Iowa (1899), Ohio St. (1912), Michigan St. (1950) and Penn St. (1993). **Withdrew later** (2): Michigan (1907, rejoined in 1917) and Chicago (1940). **Note:** Iowa belonged to both the Missouri Valley and Western Conferences from 1907 to 1910. Unofficially called the Big Ten from 1912 until after 1939, then Big Nine from 1940 until Michigan St. began conference play in 1953. Formally renamed **Big Ten** in 1984. **Current members** (11): Illinois, Indiana, Iowa, Michigan, Michigan St., Minnesota, Northwestern, Ohio St., Penn St., Purdue and Wisconsin.

Year	Champion (Record)
1896	Wisconsin (2-0-1)
1897	Wisconsin (3-0)
1898	Michigan (3-0)
1899	Chicago (4-0)
1900	Iowa (3-0-1) & Minnesota (3-0-1)
1901	Michigan (4-0) & Wisconsin (2-0)
1902	Michigan (5-0)
1903	Michigan (3-0-1), Minnesota (3-0-1) & Northwestern (1-0-2)
1904	Minnesota (3-0) & Michigan (2-0)
1905	Chicago (7-0)
1906	Wisconsin (3-0), Minnesota (2-0) & Michigan (1-0)
1907	Chicago (4-0)
1908	Chicago (5-0)
1909	Minnesota (3-0)
1910	Illinois (4-0) & Minnesota (2-0)
1911	Minnesota (3-0-1)
1912	Wisconsin (6-0)
1913	Chicago (7-0)
1914	Illinois (6-0)
1915	Minnesota (3-0-1) & Illinois (3-0-2)
1916	Ohio St. (4-0)
1917	Ohio St. (4-0)
1918	Illinois (4-0), Michigan (2-0) & Purdue (1-0)
1919	Illinois (6-1)
1920	Ohio St. (5-0)
1921	Iowa (5-0)
1922	Iowa (5-0) & Michigan (4-0)
1923	Illinois (5-0) & Michigan (4-0)
1924	Chicago (3-0-3)
1925	Michigan (5-1)
1926	Michigan (5-0) & Northwestern (5-0)
1927	Illinois (5-0)
1928	Illinois (4-1)
1929	Purdue (5-0)
1930	Michigan (5-0) & Northwestern (5-0)
1931	Purdue (5-1), Michigan (5-1) & Northwestern (5-1)
1932	Michigan (6-0)
1933	Michigan (5-0-1)
1934	Minnesota (5-0)
1935	Minnesota (5-0) & Ohio St. (5-0)
1936	Northwestern (6-0)
1937	Minnesota (5-0)
1938	Minnesota (4-1)
1939	Ohio St. (5-1)
1940	Minnesota (6-0)
1941	Minnesota (5-0)
1942	Ohio St. (5-1)
1943	Purdue (6-0) & Michigan (6-0)
1944	Ohio St. (6-0)
1945	Indiana (5-0-1)
1946	Illinois (6-1)
1947	Michigan (6-0)
1948	Michigan (6-0)
1949	Ohio St. (4-1-1) & Michigan (4-1-1)
1950	Michigan (4-1-1)
1951	Illinois (5-0-1)
1952	Wisconsin (4-1-1) & Purdue (4-1-1)
1953	Michigan St. (5-1) & Illinois (5-1)
1954	Ohio St. (7-0)

Year	Champion (Record)
1955	Ohio St. (6-0)
1956	Iowa (5-1)
1957	Ohio St. (7-0)
1958	Iowa (5-1)
1959	Wisconsin (5-2)
1960	Minnesota (5-1) & Iowa (5-1)
1961	Ohio St. (6-0)
1962	Wisconsin (6-1)
1963	Illinois (5-1-1)
1964	Michigan (6-1)
1965	Michigan St. (7-0)
1966	Michigan St. (7-0)
1967	Indiana (6-1), Purdue (6-1) & Minnesota (6-1)
1968	Ohio St. (7-0)
1969	Ohio St. (6-1) & Michigan (6-1)
1970	Ohio St. (7-0)
1971	Michigan (8-0)
1972	Ohio St. (8-0) & Michigan (7-1)
1973	Ohio St. (7-0-1) & Michigan (7-0-1)
1974	Ohio St. (7-1) & Michigan (7-1)
1975	Ohio St. (8-0)
1976	Michigan (7-1) & Ohio St. (7-1)
1977	Michigan (7-1) & Ohio St. (7-1)
1978	Michigan (7-1) & Michigan St. (7-1)
1979	Ohio St. (8-0)
1980	Michigan (8-0)
1981	Iowa (6-2) & Ohio St. (6-2)
1982	Michigan (8-1)
1983	Illinois (9-0)
1984	Ohio St. (7-2)
1985	Iowa (7-1)
1986	Michigan (7-1) & Ohio St. (7-1)
1987	Michigan St. (7-0-1)
1988	Michigan (7-0-1)
1989	Michigan (8-0)
1990	Iowa (6-2), Michigan (6-2), Michigan St. (6-2) & Illinois (6-2)
1991	Michigan (8-0)
1992	Michigan (6-0-2)
1993	Ohio St. (6-1-1) & Wisconsin (6-1-1)

BIG WEST CONFERENCE

Founded: In 1969 as the Pacific Coast Athletic Association (PCAA). **Charter members** (7): Cal St. Los Angeles, Fresno St., Long Beach St., Pacific (Cal.), San Diego St., San Jose St. and UC Santa Barb. **Admitted later** (9): Cal St. Fullerton (1974), Utah St. (1977), Nevada-Las Vegas (1982), New Mexico St. (1983), Nevada (1992), Arkansas St. (1993), Louisiana Tech (1993), Northern Ill. (1993) and Southwestern La. (1993). **Withdrew later** (5): UC Santa Barb. (1972), Cal St. Los Angeles (1974), San Diego St. (1976), Fresno St. (1991) and Long Beach St. (1991, dropped football). Renamed **Big West** in 1988. **Current members** (11): Arkansas St., Cal St. Fullerton, Louisiana Tech, Nevada, Nevada-Las Vegas, New Mexico St., Northern Ill., Pacific (Cal.), San Jose St., Southwestern La. and Utah St.

Year	Champion (Record)
1969	San Diego St. (6-0)
1970	Long Beach St. (5-1) & San Diego St. (5-1)
1971	Long Beach St. (5-1)
1972	San Diego St. (4-0)
1973	San Diego St. (3-0-1)
1974	San Diego St. (4-0)
1975	San Jose St. (5-0)
1976	San Jose St. (4-0)
1977	Fresno St. (4-0)
1978	San Jose St. (4-1) & Utah St. (4-1)
1979	Utah St. (5-0)
1980	Long Beach St. (5-0)
1981	San Jose St. (5-0)
1982	Fresno St. (6-0)
1983	Cal St. Fullerton (5-1)
1984	Cal St. Fullerton (6-1)#
1985	Fresno St. (7-0)
1986	San Jose St. (7-0)
1987	San Jose St. (7-0)
1988	Fresno St. (7-0)
1989	Fresno St. (7-0)
1990	San Jose St. (7-0)
1991	Fresno St. (6-1) & San Jose St. (6-1)
1992	Nevada (5-1)
1993	Southwestern La. (5-1) & Utah St. (5-1)

#Nevada-Las Vegas forfeited title.

MID-AMERICAN CONFERENCE

Founded: In 1946. **Charter members** (6): Butler, Cincinnati, Miami (Ohio), Ohio, Western Mich. and Western Reserve (now Case Reserve). **Admitted later**

(9): Kent St. (now Kent) (1951), Toledo (1951), Bowling Green (1952), Marshall (1954), Central Mich. (1972), Eastern Mich. (1972), Ball St. (1973), Northern Ill. (1973) and Akron (1992). **Withdrew later** (5): Butler (1950), Cincinnati (1953), Case Reserve (1955), Marshall (1969) and Northern Ill. (1986). **Current members** (10): Akron, Ball St., Bowling Green, Central Mich., Eastern Mich., Kent, Miami (Ohio), Ohio, Toledo and Western Mich.

Year	Champion (Record)
1947	Cincinnati (3-1)
1948	Miami (Ohio) (4-0)
1949	Cincinnati (4-0)
1950	Miami (Ohio) (4-0)
1951	Cincinnati (3-0)
1952	Cincinnati (3-0)
1953	Ohio (5-0-1)
1954	Miami (Ohio) (4-0)
1955	Miami (Ohio) (5-0)
1956	Bowling Green (5-0-1)
1957	Miami (Ohio) (5-0)
1958	Miami (Ohio) (5-0)
1959	Bowling Green (6-0)
1960	Ohio (6-0)
1961	Bowling Green (5-1)
1962	Bowling Green (5-0-1)
1963	Ohio (5-1)
1964	Bowling Green (5-1)
1965	Bowling Green (5-1) & Miami (Ohio) (5-1)
1966	Miami (Ohio) (5-1) & Western Mich. (5-1)
1967	Toledo (5-1) & Ohio (5-1)
1968	Ohio (6-0)
1969	Toledo (5-0)
1970	Toledo (5-0)
1971	Toledo (5-0)
1972	Kent (4-1)
1973	Miami (Ohio) (5-0)
1974	Miami (Ohio) (5-0)
1975	Miami (Ohio) (6-0)
1976	Ball St. (4-1)
1977	Miami (Ohio) (5-0)
1978	Ball St. (8-0)
1979	Central Mich. (8-0-1)
1980	Central Mich. (7-2)
1981	Toledo (8-1)
1982	Bowling Green (7-2)
1983	Northern Ill. (8-1)
1984	Toledo (7-1-1)
1985	Bowling Green (9-0)
1986	Miami (Ohio) (6-2)
1987	Eastern Mich. (7-1)
1988	Western Mich. (7-1)
1989	Ball St. (6-1-1)
1990	Central Mich. (7-1)
1991	Bowling Green (8-0)
1992	Bowling Green (8-0)
1993	Ball St. (7-0-1)

PACIFIC-10 CONFERENCE

Founded: In 1915 as the **Pacific Coast Conference** by group of four charter members. **Charter members** (4): California, Oregon, Oregon St. and Washington. **Admitted later** (6): Washington St. (1917), Stanford (1918), Idaho (1922), Southern Cal (1922), Montana (1924) and UCLA (1928). **Withdrew later** (2): Montana (1950) and Idaho (1958).

The Pacific Coast Conference dissolved in 1959 and the Athletic Association of Western Universities was founded with five charter members. **Charter members** (5): California, Southern Cal, Stanford, UCLA and Washington. **Admitted later** (5): Washington St. (1962), Oregon (1964), Oregon St. (1964), Arizona (1978) and Arizona St. (1978). Conference renamed **Pacific-8** in 1968 and **Pacific-10** in 1978. **Current members** (10): Arizona, Arizona St., California, Oregon, Oregon St., Southern Cal, Stanford, UCLA, Washington and Washington St.

Year	Champion (Record)
1916	Washington (3-0-1)
1917	Washington (3-0)
1918	California (3-0)
1919	Oregon (2-1) & Washington (2-1)
1920	California (3-0)
1921	California (5-0)
1922	California (3-0)
1923	California (5-0)
1924	Stanford (3-0-1)
1925	Washington (5-0)
1926	Stanford (4-0)
1927	Southern Cal (4-0-1) & Stanford (4-0-1)

Year	Champion (Record)
1928	Southern Cal (4-0-1)
1929	Southern Cal (6-1)
1930	Washington St. (6-0)
1931	Southern Cal (7-0)
1932	Southern Cal (6-0)
1933	Oregon (4-1) & Stanford (4-1)
1934	Stanford (5-0)
1935	California (4-1), Stanford (4-1) & UCLA (4-1)
1936	Washington (6-0-1)
1937	California (6-0-1)
1938	Southern Cal (6-1) & California (6-1)
1939	Southern Cal (5-0-2) & UCLA (5-0-3)
1940	Stanford (7-0)
1941	Oregon (7-2)
1942	UCLA (6-1)
1943	Southern Cal (4-0)
1944	Southern Cal (3-0-2)
1945	Southern Cal (6-0)
1946	UCLA (7-0)
1947	Southern Cal (6-0)
1948	California (6-0) & Oregon (6-0)
1949	California (7-0)
1950	California (5-0-1)
1951	Stanford (6-1)
1952	Southern Cal (6-0)
1953	UCLA (6-1)
1954	UCLA (6-0)
1955	UCLA (6-0)
1956	Oregon St. (6-1-1)
1957	Oregon (6-2) & Oregon St. (6-2)
1958	California (6-1)
1959	Washington (3-1), Southern Cal (3-1) & UCLA (3-1)
1960	Washington (4-0)
1961	UCLA (3-1)
1962	Southern Cal (4-0)
1963	Washington (4-1)
1964	Oregon St. (3-1) & Southern Cal (3-1)
1965	UCLA (4-0)
1966	Southern Cal (4-1)
1967	Southern Cal (6-1)
1968	Southern Cal (6-0)
1969	Southern Cal (6-0)
1970	Stanford (6-1)
1971	Stanford (6-1)
1972	Southern Cal (7-0)
1973	Southern Cal (7-0)
1974	Southern Cal (6-0-1)
1975	UCLA (6-1) & California (6-1)
1976	Southern Cal (7-0)
1977	Washington (6-1)
1978	Southern Cal (6-1)
1979	Southern Cal (6-0-1)
1980	Washington (6-1)
1981	Washington (6-2)
1982	UCLA (5-1-1)
1983	UCLA (6-1-1)
1984	Southern Cal (7-1)
1985	UCLA (6-2)
1986	Arizona St. (5-1-1)
1987	Southern Cal (7-1) & UCLA (7-1)
1988	Southern Cal (8-0)
1989	Southern Cal (6-0-1)
1990	Washington (7-1)
1991	Washington (8-0)
1992	Stanford (6-2) & Washington (6-2)
1993	UCLA (6-2)

SOUTHEASTERN CONFERENCE

Founded: In 1933 when charter members all left the **Southern Conference** to become the SEC. **Charter members** (13): Alabama, Auburn, Florida, Georgia, Georgia Tech, Kentucky, Louisiana St., Mississippi, Mississippi St., Sewanee, Tennessee, Tulane and Vanderbilt. **Admitted later** (2): Arkansas (1992) and South Caro. (1992). **Withdrew later** (3): Sewanee (1940), Georgia Tech (1964) and Tulane (1966). **Current members** (12): Alabama, Arkansas, Auburn, Florida, Georgia, Kentucky, Louisiana St., Mississippi, Mississippi St., South Caro., Tennessee and Vanderbilt.

Year	Champion (Record)
1933	Alabama (5-0-1)
1934	Tulane (8-0) & Alabama (7-0)
1935	Louisiana St. (5-0)
1936	Louisiana St. (6-0)
1937	Alabama (6-0)
1938	Tennessee (7-0)
1939	Tennessee (6-0), Georgia Tech (6-0) & Tulane (5-0)

Year	Champion (Record)
1940	Tennessee (5-0)
1941	Mississippi St. (4-0-1)
1942	Georgia (6-1)
1943	Georgia Tech (4-0)
1944	Georgia Tech (4-0)
1945	Alabama (6-0)
1946	Georgia (5-0) & Tennessee (5-0)
1947	Mississippi (6-1)
1948	Georgia (6-0)
1949	Tulane (5-1)
1950	Kentucky (5-1)
1951	Georgia Tech (7-0) & Tennessee (5-0)
1952	Georgia (6-0)
1953	Alabama (4-0-3)
1954	Mississippi (5-1)
1955	Mississippi (5-1)
1956	Tennessee (6-0)
1957	Auburn (7-0)
1958	Louisiana St. (6-0)
1959	Georgia (7-0)
1960	Mississippi (5-0-1)
1961	Alabama (7-0) & Louisiana St. (6-0)
1962	Mississippi (6-0)
1963	Mississippi (5-0-1)
1964	Alabama (8-0)
1965	Alabama (6-1-1)
1966	Alabama (6-0) & Georgia (6-0)
1967	Tennessee (6-0)
1968	Georgia (5-0-1)
1969	Tennessee (5-1)
1970	Louisiana St. (5-0)
1971	Alabama (7-0)
1972	Alabama (7-1)
1973	Alabama (8-0)
1974	Alabama (6-0)
1975	Alabama (6-0)
1976	Georgia (5-1) & Kentucky (5-1)
1977	Alabama (7-0) & Kentucky (6-0)
1978	Alabama (6-0)
1979	Alabama (6-0)
1980	Georgia (6-0)
1981	Georgia (6-0) & Alabama (6-0)
1982	Georgia (6-0)
1983	Auburn (6-0)
1984	Florida (5-0-1)*
1985	Florida (5-1)# & Tennessee (5-1)
1986	Louisiana St. (5-1)
1987	Auburn (5-0-1)
1988	Auburn (6-1) & Louisiana St. (6-1)
1989	Alabama (6-1), Tennessee (6-1) & Auburn (6-1)
1990	Florida (6-1)# & Tennessee (5-1-1)
1991	Florida (7-0)
1992	Alabama (9-0)
1993	Florida (8-1) & Auburn (8-0)#

Title vacated. #Ineligible for title (probation).

SOUTHWEST CONFERENCE

Founded: In 1914 as the Southwest Athletic Conference. **Charter members** (8): Arkansas, Baylor, Oklahoma, Oklahoma A&M (now Oklahoma St.), Rice, Southwestern (Texas), Texas and Texas A&M. **Admitted later** (5): Southern Methodist (1918), Phillips (1920), Texas Christian (1923), Texas Tech (1960) and Houston (1976). **Withdrew later** (5): Southwestern (Texas) (1917), Oklahoma (1920), Phillips (1921), Oklahoma A&M (1925) and Arkansas (1992). **Current members** (8): Baylor, Houston, Rice, Southern Methodist, Texas, Texas A&M, Texas Christian and Texas Tech.

Year	Champion (Record)
1914	No champion
1915	Oklahoma (3-0)
1916	No champion
1917	Texas A&M (2-0)
1918	Texas (4-0)
1919	Texas A&M (4-0)
1920	Texas (5-0)
1921	Texas A&M (3-0-2)
1922	Baylor (5-0)
1923	Southern Methodist (5-0)
1924	Baylor (4-0-1)
1925	Texas A&M (4-1)
1926	Southern Methodist (5-0)
1927	Texas A&M (4-0-1)
1928	Texas (5-1)
1929	Texas Christian (4-0-1)
1930	Texas (4-1)
1931	Southern Methodist (5-0-1)
1932	Texas Christian (6-0)
1933	Arkansas (4-1)*

Year	Champion (Record)
1934	Rice (5-1)
1935	Southern Methodist (6-0)
1936	Arkansas (5-1)
1937	Rice (4-1-1)
1938	Texas Christian (6-0)
1939	Texas A&M (6-0)
1940	Texas A&M (5-1)
1941	Texas A&M (5-1)
1942	Texas (5-1)
1943	Texas (5-0)
1944	Texas Christian (3-1-1)
1945	Texas (5-1)
1946	Rice (5-1) & Arkansas (5-1)
1947	Southern Methodist (5-0-1)
1948	Southern Methodist (5-0-1)
1949	Rice (6-0)
1950	Texas (6-0)
1951	Texas Christian (5-1)
1952	Texas (6-0)
1953	Rice (5-1) & Texas (5-1)
1954	Arkansas (5-1)
1955	Texas Christian (5-1)
1956	Texas A&M (6-0)
1957	Rice (5-1)
1958	Texas Christian (5-1)
1959	Texas (5-1), Texas Christian (5-1) & Arkansas (5-1)
1960	Arkansas (6-1)
1961	Texas (6-1) & Arkansas (6-1)
1962	Texas (6-0-1)
1963	Texas (7-0)
1964	Arkansas (7-0)
1965	Arkansas (7-0)
1966	Southern Methodist (6-1)
1967	Texas A&M (6-1)
1968	Texas (6-1) & Arkansas (6-1)
1969	Texas (7-0)
1970	Texas (7-0)
1971	Texas (6-1)
1972	Texas (7-0)
1973	Texas (7-0)
1974	Baylor (6-1)
1975	Arkansas (6-1), Texas A&M (6-1) & Texas (6-1)
1976	Houston (7-1) & Texas Tech (7-1)
1977	Texas (8-0)
1978	Houston (7-1)
1979	Houston (7-1) & Arkansas (7-1)
1980	Baylor (8-0)
1981	Southern Methodist (7-1)# & Texas (6-1-1)
1982	Southern Methodist (7-0-1)
1983	Texas (8-0)
1984	Southern Methodist (6-2) & Houston (6-2)
1985	Texas A&M (7-1)
1986	Texas A&M (7-1)
1987	Texas A&M (6-1)
1988	Arkansas (7-0)
1989	Arkansas (7-1)
1990	Texas (8-0)
1991	Texas A&M (8-0)
1992	Texas A&M (7-0)
1993	Texas A&M (7-0)

Arkansas forfeited title (no champion named). #Southern Methodist forfeited title (probation).

WESTERN ATHLETIC CONFERENCE

Founded: In 1962 when charter members left the Skyline and Border Conferences to form the WAC. **Charter members** (6): Arizona (from Border), Arizona St. (from Border), Brigham Young (from Skyline), New Mexico (from Skyline), Utah (from Skyline) and Wyoming (from Skyline). **Admitted later** (6): Colorado St. (1968), UTEP (1968), San Diego St. (1978), Hawaii (1979), Air Force (1980) and Fresno St. (1992). **Withdrew later** (2): Arizona (1978) and Arizona St. (1978). **Current members** (10): Air Force, Brigham Young, Colorado St., Fresno St., Hawaii, New Mexico, San Diego St., Utah, UTEP and Wyoming.

Year	Champion (Record)
1962	New Mexico (2-1-1)
1963	New Mexico (3-1)
1964	Arizona (3-1), Utah (3-1) & New Mexico (3-1)
1965	Brigham Young (4-1)
1966	Wyoming (5-0)
1967	Wyoming (5-0)
1968	Wyoming (6-1)
1969	Arizona St. (6-1)
1970	Arizona St. (7-0)
1971	Arizona St. (7-0)
1972	Arizona St. (5-1)
1973	Arizona (6-1) & Arizona St. (6-1)
1974	Brigham Young (6-0-1)
1975	Arizona St. (7-0)
1976	Brigham Young (6-1) & Wyoming (6-1)
1977	Arizona St. (6-1) & Brigham Young (6-1)
1978	Brigham Young (5-1)
1979	Brigham Young (6-1)
1980	Brigham Young (6-1)
1981	Brigham Young (7-1)
1982	Brigham Young (7-1)
1983	Brigham Young (7-0)
1984	Brigham Young (8-0)
1985	Air Force (7-1) & Brigham Young (7-1)
1986	San Diego St. (7-1)
1987	Wyoming (8-0)
1988	Wyoming (8-0)
1989	Brigham Young (7-1)
1990	Brigham Young (7-1)
1991	Brigham Young (7-0-1)
1992	Hawaii (6-2), Fresno St. (6-2) & Brigham Young (6-2)
1993	Wyoming (6-2), Fresno St. (6-2) & Brigham Young (6-2)

Division I-AA

AMERICAN WEST CONFERENCE

Founded: Started Division I-AA play in 1993 with Cal St. Northridge, Cal St. Sacramento and Southern Utah as charter I-AA members. Other members were Cal Poly SLO and UC Davis (both played as Division II members). **Admitted later** (1): Cal Poly SLO (1994). **Withdrew later** (0): None. **Current members** (5): Cal Poly SLO, Cal St. Northridge, Cal St. Sacramento, Southern Utah and UC Davis.

Year	Champion (Record)
1993	Southern Utah (3-1) & UC Davis (3-1)#

 # Participated in Division II playoffs.

BIG SKY CONFERENCE

Founded: In 1963 when six charter members—Gonzaga, Idaho, Idaho St., Montana, Montana St. and Weber St.—banded together to form the Big Sky. **Admitted later** (4): Boise St. (1970), Northern Ariz. (1970), Nevada (1979, replacing charter member Gonzaga) and Eastern Wash. (1987). **Withdrew later** (2): Gonzaga (1979) and Nevada (1992). **Current members** (8): Boise St., Eastern Wash., Idaho, Idaho St., Montana, Montana St., Northern Ariz. and Weber St.

Year	Champion (Record)
1963	Idaho St. (3-1)
1964	Montana St. (3-0)
1965	Weber St. (3-1) & Idaho (3-1)
1966	Montana St. (4-0)
1967	Montana St. (4-0)
1968	Weber St. (3-1), Montana St. (3-1) & Idaho (3-1)
1969	Montana (4-0)#
1970	Montana (5-0)
1971	Idaho (4-1)
1972	Montana St. (5-1)
1973	Boise St. (6-0)#
1974	Boise St. (6-0)#
1975	Boise St. (5-0-1)#
1976	Montana St. (6-0)#
1977	Boise St. (6-0)
1978	Northern Ariz. (6-0)
1979	Montana St. (6-1)
1980	Boise St. (6-1)
1981	Idaho St. (6-1)*
1982	Montana (5-2)*
1983	Nevada (6-1)*
1984	Montana St. (6-1)*
1985	Idaho (6-1)*
1986	Nevada (7-0)*
1987	Idaho (7-1)*
1988	Idaho (7-1)*
1989	Idaho (8-0)*
1990	Nevada (7-1)*
1991	Nevada (8-0)*
1992	Idaho (6-1)* & Eastern Wash. (6-1)*
1993	Montana (7-0)*

#Participated in NCAA Division II Championship.
*Participated in NCAA Division I-AA Championship.

GATEWAY COLLEGIATE CONFERENCE

Founded: In 1982 as a women's athletics organization by 10 Midwestern universities. Six members started as a football conference in 1985. **Charter members** (6): (Football) Eastern Ill., Illinois St., Northern Iowa, Southern Ill., Southwest Mo. St. and Western Ill. Four members—Eastern Ill., Northern Iowa, Southwest Mo. St. and Western Ill.—were members of the Mid-Continent Conference for football. **Admitted later** (1): Indiana St. (1986). **Current members** (7): Eastern Ill., Illinois St., Indiana St., Northern Iowa, Southern Ill., Southwest Mo. St. and Western Ill.

Year	Champion (Record)
1985	Northern Iowa (5-0)*
1986	Eastern Ill. (5-1)*
1987	Northern Iowa (6-0)*
1988	Western Ill. (6-0)*
1989	Southwest Mo. St. (5-1)*
1990	Northern Iowa (5-1)*
1991	Northern Iowa (5-1)*
1992	Northern Iowa (5-1)*
1993	Northern Iowa (5-1)*

*Participated in Division I-AA Championship.

IVY GROUP

Founded: In 1956 by a group of eight charter members. **Charter members** (8): Brown, Columbia, Cornell, Dartmouth, Harvard, Pennsylvania, Princeton and Yale. **Current members** (8): Brown, Columbia, Cornell, Dartmouth, Harvard, Pennsylvania, Princeton and Yale.

Year	Champion (Record)
1956	Yale (7-2)
1957	Princeton (6-1)
1958	Dartmouth (6-1)
1959	Pennsylvania (6-1)
1960	Yale (7-0)
1961	Columbia (6-1) & Harvard (6-1)
1962	Dartmouth (7-0)
1963	Dartmouth (5-2) & Princeton (5-2)
1964	Princeton (7-0)
1965	Dartmouth (7-0)
1966	Dartmouth (6-1), Harvard (6-1) & Princeton (6-1)
1967	Yale (7-0)
1968	Harvard (6-0-1) & Yale (6-0-1)
1969	Dartmouth (6-1), Yale (6-1) & Princeton (6-1)
1970	Dartmouth (7-0)
1971	Cornell (6-1) & Dartmouth (6-1)
1972	Dartmouth (5-1-1)
1973	Dartmouth (6-1)
1974	Harvard (6-1) & Yale (6-1)
1975	Harvard (6-1)
1976	Brown (6-1) & Yale (6-1)
1977	Yale (6-1)
1978	Dartmouth (6-1)
1979	Yale (6-1)
1980	Yale (6-1)
1981	Yale (6-1) & Dartmouth (6-1)
1982	Harvard (5-2), Pennsylvania (5-2) & Dartmouth (5-2)
1983	Harvard (5-1-1) & Pennsylvania (5-1-1)
1984	Pennsylvania (7-0)
1985	Pennsylvania (6-1)
1986	Pennsylvania (7-0)
1987	Harvard (6-1)
1988	Pennsylvania (6-1) & Cornell (6-1)
1989	Princeton (6-1) & Yale (6-1)
1990	Cornell (6-1) & Dartmouth (6-1)
1991	Dartmouth (6-0-1)
1992	Dartmouth (6-1) & Princeton (6-1)
1993	Pennsylvania (7-0)

METRO ATLANTIC CONFERENCE

Founded: Began in Division I-AA in 1993 with Canisius, Georgetown, Iona, Siena, St. John's (N.Y.) and St. Peter's as charter members. **Admitted later** (0): None. **Withdrew later** (0): None. **Current members** (6): Canisius, Georgetown, Iona, Siena, St. John's (N.Y.) and St. Peter's.

Year	Champion (Record)
1993	Iona (5-0)

MID-EASTERN ATHLETIC CONFERENCE

Founded: In 1970 with first playing season in 1971 by seven charter members. **Charter members** (7): Delaware St., Howard, Md.-East. Shore, Morgan St., N.C. Central, North Caro. A&T and South Caro. St. **Admitted**

later (3): Bethune-Cookman (1979), Florida A&M (1979) and Coppin St. (1985). **Withdrew later** (4): Md.-East. Shore (1979), Morgan St. (1979), N.C. Central (1979) and Florida A&M (1984). **Readmitted** (2): Morgan St. (1984) and Florida A&M (1986). **Current members** (7): Bethune-Cookman, Delaware St., Florida A&M, Howard, Morgan St., North Caro. A&T and South Caro. St.

Year	Champion (Record)
1971	Morgan St. (5-0-1)
1972	N.C. Central (5-1)
1973	N.C. Central (5-1)
1974	South Caro. St. (5-1)
1975	South Caro. St. (5-1)
1976	South Caro. St. (5-1)
1977	South Caro. St. (6-0)
1978	South Caro. St. (5-0-1)
1979	Morgan St. (5-0)#
1980	South Caro. St. (5-0)*
1981	South Caro. St. (5-0)*
1982	South Caro. St. (4-1)*
1983	South Caro. St. (4-0)
1984	Bethune-Cookman (4-0)
1985	Delaware St. (4-0)
1986	North Caro. A&T (4-1)*
1987	Howard (5-0)
1988	Bethune-Cookman (4-2), Florida A&M (4-2) & Delaware St. (4-2)
1989	Delaware St. (5-1)
1990	Florida A&M (6-0)
1991	North Caro. A&T (5-1)√
1992	North Caro. A&T (5-1)*
1993	Howard (6-0)*

#Participated in NCAA Division II Championship.
*Participated in NCAA Division I-AA Championship.
√Participated in I-AA Heritage Bowl.

OHIO VALLEY CONFERENCE

Founded: In 1948 by six charter members, five of which withdrew from the Kentucky Intercollegiate Athletic Conference (Eastern Ky., Louisville, Morehead St., Murray St. and Western Ky.) plus Evansville. **Charter members** (6): Eastern Ky., Evansville, Louisville, Morehead St., Murray St. and Western Ky. **Admitted later** (10): Marshall (1949), Tennessee Tech (1949), Middle Tenn. St. (1952), East Tenn. St. (1957), Austin Peay (1962), Akron (1979), Youngstown St. (1980), Tennessee St. (1988), Southeast Mo. St. (1991) and Tenn.-Martin (1992). **Withdrew later** (7): Louisville (1949), Evansville (1952), Marshall (1952), East Tenn. St. (1979), Western Ky. (1982), Akron (1987) and Youngstown St. (1988). **Current members** (9): Austin Peay, Eastern Ky., Middle Tenn. St., Morehead St., Murray St., Southeast Mo. St., Tenn.-Martin, Tennessee St. and Tennessee Tech.

Team	Champion (Record)
1948	Murray St. (3-1)
1949	Evansville (3-1)
1950	Murray St. (5-0-1)
1951	Murray St. (5-1)
1952	Tennessee St. (4-1) & Western Ky. (4-1)
1953	Tennessee Tech (5-0)
1954	Eastern Ky. (5-0)
1955	Tennessee Tech (5-0)
1956	Middle Tenn. St.
1957	Middle Tenn. St. (5-0)
1958	Middle Tenn. St. (5-1) & Tennessee Tech (5-1)
1959	Middle Tenn. St. (5-0-1) & Tennessee Tech (5-0-1)
1960	Tennessee Tech (6-0)
1961	Tennessee Tech (6-0)
1962	East Tenn. St. (4-2)
1963	Western Ky. (7-0)
1964	Middle Tenn. St. (6-1)#
1965	Middle Tenn. St. (7-0)
1966	Morehead St. (6-1)
1967	Eastern Ky. (5-0-2)#
1968	Eastern Ky. (7-0)
1969	East Tenn. St. (6-0-1)#
1970	Western Ky. (5-1-1)
1971	Western Ky. (5-2)
1972	Tennessee Tech (7-0)#
1973	Western Ky. (7-0)#
1974	Eastern Ky. (6-1)
1975	Tennessee Tech (6-1) & Western Ky. (6-1)#
1976	Eastern Ky. (6-1)#
1977	Austin Peay (6-1)
1978	Western Ky. (6-0)
1979	Murray St. (6-0)*
1980	Western Ky. (6-1)
1981	Eastern Ky. (8-0)*
1982	Eastern Ky. (7-0)*
1983	Eastern Ky. (6-1)*
1984	Eastern Ky. (6-1)*
1985	Middle Tenn. St. (7-0)*
1986	Murray St. (5-2)
1987	Eastern Ky. (5-1)* & Youngstown St. (5-1)
1988	Eastern Ky. (6-0)*
1989	Middle Tenn. St. (6-0)*
1990	Middle Tenn. St. (5-1)* & Eastern Ky. (5-1)*
1991	Eastern Ky. (7-0)*
1992	Middle Tenn. St. (8-0)*
1993	Eastern Ky. (8-0)*

#Participated in NCAA Division II Championship.
*Participated in NCAA Division I-AA Championship.

PATRIOT LEAGUE

Founded: In 1984 originally as the Colonial League with six charter members. **Charter members** (6): Bucknell, Colgate, Davidson, Holy Cross, Lafayette and Lehigh. **Admitted later** (1): Fordham (1990). **Withdrew later** (1): Davidson (1989). **Current members** (6): Bucknell, Colgate, Fordham, Holy Cross, Lafayette and Lehigh.

Year	Champion (Record)
1986	Holy Cross (4-0)
1987	Holy Cross (4-0)
1988	Lafayette (5-0)
1989	Holy Cross (4-0)
1990	Holy Cross (5-0)
1991	Holy Cross (5-0)
1992	Lafayette (5-0)
1993	Lehigh (4-1)

PIONEER FOOTBALL LEAGUE

Founded: Started in 1993 with Division I-AA charter members Butler, Dayton, Drake, Evansville, San Diego and Valparaiso. **Admitted later** (0): None. **Withdrew later** (0): None. **Current members** (6): Butler, Dayton, Drake, Evansville, San Diego and Valparaiso.

Year	Champion (Record)
1993	Dayton (5-0)

SOUTHERN CONFERENCE

Founded: In 1921 by 14 institutions to form the Southern Intercollegiate Conference. Roots for the conference can actually be traced back to 1894 when several football-playing schools formed a confederation known as the Southeastern Intercollegiate Athletic Association. **Charter members** (14): Alabama, Auburn, Clemson, Georgia, Georgia Tech, Kentucky, Maryland, Mississippi St., North Caro., North Caro. St., Tennessee, Virginia, Virginia Tech and Wash. & Lee. **Admitted later** (15): Florida (1922), Louisiana St. (1922), Mississippi (1922), South Caro. (1922), Tulane (1922), Vanderbilt (1922), Va. Military (1924), Citadel (1936), Furman (1936), Appalachian St. (1971), Marshall (1976), Tenn.-Chatt. (1976), Western Caro. (1976), East Tenn. St. (1978) and Ga. Southern (1992). **Withdrew later:** Since 1922, membership has changed drastically, with a total of 38 schools having been affiliated with the league, including 11 of the 12 schools currently comprising the Southeastern Conference and eight of the nine schools currently comprising the Atlantic Coast Conference. **Current members** (9): Appalachian St., Citadel, East Tenn. St., Furman, Ga. Southern, Marshall, Tenn.-Chatt., Va. Military and Western Caro.

Year	Champion (Record)
1933	Duke (4-0)
1934	Wash. & Lee (4-0)
1935	Duke (5-0)
1936	Duke (7-0)
1937	Maryland (2-0)
1938	Duke (5-0)
1939	Clemson (4-0)
1940	Clemson (4-0)
1941	Duke (5-0)
1942	William & Mary (4-0)
1943	Duke (4-0)
1944	Duke (4-0)
1945	Duke (4-0)
1946	North Caro. (4-0-1)
1947	William & Mary (7-1)
1948	Clemson (5-0)
1949	North Caro. (5-0)
1950	Wash. & Lee (6-0)
1951	Maryland (5-0) & Va. Military (5-0)
1952	Duke (5-0)
1953	West Va. (4-0)
1954	West Va. (3-0)
1955	West Va. (4-0)
1956	West Va. (5-0)
1957	Va. Military (6-0)
1958	West Va. (4-0)
1959	Va. Military (6-0-1)
1960	Va. Military (4-1)
1961	Citadel (5-1)
1962	Va. Military (6-0)
1963	Virginia Tech (5-0)
1964	West Va. (4-0)
1965	West Va. (4-0)
1966	East Caro. (4-1-1) & William & Mary (4-1-1)
1967	West Va. (4-0-1)
1968	Richmond (6-0)
1969	Davidson (5-1) & Richmond (5-1)
1970	William & Mary (3-1)
1971	Richmond (5-1)
1972	East Caro. (7-0)
1973	East Caro. (7-0)
1974	Va. Military (5-1)
1975	Richmond (5-1)
1976	East Caro. (4-1)
1977	Tenn.-Chatt. (4-1) & Va. Military (4-1)
1978	Furman (4-1) & Tenn.-Chatt. (4-1)
1979	Tenn.-Chatt. (5-1)
1980	Furman (7-0)
1981	Furman (5-2)
1982	Furman (6-1)*
1983	Furman (6-0-1)*
1984	Tenn.-Chatt. (5-1)*
1985	Furman (6-0)*
1986	Appalachian St. (6-0-1)*
1987	Appalachian St. (7-0)*
1988	Furman (6-1)* & Marshall (6-1)*
1989	Furman (7-0)*
1990	Furman (6-1)*
1991	Appalachian St. (6-1)*
1992	Citadel (6-1)*
1993	Ga. Southern (7-1)*

*Participated in NCAA Division I-AA Championship.

SOUTHLAND CONFERENCE

Founded: In 1963 by a group of five institutions. **Charter members** (5): Abilene Christian, Arkansas St., Lamar, Texas-Arlington and Trinity (Tex.). **Admitted later** (10): Louisiana Tech (1971), Southwestern La. (1971), McNeese St. (1972), North Texas (1982), Northeast La. (1982), Northwestern St. (1987), Sam Houston St. (1987), Southwest Tex. St. (1987), Stephen F. Austin (1987) and Nicholls St. (1992). **Withdrew later** (7): Trinity (Tex.) (1972), Abilene Christian (1973), Southwestern La. (1982), Texas-Arlington (1986, dropped football), Arkansas St. (1987), Lamar (1987) and Louisiana Tech (1987). **Current members** (8): McNeese St., Nicholls St., North Texas, Northeast La., Northwestern St., Sam Houston St., Southwest Tex. St. and Stephen F. Austin.

Year	Champion (Record)
1964	Lamar (3-0-1)
1965	Lamar (3-1)
1966	Texas-Arlington (3-1)
1967	Texas-Arlington (4-0)
1968	Arkansas St. (3-0-1)
1969	Arkansas St. (4-0)
1970	Arkansas St. (4-0)
1971	Louisiana Tech (4-1)
1972	Louisiana Tech (5-0)
1973	Louisiana Tech (5-0)
1974	Louisiana Tech (5-0)
1975	Arkansas St. (5-0)
1976	McNeese St. (4-1) & Southwestern La. (4-1)
1977	Louisiana Tech (4-0-1)
1978	Louisiana Tech (4-1)
1979	McNeese St. (5-0)
1980	McNeese St. (5-0)
1981	Texas-Arlington (5-0)
1982	Louisiana Tech (5-0)*
1983	North Texas (5-1)*
1984	Louisiana Tech (5-1)*
1985	Arkansas St. (5-1)*
1986	Arkansas St. (5-0)*
1987	Northeast La. (6-0)*
1988	Northwestern St. (6-0)*
1989	Stephen F. Austin (5-0-1)*
1990	Northeast La. (5-1)*
1991	McNeese St. (4-1-2)*
1992	Northeast La. (7-0)*
1993	McNeese St. (7-0)*

*Participated in NCAA Division I-AA Championship.

SOUTHWESTERN ATHLETIC CONFERENCE

Founded: In 1920 by a group of six institutions. **Charter members** (6): Bishop, Paul Quinn, Prairie View, Sam Houston College, Texas College and Wiley. **Admitted later** (9): Langston (1931), Southern-B.R. (1934), Arkansas AM&N (1936), Texas Southern (1954), Grambling (1958), Jackson St. (1958), Alcorn St. (1962), Mississippi Val. (1968) and Alabama St. (1982). **Withdrew later** (8): Paul Quinn (1929), Bishop (1956), Langston (1957), Sam Houston College (1959), Texas College (1961), Wiley (1968), Arkansas AM&N (1970) and Prairie View (1990, dropped program, readmitted 1991). **Current members** (8): Alabama St., Alcorn St., Grambling, Jackson St., Mississippi Val., Prairie View, Southern-B.R. and Texas Southern.

Year	Champion (Record√)
1921	Wiley
1922	Paul Quinn
1923	Wiley
1924	Paul Quinn
1925	Bishop
1926	Sam Houston College
1927	Wiley
1928	Wiley
1929	Wiley
1930	Wiley
1931	Prairie View
1932	Wiley
1933	Langston & Prairie View
1934	Texas College
1935	Texas College
1936	Texas College & Langston
1937	Southern-B.R. & Langston
1938	Southern-B.R. & Langston
1939	Langston
1940	Southern-B.R. & Langston
1941	No champion
1942	Texas College
1943	No champion
1944	Wiley (5-1), Texas College (5-1) & Langston (5-1)
1945	Wiley (6-0)
1946	Southern-B.R. (5-1)
1947	Southern-B.R. (7-0)
1948	Southern-B.R. (7-0)
1949	Southern-B.R. (6-0-1) & Langston (6-0-1)
1950	Southern-B.R. (7-0)
1951	Prairie View (6-1)
1952	Prairie View (6-0)
1953	Prairie View (6-0)
1954	Prairie View (6-0)
1955	Southern-B.R. (6-1)
1956	Texas Southern (5-1) & Langston (5-1)
1957	Wiley (6-0)
1958	Prairie View (5-0)
1959	Southern-B.R. (7-0)
1960	Southern-B.R. (6-1), Prairie View (6-1) & Grambling (6-1)
1961	Jackson St. (6-1)
1962	Jackson St. (6-1)
1963	Prairie View (7-0)
1964	Prairie View (7-0)
1965	Grambling (6-1)
1966	Southern-B.R. (4-2-1), Grambling (4-2-1), Texas Southern (4-2-1) & Arkansas AM&N (4-2-1)
1967	Grambling (6-1)
1968	Alcorn St. (6-1), Grambling (6-1) & Texas Southern (6-1)
1969	Alcorn St. (6-0-1)
1970	Alcorn St. (6-0)
1971	Grambling (5-1)
1972	Grambling (5-1) & Jackson St. (5-1)
1973	Grambling (5-1) & Jackson St. (5-1)
1974	Alcorn St. (5-1) & Grambling (5-1)
1975	Grambling (4-2) & Southern-B.R. (4-2)
1976	Alcorn St. (5-1)
1977	Grambling (6-0)
1978	Grambling (5-0-1)
1979	Grambling (5-1) & Alcorn St. (5-1)
1980	Grambling (5-1)* & Jackson St. (5-1)
1981	Jackson St. (5-1)*
1982	Jackson St. (6-0)*
1983	Grambling (6-0-1)
1984	Alcorn St. (7-0)*
1985	Jackson St. (6-1)* & Grambling (6-1)*
1986	Jackson St. (7-0)*
1987	Jackson St. (7-0)*
1988	Jackson St. (7-0)*
1989	Jackson St. (7-0)*
1990	Jackson St. (5-1)*
1991	Alabama St. (6-0-1)#
1992	Alcorn St. (7-0)*
1993	Southern-B.R. (7-0)#

√No records available until 1944. *Participated in NCAA Division I-AA Championship. #Participated in I-AA Heritage Bowl.

YANKEE CONFERENCE

Founded: In 1947 by six institutions from the old New England College Conference. **Charter members** (6): Connecticut, Maine, Massachusetts, New Hampshire, Rhode Island and Vermont. **Admitted later** (8): Boston U. (1971), Holy Cross (1971), Delaware (1983), Richmond (1984), Villanova (1985), James Madison (1993), Northeastern (1993) and William & Mary (1993). **Withdrew later** (2): Holy Cross (1972) and Vermont (1974, dropped football). **Current members** (12): Boston U., Connecticut, Delaware, James Madison, Maine, Massachusetts, New Hampshire, Northeastern, Rhode Island, Richmond, Villanova and William & Mary.

Year	Champion (Record)
1947	New Hampshire (4-0)
1948	New Hampshire (3-1)
1949	Connecticut (2-0-1) & Maine (2-0-1)
1950	New Hampshire (4-0)
1951	Maine (3-0-1)
1952	Connecticut (3-1), Maine (3-1) & Rhode Island (3-1)
1953	New Hampshire (3-1) & Rhode Island (3-1)
1954	New Hampshire (4-0)
1955	Rhode Island (4-0-1)
1956	Connecticut (3-0-1)
1957	Connecticut (3-0-1) & Rhode Island (3-0-1)
1958	Connecticut (4-0)
1959	Connecticut (4-0)
1960	Connecticut (3-1)
1961	Maine (5-0)
1962	New Hampshire (4-0-1)
1963	Massachusetts (5-0)
1964	Massachusetts (5-0)
1965	Maine (5-0)
1966	Massachusetts (5-0)
1967	Massachusetts (5-0)
1968	Connecticut (4-1) & New Hampshire (4-1)
1969	Massachusetts (5-0)
1970	Connecticut (4-0-1)
1971	Connecticut (3-1-1) & Massachusetts (3-1-1)
1972	Massachusetts (5-0)
1973	Connecticut (5-0-1)
1974	Maine (4-2) & Massachusetts (4-2)
1975	New Hampshire (5-0)
1976	New Hampshire (5-1)
1977	Massachusetts (5-0)
1978	Massachusetts (5-0)*
1979	Massachusetts (4-1)
1980	Boston U. (5-0)
1981	Rhode Island (4-1) & Massachusetts (4-1)
1982	Boston U. (3-2)*, Connecticut (3-2), Maine (3-2) and Massachusetts (3-2)
1983	Boston U. (4-1)* & Connecticut (4-1)
1984	Boston U. (4-1)* & Rhode Island (4-1)*
1985	Rhode Island (5-0)*
1986	Connecticut (5-2), Delaware (5-2)* & Massachusetts (5-2)
1987	Maine (6-1)* & Richmond (6-1)*
1988	Delaware (6-2)* & Massachusetts (6-2)*
1989	Connecticut (6-2), Maine (6-2)* & Villanova (6-2)*
1990	Massachusetts (7-1)*
1991	Delaware (7-1)* & Villanova (7-1)*
1992	Delaware (7-1)*
1993	Boston U. (9-0)*

*Participated in NCAA Division I-AA Championship.

1994 Schedules/ 1993 Results

1994 Schedules and 1993 Results for All Divisions

Listed alphabetically in this section are 1994 schedules and 1993 results for all football-playing NCAA member institutions. The division designation for each school is indicated to the right of the school location.

Coaching records (below head coaches' names) are for all seasons as the head coach at any four-year collegiate institution.

Game dates and starting times are subject to change. ■ Designates home games; * designates night games. Neutral sites are listed in brackets.

ABILENE CHRISTIAN

Abilene, TX 79699 II

Coach: Bob Strader, Abilene Christian '75
Record: 1 Year, 7-3-0

1994 SCHEDULE

North Texas	*Sept. 1
Mississippi Col. ■	*Sept. 10
Adams St.	Sept. 17
New Haven ■	*Sept. 24
Eastern N. Mex.	Oct. 1
Central Okla.	*Oct. 8
Angelo St. ■	Oct. 15
West Tex. A&M ■	Oct. 22
East Tex. St.	Oct. 29
Tex. A&M-Kingsville	*Nov. 5

1993 RESULTS (7-3-0)

24	Western N. Mex.	10
43	Midwestern St.	10
33	Adams St.	0
13	North Texas	33
52	Eastern N. Mex.	36
28	Central Okla.	10
20	Angelo St.	45
57	Tarleton St.	15
17	East Tex. St.	10
10	Tex. A&M-Kingsville	26
297		**195**

Nickname: Wildcats.
Stadium: Shotwell (1959), 15,000 capacity. Natural turf.
Colors: Purple & White.
Conference: Lone Star Conf.
SID: Garner Roberts, 915-674-2693.
AD: Cecil Eager.

ADAMS STATE

Alamosa, CO 81102 II

Coach: Jeff Geiser, Colorado '76
Record: 10 Years, 57-43-1

1994 SCHEDULE

Idaho St.	*Sept. 3
West Tex. A&M	*Sept. 10
Abilene Christian	Sept. 17
Northwestern Okla. ■	Sept. 24
Western St.	Oct. 1
Chadron St. ■	Oct. 8
Colorado Mines	Oct. 15
Fort Hays St.	Oct. 22
Fort Lewis ■	Oct. 29
Mesa St.	Nov. 5
N.M. Highlands ■	Nov. 12

1993 RESULTS (4-6-0)

19	Southwestern Okla.	0
0	Abilene Christian	33
26	Northwestern Okla.	37
22	Chadron St.	36
27	Colorado Mines	20
15	Fort Hays St.	30
27	Fort Lewis	17
21	Mesa St.	15
7	N.M. Highlands	14
14	Western St.	17
178		**219**

Nickname: Indians.
Stadium: Rex Field (1949), 2,800 capacity. Natural turf.
Colors: Green & White.
Conference: Rocky Mountain Ath. Conf.
SID: Lloyd Engen, 719-589-7825.
AD: Vivian Frausto.

ADRIAN

Adrian, MI 49221 III

Coach: Jim Lyall, Michigan '74
Record: 4 Years, 12-23-1

1994 SCHEDULE

Heidelberg	*Sept. 10
Defiance ■	Sept. 17
Augustana (Ill.)	Sept. 24
Wilmington (Ohio) ■	Oct. 1
Albion	Oct. 8
Kalamazoo ■	Oct. 15
Olivet ■	Oct. 22
Hope ■	Oct. 29
Alma ■	Nov. 5

1993 RESULTS (2-7-0)

0	Mount Union	42
22	Defiance	43
6	Ill. Wesleyan	7
22	Evansville	15
7	Albion	17
22	Kalamazoo	27
27	Olivet	0
12	Hope	43
19	Alma	20
137		**214**

Nickname: Bulldogs.
Stadium: Maple (1960), 5,000 capacity. Natural turf.
Colors: Gold & Black.
Conference: Michigan Inter. Ath. Assoc.
SID: Darcy Gifford, 517-265-5161.
AD: Henry Mensing.

AIR FORCE

Air Force Academy, CO 80840 ....I-A

Coach: Fisher DeBerry, Wofford '60
Record: 10 Years, 76-46-1

1994 SCHEDULE

Colorado St. ■	Sept. 3
Brigham Young ■	Sept. 10
Northwestern ■	Sept. 17
UTEP [San Antonio, Texas]	*Sept. 24
San Diego St.	*Oct. 1
Navy ■	Oct. 8
Fresno St.	Oct. 22
Wyoming	Oct. 29
Army	Nov. 5
Utah ■	Nov. 12
Notre Dame	Nov. 19
Hawaii	*Dec. 3

1993 RESULTS (4-8-0)

63	Indiana St.	21
5	Colorado St.	8
31	San Diego St.	38
3	Brigham Young	30
18	Wyoming	31
24	Navy	28
20	Fresno St.	33
35	Citadel	0
31	UTEP	10
25	Army	6
24	Utah	41
17	Hawaii	45
296		**291**

Nickname: Falcons.

Stadium: Falcon (1962), 50,049 capacity. Natural turf.
Colors: Blue & Silver.
Conference: Western Athl. Conf.
SID: Dave Kellogg, 719-472-2313.
AD: Col. Ken Schweitzer.

AKRON

Akron, OH 44325 ....I-A

Coach: Gerry Faust, Dayton '58
Record: 13 Years, 72-69-4

1994 SCHEDULE

Temple ■	*Sept. 3
Bowling Green ■	*Sept. 10
Kent	Sept. 17
Western Mich.	*Sept. 24
Miami (Ohio)	Oct. 8
Central Mich. ■	*Oct. 15
Toledo ■	*Oct. 22
Youngstown St.	Oct. 29
Eastern Mich.	Nov. 5
Ball St.	Nov. 12
Ohio ■	Nov. 19

1993 RESULTS (5-6-0)

23	Central Mich.	13
42	Kent	7
3	Western Mich.	20
14	Army	35
31	Miami (Ohio)	13
7	Bowling Green	49
31	Temple	7
13	Ohio	21
19	Eastern Mich.	7
9	Ball St.	31
0	Youngstown St.	19
192		**222**

Nickname: Zips.
Stadium: Rubber Bowl (1940), 35,202 capacity. Artificial turf.
Colors: Blue & Gold.
Conference: Mid-American Conf.
SID: Mac Yates, 216-972-7468.
AD: Michael Bobinski.

ALABAMA

University, AL 35486 ....I-A

Coach: Gene Stallings, Texas A&M '57
Record: 11 Years, 67-54-2

1994 SCHEDULE

Tenn.-Chatt. ■	Sept. 3
Vanderbilt ■	Sept. 10
Arkansas	Sept. 17
Tulane ■	Sept. 24
Georgia	Oct. 1
Southern Miss. ■	Oct. 8
Tennessee	Oct. 15
Mississippi ■	Oct. 22
Louisiana St.	*Nov. 5
Mississippi St.	Nov. 12
Auburn ■	Nov. 19

1993 RESULTS (8-3-1)

31	Tulane	17
17	Vanderbilt	6
43	Arkansas	3
56	Louisiana Tech	3
17	South Caro.	6
17	Tennessee	17
19	Mississippi	14
40	Southern Miss.	0
13	Louisiana St.	17
36	Mississippi St.	25
14	Auburn	22
13	Florida	28
316		**158**

Gator Bowl

24	North Caro.	10

Nickname: Crimson Tide.
Stadium: Bryant-Denny (1929), 70,123 capacity. Natural turf.
Colors: Crimson & White.

Conference: Southeastern Conf.
SID: Larry White, 205-348-6084.
AD: Hootie Ingram.

ALABAMA A&M
Normal, AL 35762 II

Coach: Reggie Oliver, Marshall '75
(First year as head coach)

1994 SCHEDULE
Jackson St. [Birmingham, Ala.]	*Sept. 4
North Ala.	*Sept. 10
Clark Atlanta ■	*Sept. 17
Savannah St. ■	Sept. 24
Morris Brown	*Oct. 1
Morehouse	Oct. 8
Albany St. (Ga.) ■	Oct. 15
Fort Valley St.	Oct. 22
Alabama St. [Birmingham, Ala.]	Oct. 29
Miles ■	Nov. 5
Tuskegee	Nov. 12

1993 RESULTS (4-6-1)
35	Miles	0
18	Jacksonville St.	44
7	North Ala.	49
16	Savannah St.	16
15	Morris Brown	16
14	Morehouse	0
9	Albany St. (Ga.)	34
7	Fort Valley St.	35
0	Alabama St.	7
15	Clark Atlanta	8
36	Tuskegee	18
172		**227**

Nickname: Bulldogs.
Stadium: Milton Frank, 10,000 capacity. Natural turf.
Colors: Maroon & White.
Conference: Southern Inter. Ath. Conf.
SID: Antoine Bell, 205-851-5368.
AD: Gene Bright.

ALABAMA STATE
Montgomery, AL 36195 ....I-AA

Coach: Houston Markham, Alcorn St. '65
Record: 7 Years, 49-23-4

1994 SCHEDULE
Ala.-Birmingham ■	*Sept. 3
Southern-B.R.	*Sept. 10
Alcorn St.	*Sept. 17
Troy St.	Sept. 24
Jackson St. ■	*Oct. 8
Texas Southern [Mobile, Ala.]	*Oct. 15
Prairie View	Oct. 22
Alabama A&M [Birmingham, Ala.]	Oct. 29
Grambling	Nov. 5
Mississippi Val. ■	Nov. 12
Tuskegee ■	Nov. 24

1993 RESULTS (5-4-1)
14	Southern-B.R.	23
25	Alcorn St.	28
3	Troy St.	38
15	Jackson St.	17
28	Texas Southern	26
37	Prairie View	6
7	Alabama A&M	0
16	Grambling	10
14	Mississippi Val.	14
31	Tuskegee	30
190		**192**

Nickname: Hornets.
Stadium: Cramton (1922), 24,600 capacity. Natural turf.
Colors: Black & Old Gold.
Conference: Southwestern.
SID: Peter Forest, 205-293-4511.
AD: Arthur Barnett.

ALABAMA-BIRMINGHAM
Birmingham, AL 35294 ....I-AA

Coach: Jim Hilyer, Stetson '57
Record: 3 Years, 20-8-2

1994 SCHEDULE
Alabama St.	*Sept. 3
Dayton	*Sept. 10
Jacksonville St. ■	Sept. 17
Kansas	Sept. 24
Western Ky. ■	Oct. 1
Wofford ■	Oct. 8
Mississippi Val. ■	Oct. 15
Charleston So. ■	Oct. 22
Morehead St.	Oct. 29
Butler ■	Nov. 5
Prairie View	Nov. 19

1993 RESULTS (9-2-0)
3	Troy St.	37
52	Morehead St.	14
13	Western Ky.	40
31	Miles	6
40	Lambuth	14
30	Mississippi Val.	13
48	Charleston So.	20
23	Wofford	11
31	Butler	27
27	Dayton	19
58	Prairie View	12
356		**213**

Nickname: Blazers.
Stadium: Legion Field (1927), 83,091 capacity.
 Artificial turf.
Colors: Green, Gold & White.
Conference: I-AA Independent.
SID: Grant Shingleton, 205-934-0722.
AD: Gene Bartow.

ALBANY (NEW YORK)
Albany, NY 12222 III

Coach: Robert Ford, Springfield '59
Record: 25 Years, 132-104-1

1994 SCHEDULE
Ithaca ■	*Sept. 10
St. Lawrence	Sept. 17
Brockport St.	Sept. 24
Alfred ■	*Oct. 1
Union (N.Y.) ■	*Oct. 8
Cortland St. ■	Oct. 15
Norwich	Oct. 22
Salisbury St. ■	Oct. 29
Springfield ■	*Nov. 5
Wm. Paterson	*Nov. 11

1993 RESULTS (6-4-0)
7	Ithaca	47
32	St. Lawrence	9
10	Brockport St.	13
17	Alfred	16
14	Union (N.Y.)	21
20	Cortland St.	13
19	Norwich	16
7	Salisbury St.	6
50	Western Conn. St.	6
6	Wm. Paterson	28
182		**175**

Nickname: Great Danes.
Stadium: University Field, 10,000 capacity. Natural turf.
Colors: Purple & Gold.
Conference: Division III Independent.
SID: Brian DePasquale, 518-442-3072.
AD: Milton Richards.

ALBANY STATE (GEORGIA)
Albany, GA 31705 II

Coach: Hampton Smith, Mississippi Val. '57
Record: 18 Years, 104-75-4

1994 SCHEDULE
Livingston ■	Sept. 3
Miles ■	Sept. 10
West Ga. ■	Sept. 17
Morehouse	Sept. 24
Tuskegee ■	Oct. 1

Savannah St. ■	Oct. 8
Alabama A&M	Oct. 15
Bethune-Cookman	Oct. 22
Clark Atlanta ■	Oct. 29
Morris Brown	*Nov. 5
Fort Valley St. [Columbus, Ga.]	Nov. 12

1993 RESULTS (11-0-0)
30	Livingston	21
44	Miles	0
24	West Ga.	14
39	Morehouse	0
27	Tuskegee	8
28	Savannah St.	10
34	Alabama A&M	9
14	Florida A&M	6
20	Clark Atlanta	12
31	Morris Brown	16
14	Fort Valley St.	0
305		**96**

II Championship
7	Hampton	33

Nickname: Golden Rams.
Stadium: Mills Memorial (1957), 11,000 capacity.
 Natural turf.
Colors: Blue & Gold.
Conference: Southern Inter. Ath. Conf.
SID: Rickey Walker, 912-430-4672.
AD: Wilburn Campbell.

ALBION
Albion, MI 49224 III

Coach: Pete Schmidt, Alma '70
Record: 11 Years, 74-25-4

1994 SCHEDULE
Wilmington (Ohio)	Sept. 3
Aurora ■	Sept. 10
Wabash ■	Sept. 17
DePauw ■	Sept. 24
Adrian ■	Oct. 8
Olivet	Oct. 15
Hope ■	Oct. 22
Alma	Oct. 29
Kalamazoo	Nov. 5

1993 RESULTS (9-0-0)
35	Thiel	0
45	Ohio Wesleyan	7
50	Wabash	35
28	DePauw	0
17	Adrian	7
34	Olivet	14
32	Hope	7
38	Alma	28
34	Kalamazoo	0
313		**98**

III Championship
41	Anderson	21
16	Mount Union	30

Nickname: Britons.
Stadium: Sprankle-Sprandel (1976), 5,010 capacity.
 Natural turf.
Colors: Purple & Gold.
Conference: Michigan Inter. Ath. Assoc.
SID: Robin Hartman, 517-629-0434.
AD: Pete Schmidt.

ALBRIGHT
Reading, PA 19612 III

Coach: Kevin Kiesel, Gettysburg '81
Record: 1 Year, 3-6-0

1994 SCHEDULE
King's (Pa.)	Sept. 10
Juniata ■	Sept. 17
Lycoming ■	Sept. 24
Susquehanna	Oct. 1
FDU-Madison ■	Oct. 8
Widener	Oct. 15
Moravian ■	Oct. 22
Lebanon Valley ■	Oct. 29
Delaware Valley	Nov. 5

SCHEDULES/RESULTS

Jersey City St. ....Nov. 12

1993 RESULTS (3-6-0)

31	King's (Pa.)	12
24	Juniata	14
14	Lycoming	34
7	Susquehanna	31
7	FDU-Madison	33
13	Widener	33
21	Moravian	49
13	Lebanon Valley	24
34	Delaware Valley	33
164		**263**

Nickname: Lions.
Stadium: Albright (1925), 8,000 capacity. Natural turf.
Colors: Cardinal & White.
Conference: Middle Atlantic.
SID: Stan Hyman, 215-921-7833.
AD: Sally Miller.

ALCORN STATE

Lorman, MS 39096 ....I-AA

Coach: Cardell Jones, Alcorn St. '65
Record: 3 Years, 22-9-1

1994 SCHEDULE

Grambling	*Sept. 3
Tenn.-Chatt.	*Sept. 10
Alabama St. ■	*Sept. 17
Sam Houston St. ■	*Sept. 24
Texas Southern ■	*Oct. 8
Prairie View	Oct. 15
Southern-B.R. ■	Oct. 22
Samford	Oct. 29
Mississippi Val.	Nov. 5
Troy St. ■	Nov. 12
Jackson St. ■	Nov. 19

1993 RESULTS (8-3-0)

25	Grambling	24
44	Texas Southern	41
28	Alabama St.	25
36	Howard	38
31	Sam Houston St.	24
31	Prairie View	10
31	Southern-B.R.	47
41	Jacksonville St.	36
28	Mississippi Val.	20
21	Troy St.	63
31	Jackson St.	22
347		**350**

Nickname: Braves.
Stadium: Jack Spinks (1992), 25,000 capacity. Natural turf.
Colors: Purple & Gold.
Conference: Southwestern.
SID: Derick Hackett, 601-877-6466.
AD: Cardell Jones.

ALFRED

Alfred, NY 14802 III

Coach: Jim Moretti, Alfred '72
Record: 9 Years, 54-35-2

1994 SCHEDULE

Denison ■	Sept. 3
Hartwick ■	Sept. 17
Ithaca	Sept. 24
Albany (N.Y.)	*Oct. 1
St. Lawrence	Oct. 8
Buffalo St. ■	Oct. 15
Hobart	Oct. 22
Brockport St. ■	Oct. 29
Wesley ■	Nov. 5
Catholic	Nov. 12

1993 RESULTS (4-6-0)

38	Denison	7
31	Frostburg St.	33
7	Brockport St.	14
30	Ithaca	20
16	Albany (N.Y.)	17
44	St. Lawrence	7
14	Hobart	19

14	Union (N.Y.)	30
34	Merchant Marine	28
22	LIU-C.W. Post	45
250		**220**

Nickname: Saxons.
Stadium: Merrill Field (1926), 5,000 capacity. Artificial turf.
Colors: Purple & Gold.
Conference: Division III Independent.
SID: Paul Vecchio, 607-871-2902.
AD: Hank Ford.

ALLEGHENY

Meadville, PA 16335 III

Coach: Ken O'Keefe, John Carroll '75
Record: 4 Years, 41-5-1

1994 SCHEDULE

Carnegie Mellon ■	Sept. 10
Denison	Sept. 17
Wittenberg ■	Sept. 24
Case Reserve	Oct. 1
Earlham ■	Oct. 8
Westminster (Pa.)	Oct. 15
Kenyon	Oct. 22
Wooster ■	Oct. 29
Ohio Wesleyan	Nov. 5
Oberlin ■	Nov. 12

1993 RESULTS (9-1-0)

17	Westminster (Pa.)	24
44	Wooster	3
51	Case Reserve	7
20	Carnegie Mellon	9
25	Wittenberg	14
63	Kenyon	7
48	Oberlin	7
59	Denison	7
51	Ohio Wesleyan	7
54	Earlham	6
432		**91**

III Championship

7	Mount Union	40

Nickname: Gators.
Stadium: Robertson Field (1949), 5,000 capacity. Natural turf.
Colors: Blue & Gold.
Conference: North Coast Ath. Conf.
SID: Steven Mest, 814-332-6755.
AD: Richard Creehan.

ALMA

Alma, MI 48801 III

Coach: Jim Cole, Alma '74
Record: 3 Years, 9-18-0

1994 SCHEDULE

Olivet Nazarene	Sept. 10
Elmhurst ■	Sept. 17
Franklin ■	Sept. 24
Ill. Benedictine	Oct. 1
Olivet ■	Oct. 8
Hope	Oct. 15
Kalamazoo	Oct. 22
Albion ■	Oct. 29
Adrian	Nov. 5

1993 RESULTS (2-7-0)

31	John Carroll	47
14	Franklin	35
7	Wis.-River Falls	28
16	Ill. Benedictine	28
16	Olivet	8
6	Hope	33
14	Kalamazoo	21
28	Albion	38
20	Adrian	19
152		**257**

Nickname: Scots.
Stadium: Bahlke Field (1986), 4,000 capacity. Artificial turf.
Colors: Maroon & Cream.
Conference: Michigan Inter. Ath. Assoc.

SID: Greg Baadte, 517-463-7323.
AD: Bob Eldridge.

AMERICAN INTERNATIONAL

Springfield, MA 01109 II

Coach: To be named

1994 SCHEDULE

Cheyney ■	Sept. 10
Millersville	*Sept. 17
Bloomsburg ■	Sept. 24
LIU-C.W. Post ■	Oct. 1
Ithaca ■	Oct. 8
New Haven	Oct. 15
Towson St.	Oct. 22
Southern Conn. St.	Oct. 29
Edinboro	Nov. 5
Springfield ■	Nov. 12

1993 RESULTS (3-7-0)

24	Springfield	17
10	Millersville	30
24	Bloomsburg	6
19	Southern Conn. St.	27
0	Ithaca	37
12	Wayne St. (Mich.)	27
7	Portland St.	45
10	New Haven	63
3	East Stroudsburg	42
21	Springfield	14
130		**308**

Nickname: Yellow Jackets.
Stadium: J. H. Miller Field (1964), 5,000 capacity. Natural turf.
Colors: Gold & White.
Conference: Division II Independent.
SID: Frank Polera, 413-747-6344.
AD: Robert E. Burke.

AMHERST

Amherst, MA 01002 III

Coach: Jack Siedlecki, Union (N.Y.) '74
Record: 6 Years, 39-15-1

1994 SCHEDULE

Bates ■	Sept. 24
Bowdoin	Oct. 1
Middlebury	Oct. 8
Colby ■	Oct. 15
Wesleyan	Oct. 22
Tufts ■	Oct. 29
Trinity (Conn.)	Nov. 5
Williams ■	Nov. 12

1993 RESULTS (3-5-0)

6	Hamilton	0
21	Bowdoin	0
6	Middlebury	10
0	Colby	21
6	Wesleyan	24
23	Tufts	21
19	Trinity (Conn.)	36
2	Williams	31
83		**143**

Nickname: Lord Jeffs.
Stadium: Pratt Field (1891), 8,000 capacity. Natural turf.
Colors: Purple & White.
Conference: NESCAC.
SID: Kirstin Thorne, 413-542-2321.
AD: Peter Gooding.

ANDERSON

Anderson, IN 46012 III

Coach: Mike Manley, Anderson '73
Record: 12 Years, 47-67-3

1994 SCHEDULE

Mt. Senario ■	Sept. 10
Olivet	Sept. 17
Taylor ■	Sept. 24
Rose-Hulman	Oct. 1

Franklin ■ ....Oct. 8
Hanover ....Oct. 15
Campbellsville ■ ....Oct. 22
Wabash [Indianapolis, Ind.] ....*Oct. 29
DePauw..Nov. 5
Manchester ■ ....Nov. 12

1993 RESULTS (10-0-0)

31	Aurora	12
52	Carthage	28
41	Geneva	7
21	Franklin	13
28	Hanover	21
42	Manchester	6
48	Wabash	34
35	DePauw	3
28	Rose-Hulman	21
27	Taylor	20
353		**165**

III Championship

21	Albion	41

Nickname: Ravens.
Stadium: Macholtz, 4,200 capacity. Natural turf.
Colors: Orange & Black.
Conference: Indiana Collegiate Ath. Conf.
SID: Jim Hazen, 317-641-4479.
AD: A. Barrett Bates.

ANGELO STATE

San Angelo, TX 76909 II

Coach: Jerry Vandergriff, Corpus Christi '64
Record: 12 Years, 84-45-1

1994 SCHEDULE

North Dak. St. ....*Sept. 3
Portland St. ■ ....*Sept. 10
Sam Houston St. ....*Sept. 17
Fort Lewis ....*Sept. 24
Tarleton St. ■ ....*Oct. 1
Eastern N. Mex. ■ ....*Oct. 8
Abilene Christian ....Oct. 15
Central Okla. ■ ....*Oct. 22
East Tex. St. ....Nov. 5
Tex. A&M-Kingsville ■ ....Nov. 12

1993 RESULTS (7-3-0)

7	Portland St.	45
18	Southern Utah	16
41	N.M. Highlands	10
26	Southern Ark.	16
69	Fort Lewis	0
28	Eastern N. Mex.	0
45	Abilene Christian	20
24	Central Okla.	28
31	East Tex. St.	8
7	Tex. A&M-Kingsville	16
296		**159**

Nickname: Rams.
Stadium: San Angelo (1962), 17,500 capacity. Natural turf.
Colors: Blue & Gold.
Conference: Lone Star Conf.
SID: Sean Johnson, 915-942-2248.
AD: Jerry Vandergriff.

APPALACHIAN STATE

Boone, NC 28608 ....I-AA

Coach: Jerry Moore, Baylor '61
Record: 12 Years, 61-72-2

1994 SCHEDULE

Wake Forest...*Sept. 10
North Caro. A&T ■ ....Sept. 17
Citadel ■ ....Sept. 24
East Tenn. St. ....*Oct. 1
Furman ■ ....Oct. 8
Ga. Southern ....*Oct. 15
Marshall ■ ....Oct. 22
Tenn.-Chatt. ....Oct. 29
Liberty ....Nov. 5
Western Caro. ....Nov. 12
Va. Military ■ ....Nov. 19

1993 RESULTS (4-7-0)

10	North Caro. A&T	22
14	Liberty	20
3	Wake Forest	20
14	Citadel	27
20	East Tenn. St.	16
21	Furman	27
28	Ga. Southern	34
3	Marshall	35
39	Tenn.-Chatt.	14
20	Western Caro.	16
35	Va. Military	21
207		**252**

Nickname: Mountaineers.
Stadium: Kidd Brewer (1962), 18,000 capacity. Artificial turf.
Colors: Black & Gold.
Conference: Southern Conf.
SID: Rick Covington, 704-262-3080.
AD: Roachel Laney.

ARIZONA

Tucson, AZ 85721 ....I-A

Coach: Dick Tomey, DePauw '61
Record: 17 Years, 109-77-7

1994 SCHEDULE

Georgia Tech ....*Sept. 1
New Mexico St. ■ ....*Sept. 10
Stanford ....Sept. 24
Oregon St. ■ ....*Oct. 1
Colorado St. ■ ....*Oct. 8
Washington St. ....Oct. 15
UCLA ■ ....*Oct. 22
Oregon ....Oct. 29
California ■ ....*Nov. 5
Southern Cal...Nov. 12
Arizona St. ■ ....*Nov. 25

1993 RESULTS (9-2-0)

24	UTEP	6
16	Pacific (Cal.)	13
16	Illinois	14
33	Oregon St.	0
38	Southern Cal	7
27	Stanford	24
9	Washington St.	6
17	UCLA	37
31	Oregon	10
20	California	24
34	Arizona St.	20
265		**161**

Fiesta Bowl

29	Miami (Fla.)	0

Nickname: Wildcats.
Stadium: Arizona (1928), 56,167 capacity. Natural turf.
Colors: Cardinal & Navy.
Conference: Pacific-10.
SID: Butch Henry, 602-621-4163.
AD: Jim Livengood.

ARIZONA STATE

Tempe, AZ 85287 ....I-A

Coach: Bruce Snyder, Oregon '63
Record: 14 Years, 78-72-6

1994 SCHEDULE

Oregon St. ■ ....*Sept. 3
Miami (Fla.) ■ ....*Sept. 10
Louisville ■ ....*Sept. 17
California ....Sept. 24
Stanford ■ ....*Oct. 8
Washington ....Oct. 15
Washington St. ■ ....*Oct. 22
Brigham Young ....Oct. 29
Oregon ....Nov. 5
UCLA ■ ....*Nov. 12
Arizona ....*Nov. 25

1993 RESULTS (6-5-0)

38	Utah	0
17	Louisville	35

12	Oklahoma St.	10
14	Oregon St.	30
25	Washington St.	44
36	Oregon	45
38	Stanford	30
32	Washington	17
41	California	0
9	UCLA	3
20	Arizona	34
282		**248**

Nickname: Sun Devils.
Stadium: Sun Devil (1959), 73,656 capacity. Natural turf.
Colors: Maroon & Gold.
Conference: Pacific-10.
SID: Mark Brand, 602-965-6592.
AD: Charles S. Harris.

ARKANSAS

Fayetteville, AR 72701 ....I-A

Coach: Danny Ford, Alabama '70
Record: 13 Years, 101-34-5

1994 SCHEDULE

Southern Methodist ■ ....Sept. 3
South Caro..*Sept. 10
Alabama ■ ....Sept. 17
Memphis ....*Sept. 24
Vanderbilt ■ ....Oct. 1
Tennessee ....Oct. 8
Mississippi ■ ....Oct. 15
Auburn ....Oct. 29
Mississippi St. ....Nov. 5
Northern Ill. ■ ....Nov. 12
Louisiana St. ■ ....Nov. 26

1993 RESULTS (5-5-1)

10	Southern Methodist	6
18	South Caro.	17
3	Alabama	43
0	Memphis	6
20	Georgia	10
14	Tennessee	28
0	Mississippi	19
21	Auburn	31
13	Mississippi St.	13
24	Tulsa	11
42	Louisiana St.	24
165		**208**

Nickname: Razorbacks.
Stadium: Razorback (1938), 51,000 capacity. Artificial turf.
Colors: Cardinal & White.
Conference: Southeastern Conf.
SID: Rick Schaeffer, 501-575-2751.
AD: Frank Broyles.

ARKANSAS STATE

State University, AR 72467 ....I-A

Coach: John Bobo, Maryville (Tenn.) '80
Record: 1 Year, 2-8-1

1994 SCHEDULE

Virginia Tech ....*Sept. 3
Nevada ....Sept. 10
Southern Ill. ■ ....*Sept. 17
New Mexico St..*Sept. 24
Mississippi ■ ....*Oct. 1
Southwestern La. ....Oct. 8
Memphis ....*Oct. 15
Pacific (Cal.) ■ ....*Oct. 22
Northern Ill. ■ ....Nov. 5
Colorado St. ....Nov. 12
Louisiana Tech ■ ....Nov. 19

1993 RESULTS (2-8-1)

6	Florida	44
19	New Mexico St.	22
7	Northern Ill.	23
27	Southern Ill.	6
3	Louisiana Tech	17
3	Memphis	45
3	Southwestern La.	19
15	Mississippi St.	15

10	Northeast La.	42
6	Pacific (Cal.)	20
23	Nevada	21
122		**274**

Nickname: Indians.
Stadium: Indian (1974), 33,410 capacity. Natural turf.
Colors: Scarlet & Black.
Conference: Big West.
SID: Gina Bowman, 501-972-2541.
AD: Brad Hovious.

ARMY
West Point, NY 10996 .... I-A

Coach: Bob Sutton, Eastern Mich. '74
Record: 3 Years, 15-18-0

1994 SCHEDULE

Holy Cross ■	Sept. 10
Duke	Sept. 15
Temple ■	Sept. 24
Wake Forest	Oct. 1
Rutgers [East Rutherford, N.J.]	Oct. 8
Louisville ■	Oct. 15
Citadel ■	Oct. 22
Boston College ■	Oct. 29
Air Force ■	Nov. 5
Boston U. ■	Nov. 12
Navy [Philadelphia, Pa.]	Dec. 3

1993 RESULTS (6-5-0)

30	Colgate	0
21	Duke	42
31	Va. Military	9
35	Akron	14
56	Temple	21
38	Rutgers	45
14	Boston College	41
7	Western Mich.	20
6	Air Force	25
35	Lafayette	12
16	Navy	14
289		**243**

Nickname: Cadets, Black Knights.
Stadium: Michie (1924), 39,929 capacity. Artificial turf.
Colors: Black, Gold, Gray.
Conference: I-A Independent.
SID: Robert Kinney, 914-938-3303.
AD: Al Vanderbush.

ASHLAND
Ashland, OH 44805 II

Coach: Gary Keller, Bluffton '73
(First year as head coach)

1994 SCHEDULE

Ferris St. ■	Sept. 10
Michigan Tech	Sept. 17
Grand Valley St. ■	Sept. 24
Northwood	Oct. 1
Hillsdale ■	Oct. 8
Saginaw Valley	Oct. 15
Wayne St. (Mich.) ■	Oct. 22
St. Joseph's (Ind.)	Oct. 29
Northern Mich. ■	Nov. 5
St. Francis (Ill.)	Nov. 12

1993 RESULTS (9-2-0)

13	St. Francis (Ill.)	16
6	Ferris St.	20
30	Slippery Rock	9
20	Hillsdale	18
12	Wayne St. (Mich.)	0
20	Saginaw Valley	6
12	St. Joseph's (Ind.)	0
29	Grand Valley St.	14
50	Northwood	0
27	Indianapolis	0
33	Northern Mich.	26
252		**109**

Nickname: Eagles.
Stadium: Community (1963), 5,700 capacity. Natural turf.
Colors: Purple & Gold.

Conference: Midwest Intercollegiate.
SID: Al King, 419-289-5442.
AD: Alan Platt.

ASSUMPTION
Worcester, MA 01615 II

Coach: Bernie Gaughan, Tampa '61
Record: 6 Years, 19-33-1

1994 SCHEDULE

Stonehill	Sept. 10
MIT ■	Sept. 17
Pace	Sept. 24
Nichols	Oct. 1
Mass.-Lowell ■	Oct. 8
Sacred Heart ■	Oct. 15
Curry ■	Oct. 22
Bentley	Oct. 29
Western New Eng.	Nov. 5
Salve Regina ■	Nov. 12

1993 RESULTS (6-4-0)

24	Siena	6
12	MIT	10
14	Stonehill	29
27	Nichols	0
20	Bentley	33
6	Sacred Heart	35
51	Curry	28
18	St. Peter's	13
33	Mass.-Lowell	36
30	Western New Eng.	18
235		**208**

Nickname: Greyhounds.
Stadium: Rocheleau Field (1961), 1,200 capacity. Natural turf.
Colors: Royal Blue & White.
Conference: Eastern Collegiate.
SID: Steve Morris, 508-752-5615.
AD: Rita Castagna.

AUBURN
Auburn, AL 36830 .... I-A

Coach: Terry Bowden, West Va. '78
Record: 10 Years, 75-36-1

1994 SCHEDULE

Mississippi	*Sept. 3
Northeast La. ■	*Sept. 10
Louisiana St. ■	*Sept. 17
East Tenn. St. ■	Sept. 24
Kentucky ■	*Sept. 29
Mississippi St.	*Oct. 8
Florida	Oct. 15
Arkansas	Oct. 29
East Caro. ■	Nov. 5
Georgia ■	Nov. 12
Alabama	Nov. 19

1993 RESULTS (11-0-0)

16	Mississippi	12
35	Samford	7
34	Louisiana St.	10
35	Southern Miss.	24
14	Vanderbilt	10
31	Mississippi St.	17
38	Florida	35
31	Arkansas	21
55	New Mexico St.	14
42	Georgia	28
22	Alabama	14
353		**192**

Nickname: Tigers.
Stadium: Jordan-Hare (1939), 85,214 capacity. Natural turf.
Colors: Burnt Orange & Navy Blue.
Conference: Southeastern Conf.
SID: Kent Partridge, 205-844-4750.
AD: David Housel.

AUGSBURG
Minneapolis, MN 55454 III

Coach: Jack Osberg, Augsburg '62
Record: 3 Years, 10-19-0

1994 SCHEDULE

Huron ■	Sept. 10
Concordia-M'head	Sept. 17
St. John's (Minn.) ■	*Sept. 24
Bethel (Minn.)	Oct. 1
Macalester ■	Oct. 8
Hamline ■	Oct. 15
St. Thomas (Minn.)	Oct. 22
Gust. Adolphus ■	Oct. 29
Carleton	Nov. 5
St. Olaf [Minneapolis, Minn.]	Nov. 10

1993 RESULTS (5-5-0)

22	Huron	6
7	St. John's (Minn.)	54
25	Gust. Adolphus	13
9	Hamline	29
26	Bethel (Minn.)	11
6	St. Thomas (Minn.)	27
35	Macalester	7
6	Carleton	40
0	Concordia-M'head	28
26	St. Olaf	24
162		**239**

Nickname: Auggies.
Stadium: Anderson-Nelson Field (1984), 2,000 capacity. Artificial turf.
Colors: Maroon & Gray.
Conference: Minnesota Inter. Ath. Conf.
SID: Gene McGivern, 612-330-1677.
AD: Paul Grauer.

AUGUSTANA (ILLINOIS)
Rock Island, IL 61201 III

Coach: Bob Reade, Cornell College '54
Record: 15 Years, 138-21-1

1994 SCHEDULE

Wis.-Platteville ■	Sept. 10
Adrian ■	Sept. 24
Ill. Wesleyan	Oct. 1
North Central	*Oct. 8
North Park ■	Oct. 15
Elmhurst ■	Oct. 22
Millikin	Oct. 29
Wheaton (Ill.) ■	Nov. 5
Carthage	Nov. 12

1993 RESULTS (7-2-0)

14	Loras	24
48	Drake	54
21	North Park	17
59	North Central	14
10	Ill. Wesleyan	7
46	Elmhurst	13
54	Millikin	30
48	Carthage	0
14	Wheaton (Ill.)	6
314		**165**

Nickname: Vikings.
Stadium: Ericson Field (1939), 3,500 capacity. Natural turf.
Colors: Gold & Blue.
Conference: College Conf. of Ill. & Wis.
SID: Dave Wrath, 309-794-7265.
AD: John Farwell.

AUGUSTANA (SOUTH DAKOTA)
Sioux Falls, SD 57197 II

Coach: Dennis Moller, South Dak. St. '63
Record: 1 Year, 4-7-0

1994 SCHEDULE

Winona St.	*Sept. 3
Northern Colo. ■	Sept. 17
Mankato St.	Sept. 24
South Dak. ■	Oct. 1
St. Cloud St. ■	Oct. 8
North Dak.	Oct. 15
Morningside	Oct. 22
South Dak. St. ■	Oct. 29

Nebraska-Omaha ■ ....Nov. 5
North Dak. St. ....*Nov. 12

1993 RESULTS (4-7-0)

14	Neb.-Kearney	30
35	Gust. Adolphus	0
0	Northern Colo.	24
34	Mankato St.	37
14	South Dak.	28
20	St. Cloud St.	28
20	North Dak.	7
14	Morningside	13
25	South Dak. St.	35
35	Nebraska-Omaha	14
14	North Dak. St.	31
225		**247**

Nickname: Vikings.
Stadium: Howard Wood (1957), 10,000 capacity.
Natural turf.
Colors: Blue & Yellow.
Conference: North Central Conf.
SID: Andy Ludwig, 605-336-4311.
AD: Bill Gross.

AURORA

Aurora, IL 60506 III

Coach: Jim Scott, Luther '61
Record: 8 Years, 43-25-1

1994 SCHEDULE

Albion	Sept. 10
Wheaton (Ill.)	Sept. 17
Drake ■	Sept. 24
Hope ■	Oct. 1
Olivet Nazarene	Oct. 8
Ill. Benedictine ■	Oct. 22
Trinity (Ill.) ■	Oct. 29
Valparaiso	Nov. 5
Evansville	Nov. 12

1993 RESULTS (4-5-0)

12	Anderson	31
21	Trinity (Ill.)	35
35	Elmhurst	21
14	Drake	47
28	Olivet Nazarene	21
27	MacMurray	0
14	Ill. Benedictine	19
28	Chicago	7
7	Wartburg	27
186		**208**

Nickname: Spartans.
Stadium: Aurora Field, 1,500 capacity. Natural turf.
Colors: Royal Blue & White.
Conference: Division III Independent.
SID: Dave Beyer, 708-844-5479.
AD: To be named.

AUSTIN PEAY STATE

Clarksville, TN 37044 ....I-AA

Coach: Roy Gregory, Tenn.-Chatt. '68
Record: 3 Years, 9-24-0

1994 SCHEDULE

Ky. Wesleyan ■	*Sept. 1
Western Ky.	*Sept. 17
Eastern Ky. ■	*Sept. 24
Tennessee Tech	Oct. 1
Murray St. ■	*Oct. 8
Tennessee St.	*Oct. 15
Morehead St. ■	Oct. 22
Southeast Mo. St.	Oct. 29
Middle Tenn. St. ■	Nov. 5
Samford	Nov. 12
Tenn.-Martin	Nov. 19

1993 RESULTS (1-10-0)

10	Cincinnati	42
28	Knoxville	19
27	Western Ky.	28
7	Eastern Ky.	48
17	Tennessee Tech	35
14	Murray St.	38
16	Tennessee St.	21

10	Morehead St.	23
7	Southeast Mo. St.	17
10	Middle Tenn. St.	44
33	Tenn.-Martin	39
179		**354**

Nickname: Governors.
Stadium: Governors (1946), 10,000 capacity. Artificial
turf.
Colors: Red & White.
Conference: Ohio Valley Conf.
SID: Brad Kirtley, 615-648-7561.
AD: Kaye Hart.

BALDWIN-WALLACE

Berea, OH 44017 III

Coach: Bob Packard, Baldwin-Wallace '65
Record: 13 Years, 102-28-2

1994 SCHEDULE

Moravian ■	Sept. 10
Heidelberg ■	*Sept. 17
Marietta ■	*Sept. 24
Otterbein ■	*Oct. 1
Muskingum ■	Oct. 8
Mount Union	Oct. 15
Hiram	Oct. 22
Capital ■	Oct. 29
Ohio Northern	Nov. 5
John Carroll ■	Nov. 12

1993 RESULTS (9-1-0)

25	Moravian	13
45	Hiram	13
28	Muskingum	0
7	Mount Union	35
56	Otterbein	10
17	Capital	0
31	Marietta	9
17	Heidelberg	6
62	Ohio Northern	19
28	John Carroll	13
316		**118**

Nickname: Yellow Jackets.
Stadium: George Finnie (1971), 8,100 capacity.
Artificial turf.
Colors: Brown & Gold.
Conference: Ohio Ath. Conf.
SID: Kevin Ruple, 216-826-2327.
AD: Steve Bankson.

BALL STATE

Muncie, IN 47306 ....I-A

Coach: Paul Schudel, Miami (Ohio) '66
Record: 9 Years, 55-43-3

1994 SCHEDULE

West Va.	Sept. 3
Purdue	Sept. 17
Ohio ■	Sept. 24
Central Mich. ■	Oct. 1
Toledo	*Oct. 8
Western Mich. ■	Oct. 15
Bowling Green	Oct. 22
Eastern Mich. ■	Oct. 29
Miami (Ohio)	Nov. 5
Akron ■	Nov. 12
Kent	Nov. 19

1993 RESULTS (8-2-1)

12	Syracuse	35
45	Illinois St.	30
24	Ohio	16
20	Central Mich.	17
31	Toledo	30
12	Cincinnati	44
26	Bowling Green	26
18	Eastern Mich.	13
21	Miami (Ohio)	0
31	Akron	9
28	Kent	3
268		**223**

Las Vegas Bowl

33	Utah St.	42

Nickname: Cardinals.
Stadium: Ball State (1967), 16,319 capacity. Natural
turf.
Colors: Cardinal & White.
Conference: Mid-American Conf.
SID: Joe Hernandez, 317-285-8242.
AD: Don Purvis.

BATES

Lewiston, ME 04240 III

Coach: Rick Pardy, Ithaca '83
Record: 5 Years, 17-25-2

1994 SCHEDULE

Amherst	Sept. 24
Tufts	Oct. 1
Williams ■	Oct. 8
Wesleyan ■	Oct. 15
Middlebury	Oct. 22
Colby ■	Oct. 29
Bowdoin	Nov. 5
Hamilton ■	Nov. 12

1993 RESULTS (0-8-0)

0	Trinity (Conn.)	71
14	Tufts	35
0	Williams	38
14	Wesleyan	31
16	Middlebury	33
14	Colby	53
6	Bowdoin	34
7	Hamilton	35
71		**330**

Nickname: Bobcats.
Stadium: Garcelon Field (1900), 3,000 capacity.
Natural turf.
Colors: Garnet.
Conference: NESCAC.
SID: Anne E. Whittemore, 207-786-6330.
AD: Suzanne Coffey.

BAYLOR

Waco, TX 76706 ....I-A

Coach: Chuck Reedy, Appalachian St. '71
Record: 1 Year, 5-6-0

1994 SCHEDULE

Louisiana Tech ■	*Sept. 3
San Jose St.	*Sept. 10
Oklahoma St. ■	*Sept. 17
Southern Cal	Sept. 24
Texas Christian	*Oct. 1
Southern Methodist ■	Oct. 8
Texas A&M	Oct. 15
Texas Tech	Oct. 22
Houston ■	Oct. 29
Rice	Nov. 12
Texas ■	Nov. 24

1993 RESULTS (5-6-0)

42	Fresno St.	39
21	Colorado	45
28	Utah St.	24
28	Texas Tech	26
3	Houston	24
31	Southern Methodist	12
17	Texas A&M	34
13	Texas Christian	38
27	Georgia Tech	37
38	Rice	14
17	Texas	38
265		**331**

Nickname: Bears.
Stadium: Floyd Casey (1950), 48,500 capacity.
Artificial turf.
Colors: Green & Gold.
Conference: Southwest Conf.
SID: Maxey Parrish, 817-755-1234.
AD: Dick Ellis.

SCHEDULES/RESULTS

BELOIT

Beloit, WI 53511 III

Coach: Ed DeGeorge, Colorado Col. '64
Record: 17 Years, 79-75-1

1994 SCHEDULE

Knox ■	....	Sept. 10
Cornell College	....	Sept. 17
Illinois Col.	....	Sept. 24
Monmouth (Ill.) ■	....	Oct. 1
Ripon ■	....	Oct. 8
Carroll (Wis.)	....	Oct. 15
Lawrence ■	....	Oct. 22
St. Norbert	....	Oct. 29
Lake Forest ■	....	Nov. 5

1993 RESULTS (3-6-0)

7	Concordia (Wis.)	19
9	Cornell College	13
0	Knox	3
6	Coe	41
14	Ripon	40
29	Carroll (Wis.)	28
27	Lawrence	18
14	St. Norbert	7
21	Lake Forest	28
127		**197**

Nickname: Buccaneers.
Stadium: Strong (1933), 3,500 capacity. Natural turf.
Colors: Gold & Blue.
Conference: Midwest Conf.
SID: Paul Erickson, 608-363-2229.
AD: Ed DeGeorge.

BEMIDJI STATE

Bemidji, MN 56601 II

Coach: Kris Diaz, Baldwin-Wallace '78
Record: 5 Years, 9-40-0

1994 SCHEDULE

North Dak.	....	Sept. 10
Wis.-Stout ■	....	*Sept. 17
Minn.-Duluth ■	....	*Sept. 24
Southwest St.	....	Oct. 1
Moorhead St. ■	....	Oct. 8
Winona St.	....	Oct. 15
Minn.-Morris ■	....	Oct. 22
Northern St.	....	Oct. 29
Wayne St. (Neb.) ■	....	Nov. 5

1993 RESULTS (0-10-0)

3	South Dak.	42
7	Wayne St. (Neb.)	59
23	Michigan Tech	52
0	Minn.-Duluth	20
8	Southwest St.	35
16	Moorhead St.	36
3	Winona St.	51
7	Minn.-Morris	21
20	Northern St.	35
3	Neb.-Kearney	28
90		**379**

Nickname: Beavers.
Stadium: BSU (1937), 4,000 capacity. Natural turf.
Colors: Kelly Green & White.
Conference: Northern Sun Inter. Conf.
SID: Jeff Swanson, 218-755-2763.
AD: Bob Peters.

BENTLEY

Waltham, MA 02154 II

Coach: Peter Yetten, Boston U. '71
Record: 6 Years, 38-13-1

1994 SCHEDULE

Mass.-Lowell	....	*Sept. 10
Mass. Maritime ■	....	*Sept. 16
Nichols ■	....	*Sept. 23
Curry ■	....	Oct. 1
Sacred Heart	....	Oct. 8
Siena	....	Oct. 15
Western New Eng.	....	Oct. 22
Assumption ■	....	Oct. 29
MIT ■	....	Nov. 5
Stonehill	....	Nov. 12

1993 RESULTS (10-0-0)

21	Mass.-Lowell	10
21	Mass. Maritime	12
45	Nichols	0
40	Curry	17
33	Assumption	20
47	Siena	14
34	Western New Eng.	7
30	Sacred Heart	0
22	MIT	3
27	Stonehill	26
320		**109**

Nickname: Falcons.
Stadium: Bentley Athletic Field (1990), 1,500 capacity.
 Natural turf.
Colors: Blue & Gold.
Conference: Eastern Collegiate.
SID: Dick Lipe, 617-891-2334.
AD: Bob DeFelice.

BETHANY (WEST VIRGINIA)

Bethany, WV 26032 III

Coach: Steve Campos, Indiana (Pa.) '82
Record: 1 Year, 4-4-1

1994 SCHEDULE

Malone	....	Sept. 10
St. Francis (Pa.)	....	Sept. 24
Wash. & Jeff. ■	....	Oct. 1
Thiel ■	....	Oct. 8
Grove City ■	....	Oct. 15
Waynesburg	....	Oct. 22
Gallaudet	....	Oct. 29
Robert Morris	....	Nov. 5
Gannon ■	....	Nov. 12

1993 RESULTS (4-4-1)

23	Malone	23
10	Capital	13
10	Duquesne	13
9	Wash. & Jeff.	34
10	Thiel	7
19	Grove City	23
28	Waynesburg	13
23	Gannon	20
13	Clinch Valley	7
145		**153**

Nickname: Bison.
Stadium: Bethany Field (1938), 1,000 capacity. Natural
 turf.
Colors: Green & White.
Conference: Presidents Ath. Conf.
SID: To be named, 304-829-7231.
AD: Wally Neel.

BETHEL (MINNESOTA)

St. Paul, MN 55112 III

Coach: Steve Johnson, Bethel (Minn.) '80
Record: 5 Years, 23-25-1

1994 SCHEDULE

Lake Forest ■	....	Sept. 10
St. John's (Minn.)	....	Sept. 17
Macalester ■	....	Sept. 24
Augsburg ■	....	Oct. 1
Hamline	....	Oct. 8
St. Thomas (Minn.) ■	....	Oct. 15
Gust. Adolphus	....	Oct. 22
Carleton ■	....	Oct. 29
St. Olaf	....	Nov. 5
Concordia-M'head [Minneapolis, Minn.]	....	Nov. 11

1993 RESULTS (2-8-0)

28	Central (Iowa)	38
31	Macalester	14
22	Carleton	25
15	Concordia-M'head	19
11	Augsburg	26
12	St. John's (Minn.)	77
14	Gust. Adolphus	26
3	Hamline	28
17	St. Olaf	15
41	St. Thomas (Minn.)	42
194		**310**

Nickname: Royals.
Stadium: Bremer Field, 3,000 capacity. Natural turf.
Colors: Royal Blue & Gold.
Conference: Minnesota Inter. Ath. Conf.
SID: Leland Christenson, 612-638-6394.
AD: Dave Klostreich.

BETHUNE-COOKMAN

Daytona Beach, FL 32015 ....I-AA

Coach: Jack McClairen, Bethune-Cookman '53
Record: 12 Years, 61-37-3

1994 SCHEDULE

Johnson Smith ■	....	Sept. 3
Morgan St.	....	Sept. 10
Central Fla.	....	Sept. 17
N.C. Central ■	....	Sept. 24
Delaware St. ■	....	Oct. 1
Howard	....	Oct. 8
South Caro. St.	....	Oct. 15
Albany St. (Ga.) ■	....	Oct. 22
North Caro. A&T	....	Oct. 29
Knoxville ■	....	Nov. 5
Florida A&M [Tampa, Fla.]	....	Nov. 26

1993 RESULTS (3-8-0)

31	Knoxville	33
41	Morgan St.	17
30	Johnson Smith	7
10	Samford	27
26	Delaware St.	55
7	Howard	21
27	South Caro. St.	40
14	Central Fla.	34
14	North Caro. A&T	29
33	Norfolk St.	31
22	Florida A&M	27
255		**321**

Nickname: Wildcats.
Stadium: Municipal, 10,000 capacity. Natural turf.
Colors: Maroon & Gold.
Conference: Mid-Eastern.
SID: W. Earl Kitchings, 904-255-1401.
AD: Lynn Thompson.

BLACKBURN

Carlinville, IL 62626 III

Coach: Dale Sprague, American Int'l '76
Record: 8 Years, 28-42-2

1994 SCHEDULE

Eureka ■	....	Sept. 3
N'western (Wis.)	....	Sept. 10
Illinois Col.	....	Sept. 17
Ky. Wesleyan ■	....	Oct. 1
MacMurray ■	....	Oct. 8
Principia	....	Oct. 22
Sue Bennett	....	Oct. 29
Maranatha ■	....	Nov. 5
Concordia (Ill.) ■	....	Nov. 12

1993 RESULTS (3-6-0)

6	Chicago	43
15	Maranatha	14
0	Illinois Col.	27
14	North Park	31
7	Ky. Wesleyan	49
21	Principia	22
3	MacMurray	10
22	Crown	0
19	Concordia (Ill.)	13
107		**209**

Nickname: Beavers.
Stadium: Blackburn College, 1,500 capacity. Natural
 turf.
Colors: Scarlet & Black.
Conference: Division III Independent.
SID: Karen Trader, 217-854-3231.
AD: Ira Zeff.

BLOOMSBURG

Bloomsburg, PA 17815 II

Coach: Danny Hale, West Chester '68
Record: 6 Years, 45-19-0

1994 SCHEDULE

New Haven ■	Sept. 1
Shippensburg	Sept. 10
Calif. (Pa.) ■	Sept. 17
American Int'l	Sept. 24
Mansfield ■	Oct. 1
Millersville	*Oct. 8
Lock Haven ■	Oct. 15
Kutztown ■	Oct. 22
West Chester	Oct. 29
East Stroudsburg ■	Nov. 5
Cheyney	Nov. 12

1993 RESULTS (5-6-0)

16	Bucknell	21
7	Shippensburg	30
35	Lock Haven	32
6	American Int'l	24
0	Millersville	26
18	Clarion	40
47	Kutztown	25
38	West Chester	16
6	East Stroudsburg	31
24	Cheyney	6
17	Mansfield	7
214		**258**

Nickname: Huskies.
Stadium: Redman (1974), 5,000 capacity. Natural turf.
Colors: Maroon & Gold.
Conference: Pennsylvania Conf.
SID: Jim Hollister, 717-389-4413.
AD: Mary Gardner.

BLUFFTON

Bluffton, OH 45817 III

Coach: Carlin Carpenter, Defiance '64
Record: 15 Years, 58-79-1

1994 SCHEDULE

Ohio Northern	*Sept. 10
Grove City	Sept. 17
Manchester ■	Sept. 24
Thiel ■	Oct. 1
Malone ■	Oct. 8
Urbana	Oct. 15
Mt. St. Joseph	Oct. 22
Wilmington (Ohio) ■	Oct. 29
Defiance ■	Nov. 5
Thomas More	Nov. 12

1993 RESULTS (3-7-0)

7	Ohio Northern	26
23	Hanover	33
17	Malone	9
13	Grove City	24
0	Manchester	27
21	Urbana	15
16	Mt. St. Joseph	14
14	Wilmington (Ohio)	49
14	Defiance	59
0	Thomas More	45
125		**301**

Nickname: Beavers.
Stadium: Salzman (1993), 3,000 capacity. Natural turf.
Colors: Purple & White.
Conference: Mideast Conf.
SID: Ron Geiser, 419-358-3241.
AD: Carlin Carpenter.

BOISE STATE

Boise, ID 83725 ....I-AA

Coach: Pokey Allen, Utah '65
Record: 8 Years, 65-34-2

1994 SCHEDULE

Northeastern ■	*Sept. 3
Cal St. Northridge ■	*Sept. 10
Nevada ■	*Sept. 17
Liberty ■	*Sept. 24
Northern Ariz.	*Oct. 1
Weber St. ■	*Oct. 8
Idaho St.	*Oct. 15
Montana St.	Oct. 22
Montana ■	Nov. 5
Eastern Wash.	Nov. 12
Idaho ■	Nov. 19

1993 RESULTS (3-8-0)

31	Rhode Island	10
10	Nevada	38
27	Northeastern	13
7	Stephen F. Austin	30
24	Montana	38
9	Northern Ariz.	23
14	Weber St.	21
34	Idaho St.	27
21	Montana St.	42
17	Eastern Wash.	28
16	Idaho	49
210		**319**

Nickname: Broncos.
Stadium: Bronco (1970), 22,600 capacity. Artificial turf.
Colors: Orange & Blue.
Conference: Big Sky Conf.
SID: Max Corbet, 208-385-1515.
AD: Gene Bleymaier.

BOSTON COLLEGE

Chestnut Hill, MA 02167 ....I-A

Coach: Dan Henning, William & Mary '64
(First year as head coach)

1994 SCHEDULE

Michigan	Sept. 3
Virginia Tech ■	Sept. 17
Pittsburgh	Sept. 24
Notre Dame ■	Oct. 8
Temple ■	Oct. 15
Rutgers ■	Oct. 22
Army	Oct. 29
Louisville	*Nov. 3
Syracuse ■	Nov. 12
West Va. ■	Nov. 19
Miami (Fla.)	Nov. 26

1993 RESULTS (8-3-0)

7	Miami (Fla.)	23
21	Northwestern	22
66	Temple	14
33	Syracuse	29
31	Rutgers	21
41	Army	14
42	Tulane	14
48	Virginia Tech	34
33	Pittsburgh	0
41	Notre Dame	39
14	West Va.	17
377		**227**

Carquest Bowl

31	Virginia	13

Nickname: Eagles.
Stadium: Alumni (1957), 44,500 capacity. Artificial turf.
Colors: Maroon & Gold.
Conference: Big East Conference.
SID: Reid Oslin, 617-552-3004.
AD: Chet Gladchuk.

BOSTON U.

Boston, MA 02215 ....I-AA

Coach: Dan Allen, Hanover '78
Record: 4 Years, 24-22-0

1994 SCHEDULE

Colgate	Sept. 10
Maine	Sept. 17
Villanova	Sept. 24
James Madison ■	Oct. 1
Rhode Island	Oct. 8
Northeastern ■	Oct. 15
Richmond ■	Oct. 22
Massachusetts	Oct. 29
Connecticut ■	Nov. 5
Army	Nov. 12
New Hampshire ■	Nov. 19

1993 RESULTS (11-0-0)

45	Maine	0
44	Holy Cross	18
28	Massachusetts	9
30	Villanova	15
17	Northeastern	14
44	Richmond	14
48	Rhode Island	15
24	New Hampshire	14
61	Buffalo	33
30	Connecticut	16
24	James Madison	21
395		**169**

I-AA Championship

27	Northern Iowa	21
14	Idaho	21

Nickname: Terriers.
Stadium: Nickerson Field (1930), 17,369 capacity. Artificial turf.
Colors: Scarlet & White.
Conference: Yankee.
SID: Ed Carpenter, 617-353-2872.
AD: Gary Strickler.

BOWDOIN

Brunswick, ME 04011 III

Coach: Howard Vandersea, Bates '63
Record: 17 Years, 69-78-2

1994 SCHEDULE

Williams	Sept. 24
Amherst ■	Oct. 1
Tufts ■	Oct. 8
Hamilton	Oct. 15
Trinity (Conn.) ■	Oct. 22
Wesleyan	Oct. 29
Bates ■	Nov. 5
Colby	Nov. 12

1993 RESULTS (3-4-1)

0	Middlebury	19
0	Amherst	21
24	Tufts	20
42	Hamilton	8
7	Trinity (Conn.)	63
25	Wesleyan	28
34	Bates	6
21	Colby	21
153		**186**

Nickname: Polar Bears.
Stadium: Whittier Field (1896), 6,000 capacity. Natural turf.
Colors: White.
Conference: NESCAC.
SID: To be named, 207-725-3254.
AD: Sidney J. Watson.

BOWIE STATE

Bowie, MD 20715 II

Coach: Sherman Wood, Salisbury St. '84
Record: 1 Year, 3-6-1

1994 SCHEDULE

Elizabeth City St. ■	Sept. 3
West Va. Wesleyan ■	Sept. 10
Livingstone	Sept. 17
Virginia St. ■	Sept. 24
Virginia Union ■	Oct. 1
Johnson Smith	Oct. 8
Winston-Salem	Oct. 15
Fayetteville St.	Oct. 29
New Haven ■	Nov. 5
West Liberty St. ■	Nov. 12

1993 RESULTS (3-6-1)

2	N.C. Central	30
6	Hampton	35
0	Southern Conn. St.	11
7	Virginia St.	30

7	Virginia Union	7
31	Livingstone	12
2	Elizabeth City St.	16
24	Winston-Salem	13
18	Fayetteville St.	0
19	New Haven	69
116		**223**

Nickname: Bulldogs.
Stadium: Bulldog (1992), 6,000 capacity. Natural turf.
Colors: Black & Gold.
Conference: Central Inter. Ath. Assoc.
SID: Scott Rouch, 301-464-7710.
AD: Charles Guilford.

BOWLING GREEN

Bowling Green, OH 43403 ....I-A

Coach: Gary Blackney, Connecticut '67
Record: 3 Years, 27-6-2

1994 SCHEDULE

North Caro. St.	*Sept. 1
Akron	*Sept. 10
Navy	Sept. 17
Eastern Mich.	Sept. 24
Cincinnati	*Oct. 1
Ohio ■	Oct. 8
Toledo	*Oct. 15
Ball St. ■	Oct. 22
Miami (Ohio) ■	Oct. 29
Kent	Nov. 5
Central Mich.	Nov. 12

1993 RESULTS (6-3-2)

16	Virginia Tech	33
21	Cincinnati	7
20	Navy	27
17	Toledo	10
20	Ohio	0
49	Akron	7
26	Ball St.	26
30	Miami (Ohio)	25
40	Kent	7
15	Central Mich.	17
14	Western Mich.	14
268		**173**

Nickname: Falcons.
Stadium: Doyt Perry (1966), 30,599 capacity. Natural turf.
Colors: Orange & Brown.
Conference: Mid-American Conf.
SID: Steve Barr, 419-372-7076.
AD: To be named.

BRIDGEWATER (VIRGINIA)

Bridgewater, VA 22812 III

Coach: Max Lowe, Bridgewater (Va.) '76
Record: 2 Years, 5-15-0

1994 SCHEDULE

Wesley	Sept. 10
Emory & Henry	Sept. 17
Clinch Valley ■	Sept. 24
Hampden-Sydney ■	Oct. 1
Methodist ■	Oct. 8
Guilford	Oct. 15
Frostburg St.	Oct. 22
Wash. & Lee ■	Oct. 29
Randolph-Macon	Nov. 5
Davidson ■	Nov. 12

1993 RESULTS (2-8-0)

0	Wesley	31
7	Emory & Henry	28
16	Clinch Valley	7
6	Hampden-Sydney	23
14	Methodist	17
28	Guilford	25
0	Frostburg St.	35
16	Wash. & Lee	41
13	Randolph-Macon	45
14	Davidson	55
114		**307**

Nickname: Eagles.

Stadium: Jopson Field (1971), 3,000 capacity. Natural turf.
Colors: Crimson & Gold.
Conference: Old Dominion Ath. Conf.
SID: Rob Marchiony, 703-828-5360.
AD: Tom Kinder.

BRIDGEWATER STATE (MASSACHUSETTS)

Bridgewater, MA 02324 III

Coach: Peter Mazzaferro, Centre '54
Record: 30 Years, 139-119-11

1994 SCHEDULE

Frostburg St. ■	Sept. 10
Maine Maritime	Sept. 17
Mass.-Boston ■	Sept. 24
Fitchburg St.	Oct. 1
Framingham St. ■	Oct. 8
Westfield St.	Oct. 15
Plymouth St.	Oct. 22
Worcester St. ■	Oct. 29
Mass. Maritime	Nov. 5
Mass.-Dartmouth ■	Nov. 12

1993 RESULTS (5-5-0)

16	Kean	23
14	Maine Maritime	18
37	Mass.-Boston	6
49	Fitchburg St.	0
27	Framingham St.	9
22	Westfield St.	8
3	Plymouth St.	12
8	Worcester St.	16
41	Mass. Maritime	13
10	Mass.-Dartmouth	17
227		**122**

Nickname: Bears.
Stadium: College (1974), 3,000 capacity. Natural turf.
Colors: Crimson & White.
Conference: New England.
SID: Michael Storey, 617-697-1352.
AD: John C. Harper.

BRIGHAM YOUNG

Provo, UT 84602 ....I-A

Coach: LaVell Edwards, Utah St. '52
Record: 22 Years, 197-73-3

1994 SCHEDULE

Hawaii	*Sept. 3
Air Force	Sept. 10
Colorado St. ■	Sept. 17
New Mexico ■	Sept. 24
Utah St. ■	*Sept. 30
Fresno St.	*Oct. 8
Notre Dame	Oct. 15
UTEP	*Oct. 22
Arizona St. ■	Oct. 29
Northeast La.	Nov. 5
San Diego St. ■	*Nov. 10
Utah	Nov. 19

1993 RESULTS (6-5-0)

34	New Mexico	31
41	Hawaii	38
27	Colorado St.	22
30	Air Force	3
14	UCLA	68
20	Notre Dame	45
45	Fresno St.	48
56	Utah St.	58
45	San Diego St.	44
31	Utah	34
47	UTEP	16
390		**407**

Holiday Bowl

21	Ohio St.	28

Nickname: Cougars.
Stadium: Cougar (1964), 65,000 capacity. Natural turf.
Colors: Royal Blue & White.
Conference: Western Athl. Conf.
SID: Ralph Zobell, 801-378-4911.

AD: Clayne Jensen.

BROCKPORT STATE

Brockport, NY 14420 III

Coach: Ed Matejkovic, West Chester '69
Record: 8 Years, 32-47-0

1994 SCHEDULE

Jersey City St.	Sept. 10
Merchant Marine	Sept. 17
Albany (N.Y.) ■	Sept. 24
Buffalo St. ■	Oct. 1
Cortland St.	Oct. 8
Frostburg St.	Oct. 15
St. John Fisher ■	Oct. 22
Alfred	Oct. 29
Kean ■	Nov. 5
Grove City	Nov. 12

1993 RESULTS (7-3-0)

18	Jersey City St.	12
14	Alfred	7
13	Albany (N.Y.)	10
16	Buffalo St.	18
26	Cortland St.	14
51	Norwich	17
23	St. John Fisher	20
23	Frostburg St.	36
11	Kean	26
23	St. Lawrence	14
218		**174**

ECAC Northeast

20	Maine Maritime	28

Nickname: Golden Eagles.
Stadium: Special Olympic (1979), 10,000 capacity. Natural turf.
Colors: Green & Gold.
Conference: Division III Independent.
SID: Mike Andriatch, 716-395-2380.
AD: Ed Matejkovic.

BROWN

Providence, RI 02912 ....I-AA

Coach: Mark Whipple, Brown '79
Record: 6 Years, 48-17-0

1994 SCHEDULE

Yale ■	Sept. 17
Rhode Island	Sept. 24
Colgate ■	Oct. 1
Princeton	Oct. 8
Holy Cross ■	Oct. 15
Pennsylvania ■	Oct. 22
Cornell	Oct. 29
Harvard	Nov. 5
Dartmouth ■	Nov. 12
Columbia	Nov. 19

1993 RESULTS (4-6-0)

12	Yale	3
35	Lehigh	42
7	Rhode Island	30
16	Princeton	34
21	Bucknell	12
9	Pennsylvania	34
3	Cornell	21
43	Harvard	29
16	Dartmouth	39
28	Columbia	23
190		**267**

Nickname: Bears.
Stadium: Brown (1925), 20,000 capacity. Natural turf.
Colors: Seal Brown, Cardinal & White.
Conference: Ivy League.
SID: Christopher Humm, 401-863-2219.
AD: David Roach.

BUCKNELL

Lewisburg, PA 17837 ....I-AA

Coach: Lou Maranzana, Dartmouth '70
Record: 5 Years, 21-32-0

1994 SCHEDULE

Hofstra ■	Sept. 10
Southern Conn. St. ■	Sept. 17
Harvard	Sept. 24
Princeton	Oct. 1
Towson St. ■	Oct. 8
Cornell ■	Oct. 15
Lehigh	Oct. 22
Lafayette	Oct. 29
Holy Cross	Nov. 5
Colgate ■	Nov. 12
Fordham ■	Nov. 19

1993 RESULTS (4-7-0)

21	Bloomsburg	16
14	Lafayette	31
12	Pennsylvania	42
13	Dartmouth	31
0	Hofstra	28
12	Brown	21
33	Holy Cross	23
27	Fordham	21
32	Lehigh	27
21	Towson St.	49
8	Colgate	13
193		**302**

Nickname: Bison.
Stadium: Christy Mathewson (1924), 13,100 capacity. Natural turf.
Colors: Orange & Blue.
Conference: Patriot League.
SID: Bo Smolka, 717-524-1227.
AD: Rick Hartzell.

BUENA VISTA
Storm Lake, IA 50588 III

Coach: Kevin Twait, Buena Vista '85
Record: 4 Years, 7-31-0

1994 SCHEDULE

Colorado Col.	Sept. 10
Loras ■	Sept. 17
William Penn	Sept. 24
Dubuque	Oct. 1
Luther ■	Oct. 8
Wartburg ■	Oct. 15
Upper Iowa	Oct. 22
Central (Iowa) ■	Oct. 29
Simpson	Nov. 12

1993 RESULTS (3-6-0)

20	Cornell College	34
7	Loras	26
6	Simpson	27
6	Central (Iowa)	30
21	Upper Iowa	14
10	Wartburg	28
50	William Penn	8
48	Dubuque	0
7	Luther	18
175		**185**

Nickname: Beavers.
Stadium: J. Leslie Rollins (1980), 3,500 capacity. Natural turf.
Colors: Navy Blue & Gold.
Conference: Iowa Inter. Ath. Conf.
SID: Jay Miller, 712-749-2120.
AD: Jim Hershberger.

BUFFALO
Buffalo, NY 14260 ....I-AA

Coach: Jim Ward, Md.-East. Shore '68
Record: 2 Years, 5-16-0

1994 SCHEDULE

James Madison	*Sept. 3
Towson St.	Sept. 10
Lehigh ■	*Sept. 17
Cheyney ■	Sept. 24
Colgate	Oct. 8
Illinois St. ■	*Oct. 15
Hofstra ■	*Oct. 22
Maine [Portland, Maine]	*Oct. 29

Youngstown St. ■	Nov. 5
Western Ill.	Nov. 12
Central Fla.	Nov. 19

1993 RESULTS (1-10-0)

27	Maine	30
6	New Haven	38
15	Lafayette	29
17	Edinboro	28
20	Hofstra	28
33	Fordham	14
6	Buffalo St.	13
14	Towson St.	38
12	Youngstown St.	38
33	Boston U.	61
7	Central Fla.	42
190		**359**

Nickname: Bulls.
Stadium: UB Stadium (1993), 16,500 capacity. Natural turf.
Colors: Buffalo Blue, White & Red.
Conference: I-AA Independent.
SID: Mike Rowland, 716-645-6311.
AD: Nelson E. Townsend.

BUFFALO STATE
Buffalo, NY 14222 III

Coach: Jerry Boyes, Ithaca '76
Record: 8 Years, 34-42-0

1994 SCHEDULE

Thiel ■	Sept. 10
Canisius	*Sept. 17
Cortland St. ■	Sept. 24
Brockport St.	Oct. 1
Mercyhurst ■	Oct. 8
Alfred	Oct. 15
Ithaca	Oct. 22
St. John Fisher	Nov. 5
Westminster (Pa.) ■	Nov. 12

1993 RESULTS (7-2-0)

23	Mansfield	19
20	Canisius	10
45	Cortland St.	0
18	Brockport St.	16
34	Mercyhurst	0
13	Buffalo	6
33	Ithaca	17
0	Hobart	10
7	Westminster (Pa.)	24
193		**102**

III Championship

6	Rowan	29

Nickname: Bengals.
Stadium: Coyer Field, 3,000 capacity. Natural turf.
Colors: Orange & Black.
Conference: Division III Independent.
SID: Keith Bullion, 716-878-6030.
AD: Fred Hartrick.

BUTLER
Indianapolis, IN 46208 ....I-AA

Coach: Ken LaRose, Butler '80
Record: 2 Years, 12-8-0

1994 SCHEDULE

Hofstra ■	Sept. 3
St. Xavier (Ill.)	Sept. 10
Georgetown (Ky.) ■	Sept. 17
Wis.-Stevens Point	Sept. 24
Drake	Oct. 1
Valparaiso	Oct. 8
Dayton ■	Oct. 15
San Diego	Oct. 22
Evansville ■	Oct. 29
Ala.-Birmingham	Nov. 5

1993 RESULTS (4-6-0)

19	Hofstra	20
24	Georgetown (Ky.)	21
28	Drake	3
7	Hillsdale	29
10	Valparaiso	0

6	Dayton	28
27	San Diego	28
14	Evansville	12
27	Ala.-Birmingham	31
21	Indianapolis	34
183		**206**

Nickname: Bulldogs.
Stadium: Butler Bowl (1927), 19,000 capacity. Natural turf.
Colors: Blue & White.
Conference: Pioneer Football League.
SID: Jim McGrath, 317-283-9671.
AD: John Parry.

CAL LUTHERAN
Thousand Oaks, CA 91360 III

Coach: Joe Harper, UCLA '59
Record: 21 Years, 123-86-3

1994 SCHEDULE

Claremont-M-S	Sept. 17
San Diego	*Sept. 24
Occidental	Oct. 1
La Verne ■	Oct. 8
Redlands	Oct. 15
Azusa-Pacific	Oct. 22
Pomona-Pitzer ■	Oct. 29
Whittier	Nov. 5
Chapman ■	Nov. 12

1993 RESULTS (5-4-0)

10	Azusa-Pacific	9
14	Whittier	3
10	La Verne	24
40	Menlo	20
21	San Diego	27
26	Pomona-Pitzer	13
17	Redlands	23
28	Occidental	45
44	Claremont-M-S	9
210		**173**

Nickname: Kingsmen.
Stadium: Mt. Clef (1962), 2,000 capacity. Natural turf.
Colors: Purple & Gold.
Conference: Southern Calif. Inter. Ath. Conf.
SID: John Czimbal, 805-493-3153.
AD: Robert Doering.

CAL POLY SAN LUIS OBISPO
San Luis Obispo, CA 93407 ....I-AA

Coach: Andre Patterson, Montana '83
(First year as head coach)

1994 SCHEDULE

Eastern Wash.	*Sept. 10
Humboldt St. ■	*Sept. 17
Sonoma St. ■	*Sept. 24
Montana	Oct. 1
San Fran. St.	Oct. 8
UC Davis ■	*Oct. 15
Cal St. Northridge	*Oct. 22
St. Mary's (Cal.) ■	Oct. 29
Northern Ariz.	*Nov. 5
Cal St. Sacramento	*Nov. 12
Southern Utah ■	Nov. 19

1993 RESULTS (6-4-0)

26	UC Davis	37
17	Humboldt St.	3
63	Cal St. Chico	6
53	Sonoma St.	13
46	San Fran. St.	21
38	Southern Utah	6
33	Cal St. Sacramento	35
17	Portland St.	21
14	Cal St. Northridge	22
58	St. Mary's (Cal.)	37
365		**201**

Nickname: Mustangs.
Stadium: Mustang (1935), 8,500 capacity. Natural turf.
Colors: Green & Gold.
Conference: American West.

SID: Eric McDowell, 805-756-6531.
AD: John McCutcheon.

CAL STATE CHICO
Chico, CA 95929 II

Coach: Gary Houser, Oregon St. '68
Record: 5 Years, 19-29-1

1994 SCHEDULE
Sonoma St..Sept. 10
Mesa St...Sept. 17
Cal St. Sacramento ■ ....*Sept. 24
Cal St. Northridge.............................*Oct. 1
St. Mary's (Cal.) ■ ....*Oct. 8
Humboldt St.......................................Oct. 15
San Fran. St.......................................Oct. 29
UC Davis ....*Nov. 5
Sonoma St. ■ ....*Nov. 12

1993 RESULTS (4-4-1)
42	Whittier	17
6	Cal Poly SLO	63
15	St. Mary's (Cal.)	27
10	UC Davis	35
28	Cal St. Hayward	21
24	San Fran. St.	21
7	Cal St. Northridge	21
33	Sonoma St.	27
16	Humboldt St.	16
181		**248**

Nickname: Wildcats.
Stadium: University (1952), 8,000 capacity. Natural turf.
Colors: Cardinal & White.
Conference: Northern Cal. Ath. Conf.
SID: Teresa Clements, 916-898-4658.
AD: Janet Kittell.

CAL STATE NORTHRIDGE
Northridge, CA 91330 ....I-AA

Coach: Bob Burt, Cal St. Los Angeles '62
Record: 9 Years, 52-43-0

1994 SCHEDULE
Boise St...*Sept. 10
UC Davis ■ ....*Sept. 17
Southwest Tex. St. ....*Sept. 24
Cal St. Chico ■ ....*Oct. 1
Sonoma St..Oct. 8
St. Mary's (Cal.)................................Oct. 15
Cal Poly SLO ■ ....*Oct. 22
Southern Utah ....Nov. 5
Northern Ariz. ■ ....Nov. 12
Cal St. Sacramento ....*Nov. 19

1993 RESULTS (4-6-0)
17	San Diego St.	34
12	Weber St.	27
9	Northern Ariz.	23
39	Sonoma St.	0
24	Nevada-Las Vegas	18
30	Cal St. Sacramento	31
38	UC Davis	48
21	Cal St. Chico	7
22	Cal Poly SLO	14
17	Southern Utah	20
229		**222**

Nickname: Matadors.
Stadium: North Campus (1971), 6,000 capacity. Natural turf.
Colors: Red, White & Black.
Conference: American West.
SID: Barry Smith, 818-885-3243.
AD: Bob Hiegert.

CAL STATE SACRAMENTO
Sacramento, CA 95819 ....I-AA

Coach: Mike Clemons, Cal St. Sacramento '69
Record: 1 Year, 4-6-0

1994 SCHEDULE
San Fran. St. ■ ....*Sept. 10

Stephen F. Austin ....*Sept. 17
Cal St. Chico....................................*Sept. 24
Montana St. ■ ....*Oct. 1
UC Davis ■ ....*Oct. 8
Portland St. ■ ....*Oct. 22
Southern Utah ....Oct. 29
St. Mary's (Cal.)..............................Nov. 5
Cal Poly SLO ■ ....*Nov. 12
Cal St. Northridge ■ ....*Nov. 19

1993 RESULTS (4-6-0)
34	Cal St. Hayward	17
49	San Fran. St.	10
7	Eastern Wash.	48
6	Pacific (Cal.)	30
14	St. Mary's (Cal.)	27
31	Cal St. Northridge	30
35	Cal Poly SLO	33
7	Montana	54
32	UC Davis	47
17	Southern Utah	23
232		**319**

Nickname: Hornets.
Stadium: Hornet Field, 21,418 capacity. Natural turf.
Colors: Green & Gold.
Conference: American West.
SID: Jeff Minahan, 916-278-6896.
AD: Lee McElroy.

CALIFORNIA
Berkeley, CA 94720 ....I-A

Coach: Keith Gilbertson, Central Wash. '71
Record: 5 Years, 41-20-0

1994 SCHEDULE
San Diego St. ....*Sept. 10
Hawaii ■ ....Sept. 17
Arizona St. ■ ....Sept. 24
San Jose St. ■ ....Oct. 1
UCLA ■ ....Oct. 8
Oregon ....Oct. 15
Southern Cal.....................................Oct. 22
Washington St. ■ ....Oct. 29
Arizona ....*Nov. 5
Washington ....Nov. 12
Stanford ■ ....Nov. 19

1993 RESULTS (8-4-0)
27	UCLA	25
45	San Diego St.	25
58	Temple	0
46	San Jose St.	13
42	Oregon	41
23	Washington	24
7	Washington St.	34
14	Southern Cal	42
0	Arizona St.	41
24	Arizona	20
46	Stanford	17
42	Hawaii	18
374		**300**

Alamo Bowl
37	Iowa	3

Nickname: Golden Bears.
Stadium: Memorial (1923), 75,662 capacity. Artificial turf.
Colors: Blue & Gold.
Conference: Pacific-10.
SID: Kevin Reneau, 510-642-5363.
AD: John Kasser.

CALIFORNIA (PENNSYLVANIA)
California, PA 15419 II

Coach: Kevin Donley, Anderson '73
Record: 16 Years, 107-59-1

1994 SCHEDULE
Fairmont St. ....Sept. 3
Glenville St. ■ ....Sept. 10
Bloomsburg ....Sept. 17
Kutztown ■ ....Sept. 24
Slippery Rock ■ ....Oct. 1
Indiana (Pa.) ....Oct. 8

Edinboro ■ ....Oct. 15
Clarion..Oct. 22
Lock Haven ■ ....Oct. 29
Shippensburg....................................Nov. 5
West Chester ■ ....Nov. 12

1993 RESULTS (4-7-0)
43	West Liberty St.	32
23	West Va. Wesleyan	31
31	Fairmont St.	16
28	Kutztown	31
6	East Stroudsburg	9
30	Slippery Rock	40
13	Indiana (Pa.)	52
7	Edinboro	32
26	Clarion	14
56	Lock Haven	14
6	Shippensburg	7
269		**278**

Nickname: Vulcans.
Stadium: Adamson (1970), 5,000 capacity. Natural turf.
Colors: Red & Black.
Conference: Pennsylvania Conf.
SID: Bruce Wald, 412-938-4552.
AD: Tom Pucci.

CANISIUS
Buffalo, NY 14208 ....I-AA

Coach: Barry Mynter, St. Lawrence '58
Record: 18 Years, 83-89-3

1994 SCHEDULE
Mercyhurst...Sept. 10
Buffalo St. ■ ....*Sept. 17
Siena ....Sept. 24
Georgetown ....Oct. 1
Gannon ....Oct. 8
St. John's (N.Y.) ■ ....Oct. 15
Marist ....Oct. 22
St. Peter's ■ ....Oct. 29
Iona ....Nov. 5
Duquesne ■ ....Nov. 12

1993 RESULTS (5-5-0)
12	Duquesne	16
10	Buffalo St.	20
13	Gannon	16
9	Mercyhurst	13
9	Iona	19
23	St. John's (N.Y.)	18
29	St. Peter's	20
28	St. Francis (Pa.)	10
34	Siena	19
19	Georgetown	14
186		**165**

Nickname: Golden Griffins.
Stadium: Demske Sports Complex (1990), 2,000 capacity. Artificial turf.
Colors: Blue & Gold.
Conference: Metro Atlantic.
SID: John Maddock, 716-888-2977.
AD: Daniel P. Starr.

CAPITAL
Columbus, OH 43209 III

Coach: Roger Welsh, Muskingum '64
Record: 8 Years, 37-39-4

1994 SCHEDULE
Gannon ■ ....Sept. 10
Ohio Northern ■ ....Sept. 17
Muskingum ....*Sept. 24
Heidelberg ■ ....Oct. 1
Hiram ....Oct. 8
Marietta ....Oct. 15
John Carroll ■ ....Oct. 22
Baldwin-Wallace ....Oct. 29
Mount Union ....Nov. 5
Otterbein ■ ....Nov. 12

1993 RESULTS (5-5-0)
13	Bethany (W.Va.)	10
0	John Carroll	25

31	Hiram	0
14	Marietta	10
7	Heidelberg	16
0	Baldwin-Wallace	17
28	Muskingum	21
0	Ohio Northern	14
23	Mount Union	66
31	Otterbein	10
147		**189**

Nickname: Crusaders.
Stadium: Bernlohr (1928), 1,500 capacity. Natural turf.
Colors: Purple & White.
Conference: Ohio Ath. Conf.
SID: Dave Graham, 614-236-6174.
AD: Roger Welsh.

CARLETON
Northfield, MN 55057 III

Coach: Bob Sullivan, St. John's (Minn.) '59
Record: 15 Years, 83-62-0

1994 SCHEDULE
Cornell College ■		Sept. 10
St. Thomas (Minn.) ■		Sept. 17
Gust. Adolphus		Sept. 24
Macalester		Oct. 1
St. Olaf ■		Oct. 8
Concordia-M'head		Oct. 15
St. John's (Minn.) ■		Oct. 22
Bethel (Minn.)		Oct. 29
Augsburg ■		Nov. 5
Hamline [Minneapolis, Minn.]		Nov. 11

1993 RESULTS (6-4-0)
43	Northwestern Minn.	28
31	Hamline	33
25	Bethel (Minn.)	22
14	St. Thomas (Minn.)	31
34	Macalester	12
51	St. Olaf	48
14	Concordia-M'head	45
40	Augsburg	6
14	St. John's (Minn.)	62
35	Gust. Adolphus	30
301		**317**

Nickname: Knights.
Stadium: Laird, 7,500 capacity. Natural turf.
Colors: Maize & Blue.
Conference: Minnesota Inter. Ath. Conf.
SID: Joe Hargis, 507-663-4183.
AD: Leon Lunder.

CARNEGIE MELLON
Pittsburgh, PA 15213...................................III

Coach: Rich Lackner, Carnegie Mellon '79
Record: 8 Years, 59-18-2

1994 SCHEDULE
Frank. & Marsh.		Sept. 3
Allegheny		Sept. 10
Rhodes		Sept. 17
Juniata ■		Sept. 24
Merchant Marine ■		Oct. 1
Washington (Mo.)		Oct. 15
Chicago ■		Oct. 22
Rochester ■		Oct. 29
Grove City ■		Nov. 5
Case Reserve		Nov. 12

1993 RESULTS (8-2-0)
38	Frank. & Marsh.	14
30	Washington (Mo.)	21
31	Rochester	27
29	Juniata	14
9	Allegheny	20
29	Trinity (Tex.)	30
45	Chicago	14
48	Grove City	7
55	Catholic	0
56	Case Reserve	0
370		**147**

Nickname: Tartans.
Stadium: Gesling (1990), 3,500 capacity. Artificial turf.

Colors: Cardinal, White & Gray.
Conference: University Athletic Assn.
SID: Bruce Gerson, 412-268-3087.
AD: John Harvey.

CARROLL (WISCONSIN)
Waukesha, WI 53186 III

Coach: Merle Masonholder, Northern Iowa '66
Record: 12 Years, 51-56-0

1994 SCHEDULE
Carthage		Sept. 10
North Central ■		Sept. 17
Grinnell ■		Sept. 24
Cornell College		Oct. 1
Lawrence		Oct. 8
Beloit ■		Oct. 15
Lake Forest ■		Oct. 22
Ripon		Oct. 29
St. Norbert ■		Nov. 5

1993 RESULTS (7-3-0)
45	North Central	18
13	Kalamazoo	34
24	Illinois Col.	7
20	Monmouth (Ill.)	14
24	Lawrence	6
28	Beloit	29
13	Lake Forest	12
38	Ripon	6
57	St. Norbert	41
20	Coe	47
282		**214**

Nickname: Pioneers.
Stadium: Van Male Field, 3,500 capacity. Natural turf.
Colors: Orange & White.
Conference: Midwest Conf.
SID: Shawn Ama, 414-524-7376.
AD: Merle Masonholder.

CARSON-NEWMAN
Jefferson City, TN 37760 II

Coach: Ken Sparks, Carson-Newman '68
Record: 14 Years, 132-34-2

1994 SCHEDULE
Wayne St. (Mich.)		Sept. 3
Montana		Sept. 10
Presbyterian ■		Sept. 17
Elon		Sept. 24
Catawba		Oct. 1
Wingate ■		Oct. 8
Mars Hill		Oct. 15
Gardner-Webb ■		Oct. 22
Lenoir-Rhyne		*Oct. 29
Newberry ■		Nov. 5

1993 RESULTS (8-1-1)
24	Central St. (Ohio)	24
35	Catawba	21
31	Elon	20
31	New Haven	62
46	Wingate	14
42	Mars Hill	21
47	Gardner-Webb	10
31	Lenoir-Rhyne	3
40	Howard Payne	7
28	Presbyterian	13
355		**195**

II Championship
28	North Ala.	38

Nickname: Eagles.
Stadium: Burke-Tarr (1966), 5,000 capacity. Natural turf.
Colors: Orange & Blue.
Conference: South Atlantic Conf.
SID: Eric Trainer, 615-471-3477.
AD: David Barger.

CARTHAGE
Kenosha, WI 53140 III

Coach: Mike Larry, Carthage '89
Record: 2 Years, 1-17-0

1994 SCHEDULE
Carroll (Wis.) ■		Sept. 10
Ill. Benedictine		Sept. 17
Wheaton (Ill.) ■		Oct. 1
Millikin ■		Oct. 8
Elmhurst		Oct. 15
Ill. Wesleyan		Oct. 22
North Park ■		Oct. 29
North Central		Nov. 5
Augustana (Ill.) ■		Nov. 12

1993 RESULTS (1-8-0)
28	Anderson	52
12	Ill. Benedictine	30
32	Elmhurst	40
14	Millikin	45
13	Wheaton (Ill.)	48
21	Ill. Wesleyan	20
19	North Park	26
0	Augustana (Ill.)	48
35	North Central	45
174		**354**

Nickname: Redmen.
Stadium: Art Keller Field (1965), 4,800 capacity. Natural turf.
Colors: Red & White.
Conference: College Conf. of Ill. & Wis.
SID: Greg Sorenson, 414-551-5740.
AD: Robert R. Bonn.

CASE RESERVE
Cleveland, OH 44106...............................III

Coach: To be named

1994 SCHEDULE
Rochester		Sept. 10
Chicago ■		Sept. 17
Earlham		Sept. 24
Allegheny ■		Oct. 1
Kenyon		Oct. 8
Wooster ■		Oct. 15
Ohio Wesleyan		Oct. 22
Washington (Mo.)		Oct. 29
Denison		Nov. 5
Carnegie Mellon ■		Nov. 12

1993 RESULTS (2-8-0)
9	Rochester	28
10	Washington (Mo.)	55
7	Allegheny	51
10	Wittenberg	23
16	Kenyon	23
41	Oberlin	7
28	Denison	7
13	Ohio Wesleyan	15
16	Chicago	33
0	Carnegie Mellon	56
150		**298**

Nickname: Spartans.
Stadium: E.L. Finnigan Field (1968), 3,000 capacity. Natural turf.
Colors: Blue, Gray & White.
Conference: North Coast Ath. Conf.
SID: Sue Herdle Penicka, 216-368-6517.
AD: David Hutter.

CATAWBA
Salisbury, NC 28144 II

Coach: J. D. Haglan, Clemson '79
Record: 3 Years, 16-14-0

1994 SCHEDULE
East Tenn. St.		*Sept. 1
Elon ■		Sept. 10
Mars Hill		Sept. 17
Wofford ■		Sept. 24
Carson-Newman ■		Oct. 1
Presbyterian		Oct. 8
Gardner-Webb		Oct. 15
Liberty		*Oct. 22
Newberry		Oct. 29

Wingate..Nov. 5
Lenoir-Rhyne ■..............................Nov. 12

1993 RESULTS (5-5-0)
21	Carson-Newman	35
35	Mars Hill	34
30	Wofford	31
28	Newberry	14
31	Presbyterian	38
40	Gardner-Webb	36
27	Elon	21
42	West Va. St.	8
55	Wingate	61
29	Lenoir-Rhyne	38
338		**316**

Nickname: Indians.
Stadium: Shuford Field (1926), 4,000 capacity. Natural turf.
Colors: Blue & White.
Conference: South Atlantic Conf.
SID: Dennis W. Davidson, 704-637-4720.
AD: Tom Fletcher.

CATHOLIC
Washington, DC 20064 III

Coach: Tom Clark, Maryland '86
(First year as head coach)
1994 SCHEDULE
Gettysburg..Sept. 10
Randolph-Macon ■.........................Sept. 17
Merchant Marine ....Sept. 24
Gallaudet ....Oct. 1
Coast Guard ■ ....Oct. 8
St. John Fisher.................................Oct. 15
Hampden-Sydney ....Oct. 22
Ursinus ■ ....Oct. 29
Salisbury St. ■ ....Nov. 5
Alfred ■ ....Nov. 12

1993 RESULTS (1-9-0)
6	Gettysburg	14
6	Randolph-Macon	34
6	Merchant Marine	34
6	St. John Fisher	21
0	Coast Guard	34
44	Gallaudet	13
14	Hampden-Sydney	28
0	Georgetown	10
0	Carnegie Mellon	55
0	Wash. & Lee	34
82		**277**

Nickname: Cardinals.
Stadium: CUA Field, 3,500 capacity. Natural turf.
Colors: Cardinal & Black.
Conference: Division III Independent.
SID: Gabe Romano, 202-635-5610.
AD: Robert J. Talbot.

CENTRAL (IOWA)
Pella, IA 50219..III

Coach: Ron Schipper, Hope '52
Record: 33 Years, 260-62-3
1994 SCHEDULE
Gust. Adolphus ■ ....Sept. 10
Dubuque ....Sept. 17
Wartburg ■ ....Sept. 24
Luther ....Oct. 1
Colorado Col. ■ ....Oct. 8
Loras ■ ....Oct. 15
Simpson ....Oct. 22
Buena Vista ....Oct. 29
William Penn ■ ....Nov. 5
Upper Iowa ■ ....Nov. 12

1993 RESULTS (8-1-0)
38	Bethel (Minn.)	28
49	Dubuque	0
14	Wartburg	21
30	Buena Vista	6
70	William Penn	6
43	Simpson	14
40	Loras	18

30	Upper Iowa	0
23	Luther	0
337		**93**

Nickname: Flying Dutchmen.
Stadium: Kuyper (1977), 3,500 capacity. Natural turf.
Colors: Red & White.
Conference: Iowa Inter. Ath. Conf.
SID: Larry Happel, 515-628-5278.
AD: Sam Bedrosian.

CENTRAL ARKANSAS
Conway, AR 72032 II

Coach: Mike Isom, Central Ark. '70
Record: 4 Years, 32-12-4
1994 SCHEDULE
East Tex. St. ■ ....*Sept. 3
Mo. Southern St. ■ ....*Sept. 10
McNeese St..*Sept. 17
West Ga. ■ ....Sept. 24
Delta St. ■ ....*Oct. 1
Ark.-Pine Bluff.................................*Oct. 8
Livingston ....Oct. 15
North Ala. ....Oct. 22
Henderson St. ....Oct. 29
Mississippi Col. ■ ....Nov. 5

1993 RESULTS (6-4-1)
14	Mo. Southern St.	14
13	East Tex. St.	16
28	Fort Hays St.	6
26	West Ga.	23
34	Delta St.	27
48	Ark.-Pine Bluff	37
42	Livingston	27
10	North Ala.	27
28	Henderson St.	16
14	Mississippi Col.	21
31	Portland St.	45
288		**259**

Nickname: Bears.
Stadium: Estes (1939), 7,000 capacity. Natural turf.
Colors: Purple & Gray.
Conference: Gulf South Conf.
SID: Bob Valentine, 501-450-3150.
AD: Bill Stephens.

CENTRAL CONNECTICUT STATE
New Britain, CT 06050 ....I-AA

Coach: Sal Cintorio, Central Conn. St. '86
Record: 2 Years, 6-13-0
1994 SCHEDULE
Marist ....Sept. 10
Robert Morris ■ ....Sept. 17
LIU-C.W. Post ....Sept. 24
St. Peter's ....Oct. 1
Hofstra ....Oct. 8
Springfield ....Oct. 15
St. Francis (Pa.) ■ ....Oct. 22
Wagner ■ ....Oct. 29
Southern Conn. St. ■ ....Nov. 5
Monmouth (N.J.) ■ ....Nov. 12

1993 RESULTS (5-5-0)
7	Towson St.	42
24	Iona	13
15	Wagner	22
27	St. Francis (Pa.)	29
31	Marist	33
20	Springfield	11
18	LIU-C.W. Post	72
28	Southern Conn. St.	14
9	St. Peter's	7
41	Duquesne	22
220		**265**

Nickname: Blue Devils.
Stadium: Arute Field (1969), 5,000 capacity. Natural turf.
Colors: Blue & White.
Conference: I-AA Independent.
SID: Brent Rutkowski, 203-827-7824.
AD: Judith Davidson.

CENTRAL FLORIDA
Orlando, FL 32816..I-AA

Coach: Gene McDowell, Florida St. '63
Record: 9 Years, 63-40-0
1994 SCHEDULE
Maine ....Sept. 3
Valdosta St. ■ ....Sept. 10
Bethune-Cookman ■ ....Sept. 17
Western Ky. ■ ....Sept. 24
Illinois St. ....Oct. 1
Samford ....Oct. 8
Northeast La. ....*Oct. 15
Troy St. ■ ....Oct. 22
Liberty ....*Oct. 29
East Caro. ....Nov. 12
Buffalo ■ ....Nov. 19

1993 RESULTS (9-2-0)
35	Valdosta St.	30
17	East Caro.	41
22	McNeese St.	3
42	Yale	28
48	Samford	17
35	Western Ill.	17
34	Bethune-Cookman	14
15	Troy St.	29
55	Liberty	19
42	Buffalo	7
38	Louisiana Tech	16
383		**221**

I-AA Championship
30	Youngstown St.	56

Nickname: Golden Knights.
Stadium: Florida Citrus (1936), 70,349 capacity. Natural turf.
Colors: Black & Gold.
Conference: I-AA Independent.
SID: John Marini, 407-823-2464.
AD: Steve Sloan.

CENTRAL MICHIGAN
Mt. Pleasant, MI 48859 ....I-A

Coach: Dick Flynn, Michigan St. '65
(First year as head coach)
1994 SCHEDULE
Iowa ....Sept. 3
Nevada-Las Vegas ■ ....Sept. 10
Eastern Mich. ....Sept. 17
Kent ■ ....Sept. 24
Ball St. ....Oct. 1
Western Mich. ■ ....Oct. 8
Akron ....*Oct. 15
Miami (Ohio) ■ ....Oct. 22
Ohio ....Oct. 29
Toledo ■ ....Nov. 5
Bowling Green..................................Nov. 12

1993 RESULTS (5-6-0)
13	Akron	23
38	Ohio	0
20	Nevada-Las Vegas	33
34	Michigan St.	48
17	Ball St.	20
23	Western Mich.	18
21	Eastern Mich.	28
33	Kent	28
38	Toledo	7
17	Bowling Green	15
21	Miami (Ohio)	24
275		**244**

Nickname: Chippewas.
Stadium: Kelly-Shorts (1972), 20,086 capacity. Artificial turf.
Colors: Maroon & Gold.
Conference: Mid-American Conf.
SID: Fred Stabley Jr., 517-774-3277.
AD: Herb Deromedi.

CENTRAL MISSOURI STATE
Warrensburg, MO 64093 II

Coach: Terry Noland, Southwest Mo. St. '71
Record: 11 Years, 63-52-2

1994 SCHEDULE

Upper Iowa ■	*Sept. 1
Northeast Mo. St. ■	*Sept. 17
Washburn	*Sept. 24
Mo. Western St. ■	Oct. 1
Southwest Baptist	Oct. 8
Mo. Southern St.	*Oct. 15
Pittsburg St. ■	Oct. 22
Emporia St. ■	Oct. 29
Northwest Mo. St.	Nov. 5
Missouri-Rolla ■	Nov. 12

1993 RESULTS (7-2-1)

3	Wis.-Whitewater	0
36	Northeast Mo. St.	18
41	Washburn	19
14	Mo. Western St.	14
48	Southwest Baptist	7
7	Mo. Southern St.	27
17	Pittsburg St.	19
17	Emporia St.	3
41	Northwest Mo. St.	10
24	Missouri-Rolla	21
248		**138**

Nickname: Mules.
Stadium: Vernon Kennedy (1928), 10,000 capacity. Natural turf.
Colors: Cardinal & Black.
Conference: Mid-America Intercoll. Ath. Assoc.
SID: Bill Turnage, 816-543-4312.
AD: Jerry Hughes.

CENTRAL OKLAHOMA

Edmond, OK 73034 II

Coach: Gary Howard, Arkansas '64
Record: 17 Years, 95-73-5

1994 SCHEDULE

Mesa St. ■	*Sept. 3
Southwestern Okla.	*Sept. 10
Fort Hays St.	*Sept. 17
Langston ■	Sept. 24
East Tex. St. ■	Oct. 1
Abilene Christian ■	*Oct. 8
Tex. A&M-Kingsville	*Oct. 15
Angelo St.	*Oct. 22
Neb.-Kearney ■	Nov. 5
Eastern N. Mex.	Nov. 12

1993 RESULTS (7-3-0)

37	Mesa St.	7
30	Fort Hays St.	0
21	Southern Utah	20
37	Langston	20
27	East Tex. St.	30
10	Abilene Christian	28
7	Tex. A&M-Kingsville	38
28	Angelo St.	24
14	Neb.-Kearney	7
36	Eastern N. Mex.	7
247		**181**

Nickname: Bronchos.
Stadium: Wantland (1965), 10,000 capacity. Natural turf.
Colors: Bronze & Blue.
Conference: Lone Star Conf.
SID: Mike Kirk, 405-341-2980.
AD: John "Skip" Wagnon.

CENTRE

Danville, KY 40422 III

Coach: Joe McDaniel, Muskingum '56
Record: 28 Years, 142-109-4

1994 SCHEDULE

Denison	Sept. 10
Hanover ■	Sept. 17
Wash. & Lee ■	Sept. 24
Sewanee ■	Oct. 1
Millsaps	Oct. 8
Maryville (Tenn.) ■	Oct. 15

Trinity (Tex.) ■	Oct. 22
Ky. Wesleyan ■	Oct. 29
Davidson	Nov. 5
Rhodes	Nov. 12

1993 RESULTS (4-5-0)

21	Denison	16
21	Maryville (Tenn.)	27
21	Wash. & Lee	15
26	Sewanee	27
20	Millsaps	19
10	Trinity (Tex.)	44
10	Ky. Wesleyan	21
44	Davidson	31
34	Rhodes	36
207		**236**

Nickname: Colonels.
Stadium: Farris (1925), 2,500 capacity. Natural turf.
Colors: Gold & White.
Conference: Southern Coll. Ath. Conf.
SID: Cheryl Hart, 606-238-5513.
AD: Ray Hammond.

CHADRON STATE

Chadron, NE 69337 II

Coach: Brad Smith, Western Ill. '72
Record: 6 Years, 40-31-1

1994 SCHEDULE

South Dak. Tech	*Sept. 3
Tabor ■	Sept. 10
Black Hills St.	*Sept. 17
Peru St. [Alliance, Neb.]	Sept. 24
Mesa St. ■	Oct. 1
Adams St.	Oct. 8
N.M. Highlands ■	Oct. 15
Colorado Mines ■	Oct. 22
Western St.	Oct. 29
Fort Hays St. ■	Nov. 5
Fort Lewis	Nov. 12

1993 RESULTS (5-6-0)

3	Idaho St.	52
66	South Dak. Tech	14
42	Black Hills St.	13
36	Peru St.	22
36	Adams St.	22
37	N.M. Highlands	44
28	Colorado Mines	51
20	Western St.	31
7	Fort Hays St.	35
41	Fort Lewis	3
29	Mesa St.	36
345		**323**

Nickname: Eagles.
Stadium: Elliott Field (1930), 2,500 capacity. Natural turf.
Colors: Cardinal & White.
Conference: Rocky Mountain Ath. Conf.
SID: Con Marshall, 308-432-6212.
AD: Brad Smith.

CHAPMAN

Orange, CA 92666 III

Coach: Ken Visser, Occidental '68
Record: 3 Years, 10-17-0

1994 SCHEDULE

Whittier	*Sept. 17
Claremont-M-S ■	*Sept. 24
Redlands	*Oct. 1
Azusa-Pacific	Oct. 8
Occidental	*Oct. 15
Menlo	*Oct. 22
La Verne ■	*Oct. 29
Pomona-Pitzer ■	*Nov. 5
Cal Lutheran	Nov. 12

1993 RESULTS

None—1994 is first year of football.

Nickname: Panthers.
Stadium: Chapman, 1,000 capacity. Natural turf.
Colors: Cardinal & Gray.
Conference: Division III Independent.

SID: Derek Anderson, 714-997-6900.
AD: David Currey.

CHARLESTON SOUTHERN

Charleston, SC 29423 ....I-AA

Coach: David Dowd, Guilford '76
Record: 3 Years, 8-21-0

1994 SCHEDULE

Presbyterian	Sept. 10
South Caro. St. ■	Sept. 17
Towson St. ■	Sept. 24
Morgan St.	Oct. 1
Newberry ■	Oct. 8
Troy St.	Oct. 15
Ala.-Birmingham	Oct. 22
Mars Hill ■	Oct. 29
Tenn.-Martin	Nov. 5
Wofford	Nov. 12
Liberty	*Nov. 19

1993 RESULTS (3-8-0)

20	Morgan St.	54
17	Presbyterian	16
10	South Caro. St.	44
14	Towson St.	52
0	Troy St.	56
15	Newberry	10
24	Lees-McRae	17
20	Ala.-Birmingham	48
6	Liberty	42
0	Newport News App.	21
9	Wofford	21
135		**381**

Nickname: Buccaneers.
Stadium: CSU, 3,000 capacity. Natural turf.
Colors: Blue & Gold.
Conference: I-AA Independent.
SID: Mike Hoffman, 803-863-7688.
AD: Howard Bagwell.

CHEYNEY

Cheyney, PA 19319 II

Coach: Chris Roulhac, Albany St. (Ga.) '70
Record: 2 Years, 3-19-0

1994 SCHEDULE

Delaware St.	Sept. 3
American Int'l	Sept. 10
West Va. St.	Sept. 17
Buffalo	Sept. 24
Kutztown	Oct. 1
West Chester ■	Oct. 8
East Stroudsburg	Oct. 15
Indiana (Pa.)	Oct. 22
Mansfield ■	Oct. 29
Millersville	Nov. 5
Bloomsburg ■	Nov. 12

1993 RESULTS (3-8-0)

20	Southern Conn. St.	7
12	Delaware St.	44
34	West Va. St.	10
12	Fayetteville St.	33
12	West Chester	39
12	East Stroudsburg	47
0	Slippery Rock	52
6	Mansfield	46
6	Millersville	51
6	Bloomsburg	24
30	Kutztown	19
150		**372**

Nickname: Wolves.
Stadium: O'Shield-Stevenson, 3,500 capacity. Natural turf.
Colors: Blue & White.
Conference: Pennsylvania Conf.
SID: To be named, 215-399-2287.
AD: Andrew Hinson.

CHICAGO

Chicago, IL 60637 III

Coach: Dick Maloney, Mass.-Boston '74
(First year as head coach)

1994 SCHEDULE

Lawrence ■	Sept. 10
Case Reserve	Sept. 17
Concordia (Ill.)	Sept. 24
Kalamazoo	Oct. 1
Washington (Mo.) ■	Oct. 8
Rochester ■	Oct. 15
Carnegie Mellon	Oct. 22
Oberlin ■	Oct. 29
Ky. Wesleyan	Nov. 5
Rose-Hulman	Nov. 12

1993 RESULTS (5-5-0)

43	Blackburn	6
14	Concordia (Ill.)	6
44	Lawrence	28
21	Kalamazoo	22
7	Rochester	14
19	Drake	33
14	Carnegie Mellon	45
20	Washington (Mo.)	17
7	Aurora	28
33	Case Reserve	16
222		**215**

Nickname: Maroons.
Stadium: Stagg Field (1969), 1,500 capacity. Natural turf.
Colors: White & Maroon.
Conference: University Athletic Assn.
SID: Dave Hilbert, 312-702-4638.
AD: Tom Weingartner.

CINCINNATI

Cincinnati, OH 45221 ....I-A

Coach: Rick Minter, Henderson St. '77
(First year as head coach)

1994 SCHEDULE

Indiana	Sept. 3
Syracuse ■	*Sept. 10
Miami (Ohio)	Sept. 17
Bowling Green ■	*Oct. 1
Vanderbilt ■	*Oct. 8
Rutgers	Oct. 15
Memphis	*Oct. 22
East Caro.	Oct. 29
Troy St. ■	Nov. 5
Wisconsin	Nov. 12
Tulsa ■	Nov. 19

1993 RESULTS (8-3-0)

42	Austin Peay	10
7	Bowling Green	21
30	Miami (Ohio)	23
21	Syracuse	24
22	Tulsa	15
7	Vanderbilt	17
44	Ball St.	12
31	Toledo	24
23	Memphis	20
41	Houston	17
34	East Caro.	14
302		**197**

Nickname: Bearcats.
Stadium: Nippert (1916), 35,000 capacity. Artificial turf.
Colors: Red & Black.
Conference: I-A Independent.
SID: Tom Hathaway, 513-556-5191.
AD: Rick Taylor.

CITADEL

Charleston, SC 29409 ....I-AA

Coach: Charlie Taaffe, Siena '73
Record: 7 Years, 47-33-1

1994 SCHEDULE

Wofford ■	*Sept. 10
Western Caro. ■	*Sept. 17
Appalachian St.	Sept. 24
Newberry ■	*Oct. 1
East Tenn. St. ■	Oct. 8
Furman	Oct. 15
Army	Oct. 22
Marshall	Oct. 29
Tenn.-Chatt.	Nov. 5
Va. Military	Nov. 12
Ga. Southern ■	Nov. 19

1993 RESULTS (5-6-0)

6	Wofford	20
6	Ga. Southern	16
18	Western Caro.	38
27	Appalachian St.	14
62	Lees-McRae	7
17	East Tenn. St.	20
20	Furman	10
0	Air Force	35
15	Marshall	35
41	Tenn.-Chatt.	27
34	Va. Military	33
246		**255**

Nickname: Bulldogs.
Stadium: Johnson Hagood (1948), 22,500 capacity. Natural turf.
Colors: Blue & White.
Conference: Southern Conf.
SID: To be named, 803-953-5120.
AD: Walt Nadzak.

CLAREMONT-MUDD-SCRIPPS

Claremont, CA 91711 III

Coach: John Zinda, Cal. St. Los Angeles '61
Record: 25 Years, 88-127-4

1994 SCHEDULE

Cal Lutheran ■	Sept. 17
Chapman	*Sept. 24
Trinity (Tex.) ■	Oct. 1
Whittier ■	Oct. 8
Menlo ■	Oct. 15
Occidental	*Oct. 22
Redlands	*Oct. 29
La Verne ■	Nov. 5
Pomona-Pitzer	*Nov. 12

1993 RESULTS (1-6-1)

3	Trinity (Tex.)	24
10	La Verne	46
14	Redlands	56
34	Menlo	34
12	Whittier	38
42	Occidental	68
30	Pomona-Pitzer	26
9	Cal Lutheran	44
154		**336**

Nickname: Stags.
Stadium: South Field (1955), 3,000 capacity. Natural turf.
Colors: Maroon, Gold & White.
Conference: Southern Calif. Inter. Ath. Conf.
SID: Grayle Howlett, 909-626-9855.
AD: John Zinda.

CLARION

Clarion, PA 16214 II

Coach: Malen Luke, Westminster (Pa.) '76
Record: 6 Years, 37-21-0

1994 SCHEDULE

West Chester	Sept. 10
Fairmont St. ■	Sept. 17
Westminster (Pa.) ■	Sept. 24
Millersville	Oct. 1
Lock Haven ■	Oct. 8
Shippensburg	Oct. 15
Calif. (Pa.) ■	Oct. 22
Slippery Rock	Oct. 29
Indiana (Pa.) ■	Nov. 5
Edinboro	Nov. 12

1993 RESULTS (5-5-0)

17	West Chester	19
23	New Haven	35
23	Westminster (Pa.)	20
0	Edinboro	28
40	Bloomsburg	18
37	Lock Haven	26
34	Shippensburg	32
14	Calif. (Pa.)	26
29	Slippery Rock	25
7	Indiana (Pa.)	44
224		**273**

Nickname: Golden Eagles.
Stadium: Memorial Field (1965), 5,000 capacity. Natural turf.
Colors: Blue & Gold.
Conference: Pennsylvania Conf.
SID: Rich Herman, 814-226-2334.
AD: Robert Carlson.

CLARK ATLANTA

Atlanta, GA 30314 II

Coach: Willie Hunter, Fort Valley St. '57
Record: 5 Years, 17-22-1

1994 SCHEDULE

Morris Brown ■	*Sept. 5
Alabama A&M	*Sept. 17
Valdosta St.	*Sept. 24
Fort Valley St. ■	Oct. 1
Kentucky St.	*Oct. 15
Savannah St. [Augusta, Ga.]	Oct. 22
Albany St. (Ga.)	Oct. 29
Tuskegee ■	Nov. 5
Lane	Nov. 12
Morehouse ■	Nov. 19

1993 RESULTS (2-8-0)

18	Morris Brown	42
14	Savannah St.	16
12	Valdosta St.	41
6	Fort Valley St.	10
19	Tuskegee	35
30	Kentucky St.	7
20	Miles	12
12	Albany St. (Ga.)	20
8	Alabama A&M	15
0	Morehouse	7
139		**205**

Nickname: Panthers.
Stadium: Georgia Dome (1993), 70,000 capacity. Artificial turf.
Colors: Red, Black & Gray.
Conference: Southern Inter. Ath. Conf.
SID: Roger Caruth, 404-880-8029.
AD: Richard Cosby.

CLEMSON

Clemson, SC 29633 ....I-A

Coach: Tommy West, Tennessee '76
Record: 1 Year, 5-7-0

1994 SCHEDULE

Furman ■	Sept. 3
North Caro. St. ■	Sept. 10
Virginia	Sept. 17
Maryland ■	Oct. 1
Georgia	Oct. 8
Duke	Oct. 15
Florida St.	Oct. 22
Wake Forest ■	Oct. 29
North Caro.	Nov. 5
Georgia Tech ■	Nov. 12
South Caro. ■	Nov. 19

1993 RESULTS (8-3-0)

24	Nevada-Las Vegas	14
0	Florida St.	57
16	Georgia Tech	13
20	North Caro. St.	14
13	Duke	10
16	Wake Forest	20
27	East Tenn. St.	0
29	Maryland	0

0	North Caro.	24
23	Virginia	14
16	South Caro.	13
184		**179**

Peach Bowl

14	Kentucky	13

Nickname: Tigers.
Stadium: Memorial (1942), 81,473 capacity. Natural turf.
Colors: Purple & Orange.
Conference: Atlantic Coast Conf.
SID: Tim Bourret, 803-656-2114.
AD: Bobby Robinson.

COAST GUARD
New London, CT 06320 III

Coach: Bill Schmitz, Coast Guard '76
Record: 1 Year, 4-5-0

1994 SCHEDULE

Rensselaer ■	Sept. 17
Stony Brook ■	Sept. 24
Norwich	Oct. 1
Catholic	Oct. 8
Western Conn. St. ■	Oct. 15
Union (N.Y.)	Oct. 22
Plymouth St. ■	Oct. 29
Worcester Tech	Nov. 5
Merchant Marine	Nov. 12

1993 RESULTS (4-5-0)

14	Rensselaer	53
14	Stony Brook	21
21	Norwich	8
34	Catholic	0
21	Western Conn. St.	18
10	Union (N.Y.)	52
14	Plymouth St.	31
18	Worcester Tech	21
31	Merchant Marine	23
177		**227**

Nickname: Cadets, Bears.
Stadium: Cadet Memorial Field (1932), 4,500 capacity. Natural turf.
Colors: Blue, White & Orange.
Conference: Freedom Football Conf.
SID: Shaun May, 203-437-6800.
AD: Chuck Mills.

COE
Cedar Rapids, IA 52402 III

Coach: D. J. LeRoy, Wis.-Eau Claire '79
Record: 11 Years, 83-34-2

1994 SCHEDULE

Quincy	Sept. 3
Wartburg ■	Sept. 10
St. Norbert ■	Sept. 24
Lake Forest	Oct. 1
Grinnell ■	Oct. 8
Illinois Col.	Oct. 15
Monmouth (Ill.) ■	Oct. 22
Knox	Oct. 29
Cornell College ■	Nov. 5

1993 RESULTS (10-0-0)

26	Wartburg	22
36	William Penn	7
48	Ripon	24
41	Beloit	6
69	Grinnell	7
56	Illinois Col.	12
49	Monmouth (Ill.)	14
59	Knox	14
48	Cornell College	18
47	Carroll (Wis.)	20
479		**144**

III Championship

14	St. John's (Minn.)	32

Nickname: Kohawks.
Stadium: Clark (1989), 1,100 capacity. Natural turf.
Colors: Crimson & Gold.
Conference: Midwest Conf.

SID: Alice Davidson, 319-399-8570.
AD: Barron Bremner.

COLBY
Waterville, ME 04901 III

Coach: Tom Austin, Maine '63
Record: 8 Years, 27-36-1

1994 SCHEDULE

Trinity (Conn.)	Sept. 24
Middlebury ■	Oct. 1
Wesleyan ■	Oct. 8
Amherst	Oct. 15
Hamilton ■	Oct. 22
Bates	Oct. 29
Tufts	Nov. 5
Bowdoin ■	Nov. 12

1993 RESULTS (5-2-1)

9	Williams	13
8	Middlebury	7
19	Wesleyan	21
21	Amherst	0
17	Hamilton	14
53	Bates	14
23	Tufts	13
21	Bowdoin	21
171		**103**

Nickname: White Mules.
Stadium: Seaverns (1948), 5,000 capacity. Natural turf.
Colors: Blue & Gray.
Conference: NESCAC.
SID: To be named, 207-872-3227.
AD: Richard Whitmore.

COLGATE
Hamilton, NY 13346 ....I-AA

Coach: Ed Sweeney, LIU-C.W. Post '71
Record: 9 Years, 59-30-4

1994 SCHEDULE

Boston U. ■	Sept. 10
Dartmouth ■	Sept. 17
Princeton	Sept. 24
Brown	Oct. 1
Buffalo	Oct. 8
Harvard	Oct. 15
Fordham ■	Oct. 22
Lehigh	Oct. 29
Lafayette ■	Nov. 5
Bucknell	Nov. 12
Holy Cross	Nov. 19

1993 RESULTS (3-7-1)

6	Rutgers	68
0	Army	30
22	Cornell	6
27	Columbia	24
12	Pennsylvania	30
3	Navy	31
32	Lehigh	36
7	Lafayette	7
13	Fordham	17
14	Holy Cross	27
13	Bucknell	8
149		**284**

Nickname: Red Raiders.
Stadium: Andy Kerr (1937), 10,221 capacity. Natural turf.
Colors: Maroon.
Conference: Patriot League.
SID: Bob Cornell, 315-824-7616.
AD: Mark Murphy.

COLORADO
Boulder, CO 80309 ....I-A

Coach: Bill McCartney, Missouri '62
Record: 12 Years, 82-54-5

1994 SCHEDULE

Northeast La. ■	Sept. 3
Wisconsin ■	Sept. 17
Michigan	Sept. 24
Texas	*Oct. 1
Missouri	Oct. 8
Oklahoma ■	Oct. 15
Kansas St. ■	Oct. 22
Nebraska	Oct. 29
Oklahoma St. ■	Nov. 5
Kansas	Nov. 12
Iowa St. ■	Nov. 19

1993 RESULTS (7-3-1)

36	Texas	14
45	Baylor	21
37	Stanford	41
29	Miami (Fla.)	35
30	Missouri	18
27	Oklahoma	10
16	Kansas St.	16
17	Nebraska	21
31	Oklahoma St.	14
38	Kansas	14
21	Iowa St.	16
327		**220**

Aloha Bowl

41	Fresno St.	30

Nickname: Buffaloes.
Stadium: Folsom (1924), 51,748 capacity. Artificial turf.
Colors: Silver, Gold & Black.
Conference: Big Eight Conf.
SID: David Plati, 303-492-5626.
AD: Bill Marolt.

COLORADO COLLEGE
Colorado Springs, CO 80903 III

Coach: Craig Rundle, Albion '74
Record: 8 Years, 47-30-0

1994 SCHEDULE

Buena Vista ■	Sept. 10
Pomona-Pitzer ■	Sept. 17
Millsaps	Sept. 24
Kan. Wesleyan ■	Oct. 1
Central (Iowa)	Oct. 8
Austin	Oct. 15
Rhodes	Oct. 22
Hardin-Simmons	Oct. 29
Washington (Mo.) ■	Nov. 5

1993 RESULTS (8-1-0)

44	Grinnell	17
42	Pomona-Pitzer	21
51	Rhodes	10
38	Austin	24
37	Trinity (Tex.)	6
42	Millsaps	15
31	Hardin-Simmons	29
38	Washington (Mo.)	16
21	Hastings	22
344		**160**

Nickname: Tigers.
Stadium: Washburn Field (1898), 2,000 capacity. Natural turf.
Colors: Black & Gold.
Conference: Division III Independent.
SID: Dave Moross, 719-389-6755.
AD: Max Taylor.

COLORADO SCHOOL OF MINES
Golden, CO 80401 II

Coach: Marvin Kay, Colorado Mines '63
Record: 25 Years, 80-152-5

1994 SCHEDULE

Doane	Sept. 10
Hastings ■	Sept. 17
N.M. Highlands	Oct. 1
Western St. ■	Oct. 8
Adams St. ■	Oct. 15
Chadron St.	Oct. 22
Fort Hays St.	Oct. 29
Fort Lewis ■	Nov. 5
Mesa St.	Nov. 12

1993 RESULTS (2-7-1)

17	Doane	21
0	Hastings	44
19	Eastern N. Mex.	19
25	Western St.	42
20	Adams St.	27
51	Chadron St.	28
21	Fort Hays St.	35
41	Fort Lewis	39
14	Mesa St.	31
7	N.M. Highlands	19
215		**305**

Nickname: Orediggers.
Stadium: Brooks Field (1922), 5,000 capacity. Natural turf.
Colors: Silver & Blue.
Conference: Rocky Mountain Ath. Conf.
SID: Steve Smith, 303-273-3300.
AD: R. Bruce Allison.

COLORADO STATE
Fort Collins, CO 80523 ....I-A

Coach: Sonny Lubick, Western Mont. '60
Record: 5 Years, 26-25-0

1994 SCHEDULE

Air Force	Sept. 3
Utah St. ■	Sept. 10
Brigham Young	Sept. 17
San Diego St. ■	Sept. 24
New Mexico	*Oct. 1
Arizona	*Oct. 8
UTEP ■	Oct. 15
Utah ■	Oct. 22
Wyoming ■	Nov. 5
Arkansas St. ■	Nov. 12
Fresno St.	*Nov. 19

1993 RESULTS (5-6-0)

9	Oregon	23
8	Air Force	5
22	Brigham Young	27
13	Nebraska	48
6	Kansas	24
34	Fresno St.	32
3	San Diego St.	30
21	Utah	38
21	New Mexico	20
52	UTEP	0
41	Wyoming	21
230		**268**

Nickname: Rams.
Stadium: Hughes (1968), 30,000 capacity. Natural turf.
Colors: Green & Gold.
Conference: Western Athl. Conf.
SID: Gary Ozzello, 303-491-5067.
AD: Tom Jurich.

COLUMBIA
New York, NY 10027 ....I-AA

Coach: Ray Tellier, Connecticut '73
Record: 9 Years, 27-60-1

1994 SCHEDULE

Harvard ■	Sept. 17
Lehigh	Sept. 24
Lafayette ■	Oct. 1
Fordham	Oct. 8
Pennsylvania	Oct. 15
Yale	Oct. 22
Princeton ■	Oct. 29
Dartmouth	Nov. 5
Cornell ■	Nov. 12
Brown ■	Nov. 19

1993 RESULTS (2-8-0)

3	Harvard	30
7	Fordham	0
24	Colgate	27
6	Lafayette	58
7	Pennsylvania	36
28	Yale	35
3	Princeton	14
25	Dartmouth	42

29	Cornell	24
23	Brown	28
155		**294**

Nickname: Lions.
Stadium: Lawrence A. Wien (1984), 17,000 capacity. Natural turf.
Colors: Columbia Blue & White.
Conference: Ivy League.
SID: Bill Steinman, 212-854-2534.
AD: John Reeves.

CONCORD
Athens, WV 24712 II

Coach: Bob Mullett, Concord '73
Record: 5 Years, 32-17-2

1994 SCHEDULE

Liberty	*Sept. 3
Mars Hill ■	Sept. 10
Elon	Sept. 17
Fairmont St. ■	Oct. 1
West Va. Tech	Oct. 8
Shepherd	Oct. 15
West Liberty St. ■	Oct. 22
Glenville St. ■	Oct. 29
West Va. Wesleyan	Nov. 5
West Va. St.	Nov. 12

1993 RESULTS (4-6-0)

3	Liberty	37
7	Elon	21
17	West Va. St.	0
19	Fairmont St.	15
50	West Va. Tech	6
14	Shepherd	0
0	West Liberty St.	56
7	Glenville St.	27
19	West Va. Wesleyan	20
13	Ga. Southern	51
149		**233**

Nickname: Mountain Lions.
Stadium: Callahan, 5,000 capacity. Natural turf.
Colors: Maroon & Gray.
Conference: West Va. Inter. Ath. Conf.
SID: Don Christie, 304-384-5288.
AD: Don Christie.

CONCORDIA (ILLINOIS)
River Forest, IL 60305 III

Coach: Jim Braun, Concordia (Ill.) '71
Record: 15 Years, 54-78-3

1994 SCHEDULE

Maranatha	Sept. 10
N'western (Wis.) ■	Sept. 17
Chicago ■	Sept. 24
MacMurray ■	Oct. 1
Eureka ■	Oct. 8
Quincy	Oct. 15
Lakeland ■	Oct. 22
Greenville ■	Oct. 29
Concordia (Wis.)	Nov. 5
Blackburn	Nov. 12

1993 RESULTS (0-10-0)

6	Chicago	14
7	N'western (Wis.)	34
6	Maranatha	13
14	Lakeland	19
6	Eureka	14
0	Concordia (Wis.)	41
14	Greenville	49
13	MacMurray	24
0	Principia	22
13	Blackburn	19
79		**249**

Nickname: Cougars.
Stadium: Concordia, 1,500 capacity. Natural turf.
Colors: Maroon & Gold.
Conference: Division III Independent.
SID: Jim Egan, 708-209-3116.
AD: Thomas Faszholz.

CONCORDIA-MOORHEAD
Moorhead, MN 56560 III

Coach: Jim Christopherson, Concordia-M'head '60
Record: 25 Years, 175-73-6

1994 SCHEDULE

Moorhead St.	Sept. 10
Augsburg ■	Sept. 17
Hamline	Sept. 24
St. Thomas (Minn.) ■	Oct. 1
Gust. Adolphus	Oct. 8
Carleton ■	Oct. 15
St. Olaf	Oct. 22
Macalester	Oct. 29
St. John's (Minn.) [Fargo, N.D.]	*Nov. 5
Bethel (Minn.) [Minneapolis, Minn.]	Nov. 11

1993 RESULTS (6-4-0)

0	Moorhead St.	21
13	Gust. Adolphus	6
36	Hamline	33
19	Bethel (Minn.)	15
43	St. Thomas (Minn.)	44
35	Macalester	20
45	Carleton	14
34	St. Olaf	58
28	Augsburg	0
21	St. John's (Minn.)	44
274		**255**

Nickname: Cobbers.
Stadium: Jake Christiansen, 6,000 capacity. Natural turf.
Colors: Maroon & Gold.
Conference: Minnesota Inter. Ath. Conf.
SID: Jerry Pyle, 218-299-3194.
AD: Armin Pipho.

CONNECTICUT
Storrs, CT 06269 ....I-AA

Coach: Skip Holtz, Notre Dame '86
(First year as head coach)

1994 SCHEDULE

Nicholls St. ■	Sept. 3
Troy St. ■	*Sept. 10
Richmond ■	*Sept. 17
New Hampshire	Sept. 24
Yale	Oct. 1
Villanova ■	Oct. 8
Maine ■	Oct. 15
Rhode Island ■	Oct. 22
Boston U.	Nov. 5
James Madison	Nov. 12
Massachusetts	Nov. 19

1993 RESULTS (6-5-0)

17	Furman	26
24	New Hampshire	23
45	James Madison	34
25	Yale	14
27	Towson St.	28
14	Villanova	17
17	Massachusetts	20
14	Maine	13
21	Richmond	3
41	Rhode Island	9
16	Boston U.	30
261		**217**

Nickname: Huskies.
Stadium: Memorial (1953), 16,200 capacity. Natural turf.
Colors: National Flag Blue & White.
Conference: Yankee.
SID: Tim Tolokan, 203-486-3531.
AD: Lew Perkins.

CORNELL
Ithaca, NY 14853 ....I-AA

Coach: Jim Hofher, Cornell '79
Record: 5 Years, 27-23-0

1994 SCHEDULE

Princeton ■ ....Sept. 17
Fordham...Sept. 24
Lehigh ■ ....Oct. 1
Harvard ....Oct. 8
Bucknell ....Oct. 15
Dartmouth ■ ....Oct. 22
Brown ■ ....Oct. 29
Yale ....Nov. 5
Columbia ....Nov. 12
Pennsylvania ■ ....Nov. 19

1993 RESULTS (4-6-0)

12	Princeton	18
6	Colgate	22
13	Lehigh	35
27	Harvard	0
48	Fordham	6
27	Dartmouth	28
21	Brown	3
21	Yale	0
24	Columbia	29
14	Pennsylvania	17
213		**158**

Nickname: Big Red.
Stadium: Schoellkopf (1915), 27,000 capacity. Artificial turf.
Colors: Carnelian & White.
Conference: Ivy League.
SID: Dave Wohlhueter, 607-255-3753.
AD: Laing Kennedy.

CORNELL COLLEGE

Mt. Vernon, IA 52314 III

Coach: Steve Miller, Cornell College '65
Record: 15 Years, 75-60-3

1994 SCHEDULE

Carleton ....Sept. 10
Beloit ■ ....Sept. 17
Lawrence..Sept. 24
Carroll (Wis.) ■ ....Oct. 1
Knox ■ ....Oct. 8
Monmouth (Ill.) ....Oct. 15
Grinnell ....Oct. 22
Illinois Col. ■ ....Oct. 29
Coe ....Nov. 5

1993 RESULTS (7-2-0)

34	Buena Vista	20
13	Beloit	9
26	St. Norbert	40
54	Lake Forest	0
35	Knox	21
48	Monmouth (Ill.)	32
41	Grinnell	14
26	Illinois Col.	14
18	Coe	48
295		**198**

Nickname: Rams.
Stadium: Ash Park Field (1922), 2,500 capacity. Natural turf.
Colors: Purple & White.
Conference: Midwest Conf.
SID: Ron Yoder, 319-895-4483.
AD: Ellen Whale.

CORTLAND STATE

Cortland, NY 13045 III

Coach: Dave Murray, Springfield '81
Record: 4 Years, 25-18-0

1994 SCHEDULE

Mansfield ....Sept. 3
Montclair St. ....*Sept. 10
Ferrum ■ ....Sept. 17
Buffalo St...Sept. 24
Newport News App. ■ ....Oct. 1
Brockport St. ■ ....Oct. 8
Albany (N.Y.)..Oct. 15
Springfield ■ ....Oct. 22
Wash. & Jeff. ....Oct. 29
Ithaca ■ ....Nov. 5

1993 RESULTS (1-9-0)

3	Mansfield	0
7	Montclair St.	17
10	Ferrum	21
0	Buffalo St.	45
14	Brockport St.	26
13	Albany (N.Y.)	20
33	Springfield	55
7	Wash. & Jeff.	48
14	Ithaca	32
14	Southern Conn. St.	26
115		**290**

Nickname: Red Dragons.
Stadium: Davis Field (1959), 5,000 capacity. Natural turf.
Colors: Red & White.
Conference: Division III Independent.
SID: Fran Elia, 607-753-5673.
AD: Lee Roberts.

CURRY

Milton, MA 02186 III

Coach: Jerry Varnum, Northeastern '64
Record: 1 Year, 1-8-0

1994 SCHEDULE

Fitchburg St. ....Sept. 10
Western New Eng. ■ ....Sept. 17
Framingham St. ■ ....Sept. 24
Bentley ....Oct. 1
Nichols ■ ....Oct. 8
MIT ....Oct. 15
Assumption ....Oct. 22
Stonehill ....Oct. 29
Salve Regina ■ ....Nov. 5

1993 RESULTS (1-8-0)

20	Western New Eng.	22
9	Framingham St.	39
17	Bentley	40
15	Nichols	13
16	MIT	23
28	Assumption	51
13	Stonehill	48
7	Salve Regina	14
0	Hartwick	48
125		**298**

Nickname: Colonels.
Stadium: D. Forbes Will Field, 1,500 capacity. Natural turf.
Colors: Purple & White.
Conference: Eastern Collegiate.
SID: Troy Watkins, 617-333-0500.
AD: Tom Stephens.

DARTMOUTH

Hanover, NH 03755 ....I-AA

Coach: John Lyons, Pennsylvania '74
Record: 2 Years, 15-5-0

1994 SCHEDULE

Colgate ....Sept. 17
Pennsylvania ■ ....Sept. 24
Fordham ■ ....Oct. 1
Lafayette ....Oct. 8
Yale ■ ....Oct. 15
Cornell ....Oct. 22
Harvard ■ ....Oct. 29
Columbia ■ ....Nov. 5
Brown ....Nov. 12
Princeton ....Nov. 19

1993 RESULTS (7-3-0)

6	Pennsylvania	10
7	Holy Cross	13
31	Bucknell	13
7	New Hampshire	14
31	Yale	14
28	Cornell	27
39	Harvard	34
42	Columbia	25
39	Brown	16
28	Princeton	22
258		**188**

Nickname: Big Green.
Stadium: Memorial Field (1923), 20,416 capacity. Natural turf.
Colors: Dartmouth Green & White.
Conference: Ivy League.
SID: Kathy Slattery, 603-646-2468.
AD: Dick Jaeger.

DAVIDSON

Davidson, NC 28036 ....I-AA

Coach: Tim Landis, Randolph-Macon '86
Record: 1 Year, 6-4-0

1994 SCHEDULE

Maryville (Tenn.) ....Sept. 17
Emory & Henry ■ ....Sept. 24
Guilford ■ ....*Oct. 1
Wash. & Lee ■ ....Oct. 8
Methodist ....Oct. 15
Randolph-Macon ....Oct. 22
Hampden-Sydney ....Oct. 29
Centre ....Nov. 5
Bridgewater (Va.) ....Nov. 12
Sewanee [Bermuda] ....Nov. 19

1993 RESULTS (6-4-0)

3	Sewanee	7
41	Rhodes	12
0	Emory & Henry	27
35	Guilford	24
21	Wash. & Lee	14
35	Methodist	7
16	Randolph-Macon	21
21	Hampden-Sydney	14
31	Centre	44
55	Bridgewater (Va.)	14
258		**184**

Nickname: Wildcats.
Stadium: Richardson Field (1924), 6,000 capacity. Natural turf.
Colors: Red & Black.
Conference: I-AA Independent.
SID: Emil Parker, 704-892-2374.
AD: Terry Holland.

DAYTON

Dayton, OH 45469 ....I-AA

Coach: Mike Kelly, Manchester '70
Record: 13 Years, 128-23-1

1994 SCHEDULE

Mt. St. Joseph ■ ....*Sept. 3
Ala.-Birmingham ■ ....*Sept. 10
Georgetown (Ky.)..Sept. 24
Evansville ■ ....Oct. 1
Wilmington (Ohio) ■ ....Oct. 8
Butler ....Oct. 15
Drake ■ ....Oct. 22
Valparaiso ....Oct. 29
San Diego ....*Nov. 12

1993 RESULTS (9-1-0)

31	Wis.-Platteville	14
31	Wheaton (Ill.)	8
30	San Diego	7
24	Mt. St. Joseph	23
13	Evansville	6
28	Butler	6
35	Drake	7
38	Valparaiso	10
49	Urbana	6
19	Ala.-Birmingham	27
298		**114**

Nickname: Flyers.
Stadium: Welcome (1949), 11,000 capacity. Artificial turf.
Colors: Red & Blue.
Conference: Pioneer Football League.
SID: Doug Hauschild, 513-229-4460.
AD: Ted Kissell.

DePAUW

Greencastle, IN 46135 III

Coach: Nick Mourouzis, Miami (Ohio) '59
Record: 13 Years, 81-44-4

1994 SCHEDULE

Millsaps ■	Sept. 10
Hope ■	Sept. 17
Albion	Sept. 24
Franklin	Oct. 1
Hanover ■	Oct. 8
Rose-Hulman	Oct. 15
Manchester ■	Oct. 22
Mt. St. Joseph [Indianapolis, Ind.]	Oct. 29
Anderson ■	Nov. 5
Wabash	Nov. 12

1993 RESULTS (2-8-0)

10	Hope	21
0	Millsaps	45
0	Albion	28
21	Hanover	14
23	Rose-Hulman	25
29	Taylor	26
19	Manchester	28
3	Anderson	35
18	Franklin	40
26	Wabash	40
149		**302**

Nickname: Tigers.
Stadium: Blackstock (1941), 4,000 capacity. Natural turf.
Colors: Old Gold & Black.
Conference: Indiana Collegiate Ath. Conf.
SID: Bill Wagner, 317-658-4630.
AD: Ted Katula.

DEFIANCE

Defiance, OH 43512 III

Coach: Ed Stults, Bluffton '80
(First year as head coach)

1994 SCHEDULE

Manchester	Sept. 3
Mount Union ■	Sept. 10
Adrian	Sept. 17
Olivet	Oct. 1
Mt. St. Joseph ■	Oct. 8
Wilmington (Ohio) ■	Oct. 15
Wash. & Jeff. ■	Oct. 22
Thomas More	Oct. 29
Bluffton	Nov. 5

1993 RESULTS (9-1-0)

46	Hanover	29
51	Olivet Nazarene	7
43	Adrian	22
49	Olivet	18
42	Mt. St. Joseph	0
31	Kalamazoo	14
37	Urbana	0
63	Wilmington (Ohio)	31
18	Thomas More	24
59	Bluffton	14
439		**159**

Nickname: Yellow Jackets.
Stadium: Alumni Field (1994), 4,176 capacity. Natural turf.
Colors: Purple & Gold.
Conference: Mideast Conf.
SID: To be named, 419-783-2346.
AD: Marv Hohenberger.

DELAWARE

Newark, DE 19716 ....I-AA

Coach: Harold Raymond, Michigan '50
Record: 28 Years, 232-92-2

1994 SCHEDULE

William & Mary	Sept. 10
Villanova	Sept. 17
West Chester ■	Sept. 24
Maine	Oct. 1
James Madison ■	Oct. 8
Richmond	Oct. 15
Massachusetts ■	Oct. 22
Northeastern ■	Oct. 29
Lehigh	Nov. 5
Hofstra ■	Nov. 12
Rhode Island ■	Nov. 19

1993 RESULTS (8-3-0)

62	Lehigh	21
42	William & Mary	35
32	Rhode Island	11
56	West Chester	41
38	James Madison	42
19	Villanova	7
29	Massachusetts	43
21	Maine	19
30	Towson St.	32
48	Richmond	10
28	Northeastern	23
405		**284**

I-AA Championship

49	Montana	48
31	Marshall	34

Nickname: Fightin' Blue Hens.
Stadium: Delaware (1952), 23,000 capacity. Natural turf.
Colors: Blue & Gold.
Conference: Yankee.
SID: Scott Selheimer, 302-831-2186.
AD: Edgar Johnson.

DELAWARE STATE

Dover, DE 19901 ....I-AA

Coach: William Collick, Delaware '74
Record: 9 Years, 62-34-0

1994 SCHEDULE

Cheyney ■	Sept. 3
Youngstown St. ■	Sept. 10
Towson St. [Wilmington, Del.]	Sept. 17
Bethune-Cookman	Oct. 1
Liberty	*Oct. 8
Florida A&M ■	Oct. 15
Morgan St.	Oct. 22
South Caro. St. ■	Oct. 29
North Caro. A&T ■	Nov. 5
Rhode Island	Nov. 12
Howard	Nov. 19

1993 RESULTS (6-5-0)

31	Fayetteville St.	28
44	Cheyney	12
14	Towson St.	31
55	Bethune-Cookman	26
28	Youngstown St.	42
18	Florida A&M ■	14
65	Morgan St.	42
15	South Caro. St.	38
25	North Caro. A&T	19
43	Liberty	47
33	Howard	53
371		**352**

Nickname: Hornets.
Stadium: Alumni Field (1957), 5,000 capacity. Natural turf.
Colors: Red & Blue.
Conference: Mid-Eastern.
SID: Craig Cotton, 302-739-4926.
AD: John Martin.

DELAWARE VALLEY

Doylestown, PA 18901 III

Coach: Bill Manlove, Temple '58
Record: 25 Years, 187-68-1

1994 SCHEDULE

FDU-Madison ■	Sept. 10
Moravian	Sept. 17
Lebanon Valley	Sept. 24
Wilkes	Oct. 1
Widener ■	Oct. 8
King's (Pa.)	Oct. 15
Susquehanna	Oct. 22
Upsala ■	Oct. 29
Albright ■	Nov. 5
Lycoming	Nov. 12

1993 RESULTS (2-8-0)

0	FDU-Madison	14
14	Moravian	31
10	Lebanon Valley	33
0	Wilkes	31
9	Widener	31
55	King's (Pa.)	31
8	Susquehanna	43
24	Upsala	20
33	Albright	34
0	Lycoming	31
153		**299**

Nickname: Aggies.
Stadium: James Work (1977), 4,500 capacity. Natural turf.
Colors: Green & Gold.
Conference: Middle Atlantic.
SID: Matthew Levy, 215-345-1500.
AD: Frank Wolfgang.

DELTA STATE

Cleveland, MS 38733 II

Coach: Todd Knight, Ouachita Baptist '86
Record: 1 Year, 3-7-0

1994 SCHEDULE

Northwestern St.	*Sept. 10
Harding	*Sept. 17
North Ala. ■	*Sept. 24
Central Ark.	*Oct. 1
Henderson St. ■	*Oct. 8
East Tex. St. ■	*Oct. 15
Livingston ■	*Oct. 22
Valdosta St.	*Oct. 29
West Ga. ■	Nov. 5
Mississippi Col.	Nov. 12

1993 RESULTS (3-7-0)

20	Southwest Baptist	0
20	Harding	6
17	North Ala.	58
27	Central Ark.	34
20	Henderson St.	19
14	East Tex. St.	19
55	Livingston	60
8	Valdosta St.	33
7	West Ga.	27
7	Mississippi Col.	13
195		**269**

Nickname: Statesmen.
Stadium: Delta Field (1970), 8,000 capacity. Natural turf.
Colors: Green & White.
Conference: Gulf South Conf.
SID: Rick Kindhart, 601-846-4677.
AD: Jim Jordan.

DENISON

Granville, OH 43023 III

Coach: Bill Wentworth, Purdue '80
Record: 1 Year, 3-7-0

1994 SCHEDULE

Alfred	Sept. 3
Centre ■	Sept. 10
Allegheny ■	Sept. 17
Kenyon	Sept. 24
Wooster ■	Oct. 1
Ohio Wesleyan	Oct. 8
Oberlin ■	Oct. 15
Wittenberg	Oct. 29
Case Reserve ■	Nov. 5
Earlham	Nov. 12

1993 RESULTS (3-7-0)

7	Alfred	38
16	Centre	21
31	Oberlin	0

13	Ohio Wesleyan	27
7	Earlham	14
3	Wooster	0
7	Case Reserve	28
7	Allegheny	59
0	Wittenberg	42
36	Kenyon	7
127		**236**

Nickname: Big Red.
Stadium: Deeds Field (1922), 5,000 capacity. Natural turf.
Colors: Red & White.
Conference: North Coast Ath. Conf.
SID: Jack Hire, 614-587-6546.
AD: Larry Scheiderer.

DICKINSON
Carlisle, PA 17013.............................III

Coach: Darwin Breaux, West Chester '77
Record: 1 Year, 7-4-0

1994 SCHEDULE

Hobart	Sept. 10
Muhlenberg ■	Sept. 17
Mercyhurst ■	Sept. 24
Union (N.Y.) ■	Oct. 1
Frank. & Marsh. ■	Oct. 8
Western Md.	Oct. 15
Swarthmore ■	Oct. 22
Johns Hopkins	Oct. 29
Gettysburg ■	Nov. 5
Ursinus	Nov. 12

1993 RESULTS (7-3-0)

13	Hobart	0
20	Muhlenberg	0
35	Mercyhurst	6
17	Union (N.Y.)	23
40	Frank. & Marsh.	0
33	Western Md.	19
37	Swarthmore	0
16	Johns Hopkins	0
7	Gettysburg	28
18	Ursinus	31
236		**107**

ECAC Southwest
9	Montclair St.	17

Nickname: Red Devils.
Stadium: Biddle Field (1909), 5,000 capacity. Natural turf.
Colors: Red & White.
Conference: Centennial Conference.
SID: To be named, 717-245-1652.
AD: Les Poolman.

DRAKE
Des Moines, IA 50311.......................I-AA

Coach: Rob Ash, Cornell College '73
Record: 14 Years, 83-53-4

1994 SCHEDULE

Simpson	Sept. 10
San Diego ■	Sept. 17
Aurora	Sept. 24
Butler ■	Oct. 1
Evansville	Oct. 8
Valparaiso ■	Oct. 15
Dayton	Oct. 22
Neb.-Kearney	Oct. 29
Wis.-Oshkosh ■	Nov. 5
St. Ambrose ■	Nov. 12

1993 RESULTS (8-2-0)

35	Simpson	9
54	Augustana (Ill.)	48
3	Butler	28
47	Aurora	14
33	Chicago	19
31	Valparaiso	12
7	Dayton	35
48	Ill. Benedictine	33
17	San Diego	14

29	Evansville	27
304		**239**

Nickname: Bulldogs.
Stadium: Drake (1925), 18,000 capacity. Natural turf.
Colors: Blue & White.
Conference: Pioneer Football League.
SID: Mike Mahon, 515-271-3012.
AD: Lynn King.

DUBUQUE
Dubuque, IA 52001 III

Coach: Jim Collins, Wittenberg '88
(First year as head coach)

1994 SCHEDULE

Graceland ■	Sept. 10
Central (Iowa) ■	Sept. 17
Loras	Sept. 24
Buena Vista ■	Oct. 1
Wartburg	Oct. 8
Upper Iowa ■	Oct. 15
Eureka	Oct. 22
Luther	Oct. 29
Simpson [Cedar Falls, Iowa]	Nov. 5
William Penn	Nov. 12

1993 RESULTS (2-8-0)

0	Graceland	14
0	Central (Iowa)	49
21	Eureka	17
0	Luther	33
7	Upper Iowa	41
12	Loras	13
7	Simpson	56
6	Wartburg	56
0	Buena Vista	48
27	William Penn	7
80		**334**

Nickname: Spartans.
Stadium: Chalmers Field, 2,800 capacity. Natural turf.
Colors: Blue & White.
Conference: Iowa Inter. Ath. Conf.
SID: Mike Duenser, 319-589-3225.
AD: Connie Bandy-Hodge.

DUKE
Durham, NC 27706 ....I-A

Coach: Fred Goldsmith, Florida '67
Record: 6 Years, 25-38-1

1994 SCHEDULE

Maryland ■	Sept. 3
East Caro. ■	*Sept. 10
Army ■	Sept. 15
Georgia Tech	Sept. 24
Navy	Oct. 1
Clemson ■	Oct. 15
Wake Forest	Oct. 22
Florida St.	Oct. 29
Virginia ■	Nov. 5
North Caro. St.	Nov. 12
North Caro.	Nov. 19

1993 RESULTS (3-8-0)

7	Florida St.	45
38	Rutgers	39
42	Army	21
0	Virginia	35
19	Tennessee	52
10	Clemson	13
18	Maryland	26
21	Wake Forest	13
14	Georgia Tech	47
21	North Caro. St.	20
24	North Caro.	38
214		**349**

Nickname: Blue Devils.
Stadium: Wallace Wade (1929), 33,941 capacity. Natural turf.
Colors: Royal Blue & White.
Conference: Atlantic Coast Conf.
SID: Mike Cragg, 919-684-2633.
AD: Tom Butters.

DUQUESNE
Pittsburgh, PA 15282 ....I-AA

Coach: Greg Gattuso, Penn St. '83
Record: 1 Year, 4-6-0

1994 SCHEDULE

St. Francis (Pa.) ■	*Sept. 10
Georgetown ■	Sept. 17
St. Peter's	Sept. 24
Gannon ■	Oct. 1
Robert Morris	Oct. 8
Marist ■	Oct. 15
Siena	Oct. 22
Iona ■	Oct. 29
St. John's (N.Y.)	Nov. 5
Canisius	Nov. 12

1993 RESULTS (4-6-0)

16	Canisius	12
13	Bethany (W.Va.)	10
28	Thiel	0
0	Gannon	7
24	Wagner	27
12	Marist	21
7	Mercyhurst	24
12	St. John's (N.Y.)	37
35	St. Francis (Pa.)	34
22	Central Conn. St.	41
169		**213**

Nickname: Dukes.
Stadium: Arthur J. Rooney Field (1993), 2,500 capacity. Artificial turf.
Colors: Red & Blue.
Conference: I-AA Independent.
SID: Sue Ryan, 412-396-5861.
AD: Brian Colleary.

EARLHAM
Richmond, IN 47374..............................III

Coach: Frank Carr, Albion '78
Record: 9 Years, 18-67-0

1994 SCHEDULE

Swarthmore ■	Sept. 10
Wittenberg	*Sept. 17
Case Reserve ■	Sept. 24
Principia ■	Oct. 1
Allegheny	Oct. 8
Kenyon ■	Oct. 15
Wooster	Oct. 22
Ohio Wesleyan ■	Oct. 29
Oberlin	Nov. 5
Denison ■	Nov. 12

1993 RESULTS (4-6-0)

6	Manchester	24
28	Otterbein	48
0	Wittenberg	34
10	Kenyon	17
16	Oberlin	9
14	Denison	7
18	Ohio Wesleyan	34
35	Principia	29
12	Wooster	6
6	Allegheny	54
145		**262**

Nickname: Hustlin' Quakers.
Stadium: M. O. Ross Field (1975), 1,500 capacity. Natural turf.
Colors: Maroon & White.
Conference: North Coast Ath. Conf.
SID: David Knight, 317-983-1416.
AD: Porter Miller.

EAST CAROLINA
Greenville, NC 27834 ....I-A

Coach: Steve Logan, Tulsa '75
Record: 2 Years, 7-15-0

1994 SCHEDULE

Duke	*Sept. 10
Temple	*Sept. 17

Syracuse ■ ....Sept. 24
Southern Miss. ■ ....Oct. 1
South Caro. ■ ....Oct. 8
Virginia Tech ■ ....Oct. 15
Tulsa ....*Oct. 22
Cincinnati ■ ....Oct. 29
Auburn ....Nov. 5
Central Fla. ■ ....Nov. 12
Memphis ....Nov. 19

1993 RESULTS (2-9-0)

22	Syracuse	41
41	Central Fla.	17
0	Washington	35
7	Memphis	34
3	South Caro.	27
31	Louisiana Tech	28
16	Southern Miss.	24
12	Virginia Tech	31
26	Tulsa	52
3	Kentucky	6
14	Cincinnati	34
175		**329**

Nickname: Pirates.
Stadium: Dowdy-Ficklen (1963), 35,000 capacity. Natural turf.
Colors: Purple & Gold.
Conference: I-A Independent.
SID: Charles Bloom, 919-757-4522.
AD: Dave Hart.

EAST STROUDSBURG

East Stroudsburg, PA 18301 II

Coach: Dennis Douds, Slippery Rock '63
Record: 20 Years, 124-76-3

1994 SCHEDULE

Lafayette...Sept. 10
Springfield...Sept. 17
Southern Conn. St. ■ ....Sept. 24
West Chester ....Oct. 1
Slippery Rock ■ ....Oct. 8
Cheyney ....Oct. 15
Mansfield ....Oct. 22
Millersville ■ ....Oct. 29
Bloomsburg ....Nov. 5
Kutztown ■ ....Nov. 12

1993 RESULTS (7-2-1)

45	Kutztown	14
25	Springfield	14
14	Southern Conn. St.	14
9	Calif. (Pa.)	6
47	Cheyney	12
45	Mansfield	21
7	Millersville	20
31	Bloomsburg	6
42	American Int'l	3
33	West Chester	35
298		**145**

Nickname: Warriors.
Stadium: Eiler-Martin (1969), 6,000 capacity. Natural turf.
Colors: Red & Black.
Conference: Pennsylvania Conf.
SID: Peter Nevins, 717-424-3312.
AD: Earl W. Edwards.

EAST TENNESSEE STATE

Johnson City, TN 37614 ....I-AA

Coach: Mike Cavan, Georgia '72
Record: 8 Years, 47-34-2

1994 SCHEDULE

Catawba ■ ....*Sept. 1
Morehead St. ....*Sept. 10
Va. Military ■ ....*Sept. 17
Auburn ....Sept. 24
Appalachian St. ■ ....*Oct. 1
Citadel ....Oct. 8
Ga. Southern ....Oct. 22
Furman ■ ....Oct. 29
Marshall ■ ....Nov. 5
Tenn.-Chatt. ....Nov. 12

Western Caro. ....Nov. 19

1993 RESULTS (5-6-0)

44	Wingate	17
24	Mars Hill	0
10	Va. Military	7
21	Furman	45
16	Appalachian St.	20
20	Citadel	17
24	Western Caro.	25
0	Clemson	27
9	Marshall	33
21	Tenn.-Chatt.	0
24	Ga. Southern	31
213		**222**

Nickname: Buccaneers.
Stadium: Memorial (1977), 12,000 capacity. Artificial turf.
Colors: Blue & Gold.
Conference: Southern Conf.
SID: John Cathey, 615-929-4220.
AD: Janice Shelton.

EAST TEXAS STATE

Commerce, TX 75428 II

Coach: Eddie Vowell, Southwestern Okla. '69
Record: 8 Years, 47-43-1

1994 SCHEDULE

Central Ark. ....*Sept. 3
Northwest Mo. St. ■ ....Sept. 10
Henderson St. ■ ....Sept. 17
Northwestern St. ....*Sept. 24
Central Okla. ....Oct. 1
Tex. A&M-Kingsville ■ ....Oct. 8
Delta St. ....*Oct. 15
Eastern N. Mex. ■ ....Oct. 22
Abilene Christian ....Oct. 29
Angelo St. ■ ....Nov. 5
Texas Southern ....Nov. 12

1993 RESULTS (5-6-0)

16	Central Ark.	13
45	Northwest Mo. St.	11
0	Henderson St.	7
19	Northwestern St.	30
30	Central Okla.	27
3	Tex. A&M-Kingsville	28
19	Delta St.	14
0	Eastern N. Mex.	15
10	Abilene Christian	17
8	Angelo St.	31
16	Texas Southern	7
166		**200**

Nickname: Lions.
Stadium: Memorial (1950), 10,000 capacity. Natural turf.
Colors: Blue & Gold.
Conference: Lone Star Conf.
SID: Bill Powers, 903-886-5131.
AD: Margo Harbison.

EASTERN ILLINOIS

Charleston, IL 61920 ....I-AA

Coach: Bob Spoo, Purdue '60
Record: 7 Years, 36-42-1

1994 SCHEDULE

Murray St. ■ ....*Sept. 1
UTEP ....*Sept. 10
Lock Haven ■ ....*Sept. 17
Northern Ill. ....*Sept. 24
Southwest Mo. St. ....*Oct. 1
Northern Iowa ■ ....Oct. 8
Western Ill. ....Oct. 22
Indiana St. ■ ....Oct. 29
Illinois St. ....Nov. 5
Western Ky. ■ ....Nov. 12
Southern Ill. ....Nov. 19

1993 RESULTS (3-7-1)

34	Murray St.	17
7	McNeese St.	49
10	Navy	31

14	Western Ill.	28
24	Indiana St.	27
27	Northern Iowa	31
17	Illinois St.	17
35	Southwest Mo. St.	13
26	Northwestern St.	34
14	Western Ky.	28
42	Southern Ill.	35
250		**310**

Nickname: Panthers.
Stadium: O'Brien (1970), 10,000 capacity. Natural turf.
Colors: Blue & Gray.
Conference: Gateway.
SID: Dave Kidwell, 217-581-6408.
AD: Bob McBee.

EASTERN KENTUCKY

Richmond, KY 40475 ....I-AA

Coach: Roy Kidd, Eastern Ky. '54
Record: 30 Years, 247-88-8

1994 SCHEDULE

Western Ky. ....*Sept. 1
Samford ■ ....*Sept. 10
Youngstown St. ....*Sept. 17
Austin Peay ....*Sept. 24
Middle Tenn. St. ....*Oct. 1
Tennessee St. ■ ....*Oct. 8
Murray St. ■ ....Oct. 15
Tennessee Tech ....Oct. 22
Tenn.-Martin ....*Oct. 29
Southeast Mo. St. ■ ....Nov. 5
Morehead St. ■ ....Nov. 19

1993 RESULTS (8-3-0)

10	Western Ky.	15
14	Northeast La.	40
48	Austin Peay	7
22	Youngstown St.	26
52	Tennessee St.	13
21	Murray St.	13
10	Tennessee Tech.	7
30	Tenn.-Martin	0
35	Southeast Mo. St.	21
33	Middle Tenn. St.	27
44	Morehead St.	7
319		**176**

I-AA Championship

| 12 | Ga. Southern | 14 |

Nickname: Colonels.
Stadium: Roy Kidd (1969), 20,000 capacity. Natural turf.
Colors: Maroon & White.
Conference: Ohio Valley Conf.
SID: Karl Park, 606-622-1253.
AD: Roy Kidd.

EASTERN MICHIGAN

Ypsilanti, MI 48197 ....I-A

Coach: Ron Cooper, Jacksonville St. '83
Record: 1 Year, 4-7-0

1994 SCHEDULE

Nevada-Las Vegas ....*Sept. 3
Wisconsin ....Sept. 10
Central Mich. ■ ....Sept. 17
Bowling Green ■ ....Sept. 24
Miami (Ohio) ■ ....Oct. 1
Kent ....Oct. 8
Western Mich. ....Oct. 22
Ball St. ....Oct. 29
Akron ■ ....Nov. 5
Ohio ....Nov. 12
Toledo ■ ....Nov. 19

1993 RESULTS (4-7-0)

6	West Va.	48
28	Temple	31
16	Western Ill.	14
15	Miami (Ohio)	7
20	Kent	15
28	Central Mich.	21
20	Western Mich.	21

13	Ball St.	18
7	Akron	19
10	Ohio	12
0	Toledo	14
163		**220**

Nickname: Eagles.
Stadium: Rynearson (1969), 30,200 capacity. Artificial turf.
Colors: Dark Green & White.
Conference: Mid-American Conf.
SID: Jim Streeter, 313-487-0317.
AD: Tim Weiser.

EASTERN NEW MEXICO
Portales, NM 88130 II

Coach: Bud Elliott, Baker (Kan.) '53
Record: 26 Years, 137-130-7

1994 SCHEDULE
N.M. Highlands	*Sept. 3
Fort Lewis ■	Sept. 10
Western N. Mex. ■	*Sept. 17
Southern Utah	*Sept. 24
Abilene Christian ■	Oct. 1
Angelo St.	*Oct. 8
Tarleton St. ■	Oct. 15
East Tex. St.	Oct. 22
Tex. A&M-Kingsville ■	Oct. 29
West Tex. A&M	Nov. 5
Central Okla. ■	Nov. 12

1993 RESULTS (1-8-1)
10	N.M. Highlands	15
20	Western St.	24
7	Western N. Mex.	37
19	Colorado Mines	19
36	Abilene Christian	52
0	Angelo St.	28
15	East Tex. St.	0
22	Tex. A&M-Kingsville	54
34	West Tex. A&M	35
7	Central Okla.	36
170		**300**

Nickname: Greyhounds.
Stadium: Greyhound (1969), 5,300 capacity. Natural turf.
Colors: Silver & Green.
Conference: Lone Star Conf.
SID: Wendel Sloan, 505-562-2131.
AD: Chris Gage.

EASTERN WASHINGTON
Cheney, WA 99004..............................I-AA

Coach: Mike Kramer, Idaho '77
(First year as head coach)

1994 SCHEDULE
Cal Poly SLO ■	*Sept. 10
Montana	Sept. 17
Weber St. ■	Sept. 24
Portland St.	*Oct. 1
Idaho ■	Oct. 8
Northern Ariz.	*Oct. 15
Idaho St.	Oct. 22
Montana St. ■	Oct. 29
Utah St.	Nov. 5
Boise St. ■	*Nov. 12
Northern Iowa	*Nov. 19

1993 RESULTS (7-3-0)
13	Northeast La.	34
48	Cal St. Sacramento	7
20	Montana	35
36	Weber St.	22
38	Portland St.	21
10	Idaho	49
38	Northern Ariz.	26
38	Idaho St.	7
16	Montana St.	7
28	Boise St.	17
285		**225**

Nickname: Eagles.

Stadium: Woodward (1967), 6,000 capacity. Natural turf.
Colors: Red & White.
Conference: Big Sky Conf.
SID: Dave Cook, 509-359-6334.
AD: John Johnson.

EDINBORO
Edinboro, PA 16444 II

Coach: Tom Hollman, Ohio Northern '68
Record: 10 Years, 69-30-3

1994 SCHEDULE
Hillsdale	Sept. 3
Mansfield	Sept. 10
Elizabeth City St. ■	Sept. 17
Lock Haven	Oct. 1
Shippensburg ■	Oct. 8
Calif. (Pa.)	Oct. 15
Slippery Rock ■	Oct. 22
Indiana (Pa.)	Oct. 29
American Int'l	Nov. 5
Clarion ■	Nov. 12

1993 RESULTS (8-2-0)
9	Ferris St.	23
34	Elizabeth City St.	27
28	Buffalo	17
28	Clarion	0
52	Lock Haven	20
34	Shippensburg	17
32	Calif. (Pa.)	7
41	Slippery Rock	38
24	Indiana (Pa.)	31
52	Millersville	27
334		**207**

II Championship
| 28 | New Haven | 48 |

Nickname: Fighting Scots.
Stadium: Sox Harrison (1965), 5,000 capacity. Natural turf.
Colors: Red & White.
Conference: Pennsylvania Conf.
SID: Todd Jay, 814-732-2811.
AD: Jim McDonald.

ELIZABETH CITY STATE
Elizabeth City, NC 27909 II

Coach: George Moody, Virginia St. '60
Record: 11 Years, 51-58-3

1994 SCHEDULE
Bowie St.	Sept. 3
Fayetteville St. ■	*Sept. 10
Edinboro	Sept. 17
Norfolk St. ■	*Sept. 24
N.C. Central	Oct. 1
Virginia Union ■	Oct. 8
Knoxville	Oct. 15
Virginia St. ■	Oct. 22
Hampton ■	Oct. 29
Livingstone	Nov. 5
Johnson Smith	Nov. 12

1993 RESULTS (2-8-0)
6	Winston-Salem	47
0	Fayetteville St.	38
27	Edinboro	34
12	Norfolk St.	40
14	N.C. Central	48
0	Virginia Union	67
16	Bowie St.	2
17	Virginia St.	42
0	Hampton	40
51	Lane	16
143		**374**

Nickname: Vikings.
Stadium: Roebuck, 6,500 capacity. Natural turf.
Colors: Royal Blue & White.
Conference: Central Inter. Ath. Assoc.
SID: Glen Mason, 919-335-3385.
AD: Ed McLean.

ELMHURST
Elmhurst, IL 60126 III

Coach: Paul Krohn, Mankato St. '76
Record: 1 Year, 1-7-1

1994 SCHEDULE
Alma	Sept. 17
Ill. Benedictine ■	Sept. 24
North Central ■	Oct. 1
North Park	Oct. 8
Carthage ■	Oct. 15
Augustana (Ill.)	Oct. 22
Ill. Wesleyan ■	Oct. 29
Millikin	Nov. 5
Wheaton (Ill.)	Nov. 12

1993 RESULTS (1-7-1)
28	Ill. Benedictine	47
21	Aurora	35
40	Carthage	32
14	North Park	14
22	North Central	24
13	Augustana (Ill.)	46
6	Ill. Wesleyan	58
32	Wheaton (Ill.)	49
2	Millikin	41
178		**346**

Nickname: Bluejays.
Stadium: Langhorst, 2,000 capacity. Natural turf.
Colors: Navy & White.
Conference: Division III Independent.
SID: John Quigley, 708-617-3380.
AD: Chris Ragsdale.

ELON
Elon College, NC 27244..............................II

Coach: Leon Hart, Maryville (Tenn.) '73
Record: 5 Years, 28-25-0

1994 SCHEDULE
West Ga.	Sept. 3
Catawba	Sept. 10
Concord (W.Va.) ■	Sept. 17
Carson-Newman ■	Sept. 24
Lenoir-Rhyne	*Oct. 1
Mars Hill	Oct. 8
Presbyterian ■	Oct. 15
Gardner-Webb ■	Oct. 29
Wofford ■	Nov. 5
Wingate	Nov. 12

1993 RESULTS (8-3-0)
25	West Ga.	11
60	West Va. St.	13
21	Concord (W.Va.)	7
20	Carson-Newman	31
33	Lenoir-Rhyne	9
17	Mars Hill	7
31	Presbyterian	17
21	Catawba	27
64	Gardner-Webb	21
7	Wofford	18
37	Wingate	25
336		**186**

Nickname: Fightin' Christians.
Stadium: Burlington Memorial, 10,000 capacity. Natural turf.
Colors: Maroon & Gold.
Conference: South Atlantic Conf.
SID: David Hibbard, 919-584-2316.
AD: Alan White.

EMORY AND HENRY
Emory, VA 24327 III

Coach: Lou Wacker, Richmond '56
Record: 12 Years, 89-39-0

1994 SCHEDULE
Wash. & Lee	Sept. 10
Bridgewater (Va.) ■	Sept. 17
Davidson	Sept. 24
Millsaps ■	Oct. 1

Hampden-Sydney ....Oct. 8
Randolph-Macon ■ ....Oct. 15
Guilford ....Oct. 22
Clinch Valley ■ ....Oct. 29
Ferrum ....Nov. 5
Maryville (Tenn.) ■ ....Nov. 12

1993 RESULTS (7-3-0)

15	Cumberland (Ky.)	8
36	Wash. & Lee	6
28	Bridgewater (Va.)	7
27	Davidson	0
10	Millsaps	34
10	Hampden-Sydney	7
6	Randolph-Macon	20
46	Guilford	14
16	Ferrum	13
28	Maryville (Tenn.)	29
222		**138**

Nickname: Wasps.
Stadium: Fullerton Field, 5,000 capacity. Natural turf.
Colors: Blue & Gold.
Conference: Old Dominion Ath. Conf.
SID: Nathan Graybeal, 703-944-4121.
AD: Lou Wacker.

EMPORIA STATE

Emporia, KS 66801 II

Coach: Larry Kramer, Nebraska '65
Record: 23 Years, 119-108-6

1994 SCHEDULE

Fort Hays St. ■ ....*Sept. 3
Southwest Baptist ....Sept. 17
Missouri-Rolla ■ ....*Sept. 24
Northwest Mo. St. ....Oct. 1
Northeast Mo. St. ■ ....Oct. 8
Mo. Western St. ....Oct. 15
Mo. Southern St. ■ ....Oct. 22
Central Mo. St. ....Oct. 29
Washburn ....Nov. 5
Pittsburg St. ■ ....Nov. 12

1993 RESULTS (3-7-0)

7	Fort Hays St.	17
42	Southwest Baptist	6
17	Missouri-Rolla	0
15	Northwest Mo. St.	21
13	Northeast Mo. St.	24
20	Mo. Western St.	26
17	Mo. Southern St.	39
3	Central Mo. St.	17
37	Washburn	19
14	Pittsburg St.	45
185		**214**

Nickname: Hornets.
Stadium: Welch (1937), 7,000 capacity. Natural turf.
Colors: Black & Old Gold.
Conference: Mid-America Intercoll. Ath. Assoc.
SID: J. D. Campbell, 316-341-5454.
AD: Bill Quayle.

EUREKA

Eureka, IL 61530..III

Coach: John Tully, Azusa Pacific '75
Record: 4 Years, 23-18-0

1994 SCHEDULE

Blackburn ....Sept. 3
Monmouth (Ill.) ■ ....Sept. 10
Lawrence...Sept. 17
Greenville ■ ....Sept. 24
Concordia (Wis.) ■ ....Oct. 1
Concordia (Ill.) ....Oct. 8
MacMurray ....Oct. 15
Dubuque ■ ....Oct. 22
Quincy...Oct. 29
Lakeland ....Nov. 5

1993 RESULTS (3-7-0)

14	MacMurray	17
19	Monmouth (Ill.)	21
25	North Central	31
17	Dubuque	21

23	Quincy	24
14	Concordia (Ill.)	6
34	Lakeland	8
27	Ky. Wesleyan	33
28	Concordia (Wis.)	14
21	Greenville	28
222		**203**

Nickname: Red Devils.
Stadium: McKinzie (1913), 3,000 capacity. Natural turf.
Colors: Maroon & Gold.
Conference: Division III Independent.
SID: Shellie Schwanke, 309-467-6370.
AD: Warner McCollum.

EVANSVILLE

Evansville, IN 47722 ....I-AA

Coach: Robin Cooper, Ill. Wesleyan '75
Record: 6 Years, 37-18-0

1994 SCHEDULE

Wittenberg ■ ....Sept. 3
Thomas More ■ ....Sept. 10
Ky. Wesleyan ....Sept. 17
Dayton ....Oct. 1
Drake ....Oct. 8
San Diego ....Oct. 15
Valparaiso ■ ....Oct. 22
Butler ....Oct. 29
Cumberland (Tenn.) ....Nov. 5
Aurora ■ ....Nov. 12

1993 RESULTS (6-4-0)

29	Franklin	14
35	Ky. Wesleyan	14
38	Rose-Hulman	8
15	Adrian	22
6	Dayton	13
27	San Diego	21
34	Valparaiso	28
12	Butler	14
28	Cumberland (Tenn.)	12
27	Drake	29
251		**175**

Nickname: Purple Aces.
Stadium: Arad McCutchan (1984), 3,000 capacity. Natural turf.
Colors: Purple & White.
Conference: Pioneer Football League.
SID: Bob Boxell, 812-479-2350.
AD: Jim Byers.

FAIRLEIGH DICKINSON-MADISON

Madison, NJ 07940 III

Coach: Bill Klika, Colgate '67
Record: 20 Years, 53-120-1

1994 SCHEDULE

Delaware Valley ....Sept. 10
Lycoming ■ ....*Sept. 16
Johns Hopkins..*Sept. 23
Montclair St. ....*Oct. 1
Albright ....*Oct. 8
Wilkes ■ ....*Oct. 14
Ursinus ....*Oct. 22
King's (Pa.) ■ ....*Oct. 28
Widener...Nov. 5
Upsala ....Nov. 12

1993 RESULTS (8-2-0)

14	Delaware Valley	0
21	Lycoming	20
38	Johns Hopkins	21
12	Montclair St.	22
33	Albright	7
2	Wilkes	29
30	Ursinus	25
19	King's (Pa.)	6
35	Widener	3
41	Upsala	24
245		**157**

ECAC Southeast

0	Wesley	6

Nickname: Jersey Devils.
Stadium: Jersey Devils, 4,000 capacity. Natural turf.
Colors: Columbia, Navy & White.
Conference: Middle Atlantic.
SID: Tom Bonerbo, 201-593-8965.
AD: Bill Klika.

FAIRMONT STATE

Fairmont, WV 26554 II

Coach: Doug Sams, Oregon St. '78
Record: 3 Years, 12-18-0

1994 SCHEDULE

Calif. (Pa.) ■ ....Sept. 3
Clarion ....Sept. 17
West Va. Wesleyan ....Sept. 24
Concord (W.Va.) ....Oct. 1
West Va. St. ■ ....Oct. 8
West Va. Tech ■ ....Oct. 15
Glenville St. ....Oct. 22
Shepherd ....Oct. 29
West Liberty St. ■ ....Nov. 5
Tiffin ■ ....Nov. 12

1993 RESULTS (3-7-0)

20	Presbyterian	17
6	Slippery Rock	42
16	Calif. (Pa.)	31
7	West Va. Wesleyan	11
15	Concord (W.Va.)	19
37	West Va. St.	20
48	West Va. Tech	6
7	Glenville St.	33
15	Shepherd	21
0	West Liberty St.	23
171		**223**

Nickname: Falcons.
Stadium: Rosier Field, 6,000 capacity. Natural turf.
Colors: Maroon & White.
Conference: West Va. Inter. Ath. Conf.
SID: Jim Brinkman, 304-367-4264.
AD: Colin Cameron.

FAYETTEVILLE STATE

Fayetteville, NC 28301 II

Coach: Jerome Harper, Alabama St. '74
Record: 2 Years, 11-9-1

1994 SCHEDULE

Livingstone ■ ....*Sept. 3
Elizabeth City St..*Sept. 10
Norfolk St. ....*Sept. 17
Winston-Salem ....*Oct. 1
N.C. Central ■ ....*Oct. 8
Virginia St. ■ ....*Oct. 15
Johnson Smith ....Oct. 22
Bowie St. ■ ....Oct. 29
Hampton ■ ....Nov. 12

1993 RESULTS (6-5-0)

28	Delaware St.	31
38	Elizabeth City St.	0
34	Norfolk St.	19
33	Cheyney	12
17	Winston-Salem	20
27	N.C. Central	20
6	Virginia St.	41
40	Johnson Smith	6
0	Bowie St.	18
32	Livingstone	35
20	Newberry	18
275		**220**

Nickname: Broncos.
Stadium: Bronco, 5,000 capacity. Natural turf.
Colors: White & Royal Blue.
Conference: Central Inter. Ath. Assoc.
SID: Marion Crowe Jr., 910-486-1314.
AD: Ralph Burns.

FERRIS STATE

Big Rapids, MI 49307 II

Coach: Keith Otterbein, Hillsdale '79
Record: 8 Years, 49-38-3

1994 SCHEDULE

Ashland		Sept. 10
Indianapolis ■		Sept. 17
Hillsdale ■		*Sept. 24
Grand Valley St.		Oct. 1
Northern Mich. ■		Oct. 8
Wayne St. (Mich.)		Oct. 15
Northwood ■		Oct. 22
Michigan Tech		Oct. 29
St. Joseph's (Ind.) ■		Nov. 5
Saginaw Valley		Nov. 12

1993 RESULTS (9-0-2)

23	Edinboro	9
20	Ashland	6
13	Hillsdale	13
36	Wayne St. (Mich.)	6
47	Northern Mich.	0
26	St. Francis (Ill.)	18
17	Grand Valley St.	17
47	Northwood	0
40	Indianapolis	26
34	Saginaw Valley	23
35	St. Joseph's (Ind.)	13
338		**131**

II Championship

21	Indiana (Pa.)	28

Nickname: Bulldogs.
Stadium: Top Taggart Field (1957), 9,100 capacity. Natural turf.
Colors: Crimson & Gold.
Conference: Midwest Intercollegiate.
SID: Ted Halm, 616-592-2331.
AD: Tom Kirinovic (interim).

FERRUM

Ferrum, VA 24088 III

Coach: Dave Davis, Elon '71
(First year as head coach)

1994 SCHEDULE

Rowan ■		Sept. 3
West Va. Tech		Sept. 10
Cortland St.		Sept. 17
Thomas More ■		Sept. 24
Westminster (Pa.) ■		Oct. 1
Newport News App.		Oct. 8
Chowan ■		Oct. 15
Montclair St.		Oct. 22
Emory & Henry ■		Nov. 5

1993 RESULTS (5-4-0)

16	Thomas More	8
21	Cortland St.	10
13	Lees-McRae	16
8	Westminster (Pa.)	17
22	Newport News App.	42
49	Chowan	21
24	Montclair St.	21
8	Mansfield	7
13	Emory & Henry	16
174		**158**

Nickname: Panthers.
Stadium: Adams (1969), 5,000 capacity. Natural turf.
Colors: Black & Gold.
Conference: Division III Independent.
SID: Gary Holden, 703-365-4306.
AD: Ted Kinder.

FITCHBURG STATE

Fitchburg, MA 01420 III

Coach: Mike Woessner, Massachusetts '81
Record: 1 Year, 0-8-1

1994 SCHEDULE

Curry		Sept. 10
Framingham St. ■		Sept. 17
Westfield St.		*Sept. 23
Bri'water (Mass.) ■		Oct. 1
Worcester St.		Oct. 8
Mass. Maritime ■		Oct. 15

Mass.-Dartmouth		Oct. 22
Maine Maritime ■		Oct. 29
Mass.-Boston		Nov. 5

1993 RESULTS (0-8-1)

12	Western New Eng.	12
14	Framingham St.	17
7	Westfield St.	14
0	Bri'water (Mass.)	49
7	Worcester St.	35
16	Mass. Maritime	18
0	Mass.-Dartmouth	12
8	Maine Maritime	45
2	Mass.-Boston	18
66		**220**

Nickname: Falcons.
Stadium: Robert Elliot, 1,200 capacity. Natural turf.
Colors: Green, Gold & White.
Conference: New England.
SID: David Marsh, 508-345-2151.
AD: Elizabeth Kruczek.

FLORIDA

Gainesville, FL 32604 ....I-A

Coach: Steve Spurrier, Florida '67
Record: 7 Years, 59-23-1

1994 SCHEDULE

New Mexico St. ■		*Sept. 3
Kentucky ■		*Sept. 10
Tennessee		Sept. 17
Mississippi		*Oct. 1
Louisiana St. ■		Oct. 8
Auburn ■		Oct. 15
Georgia ■		Oct. 29
Southern Miss. ■		Nov. 5
South Caro. ■		Nov. 12
Vanderbilt		Nov. 19
Florida St.		Nov. 26

1993 RESULTS (10-2-0)

44	Arkansas St.	6
24	Kentucky	20
41	Tennessee	34
38	Mississippi St.	24
58	Louisiana St.	3
35	Auburn	38
33	Georgia	26
61	Southwestern La.	14
37	South Caro.	26
52	Vanderbilt	0
21	Florida St.	33
28	Alabama	13
472		**237**

Sugar Bowl

41	West Va.	7

Nickname: Gators.
Stadium: Florida Field (1929), 83,000 capacity. Natural turf.
Colors: Blue & Orange.
Conference: Southeastern Conf.
SID: John Humenik, 904-375-4683.
AD: Jeremy Foley.

FLORIDA A&M

Tallahassee, FL 32307 ....I-AA

Coach: Billy Joe, Villanova '63
Record: 20 Years, 169-54-4

1994 SCHEDULE

Tuskegee ■		*Sept. 3
Jackson St.		Sept. 17
Howard ■		*Sept. 24
Tennessee St. [Nashville, Tenn.]		*Oct. 1
North Caro. A&T ■		*Oct. 8
Delaware St.		Oct. 15
South Caro. St. [Orlando, Fla.]		Oct. 22
Morgan St. ■		Oct. 29
Southern-B.R.		*Nov. 5
Grambling [Miami, Fla.]		Nov. 12
Bethune-Cookman [Tampa, Fla.]		Nov. 26

1993 RESULTS (5-6-0)

23	Tennessee St.	15

21	South Caro. St.	17
41	Jackson St.	19
13	Howard	32
13	North Caro. A&T	41
14	Delaware St.	18
6	Albany St. (Ga.)	14
41	Morgan St.	14
4	Southern-B.R.	26
13	Grambling	39
27	Bethune-Cookman	22
216		**257**

Nickname: Rattlers.
Stadium: Bragg Memorial (1957), 25,500 capacity. Natural turf.
Colors: Orange & Green.
Conference: Mid-Eastern.
SID: Alvin Hollins, 904-599-3200.
AD: Walter Reed.

FLORIDA STATE

Tallahassee, FL 32306 ....I-A

Coach: Bobby Bowden, Samford '53
Record: 28 Years, 239-78-3

1994 SCHEDULE

Virginia ■		Sept. 3
Maryland ■		Sept. 10
Wake Forest		*Sept. 17
North Caro. ■		*Sept. 24
Miami (Fla.)		*Oct. 8
Clemson ■		Oct. 22
Duke ■		Oct. 29
Georgia Tech		Nov. 5
Notre Dame [Orlando, Fla.]		Nov. 12
North Caro. St.		Nov. 19
Florida ■		Nov. 26

1993 RESULTS (11-1-0)

42	Kansas	0
45	Duke	7
57	Clemson	0
33	North Caro.	7
51	Georgia Tech	0
28	Miami (Fla.)	10
40	Virginia	14
54	Wake Forest	0
49	Maryland	20
24	Notre Dame	31
62	North Caro. St.	3
33	Florida	21
518		**113**

Orange Bowl

18	Nebraska	16

Nickname: Seminoles.
Stadium: Doak S. Campbell (1950), 75,000 capacity. Natural turf.
Colors: Garnet & Gold.
Conference: Atlantic Coast Conf.
SID: Rob Wilson, 904-644-1403.
AD: Bob Goin.

FORDHAM

Bronx, NY 10458 ....I-AA

Coach: Nick Quartaro, Iowa '77
Record: 2 Years, 12-8-0

1994 SCHEDULE

Villanova ■		Sept. 3
Lehigh		Sept. 10
Hofstra		Sept. 17
Cornell ■		Sept. 24
Dartmouth		Oct. 1
Columbia ■		Oct. 8
Princeton ■		Oct. 15
Colgate		Oct. 22
Holy Cross ■		Oct. 29
Lafayette ■		Nov. 12
Bucknell		Nov. 19

1993 RESULTS (1-10-0)

6	Lehigh	24
5	Villanova	25
0	Columbia	7

30	Pennsylvania	34
14	Buffalo	33
6	Cornell	48
12	Lafayette	27
21	Bucknell	27
17	Colgate	13
22	Hofstra	49
12	Holy Cross	28
145		**315**

Nickname: Rams.
Stadium: Jack Coffey Field (1930), 7,000 capacity.
  Natural turf.
Colors: Maroon & White.
Conference: Patriot League.
SID: Bill Holtz, 718-817-4240.
AD: Frank McLaughlin.

FORT HAYS STATE
Hays, KS 67601 II

Coach: Bob Cortese, Colorado '67
Record: 14 Years, 114-38-3
1994 SCHEDULE
Emporia St. ....*Sept. 3
Pittsburg St. ....*Sept. 10
Central Okla. ■ ....*Sept. 17
Neb.-Kearney ....Sept. 24
Fort Lewis ■ ....Oct. 1
N.M. Highlands ....Oct. 8
Mesa St. ....Oct. 15
Adams St. ■ ....Oct. 22
Colorado Mines ■ ....Oct. 29
Chadron St. ....Nov. 5
Western St. ■ ....Nov. 12

1993 RESULTS (8-3-0)
17	Emporia St.	7
0	Central Okla.	30
6	Central Ark.	28
32	N.M. Highlands	14
26	Neb.-Kearney	14
44	Mesa St.	14
30	Adams St.	15
35	Colorado Mines	21
35	Chadron St.	7
17	Western St.	28
44	Fort Lewis	6
286		**184**

II Championship
34	UC Davis	37

Nickname: Tigers.
Stadium: Lewis Field (1936), 7,000 capacity. Artificial
  turf.
Colors: Black & Gold.
Conference: Rocky Mountain Ath. Conf.
SID: Jack Kuestermeyer, 913-628-5903.
AD: Tom Spicer.

FORT LEWIS
Durango, CO 81301 II

Coach: Kevin Donnalley, North Dak. St. '84
Record: 2 Years, 2-18-0
1994 SCHEDULE
West Tex. A&M ■ ....*Sept. 3
Eastern N. Mex. ....Sept. 10
Montana Tech ....Sept. 17
Angelo St. ■ ....*Sept. 24
Fort Hays St. ....Oct. 1
Mesa St. ....Oct. 8
Western St. ....Oct. 15
N.M. Highlands ■ ....Oct. 22
Adams St. ....Oct. 29
Colorado Mines ....Nov. 5
Chadron St. ■ ....Nov. 12

1993 RESULTS (1-9-0)
47	West Tex. A&M	24
20	Montana St.	58
27	Mesa St.	54
0	Angelo St.	69
20	Western St.	45
34	N.M. Highlands	62

17	Adams St.	27
39	Colorado Mines	41
3	Chadron St.	41
6	Fort Hays St.	44
213		**465**

Nickname: Skyhawk.
Stadium: Ray Dennison Memorial (1958), 4,000 capac-
  ity. Natural turf.
Colors: Blue & Gold.
Conference: Rocky Mountain Ath. Conf.
SID: Chris Aaland, 303-247-7441.
AD: Bruce Grimes.

FORT VALLEY STATE
Ft. Valley, GA 31030 II

Coach: Douglas Porter, Xavier (La.) '52
Record: 24 Years, 141-93-5
1994 SCHEDULE
North Ala. [Macon, Ga.] ....*Sept. 3
Morehouse [Ypsilanti, Mich.] ....*Sept. 10
Valdosta St. ....*Sept. 17
Morris Brown [Macon, Ga.] ....*Sept. 24
Clark Atlanta ....Oct. 1
Miles ....Oct. 15
Alabama A&M ■ ....Oct. 22
Tuskegee ■ ....Oct. 29
Savannah St. ....Nov. 5
Albany St. (Ga.) [Columbus, Ga.] ....Nov. 12

1993 RESULTS (6-4-1)
14	North Ala.	36
36	Morehouse	6
24	Valdosta St.	49
17	Morris Brown	0
10	Clark Atlanta	6
13	Jacksonville St.	27
40	Miles	0
35	Alabama A&M	7
40	Tuskegee	21
14	Savannah St.	14
0	Albany St. (Ga.)	14
243		**180**

Nickname: Wildcats.
Stadium: Wildcat (1957), 7,500 capacity. Natural turf.
Colors: Royal Blue & Old Gold.
Conference: Southern Inter. Ath. Conf.
SID: Russell Boone Jr., 912-825-6437.
AD: Douglas Porter.

FRAMINGHAM STATE
Framingham, MA 01701 III

Coach: Thomas Raeke, Southern Conn. St. '71
Record: 9 Years, 31-49-0
1994 SCHEDULE
Fitchburg St. ....Sept. 17
Curry ....Sept. 24
Westfield St. ■ ....Oct. 1
Bri'water (Mass.) ....Oct. 8
Worcester St. ■ ....Oct. 15
Mass. Maritime ....Oct. 22
Mass.-Dartmouth ■ ....Oct. 29
Maine Maritime ....Nov. 5
Mass.-Boston ■ ....Nov. 12

1993 RESULTS (4-5-0)
17	Fitchburg St.	14
39	Curry	9
7	Westfield St.	28
9	Bri'water (Mass.)	27
14	Worcester St.	20
27	Mass. Maritime	6
13	Mass.-Dartmouth	27
19	Maine Maritime	28
13	Mass.-Boston	0
158		**159**

Nickname: Rams.
Stadium: Maple Street Field, 1,500 capacity. Natural
  turf.
Colors: Black & Gold.
Conference: New England.

SID: Scott Kavanagh, 508-626-4612.
AD: Lawrence Boyd.

FRANKLIN
Franklin, IN 46131 III

Coach: Mike McClure, Franklin '75
Record: 5 Years, 18-30-1
1994 SCHEDULE
Millikin ....Sept. 10
Kalamazoo ■ ....Sept. 17
Alma ....Sept. 24
DePauw ■ ....Oct. 1
Anderson ....Oct. 8
Wabash ■ ....Oct. 15
Rose-Hulman ■ ....Oct. 22
Manchester [Indianapolis, Ind.] ....Oct. 29
MacMurray ....Nov. 5
Hanover ....Nov. 12

1993 RESULTS (6-3-0)
14	Evansville	29
35	Alma	14
0	Thomas More	42
13	Anderson	21
49	Wabash	35
32	Rose-Hulman	28
30	Manchester	6
40	DePauw	18
41	Hanover	28
254		**221**

Nickname: Grizzlies.
Stadium: Goodell Field, 2,000 capacity. Natural turf.
Colors: Old Gold & Navy Blue.
Conference: Indiana Collegiate Ath. Conf.
SID: Kevin Elixman, 317-738-8184.
AD: Kerry Prather.

FRANKLIN AND MARSHALL
Lancaster, PA 17604 III

Coach: Tom Gilburg, Syracuse '61
Record: 19 Years, 128-53-2
1994 SCHEDULE
Carnegie Mellon ■ ....Sept. 3
Wash. & Jeff. ....Sept. 10
Ursinus ■ ....Sept. 17
Muhlenberg ....Sept. 24
Dickinson ....Oct. 8
Georgetown ■ ....Oct. 15
Western Md. ■ ....Oct. 22
Swarthmore ....Oct. 29
Johns Hopkins ■ ....Nov. 5
Gettysburg ....Nov. 12

1993 RESULTS (6-4-0)
14	Carnegie Mellon	38
7	Wash. & Jeff.	14
20	Ursinus	9
7	Muhlenberg	9
0	Dickinson	40
17	Georgetown	3
16	Western Md.	7
18	Swarthmore	7
13	Johns Hopkins	11
12	Gettysburg	10
124		**148**

Nickname: Diplomats.
Stadium: Williamson Field (1920), 4,000 capacity.
  Natural turf.
Colors: Blue & White.
Conference: Centennial Conference.
SID: Tom Byrnes, 717-291-3838.
AD: William A. Marshall.

FRESNO STATE
Fresno, CA 93740 ....I-A

Coach: Jim Sweeney, Portland '51
Record: 29 Years, 186-133-3
1994 SCHEDULE
Ohio St. [Anaheim, Calif.] ....*Aug. 29

San Jose St. ■		*Sept. 3
Washington St.		Sept. 10
Oregon St. ■		*Sept. 17
Hawaii		*Sept. 24
Brigham Young ■		*Oct. 8
Wyoming ■		*Oct. 15
Air Force		Oct. 22
New Mexico ■		*Oct. 29
Nevada ■		*Nov. 5
UTEP		Nov. 12
Colorado St. ■		*Nov. 19
San Diego St.		Nov. 26

1993 RESULTS (8-3-0)

39	Baylor	42
48	Oregon	30
41	New Mexico	24
30	Utah St.	14
32	Colorado St.	34
33	Air Force	20
48	Brigham Young	45
28	Wyoming	32
30	UTEP	10
45	Hawaii	21
63	San Diego St.	37
437		**309**

Aloha Bowl

30	Colorado	41

Nickname: Bulldogs.
Stadium: Bulldog (1980), 41,031 capacity. Natural turf.
Colors: Cardinal & Blue.
Conference: Western Athl. Conf.
SID: Scott Johnson, 209-278-2509.
AD: Gary Cunningham.

FROSTBURG STATE

Frostburg, MD 21532 III

Coach: Mike McGlinchey, Delaware '67
Record: 8 Years, 77-43-4

1994 SCHEDULE

Bri'water (Mass.)		Sept. 10
Mercyhurst ■		Sept. 17
Salisbury St. ■		Sept. 24
Chowan		Oct. 1
Trenton St.		Oct. 8
Brockport St. ■		Oct. 15
Bridgewater (Va.) ■		Oct. 22
Newport News App.		Oct. 29
Waynesburg		Nov. 5
Methodist ■		Nov. 12

1993 RESULTS (9-1-0)

33	Alfred	31
34	Thiel	12
34	Salisbury St.	21
27	Chowan	0
27	Trenton St.	16
35	Wesley	26
35	Bridgewater (Va.)	0
36	Brockport St.	23
22	Waynesburg	24
47	Methodist	23
330		**176**

III Championship

26	Wilkes	25
7	Wash. & Jeff.	28

Nickname: Bobcats.
Stadium: Bobcat (1974), 4,000 capacity. Natural turf.
Colors: Red, White & Black.
Conference: Division III Independent.
SID: Jeffrey P. Krone, 301-689-4371.
AD: Loyal Park.

FURMAN

Greenville, SC 29613 ....I-AA

Coach: Bobby Johnson, Clemson '73
(First year as head coach)

1994 SCHEDULE

Clemson		Sept. 3
South Caro. St. ■		*Sept. 10
William & Mary ■		*Sept. 17

Western Caro. ■		Oct. 1
Appalachian St.		Oct. 8
Citadel ■		Oct. 15
Va. Military		Oct. 22
East Tenn. St.		Oct. 29
Ga. Southern ■		Nov. 5
Marshall		Nov. 12
Tenn.-Chatt. ■		Nov. 19

1993 RESULTS (5-5-1)

26	Connecticut	17
3	Georgia Tech	37
14	Wofford	14
45	East Tenn. St.	21
20	Western Caro.	23
27	Appalachian St.	21
10	Citadel	20
24	Va. Military	0
19	Ga. Southern	31
17	Marshall	3
42	Tenn.-Chatt.	45
247		**232**

Nickname: Paladins.
Stadium: Paladin (1981), 16,000 capacity. Natural turf.
Colors: Purple & White.
Conference: Southern Conf.
SID: Hunter Reid, 803-294-2061.
AD: Ray Parlier.

GALLAUDET

Washington, DC 20002 III

Coach: Geoffrey Ciniero, Clemson '87
Record: 1 Year, 0-7-0

1994 SCHEDULE

Chowan ■		Sept. 10
Salve Regina ■		Sept. 17
Catholic		Oct. 1
Hartwick ■		Oct. 15
Methodist		Oct. 22
Bethany (W.Va.) ■		Oct. 29

1993 RESULTS (0-7-0)

0	Chowan	51
0	Salve Regina	56
6	Hartwick	38
13	Catholic	44
0	Methodist	36
7	Newport News App.	60
0	St. John Fisher	47
26		**332**

Nickname: Bison.
Stadium: Hotchkiss Field, 1,500 capacity. Natural turf.
Colors: Buff & Blue.
Conference: Division III Independent.
SID: Matt Eviston, 202-651-5602.
AD: Joe Fritsch.

GANNON

Erie, PA 16541 II

Coach: Tom Herman, Edinboro '72
Record: 5 Years, 21-24-1

1994 SCHEDULE

St. Francis (Pa.) ■		Sept. 3
Capital		Sept. 10
Rochester ■		Sept. 17
Robert Morris		Sept. 24
Duquesne		Oct. 1
Canisius ■		Oct. 8
Waynesburg		Oct. 15
Thiel ■		Oct. 29
Mercyhurst		Nov. 5
Bethany (W.Va.)		Nov. 12

1993 RESULTS (6-4-0)

20	St. Francis (Pa.)	0
9	Waynesburg	0
7	Mercyhurst	17
16	Canisius	13
7	Duquesne	0
14	LIU-C.W. Post	55
6	Wash. & Jeff.	34
20	Bethany (W.Va.)	23

16	Thiel	7
9	Grove City	3
124		**152**

Nickname: Golden Knights.
Stadium: Erie Veterans Memorial, 10,500 capacity. Natural turf.
Colors: Maroon & Gold.
Conference: Division II Independent.
SID: Bob Shreve, 814-871-7418.
AD: Howard "Bud" Elwell.

GARDNER-WEBB

Boiling Springs, NC 28017 II

Coach: Woody Fish, Gardner-Webb '73
Record: 10 Years, 59-52-1

1994 SCHEDULE

Wofford		*Sept. 3
Johnson Smith ■		Sept. 10
Tenn.-Chatt.		*Sept. 17
Newberry		*Sept. 24
Wingate ■		*Oct. 1
Lenoir-Rhyne		*Oct. 8
Catawba ■		Oct. 15
Carson-Newman		Oct. 22
Elon		Oct. 29
Presbyterian		Nov. 5
Mars Hill ■		Nov. 12

1993 RESULTS (1-9-0)

34	Lees-McRae	29
34	Tenn.-Chatt.	59
21	Newberry	23
28	Wingate	56
40	Lenoir-Rhyne	47
36	Catawba	40
10	Carson-Newman	47
21	Elon	64
30	Presbyterian	34
21	Mars Hill	40
275		**439**

Nickname: Bulldogs.
Stadium: Spangler (1972), 5,000 capacity. Natural turf.
Colors: Scarlet, White & Black.
Conference: South Atlantic Conf.
SID: Mark Wilson, 704-434-4355.
AD: Ozzie McFarland.

GEORGETOWN

Washington, DC 20057 ....I-AA

Coach: Bob Benson, Vermont '86
Record: 1 Year, 4-5-0

1994 SCHEDULE

Duquesne		Sept. 17
Iona ■		Sept. 24
Canisius ■		Oct. 1
St. John's (N.Y.)		Oct. 8
Frank. & Marsh.		Oct. 15
Johns Hopkins ■		Oct. 22
Marist ■		Oct. 29
Siena		Nov. 5
St. Peter's ■		Nov. 12

1993 RESULTS (4-5-0)

15	Iona	22
35	Siena	6
26	St. Peter's	14
3	Frank. & Marsh.	17
17	Johns Hopkins	19
10	Catholic	0
24	St. John's (N.Y.)	25
14	Canisius	19
17	Wash. & Lee	14
161		**136**

Nickname: Hoyas.
Stadium: Kehoe Field, 2,400 capacity. Artificial turf.
Colors: Blue & Gray.
Conference: Metro Atlantic.
SID: Bill Hurd, 202-687-2492.
AD: Francis X. Rienzo.

GEORGIA

Athens, GA 30602 ....I-A

Coach: Ray Goff, Georgia '78
Record: 5 Years, 34-24-0

1994 SCHEDULE

South Caro.	*Sept. 3
Tennessee ■	Sept. 10
Northeast La. ■	Sept. 17
Mississippi ■	Sept. 24
Alabama	Oct. 1
Clemson ■	Oct. 8
Vanderbilt ■	Oct. 15
Kentucky	*Oct. 22
Florida	Oct. 29
Auburn	Nov. 12
Georgia Tech ■	Nov. 25

1993 RESULTS (5-6-0)

21	South Caro.	23
6	Tennessee	38
52	Texas Tech	37
14	Mississippi	31
10	Arkansas	20
54	Southern Miss.	24
41	Vanderbilt	3
33	Kentucky	28
26	Florida	33
28	Auburn	42
43	Georgia Tech	10
328		**289**

Nickname: Bulldogs.
Stadium: Sanford (1929), 86,117 capacity. Natural turf.
Colors: Red & Black.
Conference: Southeastern Conf.
SID: Claude Felton, 706-542-1621.
AD: Vince Dooley.

GEORGIA SOUTHERN

Statesboro, GA 30460 ....I-AA

Coach: Tim Stowers, Auburn '80
Record: 4 Years, 36-14-0

1994 SCHEDULE

Miami (Fla.)	Sept. 3
West Ga. ■	*Sept. 10
Marshall ■	*Sept. 17
Tenn.-Chatt.	*Sept. 24
Va. Military ■	*Oct. 1
Western Caro.	Oct. 8
Appalachian St. ■	*Oct. 15
East Tenn. St. ■	Oct. 22
Furman	Nov. 5
Glenville St. ■	Nov. 12
Citadel	Nov. 19

1993 RESULTS (9-2-0)

35	Savannah St.	3
16	Citadel	6
3	Marshall	13
45	Tenn.-Chatt.	0
7	Miami (Fla.)	30
19	Western Caro.	18
34	Appalachian St.	28
57	Va. Military	0
31	Furman	19
51	Concord (W.Va.)	13
31	East Tenn. St.	24
329		**154**

I-AA Championship

14	Eastern Ky.	12
14	Youngstown St.	34

Nickname: Eagles.
Stadium: Paulson (1984), 18,000 capacity. Natural turf.
Colors: Blue & White.
Conference: Southern Conf.
SID: Matt Rogers, 912-681-5239.
AD: David Wagner.

GEORGIA TECH

Atlanta, GA 30332 ....I-A

Coach: Bill Lewis, East Stroudsburg '63
Record: 8 Years, 44-45-2

1994 SCHEDULE

Arizona ■	*Sept. 1
Western Caro. ■	Sept. 10
Duke ■	Sept. 24
North Caro. St.	Oct. 1
North Caro.	Oct. 8
Virginia ■	Oct. 15
Maryland ■	Oct. 22
Florida St. ■	Nov. 5
Clemson ■	Nov. 12
Wake Forest ■	Nov. 19
Georgia	Nov. 25

1993 RESULTS (5-6-0)

37	Furman	3
14	Virginia	35
13	Clemson	16
0	Florida St.	51
38	Maryland	0
3	North Caro.	41
23	North Caro. St.	28
47	Duke	14
37	Baylor	27
38	Wake Forest	28
10	Georgia	43
260		**286**

Nickname: Yellow Jackets.
Stadium: Bobby Dodd/Grant Field (1913), 46,000 capacity. Artificial turf.
Colors: Old Gold & White.
Conference: Atlantic Coast Conf.
SID: Mike Finn, 404-894-5445.
AD: Homer Rice.

GETTYSBURG

Gettysburg, PA 17325 III

Coach: Barry Streeter, Lebanon Valley '71
Record: 16 Years, 92-67-4

1994 SCHEDULE

Catholic ■	Sept. 10
Western Md.	Sept. 17
Swarthmore ■	Sept. 24
Johns Hopkins	*Sept. 30
Stony Brook ■	Oct. 8
Ursinus ■	Oct. 15
Muhlenberg	Oct. 22
Merchant Marine	Oct. 29
Dickinson	Nov. 5
Frank. & Marsh. ■	Nov. 12

1993 RESULTS (5-5-0)

14	Catholic	6
38	Western Md.	17
14	Swarthmore	15
25	Johns Hopkins	6
36	Stony Brook	43
28	Ursinus	31
28	Muhlenberg	17
6	Merchant Marine	19
28	Dickinson	7
10	Frank. & Marsh.	12
227		**173**

Nickname: Bullets.
Stadium: Musselman (1965), 6,176 capacity. Natural turf.
Colors: Orange & Blue.
Conference: Centennial Conference.
SID: Robert Kenworthy, 717-337-6527.
AD: Chuck Winters.

GLENVILLE STATE

Glenville, WV 26351 II

Coach: Rich Rodriquez, West Va. '85
Record: 4 Years, 23-27-2

1994 SCHEDULE

Calif. (Pa.)	Sept. 10
Newport News App. ■	Sept. 17
Shepherd	Sept. 24
West Liberty St.	Oct. 8

West Va. Wesleyan	Oct. 15
Fairmont St. ■	Oct. 22
Concord (W.Va.)	Oct. 29
West Va. Tech ■	Nov. 5
Ga. Southern	Nov. 12

1993 RESULTS (8-2-0)

14	Samford	20
45	Johnson Smith	0
37	Newport News App.	17
30	Shepherd	17
57	West Va. St.	0
28	West Liberty St.	17
16	West Va. Wesleyan	17
33	Fairmont St.	7
27	Concord (W.Va.)	7
50	West Va. Tech	0
337		**102**

NAIA I Championship

41	Carroll (Mont.)	24
13	Central St. (Ohio)	12
35	East Central (Okla.)	49

Nickname: Pioneers.
Stadium: Pioneer (1977), 5,000 capacity. Natural turf.
Colors: Blue & White.
Conference: West Va. Inter. Ath. Conf.
SID: Mark Loudin, 304-462-4102.
AD: Russell Shepherd.

GRAMBLING

Grambling, LA 71245 ....I-AA

Coach: Eddie Robinson, Leland '41
Record: 51 Years, 388-140-15

1994 SCHEDULE

Alcorn St. ■	*Sept. 3
Morgan St.	Sept. 17
Hampton [East Rutherford, N.J.]	*Sept. 24
Prairie View [Dallas, Texas]	*Oct. 1
Mississippi Val.	Oct. 8
Ark.-Pine Bluff [Shreveport, La.]	*Oct. 15
Jackson St. ■	Oct. 22
Texas Southern	*Oct. 29
Alabama St. ■	Nov. 5
Florida A&M [Miami, Fla.]	Nov. 12
Southern-B.R. [New Orleans, La.]	Nov. 26

1993 RESULTS (7-4-0)

24	Alcorn St.	25
33	Tennessee St.	28
26	Hampton	27
49	Prairie View	0
28	Mississippi Val.	19
45	Ark.-Pine Bluff	7
20	Jackson St.	14
50	Texas Southern	26
10	Alabama St.	16
39	Florida A&M	13
13	Southern-B.R.	31
337		**206**

Nickname: Tigers.
Stadium: Robinson (1983), 19,600 capacity. Natural turf.
Colors: Black & Gold.
Conference: Southwestern.
SID: Stanley Lewis, 318-274-2761.
AD: Eddie Robinson.

GRAND VALLEY STATE

Allendale, MI 49401 II

Coach: Brian Kelly, Assumption '83
Record: 3 Years, 23-9-2

1994 SCHEDULE

Indiana (Pa.)	Sept. 3
Indianapolis	Sept. 10
St. Francis (Ill.) ■	Sept. 17
Ashland	Sept. 24
Ferris St. ■	Oct. 1
Wayne St. (Mich.) ■	Oct. 8
Hillsdale	Oct. 15
Michigan Tech ■	Oct. 22
Northern Mich.	*Oct. 29

Saginaw Valley ■ ....Nov. 5
Northwood ....Nov. 12

1993 RESULTS (6-3-2)

38	St. Joseph's (Ind.)	14
3	Indiana (Pa.)	34
35	Northwood	0
31	Indianapolis	7
36	Saginaw Valley	17
28	Northern Mich.	28
17	Ferris St.	17
14	Ashland	29
21	Hillsdale	38
28	Wayne St. (Mich.)	25
20	St. Francis (Ill.)	18
271		**227**

Nickname: Lakers.
Stadium: Arend D. Lubbers (1979), 4,156 capacity.
   Natural turf.
Colors: Blue, Black & White.
Conference: Midwest Intercollegiate.
SID: Don Thomas, 616-895-3275.
AD: Michael Kovalchik.

GRINNELL

Grinnell, IA 50112 III

Coach: Greg Wallace, Mo. Valley '70
Record: 6 Years, 7-45-1

1994 SCHEDULE

Trinity Bible (N.D.) ■ ....Sept. 10
Principia ■ ....Sept. 17
Carroll (Wis.) ....Sept. 24
Lawrence ■ ....Oct. 1
Coe ....Oct. 8
Knox ....Oct. 15
Cornell College ■ ....Oct. 22
Monmouth (Ill.) ■ ....Oct. 29
Illinois Col. ....Nov. 5

1993 RESULTS (0-9-0)

17	Colorado Col.	44
6	Principia	34
21	Lake Forest	22
21	St. Norbert	42
7	Coe	69
21	Knox	31
14	Cornell College	41
27	Monmouth (Ill.)	55
8	Illinois Col.	38
142		**376**

Nickname: Pioneers.
Stadium: Rosenbloom (1911), 1,750 capacity. Natural
   turf.
Colors: Scarlet & Black.
Conference: Midwest Conf.
SID: Andy Hamilton, 515-269-3832.
AD: Dee Fairchild.

GROVE CITY

Grove City, PA 16127 III

Coach: Christopher Smith, Grove City '72
Record: 10 Years, 35-53-2

1994 SCHEDULE

Kenyon ■ ....Sept. 10
Bluffton ■ ....Sept. 17
Wash. & Jeff. ....Sept. 24
Waynesburg ....Oct. 1
Bethany (W.Va.) ....Oct. 15
Thiel ■ ....Oct. 22
Mercyhurst ■ ....Oct. 29
Carnegie Mellon ....Nov. 5
Brockport St. ....Nov. 12

1993 RESULTS (5-4-0)

35	Hiram	14
28	Waynesburg	22
24	Bluffton	13
23	Bethany (W.Va.)	19
14	Thiel	20
0	Wash. & Jeff.	56
7	Carnegie Mellon	48
3	Gannon	9

35	Oberlin	7
169		**208**

Nickname: Wolverines.
Stadium: Thorn Field (1981), 3,500 capacity. Natural
   turf.
Colors: Crimson & White.
Conference: Presidents Ath. Conf.
SID: Joe Klimchak, 412-458-3365.
AD: R. Jack Behringer.

GUILFORD

Greensboro, NC 27410 III

Coach: Mike Ketchum, Guilford '78
Record: 3 Years, 12-18-0

1994 SCHEDULE

Methodist ....Sept. 10
Chowan ....Sept. 17
Hampden-Sydney ....Sept. 24
Davidson ....*Oct. 1
Sewanee ....Oct. 8
Bridgewater (Va.) ■ ....Oct. 15
Emory & Henry ....Oct. 22
Randolph-Macon ....Oct. 29
Wash. & Lee ■ ....Nov. 5
Salisbury St. ■ ....Nov. 12

1993 RESULTS (2-8-0)

0	Lenoir-Rhyne	56
7	Methodist	14
28	Chowan	18
7	Hampden-Sydney	20
24	Davidson	35
25	Bridgewater (Va.)	28
14	Emory & Henry	46
13	Randolph-Macon	16
14	Wash. & Lee	13
3	Salisbury St.	41
135		**287**

Nickname: Quakers.
Stadium: Armfield Athletic (1961), 3,500 capacity.
   Natural turf.
Colors: Crimson & Grey.
Conference: Old Dominion Ath. Conf.
SID: Brett Ayers, 910-316-2107.
AD: Gayle Currie.

GUSTAVUS ADOLPHUS

St. Peter, MN 56082 III

Coach: Jay Schoenebeck, Gust. Adolphus '80
(First year as head coach)

1994 SCHEDULE

Central (Iowa) ....Sept. 10
Macalester ....Sept. 17
Carleton ■ ....Sept. 24
St. Olaf ....Oct. 1
Concordia-M'head ■ ....Oct. 8
St. John's (Minn.) ....Oct. 15
Bethel (Minn.) ■ ....Oct. 22
Augsburg ....Oct. 29
Hamline ■ ....Nov. 5
St. Thomas (Minn.) [Minneapolis, Minn.] ....*Nov. 11

1993 RESULTS (2-8-0)

0	Augustana (S.D.)	35
6	Concordia-M'head	13
13	Augsburg	25
14	St. John's (Minn.)	55
23	St. Olaf	26
3	Hamline	24
26	Bethel (Minn.)	14
6	St. Thomas (Minn.)	35
38	Macalester	29
30	Carleton	35
159		**291**

Nickname: Golden Gusties.
Stadium: Hollingsworth Field (1929), 5,500 capacity.
   Natural turf.
Colors: Black & Gold.
Conference: Minnesota Inter. Ath. Conf.
SID: Tim Kennedy, 507-933-7647.
AD: Jim Malmquist.

HAMILTON

Clinton, NY 13323 III

Coach: Steve Frank, Bridgeport '72
Record: 9 Years, 38-33-1

1994 SCHEDULE

Tufts ....Sept. 24
Wesleyan ....Oct. 1
Trinity (Conn.) ■ ....Oct. 8
Bowdoin ■ ....Oct. 15
Colby ....Oct. 22
Williams ■ ....Oct. 29
Middlebury ■ ....Nov. 5
Bates ....Nov. 12

1993 RESULTS (1-7-0)

0	Amherst	6
18	Wesleyan	22
0	Trinity (Conn.)	34
8	Bowdoin	42
14	Colby	17
3	Williams	56
17	Middlebury	33
35	Bates	7
95		**217**

Nickname: Continentals.
Stadium: Steuben Field, 3,000 capacity. Natural turf.
Colors: Buff & Blue.
Conference: NESCAC.
SID: Chris Militello, 315-859-4685.
AD: Thomas Murphy.

HAMLINE

St. Paul, MN 55104 III

Coach: Dick Tressel, Baldwin-Wallace '70
Record: 16 Years, 92-63-2

1994 SCHEDULE

Minn.-Morris ....Sept. 10
St. Olaf ....Sept. 17
Concordia-M'head ■ ....Sept. 24
St. John's (Minn.) ....Oct. 1
Bethel (Minn.) ■ ....Oct. 8
Augsburg ....Oct. 15
Macalester ■ ....Oct. 22
St. Thomas (Minn.) ■ ....Oct. 29
Gust. Adolphus ....Nov. 5
Carleton [Minneapolis, Minn.] ....Nov. 11

1993 RESULTS (7-3-0)

28	Mt. Senario	0
33	Carleton	31
33	Concordia-M'head	36
29	Augsburg	9
0	St. John's (Minn.)	69
24	Gust. Adolphus	3
21	St. Olaf	13
28	Bethel (Minn.)	3
27	St. Thomas (Minn.)	31
58	Macalester	27
281		**222**

Nickname: Pipers.
Stadium: Norton (1921), 2,000 capacity. Natural turf.
Colors: Red & Gray.
Conference: Minnesota Inter. Ath. Conf.
SID: Tim Cornwell, 612-641-2036.
AD: Dick Tressel.

HAMPDEN-SYDNEY

Hampden-Sydney, VA 23943 III

Coach: Joe Bush, Va. Military '65
Record: 9 Years, 51-37-1

1994 SCHEDULE

Muhlenberg ....Sept. 10
Clinch Valley ....Sept. 17
Guilford ■ ....Sept. 24
Bridgewater (Va.) ■ ....Oct. 1
Emory & Henry ....Oct. 8
Wash. & Lee ....Oct. 15
Catholic ■ ....Oct. 22
Davidson ■ ....Oct. 29

SCHEDULES/RESULTS

Methodist ....Nov. 5
Randolph-Macon ■ ....Nov. 12

1993 RESULTS (6-4-0)

22	Muhlenberg	21
25	Clinch Valley	28
20	Guilford	7
23	Bridgewater (Va.)	6
7	Emory & Henry	10
28	Wash. & Lee	20
28	Catholic	14
14	Davidson	21
35	Methodist	7
10	Randolph-Macon	17
212		**151**

Nickname: Tigers.
Stadium: Hundley (1964), 2,400 capacity. Natural turf.
Colors: Garnet & Grey.
Conference: Old Dominion Ath. Conf.
SID: Dean E. Hybl, 804-223-6156.
AD: Joe Bush.

HAMPTON
Hampton, VA 23668.................................II

Coach: Joe Taylor, Western Ill. '72
Record: 11 Years, 82-32-4

1994 SCHEDULE

Morehouse ■ ....Sept. 3
Howard ....Sept. 10
Virginia Union ....*Sept. 17
Grambling [East Rutherford, N.J.] ....*Sept. 24
Johnson Smith ■ ....Oct. 1
Virginia St. ....Oct. 8
Norfolk St. ■ ....Oct. 15
Livingstone ....Oct. 22
Elizabeth City St. ....Oct. 29
LIU-C.W. Post ■ ....Nov. 5
Fayetteville St. ....Nov. 12

1993 RESULTS (11-0-0)

45	Livingstone	0
35	Bowie St.	6
13	Virginia Union	0
27	Grambling	26
43	Johnson Smith	6
42	Virginia St.	14
48	Norfolk St.	21
46	Tuskegee	12
40	Elizabeth City St.	0
41	Chowan	0
49	Morris Brown	14
429		**99**

II Championship

33	Albany St. (Ga.)	7
20	North Ala.	45

Nickname: Pirates.
Stadium: Armstrong Field (1928), 11,000 capacity. Natural turf.
Colors: Royal Blue & White.
Conference: Central Inter. Ath. Assoc.
SID: LeCounte Conaway, 804-727-5757.
AD: Dennis Thomas.

HANOVER
Hanover, IN 47243.................................III

Coach: C. Wayne Perry, DePauw '72
Record: 12 Years, 74-42-2

1994 SCHEDULE

Otterbein ■ ....Sept. 10
Centre ....Sept. 17
Mt. St. Joseph ■ ....Oct. 1
DePauw ....Oct. 8
Anderson ■ ....Oct. 15
Wabash ....Oct. 22
Rose-Hulman [Indianapolis, Ind.] ....*Oct. 29
Manchester ....Nov. 5
Franklin ■ ....Nov. 12

1993 RESULTS (3-7-0)

29	Defiance	46
22	Thomas More	36
33	Bluffton	23

14	DePauw	21
21	Anderson	28
21	Wabash	55
37	Rose-Hulman	21
45	Taylor	47
45	Manchester	7
28	Franklin	41
295		**325**

Nickname: Panthers.
Stadium: L. S. Ayers Field (1973), 4,000 capacity. Natural turf.
Colors: Red & Blue.
Conference: Indiana Collegiate Ath. Conf.
SID: Carter Cloyd, 812-866-7010.
AD: Dick Naylor.

HARDIN-SIMMONS
Abilene, TX 79698 III

Coach: Jimmie Keeling, Howard Payne '58
Record: 3 Years, 18-13-0

1994 SCHEDULE

Panhandle St. ....*Sept. 10
Sul Ross St. ■ ....Sept. 24
Howard Payne ....Oct. 1
McMurry ■ ....Oct. 8
West Tex. A&M ■ ....Oct. 15
Sul Ross St. ....Oct. 22
Colorado Col. ■ ....Oct. 29
Midwestern St. ....*Nov. 5
Austin ....Nov. 12

1993 RESULTS (8-2-0)

51	Panhandle St.	13
35	Sul Ross St.	7
55	Millsaps	14
47	Howard Payne	9
38	McMurry	7
37	Tarleton St.	44
55	Sul Ross St.	9
29	Colorado Col.	31
24	Midwestern St.	13
28	Austin	3
399		**150**

NAIA II Championship

49	Evangel	21
30	Mary	20
0	Westminster (Pa.)	10

Nickname: Cowboys.
Stadium: Shelton (1993), 4,000 capacity. Natural turf.
Colors: Purple & Gold.
Conference: Division III Independent.
SID: Kevin Carson, 915-670-1273.
AD: Merlin Morrow.

HARTWICK
Oneonta, NY 13820 III

Coach: Steve Stetson, Dartmouth '73
Record: 8 Years, 23-47-2

1994 SCHEDULE

Westfield St. ....*Sept. 9
Alfred ....Sept. 17
St. John Fisher ■ ....Sept. 24
Rochester ....Oct. 1
Salve Regina ■ ....Oct. 8
Gallaudet ....Oct. 15
Rensselaer ....Oct. 22
Pace ....Oct. 29
Hobart ■ ....Nov. 5
St. Lawrence ■ ....Nov. 12

1993 RESULTS (3-3-1)

16	St. Lawrence	35
7	Westfield St.	7
21	St. John Fisher	49
38	Gallaudet	6
13	Salve Regina	15
31	Western New Eng.	21
48	Curry	0
174		**133**

Nickname: Warriors.
Stadium: AstroTurf Field, 1,500 capacity. Artificial turf.

Colors: Royal Blue & White.
Conference: Division III Independent.
SID: Tim Markey, 607-431-4703.
AD: Kenneth Kutler.

HARVARD
Cambridge, MA 02138 ....I-AA

Coach: Tim Murphy, Springfield '78
Record: 7 Years, 32-45-1

1994 SCHEDULE

Columbia ....Sept. 17
Bucknell ■ ....Sept. 24
Holy Cross ....Oct. 1
Cornell ■ ....Oct. 8
Colgate ■ ....Oct. 15
Princeton ....Oct. 22
Dartmouth ....Oct. 29
Brown ■ ....Nov. 5
Pennsylvania ....Nov. 12
Yale ■ ....Nov. 19

1993 RESULTS (3-7-0)

30	Columbia	3
17	William & Mary	45
21	Lafayette	16
0	Cornell	27
41	Holy Cross	25
10	Princeton	21
34	Dartmouth	39
29	Brown	43
20	Pennsylvania	27
31	Yale	33
233		**279**

Nickname: Crimson.
Stadium: Harvard (1903), 37,289 capacity. Natural turf.
Colors: Crimson, Black & White.
Conference: Ivy League.
SID: John Veneziano, 617-495-2206.
AD: William Cleary Jr.

HAWAII
Honolulu, HI 96822 ....I-A

Coach: Bob Wagner, Wittenberg '69
Record: 7 Years, 51-33-2

1994 SCHEDULE

Brigham Young ■ ....*Sept. 3
Oregon ■ ....*Sept. 10
California ....Sept. 17
Fresno St. ■ ....*Sept. 24
UTEP ....*Oct. 1
New Mexico ■ ....*Oct. 8
Utah ....Oct. 15
San Diego St. ....*Oct. 29
Southeast Mo. St. ■ ....*Nov. 5
Wyoming ■ ....*Nov. 19
Missouri ■ ....*Nov. 26
Air Force ■ ....*Dec. 3

1993 RESULTS (6-6-0)

35	Middle Tenn. St.	14
38	Brigham Young	41
49	Kent	17
52	UTEP	0
14	New Mexico	41
14	San Diego St.	45
10	Wyoming	48
41	Utah	30
21	Fresno St.	45
45	Air Force	17
18	California	42
56	Tulane	17
393		**357**

Nickname: Rainbow Warriors.
Stadium: Aloha (1975), 50,000 capacity. Artificial turf.
Colors: Green & White.
Conference: Western Athl. Conf.
SID: Eddie Inouye, 808-956-7523.
AD: Hugh Yoshida.

HEIDELBERG

Tiffin, OH 44883 III

Coach: Dick West, Xavier (Ohio) '73
Record: 10 Years, 49-49-2

1994 SCHEDULE

Adrian ■	*Sept. 10
Baldwin-Wallace	*Sept. 17
Hiram ■	Sept. 24
Capital	Oct. 1
John Carroll	Oct. 8
Muskingum ■	Oct. 15
Otterbein ■	Oct. 22
Mount Union	Oct. 29
Marietta	Nov. 5
Ohio Northern ■	Nov. 12

1993 RESULTS (8-2-0)

21	Olivet	19
21	Otterbein	14
28	John Carroll	17
15	Muskingum	0
16	Capital	7
7	Mount Union	24
37	Hiram	0
6	Baldwin-Wallace	17
26	Marietta	6
34	Ohio Northern	33
211		**137**

Nickname: Student Princes.
Stadium: Columbian (1936), 5,000 capacity. Natural turf.
Colors: Red, Orange & Black.
Conference: Ohio Ath. Conf.
SID: Dick Edmond, 419-448-2140.
AD: John Hill.

HENDERSON STATE

Arkadelphia, AR 71923 II

Coach: Ronnie Kerr, Henderson St. '66
(First year as head coach)

1994 SCHEDULE

Southern Ark. ■	*Sept. 3
Ark.-Monticello ■	*Sept. 10
East Tex. St.	Sept. 17
Ark.-Pine Bluff ■	*Sept. 24
Mississippi Col.	Oct. 1
Delta St.	*Oct. 8
North Ala. ■	*Oct. 15
Stephen F. Austin	Oct. 22
Central Ark. ■	Oct. 29
Livingston	Nov. 5
Valdosta St.	*Nov. 12

1993 RESULTS (4-6-0)

7	Jacksonville St.	12
35	Ark.-Monticello	22
7	East Tex. St.	0
13	Ark.-Pine Bluff	12
20	Mississippi Col.	35
19	Delta St.	20
0	North Ala.	17
16	Central Ark.	28
46	Livingston	44
20	Valdosta St.	42
183		**232**

Nickname: Reddies.
Stadium: Carpenter-Haygood, 9,600 capacity. Natural turf.
Colors: Red & Gray.
Conference: Gulf South Conf.
SID: David Worlock, 501-246-5511.
AD: Ken Turner.

HILLSDALE

Hillsdale, MI 49242 II

Coach: Dick Lowry, Baldwin-Wallace '57
Record: 20 Years, 152-62-3

1994 SCHEDULE

Edinboro ■	Sept. 3

St. Francis (Ill.)	*Sept. 10
St. Joseph's (Ind.) ■	*Sept. 17
Ferris St.	*Sept. 24
Indianapolis ■	Oct. 1
Ashland	Oct. 8
Grand Valley St. ■	Oct. 15
Northern Mich. ■	Oct. 22
Wayne St. (Mich.)	Oct. 29
Northwood ■	Nov. 5
Michigan Tech	Nov. 12

1993 RESULTS (7-3-1)

42	Saginaw Valley	7
17	St. Francis (Ill.)	18
13	Ferris St.	13
18	Ashland	20
29	Butler	7
14	Indianapolis	7
28	Northern Mich.	12
16	St. Joseph's (Ind.)	15
38	Grand Valley St.	21
37	Northwood	7
21	Wayne St. (Mich.)	23
273		**150**

Nickname: Chargers.
Stadium: Frank Waters (1982), 8,000 capacity. Natural turf.
Colors: Royal Blue & White.
Conference: Midwest Intercollegiate.
SID: Brian Boyse, 517-437-7364.
AD: Jack McAvoy.

HIRAM

Hiram, OH 44234 III

Coach: Bobby Thomas, Hiram '79
Record: 2 Years, 1-19-0

1994 SCHEDULE

Oberlin	Sept. 10
Muskingum ■	Sept. 17
Heidelberg	Sept. 24
Marietta	Oct. 1
Capital ■	Oct. 8
Otterbein	Oct. 15
Baldwin-Wallace ■	Oct. 22
Ohio Northern ■	Oct. 29
John Carroll	Nov. 5
Mount Union ■	Nov. 12

1993 RESULTS (0-10-0)

14	Grove City	35
13	Baldwin-Wallace	45
0	Capital	31
14	Otterbein	35
8	Marietta	10
13	Ohio Northern	84
0	Heidelberg	37
13	Muskingum	45
6	John Carroll	54
0	Mount Union	50
81		**426**

Nickname: Terriers.
Stadium: Charles Henry Field (1963), 3,500 capacity. Natural turf.
Colors: Red & Columbia Blue.
Conference: Ohio Athl. Conf.
SID: Tom Cammett, 216-569-5495.
AD: Cindy McKnight.

HOBART

Geneva, NY 14456 III

Coach: William Maxwell, Massachusetts '60
Record: 3 Years, 14-16-0

1994 SCHEDULE

Dickinson ■	Sept. 10
St. John Fisher	Sept. 17
Union (N.Y.) ■	Sept. 24
St. Lawrence ■	Oct. 1
Rochester ■	Oct. 8
Swarthmore	Oct. 15
Alfred ■	Oct. 22
Ithaca ■	Oct. 29
Hartwick	Nov. 5

Rensselaer ■	Nov. 12

1993 RESULTS (7-3-0)

0	Dickinson	13
14	St. John Fisher	7
3	Union (N.Y.)	26
32	St. Lawrence	7
2	Rochester	0
20	Swarthmore	13
19	Alfred	14
27	Pace	6
10	Buffalo St.	0
15	Rensselaer	20
142		**106**

Nickname: Statesmen.
Stadium: Boswell (1975), 4,500 capacity. Natural turf.
Colors: Orange & Purple.
Conference: Division III Independent.
SID: Eric T. Reuscher, 315-781-3538.
AD: Michael J. Hanna.

HOFSTRA

Hempstead, NY 11550 ....I-AA

Coach: Joe Gardi, Maryland '60
Record: 4 Years, 30-12-1

1994 SCHEDULE

Butler	Sept. 3
Bucknell	Sept. 10
Fordham ■	Sept. 17
Lafayette	Sept. 24
New Hampshire ■	Oct. 1
Central Conn. St. ■	Oct. 8
Buffalo	*Oct. 22
Towson St. ■	Oct. 29
Rhode Island ■	Nov. 5
Delaware	Nov. 12

1993 RESULTS (6-3-1)

20	Butler	19
32	Rhode Island	37
24	Lehigh	31
6	Illinois St.	16
28	Buffalo	20
28	Bucknell	0
17	Lafayette	17
40	Towson St.	12
49	Fordham	22
27	Maine	15
271		**189**

Nickname: Flying Dutchmen.
Stadium: Hofstra (1963), 7,500 capacity. Artificial turf.
Colors: Blue, Gold & White.
Conference: I-AA Independent.
SID: Jim Sheehan, 516-463-6764.
AD: James Garvey.

HOLY CROSS

Worcester, MA 01610 ....I-AA

Coach: Peter Vaas, Holy Cross '74
Record: 6 Years, 38-24-1

1994 SCHEDULE

Army	Sept. 10
Massachusetts ■	Sept. 17
Yale	Sept. 24
Harvard	Oct. 1
Pennsylvania	Oct. 8
Brown	Oct. 15
Lafayette	Oct. 22
Fordham	Oct. 29
Bucknell ■	Nov. 5
Lehigh ■	Nov. 12
Colgate	Nov. 19

1993 RESULTS (3-8-0)

7	Massachusetts	37
18	Boston U.	44
13	Dartmouth	7
0	Princeton	38
27	Yale	31
25	Harvard	41
23	Bucknell	33
10	Lehigh	17

27 Lafayette 52
27 Colgate 14
28 Fordham 12
205   **326**

Nickname: Crusaders.
Stadium: Fitton Field (1924), 23,500 capacity. Natural turf.
Colors: Royal Purple.
Conference: Patriot League.
SID: Frank Mastrandrea, 203-870-4750.
AD: Ron Perry.

HOPE
Holland, MI 49423 III

Coach: Ray Smith, UCLA '61
Record: 24 Years, 143-66-8
1994 SCHEDULE
Wheaton (Ill.) ....Sept. 10
DePauw ....Sept. 17
Wabash ■ ....Sept. 24
Aurora ....Oct. 1
Kalamazoo ....Oct. 8
Alma ■ ....Oct. 15
Albion ....Oct. 22
Adrian ■ ....Oct. 29
Olivet ■ ....Nov. 5

1993 RESULTS (5-4-0)
21 DePauw 10
28 Ill. Wesleyan 14
12 Wabash 13
14 Trinity (Ill.) 34
24 Kalamazoo 27
33 Alma 6
7   Albion 32
43 Adrian 12
32 Olivet 14
214   **162**

Nickname: Flying Dutchmen.
Stadium: Holland Municipal (1979), 5,300 capacity. Natural turf.
Colors: Orange & Blue.
Conference: Michigan Inter. Ath. Assoc.
SID: Tom Renner, 616-394-7860.
AD: Ray Smith.

HOUSTON
Houston, TX 77004 ....I-A

Coach: Kim Helton, Florida '70
Record: 1 Year, 1-9-1
1994 SCHEDULE
Kansas ■ ....*Sept. 1
Louisiana Tech ....*Sept. 10
Missouri ■ ....*Sept. 17
Ohio St. ....Sept. 24
Texas A&M ■ ....*Oct. 8
Southern Methodist ....Oct. 15
Texas Christian ■ ....*Oct. 22
Baylor ....Oct. 29
Texas ....Nov. 12
Texas Tech [San Antonio, Texas] ....*Nov. 19
Rice ■ ....*Nov. 26

1993 RESULTS (1-9-1)
7   Southern Cal 49
24 Tulsa 38
21 Michigan 42
24 Baylor 3
10 Texas A&M 34
28 Southern Methodist 28
10 Texas Christian 28
16 Texas 34
17 Cincinnati 41
7   Texas Tech 58
7   Rice 37
171   **392**

Nickname: Cougars.
Stadium: Astrodome (1965), 60,000 capacity. Artificial turf.
Colors: Scarlet & White.
Conference: Southwest Conf.

SID: To be named, 713-743-9404.
AD: Bill Carr.

HOWARD
Washington, DC 20059 ....I-AA

Coach: Steve Wilson, Howard '79
Record: 4 Years, 23-21-0
1994 SCHEDULE
Mississippi Val. ■ ....*Sept. 3
Hampton ■ ....Sept. 10
Florida A&M ....*Sept. 24
Towson St. ....Oct. 1
Bethune-Cookman ■ ....Oct. 8
N.C. Central ....Oct. 15
North Caro. A&T ■ ....Oct. 22
Morehouse ....Oct. 29
South Caro. St. ....Nov. 5
Morgan St. ■ ....Nov. 12
Delaware St. ■ ....Nov. 19

1993 RESULTS (11-0-0)
34 Virginia Union 7
31 Winston-Salem 10
38 Alcorn St. 36
32 Florida A&M 13
21 Bethune-Cookman 7
44 Towson St. 41
41 North Caro. A&T 35
34 Morehouse 9
30 South Caro. St. 14
66 Morgan St. 37
53 Delaware St. 33
424   **242**

I-AA Championship
14 Marshall 28

Nickname: Bison.
Stadium: Greene (1986), 7,500 capacity. Artificial turf.
Colors: Blue & White.
Conference: Mid-Eastern.
SID: Edward Hill, 202-806-7182.
AD: David C. Simmons.

HOWARD PAYNE
Brownwood, TX 76801 III

Coach: Vance Gibson, Austin College '75
Record: 2 Years, 11-10-0
1994 SCHEDULE
Southern Ark. ■ ....*Sept. 10
West Tex. A&M ....*Sept. 17
McMurry ■ ....Sept. 24
Hardin-Simmons ■ ....Oct. 1
Sul Ross St. ....Oct. 8
Midwestern St. ....*Oct. 22
Austin ■ ....Oct. 29
Sul Ross St. ■ ....Nov. 5
McMurry ....Nov. 12

1993 RESULTS (3-7-0)
2   Ark.-Monticello 21
40 Sul Ross St. 21
10 Southern Ark. 46
17 McMurry 27
9   Hardin-Simmons 47
20 Sul Ross St. 17
24 Midwestern St. 20
9   Austin 34
7   Carson-Newman 40
7   McMurry 35
145   **308**

Nickname: Yellow Jackets.
Stadium: Gordon Wood, 7,600 capacity. Natural turf.
Colors: Old Gold & Navy Blue.
Conference: Texas Intercollegiate.
SID: Mike Blackwell, 915-646-2502.
AD: Larry Nickell.

HUMBOLDT STATE
Arcata, CA 95521 II

Coach: Fred Whitmire, Humboldt St. '64
Record: 3 Years, 16-15-1
1994 SCHEDULE
Montana Tech ....Sept. 3
Western Mont. ■ ....*Sept. 10
Cal Poly SLO ■ ....*Sept. 17
Azusa Pacific ■ ....*Sept. 24
St. Mary's (Cal.) ....Oct. 1
Cal St. Chico ■ ....Oct. 15
San Fran. St. ....Oct. 22
UC Davis ■ ....*Oct. 29
Sonoma St. ....Nov. 5
Western N. Mex. ■ ....Nov. 12

1993 RESULTS (4-6-1)
24 Rocky Mountain 20
22 Western Mont. 7
3   Cal Poly SLO 17
0   St. Mary's (Cal.) 21
9   UC Davis 45
20 Azusa Pacific 10
21 San Fran. St. 24
15 Western N. Mex. 40
17 Sonoma St. 28
33 Cal St. Hayward 21
16 Cal St. Chico 16
180   **249**

Nickname: Lumberjacks.
Stadium: Redwood Bowl (1946), 7,000 capacity. Natural turf.
Colors: Green & Gold.
Conference: Northern Cal. Ath. Conf.
SID: Dan Pambianco, 707-826-3631.
AD: Chuck Lindemenn.

IDAHO
Moscow, ID 83843 ....I-AA

Coach: John L. Smith, Weber St. '71
Record: 5 Years, 44-18-0
1994 SCHEDULE
Southern Utah ....*Sept. 3
Nevada-Las Vegas ....*Sept. 17
Stephen F. Austin ■ ....Sept. 24
Idaho St. ■ ....Oct. 1
Eastern Wash. ....Oct. 8
Montana St. ■ ....Oct. 15
Northern Ariz. ■ ....Oct. 22
Montana ....Oct. 29
Northern Iowa ■ ....Nov. 5
Weber St. ■ ....Nov. 12
Boise St. ....Nov. 19

1993 RESULTS (9-2-0)
38 Stephen F. Austin 30
66 Southwest Tex. St. 38
56 Weber St. 0
28 Utah 17
56 Idaho St. 27
49 Eastern Wash. 10
35 Montana St. 40
34 Northern Ariz. 27
34 Montana 54
77 Lehigh 14
49 Boise St. 16
522   **273**

I-AA Championship
34 Northeast La. 31
21 Boston U. 14
16 Youngstown St. 35

Nickname: Vandals.
Stadium: Kibbie (1975), 16,000 capacity. Artificial turf.
Colors: Silver & Gold.
Conference: Big Sky Conf.
SID: To be named, 208-885-0211.
AD: Pete Liske.

IDAHO STATE
Pocatello, ID 83209 ....I-AA

Coach: Brian McNeely, Wichita St. '79
Record: 2 Years, 5-17-0

1994 SCHEDULE

Adams St. ■	*Sept. 3
Utah ■	*Sept. 10
Northern Ariz. ■	*Sept. 17
Idaho	Oct. 1
Montana St.	Oct. 8
Boise St. ■	*Oct. 15
Eastern Wash. ■	Oct. 22
Portland St. ■	*Oct. 29
Weber St.	Nov. 5
Montana ■	Nov. 12
Minn.-Duluth ■	*Nov. 19

1993 RESULTS (2-9-0)

52	Chadron St.	3
7	Portland St.	21
16	Montana	28
15	Northern Ariz.	32
59	Mesa St.	10
27	Idaho	56
24	Montana St.	25
27	Boise St.	34
7	Eastern Wash.	38
13	New Mexico	39
17	Weber St.	21
264		**307**

Nickname: Bengals.
Stadium: Holt Arena (1970), 12,000 capacity. Artificial turf.
Colors: Orange & Black.
Conference: Big Sky Conf.
SID: Glenn Alford, 208-236-3651.
AD: Randy Hoffman.

ILLINOIS

Champaign, IL 61820 ....I-A

Coach: Lou Tepper, Rutgers '67
Record: 3 Years, 11-12-1

1994 SCHEDULE

Washington St. [Chicago, Ill.]	*Sept. 1
Missouri ■	Sept. 10
Northern Ill. ■	Sept. 17
Purdue ■	Oct. 1
Ohio St.	Oct. 8
Iowa ■	Oct. 15
Michigan ■	Oct. 22
Northwestern	Oct. 29
Minnesota	*Nov. 5
Penn St. ■	Nov. 12
Wisconsin	Nov. 19

1993 RESULTS (5-6-0)

3	Missouri	31
14	Arizona	16
7	Oregon	13
28	Purdue	10
12	Ohio St.	20
49	Iowa	3
24	Michigan	21
20	Northwestern	13
23	Minnesota	20
14	Penn St.	28
10	Wisconsin	35
204		**210**

Nickname: Fighting Illini.
Stadium: Memorial (1923), 70,904 capacity. Artificial turf.
Colors: Orange & Blue.
Conference: Big Ten Conf.
SID: Mike Pearson, 217-333-1390.
AD: Ron Guenther.

ILLINOIS BENEDICTINE

Lisle, IL 60532...III

Coach: John Welty, Ill. Benedictine '77
Record: 4 Years, 14-24-1

1994 SCHEDULE

Loras	Sept. 10
Carthage ■	Sept. 17
Elmhurst	Sept. 24
Alma ■	Oct. 1
Wabash	Oct. 8

Olivet Nazarene ■	Oct. 15
Aurora	Oct. 22
Trinity (Ill.)	Nov. 5
Wittenberg ■	Nov. 12

1993 RESULTS (4-5-1)

27	Loras	27
28	Millikin	48
47	Elmhurst	28
30	Carthage	12
28	Alma	16
14	Quincy	17
14	Olivet Nazarene	50
19	Aurora	14
33	Drake	48
29	Trinity (Ill.)	49
269		**309**

Nickname: Eagles.
Stadium: Alumni Memorial (1910), 2,500 capacity. Natural turf.
Colors: Cardinal & White.
Conference: Division III Independent.
SID: J. Welty, 708-960-1500.
AD: Anthony Lascala.

ILLINOIS COLLEGE

Jacksonville, IL 62650 III

Coach: Bill Anderson, North Park '69
Record: 16 Years, 41-103-0

1994 SCHEDULE

Principia	Sept. 10
Blackburn ■	Sept. 17
Beloit ■	Sept. 24
Ripon	Oct. 1
Monmouth (Ill.)	Oct. 8
Coe ■	Oct. 15
Knox ■	Oct. 22
Cornell College	Oct. 29
Grinnell ■	Nov. 5

1993 RESULTS (3-6-0)

16	Principia	17
27	Blackburn	0
7	Carroll (Wis.)	24
26	Lawrence	20
7	Monmouth (Ill.)	13
12	Coe	56
17	Knox	28
14	Cornell College	26
38	Grinnell	8
164		**192**

Nickname: Blueboys.
Stadium: England Field (1960), 2,500 capacity. Natural turf.
Colors: Royal Blue & White.
Conference: Midwest Conf.
SID: James T. Murphy, 217-245-3048.
AD: Bill Anderson.

ILLINOIS STATE

Normal, IL 61761.....................................I-AA

Coach: Jim Heacock, Muskingum '70
Record: 6 Years, 27-38-1

1994 SCHEDULE

McNeese St.	*Sept. 3
Washburn ■	*Sept. 10
Western Ill.	Sept. 17
Indiana St.	*Sept. 24
Central Fla. ■	Oct. 1
Southwest Mo. St. ■	*Oct. 8
Buffalo	*Oct. 15
Northern Iowa ■	*Oct. 22
Southern Ill. ■	Oct. 29
Eastern Ill. ■	Nov. 5
Middle Tenn. St.	Nov. 12

1993 RESULTS (6-4-1)

23	Tennessee Tech	18
30	Ball St.	45
37	McNeese St.	27
16	Hofstra	6
12	Western Ill.	17

28	Southwest Mo. St.	40
27	Indiana St.	3
17	Eastern Ill.	17
19	Northern Iowa	20
34	Southern Ill.	16
13	Youngstown St.	10
256		**219**

Nickname: Redbirds.
Stadium: Hancock (1967), 15,000 capacity. Artificial turf.
Colors: Red & White.
Conference: Gateway.
SID: Kenny Mossman, 309-438-3825.
AD: Rick Greenspan.

ILLINOIS WESLEYAN

Bloomington, IL 61701..III

Coach: Norm Eash, Ill. Wesleyan '75
Record: 7 Years, 39-25-1

1994 SCHEDULE

Washington (Mo.)	Sept. 17
Simpson ■	Sept. 24
Augustana (Ill.) ■	Oct. 1
Wheaton (Ill.)	Oct. 8
North Central ■	Oct. 15
Carthage ■	Oct. 22
Elmhurst	Oct. 29
North Park	Nov. 5
Millikin ■	Nov. 12

1993 RESULTS (4-5-0)

14	Hope	28
7	Adrian	6
38	North Central	24
9	Wheaton (Ill.)	13
7	Augustana (Ill.)	10
20	Carthage	21
58	Elmhurst	6
17	Millikin	28
41	North Park	28
211		**164**

Nickname: Titans.
Stadium: Wesleyan (1893), 3,500 capacity. Natural turf.
Colors: Green & White.
Conference: College Conf. of Ill. & Wis.
SID: Stew Salowitz, 309-556-3206.
AD: Dennie Bridges.

INDIANA

Bloomington, IN 47405 ....I-A

Coach: Bill Mallory, Miami (Ohio) '57
Record: 24 Years, 156-108-4

1994 SCHEDULE

Cincinnati ■	Sept. 3
Miami (Ohio) ■	Sept. 10
Kentucky	*Sept. 17
Wisconsin	Sept. 24
Minnesota ■	Oct. 1
Iowa	Oct. 8
Northwestern ■	Oct. 22
Michigan St.	Oct. 29
Penn St. ■	Nov. 5
Ohio St. ■	Nov. 12
Purdue	Nov. 19

1993 RESULTS (8-3-0)

27	Toledo	0
28	Northern Ill.	10
24	Kentucky	8
15	Wisconsin	27
23	Minnesota	19
16	Iowa	10
24	Northwestern	0
10	Michigan St.	0
31	Penn St.	38
17	Ohio St.	23
24	Purdue	17
239		**152**

Independence Bowl

20	Virginia Tech	45

Nickname: Fightin' Hoosiers.
Stadium: Memorial (1960), 52,354 capacity. Artificial turf.
Colors: Cream & Crimson.
Conference: Big Ten Conf.
SID: Kit Klingelhoffer, 812-855-0847.
AD: Clarence Doninger.

INDIANA (PENNSYLVANIA)

Indiana, PA 15705 II

Coach: Frank Cignetti, Indiana (Pa.) '60
Record: 12 Years, 99-42-1

1994 SCHEDULE

Grand Valley St. ■	Sept. 3
New Haven	Sept. 17
Shippensburg	Oct. 1
Calif. (Pa.) ■	Oct. 8
Slippery Rock	Oct. 15
Cheyney ■	Oct. 22
Edinboro ■	Oct. 29
Clarion	Nov. 5
Lock Haven ■	Nov. 12

1993 RESULTS (10-0-0)

54	Kutztown	9
34	Grand Valley St.	3
37	West Chester	26
23	Liberty	7
52	Lock Haven	14
45	Shippensburg	10
52	Calif. (Pa.)	13
45	Slippery Rock	24
31	Edinboro	24
44	Clarion	7
417		**137**

II Championship

28	Ferris St.	21
38	New Haven	35
21	North Dak.	6
34	North Ala.	41

Nickname: Indians.
Stadium: Miller (1962), 8,000 capacity. Natural turf.
Colors: Crimson & Gray.
Conference: Pennsylvania Conf.
SID: Larry Judge, 412-357-2747.
AD: Frank Cignetti.

INDIANA STATE

Terre Haute, IN 47809 ....I-AA

Coach: Dennis Raetz, Nebraska '68
Record: 14 Years, 72-83-1

1994 SCHEDULE

Toledo	*Sept. 3
Lock Haven ■	*Sept. 10
West Va. Tech ■	Sept. 17
Illinois St. ■	*Sept. 24
Northern Iowa ■	Oct. 1
Southern Ill.	Oct. 8
Western Ill.	Oct. 15
Southwest Mo. St. ■	Oct. 22
Eastern Ill.	Oct. 29
Western Ky.	Nov. 5
Youngstown St. ■	Nov. 19

1993 RESULTS (4-7-0)

21	Air Force	63
10	Minnesota	27
21	Southwest Mo. St.	31
27	Eastern Ill.	24
10	Northern Iowa	17
3	Illinois St.	27
41	Western Ky.	14
26	Southern Ill.	35
10	Youngstown St.	17
49	West Va. Tech	6
16	Western Ill.	6
234		**267**

Nickname: Sycamores.
Stadium: Memorial (1970), 20,500 capacity. Artificial turf.
Colors: Blue & White.

Conference: Gateway.
SID: Eric Ruden, 812-237-4161.
AD: Brian Faison.

INDIANAPOLIS

Indianapolis, IN 46227 II

Coach: Joe Polizzi, Hillsdale '76
(First year as head coach)

1994 SCHEDULE

Grand Valley St. ■	Sept. 10
Ferris St.	Sept. 17
Wayne St. (Mich.) ■	Sept. 24
Hillsdale	Oct. 1
Michigan Tech ■	Oct. 8
Northern Mich.	Oct. 15
Saginaw Valley ■	Oct. 22
Northwood	Oct. 29
St. Francis (Ill.)	Nov. 5
St. Joseph's (Ind.)	Nov. 12

1993 RESULTS (2-9-0)

31	Wayne St. (Mich.)	34
14	Northern Mich.	20
33	St. Joseph's (Ind.)	14
7	Grand Valley St.	31
19	Northwood	24
7	Hillsdale	14
0	Saginaw Valley	14
17	St. Francis (Ill.)	20
26	Ferris St.	40
0	Ashland	27
34	Butler	21
188		**259**

Nickname: Greyhounds.
Stadium: Key (1971), 5,500 capacity. Natural turf.
Colors: Crimson & Gray.
Conference: Midwest Intercollegiate.
SID: Joe Gentry, 317-788-3494.
AD: Dave Huffman.

IONA

New Rochelle, NY 10801 ....I-AA

Coach: Harold Crocker, Central Conn. St. '74
Record: 10 Years, 42-48-1

1994 SCHEDULE

Marist	Sept. 17
Georgetown	Sept. 24
Siena ■	Oct. 1
Pace ■	Oct. 8
St. Peter's ■	Oct. 15
Wagner ■	Oct. 22
Duquesne	Oct. 29
Canisius ■	Nov. 5
St. John's (N.Y.) ■	Nov. 12

1993 RESULTS (9-1-0)

24	Sacred Heart	0
13	Central Conn. St.	24
22	Georgetown	15
30	Wagner	23
19	Canisius	9
35	St. Peter's	28
38	Pace	6
54	Siena	21
27	Marist	24
42	St. John's (N.Y.)	30
304		**180**

ECAC I-AA

0	Wagner	32

Nickname: Gaels.
Stadium: Mazzella Field (1989), 1,200 capacity. Artificial turf.
Colors: Maroon & Gold.
Conference: Metro Atlantic.
SID: Dave Torromeo, 914-633-2334.
AD: Rich Petriccione.

IOWA

Iowa City, IA 52242 ....I-A

Coach: Hayden Fry, Baylor '51
Record: 32 Years, 200-153-9

1994 SCHEDULE

Central Mich. ■	Sept. 3
Iowa St. ■	Sept. 10
Penn St.	Sept. 17
Oregon	Sept. 24
Michigan	Oct. 1
Indiana ■	Oct. 8
Illinois	Oct. 15
Michigan St. ■	Oct. 22
Purdue	Oct. 29
Northwestern ■	Nov. 12
Minnesota	*Nov. 19

1993 RESULTS (6-5-0)

26	Tulsa	25
31	Iowa St.	28
0	Penn St.	31
7	Michigan	24
10	Indiana	16
3	Illinois	49
10	Michigan St.	24
26	Purdue	17
54	Northern Ill.	20
23	Northwestern	19
21	Minnesota	3
211		**256**

Alamo Bowl

3	California	37

Nickname: Hawkeyes.
Stadium: Kinnick (1929), 70,397 capacity. Natural turf.
Colors: Old Gold & Black.
Conference: Big Ten Conf.
SID: Phil Haddy, 319-335-9411.
AD: Bob Bowlsby.

IOWA STATE

Ames, IA 50011 ....I-A

Coach: Jim Walden, Wyoming '60
Record: 16 Years, 69-102-6

1994 SCHEDULE

Northern Iowa ■	Sept. 3
Iowa	Sept. 10
Western Mich. ■	Sept. 17
Rice ■	Sept. 24
Oklahoma	Oct. 1
Kansas ■	Oct. 15
Oklahoma St.	Oct. 22
Missouri ■	Oct. 29
Kansas St.	Nov. 5
Nebraska ■	Nov. 12
Colorado	Nov. 19

1993 RESULTS (3-8-0)

54	Northern Ill.	10
28	Iowa	31
7	Wisconsin	28
21	Rice	49
7	Oklahoma	24
20	Kansas	35
20	Oklahoma St.	17
34	Missouri	37
27	Kansas St.	23
17	Nebraska	49
16	Colorado	21
251		**324**

Nickname: Cyclones.
Stadium: Cyclone-Jack Trice (1975), 50,000 capacity. Artificial turf.
Colors: Cardinal & Gold.
Conference: Big Eight Conf.
SID: Tom Kroeschell, 515-294-3372.
AD: Eugene Smith.

ITHACA

Ithaca, NY 14850 III

Coach: Michael Welch, Ithaca '73
(First year as head coach)

1994 SCHEDULE

Albany (N.Y.)	*Sept. 10

Mansfield ■ ....Sept. 17
Alfred ■ ....Sept. 24
Springfield ■ ....Oct. 1
American Int'l ....Oct. 8
St. Lawrence ■ ....Oct. 15
Buffalo St. ■ ....Oct. 22
Hobart ....Oct. 29
Cortland St. ....Nov. 5
LIU-C.W. Post ■ ....Nov. 12

1993 RESULTS (6-4-0)

47	Albany (N.Y.)	7
0	Montclair St.	29
20	Alfred	30
30	Springfield	6
37	American Int'l	0
45	St. Lawrence	7
17	Buffalo St.	33
45	Mercyhurst	25
32	Cortland St.	14
7	Wash. & Jeff.	42
280		**193**

Nickname: Bombers.
Stadium: South Hill (1958), 5,000 capacity. Natural turf.
Colors: Blue & Gold.
Conference: Division III Independent.
SID: Pete Moore, 607-274-3825.
AD: Robert Deming.

JACKSON STATE

Jackson, MS 39217 ....I-AA

Coach: James Carson, Jackson St. '63
Record: 2 Years, 12-9-1

1994 SCHEDULE

Alabama A&M [Birmingham, Ala.] ....*Sept. 4
Tennessee St. [Memphis, Tenn.] ....*Sept. 10
Florida A&M ■ ....Sept. 17
Mississippi Val. ■ ....Sept. 24
South Caro. St. [Columbia, S.C.] ....Oct. 1
Alabama St. ....*Oct. 8
Southern-B.R. ....*Oct. 15
Grambling ....Oct. 22
Texas Southern ■ ....Nov. 5
Prairie View ■ ....Nov. 12
Alcorn St. ....Nov. 19

1993 RESULTS (5-5-1)

24	Tuskegee	12
24	Tennessee St.	18
19	Florida A&M	41
7	Mississippi Val.	7
33	South Caro. St.	34
17	Alabama St.	15
3	Southern-B.R.	16
14	Grambling	20
38	Texas Southern	12
37	Prairie View	7
22	Alcorn St.	31
238		**213**

Nickname: Tigers.
Stadium: Mississippi Memorial (1949), 62,512 capacity. Natural turf.
Colors: Blue & White.
Conference: Southwestern.
SID: Samuel Jefferson, 601-968-2273.
AD: W. C. Gorden.

JACKSONVILLE STATE

Jacksonville, AL 36265 II

Coach: Bill Burgess, Auburn '63
Record: 9 Years, 72-29-4

1994 SCHEDULE

Sam Houston St. ■ ....*Sept. 3
McNeese St. ....*Sept. 10
Ala.-Birmingham [Birmingham, Ala.] ....Sept. 17
North Caro. A&T ....Sept. 24
Knoxville ■ ....Oct. 1
Western Ky. ■ ....Oct. 15
Northeast La. ....*Oct. 22
Middle Tenn. St. ■ ....Oct. 29
Western Ill. ....Nov. 5

Central St. (Ohio) ■ ....Nov. 12
Southwest Mo. St. ■ ....Nov. 19

1993 RESULTS (3-7-0)

12	Henderson St.	7
44	Alabama A&M	18
14	Northern Iowa	35
14	James Madison	35
7	Western Ky.	12
27	Fort Valley St.	13
7	Southwest Mo. St.	24
7	Montana	37
36	Alcorn St.	41
0	Central St. (Ohio)	22
168		**244**

Nickname: Gamecocks.
Stadium: Paul Snow (1947), 15,000 capacity. Natural turf.
Colors: Red & White.
Conference: Division II Independent.
SID: Mike Galloway, 205-782-5377.
AD: Jerry Cole.

JAMES MADISON

Harrisonburg, VA 22807 ....I-AA

Coach: William "Rip" Scherer, William & Mary '74
Record: 3 Years, 19-16-0

1994 SCHEDULE

Buffalo ■ ....*Sept. 3
Middle Tenn. St. ■ ....*Sept. 10
New Hampshire ....Sept. 17
Boston U. ....Oct. 1
Delaware ....Oct. 8
Villanova ■ ....Oct. 15
William & Mary ■ ....Oct. 22
Richmond ....Oct. 29
Va. Military ....Nov. 5
Connecticut ■ ....Nov. 12
Northeastern ....Nov. 19

1993 RESULTS (6-5-0)

55	Lock Haven	3
13	Richmond	20
34	Connecticut	45
35	Jacksonville St.	14
10	Massachusetts	33
42	Delaware	38
45	New Hampshire	21
26	William & Mary	31
52	Northeastern	21
42	Villanova	3
21	Boston U.	24
375		**253**

Nickname: Dukes.
Stadium: Bridgeforth (1974), 12,800 capacity. Artificial turf.
Colors: Purple & Gold.
Conference: Yankee.
SID: Gary Michael, 703-568-6154.
AD: Donald Lemish.

JERSEY CITY STATE

Jersey City, NJ 07305 III

Coach: Bill Olear, Rider '62
Record: 2 Years, 1-17-1

1994 SCHEDULE

Brockport St. ■ ....Sept. 10
Stony Brook ....Sept. 17
Rowan ....*Sept. 23
Upsala ■ ....Oct. 1
St. John Fisher ■ ....Oct. 8
Kean ■ ....Oct. 15
Trenton St. ....Oct. 22
Wm. Paterson ....*Oct. 28
Montclair St. ■ ....Nov. 5
Albright ■ ....Nov. 12

1993 RESULTS (1-7-1)

12	Brockport St.	18
22	Stony Brook	22
7	Rowan	36
28	Upsala	22

6	Kean	28
13	Trenton St.	30
6	Wm. Paterson	7
8	Montclair St.	25
24	St. Peter's	44
126		**232**

Nickname: Gothic Knights.
Stadium: Tidelands Athletic Complex (1986), 2,500 capacity. Natural turf.
Colors: Green & Gold.
Conference: New Jersey Ath. Conf.
SID: John Stallings, 201-200-3301.
AD: Larry Schiner.

JOHN CARROLL

Cleveland, OH 44118 III

Coach: Tony DeCarlo, Kent '62
Record: 7 Years, 48-19-2

1994 SCHEDULE

Ohio Wesleyan ■ ....Sept. 10
Marietta ■ ....Sept. 17
Otterbein ....Sept. 24
Mount Union ■ ....Oct. 1
Heidelberg ■ ....Oct. 8
Ohio Northern ....Oct. 15
Capital ....Oct. 22
Muskingum ■ ....Oct. 29
Hiram ■ ....Nov. 5
Baldwin-Wallace ....Nov. 12

1993 RESULTS (6-4-0)

47	Alma	31
25	Capital	0
17	Heidelberg	28
30	Ohio Northern	24
0	Mount Union	21
20	Muskingum	18
31	Otterbein	35
19	Marietta	13
54	Hiram	6
13	Baldwin-Wallace	28
256		**204**

Nickname: Blue Streaks.
Stadium: Wasmer Field (1968), 3,500 capacity. Artificial turf.
Colors: Blue & Gold.
Conference: Ohio Ath. Conf.
SID: Chris Wenzler, 216-397-4676.
AD: Tony DeCarlo.

JOHNS HOPKINS

Baltimore, MD 21218 III

Coach: Jim Margraff, Johns Hopkins '82
Record: 4 Years, 20-18-2

1994 SCHEDULE

Lebanon Valley ....Sept. 10
Swarthmore ....Sept. 17
FDU-Madison ■ ....*Sept. 23
Gettysburg ■ ....*Sept. 30
Ursinus ....Oct. 8
Muhlenberg ■ ....*Oct. 14
Georgetown ....Oct. 22
Dickinson ■ ....Oct. 29
Frank. & Marsh. ....Nov. 5
Western Md. ■ ....Nov. 12

1993 RESULTS (4-6-0)

33	Lebanon Valley	7
40	Swarthmore	17
21	FDU-Madison	38
6	Gettysburg	25
42	Ursinus	34
16	Muhlenberg	20
19	Georgetown	17
0	Dickinson	16
11	Frank. & Marsh.	13
3	Western Md.	20
191		**207**

Nickname: Blue Jays.
Stadium: Homewood Field (1906), 4,000 capacity. Artificial turf.

Colors: Blue & Black.
Conference: Centennial Conference.
SID: Andrew Bilello, 410-889-4636.
AD: Robert Scott.

JOHNSON C. SMITH

Charlotte, NC 28216 II

Coach: Ray Lee, West Va. Wesleyan '82
Record: 2 Years, 8-13-0

1994 SCHEDULE

Bethune-Cookman	Sept. 3
Gardner-Webb	Sept. 10
Winston-Salem ■	*Sept. 17
Hampton	Oct. 1
Bowie St. ■	Oct. 8
Livingstone	Oct. 15
Fayetteville St. ■	Oct. 22
Norfolk St. ■	Oct. 29
N.C. Central	Nov. 5
Elizabeth City St.	Nov. 12

1993 RESULTS (3-8-0)

14	Morehouse	†14
0	Glenville St.	45
7	Bethune-Cookman	30
6	N.C. Central	39
6	Hampton	43
20	Kentucky St.	7
29	Livingstone	12
6	Fayetteville St.	40
6	Winston-Salem	23
20	Norfolk St.	13
7	North Caro. A&T	52
†Forfeit.		
121		**318**

Nickname: Golden Bulls.
Stadium: Bullpit (1990), 7,500 capacity. Natural turf.
Colors: Blue & Gold.
Conference: Central Inter. Ath. Assoc.
SID: James Cuthbertson, 704-378-1282.
AD: Horace Small.

JUNIATA

Huntingdon, PA 16652 III

Coach: Chris Coller, Juniata '85
Record: 2 Years, 4-15-1

1994 SCHEDULE

Western Md. ■	Sept. 10
Albright	Sept. 17
Carnegie Mellon	Sept. 24
Widener ■	Oct. 1
Wilkes	Oct. 8
Lebanon Valley ■	Oct. 15
King's (Pa.) ■	Oct. 22
Moravian	Oct. 29
Lycoming ■	Nov. 5
Susquehanna	Nov. 12

1993 RESULTS (1-9-0)

14	Western Md.	16
14	Albright	24
14	Carnegie Mellon	29
12	Widener	40
14	Wilkes	28
7	Lebanon Valley	54
18	King's (Pa.)	20
0	Moravian	13
18	Lycoming	33
21	Susquehanna	13
132		**270**

Nickname: Eagles.
Stadium: Chuck Knox (1988), 3,000 capacity. Natural turf.
Colors: Yale Blue & Old Gold.
Conference: Middle Atlantic.
SID: Joseph Scialabba, 814-643-4310.
AD: William F. Berrier.

KALAMAZOO

Kalamazoo, MI 49006 III

Coach: Dave Warmack, Western Mich. '71
Record: 4 Years, 18-17-1

1994 SCHEDULE

Wooster	Sept. 10
Franklin	Sept. 17
Valparaiso	Sept. 24
Chicago	Oct. 1
Hope ■	Oct. 8
Adrian	Oct. 15
Alma ■	Oct. 22
Olivet	Oct. 29
Albion ■	Nov. 5

1993 RESULTS (7-2-0)

30	Wooster	10
34	Carroll (Wis.)	13
22	Chicago	21
14	Defiance	31
27	Hope	24
27	Adrian	22
21	Alma	14
54	Olivet	30
0	Albion	34
229		**199**

Nickname: Hornets.
Stadium: Angell Field (1946), 5,000 capacity. Natural turf.
Colors: Orange & Black.
Conference: Michigan Inter. Ath. Assoc.
SID: John Greenhoe, 616-337-7303.
AD: Bob Kent.

KANSAS

Lawrence, KS 66045 ....I-A

Coach: Glen Mason, Ohio St. '72
Record: 8 Years, 39-50-1

1994 SCHEDULE

Houston	*Sept. 1
Michigan St. ■	Sept. 10
Texas Christian	*Sept. 17
Ala.-Birmingham ■	Sept. 24
Kansas St. ■	*Oct. 6
Iowa St.	Oct. 15
Oklahoma	Oct. 22
Oklahoma St. ■	Oct. 29
Nebraska	Nov. 5
Colorado ■	Nov. 12
Missouri	Nov. 19

1993 RESULTS (5-7-0)

0	Florida St.	42
46	Western Caro.	3
14	Michigan St.	31
16	Utah	41
24	Colorado St.	6
9	Kansas St.	10
35	Iowa St.	20
23	Oklahoma	38
13	Oklahoma St.	6
20	Nebraska	21
14	Colorado	38
28	Missouri	0
242		**256**

Nickname: Jayhawks.
Stadium: Memorial (1921), 50,250 capacity. Artificial turf.
Colors: Crimson & Blue.
Conference: Big Eight Conf.
SID: Doug Vance, 913-864-3417.
AD: Bob Frederick.

KANSAS STATE

Manhattan, KS 66506 ....I-A

Coach: Bill Snyder, William Jewell '63
Record: 5 Years, 27-28-1

1994 SCHEDULE

Southwestern La. ■	*Sept. 3
Rice ■	Sept. 17
Minnesota ■	*Sept. 24
Kansas	*Oct. 6
Nebraska ■	Oct. 15

Colorado	Oct. 22
Oklahoma	Oct. 29
Iowa St. ■	Nov. 5
Missouri	Nov. 12
Oklahoma St. ■	Nov. 19
Nevada-Las Vegas	Nov. 26

1993 RESULTS (8-2-1)

34	New Mexico St.	10
38	Western Ky.	13
30	Minnesota	25
36	Nevada-Las Vegas	20
10	Kansas	9
28	Nebraska	45
16	Colorado	16
21	Oklahoma	7
23	Iowa St.	27
31	Missouri	21
21	Oklahoma St.	17
288		**210**

Copper Bowl

52	Wyoming	17

Nickname: Wildcats.
Stadium: K S U (1968), 42,000 capacity. Artificial turf.
Colors: Purple & White.
Conference: Big Eight Conf.
SID: Ben Boyle, 913-532-6735.
AD: Max Urick.

KEAN

Union, NJ 07083 III

Coach: Brian Carlson, Montclair St. '82
Record: 2 Years, 11-7-1

1994 SCHEDULE

Western Conn. St. ■	Sept. 3
Upsala ■	Sept. 17
Rensselaer	Sept. 24
Wm. Paterson ■	*Sept. 30
Montclair St. ■	Oct. 8
Jersey City St.	Oct. 15
Rowan ■	Oct. 29
Brockport St.	Nov. 5
Trenton St.	Nov. 12

1993 RESULTS (5-4-0)

14	Western Conn. St.	17
23	Bri'water (Mass.)	16
21	Upsala	18
14	Wm. Paterson	10
14	Montclair St.	16
28	Jersey City St.	6
13	Rowan	37
26	Brockport St.	11
0	Trenton St.	28
153		**159**

Nickname: Cougars.
Stadium: D'Angola, 2,200 capacity. Natural turf.
Colors: Royal Blue & Silver.
Conference: New Jersey Ath. Conf.
SID: Adam Fenton, 201-527-2435.
AD: Glenn Hedden.

KENT

Kent, OH 44242 ....I-A

Coach: Jim Corrigall, Kent '70
(First year as head coach)

1994 SCHEDULE

Rutgers	Sept. 3
Akron ■	Sept. 17
Central Mich.	Sept. 24
Western Mich.	Oct. 1
Eastern Mich. ■	Oct. 8
Youngstown St.	Oct. 15
Ohio ■	Oct. 22
Toledo ■	Oct. 29
Bowling Green ■	Nov. 5
Miami (Ohio)	Nov. 12
Ball St. ■	Nov. 19

1993 RESULTS (0-11-0)

0	Kentucky	35
7	Akron	42

17	Hawaii	49
21	Western Mich.	27
15	Eastern Mich.	20
10	Ohio	15
28	Central Mich.	33
27	Toledo	45
7	Bowling Green	40
14	Miami (Ohio)	23
3	Ball St.	28
149		**357**

Nickname: Golden Flashes.
Stadium: Dix (1969), 30,520 capacity. Natural turf.
Colors: Navy Blue & Gold.
Conference: Mid-American Conf.
SID: Dale Gallagher, 216-672-2110.
AD: To be named.

KENTUCKY
Lexington, KY 40506 ....I-A

Coach: Bill Curry, Georgia Tech '65
Record: 14 Years, 74-81-4

1994 SCHEDULE
Louisville ■		*Sept. 3
Florida		*Sept. 10
Indiana ■		*Sept. 17
South Caro. ■		*Sept. 24
Auburn		*Sept. 29
Louisiana St.		*Oct. 15
Georgia ■		*Oct. 22
Mississippi St. ■		*Oct. 29
Vanderbilt ■		Nov. 5
Northeast La. ■		Nov. 12
Tennessee		Nov. 19

1993 RESULTS (6-5-0)
35	Kent	0
20	Florida	24
8	Indiana	24
21	South Caro.	17
21	Mississippi	0
35	Louisiana St.	17
28	Georgia	33
26	Mississippi St.	17
7	Vanderbilt	12
6	East Caro.	3
0	Tennessee	48
207		**195**

Peach Bowl
13	Clemson	14

Nickname: Wildcats.
Stadium: Commonwealth (1973), 57,800 capacity. Natural turf.
Colors: Blue & White.
Conference: Southeastern Conf.
SID: Tony Neely, 606-257-3838.
AD: C. M. Newton.

KENTUCKY STATE
Frankfort, KY 40601 II

Coach: Maurice Hunt, Kentucky St. '67
Record: 15 Years, 63-86-3

1994 SCHEDULE
Southeast Mo. St.		*Sept. 1
West Va. St. ■		*Sept. 10
Livingston ■		*Sept. 17
Lane ■		*Sept. 24
Mars Hill		Oct. 1
Central St. (Ohio)		Oct. 8
Clark Atlanta ■		*Oct. 15
Knoxville ■		Oct. 22
Savannah St.		Oct. 29
Ark.-Pine Bluff		Nov. 5
Norfolk St.		Nov. 12

1993 RESULTS (2-9-0)
7	Findlay	27
0	Central St. (Ohio)	68
13	Knoxville	35
14	Lane	26
0	Mars Hill	22
7	Johnson Smith	20

7	Clark Atlanta	30
14	Ark.-Pine Bluff	27
26	Norfolk St.	24
30	N.C. Central	29
14	Southeast Mo. St.	45
132		**353**

Nickname: Thorobreds.
Stadium: Alumni Field (1978), 6,000 capacity. Natural turf.
Colors: Green & Gold.
Conference: Division II Independent.
SID: Ron Braden, 502-227-6011.
AD: Don Lyons.

KENTUCKY WESLEYAN
Owensboro, KY 42301 II

Coach: John Johnson, Northern Mich. '84
(First year as head coach)

1994 SCHEDULE
Austin Peay		*Sept. 1
Maryville (Tenn.) ■		Sept. 10
Evansville ■		Sept. 17
Sue Bennett ■		*Sept. 24
Blackburn		Oct. 1
Bethel (Tenn.) ■		Oct. 8
Baptist Christian		Oct. 15
Centre		Oct. 29
Chicago ■		Nov. 5
Valparaiso ■		Nov. 12

1993 RESULTS (6-4-0)
25	Quincy	36
7	Maryville (Tenn.)	6
14	Evansville	35
21	Rhodes	22
49	Blackburn	7
24	Bethel (Tenn.)	18
48	Principia	14
33	Eureka	27
21	Centre	10
19	Mt. Senario	21
261		**196**

Nickname: Panthers.
Stadium: Not named (1939). Natural turf.
Colors: Purple & White.
Conference: Division II Independent.
SID: Roy Pickerill, 502-683-4795.
AD: William Meadors.

KENYON
Gambier, OH 43022 III

Coach: Jim Meyer, Akron '78
Record: 5 Years, 22-25-3

1994 SCHEDULE
Grove City		Sept. 10
Oberlin		Sept. 17
Denison ■		Sept. 24
Wittenberg		Oct. 1
Case Reserve ■		Oct. 8
Earlham		Oct. 15
Allegheny ■		Oct. 22
Waynesburg ■		Oct. 29
Wooster		Nov. 5
Ohio Wesleyan ■		Nov. 12

1993 RESULTS (4-6-0)
21	Marietta	10
27	Ohio Wesleyan	32
17	Earlham	10
21	Wooster	27
23	Case Reserve	16
7	Allegheny	63
0	Wittenberg	32
12	Waynesburg	20
24	Oberlin	7
7	Denison	36
159		**253**

Nickname: Lords.
Stadium: McBride Field, 2,300 capacity. Natural turf.
Colors: Purple & White.
Conference: North Coast Ath. Conf.

SID: Joe Wasiluk, 614-427-5471.
AD: Robert D. Bunnell.

KING'S (PENNSYLVANIA)
Wilkes-Barre, PA 18711 III

Coach: Richard Mannello, Springfield '83
Record: 1 Year, 1-9-0

1994 SCHEDULE
Albright ■		Sept. 10
Widener		Sept. 17
Susquehanna ■		Sept. 24
Lycoming		Oct. 1
Upsala		Oct. 8
Delaware Valley ■		Oct. 15
Juniata		Oct. 22
FDU-Madison		*Oct. 28
Moravian ■		Nov. 5
Wilkes		Nov. 12

1993 RESULTS (1-9-0)
12	Albright	31
15	Widener	24
8	Susquehanna	51
21	Lycoming	41
13	Upsala	55
31	Delaware Valley	55
20	Juniata	18
6	FDU-Madison	19
0	Moravian	49
14	Wilkes	41
140		**384**

Nickname: Monarchs.
Stadium: Monarch Fields, 3,000 capacity. Natural turf.
Colors: Red & Gold.
Conference: Middle Atlantic.
SID: Bob Ziadie, 717-826-5934.
AD: John Dorish.

KNOX
Galesburg, IL 61401 III

Coach: Randy Oberembt, Knox '76
Record: 9 Years, 32-48-1

1994 SCHEDULE
Principia ■		Sept. 3
Beloit		Sept. 10
Lake Forest ■		Sept. 24
St. Norbert		Oct. 1
Cornell College		Oct. 8
Grinnell ■		Oct. 15
Illinois Col.		Oct. 22
Coe ■		Oct. 29
Monmouth (Ill.)		Nov. 5

1993 RESULTS (5-4-0)
7	Rose-Hulman	26
42	Concordia (St. Paul)	12
3	Beloit	0
13	Ripon	32
21	Cornell College	35
31	Grinnell	21
28	Illinois Col.	17
14	Coe	59
19	Monmouth (Ill.)	16
178		**218**

Nickname: Prairie Fire.
Stadium: Knox Bowl (1968), 6,000 capacity. Natural turf.
Colors: Purple & Gold.
Conference: Midwest Conf.
SID: Andy Gibbons, 309-343-0112.
AD: Harlan Knosher.

KUTZTOWN
Kutztown, PA 19530 II

Coach: Al Leonzi, Penn St. '64
Record: 2 Years, 4-16-1

1994 SCHEDULE
West Chester		Sept. 3
New Haven ■		Sept. 10

Calif. (Pa.) ....Sept. 24
Cheyney ■ ....Oct. 1
Mansfield ....Oct. 8
Millersville ■ ....Oct. 15
Bloomsburg ....Oct. 22
Shippensburg ■ ....Oct. 29
Towson St. ....Nov. 5
East Stroudsburg ....Nov. 12

1993 RESULTS (2-9-0)
9	Indiana (Pa.)	54
14	East Stroudsburg	45
10	Shippensburg	27
31	Calif. (Pa.)	28
21	Mansfield	24
7	Millersville	41
25	Bloomsburg	47
30	Lock Haven	52
3	West Chester	35
24	Southern Conn. St.	14
19	Cheyney	30
193		**397**

Nickname: Golden Bears.
Stadium: University Field, 5,600 capacity. Natural turf.
Colors: Maroon & Gold.
Conference: Pennsylvania Conf.
SID: Matt Santos, 610-683-4182.
AD: Clark Yeager.

LA VERNE
La Verne, CA 91750 III

Coach: Rex Huigens, La Verne '70
Record: 3 Years, 21-5-1
1994 SCHEDULE
Menlo ■ ....Sept. 10
Azusa Pacific ....*Sept. 17
Pomona-Pitzer ■ ....Oct. 1
Cal Lutheran ....Oct. 8
Whittier ....*Oct. 15
Redlands ■ ....Oct. 22
Chapman ....*Oct. 29
Claremont-M-S ....Nov. 5
Occidental ■ ....Nov. 12

1993 RESULTS (7-2-0)
28	San Diego	30
46	Claremont-M-S	10
24	Cal Lutheran	10
31	Occidental	21
38	Menlo	21
32	Azusa Pacific	37
24	Pomona-Pitzer	6
36	Redlands	6
24	Whittier	17
283		**158**

Nickname: Leopards.
Stadium: Arnett Field (1974), 1,500 capacity. Natural turf.
Colors: Orange & Green.
Conference: Southern Calif. Inter. Ath. Conf.
SID: Pam Maunakea, 909-593-3511.
AD: Jim Paschal.

LAFAYETTE
Easton, PA 18042 ....I-AA

Coach: Bill Russo, Brown '69
Record: 16 Years, 94-73-3
1994 SCHEDULE
East Stroudsburg ■ ....Sept. 10
Pennsylvania ....Sept. 17
Hofstra ■ ....Sept. 24
Columbia ....Oct. 1
Dartmouth ■ ....Oct. 8
Navy ....Oct. 15
Holy Cross ■ ....Oct. 22
Bucknell ....Oct. 29
Colgate ....Nov. 5
Fordham ....Nov. 12
Lehigh ■ ....Nov. 19

1993 RESULTS (5-4-2)
31	Bucknell	14

29	Buffalo	15
7	Princeton	21
16	Harvard	21
58	Columbia	6
17	Hofstra	17
27	Fordham	12
7	Colgate	7
52	Holy Cross	27
12	Army	35
14	Lehigh	39
270		**214**

Nickname: Leopards.
Stadium: Fisher Field (1926), 13,750 capacity. Natural turf.
Colors: Maroon & White.
Conference: Patriot League.
SID: Steve Pulver, 610-250-5122.
AD: Eve Atkinson.

LAKE FOREST
Lake Forest, IL 60045 III

Coach: Maury Waugh, Dubuque '62
Record: 13 Years, 41-75-2
1994 SCHEDULE
Bethel (Minn.) ....Sept. 10
North Park ■ ....Sept. 17
Knox ....Sept. 24
Coe ■ ....Oct. 1
St. Norbert ■ ....Oct. 8
Ripon ....Oct. 15
Carroll (Wis.) ....Oct. 22
Lawrence ■ ....Oct. 29
Beloit ....Nov. 5

1993 RESULTS (2-7-0)
7	Wheaton (Ill.)	44
19	North Park	20
22	Grinnell	21
0	Cornell College	54
14	St. Norbert	34
18	Ripon	42
12	Carroll (Wis.)	13
25	Lawrence	31
28	Beloit	21
145		**280**

Nickname: Foresters.
Stadium: Farwell Field, 2,000 capacity. Natural turf.
Colors: Red & Black.
Conference: Midwest Conf.
SID: Mark Perlman, 708-735-6011.
AD: Jackie Slaats.

LANE
Jackson, TN 38301 II

Coach: Craig Gilliam, Tennessee St. '70
(First year as head coach)
1994 SCHEDULE
Mississippi Val. [St. Louis, Mo.] ....*Sept. 10
Tenn.-Martin ....*Sept. 17
Kentucky St. ....*Sept. 24
Miles ■ ....Oct. 1
Langston ....Oct. 8
Ark.-Pine Bluff ....Oct. 22
Morris Brown ■ ....Oct. 29
Norfolk St. ....Nov. 5
Clark Atlanta ■ ....Nov. 12
Texas Southern ....Nov. 19

1993 RESULTS (1-8-0)
20	Georgetown (Ky.)	30
22	Mississippi Val.	36
26	Kentucky St.	14
8	Norfolk St.	54
3	Langston	44
13	Knoxville	34
16	Ark.-Pine Bluff	23
12	Virginia St.	48
16	Elizabeth City St.	51
136		**334**

Nickname: Dragons.
Stadium: Rothrock, 3,500 capacity. Natural turf.

Colors: Blue & Red.
Conference: Division II Independent.
SID: Sherrill Scott, 901-426-7516.
AD: J. L. Perry.

LAWRENCE
Appleton, WI 54911 III

Coach: Rick Coles, Coe '79
Record: 1 Year, 2-7-0
1994 SCHEDULE
Chicago ....Sept. 10
Eureka ■ ....Sept. 17
Cornell College ■ ....Sept. 24
Grinnell ....Oct. 1
Carroll (Wis.) ■ ....Oct. 8
St. Norbert ■ ....Oct. 15
Beloit ....Oct. 22
Lake Forest ....Oct. 29
Ripon ■ ....Nov. 5

1993 RESULTS (2-7-0)
21	N'western (Wis.)	29
28	Chicago	44
13	Monmouth (Ill.)	17
20	Illinois Col.	26
6	Carroll (Wis.)	24
36	St. Norbert	42
18	Beloit	27
31	Lake Forest	25
28	Ripon	20
201		**254**

Nickname: Vikings.
Stadium: Banta Bowl (1965), 5,255 capacity. Natural turf.
Colors: Navy & White.
Conference: Midwest Conf.
SID: Jeff School, 414-832-7346.
AD: Amy Proctor.

LEBANON VALLEY
Annville, PA 17003 III

Coach: James Monos, Shippensburg '72
Record: 8 Years, 35-43-2
1994 SCHEDULE
Johns Hopkins ■ ....Sept. 10
Wilkes ....Sept. 17
Delaware Valley ■ ....Sept. 24
Moravian ....Oct. 1
Susquehanna ■ ....Oct. 8
Juniata ....Oct. 15
Lycoming ■ ....Oct. 22
Albright ....Oct. 29
Upsala ....Nov. 5
Widener ■ ....Nov. 12

1993 RESULTS (5-5-0)
7	Johns Hopkins	33
0	Wilkes	41
33	Delaware Valley	10
15	Moravian	13
14	Susquehanna	35
54	Juniata	7
3	Lycoming	28
24	Albright	13
31	Upsala	28
26	Widener	28
207		**236**

Nickname: Flying Dutchmen.
Stadium: Arnold Field (1969), 2,500 capacity. Natural turf.
Colors: Royal Blue & White.
Conference: Middle Atlantic.
SID: John Deamer, 717-867-6033.
AD: Louis Sorrentino.

LEHIGH
Bethlehem, PA 18015 ....I-AA

Coach: Kevin Higgins, West Chester '77
(First year as head coach)

1994 SCHEDULE

Fordham ■	Sept. 10
Buffalo	*Sept. 17
Columbia ■	Sept. 24
Cornell	Oct. 1
Yale	Oct. 8
New Hampshire	Oct. 15
Bucknell ■	Oct. 22
Colgate	Oct. 29
Delaware ■	Nov. 5
Holy Cross	Nov. 12
Lafayette	Nov. 19

1993 RESULTS (7-4-0)

21	Delaware	62
24	Fordham	6
31	Hofstra	24
42	Brown	35
35	Cornell	13
23	Princeton	31
36	Colgate	32
17	Holy Cross	10
27	Bucknell	32
14	Idaho	77
39	Lafayette	14
309		**336**

Nickname: Engineers.
Stadium: Goodman (1988), 16,000 capacity. Natural turf.
Colors: Brown & White.
Conference: Patriot League.
SID: Glenn Hofmann, 215-758-3174.
AD: Joseph Sterrett.

LENOIR-RHYNE
Hickory, NC 28603 II

Coach: Charles Forbes, East Caro. '68
Record: 18 Years, 86-86-3

1994 SCHEDULE

Western Caro.	*Sept. 1
Wofford	*Sept. 17
Presbyterian	Sept. 24
Elon ■	*Oct. 1
Gardner-Webb ■	*Oct. 8
Wingate	Oct. 15
Newberry ■	Oct. 22
Carson-Newman ■	*Oct. 29
Mars Hill ■	Nov. 5
Catawba	Nov. 12

1993 RESULTS (7-3-0)

56	Guilford	0
14	Newberry	10
34	Presbyterian	27
9	Elon	33
47	Gardner-Webb	40
21	Wingate	13
27	Wofford	24
3	Carson-Newman	31
28	Mars Hill	35
38	Catawba	29
277		**242**

Nickname: Bears.
Stadium: Moretz, 8,500 capacity. Natural turf.
Colors: Red & Black.
Conference: South Atlantic Conf.
SID: Tom Neff, 704-328-7115.
AD: Keith Ochs.

LIBERTY
Lynchburg, VA 24506 ....I-AA

Coach: Sam Rutigliano, Tulsa '56
Record: 5 Years, 31-23-0

1994 SCHEDULE

Concord (W.Va.) ■	*Sept. 3
Villanova	*Sept. 9
Toledo	*Sept. 17
Boise St.	*Sept. 24
Delaware St. ■	*Oct. 8
Southwest Mo. St.	Oct. 15
Catawba ■	*Oct. 22

Central Fla. ■	*Oct. 29
Appalachian St.	Nov. 5
New Haven ■	*Nov. 12
Charleston So. ■	*Nov. 19

1993 RESULTS (6-5-0)

37	Concord (W.Va.)	3
20	Appalachian St.	14
17	Southwest Tex. St.	14
7	Indiana (Pa.)	23
30	North Caro. A&T	38
13	Troy St.	35
0	Youngstown St.	42
42	Charleston So.	6
19	Central Fla.	55
47	Delaware St.	43
27	Villanova	13
259		**286**

Nickname: Flames.
Stadium: Liberty (1989), 12,000 capacity. Artificial turf.
Colors: Red, White & Blue.
Conference: I-AA Independent.
SID: To be named, 804-582-2292.
AD: Chuck Burch.

LIVINGSTON
Livingston, AL 35470 II

Coach: Todd Stroud, Florida St. '85
(First year as head coach)

1994 SCHEDULE

Albany St. (Ga.)	Sept. 3
Nicholls St.	*Sept. 10
Kentucky St.	*Sept. 17
Mississippi Col. ■	Sept. 24
Valdosta St.	Oct. 1
West Ga.	Oct. 8
Central Ark. ■	Oct. 15
Delta St.	*Oct. 22
North Ala.	Oct. 29
Henderson St.	Nov. 5

1993 RESULTS (2-7-1)

21	Albany St. (Ga.)	30
51	Nicholls St.	42
28	Stephen F. Austin	49
22	Mississippi Col.	22
13	Valdosta St.	42
22	West Ga.	27
27	Central Ark.	42
60	Delta St.	55
15	North Ala.	65
44	Henderson St.	46
303		**420**

Nickname: Tigers.
Stadium: Tiger (1952), 8,500 capacity. Natural turf.
Colors: Red & White.
Conference: Gulf South Conf.
SID: To be appointed, 205-652-9661.
AD: Dee Outlaw.

LIVINGSTONE
Salisbury, NC 28144 II

Coach: Rudy Abhrams, Wayne St. (Neb.) '70
(First year as head coach)

1994 SCHEDULE

Fayetteville St.	*Sept. 3
Virginia Union	*Sept. 10
Bowie St. ■	Sept. 17
Winston-Salem	*Sept. 24
Virginia St.	Oct. 1
Johnson Smith ■	Oct. 15
Hampton	Oct. 22
N.C. Central	Oct. 29
Elizabeth City St. ■	Nov. 5
Knoxville	Nov. 12

1993 RESULTS (1-10-0)

0	Hampton	45
6	Virginia Union	14
0	Central St. (Ohio)	73
20	Winston-Salem	35
20	Virginia St.	36

12	Bowie St.	31
12	Johnson Smith	29
18	Savannah St.	37
18	N.C. Central	38
35	Fayetteville St.	32
7	Knoxville	10
148		**380**

Nickname: Fighting Bears.
Stadium: Alumni, 4,000 capacity. Natural turf.
Colors: Blue & Black.
Conference: Central Inter. Ath. Assoc.
SID: Clifton Huff, 704-633-7960.
AD: Delano Tucker.

LOCK HAVEN
Lock Haven, PA 17745 II

Coach: Dennis Therrell, Tennessee Tech '78
Record: 4 Years, 9-34-1

1994 SCHEDULE

Tennessee Tech	*Sept. 1
Indiana St.	*Sept. 10
Eastern Ill.	*Sept. 17
Mansfield ■	Sept. 24
Edinboro ■	Oct. 1
Clarion	Oct. 8
Bloomsburg	Oct. 15
Shippensburg ■	Oct. 22
Calif. (Pa.)	Oct. 29
Slippery Rock ■	Nov. 5
Indiana (Pa.)	Nov. 12

1993 RESULTS (2-9-0)

3	James Madison	55
14	Tennessee Tech	45
32	Bloomsburg	35
35	Mansfield	33
14	Indiana (Pa.)	52
20	Edinboro	52
26	Clarion	37
52	Kutztown	30
20	Shippensburg	31
14	Calif. (Pa.)	56
23	Slippery Rock	39
253		**465**

Nickname: Bald Eagles.
Stadium: Hubert Jack, 3,500 capacity. Natural turf.
Colors: Crimson & White.
Conference: Pennsylvania Conf.
SID: Patrick Donghia, 717-893-2350.
AD: Sharon E. Taylor.

LONG ISLAND-C.W. POST
Brookville, NY 11548 II

Coach: Tom Marshall, Detroit Mercy '62
Record: 11 Years, 58-47-2

1994 SCHEDULE

Wm. Paterson	*Sept. 9
Wagner ■	Sept. 17
Central Conn. St. ■	Sept. 24
American Int'l	Oct. 1
Rowan	Oct. 8
Trenton St. ■	Oct. 15
Mercyhurst ■	Oct. 22
Springfield	Oct. 29
Hampton	Nov. 5
Ithaca	Nov. 12

1993 RESULTS (9-1-0)

21	Wagner	27
38	Rowan	34
31	Marist	10
56	Pace	2
55	Gannon	14
28	Trenton St.	18
72	Central Conn. St.	18
23	Springfield	6
58	Salisbury St.	18
45	Alfred	22
427		**169**

ECAC II

34	Mercyhurst	3

Nickname: Pioneers.
Stadium: Hickox Field (1966), 4,000 capacity. Natural turf.
Colors: Green & Gold.
Conference: Division II Independent.
SID: Shawn Brennan, 516-299-2287.
AD: Vin Salamone.

LORAS

Dubuque, IA 52001 III

Coach: Bob Bierie, Loras '65
Record: 14 Years, 87-53-5

1994 SCHEDULE

Wis.-La Crosse	Sept. 3
Ill. Benedictine ■	Sept. 10
Buena Vista	Sept. 17
Dubuque ■	Sept. 24
Simpson	Oct. 1
William Penn ■	Oct. 8
Central (Iowa)	Oct. 15
Luther ■	Oct. 22
Upper Iowa	Nov. 5
Wartburg ■	Nov. 12

1993 RESULTS (7-2-1)

27	Ill. Benedictine	27
24	Augustana (Ill.)	14
26	Buena Vista	7
58	William Penn	0
14	Simpson	9
13	Dubuque	12
18	Central (Iowa)	40
31	Luther	28
28	Upper Iowa	3
10	Wartburg	24
249		**164**

Nickname: Duhawks.
Stadium: Rock Bowl (1945), 3,000 capacity. Natural turf.
Colors: Purple & Gold.
Conference: Iowa Inter. Ath. Conf.
SID: Howard Thomas, 319-588-7407.
AD: Bob Bierie.

LOUISIANA STATE

Baton Rouge, LA 70894 ....I-A

Coach: Curley Hallman, Texas A&M '70
Record: 6 Years, 35-32-0

1994 SCHEDULE

Texas A&M ■	*Sept. 3
Mississippi St. ■	*Sept. 10
Auburn	*Sept. 17
South Caro. ■	*Oct. 1
Florida	Oct. 8
Kentucky ■	*Oct. 15
Mississippi	Oct. 29
Alabama ■	*Nov. 5
Southern Miss. ■	*Nov. 12
Tulane	*Nov. 19
Arkansas	Nov. 26

1993 RESULTS (5-6-0)

0	Texas A&M	24
18	Mississippi St.	16
10	Auburn	34
20	Tennessee	42
38	Utah St.	17
3	Florida	58
17	Kentucky	35
19	Mississippi	17
17	Alabama	13
24	Tulane	10
24	Arkansas	42
190		**308**

Nickname: Fighting Tigers.
Stadium: Tiger (1924), 80,150 capacity. Natural turf.
Colors: Purple & Gold.
Conference: Southeastern Conf.
SID: Herb Vincent, 504-388-8226.
AD: Joe Dean.

LOUISIANA TECH

Ruston, LA 71272 ....I-A

Coach: Joe Raymond Peace, Louisiana Tech '68
Record: 6 Years, 32-30-4

1994 SCHEDULE

Baylor	*Sept. 3
Houston ■	*Sept. 10
South Caro.	*Sept. 17
Southwestern La. ■	Oct. 1
Nevada-Las Vegas	*Oct. 8
Utah St. ■	*Oct. 15
Northern Ill.	Oct. 22
West Va.	Oct. 29
Northwestern St. ■	*Nov. 5
San Jose St. ■	*Nov. 12
Arkansas St.	Nov. 19

1993 RESULTS (2-9-0)

0	Tennessee	50
3	South Caro.	34
3	Alabama	56
17	Arkansas St.	3
28	East Caro.	31
6	San Jose St.	31
17	Northern Ill.	16
23	Nevada-Las Vegas	28
13	Utah St.	24
16	Central Fla.	38
17	Southwestern La.	21
143		**332**

Nickname: Bulldogs.
Stadium: Joe Aillet (1968), 30,600 capacity. Natural turf.
Colors: Red & Blue.
Conference: Big West.
SID: Brian McCallum, 318-257-3144.
AD: Jerry Stovall.

LOUISVILLE

Louisville, KY 40292 ....I-A

Coach: Howard Schnellenberger, Kentucky '56
Record: 14 Years, 89-67-2

1994 SCHEDULE

Kentucky	*Sept. 3
Texas	*Sept. 10
Arizona St.	*Sept. 17
Pittsburgh ■	Oct. 1
North Caro. St. ■	Oct. 8
Army	Oct. 15
Navy	Oct. 22
Memphis ■	Oct. 29
Boston College ■	*Nov. 3
Texas A&M ■	Nov. 12
Tulsa ■	Nov. 26

1993 RESULTS (8-3-0)

31	San Jose St.	24
54	Memphis	28
35	Arizona St.	17
41	Texas	10
29	Pittsburgh	7
34	West Va.	36
35	Southern Miss.	27
28	Navy	0
10	Tennessee	45
7	Texas A&M	42
28	Tulsa	0
332		**236**

Liberty Bowl

18	Michigan St.	7

Nickname: Cardinals.
Stadium: Cardinal (1956), 35,500 capacity. Artificial turf.
Colors: Red, Black & White.
Conference: I-A Independent.
SID: Kenny Klein, 502-852-6581.
AD: William Olsen.

LUTHER

Decorah, IA 52101 III

Coach: Bob Naslund, Luther '65
Record: 16 Years, 82-69-0

1994 SCHEDULE

St. Olaf ■	Sept. 10
William Penn ■	Sept. 17
Upper Iowa	Sept. 24
Central (Iowa) ■	Oct. 1
Buena Vista	Oct. 8
Simpson ■	Oct. 15
Loras	Oct. 22
Dubuque ■	Oct. 29
Wartburg [Cedar Falls, Iowa]	Nov. 5
Neb. Wesleyan [Cedar Falls, Iowa]	*Nov. 10

1993 RESULTS (4-6-0)

14	St. Olaf	23
7	Simpson	17
9	Upper Iowa	20
33	Dubuque	0
7	Wartburg	21
21	Trinity (Ill.)	20
14	William Penn	0
28	Loras	31
0	Central (Iowa)	23
18	Buena Vista	7
151		**162**

Nickname: Norse.
Stadium: Carlson (1966), 5,000 capacity. Natural turf.
Colors: Blue & White.
Conference: Iowa Inter. Ath. Conf.
SID: Dave Blanchard, 319-387-1586.
AD: To be named.

LYCOMING

Williamsport, PA 17701 III

Coach: Frank Girardi, West Chester '61
Record: 22 Years, 156-55-5

1994 SCHEDULE

Susquehanna ■	Sept. 10
FDU-Madison	*Sept. 16
Albright	Sept. 24
King's (Pa.) ■	Oct. 1
Moravian ■	Oct. 8
Upsala	Oct. 15
Lebanon Valley	Oct. 22
Wilkes ■	Oct. 29
Juniata	Nov. 5
Delaware Valley ■	Nov. 12

1993 RESULTS (6-4-0)

14	Susquehanna	17
20	FDU-Madison	21
34	Albright	14
41	King's (Pa.)	21
14	Moravian	17
20	Upsala	12
28	Lebanon Valley	3
7	Wilkes	9
33	Juniata	18
31	Delaware Valley	0
242		**132**

Nickname: Warriors.
Stadium: Person Field (1962), 3,000 capacity. Natural turf.
Colors: Blue & Gold.
Conference: Middle Atlantic.
SID: Ken Weingartner, 717-321-4028.
AD: Frank Girardi.

MIT

Cambridge, MA 02139 III

Coach: Dwight Smith, Bates '75
Record: 6 Years, 16-28-1

1994 SCHEDULE

Salve Regina	Sept. 10
Assumption	Sept. 17
Western New Eng. ■	Sept. 24
Stonehill	Oct. 1
Westfield St. ■	Oct. 8
Curry	Oct. 15

Nichols ....Oct. 22
Mass.-Boston ■ ....Oct. 29
Bentley ....Nov. 5

1993 RESULTS (5-3-0)

10	Assumption	12
24	Western New Eng.	8
7	Stonehill	0
0	Westfield St.	20
23	Curry	16
43	Nichols	7
21	Mass.-Boston	6
3	Bentley	22
131		**91**

Nickname: Beavers.
Stadium: Steinbrenner (1980), 1,600 capacity. Natural turf.
Colors: Cardinal & Gray.
Conference: Eastern Collegiate.
SID: Roger F. Crosley, 617-253-7946.
AD: Richard Hill.

MacMURRAY
Jacksonville, IL 62650 III

Coach: Michael Hensley, Bowling Green '69
Record: 7 Years, 28-41-1

1994 SCHEDULE

William Penn ■ ....Sept. 10
Monmouth (Ill.) ....Sept. 17
Concordia (Wis.) ....Sept. 24
Concordia (Ill.) ....Oct. 1
Blackburn ....Oct. 8
Eureka ■ ....Oct. 15
Quincy ■ ....Oct. 22
Lakeland ■ ....Oct. 29
Franklin ■ ....Nov. 5
Greenville ....Nov. 12

1993 RESULTS (6-4-0)

17	Eureka	14
41	Manchester	14
10	Monmouth (Ill.)	7
0	Quincy	37
16	Concordia (Wis.)	41
0	Greenville	20
0	Aurora	27
10	Blackburn	3
24	Concordia (Ill.)	13
30	Lakeland	16
148		**192**

Nickname: Fighting Highlanders.
Stadium: Highlander, 1,250 capacity. Natural turf.
Colors: Navy & Scarlet.
Conference: Division III Independent.
SID: Tom Lenz, 217-479-7143.
AD: Bob Gay.

MACALESTER
St. Paul, MN 55105 III

Coach: Tom Bell, Bridgewater (Va.) '66
Record: 18 Years, 92-67-6

1994 SCHEDULE

Pomona-Pitzer ....Sept. 10
Gust. Adolphus ■ ....Sept. 17
Bethel (Minn.) ....Sept. 24
Carleton ■ ....Oct. 1
Augsburg ....Oct. 8
St. Olaf ■ ....Oct. 15
Hamline ....Oct. 22
Concordia-M'head ■ ....Oct. 29
St. Thomas (Minn.) ....Nov. 5
St. John's (Minn.) [Minneapolis, Minn.] ....*Nov. 10

1993 RESULTS (0-10-0)

13	Pomona-Pitzer	33
14	Bethel (Minn.)	31
0	St. Thomas (Minn.)	44
15	St. Olaf	28
12	Carleton	34
20	Concordia-M'head	35
7	Augsburg	35
6	St. John's (Minn.)	74

29	Gust. Adolphus	38
27	Hamline	58
143		**410**

Nickname: Scots.
Stadium: Macalester (1965), 4,000 capacity. Natural turf.
Colors: Orange & Blue.
Conference: Minnesota Inter. Ath. Conf.
SID: Andy Johnson, 612-696-6533.
AD: Ken Andrews.

MAINE
Orono, ME 04469 ....I-AA

Coach: Jack Cosgrove, Maine '78
Record: 1 Year, 3-8-0

1994 SCHEDULE

Central Fla. ■ ■ ....Sept. 3
Rhode Island ■ ....Sept. 10
Boston U. ■ ....Sept. 17
Massachusetts ....Sept. 24
Delaware ■ ....Oct. 1
Richmond ....Oct. 8
Connecticut.....................................Oct. 15
New Hampshire ■ ....Oct. 22
Buffalo [Portland, Maine] ....*Oct. 29
William & Mary ....Nov. 5
Northeastern ....Nov. 12

1993 RESULTS (3-8-0)

30	Buffalo	27
0	Boston U.	45
17	Massachusetts	13
13	New Hampshire	63
14	Richmond	17
26	Rhode Island	23
13	Connecticut	14
19	Delaware	21
23	William & Mary	47
20	Northeastern	34
15	Hofstra	27
190		**331**

Nickname: Black Bears.
Stadium: Alumni (1942), 10,000 capacity. Natural turf.
Colors: Blue & White.
Conference: Yankee.
SID: Matt Bourque, 207-581-1086.
AD: Walter Abbott.

MAINE MARITIME
Castine, ME 04420 III

Coach: Mike Hodgson
(First year as head coach)

1994 SCHEDULE

Bri'water (Mass.) ■ ....Sept. 17
Worcester St. ....Sept. 24
Mass. Maritime ■ ....Oct. 1
Mass.-Dartmouth ....Oct. 8
Plymouth St. ....Oct. 15
Mass.-Boston ■ ....Oct. 22
Fitchburg St. ....Oct. 29
Framingham St. ■ ....Nov. 5
Westfield St. ....Nov. 12

1993 RESULTS (8-1-0)

18	Bri'water (Mass.)	14
25	Worcester St.	7
6	Mass. Maritime	9
21	Mass.-Dartmouth	8
14	Plymouth St.	13
35	Mass.-Boston	6
45	Fitchburg St.	8
28	Framingham St.	19
22	Westfield St.	14
214		**98**

ECAC Northeast

28	Brockport St.	20

Nickname: Mariners.
Stadium: Ritchie (1965), 3,500 capacity. Artificial turf.
Colors: Royal Blue & Gold.
Conference: New England.

SID: Scott Fry, 207-326-4311.
AD: Bill Mottola.

MANCHESTER
North Manchester, IN 46962 III

Coach: Dale Liston, Heidelberg '66
Record: 11 Years, 45-57-0

1994 SCHEDULE

Defiance ■ ....Sept. 3
Olivet ■ ....Sept. 10
Urbana ....Sept. 17
Bluffton ....Sept. 24
Wabash ....Oct. 1
Rose-Hulman ■ ....Oct. 8
DePauw ....Oct. 22
Franklin [Indianapolis, Ind.] ....Oct. 29
Hanover ■ ....Nov. 5
Anderson...Nov. 12

1993 RESULTS (5-5-0)

24	Earlham	6
14	MacMurray	41
22	Urbana	14
7	Wabash	22
27	Bluffton	0
6	Anderson	42
28	DePauw	19
6	Franklin	30
7	Hanover	45
32	Rose-Hulman	23
173		**242**

Nickname: Spartans.
Stadium: Burt Memorial, 4,500 capacity. Natural turf.
Colors: Black & Old Gold.
Conference: Indiana Collegiate Ath. Conf.
SID: Rob Nichols, 219-982-5035.
AD: Tom Jarman.

MANKATO STATE
Mankato, MN 56001 II

Coach: Dan Runkle, Illinois Col. '68
Record: 13 Years, 72-72-2

1994 SCHEDULE

Northwest Mo. St. ....Sept. 3
Northeast Mo. St. ■ ....*Sept. 10
South Dak. ■ ....Sept. 17
Augustana (S.D.) ■ ....Sept. 24
North Dak. St. ....*Oct. 1
North Dak. ■ ....Oct. 8
Morningside ....Oct. 15
Northern Colo. ....Oct. 22
St. Cloud St. [Minneapolis, Minn.] ....Oct. 29
South Dak. St. ....Nov. 5
Nebraska-Omaha ....Nov. 12

1993 RESULTS (9-2-0)

55	Northwest Mo. St.	28
25	Northeast Mo. St.	23
44	South Dak.	31
37	Augustana (S.D.)	34
28	North Dak. St.	27
9	North Dak.	20
36	Morningside	14
35	Northern Colo.	28
49	St. Cloud St.	32
42	South Dak. St.	60
52	Nebraska-Omaha	24
412		**321**

II Championship

34	Mo. Southern St.	13
21	North Dak.	54

Nickname: Mavericks.
Stadium: Blakeslee Field (1962), 7,500 capacity. Natural turf.
Colors: Purple & Gold.
Conference: North Central Conf.
SID: Paul Allan, 507-389-2625.
AD: Don Amiot.

MANSFIELD
Mansfield, PA 16933 II

Coach: Tom Elsasser, Norwich '69
Record: 11 Years, 42-66-6

1994 SCHEDULE
Cortland St. ■	Sept. 3
Edinboro ■	Sept. 10
Ithaca	Sept. 17
Lock Haven	Sept. 24
Bloomsburg	Oct. 1
Kutztown ■	Oct. 8
West Chester	Oct. 15
East Stroudsburg ■	Oct. 22
Cheyney	Oct. 29
Millersville ■	Nov. 12

1993 RESULTS (2-8-0)
0	Cortland St.	3
19	Buffalo St.	23
33	Lock Haven	35
24	Kutztown	21
10	West Chester	29
21	East Stroudsburg	45
46	Cheyney	6
7	Ferrum	8
8	Millersville	32
7	Bloomsburg	17
175		219

Nickname: Mountaineers.
Stadium: Van Norman Field, 5,000 capacity. Natural turf.
Colors: Red & Black.
Conference: Pennsylvania Conf.
SID: Steve McCloskey, 717-662-4540.
AD: Roger Maisner.

MARIETTA
Marietta, OH 45750 III

Coach: Gene Epley, Indiana (Pa.) '65
Record: 7 Years, 23-46-2

1994 SCHEDULE
Thiel ■	*Sept. 3
John Carroll	Sept. 17
Baldwin-Wallace ■	*Sept. 24
Hiram ■	Oct. 1
Mount Union	Oct. 8
Capital ■	Oct. 15
Ohio Northern	Oct. 22
Otterbein	Oct. 29
Heidelberg ■	Nov. 5
Muskingum	Nov. 12

1993 RESULTS (2-8-0)
0	Ohio Northern	23
10	Kenyon	21
0	Mount Union	37
10	Capital	14
10	Hiram	8
0	Otterbein	10
9	Baldwin-Wallace	31
13	John Carroll	19
6	Heidelberg	26
19	Muskingum	7
77		196

Nickname: Pioneers.
Stadium: Don Drumm Field (1935), 7,000 capacity. Natural turf.
Colors: Navy Blue & White.
Conference: Ohio Ath. Conf.
SID: Jeff Schaly, 614-376-4891.
AD: Debora Lazorik.

MARIST
Poughkeepsie, NY 12601 ....I-AA

Coach: Jim Parady, Maine '84
Record: 2 Years, 9-10-1

1994 SCHEDULE
Central Conn. St. ■	Sept. 10
Iona ■	Sept. 17
Wagner	Sept. 24
St. John's (N.Y.) ■	Oct. 1
St. Peter's	Oct. 8
Duquesne	Oct. 15
Canisius ■	Oct. 22
Georgetown	Oct. 29
St. Francis (Pa.) ■	Nov. 5
Siena	Nov. 12

1993 RESULTS (5-5-0)
16	St. Francis (Pa.)	7
47	Pace	19
10	LIU-C.W. Post	31
30	St. John's (N.Y.)	31
33	Central Conn. St.	31
21	Duquesne	12
7	Rensselaer	14
6	Wagner	22
24	Iona	27
28	Siena	0
222		194

Nickname: Red Foxes.
Stadium: Leonidoff Field (1972), 2,500 capacity. Natural turf.
Colors: Black, Red & White.
Conference: Metro Atlantic.
SID: Dan Sullivan, 914-575-3000.
AD: Eugene Doris.

MARS HILL
Mars Hill, NC 28754 II

Coach: Tim Clifton, Mercer '76
Record: 1 Year, 4-6-0

1994 SCHEDULE
Newberry	*Sept. 3
Concord (W.Va.)	Sept. 10
Catawba ■	Sept. 17
Wingate	Sept. 24
Kentucky St. ■	Oct. 1
Elon ■	Oct. 8
Carson-Newman ■	Oct. 15
Presbyterian ■	Oct. 22
Charleston So.	Oct. 29
Lenoir-Rhyne	Nov. 5
Gardner-Webb	Nov. 12

1993 RESULTS (4-6-0)
21	Tusculum	3
0	East Tenn. St.	24
34	Catawba	35
28	Wingate	31
22	Kentucky St.	0
7	Elon	17
21	Carson-Newman	42
28	Presbyterian	45
35	Lenoir-Rhyne	28
40	Gardner-Webb	21
236		246

Nickname: Lions.
Stadium: Meares (1965), 5,000 capacity. Natural turf.
Colors: Blue & Gold.
Conference: South Atlantic Conf.
SID: To be named, 704-689-1373.
AD: Ed Hoffmeyer.

MARSHALL
Huntington, WV 25715 ....I-AA

Coach: Jim Donnan, North Caro. St. '67
Record: 4 Years, 40-16-0

1994 SCHEDULE
Morehead St. ■	*Sept. 3
Tennessee Tech ■	*Sept. 10
Ga. Southern	*Sept. 17
West Va. St. ■	*Sept. 24
Tenn.-Chatt. ■	*Oct. 1
Va. Military	Oct. 8
Western Caro. ■	*Oct. 15
Appalachian St.	Oct. 22
Citadel ■	Oct. 29
East Tenn. St.	Nov. 5
Furman ■	Nov. 12

1993 RESULTS (8-3-0)
56	Morehead St.	0
29	Murray St.	3
13	Ga. Southern	3
31	Tenn.-Chatt.	33
51	Va. Military	0
17	North Caro. St.	24
35	Appalachian St.	3
35	Citadel	15
33	East Tenn. St.	9
3	Furman	17
20	Western Caro.	16
323		123

I-AA Championship
28	Howard	14
34	Delaware	31
24	Troy St.	21
5	Youngstown St.	17

Nickname: Thundering Herd.
Stadium: Marshall University (1991), 28,000 capacity. Artificial turf.
Colors: Green & White.
Conference: Southern Conf.
SID: Gary Richter, 304-696-5275.
AD: William Lee Moon.

MARYLAND
College Park, MD 20740 ....I-A

Coach: Mark Duffner, William & Mary '75
Record: 8 Years, 65-22-1

1994 SCHEDULE
Duke	Sept. 3
Florida St. ■	Sept. 10
West Va.	Sept. 17
Wake Forest ■	Sept. 24
Clemson	Oct. 1
North Caro.	Oct. 15
Georgia Tech ■	Oct. 22
Tulane	Oct. 29
North Caro. St. ■	Nov. 5
Virginia	Nov. 12
Syracuse	Nov. 19

1993 RESULTS (2-9-0)
29	Virginia	43
42	North Caro.	59
37	West Va.	42
28	Virginia Tech	55
7	Penn St.	70
0	Georgia Tech	38
26	Duke	18
0	Clemson	29
20	Florida St.	49
21	North Caro. St.	44
33	Wake Forest	32
243		479

Nickname: Terrapins.
Stadium: Byrd (1950), 45,000 capacity. Natural turf.
Colors: Red, White, Black & Gold.
Conference: Atlantic Coast Conf.
SID: Herb Hartnett, 301-314-7064.
AD: To be named.

MARYVILLE (TENNESSEE)
Maryville, TN 37801 III

Coach: Phil Wilks, Marshall '70
Record: 6 Years, 29-30-0

1994 SCHEDULE
Rhodes ■	Sept. 3
Ky. Wesleyan	Sept. 10
Davidson ■	Sept. 17
Sewanee	Sept. 24
Clinch Valley ■	Oct. 1
Centre	Oct. 15
Sue Bennett	Oct. 22
Methodist ■	Oct. 29
Tusculum	Nov. 5
Emory & Henry	Nov. 12

1993 RESULTS (6-4-0)
6	Ky. Wesleyan	7

27	Centre	21
26	Sewanee	14
6	Cumberland (Tenn.)	18
30	Tenn. Wesleyan	20
10	Clinch Valley	29
16	Rhodes	12
18	Methodist	17
14	Tusculum	22
29	Emory & Henry	28
182		**188**

Nickname: Scots.
Stadium: Lloyd Thorton (1951), 2,500 capacity. Natural turf.
Colors: Orange & Garnet.
Conference: Division III Independent.
SID: Eric Etchison, 615-981-8283.
AD: Randy Lambert.

MASSACHUSETTS
Amherst, MA 01003...............................I-AA

Coach: Mike Hodges, Maine '67
Record: 2 Years, 15-6-0

1994 SCHEDULE
Richmond	Sept. 10
Holy Cross	Sept. 17
Maine ■	Sept. 24
Rhode Island ■	Oct. 1
New Hampshire	Oct. 8
William & Mary	Oct. 15
Delaware	Oct. 22
Boston U. ■	Oct. 29
Northeastern ■	Nov. 5
Youngstown St. ■	Nov. 12
Connecticut ■	Nov. 19

1993 RESULTS (8-3-0)
37	Holy Cross	7
13	Maine	17
9	Boston U.	28
33	James Madison	10
36	Rhode Island	14
20	Connecticut	17
43	Delaware	29
21	Northeastern	17
29	Richmond	24
28	William & Mary	45
15	New Hampshire	13
284		**221**

Nickname: Minutemen.
Stadium: Warren McGuirk (1965), 16,000 capacity. Natural turf.
Colors: Maroon & White.
Conference: Yankee.
SID: Bill Strickland, 413-545-2439.
AD: Bob Marcum.

MASSACHUSETTS MARITIME
Buzzards Bay, MA 02532 III

Coach: Don Ruggeri, Springfield '62
Record: 21 Years, 105-81-1

1994 SCHEDULE
Nichols ■	Sept. 10
Bentley	*Sept. 16
Mass.-Dartmouth ■	Sept. 24
Maine Maritime	Oct. 1
Mass.-Boston ■	Oct. 8
Fitchburg St.	Oct. 15
Framingham St. ■	Oct. 22
Westfield St.	*Oct. 28
Bri'water (Mass.) ■	Nov. 5
Worcester St.	Nov. 12

1993 RESULTS (4-6-0)
23	Nichols	6
12	Bentley	21
28	Mass.-Dartmouth	21
9	Maine Maritime	6
25	Mass.-Boston	33
18	Fitchburg St.	16
6	Framingham St.	27
9	Westfield St.	27
13	Bri'water (Mass.)	41

12	Worcester St.	28
155		**226**

Nickname: Buccaneers.
Stadium: Commander Ellis (1972), 3,000 capacity. Natural turf.
Colors: Blue & Gold.
Conference: New England.
SID: Leroy Thompson, 508-830-5054.
AD: Robert Corradi.

MASSACHUSETTS-BOSTON
Boston, MA 02125...............................III

Coach: Gus Giardi, Syracuse '64
(First year as head coach)

1994 SCHEDULE
Westfield St. ■	Sept. 17
Bri'water (Mass.)	Sept. 24
Worcester St.	Oct. 1
Mass. Maritime	Oct. 8
Mass.-Dartmouth ■	Oct. 15
Maine Maritime	Oct. 22
MIT	Oct. 29
Fitchburg St. ■	Nov. 5
Framingham St.	Nov. 12

1993 RESULTS (2-7-0)
0	Westfield St.	47
6	Bri'water (Mass.)	37
6	Worcester St.	27
33	Mass. Maritime	25
6	Mass.-Dartmouth	16
6	Maine Maritime	35
6	MIT	21
18	Fitchburg St.	2
0	Framingham St.	13
81		**223**

Nickname: Beacons.
Stadium: Clark Field (1986), 750 capacity. Natural turf.
Colors: Blue & White.
Conference: New England.
SID: Kevin Dolan, 617-287-7815.
AD: Charlie Titus.

MASSACHUSETTS-DARTMOUTH
North Dartmouth, MA 02747 III

Coach: William Kavanaugh, Stonehill '72
Record: 4 Years, 17-19-0

1994 SCHEDULE
Plymouth St. ■	Sept. 10
Worcester St. ■	Sept. 17
Mass. Maritime	Sept. 24
Western Conn. St. ■	Oct. 1
Maine Maritime ■	Oct. 8
Mass.-Boston	Oct. 15
Fitchburg St. ■	Oct. 22
Framingham St.	Oct. 29
Westfield St. ■	Nov. 5
Bri'water (Mass.)	Nov. 12

1993 RESULTS (5-4-0)
29	Worcester St.	17
21	Mass. Maritime	28
18	Western Conn. St.	31
8	Maine Maritime	21
16	Mass.-Boston	6
12	Fitchburg St.	0
27	Framingham St.	13
14	Westfield St.	33
17	Bri'water (Mass.)	10
162		**159**

Nickname: Corsairs.
Stadium: Not named, 1,850 capacity. Natural turf.
Colors: Blue, White & Gold.
Conference: New England.
SID: William E. Gathright, 508-999-8727.
AD: Robert A. Dowd.

MASSACHUSETTS-LOWELL
Lowell, MA 01854 II

Coach: Tom Radulski, New Hampshire '79
Record: 1 Year, 5-5-0

1994 SCHEDULE
Bentley ■	*Sept. 10
Norwich ■	*Sept. 17
Sacred Heart	Sept. 24
Plymouth St.	Oct. 1
Assumption	Oct. 8
Stonehill ■	Oct. 15
Western Conn. St. ■	Oct. 22
Worcester Tech ■	Oct. 29
Pace ■	Nov. 5
Stony Brook	Nov. 12

1993 RESULTS (5-5-0)
10	Bentley	21
28	Norwich	26
35	Pace	19
20	Plymouth St.	23
18	Sacred Heart	8
7	Stonehill	14
7	Western Conn. St.	16
7	Worcester Tech	21
36	Assumption	33
36	Stony Brook	18
204		**199**

Nickname: River Hawks.
Stadium: Cawley Memorial (1937), 7,000 capacity. Natural turf.
Colors: Red, White and Blue.
Conference: Division II Independent.
SID: B. L. Elfring, 508-934-2310.
AD: Wayne Edwards.

McNEESE STATE
Lake Charles, LA 70601.........................I-AA

Coach: Bobby Keasler, Northeast La. '70
Record: 4 Years, 30-17-2

1994 SCHEDULE
Illinois St. ■	*Sept. 3
Jacksonville St. ■	*Sept. 10
Central Ark. ■	*Sept. 17
Northern Iowa	Sept. 24
Youngstown St. ■	*Oct. 1
North Texas	Oct. 15
Sam Houston St.	Oct. 22
Stephen F. Austin ■	*Oct. 29
Southwest Tex. St. ■	*Nov. 5
Northwestern St.	*Nov. 12
Nicholls St. ■	*Nov. 19

1993 RESULTS (9-2-0)
27	Northern Iowa	10
49	Eastern Ill.	7
27	Illinois St.	37
3	Central Fla.	22
34	Northeast La.	26
18	North Texas	17
37	Sam Houston St.	14
21	Stephen F. Austin	20
27	Southwest Tex. St.	10
34	Northwestern St.	7
27	Nicholls St.	0
304		**170**

I-AA Championship
34	William & Mary	28
28	Troy St.	35

Nickname: Cowboys.
Stadium: Cowboy (1965), 17,500 capacity. Natural turf.
Colors: Blue & Gold.
Conference: Southland Conf.
SID: Louis Bonnette, 318-475-5207.
AD: Bob Hayes.

MEMPHIS
Memphis, TN 38152 ....I-A

Coach: Chuck Stobart, Ohio '59
Record: 13 Years, 63-79-3

1994 SCHEDULE
Mississippi St. ■	*Sept. 3

Tulsa ....*Sept. 10
Southern Miss. ....Sept. 17
Arkansas ■ ....*Sept. 24
Tulane ■ ....*Oct. 8
Arkansas St. ■ ....*Oct. 15
Cincinnati ■ ....*Oct. 22
Louisville ....Oct. 29
Mississippi ....Nov. 5
Tennessee ....Nov. 12
East Caro. ■ ....Nov. 19

1993 RESULTS (6-5-0)

45	Mississippi St.	35
28	Louisville	54
15	Southwestern La.	17
6	Arkansas	0
34	East Caro.	7
45	Arkansas St.	3
19	Tulsa	23
20	Cincinnati	23
19	Mississippi	3
20	Southern Miss.	9
17	Miami (Fla.)	41
268		**215**

Nickname: Tigers.
Stadium: Liberty Bowl (1965), 62,380 capacity. Natural turf.
Colors: Blue & Gray.
Conference: I-A Independent.
SID: Bob Winn, 901-678-2337.
AD: Charles Cavagnaro.

MENLO
Menlo Park, CA 94025 III

Coach: Ray Solari, California '51
Record: 8 Years, 32-39-2

1994 SCHEDULE

San Diego ■ ....Sept. 3
La Verne...Sept. 10
Occidental ■ ....Sept. 17
San Fran. St. ....Oct. 1
Redlands ■ ....Oct. 8
Claremont-M-S ....Oct. 15
Chapman ....*Oct. 22
Whittier ■ ....Oct. 29
Azusa Pacific ■ ....Nov. 12

1993 RESULTS (0-8-1)

7	San Diego	32
10	Redlands	17
0	San Fran. St.	32
20	Cal Lutheran	40
21	La Verne	38
34	Claremont-M-S	34
13	Occidental	52
14	Whittier	45
14	Azusa Pacific	42
133		**332**

Nickname: Oaks.
Stadium: Connor Field (1970), 1,000 capacity. Natural turf.
Colors: Navy Blue & White.
Conference: Division III Independent.
SID: Mark Majeski, 415-688-3780.
AD: Donald Baikie.

MERCHANT MARINE
Kings Point, NY 11024 III

Coach: Charlie Pravata, Adelphi '72
Record: 3 Years, 14-11-2

1994 SCHEDULE

Norwich ....Sept. 10
Brockport St. ■ ....Sept. 17
Catholic ■ ....Sept. 24
Carnegie Mellon ....Oct. 1
Worcester Tech ■ ....Oct. 15
Stony Brook ....Oct. 22
Gettysburg ■ ....Oct. 29
Western Conn. St. ....Nov. 5
Coast Guard ■ ....Nov. 12

1993 RESULTS (5-4-0)

35	Norwich	7
32	Western Conn. St.	2
34	Catholic	6
21	St. John Fisher	19
37	Worcester Tech	44
20	Stony Brook	21
19	Gettysburg	6
28	Alfred	34
23	Coast Guard	31
249		**170**

Nickname: Mariners.
Stadium: Capt. Tomb Field (1945), 5,840 capacity. Natural turf.
Colors: Blue & Gray.
Conference: Freedom Football Conf.
SID: Chris Brown, 516-773-5455.
AD: Susan Petersen Lubow.

MERCYHURST
Erie, PA 16546 II

Coach: Joe Kimball, Syracuse '75
Record: 9 Years, 42-42-1

1994 SCHEDULE

Canisius ■ ....Sept. 10
Frostburg St. ....Sept. 17
Dickinson ....Sept. 24
St. Francis (Pa.) ....Oct. 1
Buffalo St. ....Oct. 8
Pace ■ ....Oct. 15
LIU-C.W. Post ....Oct. 22
Grove City ....Oct. 29
Gannon ■ ....Nov. 5
Robert Morris ■ ....Nov. 12

1993 RESULTS (5-4-0)

17	Gannon	7
6	Dickinson	35
13	Canisius	9
0	Buffalo St.	34
6	Wittenberg	7
24	Duquesne	7
25	Ithaca	45
48	Pace	0
39	St. Francis (Pa.)	26
178		**170**

ECAC II

3	LIU-C.W. Post	34

Nickname: Lakers.
Stadium: Erie Veteran Memorial (1958), 10,500 capacity. Natural turf.
Colors: Blue & Green.
Conference: Division II Independent.
SID: Ed Hess, 814-824-2525.
AD: Pete Russo.

MESA STATE
Grand Junction, CO 81501 II

Coach: Jay Hood, Adams St. '65
(First year as head coach)

1994 SCHEDULE

Central Okla. ....*Sept. 3
Northern Colo. ■ ....Sept. 10
Cal St. Chico ■ ....Sept. 17
Western St. ....Sept. 24
Chadron St. ....Oct. 1
Fort Lewis ....Oct. 8
Fort Hays St. ■ ....Oct. 15
Western St. ■ ....Oct. 22
N.M. Highlands ....Oct. 29
Adams St. ■ ....Nov. 5
Colorado Mines ....Nov. 12

1993 RESULTS (5-5-0)

7	Central Okla.	37
0	Northern Colo.	49
54	Fort Lewis	27
10	Idaho St.	59
14	Fort Hays St.	44
41	Western St.	32
17	N.M. Highlands	14

15	Adams St.	21
31	Colorado Mines	14
36	Chadron St.	29
225		**326**

Nickname: Mavericks.
Stadium: Stocker, 8,000 capacity. Natural turf.
Colors: Maroon, White & Gold.
Conference: Rocky Mountain Ath. Conf.
SID: To be named, 303-248-1716.
AD: Jim Paronto.

METHODIST
Fayetteville, NC 28311 III

Coach: Jim Sypult, West Va. '67
Record: 2 Years, 4-16-0

1994 SCHEDULE

Chowan ....Sept. 3
Guilford ■ ....Sept. 10
Salisbury St. ■ ....Sept. 17
Newport News App. ....Sept. 24
Bridgewater (Va.) ....Oct. 8
Davidson ■ ....Oct. 15
Gallaudet ■ ....Oct. 22
Maryville (Tenn.) ....Oct. 29
Hampden-Sydney ■ ....Nov. 5
Frostburg St. ....Nov. 12

1993 RESULTS (4-6-0)

16	Chowan	13
14	Guilford	7
19	Salisbury St.	33
6	Newport News App.	42
17	Bridgewater (Va.)	14
7	Davidson	35
36	Gallaudet	0
17	Maryville (Tenn.)	18
7	Hampden-Sydney	35
23	Frostburg St.	47
162		**244**

Nickname: Monarchs.
Stadium: Monarch Field (1990), 1,500 capacity. Natural turf.
Colors: Green & Gold.
Conference: Division III Independent.
SID: Michael Hogan, 919-630-7175.
AD: Rita S. Wiggs.

MIAMI (FLORIDA)
Coral Gables, FL 33124 ....I-A

Coach: Dennis Erickson, Montana St. '70
Record: 12 Years, 103-38-1

1994 SCHEDULE

Ga. Southern ■ ....Sept. 3
Arizona St. ....*Sept. 10
Washington ■ ....Sept. 24
Rutgers ....Oct. 1
Florida St. ■ ....*Oct. 8
West Va. ....Oct. 22
Virginia Tech ■ ....Oct. 29
Syracuse ....Nov. 5
Pittsburgh ■ ....Nov. 12
Temple ....Nov. 19
Boston College ■ ....Nov. 26

1993 RESULTS (9-2-0)

23	Boston College	7
21	Virginia Tech	2
35	Colorado	29
30	Ga. Southern	7
10	Florida St.	28
49	Syracuse	0
42	Temple	7
35	Pittsburgh	7
31	Rutgers	17
14	West Va.	17
41	Memphis	17
331		**138**

Fiesta Bowl

0	Arizona	29

Nickname: Hurricanes.

Stadium: Orange Bowl (1935), 74,712 capacity.
Natural turf.
Colors: Orange, Green & White.
Conference: Big East Conference.
SID: Linda Venzon, 305-284-3244.
AD: Paul Dee.

MIAMI (OHIO)
Oxford, OH 45056 .... I-A

Coach: Randy Walker, Miami (Ohio) '76
Record: 4 Years, 21-20-3

1994 SCHEDULE
Western Mich. ■	Sept. 3
Indiana	Sept. 10
Cincinnati ■	Sept. 17
Michigan St.	Sept. 24
Eastern Mich.	Oct. 1
Akron ■	Oct. 8
Ohio	Oct. 15
Central Mich.	Oct. 22
Bowling Green	Oct. 29
Ball St. ■	Nov. 5
Kent ■	Nov. 12

1993 RESULTS (4-7-0)
29	Southwestern La.	28
23	Cincinnati	30
0	Western Mich.	17
7	Eastern Mich.	15
13	Akron	31
22	Toledo	19
20	Ohio	22
25	Bowling Green	30
0	Ball St.	21
23	Kent	14
24	Central Mich.	21
186		**248**

Nickname: Redskins.
Stadium: Fred C. Yager (1983), 25,183 capacity.
Natural turf.
Colors: Red & White.
Conference: Mid-American Conf.
SID: Brian Teter, 513-529-4327.
AD: To be named.

MICHIGAN
Ann Arbor, MI 48109 .... I-A

Coach: Gary Moeller, Ohio St. '63
Record: 7 Years, 42-33-6

1994 SCHEDULE
Boston College ■	Sept. 3
Notre Dame	Sept. 10
Colorado ■	Sept. 24
Iowa	Oct. 1
Michigan St. ■	Oct. 8
Penn St. ■	Oct. 15
Illinois	Oct. 22
Wisconsin ■	Oct. 29
Purdue	Nov. 5
Minnesota ■	Nov. 12
Ohio St.	Nov. 19

1993 RESULTS (7-4-0)
41	Washington St.	14
23	Notre Dame	27
42	Houston	21
24	Iowa	7
7	Michigan St.	17
21	Penn St.	13
21	Illinois	24
10	Wisconsin	13
25	Purdue	10
58	Minnesota	7
28	Ohio St.	0
300		**153**

Hall of Fame Bowl
42	North Caro. St.	7

Nickname: Wolverines.
Stadium: Michigan (1927), 102,501 capacity. Natural turf.
Colors: Maize & Blue.

Conference: Big Ten Conf.
SID: Bruce Madej, 313-763-4423.
AD: Joe Roberson.

MICHIGAN STATE
East Lansing, MI 48824 .... I-A

Coach: George Perles, Michigan St. '60
Record: 11 Years, 68-56-4

1994 SCHEDULE
Kansas	Sept. 10
Notre Dame ■	Sept. 17
Miami (Ohio) ■	Sept. 24
Wisconsin ■	Oct. 1
Michigan	Oct. 8
Ohio St. ■	Oct. 15
Iowa	Oct. 22
Indiana ■	Oct. 29
Northwestern	Nov. 5
Purdue ■	Nov. 12
Penn St.	Nov. 26

1993 RESULTS (6-5-0)
31	Kansas	14
14	Notre Dame	36
48	Central Mich.	34
17	Michigan	7
21	Ohio St.	28
24	Iowa	10
0	Indiana	10
31	Northwestern	29
27	Purdue	24
37	Penn St.	38
20	Wisconsin	41
270		**271**

Liberty Bowl
7	Louisville	18

Nickname: Spartans.
Stadium: Spartan (1957), 76,000 capacity. Artificial turf.
Colors: Green & White.
Conference: Big Ten Conf.
SID: Ken Hoffman, 517-355-2271.
AD: Merrily Baker.

MICHIGAN TECH
Houghton, MI 49931 II

Coach: Bernie Anderson, Northern Mich. '78
Record: 7 Years, 35-32-0

1994 SCHEDULE
Missouri-Rolla ■	Sept. 3
Northwood	Sept. 10
Ashland ■	Sept. 17
St. Joseph's (Ind.)	Sept. 24
Saginaw Valley ■	Oct. 1
Indianapolis	Oct. 8
St. Francis (Ill.) ■	Oct. 15
Grand Valley St.	Oct. 22
Ferris St. ■	Oct. 29
Wayne St. (Mich.)	Nov. 5
Hillsdale ■	Nov. 12

1993 RESULTS (6-4-0)
43	Wis.-Stevens Point	21
30	Northern St.	15
42	Minn.-Morris	10
52	Bemidji St.	23
24	Winona St.	13
3	Minn.-Duluth	32
21	Saginaw Valley	7
26	Wayne St. (Neb.)	34
20	Valparaiso	25
42	Southwest St.	48
303		**228**

Nickname: Huskies.
Stadium: Sherman Field (1954), 3,000 capacity.
Natural turf.
Colors: Silver & Gold.
Conference: Midwest Intercollegiate.
SID: Dave Fischer, 906-487-2350.
AD: Rick Yeo.

MIDDLE TENNESSEE STATE
Murfreesboro, TN 37132 .... I-AA

Coach: Boots Donnelly, Middle Tenn. St. '65
Record: 17 Years, 124-71-0

1994 SCHEDULE
Tennessee St.	*Sept. 3
James Madison	*Sept. 10
Murray St.	*Sept. 24
Eastern Ky. ■	*Oct. 1
Tenn.-Martin	Oct. 8
Morehead St. ■	Oct. 15
Southeast Mo. St.	Oct. 22
Jacksonville St. ■	Oct. 29
Austin Peay	Nov. 5
Illinois St. ■	Nov. 12
Tennessee Tech ■	Nov. 19

1993 RESULTS (5-6-0)
14	Hawaii	35
70	Campbellsville	13
45	Murray St.	3
33	Tennessee St.	34
14	Tenn.-Martin	24
45	Morehead St.	0
31	Southeast Mo. St.	10
17	Tulsa	38
44	Austin Peay	10
27	Eastern Ky.	33
14	Tennessee Tech	35
354		**235**

Nickname: Blue Raiders.
Stadium: Johnny Floyd (1969), 15,000 capacity.
Artificial turf.
Colors: Blue & White.
Conference: Ohio Valley Conf.
SID: Ed Given, 615-898-2450.
AD: Lee Fowler.

MIDDLEBURY
Middlebury, VT 05753 III

Coach: Mickey Heinecken, Delaware '61
Record: 21 Years, 96-70-2

1994 SCHEDULE
Wesleyan ■	Sept. 24
Colby	Oct. 1
Amherst ■	Oct. 8
Williams	Oct. 15
Bates ■	Oct. 22
Trinity (Conn.)	Oct. 29
Hamilton	Nov. 5
Tufts ■	Nov. 12

1993 RESULTS (5-3-0)
19	Bowdoin	0
7	Colby	8
10	Amherst	6
6	Williams	14
33	Bates	16
14	Trinity (Conn.)	43
33	Hamilton	17
14	Tufts	12
136		**116**

Nickname: Panthers.
Stadium: Alumni (1991), 3,500 capacity. Natural turf.
Colors: Blue & White.
Conference: NESCAC.
SID: To be named, 802-388-3711.
AD: G. Thomas Lawson.

MILES
Birmingham, AL 35208 II

Coach: Cecil Leonard, Tuskegee '69
(First year as head coach)

1994 SCHEDULE
Albany St. (Ga.)	Sept. 10
Morehouse ■	Sept. 17
Lane	Oct. 1
Morris Brown ■	Oct. 8
Fort Valley St. ■	Oct. 15

Tuskegee ....Oct. 22
Alabama A&M ■ ....Nov. 5
Savannah St. ■ ....Nov. 12

1993 RESULTS (0-10-0)

0	Alabama A&M	35
0	Albany St. (Ga.)	44
8	Tuskegee	60
6	Ala.-Birmingham	31
0	Morris Brown	37
12	Clark Atlanta	20
0	Knoxville	34
0	Fort Valley St.	40
0	Morehouse	38
6	Savannah St.	57
32		**396**

Nickname: Golden Bears.
Stadium: Alumni, 3,400 capacity. Natural turf.
Colors: Purple & Gold.
Conference: Southern Inter. Ath. Conf.
SID: Willie K. Patterson Jr., 205-923-8323.
AD: Augustus James.

MILLERSVILLE

Millersville, PA 17551 II

Coach: Gene Carpenter, Huron '63
Record: 25 Years, 167-71-5

1994 SCHEDULE

Shepherd ....Sept. 10
American Int'l ■ ....*Sept. 17
Shippensburg ....Sept. 24
Clarion ■ ....Oct. 1
Bloomsburg ■ ....*Oct. 8
Kutztown ....Oct. 15
West Chester ■ ....Oct. 22
East Stroudsburg ....Oct. 29
Cheyney ■ ....Nov. 5
Mansfield ....Nov. 12

1993 RESULTS (8-2-0)

38	Shepherd	14
30	American Int'l	10
14	Shippensburg	16
26	Bloomsburg	0
41	Kutztown	7
14	West Chester	10
20	East Stroudsburg	7
51	Cheyney	6
32	Mansfield	8
27	Edinboro	52
293		**130**

Nickname: Marauders.
Stadium: Biemesderfer (1947), 6,500 capacity. Natural turf.
Colors: Black & Gold.
Conference: Pennsylvania Conf.
SID: Greg Wright, 717-872-3100.
AD: Gene Carpenter.

MILLIKIN

Decatur, IL 62522 III

Coach: Carl Poelker, Millikin '68
Record: 12 Years, 77-32-1

1994 SCHEDULE

Franklin ■ ....Sept. 10
Valparaiso ....Sept. 17
North Park ■ ....Oct. 1
Carthage ....Oct. 8
Wheaton (Ill.) ■ ....Oct. 15
North Central ....Oct. 22
Augustana (Ill.) ■ ....Oct. 29
Elmhurst ■ ....Nov. 5
Ill. Wesleyan ....Nov. 12

1993 RESULTS (6-3-0)

48	Ill. Benedictine	28
34	Valparaiso	36
13	Wheaton (Ill.)	20
45	Carthage	14
28	North Park	7
22	North Central	21
30	Augustana (Ill.)	54

28	Ill. Wesleyan	17
41	Elmhurst	2
289		**199**

Nickname: Big Blue.
Stadium: Frank M. Lindsay Field (1987), 4,000 capacity. Natural turf.
Colors: Royal Blue & White.
Conference: College Conf. of Ill. & Wis.
SID: Mickey Smith, 217-424-6350.
AD: Merle Chapman.

MILLSAPS

Jackson, MS 39210 III

Coach: Tommy Ranager, Mississippi St. '63
Record: 5 Years, 26-18-2

1994 SCHEDULE

Austin ■ ....Sept. 3
DePauw ....Sept. 10
McMurry ■ ....Sept. 17
Colorado Col. ■ ....Sept. 24
Emory & Henry ....Oct. 1
Centre ■ ....Oct. 8
Trinity (Tex.) ■ ....Oct. 15
Sewanee ....Oct. 29
Rhodes ....Nov. 5
Greenville ....Nov. 12

1993 RESULTS (5-4-0)

30	Austin	20
45	DePauw	0
14	Hardin-Simmons	55
34	Emory & Henry	10
19	Centre	20
15	Colorado Col.	42
34	Sewanee	10
28	Rhodes	24
19	Trinity (Tex.)	21
238		**202**

Nickname: Majors.
Stadium: Alumni Field, 4,000 capacity. Natural turf.
Colors: Purple & White.
Conference: Southern Coll. Ath. Conf.
SID: Trey Porter, 601-974-1195.
AD: Ron Jurney.

MINNESOTA

Minneapolis, MN 55455 ....I-A

Coach: Jim Wacker, Valparaiso '60
Record: 23 Years, 150-107-3

1994 SCHEDULE

Penn St. ■ ....*Sept. 3
Pacific (Cal.) ■ ....*Sept. 10
San Diego St. ■ ....*Sept. 17
Kansas St. ....*Sept. 24
Indiana ....Oct. 1
Purdue ....Oct. 8
Northwestern ■ ....*Oct. 15
Wisconsin ....Oct. 22
Illinois ■ ....*Nov. 5
Michigan ....Nov. 12
Iowa ■ ....*Nov. 19

1993 RESULTS (4-7-0)

20	Penn St.	38
27	Indiana St.	10
25	Kansas St.	30
17	San Diego St.	48
19	Indiana	23
59	Purdue	56
28	Northwestern	26
28	Wisconsin	21
20	Illinois	23
7	Michigan	58
3	Iowa	21
253		**354**

Nickname: Golden Gophers.
Stadium: Metrodome (1982), 62,345 capacity. Artificial turf.
Colors: Maroon & Gold.
Conference: Big Ten Conf.
SID: Marc Ryan, 612-625-4090.

AD: McKinley Boston.

MINNESOTA-DULUTH

Duluth, MN 55812 II

Coach: James Malosky, Minnesota '51
Record: 36 Years, 231-107-12

1994 SCHEDULE

Montana St. ....Sept. 3
St. Cloud St. ■ ....Sept. 10
Portland St. ....*Sept. 17
Bemidji St. ....*Sept. 24
Wis.-River Falls ■ ....Oct. 1
Southwest St. ■ ....Oct. 8
Moorhead St. ....Oct. 15
Winona St. ■ ....Oct. 22
Minn.-Morris ....Oct. 29
Northern St. ■ ....Nov. 5
Idaho St. ....*Nov. 19

1993 RESULTS (8-3-0)

24	Wis.-Eau Claire	15
0	St. Cloud St.	47
14	Wis.-Stout	11
22	Northern St.	26
20	Bemidji St.	0
32	Michigan Tech	3
31	Southwest St.	28
23	Moorhead St.	0
15	Winona St.	17
35	Minn.-Morris	13
29	Wayne St. (Neb.)	28
245		**188**

Nickname: Bulldogs.
Stadium: Griggs Field (1966), 4,000 capacity. Artificial turf.
Colors: Maroon & Gold.
Conference: Northern Sun Inter. Conf.
SID: Bob Nygaard, 218-726-8191.
AD: Bruce McLeod.

MINNESOTA-MORRIS

Morris, MN 56267 II

Coach: Jay Mills, Western Wash. '84
Record: 1 Year, 2-9-0

1994 SCHEDULE

Hamline ■ ....Sept. 10
Northwestern (Iowa) ....Sept. 17
Moorhead St. ■ ....Sept. 24
Winona St. ....Oct. 1
Northern St. ■ ....Oct. 15
Bemidji St. ....Oct. 22
Minn.-Duluth ....Oct. 29
Southwest St. ....Nov. 5
Moorhead St. [Minneapolis, Minn.] ....Nov. 12

1993 RESULTS (2-9-0)

6	Wis.-River Falls	34
0	Wis.-Stevens Point	47
10	Michigan Tech	42
6	Southwest St.	45
14	Moorhead St.	41
9	Winona St.	40
7	Teikyo Westmar	6
21	Northern St.	44
21	Bemidji St.	7
13	Minn.-Duluth	35
14	Northern St.	50
121		**391**

Nickname: Cougars.
Stadium: UMM Field, 5,000 capacity. Natural turf.
Colors: Maroon & Gold.
Conference: Northern Sun Inter. Conf.
SID: Judy Riley, 612-589-6050.
AD: Mark Fohl.

MISSISSIPPI

University, MS 38677 ....I-A

Coach: Billy Brewer, Mississippi '61
Record: 20 Years, 124-95-6

1994 SCHEDULE

Auburn ■	*Sept. 3
Southern Ill. ■	*Sept. 10
Vanderbilt	*Sept. 17
Georgia	Sept. 24
Florida ■	*Oct. 1
Arkansas	Oct. 15
Alabama	Oct. 22
Louisiana St. ■	Oct. 29
Memphis ■	Nov. 5
Tulane	*Nov. 12
Mississippi St. ■	Nov. 26

1993 RESULTS (5-6-0)

12	Auburn	16
40	Tenn.-Chatt.	7
49	Vanderbilt	7
31	Georgia	14
0	Kentucky	21
19	Arkansas	0
14	Alabama	19
17	Louisiana St.	19
3	Memphis	19
44	Northern Ill.	0
13	Mississippi St.	20
242		**142**

Nickname: Rebels.
Stadium: Vaught-Hemingway (1941), 42,577 capacity. Natural turf.
Colors: Cardinal Red & Navy Blue.
Conference: Southeastern Conf.
SID: Langston Rogers, 601-232-7522.
AD: Warner Alford.

MISSISSIPPI COLLEGE

Clinton, MS 39058 II

Coach: Terry McMillan, Southern Miss. '69
Record: 3 Years, 17-12-3

1994 SCHEDULE

Ark.-Monticello	*Sept. 3
Abilene Christian	*Sept. 10
North Ala.	*Sept. 17
Livingston	Sept. 24
Henderson St. ■	Oct. 1
Samford	Oct. 15
Valdosta St. ■	*Oct. 22
West Ga.	Oct. 29
Central Ark.	Nov. 5
Delta St. ■	Nov. 12

1993 RESULTS (6-3-1)

31	Ark.-Monticello	6
13	Tex. A&M-Kingsville	9
28	North Ala.	38
22	Livingston	22
35	Henderson St.	20
21	Samford	14
21	Valdosta St.	42
25	West Ga.	27
21	Central Ark.	14
13	Delta St.	7
230		**199**

Nickname: Choctaws.
Stadium: Robinson Field (1985), 8,500 capacity. Natural turf.
Colors: Blue & Gold.
Conference: Gulf South Conf.
SID: Norman Gough, 601-925-3255.
AD: Terry McMillan.

MISSISSIPPI STATE

Mississippi State, MS 39762 ....I-A

Coach: Jackie Sherrill, Alabama '66
Record: 16 Years, 122-61-4

1994 SCHEDULE

Memphis	*Sept. 3
Louisiana St.	*Sept. 10
Tennessee ■	*Sept. 24
Arkansas St. ■	*Oct. 1
Auburn ■	*Oct. 8
South Caro.	Oct. 15

Tulane ■	Oct. 22
Kentucky	*Oct. 29
Arkansas	Nov. 5
Alabama ■	Nov. 12
Mississippi	Nov. 26

1993 RESULTS (3-6-2)

35	Memphis	45
16	Louisiana St.	18
36	Tulane	10
24	Florida	38
17	Auburn	31
23	South Caro.	0
15	Arkansas St.	15
17	Kentucky	26
13	Arkansas	13
25	Alabama	36
20	Mississippi	13
241		**245**

Nickname: Bulldogs.
Stadium: Scott Field (1935), 40,656 capacity. Natural turf.
Colors: Maroon & White.
Conference: Southeastern Conf.
SID: Mike Nemeth, 601-325-2703.
AD: Larry Templeton.

MISSISSIPPI VALLEY

Itta Bena, MS 38941 ....I-AA

Coach: Larry Dorsey, Tennessee St. '76
Record: 4 Years, 20-18-3

1994 SCHEDULE

Howard	*Sept. 3
Lane [St. Louis, Mo.]	*Sept. 10
Southern-B.R.	*Sept. 17
Jackson St.	Sept. 24
Grambling ■	Oct. 8
Ala.-Birmingham	Oct. 15
Texas Southern	Oct. 22
Prairie View ■	Oct. 29
Alcorn St. ■	Nov. 5
Alabama St.	Nov. 12

1993 RESULTS (4-4-2)

20	Ark.-Pine Bluff	6
36	Lane	22
7	Jackson St.	7
13	Southern-B.R.	14
19	Grambling	28
13	Ala.-Birmingham	30
42	Prairie View	6
20	Alcorn St.	28
14	Alabama St.	14
41	Texas Southern	27
225		**182**

Nickname: Delta Devils.
Stadium: Magnolia (1958), 10,500 capacity. Natural turf.
Colors: Green & White.
Conference: Southwestern.
SID: Chuck Prophet, 601-254-9041.
AD: Chuck Prophet.

MISSOURI

Columbia, MO 65201 ....I-A

Coach: Larry Smith, Bowling Green '62
Record: 17 Years, 110-80-6

1994 SCHEDULE

Tulsa ■	*Sept. 3
Illinois	Sept. 10
Houston	*Sept. 17
West Va. ■	Oct. 1
Colorado ■	Oct. 8
Oklahoma St.	Oct. 15
Nebraska ■	Oct. 22
Iowa St.	Oct. 29
Oklahoma	Nov. 5
Kansas St. ■	Nov. 12
Kansas	Nov. 19
Hawaii	*Nov. 26

1993 RESULTS (3-7-1)

31	Illinois	3
0	Texas A&M	73
3	West Va.	35
10	Southern Methodist	10
18	Colorado	30
42	Oklahoma St.	9
7	Nebraska	49
37	Iowa St.	34
23	Oklahoma	42
21	Kansas St.	31
0	Kansas	28
192		**344**

Nickname: Tigers.
Stadium: Memorial/Faurot Fld (1926), 62,000 capacity. Artificial turf.
Colors: Old Gold & Black.
Conference: Big Eight Conf.
SID: Bob Brendel, 314-882-0712.
AD: Joe Castiglione.

MISSOURI SOUTHERN STATE

Joplin, MO 64801 II

Coach: Jon Lantz, Panhandle St. '74
Record: 8 Years, 52-28-3

1994 SCHEDULE

Central Ark.	*Sept. 10
Pittsburg St.	*Sept. 17
Southwest Baptist ■	*Sept. 24
Northeast Mo. St.	Oct. 1
Mo. Western St. ■	*Oct. 8
Central Mo. St. ■	*Oct. 15
Emporia St.	Oct. 22
Washburn ■	Oct. 29
Missouri-Rolla	Nov. 5
Northwest Mo. St. ■	Nov. 12

1993 RESULTS (9-0-1)

14	Central Ark.	14
20	Pittsburg St.	3
21	Southwest Baptist	15
41	Northeast Mo. St.	37
30	Mo. Western St.	28
27	Central Mo. St.	7
39	Emporia St.	17
36	Washburn	21
47	Missouri-Rolla	33
49	Northwest Mo. St.	33
324		**208**

II Championship

13	Mankato St.	34

Nickname: Lions.
Stadium: Fred G. Hughes (1975), 7,000 capacity. Artificial turf.
Colors: Green & Gold.
Conference: Mid-America Intercoll. Ath. Assoc.
SID: Dennis Slusher, 417-625-9359.
AD: Jim Frazier.

MISSOURI WESTERN STATE

St. Joseph, MO 64507 II

Coach: Stan McGarvey, William Jewell '73
Record: 9 Years, 57-37-3

1994 SCHEDULE

Southwest St. ■	*Sept. 3
Northeastern Okla. ■	*Sept. 10
Northwest Mo. St.	Sept. 17
Pittsburg St. ■	*Sept. 24
Central Mo. St.	Oct. 1
Mo. Southern St.	*Oct. 8
Emporia St. ■	Oct. 15
Washburn	Oct. 22
Missouri-Rolla	Oct. 29
Southwest Baptist	Nov. 5
Northeast Mo. St. ■	Nov. 12

1993 RESULTS (8-2-1)

35	Southwest St.	20
46	Friends	0
21	Northwest Mo. St.	14
0	Pittsburg St.	24

14	Central Mo. St.	14
28	Mo. Southern St.	30
26	Emporia St.	20
41	Washburn	10
42	Missouri-Rolla	24
56	Southwest Baptist	0
42	Northeast Mo. St.	6
351		**162**

Nickname: Griffons.
Stadium: Spratt (1979), 6,000 capacity. Natural turf.
Colors: Black & Gold.
Conference: Mid-America Intercoll. Ath. Assoc.
SID: Paul Sweetgall, 816-271-4257.
AD: Ed Harris.

MISSOURI-ROLLA

Rolla, MO 65401 II

Coach: Jim Anderson, Missouri '69
Record: 2 Years, 5-16-0

1994 SCHEDULE

Michigan Tech	Sept. 3
Georgetown (Ky.)	Sept. 10
Washburn ■	Sept. 17
Emporia St.	*Sept. 24
Southwest Baptist ■	Oct. 1
Pittsburg St.	Oct. 8
Northwest Mo. St.	Oct. 15
Northeast Mo. St. ■	Oct. 22
Mo. Western St.	Oct. 29
Mo. Southern St. ■	Nov. 5
Central Mo. St.	Nov. 12

1993 RESULTS (3-7-0)

32	Iowa Wesleyan	0
38	Washburn	14
0	Emporia St.	17
44	Southwest Baptist	8
3	Pittsburg St.	28
20	Northwest Mo. St.	27
13	Northeast Mo. St.	21
24	Mo. Western St.	42
33	Mo. Southern St.	47
21	Central Mo. St.	24
228		**228**

Nickname: Miners.
Stadium: Jackling Field (1967), 8,000 capacity. Natural turf.
Colors: Silver & Gold.
Conference: Mid-America Intercoll. Ath. Assoc.
SID: John Kean, 314-341-4140.
AD: Mark Mullin.

MONMOUTH (ILLINOIS)

Monmouth, IL 61462 III

Coach: Kelly Kane, Ill. Wesleyan '70
Record: 10 Years, 59-34-0

1994 SCHEDULE

Eureka	Sept. 10
MacMurray ■	Sept. 17
Ripon	Sept. 24
Beloit	Oct. 1
Illinois Col. ■	Oct. 8
Cornell College ■	Oct. 15
Coe	Oct. 22
Grinnell	Oct. 29
Knox ■	Nov. 5

1993 RESULTS (4-5-0)

21	Eureka	19
7	MacMurray	10
17	Lawrence	13
14	Carroll (Wis.)	20
13	Illinois Col.	7
32	Cornell College	48
14	Coe	49
55	Grinnell	27
16	Knox	19
189		**212**

Nickname: Fighting Scots.
Stadium: Bobby Woll Field (1923), 3,000 capacity. Natural turf.

Colors: Crimson & White.
Conference: Midwest Conf.
SID: Chris Pio, 309-457-2173.
AD: Terry Glasgow.

MONMOUTH (NEW JERSEY)

W. Long Branch, NJ 07764 ....I-AA

Coach: Kevin Callahan, Rochester '77
Record: 1 Year, 2-5-0

1994 SCHEDULE

Robert Morris	Sept. 10
Pace ■	Sept. 17
St. John's (N.Y.)	Sept. 24
Wagner	Oct. 1
St. Francis (Pa.) ■	Oct. 8
Upsala ■	Oct. 22
Sacred Heart	Oct. 29
Stonehill ■	Nov. 5
Central Conn. St.	Nov. 12

1993 RESULTS (2-5-0)

8	Stonehill	13
0	Sacred Heart	12
44	St. Peter's	42
14	St. Francis (Pa.)	25
13	Hartwick	17
7	Wagner	13
15	Albright	14
101		**136**

Nickname: Hawks.
Stadium: Kessler Field, 3,000 capacity. Natural turf.
Colors: Royal Blue & White.
Conference: I-AA Independent.
SID: John Paradise, 908-571-3415.
AD: Marilyn McNeil.

MONTANA

Missoula, MT 59812 ....I-AA

Coach: Don Read, Cal St. Sacramento '59
Record: 24 Years, 130-122-1

1994 SCHEDULE

Sonoma St. ■	Sept. 3
Carson-Newman ■	Sept. 10
Eastern Wash. ■	Sept. 17
North Texas	Sept. 24
Cal Poly SLO ■	Oct. 1
Northern Ariz. ■	Oct. 8
Weber St.	Oct. 22
Idaho ■	Oct. 29
Boise St.	Nov. 5
Idaho St.	Nov. 12
Montana St. ■	Nov. 19

1993 RESULTS (10-1-0)

52	South Dak. St.	48
30	Oregon	35
28	Idaho St.	16
35	Eastern Wash.	20
38	Boise St.	24
45	Weber St.	17
38	Northern Ariz.	23
37	Jacksonville St.	7
54	Cal St. Sacramento	7
54	Idaho	34
42	Montana St.	30
453		**261**

I-AA Championship

48	Delaware	49

Nickname: Grizzlies.
Stadium: Washington-Grizzly (1986), 14,000 capacity. Natural turf.
Colors: Copper, Silver & Gold.
Conference: Big Sky Conf.
SID: Dave Guffey, 406-243-6899.
AD: Bill Moos.

MONTANA STATE

Bozeman, MT 59717 ....I-AA

Coach: Cliff Hysell, Montana St. '66
Record: 2 Years, 11-11-0

1994 SCHEDULE

Minn.-Duluth ■	Sept. 3
Stephen F. Austin	*Sept. 10
Weber St.	*Sept. 17
Northern Ariz. ■	Sept. 24
Cal St. Sacramento	*Oct. 1
Idaho St. ■	Oct. 8
Idaho	Oct. 15
Boise St. ■	Oct. 22
Eastern Wash.	Oct. 29
Western N. Mex. ■	Nov. 5
Montana	Nov. 19

1993 RESULTS (7-4-0)

29	Western Ill.	16
14	Washington St.	54
58	Fort Lewis	20
14	Weber St.	10
20	Northern Ariz.	23
32	Southern Utah	31
25	Idaho St.	24
40	Idaho	35
42	Boise St.	21
7	Eastern Wash.	16
30	Montana	42
311		**292**

Nickname: Bobcats.
Stadium: Reno H. Sales (1973), 15,197 capacity. Natural turf.
Colors: Blue & Gold.
Conference: Big Sky Conf.
SID: Bill Lamberty, 406-994-5133.
AD: Doug Fullerton.

MONTCLAIR STATE

Upper Montclair, NJ 07043 III

Coach: Rick Giancola, Rowan '68
Record: 11 Years, 84-29-2

1994 SCHEDULE

Southern Conn. St.	Sept. 3
Cortland St. ■	*Sept. 10
Western Conn. St.	*Sept. 17
FDU-Madison ■	*Oct. 1
Kean	Oct. 8
Wm. Paterson ■	*Oct. 15
Ferrum ■	Oct. 22
Trenton St. ■	*Oct. 29
Jersey City St.	Nov. 5
Rowan ■	Nov. 12

1993 RESULTS (6-3-0)

17	Cortland St.	7
29	Ithaca	0
22	FDU-Madison	12
16	Kean	14
23	Wm. Paterson	26
21	Ferrum	24
16	Trenton St.	0
25	Jersey City St.	8
15	Rowan	41
184		**132**

ECAC Southwest

17	Dickinson	9

Nickname: Red Hawks.
Stadium: Sprague (1934), 6,000 capacity. Artificial turf.
Colors: Scarlet & White.
Conference: New Jersey Ath. Conf.
SID: Al Langer, 201-655-5249.
AD: Greg Lockard.

MOORHEAD STATE

Moorhead, MN 56560 II

Coach: Ralph Micheli, Macalester '70
Record: 11 Years, 35-67-0

1994 SCHEDULE

Concordia-M'head ■	Sept. 10
Neb.-Kearney	Sept. 17
Minn.-Morris	Sept. 24
Northern St. ■	Oct. 1

Bemidji St. ....Oct. 8
Minn.-Duluth ■ ....Oct. 15
Southwest St. ....Oct. 22
Wayne St. (Neb.) ....Oct. 29
Winona St. ■ ....Nov. 5
Minn.-Morris [Minneapolis, Minn.].......Nov. 12

1993 RESULTS (6-4-0)

21	Concordia-M'head	0
17	Neb.-Kearney	16
14	Winona St.	23
41	Minn.-Morris	14
41	Northern St.	40
36	Bemidji St.	16
0	Minn.-Duluth	23
37	Southwest St.	20
0	Northern Iowa	48
20	Winona St.	23
227		**223**

Nickname: Dragons.
Stadium: Alex Nemzek (1960), 5,000 capacity. Natural turf.
Colors: Scarlet & White.
Conference: Northern Sun Inter. Conf.
SID: Larry Scott, 218-236-2113.
AD: Katy Wilson.

MORAVIAN
Bethlehem, PA 18018 III

Coach: Scot Dapp, West Chester '73
Record: 7 Years, 51-22-0

1994 SCHEDULE

Baldwin-Wallace ....Sept. 10
Delaware Valley ■ ....Sept. 17
Widener ....Sept. 24
Lebanon Valley ■ ....Oct. 1
Lycoming ....Oct. 8
Susquehanna ■ ....Oct. 15
Albright ....Oct. 22
Juniata ■ ....Oct. 29
King's (Pa.) ....Nov. 5
Muhlenberg ■ ....Nov. 12

1993 RESULTS (8-2-0)

13	Baldwin-Wallace	25
31	Delaware Valley	14
37	Widener	16
13	Lebanon Valley	15
17	Lycoming	14
17	Susquehanna	6
49	Albright	21
13	Juniata	0
49	King's (Pa.)	0
24	Muhlenberg	14
263		**125**

III Championship

7	Wash. & Jeff.	27

Nickname: Greyhounds.
Stadium: Steel Field (1917), 3,200 capacity. Natural turf.
Colors: Blue & Grey.
Conference: Commonwealth League.
SID: Mike Warwick, 610-861-1472.
AD: John Makuvek.

MOREHEAD STATE
Morehead, KY 40351 ....I-AA

Coach: Matt Ballard, Gardner-Webb '79
Record: 6 Years, 35-25-1

1994 SCHEDULE

Marshall ....*Sept. 3
East Tenn. St. ■ ....*Sept. 10
Tennessee St. ■ ....*Sept. 17
Tennessee Tech ■ ....Sept. 24
Southeast Mo. St. ■ ....Oct. 1
Middle Tenn. St. ....Oct. 15
Austin Peay ....Oct. 22
Ala.-Birmingham ■ ....Oct. 29
Murray St. ■ ....Nov. 5
Tenn.-Martin ....Nov. 12
Eastern Ky. ....Nov. 19

1993 RESULTS (3-8-0)

0	Marshall	56
14	Ala.-Birmingham	52
52	West Va. Tech	14
3	Tennessee Tech	21
23	Southeast Mo. St.	21
0	Middle Tenn. St.	45
23	Austin Peay	10
0	Tennessee St.	15
0	Murray St.	39
0	Tenn.-Martin	17
7	Eastern Ky.	44
122		**334**

Nickname: Eagles.
Stadium: Jayne (1964), 10,000 capacity. Artificial turf.
Colors: Blue & Gold.
Conference: Ohio Valley Conf.
SID: Randy Stacy, 606-783-2500.
AD: Steve Hamilton.

MOREHOUSE
Atlanta, GA 30314 II

Coach: Vincent Williams, Cheyney '86
(First year as head coach)

1994 SCHEDULE

Hampton ....Sept. 3
Fort Valley St. [Ypsilanti, Mich.] ....*Sept. 10
Miles ....Sept. 17
Albany St. (Ga.) ■ ....Sept. 24
Savannah St. ....Oct. 1
Alabama A&M ■ ....Oct. 8
Tuskegee [Columbus, Ga.] ....*Oct. 15
Morris Brown ■ ....Oct. 22
Howard ....Oct. 29
Clark Atlanta ....Nov. 19

1993 RESULTS (5-5-0)

†14	Johnson Smith	14
6	Fort Valley St.	36
0	Albany St. (Ga.)	39
19	Savannah St.	33
0	Alabama A&M	14
28	Tuskegee	23
34	Morris Brown	6
9	Howard	34
38	Miles	0
7	Clark Atlanta	0
155		**199**

†Won forfeit from Johnson Smith.

Nickname: Maroon Tigers/Tigers.
Stadium: B. T. Harvey (1983), 9,850 capacity. Natural turf.
Colors: Maroon & White.
Conference: Southern Inter. Ath. Conf.
SID: James E. Nix, 404-215-3501.
AD: Arthur J. McAfee Jr.

MORGAN STATE
Baltimore, MD 21239 ....I-AA

Coach: Ricky Diggs, Shippensburg '75
Record: 3 Years, 5-28-0

1994 SCHEDULE

Bethune-Cookman ■ ....Sept. 10
Grambling ■ ....Sept. 17
Knoxville ■ ....Sept. 24
Charleston So. ....Oct. 1
South Caro. St. ....Oct. 8
North Caro. A&T ....Oct. 15
Delaware St. ■ ....Oct. 22
Florida A&M ....Oct. 29
Samford ■ ....Nov. 5
Howard ....Nov. 12
Towson St. ....Nov. 19

1993 RESULTS (2-9-0)

54	Charleston So.	20
17	Bethune-Cookman	41
27	Youngstown St.	56
38	Virginia Union	21
13	South Caro. St.	49
33	North Caro. A&T	49
42	Delaware St.	65

14	Florida A&M	41
28	Knoxville	32
37	Howard	66
12	Towson St.	56
315		**496**

Nickname: Bears.
Stadium: Hughes, 10,000 capacity. Natural turf.
Colors: Blue & Orange.
Conference: Mid-Eastern.
SID: Joe McIver, 410-319-3831.
AD: Ken McBryde.

MORNINGSIDE
Sioux City, IA 51106 II

Coach: Charlie Cowdrey, Northwest Mo. St. '55
Record: 14 Years, 78-68-2

1994 SCHEDULE

Neb.-Kearney ....*Sept. 3
Wayne St. (Neb.) ■ ....*Sept. 10
North Dak. ■ ....Sept. 17
North Dak. St. ■ ....Sept. 24
South Dak. ....Oct. 1
Nebraska-Omaha ....*Oct. 8
Mankato St. ■ ....Oct. 15
Augustana (S.D.) ■ ....Oct. 22
South Dak. ....Oct. 29
St. Cloud St. ....Nov. 5
Northern Colo. ■ ....Nov. 12

1993 RESULTS (2-9-0)

34	Northwestern Ia.	7
17	Wayne St. (Neb.)	44
21	North Dak.	52
15	North Dak. St.	21
20	South Dak. St.	30
31	Nebraska-Omaha	14
14	Mankato St.	36
13	Augustana (S.D.)	14
20	South Dak.	31
14	St. Cloud St.	28
0	Northern Colo.	30
199		**307**

Nickname: Chiefs.
Stadium: Roberts (1939), 10,000 capacity. Natural turf.
Colors: Maroon & White.
Conference: North Central Conf.
SID: Rob Shaw, 712-274-5127.
AD: Co-Athletic Directors.

MORRIS BROWN
Atlanta, GA 30314 II

Coach: Greg Thompson, Morris Brown '73
Record: 13 Years, 53-67-4

1994 SCHEDULE

Clark Atlanta ....*Sept. 5
Tuskegee [Louisville, Ky.] ....*Sept. 17
Fort Valley St. [Macon, Ga.] ....*Sept. 24
Alabama A&M ■ ....*Oct. 1
Miles ....Oct. 8
Savannah St. ■ ....*Oct. 15
Morehouse ....Oct. 22
Lane ....Oct. 29
Albany St. (Ga.) ■ ....*Nov. 5
Ark.-Pine Bluff ....Nov. 12

1993 RESULTS (4-6-0)

42	Clark Atlanta	18
13	Ark.-Pine Bluff	20
22	Tuskegee	51
0	Fort Valley St.	17
16	Alabama A&M	15
37	Miles	0
15	Savannah St.	14
6	Morehouse	34
16	Albany St. (Ga.)	31
14	Hampton	49
181		**249**

Nickname: Wolverines.
Stadium: A.F. Herndon, 13,000 capacity. Natural turf.
Colors: Purple & Black.
Conference: Southern Inter. Ath. Conf.

SID: Cecil Mckay, 404-220-0367.
AD: Greg Thompson.

MOUNT UNION
Alliance, OH 44601 III

Coach: Larry Kehres, Mount Union '71
Record: 8 Years, 74-13-3

1994 SCHEDULE
Defiance...	Sept. 10
Otterbein ■ ....*	Sept. 17
Ohio Northern......................................	Sept. 24
John Carroll..	Oct. 1
Marietta ■	Oct. 8
Baldwin-Wallace ■	Oct. 15
Muskingum...	Oct. 22
Heidelberg ■	Oct. 29
Capital ■	Nov. 5
Hiram	Nov. 12

1993 RESULTS (10-0-0)
42	Adrian....................................	0
49	Muskingum.............................	21
37	Marietta..................................	0
35	Baldwin-Wallace......................	7
21	John Carroll.............................	0
24	Heidelberg...............................	7
49	Ohio Northern..........................	7
49	Otterbein................................	0
66	Capital...................................	23
50	Hiram....................................	0
422		**65**

III Championship
40	Allegheny................................	7
30	Albion....................................	16
56	St. John's (Minn.).....................	8
34	Rowan....................................	24

Nickname: Purple Raiders.
Stadium: Mt. Union (1915), 5,800 capacity. Natural turf.
Colors: Purple & White.
Conference: Ohio Ath. Conf.
SID: Michael De Matteis, 216-823-6093.
AD: Larry Kehres.

MUHLENBERG
Allentown, PA 18104 III

Coach: Greg Olejack, Louisville '77
(First year as head coach)

1994 SCHEDULE
Hampden-Sydney ■	Sept. 10
Dickinson..	Sept. 17
Frank. & Marsh. ■	Sept. 24
Western Md.	Oct. 1
Swarthmore ■	Oct. 8
Johns Hopkins......................................*	Oct. 14
Gettysburg ■	Oct. 22
Union (N.Y.) ■	Oct. 29
Ursinus	Nov. 5
Moravian	Nov. 12

1993 RESULTS (4-5-0)
21	Hampden-Sydney.....................	22
0	Dickinson................................	20
9	Frank. & Marsh........................	7
29	Western Md..............................	27
23	Swarthmore.............................	29
20	Johns Hopkins..........................	16
17	Gettysburg..............................	28
34	Ursinus...................................	31
14	Moravian.................................	24
167		**204**

Nickname: Mules.
Stadium: Muhlenberg Field (1928), 4,000 capacity. Natural turf.
Colors: Cardinal & Grey.
Conference: Centennial Conference.
SID: Mike Falk, 610-821-3232.
AD: Ralph Kirchenheiter.

MURRAY STATE
Murray, KY 42071 ....I-AA

Coach: Houston Nutt, Oklahoma St. '81
Record: 1 Year, 4-7-0

1994 SCHEDULE
Eastern Ill. ....*	Sept. 1
Western Ky. ■ ....*	Sept. 8
Southeast Mo. St....................................*	Sept. 17
Middle Tenn. St. ■ ....*	Sept. 24
Tenn.-Martin ■ ....*	Oct. 1
Austin Peay ....*	Oct. 8
Eastern Ky.	Oct. 15
Tennessee Tech ■	Oct. 29
Morehead St.	Nov. 5
Tennessee St. ■	Nov. 12
Western Ill.	Nov. 19

1993 RESULTS (4-7-0)
17	Eastern Ill...............................	34
3	Marshall.................................	29
17	Southeast Mo. St......................	14
3	Middle Tenn. St.......................	45
28	Tenn.-Martin...........................	21
38	Austin Peay.............................	14
13	Eastern Ky...............................	21
16	Tennessee Tech.........................	31
39	Morehead St............................	0
13	Tennessee St............................	26
14	Western Ky..............................	44
201		**279**

Nickname: Racers.
Stadium: Stewart (1973), 16,800 capacity. Artificial turf.
Colors: Blue & Gold.
Conference: Ohio Valley Conf.
SID: David Ramey, 502-762-4270.
AD: Mike Strickland.

MUSKINGUM
New Concord, OH 43762 III

Coach: Jeff Heacock, Muskingum '76
Record: 13 Years, 66-58-3

1994 SCHEDULE
Wittenberg ....*	Sept. 10
Hiram	Sept. 17
Capital ■ ....*	Sept. 24
Ohio Northern ■	Oct. 1
Baldwin-Wallace	Oct. 8
Heidelberg	Oct. 15
Mount Union ■	Oct. 22
John Carroll..	Oct. 29
Otterbein	Nov. 5
Marietta ■	Nov. 12

1993 RESULTS (2-7-1)
7	Wittenberg..............................	29
21	Mount Union...........................	49
0	Baldwin-Wallace......................	28
0	Heidelberg...............................	15
21	Ohio Northern..........................	21
18	John Carroll.............................	20
21	Capital...................................	28
45	Hiram....................................	13
32	Otterbein................................	29
7	Marietta..................................	19
172		**251**

Nickname: Fighting Muskies.
Stadium: Mc Conagha (1925), 5,000 capacity. Natural turf.
Colors: Black & Magenta.
Conference: Ohio Ath. Conf.
SID: Jacquie Nelson, 614-826-8134.
AD: Al Christopher.

NAVY
Annapolis, MD 21402 ....I-A

Coach: George Chaump, Bloomsburg '58
Record: 12 Years, 67-66-2

1994 SCHEDULE
San Diego St.	Sept. 3
Virginia ■ ....*	Sept. 10
Bowling Green.......................................	Sept. 17
Duke ■	Oct. 1
Air Force	Oct. 8
Lafayette ■	Oct. 15
Louisville ■	Oct. 22
Notre Dame	Oct. 29
Tulane ....*	Nov. 5
Rice ■	Nov. 19
Army [Philadelphia, Pa.].........................	Dec. 3

1993 RESULTS (4-7-0)
0	Virginia..................................	38
31	Eastern Ill...............................	10
27	Bowling Green..........................	20
25	Tulane...................................	27
28	Air Force................................	24
31	Colgate..................................	3
0	Louisville................................	28
27	Notre Dame.............................	58
7	Vanderbilt...............................	41
13	Southern Methodist...................	42
14	Army.....................................	16
203		**307**

Nickname: Midshipmen.
Stadium: Navy-Marine Corps Mem. (1959), 30,000 capacity. Natural turf.
Colors: Navy Blue & Gold.
Conference: I-A Independents.
SID: Tom Bates, 410-268-6226.
AD: Jack Lengyel.

NEBRASKA
Lincoln, NE 68588 ....I-A

Coach: Tom Osborne, Hastings '59
Record: 21 Years, 206-47-3

1994 SCHEDULE
West Va. [East Rutherford, N.J.]	Aug. 28
Texas Tech ....*	Sept. 8
UCLA ■	Sept. 17
Pacific (Cal.) ■	Sept. 24
Wyoming ■	Oct. 1
Oklahoma St. ■	Oct. 8
Kansas St.	Oct. 15
Missouri ■	Oct. 22
Colorado ■	Oct. 29
Kansas ■	Nov. 5
Iowa St.	Nov. 12
Oklahoma	Nov. 25

1993 RESULTS (11-0-0)
76	North Texas.............................	14
50	Texas Tech..............................	27
14	UCLA....................................	13
48	Colorado St.............................	13
27	Oklahoma St............................	13
45	Kansas St................................	28
49	Missouri.................................	7
21	Colorado................................	17
21	Kansas...................................	20
49	Iowa St...................................	17
21	Oklahoma...............................	7
421		**176**

Orange Bowl
16	Florida St................................	18

Nickname: Cornhuskers.
Stadium: Memorial (1923), 72,700 capacity. Artificial turf.
Colors: Scarlet & Cream.
Conference: Big Eight Conf.
SID: Chris Anderson, 402-472-2263.
AD: Bill Byrne.

NEBRASKA WESLEYAN
Lincoln, NE 68504 III

Coach: Steve Standards, Nebraska '89
(First year as head coach)

1994 SCHEDULE
Mary ■	Sept. 3

Carroll (Mont.) ....Sept. 10
St. Ambrose ■ ....Sept. 17
Concordia (Neb.) ■ ....Sept. 24
Northwestern Ia. ....Oct. 1
Hastings ■ ....Oct. 8
Dana ....Oct. 15
Doane ....Oct. 29
Midland Lutheran ■ ....Nov. 5
Luther [Cedar Falls, Iowa] ....*Nov. 10

1993 RESULTS (7-3-0)

49	Austin	35
45	Kan. Wesleyan	14
17	Carroll (Mont.)	20
40	Northwestern Ia.	25
5	Hastings	33
49	Dana	17
14	Doane	41
56	Midland Lutheran	25
41	Concordia (Neb.)	13
13	Peru St.	7
329		**230**

Nickname: Plainsmen.
Stadium: Abel (1986), 2,000 capacity. Natural turf.
Colors: Yellow & Brown.
Conference: Nebraska-Iowa Athletic.
SID: Jim Angele, 402-465-2151.
AD: Mary Beth Kennedy.

NEBRASKA-KEARNEY

Kearney, NE 68849 II

Coach: Claire Boroff, Neb.-Kearney '59
Record: 22 Years, 132-81-4

1994 SCHEDULE

Morningside ■ ....*Sept. 3
Nebraska-Omaha ....Sept. 10
Moorhead St. ....Sept. 17
Fort Hays St. ■ ....Sept. 24
Western N. Mex. ■ ....*Oct. 1
Wayne St. (Neb.) ....Oct. 8
Portland St. ■ ....*Oct. 15
Northern St. ■ ....Oct. 22
Drake ■ ....Oct. 29
Central Okla. ....Nov. 5
Winona St. [Minneapolis, Minn.] ....Nov. 12

1993 RESULTS (3-7-0)

30	Augustana (S.D.)	14
29	Nebraska-Omaha	38
16	Moorhead St.	17
24	Western St.	31
14	Fort Hays St.	26
9	Wayne St. (Neb.)	28
14	Portland St.	24
33	Northern St.	0
7	Central Okla.	14
28	Bemidji St.	3
204		**195**

Nickname: Antelopes.
Stadium: Foster Field (1929), 6,500 capacity. Natural turf.
Colors: Royal Blue & Old Gold.
Conference: Rocky Mountain Ath. Conf.
SID: Brent Robinson, 308-234-8334.
AD: Dick Beechner.

NEBRASKA-OMAHA

Omaha, NE 68182 II

Coach: Pat Behrns, Dakota St. '72
Record: 6 Years, 36-26-0

1994 SCHEDULE

Wayne St. (Neb.) ....Sept. 3
Neb.-Kearney ■ ....Sept. 10
North Dak. St. ■ ....*Sept. 17
South Dak. ....Sept. 24
St. Cloud St. ....Oct. 1
Morningside ■ ....*Oct. 8
South Dak. St. ■ ....*Oct. 15
North Dak. ....Oct. 22
Northern Colo. ■ ....*Oct. 29
Augustana (S.D.) ....Nov. 5

Mankato St. ■ ....Nov. 12

1993 RESULTS (2-9-0)

19	Wayne St. (Neb.)	32
38	Neb.-Kearney	29
7	North Dak. St.	28
10	South Dak.	27
37	St. Cloud St.	18
14	Morningside	31
10	South Dak. St.	50
8	North Dak.	17
7	Northern Colo.	49
14	Augustana (S.D.)	35
24	Mankato St.	52
188		**368**

Nickname: Mavericks.
Stadium: Al F. Caniglia Field (1949), 9,500 capacity. Artificial turf.
Colors: Black & Crimson.
Conference: North Central Conf.
SID: Gary Anderson, 402-554-2305.
AD: Robert Gibson.

NEVADA

Reno, NV 89557 ....I-A

Coach: Chris Ault, Nevada '68
Record: 17 Years, 145-58-1

1994 SCHEDULE

Northern Ariz. ■ ....Sept. 3
Arkansas St. ■ ....Sept. 10
Boise St. ....*Sept. 17
Northeast La. ■ ....Sept. 24
Northern Ill. ....Oct. 1
Pacific (Cal.) ■ ....Oct. 8
New Mexico St. ■ ....Oct. 15
San Jose St. ....*Oct. 22
Fresno St. ....*Nov. 5
Utah St. ■ ....Nov. 12
Nevada-Las Vegas ....Nov. 19

1993 RESULTS (7-4-0)

17	Wisconsin	35
38	Boise St.	10
63	Texas Southern	14
42	Northern Ill.	46
49	Nevada-Las Vegas	14
48	Utah St.	44
30	Weber St.	47
31	Pacific (Cal.)	23
46	San Jose St.	45
34	New Mexico St.	14
21	Arkansas St.	23
419		**315**

Nickname: Wolf Pack.
Stadium: Mackay (1965), 31,545 capacity. Natural turf.
Colors: Silver & Blue.
Conference: Big West.
SID: Paul Stuart, 702-784-4600.
AD: Chris Ault.

NEVADA-LAS VEGAS

Las Vegas, NV 89154 ....I-A

Coach: Jeff Horton, Nevada '81
Record: 1 Year, 7-4-0

1994 SCHEDULE

Eastern Mich. ■ ....*Sept. 3
Central Mich. ....Sept. 10
Idaho ■ ....*Sept. 17
Utah St. ■ ....*Sept. 24
New Mexico St. ....*Oct. 1
Louisiana Tech ■ ....*Oct. 8
Tulsa ....*Oct. 15
San Jose St. ■ ....*Oct. 29
Southwestern La. ....Nov. 5
Nevada ■ ....Nov. 19
Kansas St. ■ ....Nov. 26

1993 RESULTS (3-8-0)

14	Clemson	24
24	UTEP	41
33	Central Mich.	20

20	Kansas St.	36
14	Nevada	49
18	Cal St. Northridge	24
26	Utah St.	33
40	New Mexico St.	52
28	Louisiana Tech	23
28	San Jose St.	14
14	Southwestern La.	31
259		**347**

Nickname: Rebels.
Stadium: Sam Boyd (1971), 32,000 capacity. Artificial turf.
Colors: Scarlet & Gray.
Conference: Big West.
SID: Tommy Sheppard, 702-895-3764.
AD: Jim Weaver.

NEW HAMPSHIRE

Durham, NH 03824 ....I-AA

Coach: Bill Bowes, Penn St. '65
Record: 22 Years, 142-83-5

1994 SCHEDULE

Northeastern ....Sept. 10
James Madison ■ ....Sept. 17
Connecticut ■ ....Sept. 24
Hofstra ....Oct. 1
Massachusetts ■ ....Oct. 8
Lehigh ■ ....Oct. 15
Maine ....Oct. 22
Rhode Island ....Oct. 29
Richmond ....Nov. 5
Villanova ■ ....Nov. 12
Boston U. ....Nov. 19

1993 RESULTS (6-5-0)

14	William & Mary	27
23	Connecticut	24
31	Richmond	20
63	Maine	13
14	Dartmouth	7
21	James Madison	45
21	Northeastern	6
14	Boston U.	24
45	Villanova	14
51	Rhode Island	33
13	Massachusetts	15
310		**228**

Nickname: Wildcats.
Stadium: Cowell (1936), 9,571 capacity. Natural turf.
Colors: Blue & White.
Conference: Yankee.
SID: Pete Dauphinais, 603-862-2585.
AD: Gilbert Chapman.

NEW HAVEN

West Haven, CT 06516 II

Coach: Tony Sparano, New Haven '82
(First year as head coach)

1994 SCHEDULE

Bloomsburg ....Sept. 1
Kutztown ....Sept. 10
Indiana (Pa.) ■ ....Sept. 17
Abilene Christian ....*Sept. 24
Valdosta St. ....Oct. 8
American Int'l ■ ....Oct. 15
Southern Conn. St. ■ ....Oct. 22
Knoxville ....Oct. 29
Bowie St. ....Nov. 5
Liberty ....*Nov. 12

1993 RESULTS (10-0-0)

45	West Chester	33
38	Buffalo	6
35	Clarion	23
62	Springfield	3
62	Carson-Newman	31
71	Virginia Union	28
47	Southern Conn. St.	14
63	American Int'l	10
69	Bowie St.	19
55	Shepherd	0
547		**167**

II Championship

48	Edinboro	28
35	Indiana (Pa.)	38

Nickname: Chargers.
Stadium: Robert B. Dodds, 3,500 capacity. Natural turf.
Colors: Blue & Gold.
Conference: Division II Independent.
SID: Jack Jones, 203-932-7025.
AD: Deborah Chin.

NEW MEXICO
Albuquerque, NM 87131 ....I-A

Coach: Dennis Franchione, Pittsburg St. '73
Record: 11 Years, 89-32-2

1994 SCHEDULE

Texas Tech	Sept. 3
Texas Christian ■	*Sept. 10
Southern Methodist	*Sept. 17
Brigham Young	Sept. 24
Colorado St. ■	*Oct. 1
Hawaii	*Oct. 8
San Diego St. ■	*Oct. 15
New Mexico St. ■	*Oct. 22
Fresno St.	*Oct. 29
Utah ■	Nov. 5
Wyoming	Nov. 12
UTEP	Nov. 19

1993 RESULTS (6-5-0)

31	Brigham Young	34
34	Texas Christian	35
24	Fresno St.	41
42	New Mexico St.	7
41	Hawaii	14
42	Utah	35
17	San Diego St.	20
20	Colorado St.	21
39	Idaho St.	13
10	Wyoming	7
35	UTEP	29
335		**256**

Nickname: Lobos.
Stadium: University (1960), 30,646 capacity. Natural turf.
Colors: Cherry & Silver.
Conference: Western Ath. Conf.
SID: Greg Remington, 505-277-2026.
AD: Rudy Davalos.

NEW MEXICO HIGHLANDS
Las Vegas, NM 87701 II

Coach: Jim Ewan, Arizona St. '72
Record: 2 Years, 13-7-1

1994 SCHEDULE

Eastern N. Mex. ■	*Sept. 3
Western N. Mex.	*Sept. 10
West Tex. A&M	Sept. 24
Colorado Mines ■	Oct. 1
Fort Hays St. ■	Oct. 8
Chadron St.	Oct. 15
Fort Lewis	Oct. 22
Mesa St. ■	Oct. 29
Western St.	Nov. 5
Adams St.	Nov. 12

1993 RESULTS (6-4-0)

15	Eastern N. Mex.	10
40	Western N. Mex.	42
10	Angelo St.	41
14	Fort Hays St.	32
44	Chadron St.	37
62	Fort Lewis	34
14	Mesa St.	17
49	Western St.	30
14	Adams St.	7
19	Colorado Mines	7
281		**257**

Nickname: Cowboys.
Stadium: Perkins, 5,000 capacity. Natural turf.
Colors: Purple & White.
Conference: Rocky Mountain Ath. Conf.

SID: Jesse Gallegos, 505-454-3368.
AD: Rob Evers.

NEW MEXICO STATE
Las Cruces, NM 88003 ....I-A

Coach: Jim Hess, Southeastern Okla. '59
Record: 19 Years, 126-83-5

1994 SCHEDULE

Florida	*Sept. 3
Arizona	*Sept. 10
UTEP	*Sept. 17
Arkansas St. ■	*Sept. 24
Nevada-Las Vegas ■	*Oct. 1
Northern Ill.	Oct. 8
Nevada	Oct. 15
New Mexico ■	*Oct. 22
San Jose St.	*Nov. 5
Pacific (Cal.) ■	*Nov. 12
Utah St.	Nov. 19

1993 RESULTS (5-6-0)

10	Kansas St.	34
22	Arkansas St.	19
31	UTEP	14
7	New Mexico	42
24	Northern Ill.	17
13	San Jose St.	52
27	Pacific (Cal.)	23
52	Nevada-Las Vegas	40
14	Auburn	55
14	Nevada	34
17	Utah St.	20
231		**350**

Nickname: Aggies.
Stadium: Aggie Memorial (1978), 30,343 capacity. Natural turf.
Colors: Crimson & White.
Conference: Big West.
SID: Steve Shutt, 505-646-3929.
AD: Al Gonzales.

NEWBERRY
Newberry, SC 29108 II

Coach: Mike Taylor, Newberry '76
Record: 2 Years, 7-14-0

1994 SCHEDULE

Mars Hill ■	*Sept. 3
Wingate	Sept. 10
West Liberty St.	Sept. 17
Gardner-Webb ■	*Sept. 24
Citadel	*Oct. 1
Charleston So.	Oct. 8
Wofford ■	*Oct. 15
Lenoir-Rhyne	Oct. 22
Catawba ■	Oct. 29
Carson-Newman	Nov. 5
Presbyterian	Nov. 12

1993 RESULTS (2-8-0)

0	South Caro. St.	38
10	Lenoir-Rhyne	14
13	Presbyterian	30
23	Gardner-Webb	21
14	Catawba	28
10	Charleston So.	15
3	Wofford	29
10	Western Caro.	56
27	Lees-McRae	24
18	Fayetteville St.	20
128		**275**

Nickname: Indians.
Stadium: Setzler Field (1930), 4,000 capacity. Natural turf.
Colors: Scarlet & Gray.
Conference: Division II Independent.
SID: To be named, 803-321-5169.
AD: To be named.

NICHOLLS STATE
Thibodaux, LA 70301 ....I-AA

Coach: Rick Rhoades, Central Mo. St. '70
Record: 5 Years, 35-22-1

1994 SCHEDULE

Connecticut	Sept. 3
Livingston ■	*Sept. 10
Northwestern St. ■	*Sept. 17
Samford	*Oct. 1
Troy St.	Oct. 8
Stephen F. Austin ■	Oct. 15
Southwest Tex. St.	*Oct. 22
Southern-B.R. ■	*Oct. 29
Sam Houston St.	*Nov. 5
North Texas ■	Nov. 12
McNeese St.	*Nov. 19

1993 RESULTS (3-8-0)

42	Livingston	51
17	Troy St.	24
30	Northeast La.	51
6	Samford	21
21	Northwestern St.	35
21	Stephen F. Austin	35
63	Southwest Tex. St.	37
28	Southern-B.R.	14
20	Sam Houston St.	19
21	North Texas	63
0	McNeese St.	27
269		**377**

Nickname: Colonels.
Stadium: John L. Guidry (1972), 12,800 capacity. Natural turf.
Colors: Red & Gray.
Conference: Southland Conf.
SID: Ron Mears, 504-448-4282.
AD: Mike Knight.

NICHOLS
Dudley, MA 01570 III

Coach: Jim Crowley, Villanova '51
Record: 1 Year, 1-8-0

1994 SCHEDULE

Mass. Maritime	Sept. 10
Stonehill ■	Sept. 17
Bentley	*Sept. 23
Assumption ■	Oct. 1
Curry	Oct. 8
Salve Regina	Oct. 15
MIT ■	Oct. 22
Western New Eng. ■	Oct. 29
Worcester St.	Nov. 5

1993 RESULTS (1-8-0)

6	Mass. Maritime	23
6	Stonehill	36
0	Bentley	45
0	Assumption	27
13	Curry	15
20	Salve Regina	18
7	MIT	43
13	Western New Eng.	17
11	Worcester St.	40
76		**264**

Nickname: Bison.
Stadium: Bison Bowl (1961), 3,000 capacity. Natural turf.
Colors: Black & Green.
Conference: Eastern Collegiate.
SID: Bob Flannery, 508-943-1560.
AD: Thomas R. Cafaro.

NORFOLK STATE
Norfolk, VA 23504 II

Coach: To be named

1994 SCHEDULE

Virginia St.	*Sept. 3
N.C. Central ■	*Sept. 10
Fayetteville St. ■	*Sept. 17
Elizabeth City St.	*Sept. 24
Winston-Salem	Oct. 8
Hampton	Oct. 15
Virginia Union ■	Oct. 22

Johnson Smith ....Oct. 29
Lane ■ ....Nov. 5
Kentucky St. ■ ....Nov. 12

1993 RESULTS (3-7-1)

7	Virginia St.	21
20	N.C. Central	30
19	Fayetteville St.	34
40	Elizabeth City St.	12
54	Lane	8
54	Winston-Salem	54
21	Hampton	48
21	Virginia Union	9
24	Kentucky St.	26
13	Johnson Smith	20
31	Bethune-Cookman	33
304		**295**

Nickname: Spartans.
Stadium: Foreman Field (1935), 26,000 capacity. Artificial turf.
Colors: Green & Gold.
Conference: Central Inter. Ath. Assoc.
SID: John Holley, 804-683-8444.
AD: William "Dick" Price.

NORTH ALABAMA

Florence, AL 35630.....................................II

Coach: Bobby Wallace, Mississippi St. '76
Record: 6 Years, 40-27-1

1994 SCHEDULE

Fort Valley St. [Macon, Ga.] ....*Sept. 3
Alabama A&M ■ ....*Sept. 10
Mississippi Col. ■ ....*Sept. 17
Delta St. ....*Sept. 24
Youngstown St. ....*Oct. 8
Henderson St. ....*Oct. 15
Central Ark. ■ ....Oct. 22
Livingston ....Oct. 29
Valdosta St. ■ ....*Nov. 5
West Ga. ....Nov. 12

1993 RESULTS (10-0-0)

36	Fort Valley St.	14
49	Alabama A&M	7
58	Delta St.	17
44	Portland St.	32
38	Mississippi Col.	28
17	Henderson St.	0
27	Central Ark.	10
65	Livingston	15
31	Valdosta St.	21
41	West Ga.	14
406		**158**

II Championship

38	Carson-Newman	28
45	Hampton	20
27	Tex. A&M-Kingsville	25
41	Indiana (Pa.)	34

Nickname: Lions.
Stadium: Braly, 13,000 capacity. Natural turf.
Colors: Purple & Gold.
Conference: Gulf South Conf.
SID: Jeff Hodges, 205-760-4595.
AD: Bill Jones.

NORTH CAROLINA

Chapel Hill, NC 27514 ....I-A

Coach: Mack Brown, Florida St. '74
Record: 10 Years, 51-62-1

1994 SCHEDULE

Texas Christian ■ ....*Sept. 3
Tulane ■ ....Sept. 17
Florida St. ....*Sept. 24
Southern Methodist ....Oct. 1
Georgia Tech ■ ....Oct. 8
Maryland ■ ....Oct. 15
Virginia ....Oct. 22
North Caro. St. ■ ....Oct. 29
Clemson ■ ....Nov. 5
Wake Forest ....Nov. 12
Duke ....Nov. 19

1993 RESULTS (10-2-0)

31	Southern Cal	9
44	Ohio	3
59	Maryland	42
7	Florida St.	33
35	North Caro. St.	14
45	UTEP	39
45	Wake Forest	35
41	Georgia Tech	3
10	Virginia	17
24	Clemson	0
42	Tulane	10
38	Duke	24
421		**229**

Gator Bowl

10	Alabama	24

Nickname: Tar Heels.
Stadium: Kenan (1927), 52,000 capacity. Natural turf.
Colors: Blue & White.
Conference: Atlantic Coast Conf.
SID: Rick Brewer, 919-962-2123.
AD: John Swofford.

NORTH CAROLINA A&T

Greensboro, NC 27411 ....I-AA

Coach: Bill Hayes, N.C. Central '65
Record: 18 Years, 131-66-2

1994 SCHEDULE

N.C. Central ■ ....Sept. 3
Winston-Salem ■ ....Sept. 10
Appalachian St. ....Sept. 17
Jacksonville St. ....Sept. 24
Southern-B.R. [Indianapolis, Ind.] ....*Oct. 1
Florida A&M ....*Oct. 8
Morgan St. ■ ....Oct. 15
Howard ....Oct. 22
Bethune-Cookman ■ ....Oct. 29
Delaware St. ....Nov. 5
South Caro. St. ....Nov. 19

1993 RESULTS (8-3-0)

22	Appalachian St.	10
49	Winston-Salem	21
34	Western Caro.	7
38	Liberty	30
41	Florida A&M	13
49	Morgan St.	33
35	Howard	41
29	Bethune-Cookman	14
19	Delaware St.	25
52	Johnson Smith	7
52	South Caro. St.	58
420		**259**

Nickname: Aggies.
Stadium: Aggie (1981), 17,500 capacity. Natural turf.
Colors: Blue & Gold.
Conference: Mid-Eastern.
SID: Charles E. Mooney, 919-334-7141.
AD: Willie Burden.

NORTH CAROLINA CENTRAL

Durham, NC 27707....................................II

Coach: Larry Little, Bethune-Cookman '66
Record: 10 Years, 48-55-1

1994 SCHEDULE

North Caro. A&T ....Sept. 3
Norfolk St. ....*Sept. 10
Virginia St. ■ ....*Sept. 17
Bethune-Cookman ....Sept. 24
Elizabeth City St. ■ ....Oct. 1
Fayetteville St. ....*Oct. 8
Howard ■ ....Oct. 15
Winston-Salem ■ ....Oct. 22
Livingstone ....Oct. 29
Johnson Smith ■ ....Nov. 5
Virginia Union ■ ....Nov. 12

1993 RESULTS (6-5-0)

30	Bowie St.	2
30	Norfolk St.	20
17	Virginia St.	40

39	Johnson Smith	6
48	Elizabeth City St.	14
20	Fayetteville St.	27
28	Winston-Salem	46
13	South Caro. St.	42
38	Livingstone	18
29	Kentucky St.	30
20	Virginia Union	13
312		**258**

Nickname: Eagles.
Stadium: O'Kelly-Riddick, 11,500 capacity. Natural turf.
Colors: Maroon & Gray.
Conference: Central Inter. Ath. Assoc.
SID: To be named, 919-560-6573.
AD: Carey Hughley.

NORTH CAROLINA STATE

Raleigh, NC 27695 ....I-A

Coach: Mike O'Cain, Clemson '77
Record: 1 Year, 7-5-0

1994 SCHEDULE

Bowling Green ■ ....*Sept. 1
Clemson ....Sept. 10
Western Caro. ■ ....*Sept. 24
Georgia Tech ■ ....Oct. 1
Louisville ....Oct. 8
Wake Forest ■ ....Oct. 15
North Caro. ■ ....Oct. 29
Maryland ....Nov. 5
Duke ■ ....Nov. 12
Florida St. ■ ....Nov. 19
Virginia ....Nov. 25

1993 RESULTS (7-4-0)

20	Purdue	7
34	Wake Forest	16
14	North Caro.	35
14	Clemson	20
36	Texas Tech	34
24	Marshall	17
28	Georgia Tech	23
34	Virginia	29
20	Duke	21
44	Maryland	21
3	Florida St.	62
271		**285**

Hall of Fame Bowl

7	Michigan	42

Nickname: Wolfpack.
Stadium: Carter-Finley (1966), 50,000 capacity. Natural turf.
Colors: Red & White.
Conference: Atlantic Coast Conf.
SID: Mark Bockelman, 919-515-2102.
AD: Todd Turner.

NORTH CENTRAL

Naperville, IL 60540 III

Coach: Bill Mack, Beloit '58
Record: 1 Year, 3-6-0

1994 SCHEDULE

Quincy ■ ....*Sept. 10
Carroll (Wis.) ....Sept. 17
Elmhurst ....Oct. 1
Augustana (Ill.) ■ ....*Oct. 8
Ill. Wesleyan ....Oct. 15
Millikin ■ ....Oct. 22
Wheaton (Ill.) ....Oct. 29
Carthage ■ ....Nov. 5
North Park ....Nov. 12

1993 RESULTS (3-6-0)

18	Carroll (Wis.)	45
31	Eureka	25
24	Ill. Wesleyan	38
14	Augustana (Ill.)	59
24	Elmhurst	22
21	Millikin	22
12	Wheaton (Ill.)	56
16	North Park	29

| 45 | Carthage | 35 |
| **205** | | **331** |

Nickname: Cardinals.
Stadium: Kroehler Field, 3,000 capacity. Natural turf.
Colors: Cardinal & White.
Conference: College Conf. of Ill. & Wis.
SID: Mike Koon, 708-420-3440.
AD: Allen Carius.

NORTH DAKOTA
Grand Forks, ND 58202 II

Coach: Roger Thomas, Augustana (Ill.) '69
Record: 10 Years, 48-53-2

1994 SCHEDULE
Bemidji St. ■		Sept. 10
Morningside		Sept. 17
St. Cloud St. ■		Sept. 24
Northern Colo.		Oct. 1
Mankato St.		Oct. 8
Augustana (S.D.) ■		Oct. 15
Nebraska-Omaha ■		Oct. 22
North Dak. St.		*Oct. 29
South Dak.		Nov. 5
South Dak. St. ■		Nov. 12

1993 RESULTS (8-2-0)
52	Southern Conn. St.	0
52	Morningside	21
10	St. Cloud St.	0
14	Northern Colo.	10
20	Mankato St.	9
7	Augustana (S.D.)	20
17	Nebraska-Omaha	8
22	North Dak. St.	21
42	South Dak.	7
0	South Dak. St.	28
236		**124**

II Championship
17	Pittsburg St.	14
54	Mankato St.	21
6	Indiana (Pa.)	21

Nickname: Sioux.
Stadium: Memorial (1927), 10,000 capacity. Artificial turf.
Colors: Kelly Green & White.
Conference: North Central Conf.
SID: Justin Doherty, 701-777-2985.
AD: Terry Wanless.

NORTH DAKOTA STATE
Fargo, ND 58105 II

Coach: Rocky Hager, Minot St. '74
Record: 7 Years, 66-15-1

1994 SCHEDULE
Angelo St. ■		*Sept. 3
Nebraska-Omaha ■		*Sept. 17
Morningside		Sept. 24
Mankato St. ■		*Oct. 1
South Dak. St. ■		Oct. 8
South Dak.		Oct. 15
St. Cloud St. ■		*Oct. 22
North Dak. ■		*Oct. 29
Northern Colo.		Nov. 5
Augustana (S.D.) ■		*Nov. 12

1993 RESULTS (7-3-0)
35	Pittsburg St.	16
28	Nebraska-Omaha	7
21	Morningside	15
27	Mankato St.	28
30	South Dak. St.	42
35	South Dak.	14
32	St. Cloud St.	24
21	North Dak.	22
40	Northern Colo.	14
31	Augustana (S.D.)	14
300		**196**

Nickname: Bison.
Stadium: FargoDome (1992), 18,900 capacity. Artificial turf.
Colors: Yellow & Green.

Conference: North Central Conf.
SID: George Ellis, 701-237-8331.
AD: Robert Entzion.

NORTH PARK
Chicago, IL 60625 III

Coach: Tim Rucks, Carthage '83
Record: 4 Years, 6-27-3

1994 SCHEDULE
Concordia (Wis.) ■		Sept. 10
Lake Forest		Sept. 17
Millikin		Oct. 1
Elmhurst ■		Oct. 8
Augustana (Ill.)		Oct. 15
Wheaton (Ill.) ■		Oct. 22
Carthage		Oct. 29
Ill. Wesleyan ■		Nov. 5
North Central ■		Nov. 12

1993 RESULTS (4-4-1)
20	Lake Forest	19
31	Blackburn	14
17	Augustana (Ill.)	21
14	Elmhurst	14
7	Millikin	28
7	Wheaton (Ill.)	41
26	Carthage	19
29	North Central	16
28	Ill. Wesleyan	41
179		**213**

Nickname: Vikings.
Stadium: Athletic Field (1955), 2,500 capacity. Natural turf.
Colors: Blue & Gold.
Conference: College Conf. of Ill. & Wis.
SID: To be named, 312-509-5840.
AD: Jerry Chaplin.

NORTH TEXAS
Denton, TX 76203 ....I-AA

Coach: Matt Simon, Eastern N. Mex. '76
(First year as head coach)

1994 SCHEDULE
Abilene Christian ■		*Sept. 1
Southwest Mo. St. ■		*Sept. 10
Montana ■		Sept. 24
Oklahoma St.		*Oct. 1
Southwest Tex. St.		*Oct. 8
McNeese St. ■		Oct. 15
Northwestern St.		Oct. 22
Sam Houston St. ■		Oct. 29
Stephen F. Austin		Nov. 5
Nicholls St.		Nov. 12
Northeast La.		*Nov. 19

1993 RESULTS (4-7-0)
14	Nebraska	76
23	Northern Ariz.	24
34	Southwest Mo. St.	33
33	Abilene Christian	13
35	Southwest Tex. St.	28
17	McNeese St.	18
37	Northwestern St.	38
14	Sam Houston St.	24
27	Stephen F. Austin	29
63	Nicholls St.	21
31	Northeast La.	61
328		**365**

Nickname: Mean Green, Eagles.
Stadium: Fouts Field (1952), 30,500 capacity. Artificial turf.
Colors: Green & White.
Conference: Southland Conf.
SID: Brian Briscoe, 817-565-2664.
AD: Craig Helwig.

NORTHEAST LOUISIANA
Monroe, LA 71209 ....I-A

Coach: Ed Zaunbrecher, Middle Tenn. St. '71
(First year as head coach)

1994 SCHEDULE
Colorado		Sept. 3
Auburn		*Sept. 10
Georgia		Sept. 17
Nevada		Sept. 24
Weber St. ■		*Oct. 1
Wyoming		Oct. 8
Central Fla. ■		*Oct. 15
Jacksonville St. ■		*Oct. 22
Brigham Young		Nov. 5
Kentucky		Nov. 12
North Texas ■		*Nov. 19

1993 RESULTS (9-2-0)
34	Eastern Wash.	13
40	Eastern Ky.	14
37	Southern Miss.	44
51	Nicholls St.	30
26	Northwestern St.	24
26	McNeese St.	34
40	Southwest Tex. St.	21
26	Stephen F. Austin	10
42	Arkansas St.	10
48	Sam Houston St.	10
61	North Texas	31
431		**241**

I-AA Championship
31	Idaho	34

Nickname: Indians.
Stadium: Malone (1978), 30,427 capacity. Natural turf.
Colors: Maroon & Gold.
Conference: I-A Independent.
SID: To be named, 318-342-5460.
AD: Richard Giannini.

NORTHEAST MISSOURI STATE
Kirksville, MO 63501 II

Coach: Eric Holm, Northeast Mo. St. '81
Record: 4 Years, 29-16-0

1994 SCHEDULE
Mankato St.		*Sept. 10
Central Mo. St.		*Sept. 17
Northwest Mo. St. ■		*Sept. 24
Mo. Southern St. ■		Oct. 1
Emporia St.		Oct. 8
Washburn ■		Oct. 15
Missouri-Rolla		Oct. 22
Southwest Baptist ■		Oct. 29
Pittsburg St.		Nov. 5
Mo. Western St.		Nov. 12

1993 RESULTS (6-5-0)
17	Iowa Wesleyan	13
23	Mankato St.	25
18	Central Mo. St.	36
38	Northwest Mo. St.	16
37	Mo. Southern St.	41
24	Emporia St.	13
34	Washburn	0
21	Missouri-Rolla	13
42	Southwest Baptist	14
0	Pittsburg St.	15
6	Mo. Western St.	42
260		**228**

Nickname: Bulldogs.
Stadium: Stokes (1930), 4,000 capacity. Natural turf.
Colors: Purple & White.
Conference: Mid-America Intercoll. Ath. Assoc.
SID: William Cable, 816-785-4127.
AD: To be named.

NORTHEASTERN
Boston, MA 02115 ....I-AA

Coach: Barry Gallup, Boston College '69
Record: 3 Years, 11-21-1

1994 SCHEDULE
Boise St.		*Sept. 3
New Hampshire ■		Sept. 10
Rhode Island ■		Sept. 17
Richmond ■		Sept. 24
William & Mary		Oct. 8

Boston U. ....Oct. 15
Villanova ■ ....Oct. 22
Delaware ....Oct. 29
Massachusetts ....Nov. 5
Maine ■ ....Nov. 12
James Madison ....Nov. 19

1993 RESULTS (2-9-0)

27	Villanova	3
13	Boise St.	27
13	Rhode Island	15
21	Richmond	24
14	Boston U.	17
6	William & Mary	53
6	New Hampshire	21
17	Massachusetts	21
21	James Madison	52
34	Maine	20
23	Delaware	28
195		**281**

Nickname: Huskies.
Stadium: E.S. Parsons (1933), 7,000 capacity. Artificial turf.
Colors: Red & Black.
Conference: Yankee.
SID: Jack Grinold, 617-373-2691.
AD: Barry Gallup.

NORTHERN ARIZONA
Flagstaff, AZ 86011 ....I-AA

Coach: Steve Axman, LIU-C. W. Post '69
Record: 4 Years, 19-25-0

1994 SCHEDULE

Nevada ....Sept. 3
Southern Utah ■ ....*Sept. 10
Idaho St. ■ ....*Sept. 17
Montana St. ....Sept. 24
Boise St. ■ ....*Oct. 1
Montana ....Oct. 8
Eastern Wash. ■ ....*Oct. 15
Idaho ....Oct. 22
Weber St. ■ ....*Oct. 29
Cal Poly SLO ■ ....*Nov. 5
Cal St. Northridge ....Nov. 12

1993 RESULTS (7-4-0)

31	Southern Utah	27
24	North Texas	23
23	Cal St. Northridge	9
32	Idaho St.	15
23	Montana St.	20
23	Boise St.	9
23	Montana	38
26	Eastern Wash.	38
27	Idaho	34
28	Weber St.	67
55	Valparaiso	13
315		**293**

Nickname: Lumberjacks.
Stadium: Walkup Skydome (1978), 15,300 capacity. Artificial turf.
Colors: Blue & Gold.
Conference: Big Sky Conf.
SID: Chris Burkhalter, 602-523-6792.
AD: Steve Holton.

NORTHERN COLORADO
Greeley, CO 80639 II

Coach: Joe Glenn, South Dak. '71
Record: 9 Years, 56-37-1

1994 SCHEDULE

Western St. ■ ....Sept. 3
Mesa St. ....Sept. 10
Augustana (S.D.) ....Sept. 17
South Dak. St. ....Sept. 24
North Dak. ■ ....Oct. 1
South Dak. ■ ....Oct. 8
St. Cloud St. ....Oct. 15
Mankato St. ■ ....Oct. 22
Nebraska-Omaha ....*Oct. 29
North Dak. St. ■ ....Nov. 5
Morningside ....Nov. 12

1993 RESULTS (8-3-0)

38	Western St.	0
49	Mesa St.	0
24	Augustana (S.D.)	0
38	South Dak. St.	17
10	North Dak.	14
24	South Dak.	14
20	St. Cloud St.	16
28	Mankato St.	35
49	Nebraska-Omaha	7
14	North Dak. St.	40
30	Morningside	0
324		**143**

Nickname: Bears.
Stadium: Jackson Field (1926), 7,500 capacity. Natural turf.
Colors: Navy & Gold.
Conference: North Central Conf.
SID: Scott Leisinger, 303-351-2150.
AD: Jim Fallis.

NORTHERN ILLINOIS
De Kalb, IL 60115 ....I-A

Coach: Charlie Sadler, Northeastern Okla. '71
Record: 3 Years, 11-22-0

1994 SCHEDULE

Oklahoma St. ■ ....*Sept. 1
Southwestern La. ....*Sept. 10
Illinois ....Sept. 17
Eastern Ill. ■ ....*Sept. 24
Nevada ■ ....Oct. 1
New Mexico St. ■ ....Oct. 8
Pacific (Cal.) ....*Oct. 15
Louisiana Tech ■ ....Oct. 22
Vanderbilt ....Oct. 29
Arkansas St. ....Nov. 5
Arkansas ....Nov. 12

1993 RESULTS (4-7-0)

10	Iowa St.	54
10	Indiana	28
23	Arkansas St.	7
46	Nevada	42
45	Southern Ill.	15
17	New Mexico St.	24
21	Pacific (Cal.)	16
19	Southwestern La.	33
16	Louisiana Tech	17
20	Iowa	54
0	Mississippi	44
227		**334**

Nickname: Huskies.
Stadium: Huskie (1965), 30,998 capacity. Artificial turf.
Colors: Cardinal & Black.
Conference: Big West.
SID: Mike Korcek, 815-753-1706.
AD: To be named.

NORTHERN IOWA
Cedar Falls, IA 50613 ....I-AA

Coach: Terry Allen, Northern Iowa '79
Record: 5 Years, 47-15-0

1994 SCHEDULE

Iowa St. ....Sept. 3
Southwest Tex. St. ....*Sept. 8
Southwest Mo. St. ■ ....*Sept. 17
McNeese St. ■ ....Sept. 24
Indiana St. ....Oct. 1
Eastern Ill. ....Oct. 8
Illinois St. ■ ....*Oct. 22
Western Ill. ■ ....*Oct. 29
Idaho ....Nov. 5
Southern Ill. ....Nov. 12
Eastern Wash. ....*Nov. 19

1993 RESULTS (8-3-0)

10	McNeese St.	27
42	Wyoming	45
35	Jacksonville St.	14
34	Southwest Tex. St.	13
20	Southwest Mo. St.	14
17	Indiana St.	10

31	Eastern Ill.	27
23	Western Ill.	25
20	Illinois St.	19
48	Moorhead St.	0
49	Southern Ill.	17
329		**211**

I-AA Championship

21	Boston U.	27

Nickname: Panthers.
Stadium: U.N.I.-Dome (1976), 16,324 capacity. Artificial turf.
Colors: Purple & Old Gold.
Conference: Gateway.
SID: Nancy Justis, 319-273-6354.
AD: Christopher Ritrievi.

NORTHERN MICHIGAN
Marquette, MI 49855 II

Coach: Mark Marana, Northern Mich. '81
Record: 3 Years, 9-19-2

1994 SCHEDULE

Saginaw Valley ....Sept. 10
Northwood ■ ....*Sept. 17
St. Francis (Ill.) ....Sept. 24
St. Joseph's (Ind.) ■ ....Oct. 1
Ferris St. ....Oct. 8
Indianapolis ■ ....Oct. 15
Hillsdale ....Oct. 22
Grand Valley St. ■ ....*Oct. 29
Ashland ....Nov. 5
Wayne St. (Mich.) ■ ....Nov. 12

1993 RESULTS (5-4-1)

14	Northwood	13
20	Indianapolis	14
28	Saginaw Valley	14
26	St. Francis (Ill.)	16
0	Ferris St.	47
28	Grand Valley St.	28
12	Hillsdale	28
18	Wayne St. (Mich.)	28
24	St. Joseph's (Ind.)	7
26	Ashland	33
196		**228**

Nickname: Wildcats.
Stadium: Superior Dome (1991), 8,000 capacity. Artificial turf.
Colors: Old Gold & Olive Green.
Conference: Midwest Intercollegiate.
SID: Jim Pinar, 906-227-2720.
AD: Rick Comley.

NORTHERN STATE
Aberdeen, SD 57401 II

Coach: Dennis Miller, St. Cloud St. '81
Record: 8 Years, 57-31-0

1994 SCHEDULE

Wis.-Eau Claire ■ ....*Sept. 3
South Dak. ■ ....*Sept. 10
Wayne St. (Neb.) ....Sept. 17
Southwest St. ■ ....Sept. 24
Moorhead St. ....Oct. 1
Winona St. ■ ....Oct. 8
Minn.-Morris ....Oct. 15
Neb.-Kearney ....Oct. 22
Bemidji St. ■ ....Oct. 29
Minn.-Duluth ....Nov. 5
Wis.-River Falls [Minneapolis, Minn.] ....Nov. 12

1993 RESULTS (6-5-0)

0	South Dak.	59
15	Michigan Tech	30
40	Minot St.	37
26	Minn.-Duluth	22
28	Southwest St.	22
40	Moorhead St.	41
14	Winona St.	42
44	Minn.-Morris	21
0	Neb.-Kearney	33
35	Bemidji St.	20

50 Minn.-Morris....14
292 **341**

Nickname: Wolves.
Stadium: Swisher (1975), 6,000 capacity. Natural turf.
Colors: Maroon and Gold.
Conference: Northern Sun Inter. Conf.
SID: Deb Smith, 605-622-7748.
AD: Jim Kretchman.

NORTHWEST MISSOURI STATE

Maryville, MO 64468 II

Coach: Mel Tjeerdsma, Southern St. '67
Record: 10 Years, 59-39-4

1994 SCHEDULE

Mankato St. ■ ....Sept. 3
East Tex. St....Sept. 10
Mo. Western St. ■ ....Sept. 17
Northeast Mo. St. ....*Sept. 24
Emporia St. ■ ....Oct. 1
Washburn ....*Oct. 8
Missouri-Rolla ■ ....Oct. 15
Southwest Baptist ....Oct. 22
Pittsburg St. ■ ....Oct. 29
Central Mo. St. ■ ....Nov. 5
Mo. Southern St. ....Nov. 12

1993 RESULTS (3-8-0)

28 Mankato St. 55
11 East Tex. St. 45
14 Mo. Western St. 21
16 Northeast Mo. St. 38
21 Emporia St. 15
61 Washburn....36
27 Missouri-Rolla 20
17 Southwest Baptist....21
12 Pittsburg St. 38
10 Central Mo. St....41
33 Mo. Southern St. 49
250 **379**

Nickname: Bearcats.
Stadium: Rickenbrode, 7,500 capacity. Natural turf.
Colors: Green & White.
Conference: Mid-America Intercoll. Ath. Assoc.
SID: Larry Cain, 816-562-1118.
AD: Jim Redd.

NORTHWESTERN

Evanston, IL 60208 ....I-A

Coach: Gary Barnett, Missouri '69
Record: 4 Years, 13-28-1

1994 SCHEDULE

Notre Dame ■ ....*Sept. 3
Stanford ■ ....Sept. 10
Air Force ....Sept. 17
Ohio St. ■ ....Oct. 1
Wisconsin ■ ....Oct. 8
Minnesota ....*Oct. 15
Indiana ....Oct. 22
Illinois ■ ....Oct. 29
Michigan St. ■ ....Nov. 5
Iowa ....Nov. 12
Penn St....Nov. 19

1993 RESULTS (2-9-0)

12 Notre Dame....27
22 Boston College....21
26 Wake Forest 14
3 Ohio St....51
14 Wisconsin....53
26 Minnesota....28
0 Indiana....24
13 Illinois....20
29 Michigan St. 31
19 Iowa....23
21 Penn St. 43
185 **335**

Nickname: Wildcats.
Stadium: Dyche (1926), 49,256 capacity. Artificial turf.
Colors: Purple & White.
Conference: Big Ten Conf.
SID: Greg Shea, 708-491-8816.
AD: Rick Taylor.

NORTHWESTERN (WISCONSIN)

Watertown, WI 53094....III

Coach: Dennis Gorsline, Northern Mich. '65
Record: 23 Years, 83-85-0

1994 SCHEDULE

Blackburn ■ ....Sept. 10
Concordia (Ill.)....Sept. 17
Concordia (Minn.)....Sept. 24
Crown ■ ....Oct. 1
Northwestern Minn. ■ ....Oct. 8
Dr. Martin Luther....Oct. 15
Mt. Senario ....Oct. 22
Maranatha ■ ....Oct. 29

1993 RESULTS (7-1-0)

29 Lawrence 21
34 Concordia (Ill.) 7
24 Principia 14
36 Maranatha....14
44 Concordia (Minn.) 13
56 Northwestern Minn. 20
39 Dr. Martin Luther....26
20 Mt. Senario....21
282 **136**

Nickname: Trojans.
Stadium: Northwestern (1953), 2,000 capacity. Natural turf.
Colors: Black & Red.
Conference: Division III Independents.
SID: Tim Dolan, 414-262-8117.
AD: Jerome Kruse.

NORTHWESTERN STATE

Natchitoches, LA 71497 ....I-AA

Coach: Sam Goodwin, Henderson St. '66
Record: 13 Years, 71-69-4

1994 SCHEDULE

Southern-B.R. ■ ....*Sept. 3
Delta St. ■ ....*Sept. 10
Nicholls St.....*Sept. 17
East Tex. St. ■ ....*Sept. 24
Troy St. ■ ....*Oct. 1
Sam Houston St. ■ ....*Oct. 15
North Texas ■ ....Oct. 22
Southwest Tex. St. ....Oct. 29
Louisiana Tech ....*Nov. 5
McNeese St. ■ ....*Nov. 12
Stephen F. Austin ....Nov. 19

1993 RESULTS (5-6-0)

13 Southern-B.R....30
14 Troy St....21
30 East Tex. St. 19
24 Northeast La. 26
35 Nicholls St. 21
34 Sam Houston St....27
38 North Texas 37
15 Southwest Tex. St....22
34 Eastern Ill....26
7 McNeese St....34
20 Stephen F. Austin....51
264 **314**

Nickname: Demons.
Stadium: Turpin (1976), 15,971 capacity. Artificial turf.
Colors: Purple & White.
Conference: Southland Conf.
SID: Doug Ireland, 318-357-6467.
AD: Tynes Hildebrand.

NORTHWOOD

Midland, MI 48640 II

Coach: Pat Riepma, Hillsdale '83
Record: 1 Year, 3-7-1

1994 SCHEDULE

Michigan Tech ■ ....Sept. 10
Northern Mich. ....*Sept. 17
Saginaw Valley....Sept. 24
Ashland ■ ....Oct. 1
St. Francis (Ill.) ....*Oct. 8
St. Joseph's (Ind.) ■ ....Oct. 15
Ferris St.....Oct. 22
Indianapolis ■ ....Oct. 29
Hillsdale ....Nov. 5
Grand Valley St. ■ ....Nov. 12

1993 RESULTS (3-7-1)

13 Northern Mich....14
13 St. Joseph's (Ind.)....13
0 Grand Valley St....35
22 Findlay 21
24 Indianapolis 19
14 Wayne St. (Mich.) 32
31 St. Francis (Ill.)....22
0 Ferris St. 47
0 Ashland....50
7 Hillsdale....37
7 Saginaw Valley....13
131 **303**

Nickname: Northmen.
Stadium: Louis Juillerat, 2,500 capacity. Natural turf.
Colors: Columbia Blue & White.
Conference: Midwest Intercollegiate.
SID: Fritz Reznor, 517-837-4239.
AD: Dave Coffey.

NORWICH

Northfield, VT 05663 III

Coach: Steve Hackett, Canisius '76
Record: 3 Years, 5-23-0

1994 SCHEDULE

Merchant Marine ■ ....Sept. 10
Mass.-Lowell ....*Sept. 17
Plymouth St.....Sept. 24
Coast Guard ■ ....Oct. 1
Worcester Tech ■ ....Oct. 8
Stony Brook....Oct. 15
Albany (N.Y.) ■ ....Oct. 22
St. Lawrence....Oct. 29
Western Conn. St....Nov. 12

1993 RESULTS (0-9-0)

7 Merchant Marine....35
26 Mass.-Lowell....28
19 Plymouth St. 44
8 Coast Guard....21
21 Worcester Tech 41
17 Brockport St. 51
16 Albany (N.Y.)....19
19 St. Lawrence 34
21 Western Conn. St. 33
154 **306**

Nickname: Cadets.
Stadium: Sabine Field (1921), 5,000 capacity. Natural turf.
Colors: Maroon & Gold.
Conference: Freedom Football Conf.
SID: Todd Bamford, 802-485-2160.
AD: Tony Mariano.

NOTRE DAME

Notre Dame, IN 46556 ....I-A

Coach: Lou Holtz, Kent '59
Record: 24 Years, 193-84-6

1994 SCHEDULE

Northwestern ....*Sept. 3
Michigan ■ ....Sept. 10
Michigan St.....Sept. 17
Purdue ■ ....Sept. 24
Stanford ■ ....Oct. 1
Boston College....Oct. 8
Brigham Young ■ ....Oct. 15
Navy ■ ....Oct. 29
Florida St. [Orlando, Fla.] ....Nov. 12
Air Force ■ ....Nov. 19
Southern Cal....*Nov. 26

1993 RESULTS (10-1-0)

27 Northwestern....12

27	Michigan	23
36	Michigan St.	14
17	Purdue	0
48	Stanford	20
44	Pittsburgh	0
45	Brigham Young	20
31	Southern Cal	13
58	Navy	27
31	Florida St.	24
39	Boston College	41
403		**194**

Cotton Bowl

24	Texas A&M	21

Nickname: Fighting Irish.
Stadium: Notre Dame (1930), 59,075 capacity.
   Natural turf.
Colors: Gold & Blue.
Conference: I-A Independent.
SID: John Heisler, 219-631-7516.
AD: Dick Rosenthal.

OBERLIN

Oberlin, OH 44074 III

Coach: Pete Peterson, Gettysburg '83
(First year as head coach)

1994 SCHEDULE

Hiram ■	Sept. 10
Kenyon ■	Sept. 17
Wooster	Sept. 24
Ohio Wesleyan ■	Oct. 1
Denison	Oct. 15
Wittenberg ■	Oct. 22
Chicago	Oct. 29
Earlham ■	Nov. 5
Allegheny	Nov. 12

1993 RESULTS (0-10-0)

0	Thiel	37
0	Denison	31
0	Ohio Wesleyan	35
9	Earlham	16
3	Wooster	31
7	Case Reserve	41
7	Allegheny	48
6	Wittenberg	55
7	Kenyon	24
7	Grove City	35
46		**353**

Nickname: Yeomen.
Stadium: Dill Field (1925), 3,500 capacity. Natural turf.
Colors: Crimson & Gold.
Conference: North Coast Ath. Conf.
SID: Scott Wargo, 216-775-8503.
AD: Donald Hunsinger.

OCCIDENTAL

Los Angeles, CA 90041 III

Coach: Dale Widolff, Indiana Central '75
Record: 12 Years, 79-32-2

1994 SCHEDULE

Menlo	Sept. 17
Whittier ■	*Sept. 24
Cal Lutheran	Oct. 1
Pomona-Pitzer ■	*Oct. 8
Chapman ■	*Oct. 15
Claremont-M-S ■	*Oct. 22
Azusa Pacific	*Oct. 29
Redlands	*Nov. 5
La Verne	Nov. 12

1993 RESULTS (8-1-0)

14	Azusa Pacific	6
17	Trinity (Tex.)	13
21	La Verne	31
37	Whittier	25
51	Pomona-Pitzer	21
52	Menlo	13
68	Claremont-M-S	42
45	Cal Lutheran	28
21	Redlands	14
326		**193**

Nickname: Tigers.
Stadium: Patterson Field (1900), 4,000 capacity.
   Natural turf.
Colors: Orange and Black.
Conference: Southern Calif. Inter. Ath. Conf.
SID: James Kerman, 213-259-2699.
AD: Dale Widolff.

OHIO

Athens, OH 45701 ....I-A

Coach: Tom Lichtenberg, Louisville '62
Record: 7 Years, 26-48-3

1994 SCHEDULE

Pittsburgh	*Sept. 10
Utah St. ■	Sept. 17
Ball St.	Sept. 24
Toledo ■	Oct. 1
Bowling Green	Oct. 8
Miami (Ohio) ■	Oct. 15
Kent	Oct. 22
Central Mich. ■	Oct. 29
Western Mich.	Nov. 5
Eastern Mich. ■	Nov. 12
Akron	Nov. 19

1993 RESULTS (4-7-0)

3	North Caro.	44
0	Central Mich.	38
16	Ball St.	24
10	Toledo	28
7	Virginia	41
0	Bowling Green	20
15	Kent	10
22	Miami (Ohio)	20
21	Akron	13
28	Western Mich.	34
12	Eastern Mich.	10
134		**282**

Nickname: Bobcats.
Stadium: Peden (1929), 20,000 capacity. Natural turf.
Colors: Green & White.
Conference: Mid-American Conf.
SID: Pam Fronko, 614-593-1299.
AD: Harold McElhaney.

OHIO NORTHERN

Ada, OH 45810 III

Coach: Tom Kaczkowski, Illinois '78
Record: 8 Years, 29-48-2

1994 SCHEDULE

Bluffton ■	*Sept. 10
Capital	Sept. 17
Mount Union ■	Sept. 24
Muskingum	Oct. 1
Otterbein	Oct. 8
John Carroll ■	Oct. 15
Marietta ■	Oct. 22
Hiram	Oct. 29
Baldwin-Wallace ■	Nov. 5
Heidelberg	Nov. 12

1993 RESULTS (5-4-1)

26	Bluffton	7
23	Marietta	0
41	Otterbein	16
24	John Carroll	30
21	Muskingum	21
84	Hiram	13
7	Mount Union	49
14	Capital	0
19	Baldwin-Wallace	62
33	Heidelberg	34
292		**232**

Nickname: Polar Bears.
Stadium: Ada Memorial (1948), 4,000 capacity.
   Natural turf.
Colors: Orange & Black.
Conference: Ohio Ath. Conf.
SID: Cort Reynolds, 419-772-2046.
AD: Gale Daugherty.

OHIO STATE

Columbus, OH 43210 ....I-A

Coach: John Cooper, Iowa St. '62
Record: 17 Years, 126-63-6

1994 SCHEDULE

Fresno St. [Anaheim, Cal.]	*Aug. 29
Washington	Sept. 10
Pittsburgh ■	Sept. 17
Houston ■	Sept. 24
Northwestern	Oct. 1
Illinois ■	Oct. 8
Michigan St.	Oct. 15
Purdue ■	Oct. 22
Penn St.	Oct. 29
Wisconsin ■	Nov. 5
Indiana	Nov. 12
Michigan ■	Nov. 19

1993 RESULTS (9-1-1)

34	Rice	7
21	Washington	12
63	Pittsburgh	28
51	Northwestern	3
20	Illinois	12
28	Michigan St.	21
45	Purdue	24
24	Penn St.	6
14	Wisconsin	14
23	Indiana	17
0	Michigan	28
323		**172**

Holiday Bowl

28	Brigham Young	21

Nickname: Buckeyes.
Stadium: Ohio (1922), 91,470 capacity. Natural turf.
Colors: Scarlet & Gray.
Conference: Big Ten Conf.
SID: Steve Snapp, 614-292-6861.
AD: Andy Geiger.

OHIO WESLEYAN

Delaware, OH 43015 III

Coach: Mike Hollway, Michigan '74
Record: 11 Years, 61-46-2

1994 SCHEDULE

John Carroll	Sept. 10
Wooster ■	Sept. 17
Olivet ■	Sept. 24
Oberlin	Oct. 1
Denison ■	Oct. 8
Wittenberg	Oct. 15
Case Reserve ■	Oct. 22
Earlham	Oct. 29
Allegheny ■	Nov. 5
Kenyon	Nov. 12

1993 RESULTS (6-4-0)

7	Albion	45
32	Kenyon	27
35	Oberlin	0
27	Denison	13
0	Wilmington (Ohio)	7
34	Earlham	18
48	Wooster	0
15	Case Reserve	13
7	Allegheny	51
21	Wittenberg	28
226		**202**

Nickname: Battling Bishops.
Stadium: Selby (1929), 9,600 capacity. Natural turf.
Colors: Red & Black.
Conference: North Coast Ath. Conf.
SID: Mark Beckenbach, 614-368-3340.
AD: John Martin.

OKLAHOMA

Norman, OK 73019 ....I-A

Coach: Gary Gibbs, Oklahoma '75
Record: 5 Years, 38-17-2

1994 SCHEDULE

Syracuse	*Sept. 3
Texas A&M	Sept. 10
Texas Tech ■	Sept. 17
Iowa St. ■	Oct. 1
Texas [Dallas, Tex.]	Oct. 8
Colorado	Oct. 15
Kansas	Oct. 22
Kansas St. ■	Oct. 29
Missouri ■	Nov. 5
Oklahoma St.	Nov. 12
Nebraska ■	Nov. 25

1993 RESULTS (8-3-0)

35	Texas Christian	3
44	Texas A&M	14
41	Tulsa	20
24	Iowa St.	7
38	Texas	17
10	Colorado	27
38	Kansas	23
7	Kansas St.	21
42	Missouri	23
31	Oklahoma St.	0
7	Nebraska	21
317		**176**

John Hancock Bowl

41	Texas Tech	10

Nickname: Sooners.
Stadium: Owen Field (1924), 75,004 capacity. Natural turf.
Colors: Crimson & Cream.
Conference: Big Eight Conf.
SID: Mike Prusinski, 405-325-8228.
AD: Donnie Duncan.

OKLAHOMA STATE

Stillwater, OK 74078 ....I-A

Coach: Pat Jones, Arkansas '69
Record: 10 Years, 59-53-2

1994 SCHEDULE

Northern Ill.	*Sept. 1
Baylor	*Sept. 17
Tulsa ■	*Sept. 24
North Texas ■	*Oct. 1
Nebraska	Oct. 8
Missouri ■	Oct. 15
Iowa St. ■	Oct. 22
Kansas	Oct. 29
Colorado	Nov. 5
Oklahoma ■	Nov. 12
Kansas St.	Nov. 19

1993 RESULTS (3-8-0)

45	Southwest Mo. St.	7
16	Tulsa	10
10	Arizona St.	12
27	Texas Christian	22
13	Nebraska	27
9	Missouri	42
17	Iowa St.	20
6	Kansas	13
14	Colorado	31
0	Oklahoma	31
17	Kansas St.	21
174		**236**

Nickname: Cowboys.
Stadium: Lewis (1920), 50,614 capacity. Artificial turf.
Colors: Orange & Black.
Conference: Big Eight Conf.
SID: Steve Buzzard, 405-744-5749.
AD: Dave Martin.

OLIVET

Olivet, MI 49076 III

Coach: Dallas Hilliar, Central Mich. '68
Record: 1 Year, 1-8-0

1994 SCHEDULE

Manchester	Sept. 10
Anderson ■	Sept. 17
Ohio Wesleyan	Sept. 24

Defiance ■	Oct. 1
Alma	Oct. 8
Albion ■	Oct. 15
Adrian	Oct. 22
Kalamazoo ■	Oct. 29
Hope	Nov. 5

1993 RESULTS (1-8-0)

19	Heidelberg	21
47	Taylor	22
18	Defiance	49
25	Wilmington (Ohio)	29
8	Alma	16
14	Albion	34
0	Adrian	27
30	Kalamazoo	54
14	Hope	32
175		**284**

Nickname: Comets.
Stadium: Griswold Field (1972), 3,500 capacity. Natural turf.
Colors: Red & White.
Conference: Michigan Inter. Ath. Assoc.
SID: Tom Shaw, 616-749-7189.
AD: Jackie Shimp.

OREGON

Eugene, OR 97401 ....I-A

Coach: Rich Brooks, Oregon St. '63
Record: 17 Years, 82-105-4

1994 SCHEDULE

Portland St. ■	Sept. 3
Hawaii	*Sept. 10
Utah	Sept. 17
Iowa ■	Sept. 24
Southern Cal	Oct. 1
Washington St.	Oct. 8
California ■	Oct. 15
Washington ■	Oct. 22
Arizona ■	Oct. 29
Arizona St. ■	Nov. 5
Stanford	Nov. 12
Oregon St.	Nov. 19

1993 RESULTS (5-6-0)

23	Colorado St.	9
35	Montana	30
13	Illinois	7
41	California	42
13	Southern Cal	24
45	Arizona St.	36
6	Washington	21
46	Washington St.	23
10	Arizona	31
34	Stanford	38
12	Oregon St.	15
278		**276**

Nickname: Ducks.
Stadium: Autzen (1967), 41,678 capacity. Artificial turf.
Colors: Green & Yellow.
Conference: Pacific-10.
SID: Steve Hellyer, 503-346-5488.
AD: Rich Brooks.

OREGON STATE

Corvallis, OR 97331 ....I-A

Coach: Jerry Pettibone, Oklahoma '63
Record: 9 Years, 39-58-2

1994 SCHEDULE

Arizona St.	*Sept. 3
Wyoming ■	Sept. 10
Fresno St.	*Sept. 17
Arizona	*Oct. 1
Southern Cal ■	Oct. 8
UCLA	Oct. 15
Stanford ■	Oct. 22
Washington	Oct. 29
Pacific (Cal.) ■	Nov. 5
Washington St. ■	Nov. 12
Oregon ■	Nov. 19

1993 RESULTS (4-7-0)

27	Wyoming	16
30	Fresno St.	48
6	Washington St.	51
0	Arizona	33
30	Arizona St.	14
42	Pacific (Cal.)	7
9	Southern Cal	34
17	UCLA	20
27	Stanford	31
21	Washington	28
15	Oregon	12
224		**294**

Nickname: Beavers.
Stadium: Parker (1953), 35,547 capacity. Artificial turf.
Colors: Orange & Black.
Conference: Pacific-10.
SID: Hal Cowan, 503-737-3720.
AD: Dutch Baughman.

OTTERBEIN

Westerville, OH 43081 III

Coach: John Hussey, Otterbein '78
Record: 3 Years, 9-19-2

1994 SCHEDULE

Hanover	Sept. 10
Mount Union	*Sept. 17
John Carroll ■	Sept. 24
Baldwin-Wallace	*Oct. 1
Ohio Northern ■	Oct. 8
Hiram ■	Oct. 15
Heidelberg	Oct. 22
Marietta ■	Oct. 29
Muskingum ■	Nov. 5
Capital	Nov. 12

1993 RESULTS (4-6-0)

48	Earlham	28
14	Heidelberg	21
16	Ohio Northern	41
35	Hiram	14
10	Baldwin-Wallace	56
10	Marietta	0
35	John Carroll	31
0	Mount Union	49
29	Muskingum	32
10	Capital	31
207		**303**

Nickname: Cardinals.
Stadium: Memorial (1946), 4,000 capacity. Natural turf.
Colors: Tan & Cardinal.
Conference: Ohio Ath. Conf.
SID: Ed Syguda, 614-823-1600.
AD: Dick Reynolds.

PACE

Pleasantville, NY 10570 II

Coach: Gregory Lusardi, Slippery Rock '75
(First year as head coach)

1994 SCHEDULE

Stony Brook	Sept. 10
Monmouth (N. J.)	Sept. 17
Assumption ■	Sept. 24
Iona ■	Oct. 8
Mercyhurst	Oct. 15
Salve Regina ■	Oct. 22
Hartwick ■	Oct. 29
Mass.-Lowell	Nov. 5
Sacred Heart ■	Nov. 12
St. John's (N.Y.)	Nov. 24

1993 RESULTS (0-10-0)

2	Stony Brook	20
19	Marist	47
19	Mass.-Lowell	35
2	LIU-C.W. Post	56
16	St. John's (N.Y.)	44
10	Wagner	47
6	Iona	38
6	Hobart	27
0	Mercyhurst	48

| 0 | Sacred Heart | 36 |
| **80** | | **398** |

Nickname: Setters.
Stadium: Finnerty Field, 1,200 capacity. Natural turf.
Colors: Blue & Gold.
Conference: Division II Independent.
SID: John Balkam, 914-773-3411.
AD: Chris Bledsoe.

PACIFIC (CALIFORNIA)
Stockton, CA 95211 ....I-A

Coach: Chuck Shelton, Pittsburg St. '61
Record: 17 Years, 72-114-1
1994 SCHEDULE
UC Davis ■	*Sept. 3
Minnesota	*Sept. 10
Southwest Tex. St. ■	*Sept. 17
Nebraska	Sept. 24
Nevada	Oct. 8
Northern Ill. ■	*Oct. 15
Arkansas St.	*Oct. 22
Utah St. ■	Oct. 29
Oregon St.	Nov. 5
New Mexico St.	*Nov. 12
San Jose St.	Nov. 19

1993 RESULTS (3-8-0)
7	Texas Tech	55
13	Arizona	16
30	Cal St. Sacramento	6
0	Washington St.	12
7	Oregon St.	42
16	Northern Ill.	21
23	New Mexico St.	27
23	Nevada	31
21	Utah St.	24
20	Arkansas St.	6
24	San Jose St.	20
184		**260**

Nickname: Tigers.
Stadium: Amos Alonzo Stagg (1950), 30,000 capacity. Natural turf.
Colors: Orange & Black.
Conference: Big West.
SID: Kevin Messenger, 209-946-2479.
AD: Bob Lee.

PENN STATE
University Park, PA 16802 ....I-A

Coach: Joe Paterno, Brown '50
Record: 28 Years, 257-69-3
1994 SCHEDULE
Minnesota	*Sept. 3
Southern Cal ■	Sept. 10
Iowa ■	Sept. 17
Rutgers ■	Sept. 24
Temple [Franklin Field]	Oct. 1
Michigan	Oct. 15
Ohio St. ■	Oct. 29
Indiana	Nov. 5
Illinois	Nov. 12
Northwestern ■	Nov. 19
Michigan St. ■	Nov. 26

1993 RESULTS (9-2-0)
38	Minnesota	20
21	Southern Cal	20
31	Iowa	0
31	Rutgers	7
70	Maryland	7
13	Michigan	21
6	Ohio St.	24
38	Indiana	31
28	Illinois	14
43	Northwestern	21
38	Michigan St.	37
357		**202**

Citrus Bowl
| 31 | Tennessee | 13 |

Nickname: Nittany Lions.
Stadium: Beaver (1960), 93,967 capacity. Natural turf.

Colors: Blue & White.
Conference: Big Ten Conf.
SID: Jeff Nelson, 814-865-1757.
AD: Tim Curley.

PENNSYLVANIA
Philadelphia, PA 19104 ....I-AA

Coach: Al Bagnoli, Central Conn. St. '74
Record: 12 Years, 103-22-0
1994 SCHEDULE
Lafayette ■	Sept. 17
Dartmouth	Sept. 24
Holy Cross ■	Oct. 8
Columbia ■	Oct. 15
Brown	Oct. 22
Yale ■	Oct. 29
Princeton	Nov. 5
Harvard ■	Nov. 12
Cornell	Nov. 19

1993 RESULTS (10-0-0)
10	Dartmouth	6
42	Bucknell	12
34	Fordham	30
30	Colgate	12
36	Columbia	7
34	Brown	9
48	Yale	7
30	Princeton	14
27	Harvard	20
17	Cornell	14
308		**131**

Nickname: Red & Blue, Quakers.
Stadium: Franklin Field (1895), 60,546 capacity. Artificial turf.
Colors: Red & Blue.
Conference: Ivy League.
SID: B. Hurlbut & G. Stasulli, 215-898-6128.
AD: Steve Bilsky.

PITTSBURG STATE
Pittsburg, KS 66762 II

Coach: Chuck Broyles, Pittsburg St. '70
Record: 4 Years, 47-6-1
1994 SCHEDULE
Fort Hays St. ■	*Sept. 10
Mo. Southern St. ■	*Sept. 17
Mo. Western St. ■	*Sept. 24
Washburn ■	*Oct. 1
Missouri-Rolla	Oct. 8
Southwest Baptist ■	Oct. 15
Central Mo. St.	Oct. 22
Northwest Mo. St.	Oct. 29
Northeast Mo. St. ■	Nov. 5
Emporia St.	Nov. 12

1993 RESULTS (8-2-0)
16	North Dak. St.	35
3	Mo. Southern St.	20
24	Mo. Western St.	0
55	Washburn	18
28	Missouri-Rolla	3
17	Southwest Baptist	0
19	Central Mo. St.	17
38	Northwest Mo. St.	12
15	Northeast Mo. St.	0
45	Emporia St.	14
260		**119**

II Championship
| 14 | North Dak. | 17 |

Nickname: Gorillas.
Stadium: Carnie Smith (1924), 5,600 capacity. Natural turf.
Colors: Crimson & Gold.
Conference: Mid-America Intercoll. Ath. Assoc.
SID: Shawn Ahearn, 316-235-4148.
AD: Bill Samuels.

PITTSBURGH
Pittsburgh, PA 15213 ....I-A

Coach: Johnny Majors, Tennessee '57
Record: 26 Years, 176-113-10
1994 SCHEDULE
Texas ■	Sept. 3
Ohio ■	*Sept. 10
Ohio St.	Sept. 17
Boston College ■	Sept. 24
Louisville	Oct. 1
Syracuse	Oct. 8
West Va. ■	Oct. 15
Virginia Tech	Oct. 22
Temple ■	Oct. 29
Miami (Fla.)	Nov. 12
Rutgers ■	Nov. 19

1993 RESULTS (3-8-0)
14	Southern Miss.	10
21	Virginia Tech	63
28	Ohio St.	63
7	Louisville	29
0	Notre Dame	44
21	Syracuse	24
21	West Va.	42
21	Rutgers	10
7	Miami (Fla.)	35
0	Boston College	33
28	Temple	18
168		**371**

Nickname: Panthers.
Stadium: Pitt (1925), 56,500 capacity. Artificial turf.
Colors: Blue & Gold.
Conference: Big East Conference.
SID: Ron Wahl, 412-648-8240.
AD: L. Oval Jaynes.

PLYMOUTH STATE
Plymouth, NH 03264 III

Coach: Don Brown, Norwich '77
Record: 1 Year, 6-4-0
1994 SCHEDULE
Mass.-Dartmouth	Sept. 10
Norwich ■	Sept. 24
Mass.-Lowell ■	Oct. 1
Western Conn. St.	Oct. 8
Maine Maritime ■	Oct. 15
Bri'water (Mass.) ■	Oct. 22
Coast Guard	Oct. 29
Stony Brook ■	Nov. 5
Worcester Tech ■	Nov. 12

1993 RESULTS (6-3-0)
7	Wilkes	17
44	Norwich	19
23	Mass.-Lowell	20
33	Western Conn. St.	14
13	Maine Maritime	14
12	Bri'water (Mass.)	3
31	Coast Guard	14
26	Stony Brook	9
17	Worcester Tech	35
206		**145**

ECAC Northwest
| 0 | Rensselaer | 13 |

Nickname: Panthers.
Stadium: Currier Memorial Field, 3,000 capacity. Natural turf.
Colors: Green & White.
Conference: Freedom Football Conf.
SID: To be named, 603-535-2477.
AD: Steve Bamford.

POMONA-PITZER
Claremont, CA 91711 III

Coach: To be named
1994 SCHEDULE
Macalester ■	Sept. 10
Colorado Col.	Sept. 17
Redlands ■	Sept. 24
La Verne	Oct. 1
Occidental	*Oct. 8
Whittier ■	*Oct. 22

Cal Lutheran ....Oct. 29
Chapman ....*Nov. 5
Claremont-M-S ■ ....*Nov. 12

1993 RESULTS (1-7-0)

33	Macalester	13
25	Redlands	58
21	Colorado Col.	42
25	Whittier	26
21	Occidental	51
13	Cal Lutheran	26
6	La Verne	24
26	Claremont-M-S	30
170		270

Nickname: Sagehens.
Stadium: Merritt Field, 5,000 capacity. Natural turf.
Colors: Blue, White & Orange.
Conference: Southern Calif. Inter. Ath. Conf.
SID: Kirk Reynolds, 909-621-8429.
AD: Curt Tong.

PORTLAND STATE

Portland, OR 97201 II

Coach: Tim Walsh, UC Riverside '77
Record: 5 Years, 35-17-0

1994 SCHEDULE

Oregon ....Sept. 3
Angelo St. ....*Sept. 10
Minn.-Duluth ■ ....*Sept. 17
Tex. A&M-Kingsville ■ ....*Sept. 24
Eastern Wash. ■ ....*Oct. 1
Western Ky. ....Oct. 8
Neb.-Kearney ■ ....*Oct. 15
Cal St. Sacramento ■ ....*Oct. 22
Idaho St. ....*Oct. 29
Southern Utah ■ ....*Nov. 12

1993 RESULTS (8-2-0)

45	Angelo St.	7
21	Idaho St.	7
22	Tex. A&M-Kingsville	17
32	North Ala.	44
21	Eastern Wash.	38
24	Neb.-Kearney	14
45	American Int'l	7
21	Cal Poly SLO	17
24	Southern Utah	14
45	Central Ark.	31
300		196

II Championship

15	Tex. A&M-Kingsville	50

Nickname: Vikings.
Stadium: Civic (1928), 23,150 capacity. Artificial turf.
Colors: Green & White.
Conference: Division II Independent.
SID: Larry Sellers, 503-725-2525.
AD: Randy Nordlof.

PRAIRIE VIEW A&M

Prairie View, TX 77445 ....I-AA

Coach: Ronald Beard, Eastern Mich. '74
Record: 3 Years, 0-33-0

1994 SCHEDULE

Texas Southern [Houston, Texas] ....*Sept. 3
Ark.-Pine Bluff ....*Sept. 10
Langston ....*Sept. 17
Grambling [Dallas, Tex.] ....*Oct. 1
Southern-B.R. [Houston, Texas] ....Oct. 8
Alcorn St. ....Oct. 15
Alabama St. ■ ....Oct. 22
Mississippi Val. ....Oct. 29
Tarleton St. ■ ....Nov. 5
Jackson St. ....Nov. 12
Ala.-Birmingham ■ ....Nov. 19

1993 RESULTS (0-11-0)

8	Texas Southern	38
8	Langston	45
6	Southern-B.R.	46
0	Grambling	49
6	West Tex. A&M	28
10	Alcorn St.	31

6	Alabama St.	37
6	Mississippi Val.	42
8	Ark.-Pine Bluff	12
7	Jackson St.	37
12	Ala.-Birmingham	58
77		423

Nickname: Panthers.
Stadium: Blackshear (1960), 6,000 capacity. Natural turf.
Colors: Purple & Gold.
Conference: Southwestern.
SID: Jacqueline Davis, 409-857-2114.
AD: Barbara Jacket.

PRESBYTERIAN

Clinton, SC 29325 II

Coach: John Perry, Presbyterian '72
Record: 10 Years, 48-62-0

1994 SCHEDULE

Newport News App. ....Sept. 3
Charleston So. ....Sept. 10
Carson-Newman ....Sept. 17
Lenoir-Rhyne ■ ....Sept. 24
Wofford ....*Oct. 1
Catawba ■ ....Oct. 8
Elon ....Oct. 15
Mars Hill ....Oct. 22
Wingate ■ ....Oct. 29
Gardner-Webb ■ ....Nov. 5
Newberry ■ ....Nov. 12

1993 RESULTS (5-6-0)

17	Fairmont St.	20
16	Charleston So.	17
30	Newberry	13
27	Lenoir-Rhyne	34
13	Wofford	20
38	Catawba	31
17	Elon	31
45	Mars Hill	28
35	Wingate	6
34	Gardner-Webb	30
13	Carson-Newman	28
285		258

Nickname: Blue Hose.
Stadium: Bailey Memorial, 5,000 capacity. Natural turf.
Colors: Garnet & Blue.
Conference: South Atlantic Conf.
SID: Art Chase, 803-833-8252.
AD: Allen Morris.

PRINCETON

Princeton, NJ 08544 ....I-AA

Coach: Steve Tosches, Rhode Island '79
Record: 7 Years, 46-23-1

1994 SCHEDULE

Cornell ....Sept. 17
Colgate ■ ....Sept. 24
Bucknell ■ ....Oct. 1
Brown ■ ....Oct. 8
Fordham ....Oct. 15
Harvard ■ ....Oct. 22
Columbia ■ ....Oct. 29
Pennsylvania ■ ....Nov. 5
Yale ....Nov. 12
Dartmouth ■ ....Nov. 19

1993 RESULTS (8-2-0)

18	Cornell	12
21	Lafayette	7
38	Holy Cross	0
34	Brown	16
31	Lehigh	23
21	Harvard	10
14	Columbia	3
14	Pennsylvania	30
28	Yale	7
22	Dartmouth	28
241		136

Nickname: Tigers.
Stadium: Palmer (1914), 45,725 capacity. Natural turf.

Colors: Orange & Black.
Conference: Ivy League.
SID: Kurt Kehl, 609-258-3568.
AD: Robert Myslik.

PRINCIPIA

Elsah, IL 62028 III

Coach: Michael Barthelmess, Principia '83
Record: 4 Years, 8-24-1

1994 SCHEDULE

Knox ....Sept. 3
Illinois Col. ■ ....Sept. 10
Grinnell ....Sept. 17
Maranatha ■ ....Sept. 24
Earlham ....Oct. 1
Bapt. Christian ■ ....Oct. 8
Blackburn ■ ....Oct. 22
Trinity (Tex.) ■ ....Oct. 29
Crown ....Nov. 5

1993 RESULTS (4-4-0)

17	Illinois Col.	16
34	Grinnell	6
14	N'western (Wis.)	24
22	Blackburn	21
14	Ky. Wesleyan	48
29	Earlham	35
33	Washington (Mo.)	49
22	Concordia (Ill.)	0
185		199

Nickname: Panthers.
Stadium: Clark Field (1937), 1,000 capacity. Natural turf.
Colors: Navy Blue & Gold.
Conference: Division III Independent.
SID: Phil Webster, 618-374-5372.
AD: Seth Johnson.

PURDUE

West Lafayette, IN 47907 ....I-A

Coach: Jim Colletto, UCLA '67
Record: 8 Years, 26-62-1

1994 SCHEDULE

Toledo ■ ....*Sept. 10
Ball St. ■ ....Sept. 17
Notre Dame ....Sept. 24
Illinois ....Oct. 1
Minnesota ■ ....Oct. 8
Wisconsin ■ ....Oct. 15
Ohio St. ....Oct. 22
Iowa ■ ....Oct. 29
Michigan ■ ....Nov. 5
Michigan St. ....Nov. 12
Indiana ■ ....Nov. 19

1993 RESULTS (1-10-0)

7	North Caro. St.	20
28	Western Mich.	13
0	Notre Dame	17
10	Illinois	28
56	Minnesota	59
28	Wisconsin	42
24	Ohio St.	45
17	Iowa	26
10	Michigan	25
24	Michigan St.	24
17	Indiana	24
221		326

Nickname: Boilermakers.
Stadium: Ross-Ade (1924), 67,861 capacity. Natural turf.
Colors: Old Gold & Black.
Conference: Big Ten Conf.
SID: Mark Adams, 317-494-3197.
AD: Morgan Burke.

QUINCY

Quincy, IL 62301 II

Coach: Ron Taylor, Missouri '61
Record: 5 Years, 35-14-2

1994 SCHEDULE

Coe ■	Sept. 3
North Central	*Sept. 10
Lakeland ■	Sept. 17
Greenville	Oct. 1
Concordia (Wis.)	Oct. 8
Concordia (Ill.) ■	Oct. 15
MacMurray ■	Oct. 22
Eureka ■	Oct. 29
Culver-Stockton ■	Nov. 12

1993 RESULTS (9-0-0)

36	Ky. Wesleyan	25
35	Central Meth.	21
37	MacMurray	0
24	Eureka	23
17	Ill. Benedictine	14
49	Greenville	14
65	Lakeland	6
42	Concordia (Wis.)	21
21	Culver-Stockton	20
326		**144**

Nickname: Hawks.
Stadium: QU (1938), 2,500 capacity. Natural turf.
Colors: Brown, White & Gold.
Conference: Division II Independent.
SID: Damiam Becker, 217-228-5277.
AD: Jim Naumovich.

RANDOLPH-MACON
Ashland, VA 23005 III

Coach: Joe Riccio, Miami (Fla.) '76
Record: 3 Years, 15-14-1

1994 SCHEDULE

Catholic	Sept. 17
Wesley ■	Sept. 24
Wash. & Lee	Oct. 1
Western Md. ■	Oct. 8
Emory & Henry ■	Oct. 15
Davidson ■	Oct. 22
Guilford ■	Oct. 29
Bridgewater (Va.) ■	Nov. 5
Hampden-Sydney	Nov. 12

1993 RESULTS (7-2-1)

17	Swarthmore	24
34	Catholic	6
8	Wesley	27
35	Wash. & Lee	14
27	Western Md.	27
20	Emory & Henry	6
21	Davidson	16
16	Guilford	13
45	Bridgewater (Va.)	13
17	Hampden-Sydney	10
240		**156**

Nickname: Yellow Jackets.
Stadium: Day Field (1953), 5,000 capacity. Natural turf.
Colors: Lemon & Black.
Conference: Old Dominion Ath. Conf.
SID: Todd Hilder, 804-798-8372.
AD: Ted Keller.

REDLANDS
Redlands, CA 92373 III

Coach: Mike Maynard, Ill. Wesleyan '80
Record: 6 Years, 38-18-0

1994 SCHEDULE

Azusa Pacific ■	*Sept. 10
Pomona-Pitzer	Sept. 24
Chapman ■	*Oct. 1
Menlo	Oct. 8
Cal Lutheran ■	Oct. 15
La Verne	Oct. 22
Claremont-M-S ■	*Oct. 29
Occidental ■	*Nov. 5
Whittier	*Nov. 12

1993 RESULTS (6-3-0)

17	Menlo	10
58	Pomona-Pitzer	25

27	Cal St. Hayward	23
56	Claremont-M-S	14
21	Whittier	28
48	Azusa Pacific	18
23	Cal Lutheran	17
6	La Verne	36
14	Occidental	21
270		**192**

Nickname: Bulldogs.
Stadium: Ted Runner (1968), 7,000 capacity. Natural turf.
Colors: Maroon & Gray.
Conference: Southern Calif. Inter. Ath. Conf.
SID: Chuck Sadowski, 909-335-4004.
AD: Greg Warzecka.

RENSSELAER
Troy, NY 12180 III

Coach: Joe King, Siena '70
Record: 5 Years, 28-16-2

1994 SCHEDULE

Coast Guard	Sept. 17
Kean ■	Sept. 24
Worcester Tech ■	Oct. 1
Siena	Oct. 8
Union (N.Y.)	*Oct. 15
Hartwick ■	Oct. 22
St. John Fisher ■	Oct. 29
St. Lawrence ■	Nov. 5
Hobart	Nov. 12

1993 RESULTS (7-2-0)

0	St. John Fisher	17
53	Coast Guard	14
31	Worcester Tech	14
56	Siena	6
16	Union (N.Y.)	19
14	Marist	7
16	Rochester	8
34	St. Lawrence	7
20	Hobart	15
240		**107**

ECAC Northwest

13	Plymouth St.	0

Nickname: Engineers.
Stadium: '86 Field (1912), 3,000 capacity. Natural turf.
Colors: Cherry & White.
Conference: Division III Independent.
SID: Kelly Vergin, 518-276-6536.
AD: Bob Ducatte.

RHODE ISLAND
Kingston, RI 02881 ....I-AA

Coach: Floyd Keith, Ohio Northern '70
Record: 5 Years, 26-25-2

1994 SCHEDULE

William & Mary ■	Sept. 3
Maine	Sept. 10
Northeastern	Sept. 17
Brown ■	Sept. 24
Massachusetts	Oct. 1
Boston U. ■	Oct. 8
Connecticut	Oct. 22
New Hampshire ■	Oct. 29
Hofstra	Nov. 5
Delaware St. ■	Nov. 12
Delaware	Nov. 19

1993 RESULTS (3-8-0)

10	Boise St.	31
37	Hofstra	32
11	Delaware	32
15	Northeastern	13
30	Brown	7
14	Massachusetts	36
23	Maine	26
15	Boston U.	48
10	Villanova	14
9	Connecticut	41
33	New Hampshire	51
207		**331**

Nickname: Rams.
Stadium: Meade Stadium (1928), 8,000 capacity. Natural turf.
Colors: Blue & White.
Conference: Yankee.
SID: Chuck Lamendola, 401-792-2409.
AD: Ronald J. Petro.

RHODES
Memphis, TN 38112 III

Coach: Mike Clary, Rhodes '77
Record: 10 Years, 61-27-5

1994 SCHEDULE

Maryville (Tenn.)	Sept. 3
Lambuth	Sept. 10
Carnegie Mellon ■	Sept. 17
Bethel (Tenn.)	Sept. 24
Washington (Mo.) ■	Oct. 1
Trinity (Tex.)	*Oct. 8
Sewanee	Oct. 15
Colorado Col. ■	Oct. 22
Millsaps ■	Nov. 5
Centre ■	Nov. 12

1993 RESULTS (3-7-0)

13	Lambuth	37
12	Davidson	41
22	Ky. Wesleyan	21
10	Colorado Col.	51
10	Washington (Mo.)	28
31	Sewanee	13
12	Maryville (Tenn.)	16
10	Trinity (Tex.)	13
24	Millsaps	28
36	Centre	34
180		**282**

Nickname: Lynx.
Stadium: Fargason, 5,000 capacity. Natural turf.
Colors: Cardinal & Black.
Conference: Southern Coll. Ath. Conf.
SID: Matthew V. Dean, 901-726-3940.
AD: Mike Clary.

RICE
Houston, TX 77005 ....I-A

Coach: Ken Hatfield, Arkansas '65
Record: 15 Years, 113-62-3

1994 SCHEDULE

Tulane ■	*Sept. 10
Kansas St.	Sept. 17
Iowa St.	Sept. 24
Texas Tech ■	Oct. 8
Texas ■	Oct. 15
Texas A&M ■	Oct. 22
Texas Christian	Oct. 29
Southern Methodist ■	Nov. 5
Baylor ■	Nov. 12
Navy	Nov. 19
Houston	*Nov. 26

1993 RESULTS (6-5-0)

7	Ohio St.	34
34	Tulane	0
14	Sam Houston St.	13
49	Iowa St.	21
38	Texas	55
34	Texas Christian	19
16	Texas Tech	45
10	Texas A&M	38
31	Southern Methodist	24
14	Baylor	38
37	Houston	7
284		**294**

Nickname: Owls.
Stadium: Rice (1950), 70,000 capacity. Artificial turf.
Colors: Blue & Gray.
Conference: Southwest Conf.
SID: Bill Cousins, 713-527-4034.
AD: J. R. "Bobby" May.

SCHEDULES/RESULTS

RICHMOND
Richmond, VA 23173 ....I-AA

Coach: Jim Marshall, Tenn.-Martin '69
Record: 5 Years, 16-39-0

1994 SCHEDULE
Va. Military	Sept. 3
Massachusetts ■	Sept. 10
Connecticut....................................	*Sept. 17
Northeastern	Sept. 24
Villanova	Oct. 1
Maine ■	Oct. 8
Delaware ■	Oct. 15
Boston U. ■	Oct. 22
James Madison ■	Oct. 29
New Hampshire ■	Nov. 5
William & Mary ■	Nov. 19

1993 RESULTS (5-6-0)
38	Va. Military	14
20	James Madison	13
20	New Hampshire	31
21	Villanova	7
24	Northeastern	21
17	Maine.......................................	14
14	Boston U.	44
3	Connecticut	21
24	Massachusetts	29
10	Delaware	48
17	William & Mary	31
208		**273**

Nickname: Spiders.
Stadium: Richmond (1929), 22,611 capacity. Natural turf.
Colors: Red & Blue.
Conference: Yankee.
SID: Phil Stanton, 804-289-8320.
AD: Chuck Boone.

RIPON
Ripon, WI 54971 III

Coach: Ron Ernst, Neb. Wesleyan '80
Record: 3 Years, 15-12-0

1994 SCHEDULE
Lakeland ■	*Sept. 10
Upper Iowa	Sept. 17
Monmouth (Ill.)	Sept. 24
Illinois Col. ■	Oct. 1
Beloit...	Oct. 8
Lake Forest ■	Oct. 15
St. Norbert	Oct. 22
Carroll (Wis.) ■	Oct. 29
Lawrence..	Nov. 5

1993 RESULTS (5-4-0)
38	Lakeland	20
33	Northwestern Minn.	7
24	Coe	48
32	Knox	13
40	Beloit	14
42	Lake Forest	18
22	St. Norbert	26
6	Carroll (Wis.)	38
20	Lawrence	28
257		**212**

Nickname: Red Hawks.
Stadium: Ingalls Field (1888), 2,000 capacity. Natural turf.
Colors: Crimson & White.
Conference: Midwest Conf.
SID: Bret Atkins, 414-748-8133.
AD: Bob Gillespie.

ROBERT MORRIS
Coraopolis, PA 15108..............................III

Coach: Joe Walton, Pittsburgh '57
(First year as head coach)

1994 SCHEDULE
Waynesburg.......................................	Sept. 3
Monmouth (N.J.) ■	Sept. 10
Central Conn. St.	Sept. 17
Gannon ■	Sept. 24
Duquesne ■	Oct. 8
Wagner	Oct. 15
St. Francis (Pa.)	Oct. 29
Bethany (W.Va.) ■	Nov. 5
Mercyhurst	Nov. 12

1993 RESULTS
None—1994 is first year of football.

Nickname: Colonials.
Stadium: Moon, 1,000 capacity. Natural turf.
Colors: Blue & White.
Conference: Division III Independent.
SID: Marty Galosi, 412-262-8314.
AD: Robert McBee.

ROCHESTER
Rochester, NY 14627 III

Coach: Rich Parrinello, Rochester '72
Record: 6 Years, 36-21-0

1994 SCHEDULE
Case Reserve ■	Sept. 10
Gannon	Sept. 17
St. Lawrence	Sept. 24
Hartwick	Oct. 1
Hobart	Oct. 8
Chicago	Oct. 15
Washington (Mo.) ■	Oct. 22
Carnegie Mellon	Oct. 29
Union (N.Y.)	Nov. 5

1993 RESULTS (5-4-0)
28	Case Reserve	9
27	Carnegie Mellon	31
14	Washington (Mo.)	6
14	Chicago	7
0	Hobart.....................................	2
32	St. John Fisher	14
43	St. Lawrence	0
8	Rensselaer	16
6	Union (N.Y.)...............................	24
172		**109**

Nickname: Yellowjackets.
Stadium: Fauver (1930), 5,000 capacity. Artificial turf.
Colors: Yellow & Blue.
Conference: University Athletic Assn.
SID: Dennis O'Donnell, 716-275-5955.
AD: Jeff Vennell.

ROSE-HULMAN
Terre Haute, IN 47803 III

Coach: Scott Duncan, Northwestern '80
Record: 8 Years, 47-32-1

1994 SCHEDULE
Washington (Mo.) ■	Sept. 3
Greenville...	Sept. 10
Sewanee	Sept. 17
Anderson ■	Oct. 1
Manchester	Oct. 8
DePauw ■	Oct. 15
Franklin	Oct. 22
Hanover [Indianapolis, Ind.]...............	*Oct. 29
Wabash ■	Nov. 5
Chicago ■	Nov. 12

1993 RESULTS (3-7-0)
7	Washington (Mo.)	28
26	Knox..	7
8	Evansville	38
16	Greenville	13
25	DePauw	23
28	Franklin	32
21	Hanover	37
13	Wabash	17
21	Anderson	28
23	Manchester	32
188		**255**

Nickname: Fightin' Engineers.
Stadium: Phil Brown Field, 2,000 capacity. Natural turf.
Colors: Red & White.
Conference: Indiana Collegiate Ath. Conf.
SID: Dale Long, 812-877-8418.
AD: Scott Duncan.

ROWAN
Glassboro, NJ 08028 III

Coach: K. C. Keeler, Delaware '81
Record: 1 Year, 11-2-0

1994 SCHEDULE
Ferrum...	Sept. 3
Newport News App. ■	Sept. 10
Jersey City St. ■	*Sept. 23
Trenton St.	*Sept. 30
LIU-C.W. Post ■	Oct. 8
Southern Conn. St.	*Oct. 14
Kean	Oct. 29
Wm. Paterson ■	Nov. 5
Montclair St.	Nov. 12

1993 RESULTS (8-1-0)
54	Newport News App.	7
34	LIU-C.W. Post	38
36	Jersey City St.	7
14	Trenton St.	13
71	Salisbury St.	14
41	Southern Conn. St.	20
37	Kean	13
46	Wm. Paterson	22
41	Montclair St.	15
374		**149**

III Championship
29	Buffalo St.	6
37	Wm. Paterson	0
23	Wash. & Jeff.	16
24	Mount Union	34

Nickname: Profs.
Stadium: John Page (1969), 6,000 capacity. Natural turf.
Colors: Brown & Gold.
Conference: New Jersey Ath. Conf.
SID: Sheila Stevenson, 609-863-7080.
AD: Joy Reighn.

RUTGERS
New Brunswick, NJ 08903........................I-A

Coach: Doug Graber, Wayne St. (Mich.) '66
Record: 5 Years, 26-29-0

1994 SCHEDULE
Kent ■	Sept. 3
West Va. ■	Sept. 10
Syracuse	Sept. 17
Penn St.	Sept. 24
Miami (Fla.) ■	Oct. 1
Army ■ [East Rutherford, N.J.]	Oct. 8
Cincinnati ■	Oct. 15
Boston College..................................	Oct. 22
Temple ■	Nov. 5
Virginia Tech	Nov. 12
Pittsburgh...	Nov. 19

1993 RESULTS (4-7-0)
68	Colgate.....................................	6
39	Duke	38
7	Penn St.	31
62	Temple	0
21	Boston College	31
45	Army	38
42	Virginia Tech	49
10	Pittsburgh	21
22	West Va.	58
17	Miami (Fla.)	31
18	Syracuse	31
351		**334**

Nickname: Scarlet Knights.
Stadium: Rutgers (1994), 41,500 capacity. Natural turf.
Colors: Scarlet.
Conference: Big East Conference.
SID: Peter Kowalski, 908-932-4200.
AD: Frederick E. Gruninger.

SACRED HEART
Fairfield, CT 06432..............................II

Coach: Gary Reho, Springfield '76
Record: 3 Years, 7-20-0

1994 SCHEDULE
St. John's (N.Y.) ■ ....Sept. 10
St. Francis (Pa.) ....Sept. 17
Mass.-Lowell ■ ....Sept. 24
Stony Brook ....Oct. 1
Bentley ■ ....Oct. 8
Assumption ....Oct. 15
Stonehill ■ ....Oct. 22
Monmouth (N.J.) ■ ....Oct. 29
Pace ....Nov. 12

1993 RESULTS (2-7-0)
0	Iona	24
14	St. Francis (Pa.)	16
13	Stony Brook	20
8	Mass.-Lowell	18
35	Assumption	6
0	St. John's (N.Y.)	30
0	Bentley	30
26	Stonehill	30
36	Pace	0
132		**174**

Nickname: Pioneers.
Stadium: Campus Field, 2,000 capacity. Artificial turf.
Colors: Scarlet & White.
Conference: Eastern Collegiate.
SID: Don Harrison, 203-371-7970.
AD: Don Cook.

SAGINAW VALLEY STATE
University Center, MI 48710..............................II

Coach: Jerry Kill, Southwestern Kan. '83
(First year as head coach)

1994 SCHEDULE
Northern Mich. ■ ....Sept. 10
Wayne St. (Mich.) ....Sept. 17
Northwood ■ ....Sept. 24
Michigan Tech ....Oct. 1
St. Joseph's (Ind.) ....Oct. 8
Ashland ■ ....Oct. 15
Indianapolis....................................Oct. 22
St. Francis (Ill.) ■ ....Oct. 29
Grand Valley St. ....Nov. 5
Ferris St. ■ ....Nov. 12

1993 RESULTS (4-7-0)
7	Hillsdale	42
32	Wayne St. (Mich.)	31
14	Northern Mich.	28
13	St. Joseph's (Ind.)	3
17	Grand Valley St.	36
6	Ashland	20
14	Indianapolis	0
7	Michigan Tech	21
33	St. Francis (Ill.)	54
23	Ferris St.	34
13	Northwood	7
179		**276**

Nickname: Cardinals.
Stadium: Harvey R. Wickes (1990), 4,028 capacity.
   Natural turf.
Colors: Red, White & Blue.
Conference: Midwest Intercollegiate.
SID: Tom Waske, 517-790-4053.
AD: Bob Becker.

SALISBURY STATE
Salisbury, MD 21801..............................III

Coach: Joe Rotellini, Bethany (W.Va.) '77
Record: 4 Years, 6-31-0

1994 SCHEDULE
Trenton St. ■ ....Sept. 10
Methodist ....Sept. 17
Frostburg St. ....Sept. 24
Chowan ■ ....Oct. 8

Newport News App. ■ ....Oct. 15
Wesley ■ ....Oct. 22
Albany (N.Y.) ....Oct. 29
Catholic....................................Nov. 5
Guilford....................................Nov. 12

1993 RESULTS (2-7-0)
0	Trenton St.	24
33	Methodist	19
21	Frostburg St.	34
14	Rowan	71
21	Newport News App.	35
30	Wesley	45
6	Albany (N.Y.)	7
18	LIU-C.W. Post	58
41	Guilford	3
184		**296**

Nickname: Sea Gulls.
Stadium: Sea Gull (1980), 3,000 capacity. Natural turf.
Colors: Maroon & Gold.
Conference: Division III Independent.
SID: G. Paul Ohanian, 410-543-6016.
AD: Michael Vienna.

SALVE REGINA
Newport, RI 02840..............................III

Coach: Tim Coen, Salve Regina '76
Record: 2 Years, 9-5-0

1994 SCHEDULE
MIT ■ ....Sept. 10
Gallaudet ....Sept. 17
Stonehill ■ ....Sept. 24
Western New Eng. ■ ....Oct. 1
Hartwick ....Oct. 8
Nichols ■ ....Oct. 15
Pace ....Oct. 22
Curry ....Nov. 5
Assumption ....Nov. 12

1993 RESULTS (4-2-0)
56	Gallaudet	0
35	Western New Eng.	6
15	Hartwick	13
18	Nichols	20
0	St. John Fisher	27
14	Curry	7
138		**73**

Nickname: Newporters.
Stadium: Toppa Field, 1,500 capacity. Natural turf.
Colors: Blue, White & Green.
Conference: Division III Independent.
SID: Ed Habershaw, 401-847-6650.
AD: Lynn Sheedy.

SAM HOUSTON STATE
Huntsville, TX 77341..............................I-AA

Coach: Ron Randleman, William Penn '64
Record: 25 Years, 155-105-6

1994 SCHEDULE
Jacksonville St. ....*Sept. 3
Southeast Mo. St. ■ ....*Sept. 10
Angelo St. ■ ....*Sept. 17
Alcorn St. ■ ....*Sept. 24
Texas Southern ■ ....Oct. 1
Stephen F. Austin ....Oct. 8
Northwestern St. ....*Oct. 15
McNeese St. ■ ....Oct. 22
North Texas ....Oct. 29
Nicholls St. ■ ....*Nov. 5
Southwest Tex. St. ■ ....Nov. 19

1993 RESULTS (4-7-0)
40	Southeast Mo. St.	7
13	Rice	14
34	Tex. A&M-Kingsville	20
24	Alcorn St.	31
20	Stephen F. Austin	24
27	Northwestern St.	34
14	McNeese St.	37
24	North Texas	14
19	Nicholls St.	20
10	Northeast La.	48

35	Southwest Tex. St.	10
260		**259**

Nickname: Bearkats.
Stadium: Elliott T. Bowers (1986), 14,885 capacity.
   Artificial turf.
Colors: Orange & White.
Conference: Southland Conf.
SID: Paul Ridings Jr., 409-294-1764.
AD: Ronnie Choate.

SAMFORD
Birmingham, AL 35229..............................I-AA

Coach: Pete Hurt, Mississippi Col. '78
(First year as head coach)

1994 SCHEDULE
Bethel (Tenn.) ■ ....*Sept. 3
Eastern Ky. ....*Sept. 10
Tennessee Tech ....Sept. 17
Nicholls St. ■ ....*Oct. 1
Central Fla. ■ ....Oct. 8
Mississippi Col. ■ ....Oct. 15
Southern Miss. ....Oct. 22
Alcorn St. ■ ....Oct. 29
Morgan St. ....Nov. 5
Austin Peay ■ ....Nov. 12
Troy St. ....Nov. 19

1993 RESULTS (5-6-0)
20	Glenville St.	14
7	Auburn	35
30	Tennessee Tech	3
27	Bethune-Cookman	10
21	Nicholls St.	6
17	Central Fla.	48
14	Mississippi Col.	21
7	Youngstown St.	24
10	Tenn.-Martin	0
14	Southwest Mo. St.	42
24	Troy St.	52
191		**255**

Nickname: Bulldogs.
Stadium: Seibert (1960), 6,700 capacity. Natural turf.
Colors: Crimson & Blue.
Conference: I-AA Independent.
SID: Riley Adair, 205-870-2799.
AD: Steve Allgood.

SAN DIEGO
San Diego, CA 92110..............................I-AA

Coach: Brian Fogarty, Cal St. Los Angeles '75
Record: 11 Years, 56-45-3

1994 SCHEDULE
Menlo ....Sept. 3
St. Mary's (Cal.) ■ ....*Sept. 10
Drake ....Sept. 17
Cal Lutheran ■ ....*Sept. 24
Valparaiso ■ ....*Oct. 1
Wagner ....Oct. 8
Evansville ■ ....Oct. 15
Butler ....Oct. 22
Azusa Pacific ....*Nov. 5
Dayton ■ ....*Nov. 12

1993 RESULTS (6-4-0)
32	Menlo	7
30	La Verne	28
7	Dayton	30
25	Valparaiso	35
27	Cal Lutheran	21
21	Evansville	27
28	Butler	27
24	Azusa Pacific	21
14	Drake	17
44	Wagner	14
252		**227**

Nickname: Toreros.
Stadium: USD Torero (1955), 4,000 capacity. Natural
   turf.
Colors: Columbia Blue, Navy & White.
Conference: Pioneer Football League.

SID: Ted Gosen, 619-260-4745.
AD: Tom Iannacone.

SAN DIEGO STATE

San Diego, CA 92182 ....I-A

Coach: Ted Tollner, Cal Poly SLO '62
Record: 4 Years, 26-20-1

1994 SCHEDULE

Navy ■ ....Sept. 3
California ■ ....*Sept. 10
Minnesota ....*Sept. 17
Colorado St. ....Sept. 24
Air Force ■ ....*Oct. 1
Utah ■ ....*Oct. 8
New Mexico ....*Oct. 15
Wyoming ....Oct. 22
Hawaii ■ ....*Oct. 29
Brigham Young ....*Nov. 10
Fresno St. ■ ....Nov. 26

1993 RESULTS (6-6-0)

34	Cal St. Northridge	17
25	California	45
38	Air Force	31
48	Minnesota	17
13	UCLA	52
45	Hawaii	14
30	Colorado St.	3
20	New Mexico	17
41	Utah	45
44	Brigham Young	45
37	Fresno St.	63
38	Wyoming	43
413		**392**

Nickname: Aztecs.
Stadium: Jack Murphy (1967), 60,049 capacity.
  Natural turf.
Colors: Scarlet & Black.
Conference: Western Ath. Conf.
SID: John Rosenthal, 619-594-5547.
AD: Fred Miller.

SAN FRANCISCO STATE

San Francisco, CA 94132 II

Coach: Dick Mannini, Cal Poly SLO
Record: 9 Years, 51-37-1

1994 SCHEDULE

St. Mary's (Cal.)..................................Sept. 3
Cal St. Sacramento ....*Sept. 10
Western N. Mex. ....*Sept. 24
Menlo ■ ....Oct. 1
Cal Poly SLO ■ ....Oct. 8
Sonoma St. ....Oct. 15
Humboldt St. ■ ....Oct. 22
Cal St. Chico ■ ....Oct. 29
UC Davis ■ ....Nov. 12

1993 RESULTS (3-7-0)

6	St. Mary's (Cal.)	27
10	Cal St. Sacramento	49
32	Menlo	0
32	Western N. Mex.	12
21	Cal Poly SLO	46
24	Humboldt St.	21
21	Cal St. Chico	24
21	Cal St. Hayward	28
14	UC Davis	45
31	Sonoma St.	34
212		**286**

Nickname: Gators.
Stadium: Cox (1948), 6,200 capacity. Natural turf.
Colors: Purple & Gold.
Conference: Northern Cal. Ath. Conf.
SID: Kyle McRae, 415-338-1579.
AD: Elizabeth Alden.

SAN JOSE STATE

San Jose, CA 95192 ....I-A

Coach: John Ralston, California '51
Record: 14 Years, 88-56-4

1994 SCHEDULE

Fresno St. ....*Sept. 3
Baylor ■ ....*Sept. 10
Stanford ....Sept. 17
Southwestern La. ■ ....*Sept. 24
California ....Oct. 1
Washington ....Oct. 8
Nevada ■ ....*Oct. 22
Nevada-Las Vegas ....*Oct. 29
New Mexico St. ■ ....*Nov. 5
Louisiana Tech ....*Nov. 12
Pacific (Cal.) ....Nov. 19

1993 RESULTS (2-9-0)

24	Louisville	31
28	Stanford	31
25	Wyoming	36
13	California	46
17	Washington	52
52	New Mexico St.	13
31	Louisiana Tech	6
13	Southwestern La.	24
45	Nevada	46
14	Nevada-Las Vegas	28
20	Pacific (Cal.)	24
282		**337**

Nickname: Spartans.
Stadium: Spartan (1933), 31,218 capacity. Natural
  turf.
Colors: Gold, White & Blue.
Conference: Big West.
SID: Lawrence Fan, 408-924-1217.
AD: Thomas Brennan.

SAVANNAH STATE

Savannah, GA 31404................................II

Coach: Joseph Crosby, North Caro. A&T '77
Record: 1 Year, 5-3-2

1994 SCHEDULE

Virginia Union ■ ....Sept. 3
Tuskegee ■ ....Sept. 10
Texas Southern ■ ....Sept. 17
Alabama A&M ■ ....Sept. 24
Morehouse ■ ....Oct. 1
Albany St. (Ga.) ....Oct. 8
Morris Brown ....*Oct. 15
Clark Atlanta [Augusta, Ga.]................Oct. 22
Kentucky St. ■ ....Oct. 29
Fort Valley St. ■ ....Nov. 5
Miles..Nov. 12

1993 RESULTS (5-3-2)

3	Ga. Southern	35
32	Tuskegee	16
16	Clark Atlanta	14
16	Alabama A&M	16
33	Morehouse	19
10	Albany St. (Ga.)	28
14	Morris Brown	15
37	Livingstone	18
14	Fort Valley St.	14
57	Miles	6
232		**181**

Nickname: Tigers.
Stadium: Ted Wright (1967), 7,500 capacity. Natural
  turf.
Colors: Blue & Orange.
Conference: Southern Inter. Ath. Conf.
SID: Lee Grant Pearson, 912-356-2446.
AD: Kenneth Taylor.

SEWANEE (UNIVERSITY OF THE SOUTH)

Sewanee, TN 37375..................................III

Coach: Alan Logan, Muskingum '82
(First year as head coach)

1994 SCHEDULE

Rose-Hulman ■ ....Sept. 17
Maryville (Tenn.) ....Sept. 24
Centre ....Oct. 1
Guilford ■ ....Oct. 8

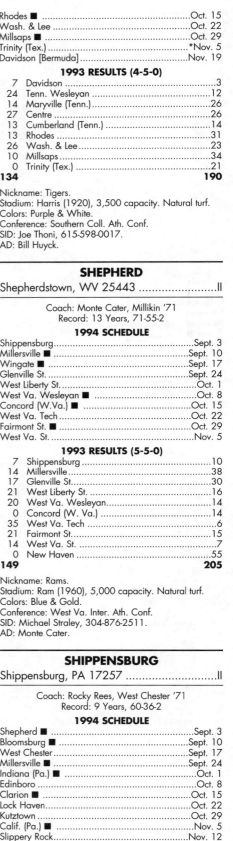

Rhodes ■ ....Oct. 15
Wash. & Lee ....Oct. 22
Millsaps ■ ....Oct. 29
Trinity (Tex.) ....*Nov. 5
Davidson [Bermuda]............................Nov. 19

1993 RESULTS (4-5-0)

7	Davidson	3
24	Tenn. Wesleyan	12
14	Maryville (Tenn.)	26
27	Centre	26
13	Cumberland (Tenn.)	14
13	Rhodes	31
26	Wash. & Lee	23
10	Millsaps	34
0	Trinity (Tex.)	21
134		**190**

Nickname: Tigers.
Stadium: Harris (1920), 3,500 capacity. Natural turf.
Colors: Purple & White.
Conference: Southern Coll. Ath. Conf.
SID: Joe Thoni, 615-598-0017.
AD: Bill Huyck.

SHEPHERD

Shepherdstown, WV 25443 II

Coach: Monte Cater, Millikin '71
Record: 13 Years, 71-55-2

1994 SCHEDULE

Shippensburg..Sept. 3
Millersville ■ ....Sept. 10
Wingate ■ ....Sept. 17
Glenville St. ....Sept. 24
West Liberty St. ....Oct. 1
West Va. Wesleyan ■ ....Oct. 8
Concord (W.Va.) ■ ....Oct. 15
West Va. Tech ....Oct. 22
Fairmont St. ■ ....Oct. 29
West Va. St. ....Nov. 5

1993 RESULTS (5-5-0)

7	Shippensburg	10
14	Millersville	38
17	Glenville St.	30
21	West Liberty St.	16
20	West Va. Wesleyan	14
0	Concord (W. Va.)	14
35	West Va. Tech	6
21	Fairmont St.	15
14	West Va. St.	7
0	New Haven	55
149		**205**

Nickname: Rams.
Stadium: Ram (1960), 5,000 capacity. Natural turf.
Colors: Blue & Gold.
Conference: West Va. Inter. Ath. Conf.
SID: Michael Straley, 304-876-2511.
AD: Monte Cater.

SHIPPENSBURG

Shippensburg, PA 17257 II

Coach: Rocky Rees, West Chester '71
Record: 9 Years, 60-36-2

1994 SCHEDULE

Shepherd ■ ....Sept. 3
Bloomsburg ■ ....Sept. 10
West Chester ....Sept. 17
Millersville ■ ....Sept. 24
Indiana (Pa.) ■ ....Oct. 1
Edinboro ....Oct. 8
Clarion ■ ....Oct. 15
Lock Haven ....Oct. 22
Kutztown ....Oct. 29
Calif. (Pa.) ■ ....Nov. 5
Slippery Rock ....Nov. 12

1993 RESULTS (6-5-0)

10	Shepherd	7
30	Bloomsburg	7
27	Kutztown	10
16	Millersville	14
7	Slippery Rock	36

10	Indiana (Pa.)	45
17	Edinboro	34
32	Clarion	34
31	Lock Haven	20
19	West Chester	24
7	Calif. (Pa.)	6
206		**237**

Nickname: Red Raiders.
Stadium: Grove (1972), 8,200 capacity. Natural turf.
Colors: Red & Blue.
Conference: Pennsylvania Conf.
SID: John R. Alosi, 717-532-9121.
AD: James Pribula.

SIENA

Loudonville, NY 12211 ....I-AA

Coach: Jack DuBois, Oneonta St. '58
Record: 7 Years, 13-49-0

1994 SCHEDULE

St. Peter's	Sept. 17
Canisius	Sept. 24
Iona	Oct. 1
Rensselaer ■	Oct. 8
Bentley ■	Oct. 15
Duquesne ■	Oct. 22
St. John's (N.Y.)	Oct. 29
Georgetown ■	Nov. 5
Marist ■	Nov. 12

1993 RESULTS (0-10-0)

6	Assumption	24
0	St. Peter's	31
6	St. John's (N.Y.)	28
6	Georgetown	35
6	Rensselaer	56
14	Bentley	47
13	Stonehill	28
21	Iona	54
19	Canisius	34
0	Marist	28
91		**365**

Nickname: Saints.
Stadium: Siena Field, 500 capacity. Natural turf.
Colors: Green & Gold.
Conference: Metro Atlantic.
SID: Chris Caporale, 518-783-2528.
AD: John D'Argenio.

SIMPSON

Indianola, IA 50125 III

Coach: Jim Williams, Northern Iowa '60
Record: 7 Years, 49-21-1

1994 SCHEDULE

Drake ■	Sept. 10
Wartburg	Sept. 17
Ill. Wesleyan	Sept. 24
Loras ■	Oct. 1
Upper Iowa	Oct. 8
Luther	Oct. 15
Central (Iowa) ■	Oct. 22
William Penn	Oct. 29
Dubuque [Cedar Falls, Iowa]	Nov. 5
Buena Vista ■	Nov. 12

1993 RESULTS (5-5-0)

9	Drake	35
17	Luther	7
27	Buena Vista	6
6	Wartburg	24
9	Loras	14
14	Central (Iowa)	43
56	Dubuque	7
7	Wis.-La Crosse	46
62	William Penn	8
33	Upper Iowa	7
240		**197**

Nickname: Storm.
Stadium: Simpson/Indianola Field (1990), 5,000 capacity. Natural turf.
Colors: Red & Gold.
Conference: Iowa Inter. Ath. Conf.

SID: To be named, 515-961-1577.
AD: John Sirianni.

SLIPPERY ROCK

Slippery Rock, PA 16057 II

Coach: George Mihalik, Slippery Rock '74
Record: 6 Years, 33-25-4

1994 SCHEDULE

South Dak. St.	Sept. 3
West Va. Wesleyan ■	Sept. 17
Youngstown St.	*Sept. 24
Calif. (Pa.)	Oct. 1
East Stroudsburg	Oct. 8
Indiana (Pa.) ■	Oct. 15
Edinboro	Oct. 22
Clarion ■	Oct. 29
Lock Haven	Nov. 5
Shippensburg ■	Nov. 12

1993 RESULTS (6-4-0)

10	West Va. Wesleyan	6
42	Fairmont St.	6
9	Ashland	30
36	Shippensburg	7
40	Calif. (Pa.)	30
52	Cheyney	0
24	Indiana (Pa.)	45
38	Edinboro	41
25	Clarion	29
39	Lock Haven	23
315		**217**

Nickname: Rockets, The Rock.
Stadium: N. Kerr Thompson (1974), 10,000 capacity. Natural turf.
Colors: Green & White.
Conference: Pennsylvania Conf.
SID: Jeff Michaels, 412-738-2777.
AD: To be named.

SONOMA STATE

Rohnert Park, CA 94928 II

Coach: Frank Scalercio, UC Davis '83
Record: 1 Year, 2-7-0

1994 SCHEDULE

Montana	Sept. 3
Cal St. Chico ■	Sept. 10
St. Mary's (Cal.)	Sept. 17
Cal Poly SLO	*Sept. 24
Southwest Tex. St.	*Oct. 1
Cal St. Northridge ■	Oct. 8
San Fran. St. ■	Oct. 15
UC Davis	*Oct. 22
Humboldt St. ■	Nov. 5
Cal St. Chico	*Nov. 12

1993 RESULTS (2-7-0)

28	Weber St.	40
23	St. Mary's (Cal.)	44
0	Cal St. Northridge	39
13	Cal Poly SLO	53
21	UC Davis	31
19	Cal St. Hayward	20
28	Humboldt St.	17
27	Cal St. Chico	33
34	San Fran. St.	31
193		**308**

Nickname: Cossacks.
Stadium: Cossack, 2,500 capacity. Natural turf.
Colors: Navy Blue & White.
Conference: Northern Cal. Ath. Conf.
SID: Mitch Cox, 707-664-2701.
AD: Ralph Barkey.

SOUTH CAROLINA

Columbia, SC 29208 ....I-A

Coach: Brad Scott, South Fla. '79
(First year as head coach)

1994 SCHEDULE

Georgia ■	*Sept. 3

Arkansas ■		*Sept. 10
Louisiana Tech ■		*Sept. 17
Kentucky ■		*Sept. 24
Louisiana St.		*Oct. 1
East Caro. ■		Oct. 8
Mississippi St. ■		Oct. 15
Vanderbilt		Oct. 22
Tennessee ■		Oct. 29
Florida		Nov. 12
Clemson		Nov. 19

1993 RESULTS (4-7-0)

23	Georgia	21
17	Arkansas	18
34	Louisiana Tech	3
17	Kentucky	21
6	Alabama	17
27	East Caro.	3
0	Mississippi St.	23
22	Vanderbilt	0
3	Tennessee	55
26	Florida	37
13	Clemson	16
188		**214**

Nickname: Fighting Gamecocks.
Stadium: Williams-Brice (1934), 72,400 capacity. Natural turf.
Colors: Garnet & Black.
Conference: Southeastern Conf.
SID: Kerry Tharp, 803-777-5204.
AD: Mike McGee.

SOUTH CAROLINA STATE

Orangeburg, SC 29117 ....I-AA

Coach: Willie E. Jeffries, South Caro. St. '60
Record: 21 Years, 132-92-6

1994 SCHEDULE

Winston-Salem ■	*Sept. 3
Furman	*Sept. 10
Charleston So.	Sept. 17
Tennessee St. [Atlanta, Ga.]	Sept. 24
Jackson St. [Columbia, S.C.]	Oct. 1
Morgan St. ■	Oct. 8
Bethune-Cookman ■	Oct. 15
Florida A&M [Orlando, Fla.]	Oct. 22
Delaware St.	Oct. 29
Howard ■	Nov. 5
North Caro. A&T	Nov. 19

1993 RESULTS (8-3-0)

38	Newberry	0
17	Florida A&M	21
44	Charleston So.	10
10	Southern-B.R.	14
34	Jackson St.	33
49	Morgan St.	13
40	Bethune-Cookman	27
42	N.C. Central	13
38	Delaware St.	15
14	Howard	30
58	North Caro. A&T	52
384		**228**

Heritage Bowl

0	Southern-B.R.	11

Nickname: Bulldogs.
Stadium: Dawson Bulldog (1955), 22,000 capacity. Natural turf.
Colors: Garnet & Blue.
Conference: Mid-Eastern.
SID: Bill Hamilton, 803-536-7060.
AD: James Martin Sr.

SOUTH DAKOTA

Vermillion, SD 57069 II

Coach: Dennis Creehan, Edinboro '71
Record: 9 Years, 51-41-1

1994 SCHEDULE

Wis.-Whitewater ■	Sept. 3
Northern St.	*Sept. 10
Mankato St.	Sept. 17
Nebraska-Omaha ■	Sept. 24

Augustana (S.D.) ....Oct. 1
Northern Colo. ....Oct. 8
North Dak. St. ■ ....Oct. 15
South Dak. St. ....Oct. 22
Morningside ■ ....Oct. 29
North Dak. ■ ....Nov. 5
St. Cloud St. ....Nov. 12

1993 RESULTS (6-5-0)

59	Northern St.	0
42	Bemidji St.	3
31	Mankato St.	44
27	Nebraska-Omaha	10
28	Augustana (S.D.)	14
14	Northern Colo.	24
14	North Dak. St.	35
29	South Dak. St.	7
31	Morningside	20
7	North Dak.	42
10	St. Cloud St.	21
292		**220**

Nickname: Coyotes.
Stadium: DakotaDome (1979), 10,000 capacity.
  Artificial turf.
Colors: Red & White.
Conference: North Central Conf.
SID: Kyle Johnson, 605-677-5927.
AD: Jack Doyle.

SOUTH DAKOTA STATE
Brookings, SD 57007 II

Coach: Mike Daly, Augustana (S.D.) '71
Record: 3 Years, 20-11-0

1994 SCHEDULE

Slippery Rock ■ ....Sept. 3
South Dak. Tech ■ ....Sept. 10
St. Cloud St. ....Sept. 17
Northern Colo. ■ ....Sept. 24
Morningside ■ ....Oct. 1
North Dak. ■ ....Oct. 8
Nebraska-Omaha ■ ....*Oct. 15
South Dak. ■ ....Oct. 22
Augustana (S.D.) ....Oct. 29
Mankato St. ■ ....Nov. 5
North Dak. ....Nov. 12

1993 RESULTS (7-4-0)

48	Montana	52
56	Southwest St.	12
21	St. Cloud St.	30
17	Northern Colo.	38
30	Morningside	20
42	North Dak. St.	30
50	Nebraska-Omaha	10
7	South Dak.	29
35	Augustana (S.D.)	25
60	Mankato St.	42
28	North Dak.	0
394		**288**

Nickname: Jackrabbits.
Stadium: Coughlin-Alumni (1962), 16,000 capacity.
  Natural turf.
Colors: Yellow & Blue.
Conference: North Central Conf.
SID: Ron Lenz, 605-688-4623.
AD: Fred Oien.

SOUTHEAST MISSOURI STATE
Cape Girardeau, MO 63701 ....I-AA

Coach: John Mumford, Pittsburg St. '79
Record: 4 Years, 15-28-0

1994 SCHEDULE

Kentucky St. ■ ....*Sept. 1
Sam Houston St. ....*Sept. 10
Murray St. ■ ....*Sept. 17
Tenn.-Martin ■ ....*Sept. 24
Morehead St. ....Oct. 1
Tennessee Tech ....Oct. 8
Southern Ill. ....Oct. 15
Middle Tenn. St. ■ ....Oct. 22
Austin Peay ■ ....Oct. 29
Eastern Ky. ....Nov. 5

Hawaii ....*Nov. 12
Tennessee St. ....Nov. 19

1993 RESULTS (3-8-0)

10	Southwest Mo. St.	24
7	Sam Houston St.	40
14	Murray St.	17
14	Tenn.-Martin	17
21	Morehead St.	23
3	Tennessee Tech	24
10	Middle Tenn. St.	31
17	Austin Peay	7
21	Eastern Ky.	35
45	Kentucky St.	14
14	Tennessee St.	13
176		**245**

Nickname: Indians.
Stadium: Houck (1930), 10,000 capacity. Natural turf.
Colors: Red & Black.
Conference: Ohio Valley Conf.
SID: Ron Hines, 314-651-2294.
AD: Richard McDuffie.

SOUTHERN CALIFORNIA
Los Angeles, CA 90089 ....I-A

Coach: John Robinson, Oregon '58
Record: 8 Years, 75-19-2

1994 SCHEDULE

Washington ■ ....Sept. 3
Penn St. ....Sept. 10
Baylor ■ ....Sept. 24
Oregon ■ ....Oct. 1
Oregon St. ....Oct. 8
Stanford ....Oct. 15
California ■ ....Oct. 22
Washington St. ....Nov. 5
Arizona ■ ....Nov. 12
UCLA ....Nov. 19
Notre Dame ■ ....*Nov. 26

1993 RESULTS (7-5-0)

9	North Caro.	31
49	Houston	7
20	Penn St.	21
34	Washington St.	3
7	Arizona	38
24	Oregon	13
34	Oregon St.	9
13	Notre Dame	31
42	California	14
45	Stanford	20
22	Washington	17
21	UCLA	27
320		**231**

Freedom Bowl

28	Utah	21

Nickname: Trojans.
Stadium: L.A. Coliseum (1923), 68,000 capacity.
  Natural turf.
Colors: Cardinal & Gold.
Conference: Pacific-10.
SID: Tim Tessalone, 213-740-8480.
AD: Mike Garrett.

SOUTHERN CONNECTICUT STATE
New Haven, CT 06515 II

Coach: Richard Cavanaugh, American Int'l '76
Record: 9 Years, 35-53-1

1994 SCHEDULE

Montclair St. ■ ....Sept. 3
Wilkes ■ ....Sept. 10
Bucknell ....Sept. 17
East Stroudsburg ....Sept. 24
Springfield ....Oct. 8
Rowan ■ ....*Oct. 14
New Haven ....Oct. 22
American Int'l ■ ....Oct. 29
Central Conn. St. ....Nov. 5
Towson St. ■ ....Nov. 12

1993 RESULTS (3-7-1)

7	Cheyney	20

0	North Dak.	52
11	Bowie St.	0
14	East Stroudsburg	14
27	American Int'l	19
29	Springfield	30
20	Rowan	41
14	New Haven	47
14	Central Conn. St.	28
14	Kutztown	24
26	Cortland St.	14
176		**289**

Nickname: Owls.
Stadium: Jess Dow Field (1988), 6,000 capacity.
  Artificial turf.
Colors: Blue & White.
Conference: Division II Independent.
SID: Richard Leddy, 203-397-4223.
AD: Darryl Rogers.

SOUTHERN ILLINOIS
Carbondale, IL 62901 ....I-AA

Coach: Shawn Watson, Southern Ill. '82
(First year as head coach)

1994 SCHEDULE

Tenn.-Martin ■ ....Sept. 3
Mississippi ....*Sept. 10
Arkansas St. ....*Sept. 17
Western Ill. ■ ....Oct. 1
Indiana St. ■ ....Oct. 8
Southeast Mo. St. ■ ....Oct. 15
Western Ky. ....Oct. 22
Illinois St. ....Oct. 29
Southwest Mo. St. ....Nov. 5
Northern Iowa ■ ....Nov. 12
Eastern Ill. ....Nov. 19

1993 RESULTS (2-9-0)

46	Washburn	14
28	Toledo	49
6	Arkansas St.	27
15	Northern Ill.	45
13	Western Ill.	14
24	Western Ky.	51
17	Southwest Mo. St.	22
35	Indiana St.	26
16	Illinois St.	34
17	Northern Iowa	49
35	Eastern Ill.	42
252		**373**

Nickname: Salukis.
Stadium: McAndrew (1975), 17,324 capacity. Artificial
  turf.
Colors: Maroon & White.
Conference: Gateway.
SID: Fred Huff, 618-453-7235.
AD: Jim Hart.

SOUTHERN METHODIST
Dallas, TX 75275 ....I-A

Coach: Tom Rossley, Cincinnati '69
Record: 3 Years, 8-23-2

1994 SCHEDULE

Arkansas ....Sept. 3
UCLA ....Sept. 10
New Mexico ■ ....*Sept. 17
Texas Tech ....Sept. 24
North Caro. ■ ....Oct. 1
Baylor ....Oct. 8
Houston ■ ....Oct. 15
Texas ....Oct. 22
Texas A&M [San Antonio, Texas] ....Oct. 29
Rice ....Nov. 5
Texas Christian ■ ....Nov. 12

1993 RESULTS (2-7-2)

6	Arkansas	10
16	Wisconsin	24
21	Texas Christian	15
10	Missouri	10
12	Baylor	31
28	Houston	28
10	Texas	37

13	Texas A&M	37
24	Rice	31
24	Texas Tech	41
42	Navy	13
206		**277**

Nickname: Mustangs.
Stadium: Ownby (1926), 23,783 capacity. Artificial turf.
Colors: Red & Blue.
Conference: Southwest Conf.
SID: Ed Wisneski, 214-768-2883.
AD: To be named.

SOUTHERN MISSISSIPPI

Hattiesburg, MS 39406 ....I-A

Coach: Jeff Bower, Southern Miss. '76
Record: 3 Years, 13-20-1

1994 SCHEDULE

Tulane		*Sept. 3
Virginia Tech ■		Sept. 10
Memphis ■		Sept. 17
Texas A&M		Sept. 24
East Caro.		Oct. 1
Alabama		Oct. 8
Southwestern La. ■		Oct. 15
Samford ■		Oct. 22
Tulsa ■		Oct. 29
Florida		Nov. 5
Louisiana St.		*Nov. 12

1993 RESULTS (2-8-1)

10	Pittsburgh	14
44	Northeast La.	37
24	Auburn	35
7	Southwestern La.	13
24	Georgia	54
27	Louisville	35
24	East Caro.	16
0	Alabama	40
15	Tulane	17
9	Memphis	20
30	Tulsa	30
214		**311**

Nickname: Golden Eagles.
Stadium: Roberts (1976), 33,000 capacity. Natural turf.
Colors: Black & Gold.
Conference: I-A Independent.
SID: M.R. Napier, 601-266-4503.
AD: Bill McLellan.

SOUTHERN UTAH

Cedar City, UT 84720 ....I-AA

Coach: Jack Bishop, Southern Utah '69
Record: 13 Years, 74-58-4

1994 SCHEDULE

Idaho ■		*Sept. 3
Northern Ariz.		*Sept. 10
Western St. ■		*Sept. 17
Eastern N. Mex. ■		*Sept. 24
UC Davis		*Oct. 1
Weber St. ■		Oct. 15
St. Mary's (Cal.) ■		Oct. 22
Cal St. Sacramento ■		Oct. 29
Cal St. Northridge ■		Nov. 5
Portland St.		*Nov. 12
Cal Poly SLO		Nov. 19

1993 RESULTS (3-7-1)

27	Northern Ariz.	31
16	Angelo St.	18
20	Central Okla.	21
28	UC Davis	27
31	Montana St.	32
6	Cal Poly SLO	38
35	St. Mary's (Cal.)	35
39	Weber St.	43
14	Portland St.	24
20	Cal St. Northridge	17
23	Cal St. Sacramento	17
259		**303**

Nickname: Thunderbirds.

Stadium: Coliseum of Southern Utah (1967), 6,500 capacity. Natural turf.
Colors: Scarlet, Royal Blue & White.
Conference: American West.
SID: Neil Gardner, 801-586-7753.
AD: Jack Bishop.

SOUTHERN-BATON ROUGE

Baton Rouge, LA 70813 ....I-AA

Coach: Pete Richardson, Dayton '68
Record: 6 Years, 52-15-1

1994 SCHEDULE

Northwestern St.		*Sept. 3
Alabama St. ■		*Sept. 10
Mississippi Val. ■		*Sept. 17
Texas Southern ■		*Sept. 24
North Caro. A&T [Indianapolis, Ind.]		*Oct. 1
Prairie View [Houston, Texas]		*Oct. 8
Jackson St. ■		*Oct. 15
Alcorn St.		Oct. 22
Nicholls St. ■		*Oct. 29
Florida A&M ■		*Nov. 5
Grambling [New Orleans, La.]		Nov. 26

1993 RESULTS (10-1-0)

30	Northwestern St.	13
23	Alabama St.	14
46	Prairie View	6
14	South Caro. St.	10
14	Mississippi Val.	13
48	Texas Southern	7
16	Jackson St.	3
47	Alcorn St.	31
14	Nicholls St.	28
26	Florida A&M	4
31	Grambling	13
309		**142**

Heritage Bowl

11	South Caro. St.	0

Nickname: Jaguars.
Stadium: A.W. Mumford (1928), 24,000 capacity. Natural turf.
Colors: Blue & Gold.
Conference: Southwestern.
SID: Rodney Lockett, 504-771-4142.
AD: Marino Casem.

SOUTHWEST BAPTIST

Bolivar, MO 65613 II

Coach: Wayne Haynes, Pittsburg St. '76
Record: 1 Year, 2-9-0

1994 SCHEDULE

Ouachita Bapt.		*Sept. 3
Emporia St. ■		Sept. 17
Mo. Southern St. ■		*Sept. 24
Missouri-Rolla ■		Oct. 1
Central Mo. St. ■		Oct. 8
Pittsburg St.		Oct. 15
Northwest Mo. St. ■		Oct. 22
Northeast Mo. St.		Oct. 29
Mo. Western St.		Nov. 5
Washburn		Nov. 12

1993 RESULTS (2-9-0)

0	Ouachita Bapt.	7
0	Delta St.	20
6	Emporia St.	42
15	Mo. Southern St.	21
8	Missouri-Rolla	44
7	Central Mo. St.	48
0	Pittsburg St.	17
21	Northwest Mo. St.	17
14	Northeast Mo. St.	42
0	Mo. Western St.	56
25	Washburn	20
96		**334**

Nickname: Bearcats.
Stadium: Plaster (1986), 2,200 capacity. Natural turf.
Colors: Purple & White.
Conference: Mid-America Intercoll. Ath. Assoc.
SID: Christopher Johnson, 417-326-1799.

AD: Rex Brown.

SOUTHWEST MISSOURI STATE

Springfield, MO 65804 ....I-AA

Coach: Jesse Branch, Arkansas '64
Record: 8 Years, 51-37-1

1994 SCHEDULE

North Texas ■		*Sept. 10
Northern Iowa ■		*Sept. 17
Western Ill. ■		*Sept. 24
Eastern Ill. ■		*Oct. 1
Illinois St.		*Oct. 8
Liberty ■		Oct. 15
Indiana St.		Oct. 22
Central St. (Ohio) ■		Oct. 29
Southern Ill. ■		Nov. 5
Tulsa		Nov. 12
Jacksonville St.		Nov. 19

1993 RESULTS (7-4-0)

24	Southeast Mo. St.	10
7	Oklahoma St.	45
33	North Texas	34
31	Indiana St.	21
14	Northern Iowa	20
40	Illinois St.	28
24	Jacksonville St.	7
22	Southern Ill.	17
13	Eastern Ill.	35
21	Western Ill.	18
42	Samford	14
271		**249**

Nickname: Bears.
Stadium: Plaster Field (1941), 16,300 capacity. Artificial turf.
Colors: Maroon & White.
Conference: Gateway.
SID: Mark Stillwell, 417-836-5402.
AD: Bill Rowe.

SOUTHWEST STATE

Marshall, MN 56258 II

Coach: Brent Jeffers, Bemidji St. '85
Record: 1 Year, 4-6-0

1994 SCHEDULE

Mo. Western St.		*Sept. 3
Wis.-Stevens Point		*Sept. 10
Northern St.		Sept. 24
Bemidji St. ■		Oct. 1
Minn.-Duluth		Oct. 8
Wayne St. (Neb.)		Oct. 15
Moorhead St. ■		Oct. 22
Winona St.		Oct. 29
Minn.-Morris ■		Nov. 5
Wis.-Stout [Minneapolis, Minn.]		Nov. 12

1993 RESULTS (4-6-0)

20	Mo. Western St.	35
12	South Dak. St.	56
45	Minn.-Morris	6
22	Northern St.	28
35	Bemidji St.	8
28	Minn.-Duluth	31
34	Wayne St. (Neb.)	63
20	Moorhead St.	37
25	Winona St.	18
48	Michigan Tech	42
289		**324**

Nickname: Golden Mustangs.
Stadium: Mattke Field (1971), 5,000 capacity. Natural turf.
Colors: Brown & Gold.
Conference: Northern Sun Inter. Conf.
SID: Bob Otterson, 507-537-7177.
AD: Gary Carney.

SOUTHWEST TEXAS STATE

San Marcos, TX 78666 ....I-AA

Coach: Jim Bob Helduser, Texas Lutheran '79
Record: 2 Years, 7-14-1

1994 SCHEDULE

Tex. A&M-Kingsville ■	*Sept. 1
Northern Iowa ■	*Sept. 8
Pacific (Cal.)	*Sept. 17
Cal St. Northridge ■	*Sept. 24
Sonoma St. ■	*Oct. 1
North Texas ■	*Oct. 8
Nicholls St. ■	*Oct. 22
Northwestern St. ■	Oct. 29
McNeese St.	*Nov. 5
Stephen F. Austin ■	Nov. 12
Sam Houston St.	Nov. 19

1993 RESULTS (2-9-0)

20	Tex. A&M-Kingsville	14
38	Idaho	66
14	Liberty	17
13	Northern Iowa	34
28	North Texas	35
21	Northeast La.	40
37	Nicholls St.	63
22	Northwestern St.	15
10	McNeese St.	27
7	Stephen F. Austin	29
10	Sam Houston St.	35
220		**375**

Nickname: Bobcats.
Stadium: Bobcat (1981), 14,104 capacity. Natural turf.
Colors: Maroon & Gold.
Conference: Southland Conf.
SID: Tony Brubaker, 512-245-2966.
AD: Richard Hannan.

SOUTHWESTERN LOUISIANA
Lafayette, LA 70506 .... I-A

Coach: Nelson Stokley, Louisiana St. '68
Record: 8 Years, 42-45-1

1994 SCHEDULE

Kansas St.	*Sept. 3
Northern Ill. ■	*Sept. 10
Troy St. ■	*Sept. 17
San Jose St. ■	*Sept. 24
Louisiana Tech	Oct. 1
Arkansas St. ■	Oct. 8
Southern Miss.	Oct. 15
Utah St.	*Oct. 22
Nevada-Las Vegas ■	Nov. 5
Texas Tech	Nov. 12
Western Mich. ■	*Nov. 19

1993 RESULTS (8-3-0)

13	Utah St.	34
28	Miami (Ohio)	29
17	Memphis	15
13	Southern Miss.	7
36	Tulane	15
19	Arkansas St.	3
33	Northern Ill.	19
24	San Jose St.	13
14	Florida	61
31	Nevada-Las Vegas	14
21	Louisiana Tech	17
249		**227**

Nickname: Ragin' Cajuns.
Stadium: Cajun Field (1971), 31,000 capacity. Natural turf.
Colors: Vermilion & White.
Conference: Big West.
SID: Dan McDonald, 318-231-6331.
AD: Nelson Schexnayder.

SPRINGFIELD
Springfield, MA 01109 II

Coach: Mike DeLong, Springfield '74
Record: 12 Years, 55-58-2

1994 SCHEDULE

Wagner ■	*Sept. 9
East Stroudsburg ■	Sept. 17
Trenton St.	*Sept. 23
Ithaca	Oct. 1
Southern Conn. St. ■	Oct. 8
Central Conn. St. ■	Oct. 15
Cortland St.	Oct. 22
LIU-C.W. Post ■	Oct. 29
Albany (N.Y.)	*Nov. 5
American Int'l	Nov. 12

1993 RESULTS (3-7-0)

17	American Int'l	24
14	East Stroudsburg	25
3	New Haven	62
6	Ithaca	30
30	Southern Conn. St.	29
11	Central Conn. St.	20
55	Cortland St.	33
6	LIU-C.W. Post	23
21	Trenton St.	18
14	American Int'l	21
177		**285**

Nickname: Chiefs.
Stadium: Benedum Field (1971), 2,500 capacity. Artificial turf.
Colors: Maroon & White.
Conference: Division II Independent.
SID: Ken Cerino, 413-748-3341.
AD: Edward Bilik.

ST. CLOUD STATE
St.Cloud, MN 56301 II

Coach: Noel Martin, Nebraska '63
Record: 11 Years, 65-54-0

1994 SCHEDULE

Minn.-Duluth	Sept. 10
South Dak. St. ■	Sept. 17
North Dak.	Sept. 24
Nebraska-Omaha ■	Oct. 1
Augustana (S.D.)	Oct. 8
Northern Colo. ■	Oct. 15
North Dak. St.	*Oct. 22
Mankato St. [Minneapolis, Minn.]	Oct. 29
Morningside ■	Nov. 5
South Dak. ■	Nov. 12

1993 RESULTS (5-5-0)

47	Minn.-Duluth	0
30	South Dak. St.	21
0	North Dak.	10
18	Nebraska-Omaha	37
28	Augustana (S.D.)	20
16	Northern Colo.	20
24	North Dak. St.	32
32	Mankato St.	49
28	Morningside	14
21	South Dak.	10
244		**213**

Nickname: Huskies.
Stadium: Selke Field (1939), 4,000 capacity. Natural turf.
Colors: Cardinal & Black.
Conference: North Central Conf.
SID: Anne Abicht, 612-255-2141.
AD: Morris Kurtz.

ST. FRANCIS (ILLINOIS)
Joliet, IL 60435 II

Coach: Mike Slovick, Lewis '71
(First year as head coach)

1994 SCHEDULE

Central St. (Ohio)	Sept. 3
Hillsdale ■	*Sept. 10
Grand Valley St.	Sept. 17
Northern Mich.	Sept. 24
Wayne St. (Mich.)	*Oct. 1
Northwood ■	*Oct. 8
Michigan Tech	Oct. 15
St. Joseph's (Ind.) ■	Oct. 22
Saginaw Valley	Oct. 29
Indianapolis	Nov. 5
Ashland ■	Nov. 12

1993 RESULTS (5-6-0)

16	Ashland	13
18	Hillsdale	17
7	Wayne St. (Mich.)	21
16	Northern Mich.	26
29	St. Joseph's (Ind.)	0
18	Ferris St.	26
22	Northwood	31
20	Indianapolis	17
54	Saginaw Valley	33
23	Central St. (Ohio)	43
18	Grand Valley St.	20
241		**247**

Nickname: Fighting Saints.
Stadium: Joliet Memorial (1951), 10,000 capacity. Natural turf.
Colors: Brown & Gold.
Conference: Midwest Intercollegiate.
SID: Dave Laketa, 815-740-3842.
AD: Pat Sullivan.

ST. FRANCIS (PENNSYLVANIA)
Loretto, PA 15940 .... I-AA

Coach: Frank Pergolizzi, Williams '78
Record: 5 Years, 22-26-1

1994 SCHEDULE

Gannon	Sept. 3
Duquesne	*Sept. 10
Sacred Heart ■	Sept. 17
Bethany (W.Va.) ■	Sept. 24
Mercyhurst ■	Oct. 1
Monmouth (N.J.)	Oct. 8
Central Conn. St.	Oct. 22
Robert Morris ■	Oct. 29
Marist	Nov. 5
Wagner ■	Nov. 12

1993 RESULTS (2-7-0)

0	Gannon	20
7	Marist	16
16	Sacred Heart	14
14	St. Peter's	17
29	Central Conn. St.	27
21	Wagner	31
10	Canisius	28
34	Duquesne	35
26	Mercyhurst	39
157		**227**

Nickname: Red Flash.
Stadium: Pine Bowl (1979), 1,500 capacity. Natural turf.
Colors: Red & White.
Conference: I-AA Independent.
SID: Kevin Southard, 814-472-3128.
AD: Frank Pergolizzi.

ST. JOHN FISHER
Rochester, NY 14618 III

Coach: Paul Vosburgh, William Penn '75
Record: 3 Years, 9-19-0

1994 SCHEDULE

Western Conn. St. ■	Sept. 10
Hobart ■	Sept. 17
Hartwick	Sept. 24
Jersey City St.	Oct. 8
Catholic ■	Oct. 15
Brockport St.	Oct. 22
Rensselaer	Oct. 29
Buffalo St. ■	Nov. 5
Thiel	Nov. 12

1993 RESULTS (5-4-0)

17	Rensselaer	0
7	Hobart	14
49	Hartwick	21
21	Catholic	6
19	Merchant Marine	21
14	Rochester	32
20	Brockport St.	23
27	Salve Regina	0
47	Gallaudet	0
221		**117**

Nickname: Cardinals.
Stadium: Cardinal Field, 1,000 capacity. Natural turf.

Colors: Cardinal & Gold.
Conference: Division III Independent.
SID: Michele Morano, 716-385-8309.
AD: Bob Ward.

ST. JOHN'S (MINNESOTA)
Collegeville, MN 56321 III

Coach: John Gagliardi, Colorado Col. '49
Record: 45 Years, 306-96-10

1994 SCHEDULE
Mayville St.	*Sept. 10
Bethel (Minn.) ■	Sept. 17
Augsburg	*Sept. 24
Hamline ■	Oct. 1
St. Thomas (Minn.)	Oct. 8
Gust. Adolphus ■	Oct. 15
Carleton	Oct. 22
St. Olaf ■	Oct. 29
Concordia-M'head [Fargo, N.D.]	*Nov. 5
Macalester [Minneapolis, Minn.]	*Nov. 10

1993 RESULTS (10-0-0)
40	Mayville St.	0
54	Augsburg	7
71	St. Olaf	10
55	Gust. Adolphus	14
69	Hamline	0
77	Bethel (Minn.)	12
69	St. Thomas (Minn.)	13
74	Macalester	6
62	Carleton	14
44	Concordia-M'head	21
615		**97**

III Championship
32	Coe	14
47	Wis.-La Crosse	25
8	Mount Union	56

Nickname: Johnnies.
Stadium: St. John's (1908), 5,000 capacity. Natural turf.
Colors: Red & White.
Conference: Minnesota Inter. Ath. Conf.
SID: Tom Nelson, 612-363-2595.
AD: John Gagliardi.

ST. JOHN'S (NEW YORK)
Jamaica, NY 11439 ....I-AA

Coach: Bob Ricca, LIU-C.W. Post '69
Record: 16 Years, 99-62-1

1994 SCHEDULE
Sacred Heart	Sept. 10
Monmouth (N.J.) ■	Sept. 24
Marist	Oct. 1
Georgetown ■	Oct. 8
Canisius	Oct. 15
St. Peter's	Oct. 22
Siena ■	Oct. 29
Duquesne ■	Nov. 5
Iona	Nov. 12
Pace ■	Nov. 24

1993 RESULTS (8-3-0)
29	St. Peter's	28
9	Wagner	34
28	Siena	6
31	Marist	30
44	Pace	16
18	Canisius	23
30	Sacred Heart	0
37	Duquesne	12
25	Georgetown	24
30	Iona	42
17	Stony Brook	14
298		**229**

Nickname: Red Storm.
Stadium: Redmen Field (1961), 3,000 capacity. Artificial turf.
Colors: Red & White.
Conference: Metro Atlantic.
SID: Frank Racaniello, 718-990-6367.
AD: John Kaiser.

ST. JOSEPH'S (INDIANA)
Rensselaer, IN 47978 II

Coach: Bill Reagan, St. Joseph's (Ind.) '73
Record: 9 Years, 30-57-3

1994 SCHEDULE
Wayne St. (Mich.) ■	Sept. 10
Hillsdale	*Sept. 17
Michigan Tech ■	Sept. 24
Northern Mich.	Oct. 1
Saginaw Valley ■	Oct. 8
Northwood	Oct. 15
St. Francis (Ill.)	Oct. 22
Ashland	Oct. 29
Ferris St.	Nov. 5
Indianapolis ■	Nov. 12

1993 RESULTS (1-8-1)
14	Grand Valley St.	38
13	Northwood	13
14	Indianapolis	33
3	Saginaw Valley	13
0	St. Francis (Ill.)	29
0	Ashland	12
15	Hillsdale	16
38	Wayne St. (Mich.)	24
7	Northern Mich.	24
13	Ferris St.	35
117		**237**

Nickname: Pumas.
Stadium: Alumni Field (1947), 4,000 capacity. Natural turf.
Colors: Cardinal & Purple.
Conference: Midwest Intercollegiate.
SID: Ron Fredrick, 219-866-6141.
AD: Keith Freeman.

ST. LAWRENCE
Canton, NY 13617 III

Coach: Dennis Riccio, Illinois St. '68
Record: 7 Years, 36-33-0

1994 SCHEDULE
Union (N.Y.)	Sept. 10
Albany (N.Y.) ■	Sept. 17
Rochester ■	Sept. 24
Hobart	Oct. 1
Alfred ■	Oct. 8
Ithaca	Oct. 15
Norwich ■	Oct. 29
Rensselaer	Nov. 5
Hartwick	Nov. 12

1993 RESULTS (2-8-0)
35	Hartwick	16
7	Union (N.Y.)	48
9	Albany (N.Y.)	32
7	Hobart	32
7	Alfred	44
7	Ithaca	45
0	Rochester	43
34	Norwich	19
7	Rensselaer	34
14	Brockport St.	23
127		**336**

Nickname: Saints.
Stadium: Weeks Field (1906), 3,000 capacity. Natural turf.
Colors: Scarlet & Brown.
Conference: Division III Independent.
SID: Wally Johnson, 315-379-5588.
AD: John Clark.

ST. MARY'S (CALIFORNIA)
Moraga, CA 94575 ....I-AA

Coach: Mike Rasmussen, Michigan St. '72
Record: 4 Years, 24-15-1

1994 SCHEDULE
San Fran. St.	Sept. 3
San Diego	*Sept. 10
Sonoma St. ■	Sept. 17
UC Davis	*Sept. 24
Humboldt St. ■	Oct. 1
Cal St. Chico	*Oct. 8
Cal St. Northridge ■	Oct. 15
Southern Utah	Oct. 22
Cal Poly SLO	Oct. 29
Cal St. Sacramento ■	Nov. 5

1993 RESULTS (6-3-1)
27	San Fran. St.	6
44	Cal St. Hayward	0
44	Sonoma St.	23
21	Humboldt St.	0
27	Cal St. Chico	15
27	Cal St. Sacramento	14
35	Southern Utah	35
21	UC Davis	28
15	Western N. Mex.	42
37	Cal Poly SLO	58
298		**221**

Nickname: Gaels.
Stadium: St. Mary's (1973), 5,000 capacity. Natural turf.
Colors: Red & Blue.
Conference: I-AA Independent.
SID: Steve Janisch, 510-631-4402.
AD: Rick Mazzuto.

ST. NORBERT
DePere, WI 54115 III

Coach: Greg Quick, Baldwin-Wallace '79
Record: 5 Years, 11-38-0

1994 SCHEDULE
Wis.-Oshkosh	*Sept. 10
Concordia (Wis.) ■	*Sept. 17
Coe	Sept. 24
Knox ■	Oct. 1
Lake Forest	Oct. 8
Lawrence	Oct. 15
Ripon ■	Oct. 22
Beloit ■	Oct. 29
Carroll (Wis.)	Nov. 5

1993 RESULTS (6-3-0)
12	Wis.-Oshkosh	28
17	Concordia (Wis.)	16
40	Cornell College	26
42	Grinnell	21
34	Lake Forest	14
42	Lawrence	36
26	Ripon	22
7	Beloit	14
41	Carroll (Wis.)	57
261		**234**

Nickname: Green Knights.
Stadium: Minahan (1937), 3,079 capacity. Natural turf.
Colors: Green & Gold.
Conference: Midwest Conf.
SID: Len Wagner, 414-337-4077.
AD: Larry Van Alstine.

ST. OLAF
Northfield, MN 55057 III

Coach: Don Canfield, St. Olaf '63
Record: 21 Years, 112-85-1

1994 SCHEDULE
Luther	Sept. 10
Hamline ■	Sept. 17
St. Thomas (Minn.)	Sept. 24
Gust. Adolphus ■	Oct. 1
Carleton	Oct. 8
Macalester	Oct. 15
Concordia-M'head ■	Oct. 22
St. John's (Minn.)	Oct. 29
Bethel (Minn.) ■	Nov. 5
Augsburg [Minneapolis, Minn.]	Nov. 10

1993 RESULTS (4-6-0)
23	Luther	14
12	St. Thomas (Minn.)	35
10	St. John's (Minn.)	71
28	Macalester	15

26	Gust. Adolphus	23
48	Carleton	51
13	Hamline	21
58	Concordia-M'head	34
15	Bethel (Minn.)	17
24	Augsburg	26
257		**307**

Nickname: Oles.
Stadium: Manitou Field (1930), 5,000 capacity. Natural turf.
Colors: Black & Old Gold.
Conference: Minnesota Inter. Ath. Conf.
SID: Nancy Moe, 507-646-3834.
AD: Whitey Aus.

ST. PETER'S
Jersey City, NJ 07306 ....I-AA

Coach: Mark Collins, Central Conn. St. '80
(First year as head coach)
1994 SCHEDULE
Siena ■ ....Sept. 17
Duquesne ■ ....Sept. 24
Central Conn. St. ■ ....Oct. 1
Marist ■ ....Oct. 8
Iona ....Oct. 15
St. John's (N.Y.) ■ ....Oct. 22
Canisius ....Oct. 29
Wagner ....Nov. 5
Georgetown ....Nov. 12

1993 RESULTS (3-6-0)
28	St. John's (N.Y.)	29
31	Siena	0
17	St. Francis (Pa.)	14
14	Georgetown	26
28	Iona	35
20	Canisius	29
13	Assumption	18
7	Central Conn. St.	9
44	Jersey City St.	24
202		**184**

Nickname: Peacocks.
Stadium: JFK Stadium (1990), 4,000 capacity. Artificial turf.
Colors: Blue & White.
Conference: Metro Atlantic.
SID: Tim Camp, 201-915-9101.
AD: William Stein.

ST. THOMAS (MINNESOTA)
St. Paul, MN 55105 III

Coach: Mal Scanlan, St. Thomas (Minn.) '65
Record: 1 Year, 8-2-0
1994 SCHEDULE
Wis.-River Falls ■ ....Sept. 10
Carleton ....Sept. 17
St. Olaf ■ ....Sept. 24
Concordia-M'head ....Oct. 1
St. John's (Minn.) ■ ....Oct. 8
Bethel (Minn.) ....Oct. 15
Augsburg ■ ....Oct. 22
Hamline ....Oct. 29
Macalester ■ ....Nov. 5
Gust. Adolphus [Minneapolis, Minn.].............*Nov. 11

1993 RESULTS (8-2-0)
16	Wis.-River Falls	34
35	St. Olaf	12
44	Macalester	0
31	Carleton	14
44	Concordia-M'head	43
27	Augsburg	6
13	St. John's (Minn.)	69
35	Gust. Adolphus	6
31	Hamline	27
42	Bethel (Minn.)	41
318		**252**

Nickname: Tommies.
Stadium: O'Shaughnessy Field (1940), 5,500 capacity. Natural turf.
Colors: Purple & Gray.

Conference: Minnesota Inter. Ath. Conf.
SID: Greg Capell, 612-962-5903.
AD: Steve Fritz.

STANFORD
Stanford, CA 94305 ....I-A

Coach: Bill Walsh, San Jose St. '59
Record: 4 Years, 31-17-0
1994 SCHEDULE
Northwestern ....Sept. 10
San Jose St. ■ ....Sept. 17
Arizona ■ ....Sept. 24
Notre Dame ....Oct. 1
Arizona St. ....*Oct. 8
Southern Cal ■ ....Oct. 15
Oregon St. ....Oct. 22
UCLA ....Oct. 29
Washington ■ ....Nov. 5
Oregon ■ ....Nov. 12
California ....Nov. 19

1993 RESULTS (4-7-0)
14	Washington	31
31	San Jose St.	28
41	Colorado	37
25	UCLA	28
20	Notre Dame	48
24	Arizona	27
30	Arizona St.	38
31	Oregon St.	27
20	Southern Cal	45
38	Oregon	34
17	California	46
291		**389**

Nickname: Cardinal.
Stadium: Stanford (1921), 85,500 capacity. Natural turf.
Colors: Cardinal & White.
Conference: Pacific-10.
SID: Gary Migdol, 415-723-4418.
AD: Ted Leland.

STEPHEN F. AUSTIN
Nacogdoches, TX 75962 ....I-AA

Coach: John Pearce, East Tex. St. '70
Record: 2 Years, 11-12-0
1994 SCHEDULE
Youngstown St. ....*Sept. 1
Montana St. ■ ....*Sept. 10
Cal St. Sacramento ■ ....*Sept. 17
Idaho ....Sept. 24
Sam Houston St. ■ ....Oct. 8
Nicholls St. ....Oct. 15
Henderson St. ■ ....Oct. 22
McNeese St. ....*Oct. 29
North Texas ■ ....Nov. 5
Southwest Tex. St. ....Nov. 12
Northwestern St. ■ ....Nov. 19

1993 RESULTS (8-3-0)
30	Idaho	38
35	Youngstown St.	15
49	Livingston	28
30	Boise St.	7
24	Sam Houston St.	20
35	Nicholls St.	21
10	Northeast La.	26
20	McNeese St.	21
29	North Texas	27
29	Southwest Tex. St.	7
51	Northwestern St.	20
342		**230**

I-AA Championship
| 20 | Troy St. | 42 |

Nickname: Lumberjacks.
Stadium: Homer Bryce (1973), 14,575 capacity. Artificial turf.
Colors: Purple & White.
Conference: Southland Conf.
SID: Gregg Fort, 409-568-2606.
AD: Steve McCarty.

STONEHILL
North Easton, MA 02356 II

Coach: Connie Driscoll, Mass.-Dartmouth '76
Record: 1 Year, 7-2-0
1994 SCHEDULE
Assumption ■ ....Sept. 10
Nichols ....Sept. 17
Salve Regina ....Sept. 24
MIT ■ ....Oct. 1
Western New Eng. ■ ....Oct. 8
Mass.-Lowell ....Oct. 15
Sacred Heart ....Oct. 22
Curry ■ ....Oct. 29
Monmouth (N.J.) ....Nov. 5
Bentley ■ ....Nov. 12

1993 RESULTS (7-2-0)
36	Nichols	6
29	Assumption	14
0	MIT	7
13	Western New Eng.	7
14	Mass.-Lowell	7
28	Siena	13
48	Curry	13
30	Sacred Heart	26
26	Bentley	27
224		**120**

Nickname: Chieftains.
Stadium: Stonehill (1970), 1,200 capacity. Natural turf.
Colors: Purple & White.
Conference: Eastern Collegiate.
SID: Bob Richards, 508-230-1384.
AD: Ray Pepin.

STONY BROOK
Stony Brook, NY 11794 III

Coach: Sam Kornhauser, Missouri Valley '71
Record: 10 Years, 43-49-2
1994 SCHEDULE
Pace ■ ....Sept. 10
Jersey City St. ■ ....Sept. 17
Coast Guard ....Sept. 24
Sacred Heart ■ ....Oct. 1
Gettysburg ....Oct. 8
Norwich ■ ....Oct. 15
Merchant Marine ■ ....Oct. 22
Western Conn. St. ....Oct. 29
Plymouth St. ....Nov. 5
Mass.-Lowell ■ ....Nov. 12

1993 RESULTS (6-3-1)
20	Pace	2
22	Jersey City St.	22
21	Coast Guard	14
20	Sacred Heart	13
43	Gettysburg	36
21	Merchant Marine	20
33	Western Conn. St.	6
9	Plymouth St.	26
18	Mass.-Lowell	36
14	St. John's (N.Y.)	17
221		**192**

Nickname: Seawolves.
Stadium: Seawolf Field (1978), 2,000 capacity. Natural turf.
Colors: Scarlet & Gray.
Conference: Freedom Football Conf.
SID: Kenneth Alber, 516-632-7205.
AD: Sam Kornhauser.

SUSQUEHANNA
Selinsgrove, PA 17870 III

Coach: Steve Briggs, Springfield '84
Record: 4 Years, 33-10-0
1994 SCHEDULE
Lycoming ....Sept. 10
Wash. & Jeff. ■ ....Sept. 17
King's (Pa.) ....Sept. 24
Albright ■ ....Oct. 1

Lebanon Valley ....Oct. 8
Moravian ....Oct. 15
Delaware Valley ■ ....Oct. 22
Widener ....Oct. 29
Wilkes ■ ....Nov. 5
Juniata ■ ....Nov. 12

1993 RESULTS (6-4-0)

17	Lycoming	14
9	Wash. & Jeff.	13
51	King's (Pa.)	8
31	Albright	7
35	Lebanon Valley	14
6	Moravian	17
43	Delaware Valley	8
12	Widener	10
0	Wilkes	27
13	Juniata	21
217		**139**

Nickname: Crusaders.
Stadium: Amos Alonzo Stagg, 4,600 capacity. Natural turf.
Colors: Orange & Maroon.
Conference: Middle Atlantic.
SID: Mike Ferlazzo, 717-372-4119.
AD: Don Harnum.

SWARTHMORE

Swarthmore, PA 19081 III

Coach: Karl Miran, Middlebury '77
Record: 4 Years, 17-19-1

1994 SCHEDULE

Earlham ....Sept. 10
Johns Hopkins ■ ....Sept. 17
Gettysburg..Sept. 24
Ursinus ■ ....Oct. 1
Muhlenberg ....Oct. 8
Hobart ■ ....Oct. 15
Dickinson..Oct. 22
Frank. & Marsh. ■ ....Oct. 29
Western Md. ....Nov. 5
Wash. & Lee ■ ....Nov. 12

1993 RESULTS (3-6-0)

24	Randolph-Macon	17
17	Johns Hopkins	40
15	Gettysburg	14
16	Ursinus	57
29	Muhlenberg	23
13	Hobart	20
0	Dickinson	37
7	Frank. & Marsh.	18
27	Western Md.	36
148		**262**

Nickname: Garnet.
Stadium: Clothier (1923), 4,000 capacity. Natural turf.
Colors: Garnet & White.
Conference: Centennial Conference.
SID: Rose Smith, 610-328-8206.
AD: Robert Williams.

SYRACUSE

Syracuse, NY 13244 ....I-A

Coach: Paul Pasqualoni, Penn St. '72
Record: 8 Years, 60-25-1

1994 SCHEDULE

Oklahoma ■ ....*Sept. 3
Cincinnati..*Sept. 10
Rutgers ■ ....Sept. 17
East Caro. ....Sept. 24
Virginia Tech ■ ....Oct. 1
Pittsburgh ■ ....Oct. 8
Temple ....*Oct. 22
Miami (Fla.) ■ ....Nov. 5
Boston College ....Nov. 12
Maryland ■ ....Nov. 19
West Va. ■ ....*Nov. 24

1993 RESULTS (6-4-1)

35	Ball St.	12
41	East Caro.	22
21	Texas	21

24	Cincinnati	21
29	Boston College	33
24	Pittsburgh	21
0	Miami (Fla.)	49
0	West Va.	43
52	Temple	3
24	Virginia Tech	45
31	Rutgers	18
281		**288**

Nickname: Orangemen.
Stadium: Carrier Dome (1980), 50,000 capacity. Artificial turf.
Colors: Orange.
Conference: Big East Conference.
SID: Larry Kimball, 315-443-2608.
AD: Jake Crouthamel.

TARLETON STATE

Stephenville, TX 76402 II

Coach: Ronnie Roemisch, Tarleton St. '79
Record: 1 Year, 5-5-0

1994 SCHEDULE

Southeastern Okla. ■ ....*Sept. 3
Midwestern St. ■ ....*Sept. 10
Southern Arkansas ....*Sept. 17
Ouachita Baptist ■ ....*Sept. 24
Angelo St. ....*Oct. 1
Eastern N. Mex. ....Oct. 15
Tex. A&M-Kingsville ....*Oct. 22
West Tex. A&M ■ ....Oct. 29
Prairie View ....Nov. 5
Southwestern (Kan.) ■ ....Nov. 12

1993 RESULTS (5-5-0)

24	East Central (Okla.)	21
16	Northeastern St.	38
34	Southern Arkansas	31
23	Ouachita Baptist	49
7	Southwestern St.	12
10	Valdosta St.	68
44	Hardin-Simmons	37
15	Abilene Christian	57
28	West Tex. A&M	27
31	Lindenwood	14
232		**354**

Nickname: Texans.
Stadium: Memorial (1976), 5,500 capacity. Natural turf.
Colors: Purple & White.
Conference: Lone Star Conference.
SID: Reed Richmond, 817-968-9077.
AD: Lonn Reisman.

TEMPLE

Philadelphia, PA 19122 ....I-A

Coach: Ron Dickerson, Kansas St. '71
Record: 1 Year, 1-10-0

1994 SCHEDULE

Akron..*Sept. 3
East Caro. ■ ....*Sept. 17
Army..Sept. 24
Penn St. [Franklin Field] ....Oct. 1
Virginia Tech ....Oct. 8
Boston College ....Oct. 15
Syracuse ■ ....*Oct. 22
Pittsburgh...Oct. 29
Rutgers ....Nov. 5
West Va. ■ ....Nov. 12
Miami (Fla.) ■ ....Nov. 19

1993 RESULTS (1-10-0)

31	Eastern Mich.	28
0	California	58
14	Boston College	66
0	Rutgers	62
21	Army	56
7	Virginia Tech	55
7	Akron	31
7	Miami (Fla.)	42
3	Syracuse	52
7	West Va.	49

18 Pittsburgh 28
115   **527**

Nickname: Owls.
Stadium: Veterans (1971), 66,592 capacity. Artificial turf.
Colors: Cherry & White.
Conference: Big East Conference.
SID: Al Shrier, 215-204-7445.
AD: R. C. Johnson.

TENNESSEE

Knoxville, TN 37996 ....I-A

Coach: Phillip Fulmer, Tennessee '72
Record: 2 Years, 13-2-1

1994 SCHEDULE

UCLA...Sept. 3
Georgia ....Sept. 10
Florida ■ ....Sept. 17
Mississippi St. ....*Sept. 24
Washington St. ■ ....Oct. 1
Arkansas ■ ....Oct. 8
Alabama ■ ....Oct. 15
South Caro. ■ ....Oct. 29
Memphis ■ ....Nov. 12
Kentucky ■ ....Nov. 19
Vanderbilt..Nov. 26

1993 RESULTS (9-1-1)

50	Louisiana Tech	0
38	Georgia	6
34	Florida	41
42	Louisiana St.	20
52	Duke	19
28	Arkansas	14
17	Alabama	17
55	South Caro.	3
45	Louisville	10
48	Kentucky	0
62	Vanderbilt	14
471		**144**

Citrus Bowl

13	Penn St.	31

Nickname: Volunteers.
Stadium: Neyland (1921), 91,902 capacity. Natural turf.
Colors: Orange & White.
Conference: Southeastern Conf.
SID: Bud Ford, 615-974-1212.
AD: Doug Dickey.

TENNESSEE STATE

Nashville, TN 37203 ....I-AA

Coach: Bill Davis, Johnson Smith '65
Record: 15 Years, 104-58-1

1994 SCHEDULE

Middle Tenn. St. ■ ....*Sept. 3
Jackson St. [Memphis, Tenn.] ....*Sept. 10
Morehead St. ....*Sept. 17
South Caro. St. [Atlanta, Ga.] ....Sept. 24
Florida A&M [Nashville, Tenn.] ....*Oct. 1
Eastern Ky. ....*Oct. 8
Austin Peay ■ ....*Oct. 15
Tenn.-Martin ■ ....*Oct. 22
Tennessee Tech ....Nov. 5
Murray St. ....Nov. 12
Southeast Mo. St. ■ ....Nov. 19

1993 RESULTS (4-7-0)

15	Florida A&M	23
18	Jackson St.	24
28	Grambling	33
34	Middle Tenn. St.	33
13	Eastern Ky.	52
21	Austin Peay	16
14	Tenn.-Martin	21
15	Morehead St.	0
21	Tennessee Tech	24
26	Murray St.	13
13	Southeast Mo. St.	14
218		**253**

Nickname: Tigers.

Stadium: W.J. Hale (1953), 16,000 capacity. Natural turf.
Colors: Blue & White.
Conference: Ohio Valley Conf.
SID: Johnny M. Franks, 615-320-3596.
AD: William A. Thomas.

TENNESSEE TECH
Cookeville, TN 38505 ....I-AA

Coach: Jim Ragland, Tennessee Tech '64
Record: 8 Years, 33-53-0
1994 SCHEDULE
Lock Haven ■ ....*Sept. 1
Marshall.....................................*Sept. 10
Samford ■ ....Sept. 17
Morehead St. ....Sept. 24
Austin Peay ■ ....Oct. 1
Southeast Mo. St. ■ ....Oct. 8
Tenn.-Martin ....*Oct. 15
Eastern Ky. ■ ....Oct. 22
Murray St. ....Oct. 29
Tennessee St. ■ ....Nov. 5
Middle Tenn. St. ....Nov. 19

1993 RESULTS (8-3-0)
18	Illinois St.	23
45	Lock Haven	14
3	Samford	30
21	Morehead St.	3
35	Austin Peay	17
24	Southeast Mo. St.	3
20	Tenn.-Martin	3
7	Eastern Ky.	10
31	Murray St.	16
24	Tennessee St.	21
35	Middle Tenn. St.	14
263		**154**

Nickname: Golden Eagles.
Stadium: Tucker (1966), 16,500 capacity. Artificial turf.
Colors: Purple & Gold.
Conference: Ohio Valley Conf.
SID: Rob Schabert, 615-372-3088.
AD: David Larimore.

TENNESSEE-CHATTANOOGA
Chattanooga, TN 37402 ....I-AA

Coach: Buddy Green, North Caro. St. '76
(First year as head coach)
1994 SCHEDULE
Alabama......................................Sept. 3
Alcorn St. ■ ....*Sept. 10
Gardner-Webb ■ ....*Sept. 17
Ga. Southern ■ ....*Sept. 24
Marshall......................................*Oct. 1
Va. Military ■ ....*Oct. 15
Western Caro. ....Oct. 22
Appalachian St. ■ ....Oct. 29
Citadel ....Nov. 5
East Tenn. St. ■ ....Nov. 12
Furman.......................................Nov. 19

1993 RESULTS (4-7-0)
26	Tenn.-Martin	7
7	Mississippi	40
59	Gardner-Webb	34
0	Ga. Southern	45
33	Marshall	31
29	Va. Military	35
10	Western Caro.	41
14	Appalachian St.	39
27	Citadel	41
0	East Tenn. St.	21
45	Furman	42
250		**376**

Nickname: Moccasins.
Stadium: Chamberlain Field (1947), 10,501 capacity. Natural turf.
Colors: Navy Blue & Gold.
Conference: Southern Conf.
SID: Neil Magnussen, 615-755-4618.
AD: Ed Farrell.

TENNESSEE-MARTIN
Martin, TN 38238 ....I-AA

Coach: Don McLeary, Tennessee '70
Record: 10 Years, 49-59-0
1994 SCHEDULE
Southern Ill. ....Sept. 3
Lane ■ ....*Sept. 17
Southeast Mo. St. ....*Sept. 24
Murray St. ....*Oct. 1
Middle Tenn. St. ....Oct. 8
Tennessee Tech ■ ....*Oct. 15
Tennessee St. ■ ....*Oct. 22
Eastern Ky. ■ ....*Oct. 29
Charleston So. ■ ....Nov. 5
Morehead St. ■ ....Nov. 12
Austin Peay ■ ....Nov. 19

1993 RESULTS (6-5-0)
7	Tenn.-Chatt.	26
20	West Ga.	12
17	Southeast Mo. St.	14
21	Murray St.	28
24	Middle Tenn. St.	14
3	Tennessee Tech	20
21	Tennessee St.	14
0	Eastern Ky.	30
0	Samford	10
17	Morehead St.	0
39	Austin Peay	33
169		**201**

Nickname: Pacers.
Stadium: Pacer (1964), 7,500 capacity. Natural turf.
Colors: Orange, White & Royal Blue.
Conference: Ohio Valley Conf.
SID: Lee Wilmot, 901-587-7630.
AD: Benny Hollis.

TEXAS
Austin, TX 78712 ....I-A

Coach: John Mackovic, Wake Forest '65
Record: 9 Years, 55-46-2
1994 SCHEDULE
Pittsburgh...................................Sept. 3
Louisville ■ ....*Sept. 10
Texas Christian ....*Sept. 24
Colorado ■ ....*Oct. 1
Oklahoma [Dallas, Texas] ....Oct. 8
Rice ....Oct. 15
Southern Methodist ■ ....Oct. 22
Texas Tech ....Oct. 29
Texas A&M ■ ....Nov. 5
Houston ■ ....Nov. 12
Baylor ....Nov. 24

1993 RESULTS (5-5-1)
14	Colorado	36
21	Syracuse	21
10	Louisville	41
55	Rice	38
17	Oklahoma	38
37	Southern Methodist	10
22	Texas Tech	31
34	Houston	16
24	Texas Christian	3
38	Baylor	17
9	Texas A&M	18
281		**269**

Nickname: Longhorns.
Stadium: Memorial (1924), 77,809 capacity. Artificial turf.
Colors: Burnt Orange & White.
Conference: Southwest Conf.
SID: Bill Little, 512-471-7437.
AD: DeLoss Dodds.

TEXAS A&M
College Station, TX 77843 ....I-A

Coach: R. C. Slocum, McNeese St. '67
Record: 5 Years, 49-12-1

1994 SCHEDULE
Louisiana St. ....*Sept. 3
Oklahoma ■ ....Sept. 10
Southern Miss. ■ ....Sept. 24
Texas Tech ■ ....Oct. 1
Houston ....*Oct. 8
Baylor ■ ....Oct. 15
Rice ■ ....Oct. 22
Southern Methodist [San Antonio, Texas] ....Oct. 29
Texas ....Nov. 5
Louisville ....Nov. 12
Texas Christian ■ ....Nov. 19

1993 RESULTS (10-1-0)
24	Louisiana St.	0
14	Oklahoma	44
73	Missouri	0
31	Texas Tech	6
34	Houston	10
34	Baylor	17
38	Rice	10
37	Southern Methodist	13
42	Louisville	7
59	Texas Christian	3
18	Texas	9
404		**119**

Cotton Bowl
21	Notre Dame	24

Nickname: Aggies.
Stadium: Kyle Field (1925), 70,210 capacity. Artificial turf.
Colors: Maroon & White.
Conference: Southwest Conf.
SID: Alan Cannon, 409-845-5725.
AD: Wally Groff.

TEXAS A&M-KINGSVILLE
Kingsville, TX 78363 II

Coach: Ron Harms, Valparaiso '59
Record: 24 Years, 163-94-4
1994 SCHEDULE
Southwest Tex. St. ....*Sept. 1
East Central (Okla.) ■ ....*Sept. 17
Portland St. ....*Sept. 24
Central St. (Ohio) ■ ....*Oct. 1
East Tex. St. ....Oct. 8
Central Okla. ■ ....*Oct. 15
Tarleton St. ■ ....*Oct. 22
Eastern N. Mex. ....Oct. 29
Abilene Christian ■ ....*Nov. 5
Angelo St. ....Nov. 12

1993 RESULTS (5-5-0)
14	Southwest Tex. St.	20
9	Mississippi Col.	13
17	Portland St.	22
20	Sam Houston St.	34
19	Central St. (Ohio)	36
28	East Tex. St.	3
38	Central Okla.	7
54	Eastern N. Mex.	22
26	Abilene Christian	10
16	Angelo St.	7
241		**174**

II Championship
50	Portland St.	15
51	UC Davis	28
25	North Ala.	27

Nickname: Javelinas.
Stadium: Javelina (1950), 15,000 capacity. Natural turf.
Colors: Blue & Gold.
Conference: Lone Star Conf.
SID: Fred Nuesch, 512-595-3908.
AD: Ron Harms.

TEXAS CHRISTIAN
Fort Worth, TX 76129 ....I-A

Coach: Pat Sullivan, Auburn '72
Record: 2 Years, 6-15-1

1994 SCHEDULE

North Caro.		*Sept. 3
New Mexico		*Sept. 10
Kansas ■		*Sept. 17
Texas ■		*Sept. 24
Baylor ■		*Oct. 1
Tulane		*Oct. 15
Houston		*Oct. 22
Rice ■		Oct. 29
Southern Methodist		Nov. 12
Texas A&M		Nov. 19
Texas Tech ■		Nov. 25

1993 RESULTS (4-7-0)

3	Oklahoma	35
35	New Mexico	34
15	Southern Methodist	21
22	Oklahoma St.	27
19	Rice	34
14	Tulane	7
38	Baylor	13
28	Houston	10
21	Texas Tech	49
3	Texas	24
3	Texas A&M	59
201		**313**

Nickname: Horned Frogs.
Stadium: Amon G. Carter (1929), 46,000 capacity. Natural turf.
Colors: Purple & White.
Conference: Southwest Conf.
SID: Glen Stone, 817-921-7969.
AD: Frank Windegger.

TEXAS SOUTHERN

Houston, TX 77004 ....I-AA

Coach: Bill Thomas, Tennessee St. '70
Record: 5 Years, 34-20-3

1994 SCHEDULE

Prairie View ■		*Sept. 3
Savannah St.		Sept. 17
Southern-B.R.		*Sept. 24
Sam Houston St.		Oct. 1
Alcorn St.		*Oct. 8
Alabama St. [Mobile, Ala.]		*Oct. 15
Mississippi Val. ■		Oct. 22
Grambling ■		*Oct. 29
Jackson St.		Nov. 5
East Tex. St. ■		Nov. 12
Lane ■		Nov. 19

1993 RESULTS (2-9-0)

38	Prairie View	8
41	Alcorn St.	44
14	Nevada	63
6	Central St. (Ohio)	55
39	Knoxville	26
7	Southern-B.R.	48
26	Alabama St.	28
26	Grambling	50
12	Jackson St.	38
7	East Tex. St.	16
27	Mississippi Val.	41
243		**417**

Nickname: Tigers.
Stadium: Robertson (1965), 25,000 capacity. Natural turf.
Colors: Maroon & Gray.
Conference: Southwestern.
SID: Andre Smith, 713-527-7270.
AD: To be named.

TEXAS TECH

Lubbock, TX 79409 ....I-A

Coach: Spike Dykes, Stephen F. Austin '59
Record: 7 Years, 41-38-1

1994 SCHEDULE

New Mexico		Sept. 3
Nebraska ■		*Sept. 8
Oklahoma		Sept. 17
Southern Methodist ■		Sept. 24
Texas A&M		Oct. 1

Rice		Oct. 8
Baylor ■		Oct. 22
Texas ■		Oct. 29
Southwestern La. ■		Nov. 12
Houston [San Antonio, Texas]		*Nov. 19
Texas Christian		Nov. 25

1993 RESULTS (6-5-0)

55	Pacific (Cal.)	7
27	Nebraska	50
37	Georgia	52
26	Baylor	28
6	Texas A&M	31
34	North Caro. St.	36
45	Rice	16
31	Texas	22
49	Texas Christian	21
41	Southern Methodist	24
58	Houston	7
409		**294**

John Hancock Bowl

10	Oklahoma	41

Nickname: Red Raiders.
Stadium: Jones (1947), 50,500 capacity. Artificial turf.
Colors: Scarlet & Black.
Conference: Southwest Conf.
SID: Joe Hornaday, 806-742-2770.
AD: Bob Bockrath.

THIEL

Greenville, PA 16125 III

Coach: Charles Giangrosso, Friends '82
Record: 5 Years, 21-26-0

1994 SCHEDULE

Marietta		*Sept. 3
Buffalo ■		Sept. 10
Waynesburg ■		Sept. 24
Bluffton		Oct. 1
Bethany (W.Va.)		Oct. 8
Wash. & Jeff. ■		Oct. 15
Grove City		Oct. 22
Gannon		Oct. 29
Malone ■		Nov. 5
St. John Fisher ■		Nov. 12

1993 RESULTS (2-7-0)

0	Albion	35
37	Oberlin	0
12	Frostburg St.	34
0	Duquesne	28
7	Bethany (W.Va.)	10
7	Wash. & Jeff.	48
20	Grove City	14
7	Waynesburg	32
7	Gannon	16
97		**217**

Nickname: Tomcats.
Stadium: Stewart Field (1954), 5,000 capacity. Natural turf.
Colors: Blue & Gold.
Conference: Presidents Ath. Conf.
SID: Joseph Michalski, 412-589-2187.
AD: John A. Dickason.

THOMAS MORE

Crestview Hills, KY 41017 III

Coach: Vic Clark, Indiana St. '71
Record: 4 Years, 30-10-0

1994 SCHEDULE

Mt. Senario ■		Sept. 3
Evansville		Sept. 10
Wilmington (Ohio)		Sept. 17
Ferrum		Sept. 24
Wesley		Oct. 1
Union (Ky.)		Oct. 8
Wis.-Stevens Point ■		Oct. 15
Defiance		Oct. 29
Mt. St. Joseph		Nov. 5
Bluffton ■		Nov. 12

1993 RESULTS (8-2-0)

8	Ferrum	16

36	Hanover	22
42	Wilmington (Ohio)	24
42	Franklin	0
24	Wesley	8
29	Waynesburg	14
17	Wis.-Stevens Point	20
24	Defiance	18
54	Mt. St. Joseph	21
45	Bluffton	0
321		**143**

Nickname: Saints.
Stadium: Lackland (1945), 6,500 capacity. Natural turf.
Colors: Royal Blue & White.
Conference: Mideast Conf.
SID: Ted Kiep, 606-344-3673.
AD: Vic Clark.

TOLEDO

Toledo, OH 43606 ....I-A

Coach: Gary Pinkel, Kent '75
Record: 3 Years, 17-15-1

1994 SCHEDULE

Indiana St. ■		*Sept. 3
Purdue		*Sept. 10
Liberty ■		*Sept. 17
Ohio		Oct. 1
Ball St. ■		*Oct. 8
Bowling Green ■		*Oct. 15
Akron		*Oct. 22
Kent ■		Oct. 29
Central Mich.		Nov. 5
Western Mich. ■		Nov. 12
Eastern Mich.		Nov. 19

1993 RESULTS (4-7-0)

0	Indiana	27
49	Southern Ill.	28
28	Ohio	10
10	Bowling Green	17
30	Ball St.	31
19	Miami (Ohio)	22
24	Cincinnati	31
45	Kent	27
7	Central Mich.	38
26	Western Mich.	39
14	Eastern Mich.	0
252		**270**

Nickname: Rockets.
Stadium: Glass Bowl (1937), 26,248 capacity. Artificial turf.
Colors: Blue & Gold.
Conference: Mid-American Conf.
SID: Rod Brandt, 419-537-3790.
AD: Allen Bohl.

TOWSON STATE

Towson, MD 21204 ....I-AA

Coach: Gordy Combs, Towson St. '72
Record: 2 Years, 13-7-0

1994 SCHEDULE

Buffalo ■		Sept. 10
Delaware St. [Wilmington, Del.]		Sept. 17
Charleston So.		Sept. 24
Howard		Oct. 1
Bucknell		Oct. 8
American Int'l ■		Oct. 22
Hofstra		Oct. 29
Kutztown ■		Nov. 5
Southern Conn. St.		Nov. 12
Morgan St. ■		Nov. 19

1993 RESULTS (8-2-0)

42	Central Conn. St.	7
31	Delaware St.	14
52	Charleston So.	14
28	Connecticut	27
41	Howard	44
38	Buffalo	14
12	Hofstra	40
32	Delaware	30
49	Bucknell	21

56	Morgan St.	12
381		**223**

Nickname: Tigers.
Stadium: Minnegan Stadium (1978), 5,000 capacity. Natural turf.
Colors: Gold & White.
Conference: I-AA Independent.
SID: Peter Schlehr, 410-830-2232.
AD: Bill Hunter.

TRENTON STATE
Trenton, NJ 08650 III

Coach: Eric Hamilton, Trenton St. '75
Record: 17 Years, 101-63-5

1994 SCHEDULE
Wesley ....Sept. 3
Salisbury St. ....Sept. 10
Wm. Paterson ■ ....*Sept. 16
Springfield ■ ....*Sept. 23
Rowan ■ ....*Sept. 30
Frostburg St. ■ ....Oct. 8
LIU-C.W. Post ....Oct. 15
Jersey City St. ■ ....Oct. 22
Montclair St. ■ ....*Oct. 29
Kean ■ ....Nov. 12

1993 RESULTS (3-6-1)
10	Wesley	10
24	Salisbury St.	0
19	Wm. Paterson	24
13	Rowan	14
16	Frostburg St.	27
18	LIU-C.W. Post	28
30	Jersey City St.	13
0	Montclair St.	16
18	Springfield	21
28	Kean	0
176		**153**

Nickname: Lions.
Stadium: Lions (1984), 5,000 capacity. Artificial turf.
Colors: Blue & Gold.
Conference: New Jersey Ath. Conf.
SID: Ann Bready, 609-771-2517.
AD: Kevin McHugh.

TRINITY (CONNECTICUT)
Hartford, CT 06106 III

Coach: Don Miller, Delaware '55
Record: 27 Years, 148-63-5

1994 SCHEDULE
Colby ■ ....Sept. 24
Williams ....Oct. 1
Hamilton ....Oct. 8
Tufts ■ ....Oct. 15
Bowdoin ....Oct. 22
Middlebury ■ ....Oct. 29
Amherst ■ ....Nov. 5
Wesleyan ....Nov. 12

1993 RESULTS (8-0-0)
71	Bates	0
21	Williams	7
34	Hamilton	0
55	Tufts	30
63	Bowdoin	7
43	Middlebury	14
36	Amherst	19
32	Wesleyan	8
355		**85**

Nickname: Bantams.
Stadium: Jessee Field (1900), 6,500 capacity. Natural turf.
Colors: Blue & Gold.
Conference: NESCAC.
SID: Kevin Kavanagh Jr., 203-297-2137.
AD: Rick Hazleton.

TRINITY (TEXAS)
San Antonio, TX 78212 III

Coach: Steven Mohr, Denison '76
Record: 4 Years, 10-30-0

1994 SCHEDULE
McPherson ■ ....*Sept. 10
Austin ■ ....*Sept. 17
Washington (Mo.) ....*Sept. 24
Claremont-M-S ....Oct. 1
Rhodes ■ ....*Oct. 8
Millsaps ....Oct. 15
Centre ....Oct. 22
Principia ■ ....Oct. 29
Sewanee ■ ....*Nov. 5
Wooster ....Nov. 12

1993 RESULTS (6-4-0)
24	Claremont-M-S	3
0	Austin	31
13	Occidental	17
10	Washington (Mo.)	34
30	Carnegie Mellon	29
6	Colorado Col.	37
44	Centre	10
13	Rhodes	10
21	Sewanee	0
21	Millsaps	19
182		**190**

Nickname: Tigers.
Stadium: E. M. Stevens (1972), 3,500 capacity. Natural turf.
Colors: Maroon & White.
Conference: Southern Coll. Ath. Conf.
SID: Tony Ziner, 210-736-8406.
AD: Bob King.

TROY STATE
Troy, AL 36081 ....I-AA

Coach: Larry Blakeney, Auburn '70
Record: 3 Years, 27-8-1

1994 SCHEDULE
Connecticut ....*Sept. 10
Southwestern La. ....*Sept. 17
Alabama St. ....Sept. 24
Northwestern St. ....*Oct. 1
Nicholls St. ■ ....Oct. 8
Charleston So. ■ ....Oct. 15
Central Fla. ....Oct. 22
Western Ky. ....*Oct. 29
Cincinnati ....Nov. 5
Alcorn St. ....Nov. 12
Samford ....Nov. 19

1993 RESULTS (10-0-1)
37	Ala.-Birmingham	3
21	Northwestern St.	14
24	Nicholls St.	17
38	Alabama St.	3
56	Charleston So.	0
35	Liberty	13
21	Central St. (Ohio)	21
29	Central Fla.	15
31	Western Ky.	24
63	Alcorn St.	21
52	Samford	24
407		**155**

I-AA Championship
42	Stephen F. Austin	20
35	McNeese St.	28
21	Marshall	24

Nickname: Trojans.
Stadium: Memorial (1950), 12,000 capacity. Natural turf.
Colors: Cardinal, Gray & Black.
Conference: I-AA Independent.
SID: Tom Ensey, 205-670-3480.
AD: John D. Williams.

TUFTS
Medford, MA 02155 III

Coach: Bill Samko, Connecticut '73
Record: 7 Years, 35-27-1

1994 SCHEDULE
Hamilton ■ ....Sept. 24
Bates ■ ....Oct. 1
Bowdoin ....Oct. 8
Trinity (Conn.) ....Oct. 15
Williams ■ ....Oct. 22
Amherst ....Oct. 29
Colby ■ ....Nov. 5
Middlebury ....Nov. 12

1993 RESULTS (1-7-0)
6	Wesleyan	27
35	Bates	14
20	Bowdoin	24
30	Trinity (Conn.)	55
14	Williams	35
21	Amherst	23
13	Colby	23
12	Middlebury	14
151		**215**

Nickname: Jumbos.
Stadium: Ellis Oval (1923), 6,000 capacity. Natural turf.
Colors: Brown & Blue.
Conference: NESCAC.
SID: Paul Sweeney, 617-627-3586.
AD: Rocco Carzo.

TULANE
New Orleans, LA 70118 ....I-A

Coach: Buddy Teevens, Dartmouth '79
Record: 9 Years, 44-49-2

1994 SCHEDULE
Southern Miss. ■ ....*Sept. 3
Rice ....*Sept. 10
North Caro. ....Sept. 17
Alabama ....Sept. 24
Memphis ....*Oct. 8
Texas Christian ■ ....*Oct. 15
Mississippi St. ....Oct. 22
Maryland ....Oct. 29
Navy ■ ....*Nov. 5
Mississippi ■ ....*Nov. 12
Louisiana St. ■ ....*Nov. 19

1993 RESULTS (3-9-0)
17	Alabama	31
0	Rice	34
10	William & Mary	0
10	Mississippi St.	36
27	Navy	25
15	Southwestern La.	36
7	Texas Christian	14
14	Boston College	42
17	Southern Miss.	15
10	North Caro.	42
10	Louisiana St.	24
17	Hawaii	56
154		**355**

Nickname: Green Wave.
Stadium: Superdome (1975), 69,065 capacity. Artificial turf.
Colors: Olive Green & Sky Blue.
Conference: I-A Independent.
SID: Lenny Vangilder, 504-865-5506.
AD: Kevin White.

TULSA
Tulsa, OK 74104 ....I-A

Coach: David Rader, Tulsa '80
Record: 6 Years, 31-36-1

1994 SCHEDULE
Missouri ....*Sept. 3
Memphis ■ ....*Sept. 10
Wyoming ....Sept. 17
Oklahoma St. ....*Sept. 24
UTEP ■ ....*Oct. 8
Nevada-Las Vegas ■ ....*Oct. 15
East Caro. ....*Oct. 22
Southern Miss. ....Oct. 29
Southwest Mo. St. ■ ....Nov. 12
Cincinnati ....Nov. 19

Louisville ....Nov. 26

1993 RESULTS (4-6-1)

25	Iowa	26
38	Houston	24
10	Oklahoma St.	16
20	Oklahoma	41
15	Cincinnati	22
23	Memphis	19
38	Middle Tenn. St.	17
52	East Caro.	26
11	Arkansas	24
30	Southern Miss.	30
0	Louisville	28
262		**273**

Nickname: Golden Hurricane.
Stadium: Skelly (1930), 40,385 capacity. Artificial turf.
Colors: Blue & Gold.
Conference: I-A Independent.
SID: Don Tomkalski, 918-631-2395.
AD: Christopher Small.

TUSKEGEE
Tuskegee Institute, AL 36088 II

Coach: Haney Catchings, Alcorn St. '72
Record: 4 Years, 12-26-0

1994 SCHEDULE

Florida A&M	*Sept. 3
Savannah St.	Sept. 10
Morris Brown [Louisville, Ky.]	*Sept. 17
Albany St. (Ga.)	Oct. 1
Morehouse [Columbus, Ga.]	*Oct. 15
Miles ■	Oct. 22
Fort Valley St.	Oct. 29
Clark Atlanta	Nov. 5
Alabama A&M ■	Nov. 12
Alabama St.	Nov. 24

1993 RESULTS (3-8-0)

12	Jackson St.	24
16	Savannah St.	32
51	Morris Brown	22
60	Miles	8
8	Albany St. (Ga.)	27
35	Clark Atlanta	19
23	Morehouse	28
12	Hampton	46
21	Fort Valley St.	40
18	Alabama A&M	36
30	Alabama St.	31
286		**313**

Nickname: Golden Tigers.
Stadium: Alumni Bowl (1925), 10,000 capacity. Natural turf.
Colors: Old Gold & Crimson.
Conference: Southern Inter. Ath. Conf.
SID: Arnold Houston, 205-727-8150.
AD: H. Frank Leftwich.

UC DAVIS
Davis, CA 95616 II

Coach: Bob Biggs, UC Davis '73
Record: 1 Year, 10-2-0

1994 SCHEDULE

Pacific (Cal.)	*Sept. 3
Cal St. Northridge	*Sept. 17
St. Mary's (Cal.) ■	*Sept. 24
Southern Utah ■	*Oct. 1
Cal St. Sacramento ■	*Oct. 8
Cal Poly SLO	*Oct. 15
Sonoma St. ■	*Oct. 22
Humboldt St.	*Oct. 29
Cal St. Chico ■	*Nov. 5
San Fran. St.	Nov. 12

1993 RESULTS (9-1-0)

37	Cal Poly SLO	26
52	Cal St. Hayward	13
27	Southern Utah	28
45	Humboldt St.	9
35	Cal St. Chico	10
31	Sonoma St.	21
48	Cal St. Northridge	38
28	St. Mary's (Cal.)	21
45	San Fran. St.	14
47	Cal St. Sacramento	32
395		**212**

II Championship

37	Fort Hays St.	34
28	Tex. A&M-Kingsville	51

Nickname: Aggies.
Stadium: Toomey Field (1949), 9,400 capacity. Natural turf.
Colors: Blue & Gold.
Conference: Division II Independent.
SID: Doug Dull, 916-752-3505.
AD: Keith Williams.

UCLA
Los Angeles, CA 90024 ....I-A

Coach: Terry Donahue, UCLA '67
Record: 18 Years, 139-63-8

1994 SCHEDULE

Tennessee ■	Sept. 3
Southern Methodist ■	Sept. 10
Nebraska	Sept. 17
Washington St. ■	Sept. 24
Washington	Oct. 1
California	Oct. 8
Oregon St. ■	Oct. 15
Arizona	*Oct. 22
Stanford	Oct. 29
Arizona St.	*Nov. 12
Southern Cal ■	Nov. 19

1993 RESULTS (8-3-0)

25	California	27
13	Nebraska	14
28	Stanford	25
52	San Diego St.	13
68	Brigham Young	14
39	Washington	25
20	Oregon St.	17
37	Arizona	17
40	Washington St.	27
3	Arizona St.	9
27	Southern Cal	21
352		**209**

Rose Bowl

16	Wisconsin	21

Nickname: Bruins.
Stadium: Rose Bowl (1922), 98,101 capacity. Natural turf.
Colors: Blue & Gold.
Conference: Pacific-10.
SID: Marc Dellins, 310-206-6831.
AD: Peter Dalis.

UTEP
El Paso, TX 79968 ....I-A

Coach: Charlie Bailey, Tampa '62
Record: 3 Years, 12-25-1

1994 SCHEDULE

Wyoming	Sept. 3
Eastern Ill. ■	*Sept. 10
New Mexico St. ■	*Sept. 17
Air Force [San Antonio, Texas]	*Sept. 24
Hawaii ■	*Oct. 1
Tulsa	*Oct. 8
Colorado St.	Oct. 15
Brigham Young ■	*Oct. 22
Utah	Oct. 29
Fresno St. ■	Nov. 12
New Mexico	Nov. 19

1993 RESULTS (1-11-0)

6	Arizona	24
41	Nevada-Las Vegas	24
14	New Mexico St.	31
0	Hawaii	52
39	North Caro.	45
26	Wyoming	33
29	Utah	45
10	Air Force	31
10	Fresno St.	30
0	Colorado St.	52
29	New Mexico	35
16	Brigham Young	47
220		**449**

Nickname: Miners.
Stadium: Sun Bowl (1963), 51,270 capacity. Artificial turf.
Colors: Orange, White & Blue.
Conference: Western Ath. Conf.
SID: Eddie Mullens, 915-747-5330.
AD: John Thompson.

UNION (NEW YORK)
Schenectady, NY 12308 III

Coach: John Audino, Notre Dame '75
Record: 4 Years, 24-17-0

1994 SCHEDULE

St. Lawrence ■	Sept. 10
Worcester Tech	Sept. 17
Hobart ■	Sept. 24
Dickinson	Oct. 1
Albany (N.Y.)	*Oct. 8
Rensselaer ■	*Oct. 15
Coast Guard ■	Oct. 22
Muhlenberg	Oct. 29
Rochester	Nov. 5

1993 RESULTS (9-0-0)

48	St. Lawrence	7
44	Worcester Tech	0
26	Hobart	3
23	Dickinson	17
21	Albany (N.Y.)	14
19	Rensselaer	16
52	Coast Guard	10
30	Alfred	14
24	Rochester	6
287		**87**

III Championship

7	Wm. Paterson	17

Nickname: Dutchmen.
Stadium: Frank Bailey Field (1981), 4,000 capacity. Artificial turf.
Colors: Garnet.
Conference: Division III Independent.
SID: George Cuttita, 518-388-6170.
AD: Richard Sakala.

UPPER IOWA
Fayette, IA 52142 III

Coach: Paul Rudolph, Minot St. '88
Record: 3 Years, 11-19-0

1994 SCHEDULE

Central Mo. St.	*Sept. 1
Ripon ■	Sept. 17
Luther ■	Sept. 24
William Penn	Oct. 1
Simpson ■	Oct. 8
Dubuque	Oct. 15
Buena Vista ■	Oct. 22
Wartburg	Oct. 29
Loras ■	Nov. 5
Central (Iowa)	Nov. 12

1993 RESULTS (3-7-0)

8	Wis.-Whitewater	38
12	Wartburg	20
20	Luther	9
46	William Penn	7
41	Dubuque	7
14	Buena Vista	21
28	Mid-America Nazarene	35
0	Central (Iowa)	30
3	Loras	28
7	Simpson	33
179		**228**

Nickname: Peacocks.
Stadium: Upper Iowa (1993), 3,500 capacity. Natural turf.

Colors: Blue & White.
Conference: Iowa Inter. Ath. Conf.
SID: Julie Lentz, 319-425-5307.
AD: Mike McCready.

UPSALA
East Orange, NJ 07019 III

Coach: Mike Walsh, Central Conn. St. '77
Record: 5 Years, 15-33-1

1994 SCHEDULE
Widener ■ ....Sept. 10
Kean ....Sept. 17
Wilkes ....Sept. 24
Jersey City St. ....Oct. 1
King's (Pa.) ....Oct. 8
Lycoming ■ ....Oct. 15
Monmouth (N.J.) ....Oct. 22
Delaware Valley ....Oct. 29
Lebanon Valley ■ ....Nov. 5
FDU-Madison ....Nov. 12

1993 RESULTS (1-8-0)
24	Widener	27
18	Kean	21
14	Wilkes	23
22	Jersey City St.	28
55	King's (Pa.)	13
12	Lycoming	20
20	Delaware Valley	24
28	Lebanon Valley	31
24	FDU-Madison	41
217		228

Nickname: Vikings.
Stadium: Walker Field (1949), 3,500 capacity. Natural turf.
Colors: Blue & Gray.
Conference: Middle Atlantic.
SID: Rich Carroll, 201-266-7226.
AD: Mike Walsh.

URSINUS
Collegeville, PA 19426...........................III

Coach: Steve Gilbert, West Chester '79
Record: 6 Years, 26-32-0

1994 SCHEDULE
Worcester Tech ■ ....Sept. 10
Frank. & Marsh. ....Sept. 17
Western Md. ■ ....Sept. 24
Swarthmore ....Oct. 1
Johns Hopkins ■ ....Oct. 8
Gettysburg...Oct. 15
FDU-Madison ....Oct. 22
Catholic ....Oct. 29
Muhlenberg ■ ....Nov. 5
Dickinson ■ ....Nov. 12

1993 RESULTS (5-4-0)
21	Worcester Tech	14
9	Frank. & Marsh.	20
42	Western Md.	33
57	Swarthmore	16
34	Johns Hopkins	42
31	Gettysburg	28
25	FDU-Madison	30
31	Muhlenberg	34
31	Dickinson	18
281		235

Nickname: Bears.
Stadium: Patterson Field (1923), 2,500 capacity. Natural turf.
Colors: Old Gold, Red & Black.
Conference: Centennial Conference.
SID: David M. Sherman, 215-489-4111.
AD: Robert Davidson.

UTAH
Salt Lake City, UT 84112 ....I-A

Coach: Ron McBride, San Jose St. '63
Record: 4 Years, 24-24-0

1994 SCHEDULE
Utah St. ....*Sept. 3
Idaho St. ■ ....*Sept. 10
Oregon ....Sept. 17
Wyoming ■ ....*Sept. 24
San Diego St. ....*Oct. 8
Hawaii ■ ....Oct. 15
Colorado St. ....Oct. 22
UTEP ■ ....Oct. 29
New Mexico ....Nov. 5
Air Force ....Nov. 12
Brigham Young ■ ....Nov. 19

1993 RESULTS (7-5-0)
0	Arizona St.	38
31	Utah St.	29
41	Kansas	16
12	Wyoming	28
17	Idaho	28
35	New Mexico	42
45	UTEP	29
38	Colorado St.	21
45	San Diego St.	41
30	Hawaii	41
41	Air Force	24
34	Brigham Young	31
369		368

Freedom Bowl
| 21 | Southern Cal | 28 |

Nickname: Utes.
Stadium: Robert Rice (1927), 32,500 capacity. Artificial turf.
Colors: Crimson & White.
Conference: Western Ath. Conf.
SID: Liz Abel, 801-581-3510.
AD: Chris Hill.

UTAH STATE
Logan, UT 84322 ....I-A

Coach: Charlie Weatherbie, Oklahoma St. '77
Record: 2 Years, 12-11-0

1994 SCHEDULE
Utah ■ ....*Sept. 3
Colorado St. ....Sept. 10
Ohio ....Sept. 17
Nevada-Las Vegas ■ ....*Sept. 24
Brigham Young ....*Sept. 30
Louisiana Tech ....*Oct. 15
Southwestern La. ■ ....*Oct. 22
Pacific (Cal.) ....Oct. 29
Eastern Wash. ■ ....Nov. 5
Nevada ....Nov. 12
New Mexico St. ■ ....Nov. 19

1993 RESULTS (6-5-0)
34	Southwestern La.	13
29	Utah	31
24	Baylor	28
14	Fresno St.	30
17	Louisiana St.	38
44	Nevada	48
33	Nevada-Las Vegas	26
58	Brigham Young	56
24	Pacific (Cal.)	21
24	Louisiana Tech	13
20	New Mexico St.	17
321		321

Las Vegas Bowl
| 42 | Ball St. | 33 |

Nickname: Aggies.
Stadium: E.L. Romney (1968), 30,257 capacity. Natural turf.
Colors: Navy Blue & White.
Conference: Big West.
SID: John Lewandowski, 801-797-1361.
AD: Chuck Bell.

VALDOSTA STATE
Valdosta, GA 31698...................................II

Coach: Hal Mumme, Tarleton St. '75
Record: 5 Years, 37-18-1

1994 SCHEDULE
Knoxville ■ ....*Sept. 3
Central Fla. ....Sept. 10
Fort Valley St. ■ ....*Sept. 17
Clark Atlanta ■ ....*Sept. 24
Livingston ....Oct. 1
New Haven ■ ....Oct. 8
West Ga. ■ ....Oct. 15
Mississippi Col. ....*Oct. 22
Delta St. ■ ....*Oct. 29
North Ala. ....*Nov. 5
Henderson St. ■ ....*Nov. 12

1993 RESULTS (8-3-0)
65	Mt. Senario	0
30	Central Fla.	35
49	Fort Valley St.	24
41	Clark Atlanta	12
42	Livingston	13
68	Tarleton St.	10
16	West Ga.	23
42	Mississippi Col.	21
33	Delta St.	8
21	North Ala.	31
42	Henderson St.	20
449		197

Nickname: Blazers.
Stadium: Cleveland Field (1922), 11,798 capacity. Natural turf.
Colors: Red & Black.
Conference: Gulf South Conf.
SID: Steve Roberts, 912-333-5890.
AD: Herb Reinhard.

VALPARAISO
Valparaiso, IN 46383 ....I-AA

Coach: Tom Horne, Wis.-La Crosse '76
Record: 8 Years, 27-53-2

1994 SCHEDULE
St. Ambrose ■ ....Sept. 3
Millikin ■ ....Sept. 17
Kalamazoo ■ ....Sept. 24
San Diego ....*Oct. 1
Butler ■ ....Oct. 8
Drake ....Oct. 15
Evansville ....Oct. 22
Dayton ■ ....Oct. 29
Aurora ■ ....Nov. 5
Ky. Wesleyan ....Nov. 12

1993 RESULTS (5-5-0)
37	St. Ambrose	30
43	St. Xavier (Ill.)	6
36	Millikin	34
35	San Diego	25
0	Butler	10
12	Drake	31
28	Evansville	34
10	Dayton	38
25	Michigan Tech	20
13	Northern Ariz.	55
239		283

Nickname: Crusaders.
Stadium: Brown Field (1947), 5,000 capacity. Natural turf.
Colors: Brown & Gold.
Conference: Pioneer Football League.
SID: Bill Rogers, 219-464-5232.
AD: William Steinbrecher.

VANDERBILT
Nashville, TN 37212 ....I-A

Coach: Gerry DiNardo, Notre Dame '75
Record: 3 Years, 13-20-0

1994 SCHEDULE
Wake Forest ■ ....*Sept. 3
Alabama ....Sept. 10
Mississippi ■ ....*Sept. 17
Arkansas ....Oct. 1
Cincinnati ....*Oct. 8
Georgia ....Oct. 15

South Caro. ■ ....Oct. 22
Northern Ill. ■ ....Oct. 29
Kentucky.....................................Nov. 5
Florida ■ ....Nov. 19
Tennessee ■ ....Nov. 26

1993 RESULTS (4-7-0)
27	Wake Forest	12
6	Alabama	17
7	Mississippi	49
10	Auburn	14
17	Cincinnati	7
3	Georgia	41
0	South Caro.	22
12	Kentucky	7
41	Navy	7
0	Florida	52
14	Tennessee	62
137		**290**

Nickname: Commodores.
Stadium: Vanderbilt Stadium (1981), 41,000 capacity.
  Artificial turf.
Colors: Black & Gold.
Conference: Southeastern Conf.
SID: To be named, 615-322-4121.
AD: Paul Hoolahan.

VILLANOVA
Villanova, PA 19085 ....I-AA

Coach: Andy Talley, Southern Conn. St. '67
Record: 14 Years, 87-50-2

1994 SCHEDULE
Fordham......................................Sept. 3
Liberty ■ ....*Sept. 9
Delaware ■ ....Sept. 17
Boston U. ■ ....Sept. 24
Richmond ■ ....Oct. 1
Connecticut..................................Oct. 8
James Madison...............................Oct. 15
Northeastern................................Oct. 22
William & Mary ■ ....Oct. 29
West Chester ■ ....Nov. 5
New Hampshire...............................Nov. 12

1993 RESULTS (3-8-0)
3	Northeastern	27
25	Fordham	5
7	Richmond	21
15	Boston U.	30
17	Connecticut	14
7	Delaware	19
17	William & Mary	51
14	Rhode Island	10
14	New Hampshire	45
3	James Madison	42
13	Liberty	27
135		**291**

Nickname: Wildcats.
Stadium: Villanova (1927), 12,000 capacity. Artificial
  turf.
Colors: Blue & White.
Conference: Yankee.
SID: James H. DeLorenzo, 610-519-4120.
AD: Gene DeFilippo.

VIRGINIA
Charlottesville, VA 22903.........................I-A

Coach: George Welsh, Navy '56
Record: 21 Years, 135-102-4

1994 SCHEDULE
Florida St....................................Sept. 3
Navy ■ ....*Sept. 10
Clemson ■ ....Sept. 17
William & Mary ■ ....Oct. 1
Wake Forest.................................*Oct. 8
Georgia Tech ....Oct. 15
North Caro. ■ ....Oct. 22
Duke...Nov. 5
Maryland ■ ....Nov. 12
Virginia Tech ....Nov. 19
North Caro. St. ■ ....Nov. 25

1993 RESULTS (7-4-0)
43	Maryland	29
38	Navy	0
35	Georgia Tech	14
35	Duke	0
41	Ohio	7
14	Florida St.	40
17	North Caro.	10
29	North Caro. St.	34
21	Wake Forest	9
14	Clemson	23
17	Virginia Tech	20
304		**186**

Carquest Bowl
13	Boston College	31

Nickname: Cavaliers.
Stadium: Scott (1931), 40,000 capacity. Artificial turf.
Colors: Orange & Blue.
Conference: Atlantic Coast Conf.
SID: Rich Murray, 804-982-5500.
AD: Jim Copeland.

VIRGINIA MILITARY
Lexington, VA 24450............................I-AA

Coach: Bill Stewart, Fairmont St. '75
(First year as head coach)

1994 SCHEDULE
Richmond ■ ....Sept. 3
East Tenn. St. ....*Sept. 17
William & Mary..............................Sept. 24
Ga. Southern ....*Oct. 1
Marshall.....................................Oct. 8
Tenn.-Chatt. ....*Oct. 15
Furman.......................................Oct. 22
Western Caro. ■ ....Oct. 29
James Madison ....Nov. 5
Citadel ■ ....Nov. 12
Appalachian St. ....Nov. 19

1993 RESULTS (1-10-0)
14	Richmond	38
7	East Tenn. St.	10
9	Army	31
6	William & Mary	49
0	Marshall	51
35	Tenn.-Chatt.	29
0	Ga. Southern	57
0	Furman	24
14	Western Caro.	38
33	Citadel	34
21	Appalachian St.	35
139		**396**

Nickname: Keydets.
Stadium: Alumni Field (1962), 10,000 capacity.
  Natural turf.
Colors: Red, White & Yellow.
Conference: Southern Conf.
SID: Wade Branner, 703-464-7253.
AD: Davis Babb.

VIRGINIA STATE
Ettrick, VA 23806 II

Coach: Louis Anderson, Claflin '61
Record: 3 Years, 16-15-0

1994 SCHEDULE
Norfolk St. ■ ....*Sept. 3
Central St. (Ohio)...........................Sept. 10
N.C. Central ....*Sept. 17
Bowie St.....................................Sept. 24
Livingstone ■ ....Oct. 1
Hampton ■ ....Oct. 8
Fayetteville St. ....*Oct. 15
Elizabeth City St. ....Oct. 22
Virginia Union ....Oct. 29
Winston-Salem ■ ....Nov. 12

1993 RESULTS (10-1-0)
21	Norfolk St.	7
10	West Liberty St.	7
0	N.C. Central	17
30	Bowie St.	7

36	Livingstone	20
14	Hampton	42
41	Fayetteville St.	6
42	Elizabeth City St.	17
41	Virginia Union	6
48	Lane	12
48	Winston-Salem	24
371		**165**

Nickname: Trojans.
Stadium: Rogers, 13,500 capacity. Natural turf.
Colors: Orange & Navy Blue.
Conference: Central Inter. Ath. Assoc.
SID: Gregory C. Goings, 804-524-5028.
AD: Alfreeda Goff.

VIRGINIA TECH
Blacksburg, VA 24061 ....I-A

Coach: Frank Beamer, Virginia Tech '69
Record: 13 Years, 75-66-4

1994 SCHEDULE
Arkansas St. ■ ....*Sept. 3
Southern Miss................................Sept. 10
Boston College...............................Sept. 17
West Va. ■ ....*Sept. 22
Syracuse.....................................Oct. 1
Temple ■ ....Oct. 8
East Caro. ....Oct. 15
Pittsburgh ■ ....Oct. 22
Miami (Fla.) ....Oct. 29
Rutgers ■ ....Nov. 12
Virginia ■ ....Nov. 19

1993 RESULTS (8-3-0)
33	Bowling Green	16
63	Pittsburgh	21
2	Miami (Fla.)	21
55	Maryland	28
13	West Va.	14
55	Temple	7
49	Rutgers	42
31	East Caro.	12
34	Boston College	48
45	Syracuse	24
20	Virginia	17
400		**250**

Independence Bowl
45	Indiana	20

Nickname: Gobblers, Hokies.
Stadium: Lane (1965), 51,000 capacity. Natural turf.
Colors: Orange & Maroon.
Conference: Big East Conference.
SID: Dave Smith, 703-231-6726.
AD: Dave Braine.

VIRGINIA UNION
Richmond, VA 23220..............................II

Coach: Henry Lattimore, Jacksonville St. '57
Record: 15 Years, 83-72-5

1994 SCHEDULE
Savannah St. ....Sept. 3
Livingstone ■ ....*Sept. 10
Hampton ■ ....*Sept. 17
Bowie St.....................................Oct. 1
Elizabeth City St. ....Oct. 8
Central St. (Ohio) ■ ....Oct. 15
Norfolk St...................................Oct. 22
Virginia St. ■ ....Oct. 29
Winston-Salem ....Nov. 5
N.C. Central ....Nov. 12

1993 RESULTS (2-8-1)
7	Howard	34
14	Livingstone	6
0	Hampton	13
21	Morgan St.	38
7	Bowie St.	7
67	Elizabeth City St.	0
28	New Haven	71
9	Norfolk St.	21
6	Virginia St.	41
27	Winston-Salem	35

13	N.C. Central	20
199		**286**

Nickname: Panthers.
Stadium: Hovey Field, 10,000 capacity. Natural turf.
Colors: Steel Gray & Maroon.
Conference: Central Inter. Ath. Assoc.
SID: Paul Williams, 804-257-5890.
AD: James Battle.

WABASH

Crawfordsville, IN 47933 III

Coach: Greg Carlson, Wis.-Oshkosh '70
Record: 11 Years, 68-32-2

1994 SCHEDULE

Albion ■	Sept. 17
Hope	Sept. 24
Manchester ■	Oct. 1
Ill. Benedictine ■	Oct. 8
Franklin	Oct. 15
Hanover ■	Oct. 22
Anderson [Indianapolis, Ind.]	*Oct. 29
Rose-Hulman	Nov. 5
DePauw ■	Nov. 12

1993 RESULTS (5-4-0)

19	Wis.-Eau Claire	29
35	Albion	50
13	Hope	12
22	Manchester	7
35	Franklin	49
55	Hanover	21
34	Anderson	48
17	Rose-Hulman	13
40	DePauw	26
270		**255**

Nickname: Little Giants.
Stadium: Little Giant (1969), 4,500 capacity. Natural turf.
Colors: Scarlet.
Conference: Indiana Collegiate Ath. Conf.
SID: Jim Amidon, 317-364-4364.
AD: Max Servies.

WAGNER

Staten Island, NY 10301 ....I-AA

Coach: Walt Hameline, Brockport St. '75
Record: 13 Years, 103-32-2

1994 SCHEDULE

Springfield	*Sept. 9
LIU-C.W. Post	Sept. 17
Marist ■	Sept. 24
Monmouth (N.J.) ■	Oct. 1
San Diego ■	Oct. 8
Robert Morris ■	Oct. 15
Iona	Oct. 22
Central Conn. St.	Oct. 29
St. Peter's ■	Nov. 5
St. Francis (Pa.)	Nov. 12

1993 RESULTS (7-2-0)

27	LIU-C.W. Post	21
34	St. John's (N.Y.)	9
22	Central Conn. St.	15
23	Iona	30
27	Duquesne	24
47	Pace	10
31	St. Francis (Pa.)	21
22	Marist	6
14	San Diego	44
247		**180**

ECAC I-AA

32	Iona	0

Nickname: Seahawks.
Stadium: Fischer Memorial Field (1967), 5,000 capacity. Natural turf.
Colors: Green & White.
Conference: I-AA Independent.
SID: Scott Morse, 718-390-3227.
AD: Walt Hameline.

WAKE FOREST

Winston-Salem, NC 27109 ....I-A

Coach: Jim Caldwell, Iowa '77
Record: 1 Year, 2-9-0

1994 SCHEDULE

Vanderbilt	*Sept. 3
Appalachian St. ■	*Sept. 10
Florida St. ■	*Sept. 17
Maryland	Sept. 24
Army ■	Oct. 1
Virginia ■	*Oct. 8
North Caro. St.	Oct. 15
Duke ■	Oct. 22
Clemson	Oct. 29
North Caro. ■	Nov. 12
Georgia Tech	Nov. 19

1993 RESULTS (2-9-0)

12	Vanderbilt	27
16	North Caro. St.	34
20	Appalachian St.	3
14	Northwestern	26
35	North Caro.	45
20	Clemson	16
13	Duke	21
0	Florida St.	54
9	Virginia	21
28	Georgia Tech	38
32	Maryland	33
199		**318**

Nickname: Demon Deacons.
Stadium: Groves (1968), 31,500 capacity. Natural turf.
Colors: Old Gold & Black.
Conference: Atlantic Coast Conf.
SID: John Justus, 910-759-5640.
AD: Ron Wellman.

WARTBURG

Waverly, IA 50677 III

Coach: Bob Nielson, Wartburg '82
Record: 5 Years, 29-19-1

1994 SCHEDULE

Coe	Sept. 10
Simpson ■	Sept. 17
Central (Iowa)	Sept. 24
Concordia (Minn.)	Oct. 1
Dubuque ■	Oct. 8
Buena Vista	Oct. 15
William Penn	Oct. 22
Upper Iowa ■	Oct. 29
Luther [Cedar Falls, Iowa]	Nov. 5
Loras	Nov. 12

1993 RESULTS (9-1-0)

22	Coe	26
20	Upper Iowa	12
21	Central (Iowa)	14
24	Simpson	6
21	Luther	7
52	William Penn	3
28	Buena Vista	10
56	Dubuque	6
27	Aurora	7
24	Loras	10
295		**101**

III Championship

26	Wis.-La Crosse	55

Nickname: Knights.
Stadium: Schield (1957), 2,500 capacity. Natural turf.
Colors: Orange & Black.
Conference: Iowa Inter. Ath. Conf.
SID: Duane Schroeder, 319-352-8277.
AD: Bob Nielson.

WASHBURN

Topeka, KS 66621 II

Coach: Tony DeMeo, Iona '71
Record: 11 Years, 63-31-4

1994 SCHEDULE

Illinois St.	*Sept. 10
Missouri-Rolla	Sept. 17
Central Mo. St. ■	*Sept. 24
Pittsburg St.	*Oct. 1
Northwest Mo. St. ■	*Oct. 8
Northeast Mo. St.	Oct. 15
Mo. Western St. ■	Oct. 22
Mo. Southern St.	Oct. 29
Emporia St. ■	Nov. 5
Southwest Baptist ■	Nov. 12

1993 RESULTS (0-10-0)

14	Southern Ill.	46
14	Missouri-Rolla	38
19	Central Mo. St.	41
18	Pittsburg St.	55
36	Northwest Mo. St.	61
0	Northeast Mo. St.	34
10	Mo. Western St.	41
21	Mo. Southern St.	36
19	Emporia St.	37
20	Southwest Baptist	25
171		**414**

Nickname: Ichabods.
Stadium: Moore Bowl (1928), 7,200 capacity. Natural turf.
Colors: Yale Blue & White.
Conference: Mid-America Intercoll. Ath. Assoc.
SID: Mary Beth Brutton, 913-231-1010.
AD: Richard Johanningmeier.

WASHINGTON

Seattle, WA 98195 ....I-A

Coach: Jim Lambright, Washington '65
Record: 1 Year, 7-4-0

1994 SCHEDULE

Southern Cal	Sept. 3
Ohio St. ■	Sept. 10
Miami (Fla.)	Sept. 24
UCLA ■	Oct. 1
San Jose St. ■	Oct. 8
Arizona St. ■	Oct. 15
Oregon	Oct. 22
Oregon St. ■	Oct. 29
Stanford	Nov. 5
California ■	Nov. 12
Washington St.	Nov. 19

1993 RESULTS (7-4-0)

31	Stanford	14
12	Ohio St.	21
35	East Caro.	0
52	San Jose St.	17
24	California	23
25	UCLA	39
21	Oregon	6
17	Arizona St.	32
28	Oregon St.	21
17	Southern Cal	22
26	Washington St.	3
288		**198**

Nickname: Huskies.
Stadium: Husky (1920), 72,500 capacity. Artificial turf.
Colors: Purple & Gold.
Conference: Pacific-10.
SID: Jim Daves, 206-543-2230.
AD: Barbara Hedges.

WASHINGTON (MISSOURI)

St. Louis, MO 63130 III

Coach: Larry Kindbom, Kalamazoo '74
Record: 11 Years, 55-52-1

1994 SCHEDULE

Rose-Hulman	Sept. 3
Central Meth. ■	*Sept. 10
Ill. Wesleyan ■	Sept. 17
Trinity (Tex.) ■	*Sept. 24
Rhodes	Oct. 1
Chicago	Oct. 8
Carnegie Mellon ■	Oct. 15
Rochester	Oct. 22

Case Reserve ■ ....Oct. 29
Colorado Col. ....Nov. 5

1993 RESULTS (6-4-0)

28	Rose-Hulman	7
21	Carnegie Mellon	30
55	Case Reserve	10
6	Rochester	14
34	Trinity (Tex.)	10
28	Rhodes	10
36	Central Meth.	3
17	Chicago	20
49	Principia	33
16	Colorado Col.	38
290		**175**

Nickname: Bears.
Stadium: Francis Field (1904), 4,000 capacity. Natural turf.
Colors: Red & Green.
Conference: University Athletic Assn.
SID: Mike Wolf, 314-935-5077.
AD: John Schael.

WASHINGTON STATE
Pullman, WA 99164 ....I-A

Coach: Mike Price, Puget Sound '69
Record: 13 Years, 73-73-0

1994 SCHEDULE

Illinois [Chicago, Ill.]	*Sept. 1
Fresno St. ■	Sept. 10
UCLA	Sept. 24
Tennessee	Oct. 1
Oregon ■	Oct. 8
Arizona ■	Oct. 15
Arizona St.	*Oct. 22
California	Oct. 29
Southern Cal ■	Nov. 5
Oregon St.	Nov. 12
Washington ■	Nov. 19

1993 RESULTS (5-6-0)

14	Michigan	41
54	Montana St.	14
51	Oregon St.	6
3	Southern Cal	34
12	Pacific (Cal.)	0
44	Arizona St.	25
34	California	7
6	Arizona	9
23	Oregon	46
27	UCLA	40
3	Washington	26
271		**248**

Nickname: Cougars.
Stadium: Clarence D. Martin (1972), 40,000 capacity. Artificial turf.
Colors: Crimson & Gray.
Conference: Pacific-10.
SID: Rod Commons, 509-335-0270.
AD: Rick Dickson.

WASHINGTON AND JEFFERSON
Washington, PA 15301 III

Coach: John Luckhardt, Purdue '67
Record: 12 Years, 97-25-2

1994 SCHEDULE

Frank. & Marsh. ■	Sept. 10
Susquehanna	Sept. 17
Grove City ■	Sept. 24
Bethany (W.Va.)	Oct. 1
Waynesburg ■	Oct. 8
Thiel	Oct. 15
Defiance	Oct. 22
Cortland St. ■	Oct. 29
Wesley	Nov. 12

1993 RESULTS (9-0-0)

14	Frank. & Marsh.	7
13	Susquehanna	9
34	Bethany (W.Va.)	9
41	Waynesburg	3
48	Thiel	7

34	Gannon	6
56	Grove City	0
48	Cortland St.	7
42	Ithaca	7
330		**55**

III Championship

27	Moravian	7
28	Frostburg St.	7
16	Rowan	23

Nickname: Presidents.
Stadium: College Field (1958), 5,000 capacity. Natural turf.
Colors: Red & Black.
Conference: Presidents Ath. Conf.
SID: Susan Isola, 412-223-6074.
AD: John Luckhardt.

WASHINGTON AND LEE
Lexington, VA 24450 III

Coach: Gary Fallon, Syracuse '62
Record: 16 Years, 71-81-1

1994 SCHEDULE

Emory & Henry ■	Sept. 10
Centre	Sept. 24
Randolph-Macon ■	Oct. 1
Davidson	Oct. 8
Hampden-Sydney ■	Oct. 15
Sewanee	Oct. 22
Bridgewater (Va.)	Oct. 29
Guilford	Nov. 5
Swarthmore	Nov. 12

1993 RESULTS (2-8-0)

6	Emory & Henry	36
15	Centre	21
14	Randolph-Macon	35
14	Davidson	21
20	Hampden-Sydney	28
23	Sewanee	26
41	Bridgewater (Va.)	16
13	Guilford	14
34	Catholic	0
14	Georgetown	17
194		**214**

Nickname: Generals.
Stadium: Wilson Field (1930), 7,500 capacity. Natural turf.
Colors: Royal Blue & White.
Conference: Old Dominion Ath. Conf.
SID: Brian Logue, 703-463-8676.
AD: Mike Walsh.

WAYNE STATE (MICHIGAN)
Detroit, MI 48202 II

Coach: Brian VanGorder, Wayne St. (Mich.) '91
Record: 2 Years, 10-12-0

1994 SCHEDULE

Carson-Newman ■	Sept. 3
St. Joseph's (Ind.)	Sept. 10
Saginaw Valley ■	Sept. 17
Indianapolis	Sept. 24
St. Francis (Ill.) ■	Oct. 1
Grand Valley St.	Oct. 8
Ferris St. ■	Oct. 15
Ashland	Oct. 22
Hillsdale ■	Oct. 29
Michigan Tech	Nov. 5
Northern Mich.	Nov. 12

1993 RESULTS (6-5-0)

34	Indianapolis	31
31	Saginaw Valley	32
21	St. Francis (Ill.)	7
6	Ferris St.	36
0	Ashland	12
32	Northwood	14
27	American Int'l	12
28	Northern Mich.	18
24	St. Joseph's (Ind.)	38
25	Grand Valley St.	28

23	Hillsdale	21
251		**249**

Nickname: Tartars.
Stadium: Wayne State (1968), 6,000 capacity. Natural turf.
Colors: Green & Gold.
Conference: Midwest Intercollegiate.
SID: Richard Thompson Jr., 313-577-7542.
AD: Bob Brennan.

WAYNE STATE (NEBRASKA)
Wayne, NE 68787 II

Coach: Dennis Wagner, Utah '80
Record: 5 Years, 28-23-1

1994 SCHEDULE

Nebraska-Omaha ■	Sept. 3
Morningside	*Sept. 10
Northern St.	Sept. 17
Winona St.	Sept. 24
Iowa Wesleyan ■	Oct. 1
Neb.-Kearney ■	Oct. 8
Southwest St. ■	Oct. 15
Moorhead St. ■	Oct. 29
Bemidji St.	Nov. 5
Peru St.	Nov. 12

1993 RESULTS (9-1-0)

32	Nebraska-Omaha	19
44	Morningside	17
59	Bemidji St.	7
91	Mayville St.	12
41	Iowa Wesleyan	12
28	Neb.-Kearney	9
63	Southwest St.	34
34	Michigan Tech	26
27	Peru St.	0
28	Minn.-Duluth	29
447		**165**

Nickname: Wildcats.
Stadium: Memorial, 3,500 capacity. Natural turf.
Colors: Black & Gold.
Conference: Division II Independent.
SID: Dean Watson, 402-375-7520.
AD: Pete Chapman.

WAYNESBURG
Waynesburg, PA 15370 III

Coach: Dan Baranik, Shippensburg '84
(First year as head coach)

1994 SCHEDULE

Robert Morris ■	Sept. 3
Wesley	Sept. 17
Thiel	Sept. 24
Grove City ■	Oct. 1
Wash. & Jeff.	Oct. 8
Gannon ■	Oct. 15
Bethany (W.Va.) ■	Oct. 22
Kenyon	Oct. 29
Frostburg St. ■	Nov. 5

1993 RESULTS (3-6-0)

0	Gannon	9
22	Grove City	28
3	Wash. & Jeff.	41
14	Thomas More	29
13	Bethany (W.Va.)	28
32	Thiel	7
20	Kenyon	12
24	Frostburg St.	22
15	Wesley	22
143		**198**

Nickname: Yellow Jackets.
Stadium: College Field (1904), 1,300 capacity. Natural turf.
Colors: Orange & Black.
Conference: Presidents Ath. Conf.
SID: To be named, 412-852-3230.
AD: Rudy Marisa.

SCHEDULES/RESULTS

WEBER STATE

Ogden, UT 84408 ....I-AA

Coach: Dave Arslanian, Weber St. '72
Record: 5 Years, 29-27-0

1994 SCHEDULE

Western Mont. ■	*Sept. 3
Montana Tech ■	*Sept. 10
Montana St. ■	*Sept. 17
Eastern Wash.	Sept. 24
Northeast La.	*Oct. 1
Boise St.	*Oct. 8
Southern Utah	Oct. 15
Montana	Oct. 22
Northern Ariz.	*Oct. 29
Idaho St. ■	Nov. 5
Idaho	Nov. 12

1993 RESULTS (7-4-0)

40	Sonoma St.	28
27	Cal St. Northridge	12
0	Idaho	56
10	Montana St.	14
22	Eastern Wash.	36
17	Montana	45
21	Boise St.	14
47	Nevada	30
43	Southern Utah	39
67	Northern Ariz.	28
21	Idaho St.	17
315		**319**

Nickname: Wildcats.
Stadium: Wildcat (1966), 17,500 capacity. Natural turf.
Colors: Royal Purple & White.
Conference: Big Sky Conf.
SID: Brad Larsen, 801-626-6010.
AD: Tom Stewart.

WESLEY

Dover, DE 19901 III

Coach: Mike Drass, Mansfield '83
Record: 1 Year, 7-3-1

1994 SCHEDULE

Trenton St. ■	Sept. 3
Bridgewater (Va.) ■	Sept. 10
Waynesburg ■	Sept. 17
Randolph-Macon	Sept. 24
Thomas More ■	Oct. 1
Wm. Paterson	Oct. 8
Salisbury St.	Oct. 22
Chowan	Oct. 29
Alfred	Nov. 5
Wash. & Jeff. ■	Nov. 12

1993 RESULTS (6-3-1)

10	Trenton St.	10
31	Bridgewater (Va.)	0
21	Geneva	18
27	Randolph-Macon	8
8	Thomas More	24
7	Wm. Paterson	21
26	Frostburg St.	35
45	Salisbury St.	30
43	Chowan	6
22	Waynesburg	15
240		**167**

ECAC Southeast

6	FDU-Madison	0

Nickname: Wolverines.
Stadium: Wesley, 1,500 capacity. Natural turf.
Colors: Blue & White.
Conference: Division III Independent.
SID: Richard Biscayart, 302-736-2354.
AD: To be named.

WESLEYAN

Middletown, CT 06457 III

Coach: Frank Hauser, Wesleyan '79
Record: 2 Years, 10-6-0

1994 SCHEDULE

Middlebury	Sept. 24
Hamilton ■	Oct. 1
Colby	Oct. 8
Bates	Oct. 15
Amherst ■	Oct. 22
Bowdoin ■	Oct. 29
Williams	Nov. 5
Trinity (Conn.) ■	Nov. 12

1993 RESULTS (6-2-0)

27	Tufts	6
22	Hamilton	18
21	Colby	19
31	Bates	14
24	Amherst	6
28	Bowdoin	25
16	Williams	54
8	Trinity (Conn.)	32
177		**174**

Nickname: Cardinals.
Stadium: Andrus Field (1881), 8,000 capacity. Natural turf.
Colors: Red & Black.
Conference: NESCAC.
SID: Brian Katten, 203-347-9411.
AD: John Biddiscombe.

WEST CHESTER

West Chester, PA 19383 II

Coach: Rick Daniels, West Chester '75
Record: 5 Years, 35-19-0

1994 SCHEDULE

Kutztown	Sept. 3
Clarion ■	Sept. 10
Shippensburg ■	Sept. 17
Delaware	Sept. 24
East Stroudsburg ■	Oct. 1
Cheyney	Oct. 8
Mansfield ■	Oct. 15
Millersville	Oct. 22
Bloomsburg ■	Oct. 29
Villanova	Nov. 5
Calif. (Pa.)	Nov. 12

1993 RESULTS (6-5-0)

33	New Haven	45
19	Clarion	17
26	Indiana (Pa.)	37
41	Delaware	56
39	Cheyney	12
29	Mansfield	10
10	Millersville	14
16	Bloomsburg	38
35	Kutztown	3
24	Shippensburg	19
35	East Stroudsburg	33
307		**284**

Nickname: Golden Rams.
Stadium: Farrell (1970), 7,500 capacity. Natural turf.
Colors: Purple & Gold.
Conference: Pennsylvania Conf.
SID: Tom Di Camillo, 610-436-3316.
AD: William Lide.

WEST GEORGIA

Carrollton, GA 30118 II

Coach: Charlie Fisher, Springfield '81
Record: 1 Year, 4-6-0

1994 SCHEDULE

Elon ■	Sept. 3
Ga. Southern	*Sept. 10
Albany St. (Ga.)	Sept. 17
Central Ark.	Sept. 24
Union (Ky.) ■	Oct. 1
Livingston ■	Oct. 8
Valdosta St.	Oct. 15
Mississippi Col. ■	Oct. 29
Delta St.	Nov. 5
North Ala. ■	Nov. 12

1993 RESULTS (4-6-0)

11	Elon	25
12	Tenn.-Martin	20
14	Albany St. (Ga.)	24
23	Central Ark.	26
19	Harding	22
27	Livingston	22
23	Valdosta St.	16
27	Mississippi Col.	25
27	Delta St.	7
14	North Ala.	41
197		**228**

Nickname: Braves.
Stadium: Grisham (1966), 6,500 capacity. Natural turf.
Colors: Red & Blue.
Conference: Gulf South Conf.
SID: Ken Skinner, 404-836-6542.
AD: Ed Murphy.

WEST LIBERTY STATE

West Liberty, WV 26074 II

Coach: Bob Eaton, Glenville St. '78
Record: 4 Years, 16-23-1

1994 SCHEDULE

Findlay ■	Sept. 3
Newberry ■	Sept. 17
West Va. Tech	Sept. 24
Shepherd ■	Oct. 1
Glenville St. ■	Oct. 8
West Va. St.	Oct. 15
Concord (W.Va.)	Oct. 22
West Va. Wesleyan ■	Oct. 29
Fairmont St.	Nov. 5
Bowie St.	Nov. 12

1993 RESULTS (5-5-0)

32	Calif. (Pa.)	43
7	Virginia St.	10
51	West Va. Tech	12
16	Shepherd	21
17	Glenville St.	28
38	West Va. St.	9
56	Concord (W.Va.)	0
19	West Va. Wesleyan	16
23	Fairmont St.	0
14	Findlay	38
273		**177**

Nickname: Hilltoppers.
Stadium: Russek Field (1960), 4,000 capacity. Natural turf.
Colors: Gold & Black.
Conference: West Va. Inter. Ath. Conf.
SID: Lynn Ullom, 304-336-8320.
AD: James Watson.

WEST TEXAS A&M

Canyon, TX 79016 II

Coach: Morris Stone, Midwestern St. '87
(First year as head coach)

1994 SCHEDULE

Fort Lewis	*Sept. 3
Adams St. ■	*Sept. 10
Howard Payne ■	*Sept. 17
N.M. Highlands ■	Sept. 24
Midwestern St.	Oct. 1
Western N. Mex. ■	*Oct. 8
Hardin-Simmons	Oct. 15
Abilene Christian	Oct. 22
Tarleton St.	Oct. 29
Eastern N. Mex. ■	Nov. 5
Panhandle St.	Nov. 12

1993 RESULTS (3-6-0)

24	Fort Lewis	47
69	Panhandle St.	8
24	Southwestern Okla.	47
12	Midwestern St.	31
28	Prairie View	6
14	Southeastern Okla.	44
27	Tarleton St.	28
35	Eastern N. Mex.	34

16	Western N. Mex.	41
249		**286**

Nickname: Buffaloes.
Stadium: Kimbrough (1959), 20,000 capacity. Natural turf.
Colors: Maroon & White.
Conference: Division II Independent.
SID: Bill Kauffman, 806-656-2687.
AD: Mike Chandler.

WEST VIRGINIA
Morgantown, WV 26505 ....I-A

Coach: Don Nehlen, Bowling Green '58
Record: 23 Years, 156-91-8

1994 SCHEDULE
Nebraska [East Rutherford, N.J.] ....Aug. 28
Ball St. ■ ....Sept. 3
Rutgers ....Sept. 10
Maryland ■ ....Sept. 17
Virginia Tech ....*Sept. 22
Missouri ....Oct. 1
Pittsburgh ....Oct. 15
Miami (Fla.) ■ ....Oct. 22
Louisiana Tech ■ ....Oct. 29
Temple ....Nov. 12
Boston College ■ ....Nov. 19
Syracuse ■ ....*Nov. 24

1993 RESULTS (11-0-0)
48	Eastern Mich.	6
42	Maryland	37
35	Missouri	3
14	Virginia Tech	13
36	Louisville	34
42	Pittsburgh	21
43	Syracuse	0
58	Rutgers	22
49	Temple	7
17	Miami (Fla.)	14
17	Boston College	14
401		**171**

Sugar Bowl
7	Florida	41

Nickname: Mountaineers.
Stadium: Mountaineer Field (1980), 63,500 capacity. Artificial turf.
Colors: Old Gold & Blue.
Conference: Big East Conference.
SID: Shelly Poe, 304-293-2821.
AD: Ed Pastilong.

WEST VIRGINIA TECH
Montgomery, WV 25136 II

Coach: Bob Gobel, West Va. Tech '79
Record: 5 Years, 17-32-1

1994 SCHEDULE
West Va. St. [Charleston, W.Va.] ....*Sept. 3
Ferrum ■ ....Sept. 10
Indiana St. ....Sept. 17
West Liberty St. ■ ....Sept. 24
West Va. Wesleyan ....Oct. 1
Concord (W.Va.) ■ ....Oct. 8
Fairmont St. ....Oct. 15
Shepherd ■ ....Oct. 22
Glenville St. ....Nov. 5
Geneva ....Nov. 12

1993 RESULTS (0-10-0)
10	West Va. St.	12
14	Tiffin	28
14	Morehead St.	52
12	West Liberty St.	51
22	West Va. Wesleyan	48
6	Concord (W.Va.)	50
6	Fairmont St.	48
6	Shepherd	35
0	Glenville St.	50
6	Indiana St.	49
96		**423**

Nickname: Golden Bears.
Stadium: Martin, 3,000 capacity. Artificial turf.

Colors: Gold & Blue.
Conference: West Va. Inter. Ath. Conf.
SID: Jeff Kepreos, 304-442-3308.
AD: Terry Rupert.

WEST VIRGINIA WESLEYAN
Buckhannon, WV 26201 II

Coach: Bill Struble, West Va. Wesleyan '76
Record: 11 Years, 47-62-0

1994 SCHEDULE
Geneva ■ ....*Sept. 3
Bowie St. ■ ....Sept. 10
Slippery Rock ■ ....Sept. 17
Fairmont St. ■ ....Sept. 24
West Va. Tech ■ ....Oct. 1
Shepherd ....Oct. 8
Glenville St. ■ ....Oct. 15
West Va. St. ....Oct. 22
West Liberty St. ....Oct. 29
Concord (W.Va.) ■ ....Nov. 5

1993 RESULTS (7-3-0)
6	Slippery Rock	10
31	Calif. (Pa.)	23
11	Fairmont St.	7
48	West Va. Tech	22
14	Shepherd	20
17	Glenville St.	16
41	West Va. St.	6
16	West Liberty St.	19
20	Concord (W.Va.)	19
9	Geneva	0
213		**142**

Nickname: Bobcats.
Stadium: Cebe Ross Field, 4,000 capacity. Natural turf.
Colors: Orange & Black.
Conference: West Va. Inter. Ath. Conf.
SID: Robert Blake, 304-473-8102.
AD: George Klebez.

WESTERN CAROLINA
Cullowhee, NC 28723 ....I-AA

Coach: Steve Hodgin, North Caro. '71
Record: 4 Years, 18-26-0

1994 SCHEDULE
Lenoir-Rhyne ■ ....*Sept. 1
Georgia Tech ....Sept. 10
Citadel ■ ....*Sept. 17
North Caro. St. ....*Sept. 24
Furman ....Oct. 1
Ga. Southern ■ ....Oct. 8
Marshall ....*Oct. 15
Tenn.-Chatt. ■ ....Oct. 22
Va. Military ....Oct. 29
Appalachian St. ■ ....Nov. 12
East Tenn. St. ■ ....Nov. 19

1993 RESULTS (6-5-0)
3	Kansas	46
38	Citadel	18
7	North Caro. A&T	34
23	Furman	20
18	Ga. Southern	19
25	East Tenn. St.	24
41	Tenn.-Chatt.	10
56	Newberry	10
38	Va. Military	14
16	Appalachian St.	20
16	Marshall	20
281		**235**

Nickname: Catamounts.
Stadium: E.J. Whitmire (1974), 12,000 capacity. Artificial turf.
Colors: Purple & Gold.
Conference: Southern Conf.
SID: Steve White, 704-227-7171.
AD: Larry B. Travis.

WESTERN CONNECTICUT STATE
Danbury, CT 06810 III

Coach: John Cervino, West Va. Wesleyan '82
Record: 2 Years, 6-14-0

1994 SCHEDULE
Kean ....Sept. 3
St. John Fisher ....Sept. 10
Montclair St. ■ ....*Sept. 17
Mass.-Dartmouth ....Oct. 1
Plymouth St. ■ ....Oct. 8
Coast Guard ....Oct. 15
Mass.-Lowell ....Oct. 22
Stony Brook ■ ....Oct. 29
Merchant Marine ■ ....Nov. 5
Norwich ■ ....Nov. 12

1993 RESULTS (4-6-0)
17	Kean	14
2	Merchant Marine	32
21	Wm. Paterson	28
31	Mass.-Dartmouth	18
14	Plymouth St.	33
18	Coast Guard	21
16	Mass.-Lowell	7
6	Stony Brook	33
6	Albany (N.Y.)	50
33	Norwich	21
164		**257**

Nickname: Colonials.
Stadium: Midtown Campus Field, 2,500 capacity. Artificial turf.
Colors: Blue & White.
Conference: Freedom Football Conf.
SID: Scott Ames, 203-797-2777.
AD: Ed Farrington.

WESTERN ILLINOIS
Macomb, IL 61455 ....I-AA

Coach: Randy Ball, Northeast Mo. St. '73
Record: 4 Years, 21-23-1

1994 SCHEDULE
Iowa Wesleyan ■ ....*Sept. 3
Western Mich. ....Sept. 10
Illinois St. ■ ....Sept. 17
Southwest Mo. St. ....*Sept. 24
Southern Ill. ....Oct. 1
Indiana St. ■ ....Oct. 15
Eastern Ill. ■ ....Oct. 22
Northern Iowa ....*Oct. 29
Jacksonville St. ■ ....Nov. 5
Buffalo ■ ....Nov. 12
Murray St. ■ ....Nov. 19

1993 RESULTS (4-7-0)
16	Montana St.	29
14	Eastern Mich.	16
28	Eastern Ill.	14
17	Illinois St.	12
14	Southern Ill.	13
17	Central Fla.	35
25	Northern Iowa	23
9	Western Ky.	41
18	Southwest Mo. St.	21
25	St. Ambrose	27
6	Indiana St.	16
189		**247**

Nickname: Leathernecks.
Stadium: Hanson Field (1948), 15,000 capacity. Natural turf.
Colors: Purple & Gold.
Conference: Gateway.
SID: Michael McFarland, 309-298-1133.
AD: Helen Smiley.

WESTERN KENTUCKY
Bowling Green, KY 42101 ....I-AA

Coach: Jack Harbaugh, Bowling Green '61
Record: 10 Years, 48-57-3

1994 SCHEDULE
Eastern Ky. ■ ....*Sept. 1
Murray St. ....*Sept. 8
Austin Peay ■ ....*Sept. 17
Central Fla. ....Sept. 24

Ala.-Birmingham		Oct. 1
Portland St. ■		Oct. 8
Jacksonville St.		Oct. 15
Southern Ill. ■		Oct. 22
Troy St. ■		*Oct. 29
Indiana St. ■		Nov. 5
Eastern Ill.		Nov. 12

1993 RESULTS (8-3-0)

15	Eastern Ky.	10
13	Kansas St.	38
28	Austin Peay	27
40	Ala.-Birmingham	13
12	Jacksonville St.	7
51	Southern Ill.	24
14	Indiana St.	41
41	Western Ill.	9
24	Troy St.	31
28	Eastern Ill.	14
44	Murray St.	14
310		**228**

Nickname: Hilltoppers.
Stadium: L. T. Smith (1968), 17,500 capacity. Natural turf.
Colors: Red & White.
Conference: I-AA Independent.
SID: Paul Just, 502-745-4298.
AD: Jim Richards.

WESTERN MARYLAND

Westminster, MD 21157 III

Coach: Tim Keating, Bethany (W.Va.) '75
Record: 6 Years, 29-28-1

1994 SCHEDULE

Juniata		Sept. 10
Gettysburg ■		Sept. 17
Ursinus		Sept. 24
Muhlenberg ■		Oct. 1
Randolph-Macon		Oct. 8
Dickinson ■		Oct. 15
Frank. & Marsh.		Oct. 22
Swarthmore ■		Nov. 5
Johns Hopkins		Nov. 12

1993 RESULTS (3-5-1)

16	Juniata	14
17	Gettysburg	38
33	Ursinus	42
27	Muhlenberg	29
27	Randolph-Macon	27
19	Dickinson	33
7	Frank. & Marsh.	16
36	Swarthmore	27
20	Johns Hopkins	3
202		**229**

Nickname: Green Terror.
Stadium: Scott S. Bair (1981), 4,000 capacity. Natural turf.
Colors: Green & Gold.
Conference: Centennial Conference.
SID: Scott E. Deitch, 410-857-2291.
AD: J. Richard Carpenter.

WESTERN MICHIGAN

Kalamazoo, MI 49008 .... I-A

Coach: Al Molde, Gust. Adolphus '66
Record: 23 Years, 152-87-8

1994 SCHEDULE

Miami (Ohio)		Sept. 3
Western Ill. ■		Sept. 10
Iowa St.		Sept. 17
Akron ■		*Sept. 24
Kent ■		Oct. 1
Central Mich.		Oct. 8
Ball St.		Oct. 15
Eastern Mich. ■		Oct. 22
Ohio ■		Nov. 5
Toledo		Nov. 12
Southwestern La.		*Nov. 19

1993 RESULTS (7-3-1)

13	Youngstown St.	17

13	Purdue	28
20	Akron	3
17	Miami (Ohio)	0
27	Kent	21
18	Central Mich.	23
21	Eastern Mich.	20
20	Army	7
34	Ohio	28
39	Toledo	26
14	Bowling Green	14
236		**187**

Nickname: Broncos.
Stadium: Waldo (1939), 30,000 capacity. Natural turf.
Colors: Brown & Gold.
Conference: Mid-American Conf.
SID: John Beatty, 616-387-4104.
AD: Dan Meinert.

WESTERN NEW ENGLAND

Springfield, MA 01119 III

Coach: Gerry Martin, Connecticut '80
Record: 3 Years, 9-17-1

1994 SCHEDULE

Worcester St. ■		Sept. 10
Curry		Sept. 17
MIT		Sept. 24
Salve Regina		Oct. 1
Stonehill		Oct. 8
Bentley ■		Oct. 22
Nichols		Oct. 29
Assumption ■		Nov. 5

1993 RESULTS (2-6-1)

12	Fitchburg St.	12
22	Curry	20
8	MIT	24
6	Salve Regina	35
7	Stonehill	13
7	Bentley	34
17	Nichols	13
21	Hartwick	31
18	Assumption	30
118		**212**

Nickname: Golden Bears.
Stadium: WNEC, 1,500 capacity. Natural turf.
Colors: Blue & Gold.
Conference: Eastern Collegiate.
SID: Gene Gumbs, 413-782-1377.
AD: Eric Geldart.

WESTERN NEW MEXICO

Silver City, NM 88061 II

Coach: Charley Wade, Southwest Mo. St. '64
(First year as head coach)

1994 SCHEDULE

N.M. Highlands ■		*Sept. 10
Eastern N. Mex.		*Sept. 17
San Fran. St. ■		*Sept. 24
Neb.-Kearney		Oct. 1
West Tex. A&M		*Oct. 8
Sul Ross St.		Oct. 29
Montana St.		Nov. 5
Humboldt St.		Nov. 12

1993 RESULTS (7-2-0)

10	Abilene Christian	24
42	N.M. Highlands	40
37	Eastern N. Mex.	7
12	San Fran. St.	32
35	Northwestern Okla.	16
40	Humboldt St.	15
47	Sul Ross St.	7
42	St. Mary's (Cal.)	15
41	West Tex. A&M	16
306		**172**

Nickname: Mustangs.
Stadium: Silver Sports Complex, 2,000 capacity. Natural turf.
Colors: Old Gold & Purple.
SID: Scott Woodard, 505-538-6233.
AD: Dick Drangmeister.

WESTERN STATE

Gunnison, CO 81231 II

Coach: Carl Iverson, Whitman '62
Record: 11 Years, 70-38-2

1994 SCHEDULE

Northern Colo.		Sept. 3
Southern Utah		*Sept. 17
Mesa St. ■		Sept. 24
Adams St. ■		Oct. 1
Colorado Mines		Oct. 8
Fort Lewis ■		Oct. 15
Mesa St.		Oct. 22
Chadron St. ■		Oct. 29
N.M. Highlands ■		Nov. 5
Fort Hays St.		Nov. 12

1993 RESULTS (8-3-0)

0	Northern Colo.	38
24	Eastern N. Mex.	20
49	Western Mont.	28
31	Neb.-Kearney	24
42	Colorado Mines	25
45	Fort Lewis	20
32	Mesa St.	41
31	Chadron St.	20
30	N.M. Highlands	49
28	Fort Hays St.	17
17	Adams St.	14
329		**296**

Nickname: Mountaineers.
Stadium: Mountaineer Bowl (1950), 2,400 capacity. Natural turf.
Colors: Crimson & Slate.
Conference: Rocky Mountain Ath. Conf.
SID: J. W. Campbell, 303-943-3035.
AD: To be named.

WESTFIELD STATE

Westfield, MA 01085 III

Coach: Steve Marino, Westfield St. '71
Record: 4 Years, 20-18-1

1994 SCHEDULE

Hartwick ■		*Sept. 9
Mass.-Boston		Sept. 17
Fitchburg St. ■		*Sept. 23
Framingham St.		Oct. 1
MIT		Oct. 8
Bri'water (Mass.) ■		Oct. 15
Worcester St.		Oct. 22
Mass. Maritime ■		*Oct. 28
Mass.-Dartmouth		Nov. 5
Maine Maritime ■		Nov. 12

1993 RESULTS (7-2-1)

7	Hartwick	7
47	Mass.-Boston	7
14	Fitchburg St.	7
28	Framingham St.	7
20	MIT	0
8	Bri'water (Mass.)	22
33	Worcester St.	6
27	Mass. Maritime	9
33	Mass.-Dartmouth	14
14	Maine Maritime	22
231		**94**

Nickname: Owls.
Stadium: Alumni Field (1982), 4,000 capacity. Artificial turf.
Colors: Navy & White.
Conference: New England.
SID: Mickey Curtis, 413-572-5433.
AD: F. Paul Bogan.

WHEATON (ILLINOIS)

Wheaton, IL 60187 III

Coach: J. R. Bishop, Franklin '61
Record: 12 Years, 67-40-1

1994 SCHEDULE

Hope ■		Sept. 10

Aurora ■ ....Sept. 17
Carthage ....Oct. 1
Ill. Wesleyan ■ ....Oct. 8
Millikin ....Oct. 15
North Park ....Oct. 22
North Central ■ ....Oct. 29
Augustana (Ill.) ....Nov. 5
Elmhurst ■ ....Nov. 12

1993 RESULTS (7-2-0)

44	Lake Forest	7
8	Dayton	31
20	Millikin	13
13	Ill. Wesleyan	9
48	Carthage	13
41	North Park	7
56	North Central	12
49	Elmhurst	32
6	Augustana (Ill.)	14
285		**138**

Nickname: Crusaders.
Stadium: McCully Field (1955), 7,000 capacity. Natural turf.
Colors: Orange & Blue.
Conference: College Conf. of Ill. & Wis.
SID: Steve Schwepker, 708-752-5747.
AD: Tony Ladd.

WHITTIER

Whittier, CA 90608 III

Coach: Kirk Hoza, Slippery Rock '85
(First year as head coach)

1994 SCHEDULE

Chapman ■ ....*Sept. 17
Occidental ....*Sept. 24
Azusa Pacific ■ ....*Oct. 1
Claremont-M-S ....Oct. 8
La Verne ■ ....*Oct. 15
Pomona-Pitzer ....*Oct. 22
Menlo ....Oct. 29
Cal Lutheran ■ ....Nov. 5
Redlands ■ ....*Nov. 12

1993 RESULTS (4-5-0)

17	Cal St. Chico	42
3	Cal Lutheran	14
10	Azusa Pacific	14
26	Pomona-Pitzer	25
25	Occidental	37
28	Redlands	21
38	Claremont-M-S	12
45	Menlo	14
17	La Verne	24
209		**203**

Nickname: Poets.
Stadium: Memorial, 7,000 capacity. Natural turf.
Colors: Purple & Gold.
Conference: Southern Calif. Inter. Ath. Conf.
SID: Rock Carter, 310-907-4271.
AD: Dave Jacobs.

WIDENER

Chester, PA 19013 III

Coach: Bill Cubit, Delaware '75
Record: 2 Years, 9-10-1

1994 SCHEDULE

Upsala ....Sept. 10
King's (Pa.) ■ ....Sept. 17
Moravian ■ ....Sept. 24
Juniata ....Oct. 1
Delaware Valley ....Oct. 8
Albright ■ ....Oct. 15
Wilkes ....Oct. 22
Susquehanna ....Oct. 29
FDU-Madison ■ ....Nov. 5
Lebanon Valley ....Nov. 12

1993 RESULTS (6-4-0)

27	Upsala	24
24	King's (Pa.)	15
16	Moravian	37
40	Juniata	12

31	Delaware Valley	9
33	Albright	13
15	Wilkes	36
10	Susquehanna	12
3	FDU-Madison	35
28	Lebanon Valley	26
227		**219**

Nickname: Pioneers.
Stadium: Leslie Quick Jr. (1994), 5,000 capacity. Natural turf.
Colors: Widener Blue & Gold.
Conference: Commonwealth League.
SID: Susan Fumagalli, 610-499-4436.
AD: Bruce Bryde.

WILKES

Wilkes-Barre, PA 18766 III

Coach: Joe DeMelfi, Delta St. '66
Record: 4 Years, 17-23-1

1994 SCHEDULE

Southern Conn. St. ....Sept. 10
Lebanon Valley ■ ....Sept. 17
Upsala ■ ....Sept. 24
Delaware Valley ....Oct. 1
Juniata ■ ....Oct. 8
FDU-Madison ....*Oct. 14
Widener ■ ....Oct. 22
Lycoming ....Oct. 29
Susquehanna ....Nov. 5
King's (Pa.) ■ ....Nov. 12

1993 RESULTS (10-0-0)

17	Plymouth St.	7
41	Lebanon Valley	0
23	Upsala	14
31	Delaware Valley	0
28	Juniata	14
29	FDU-Madison	2
36	Widener	15
9	Lycoming	7
27	Susquehanna	0
41	King's (Pa.)	14
282		**73**

III Championship

25	Frostburg St.	26

Nickname: Colonels.
Stadium: Ralston Field (1965), 4,000 capacity. Natural turf.
Colors: Navy & Gold.
Conference: Middle Atlantic.
SID: Thomas McGuire, 717-831-4777.
AD: Phil Wingert.

WILLIAM PATERSON

Wayne, NJ 07470 III

Coach: Gerry Gallagher, Wm. Paterson '74
Record: 8 Years, 38-38-1

1994 SCHEDULE

LIU-C.W. Post ■ ....*Sept. 9
Trenton St. ....*Sept. 16
Kean ■ ....*Sept. 30
Wesley ....Oct. 8
Montclair St. ....*Oct. 15
Worcester Tech ....Oct. 22
Jersey City St. ■ ....*Oct. 28
Rowan ....Nov. 5
Albany (N.Y.) ■ ....*Nov. 11

1993 RESULTS (7-3-0)

9	Geneva	10
24	Trenton St.	19
28	Western Conn. St.	21
10	Kean	14
21	Wesley	7
26	Montclair St.	23
31	Worcester Tech	14
7	Jersey City St.	6
22	Rowan	46
28	Albany (N.Y.)	6
206		**166**

III Championship

17	Union (N.Y.)	7
0	Rowan	37

Nickname: Pioneers.
Stadium: Wightman Field, 2,000 capacity. Natural turf.
Colors: Orange & Black.
Conference: New Jersey Ath. Conf.
SID: Joe Martinelli, 201-595-2705.
AD: Arthur Eason.

WILLIAM PENN

Oskaloosa, IA 52577 III

Coach: Ralph Young, Parsons '68
Record: 8 Years, 22-51-0

1994 SCHEDULE

MacMurray ....Sept. 10
Luther ....Sept. 17
Buena Vista ■ ....Sept. 24
Upper Iowa ■ ....Oct. 1
Loras ....Oct. 8
Central Meth. ■ ....Oct. 15
Wartburg ■ ....Oct. 22
Simpson ....Oct. 29
Central (Iowa) ....Nov. 5
Dubuque ■ ....Nov. 12

1993 RESULTS (1-9-0)

31	Concordia (Minn.)	19
7	Coe	36
0	Loras	58
7	Upper Iowa	46
6	Central (Iowa)	70
3	Wartburg	52
0	Luther	14
8	Buena Vista	50
8	Simpson	62
7	Dubuque	27
77		**434**

Nickname: The Statesmen.
Stadium: Community, 5,000 capacity. Natural turf.
Colors: Navy Blue & Gold.
Conference: Iowa Inter. Ath. Conf.
SID: John Eberline, 515-673-1046.
AD: Mike Laird.

WILLIAM AND MARY

Williamsburg, VA 23185 ....I-AA

Coach: Jimmye Laycock, William & Mary '70
Record: 14 Years, 90-67-2

1994 SCHEDULE

Rhode Island ....Sept. 3
Delaware ■ ....Sept. 10
Furman ....*Sept. 17
Va. Military ■ ....Sept. 24
Virginia ....Oct. 1
Northeastern ■ ....Oct. 8
Massachusetts ■ ....Oct. 15
James Madison ....Oct. 22
Villanova ....Oct. 29
Maine ■ ....Nov. 5
Richmond ....Nov. 19

1993 RESULTS (9-2-0)

27	New Hampshire	14
35	Delaware	42
0	Tulane	10
45	Harvard	17
49	Va. Military	6
53	Northeastern	6
51	Villanova	17
31	James Madison	26
47	Maine	23
45	Massachusetts	28
31	Richmond	17
414		**206**

I-AA Championship

28	McNeese St.	34

Nickname: Indians, Tribe.
Stadium: Walter Zable (1935), 15,000 capacity. Natural turf.
Colors: Green, Gold & Silver.

SCHEDULES/RESULTS

Conference: Yankee.
SID: Jean Elliott, 804-221-3344.
AD: John Randolph.

WILLIAMS
Williamstown, MA 01267 III

Coach: Dick Farley, Boston U. '68
Record: 7 Years, 45-9-2

1994 SCHEDULE
Bowdoin ■ ....Sept. 24
Trinity (Conn.) ■ ....Oct. 1
Bates ....Oct. 8
Middlebury ■ ....Oct. 15
Tufts ....Oct. 22
Hamilton ....Oct. 29
Wesleyan (Conn.) ■ ....Nov. 5
Amherst ....Nov. 12

1993 RESULTS (7-1-0)
13	Colby	9
7	Trinity (Conn.)	21
38	Bates	0
14	Middlebury	6
35	Tufts	14
56	Hamilton	3
54	Wesleyan (Conn.)	16
31	Amherst	2
248		**71**

Nickname: Ephs.
Stadium: Weston Field (1875), 7,000 capacity. Natural turf.
Colors: Purple.
Conference: NESCAC.
SID: Dick Quinn, 413-597-4982.
AD: Robert R. Peck.

WILMINGTON (OHIO)
Wilmington, OH 45177 III

Coach: Mike Wallace, Bowling Green '68
Record: 3 Years, 9-21-0

1994 SCHEDULE
Albion ■ ....Sept. 3
Thomas More ■ ....Sept. 17
Tiffin ■ ....Sept. 24
Adrian ....Oct. 1
Dayton ....Oct. 8
Defiance ....Oct. 15
Geneva ■ ....Oct. 22
Bluffton ....Oct. 29
Urbana ....Nov. 5
Mt. St. Joseph ■ ....Nov. 12

1993 RESULTS (6-4-0)
17	Cumberland (Ky.)	14
24	Thomas More	42
26	Tiffin	38
29	Olivet	25
7	Ohio Wesleyan	0
31	Defiance	63
21	Geneva	31
49	Bluffton	14
41	Wooster	19
42	Mt. St. Joseph	31
287		**277**

Nickname: Quakers.
Stadium: Williams (1983), 3,250 capacity. Natural turf.
Colors: Green & White.
Conference: Mideast Conf.
SID: Brian Neal, 513-382-6661.
AD: Richard Scott.

WINGATE
Wingate, NC 28174 II

Coach: Doug Malone, Carson-Newman '83
(First year as head coach)

1994 SCHEDULE
Newberry ■ ....Sept. 10
Shepherd ....Sept. 17
Mars Hill ■ ....Sept. 24

Gardner-Webb ....Oct. 1
Carson-Newman ....Oct. 8
Lenoir-Rhyne ■ ....Oct. 15
Wofford ....Oct. 22
Presbyterian ....Oct. 29
Catawba ■ ....Nov. 5
Elon ■ ....Nov. 12

1993 RESULTS (6-5-0)
17	East Tenn. St.	44
21	Wofford	17
45	Lees-McRae	28
31	Mars Hill	28
56	Gardner-Webb	28
14	Carson-Newman	46
13	Lenoir-Rhyne	21
63	Chowan	21
6	Presbyterian	35
61	Catawba	55
25	Elon	37
352		**360**

Nickname: Bulldogs.
Stadium: Walter Bickett, 5,000 capacity. Natural turf.
Colors: Navy Blue & Old Gold.
Conference: South Atlantic Conf.
SID: David Sherwood, 704-233-8194.
AD: John Thurston.

WINONA STATE
Winona, MN 55987 II

Coach: Tom Hosier, DePauw '66
Record: 20 Years, 75-118-3

1994 SCHEDULE
Augustana (S.D.) ■ ....*Sept. 3
Wis.-La Crosse ....Sept. 10
Wis.-Eau Claire ....*Sept. 17
Wayne St. (Neb.) ■ ....Sept. 24
Minn.-Morris ■ ....Oct. 1
Northern St. ....Oct. 8
Bemidji St. ■ ....Oct. 15
Minn.-Duluth ....Oct. 22
Southwest St. ■ ....Oct. 29
Moorhead St. ....Nov. 5
Neb.-Kearney [Minneapolis, Minn.] ....Nov. 12

1993 RESULTS (7-3-0)
21	Wis.-La Crosse	26
24	Wis.-Eau Claire	16
23	Moorhead St.	14
13	Michigan Tech	24
40	Minn.-Morris	9
42	Northern St.	14
51	Bemidji St.	3
17	Minn.-Duluth	15
18	Southwest St.	25
23	Moorhead St.	20
272		**166**

NAIA I Championship
7	Central St. (Ohio)	58

Nickname: Warriors.
Stadium: Maxwell, 3,000 capacity. Natural turf.
Colors: Purple & White.
Conference: Northern Sun Inter. Conf.
SID: Michael R. Herzberg, 507-457-5576.
AD: Stephen Juaire.

WINSTON-SALEM STATE
Winston-Salem, NC 27102 II

Coach: Kermit Blount, Winston-Salem '80
Record: 1 Year, 6-4-1

1994 SCHEDULE
South Caro. St. ....*Sept. 3
North Caro. A&T ....Sept. 10
Johnson Smith ....*Sept. 17
Livingstone ■ ....*Sept. 24
Fayetteville St. ■ ....*Oct. 1
Norfolk St. ....Oct. 8
Bowie St. ■ ....Oct. 15
N.C. Central ....Oct. 22
Wofford ■ ....Oct. 29
Virginia Union ■ ....Nov. 5

Virginia St. ....Nov. 12

1993 RESULTS (6-4-1)
47	Elizabeth City St.	6
21	North Caro. A&T	49
10	Howard	31
35	Livingstone	20
20	Fayetteville St.	17
54	Norfolk St.	54
46	N.C. Central	28
13	Bowie St.	24
23	Johnson Smith	6
35	Virginia Union	27
24	Virginia St.	48
328		**310**

Nickname: Rams.
Stadium: Bowman-Gray (1940), 18,000 capacity. Natural turf.
Colors: Scarlet & White.
Conference: Central Inter. Ath. Assoc.
SID: Kevin Manns, 919-750-2143.
AD: Albert L. Roseboro.

WISCONSIN
Madison, WI 53711 ....I-A

Coach: Barry Alvarez, Nebraska '69
Record: 4 Years, 21-23-1

1994 SCHEDULE
Eastern Mich. ■ ....Sept. 10
Colorado ....Sept. 17
Indiana ■ ....Sept. 24
Michigan St. ....Oct. 1
Northwestern ....Oct. 8
Purdue ■ ....Oct. 15
Minnesota ■ ....Oct. 22
Michigan ....Oct. 29
Ohio St. ....Nov. 5
Cincinnati ■ ....Nov. 12
Illinois ■ ....Nov. 19

1993 RESULTS (9-1-1)
35	Nevada	17
24	Southern Methodist	16
28	Iowa St.	7
27	Indiana	15
53	Northwestern	14
42	Purdue	28
21	Minnesota	28
13	Michigan	10
14	Ohio St.	14
35	Illinois	10
41	Michigan St.	20
333		**179**

Rose Bowl
21	UCLA	16

Nickname: Badgers.
Stadium: Camp Randall (1917), 77,745 capacity. Artificial turf.
Colors: Cardinal & White.
Conference: Big Ten Conf.
SID: Steve Malchow, 608-262-1811.
AD: Pat Richter.

WISCONSIN-EAU CLAIRE
Eau Claire, WI 54702 III

Coach: Greg Polnasek, Wis.-Eau Claire '79
Record: 2 Years, 8-11-0

1994 SCHEDULE
Northern St. ....*Sept. 3
Winona St. ■ ....*Sept. 17
Wis.-Oshkosh ■ ....*Sept. 24
Teikyo Westmar ■ ....Oct. 1
Wis.-Stevens Point ■ ....Oct. 8
Wis.-River Falls ....Oct. 15
Wis.-Whitewater ■ ....Oct. 22
Wis.-Platteville ....Oct. 29
Wis.-Stout ....Nov. 5
Wis.-La Crosse ....Nov. 12

1993 RESULTS (4-6-0)
15	Minn.-Duluth	24
29	Wabash	19

16	Winona St.	24
35	Wis.-Oshkosh	26
23	Wis.-Stevens Point	47
33	Wis.-River Falls	6
10	Wis.-Whitewater	27
29	Wis.-Platteville	40
31	Wis.-Stout	20
32	Wis.-La Crosse	42
253		**275**

Nickname: Blugolds.
Stadium: Carson Park, 6,500 capacity. Natural turf.
Colors: Navy Blue & Old Gold.
Conference: Wisconsin St. U. Conf.
SID: Tim Petermann, 715-836-4184.
AD: Mel Lewis.

WISCONSIN-LA CROSSE

La Crosse, WI 54601 III

Coach: Roger Harring, Wis.-La Crosse '58
Record: 25 Years, 210-60-7

1994 SCHEDULE

Loras ■	Sept. 3
Winona St. ■	Sept. 10
Wis.-Oshkosh	*Sept. 17
Wis.-Platteville ■	Sept. 24
Wis.-Stevens Point	Oct. 1
St. Ambrose	Oct. 8
Wis.-Stout ■	Oct. 15
Wis.-River Falls	Oct. 22
Wis.-Whitewater	Nov. 5
Wis.-Eau Claire ■	Nov. 12

1993 RESULTS (10-0-0)

26	Winona St.	21
54	Wis.-Oshkosh	8
7	Wis.-Platteville	0
21	Wis.-Stevens Point	14
35	St. Ambrose	28
24	Wis.-Stout	14
42	Wis.-River Falls	13
46	Simpson	7
31	Wis.-Whitewater	23
42	Wis.-Eau Claire	32
328		**160**

III Championship

55	Wartburg	26
25	St. John's (Minn.)	47

Nickname: Eagles.
Stadium: Memorial (1937), 5,500 capacity. Natural turf.
Colors: Maroon & Gray.
Conference: Wisconsin St. U. Conf.
SID: Todd Clark, 608-785-8493.
AD: Bridget Belgiovine.

WISCONSIN-OSHKOSH

Oshkosh, WI 54901 III

Coach: Ron Cardo, Wis.-Oshkosh '71
Record: 10 Years, 37-59-4

1994 SCHEDULE

St. Norbert ■	*Sept. 10
Wis.-La Crosse ■	*Sept. 17
Wis.-Eau Claire	*Sept. 24
Wis.-Stout	Oct. 1
Wis.-River Falls ■	Oct. 8
Wis.-Platteville ■	Oct. 15
St. Ambrose	Oct. 22
Wis.-Stevens Point	Oct. 29
Drake	Nov. 5
Wis.-Whitewater ■	Nov. 12

1993 RESULTS (3-7-0)

21	St. Xavier (Ill.)	19
28	St. Norbert	12
8	Wis.-La Crosse	54
26	Wis.-Eau Claire	35
44	Wis.-Stout	34
13	Wis.-River Falls	34
19	Wis.-Platteville	30
38	St. Ambrose	48
6	Wis.-Stevens Point	76

0	Wis.-Whitewater	26
203		**368**

Nickname: Titans.
Stadium: Titan (1970), 9,680 capacity. Natural turf.
Colors: Gold, Black & White.
Conference: Wisconsin St. U. Conf.
SID: Kennan Timm, 414-424-0365.
AD: Allen Ackerman.

WISCONSIN-PLATTEVILLE

Platteville, WI 53818 III

Coach: Jim Kinder, Wisconsin '73
Record: 1 Year, 3-7-0

1994 SCHEDULE

Augustana (Ill.)	Sept. 10
Wis.-River Falls ■	Sept. 17
Wis.-La Crosse	Sept. 24
Wis.-Whitewater ■	Oct. 1
Wis.-Stout ■	Oct. 8
Wis.-Oshkosh	Oct. 15
Iowa Wesleyan	Oct. 22
Wis.-Eau Claire ■	Oct. 29
St. Ambrose ■	Nov. 5
Wis.-Stevens Point	Nov. 12

1993 RESULTS (3-7-0)

14	Dayton	31
29	Wis.-River Falls	43
0	Wis.-La Crosse	7
14	Wis.-Whitewater	23
16	Wis.-Stout	24
30	Wis.-Oshkosh	19
21	Iowa Wesleyan	31
40	Wis.-Eau Claire	29
34	St. Ambrose	14
7	Wis.-Stevens Point	21
205		**242**

Nickname: Pioneers.
Stadium: Ralph E. Davis Pioneer (1972), 10,000 capacity. Natural turf.
Colors: Orange & Blue.
Conference: Wisconsin St. U. Conf.
SID: Becky Bohm, 608-342-1574.
AD: Daryl Leonard.

WISCONSIN-RIVER FALLS

River Falls, WI 54022 III

Coach: John O'Grady, Wis.-River Falls '79
Record: 5 Years, 28-18-3

1994 SCHEDULE

Wis.-Stout ■	Sept. 3
St. Thomas (Minn.)	Sept. 10
Wis.-Platteville	Sept. 17
Minn.-Duluth	Oct. 1
Wis.-Oshkosh	Oct. 8
Wis.-Eau Claire ■	Oct. 15
Wis.-La Crosse ■	Oct. 22
Wis.-Whitewater	Oct. 29
Wis.-Stevens Point ■	Nov. 5
Northern St. [Minneapolis, Minn.]	Nov. 12

1993 RESULTS (6-4-0)

34	Minn.-Morris	6
34	St. Thomas (Minn.)	16
43	Wis.-Platteville	29
28	Alma	7
34	Wis.-Oshkosh	13
6	Wis.-Eau Claire	33
13	Wis.-La Crosse	42
9	Wis.-Whitewater	20
22	Wis.-Stevens Point	36
44	Wis.-Stout	6
267		**208**

Nickname: Falcons.
Stadium: Ramer Field (1966), 4,800 capacity. Natural turf.
Colors: Red & White.
Conference: Wisconsin St. U. Conf.
SID: Jim Thies, 715-425-3846.
AD: Rick Bowen.

WISCONSIN-STEVENS POINT

Stevens Point, WI 54481 III

Coach: John Miech, Wis.-Stevens Point '75
Record: 6 Years, 40-19-2

1994 SCHEDULE

Southwest St. ■	*Sept. 10
Wis.-Whitewater	Sept. 17
Butler ■	Sept. 24
Wis.-La Crosse ■	Oct. 1
Wis.-Eau Claire	Oct. 8
Thomas More	Oct. 15
Wis.-Stout	Oct. 22
Wis.-Oshkosh ■	Oct. 29
Wis.-River Falls	Nov. 5
Wis.-Platteville ■	Nov. 12

1993 RESULTS (8-2-0)

21	Michigan Tech	43
47	Minn.-Morris	0
31	Wis.-Whitewater	6
14	Wis.-La Crosse	21
47	Wis.-Eau Claire	23
20	Thomas More	17
45	Wis.-Stout	12
76	Wis.-Oshkosh	6
36	Wis.-River Falls	22
21	Wis.-Platteville	7
358		**157**

Nickname: Pointers.
Stadium: Goerke Field (1932), 4,000 capacity. Natural turf.
Colors: Purple & Gold.
Conference: Wisconsin St. U. Conf.
SID: Terry Owens, 715-346-2840.
AD: Frank O'Brien.

WISCONSIN-STOUT

Stout, WI 54751 III

Coach: Ed Meierkort, Dakota Wesleyan
Record: 1 Year, 2-8-0

1994 SCHEDULE

Wis.-River Falls	Sept. 3
St. Ambrose ■	*Sept. 10
Bemidji St. ■	*Sept. 17
Wis.-Whitewater ■	Sept. 24
Wis.-Oshkosh ■	Oct. 1
Wis.-Platteville	Oct. 8
Wis.-La Crosse	Oct. 15
Wis.-Stevens Point ■	Oct. 22
Wis.-Eau Claire	Nov. 5
Southwest St. [Minneapolis, Minn.]	Nov. 12

1993 RESULTS (2-8-0)

30	Mayville St.	0
11	Minn.-Duluth	14
7	Wis.-Whitewater	14
34	Wis.-Oshkosh	44
24	Wis.-Platteville	16
14	Wis.-La Crosse	24
12	Wis.-Stevens Point	45
18	St. Ambrose	35
20	Wis.-Eau Claire	31
6	Wis.-River Falls	44
176		**267**

Nickname: Blue Devils.
Stadium: Nelson Field, 5,000 capacity. Natural turf.
Colors: Navy Blue & White.
Conference: Wisconsin St. U. Conf.
SID: Glen McMicken, 715-232-2224.
AD: Rita Slinden.

WISCONSIN-WHITEWATER

Whitewater, WI 53190 III

Coach: Bob Berezowitz, Wis.-Whitewater '67
Record: 9 Years, 59-33-4

1994 SCHEDULE

South Dak.	Sept. 3
Wis.-Stevens Point ■	Sept. 17
Wis.-Stout	Sept. 24

Wis.-Platteville		Oct. 1
Mt. Senario ■		Oct. 8
St. Ambrose		Oct. 15
Wis.-Eau Claire		Oct. 22
Wis.-River Falls ■		Oct. 29
Wis.-La Crosse ■		Nov. 5
Wis.-Oshkosh		Nov. 12

1993 RESULTS (6-4-0)

0	Central Mo. St.	3
38	Upper Iowa	8
6	Wis.-Stevens Point	31
14	Wis.-Stout	7
23	Wis.-Platteville	14
6	St. Ambrose	7
27	Wis.-Eau Claire	10
20	Wis.-River Falls	9
23	Wis.-La Crosse	31
26	Wis.-Oshkosh	0
183		**120**

Nickname: Warhawks.
Stadium: Warhawk (1970), 11,000 capacity. Natural turf.
Colors: Purple & White.
Conference: Wisconsin St. U. Conf.
SID: Tom Fick, 414-472-1147.
AD: Willie Myers.

WITTENBERG
Springfield, OH 45501 III

Coach: Doug Neibhur, Millikin '74
Record: 5 Years, 32-15-1

1994 SCHEDULE

Evansville		Sept. 3
Muskingum ■		*Sept. 10
Earlham ■		*Sept. 17
Allegheny		Sept. 24
Kenyon ■		Oct. 1
Wooster		Oct. 8
Ohio Wesleyan ■		Oct. 15
Oberlin ■		Oct. 22
Denison ■		Oct. 29
III. Benedictine		Nov. 12

1993 RESULTS (9-1-0)

29	Muskingum	7
34	Earlham	0
33	Wooster	6
23	Case Reserve	10
14	Allegheny	25
7	Mercyhurst	6
32	Kenyon	0
55	Oberlin	6
42	Denison	0
28	Ohio Wesleyan	21
297		**81**

Nickname: Tigers.
Stadium: Edwards-Maurer (1923), 3,000 capacity. Artificial turf.
Colors: Red & White.
Conference: North Coast Ath. Conf.
SID: Alan Aldinger, 513-327-6114.
AD: Carl Schraibman.

WOFFORD
Spartanburg, SC 29303 II

Coach: Mike Ayers, Georgetown (Ky.) '74
Record: 9 Years, 53-45-2

1994 SCHEDULE

Gardner-Webb ■		*Sept. 3
Citadel		*Sept. 10
Lenoir-Rhyne ■		*Sept. 17
Catawba		Sept. 24
Presbyterian ■		*Oct. 1
Ala.-Birmingham		Oct. 8
Newberry		*Oct. 15
Wingate ■		Oct. 22
Winston-Salem		Oct. 29
Elon		Nov. 5
Charleston So. ■		Nov. 12

1993 RESULTS (7-3-1)

20	Citadel	6
17	Wingate	21
14	Furman	14
31	Catawba	30
20	Presbyterian	13
46	Lees-McRae	13
29	Newberry	3
24	Lenoir-Rhyne	27
11	Ala.-Birmingham	23
18	Elon	7
21	Charleston So.	9
251		**166**

Nickname: Terriers.
Stadium: Snyder Field (1930), 6,500 capacity. Natural turf.
Colors: Old Gold & Black.
Conference: Division II Independent.
SID: Mark Cohen, 803-597-4093.
AD: Danny Morrison.

WOOSTER
Wooster, OH 44691 III

Coach: Bob Tucker, Wooster '65
Record: 9 Years, 28-57-1

1994 SCHEDULE

Kalamazoo		Sept. 10
Ohio Wesleyan		Sept. 17
Oberlin ■		Sept. 24
Denison		Oct. 1
Wittenberg ■		Oct. 8
Case Reserve		Oct. 15
Earlham ■		Oct. 22
Allegheny		Oct. 29
Kenyon ■		Nov. 5
Trinity (Tex.) ■		Nov. 12

1993 RESULTS (2-7-0)

10	Kalamazoo	30
3	Allegheny	44
6	Wittenberg	33
27	Kenyon	21
31	Oberlin	3
0	Denison	3
0	Ohio Wesleyan	48
6	Earlham	12
19	Wilmington (Ohio)	41
102		**235**

Nickname: Fighting Scots.
Stadium: John P. Papp (1991), 4,500 capacity. Natural turf.
Colors: Black & Old Gold.
Conference: North Coast Ath. Conf.
SID: John Finn, 216-263-2374.
AD: Bill McHenry.

WORCESTER POLYTECHNIC
Worcester, MA 01609 III

Coach: Kevin Morris, Williams '86
Record: 1 Year, 5-4-0

1994 SCHEDULE

Ursinus		Sept. 10
Union (N.Y.) ■		Sept. 17
Rensselaer		Oct. 1
Norwich		Oct. 8
Merchant Marine		Oct. 15
Wm. Paterson ■		Oct. 22
Mass.-Lowell		Oct. 29
Coast Guard ■		Nov. 5
Plymouth St.		Nov. 12

1993 RESULTS (5-4-0)

14	Ursinus	21
0	Union (N.Y.)	44
14	Rensselaer	31
41	Norwich	21
44	Merchant Marine	37
14	Wm. Paterson	31
21	Mass.-Lowell	7
21	Coast Guard	18
35	Plymouth St.	17
204		**227**

Nickname: Engineers.
Stadium: Alumni Field (1916), 2,300 capacity. Artificial turf.
Colors: Crimson & Gray.
Conference: Freedom Football Conf.
SID: Chris Gonzales, 508-831-5328.
AD: Raymond Gilbert.

WORCESTER STATE
Worcester, MA 01602 III

Coach: Brien Cullen, Worcester St. '77
Record: 9 Years, 41-39-0

1994 SCHEDULE

Western New Eng.		Sept. 10
Mass.-Dartmouth		Sept. 17
Maine Maritime ■		Sept. 24
Mass.-Boston		Oct. 1
Fitchburg St. ■		Oct. 8
Framingham St.		Oct. 15
Westfield St. ■		Oct. 22
Bri'water (Mass.)		Oct. 29
Nichols ■		Nov. 5
Mass. Maritime ■		Nov. 12

1993 RESULTS (6-3-0)

17	Mass.-Dartmouth	29
7	Maine Maritime	25
27	Mass.-Boston	6
35	Fitchburg St.	7
20	Framingham St.	14
6	Westfield St.	33
16	Bri'water (Mass.)	8
40	Nichols	11
28	Mass. Maritime	12
196		**145**

Nickname: Lancers.
Stadium: John Coughlin Memorial (1976), 2,500 capacity. Natural turf.
Colors: Royal Blue & Gold.
Conference: New England.
SID: Bruce Baker, 508-793-8128.
AD: Susan E. Chapman.

WYOMING
Laramie, WY 82071 ....I-A

Coach: Joe Tiller, Montana St. '65
Record: 3 Years, 17-17-1

1994 SCHEDULE

UTEP ■		Sept. 3
Oregon St.		Sept. 10
Tulsa ■		Sept. 17
Utah		*Sept. 24
Nebraska		Oct. 1
Northeast La. ■		Oct. 8
Fresno St.		*Oct. 15
San Diego St. ■		Oct. 22
Air Force ■		Oct. 29
Colorado St.		Nov. 5
New Mexico ■		Nov. 12
Hawaii		*Nov. 19

1993 RESULTS (8-3-0)

16	Oregon St.	27
45	Northern Iowa	42
36	San Jose St.	25
28	Utah	12
31	Air Force	18
33	UTEP	26
48	Hawaii	10
32	Fresno St.	28
7	New Mexico	10
21	Colorado St.	41
43	San Diego St.	38
340		**277**

Copper Bowl

17	Kansas St.	52

Nickname: Cowboys.
Stadium: War Memorial (1950), 33,500 capacity. Natural turf.
Colors: Brown & Yellow.
Conference: Western Ath. Conf.

SID: Kevin McKinney, 307-766-2256.
AD: Paul Roach.

YALE

New Haven, CT 06520 ....I-AA

Coach: Carmen Cozza, Miami (Ohio) '52
Record: 29 Years, 169-99-5

1994 SCHEDULE

Brown	Sept. 17
Holy Cross ■	Sept. 24
Connecticut ■	Oct. 1
Lehigh ■	Oct. 8
Dartmouth	Oct. 15
Columbia ■	Oct. 22
Pennsylvania	Oct. 29
Cornell ■	Nov. 5
Princeton ■	Nov. 12
Harvard	Nov. 19

1993 RESULTS (3-7-0)

3	Brown	12
14	Connecticut	25
28	Central Fla.	42
31	Holy Cross	27
14	Dartmouth	31
35	Columbia	28
7	Pennsylvania	48
0	Cornell	21
7	Princeton	28
33	Harvard	31
172		**293**

Nickname: Elis, Bulldogs.
Stadium: Yale Bowl (1914), 70,896 capacity. Natural turf.
Colors: Yale Blue & White.
Conference: Ivy League.
SID: Steve Conn, 203-432-1456.
AD: Tom Beckett.

YOUNGSTOWN STATE

Youngstown, OH 44555 ....I-AA

Coach: Jim Tressel, Baldwin-Wallace '75
Record: 8 Years, 70-33-1

1994 SCHEDULE

Stephen F. Austin ■	*Sept. 1
Delaware St.	Sept. 10
Eastern Ky. ■	*Sept. 17
Slippery Rock ■	*Sept. 24
McNeese St. ■	*Oct. 1
North Ala. ■	*Oct. 8
Kent ■	Oct. 15
Akron ■	Oct. 29
Buffalo	Nov. 5
Massachusetts	Nov. 12
Indiana St.	Nov. 19

1993 RESULTS (9-2-0)

17	Western Mich.	13
15	Stephen F. Austin	35
56	Morgan St.	27
26	Eastern Ky.	22
42	Delaware St.	28
42	Liberty	0
24	Samford	7
38	Buffalo	12
17	Indiana St.	10
10	Illinois St.	13
19	Akron	0
306		**167**

I-AA Championship

56	Central Fla.	30
34	Ga. Southern	14
35	Idaho	16
17	Marshall	5

Nickname: Penguins.
Stadium: Arnold D. Stambaugh (1982), 16,000 capacity. Artificial turf.
Colors: Red & White.
Conference: I-AA Independent.
SID: Greg Gulas, 216-742-3192.
AD: Jim Tressel.

1994 Divisions I-A and I-AA Schedules by Date

This listing by dates includes all 1994 season games involving Divisions I-A and I-AA teams, as of printing deadline.

Neutral sites, indicated by footnote numbers, are listed at the end of each date. Asterisks (*) before the visiting team indicate night games.

Game dates and starting times are subject to change.

SUNDAY, AUGUST 28

HOME	OPPONENT
Nebraska [1]	West Va.

[1] East Rutherford, N.J.

MONDAY, AUGUST 29

HOME	OPPONENT
Fresno St. [1]	*Ohio St.

[1] Anaheim, Calif.

THURSDAY, SEPTEMBER 1

HOME	OPPONENT
Austin Peay	*Ky. Wesleyan
East Tenn. St.	*Catawba
Eastern Ill.	*Murray St.
Georgia Tech	*Arizona
Houston	*Kansas
Illinois [1]	*Washington St.
North Caro. St.	*Bowling Green
North Texas	*Abilene Christian
Northern Ill.	*Oklahoma St.
Southeast Mo. St.	*Kentucky St.
Southwest Tex. St.	*Tex. A&M-Kingsville
Tennessee Tech	*Lock Haven
Western Caro.	*Lenoir-Rhyne
Western Ky.	*Eastern Ky.
Youngstown St.	*Stephen F. Austin

[1] Chicago, Ill.

SATURDAY, SEPTEMBER 3

HOME	OPPONENT
Air Force	Colorado St.
Akron	*Temple
Alabama	Tenn.-Chatt.
Alabama St.	*Ala.-Birmingham
Arizona St.	*Oregon St.
Arkansas	Southern Methodist
Baylor	*Louisiana Tech
Bethune-Cookman	Johnson Smith
Boise St.	*Northeastern
Butler	Hofstra
Clemson	Furman
Colorado	Northeast La.
Connecticut	Nicholls St.
Dayton	*Mt. St. Joseph
Delaware St.	Cheyney
Duke	Maryland
Evansville	Wittenberg
Florida	*New Mexico St.
Florida A&M	*Tuskegee
Florida St.	Virginia
Fordham	Villanova
Fresno St.	*San Jose St.
Gannon	St. Francis (Pa.)

HOME	OPPONENT
Grambling	*Alcorn St.
Hawaii	*Brigham Young
Howard	*Mississippi Val.
Idaho St.	*Adams St.
Indiana	Cincinnati
Iowa	Central Mich.
Iowa St.	Northern Iowa
Jacksonville St.	*Sam Houston St.
James Madison	*Buffalo
Kansas St.	*Southwestern La.
Kentucky	*Louisville
Liberty	*Concord (W.Va.)
Louisiana St.	*Texas A&M
Maine	Central Fla.
Marshall	*Morehead St.
McNeese St.	*Illinois St.
Memphis	*Mississippi St.
Menlo	San Diego
Miami (Fla.)	Ga. Southern
Miami (Ohio)	Western Mich.
Michigan	Boston College
Minnesota	*Penn St.
Mississippi	*Auburn
Missouri	*Tulsa
Montana	Sonoma St.
Montana St.	Minn.-Duluth
Nevada	Northern Ariz.
Nevada-Las Vegas	*Eastern Mich.
North Caro.	*Texas Christian
North Caro. A&T	N.C. Central
Northwestern	*Notre Dame
Northwestern St.	*Southern-B.R.
Oregon	Portland St.
Pacific (Cal.)	*UC Davis
Pittsburgh	Texas
Rhode Island	William & Mary
Rutgers	Kent
Samford	*Bethel (Tenn.)
San Diego St.	Navy
South Caro.	*Georgia
South Caro. St.	*Winston-Salem
Southern Cal	Washington
Southern Ill.	Tenn.-Martin
Southern Utah	*Idaho
St. Mary's (Cal.)	San Fran. St.
Syracuse	*Oklahoma
Tennessee St.	*Middle Tenn. St.
Texas Southern	*Prairie View
Texas Tech	New Mexico
Toledo	*Indiana St.
Tulane	*Southern Miss.
UCLA	Tennessee
Utah St.	*Utah
Va. Military	Richmond
Valparaiso	St. Ambrose
Vanderbilt	*Wake Forest
Virginia Tech	*Arkansas St.
Weber St.	*Western Mont.
West Va.	Ball St.
Western Ill.	*Iowa Wesleyan
Wyoming	UTEP

SUNDAY, SEPTEMBER 4

HOME	OPPONENT
Alabama A&M [1]	*Jackson St.

[1] Birmingham, Ala.

THURSDAY, SEPTEMBER 8

HOME	OPPONENT
Murray St.	*Western Ky.
Southwest Tex. St.	*Northern Iowa
Texas Tech	*Nebraska

FRIDAY, SEPTEMBER 9

HOME	OPPONENT
Springfield	*Wagner
Villanova	*Liberty

SATURDAY, SEPTEMBER 10

HOME	OPPONENT
Air Force	Brigham Young
Akron	*Bowling Green
Alabama	Vanderbilt
Arizona	*New Mexico St.
Arizona St.	*Miami (Fla.)
Ark.-Pine Bluff	*Prairie View
Army	Holy Cross
Auburn	*Northeast La.
Boise St.	*Cal St. Northridge
Bucknell	Hofstra
Cal St. Sacramento	*San Fran. St.
Central Fla.	Valdosta St.
Central Mich.	Nevada-Las Vegas
Cincinnati	*Syracuse
Citadel	*Wofford
Clemson	North Caro. St.
Colgate	Boston U.
Colorado St.	Utah St.
Connecticut	Troy St.
Dayton	*Ala.-Birmingham
Delaware St.	Youngstown St.
Duke	*East Caro.
Duquesne	*St. Francis (Pa.)
Eastern Ky.	*Samford
Eastern Wash.	*Cal Poly SLO
Evansville	Thomas More
Florida	*Kentucky
Furman	*South Caro. St.
Ga. Southern	*West Ga.
Georgia	Tennessee
Georgia Tech	Western Caro.
Hawaii	*Oregon
Howard	Hampton
Illinois	Missouri
Illinois St.	*Washburn
Indiana	Miami (Ohio)
Indiana St.	*Lock Haven
Iowa	Iowa St.
James Madison	*Middle Tenn. St.
Kansas	Michigan St.
Lafayette	East Stroudsburg
Lehigh	Fordham
Louisiana St.	*Mississippi St.
Louisiana Tech	*Houston
Maine	Rhode Island
Marist	Central Conn. St.
Marshall	*Tennessee Tech
Maryland	Florida St.
McNeese St.	*Jacksonville St.
Mercyhurst	Canisius
Minnesota	*Pacific (Cal.)
Mississippi	*Southern Ill.
Mississippi Val. [1]	*Lane
Montana	Carson-Newman
Morehead St.	*East Tenn. St.
Morgan St.	Bethune-Cookman
Navy	*Virginia
Nevada	Arkansas St.
New Mexico	*Texas Christian
Nicholls St.	*Livingston
North Caro. A&T	Winston-Salem
Northeastern	New Hampshire
Northern Ariz.	*Southern Utah
Northwestern	Stanford
Northwestern St.	*Delta St.
Notre Dame	Michigan
Oregon St.	Wyoming
Penn St.	Southern Cal
Pittsburgh	*Ohio
Presbyterian	Charleston So.
Purdue	*Toledo
Rice	*Tulane
Richmond	Massachusetts
Robert Morris	Monmouth (N.J.)
Rutgers	West Va.
Sacred Heart	St. John's (N.Y.)
Sam Houston St.	*Southeast Mo. St.
San Diego	*St. Mary's (Cal.)
San Diego St.	*California
San Jose St.	*Baylor
Simpson	Drake
South Caro.	*Arkansas

HOME	OPPONENT
Southern Miss.	Virginia Tech
Southern-B.R.	*Alabama St.
Southwest Mo. St.	*North Texas
Southwestern La.	*Northern Ill.
St. Xavier (Ill.)	Butler
Stephen F. Austin	*Montana St.
Tenn.-Chatt.	*Alcorn St.
Tennessee St. [2]	*Jackson St.
Texas	*Louisville
Texas A&M	Oklahoma
Towson St.	Buffalo
Tulsa	*Memphis
UCLA	Southern Methodist
Utah	*Idaho St.
UTEP	*Eastern Ill.
Wake Forest	*Appalachian St.
Washington	Ohio St.
Washington St.	Fresno St.
Weber St.	*Montana Tech
Western Mich.	Western Ill.
William & Mary	Delaware
Wisconsin	Eastern Mich.

[1] St. Louis, Mo.
[2] Memphis, Tenn.

THURSDAY, SEPTEMBER 15

HOME	OPPONENT
Duke	Army

SATURDAY, SEPTEMBER 17

HOME	OPPONENT
Air Force	Northwestern
Ala.-Birmingham	Jacksonville St.
Alcorn St.	*Alabama St.
Appalachian St.	North Caro. A&T
Arizona St.	*Louisville
Arkansas	Alabama
Arkansas St.	*Southern Ill.
Auburn	*Louisiana St.
Baylor	*Oklahoma St.
Boise St.	*Nevada
Boston College	Virginia Tech
Bowling Green	Navy
Brigham Young	Colorado St.
Brown	Yale
Bucknell	Southern Conn. St.
Buffalo	*Lehigh
Butler	Georgetown (Ky.)
Cal Poly SLO	*Humboldt St.
Cal St. Northridge	*UC Davis
California	Hawaii
Canisius	*Buffalo St.
Central Conn. St.	Robert Morris
Central Fla.	Bethune-Cookman
Charleston So.	South Caro. St.
Citadel	*Western Caro.
Colgate	Dartmouth
Colorado	Wisconsin
Columbia	Harvard
Connecticut	Richmond
Cornell	Princeton
Delaware St. [1]	Towson St.
Drake	San Diego
Duquesne	Georgetown
East Tenn. St.	*Va. Military
Eastern Ill.	*Lock Haven
Eastern Mich.	Central Mich.
Fresno St.	*Oregon St.
Furman	*William & Mary
Ga. Southern	*Marshall
Georgia	Northeast La.
Hofstra	Fordham
Holy Cross	Massachusetts
Houston	*Missouri
Illinois	Northern Ill.
Indiana St.	West Va. Tech
Iowa St.	Western Mich.
Jackson St.	Florida A&M
Kansas St.	Rice
Kent	Akron
Kentucky	*Indiana

HOME	OPPONENT
Ky. Wesleyan	Evansville
Langston	*Prairie View
LIU-C.W. Post	Wagner
Maine	Boston U.
Marist	Iona
Maryville (Tenn.)	Davidson
McNeese St.	*Central Ark.
Miami (Ohio)	Cincinnati
Michigan St.	Notre Dame
Minnesota	*San Diego St.
Monmouth (N.J.)	Pace
Montana	Eastern Wash.
Morehead St.	*Tennessee St.
Morgan St.	Grambling
Nebraska	UCLA
Nevada-Las Vegas	*Idaho
New Hampshire	James Madison
Nicholls St.	*Northwestern St.
North Caro.	Tulane
Northeastern	Rhode Island
Northern Ariz.	*Idaho St.
Northern Iowa	*Southwest Mo. St.
Ohio	Utah St.
Ohio St.	Pittsburgh
Oklahoma	Texas Tech
Oregon	Utah
Pacific (Cal.)	*Southwest Tex. St.
Penn St.	Iowa
Pennsylvania	Lafayette
Purdue	Ball St.
Sam Houston St.	*Angelo St.
South Caro.	*Louisiana Tech
Southeast Mo. St.	*Murray St.
Southern Methodist	*New Mexico
Southern Miss.	Memphis
Southern Utah	*Western St.
Southern-B.R.	*Mississippi Val.
Southwestern La.	*Troy St.
St. Francis (Pa.)	Sacred Heart
St. Mary's (Cal.)	Sonoma St.
St. Peter's	Siena
Stanford	San Jose St.
Stephen F. Austin	*Cal St. Sacramento
Syracuse	Rutgers
Temple	*East Caro.
Tenn.-Chatt.	*Gardner-Webb
Tenn.-Martin	*Lane
Tennessee	Florida
Tennessee Tech	Samford
Texas Christian	*Kansas
Toledo	*Liberty
UTEP	*New Mexico St.
Valparaiso	Millikin
Vanderbilt	*Mississippi
Villanova	Delaware
Virginia	Clemson
Wake Forest	*Florida St.
Weber St.	*Montana St.
West Va.	Maryland
Western Ill.	Illinois St.
Western Ky.	*Austin Peay
Wyoming	Tulsa
Youngstown St.	*Eastern Ky.

[1] Wilmington, Del.

THURSDAY, SEPTEMBER 22

HOME	OPPONENT
Virginia Tech	*West Va.

SATURDAY, SEPTEMBER 24

HOME	OPPONENT
Alabama	Tulane
Appalachian St.	Citadel
Army	Temple
Auburn	East Tenn. St.
Aurora	Drake
Austin Peay	*Eastern Ky.
Ball St.	Ohio
Bethune-Cookman	N.C. Central
Boise St.	*Liberty
Brigham Young	New Mexico

Buffalo ....Cheyney
Cal Poly SLO ....*Sonoma St.
Cal St. Chico ....*Cal St. Sacramento
California ....Arizona St.
Canisius ....Siena
Central Fla. ....Western Ky.
Central Mich. ....Kent
Charleston So. ....Towson St.
Colorado St. ....San Diego St.
Dartmouth ....Pennsylvania
Davidson ....Emory & Henry
Delaware ....West Chester
East Caro. ....Syracuse
Eastern Mich. ....Bowling Green
Eastern Wash. ....Weber St.
Florida A&M ....*Howard
Florida St. ....North Caro.
Fordham ....Cornell
Georgia ....Mississippi
Georgia Tech ....Duke
Grambling [1] ....*Hampton
Harvard ....Bucknell
Hawaii ....*Fresno St.
Idaho ....Stephen F. Austin
Indiana St. ....*Illinois St.
Iowa St. ....Rice
Jackson St. ....Mississippi Val.
Kansas ....Ala.-Birmingham
Kansas St. ....Minnesota
Kentucky ....*South Caro.
Lafayette ....Hofstra
Lehigh ....Columbia
LIU-C.W. Post ....Central Conn. St.
Marshall ....*West Va. St.
Maryland ....Wake Forest
Massachusetts ....Maine
Memphis ....*Arkansas
Miami (Fla.) ....Washington
Michigan ....Colorado
Michigan St. ....Miami (Ohio)
Mississippi St. ....*Tennessee
Montana St. ....Northern Ariz.
Morehead St. ....Tennessee Tech
Morgan St. ....Knoxville
Murray St. ....*Middle Tenn. St.
Nebraska ....Pacific (Cal.)
Nevada ....Northeast La.
New Hampshire ....Connecticut
New Mexico St. ....*Arkansas St.
North Caro. A&T ....Jacksonville St.
North Caro. St. ....*Western Caro.
North Texas ....Montana
Northeastern ....Richmond
Northern Ill. ....*Eastern Ill.
Northern Iowa ....McNeese St.
Northwestern St. ....*East Tex. St.
Notre Dame ....Purdue
Ohio St. ....Houston
Oklahoma St. ....*Tulsa
Oregon ....Iowa
Penn St. ....Rutgers
Pittsburgh ....Boston College
Princeton ....Colgate
Rhode Island ....Brown
Sam Houston St. ....*Alcorn St.
San Diego ....*Cal Lutheran
San Jose St. ....*Southwestern La.
Southeast Mo. St. ....*Tenn.-Martin
Southern Cal ....Baylor
Southern Utah ....*Eastern N. Mex.
Southern-B.R. ....*Texas Southern
Southwest Mo. St. ....*Western Ill.
Southwest Tex. St. ....*Cal St. Northridge
St. Francis (Pa.) ....Bethany (W.Va.)
St. John's (N.Y.) ....Monmouth (N.J.)
St. Peter's ....Duquesne
Stanford ....Arizona
Tenn.-Chatt. ....*Ga. Southern
Tennessee St. [2] ....South Caro. St.
Texas A&M ....Southern Miss.
Texas Christian ....*Texas
Texas Tech ....Southern Methodist
Troy St. ....Alabama St.
UC Davis ....*St. Mary's (Cal.)

UCLA ....Washington St.
Utah ....*Wyoming
Utah St. ....*Nevada-Las Vegas
UTEP [3] ....*Air Force
Valparaiso ....Kalamazoo
Villanova ....Boston U.
Wagner ....Marist
Western Mich. ....*Akron
William & Mary ....Va. Military
Wis.-Stevens Point ....Butler
Wisconsin ....Indiana
Yale ....Holy Cross
Youngstown St. ....*Slippery Rock
[1] East Rutherford, N.J.
[2] Atlanta, Ga.
[3] San Antonio, Texas

THURSDAY, SEPTEMBER 29

HOME	OPPONENT
Auburn	*Kentucky

FRIDAY, SEPTEMBER 30

HOME	OPPONENT
Brigham Young	*Utah St.

SATURDAY, OCTOBER 1

HOME	OPPONENT
Ala.-Birmingham	Western Ky.
Alabama	Georgia
Arizona	*Oregon St.
Arkansas	Vanderbilt
Ball St.	Central Mich.
Bethune-Cookman	Delaware St.
Boston U.	James Madison
Brown	Colgate
Cal St. Northridge	*Cal St. Chico
Cal St. Sacramento	*Montana St.
California	San Jose St.
Charleston So.	Morgan St.
Cincinnati	*Bowling Green
Citadel	*Newberry
Clemson	Maryland
Columbia	Lafayette
Cornell	Lehigh
Dartmouth	Fordham
Davidson	*Guilford
Dayton	Evansville
Drake	Butler
Duquesne	Gannon
East Caro.	Southern Miss.
East Tenn. St.	*Appalachian St.
Eastern Mich.	Miami (Ohio)
Furman	Western Caro.
Ga. Southern	*Va. Military
Georgetown	Canisius
Hofstra	New Hampshire
Holy Cross	Harvard
Howard	Towson St.
Idaho	Idaho St.
Illinois	Purdue
Illinois St.	Central Fla.
Indiana	Minnesota
Indiana St.	Northern Iowa
Iona	Siena
Iowa	Michigan
Louisiana St.	*South Caro.
Louisiana Tech	Southwestern La.
Louisville	Pittsburgh
Maine	Delaware
Marist	St. John's (N.Y.)
Marshall	*Tenn.-Chatt.
Massachusetts	Rhode Island
Michigan St.	Wisconsin
Middle Tenn. St.	*Eastern Ky.
Mississippi	*Florida
Mississippi St.	*Arkansas St.
Missouri	West Va.
Montana	Cal Poly SLO

Morehead St. ....Southeast Mo. St.
Murray St. ....*Tenn.-Martin
Navy ....Duke
Nebraska ....Wyoming
New Mexico ....*Colorado St.
New Mexico St. ....*Nevada-Las Vegas
North Caro. St. ....Georgia Tech
Northeast La. ....*Weber St.
Northern Ariz. ....*Boise St.
Northern Ill. ....Nevada
Northwestern ....Ohio St.
Northwestern St. ....*Troy St.
Notre Dame ....Stanford
Ohio ....Toledo
Oklahoma ....Iowa St.
Oklahoma St. ....*North Texas
Portland St. ....*Eastern Wash.
Prairie View [1] ....*Grambling
Princeton ....Bucknell
Rutgers ....Miami (Fla.)
Sam Houston St. ....Texas Southern
Samford ....*Nicholls St.
San Diego ....*Valparaiso
San Diego St. ....*Air Force
South Caro. St. [2] ....Jackson St.
Southern Cal ....Oregon
Southern Ill. ....Western Ill.
Southern Methodist ....North Caro.
Southern-B.R. [3] ....*North Caro. A&T
Southwest Mo. St. ....*Eastern Ill.
Southwest Tex. St. ....*Sonoma St.
St. Francis (Pa.) ....Mercyhurst
St. Mary's (Cal.) ....Humboldt St.
St. Peter's ....Central Conn. St.
Syracuse ....Virginia Tech
Temple [4] ....Penn St.
Tennessee ....Washington St.
Tennessee St. [5] ....*Florida A&M
Tennessee Tech ....Austin Peay
Texas ....*Colorado
Texas A&M ....Texas Tech
Texas Christian ....*Baylor
UC Davis ....*Southern Utah
UTEP ....*Hawaii
Villanova ....Richmond
Virginia ....William & Mary
Wagner ....Monmouth (N.J.)
Wake Forest ....Army
Washington ....UCLA
Western Mich. ....Kent
Yale ....Connecticut
Youngstown St. ....*McNeese St.
[1] Dallas, Texas
[2] Columbia, S.C.
[3] Indianapolis, Ind.
[4] Franklin Field
[5] Nashville, Tenn.

THURSDAY, OCTOBER 6

HOME	OPPONENT
Kansas	*Kansas St.

SATURDAY, OCTOBER 8

HOME	OPPONENT
Air Force	Navy
Ala.-Birmingham	Wofford
Alabama	Southern Miss.
Alabama St.	*Jackson St.
Alcorn St.	*Texas Southern
Appalachian St.	Furman
Arizona	*Colorado St.
Arizona St.	*Stanford
Austin Peay	*Murray St.
Baylor	Southern Methodist
Boise St.	*Weber St.
Boston College	Notre Dame
Bowling Green	Ohio
Bucknell	Towson St.
Buffalo	Colgate
Cal St. Chico	*St. Mary's (Cal.)
California	UCLA

Central Mich.	Western Mich.
Charleston So.	Newberry
Cincinnati	*Vanderbilt
Citadel	East Tenn. St.
Connecticut	Villanova
Davidson	Wash. & Lee
Dayton	Wilmington (Ohio)
Delaware	James Madison
Eastern Ill.	Northern Iowa
Eastern Ky.	*Tennessee St.
Eastern Wash.	Idaho
Evansville	Drake
Florida	Louisiana St.
Florida A&M	*North Caro. A&T
Fordham	Columbia
Fresno St.	*Brigham Young
Gannon	Canisius
Georgia	Clemson
Harvard	Cornell
Hawaii	*New Mexico
Hofstra	Central Conn. St.
Houston	*Texas A&M
Howard	Bethune-Cookman
Illinois St.	*Southwest Mo. St.
Iowa	Indiana
Kent	Eastern Mich.
Lafayette	Dartmouth
Liberty	*Delaware St.
Louisville	North Caro. St.
Memphis	*Tulane
Miami (Fla.)	Florida St.
Miami (Ohio)	Akron
Michigan	Michigan St.
Middle Tenn. St.	Tenn.-Martin
Mississippi St.	*Auburn
Mississippi Val.	Grambling
Missouri	Colorado
Monmouth (N.J.)	St. Francis (Pa.)
Montana	Northern Ariz.
Montana St.	Idaho St.
Nebraska	Oklahoma St.
Nevada	Pacific (Cal.)
Nevada-Las Vegas	*Louisiana Tech
New Hampshire	Massachusetts
North Caro.	Georgia Tech
Northern Ill.	New Mexico St.
Northwestern	Wisconsin
Ohio St.	Illinois
Oregon St.	Southern Cal
Pace	Iona
Pennsylvania	Holy Cross
Prairie View [1]	Southern-B.R.
Princeton	Brown
Purdue	Minnesota
Rhode Island	Boston U.
Rice	Texas Tech
Richmond	Maine
Robert Morris	Duquesne
Rutgers [2]	Army
Samford	Central Fla.
San Diego St.	*Utah
San Fran. St.	Cal Poly SLO
Siena	Rensselaer
Sonoma St.	Cal St. Northridge
South Caro.	East Caro.
South Caro. St.	Morgan St.
Southern Ill.	Indiana St.
Southwest Tex. St.	*North Texas
Southwestern La.	Arkansas St.
St. John's (N.Y.)	Georgetown
St. Peter's	Marist
Stephen F. Austin	Sam Houston St.
Syracuse	Pittsburgh
Tennessee	Arkansas
Tennessee Tech	Southeast Mo. St.
Texas [3]	Oklahoma
Toledo	*Ball St.
Troy St.	Nicholls St.
Tulsa	*UTEP
UC Davis	*Cal St. Sacramento
Va. Military	Marshall
Valparaiso	Butler
Virginia Tech	Temple
Wagner	San Diego
Wake Forest	*Virginia
Washington	San Jose St.
Washington St.	Oregon
Western Caro.	Ga. Southern
Western Ky.	Portland St.
William & Mary	Northeastern
Wyoming	Northeast La.
Yale	Lehigh
Youngstown St.	*North Ala.

[1] Houston, Texas
[2] East Rutherford, N.J.
[3] Dallas, Texas

SATURDAY, OCTOBER 15

HOME	OPPONENT
Akron	*Central Mich.
Ala.-Birmingham	Mississippi Val.
Alabama St. [1]	*Texas Southern
Arkansas	Mississippi
Army	Louisville
Ball St.	Western Mich.
Boston College	Temple
Boston U.	Northeastern
Brown	Holy Cross
Bucknell	Cornell
Buffalo	*Illinois St.
Butler	Dayton
Cal Poly SLO	*UC Davis
Canisius	St. John's (N.Y.)
Colorado	Oklahoma
Colorado St.	UTEP
Connecticut	Maine
Dartmouth	Yale
Delaware St.	Florida A&M
Drake	Valparaiso
Duke	Clemson
Duquesne	Marist
East Caro.	Virginia Tech
Eastern Ky.	Murray St.
Florida	Auburn
Fordham	Princeton
Frank. & Marsh.	Georgetown
Fresno St.	*Wyoming
Furman	Citadel
Ga. Southern	*Appalachian St.
Georgia	Vanderbilt
Georgia Tech	Virginia
Grambling [2]	*Ark.-Pine Bluff
Harvard	Colgate
Idaho	Montana St.
Idaho St.	*Boise St.
Illinois	Iowa
Iona	St. Peter's
Iowa St.	Kansas
Jacksonville St.	Western Ky.
James Madison	Villanova
Kansas St.	Nebraska
Louisiana St.	*Kentucky
Louisiana Tech	*Utah St.
Marshall	*Western Caro.
Memphis	*Arkansas St.
Methodist	Davidson
Michigan	Penn St.
Michigan St.	Ohio St.
Middle Tenn. St.	Morehead St.
Minnesota	*Northwestern
Navy	Lafayette
N.C. Central	Howard
Nevada	New Mexico St.
New Hampshire	Lehigh
New Mexico	*San Diego St.
Nicholls St.	Stephen F. Austin
North Caro.	Maryland
North Caro. A&T	Morgan St.
North Caro. St.	Wake Forest
North Texas	McNeese St.
Northeast La.	*Central Fla.
Northern Ariz.	*Eastern Wash.
Northwestern St.	*Sam Houston St.
Notre Dame	Brigham Young
Ohio	Miami (Ohio)
Oklahoma St.	Missouri
Oregon	California
Pacific (Cal.)	*Northern Ill.
Pennsylvania	Columbia

Pittsburgh	West Va.
Prairie View	Alcorn St.
Rice	Texas
Richmond	Delaware
Rutgers	Cincinnati
Samford	Mississippi Col.
San Diego	Evansville
Siena	Bentley
South Caro.	Mississippi St.
South Caro. St.	Bethune-Cookman
Southern Ill.	Southeast Mo. St.
Southern Methodist	Houston
Southern Miss.	Southwestern La.
Southern Utah	Weber St.
Southern-B.R.	*Jackson St.
Southwest Mo. St.	Liberty
Springfield	Central Conn. St.
St. Mary's (Cal.)	Cal St. Northridge
Stanford	Southern Cal
Tenn.-Chatt.	*Va. Military
Tenn.-Martin	*Tennessee Tech
Tennessee	Alabama
Tennessee St.	*Austin Peay
Texas A&M	Baylor
Toledo	*Bowling Green
Troy St.	Charleston So.
Tulane	*Texas Christian
Tulsa	*Nevada-Las Vegas
UCLA	Oregon St.
Utah	Hawaii
Wagner	Robert Morris
Washington	Arizona St.
Washington St.	Arizona
Western Ill.	Indiana St.
William & Mary	Massachusetts
Wisconsin	Purdue
Youngstown St.	Kent

[1] Mobile, Ala.
[2] Shreveport, La.

SATURDAY, OCTOBER 22

HOME	OPPONENT
Air Force	Fresno St.
Akron	*Toledo
Ala.-Birmingham	Charleston So.
Alabama	Mississippi
Alcorn St.	Southern-B.R.
Appalachian St.	Marshall
Arizona	*UCLA
Arizona St.	*Washington St.
Arkansas St.	*Pacific (Cal.)
Army	Citadel
Austin Peay	Morehead St.
Bethune-Cookman	Albany St. (Ga.)
Boston College	Rutgers
Boston U.	Richmond
Bowling Green	Ball St.
Brown	Pennsylvania
Buffalo	*Hofstra
Butler	San Diego
Cal St. Northridge	*Cal Poly SLO
Central Conn. St.	St. Francis (Pa.)
Central Fla.	Troy St.
Central Mich.	Miami (Ohio)
Colgate	Fordham
Colorado	Kansas St.
Colorado St.	Utah
Connecticut	Rhode Island
Cornell	Dartmouth
Dayton	Drake
Delaware	Massachusetts
Evansville	Valparaiso
Florida A&M [1]	South Caro. St.
Florida St.	Clemson
Ga. Southern	East Tenn. St.
Georgetown	Johns Hopkins
Grambling	Jackson St.
Houston	*Texas Christian
Howard	North Caro. A&T
Idaho	Northern Ariz.
Idaho St.	Eastern Wash.
Illinois	Michigan
Indiana	Northwestern

Indiana St.	Southwest Mo. St.
Iona	Wagner
Iowa	Michigan St.
James Madison	William & Mary
Kansas	Oklahoma
Kent	Ohio
Kentucky	*Georgia
Lafayette	Holy Cross
Lehigh	Bucknell
Liberty	*Catawba
Maine	New Hampshire
Marist	Canisius
Maryland	Georgia Tech
Memphis	*Cincinnati
Mississippi St.	Tulane
Missouri	Nebraska
Monmouth (N.J.)	Upsala
Montana St.	Boise St.
Morgan St.	Delaware St.
Navy	Louisville
New Mexico St.	*New Mexico
Northeast La.	*Jacksonville St.
Northeastern	Villanova
Northern Ill.	Louisiana Tech
Northern Iowa	*Illinois St.
Northwestern St.	North Texas
Ohio St.	Purdue
Oklahoma St.	Iowa St.
Oregon	Washington
Oregon St.	Stanford
Portland St.	*Cal St. Sacramento
Prairie View	Alabama St.
Princeton	Harvard
Randolph-Macon	Davidson
Sam Houston St.	McNeese St.
San Jose St.	*Nevada
Siena	Duquesne
Southeast Mo. St.	Middle Tenn. St.
Southern Cal	California
Southern Miss.	Samford
Southern Utah	St. Mary's (Cal.)
Southwest Tex. St.	*Nicholls St.
St. Peter's	St. John's (N.Y.)
Stephen F. Austin	Henderson St.
Temple	*Syracuse
Tennessee St.	*Tenn.-Martin
Tennessee Tech	Eastern Ky.
Texas	Southern Methodist
Texas A&M	Rice
Texas Southern	Mississippi Val.
Texas Tech	Baylor
Towson St.	American Int'l
Tulsa	*East Caro.
Utah St.	*Southwestern La.
UTEP	*Brigham Young
Va. Military	Furman
Vanderbilt	South Caro.
Virginia	North Caro.
Virginia Tech	Pittsburgh
Wake Forest	Duke
Weber St.	Montana
West Va.	Miami (Fla.)
Western Caro.	Tenn.-Chatt.
Western Ill.	Eastern Ill.
Western Ky.	Southern Ill.
Western Mich.	Eastern Mich.
Wisconsin	Minnesota
Wyoming	San Diego St.
Yale	Columbia

[1] Orlando, Fla.

SATURDAY, OCTOBER 29

HOME	OPPONENT
Alabama A&M [1]	Alabama St.
Army	Boston College
Auburn	Arkansas
Ball St.	Eastern Mich.
Baylor	Houston
Bowling Green	Miami (Ohio)
Brigham Young	Arizona St.
Bucknell	Lafayette
Butler	Evansville
Cal Poly SLO	St. Mary's (Cal.)
California	Washington St.
Canisius	St. Peter's
Central Conn. St.	Wagner
Charleston So.	Mars Hill
Clemson	Wake Forest
Columbia	Princeton
Cornell	Brown
Dartmouth	Harvard
Delaware	Northeastern
Delaware St.	South Caro. St.
Duquesne	Iona
East Caro.	Cincinnati
East Tenn. St.	Furman
Eastern Ill.	Indiana St.
Eastern Wash.	Montana St.
Florida	Georgia
Florida A&M	Morgan St.
Florida St.	Duke
Fordham	Holy Cross
Fresno St.	*New Mexico
Georgetown	Marist
Hampden-Sydney	Davidson
Hofstra	Towson St.
Idaho St.	*Portland St.
Illinois St.	Southern Ill.
Iowa St.	Missouri
Kansas	Oklahoma St.
Kentucky	*Mississippi St.
Lehigh	Colgate
Liberty	*Central Fla.
Louisville	Memphis
Maine [2]	*Buffalo
Marshall	Citadel
Maryland	Tulane
Massachusetts	Boston U.
McNeese St.	*Stephen F. Austin
Miami (Fla.)	Virginia Tech
Michigan	Wisconsin
Michigan St.	Indiana
Middle Tenn. St.	Jacksonville St.
Mississippi	Louisiana St.
Mississippi Val.	Prairie View
Montana	Idaho
Morehead St.	Ala.-Birmingham
Morehouse	Howard
Murray St.	Tennessee Tech
Neb.-Kearney	Drake
Nebraska	Colorado
Nevada-Las Vegas	*San Jose St.
Nicholls St.	*Southern-B.R.
North Caro.	North Caro. St.
North Caro. A&T	Bethune-Cookman
North Texas	Sam Houston St.
Northern Ariz.	*Weber St.
Northern Iowa	*Western Ill.
Northwestern	Illinois
Notre Dame	Navy
Ohio	Central Mich.
Oklahoma	Kansas St.
Oregon	Arizona
Pacific (Cal.)	Utah St.
Penn St.	Ohio St.
Pennsylvania	Yale
Pittsburgh	Temple
Purdue	Iowa
Rhode Island	New Hampshire
Richmond	James Madison
Sacred Heart	Monmouth (N.J.)
Samford	Alcorn St.
San Diego St.	*Hawaii
South Caro.	Tennessee
Southeast Mo. St.	Austin Peay
Southern Methodist [3]	Texas A&M
Southern Miss.	Tulsa
Southern Utah	Cal St. Sacramento
Southwest Mo. St.	Central St. (Ohio)
Southwest Tex. St.	Northwestern St.
St. Francis (Pa.)	Robert Morris
St. John's (N.Y.)	Siena
Tenn.-Chatt.	Appalachian St.
Tenn.-Martin	*Eastern Ky.
Texas Christian	Rice
Texas Southern	*Grambling
Texas Tech	Texas
Toledo	Kent
UCLA	Stanford
Utah	UTEP
Va. Military	Western Caro.
Valparaiso	Dayton
Vanderbilt	Northern Ill.
Villanova	William & Mary
Washington	Oregon St.
West Va.	Louisiana Tech
Western Ky.	*Troy St.
Wyoming	Air Force
Youngstown St.	Akron

[1] Birmingham, Ala.
[2] Portland, Maine
[3] San Antonio, Texas

THURSDAY, NOVEMBER 3

HOME	OPPONENT
Louisville	*Boston College

SATURDAY, NOVEMBER 5

HOME	OPPONENT
Ala.-Birmingham	Butler
Appalachian St.	Liberty
Arizona	*California
Arkansas St.	Northern Ill.
Army	Air Force
Auburn	East Caro.
Austin Peay	Middle Tenn. St.
Azusa Pacific	*San Diego
Bethune-Cookman	Knoxville
Boise St.	Montana
Boston U.	Connecticut
Brigham Young	Northeast La.
Buffalo	Youngstown St.
Central Conn. St.	Southern Conn. St.
Central Mich.	Toledo
Cincinnati	Troy St.
Citadel	Tenn.-Chatt.
Colgate	Lafayette
Colorado	Oklahoma St.
Colorado St.	Wyoming
Cumberland (Tenn.)	Evansville
Dartmouth	Columbia
Davidson	Centre
Delaware St.	North Caro. A&T
Drake	Wis.-Oshkosh
Duke	Virginia
East Tenn. St.	Marshall
Eastern Ky.	Southeast Mo. St.
Eastern Mich.	Akron
Florida	Southern Miss.
Fresno St.	*Nevada
Furman	Ga. Southern
Georgia Tech	Florida St.
Grambling	Alabama St.
Harvard	Brown
Hofstra	Rhode Island
Holy Cross	Bucknell
Idaho	Northern Iowa
Illinois St.	Eastern Ill.
Indiana	Penn St.
Iona	Canisius
Jackson St.	Texas Southern
Kansas St.	Iowa St.
Kent	Bowling Green
Kentucky	Vanderbilt
Lehigh	Delaware
Louisiana St.	*Alabama
Louisiana Tech	*Northwestern St.
Marist	St. Francis (Pa.)
Maryland	North Caro. St.
Massachusetts	Northeastern
McNeese St.	*Southwest Tex. St.
Miami (Ohio)	Ball St.
Minnesota	*Illinois
Mississippi	Memphis
Mississippi St.	Arkansas
Mississippi Val.	Alcorn St.
Monmouth (N.J.)	Stonehill
Montana St.	Western N. Mex.
Morehead St.	Murray St.
Morgan St.	Samford

SCHEDULES/RESULTS

Nebraska ....Kansas
New Mexico ....Utah
North Caro..Clemson
Northern Ariz.................................*Cal Poly SLO
Northwestern ....Michigan St.
Ohio St...Wisconsin
Oklahoma...Missouri
Oregon ....Arizona St.
Oregon St. ....Pacific (Cal.)
Prairie View ....Tarleton St.
Princeton ....Pennsylvania
Purdue ....Michigan
Rice ....Southern Methodist
Richmond...............................New Hampshire
Rutgers ....Temple
Sam Houston St.............................*Nicholls St.
San Jose St. ....*New Mexico St.
Siena..Georgetown
South Caro. St...Howard
Southern Utah.................Cal St. Northridge
Southern-B.R.................................*Florida A&M
Southwest Mo. St...........................Southern Ill.
Southwestern La.................Nevada-Las Vegas
St. John's (N.Y.) ....Duquesne
St. Mary's (Cal.) ....Cal St. Sacramento
Stanford ....Washington
Stephen F. Austin ....North Texas
Syracuse......................................Miami (Fla.)
Tenn.-Martin ....Charleston So.
Tennessee Tech ....Tennessee St.
Texas ....Texas A&M
Towson St. ....Kutztown
Tulane ....*Navy
Utah St. ....Eastern Wash.
Va. Military ....James Madison
Valparaiso ....Aurora
Villanova ....West Chester
Wagner ....St. Peter's
Washington St........................Southern Cal
Weber St. ....Idaho St.
Western Ill. ....Jacksonville St.
Western Ky. ....Indiana St.
Western Mich. ....Ohio
William & Mary ....Maine
Yale ....Cornell

THURSDAY, NOVEMBER 10

HOME	OPPONENT
Brigham Young	*San Diego St.

SATURDAY, NOVEMBER 12

HOME	OPPONENT
Air Force	Utah
Alabama St.	Mississippi Val.
Alcorn St.	Troy St.
Arizona St.	*UCLA
Arkansas	Northern Ill.
Army	Boston U.
Auburn	Georgia
Ball St.	Akron
Boston College	Syracuse
Bowling Green	Central Mich.
Bridgewater (Va.)	Davidson
Brown	Dartmouth
Bucknell	Colgate
Cal St. Northridge	Northern Ariz.
Cal St. Sacramento	*Cal Poly SLO
Canisius	Duquesne
Central Conn. St.	Monmouth (N.J.)
Clemson	Georgia Tech
Colorado St.	Arkansas St.
Columbia	Cornell
Delaware	Hofstra
Drake	St. Ambrose
East Caro.	Central Fla.
Eastern Ill.	Western Ky.
Eastern Wash.	Boise St.

Evansville ....Aurora
Florida ....South Caro.
Florida A&M [1] ....Grambling
Fordham ....Lafayette
Ga. Southern ....Glenville St.
Georgetown ....St. Peter's
Hawaii ....*Southeast Mo. St.
Holy Cross ....Lehigh
Howard ....Morgan St.
Idaho...Weber St.
Idaho St. ....Montana
Illinois ....Penn St.
Indiana ....Ohio St.
Iona ....St. John's (N.Y.)
Iowa ....Northwestern
Iowa St. ....Nebraska
Jackson St. ....Prairie View
James Madison ....Connecticut
Kansas ....Colorado
Kentucky ....Northeast La.
Ky. Wesleyan ....Valparaiso
Liberty ....*New Haven
Louisiana St. ....*Southern Miss.
Louisiana Tech ....*San Jose St.
Louisville ....Texas A&M
Marshall ....Furman
Massachusetts ....Youngstown St.
Miami (Fla.) ....Pittsburgh
Miami (Ohio) ....Kent
Michigan ....Minnesota
Michigan St. ....Purdue
Middle Tenn. St. ....Illinois St.
Mississippi St. ....Alabama
Missouri ....Kansas St.
Murray St. ....Tennessee St.
Nevada ....Utah St.
New Hampshire ....Villanova
New Mexico St. ....*Pacific (Cal.)
Nicholls St. ....North Texas
North Caro. St. ....Duke
Northeastern ....Maine
Northwestern St. ....*McNeese St.
Notre Dame [2] ....Florida St.
Ohio...Eastern Mich.
Oklahoma St. ....Oklahoma
Oregon St. ....Washington St.
Pennsylvania ....Harvard
Portland St. ....*Southern Utah
Rhode Island ....Delaware St.
Rice ....Baylor
Samford ....Austin Peay
San Diego ....*Dayton
Siena ....Marist
Southern Cal ....Arizona
Southern Conn. St. ....Towson St.
Southern Ill. ....Northern Iowa
Southern Methodist ....Texas Christian
Southwest Tex. St. ....Stephen F. Austin
St. Francis (Pa.) ....Wagner
Stanford ....Oregon
Temple ....West Va.
Tenn.-Chatt. ....East Tenn. St.
Tenn.-Martin ....Morehead St.
Tennessee ....Memphis
Texas ....Houston
Texas Southern ....East Tex. St.
Texas Tech ....Southwestern La.
Toledo ....Western Mich.
Tulane ....*Mississippi
Tulsa ....Southwest Mo. St.
UTEP ....Fresno St.
Va. Military ....Citadel
Virginia ....Maryland
Virginia Tech ....Rutgers
Wake Forest ....North Caro.
Washington ....California
Western Caro. ....Appalachian St.
Western Ill. ....Buffalo
Wisconsin ....Cincinnati
Wofford ....Charleston So.
Wyoming ....New Mexico
Yale ....Princeton
[1] Miami, Fla.
[2] Orlando, Fla.

SATURDAY, NOVEMBER 19

HOME	OPPONENT
Akron	Ohio
Alabama	Auburn
Alcorn St.	Jackson St.
Appalachian St.	Va. Military
Arkansas St.	Louisiana Tech
Boise St.	Idaho
Boston U.	New Hampshire
Bucknell	Fordham
Cal Poly SLO	Southern Utah
Cal St. Sacramento	*Cal St. Northridge
California	Stanford
Central Fla.	Buffalo
Cincinnati	Tulsa
Citadel	Ga. Southern
Clemson	South Caro.
Colgate	Holy Cross
Colorado	Iowa St.
Columbia	Brown
Cornell	Pennsylvania
Davidson [1]	Sewanee
Delaware	Rhode Island
Duke	North Caro.
Eastern Ill.	Southern Ill.
Eastern Ky.	Morehead St.
Eastern Mich.	Toledo
Fresno St.	*Colorado St.
Furman	Tenn.-Chatt.
Georgia Tech	Wake Forest
Harvard	Yale
Hawaii	*Wyoming
Howard	Delaware St.
Idaho St.	*Minn.-Duluth
Indiana St.	Youngstown St.
Jacksonville St.	Southwest Mo. St.
James Madison	Northeastern
Kansas St.	Oklahoma St.
Kent	Ball St.
Lafayette	Lehigh
Liberty	*Charleston So.
Massachusetts	Connecticut
McNeese St.	*Nicholls St.
Memphis	East Caro.
Middle Tenn. St.	Tennessee Tech
Minnesota	*Iowa
Missouri	Kansas
Montana	Montana St.
Navy	Rice
Nevada-Las Vegas	Nevada
New Mexico	UTEP
North Caro. A&T	South Caro. St.
North Caro. St.	Florida St.
Northeast La.	*North Texas
Northern Iowa	*Eastern Wash.
Notre Dame	Air Force
Ohio St.	Michigan
Oregon St.	Oregon
Pacific (Cal.)	San Jose St.
Penn St.	Northwestern
Pittsburgh	Rutgers
Prairie View	Ala.-Birmingham
Princeton	Dartmouth
Purdue	Indiana
Richmond	William & Mary
Sam Houston St.	Southwest Tex. St.
Southwestern La.	*Western Mich.
Stephen F. Austin	Northwestern St.
Syracuse	Maryland
Temple	Miami (Fla.)
Tenn.-Martin	Austin Peay
Tennessee	Kentucky
Tennessee St.	Southeast Mo. St.
Texas A&M	Texas Christian
Texas Southern	Lane
Texas Tech [2]	*Houston
Towson St.	Morgan St.
Troy St.	Samford
Tulane	*Louisiana St.
UCLA	Southern Cal
Utah	Brigham Young
Utah St.	New Mexico St.
Vanderbilt	Florida
Virginia Tech	Virginia

Washington St. ....Washington
West Va. ....Boston College
Western Caro. ....East Tenn. St.
Western Ill. ....Murray St.
Wisconsin ....Illinois
[1] Bermuda
[2] San Antonio, Texas

THURSDAY, NOVEMBER 24

HOME	OPPONENT
Alabama St.	Tuskegee
Baylor	Texas
St. John's (N.Y.)	Pace
West Va.	*Syracuse

FRIDAY, NOVEMBER 25

HOME	OPPONENT
Arizona	*Arizona St.
Georgia	Georgia Tech
Oklahoma	Nebraska
Texas Christian	Texas Tech
Virginia	North Caro. St.

SATURDAY, NOVEMBER 26

HOME	OPPONENT
Arkansas	Louisiana St.
Florida A&M [1]	Bethune-Cookman
Florida St.	Florida
Hawaii	*Missouri
Houston	*Rice

Louisville ....Tulsa
Miami (Fla.) ....Boston College
Mississippi ....Mississippi St.
Nevada-Las Vegas ....Kansas St.
Penn St. ....Michigan St.
San Diego St. ....Fresno St.
Southern Cal ....*Notre Dame
Southern-B.R. [2] ....Grambling
Vanderbilt ....Tennessee
[1] Tampa, Fla.
[2] New Orleans, La.

SATURDAY, DECEMBER 3

HOME	OPPONENT
Hawaii	*Air Force
Navy [1]	Army

[1] Philadelphia, Pa.

SCHEDULES/RESULTS